TWENTY-F

MW00561112

KOVELS'

Antiques &
Collectibles
PRICE LIST

For the 1989 Market

ILLUSTRATED

Crown Publishers, Inc.
New York

BOOKS BY RALPH AND TERRY KOVEL

Dictionary of Marks—Pottery and Porcelain
Kovels' New Dictionary of Marks
A Directory of American Silver, Pewter and Silver Plate
American Country Furniture 1780–1875
Kovels' Antiques & Collectibles Price List
Kovels' Bottle Price List
The Kovels' Collector's Guide to American Art Pottery
Kovels' Organizer for Collectors
The Kovels' Price Guide for Collector Plates, Figurines,
    Paperweights, and other Limited Editions
The Kovels' Illustrated Price Guide to Royal Doulton
Kovels' Depression Glass & American Dinnerware
    Price List
Kovels' Know Your Antiques
Kovels' Know Your Collectibles
The Kovels' Book of Antique Labels
The Kovels' Collectors' Source Book
Kovels' Advertising Collectibles Price List
Kovels' Guide to Selling Your Antiques & Collectibles

Published by Crown Publishers, Inc., 225 Park Avenue South,
New York, New York 10003, and represented in Canada by the Canadian
MANDA Group
CROWN is a trademark of Crown Publishers, Inc.
Manufactured in the United States of America
Library of Congress Catalog Card Number: 83–643618

ISBN: 0-517-56985-X
10 9 8 7 6 5 4 3 2 1
First Edition

Dear Reader,

Twenty-one years of reporting prices! 1988 will probably be known as the year of the collector. The publicity generated by the Andy Warhol collectibles auction in New York made cookie jars and junk jewelry important enough to be news in the *Wall Street Journal*, *New York Times*, *Newsweek*, *Time*, and almost every local newspaper. For years we have purchased minor collectibles like store advertising, while writing for others with similar interests. Serious collectors of Chippendale chairs and eighteenth-century English porcelains (we collect those, too) often told us how strange our interests were. Now at last it is "in" to collect almost anything. Although we predicted rises in prices of iron doorstops, art pottery, and Japanese-inspired silver, we never imagined that costume jewelry from the thirties would be worth more than real Victorian jewelry. What this year has proved is that collectors must buy out of love, a passion for the objects. The "investment" potential of antiques is as unpredictable as the stock market and almost any item can be the one that goes up in price.

Over the years we have read millions of prices and used thousands of pictures in *Kovels' Antiques & Collectibles Price List*. Prices listed here include a random selection of pieces offered for sale *this* year. We report on the everyday antiques like pressed glass and oak furniture, the exotic Tiffany and Lalique, and the uncommon skorps and roemers. The smallest item is probably an earring, the largest a 27-foot post office stairwell. The least expensive is a Bonzo's beer can from Pittsburgh for $.50, the most expensive a Gallé punch bowl for $13,200.

The book is changed slightly each year. Categories are arranged, added, or omitted to make it easier for you to find your antiques. The book remains about 800 pages long because it is written to go with you to the sales. We try to have a balanced format, not too much glass, pottery, or collectibles, not too many items that sell for over $5,000. The prices are *from* the American market *for* the American market. No European sales are reported. We take the editorial privilege of not including any prices that seem to result from "auction fever."

Old *Kovels'* price books should be saved for reference, tax, and appraisal information. The index, written by a special computer program, is so complete it amazes us. Use it often. An internal alphabetical index is also included. For example, there is a category for "celluloid." Most items will be found there, but if there is a toy made of celluloid, it will be listed under "toy" and also indexed under "celluloid."

All pictures and prices are new every year, except pictures that are pattern examples shown in Depression Glass and Pressed Glass. Pictured antiques are not museum pieces but items recently offered for sale.

The hints are set in easy-to-notice special type. Leaf through the book and learn how to wash porcelains, store textiles, guard against theft, and much more.

RECORD PRICES

Biggest newsmakers of the year were the cookie jars sold at the Andy Warhol collection auction. The top-priced lot with the black chef jar marked "Cooky" and a black mammy cookie jar sold for $23,100. A retail store would have charged less than $500. Another stunning record was $22,000 for a Haskell minnow fishing lure, a continuation of the increased interest in sporting items.

Other unusual records include $16,500 for a painted leather fire bucket; $27,500 for a hand-painted ceremonial parade leather fire hat circa 1840; and $14,300 for a cranberry glass presentation fire trumpet. Fire items are hot. A smoking tobacco tin depicting the Lime Kiln club sold for $13,200; and a set of James Taddy & Co. tobacco cards for $25,575. An eager bidder paid $52,800 for a 1756 carved powder horn; another bid $9,900 for a Garrison model 201 trout fishing rod made in 1944; and $9,350 for a G. W. Gayle & Son trout fly reel. But a 1910 Honus Wagner baseball card brought $19,800, perhaps proving that spectator sports are as valued as physical activities.

Eating seems to be popular with collectors. A heart-shaped ice-cream scoop sold for $4,620; soda fountain strawholder for $1,540; Dr. Pepper Phos-Ferrate syrup dispenser for $9,900; and Blinkey Eye gum vending machine for $5,720. Full-size cars always sell well. A 1932 Hispano Suiza J12 phaeton and 1973 Ferrari Daytona Spyder each brought over a million dollars. Any automotive item is in demand, but the record $4,150 for Liberace's driver's license, $9,900 for an Arcade Yellow Cab baggage express iron toy, and $17,500 for a Jordan pedal car of the late 1920s surprised many.

Furniture, as always, set records; this year it was the twentieth-century makers that had the publicity. A Mackintosh center table went for $275,000; Pierre Legrain console for $209,000; Ruhlmann ivory inlaid armchair for $154,00; Gustav Stickley secretary for $102,300; Limbert settee for $3,850; and Frank Lloyd Wright dining-room set for $1,600,000. Eighteenth-century records included a Windsor high-chair for $85,250; Queen Anne high chest for $115,500; and pair of Newport card tables for $363,000. Nineteenth-century furniture included $104,500 for an 1820 Philadelphia sideboard; $94,600 for a Shaker tiger maple dining table; $88,000 for a revolving Shaker chair; $77,000 for a Belter sofa; and $39,600 for a Belter bed.

Record-setting toys included $4,200 for a double sulfide marble with a lion and a dog; Marklin tin Central Railroad station, $20,500; Donald Duck keywind carousel for $5,500; baby elephant mechanical bank for $20,350; and 21-inch Jumeau whistler doll for $29,000.

Pottery and porcelain records were set for a 4-gallon stoneware deer crock for $11,500; $4,500 for a 4-gallon star face stoneware jug; $22,550 for a pair of Mettlach plaques; $132,000 for a Chinese export armorial charger; $90,200 for a Chinese export Hong bowl; and $6,600 for a Newcomb Pottery plaque. There were only a few glass records. A stained glass window by LaFarge brought $242,000; blue Columbia-eagle portrait flask GI-118 sold for $40,700; glass label bottle for Brown's Celery Phosphate went for $1,540; blue Wynkoop's Sarsaparilla bottle for $13,000; Pairpoint puffy lamp for $22,000; and Lalique perfume bottle for $20,000.

A few other interesting records should be noted. An oculist's advertising sign shaped like a pince-nez went for $34,100; Sleepy Eye flour sign for $6,200; and Buster Brown sign for $14,300. A 142-piece set of Tiffany silver sold for $99,000; carousel horse for $57,200; carved meerschaum pipe for $13,090; and 1899 charge coin for Abraham & Straus for $137.50.

Record prices are often reported in newspapers and on TV because they are so surprising to the non-collector. Those who follow the antiques market know dozens of records are set each year as collectors find new interests; and the changing values of money, silver, and stocks influence prices.

The prices in this book are reports of the general antiques market, not the record-setting examples. Each year every price in the book is new. We do *not* estimate or "update" prices. Prices are the actual asking price, although the buyer may have negotiated to a lower figure. No price is an estimate. *We do not ask dealers and writers to estimate prices.* Experience has shown that a collector of one type of antique is prejudiced in favor of that item, and prices are usually high or low, but rarely a true report. If a price range is given, it is because at least two identical items were offered for sale at different places. The computer records the prices and prints the high and low figures. Price ranges are found only in categories like "pressed glass," where identical items can be identified. Some prices in *Kovels' Antiques & Collectibles Price List* may seem high and some may seem low because of regional variations. But each price is one you could have paid for the object.

If you are selling your collection, do *not* expect to get retail value unless you are a dealer. Wholesale prices for antiques are from 20 to 50 percent less than retail. Remember, the antiques dealer must make a profit or go out of business.

HOW TO USE THIS BOOK

There are a few rules for using this book. Each listing is arranged in the following manner: CATEGORY (such as pressed glass or furniture), OBJECT (such as vase), DESCRIPTION (as much information as possible about size, age, color, and pattern). Some types of glass are exceptions to this rule. These are listed CATEGORY, PATTERN, OBJECT, DESCRIPTION. All items are presumed to be in good condition, undamaged, unless otherwise noted.

Several special categories were formed to make a more sensible listing possible. "Kitchen" and "Tool" include special equipment. The casual collector might not know the proper name for an "adze" or "trephine," so we have created special categories. A new general category is "Sports." Masonic has been put into the larger category of "Fraternal." The index can help you locate items.

Several idiosyncrasies of style appear because the book is printed by computer. Everything is listed according to the computer alphabetizing system. This means words such as "Mt." are alphabetized as "M-T," not as "M-O-U-N-T." All numerals are before all letters, thus 2 comes before Z. A quick glance will make this clear, as it is consistent throughout the book.

We made several editorial decisions. A bowl is a "bowl" and not a dish unless it is a special dish, such as a pickle dish. A butter dish is a "butter." A salt dish is called a "salt" to differentiate it from a saltshaker. It is always "sugar and creamer," never "creamer and sugar." Where one dimension is given, it is the height; or if the object is round, the dimension is the diameter. Height of a picture is listed before width. Glass is clear unless a color is indicated.

Every entry is listed alphabetically. The problem of language remains. Some antiques terms, like "Sheffield" or "snow baby," have two meanings. Be sure to read the paragraph headings to know the meaning used. All category headings are based on the language of the average person at an average show, and we use terms like "mud figures" even if not technically correct.

This book does not include price listings of fine art paintings, books, comic books, stamps, coins, and a few other special categories.

All pictures in *Kovels' Antiques & Collectibles Price List* are listed with the prices asked by the seller. "Illus" (illustrated on the page) is part of the description if a picture is shown.

There have been misinformed comments about how this book is written. We *do* use the computer. It alphabetizes, ranges prices, sets type, and does other time-consuming jobs. Because of the computer, the book can be produced quickly. The last entries are added in June; the book is available in October. This is six months faster than would be possible any other way. But it is human help that finds prices and checks accuracy. We read everything at least twice, sometimes more. We edit from 100,000 entries to the 50,000 entries found here. We correct spelling, remove incorrect data, write category headings, and decide on new categories. We sometimes make errors.

Prices are reports of sales from all parts of the United States or Canada (translated to U.S. dollars) between June 1987 and June 1988. A few prices are from auctions, but most are from shops and shows. Every price is checked for accuracy, but we are not responsible for errors.

It is unprofessional for an appraiser to set a value for an unseen item. Because of this we cannot answer your letters asking for specific price information. But please write if you have any requests for categories to be included in future editions.

When you see us at the shows, stop and say hello. Since our television show has been on public television stations in all parts of the country, we find we can no longer be anonymous buyers. It may mean we pay more for items because the dealers know us, but it has been wonderful to meet all of you. Don't be surprised if we ask for your suggestions for the next edition of *Kovels' Antiques & Collectibles Price List*. Or you can write us at P.O. Box 22200, Beachwood, Ohio 44122.

Ralph & Terry Kovel,
Senior Members, American Society of Appraisers
June 1988

ACKNOWLEDGMENTS

Special thanks should go to those who helped us with pictures and deeds: David & Linda Arman, Della Graham (Neal Alford), Noel Barrett, Bill Bertoia, Betty Bagshaw (Richard A. Bourne Co. Inc.), Nancy Brown (Butterfield & Butterfield), Roberta Maneker (Christie's), Lee Ann Fahey (Christie's East), Jim Hagenbuch (The Glassworks), Morton M. Goldberg Auction Gallery, Barbara Mintz (Guernseys), Gene Harris, Inc., Willis Henry Auctions, Richard W. Oliver, Phillips, David Rago, Brian Riba, Lloyd Ralston, Ginger Rosa and Sarah Hamill (Robert Skinner, Inc.), Magda Grigorian (Sotheby's), Theriault's, Wolf's Gallery, and Woody Auction Company. Denis Jackson wrote us about Parrish prints and Lee Markley has once again made suggestions for the Carnival glass problems.

To the others in the antiques trade who knowingly or unknowingly contributed prices or pictures to this book, we say "Thank You!" We cannot do it without you. Some of you are: American Clay Exchange, American Pin Collection, American Vignette, Dianne Anglin, The Antique Co., Antiques & Collecting, Ark Antiques, Avon Times, Ballentine, Dee Baston, Be In Buttons, Dorothy Becker, Birchland Antiques, Brett Bollinger, Walt Brace, Brookside Antiques, Henry W. Burkhardt, Burns Auction Service, J.R. Burns Print Shop, Pat Call, Bobbie Camp-Gomez, Cerebro Lithographs, H.W. Cole Enterprises, Tod Connell, Aaron Corenman, Vernon Creech, Meredith J. DeGood, Dr. Roy DeSelms, Richard Diehl, Craig Dinner, Jeannine Dobbs, The Duke, Robert Eldred, Eileen Elfant, William Fagan, Fantasmagoria, Finders-Keepers, K.W. Fitzsimmons Contemporary & Antique Paperweights, N. Flayderman & Co., Inc., Frank's Antiques, Don Fritschel, Garth's Auctions, Inc., Mike's General Store, Jan Getz, Leigh Giarde, Gifts and Things, Ann Gilbert McDonald, Lee & Bob Gustavson, Henry F. Hain III, James L. Hamon, Peggy & Stan Hecker, Heirloom & Howard Limited, Heisey News, Hell Gate Newsletter, The Hobstar, Dennis Hopkins, Hummel Collector's Club Inc., E.B. Jesse, Ray Johnson, Brian Kathenes Autographs & Collectibles, C.J. Kilanowicz, Krafts & Kollectors, Dave Kreuzenstein, Louise's Old Things, Lyons Ltd. Antique Prints, M.T. Dairy Bottles, Jerry

Madsen, The Maine Idea, Manion's International Auction House Inc., Beverly Marmon, B.J. Macey, David Metz, Milwaukee Auction Galleries, Jackson Mitchell, Mark E. Mitchell, Inc., Joan Mogensen Antiques, Bill Monthie, Mystic Light of the Aladdin Knights, Louis E. Neuman & Co., The New Glaze, Of Dice and Men, Old Bottle Magazine, Old Sleepy Eye, The Opener, Richard Opfer Auctioneering, Inc., Ornament Trader, Bruce & Elaine Overby, Paper Collectors' Marketplace, Paper Pile Quarterly, Parker Enterprises, Payton Place Antiques, Paper Collectors' Marketplace, The Penn Central Collection, J. Peters, The Political Bandwagon, The Post Card Wholesaler, R & L Watches, Connie Rausch, The Ravenstree Company, Michael L. Raymond, Kenneth W. Rendell Gallery Inc., Ruth Ricker, Rocky Mountain Brewery Collectibles, Elise & Martin Roenig, Arlene Romoff, Ronelle Sales, Ronin Gallery, Roscha's, Rudisill's Alt Print Haus, Brian Russell, Darlene Schnitzer, Shadow Hills Antiques, Silver Magazine, Inc., The Soda Mart/Can World, Springhill Antiques & Cut Glass, St. James Place, Stebbins, Tony Steffen, Mark Supnick, Irv Taras, Team Antiques, Grace M. Trabosh, Harry A. Victor, Vintage Posters & Graphics, Whirligig Antiques, Windward Gallery, Tom Witte's Antiques, Richard Wood, Yesterdaze Toys, Audrey B. Zeder.

MORE ANTIQUE PRICE NEWS

Each year *Kovels' Antiques & Collectibles Price List* is completely rewritten. Every entry is new because of the changing antiques market. Many collectors need more current information about prices, trends, and sales. We have been writing a monthly newsletter, *Kovels on Antiques and Collectibles* for the collector and investor for fourteen years. Our newsletter includes reviews of price books, information about what to buy and sell, tips on refinishing, and articles on marks, fakes, and more. It is a 12-page, picture-filled newsletter about antiques that interest the collector and dealer. For more information about *Kovels on Antiques and Collectibles*, send a stamped, self-addressed envelope to Kovels, P.O. Box 22200-K, Beachwood, Ohio 44122.

We are now appearing on public television in a 13-week series about collecting. The show includes news, prices, and information. Watch "Kovels on Collecting" to see antiques and antiquers from all parts of the country.

TWENTY-FIRST EDITION

KOVELS'
Antiques &
Collectibles
PRICE LIST

To test the age of engraving on glass, place a white handkerchief on the inside. If the engraving is old, the lines will usually show up darker than the rest of the glass. New engraving has a bright powderlike surface.

A. Walter, Box, Pate-De-Verre,
A. Walter Nancy, 3¼ In.

Almaric Walter made pate–de–verre glass under contract at the Daum glassworks from 1908 to 1914. He started his own firm in Nancy, France, in 1919. Pieces made before 1914 are signed "Daum, Nancy" with a cross. After 1919 the signature is "A. Walter Nancy."

A.WALTER, Ashtray, Duck, Fish In Beak, Lily Pad Form, Signed, 6 1/2 In. 2750.00
Box, Pate–De–Verre, A.Walter Nancy, 3 1/4 In. .... *Illus* 2200.00
Figurine, Pate–De–Verre, Woman, Seminude, Tilted Head, 8 In. 6500.00
Figurine, Turtle, Tortoise, Green, Signed, C.1925, 4 1/4 In. 2450.00
Figurine, Woman, Pate–De–Verre, Sitting, Bench 5500.00

ABC plates, or children's alphabet plates, were most popular from 1780 to 1860, but are still being made. The letters on the plate were meant as teaching aids for children learning to read. The plates were made of pottery, porcelain, metal, or glass.

ABC, Book, Daisy Dell Farm Series, Linen, 7 X 8 3/4 In. 28.50
Bowl, Attached Underplate, Mug, Glass, Enameled Lamb, Boy Blue On Mug 55.00
Bowl, Ironstone, Germany, Hallmarked, 8 In. 68.00
Cereal Set, Panther, Bowl & Plate, Carnival Glass, Marigold, 9 In. 125.00
Cup Plate, Woman, On Horse, Porcelain 55.00
Cup, Humpty–Dumpty, Pottery 6.00
Cup, Raised Alphabet & Florals, Strap Handle, Tin 165.00
Dish, Divided, Little Tommy Tucker, Pottery 7.50
Dish, Dogs & Cat Playing Ball, 6 1/2 X 1 1/2 In. 30.00
Dish, Feeding, Jolly Jinks, 3 Bears, Pottery 48.00
Dish, Feeding, Raggedy Ann, Crooksville 25.00
Mug, Germany, White, Gold Trim, Pottery 25.00
Pitcher, Milk, Child's, Golliwog, Hobby Horse, Girl, Wagon, Dog, Pottery 24.00
Plate, 2 Girls, Leaving House Under Umbrella, Polychrome, Pottery 85.00
Plate, 2 Kittens, Skipping Rope, Hand Signals Alphabet, Pottery, 8 In. 140.00
Plate, 3 Boys, Playing Ball, Pottery 22.00
Plate, 3 Girls, Jumping Rope, Glass 49.00
Plate, Alphabet In Capitals, Floral Rim, Children, Pottery, 5 3/4 In. 125.00
Plate, Alphabet, General Grant Center, Staffordshire 150.00
Plate, Baby Bunting, Pottery .... 20.00 To 44.00
Plate, Bear, Roller Skating, Pottery, 7 1/2 In. 25.00
Plate, Boy & Girl Rolling Hoops, Tin, 3 1/2 In. 45.00
Plate, Branches, Ferns, Cattails, A.Shaw, Burslem, England, 7 1/4 In. 48.00
Plate, Bunnykins, Stoke On Trent Box, Bowl & Mug, 3 Piece 65.00
Plate, Canary, Bullfinch & Goldfinch, Porcelain 65.00
Plate, Cats, Polychrome, Tin, Small 90.00
Plate, Chicken Litho, Tin, Germany 35.00

Plate, Children Playing Skip Rope, Tin, Germany, 7 In.	45.00
Plate, Clock Face, Caboose, Yellow, Glass	17.00
Plate, Clock, Glass, Amber	14.50
Plate, Crusoe Rescues Friday, Glass	58.00
Plate, Donkey, Green Transfer, Pottery, 6 In.	60.00
Plate, Elephant, Figures In Howdah, Waving Flag, Alphabet Border, 6 In.	150.00
Plate, Evening Bathing Scene At Manhattan Beach, Pottery, 7 1/2 In.	85.00
Plate, Feeding, See Saw Margery Daw, Divided, Green, Glass	35.00
Plate, Flowers, Perched Bird, Alphabet Between, England, 7 1/4 In.	55.00
Plate, Fox & Geese, Forest, Meadow, Stream, Polychrome, 8 In.	85.00
Plate, Franklin's Proverbs, Pottery, 5 1/4 In.	45.00
Plate, Girl At Piano, Staffordshire	105.00
Plate, Guardian, Dog Watching Sleeping Girl Under Tree, 7 In.	95.00
Plate, How Glorious Is Our Heavenly King, Staffordshire, 7 In.	55.00
Plate, Humpty–Dumpty, Glass, 8 In.	38.00
Plate, Hunt Scene, Horses, Riders, Lady Sidesaddle & Man, 7 1/2 In.	95.00
Plate, Independence Hall, Glass	95.00
Plate, London Dog Seller, Staffordshire	125.00
Plate, Major General Ulysses S.Grant, Porcelain	250.00
Plate, Margery Daw, Divided, Glass, Amber	40.00
Plate, Newspaper Boy, Polychrome, City Street Scene, 7 In.	85.00
Plate, Niagara From Edge of American Fall, 7 1/2 In.	85.00
Plate, Now I Have A Sheep, Staffordshire	95.00
Plate, Nursery Rhyme, Goofus Glass	40.00
Plate, Organ Grinder, Alphabet Rim, Staffordshire	115.00
Plate, Oriental Hotel, Ocean, People On Beach, Porcelain, 7 1/2 In.	75.00
Plate, Panza & Dapple, Frosted Glass	58.00
Plate, Playing Cricket, Staffordshire	125.00
Plate, Poor Richard's Maxims, Handle Your Tools With Mittens, 6 In.	95.00
Plate, Punch & Judy, Staffordshire, 7 1/2 In.	42.00
Plate, Rabbit, Lamp & Children Seesawing, 3 Sections	39.00
Plate, Robinson Crusoe, Viewing Island, Staffordshire	145.00
Plate, Roosters & Chicks, Pottery, German	45.00
Plate, School Master, Hold Your Hand Out You Rascal, 4 1/2 In.	110.00
Plate, Sign Language, Alphabet Border, Staffordshire	110.00
Plate, Sign Language, Alphabet Center, Dutch Boy & Girl, 8 1/4 In.	125.00
Plate, Sioux Indian Chief, On Horseback, Pottery, 6 3/4 In.	85.00
Plate, Stork, Carnival Glass, Marigold	75.00
Plate, Thousand Eye Pattern, Clock Center, Blue, 6 In.	70.00
Plate, Thousand Eye, Clock Face Center, Blue, Glass	65.00
Plate, Who Killed Cock Robin, Tin, 7 7/8 In.	65.00
Plate, Wild Animals, Leopard, Brown & Green, Pottery	75.00
Plate, Woman Selling Baked Goods, Girl Peeking Into Basket, 6 In.	75.00
Table Set, Menagerie, Clear Glass, Bryce Higbee Co., 1885, 4 Piece	220.00

ABINGDON

Abingdon Pottery was established in 1934 by Raymond E. Bidwell as the Abingdon Sanitary Manufacturing Company. The company made art pottery and other wares. Sixteen varieties of cookie jars are known. The factory ceased production of art pottery in 1950.

ABINGDON, Bookends, Horse	85.00
Bookends, Horsehead	34.00
Bookends, Horsehead, Black & White	50.00
Bowl, No.528, Hibiscus, Green	40.00
Cookie Jar, 3 Bees In Relief	50.00
Cookie Jar, Bear	45.00
Cookie Jar, Bopeep	88.00
Cookie Jar, Choo Choo, Yellow, Black Trim	85.00
Cookie Jar, Clock	40.00 To 45.00
Cookie Jar, Cookie Time	17.50
Cookie Jar, Daisy, Blue Top	35.00
Cookie Jar, Daisy, Blue, Yellow Trim	65.00
Cookie Jar, Granny	75.00 To 90.00
Cookie Jar, Hippo	65.00
Cookie Jar, Humpty–Dumpty	35.00 To 65.00

Cookie Jar, Jack–In–The–Box ....70.00 To 100.00
Cookie Jar, Jack–O'–Lantern .... 50.00 To 55.00
Cookie Jar, Little Miss Muffet .... 75.00 To 95.00
Cookie Jar, Money Bag, White .... 35.00 To 45.00
Cookie Jar, Old Lady 70.00
Cookie Jar, Pineapple .... 35.00 To 50.00
Cookie Jar, Rocking Horse, Pink Trim 95.00
Cookie Jar, Three Bears 50.00
Cookie Jar, Train ....45.00 To 60.00
Figurine, Flamingo, Pink 6.00
Figurine, Goose, White 20.00
Figurine, Scarf Dancer, 14 In. 300.00
Salt & Pepper, Daisy, Blue, Yellow Trim 22.00
Vase, 2 Handles, Blue Glaze, No.522, 8 1/2 In. 14.00
Vase, Daisies, Handles, Gold Trim, 9 In. 25.00
Vase, Design, Gold Trim, 9 In. 25.00
Vase, Stars, Clouds, Star Forms Handle, Blue, Marked 12.00
Wall Pocket, Daisy, Brown & Yellow 55.00
Wall Pocket, Green 12.00
Wall Pocket, Ionic, Matte Raspberry 60.00

Adams china was made by William Adams and Sons of Staffordshire, England. The firm was founded in 1769 and is still working. All types of tablewares and useful wares have been made through the years. Other pieces of Adams will be found listed under Flow Blue.

ADAMS, Bowl, Cries of London, Large 60.00
Creamer, Milkmaids, Cries of London 27.00
Plate, Columbus, Man, With Horse & 2 Indians, Pink, Signed, 8 3/8 In. 75.00
Plate, Merchant, 10 1/2 In. 42.00
Plate, Richard III, 10 1/2 In. 42.00
Plate, U.S.Capitol, Blue, Marked, 10 In. 55.00

The old country store with the crackers in a barrel and a potbellied stove is a symbol of an earlier, less hectic time. The advertisements, containers, and products sold in these stores are now all collectibles. We have tried to list items in the logical places, so large store fixtures will be found under the Architectural category, enameled tin dishes under Graniteware, etc. Listed here are many of the advertising items. Other similar pieces may be found under the product name such as Planters Peanuts.

ADVERTISING, see also Paper
ADVERTISING, Ashtray, Breyers Ice Cream 15.00
Ashtray, Coors 6.00
Ashtray, Dobbs, Hat Shape, Black Amethyst Glass, 2 X 4 In. 35.00
Ashtray, Empire Cream Separator, Brass 55.00
Ashtray, Firestone Tire 7.00
Ashtray, Firestone, International Expo., 1939 .... 27.50
Ashtray, Fleck Bros., Indian, Cast Iron 45.00
Ashtray, Genever Liquers Bols, Gouda 9.00
Ashtray, Goodyear Tire 20.00
Ashtray, Griesdieck Brothers Beer 10.00
Ashtray, H.Fendrick Cigar Co., Brass, Large 15.00
Ashtray, Hat Shape, Lowell Hand Cream, Cobalt Glass 18.00
Ashtray, Johnnie Walker 8.00
Ashtray, Kelly Heavy Duty Tire, Green Glass 25.00
Ashtray, La Fendrich Cigar, Brass, Etched Factory, Cigar, Large 18.00
Ashtray, Lem Beer 35.00
Ashtray, Match Holder, Shenango China, Indian Logo Front 35.00
Ashtray, Providence Ins. Co., Brass 15.00
Ashtray, Provident Life & Accident, Brass, 8 X 4 In. 12.00
Ashtray, RCA, Nipper, Glass 8.00
Ashtray, Seiberling, Patrician, Tire, Green Glass, 3 1/2 In. 12.00

Ashtray, Sullivan's Cigars, Porcelain 21.00
Ashtray, United States Tires Are Good Tires, Treads 35.00
Ashtray, Viceroy, China 10.00
Ashtray, Winston, Metal 8.00
Badge, A.B.C. Parrot Brand Biscuit, 7/8 In. 11.00
Badge, Bullfrog, Silk Fish Line, R.J.Hillinger & Co., Chicago 100.00
Badge, Dr Pepper, Brass, Enameled 61.50
Bag, Newsboy, Colliers 40.00
Banner, Dr.A.C.Daniels Horse Renovator, Cloth, 24 X 12 In. 75.00
Banner, Kendall Oil, 3 Colors, 1940s, 29 X 44 1/2 In. 35.00
Banner, Mayo's Plug Tobacco, Cloth, 60 X 24 In. 75.00
Banner, Superior Northwest Paint, Cloth, Dog, Can, 36 X 48 In. 75.00
Barrel, Jack Daniel's, Wooden, Top, Large 45.00
Barrel, Red Keg, 5 Cents, Push–Type Dispenser Top 1100.00
Beer Foam Scraper, Ruppert, Bakelite 19.00
Bill Holder, Rock Island Plow, Canvas 28.00
Bill Hook, Hilgemeirs Ham, Bacon, Lard 18.00
Bin, Arbuckle Bros., ABC Brand Japan Tea, Slant Top, Rose Logo 330.00
Bin, Beechnut Tobacco, Slant Front, Red & Yellow ....75.00 To 135.00
Bin, Coffee, Lake Shore Coffee, Steamship 1300.00
Bin, Dibbitt's Toffees, Slant Front 695.00
Bin, Game Tobacco, Tin ....275.00 To 425.00
Bin, High–Grade Tea, Picturing Factory, Horses & Buggies 550.00
Bin, Honest Scrap Tobacco, Straight, Cover 1050.00
Bin, Hoosier Boy Coffee 275.00
Bin, Jersey Coffee, Wooden, Red & Black Paint 495.00
Bin, Luxury Coffee, Stenciled, Mustard Paint, 32 X 22 In. 330.00
Bin, Mail Pouch, Picturing Package 850.00
Bin, McClaren's Coffee, Woman Holding Coffee Can 450.00
Bin, Mohican Coffee, Indian 85.00
Bin, Old English Curve Cut Tobacco ....395.00 To 450.00
Bin, Pastime Tobacco 135.00
Bin, Paxton & Gallagher Coffee, Store 450.00
Bin, Plow Boy Tobacco, Cover 895.00
Bin, R.J.Allens, Cigar Maker, Slant Front 85.00
Bin, Sterling Tobacco, Store, Green 150.00
Bin, Sure Shot Tobacco 395.00
Bin, Sweet Cuba Tobacco, Store, Yellow 135.00
Bin, Tennyson Tobacco, Slant Front 85.00
Bin, Wampum Coffee 375.00
Bin, White Lion Tobacco, Slant Front 115.00
Birdhouse, Burger Chef 35.00
Blotter, American Woodworking Lathes, Celluloid 18.00
Blotter, Chase & Sanborn's Seal Brand, Unused, 3 1/4 X 6 In. 2.00
Blotter, Glenmore Whiskey 3.00
Blotter, Kellogg's Whole Wheat Krumbles, 1940s 2.50
Blotter, National Hearse, Picture, Stand–Up, 1950s 8.00
Blotter, Smith Brothers Cough Drops, Red & Black, Unused 5.00
Blotter, Stetson Hats, Cowgirl's Face, 10 Gallon Hat 2.50
Blotter, Wampole's Creo–Terpin Compound, Birds, Orange, Unused 3.00
Blotter, Wampole's Preparations, Zodiac Design, Color 2.00
ADVERTISING, BOOK, see Paper, Book
Booklet, Alka–Seltzer, 25 Popular Songs of '30s, 1937 .... 3.00
Booklet, Clark's ONT Thread, Illustrations, 12 Page, C.1880 .... 8.00
Booklet, Game Book, Dupont, Author, Lynn Bouge Hunt 25.00
Booklet, Hood's Sarsaparilla, Flags of All Nations, 16 Pages 15.00
Booklet, Jerry Jones Jolly Jingles, Black Flag Powder, 1914 .... 1.50
Booklet, Jingle, Burma Shave, 1936 .... 18.00
Booklet, Kellogg's Fairy Tales, Singing Lady, 1930s 7.00
Booklet, Kelloggs, Mother Goose, 1935 .... 5.00
Booklet, New Victor Records, 30 Pages 5.00
Booklet, Niagara Falls Power Co., 16 Pages, 5 X 9 In. 4.50
Booklet, Quaker Oats, Full–O–Pep, Hen Laying, 1937, 31 Pages 10.00
Booklet, Sinclair, Premium, Unused, 1930s 2.50

Booklet, Story of Money, Alka Seltzer, Late 1930s, 16 Pages 5.00
Booklet, Tait's Wire Check Rower, 4 Pages, 1882 Testimonials 7.50
Booklet, Today's Children Story Book, Pillsbury, 1934 .... 15.00
Bookmark, Summit Stoves & Ranges, Floral Design, 1890, 6 In. 4.50
Bootjack, Use Musselman's Bootjack Plug Tobacco, Iron 150.00
   ADVERTISING, BOTTLE, see Bottle
Bowl, Quaker Oats, Flowers, Border, Quaker Man Center 75.00
Bowl, Ralston Purina, Find The Bottom, Rabbit, 6 1/8 In. 45.00
Bowl, Wooden, Merrick Sewing, Black Enameled Flowers, 2 1/2 In. 35.00
   ADVERTISING, BOX, see also Box
Box, Avon Perfection Powdered Cleaner, Unopened 50.00
Box, Bakers Chocolate, Wooden, Brass Handles, 9 X 5 1/2 In. 35.00
Box, Brillian Needles, Cardboard, Red, White, 200 Needles 3.00
Box, Bulldog Tobacco, Wooden, Hinged Lid, Lovell–Buffington 70.00
Box, Cigar, Red Ranger, Wooden, Litho, 2 For 5 Cents, 9 3/4 In. 4.00
Box, Conestoga Scrap 5 Cents, 1926 Stamp, Contents 15.00
Box, Cracker, Metal, Glass Insert, Dane–T–Bits, 10 1/4 In. 18.00
Box, Day & Night Tobacco, 1910 Stamp, Contents 10.00
Box, Deet's Mechanics Soap, Wooden, Label 65.00
Box, Display, Chiclets, Glass Lid, Counter 33.00
Box, Dobbs Hat, Sample, With Hat 20.00
Box, Dr.Thacker's Magnetic Ointment 8.00
Box, Dunham's Coconut, 1920s, Lady Baker, Sample 20.00
Box, Fairy Cigars, 3 For 10 Cents, Brass Nails, Hinges, Wooden 26.00
Box, Ferry Seed, Label, Oak, 6 X 12 X 3 In. 85.00
Box, Gold Dust Twins, Content, C.1930 .... 7.25
Box, Grandpa's Tar Soap, Picture of Grandpa 4.00
Box, Heide's Licorice Gumdrops, Winter Scene, 5 Lbs. 10.00
Box, Jack Sprat Cheese, Wooden, 5 Lbs. 12.00
Box, Jack Sprat Prunes, Wooden 12.00
Box, Jello–O, Wooden, 14 X 7 3/4 X 8 In. 45.00
Box, Jewel Tea Grano, Soap, Unopened, 1 2/2 Lb. 25.00
Box, Kellogg's Toasted Cornflakes, Says Send 10 Cents, Sample 10.00
Box, Knox Hat, Sample, Box With Hat 15.00
Box, Little Buster Brownies Popcorn, 1920s 15.00
Box, Mel–O–Brick Cheese, Wooden, 2 Lb. 5.00
Box, Milky Way, 11 1/2 X 6 1/2 In. 11.00
Box, Mitchell's Kidney Plaster, Lowell, MA, Wood, 1 Drawer 125.00
Box, Mouston, Brass & Glass 80.00
Box, National, Brass & Glass 80.00
Box, Oh Henry, 5 Cents, 11 1/2 X 8 In. 18.00
Box, Pennsylvania Soap Company, Baby 35.00
Box, Peters Target, Shot Shell, No.16 Gauge 24.00
Box, Post Toasties, Cardboard, 1935, Large 8.00
Box, Raymon's Caffeine Tabs, Little Doctor Picture 20.00
Box, Red Ranger Cigar, 2 For 5 Cents, 9 3/4 X 5 1/4 X 4 In. 4.50
Box, Seed, 27 Different Types of Peas, Dovetailed Drawers 700.00
Box, Seed, D.M.Ferry & Co. 55.00
Box, Sheik Prophylactics, Wartime Package, Cardboard 25.00
Box, Tea, Red Moon, Hinged Lid, Hillman, Waterloo, 18 X 11 In. 40.00
Box, U.S.Defiance, No.6 Shot, 12 Gauge 15.00
Box, Uneeda Bakers, Graham Crackers, Wheat, Nabisco, Sample 15.00
Box, Walter Baker Cocoa, Wooden, 3 1/2 X 6 1/2 X 10 1/2 In. 45.00
Box, Wheatena, Contents, Unopened, 1930, Sample 25.00
Box, Willimantic Spool Cotton, Lid Handle, Walnut, 13 In. 115.00

Any lithographed can with a picture is of more value to the collector than a lithographed can with just names.

Box, Wilson's Faultless Biscuits, Cardboard, 12 X 14 X 20 In. 38.00
Box, Worm Powder, Dr.LeGear's, For Hogs, Cardboard 5.00
Bridge Pad, Chesterfield Cigarettes, Beautiful Women, 1930s 15.00
Brush, Crescent Ice Cream 15.00
Bucket, Chicken In The Rough, Tin, 1937 .... 12.00
Bucket, Hiawatha Chewing Tobacco, Wood, Topless Minnehaha 355.00
Bucket, Soilax Soap 35.00
Bucket, Wisconsin Butter Tub Co., Wooden, Cover 32.00
Bust, Chief Watta Pop, Chalkware 95.00
Butter Box, Norge 65.00
Buttonhook, Walk Over Shoes 8.00
Cabinet, Boye Needle–Shuttle, Metal, Some Contents, 1920s 100.00
Cabinet, Brook's, Spool, 2 Drawers, Reverse Glass Insert 265.00
Cabinet, Bus Fuses, Man, With 1930s Car, Tin 65.00
Cabinet, Bus Fuses, Tin, Man With 1930s Car 65.00
Cabinet, Clark's Christmas, Spool, 6 Drawers 650.00
Cabinet, Corticelli, Spool, 2 Drawers, Thread 160.00
Cabinet, Counter, Eversharp Fountain Pens, Holds 64 Pens 200.00
Cabinet, Diamond Dyes, Balloon 575.00
Cabinet, Diamond Dyes, Mansion 500.00
Cabinet, Dutch Boy, Embossed Metal, Sample 27.00
Cabinet, Hardware, Pine, Rotates, 80 Drawers, Octagonal 1200.00
Cabinet, Humphrey's Veterinary Specifics, Oak 995.00
Cabinet, James, Needles, 2 Drawers, Oak, 16 X 8 X 5 1/2 In. 165.00
Cabinet, Peerless Dye, Veiled Dancing Lady, Rolltop Opening 1200.00
Cabinet, Putnam Dye, Tin, With Booklet, 1931 .... 150.00
Cabinet, Ritt Dye, Tin, Late 1930s 100.00
Cabinet, Spool, 3 Drawers, Accessories, Walnut, 9 X 22 In. 100.00
Cabinet, Spool, Belding's Silk, Oak, 3 Drawers, Brass Handles 260.00
Cabinet, Spool, Coats, Labels On All Sides 650.00
Cabinet, Spool, J & P Coats, 4 Drawers 595.00
Cabinet, Spool, Ribbon, 48 Spools, Selector Mechanism, Oak 775.00
Cabinet, Spool, Star Twist, Metal, 4 Drawers 62.50
Can Opener, Pet Milk, Round 8.00
Candy Dish, Baker's Chocolate, Pressed Glass, Engraved 50.00
    ADVERTISING, CANISTER, see Advertising, Tin
Carrying Case, White Rock Beverages, Wood Nymph, Unused 10.00
Carton, Orange Crush 5.00
Case, Brass, Glass, Wood, General Case Co., Salesman's Sample 245.00
Case, Licorice Lozenges, Sommers Bros., Glass Front, 1879 .... 175.00
Case, Parker Lucky Curve Fountain Pen, 1/4 Sawn Oak, Glass 450.00
Case, Timex Quartz, Lighted Logo, 10 1/2 X 14 In. 42.50
Chair, Piedmont Tobacco, Folding 195.00
Change Holder, Clix Razor Blades, Embossed Concave Glass 15.00
    ADVERTISING, CHANGE RECEIVER, see also Advertising, Tip Tray
Change Receiver, Baby Ruth Candy 125.00
Change Receiver, Baby Ruth, Gum Dispenser 90.00
Change Receiver, Black Man, White Servants 12.75
Change Receiver, Cuticura Soap, Glass .... 20.00 To 35.00
Change Receiver, Kool Cigarettes, Rubber 20.00
Change Receiver, Rockford Pocket Watches 37.50
Change Receiver, Rockford Watches 45.00
Change Receiver, Rockford Watches, Rectangular 45.00
Change Receiver, Smoke Goddard's 1872 Cigars, Glass 95.00
Change Receiver, Teaberry Gum, Glass 30.00
Change Receiver, Whitman's Candy, Glass 40.00
Checkerboard, Canadian Club Whiskey, Wooden, 1910, 4 X 8 In. 88.00
Chess Set, Old Crow 1500.00
Chest, Esquire Shoe Care, Logo, Dovetailed, Wooden 35.00
Chest, Razor, Eveready, Wooden, Little 15.00
Cigar Cutter, A.S.Valentine & Sons, Betsy Ross 600.00
Cigar Cutter, African Women In Costume, Iron, 6 X 7 In. 165.00
Cigar Cutter, Barry Lyndon, Windup, Cast Iron, 8 X 6 X 4 In. 240.00
Cigar Cutter, Blackstone, Spring Wound Motor, Counter Top 350.00

Cigar Cutter, Brunhoff Co., Dated 1902	295.00
Cigar Cutter, Cafe Herwig, Cardinal, Knife & Corkscrew	17.50
Cigar Cutter, Dawson's Scotch	12.00
Cigar Cutter, King of Havan Cigars, Pat.Dec.9, '02	12.50
Cigar Cutter, National Fire Hartford, Knife & Nail File	55.00
Cigar Cutter, Pico Grande 5 Cent Cigar, Dated 1902	250.00
Cigar Cutter, Smoke El Gusto Cigars, Pump Handle Shape	295.00
Cigar Cutter, Tom Benton Cigars	295.00
Cigar Cutter, Traiser's Harvard 10 Cent Cigar, Case, C.1900	300.00
Cigarette Roller, Brown & Williamson Tobacco, Metal	12.50
Cigarette Silk, Domestic Animals, Shetland Pony	2.50
Circus Set, Post Toasties, Cardboard	4.00
Clicker, Leichtman's Ice Cream, Yellow & Black	5.00
Clicker, Red Goose Shoe, Full Head	8.00
Cloth, Cream of Wheat, Rastus Doll, Uncut	85.00
Clothespin Bag, Purina	20.00
Clothespin, Maytag Washers	10.00
Coaster, German Beer, Fiberboard, All Different, 1960, 6 Piece	2.00
Coaster, Keubler Beer, Tin	15.00
Coaster, Stegmaiers Beer, 4 1/2 In.	12.00
Coaster, Wiedeman Beer	3.00
ADVERTISING, COFFEE GRINDER, see Coffee Grinder	
Coffeepot, Blanke's Drip Coffeepot, Faust Blend, Devil	345.00
Coin Holder, Lucky Mo–Jo	8.00
Container, Bull Meat Brand Flour, Cardboard, Round, 18 In.	75.00
Container, Figural, Frankenstein, Colgate–Palmolive	40.00
Container, Rheingold Beer, Metal, 10 X 6 In.	20.00
Cookie Cutter, Robin Hood Flour, Set of 4	25.00
Cookie Cutter, The Muffin Man	5.00
Cooler, Moxie Bottle, 36 In.	825.00
Corkscrew, Keen Kutter, Metal, Wood	22.00
Creamer, Kellogg Correct Cereal	17.50
Creamer, Lenick's Dairy, Meadow Gold, Individual	12.50
Creamer, Meadow Gold	8.00
Creamer, Sanitary Dairy, Ft.Dodge, Iowa, Miniature	7.50
Crock, Apple Butter, Heinz, Labels	300.00
Crock, Heinz, Incised Design On Front	225.00
Crowbar, Beechnut Gum, Cast Iron	40.00
Crumb Tray, & Scraper, Steinklein Furniture, Brass, 1900s	35.00
Cuff Links, Fram Filter	15.00
Cuff Links, Greyhound Bus	5.00
Cuff Links, Lucky Strike Cigarettes, 1930s	20.00 To 100.00
Cup & Saucer, House of Pancakes, Lamppost Logo On Both	20.00
Cup & Saucer, Johnston Hot Chocolate, 1930s	15.00
Cup, Colgate Dental Cream, Captain Kangaroo, Blue, 1961	11.00
Cup, Collapsible, Worcester Salt, Cover	10.00
Cup, Gerber Baby Food, Babies Are Our Business, Pair	10.00
Cup, McDonald, Ronald McDonald Head Shape	6.00
Cup, Measuring, Cream Dove Peanut Butter, Clear	30.00
Cup, Measuring, Milk Glass, Snowflake, 4 Cups	95.00
Cup, Measuring, Urban Liberty Flour, Yellow	75.00
Cup, Ovaltine, Uncle Wiggily, Porcelain	35.00
Cup, Paper, Heinz, Pickle Picture, Miniature	20.00
Cup, Texaco, Red Star Logo, On Green Flag, Mayer China	20.00
Cup, Uncle Wiggily Ovaltine, 1924	65.00
Cuspidor, Redskin Brand Chewing Tobaacco, Chief, Headdress	75.00
Cylinder, Dr.LeGear's Chick Diarrhoea Tablet, Cardboard, 4 In.	3.00
Decal Set, Li'L Abner, Orange Crush, 1950, Set of 8	10.00
Decal, Old Dutch Cleanser, Original Envelope, 1937	7.50
Decal, Window, Shell, 1920s	2.00
Decanter, Burgie, Man, In Black & White, Hat Cover, 1971, 10 In.	50.00
Decanter, Hamm, Bear Standing At Bar, Head Cover, 1973, 11 In.	50.00
Desk Pen, Match Holder & Ashtray, Purina Chow	65.00
Dial Chart, Boye Needles, Shuttles, Bobbins, Tin	50.00

Dial, Ruhl's Bread, Help Kids With Arithmetic, 8 In. 14.00
Dice, 7–Up, Ivory 16.00
Dice, Poker, Cream of The Barley 15.00
Dispenser, Alka Seltzer, Marked 100.00
Dispenser, Bromo–Seltzer, Cobalt Blue Bottle & Base, Stand 150.00
Dispenser, Cherry Smash 1900.00
Dispenser, Dixie Cups, Chrome & Glass, Scroll Design 27.50
Dispenser, Fan–Jaz Drink, 5 Cents ....*Illus* 2750.00
Dispenser, Green River Soda, Ceramic, Yellow & Green 425.00
Dispenser, Heinz, Barrel On Glass Base 300.00
Dispenser, Hires Syrup 400.00
Dispenser, Johnston's Hot Chocolate 75.00
Dispenser, Lash's Orangeade, C.1920 .... 395.00
Dispenser, Magnus California Concordia Punch, C.1920 .... 195.00
Dispenser, Mission Orange, Counter Top 145.00
Dispenser, Mission Orange, Pink, Black Base 195.00
Dispenser, Orange Crush 525.00
Dispenser, Razor Blade, Hand Painted Hunter, Trenton Pottery 17.00
Dispenser, Straw, Hires 750.00
Dispenser, Ward's Lemon Crush ....*Illus* 500.00
Dispenser, Ward's Orange Crush ....*Illus* 500.00
Door Pull, Kist, With Handle 45.00
Door Push, Emerson Cigar 35.00
Door Push, Junge's Bread, 1930s 20.00
Door Push, Perry's Beverage 38.00
Door Push, Pulver Chewing Gum, Porcelain 85.00
Door Push, Seanate Beer 70.00
Door Push, Swanson Bread 17.50
Door Push, Vicks, Porcelain 100.00
Door, Screen, Ideal Bread 100.00
Egg Separator, South Bend Range, Tin 8.00
Fan, 7–Up, Bathing Beauty 12.00
Fan, Coon Chicken Inn 20.00
Fan, Dingman Soap, Palette Shape 10.00
Fan, Moxie, Girl & Soda Jerk, Cardboard 36.50
Fan, Pooler's Clothing Store, Pig Design, 3 Part, C.1929 .... 7.50
Figure, Bartender, Holding Mugs of Schmidt's Beer, 12 In. 65.00
Figure, Bathtub & Sink, Porcelain, Iron, S M Co., 6 In. 265.00
Figurine, Dog, Nipper, RCA, Papier–Mache, 3 Ft. 550.00
Figurine, 7–Up Bottle, 1953, 5 X 9 In. 5.00
Figurine, Black & White Scotch, Electric, Dogs Barking 75.00
Figurine, Dog, Nipper, Papier–Mache, 18 In. 165.00

Advertising, Dispenser,
Ward's Lemon Crush

Advertising, Dispenser,
Fan–Jaz Drink, 5 Cents

Advertising, Dispenser,
Ward's Orange Crush

Figurine, Dog, RCA, Glass Eyes, Tin, 17 1/2 In.	500.00
Figurine, Dog, Scotties, Buchanan's Scotch, 6 1/2 X 5 1/4 In.	49.00
Figurine, Dr.Johnson, Gesso Covered Papier–Mache, 1910	330.00
Figurine, Happy Prospector, Safe Co., Insurance, Spelter, 9 In.	13.00
Figurine, Heidelberg Beer, Student Prince, Chalkware, 1940s	85.00
Figurine, Hennessey Cognac, St.Bernard, Keg, Chalkware, 11 In.	90.00
Figurine, Horsehead, Johnson Halters, Life–Size	450.00
Figurine, Pig, Moorman Feeds, Metal, Dated 1957, Small	8.00
Figurine, Professor, Scroll, Teacher's Scotch Whiskey, 13 In.	40.00
Figurine, St.Bernard, Keg, Hennessy Cognac, Chalkware, 11 In.	50.00
Figurine, Windmill, Heineken Beer, Large	150.00
Flask, Pine Cone Gin, Kidney, Bladder & Rheumatic, Cork, 1906	35.00
Fly Swatter, Socony, Litho Tin, Fly Swatter For Your Car	35.00
Fork, Childs, Little Dutch Milk Maid, Maid Scene On Handle	35.00
Fork, McDonald, Ronald McDonald Figure Handle	2.00
Fork, Pickle, Heinz, Long	30.00
Goblet, Meorlein's Cincinnati Lager Beer, Good Luck	45.00
Gum Stand, Teaberry, Vaseline	44.00
Handkerchief, Coor's Beer, Square, 20 In.	4.50
Holder, Broom, Hanging, Wire	85.00
Holder, Ice–Cream Cones, Glass Sides, Metal Back, Wall Mount	85.00
Holder, Pocket Watch, Baldwin Locomotive Works, Engine Shape	325.00
Holder, Sucker, Morse's Pure Pops, Dog	65.00
Holder, Wall, Old Dutch Cleanser, Metal	30.00
Humidor, Figural, Man Drinking Gaussig Pilsner, Bisque	155.00
Humidor, Prince Albert, Glass	25.00
Ice Chest, Dr Pepper, Metal, Green	38.00
Jar, Bulldog Rubbers, Full Box	10.00
Jar, Colgan's Gum, Paper Label	19.00
Jar, Horlick's Malt, Stoneware, Tin Lid	32.00
Jar, Kimball Tobacco, Rochester, N.Y., Amber	36.00
Jar, Kisseme Gum, Purple Glass	110.00
Jar, Lutter Cough Drop, Glass, 11 1/2 In.	150.00
Jar, Mayonnaise Mixer, Wesson Oil, Directions On Side	20.00
Jar, Virol, A Preparation of Bone Marrow, Stoneware, 5 In.	12.00
Jar, W & S Cough Drops, Pressed Glass	155.00
Keg, Dupont Powder, With Hunting Dog, 1897	75.00
Knife, Anheuser–Busch, Pocket	190.00
Knife, City Ice & Fuel Co., Clinton, Iowa, Wooden Handle, 1900	8.50
Knife, Firestone, Bone & Silver Inlay, Pocket	38.00
Knife, Grain Belt Beer, Plastic	3.00
Knife, Gulf Gas	13.00
Knife, Johnson Wax, Pocket	24.00
Knife, Star Brand Shoes	75.00
Knife, Traveler's Insurance Co., Pocket	28.00
Knife, Westinghouse Coolers, Embossed, Pocket	30.00
Label, Asbury Park, 1979, 12 Oz.	.50
Label, Ballantine Bicentennial, 3 Ring Sign, Falstaff	.75
Label, Battle of Germantown, 12 Oz.	1.00
Label, Black Label Non–Alcoholic	.75
Label, Blatz Low Alcohol, 12 Oz.	.50
Label, Bock, 12 Oz.	.75
Label, Buffalo Ammonia, Arched Top, 3 1/2 X 5 1/2 In.	3.00
Label, Cora, Tobacco, 1890s, 14 X 7 In.	20.00
Label, Declaration of Independence, 12 Oz.	.50
Label, Dixie Worlds Expo, 1984, 12 Oz.	.75
Label, Fischer's Beer, 12 Oz.	.50
Label, Golden Heart, Citrus, Sanford	11.00
Label, Hamm's Special Light, 12 Oz.	.50
Label, Happy New Year, 1979, 12 Oz.	.50
Label, Heritagefest, 1980, 12 Oz.	.50
Label, Iron City Beer, Pittsburgh Bicentennial, 1787–1987	.50
Label, Jungle River, Citrus, Napier, Vero Beach	6.00
Label, Kentucky Derby, 1984, 12 Oz.	.75

Label, Mardi Gras, 1984, 12 Oz. .... .75
Label, Meister Brau Draft, 12 Oz. 1.00
Label, Mug, Dinkel Acker Beer, Glass, Label, 13 Oz. 4.00
Label, Oktoberfest, 1979, 12 Oz. .... .50
Label, Old Bohemian Light, 12 Oz. .... .50
Label, Old Dutch Beer, Pittsburg .... .50
Label, Persian Apple, White Persian Cat, Red Ground 100.00
Label, Real Ripe, Citrus, Leesburg 2.00
Label, Sarsaparilla, A Pure Beverage, Drug Act of 1906 .... .50
Label, Schlitz 1980 Olympic Games .... .50
Label, St.Patrick's Day, 1980, 12 Oz. .... .50
Label, Stroh's Light Liberty, 1886–1986 .... .75
Label, Sunshine Fruits, Miami–Burdines 6.00
Label, Wise Bird, Citrus, Winter Garden 6.00
Lamp, Charlie The Tuna 50.00
Lamp, Elsie The Cow & Baby 95.00
Lamp, Student, Brass, Budweiser On Shade 75.00
Lamp, Winchester Rubber Enclosed Mine Safety Light, 3 Cells 45.00
Leaflet, Victor Records By Galli–Curci, 11–24–16, 4 Pages 2.00
Light Pull, Canadian Club Cigar 5.00
Luggage Tag, McDonald 6.50
ADVERTISING, LUNCH BOX, see Lunch Box
Lunch Pail, Nigger Hair Tobacco, Brown 195.00
Match Box, Bartel's Syracuse Beer, Wooden 20.00
Match Holder, DeLaval, Tin 47.00
Match Holder, Juicy Fruit Gum, Wall 100.00
Match Holder, Kool 20.00
Match Safe, Somers Bros., Man Fishing In Rain, Late 1800s 15.00
Match Safe, Valblatz Brewery 13.00
Match Safe, Welch's Overalls, Sample 75.00
Measure, Fleet Buffered Laxative, Marked Spoons, Ounces, Glass 6.00
Measure, Foot, Sliding, Dr.Scholls 35.00
Memo Book, Pocket, Koehler's Grocery, Black Cardboard 15.00
Menu Holder, Pioneer Ice Cream, Celluloid Base, 2 1/2 In. 15.00
Menu Sign, Cheer–Up, Tin, 1930s, 24 X 10 In. 95.00
Menu, Coon Chicken Inn, 12 In. 65.00

Pocket mirrors range in size from 1 1/2 to 5 inches in diameter.
Most of these mirrors were given away as advertising promotions.

Mirror, Angelus Marshmallow, Winged Girl, Oval, Pocket 40.00
Mirror, Angelus Marshmallows, Oval, Pocket 45.00
Mirror, Applegarths Oysters, Boston, Pocket, 3 1/2 In. 15.00
Mirror, Atlanta Paper Co., Atlanta, Ga., Pocket 14.00
Mirror, Atlantic Journal, Covers Dixie Like Dew, Pocket 5.00
Mirror, B.J.Milleysack Cigars & Tobacco, Pocket 35.00
Mirror, Bartlett Hardware, Hibbard, Spencer, Pocket 25.00
Mirror, Bell Coffee, Pocket 30.00
Mirror, Bennett's Vaudeville, Celluloid, Pocket 25.00
Mirror, Boot & Shoe Worker's Union, Pocket 20.00
Mirror, Boot & Shoe Workers Union, Pocket, Oval, 2 3/4 In. 30.00
Mirror, Campbell's Soup, Can Picture At 10 Cents, Pocket 95.00
Mirror, Casey's Tool Works, Pocket 40.00
Mirror, Celluloid Advertising Specialties, Thermometer 10.00
Mirror, Ceresota Flour, Boy Cutting Bread, Pocket, 2 In. 40.00
Mirror, Colby's Clothing House, Taunton, Mass., 1876, Pocket 30.00
Mirror, Columbia Tool Steel, Pocket 20.00
Mirror, Copper Clad Stoves, Pocket 40.00
Mirror, Decatur Coffin Co., Birthstones of Months, Pocket 30.00
Mirror, Dental Supply, 3 1/4 In. 40.00
Mirror, Dixie Tailoring, Statue of Liberty, Pocket 85.00
Mirror, Dueber Watch Co., Pocket 45.00
Mirror, Duffy's Pure Malt Whiskey, Picture of Chemist, Pocket 18.00
Mirror, Eat Checkers, Pocket 60.00
Mirror, G & M Lines, Grand Rapids, Oval, 2 3/4 In. 30.00

Mirror, G & M Lines, Red & Blue, On White, Oval, Pocket	27.50
Mirror, Gaier Mirror Hats, Celluloid, 2 In.	22.00
Mirror, Gem Razor, Man Shaving, Baby, Display	425.00
Mirror, Ghirardelli's Chocolate, Pocket	55.00
Mirror, Golden Pheasant Inn Co., Pocket, Oval, 2 3/4 In.	19.00
Mirror, Goodrich Sewing Machines, Pocket ....23.50 To 37.00	
Mirror, Haines Shoes, Pocket	18.00
Mirror, Hand, Red Jacket Shaft, Calumet, Mich., Brass, Miniature	45.00
Mirror, Heineken Beer, Green Letters, Framed, 13 1/2 X 20 In.	62.00
Mirror, Henry Siegel Co., Boston, Gold Finish, 2 In.	30.00
Mirror, J & P Coates, Square, Pocket	12.50
Mirror, John Morrell, Pocket	12.00
Mirror, Joplin Bank, Silver Plated, Child's, Hand	12.50
Mirror, Kansas Expansion Flour, Flower, 2 1/4 In.	16.00
Mirror, Kansas Expansion Flour, Sunflower, 2 1/4 In.	12.00
Mirror, Keystone State Normal School Basketball Team, Pocket	9.00
Mirror, Lady Laurel Stoves, Pocket	155.00
Mirror, Lava Soap, Pocket	30.00
Mirror, Liberty State Bank, Bloomington, Illinois, Pocket	5.00
Mirror, Lucky Tiger Cures Dandruff, Girl, Hugs Tiger, Pocket	75.00
Mirror, Maccabees Insurance Co., 2 In.	30.00
Mirror, Maryland Casualty Insurance, Round, 1961	12.00
Mirror, Maryland Casualty, Pocket	22.00
Mirror, Mascot Tobacco, Pocket ....38.00 To 50.00	
Mirror, Menz Lumber Co., Minneapolis, Pocket	15.00
Mirror, Minneapolis Dry Goods Co., Pocket	20.00
Mirror, Morton Salt	12.00
Mirror, Nature's Remedy, Pocket	30.00
Mirror, Oliver Chilled Plow Works, 3 In.	70.00
Mirror, Paul Vallette Swiss Watches of Quality, Pocket	28.00
Mirror, Pennisular Stoves & Ranges, Factory Scene, Pocket	75.00
Mirror, Red Seal Lye, Pocket	28.00
Mirror, Reed Jewelry Co., Poplar Bluff, Mo., Pocket	17.00
Mirror, Reed Jewelry Company, Pocket	9.00
Mirror, Remington Typewriter, Enameled, 3 1/2 In.Diam.	65.00
Mirror, Rexal, Beveled, 4 1/2 In.	38.00
Mirror, Rock Island, Ill.Stove Co., Pocket, 1 3/4 In.	12.00
Mirror, Roman Meal Bread, Pocket ....9.00 To 17.00	
Mirror, Rosell's Zizelbread, Pre–Nabisco, Pocket	22.00
Mirror, Schaefer Pianos, Pocket	45.00
Mirror, Schoettelkotte Bros., 1940s Girl	11.00
Mirror, Sharples Separators, Pocket	45.00
Mirror, Smith Piano Co., Milwaukee, Pocket, 2 1/4 In.	21.00
Mirror, Socony Motor Gasoline, Pocket	35.00
Mirror, Socony, Pocket	35.00
Mirror, St. Joseph Steamship Line, Red, Blue, White, Pocket	28.00
Mirror, Star Soap, Pocket	8.00
Mirror, Travelers Insurance, Pocket	35.00
Mirror, Tujague Restaurant, New Orleans, Pocket	16.50
Mirror, Vess Cola, Pocket ....7.00 To 11.00	
Mirror, W.I.Hartenstine Watchmaker & Jeweler, Pocket	24.00
Mirror, Whirlpool Appliances, Pocket	7.00
Mirror, Whirlpool Washer, Pocket	11.00
Mirror, White Pearl Macaroni, Pocket	18.00
Mirror, Yellow Cab, 1920s, Pocket	85.00
Mirror, Zizel Bread, Rosen's Pure Rye, Pocket, 2 In.	25.00
Mixing Bowl, Diamond Salt, Depression Glass, Ornate Handles	15.00
Money Clip, Champion Sparkplug, Figural	16.00
Money Clip, Kodak Camera, With Knife & File, Silver Plate	8.00
Money, Poll Parrott Shoe, 10, 25 & 50 Cent, $1, 4 Piece	13.00
Movie, Flip, Babe Ruth, Quaker Oats Premium, 1934	100.00
Mug, Armour Vigoral, Carnations, China	15.00
Mug, Arrow Beer, Stoneware	15.00

Mug, Bismarck Hotel–Restaurant, Chicago, Monk Transfer, Blue 85.00
Mug, Bosco, Bear, 1950s 18.00
Mug, Budweiser Clydesdale 20.00
Mug, Chase & Sanborn 10.00
Mug, Cream of Wheat, Rastus Picture 25.00
Mug, Dad's Root Beer, Barrel Shape 25.00
Mug, Dad's Root Beer, Glass 25.00
Mug, Doe–Wah–Jack, Handle, Oak 75.00
Mug, Doe–Wah–Jack, Standing Indian 125.00
Mug, Elsie, Borden Co. 20.00
Mug, Good–Cheer Cigars, Tin 85.00
Mug, Henn Gabler Old Timers, Chicago 295.00
Mug, Hires, Branch Handle 250.00
Mug, Howel's Root Beer 20.00
Mug, Nestle Cocoa, Etched Maps of The World 10.00
Mug, Nestle's Quick 3.00
Mug, Pabst Beer, Elves 35.00
Mug, Quaker Oats 15.00
Mug, Richardson's Root Beer, Embossed 18.00
Mug, Royal Brewing Co., Pre–Prohibition 65.00
Mug, Schlitz Beer, Stoneware, Gray, Blue 125.00
Mug, Stang Sandusky Brewery, Scene 175.00
Mug, Sterns Root Beer, Blue & White Bands, Blue Printing 185.00
Mug, Tony Tiger 6.00
Mug, Weger's Brewery, Ceramic 60.00
Napkin Holder, 4 Roses, With Napkins 15.00
Needle Case, Lydia Pinkham, Match Book Style, 5 Threads 3.50
Oilcan, Maytag 12.00
Opener, Carton, Beechnut Gum, Cast Iron, 13 In. 55.00
Opener, Cigar Box, Arion Cigar, Pat.12/7/97 .... 17.50
Opener, Cigar Box, Coony Bayer Cigar Co., Pat.Pending 25.00
Opener, Cigar Box, Donatus Solingen, Brass, Western Germany 25.00
Opener, Cigar Box, Front Rank Furnace 9.00
Opener, Cigar Box, Geo.L.Schulz, Stag Horn Handle 25.00
Opener, Cigar Box, Hamilton Harris & Co, Bottle Opener 8.50
Opener, Cigar Box, La Saramita Cigars, Serrated Edge 15.00
Opener, Cigar Box, Red Lion 5 Cent Cigar, Folding Blade 22.50
Opener, Cigar Box, U.S.Club House, The Nations Choice, Hammer 27.50
Package, Nipples, For Baby Bottles, Sessions, 9 1/2 X 11 In. 5.00
Pail, 'Twas The Night Before Christmas 59.00
Pail, After Glow Coffee, Handle, 4 Lb. 45.00
Pail, Aladdin, Fire Truck, Firemen At Fire 35.00
Pail, Armour's Peanut Butter 35.00
Pail, Bagdad Coffee 100.00
Pail, Brotherhood Tobacco 110.00
Pail, Buffalo Peanut Butter, 20 Lb. 195.00
Pail, Campbell's Coffee, Lid, Bail, 4 Lb. 45.00
Pail, Candy, Lovell & Coval, Peter Rabbit 125.00
Pail, Creme Dove Peanut Butter, 1 Lb. 50.00
Pail, Crystal Flake Shortening, Red, White, Blue, Gold, 8 Lb. 30.00
Pail, Delmonico Coffee 35.00
Pail, Dutch Boy Paint 8.00
Pail, Eight Brothers Tobacco 125.00
Pail, French Opera Coffee 35.00
Pail, George Washington Tobacco 100.00
Pail, Iten Biscuit Co., Omaha, Child's, Animals 68.00
Pail, Jack & Jill Peanut Butter, Red, White, Blue, 1 Lb. 225.00
Pail, Just Suits Tobacco 75.00
Pail, Lighthouse Peanut Butter, 1 Lb. 110.00
Pail, Maverick Coffee 28.00
Pail, Maxi–Mum Peanut Butter, 1 Lb. 200.00
Pail, Meadow Sweet Peanut Butter, 1 Lb. 150.00
Pail, Mica Axle Grease, Standard Oil Co., Red Letters, Sample 35.00
Pail, Monarch Teenie Weenie Peanut Butter, 10 Oz. .... 60.00 To 65.00

> Tin signs and cans will fade from the ultraviolet rays coming in a window or from a fluorescent light. Plexiglass UF-1 or UF-3 will cover the window and keep the rays away from your collection. There are also plastic sleeves to cover fluorescent tubes.

Pail, Monsson Peanut Butter 25.00
Pail, Morris Supreme Peanut Butter, 1 Lb. 250.00
Pail, Mosemann's Peanut Butter, Animals, 1 Lb. ....85.00 To 100.00
Pail, Mt.Cross Coffee, 10 Lb. 100.00
Pail, Nigger Hair Tobacco, Tin 175.00
Pail, Nigger Hair Tobacco, Yellow 245.00
Pail, Nursery Candies Expressly For Little Folks 50.00
Pail, Ojibwa Tobacco .... 195.00 To 200.00
Pail, Old Squire 55.00
Pail, Ox Heart Peanut Butter, 1 Lb. 50.00
Pail, Peerless Tobacco 125.00
Pail, Peter Rabbit 60.00
Pail, Peter Rabbit Peanut Butter 150.00
Pail, Prairie Queen Baking Powder 135.00
Pail, Red Seal Peanut Butter, 1 Lb. 25.00
Pail, Schoolboy Peanut Butter 65.00
Pail, Southern Star Pure Lard, 8 Lb. 10.00
Pail, Sultana Peanut Butter, A.& P., Orange, 1 Lb. 30.00
Pail, Sultana Peanut Butter, Dogs & Rabbits, Blue 85.00
Pail, Sunny Boy Peanut Butter, Red & White, 1 Lb. 68.00
Pail, Sweet Girl Peanut Butter, 1 Lb. 450.00
Pail, Swift's Silverleaf Lard, Cover, 8 Lb. 8.00
Pail, Uncle Wiggly Peanut Butter, 1 Lb. 400.00
Pail, Union Leader Cut Plug 75.00
Pail, Veribest Peanut Butter, 1 Lb. 100.00
Pail, Winner Tobacco 75.00
Pail, Wishbone Coffee, 4 Lb. .... 45.00 To 55.00
Pail, Yacht Club Peanut Butter, 1 Lb. 250.00
Pail, Yorkshire Farm Peanut Butter, 1 Lb. 325.00
Pan, Cake, Swans Down 10.00
Pan, Frying, Mt.Penn Stoves & Ranges, Miniature, 2 1/2 In. 15.00
Pastry Cutter, Calumet 8.00
Patch, Pocket, Borden's Milk & Ice Cream, Elsie's Picture 15.00
Pencil Box, Good Luck The Winchester Store 85.00
Pencil Box, Red Goose Shoes, Tube .... 50.00 To 75.00
Pencil Box, Television Future Electrical Eyes .... 25.00 To 35.00
Pencil Sharpener, Bakers Chocolate 35.00
Pencil, Mechanical, Borden's, Milk Bottle On Top 20.00
Pencil, Mechanical, Indian Motorcycle 30.00
Pendant, Elsie The Cow, Plastic 2.00
Penny Holder, Dr.Drake's Cough Syrup 10.00
Pill Case, McKesson Robbins, Salesman's Sample, 1800s 35.00
Pin & Earrings, Reddi–Kilowatt, Original Card 30.00
Pin Tray, Souvenir Krohn Mdse.Co., Chamois, Missouri 28.00
Pin, Barber Bill Happyland Barber Shop, Boy, Horse 20.00
Pin, Bond Bread Brings You Sunshine 3.00
Pin, Bond Bread, Brings You Sunshine Vitamin D 3.00

14

Pin, Bucher & Gibbs Imperial Plows 25.00
Pin, Cub Shoe Polish, Red, Tin 42.00
Pin, Elsie The Cow, Original Display Card, 2 In. 20.00
Pin, Figural, Crab, Goes Good With National Beer, 2 In. 10.00
Pin, Ford, 1932, 3/4 In. 8.00
Pin, Gamossi Kid Clu, Boy In Western Garb 10.00
Pin, GE Radio, Brass, Enameled 5.00
Pin, Great Minneapolis Line, Tractor 30.00
Pin, Hassan Cigarettes, Mutt & Jeff 10.00
Pin, Let's Go To Luna Park, Large Comic 25.00
Pin, Miller's High Life Beer, Celluloid Attached Lady 30.00
Pin, Parlin & Orendorff Farm Implements, Lapel 30.00
Pin, Ralston Straight Shooters, Wash Portrait 6.00
Pin, Ritz Crackers, Yellow, Red, White & Blue, 7/8 In. 5.00
Pin, Shamrock, Schlitz, Plastic 4.00
Pin, Sharples Separator 15.00
Pin, Ski-U-Mah, Football Player, 1906 .... 30.00
Pin, Spiegel's Ice Cream Soda, Plankton Drug Store, 1899 .... 50.00
Pin, St.Paul Curling & Skating Club, 1915 .... 15.00
Pin, Stahl's Puncture Proof Tires, Quincy, Illinois, Lapel 30.00
Pin, Staver & Abbott Mfg.Co., Old Buggy, Lapel 30.00
Pin, Straight Shooters, Jane Mix, Ralston 10.00
Pin, Uncle Jerry's Pancake Flour, New England, Lapel 50.00
Pitcher, Armour & Co., Chicago, Ironstone 50.00
Pitcher, Jack Daniels Whiskey, Stoneware 22.00
Pitcher, Seagram's VO, Cobalt Blue .... 10.00 To 20.00
Plate, Coon Chicken Inn, 9 3/4 In. 150.00
Plate, Ojibway Indian Brave Picture, Greek American Fruit Co. 40.00
Plate, Union Pacific Tea Co., Tin Litho, Dated 1907, 7 1/2 In. 50.00
Postcard, Shredded Wheat, Niagara Falls, Factory 4.00
Pot Scraper, Junket 145.00
Pot Scraper, Penn Stoves 35.00
Powder Keg, Wooden, Oliver M.Whipple Co., 25 Lb. 99.00
Print, Orange Crush, Soda Fountain, Rockwell, 1940, 11 X 14 In. 35.00
Punchboard, Benrus Watches, of Famous Airlines, 1940s, Unused 10.00
Punchboard, Great Smokes, Round, 10 In. 20.00
Puppet, Dancing Bear, Capt.Kangaroo, Oscar Mayer Premium, 1966 .... 20.00
Puzzle, Chase & Sanborn Teas, 4 Girls Picking Tea, 8 X 6 In. 30.00
Puzzle, Dutch Masters Cigars, Christmas 25.00
Puzzle, Hood's Sarsaparilla Cures, Man, Wagon, Horses, 15 In. 25.00
Puzzle, Hood's Sarsaparilla, Rainy Day 90.00
Puzzle, Singer, Man, Wagon, Treadle Machine, Buffalo Pulled 25.00
Puzzle, Sundrop Cola, Children On Picnic, 12 X 8 In. 10.00
Rack, Campbell's Soup Can, 4 Shelves, Tin 150.00
Rack, Display, Beech-Nut Gum, 2 Shelves, Metal, 8 X 8 X 12 In. 45.00
Rack, Grocery Store Bag, 9 Graduated Sections, With Bags 90.00
Rack, Prince Albert, Pocket, Tin 20.00
Rack, St.Joseph Aspirin, Counter Top 75.00
Rack, Wrigley's Gum, Celluloid Moon Face 395.00
Rattle, Baby's, Heinz 57 Baby Foods 15.00
Ribbon, Utica Daily Press, Excursion, July 17, 1885, Silk, 6 In. 3.00
Richmond Cigarettes, Tin, Self-Framed, 1900, 28 X 22 In. 1250.00
Ring, Post Toastie, Mama, Cellophane Wrappers, 1949 .... 25.00
Ring, Tom Corbett Space Cadet, Kellogg, Thunderceptor Picture 20.00
Roller, Dennison's Adhesive Tape, Wooden, Tin, Dated 1910 .... 10.00
Ruler, Baby Bear Bread, 12 In. 8.00
Ruler, Banbury Baking Co., Penbrook, Pa., 12 In. 1.50
Ruler, Pevely Milk, 6 In. 4.00
Sack, Feed, Rooster Design, White 8.00
Sack, Fisher's Cake Flour, Chef, 2 Lbs. 35.00
Sack, Flour, Jones Dairy Farm, 1 Lb. 4.00
Sack, Flour, Log Cabin Grits, Cabin, With Smoking Chimney 7.00
Sack, Flour, Log Cabin, Paper 10.00
Sack, Flour, Southern Best, Logo 3.50

Sack, Flour, Temptation, Plate of Warm Biscuits, Logo	3.50
Sack, Flour, Texas Pioneer, U.S.Pat.Office 1906, 2 Lbs.	2.50
Sack, Flour, Town Crier, Cloth, 49 Lbs.	30.00
Sack, Popps Egg Mash, 100 Lb.	30.00
Sack, Texas Pioneer Flour, Paper, Man In Wreath, 9 X 6 1/2 In.	2.50
Sadiron, Grand Union Tea Co., 1897	95.00
Salt & Pepper, Ball Perfect Mason, Round	14.00
Salt & Pepper, Budweiser Beer, Original Box	9.50
Salt & Pepper, Esslinger, Miniature	25.00
Salt & Pepper, Esso, Figural, Gas Pumps	15.00
Salt & Pepper, Ft.Pitt Beer	15.00
Salt & Pepper, GE Refrigerator, Opaque Glass, Original Top	25.00
Salt & Pepper, Nipper	18.00 To 25.00
Salt & Pepper, Old Export Beer	35.00
Salt & Pepper, Schlitz Beer, Figural, Box	10.00
Salt & Pepper, Sinclair Gas Pump	12.50
ADVERTISING, SCALE, see Scale	
Scoop, French Chef, Lindy, Nebr., Celluloid	4.00
Scoop, Ice Cream, Probst, Aluminum	10.00
Scoop, Measuring, C.D.Kenny Coffee, Embossed	15.00
Scraper, Car Windshield, Firestone	10.00
Scraper, Foam, Ober Bros., Pittsburg Brewing	45.00
Screwdriver, Old Farm Machinery	15.00
Sharpener, Knife, Sears, Roebucks & Co.	15.00
Sharpener, Pencil, Baker's Chocolate Lady	18.00
Sheet Music, Bromo Seltzer, C.1900	12.00
Sheet Music, Moxie Song, Moxie Man Cover, 1921	15.00
Shelf Grabber, Octagon Soap, On Handle & Paper Label	48.00
Shoehorn, Bon Ton Shoe Store	7.00
Shoehorn, Red Goose, Picture	10.00
Shot Glass, Belle of Kentucky 1869 Bourbon, Etched	27.50
Shot Glass, Hayner Beer, Etched	9.00
Shot Glass, Oklahoma Vinegar Co., Ft.Smith, Ark., Etched, 6 In.	22.00
Sign, 7–Up, Silver & Red, Canada, 7 X 30 In.	35.00
Sign, 7–Up, Tin, 19 X 54 In.	50.00
Sign, A.B.C.Beer, Seminude Riding Eagle, 1900, 27 X 20 In.	650.00
Sign, ABC Baking Powder, Tin, 1950s, 12 X 28 In.	25.00
Sign, Admiration Cigar, With Lady, Tin, 7 1/2 X 5 1/2 In.	130.00
Sign, Advance Thresher, Knight, Flag, Tin, 1900, 26 X 18 In.	550.00
Sign, All Jack's Cigarettes, Sheet Metal, 9 3/4 X 3 3/4 In.	40.00
Sign, American Brewing Co., Tin, Self–Framed, 15 X 19 1/2 In.	200.00
Sign, American Red Cross, R.Williams, Cardboard, 13 X 21 In.	15.00
Sign, Anheuser–Busch, Indians On Raft, Litho, Framed, 15 X 5 In.	125.00
Sign, Armour's Star, The Ham What Am, 9 X 20 In.	165.00
Sign, B–L Lemon Soda, Standup, Cardboard, 7 X 10 In.	6.00
Sign, Bachmann Brewing, Factory & Hotel, 1890s, 2 X 3 Ft.	2100.00
Sign, Baer Bros.Paint, Double–Sided, C.1900, 17 1/2 X 12 In.	695.00
Sign, Bank, Man With Bankbook In Hand, Motor, Wooden, 3 Ft.	275.00
Sign, Barrister Cigar, Man Smoking, Cardboard, 27 X 37 In.	550.00
Sign, Bartels 5,000 Pure Beer, Tin, 27 X 40 In.	425.00
Sign, Bauer Whiskey, Cowboy, Paper, Framed, 1870s, 28 X 21 In.	650.00
Sign, Beech–Nut Tobacco, John & Demijohn, Framed, 15 X 22 In.	75.00
Sign, Beer, Man With Beer Glass, 1930s, 7 X 17 In.	185.00
Sign, Betsy's Best Flour, New Frame, 42 X 24 In.	375.00
Sign, Biltrite Heels & Shoes, Shoemaker In Heel, 4 X 15 In.	85.00
Sign, Blackstone Cigar, Porcelain, Blue & Yellow, 12 X 36 In.	95.00
Sign, Borax Mule Team, Self–Framed, 32 X 21 In.	70.00
Sign, Botl' O Grape, Embossed, Tin, 1940s, 12 X 20 In.	30.00
Sign, Bouquet Cigars, Reverse Painted, Framed, 10 X 18 In.	350.00
Sign, Brooke Bond Tea, Enameled Sheet Iron, 20 X 30 In.	85.00
Sign, Brownie Soda, Cardboard, Wooden Frame, 5 Ft.	275.00
Sign, Budd's Gingerale, Tin, Menu Slots, 19 X 9 In.	20.00
Sign, Budweiser, Porcelain, 1920s, 12 X 26 In.	135.00
Sign, Bunker Hill Brewing, Woman, Low–Cut Dress, 20 X 30 In.	600.00

Sign, Butter Nut Bread, Embossed, Tin, 1930s, 12 X 26 In. 35.00
Sign, C.H.Case Drugs, Mortar & Pestle, 40 1/2 X 21 1/2 In. 125.00
Sign, California Champagne, Tin, C.1910, 13 X 19 In. 195.00
Sign, Call Again, Embossed, Tin, 1930s, 12 X 32 In. 45.00
Sign, Calotabs For Biliousness Due To Torpidity, 19 X 13 In. 45.00
Sign, Camel, The Better Cigarette, Yellow Canvas, 43 X 93 In. 63.00
Sign, Canada Dry, Porcelain, 5 X 24 In. 45.00
Sign, Carlsberg Beer, Label Picture, Celluloid, 10 X 5 In. 10.00
Sign, Carnation Milk, Enamel On Porcelain, C.1930, 15 X 14 In. 75.00
Sign, Cashmere Bouquet Talcum, Stand–Up, 22 X 12 In. 95.00
Sign, Cataract Beer, Round, 12 In. 65.00
Sign, Cer–Ola, Kolb Brewery, Cardboard, Prohibition, 12 X 18 In. 45.00
Sign, Champagne Velvet Beer, Fishing Scene, Tin, 20 X 14 In. 85.00
Sign, Champion Spark Plug, Plug Shape, 23 1/2 X 14 In. 175.00
Sign, Cherry Pepsin, Quiets Nerves, Tin, 14 X 10 In. 150.00
Sign, Chesapeake Steamship Co., Litho, 1915, 31 X 40 In. 425.00
Sign, Chesterfield, Buy Here, 2 Packs, Tin, 12 X 18 In. 25.00
Sign, Chesterfield, Lady, Cardboard, 1940s, 24 X 24 In. 55.00
Sign, Chi–Namel, Cardboard, Standup, 17 1/2 X 29 In. 20.00
Sign, Clabber Girl, 1940s, 12 X 36 In. 25.00
Sign, Climax Tobacco, Red, White & Blue, Porcelain, 15 X 15 In. 195.00
Sign, Cliquot Club, Cardboard, 1940s, 42 X 18 In. 30.00
Sign, Cobake, Best In Bread, Boy, Leaf On Head, Tin, 4 X 19 In. 35.00
Sign, Coburger Beer, Barmaid With Mugs, Tin, 1900, 22 X 16 In. 175.00
Sign, Colgate, Framed, 21 X 11 In. 135.00
Sign, Colonial Is Good Bread, Red & Gold, Tin, 19 X 13 In. 24.00
Sign, Concordia Fire Inc.Co., Milwaukee, Porcelain, 14 X 20 In. 150.00
Sign, Connermade, Embossed, Tin, 1920s, 16 X 20 In. 35.00
Sign, Continental Automobile Ins., Tin Litho, 13 X 19 In. 150.00
Sign, Cooks Beer, Tin, 1940s, 16 X 20 In. 25.00
Sign, Cork Whiskey, Self–Framed, Tin, 1885, 18 X 24 In. 65.00
Sign, Croft Ale, Tin, 9 X 13 In. 25.00
Sign, Crown Gasoline, Flange, Porcelain, 26 X 26 In. 350.00
Sign, Dad's Root Beer, Tin, 28 In. 70.00
Sign, Dairy, Garden, Poultry, Oakdale Farm, Iron, 20 X 33 In. 185.00
Sign, Dancing Girls Upstairs, Neon, Blue & Red, 28 X 18 In. 195.00
Sign, Dandy Shandy Non–Alcoholic Beverage, 12 X 9 In. 10.00
Sign, DeLaval Cream Separators, Lady, With Cow, Tin, 31 X 20 In. 200.00
Sign, DeLaval, Figural, Holstein Cow, Tin, 5 1/2 In 75.00
Sign, DeLaval, Window, Separator Both Sides, 18 X 27 In. 200.00
Sign, Delco, Tin, Round, 70 In. 40.00
Sign, Diamond Edge, Embossed, Tin, 1940s, 11 X 27 In. 25.00
Sign, Diamond Horseshoes, Horses, Wagon, Tin, 36 X 24 In. 375.00
Sign, Diamond Kerosene, Porcelain, 14 X 20 In. 100.00
Sign, Diamond Portland Cement, Porcelain, Round, 18 In. 95.00
Sign, Dill's Best Tobacco, Girl On Tobacco Can, 20 X 25 In. 65.00
Sign, Dr.Gahring, Osteopathic Physician, Tin, 15 3/4 X 57 In. 55.00
Sign, Drink Dr Pepper, Tin, 11 1/2 X 16 In. 18.00
Sign, Drink Frostie Root Beer, Man & Bottle, Tin, 20 X 20 In. 60.00
Sign, Drink Polly's Soda, Tin, Orange, Red, Parrot, 11 X 26 In. 85.00
Sign, Drink Upper 10, Bottle, Red & Yellow, Tin, 10 In. 20.00
Sign, Drost Cocoa, Stand–Up, 13 X 9 In. .... 20.00 To 20.00
Sign, Dupont Duco Wax, 22 X 28 In. 20.00
Sign, Dupont Powders, Hunting Dogs, Tin, 1903, 28 X 23 In. 750.00
Sign, Dutch Boy Paint, Cardboard, Standup, 1930s, 51 X 45 In. 150.00
Sign, Early Times Whiskey, Distillery, Plaster, 23 X 27 In. 350.00
Sign, East Grand Forks Brewing, Tin, 14 X 14 In. 100.00
Sign, Edison Phonograph, Embossed On Tin, 11 3/4 X 23 1/2 In. 295.00
Sign, El Wadora, Tin, 1930s, 24 X 36 In. 45.00
Sign, Elgin Watches, Boy Holding Watch, Wood, 1910, 23 X 15 In. 285.00
Sign, Employer's Liability Assurance, Ltd., Framed, 24 X 13 In. 225.00
Sign, English Pub, Viscount Lord Nelson, 47 1/2 X 34 In. 770.00
Sign, Enterprise Brewing Co., 3 Monk, Mugs, Tin, Round, 12 In. 220.00
Sign, Everready Radio Steel Blades, Man, Tin Litho, 3 X 11 In. 185.00

Sign, Fairbanks, Morse Scales, Porcelain, 9 X 52 In. 135.00
Sign, Fame & Fortune, Tin Litho, 3 Cent Cigars, 8 X 14 In. 45.00
Sign, For Sale, Butte Land Co., Tin, Red, White, 10 X 28 In. 30.00
Sign, Fred Husemann Bottling, Miss Liberty, 8 X 11 In. 9.00
Sign, Friedman Keiler & Co., Paducah, Ky., 9 X 13 In. 195.00
Sign, G.Hartz Saloon, Rupert's Lager, 2 Sides, Wooden, 36 In. 2200.00
Sign, Ganong's Chocolates, Framed, Art Deco, 1920s, 22 X 13 In. 95.00
Sign, Gay Rock Clothing, Paper Hanger, 1901, 28 X 21 In. 29.00
Sign, Gillette Safety Razor, Tin Litho Die Cut, 13 3/8 X 15 In. 875.00
Sign, Glidden Paints, Neon, Red, Gold & Green, 27 X 11 In. 125.00
Sign, Globe Wernicke Bookcases, Man & Woman, Tin, 29 X 40 In. 200.00
Sign, Goldyrock, Embossed, Tin, 1930s, 11 X 22 In. 25.00
Sign, Grand Council Cigars, Generals, Framed, 1870s, 17 X 14 In. 185.00
Sign, Grange Silos, Red Block Letters, White, 9 X 16 In. 130.00
Sign, Grape–Nuts, To School Well Fed, Tin, 20 1/4 X 30 1/2 In. 950.00
Sign, Grapette Soda, Tin, 1920s, 12 X 41 In. 95.00
Sign, Grapette, Embossed, Tin, 1940s, 12 X 24 In. 25.00
Sign, Green River Whiskey, Cardboard, 1959, 22 X 32 In. 25.00
Sign, Gunsmith, Double–Barrel Shot Gun, Wood, 8 Ft.4 In. 1000.00
Sign, Handy Package Dyes, Paper Board, 1880s, 19 X 15 In. 175.00
Sign, Harley Davidson, Embossed, Tin, 29 1/2 X 23 1/4 In. 700.00
Sign, Hartford Fire Insurance Co., Stag, Tin, 12 X 18 In. 100.00
Sign, Hazel Club, Round, 8 3/4 In. 15.00
Sign, Hemricks Beer, Double–Sided, Lighted Glass, Round, 16 In. 165.00
Sign, Hires Root Beer, Child, Cardboard, 14 X 11 In., 2 Piece 125.00
Sign, Hires Root Beer, Enamel, Red Center, Blue Border, 12 In. 22.00
Sign, Hires Root Beer, Tin, 6 X 15 In. 50.00
Sign, Hires Root Beer, Tin, Nail Holes, 14 X 20 In. 396.00
Sign, Honeymoon Tobacco, Couple, Moon, Embossed Tin, 7 X 9 In. 295.00
Sign, Howel's Root Beer, Tin, 1920s, 16 X 57 In. 150.00
Sign, I'm Proud of Suncrest, Bottle, Head of Man, 11 X 26 In. 50.00
Sign, I.W. Harper Whiskey, Milk Glass, Cabin ....*Illus* 1050.00

Advertising, Sign, I.W. Harper Whiskey,
Milk Glass, Cabin

Sign, Icy Pi, Metal & Glass, Lighted, 1920s, 17 X 10 X 5 In. 125.00
Sign, Ingersoll Watches, 2 Sides, Blue & White, 7 X 16 In. 75.00
Sign, International Harvester Gasoline Engines, 23 X 16 In. 375.00
Sign, Interstate Oil 50th Anniversary, Tin, 1937, 9 X 15 In. 45.00
Sign, Japanese Rose Soap, Kids Bathing Doll, 1910, 28 X 38 In. 285.00
Sign, Jeweler's Watch, Cast Iron Frame, Tin Dials, 1900s, 40 In. 1200.00
Sign, Keds, Basketball, Die Cut, Stand–Ups, 1915, 17 In., Pair 45.00
Sign, Keen Kutter Tools, Tin, 27 X 9 In. 39.00
Sign, Kendall's Spavin Cure, Stone Litho, 26 X 20 In. 400.00
Sign, Kinney Bros., High Class Cigarettes, Framed, 20 X 31 In. 280.00
Sign, Kis–Me Gum, Die Cut, Lady, Flowers, Coins, 19 X 13 In. 400.00
Sign, Kist Orange, Bottle Shape, C.1930, 55 X 16 In. 125.00
Sign, Kramer's Beverage, Tin, 1950s, 12 X 4 In. 12.00
Sign, La Raphaelle, Stone Litho, 1908, 30 X 42 In. 250.00
Sign, Laflin & Rand, Soldiers, Branches, 1900, 24 X 43 In. 290.00
Sign, Lancashie Insurance Co., London, Tin Litho, 22 X 26 In. 145.00
Sign, Le Nil Cigarette Papers, Lithographed, 47 X 58 In. 195.00
Sign, Lemp Beer, Falstaff, Maidens, Pre–Prohibition, 24 In. 450.00
Sign, Libbey Glasses, Cardboard, Standup, 1948, 23 X 24 In. 45.00
Sign, Lowneys Chocolate, People, Candy Display, Tin, 27 X 20 In. 550.00
Sign, Lucky Lager Beer, 2 For 25 Cents, Tin, 7 X 13 1/2 In. 65.00
Sign, Lucky Strike, Embossed, Tin, 1950s, 12 X 4 In. 25.00
Sign, Lucky Teter, 1940s, 42 X 26 In. 25.00
Sign, M.Knap, Tavern, Pine, Iron, Hanging, 1820, Oval, 24 X 41 In. 8525.00
Sign, Ma's Root Beer, Tin, 1940s, 12 X 24 In. 25.00
Sign, Ma's Root Beer, Tin, 27 1/2 X 19 1/2 In. 45.00
Sign, Majestic Hams, Cook With Product, Tin, 1905, 38 X 25 In. 1450.00
Sign, Market Street Railway Co., Shield, Porcelain, 8 X 10 In. 165.00
Sign, McVitie & Price's Biscuits, Child, Tin, 19 X 14 In. 375.00
Sign, Meerschaum Tobacco, Cat Sitting, Cardboard, 24 In. 85.00
Sign, Member of Combes Citrus Assn., Metal, 6 X 12 In. 12.00
Sign, Miller Beer, Girl On Box, Wooden, Oval, 13 X 17 In. 175.00
Sign, Model T, Car's Side, Tin, 22 In. 40.00
Sign, Monarch Paint, Porcelain, 2 Sides, 15 X 17 In. 35.00
Sign, Mortar & Pestle, Wooden, Sheet Zinc Cover On Top, 16 In. 250.00
Sign, Mother's Best Flour, Lighted, Round, C.1930, 17 In. 250.00
Sign, Mound City Horseshoe Paints, Tin, 6 1/2 X 28 In. 21.00
Sign, Mule Beer, McGovern Brewery, Mo., 1930s, 8 X 10 In. 8.00
Sign, Nature's Remedy, Porcelain, 5 X 27 In. 150.00
Sign, Neon, Samda Ice Cream, Pink, Blue & Orange, 31 By 18 In. 400.00
Sign, Nesbitt, Embossed, Tin, 1940s, 24 X 24 In. 30.00
Sign, New Haven Dairy Ice Cream, Tin, Framed, 24 X 36 In. 95.00
Sign, New York Plate Glass Inc., Brooklyn Bridge, 15 X 12 In. 285.00
Sign, Nichol 5 Cent Kola, Tin, 12 X 36 In. 26.00
Sign, Nichol Kola, 5 Cents, Embossed Tin, 12 X 4 In. 20.00
Sign, Nichol Kola, America's Taste Sensation, Tin, 28 X 20 In. 20.00
Sign, Nichol Kola, Man & Bottle, Tin, 11 1/2 X 29 1/2 In. 30.00
Sign, Nichol Kola, Man Serving, Embossed Tin, 35 X 12 In. 45.00
Sign, Nicklas Ice Delivery, Wooden, 1910, 24 X 34 In. 250.00
Sign, Normandy Rye, Louisville, Ky., Bottle On Pedestal, 20 In. 225.00
Sign, O.F.C.Bourbon, 2 Hunters, Paper Board, 1890s, 31 X 22 In. 375.00
Sign, O.F.C.Bourbon, Deer Hunters, 1890s, 31 X 22 In. 350.00
Sign, Odo–Ro–No, Bottle Shape, Cardboard, Art Deco, 30 In. 45.00
Sign, Old Barbee Whiskey, Old Man, Girls, Tin, 1905, 38 X 26 In. 575.00
Sign, Old English Tobacco, Man At Fireplace, 1900, 31 X 24 In. 225.00
Sign, Old Honesty Tobacco, New Frame, 28 X 28 In. 550.00
Sign, Old Overholt Whiskey, Hunter, Dog, 1900, 35 X 26 In. 650.00
Sign, Old Overholt, Trespassing Hunter, Tin, 1900, 35 X 26 In. 650.00
Sign, Old Schenley Whiskey, Man, Rifle, Tin, 1900, 33 X 25 In. 1250.00
Sign, Old Schenley, Daniel Boone, Canoe, Tin, 1900, 31 X 23 In. 9500.00
Sign, Omar Cigarette, Original Frame, C.1900, 18 X 24 1/2 In. 295.00
Sign, Omega Watch of Matchless Merit, Tin, Pre–1930, 13 X 5 In. 16.00
Sign, Orange Kist, Embossed, Tin, 1930s, 3 X 20 In. 20.00
Sign, Ourlda, Tin, 1879, 14 X 8 In. 50.00

Sign, Pabst Beer, Sexy Girl Sipping Beer, 1899, 17 X 22 In. 225.00
Sign, Pabst Blue Ribbon, Mirrored, C.1910, 12 X 20 In. 100.00
Sign, Pacific Beer, Tacoma, Porcelain, C.1904, 22 X 15 1/2 In. 200.00
Sign, Paine's Celery Compound, Box, Tin, 14 X 10 In. 320.00
Sign, Paul Jones Whiskey, Farmer, Tin Frame, 1900, 28 X 22 In. 950.00
Sign, Peter Pan Ice Cream, Embossed, Tin, 1940s, 30 X 20 In. 40.00
Sign, Peters Shoes, High Top Shoe Picture, Tin, 13 X 19 1/2 In. 75.00
Sign, Piedmont Cigarettes, Porcelain, 12 X 12 In. 75.00
Sign, Pince–Nez Shape, Brass, 1 Blue Glass & 1 Red, 15 X 25 In. 225.00
Sign, Plymouth Rope, Cardboard, Stand–Up, 1941, 19 1/2 .... 24.00
Sign, Pocket Watch, Ring Top, Wooden, 2 Sides, 21 In.Diam. 850.00
Sign, Poll–Parrot Shoes, Cardboard, Framed, 6 X 12 In. 65.00
Sign, Ponchartrain Beach, Embossed, Tin, 1930s, 21 X 27 In. 85.00
Sign, Postal Telegraph, Porcelain, 2 Sides, Flange, 10 X 8 In. 65.00
Sign, Pride of The Rockies Flour, New Frame, 8 1/2 X 16 In. 50.00
Sign, Priscilla Ware Utensils, Metal, 1920s, 10 X 5 In. 12.00
Sign, Providence Insurance, George Washington, Tin, 18 X 24 In. 500.00
Sign, Pub, English, The Greyhound, 60 X 49 In. 55.00
Sign, Pub, English, Viscount Lord Nelson, 47 X 34 In. 770.00
Sign, Pub, French, Heraldic Design, Enamels, 39 X 31 In. 310.00
Sign, Pub, Wheat Sheaf, Landscape, Wood, Iron, 1900, 39 X 26 In. 900.00
Sign, Quaker Oats, Bike Club Coupons, Stand–Up, 1934, 1 .... 85.00
Sign, Quality Hardware, Master Lock, Wooden, Brass, 10 X 14 In. 42.00
Sign, Quiky, Cardboard, 1950s, 40 X 18 In. 30.00
Sign, R Pep, Embossed, Tin, 1940s, 48 X 12 In. 115.00
Sign, Rainier Beer & Ale, Aluminum, C.1930, 5 X 14 In. 60.00
Sign, Red Fox, Tin, 1940s, 13 X 4 In. 10.00
Sign, Red Jacket Tobacco, Baseball, Cardboard, 22 X 28 In. 125.00
Sign, Reid Mfg. Co., Machinist's Vice, Tin, 1907, 14 X 22 In. 125.00
Sign, Riding Hunt Club, Cooperstown N.Y., 1880, 14 X 26 In. 250.00
Sign, Rochelle Club Ginger Ale, Bottle Shape, Cardboard, 36 In. 30.00
Sign, Rochester Root Beer, 23 1/2 X 17 1/2 In. 35.00
Sign, Rochester Special Beer, Red, 25 X 42 In. 75.00
Sign, Rockford Watches, 20 Cities Time, Tin, 1900, 23 X 17 In. 550.00
Sign, Roxbury Rye, Reverse Painted Glass, Framed, 15 X 17 In. 375.00
Sign, Royal Baking Powder, 1920s, 26 X 20 In. 30.00
Sign, Royal Crown Cola, Santa, Cardboard, 1940, 28 X 11 In. 45.00
Sign, Royal Crown, Embossed, Tin, 1940s, 2 X 20 In. 20.00
Sign, Russell's Ales, Tin, Self–Framed, 1930s, 29 X 21 In. 195.00
Sign, Salzburger Beer, Lobster, Flowers, Round, Metal, 24 In. 550.00
Sign, San Felice 5 Cent Cigar, C.1900, 7 1/2 X 11 1/2 In. 125.00
Sign, San Felice Cigars, Gentlemen, Good Taste, Tin, 15 X 8 In. 18.00
Sign, Scandinavian American Line, R.Valentino, Tin, 8 In.Diam. 45.00
Sign, Schlitz Beer, Man & Woman, Picnic, Cardboard, 35 X 54 In. 150.00
Sign, Schlitz Beer, Winged Woman, Cardboard, 22 X 29 In. 55.00
Sign, Sedgwick Rye, Black Man, Gambling, 1925, 22 X 13 In. 250.00
Sign, Sedgwick Rye, Gambling Man, Paperboard, 1925, 22 X 13 In. 250.00
Sign, Shop, Eye Glass Shape, Tin, Reverse Painted, 23 1/2 In. 1760.00
Sign, Sir Walter Raleigh Tobacco, Metal, 16 X 26 In. 25.00
Sign, Sky Chief Texaco, Porcelain, 12 X 18 In. 60.00
Sign, Snow King, 1930s, Cardboard, 10 X 14 In. 40.00
Sign, Socony Aircraft Oils, Porcelain, 1930s, 10 X 14 In. 50.00
Sign, Socony Vacuum, Porcelain, 2 Sides, Shield Shape, 42 In. 225.00
Sign, Southern Bread, Tin, 28 X 5 1/2 In. 40.00
Sign, Spearmint Toothpaste Box, Wrigley, 1922, 5 X 5 X 4 In. 10.00
Sign, Speedboat, Marine, Gasoline, 2 Pilots, 4 X 2 1/2 In. 375.00
Sign, Spitz Cider, Tin, American Art Works, C.1900, 9 X 13 In. 300.00
Sign, Squires Hams, Pig, Human Features, Tin, Oval, 1906, 19 In. 1250.00
Sign, Standard Brewing, Sioux Execution, 1862, Tin, 26 X 18 In. 3800.00
Sign, Standard Home Sewing Machine, Cardboard, 12 1/4 X 20 In. 225.00
Sign, Standard White Crown, Flame Log, Porcelain, 12 X 15 In. 35.00
Sign, Star Soap Bar, Extra Large & Good, Porcelain, 20 X 28 In. 150.00
Sign, Star Soap, Girl & Mastiff, Tin, 1890s, 15 X 19 In. 365.00
Sign, Stephenson Underwear, 3–D Die Cut, Man, 1910, 37 In. 1150.00

Sign, Sun Crest, Embossed, Tin, 1940s, 21 X 7 In. 25.00
Sign, Sunbeam Bread, Tin, Embossed, 29 1/2 X 12 In. 100.00
Sign, Sunbeam, Cardboard, 21 X 23 In. 45.00
Sign, Sunsweet, Tin, 1940s, 26 X 20 In. 20.00
Sign, Swift's, Cardboard, 8 X 10 In. 11.00
Sign, Tasty Dixie Milk, Neon, 22 In. 350.00
Sign, Texaco Fire Chief Gasoline, Porcelain, 12 X 18 In. 50.00
Sign, Texaco Gasoline, Cardboard, 1936, 10 X 25 In. 12.00
Sign, Texaco Sky Chief, 11 X 18 In. 35.00
Sign, Texaco, Stained Glass, 24 In.Diam. 495.00
Sign, Tom Moore Cigars, Portrait of Man, 15 1/2 X 11 In. 110.00
Sign, Tru–Ade, Cold N' Golden Not Carbonated, 28 X 12 In. 18.00
Sign, True–Temper, Die Cut Cardboard, 18 X 24 In. 40.00
Sign, Tutti Frutti Gum, Adams, Lady With Flowers, 14 X 10 In. 300.00
Sign, U.M.C.Cartridges, Bull's Head, Metal, 1910, 26 X 18 In. 1250.00
Sign, U.S.Steel American Quality Nails, Tin, 20 X 29 In. 30.00
Sign, Uneeda Biscuit, NBC, Framed, 21 X 11 In. 190.00
Sign, Uniform Cut Plug, Tin, 4 X 6 In. 125.00
Sign, Use Garland Flour, Sewn Bamboo Sticks, 18 X 30 In. 45.00
Sign, Utica Club Ginger Ale, Tin, 11 X 24 In. 55.00
Sign, Utica Club, Cardboard, Standup, 10 X 21 In. 15.00
Sign, Vaseline, Toonerville Town, Characters, 20 X 10 In. 75.00
Sign, Veedol, Porcelain, Round, 23 In. 40.00
Sign, Velvet Tobacco, Porcelain, 12 X 39 In. 250.00
Sign, Velvet Tobacco, Porcelain, 12 X 42 In. 400.00
Sign, Vernar's, Embossed, Tin, 1940s, 18 X 54 In. 75.00
Sign, Viceroy Cigarettes, Metal, 26 X 17 In. 23.00
Sign, Victor Talking Machine Co., Record Shape, 1927, 30 In. 265.00
Sign, Voigt's Royal Patent Flour, Porcelain, 5 X 7 In. 75.00
Sign, Wells Fargo, Cardboard, 12 X 12 In. 20.00
Sign, Whistle, Cardboard, 1940s, 36 X 24 In. 35.00
Sign, Whistle, Tin, 1950s, 6 X 24 In. 15.00
Sign, Willard & Co., Brush Manufactures, Wood, 23 1/2 X 36 In. 150.00
Sign, Winchester, Game & Guns, Tin, 1909, 3 X 3 1/2 Ft. 110.00
Sign, Winchester, Guns & Dead Mallards, Tin, 1913, 30 X 36 In. 1450.00
Sign, Winne's Ice Cream, Tin, 2 Sides, 20 X 28 In. 25.00
Sign, Woonsocket, Embossed, Tin, 1920s, 6 X 18 In. 30.00
Sign, Zenith Radio, Porcelain, 1930s, 3 X 5 Ft. 275.00
Skillet, Niferex Tablets, Cast Iron, Miniature 10.00
Soap Dish, Kirkman's Soap, Floral, Says Save The Wrappers 15.00
Soap, Figural, Tank Truck, Sinclair Gasoline, Giveaway 10.00
Spittoon, Redskin Cut Plug Chewing Tobacco, Brass 110.00
Spoon, A & P, Tin 7.00
Spoon, Chiclets 6.00
Spoon, Cream Top 8.00
Spoon, Doe Wah Jack, Silver Plate 60.00
Spoon, Figural, Log Cabin 17.50
Spoon, Gerber Boy, Child's, Silver Plate, Round Bowl 12.50
Spoon, Kellogg's, Wooden, Long Handle 5.00
Spoon, Log Cabin Syrup, Demitasse 15.00
Spoon, Norge, Painted 38.00
Spoon, Northern Rock Island Plow Co., Metal 18.00
Spoon, Rolex, Lion In Bowl, Demitasse 15.00
Stickpin, Doe Wah Jack 20.00
Stickpin, Old Dutch Cleanser, Enameled Figure 35.00
Stickpin, Whiskbroom Cigars 29.00
Straw Dispenser, Hires Root Beer 750.00
String Holder, Red Goose Shoes 1300.00
Sugar & Creamer, Borden's Elsie & Elmer, Plastic 20.00
Sugar & Creamer, Tappan 25.00
Sugar, Lipton Tea, Blue, Cover 15.00
Syrup, Cup, Sheeham's Orange Ade, Reverse Curved Glass, 12 In. 285.00
Tap Handle, Miller High Life Beer, Wood 12.00
Tap Knob, Iron City 8.00

Teapot, Lipton, Porcelain, Individual	25.00
ADVERTISING, THERMOMETER, see Thermometer	
Thermos, Panama Pacific Expo, San Fran., Chrome, 1915, 14 In.	120.00
Tie Bar, Fleers Bubble Gum	8.00
Tile, Winchester, Presentation, Horse & Rider, White, 6 X 6 In.	89.50

 The English language is sometimes confusing. Tin cans or canisters were first used commercially in the United States in 1819 and were called "tins." Today the word "tin" is used by most collectors to describe many types of containers, including food tins, biscuit boxes, roly poly tobacco containers, gunpowder cans, talcum powder sprinkle–top cans, cigarette flat–fifty tins, and more. Beer cans are listed in their own section. Things made of undecorated tin are listed under Tinware.

Tin, 3 Knights, Condom	50.00
Tin, 666 Salve, Monticello Drug Co., Red, On Yellow, 1 In.	2.00
Tin, Aero Eastern Oil, DC–3 Airplane, 2 Gal.	50.00
Tin, Aero Eastern Oil, Single Engine Plane, 2 Gal.	50.00
Tin, American Ace Coffee, Pictures Pilot	75.00
Tin, American Powder Co., 1/2 Lb.	55.00
Tin, Angelus Marshmallows, 5 Lb.	24.00
Tin, Apex Cocoa, 1/2 Lb.	10.00
Tin, Aristocrat Condoms	100.00
Tin, Arkogast & Bastian Co., Allentown, Pa., Pig, 50 Lb.	16.00
Tin, Artstyle Candy, Butterflies, Yellow, 2 Lb.	15.00
Tin, Astor House Coffee, Blue Printing, Cream, 1 Lb.	33.00
Tin, Bagley's Wild Fruit Tobacco	65.00
Tin, Baker's Cocoa, Paper Label, 1904, 3 X 3 X 6 In.	145.00
Tin, Banquet Tea, McCormick & Co., 1 Lb.4 Oz.	20.00
Tin, Barrus Mustard, Eagle, Litho Child Sides, Canister, 10 In.	33.00
Tin, Battleship Coffee, Graphics of Battleship, 3 Lb.	20.00
Tin, Bee Brand Insect Powder, McCormick & Co., 4 3/4 In.	12.00
Tin, Beechnut Factory Scenes, Tin, 6 X 12 In., Set of 5	50.00
Tin, Ben–Hur Nutmeg, Yellow & Black, Red Ground, 3 1/4 In.	9.00
Tin, Best Talking Machine, Needle, Contents	7.00
Tin, Big Ben Tobacco, Horse, Pocket	20.00
Tin, Big Horn Coffe, 1 Lb.	25.00
Tin, Bigger Hair Tobacco, Brown, Canister	75.00
Tin, Blue Hill Coffee, 10 Lb.	55.00
Tin, Bokar Coffee, Screw Lid, 1 Lb.	20.00
Tin, Bon Ami, 1937 Instruction Sheet, Sample, Contents	15.00
Tin, Bon Ami, Housewife Washing Windows, 1930s, Sample, Unused	15.00
Tin, Bouquet Coffee, 1 Lb.	30.00
Tin, Bowl of Roses Tobacco, Pocket, 3 X 2 In.	140.00
Tin, Breakfast Call Coffee, 1 Lb.	40.00
Tin, Britannia Plug Tobacco, Picture of Ship	40.00
Tin, Brundage Peanuts, 10 Lb.	40.00
Tin, Buckingham Cut Plug Smoking Tobacco, Orange, Round	85.00
Tin, Buckingham, Bright Cut Plug Tobacco, 4 X 4 1/2 In.	40.00
Tin, Buckingham, Pocket, 4 X 2 In. .... 40.00 To	75.00
Tin, Budweiser Tobacco, Pocket	250.00
Tin, Buffalo Brand Peanuts	85.00
Tin, Bugle Cigars, Canister, 6 X 4 In.	75.00
Tin, Bugler Tobacco, 2 X 2 In.	15.00
Tin, Bull's Head Motor Oil, Pictures Bull, 1920s, 2 Gal.	45.00
Tin, Bungalow Wagers, 1920s Bungalow, Denver, 9 X 9 X 7 In.	65.00
Tin, Bushel's Tea, Embossed Animals, Canister, Dome Top	135.00
Tin, Butter–Nut Brand Coffee, Graphics, 2 Lb.	8.00
Tin, Butternut Coffee, 1 Lb.	10.00
Tin, Butternut Coffee, 2 Lb.	18.00
Tin, California Nugget Tobacco, 4 X 2 In.	85.00
Tin, California Nugget Tobacco, Nugget Shape, 3 X 2 In.	130.00
Tin, Calumet Baking Powder, Canister, No.10, Store	100.00
Tin, Calumet Baking Powder, Indian Picture, 1 Lb.	12.00

Any paper-labeled can that can be dated before 1875 is rare.

Tin, Camel Cigars, Pocket, 5 1/2 X 4 1/2 X 2 1/2 In.	45.00
Tin, Campfire Coffee, San Francisco, Ca., 1931, 2 Lb.	195.00
Tin, Campfire Lard, Cowpoke At Campfire, 50 Lb.	45.00 To 45.00
Tin, Campfire Marshmallow, Round, 5 Lb.	18.00
Tin, Caraven Prophylactics, Arabs On Camels	55.00
Tin, Checkers Tobacco, Upright, Pocket, Unopened	450.00
Tin, Cherry Blossom Coffee, 1 Lb.	45.00
Tin, Chesterfield, Canister, Round, Fifty	25.00
Tin, Chesterfield, Flat, Fifty	8.50
Tin, Class Cigars, 6 X 5 X 3 In.	35.00
Tin, Club Lido Tobacco, Pocket	200.00 To 300.00
Tin, Coach & Four, Pocket	350.00
Tin, Colgate Baby Talc, Picture of Baby	48.00
Tin, Colgate's Rapid Shave Powder, Dome Top, 1920s	20.00
Tin, Conrad's Eagle Brand Coffee, 1 Lb.	12.00
Tin, Country Club Cigars, 6 X 5 X 4 In.	135.00
Tin, Cutex Nail Care, Art Deco, 1930s	10.00
Tin, Dan Patch Tobacco, 4 X 6 In.	35.00 To 50.00
Tin, Dean's Peacocks, Prophylactic, Peacock Cover	27.50
Tin, Del Monte Peas, Sample	10.00
Tin, Dereszke Tobacco, Oval, Pictures Dracula, Pocket	35.00
Tin, Dilling Candy, Red & Yellow, 15 Lb.	28.00
Tin, Dixie Queen Tobacco, Red Letters, Small	150.00
Tin, Dixie Queen, Light Blue, 6 X 4 In.	375.00
Tin, Dolly Dimple Hair Dressing, Buy U.S.War Stamps	35.00
Tin, Don Sebastian Cigars, Round, Paper Label	13.00
Tin, Dr.Johnson's Educator Crackers	35.00
Tin, Dr.LeGear's Fly Chaser, Contents, 1/4 Gal.	5.00
Tin, Droste Cocoa, 2 Lb.	20.00
Tin, Droste Cocoa, 5 Lb.	45.00
Tin, DuPont Gun Powder, Black & White, 5 X 4 X 2 In.	50.00
Tin, DuPont Gun Powder, Dated 1924	50.00
Tin, Dutch Masters Cigars, 6 X 3 X 3 In.	10.00
Tin, E.C.Harley Co.Tea, Red, 2 Lb.	40.00
Tin, Edgeworth Tobacco, Blue, 3 X 4 In.	20.00
Tin, Edgeworth Tobacco, Pocket, 4 X 2 In.	5.00
Tin, Edgeworth, Sample	45.00
Tin, Elephant Coffee, 4 Lb.	150.00
Tin, Elephant Salted Peanuts, 10 In.	65.00
Tin, Elgin Watch Co., Main Springs, Father Time, 5 X 2 X In.	20.00
Tin, Epicure Tobacco, Hinged Top, Embossed Flowers	40.00
Tin, Epicure Tobacco, Pocket, 4 X 2 In.	70.00
Tin, Euclid Peanut Butter, 25 Lb.	65.00
Tin, Eureka Coffee, 1 Lb.	30.00
Tin, Eureka Knitting Needles, 9 In.Needles, Germany	25.00
Tin, Eve Tobacco, Pocket	250.00
Tin, Fairy Marshmallow, Cover, Dated June 30, 1906, Label	35.00
Tin, Farmer's Brand Coffee, 5 Lb.	18.00
Tin, Fathom Fish, Embossed Box, 5 X 10 X 16 In.	12.50
Tin, Flaroma Coffee, Screw Lid, 1 Lb.	20.00
Tin, Folger's Coffee, 1 Lb.	10.00
Tin, Forest & Stream Tobacco, Ducks, Pocket	55.00 To 70.00

Tin, Forest & Stream Tobacco, Fisherman, Pocket	50.00
Tin, Forster's Peanut Butter, Little Girl & Dog, 1 Lb.	75.00
Tin, Four Roses Tobacco, Flat Top, Pocket	350.00
Tin, Franco–American Coffee, 1 Lb.	85.00
Tin, Friends Smoking Tobacco, Pocket	25.00
Tin, Friends Tobacco, 1 Lb.	32.00
Tin, Glendora Coffee, 5 Lb.	50.00
Tin, Gold Band Coffee, 1 Lb.	10.00
Tin, Gold Standard Tea, Graphics, 4 X 6 X 9 In.	100.00
Tin, Golden Dome Coffee, 1 Lb.	20.00
Tin, Golden Pheasant Prophylactics	45.00
Tin, Golden Sceptre Tobacco, Red Arm, Pocket	300.00
Tin, Golden Sceptre, Surbrug's, Fat Pocket	50.00
Tin, Grandmother's Tea, A.& P.	18.00
Tin, Granger Pipe Tobacco, Pointer On Lid, 6 X 4 3/4 In.	8.00
Tin, Granger Tobacco, Pointer Dog, Canister, 5 X 3 In.	15.00
Tin, Grape–Nut	90.00
Tin, Green Seal Sliced Plug, Flat, Pocket	60.00
Tin, Guide, Pocket	150.00
Tin, Gumbert's Raspberry Dessert, Large Dessert Glass, 12 In.	75.00
Tin, Half & Half, Pocket, Sample	65.00
Tin, Handmade Tobacco, Canister, 6 X 2 In.	85.00
Tin, Handmade Tobacco, Globe, Flat Pocket	295.00
Tin, Handsome Dan, Bulldog, 5 X 7 X 3 In.	135.00
Tin, Harvard Jumbo Peanuts, No.5	75.00
Tin, Havana Cadet Cigars	65.00
Tin, Havana Favors Cigars, Counter Top Display	60.00
Tin, Havoline Oil, 1 Gal.	15.00
Tin, Hi Plane Tobacco, 2 Engine, Pocket	85.00
Tin, Hiawatha Tobacco, 2 X 3 X 5 In.	55.00
Tin, Hill's Brothers, Picture of Man, 10 Lb.	60.00
Tin, HMV, Needle, Loud, Red, White, Black, Brown	8.00
Tin, Holiday, Pocket, Flat Top, Contents	65.00
Tin, Holland House Coffee, 1 Lb.	40.00
Tin, Honeymoon Tobacco, Man, Moon, Pocket	75.00
Tin, Huntley & Palmer, Book Shape, Christmas, 1901	450.00
Tin, Huntley & Palmer, Twilight Nature Scene	35.00
Tin, Iona Cocoa	25.00
Tin, Jack Sprat Peanut Butter, 25 Lb.	85.00
Tin, Jack Sprat Tea, Jack's Picture	35.00
Tin, Jacobs, Coronation Coach, Wheels, Biscuit, 1936, 8 3/4 In.	100.00
Tin, Johnson Mustard Plasters, Somers Bros., 4 X 5 X 1/4 In.	45.00
Tin, Johnson's Baby Powder, 1930s, 3 3/4 In.	7.00
Tin, Jumbo Dixie Brand Peanuts, Black Advertising, 10 Lb.	150.00
Tin, Jumbo Popcorn, Orange & Blue, Picture, 10 Lb.	25.00
Tin, Just Suits, 5 X 4 In.	65.00
Tin, Kaffee Hag, Kellogg Co., Battle Creek, Mich., 8 Oz.	10.00
Tin, Kar–A–Van Coffee Co., Camel, Blue Ground, 1 Lb.	30.00
Tin, Kaupke Coffee, Cedar Rapids, Ia., 1 Lb.	10.00
Tin, Keen's Mustard, 8 Sides, Lord Nelson's Life	120.00
Tin, Keen's Mustard, Military Scenes, English, 7 1/2 In.	60.00
Tin, Kelly's Slide Shoe Polish, Baseball Players	20.00
Tin, King Cole, 1/2 Lb.	75.00
Tin, King Edward Tobacco, Pocket	700.00
Tin, King Leo Stick Candy, Lion Standing On Candy Stick, 2 Lb.	12.75
Tin, Kohrs Lard, Red, 4 Lb.	40.00
Tin, Krispy Crackers Sunshine Biscuits, Lift Top, 9 X 8 In.	32.50
Tin, La Fendrich Cigars, Man, Gold Medals, 5 X 4 X 1 In.	22.00
Tin, Lady Helen Coffee, 1 Lb.	25.00
Tin, Laredo Cut Plug Tobacco, 4 X 6 In.	25.00
Tin, Laurel Biscuit Co., Blue & Yellow, 11 In.	32.00
Tin, Le Gears Lice Powder, Trial Size	32.00
Tin, Libby's Corned Beef, Cattle, 1915, Sample	35.00
Tin, Lipton Coffee, Yellow Label, Screw Lid, 1 Lb.	70.00

Tin, Lipton Tea, 1 Lb. 15.00
Tin, Little Teaser Twist, Tintype With Sexual Overtones 450.00
Tin, Log Cabin Syrup, Cartoon On All Sides 110.00
Tin, Log Cabin Syrup, Cartoon Style, Dr.R.U.Well 120.00
Tin, Log Cabin Syrup, Girl, Mother Flipping Pancakes, 1930s 150.00
Tin, Log Cabin Syrup, Girl, Mother, Window, 58 Oz. 150.00
Tin, Log Cabin Syrup, Home Sweet Home, Small 75.00
Tin, Log Cabin Syrup, Kid At Door, 1914 .... 120.00
Tin, Log Cabin Syrup, Red, 5 Lb. 50.00
Tin, Log Cabin Syrup, Sample 450.00
Tin, London Dock, 5 X 3 X 3 In. 10.00
Tin, Lucky Strike Cigarettes, Flat, Pocket, 5 X 3 In. 12.00
Tin, Lucky Strike Cut Plug, Hinged Lid 8.00
Tin, Lucky Strike, Flat, Fifty 8.50
Tin, Lucky Strike, Pocket, White 275.00
Tin, Luter's Lard, 4 Lb. 25.00
Tin, Magic Shaving Powder 22.00
Tin, Mammy's Favorite Coffee, 4 Lb. .... 110.00 To 150.00
Tin, Man–Zan Rectal Cream, Sample, Original Box 15.00
Tin, Master Mason Tobacco, Pocket 1150.00
Tin, Maxwell House Coffee, Key Lid 8.00
Tin, Mayo's Mixture, Red Ribbon, Pocket 75.00
Tin, McCormack Tea, 5 In. 7.00
Tin, McKesson's Talc, Picture of Nude Babies 35.00
Tin, Mecca Tobacco, Pocket 25.00
Tin, Menthol Cough Drops, Eagles 75.00
Tin, Merry Widow Prophylactic .... 25.00 To 48.00
Tin, Mocha & Java Coffee, Harper Brass Co., 10 In. 26.00
Tin, Monadnock Coffee, 1 Lb. 50.00
Tin, Monarch Cocoa, Lion's Head, Sample 20.00
Tin, Monarch Tea 38.00
Tin, Montgomery Ward's Best Tobacco, Paper Label 35.00
Tin, Montgomery Ward's Oriental Tea, Lady On 4 Sides, 5 Lb. 125.00
Tin, Morning Sip Coffee, 1 Lb. 50.00
Tin, Mother's Joy Coffee, Philadelphia, 1 Lb. 17.50
Tin, Mount Cross Coffee, 3 Lb. 38.00
Tin, Murad Cigarettes, Paper Label, Pocket 85.00
Tin, Murrays Cookie Container, Red, White & Blue, 12 In. 24.00
Tin, Needle Box, Victrola, Pictures Nipper, Tin 10.00
Tin, New Era Coffee, 1 Lb. 22.0a
Tin, No–To–Bac Tobacco 45.00
Tin, Nutrena Dog Food, Bail, Orange, Dog Picture, 10 Lb. 45.00
Tin, Nutrine Candy, Blue, 20 Lb. 55.00
Tin, O'Cedar Mop, Picture of Lady 25.00
Tin, Oceanic Tobacco, Pocket, 6 X 4 In. 50.00
Tin, Oh Boy Peanut Butter, 2 Lb. 125.00
Tin, Old English Talc 120.00
Tin, Old Gold Cigarettes, Litho, Box, 4 1/2 X 3 X 2 In. 11.50
Tin, Old King Cole Cigars, Maxfield Parrish, 5 X 4 In. 1000.00
Tin, Old Southern Coffee, 1 Lb. 65.00
Tin, Orcico Cigars, Square 60.00
Tin, Oriental Tea, 5 Lb. 105.00
Tin, Ovaltine, 4 Lb. 28.00
Tin, Ox–Heart Peanut Butter 35.00
Tin, Ox–Heart Peanuts, 10 Lb. 125.00
Tin, Oxo Cubes, Woman Drinking, Gold, Black, On Red, 3 X 2 In. 4.50
Tin, Packer's Tar Soap 10.00
Tin, Peacock Food Coloring, Dome Top, Peacock Picture 15.00
Tin, Peak Coffee, 1 Lb. 12.00
Tin, Pegasus Original, Needle, La Qualitat, Flying Horse 5.00
Tin, Pep Boys Oil, Cartoon Pepboys On Bronco, 2 Gal. 65.00
Tin, Perfect Brand Fine Teas 45.00
Tin, Persian Garden Talcum Powder, Girl, Flowers, Full 60.00
Tin, Peter Rabbit, Tindeco, 1920s 55.00

| Advertising, Tin, Roly Poly, Satisfied Customer, Mayo | Advertising, Tin, Roly Poly, Mammy, Mayo's Tobacco | Advertising, Tin, Roly Poly, Dutchman, Dixie Queen Tobacco | Advertising, Tin, Roly Poly, Storekeeper, U.S.Marine Tobacco |

Tin, Phillies 5 Cent Perfecto	8.00
Tin, Phoenix Violet Talc	20.00
Tin, Picobac, Pocket, Hand Holding Leaf	65.00
Tin, Pike's Centennial Salve, Chelsea, Mass., 1876, Box, 3 In.	18.00
Tin, Pilot Tobacco, Gyrocopter Picture, 1 Lb.	120.00
Tin, Pippins Cigars, 3 X 3 X 6 In.	85.00
Tin, Players Navy Cut Cigarettes, 6 1/2 X 3 1/2 X 1 1/2 In.	40.00
Tin, Possum Cigars, Pocket	45.00
Tin, Postmaster Cigars, Canister, 6 X 5 In.	42.00
Tin, Pride of Virginia Tobacco, Pocket, 4 1/2 X 2 3/4 X 1 In.	25.00
Tin, Princess Pat Rouge, Art Deco, Girl Picture, Concave	10.00
Tin, Puritan Tobacco, Pocket	150.00
Tin, Queen Mary Candy	15.00
Tin, Quickshine Stove Polish, Little Girl With Stove	20.00
Tin, R.J.Allens, Cigar Maker	85.00
Tin, Raleigh, Pocket	4.00
Tin, Red Belt, Striker, Pocket	27.50
Tin, Red Dot Cigars, Large	35.00
Tin, Red Indian Oil, Picture of Indian, 5 Qt.	22.00
Tin, Red Indian Tobacco, Canister, 6 X 5 In.	250.00
Tin, Red Indian Tobacco, Cylindrical	375.00
Tin, Red Jacket Tobacco, Pocket	25.00
Tin, Red Wolf Coffee, Bail & Lid, Tin, 6 Lb.	49.50
Tin, Revelation, Trial Size	35.00
Tin, Rex Tobacco, Pocket	80.00
Tin, Roly Poly, Dutchman, Dixie Queen Tobacco ....*Illus*	595.00
Tin, Roly Poly, Dutchman, Mayo	550.00
Tin, Roly Poly, Happy Hooligan Tobacco, Musical, 10 In.	100.00
Tin, Roly Poly, Indian Mammy, Red Indian	595.00
Tin, Roly Poly, Mammy, Mayo's Tobacco ....*Illus*	400.00
Tin, Roly Poly, Satisfied Customer, Mayo ....*Illus*	495.00
Tin, Roly Poly, Singing Waiter, Mayo	500.00
Tin, Roly Poly, Storekeeper, U.S.Marine Tobacco ....*Illus*	400.00
Tin, Rooster Snuff	15.00
Tin, Rose Leaf Tobacco, With Compass, Flat, Pocket	50.00
Tin, Rosebud Face Powder, Little Girl, Roses, Dated 1914	15.00
Tin, Royal Dutch Coffee, 1 Lb.	30.00
Tin, Royal Tooth Powder, Contents, 4 In.	105.00
Tin, Sanitol Tooth Powder, Dome Top, Dated 1906	20.00
Tin, Saratoga Chips, Box, 3 3/16 X 2 7/16 In.	14.00
Tin, Savarin Tea	25.00

Tin, Seal of North Carolina, 6 X 4 In.	125.00
Tin, Senate Coffee, 1 Lb.	28.00
Tin, Sensation, Gold, Blue	38.00
Tin, Sensible Tobacco, Box, 4 1/2 X 3 1/2 X 3 1/4 In.	9.00
Tin, Shakespeare Tobacco, Pocket	75.00
Tin, Shot Tobacco, Pocket	350.00
Tin, Silver Tex Prophylactics	38.00
Tin, Singer Household Oil	10.00
Tin, Sir Walter Raleigh Tobacco, Dummy, Canister, Large	45.00
Tin, Smith's Rosebud Talc	95.00
Tin, Solitaire Coffee, 5 Lb.	18.00
Tin, Squirrel Peanut Butter, 1 Lb.	100.00
Tin, Stag Tobacco, Canada, 2 Lb.	35.00
Tin, Star Maid Peanuts, Picture of Woman	65.00
Tin, Starless Gall Salve, Horse Team Logo, Unused, 2 3/4 In.	9.00
Tin, Stewart's Chips, Red, White & Blue, 12 In.	26.00
Tin, Stillboma Oriental Polish, Deer Picture, 5 X 1 1/2 In.	15.00
Tin, Sunset Trail Cigars, Cow Persons, 4 X 6 X 6 In.	95.00
Tin, Sunset Trail Tobacco, Dark Blue	295.00
Tin, Sunshine Biscuits, White House On Cover, 12 1/2 X 11 In.	15.00
Tin, Swee–Touch–Nee Tea, Trunk Shape, Tin, 4 3/4 X 6 In.	18.00
Tin, Sweet Burley Tobacco, Canister, 11 In.	60.00
Tin, Sweet Burley, Store, Red, Round	138.00
Tin, Sweet Burley, Store, Yellow, Round	165.00
Tin, Sweet Cuba Tobacco, Flat, Round, 2 X 8 In.	50.00
Tin, Sweet Cuba Tobacco, Round	39.00
Tin, Sweet Mist, Store, Cardboard, Round	225.00
Tin, Sweet Pea Talc	12.00
Tin, Sweet Violet Tobacco, Pocket	650.00
Tin, Swift's Peanut Butter, 5 Lb.	10.00
Tin, Talc, Vogue Perfumery Co., Painted, Shakes, 3 X 4 In.	75.00
Tin, Taxi Tobacco, Pocket	2250.00
Tin, Temple Bar Tobacco, Flat	20.00
Tin, Tennyson Cigars, 6 X 3 X 3 In.	45.00
Tin, Testers Coffee, Screw Lid, 1 Lb.	33.00
Tin, Tex Ret Tablets, Black, Olive Green, 1 3/4 X 1 1/2 In.	5.00
Tin, Texaco, Star, 1930's, 1 Qt.	25.00
Tin, Texide Prophylactics, Negroes On Rubber Plantation	38.00
Tin, Three States Mixture, Oval, Pocket	300.00
Tin, Three States Tobacco, Flat, Pocket, Oval	275.00
Tin, Tiger Tobacco, Upright Pocket, 1910 Stamp	150.00
Tin, Timur Coffee, 1 Lb.	160.00
Tin, Torpedo Tobacco, Destroyer, Pocket	1250.00
Tin, Tray, Welch's, Lace Doily Effect, Oval	30.00
Tin, Triangle Club Peanut Butter, 5 Lb.	85.00
Tin, Trojans Prophylactics	25.00
Tin, Trout Line Tobacco, Pocket	400.00
Tin, Try Moses Cough Drops, Tin, Small	115.00
Tin, Tube Rose Scotch Snuff, Round, 1 1/2 X 2 1/2 In.	4.00
Tin, Tuxedo Tobacco, Pocket	17.00
Tin, Tuxedo, Vacuum, Canister, 4 X 4 In.	40.00
Tin, Twin Oaks Tobacco, Flat, Pocket	100.00
Tin, Twin Oaks Tobacco, Flip Top	65.00
Tin, U.S.Marine Tobacco, Pocket	185.00
Tin, Uncle Daniel Tobacco, Detroit, Red, Printing, 8 X 2 In.	44.00
Tin, Uncle Daniel Tobacco, Yellow, 2 X 8 In.	300.00
Tin, Uniform Cut Plug, 4 X 6 In.	125.00
Tin, Union Leader Cut Plug Tobacco, Gold & Red, Eagles, Smoke	100.00
Tin, Union Leader Tobacco, Uncle Sam, Pocket	28.00
Tin, Union Leader, Eagle, Pocket	165.00
Tin, United Biscuit Co., Ye Christmas Feast, 10 In.	30.00
Tin, Van Dyke Coffee, Screw Lid, 1 Lb.	24.00
Tin, Vanko Cigars	30.00
Tin, Vanko Cigars, Horserace	95.00

Tin, Veribest Mince Meat, 4 In. 20.00
Tin, Vick's, Sample 10.00
Tin, Victoria Cavendish Tobacco, Pocket 35.00
Tin, Wagon Wheel, Pocket 875.00
Tin, Wallen's Coffee, Pry Lid, 5 Lb. 80.00
Tin, Walter Baker & Co., Ltd., Breakfast Cocoa, Label, 1/5 Lb. 15.00
Tin, War Eagle Cigar 50.00
Tin, War Eagle, Red, Canister, 5 X 3 In. 75.00
Tin, Watkin's Malted Milk 23.00
Tin, Watkins Egyptian Bouquet Talc 45.00
Tin, Webster Cigars, Hinged Lid, Pocket 13.00
Tin, Webster Savoy 10 Cent Size, Lid, 4 1/2 X 3 1/4 X 1 In. 9.50
Tin, Webster Thomas Tea 32.00
Tin, Wedding Breakfast Coffee, 1 Lb. 34.00
Tin, Wedding Breakfast Coffee, 3 Lb. 18.00
Tin, Wellington Tobacco, Pocket 95.00
Tin, Wellington, Pocket 85.00
Tin, Whip Tobacco, Octagonal 300.00
Tin, White Lion 115.00
Tin, White Manor, Pocket 190.00
Tin, Whitman's Candy, Gold & Black, 2 Lb. 20.00
Tin, Whitman's Salamagundi, Art Nouveau Girl, 1 Lb. 22.00
Tin, Whittles Marshmallow, Orange, Brown, White, 10 X 6 In. 28.00
Tin, Wishbone Coffee, 1 Lb. 75.00
Tin, Wishbone Coffee, 2 Lb. 60.00
Tin, Wood's Improved Lollacapop, Mosquito, 3 1/4 In. 8.00
Tin, Woodward's Marshmallow, Blues 37.50
Tin, Y & S Licorice Wafers, Hinged Lid, Enjoyed By Smokers 10.00
Tin, Yacht Club Marshmallows, 5 Lb. 50.00
Tin, Yankee Boy Tobacco, Pocket .... 395.00 To 425.00
Tin, Yellow Bonnet Coffee, 1 Lb. 25.00
Tin, Zeno Pepsin Gum 175.00

A tip tray is a decorated metal tray less than 5 inches in diameter. It was placed on the table or counter to hold either the bill or the coins that were left as a tip. A change receiver could be made of glass, plastic or metal. It was kept on the counter near the cash register and held the money passed back and forth by the cashier.

ADVERTISING, TIP TRAY, see also Advertising, Change Receiver

Tip Tray, Andrew White Cigars, Litho 75.00
Tip Tray, Angeles Brewing & Malting Co., 1909, 4 1/4 In. 101.00
Tip Tray, Baby Ruth Gum, With Gum Rack 150.00
Tip Tray, Ballentine Beer 45.00
Tip Tray, Bartel Lager, Ale, Porter, Nightwatchman, 1907, 4 In. 115.00
Tip Tray, Bartels, Viking, Syracuse, New York 75.00
Tip Tray, Batholomay's Brewery 60.00
Tip Tray, Benjamin Franklin Insurance 15.00
Tip Tray, Bettendorf Axle Co., Farm Wagon 60.00
Tip Tray, Booth Shoes 37.50
Tip Tray, C.D.Kenny, Star Spangled Banner, Center Hole, 1914 .... 35.00
Tip Tray, C.D.Kenny, Thanksgiving 20.00
Tip Tray, Canada Dry 17.00
Tip Tray, Carnation Dairy 70.00
Tip Tray, Carnation Milk 50.00
Tip Tray, Cortez Cigar, C.1915 .... 15.00
Tip Tray, Cottolene, Blacks Picking Cotton .... 65.00 To 100.00
Tip Tray, DeLaval Cream Separators, 1906 .... 75.00
Tip Tray, Dixie Queen Tobacco 35.00
Tip Tray, Don't Gamble–Drink Quevic, Dimple Center, 4 1/4 In. 9.00
Tip Tray, Evinrude Rowboat & Canoe Motors, 4 In. 100.00
Tip Tray, Fairy Soap, Little Girl, Sitting On Bar of Soap .... 45.00 To 65.00
Tip Tray, Feigenspan Beer, 1910 .... 48.00
Tip Tray, Feigenspan Brewery, 1910 .... 110.00
Tip Tray, Fox Head 400 Beer 10.00

Tip Tray, Franklin Life Insurance Company 13.95
Tip Tray, Globe, Wernicke Bookcases 25.00
Tip Tray, Gobel Beer, Dutch Scene 45.00
Tip Tray, Grain Belt Beer 20.00
Tip Tray, Grain Belt Beer, Minneapolis 25.00
Tip Tray, International Harvester 22.00
Tip Tray, Jack Daniels Whiskey .... 27.50 To 37.50
Tip Tray, Kentucky Cardinal, Glass, Round 95.00
Tip Tray, Kentucky Derby, Spins, Original Package, Instructions 12.00
Tip Tray, Los Angeles Brewing, Factory 115.00
Tip Tray, Mascot Tobacco 30.00
Tip Tray, Miller Beer, Dated 1952 .... 15.00
Tip Tray, Miller High Life Beer, Black Waiter, 6 1/2 In. 15.00
Tip Tray, Mokaine, Man In Outdoor Cafe, France, 3 X 4 1/2 In. 27.00
Tip Tray, Montezuma Cerveza, Senorita 35.00
Tip Tray, Montgomery Ward 25.00
Tip Tray, Moxie, 6 In. 137.00
Tip Tray, Moxie, Lady, Yellow Dress, Green Ground 125.00
Tip Tray, Moxie, Picture of Girl 250.00
Tip Tray, Moxie, Purple Flowers, Lady 150.00
Tip Tray, Moxie, Violets & Girl 125.00
Tip Tray, Muriel Cigar 28.00
Tip Tray, Newsweek, Cast Iron, Counter Top 25.00
Tip Tray, Oak Stove 18.00
Tip Tray, Prudential Insurance Co. 15.00
Tip Tray, Quandts Beer & Ales, Blue, Yellow & White, 4 In. 18.00
Tip Tray, Red Cross Ranges 32.00
Tip Tray, Red Raven Splits 65.00
Tip Tray, Rockford Watch Co., Girl's Portrait 40.00
Tip Tray, Rockford Watches, Rectangular 45.00
Tip Tray, Ruppert's Beer 35.00
Tip Tray, S & H Green Stamps 60.00
Tip Tray, Saver's Extracts 85.00
Tip Tray, Sears Roebuck, Sears Building, 1920s, 6 In. .... 35.00 To 50.00
Tip Tray, Smith Brothers 20.00
Tip Tray, Stegmaier Beer, Oval, Factory, Street Scene .... 55.00 To 85.00
Tip Tray, Sterling Beer, 1915 .... 20.00
Tip Tray, Tom Moore Cigars 20.00
Tip Tray, Universal Stoves 60.00
Tip Tray, White Rock, Nude 35.00
Tip Tray, Yeoman Insurance 25.00
Tire Patch Kit, Dutch Brand, Forever Tight, Never Loosens, Full 10.00
Tobacco Cutter, Bottle Base, Cast Iron 225.00
Tobacco Cutter, Brighton Little Imp 55.00
Tobacco Cutter, Brown's Mule 60.00
Tobacco Cutter, Champagne Flavor, Champagne Bottle Base 200.00
Tobacco Cutter, Counter Top, Brown's Mule, Iron 55.00
Tobacco Cutter, Crescent Shaped Blade, Iron & Sheet Metal 45.00
Tobacco Cutter, Griswold, 1883 .... 90.00
Tobacco Cutter, Griswold, No.3 .... 75.00
Tobacco Cutter, Guillotine Type 200.00
Tobacco Cutter, Heidsieck Champagne Flavor, Bottle Base 275.00
Tobacco Cutter, Lorillard's Tomahawk, Iron 45.00
Tobacco Cutter, Piper Heidsieck, Bottle Base, Iron 275.00
Tobacco Cutter, Star 50.00
Tobacco Cutter, Star, Iron 30.00
Tobacco Cutter, W.H.L.Hayes, Iron 45.00
Tobacco Cutter, W.H.L.Hayes, Original Paint, Iron 55.00
Tobacco Cutter, Wilson & McGalley, Guillotine Model 120.00
Tobacco Cutter, Wooden Base, Iron 75.00
Tobacco Pouch, Yankee Girl Scrap, Paper, 11 Cent 15.00
Tobacco Tag, Best Navy, Tin 3.00
Tobacco Tag, Dewey Twist, Tin 6.50
Tobacco Tag, Red Rabbit, Yellow Ground, Tin 18.00

Tobacco Tag, Sweet Marie, Mt.Airy, N.C., Tin 22.00
Tobacco Tag, To Success, Key, Tin 5.50
Toy, Lunch Pail, Pull Toy, Marked Iten Biscuit, Omaha 88.50
Tray, 7–Up, Block of Ice With Bottle 125.00
Tray, 7–Up, The Uncola, Round 6.00
Tray, Akron Brewery, Scene, Oval 795.00
Tray, American Brewery, New Orleans, Girl With Tiger 450.00
Tray, Bartel's $5,000 Beer, Lady & Bottle, Pre–Prohibition 600.00
Tray, Bartel's Beer, Edwardsville, Pa., White & Blue, 16 In. 65.00
Tray, Budweiser Beer, Levee Scene, 1914 .... 75.00 To 195.00
Tray, Budweiser, Wooden, 11 X 18 In. 22.00
Tray, Burkhardt's Beer, Factory, Pre–Prohibition 450.00
Tray, C.D.Kenney Co., Bust of George Washington 30.00
Tray, Candy Brothers Candy Company 185.00
Tray, Capedine 225.00
Tray, Chero–Cola, 9 In. 65.00
Tray, Congress Beer, Brass Rim, Eagle, Pre–1900 .... 650.00
Tray, Consumers Brewery, New Orleans, Factory, Oval 1100.00
Tray, Coor's Beer, Moutain Scene, Pre–Prohibition 200.00
Tray, Coor's Brewery, Golden, Colorado, Logo 300.00
Tray, Crescent Brewing, Nampa, Idaho, Factory, Pre–Prohibition 295.00
Tray, Crystal Spring Brewing Co., Porcelain Insert, Brass Rim 150.00
Tray, Curtis & Moore's Crushed Fruits, Lady & Horse Head 500.00
Tray, Dawson's Ale & Beer 75.00
Tray, Dick's Brewery, Quincy, Scene 825.00
Tray, Dr Pepper, Circle A Soda Water 250.00
Tray, Dr Pepper, Girl In Green Dress Holding Bottle 245.00
Tray, Dr Pepper, Girl In Green Dress, Holding 2 Dr Peppers 245.00
Tray, Dr Pepper, Girl With Bottle 105.00
Tray, Drink Orange Crush, Carbonated Beverage, 1948 .... 20.00
Tray, Duquesne Pilsner, Face of Student Prince 12.00
Tray, Edelweiss Beer, 1913, 13 In. 120.00
Tray, Ehret's Hellgate Brewery, Pre–Prohibition 95.00
Tray, Enterprise Brewing, Lady & Horse 350.00
Tray, Fairs Malt & Tonic, Louisville, Ky, Lady, Cherubs, Large 630.00
Tray, Falls City Ice & Beverage 45.00
Tray, Frank Schwab Co., Buffalo, Boy Carrying Wooden Keg 245.00
Tray, Fredericksburg Beer, Girl Carrying Beer, Pre–Prohibition 450.00
Tray, Garret Wine, Paul & Virginia Dare 195.00
Tray, Genesee Beer, Brass 165.00
Tray, George Brehm Beer, Porcelain, Oval 150.00
Tray, Golden State Beer, San Francisco, Eagle & Fair 160.00
Tray, Golden West Brewery, Oakland, California, Factory 175.00
Tray, Granite City Ice Cream, 1920s, 13 In. 50.00
Tray, Gretz Beer, Comic 45.00
Tray, Harvard Beer, Woman In Long Dress, Pre–Prohibition 350.00
Tray, Hires Root Beer, Ladies, Square 200.00
Tray, Huebner Beer, Toledo, Ohio, Lady 250.00
Tray, Jacob Ruppert Beer, Oval 45.00
Tray, Juarez Beer, Oval 55.00
Tray, Jung Brewing, Factory, Pre–Prohibition, 13 In. 750.00
Tray, Koppitz–Melcher Beer, Elves, Oval, Small 350.00
Tray, Leisen & Henes Beer, Factory, Oval, Pre–Prohibition 600.00
Tray, Lemp Brewery, St.Louis, Logo 500.00
Tray, Lipp's Brewery, Cincinnati, Dresden Art 100.00
Tray, Lord Calvert Whiskey, Tin, 23 In. 48.00
Tray, Louis Obert Beer, St.Louis 95.00
Tray, Maiers Brewery, Scene 1400.00
Tray, Malt Sinew Beer, Girl With Braids 250.00
Tray, Mathie Brewery, Lady In Black 495.00
Tray, Maxwell House Coffee 50.00
Tray, McAvoy's Malt Marrow, Round 150.00
Tray, McDonald Hamburgers, Captain Crook Picture, Plastic 10.00
Tray, Miller Beer, Girl Sitting On Moon 25.00

Tray, Miller High Life Beer, Gold & White	25.00
Tray, Miller Liquors, Germantown, Pa	85.00
Tray, Miller's Beer, Lady In Moon, Pre–Prohibition, 13 In.	150.00
Tray, Moore–McCormack, Ss Argentina, Porcelain, 1958, 7 X 5 In.	20.00
Tray, Narragansett Chief Gansett, By Dr.Seuss	37.00 To 65.00
Tray, Neuweiler's Beer, Pre–Prohibition	40.00 To 67.50
Tray, Nu–Grape, Flapper Girl	125.00
Tray, Old Forester Whiskey, Brass	18.00
Tray, Old Milwaukee Beer, Round	18.00
Tray, Orange Julep	128.00
Tray, Ortlieb's, Lager Beer & Ale, Round	25.00
Tray, Pabst, Man	35.00
Tray, Pacific Beer, Tacoma, Wa., C.1910, 12 In.	50.00
Tray, Pacific Beer, Tacoma, Washington, Mt.Tacoma	125.00
Tray, Palasades Beer, Factory	125.00
Tray, Peerless Ale	65.00
Tray, Peerless Ice Cream	85.00
Tray, Peoples Beer, Hits The Spot	25.00
Tray, Perfect Brew, Bulldog, 1900	225.00
Tray, Piels Beer, Pictures Piels Brothers, 1957	12.00
Tray, Pin, Oakland Auto, Shield Shape, Logo & Eagle, Copper	45.00
Tray, Rainier Beer, Lady & Bear, Pre–Prohibition	185.00 To 250.00
Tray, Red Raven Splits	350.00
Tray, Red Raven Whiskey, 13 X 13 In.	135.00
Tray, Red Raven, Lady Hugging Raven	250.00
Tray, Red Raven, Papa Has A Headache	525.00
Tray, Robin Hood Ale, Scranton, Pennsylvania, Oval	95.00
Tray, Rock Island Brewing Beer, Indian In Canoe, 12 In.	275.00
Tray, Rock Spring Sparkling Water Soda, Round	14.00
Tray, Rome Brewery, Roman Soldier	350.00
Tray, Ruppert Beer, 2 Hands With Steins, 1938	45.00
Tray, Schlitz Brewery, Wood Burning Train	500.00
Tray, Schuller's Ice Cream, 3 Women Eating, 13 X 11 In.	200.00
Tray, Seitz Beer, Spread Winged Eagle, 13 In.	25.00
Tray, Sheboygan Mineral Water, Indian, 2 Black Waiters	100.00
Tray, Sparks Kidney & Liver, Mrs.Grover Cleveland, Ceramic	275.00
Tray, Spokane Brew & Malt, Lady With Butterfly	475.00
Tray, Standard Breu Mankato Indian Execution	650.00
Tray, Star Brewing Co. Prize Ale & Lager, Pre–Prohibition	150.00
Tray, Star Brewing Company, Tavern Scene	65.00
Tray, Stegmaier's Beer, Wilkes–Barre, Pa., 13 1/4 In.	12.00
Tray, Sterling Ale	30.00
Tray, Sterling Beer	25.00
Tray, Student Prince Beer	15.00
Tray, Superior XX Beer, Indian	50.00
Tray, Temple Table Water	50.00
ADVERTISING, TRAY, TIP, see Advertising, Tip Tray	
Tray, Utica Blue, Hand Holding Glass	15.00
Tray, Utica Club, No.2, Character Steins	20.00
Tray, Vogue Fashion, 1921, 4 X 5 1/2 In.	15.00
Tray, White Cap Ale, Porcelain	55.00 To 85.00
Tray, White Rock Brewery, Lady On Tiger	200.00
Tray, With Bottle Opener, Iron City Beer	22.00
Tray, Y & B Cigars, Vienna Art	95.00
Tray, Yu–Say Beer	20.00

Any ad that pictures an American flag or a black has added value. Known brand names are also of greater value.

Tube, Dr.Hobson's Sunburn Cream, Box, 5 1/4 In. 10.00
Tumbler, Booth Bros. Ginger Ale, Liberty Bell 45.00
Tumbler, Coon Chicken Inn, Black Face With Logo 35.00
Tumbler, Dr.Brown's Celery Tonic, Federal, 6 Piece 35.00
Tumbler, Duquesne 5.00
Tumbler, Elsie, Borden Inc., Embossed, 3 1/4 In. 15.00
Tumbler, German Brewing 18.00
Tumbler, Harrisburg Dairies 9.00
Tumbler, Hires Root Beer, Thin Glass, Syrup Line 22.00
Tumbler, Howard Johnson, Boy, Dog, Pie Man Restaurant Picture 20.00
Tumbler, Jack Daniel No.7, Cut Glass Letters, Pair 45.00
Tumbler, Lion Export, Embossed 15.00
Tumbler, Moerlein Beer, Embossed 12.00
Tumbler, Moxie, Embossed, Fountain 25.00
Tumbler, National Steelton, Pa. 115.00
Tumbler, Old Crow Distilliers, Enameled 7.00
Tumbler, Old Dutch 12.00
Tumbler, Parade, Union Fire Co., Smokey The Bear, 1965 .... 10.00
Tumbler, Pillsbury's Flour, Victory Star, Carrier, 1940s, 4 Pc. 35.00
Tumbler, Quality Checked Ice Cream, Glass, 1940–50 .... 4.00
Tumbler, Schlitz Beer, Box, 9 Oz., Set of 6 .... 45.00
Tumbler, Welch's Grape Juice, Etched Grapes & Letters 25.00
Tumbler, Werner Pilsener, Boot Shape, German, 8 In. 15.00
Wallet, Campbell's Soup, Lassie, Giveaway, 1959, Unused Mailer 10.00
Whistle, Kraft, Tin 5.00
Whistle, Rochester Dairy 5.00
Whistle, Weiner Shape, Oscar Mayer 5.00
Windshield Scraper, Firestone 10.00
Wooden Shoe, Heineken Beer, Holland, 1950s 20.00
Wrapper, Beechnut Gum 5.00
Yo–Yo, Cheerio, Blue .... ˙6.00

Agata glass was made by Joseph Locke of the New England Glass Company of Cambridge, Massachusetts, after 1885. A metallic stain was applied to New England Peachblow and the mottled design characteristic of agata appeared.

AGATA, Bowl, Ruffled, 2 1/2 X 5 1/2 In. 700.00
Tumbler, Allover Pattern, Peachblow 585.00
Tumbler, Gold Tracery, 3 3/4 In. 685.00
Tumbler, Gold Tracery, Mottled, 3 3/4 In. 685.00
Tumbler, Gold Tracery, Peachblow Ground, New England 785.00
Tumbler, Lemonade, Handle At Lower Edge, Gold Tracery, 5 1/8 In. 1350.00
Vase, Buttercups, Opaque Green, Mottling, 6 1/4 In. 1500.00

Akro agate glass was made in Clarksburg, West Virginia, from 1932 to 1951. Before that time, the firm made children's glass marbles. Most of the glass is marked with a crow flying through the letter A.

AKRO AGATE, Bowl, Cereal, White, Marbelized 16.00
Cigarette Set, Swirl Pattern, Green, 5 Piece 25.00
Cup, Child's, Blue, 1 1/2 In. 10.00
Cup, Child's, Octagonal, Closed Handle, Pumpkin 15.00
Dish, Southern Belle, Cover, 6 X 4 In. 50.00
Lemonade Set, Child's, Octagonal, Ox Blood, Box, 20 Piece 275.00
Pitcher, Water, Octagonal, Blue 11.00
Plate, Child's, Blue, 4 1/4 In. 2.00
Powder Box, Scotty, Pink Base, White Top 75.00
Powder Jar, Scotty .... 40.00 To 65.00
Saucer, Child's, Pink, 3 1/2 In. 2.00
Sugar, Child's, Yellow, White Cover, 1 1/2 In. 12.00
Tea Set, Child's, Concentric Rings, Pumpkin Cups, 16 Piece 85.00
Tea Set, Raised Daisy, Box, 13 Piece 225.00
Teapot, Open Handle, Octagonal, Blue 12.50
Vase, Green, Iron Holder 35.00
Water Set, Transparent Green, 7 Piece 45.00

Alabaster is a very soft form of gypsum, a stone that resembles marble. It was often carved into vases or statues in Victorian times. There are alabaster carvings being made even today. Because the alabaster is very porous, it will dissolve if kept in water, so do not use alabaster vases for flowers.

ALABASTER, Box, Pale Blue, Added Color, 4 X 6 In. 30.00
    Figurine, Boy, Knickers, 12 In. 60.00
    Figurine, Girl, Classical Dress, Signed Marron, 13 1/2 In. 100.00

Alexandrite is a name with many meanings. It is a form of the mineral chrysoberyl that changes from green to red under artificial light. A man–made version of this mineral is sold in Mexico today. It changes from deep purple to aquamarine blue under artificial light. The Alexandrite listed here is glass made in the late nineteenth and twentieth centuries. Thomas Webb & Sons sold their transparent glass shaded from yellow to rose to blue under the name Alexandrite. Stevens and Williams had a cased Alexandrite of yellow, rose, and blue. A. Douglas Nash Corporation made an amethyst–colored Alexandrite. Several American glass companies of the 1920s made a glass that changed color under electric lights and these were called Alexandrite too.

ALEXANDRITE, Bowl, Nut, Optic Diamond–Quilted, Webb, Blue, 2 9/16 In. 985.00
    Compote, Honeycomb, Fluted Top, Amber Stem & Foot, 6 3/4 In. 1475.00
    Goblet, Wafer Base, Leaves On Twisted Stem, 8 1/2 In. 1750.00
    Tumbler, Juice, Rose To Amber 365.00

Alhambra is a pattern of tableware made in Vienna, Austria, in the twentieth century. The geometric designs are in applied gold, red, and dark green. Full sets of dishes can be found in this pattern.

ALHAMBRA, Cup, Mottled, 3 In. 25.00
    Pitcher, 6 In. 120.00
    Plate, 9 In. 30.00

Aluminum was more expensive than gold or silver until the 1850s. Chemists learned how to refine bauxite to get aluminum. Jewelry and other small objects were made of the valuable metal until 1914 when an inexpensive smelting process was invented. The aluminum collected today dates from the 1930s through 1950s. Hand–hammered pieces are the most popular.

ALUMINUM, Bowl, Enameled Fruit Design, Pedestal, Cellini Craft, 5 3/4 In. 120.00
    Broiler, Griddle, Guardian Service 10.00
    Butter Tub, Butterbean Knot On Lid, Embossed Butterbean Leaves 16.00
    Cup, Collapsible, Embossed Couple On Tandem Bicycle On Top 17.50
    Lazy Susan, 2 Butters, 2 Jam Jars, Toast Rack 25.00
    Mold, Cake, Lamb, 2 Piece 40.00
    Roaster, Cover, Guardian Service 35.00
    Tray, Hammered, Handles, 20 In. 10.00
    Tray, Round, Large, Guardian Service 10.00
    Tumbler, Colored, 1940s, Set of 6 .... 15.00
    AMBER, see Jewelry

Amber glass is the name of any glassware with the proper yellow–brown shading. It was a popular color just after the Civil War and many pressed glass pieces were made of amber glass. Depression glass of the 1930s–1950s was also made in shades of amber glass. All types are being reproduced.

AMBER GLASS, Basket, Applied Braided Handle, 6 Panels, 8 3/4 In. 28.00
    Basket, Sandwich Pattern, Flared Rim, Handle, 10 In. 58.00
    Bowl, Three Panels, Footed, 10 In. 50.00
    Bride's Bowl, Shell & Tassel, Original Frame 195.00
    Cruet, Hercules Pillar 125.00
    Cruet, Log & Star, Original Stopper 25.00
    Cruet, Ribbed, Blue Handle & Stopper, 7 1/4 In. 65.00

Cruet, Winged Griffin Bust On Handle, Pewter Mounts, 9 1/8 In. 225.00
Decanter, Art Nouveau, Pewter Holder, 14 In. 175.00
Decanter, Wine, Pewter Stopper, Woman's Head On Handle, 11 In. 195.00
Flower Frog, Brown Streaks, 2 1/2 In.Diam. 25.00
Mug, Child's, Our Boy, Monkey Riding Pig, 3 1/4 In. 42.00
Pitcher, Inverted Thumbprint, Clear Rope Handle, 6 1/4 In. 150.00
Pitcher, Water, Swirled, Blue Handles, 10 In. 95.00
Rose Bowl, Enameled Flowers, Gold Tracery Leaves, Ruffled Rim 48.50
Sugar & Creamer, Thousand Eye, C.1880, 4 1/2 In. 75.00
Tray, Fan Shape, Button & Bows Pattern 35.00
　　　AMBERETTE, see Pressed Glass, Klondike

Amberina is a two-toned glassware made from 1883 to about 1900.
It was patented by Joseph Locke of the New England Glass
Company. The glass shades from red to amber.

AMBERINA, see also Baccarat; Bluerina; Plated Amberina
AMBERINA, **Bowl,** Applied Threading, Ruffled Rim, 5 5/8 In. 65.00
Bowl, Ruffled Rim, 9 1/2 In. 175.00
Bread Tray, Daisy & Button, 13 X 9 In. 135.00
Candlestick, Eiffel Tower, 11 In., Pair 75.00
Canoe, Daisy & Button 395.00
Carafe, Diamond–Quilted, Pinched Sides, Amber Rigaree, 8 1/2 In. 325.00
Carafe, Optic Pattern, Matching Tumbler, 7 In. 175.00
Celery, Diamond–Quilted, Scalloped Rim, New England, 6 1/2 In. 325.00
Celery, Inverted Thumbprint, Amber To Cranberry, 6 1/2 In. 510.00
Celery, Inverted Thumbprint, Scalloped Rim, 5 3/4 In. 160.00
Celery, Inverted Thumbprint, Square Rim, New England, 6 1/2 In. 375.00
Compote, Dolphin Footed, Northwood Mold, 6 In. 18.00
Creamer, Inverted Thumbprint, Clear Reeded Handle 40.00
Cruet, Diamond–Quilted, Faceted Stopper, 6 1/2 In. 175.00
Cruet, Drape Pattern, Original Stopper 395.00
Cruet, Inverted Thumbprint, Amber Reeded Handle, Faceted Stopper 350.00
Cruet, Vinegar, Inverted Thumbprint, 7 1/2 In. 195.00
Dish, Cheese, Cover, Inverted Thumbprint, Amber Finial, 9 In. 325.00
Dish, Daisy & Button, Square, 4 3/4 In. 75.00
Finger Bowl, Swirl, New England, 4 3/8 In. 145.00
Lemonade Set, Enameled Red Holly Berries, Leaves, 10 In., 5 Piece 795.00
Mug, Barrel Shape, Swirl, Amber Handle, 4 1/4 In. 60.00
Paperweight, Apple 20.00
Pitcher, Applied Amber Ribbed Handle, 7 1/2 In. 275.00
Pitcher, Inverted Thumbprint, 8 1/2 In. 295.00
Pitcher, Inverted Thumbprint, Clear Handle, 6 In. 250.00
Pitcher, Inverted Thumbprint, Threaded Handle, 10 1/2 In. 225.00
Pitcher, Water, Inverted Thumbprint, Amber Handle, 7 1/2 In. 375.00
Powder Box, Swan 10.00
Reamer, Handle, Large 35.00
Saltshaker, Ribbed, Original Top, 3 3/4 In. 125.00
Spooner, Inverted Thumbprint, 5 1/2 In. 125.00
Sugar, Inverted Thumbprint, Boston & Sandwich Glass Co., 6 In. 350.00
Toothpick, Daisy & Button, 3–Footed 165.00
Toothpick, Diamond–Quilted, Fuchsia 225.00
Toothpick, Inverted Thumbprint 400.00
Toothpick, Reverse Amberina, Raised Diamond Pattern, Pedestal 265.00
Toothpick, Venetian Diamond, Tricornered 235.00
Tumbler, Diamond Optic, Ruby To Amber, 1920, Set of 6 .... 115.00
Tumbler, Diamond–Quilted, New England, 3 5/8 In. 88.00
Tumbler, Inverted Thumbprint 95.00
Tumbler, Optic Swirl 145.00
Vase, 12 Molded Ribs, Footed, Libbey, C.1917, 8 In. 685.00
Vase, Amber–Footed, Cylindrical, Amber Spiral Trim, 10 1/8 In. 160.00
Vase, Crystal Ruffled Top, Crystal Leaves, Crackled, 6 1/8 In. 395.00
Vase, Daisies, Poppies, Leaves, Ruffled Top, 11 3/4 In. 175.00
Vase, Daisies, White Flowers, Leaves, Ribbon, Fluted, 9 1/2 In. 165.00
Vase, Free–Form Lip, Amber Crackle To Base, 4 3/4 In. 250.00

Vase, Hobnail, Ruffled, 9 In. 45.00
Vase, Jack–In–The–Pulpit Top, Gold Flowers, 10 In. 210.00
Vase, Lily, 7 In. 275.00
Vase, Lily, 9 3/4 In. 195.00
Vase, Swirl Pattern, Enameled Flowers, Birds, 10 1/2 In. 650.00
Vase, Thumbprint, Ruffled Top, 8 In. 150.00
Water Set, Enameled Flowers, Lacy Gold Foliage, 6 Piece 495.00
Water Set, Inverted Thumbprint, Clear Reed Handle, 7 Piece 580.00
Whiskey, Venetian Diamond, New England, 2 3/4 In. 125.00
Wine, Diagonal Swirl, Square Rim 165.00

The American Encaustic Tiling Company was founded in Zanesville, Ohio, in 1875. The company planned to make a variety of tiles to compete with the English tiles that were selling in the United States for use in fireplaces and other architectural needs. The first glazed tiles were made in 1880, embossed tiles were added in 1881, faience tiles in the 1920s. The firm closed in 1935 and reopened in 1937 as the Shawnee Pottery.

AMERICAN ENCAUSTIC TILING CO., Figurine, Art Deco Woman, Celadon, 7 In. 85.00
Tile, Chicken, Brown, 4 In. 25.00
Tile, Fleur–De–Lis, Tan Relief, Blue, 6 In. 45.00
Tile, Polly Put The Kettle On, 6 In. 125.00

Amethyst glass is any of the many glasswares made in the dark purple color of the gemstone called amethyst. Included in this section are many pieces made in the nineteenth and twentieth centuries. Very dark pieces are called black amethyst and are listed under that heading.

AMETHYST GLASS, Basket, Vaseline Edge, 7 3/8 In. 175.00
Canoe, Daisy & Button, Scalloped Edge, Bryce Bros., 12 In. 60.00
Decanter, Flowers, Gold Enameling, Blown Stopper 48.00
Honey Jar, Fly, Silver Plated Head, Wings, Mappin Webb, 6 In. 125.00
Pitcher, Melon Shape, Blown, Bulbous, Applied Handle, 6 In. 22.00
Sugar, Hexagonal Cover, Panels of Bellflowers, 1835, 6 In. 750.00
Vase, Tulip, Hexagonal, 19th Century, 9 3/4 In., Pair 1700.00
AMPHORA, see Teplitz
ANDIRON AND RELATED FIREPLACE ITEMS, see Fireplace

Stuffed animals or fish, rugs made of animal skins, and other similar collectibles are listed in this section. Collectors should be aware of the endangered species laws that make it illegal to buy and sell some of these items. Any eagle feathers, many types of cats, such as leopard, and many forms of tortoiseshell can be confiscated if discovered by the government.

ANIMAL TROPHY, Alligator, Mounted, 5 Ft. 275.00
Bear, Black, North American, Brown Phase, Full Body 1000.00
Bear, Full Body, 6 1/2 Ft. 1395.00
Bear, Grizzly, North American, Dark Blond Phase, Full Body 2800.00
Bearskin Rug, 4 X 6 Ft. 125.00
Bearskin Rug, Black, 3 X 5 Ft. 300.00
Bearskin Rug, Head & Claws, 5 Ft. 350.00
Beaver, North American, Standing By Chewed Birch, Full Body 95.00
Buffalo Hide Rug, 72 X 80 In. 50.00
Buffalo, American, Shoulder Mount 695.00
Calf Skin, 2–Headed, Freak 48.00
Calf, 2–Headed 350.00
Coyote Skin, Mounted On Black Felt 75.00
Deer Head, Antlers 75.00
Eland, Mounted 110.00
Fallow Deer Stag, Shoulder Mount 75.00
Fox, Arctic, Mature, Full Mount, Glass & Wooden Display Case 550.00
Goat Head, Mounted 350.00
Ibex 577.00
Lake Trout, Mounted 50.00

Always vacuum your moose from the snout up and scrub your
pheasant with fresh white bread, torn not sliced. Vacuum your
moose head with the furniture attachment but go with, not against,
the grain. Rinse the head every five years. Careful—too much water
will make a mildewed moose.

Large Mouth Bass, Mounted	30.00
Leopard Rug, Head & Feet	1275.00
Lynx, Crouched Over Snowshoe Hare, Full Mount	275.00
Mink, Upright	85.00
Moose Head, Mounted	375.00
Moose, Alaskan, Shoulder Mount, 60 In. Back	1250.00
Mountain Goat, Female, Neck Mount	70.00
Mountain Lion Rug	375.00
Muskie, Mounted	45.00
Northern Pike, Mounted	60.00
Owl, Arctic, Stuffed	175.00
Pronghorn Antelope, North American, Full Body, 13 In.Horns	450.00
Rocky Mountain Elk, Royal Rack, Shoulder Mount	400.00
Russian Boar, Neck Mount	100.00
Sitatunga, African Antelope	250.00
Small Mouth Bass, Mounted	40.00
Stag Hide	65.00
Timber Wolf, North American, Dark Phase, Full Body	550.00
Ural Sheep	635.00
White–Tailed Deer, 13–Point Rack, Plaque	110.00
Wild Boar, Dark Brown, Shoulder Mount	70.00
Wolf, Arctic, Standing & Howling, White & Gray, Full Body	1200.00
Zebra Skin, 4 Ft. 6 In. X 6 Ft. 6 In.	500.00

Animation cels are painted drawings on celluloid that are needed to
make an animated cartoon. Hundreds of cels are made, then
photographed in sequence to make a cartoon showing moving
figures. Early examples made by the Walt Disney Studios are
popular with collectors today.

ANIMATION ART, Cel, Alice In Wonderland, 1951, Framed, 10 1/4 X 13 1/4 In.	1650.00
Cel, Baby Smurf, Dreaming of Teddy Bear, Jack–In–The–Box	75.00
Cel, Donald Duck & Jose Carioca, Disney, 1945	995.00
Cel, Dumbo, 2 Crows Dancing, Signed By Walt Disney	1000.00
Cel, Dwarves Pulling Mining Cart, Wood Veneer Ground	3500.00
Cel, Edgar, Putting On Pants, From Aristocats, Disney	100.00
Cel, Fantasia, Night On Bald Mountain, 1940, 10 X 14 In.	330.00
Cel, Fritz The Cat, Matted, 3 Cels, 1971, 9 1/2 X 12 1/2 In.	385.00
Cel, Frog & Texas Toad, Colors	35.00
Cel, George Jetson, Wife & Robot, Matted	75.00
Cel, Jetson, Elroy & Astro, Elroy Meets Orbity, Hand Painted	145.00
Cel, Jetson, George, Mr.Spacely, Robot Dog, Matted	125.00
Cel, Jungle Book Figures, Mowgli & Baloo, Jungle Ground	2750.00
Cel, Mother Goose, Framed, 1938, 8 X 9 1/2 In.	770.00
Cel, Mr.Magoo	75.00
Cel, Peter Pan, Princess Tiger Lily, 1953, 7 1/2 X 9 1/4 In.	715.00
Cel, Pinocchio, Giddy & Foulfellow, 1939, 7 1/4 X 7 1/2 In.	1870.00
Cel, Rescuers, With Seal, Disney	400.00

Cel, Scooby–Doo, With Scrappy, Barbecuing 75.00
Cel, Sleeping Beauty, Evil Malificent & Her Crow 2000.00
Cel, Sleeping Beauty, Matted, 1959, 9 X 12 In. 825.00
Cel, Snow White & 7 Dwarfs, Disney 5500.00
Cel, Superman, Close–Up 45.00
Cel, The Ugly Duckling, Airbrushed, 1931, 6 1/2 X 7 3/8 In. 1320.00
Cel, Three Little Pigs, Framed, 1932, 9 X 11 1/2 In. 6600.00
Cel, Turtle & Chipmunk, From Snow White & 7 Dwarfs, 5 In. 950.00
    APPLE PEELER, see Kitchen, Peeler, Apple

 This section includes a variety of collectibles, usually very large, that have been removed from buildings. Hardware, backbars, doors, paneling, and even old bathtubs are now wanted by collectors. Pieces of the Victorian, Art Nouveau, and Art Deco styles are in greatest demand.

ARCHITECTURAL, Altar Frontal, Birds, Foxes, 18th Century, Italy, 180 X 84 In. 2250.00
Backbar, 2 Posters, Mirror, Oak, 16 Ft. 2000.00
Backbar, 3 Mirrors, 2 Columns, Brass Chandelier, 8 X 16 Ft. 6500.00
Backbar, Brunswick, Balke & Collender, Cherry, 8 Ft. 3000.00
Backbar, Cherry, Marble Top, Columns, Doors Below, 1922, 14 Ft. 6000.00
Backbar, Cherrywood, Leaded Glass Doors, Marble, 10 X 8 Ft. 2000.00
Backbar, Marble Top, Bonneted Back, Phosphates Sign, 1890 .... 3500.00
Backbar, Marble, Oak, Stained Glass Panels, 10 Ft. 4250.00
Backbar, Oak, Hanging Shades, Marble Top, 54 In. 2800.00
Backbar, Sliding Door Cabinets, 5 Glass Doors, 6 X 8 Ft. 1500.00
Balustrade, Chicago Stock Exchange, L.Sullivan, Iron, 7 Ft. 2200.00
Bathtub, Claw Feet, Original Faucet & Brass 200.00
Bathtub, Copper, Oak Rim, Engraved Cast Legs 800.00
Bathtub, Enameled Copper, Brass Feet, Fixtures & Trim 4000.00
Bathtub, Folding, Copper, Kerosene Heater, Oak Cabinet 1500.00
Bean Counter, 6 Bins 1125.00
Brick, Handmade, From Civil War Hospital, C.1830 .... 10.00
Cornice, Ceiling, Giltwood, Laurel Leaves, 19 & 15 Ft. 550.00
Cupola, Barn, Pennsylvania Dutch, Metal, 1940s, 6 Ft.X 40 In. 125.00
Door Handle, Brass, Ornamental, Large 19.00
Door, Iron, Scrolling, 18th Century, 38 In., Pair 2200.00
Door, Leaded Glass, Prairie School Style, Oak Frame, 84 In. 500.00
Door, Post Office Box, Brass, Combination Lock, 5 X 6 In. 15.00
Door, Post Office Box, Brass, With Glass 20.00
Doorbell, Turn Handle, Bell Rings, C.1880 .... 75.00
Doorknob, Black Porcelain, Pair 6.00
Doorknob, Millefiori Glass Paperweight, Pair 75.00
Doorknob, Painted Flowers, Screws, Drapery Tieback, 4 Piece 35.00
Eagle, Copper, Traces of Gilding, 48 In. 2250.00
Eave, House, Pine, Red & Green Paint Traces, 45 X 116 In. 275.00
Fountain Head, Cherub With Fish, Cast Zinc, 26 1/2 In. 275.00
Fountain, Garden, 2 Fish Forming Circle, Plinth, Lead, 35 In. 2750.00
Fountain, Heron, Outstretched Wings, Painted Zinc, 38 In. 2475.00
Gate, Victorian, Iron, 8 X 14 Ft. 1200.00
Hinge, Iron, Bird's Head Design, 11 In., Pair 75.00
Hinge, L–Form, Iron, Pair 12.50
Lamp, Street, Globes, Cast Iron, 12 Ft. 250.00
Lamp, Street, Pioneer, Dietz, On Post Socket, Green Paint 425.00
Latch, F–Form, Iron, 4 1/2 In. 95.00
Latch, Thumb, Iron 4.50
Lightning Rod, Horse, Arrow, Marked James, Tin 275.00
Lock, Bathroom Door, Coin–Operated, English 90.00
Lock, Door, Kamindore Lock Co., Box, 1910 .... 30.00
Lock, Door, Key, Scrolled, Iron, French, 18th Century, 16 In. 1100.00
Lock, Turned Bolt, Key, Iron, German, 11 5/8 In. 125.00
Mailbox Cluster, 36 Brass Front Encased 295.00
Mantel, Carved, Incised, Bronze Plaque Inserts, 80 In. 2530.00
Mantel, Faux Marble Painted, New England, C.1830, 54 3/4 In. 375.00
Mantel, Federal, White Paint, Poplar, 57 3/4 X 68 1/4 In. 325.00

Mantel, Leaded Glass Doors, Oak, 72 X 57 In. 750.00
Mantel, Pine, Grain Painted, Serpentine, 19th Century, 52 In. 248.00
Panel, Continental, Shepherdess, Marquetry, Enameled Frame 135.00
Panel, Spread Eagle, Flower Baskets, Wooden, 27 X 32 In. 900.00
Panel, Stained Glass, Armorial, Burger & Wife, 13 X 9 In. 990.00
Panel, Stained Glass, Noblemen, Armor, 19th Century, 20 In. 2090.00
Panel, Stained Glass, St.Catherine, 19th Century, 20 In. 935.00
Pedestal, Eagle Picture, Pair 440.00
Pedestal, Oak, Marble Top, Box Base, Flared, 37 X 22 In., Pair 1000.00
Pediment, Shadow-Form Letters, Swags, 4 Parts, 31 In.X 7 Ft. 475.00
Podium, Hand Carved Eagle, 31 X 22 In. 750.00
Radiator, Cast Iron, Painted Designs, Marble Top 110.00
Screen Door Frame, Relief Carved Floral, 32 X 81 In. 50.00
Seed Counter, Display Windows, Curved Lower Bay, 10 1/2 Ft. 1500.00
Seed Counter, Oak, 6 Ft. 600.00
Sink, Bar, Copper Lined 325.00
Sink, Built-In, Victorian, Rounded Front 275.00
Soda Fountain, 4 Brass Spigots, 8 Flavors, 1832, 4 X 10 Ft. 6000.00
Stairwell, Post Office, Circular, Cast Iron, 1912, 27 Ft. 2000.00
Streetlight, Gas, Copper Top, Iron, 10 Ft. 110.00
Sundial, Stone, 4 Monks, Iron Numerals, 16th Century, 10 In. 1100.00
Toilet Seat, Mahogany 48.00
Windowpane, Floral, Blue, 7 7/8 X 3 15/16 In. 125.00
Windowpane, Foliate Pattern, Amber, Square, 5 5/8 In. 175.00

Arequipa Pottery was produced from 1911 to 1918 by the patients of the Arequipa Sanitorium in Marin County Hills, California.

AREQUIPA, Vase, Berry and Leaf Carved Design, Purple, 3 1/2 In. 375.00
Vase, Crystalline Glaze, Incised Geometric Design, Blue, 6 In. 275.00
Vase, Green Matte Glaze, 6 In. 250.00
Vase, Incised Flowers, Blue, 6 In. 325.00
Vase, Pink Mottled Glaze, Marked, Numbered, 5 In. 295.00
ARGY-ROUSSEAU, see G. Argy-Rousseau

Art Deco, or Art Moderne, a style started at the Paris Exposition of 1925, is characterized by linear, geometric designs. All types of furniture and decorative arts, jewelry, book bindings, and even games were designed in this style.

ART DECO, Ashtray, Nude, Reclining, Bisque, White, Gold, Porzellan, 6 1/2 In. 175.00
Biscuit Jar, Flowers, Leaves, Green, Wicker Handle, 7 1/4 In. 150.00
Bottle, Liquor, Chrome, Glass, Musical 20.00
Bowl & Pitcher, Coronaware, Cairo Pattern, S.Hancock & Sons 250.00
Box, Cigarette, Bronze, Classical Figure, Goats, R.Kent, 6 1/2 In. 500.00
Brush, Man's, Black, Silver, Monogram M.H., Pair 38.00
Candlestick, Brass, 10 In., Pair 60.00
Candy Dish, Cover, Yellow & Black, Exotic Birds, Shelley 49.00
Cigarette Holder, Cylinder, Cigarette Presented By Handle, 6 In. 35.00
Cocktail Shaker Set, Enameled Camels, Palm Trees, 7 Piece 39.00
Coffee Urn, Sugar, Creamer & Tray, Chrome Plated, 1930-40 .... 40.00
Coffeepot, Drip, White, Blue Stars, 8 In. 95.00
Figurine, Dancer, Harem, Ivory, Gold Trim, 10 In. 125.00
Figurine, Dancing Lady, Moriama, 13 In. 145.00
Figurine, Flamingo, Brad Keeler, 10 In., Pair 100.00
Figurine, Leda & The Swan, China, Paper Label, Akro, 15 In. 350.00
Figurine, Oriental Lady & Man, Mandolin, Porcelain, 12 1/4 In., Pr. 45.00
Figurine, Theatrical Lady, Cape, Cap Hair, Erphila, 1886, 12 In. 495.00
Head, Erotica, White 70.00
Humidor, Bronze, Wood Lined, 5 X 7 1/2 In. 65.00
Incense Burner, Girl, Flower Basket, Bronzed Metal, Vantine, 5 In. 35.00
Jam Jar, Apple Shape, Green, Blue, Flowers, Cover, 3 1/2 In. 98.00
Jar, Powder, Pink Frosted, Egyptian Head Finial 45.00
Lamp, 2 Nude Women, Pagoda, Stained Glass, Dragons, Old Man, Birds 275.00
Lamp, Indian Maiden, Dog, Blue Glass Shade 47.50
Lamp, Satellite, Green 75.00

Lamp, Spanish Dancers, Bronze Washed Metal, Rumba On Base, 17 In.	95.00
Plaque, Orchids, Yellow Ground, Satin Glass, Signed Seyt	175.00
Powder Box, Blue Enamel, Silver Butterfly Design	25.00
Powder Box, Girl & 2 Dogs On Cover, Green Frosted	65.00
Smoking Stand, Greyhound Handle	75.00
Vase, Bizarre Style Painted Lady & Man, Haynes, 14 In.	50.00
Vase, Blue Flamingos, Milk Glass, 9 In.	20.00
Vase, Bronze, Signed Carl Sorensen, 8 In., Pair	225.00
Vase, Draped Lady, Green Glass, 9 1/2 In.	70.00
Vase, Green, Girl Inside Circular Cutout, Howard Pierce	50.00
Wall Pocket, Figural, Flapper Style Lady, Rose Grapes, German Mark	42.00

 Art glass means any of the many forms of glassware made during the late nineteenth century or early twentieth century. These wares were expensive and production was limited. Art glass is not the typical commercial glass that was made in large quantities, and most of the art glass was produced by hand methods.

ART GLASS, see also separate headings such as Burmese; Cameo Glass; Tiffany; etc.

ART GLASS, Basket, Cranberry Threading, Clear, 8 Point Form, Handle, 12 In.	660.00
Basket, Horned Handle, Pink Inside, Bristol Outside, 5 3/4 In.	395.00
Basket, Opaque Cream, Applied Flowers, Ribbon Candy Top, 7 In.	148.00
Basket, Peppermint Striped, Ruffled, Thorn Handle	175.00
Basket, Pink & White Spatter Overlay, Thorn Handle, 7 In.	125.00
Biscuit Jar, Pink, Birds, Raspberry Branches, 5 1/2 In.	375.00
Bottle, Perfume, Art Deco Floral Overlay, Ground Glass Stopper	95.00
Bottle, Perfume, Diamond–Quilted, Yellow To White, 6 In.	395.00
Bottle, Perfume, Floral Overlay, Glass Stopper, Art Deco	95.00
Bowl, Amber, Iridescent, Ruffled Edge, 8 In.	80.00
Bowl, Enameled, Candy Ribbon Edge, Yellow, Green Trim, 11 In.	225.00
Bowl, Oval Bands, Overlapping Circles, Decorchemont, 7 1/4 In.	6600.00
Candlestick, Emerald, Gold Overlay Bands, Acorn Shape, 11 In.	80.00
Cigarette Holder, Blue Glass Base, Chase	20.00
Epergne, Lily, Rainbow Base	150.00
Pitcher, Ducks On Water, White Satin, Pink Interior, 9 1/4 In.	405.00
Salt, Cranberry, Crystal 8–Point Edge, Silver Holder, 2 X 4 In.	150.00
Sugar & Creamer, Diamond–Quilted, Amberina, Shell Handles	395.00
Sugar Shaker, Mushroom, Allover Asters, Signed Albertine	550.00
Vase, Art Deco, Bulbous, Odetta, 12 In.	550.00
Vase, Blue, Bluebirds, Flowers Between Layers, Pedestal, 10 In.	450.00
Vase, Clear, Emerald Green Spiral Ribbing, Crimped, 13 1/2 In.	60.00
Vase, Jack–In–The–Pulpit, Ruby Iridescent, Crider	35.00
Vase, Latticinio, Pale Pink Satin Finish, Translucent, 13 In.	110.00
Vase, Stylized Flowers Over Mottled Ground, Charder, 7 1/2 In.	375.00

 Art Nouveau is a style of design that was at its most popular from 1895 to 1905. Famous designers, including Rene Lalique and Emile Galle, produced furniture, glass, silver, metalwork, and buildings in the new style. Ladies with long flowing hair and elongated bodies were among the more easily recognized design elements. Copies of this style are being made today. Many modern pieces of jewelry can be found.

ART NOUVEAU, see also Furniture; various glass categories; etc.

ART NOUVEAU, Brush, Clothes, Sterling Silver Top, Floral, Set of 3	125.00
Candleholder, Figural, Lady, Standing, Cameo Mirror, Pair	1200.00
Candlestick, Lady Holds Candle, Iron, Bronze Patina, 16 In., Pr.	105.00
Candlestick, Nude Lady, Stands On Foot, Holds Flower, 15 In.	105.00
Decanter, Amber Glass, Silver Plated Mounts, 1890	50.00
Figurine, Herodian, Metal Bust, Plaster Base, Signed, 21 In.	750.00
Jewelry Box, Victorian, Metal, Floral Design, 4 X 4 X 5 In.	75.00
Lighter, Cigar, Monkey	25.00
Match Safe, Raised Head of Lady, Sterling	75.00
Spoon, Nude Handle, Sterling Silver	75.00
Tray, Card, Pewter–Type Metal, Nude, Flowing Hair, 4 X 7 In.	72.00

Vase, Silver Overlay, Etched Floral, Bulbous, DKG, 12 1/4 In. 850.00
Vase, Water Lilies, Sterling Silver, Scroll Handles, 10 1/2 In. 450.00

The first American art pottery was made in Cincinnati, Ohio, during the 1870s. The pieces were hand thrown and hand decorated. The art pottery tradition continued until the 1920s when studio potters began making the more artistic wares.

ART POTTERY, see also under factory name

ART POTTERY, Coffee Server, 4 Mugs, Turquoise, 4 Mugs, Metal Handles, Deco 88.00
Decanter, Bretby, Moths, Handle, 1883, 16 1/2 In., Pair 250.00
Jug, Corn Design, Standard Glaze, Signed Olympia 125.00
Lamp, Bamboo Brush Sketch, Crackle Ground, Japan, 15 1/8 In. 125.00
Mug, Motto, Cutout Square Handle, Jervis Mark, 5 3/4 X 4 In. 200.00
Pitcher, Gold, Green, Stockton 85.00
Pitcher, Mottled Blue & Brown Drip Glaze, Lachenal, 15 3/4 In. 400.00
Salt, MacInyre, Open, Cream, Marbelized Brown, Dated 1878 .... 60.00
Vase, Band of Monkeys, Squigglework, Mayodon, C.1925, 9 1/2 In. 770.00
Vase, Crackled Turquoise, Robineau, 7 3/8 X 4 In. 7000.00
Vase, Green, Bellflowers & Broad Leaves In Relief, 10 In. 60.00
Vase, Low Handles, Zark 225.00
Vase, Milk White, Amber & Blue Flambe, T.Doat, 1900, 8 In. 500.00
Vase, Omar Khayyam, Dated & Stamped OLB, 20 In. 2100.00
Vase, Pink & Mauve Iris Blossoms, Pointons, 1883–90, 20 5/8 In. 150.00
Vase, Scene On Yellow, Applied Cicada, Valluris, 3 1/2 In. 55.00
Vase, Silver Snowflake Crystals, Flared, Robineau ....*Illus* 7500.00
Vase, Silver Snowflake Crystals, Robineau, 6 In. ....*Illus* 7500.00
Vase, Standing Maiden, Pastoral Setting, French, 5 3/4 In. 595.00
Vase, Turquoise, Robertson, 3 1/2 In. 45.00
Vase, Yellow, Brown, Goldenrod, Brouwer, 12 1/2 In. ....*Illus* 8000.00

AURENE

Aurene glass was made by Frederick Carder of New York about 1904. It is an iridescent gold or blue glass, usually marked "Aurene" or "Steuben."

AURENE, Bowl, Blue, Fold–In Top, 3–Footed, Numbered, 3 X 12 In. 750.00
Bowl, Blue, Signed, Numbered, 3 X 12 In. 675.00
Bowl, Fluted, Signed, 6 1/4 In. 375.00
Bowl, Pedestal, Gold, Signed, 10 In. 325.00
Compote, Gold, Signed, 6 1/4 In. 415.00
Perfume Bottle, Matching Stopper, Blue, 5 1/2 In. 475.00
Perfume Bottle, Teardrop Stopper, Signed, 6 In. 495.00
Powderbox, Calcite Interior, Star Design Cover 650.00

Art Pottery, Vase, Silver Snowflake Crystals, Flared, Robineau

Art Pottery, Vase, Silver Snowflake Crystals, Robineau, 6 In.

Art Pottery, Vase, Yellow, Brown, Goldenrod, Brouwer, 12 1/2 In.

Rose Bowl, Alabaster, Gold Pulled Feathers, Signed, 3 1/4 In.	975.00
Salt, Blue	250.00
Spittoon, Lady's, Gold	475.00
Vase, Blue, Ribbed Body, Signed, 5 In.	475.00
Vase, Flower Form, Narrow Stem, Blue, 6 In.	425.00
Vase, Pinched Top, Signed, 8 1/4 In.	425.00
Vase, White Ground, Heart Shape Leaves & Random Vines, Signed, 6 In.	675.00

AUSTRIA, see Royal Dux; Kauffmann; Porcelain

Auto parts and accessories are collectors' items today. Gas pump globes and license plates are part of this specialty. Prices are determined by age, rarity, and condition.

AUTO, Ammeter, Eveready, Pat.1910, Box	60.00
Ashtray, Chrome, Flip Top	4.00
Banner, Kendall Motor Oil, 3 Colors	35.00
Battery Charger, GE, C.1920	35.00
Blue Book, 1926	15.00
Brochure, 1946 Hudson	16.00
Bumper Emblem, Metal, Chicago Motor Club	9.00
Bumper Jack, Hydraulic	15.00
Bumper, Model A Ford, Pair	37.50
Can, Oil, Purelube, Pure Oil 10 W, 1 Qt.	10.00
Can, Oil, Skelly, Primrose, 1 Qt.	10.00
Can, Prestone Antifreeze, 1929, 1 Gal.	20.00
Can, Pyroil, 1936, 1 Gal.	25.00
Catalog, Chalmers, 1914, Delux, Color, 32 Pages, 7 X 9 In.	50.00
Catalog, Chevrolet, 1955	20.00
Catalog, Ford Motor Car, 1911	55.00
Catalog, Nash For 1924, 12 Pages, 3 1/2 X 6 In.	15.00
Catalog, Pontiac, 1957	20.00
Catalog, White Trucks, 1500 Photos, 225 Pages, 9 X 12 In.	125.00
Clock, Waltham, 8–Day, 7 Jewel, Nickel Movement, Size 32	30.00
Clock, Waltham, Hudson Super 6, 8–Day	110.00
Clock, Westclox, Fits Into Rear View Mirror	60.00
Gas Pump Globe, Amaco, Glass Lenses, Tin Frame, 15 In., Pair	275.00
Gas Pump Globe, Ashland Diesel, Milk Glass	110.00
Gas Pump Globe, Kendall	165.00
Gas Pump Globe, Marathon, Runner, Glass Frame & Inserts	285.00
Gas Pump Globe, Mobil Eagle	575.00
Gas Pump Globe, Mobil Gas, Glass On Glass	175.00
Gas Pump Globe, Pan–Am	225.00
Gas Pump Globe, Red Crown Gasoline, Embossed Letters	375.00
Gas Pump Globe, Richfield Hi–Octane Gasoline	250.00
Gas Pump Globe, Sinclair	65.00
Gas Pump Globe, Sinclair Power–X Over 100 Octane	165.00
Gas Pump Globe, Socony Motor Gasoline, Shipping Box, 15 In.	270.00
Gas Pump Globe, Standard Oil, Crown, Blue & Green	300.00
Gas Pump Globe, Standard Oil, Gold Crown	1500.00
Gas Pump Globe, Super Shell	400.00
Gas Pump Globe, Super Shell, Ethyl	375.00
Gas Pump Globe, Wagner, Visible Glass	300.00
Gas Pump Globe, White Eagle	450.00
Gas Pump Globe, Zephyr	60.00
Gauge Stick, Gasoline, Atwater Kent, For 1909 Ford	25.00
Headlight, Ford Two–Lite, Dome Shape, 9 In.Diam., Pair	16.00
Headlight, Glass Lens, Concave Circle, 9 1/4 In.	5.00
Headlight, Kerosene, C.1900, Pair	165.00
Headlight, Model T Ford, Pair	50.00

AUTO, HOOD ORNAMENT, see also Lalique

Hood Ornament, Chevrolet, 1932	25.00
Hood Ornament, Chevrolet, 1935	30.00
Hood Ornament, Eagle	75.00
Hood Ornament, Eagle, Temperature Gauge, Brass, 1920s, 5 3/4 In.	125.00
Hood Ornament, Figural, Woman, Flowing Hair, Chrome	47.50

Hood Ornament, Indian Chief, Light, Pontiac	35.00
Hood Ornament, Model A, Quail	250.00
Hood Ornament, Nude Woman, Art Deco	45.00
Hood Ornament, Plymouth, Brass, 1937	25.00
Hood Ornament, Ram, Dodge	35.00
Hood Ornament, Super Chief, 1950	45.00
Hood Ornament, Uncle Sam & Eagle	275.00
Hood Ornament, Uncle Sam & Eagle, 1919	220.00
Hood Ornament, Winged Lady	50.00
Horn, Brass, Original Bulb, 1909	105.00
Hubcap, Buick, 5 In., Pair	12.50
Inspection Sticker, Pennsylvania, Unused, 1936–37	20.00
Kerosene Pump, Brass, 11 In.	15.00
Knob, Gearshift, Marble	22.50
Knob, Gearshift, Swirl	35.00
Knob, Steering Wheel, Blue	6.50
Lamp Kit, Eveready, Metal, 2 Bulbs	40.00
Lens Tail, Ford, Passenger Car, Dietz, Box, 1956, Pair	30.00
License Plate Attachment, Advertising, Tydol, Metal, 5 X 6 1/2 In.	30.00
License Plate, Alabama, 1949	8.50
License Plate, Arizona, 1933, Copper	55.00
License Plate, California, 1925, Pair	52.00
License Plate, California, 1936	8.50
License Plate, Colorado, 1920, Stamped	50.00
License Plate, Connecticut, 1919	12.50
License Plate, Idaho, 1942, Pair	40.00
License Plate, Illinois, 1923	12.50
License Plate, Iowa, 1913	20.50
License Plate, Maine, 1921	10.50
License Plate, Massachusetts, 1917	12.50
License Plate, Massachusetts, 1931	6.00
License Plate, Minnesota, 1912	15.00
License Plate, Minnesota, 1927	15.00
License Plate, Montana, 1923	32.00
License Plate, New Hampshire, 1920	14.50
License Plate, New York, 1922	7.50
License Plate, Ohio, 1917	14.50
License Plate, Oklahoma, 1928	10.00
License Plate, Ontario, Canada, 1924	15.50
License Plate, Oregon, 1921	12.00
License Plate, Oregon, 1936	12.00
License Plate, Pennsylvania, 1908, Porcelain	220.00
License Plate, Pennsylvania, 1922	20.00
License Plate, South Dakota, 1922	10.50
License Plate, Vermont, 1917	16.50
License Plate, West Virginia, 1923	22.50
License Plate, Wyoming, 1923	30.00
Manual, Ford, 1927, 1928, 1929, 3 Piece	35.00
Mirror, Motorcycle, Brass Frame, Seesall, Mirror, Dated 1922, 2 Piece	35.00
Motometer, With Dogbone	65.00
Nozzle, Gas Pump, Brass	24.50 To 35.00
Pump, Kerosene Or Gas, Hand Crank, Cast Iron, 1915, 5 Ft.	195.00
Radiator Cap, Eagle, Chevrolet, 1933	65.00
Radiator Cap, Willys, Knight	45.00
Stoplight, Cast Aluminum, 1920s, 5 Ft.	250.00
Thermometer, Prestone Antifreeze, Porcelain, 36 In.	47.50
Tire Gauge, Gas Station, Oak Box, Directions	75.00
Tire Gauge, Leather Case	18.00
Tire Gauge, Model A Ford	35.00 To 40.00
Tire Gauge, Pouch, Studebaker	145.00
Tire Gauge, Schrader, C.1916	10.00
Tool Box, Running Board, Model T	40.00
Tune–Up Kit, Chevrolet, Brass & Steel, Pocket	150.00
Vase, Bud, Holder, Carnival Glass, Orange	65.00

Vase, Cornucopia, Pressed Glass, 11 In.	75.00
Wheel Cover, Spinners, For Classic & Ambassador, Unused, Box	42.00
Wrench, Monkey, Ford Script	15.00
AUTOMOBILE, Battery Charger, GE, C.1920	35.00

Autumn Leaf pattern china was made for the Jewel Tea Company from 1933. Hall China Company of East Liverpool, Ohio, Crooksville China Company of Crooksville, Ohio, Harker Potteries of Chester, West Virginia, and Paden City Pottery, Paden City, West Virginia, made dishes with this design. Autumn Leaf has remained popular and was still being made by Hall China Company until 1978. Some other pieces in the Autumn Leaf pattern are still being made.

AUTUMN LEAF, Baker, Individual, Swirl, 10 Oz.	50.00
Bean Pot, 2 Handles	65.00
Bean Pot, Handle, Jewel Tea, 6 X 7 In.	275.00
Bowl, Cereal	8.00
Bowl, Cover, Round, 6 1/2 In.	30.00
Bowl, Fruit, 5 In.	6.00
Bowl, Salad, Jewel Tea	12.00
Bowl, Vegetable, Cover, Handles, 11 1/2 In.	40.00
Bowl, Vegetable, Jewel Tea, Round	22.00
Bowl, Vegetable, Oval, 2 Sections	50.00
Butter, Cover, No.1, Box	150.00
Cake Carrier, Handle, Jewel Tea	85.00
Cake Plate, Metal Base	135.00
Cake Plate, Metal Base, Jewel Tea	195.00
Candy Dish, Hall	300.00
Candy Dish, Metal Base, Jewel Tea	300.00
Casserole, Orange Poppy, Oval	22.50
Casserole, Swirl, Hall, Individual	6.00
Clock, Electric, Hall	350.00
Coaster Set	40.00
Coaster, Round	5.00
Coffee Dispenser, Jewel Tea	45.00
Coffeepot, Jewel Tea, All China	195.00
Cookie Jar, Big Ears	75.00
Cookie Jar, Jewel Tea, Ziesel	80.00
Creamer, Ruffled, D Shape	9.00
Cup & Saucer ....6.00 To	12.00
Cup & Saucer, No Handle, Tea Leaf	60.00
Drip Jar & Range Shakers, 3 Piece	30.00
Gravy Boat ....12.00 To	20.00
Hot Pad, Round, 7 In.	9.00
Hot Plate, 9 1/2 In.	35.00
Jam Jar, 3 Piece	45.00
Mixing Bowl Set, 3 Piece	45.00
Mixing Bowl, 6 In. ....6.00 To	8.00
Mug, Irish Coffee, 4 Piece	70.00
Percolator, Electric ....150.00 To	200.00
Pitcher, 5 3/4 In.	17.00
Pitcher, Ball Jug ....20.00 To	28.00
Plate, 6 In.	7.00
Plate, 8 In.	8.00
Plate, Hall, 9 In.	9.00
Plate, Hall, 10 In.	10.00
Platter, 11 In. ....12.00 To	14.00
Platter, 14 In. ....15.00 To	22.50
Playing Cards, Canasta	115.00
Range Set, Jewel Tea, 3 Piece	35.00
Salt & Pepper, Casper	10.00
Salt & Pepper, Mug Shape	18.00
Salt & Pepper, Range	20.00
Sifter, Metal	140.00

Soup, Dish	10.00 To 15.00
Stack Set, Cover, 3 Piece	45.00
Sugar & Creamer, Cover	18.00
Tablecloth, 54 X 72 In.	75.00
Tablecloth, Sailcloth, 54 X 54 In.	50.00
Teapot, Aladdin	25.00 To 35.00
Teapot, Aladdin, Infuser, Hall	48.00
Teapot, Long Spot, Hall	40.00
Tidbit, 3 Tier	45.00
Tray, Glass, Wooden Handles	75.00
Tray, Metal, Hall, 18 3/4 In.	55.00
Tray, Red Border	48.00
Tumbler, 9 Oz., 5 Piece	100.00
Tumbler, 12 Oz., 7 Piece	77.00
Tumbler, Frosted, 9 Oz.	22.00
Tumbler, Frosted, Flat, 5 1/2 In.	12.00
Tumbler, Hall, 14 Oz.	12.00
Vase, Bud	150.00
Warmer, Candle, Jewel Tea, Round, Box	100.00
Warmer, Jewel Tea, Oval	90.00

AVON, see Bottle, Avon

Baccarat glass was made in France by La Compagnie des Cristalleries de Baccarat, located 150 miles from Paris. The factory was started in 1765. The firm went bankrupt and began operating again about 1822. Cane and millefiori paperweights were made during the 1860 to 1880 period. The firm is still working near Paris making paperweights and glasswares.

BACCARAT, Bowl, Diamond Point Band, Silver Plated Cradle, Signed, 8 1/2 In.	135.00
Candelabra, 3–Branch, Center Stem, Flower Form, France, 20 In., Pr.	850.00
Celery, Amberina Swirl, Signed, 3 1/2 X 9 1/2 In.	55.00
Dish, Rose Teinte, Oblong	58.00
Fairy Lamp, Saucer Base, Rose Teinte, Marked, 4 X 5 1/4 In.	235.00
Figurine, Dolphin, Crystal	39.00
Figurine, Duck, Crystal	39.00
Figurine, Sparrow, Crystal	39.00
Goblet, Cobalt Blue, Clear Stem, Signed, 7 3/4 In.	49.00
Inkwell, Engraved Hinged Silver Plated Cover, Square, 2 3/4 In.	80.00
Inkwell, Mermaid On Crest of Wave, Bronze, Glass, C.1900, 14 In.	4125.00
Lamp, Kerosene, Clear To Cranberry, Signed, 11 In.	110.00
Nappy, Blue, Clear Handle, Signed	60.00
Paperweight, 6 Concentric Circles	275.00
Paperweight, Aquarius, Diamond Cut Base, Sulfide, 1956, 3 In.	80.00
Paperweight, Center Flower, Millefiori Ring, Base Star	1350.00
Paperweight, Concentric Millefiori, Dated 1968, 2 3/4 In.	125.00
Paperweight, Millefiori Garland, Clear, 6 In.	350.00
Paperweight, Pansy, 7 Leaves, 1 Bud	550.00
Paperweight, Ring Millefiori	195.00
Paperweight, Salamander, On Rock Ground, C.1973, Signed	375.00
Paperweight, Scattered Millefiori On Lace	195.00
Paperweight, Scattered, On Lace	195.00
Paperweight, Sulfide, Abraham Lincoln	125.00
Paperweight, Sulfide, Andrew Jackson	115.00
Paperweight, Sulfide, Coronation	300.00
Paperweight, Sulfide, Dwight Eisenhower	275.00
Paperweight, Sulfide, Eleanor Roosevelt, Box	85.00
Paperweight, Sulfide, Herbert Hoover, Box	85.00
Paperweight, Sulfide, John F. Kennedy	150.00
Paperweight, Sulfide, President Jackson, Box	85.00
Paperweight, Sulfide, Theodore Roosevelt, Amethyst, Box, 1966	225.00
Paperweight, Sulfide, Winston Churchill	575.00
Paperweight, Zodiac Signs, Millefiori, Multicolor, 1967, 3 1/2 In.	175.00
Perfume Bottle, Allover Design, Pale Green, Square, 5 1/2 In.	55.00
Perfume Bottle, Allover Design, Rose Amber, Square, 6 In.	60.00

Perfume Bottle, Bulldog On Pillow	125.00
Perfume Bottle, Clear To Cranberry, Jewel In Cap, Signed, 6 In.	145.00
Perfume Bottle, Clear To Cranberry, Stopper, Signed, 6 1/2 In.	185.00
Perfume Bottle, Diagonal Cut Glass, 4 In.	28.00
Perfume Bottle, Sunburst Swirl, Rose Teinte, 6 1/2 In.	85.00
Perfume Bottle, Sunburst Swirl, Stopper, Shaded Amber, 6 1/4 In.	90.00
Perfume Bottle, White To Cranberry, Faceted Stopper, Signed	185.00
Pitcher, Bulbous, Signed, Crystal, 11 In.	95.00
Pitcher, Horizontal Ribbing, Etched Designs, Pedestal, 10 In.	195.00
Salt, Faceted, Signed	35.00

Badges have been used since before the Civil War. Collectors search for examples of all types, including law enforcement and company identification badges. Well–known prison or law enforcement badges are most desirable. Most are made of nickel or brass. Many recent reproductions have been made.

BADGE, B.P.O.E., Beaded	15.00
Capt.Frank's Air Hawks, Premium	25.00
Captain Wyckoff, Police, Wyckoff, N.J., Starburst Shape, 2 1/2 In.	40.00
Chauffeur, California, 1930	18.00
Chauffeur, Illinois, 1928	20.00
Chauffeur, Iowa, 1923	15.00
Chauffeur, Kansas, 1939	3.00
Chauffeur, Missouri, 1918	15.00
Chauffeur, Missouri, Brass, 1924	15.00
Chauffeur, New Hampshire, Bronze, 1918	7.00
Chauffeur, New York, 1923	7.00
Chauffeur, New York, 1927	10.00
Chauffeur, Oregon, 1912	35.00
Chauffeur, Quebec, Enameled, 1919	28.00
Chauffeur, Texas	15.00
Civil Defense, Special Officer, Kansas, State Seal, 2 1/2 In.	15.00
Deputy Sheriff, Putnam County, Black Lettering, Gold, 2 1/2 In.	38.00
Deputy Sheriff, Westchester County, N.Y., 14K Gold	175.00
Employee, American Cyanamid	10.00
Employee, Oliver Shilled Plow Works	35.00
G.A.R., Memorial, Mauston, Wisconsin, Celluloid	15.00
Game Warden, Iowa State Park Police	30.00
Game Warden, Nevada	30.00
Game Warden, North Dakota	30.00
Graf Zeppelin, Enameled	145.00
Highway Patrol, Oklahoma, Black & Gold	200.00
Hindenburg, Zeppelin, Iron Cross, Landing Crew, Lakehurst, Brass	300.00
Norfolk & Western Veterans Ass., Meeting of 1940, Celluloid, Ribbon	15.00
Police, Chicago, 1910	95.00
Police, Marlborough, Shield Shape, New Hampshire, Nickel Finish, 3 In.	26.00
Police, Metropolitan, D.C., Sterling Silver, 1/2 In.	10.00
Police, Selma, Ala., Shield Shape, Eagle Top	95.00
Police, Special, N.Y.Street, N.Y.State Seal, Cutout Numbers, 1930s	100.00
Police, Worcester, Mass., Silver, Spread Winged Eagle, Enameled, 2 In.	18.00
Post Office Maintenance	12.00
Post Office Motor Vehicle Operator	22.00
Texas Ranger, Brass, 3 1/2 In.	25.00

BAG, BEADED, see Purse

Never repaint an old bank. It lowers the resale value.

Metal banks have been made since 1868. There are still banks, mechanical banks, and registering banks (those which show the total money deposited on the face of the bank). Many old banks have been reproduced since the 1950s in iron or plastic.

BANK, American Can Co., Declaration of Independence Scene, Tin	15.00
Amish Boy, On Bale of Straw, White Metal, Painted, KLT, 4 1/2 In.	60.50
Andy Gump Thrift	225.00
Atlas Batteries, Tin	15.00
Bank Building, With Cupola, Cast Iron	30.00
Bank, Faro's, Buff Clay, Gray Brown Matte, L.H.Halle Label, 6 1/2 In.	110.00
Barrel, White City Savings, 1894	48.00
Barrel, Wooden, Black Stain, 3 1/2 In.	5.00
Baseball Player, Metal, 5 3/4 In.	150.00
Baseball, Los Angeles Dodgers, Ceramic	15.00
Baseball, Mobil Gasoline, Flying Horse, Glass, 3 In.	15.00
Battleship, Cast Iron	250.00
Bear, Figural, Glass	15.00
Bear, Hinged Head, Brown, White Metal, Marked Germany, 2 5/8 In.	105.00
Bear, Holding Pig, Brass, 5 3/8 In.	35.00
Bear, Standing, Cast Iron, 5 1/2 In.	75.00
Bear, With Honey Pot, Cast Iron, 6 1/2 In.	45.00
Bears, Three, Bronze, Bush Metal Products, 1920s	30.00
Beehive, Wooden, 3 Wire Figural Bees, Locked Door	45.00
Ben Franklin, Marx	43.00
Billiken, Good Luck, 4 1/8 In.	50.00
Billiken, On Throne, 6 1/4 In.	125.00
Billiken, Shoes Bring Luck, Gold, Cast Iron, 4 1/8 In.	65.00
Birdhouse, Cast Iron, Germany	20.00
Black Boy On Cotton Base, Nodder	60.00
Black Girl, 2 Faces, 3 In.	125.00
Black Mammy, Cast Iron	110.00
Black Man, 2 Faces, Cast Iron	95.00
Black Man, Lucky Joe	60.00
Blackpool Tower, Japanned, Cast Iron, 7 1/2 In.	55.00
Boat, 2 Stacks, 2 Paddle Wheels, 8 In.	250.00
Boat, Oregon, Cast Iron, Medium	150.00
Book, Picture & Rhyme, Tom, Tom, The Piper's Son, Tin	35.00
Book, Prudential Insurance Co.	17.50
Boy, With Basketball, Germany, Cast Iron	90.00
Bozo, Vinyl Head	15.00
Buffalo	110.00
Buffalo, Gold Repaint, 4 3/8 In.	50.00
Bugs Bunny, Barrel, Cast Iron	37.50
Building, 4 Towers, Cast Iron	32.50
Building, Bank, Cast Iron	65.00
Building, Columbia, Painted, 6 In.	165.00
Building, Flat Top, Cast Iron	100.00
Bullet, Decal of Admiral George Dewey, Souvenir, Wooden, 6 1/2 In.	65.00
Bungalow, With Porch, Polychrome Paint, Cast Iron, 3 3/4 In.	175.00
Bunny, Papier–Mache, 12 In.	25.00
Buster Brown, Good Luck, Cast Iron	90.00
Cannon, Big Bang, 17 In.	28.00
Captain Kidd, Iron	300.00
Car, 1910 Baker Electric, Banthrico	15.00
Car, 1910 Stanley, Banthrico	15.00
Car, 1930 Duesenberg, Banthrico	15.00
Car, 1950 Cadillac	75.00
Car, Armored, Tin, Japanese, 10 In.	80.00
Car, Buick Fireball, Tin	18.00
Car, Cadillac, Banthrico	15.00
Car, Duesenberg, 1930, Metal	12.00
Casper, Brush Pottery	80.00
Cat & Mouse, Cast Iron, 1880s	225.00

Cat, Black, Ceramic	12.00
Cat, Seated, Cast Iron	175.00
Cat, Sitting, Original White Paint, Cast Iron, 5 In.	65.00
Cat, With Ball, Cast Iron	95.00 To 135.00
Cat, With Ball, White Clay, Brown Glaze, 5 1/2 In.	65.00
Children's Crusade, Tin, Norman Rockwell Design, 1940	50.00
Clock Tower, Pen On Side, Williamsburgh Savings Bank, Ceramic	35.00
Clock, Kingsbury	200.00
Clock, Time Is Money, Save It, Ohio Foundry, Cleveland, Ohio, Cast Iron	85.00
Clown, Aluminum Paint, Red, Iron	125.00
Clown, Banthrico	68.00
Clown, Cast Iron, 6 In.	85.00
Clown, Chalkware, 13 In.	45.00
Clown, Chein, 6 1/8 In.	75.00
Clown, Iron	75.00
Coin Saver, Glass, Square	10.00
Colonial House, Polychrome Paint, Cast Iron, 4 In.	185.00
Cook, Black Woman, Cast Iron	75.00
Cow, Borden's Elsie, 1940s	60.00
Cow, Cast Iron, 3 1/4 X 5 1/4 In.	100.00
Cow, Sirloin Stockade Steak Houses	25.00
Cow, Sirloin Stockade Steak Houses, Ceramic	25.00
Cow, Standing, Original Gilt Paint, Cast Iron, 3 1/4 X 5 1/4 In.	95.00
Cradle	100.00 To 125.00
Daffy Duck, Warner Bros., Cast Iron	40.00
Deer, Antlers, Cast Iron, 6 In.	75.00
Deer, Cast Iron, 6 In.	35.00
Deer, Cast Iron, 9 In.	90.00
Deer, Cast Iron, 10 In.	125.00
Deer, Cast Iron, 1930s, 10 X 5 In.	100.00
Derby Hat, Cast Iron	85.00
Devil, 2 Faces, Cast Iron	270.00
Dime Register, B & R Mfg.Co., New York	9.00
Dime Register, Barrel, Cast Iron, Painted, Label	55.00
Dime Register, Cash Register, 3–Coin, Blue, Tin	45.00
Dime Register, Cash Register, Iron	40.00
Dime Register, Chase Brass, Chrome, Box	22.00
Dime Register, Picture of Pig	20.00
Dime Register, Popeye	27.00
Dime Register, Uncle Sam, 3 Coin, Tin	35.00
Dime Register, Uncle Sam, Western Stamping Corp., 3 Coins	75.00
Dinah, Yellow, Black, Cast Iron, 6 1/2 In.	100.00
Dinosaur, Copper, Sinclair, 1950s, 8 In.	45.00
Dog's Head, Brown & Green Sponging, White Clay, 3 7/8 In.	135.00
Dog, Boston Bull, Seated, Polychrome Paint, Cast Iron, 4 3/8 In.	85.00
Dog, Boston Bull, Standing, Polychrome, Cast Iron, 5 1/4 In.	125.00
Dog, Boston Bulldog, Standing, Cast Iron, 5 In.	75.00
Dog, Bulldog, Cast Iron	85.00
Dog, Bulldog, Metal	60.00
Dog, Bulldog, Sitting, Cast Iron	45.00
Dog, Chalkware	35.00
Dog, Irish Setter, Cast Iron	100.00
Dog, Newfoundland, Black, Cast Iron, 3 5/8 In.	40.00
Dog, On Pillow With Bee, Cast Iron	110.00
Dog, On Tub, Iron	125.00
Dog, Poodle, Gray, Removable Head, Pottery, Padlock On Collar, 10 In.	20.00
Dog, Retriever, Cast Iron	195.00
Dog, Retriever, With Pack, Black & Silver, Cast Iron, 3 3/4 In.	45.00
Dog, Scotty In Barrel, Composition, 6 In.	25.00
Dog, Scotty, Seated, Black, Red Collar, Cast Iron, 5 In.	75.00
Dog, Scotty, Slot In Tin Trap, White, 2 7/8 In.	37.50
Dog, St.Bernard, With Pack, Cast Iron	85.00
Dog, Terrier, Sitting, Hubley	65.00
Dog, With Backpack, Black Paint, Cast Iron, 5 1/2 In.	55.00

Dog, With Pack	80.00
Doghouse, Snoopy, Marked, 1958	25.00
Dome, Embossed Flowers, 2 Side Handles, Key, Brass, Large	35.00
Donald Duck, Ceramic	55.00
Donkey, Brown, Brush Pottery	60.00
Donkey, Green, Cast Iron, 4 1/2 In.	50.00
Donkey, Saddled, Cast Iron	75.00
Donkey, With Saddle & Blanket, Cast Iron, 5 In.	40.00
Dreadnought, United We Stand, Cast Iron, 7 1/4 X 7 1/2 In.	100.00
Drum, Remember Pearl Harbor, Ohio Art	38.00 To 45.00
Duck, On Barrel, Cast Iron	110.00
Duck, On Tub	90.00
Dutch Boy, On Barrel, Cast Iron	75.00
Eagle's Head, Spongeware, 3 1/2 In.	250.00
Eagle, On Globe, Iron	295.00
Eight O'Clock Coffee, Tin, 4 In.	9.00
Electrolux, Calendar	15.00
Elephant, Black, White Metal, 5 In.	17.50
Elephant, Circus, Cast Iron	140.00 To 175.00
Elephant, On Bench, Cast Iron, 4 In.	55.00
Elephant, Painted Gold, Cast Iron, 2 1/2 In.	55.00
Elephant, Rexall Drug, Jumbo Value	3.00
Elephant, Swivel Trunk, Cast Iron, 2 1/2 In.	60.00 To 195.00
Elephant, Three, Cast Iron, 5 1/8 In.	48.00
Elephant, With Howdah, 3 In.	45.00
Elephant, With Howdah, Cast Iron, Painted, 6 1/2 In.	71.50
Elf, Painted, Cast Iron	325.00
Esso, Glass, 1940	27.50
Face, Frowning, Cast Iron, 5 3/4 In.	485.00
Ferdinand The Bull	90.00
Flatiron Building, New York City, Cast Iron, 6 In.	60.00
Foxy Grandpa, Cast Iron	95.00
Frigidaire, White, 4 In.	33.00
Frog, Cast Iron	325.00
G.E.Refrigerator, Door Logo, Cast Iron, Painted, 3 3/4 In.	44.00
General Butler, Polychrome Paint, Cast Iron, 6 1/2 In.	850.00
General Pershing, Cast Iron, 1918	95.00
George Washington	75.00
Gerber's Orange Juice, Tin	7.00
Globe, Chein, Tin	10.00
Globe, Glass	36.00
Globe, Tin, Marked Globe Bank, Slot In North Atlantic, 1940s	13.50
Globe, Tin, Yellow & Brown Base, 1940s, 4 1/2 In.	15.00
Golliwog, No.3, Cast Iron	175.00
Golliwog, Painted Aluminum	135.00
Golliwog, Polychrome Paint, Cast Iron, 6 1/4 In.	250.00
Good Luck, Horse, Cast Iron	100.00
Goose, Cast Iron, 4 7/8 In.	95.00
Goose, Red Goose School Shoes On Side, 3 3/4 In.	150.00
Graf Zeppelin, Cast Iron	70.00 To 125.00
Heinz, Tin Can, Facsimile Paper Label of Canned Tomatoes, 1970	10.00
Heinz, Vegetable Soup, Tin, Round, 2 In.	15.00
Hershey Bar, Vending Machine, 1 Cent, Key, Box	110.00
Horse, Prancing	45.00
Horse, Standing On Rear Legs, Oval Donut Base, Cast Iron	75.00
Horse, Standing, Cast Iron	30.00
House, 2 Story, Cast Iron, Worn Gold Paint, 3 1/8 In.	35.00
House, 2 Story, Silver, Red Roof, Cast Iron	60.00
Humpty–Dumpty, Brush Pottery	23.00
Humpty–Dumpty, Cast Iron, 5 1/2 In.	120.00
Ideal Safe Deposit, Cast Iron, 4 In.	75.00
Indian, Bust, Full Headdress, White Metal, Painted, 4 3/4 In.	88.00
Indian, Cast Iron, 3 1/2 In.	25.00
Indian, Cast Iron, 6 In.	75.00

> To clean lithographed tin banks, try using Sani-wax and 0000 grade steel wool, but use with extreme caution.

Indian, Chief, Bronze Pot Metal, Japan	30.00
Indian, Shawnee, Marblehead Pottery	100.00
Interlocking Key Design, Appears Like Baby Rattle, Wooden, 4 1/2 In.	130.00
Katzenjammer Kids, Ceramic	110.00
Kiddie Clock, Dime, Crosetti Co., Tin	18.00
Kitten, Green Eyes, Porcelain, 7 In.	35.00
Kitten, Sitting, Blue Ribbon & Bow At Neck, Cast Iron, 4 3/4 In.	80.00
Kitty, Green Eyes, Porcelain	30.00
Kitty, Pink Ribbon Around Neck, Cast Iron, 5 In.	35.00
Kola Bear, Glass Eyes	15.00
Liberty Bell, Sheet Metal, Bronze Finish, Wood Trim, 3 7/8 In.	2.00
Liberty Bell, Tin, Key, 1919	15.00
Lincoln, Bust, Plastic, 6 In.	8.00
Lindy, 1928, Gold, Aluminum, 6 3/8 In.	40.00
Lion	50.00
Lion On Drum, Gold, Cast Iron, 5 1/2 In.	65.00
Lion, Cast Iron, 2 1/2 In.	40.00
Lion, Cast Iron, 5 In.	40.00
Lion, Gold Paint, Cast Iron, 5 In.	72.50
Lion, Harris Trust & Savings Bank, Bronze Finish	40.00
Lion, On Back, Cast Iron, 4 1/4 In.	35.00
Lion, On Tub, Cast Iron	55.00 To 85.00
Lion, Standing, Cast Iron, 4 1/2 In.	30.00
Lion, Standing, Gold Color, Cast Iron, 5 1/2 In.	35.00
Little Brown Church, Metal	12.00
Little Red Riding Hood, With Green Basket, Regal	145.00
Log Cabin, Glass	25.00
Log Cabin, Van Dyke Teas, Ceramic, C.1930, 2 1/2 X 3 1/2 In.	35.00
Lucas Paint, Tin	10.00
Lucky Joe, Mustard	12.00
Mailbox, All American, Dark Green, Bottom Slides Out, Marked, 9 In.	20.00
Mailbox, Cast Iron	75.00
Mailbox, Movable Slot, Cast Iron, Green	25.00
Mailbox, Rural, Dean's Dairy, Metal	20.00
Mailman, Metal	15.00
Mammy, Cast Iron, Hubley, 12 In.	290.00
Mammy, Ceramic, 8 In.	58.00
Mammy, With Spatula, Iron	145.00
Man's Face, With Ruff, Majolica, 3 In.	47.50
Mary & Lamb, Polychrome Paint, Cast Iron, 4 3/8 In.	285.00
Mason Jar, Zinc Slotted Lid, Atlas, Clear	10.00
Mausoleum, Cast Iron	32.00

Mechanical banks were first made about 1870. Any bank with moving parts is considered mechanical. The metal banks made before World War I are the most desirable. Copies and new designs of mechanical banks have been made in metal or plastic since the 1920s.

Mechanical, Advertising, Kool Aid Man 20.00
Mechanical, Air Force Rocket 55.00
Mechanical, Always Did 'Spise A Mule .... 200.00 To 400.00
Mechanical, Bad Accident, Upside Down, Cast Iron, 1891, 10 In. 1100.00
Mechanical, Balking Mule, Clown, Yellow Blouse, Lehmann, 7 In. 85.00
Mechanical, Baseball, Downtown Battery, 1 Color, 5 1/2 In. 77.00
Mechanical, Bear Stealing Pig, Cast Iron, 5 5/8 In. 535.00
Mechanical, Big Chief, Cast Iron 900.00
Mechanical, Black Man, High Hat, Money, Hand To Mouth, Pat.Mar.14, 1882 .... 195.00
Mechanical, Boy & Girl, Cast Iron, 1882 .... 485.00
Mechanical, Boy On Trapeze, Cast Iron 1350.00
Mechanical, Bucking Mule, Cast Iron, Painted, 4 In. 2450.00
Mechanical, Bulldog On Pillow 460.00
Mechanical, Bulldog, Standing, Cast Iron, Gold Wash, 7 In. 415.00
Mechanical, Cabin, Polychrome Paint, Cast Iron, 3 5/8 In. 350.00
Mechanical, Calumet, Baby's Head On Top, Cardboard, 4 In. 88.00
Mechanical, Cat & Mouse, Cat Balancing, Polychrome Paint, 8 1/4 In. 150.00
Mechanical, Chief Big Moon, J & E Stevens, Pat.1899, 10 In. 1200.00
Mechanical, Chimpanzee, Cast Iron, Painted, 5 1/2 In. 2090.00
Mechanical, Church, Tin Litho, Chein, 6 1/2 In. 88.00
Mechanical, Circus, Cast Iron, Painted, Original Crank, 7 In.Diam. 4950.00
Mechanical, Clown, On Globe, Cast Iron, Painted, 9 In. 3530.00
Mechanical, Columbian Exposition, Cast Iron, 1492, 1892 .... 225.00
Mechanical, Creedmore 400.00
Mechanical, Creedmore, J & E Stevens Co., Pat.1877, Cast Iron, 10 In. 300.00
Mechanical, Darkie In Cabin 395.00
Mechanical, Darktown Battery, Iron .... 850.00 To 1275.00
Mechanical, Destination Moon, Model 100, April 26, 1962 .... 65.00
Mechanical, Dinah, Aluminum, Painted, 6 1/4 In. 121.00
Mechanical, Dinah, Long Sleeves, Cast Iron, Painted, 6 1/2 In. 495.00
Mechanical, Dog On Turntable, Cast Iron, Black Enameled, 4 3/4 In. 457.00
Mechanical, Eagle & Eaglets, Cast Iron ....*Illus* 400.00
Mechanical, Eagle, On Globe, Cast Iron, Painted, Bell Works, 5 3/4 In. 71.50
Mechanical, Elephant, Gar-Ru 50.00
Mechanical, Elephant, Pull Tail, Cast Iron, Painted, Hubley, 8 1/2 In. 415.00
Mechanical, Elephant, Tin Litho, Chein, 5 In. 88.00
Mechanical, Elephant, Trunk Swings, Cast Iron, 6 1/4 In. .... 150.00 To 275.00
Mechanical, Fort, Cast Iron, Painted, Octagonal, 11 In.Base 2420.00
Mechanical, Frog, 2 Frogs 625.00
Mechanical, Full Dog, J & E Stevens, Pat.1880, Glass Eyes, Iron, 7 In. 500.00
Mechanical, Guided Missle, Box 50.00
Mechanical, Hall's Liliput Bank, Sheet Metal Tray, 4 1/4 In. 575.00
Mechanical, Hen & Chick, Cast Iron, Old Repaint, 9 3/4 In. 1375.00
Mechanical, Horse Race 400.00
Mechanical, Indian and Bear 1100.00
Mechanical, Indian, Big Chief, Cast Iron ....*Illus* 900.00
Mechanical, Joe Socko, Tin Litho, 5 In. 300.00
Mechanical, John Deere, Blacksmith, Cast Iron, Painted, 9 1/2 In. 220.00
Mechanical, Jolly Nigger, Aluminum, Ears Move, Starkies, 6 In. 125.00
Mechanical, Jolly Nigger, Skimmer Hat, Aluminum, Repainted, 6 1/4 In. 70.50
Mechanical, Jolly Nigger, Top Hat, Cast Iron, Painted, 6 5/8 In. 275.00
Mechanical, Jonah & The Whale, Boat, Cast Iron, Repainted, 10 1/4 In. 935.00
Mechanical, Lion & Two Monkeys, Polychrome Paint, Cast Iron, 9 1/4 In. 150.00
Mechanical, Man Holding Bankbook, Window Signs, $20, Revolves, 3 In. 225.00
Mechanical, Man, Guessing Weight, White Metal, Iron Base, 9 3/4 In. 3850.00
Mechanical, Merry-Go-Round, Cast Iron, Painted, 6 In. 7920.00
Mechanical, Mickey Mouse, On Drum, Hand Puts Coin Into Drum 175.00
Mechanical, Monkey, Tin Litho, Chein 110.00
Mechanical, Mule Entering Barn, Iron, 1880, 8 5/8 In. .... 275.00 To 550.00
Mechanical, New Creedmore, Cast Iron, Painted, 10 1/2 In. 467.00
Mechanical, Organ Monkey, Cast Iron, C.1882, 7 In. .... 375.00 To 700.00

Bank, Mechanical, Indian, Big Chief, Cast Iron

Bank, Mechanical, Trick Pony, Cast Iron   Bank, Mechanical, Eagle & Eaglets, Cast Iron

Mechanical, Organ, Cast Iron, Painted, 4 In. 265.00
Mechanical, Organ, Cat & Dog, 7 3/4 In. .... 435.00 To 575.00
Mechanical, Organ, Polychrome Paint, Cast Iron, 7 3/4 In. 225.00
Mechanical, Owl Turns Head, Brown, Gray 390.00
Mechanical, Owl, J & E Stevens, Pat.1880, Cast Iron, 7 In. 200.00
Mechanical, Paddy & Pig, Cast Iron, Painted, 8 In. 2000.00
Mechanical, Pay Phone, Nickel Cast Iron, 7 1/4 In. 225.00
Mechanical, Peg–Leg Beggar, Cast Iron, 5 1/4 In. 2420.00
Mechanical, Professor Pug Frog, Mother Goose, Cast Iron, Painted 3000.00
Mechanical, Punch & Judy, Iron 1050.00
Mechanical, Punch & Judy, Tin Litho, 4 1/4 In. 55.00
Mechanical, Punch & Judy, Tin, Original Box 250.00
Mechanical, Rabbit, Standing, Cast Iron, Painted, 5 3/4 In. 635.00
Mechanical, Ram, Butting, Cast Iron, Old Repaint, 6 3/4 In. 6600.00
Mechanical, Rocket Ship, Die Cast Metal, Gold, Astro, 1960s 12.00

Mechanical, Santa Claus, Cast Iron, Painted, 5 3/4 In. 825.00
Mechanical, Santa Claus, Charles Shepard Hardware Co., Iron, 6 In. 450.00
Mechanical, Santa Claus, Marked J.M.Harper, Cast Iron 4700.00
Mechanical, Southern Comfort, Union Soldier Shoots Coin Into Bottle 85.00
Mechanical, Speaking Dog, Rectangular Trap, Cast Iron, 7 In. .... 375.00 To 575.00
Mechanical, Squirrel & Tree Stump, Cast Iron, Painted, 6 3/4 In. 577.00
Mechanical, Stump Speaker, Key Lock Trap, Iron, 9 3/4 In. 750.00
Mechanical, Stump Speaker, Key Lock Tray, Iron, 9 3/4 In. 1575.00
Mechanical, Sweet Thrift, Tin Litho, 6 In. 132.00
Mechanical, Tammany, Cast Iron, Painted, Round Trap, 5 5/8 In. 300.00
Mechanical, Tammany, Iron, Polychrome, 5 3/4 In. 150.00
Mechanical, Teddy & Bear, Cast Iron 995.00
Mechanical, Tiger, Rollover, Windup, Tin, C.K.Japan 65.00
Mechanical, Trick Dog, 1888 .... 495.00
Mechanical, Trick Dog, Hubley, 1920s, 7 In. .... 145.00 To 295.00
Mechanical, Trick Pony, Cast Iron ....*Illus* 400.00
Mechanical, Uncle Remus, Cast Iron, Painted, 5 3/4 In. 2970.00
Mechanical, Uncle Sam, With Satchel, Cast Iron 450.00
Mechanical, Uncle Wiggly, Tin Litho, Chein 165.00
Mechanical, Weeden's Plantation Darky, Painted Tin, Wood, Label, 5 In. 495.00
Mechanical, William Tell, J & E Stevens, Pat, 1896, 10 In. 355.00
Mechanical, William Tell, J & E Stevens, Pat.1896, 10 In. 425.00
Mechanical, World's Fair, J & E Stevens, Pat.1893, Cast Iron, 8 In. 600.00
Mechanical, Zoo, Cast Iron, Painted, 4 1/4 In. 1550.00
Menier Chocolate, Tin Litho 650.00
Mickey Mouse, Action, Box 20.00
Middy, Trace of Black, Cast Iron, 5 1/4 In. 85.00
Minnesota Twins Bobble–Head, Composition 35.00
Monk, Brown Robe, Black Hat, Gloves, Belt, China, 5 1/2 In. 40.00
Monkey & Parrot, Cast Iron 240.00
Monkey, Circus, C.Miller, Regal China, Large 75.00
Monkey, Tin 15.00
Monkey, With Fez, Roseville, Green 75.00
Mr.Zip, Ohio Art, Tin 5.00
Mule 55.00
Mutt & Jeff, Cast Iron ....75.00 To 225.00
My Loot Box, Book Shape 12.00
Nash Car, Banthico, 1953 .... 75.00
Nevada Jackpot 14.00
Nigger, Cast Iron, 1915 .... 175.00
Nipper, White Flocking, Glass Eyes 145.00
Ocean Spray Cranberry Sauce, Tin 20.00
Old Dutch Cleanser 30.00
Old Mother Hubbard 25.00
Olive Oyl, Wood, French, 9 In. 12.00
Orange Bird, Florida 18.00
Oriental Camel, Cast Iron 950.00
Owl, Be Wise, Save Money, Cast Iron, 5 In. ....75.00 To 150.00
Owl, Figural, Bisque, Occupied Japan 60.00
Owl, Royal Ruby 145.00
Owl, Wire Glasses, Ceramic 14.00
Palace, Key, Cast Iron, 7 5/8 In. 375.00
Panda, Brush 125.00
Patton Paint Co., Litho 35.00
Pay Phone, Tin, Structo, 10 1/4 In. 20.00
Pickle, Green Glaze, Pottery, 6 1/2 In. 75.00
Pig Doing Handstand, Ceramic 25.00
Pig, Brush Pottery 85.00
Pig, Chrome, Large, 1930s 27.00
Pig, Decker's Iowana, Cast Iron ....60.00 To 85.00
Pig, Marbleized Glaze, Pottery, 6 3/8 In. 40.00
Pig, Overalls & Felt Hat, Bisque, 5 3/4 In. 45.00
Pig, Papier–Mache, 1930s 22.00

Pig, R.B.Rice Sausage Co., Cellulite 30.00
Pig, Seated, Cast Iron 25.00
Pig, Sitting, Cast Iron 70.00
Pig, Standing, Glass, 8 In. 45.00
Pig, White, Brown Sponging, Pottery, 5 3/4 In. 65.00
Pig, Wise, Thrifty, Cast Iron 40.00
Pig, With Leper Tag, Cast Iron 45.00
Pig, Yellowware Belly, Blue, Rust, Cream Stripe, Swirl, 4 X 2 1/4 In. 75.00
Pigs, Graduated Group of 3, Pottery, 5 1/2, 6 & 7 In. 270.00
Pink Pig Purse, Porcelain, Germany 45.00
Pinocchio, Pot Metal 35.00
Pirate On Chest, Pot Metal 25.00
Pirate's Treasure Chest, Metal 12.00
Pirate, Domed Chest, Lock & Key 35.00
Pirate, Sitting On Treasure Chest, Bronze .... 300.00 To 450.00
Plane, Spirit of St. Louis 200.00
Planet of The Apes, Galen, Plastic, 1974, 11 In. 10.00
Policeman, Cast Iron 85.00
Pony, Prancing, 4 In. 45.00
Popeye, Brush Pottery 135.00
Porky Pig, Hubley, Cast Iron, 5 3/4 In. .... 100.00 To 375.00
Post Office Box, English, Tin 35.00
Potbelly Stove, Metal 15.00
Prince Valiant, Register 35.00
Rabbit, Gray & Pink, Cast Iron, 4 3/4 In. 100.00
Rabbit, Gray, Traces of White, Cast Iron, 4 3/4 In. 105.00
Rabbit, Lying Down, Gold, Cast Iron, 5 1/8 In. 345.00
Rabbit, Oval Base Marked Bank & 1888, Cast Iron, 2 3/8 In. 415.00
Rabbit, Standing, Cast Iron 70.00
Rabbit, With Carrot, White, Colored Detail, 3 3/8 In. 75.00
Radio, 2 Dials, Nickel Cast Iron, Steel Sides & Back, 4 1/2 In. 88.00
Radio, G.E., Cast Iron 75.00
Radio, Majestic, Cast Iron 45.00
Radio, Red, Gold Trim, Nickel Door, Cast Iron, Kenton Toyo, 4 3/4 In. 85.00
Raggedy Ann, Nodder 45.00
Railroad Tanker, Glass 32.00
Red Circle Coffee, Yellow, Black Letters, Tin, 3 7/8 In. 15.00
Red Goose School Shoes, Figural, Maroon & Gold, Cast Iron, 3 3/4 In. 160.00
Red Goose Shoes, Cast Iron, 4 1/2 In. 85.00
Red Goose Shoes, Figural, Cast Iron, 3 7/8 In. 305.00
Red Goose Shoes, Figural, Cast Iron, 4 1/2 In. 125.00
Red Goose Shoes, Figural, Red & Gold, Cast Iron, 3 3/4 In. 165.00
Red Goose Shoes, Red, 4 1/2 In. 175.00
Red Riding Hood, Metal 155.00
Refrigerator, Electrolux, Figural .... 40.00 To 50.00
Refrigerator, Frigidaire, Pot Metal, 4 1/2 In. 35.00
Register, 3 Coin, Universal 50.00
Register, Reno Slot Machine 28.00
Retriever, Cast Iron 195.00
Rex Water Heater 110.00
Rival Dog Food .... 10.00 To 12.00
Robin, Ceramic 45.00
Roosevelt, Cast Iron 130.00
Rooster 50.00
Rooster, Cast Iron ....6.50 To 80.00
Rooster, Standing, With Top Knot, Cast Iron, 5 1/2 In. 350.00
Royal Safe Deposit, Combination, Cast Iron, 6 In. 115.00
Safe Boom, Kenton 95.00
Safe, Barking Dog On Door, Soldiers On Sides, Cast Iron 300.00
Safe, Cast Iron, 5 In. 40.00
Safe, Embossed Animals, Nickeled Steel, 3 1/8 In. 75.00
Safe, Ideal Trust, Iron, Bronze Finish, 7 In. 115.00
Safe, Security, Cast Iron 200.00
Safe, Star, Cast Iron, 3 In. 50.00

Safe, Tin	25.00
Safe, Treasure, Nickel Cast Iron, 5 In.	467.00
Safe, Union, Cast Iron, Kenton, 3 1/4 In.	33.00
Safe, Watch Dog Safe, Norman No.5890	325.00
Safe, With Key, Aug.24, '87	65.00
Sailor, Seamans Savings, Porcelain	20.00
San Francisco Trolley, Embossed People, Street Names, 6 1/4 In.	40.00
Santa Claus, Sack of Toys, Atop Chimney, Chalkware, Dated 1943	35.00
Santa Claus, Seated In Armchair, Metal	25.00 To 35.00
Santa Claus, Sleeping, Banthrico, Metal	65.00
Santa Trim–A–Tree	120.00
Santa, Holding Christmas Tree, Iron	55.00
Save & Have, Calendar, Metal, Dated 1920	65.00
Savings, Buddy L	65.00
Schlitz Beer	12.00
Schnozzola, Jimmy Durante, Metal, Abbot Wares, 6 3/4 In.	140.00
Servicemen, Saluting, Globe, Glass, World War II	40.00
Sharecropper, Black Man, Cast Iron, 5 1/2 In.	55.00 To 75.00
Shoe, Wooden, Bank On Dutch Brand Products, 4 1/2 In.	12.00
Skyscraper, 4 Towers, Cast Iron, 5 1/2 In.	45.00
Squirrel, Upright, With Nut, Original Gold Paint, 4 In.	300.00
Stagecoach, Banthrico	10.00
Statue of Liberty, Cast Iron	85.00
Stollwerch's Candies, Litho Tin	850.00
Stoneware, Dark Brown Albany Slip, 4 3/4 In.	40.00
Stove, Wood Burning, Cast Iron	25.00
Suitcase, Batesville, Indiana, Cast Iron	30.00
Suitcase, Burns, Chicago, Cast Iron	25.00
Tang, Kitten	2.00
Tank, Litho Metal, Cast Iron, 6 In.	40.00
Tasmanian Devil, Ceramic	12.00
Teddy Bear, Cast Iron, 5 1/2 In.	55.00
Telephone Booth	50.00
Texas Ringer, Plastic Horseshoe On Top, Tin	20.00
Time Popcorn, Metal	8.00
Tiny Mite, Aluminum, Combination	25.00
Tootsie Roll	2.00
Tower, Polychrome Paint, Cast Iron, 1890, 6 7/8 In.	265.00
Trolley, Banthrico	15.00
Trolley, Main Street, Cast Iron, 6 1/2 In.	350.00
Truck, Armored, Buddy L, Tin	15.00
Turkey, Cast Iron, Large	225.00
Turkey, Cast Iron, Small	70.00
Turtle, Pottery, Brown	20.00
Typewriter, New York World's Fair, Metal, 1940	65.00
U.S.Mail, Cast Iron	30.00
Uncle Sam, Bust, Cast Iron, Painted, 5 1/4 In.	825.00
Uncle Sam, Poll Parrot Shoes, Red, White & Blue	20.00
Uncle Sam, Red, White & Blue Top Hat, Chein	45.00
Uncle Sam, Roseville	78.50 To 95.00
Vault, Tin, Combination Tag	75.00
Vault, Tin, Original Combination Tag	45.00
Vending Machine, Plastic, Box, 1950s	95.00
Washington Bust, White Metal, Advertising, East River Savings, 6 In.	22.00
Water Heater, Tin	80.00
Wolf's Head Motor Oil, Tin	20.00
World War I Tank, Cast Iron, Painted, 1918, 4 X 2 X 2 In.	85.00
Yellow Cab, Arcade, Cast Iron, 8 In.	550.00

There is much confusion about the terms Banko, Korean ware, and Sumida. We are using the terms in the way most often used by antiques dealers and collectors. Korean ware is now called "Sumida" and is listed in this book under that heading. Banko is a group of rustic Japanese wares made in the nineteenth and twentieth

centuries. Some pieces are made of mosaics of colored clay, some
are fanciful teapots. Redware and other materials were also used.

BANKO, Bowl, Painted Morning Glories, Brown, 5 In.	85.00
Dish, Fish, Figural Cat At Side	68.00
Group, Monkey, With Bowl, C.1900	195.00
Humidor, 7 Gods of Good Luck In Relief, C.1900	425.00
Jar, Applied Peaches & Leaves, Painted Flowers, Cover	165.00
Nodder, Fukusukesan, C.1900, 3 In.	295.00
Pitcher, Applied Flowers, 3 In.	25.00
Pitcher, Man, Seal, 8 In.	80.00
Teapot, 7 Gods of Good Luck	135.00
Teapot, Sugar & Creamer, Flying Cranes, Yellow Enamel, Covers	145.00
Vase, Boy With Ball, 8 In.	115.00
Vase, Matte Glaze, Applied Design, 12 In.	150.00
Vase, Paneled, Ring Handles, Enameled Birds, Hexagonal, 7 1/2 In.	125.00
Vase, Wasps, Gray, 7 1/4 In.	375.00

Barbershop collectibles range from the popular red and white striped
pole that used to be found in front of every shop to the small
scissors and tools of the trade. Barber chairs are wanted, especially
the older models with elaborate iron trim.

BARBER, Basin, Cut To Fit Around Neck, Footed, Ring, 18th Century, 6 In.	175.00
Box, Razor, 12 Sections	85.00
Brush, Figural, Lady	75.00
Cabinet, Shelves, Mirror, Baltimore Towel Supply Co.On Door, 27 In.	135.00
Chair, Burgundy Upholstery, Brass	2250.00
Chair, Child's, Carved Horse Head, Koken	1200.00
Chair, Child's, Wooden Horse	1650.00
Chair, Elephant, Gold Trim, Wooden, Child's	5500.00
Chair, Fleur-De-Lis, Koken, Wooden	2750.00
Chair, Kochs, Dated 1908	500.00
Chair, Kochs, Eureka, Walnut & Velvet, Patent 1880	550.00
Chair, Koken, Cast Iron Legs, Horse Hoof Feet	900.00
Chair, Koken, Porcelain, Matching Pair	475.00
Chair, Koken, Round Seat & Back, Restored	2250.00
Chair, Round Seat, Tufted Leather	3400.00
Clippers, Beard, Germany	20.00
Clippers, Chrome	7.50
Clippers, Hair, Oster	10.00
Hat Rack, Koken	1850.00
Pole, Black Face, On Ball Top, Collar, Bib & Tie, 48 In.	3900.00
Pole, Padar	850.00
Pole, Red, White & Blue Spiral, Iowa, 19th Century, 8 Ft.6 In.	2475.00
Pole, Red, White & Blue, Ball Top, Crown, 44 In.	495.00
Pole, Revolving, Fired-On Porcelain Paint	1650.00
Pole, Revolving, Milk Glass Globe	1950.00
Pole, Wall Mount, Electric, 1951	325.00
Pole, Wall Mount, Koken, Art Glass	1000.00
Pole, Wooden Turned, Weathered Red, White & Blue, Dish Base, 77 In.	470.00
Pole, Wooden, 3 Ft.	150.00
Seat, Booster	35.00
Sharpener, Blade, Kriss Kross, Original Box, Directions	15.00
Shaving Cloth, Turkey Red, Straight Razor, Mug, Brush	15.00
Sign, Ask For Wildroot, Red, White & Blue, 39 X 13 In.	45.00
Sign, Barber Shop, Porcelain, Look Better, Feel Better, 8 X 48 In.	95.00
Sign, Porcelain On Steel, 24 X 15 In.	90.00

Barometers are used to forecast the weather. Antique barometers
with elaborate wooden cases and brass trim are the most desirable.
Mercury column barometers are popular with collectors. It is
difficult to find someone to repair a broken example so be sure your
barometer is in working condition.

BAROMETER, Aneroid, Mahogany Veneer, D.Rivolta, Edinburgh, 38 1/2 In.	200.00

Banjo, Pediment Over Thermometer & Barometer, Mahogany, 38 In.	175.00
Carved, Ebonized, E.C.Spooner, Boston, With Thermometer	650.00
Continental, Neoclassical, Madrid, Obelisk Form, 39 1/2 In.	3575.00
Louis XVI, Thermometer, Gilt-Bronze, Porcelain, C.1870, 49 In.	1450.00
Metabolism, Sea Level To 8, 000 Ft., Germany	25.00
Open Face, Beveled Glass, Brass, English, C.1870, 7 In.	165.00
Stick, C.Wilder, Petersborough, N.H., Patent 1860, 38 1/4 In.	1000.00
Timby, Ripple Molding, No Thermometer, Pat.1857	175.00
Victorian, Walnut, C.1880	575.00
Wheel, Rosewood Veneer, Victorian, Mid-19th Century, 37 1/2 In.	330.00

Basalt is a special type of ceramic invented by Josiah Wedgwood in the eighteenth century. It is a fine-grained, unglazed stoneware.

BASALT, Bust, Washington, Wedgwood, C.1840	1650.00
Pitcher, Globular, Pinched Mouth, Ribbon Handle, Black, 10 1/2 In.	50.00
Teapot, Cyples, Glazed, 1830	110.00

Baskets of all types are popular with collectors. Indian, Japanese, African, Shaker, and many other kinds of baskets can be found. Of course, baskets are still being made; so the collector must learn to tell the age and style of the basket to determine the value.

BASKET, Animals & Figural Bands, Woven, Indian, E.B., 1916, 8 X 10 In.	450.00
Apple, Splint Oak, 19 In.	40.00
Apple, Woven Splint, Iron Hanger, Bentwood Handle, 1860, 11 X 13 In.	220.00
Basket, Papago, Split Stitch, Cover, 3 1/2 X 5 1/2 In.	40.00
Bentwood Staves, Wood & Metal Bands, Bentwood Handle, 3 X 5 1/2 In.	325.00
Berry Picker's, Splint, Handle	85.00
Bowl Shape, Leather Binding At Rim, Geometric Band, African, 17 In.	35.00
Bushel, Bentwood Staves, Wooden Bottom, 11 X 19 In.	45.00
Buttocks, 2-Color Splint, Center Handle, 7 1/2 X 6 1/2 In.	220.00
Buttocks, Deep Cleft, 19th Century, 6 1/2 X 8 In.	250.00
Buttocks, Splint, Fixed Handle, Fabric Lined For Sewing Accessories	90.00
Buttocks, Woven Reed, Bentwood Handle, 5 1/2 X 5 X 8 1/2 In.	65.00
Candy, Heart Shape, Braided Straw & Wood, Satin Lined, Germany	20.00
Cheese, 16 In.	350.00
Clam, Slatted, Wooden, Bentwood Handle	80.00
Coiled, Vertical Wraps, Animal Design, India, 5 1/2 X 8 1/2 In.	310.00
Double-Wrapped Rim, Natural Patina, Albra Lord, Me., 10 3/4 In., Pr.	850.00
Drying, Blueberry-Dyed Weavers, C.1930, 5 X 8 In.	225.00
Egg, Woven Splint, Bentwood Handle, 4 X 7 1/2 In.	135.00
Egg, Woven Splint, Initialed ACF, Bentwood Handle, 9 1/2 X 10 In.	275.00
Featherbed	192.50
Firkin, Wood, Swing Handle, Blue Paint, C.Alleder & Son, 10 X 9 In.	385.00
Fixed Overhandle, Original Brownish Red Paint, 4 3/4 X 8 /12 In.	360.00
Flower Gathering, Wooden Runners, 23 1/2 X 17 1/2 In.	60.00
Fruit, Wood Slat, 18 X 9 X 4 In.	35.00
Gathering, Wicker, Handles, 14 In.	25.00
Gizzard, 28 Ribs, Handle, Large	195.00
Laundry, Woven Splint, 2 Bentwood Handles, New England, 7 X 16 In.	440.00
Laundry, Woven Splint, Oblong, 18 X 24 1/2 In.	55.00
Laundry, Woven Splint, Pierced Handles, IA, 19th Century, 22 X 23 In.	138.00
Lid Attached With Leather Thong, Coiled, African, 10 X 6 1/2 In.	45.00
Loom, Woven Splint, 7 1/2 In.	165.00
Melon, Wall Pocket, Double, 1 Above The Other, 27 1/2 X 11 1/2 In.	1000.00
Nantucket, Capt.Thomas James, Ash, Willow, 12 X 18 In. ....*Illus*	1870.00
Nantucket, Lightship, Cylindrical, Swing Handle, 10 1/2 In.	650.00
Nantucket, Lightship, Shape of Handbag, Ivory Whale On Lid, C.1950	450.00
Nantucket, Mitchell Ray, Early 20th Century, 3 1/4 In.	1050.00
Nantucket, Swing Handle, Brass Ears, Turned Wooden Bottom, 5 X 7 In.	550.00
Nantucket, Woven Splint, Swing Handles, 5 3/4 X 7 1/2 In.	495.00
Oak Splint, Gizzard, Large	275.00
Peach, Green Crisscross Diamond Bands, Wooden Bottom	295.00
Picnic, Double Swing Handle, Splint, Painted Bands, C.1860`	195.00
Picnic, Woven Splint, Gray Paint, Cover, Handle, 8 1/4 X 15 1/2 In.	110.00

Rye Straw, 3 1/2 X 12 In.	40.00
Rye Straw, Ovoid, 10 X 15 In.	45.00
Splint Nose, For Feeding Livestock, 19th Century	325.00
Splint, Dark Green Paint, Oblong, 19th Century, 7 1/2 X 16 In.	550.00
Splint, Fixed Handle, Double Wrapped Rim, Old Red, 16 1/2 X 15 In.	540.00
Splint, Hanging, Loom, Step Down Back & Sides, 10 1/2 X 11 In.	125.00
Splint, Oak, Painted White, Handle, 11 1/2 X 5 In.	85.00
Splint, Ovoid, 23 1/2 X 10 1/2 In.	125.00
Swing Handle, 19th Century, Round, 13 1/2 In.	260.00
Swing Handle, A.Lord, Maine	522.50
Taghkanic, Coiled Bottom, Ash	375.00
Tobacco Picker's	110.00
Utility, Splint, White Oak, 12 X 14 In.	20.00
Wicker, Locking Cover, Leather Handles, 14 X 22 In.	55.00
Winnower, Bentwood, Handles, 3 Board Base, 4 Ft.8 In.	165.00
Wooden Stave Constructed, Swivel Handle, 1/2 Bushel	55.00
Woven Hickory Splint, Bentwood Handle, Cylindrical, 7 1/2 X 14 In.	137.00
Woven Splint, 2 Handles, Bound Rim, Domed Center Base, 11 1/2 In.	192.00
Woven Splint, Bentwood Handle, 3 X 5 1/2 In.	425.00
Woven Splint, Bentwood Handle, 5 1/4 X 8 In.	55.00
Woven Splint, Bentwood Handle, 9 X 17 In.	65.00
Woven Splint, Bentwood Handle, Dark Green, 6 X 15 In.	275.00
Woven Splint, Bentwood Handle, Worn Orange Paint, 9 In.	215.00
Woven Splint, Bentwood Rim Handles, 3 1/4 X 6 X 8 In.	135.00
Woven Splint, Bentwood Rim Handles, Old Blue Paint, 14 1/2 In.	325.00
Woven Splint, Bentwood Rim Handles, Round, 18 X 12 1/2 In.	225.00
Woven Splint, Bentwood Rim, Gooseneck Handles, 13 1/2 X 18 In.	137.00
Woven Splint, Bulging Body, Bentwood Loop Handles, 25 X 50 In.	522.00
Woven Splint, Buttocks, Bentwood Handle, Varnished, 15 X 17 In.	75.00
Woven Splint, Cheese Curd, Hexagonal Design, Round, 8 X 20 In.	330.00
Woven Splint, Curliques, Old White Paint, Oblong, 7 1/4 X 11 In.	45.00
Woven Splint, Divider, Watercolor Designs, 3 3/4 X 9 X 13 In.	25.00
Woven Splint, Domed Center Base, Pierced With Handles, 11 1/2 In.	192.00
Woven Splint, Egg, Bentwood Handle, Green Paint, 8 3/4 X 13 In.	220.00
Woven Splint, Geometric, Potato Stamped, Sturtivant, 8 X 13 In.	137.00
Woven Splint, Green Paint, Oval Rim, 19th Century, 1 3/4 X 9 1/2 In.	77.00
Woven Splint, Green Stripes, Potato Print Design, Round, 9 In.	55.00
Woven Splint, Handle, Black & Green Paneled Rim, 7 X 12 In.	247.00
Woven Splint, Heart Shaped Bentwood Handles, 13 X 25 In.	165.00
Woven Splint, Lid Flaps, Bentwood Handle, 10 1/2 X 22 In.	175.00
Woven Splint, Lid, Old Green Paint, 12 In.	325.00
Woven Splint, Melon Rib, Bentwood Handles, Reddish Paint, 20 In.	40.00

Basket, Nantucket, Capt.Thomas James, Ash,
Willow, 12 X 18 In.

Let your baskets share the bathroom with you when you take a shower. The hot moist air is good for the basket.

Woven Splint, Melon Rib, Rim Handles, 11 1/2 X 23 X 25 In.	75.00
Woven Splint, Painted Dark Green, Rectangular Base, 12 1/2 X 8 In.	100.00
Woven Splint, Red Paint, Handle, 19th Century, American, 5 X 8 In.	357.00
Woven Splint, Red Paint, Square Base, Bentwood Handle, 16 X 9 In.	205.00
Woven Splint, Round Top, Square Base, Handle, 12 1/2 X 11 1/2 In.	495.00
Woven Splint, Salmon Paint, Bentwood Frame & Handle, 7 3/4 X 22 In.	192.00
Woven Splint, Short Wooden Feet, H Shaped Frame, 13 1/2 X 27 In.	170.00
Woven Splint, Square Base, Rounded Top, 4 Rim Handles, 16 X 33 In.	175.00
Woven Splint, Wall, 2 Eared Hangers, Split Ash, Green Paint, 13 In.	1045.00
Woven Twig, Red & Green Paint, 2 Button Feet, 4 1/2 X 10 1/2 In.	192.00
Woven Willow, Chicken, Ovoid, Wide Everted Rim, 6 X 14 In.	55.00

BATCHELDER Ernest Batchelder made ceramic and copper items in Los Angeles,
LOS ANGELES California. He died in 1957.

BATCHELDER, Bowl, Advertising For Tiles	175.00
Tile, Grape Design, 7 X 12 In.	85.00
Vase, Blue & White Drip Glaze, Black Ground, Cylindrical, 8 In.	195.00
Vase, Green Shading, 6 1/2 In.	85.00

Batman and Robin are characters from a comic strip by Bob Kane
that started in 1939. In 1966, the characters became part of a
popular television series. There have been radio and movie serials
that featured the pair.

BATMAN, Bank, Figural, Bust	20.00
Bank, National Periodical Publicatons, 1966	40.00
Banner, 1966	10.00
Bat Ring, 1960 Premium	15.00
Batmobile, Tin, Battery Operated ....35.00 To 100.00	
Batmobile, With Robin, 1972	95.00
Book, Comic No.7, 1941	99.00
Box, Slam Bang Vanilla Ice Cream	50.00
Bracelet, Charm	10.00
Button, Charter Member Batman & Robin Society	12.00
Cape & Mask, In Package, 1966	15.00
Cape & Mask, POW, Felt	5.00
Car, Batmobile, 1974	10.00
Clock	25.00
Comic Book, Batman Vs.Joker, No.40	205.00
Container, Orange Drink	10.00
Flasher, Advertising For Vending Machine	55.00
Fork, Stainless, 1966	3.00
Game, Board	18.00
Helmet & Cape, Box, 1966	30.00
Lamp, Batcave	28.00
Mask, Papier–Mache	20.00
Mug, Atlantic Mold	125.00
Night–Light	25.00
Poster, Movie, Chapter No.1, Batman Takes Over	350.00
Puzzle, Jigsaw, Golden Age of Comics	400.00
Record Album, Power Records	3.00
Ring, Bat, Premium, 1960s	15.00
Ring, Official	4.00
Shade, Mask, Bat	37.50
Toothbrush Holder	9.00
Toy, Batcave	28.00
Toy, Batmobile	35.00
Toy, Penguin Car, Corgi	4.00
Toy, Shazam Car, Corgi	4.00
Tumbler, 1966	7.50

Battersea enamels are enamels painted on copper and made in the
Battersea district of London from about 1750 to 1756. Many similar
enamels are mistakenly called "Battersea."

BATTERSEA, Box, Floral Design On Lid, Pink, Gilt Brass Fittings, 4 In.	140.00

Box, Hunt Scene On Lid, Floral Design All Around, 5 5/8 In. 500.00
Box, Polychrome Florals, Enameled, Brass Fittings, 2 5/8 In. 200.00
Candlestick, Blue Reserves, Polychrome Florals, 9 In., Pair 900.00

J.A. Bauer moved his Kentucky pottery to Los Angeles, California, in 1909. The company made art pottery after 1912 and dinnerwares after 1929.

BAUER, Bowl, Batter, Pouring Spout, Blue 26.00
Bowl, Boat Shape, Green, 16 1/4 In. 520.00
Bowl, Carmel, No.18, 8 1/2 In. 9.00
Bowl, Mixing, Ring, Green, No.9, 11 1/2 In. 25.00
Bowl, Mixing, Ring, Orange, No.12, 9 1/2 In. 25.00
Bowl, Pudding, Black, No.1 .... 30.00
Bowl, Rings, Cover, Green, 6 In. 30.00
Butter, Cover, Monterey, Red 37.00
Butter, Ring, Orange–Red Cover 85.00
Butter, Ring, Red 85.00
Carafe, Coffee, Ring, Orange 20.00
Casserole, Copper Holder, Cover, Pink 20.00
Casserole, Cover, Green, 7 In. 30.00
Casserole, Cover, Individual 55.00
Casserole, Ring, Red, Cover, Individual 55.00
Casserole, Rings, Large 25.00
Coffee Server, Wooden Handle, Turquoise 30.00
Container, Refrigerator, Monterey, Burnt Orange 65.00
Cookie Jar, Pastel Green Gloss 48.00
Cookie Jar, Ring 18.00
Cornucopia, Art Deco 10.00
Creamer, Green, Ringware 7.00
Custard Cup, Ringware, Red 8.00
Mixing Bowl, Aladdin, Rust 22.00
Mixing Bowl, Yellow, Ring, No.18 .... 20.00
Pitcher, Ice Lip, 7 In. 65.00
Pitcher, Red, 2 Qt. 35.00
Pitcher, Red, Ring Pattern 35.00
Pitcher, Ringware, Green, 1 1/2 Pt. 12.00
Pitcher, Yellow, 1 Pt. 25.00
Plate, Yellow, 9 1/2 In. 4.50
Sherbet, Ring, Black 85.00
Sherbet, Ring, Cobalt Blue 42.00
Sugar & Creamer, Cover, Cobalt Blue, Miniature 25.00
Sugar & Creamer, Ring Pattern, Red 35.00
Teapot, Aladdin, Rust, 4 Cup 32.00
Teapot, Aladdin, Yellow 35.00
Tumbler, Aqua, 6 Oz. 7.00
Tumbler, Burgundy, 6 Oz. .... 10.00 To 20.00
Vase, Horn-of-Plenty, Pair 15.00
Vase, Light Green, 8 In. 8.00

Porcelains of all types were made in the region known as Bavaria. In the nineteenth century, the mark often included the word "Bavaria." After 1871, the words "Bavaria, Germany" were used. Listed here are pieces that include the name Bavaria in some form, but major porcelain makers such as Rosenthal are listed in their own categories.

BAVARIA, Bowl, Hummingbird, Schwarzenhammer, 9 In. 45.00
Chocolate Set, Floral Design, Bulbous, 13 Piece 125.00
Cocoa Pot, Windmill & People Front, Castle Back, J.P.S.V., 9 In. 100.00
Plate, Gold Encrusted Rim Design, Ivory, Bavaria, 8 3/4 In. 15.00
Plate, Melon Boys, Floral Border, Gold Beading, 1873, 10 In. 175.00

The Beatles became a famous music group in the 1960s. They first appeared on American network television in 1964. The group disbanded in 1971. Collectors search for any items picturing the four members of the group or any recordings. Because these items are so new, the condition is very important and top prices are paid only for items in mint condition.

BEATLES, Bank, 4 Beatles, Orange Plastic, Round, 1964, Nems	30.00
Bank, Drum	8.00
Book Cover, School	5.00
Book, Comic, No.4, Marvel	30.00
Book, Pop–Up, Yellow Submarine, 9 1/2 X 15 In.	15.00
Book, The Beatle Book, Paperback, 1964	15.00
Button, Booster, Picture of 4 Beatles, 2 1/2 In.	2.50
Button, Character, Yellow Submarine, 1968, Large, Set of 4	14.00
Button, I'm A Beatles Fan	75.00
Button, Ringo, Metal Head	12.00
Button, With Chain, 7/8 In.	55.00
Cake Decoration Set	20.00
Cap, Wool, Ringo	15.00
Card, Arcade, 3 1/2 X 5 1/2 In., 25 Piece	8.00
Card, Playing	55.00
Carrying Case, Black, Plastic	25.00
Case, Pencil	12.00
Doll Set, Remco, 4 Piece	150.00
Doll, George Harrison, Nems, 1964	55.00
Doll, Rooted Hair, Set of 4	200.00
Figure Set, Standing, 3 1/2 In., 4 Piece	9.00
Gum Wrapper	12.00
Knife, Pocket, Commemorative, 4 Pictures	3.50
Lunch Box, Yellow Submarine, Child's, Dated 1968	58.00
Lunch Box, Yellow Submarine, Dated 1969	52.00
Magazine, Rolling Stone, John Lennon As Man of The Year 1970	50.00
Magazine, Swedish Tour, 1963, 10 X 13 In.	65.00
Model, Yellow Submarine, Box	42.00
Nodder, Box, 8 In., Set of 4	250.00 To 500.00
Paperback, Hard Day's Night, True Story of Beatles, 1964, 2 Piece	28.00
Pillow, Faces, Blue Suits, Red Ties, Signatures, Square, 12 In.	68.00
Pin, Flasher Portrait, 2 1/2 In.	15.00
Pin, I'm A Beatle Bug	7.50
Pin, Name, Guitar, Drum & Wig, English, Nems	160.00
Pinback, Flasher	20.00
Poster, Facsimile Autographs, 1964, 5 Ft.	55.00
Poster, Nems, 4 Ft.	10.00
Puppet Marionette, Pelham, Box	200.00
Puzzle, Ringo, With Drum, Remco	35.00
Puzzle, Yellow Submarine, Sealed	35.00
Record, 7 Songs, 45 RPM	8.00
Record, Let It Be, Slip Cover	7.50
Scarf, Images of Beatles, White, Black Logo	40.00
Sheet Music, Help	18.00
Sheet Music, Something	18.00
Stockings, Nylon, Original Package, 1960s	25.00
Ticket, Crosley Field Concert, Unused, 1966	75.00
Wallet	10.00

"Beehive, Austria," or "Beehive, Vienna," are terms used in English–speaking countries to refer to the many types of decorated porcelain bearing a mark that looks like a beehive. The mark is actually a shield, viewed upside down. It was first used in 1744 by the Royal Porcelain Manufactory of Vienna. The firm made porcelains, called "Royal Vienna" by collectors, until it closed in 1864. Many other German, Austrian, and Japanese factories have reproduced Royal Vienna wares, complete with the original shield or "beehive" mark. This listing includes the expensive, original Royal Vienna porcelains and many other types of beehive porcelain. The Royal Vienna pieces include that name in the description.

BEEHIVE, see also Royal Vienna

BEEHIVE, Charger, Tannhauser & Venus Scene, A.Heer, C.1910, 14 5/8 In. 1325.00
Demitasse Set, Watteau Scenes, Cobalt Blue, Sepia, 15 Piece 275.00
Dish, Octagonal, Lacy 225.00
Dresser Set, Yellow Roses, Ring Tree, Tray, Pin Tray 75.00
Ewer, Allegorical Scene, Artist Signed, 8 In. 150.00
Ewer, Blue, Portrait of Ladies, 5 Cherubs, 9 X 7 In. 150.00
Ewer, Maiden & Cupid In Reserve, Signed Kauffmann, 6 1/4 In. 195.00
Ewer, Maiden & Cupid, Gold, Maroon, Dark Green, Marked, 6 In. 195.00
Ewer, Portrait, Vertical Gold Stripes, Marked, 9 1/2 In. 375.00
Pitcher, Cherub Design, Cobalt Blue, Marked, 4 1/2 In. 25.00
Pitcher, Water, Painted Flower Pictures, Signed, 4 1/2 In. 80.00
Plaque, Psyche, Maiden, Carried By Mercury, 15 1/4 X 10 In. 5500.00
Plaque, Winter Bison, Woman, Green Dress, 4 X 3 In. 625.00
Plaque, Wood Nymph, White Gown, Forest, 11 X 6 5/8 In. 2550.00
Plate, 2 Ladies & Cupid Garden Scene, Hand Painted 100.00
Plate, Cupid & Venus Panel, Shield Mark, 9 5/8 In. 1450.00
Plate, Devonshire, Woman, Magenta Dress, White Shawl, 9 In. 475.00
Plate, Lady, Maroon, Gold, Brown Hair, 1901 .... 125.00
Plate, Maiden, Flowing Brown Hair, Rose Kimono, 9 1/2 In. 885.00
Tete-A-Tete, Child's, Stripes, Wreath Medallion, 7 Piece 775.00
Tray, 3 Classical Maidens, Shield, C.1910, Round, 20 1/2 In. 1200.00
Vase, Diana The Huntress, Gold Medallion, 8 In. 345.00
Vase, Echo, Maiden, Brown Ground, 2 Handles, 19 In. 2400.00
Vase, Flora Design, Lavender, Handle, 4 1/2 In. 295.00
Vase, Florals, Signed, 15 In. 190.00
Vase, Klea, Maiden, Pink Classic Dress, C.1900, 14 In. 885.00
Vase, Orchids, Gold Outlined, Green & Brown Handles, 14 In. 225.00
Vase, Portrait, Floral, Cover, Signed Ferd, 34 3/4 In. 2200.00
Vase, Portrait, Maiden, Green To Tan, Cover, Shield, 14 7/8 In. 2200.00
Vase, The Bride, Maiden, Wreath of Leaves, Brown, Marked, 11 In. 900.00

Beer was sold in kegs or returnable bottles until 1934. The first patent for a can was issued to the American Can Company in September of that year; and Gotfried Kruger Brewing Company, Newark, New Jersey, was the first to use the can. The cone–top can was first made in 1935, the aluminum pop–top in 1962. Collectors should look for cans in good condition, with no dents or rust. Serious collectors prefer cans that have been opened from the bottom.

BEER CAN, ABC Ale, Hammonton, N.J., 12 Oz. .... .75
Alligator Light, Florida, 12 Oz. .... .75
Alps Brau, Maier 75.00
Andy's Minnesota Map, 1978, 6 Piece 6.00
Balinger's, Forrest, New Bedford 3.00
Ballantine Ale, Ballantine, Newark, Tab 5.00
Ballantine Draft, Tab 2.00
Ballantines Ale, 2 Face, Flat, 16 Oz. 24.00
Battling Bulldog 5.00
Beer Can, Lucky Draft Beer 9.00
Billy Beer, Utica, New York, 12 Oz. 1.00
Billy, Cold Spring–Steel 3.00
Black Horse Ale .... .75
Black Label, 16 Oz. .... .65
Blatz Color Can, Green, Flat, 16 Oz. 45.00
Blatz Old Heidelberg Castle, Cone 45.00
Blatz, No Opener Needed, 16 Oz. 8.00
Blitz Weinhard, 50th Anniversary, 16 Oz. .... .75
Bonzo's, Pittsburgh, 12 Oz. .... .50
Burgermeister, Flat Top, 16 Oz. 25.00
Busch, Los Angeles, Zip Tab 10.00

Camden Lager	125.00
Canadian Ace Ale, Flat Top	60.00
Carling National, Colt 45, 16 Oz.	.50
Carling's Ale, Line of Writing At Bottom, Cone	45.00
Champale Extra Dry, 12 Oz.	.50
Chippewa Pride	.85
Christian Moerlein, Hudepohl, 12 Oz.	.50
Coors, 15 Oz.	5.00
Coors, Golden, 16 Oz.	.50
Coors, Masters III, 12 Oz.	.75
Dixie Light, 10 Oz.	.75
E & B Light Lager, IRTP, Cone	50.00
Ebling White Head Ale, IRTP, Crowntainer	275.00
Edelweiss	3.00
Einbock Bock, Maier, Los Angeles	10.00
Encore, Dated 1968, Tab	6.00
Falstaff Draft, Ft.Wayne	20.00
Falstaff, Cone	40.00
Fitzgeralds Lager Beer, IRTP, Crowntainer	50.00
Fox Deluxe, Cone Top	45.00
Genesee 12 Horse Ale, Flat, 16 Oz.	40.00
Genesee, Natural More Refreshing, Zip Tab	3.00
Genesee, Rochester, Beer In White, Flat Top	6.00
Goetz, Cone Top	40.00
Golden Glow Beer, IRTP	100.00
Grain Belt Premium	1.25
Griesedieck M.L., St.Louis	5.00
Guiness, England, Flat Top, Green	5.00
Hamm's Draft, Tab	9.00
Hamm's Special Light	.50
Heileman's Special Export, Flat, 12 Oz.	8.00
Hoffman House	8.00
Holiday Bock, Tab, 12 Oz.	7.00
Huber's Historical Pa.Breweries, All Different, Set of 6	5.00
Hudepohl	7.00
Hynne	9.00
Iron City, Christmas, 3 Different Scenes, 3 Piece	5.00
Iron City, Pittsburgh, Zip Tab	8.00
Iron City, Steelers Autographs, Pittsburgh, Pa., 1986, 12 Oz.	.50
Iron City, Winter Scenes, 1974, Set of 3	6.00
Iroquois Indian Head Beer, Columbus, Tab	6.00
Knickerbocker Natural, 12 Oz.	.65
Koehler Blue	.75
Labott's Extra Stock, Canadian	.65
Lion Brown, New Zealand, Flat Top	10.00
Little Kings Cream Ale, 12 Oz.	.50
Lone Star	.50
Lucky Lager, Colorado	5.00
Markmeister	8.00
Meister Brau Bock	3.00
Meister Brau Draft	1.50
Meister Brau Premium, 16 Oz.	3.00

Billy Beer cans are not worth hundreds of dollars even though this myth appears in newspapers about every six months.

Meister Brau, 14 Oz. .... .75
Miller $1000, Tab 5.00
Miller, Bank Top, 12 Oz. 2.00
Miller, Eagle Logo, 16 Oz. .... .50
Mr.Lager Beer, Grade 1 .... 175.00
Narragansett, Falstaff, 12 Oz. .... .50
Narragansett, Wake Up America, 12 Oz. .... .50
National Bohemian Bock .... .85
National Bohemian, IRTP, Crowntainer 400.00
National Bohemian, North Star, Cold Spring, 12 Oz. .... .50
New Yorker Beer 450.00
Old Bohemian Light Beer, Harvard, Flat, 16 Oz. 15.00
Old Crown .... .85
Old German, IRTP, Cone 42.00
Old Imperial, Crowntainer 65.00
Old Milwaukee, Schlitz, Zip Tab, Green 3.00
Old Milwaukee, Zip Tab 4.00
Old Timers, Wisconsin .... .85
Olympia Gold .... .50
Ortlieb's Bicentennial, Set of 12 .... 15.00
Ortlieb's, Bicentennial, Independence Hall, 12 Oz. 1.00
Ortlief's Bock, 12 Oz. .... .50
Ortlief's, Bicentennial, World's Fair, San Antonio, 1984, 12 Oz. ... 1.00
Ortlief's, Mummer's Parade, 12 Oz. .... .75
Pfeiffer, Detroit, Flat Top 10.00
Phartz Milwaukee Beer, Novelty, 12 Oz. .... .50
Pilsener's Brewing Company, Cone Top, 32 Oz. 50.00
Polish Countess, Schell, 12 Oz. .... .50
Rams Head Ale 90.00
Ranier Old Stock Ale, Cone 90.00
Red Cap Ale, Flat, 16 Oz. 7.00
Red Top Ale, Cone Top, 12 Oz. 5.00
Renner Old German, Ft.Wayne 2.00
Rheingold, Kool Mule, 12 Oz. .... .75
Rhinelander 6.00
Ruppert Beer, IRTP 50.00
Schell Brewing Co., Deer Brand, Black, Gold & Red, 12 Oz. .... .75
Schell's Deer Brand Export I 2.00
Schell's, Golden 16, Pull Tab 25.00
Schlitz, 1980 Olympic Games, 12 Oz. .... .50
Schlitz, Dated 1949, Flat, 16 Oz. 4.00
Schlitz, Tab, Dated 1968, 12 Oz. 1.50
Schmidt Draft, Heileman, 16 Oz. 3.00
Schmidt's Anniversary, Seven Springs, Green, 12 Oz. .... .50
Spirit of Dubuque 1.25
Standard Dry Ale 1.25
Storz, Omaha, Green 15.00
Strohs, Piels Draft, 16 Oz. .... .50
Tacoma Pale Beer, IRTP, Flat, 16 Oz. 75.00
Tam O'Shanter Ale Dry Hopped 125.00
Tivoli, Denver 25.00
Tru Blu White Seal Beer, IRTP, Crowntainer 200.00
Tuborg Gold .... .50
Utica Club, 16 Oz. .... .85
Walter's Beer, Zip Tab 10.00
Walter, Owen Brew, Old Style Light, Silver, 12 Oz. .... .75
West Virginia 4.00
Western Gold 75.00
White Cap, Cone 85.00

Bells have been made of porcelain, china, or metal through the centuries. All types are collected. Favorites include glass bells, figural bells, school bells, and cowbells. Be careful not to buy a bell made from an old glass goblet.

BELL, Brass, Good & Moores 300.00
 Butler's, Brass 17.50
 Cambridge Glass, Souvenir, Coney Island, Rose Design, Gold 150.00
 Christmas, New England Society, Silver Plate, Angel Handle, 1982 .... 5.00
 Cow, Brass, 6 1/2 In. 12.50
 Crystal, Floral Design, German 10.00
 Cut Glass, Hobstar Pattern, German 15.00
 Felix The Cat, Figural Handle, Brass, 4 3/4 In. 75.00
 Figural Head Handle, Neville Chamberlain, Brass, 5 1/4 In. 65.00
 Figural, Witch From Hansel & Gretel, Brass 145.00
 Floral Design, Amber To Clear Cut, Bohemian 5.00
 Frosted, Blue, Green Leaves, Red Rim & Stem 15.00
 Graduated, Bronze, Amish, Set of 8 .... 250.00
 Hemony, Crowned Bear Holding Shield Handle, Brass, 5 5/8 In. 110.00
 Hemony, Knight Holding Sword & Shield Handle, Brass, 6 1/4 In. 110.00
 Hotel Desk, Turtle, Clock Wound, 7 In. 325.00
 Locomotive, Yoke & Cradle, Bronze, 17 In. 875.00
 Medieval Scenes, Brass, 4 In. 22.00
 Millefiori Design, Animal Shaped Handles, Murano Glass, Set of 4 .... 25.00
 Napoleon, Figural Handle, Brass, 7 X 3 3/8 In. 70.00
 Napoleon, Figural Handle, Waterloo Battle Scenes, Brass, 6 1/4 In. 70.00
 Northwestern Casket Co., Metal 12.00
 Pink Flamingo, Florida Souvenir, China 10.00
 Ruby To Clear, Etched, Inscribed West Allis, Wisc.1914, Clear Handle 10.00
 Saignelegier, 1878, 3 In. 55.00
 School, Brass, 19th Century 50.00
 School, Brass, 9 In. 35.00
 School, Brass, Wooden Handle, 10 In. 100.00
 School, Iron, With Rope Wheel 300.00
 School, Turned Cherry Handle, Stamped 6, Metal, 8 In. 40.00
 Sheep's, Strap Handle, Brass, 1910 .... 45.00
 Sleigh, Cast Brass, Graduated 235.00
 Sleigh, On Fancy Edged Buckled Strip, 1870s 225.00
 Smoke, Daisy & Button, Amber 70.00
 Souvenir, Columbia Liberty, Cast 1893, McShang Foundry 45.00
 Spaniels, Figural Handle, Word Spaniels, Brass, 4 In. 70.00
 Stag Design, Ruby To Clear Cut Glass, Bohemian 15.00
 Sterling Silver, FWK Etched, Wooden Handle, Signed B.Altman, 3 5/8 In. 65.00
 Suffragette, Votes For Women, Thou Shall Have A Vote, Arcadian Janus 175.00
 Temple, Cast Iron, Geometric, Calligraphy, Cylindrical, Japan, 4 3/8 In. 75.00
 Thumbprint Design, Clear Handle, Green Crystal, Bohemia, Large 10.00
 Victorian Belle, Heisey 125.00

Belleek china is made in Ireland, other European countries, and the
United States. The glaze is creamy yellow and appears wet. The first
Belleek was made in 1857. All pieces listed here are Irish Belleek.
The mark changed through the years. The first mark, black, dates
from 1863 to 1890. The second mark, black, dates from 1891 to
1926 and includes the words "Co. Fermanagh, Ireland." The third
mark, black, dates from 1926 to 1946 and has the words "Deanta in
Eirinn." The fourth mark, same as the third mark but green, dates
from 1946 to 1955. The fifth mark, green, dates from 1955 to 1965
and has an R in a circle added in the upper right. The sixth mark,
green, dates after 1965 and the words "Co. Fermanagh" have been
omitted.

 **BELLEEK, see also Ceramic Art Co.; Haviland; Lenox; Ott & Brewer;
Willets**
BELLEEK, Basket, Buds, Flowers, 3 Strand, Henshall, 8 In. 2800.00
 Basket, Buds, Flowers, Cover, 3 Strand, Oval, 8 1/2 In. 4800.00
 Basket, Erne, Shamrock Shape, Border Florals, 6 3/4 In. 475.00
 Bowl, Flying Fish, Pearl, 1st Black Mark, 5 In. 650.00
 Bowl, Quilted Diamond, 1st Green Mark 65.00
 Butter Tub, Aberdeen, 3rd Green Mark 22.00

Butter, Cover, Figural, Cottage, Branch Handle, 1st Green Mark, 5 In.	185.00
Butter, Shell, Cover, Green Mark	65.00
Cake Plate, Art Deco, Silver Overlay, Cocktail Glass Shape, 11 In.	115.00
Cake Plate, Basket Weave Ware, Twig Handles, 10 3/4 In.	650.00
Cake Plate, Limpet, 3rd Black Mark	90.00
Cauldron, 3–Footed, 2nd Black Mark	95.00
Cheese Dish, Figural Cottage, Yellow Luster, 1st Green Mark	175.00
Compote, Greek, Aqua Trim, 2nd Black Mark, 4 3/4 X 9 3/4 In.	650.00
Compote, Tri–Dolphin, 1st Black Mark, 4 7/8 X 10 In.	650.00
Creamer, Girl's Face, Flowing Hair, 6 In.	125.00
Creamer, Lily, 1st Black Mark	70.00
Creamer, Lily, 1st Green Mark	33.00
Creamer, Nautilus, 1st Black Mark	200.00
Creamer, Scale, 1st Black Mark	70.00
Creamer, Shamrock, Twig Handle, Black Mark	50.00
Creamer, Shell, 1st Black Mark, 3 X 5 1/2 In.	325.00
Cup & Saucer, Chocolate, Cobalt Blue, Unicorn Mark	20.00
Cup & Saucer, Demitasse, Blue Mark	25.00
Cup & Saucer, Erne, 1st Black Mark	85.00
Cup & Saucer, Grass, 1st Black Mark	135.00
Cup & Saucer, Hawthorne, White, Gold Trim, 1st Black Mark	175.00
Cup & Saucer, Mandarin	20.00
Cup & Saucer, Mandarin, Demitasse	15.00
Cup & Saucer, Neptune, Green Trim, Shell Feet, 1st Black Mark	77.00
Cup & Saucer, Ring Handle, Flowers, Last Black Mark, Demitasse	225.00
Cup & Saucer, Shamrock, 3rd Black Mark	55.00
Cup & Saucer, Shamrock, 3rd Black Mark, Demitasse	68.00
Cup & Saucer, Tridacna, Blue Trim, 1st Blue Mark	215.00
Cup & Saucer, Tridacna, Eggshell	50.00
Cup & Saucer, Tridacna, Green Trim, 2nd Black Mark	85.00
Cup & Saucer, Tridacna, Pearl Luster, Gold Rim, 1st Black Mark	95.00
Cup & Saucer, Tridacna, Pink Trim, 2nd Black Mark	85.00
Cup, Saucer & Tea Plate, Tridacna, 1st Black Mark	150.00
Dejeuner Set, Echinus, Pink Trim, Tray, 1st Black Mark, 6 Piece	1750.00
Dish, Heart Shape, 6th Mark	30.00
Dish, Sycamore Leaf, 3rd Black Mark, 4 1/2 In.	45.00
Ewer, Aberdeen, Applied Floral Design, 2nd Green Mark, Pair	845.00
Figurine, Affection, 3rd Green Mark, 15 In.	495.00
Figurine, Dog, Sitting, 6th Mark	25.00
Figurine, Erin, 1st Black Mark	4200.00
Figurine, Leprechaun, Good Luck, English & Irish, 2nd Black Mark	325.00
Figurine, Meditation, 3rd Black Mark, 15 In.	1275.00
Figurine, Pit, 3rd Black Mark	220.00
Figurine, Praying Madonna, 1st Green Mark, 12 In.	500.00
Flower Holder, Seahorse, 4th Green Mark	135.00
Flower Spill, 4 Footed, 2nd Black Mark, 5 In.	250.00
Frame, Lily, Beaded, 1st Black Mark, Oval, 6 1/2 In.	1750.00
Gravy, Attached Underplate, Boulevard	425.00
Honey Pot, Grass, 1st Black Mark	350.00
Honey Pot, Shamrock, 2nd Black Mark	500.00
Honey Pot, Shamrock, Basket Weave, 3rd Black Mark	145.00
Jug & Bowl, Thistle, 1st Production	1050.00
Mug, Monk In Wine Cellar, Monochromatic Blue, 6 3/4 In.	120.00
Mug, Thistle	85.00
Pitcher, Cider, Lily Pad, Hobnail Handle, Signed	295.00
Pitcher, Girl, Gold Braided Hair Handle, Green Mark, 5 In.	49.00
Plaque, Figural, Communion	22.00
Plate, Dinner, Boulevard, 10 1/2 In.	200.00
Plate, Green, Gold Rim, Gold Berries, Black Mark, 5 1/2 In.	57.00
Plate, Pink Shells, Gold Rim, 1st Green Mark, 7 In.	54.00
Plate, Shamrock, 2nd Black Mark, 6 1/2 In.	40.00
Plate, Shell, 1st Black Mark, 8 1/2 In.	85.00
Plate, Shell, Green Trim, 2nd Black Mark, 4 X 5 In.	75.00
Plate, Sycamore Leaf, 3rd Black Mark	42.00

Plate, Thistle, Pink Trim, 2nd Black Mark, 6 3/4 In.	75.00
Plate, Tridacna, Coral Rim, 1st Black Mark, 6 In.	90.00
Platter, Boulevard, Oval, 17 1/2 In.	300.00
Spill, Lily, 2nd Black Mark	85.00
Sugar & Creamer, Ivy, 1st Green Mark	85.00
Sugar & Creamer, Lotus, 1st Green Mark	85.00
Sugar & Creamer, Lotus, Black Mark	165.00
Sugar & Creamer, Lotus, Green, 2nd Black Mark	100.00
Sugar & Creamer, Mask, Black Mark	145.00
Sugar & Creamer, Shamrock, 1st Green Mark	60.00 To 65.00
Sugar & Creamer, Shamrock, 2nd Black Mark	85.00
Sugar & Creamer, Tridacna, Yellow Luster Interior, 3rd Green Mark	20.00
Sugar, Hexagon, 2nd Black Mark	35.00
Sugar, Neptune, Green, 2nd Black Mark	80.00
Sugar, Ribbon, 3rd Green Mark	12.50
Sugar, Swirl Pattern, White, Green Trim, 2nd Black Mark	70.00
Sugar, Tridacna, Green, 2nd Black Mark	75.00
Tankard, Musicians, Blue, Green Mark, 7 In.	95.00
Tea Kettle, Tridacna, Green Trim, 2nd Black Mark, 5 1/2 In.	345.00
Tea Set, Basket Weave, Green Mark, 3 Piece	85.00
Tea Set, Basket Weave, Shamrock Pattern, Black Mark, 5 Piece	350.00
Tea Set, Harp Shamrock, Green, Pearl Glaze, 2nd Black Mark, 5 Piece	1950.00
Tea Set, Morning, Woman's, Erne Pattern, C.1890, 2nd Black Mark	1500.00
Tea Set, Shamrock Basket Weave, Black Mark	245.00
Tea Set, Shell Pattern, 2nd Black Mark, 16 Piece	600.00
Tea Set, Woven Textured Ground With Shamrocks, C.1900, 17 Piece	375.00
Teapot, Bamboo, 1st Black Mark	450.00
Teapot, Echinus, 1st Black Mark	300.00
Teapot, Erne, 1st Black Mark	300.00
Teapot, Limpet, 3rd Black Mark	175.00 To 325.00
Teapot, Neptune, Green Trim, 2nd Black Mark, 4 3/4in.	245.00
Teapot, Neptune, Yellow, 2nd Black Mark	250.00 To 270.00
Teapot, Shell, 2nd Black Mark	345.00
Teapot, Tridacna, 2nd Black Mark	245.00
Tray, Tea, Tridacna, Green Trim, Black Mark, 14 1/4 X 15 1/2 In.	595.00
Tray, Tridacna, 1st Black Mark	500.00
Tray, Trinket, Open, Fan Shape, 2nd Black Mark	65.00
Tumbler, 2nd Black Mark	110.00
Tumbler, Tridacna, Yellow Trim, 2nd Black Mark	95.00
Vase, Aberdeen, Applied Flowers, 2nd Black Mark, 10 In.	495.00
Vase, Applied Floral Design, Green Mark, 9 In.	50.00
Vase, Double Fish, 1st Black Mark, 12 In.	3000.00
Vase, Elm, 3rd Green Mark	65.00
Vase, Figural, Corn, All White, 1st Black Mark, 6 In., Pair	385.00
Vase, Figural, Owl, Marked, 8 In.	40.00
Vase, Flying Fish, Shell Form, 2nd Black Mark, 2 3/8 In.	425.00
Vase, Frog, Black Eye, 2nd Black Mark, 6 In.	1375.00
Vase, Gold Celtic Tara, 3rd Black Mark, 7 1/2 In.	250.00
Vase, Hippiritus, 1st Black Mark, 6 3/4 In.	225.00
Vase, Incised Salamander Pattern, Elephant Head Handles, 7 In.	85.00
Vase, Ivory, 8 In.	37.50
Vase, Lizard, 1st Black Mark, 8 1/4 In.	1500.00
Vase, Melvin, 3rd Green Mark	85.00
Vase, Moore, Green Mark, 7 In.	55.00
Vase, Nile Pattern, Fluted Top, 2nd Black Mark, 13 In.	495.00
Vase, Princess, Colored Flowers, 2nd Black Mark, 9 In.	795.00
Vase, Ram's Horn, White	1600.00
Vase, Rose Isle, Handmade Porcelain Flowers, 13 In.	675.00
Vase, Shamrock & Harp, 2nd Black Mark, 9 In.	300.00
Vase, Trellis, Roses, 2nd Black Mark, 4 In.	135.00

Bennington ware was the product of two factories working in Bennington, Vermont. Both firms were out of business by 1896. The wares include brown and yellow mottled pottery, Parian, scroddled ware, stoneware, graniteware, yellowware, and Staffordshirelike vases.

BENNINGTON, Bowl, 8 In. 65.00
   Bowl, 10 In. 75.00
   Bowl, 4 X 9 In. 68.00
   Bowl, Milk, 10–Footed, Lead Glaze, Canted Sides, 11 1/4 In. 155.00
   Bowl, Mixing, 4 X 9 1/2 In. 90.00
   Bowl, Sawtooth Pattern, Brown & Yellow, 9 1/2 In. 120.00
   Crock, Cobalt Blue Leaf Design, Norton, 2 Gal., 13 1/2 In. 248.00
   Cuspidor, 1849 Mark & Rockingham Glaze, 8 In. 110.00
   Cuspidor, Shell Pattern, Side Vent, 8 1/2 In. 110.00
   Custard, Set of 6 .... 85.00
   Flowerpot, Underplate, Cattails, Dark Brown Glaze, 5 3/8 In. 55.00
   Inkwell, Child Asleep, Holding Hat In Hand, Brown Glaze 150.00
   Jug, Albany Slip, L.Norton & Sons, 1830–38 .... 150.00
   Mug, Brown, Impressed Mark, Pair 85.00
   Pie Plate 65.00
   Pie Plate, 11 1/4 In. 130.00
   Pitcher, 6–Sided Panels 95.00
   Pitcher, Flowers, Brown Mottled, 9 1/2 In. 125.00
   Pitcher, Hunt Scene 85.00
   Pitcher, Milk, Mottled Brown & Yellow, 3 Qt. 195.00
   Pitcher, Peacock 50.00
   Pitcher, President's Portraits On Sides, 11 In. 150.00
   Pitcher, Wreath, With Game 95.00
   Salt Box, Peacock At Fountain 215.00
   Spittoon, Shell, Side Vent, 8 1/2 X 3 1/2 In. 95.00
   Teapot, Chinaman, 10 1/2 In. 115.00
   Vase, Corn, With Grapes, Parian, 9 In. 70.00

If you live in an old house and the locks are old, check the new types. There have been many improvements and new locks give much better security.

John Beswick started making earthenware in Staffordshire, England, in 1936. The company is now part of Royal Doulton Tableware, Ltd. Figurines of animals, especially dogs and horses, Beatrix Potter animals, and other wares are still being made.

BESWICK, Character Jug, Captain Cuttle, 5 1/2 In. 40.00
   Character Jug, Sairey Gamp, 7 In. 40.00
   Figurine, Bulldog, 4 In. 12.00
   Figurine, Cat, Nestling Siamese Kittens, 4 1/2 In. 40.00
   Figurine, Ziggy, Lion 20.00
   Mug, Captain Cuttle 42.00
   Mug, Hamlet, To Be Or Not To Be 24.00
   Mug, Juliet, Parting Is Such Sweet Sorrow 24.00
   Pitcher, Blown–Out Palm Tree, Maroon, 7 1/4 In. 50.00
   Pitcher, Sairey Gamp 60.00
   Toby, Mr.Varden, No.9204 .... 32.00
   Toby, Mrs.Varden 30.00
   Vase, Blown–Out Palm Tree 35.00

Betty Boop, the cartoon figure, first appeared on the screen in 1931. Her face was modeled after the famous singer Helen Kane and her body after Mae West. In 1935 a comic strip was started. Although the Betty Boop cartoons were ended by 1938, there has been a

revival of interest in the Betty Boop image in the 1980s and new
pieces are being made.

BETTY BOOP, Bank, Papier–Mache, 8 In.	75.00
Bottle, Perfume, Figural, Clear Glass, 3 1/2 In.	55.00
Button, Picture With Krazy Cat	1.00
Decal, Sheet, 1920s, 4 X 8 In.	4.00
Doll, Bisque, Jointed, Box, 12 In.	25.00
Doll, Cameo	1000.00
Doll, Celluloid, Movable Arms, 8 In.	95.00
Doll, Jointed, Wooden, 4 1/2 In.	65.00
Doll, Rag, Colorforms, 1978, Box, 17 In.	35.00
Doll, Vinyl, Jointed, 7 Different Outfits, 1986, Box, 11 1/2 In.	25.00
Figurine, Chalkware	32.00
Light Bulb, Christmas	65.00 To 70.00
Perfume Bottle	15.00
Pin, Scotty Dog	10.00
Playing Card, Cinderella	100.00
Playing Cards, Box	75.00
Vase, Wall, Betty Twisting Bimbo's Ear	275.00
Vase, Wall, Ceramic	135.00
Watch, Betty In Center, Bimbo On Back, 1930s	200.00
Watch, Pocket	150.00

 The bicycle was invented in 1839. The first manufactured bicycle
was made in 1861. Special ladies' bicycles were made after 1874.
The modern safety bicycle was not produced until 1885. Collectors
search for all types of bicycles and tricycles.

BICYCLE, Columbia, 3 Star Deluxe, Horn Tank, Front Fender Light	175.00
Columbia, High Wheel, 56 In.	1800.00
Columbia, High Wheel, C.1883, Pope Co.	2850.00
Columbia, Lady's, Wood Rims, Block Chain, Coaster Brake	125.00
Dunelt, Boy's, White Grips, Tear Coaster Brake, Front Hand Brake	50.00
E.C.Simmons, Wood Wheels	275.00
Firestone, Man's, Rear Carrier, Light, Chrome Fenders	75.00
Firestone, Special Cruiser, Lady's, Front Fender Light	75.00
Huffy, Eldorado, Lady's, Front Light, Rear Carrier, Chrome Fenders	100.00
Iroquois, Woman's, Wooden Wheel Rims, Wooden Fender, Pinstriping	375.00
Philips, Man's, Metal Rims, Hand Brakes, English	75.00
Red Wing, Lady's, Coaster Brake, Worcester, Mass., C.1918	125.00
Remington Arms, Built For 2, Chain Drive Steering	400.00
Road Queen, Woman's, A.Featherstone & Co., Wooden Rims, Fenders	210.00
Roadmaster, Luxury Liner, Man's, Front Light, Carrier, Chrome Trim	650.00
Roadmaster, Man's, Deluxe, Long Rear Carrier, New Tires	150.00
Roller Tricycle, Wooden Seat & Handlebars, 1930s	125.00
Ross, Custom Deluxe, Girl's, Red Rear Carrier, Red Tank, Truss Rods	125.00
Rouse Hazard Overland, Peoria, Illinois, Wooden Wheels, Fenders	225.00
Royal Racer, Red Paint, Seat Above Gears & 4 Spoked Wheels, 39 In.	660.00
Schwinn, Balloon Tires, 1940	20.00
Schwinn, Black Phantom, Boy's	750.00
Schwinn, Hornet, Man's, Front Fender Light, Rear Carrier	400.00
Schwinn, Woman's, Black Panther	290.00
Scooter, Cushman, 1958	1500.00
Sears, Man's, Red Paint, Rear Carrier, Chrome Fenders	100.00
Siren, Child's, Fire Chief	20.00
Siren, Spiderman	7.50
Tandem, Boy's & Girl's Junior, Balloon Tires, Red Paint	200.00
Tandem, Remington	500.00 To 750.00
Tricycle, 1902	975.00
Tricycle, Laminated Wood, Fabric Covered Saddle Seat, 4 Ft.10 In.	660.00
Velocipede, Fairy, Elyria	675.00
Velocipede, Original Red Paint	675.00
Velocipede, Toledo, Original Paint	1050.00

Bing and Grondahl is a famous Danish factory making fine porcelains from 1853 to the present. Underglaze blue decoration was started in 1886. The annual Christmas plate series was introduced in 1895. Dinnerwares, stoneware, and figurines are still being made today. The firm has used the initials B & G and a stylized castle as part of the mark since 1898.

B & G / TJØBENHAVN / MADE IN DENMARK

BING & GRONDAHL, Bell, Christmas, St.Paul's Cathedral, Porcelain	10.00
Coffeepot, Seagull	95.00
Figurine, Ballerina, Dove, No.2300, 12 In.	225.00
Figurine, Boy With Pet, No.2334	93.00
Figurine, Girl With Cat, No.2249	70.00
Figurine, Girl, With Calves	295.00
Figurine, Love Refused, No.2162, 1920s Mark, 7 1/2 In.	145.00
Figurine, Peacock, No.1628, 15 In.	325.00
Figurine, Pheasant, No.2389	300.00
Figurine, Pierrot Clown, No.2353	150.00
Figurine, Seagull, 4 In.	30.00
Nappy, Leaf Shape, Seagull, Handle, 9 1/2 In.	45.00
Plate, Christmas, 1922	65.00
Plate, Christmas, 1924	65.00
Plate, Christmas, 1967	29.50
Plate, Christmas, 1971	7.50
Plate, Mother's Day, 1972, 6 In.	7.50
Vase, Bluebird On Branch, Hand Painted, 15 1/2 In.	295.00
Vase, Dandelions, 10 In.	50.00
Vase, Lily-of-The-Valley, 4 1/2 In.	27.50
Vase, Seagull, 5 1/4 In.	40.00
Vase, Seagull, Gold Wing Tips, Blue, 8 In.	95.00

All types of old binoculars are wanted by collectors. Those made in the eighteenth and nineteenth centuries are favored by serious collectors. The small, attractive binoculars called opera glasses are listed in their own section.

BINOCULARS, Busch Tenni Special, Brass, Leather Covered Barrels, 6 In.	15.00
Hunter's, Carl Zeiss	25.00
Ivory With Brass Fittings, 3 1/2 In.	130.00
Jockey Club Paris, Nickel Plated Brass, Brown Leather, 4 In.	15.00
World War I, Signal Corps, Case	65.00

Old birdcages are collected for use as homes for pet birds and as decorative objects of folk art. Elaborate wooden cages of the past centuries can still be found. The brass or wicker cages of the 1930s are popular with bird owners.

BIRDCAGE, Bin, Top Handle	88.00
Brass, Stand, 6 Ft.	65.00
Canary, Wooden, Handmade	30.00
Domed, Wire Sides, Wooden, Blue Paint, American, 19 X 20 3/4 In.	100.00
Domed, Wirework, Hanging Handle, American, Gray, 24 1/2 In.	192.50
Hartz Mountain, Wooden	45.00
Hendryx, Brass	65.00
Hendryx, Brass, With Wheel	75.00
Hendryx, Copper	125.00
Mustard Ground, Red & Green, Pine & Metal, C.1860, 25 In.	2200.00
Parrot, Victorian, Twisted Wire & Tin	75.00
Tin & Wood	80.00
Tin & Wood, Rectangular, Red Paint, 19 X 26 1/4 In.	137.00
Tin, Domed, Round Cupola, Pierced Galleried Tray, U.S., 18 X 14 In.	302.00
Tole, Acorn Finial, Hanging Loop, American, 10 In.	110.00
Wicker	35.00
Windsor	235.00

Bisque is an unglazed baked porcelain. Finished bisque has a slightly sandy texture with a dull finish. Some of it may be decorated with various colors. Bisque gained favor during the late Victorian era when thousands of bisque figurines were made. It is still being made.

BISQUE, see also named porcelain factories

BISQUE, Bust, Marie Antoinette, Mounted Now As Table Lamp, 26 3/4 In. 1760.00
  Candlestick, Girl On Swing, Blue & White, Gold Trim, 8 3/4 In. 175.00
  Figurine, Bathing Beauty, Diving Pose, 1910, Heubach, 21 In. 1300.00
  Figurine, Bathing Beauty, Lying On Stomach, German, 5 In. 75.00
  Figurine, Boy & Girl On Swing, Tan & White, 5 1/2 In. 95.00
  Figurine, Boy & Girl With Basket, German, 5 1/2 In., Pair 75.00
  Figurine, Boy With Mandolin, 21 In. 1200.00
  Figurine, Girl On Swing, Holding Dog, Blue Dress, 4 5/8 In. 88.00
  Figurine, Girl, Boy, Coral & Rust Clothes, English, 14 1/2 In., Pair 175.00
  Figurine, Kate Greenaway Type Girl, Costume, German, 4 In. 24.00
  Figurine, Man In Plumed Hat & Maiden, French, 25 In., Pair 950.00
  Figurine, No.554, Crown MAF Mark, 10 In., Pair 365.00
  Figurine, Old King Cole, On Throne, German, 4 In. 28.50
  Figurine, Peasant Children, White, Lavender & Green, 9 3/8 In., Pair 135.00
  Figurine, Persian Harem Dancer, White, Artist Signed, 9 1/2 In. 95.00
  Figurine, Sailor Boy, Colored, Germany, C.1870, 13 In. 135.00
  Figurine, Smokey The Bear, 2 In. 12.00
  Figurine, Young Man and Woman, Elizabethan Costumes, 19 In., Pair 300.00
  Group, Young Man & Woman, Under Umbrella, 6 In. 175.00
  Holder, Toothbrush, 3 Little Pigs 50.00
  Plaque, Heart, Valentine, 2 Cherubs, 5 1/2 X 5 In. 30.00
  Tobacco Jar, Black Man, Head, Smoking Pipe, 4 1/4 In. 85.00
  Toothpick, Rabbit, Intaglio Eyes, Victorian Dressed, Open Top Egg 115.00

Black amethyst glass appears black until it is held to the light, then a dark purple can be seen. It has been made in many factories from 1860 to the present.

BLACK AMETHYST, Bottle, Pinched, Silver Deposit, Sterling Silver Stopper 50.00
  Bowl, Console, Thorn & Clover, 11 In. 35.00
  Bowl, Cover, 6 In. 25.00
  Bowl, Impressed Florals, 10 3/4 In. 25.00
  Bowl, World's Fair, Monsoric Patrol, 1933, 10 In. 85.00
  Box, Dresser, Hinged Top, Blue Forget–Me–Nots, 3 1/2 In. 95.00
  Box, Lady, Long Dress, On Lid, Enameled, 3 3/4 X 5 5/8 In. 245.00
  Box, Patch, Butterfly On Lid, 1 1/4 X 2 1/4 In. 125.00
  Candlestick, Pair 50.00
  Dish, Flared, Scalloped Top, 3 Corners, 3–Footed 23.50
  Dish, Hen On Nest Cover 25.00
  Ice Bucket, With 6 Tumblers 65.00
  Inkwell, Insert, Egg Shape, Square, 4 In. 80.00
  Loving Cup, Dancing Girls, 7 1/2 In. 35.00
  Powder Jar 18.00
  Salt & Pepper, Art Deco 25.00
  Sugar 10.00
  Toothpick, Bees On Basket 60.00
  Tray, Round, 14 1/2 In. 65.00
  Vase, Applied Grecian Figures, Matte Ocher, 12 1/2 In. 205.00
  Vase, Enameled Stork & Plants, Beading, 9 In. 90.00
  Vase, Forest, 7 In. 65.00
  Vase, Greek Key Pattern Around Rim, Mirror Bottom, 6 In. 17.50
  Vase, Greek Key Rim, 6 In. 17.50
  Vase, Mary Gregory Type, 11 In. 145.00
  Vase, Mirror Bottom, 6 1/2 In. 12.00
  Vase, Young Girl, Umbrella, Cover, Mary Gregory, 17 In. 450.00

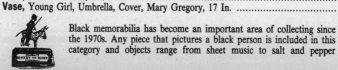

Black memorabilia has become an important area of collecting since the 1970s. Any piece that pictures a black person is included in this category and objects range from sheet music to salt and pepper shakers. The best material dates from past centuries, but many recent items are of interest even if not yet expensive.

BLACK, Amos & Andy, Cardboard Stand–Up, 1930 Colgate Premium, 8 1/2 In.	78.00
Amos & Andy, Toy, Lithographed, Tin, 11 1/2 In.	650.00
Ashtray, Amos & Andy	75.00
Ashtray, Bass Ale, Comic Scene, Blacks Cooking White Man In Pot	35.00
Ashtray, Bass Ale, Comic Scene, Newhall China	40.00
Ashtray, Black Boy, On Toilet	10.00
Ashtray, Black Boy, With Donkey	12.00
Ashtray, Boy On Pot, Scram Bee This Ain'T Yo Hive	30.00
Ashtray, Clown	20.00
Ashtray, Figural, Goose, Grabbing Black Boy's Plumbing	45.00
Ashtray, Georgia Restaurant, Home of The World's Best Pecan Pie	50.00
Ashtray, Man With Basket, Glass Insert, Wooden Head, Metal, 6 X 5 In.	22.00
Ashtray, Uncle Mose, Iron	95.00
Aunt Jemima, Creamer, Plastic	20.00
Aunt Jemima, Plate, Paper	45.00
Aunt Jemima, Shaker, Pancake	45.00
Bank, Boy On Potty, Iron	100.00
Bank, Double Faced	100.00
Bank, Give Me A Penny	150.00
Bank, Mammy, Iron, Hubley, 12 In.	290.00
Block, Printer's, Carbon Copies, Mammy & Parade of Children	35.00
Book, 100 Amazing Facts About The Negro, 1934	20.00
Book, Adventures of Rufus Rastus Brown In Darktown, 1906	75.00
Book, All About Amos & Andy, Gosden & Correll	55.00
Book, Billie Whiskers In The South	65.00
Book, Little Black Sambo, Bannerman	27.50
Book, Little Black Sambo, Christmas Stocking Series, 3 X 4 In.	50.00
Book, Little Black Sambo, Colored, Saalfield, 1928	25.00
Book, Little Black Sambo, Platt & Munk, 28 Pages, Copyright 1955	25.00
Book, Little Black Sambo, Whitman	10.00
Book, Piccaninny Twins, 1931	12.00
Book, Ten Little Colored Boys, 1942, 10 1/2 X 8 1/2 In.	28.00
Book, Ten Little Niggers, Fold Up, Pictures, Story, 2 1/4 X 3 1/4 In.	10.00
Book, Ten Little Niggers, Hayes–Buffalo	65.00
Book, Topsy–Turvy Easter Bunny, McNally, Esther Fiske, 1939	25.00
Book, Turkey Trot & The Black Santa, Platt & Munk, 1942, 36 Pgs.	50.00
Book, Uncle Tom's Cabin, F.M.Lupton Issue	12.00
Bookends, Boy, Cast Iron	90.00
Booklet, Aunt Jemima Recipe, 1928	12.00
Bottle Opener, Negro, Brass	16.00
Bottle Opener, Wooden Minstrel, Top Hat, Banjo Opener, 7 In.	18.00
Bottle Stopper, Sambo Head, 1940s	25.00
Bottle, Shoe Polish, Mason's	32.00
Bowl, Coon Chicken Inn, 3 1/2 In.	40.00

When buying antiques, beware of stickers, magic marker numbers, and other dealer-added labels that may damage the antique. Any type of sticky tape or label will leave marks on paper or paint finishes. Metal with an oxidized finish is damaged when ink marks are removed. Pencil or pen notations often leave indentations.

Box, 3 Alabama Coons, Cardboard, Engraved, 3 Children 40.00
Box, Cigarette, Inlaid, Sliding Lid, Black Pops Up With Cigarette 75.00
Box, Mason's Shoe–Black, Black's Picture, Partial Label 28.00
Box, Watermelon Boy On Pile of Cotton, 1930s 45.00
Box, White Chalk, Black Face, Chalk Make White Teeth 20.00
Brush, Bellhop, Figural, 8 In. 27.00
Brush, Clothes, Male, Figural 23.00
Brush, Clothes, Mammy, Large 35.00
Brush, Mammy, Boar Bristled, Pre–1940, 4 In. 28.00
Button, Aunt Jemima I'se In Town Honey, 7/8 In. 30.00
Calendar, Perpetual Laundry List, 1937 .... 60.00
Canister Set, Black Eating Watermelon, Bakelite Handles, 2 Piece 67.00
Card, Bending Machine, Amos & Andy, 5 1/4 X 3 1/4 In., 16 Piece 75.00
Cigar Wrapper, Old Cheroots, With Black Head 12.00
Clock, Aunt Jemima, Ceramic, Red Wing 100.00
Clock, Blue Striped Apron 95.00
Clock, Kitchen, Aunt Jemima, Ceramic, Red Wing 100.00
Clothes Bag, Mammy, Paper Label, 17 X 12 In. 45.00
Clothespin Bag, Cloth, Mammy Oilcloth Head 35.00
Coat Hanger, Figural, Black Girl 15.00
Cookbook, Aunt Caroline's Dixieland Recipes, 1922 .... 38.00
Cookbook, Kitchen & The Cotton Patch, 1948 .... 20.00
Cookie Jar, Aunt Jemima's Cookie Jar On Apron, 10 1/2 In. 58.00
Cookie Jar, Aunt Jemima, Plastic, F & F Mold & Die Works .... 100.00 To 125.00
Cookie Jar, Chef, Pearl China 95.00
Cookie Jar, Mammy, Mosaic 145.00
Cookie Jar, Mammy, Pearl China .... 200.00 To 275.00
Cruet, Mammy & Chef, V & O 69.00
Cruet, Oil, Black Chef, Figural, China 65.00
Decal, Black, With Watermelon 8.50
Display, Black Man, Sitting, Watermelon, Papier–Mache, 1922, 14 In. 150.00
Doll, Aunt Jemima, Cloth 85.00
Doll, Aunt Jemima, Oilcloth, 1940s .... 17.00 To 25.00
Doll, Aunt Jemima, Vinyl, 1950s 40.00
Doll, Baby Bottle, Button Eyes, Lace Cap, Gingham Dress, 11 1/2 In. 110.00
Doll, Baby, Painted, Yarn Hair, Red Dress, C.1930, 10 1/4 In. 220.00
Doll, Baby, Red Hat, Melon, On Burlap, Way Down Yonder, New Orleans 35.00
Doll, Cloth, Yarn Hair, Blue Floral Dress, Earrings, C.1930, 12 1/2 In. 165.00
Doll, Clown, Bean Bag 25.00
Doll, Cream of Wheat, Cloth 65.00
Doll, Dinah, Wooden, Red Polka Dot Dress, Cotton Bundle On Head, Box 50.00
Doll, Girl, Stuffed, Embroidered Eyebrows, Print Dress, 12 In. 192.00
Doll, Girl, Stuffed, Embroidered Eyes, Button Hair, 1930, 13 1/2 In. 302.00
Doll, Hula, Jointed 11.00
Doll, Mammy, Celluloid, Marked Jamaica, 7 In. 35.00
Doll, Mammy, Stockinette, 1940, 14 In. 58.00
Doll, Mammy, Walker, Wilson 50.00
Doll, Pickaninny Style, Hair Clusters 45.00
Doll, Potholder, Mammy 28.00
Doll, Sachet, Mammy, Honeysuckle, Mammy Picture On Box, 6 In. 45.00
Doll, Uncle Mose, Cloth 85.00
Doorstop, Aunt Jemima, Full–Bodied, Iron, Polychrome Paint, 8 3/4 In. 175.00
Doorstop, Aunt Jemima, Wedge, Original Paint 220.00
Doorstop, Bellhop, Painted Wood, Iron Wedge 85.00
Doorstop, Frog, With Black Boy, Solid Iron, 5 1/2 X 6 1/2 In. 655.00
Doorstop, Major Domo 190.00
Doorstop, Mammy, 1–Piece Cast Iron, 10 In. 425.00
Egg, Blown–Out Black Face, Says More Chicken, Open Bottom 200.00
Figurine, 3 Boys Eating Watermelon, Chalkware, Large 120.00
Figurine, Alligator Head, Black Person In Mouth, Celluloid 30.00
Figurine, Alligator With Black Baby In Jaws, Lead 55.00
Figurine, Black Boy, Throwing Dice, On Platform, Celluloid, 2 X 1 In. 115.00
Figurine, Boy Hugging Commode, 2 X 3 1/2 In. 12.00
Figurine, Boy In Outhouse, & Boy Waiting, Porcelain, Japan, 3 In. 8.00

Black, Humidor,
Lady With Kerchief

Figurine, Boy With Watermelon, Sitting On Fence, Metal, 2 1/2 In.	67.00
Figurine, Chef, Porcelain, Germany	35.00
Figurine, Fat Albert	10.00 To 15.00
Figurine, Female Seated, Nightgown, Nightcap, German	85.00
Figurine, Goose, Black Boy, In Odd Predicament	55.00
Figurine, Kids On Sled, Iron	95.00
Figurine, Lucky Joe, Brayton	35.00
Figurine, Mammy, Cast Iron, Original Paint, 2 In.	50.00
Figurine, On White Bird, Blown Glass, 1940s, Miniature	12.00
Figurine, Porter, Red Cap, Syrocco	85.00
Game, Snake Eyes, Selchow & Righter Co., 1930s	60.00
Holder, Scrub Pad, Mammy Head	49.00
Holder, String, Mammy's Head, Tie Me, Plaster, 1936	90.00
Holder, String, National Silver	65.00
Holder, String, Young Mammy, Wooden, Cloth	95.00
Humidor, Lady With Kerchief ....*Illus*	145.00
Kazoo, Lips & Teeth	25.00
Key Rack, Mammy, Wooden Board	34.00
Label, Can, Old Black Joe	2.50
Lantern Slide, 6 Minutes With Mule, Comic Ink Drawings, Box, Set of 6	100.00
Lantern Slide, Black Couple, Umbrella, Wooden Frame, 7 X 4 In.	60.00
Laundry Bag, Mammy, Kerchief Head, Painted Face, Fiberboard	22.00
Lawn Ornament, Seated, Holding Lunchbox, Cast Iron, 1950s	125.00
Lawn Sprinkler, Black Sambo, Wooden, 35 In.	275.00
Letter Opener, Black Head On Pencil, Alligator's Mouth, Celluloid	50.00
Lighter, Bartender, Art Deco Bar	665.00
Map, Webster City, MIE, Amos & Andy	30.00
Marionette, Tap Dancer	195.00
Match Holder, Chalk, Boy Eating Melon	65.00
Match Holder, Mammy On Washing Machine, Ceramic	30.00
Memo Board, Oh! I Needs, Mammy, Wooden, With Pegs	22.00
Memo Holder, Mammy, Great Falls, Montana, Wooden Pegs	32.00
Memo Pad, Mammy, Plastic, 10 1/2 In.	35.00
Mug, Satin Glass, Painted Black Caricatures, Pair	59.00
Nodder, Barefoot Boy, Smoking Cigar, Straw Hat, Metal, Austria, 4 In.	75.00
Paper Doll, Aunt Jemima, Set of 5, Clothes, Framed	50.00
Paperweight, Aunt Jemima, Figural, Lead, 2 1/2 In.	50.00
Paperweight, Mammy	75.00
Pen Holder, Black Boy Under Palm Tree, Ceramic	20.00
Pencil Sharpener, Black Face, Sharpener In Mouth	115.00
Photograph, Comic, Skin Game, Playing Cards & Cheating, 11 X 13 In.	25.00
Photograph, Wedding Scene, Honey Does You Lub Your Man, 10 X 13 In.	150.00
Picture, Couple, We's Free, Cross–Stitch, Post–Civil War, 4 X 6 In.	85.00
Pie Bird, Chef	50.00 To 55.00
Pin, Alligator & Black Boy's Head, Figural, Sterling Silver, 2 Piece	100.00
Pin, Negro's Head, Mechanical Tip, German, 1900s	18.00
Pin, Slave, Town & Country Waiter, Heavy Metal	10.00
Pincushion, Bisque Child, Melon, Cotton Blossom, Marked, Dated, Box	50.00

Pincushion, Black, Holding Pumpkin, Sitting, Handstitched, 1890s 145.00
Pincushion, Mammy, 1930s 20.00
Pincushion, Pecan Head, Mammy 37.00
Pincushion, Pickaninny, Bisque, Boy Eating Watermelon, Box, Dated 1939 .... 55.00
Pineback, Googly–Eye, German 55.00
Placemat, Coon Chicken Inn, Framed 35.00
Planter, Black Boy, With Watermelon 22.00
Planter, Musician, Black Girl 29.00
Plaque, Boy & Girl, Holding Umbrellas, Pair 60.00
Plaque, Wall, Boy With Umbrella, 8 In. 25.00
Plate, Aunt Jemima's Kitchen, 10 In. 58.00
Postcard Set, Christmas, New York, Raphael Tuck, Black, White Statues 69.00
Postcard, Big Lips & Bulging Eyes, Comical, Black Saying, 6 Piece 25.00
Postcard, Blacks In Comical Scenes, 1905, 5 Piece 55.00
Postcard, Leather, Black Boy, Fence, Watermelons, Bulldog, 1905 .... 20.00
Postcard, Mammy, Boy Hiding Stolen Rooster, Overcoat, Feather 75.00
Postcard, Man, Feather Out of Overcoat, No Stray Rooster Heah' 100.00
Postcard, Sambo Restaurant, Set of 8 .... 15.00
Postcard, Walker & Williams, Cakewalk Dancers, Color, 1898, 3 Piece 50.00
Poster, Gorton's Original New Orleans Minstrels 1300.00
Print, Uncle Remus, Color, Framed, 1923 .... 45.00
Program, Minstrel, Vaudeville, Buckley's Ethiopian Opera House, 1840 .... 25.00
Puppet, Black Man, Papier–Mache 225.00
Puppet, String, Jambo The Jiver, Wooden, Talentoy 34.00
Puzzle, Little Black Sambo, C.1930 .... 38.00
Puzzle, Pickaninny, Children of All Nations, Box, 7 1/2 X 9 1/2 In. 18.00
Recipe Box, Mammy 65.00
Record Set, Moran & Mack, 2 Black Crows, Columbia, Set of 4 .... 75.00
Record, Amos & Andy, Carrell & Godsen, Victor, 2 Piece 45.00
Record, Basin Street Blues, Blacks Dancing In Street 35.00
Rug, Hooked, Black Figures, Star Alternating With Blocks, 7 Ft.11 In. 800.00
Salt & Pepper Shaker, Black Boy & Girl Sitting In A Basket 12.00
Salt & Pepper Shaker, Boy On Potty 65.00
Salt & Pepper Shaker, Boy With Hat & Watermelon Slice 42.00
Salt & Pepper Shaker, Mammy & Chef 28.00
Salt & Pepper, Aunt Jemima & Uncle Mose, 5 1/4 In. 15.00
Salt & Pepper, Aunt Jemima, Large 20.00
Salt & Pepper, Aunt Jemima, Small 15.00
Salt & Pepper, Butler & Mammy, 4 1/2 In. 45.00
Salt & Pepper, Chef & Maid 24.00
Salt & Pepper, Chef In White Uniform, Mammy With Red Bandana 36.00
Salt & Pepper, Chef, Mammy, Ceramic, 8 In. 55.00
Salt & Pepper, Chef, Mammy, Waving, F & F, Plastic, 3 In. 24.00
Salt & Pepper, Chef, White Chef, Tall Hats 19.50
Salt & Pepper, Luizianne Mammy 25.00
Salt & Pepper, Mammy's Salt, Orange & Blue Tops, 3 1/4 In. 32.00
Salt & Pepper, Mammy, Gold, Green & Maroon Dotted Dress, 3 In. 45.00
Salt & Pepper, Policeman 32.00
Salt, Pepper & Sugar, Stacking, Figural, Sitting Chef 46.00
Sat & Pepper, Porter Carrying Black Suitcases 25.00
Sheet Music, 3 Little Words, Amos & Andy 18.00
Sheet Music, and They Called It Dixieland, Mammy 5.35
Sheet Music, At Uncle Tom's Cabin Door, 1912 .... 15.00
Sheet Music, Baby 5.00
Sheet Music, By The Watermelon Vine, 1904 .... 15.00
Sheet Music, Carolina Mammy, Oak Frame, Pink & Black 35.00
Sheet Music, Crabapples, Ragtime 2–Step, 1905 .... 15.00
Sheet Music, Girl With Golliwog 5.00
Sheet Music, Pickaninny It's Time You Was In Bed, 1898 .... 12.00
Sheet Music, Sentimental Sal, Koon 2–Step March 12.00
Spice Set, Aunt Jemima, F & F, Plastic, 6 Piece 135.00
Spoon Holder, Mammy, Arms Out 49.00
Spoon, Sterling Silver, Black Boy Handle 95.00

Spoon, Sterling Silver, Sunny Jim 95.00
Sprinkler, Black Sambo, Firestone Rubber Co., Wood, Metal .... 225.00 To 275.00
Stereo Card, Black Children, Playing Dice 20.00
String Holder, Mammy Head, Plaster ....65.00 To 100.00
String Holder, Mammy, National Silver 60.00
String Holder, Mammy, Yellow Dress, Green Trim 55.00
String Holder, Teapot Shape, Removable Lid, Chef's Head Decal 58.00
Sugar & Creamer, Aunt Jemima, F & F .... 65.00 To 80.00
Swizzle Stick, Zuzu Lulu 29.00
Syrup, Aunt Jemima .... 25.00 To 45.00
Tape Measure, Mammy 35.00
Tea Towel, Linen, Children In Watermelon Patch, 28 X 15 In. 30.00
Teapot, Salt & Pepper, Chef Decal, Plastic, 3 Piece 27.00
Thermometer, Black Boy, Pressed Wood 12.00
Timer, Sitting Chef, Figural, Glass 68.00
Tin, Hair Pomade, Sweet Georgia Brown 15.00
Tin, International Harness Soap Tin, Boy Polishing Harness 75.00
Tin, Tobacco, Brown Beauty 125.00
Tin, Tobacco, Nigger Hair 80.00
Toaster Cover, Mammy 38.00
Toothpick, Black Boy Holding Whiskey Bottle, Germany 59.00
Toothpick, Coon Chicken Inn, Metal, Black, Red & White, 3 1/2 In. 125.00
Towel, Black Mammy, With Watermelon 22.00
Towel, Dish, Mammy, Doing Different Chores, Set of 7 .... 95.00
Towel, Kitchen, Mammy, 30 In. 12.50
Towel, Linen, Children Eating Watermelons, 28 X 15 In. 40.00
Toy, 2 Blacks Playing Instruments, Gunthermann Platform Clockwork 1650.00
Toy, Amos & Andy Taxi, Marx, 1930 .... 650.00
Toy, Amos & Andy, Walker, Rolling Eyes, Box 1400.00
Toy, Baby, With Watermelon, Dog, Celluloid, Windup, 6 In. 950.00
Toy, Black Boy, Wooden, Jointed, Little Jasper Toy, 1950s, 7 In. 75.00
Toy, Boy, Eating Watermelon, With Biting Dog, Celluloid, Windup 225.00
Toy, Coon Jigger, Tin, Lehmann 250.00
Toy, Little Black Sambo, Little Playette Theater, Box 88.00
Toy, Man Dancing, Carved Wood, Military Uniform, Jointed, 1863, 9 In. 750.00
Toy, Man, Dancing, Jointed, Standing, On Paddle, C.1930, 16 In. 135.00
Toy, Man, Dancing, Jointed, Stenciled Wood, C.1930, 11 1/2 In. 88.00
Toy, Man, Papier–Mache, Jointed Arms & Legs, Curly Wig, 9 In. 160.00
Toy, Musician, With Banjo 26.00
Tumbler, Old Folks At Home, Blacks, Cabin, Song On Reverse 15.00
Valentine, Mechanical, Children, Chicken, With Basket, Large 35.00
Whiskbroom, Black Face Mammy 25.00

Blown glass was formed by forcing air through a rod into molten glass. Early glass and some forms of art glass were hand blown. Other types of glass were molded or pressed.

BLOWN GLASS, Beaker, Enameled, Pewter Base, 3/10 Liter 115.00
Bird Fountain, Cobalt Finial, Clear, 5 1/4 In. 105.00
Bottle, 16 Swirled Ribs, Amber, 7 1/4 In. 75.00
Bottle, 24 Ribs, Broken Swirl, Zanesville, Aqua, 8 1/4 In. 150.00
Bottle, 24 Swirled Ribs, Globular, Zanesville, Aqua, 7 1/2 In. 255.00
Bottle, Applied Lip, Dark Olive Green, 10 In. 80.00
Bottle, Bar, Engraved Label, Wine, 2 Applied Rings, 8 1/4 In. 65.00
Bottle, Condiment, Pewter Collar, Double Spout, 4 3/8 In. 25.00
Bottle, Double, Applied Rigaree, 9 In. 25.00
Canister, Applied Cobalt Blue Rings, Finial, 10 1/4 In. 485.00
Canister, Applied Rings, Patent 1866, 9 In. 55.00
Cruet, 21 Swirled Ribs, Pale Green, 10 In. 90.00
Decanter, 3 Applied Rings, Clear, 8 1/4 In. 115.00
Decanter, 3–Mold, Embossed Gin Label, Folded Lip, 8 1/4 In. 175.00
Decanter, 3–Mold, Pouring Spout Lip, Wheel Stopper, 7 In., Pair 250.00
Goblet, Enameled, Cavalier, Amber, 8 1/2 In. 55.00
Goblet, Enameled, Crest, Green, 7 1/4 In. 60.00
Goblet, Threaded Design, Gold Floral Enamel, 9 1/2 In. 116.00

Hat, Amber, 7 In.	25.00
Jar, Apothecary, Tin Cover, 10 In.	55.00
Jar, Olive Amber, 4 3/8 In.	110.00
Jar, Tin Lid, Light Aqua, 7 3/4 In.	125.00
Pitcher, Diamond Panel Cutting, 7 1/4 In.	250.00
Pitcher, Green, 4 3/4 In.	25.00
Pitcher, South Jersey, Handle, Cobalt Blue, C.1850, 5 1/2 In.	225.00
Pitcher, Tooled Rim, Applied Foot & Handle, Clear, 7 5/8 In.	450.00
Shot Glass, 6–Panel, Cobalt Blue, C.1865	80.00
Sugar, Copper Wheel Engraved Design, Cover, 8 1/4 In.	45.00
Syrup, Amethyst, 4 Sides, Clear Handle	125.00
Toothpick, Hat Shape, Ribs, Diamonds & Sunburst	235.00
Tumbler, Vertical Ribs, Zanesville	275.00
Vase, Applied Foot, Bulbous Stem, Grass Green, 8 5/8 In.	85.00
Vase, Flared, Monteith Rim, 12 Scallops, Clear To White, 5 In.	395.00
Vase, Hyacinth, Emerald Green, 7 5/8 In.	110.00
Vase, Opalescent Loopings, Clear Base & Stem, Clear, 13 1/2 In.	325.00
Vase, Poppies, Roses, Opaque, Hand Painted, 15 In., Pair	1500.00
Wine, Cut Stem, 4 1/2 In., Pair	75.00
Wine, Folded Rim Foot, Gold Stripes, White & Blue Latticino	55.00

BLUE AMBERINA, see Bluerina
BLUE GLASS, see Cobalt Blue
BLUE ONION, see Onion

Blue Willow pattern has been made in England since 1780. The pattern has been copied by factories in many countries, including Germany, Japan, and the United States. It is still being made. Willow was named for a pattern that pictures a bridge, birds, willow trees, and a Chinese landscape.

BLUE WILLOW, Ashtray Set, Holder, Set of 4	8.00
Bank, Pig Shape, 3 1/2 X 2 1/2 In.	6.00
Bank, Pig Shape, 5 X 4 In.	10.00
Basket, Chestnut, Spode, C.1810	525.00
Bowl, Vegetable, Cover, Lion Finial, C.1840, 9 1/4 X 11 In.	195.00
Bowl, Vegetable, Open, Allerton	30.00
Bowl, Vegetable, Rectangular, Marked, 9 X 7 1/2 In.	22.50
Bowl, Vegetable, Ridgway	50.00
Butter, Cover, 1/4 Lb.	45.00
Butter, Word Butter On Border, White Rim, 6 1/2 X 4 In.	135.00
Candle Holder, 3 3/4 In., Pair	37.50
Canister Set, Wedgwood, 3 Piece	175.00
Canister, Oval, Wedgwood	65.00
Chocolate Pot	29.00
Clock, Tin, Key, Round	185.00
Coffeepot, Blue Willow, Johnson Brothers	90.00
Condiment Set, Cover	60.00
Cracker Barrel, Bail Handle, Tin	10.00
Cracker Jar, Wicker Handle, English	125.00
Creamer, Ridgway	45.00
Cruet, Handle, 4 1/2 In., Pair	18.50
Cup & Saucer, Adderley, Demitasse	14.00
Cup & Saucer, Auld Lang Syne, Copeland	18.00
Cup & Saucer, Inside Design, Japan	10.00
Cup & Saucer, Japan	14.00
Cup & Saucer, Wedgwood, Unicorn Mark	20.00
Cup, Handleless, Embossed England Mark	20.00
Eggcup, Double, Burleigh	6.50
Gravy Boat, Attached Plate	45.00
Gravy Boat, Gravy Fat–Gravy Lean	35.00
Gravy, Underplate, Staffordshire	35.00
Grill Plate	48.00
Hatpin Holder	18.00
Holder, Soap Pad, Japanese, C.1950	35.00
Juicer, Cover, 2 Piece	12.00

> Put up glass shelves, fill them with inexpensive, colorful bottles. A
> burglar would have to break all of it, with accompanying noise, to
> get in.

Ladle, Sauce, 6 3/4 In.	15.00
Lamp, Hurricane, 9 In.	28.00
Lamp, Kerosene, 8 In.	33.00
Lamp, Kerosene, With Plate Behind, 9 In.	20.00
Matchbox Holder, Hanging	15.00
Mustard Pot, Barrel Shape, 2 1/2 In.	32.00
Mustard Pot, Ladle	55.00
Pitcher, Border Inside & Out, C.1870, 26 Oz., 7 3/4 In.	185.00
Pitcher, Bow Knot, Cobalt Decal	85.00
Pitcher, Castle	125.00
Pitcher, Light & Dark Blue, Gold, Myott, C.1936, 14 In.	175.00
Pitcher, Milk	45.00
Pitcher, Snake Handle, Octagonal, Mason	45.00
Placemats, Plastic, 16 1/4 X 11 In.	2.00
Plate, Japan, 9 In.	7.00
Plate, Meakin, 10 In.	11.00
Plate, Royal China, 10 In.	5.00
Plate, Scalloped Edge, Allerton, 7 In.	14.00
Plate, Wedgwood, Unicorn Mark, 7 In.	9.00
Platter, 18 In.	115.00
Platter, Allerton, 7 X 6 In.	45.00
Platter, Bacon, Allerton	50.00
Platter, Blue & White, 18 1/2 In.	121.00
Platter, Dark Blue, Oval, 12 1/2 X 8 1/2 In.	20.00
Platter, England, 16 In.	65.00
Platter, Homer Laughlin, 12 X 9 In.	15.00
Platter, Octagonal, Scalloped, Patterson, C.1870, 17 1/2 In.	165.00
Platter, Ridgway, 13 In.	55.00
Platter, Scalloped Edge, Booth, 17 X 13 In.	110.00
Platter, Vermacelli, Blue & White, WRS & Co.	143.00
Platter, Wood, 16 In.	75.00
Pudding Bowl Set, English, 4 1/4 To 3 1/8 In., 4 Piece	150.00
Rolling Pin, Earthenware, 13 1/2 In.	18.00
Rolling Pin, Wildflower	235.00
Salt & Pepper, 3 In.	15.50
Salt & Pepper, Moriama, Japan, 3 1/2 In.	58.00
Salt Bowl	40.00
Salt Box, Hanging, Wooden Cover	45.00
Salt, Cover, Eagle	325.00
Sauce Tureen, Underplate, Cover, English, C.1860, 5 1/2 X 7 In.	195.00
Sauce, Booths	8.00
Sauce, Grimwald	3.00
Server, Asparagus, 19th Century	78.00
Snack Hound, Japanese, C.1950, 5 Piece	18.00
Soap Dish, Lion	125.00
Soup Dish, Japan	7.00
Soup Dish, Maastrich, 9 In.	15.00
Sugar & Creamer, Cover, Tray, Japan, 3 1/2 In.	16.00
Sugar, Cover, Ridgway	55.00
Tea Set, Child's, 15 Piece	65.00
Tea Set, Child's, Box, 17 Piece	125.00
Tea Set, Child's, Platter, Casserole, Occupied Japan, 16 Piece	125.00

Tea Set, Edge Malkin & Co., Child's, C.1870, 7 Piece	165.00
Teapot, Raised Design On Spout & Handle, 18th Century, 6 In.	395.00
Tidbit, Man On Bridge, 4 1/8 In.	3.00
Tile, 4 In.	3.00
Tile, 6 In.	3.50
Toothbrush Holder, Hanging, Holds 3 Brushes	7.00
Tray, Square, Tin, 13 1/2 X 13 1/2 In.	6.00
Tumbler, Burleigh, 3 3/4 In.	12.00
Warmer, Japan	30.00

Bluerina is a type of art glass which shades from light blue to ruby. It is often called blue amberina.

BLUERINA, Dish, Hen On Basket Cover, Marked	135.50

Osso China Company was reorganized as Edward Marshall Boehm, Inc., in 1953. The company is still working in England and New Jersey. In the early days of the factory, dishes were made, but the elaborate and lifelike bird figurines are the best known ware. Edward Marshall Boehm, the founder, died in 1961; but the firm has continued to design and produce porcelain. Today, the firm makes both limited and unlimited editions of figurines and plates.

BOEHM, Figurine, Baby Bluejay	150.00
Figurine, Baby Cedar Waxwing, No.433	150.00
Figurine, Black Burnian Warbler	160.00
Figurine, Black Capped Chickadee, No.438E	695.00
Figurine, Black Capped Chickadee, On Holly Branch, 9 In.	450.00
Figurine, Chipmunk, Sitting	150.00 To 185.00
Figurine, Cocker Spaniel, Black, 1980	175.00
Figurine, Don Quixote	140.00
Figurine, Fledgling, Baby Crested Flycatcher	150.00
Figurine, Giselle	140.00
Figurine, La Pieta Madonna, White, 1950s, 10 In.	350.00
Figurine, Lesser Prairie Chicken, 1974, Pair	1450.00
Figurine, Nutcracker	140.00
Figurine, Nuthatch	650.00
Figurine, Pheasant, Male & Female, Pair	550.00
Figurine, Poodle, Reclining, 3 1/2 X 5 In.	140.00
Figurine, Prothonotary Warbler, No.445N	550.00
Figurine, Sitting Chipmunk	170.00
Figurine, Swan Lake	140.00
Figurine, White Throated Sparrow, No.430E	695.00
Pitcher, 7 1/2 In.	40.00
Plate, Annual, 1973, Wildlife, Raccoons	45.00
Plate, Owl, Box	65.00

Bohemian glass is an ornate overlay or flashed glass made during the Victorian era. It has been reproduced in Bohemia, which is now a part of Czechoslovakia. Glass made from 1875 to 1900 is preferred by collectors.

BOHEMIAN GLASS, Bowl, Amber Cut To Clear, Deer & Castle, Footed, 9 In.	85.00
Centerpiece, Oval Form, Amber Overlay, Cut Florals, 14 In.	90.00
Compote, Florals, White Cut To Green, Overlay, 9 1/2 In.	80.00
Decanter, Amber, Castles, 8 1/2 In.	22.50
Decanter, Cut Panel, Acid Design, Ruby, 5 Goblets	250.00
Decanter, Deer & Castle, Red Cut To Clear, Stopper, 15 In.	50.00
Decanter, Deer & Castle, Red To Clear, Stopper, 15 In.	50.00
Decanter, White Enameled Flowers & Gilt, Ruby, 7 1/4 In.	95.00
Goblet, Red, Deer In Forest	195.00
Lamp, Deer & Castle, Brass & Marble Base, Red	250.00
Lamp, Red Cut Glass, Luster, 24 In., Pair	750.00
Pitcher Set, Red Floral & Leaf Design, 6 Piece	250.00
Pitcher, Frosted Deer & Trees, Gold Bands, 5 1/2 In.	90.00
Tantalus, Cobalt Blue, Metal Spigot & Trim, Floral, 15 In.	100.00
Vase, Diamond & Oval Pattern, Cranberry To Clear, 5 In.	135.00

Vase, Painted Flowers, White Cut Over Blue, 1875, 6 In. 60.00
Vase, Strapwork, Arabesques, Key Border, 26 3/8 In., Pair 1325.00

 Bookends have probably been used since books became inexpensive. Early libraries kept books in cupboards, not on open shelves. By the 1870s bookends appear, especially homemade fretcarved wooden examples. Most bookends listed in this book date from the twentieth century.

BOOKENDS, Abraham Lincoln, Cast Iron, Copper Finish 45.00
   Amish Couple, Seated, Green Clothes, Cast Iron 35.00
   Amish Man & Woman, Full Figure, Woman Quilting, Iron 250.00
   Angelus, Raised Figures, Bronze Color 38.00
   Ann Hathaway's Cottage, Stratford On Avon, Bronze 45.00
   Archer, Female, Oversized Bow, Wild Hair, Bronze Wash, 8 In. 55.00
   Aviator, Iron, 1922 .... 75.00
   Bears, Hand Carved From 1 Piece, German, 13 1/2 In. 85.00
   Bust of Lincoln, Iron, Parson's Casket Hardware Co., 5 1/2 In. 58.00
   Cat, Art Deco 40.00
   Cupid & Psyche, Iron 40.00
   Dog Head, Dachshund 8.00
   Dog, Drunken, Singing, Cast Iron, Painted 34.00
   Dog, German Shepherd, Cast Iron .... 20.00 To 35.00
   Dog, German Shepherd, Sitting, Iron 30.00
   Dog, Scotty Head, Silvered Spelter, 1960s, 4 1/2 X 5 In. 50.00
   Dog, Scotty, Black & White, Ceramic 18.00
   Dog, Scotty, Cast Iron, Dated 1929 .... 22.50
   Dog, Scotty, Dark Gray, Syroco, Pair 28.00
   Dog, Terrier, Black, Cast Iron 40.00
   Dragon Design, Circle Panel, Chinese, Brass, 7 In. 20.00
   Dying Gaul 13.00
   Eagle, Cambridge, 1934 .... 150.00
   Elephants, Full Figure, Bronze 30.00
   End of The Trail, Indian Design, Brass Color 26.00
   Fawn Head, Silver Plate, 6 In. 15.00
   Floral, Embossed Design, Hammered Copper, Karl Kipp, 5 In. 85.00
   Football Players, Ceramic, Sears & Roebuck, 1974 .... 25.00
   Girl Holds Dress Tail, Art Nouveau, Cast Iron, 7 In. 27.00
   Hartford Insurance, 1933 .... 23.00
   Horse's Head, Art Deco, Onyx, 9 In. 40.00
   Horse's Head, Metal, Walnut, 5 X 6 In. 20.00
   Horse, Abingdon, Label 75.00
   Horse, Bucking, Cast Iron, Polychrome Paint, Marked A–C, 5 3/4 In. 5.00
   Horse, Glass, 5 X 5 1/2 In. 25.00
   Horse, Rearing 75.00
   Horse, Rearing, Brass 60.00
   Horse, Saddled, Cast Iron 10.00
   Horses, Rearing, Glass, 8 In. 45.00
   Indian Chief, Wooden 15.00
   Indian Heads, Bronze 50.00
   Indian In Headdress, Metal 45.00
   Indian, Bust, Cast Iron, White Paint, 5 1/4 In. 30.00
   Indian, Carrying Deer, Bronze, Relief 50.00
   Indian, On Horse, Cast Iron 20.00
   Irish Setter, Black & White Paint 105.00
   Jacks, Iron 12.00
   Knight On Horse, Shield, Lance 60.00
   Knight, Slaying Dragon, Hubley 35.00
   Knute Rockne, White Bust, Brown Base, Pottery, 6 X 7 1/2 In. 55.00
   Liberty Bell, Cast Iron 38.50
   Lincoln Memorial, Bradley & Hubbard 25.00
   Lincoln, Bust, Bronzed Metal, Parson's Casket Hdw.Co., 5 1/2 In. 55.00
   Lindbergh, The Aviator, Cast Iron, 1927 .... 25.00

Lion In Relief, Cast Iron 25.00
Lion, Victorian, Cast Iron, 1840s 25.00
Longfellow, Cast Iron 8.00
Mary Quite Contrary, Pink Dress, Bonnet, Watering Can, Cast Iron 65.00
Medieval Man & Woman, Silver On Copper Plated, 11 1/2 In. 250.00
Musicians, Male & Female, Art Deco, Green Onyx 125.00
Nautical, Chase Chrome 85.00
Nude, Arched Back, Flowing Hair, Bronze Wash, 7 In. 80.00
Nude, Kneeling, Gold Satin Finish, 5 In. 65.00
Nude, Thinker, Dated, Bronze Color, Pot Metal, 1928 .... 25.00
Owl, Bronzed, Expandable 30.00
Owl, Carved Alabaster 25.00
Owl, Iron 37.50
Pirates, Ivory Faces, Bronze 225.00
Pointer, Bronze, Color 23.00
Polo Player, On Galloping Pony, Brass 58.00
Prancing Horse, Glass 65.00
Ram's Head, Metal 42.00
Roman Soldier, Alabaster 35.00
Rooster, Glass, 11 1/2 In. 85.00
Scottie, Sitting, Cast Iron, Hubley 85.00
Sea Horse, Seashell Base, 8 1/4 In. 50.00
Stag, Hartford Fire Ins., Brass, Dated 1935 .... 35.00
Stag, Hartford Insurance Co., Brass, Dated 1935 .... 65.00
Terrior, Standing, Cast Iron 95.00
Thinker, Bronze, 4 In. 25.00
Thinker, Iron, Gold Wash, 6 In. 15.00
Tillers, Bronze, Theodore B.Starr, Signed, 5 1/2 In. 275.00
Viking Ships, Brass 22.00
Woman & Man, Bust, Roman Attire, Bronze 38.50

Bookmarks were originally made of parchment, cloth, or leather. Soon woven silk ribbon, thin cardboard, celluloid, wood, silver, tortoiseshell, and metals were used. Examples made before 1850 are scarce, but there are many to be found dating before 1920.

BOOKMARK, 5 Cherubs & Angels, Wishbone, Silver, Kerr 350.00
Amber Thistle, Sterling, 1910 .... 45.00
Art Nouveau, Stylized Flowers, Loop, German, Silver, 1 5/8 In. 75.00
Commemoration of Landing of Columbus, Silk, 1892 .... 75.00
Dog 15.00
Double Roman Head, Shiebler Type, Silver 55.00
English Hunt Scenes, Woven 15.00
Montabert Co., Woven Label 12.00
Needlepoint, Verse 15.00
Owl, Figural, Sterling Silver, Marked, 3 In. 45.00
Packard Organ, Fort Wayne, Ind., 1903 Calendar Back 3.50
Pickel, Figural, Heinz, Pictures Little Girl 10.00
Red Grosgrain Ribbon, Silver, Leonore Doskow, 2 In. 22.00
Roses, Sterling, Kirk 45.00
Tom Pinch, Silver 45.00
Washington Bicentennial, 1932 Calendar, Woven 22.00
Woven Swirl Design, Silver, 2 3/4 X 1 1/2 In. 90.00
BOSTON & SANDWICH CO., see Sandwich Glass

As soon as the commercial bottle was invented, the opener to be used with the new types of closures became a necessity. Many types of bottle openers can be found, most dating from the twentieth century. Collectors prize advertising and comic openers.

BOTTLE OPENER, 4-Eyed Lady, Cast Iron .... 11.00 To 40.00
4-Eyed Man, Brass 5.00
4-Eyed Man, Cast Iron, Wall Mount 26.00
4-Eyed Man, Open Mouth, Cast Iron, 4 In. 15.00
Albera Breweries, For Beer 4.00
Alligator, Cast Iron 95.00

Alligator, Cast Iron, Badly Worn Paint	35.00
Amish Boy	185.00
Anheuser–Busch, Bottle Shape, Brass	20.00
Animal Horn	12.50
Auto Jack, Cast Iron	32.00
Baseball Cap, New York Mets, Cast Iron	20.00
Beaded, Georg Jensen	65.00
Beaver, Cast Iron	45.00
Billy Goat, Cast Iron	14.00
Black Boy, Cast Iron	12.00
Black Boy, With Alligator, Cast Iron	100.00 To 125.00
Black Face, Large Smile, White Teeth, Red Bowtie, Cast Iron	75.00
Braying Donkey, Cast Iron	35.00
Canada Goose, Rubal, N.Y.	22.00 To 29.00
Canvasback Duck, Cast Iron	85.00
Canvasback, Duck, Cast Iron	70.00
Chinaman, Smiling, Brass	35.00
Clown Face, Metal	45.00
Clown Head, Brass, Small	6.00
Clown, Cast Iron, Wall Mount	35.00
Clown, Wall Mount, Brass	20.00
Cobwoy With Guitar	145.00
Cow Boy, Aluminum	20.00
Diamond Ginger Ale, 1901	4.00
Dinky Dan	125.00
Dog, Bird Dog, Paw Uplifted, Cast Iron	45.00
Dog, Bulldog, Cast Iron	28.00
Dog, Cocker Spaniel, Brass	20.00
Dog, Cocker, Black	4.00
Dog, Dachshund, Brass	25.00
Dog, Dachshund, With Stud Holes In Collar, Brass	85.00
Dog, English Setter, Pointing, Spelter, 3 2/3 X 6 1/2 In.	58.00
Dog, Pointer, Cast Iron	55.00
Dog, Setter	20.00
Dog, Setter, Brass	25.00
Dog, Springer Spaniel, Iron	65.00
Donkey Head	20.00
Donkey, Brass	22.00
Donkey, Cast Iron	20.00 To 38.00
Donkey, Wide–Eared	42.00
Double Fish, Brass	10.00
Drunk, At Sign Post, St.Petersburg, Florida, Cast Iron	14.00
Drunk, Hanging, Cast Iron	25.00
Drunk, Leg Up, Lamp Post, Die Cast	20.00
Drunk, On Ashtray	3.00
Drunk, Tiny	20.00
Dumbo The Elephant, Brass	15.00
Early Times Distillery, Brass	12.00
Edlund, Pat.1929	4.00
Fish, Brass	20.00
Fish, With Scales, Brass	18.00
Flamingo	65.00
Fox, Riding Habit, 3–D, 7 In.	64.00
Goat, Cast Iron	65.00
Grand Prize Beer Stationary	12.00

To dry a small-necked bottle, give it a last rinse with alcohol.

Hawk Head, With Corkscrew, Stainless Steel 35.00
Horse's Rear End, Cast Iron .... 32.00 To 40.00
Key, Brass 2.00
Lamppost Drunk 4.00
Lobster, Cast Iron .... 12.00 To 22.00
Mademoiselle, Cast Iron, Japan .... 17.00 To 20.00
Mallard Duck, Brass 20.00
Mallard Duck, Cast Iron 65.00
Monkey, Aluminum 10.00
Monkey-Shine, Corkscrew, Brass 45.00
Monkeys, Cast Iron 195.00
Motorcycle Equipment Co., Cigar Cutter & Screw Driver 18.00
Mule, Cast Iron 45.00
Necktie, Iron 25.50
Nu-Grape, Figural 9.00
Nude, Brass 16.00
Nude, Female, Bronze, 7 1/2 In. 85.00
Nude, Standing, Arms Raised, Gilt Metal, 4 1/2 In. 15.00
Old Miner, Corkscrew 28.00
Paddy The Pledgemaster, Cast Iron 235.00
Palm Tree ....75.00 To 125.00
Palm Tree, Drunk, With Bald Head 27.00
Parrot, Cast Iron 32.00
Parrot, Corkscrew, Gold Tone, Ruby Eyes 15.00
Parrot, On Perch, Cast Iron, 5 In. .... 12.00 To 25.00
Parrot, With Corkscrew, Aluminum 15.00
Pelican, Bronze 40.00
Pelican, Cast Iron .... 18.00 To 30.00
Penis, Brass 25.00
Pheasant Head, Colored, Cast Iron, 4 In. 40.00
Pheasant, Cast Iron 110.00
Pretzel, Cast Iron 25.00
Rooster, Pot Metal, Large 40.00
Sea Gull, Brass .... 17.00 To 22.00
Sea Horse 55.00
Set of Teeth, Pink & White Paint, 3 1/2 In. 10.00
Shark, Aluminum 15.00
Skull, Bronze 53.00
Squirrel, Cast Iron .... 35.00 To 75.00
Stag Handle, Sterling Silver Ferrule .... 25.00 To 32.00
Stegmaier Beer, Retractable, Black Chrome 15.00
Sterling Silver, Repouse, Kirk 35.00
Stoner's Ginger Ale, Metal, 3 1/2 In. 1.50
Streetwalker 40.00
Tennis Racquet, 6 1/4 In. 22.00
Three Star Cigars, Julius Fecht, Inc., Cigar Opener 16.00
Turtle, Cast Iron 25.00
Wehr Milwaukee, Brass, Cigar Opener 25.00
Whale, Aluminum 6.00

Bottle collecting has become a major American hobby. There are several general categories of bottles, such as historic flasks, bitters, household, and figural. For modern bottle prices and more old bottle prices, see the book "The Kovels' Bottles Price List" by Ralph and Terry Kovel.

BOTTLE, Apothecary, Clear Stopper, 4 In. 45.00
Apothecary, Cobalt Blue, Stopper 95.00

Avon started in 1886 as the California Perfume Company. It was not until 1929 that the name Avon was used. In 1939, it became Avon Products, Inc. Each year Avon sells figural bottles filled with cosmetic products. Ceramic, plastic, and glass bottles are made in limited editions.

Avon, Army Jeep 4.00

Avon, Cable Car	3.50
Avon, Cadillac, Gold	10.00
Avon, Car, 1948 Chrysler	3.00
Avon, Car, Cable, 1974	4.00
Avon, Car, Touring T, Silver	4.00
Avon, Checker Cab	4.00
Avon, Chess Set, Box	75.00
Avon, Dog, German Shepherd	20.00
Avon, Dog, Pointer, Brown Spots	20.00
Avon, Dog, Schnauzer	20.00
Avon, Ford Ranger Pickup	4.00
Avon, Gun, Twenty Paces	3.00
Avon, Hard Hat	4.00
Avon, Orioles, Miniature	20.00
Avon, Pipe, Dutch	6.00
Avon, Pipe, Pony	10.00
Avon, Pipe, Uncle Sam	6.00
Avon, Pot Belly Stove	4.00
Avon, Rabbits, Miniature	20.00
Avon, Rolls–Royce, 1972	4.00
Avon, Snowmobile, 1973	5.00
Avon, Stanley Steamer, 1978, Silver	4.00
Avon, Steer Horns	8.00
Avon, Western Roundup, 1983	5.00
Barber, Amber Hobnail, Pontil	95.00
Barber, Barbers Supply Co., Atlanta, Ga., Round, Quart	28.50
Barber, Cranberry & Opalescent, Blown, Pewter Stopper, 10 1/4 In.	132.00
Barber, Faceted Stopper, Pressed Glass	25.00

 Beam bottles are made to hold Kentucky Straight Bourbon, made by the James B. Beam Distilling Company. The Beam series of ceramic bottles began in 1953.

Bottle, Bitters, Columbo, L.E. Jung, New Orleans

Bottle, Poison, Nichols Bed–Bug Liquid, Chicago, 6 In.

Beam, Black Katz, Figural, Label, 1968, 14 In. 30.00
Beam, Blue Cherub 75.00
Beam, Circus Wagon 35.00
Beam, Executive, 1961 .... 39.00
Beam, King Kong, Decanter 25.00
Beam, Muskie 10.00
Beam, Mustang, Red 59.00
Beam, Phone, French Cradle 45.00
Beam, Police Car 65.00
Beam, Sailfish 15.00
Beam, Telephone, Antique 50.00
Beer, Anderson Co., Home Brewed Ale, Albany, NY, Amber, 7 In. 47.50
Beer, Atlantic Ale, Black Waiter, With Tray Label 25.00
Beer, Blatz, Logo, 1st Bottle After Prohibition, 28 Oz. 18.00
Beer, Elgin Eagle 8.00
Beer, Guinness Extra Stout, Paper Label, Contents, Miniature 1.50
Beer, Guinness, Bi–Century, Contents, 3 1/4 In. 15.00
Beer, John Rapp & Son, Rainier Beer, San Francisco, 1918 .... 5.00
Beer, Picnic, Blue, Chicago 25.00
Beer, Ruby Red, No Deposit, No Return, Not To Be Refilled, 1950s 20.00
Bininger, Medium Amber, OP, Barrel, Small 175.00
Bitters, Abbots, Contents, Label, Miniature 20.00
Bitters, Capitol Bitters, Aqua 47.50
Bitters, Columbo, L.E. Jung, New Orleans ....*Illus* 40.00
Bitters, Doyle's, Hop, Bitters, Honey Amber, Square, 1872, 9 5/8 In. 28.00
Bitters, Dr.Harter's Wild Cherry, Dayton 23.00
Bitters, Dr.J.Hostetters Stomach Bitters, Amber 20.00
Bitters, Fish Bitters, W.H.Ware, Patented 1866, Honey Amber, 11 In. 250.00
Bitters, Fish Shape, Fish Bitters, W.H.Ware, Amber 85.00
Bitters, Great Western Tonic, 1886 .... 128.00
Bitters, Holtzerman Stomach, Cabin Shape, Amber 140.00
Bitters, Hostetter's Stomach, Yellow 35.00
Bitters, Hostetter's, Amber 15.00
Bitters, Indian Princess, Brown's Celebrated Indian Herb, Amber 75.00
Bitters, James Dingley & Co., Boston, Amber, Square, 9 1/2 In. 12.00
Bitters, Kelly's Old Cabin Bitters, Patented 1863, Amber, 9 In. 490.00
Bitters, L.E.Jung, Columbia 125.00
Bitters, Lash's Bitters, Contents, Label 35.00
Bitters, Lash's, Light Amber, Square 10.00
Bitters, Leidiard's Celebrated Stomach Bitters, Dark Green 600.00
Bitters, M.G.Landsberg, 13 Stars At Shoulder, Flag, Amber 425.00
Bitters, Morley's Liver & Kidney Cordial, Amber, Square, 9 In. 30.00
Bitters, Morning Star, Yellow Amber 200.00
Bitters, Suffolk Bitters, Honey Amber, Sheared Lip, 9 In. 400.00
Bitters, Tippecanoe, Warner, Amber 85.00
Blown, 3–Part Mold, Applied Sloping Lip, Green, 12 3/4 In. 60.00
Blown, Midwestern, Club Shape, Aqua, 9 In. 35.00
Bottle, Whiskey, 24 Ribs, Green, Cylindrical, Zanesville, 7 3/4 In. 300.00
Bromo Seltzer, Blue, 6 1/2 In. 12.00
Brownhill's Indian, Sauce, Leeds, Deep Aqua, Burst Li, 5 3/4 In. 7.50
    BOTTLE, COCA–COLA, see Coca–Cola, Bottle
Cologne, 12 Sides, Cobalt, 7 1/4 In. 125.00
Cologne, 12 Sides, Opaque Light Blue, 8 3/4 In. 175.00
Cologne, Clear Cut, Metal Flip, Chatelaine, 2 1/4 In. 85.00
Cologne, Clear Overshot 38.00
Cologne, Cobalt Blue, Sandwich Type, 39 Verticle Ribs, 5 5/8 In. 155.00
Cologne, White, Floral Design, 6 In. 110.00
Cosmetic, Ayer's Hair Vigor, Peacock Blue, No Stopper, 6 1/2 In. 14.00
Cosmetic, Egyptian Lotusia, Harem's Secret, For Complexion, 6 In. 11.00
Cosmetic, Gouraud's Oriental Cream, London, New York, 2 1/2 In. 2.00
Cosmetic, Metamorphic, Buckingham Dye For The Whiskers 12.50
Creamer, Ewald Bros.Golden Guernsey, Red, 1/2 Oz. 15.00
Creamer, Lone Oak Farm, Emblem, 2 Oz. 18.00
Cure, Foley's Kidney & Liver Cure, Label, Contents 36.00

Cure, Great Shoshonies Remedy of Dr.Josephus, Aqua, 9 In. 65.00
Decanter, Clear Cut, Cut Citron Stopper, Czechoslovakia, 1 3/4 In. 85.00
Decanter, Cut Glass, Sandwich Blown, Greek Key, Bellflower, 13 In. 198.00
Drug, Burnett's Cocaine, Aqua 12.50
Drug, Vial, Light Green, Applied Foot, 2 5/8 In. 90.00
Figural, Buddha, Porcelain, Germany, 2 3/8 In. 75.00
Figural, Clown, Bank, Clear, Cap For Money, 7 1/4 In. 8.00
Figural, Clown, Grapette Products Co., Bank, Metal Cap, 7 1/4 In. 7.00
Figural, Cluster of Grapes, France, 1/2 Pt. 20.00
Figural, JSP Monogram, Teal, Long Neck, Applied Lip, 8 3/4 In. 17.50
Figural, Man, Hat Stopper, Ceramic, Red Eye 18.00
Figural, Pineapple, Deep Amber, 9 In. 150.00
Figural, Poland Water, Moses, Emerald, Medicine Type Lip, 11 In. 30.00
Figural, Violin, Cobalt Blue, ABM, 8 In. 14.00
Figural, Volkswagen, Liquor Decanter, Music Box, Red, Japanese 90.00
Flask, Chapman Montreal, Honey Amber, Teardrop Shape 75.00
Flask, Chestnut, 16 Ribs, Light Citron, Swirl, Mantua, Ohio, 6 3/8 In. 1800.00
Flask, Chestnut, Medium Green, Sheared Lip, Flared Neck, 6 3/4 In. 75.00
Flask, Chestnut, Olive Green, Ludlow, 12 1/2 In. 175.00
Flask, Chestnut, Olive Green, Ludlow, 5 1/4 In. 125.00
Flask, Cornucopia Urn, Olive Green, Sheared Pontil, 6 3/4 In. 44.00
Flask, Double Eagle, Cunningham & Co., Pittsburgh, Aqua, Qt. 45.00
Flask, Expanded Diamond Pattern, Chestnut, German, 5 1/4 In. 55.00
Flask, Figural, Glad Hand, Ceramic, Painted, 7 In. 75.00
Flask, Flattened Beehive, Chestnut, Golden Amber, 10 In. 110.00
Flask, Flattened, Chestnut, Sage Green, Thick Collar, 10 3/4 In. 90.00
Flask, Flora Temple, Pale Amber, Handle 400.00
Flask, Henry Chapman & Co., Red Amber, Ovoid, Pocket 40.00
Flask, Henry Chapman & Co., Red Amber, Pocket, Applied Lip, Ovoid 32.00
Flask, McK G I–031, Green 100.00
Flask, McK G I–051, Cornflower Blue 500.00
Flask, McK G I–112, Calabash 300.00
Flask, McK G III–004, Horn, Olive Amber 75.00
Flask, McK G XIII–004, Calabash 55.00
Flask, McK G–102, Whiskey, Greeley's Bourbon 300.00
Flask, Painted Woman, Light Green, Inscription, Bohemian, 7 1/2 In. 770.00
Flask, Red Amber, 24 Ribs, Zanesville, 8 1/2 In. 475.00
Flask, Samuel Westheimer, Red Amber, Oval Flattened, 6 7/8 In. 12.00
Flask, Samuel Westheimer, St.Joseph, Mo., Red Amber, 1/2 Pt. 13.00
Flask, Scroll, Iron Pontil, Aqua, Qt. .... 40.00 To 45.00
Flask, Shot, Embossed Dog, Pheasants, Copper, Brass Spout, 6 1/8 In. 30.00
Flask, Silver, Winged Shoulders, Bowed Sides, Bright Cut, 6 X 4 In. 150.00
Flask, Wharton's Whiskey, Chestnut Grove 1850, Sapphire Blue 150.00
Food, Beechnut, Nut & Leaf, No Lid, 1/2 Pt. 4.00
Food, Bovril Limited, Striated Amber, 2 Oz., Bulbous, 3 In. 4.50
Food, Bovril, Limited, Bulbous, Striated Amber, 2 Oz. 5.00
Food, Captain Post Pure Horseradish, New York City, Aqua, Qt. 75.00
Food, Coffee, Sunshine Brand, Springfield, Mo., Lion, Qt. 5.00
Food, Heinz Manzanilla, Olive, Dated 1883 .... 60.00
Food, Horseradish, As You Like It, Stoneware, No Lid, 1/2 Pt. 15.00
Food, Jumbo Peanut Butter, Elephant 25.00
Food, Pure Horseradish, A.S.Keyes, Medfield, Mass., 1/2 Pt. 15.00
Food, Pure Horseradish, L.M.Lyon Market Gardner, 1/2 Pt. 20.00
Food, Royal Mint Sauce, Emerald Green, Bulbous, Keyslot Mold, 7 In. 20.00
Food, Royal Mint Sauce, Emerald Green, Bulbous, Long Neck, 7 In. 18.00
Food, Snappy Horseradish, John Lang, Cuba, Glass Lid, 1/2 Pt. 15.00
Food, Strickley Pure Radish, Black Horse, J.H.Parker, Aqua, 1/2 Pt. 20.00
Food, Syrup, Allen's Red Tame Cherry 775.00
Food, Tic Tic Relish, Nash Underwood, Inc., Chicago, Ill., 1/2 Pt. 17.50
Food, Vanilla Extract, Embossed A & P, Cork, Contents 20.00
Food, Wan–Eta Cocoa, Boston, Amber, 1/2 Pt. 15.00
Food, Wan–Eta Cocoa, Boston, Amber, Qt. 58.00
Fruit Jar, Ball Deluxe, Mold Numbers On Front, Clear, Qt. 3.50
Fruit Jar, Ball Freeezer Jar, Zinc Lid, Pt. 4.00

Bottle, Fruit Jar, E I, Newark, Ohio, 1860, Yellow Green, 1/2 Gal.

Bottle, Ink, Carter, Cobalt Blue, Qt.

Fruit Jar, Ball Perfect Mason, Salesman's Sample, Square	35.00
Fruit Jar, Ball Sanitary Sure Seal, Blue, Qt.	5.00
Fruit Jar, Ball, Ideal, Blue, 1/2 Pt.	45.00
Fruit Jar, C.F.Spencer's Patent	90.00
Fruit Jar, Canton Domestic Fruit Jar, Pt.	150.00
Fruit Jar, Clark's Peerless, Aqua, Qt.	5.00
Fruit Jar, Clarke Fruit Jar Co., Cleveland, Ohio, Aqua, 1/2 Gal.	60.00
Fruit Jar, Crown, Made In Canada, Pt.	5.00
Fruit Jar, Crystal Jar, Qt.	35.00
Fruit Jar, Crystal Jar, Screw On Lid, Pat.Dec.17, 1878, 7 1/2 In.	10.00
Fruit Jar, Drey, Improved Ever Seal, Pat.1920, Qt.	3.00
Fruit Jar, E I, Newark, Ohio, 1860, Yellow Green, 1/2 Gal. ....*Illus*	85.00
Fruit Jar, E.T.Cowdrey, Amber, Qt.	75.00
Fruit Jar, Easy Trade VJC Co., Aqua, Qt.	25.00
Fruit Jar, Electric, World Globe, Wire Clamp, Aqua	125.00
Fruit Jar, Fruit Keeper GC Co., Aqua, Qt.	40.00
Fruit Jar, Globe, 75 On Base, Light Green Aqua, Clamp Closure, Qt.	18.00
Fruit Jar, Ideal, Aqua, Qt.	25.00
Fruit Jar, Jos.Middleberry Jr., Inc., 1/2 Gal.	12.00
Fruit Jar, King, Banner Below King's Head, Pt.	15.00
Fruit Jar, Lightning, Lid, Wire Fastener, Amber, 8 In.	20.00
Fruit Jar, Lightning, Medium Amber	45.00
Fruit Jar, Mason's Patent Nov.30th 1858, Deep Aqua	20.00
Fruit Jar, Mason's Patent, Anchor, Qt.	20.00
Fruit Jar, Mason's, Pat.Nov.30th 1858, Aqua, Zinc Lid, 2 Qt.	10.00
Fruit Jar, Mason, Pat.1858, Qt.	14.00
Fruit Jar, Mason, Pat.Nov 30th 1858, Keystone, Aqua, 1/2 Gal.	15.00
Fruit Jar, Millville Atmospheric, Aqua, Qt.	38.00
Fruit Jar, Peerless, Aqua, Qt.	125.00
Fruit Jar, Pitman, Aqua, Qt.	115.00
Fruit Jar, Safety Valve, Pat.May 21 1895, Aqua, Qt.	5.00
Fruit Jar, Swayzee's, Olive, 1/2 Gal.	45.00
Fruit Jar, Swirls of Olive At Neck, Aqua, A.W.Pinkerhuff's, 1876	400.00
Fruit Jar, Victory, Glass Lid, Pat.1929, Pt.	20.00
Fruit Jar, Wears Jar, Tight Embossed At Neck, Clamp, Lid, Pt.	8.00
Fruit Jar, Wears, Smalley, Kivlan & Onthank, Pat.Feb.23, '09, Pt.	12.00
Fruit Jar, Western Pride, Contents	210.00
Fruit Jar, Whitneymason, Pat.1858, Aqua, Pt.	15.00
Fruit Jar, Winslow Improved Valve Jar, Original Spring, Qt.	400.00
Fruit Jar, Winslow Jar, Aqua, Crown, Aqua Lid, Midget	12.00
Fruit Jar, Winslow Jar, Aqua, Mason's Pat.Nov 30th 1858, Aqua, Midget	275.00
Fruit Jar, Winslow Jar, Aqua, Pt.	50.00

Gin, Avan Hoboken & Co., Rotterdam, Beveled Base, 10 3/4 In. 35.00
Gin, Blankenheym & Nolet, 9 1/8 In. 25.00
Gin, Kenaway & Co., Green, Bubbly, Crude .... · 55.00
Gin, Old London Dock, A.M.Bininger, Olive Amber 80.00
Gin, P.Loopayt & Co., Amber, 9 1/4 In. 35.00
Ginger, E.G.Lyons & Co., Ess.Jamaica Ginger, Green Aqua, 5 3/4 In. 16.00
Glue, Spalding's, Aqua, Rolled Lip, Cylinder, 3 1/4 In. 10.50
Hires Root Beer, Blob Top, C.1880 .... 30.00
Ink, Bertinquoit, Deep Olive Green, Sheared Lip, Embossed 94.00
Ink, Carter's Ink, Figural, Grandma, German 65.00
Ink, Carter's, Aqua, Contents, 1/2 Pt. 9.00
Ink, Carter's, Cathedral, Cobalt Blue, 9 1/2 In. 115.00
Ink, Carter's, Cobalt Blue, Gothic Style, 9 3/4 In. 20.00
Ink, Carter's, Cone, Light Amber, BIMAL, 2 1/2 In. 14.00
Ink, Carter's, Grandma, Pottery 48.00
Ink, Carter's, Grandpa, Pat.Jan.1914, Germany, Pottery 100.00
Ink, Carter, Cobalt Blue, Qt. ....*Illus* 85.00
Ink, Cone, Jagged Open Pontil, Amber, Sheared Lip 90.00
Ink, Harrison's Columbian, Aqua, 3 In. 28.00
Ink, Lyon's, Aqua, 4 1/2 In. 10.00
Ink, Pinched Pour Lip, Coblat Blue, 16 Sides 40.00
Ink, Sanford's, Fountain Pen, Inks, Clear, Square Base, ABM, 2 X 2 In. 14.00
Ink, Signet, Cobalt Blue, Qt. 30.00
Ink, Standardized, Cobalt Blue, Master, Cylinder, Label, 9 1/2 In. 35.00
Ink, Teapot, Amethyst 260.00
Ink, Thomas & Co., Aqua Blue, Square, 1900, 2 1/4 In. 5.00
Ink, Umbrella, Aqua, 8 Sides, Open Pontil, Rolled Lip, 2 3/8 In. 24.00
Ink, Waterman, Pour Spout, Box, 6 In. 30.00
Jar, Apothecary, Blown Glass, Tin Cover, 10 In. 55.00
Jug, Grant's Scotch, 8 1/2 In. 22.00
Jug, Purple, Wicker Design, Applied Handle, Cylinder, OP, 5 1/4 In. 50.00
Jug, Whiskey, Happy Days, Qt. 40.00
Kitchen, Bear Bluing, Paper Lable, Octagonal Glass 20.00
Liqueur, Lighthouse Shape, Dome Lights Up, 12 In. 35.00
Madam Yales Fruit Cure, Rectangular, Clear 25.00
Medicine, Baltimore Pills, Sealed, Paper Wrapper, 1900s, 2 1/2 In. 30.00
Medicine, Cactus Oil, Prof.Deans, Great Barbed Wire, 6 1/2 In. 24.00
Medicine, Clay's Sure Cure For Rheumatism, Savannah, Georgia, Amber 75.00
Medicine, Corslene's Catarrh Cure, Athens, Ohio, Amber 75.00
Medicine, Davis Vegetable Pain Killer, Aqua, Indented Panels, 5 In. 38.00
Medicine, Dr. Hobson's Sunburn Cream, 5 1/4 In. 10.00
Medicine, Dr. Thatcher's Liver Pills, Unopened, 2 1/4 In. 25.00
Medicine, Dr.Caldwell's Syrup Pepsin, Aqua, Embossed 10.00
Medicine, Dr.D.Jayne's Carminative Balsam, Aqua, Cylinder, 5 In. 11.00
Medicine, Dr.Jayne's Expectorant, Aqua, Embossed, Cork 12.00
Medicine, Dr.Jayne's Tonic Vermifuge, Strength Giver 7.50
Medicine, Dr.Kilmer's Swamp Root, Embossed, Full, Original Box 15.00
Medicine, Dr.Kilmer's, Swamp Root Cure, Sample 65.00
Medicine, Dr.L.E.Keeley's Gold Cure For Drunkenness, Clear, Pour Lip 55.00
Medicine, Dr.Pierce's Favorite Prescription For Women, Full, Box 20.00
Medicine, Dr.S.S.Fitch, Blue Aqua, OP, Oval, 8 1/2 In. 45.00
Medicine, Dr.Steeling's Pulmonary Syrup, Indented Panels, 6 In. 275.00
Medicine, Dr.Thatcher's Liver Pills, Unopened, 2 3/4 In. 25.00
Medicine, Fritzsche Brothers Inc., New York, Amber, Label 5.00
Medicine, Frye's Pepsin Dyspepsia Remedy, Full, Box 25.00
Medicine, Great Barber Wire Remedy, Amber, Round, 9 1/2 In. 54.00
Medicine, H.G.Farrell's Arabian Liniment, Chicago, Ill., 5 In. 125.00
Medicine, Hall's Catarrh Cure, Aqua, Round, 4 5/8 In. 3.00
Medicine, Handysides Blood Purifier, Block Glass 75.00
Medicine, Hart Swedish Asthma Cure, Amber, 5 In. 18.00
Medicine, Jackson's Fever Cure, Aqua 16.00
Medicine, Kickapoo Cough Cure, Round, Aqua 7.00
Medicine, Kickapoo Cough Syrup, Round, Aqua 6.00
Medicine, L.Wishart's Pine Tree Tar Cordial, Green, 7 1/2 In. 29.50

Medicine, Laxated Pepsin Tablets, Amber, Label, Box, 3 In. 3.00
Medicine, Leslie E. Keeley Co., 4 1/2 In. 8.00
Medicine, Lord's Opodeldoc, Deep Aqua, Man, Breaking Crutches, 5 In. 16.00
Medicine, Milk's Emulsion, Brown, Label, Box, 8 1/2 In. 20.00
Medicine, Morley's Liver and Kidney Cordial, Amber, 9 In. 32.00
Medicine, Olive Green, USA Hospital Dept., Qt., 9 In. 125.00
Medicine, Pancreobismuth & Pepsin, Embossed Mortar & Pestle 15.00
Medicine, Pineoleum, Physician's Sample, Aqua, Embossed, Small 20.00
Medicine, Piso's Cure For Consumption, Hazeltine & Co., Green, 5 In. 6.50
Medicine, Smith's Green Mountain Renovator, Aqua, Oval, 7 3/4 In. 35.00
Medicine, Sperry's Rheumatic Liniment, Blue Aqua, 4 In. 135.00
Medicine, Spohn's Distemper Cure, Label, Content 18.00
Medicine, Swift's Syphilitic, Cobalt Blue, 9 In. 350.00
Medicine, W.H.Bull's, Honey Amber, Chamfered Corners, Corked, 8 In. 8.00
Medicine, Wakefield's Cough Syrup, Aqua, Rectangular, 5 In. 6.00
Medicine, Warner's Safe Cure, Frankfurt 350.00
Medicine, Warner's Safe Kidney & Liver Cure, Rochester, Amber, Pt. 17.50
Medicine, Warner's Safe, Melbourne, BT, Red Amber, Embossed, Pt. 70.00
Medicine, Winersmith, Louisville, Ky, Amber, ABM, 5 3/4 In. 2.00
Medicine, Wyeth, Cobalt Blue, Dose Cap 15.00
Milk, A & T College, Greensboro, N.C., Red, Square, 1/2 Pt. 12.00
Milk, A.W.Mayer, Cap, Round, Amber 55.00
Milk, Alfafa Farm Dairy, Clear, Pint 6.50
Milk, Annapolis Dairy Products Co., Dolly Madison, Cream Top, Qt. 22.00
Milk, Baby Face, Sunshine Dairy, Square, Qt. 35.00
Milk, Bennet Co., Athens–Nelsonville, Ohio, ISP, Emblem, 1/2 Pt. 10.00
Milk, Bentley & Sons Farm Dairy, Fairbanks, Pyro, Red, 1/4 Pt. 60.00
Milk, Biemiller Dairy, Baltimore, Md., Health Dept.Permit, Pt. 15.00
Milk, Brookfield Dairy, O Shoulders, Emblem, Baby Top, 1/2 Pt. 40.00
Milk, Clover Leaf Creamery, Anaconda, Mont., Red Pyro, 1/2 Pt. 12.00
Milk, Cole Farm Dairy, Biddeford, Me., Maroon Pyro, Square, Qt. 8.00
Milk, Cranford Dairy, Cranford, N.J., ISP, Original Cap, 1/4 Pt. 12.00
Milk, Crescent Dairy, Schenectady, N.Y., Crescent Moon Emblem, Qt. 15.00
Milk, Dairy Lee, Double Baby Face, Qt. 45.00
Milk, Drew's Dairy, Augusta, Me., Uncle Sam, Orange & Black Pyro, Qt. 38.00
Milk, Drink Hoffman's Milk, Cream Top, 1/2 Pt. 13.00
Milk, E.J.Dawson Dairy, Ogdensburg, N.Y., Dimpled Neck, 1/2 Pt. 7.50
Milk, Franklin Farms & Dairies, Franklin, Me., Round Emblem, Pt. 9.00
Milk, Golden Guernsey Products, Bell Shape, Squat, Emblem, Qt. 20.00
Milk, Guadalupe Valley Creamery, Sequin, Texas, Orange Pyro, Pt. 5.00
Milk, H.P.Hood & Sons, Cone Shape, Lines In Top & Bottom 9.00
Milk, Happy Valley Farms, Clear, 1/2 Pint 10.00
Milk, Hillyland Farm Dairy, Scotland, Conn., Maroon Pyro, Square, Qt. 15.00
Milk, Hygienic Dairy Co., R Quality Service, Red, 1/4 Pt. 9.00
Milk, Ka Vee Ice Cream Dairy Co. 8.00
Milk, Kern County Hospital, ISP, Pyro, 1/4 Pt. 25.00
Milk, Little Joe's Dairy, Herkimer, N.Y., Red Pyro, 1/2 Pt. 12.00
Milk, Mack Farm Dairy, Batesville, Ark., O & R Shoulders, Qt. 18.50
Milk, Macomber's Dairy, Cow & Child With Doll, Red Pyro, 1/2 Pt. 9.00
Milk, Noble Dairy, Baseball, Drink For Muscle & Strength 12.00
Milk, Oakhurst Dairy, Portland, Me., Children, Green, Pyro, Qt. 14.00
Milk, Pleasant View Dairy, A.W.Croscut & Sons, Red Pyro, Pt. 12.00
Milk, Quaker Maid Dairy Products, Philadelphia, Neck Chain, 1/2 Pt. 9.00
Milk, Queen City Dairy Inc., Cumberland, Md., ISP, Stippled, Qt. 15.00
Milk, R.O. Stockman, Portland, Maine, Round, Qt. 9.00
Milk, Round Top Farms Quality Dairy Products, Cream Top, 1/2 Pt. 28.00
Milk, S.Castagna Dairy, Johnstown, Pa., Fluted Neck, Clear, Pt. 6.00
Milk, Shrewsbury Dairy Co., New Jersey 10.00
Milk, Silver Lake Farm Eastlake Weir, Fla., ISP, Ribs On Neck, Qt. 12.00
Milk, Southland Dairies Ltd., In Triangle, ISP, Paneled, Pt. 7.50
Milk, Sun Valley Dairy Multi-Vitamin, Green, Yellow Pyro, 1/2 Gal. 20.00
Milk, Sunnyside Farm, Newport, N.H., Clear, 1/2 Pt. 5.00
Milk, Sunshine Dairy, St.Johns, Newfoundland, Red, Qt. 15.00
Milk, Turner Centre Creamery, Mas Seal 8.00

Milk, V.M.& I.C., Amber, Qt. 75.00
Milk, Wakefield Dairy, Washington, D.C., Gen.Washington Profile, Qt. 16.00
Milk, Wilber Farms, Buffalo, N.Y., Smiling Calf, Red, Square, Pt. 10.00
Milk, Wm.F.McKenzie Co., Portland, Me., Round Emblem, Qt. 18.00
Mineral Water, Congress & Empire Spring Co., Green 35.00
Mineral Water, Haas Bros.Natural, Napa Soda, Cobalt Blue, Qt. 125.00
Mineral Water, Hawthorn Spring, Amber, Quart 18.00
Mineral Water, Hopkins Chalybeate, Medium Green, Pint 85.00
Mineral Water, Oak Orchard, Acid Spring, Lockport, N.Y., Green, 9 In. 55.00
Nurser, 16 Ribs, Vertical, Aqua, Pocket, 6 7/8 In 210.00
Nurser, Peter Rabbit, Oval 22.00
Oil, Wolf Head, Embossed Logo, Paper Logo, Qt. 20.00
    BOTTLE, PERFUME, see Perfume Bottle
Pickle, Bunker Hill, Light Amber 26.50
Pickle, Cathedral, Aqua, Rolled Lip, Open Pontil, 9 In. 135.00
Pickle, Hayward's Military 15.00
Pickle, Skilton Foote Bunker Hill, Cork Closure, Aqua, 1/2 Pt. 5.00
Poison, Abortion Remedy, Saves The Calves, Cow Picture, Cork 40.00
Poison, Martins, English, Ice Blue 240.00
Poison, Nichols Bed–Bug Liquid, Chicago, 6 In. ....*Illus*   5.00
Poison, Pill, Cobalt Blue, Embossed 1 Side, ABM, Flat, Ovoid, 3 In. 18.00
Sarsaparilla, Dr.Townsend's, Square, Green, 8 3/4 In. 55.00
Snuff, 24 Ribs, Green Aqua, Amber Swirl 3 Sides, Zanesville, 6 In. 950.00
Snuff, Agate, 19th Century 55.00
Snuff, Cameo Glass, Red Floral, White, Peking 175.00
Snuff, Carved Turquoise, Florals, Chinese 45.00
Snuff, Doctor Marshall's, Aqua, Bubbles, Rolled Lip, 3 1/4 In. 18.00
Snuff, Double Fish, Cloisonne 80.00
Snuff, Enameled Floral Design, Wooden Spoon, 3 1/4 In. 10.00
Snuff, Geometric Design, Burgute Lacquer 50.00
Snuff, Grape Cluster Shape, Peking Glass 195.00
Snuff, Inside Painted With 2 Pairs of Tigers 120.00
Snuff, Olive Green Glass, Blown, 18th Century, 4 3/4 In. 140.00
Snuff, Opal Gemstone, Carved Fish 250.00
Snuff, Oriental Etching On Sides, Dark Red 190.00
Snuff, P.Lorillar, Amber, Pat.1872 .... 20.00
Snuff, Painted Figural & Scenic Design Interior, Red Top, 4 In. 25.00
Snuff, Painted Inside, Calligraphy On Panels, Oriental, 3 In. 400.00
Snuff, Pear Shape, Carved Leaves, Berry Top, 3 1/4 In. 245.00
Snuff, Polychrome, Jade Stopper, Chien Lung Seal 150.00
Snuff, Relief Polychrome, Chien Lung Seal, Sealed Stopper 100.00
Snuff, Relief Polychrome, Metallic Stopper 95.00
Snuff, Rock Crystal, Silver Cover, Spoon With Turquoise Top, 3 In. 80.00
Soda, Canada Dry, Top & Bottom Paper Labels, 1920s, Green Glass 10.00
Soda, Carolina Sparkling Beverage, Painted Label, Orange Crush 7.00
Soda, Cliquot Club, Embossed, Paper Label 8.00
Soda, Coca–Cola, Charleston, S.C., Embossed Front, Aqua 18.00
Soda, Coca–Cola, Mint Cola, Salisbury, N.C., C.1910, 6 1/2 Oz. 12.00
Soda, Codd, Marble Stopper, Embossed Castle Turret, Flag, Green 37.00
Soda, Donald Duck Cola 8.00
Soda, Dove Root Beer Extract, Full, Cork Stopper, Original Box 15.00
Soda, Dr Pepper, 1924, 6 Oz. 8.00
Soda, Orange Crush, Amber 7.00
Soda, Parfay, Selma, N.C., Worley–Selma, N.C., C.1915 .... 12.00
Soda, Pepsi–Cola, Birmingham, Alabama, Old Script On Front, Aqua 16.00
Soda, Pepsi–Cola, Petersburg, Virginia, Red, White Label, 1956, 10 Oz. 3.00
Soda, Royal Crown Cola, Pyramids, Dated 1936 .... 10.00
Soda, Sand Springs, Painted Label 3.00
Soda, Try Me, Embossed 15.00
Spirit, Black Glass, Squat, Pontil, Holland, 1700–30, 5 3/4 In. 200.00
Spirit, Black, Squat, Sheared Mouth, Neck Ring, Holland, 1700–30, 6 In. 200.00
Stove Polish, Black Cat, Contents 20.00
Vinegar, Champions, Aqua, Tapered, 5 In. 45.00
Whiskey Jug, Rose Distiller, Atlanta, Cobalt Rose, C.1875 .... 120.00

Whiskey, Belle of Anderson, Milk Glass 80.00
Whiskey, Canadian Mist, Full Figure Mountie 20.00
Whiskey, Duffy Malt Whiskey, Amber, Round, Pat.Aug.24, 1886, 10 In. 11.00
Whiskey, Embossed Bust of Paul Jones, Sailing Ship, Label, Amber 75.00
Whiskey, Figural, Boy, Googly–Eye, Scotty, All Scotch, Bisque 75.00
Whiskey, Golden Wedding, Old Rye, Box, 4 In. ....*Illus* 18.00
Whiskey, I.W. Harper, Porcelain, 15 In. ....*Illus* 25.00
Whiskey, I.W.Harper Gold Medal, Square Anchors, Qt. 75.00
Whiskey, J.Rieger & Co., Kansas City, Fluted Neck, Label, 4 1/2 In. 27.50
Whiskey, Judge Thorn's Straight Bourbon Whiskey, Label, 9 1/2 In. 6.00
Whiskey, Jug, Harper's, Black, Miniature 60.00
Whiskey, Kellerstrass Distilling, Fancy, Qt. 15.00
Whiskey, Meadville, Pa.Distillery, Qt. 55.00
Whiskey, Udolpho Wolfe's Aromatic Schnapps, Dark Amber 28.50
Wine, Cordon Rouge, C.H.Mumm & Co., 1913 .... 45.00
Wine, Moet & Chandon Dry Imperial Champagne, Label, 1904, 1/2 Bottle 30.00
Zanesville, 24 Ribs, Swirl, Citron, Globular, 7 1/2 In. 2200.00
Zanesville, 24 Ribs, Swirl, Dark Red Amber, Globular, 8 In. 425.00
Zanesville, 24 Vertical Ribs, Aqua, Globular, 7 1/2 In. 550.00

Boxes of all kinds are collected. They were made of thin strips of inlaid wood, metal, tortoiseshell, embroidery, or other material.

BOX, see also Advertising, Box; Ivory, Box; Porcelain, Box; Shaker, Box; Tinware, Box; and various Porcelain categories.
BOX, 2 Cutout Hearts Front, Dark Green Paint, Early 19th Century, 4 X 9 In. 1320.00
2 Sliding Lids, Chip Carved, Brass Tack Trim 150.00
2 Tier, Drawer Over 6 Divided Drawers, Painted, 14 1/2 X 13 3/4 In. 1300.00
Academy Painted, American, Bird's–Eye Maple, 6 1/4 X 12 1/4 In. 3600.00
Apple, Poplar, Dark Finish, Octagonal, 8 1/2 In. 85.00
Ballot, 1922 .... 10.00
Band, Floral Wallpaper, New England, Cylindrical, 4 X 6 1/4 In. 220.00
Band, Fruit Wallpaper, Oval, 19th Century, 4 1/2 X 8 X 5 1/2 In. 325.00
Band, Wallpaper Stenciled, New Hampshire, C.1840, 6 X 12 1/2 In. 165.00
BOX, BATTERSEA, see Battersea, Box
Bentwood, Green Paint, Metal Plate 1 End, Iron Ring Handles, 6 X 15 In. 137.00
Bentwood, Green Stain, Polychrome Dots, Zigzag, Oval, 6 1/2 In. 55.00
Bentwood, Laced Seams, Old Varnish, Decoupage Floral Lid, Oval, 6 In. 45.00
Bentwood, Laced Seams, Wooden Lid, Floral & Geometric Burnt, 13 In. 300.00
Bentwood, Single Finger Construction In Lid, Round, 12 3/4 In. 220.00
Bentwood, Single Finger On Base & Lid, Iron Tacks, B.Smith, 7 In. 85.00
Bentwood, Single Finger On Base & Lid, Iron Tacks, Oval, 6 3/8 In. 65.00
Bentwood, Storage, Copper Tack Construction, Bentwood, Round, 7 1/4 In. 55.00

Bottle, Whiskey, Golden Wedding,
Old Rye, Box, 4 In.

Bottle, Whiskey, I.W. Harper,
Porcelain, 15 In.

Bentwood, Storage, Overlapping Seam, Copper Tacks, 6 1/4 In. 100.00
Bentwood, Stylized Floral Design, 2 Finger Constructions, 5 1/4 In. 45.00
Bentwood, Turned Wood Handle, Copper Tack Construction, Round 55.00
Bible, Bible Shape, Walnut 25.00
Bible, Fluted Carvings, English, Oak, 23 In. 130.00
Bible, Pine, Iron Strap Hinges, Till, Refinished, White Paint, 21 In. 75.00
Bible, Thumbnail Beading Front, Back, Carved Pine, 9 1/4 X 16 1/2 In. 5500.00
Black Striping, Stenciled & Freehand Vines, Pine, 13 In. 95.00
Bonnet, Pennsylvania, Pine, C.1880 .... 450.00
Brass Bale Handle, Divided Interior, Flame Mahogany Veneer, 13 1/2 In. 200.00
Brass Handles & Corners, Medallion Lock, Rosewood, 8 1/4 X 18 In. 185.00
Brass, Pixie On Hinged Lid, Says Exmoor Pixie, 3 1/4 X 1 In. 90.00
Brass, Spring Action, Carved, Lancet 85.00
Bread, Metal, Brick Red, Square, Large 12.00
Bride's, Bentwood, Blue, Floral Sprig, PA, 19th Century, Oval, 6 X 14 In. 715.00
Bride's, Bentwood, Man & Woman Walking, New England, 7 X 15 5/8 In. 1045.00
Bride's, Bentwood, Oval Locking Lid, Scandinavian, 1 1/2 X 2 1/8 In. 77.00
Bride's, Pine, Laced Seams, Black Ground, Design On Cover, 17 In. 2800.00
Bride's, Pine, Laced Seams, Red Paint, Floral Sides, Verse, Oval, 18 In. 1900.00
Brown Sponging, Daubs of Red, Original Lock & Hasp, 17 3/4 In. 775.00
Candle, Beveled Slide Cover, Cut Nails, 1820, 5 1/2 X 7 1/2 In. 65.00
Candle, Carved Birds, Walnut, American, 19th Century, 6 1/4 X 15 1/8 In. 275.00
Candle, Curly Maple, Dovetailed, Pegged With Rooster Pull Lid 340.00
Candle, Hanging, Gray Paint, Wire Nail Construction, 12 3/4 In. 65.00
Candle, Oak, Carved, Hex Design, American, 19th Century, 5 X 14 1/4 In. 412.00
Candle, Pine, Dovetailed, Slide Cover, C.1800, 6 X 9 X 11 In. 260.00
Candle, Pine, Dovetailed, Slide Cover, Dry Red, C.1880, 4 X 7 X 10 In. 120.00
Candle, Pine, Hanging, Divided Drawer 320.00
Candle, Pine, Salmon Paint, Arched Back, New England, 5 X 14 X 13 In. 220.00
Candle, Pine, Slide Cover, Red Paint, C.1820, 6 X 7 X 13 In. .... 250.00 To 265.00
Candle, Red & Yellow Sponged, Pierced, Early 19th Century, 8 X 12 In. 467.00
Candle, Tin, Hanging, Japanned, Hinged Lid & Hasp, Hanging Rings, C.1820 .... 350.00
Cardboard, Floral Wallpaper Covered, Oval, Cover, 9 1/4 In. 215.00
Cast Brass, Oriental, Dragons In High Relief, 8 3/4 In. 95.00
Ceremonial, Japanese, Silver, Fan Design, 6–Footed, 3 1/2 X 2 1/2 In. 325.00
Ceremonial, Silver, Enameled Japanese & American Flags, Miyamoto 225.00
Cheese, Wooden, Dark Green, Cover, Carved S.Taylor, New Eng., 7 X 16 In. 275.00
Child's, Postcard Like Scenes In 12 Blocks, Cards, Hinged, German 155.00
Chippendale, Sliding Cover, Pinwheel Carving, Initials, 2 3/4 X 11 In. 475.00
Cigar, Wooden, Copper Lining 20.00
Cover, Aladdin Alacite, Handles, 3 3/4 X 5 In. 125.00
Cutlery, Bird's–Eye Maple, Divided, Flared, Oval Handle, 12 X 8 In. 99.00
Cutlery, Keen Kutter 18.00
Cutlery, Pine, Gray Paint, Divided, Pierced Handle, 17 1/2 In. 137.00
Desk, Rosewood, Inkwell, Pen Tray, 3 Secret Drawers, 7 X 19 In. 225.00
Document, Birch Marquetry, Hinged Cover, Karelian Russian, 10 3/4 In. 1320.00
Document, Domed Top, Brass Handle, American, 19th Century, 14 1/8 In. 45.00
Document, Dovetailed, Pomegranate Design, Brass Handle, C.1825 .... 1350.00
Document, Hex Design, Geometric, Handles, PA, 19th Century, 6 X 11 In. 1320.00
Document, Inlaid Mahogany, Hepplewhite, Bow–Front, C.1800 .... 1760.00
Document, Iron Lock, Brass Heads, Original Paper Lining, C.1860 .... 45.00
Document, Leather, Studded, N.W.Marsh, Sadler, Paper Interior, 6 X 14 In. 330.00
Document, Pine, Dark Green, Scattered Flower Heads, Border, 7 X 18 In. 88.00
Document, Salmon Flowers, Leaves, 19th Century, 6 1/2 X 12 1/2 In. 1250.00
Document, Tin, Dome Cover, Brown Asphaltum, Ocher Leaves, 5 X 4 X 9 In. 350.00
Document, Tin, Domed Cover, Handle, Upson Style Cherries, 1840, 9 1/2 In. 250.00
Dome Top, Allover Wheel Design, Lines, Dots, Painted, 11 1/2 X 13 In. 400.00
Dome Top, American, Putty Grained, C.1835, 8 3/4 X 20 In. 250.00
Dome Top, Black Graining Over Red, Iron Lock & Hasp, 30 1/4 In. 180.00
Dome Top, Brush Strokes In Whirlwind Design, Grain Painted, 12 In. 1100.00
Dome Top, Dovetailed & Square Nail Construction, 30 X 17 1/2 In. 100.00
Dome Top, Floral Wallpaper Covering, Tin Hinges, 18 In. 105.00
Dome Top, Freehand Design, Painted, C.1825, 13 X 32 In. 450.00
Dome Top, Large Flower, Corner Leaves, Painted, C.1835, 6 1/4 X 14 In. 650.00

Dome Top, Old Red With Mustard & Black, Dated 1844, 10 3/4 X 24 In. 950.00
Dome Top, Painted Tree of Life, American, C.1840, 33 X 33 In. 1900.00
Dome Top, Paneled Sides, Black Combed Graining, 9 1/2 X 20 1/4 In. 1000.00
Dome Top, Poplar, Brown Flame Graining, 24 In. 75.00
Dome Top, Poplar, Dovetailed, Brown Vinegar Graining, Carved Lid, 24 In. 395.00
Dome Top, Smoke Grained Flower & Fruit, Ocher Ground, 8 X 18 1/4 In. 1200.00
Dome Top, Vinegar Graining, Original Iron Lock, Poplar, 21 3/4 In. 225.00
Dome Top, Wallpaper Covered, 21 In. 200.00
Dome Top, Wooden, Painted, Leafy Sprays, Green, C.1830, 8 X 20 X 10 In. 900.00
Dough, French Country, Large Turned Legs, Rectangular, 24 X 42 X 31 In. 400.00
Dough, Lift Top, Breadboard Top, Splay Legs, Early 19th Century, 55 In. 633.00
Dough, Pine, Blue, Painted Train Side, Leather Hinges, Breadboard Top 600.00
Dough, Poplar, Cut Out Handle On Cover, Blue Repaint, 24 In. 150.00
Dough, Poplar, Slanted Sides, Red, Lid, 27 In. 100.00
Dough, Primitive, Pine, Black, Cutout Feet, Square Nails, 18 X 36 In. 80.00
Dovetailed Striped Tiger Maple, Wooden Pins, C.1820, 5 1/2 X 9 In. 350.00
Edge Inlay, Ivory Escutcheon, Brass Bale, Mahogany, 12 In. 175.00
Enameled, Repousse Fish, Wood Interior, Peking, 2 1/2 X 3 X 4 7/8 In. 85.00
Fitted Lid, Painted Man On Horseback, Boy, C.1780, 7 1/2 X 18 3/4 In. 1750.00
Floral Wallpaper Covered, Oval, 19th Century, 5 1/2 X 9 3/4 In. 400.00
Friesian Carved, 2 Sliding Lids, Chip Carved, C.1725, 5 In. 800.00
Geometric Pin Stripe Design, American, 19th Century, 5 X 17 In. 375.00
Glove, Paper Covered, Wooden, Picture of Cherubs On Lid 20.00
Grain Painted, 4 Triangular Sections, Stencil, Wallpaper Lined, 14 In. 250.00
Handkerchief, Art Nouveau Woman's Head On Lid, Pyrography 17.50
Handkerchief, Dresser, English Country Scene, Lined 12.00
Hanging, 2 Open Compartments, Square Nails, Poplar, 12 In. 255.00
Hanging, Square Nails, Dark Patina, Pine, 14 3/4 In. 95.00
Hat, Wallpaper Covered, Merchants Exchange, N.Y., C.1842, 18 1/2 In. 950.00
Heart Shape, Hand Carved, U.S.Franklin, Dated 1853 ....95.00 To 135.00
Hide Covered, Iron Lock & Hasp, Brass Studs, Brass Handle, 10 In. 25.00
Hinged With Cotterpins, Painted Lattice Pattern, 7 5/8 X 6 3/4 In. 300.00
Initialed Cover, Stylized Design, Floral Band, C.1830, 30 X 16 In. 2750.00
Jewelry, Art Deco, Glass, Silhouettes of Woman & Greyhound 40.00
Jewelry, Mother–of–Pearl, Inlaid Rosewood, Fitted, 11 X 7 1/2 X 6 In. 40.00
Jewelry, Silk Lined, Fitted Interior, Oriental, 17 In. 85.00
Knife, Arched Divider, Cut Out Handle, Cherry, 8 1/2 X 11 1/2 In. 100.00
Knife, George III, Mahogany, Serpentine, Hinged Lid, 13 In., Pair 2750.00
Knife, George III, Serpentine Fronted, Inlaid Mahogany, 14 1/2 In. 440.00
Knife, George III, Sloping Lid, Serpentine Front, Mahogany, 14 1/2 In. 825.00
Knife, Hepplewhite, Frame Grain Mahogany Veneer, Divided, 13 3/4 In. 350.00
Knife, Odd Fellows, Inlaid Star, Walnut, 5 1/4 X 20 In. 375.00
Knife, Orange Striping, Black Trim, 8 1/2 X 13 In. 195.00
Knife, Painted Birds, Leafy Sprigs, Copper Handle, July 30, 1833 .... 800.00
Mahogany, 1 Drawer, White Porcelain Pull, 10 3/4 In. 35.00
Manicure Set, Art Deco, Red & White Bakelite, Glico, Germany 25.00
Marquetry, Flower Basket, Birds, Pleat Design, Hinged Lid, 15 X 10 In. 475.00
Mitten, Nursery Rhyme 13.00
Painted & Freehand Design, Pennsylvania, C.1830, 5 1/2 X 12 X 7 In. 6500.00
Painted, Compote of Fruit Top, Cornucopias, Bird's–Eye Maple, 8 1/4 In. 3600.00
Pantry, Bentwood, Plank Base, Red Paint, America, 19th Century, 3 X 7 In. 137.00
Pantry, Dark Green, Side Swing Fasteners, 7 1/4 X 11 3/4 In. 165.00
Pantry, Green, Nailed Ends, Circular Top, 19th Century, 7 X 16 In. 165.00
Pantry, Wooden, Dated 1799, 3 X 2 1/2 In. 200.00
Pantry, Wooden, Natural Finish, Copper Nails, 7 1/2 X 3 1/2 In. 52.00
Patch, Moss Agate Top, Pierced Brass Sides, 1 5/8 X 1 7/8 In. 75.00
Patch, Snowflake Agate Pattern, Pillow Shape Top, Scotch, 2 X 5/8 In. 200.00
Pencil, Child's, Wood & Leather, Children & Verse, Sections, C.1850 .... 95.00
Pencil, Child's, Wooden, Rose Decal Cover, 2 Layer, 1 1/2 X 2 X 9 In. 25.00
Pencil, Child's, Wooden, Sliding Top, Germany 17.00
Pencil, Jackie Coogan As A Child, Tin 20.00
Pencil, Simple Simon, Lithographed Lid 25.00
Pine, Dovetailed, Poplar Lid, Iron Hinges, 33 In. 75.00

Pine, Dovetailed, Red Graining, Black Edge, 1841 Newspaper Lined, 12 In. 250.00
Pine, Dovetailed, Sliding Lid, 22 3/4 In. 82.50
Pine, Dovetailed, Sliding Lid, Floral, Blue Paint, Red Trim, 8 X 12 In. 200.00
Pine, Geometric Inlay On All Sides, 19 1/4 In. 75.00
Pine, Rose Mulled Floral Design On Lid, Iron Bound, 23 1/2 In. 425.00
Pine, Salmon Paint, Geometric & Flower Border Designs, 13 1/2 In. 110.00
Pine, Sliding Lid, 2 Interior Compartments, Dark Green, 5 1/2 In. 115.00
Pipe, Carved Maple, Shaped Back, Scrolled Sides, Drawer, 19 1/2 In. 2200.00
Pipe, Cherry, Applied Edge Molding, Heart Cutout, Hanging Hole, 22 In. 4100.00
Pipe, Pine, Hanging, C.1800, 32 In. 255.00
Pipe, Pine, Pierced, Drawer, Deep Well, New Eng., 18th Century, 22 X 8 In. 385.00
Poplar, Wire Nail Construction, 2 Drawers, 8 X 10 1/2 X 12 In. 80.00
Portrait, Pine, Gentleman, Black Coat, Grain Painted, C.1830, 10 X 30 In. 3520.00
Quarter Sawed Oak, Mahogany Inlaid, Divided, Brass Feet, 7 3/8 In. 55.00
Red Flame Graining, Gold Stenciled Initials, Wallpaper Lined, 13 In. 65.00
Robe, Parchment, Hand Painted Leaf Design, Brass Hinges, Chinese, 38 In. 125.00
Salt, Blue Willow, Blue Painted Cover, Mariyama 225.00
Salt, Hanging, Blue Paint, Inscribed Black Braids, Blue Green, 10 In. 137.00
Salt, Pine, Primitive, Crest, Wrought Iron Nails, Hanging, 12 X 20 In. 145.00
Salt, Pine, Zinc Liner 90.00
Salt, Tulip Form Backboard, Square Base, Lid, Polychrome, C.1830 .... 350.00
Scouring, Hanging, Chestnut Backboard, Old Red & Blue Paint, 21 In. 300.00
Sewing Machine, Oak, Pat.February 19, 1889 .... 15.00
Silver Gilt, Brown Agate Bead On Lid, Asprey, Round, 2 1/2 X 7/8 In. 110.00
Spice, 2 Finger, Rose Head Nails, 18th Century, 1 3/4 X 3 In. 130.00
Spice, Bentwood, 8 Tin Black Canisters, Round, 9 1/4 In. 75.00
Spice, Dark Green Paint, Gold Leaf Band, Initials S.J.L., Ma., 4 X 6 In. 450.00
Spice, Mulberry Paint, Side Dots, Earthworm Design Cover, 5 X 10 In. 425.00
Spice, White, Blue Trim, 6 Drawers, Hanging, 19th Century, 14 X 8 In. 275.00
Stamp, Sterling Silver, Ebonized Fruitwood, Halo Sterling, 2 1/4 In. 250.00
Stenciled Silver Powder Leaf Design On Cover, Pinstriped, 14 In. 450.00
Stenciled Sprays, Martha's Vineyard, Rosewood Graining, C.1844, 12 In. 600.00
Strong, Wells Fargo, Virginia City, Nevada, Metal 500.00
Tambour Sliding Lid, Brass Knob, Walnut, 3 1/2 X 5 3/4 X 10 3/8 In. 450.00
BOX, TEA CADDY, see Tea Caddy
Tinder, Sheet Iron, Wooden Frame, Punched Holes Top & Sides, 1880 .... 50.00
Trinket, House Shape, Made From Cigar Boxes, Shell Covered, 9 In. 40.00
Trinket, Tree Lined Road, Pyrographic, Olive, 1910, 3 X 16 X 9 In. 225.00
Wall, Pine, Concentric Hearts, Wrigglework, Black, New Eng., 19 X 10 In. 440.00
Wall, Pine, Open, Hanging, Apple Green, Lollipop Top, 10 X 12 1/2 In. 295.00
Walnut Trim, Green Paint, Pine, 18 1/4 In. 70.00
Walnut, Sliding Lid Has Underside Latch, Old Finish, 8 3/4 In. 95.00
Wooden, Grain Painted, Red, Black, Lid, New Eng., 1820, 15 X 30 X 16 In. 175.00
Writing, Bird's-Eye Veneer, Brass & Nacre Inlaid, 11 In. 50.00
Writing, Brass Bound, Fitted Drawer, Richard Yaxley, 1818, 19 1/2 In. 200.00
Writing, Red Flame Graining, Cloth Covered, Poplar, 18 In. .... 105.00 To 155.00

The Boy Scout movement in the United States started in 1910. The first Jamboree was held in 1937. Collectors search for any material related to scouting, including patches, manuals, and uniforms. Girl Scouts are listed under their own heading.

BOY SCOUT, Ax, Plumb, Original Handle, Leather Sheaf 35.00
Badge, Hat, Senior Patrol Leader, Green Enameled, Screw Back 29.00
Badge, Ribbon, Sterling Silver Eagle, Be Prepared 65.00
Bank, Boy Scout Camp, Mechanical, Cast Iron, Painted, 10 In. 2640.00
Bank, Cast Iron, 5 3/4 In. .... 80.00 To 95.00
Bead Craft Kit, Box 25.00
Binoculars, Brass 45.00
Binoculars, Tan Leather, 1920s 85.00
Book, Crooked Trails, Remington 10.00
Book, Golden Anniversary Book of Scouting, Rockwell, 1959 .... 35.00
Book, In An Airship, Early Biplane 11.00
Book, Key To Treaty Box 9.00
Book, Rope Knowledge For Boy Scouts, 1933 .... 9.00

To remove a musty odor from a book, sprinkle talcum powder between the pages, then wrap the book and store it for a few months. When you open it again brush out all the powder and the musty smell will be gone.

Book, Through The Big Timber	8.00
Booklet, Bird Study For Merit Badge, 35 Pages, 1938	3.50
Booklet, Indian Sign Language, Jamboree, England, 1929	20.00
Booklet, Requirements, 1964	2.00
Bracelet, 5 Charms, Sterling	30.00
Bugle, Rexcraft, Brass	75.00
Calendar, 1925	30.00
Calendar, 1936	10.00
Calendar, 1954	6.00
Calendar, A Scout Is Reverent, Norman Rockwell, 1940, 11 X 24 In.	30.00
Camera, Folding, Green	25.00
Camping Set, Knife, Fork & Spoon	12.50
Cannon, 12–In.Barrel, Wood Wheels	225.00
Canteen, 1950s	10.00
Cap, Cub, All Wool	5.50
Card, Member, For Year Ending 1919	10.00
Catalog, 1929	12.00
Celluloid, 1917 Series, Boy Scouts of America, With Codes	20.00
Compass, Bakelite Case, Box	22.00
Compass, Box, 1940s	35.00
Cup, Folding, Aluminum	15.00
Diary, 1917, 192 Pages	10.00
Diary, Silver Jubilee Edition, Pocket, Unused, 1935	14.00
Handbook, 1910	150.00
Handbook, 1922	15.00
Handbook, 1929	10.00
Handbook, 1943	12.00
Handbook, 1954, 568 Pages	20.00
Handbook, Den Mother's, 1943 Copyright	5.00
Handbook, For Patrol Leaders, 1949	8.00
Handbook, Rockwell Cover, 1932	13.00
Handbook, Rockwell Cover, 1962	7.00
Handbook, Scout Master's, 1947	6.50
Hatpin, Enameled, Oval, 3/4 In.	60.00
Indian Beadcraft Outfit, Official, 1935	20.00
Kit, Crystal Radio	22.00
Kit, Firemaking	25.00
Knife, Camillus Cutlery Company	10.00
Knife, Cattaraugus Cutlery Company	75.00
Knife, Imperial Knife Company	15.00
Knife, Pocket, Ulster	20.00
Knife, Sheath, 1929, Box	25.00
Knife, Ulster Knife Company, Pre–1970	30.00
Knife, Western Cutlery Company	15.00
Medal, Eagle Scout, Sterling, Red, White & Blue Ribbon	32.00
Medal, George Washington, Embossed	15.00
Medal, God & Country, Blue Ribbon, Enameled Back Bar	5.00

Medal, War Service, 1917	55.00
Merit Badge, Carved Wings, 1930s	60.00
Morse Code Signaller, Box	12.00
Neckerchief, 1935, National Jamboree	75.00
Neckerchief, 1937, National Jamboree	85.00
Neckerchief, 1950, National Jamboree, Bottom Triangle	20.00
Neckerchief, 1953, National Jamboree	15.00
Neckerchief, 1957, National Jamboree	10.00
Neckerchief, 1960, National Jamboree	10.00
Neckerchief, 1973, National Jamboree	3.00
Pack, 1950s	10.00
Patch, 1935, National Jamboree	100.00
Patch, 1950, National Jamboree	20.00
Patch, 1957, National Jamboree	12.00
Pin, 1st Class, Gilt Finish	10.00
Pin, Collar, Commissioner, Silver Wreath, Eagle, Purple Enameled	27.00
Pin, Collar, Scoutmaster, Silver, Green Enameled Ground, 7/8 In.	10.00
Pin, Den Mother	7.00
Pin, Heart Shape, Enameled	8.00
Print, Boy, Campfire, Vision, T.Roosevelt, Hintermeister, 20 In.	75.00
Ring, 1st Class, Sterling, Square Knots On Sides	5.00
Ring, Cub Scout, Sterling Silver	10.00
Ring, Eagle Scout, Sterling, Eagle, Blue & White Enameled	14.00
Sheet Music, March of Boy Scouts, 1912	12.00
Signal Set, Box, 1948	15.00
Tie Hanger, Cub Scout, Plaster	14.00
Tie Holder, String, Statue of Liberty	12.00
Uniform, Air Explorer, Topeka, Kansas	40.00
Watch, 1930's	50.00
Watch, Ansonia, Sun, Box	85.00

Bradley & Hubbard Manufacturing Company made lamps and other metalwork in Meriden, Connecticut, from the 1840s. Their lamps are especially prized by collectors.

BRADLEY & HUBBARD, Bookends, John Alden & Priscilla	65.00
Bookends, Lion	45.00
Box, Stamp, Century of Progress, Chicago, 1934, 3 1/2 In.	45.00
Candlestick, Brass, 12 In.	18.00
Chandelier, 3–Light, Brass, Patent 1894, 36 X 27 In.	850.00
Desk Set, Signed, 5 Piece	95.00
Humidor, 7 In.	20.00
Inkwell, Milk Glass Inserts, Brass, 4 X 8 1/2 In.	100.00
Lamp, 8 Slag Paneled Shade, Orchid & White, 19 In.	500.00
Lamp, 8–Panel Shade, 18 1/2 In.	195.00
Lamp, Double, Student, Electrified	365.00
Lamp, Floor, Attached Ashtray & Drink Holder	195.00
Lamp, Gold Iridescent Domed Shade, 1910, 15 X 11 1/2 In.	700.00
Lamp, Green Marbelized, Brass Acanthus Leaves, 18 In.	650.00
Lamp, Orchid & White, 8 Slag Shade, Pat.Pending, 19 In.	500.00
Lamp, Pattern On Clear Glass	95.00
Lamp, Pyramid Shape Shade, Slag Glass, Brass Stem, Trim	400.00
Lamp, Reverse Painted, Cabbage Roses, Gold, Marked, 12 In.	185.00
Lamp, Slag Glass, Lily Overlay, Brass Base, Signed, 20 In.	425.00
Lamp, Table, Multicolor Slag Glass Shade, Signed	650.00
Lamp, Tin Shade, Embossed Brass Font, Signed, 36 In.	350.00
Letter Holder, Cherubs	48.00
Letter Holder, Stag, Dogs, Fence, Brass	60.00
Match Holder, Knight's Helmet, Spears, Halberd, 6 In.	75.00
Mirror, Dolphins, Brass, Beveled Glass, 16 X 6 In.	45.00
Plaque, Woman, Flowing Blue Gown, 10 X 13 In.	385.00

Brass has been used for decorative pieces and useful tablewares since ancient times. It is an alloy of copper, zinc, and other metals.

BRASS, see also Bell; Tool; Trivet; etc.

BRASS, Ashtray, Armadillo, 5 1/2 In. 15.00
  Bed Warmer, Engraved Floral Lid, Wooden Handle, 41 1/2 In. 170.00
  Bed Warmer, Engraved Lid, Turned Wooden Bands, 46 In. 275.00
  Bed Warmer, Punched & Engraved Lid, Wooden Handle, 41 1/2 In. 225.00
  Bed Warmer, Rose Chased Design, Turned Handle 150.00
  Bed, Cannon Ball, Claw & Ball Feet, Miniature, 10 X 14 In. 75.00
  Bowl, Fruit, Solid, 9 X 3 In. 35.00
  Box, Hinged Cover, Engraved VP, 1911, 3 1/4 X 5 1/2 In. 35.00
  Box, Inlaid Wooden Lid, Germany, 4 3/4 In. 70.00
  Box, Renaissance Design, Wood Lined, Bail Handle & Latch, 9 X 6 In. 175.00
  Box, Writing, Victorian, Hinged Lid, Velvet Lined, 7 X 15 X 11 In. 850.00
  Bucket, Peat, Reeded Mahogany, Loop Handle, 19th Century, 17 In. 2750.00
  Buckle, Eagle, With Cross & Crown, Original Belt 39.00
  Candle Snuffer, English, On Stand 1100.00
  Candleholder, Cobra Snake Shape, Wall Mount, 18 In., Pair 30.00
    BRASS, CANDLESTICK, see Candlestick
  Cauldron, American, Spun, 16 X 21 In. 209.00
  Chamberstick, Carrying Handle, Push Up, 6 X 4 In. 110.00
  Chandelier, 3-Light, Glass Fonts, Frosted Rim Bowl Shade, 38 In. 500.00
  Chandelier, Bell Form Shades, Green Feather Design, 4 Supports 800.00
  Cigarette Case, Egyptian Design 35.00
  Dispenser, Gunpowder, Crossed Pistol & Eagle Insignia 80.00
  Door Knocker, Figural, Cat's Head, 1910 .... 60.00
  Door Knocker, Kewpie, Figural, 1920s 78.00
  Door Knocker, Kissing Couple, Roses, 5 1/2 In. 50.00
  Door Knocker, Lion's Head, 1890s 65.00
  Doorbell, English Shop, C.1865 .... 35.00
  Figure, Heron, Removable Legs, Dark Patina, Japan, 25 1/2 In. 70.00
  Frame, Scrolled Foliate Design, 18 X 15 In. 130.00
  Gas Light, Height Adjustment, Focusing Lens, Adjusts From 15 In. 85.00
  Gong, China, 7 In. 200.00
  Hat Rack, Porcelain Knobs, Butterfly Hooks 140.00
  Holder, Flag Pole, Wall 36.50
  Holder, Whiskbroom, Rolled, Hanging 65.00
  Hooks, Long Winged Dragonfly, Resting On Lotus, 1900, Set of 4 .... 1650.00
  Inkwell, Crab, Figural 85.00
  Jardiniere, 3 Lion Head Handles, 3 Ball Feet, 10 X 11 1/2 In. 65.00
  Kettle, Handle Ears, Bail, Flat Bottom, 18th Century, 10 3/4 In. 75.00
  Kettle, Iron Bail, Dated On Bottom, 1852 .... 120.00
  Kettle, Tea, Tilting, Warmer Base, 12 In. 125.00
  Lamp, Whale Oil, Russian 100.00
  Lantern, Shop's, 4 Glass Panels, Onion Shape Chimney, 15 In. 185.00
  Letter Holder, Desk, Dragons, 3 Sections, 9 1/2 X 6 In. 135.00
  Letter Holder, Shape of Owl, 4 1/4 In. 20.00
  Match Box, Embossed Bust of McKinley, 3 In. 125.00
  Match Safe, Bulldog, Figural, 1910 .... 50.00
  Mortar & Pestle, 3 3/4 In. 105.00
  Mortar & Pestle, Embossed Band of Women's Faces, 2 3/4 In. 50.00
  Pail, Ansonia Brass Co.Label, Iron Bale Handle, Spun, 12 1/2 X In. 50.00
  Pail, Iron Bale Handle, Label On Bottom, Spun, 10 3/4 In. 30.00
  Pail, Iron Bale Handle, Label, Hayden's Patent, Spun, 10 3/4 In. 45.00
  Pail, Iron Bale Handle, Partial Stamped Label, Spun, 13 In. 35.00
  Pail, Wrought Iron Hole Handle, 5 X 10 In. 25.00
  Pie Bird, Water Base, Beak & Tail Move & Whistle When Steams 55.00
  Pin Tray, Rabbit In Field Design, G.W.Frost, 3 1/2 In. 75.00
  Plaque, Dragons, Chinese, 1930, 12 In. 48.00
  Pot, Jelly, Wrought Iron Swing Handle, 8 1/2 X 13 1/4 In. 132.00
  Roaster, Chestnut, Brass Handle 125.00
  Roaster, Chestnut, Coat of Arms On Handle, Registry Mark, 22 In. 95.00
  Salver, Engraved Egyptian Scenes, 24 1/2 In. 20.00
  Salver, Tooled, Star Center, Wooden Stand, 38 In. 70.00
  Scissor, Wick Trimmer, Tray, 9 1/4 In. 45.00
  Sconce, 3 Removable Arms, Lyre & Scroll, Handmade, 10 In. 65.00
  Silent Butler, Embossed Roses 10.00

Skimmer, Round, Pierced Bowl, 5 1/2 In. 130.00
Snuffer, Tray, 1800–30 .... 110.00
Spittoon, Redskin Cut Plug Chewing Tobacco 50.00
Spittoon, Saloon Style, Concave Lid, 4 X 9 1/2 In. 45.00
Stand, Umbrella, Hammered, Pitcher Shape, 19 In. 15.00
Stencil, Capital Letters & Numbers, 2 X 4 In., 50 Piece 35.00
Stencil, Patch & Roberts, 3866, Boston, 2 1/2 X 6 In. 15.00
Sugar Shaker, Boy On Dolphin, Holding Trident On Top, 8 1/2 In. 68.00
Sundial, Analemmatic, English, Sliding Cursor, C.1800, 5 1/2 In. 2310.00
Sundial, Nocturnal, Months, Days, Zodiac Signs, 4 Quadrants, 4 1/4 In. ... 4675.00
Table, Tilt Top, Miniature, 3 In. 45.00
Tea Set, Samovar, Encrusted With Colored Stones, Russia, 8 Piece 65.00
Teakettle, Marked Empress, 5 1/2 In. 155.00
Teakettle, Tilting, Over Oil Burning Base, 12 In. 125.00
Teapot, Applied Brass Medallion, Swing Handle, 6 In. 25.00
Teapot, Long Spout, Japanese, 6 In. 400.00
Telescope, 3–Draw, Extended Length 17 In. 88.00
Telescope, 5 Sections 120.00
Telescope, Extends To 28 Ft. 195.00
Tray, British Royalty, Profiles, Jubilee, 1935, 11 In. 28.00
Tray, Etched Iris, Carence Crafters, 5 3/4 X 2 5/8 In. 195.00
Tray, Floral & Bird Design, Scalloped, Chinese, Round, 30 In. 20.00
Tray, Flowers & Peacocks, Inlaid, Indian, 25 In.Diam. 10.00
Trivet, Lyre Design, 11 In. 35.00
Warming Pan, Geometric Design, Maple Handle 340.00
Warming Pan, Geometric Design, Turned Maple Handle, American 341.00
Warming Pan, Stylized Floral, Gadrooned Rim, 18th Century, 42 1/2 In. .. 275.00
Whistle, Steam Engine 85.00

BREAD PLATE, see various Pressed Glass patterns

Brides' baskets of glass were usually one–of–a–kind novelties made in American and European glass factories. They were especially popular about 1880 when the decorated basket was often given as a wedding gift. Cut glass baskets were popular after 1890. All brides' baskets lost favor about 1905.

BRIDE'S BASKET, Apricot Ruffled, Flowers, Silver Plated Frame, 10 3/4 In. 250.00
Cased Bowl, Enameled Flowers, Silver Plated Holder 225.00
Cased Ruffled Bowl, Cinnamon To Pink, Enameled Flowers 225.00
Cranberry, Pink, Cased White, Fluted, Blown, 11 1/2 X 4 In. 75.00
Enameled Flowers, Silver Plated Holder 150.00
Flowers & Scrolls, Adelphi Holder, Bowl, 11 3/4 In. 600.00
Fluted, 4 Floral Arms, Butterscotch, 10 1/2 In. 375.00
Fluted, Pink Overlay, Enameled Flowers, Gold Band, 12 In. 325.00
Lady, Figural, Rubina Verde Edge, 16 1/2 In. 895.00
Opaque Red Bowl, Silver Plate Frame, Bowl, 9 In. 300.00
Pink Satin Glass, Enameled Flowers, Silver Plated Holder 150.00
Ruffled & Crimped, Pink, Silver Plated Holder 235.00
Victorian Silver Plate, Filigree, Floral Design 48.00
White Flowers, Gold Overlay, Plated Holder, 11 1/2 In. 550.00
White Opaline Ruffled, Pink Trim, Pairpoint Frame 225.00
BRIDE'S BOWL, Fluted, Pink, Lime, Mica Flakes, Silver Plated Holder, 10 In. 245.00
Frosted Ruffled Edge, Square Frosted Handles 150.00
Pink To Yellow Interior, White Exterior, Floral, Stand 380.00
Quilted, Blue Satin 400.00

Bristol glass was made in Bristol, England, after the 1700s. The Bristol glass most often seen today is a Victorian, lightweight opaque glass that is often blue. Some of the glass was decorated with enamels.

BRISTOL, Biscuit Jar, Allover Florals, Gray Opaque, Silver Plated Fittings 110.00
Biscuit Jar, Enameled Flowers, Gold Stems, Gray, 6 In. 110.00
Biscuit Jar, Enameled Leaves, Colored Flowers, Silver Plated Lid 110.00
Biscuit Jar, Glass, Flowers, Silver Plated, Gray, 6 In. 110.00
Biscuit Jar, Pink Overlay, Enameled Flowers, Leaves, 6 In. 145.00

Bottle, Floral Scene, Hand Painted, Gold Trim, Stopper, 10 In. 10.00
Box, Scenes, Ladies & Gentlemen, Hinged Lid, Ormolu Feet, 3 3/4 In. 95.00
Compote, Playful Kitten In Grass, Fluted 65.00
Decanter, Cobalt Blue, White & Gold Enameling, Large 375.00
Lamp, Kerosene, Blue, Clear Chimney, Enameled Floral, 3 1/2 X 5 In. 85.00
Perfume Bottle, Pink, Blue Flowers, Teardrop Stopper, 8 1/4 In. 100.00
Perfume Bottle, White, Orange Flowers, Green Leaves, Blue, 5 3/4 In. 60.00
Perfume Bottle, White, Yellow & Orange Flowers, Leaves, Blue, 6 In. 65.00
Pitcher, Enameled Bird & Flowers, Opaque Green, 8 1/2 In. 40.00
Punch Bowl, Frosted, Enameled Floral, 19th Century, 12 In. 100.00
Rose Bowl, Crimped Top, Gold Design, Garlands & Tassels, 4 1/8 In. 75.00
Salt & Pepper, Pewter Tops 30.00
Tray, Dresser, Allover Gold & Yellow Flowers, 7 3/4 X 11 In. 118.00
Urn, Portrait of Lady, 20 In. 198.00
Vase, Bud, Hand Painted, Blue, Pair 65.00
Vase, Child's, Blue, Tan, Gold Trim, Pair 75.00
Vase, Enameled Jeweling, Pedestal, White Satin Ground, 12 In., Pair 225.00
Vase, Floral & Bird Design, Ruffled Rim, 11 1/2 In., Pair 60.00
Vase, Hand Painted Florals, Pink, 14 In. 265.00
Vase, Mid–Gold Band, Enameled Flowers, Turquoise, 6 1/2 In., Pair 135.00
    BRITANNIA, see Pewter

Bronze is an alloy of copper, tin, and other metals. It is used to make figurines, lamps, and other decorative objects.

BRONZE, Ashtray, Cat, Green Onyx 55.00
Ashtray, Elephant 375.00
Ashtray, Figural, Bucking Bronco, Rider, Armor 70.00
Ashtray, Vienna, Full Figure Standing Bison, 8 In. 260.00
Bookends, Seated Sphinx, Austria, 6 1/2 In. 225.00
Bowl, Tripod, Everted Rim, 3 Stick Legs, Ming Dynasty, 4 In. 125.00
Box, Cigarette, Champleve Enamel, Geometric Border, 4 7/16 In. 175.00
Bust, Anna Coleman Ladd, Amelia Earhart, Marble Stand, 13 In. 2900.00
Bust, Carrier–Belleuse, William Shakespeare, 19th Century 2750.00
Bust, Laughing Boy, Stepped Rectangular Marble Base, 14 In. 425.00
Bust, LeCourtier, Head of Bloodhound, Medallion With Elk, 20 In. 2650.00
Bust, Savine, Woman, Peacock Feathers On Breast, 1900, 22 In. 1650.00
Bust, Smiling Boy, Hat, Dark Brown Patina, 12 3/4 In. 550.00
Casket, Jewel, Foliate Design, Painted Porcelain Panel, Harem Scene 550.00
Clock, Louis Chalon, Pansy Blossoms, Maiden, Robed, 1900, 22 In. 7425.00
Desk Set, Calendar, Blotter, Pen Tray, Silvercrest, 1915, 6 Piece 100.00
Desk Set, Gold Washed Elk, Marble, Signed H.Muller 300.00
Desk Set, Hinged Well, Pen Tray, Letter Holder, Jenning Bros. 125.00
Figurine, A.Carrier–Belleuse, Melodie, Holding Lyre, 32 In. 3300.00
Figurine, A.Pope, Polo Pony, Ears Raised, Saddle, 14 3/4 In. 5280.00
Figurine, Adolph, Nude, Leaded Glass Butterfly Wings, 15 In. 1500.00
Figurine, Andoz, Rabbit, Crouching, 1920, 3 In. 825.00
Figurine, Anna Colemann Ladd, Woman Triumphant, C.1920, 23 In. 2300.00
Figurine, Art Deco, Crane, 34 In., Pair 800.00
Figurine, Athlete, Arms Uplifted, 1930, 28 In. 1750.00
Figurine, Austria, Indian Brave, Reclining, Blanket, 1900, 8 In. 650.00
Figurine, Austria, Jester, Carved Ivory Face, C.1900, 5 In. 250.00
Figurine, Austria, Stag, Cold Painted, Marble Base, 11 3/4 In. 300.00

If you buy an Art Deco bronze and ivory figure, be very careful to examine the ivory. Even slight cracks or damage can lower the value.

Figurine, Barrias, Nature Before Science, 1900, 23 In. 5000.00
Figurine, Barrias, Winged Victory, C.1900, Laurel Wreath, 33 1/2 In. 5500.00
Figurine, Barrias, Winged Victory, Onyx Pedestal, 1900, 37 1/2 In. 1980.00
Figurine, Barye, Hunting Dog, 7 1/2 In. 300.00
Figurine, Barye, Jaguar, Standing, Oval Base, 11 1/2 In. 3300.00
Figurine, Barye, Lion Crushing Snake, 1890, 14 In. 600.00
Figurine, Barye, Tiger, Walking, Curling Tail, 10 1/8 In. 2750.00
Figurine, Barye, Walking Lion, Rectangular Base, 15 1/2 In. 2530.00
Figurine, Bergman, Cat Band, C.1890, 1 1/2 In., 10 Piece ....850.00 To 1000.00
Figurine, Bergman, French Soldier, Backpack, Rifle, French, 4 In. 475.00
Figurine, Bonheur, Horse & Jockey, Jumping, 36 In. 4000.00
Figurine, Bonheur, Stag, Standing, Rectangular Base, 31 5/8 In. 5500.00
Figurine, Bonheur, Tiger, Sitting, Contented Expression, 16 1/2 In. 2400.00
Figurine, Boucher, Chinese Sorceress, 1913, 26 In. 2600.00
Figurine, Bouret, Farm Girl, Kerchief On Head, 27 1/4 In. 1430.00
Figurine, Bouret, Woman, Dressed As Scribe, Book At Side, 21 In. 575.00
Figurine, Bouval, Hunter, Loin Cloth, Walking, 1900, 27 1/4 In. 825.00
Figurine, Boy, Columnar Marble Base, 17th Century, 3 1/4 In. 495.00
Figurine, Bronco Buster, Cowboy, Wire Rope, Rearing Horse, 22 In. 600.00
Figurine, Buddha, 4 In. 175.00
Figurine, Buddha, 8 In. 170.00
Figurine, Buddha, On Lotus Throne, 4 3/8 In. 25.00
Figurine, Burger, Ladies, 1 Bowling, 1 Playing Blind Man's Bluff, Pr. 495.00
Figurine, Burger, Woman, Throwing Ball, Flowing Gown, 5 1/4 In. 295.00
Figurine, Carl E.Akeley, Elephant, Snake Twining Around Leg, 9 In. 4250.00
Figurine, Carl Kauba, Running Fire, Signed, 1865–1922, 11 In. 4500.00
Figurine, Carrier–Belleuse, Woman Reading, Medieval Clothes, 24 In. 3850.00
Figurine, Carvin, German Shepherd, French, 14 1/2 X 18 In. 650.00
Figurine, Charles Frace, Snow Leopard 800.00
Figurine, Charles Richefen, Gentleman, Dueling Pistol, 9 In. 625.00
Figurine, Chinese, Elephant, Standing, Ivory Tusks, Brown, 6 In. 210.00
Figurine, Chinese, Mythological Dog, 18th Century, 3 In. 1100.00
Figurine, Clara, Girl On Footstool, Holds Shoe, 1900, 13 In. 1350.00
Figurine, Contenot, Roman Shepherd, Seated, Straw Hat, 26 In. 770.00
Figurine, Couple Dancing, 18th Century, 1920, 10 In. 2090.00
Figurine, D.H.Chiparus, Javelin Thrower, C.1925, 34 In. 2475.00
Figurine, Dalton, Indian 2145.00
Figurine, DeLucca, Riders On Horseback, Marble Plinth, 18 In., Pair 975.00
Figurine, Descomps, Dancer, Ivory & Bronze, 18 1/4 In. 3850.00
Figurine, Drouot, Soldier, 18th–Century Uniform, Plaque, 15 3/4 In. 660.00
Figurine, E.Stillman, Jockey On Horse, Standing Horse, 14 In. 800.00
Figurine, Egyptian, Cat, Upright, Seated, Oxidized Patina, 5 In. 675.00
Figurine, Egyptian, Holding Incense, Homeric Bronze, 13 In. 125.00
Figurine, Emperor, Classical Armor, Italy, C.1700, 4 3/4 In. 660.00
Figurine, Exotic Dancer, Ivory Body, Jeweled Cloth, 19 In. 5500.00
Figurine, F.D.Fondeur, Female, Raised Arms, Holding Bowl, 19 1/2 In. 495.00
Figurine, F.David, Nude Woman, Bowl In Upraised Arms, 19 1/2 In. 695.00
Figurine, France, Napoleon On Horse, Military Clothes, 16 In. 1500.00
Figurine, Francesco Fanelli, Female Nude, 6 3/8 In. 3300.00
Figurine, French, Cherubs Reading & Writing, White Marble Base, 1870 .... 550.00
Figurine, G.Allan Wright, Bear, Hammered, 1964, 15 In. 100.00
Figurine, Gabbrielli, Fountain, Laughing Boy, Pouring Water From Jar 1200.00
Figurine, Garnier, Boy, Violin Under Arm, 15 In. 495.00
Figurine, Gautier, Mephistopheles, Rocky Base, 34 1/2 In. 2640.00
Figurine, German, Dancer Throwing Knife, 1925, 16 1/2 In. 3190.00
Figurine, Gerome, Woman, Upswept Hair, Long Skirt, 1900, 25 In. 4400.00
Figurine, Gladenbeck, Resting Soldier, Pensive Pose, 1900, 20 1/2 In. 660.00
Figurine, Gratchev, The Kiss, Soldier Kissing Sweetheart, 9 1/4 In. 1650.00
Figurine, Greyhound, Recumbent, English, 19th Century, 3 X 6 1/2 In. 495.00
Figurine, Halko, Flying Canada Goose, 8 1/2 In. 650.00
Figurine, Harpist, Empire Style Gown, 1910, 15 In. 1650.00
Figurine, Herbert Hazeltine, Horse, 11 In. 1000.00
Figurine, Hiolin, Aguador, Slave, Carrying Water Jug, 13 1/2 In. 660.00
Figurine, Holland, Clad Large Bull, Signed, 24 In. 260.00

Bronze, Figurine, Japanese, Stallion, Musculature, 40 In.

Bronze, Figurine, Standish, Elephant Head, Ivory Tusks, 11 In.

Figurine, Husset, Panther, Stalking Jungle Animals, 1925, 24 In. 1760.00
Figurine, Italian, Venus Marina, Nude, Standing On Waves, 17 1/2 In. 4500.00
Figurine, Japanese, Rabbit, Amusing Pose, 22 In. 500.00
Figurine, Japanese, Stallion, Musculature, 40 In. ....*Illus* 900.00
Figurine, Kauba, Crouching Indian, 4 1/2 X 3 In. 150.00
Figurine, Kauba, George, Dragon, Rearing House, Armor, 10 In. 1395.00
Figurine, Kauba, Indian On Horseback 2750.00
Figurine, Kauba, Over The Top, Horse & Cowboy, Cliff, 1912 .... 1500.00
Figurine, Lavergne, Snake Charmer, Man, Serpent, C.1880, 11 In. 850.00
Figurine, Leiberich, Borzoi Hound, Standing, Woerffel Foundry, 12 In. 2420.00
Figurine, Leroux, Aida, Egyptian Slave, Seated, Sphinx, 30 1/2 In. 8525.00
Figurine, Lion, Stylized, Seated, Gilded Traces, 2 3/4 In. 330.00
Figurine, M.Nunez Del Prado, Bull, Standing, 9 3/8 X 13 In. 650.00
Figurine, Mariotton, Winged Angel, Globe, Laurel Wreath, 1900, 34 In. 1580.00

Figurine, Mars, Classical Armor, Venetian, 17th Century, 6 3/4 In. 1540.00
Figurine, Masson, Equestrian Group, Napoleon, Seated On Horse, 24 In. 4125.00
Figurine, Mene, Dog, Playing With Ball, 5 X 5 1/2 In. 650.00
Figurine, Mene, Horse & Hound, Bending Down, 19th Century, 18 1/2 In. 3300.00
Figurine, Mene, Mare & Foal, 12 X 21 In. 1100.00
Figurine, Mene, Stag, Browsing, Large Tree Stump, 15 1/4 In. 2000.00
Figurine, Moigniez, Tigeress, Walking, Oval Base, 7 1/4 In. 650.00
Figurine, Moreau, Nymph, 1890, 31 In. 2500.00
Figurine, Mountain Goat, 9 X 4 In.Base 450.00
Figurine, Nicolai Schmidt, Veils, Ivory, Marble Socle, 14 3/4 In. 4020.00
Figurine, Paul Perret, Nude, Life Size 4950.00
Figurine, Pendaries, Farmer, Child, Hoe At Feet, 34 In. 3300.00
Figurine, Phillipe, Dancey, Polychrome, Signed, 16 In. 300.00
Figurine, Priess, Dancer, Marble Base, Rhinestones On Dress, 15 In. 425.00
Figurine, Prof.A.Miniati, Oxen Pulling Cart, Grape Pickers, 13 In. 450.00
Figurine, Rancoulet, Diane, Running, Holding Bow & Arrow, 7 In. 245.00
Figurine, Rebecca, Belted Robe, Shawl, Holding Bucket, 22 In. 980.00
Figurine, Remington, Mountain Man, Recast 1100.00
Figurine, Remington, Savage, No.15, Bill of Sale, 1918 .... 9500.00
Figurine, Ripamonte, Napoleon After Waterloo 2970.00
Figurine, Rodriguez, Nude Dancer, Clutches Head of St.John, 48 In. 4125.00
Figurine, Roman, Apis Bull, Red Marble Base, 3 1/4 In. 2000.00
Figurine, Sino–Tibetan, Young Buddha, Standing, 7 1/4 In. 400.00
Figurine, Spanish Dancer, Long Dress, Castanets, 1920, 10 In. 1100.00
Figurine, Standish, Elephant Head, Ivory Tusks, 11 In. .... *Illus*   850.00
Figurine, Stouffer, Interrupted Wooing, Couple On Monster, 3 1/2 In. 350.00
Figurine, Straeten, Woman, Pick Blossom From Tree, Basket, 30 In. 1650.00
Figurine, Thailandcrane, 1 With Erect Head, 1 Preening, 49 In., Pair 400.00
Figurine, Tourgueneff, Stallion, Rectangular Base, 18 1/2 In. 2200.00
Figurine, Two Women Fencing, Revealing Blouses, Petticoats, 19 In. 1980.00
Figurine, Venus De Milo, Late 19th Century, 13 3/4 In. 130.00
Figurine, Venus, Crouching, Marble Socle, 5 3/8 In. 660.00
Figurine, Vienna, Bear, On Ivory Pot, 1 1/8 In. 175.00
Figurine, Vienna, English Bulldog, Brownish Tan, Collar, 4 1/4 In. 650.00
Figurine, Vienna, Flapper At Rest, Pillow, 1900, 10 In. 1430.00
Figurine, Vienna, Polar Bear, Green–Brown Patina, 7 1/2 X 3 5/8 In. 450.00
Figurine, Vienna, Swordsman, 1880s 155.00
Figurine, Whippet, Double, Standing, Lying, Marble Base, 6 X 10 In. 750.00
Figurine, Willis Goode, Horse, Jockey, Groom, 12 In. 775.00
Figurine, Woman Bathing, Engraved A.D.N., Marble Plinth, 5 1/8 In. 1650.00
Figurine, Woman, Kissing Child, 1920, 9 In. 995.00
Figurine, Woman, Nude, Hands Clasped, 1930, 23 In. 1100.00
Figurine, Zack, Woman, Tea Dress, Upswept Hair, 1925, 15 In. 2200.00
Garniture, Louis XVI, Porcelain, Winged Putto, 4–Light, 1870, 3 Piece 4125.00
Garniture, Napoleon III, Gilt, Marble, Eagle, 6–Light, C.1860, 3 Piece 5775.00
Grand D'Illiers, Huntsman & Hounds, 9 7/8 In. 605.00
Group, Barye, Hero, On Centaur, Holds Mallet Overhead, 13 1/2 In. 6600.00
Group, Bouraine, Nude Woman, Child Seated, 1925, 22 In. 2750.00
Group, Gratchev, Cossack, Holding Maiden, On Horse, 13 7/8 In. 3200.00
Group, Gratchev, Troika, Over Snow, Woerffel Foundry Mark, 9 1/2 In. 1550.00
Group, Kauba, Mare & Foal, Paddock, Green Marble Base, 10 1/4 In. 1540.00
Group, Lanceray, Equestrian, Jockey, Resting On Mount, 15 1/2 In. 3025.00
Group, Leon Hermant, Lady Godiva, C.1931, 16 In. 1985.00
Group, Ludovisi, On Rock, Late 18th Century, Italy, 7 7/8 In. 2200.00
Group, Mene, Cow, Resting Chin, On Nursing Calf, 9 In. 1100.00
Group, Mene, L'Accolade, 2 Horses, 21 In. 7700.00
Group, Mene, Wolf, Attacking A Horse, 6 1/2 In. 605.00
Group, Mercie, Angel of Victory, Carrying Soldier, 4 Ft.7 1/2 In. 3520.00
Group, Pheasant & Fox, Rocky Mound, Vines & Stumps, 1880, 27 1/2 In. 4125.00
Group, S.DaRavenna, Neptune Riding Sea Monster, Marble Base, 17 In. 3575.00
Group, Tegner, Nude Cupid Shooting Arrow, On Mother's Knee, 41 In. 9350.00
Group, Vienna, Generals, Seated, Uniform, Hat & Sword, Vienna 140.00
Group, Woman & Gazelle, C.1935, 26 1/2 In. 1100.00
Incense Burner, Dragon Design, Foo Dog Finial, Chinese, 7 In. 80.00

Jar, Cover, Woman Amid Grape Vines, Branch Handles, Patinated, 8 In. 300.00
Jardiniere, Brass Strap Handle, Paw Feet, Russian, Marked, 12 1/2 In. 200.00
Jardiniere, Molded Crane Handles, Japanese, C.1900, 9 1/2 In., Pair 200.00
Jardiniere, Woman, Closed Eyes, Lily Headdress, 19 In. 2250.00
Lamp, Figural, 2 Nymphs, Entwined In Tree, Alice Maria Nordin, 20 In. 2750.00
Lamp, Figural, Greek Lady Playing Pipes, Iridescent Glass, 23 In. 3850.00
Lamp, Figural, Loie Fuller, Dancer, Draped, R.F.Larche, C.1900, 18 In. 6600.00
Lamp, Sculptured, 24K Gold, Golden Bee, Art Glass Wings, 20 In. 650.00
Mortar, Putti, Floral, 2 Handles, French, 18th Century, 16 X 17 In. 3575.00
Paperweight, Good Luck, Elf On Horseshoe 90.00
Pen Stand, Church Center, 2 Wells, Made For Long Wooden Pens, France 80.00
Plaque, E.Fraser, Teddy Roosevelt, Profile, Dated 1920, 10 X 13 In. 800.00
Plaque, Scenic Figures In Relief, Round, 9 In. 125.00
Plate, Art Nouveau, Nude Lady, Pond, Flowers 350.00
Sconce, Figural, Bacchante, 2–Light, Patinated Leafage, 35 In., Pair 4950.00
Sconce, Wall, Holds 10 Candlelights, Silk Shades, Pair 2500.00
Stand, Egyptian, Tripod Form, Wire Supports, 6 In. 225.00
Sundial, Roman Numeral, Mars, Achilles, English, 19th Century, 24 In. 1425.00
Urn, Birds In Trees, Applied Seahorse Handles, Footed, 9 1/4 In. 165.00
Urn, Champleve Iris Inlay, Elephant Handle, Drilled For Lamp 275.00
Urn, Charpentier, Nude Nymph On Top, Flower Handles, 26 In. 5225.00
Urn, Double Handles, Raised Florals, High Stand, Oriental, 14 In. 225.00
Urn, Greek Key Design, Loop & Angular Handles, French, 12 In., Pair 5500.00
Urn, Louis XV, Molded Glass, Lamp Mounted, Late 19th Century, 20 In. 1540.00
Urn, Louis XVI, Rouge Marble, Tripod Support, Ram's Heads, 25 In., Pr. 5775.00
Urn, Renaissance, Baluster, Strap Handles, Cover, 1875, 14 In., Pair 500.00
Vase, Art Deco, Carl Sorensen, 8 In., Pair 225.00
Vase, Dancers, Bird, Flower, Club Form, Bird Handles, Japanese, 11 In. 99.00
Vase, Floral Top, Allover Hammer Marks, Arts & Crafts, 9 3/4 In. 395.00
Vase, Phoenix Birds, Chinese, C.1800, 10 In., Pair 650.00
Vase, Sprays of Irises, Green, Handles, Cold Painted, 1902, 13 In. 525.00
Vase, Sterling Silver Windmill Design, Heintz Art, 3 1/2 In. 175.00
Vase, Symbolic Design Medallions, Chinese, 5 1/2 In. 100.00

Brownies were first drawn in 1883 by Palmer Cox. They are
characterized by large round eyes, downturned mouths, and skinny
legs. Toys, books, dinnerware, and other objects were made with the
Brownies as part of the design.

BROWNIES, Almanac, Palmer Cox, G.Green Woodbury, 1890 .... 18.00
Almanac, Palmer Cox, Illustrated, 1890 .... 35.00
Block Set, 6 Figures, Brownies, 9 Piece 75.00
Book, Bomba The Merry Old King, Palmer Cox, 1903 .... 25.00
Book, Jolly Chinee, Palmer Cox, 1903 .... 25.00
Book, Jolly Chinese, 1903 .... 25.00
Book, Monk's Victory, Funny Animals, Palmer Cox, 1911 .... 25.00
Book, Queerie Queers With Hands, Palmer Cox 30.00
Book, Wings & Claws, Palmer Cox 30.00
Box, Oatmeal, Tosting Oats Over Fire, Round 45.00
Doll, Hand Painted, 8 In. 25.00
Doll, Printed Cloth, Uncut, 6 Dolls 450.00
Game, Marble, Auto Race, Palmer Cox, Tin 35.00
Game, Palmer Cox, Dice & Sticks, Wooden Box 55.00
Humidor, Figural Head, Brownie Sailor, Hat Forms Cover, Majolica 150.00
Jigsaw Set, Litho Paper On Wood, Palmer Cox, 1892, 12 In. 400.00
Napkin Ring, Brownie, Signed 195.00
Napkin Ring, Silver Plate, Palmer Cox 25.00
Pencil Case 25.00
Pin, Blue & Gold, 1960s 5.00
Pitcher, 2 Brownies On Front, 3 On Back, 4 1/2 In. 65.00
Puzzle, Jigsaw, Uncle Sam, Canadian, Indian, Palmer Cox, 1892, 9 Pc. 400.00
Saucer, Palmer Cox 15.00
Sheet Music, 1909 .... 24.00
Stamp, Rubber, Brownie & Animal, Pad & Box 25.00
Syrup, Brownies Playing Soccer, Hinged Pewter Top, 6 In. 225.00

George Brush started working in 1901 in Zanesville, Ohio. He started his own pottery in 1907, but it burned to the ground and he joined McCoy in 1909. After a series of name changes, the company became The Brush Pottery in 1925. Collectors favor the figural cookie jars made by this company.

BRUSH, Cookie Jar, Brown Cow	48.00
Cookie Jar, Cinderella's Pumpkin	20.00 To 48.00
Cookie Jar, Circus Horse	75.00 To 100.00
Cookie Jar, Clown Bust, 1970	43.00 To 100.00
Cookie Jar, Covered Wagon, 1962	90.00 To 135.00
Cookie Jar, Cow, Cat On Back, 1970	24.00
Cookie Jar, Donkey & Cart, 1964	75.00 To 85.00
Cookie Jar, Elephant	60.00 To 110.00
Cookie Jar, Granny	75.00
Cookie Jar, Humpty–Dumpty	50.00
Cookie Jar, Little Boy Blue, Gold Trim	345.00
Cookie Jar, Panda	68.00
Cookie Jar, Peter Pan	110.00 To 195.00
Cookie Jar, Peter Peter Pumpkin Eater	125.00
Cookie Jar, Rabbit	55.00
Cookie Jar, Raggedy Ann, White Skirt With Patches	90.00
Cookie Jar, Teddy Bear, Feet Apart	40.00
Cookie Jar, Treasure Chest	32.00
Sun Dial, Pottery & Brass	425.00

BRUSH MCCOY, see McCoy

Buck Rogers was the first American science fiction comic strip. It started in 1929 and continued until 1965. Buck has also appeared in comic books, movies, and, in the 1980s, in a television series. Any memorabilia connected with the character Buck Rogers is collectible.

BUCK ROGERS, Atomic Gun, Tin Litho	55.00
Atomic Pistol, Atomic Adventure Comic Book, Box	250.00
Badge, Solar Scout, Brass, 1 1/2 In.	48.00
Book, Big Little Book, In The 25th Century, 1933	50.00
Book, Big Little Book, War With The Planet Venus, 1938	40.00
Card, Membership, Satellite Pioneers	60.00
Comic Strip, Full Page, Sunday, Dick Calkins, Late 1930s	10.00
Destroyer, Tootsietoy, Box	225.00
Doll, 12 In.	30.00
Doll, Mego, 1979, Box, 12 In.	30.00
Game Board, 1934	50.00
Gun, 25th Century	45.00
Gun, Clicker	95.00
Gun, Disintegrator	45.00 To 100.00
Gun, Rubber Band, Cardboard, To Be Punched Out, 1940	45.00
Gun, Squirt	60.00
Kite, Original Package, Unopened, 1946	65.00
Lunch Box, Thermos	22.00
Map, Planet of Venus, Black & White, 17 X 17 1/2 In.	75.00
Outfit, Rangers, Vest, Pants & Hat	65.00 To 100.00
Pinback, Celluloid, 1 In.	42.00
Popgun, Daisy	40.00 To 70.00
Punch–O–Bag, Radio Premium, Envelope	30.00
Puzzle, In The 25th Century, Inlaid, Frame & Tray, Wrapper	65.00
Puzzle, Inlaid, Box, Early 1950s	55.00
Ray Gun, Sonic, Norton Honer, Box, 1952	80.00
Ring of Saturn, Box	350.00
Ring, Repeller Ray	500.00
Rocket Ship, Windup, Marx	425.00
Space Figures, Metal, 3 In., 14 Piece	49.00
Spaceship	950.00
Toy, Rocket Police Patrol	425.00
Toy, Twiki, Silver Plastic, Battery Operated, Light, 10 In.	30.00

Watch, Pocket, 1935 .... 225.00 To 400.00

 Buffalo pottery was made in Buffalo, New York, after 1902. The company was established by the Larkin Company, famous manufacturers of soap. The wares are marked with a picture of a buffalo and the date of manufacture. Deldare ware is the most famous pottery made at the factory. It is khaki-colored transfer-decorated ware.

BUFFALO POTTERY DELDARE, Bowl, Fallowfield Hunt, 9 In. .... 425.00 To 450.00
Bowl, Ye Village Tavern, 9 In. 425.00
Candlestick, Ye Olden Days, Pair 575.00
Charger, Fallowfield Hunt, The Start, Hole, 14 In. 350.00
Chop Plate, Fallowfield Hunt, The Start .... 495.00 To 525.00
Cream & Sugar, Life In Ye Olden Days, Octagon 335.00
Creamer, Breaking Cover, 1908 .... 150.00
Cup & Saucer, Ye Olden Days .... 150.00 To 165.00
Fruit Bowl, Ye Olden Days, 3 1/2 X 9 In. 325.00
Fruit Bowl, Ye Village Tavern, 1908, 9 In. 370.00
Humidor, Lion Inn, Octagonal, 7 In. 650.00
Humidor, Sailor .... 700.00 To 750.00
Humidor, Ye Lion Inn .... 500.00 To 625.00
Humidor, Ye Olden Days 300.00
Mug, At Three Pigeons, 1908 .... 200.00
Mug, At Three Pigeons, 1909, 4 1/2 In. 280.00
Mug, Fallowfield Hunt, 1908, 2 1/4 In. 315.00
Mug, Ye Lion Inn, 1908, 4 1/2 In. 200.00
Mug, Ye Lion Inn, 1909, 4 1/2 In. 280.00
Mug, Ye Olden Days, Set of 4 .... 675.00
Nut Bowl, Ye Lion Inn 400.00
Pitcher, Breaking Cover, 7 In. 500.00
Pitcher, Dr.Syntax, 8 In. 675.00
Pitcher, George Washington .... 195.00 To 400.00
Pitcher, Great Controversy, 12 1/2 In. 725.00
Pitcher, Superior Air, 9 In. 525.00
Pitcher, To Spare An Old Broken Soldier, 7 In. 425.00
Plaque, Breakfast At Three Pigeons, 1908, 12 In. 475.00
Plaque, Ye Lion Inn, 1908, 12 In. .... 400.00 To 475.00
Plate, Art Nouveau, 8 1/4 In. 350.00
Plate, Dr.Syntax Loses His Wig, 9 1/4 In. 425.00
Plate, Evening At Ye Lion Inn, 1908, 13 1/2 In. 465.00
Plate, Fallowfield Hunt To Death, 1908, 8 1/2 In. 140.00
Plate, Fallowfield Hunt, Breaking Cover, 10 In. 180.00
Plate, Fallowfield Hunt, Start, 14 In. 510.00
Plate, Fallowfield, Start, 9 1/2 In. 190.00
Plate, Olden Times, 9 1/2 In. 150.00
Plate, Start, 9 1/2 In. 150.00
Plate, Ye Olden Times, 1908, 7 1/4 In. 145.00
Plate, Ye Olden Times, 1909, 9 1/4 In. 175.00
Plate, Ye Town Crier, 1908, 8 1/2 In. .... 125.00 To 150.00
Plate, Ye Village Gossips, 1909, 10 In. 155.00
Plate, Ye Village Street, 6 In. 185.00
Plate, Ye Village Street, 7 In. 180.00
Punch Bowl, Fallowfield Hunt, 14 1/2 In. 4000.00
Relish, Ye Olden Days, Signed, 1908, 12 X 6 In. 395.00
Saucer, Ye Olden Days .... 70.00 To 95.00
Soup, Dish, Ye Village Street, 9 In. 250.00
Tankard, Fallowfield Hunt, Supper, 12 1/2 In. 900.00
Tankard, Teach Dutchman English, 12 1/2 In. 725.00
Tankard, Ye Olden Days, Olive Green Base 650.00
Tea Set, Ye Olden Days, 3 Piece 325.00
Teapot, Village Scenes 350.00
Tray, Calling Card, Hunt 325.00
Tray, Calling Card, Ye Olden Days 200.00
Tray, Card, Dr.Syntax, Emerald 500.00

Vase, Ye Olden Days, Dated 1925	250.00
BUFFALO POTTERY, Butter Chip, Blue Willow	18.00
Chocolate Pot, Flower Design, Orange To Buff Ground	95.00
Creamer, Blue Willow, 1909	25.00
Dish, Feeding, Campbell Kids	75.00
Game Plate, Dusky Grouse, 9 In.	65.00
Grill Plate, Blue Willow	10.00
Pitcher, Chicago, 1907, 16 Oz.	70.00
Pitcher, Cinderella	400.00
Pitcher, Cover, Blue Willow, 1910, 6 In.	75.00
Pitcher, George Washington	225.00
Pitcher, Geranium, 3 1/2 In.	125.00
Pitcher, Geranium, 4 1/2 In.	175.00
Pitcher, Geranium, Blue, 6 1/2 In.	185.00
Pitcher, John Paul Jones	425.00
Pitcher, Pilgrim	500.00
Pitcher, Robin Hood	345.00
Pitcher, Sailor	525.00
Plate, 3 Ducks, Blue & White, Dated 1908, 9 1/4 In.	37.50
Plate, Abino, 9 1/2 In.	500.00
Plate, American Scenery, Niagara Falls Center, 10 In.	100.00
Plate, Christmas, 1953	60.00
Plate, Christmas, 1958	25.00
Plate, Christmas, 1962, Hample Equipment Co.	135.00
Plate, Fish, Marked, 9 In.	15.00
Plate, Gaudy Willow, 7 In.	75.00
Plate, Independence Hall	35.00 To 45.00
Plate, Mt.Vernon, 10 In.	45.00
Plate, New Bedford	35.00
Plate, Niagara, 10 In.	45.00
Plate, Purple Scene of Niagara Falls, Scalloped, 7 1/2 In.	35.00
Plate, St.Mary Magdelen Church Dedication	35.00
Plate, White House	45.00
Platter, Blue Willow, 10 3/4 X 8 1/2 In.	32.50
Platter, Blue Willow, 14 In.	50.00
Platter, Blue Willow, Dated 1919, 14 X 11 In.	45.00
Platter, Blue Willow, Rectangular, 1909, 14 In.	85.00
Platter, Deer, Green Border, Signed, 15 X 11 In.	50.00
Teapot, Argyle, With Tea Ball	125.00

Burmese glass was developed by Frederick Shirley at the Mt. Washington Glass Works in New Bedford, Massachusetts, in 1885.

Feel the edges of the design of the glass. Cut glass has sharp edges; pressed glass designs were molded into the glass.

Burmese, Bride's Bowl

It is a two–toned glass, shading from peach to yellow. Some have a pattern mold design. A few Burmese pieces were decorated with pictures or applied glass flowers of colored Burmese glass.

BURMESE, see also Gunderson

BURMESE, Basket, Hand Painted By D.Hill, 6 1/2 In.	750.00
Bowl, Floral Design, Applied Glass Rim, Marked, 3 3/4 X 6 1/4 In.	1110.00
Bowl, Piecrust Edge, 3 X 6 In.	350.00
Bride's Bowl ....*Illus*	2600.00
Cruet	250.00
Lamp, Fairy, Hand Painted Flowers & Butterfly	225.00
Pitcher, Crimped Rim, 5 1/2 In.	365.00
Sugar & Creamer, Applied Handles, 2 3/4 In.	785.00
Sugar & Creamer, Third Firing, Squat, 2 1/4 In.	495.00
Sweetmeat, Silver Plated, Basket Frame, Glossy Finish, 7 In.	335.00
Toothpick, Optic Diamond Quilt, Square Top, 2 3/4 In.	335.00
Toothpick, Square, 2 3/4 X 2 1/2 In.	175.00
Tumbler, Whiskey, Diamond Quilted, Mt.Washington, 2 5/8 In.	325.00
Vase, Bulbous Base, Tapering To Slim Neck, 13 In.	450.00
Vase, Clover–Shaped Top, Slender Neck, Bulbous, 13 In.	375.00
Vase, Cream To Pink, Bulbous, 10 In.	295.00
Vase, Fern Frond, Beading On Gold, 8 1/2 In.	195.00
Vase, Floral Design, Silver Plated Frame, 8 1/4 In.	510.00
Vase, Flower Petal Top, Brown Foliage, Pedestal Foot, 4 1/8 In.	295.00
Vase, Pleated Piecrust Rim, Acorn & Oak Leaves, 4 1/2 In.	395.00
Vase, Ruffled Rim, Acid Finish, 13 In.	850.00
Vase, Ruffled Rim, Acorn & Leaf Design, 4 1/2 In.	295.00

BURMESE, WEBB, see Webb Burmese

Buster Brown, the comic strip, first appeared in color in 1902. Buster and his dog Tige remained a popular comic and soon became even more famous as the emblem for a shoe company, a textile firm, and others. The strip was discontinued in 1920, but some of the advertising is still in use.

BUSTER BROWN, Bank, Buster Brown & Tige, Iron, Painted, Wooden Base, 6 In.	33.00
Book, Bill, Advertising	5.00
Book, Comic, No.36	10.00
Buckle, Belt, Tige	10.00
Card, Playing, Leather Case	75.00
Card, Valentine, Tuck, 1903	18.00
Clapper, Molded Paper, Advertising, Germany	55.00
Clock, America's Favorite Children's Shoes, Lighted, 15 In.	585.00
Comic 1/2 Page, Cincinnati Enquirer, May 6, 1934	15.00
Comic Page, & Tige, Time, Picaynune, New Orleans, 1917	10.00
Cup & Saucer	60.00
Dog, Stuffed, Tige, Steiff	125.00
Figure, Dog, Tige, 18 In.	125.00
Fork, Silver Plate	22.50
Game, Pin Tie On Buster Brown, Oil Cloth, 12 Ties, 30 X 27 In.	375.00
Knife, 3 Blades	25.00
Krazyskope	5.00
Mirror, Pocket, 1946	10.00
Pin, Buster Brown Bread	20.00
Pin, Membership ....8.00 To	20.00
Plate, 5 In. .... 25.00 To	40.00
Plate, 8 In.	35.00
Plate, Buster & Girlfriend, 6 In.	60.00
Plate, Buster With Tige, German	40.00
Plate, Tige & Buster Having Tea, 6 In.	60.00
Ruler	6.00
Shoe Trees, Figural .... 13.00 To	15.00
Shoehorn	15.00
Sign, Dealer, Pressed Board, 14 1/2 X 14 In.	35.00
String Holder, Counter Top, Buster & Tige, Cast Iron, 15 In.	550.00

Calendar Paper, 1900, Hancock Insurance Co.,
13 1/2 X 16 1/2 In.

Tinware, Pots, Pans, Skillets, Red Handles	125.00
Tool, Hatchet, Buster Brown Shoes	95.00
Tray, Pin, China	35.00
Yo–Yo	5.00

BUTTER MOLD, see Kitchen, Mold, Butter
BUTTERMILK GLASS, see Custard Glass

Buttons have been known throughout the centuries, and there are millions of styles. Gold, silver, or precious stones were used for the best buttons but most were made of natural materials like bone or shell, or from inexpensive metals. Only a few types are listed for comparison.

BUTTON, Civil War Uniform	10.00
Embossed Face Top, Sterling Silver, English, Box, 1901, Set of 6	175.00
Nouveau, Inset Coral Cents, Silver Rims, Set of 6	125.00
Painted Gold Flowers, Satsuma	45.00
Sharpsburg, Penna.Fire Department, C.1900, 6 Piece	20.00

Buttonhooks have been a popular collectible in England for many years but only recently have gained the attention of American collectors. The buttonhooks were made to help fasten the many buttons of the old-fashioned high-button shoes and other items of apparel.

BUTTONHOOK, Art Nouveau, Lady's Head, Flowing Hair Sterling Silver, 6 In.	65.00
Double Faced Cherubs Handle, Brass, 6 In.	37.50
Engraved Floral Handle, Marked, Gorham, Sterling Sterling, 8 In.	22.00
Figural, Woman's Head, Flowing Hair Forms Handle, Simons Bros.	65.00
Glove, Sterling Silver	38.00
Home Sweet Home, Larkin	10.00
Ivory, Spiral Carved	32.00
Keene & Mumma, Lancaster, Pa., Steel	4.50
Staub & Co., Lancaster, Pa., Steel, 5 In.	6.00

Unger Bros., Hollow Handle, Cupid, Dolphin, 8 In. 75.00
Walkover Shoes 8.00

Calendars made to hang on the wall or to be displayed on a desk top have been popular since the last quarter of the nineteenth century. Many were printed with advertising as part of the artwork and were given away as premiums. Calendars with gun or gunpowder or Coca–Cola advertising are most prized.

CALENDAR PAPER, 1881, Pierce Paints & Varnishes, Blacks Painting House 55.00
1882, Youth's Companion, Foldout, 5 1/2 X 17 1/2 In. 10.00
1886, Hood's Sarsaparilla, 5 X7 In. 50.00
1889, E.W.Hoyt & Co., Picture of Girl 25.00
1891, Arm & Hammer, Ruler Shape 5.00
1892, Hood's Sarsaparilla, Creased Top 80.00
1893, Hoyt's German Cologne, Girl, Fan, 3 1/2 X 5 1/2 In. 3.50
1895, Morrison Machine Co., Black Boy, Thorn In Pal's Foot 60.00
1897, Hood's Sarsaparilla .... 27.50 To 30.00
1898, Fairbanks 50.00
1898, Hoffman Hardware, Otterville, Mo., Black Scene, Framed 65.00
1898, Hood's Sarsaparilla .... 30.00 To 35.00
1898, Merchant's Gargling Oil Dream Fate, Songster 10.00
1898, Winchester Repeating Arms, Framed 325.00
1899, John Hancock Life Insurance, Girl In Middle 35.00
1899, Ludwig Pianos, Mother, Transparent Celluloid, Window 20.00
1900, Hancock Insurance Co., 13 1/2 X 16 1/2 In. ....*Illus* 33.00
1900, Youth's Companion 35.00
1904, Continental Insurance 17.00
1904, Hood's Sarsaparilla, Beautiful Women 42.00
1904, Youth's Companion 35.00
1905, Black Girl, Says Hush Yo'Bizness Bee, 10 X 14 In. 35.00
1905, Larkin Perfume Co., Die Cut 95.00
1906, Fidelity, Raphael Beck, Girl & Dog, 20 X 10 In. 11.00
1906, Larkin, Art Nouveau 35.00
1908, Clark's Thread, Victorian Children 31.00
1908, H.Tegtmeier & Sons, Fitzhugh Lee, 6 X 9 In. 28.00
1909, Metropolitan Life Insurance 55.00
1910, Cardui Medicines 20.00
1910, Hood's Sarsaparilla 20.00
1910, N.C. & St.Louis, Locomotives, 27 X 22 In. 350.00
1910, Stegmaier, Brewery Scene 850.00
1911, Iowa Store, Cawker City, Kansas 12.50
1911, Western Carbon & Ribbon Co., Girl, Holding Golf Club 18.00
1913, Crockery City Brewery, E.Liverpool, Ohio, 15 X 20 In. 275.00
1913, Pabst Extract, Woman With Parasol 85.00
1915, F.Schneider, Waltham Watches, Diamonds, 3 1/2 X 6 In. 6.00
1915, Hood's Sarsaparilla, School Days 48.00
1916, Twelvetrees, Small 8.00
1917, Army Recruiting Office, Perpetual, Tin Panel, 14 In. 395.00
1917, Little Fairies Bath Powder, Mother, Child, 9 X 10 In. 7.00
1918, Swift's Premium 45.00
1918, Swift's, Artist's Photos, 4 Pages, 8 1/2 X 15 In. 145.00
1920, Chevrolet Motor Cars, 14 X 30 In. 275.00
1920, Hood's Sarsaparilla 75.00
1920, J.W.Smith, Diamond & His Mother, Ocean, Signed, 12 In. 15.00
1921, Musselman, Outdoor–Type Girl Riding 20.00
1921, Winchester 325.00
1922, Baby & Mother, Color, 14 X 19 In. 25.00
1924, Wrigley's Gum 20.00
1925, Rexall Drugs 15.00
1925, Winchester Repeating Arms Co. 742.50
1926, Boy & Bluebird, Signed, 12 X 15 In. 32.50
1926, Farmers Trust Co., Anderson, Ind., Boy With Dog 22.50
1926, McCreight Lumber, When Storm Clouds Gather, 11 In. 35.00
1927, American Art Works, Girl, With Roses, Wade Traver 65.00

1927, U.S.Cartridge, Ducks 450.00
1927, U.S.S.West Virginia Battleship, Flags, Natives, Canoe 60.00
1928, St.Kerr Plumbing & Windmills, 8 1/2 X 17 In. 15.00
1928, Winchester 235.00
1929, Frigidaire 35.00
1929, Hercules Powder, Hunting Dogs By Fire 150.00
1929, Horse Review Calendar of Champions, Trotters, 12 Pgs. 36.00
1929, Land, Water, Air, Touring Car, 17 X 35 In. ....*Illus* 61.00
1930, DeLaval, Farm Pictures 18.00
1930, Rexall 15.00
1930, U.S.Ammunition 395.00
1931, McCormick–Deering, N.C.Wyeth, 1931, 14 X 21 In. 26.60
1931, Standard Auto Parts Co., Quincy, Ill. 28.00
1932, Santa Fe R.R. 55.00
1933, Doe–Wah–Jack, Fills His Creel 100.00
1933, Fairbank's Gold Dust Washing Powder, 7 X 10 1/2 In. 45.00
1935, Apple Blossom Scene, Card, Wallace Nutting, Envelope 50.00
1935, Keen Kutter 15.00
1936, Grocery, Yorkville, Ohio, 12 Pages, 12 X 16 In. 15.00
1938, Case Farm Mahinery 25.00
1939, En–Ar–Co, Little Boy 20.00
1939, John Rogers Group, Travelers Insurance 12.00
1939, Morrell Hams 10.00
1939, Skelly Oil Co. 12.00
1940, Lady, Sitting, Looking Up At Orange Parrot, Parrish 47.50
1941, Farm Boy & Dog, Norman Rockwell, Complete 100.00
1941, Gaynon's Dairy, Milk Bottle Shape .... 4.00 To 5.00
1941, Morrell, N.C.Wyeth, Story of Furs 25.00
1942, Vargas 50.00
1943, Ruppert 15.00
1943, United Airlines, 13 Scenes, Unused 20.00
1943, Utica Club Beer, 13 X 20 In. 30.00
1944, Gromman Aircraft, Planes, Spiral Book, 6 X 7 In. 25.00
1944, Vargas, Accordian, 6 Months Front, 6 Back, 4 3/4 In. 37.50
1945, Vargas 50.00
1946, Massey Harris 18.00
1946, Moran, Small 12.00
1946, Petty Girls 35.00
1947, Dionne Quints, Everybody Helps 18.00
1947, Ehret Brewery 24.00
1947, International Harvester, Caterpillar 45.00
1947, Pan American Airlines 15.00
1947, Petty Girls, Original Envelope 50.00
1947, St.Louis Browns, Baseball, 8 X 12 In. 13.00
1947, Vargas, Esquire 45.00
1947, Veedol Flying A Gasoline & Motor Oil, 18 In. 12.00
1948, Dr Pepper, 4 Pages, 13 1/2 X 44 In. 36.00
1948, Petty Girls, 6 Prints 75.00
1948, Seminude Lady, Sitting, Dog, Parrish, Large 120.00
1948, Vargas, Envelope 125.00
1949, Gulf Oil 20.00
1949, New Idea Form Equipment, 50th Anniversary 15.00
1950, 12 Different Pinup Girls, Earl Moran, 14 X 8 In. 65.00
1950, De Forest's Training, Girl In Front of TV 12.50
1950, General Motors, Pocket 25.00
1951, Esquire, Al Moore, Original Envelope 22.50
1952, 12 Different Pinup Girls, Earl Moran, 14 X 8 In. 52.00
1952, Tydol–Veedol 7.50
1953, Audubon 20.00
1953, Ford's 50th Anniversary, Rockwell Illustration 85.00
1954, Marilyn Monroe, Nude 30.00
1955, Marilyn Monroe, Nude, 10 X 17 In. 22.00
1955, Petty 35.00
1956, Knave of Hearts 325.00

1956, Penna.R.R., Pocket, Mountain Scene 8.00
1956, Petty, Esquire 30.00
1957, Nude, Advertising 8.00
1958, National Life Insurance 8.00
1958, Rock Island Lines, 13 X 20 In. 10.00
1960, Each Month Has Train From Different R.R. 6.00
1961, Chesapeake & Ohio Railroad 18.00
1965, Fischer Quints 18.00
1965, Maidens 5.00
1966, Nudist Daily, Day By Day, 365 Unretouched Photos 12.00
1967, Nude Living 5.00
1968, 12 Photographic Pinup Girls, Tiparillo, 17 X 12 In. 15.00
1972, Four Seasons, Norman Rockwell 5.00
1976, Hummel 10.00
1978, Ronald McDonald 3.00

Calendar plates were very popular in the United States from 1906 to 1929. Since then, plates have been made every year. A calendar and the name of a store, a picture of flowers, a girl, or a scene were featured on the plate.

CALENDAR PLATE, 1904, Holly & Berries 22.00
1907, Gypsy Girl, Canal Dover, Ohio 48.50
1908, Santa Monica, Advertising 35.00
1909, Gibson Girl, Peterson, Iowa 16.00
1909, Jamestown, Ohio 12.00
1909, Roses 25.00
1909, Santa Claus 38.00
1909, Woman Driving Car Center 35.00
1910, Cupid, Advertising 25.00
1910, Gibson Girl 20.00
1910, Use Mother's Pride Products 35.00
1911, Ducks In Flight, 7 1/2 In. 32.50
1911, Indian, Advertising 25.00
1911–12, Bosco's Cash Grocery & Market, Jacksonville, Fla. 45.00
1912, Biplane 40.00
1912, Mountains, Aviation Balloon, Advertising 30.00
1913, Airplane 35.00
1914, Horse Jumping, Dolan's Wine Store, Crazing 20.00
1914, Woman On Horse, Kansas 18.00
1915, Owl Center 25.00
1915, Owl On Book 18.00
1915, Panama Canal 123.00

Calendar Paper, 1929,
Land, Water, Air,
Touring Car, 17 X 35 In.

1916, Flags 15.00
1917, Battleship, Advertising 37.50
1917, Flag, Advertising 30.00
1918, Clock Design 22.00
1928, Good Luck, Blue & White 47.50
1955, Fiesta, Gold 27.50
1964, Nevada Centennial 10.00

Camark Pottery started in 1924 in Camden, Arkansas. Jack Carnes founded the firm and made many types of glazes and wares. The company was bought by Mary Daniel, who still owns the firm. Production was halted in 1983.

CAMARK, Candleholder, Triple 23.00
Console Set, Triangular, Green Drip On Pink, Label, 4 Piece 55.00
Figurine, Wistful Kitten, Powder Blue 22.00
Pitcher, Chocolate, Colonial Man 20.00
Salt & Pepper, Black Man & Woman 10.00
Sugar & Creamer, Pink 18.00
Vase, Blue & Green Matte Glaze, 16 In. 150.00
Vase, Blue, 2 Handles, 6 In. 8.00
Vase, Plum Red, High Glaze, 6 1/2 In. 50.00
Vase, Ruffled Top, 5 In. 50.00
Vase, Turquoise, Ruffled, 5 In. 22.00
Wall Pocket, Window Box, Burgundy 7.50

Cambridge art pottery was made in Cambridge, Ohio, from about 1895 until World War I. The factory made brown glazed decorated wares with a variety of marks including an acorn, the name "Cambridge," the name "Oakwood," or the name "Terrhea."

CAMBRIDGE POTTERY, Flower Holder, Figural, Green, 8 1/2 In. 65.00
Tile, Night & Morning, Pair 350.00
Vase, Green, Yellow, Cream, Oakwood, 8 In. 75.00
Vase, Honeysuckle, Terrhea, 9 In. 175.00

Cambridge Glass Company was founded in 1901 in Cambridge, Ohio. The company closed in 1954, reopened briefly, and closed again in 1958. The firm made all types of glass. Their early wares included heavy pressed glass with the mark "Near Cut." Later wares included Crown Tuscan, etched stemware, clear and colored glass. The firm used a C in a triangle mark after 1920.

CAMBRIDGE, see also Depression Glass
CAMBRIDGE, Adonis, Goblet, Water 28.00
Apple Blossom, Ashtray, 2–Footed 23.00
Apple Blossom, Bowl, Yellow, 12 1/2 In. 30.00
Apple Blossom, Butter, Cover, Crystal 90.00
Apple Blossom, Candleholder, Single, Keyhole, Pair 30.00
Apple Blossom, Candlestick, Keyhole, 1–Light, Pair 40.00
Apple Blossom, Compote, Mandarin, 7 In. 66.00
Apple Blossom, Cup & Saucer, Crystal 15.00
Apple Blossom, Goblet, Topaz 22.00
Apple Blossom, Puff Box, 3 1/2 In. 45.00
Apple Blossom, Relish, 3 Sections, Amber 25.00
Athena, Wine 12.00
Bashful Charlotte, Candleholder, Emerald Green, 13 In. 350.00
Bashful Charlotte, Cigarette Holder, Amethyst 40.00
Bashful Charlotte, Cigarette Holder, Carmen 65.00
Bashful Charlotte, Flower Frog, 8 1/2 In. .... 35.00 To 60.00
Bashful Charlotte, Flower Frog, Amber, 13 In. 180.00
Bashful Charlotte, Flower Frog, Crystal, 8 1/2 In. 55.00
Bashful Charlotte, Flower Holder, Pink, 13 1/2 In. 200.00
Bashful Charlotte, Plate, Green, 9 In. 75.00
Blue Jay, Flower Frog 62.00
Bookends, Eagle, Cobalt Blue 30.00
Bookends, Lion, Amber .... 38.00 To 75.00

Bookends, Scotty, Black Frosted	30.00
Buzz Saw, Tumbler	12.50
Canterbury, Tumbler, 12 Oz.	8.00
Caprice, Ashtray, Blue, 5 In.	20.00
Caprice, Bonbon, Crystal, 8 In.	12.00
Caprice, Bonbon, Handle, 6 In. ....8.00 To	12.00
Caprice, Bonbon, Square, 6 In.	9.00
Caprice, Bowl, 10 1/4 In.	24.00
Caprice, Bowl, 3 1/2 In.	45.00
Caprice, Bowl, Blue, Tab Handles, 4–Footed, 12 In.	35.00
Caprice, Bowl, Centerpiece, Ruffled & Fluted Rim, 12 In.	45.00
Caprice, Bowl, Cigarette, 4 Dolphin Feet, 4 1/2 X 3 1/2 In.	22.00
Caprice, Bowl, Cupped, 4–Footed, Blue, 13 In.	57.00
Caprice, Bowl, Footed, 10 In.	22.00
Caprice, Bowl, Sterling Silver Overlay, 3–Footed, 11 In.	35.00
Caprice, Candlestick, 2 1/2 In.	9.00
Caprice, Candlestick, 3–Light, Blue, Pair	98.00
Caprice, Candlestick, 3–Light, Tri–Level, Pair	40.00
Caprice, Candlestick, Prisms, Blue, 7 In., Pair	54.00
Caprice, Candy Dish, 3–Footed, Cover	40.00
Caprice, Cigarette Box, Blue	35.00
Caprice, Cocktail, Oyster, 4 1/2 Oz.	12.00
Caprice, Creamer, Blue	15.00
Caprice, Cup & Saucer ....9.00 To	35.00
Caprice, Cup & Saucer, Mocha	25.00
Caprice, Dish, Jelly, Crimped, Blue, 7 In.	40.00
Caprice, Dish, Mayonnaise, Underplate, Divided	79.00
Caprice, Goblet	15.00
Caprice, Jug, Blue, 32 Oz.	195.00
Caprice, Mayonnaise Set, 3 Piece	24.00
Caprice, Plate, 7 In.	7.50
Caprice, Plate, 8 1/2 In.	9.00
Caprice, Plate, 9 In.	25.00
Caprice, Plate, 14 In.	20.00
Caprice, Plate, Blue, 7 1/2 In.	15.00
Caprice, Plate, Blue, 8 1/2 In.	18.00
Caprice, Plate, Blue, 11 1/2 In.	35.00
Caprice, Plate, Blue, 17 In.	55.00
Caprice, Relish, 3 Sections, 8 In.	35.00
Caprice, Salad Bowl, 12 3/4 In.	24.00
Caprice, Sherbet, 7 Oz.	14.00
Caprice, Sherbet, Footed	25.00
Caprice, Stein, Blue, Clear Stem, 6 1/2 In.	25.00
Caprice, Sugar & Creamer	14.00
Caprice, Sugar & Creamer, Blue	30.00
Caprice, Sugar, Blue, Individual	14.00
Caprice, Tumbler, Blue, 12 Oz.	37.50
Caprice, Tumbler, Footed, 5 Oz.	9.00
Caprice, Tumbler, Footed, 12 Oz.	20.00
Caprice, Tumbler, Footed, Blue, 10 Oz.	35.00
Caprice, Tumbler, Juice, Blue, Flat	20.00
Caprice, Vase, 9 1/2 In.	45.00
Caprice, Vase, Blue, Round, 4 1/2 In.	80.00
Caprice, Vase, Globe, Blue, 5 In.	48.00
Carmen, Decanter, Crystal Stopper, 32 Oz.	65.00
Carmen, Vase, Gold Portia Etch, 10 3/4 In.	95.00
Cascade, Compote, 5 1/2 In.	12.50
Cascade, Cup & Saucer	5.00
Cascade, Goblet, Footed, 5 1/2 In.	4.00
Cascade, Goblet, Water	10.00
Cascade, Sherbet ....3.50 To	9.00
Cascade, Vase, 9 3/4 In.	20.00
Cascade, Vase, Green, 9 In.	18.00
Chantilly, Candlestick, 2–Light, Pair	50.00

> If two tumblers get stuck when stacked, try putting cold water into the inside glass, then put both into hot water up to the lower rim.

Chantilly, Candy Dish, Cover, 3 Sections	43.00
Chantilly, Cocktail Shaker	90.00 To 110.00
Chantilly, Compote, 5 1/2 In.	36.00
Chantilly, Goblet, Water	18.00
Chantilly, Ice Bucket	60.00
Chantilly, Mayonnaise Set, Sterling Silver Base, Lid & Spoon	65.00
Chantilly, Pitcher, 76 Oz.	145.00
Chantilly, Salt & Pepper, Sterling Silver Base	40.00
Chantilly, Sherbet	13.00
Chantilly, Sugar & Creamer	20.00
Chantilly, Sugar & Creamer, Farberware Holdler, Chrome Tray	15.00
Chantilly, Wine	38.00
Chrysanthemum, Pitcher, 4 Tumbler, Green	95.00
Cleo, Dish, Handles, Green, 11 In.	20.00
Cleo, Dish, Serving, Curved Sides, Handle, 11 In.	35.00
Cleo, Plate, Green, 7 In.	10.00
Cleo, Sugar, Blue	15.00
Coin Spot, Compote, Black, Dugan	10.00
Colonial, Serving Set, Child's, Cobalt Blue, 4 Piece	60.00
Colonial, Spooner, Child's, Cobalt Blue	35.00
Colonial, Spooner, Child's, Green	25.00
Colonial, Toothpick	30.00
Crown Tuscan, Basket, 2 Handles, Etched, Signed, 11 1/2 In.	35.00
Crown Tuscan, Bowl, 11 1/2 In.	50.00
Crown Tuscan, Bowl, 3–Footed, 11 In.	45.00
Crown Tuscan, Dish, Oval, 8 In.	40.00
Crown Tuscan, Ivy Ball	50.00
Crown Tuscan, Nut Dish	20.00
Crown Tuscan, Swan, 8 1/2 In.	155.00
Crown Tuscan, Urn, Chintz Gold, Cover, 10 In.	135.00
Crown Tuscan, Vase, Globe, 5 In.	44.00
Cup, Measuring, Pink	200.00
Cut Log, Creamer	20.00
Decagon, Bowl, Amber, 10 In.	25.00
Decagon, Creamer, Blue	14.00
Decagon, Creamer, Pink	7.00
Decagon, Cup & Saucer, Black Saucer, Crystal Cup	55.00
Decagon, Cup & Saucer, Green	6.00
Decagon, Cup, Amber	6.50
Decagon, Cup, Bouillon, Yellow	2.00
Decagon, Cup, Pink	6.00
Decagon, Goblet, Topaz, 8 Oz.	17.00
Decagon, Ice Bucket, Amber	25.00
Decagon, Ice Bucket, Amethyst	45.00
Decagon, Saucer, Pink	3.00
Decagon, Sugar & Creamer, Amber	20.00
Decagon, Sugar & Creamer, Tray, Green	35.00
Decagon, Sugar & Creamer, Tray, Pink	26.00
Decagon, Sugar, Footed, Pink	6.00
Decagon, Tray, Center Handle	12.00
Diane, Cocktail, Crystal	18.00
Diane, Goblet, Footed, 11 Oz.	9.00
Diane, Mayonnaise Set, 3 Piece	25.00
Diane, Relish, 3 Sections, 8 In.	24.00
Diane, Relish, 5 Sections	40.00

Diane, Server, Closed Handle, Amber 95.00
Diane, Tray, Center Handle, Heatherbloom 95.00
Dolphin, Candlestick, Pair .... 185.00 To 225.00
Draped Lady, Bowl, Pink, 9 In. 70.00
Draped Lady, Console Set, Emerald Green 250.00
Draped Lady, Flower Frog, 8 1/2 In. 75.00
Draped Lady, Flower Frog, Amber, 8 In. 125.00
Draped Lady, Flower Frog, Amber, 13 In. 195.00
Draped Lady, Flower Frog, Apple Green, 8 1/4 In. 25.00
Draped Lady, Flower Frog, Blue, 8 1/2 In. 350.00
Draped Lady, Flower Frog, Pink, 8 In. 115.00
Draped Lady, Flower Frog, Pink, 13 In. 185.00
Draped Lady, Flower Holder, Green, Marked, 8 1/2 In. 135.00
Eagle, Full Figure, 6 In., Pair 155.00
Elaine, Center Bowl, Gold Trim 45.00
Elaine, Champagne 22.50
Elaine, Compote, Jelly 20.00
Elaine, Console Set, Green Etched, 1–Light Candlestick, 3 Piece 47.50
Elaine, Pitcher, Tally–Ho Blank 130.00
Elaine, Relish, 5 Sections, Crystal 38.00
Elaine, Sherbet 22.50
Elaine, Tumbler, Iced Tea 22.50
Elaine, Vase, Footed, 8 In. 67.00
English Hobnail, Bowl, Amber, 6 In. 5.00
Everglades, Candelabrum, Double, 6 In., Pair 65.00
Everglades, Sugar & Creamer 35.00
Everglades, Vase, 10 In. 60.00
Feather, Cruet, Near Cut 30.00
Feather, Pitcher, Near Cut 50.00
Feather, Tumbler, Near Cut 12.00
Fernland, Breakfast Set, Child's, Box 135.00
Fernland, Creamer, Cobalt Blue 20.00
Fernland, Creamer, Green 20.00
Flower Frog, Turtle 125.00
Flying Nude, Bowl, Conch Shell 350.00
Gadroon, Bonbon, Yellow Square Handles 14.00
Gadroon, Relish, 6 Sections, Adonis Cutting 65.00
Georgian, Tumbler, Blue 12.50
Georgian, Tumbler, Emerald 12.50
Georgian, Tumbler, Red, 9 Oz. 15.00
Georgian, Tumbler, Yellow 12.50
Heatherbloom, Jug, Ball 225.00
Heirloom–5000, Bowl, Footed 19.00
Heirloom–5000, Creamer 7.50
Heirloom–5000, Sugar 7.50
Helios, Bowl 80.00
Heron, 8 1/4 In. 65.00
Heron, Flower Frog, Sticker, 9 In. 68.00
Honeycomb, Compote, Rubena, 8 1/4 In. 60.00
Inverted Strawberry, Tumbler 18.00
Keyhole, Candleholder, Stem, Amethyst.C.1920, Pair 35.00
Keyhole, Vase, Forest Green, 9 3/4 In. 35.00
Keyhole, Vase, Forest Green, 13 3/4 In. 60.00
Keyhole, Vase, Ivy, Carmen 55.00
Laurel Wreath, Bowl, 8 In. 10.00
Laurel Wreath, Plate, 8 In. 5.00
Laurel Wreath, Wine .... 16.00 To 18.00
Lily–of–The–Valley, Sugar & Creamer, Frosted 130.00
Magnolia, Cruet 20.00
Marjorie, Cracker Jar 90.00
Mt.Vernon, Wine, 3 Oz. 8.00
Nautilus, Decanter, Amber, 28 Oz. 34.00
Nude Stem, Ashtray, Amber .... 175.00 To 325.00
Nude Stem, Ashtray, Amethyst 90.00

Nude Stem, Ashtray, Crystal 150.00
Nude Stem, Ashtray, Dark Green 175.00
Nude Stem, Box, Cigarette, Amethyst, Short Stem 185.00
Nude Stem, Box, Cigarette, Amethyst, Tall Stem 310.00
Nude Stem, Box, Cigarette, Cover, Crystal 175.00
Nude Stem, Box, Cigarette, Crown Tuscan, Short Stem 200.00
Nude Stem, Box, Cigarette, Green, Short Stem 185.00
Nude Stem, Brandy Bowl, Blue Bowl, Moonlight 250.00
Nude Stem, Candlestick, Crown Tuscan, Pair 350.00
Nude Stem, Candlestick, Rose Point Etch On Base 775.00
Nude Stem, Champagne, Amber 110.00
Nude Stem, Champagne, Amethyst .... 100.00 To 110.00
Nude Stem, Champagne, Forest Green 100.00
Nude Stem, Claret, Carmen 350.00
Nude Stem, Clear Bowl, Ebony Stem 75.00
Nude Stem, Cocktail, Black 65.00
Nude Stem, Cocktail, Blue Bowl, Moonlight 200.00
Nude Stem, Cocktail, Clear Bowl & Foot, 3 Oz. 50.00
Nude Stem, Cocktail, Frosted Nude 175.00
Nude Stem, Cocktail, Gold Bowl, Crown Tuscan 80.00
Nude Stem, Cocktail, Smoke Bowl 250.00
Nude Stem, Cocktail, Yellow 150.00
Nude Stem, Compote, Crown Tuscan, 7 In. 125.00
Nude Stem, Compote, Cupped, Crystal, 7 In. 110.00
Nude Stem, Compote, Forest Green, 8 1/4 In. 125.00
Nude Stem, Creamer, Topaz 200.00
Nude Stem, Goblet, Banquet, Emerald Green 175.00
Nude Stem, Goblet, Water, Amethyst 160.00
Nude Stem, Ivy Ball, Amethyst 275.00
Nude Stem, Ivy Ball, Crown Tuscan 175.00
Nude Stem, Ivy Ball, Crystal .... 80.00 To 125.00
Nude Stem, Vase, Bud, Amethyst 650.00
Palm Wreath, Goblet 25.00
Peacock & Rose, Vase, Pink, 12 In. 65.00
Petal Swirl, Salad Bowl, Delfite, 9 In. 10.00
Pilsner, Cobalt, Footed, 7 1/2 In. 10.00
Portia, Cocktail Shaker 80.00
Portia, Plate, 6 1/2 In. 5.00
Portia, Plate, Handles, 7 In. 7.00
Rooster, Muddler, 6 Piece 95.00
Rosalie, Console Set, Footed Bowl, Pink 65.00
Rosalie, Mayonnaise, Pink 110.00
Rosalie, Relish, 3 Sections, Ebony 85.00
Rose Point, Bonbon, 2 Handles 25.00
Rose Point, Bonbon, 5 1/4 In. 25.00
Rose Point, Bonbon, 6 In. 25.00
Rose Point, Bowl, Footed, Gold Trim, 6 In. 35.00
Rose Point, Bowl, Handle, 9 1/2 In. 55.00
Rose Point, Butter, Cover, 5 In. .... 185.00 To 220.00
Rose Point, Candleholder, Keyhole, Single 50.00
Rose Point, Candlestick, 2–Light, Pair 75.00
Rose Point, Candlestick, 3–Light 35.00
Rose Point, Candlestick, Double, Pair 60.00
Rose Point, Candlestick, Low, Pair 60.00
Rose Point, Candy Dish, 3 Sections 85.00
Rose Point, Candy Dish, 3 Sections, Crown Tuscan 85.00
Rose Point, Candy Dish, Cover, 3 Sections .... 90.00 To 95.00
Rose Point, Cocktail 36.00
Rose Point, Cocktail, Oyster, Blue, 4 1/2 Oz. 28.00
Rose Point, Cocktail, Stemmed 30.00
Rose Point, Compote, 5 1/2 In. 42.50
Rose Point, Cordial, Stem, 1 Oz. 55.00
Rose Point, Creamer, Footed 18.00

Rose Point, Cruet	75.00
Rose Point, Cruet, Loop Handle, 6 Oz.	70.00
Rose Point, Decanter, 13 In.	250.00
Rose Point, Decanter, Gold Encrusted, 28 Oz.	200.00
Rose Point, Flip Vase, Amber, 8 In.	450.00
Rose Point, Goblet, 10 Oz.	21.00
Rose Point, Goblet, Blue, Footed, 10 Oz.	22.00
Rose Point, Goblet, Iced Tea, Footed, 12 Oz.	28.00
Rose Point, Goblet, Water	32.00
Rose Point, Mustard, Footed, Sterling Silver Lid, Crystal	170.00
Rose Point, Night Set, Crystal, 2 Piece	450.00
Rose Point, Pitcher, 80 Oz.	295.00
Rose Point, Pitcher, Flared, 64 Oz.	175.00
Rose Point, Pitcher, Ice Lip	175.00
Rose Point, Pitcher, Martini, Crystal, 32 Oz.	400.00
Rose Point, Plate, 6 In.	9.50
Rose Point, Plate, 7 1/2 In.	18.00
Rose Point, Plate, 8 In.	18.00
Rose Point, Plate, 13 In.	65.00
Rose Point, Plate, 14 In.	55.00
Rose Point, Plate, Center Handle, 11 In.	125.00 To 145.00
Rose Point, Plate, Handles, 11 In.	50.00
Rose Point, Relish, 2 Sections, 7 In.	25.00
Rose Point, Relish, 3 Sections, 6 1/2 In.	22.00
Rose Point, Relish, 3 Sections, 9 In.	35.00
Rose Point, Relish, 3 Sections, Handle, 6 1/2 In.	42.00
Rose Point, Relish, 4 Sections	125.00
Rose Point, Salt & Pepper	55.00
Rose Point, Sherbet	18.00 To 30.00
Rose Point, Sugar & Creamer, 3 In.	48.00
Rose Point, Sugar & Creamer, 5 In.	45.00
Rose Point, Sugar, Footed	17.00
Rose Point, Tray, Handles, 13 1/2 In.	47.50
Rose Point, Tumbler, 13 Oz.	40.00
Rose Point, Tumbler, Juice, Footed	35.00
Rose Point, Vase, Bud, Black	350.00
Rose Point, Vase, Footed, 10 In.	50.00 To 55.00
Rose Point, Vase, Globe, Gold Trim, Crown Tuscan, 5 In.	120.00
Rose Point, Vase, Gold, 8 1/2 In.	38.00
Rose Point, Wine	38.00
Rosylon, Butter, Cover	90.00
Rosylon, Sugar & Creamer	25.00
Seagull, Flower Frog	50.00
Seashell, Candy Dish, Cover, Shell Finial, Crown Tuscan	35.00
Seashell, Candy Dish, Footed, Crown Tuscan, Pink	35.00
Seashell, Candy Dish, Shell Finial, Cover, Crown Tuscan, 6 In.	65.00
Seashell, Compote, Enameled, Crown Tuscan, 7 In.	75.00 To 125.00
Seashell, Compote, Red Flower, Green Leaves, Gold, 8 In.	75.00
Seashell, Sugar & Creamer, Crystal	24.00
Shell, Bowl, Shell, Crown Tuscan, Decal, 8 X 8 1/2 In.	55.00
Star, Candleholder, Light Blue	7.50
Stradivari, Cocktail, Light Green	20.00
Swan, 3 In.	18.00
Swan, 8 1/2 In.	45.00
Swan, 8 In.	55.00
Swan, Head Turned, 3 1/2 In.	22.00
Swan, Mandarin Gold, Marked, 8 2/3 In.	85.00
Swan, Marked, 3 1/2 In.	25.00
Swan, Marked, 9 In.	75.00
Swan, Pink, Marked, 3 1/2 In.	25.00
Swan, Pink, Signed, 9 In.	225.00
Swan, Salt, Red, Individual	95.00
Tally Ho, Punch Bowl, With Ladle	100.00
Tally Ho, Tumbler, Footed, Royal Blue, 12 Oz.	28.00

Cameo Glass, Bowl, Orange & White,
Base Marked Jatt, 6 1/4 In.

The best time to buy an antique is when you see it.

Tally Ho, Wine	5.00
Teardrop, Candlestick, Double, Pair	58.00
Thumbprint, Compote, 7 In.	150.00
Twist, Candlestick, Jade, 8 1/2 In., Pair	95.00
Valencia, Sherbet, Low, Crystal	10.00
Wildflower, Candleholder, 2–Light, Pair	45.00
Wildflower, Candlestick, 2–Light, Gold Rim, Pair	45.00
Wildflower, Candlestick, 2–Light, Pair	20.00
Wildflower, Candy Dish, Cover, Gold Trim, Footed	68.00
Wildflower, Cocktail, Stem, Footed, 4 Oz.	25.00
Wildflower, Cup & Saucer	22.00
Wildflower, Goblet, Gold Trim	18.00
Wildflower, Ice Bucket, Handles	40.00
Wildflower, Plate, Gold Rim, 7 1/2 In.	12.00
Wildflower, Sherbet, Gold Trim	14.00

Cameo glass was made in much the same manner as a cameo in jewelry. Parts of the top layer of glass were cut away to reveal a different colored glass beneath. The most famous cameo glass was made during the nineteenth century.

CAMEO GLASS, see also under factory names

CAMEO GLASS, Biscuit Jar, English, Berries, Leaves, Frosted Vaseline, 6 In.	1995.00
Bonbon, Enameled, Blue, White & Gold Lace, Lobmeyer, 3 1/2 In.	185.00
Bottle, Cent, Simulated Ivory, English	495.00
Bottle, Perfume, English, White Cherries On Red, Engraved Lid	485.00
Bottle, Perfume, White Opaque Satin Ground, Floral, 3 1/2 In.	850.00
Bowl, Blossoming Prunus Branches, Burgun & Schverer, 8 In.	2750.00
Bowl, Orange & White, Base Marked Jatt, 6 1/4 In. ....*Illus*	175.00
Bowl, White, Pink Ground, Flowers, Leaves, Butterfly, 4 X 3 In.	1800.00
Dish, Sweetmeat, English, Plants On Sides, Square, 3 1/2 In.	1800.00
Inkwell, Citron, White Floral, Domed Silver Lid, 4 1/2 X 3 In.	1350.00
Jug, Claret, White On Cranberry Leaves, English, 12 In.	3450.00
Jug, Wine, Cranberry, White Leaves, Silver Top, England, 12 In.	3450.00
Perfume Bottle, 4 Carved Panels, Flowers, Leaves, English, 5 In.	1250.00
Perfume Bottle, Appears Like Ivory, English, 3 1/2 In.	595.00
Rose Bowl, English, White Leaves & Berries Cut To Blue, 2 In.	850.00
Shade, English, Spray of Maidenhair Fern, Blue, Pair	1500.00
Sweetmeat, Light Blue, White Plants On Sides, Square, 5 3/4 In.	1800.00
Vase, 3 Acid Cut Scenes, Sailboats, Michel Paris, 8 1/2 In.	750.00
Vase, 3 Layers, Trees & Mountains, De Vez, 5 1/2 In.	740.00
Vase, Amber Ground, Daisies, Leaf, Bud, 5 In.	1150.00
Vase, Arabesque Collar, Stippled Flowers, 12 1/2 In.	2500.00

Vase, Blossoms, White Over Indigo, Converted To Lamp, 12 In.	1250.00
Vase, Bulbous, Burgundy Leaves, Pumpkin Ground, 7 1/2 In.	395.00
Vase, Citron, Flowers, Elaborate Collar, Bulbous Base, 9 In.	1750.00
Vase, English, Blue Overlay, Carved Flowers, Leaves, 4 3/4 In.	895.00
Vase, English, Flowers, Leaves, Dragonfly, Citron, 7 1/4 In.	1100.00
Vase, English, Passion Flower, Butterfly, Blue, 8 1/2 In.	1450.00
Vase, English, White Flowers, Frosted Citron, 2 3/4 In.	550.00
Vase, English, White Irises & Leaves, Bottom Bands, Blue, 12 In.	2250.00
Vase, Florentine, Persimmon, Enameled Maiden, 10 1/2 In.	325.00
Vase, Florentine, Pink Overlay, Thorn Handles, 12 1/8 In., Pair	995.00
Vase, Flower, Leaves, Green, Black On Pink, 1900, Signed, 6 In.	595.00
Vase, French, Florals, Cherries, Brown, Gray, Pink, Arsall, 5 In.	395.00
Vase, Green & Peach Flowers On White, Signed Weis, 1 1/2 In.	650.00
Vase, Leaves, Cherries, Black To Maroon Base, Arsall, 5 1/2 In.	435.00
Vase, Lilies, Pads, Leaves Frame Top, De Vez, 5 1/2 X 3 3/4 In.	750.00
Vase, Red Overlay, White Carved Leaves, 3 5/8 In.	795.00
Vase, Red Spirals, Branches, Burgun & Schverer, C.1900, 10 In.	4400.00
Vase, Sailing Ship One Side, Lighthouse, Michel, 10 1/4 In.	1215.00
Vase, Spring Blossoms, Lappets Band, English, C.1900, 7 12 In.	820.00
Vase, Tulips, Deep Purple, Frosted Ground, 9 1/2 In.	575.00
Vase, White Leaves, Bird, Citron, Florentine, 5 In.	45.00
Water Set, English, Allover Enameld Design, Cranberry, 3 Piece	325.00

CAMPAIGN, see Political

The Campbell Kids were first used as part of an advertisement for the Campbell Soup Company in 1906. The kids were created by Grace Drayton, a popular illustrator of the day. The kids were used in magazine and newspaper ads until about 1951. They were presented again in 1966; and in 1983, they were redesigned with a slimmer, more contemporary appearance.

CAMPBELL KIDS, Ad, Full Page, Color	10.00
Ashtray	25.00
Book, Coloring	8.00
Cup & Saucer, Plate	110.00
Dish, Juvenile, Buffalo Pottery	48.00
Doll, Boy, Campbell's Soup	60.00
Doll, Squeeze, Rubber, 5 1/2 In.	10.00
Doorstop, Pink Dress, Blue Pants, Gray Dog, Cast Iron	145.00
Kaleidoscope, Vegetable Soup Can	32.00
Napkin, Paper, Kids Stirring Soup In Kettle, 1950s	4.00
Salt & Pepper	38.00
Spoon, Girl, Silver Plate	10.00
Toy, Farm Truck, Pull Toy, Wooden, Fisher Price, 1950s	79.00
Toy, Tool Set, Carpenter, Unused	60.00

Camphor glass is a cloudy white glass that has been blown or pressed. It was made by many factories in the Midwest during the mid–nineteenth century.

CAMPHOR GLASS, Bookends, Seal & Ball	125.00
Candlestick, 3 In., Pair	10.00
Plate, Kitten	37.50
Toothpick, Chicken & Egg	65.00

CANARY GLASS, see Vaseline Glass

A candlestick is designed to hold one candle; a candelabrum has more than one arm and holds many candles. The eccentricity of the English language makes the plural of candelabrum into candelabra.

CANDELABRUM, 2–Branch, Baluster Cups, Wide Saucers, Brass, 11 5/8 In., Pair	450.00
2–Light, 3 Tiers Glass Drops, Pineapple Finial, 19 1/2 In.	2200.00
2–Light, Gilt-Bronze Leaf Mounts, Floriform Holders, 14 In.	1650.00
2–Light, Iron & Oak, Adjustable, Chamfered Base, 41 1/2 In.	825.00
2–Light, Louis XV, Gilt-Bronze, Bisque Foo Dog, 18 In., Pair	2200.00
2–Light, Scrolling Leafage, Iron, 14 In., Pair	880.00
3–Light, Louis XVI, Bronze, Putto, Marble Pedestal, 16 In., Pair	825.00

3–Light, Louis XVI, Ormolu, Satyrs' Mask, Hoof Feet, 20 In., Pr.	4400.00
3–Light, Louis XVI, Putti, Ormolu, Marble Base, 23 1/4 In., Pair	8800.00
3–Light, Silver, 13 X 13 1/2 In.	55.00
3–Socle, Convertible To Candlesticks, Foliate & Shell, 24 In.	500.00
4–Light, Acanthus Leaf, Scrolled Arms, Gorham, 8 3/4 In., Pair	60.00
4–Light, Neoclassical, Held By Female Figure, 21 In.	900.00
4–Light, Parcel Gilt, Bronze, Marble Base, 1880, 21 In., Pair	225.00
5–Light, Empire, Gilt–Bronze, Lamp Mounted, C.1910, 29 In., Pair	2750.00
5–Light, Louis XV, Brass & Glass, Faceted Pendants, 25 1/4 In.	1540.00
5–Light, Louis XV, Gilt–Bronze, Dolphin, C.1870, 19 In., Pair	660.00
5–Light, Victorian, Bronze, Marble Base, Urn Shape, 33 In., Pair	300.00
6–Light, Brass Acanthus Scroll, Marble Columns, 29 In., Pair	350.00
6–Light, Louis XVI, Bronze, Crystal, Amethyst Drop, 30 In., Pair	4400.00
7–Light, Bobeches, Faceted Prisms, Central Arm, 32 In.	1980.00
7–Light, Silver Plated, Victorian, Grapevine Stem, 24 In., Pair	2475.00
8–Light, Louis XVI, Gilt–Bronze, White Marble, 25 In., Pair	2475.00
9–Light, Barbedienna, Bronze, Champleve Enameled, 30 In., Pair	5500.00
10–Light, Regency, Gilt–Bronze, Rouge Marble, Prisms, 40 In., Pr.	4950.00
Bronze, First Empire, French, Pair	3250.00
Clear Cut Prisms, Black Slate & Marble Base, 13 1/2 In.	25.00

Candlesticks were made of brass, pewter, Sandwich glass, sterling silver, plated silver, and all types of pottery and porcelain. The earliest candlesticks, dating from the sixteenth century, held the candle on a pricket (sharp pointed spike). These lost favor because in times of strife the large church candlesticks with prickets became formidable weapons, so the socket was mandated. Candlesticks changed in style through the centuries and designs range from classic to rococo to Art Nouveau to Art Deco.

CANDLESTICK, 3 Lion's Paws, Victorian, Brass, 7 In., Pair	48.00
Baluster, English, Brass, C.1850, 9 In., Pair	130.00
Brass, Baluster, Iron Pricket, Italy, 17th Century, 18 In., Pair	715.00
Brass, Candle Cup, Mid Drip, 18th Century, 9 In., Pr. ......*Illus*	1760.00
Brass, Initialed Base, 1 Piece Stem, 6 1/2 In.	180.00
Brass, Nuremberg, Mid Drip, 16th Century	1500.00
Brass, Oval Base, 6 In., Pair	50.00
Brass, Primitive, Rope Spiral Stem, 7 In.	40.00
Brass, Push–Up, 11 In., Pair	231.00
Brass, Push–Up, Beehive & Diamond Quilted, English, 8 In., Pair	90.00
Brass, Push–Up, Neoclassical, 6 3/4 In.	85.00
Brass, Push–Up, Round Base, Marked, 4 1/4 In., Pair	150.00
Brass, Victorian, 3 Lion's Paws, 7 In., Pair	48.00

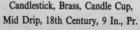

Candlestick, Brass, Candle Cup,
Mid Drip, 18th Century, 9 In., Pr.

Candelabrum, Bronze, Neoclassical, Female,
21 In., Pair

Brass, Victorian, Push–Up, Beehive, Quilted, England, 10 In., Pair 150.00
Bronze, Arts & Crafts, Copper, Nailhead, Eiffel Tower, 8 1/2 In. 425.00
Bronze, Dolphin, 14 In., Pair 685.00
Bronze, Figural, Woman, Holds Stick In Each Arm, C.1900, 16 In. 6050.00
Bronze, George III, Prism Chains, Wedgwood Standard, 11 In., Pr. 1325.00
Bronze, Gothic Style, 22 In., Pair 190.00
Bronze, Leaf Molded Socket, Green–Brown Patina, 7 In., Pair 1200.00
Bronze, Seahorse Standard, E.T.Hurley, 1916, 12 1/2 In., Pair 800.00
Bronze, Winged Harpies, 17th Century, Venetian, 7 1/4 In., Pair 8250.00
Copper, Hammered, L.C.Shellabarger, 1910, 14 1/4 In., Pair 495.00
Dancing Monkey, Brass, Pair 300.00
English, Brass, C.1740, 9 In., Pair 1870.00
Gilt–Bronze, Lion, Scrolling Arm, 19th Century, 10 In., Pair 2100.00
Gothic Style, English Registry Mark, Brass, 5 1/2 In., Pair 45.00
Hogscraper, Lift, 18th Century, Brass, 7 1/2 In., Pair 350.00
Iron Pricket, Stepped Base, Flemish, Brass, 20 In., Pair 3400.00
Iron, Hog Scraper, Iron, 6 1/2 In., Pair 80.00
Iron, Hog Scraper, Wedding Band, Brass 285.00
Iron, Hog Scraper, Wedding Band, Shaw, 7 1/2 In. 260.00
Iron, Spiral, Push–Up, Turned Wooden Base, 7 3/4 In. 175.00
Molded Cup, Shaped Standard, Domed Base, Brass, 10 In., Pair 2090.00
Parcel Gilt, Enamel, Floral, So.Staffordshire, 10 In., Pair 2420.00
Pewter, Push–Up, 9 3/4 In. 75.00
Porcelain Kneeling Children, 20th Century, 9 1/4 In., Pair 300.00
Pressed Glass, Honeycomb Variant, Flint, 7 3/4 In. 75.00
Push–Up, Beehive & Diamond, England, Brass, 11 3/4 In., Pair 190.00
Push–Up, Bobeches, England, Brass, C.1800, 7 1/2 In., Pair 175.00
Push–Up, Brass, 10 5/8 In., Pair 65.00
Push–Up, Threaded Band At Base, Brass, 8 In. 20.00
Push–Up, Victorian, Brass, 7 3/8 In., Pair 65.00
Push–Up, Victorian, Brass, 9 In., Pair 130.00
Sausage–Turned Stem, Trumpet Base, Brass, C.1690, 5 1/4 In. 1900.00
Sconce, Star Shaped Mirrored Reflectors, 2 Arms, 15 In., Pair 3800.00
Silver On Copper, Ship, Benedict, Viking, Triangular, 1927, 6 In. 275.00
Silver Plate, Blue Enameled, 7 1/2 In., Pair 20.00
Silver Plate, Elongated Pear Stems, Sheffield, 11 1/4 In., Pr. 995.00
Silver Plate, Knop, Campana Sconce, Sheffield, 12 In., 4 Pc. 1650.00
Silver Plate, Square Base, Acanthus, Thom.Law, 11 3/4 In., Pair 995.00
Silver Plate, Urn Shaped Nozzles, Domed Foot, 12 In., Set of 4 .... 775.00
Silver, George II, Campana Sconce, John Cafe, 9 7/8 In., Pair 3100.00
Silver, George III, 13 In., Pair 9460.00
Steel, Spiral Push–Up, Turned Wooden Base, 8 1/2 In. 165.00
Sterling Silver, Floral, Kirk, 3 In. 210.00
Sterling Silver, Gorham, 3 1/2 In., Pair 150.00
Sterling Silver, Towle, 3 3/4 In., Pair 150.00
Tin, 2–Light, Conical Base, Adjustable Pan, Repainted, 28 In. 80.00
    CANDLEWICK, see Imperial; Pressed Glass

 Candy containers have been popular since the late Victorian era. Collectors have long favored the glass containers; but now all types, including tin and papier-mache, are collected. Probably the earliest glass container sold commercially was the Liberty Bell made in 1876 for sale at the Centennial Exposition. Thousands of designs were made until the cost became too high in the 1960s. By the late 1970s, reproductions were being made and sold without the candy.

CANDY CONTAINER, Airplane, Army Bomber .... 22.00 To 35.00
  Airplane, Spirit of Goodwill ....95.00 To 115.00
  Amos & Andy 395.00
  Angel, Papier–Mache, Wax Face, Fur, German, 10 In. 575.00
  Army Hat, 3 In. 8.00
  Auto Lamp, Papier–Mache, Contents 80.00
  Baby Dear 20.00
  Baby Doll's Head, Composition, Round Box, Germany, 4 In. 350.00
  Baby Head, Wax, Screaming, Bonnet, Glass Eyes, Blond 350.00

Baby Nurser 20.00
Barney Google, Pedestal 175.00
Basket, Grape Design 35.00
Battleship, Glass, 5 1/2 In. 20.00
Battleship, Maine 15.00
Battleship, On Waves 85.00
Bear, On Circus Tub 250.00
Bear, Removable Head 295.00
Bell, With 3-D Santa Claus, Papier-Mache & Cotton, 4 In. 65.00
Boat With Sail 5.00
Boat, Colorado, E & A No.102, Glass, 1915-16 .... 75.00
Boot, Dress 35.00
Boot, Goodyear 75.00
Boot, Paper, German, 6 In. 45.00
Boot, Santa's, Merry Christmas Label 10.00
Boot, Santa's, Red Papier-Mache, Germany, 8 In. 20.00
Bristol Dice Mints, Square Shape 16.50
Brownie, Hatching From Egg, Wooden Legs, 6 In. 395.00
Bucket 15.00
Buddy Bank 495.00
Bug, Top Hat, Glasses, Composition, Germany, 8 1/2 In. 125.00
Bugle, Clear 20.00
Bunny Top & 2 Separate Bunnies, Cardboard, 1920s 25.00
Bunny, Composition, Pack On Back, Candy Box Base 125.00
Bunny, Papier-Mache, Brown, Glass Eyes, Removable Head 70.00
Bunny, Sailor Shirt, Composition, Germany, 6 In. 85.00
Bus, Victory Lines 65.00
Bust, George Washington 90.00
Camel, Lying Down 15.00
Camera, Tripod, No Bulb & Back 275.00
Candy Cane 50.00
Cap, Military 15.00
Car, Chevrolet Sedan, 1947 .... 35.00
Car, Lincoln Coupe 25.00
Car, Station Wagon 20.00
Car, Tassels 35.00
Car, Volkswagen 35.00
Cat, Black, Halloween, Germany 150.00
Cat, Black, On Box, Papier-Mache, Germany 95.00
Cat, Black, Pressed Cardboard, Painted, 1930s, 7 In. 95.00
Cat, On Pumpkin, Halloween, Germany 125.00
Cat, Sitting, Amber Glass Eyes 80.00
Cat, White, Papier-Mache, Glass Eyes, 7 In. 69.00
Charlie Chaplin, Next To Barrel 75.00
Chick, Pressed Cardboard, Glass Eyes, 8 In. 65.00
Chicken, On Basket 45.00
Chicken, On Basket, Original Paint, E & A No.147 .... 18.00
Chicken, On Nest 12.00
Chicken, On Nest, Cardboard Closure, 4 5/8 In. 35.00
Chicken, On Oblong Basket 35.00
Chicks & Mother Hen, Basket, Cotton, 2 1/2 X 3 1/2 In. 65.00
Child, Naked, 3 In. 25.00
Chinaman, Sitting On Log, Papier-Mache, Germany, 4 In. 245.00
Cigar, Pull Top Makes Flag, 4th of July 8.00
Clock, Mantel, Octagon 125.00
Clock, Oval, Milk Glass 85.00
Clown, Chalk Face, Ruffled Neckpiece, Pointed Hat, C.1860 .... 145.00
Clown, Papier-Mache, Nodder Nose, C.1900, 6 In. 350.00
Coach, Milk Glass 55.00
Cockatoo, Papier-Mache 32.00
Deer, Glass Eyes, Pewter Horns, Velvet, 9 1/2 In. 375.00
Dog Sitting, Round Base 100.00
Dog, Bulldog .... 25.00 To 30.00

Dog, Dachshund, Wooden, Tin Eyes, Felt Ears, Large 12.00
Dog, English Bulldog 22.50
Dog, Glass Eyes, Papier-Mache, 12 1/2 X 18 In. 650.00
Dog, Painted, Cohodas, Inc. 22.00
Dog, Scotty ....5.00 To 20.00
Dog, Shepherd, Papier-Mache, Germany 65.00
Donkey Pulling Cart 20.00
Donkey, Glass Eyes, Papier-Mache, Germany .... 185.00 To 215.00
Donkey, With Cart 15.00
Duck, On Basket, Yellow, Tin Closure, Some Paint 65.00
Duck, On Nest 60.00
Duck, On Rectangular Basket .... 45.00 To 50.00
Duck, On Rectangular Nest, Victoria Glass Company 70.00
Duck, Papier-Mache, Spring Neck, West Germany, 10 In. 55.00
Duck, Papier-Mache, Wing Lifts For Candy, Germany 30.00
Duck, Round Base 425.00
Duckling 25.00
Ducks Swimming, 3 .... 35.00
Ear of Corn, Painted, Tin Lid 35.00
Egg, Emerging Chick, Composition, Germany, 4 1/2 In. 135.00
Electric Iron 25.00
Elephant, G.O.P., Convention, Plastic, 1968 .... 18.00
Elephant, Howdah, Frosted Glass 100.00
Elephant, In Swallowtail Suit 325.00
Elephant, Sitting On Egg, Glass Tusks & Cup, 4 In. 225.00
Father Christmas, 18 In. 475.00
Felix, By Barrel, Mitten Glove 250.00
Fire Engine, Pumper, Glass 30.00
Fire Truck, Ladder 100.00
Football, 1930s ....8.50 To 10.00
Foxy Grandpa, Hatching From Egg, Papier-Mache, 5 In. 295.00
Foxy Grandpa, Jointed Arms & Legs, Removable Head, 7 In. 395.00
Foxy Grandpa, Squeaker, 1910, 8 In. 145.00
Girl, Draped In Flag, Kirk Soap, Hangs, 1897 .... 45.00
Glass, Fire Engine Pumper 30.00
Golliwog, Figural, Tin, 5 In. 125.00
Gun, Amber 40.00
Gun, Revolver, Amethyst 12.00
Hat, Army, World War II 12.00
Hat, Fedora 45.00
Hat, Military .... 10.00 To 28.00
Hen, Gray, Chicks, Papier-Mache, 2 In. 85.00
Hen, On Nest, Glass, Bottom Closure, Millstein 35.00
High Hat 20.00
Horn 20.00
Horse, Sparkplug, 1923 ....85.00 To 125.00
Irish Boy, Standing, Composition, Germany, 4 In. 95.00
Jack-O'-Lantern, Papier-Mache 28.00
Jeep, Cardboard Closure 15.00
Jeep, No Closure 15.00
Kettle, Green Flashed, Harbor Beach, Mich. 26.00
Kewpie, Standing Beside Barrel, Original Paint 50.00
Koala Bear 25.00
Lady Duck, Composition, Pink Bonnet, Germany, 7 In. 85.00
Lantern, Barn 35.00
Lantern, Beaded 20.00
Lantern, Dated 12-20-1904 .... 15.00
Lantern, Green Glass 10.00
Lantern, Red, Victor Glass, Complete 18.00
Liberty Bell 350.00
Liberty Bell, Amber, Tin Closure 18.00
Liberty Bell, Milk Glass, Dated 1885, 4 1/2 In. 195.00
Little Red Riding Hood 250.00
Locomotive, Jeannette, Pa. 27.00

Locomotive, Lithograph Closure, E & A No.496 .... 66.00
Locomotive, No.888 .... 75.00
Locomotive, Single Window 22.00
Locomotive, Tin Litho Closure, Papier–Mache 150.00
Mailbox 225.00
Man, On Motorcycle 275.00
Mickey Mouse's Bank, Filled, Box 25.00
Milk Can, Huylers, 4 In. 45.00
Mug 15.00
Opera Glasses, Milk Glass, No Closure 65.00
Owl, On Branch 55.00
Parrot, Papier–Mache 35.00
Pencil, Label, Candy, 5 1/2 In. 45.00
Peter Cottontail 225.00
Peter Rabbit .... 20.00 To 35.00
Potato, Painted, Tin Lid 25.00
Pumpkinhead, Halloween, Germany 125.00
Pure Milk, 4 Bottles, Wire Rack 60.00
Queen of Hearts 100.00
Queen Victoria, Blue Glass 70.00
Rabbit Head 14.00
Rabbit, Basket On Arm .... 50.00 To 65.00
Rabbit, Begging 5.00
Rabbit, Dressed As Baseball Player, Fabric Clothes, 8 In. 795.00
Rabbit, Eating Carrot 45.00
Rabbit, Glass Eyes, Papier–Mache, Germany, 6 X 7 In. 45.00
Rabbit, Glass, Millstein Co., Large 12.00
Rabbit, Head In Tree, Papier–Mache, Germany .... 195.00 To 245.00
Rabbit, In Dress 95.00
Rabbit, In Eggshell, Closure 85.00
Rabbit, Lop–Eared, With Basket, Papier–Mache 28.00
Rabbit, Mother & Daughter 595.00
Rabbit, On All Fours, Papier–Mache, Germany 24.00
Rabbit, Papier–Mache, Blue 18.00
Rabbit, Papier–Mache, Brown 20.00
Rabbit, Papier–Mache, Germany, 5 In. 25.00
Rabbit, Papier–Mache, Removable Head, 1919 .... 20.00
Rabbit, Pulling Girl In Cart .... 450.00 To 495.00
Rabbit, Pushing Chick In Shell Cart 350.00
Rabbit, Pushing Wheelbarrow 35.00
Rabbit, With Cart, Papier–Mache 18.00
Rabbit, With Little Girl Face, Mohair Cover 240.00
Railroad Lantern, Victory Glass Co. 12.00
Revolver, Waffle Grip, 8 1/2 In. 25.00
Rocking Horse 250.00
Roosevelt .... 200.00 To 250.00
Roosevelt Bears, Suitcase 95.00
Sailboat, Gold, Flat, Dresden 50.00
Santa Claus, Avon, 4 1/2 In. 85.00
Santa Claus, Bag Pack, Red, Chalkware, Paper, Germany, 8 In. 85.00
Santa Claus, Banded Coat, E & A No.669 .... 137.00
Santa Claus, Basket On Back, Papier–Mache 565.00
Santa Claus, Cardboard, Flannel Cape, Japan, 7 3/4 In. 100.00
Santa Claus, Composition Face & Feet, Fur Beard, Felt Coat 275.00
Santa Claus, Double Cuffs .... 52.00 To 75.00

Santa Claus, Full Figure, Head Closure	45.00
Santa Claus, In Boot, Cardboard, Papier–Mache Face	85.00
Santa Claus, In Sleigh, Rabbit Fur Beard, 6 In.	265.00
Santa Claus, Jolly, Screw–On Plastic Head, Papier–Mache	60.00
Santa Claus, Next To Chimney, Papier–Mache	55.00
Santa Claus, Nodder, Papier–Mache	550.00
Santa Claus, On House	55.00
Santa Claus, On House, Cotton	50.00
Santa Claus, On Woodpile, Germany	125.00
Santa Claus, Papier–Mache, C.1930	165.00
Santa Claus, Papier–Mache, Germany, 7 1/2 In.	50.00
Santa Claus, Papier–Mache, White	45.00
Santa Claus, Pointed Cap, Papier–Mache	125.00
Santa Claus, Slender, Blue Eyes, Papier–Mache	55.00
Santa Claus, Tree, Spring Nodding Head, W.Germany, 7 In.	55.00
Shoe, High	29.00
Shooting Stars, Gold, Flat, Dresden	50.00
Skull, Halloween, Germany	165.00
Snowball, Santa Claus Face, U.S.Zone, 3 3/4 In.	85.00
Snowman, Blue Hat, Removable Bottom	75.00
Street Lamp On Post	200.00
Submarine	295.00
Suitcase, Clear	35.00
Suitcase, Hand Painted Bears, Tin Closure, Milk Glass	65.00
Suitcase, Milk Glass, Tin Closure	60.00
Tank, 2 Guns ....22.00 To	25.00
Tank, Glass	12.00
Tank, Victory, With Driver, Glass	45.00
Tank, World War I, Electric Blue	155.00
Telephone, Candlestick	20.00
Telephone, Candlestick, Wooden Receiver	25.00
Telephone, Dial, Label, Jeannette Glass Co.	45.00
Telephone, Pewter Screw Top, Wooden Receiver, 4 1/4 In.	95.00
Telephone, Victory Glass Co.	22.00
This Little Pig	100.00
Toonerville Trolley ....300.00 To	675.00
Train ....20.00 To	60.00
Trunk, Gold & Floral, Bryon, Illinois, Milk Glass	125.00
Trunk, Hand Painted Teddy Bears, Milk Glass	65.00
Turkey, 6 In.	45.00
Turkey, Papier–Mache, 5 In.	30.00
Turkey, Papier–Mache, 8 In.	25.00
Turkey, Papier–Mache, 10 In.	35.00
U.S.Mail	95.00
Uncle Sam, By Barrel	275.00
Vegetable Head, Papier–Mache ....95.00 To	120.00
Watch	20.00
Windmill, Contents, Label	55.00
Witch, Halloween, Germany	285.00
World Globe	350.00

Canes and walking sticks were used by every well–dressed man in the nineteenth century, but by World War I the style had changed. Today canes are used by few but the infirm. Collectors prize old canes made with special features such as hidden swords, whiskey flasks, or risque pictures seen through peepholes. Examples with solid gold heads or made from exotic materials such as walrus vertebrae are among the higher priced canes.

CANE, 2 Handles, Folding, Amber & Silver, Case	785.00
Animated, Uncle Sam, Ivory, Button On Head Pressed, Jaw Drops, 35 In.	1400.00
Bamboo Type, Umbrella Inside	60.00
Bird's–Eye Maple	25.00
Blown Glass, Green, C.1910	95.00
Bronze Eagle Handle, Mounted On Lapis	200.00

Cane, Ivory, Uncle Sam,
Brass Tip, 35 In.

Carnival Glass, Good Luck, Bowl,
Piecrust Edge, Aqua

Bulb Head, Barber Pole Style, Glass, 57 In.	225.00
Bulbous Top, Threaded Glass, Pointed Tip	95.00
Bulldog Head	25.00
Candleholder & Matchstick Container	585.00
Carved Bulldog Handle, Glass Eyes, Silver Trim, 37 In.	275.00
Carved Horn, Ivory Inlay, Prussian Naval Officer	750.00
Carved Ivory Handle, Dragon, Clouds, Butterfly, Japan	500.00
Carved Ivory Knob, Fist, Horn Divider, 34 3/4 In.	225.00
Glass, Aqua	75.00
Glass, Swirl Pattern, Red & White Stripes Inside, 36 In.	145.00
Greyhound Head, Glass Eyes, Silver Band, Ivory	485.00
Ivory Bulldog Head Handle, Silver Collar, Garnet Eyes	575.00
Ivory, Late 1800s, 34 1/2 In.	350.00
Ivory, Uncle Sam, Brass Tip, 35 In. ....*Illus*	1400.00
Parade, Swirl Pattern, Red & White Stripes Inside, 36 In.	145.00
Riding Crop, Carved Animal Leg & Hoof Bone Handle, 27 In.	20.00
Sandwich Glass	330.00
Snake Wrapped Around Art Nouveau Log, Silver & Wood	495.00
Sterling Silver, Bird Head Handle	125.00
Sword, Carved Bone, Lion Head Top, 35 3/4 In.	65.00
Telescope, Ivory Knob, Brass Telescope	850.00
Walking Stick, 2 Spiraling Snakes, Black Stripes, 33 3/4 In.	110.00
Walking Stick, Amber Blown, Swirled Ribs, Hollow Bulbous Head, 41 In.	50.00
Walking Stick, Aultman Co.Mfgr's Threshers, Engines, Canton, Ohio	15.00
Walking Stick, Burlwood, Smiling Black Man's Face, 35 1/2 In.	880.00
Walking Stick, Carved Indian Head, Polychrome Paint, 37 In.	100.00
Walking Stick, Carved Pine, Serpents, Bullfrog, 37 In.	3740.00
Walking Stick, Double Spiral Snakes, Gold Paint, Black Shaft, 33 In.	175.00
Walking Stick, Female Acrobat Mounted On Ball In Cage, C.1900	900.00
Walking Stick, Fist, Clutching Scroll, Carved Date 1931, 39 In.	170.00
Walking Stick, Gnarled Knobby Shank, Relief Carving, Xmas, 1898, 33 In.	125.00
Walking Stick, Gnarled Sapling, Root & Burl Handle, Carved, 35 1/2 In.	105.00
Walking Stick, Gold Head, C.Engalls 70th Birthday, Friends, 1808–78	175.00
Walking Stick, Ivory Knob, Brass Ferule, 32 3/4 In.	100.00
Walking Stick, Ivory Tip, Bulbous Knob, Mahogany, 33 In.	275.00
Walking Stick, Rattlesnake Curled Around Stick, Open Mouth, C.1900	325.00
Walking Stick, Root Head, Horned Animal Shape, Glass Eyes, 34 In.	115.00
Walking Stick, Spiraling Snake, Ink Drawn Scales, Ash, 36 In.	100.00
Walking Stick, Tooled Gold Finish Knob, Presentation, 1885, 34 In.	90.00
Walking Stick, Twisted Carved Snake, Grape Vine, Natural Shaft	120.00
Walking Stick, Vertebrae, Horn Segments & Knob, 33 1/2 In.	35.00
Walking Stick, World's Fair, 1939	55.00

Western Dance Hall Girl, Sitting At Top, Ivory 575.00

Caneware is a tan–colored, unglazed stoneware that was first developed by Josiah Wedgwood about 1770. It has been made by many companies since that time and is often used for cooking or serving utensils.

CANEWARE, Basket, Chestnut, Cover, Twisted Handle, C.1800, 4 X 7 3/4 In. 100.00
Tureen, Rabbits, Grapes, 10 In. 150.00

Canton china is blue–and–white ware made near Canton, China, from about 1785 to 1895. It is hand decorated with Chinese scenes.

CANTON, Bowl, Cut–Corner, Pagoda Pattern, Cloud Border, Teak Stand, 10 In. 300.00
Bowl, Salad, Scene, Shaped Rim, Notched Corners, 41 3/4 X 10 1/2 In. 650.00
Bowl, Vegetable, Lozenge, Cover 250.00
Butter Pat, Blue & White, 2 3/4 In., Set of 4 .... 110.00
Cache Pot, Underplate, Blue & White, Hexagonal, 14 In., Pair 400.00
Dish, Serving, Canton Scene, Rain Cloud Border, Oval, 10 3/4 In. 175.00
Dish, Serving, Scene, Rain Cloud Border, Scalloped, Domed Base, 10 In. 325.00
Dish, Shrimp, Fan Shaped Handle Top, Rain Cloud Border, 10 3/8 In. 275.00
Ewer, 12 In. 1210.00
Jar, Ginger, 6 In. 155.00
Jar, Ginger, Blue & White, 4 1/2 In. 10.00
Jar, Ginger, Cover, Pagoda Pattern, Blue & White, 7 In. 85.00
Plate, Pagoda Pattern, Blue & White, 8 1/2 In. 20.00
Platter, 10 X 6 1/2 In. 110.00
Platter, Orange Peel Glaze, Blue & White, 16 In. 375.00
Platter, Orange Peel Glaze, Blue & White, 18 1/2 In. 550.00
Platter, Pagoda, Mountains, Squared Corners, 10 1/2 In. 150.00
Platter, Rain Cloud Border, 19th Century, 10 1/2 X 13 1/2 In. 200.00
Sauce, Blue & White, 5 In. 10.00
Soap Dish, 3–Part 880.00
Teapot, Pagoda Finial, Square 1650.00
Tureen, Domed Cover, Boar's Head Handles, Octagonal, 6 1/2 X 12 In. 450.00
Vegetable, Lotus Bud Finial, Rain Cloud Border, Cover, 11 In. 225.00

N

Capo–di–Monte porcelain was first made in Naples, Italy, from 1743 to 1759. The factory moved near Madrid, Spain, and reopened in 1771 and worked to 1834. Since that time the Doccia factory of Italy acquired the molds and is using the N and crown mark. Societe Richard Ceramica is a modern–day firm often referred to as Ginori or Capo–di–Monte. This company uses the crown and N mark.

CAPO-DI-MONTE, Bowl, Bacchanalian Scene, Leopards, 1860, 14 In. 175.00
Card Holder, Figural, Art Deco, Pearlized, Black 30.00
Clock, Tinted Children, Gold, Queen Anne Legs, 9 In. 95.00
Cup & Saucer, Chocolate, Miniature Figures, Cover, 1860 .... 100.00
Cup, Chocolate, Cupid Cover, Miniature Figures, 1870 .... 140.00
Ewer, Sea Horse & Mermaids, 16 In., Pair 75.00
Figurine, African Crowned Crane, Foot In Water, 14 In. 150.00
Figurine, Clown, Playing A Violin, 12 In. 450.00
Figurine, Girl, Holding Bouquet, Signed, 10 In. 125.00
Figurine, Pearl Fisherman, Bonalberti, 9 1/2 In. 175.00
Group, Lovers, With Dog, C.1750, X Mark, 7 11/16 In. 4400.00
Lamp, Urn Form, Young Maiden, Cherubs, 17 In., Pair 350.00
Mug, Satyr, 1900 .... 85.00
Tureen, Cherubs, Blue, Crown Mark 145.00
Urn & Bowl, Bas Relief Figures, Gold, Pedestal, Cover, 3 Pc. 100.00
Urn, Bacchanalian Scenes, 8 In., Pair 200.00
Urn, Classical Women & Cherubs, Gold Trim, Marked, 7 In. 165.00

Captain Marvel was introduced in February 1940 in Whiz comic books. An orphan named Billy Batson met the wizard Shazam and whenever he said the magic word he was transformed into a superhero. A movie serial was released in 1940. The comic was

discontinued in 1954. A second Captain Marvel appeared in 1966, a
third in 1967. Only the original was transformed by shouting
"Shazam."

CAPTAIN MARVEL, Bank, Dime, Magic	140.00
Button, Clu Shazam, Red & Yellow, 1 3/4 In.	25.00
Car, Race, Windup, Fawcett, 1947, 4 In.	240.00
Card, Club Membership, 1941	75.00
Cutout, Original Envelope	7.50
Decoder	35.00
Paper Doll, Flying Marvel Family, Folder, Uncut	14.00
Pennant	30.00
Photograph, Movie Promotional, 1940s	95.00
Pin, Club, Shazam	28.00
Puzzle, Find The Heroes, Paper	30.00
Tie Clip, On Original Card, Dated 1946	110.00
Wristwatch	150.00

Captain Midnight began as a radio show in September 1940. The
first comic book appeared in July 1941. Captain Midnight was really
the aviator Captain Albright, who was to defeat the Nazis. A movie
serial was made in 1942 and a comic strip was published for a short
time. The comic book Captain Midnight ended his career in 1948.
The radio premiums are the prized collector memorabilia today.

CAPTAIN MIDNIGHT, Album, Stamp, Skelly Oil, All Stamps	45.00
Badge, Decoder, 1949	15.50
Decoder Whistle, 1947	35.00
Decoder, 1941	32.00 To 40.00
Decoder, 1947	28.00
Manual, 1947	22.00
Medal, Flight Patrol, 1940	7.00
Medal, Membership, 1940	25.00 To 40.00
Membership Medal, Chain Fob, Skelly Oil Co., 1940	15.00
Mug, Ovaltine	25.00
Watch Fob, Spinner, Brass, 1940	37.50

CARAMEL SLAG, see Chocolate Glass

The cards listed here include advertising cards, greeting cards,
baseball cards, playing cards, valentines, and others. Color pictures
were rare in the nineteenth century, so companies gave away
colorful cards with pictures of children, flowers, products, or related
scenes that promoted the company name. These were often collected
and stored in albums. Greeting cards are also a nineteenth–century
idea that has remained popular. Baseball cards also date from the
nineteenth century when they were used by tobacco companies as
giveaways. The gum cards were started in 1933, but it was not until
after World War II that the bubble gum cards favored today were
produced. Today over 1,000 cards are issued each year by the gum
companies.

CARD, see also Postcard

CARD, Advertising, Adriance Rear Discharge Binder, 5 X 7 1/2 In.	5.50
Advertising, Anglo Swiss Condensed Milk, Paris	10.00
Advertising, Arbuckle Bros., Animal Series, Color, 1892	4.00
Advertising, Armour Extract Soup	4.00
Advertising, Aunt Jemima, C.1880	8.00
Advertising, Ayers Cherry Pectoral, C.1878	8.00
Advertising, Ayers Pills, Girl Holding Cat	5.00
Advertising, Bird, Arm & Hammer, 9th Series, 15 Cards	10.00
Advertising, C.C.C.Certain Chill Cure, Cottage, Texas Dealer's Name	6.00
Advertising, C.I.Hood & Co., Sarsaparilla, Stag, Blue Print	4.50
Advertising, Cigarette Girl, Actress, C.1890, 14 Piece	20.00
Advertising, Clark's O.N.T.Spool Cotton, Delaware Water Gap, 5 In.	4.00
Advertising, Cleveland's Baking Powder, Donaldson Bros.	10.00

Advertising, Consolidated Coffee, German Hop Yeast, 3 X 5 In. 4.00
Advertising, Currier & Ives, Blood Will Tell, 1879 .... 65.00
Advertising, Currier & Ives, Boss of The Road, 1880 .... 65.00
Advertising, Currier & Ives, Hung Up With The Starch Out, 1878 .... 65.00
Advertising, Currier & Ives, Jolly Smoker, 1880 .... 70.00
Advertising, Currier & Ives, La Cigarita 70.00
Advertising, Currier & Ives, Where Do You Buy Your Cigars, 1880 .... 65.00
Advertising, Dr. Kilmer's Indian Cough Cure 7.00
Advertising, Dr.Hand's Remedies For Children 12.00
Advertising, Dr.Sanford's Liver Invigorator, Stag Picture, Foldout 7.50
Advertising, Drummond Tobacco Co. 10.00
Advertising, Duryea's Corn Starch, Major Knapp Lithograph, C.1879 .... 12.00
Advertising, Edison's Polyform, Cures Himself, Lithograph 9.50
Advertising, Eulalie Flour, Girl On Front, Advertising Back, 1895 .... 5.00
Advertising, Everett Piano, People Looking In Window, Piano Player 25.00
Advertising, Fail & Ax Navy Long Cut Tobacco, Lady, Advertising Back 6.00
Advertising, Fur Company, Black Boy Grabbing Fur Tail, 6 X 4 In. 45.00
Advertising, Garland Stoves & Ranges, Black Entering Messed Up Room 8.00
Advertising, Hecker's Flour, Hatch Lithograph, 1881 .... 5.00
Advertising, Heinz Pickle, 2 X 5 1/2 In. 16.00
Advertising, Hershey Chocolate & Cocoa, Dressed Cat 3.50
Advertising, Hood's Pills, Cure Liver Ills, Die Cut Card 8.00
Advertising, Hoyt's German Cologne, 4 1/2 X 2 3/4 In. 5.00
Advertising, Hunt's Remedy, Boy In Sailor Hat 6.00
Advertising, Huyler's Chocolates, Lake, 1880 .... 7.50
Advertising, International Industrial Fair, Buffalo, 1888 .... 7.50
Advertising, Jackson's Best Chewing Tobacco, Mechanical, 1880s 37.50
Advertising, Jockey Club, Man With Huge Cigar 70.00
Advertising, Just Because–Cherry Beauty Sunday, Ice Cream, 1912 .... 95.00
Advertising, Ladies Visiting G.A.R.Encampment, St.Paul, 1896 .... 7.00
Advertising, Lawrence's Bread, Kiddie Cutout, Peter Pan, Santa, 5 Pc. 15.00
Advertising, Liebig Extract, Paris 10.00
Advertising, Lion Coffee, Santa Claus, Large 10.00
Advertising, Mennen's Talcum Powder, C.1884 .... 10.00
Advertising, Monitor Rake, Horse–Drawn Riding Rake, Full Color 8.50
Advertising, Moody Hotel & Bath House, Hot Springs, Ark., Lithograph 5.00
Advertising, Niagara Starch & Sweet, C.1887 .... 6.00
Advertising, Patented Illumination Candlesticks, 1861, 10 X 8 In. 400.00
Advertising, Patrons of Husbandry, Political Group, Foldover, 1884 .... 27.50
Advertising, Perfect Cereals, C.1888, 3 X 5 In. 12.00
Advertising, Pillsbury, 3 Ladies Standing On Top, 3 X 5 In. 5.00
Advertising, Playing, Busch, Blue & Red Logo 2.50
Advertising, Playing, Christo Cola 8.00
Advertising, Playing, Hard–A–Port 45.00
Advertising, Puzzle, Toll Gate No.2, Man Talking To Face, 1879 .... 4.00
Advertising, Quaker Oats, Copyright 1893, American Caral Co. 8.00
Advertising, Red Cross Cough Drops, Cure Your Cold, Steel Engraving 3.50
Advertising, Saved By Dr.Wm.Hall's Balsam For Lungs, 2 3/4 X 3 In. 10.00
Advertising, Soapine, Illustration of Wizard 5.00
Advertising, St.Jacobs Oil Conquers Pain, Young Woman 4.00
Advertising, Syracuse Chilled Plow Co., 3 Cherubs, On Plowshare 5.50
Advertising, T.Trifet, Wholesale & Retail Dealer, 1880s 4.50
Advertising, Trix Perfume, 4 1/4 X3 In., C.1860 .... 5.00
Advertising, Twin Match Safe, Embossed Eagle, Pat.April 30, 1861 .... 400.00
Advertising, Union Pacific Tea Company, We Had A High Old Time 4.00
Advertising, Van Houten's Cocoa, Bird, 8 Piece 18.00
Advertising, Velvet Candy, Monkey Chewing Candy, Mechanical 25.00
Advertising, Waterbury Watch Co., Century Clock, 20 Ft.Tall Photo 4.50
Advertising, Wilson & McCallay's Tobacco, Mechanical, 1880s 37.50
Advertising, Wright's Indian Vegetable Pills, 3 Black Women, 1880s 15.00
Christmas, Maxwell Parrish 35.00
Cigarette, Actresses, Our Little Beauties, 1 Card 10.00
Cigarette, Henry, Comic Character, Set of 50 .... 120.00
Cigarette, Quadrupeds, Set of 9 .... 25.00

> **Advertising card collectors should be careful how the cards are displayed. Don't use photo albums with plastic envelopes and a sticky cardboard backing (sometimes called magnetic albums). The cards will stick and the backs will be ruined. Pure pharmacy acetone, carefully dripped under the corner of the card, will help free it with minimal damage. Do not use nail polish remover.**

Cigarette, Red Cloud, American Indian Chiefs	3.50
Cigarette, World's Racers, Connemara	1.00
Easter, Eggs In Basket, Honeycomb, Foldout, 9 In.	10.00
Game, Blondie, Original Box, 1941	70.00
Gypsy, Fortune-Telling	17.00
Lobby, Behind The Front, Wallace Beery, 1926	200.00
Lobby, Countess Dracula, 1960s	4.00
Lobby, Elvis Presley, King Allahad	20.00
Lobby, Love Affair, Humphrey Bogart, Dorothy McCaill, 1932, 14 In.	125.00
Lobby, Outlaw Express, Leo Maloney, 1926	12.50
Lobby, Sun Valley Serenade, Sonja Henie, 1941	35.00
Lobby, Suspicion, Cary Grant, Joan Fontaine, 1941	65.00
Lobby, The King On Main Street, Adolph Menjou, 1925, Set of 7	100.00
Lobby, The Unknown Soldier, 1926, Set of 8	75.00
Mutoscope, Pinup Girls, Artist Signed, Caption	2.00
Playing, Airplane Spotter, Box, 1940s	57.50
Playing, Alka-Seltzer	6.00
Playing, American Made Rubber Pharis Tires, Box, 1945	6.50
Playing, Atwater Kent Radio, 2 Decks, Box	25.00
Playing, Budweiser Beer	1.80
Playing, Caleb Bartlett, Eagle, 15 Stars, C.1812	450.00
Playing, Century of Progress, 1934	18.00
Playing, Conrail Railroad	9.00
Playing, Coors Beer	180.00
Playing, Edelweiss Beer, Chicago, Box	22.00
Playing, Esquire, Double Deck, 2 Different Girls, Esquire, Inc., 1941	60.00
Playing, Faro, Western Gambling, Hart's Squared Linen Eagle, 1868	125.00
Playing, Florida East Coast Railroad, 1945	25.00
Playing, Frisco R.R.	9.00
Playing, G.N.R.R., Indian	15.00
Playing, GE Coil Top Refrigerator, Double Deck	29.00
Playing, Goodyear	18.00
Playing, Petty Pippins, Indian Headdress, Bob Elsons	85.00
Playing, Philips Radio, Belgium	17.00
Playing, Santa Fe Railroad, 1968	17.50
Playing, Santa Fe Railroad, Each Card Different, Box	10.00
Playing, Soldier's, 2-34 Star Flags, Civil War, 2 1/2 X 3 1/2 In.	125.00
Playing, Southern Pacific, Golden West Series	60.00
Playing, United Airlines	2.50
Playing, Van Camp's Pork & Beans	35.00
Playing, Warren's Chewing Gum, Box	6.00
Playing, Western Pacific, 1922	35.00
Tarot, Switzerland, Box, 1970	20.00
Thanksgiving, Pickaninny	5.00
Valentine, Bear, Movable Arms	18.00
Valentine, Cupid & Urn, Foldout, C.1920, 8 In.	12.00
Valentine, Felix, Mechanical, Germany, Framed	60.00

Valentine, Girl In Garden Scene, Foldout, Pair 10.00
Valentine, Kewpies, Signed Rose O'Neill 12.00
Valentine, Layered Stand–Up, Germany, 6 1/2 X 11 In. 25.00
Valentine, Li'L Abner, 1950 .... 7.50
Valentine, Little Nemo, Chromo, 1907 .... 65.00
Valentine, Loving Cup, Honeycombed, Foldout, 1925, 10 In. 10.00
Valentine, Made From Different Sized Shells, Hanging Holes, 1800s 10.00
Valentine, Mammy, Eyes Roll As She Reads, Stand–Up 15.00
Valentine, Marine, In Uniform, Die Cut, World War II 15.00
Valentine, Move Dog's Ear, Girl's Eyes Move, Black 10.00
Valentine, Pinnochio, Mechanical, 1939 .... 8.00
Valentine, Postal, Changing Face, Mechanical 22.00
Valentine, Snow White, Mechanical, 1938 .... 12.00
Valentine, U.S.S.Mississippi, Handmade, Feb.14, 1937, 8 X 14 In. 25.00
Valentine, Woman, Pierced Border, Die Cut, 10 X 13 In. 25.00
Valentine, Zeppelin & Angel 30.00
    CARDER, see Aurene; Steuben

Carlsbad, Germany, is a mark found on china made by several factories in Germany. Most of the pieces available today were made after 1891.

CARLSBAD, Dish, Sardine, Fish Finial, Franz Mehlem, Bonn, C.1890 .... 55.00
Lamp, Kerosene, Art Nouveau 195.00
Match Holder, Devil 40.00
Pitcher, Ivory, Lily, Gold Trim, 8 In. 50.00
Plate, Cherry, Beaded, Scalloped 20.00
Plate, Dessert, Hand Painted Snow Scenes, Set of 5 .... 48.00

Carlton ware was made at the Carlton Works of Stoke–on–Trent, England, about 1890. The firm traded as Wiltshaw & Robinson until 1957. It was renamed Carlton Ware Ltd. in 1958.

CARLTON WARE, Ashtray, Advertising, Gordon's Dry Gin 16.00
Bookends, Art Deco, Multicolored 65.00
Bookends, Figural, Ladies With Shields & Serpents 165.00
Bowl, Raised Enamel Flowers, Birds, Oval, Handles, 12 1/2 In. 170.00
Bowl, Raised Tree, Ribbed, Twig Handle, Blue, 11 In. 75.00
Cup & Saucer, Gold Chinoiserie, Rouge Royale 50.00
Cup & Saucer, Oriental Design, Gold–Lined Cup, Blue Luster 55.00
Cup & Saucer, Rouge Royale, Gold Chinoiserie 45.00
Dish, Cheese, Stylized Flowers, Beige Ground 45.00
Inkwell, Birds In Flight, Lusterware 95.00
Jam Jar, Art Deco, Orange 65.00
Tray, Tidbit, 2 Tier 28.00
Vase, Chrysanthemums, Scroll–Footed, Gilt, 9 1/2 In. 98.00
Vase, Pink Chinoiserie, Jeweled, 6 In. 85.00
Vase, Raised Enamel Flowers, Birds, 6 In. 80.00
Vase, Rouge Royale, 8 In. 90.00
Vase, Vert Royale, 6 In. 45.00

Carnival, or taffeta, glass was an inexpensive, pressed, iridescent glass made from about 1907 to about 1925. Over 1,000 different patterns are known. Carnival glass is currently being reproduced.

    CARNIVAL GLASS, see also Northwood
    ACORN BURRS & BARK, see Acorn Burrs
CARNIVAL GLASS, Acorn Burrs, Pitcher, Marigold 135.00
Acorn Burrs, Punch Cup, Marigold 15.00
Acorn Burrs, Punch Set, Marigold, 7 Piece 675.00
Acorn Burrs, Tumbler, Green 65.00
Acorn Burrs, Tumbler, Marigold 35.00
Acorn Burrs, Water Set, Marigold, 5 Piece 450.00
Acorn Burrs, Water Set, Purple, 5 Piece 475.00
    AMERICAN BEAUTY ROSES, see Wreath of Roses
    APPLE & PEAR, see Two Fruits
Apple Blossom Twigs, Dish, Ice Cream, Smokey 145.00

Apple Blossom Twigs, Plate, Purple, 9 1/8 In. 140.00
Apple Panels, Sugar & Creamer, Marigold 40.00
Apple Tree, Pitcher, Water, Marigold 150.00
Apple Tree, Water Set, Marigold, 7 Piece 175.00
Arched Flute, Toothpick, Marigold 50.00
    ASTRAL STAR, see Curved Star
Australian Swan, Bowl, Marigold, 5 1/2 In. 50.00
    BANDED MEDALLION & TEARDROP, see Beaded Bull's Eye
    BATTENBURG LACE NO.1, see Hearts & Flowers
    BATTENBURG LACE NO.2, see Captive Rose
Beaded Acanthus, Pitcher, Milk, Marigold 65.00
Beaded Bull's Eye, Vase, Amethyst, 7 1/2 In. 39.00
Beaded Cable, Candy Dish, Footed, Marigold 35.00
Beaded Cable, Rose Bowl, Aqua .... 350.00 To 375.00
Beaded Cable, Rose Bowl, Marigold .... 42.00 To 50.00
Beaded Cable, Rose Bowl, Purple .... 60.00 To 75.00
Beaded Cable, Rose Bowl, White .... 500.00 To 750.00
    BEADED MEDALLION & TEARDROP, see Beaded Bull's Eye
Beaded Shell, Mug, Amethyst 75.00
Beaded Shell, Mug, Marigold .... 110.00 To 190.00
Beaded Shell, Mug, Purple .... 55.00 To 75.00
Beaded Shell, Tumbler, Purple 85.00
    BEADED STAR & SNAIL, see Constellation
Beaded Stars, Rose Bowl, Marigold 45.00
Bearded Berry, Bowl, Marigold, 9 In. 68.00
Birds & Cherries, Bonbon, Green 58.00
Birds & Cherries, Bonbon, Marigold, 2 Handles 125.00
    BIRDS ON BOUGH, see Birds & Cherries
    BLACKBERRY B., see Blackberry Spray
Blackberry Spray, Hat, Aqua .... 65.00 To 85.00
Blackberry Spray, Hat, Marigold, Over Vaseline 55.00
Blackberry Wreath, Bowl, Green, 9 In. 65.00
Blackberry Wreath, Sauce, Marigold 35.00
Blossom Time, Compote, Green 275.00
Blossoms & Spears, Plate, Marigold, 8 In. 35.00
Bo–Peep, Mug, Marigold .... 45.00 To 90.00
Bouquet, Water Set, Marigold, 5 Piece 325.00
Brocaded Palms, Bonbon, Ice Green 18.00
Butterflies, Bonbon, 2 Handles, Purple 65.00
Butterfly & Berry, Berry Set, Marigold, 6 Piece 170.00
Butterfly & Berry, Berry Set, Marigold, 7 Piece 195.00
Butterfly & Berry, Bowl, Footed, Marigold, 5 In. 35.00
Butterfly & Berry, Bowl, Marigold, 9 In. 250.00
Butterfly & Berry, Creamer, Marigold .... 50.00 To 55.00
Butterfly & Berry, Fernery, Cobalt Blue 895.00
Butterfly & Berry, Spooner, Marigold 60.00
Butterfly & Berry, Tumbler, Marigold .... 23.50 To 35.00
Butterfly & Berry, Water Set, Marigold, 5 Piece 350.00
Butterfly & Fern, Pitcher, Marigold, 11 In. 275.00
Butterfly & Fern, Tumbler, Green 40.00
Butterfly & Fern, Tumbler, Marigold .... 22.50 To 35.00
    BUTTERFLY & GRAPE, see Butterfly & Berry
    BUTTERFLY & PLUME, see Butterfly & Fern
    BUTTERFLY & STIPPLED RAYS, see Butterfly
Butterfly, Hatpin, Green 75.00
Buzz Saw, Cruet, Green, 4 In. 400.00
    CABBAGE ROSE & GRAPE, see Wine & Roses
    CACTUS LEAF RAYS, see Leaf Rays
Cactus, Rose Bowl, Aqua 40.00
Captive Rose, Bowl, Ruffled, Amethyst, 8 In. 45.00
Captive Rose, Plate, Blue, 9 In. .... 165.00 To 175.00
Carolina Dogwood, Plate, Peach 615.00
Caroline, Basket, Purple 275.00
    CATTAILS & FISH, see Fisherman's Mug

CATTAILS & WATER LILY, see Water Lily & Cattails
Chatelaine, Tumbler, Purple 350.00
Checkerboard, Water Set, 7 Piece 165.00
    CHERRIES & MUMS, see Mikado
Cherry Chain Variant, Bowl, Cobalt Blue, 9 1/2 In. 45.00
Cherry Chain, Dish, Ice Cream, Marigold 35.00
Cherry Chain, Plate, Cobalt Blue, 5 In. 85.00
    CHERRY WREATHED, see Wreathed Cherry
Cherry, Bowl, Green, 7 In. 75.00
Cherry, Bowl, Peach, 5 In. 40.00
Cherry, Compote, 3–Footed, Marigold 90.00
Cherry, Tumbler, Marigold 25.00
    CHRISTMAS CACTUS, see Thistle
    CHRISTMAS PLATE, see Poinsettia
    CHRISTMAS ROSE & POPPY, see Six–Petals
    CHRYSANTHEMUM WREATH, see Ten Mums
Chrysanthemum, Bowl, Green, 9 In. 75.00
Chrysanthemum, Bowl, Marigold, 11 In. 55.00
Chrysanthemum, Chop Plate, Purple .... 950.00 To 975.00
Circled Scroll, Creamer, Marigold 45.00
Circled Scroll, Tumbler, Marigold .... 150.00 To 200.00
Circled Scroll, Tumbler, Purple 11.50
    COMET, see Ribbon Tie
Constellation, Compote, White 120.00
    CONSTITUTION, see God & Home
Corinth, Vase, Aqua, 8 In. 37.50
Cosmos & Cane, Bowl, Ruffled, White, 11 In. 185.00
Cosmos & Cane, Tumbler, White 130.00
Cosmos, Dish, Ice Cream, Green 49.00
Curved Star, Compote, Ruffled, Marigold 15.00
Dahlia, Berry Set, White, 5 Piece 595.00
    DAISY & LATTICE BAND, see Lattice & Daisy
Daisy & Plume, Rose Bowl, Marigold 45.00
Daisy, Bell, Marigold 365.00
    DANDELION VARIANT, see Paneled Dandelion
Dandelion, Mug, Aqua 450.00
Dandelion, Tumbler, Amethyst .... 65.00 To 75.00
Dandelion, Tumbler, Marigold 35.00
    DIAMOND BAND, see Diamond
Diamond Lace, Bowl, Ruffled, Purple, 9 In. 65.00
Diamond Lace, Epergne, Amethyst, 4 Piece 75.00
Diamond Lace, Pitcher, Amethyst 250.00
Diamond Lace, Pitcher, Purple, 9 1/2 In. 350.00
Diamond Ovals, Butter, Cover, Marigold 40.00
    DIAMOND POINT & DAISY, see Cosmos & Cane
Diamond Point, Vase, Aqua, 10 1/2 In. 225.00
Diamond Ring, Sauce, Ruffled, Amethyst, 6 In. 35.00
Diamond, Tumbler, Amethyst 35.00
    DOGWOOD & MARSH LILY, see Two Flowers
Dogwood Spray, Compote, Marigold, 9 In. 40.00
Double–Stem Rose, Bowl, Marigold, 9 In. 35.00
Dragon & Berry, Bowl, Fluted, Marigold, 10 In. 195.00
Dragon & Lotus, Bowl, Amethyst, 9 In. 48.00
Dragon & Lotus, Bowl, Cobalt Blue, 8 3/4 In. 45.00
Dragon & Lotus, Bowl, Footed, Green, 7 1/2 In. 40.00
Dragon & Lotus, Bowl, Marigold, 9 In. 50.00
Dragon & Lotus, Bowl, Purple, 9 In. 75.00
Dragon & Lotus, Bowl, Ruffled, Collar Base, Vaseline, 8 In. 375.00
Dragon & Lotus, Bowl, Ruffled, Marigold, 9 In. 40.00
Dragon & Lotus, Bowl, Scalloped Rim, Marigold, 9 In. 70.00
Dragon & Lotus, Dish, Ice Cream, Marigold 39.00
Drapery, Candy Dish, Ice Blue .... 85.00 To 175.00
Drapery, Candy Dish, Ice Green 175.00
Drapery, Candy Dish, White 135.00

Drapery, Rose Bowl, Ice Blue 450.00
    DUTCHMAN, see Sailing Ship
Eastern Star, Bowl, Purple, 7 In. 58.00
Eastern Star, Plate, Purple, 9 1/4 In. 115.00
    EGYPTIAN BAND, see Round–Up
    EMALINE, see Zippered Loop Lamp
Estate, Sugar, Aqua 85.00
    FAN & ARCH, see Persian Garden
Fans, Pitcher, Milk, Marigold 25.00
    FANTASY, see Question Marks
Fashion, Punch Cup, Marigold 16.00
Fashion, Rose Bowl, Marigold 900.00
Fashion, Tumbler, Purple 55.00
    FIELD ROSE, see Rambler Rose
Fieldflower, Pitcher, Water, Marigold 250.00
Fieldflower, Water Set, Marigold, 7 Piece 275.00
File, Tumbler, Marigold 145.00
Fine Cut & Roses, Candy Dish, Footed, Purple 75.00
Fine Cut & Roses, Rose Bowl, Aqua 950.00
Fine Cut & Roses, Rose Bowl, Ice Blue 295.00
Fine Cut & Roses, Rose Bowl, Marigold 65.00
Fine Cut & Roses, Rose Bowl, Purple 120.00
Fine Rib, Vase, Green, 11 In. 30.00
    FINECUT & STAR, see Star & File
    FISH & FLOWERS, see Trout & Fly
Fisherman's Mug, Amber 150.00
Fisherman's Mug, Marigold ....65.00 To 130.00
Fisherman's Mug, Purple 125.00
    FISHERMAN'S NET, see Treebark
Fishscale & Beads, Plate, White, 7 In. 75.00
    FLORAL & DIAMOND POINT, see Fine Cut & Roses
Floral & Grape, Pitcher, Water, Blue 155.00
Floral & Grape, Pitcher, Water, Marigold 100.00
Floral & Grape, Tumbler, Amethyst 45.00
Floral & Grape, Tumbler, Purple 30.00
Floral & Grape, Water Set, Blue, 7 Piece 315.00
Floral & Grape, Water Set, White, 5 Piece 695.00
    FLORAL & GRAPEVINE, see Floral & Grape
    FLOWERING ALMONDS, see Peacock Tail
Flowers & Spades, Bowl, Ruffled, Purple, 9 In. 425.00
    FLUFFY BIRD, see Peacock
Fluffy Peacock, Tumbler, Marigold 45.00
Flute, Salt, Master, Blue 45.00
Flute, Sugar & Creamer, Amethyst 165.00
Flute, Table Set, Marigold, 4 Piece 65.00
Flute, Toothpick, Marigold 65.00
Flute, Toothpick, Purple 100.00
Flying Bat, Hatpin Holder, Purple 65.00
Four Flowers, Bowl, Marigold, 8 3/4 In. 45.00
Four Flowers, Chop Plate, Peach 400.00
Four Flowers, Plate, Peach, 6 1/2 In. 125.00
French Knots, Candy Dish, Blue 45.00

To clean carnival glass, try using a mixture of 1/2 cup ammonia and 1/8 cup white vinegar.

Frolicking Bears, Spittoon, Aqua	50.00
Fruits & Flowers, Bonbon, Handle, Marigold	38.00
Fruits & Flowers, Bonbon, Handles, Cobalt Blue	95.00
Fruits & Flowers, Bonbon, Handles, White	400.00
Fruits & Flowers, Bonbon, Ice Blue	450.00
Fruits & Flowers, Bonbon, Stemmed, Aqua	400.00
Fruits & Flowers, Bowl, Basketweave, Amethyst, 9 1/2 In.	60.00
Fruits & Flowers, Punch Bowl, Base, Marigold	600.00
Garden Path Variant, Dish, Ice Cream, White, 10 In.	275.00
Garland, Rose Bowl, Footed, Green	60.00
God & Home, Water Set, Amethyst	100.00
Golden Harvest, Wine Set, Amethyst, 6 Piece	395.00
Golden Harvest, Wine Set, Grape Stopper, Marigold, 7 Pc.	195.00
Good Luck, Bowl, Fluted, Cobalt Blue, 8 3/4 In.	165.00
Good Luck, Bowl, Green, 9 In.	185.00
Good Luck, Bowl, Piecrust Edge, Aqua *Illus*	1900.00
Good Luck, Bowl, Piecrust Edge, Blue, 8 3/4 In.	215.00
Good Luck, Bowl, Purple, 9 In.	165.00
Grape & Cable, Banana Boat, Amethyst	200.00
Grape & Cable, Banana Boat, Blue	575.00
Grape & Cable, Banana Boat, Ice Green	750.00
Grape & Cable, Banana Boat, Marigold	150.00
Grape & Cable, Banana Boat, Purple	200.00
Grape & Cable, Berry Bowl, Master, Green	125.00
Grape & Cable, Bonbon, 2 Handles, Marigold	48.00
Grape & Cable, Bonbon, Stippled, Handles, Green	55.00
Grape & Cable, Bottle, Perfume, Purple	50.00
Grape & Cable, Bowl, Basket Weave Exterior, Green, 11 In.	150.00
Grape & Cable, Bowl, Cobalt Blue, 11 In.	595.00
Grape & Cable, Bowl, Console, Purple	250.00
Grape & Cable, Bowl, Fluted, Amethyst, 9 In.	60.00
Grape & Cable, Bowl, Footed, Cobalt Blue, 7 In.	80.00
Grape & Cable, Bowl, Purple, 5 In.	25.00
Grape & Cable, Bowl, Ruffled, Marigold, 7 In.	18.00
Grape & Cable, Bowl, Scroll Feet, Scalloped, Green, 7 3/4 In.	70.00
Grape & Cable, Breakfast Set, Purple, 4 Piece	400.00 To 500.00
Grape & Cable, Butter, Cover, Green	130.00
Grape & Cable, Butter, Cover, Marigold	120.00 To 165.00
Grape & Cable, Butter, Cover, Purple	185.00 To 200.00
Grape & Cable, Candlestick, Marigold	45.00
Grape & Cable, Candlestick, Purple, Pair	250.00
Grape & Cable, Compote, Ice Cream, Red, 6 7/8 In.	425.00
Grape & Cable, Cracker Jar, Amethyst	295.00
Grape & Cable, Cracker Jar, Marigold	225.00
Grape & Cable, Cracker Jar, Marigold, 8 1/4 In.	375.00
Grape & Cable, Cracker Jar, White	800.00
Grape & Cable, Creamer, Green	90.00
Grape & Cable, Creamer, Marigold	40.00 To 60.00
Grape & Cable, Cup & Saucer, Marigold	195.00
Grape & Cable, Decanter, Whiskey, Amethyst	695.00
Grape & Cable, Decanter, Whiskey, Marigold	600.00
Grape & Cable, Fernery, Purple	300.00
Grape & Cable, Hat, Green	45.00
Grape & Cable, Hatpin Holder, Green	150.00 To 235.00
Grape & Cable, Hatpin Holder, Marigold	125.00 To 150.00
Grape & Cable, Hatpin Holder, Purple	175.00 To 195.00
Grape & Cable, Humidor, Stippled, Marigold	285.00
Grape & Cable, Nappy, Green	75.00
Grape & Cable, Orange Bowl, Green	195.00
Grape & Cable, Orange Bowl, Marigold	235.00
Grape & Cable, Orange Bowl, Purple	185.00
Grape & Cable, Pitcher, Ice Green, 9 1/2 In.	2500.00
Grape & Cable, Pitcher, Water, Green	350.00
Grape & Cable, Pitcher, Water, Marigold	125.00

Grape & Cable, Powder Box, Cover, Marigold 60.00
Grape & Cable, Powder Box, Cover, Northwood, Amethyst 25.00
Grape & Cable, Powder Box, Purple 135.00
Grape & Cable, Powder Jar, Purple 55.00
Grape & Cable, Punch Cup, Ice Blue 50.00
Grape & Cable, Punch Cup, Stippled, Green 50.00
Grape & Cable, Punch Cup, White .... 40.00 To 50.00
Grape & Cable, Punch Set, Marigold, 11 Piece 325.00
Grape & Cable, Salad Bowl, 3–Footed, White 595.00
Grape & Cable, Sauce, Ruffled, Amethyst 18.00
Grape & Cable, Sugar, Handle, Purple 65.00
Grape & Cable, Tankard, Purple 550.00
Grape & Cable, Tobacco Jar, Marigold 295.00
Grape & Cable, Tumbler, Amethyst 30.00
Grape & Cable, Tumbler, Marigold .... 25.00 To 45.00
Grape & Cable, Tumbler, Purple 25.00
Grape & Cable, Water Set, Marigold, 5 Piece 300.00
Grape & Cable, Water Set, Purple, 7 Piece 395.00
Grape & Gothic Arches, Berry Bowl, Marigold, Master 48.00
Grape & Gothic Arches, Pitcher, Water, Marigold 175.00
Grape & Gothic Arches, Punch Cup, Marigold 35.00
Grape & Gothic Arches, Tumbler, Blue 50.00
Grape & Gothic Arches, Tumbler, Marigold .... 28.00 To 48.00
Grape & Gothic Arches, Water Set, Blue, 7 Piece 425.00
Grape & Gothic Arches, Water Set, Marigold, 7 Piece 180.00
Grape Arbor, Tumbler, Marigold .... 30.00 To 50.00
Grape Arbor, Tumbler, White 75.00
Grape Arbor, Water Set, Amethyst, 7 Piece .... 575.00 To 650.00
Grape Arbor, Water Set, White, 7 Piece 1800.00
GRAPE DELIGHT, see Vintage
Grape Leaves, Bowl, Purple, 8 In. 55.00
Grape, Bowl, Amethyst, 8 1/2 In. 45.00
Grape, Bowl, Green, 11 1/2 In. 125.00
Grape, Bowl, Green, 9 In. 45.00
Grape, Candlestick, Amethyst 165.00
Grape, Chop Plate, Amethyst 395.00
Grape, Goblet, Amber, 10 Oz. 18.00
Grape, Nappy, Orange, 6 In. 15.00
Grape, Pitcher, Water, Green 150.00
Grape, Plate, Purple, 8 1/4 In. 85.00
Grape, Spooner, Purple 75.00
Grape, Sugar, Cover, Purple 95.00
Grape, Tumbler, Amethyst 34.00
Grape, Water Set, Amber 85.00
GRAPEVINE DIAMONDS, see Grapevine Lattice
Grapevine Lattice, Bowl, White, 7 In. 40.00
Grapevine Lattice, Tumbler, Marigold 38.00
Greek Key, Tumbler, Purple 75.00
HARVEST TIME, see Golden Harvest
Heart & Vine, Bowl, Blue, 9 In. 48.00
Heart & Vine, Bowl, Green, 9 In. 48.00
Heart Band, Mug, Marigold 65.00
Hearts & Flowers, Bowl, Ice Blue, 9 In. 395.00
Hearts & Flowers, Compote, Aqua .... 350.00 To 425.00
Hearts & Flowers, Compote, Stemmed, Cobalt Blue 310.00
Hearts & Flowers, Compote, White 145.00
Heavy Grape, Bowl, Amethyst, 10 1/2 In. 200.00
Heavy Grape, Bowl, Green, 9 In. 60.00
HERON & RUSHES, see Stork & Rushes
HOBNAIL, see also Hobnail category
Hobstar & Feather, Punch Cup, Purple 65.00
Hobstar & Feather, Punch Set, Tulip Top, Amethyst, 11 Piece 4850.00
Hobstar, Cookie Jar, Marigold 50.00
Hobstar, Creamer, Marigold 35.00

To remove the musty smell from a closed cupboard or box, try using rice. Parch several handfuls of uncooked rice in a shallow pan in the oven. Then put the pan and rice in the musty drawer. You may have to repeat the parching to keep the moisture and mildew from reappearing.

Holly Sprig, Bonbon, 2 Handles, Green 32.50
Holly Whirl, Bonbon, Marigold 75.00
Holly, Bowl, Candy Ribbon Rim, Amethyst, 9 In. 42.50
Holly, Bowl, Fluted, Marigold, 6 1/2 In. 35.00
Holly, Bowl, Green, 9 In. 45.00
Holly, Hat, Marigold Over Green 45.00
Holly, Plate, Amethyst, 9 1/2 In. 225.00
Holly, Plate, Blue, 9 In. 200.00
Holly, Plate, Marigold, 9 1/2 In. 95.00
Holly, Sherbet, Pedestal, Fluted Rim, Marigold 22.00
    HONEYCOMB COLLAR, see Fishscale & Beads
Honeycomb, Rose Bowl, Peach 250.00
Honeycomb, Sugar & Creamer, Marigold, 3 In. 20.00
    HORSE MEDALLIONS, see Horses' Heads
Horses' Heads, Bowl, 3–Footed, Cobalt Blue, 7 1/2 In. 100.00
Horses' Heads, Bowl, 3–Footed, Marigold, 6 1/2 In. 75.00
Horses' Heads, Bowl, Marigold, 7 In. .... 50.00 To 58.00
Horses' Heads, Plate, Marigold, 8 In. 125.00
Horses' Heads, Rose Bowl, Marigold 75.00
Horses' Heads, Vase, Jack–In–The–Pulpit, Marigold 110.00
Imperial Grape, Bottle, Water, Amethyst 200.00
Imperial Grape, Bottle, Water, Purple 95.00
Imperial Grape, Chop Plate, Purple, 11 1/8 In. 345.00
Imperial Grape, Decanter, Marigold 110.00
Imperial Grape, Decanter, Purple 160.00
Imperial Grape, Goblet, Ribbed Interior, Purple 35.00
Imperial Grape, Goblet, Wine, Green 27.50
Imperial Grape, Goblet, Wine, Marigold .... 12.50 To 20.00
Imperial Grape, Pitcher, Water, Marigold .... 95.00 To 110.00
Imperial Grape, Plate, Ruffled, Clambroth, 8 In. 48.00
Imperial Grape, Punch Set, Marigold, 6 Piece 235.00
Imperial Grape, Tumbler, Purple 35.00
Imperial Grape, Water Set, Marigold, 5 Piece 195.00
Imperial Grape, Water Set, Marigold, 6 Piece 135.00
    INTAGLIO, see Hobstar & Feather
    INTERIOR OF CHERRIES & MUMS, see Mikado
Inverted Coin Dot, Tumbler, Marigold 55.00
Inverted Strawberry, Candlestick, Green, Pair 225.00
Inverted Strawberry, Spittoon, Purple 650.00
Iris, Goblet, Buttermilk, Ice Blue 150.00
Iris, Goblet, Green 69.00
Iris, Tumbler, Purple, Enameled 35.00
    IRISH LACE, see Louisa
Jeweled Heart, Bowl, Peach, 10 In. 145.00
Kittens, Banana Boat, Amethyst 425.00
Kittens, Bowl, Ruffled, Marigold, 6 In. 115.00
Kittens, Cup, Marigold 150.00
Kittens, Spooner, Marigold 30.00
Kittens, Vase, Whimsey, Marigold, 2 1/2 In. 85.00
    LABELLE POPPY, see Poppy Show
    LABELLE ROSE, see Rose Show
Lattice & Daisy, Tumbler 55.00

Lattice & Grape, Tumbler, Blue 35.00
Lattice & Grape, Tumbler, Marigold 25.00
    LATTICE & GRAPEVINE, see Lattice & Grape
Leaf & Beads, Dish, Flared, Green 65.00
Leaf & Beads, Rose Bowl, Aqua .... 235.00 To 350.00
Leaf & Beads, Rose Bowl, Blue 55.00
Leaf & Beads, Rose Bowl, Marigold 45.00
Leaf & Beads, Rose Bowl, Purple 95.00
Leaf Chain, Bowl, White, 6 1/2 In. 55.00
Leaf Chain, Plate, Green, 9 In. 200.00
Leaf Chain, Plate, Marigold, 7 In. 35.00
    LEAF MEDALLION, see Leaf Chain
    LEAF PINWHEEL & STAR FLOWER, see Whirling Leaves
Leaf Rays, Nappy, Amethyst 22.00
Leaf Rays, Nappy, Purple 75.00
Lion, Bowl, Ruffled, Marigold, 7 In. 110.00
Little Beads, Compote, Purple 55.00
Little Flowers, Bowl, Amethyst, 8 1/2 In. 85.00
Little Flowers, Bowl, Marigold, 6 In. 25.00
Little Flowers, Bowl, Purple, 6 In. 30.00
Little Stars, Bowl, Marigold, 8 In. 110.00
Long Thumbprint, Sugar & Creamer, Marigold 65.00
Lotus & Grape, Bonbon, 2 Handles, Marigold 55.00
Louisa, Rose Bowl, Green 45.00
Lustre Rose, Berry Bowl, Marigold, 10 1/4 In. 65.00
Lustre Rose, Bowl, Marigold, 8 In. 40.00
Lustre Rose, Bowl, Smokey, 9 In. 38.00
Lustre Rose, Console, 3-Footed, Marigold 89.00
Lustre Rose, Creamer, Marigold 30.00
Lustre Rose, Plate, Marigold, 9 In. 25.00
Lustre Rose, Tumbler, Aqua 55.00
Lustre Rose, Tumbler, Olive Green, Ribbed Interior 35.00
Lustre Rose, Water Set, Purple, 5 Piece 525.00
    MAGNOLIA & POINSETTIA, see Water Lily
    MAINE COAST, see Seacoast
Many Fruits, Punch Bowl, Cobalt Blue 575.00
Many Fruits, Punch Bowl, Marigold 500.00
Many Fruits, Punch Set, Amethyst, Base, 8 Piece 600.00
Many Fruits, Punch Set, Green, 6 Piece 1675.00
Maple Leaf, Table Set, Marigold, 4 Piece 195.00
Maple Leaf, Water Set, Purple, 7 Piece 195.00
    MARYLAND, see Rustic
    MELINDA, see Wishbone
Memphis, Punch Bowl, Purple 65.00
Memphis, Punch Cup, Marigold 20.00
Memphis, Punch Cup, Purple 135.00
Memphis, Punch Set, Marigold, 7 Piece 450.00
Mikado, Compote, Ice Cream, Marigold 395.00
Milady, Pitcher, Water, Blue, 11 In. 550.00
Milady, Tumbler, Marigold 55.00
Morning Glory, Vase, Smokey, 7 1/2 In. 25.00
    MULTI FRUIT & FLOWERS, see Many Fruits
Nippon, Bowl, Ice Blue, 8 In. 150.00
Octagon, Goblet, Marigold 35.00
Octagon, Pitcher, Water, Purple 650.00
    OLD FASHION FLAG, see Iris
Open Rose, Plate, Marigold, 9 In. 50.00
    ORANGE TREE & CABLE, see Orange Tree Orchard
Orange Tree & Scroll, Pitcher, Marigold 325.00
Orange Tree Orchard, Pitcher, Water, Marigold 45.00
Orange Tree Orchard, Water Set, Marigold, 7 Piece 395.00
Orange Tree, Bowl, Fluted, White, 8 1/2 In. 115.00
Orange Tree, Bowl, Footed, Marigold, 10 In. 100.00
Orange Tree, Bowl, Footed, White, 8 1/2 In. 85.00

Orange Tree, Bowl, Purple, 8 1/2 In. 75.00
Orange Tree, Bowl, Scalloped, Footed, Blue, 10 In. 150.00
Orange Tree, Bowl, White, 8 1/2 In. 58.00
Orange Tree, Creamer, White 110.00
Orange Tree, Cup, Blue, 3 1/2 In. 37.50
Orange Tree, Dish, Ice Cream, White, 8 1/2 In. 135.00
Orange Tree, Goblet, Wine, Blue .... 50.00 To 55.00
Orange Tree, Hatpin Holder, Cobalt Blue 158.00
Orange Tree, Loving Cup, Marigold .... 150.00 To 225.00
Orange Tree, Mug, Amber 150.00
Orange Tree, Mug, Amethyst .... 225.00 To 350.00
Orange Tree, Mug, Blue .... 25.00 To 65.00
Orange Tree, Mug, Marigold 25.00
Orange Tree, Mug, Red 475.00
Orange Tree, Mug, Vaseline 165.00
Orange Tree, Orange Bowl, Footed, Blue 225.00
Orange Tree, Pitcher, Footed, Marigold 250.00
Orange Tree, Plate, Blue .... 300.00 To 350.00
Orange Tree, Powder Jar, Cover, Blue 85.00
Orange Tree, Punch Set, Blue, 8 Piece .... 400.00 To 635.00
Orange Tree, Punch Set, Marigold, 6 Piece 365.00
Orange Tree, Rose Bowl, Purple, 4 In. 95.00
Orange Tree, Shaving Mug, Amber 125.00
Orange Tree, Shaving Mug, Blue 55.00
Orange Tree, Shaving Mug, Red 425.00
Oriental Poppy, Pitcher, Green 700.00
Oriental Poppy, Tumbler, Blue 275.00
Palm Beach, Berry Bowl, Marigold 15.00
Palm Beach, Creamer, White 150.00
Palm Beach, Rose Bowl, Amethyst, Marigold Overlay 300.00
PANELED BACHELOR BUTTONS, see Milady
Paneled Dandelion, Pitcher, Cobalt Blue 475.00
Paneled Dandelion, Water Set, Marigold, 6 Piece 375.00
Paneled Holly, Bonbon, 2 Handles, Green 30.00
Pansy Spray, Creamer, Green 35.00
Pansy Spray, Nappy, Handle, Green 25.00
Pansy Spray, Relish, Oval, Green 45.00
Pansy, Sugar, Amethyst 58.00
Panther, Berry Bowl, Master, Green 550.00
Panther, Bowl, 3–Footed, Marigold, 5 1/2 In. 35.00
Panther, Bowl, Clawfoot, Marigold, 5 In. 60.00
Panther, Bowl, Clawfoot, Marigold, 9 In. 150.00
Panther, Bowl, Footed, Marigold, 5 In. .... 45.00 To 60.00
Peacock & Dahlia, Bowl, Blue, 6 3/4 In. 95.00
Peacock & Grape, Bowl, Beaded Berry Outside, Marigold, 9 In. 200.00
Peacock & Grape, Bowl, Marigold, 7 1/2 In. 30.00
Peacock & Grape, Bowl, Marigold, 8 In. 65.00
Peacock & Grape, Bowl, Purple, 8 In. 65.00
Peacock & Grape, Bowl, Ruffled, Vaseline, 8 1/2 In. 325.00
Peacock & Grape, Dish, Ice Cream, Green, 8 1/4 In. 50.00
Peacock & Grape, Plate, Green, 8 1/4 In. 40.00
Peacock & Grape, Water Set, Smokey, 7 Piece 75.00
Peacock & Urn, Bowl, Marigold, 9 In. .... 68.00 To 70.00
Peacock & Urn, Bowl, Purple, 10 In. 375.00
Peacock & Urn, Bowl, Ruffled, Blue, 9 In. 150.00
Peacock & Urn, Compote, Footed, Marigold 32.00
Peacock & Urn, Dish, Ice Cream, Master, White 475.00
Peacock At The Fountain, Compote, White .... 550.00 To 750.00
Peacock At The Fountain, Orange Bowl, 3–Footed, Marigold 160.00
Peacock At The Fountain, Pitcher, Amethyst 295.00
Peacock At The Fountain, Pitcher, Water, Cobalt Blue 250.00
Peacock At The Fountain, Pitcher, White 650.00
Peacock At The Fountain, Spooner, White 90.00
Peacock At The Fountain, Tumbler, Blue 55.00

Peacock At The Fountain, Tumbler, Marigold 40.00
Peacock At The Fountain, Tumbler, Purple 50.00
Peacock At The Fountain, Water Set, Marigold, 7 Piece 695.00
Peacock At The Fountain, Water Set, Purple, 5 Piece 495.00
    PEACOCK EYE & GRAPE, see Vineyard
    PEACOCK ON FENCE, see Peacock
Peacock Tail Variant, Compote, Amethyst 95.00
Peacock Tail, Bowl, Crimped, Green, 8 3/4 In. 65.00
Peacock Tail, Bowl, Marigold, 6 1/2 In. 20.00
Peacock Tail, Compote, Green 39.00
Peacock, Bowl, 3–Footed, Crimped, Amber, 11 1/2 In. 48.00
Peacock, Bowl, Blue, 9 In. 300.00
Peacock, Bowl, Marigold, 8 3/4 In. 100.00
Peacock, Bowl, Piecrust Edge, Blue, 8 3/4 In. 375.00
Peacock, Bowl, Ruffled, Amethyst, 8 3/4 In. 300.00
Peacock, Bowl, Ruffled, Cobalt Blue, 8 1/2 In. 290.00
Peacock, Bowl, Ruffled, Purple, 9 In. 250.00
Peacock, Plate, White 365.00
Peacock, Water Set, Purple, 5 Piece 900.00
Persian Garden, Bowl, White, 6 In. 52.00
Persian Garden, Dish, Ice Cream, Purple 800.00
Persian Garden, Dish, Ice Cream, White, 11 In. 200.00
Persian Garden, Plate, Marigold, 6 In. 55.00
Persian Garden, Plate, White, 6 1/2 In. 95.00
Persian Garden, Plate, White, 7 1/2 In. 125.00
Persian Medallion, Bonbon, 2 Handles, Blue 65.00
Persian Medallion, Bonbon, Handles, Marigold 67.50
Persian Medallion, Bowl, Amethyst, 10 In. 80.00
Persian Medallion, Chop Plate, Blue .... 300.00 To 425.00
Persian Medallion, Compote, Ruffled, Orange 24.00
Persian Medallion, Plate, Marigold, 6 In. 40.00
Persian Medallion, Sauce, Marigold 25.00
    PINE CONE WREATH, see Pine Cone
Pine Cone, Plate, Amethyst, 6 1/2 In. 70.00
Pine Cone, Plate, Green, 6 In. 95.00
Pine Cone, Plate, Marigold, 6 In. 30.00
Plume Panels, Vase, Red, 10 In. 750.00
Pods & Posies, Bowl, Purple, 9 1/8 In. 95.00
    POINSETTIA & LATTICE, see Poinsettia
Poinsettia Interior, Tumbler, Marigold 325.00
    POLKA DOT, see Inverted Coin Dot
Pond Lily, Bonbon, 2 Handles, White 75.00
    POPPY SCROLL, see Poppy
Poppy Show, Plate, Marigold .... 375.00 To 400.00
Poppy Show, Plate, Purple 850.00
Poppy Show, Vase, Marigold .... 225.00 To 245.00
Poppy, Tumbler, Green 45.00
Premium, Candleholder, Marigold, Pair 40.00
    PRINCESS LACE, see Octagon
Princess Lamp, Lamp, Purple 175.00
Quartered Block, Butter, Cover, Diamond Shape, Marigold 17.50
Question Marks, Bonbon, Footed, Handles, Amethyst 55.00
Question Marks, Bonbon, Footed, Handles, Marigold 40.00
Raindrops, Bowl, Peach, 9 1/2 In. 75.00
Rambler Rose, Pitcher, Water, Marigold 95.00
Rambler Rose, Tumbler, Marigold 15.00
Raspberry, Bonbon, Hat Shape, Marigold 30.00
Raspberry, Pitcher, Basket Weave Base, Purple, 9 In. 215.00
Raspberry, Pitcher, Northwood, Purple 125.00
Raspberry, Pitcher, Water, Purple 195.00
Raspberry, Tumbler, Purple 35.00
Ribbon Tie, Bowl, Cobalt Blue, 8 In. 50.00
Ribbon Tie, Bowl, Cobalt Blue, 9 In. 67.50
Ripple, Vase, Flared Scalloped Rim, Purple, 8 3/4 In. 45.00

Ripple, Vase, Marigold, 7 1/4 In. 85.00
  ROBIN RED BREAST, see Robin
Robin, Mug, Amber 45.00
Robin, Mug, Marigold 25.00
Robin, Pitcher, Water, Blue 65.00
Robin, Water Set, White 85.00
  ROSE & RUFFLES, see Open Rose
Rose Show, Plate, Purple, 9 1/2 In. 950.00
  ROSES & LOOPS, see Double–Stem Rose
Round–Up, Plate, Blue 225.00
Rustic, Vase, Cobalt Blue, 9 1/2 In. 40.00
Rustic, Vase, Funeral, Marigold, 18 In. 200.00
Rustic, Vase, Funeral, Purple, 21 In. 250.00
Rustic, Vase, Purple, 11 In. 37.00
S–Repeat, Punch Cup, Purple 22.00
S–Repeat, Punch Set, Purple, 14 Piece 2900.00
  SAILBOAT & WINDMILL, see Sailboats
Sailboats, Goblet, Wine, Marigold 95.00
Sailboats, Sauce, Ruffled, Aqua 95.00
Sailing Ship, Goblet, Wine, Marigold 30.00
  SCROLL EMBOSSED, see Eastern Star
  SCROLL–CABLE, see Estate
Seacoast, Tray, Pin, Amethyst 295.00
  SHELL & WILD ROSE, see Wild Rose
Singing Birds, Berry Bowl, Marigold, 5 In. 30.00
Singing Birds, Berry Set, Green, 7 Piece 395.00
Singing Birds, Mug, Green .... 135.00 To 145.00
Singing Birds, Mug, Marigold 45.00
Singing Birds, Mug, Purple 95.00
Singing Birds, Mug, Stippled, Marigold 110.00
Singing Birds, Spooner, Purple 63.00
Singing Birds, Sugar & Creamer, Amethyst 150.00
Singing Birds, Tumbler, Green 40.00
Singing Birds, Tumbler, Purple 40.00
Singing Birds, Water Set, Green, 6 Piece 535.00
Single Flower, Bowl, Peach, 9 In. 75.00
Six–Petals, Bowl, Peach, 7 1/2 In. 95.00
Ski Star, Bowl, Ruffled, Peach, 11 In. 95.00
  SPRING FLOWERS, see Bouquet
Stag & Holly, Bowl, 3–Footed, Blue, 11 In. 225.00
Stag & Holly, Bowl, 3–Footed, Green, 8 In. 150.00
Stag & Holly, Bowl, 3–Footed, Marigold, 10 In. 175.00
Stag & Holly, Bowl, Blue, 8 In. 165.00
Stag & Holly, Bowl, Cobalt Blue, 10 3/4 In. 210.00
Stag & Holly, Bowl, Footed, Marigold, 10 In. 145.00
Stag & Holly, Bowl, Footed, Red, 10 1/2 In. 750.00
Stag & Holly, Bowl, Marigold, 9 In. 50.00

Be careful about putting antique china or glass in the dishwasher.
Glass will sometimes crack from the heat. Porcelains with gold
overglaze decoration often lose the gold. Damaged or crazed glass
will sometimes pop off the plates in large pieces.

Stag & Holly, Bowl, Spatula–Footed, Green, 8 In.	165/.00
Stag & Holly, Dish, Ice Cream, Footed, Amethyst, 11 In.	450.00
Star & File, Goblet, Wine, Marigold	35.00 To 40.00
Star & File, Pitcher, Water, Marigold	135.00
Star Medallion, Bowl, Marigold, 6 In.	20.00
Star Medallion, Bowl, Marigold, 8 In.	25.00
Star Medallion, Goblet, Ice Blue	50.00
Star Medallion, Pitcher, Milk, Marigold	32.00
Star of David & Bows, Bowl, Amethyst, 8 In.	40.00
Star of David & Bows, Bowl, Purple, 8 1/2 In.	75.00
STAR OF DAVID MEDALLION, see Star of David & Bows	
Starfish, Compote, Peach	50.00
STIPPLED CLEMATIS, see Little Stars	
STIPPLED DIAMOND & FLOWER. see Little Flowers	
STIPPLED LEAF & BEADS, see Leaf & Beads	
Stippled Petals, Banana Boat, Crimped, Purple	75.00
Stippled Petals, Banana Boat, Marigold	95.00
STIPPLED POSY & PODS, see Four Flowers	
Stippled Rays, Berry Set, Marigold, 7 Piece	95.00
Stippled Rays, Bowl, Amethyst, 10 In.	300.00
Stippled Rays, Bowl, Ruffled, Amethyst, 7 3/4 In.	25.00
Stippled Rays, Bowl, Ruffled, Amethyst, 9 In.	50.00
Stippled Rays, Bowl, Ruffled, Marigold, 8 In.	35.00
Stippled Rays, Creamer, Green	40.00
Stippled Rays, Plate, Marigold, 7 In.	42.50
Stippled Rays, Plate, Scale Band Exterior, Marigold, 7 In.	40.00
Stippled Rays, Sugar, Marigold	35.00
Stork & Rushes, Mug, Amethyst	250.00
Stork & Rushes, Mug, Marigold	35.00
Stork & Rushes, Punch Set, Marigold, 8 Piece	250.00
Stork & Rushes, Tumbler, Blue	40.00
Strawberry, Bonbon, 2 Handles, Marigold	30.00
Strawberry, Bonbon, Green, 5 In.	55.00
Strawberry, Bowl, Fluted, Amethyst, 9 1/2 In.	55.00
Strawberry, Plate, Handles, Green, 7 In.	65.00
Strutting Peacock, Sugar, Purple	30.00
SUNFLOWER, see Dandelion	
SUNFLOWER & WHEAT, see Fieldflower	
Swirl Hobnail, Rose Bowl, Amethyst	315.00
TEARDROPS, see Raindrops	
Ten Mums, Bowl, Green, 10 In.	90.00
Ten Mums, Bowl, Ruffled, Amethyst.10 In.	95.00
Thistle, Banana Boat, Blue	185.00
Thistle, Bowl, Ruffled, Amber, 9 In.	80.00
Thistle, Bowl, Ruffled, Amethyst, 8 In.	40.00
Thistle, Bowl, Ruffled, Blue, 9 In.	59.00
Thistle, Plate, Marigold	1700.00
Three Fruits, Bonbon, Basket Weave Exterior, Clambroth	25.00
Three Fruits, Bowl, Amethyst, 9 3/4 In.	60.00
Three Fruits, Bowl, Marigold, 8 1/2 In.	45.00
Three Fruits, Plate, 9 In.	115.00
Three Fruits, Plate, Amethyst, 9 In.	125.00
Three Fruits, Plate, Clambroth, 9 In.	100.00
Three Fruits, Plate, Marigold, 9 In.	45.00
Three Fruits, Plate, Purple, 9 In.	135.00
Three Fruits, Plate, Ruffled, Purple, 6 1/4 In.	20.00
Town Pump, Pitcher, Marigold	1375.00
Tree of Life, Basket, Handle, Marigold	25.00
Tree Trunk, Vase, Cobalt Blue, 8 In.	45.00
Treebark, Pitcher, Marigold	55.00
Treebark, Pitcher, Water, Marigold	60.00
Treebark, Pitcher, Water, Smokey	50.00
Trout & Fly, Bowl, Purple, 8 In.	400.00
Two Flowers, Bowl, Blue, 7 In.	65.00

Two Flowers, Bowl, Blue, Footed, 11 In. 100.00
Two Flowers, Bowl, Marigold, 9 In. 85.00
Two Flowers, Bowl, Ruffled, Footed, Aqua, 10 In. 350.00
Two Flowers, Bowl, Spatula-Footed, Purple, 7 In. 135.00
Two Flowers, Chop Plate, Footed, Marigold 625.00
Two Flowers, Plate, Marigold, 6 1/2 In. 125.00
Two Flowers, Rose Bowl, Blue ....95.00 To 110.00
Two Flowers, Rose Bowl, Marigold 59.00
Two Fruits, Candy Dish, Divided, Blue 75.00
Vineyard, Pitcher, Water, Marigold 95.00
Vineyard, Tumbler, Marigold 25.00
Vineyard, Water Set, Marigold, 7 Piece 295.00
Vintage Banded, Mug, Marigold .... 20.00 To 30.00
Vintage, Bowl, Nut, Amethyst 75.00
Vintage, Goblet, Wine, Amethyst 25.00
Vintage, Powder Jar, Cover, Marigold 65.00
Vintage, Punch Cup, Amethyst 10.00
Vintage, Rose Bowl, 6-Footed, White .... 50.00 To 75.00
Vintage, Rose Bowl, Marigold 42.00
Vintage, Rose Bowl, Purple 50.00
Waffle Block, Basket, Clambroth 45.00
Water Lily & Cattails, Tumbler, Marigold .... 25.00 To 45.00
Water Lily & Cattails, Water Set, Marigold, 7 Piece 600.00
Water Lily, Bowl, Footed, Green, 10 In. 125.00
Water Lily, Bowl, Footed, Marigold, 10 In. 75.00
Whimsey, Mug, Aqua 50.00
Whimsey, Sugar & Creamer, Aqua 150.00
Whirling Leaves, Bowl, Amethyst, 9 In. 125.00
Whirling Leaves, Bowl, Marigold, 9 1/2 In. 65.00
Wide Panel, Epergne, 4-Lily, Green 1275.00
   WILD GRAPES, see Grape Leaves
Wild Rose, Bowl, Footed, Open Heart Rim, Green, 7 In. 45.00
Windflower, Plate, Blue, 9 In. 125.00
Windmill & Mums, Bowl, Cobalt Blue, 10 1/2 In. 135.00
   WINDMILL MEDALLION, see Windmill
Windmill, Pitcher, Milk, Marigold .... 50.00 To 70.00
Windmill, Water Set, Green, 7 Piece 110.00
Windmill, Water Set, Marigold, 7 Piece ....90.00 To 165.00
Wine & Roses, Goblet, Blue 75.00
Wine & Roses, Goblet, Purple 35.00
Wine & Roses, Goblet, Wine, Marigold 25.00
Wishbone & Spades, Bowl, Ruffled, Peach, 6 In. 55.00
Wishbone & Spades, Chop Plate, Purple ....850.00 To 950.00
Wishbone, Bowl, Footed, Amethyst, 8 1/2 In. 70.00
Wishbone, Chop Plate, Marigold 500.00
Wishbone, Chop Plate, Purple 675.00
Wishbone, Plate, Amethyst, 9 In. 235.00
Wishbone, Plate, Footed, Purple, 8 1/4 In. 245.00
Wreath of Roses, Rose Bowl, Marigold ....35.00 To 40.00
Wreathed Cherry, Banana Boat, Amethyst 135.00
Wreathed Cherry, Banana Boat, White 250.00
Wreathed Cherry, Sauce, Marigold 32.00
Zippered Loop Lamp, Lamp, Marigold 200.00

The first carousel or merry-go-round figures carved in the United States were made in 1867 by Gustav Dentzel. Collectors discovered the charm of the hand-carved figures in the 1970s and they were soon classed as folk art. Most desirable are the figures other than horses, such as pigs, camels, lions, or dogs. A jumper is a figure that was made to move up and down on a pole, a stander was placed in a stationary position.

CAROUSEL, Figure, Laughing Lady, Animated Fat Lady, 1920s, Full Size 3200.00
Flying Horses, W.H.Dentzel, Hand Crank, 5 Animals, 14 Ft. Diam. 3500.00
French Camel, Bayol Company, C.1880 .... 3600.00

Giraffe, Prancer, Carved Wood, Early 1900s, 58 In.	5775.00
Horse, Brown & White, Over Red, French, C.1880, Life Size	4400.00
Horse, Carved Mane To Side, Stripped Pine, 19th Century, 53 In.	1650.00
Horse, Cast Iron, From Natzen Beach Amusement Park, Ore., 1936	625.00
Horse, Horsehair Tail, Open Mouth, Wood, Polychrome, American, 5 Ft.	2200.00
Horse, Inner–Row Prancer, Gustav Dentzel, C.1900	7500.00
Horse, Jumper, C.W.Parker, Large, 1917	3000.00
Horse, Jumper, Park Paint, Spillman	1350.00
Horse, Jumper, Stein & Goldstein, Stripped	7500.00
Horse, Jumper, Track Style, Armitage Herschell, Small	1100.00
Horse, Mirrored Tiles, Eagle Head Saddle, Heyn, 46 In. ....*Illus*	5000.00
Horse, Outer Row, Looff	8500.00
Horse, Polychrome, Zinc Alloy, 57 In.	1250.00
Horse, Prancer, Jewels, Looff, 1885	800.00
Horse, Prancing, Open Mouth, Herschell–Spillman, C.1880, 48 In.	1430.00
Horse, Prancing, Restored, Stein & Goldstein, 1915	7200.00
Horse, Second Row, Looff	6000.00
Horse, Stander, Original Paint, Jeweled Saddle, C.1900, 27 X 29 In.	1500.00
Horse, Stander, Outside, Jewels, Looff	1900.00
Horse, Third Row, Looff	5000.00
Horse, Yellow, Red & Blue Trim, 4 Ft.	800.00
Jumper, Armitage Herschell, No.77, C.1890	1900.00
Pig, Dentzel	9500.00
Punch & Judy, Herschell–Spillman	3000.00
Rooster, Herschell–Spillman	5200.00
Woody Woodpecker, Wooden	950.00

The word "carriage" has several meanings, so this section lists baby carriages, buggies for adults, horse–drawn sleighs, and even strollers. Doll–sized carriages are listed under "toy."

CARRIAGE, Baby Buggy, Amish	600.00
Baby Buggy, Attached Parasol, Wicker	375.00

Carousel, Horse, Mirrored Tiles, Eagle Head Saddle, Heyn, 46 In.

Baby Buggy, Hood, Painted, 2 Large Wheels & 2 Small, 1860–80 .... 1350.00
Cart, Horse–Drawn, Child's, Victorian, Hide Covered, Wicker Wheels 1350.00
Goat Cart, Red & Green, Wheels Or Runners, D & J Furniture 775.00
Pram, English, Wilson 35.00

An eye on the cash was a necessity in stores of the nineteenth century, too. The cash register was invented in 1884. John and James Ritty invented a large clocklike model that kept a record of the dollars and cents exchanged in the store. John Patterson improved the cash register with a paper roll to record the money. By the early 1900s, elaborate brass registers were made. About World War I, the fancy case was exchanged for the more modern types.

CASH REGISTER, Michigan, Amount Purchase Sign, Brass 300.00
National, Model 4, Brass 1000.00
National, Model 30, Autographic 1200.00
National, Model 130 .... 550.00
National, Model 143, Brass 595.00
National, Model 213, Brass 550.00
National, Model 225, Fleur–De–Lis, Bronze 875.00
National, Model 250, Candy Store 1250.00
National, Model 313, Candy Store .... 595.00 To 795.00
National, Model 327, Brass 950.00
National, Model 332, Brass 595.00
National, Model 337, Bronze .... 495.00 To 650.00
National, Model 348–2, 2 Drawers 475.00
National, Model 421, Top Bonnet Marked Archie Marshall 600.00
National, Model 442, Bronze & Brass, 1912 .... 1275.00
National, Model 452 .... 135.00
National, Model 582 E 850.00
National, Model 592, 9 Drawers, Bombay Base, Oak, 5 1/2 Ft. 675.00
Ohmer, Green, Small 395.00
Standard, Oak, 1890 .... 350.00

Castor sets holding just salt and pepper castors were used in the seventeenth century. The sugar castor, mustard pot, spice dredger, bottles for vinegar and oil, and other spice holders became popular by the eighteenth century. These sets were usually made of sterling silver. The American Victorian castor set, the type most collected today, was made of silver plated Britannia metal. Colored glass bottles were introduced after the Civil War. The sets were out of fashion by World War I. Be careful when buying sets with colored bottles; many are reproductions.

CASTOR SET, see also various Porcelain and Glass categories
CASTOR SET, 3–Bottle, Bell Flower Pattern, Pewter Frame, 11 In. 125.00
4–Bottle, Pewter Frame, Revolving, Child's, 9 1/2 In. 155.00
5–Bottle, Daisy & Button, Meriden Holder, Amber 195.00
5–Bottle, Silver Plated Holder 110.00
6–Bottle, Allover Diamond Perforated Silver Plated Frame 125.00
6–Bottle, Grape & Foliage In Bas Relief, Cameo–Shaped Handle 175.00

The pickle castor was a glass jar about six inches in height, held in a special metal holder. It became a popular dinner table accessory about 1890. The jar had a top that was usually silver or silver plate. The frame, also of a silver metal, had a handle that arched above the jar and a hook that held a pair of tongs. By 1900, the pickle castor was out of fashion. Many examples found today have reproduced glass jars in old holders.

CASTOR, PICKLE, see also various Glass categories
CASTOR, Pickle, Beaded Dart, Webster Frame 195.00
Pickle, Canary Pattern Insert, Silver Frame, Tongs, Lid 185.00
Pickle, Carmen Pattern, Silver–Plated Frame, Tongs, Fostoria 95.00
Pickle, Clear Paneled Glass, Silver–Plated Frame, Signed 160.00
Pickle, Coin Dot, Eagle Finial, Silver–Plated Holder 300.00

Pickle, Cranberry Glass, Inverted Diamond, Plated Frame, 11 In. 380.00
Pickle, Cranberry Glass, Inverted Honeycomb Insert, Homan Frame 395.00
Pickle, Cranberry Glass, Thumbprint, Enameled Daisies 325.00
Pickle, Cranberry Glass, Tongs, Enameled, Poole 300.00
Pickle, Cupid & Venus, Pairpoint Frame, Stylized Swan Heads 85.00
Pickle, Daisy & Button, Silver-Plated Frame & Tongs 210.00
Pickle, Daisy & Button, Vaseline, Silver-Plated Holder 145.00
Pickle, Egg-Shaped, White Interior, Enameled Gold Flowers 395.00
Pickle, Enameled Florals, Foliage, Vaseline, Silver Fork & Frame 425.00
Pickle, Enameled, Cranberry, Figural Bird On Frame, Sterling Silver 385.00
Pickle, Inverted Thumbprint, Enameled, Interior Ribs, 2 13/16 In. 130.00
Pickle, Inverted Thumbprint, Hourglass Shape, Silver-Plated Holder 95.00
Pickle, Inverted Thumbprint, Tongs, Silver Plate 155.00
Pickle, Maidenhair & Fern, Cranberry, 2 5/8 In. 70.00
Pickle, Medallion Sprig, Cranberry To Clear 210.00
Pickle, Melon Rib Swirl, Derby Silver Plate 135.00
Pickle, Mums, Frosted, Silver Plated Frame, Royal Flemish, 9 1/2 In. 1265.00
Pickle, Pairpoint Glass, Rubena's Vertical Optic 225.00
Pickle, Paneled Cranberry, Fork 225.00
Pickle, Pinched, Gold, Tufts Frame 245.00
Pickle, Pineapple & Fan, Silver-Plated Holder & Tongs 65.00
Pickle, Royal Oak, Rubina 210.00
Pickle, Rubina, Diamond Pattern, Floral, 4 1/2 In. 165.00
Pickle, Ruby Glass, Torquay Pattern 295.00
Pickle, Vaseline Glass, Allover White Design, Footed Frame 450.00
Pickle, Vaseline Glass, Meriden 145.00
Pickle, Venus & Cupid, Fork 145.00
    CATALOG, see Paper, Catalog
    CAUGHLEY, see Salopian

The firm Cauldon Limited worked in Staffordshire, Great Britain, and went through many name changes. John Ridgway made porcelain at Cauldon Place, Hanley, until 1855. The firm of John Ridgway, Bates and Co. of Cauldon Place worked from 1856 to 1859. It became Bates, Brown-Westhead, Moore and Co. from 1859 to 1862. Brown-Westhead, Moore and Co. worked from 1862 to 1904. About 1890, this firm started using the words "Cauldon" or "Cauldon ware" as part of the mark. Cauldon Ltd. worked from 1905 to 1920, Cauldon Potteries from 1920 to 1962.

    CAULDON, see also Indian Tree
CAULDON, Cup & Saucer, Cobalt Blue & Gold, Gold Handles, 14 Piece 60.00
  Plate, Hunt Scene, 10 3/4 In. 75.00
  Tea Set, Westhead Moore 225.00

Celadon is a Chinese porcelain having a velvet-textured green-gray glaze. Japanese, Korean, and other factories also made a celadon-colored glaze.

CELADON, Ginger Jar, Cabbage Leaf, Celadon, Domed Top, 12 In. 415.00
  Jar, Cabbage Leaf, Butterfly, C.1900, 8 In. 55.00
  Plate, American Eagle, C.1900, 10 In. 55.00
  Plate, Red Flowers, Birds, Butterflies, Marked, 7 In. 125.00
  Rose Jar, Flowers, Molded Leaves, Gold Trim, Cover, 5 1/2 In. 95.00
  Vase, Applied Blue & White Prunus Design, 11 1/2 In. 67.50

Celluloid is a trademark for a plastic developed in 1868 by John W. Hyatt. Celluloid Manufacturing Company, the Celluloid Novelty Company, Celluloid Fancy Goods Company, and American Xylonite Company all used Celluloid to make jewelry, games, sewing equipment, false teeth, and piano keys. Eventually, the Hyatt Company became the American Celluloid and Chemical Manufacturing Company—the Celanese Corporation. The name "Celluloid" was often used to identify any similar plastic. Celluloid toys are listed under toys.

CELLULOID, Box, Collar 25.00

Box, Dresser, Scenic, Scalloped, Oblong 40.00
Box, Girl & Dog Playing Piano, Lady With Hat 25.00
Comb, Brown, Butterfly Shape 20.00
Comb, Lavender Stone 18.00
Comb, Red Rhinestones, 4 In. 22.00
Dancer, Hawaiian, Windup, 1940s 125.00
Dresser Set, Brass, Mirror, Brush, Comb & Box, 1930, 4 Piece 65.00
Dresser Set, LaBelle, 3 Piece 40.00
Dresser Set, Light Green, Designs, Gold Trim, 9 Piece 45.00
Dresser Set, Mirror, Brush & Comb, Art Deco, Green, Black, Silver 23.00
Hairbrush, Child's 4.00
Mustache Comb, Tortoise–Type, Silver Casing 15.00
Powder Box & Hand Mirror, Ivory Color, Beveled, Cover 25.00
Rattle, Googly Eyes, 1927 .... 18.00
Traveling Kit, Man's Leather Case, 7 Piece 55.00

The Ceramic Art Company of Trenton, New Jersey, was established in 1889 by J. Coxon and W. Lenox and was an early producer of American Belleek porcelain. Pieces made by this company are listed here. Do not confuse this ware with the pottery made by the Ceramic Arts Studio of Madison, Wisconsin, from 1941 to 1957.

CERAMIC ART CO., Coffee Set, Palette Mark, 1898–1906, 3 Piece 187.00
Creamer, Gold Gilded Floral Allover, 3 3/4 In. 105.00
Salt, Individual, Floral Design, 1 1/2 In., 5 Piece 20.00
Tankard, Green Leaves, With Monk, Purple Mark, 14 In. 375.00
Vase, Autumn Leaves, CAC, C.1879, 12 1/2 In. 145.00

Chalkware is really plaster of Paris decorated with watercolors. One type was molded from Staffordshire and other porcelain models and painted and sold as inexpensive decorations in the nineteenth century. Figures of plaster, made from about 1910 to 1940 for use as prizes at carnivals, are also known as chalkware.

CHALKWARE, Ashtray, Scotty Dog, Gold, Marked Basons Fala, 1943 On Front 35.00
Bank, Cupid, 12 In. 100.00
Bank, Dog 35.00
Bank, Santa Claus 58.00
Billiken, On Throne 25.00
Bookends, Dog 8.00
Bust, Lincoln, Wooden Base, White Paint, 13 1/2 In. 35.00
    CHALKWARE, FIGURINE, see also Kewpie
Figurine, Bird, On Plinth, Original Polychrome Paint, 6 1/2 In. 210.00
Figurine, Blatz Beer Dancer, On Barrel 225.00
Figurine, Bride & Groom, 1930s, 5 In. 17.50
Figurine, Cat, Seated, Smoke Grain Painted, 10 3/4 In. 850.00
Figurine, Cat, Seated, Yellow, Red Collar, Pa., 15 3/4 In. 1540.00
Figurine, Cat, Shellac Finish 935.00
Figurine, Child, Reading Book, Eyelet Bonnet, Brown Patina 65.00
Figurine, Clark Gable 85.00
Figurine, Dog, Freestanding Front Legs, 8 In. 185.00
Figurine, Dog, Seated, Black & Yellow, With Red, 5 1/2 In., Pair 250.00
Figurine, Dove, Painted, 1800s 55.00
Figurine, Dove, Pink Paint, 11 In., Pair 410.00
Figurine, Dutch Boy & Girl 20.00
Figurine, Jockey, On Horse, Carnival 22.50
Figurine, Lady, Upswept Hair, Deep Browns, 8 In. 75.00
Figurine, Mae West 35.00
Figurine, Ram, Original Red & Black Painted Trim, 3 3/8 In. 225.00
Figurine, Snow White, Carnival .... 40.00 To 85.00
Figurine, Uncle Sam, Carnival, Large 45.00
Frame, Picture, Fancy, Oval, 18 X 24 In. 125.00
Garniture, Fruit & Foliage, Polychrome Paint, 13 1/2 In. 95.00
Garniture, Pineapple, Yellow & Green, 12 In. 40.00
Lamp, Electric, Indian On Horse 40.00

Lamp, Figural, Will Rogers, On Rearing Horse, 14 In.	59.00
Match Safe, Smiling Black Face, Wall–Type	85.00
Potholder, Wall, Black Chef & Girl, Pair	28.50
String Holder, Boy With Pipe	11.25
String Holder, French Chef	15.00
String Holder, Mexican With Red Hat	20.00
String Holder, Spanish Senor & Senorita, Pair	50.00
String Holder, Top Hat With Face	35.00
Vase, Tree, With Owls, Birds & Flowers, 8 In.	50.00

Charlie Chaplin, the famous comic and actor, lived from 1889 to 1977. He made his first movie in 1913. He did the movie "The Tramp" in 1915. The character of the Tramp has remained famous and is in use today in a series of television commercials for computers. Dolls, candy containers, and all sorts of memorabilia picture Charlie Chaplin. Pieces are being made even today.

CHARLIE CHAPLIN, Candy Container	125.00
Doll, Cadeaux, Bubbles Inc., 1972, Box, 17 In.	75.00
Doll, Composition, Straw–Filled Muslin Body, 1920, 30 In.	400.00
Doll, Tin Body, Papier–Mache Head, Cloth Outfit, 7 1/2 In.	235.00
Doorstop	350.00
Figurine, Plays Song Smile, Revolving, 1973, 7 1/2 In.	28.00
Photograph, Young Man, Signed, Framed, 6 1/4 X 4 1/2 In.	650.00
Poster, City Lights, French Release, C.1958, 60 X 46 In.	80.00
Toy, Twirls Cane, Schuco, 1920s	650.00
Toy, Walking, Fully Dressed, Tin, Key Wind, Germany, 8 In.	950.00
Toy, Windup, Tips Hat, Tin, 4 In.	65.00

Charlie McCarthy was the ventriloquist's dummy used by Edgar Bergen from the 1930s. He was famous for his work in radio, movies, and television. The act was retired in the 1970s.

CHARLIE MCCARTHY, Book, Adventures, Charlie McCarthy & Edgar Bergen, 1933	20.00
Book, Comic, In The Haunted Hideout, 1948	15.00
Doll, Composition, Pull String, Mouth Opens, 20 In.	295.00
Doll, Tuxedo, 1933, 28 In.	325.00
Doll, Ventriloquist, Composition, 22 1/2 In.	265.00 To 375.00
Doll, Walker	275.00
Game, Bingo, 1938	27.00
Game, Radio Party, Die Cut Figures, Complete	45.00
Gum Wrapper, Edgar Bergen, Better Bubble Gum	20.00
Paper Doll, 12 In.	25.00
Pencil Sharpener	40.00
Pin, Mechanical	35.00
Radio, Majestic, Beige, Art Nouveau Plastic, 7 X 7 In.	500.00
Radio, White Bakelite, Charlie Sitting On Front	445.00
Spoon, Silver Plate	9.00
Toy, Benzine Buggy, Tin, Louis Marx, Box, 7 In.	400.00
Toy, Car, Marx	285.00
Toy, Mortimer Snerd, Tin, Walker, Key Wind, Marx, 7 3/4 In.	200.00

Chelsea grape pattern was made before 1840. A small bunch of grapes in a raised design, colored with purple or blue luster, is on the border of the white plate. Most of the pieces are unmarked. The pattern is sometimes called "Aynsley" or "Grandmother." Chelsea sprig is similar but has a sprig of flowers instead of the bunch of grapes.

CHELSEA GRAPE, Bowl, 8 In.	50.00
Creamer	20.00
Cup & Saucer	30.00
CHELSEA KERAMIC ART WORKS, see Dedham	
CHELSEA SPRIG, Bowl, 7 In.	20.00
Cup & Saucer	25.00

Chelsea porcelain was made in the Chelsea area of London from about 1745 to 1784. Ceramic designs were borrowed from the Meissen models of the day. Pieces were made of soft paste. The gold anchor was used as the mark but it has been copied by many other factories. Recent copies of Chelsea have been made from the original molds.

CHELSEA, Dish, Leaf Shape, Serrated, Green To Yellow, Brown Anchor, 11 In.	2750.00
Figurine, Lady, Purple, Hat & Apron, Holding Hat, Gold Anchor, 7 In.	175.00
Perfume Bottle, Girl In A Swing, Stopper, Gold Mounted, 3 7/8 In.	1650.00
Perfume Bottle, Harlequin & Columbine, Stopper, 1760–65, 3 3/4 In.	7150.00
Perfume Bottle, Wine Flask, Basket, Stopper, Gold Mounted, 3 5/8 In.	550.00
Tea Jar, Chinaman, Seated, Smiling, 1745–49, Triangle Mark, 6 In.	1350.00
Teapot, Gothic Shape	75.00
Tureen, Asparagus, Figural, Cover, C.1755, Red Anchor Mark, 7 1/4 In.	8250.00
Vase, Pillow, Blue, Cherry Red Glaze, Impressed, 3 In.	550.00

Chinese export porcelain comprises all the many kinds of porcelain made in China for export to America and Europe in the eighteenth and nineteenth centuries.

CHINESE EXPORT, see also Canton; Celadon; Nanking; Rose Medallion

CHINESE EXPORT, Basket, Fruit, Armorial, Blunt Center, C.1785, 3 X 8 In.	3850.00
Bowl, Cabbage Leaf, Insects, C.1900, 12 In.	40.00
Bowl, Dutch Ship Vryburg, Square, 10 In.	80.00
Bowl, Masonic Emblems, 10 In.	400.00
Brush Pot, 2 Birds On Prunus Bough, C.1720, 5 In.	2950.00
Brush Pot, Scholar, Lady On Either Side of Table, C.1700	2250.00
Butter Tub, Armorial, St.John, Cover, C.1800, 7 1/2 In.	4350.00
Candlestick, Armorial, Steensen, Yung Cheng, 5 In., Pair	7500.00
Dish, 2 Ladies On Terrace, C.1710, 11 In.	4200.00
Dish, Birds & Flowering Plants, C.1710, 14 1/2 In.	680.00
Dish, Butterfly Hovering Over Flowers, C.1720, 4 1/2 In.	325.00
Dish, Floral, Peach Form Finial, Cover, Oval, 5 In.	155.00
Dish, Warming, Fitzhugh, Oval, Flower Clusters, 17 1/2 In.	1300.00
Fan, Carved Ivory & Feather, Lacquer Box	50.00
Figurine, Foo Dogs, Green, Brown, Marked, 1930, 10 In., Pair	95.00
Ginger Jar, Famille Rose, Florals, Calligraphy, 12 In.	125.00
Jar, Melon Form, Famille Noire, Duck & Lotus, 8 In., Pair	115.00
Mug, Blue Floral Design, Porcelain, 18th Century, 7 1/4 In.	450.00
Mug, Demi–Lion Crest, Blue Flowers, 1795, 7 1/4 In.	1850.00
Mug, Floral Spray, Dragon Handle, C.1780, 5 In., Pair	1300.00
Mug, Heart Thumb Rest On Handle, 19th Century, 5 3/4 In.	325.00
Mug, Orange Fish Scale, Floral Panels, 5 3/4 In. ....*Illus*	325.00
Pitcher, Milk, Porcelain, Green, Gold, Fitzhugh Design, 9 In.	385.00
Plate, Armorial, Gibbon of Bishop's Bourne, Kent, 1727, 9 In.	1850.00
Plate, Armorial, Harrison, Fort St.George, C.1720, 14 In.	885.00
Plate, Armorial, Hutchinson, Boston, C.1755, 9 In.	1500.00
Plate, Armorial, Marquis De Coetlogan, C.1750, 11 In.	5500.00
Plate, Armorial, Monro of Foulis, C.1745, 9 In.	1850.00
Plate, Chinese Terrace Scene, Crest, G.H., 1810, 9 1/2 In.	450.00
Plate, Famille Rose, Flower Sprays At Rim, C.1745	420.00
Platter, Armorial, Crest of Boswell, C.1800, 19 In.	1800.00
Punch Bowl, Famille Rose, Mandarin Scenes, 5 X 16 In.	850.00
Punch Bowl, Mandarin Pattern, Porcelain, 6 1/2 X 15 3/4 In.	3100.00
Soup, Dish, Armorial, C.1735, 9 In.	4200.00
Soup, Dish, Armorial, Octagonal, C.1765, 9 In.	1450.00
Tea Caddy, Famille Rose Flowers, 5 In. ....*Illus*	50.00
Teapot Stand, Armorial, Blue Enameled, C.1740	480.00
Teapot, Oriental People, Flattened Shape, 10 3/4 In.	350.00
Tureen, Cover, Stand, Branch Handles, Fish, 14 1/2 In.	3850.00
Tureen, Tray, Bombe Form, Famille Rose, 15 In.	2750.00
Tureen, Tray, Coral Red Floral, Cover, 15 In.	440.00
Umbrella Stand, Cross Hatched Bands, Birds, 23 1/2 In.	400.00
Umbrella Stand, Famille Rose, Dragons, Flowers, 24 1/2 In.	1300.00

Chinese Export, Mug,   Chinese Export, Tea Caddy,   Chinese Export, Vase, Temple,
Orange Fish Scale,   Famille Rose Flowers, 5 In.   Exotic Birds, Flowers,
Floral Panels, 5 3/4 In.   25 In., Pair

Urn, Sepia River Scene Front & Back, 13 1/4 In.	225.00
Vase, Double Gourd, Flowers & Insects, 12 1/2 In.	2200.00
Vase, Lamp, Allover Flowerheads, Vines, 28 In., Pair	1650.00
Vase, Lamp, Famille Jaune, Lion Lid, Electric, 20 In., Pair	3300.00
Vase, Temple, Exotic Birds, Flowers, 25 In., Pair ....*Illus*	400.00

 Chocolate glass, sometimes mistakenly called caramel slag, was made by the Indiana Tumbler and Goblet Company of Greentown, Indiana, from 1900 to 1903.

CHOCOLATE GLASS, Berry Bowl, Cactus, Individual	30.00
Berry Bowl, Wild Rose & Bowknot	85.00
Berry Set, Cactus, 7 Piece	265.00
Bowl, 6 Points, Large	185.00
Bowl, Beaded Triangle, 4 1/2 In.	265.00
Bowl, Cactus, 4 X 9 1/2 In.	75.00
Breakfast Set, Wild Rose With Scrolling, Child's, 4 Piece	1450.00
Butter, Cactus, Cover	165.00
Butter, Cactus, Stemmed	800.00
Butter, Daisy, Cover	215.00
Butter, Dewey, Cover, 1/4 Lb.	150.00
Butter, Fleur–De–Lis, Cover	350.00
Butter, Leaf Bracket, Cover	100.00
Candy Dish, Cover, Cactus, 6–Footed, 6 X 5 In.	138.00
Compote, Cactus, 5 1/2 In.	150.00
Compote, Eagle, Footed, Cover	65.00
Creamer, Geneva	350.00
Creamer, Shuttle	110.00
Creamer, Sultan, Child's	250.00
Cruet, Cactus, Original Stopper	155.00
Cruet, Leaf Bracket, Stopper	135.00 To 175.00
Cruet, Wild Rose With Bowknot, Original Stopper	265.00
Dish, Bird With Berry, Cover	675.00
Dish, Cat On Hamper Cover	275.00
Dish, Hen On Nest Cover	365.00 To 375.00
Dish, Rabbit Cover	425.00
Dish, Rooster Cover	95.00
Dish, Turkey Mystery, Cover	50.00
Mug, Cactus	68.00 To 95.00
Mug, Herringbone, 4 3/4 In.	55.00
Mug, Indoor Drinking Scene, Master	525.00
Mug, Indoor Drinking Scene, Pouring Spout	135.00
Mug, Outdoor Drinking Scene, Castle	110.00

Mug, Serenade, Master 750.00
Mug, Shuttle 55.00
Mustard, Wild Rose & Bowknot, Cover 40.00
Nappy, Cactus 100.00
Nappy, Leaf Bracket .... 40.00 To 65.00
Pitcher, Milk, Feather 650.00
Pitcher, Water, Wild Rose With Bowknot 550.00
Relish, Leaf Bracket 55.00
Salt & Pepper, Cactus, Original Tops 95.00
Saltshaker, Cactus 60.00
Spooner, Cactus 95.00
Spooner, Geneva 135.00
Spooner, Leaf Bracket 90.00
Spooner, Sultan, Child's 225.00
Sugar, Cactus 120.00
Syrup, Shuttle .... 65.00 To 95.00
Table Set, Leaf Bracket, 4 Piece 450.00
Toothpick, Cactus 40.00
Tray, Dresser, Wild Rose & Bowknot 275.00
Tumbler, Cactus, Straight–Sided 55.00
Tumbler, Cord Drapery, Greentown 225.00
Tumbler, Leaf Bracket 55.00
Tumbler, Lemonade, Cactus 65.00
Tumbler, Sawtooth, Greentown 85.00
Tumbler, Uneeda Biscuit 125.00
Water Set, Allover Pears & Leaves, 5 Piece 150.00

The first decorated Christmas tree in America is claimed by many states, including Pennsylvania (1747), Massachusetts (1832), Illinois (1833), Ohio (1838), and Iowa (1845). The first glass ornaments were imported from Germany about 1860. Manufacturers in the United States were making ornaments in the early 1870s. Electric lights were first used on a Christmas tree in 1882. Character light bulbs became popular in the 1920s, bubble lights in the 1940s, twinkle bulbs in the 1950s, plastic bulbs by 1955. In this book a Christmas light is a holder for a candle used on the tree. Other forms of lighting include light bulbs.

CHRISTMAS TREE, Feather, 18 In. 52.00
Feather, 2 Sections, 5 1/2 In. 500.00
Feather, 5 Ft. 275.00
Feather, Berries, Stenciled Base, Germany, 96 In., 2 Piece 1500.00
Feather, Box, 20 In. 175.00
Feather, Cotton Ornaments, Die Cut Santa Claus, 15 1/2 In. 225.00
Feather, Germany, 8 In. 88.00
Feather, Germany, 22 In. 125.00
Feather, Goose, Handmade, Berries, Wooden Base, 3 Ft. 135.00
Feather, Green, 4 Ft. 230.00
Feather, On Turned Wooden Base, Clips At Tips, 52 In. 90.00
Feather, Red Berries, 15 In. 75.00
Feather, Red Berries, No Base, 6 Ft. 500.00
Feather, Silver Green, Crepe Paper Trunk, 70 In. 65.00
Feather, Simulated, Green Wooden Base, 32 In. 250.00
Feather, With Berries, Painted Wood Base, 3 Ft. 280.00
Feather, With Candleholders, 2 Ft. 130.00
Fence, 4 Sections, 6 In. 65.00
Fence, 2 Gates, 2 8–In. Sections, 6 12–In. Sections, Iron 350.00
Fence, 4 Green Sections, Red Corner Post, Wooden 62.00
Fence, Accordian Style, 16 Sections, Wooden, 96 In. 30.00
Fence, Gate, Green Paint, Gold Trim 275.00
Fence, Iron, Green, 8 Ft. 300.00
Fence, Pickets, Gate, Red & Green, Wooden, 40 X 20 In. 73.00
Fence, Red & Green, 14 Sections, Wooden 85.00
Fence, Red & Green, Square, 22 In. 80.00
Fence, Twig, Gate, Square, 22 In. 85.00

Fence, Victorian, Swinging Gate, Cast Iron	265.00
Fence, White Picket, Post, Double Gate, 35 Ft.	125.00
Light Bulb, 3 Father Christmas Faces, Milk Glass	12.00
Light Bulb, Andy Gamp	35.00
Light Bulb, Apple	15.00
Light Bulb, Baby In Stocking	12.00
Light Bulb, Basket of Fruit, Noma	25.00
Light Bulb, Bell, Red	10.00
Light Bulb, Betty Boop	70.00
Light Bulb, Birds, Pastel	10.00
Light Bulb, Bluebird	9.50
Light Bulb, Boy With Bat	20.00
Light Bulb, Candle, Series Type	10.00
Light Bulb, Cat In Stocking	35.00
Light Bulb, Cat With Mandolin, Milk Glass	35.00
Light Bulb, Chinese Lantern	5.00
Light Bulb, Coach Lamp	5.00
Light Bulb, Cottage With Snow	10.00
Light Bulb, Dog, Flop–Earred	40.00
Light Bulb, Drummer Boy, Milk Glass	45.00
Light Bulb, Elephant On Ball	35.00
Light Bulb, Elephant With Trunk Up	15.00
Light Bulb, Fish	15.00
Light Bulb, Girl With Muff, Milk Glass	20.00
Light Bulb, Grapes	9.00 To 15.00
Light Bulb, Hound Dog	25.00
Light Bulb, House, With Snow	10.00
Light Bulb, Humpty–Dumpty, Standing	40.00
Light Bulb, Japanese Lantern	5.00 To 10.00
Light Bulb, Kayo, Squatting	35.00
Light Bulb, Lantern Shape, Hobnail, Wire Handle, 4 1/4 In.	20.00
Light Bulb, Little Red Riding Hood	30.00
Light Bulb, Moon Mullins	30.00
Light Bulb, Orphan Annie	20.00 To 45.00
Light Bulb, Pine Cone	10.00
Light Bulb, Pocket Watch	25.00
Light Bulb, Princess Summer Fall Winter Spring	115.00
Light Bulb, Rose, Open, Red	20.00
Light Bulb, Sandy	30.00
Light Bulb, Santa Claus Face, Double–Sided	11.00
Light Bulb, Santa Claus, 8 1/2 In.	135.00
Light Bulb, Santa Claus, Milk Glass	8.00 To 17.50
Light Bulb, Santa, Sleigh & Reindeer	15.00
Light Bulb, Smitty	35.00
Light Bulb, Snowball	5.00
Light Bulb, Snowman	11.00 To 22.50
Light Bulb, Snowman, With Holly, Milk Glass	8.00
Light Bulb, Squirrel	30.00
Light Bulb, Stiegel Type, Infold Rim, Expanded Diamond	110.00
Light Bulb, String, Reliance, 6 Original Bulbs, Box	100.00
Light Bulb, Three Bears, Milk Glass	20.00
Light Bulb, Zeppelin, Milk Glass	45.00
Light, Basket, Quilted, Bail, Amber, 3 1/4 In.	9.00
Light, Basket, Quilted, Emerald Green, 3 1/4 In.	16.00
Ornament, 3 Masted Ships, Red Hull, Dresden, 4 1/2 In.	190.00
Ornament, Air Balloon, Spun Glass, Die Cut Cupids	55.00
Ornament, Alligator, Iridescent Green, Gold, Dresden, 4 In.	200.00
Ornament, Andy Gump	45.00
Ornament, Angel, Blown, Hand Painted, Germany	6.50
Ornament, Angel, Spun Glass	10.00
Ornament, Automobile	100.00
Ornament, Aviator	35.00
Ornament, Baby In Cradle	20.00
Ornament, Ball, Santa Claus In The Moon, Glass	55.00

Ornament, Ball, Whistling Boy, Glass	65.00
Ornament, Banana, 4 In.	85.00
Ornament, Banjo, Silver & Gold Glass, 7 In.	12.00
Ornament, Basket Cart, Goat, 2 Wheels, Silver, Dresden, 4 In.	450.00
Ornament, Basket, Tinsel Wrapped, Magenta, Swan, 5 1/2 In.	65.00
Ornament, Beads, Glass, 7 Ft.	20.00
Ornament, Begging Cat	45.00
Ornament, Bell, Santa Claus Face, Chenille, 4 In.	65.00
Ornament, Bell, Tinsel Wrapped	24.00
Ornament, Betty Boop	60.00
Ornament, Bird, Blown, Hand Painted, Germany	5.50
Ornament, Cannon On Wheels, Gun Crew, Silver, Dresden, 3 In.	200.00
Ornament, Carousel	35.00
Ornament, Carrot, 4 In.	85.00
Ornament, Cat In Sack, Glass	65.00
Ornament, Child's Face, Glass Eyes	85.00
Ornament, Child's Head, Blown Glass, 2 1/2 In.	20.00
Ornament, Child, Clown Hat, Silver, Faded Colors, 3 1/4 In.	45.00
Ornament, Chinese Lantern	10.00
Ornament, Circus Elephant, Silver, Red, Gold, 3 In.	70.00
Ornament, Clown In Barrel, Cotton Batting	65.00
Ornament, Clown, Double-Faced, Silvered, 5 1/2 In.	95.00
Ornament, Cockatoo In Hoop, Rose Iridescent, Dresden, 4 In.	175.00
Ornament, Coffeepot, Red	10.00
Ornament, Comic Figure of Black Man, Long Legs, 5 In.	25.00
Ornament, Corn, Glass	65.00
Ornament, Cornucopia, With Doll	52.00
Ornament, Cross, With Star	25.00
Ornament, Dog, On Ball	95.00
Ornament, Doll In Basket	55.00
Ornament, Donkey, Pulls Sleigh, Dry Flowers, Dresden, 4 In.	500.00
Ornament, Duck	40.00
Ornament, Ear of Corn, Silvered With Gold Stain, 3 3/4 In.	40.00
Ornament, Elephant	25.00
Ornament, Fat Man, With Accordion	45.00
Ornament, Fish, 6 In.	60.00
Ornament, Fish, Blown Glass	25.00
Ornament, Fish, Blue	10.00
Ornament, Flower, On Tin Clip, Frosted Mica, 3 In.	45.00
Ornament, Football Player, Celluloid Head, Straw Body	58.00
Ornament, Frog, Pink, Glass	40.00
Ornament, Girl In Beehive, Glass	55.00
Ornament, Girl With Muff, Milk Glass	20.00
Ornament, Girl's Head, Glass Eyes	130.00
Ornament, Glass, Max Eckardt, Box, 1930s, 12 Piece	22.00
Ornament, Goldilocks, Glass	65.00
Ornament, Grapes, Green, Blown Glass, Brass Hook, 4 1/2 In.	225.00
Ornament, Heart, Blue, Small	6.00
Ornament, Heart, Figural, Silvered	5.00
Ornament, Horse, Running, Pulling Farm Wagon, Dresden, 5 In.	400.00
Ornament, Hound Dog	35.00
Ornament, Humpty-Dumpty, On Wall	35.00
Ornament, Icicle, Cotton Batting	10.00
Ornament, Icicle, Swirled, 13 1/2 In.	20.00
Ornament, Indian Head, Silvered, 3 1/2 In.	135.00
Ornament, Indian, Bust	135.00
Ornament, Jack-O'-Lantern, Deep Red, White, Black, 2 1/2 In.	105.00
Ornament, Jockey On Horse, Jumping, Silver, Dresden, 2 In.	150.00
Ornament, Kayo	45.00
Ornament, Lamb, Wood, Papier-Mache, Wooly, Germany, 3 In., Pair	90.00
Ornament, Little Boy Blue	35.00
Ornament, Little Miss Muffet	35.00
Ornament, Little Orphan Annie	50.00
Ornament, Little Red Riding Hood	35.00

Ornament, Lyre	65.00
Ornament, Madonna & Child	75.00
Ornament, Man In Carriage, Horse, Polychrome, Dresden, 4 In.	700.00
Ornament, Mandolin, Blown Glass	25.00
Ornament, Moon Mullins	45.00
Ornament, Mother Goose	35.00
Ornament, My Darling Dog, In Sack	115.00
Ornament, Old Lady In Shoe	25.00
Ornament, Owl, Glass	55.00
Ornament, Pelican, Glass	55.00
Ornament, Pine Cone, Silver	3.00
Ornament, Pine Cone, With Santa Claus Face	65.00
Ornament, Pinocchio	50.00
Ornament, Poodle, White, Red Silk Ribbon, Dresden, 3 1/4 In.	225.00
Ornament, Potbelly Stove, Papier–Mache	15.00
Ornament, Purse	35.00
Ornament, Rabbit, Eating Carrot, Glass	50.00
Ornament, Raspberries	3.00
Ornament, Retriever, Holds Riding Crop, Dresden, 2 3/4 In.	300.00
Ornament, Roly Poly	45.00
Ornament, Rooster, Brown Over Gold, Dresden, 3 1/2 In.	140.00
Ornament, Rooster, Composition, Clip–On, Germany	28.00
Ornament, Saddle Shoes	60.00
Ornament, Sailor Doll, Holland American Lines, Composition	45.00
Ornament, Sandy	50.00
Ornament, Santa Claus Head, Celluloid, Movable Eyes, Rattle	39.00
Ornament, Santa Claus Head, Papier–Mache	20.00
Ornament, Santa Claus, Ball, Hand Painted, Germany, 5 In.	7.50
Ornament, Santa Claus, Celluloid, Irwin, 4 1/2 In.	35.00
Ornament, Santa Claus, Cotton, Glass	25.00
Ornament, Santa Claus, On Bell, Clapper, Silvered, 4 1/2 In.	55.00
Ornament, Santa Claus, On Oak Leaf	45.00
Ornament, Santa Claus, On Swing, Tinsel	25.00
Ornament, Santa Claus, Plaster Face, Chenille, Skinny, 5 In.	15.00
Ornament, Santa Claus, With Tree, Glass	65.00
Ornament, Santa Claus, With Tree, Sanded Trim	22.50
Ornament, Santa Claus, With Tree, Silver, Gold, 4 1/2 In.	55.00
Ornament, Scotty Dog, Silvered, 3 3/4 In.	35.00
Ornament, Shoe On Wheels	65.00
Ornament, Silver Fish	20.00
Ornament, Skier, Cotton Batting	28.00
Ornament, Slipper, Dresden, Marked, 3 5/8 In.	65.00
Ornament, Snowman, With Broom, Blown Glass	65.00
Ornament, Steamship, Blown Glass	85.00
Ornament, Steamship, Paper Anchor	185.00
Ornament, Street Lamp, Sanded Snow Trim	7.00
Ornament, Swan, Glass, Hook, 6 In.	16.00
Ornament, Three Men In A Tub	55.00
Ornament, Tomato, Red	95.00
Ornament, Tree Top, Painted Gold Flakes, Papier–Mache	15.00
Ornament, Trumpet	55.00
Ornament, Turnip	60.00
Ornament, Umbrella, Closed, Blown Glass, 10 In.	20.00
Ornament, Umbrella, Wire–Wrapped	95.00
Stand, Adjustable, Case Iron, 10 1/2 In.	45.00
Stand, Cast Iron & Tin, Original Green Paint	45.00
Stand, Cast Iron, White Co., Box	15.00
Stand, Embossed Trunk & Root Design, Green, Iron, 11 In.	75.00
Stand, Green, Stenciled, Tin, 1915	35.00
Stand, Ornamental, Cast Iron, C.1900	125.00
Stand, Revolving, 2 Song	55.00
Stand, Santa Claus & Reindeer	150.00
Stand, Scenes of Girl With Halo, German Inscription, Iron	75.00
Stand, Stenciled, Tin, Dated 1915	50.00

If you are a collector of old Christmas tree ornaments or Christmas lights, use these on the tree. Do not use burning candles—It is too dangerous.

Stand, Tripod Legs, Santas On Sides, 10 In.	150.00
Stand, White Co., Cast Iron	15.00
Wooden, Aluminum Branches, Box, 1950s	10.00

Almost anything connected with Christmas is collected. Ornaments, feather trees, tree stands, santa claus figures, special dishes, even games and wrapping paper.

CHRISTMAS, Banner, Store, Headquarters For Holiday Goods, 1920, 10 Ft.	400.00
Belsnickels, Composition, Standing, Red, 1920, Germany, 4 1/4 In.	130.00
Book, Coloring, Hi Santa, 48 Pages, 1950	10.00
Book, Santa Claus Visit, Blue Santa On Cover, Donahue	16.00
Candleholder, Holly, Iron, Pair	24.00
Candy Box, Bell, Cardboard	10.00
Candy Box, Children At Fireplace, Santa Claus, Cardboard, 1930s	25.00
Card, Fringed, Square, 8 In.	12.00
Cigar Box, Girl, With Holly, Merry Christmas, 5 1/4 In.	30.00
Costume, Santa Claus, With Mask	25.00
Display, Music Box, Snap, Crackle, Pop, Jingle Bells, 11 In.	185.00
Doll, English, St.Nicholas, Poured Wax, Muslin Body, 18 In.	800.00
Lamp, Kerosene, Santa Claus, Figural Chimney, Hanging	165.00
Marionette, Santa Claus, 1950	25.00
Mask, Santa Claus, Canvas & Cotton	30.00
Music Box, Figural, Santa's Face, Celluloid	35.00
Nodder, Father Christmas, Key Wind, Papier–Mache, 24 In.	2500.00
Party Hat & Surprise, FAO Schwartz, Box, 6 In.	50.00
CHRISTMAS, PLATE, see Collector Plate	
Puppet, Santa Claus, Push Button, Kohner, 1972	25.00
Rattle, Santa On Ring, Celluloid	8.00
Santa Claus Head, Molded, 1938, 24 In.	75.00
Santa Claus, Accordion Crepe Paper, Life Size	100.00
Santa Claus, Brown, Pele Nichols, 15 In.	50.00
Santa Claus, Celluloid Face, With Sack, 7 1/2 In.	85.00
Santa Claus, Composition, Red Sparkle Coat, Germany, 9 In.	225.00
Santa Claus, Fur Beard, In Sleigh, Papier–Mache, 4 In.	150.00
Santa Claus, Holding Bag of Toys, Die Cut, 16 In.	125.00
Santa Claus, Holding Feather Tree, 6 In.	190.00
Santa Claus, Light Bulb Eyes, 1920, 29 In.	225.00
Santa Claus, Paper, 8 In.	25.00
Santa Claus, Papier–Mache, Japan, 8 In.	125.00
Santa Claus, Pressed Cardboard, Germany, 1910, 18 In.	85.00
Santa Claus, Printed Cardboard, Feet That Go Around, 12 In.	30.00
Santa Claus, Red, Pele Nichols, 11 In.	40.00
Santa Claus, Reindeer, Teddy Bear At Feet, Die Cut, 15 In.	200.00
Santa Claus, Sleigh, Papier–Mache, Wooden, Germany, 10 In.	200.00
Santa Claus, Sleigh, Reindeer, Celluloid, 4 1/2 In.	25.00
Santa Claus, Straw–Stuffed, In Wicker Sleigh, 9 In.	335.00
Sheep, Wooden, Papier–Mache, Fleece, Victorian, 4 X 4 In.	45.00
Sign, Santa Claus, Service With A Smile, Lighted, 18 3/4 X 19 In.	335.00
Suit, Santa Claus, Chintz, Linen–Type Mask	45.00
Tablecloth, Merry Christmas, 1920s, 26 X 20 In.	25.00
Wreath, Foil Covered, Papier–Mache Bells, 8 In.	10.00
Wreath, Tree Branch Trim, Crepe Paper, 1920s	15.00

Art Deco chrome items became popular in the 1930s. Collectors are most interested in pieces made by the Chase Brass and Copper Company of Waterbury, Connecticut.

CHROME, Ashtray, Bulldog, Mack	20.00
Ashtray, Twirlaway, Box	25.00
Bell, Table, Art Deco	15.00
Bottle Opener, Corkscrew, Parrot	12.00
Box, Cigarette, Art Deco, Celluloid & Chrome, Chase Brass Co.	85.00
Candlestick, Tubular, Art Deco, Pair	15.00
Cigar Cutter, Fob, Dyed Agate	20.00
Cocktail Set, Art Deco, Shaker, Red Handle, 5 Stemmed Tumblers	65.00
Cocktail Set, Black Bands, 18 Cups, Tray, Swizzle Sticks	150.00
Cocktail Set, Zeppelin Shaker, Plated, Cups, Spoons & Squeezer	350.00
Cocktail Shaker, Red Bakelite Handle	40.00
Coffee Set, Bakelite Handles, Krome–Kraft, Electric, 3 Piece	140.00
Coffee Set, Bakelite, Hotpoint, 1940s, 4 Piece	45.00
Coffeepot, Art Deco, Manning Bowman & Co.	35.00
Coin Changer, Belt, 1930	9.00
Decanter, Cocktail, Art Deco, Chase	18.00
Decanter, Water, Bakelite Handles, Farber Bros.	45.00
Flask, Art Deco, Attached Cap, Germany, Pocket	8.00
Goblet, Snifter, Dimpled, 6 Piece	135.00
Hair Waver, Tiny Water Tank	10.00
Ice Cream Set, Chase, 7 Piece	47.00
Ice Pail, Chase	15.00
Lamp, Floor, 4 Rectangular Panels, Square Base, 1935, 6 Ft.	2750.00
Lighter, Table, World's Fair, Chase Brass, 1939	32.50
Mirror, Jeweler's, Art Deco, 1930s, 21 In.	145.00
Mustard, Chase	10.00
Plate, Hors D'Oeuvre, Chase	15.00
Plate, Pancake, Floral Design, Chrome Dome, Farberware, 10–In. Plate	30.00
Sailboat, Art Deco, 5 In.	12.50
Sugar & Creamer, Tray, Chase	25.00 To 40.00

Carved wooden or cast iron figures were used as advertisements in front of the Victorian cigar store. The carved figures are now collected as folk art. They range in size from counter type, about three feet, to over eight feet high.

CIGAR STORE FIGURE, Bust, Indian Chief, Plaster, C.1900	575.00
Indian, 1940s, 42 In.	165.00
Indian, Wooden Carved, Early 1900s, 73 1/2 In.	1200.00

Cinnabar is a vermilion or red lacquer. Some pieces are made with hundreds of thicknesses of the lacquer that is later carved.

CINNABAR, Button, Carved Chrysanthemum, 1 1/2 In.	55.00
Lamp, Monks, Temple & Trees, Upper Part Copper	125.00
Vase, Red, Carved, Bulbous Middle, Oriental, 12 1/2 In., Pair	395.00

Civil War mementos are important collectors' items. Most of the pieces are military items used from 1861 to 1865.

CIVIL WAR, Army Regulations, George W.Childs Pub., 1863	35.00
Book, Maps, Battle of Shiloh, 1902	45.00
Book, Song, Soldier's Name & Date, 1863, Pocket	39.00
Book, Southern War Songs, Campfire, Patriotic, Sentimental, Fagan	35.00
Book, What A Boy Saw In The Army, Jessie Young, 100 Drawings	20.00
Canteen, Infantry, Pewter Spout, Double Side Bands	37.50
Chair, Camp	75.00
Cloak, Officer's, Confederate	440.00
Condiment Tin, Union, Soldier's Name, Regiment, Iron, 4 X 6 In.	225.00
Cup, Collapsible, Hard Rubber, Gutta Percha, Niles, 1860	145.00
Cup, Collapsible, Pewter–Like, Graduated Size, Box, 3 1/2 In.	94.50
Cup, Pewter, Tin Case, 20th Maine	45.00
Document, Desertion, Pvt.George W.Payne, General Orders, 1864	7.00

Dog Tag, Thomas W.Shields, 2nd Kentucky Guard, Pewter 100.00
Drum, Parade, 11 X 14 1/2 In. 100.00
Fife 35.00
Flag, Made For Col.Whiton of 58th Massachusetts, 35 Stars 475.00
Flag, Union, 34 Stars, 1861 .... 100.00
Foot Locker, Maine Cavalry, Lieutenant's Name On Front 577.00
Fork, Dated 1850 .... 20.00
Fork, John Brown, Sterling Silver, Bone Handle, Dated 1862 .... 35.00
Handcuffs, Figure Eight, Single Drum Lock, Rigged Frame 65.00
Hat, Slouch, Chaplain 2700.00
Holster, For Colt Root Revolver, Belt Loop, 3 1/2 X 4 In. 57.50
Horse Bit, U.S. 80.00
Kepi, Officer's, Blue, Twisted Gold Cord & Wreath, No.16 Center 225.00
Kepi, U.S.Army Issue, Blue Wool Serge, Tilt Forward Crown 550.00
Knife, Bowie, Spearpoint Blade, German Silver Guard, 10 3/4 In. 650.00
Knife, Wooden Handle, Dated 1850 .... 25.00
Marker, Grave, Star, Brass, G.A.R. 30.00
Mess Gear, Folding, Knife–Like, Marked Camillus, N.Y., 3 1/2 In. 49.50
Mess Gear, Tin, J.W.Sleeper, N.H.Cavalry, 4 1/2 In. 350.00
Mirror, Hand 20.00
Mirror, Shaving, Paddle Shape, U.S.Stamp, 2 X 4 In. 97.50
Model, Monument, Citizen Soldiers, Wooden, 1861–65, 11 X 40 In. 220.00
Pay Document, Dated Sept.18, 1780, Hartford, 7 X 7 In. 31.00
Pay Voucher, E.W.Hawkins, 6th District, Ky., 1864 .... 15.00
Plate, Pewter, Depressed Medial, Raised Flat Edge, 10 In. 55.00
Pouch, For Percussion Caps, Marked USN, Black Leather, Flap Cover 250.00
Quilt, Red, Beige, 75 X 72 In. 250.00
Receipt, Slave, Harry, George, Spotswood Plantation, 1862 .... 15.00
Shaving Mug, Side Brush Pocket, Tin 75.00
Sheet Music, Drummer Boy of Shiloh, 1863 .... 21.00
Sheet Music, Tramp, Tramp, Tramp, Prisoner's Hope Song, 1864 .... 17.50
Spurs, Officers, Brass, Iron Spike In Heel of Boot, Pair 40.00
Star, Grave Marker, Brass 30.00
Stickpin, U.S.Grant Photograph 70.00
Trunk, 10th Regiment 42.50
CKAW, see Dedham

Clambroth glass, popular in the Victorian era, is a grayish color and is semiopaque like clambroth.

CLAMBROTH, Candlestick, Ribbed Swirl Pattern Base, 8 In. 45.00
Creamer, Swan 22.00
Eggcup, Cable 550.00
Perfume Bottle, Corset Shape, Threaded, Stopper, 5 1/4 In. 195.00
Plate, Persian Medallion, 6 In. 48.00
Rose Bowl, Flowers, Footed, Fenton 170.00
Tumbler, Lustre Rose, Imperial 42.50
Vase, Palmetto Leaf Around Rim, 6 In. 10.00

Clarice Cliff was a designer who began working at several English factories in the 1920s. She died in 1972.

CLARICE CLIFF, Bowl, Balloon Trees, House, Handle, 5 In. 125.00
Bowl, Bizarre, 9 In. 100.00
Bowl, Molded Flowers Base, 8 1/2 In. 85.00
Bowl, Waterlily Shape, Molded Lily Pads, Marked, 9 X 5 In. 32.50
Candleholder, Crocus Pattern 75.00
Coffee Set, Cream Matte, Green Interiors, C.1940, 15 Piece 140.00
Coffee Set, Fantasque, Geometric, 11 Piece 325.00
Coffeepot, Bizarre, Crocus 135.00
Creamer, Bizarre 90.00
Creamer, Crocus 80.00
Creamer, Royal Staffordshire 18.50
Creamer, Sailboats 85.00
Cup & Saucer, Tonquin 5.00
Dish, Novota, Royal Staffordshire, 10 In. 58.00

Eggcup, Moderne	35.00
Mayonnaise Set, Charlotte, 3 Piece	20.00
Pepper, Bullet, 2 1/2 In.	55.00
Pitcher, Bizarre, Orange Circles, Blue & Green Petals, 5 In.	300.00
Pitcher, Tree & Houses Landscape, Octagonal, 6 1/2 In.	150.00
Plate, Balloon Tree Fantasy, 8 In.	125.00
Plate, Bizarre, 6 1/2 In.	25.00
Plate, Black Balloon Tree, House, Oval, 10 In.	150.00
Plate, Bullet, 6 1/2 In.	20.00
Plate, Bullet, 10 In.	30.00
Plate, Canterbury Bells, 9 In.	18.00 To 25.00
Plate, Day & Night, 6 In.	65.00
Plate, Tonquin, 6 In.	2.00
Plate, Tonquin, 10 1/4 In.	3.00
Platter, Charlotte, 14 In.	10.00
Soup, Dish, Tonquin	4.00
Sugar & Creamer, Crocus Pattern	125.00
Sugar & Creamer, Flower, Trees, Small	75.00
Sugar, Fantasque	70.00 To 80.00
Vase, Lotus, Wicker, Handle, 8 In.	125.00
Vase, Viscaria, 8 In.	115.00
Vase, Wisteria Pattern, 12 In.	190.00

Clewell ware was made in limited quantities by Charles Walter Clewell of Canton, Ohio, from 1902 to 1955. Pottery was covered with a thin coating of bronze, then treated to make the bronze turn different colors. Pieces covered with copper, brass, or silver were also made. Mr. Clewell's secret formula for blue patina bronze was burned when he died in 1965.

CLEWELL, Tankard Set, Strapped, 6 Piece	625.00
Vase, Blue–Green, Flared Lip, Bulbous Bottom, 7 In.	250.00
Vase, Brown & Green Patina, Long Neck, Tapered, 10 In.	385.00
Vase, Bud, Green Patina, 4 In.	90.00
Vase, Green, Orange Patina, 6 1/2 In.	275.00
Vase, Reticulated Form, Large Molded Poppies, 8 In.	3300.00

Clews pottery was made by George Clews & Co. of Brownhill Pottery, Tunstall, England, from 1806 to 1861.

CLEWS, see also Flow Blue

CLEWS, Plate, Toddy, Landing of Lafayette, Dark Blue, 5 3/8 In.	325.00
Plate, Wilkie Series, Valentine, Deep Blue, 10 In.	165.00
Soup, Dish, Landing of Lafayette, 9 3/4 In.	295.00

Clifton Pottery was founded by William Long in Clifton, New Jersey, in 1905. He worked there until 1908 making a line called "Crystal Patina." Clifton Pottery made art pottery. Another firm, Chesapeake Pottery, sold majolica marked "Clifton ware."

CLIFTON, Bowl, Robin's–Egg Blue, Dated 1905, 4 1/2 In.	90.00
Bowl, Squirrels, Footed, 3 X 6 In.	25.00
Cookie Jar, Cookie Truck	28.00
Jardiniere, Ivory, Swans, 5 In.	45.00
Tobacco Jar, Redware, 4 In.	35.00
Vase, Green Patina, Dated 1906, 8 1/2 In.	175.00
Vase, Indian Ware, Angled Rim, Squat Bulbous, 1910, 10 1/2 X 12 In.	300.00
Vase, Indian Ware, Geometric, Homolobi Tribe, 1910, 8 X 10 In.	325.00
Vase, Teardrop Shape, Tab Handles, 4 1/2 In.	120.00

Clocks of all types have always been popular with collectors. The eighteenth–century tall case, or grandfather's clock, was designed to house a works with a long pendulum. In 1816, Eli Terry patented a new, smaller works for a clock; and the case became smaller. The clock could be kept on a shelf instead of on the floor. By 1840, coiled springs were used and even smaller clocks were made. Battery–powered electric clocks were made in the 1870s.

CLOCK, Advertising, 7–Up, Porcelain	50.00
Advertising, Airmail Nylons, Woman's Legs, Reverse Painted Glass	375.00
Advertising, Allis–Chalmers Tractors–Machinery, Neon, 8 Sides, 18 In.	275.00
Advertising, Aunt Jemima, Ceramic, Kitchen, Red Wing	100.00
Advertising, Bachelor Cigars 5 Cents, 2 Faces, Window Hung	2650.00
Advertising, Ballantine Beer, Electric, Pendulum, Lights Up	35.00
Advertising, Bireley's Soda	40.00
Advertising, Blatz Beer, Barrel, Drummer, Electric	50.00
Advertising, Blatz Beer, Man Drinking, Lighted	75.00
Advertising, Bluebird, Moves Back & Forth, Keebler, Key Wind	35.00
Advertising, Borden's, Pictures Elsie, Lighted, Electric	85.00
Advertising, Breyer's Ice Cream, Electric	150.00
Advertising, Budweiser Beer, Pocket Watch Shape, Picture Lights Up	55.00
Advertising, Buy St.Joseph Aspirin, Electric, Giant Aspirin	85.00
Advertising, Calumet Baking Powder, Calendar, Oak Case	995.00
Advertising, Calumet Cake, Let Us Bake Your Cake, Wall, 39 In.	675.00
Advertising, Canada Dry	53.00
Advertising, Charlie The Tuna, Alarm	22.00
Advertising, Del Miles Garage, Round	185.00
Advertising, Double Cola	65.00
Advertising, Dr Pepper, Drink A Bite To Eat, Warren Telechron Co.	250.00
Advertising, Dr Pepper, Good For Life, Red Grid	85.00
Advertising, Embassy Dairy, Pam Clock Company	35.00
Advertising, Evinrude Parts & Service, Uses Light Bulbs, 14 In.	10.00
Advertising, Four Roses Whiskey, 1940s	65.00
Advertising, Garfield Tea & Syrup, Seth Thomas Movement	875.00
Advertising, Garfield Tea, Regulator, Wooden Case, Brass Trim, C.1900	1150.00
Advertising, Grapette, Wall, Second Hand, Round, 10 In.	125.00
Advertising, Headlight Overalls, Steaming Train, Neon ....275.00 To 375.00
Advertising, Keebler, Cat's Head, Glass Eyes	450.00
Advertising, Lowenbrau, Cube, Electric, Logo, 5 1/4 X 9 1/4 In.	22.50
Advertising, Lucky Strike Cigarettes	575.00
Advertising, Mark Twain Flour, Wall	400.00
Advertising, Miller High Life Beer, Electric	75.00
Advertising, Miller Lite Beer, Cube Clock, Shelf Or Wall, Lighted	30.00
Advertising, National Beer, Lighted	25.00
Advertising, Nu Grape	45.00
Advertising, Old Mr. Boston, Windup	175.00
Advertising, Orange Crush, Lights Up, 13 X 15 In.	25.00
Advertising, Pabst Blue Ribbon	35.00
Advertising, People's Band, Time To Save, Neon	295.00
Advertising, Philadelphia Inquirer, Bakelite, Pictures Bulldog	35.00
Advertising, Pillsbury's Best Foods, Neon	185.00
Advertising, Postal Telegraph ....110.00 To 185.00
Advertising, Procter & Gamble, Electric Time, C.1920	90.00
Advertising, Purina Chow Food, Alarm	12.50
Advertising, RCA, Gold Record, Display	150.00
Advertising, Red Goose School Shoes, Goose	1050.00
Advertising, Reminder Clock Co., 11 Panels, Battery Operated, C.1885	800.00
Advertising, Rival Dog Food, Electric	45.00
Advertising, Royal Crown Cola, Electric, Wall, Lighted, 1950s	65.00
Advertising, Royal Crown Cola, Neon	400.00
Advertising, Sauers Extract, Regulator, Gold Leaf Reverse Glass	950.00
Advertising, Schlitz Beer, Diver's Helmet, 4 Sides, Tin	200.00
Advertising, Schlitz Beer, Words At Base, Electric, 1955	125.00
Advertising, Sessions Pottery, Electric, Birdhouse Shape	25.00
Advertising, Sprite, Plastic	18.00
Advertising, Star Brand Shoes, Alarm	20.00
Advertising, Vat 69 Scotch	35.00
Advertising, Western Union, Wall	150.00
Advertising, Woody's Cafe, Woody Woodpecker, Animated, Alarm	100.00
Advertising, Work Clothes, Key Wind	85.00
Alarm, Bakelite, Steeple–Shaped Radio, Electric, 1930s, 6 In.	25.00
Alarm, Cinderella, Pink Enamel	50.00

Alarm, Mickey Mouse, Bradley, Hand Wind, Double Bell	20.00
Alarm, Musical, Junghan	95.00
Alarm, National Call, 8–Day, 6 In.	17.00
Alarm, Night, Louis XV, Gilt Metal, Revolving Ring, Marked, 11 1/2 In.	4400.00
Alarm, Pencil Sharpener, Miniature	6.00
Alarm, Raggedy Ann & Andy, Talking	25.00
Alarm, Woody Woodpecker, Animated	110.00
American Clock Co., Regulator, Wall, Carved Oak Case, 1895	850.00
Ansonia, Alarm, 8–Day, Interval, 1910	35.00
Ansonia, Alarm, With Bell, 5 1/2 In.	15.00
Ansonia, Boudoir, Gothic Design, 8–Day, Porcelain Face, 3 X 5 In.	75.00
Ansonia, Calendar, Rosewood, Round Drop, 8–Day Time & Strike, 26 In.	1200.00
Ansonia, Crystal Palace, Domed	575.00
Ansonia, Crystal Regulator, Visible Escapement	235.00
Ansonia, Gilt Bronze, Crystal Regulator, 1840s	850.00
Ansonia, Gravity, 30–Hour, Gold Paint, C.1900, 10 1/4 In.	175.00
Ansonia, Kitchen, Gingerbread, 22 In.	195.00
Ansonia, Louis XIV–Style, Cast Iron	350.00
Ansonia, Mantel, Cathedral, 8–Day, Porcelain Dial, C.1918	150.00
Ansonia, Mantel, Slate & Carrera Marble, C.1880	245.00
Ansonia, Mantel, The Thinker, Bronze, China Face	350.00
Ansonia, Newton Statue, Outside Escapement	325.00
Ansonia, Porcelain Dial, Royal Bonn Case	250.00
Ansonia, Queen Anne, Regulator	600.00
Ansonia, Regulator, Crystal Palace Extra, 17 In. ....*Illus*	350.00
Ansonia, School, Time & Strike, Oak	425.00
Ansonia, Shelf, Calendar, Oak	175.00
Ansonia, Shelf, Porcelain With Brass, Polychrome Scenes, 12 1/2 In.	95.00
Ansonia, Statue, Opera, 1886, 16 1/4 In.	350.00
Ansonia, Wall, Oak, Round, 16 In.	270.00
Art Deco, Marbled, Bronze Bird, Wings Up, Brass, Round, 3 Piece	315.00
Austrian, Repeating, Steel Hands, Seated Figure Finial, 14 7/8 In.	1450.00
Banjo, Abner Rogers, Carved Brackets, 2 Painted Tablets, Mahogany	3750.00
Banjo, Federal, Mahogany, Eglomise, 8–Day, New England, 1820, 35 In.	600.00
Banjo, J.Sawin, Presentation, 8–Day, Weight Driven, C.1815, 41 1/2 In.	1100.00
Banjo, Mahogany, Reverse Painted, Brass Arms, Weight Driven, 33 In.	770.00
Banjo, New Haven, Strike, 8–Day	275.00
Banjo, Rosewood, 8–Day, Black Eglomise Tablet, 32 In.	750.00
Banjo, Roxbury School, Mahogany, Glass Tablets, 8–Day, C.1810, 30 In.	500.00
Banjo, Seward, Painted Tablet, Brass Side Arms, 8–Day	1600.00
Banjo, Treasure Island	395.00
Banjo, War of 1812 Depicted On Reverse Glass, C.1815	6500.00
Barometer, Louis XVI, Gilt, Patinated Bronze, Rose Vines, Paris, 26 In.	2090.00
Bird In Cage, On Stand, Japan, 1925, 8 1/2 In.	40.00
Birge & Fuller, Steeple On Steeple, Wagon, Spring	1400.00
Birge, Peck & Co., Empire, Shelf, 3 Decker, Time & Strike, 34 X 16 In.	880.00
Bishop & Bradley, Pillar & Scroll, Mahogany, Reverse Painted, 28 In.	1210.00
Black Sambo, Quartz Movement, Iron, 15 In.	50.00
Blinking Eye, Topsy, 30–Hour Movement, C.1858, 16 1/2 In. ....*Illus*	1600.00
Bracket, Musical, George III Style, Ebonized & Gilt Brass, 21 1/2 In.	1870.00
Bradley & Hubbard, Blinking Eye	1150.00
Buckingham, Lantern, William & Mary, Brass, Oak, C.1670, 12 3/8 In.	825.00
Butler & Henderson, Pillar & Scroll, Terry Movement	1500.00
Carriage, Boston, Brass, Porcelain Dial, 8–Day, 6 3/4 In.	300.00
Carriage, Cartier, Hour & Quarter Hour Strike, Gold Mounted, 8 In.	7700.00

If you find a clock with a complete, original paper label, add 35 percent to the value.

Carriage, Repeat, Gilt Minute Dots, Fluted Columns, C.1900, 3 1/8 In. 1650.00
Carriage, Repeater, Gilt Metal, Champleve Enamel, Quarter Strike 4125.00
Carriage, Repeater, Seconds, Alarm, Calendar, Brass, 6 1/8 In. 6325.00
Chelsea, Desk Set, With Barometer, Brass, 8 1/4 X 16 In. 350.00
Chelsea, Regulator, Oak, Made For D.Pratt's Son, Boston, 33 In. 1430.00
Chinese, Mantel, Cloisonne, Portrait Side Panels, 7 1/2 In. 300.00
Chinese, Table, Drum Form, Revolving Disc, Calendar, Round, 5 1/8 In. 1870.00
Continental, Bronze, Brass, Paw Feet, Key Wind, 17 In. 425.00
Cowboy, Waving Hat, Rearing Bronco, Deco, Copper Wash, 18 X 18 In. 95.00
Cuckoo, Brass, Gilt Wash, Pierced Fret, 8–Day, Germany, C.1880, 21 In. 1050.00
David Wood, Shelf, Federal, Inlaid Mahogany, 34 1/2 X 11 1/2 In. 5225.00
Desk, Empire, Lapis Lazuli, Silver Gilt, Enameled, Viennese, 5 5/8 In. 3190.00
Desk, Silver Gilt, Gilt Jeweled Movement, Round Dial, Floral Design 450.00
Desk, Traveling, Brass Bound, Carleton College, Pigeonhole, 1913 .... 375.00
Dutch, Wall, Animations of Windmill & Fisherman With Fish, 1790 .... 1150.00
Eastlake, Wall, Time & Strike, Brass Pendulum, 23 In. 90.00
Egyptian Style, Garniture, Bronze Basalt, Marble, C.1890, 3 Piece 2310.00
Eli Terry, Alarm, Cast Brass, 30–Hour, Pat.1881 & 1883, 9 1/4 In. 175.00
Eli Terry, Federal, Pillar & Scroll, Eglomise, 30–Hour, 29 In. 1500.00
Eli Terry, Mantel, Pillar & Scroll, Reverse Painting, Mahogany 1540.00
Eli Terry, Pillar & Scroll, Gilt Stenciling, Wooden Works, 31 1/2 In. 800.00
Eli Terry, Pillar & Scroll, Mahogany, C.1830, 31 1/2 In. ....Illus 3410.00
Eli Terry, Regulator, 8–Day, Weight–Driven Movement, Mahogany 3500.00
Eli Terry, Shelf, Pillar & Scroll, Wooden Works, Reverse Glass, 13 In. 700.00
Eli Terry, Skeleton, Dome 550.00
Elmer Stennes, Banjo, Presentation 3250.00
English, Gravity, Nickel Case, Glass Dial, C.1920, 10 1/4 In. 200.00
Faller, Mechanical, Napoleon Pacing In Room, French Empire 2310.00
Fiddle, Walnut, 19th Century, 29 1/2 In. 1188.00
Figural, Bicycle, Brass, Germany, C.1898, 4 1/2 In. ....Illus 1760.00
Forestville, Beehive, Rosewood, Piecrust Molded, 8–Day, Strike, 19 In. 1700.00
Forestville, Ogee, Mahogany, 2 Doors, 8–Day Time & Strike, 31 In. 550.00
Forestville, Steeple, Mahogany, 8–Day Fusee Time & Strike, 19 3/4 In. 950.00
Forestville, Steeple, Rosewood, Ripple Molded, 8–Day & Strike, 20 In. 1500.00
Forestville, Zinc Dial, 8–Day, C.1850, 19 3/4 In. ....Illus 1500.00
French, Art Nouveau, 2 Ladies Standing, Looking At Clock Face, Metal 800.00
French, Coal Furnace Shape, Brass, Silver Plate, 8–Day, C.1880, 18 In. 2700.00
French, Crystal, Mercury Pendulum, Beaded Case 265.00
French, Empire, Bronze & Crystal Door, Honeycomb Columns, 14 1/2 In. 850.00
French, Figural, Gilt Bronze & Silver Plate, Cupids, Birds, 22 1/2 In. 1700.00
French, Garniture, Louis XVI, Jeweled Sevres, Gilt Bronze, 3 Piece 4950.00
French, Industry, Animated, C.1880 .... 2700.00
French, Lady Figurine, Red Marble Case, 23 In. 975.00
French, Mantel, Enameled Face, Marble & Gilt Base, Tiffany 650.00
French, Mantel, Ormolu, Porcelain, 19th Century, 8 3/4 In. 175.00
French, Night, Figural, Troubadour, Lighted Globe, C.1850 .... 1100.00
French, Open Escapement, Beveled Face & Back Cover, Onyx, Tall 350.00
French, Regulator, Crystal, Torsion Balance Movement, Brass & Glass 185.00

Clock, Ansonia, Regulator,
Crystal Palace Extra, 17 In.

Clock, Figural, Bicycle, Brass, Germany,
C.1898, 4 1/2 In.

French, Shelf, 8–Day Time & Strike, Porcelain, Beveled Bezel	325.00
French, Shelf, Marble, Brass Columns, Marley Horse Figures, 31 In.	250.00
French, Shelf, Mercury Pendulum, Glass & Brass Case, 11 In.	175.00
French, Shelf, Mercury Weight, Painted Porcelain, 11 In.	20.00
French, Steam Hammer Shape, Brass, Marble, 8–Day Time & Strike, 8 In.	1200.00
French, Warrior On Horse, Ormolu, Marble & Bronze, Key Wind	975.00
French, Windmill Shape, Brass, 8–Day, 2 Thermometers, C.1880, 18 In.	1700.00
Geddes, Stoneware, Gray, Blue Feather, Brown Glazed Interior, 8 In.	80.00
George Hills, Mirror, Inverted Ogee, Rosewood, 30–Hour, C.1842, 26 In.	200.00
Gilbert, Balloon, Mahogany, Inlaid Edge, 8–Day, Lever Escapement, 9 In.	150.00
Gilbert, Calendar, Walnut, Reverse Painted Drop, Label, 24 X 17 In.	715.00
Gilbert, Kitchen, Oak, 8–Day	150.00
Gilbert, Mantel, 8–Day Time & Strike, 1920s	25.00
Gilbert, Mantel, 8–Day Time & Strike, Reverse Painted Panel, 13 In.	140.00
Gilbert, Mantel, Cast Feet & Pillars, Black Wood	125.00
Gilbert, Regulator, Brass, Enamel Dial, Open Escapement, 9 1/2 In.	209.00
Gilbert, Regulator, No.3 Weight, Rosewood Case, C.1870	1200.00
Gilbert, Regulator, Walnut Veneer, Octagon Drop, 26 X 16 1/2 In.	303.00
Gilbert, Regulator, Weight Driven, Bird's-Eye Maple & Ash	785.00
Gorham, Mantel, Brass, Large	950.00
Gustav Becker, Mantel, Bim–Bam Tambour	115.00
Gustav Becker, Regulator, Barometer & Thermometer, Horse On Top	3950.00
Gustav Becker, Vienna Regulator, 2 Weight, 50 In.	550.00
Henry Sperry, Cottage, Black Paint, Stenciled Eagle, 30–Hour, 12 In.	150.00
Howard, Banjo, No.4	1350.00
Howard, Figure Eight, 44 In.	4200.00
Howard, No.11, Regulator, Keyhole, Grained, 8–Day, C.1880, 31 1/2 In.	1950.00
Howard, No.27, Pine, White Enameled, Marble Front, 8–Day, 35 1/2 In.	1500.00
Howard, Regulator, Keyhole Model, No.11, Cherry	1950.00
Howard, Tall Case, Westminster, Wittington & St.Michael's Chimes	575.00
Ingersoll, Art Deco, Folding, Box, 1 3/4 X 1 3/8 In.	25.00
Ingraham, Calendar, Fancy Case	425.00
Ingraham, Calendar, Store, Regulator, 8–Day	350.00
Ingraham, Mantel, 8–Day, Pat.1885	85.00
Ingraham, Mantel, Pillar, 1890, 14 In.	60.00
Ingraham, Meridan, 8 Day Time, Calendar, Grain–Painted Rosewood	325.00
Ingraham, Occidental Mirror Side	375.00
Ingraham, Regulator, 8–Day, Octagon Schoolhouse Style, Oak, 32 In.	50.00
Ingraham, Regulator, Calendar, Oak	325.00
Ingraham, Yankee Clipper, Time & Strike, Pendulum	160.00
Ithaca, Mantel, 8–Day Time & Strike, Carved Oak Case	500.00
Ithaca, Model No. 6, Hanging Library, C.1870, 25 1/2 In. ....*Illus*	700.00
Ithaca, Office, Wall, No.4, Nickel Plated, Double Spring Movement	750.00
Ithaca, Shelf, Cottage, Walnut, 8–Day Time & Strike, 24 In.	800.00
Japanese, Alarm, Brass & Steel Movement, Rosewood Stand, 38 3/4 In.	5500.00
Japanese, Lantern, Iron Movement, Adjustable Weights, 11 1/2 In.	990.00
Jappe, Onyx, Bronze, French	875.00
Japy Freres, Wall, Tole, Striking, Octagonal, 15 1/2 In.	385.00
Jerome, Mini–Empire, Time, Strike & Alarm	245.00
Jerome, Painted Tablet, Fusee Movement, C.1850, 21 In. ....*Illus*	200.00
Jerome, Shelf, Rosewood, 8–Day Time & Strike Fusee, 18 In.	650.00
Jerome, Steeple, Mahogany, Reverse Painted, 30–Hour Alarm, 15 1/2 In.	198.00
Jeweler's, Regulator, No.70	1700.00
Jeweler's, Regulator, Pinwheel Movement, Lyre Pendulum, Walnut, 80 In.	3250.00
John Jackson, Bracket, George I, Mahogany, Domed Lid, 13 3/4 In.	2860.00
John Peck, Chimney, Wooden Works, 30–Hour	800.00
John Swain, Lyre, Eagle Finial	1000.00
John Swain, Shelf, 30–Day Torsion Pendulum	1600.00
Junghans, Bracket, 1/4 Hour Westminster Chimes	250.00
Junghans, Desk, White Metal, Marble Base, 30–Hour, C.1900, 8 1/4 In.	175.00
Kit–Kat, Eye & Tail Move, Glows In Dark	39.00
Kit–Kat, Tail Moves, Rhinestone Eyes, Tan	17.50
Kitchen, Aunt Jemima, Red Wing, Ceramic	100.00
Kitchen, Dutch Boy & Girl On Face, Tin, Electric	22.00

Clock, Blinking Eye, Topsy,
30–Hour Movement, C.1858, 16 1/2 In.

To set the time, push the minute hand clockwise. If the clock chimes, be sure to wait until it stops striking before you advance the hands again.

LeCoultre, Travel, 8–Day, Maroon Enamel, Brass Trim	60.00
LeCoultre, Visible Movement, Brushed Gold Case, 6 1/2 In.	55.00
Louis XVI, Garniture, Garland Drapery, Enameled Dial, C.1870, 8 In.	1980.00
Lux, ABC	425.00
Lux, Alarm, Beer Drinkers	100.00
Lux, Boy Scout, Pendulette	375.00
Lux, Bungalow, 10 In.	45.00 To 75.00
Lux, Cat, Animated	285.00
Lux, Clown, With Tie, Pendulette	425.00
Lux, Cuckoo, Red	40.00
Lux, Desk	35.00
Lux, Dixie Boy, Pendulette	300.00
Lux, Green, Black Checks, Tin	150.00
Lux, Sally Rand, Fan Dancer, Pendulette	365.00
Lux, Seven Dwarfs, Pendulette	125.00
Lux, Ship's Wheel, Pendulette	120.00
Lux, Shmoo, Pendulette	85.00
Mancell, Statue, Under Dome, Mid–1800s	2000.00
Mantel, Animated, 30–Hour, Calendar, C.1825, 23 1/2 In. ....*Illus*	450.00
Mantel, Arts & Crafts, Hammered Copper, Motto, England, 1910, 13 In.	100.00
Mantel, Arts & Crafts, Mahogany, 3 Glass Inserts, 1900, 12 In.	500.00
Mantel, Champleve Enameled, Gilt Bronze, Scrolls, C.1900, 16 1/2 In.	1760.00
Mantel, Empire Ormolu, Eros & Psyche Over Clock, Paris, 22 1/4 In.	2750.00
Mantel, Gothic, Gilt Bronze, Glass Base, Winged Animal Feet, 23 In.	2750.00
Mantel, Jacques Vaillant, Red Shades, Angel Figure Top, 8–Day, 18 In.	800.00
Mantel, L.Philippe, Classical Male, Sword, Marble Plinth, 27 In.	1210.00
Mantel, Louis XVI, 8–Day, Bronze, Marble, Porcelain, Paris, 1800, 17 In.	825.00
Mantel, Marble, Eastlake, Black, Gold Details, 19 1/2 In.	500.00
Mantel, McKinley Portrait Top, Gingerbread, 23 X 15 In.	300.00
Mantel, Napoleon III, Gilt, Bronze, Men In Armour, 1860, Paris, 18 In.	1540.00
Mantel, Norma Shearer, With Presentation Plaque	1500.00
Mantel, Renaissance, Revival, Walnut, 8–Day Time, Floral, 24 In.	325.00
Mantel, Upright Case, Mercury Glass Pendulum, Tiffany, Brass, 13 In.	300.00
New Haven, Alabaster Case, 1900–20	125.00
New Haven, Ball, Brass Band, Crystal, Crescent Shape, 2 1/2 In.	176.00
New Haven, Banjo, Key Wind, 36 In.	450.00
New Haven, Banjo, Oval Bottom, 12–Day Movement, Miniature	140.00
New Haven, Banjo, Reverse Glass, 25 In.	135.00
New Haven, Banjo, Time & Strike, Pendulum Movement, 29 In.	150.00
New Haven, Banjo, Winnetka Model, Time & Strike, 18 In.	235.00
New Haven, Beehive Type, 8–Day, Wood, 4 1/2 X 3 In.	60.00
New Haven, Carriage, Repeater, 1890s	350.00

New Haven, Desk, Iron Case, 30–Hour, Fixed Pendulum, C.1875, 6 In. 40.00
New Haven, Hand Painted Garden Scene, Bronze, Time & Strike, C.1880 .... 675.00
New Haven, Kitchen, Walnut, Pendulum, Key, Carved Crown 65.00
New Haven, Mouse Climbs Up & Down Face 1600.00
New Haven, Open Escapement, Cast Iron 200.00
New Haven, Saturn No.2, Weight Regulator, Oak 750.00
New Haven, Shelf, 4 Column, Mahogany, 8–Day Time & Strike, 19 In. 275.00
New Haven, Shelf, Black Metal Case, Brass & Porcelain Face, 12 In. 200.00
New Haven, Shelf, Rosewood, 8–Day Time & Strike, C.1860, 14 1/2 In. 325.00
New Haven, Steeple, 30 Hours, Time & Strike 45.00
New Haven, Time & Strike, Garden Scene, Man, Woman, 1880 .... 675.00
New Haven, Time & Strike, Iron, 9 X 10 In. 65.00
New York Standard, Regulator, Electric, Cherry, Pendulum, 80 1/2 In. 800.00
Noiseless Rotary Pendulum, Dome 2100.00
Oriental, Carriage, Repeat, Seconds, Alarm, Exposed Bell, 5 5/8 In. 1210.00
Pillar & Scroll, Spring Wound Movement, Walnut Case 750.00
Raggedy Ann & Andy, Talking, Box 20.00
Red Wing, Aunt Jemima 100.00
Regency Style, Gilt Bronze Putto, Boulle Brass Marquetry, 32 In. 1870.00
Regulator, James Hamblet, Walnut, 8–Day, Dead Beat Escapement, 78 In. 1700.00
Root, Desk, 30–Hour, Paper On Zinc Dial, C.1880, 6 In. 80.00
Schatz, 400–Day 85.00
Sessions, Mantel, Strikes On Hour & 1/2 Hour 120.00
Sessions, Mantel, Striking, 8–Day, Pillar Trim 90.00
Sessions, Regulator, 8–Day, Oak, Octagon School Style, 26 In. 50.00
Seth Thomas, Alarm, Road Runner, Yellow Case 25.00
Seth Thomas, Banjo, 28 In. 175.00
Seth Thomas, Banjo, Time & Strike .... 190.00 To 475.00
Seth Thomas, Boudoir No.1, Brass Dial, 1920 .... 48.00
Seth Thomas, Calendar, Double Dial, Parlor, No.4 .... 850.00
Seth Thomas, Calendar, Double Dial, Weight Driven 275.00
Seth Thomas, Calendar, Rosewood Case, Weight Driven 1125.00
Seth Thomas, Calendar, Walnut, 8–Day Time & Strike, 24 In. 850.00
Seth Thomas, Cottage, 8–Day, Time, Strike & Alarm 100.00
Seth Thomas, Cottage, Rosewood, Reverse Painted Throat, Alarm, 9 In. 264.00
Seth Thomas, Crystal Regulator, Porcelain Dial, 10 3/4 In. 235.00
Seth Thomas, Figural, Rebekah At The Well, 15 1/2 In. 350.00
Seth Thomas, Gallery, 8–Day, Brass, Miniature 125.00
Seth Thomas, Kitchen, Ball Top, 8–Day Time, Strike & Alarm 285.00
Seth Thomas, Kitchen, Great White Fleet 155.00
Seth Thomas, Locomotive, Brass, Dated 1876 .... 125.00
Seth Thomas, Mantel, Gingerbread 240.00

Clock, Eli Terry, Pillar & Scroll,
Mahogany, C.1830, 31 1/2 In.

Clock, Forestville, Zinc Dial,
8–Day, C.1850, 19 3/4 In.

Clock, Jerome, Painted Tablet,
Fusee Movement, C.1850, 21 In.

Seth Thomas, Mantel, Marbelized Wood, Claw Feet, Lion Head At Sides 60.00
Seth Thomas, Mantel, Westminster Chime, Mahogany Case 95.00
Seth Thomas, Miniature Ogee 175.00
Seth Thomas, Oak, Key Wind, 30–Day, 15 In. 275.00
Seth Thomas, Oak, Key, Pendulum, Glass, Fruit Spilling From Basket 95.00
Seth Thomas, Office Calendar, Rosewood, Pat.Feb.15, 1876, 40 3/4 In. 1050.00
Seth Thomas, Ogee, Mahogany, 8–Day Time & Strike, C.1870, 16 1/2 In. 350.00
Seth Thomas, Peach Glass, C.1940, 7 1/8 In. 85.00
Seth Thomas, Perpetual Calendar, Rosewood Case, 1876 .... 650.00
Seth Thomas, Pillar & Scroll, Mantel, Reverse Painting, Brass Finials 825.00
Seth Thomas, Pillar, Weight Driven .... 150.00 To 165.00
Seth Thomas, Regulator, 2 Weight, Oak 795.00
Seth Thomas, Regulator, No.1 .... 1050.00
Seth Thomas, Regulator, No.18, 8–Day, Dead Beat Escapement, 54 In. 1350.00
Seth Thomas, Regulator, No.18, Walnut, 54 In. 1350.00
Seth Thomas, Regulator, Rosewood Veneer, Long Drop, 32 X 17 In. 358.00
Seth Thomas, Regulator, Weight Driven, Oak 765.00
Seth Thomas, Shelf, 8–Day Ship's Bell Movement, Mahogany 200.00
Seth Thomas, Shelf, 8–Day Time, Strike & Alarm, Golden Oak 195.00
Seth Thomas, Shelf, Brass Design, Woman's Head, Oak 150.00
Seth Thomas, Shelf, Empire, Label, 15 1/2 X 10 In. 341.00
Seth Thomas, Shelf, Tudor, Rosewood, 8–Day Time & Strike, 15 In. 200.00
Seth Thomas, Sonora Chime, 5 Bells, Inlaid Mahogany Case 350.00
Seth Thomas, Sonora, 8 Bells, 2 Tunes 800.00
Seth Thomas, Steeple, Time, Strike & Alarm 250.00
Seth Thomas, Tall Case, Chippendale, Mahogany, No Pendulum, 95 In. 900.00
Seth Thomas, Tower, Green Painted Iron Frame 1200.00
Seth Thomas, Watchman's, Oak, Nickel Trim, 1898, 5 Ft. 1000.00
Seth Thomas, Westminster, Lancet Style, Silvered Dial 325.00
Seth Thomas, Wooden Case, 8–Day, 6 1/4 In. 20.00
Sharpentier & Cie, Double–Faced, Gilt Bronze, 19th Century, 3 In. 8500.00
Shelf, C.Goodrich, Cast Iron, Mother–of–Pearl, 8–Day, 1857, 21 3/4 In. 150.00
Shelf, French Rococo Style, Painted, Ormolu Mounts, 21 In. 400.00
Shelf, J.C.Brown, Shelf, Rosewood, 8–Day Time & Strike, C.1855, 15 In. 1000.00
Shelf, Maple, Red Paint, White Dial, New England, 6 1/4 X 4 In. 2200.00
Shelf, Miles Morse, Black, Mother–of–Pearl, 8–Day & Strike, 16 In. 250.00
Ship's Bell, Brass, 6 In. 245.00
Skeleton, Brass Pendulum, Glass Dome, 8–Day, England, 1850, 15 1/4 In. 900.00
Southern Calendar Clock Co., Calendar, Fashion Model No.3, Walnut 1700.00
Spaulding, Carriage, Repeat & Alarm, Curved Glass, C.1900, 5 1/2 In. 1430.00
Sperry, Cottage, Pine, Zinc Dial, 30–Hour, Pendulum, C.1860, 12 In. 200.00
Stennes, Looking Glass 1100.00
Stromberg, Oak, Master, 1915 .... 625.00
Swiss, Carved, Organ Music Box 6500.00
T.D.R. & Co., Cast Iron, Mother–of–Pearl Inlay, 10 1/2 In. ....*Illus* 150.00
Tall Case, 3–Weight, Austrian Baroque Style, Walnut, C.1890, 87 In. 5200.00
Tall Case, A.Miller, Pennsylvania, Rocking Ship Movement, 93 In. 8800.00
Tall Case, Alex Gordon, Chippendale, Mahogany, Calendar, 95 In. 2100.00
Tall Case, Alexander McRae, 8–Day 2100.00
Tall Case, Benjamin Swan, Federal, Maple, Birch, Mahogany Veneer 6500.00
Tall Case, Brass Ball Finials, Inlaid Cherry, C.1800, 94 In. 7000.00
Tall Case, Cherry, 74 In. 2970.00
Tall Case, Cincinnati, 5 Tubes, 1915, 7 Ft. 1500.00
Tall Case, Duplock, Signed 3100.00
Tall Case, English, Calendar & Moon Face, 18th Century 2100.00
Tall Case, English, Calendar, Quarter Columns, Brass Works, 81 In. 700.00
Tall Case, English, Painted Face, Lion's Eyes, Oak, C.1840, 83 1/2 In. 2600.00
Tall Case, Federal, Mahogany, Fretwork, 3 Plinths, Ma., 1790, 91 In. 7000.00
Tall Case, Federal, Mahogany, Swan's Neck Crest, 1800, 8 Ft.5 1/2 In. 4675.00
Tall Case, Frederick Wingate, Moon Dial 8500.00
Tall Case, French, Ormolu Mounted Glass, Mahogany, 100 In. 7500.00
Tall Case, German, Austrian Baroque, 3 Weight, Walnut, C.1890, 87 In. 5200.00
Tall Case, Hepplewhite, Fretwork, Brass Finial, Inlaid Cherry Case 7250.00
Tall Case, Inlaid Cherry Case, Connecticut, C.1800, 85 In. 4000.00

Clock, Ithaca, Model No. 6, Hanging Library, C.1870, 25 1/2 In.

Clock, Mantel, Animated, 30-Hour, Calendar, C.1825, 23 1/2 In.

Clock, T.D.R. & Co., Cast Iron, Mother-of-Pearl Inlay, 10 1/2 In.

Tall Case, Italian Renaissance, Walnut, Circular Dial, 91 3/4 In.	1400.00
Tall Case, J.Pratt, Federal, Curly Maple, J.Nicholl Works, 1824, 7 Ft.	7150.00
Tall Case, John Hall, George I, Walnut, Caddy Top Hood, 7 Ft.11 In.	4675.00
Tall Case, John Telford, George III, Inlaid Mahogany, Striking, 8 Ft.	4675.00
Tall Case, L.Furtwangler Sohme Mark, 1836–95	3200.00
Tall Case, Noah Rantlet, Mahogany	8000.00
Tall Case, Oak, George III, Arched Cornice Crest, Brass Dial, 81 In.	1400.00
Tall Case, Pietre Thymen, Dutch Rococo, Burl Walnut, 8 Ft.10 In.	5225.00
Tall Case, Pine, Original 8–Day Movement, Lancaster County, Pa.	3850.00
Tall Case, Poplar, Arch Pediment, German Movement, C.1825, 91 In.	1000.00
Tall Case, R.Whiting, Pine, Red Paint, C.1820, 81 X 17 In.	2750.00
Tall Case, Scottish, Oak, Flat Top, Painted Dial, Brass Works, 82 In.	1100.00
Tall Case, Silas Hoadley, Federal, Maple, C.1820, 81 In.	1800.00
Tall Case, Silas Hoadley, Fretwork Hood, Painted Pine, C.1825, 93 In.	9000.00
Tall Case, T.Noon, Calendar, Greek Key, Brass Works, Oak, 79 In.	900.00
Tall Case, Thomas Harland, Cherry	6490.00
Tall Case, Westminster Movement, Colonial, 1915	875.00
Tall Case, Westminster, 2 Large Pillars, 1915	1200.00
Tall Case, Whiting, Federal, Pine, Red Paint, Glazed Door, 6 Ft.11 In.	1100.00
Tall Case, Willard, Mahogany, Domed Top, Chime Movement, 93 In.	2750.00
Tall Case, William J.Leslie, Moon Phases Dial, 92 In.	6600.00
Tall Case, Wingate–Type, Bird's–Eye Maple, Maple Door	3850.00
Tall Case, Wm.Burnall, Painted Pine, Bonnet, Painted Dial, 81 In.	715.00
Tall Case, Wm.Gill, Queen Anne, Burl Walnut, Brass Dial, 5 Ft.	6050.00
Terry, Ogee, Double Door	275.00
Terry, Shelf, Cast Iron, Mother–of–Pearl, Pat.Oct.5, 1852, 10 In.	650.00
Terry, Steeple, Mahogany & Rosewood Case, Oversized	3750.00
CLOCK, TIFFANY, see Tiffany, Clock	
Topsy, Blinking Eye, Round Clock In Skirt, Iron, C.1875	2200.00
Tower, Stone Pendulum, 3 Rains, 17th Century	3400.00
Viennese Regulator, 2 Weights, 30–Day, 1890	1600.00
Viennese, Enamel & Gilt Bronze, Easel, 8 In.	250.00
Viennese, Triptych, Metal & Enamel, Cherubs, Figures, 5 1/2 In.	1100.00
Wag–On–The–Wall, Brass Works, Pine Cone Weights, Pendulum, 18 In.	350.00
Wag–On–The–Wall, Felix The Cat, Tail & Eyes Move	250.00
Wall, Eyes Move Back & Forth, Pendulum Driven, Wooden	15.00
Wall, Mahogany, Beveled Glass Door, 36 In.	250.00
Waltham, Auto, 8–Day	45.00
Waltham, Banjo, Reverse Painted, Perry's Victory On Lake Erie, 40 In.	1210.00
Waltham, Car, 8–Day, Size 37	30.00
Watchman's, Oak, 7 Ft.	1000.00
Waterbury, Alarm, Victorian, Metal	40.00

Waterbury, Calendar, Double Dial, No.44 .... 775.00
Waterbury, Carriage, 1890s 275.00
Waterbury, Carriage, Porcelain Face, 1891 .... 150.00
Waterbury, Figural, Train, Brass, 1889, 13 1/4 In. ....*Illus* 1500.00
Waterbury, Gingerbread, 8–Day Time & Strike, Oak 175.00
Waterbury, Mantel, Baseball, Scorekeeper, Gilded White Metal 8250.00
Waterbury, Mother–of–Pearl Inserts, Painted, C.1895, 20 1/4 In. 425.00
Waterbury, No.73, Parlor, Carlsbad Floral Porcelain Painted Case 150.00
Waterbury, Pinwheel, No.7, Jeweler's Regulator, Walnut 1900.00
Waterbury, Regulator, No.61, Floor Model, 1898 .... 4000.00
Waterbury, Shelf, Calendar, Walnut, Gingerbread Style, 21 In. 193.00
Waterbury, Shelf, Gilt Face, Beveled Lens, Brass Works, Green Onyx 75.00
Waterbury, Shelf, Octagon, Spool Pendulum 100.00
Waterbury, Wall, Octagon, Rosewood, 30–Hour Time & Alarm, 1860, 11 In. 100.00
Welch, Calendar, Golden Oak .... 400.00 To 450.00
Welch, Ogee, Reverse Painting On Glass, Merchants Exchange, 30–Hour 99.00
Welch, Shelf, 8–Day Time & Strike, Rosewood 750.00
Welch, Shelf, Gothic, Rosewood Veneer, 8–Day & Strike, 19 1/2 In. 1900.00
Welch, Shelf, Gothic, Round, Ripple Front 1900.00
Westclox, Alarm, Big Ben, 6 In. 17.00
Westclox, Gray Plastic, Art Deco, Electric 27.50
Westclox, Sleep–Meter, 4 In. 20.00
Willard, Banjo, Acorn Finial, Painted Tablets, Iron Face 1750.00
Willard, Banjo, Mahogany, Reverse Painted, Brass Arms, 33 In. 1540.00

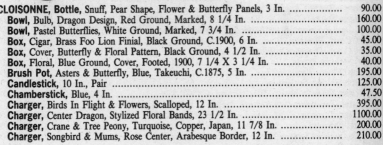

Cloisonne enamel was developed during the tenth century. A glass enamel was applied between small ribbonlike pieces of metal on a metal base. Most cloisonne is Chinese or Japanese. Pieces marked "China" are twentieth–century examples.

CLOISONNE, Bottle, Snuff, Pear Shape, Flower & Butterfly Panels, 3 In. 90.00
Bowl, Bulb, Dragon Design, Red Ground, Marked, 8 1/4 In. 160.00
Bowl, Pastel Butterflies, White Ground, Marked, 7 3/4 In. 100.00
Box, Cigar, Brass Foo Lion Finial, Black Ground, C.1900, 6 In. 45.00
Box, Cover, Butterfly & Floral Pattern, Black Ground, 4 1/2 In. 35.00
Box, Floral, Blue Ground, Cover, Footed, 1900, 7 1/4 X 3 1/4 In. 40.00
Brush Pot, Asters & Butterfly, Blue, Takeuchi, C.1875, 5 In. 195.00
Candlestick, 10 In., Pair 125.00
Chamberstick, Blue, 4 In. 47.50
Charger, Birds In Flight & Flowers, Scalloped, 12 In. 395.00
Charger, Center Dragon, Stylized Floral Bands, 23 1/2 In. 1100.00
Charger, Crane & Tree Peony, Turquoise, Copper, Japan, 11 7/8 In. 200.00
Charger, Songbird & Mums, Rose Center, Arabesque Border, 12 In. 210.00

Clock, Waterbury, Figural, Train, Brass, 1889, 13 1/4 In.

Never hang a knit garment, one cut on the bias, or ornately beaded clothing. Store flat in an acid-free cardboard box.

Cloisonne, Figurine, Rooster,
Crowing, Rocky Base, 39 In.

Cocoa Pot, Butterflies, Goldstone, Scalloped, Open, Japan, 6 In.	85.00
Crumber, Brass, People, Flowers, Animals, China	65.00
Figurine, Rooster, Crowing, Rocky Base, 39 In. ....*Illus*	650.00
Ginger Jar, Allover Wirework On White	85.00
Ginger Jar, Cover, Floral Design, C.1910, 7 3/4 In., Pair	85.00
Humidor, Floral Design, Brown Ground, Stand, 8 In.	100.00
Humidor, Multicolored Florals, Yellow Ground, C.1900, 6 3/4 In.	265.00
Incense Burner, Animal Finial, Tripod Base, 7 In.	50.00
Incense Burner, Green & Blue Ground, 2 Handles, 1920, 7 1/2 In.	100.00
Jar, Bird & Flower, Black Ground, Yasuyuki Namikawa, 4 1/2 In.	7920.00
Jar, Cover, Blossoms, Blues, Red, Yellow & White, 7 1/2 In.	200.00
Jar, Cover, Dragons On Blue, 9 In.	60.00
Jar, Satsuma Panels, 5 In.	245.00
Lamp, Floor, Islamic, 66 In.	200.00
Match Holder, Butterflies .... 35.00 To 70.00	
Pitcher, Butterfly Design, Blue Ground, C.1900, 5 In.	60.00
Planter, Red, Blue, 19th Century, Japan, 10 X 7 1/4 X 4 3/4 In.	475.00
Planter, Turquoise, Pink, Still–Life Design, Chinese, 1960, 8 In.	325.00
Plate, Dragon Design, 7 1/4 In.	35.00
Plate, Imperial Dragon Over Multicolor Mountains, 8 1/2 In.	200.00
Plate, Prunus Tree, Spring Coil Border, Dark Blue, Signed, 7 In.	295.00
Saltshaker, Flowers, White Ground, Copper Base	65.00
Snuff Bottle, Chinese	35.00
Teapot, Butterfly Design, Black Ground, Stand, 2 1/2 In.	45.00
Teapot, Floral Design, Green Ground, C.1910, 6 In.	40.00
Teapot, Paneled, Butterflies, Cranes, Gold Stones, 3–Footed	240.00
Teapot, Polychrome Flowers, Black Ground, Stand, 2 1/4 In.	37.50
Teapot, Swing Handle, Floral Design, Fitted Stand, 5 3/4 In.	25.00
Teapot, Swing Handles, Various Designs, 3 1/2 X 6 1/2 In.	385.00
Tray, Bronze Sides & Feet, Blue Underside, 8 In.	90.00
Tray, Fish & Dragon Design, Floral On Reverse, 6 1/2 X 10 In.	250.00
Tumbler, Dragon, Black, 19th Century, Chinese, 3 7/8 In., 7 Piece	475.00
Urn, Floral Design, Green Ground, C.1920, 5 In., Pair	35.00
Vase, Allover Silver & Pink Flowers, Foil Ground, 2 1/2 In.	60.00
Vase, Birds, Flowers, Dark Blue Ground, Signed Gyoku, 7 In.	302.50
Vase, Black Dragon, Putty Ground, 5 1/4 In.	7.50
Vase, Branches, Pink Blossoms, Flecked Black Ground, 8 In., Pair	425.00
Vase, Butterflies, Black Ground, 6 In.	97.50
Vase, Confronting Dragons, Black Ground, 9 1/4 In.	40.00
Vase, Cranes, Iris, Tree, Black Ground, Japan, Square, 6 In.	495.00
Vase, Dragon & Phoenix Cartouche, Blue, Namikawa, Square, 12 In.	6500.00
Vase, Dragon Design On Brown, Gold Flecks, Stand, 9 3/4 In.	100.00

Vase, Dragon Design, Black Ground, C.1870, 4 1/2 In., Pair 55.00
Vase, Exotic Birds, Dragons, Goldstone, 6 Panels, 9 1/2 In. 375.00
Vase, Fishscale, Blossoms, Yellow Base, 9 1/2 In. 165.00
Vase, Geometric, Floral Panels, Blue, 2 Dragon Handles, 14 1/2 In. 200.00
Vase, Goldstone, 6 Panels, Japanese, 12 In. 300.00
Vase, Gray Dragon, Midnight Blue, Teardrop Form, Japan, 12 1/4 In. 770.00
Vase, Melon Shape, 6 In. 75.00
Vase, Pale Blue, 7 1/2 In., Pair 192.50
Vase, Panels of Dragons, Phoenix Birds, Goldstone, 14 1/2 In. 450.00
Vase, Pink Blossoms, Gold-Flecked Black Ground, 8 1/2 In., Pair 425.00
Vase, Pink Mums, Green Ground, 9 1/2 In. 295.00
Vase, Polychrome Dragon, 8 7/8 In. 30.00
Vase, Polychrome Floral Design, C.1920, 10 1/2 In. 65.00
Vase, Prunus, Bird In Flight, Blue Ground, 6 In. 425.00
Vase, Shield Design, Stand, 8 1/2 In. 90.00
Vase, Silver Wire, Floral Design, Green Ground, 6 1/4 In. 40.00
Vase, Thousand Flower, White Ground, Double Gourd, 9 1/2 In. 295.00
Vase, Treebark, Japan, C.1890, 24 3/4 In. 3500.00

Antique and collectible clothes of all types are listed in this section.
Dresses, hats, shoes, underwear and more are found here. Other
textiles are to be found in the Textile, World War I, World War II,
Quilt, and Coverlet sections.

CLOTHING, Apron, Appliqued Gray Chickens, Salmon Red, Handmade, 1930 .... 90.00
Apron, Dark Blue Checked Homespun, Gored, Gathered, Long 45.00
Baby Outfit, Silk Coat, Bonnet, Matching Dress, Leather Shoes 35.00
Bathing Costume, Black, 1910, 2 Piece 25.00
Bathing Costume, With Bloomers, Black Sateen, 1910 .... 36.00
Bathing Suit, Woman's, Black Wool, Lattice Sides, 1920-30 .... 35.00
Belt, Turquoise Stones Linked Together, Silver Plate, Brass 40.00
Bloomers, Gym, Black 20.00
Blouse, Dress, U.S.Militia, 5th Maryland, 3 Rows Brass Buttons 39.50
Blouse, Lamb's Wool, Pearl Beaded, Sequins, Sleeveless, Small 16.00
Blouse, Sailor's, U.S.Navy, White Cotton, Pullover, Civil War 350.00
Blouse, Side Slits, Wrap-Around Front, White Organdy 48.00
Blouse, White Voile, Lace, Long Sleeves, Drawstring, Size 10 .... 28.00
Boa, Medium Brown Mink 25.00
Bonnet, Amish 25.00
Bonnet, Baby's, 8 1/4 In.Wallpaper-Covered Cardboard Box 150.00
Bonnet, Black Velvet 9.00
Bonnet, Child's, Wine Velvet 22.00
Bonnet, Christening, Embroidered IHS, Ivory Satin, 19th Century 880.00
Bonnet, Crocheted 10.00
Bonnet, Handmade, Hand Crocheted Lace, Silk, Pre-1900 .... 35.00
Bonnet, Tatting Ribbon Rosettes, Lined 12.00
Booties, Baby's, White Linen, Embroidered, 1900s 6.00
Boots, Rubber, Red, Peanuts, Embossed Snoopys 15.00
Bunting, Silk, Pink Flower, With Hat 15.00
Camisole, Cutwork, Embroidered, Tucked Peplum 20.00
Cap, Baby's, Crocheted, Pineapple Design 15.00
Cap, Baby's, Irish Rose, Crocheted 12.00
Cap, Doll's, Handmade Tatting 24.00
Cap, Juliet, Rhinestone & Pearl Trim 8.00
Cape, Opera, Hood, Black Velvet, Silk Lining 85.00
Cape, Scotch Plaid, Linen, Homespun Lining, American, 19th Century 825.00
Cape, Seal Fur 90.00
Cape, Squirrel, 1940s 35.00
Cape, Velvet, Fuchsia Silk, Fox Collar, 1920s 60.00
Cape, Velvet, Hunter Green, Floor Length, Chinchilla Collar, 1920s 50.00
Chemise, Crocheted Yoke, Batiste, Size 10 .... 18.00
Clogs, Child's, Pair 145.00
Coat, Amish, Man's 95.00
Coat, Beige Mouton, 1940s, Size 14 .... 20.00
Coat, Black Velvet, Artichoke Pattern, Knee-Length, C.1920 .... 6000.00

Coat, Black, Lincoln Style, C.1880	95.00
Coat, Cashmere, Man's, With Bowler Hat	185.00
Coat, Child's, Pique, 1930	20.00
Coat, Chinese Silk, Cream, Hand Embroidered, Size 10–12	60.00
Coat, Christening, Yellow Embroidery Around Skirt & Cape	25.00
Coat, Evening, Shrimp Velvet, Fox Cuffs, 1920s	65.00
Coat, Gambler's, Double–Breasted, Long Tail	21.50
Coat, Girl's, Shawl Collar, Satin–Stitch Florals, White Linen	40.00
Coat, Horse Fur, Man's	300.00
Coat, Mouton, Beige, 1940s, Size 14	10.00
Coat, Mouton, Black, Size 9–10	65.00
Coat, Muskrat, Medium, Full, 1940s	25.00
Coat, Opera, Red Silk Velvet, Ermine Collar, Full Length	95.00
Coat, Raccoon, Man's, Large	450.00
Coat, Raccoon, Woman's, Long	250.00
Coat, Silk, Bonnet & Dress, Baby's, 1940s, 3 Piece	35.00
Coat, Silk, Gilt Buttons, Lamb's Wool Lined, Chinese, 41 In.	75.00
Coat, Woman's, Red Cross, World War II	28.00
Coatee, U.S.Navy, Sailing Master's, Blue Wool Serge, 1833	1450.00
Collar, Black Beaded, Wide	15.00
Collar, Irish Rose, Crocheted	11.00
Collar, Shell–Shaped Pearls, Crystal Bead Fringe, 1950s	18.00
Collar, Silver–Gray Fox	40.00
Corset, Print, Silver & Black, Lace Trim, 1920–30	35.00
Corset, White, Long	20.00
Costume, Scout's, Hide, Bone & Metal Buttons, C.1900, 33 In.Waist	600.00
Costume, Stripper's	55.00
Dress, Applique, Lace Accents, Mauve, 2 Piece	85.00
Dress, Beadwork, Matching Cape, Black	225.00
Dress, Black & White Houndstooth, Peter Pan Collar, Front Zip	20.00
Dress, Black Jet Beaded	150.00
Dress, Black Velvet, Long, 1930s, Size 8	55.00
Dress, Black Velvet, Matching Coat, Cluster Rhinestone Buttons	65.00
Dress, Blue Velvet, Blue Rhinestones	25.00
Dress, Brocade, Lace Accents, National Cloak Co., N.Y., 2 Piece	120.00
Dress, Child's, Brown & White Calico	24.00
Dress, Child's, Dotted Batiste, Handmade, Size 7	4.00
Dress, Child's, Pink & White Calico	22.00
Dress, Child's, Selfdot Pattern, Sleeveless, Pink Rayon	2.00
Dress, Cocktail, Beaded, 1920s	75.00
Dress, Dotted Crepe De Chine, Ecru, Lace Inserts, 2 Piece	100.00
Dress, Dropped Waistband, Braid Trim; Brown & Beige	15.00
Dress, Embroidered Collar, White Lawn, 1910	15.00
Dress, Empire, Red & White, Cotton, Drawstring Neck, C.1825	325.00
Dress, Evening, Bias Cut, Lined, Blue Silk Velvet, Size 13	150.00
Dress, Flapper, Allover Glass Beading, Edged With Silver Beads	75.00
Dress, Flapper, Beaded Girdle, Green Chiffon & Satin Underslip	65.00
Dress, Flapper, Beaded, Sleeveless, Size 12	35.00
Dress, Flapper, Beadwork Front & Back, Size 14	85.00
Dress, Flapper, Burnt Orange, Heavily Beaded	195.00
Dress, Flapper, Green Chiffon, Black & Silver Beaded Girdle	75.00
Dress, Flapper, Lame Insert, Magenta Velvet, 1920s	70.00
Dress, Flapper, Pink Print, Chiffon	35.00
Dress, Flapper, Purple, Silk Velvet, 1920s	85.00
Dress, Flapper, Rows of Lace, Ecru Georgette, Size 16	5.00
Dress, Lace Front, Ribbons, Leg O'Mutton Sleeves, Silk, 1895	195.00
Dress, Nelly Don, Horizontal Stripes, Sleeveless, Size 8	15.00
Dress, Prom, Embroidered Organza, Cotton Underdress, Strapless	20.00
Dress, Shaker, Homespun Linen, Pale Brown, Wide Double Collar	192.00
Dress, Silk Taupe, 10 Rhinestone Buttons On Front, Cowl Neckline	35.00
Dress, Sun, Beige	20.00
Dress, Tea, Pleated Black Silk, Gold Geometric Belt, Fortuny	3575.00
Dress, Tea, Pleated Tan Silk, Fortuny, Box, Late 1920s	5500.00
Dress, Tea, Purple & Black Floral Challis Print	155.00

Dress, Victorian, Batiste, Print, 2 Piece 70.00
Dress, Victorian, Rows of White Beading, Tiered Look 65.00
Dress, Victorian, Shawl Collar, White Organdy, Lace Trim, Size 14 ...... 60.00
Dress, Wedding Attendant, Batiste & Lace, White, C.1920, Size 8 .... 50.00
Dress, Wedding, Cotton Lace & Eyelet, White, 1900, Size 12 .... 165.00
Dress, Wedding, Embroidered, Tucks, White Lawn, 1900–05 .... 175.00
Dress, Wedding, Lace Trim, 1890s 95.00
Dress, Wedding, Lace, Capped Sleeves, Finger–Tip Veil, Hoop, 1953 ..... 115.00
Dress, Wedding, Satin, Lace Inserts, Long Train, C.1935, Size 10 .... 58.00
Dress, Wedding, Victorian, Silk, Lace Trim, Size 10 .... 55.00
Dress, Wedding, Wool & Lace, 1890, 2 Piece 78.00
Duster, Square Collar, Pleated, Calico 80.00
Duster, Woman's, 1910 .... 30.00
Fencing Outfit, White Canvas Jacket, Knickers, Mask, 2 Foils, Case 125.00
Garter Belt, Velvet, Black, Fancy, 1920–30 .... 25.00
Garters, Man's, Paris, Box 10.00
Glove, Rubber, Gauntlet Type, For Acid Or Stripping, American 8.00
Gloves, Bear Fur 65.00
Gloves, Gauntlet Type, U.S.Army, Buffalo Fur, 15 In. 150.00
Gloves, Hand Crocheted, Long 30.00
Gloves, Leather, White, Opera Length, 1910 .... 18.00
Gloves, Woman's, Hand Knitted Wool, C.1900, Long 15.00
Gloves, Woman's, Kid, 1920–30, Long 12.50
Hairnet, Elite, 1940s 4.00
Handkerchief, Sepia, Thomas Nast 115.00
Hat, Amish, Man's 25.00
Hat, Beaver, Man's, Pa's High Silk Hat Label On Box 45.00
Hat, Coolie, Woven Reed 4.00
Hat, Felt, Boy's 125.00
Hat, Man's, Bowler, Stetson, Box 30.00
Hat, Officer's, Black Beaver, U.S.Army, Cockade, Box, 1800–12 .... 1750.00
Hat, Straw, Man's 20.00
Hat, Straw, Stetson, Salesman Sample 12.00
Helmet, Indian War, Eagle Front, Buff Tan, Horsehair Plume, 1880s 100.00
Helmet, Iron Plated, Late 17th Century, 11 In. 2640.00
Helmet, US Army, Leather, Silver Eagle Shield, Chin Strap, 1821–32 ..... 1250.00
Hose, Woman's, Silk, Seams, Miss Liberty, Box 10.00
Jabot, Lace 35.00
Jacket, Allover Sequins, Chanel Style, Size 14 .... 75.00
Jacket, Band, Wool, University of Illinois, 1929 .... 30.00
Jacket, Black Velvet, Glass Bead Closing, Lined, Fortuny, 1930s 3500.00
Jacket, Gray Mink, 1950s 95.00
Jacket, Jaguar 550.00
Jacket, White Damask Cuffs, Embroidered, Black Silk, Oriental 165.00
Jodphurs, Woman's, Riding, 1880s 60.00
Jumpsuit, Black Satin, Matching Velvet Cape 28.00
Kimono, Ceremonial, White, Silver Threads, Japanese, Full Length 300.00
Kimono, Clusters of Flowers, Figures, Purple Silk, Gold Lined 47.00
Kimono, Embroidered Panel Trim, Padded, Blue Cotton 5.00
Kimono, Royal Blue Brocade 10.00
Kimono, Silk, Painted Pattern, Red Lining, Japanese 25.00
Lederhosen, Child's, Swiss, Leather, Size 6–8 .... 26.00
Lederhosen, With Suspenders, German, Adjustment For Expansion 150.00
Leggings, Cavalry 25.00
Middy, Woman's, Sailor, Wool, 1910 .... 20.00
Mittens, Child's, Leather 4.00
Negligee, French Silk, Handmade, C.1940 .... 55.00
Night Cap, Silk & Lace 10.00
Nightgown, Cotton, Crocheted Bodice, White 22.50
Nightgown, Cotton, Tatted & Tucked, White 85.00
Nightgown, Embroidered, Lace, Pink, 1930s 15.00
Nightgown, White Cotton, Lace Trim, Girl's Size 10 .... 12.75
Nightgown, White, Cap Sleeve, Pink Ribbon Embroidery, 1900, Size 17 ... 25.00
Pajamas, Woman's, Embroidered Front, Oriental, World War II 75.00

Stuff hats with acid-free tissue for storage. Try to make the stuffing deep enough so the hat brim does not touch the shelf.

Pants, Uniform, U.S.Militia, 5th Maryland, Gray Wool, Black Stripe	34.50
Petticoat, Hand Quilted, Black, 1860	68.00
Petticoat, Machine Quilted, Black & Blue Calico	65.00
Petticoat, Victorian, Child's, Size 7–9	40.00
Robe, Embroidered Dragon On Back, Black Velvet	25.00
Robe, Embroidered, Blue & Green, Japanese, 1930s	45.00
Scarf, Gold, Woven, Square, 18 In.	35.00
Scarf, Partridge In Pear Tree, Neiman Marcus, 30 X 30 In.	30.00
Shawl, Black & White, Hand Woven, C.1890	72.00
Shawl, Black Center, Embroidered Border, Square, 64 In.	90.00
Shawl, Black Lace, C.1925, 12 X 66 In.	20.00
Shawl, Black, Floral, Teal Border, 12 X 9 Ft.	990.00
Shawl, Blue Silver Mesh, 1920–30	65.00
Shawl, Brown Wool, Reversible Pattern, Fringe, Late 1880s	35.00
Shawl, Calico, Net Trim, White Linen, Victorian	95.00
Shawl, Floral, Silk, Ecru On Ecru, Ornate Fringe, French, 1930s	275.00
Shawl, Kashmir, Rectangular Design, Ivory, 4 Ft. X 10 Ft.7 In.	500.00
Shawl, Kashmir, Red Center, Floral, Vines, 5 Ft.2 In. X 5 Ft.6 In.	200.00
Shawl, Multicolored Red Woven Design, Paisley, 68 X 70 In.	120.00
Shawl, Paisley, Black Center, 72 X 72 In.	85.00
Shawl, Paisley, Kashmiri Pine Design, C. 1860, 78 X 76 In.	240.00
Shawl, Paisley, Red Center, 69 X 69 In.	95.00
Shawl, Paisley, Red, Black, Medallion, 62 X 65 In.	225.00
Shawl, Paisley, White Center, Woven Design, 60 X 66 In.	55.00
Shawl, Paisley, Woven Design, White Center, 66 X 130 In.	75.00
Shawl, Paisley, Woven Design, Red Center, 42 X 46 In.	95.00
Shawl, Spanish Lace, Black, Tri–Cornered, 52 1/2 X 66 1/2 In.	260.00
Shawl, White Satin Stitch Embroidery, Hand–Tied Fringe, Silk	98.00
Shirt, Man's, Gray, Long Tail, Flannel	15.00
Shoes, Boy's, Red Goose, Box	19.00
Shoes, Woman's, High Top, Victorian	125.00
Skirt, Poodle, Red Felt	35.00
Skirt, White Muslin, Embroidered, Flounced, Tucked, 26 In.Waist	38.00
Slip & Bloomers, Nightgown, Set, 3 Piece	125.00
Snowshoes, Bentwood, Rawhide, Pair	50.00
Stole, Skunk	65.00
Suit, Amish, Boy's, Wool	45.00
Suit, Amish, Man's	75.00
Suit, Buster Brown, Boy's, Black Velvet, Pearl Buttons	10.00
Suit, Lady's, Lilly Ann, Wine, Size 12, 2 Piece	48.00
Suit, Man's, White Linen, Mother–of–Pearl Buttons, Size 34	55.00
Suit, Rhinestone Buttons On Back, Kick Pleat, 2 Piece	25.00
Sweater Set, Baby's, 3 Piece	25.00
Teddie, Silk, Lace Trim, 1920–30	20.00
Toby Jack, Leather, Boot Worn In 17th Century, Above The Knee	850.00
Top Hat, Abe Lincoln Type	60.00
Trousers, US Navy, White, Summer, Bone Buttons, 1860–70	225.00

Uniform, Ringling Bros., Big Top On Shoulders of Jacket, Hat 90.00
Vest, Man's, Printed Silk, 1850s 38.00

Cluthra glass is a two–layered glass with small air pockets that form white spots. The Steuben Glass Works of Corning, New York, made it after 1903. Kimball Glass Company of Vineland, New Jersey, made Cluthra from about 1925.

CLUTHRA, see also Steuben
CLUTHRA, Chalice, Green & White, Signed Stanhope, 10 1/2 In. 110.00
Vase, Acid Marked, France, 6 5/8 In. 600.00

Coalport ware has been made by the Coalport Porcelain Works of England from 1795 to the present time. Early pieces were unmarked. About 1810–1825 the pieces were marked with the name "Coalport" in various forms. Later pieces also had the name "John Rose" in the mark. The crown mark has been used with variations since 1881.

COALPORT, Butter Chip, Green 18.00
Butter Chip, Rust 18.00
Creamer, Beaded Gold Over Cobalt Exterior, Gold Interior 37.50
Cup & Saucer, Cairo, Pink 12.00
Cup & Saucer, Flowers, Maroon & Gold, Hand Painted, Demitasse 15.00
Ginger Jar, Blue Willow 25.00
Mustache Cup, Saucer, Blue Bamboo, Birds, 1880s 110.00
Plate, Admiral Dewey, Manila, Blue & White, 10 In. 75.00
Plate, Floral Medallions, Allover Gold, 1895, 9 1/2 In., Pair 165.00
Plate, Orange & Gold Flowers, C.1820, 9 In. 60.00
Plate, Scalloped Rim, Gold Shells, Enameled Flowers, 9 1/2 In. 75.00
Plate, Wells Cathedral, Signed J.H.Plant, 9 1/4 In. 85.00
Soup, Dish, Hong Kong Pattern 9.00
Sugar & Creamer, Gold Handle, Chicago, 1893 .... 150.00
Tea Caddy, Allover Enameled Circles, Jewels, Signed, 5 1/2 In. 175.00
Toothpick, Ming Rose 15.00

Cobalt blue glass was made using oxide of cobalt. The characteristic bright dark blue identifies it for the collector. Most cobalt glass found today was made after the Civil War.

COBALT BLUE, Ashtray, Hat 12.00
Candlestick, Hexagonal, 7 5/8 In. 225.00
Cuspidor, Blown Glass, Mid–19th Century, 5 X 9 In. 250.00
Ewer, Gold & Enameled Flowers, 9 1/2 In. 15.00
Lamp, Finger, Applied Handle 125.00
Luncheon Set, Sandwich Tray, 15 Piece 130.00
Pitcher & Bowl, Paneled, Miniature 800.00
Pitcher, Handle, Gold Foliage, Forget–Me–Nots, 2 1/2 In. 70.00
Pitcher, Lemonade, Threaded, Clear Handle, 7 1/2 In. 32.50
Pitcher, Swirl, 5 1/2 In. 25.00
Pitcher, Water, Applied Crystal Handle, 3 Goblets 165.00
Sugar, Enameling, C.1790 .... 375.00
Tumbler, Atlantic City, Beach Scenes, Set of 5 .... 35.00
Tumbler, Gold Design, Large 22.50
Tumbler, King's 500, Parrot, Gold Trim 50.00
Vase, 5 1/2 In. 7.00
Vase, Bird Design, 9 In. 10.00
Vase, Fan, Silver Resist Design, 8 In. 15.00
Vase, Hand Painted Butterflies, 12 In. 22.50
Vase, Swirl, Scalloped Rim, 10 In. 12.50

Coca–Cola was first served in 1886 in Atlanta, Georgia. It was advertised through signs, newspaper ads, coupons, bottles, trays, calendars, and even lamps and clocks. Collectors want anything with the word "Coca–Cola," including a few rare products like gum wrappers and cigar bands. The famous trademark was patented in

1893, the "Coke" mark in 1945. Many modern items and reproductions are being made.

COCA–COLA, Ad, Black & White, 1st Drive–In, Munsey's, 1905	25.00
Ad, Girl Water Skiing, Color, Matted, 1922, 18 X 14 In.	30.00
Band, Cigar, 2 Piece	135.00
Bank, Can	4.00
Beach Seat, Child's, Aluminum Frame, Cloth Cover	85.00
Blotter, 1932–33, 3 1/2 X 7 3/4 In.	39.00
Blotter, Black Boy, Serving White Boy, 1932	50.00
Blotter, Boy & Girl, 1927	42.00
Blotter, Refresh Yourself, 1920s	15.00
Book Cover, 1930s	12.00
Book, Copyright 1950, 59 & 60, 8 1/4 X 5 1/2 In.	22.50
Booklet, Paper Doll, Coke Crown, Teenagers Holding Bottle, 1946	90.00
Booklet, Pause For Living, 1957	5.00
Booklet, Pause For Living, 1960	22.50
Booklet, When You Entertain Book, 1932	17.50
Bookmark, Dated 1904	250.00
Bottle Holder, Shopping Cart	25.00
Bottle Opener, Brass, 1910	30.00
Bottle Opener, Drink Coke In Bottles, Milwaukee Bottling Co.	40.00
Bottle Opener, Wall, Sprite Boy, Cap Catcher, 1950	9.00
Bottle Opener, Wooden Ice Pick	24.00
Bottle, 75th Anniversary Eng.Dept.Convention, Multicolored, 1961	85.00
Bottle, Embossed, Straight, 24 Oz.	45.00
Bottle, Jonesboro, Ark., Amber	250.00
Bottle, Knoxville, Amber	35.00
Bottle, Tin, Front Half, Embossed Bottle, Pat.Dec.25, 1923	30.00
Box, Pencil, 1937	28.00
Box, Pencil, 75th Anniversary, Box	55.00
Calendar, 1926	475.00
Calendar, 1937, Boy With Fishing Pole, 12 X 25 In.	275.00
Can, Syrup, Paper Label, 1939, 1 Gal.	67.50
Cap, Visor, Leather, Embossed Lilian Nordica On Visor	130.00
Card, Playing, Girl In Water, 1959, Box	35.00
Card, Playing, Girl With Dog, 1943	50.00
Carrier, 6 Pack, Cardboard, Dated 1924	55.00
Change Purse, Gold Lettering, Black Leather, 1920s, 4 In.	50.00
Charm, Bracelet, Coke, Enameled Bottle, Brass	15.00
Chest, Picnic, 1930's	125.00
Clock, Enjoy Coke, Electric, 1970s	60.00
Clock, Indoor, Illuminated Bottle, Neon, 1942, 15 In.	475.00
Coin Wrapper, Nickel & Half Dollar, 1940s, 2 Piece	2.50
Coin–Operated Machine, 6 1/2 Oz.Bottle	185.00
Compact	10.00
Cookie Jar, Coke Bottle, Brown	15.00
Cuff Links, Red Celluloid, C.1920	85.00
Cuff Links, Sterling Silver, Celluloid, 1925	40.00
Display, Witch	85.00
Doll, Box	12.00
Dominoes	15.00
Door Handle	125.00
Door Push, Coke, Porcelain	85.00
Frisbee, 1970	65.00
Game, Ping–Pong Set	50.00
Golf Ball, Arnold Palmer	20.00
Ice Chest, Drink Coca–Cola In Bottles, Red, 1930s .... 50.00 To	60.00
Ice Pick & Bottle Opener, Drink Coca–Cola, Script, 10 1/4 In.	13.00
Jar, Chewing Gum, Franklin Card Co.Lid, 11 1/2 X 4 1/2 In.	200.00
Jug, Syrup, 1930s, Paper Label	16.00
Knife, Drink Coca–Cola In Bottles, Bone Handle, Pocket	95.00
Knife, Lock Blade, Leather Case, 3 In.	20.00
Knife, World's Fair, Pocket, 1933	40.00

Letterhead, Lexington, Ky., 1907, 8 1/2 X 11 In. 21.60
Lighter, Cigarette, Bottle Shape .... 15.00 To 18.00
Lighter, Cigarette, Musical, 1950 .... 100.00
Lillian Nordica Ad, Coupon, 1904 .... 125.00
Marbles, See–Through Bag, Unopened 30.00
Marker, Golf Tee, Metal, In Paper, 1940s 250.00
Menu Sign, Fishtail, Light–Up 50.00
Mirror, Girl With Big Hat, Pocket 50.00
Mirror, Pocket, 1911 .... 155.00
Money Clip, St.Louis World's Fair, Tiffany, Pat.Pending, 1904 .... 575.00
Paddles, Ping–Pong, 1940s, Set of 4 .... 65.00
Paperweight, Round 34.50
Pencil Sharpener 25.00
Pin, German Coke Soccer Sponsor 20.00
Pin, Safety, 2 Year Driver, 1930s 35.00
Pin, Statue of Liberty Sponsor 7.00
Pin, Superbowl Sponsor 5.00
Plate, Sandwich, With Bottle & Tumbler 125.00
Poster, Edwards & Deutsch, Chicago, Litho, 27 X 56 In. 165.00
Poster, Rock Hudson, Woman Poolside, 56 X 27 In. 115.00
Radio, Can Shape, Box, 1970 .... 15.00
Ruler, 1933 .... 15.00
Santa Claus, Coca–Cola In Hand, Cardboard 25.00
Sign Set, U.S.Army Fighter Planes, 1943, 20 Piece, 13 X 15 In. 600.00
Sign, 3–D, With Hot Dog, Cardboard, 1932 .... 100.00
Sign, Bottle, Each End, Waxed Cardboard, 1915, 21 X 60 In. 750.00
Sign, Coca–Cola 6 Cents, 1950, Cardboard, 11 X 14 In. 15.00
Sign, Coca–Cola No Drip Protector, Dated June 14, 1927, Framed 15.00
Sign, Coke, Embossed Gold Bottle, 1937, 7 X 16 In. 75.00
Sign, Golf Course, Tin, Cast Iron, 1940s 200.00
Sign, Know Your War Planes, Civil Defense Office, 1943 .... 25.00
Sign, Lighted, Multicolor, 1950s 150.00
Sticker Set, Uncut Lithos, For Motion Picture, 3 X 4 In., 1953 .... 24.00
Thermometer, Bottle Shape, Brass, 50th Anniversary 100.00
Thermometer, Drink Coca–Cola, 5 Cents, Wooden, 14 3/4 X 3 3/4 In. 180.00
Thermometer, Wooden, 5 Cents, 1906 .... 250.00
Thermos, Tin, Gold, Silver, 1941, Set of 2 .... 250.00
Thimble, Aluminum, 1920s 30.00
Tip Tray, 1906, Relieves Fatique 150.00
Tip Tray, 1909, Coca–Cola Girl 195.00
Tip Tray, 1912, Hamilton King Girl .... 125.00 To 140.00
Tip Tray, 1914, Betty .... 65.00 To 200.00
Tip Tray, 1917, Elaine .... 50.00 To 125.00
Tip Tray, Oval, 1917 .... 120.00
Toy, Delivery Truck, Yellow, Red, Tin, Crates, 1947, 8 1/4 In. 110.00
Toy, Kazoo, 1971 .... 2.50
Toy, Truck, Steel, 10 Glass Bottles, Metalcraft, 11 In. 475.00
Toy, Vending Machine, Battery Operated, Linemar, Box 650.00
Tray, 1904, With Glass, Oval .... 650.00 To 850.00
Tray, 1909, Hamilton King Girl, Rectangular 550.00
Tray, 1912, Woman With Large Hat ....*Illus* 250.00
Tray, 1914, Betty ....*Illus* 200.00
Tray, 1914, Betty, Oval 290.00
Tray, 1917, Elaine, 8 1/2 X 19 In. 175.00
Tray, 1920, Garden Girl ....*Illus* 300.00
Tray, 1920, Garden Girl, Oval 400.00
Tray, 1927, Girl With Bobbed Hair .... 150.00 To 175.00
Tray, 1930, Bathing Beauty 160.00
Tray, 1930, Girl With Telephone .... 135.00 To 180.00
Tray, 1932, Yellow Bathing Suit Girl 200.00
Tray, 1933, Francis Dee 125.00
Tray, 1934, Weismuller & O'Sullivan .... 155.00 To 265.00
Tray, 1935, Madge Evans .... 90.00 To 100.00
Tray, 1936, Hostess 125.00

Coca–Cola, Tray, 1912, Woman With Large Hat   Coca–Cola, Tray, 1914, Betty   Coca–Cola, Tray, 1920, Garden Girl

Tray, 1937, Running Girl	79.50
Tray, 1938, Woman In Yellow Dress	68.00 To 85.00
Tray, 1940, Sailor Girl	55.00
Tray, 1941, Girl Ice Skater	50.00 To 75.00
Tray, 1943, Girl With Wind In Her Hair	22.00
Tray, 1950, Girl With Menu	20.00 To 47.00
Tumbler, Santa Claus, Rockwell, Set of 6	25.00
Tumbler, White Lettering, Large	7.00
Urn, Pencil, 75th Anniversary, Ceramic, Box	55.00
Vest, Wool, With Zipper, 1940s	60.00
Wallet, Pigskin, Embossed Bottle & Logo, Box	75.00
Watch Fob, 1908	150.00 To 275.00
Yo–Yo, Whistling, Metal	125.00

Coffee grinders of home size were first made about 1894. They lost favor by the 1930s. Large floor–standing or counter model coffee grinders were used in the nineteenth–century country store. The renewed interest in fresh–ground coffee has produced many modern electric and hand grinders; and reproductions of the old styles are being made.

COFFEE GRINDER, Arcade, Glass Base, Cast Iron Top	30.00
Arcade, No. 25, Wall	54.00
Bridgton, Wall Mount, Cast Iron	42.50
Charles Parker, Double Wheels, Cast Iron, 21 1/2 In.	275.00
Charles Parker, Model 5000, Repainted	195.00
Clark & Co., Lap Model, Brass Cup, Mounted On Board	130.00
Elgin National Coffee Mill, Iron, Red Paint, No Handle	85.00
Enterprise, No.1, Counter Model, Black Cast Iron Crank	250.00
Enterprise, No.9	900.00
Hobart, Electric, Glass Dome Top	200.00
Landers, Clary, Iron & Brass, Lap	130.00
Lap Style, Pewter Cup, Hand Dovetailed, Pennsylvania	95.00
Lap, Elma, Drawer, Red Tin	35.00
Lap, Grand Union Tea Co., Red Paint, Cast Iron	275.00
Lap, Patent July 20, 1886	65.00
Morning Glory, Kansas City, Tin, 19 In.	149.00
Peugeot Freres Brevetes, Cast Iron, Painted, French, 20 In.	70.00
Royal, Mill	150.00
Royal, Wall Mount, Cast Iron	35.00
Star Coffee, Floor Model, Original Paint	1095.00
Swift Mill, Original Red Paint, 29 1/2 In.	358.00
Universal, No.109, Black Metal, Pat.Feb.1905	35.00
Wooden, Brass Hopper	80.00

Coin spot is a glass pattern that was named by the collectors. It, of course, features coinlike spots as part of the glass. Colored, clear, and opalescent glass was made with the spots. Many companies used

the design in the 1870–90 period. It is so popular that reproductions are still being made.

COIN SPOT, Celery, Ribbed, Cranberry .... 110.00 To 150.00
   Ewer, Clear & Opalescent, Fenton 35.00
   Hat, Cranberry, 4 In. 40.00
   Hat, Ruffled Rim, 3 In. 35.00
   Lamp, Cranberry, 18 In. 100.00
   Lamp, Oil, Clear Base, Vaseline 260.00
   Pitcher, Ruffled Top, Clear Handle, 8 1/2 In. 85.00
   Pitcher, Ruffled Top, Vaseline 110.00
   Pitcher, Ruffled, Blue 120.00
   Pitcher, Trefoil Rim, Frosted Handle, Dimpled, 9 1/4 In. 175.00
   Pitcher, Triangular Mouth, Cranberry, With 2 Tumblers 165.00
   Pitcher, Water, Opalescent Crystal 75.00
   Pitcher, Water, Ruffled, Hexagonal, Blue 65.00
   Rose Bowl, Ruffled Rim 35.00
   Sugar Shaker, 9 Panel Mold, Blue 75.00
   Sugar Shaker, Blue, 9 Ribs 85.00
   Sugar Shaker, Daisy & Fern, 9 Panels, Blue Opalescent 110.00
   Syrup, Pear Shape, Silver Plated Lid, Blue, 7 In. 77.50
   Syrup, Ring Neck, Northwood 210.00
   Syrup, Ring Neck, Rubina, Opalescent 150.00
   Syrup, Silver Plated Lid, 9 Panels, Clear, 6 In. 48.50
   Syrup, Silver Plated Lid, 9 Panels, Green, 6 In. 77.50
   Syrup, White Spots, Tapered, Applied Handle, Original Top 65.00
   Tumbler, Blue 30.00
   Tumbler, Enameled Foliage & Insects, Colors & Gold, 3 3/4 In. 35.00
   Tumbler, Northwood, Cranberry 295.00
   Vase, Green, 7 X 7 In. 32.00
   Vase, Mother–of–Pearl, Peach, Ruffled, White Lining, 8 1/2 In. 550.00
   Vase, Mother–of–Pearl, White Lining, Fluted Top, Blue, 7 3/8 In. 195.00
   Vase, Ruffled Top, Cranberry, 4 In. 40.00
   Vase, Ruffled Top, Cranberry, 7 In. 45.00
   Water Set, Cranberry, 7 Piece 225.00

The vending machine is an ancient invention dating back to 200 B.C. when holy water was dispensed in a coin–operated vase. Smokers in seventeenth–century England could buy tobacco from a coin–operated box. It was not until after the Civil War that the technology made modern coin–operated games and vending machines plentiful. Slot machines, arcade games, and dispensers are all collected.

COIN–OPERATED MACHINE, Abbey, Chlorophyll 75.00
   Art Pistol Shoot 200.00
   Basketball, Topper, C.1944 .... 40.00
   Blink's Whiz Bowler, Counter Top, 1940s 225.00
   Cailoscope, Caille, Peep Show, 1 Cent 1850.00
   Coin Changer, Patent Date 1890 .... 150.00
   Comb, Pocket, 10 Cent 38.00
   Digger Claw, Exhibit Supply & Novelty, 25 Cent 1200.00
   Digger, Iron Claw 1850.00
   Dixie Cup Dispenser, Glass Dome 185.00
   Door Lock, Restroom, Brass, With Keys 100.00
   Fems Sanitary Napkin, White Porcelain, 1930s 235.00
   Football Game, Arcade, Floor Model, 1930s 310.00
   Gum, Adams 165.00
   Gum, Advance 35.00
   Gum, Baker's Chocolate, Wall, Porcelain 175.00
   Gum, Chicklets, Dentyne, L Shape 650.00
   Gum, Mechanical Cloth Yellow Kid Inside 700.00
   Gum, Pepsin, Mansfield 550.00
   Gum, Pulver, 1 Cent, Yellow Kid Type, 1930s 475.00
   Gum, Pulver, Policeman 550.00

Gum, Zeno	250.00
Gumball, Advance, Original Decal, C.1923	125.00
Gumball, Baby Grand, Penny, Oak, C.1939	55.00
Gumball, Baldwin, Tin Chicken, Turn Crank, Cackles	95.00
Gumball, Baseball Target Shooter	395.00
Gumball, Berkshire, Decal	450.00
Gumball, Dice Game, Bluebird Co., 1920s, 11 1/2 In.	250.00
Gumball, Dietz, Gambling	165.00
Gumball, Ford, 1 Cent, 1920s	65.00
Gumball, Hunter Duck Shoot, 1 Cent	325.00
Gumball, Jawbreaker, Atlas Master, 1 Cent	65.00
Gumball, Master, Short Coin Entry, 1 & 5 Cent	190.00
Gumball, Mills, Cast Iron, Glass Globe	375.00
Gumball, Mills, In 1919 Mills Catalog	425.00
Gumball, Northwestern, 1 Cent	150.00
Gumball, Penny Pack, Counter Top, 1930s, 10 1/2 In.	195.00
Gumball, Simmons, Red Porcelain, Embossed Globe	145.00
Gumball, Topper, 1 Cent	55.00
Gumball, Watling, 1 Cent	3000.00
Hawkeye, Bell, Original Decal	275.00
Horse Race, Baker's Pacers	4250.00
Jennings, Little Duke, 1 Cent	2175.00
Jennings, Woman's Model, Push—Down Handle, 50 Cent	6500.00
Jergens Lotion Dispenser, 1 Cent	175.00
Lucky Strike, Wilson	795.00
Match Vendor, Cast Iron, C.1911	395.00
Matchbox, Barrett & Barrett, Oak, Iron, Glass, 1 Cent	185.00
Paper Cups, Dixie, 1 Cent	500.00
Peanut, Brice Williams, Coin Rejector	325.00
Peanut, Columbus, Model A	145.00
Peanut, Double Nugget, 1 Cent	175.00 To 225.00
Peanut, Leebold	225.00
Peanut, Maroon, Lighted Red Top, 5 Cent, 1930s	125.00
Peanut, Northwestern, Table Model, Key, 10 Cent	40.00
Peanut, Or—Bits, Cylinder Globe	115.00
Peanut, Selmor, Cast Iron, 1 Cent	200.00
Peanut, Sun	45.00
Pencil, Stamps Your Name, Slot Machine Look	395.00
Peppy The Musical Clown, Arcade, 10 Cent	950.00
Perfume Vendor, Mills, Original Bottles, 1 Cent	3800.00
Perk—Up Peanut, 5 Cent	75.00
Pinball, Atlantis	450.00
Pinball, Cadet, 5 Cent	195.00
Pinball, Eldorado	450.00
Pinball, Genco, Monte Carlo, 1 Cent	225.00
Pistol Shoot, Challenger, 1 Cent	350.00
Play Football, Chester Pollard, Upright	1200.00
Popcorn, Holcomb & Hoke	3550.00
Radio, Wooden	190.00
Roulette, Acme, Automatic, C.1900	1250.00
Shock, Arcade, 5 Cent, Table Top	275.00
Shoeshine, National, 1914	2100.00
Shooting Gallery, Target Skill, 1940s	110.00
Shooting Gallery, U.S.Marshal, 1950s	200.00
Slot, Apache Olla Jar	500.00
Slot, Bally, Double Bell, 5 & 25 Cents	3000.00
Slot, Bally, Double Bell, 5 Cents to 15 Cents	3000.00
Slot, Bally, Electric Double Up, 1 Or 2 Quarters	700.00
Slot, Bally, Tic—Tac—Toe, 1 To 5 Quarters	700.00
Slot, Bally, Triple Bell, 5 & 25 Cent	750.00
Slot, Buckley, A Guaranteed $7.50 Jackpot	950.00
Slot, Buckley, Track Odds	2000.00
Slot, Bursting Cherry	850.00

Slot, C.& F., Baby Grand 1800.00
Slot, Caille, Art Deco, Wood, Floor Medal, 5 Cent 4500.00
Slot, Caille, Doughboy 5 Cent, 1935 .... 675.00
Slot, Caille, Nude, 25 Cent 1500.00
Slot, Caille, Silent Sphinx, 1920s 950.00
Slot, Davon Penny Pack, Cigarette, Gum Dispenser 225.00
Slot, Fey, Liberty Bell 1800.00
Slot, Harolds Club 950.00
Slot, Hennings, Galaxy, 2 Plays 25 Cents, 3 Reels 780.00
Slot, Icart, Model II 3500.00
Slot, Jennings, Operator Bell, Future Pay, Iron 1800.00
Slot, Jennings, Triplex, 1937 .... 4000.00
Slot, Jennings, Victoria Silent Bell, Peacock, 1932 .... 1750.00
Slot, Keeney Pyramid 2200.00
Slot, Mills, 4 Bells 850.00
Slot, Mills, Cherry Spray, Watermelon Top Jackpot 870.00
Slot, Mills, Extraordinary, Table Model, 25 Cent 1250.00
Slot, Mills, Firebird QT, 1 Cent 925.00
Slot, Mills, Golden Falls, 10 Cent 1150.00
Slot, Mills, Lion Front, 25 Cent 1850.00
Slot, Mills, Operator Bell, Cast Iron, 5 Cent 4800.00
Slot, Mills, Skyscraper, 1 Cent 1250.00
Slot, Mills, Triple Bells 600.00
Slot, Mills, Vest Pocket, Chrome, 5 Cent 560.00
Slot, Pace, Bantam, 1 Cent, 1928 .... 1500.00
Slot, Pace, Royal Deluxe Twin, C.1940, 5 & 25 Cent 6200.00
Slot, Reel 21, Blackjack, Gum Payout, Counter, 1930s 250.00
Slot, Rock–Ola, 1 Cent 950.00
Slot, Rock–Ola, Four Aces 1195.00
Slot, Seeburg Barrel 775.00
Slot, Superior, Automat 3200.00
Slot, Superior, Extra Bell, 5 Cent 1800.00
Slot, Universal, Arrow Bell, 2–Way, 5 & 25 Cent 300.00
Slot, Watling, Cherry Front Rol–A–Top, 5 Cent 950.00
Slot, Watling, Rol–A–Top, 5 Cent .... 2500.00 To 2600.00
Slot, Watling, Treasury, 10 Cent 4250.00
Sorter & Counter, Coin, Brandt Cashier Co. 500.00
Stamp, Shermack, Embossed Sign of Uncle Sam 350.00
Stereoscope, Mills, Bowfront, Peep Show, 1 Cent 1850.00
Strength Tester, Caille, Hercules 3500.00
Strength Tester, Caille, Mickey Finn 4500.00
Test Your Grip, Penny 175.00
Trade Stimulator, Ad Lib Try It 500.00
Trade Stimulator, Ball Game 185.00
Trade Stimulator, Jennings Target 325.00
Trade Stimulator, Mills, Dial 1200.00
Trade Stimulator, Mills, Dial, Airplane Front, Map 1000.00
Trade Stimulator, Mills, Target Practice 200.00
Trade Stimulator, Puritan Baby Bell, 1928 .... 375.00
Trade Stimulator, Race Track, Excelsior 1750.00
Trade Stimulator, Spin–It 180.00
Trade Stimulator, Steeple Chase, Horse Race, Keeney 375.00
Trade Stimulator, Wheel of Fortune, Pat.1893 .... 250.00
Victory Fruit Gum, Penny Drop 300.00
Yu–Chu Breath Mint, Original Decal 275.00

 Collector plates are modern plates produced in limited editions. Some will be found listed under the factory name, such as Bing & Grondahl, Royal Copenhagen, Royal Doulton, and Wedgwood. Pictures and more price information can be found in "Kovels' Price Guide for Collector Plates, Figurines, Paperweights and Other Limited Editions."

COLLECTOR PLATE, Avon, Christmas, 1973, Box, 1st Edition 95.00
Holly Hobbie, Mother's Day, 1975 .... 9.50

Knowles, Annie & Sandy, Annie Series	10.00
Porsgrund, Christmas, 1970	2.50
Porsgrund, Christmas, 1971	5.00
Rockwell Kent, Map of U.S., 17 In.	275.00
Rockwell Kent, Our American Plates, Pacific, Brown, 14 In.	225.00
Rockwell, 4 Seasons, 1972, 4 Piece	125.00
Rockwell, Christmas, 1974	65.00
Rockwell, Christmas, 1975	45.00

Comic art, or cartoon art, is a relatively new field of collecting. Original comic strips, magazine covers, and even printed strips are collected. The first daily comic strip was printed in 1907. The paintings on celluloid used for movie cartoons are listed in this book under Animation Art.

COMIC ART, Book, Tarzan, Tip–Top Comics, No.41, Sept.'37	65.00
Book, Terry & The Pirates, No.17, Harvey	30.00
Cartoon, Dennis The Menace, Hank Ketcham	100.00
Cartoon, Felix The Cat, Pen & Ink, Matted, 1950s	95.00
Full Page, Dick Tracy, Sunday Section, Chester Gould, 1940s	8.00
Strip, Blondie, Chic Young, October, 1930	350.00
Strip, Bringing Up Father, George McManus, January, 1942	150.00
Strip, Bringing Up Father, George McManus, June, 1941	175.00
Strip, Sambo, Sunday Newspaper, Baltimore, Sept.19, 1909	20.00
Strip, Steve Canyon, Milton Caniff, 1971, 6 1/2 X 22 In.	113.00
Title Page From Book, Conan The Barbarian, John Buscema	80.00

Commemorative items have been made to honor members of royalty and those of great national fame. World's fairs and important historical events are also remembered with commemorative pieces.

COMMEMORATIVE, see also Coronation; World's Fair

COMMEMORATIVE, Beaker, Queen Victoria, Banners Above Portrait Head	85.00
Beaker, Queen Victoria, Young & Old Portraits, 1839, 1897	75.00
Bowl, Prince, Princess of Wales, Silver Wedding, 1888, 2 In.	40.00
Box, Cover, Queen's Silver Jubilee, 1952–1977, 3 In.	100.00
Card, Playing, Silver Jubilee, King George V, De LaRue	75.00
Cup & Saucer, Edward VIII Abdication, 1936, Sepia Portrait	125.00
Cup & Saucer, Prince Andrew's Wedding, 1986, Jasperware	40.00
Cup & Saucer, Prince Philip's 60th Birthday, 1981	35.00
Cup & Saucer, Queen Elizabeth, 60th Birthday, Coalport	45.00
Cup, Elizabeth & George VI, 1939	30.00
Cup, George V, Silver Gilt, Panel of Horses, 1823, 18 In.	3250.00
Dish, Cover, Queen Elizabeth, 60th Birthday, Coalport	20.00
Loving Cup, Prince William, 1st Birthday, 1983, Coronet	25.00
Loving Mug, Elizabeth II, 25th Coronation, Paragon, 3 1/2 In.	100.00
Mug, Cider, Elizabeth II, Silver Wedding, Wedgwood	35.00
Mug, Diamond Jubilee Victoria, 1897, Brown Transfer, Aynsley	110.00
Mug, Edward VII, Cobalt Blue, Stoneware, Royal Doulton	145.00
Mug, Edward VIII, Portrait, Jasperware, Wedgwood, 4 In.	350.00
Mug, Queen Victoria, Diamond Jubilee, Green Transfer	65.00
Photograph, Edward VIII, Signed, Framed, 5 1/4 X 3 In.	500.00
Pin Dish, Prince of Wales Investiture, Coronet, 1969, 5 In.	25.00
Pitcher, Music, Edward VIII, Creamware, Crown Devon, 8 In.	400.00

Keep art, paintings, prints, and textiles away from sunny windows.

Pitcher, Queen Victoria Jubilee, 1897, 8 In.	165.00
Pitcher, Queen Victoria Jubilee, 1897, Royal Doulton, 10 In.	525.00
Plaque, Queen Victoria, Royal Doulton	225.00
Plate, King George VI & Queen Elizabeth, U.S. Visit, 1939	25.00
Plate, Memorial, Edward VIII	125.00
Plate, Queen Victoria, Jubilee, Advertising On Reverse, 1897	75.00
Spoon, Tea Caddy, Edward VIII, Holder	25.00
Tea Canister, Russian–Japanese Peace Comm., 1903, 10 In.	110.00
Tea Set, George VI & Queen Elizabeth, Visit, 1939, 7 Piece	135.00
Tea Set, Sepia Transfer, Queen Victoria, RHP, 1887, 15 Piece	1200.00
Tin, Queen Victoria, 1897, Ivory Gloss Starch, 9 In.	165.00
Toothpick, Charles & Diana Portraits, White, 1981, 2 3/4 In.	15.00
Tray, King & Queen, British Jubilee, Brass, 1935, 11 In.	28.00

A woman did not powder her face in public until after World War I. By 1920 the beauty parlor, permanent waves, and cosmetics had become acceptable. A few companies sold cake face powder in a box with a mirror and a pad or puff. Soon the compact was being designed by jewelers and made of gold, silver, and precious materials. Cosmetic companies began to sell powder in attractive compacts of less valuable metal or plastic. Collectors today search for Art Deco designs, commemorative compacts from world's fairs or political events, and unusual examples. Many were made with companion lipsticks and other fittings.

COMPACT, Art Deco, 2 Deer, 3 3/4 In.	20.00
Art Deco, Floral Design, Sterling Silver, 4 In.	50.00 To 85.00
Art Deco, Sterling Silver Deposit Top	22.00
Art Deco, Sterling Silver, Hand Chased Floral, Round	75.00
Century of Progress	18.00
Chain, Rectangular, Sterling Silver	57.50
Commemorative, King George V & Queen Portraits, Powder, 2 In.	35.00
Double, Powder & Rouge, Sterling Silver, Enamel Ring, 2 In.	60.00
Eastern Star, Brass	10.00
Elgin American, Pear Shape, Unused, 1940s	37.00
Elgin, 14K Gold Inlaid, Sterling, Yellow, Gold, Round	70.00
Elgin, Bakelite	8.00
Floral Design, Sterling Silver, Round, Art Deco	75.00
Floral Etched, ECB Monogram, 14K Gold, C.1915	450.00
Flower Basket On Cover	8.00
Gold, Black, With Lipstick, H. Rubenstein	15.00
Golden Gate Expo, 1939	17.50
Goldtone, Stratton, England, Round	12.00
Grey, World's Fair, Chicago, 1933	14.00
Hand Chased Floral Design, Art Deco, Sterling, Round	75.00
Helena Rubenstein, Gold, Black, Lipstick	15.00
Kremola Skin Cream, Girl Picture, Mirror Inside, Celluloid, 1915	15.00
Lipstick Holder & Music Box, Silver Plate, 2 1/2 In.	55.00
Lipstick, Corset Shape, Middle Band of Rhinestones, 2 3/4 In.	18.50
Lucite, Blue Mirror Top, Round	40.00
Marcasite Set Bells, V Initial, Heart Shape	45.00
Marcasite Set, Heart Shape, Initial V	50.00
Mary Dunhill, Oval, Sterling Silver	65.00
Multicolor Jewels, Filigree Both Sides	45.00
Powder & Rouge, Mirror, Silver Plate, C.1910	25.00
Rhinestone Top, Marhill 5th Avenue	35.00
Rhinestones, Lipstick Holder, Volupte	20.00
Rouge & Lipstick Compartment, Rhinestones On Celluloid, 1920s	40.00
Snake Skin Cover	15.00
Sterling Silver, Early 1900s	65.00
Trifari, Jeweled Top	55.00
Turquoise Enamel, World's Fair, Square, 1939	40.00
USN Insignia, Black Metal	8.00

We Want Willkie, With Lipstick	15.00
World's Fair, 1939	10.00

> The term "contemporary glass" refers to art glass made since 1950. Some contemporary glass factories, such as Orrefors or Baccarat, are listed under their own categories.

CONTEMPORARY GLASS, Figurine, Black Jazz Musician With Clarinet, 6 In.	150.00
Figurine, Murano, Snake Charmer and Snake, 8 In.	75.00
Vase, Basket Weave, Red, Barovier & Toso, 12 In.	500.00
Vase, Engraved Birds, Kosta, 10 In.	115.00
Vase, Handkerchief Shape, Red Line, Venini, 12 In.	750.00
Vase, Teardrop, Green, Blue, White, Ferro, 1956, 10 In.	550.00
Vase, Woman With Laundry, Lindstrand, Kosta, 1940, 11 In.	1000.00

> Cookbooks are collected for various reasons. Some are wanted for the recipes, some for investment, and some as examples of advertising. Cookbooks and recipe pamphlets are included in this section.

COOKBOOK, A & P, 288 Pages, 1975	7.00
American Cooking, 1915–31, 12 Volumes	95.00
American Pure Food Cookbook, Sears Roebuck, 500 Pages, 1899	32.50
Arm & Hammer, Recipe & Almanac	50.00
Aunt Jane's, McCannon & Co., 1889–1928, 50th Anniversary	10.00
Baker's Chocolate, 1932	5.00
Baker's Chocolate, Famous Recipes, 1928, 63 Pages	4.50
Best Foods, 1935	15.00
Better Homes & Gardens, 1968	10.00
Betty Crocker's Picture Cookbook, 1950	15.00
Bisquick All–Star, 1935	10.00
Bond Bread, 1933	5.00
Boston Cooking School, 1942	13.50
Calumet Baking Powder, 1922, 80 Pages	12.00
Calumet, 1929	2.00
Calumet, Figural, 1920s	6.00
Campbell Soup, Campbell Soup Can Shaped	5.00
Carnation, 1939	5.00
Carving & Serving, 1914, Mrs. Lincoln	25.00
Cheese Making, 1909, Decker	35.00
Crisco, 1916	5.00
Cutco, Meat, 1961	2.50
Desert, Susse Speisen Und Eisbomden, Nordhausen, 1907	125.00
Economy Administration Cookbook, 696 Pages, 1913	45.00
Enterprising Housekeeper, 1913	8.00
F.W.McNess, 1933, 63 Pages	4.50
Fanny Farmer, 1920	17.00
Fanny Farmer, Boston Cooking School, 808 Pages, 1928	18.00
Fine Old Dixie Recipes, 1939	45.00
Frigidaire Recipes, 91 Pages, 1929	6.00
General Foods, 1940	4.00
Gold Cross Milk, 1938	5.00
Gold Medal Flour, Giveaway, 1917	7.50
Gone With The Wind, Pebeco Toothpaste, Illustrated, 1940	22.50
Good Housekeeping, 1956	3.00
Good Luck Margarine, 1932	5.00
Greer, Hardbound, 1915	7.00
Heinz, 210 Pages, 1939	8.00
Hellman, 1930	5.00
Hershey Recipe Book, 1930	8.00
Hood's Cookbook Number One, 1879, 32 Pages	7.00
Housekeeping In Old Virginia, John Morton & Co., Dated 1879	98.00
Inglenook, 1913	15.00
Jell–O, 23 Pages, 1930	3.50
Jell–O, Through The Menu With Jell–O, 1927	4.00
Jewel Tea, Mary Dunbar's New Cookbook, 1933	15.00

K.C.Baking Powder, Cook's Book, 1931	5.00
Kate Smith, 55 Cake Recipes, 1962	4.00
Kingsford Corn Starch Recipe Book, 1907	3.00
Knox Gelatin Recipes, 1914	7.50
Larkin, 1909	5.00
Let's Eat, 1931	8.25
Lowney's, 1912	10.00
Margaret Rudkin Pepperidge Farm Cookbook, 1963	7.50
Mary Arnold's Century, 1895	20.00
Mary Dunbar's New Cook Book, Jewel Tea, 1933	4.00
Mary Dunbar's New Cookbook, 1933	5.00
Mary Lee Taylor, Pet Milk Recipes, 1949	4.00
McCormick & Co., Selected Recipes That Keep Family Happy, 1924	2.00
Methodist, 1924	15.00
Miss Parola's Cookbook, 1881	20.00
Mrs.Lincoln's Boston Cookbook, 1899	45.00
New Delineator Recipes, Hardback, 1930s	9.25
Occident Flour, 1930s	5.00
Peerless Cookbook, 1901, Lincoln	20.00
Pillsbury, 1914	22.50
Pillsbury, 3rd Bake–Off	5.00
Pure Food, 1907	8.00
Recipes To Match Your Sugar Ration, 1942	5.00
Redding's, Paper Cover, 1886	8.00
Royal Desserts, Ginger Rogers Cover, 1940	10.00
Successful Housekeeper, 1886	25.00
Swans Down Cake Flour, 1934	5.00
The Modern Cookbook, 1930	12.00
Thirty Cent Bread, 1917, McCann	20.00
Town Crier Flours, 1938	4.00
Watkins Salad Book, 1940	12.00
Watkins, 46 Pages, Dated 1903	5.00
Westinghouse Electric Range Recipes, 80 Pages, 1954	4.00
White House, 1926	27.50
White House, Mrs.Roosevelt, 1907	12.50
Woman's World, 1939	12.00

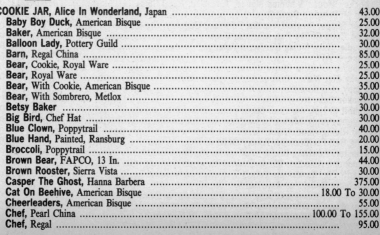

Cookie jars with brightly painted designs or amusing figural shapes became popular in the mid–1930s. Many companies made them and collectors search for cookie jars either by design or by maker's name. Listed here are examples by the less common makers. Major factories are listed under their own names in other sections of the book.

COOKIE JAR, Alice In Wonderland, Japan	43.00
Baby Boy Duck, American Bisque	25.00
Baker, American Bisque	32.00
Balloon Lady, Pottery Guild	30.00
Barn, Regal China	85.00
Bear, Cookie, Royal Ware	25.00
Bear, Royal Ware	25.00
Bear, With Cookie, American Bisque	35.00
Bear, With Sombrero, Metlox	30.00
Betsy Baker	30.00
Big Bird, Chef Hat	30.00
Blue Clown, Poppytrail	40.00
Blue Hand, Painted, Ransburg	20.00
Broccoli, Poppytrail	15.00
Brown Bear, FAPCO, 13 In.	44.00
Brown Rooster, Sierra Vista	30.00
Casper The Ghost, Hanna Barbera	375.00
Cat On Beehive, American Bisque	18.00 To 30.00
Cheerleaders, American Bisque	55.00
Chef, Pearl China	100.00 To 155.00
Chef, Regal	95.00

> For emergency repairs to chipped pottery, try coloring the spot with a wax crayon or oil paint. It will look a little better.

Cookie Cop, Pfaltzgraff	65.00
Cookie Monster, California Originals	30.00
Cookie Train, American Bisque	32.00
Cow, American Bisque	20.00
Cup & Cookies, Coffeepot, American Bisque	22.00
Davy Crockett, American Bisque	100.00
Donkey, With Milk Wagon, American Bisque	30.00
Dumbo, American Pottery	65.00
Dumbo, Turnabout, Disney	22.00 To 55.00
Dutch Boy, American Bisque	25.00
Dutch Girl, American Bisque	20.00
Dutch Girl, Pottery Guild	50.00
Dutch Girl, Regal China	95.00
Ear of Corn, Stanfordware	35.00
Elephant, Twin Winton	10.00
Elf's Schoolhouse, California	10.00
Elsie In Barrel, Regal	58.00
French Chef, Black Mustache & Goatee, White Hat, Metlox	42.00
Girl, Pottery Guild	32.00
Goldilocks, Cookie Head, Regal	45.00 To 70.00
Grandma, Brayton Laguna	195.00
House, With Carlil Restaurant Above Door, Sierra Vista	30.00
Indian, Light Brown Ears, USA Stoneware	35.00
Kitten, On Beehive, American Bisque	25.00
Kraft Bear, Regal	75.00
Lamb, American Bisque	25.00
Little Red Riding Hood, Napco	25.00 To 50.00
Little Red Riding Hood, Pottery Guild	50.00 To 95.00
Majorette, American Bisque	26.00
Mammy Cook, Blue Polka Dots, Metlox	65.00
Mammy, Blue Polka Dots, Metlox	85.00
Mammy, Pearl China	200.00 To 250.00
Matilda, Brayton Laguna	165.00
Melon Ribbed, Smith Bros.	310.00
Mickey Mouse & Minnie Mouse, Turnabout, Regal China	95.00 To 125.00
Old McDonald's Barn, Regal	100.00
Pear Shape, Rosebud Handles, Porcelain, Germany, Crown, 8 In.	250.00
Pine Cone Coffee Pot, American Bisque	27.00
Poodle, Gray, Sitting Up, Sierra Vista	45.00
Popeye, ABC	160.00
Popeye, American Bisque	275.00
Porky Pig, Warner Bros.	25.00
Puppy, American Bisque	18.00
Quaker Oats, Regal China	40.00 To 65.00
Rabbit In Hat, American Bisque	25.00 To 36.00
Raggedy Andy, Metlox	25.00
Red Riding Hood, U.S.A.	65.00
Ring Bell For Cookies, Pottery Guild	30.00
Rooster, American Bisque	35.00 To 38.00
Sandman, American Bisque	45.00
Sheriff Pig, Ransbottom Pottery	30.00
Southern Belle, Pan American	40.00
Spaceship, American Bisque	50.00
Star Wars, R2D2, Ceramic, 20th Century Fox, 1977, 13 In.	60.00
Strawberry, Maurice	12.00

Coors, Plate, Rosebud, Green, 8 In.

Don't cook acid foods in copper pots unless they have tin linings. The combination of acid and copper creates a poison.

Teddy Bear, Lying On Top of Lid, Purple Drip Glaze, Winfield	50.00
Thumper, Disney	25.00
Tigger, Disney	55.00 To 85.00
Topsy, Metlox	80.00 To 85.00
Train, Pfaltzgraff	45.00
Treehouse, Keebler	30.00
Truck, American Bisque	30.00
Umbrella Kids, American Bisque	55.00
White Owl, Arnel	25.00
Winnie–The–Pooh, Marcia of California	24.00
Wooden Soldier, American Bisque	40.00
Yarn Doll, American Bisque	22.00 To 30.00
Yogi Bear, Hanna Barbera, 14 In.	70.00

COORS U.S.A.

Coors ware was made by a pottery in Golden, Colorado, owned by the Coors Beverage Company. It was produced from the turn of the century until the pottery was destroyed by fire in the 1930s. The name "Coors" is marked on the back.

COORS, Batter Bowl, Rosebud, Maroon	40.00
Bowl, Maroon, 7 In.	25.00
Bowl, Rosebud, Tab Handle, Maroon, 6 1/2 In.	6.00
Cup & Saucer, Rosebud, Blue	30.00
Cup & Saucer, Rosebud, Orange	12.00
Mortar & Pestle	37.00
Mortar & Pestle, Marked, Small	45.00
Mug, Coors U.S.A., Signed	20.00
Pitcher, Rosebud, Orange, Cork & Label	45.00
Plate, Mellow Tone, Pastel	7.00
Plate, Rosebud, Blue, 9 In.	40.00
Plate, Rosebud, Cobalt Blue, 8 In.	6.00
Plate, Rosebud, Green, 8 In. ....*Illus*	6.00
Plate, Rosebud, Maroon, 8 In.	6.00
Plate, Rosebud, Orange, 8 In.	6.00
Plate, Rosebud, Yellow, 6 In.	5.00
Plate, Rosebud, Yellow, 9 In.	7.00
Salt & Pepper, Rosebud, 4 1/2 In.	25.00
Scoop, Pouring, China Handle	20.00
Vase, Beige, 8 1/2 In.	23.00
Vase, Blue, 6 In.	20.00
Vase, Brown & White, Signed, 7 In.	20.00
Vase, Burnt Orange Matte, Turquoise Lining, Ring Pattern, 5 1/2 In.	65.00
Vase, Magenta, 10 Sides, 5 1/2 In.	22.00
Vase, Round Handles, Brown Matte, 8 In.	30.00
Vase, Turquoise & Buff Matte, 5 In.	10.00
Vase, Turquoise, 9 In.	22.00

Josiah Spode established a pottery at Stoke–on–Trent, England, in 1770. In 1833, the firm was purchased by William Copeland and

Thomas Garrett and the firm mark was changed. In 1847, Copeland became the sole owner and the mark changed again. W. T. Copeland & Sons continued until a 1976 merger when it became Royal Worcester Spode. Pieces are listed in this book under the name that appears in the mark. Copeland Spode, Copeland, and Royal Worcester have separate listings.

COPELAND SPODE, Bowl, Italian, 9 1/2 In.	60.00
Bowl, Vegetable, Bridal Rose, Open	100.00
Bread & Butter, Bridal Rose	25.00
Creamer, Bridal Rose	55.00
Cup & Saucer, Bridal Rose	45.00
Cup & Saucer, Castelton, Royal	35.00
Dinner Set, Wicker Lane Pattern, Service For 8, 51 Piece	210.00
Figurine, Bluebird, Signed, 5 1/4 In.	45.00
Gravy Boat, Attached Underplate, Patricia	35.00
Gravy Boat, Bridal Rose, With Stand	140.00
Pitcher, Chicago Scenes, Fire, Mrs.O'Leary's Cow	375.00
Pitcher, Tower	65.00
Plate, Bryon Series, Divided	30.00
Plate, Buildings, Universtiy of Chicago, 1931, Set of 12	800.00
Plate, Dinner, Castelton, Royal	30.00
Plate, Patricia, 8 In.	48.00
Plate, Royal Jasmine, Brown Flowers, 1925, 10 1/2 In., 12 Pc.	145.00
Plate, Spanish Festivities, 10 1/4 In.	30.00
Plate, Tower, 10 1/2 In.	22.00
Platter, Bridal Rose, 15 1/2 In.	150.00
Platter, Tree, Turquoise, Embossed, 1830s	225.00
Punch Bowl, 15 1/2 In.	265.00
Sugar & Creamer, Patrician	30.00
Sugar, Bridal Rose, Cover	780.00
Teapot, Patricia	55.00
Vase, Bulbous, Blue & White, 8 In.	30.00
COPELAND, Bowl, Figural, Center, Classical Maidens, Flowing Tresses, 18 In.	715.00
Bowl, Vegetable, Brown Transfer, Cattle Scene On Cover, 10 In.	50.00
Figurine, Mending The Net, Woman, Repairing Seine, Parian, 17 In.	250.00
Pancake Dish, Blue Willow, Gilt Trim, Cover, 1851–85, 9 In.	265.00
Pitcher, Milk, Spode's Tower, Red	45.00
Plate, Brown Transfer, Sheep, Flock, C.1840, 7 1/2 In.	18.00
Platter, Fish, Drain Insert, 1847 Mark	385.00
Tile, Flow Blue, Shakespeare Scene, 6 In.	70.00

COPPER LUSTER, see Luster, Copper

Utilitarian items, such as teakettles and cooking pans, have been handcrafted from copper in America since the days of the early colonists. Copper became a popular metal with the Arts and Crafts makers of the early 1900s and decorative pieces such as bookends and desk sets were made. Other pieces of copper may be found in the Bradley & Hubbard, Roycroft, and Kitchen categories.

COPPER, Ashtray, Floor, Hammered, S–Scroll, L.Hansen On Tray, 22 1/2 In.	90.00
Ashtray, Match Holder, Triangular, Windmill Logo, C.1910, 4 3/4 In.	300.00
Beaker, Coronation of Nicolas & Alexandra, Enameled, C.1896, 4 In.	110.00
Bed Warmer, Floral Engraved Lid, Turned Wooden Handle, 46 1/2 In.	120.00
Bed Warmer, Insert For Bottle, Oval, Germany, 7 1/2 X 11 In.	140.00
Bed Warmer, Pierced, Turned Wooden Handle	231.00
Bed Warmer, Tooled Star Flower Cover, Handle, 42 In.	175.00
Bedwarmer, Incised Design, Original Handle	279.00
Bell, Tulip Shape, Jarvie In Script, C.1910, 7 3/4 In.	1200.00
Bottle, Hot Water, Brass Stopper, Normal–Warmflasche, Marked	75.00
Bowl, Frog On Side	321.00
Bowl, Scalloped Rim, Medium Blue Enameled Lined, 1 3/4 X 6 1/2 In.	65.00
Bowl, Scroll Feather & Loop, Squat, Bulbous, A.Stone, 1910, 3 X 5 In.	3000.00
Box, Cigar, Medieval Style Hinges, Rivet Design, 4 X 13 X 9 1/4 In.	250.00
Candlestick, Disc Base, Cylindrical, Karl Kipp, 6 1/4 In., Pair	225.00

Candlestick, Flared Bobeche, 1910, 14 1/2 In., Pair 495.00
Candlestick, Signed Heinrichs, Pair 125.00
Candlestick, Tulip Shaped Socket, Sternau & Co., 16 1/2 In., Pair 100.00
Chaffing Dish, Stand, Wood Handle 25.00
Chalice, Polychrome Floral Design, Enameled, 8 In. 45.00
Coffeepot, Dovetailed, Charred Bottom Wooden Handle, 11 In. 45.00
Coffeepot, Percolator, Hammered, Trifid Base, Jos.Heinrichs, 15 In. 250.00
Coffeepot, Pewter Spout & Handle, Rochester, 8 In. 95.00
Coffeepot, White Metal Spout & Handle, Rochester Stamping, 8 In. 45.00
Cooker, 4 Pot, Cover, Carrying Handles, 14 X 20 In. 165.00
Crayfish, Joints Move, Japanese, 10 In. 300.00
Cup, Geometric Silver Band, Cylindrical, C.1910, 3 1/4 X 3 1/2 In. 170.00
Desk Set, Blue Floral Enameled, Art Crafts Shop, C.1910, 7 Piece 150.00
Dipper, Cider 55.00
Flask, Colt, Marked Navy, Crossed Flags, Rifles, Cannon, Lacquer 395.00
Flask, For Walker Revolver, Colt, 9 In. 895.00
Flask, Pistol, Eagle, Wings Down, American Shield, Lacquer, 4 3/4 In. 145.00
Frame, Standup, Ornate, 3 X 5 In. 78.00
Horsehead, Green Patina, 10 1/2 In. 125.00
Humidor, Enameled Ship, Signed Cauman, 1925, 6 1/2 X 5 1/2 In. 425.00
Humidor, Threaded Button Finial, Mission Kopper Kraft, 1910, 6 In. 70.00
Inkwell, Gustav Stickley, Hinged Cover 145.00
Jardiniere, Flat Cutout Handles, Straight Side, 6 1/2 X 13 In. 140.00
Jardiniere, Incised Indian Style Design, Squat Bulbous, 4 3/4 In. 150.00
Kettle, Candy, 19 In. 95.00
Kettle, Hammered, Foldover Rim, Wrought Iron Handles, 22 1/2 In. 220.00
Kettle, Hanging, Fireplace, 18 X 12 In. 25.00
Kettle, Tea, Cover, Swing Handle, 13 1/2 In. 145.00
Kettle, Tea, Dovetailed, Brass Trim, 12 In. 100.00
Kettle, Tea, Dovetailed, H.R.Eigart, Repaired, 12 1/4 In. 385.00
Kettle, Tea, Stand & Tray, Heinrich 70.00
Lantern, Swiss, Glass Sides, 30 In. 65.00
Lanterns, Wall, Brass, 26 In., Pair 100.00
Lavabo, Chased Armorial Design 50.00
Lightning Rod, Tin Arrow & Horse, Milk Glass Insulator, 60 In. 75.00
      COPPER, MOLD, see Kitchen, Mold
Pan, Warming, Turned Wooden Handle 220.00
Pitcher, Classic Design, Dovetailed, 12 In. 110.00
Pitcher, Putti, Floral, Bulbous, Loop Handle, French, 1754, 15 1/4 In. 1650.00
Pitcher, Water, Floral Design Feet & Handles, Footed, Silver 100.00
Plaque, Crucified Christ, Praying Woman, Enamel, Frame, 10 X 10 In. 190.00
Pot, Handle, 10 1/2 X 14 1/4 In. 99.00
Pot, Handle, E.M., New York, 6 X 9 1/4 In. 121.00
Salver, Brass Rim, Center Tooled Design, Middle Eastern, 39 In. 150.00
Sconce, Wall, Hammered, Flared Socket, D Shape Shelf, 11 X 9 In. 125.00
Skillet, Tin Lined, Brass Handle, France, 29 In. 45.00
Spoon, Nut, Sterling Silver Celtic Design, Overlay Handle, 5 In. 115.00
Tea Kettle, Dovetailed, Cover, 10 In. 66.00
Tea Kettle, Gooseneck Spout, Brass Handle, 5 X 6 In. 56.00
Teakettle, Brass Trim, Dovetailed Construction, 11 1/2 In. 185.00
Teakettle, Brass Trim, Label On Bottom, 12 In. 45.00
Tobacco Jar, Sterling Rivets, Monogrammed Medallion, 4 1/2 In. 195.00
Tray, Allover Floral, Silver, Round, 10 1/2 In. 50.00
Tray, G.Stickley, Oval Loop Handles, C.1910, 23 X 11 1/2 In. 275.00
Tray, Hammered, Loop Handles, G.Stickley, Craftsman Logo, 24 X 11 In. 350.00
Tsuba, Figure, Under Umbrella, Spider On Reverse, Joryu, 19th Century 302.50
Tsuba, God of Good Fortune, Alloyed Silver & Gold, Stippled, Ebisu 247.50
Vase, Angled Shoulder, Bulbous, Hammered, Dirk Van Erp, 8 X 7 In. 475.00
Vase, Geometric Design, Pink, White, Lavender, Purple, 1925, 9 In. 1980.00
Vase, Strap Handles, Bulbous, Wide Mouth, 20th Century, 9 X 9 In. 75.00
Warming Pan, Pierced Brass Cover, Wooden Handle, 3 1/2 Ft. 275.00

Coralene glass was made by firing many small colored beads on the outside of glassware. It was made in many patterns in the United States and Europe in the 1880s. Reproductions are made today.

CORALENE, Bride's Bowl, 7 In.	225.00
CORALENE, JAPANESE, see Japanese Coralene	
Plate, Poppy, Green, Bisque, Gold Enamel, Beaded Rim, 7 3/4 In.	100.00
Sugar Shaker, White Frosted Glass, Orange Seaweed	165.00
Tumbler, Seaweed Design, Frosted Cranberry	80.00
Urn, Purple Flowers, Corinthian Base, 2 Handles, Japan, 8 In.	225.00
Vase, Coralene Flowers, Gold Trim, 3 Handles, 5 In.	185.00
Vase, Gold & Black Ornaments, Florals, Frosted, 12 In.	175.00
Vase, Gold Design, Bulbous, 2 Handles, 11 In.	190.00
Vase, Green, Yellow, Purple Beading, Marked, Double Handle, 5 In.	169.00
Vase, Purple Beading, Double Handles, Marked, 4 1/2 In.	170.00
Vase, Wheat Pattern, Pink Overlay, White Inside, 6 3/4 In.	450.00

The Cordey China Company was founded in 1942 by Boleslaw Cybis in Trenton, New Jersey. The firm produced gift shop items. Production stopped in 1950 and Cybis Porcelains was founded.

CORDEY, Box, Roses In Relief On Cover, Square, 5 1/2 In.	65.00
Bust, Girl, Curls, Lacy Jabot, Tricorned Hat, 7 In., Pair	75.00
Bust, Lady, Green Hat & Flowers, Yellow Collar, Holding Rose, 6 In.	40.00
Bust, Lady, No.4015	75.00
Bust, Lady, No.5005	48.00
Bust, Lady, No.5010	65.00
Bust, Lady, No.5026	85.00
Dish, Cover, No.6029	35.00
Figurine, Chinese Coquette, Full Figure, Long Skirt, 11 3/4 In.	140.00
Figurine, Colonial Man, 16 1/2 In.	125.00
Figurine, Colonial Woman, 16 1/2 In.	125.00
Figurine, Girl, With Jug On Shoulder, No.5047, 10 In.	125.00
Figurine, Grape Harvesters, No.304, 305, Dressed Alike, 16 In.	155.00
Figurine, Man & Woman, Victorian, 16 In., Pair	235.00
Lamp, Base, Oriental Dragon	150.00
Lamp, Boudoir, Matching Art Deco Busts, Pair	195.00
Lamp, Madame & Monsieur, Lace, Roses, Paper Labels, Pair	150.00
Plaque, Lady's Face, 10 In.	125.00 To 135.00
Salt & Pepper, Doghouse & Spaniel, Full Bee Mark	60.00
Scone, Cherubs & Flowers, Pair	95.00

There has been a need for a corkscrew since the first bottle was sealed with a cork, probably in the seventeenth century. Today collectors search for the early, unusual patented examples or the figural corkscrews of recent years.

CORKSCREW, Anheuser–Busch Beer, Letters & Eagle Logo, 6 In.	6.00
Austrian, Steel Handle, Grey Horn, C.1920	20.00
Bird's Clenched Claws Form, Molded Plastic, Canada	18.00
Boar's Tusk, Sterling Silver Pierced Floral Design, 4 1/2 In.	125.00
Brass, Double Lever, Italian, C.1930	28.00
Brass, Finger Signet Ring, Steel Helix Worm, England, C.1780	150.00
Cat, Black, With Opener, Brass, Box	95.00
Cigar Shaped Wooden Handle, Walker, Pat.1900	6.00
Compound Lever, English, Eir's Patent 1884	130.00
Concertina, Lazy Tong, Perfect Brevete S.G.D.G., French, 1900	120.00
Dog, Figural, Carved Rosewood, Cap Lifter, France, 1930, 5 1/2 In.	35.00
E–Z Cork Puller, Push In, Pull, U.S.	20.00
Elephant, Ivory Handle, Polished Steel, Helix Worm, English, 1890	75.00
Fish, Brass, Art Nouveau, Foldout Helix Worm, Cap Lifter, 1920	28.00
G.H.Mumm & Co. Dry Verzenay, French, C.1890, 7 In.	65.00
Green River Whiskey, Collapsible, Dated 1904	15.00
Hercules, Spring Over Shaft, Open Barrel, German, C.1900	18.00
Horn Handle, Sterling Base, 5 3/4 In.	80.00
Hotel DeSoto, Bottle Opener, Folding	25.00

Ivory Handle, Embossed Lion & Unicorn Label, Brass, 7 In. 200.00
Jack Tar Hotel, Bottle Opener, Folding 25.00
John S.Low, Fine Wines, Carlisle, Pa., Twisted Wire, Wood Sheath 18.00
Kessler Whiskey, Bottle Opener, Folding 30.00
King's Screw, Steel, Bone Handle, Dusting Brush, C.1800 .... 450.00
Lady's Legs, Figural, Green Striped 175.00
Lazy Tong, Marked Perfect Brevete S.G.D.G., C.1900 .... 120.00
Lund Patentee London, Steel Lund Lever, 1855 .... 120.00
Mermaid, Nude, Celluloid, 4 In. 200.00
Monopoly, Self Lifting, Ball Bearings, German, C.1880 .... 15.00
Old Forester Whiskey, Bullet Shape 42.00
Picnic Set, Pocket, Horn Slab Handles, Box, Austria, 1900, 4 Piece 125.00
Punch & Judy, Brass Head, C.1840, 6 In. 95.00
Scrimshaw Handle, Dated 1871 .... 275.00
Senator Volstead, Figural 65.00
Silver, Applied Spiral Scrolls, Dutch, C.1760, 4 In. ....*Illus* 748.00
Silver, Applied Urns & Swags, Dutch, C.1785, 3 1/2 In. ....*Illus* 770.00
Silver, Chased Maidens, Dutch, C.1745, 3 1/8 In. ....*Illus* 880.00
Spring Barrel, Wood Handle, German, C.1890 .... 29.00
Staghorn, Dusting Brush, Faceted Shaft, Center Worm, German, 4 In. 48.00
Turned Chipped Wooden Handle, Tapers, Helix Worm, English, C.1880 .... 10.00
U.S.Clough, Pat.1875 .... 15.00
Viking Ship, Norge, Sail Lifts To Center Worm, Norwegian, 1910 .... 110.00
Waiter's, Center Worm, Notched Lifter, German, C.1900 .... 20.00
Walnut Acorn Handle, Square To Round Shaft, Will & Finck, 1880 .... 175.00
Walrus Tusk, Sterling Ends, Floral Design, C.1900, 11 In. 275.00
Whale's Tooth Handle, Tapering Steel Shaft, Hole, English 95.00
Wooden Handle, Open Barrel, Hercules, C.1900 .... 18.00

Coronation cups have been made since the 1800s. Pottery or glass with a picture of the monarch and date have been souvenirs for many coronations. The pieces that mention King Edward VIII, the king who was never crowned, are not rare; and collectors should be sure to check values before buying.

CORONATION, see also Commemorative
CORONATION, Bookmark, Edward VIII, Metal, Birmingham 15.00
Cup & Saucer, Queen Elizabeth II, 2 Children's Photograph 12.00
Cup, Queen Elizabeth, 1953 .... 18.00
Elizabeth II & Philip, Portrait In Blue Oval, Burleigh 50.00
Handkerchief, Queen Elizabeth, 1937 .... 20.00
Loving Cup, Elizabeth II, Royal Doulton, 10 In. 875.00
Mug, Edward VIII, May 1937, Copeland 100.00
Mug, Edward VIII, May, 1937, Spode 27.00
Pincushion, Crown Shape, Red Velvet, Elizabeth II, 1953 .... 48.00
Pitcher, Embossed Queen Elizabeth, Pink 30.00
Pitcher, George V, 1910, Royal Doulton, 5 In. 115.00
Pitcher, King George V & Queen, 1910, Royal Doulton, 5 In. 115.00
Pitcher, Queen Elizabeth, Pink With White Silhouette, 1953 .... 45.00

Corkscrew, Silver, Chased Maidens, Dutch,
C.1745, 3 1/8 In.

Corkscrew, Silver, Applied Urns & Swags,
Dutch, C.1785, 3 1/2 In.

Corkscrew, Silver, Applied Spiral Scrolls,
Dutch, C.1760, 4 In.

Plate, Queen Elizabeth II, 1953, 7 1/2 In.	12.00
Plate, Queen Elizabeth, Johnson Bros., 10 In.	30.00
Program, Queen Elizabeth & King George VI, U.S.Edition	12.00
Program, Queen Elizabeth II, 40 Pages	10.00
Scarf, Queen Elizabeth	15.00
Tea Set, Royal Blue, Wedgwood, 1953, 3 Piece	750.00
Teapot, Crown Shape, Elizabeth II, Cromaline, 1 Cup	35.00

Cosmos is a pressed milk glass pattern with colored flowers made from 1894 to 1915 by the Consolidated Lamp and Glass Company. Tablewares and lamps were made. A few pieces were also made of clear glass with painted decorations.

COSMOS, Butter, Cover	165.00
Butter, Pink Band, Cover .... 210.00 To	225.00
Castor, Pickle, Pink Band, Racine Triple Plate Frame	300.00
Compote, Classic, Cover, 7 1/2 In.	185.00
Condiment Set, Cosmos Frame, 3 Piece	295.00
Creamer, Pink Band	225.00
Lamp, Miniature	165.00
Pitcher, Water, Pink Band	250.00
Salt & Pepper, Pink Band	110.00
Spooner, Pink Band	200.00
Sugar, Pink Band, Cover	200.00
Table Set, 4 Piece	440.00
Tumbler, Pink Band	55.00
Water Set, Pink Band, 5 Piece	460.00

Linen or wool coverlets were made during the nineteenth century. Most of the coverlets date from 1800 to 1850. Four types were made: the double woven, jacquard, summer and winter, and overshot. Later coverlets were made of a variety of materials. Quilts are listed in this book in their own section.

COVERLET, Baby Elephant Design, Summer, Baby's	18.00
Blue & Cream, Summer/Winter, Snowflake & Pine Tree, 1840	285.00
Double Weave, Pine Tree & Snowflake Pattern, 80 X 86 In.	250.00
Double Weave, Pine Tree & Snowflake, Red, White, Blue, 72 X 88 In. ..	350.00
Floral, 3–Color, Made By Hausman, Lobachsville, 1846, 1 Piece	795.00
Geometric Design, Reversible, Wool, 72 X 84 In.	225.00
Jacquard, 2 Piece, Floral, 1837, Red, Blue, Green, 96 X 80 In.	625.00
Jacquard, Blue & White Floral, Single Weave, 72 X 86 In., 2 Piece	90.00
Jacquard, Blue & White, Lady's Fancy, Stars, Seam, 1842, 80 X 88 In. ..	375.00
Jacquard, Center Floral Urn, Flanked By Pheasants, 86 X 90 In.	250.00
Jacquard, Central Cartouche, Blue & White, 6 Ft.4 In. X 6 Ft.	192.00
Jacquard, Central Floral Medallion, Single Weave, 76 X 82 In.	75.00
Jacquard, Eagle Corners, Blue & White, Dated 1844, 80 X 88 In.	700.00
Jacquard, Floral & Foliage, Snowflake Border, 1841, 80 X 88 In.	175.00
Jacquard, Floral Design In Blue & White, 82 X 85 In.	100.00
Jacquard, Floral Design, Blue & White, 73 X 90 In.	300.00
Jacquard, Floral Design, Indiana, Corners Dated 1851, 79 X 86 In.	300.00
Jacquard, Floral Medallions, C.Ardner, 1852, 78 X 84 In., 2 Piece	375.00
Jacquard, Floral Medallions, For Mary Habbes, 1839, 84 X 104 In.	150.00
Jacquard, Floral Medallions, Rebecca Hofman, Nov.1839, 72 X 92 In. ..	400.00
Jacquard, Floral Medallions, Signed C.O.E. 1851, 72 X 88 In.	225.00
Jacquard, Floral Stripe Pattern, Blue & White, 74 X 88 In.	250.00
Jacquard, Floral Wreaths, Compass Star, DI Grave, 1841, 72 X 82 In. ..	275.00
Jacquard, Floral, Borders, M.Harham, 1867, 72 X 90 In., 2 Piece	300.00
Jacquard, Flower Medallion, Borders, A.& T.Fehr, 76 X 88 In.	165.00
Jacquard, For Margaret Smith, C.K.Hinkel, 1843, 92 X 84 In.	900.00
Jacquard, Liberty Theme, Dated 1876	350.00
Jacquard, Made By S.Kuter, Trexlertown, Pa., 1845, 81 X 96 In.	725.00
Jacquard, Medallions, Bird Border, 1842, G.E.Goodman, 82 X 96 In. ...	150.00
Jacquard, Medallions, Jacob Snyder, Indiana, 1856, 66 X 84 In.	325.00
Jacquard, Salmon, Blue, Overshot, Joined Circles, Flowers, 8 X 6 Ft. ...	165.00
Jacquard, Signed Jacob Stephen Springvil, 1853, 78 X 88 In.	495.00

Cowan, Figurine, Dancer, Cowan, Flower Frog,
Maroon Pants, 9 In. Elf On Mushroom

Jacquard, Star Medallion, North Lima, Ohio, 1850, 76 X 88 In.	160.00
Jacquard, Stylized Floral, 1902 K.M.M., 56 X 84 In.	250.00
Jacquard, White & Tomato Red, Floral Medallions, 78 X 98 In.	425.00
Linsey-Woolsey, Alternating Squares, 19th Century, 94 X 102 In.	1100.00
Overshot, Blue, White, Stylized Flowerhead, Panels, Mo., 90 X 70 In.	137.00
Overshot, Geometric Field, Red, Indigo, Natural, Seam, 70 X 80 In.	275.00
Overshot, White, Red & Beige, 62 X 80 In.	35.00
Red & Green, Signed Ph.Schum, Lancaster, Pa., Wool, 82 X 72 In.	350.00
Red, Green & Dark Navy On Cream, Dated 1848, 70 X 95 In.	450.00
White-On-White, Cotton, 76 X 82 In.	68.00

Guy Cowan made pottery in Rocky River, Ohio, a suburb of Cleveland, from 1913 to 1931. The Cowan Pottery made art pottery and wares for florists. A stylized mark with the word "Cowan" was used on most pieces. A commercial, mass-produced line was marked "Lakeware." Collectors today search for the Art Deco pieces by Guy Cowan, Viktor Schreckengost, Waylande Gregory, or Thelma Frazier Winter.

COWAN, Ashtray, Clown	36.00
Ashtray, Figural, Duck, Signed	28.00
Ashtray, Gazelle	45.00
Bookends, Elephant, Push & Pull, Dusty Rose, Cream	375.00
Bowl, Console, Seahorse Handle	50.00
Bowl, Flared & Fluted Rim, Green Interior, White Exterior, 11 3/4 In.	12.50
Bowl, Wide Flared Rim, Blue, 11 3/4in.	20.00
Bowl, Yellow & Black, 8 In.	45.00
Candlestick, Lyre Shape, Silver On Copper, Marked, 1900s, 12 In., Pair	125.00
Candlestick, Seahorse, 4 1/4 In., Pair	22.00
Console Set, Birds, Footed, 3 Piece	35.00
Figurine, Dancer, Maroon Pants, 9 In. *Illus*	195.00
Figurine, Flamingo, Ivory, 11 In.	195.00
Flower Frog, 2 Dancing Figures	250.00
Flower Frog, Elf On Mushroom *Illus*	100.00
Flower Frog, Nude	100.00
Lamp, Waylande Gregory	450.00
Teapot, Flame Finial, Celadon, Straight-Sided	65.00
Trivet, Multicolored, High Relief Floral, Hexagonal	325.00
Urn, Cover, Gold Details, Aqua, 10 1/2 In.	40.00
Vase, Blue Metallic Iridescent, Squat, 2 3/4 X 5 In.	15.00
Vase, Flared, Flower In Handles, Orange, 8 In.	85.00
Vase, Green & Gold, Twig Handle, Flowers, 8 In.	35.00
Vase, Lustre, 7 In.	35.00
Vase, Mythical Figures At Base, Royal Blue Crackle, 12 In.	250.00
Vase, Seahorses At Base, Turquoise & Green	35.00

Cracker Jack, the molasses-flavored popcorn mixture, was first made in 1896 in Chicago, Illinois. A prize was added to each box in

1912. Collectors search for the old boxes and toys and advertising materials. Many of the toys are unmarked.

CRACKER JACK, Badge, Catcher	45.00
Badge, Police, Pot Metal	18.00
Bear, Standing, Tin, 2 1/2 In.	17.50
Book, Business History	65.00
Book, Riddle	18.00
Booklet, Recipe, Angelus	35.00
Bookmark, Dog	12.00 To 13.00
Bookmark, Dog, Tin	20.00
Bottle Opener	45.00
Chester, Standup, Oval, Tin	55.00
Clicker	32.00 To 35.00
Counter, Baseball Score	50.00
Fortune Wheel	20.00 To 25.00
Frog, Green	30.00
Horse & Wagon	25.00 To 32.00
Mystery Top	17.00
Orphan Annie, Tin, Standup	45.00
Pie Plate	12.00
Riddles	15.00
Ring, Davy Crocket, Gold, Adjustable, Box	28.00
Spinner, Rainbow	12.00
Standing Bear, Tin, 2 1/2 In.	40.00
Token, Gum, 40 Piece	18.00
Tokens, Presidents, Set of 9	20.00
Top, Spinning	45.00 To 55.00
Toy, Delivery Truck	50.00 To 65.00
Toy, Horse & Wagon	60.00
Toy, Midget Auto Racer, Paper	10.00
Toy, Truck, Tin	25.00 To 35.00
Train, Plastic, 2 Piece	10.00
Trolley, Toonerville	275.00
Truck, Delivery	65.00
Wagon, Yellow, Green, 4 1/2 In.	35.00
Watch, Pocket, Tin	15.00
Whistle	7.00 To 15.00
Whistle, Barrel	20.00
Whistle, Screamer, Tin	12.00
World's Smallest Bible, Paper Container	25.00

Crackle glass was originally made by the Venetians, but most of the ware found today dates from the 1800s. The glass was heated, cooled, and refired so that many small lines appeared inside the glass. It was made in many factories in the United States and Europe.

CRACKLE GLASS, Decanter, Cranberry, Amber, Stopper, 5 In.	25.00
Perfume Bottle, Bird With Long Tail Stopper, 10 1/2 In.	75.00
Pitcher, Lemonade, Cover, Amber	67.00
Pitcher, Water, Amber Handle, Ground Pontil, Blue	165.00
Powder Box, Elephant Finial, Germany	25.00
Vase, Blue Flowers, Green Leaves, Tantin	325.00

Cranberry glass is an almost transparent yellow–red glass. It resembles the color of cranberry juice. The glass has been made in Europe and America since the Civil War. It is still being made and reproductions can fool the unwary.

CRANBERRY GLASS, see also Northwood; Rubena Verde; etc.

CRANBERRY GLASS, Basket, Clear Wishbone Feet, Clear Trim, 12 In.	275.00
Basket, Diamond Quilted, Clear Applied Top, Handle, 7 In.	225.00
Basket, Honeycomb Pattern, Clear Thorn Handle, 7 1/2 In.	235.00
Bottle, Opaque White Flowers, Green Leaves, Stopper, 4 In.	265.00
Bowl, Applied Crystal Rim, Berry Pontil, 6 3/4 X 3 In.	225.00

Bowl, Clear Rigaree Trim, 4 In.	55.00
Bowl, Crystal Garlands & Berry Prunts, 4 3/4 In.	325.00
Bowl, Crystal Leaves & Branches, 8–Crimp Top, 6 1/4 In.	245.00
Box, Dot Enameled Sprays, Brass Rings, 6 X 4 7/8 In.	325.00
Box, Enameled Florals, Leaves, Hinged Lid, 3 1/4 In.	175.00
Box, Jewelry, Beveled Hinged Top, Brass Trim, Scenes	135.00
Box, Lift–Off Lid, Butterfly, Flowers, Dots, 4 3/8 In.	135.00
Bride's Basket, Hobnail	500.00
Butter, Chrysanthemum Swirl, Cover	225.00
Butter, Classic, Footed, Cover	225.00
Candlestick, 11 In.	78.50
Castor, Pickle, Thumbprint, Enameled Design	285.00
Champagne, D.K.Mumm & Co., Trumpet Shape, 22 In.	275.00
Cocktail Shaker, Frosted Ducks, Clouds & Cattails	30.00
Compote, Scalloped Edge, Gold Trim, 9 X 9 1/2 In.	275.00
Cracker Jar, Figural Bear Finial, Silver Plated Fittings	235.00
Cruet, Cased White Interior, Original Stopper	75.00
Cruet, Clear Flattened Stopper, Engraved, 10 1/2 In.	128.00
Cruet, Paneled, Enameled Daisies, Clear Handle, 8 In.	145.00
Cruet, Pewter Holder, Cherub Stopper, 9 In.	295.00
Decanter, Clear Handle & Foot, Flowers, Leaves, 9 1/2 In.	158.00
Decanter, French Pewter, Stopper, Handle, Encased, 13 In.	375.00
Decanter, Gold Scrolls, Bows, Blown Petal Stopper, 11 In.	128.00
Decanter, Wine, Yellow Flowers, Leaves, Dots, 11 3/4 In.	175.00
Epergne, 3–Lily, Crystal Trim, Cranberry, 15 3/4 In.	295.00
Epergne, 4–Lily, Applied Rigaree To Lilies, 19 In.	475.00
Epergne, 7–Trumpet, Spiral Crystal Rigaree, 22 In.	625.00
Inkwell, Draped Raised Rib, Mushroom Shape, Brass Cover	225.00
Jar, Sweetmeat, Verre Moire, Silver Plated Top, 4 In.	195.00
Lamp, Finger, Clear Handle, Complete, 5 1/4 In.	135.00
Lamp, Kerosene, Opalescent Stripe Fonts, Clear Base, Pair	595.00
Loving Cup, Silver Overlay, 3 Handles, 3 1/2 In.	495.00
Perfume Bottle, Enameled Flowers, Gold Trim, 5 3/4 In.	118.00
Perfume Bottle, Gold Band, Enameled Flowers, 5 5/8 In.	115.00
Perfume Bottle, White & Yellow Flowers, Gold Outlined	110.00
Pitcher, Diamond–Quilted, 11 In.	125.00
Pitcher, Diamond–Quilted, Clear Handle, 3 3/4 In.	65.00
Pitcher, Enameled Allover, 8 In.	245.00
Pitcher, Inverted Thumbprint, Clear Handle, 6 3/4 In.	140.00
Pitcher, Inverted Thumbprint, Clear Reeded Handle, 6 In.	60.00
Pitcher, Rippled Thumbprint, Allover Pattern, 6 1/2 In.	110.00
Pitcher, Rippled Thumbprint, Clear Handle, 6 1/2 In.	110.00
Pitcher, Water, Bulbous, 8 In.	95.00
Pitcher, Water, Rope Handle, Bulbous, 7 3/8 In.	245.00
Salt & Pepper	100.00
Salt, Crystal Rigaree, Vaseline Leaves, 4 In.	55.00
Salt, Crystal Shell Feet, Center Rigaree, 2 X 3 1/4 In.	70.00
Salt, Master, Heart Shape, Clear Ring Handle & Shell Feet	95.00
Salt, Optic Pattern, Applied Wishbone Feet, Silver Spoon	60.00
Salt, Twisted Clear Rigaree At Middle, 2 1/4 In.	45.00
Salt, White Enameled Flowers, Master, 1 3/4 In.	55.00
Salt, White Threading, Shell Feet, 1 7/8 In.	60.00
Saltshaker, Erie Twist	42.50
Saltshaker, Reverse Swirl	45.00
Sugar Shaker, Cut Panels, Silver Plated Top, 5 1/2 In.	55.00
Sugar Shaker, Leaf Umbrella	225.00
Sugar Shaker, Molded Panels, Silver Plated Top, 5 3/4 In.	55.00
Sugar Shaker, Ring Neck	95.00
Syrup, Daisy & Fern	90.00
Tankard, Milk, Overshot, Clear Reeded Handle, 7 1/8 In.	135.00
Tankard, Water, Overshot, Clear Reeded Handle, 9 1/8 In.	165.00
Thumbprint, Pitcher Set, 4 Tumblers, 5 Piece	200.00
Toothpick, Chrysanthemum, Base Swirl	115.00
Toothpick, Leaf Umbrella	120.00

Tumbler, Top Gold Band, Gold Flowers At Base, 3 3/4 In.	58.00
Vase, Applied Crystal Foot & Leaves, 3 Melon Top, 7 In.	95.00
Vase, Bud, Clear, Cone Shape, 6 In.	35.00
Vase, Crystal Branch Feet, Go Up To Form Branches, 5 In.	125.00
Vase, Crystal Leaves, Feet & Rim, Berry Pontil, 5 1/2 In.	335.00
Vase, Enameled Dots & Scrolls, Red Jewels, 4 1/4 In.	40.00
Vase, Gold Band At Top, Enameled Flowers, 2 3/4 In.	30.00
Vase, Gold Florals, White Enamel Trim, 10 3/4 In.	225.00
Vase, Gold Flowers, Leaves, Gold Bands, 4 7/8 In., Pair	118.00
Vase, Gold Leaves Outlined In White Enamel, 9 1/2 In.	148.00
Vase, Inverted Panel, Enameled Flowers, Vines, 12 In.	150.00
Vase, Inverted Thumbprint, Applied Icicles, 4 5/8 In.	250.00
Vase, Jack-In-The-Pulpit, Pink, Applied Flowers, 7 In.	145.00
Vase, Ormolu Feet, Banded Scallops, Grapes, 12 1/4 In., Pr.	395.00
Vase, Sanded Gold Flowers, White Outlining, 2 3/8 In., Pr.	105.00
Vase, Sanded Gold Leaves, Enameled Flowers, 8 1/8 In.	118.00
Vase, Sanded Gold Leaves, Flowers, 11 1/4 In.	245.00
Vase, Swirl Pattern, Bulbous, Ruffled Top, 9 In.	95.00
Vase, Tricornered, Rigaree, 11 In.	145.00
Vase, Trumpet Shape, Gold Trim, 7 In., Pair	150.00
Vase, Urn Shape, Crystal Applied Handle, 7 3/8 In., Pair	148.00
Wine, Notched Stem, Signed, 7 1/2 In.	80.00

Creamware, or queensware, was developed by Josiah Wedgwood about 1765. It is a cream-colored earthenware that has been copied by many factories.

CREAMWARE, see also Wedgwood

CREAMWARE, Bowl, Fruit, Reticulated, Floral, Monogram, Underplate, 9 X 10 In.	155.00
Chamber Pot, Seaweed, Blue Banded, Miniature	325.00
Dish, Serving, Swag Design Around Border, 10 1/2 X 9 In., Pair	750.00
Gravy, Melon Form, Attached Leaf Undertray, 18th Century, 8 In.	575.00
Match Holder, Dog By Barrel, Molded Striker, 4 X 3 In.	75.00
Mug, Dutch, 5 In.	38.00
Mug, Eagle	85.00
Pitcher, Cover, Button Finial, Checkerboard Pattern, 6 1/4 In.	125.00
Plate, Black Transfer Initials, Border, Pierced Rim, 9 In., Pair	150.00
Plate, Enameled Flowers, Lavender, C.1820, 8 In.	48.00
Plate, Pierced Border, Enamel Trim, Basket Weave, 1765, 9 3/4 In.	120.00
Plate, Toddy, Floral Rim, Blue Transfer Verse Center, 5 1/2 In.	100.00
Plate, Truth, Liberty, Justice, Balancing Scale, Crazed, 9 In.	150.00
Soup, Dish, Rowboat Under Bridge Scene, Anchor Mark, 9 1/4 In.	50.00
Stein, Munich Child, Twin Towers Thumblift, 1/2 Liter	72.00
Teapot, Oriental Floral Transfer, 6 1/8 In.	45.00

Crown Derby is the nickname given to the works of the Royal Crown Derby factory, which began working in England in 1859. An earlier and more famous English Derby factory existed from 1750 to 1848. The two factories were not related. Most of the porcelain found today with the Derby mark is the work of the later Derby factory.

CROWN DERBY, see also Derby; Royal Crown Derby

CROWN DERBY, Asparagus Server, Pagoda, Tree, Hand Painted, C.1760, 3 1/4 In.	195.00
Bowl, Mansion House Dwarf, C.1780, 7 In.	450.00
Cake Stand, Imari, No.2451, 5 In.	75.00
Cup & Saucer, Kakiemon, C.1815	65.00
Cup & Saucer, Tea, Imari Pattern No.2451	75.00
Maroon & Yellow, 2 Handle, 7 In.	225.00
Pitcher, Imari, Octagonal, No.1451, C.1881, 8 In.	135.00
Teapot, Imari, No.2451, C.1750, 6 In.	195.00

Crown Milano glass was made by Frederick Shirley about 1890. It had a plain biscuit color with a satin finish. It was decorated with flowers and often had large gold scrolls.

CROWN MILANO, Biscuit Jar, Allover Bouquets, Beige Ground, Cover, Signed 875.00
   Bowl, Melon Ribbed, Reeded Rim, Glossy Roses, Cover, 5 1/2 In. 390.00
   Castor, Pickle, Pastel Swags, Blossoms, Silver Holder & Tongs 845.00
   Cookie Jar, Raised Daisies, Signed Pairpoint In Lid 300.00
   Cracker Jar, Blossom Sprays, Pairpoint Fittings, 8 1/2 In. 785.00
   Cracker Jar, Enameled Bouquets, Gold Trim, Metal Bail 785.00
   Dish, Sweetmeat, Melon Ribbed, Gold Scrolls, Marked, 4 In. 825.00
   Ewer, Gold Outlined Scrolling, Gold Chrysanthemums, 12 In. 875.00
   Jar, Melon Shape, Multi-Florals, White, Signed, 6 In. 425.00
   Mustard, Florals & Gold Designs, Cover 563.00
   Pitcher, Water, Snail Handle, Beige, Allover Pond Lilies, 9 In. 1800.00
   Salt, Molded-In Ribs, Flowers & Scrolls 95.00
   Salt, Open, Roses, Floral, Shiny 100.00
   Sugar & Creamer, Violets, Lusterless White, Gold Trim, Label 900.00
   Sweetmeat, Jeweled Starfish, Plated Bail & Lid, 6 1/2 In. 735.00
   Sweetmeat, Melon Ribbed, Pink, Flowers, Marked, 5 1/2 In. 825.00
   Vase, Cherubs, Raised Gold, Signed, 11 In. 585.00
   Vase, Enameled Dot Design, Floral & Scroll, 12 1/2 In. 930.00
   Vase, Enameled Floral Design, Pink To Cream, 12 In. 300.00
   Vase, Gold Overlay, Eggshell White, Signed, 5 1/4 In. 310.00
   Vase, Maiden, Ferns, Gold Medallions, 9 In. 450.00
   Vase, Raised Gold Design, Cherubs In Wreath, Signed, 11 In. 585.00
      CROWN TUSCAN, see Cambridge

Cruets of glass or porcelain were made to hold vinegar, oil, and other condiments. They were especially popular during Victorian times but have been made in a variety of styles since the eighteenth century.

   CRUET, see also Castor Set
CRUET, Amberina Verde, Hobnail Opalescent Lip 325.00
   Amethyst Nestor 75.00
   Cranberry Glass, Avon 8.00
   Cut Glass, Victorian, Silver Plate, 1880s, 5 Piece 75.00
   Daisy & Fern, White Opalescent, Parian Mold 85.00
   Diamond Fountain, Higby Glass 90.00
   Georgia Gem, Green 125.00
   Nestor, Amethyst 95.00
   Oil & Vinegar, Floral Design, Engraved, H.Hawkes, 7 In. 55.00
   Sapphire Blue, Gold Bird, Crystal Twisted Handle, Stopper, 8 In. 230.00
   Shoshone, Clear, Stopper 55.00
   Shoshone, Green, Stopper 95.00
   Verre De Soi, Ribbons & Scrolls, Stopper, Steuben, Hawkes, 6 1/2 In. 335.00
   Vinegar, Double Circle, Apple Green, Riverside Glass, No Stopper 100.00

There are many marks that include the words "CT Germany." The first mark with those words was used by a company in Altwasser, Germany, in 1845. The initials stand for C. Thielsch, a partner in the firm. The Hutschenreuther firm took over the company in 1918 and continued to use the "CT."

C.T.

CT GERMANY, Bowl, Fruit, Peaches, Plums, Grapes, Eagle Mark, 8 In. 65.00
   Bowl, Multicolor Flowers, Gold Border, 10 In. 75.00
   Plate, Queen Louisa, Scarf On Neck, Pink Dress, 10 1/2 In. 50.00
   Tray, Dresser, Pink Roses, Green Leaves, Gold Border, 10 X 8 In. 50.00

Cup plates are small glass or china plates that held the cup while a gentleman of the mid-nineteenth century drank his coffee or tea from the saucer. The most famous cup plates were made of glass at the Boston and Sandwich factory located in Sandwich, Massachusetts. There have been many new glass cup plates made in recent years for sale to the gift shops or the limited edition collectors. These are similar to the old plates but can be identified.

CUP PLATE, 16–Rib Pattern, Green Aqua, Folded Rim, Pontil, 4 3/8 In.	425.00
Allegheny, Mulberry	45.00
Anchor, Clear	180.00
Beehive, Greenish Tint	650.00
Black, Staffordshire Transfer	35.00
Blue Eagle	275.00
Blue Feather Rim, Leeds, C.1790, 4 1/2 In.	55.00
Bunker Hill	20.00
Child & Bird, Creamware, Staffordshire, Wood	155.00
Copper Lustre Rim, Staffordshire	90.00
Country Scene, Black Framed, Staffordshire	55.00
Eagle	55.00
Eagle, Wheeling, Clear	350.00
General Harrison, Clear	75.00
Heart, Blue Tint	375.00
Heart, Canary Yellow	225.00
Henry Clay, Blue	150.00
Henry Clay, Medium Blue	190.00
Hound, Clear	110.00
Hudson River Near Sandy Hill, Pink, Clews	150.00
Log Cabin, Amber	475.00
Log Cabin, Eastern, Clear	215.00
Log Cabin, Midwestern, Clear	60.00
Log Cabin, Opalescent	340.00
Log Cabin, Scalloped, Clear	150.00
Lyre Pattern, Blue, 3 1/2 In.	170.00
Lyre, Clear	550.00
Lyre, Smoky Gray	900.00
Marriage, Green Tint	150.00
Massacre & Innocence, Pearlware, C.1840	32.00
Plow, Clear	425.00
Roman Rosette	55.00
Ship, Blue	600.00
Ship, Medium Blue	800.00
Ship, Violet Blue	625.00
Sunburst, Amethyst	150.00
Sunburst, Flint, Light Green	275.00
Sunburst, Peacock Blue	210.00
Sunburst, Red Amber	375.00
Waffle, Clear	35.00
Washington	27.50

Currier & Ives made the famous American lithographs marked with their name from 1857 to 1907. The mark used on the print included the street address in New York City, and it is possible to date the year of the original issue from this information. Earlier prints were made by N. Currier and use that name from 1835 to 1847. Many reprints of the Currier or Currier & Ives prints have been made and it is the undamaged, untrimmed originals that are priced here unless otherwise noted. Many collectors also buy the insurance calendars that were based on the old prints. The words large, small, or medium folio refer to size.

CURRIER & IVES, American Farm Scenes No.2, Summer, 21 X 28 In. ....*Illus*	2200.00
American Farm Scenes No.3, Frame, 23 1/4 X 29 1/2 In.	2150.00
American Game, 19 1/2 X 27 5/8 In.	1550.00
American Homestead, Autumn, Small Folio	395.00
American Homestead, Summer, Small Folio	350.00
American Winter Scenes, Morning, Gilt Frame, 31 X 25 In.	7500.00

Assassination of President Lincoln, Black & White 50.00
Autumn Fruits, Framed, 17 1/2 X 22 In. 275.00
Autumn Fruits, Gilded & Button Frame, 15 1/2 X 20 In. 175.00
Belle of New York 50.00
Brook Trout, Just Caught, 14 3/4 X 20 In. ....*Illus* 770.00
Burning of Chicago 225.00
Celebrated Boston Team Mill Boy & Blondine, 1822, Large 380.00
Celebrated Horse, 16 3/4 X 26 1/2 In. ....*Illus* 140.00
Celebrated Trotting Horse Henry, Driven By John Murphy 195.00
Champion Pacer Johnson 1870.00
Clipper Ship Cosmos, 9 7/8 X 14 In. ....*Illus* 1540.00
Coming From The Trot, Framed 3100.00
Darktown Hook & Ladder Corps, Comicla, 1884 .... 290.00
Deer Hunting On The Susquehanna, Medium 400.00
Ethan Allen & Mate & Dexter, Large 1600.00
First Lesson, Large 195.00
Four Seasons of Life, Copyright 1868, Large 1600.00
Fruit Vase, Framed, 15 1/2 X 19 1/2 In. 165.00
Good Times On Old Plantation, Frame, 14 1/4 X 18 In. 375.00
Grand New Steamboat Pilgrim, Oak Frame, Large 2100.00
Grand Trotter Nelson 1870.00
Great Fire At Boston 195.00
Great Mississippi Steamboat Race, Frame, 15 X 11 In. 225.00
Home of Washington, 14 X 18 In. 200.00
Home On The Mississippi, Beveled Frame, 14 1/2 X 15 In. 175.00
Hudson, From West Point, 1862, Framed, Medium 800.00
Indian Beauty, Porcelain Knob Carved X Frame 75.00
James Polk, George M.Dallas, Grand Nat'l Democratic Banner 190.00
John C.Heenan, Champion of The World, Boxer, 1860s, Small 220.00
King of The House 40.00
Lake Memphremagog, Owls Head, 10 X 14 In. 200.00
Life & Age of Man, 10 X 14 In. ....*Illus* 170.00

AMERICAN FARM SCENES.

Currier & Ives, American Farm Scenes No.2, Summer, 21 X 28 In.

Currier & Ives, Brook Trout, Just Caught, 14 3/4 X 20 In.

Currier & Ives, Clipper Ship Cosmos, 9 7/8 X 14 In.

Currier & Ives, Celebrated Horse,
16 3/4 X 26 1/2 In.

Currier & Ives, Life & Age of Man,
10 X 14 In.

Little Annie, Framed, 13 1/2 X 15 1/2 In. 100.00
Little Daisy 45.00
Marriage Morning 55.00
Morning of Life, 11 1/2 X 15 In. 50.00
My Little White Kitties, Playing Dominoes 75.00
My Pet Bird, Medium 85.00
Narrows, New York Bay, From Staten Island, Small 400.00
New England Winter Scene, Frame, 25 1/4 X 31 1/4 In. 6000.00
Newport Beach, Framed, Small 300.00
Niagara Falls, From Goat Island, Small 190.00
Pair of Nutcrackers, Frame, 14 X 17 In. 145.00
Pride of The Garden, Grained Frame, 13 1/2 X 17 1/2 In. 55.00
Roadside Mill, Framed, 11 X 15 In. 225.00
Sailor's Bride 125.00
Scene In Old Ireland, Curly Maple Frame, 15 3/4 X 20 In. 105.00
Scenery of The Upper Mississippi, 11 X 14 In. 200.00
Scenery of The Wissahickon, Small 200.00
Season of Joy, Frame, 12 5/8 X 16 1/2 In. 400.00
Sleigh Race, C.1848, Framed 240.00
Spirit of '61, Medium 225.00
Spring, Small 90.00
Star Spangled Banner, Framed, 13 1/2 X 17 1/2 In. 95.00
Summer Shades, Framed, 21 1/2 X 29 1/2 In. 550.00
Through To The Pacific, 1870, Small 1320.00
Tom Thumb 65.00
Trade Card, A Crack Trotter, In Harness, Dated 1880 .... 65.00
Trade Card, Cupid's Own, Carrying Cigars, Dated 1880 .... 55.00
Trade Card, Hat That Makes The Man, Dated 1880 .... 75.00
Trade Card, Please Give A Light Sir, Dated 1880 .... 70.00
Trade Card, Trotters On The Snow, Man In Sleigh 65.00
Tree of Temperance, Curly Maple Frame, 13 1/2 X 17 1/2 In. 275.00
U.S.Sloop of War Albany, 22 Guns, Title Plate 525.00
View From Fort Putnam–West Point 275.00
Washington At Home, Black & White, 1867, Large 250.00
Washington, Black Beveled Frame, 14 1/4 X 18 1/2 In. 35.00
Woodcock Shooting, 1870, Small 450.00
Woodcock, 11 X 14 In. 150.00
Woodlands In Winter 225.00

> Custard glass is an opaque glass sometimes called "buttermilk glass."
> It was first made in the United States after 1886 at the La Belle
> Glass Works, Bridgeport, Ohio. It is being reproduced.

CUSTARD GLASS, see also Maize
CUSTARD GLASS, Argonaut Shell, Berry Bowl, Goofus Trim, Small 40.00
Argonaut Shell, Butter, Cover, Gold Trim 265.00
Argonaut Shell, Creamer .... 95.00 To 120.00
Argonaut Shell, Toothpick 275.00
Argonaut Shell, Water Set, Gold & Enamel Trim, 5 Piece 575.00
Beaded Circle, Butter, Cover, Gold & Enamel .... 95.00 To 310.00
Beaded Circle, Butter, Cover, Gold Trim 110.00
Beaded Circle, Spooner 75.00
Beaded Roses, Goblet, Huron, South Dakota 60.00
Beaded Swag, Butter, Cover 60.00
Beggar's Hand, Toothpick 17.50
Berry & Leaf, Plate, 9 In. 10.00
Blackberry, Dish, Deep, 7 In. 20.00
Chrysanthemum Sprig, Butter, Cover .... 200.00 To 275.00
Chrysanthemum Sprig, Celery .... 700.00 To 850.00
Chrysanthemum Sprig, Compote, Jelly 37.50
Chrysanthemum Sprig, Creamer, Blue, Gold Trim 235.00
Chrysanthemum Sprig, Cruet .... 125.00 To 285.00
Chrysanthemum Sprig, Jam Jar, Cover 110.00
Chrysanthemum Sprig, Pitcher, Water 375.00
Chrysanthemum Sprig, Salt & Pepper 150.00

Chrysanthemum Sprig, Sauce, Blue ....75.00 To 100.00
Chrysanthemum Sprig, Spooner, Blue, Gold Trim 265.00
Chrysanthemum Sprig, Table, Set, Gold Trim, 4 Piece 575.00
Chrysanthemum Sprig, Toothpick 195.00
Chrysanthemum Sprig, Tumbler 65.00
Chrysanthemum Sprig, Tumbler, Blue, Gold Trim 185.00
Chrysanthemum Sprig, Water Set, Gold Trim, 7 Piece 670.00
Delaware, Creamer, Rose, Gold Trim 30.00
Delaware, Ring Tray, Blue Design 70.00
Diamond With Peg, Decanter, Rose 38.00
Diamond With Peg, Toothpick ....40.00 To 50.00
Diamond With Peg, Wine, Rose 55.00
Fan, Dish, Ice Cream ....40.00 To 45.00
Fluted Scroll, Cruet 90.00
Geneva, Banana Boat 135.00
Geneva, Banana Boat, Green 115.00
Geneva, Berry Bowl, Green, Gold Trim, Master 95.00
Geneva, Butter, Cover 125.00
Geneva, Creamer ....70.00 To 75.00
Geneva, Pitcher, Water, Gold Trim 90.00
Geneva, Saltshaker, Original Lid 75.00
Geneva, Spooner ....50.00 To 90.00
Geneva, Tumbler, Green & Gold 60.00
Geneva, Tumbler, Red & Green Enameled Design 50.00
Georgia Gem, Butter, Cover, Green 200.00
Georgia Gem, Mug, Souvenir, Green 45.00
Georgia Gem, Spooner, Green 85.00
Georgia Gem, Sugar 70.00
Georgia Gem, Sugar & Creamer 125.00
Georgia Gem, Sugar, Green Leaves, Blue Flowers 135.00
Georgia Gem, Sugar, Souvenir, Cody, Nebraska 55.00
Georgia Gem, Toothpick, Footed, Gold 60.00
Georgia Gem, Toothpick, Pink, C.1905 .... 250.00
Georgia Gem, Tumbler, Green, Gold Trim 30.00
Grape & Cable, Pin Tray, Nutmeg Stain 120.00
Grape & Gothic Arches, Goblet, Nutmeg Stain 50.00
Grape & Gothic Arches, Tumbler, Gold Carnival Finish 55.00
Grape & Gothic Arches, Water Set, 7 Piece 475.00
Harvard, Toothpick, Painted Flowers, 2 1/4 In. 30.00
Heart & Thumbprint, Lamp, Finger, Green ....325.00 To 345.00
Heart & Thumbprint, Lamp, Oil, 8 1/2 In. 550.00
Heart & Thumbprint, Sugar 75.00
Honeycomb, Wine 55.00
Intaglio, Bowl, Fruit, Footed 165.00
Intaglio, Butter, Cover ....140.00 To 175.00
Intaglio, Compote, Jelly, Green, Gold Trim 70.00
Intaglio, Maple Leaf, Spooner 75.00
Intaglio, Sauce, Green Trim 60.00
Intaglio, Spooner 70.00
Intaglio, Table Set, Blue Design, 4 Piece 575.00
Intaglio, Table Set, Green, Gold Trim, 4 Piece 550.00
Intaglio, Water Set, Green Trim, 7 Piece 475.00
Inverted Fan & Feather, Berry Bowl, Gold Trim, Master 295.00
Inverted Fan & Feather, Salt & Pepper, Gold Trim 450.00
     IVORINA VERDE, see Winged Scroll
Jackson, Creamer 73.00
Jackson, Creamer, Goofus Trim 55.00
Jackson, Cruet 150.00
Jackson, Tumbler 25.00
     LITTLE GEM, see Georgia Gem
Louis XV, Banana Bowl, Green, Gold Trim 85.00
Louis XV, Berry Bowl, Gold Trim 40.00
Louis XV, Berry Bowl, Gold Trim, Master 125.00
Louis XV, Butter, Cover 140.00

Louis XV, Creamer	50.00 To 90.00
Louis XV, Pitcher, Water, Gold Trim	150.00
Louis XV, Sugar & Creamer	125.00
Louis XV, Sugar, Cover	100.00
Louis XV, Table Set, 4 Piece	350.00 To 640.00
Louis XV, Tumbler	55.00
Louis XV, Water Set, 7 Piece	400.00 To 450.00
MAIZE, see Maize category	
Maple Leaf, Berry Bowl, Pedestal, Gold Trim, Decal, Master	200.00
Maple Leaf, Creamer, Gold Trim	105.00
Maple Leaf, Pitcher, Water	350.00
Maple Leaf, Spooner, Green, Gold Trim	100.00 To 105.00
Maple Leaf, Table Set, Gold Trim, 4 Piece	550.00
Peacock At Urn, Bowl, Ice Cream, Master	175.00
Pineapple & Fan, Saltshaker, Sterling Silver Lid	20.00
Poppy, Bowl, Ruffled, Nutmeg Stain	45.00
Ring Band, Creamer, Rose Design	70.00
Ring Band, Pitcher, Rose Design, 7 1/2 In.	240.00
Ring Band, Toothpick, Rose Design	75.00
Rose, Hair Receiver, Woodson, Kansas	35.00
Singing Bird, Mug	80.00
Vermont, Pitcher, Water, Green Design	275.00
Winged Scroll, Ash Receiver	100.00
Winged Scroll, Berry Bowl	150.00
Winged Scroll, Celery, Gold Trim	435.00
Winged Scroll, Cruet	150.00
Winged Scroll, Pitcher	250.00
Winged Scroll, Spooner, Gold Trim	75.00
Winged Scroll, Sugar & Creamer	275.00
Winged Scroll, Table Set, 4 Piece	440.00
Winged Scroll, Toothpick	65.00
Winged Scroll, Tumbler	50.00

Cut glass has been made since ancient times, but the large majority of the pieces now for sale date from the brilliant period of glass design, 1880 to 1905. These pieces have elaborate geometric designs with a deep miter cut. Modern cut glass with a similar appearance is being made in England and Ireland. Chips and scratches are often difficult to notice but lower the value dramatically.

CUT GLASS, see also listings under factory name

CUT GLASS, Ashtray, Cobalt To Clear, 6 In.	25.00
Ashtray, Diamond Miters, Serrated Rim, Star Bottom, 2 X 3 In.	25.00
Basket, Bonbon, 8 In.	110.00
Basket, Miters, Fans & Stars, 9 1/2 X 7 1/4 X 10 In.	225.00
Berry Bowl, Pinwheels & Hobstars, 9 In.	55.00
Boat, Russian, Starred Buttons, 13 1/2 In.	525.00
Bonbon, Divided, Ring Handle, Hobstars, Strawberry, 6 3/4 In.	235.00
Bonbon, Fan & Diamond, Openwork, Rococo Design, 4 1/2 In., Pair	600.00
Bottle, Diamond Quilted, Velvet, 6 In.	110.00
Bottle, Perfume, Cane, Pointed Stopper, 7 In.	95.00
Bowl, Allover Cut, Sterling Silver Beaded Rim, 8 1/2 In.	225.00
Bowl, Brilliant, Shallow, 10 In. ....*Illus*	140.00
Bowl, Diamond & Fan, Scalloped Sawtooth Rim, 9 In.	80.00
Bowl, Eggnog, Prism, Hobs, Crosshatch, Hob Base, 10 3/4 In.	1350.00
Bowl, Fruit, Floral, 2 In. Panels & Daisy & Button, 8 X 7 In.	185.00
Bowl, Harvard, 3 1/2 X 10 In.	125.00
Bowl, Heart, 3 1/2 X 8 In.	310.00
Bowl, Hobstar & Swirl, Notched Rim, Signed, 9 In.	225.00
Bowl, Hobstar, 4 X 9 In.	225.00
Bowl, Hobstar, Scalloped Sawtooth Rim, 9 In.	55.00
Bowl, Hobstars & Pinwheel, 10 In., 2 Part	400.00
Bowl, Jubilee, Dorflinger, 10 X 4 In.	475.00
Bowl, Kohinoor & Hobstars, 10 In. ....*Illus*	1650.00
Bowl, Miters, Hobstars, 8 In.	100.00

Cut Glass, Bowl, Kohinoor & Hobstars, 10 In.

Cut Glass, Bowl, Nautilus

Cut Glass, Bowl, Wedding Ring, J. Hoare

Cut Glass, Plate, Panel, Hawkes

Bowl, Nautilus	*Illus*	475.00
Bowl, Pineapple & Fan, Sawtooth Rim, 8 In.		50.00
Bowl, Wedding Ring, J. Hoare	*Illus*	2000.00
Box, Dresser, Sterling Silver Rim, Signed C.F.Monroe, 7 1/2 In.		695.00
Box, Glove, Harvard Border, Intaglio Cut Floral, Hinged Lid		750.00
Box, Hinged Cover, Thumbprints At Base, Star Bottom, 5 1/2 In.		325.00
Box, Pinwheel Covers Entire Lid, Hobstars & Crosshatch, 6 In.		275.00
Butter, Cornell, Dark Green, Gold Trim		65.00
Butter, Underplate, Signed Hawkes, 8 In.		265.00
Candlestick, Faceted Knob Stem, Hobstar Base, 8 1/4 In., Pair		645.00
Candlestick, Hobstars, Hobnail, Fans, Star Foot, 8 In., Pair		975.00
Candy Jar, Athens, Cover, Straus, 8 X 6 1/4 In.		875.00
Carafe, Water, Harvard, 24–Rayed Base, 8 X 6 In.		225.00
Celery, Hobstar, 14 In.		175.00
Celery, Russian, Rolled Rim, 11 1/2 In.		195.00
Celery, Scalloped Rim, Hobs, Rosettes, Crossed Vesicas, 12 In.		250.00
Cheese Dish, Dome Cover, Hobstars		450.00
Clock, Harvard, Horizontal Step & Line Cut, 10 X 5 In.		975.00
Compote, Buzz Stars & Cane, Star Base, Notched Stem, 10 In.		105.00
Compote, Cosmos, 6 X 9 In.		95.00
Compote, Cover, Arcadia, J.D.Bergen, 9 X 6 1/2 In.		1650.00
Compote, Daisies & Foliage, 8 In.		80.00
Compote, Hobstars, Elmira Cut Glass Co., 12 In.		795.00
Compote, Teardop Stem, Star Foot, Elmira Cut Glass Co., 9 In.		470.00
Creamer, Eulalia		75.00
Cruet, Drape		70.00
Cruet, Fans & Miters		75.00
Cruet, Lighthouse Shape, Hobstars, Fans & Pinwheel, 9 1/2 In.		68.00
Cruet, Strawberry & Fan		75.00
Cruet, Strawberry Diamond Fan		75.00
Decanter, Demijohn Handle, C.Dorflinger, 13 In.		750.00
Decanter, Greek Key & Bellflower, 13 1/2 In.		75.00
Decanter, Hobnail, Matching Stopper & Ring Neck, 10 1/2 In.		550.00
Decanter, Orloff, Clarke, 11 1/2 In.		1450.00
Decanter, Waffle, Cut Panels, 10 1/2 In., Pair		80.00
Decanter, Wine, Hawkes, 11 1/2 In.		195.00
Eggnog Bowl, Stand, Hobstar, Cane & Strawberry Diamond, 10 In.		650.00
Ewer, Russian, Sterling Art Nouveau Collar, Fish Handle		4200.00
Ferner, Hunt's Royal, 3 Footed		195.00
Finger Bowl, Cranberry, Clear, Heraldic Crest, 2 1/2 X 5 1/8 In.		135.00
Fruit Bowl, Daisy & Button Panels, Footed, 7 X 8 In.		185.00
Fruit Bowl, Imperial Pattern, 9 In.		195.00
Hair Receiver, Engraved Sterling Top, Floral, Buds, 3 In.		75.00
Horseradish Jar, Allover Hobstars, Ladder Cutting, 5 1/2 In.		135.00
Ice Bucket, Hawkes, 7 In.		195.00
Inkwell, Brass Hinged Collar, Cane, 3 1/2 X 4 In.		195.00
Jar, Hobstars, Cover, 6 In.		295.00
Jar, Horseradish, Hobstars, Ladder Cutting Panels, 5 1/2 In.		135.00

Lamp, Boudoir, Mushroom Shade, Pinwheel, Fan & Strawberry, 13 In.	650.00
Lamp, Mushroom Shade, Electrified, 23 1/2 In.	1500.00
Mustard, Sultana, Sterling Silver Lid, Dorflinger, 2 3/4 In.	165.00
Nappy, Hobstar With Buttons, Floral Rim, Footed, Handle, 5 In.	65.00
Nappy, Hobstar, Feather Cut Leaves, Double Notched Handle, 6 In.	58.00
Nappy, Painted Loops Center Design, Hobstars & Cane, 9 In.	410.00
Nappy, Pinwheels & Fans, Divider, Handle, 6 In.	50.00
Oil & Vinegar Bottle, Signed Hawkes, 1916	55.00
Pitcher, Alhambra, Meriden Cut Glass Co., 12 1/2 In.	1850.00
Pitcher, Cane, 9 In.	225.00
Pitcher, Champagne, Hobstars, Triple Notch Handle, 13 In.	245.00
Pitcher, Cider, Signed Hoare, 7 1/2 In.	185.00
Pitcher, Crosshatch & Swag Body, Thumbprint Neck, 6 1/2 In.	70.00
Pitcher, Engraved Silver Plate Top, Flower, Leaves, 5 3/4 In.	125.00
Pitcher, Hobs, Cane, Notched Prism, 8 1/2 In.	200.00
Pitcher, Hobstar, Pinwheel & Fan, Honeycomb Holder, 10 In.	295.00
Pitcher, Keystone Rose, 10 In.	135.00
Pitcher, Lemonade, Hobstars, Crosshatch, Curved Handle, 11 In.	250.00
Pitcher, Straw Pattern, 11 In.	300.00
Pitcher, Water, Floral & Diamond Point Panels, 32 Rays, 9 In.	155.00
Pitcher, Water, Hobstars, Cane, Double Thumbprint Handle, 8 In.	225.00
Pitcher, Water, Napoleon, Cut Handle, O'Connor, 9 In.	395.00
Pitcher, Water, Pluto, Single Star Base, Hoare, 9 In.	435.00
Pitcher, Water, Signed Clarke, 10 In.	175.00
Plate, Colonial, Dorflinger, 7 In.	38.00
Plate, Empress Eugenie, J.D.Bergen, 9 In.	1175.00
Plate, Murillo, Serrated Rim, 10 In.	250.00
Plate, Panel, Hawkes ....*Illus*	3050.00
Plate, Rex, 7 In.	1500.00
Platter, Etched Pear & Leaf, Cut Diamond Point, 11 1/2 In.	125.00
Platter, Ice Cream, Hobnail & Fans, 11 1/2 X 8 In.	175.00
Powder Box, Hawkes, 7 In.Diam.	165.00
Punch Bowl Set, Star, 8 X 12 In.Bowl, 11 Cups	85.00
Punch Bowl, Signed Clarke, 16 Goblets, Ladle ....*Illus*	1500.00
Salt & Pepper, Sterling Tops, Irregular Notched Prisms, 4 In.	36.00
Salt, Russian, Boat Shape, Turned–In Sides, Master	125.00
Shaving Mug, Cane, Blazed Stars, Fans, 5 In.	95.00
Sherbet, Stemmed, Signed Egginton	35.00
Shot Glass, Quill, Gilded Top, Faceted Base, Floral Enameled	125.00
Spooner, Pinwheel, Handles	80.00
String Holder, Notched Prism, Pierced Sterling Silver Top	125.00
Sugar & Creamer, Cover, Buzz, Hobnail, Fans, Pedestal, 5 In.	975.00

Cut Glass, Bowl, Brilliant, Shallow, 10 In.

Cut Glass, Punch Bowl, Signed Clarke,
16 Goblets, Ladle

Sugar & Creamer, Flute Cut Lip & Stem, Double Notch Handle	325.00
Sugar & Creamer, Hobstar, 3 In.	150.00
Sugar & Creamer, Hobstar, Fans, 8 Point Star & Hobstar Bottom	90.00
Sugar & Creamer, Pedestal, Hobstars	475.00
Sugar & Creamer, Pinwheel, Applied Handles	35.00
Sugar & Creamer, Prima Donna, Pedestal, Clark, 4 3/4 In.	330.00
Syrup, Vertical Notched Prism	115.00
Tankard, Hobstar & Cane, 24 Point Hobstar Base, 7 1/2 In.	895.00
Toothpick, Empress, Green	85.00
Toothpick, Fluted Diamonds	38.00
Tray, Butterfly, Leaves & Flowers, Center Handle, 10 In.	195.00
Tray, Ice Cream, Columbia, Blackmet, 17 1/2 X 10 In.	1895.00
Tray, Ice Cream, Hobstar, Cane, Fine Diamond, 12 X 9 In.	335.00
Tray, Ice Cream, Interlocking Circles, 9 In.	275.00
Tray, Leaf Sprays, Pinwheels, Daisies, Star Centers, 12 1/2 In.	195.00
Tray, Marlboro, Dorflinger, 15 1/2 In.	795.00
Tray, Russian Cut, Round, 11 1/8 In.	125.00
Tray, Sugar Cube, Cane, 9 In.	75.00
Tray, Sunbursts & Leaves, Handles, 13 X 8 1/2 In.	250.00
Tray, Trellis, Signed Egginton, Oval, 10 1/4 X 7 In.	2500.00
Vase, 3 Etched Floral Panels, Signed Clark, 14 1/2 In.	225.00
Vase, Cut Flowers, Vines, Notched Prisms On Sides, 11 3/4 In.	135.00
Vase, Hobstar Bottom, Square, 10 1/4 In., Pair	950.00
Vase, Honeycomb, 9 In.	175.00
Vase, Jack–In–The–Pulpit, Russian Cut Foot, Dorflinger, 13 In.	1850.00
Vase, Pinwheel, Allover Hobstars, Sawtooth Rim, Rayed Base, 10 In.	150.00
Vase, Russian, Pillar, 12 In.	900.00
Vase, Scalloped & Serrated Rim, Rayed Base, Corset Shape, 8 In.	100.00
Vase, Trumpet, Diamonds & Fans, 10 In.	38.00
Wine Cooler, Queens, Signed Hawkes, 9 X 9 In.	3950.00
Wine, Bakers Gothic, Signed Clarke, 4 In., 8 Piece	400.00

CYBIS

Boleslaw Cybis came to the United States from Poland in 1939. He started making porcelains in Long Island, New York, in 1940. He moved to Trenton, New Jersey, in 1942 to work for Cordey and started his own Cybis Porcelains in 1950. The firm is still working.

CYBIS, Figurine, Baby Owl, White, 1950s	45.00
Figurine, Beatrice	750.00
Figurine, Blueheaded Vireo, Building Nest, 1965	450.00
Figurine, Calla Lily	1125.00
Figurine, Cat	95.00
Figurine, Cinderella, Broom	500.00
Figurine, Circus Elephant	250.00
Figurine, Deer Mouse In Clover	130.00 To 150.00
Figurine, First Flight	175.00
Figurine, Foal, Standing	150.00 To 175.00
Figurine, Funny Face	250.00
Figurine, Goldilocks & Three Bears	400.00
Figurine, Guinevere	500.00
Figurine, Hansel	350.00
Figurine, Heidi	225.00
Figurine, Holly Boy	375.00
Figurine, Little Princess	350.00 To 450.00
Figurine, Little Red Riding Hood	250.00 To 295.00
Figurine, Peter Pan, 1970	285.99
Figurine, Queen Esther	1200.00
Figurine, Raccoon	225.00 To 350.00
Figurine, Robin Hood	600.00
Figurine, Snail	225.00
Figurine, Wendy	150.00

There are some collectibles that are identified by the name of the country, not a factory mark. Anything marked "Czechoslovakia" is popular today. The name, first used as a mark after the country was

D'Argental, Vase, Cameo, Olive
Wild Flowers, Pale Green, 6 In.

You can date an old bottle from the spelling of the word Pittsburgh. From 1891 to 1911 the "h" was removed by the United States Board of Geographic names. The old spelling was resumed because of complaints from those who lived in Pittsburg.

formed in 1918, appears on glass and porcelain and other decorative items. The name is still used in some trademarks.

CZECHOSLOVAKIA, Bottle, Perfume, Cut Glass, Amethyst	35.00
Bottle, Perfume, Frosted Floriform Stopper, 4 1/4 In.	60.00
Bowl & Platter, Silver Maple Leaf, Gold Trim, Cover, Signed	85.00
Bowl, Scalloped Rim, Iridescent Finish, Signed, 2 X 12 In.	75.00
Creamer, Parrot, Figural	25.00
Figurine, Rooster & Hen, Porcelain, Painted, 7 In., Pair	38.00
Juice Set, Flared Pitcher, Pottery, 4 Tumblers	55.00
Lamp, Perfume, Cone Shape, Enameled Flowers, 4 In.	85.00
Perfume Bottle, Fan Shape Stopper, Crystal, 4 In.	75.00
Perfume Bottle, Floral, Mesh, White Enameled Flowers, 2 In.	55.00
Perfume Bottle, Green Top, Crystal Bottle, 2 In.	45.00
Pitcher, Water, Millefiori Canes, Vaseline, Large	75.00
Plate, Bird Center, White Ground, Art Deco, 12 In.	12.00
Plate, Floral, Cobalt Border, Gold Tracery, 11 In.	300.00
Rose Bowl, Daisy & Fern Style, Opalescent, Signed	35.00
Tumbler, Maud's Flour, Glazed, Blue Scene	22.50
Vase, Art Deco, Marked Ditmar Urbach, 1930s	65.00
Vase, Cobalt Blue Slip Design, Geometric, 7 In.	35.00
Vase, Fan, Glass, Pink, Black, Signed	95.00
Vase, Gold Web, Red Stones, Rose, Bulbous, Label, 5 In.	90.00
Vase, Relief Birds, Signed, 10 In.	175.00
Vase, Silver Overlay, Ship, Black Amethyst, 6 1/2 In.	55.00
Wall Pocket, Birds & Fruit	10.00

D'Argental is a mark used by the St. Louis, France, glassworks. The firm made multilayered, acid-cut cameo glass in the late nineteenth and twentieth centuries. D'Argental is the French name for the city of Munzthal, home of the glassworks. Later they made enameled etched glass. Compagnie des Cristalleries de St. Louis is still working.

D'ARGENTAL, Box, Floral, Cuttings, Cover	750.00
Box, Flower Branch Cover, Band of Leaves Around, 4 1/4 In.	835.00
Lamp, Cameo, Lemon Yellow, Crimson, Foliate Fiddlehead, 20 In.	6600.00
Vase, Acid-Cut Flowers, Caramel Ground, Signed, 9 1/4 In.	795.00
Vase, Brown Cut To Amber Orchids, 14 In.	900.00
Vase, Cameo, Olive Wild Flowers, Pale Green, 6 In. ....*Illus*	550.00
Vase, Floral, All Brown Tones, 14 In.	775.00
Vase, Harbor Scene, Men In Sailboats, 3–Dimensional, 11 3/4 In.	1650.00
Vase, Landscape Scenes, Cameo, Mauve, Brown, Signed, 9 3/4 In.	650.00

Vase, Pine Cones, Brown, Mushrooms, Amber Ground, 7 In. 950.00
Vase, Scenic Cameo, Rocky Shore, Lighthouse, 5 In. 675.00
Vase, Scenic, Venice, Man In Gondola, Signed, 5 5/8 In. 650.00
Vase, Woman Washing Clothes At Lake, Signed, 3 1/2 In. 550.00

DAUM NANCY Jean Daum started a glassworks in Nancy, France, in 1875. The
company, now called "Cristalleries de Nancy," is still working. The
"Daum Nancy" mark has been used in many variations. The name
of the city and the artist are usually both included.

DAUM NANCY, Ashtray, Yellow Orange, Signed, 4 1/2 In. 140.00
Bottle, Cone Shape, Faceted Stopper, Signed, 14 1/2 In. 245.00
Bowl, Bare Trees, Bushes, Snow On Ground, Signed, 2 3/4 In. 700.00
Bowl, Scenic, Cameo & Enamel, Blue, 2 1/2 X 6 In. 975.00
Box, Carved Dragons On Cover, Signed, C.1900, 6 In. 3025.00
Box, Double Scenic, Enameling 750.00
Compote, Sculptured Deco Pattern, Footed, Signed, 4 1/4 In. 450.00
Ewer, Amethyst, Silver Plated Mount 975.00
Jar, Trinket, Cameo, White To Cranberry, Cover, 3 1/2 In. 185.00
Jardiniere, Green Leaves, Orange Berries, Signed, 11 1/4 In. 300.00
Lamp, Acid Etched, Onion Shape Shade, Winter Scene, 14 In. 2000.00
Lamp, Boudoir, Cameo, Floral Shade, 13 In., Pair ....*Illus* 7000.00
Lamp, Cameo, Winter Scene, Signed, 18 In. 5000.00
Lamp, Desk, Sylvan Pond Setting, 19 In. 9240.00
Lamp, Dutch Shipping, Glass & Wrought Iron, C.1910, 19 3/4 In. 9350.00
Lamp, Floral Shade, Blue, Green & Yellow Pedestal, 12 3/4 In. 7700.00
Perfume Bottle, Cameo Cut Circle Pattern, Signed, 3 In. 350.00
Perfume Bottle, Woodland Scene, Orange, Swirl Stopper, 5 1/4 In. 750.00
Salt, Winter Scene, Yellow Orange Ground, Oval, 2 X 1/4 X 1 In. 580.00
Shade, For Bedroom Lamp, Purple Flowers, Signed 400.00
Shot Glass, 3 Green, 3 Amber, Different Plants, Box 1600.00
Tumbler, Violets, Rust Ground, 3 1/2 In. 150.00
Vase, Acid Cut–Back Foliate, Green, Enamel, 10 3/4 In. ....*Illus* 200.00
Vase, Applied Rope Twist, Signed, 9 1/2 In. 495.00
Vase, Brown & Violet Foliage, Enamel, 8 1/4 In. ....*Illus* 300.00
Vase, Brown Tree Scene, Red, Mottled Yellow Interior, 9 1/4 In. 1670.00
Vase, Cameo, 4 Colors, 4 3/4 In. ....*Illus* 1760.00
Vase, Crystal & Frosted Green, Gold, Signed, 7 1/2 In. 425.00
Vase, Enameled Orchids, Leaves, Spider Webs, Signed, 15 1/4 In. 2100.00
Vase, Flowers, Frosted Ground, 4–Sided Tapered, 6 In. 750.00
Vase, Forest Landscape, White To Yellow, Signed, 23 3/4 In. 1300.00
Vase, Frosted Green, Gold, Signed, 14 In. 425.00
Vase, Landscape, River, Boat, Trees, Signed, 19 In. 2640.00

Daum Nancy, Vase, Acid
Cut–Back Foliate, Green,
Enamel, 10 3/4 In.

Daum Nancy, Vase,
Brown & Violet Foliage,
Enamel, 8 1/4 In.

Daum Nancy, Vase, Cameo, 4 Colors,
4 3/4 In.

Daum Nancy, Lamp, Boudoir, Cameo, Floral Shade, 13 In., Pair   Daum Nancy, Vase, Scenic, Brown On Streaked Amber, 9 In.   De Vez, Vase, Bud, 6 1/4 In.

Vase, Mounted As Lamp, Floral Design, Frosted, 33 1/2 In. 1200.00
Vase, Orange Fruit, Leaves, Numbered 2024, 19 In. 1950.00
Vase, Pinched In & Out, Red Ground, Mottled, Signed, 14 In. 350.00
Vase, Purple Flowers, Green Center, Buds, Gold, Signed, 16 In. 2500.00
Vase, Scenic, Brown On Streaked Amber, 9 In. .... *Illus* 800.00
Vase, Squared Greek Form Handles, Spattered, Signed, 10 In. 325.00
Vase, Stylized Mistletoe Branches, Signed, 16 1/2 In. 4400.00
Vase, Summer Scene, Trees, Water, Oval, 4 3/4 X 5 1/4 In. 1015.00
Vase, Sunset Landscape, Baluster Form, Signed, 23 In. 900.00
Vase, Thistle & Leaf Cameo, Hammered Ground, Signed, 12 1/4 In. 3000.00
Vase, Winter Landscape, Black Birds, Signed, C.1900, 5 In. 4125.00
Vase, Winter Scene, Flattened Oval Shape, 4 3/4 In. 755.00

DAVENPORT
LONGPORT
STAFFORDSHRE

Davenport pottery and porcelain were made at the Davenport factory in Longport, Staffordshire, England, from 1793 to 1887. Earthenwares, creamwares, porcelains, ironstone, and other ceramics were made. Most of the pieces are marked with a form of the word "Davenport."

DAVENPORT, Creamer, Tavern Scene, Brown Top Band, White Base, 5 In. 150.00
Cup & Saucer, Cyprus, Mulberry, Handleless 55.00
Tureen, Sauce, Cover, Gilt & Floral Design, C.1810, 5 X 8 In. 160.00

Davy Crockett, the American frontiersman, was born in 1786 and died in 1836. He became popular again in 1954 with the introduction of a television series about his life. Coonskin caps and buckskins became popular and hundreds of different Davy Crockett items were made.

DAVY CROCKETT, Badge, Hero of The Alamo 12.00
Bank, Kill The Bear, Amusement Machine, Large 95.00
Belt, Original Package 20.00
Bowl & Plate, Pottery 25.00
Cap, Coonskin 12.00
Card, Trolley, York Peanut Butter, Disney, 21 X 11 In. 46.00
Clock, Animated 125.00
Comic Book, 1955 .... 8.00
Doll, Stuffed, Ideal, 1950s, 29 In. 48.00
Fishing Set, Original Card 85.00
Handkerchief 12.00
Hatchet Knife 55.00
Indian Fighter Hat, Real Fur, Box, 1950s 75.00
Lamp .... 40.00 To 55.00
Lunch Box 22.00

Mug, Figural, 5 In.	25.00
Neckerchief	18.00 To 25.00
Pin	6.00
Pistol, Full Size, 1950, Box	18.00
Pitcher, Water, 6 Tumblers	105.00
Plate	15.00
Powder Horn	25.00
Pup Tent, Box	80.00
Scarf, With Slide	9.00
Shirt, Child's, Size 6X, Disney	25.00
Stool, Vinyl Upholstered	45.00
Suspenders, Original Card	25.00

William de Morgan made art pottery in England from the 1860s to 1907. He is best known for his luster–glazed Moorish–inspired pieces. The pottery used a variety of marks.

DE MORGAN, Charger, Iridescent Red, Black Geometrics, C.1890, 18 In.	8000.00
Tile, Leaves & Cherries, 8 X 8 In.	275.00
Vase, Iridescent Red, Crouching Lion, 12 In.	4000.00

De Vez is a name found on special pieces of French cameo glass made by the Cristallerie de Pantin about 1890. Monsieur de Varreaux was the art director of the glassworks and he signed pieces "de Vez."

DE VEZ, Night–Light, Scenic, Cameo Glass	1295.00
Vase, Blue Satin, Cameo, Green Cut To Pink Tree Scene, 5 1/2 In.	650.00
Vase, Boat & Village Scene, 3 Acid Cuttings, Signed, 7 1/2 In.	495.00
Vase, Bud, 6 1/4 In. *Illus*	250.00
Vase, Foreground Trees, Mountains, Island Ground, Signed, 5 1/2 In.	650.00
Vase, Islands, Mountains, Branches Frame Scene, Signed, 6 X 2 3/4 In.	550.00
Vase, Sailboats, Branches Drape Scene, Signed, 9 5/8 In.	775.00
Vase, Sailboats, Leafy Branches Frame Scene, Signed, 4 1/4 In.	450.00
Vase, Tree Landscape, Mountains In Background, Signed, 5 1/4 In.	495.00
Vase, Trees, Shore, Islands, Navy Blue Cut To Yellow, Signed, 6 In.	550.00
Vase, Woman, Flowing Scarves, Fringed Dress, Signed, C.1920, 19 In.	3025.00

Decoys are carved or turned wooden copies of birds or fish. The decoy was placed in the water or propped on the shore to lure flying birds to the pond for hunters. Some decoys are handmade, some are commercial products. Today there is a group of artists making modern decoys for display, not use in a pond.

DECOY, Bird, Natural Root Growth, Tin Wings, Bead Eyes, 12 1/2 In.	150.00
Black Bellied Plover, Russ Burr	2300.00
Black Duck, Balsa, Wooden Head, Wild Fowler Decoys, 19 1/2 In.	80.00
Black Duck, Cork Body, Thomas Gelston, Long Island	100.00
Black Duck, Cork, Charles Disbrow, Connecticut	55.00
Black Duck, Elongated Body, Carved Head, Glass Eyes, 17 1/2 In.	105.00
Black Duck, Ken Anger, Ontario	650.00
Black Duck, Turned Head, Glass Eyes, Original Paint, 15 1/2 In.	115.00
Black Duck, Wildfowler Co., Cork	60.50
Blue–Winged Teal, Hollow, Paul Lipke	2200.00
Blue–Winged Teal, Illinois River, 11 1/2 In.	95.00
Bluebill Drake, Primitive, Old Repaint, Glass Eyes, Michigan, 13 In.	750.00
Bluebill Drake, Primitive, Snakey Head, Worn Paint, 12 1/2 In.	155.00
Bluebill Drake, Tack Eyes, Removable Wire Props, 14 3/4 In.	85.00
Bluebill Hen, Hollow Body, Glass Eyes, Mason's, 13 1/2 In.	135.00
Bluebill Hen, Nate Quilon, Rockwood, Michigan, 13 In.	185.00
Brant Goose, Hollow Body, Whittled Head, Black & White, 18 3/4 In.	85.00
Bufflehead Drake Sleeper, Mid–20th Century, 11 In.	75.00
Canada Goose, Canvas Cover, George Boyd	8525.00
Canada Goose, Glass Eyes, Original Paint, 23 1/2 In.	200.00
Canada Goose, Hissing, Lincoln, Miniature	1050.00
Canada Goose, Primitive, Mid–20th Century, 20 1/2 In.	110.00
Canada Goose, Robert F.McGaw, Maryland	3000.00

Canada Goose, Swimmer, Snakey Head, Primitive, Age Cracks, 29 In. 300.00
Canvasback Drake, Balsa Body, Turned Head, Original Paint, 14 In. 65.00
Canvasback Drake, Ben Dye, Maryland, 15 1/4 In. 150.00
Canvasback Drake, Glass Eyes, Original Paint, 16 1/4 In. 55.00
Canvasback Drake, Hollow Body, Glass Eyes, Lake St.Clair, 15 In. 130.00
Canvasback Drake, Sinclair Flats, Michigan, 15 1/2 In. 75.00
Canvasback Drake, Turned Head, Fred Bradshaw, 1967, 16 3/4 In. 145.00
Canvasback Hen, Nick Purdo, Worn Paint, Glass Eyes, 15 1/2 In. 140.00
Canvasback, Ward Brothers, Crisfield, Maryland, Pair 2700.00
Coot, Hollow Body, Inset Head, Black & White, 9 3/4 In. 45.00
Crow, Folding Wings, Tin 125.00
Crow, Glass Eyes, Wire Stand, 14 1/2 In. 35.00
Crow, Herters, Balsa Wood 120.00
Crow, Stick-Up, Black Sheet Iron, C.1920, Life Size, Pair 175.00
Curlew, Long Island, 1940s 1350.00
Dove, Papier-Mache, Carrylite Products, 9 In. 125.00
Fish, Red & White 25.00
Goldeneye Drake, Glass Eyes, William E.Pratt Mfg.Co., 13 In. 150.00
Goose, Canvas, Minnesota 130.00
Goose, Feeding, Clarence Glass, Wisc., 1940, Pair 375.00
Goose, Fold-Type, Johnson, Original Field Bag 20.00
Goose, Tin, Stick-Up 55.00
Green-Winged Teal, Wood, Canvas, Plank Base, E.Martin, LaCrosse, 14 In. 20.00
Heron, Wooden, Stylized Body, Gray Stain, Over White Paint, Rod, 24 In. 175.00
Long-Billed Curlew, Mason Decoy Factory, Detroit 2400.00
Loon, Primitive, Whittled, Original Paint, 16 In. 175.00
Mallard Drake, Glass Eyes, Snakey Head, Mason's, 16 1/4 In. 335.00
Mallard Drake, Hollow Body & Head, Tack Eyes, Illinois River, 15 In. 100.00
Mallard Drake, Hollow Body, Wilfred Bush, 16 5/8 In. 275.00
Mallard Drake, Original Paint, Mason Premiere 400.00
Mallard Drake, Wood & Cork, Glass Eyes, Marked N.Y.State, 17 In. 40.00
Mallard Hen, Carl Sattler, Iowa 1155.00
Mallard Hen, Cork Body, A.E.Crowell 3850.00
Mallard Hen, Hayes Decoy Co., Missouri, 16 1/2 In. 120.00
Mallard, Raised Wings, Gus Wilson 8800.00
Merganser Hen, Stylized Body, Original Brown & White Paint, 18 In. 350.00
Merganser, Driftwood Head, Branded Seidel, 16 1/2 In. 65.00
Merganser, Hooded, Dr.Woods, Orillia, Ontario 2200.00
Merganser, Hooded, Miles Hancock, Chesapeake Bay, Pair 1450.00
Owl, Composition, Sculptured Features, Glass Eyes, 14 1/2 In. 175.00
Owl, Papier-Mache, Glass Eyes, 17 In. 20.00
Pintail Drake, Hollow Body, Glass Eyes, 17 In. 45.00
Pintail Drake, Repaint, Glass Eyes, Factory, 16 1/2 In. 75.00
Pintail Duck, Mason's 200.00
Plover, Golden, Spring Plumage, Split Tail 700.00
Red Breasted Merganser Drake, Glass Eyes, Chuck Fluka, 16 3/4 In. 375.00
Redhead Drake, Glass Eyes, Ralph Reghie, Michigan, 14 1/2 In. 60.00
Redhead Drake, Hollow Body, Dipper Ortley, 14 1/2 In. 135.00
Redhead Drake, Hollow Body, Glass Eyes, John Wells, 14 1/4 In. 225.00
Redhead Drake, Low-Headed, Branded Hy-Dahlka, 15 In. 75.00
Redhead Drake, Marked Evans Decoy, Original Paint, 14 1/2 In. 225.00
Redhead Hen, Hollow Body, Glass Eyes, Chris Smith, 15 1/2 In. 200.00
Redhead Hen, Preening, Hollow, Paul Lipke 1100.00
Redhead, Crowell, Miniature 600.00
Redhead, Mason Factory Premier, Pair 2550.00
Roothead, 19th Century, Pine Base 1000.00
Ruddy Duck, Canvas, Wood & Wire Frame, Original Paint, 10 3/4 In. 185.00
Ruddy Duck, Glass Eyes, Original Paint, 10 1/2 In. 45.00
Screaming Eider, Signed, Canada 195.00
Sea Gull, Hollow Body, Glass Eyes, 14 1/2 In. 20.00
Shorebird, Carved Cork, Whittled Wooden Bill, Paint, Rod, Base, 14 In. 100.00
Shorebird, Impressed Walker, 10 In. 55.00
Shorebird, Tin, Folding, Original Paint, Rod, 9 1/2 In. 90.00
Stylized Detail, Relief Carving, Screw Head Eyes, 11 In. 85.00

Surf Scoter, Samuel Fabens	6875.00
Surf Scoter, Ward Brothers, 1970	1760.00
Whistler Drake, Black & White Paint, 15 In.	35.00
Wisconsin Coot, Black & White, Branded Hall, 13 1/4 In.	75.00
Wood Duck Drake, Original Paint, Mid–20th Century, 15 In.	65.00
Yellowlegs, Maryland	900.00

Chelsea Keramic Art Works was established in 1872 in Chelsea, Massachusetts, by members of the Robertson family. The factory closed in 1889 and was reorganized as the Chelsea Pottery U.S. in 1891. It became the Dedham Pottery of Dedham, Massachusetts, in 1895. The factory closed in 1943. It was famous for its crackleware dishes, which picture blue outlines of animals, flowers, and other natural motifs.

DEDHAM, Ashtray, Elephant, Stamped, 4 In.	300.00
Creamer, Rabbit .... 125.00 To	295.00
Cup & Saucer, Azalea, Demitasse, 5 In.	210.00
Cup & Saucer, Swan, Stamped, 4 In.	200.00
Jar, Honeycomb, Olive Glaze, 2 Handles, Bulbous, Cover, CKAW, 5 1/2 In.	150.00
Jar, Marmalade, Cover, Rabbit, Stamped, 5 In.	200.00
Pitcher, Owl & Chicken, 5 In.	150.00
Pitcher, Rabbit, 4 1/2 In.	225.00
Plate, Azalea, 6 In.	125.00
Plate, Clover, Stamped, 10 In.	650.00
Plate, Horsechestnut, 6 In.	95.00
Plate, Horsechestnut, 8 1/2 In.	150.00
Plate, Lily, 8 3/4 In.	150.00
Plate, Lily, Stamped, 6 1/8 In.	300.00
Plate, Mushroom, Stamped, 8 1/2 In.	85.00
Plate, Pineapple, Stamped, 10 In.	225.00
Plate, Rabbit, 8 1/2 In.	85.00
Plate, Snowtree, Stamped, 9 3/4 In.	225.00
Plate, Swan, Stamped, Impressed, 10 1/2 In.	225.00
Plate, Turkey, Stamped, 10 In.	225.00
Saltshaker, Rabbit, Tall	195.00
Saucer, Rabbit	30.00
Vase, Brown, Green & Dark Blue Drip Glaze, Experimental, 7 In.	375.00
Vase, Crackleware, Flying Cranes, Bulbous, Artist, 7 1/2 X 6 In.	2000.00
Vase, Dragon's Blood, Incised Mark, 2 7/8 In.	650.00
Vase, Dragon's Blood, Wide Mouth, Cylindrical, HCR, 2 7/8 In.	650.00
Vase, Iridescent Red, Green & Taupe, Experimental, H.R., 8 In.	1300.00
Vase, Mottled Iridescent Red Glaze, Over Rose, Experimental, 4 In.	350.00
Vase, Oxblood, Orange Peel Texture, Chelsea Keramic Art Works, 8 In.	2000.00
Vase, Volcanic Drip, Signed Hugh Robertson, Marked 10 In.	550.00

Degue

Degue is a signature found acid–etched on pieces of French glass made in the early 1900s. Cameo, mold blown, and smooth glass with contrasting colored rims are the types most often found.

DEGUE, Vase, Trees On Shore, Sailboats, Maroon Scene, Signed, 5 3/8 X 3 In.	450.00

DELATTE NANCY

Delatte glass is a French cameo glass made by Andre Delatte. It was first made in Nancy, France, in 1921. Lighting fixtures and opaque glassware in imitation of Bohemian opaline were made. There were many French cameo glass makers, so be sure to look in other appropriate sections.

DELATTE, Vase, 3 Colors, 10 In.	900.00
Vase, Tree Landscape At River, Ears Form Handles, Signed, 9 1/4 In. ...	895.00
DELAWARE, see Custard Glass; Pressed Glass	
DELDARE, see Buffalo Pottery Deldare	

Delft is a tin–glazed pottery that has been made since the seventeenth century. It is decorated with blue on white or with colored decorations. Most of the pieces sold today were made after 1891, and the name "Holland" appears with the Delft factory marks.

DELFT, Ashtray, Windmill Scene, Chrome Top 20.00
  Bank, Rabbit, Polychrome Enameling, 4 In. 250.00
  Basket, Peonies, Prunus, Reticulated, Blue, White, Liverpool, 12 In. 650.00
  Brick, Flower, Mauve Blue, Castle, Ships 45.00
  Candlestick, Polychrome, C.1790, 9 1/2 In. 275.00
  Charger, Ann Gomm Pattern, Lambeth, Polychrome, 13 3/4 In. 100.00
  Charger, Stylized Design, Yellow Trim On Rim, 18th Century, 14 In. 300.00
  Cigarette Holder, House With Chimney, Marked, 4 In., Pair 60.00
  Compote, Turquoise & Green, Polychrome Gold Foot, Sticker, 6 3/4 In. 25.00
  Figurine, Bagpiper, Sitting, Polychrome, V Duyn Mark, 10 3/8 In. 1980.00
  Figurine, Bird, Open Base, Marked AK, 6 3/4 In. 85.00
  Figurine, Little Girls, Flower Bouquets, 5 In., Pair 95.00
  Fruit, Polychrome Enameled, 4 In., Pair 80.00
  Inkwell, Polychrome Flowers, White, 4 X 4 X 2 In. 175.00
  Jar, Apothecary, Brown Black Enameled Label, 9 3/4 In. 300.00
  Jar, Polychrome Floral Design, Brass Domed Lid, 8 In. 375.00
  Pitcher, Figural, Cow, Floral On Back & Base, 6 X 8 1/2 In. 75.00
  Plaque, 11 Figures Around Table, Blue & White, MVK, 10 7/8 In. 2450.00
  Plaque, Bamboo, Chinese Pheasant, Blue & White, C.1720, 9 1/8 In. 1375.00
  Plate, Blue, White, Flower, Lambeth, 1740–50, 10 In. 295.00
  Pot, Crocus, Tin Glaze, Polychrome Design of Birds, 4 1/4 In., Pair 130.00
  Punch Bowl, Tin Glazed Body, Floral Sprays, 3 1/4 X 7 3/4 In. 125.00
  Sauceboat, Couple In Garden, Fox Handles, C.1740, 8 11/16 In. 2100.00
  Tankard, Blue & White Floral, Sponged Purple, Marked B.P., 7 1/2 In. 450.00
  Tile, Windmills, Polychrome, Marked, 6 In. 20.00
  Vase, Chinese Warriors On Horseback, Figure With Parasol, Octagonal 3100.00

Dental cabinets, chairs, equipment, and other related items are listed
here. Other objects may be found listed under Medical.

DENTAL, Air Compressor, Dental Mfg., 1916, Automatic, Leather Belt 375.00
  Book, Artificial Crown & Bridge Work, Color Pages, 450 Pages, 1905 .... 16.00
  Cabinet, Cut Glass Knobs, Marble Top, 5 Drawers, Lap Size 175.00
  Cabinet, Pearl Pulls, 7 Drawers, Oak, Lap Size 225.00
  Chair, Dentist, Late 18th Century 275.00
  Jar, Dental Snuff, Tooth Picture, Label, Stamp, Tin Lid, 1879 .... 35.00
  Lamp, Alcohol, Pair 35.00
  Mold, False Teeth, Brass 50.00
  Pliers, Tooth Pulling 11.00
  Teeth, Trubyte Dentist Supply Co., 34 Teeth Mounted, Case 125.00
  Tooth Forms, New Century Steel, Central Tool Co., 150 Steel Teeth 200.00

Depression glass was an inexpensive glass manufactured in large
quantities during the 1920s and early 1930s. It was made in many
colors and patterns by dozens of factories in the United States. The
name "Depression glass" is a modern one. For more descriptions,
history, pictures, and prices of Depression glass, see the book
"Kovels' Depression Glass & American Dinnerware Price List."

DEPRESSION GLASS, Adam, Bowl, Green, 4 3/4 In. 9.50
  Adam, Bowl, Pink, 5 3/4 In. 25.00
  Adam, Butter, Cover, Pink 38.00
  Adam, Cake Plate, Green 13.00
  Adam, Candy Dish, Cover, Pink .... 40.00 To 55.00
  Adam, Creamer, Green 10.50
  Adam, Creamer, Pink .... 10.00 To 12.00
  Adam, Grill Plate, Green 11.00
  Adam, Grill Plate, Pink 10.00
  Adam, Plate, Green, 6 In. 2.50
  Adam, Plate, Green, 7 3/4 In. 7.00
  Adam, Plate, Square, Pink, 8 In. 5.00
  Adam, Relish, Divided, Pink 10.00
  Adam, Salt & Pepper, Footed, Pink 45.00
  Adam, Saucer, Green 2.00
  Adam, Saucer, Pink 4.00
  Adam, Sugar, Cover, Pink .... 15.00 To 22.00

Adam, Tumbler, Footed, Pink, 4 1/2 In. 12.00
Adam, Tumbler, Green, 5 1/2 In. .... 25.00 To 30.00
Adam, Vase, Pink 155.00
Alpine Caprice, Candy Jar, Cover, 3–Footed, Crystal, 6 In. 48.00
    AMERICAN BEAUTY, see English Hobnail
American Pioneer, Lamp, Pink, 8 1/2 In. 50.00
American Pioneer, Plate, Green, 11 1/2 In. 10.00
American Sweetheart, Berry Bowl, Monax, 9 In. 30.00
American Sweetheart, Berry Bowl, Pink, 3 3/4 In. 25.00
American Sweetheart, Bowl, Monax, 6 In. 18.00
American Sweetheart, Creamer, Pink .... 6.00 To 7.00
American Sweetheart, Cup & Saucer, Pink .... 9.50 To 10.00
American Sweetheart, Cup & Saucer, Red 90.00
American Sweetheart, Cup, Pink .... 6.50 To 7.50
American Sweetheart, Plate, Blue, 8 In. 63.00
American Sweetheart, Plate, Green, 9 3/4 In. 12.00
American Sweetheart, Plate, Monax, 6 1/2 In. 2.00
American Sweetheart, Plate, Monax, 8 In. 4.50
American Sweetheart, Plate, Monax, 10 1/4 In. .... 9.50 To 12.00
American Sweetheart, Plate, Pink, 6 In. 2.50
American Sweetheart, Plate, Pink, 9 3/4 In. 15.00
American Sweetheart, Plate, Pink, 11 In. 11.00
American Sweetheart, Plate, Red, 8 In. 60.00
American Sweetheart, Platter, Pink 14.00
American Sweetheart, Salt & Pepper, Pink 250.00
American Sweetheart, Saltshaker, Pink .... 95.00 To 100.00
American Sweetheart, Sugar & Creamer, Red 165.00
American Sweetheart, Sugar, Monax .... 3.50 To 6.00
American Sweetheart, Sugar, Pink 6.00
American Sweetheart, Sugar, Red 65.00
American, Bowl, Vegetable, Crystal 10.00
American, Candy Jar, Cover, Pink 95.00
American, Mayonnaise, Ladle 25.00
American, Relish, Divided, Crystal 12.00
American, Sugar & Creamer, Crystal 12.00
    APPLE BLOSSOM, see Dogwood
Aunt Polly, Butter, Cover, Blue 125.00
Aunt Polly, Vase, Green 12.00
    AURORA, see Petalware
Avocado, Cup, Green 21.00
Avocado, Dish, Pickle 8.00
Avocado, Relish, Green, 6 In. 20.00
    B PATTERN, see Dogwood
    BALLERINA, see Cameo
    BANDED CHERRY, see Cherry Blossom
    BANDED FINE RIB, see Coronation
    BANDED PETALWARE, see Petalware

If you move glass in cold weather be sure to let it sit at room temperature for several hours before you try unpacking it. The glass will break more easily if there is an abrupt temperature change.

BANDED RAINBOW, see Ring
BANDED RIBBON, see New Century
BANDED RINGS, see Ring
BASKET, see No. 615
Beaded Block, Dish, Jelly, Iridescent, 4 1/2 In. 10.00
Beaded Block, Plate, Amber, 7 3/4 In. 4.50
BERWICK, see Boopie
BEVERAGE WITH SAILBOAT, see White Ship
BIG RIB, see Manhattan
BLOCK, see Block Optic
Block Optic, Bowl, Green, 5 1/4 In. 7.00
Block Optic, Butter, Cover, Green 35.00
Block Optic, Cup & Saucer, Green 11.50
Block Optic, Cup, Pink 2.50
Block Optic, Cup, Yellow 6.00
Block Optic, Goblet, Wine, Green 10.00
Block Optic, Ice Tub, Green 35.00
Block Optic, Mug, Green 23.00
Block Optic, Pitcher, Green, 8 In. 25.00
Block Optic, Plate, Green, 6 In. 1.25
Block Optic, Plate, Green, 8 In. 2.25
Block Optic, Plate, Green, 9 In. .... 10.00 To 12.00
Block Optic, Plate, Green, 10 1/4 In. 9.50
Block Optic, Plate, Yellow, 8 In. 4.00
Block Optic, Salt & Pepper, Pink 35.00
Block Optic, Saucer, Pink 3.00
Block Optic, Sherbet, 3 1/4 In. 3.50
Block Optic, Sherbet, Green, 3 1/4 In. 3.00
Block Optic, Sherbet, Green, 4 3/4 In. 5.00
Block Optic, Sugar & Creamer, Cone, Green 18.00
Block Optic, Sugar & Creamer, Cone, Pink 30.00
Block Optic, Sugar, Cover, Green 30.00
Block Optic, Sugar, Yellow 9.50
Block Optic, Tumbler, Flat, Pink, 9 Oz. 95.00
Boopie, Sherbet, Red 5.00
BOUQUET & LATTICE, see Normandie
BRIDAL BOUQUET, see No. 615
Bubble, Bowl, Blue, 5 1/4 In. .... 4.50 To 8.00
Bubble, Bowl, Crystal, 5 1/4 In. .... 2.00 To 3.50
Bubble, Bowl, Crystal, 8 3/8 In. 4.00
Bubble, Bowl, Green, 5 1/4 In. 5.00
Bubble, Creamer, Blue .... 15.00 To 18.00

American Sweetheart

Bubble

Bubble, Cup & Saucer, Red 5.50
Bubble, Cup, Blue .... 2.50 To 3.50
Bubble, Dinner Set, Blue, 43 Piece 95.00
Bubble, Grill Plate, Blue 7.50
Bubble, Plate, Blue, 6 3/4 In. 5.00
Bubble, Plate, Blue, 9 3/8 In. 5.00
Bubble, Platter, Blue .... 7.00 To 8.00
Bubble, Soup, Dish, Blue .... 7.00 To 8.00
Bubble, Sugar & Creamer, Blue 30.00
Bubble, Sugar, Green 5.00
Bubble, Tumbler, Red, 9 Oz. 5.50
Bubble, Tumbler, Red, 16 Oz. 12.00
    BULLSEYE, see Bubble
    BUTTERFLIES & ROSES, see Flower Garden with Butterflies
    BUTTONS & BOWS, see Holiday
    CABBAGE ROSE, see Sharon
    CABBAGE ROSE WITH SINGLE ARCH, see Rosemary
Cameo, Berry Bowl, Green, 8 1/4 In. .... 20.00 To 25.00
Cameo, Bottle, Water, Green 15.00
Cameo, Bowl, Green, 7 1/4 In. 25.00
Cameo, Bowl, Vegetable, Oval, Green, 10 In. .... 11.00 To 13.50
Cameo, Butter, Cover, Green .... 95.00 To 130.00
Cameo, Candlestick, Green, Pair 60.00
Cameo, Candy Jar, Cover, Green, 6 1/2 In. 75.00
Cameo, Cookie Jar, Cover, Green .... 20.00 To 35.00
Cameo, Creamer, Green, 4 1/4 In. 14.00
Cameo, Cup & Saucer, Yellow 7.00
Cameo, Decanter, Stopper, Green 82.50
Cameo, Goblet, Green, 6 In. 35.00
Cameo, Grill Plate, Green .... 7.00 To 7.50
Cameo, Grill Plate, Yellow .... 4.00 To 6.00
Cameo, Jam Jar, Cover, Green, 2 In. 120.00
Cameo, Pitcher, Green, 5 3/4 In. 135.00
Cameo, Plate, Green, 8 In. .... 5.00 To 7.00
Cameo, Plate, Pink, 10 In. 32.00
Cameo, Plate, Square, Green, 8 1/2 In. 25.00
Cameo, Plate, Yellow, 6 In. 1.75
Cameo, Plate, Yellow, 9 1/2 In. 5.00
Cameo, Platter, Green, 12 In. 11.00
Cameo, Relish, 3 Sections, Footed, Green 15.00
Cameo, Salt & Pepper, Green .... 36.00 To 55.00
Cameo, Sherbet, Green, 4 7/8 In. 22.50
Cameo, Sherbet, Yellow, 4 7/8 In. 25.00
Cameo, Sugar & Creamer, Green, 3 1/4 In. 18.00
Cameo, Sugar & Creamer, Yellow, 3 1/4 In. 22.00
Cameo, Sugar, Green 5.00
Cameo, Tumbler, Footed, Green, 3 Oz. 30.00
Cameo, Tumbler, Footed, Green, 5 3/4 In. .... 29.50 To 40.00
Cameo, Tumbler, Footed, Yellow, 5 In. 9.00
Cameo, Vase, Green, 8 In. .... 15.00 To 18.50
Candlewick, Basket, Crystal, 6 1/2 In. 15.00
Candlewick, Butter, Cover, Beaded Base, Crystal, 1 Lb. 30.00
Candlewick, Goblet, Beaded Stem, Crystal, 7 In. 9.00
Candlewick, Jam Jar, Cover, Spoon, Beaded, Crystal 25.00
Candlewick, Plate, Crystal, 8 In. 6.00
Candlewick, Relish, 2 Sections, Crystal, 6 1/2 In. 12.00
Cape Cod, Cup, Crystal 6.00
    CAPRICE, see Cambridge
Caprice, Bowl, Nut, Square, Blue, 4 In. 22.00
Caprice, Candlestick, 3–Light, Blue 64.00
Caprice, Relish, 3 Sections, Blue, 8 In. 47.50
Century, Mayonnaise, Spoon, Divided, Crystal 20.00
    CHAIN DAISY, see Adam
    CHERRY, see Cherry Blossom

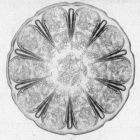

Cherry Blossom

Cameo

Cubist

Cherry Blossom, Berry Bowl, Pink, 4 3/4 In.	7.00
Cherry Blossom, Bowl, Delphite, 9 In.	25.00
Cherry Blossom, Butter, Cover, Green	35.00 To 65.00
Cherry Blossom, Cake Plate, Green	12.00 To 14.50
Cherry Blossom, Coaster, Green	7.50
Cherry Blossom, Creamer, Child's, Pink	22.00
Cherry Blossom, Cup & Saucer, Pink	16.00
Cherry Blossom, Grill Plate, Green	14.50
Cherry Blossom, Plate, Green, 6 In.	4.00
Cherry Blossom, Plate, Green, 9 In.	15.00
Cherry Blossom, Plate, Pink, 7 In.	11.00
Cherry Blossom, Platter, Pink, 13 In.	22.00 To 35.00
Cherry Blossom, Saucer, Green	2.00
Cherry Blossom, Saucer, Pink	2.00 To 2.50
Cherry Blossom, Sherbet, Pink	8.00 To 10.00
Cherry Blossom, Sugar & Creamer, Cover, Green	20.00 To 32.00
Cherry Blossom, Tray, Sandwich, Delphite	25.00
Cherry Blossom, Tray, Sandwich, Pink	15.00
Cherry Blossom, Tumbler, Footed, Green, 4 1/2 In.	15.00
Cherry Blossom, Tumbler, Footed, Pink, 3 3/4 In.	7.00
Cherry Blossom, Tumbler, Pink, 3 1/2 In.	8.00
Cherry Blossom, Tumbler, Scalloped Foot, Green, 4 1/2 In.	22.00
CHERRY–BERRY, see Strawberry	
Chico, Tumbler, Cobalt Blue, 9 Oz.	7.00
Chico, Tumbler, Cobalt Blue, 14 Oz.	8.00
Circle, Cup, Green	2.50
Circle, Goblet, Green, 8 Oz.	6.00
CIRCULAR RIBS, see Circle	
Cloverleaf, Ashtray, Black	42.00 To 55.00
Cloverleaf, Candy Dish, Cover, Green	25.00
Cloverleaf, Candy Dish, Cover, Yellow	85.00
Cloverleaf, Cup & Saucer, Black	13.50
Cloverleaf, Cup & Saucer, Green	4.00 To 8.50
Cloverleaf, Cup, Black	7.00
Cloverleaf, Cup, Pink	5.00
Cloverleaf, Grill Plate, Yellow	15.00
Cloverleaf, Plate, Black, 8 In.	10.00
Cloverleaf, Salt & Pepper, Black	52.00
Cloverleaf, Salt & Pepper, Green	25.00
Cloverleaf, Sherbet, Green	2.50 To 4.00
Cloverleaf, Sherbet, Yellow	8.00
Cloverleaf, Sugar & Creamer, Black	17.50 To 25.00

Cloverleaf, Tumbler, Footed, Yellow, 5 3/4 In. 20.00
Colonial Block, Creamer, Green 5.00
Colonial, Butter, Cover, Green 50.00
Colonial, Cup, Crystal 7.00
Colonial, Cup, Pink 3.00
Colonial, Goblet, Green, 4 In. .... 15.00 To 20.00
Colonial, Goblet, Green, 5 1/4 In. 17.00
Colonial, Goblet, Green, 5 3/4 In. 18.00
Colonial, Plate, Green, 6 In. .... 2.00 To 2.50
Colonial, Plate, Pink, 8 1/2 In. 4.00
Colonial, Saucer, Green 2.50
Colonial, Soup, Cream, Pink 25.00
Colonial, Sugar, Cover, Crystal 16.00
Colonial, Whiskey, Green 8.00
Columbia, Butter, Cover, Crystal .... 10.00 To 15.00
Columbia, Cup & Saucer, Crystal 4.00
Columbia, Plate, Crystal, 6 In. 1.00
Coronation, Berry Bowl, Ruby, 8 In. 10.00
Coronation, Bowl, Handle, Red, 4 1/2 In. 9.50
Coronation, Bowl, Red, 4 1/2 In. 3.50
Coronation, Sherbet, Pink 3.00
    CUBE, see Cubist
Cubist, Butter, Green 7.00
Cubist, Butter, Pink 10.00
Cubist, Candy Jar, Cover, Green 20.00
Cubist, Coaster, Pink 2.00
Cubist, Creamer, Pink, 3 In. 3.00
Cubist, Cup & Saucer, Green 5.00
Cubist, Pitcher, Pink .... 100.00 To 125.00
Cubist, Saltshaker, Pink 9.00
Cubist, Saucer, Green 1.00
Cubist, Sugar & Creamer, Pink, 2 In. 4.00
    DAISY, see No. 620
    DAISY PETALS, see Petalware
    DANCING GIRL, see Cameo
    DIAMOND, see Windsor
    DIAMOND PATTERN, see Miss America
    DIAMOND POINT, see Petalware
Diamond Quilted, Bowl, Green, 5 1/2 In. .... 3.00 To 4.00
Diamond Quilted, Saucer, Pink 2.00
Diamond Quilted, Sugar & Creamer, Pink 9.00
Diamond Quilted, Tumbler, Footed, 12 Oz. 10.00
Diana, Bowl, Crystal, 12 In. 3.00
Diana, Bowl, Pink, 5 In. 3.50
Diana, Candy Dish, Amber 24.00
Diana, Plate, Amber, 11 3/4 In. 4.00
Diana, Plate, Crystal, 11 3/4 In. .... 2.50 To 3.00
Dogwood, Cake Plate, Monax, 12 In. 20.00
Dogwood, Creamer, Pink 8.00
Dogwood, Cup & Saucer, Pink 12.50
Dogwood, Grill Plate, Pink 12.50
Dogwood, Plate, Green, 8 In. 5.50
Dogwood, Plate, Pink, 6 In. 3.00
Dogwood, Plate, Pink, 8 In. 4.00
Dogwood, Saucer, Pink .... 2.00 To 4.00
Dogwood, Sherbet, Pink 18.00
Dogwood, Sugar & Creamer, Pink, 2 1/2 In. 17.00
Doric & Pansy, Creamer, Child's, Pink .... 15.00 To 25.00
Doric & Pansy, Fruit Bowl, Handles, Ultramarine, 9 In. 35.00
Doric & Pansy, Plate, Sherbet, Ultramarine, 6 In. 5.00
Doric & Pansy, Saucer, Pink 2.00
    DORIC WITH PANSY, see Doric & Pansy
Doric, Berry Bowl, Green, 4 1/2 In. 5.50
Doric, Butter, Cover, Pink 55.00

Doric, Coaster, Pink .... 7.00 To 8.00
Doric, Cup, Green 5.00
Doric, Pitcher, Green, 6 In. 30.00
Doric, Plate, Pink, 9 In. 5.00
Doric, Relish, 4 Sections, Green 35.00
Doric, Salt & Pepper, Pink 20.00
Doric, Saucer, Pink 2.00
Doric, Sherbet, Footed, Delphite 4.00
Doric, Sugar, Cover, Pink 14.00
Doric, Tumbler, Pink, 4 1/2 In. 22.50
    DOUBLE SHIELD, see Mt. Pleasant
    DOUBLE SWIRL, see Swirl
    DRAPE & TASSEL, see Princess
    DUTCH, see Windmill
    DUTCH ROSE, see Rosemary
    EARLY AMERICAN HOBNAIL, see Hobnail
    EARLY AMERICAN ROCK CRYSTAL, see Rock Crystal
    ENGLISH HOBNAIL, see also Miss America
English Hobnail, Lamp, Pink, 9 1/4 In. 65.00
Fairfax, Saucer, Amber 3.00
    FAN & FEATHER, see Adam
    FINE RIB, see Homespun
    FLAT DIAMOND, see Diamond Quilted
Floragold, Butter, Cover, Oblong, Iridescent, 1/4 Lb. 15.00
Floragold, Candy Dish, Cover, Iridescent 35.00
Floragold, Pitcher, Pink 20.00
Floragold, Platter, Iridescent 12.00
Floragold, Salt & Pepper, Iridescent 40.00
Floragold, Sugar & Creamer, Cover, Iridescent 12.00
Floragold, Tumbler, Iridescent, 11 Oz. 10.00
Floral, Creamer, Green 9.00
Floral, Pitcher, Pink, 8 In. 11.00
Floral, Plate, Green, 9 In. 10.00
Floral, Salt & Pepper, Pink 26.00
Floral, Sherbet, Pink 7.00
Floral, Sugar, Cover, Pink 16.00
Floral, Tumbler, Footed, 5 1/4 In., 6 Piece 160.00
Floral, Tumbler, Footed, Pink, 4 3/4 In. 12.00
Florentine No.1, Berry Bowl, Pink, 5 In. 6.00
Florentine No.1, Berry Bowl, Pink, 8 1/2 In. 22.00
Florentine No.1, Butter, Cover, Green .... 95.00 To 100.00
Florentine No.1, Pitcher, Water, Green, 7 1/2 In. 45.00
Florentine No.1, Plate, Green, 10 In. 8.00
Florentine No.1, Plate, Pink, 8 1/2 In. 7.00
Florentine No.1, Platter, Oval, Green, 11 1/2 In. 8.00
Florentine No.1, Salt & Pepper, Yellow .... 40.00 To 45.00
Florentine No.1, Sherbet, Yellow 7.00
Florentine No.1, Sugar & Creamer, Pink 15.00
Florentine No.1, Sugar, Yellow 8.00
Florentine No.1, Tumbler, Footed, Yellow, 3 1/4 In. 13.00
Florentine No.2, Berry Bowl, Green, 4 1/2 In. 10.00
Florentine No.2, Candy Dish, Cover, Green 39.00
Florentine No.2, Cup & Saucer, Green 9.50
Florentine No.2, Custard Cup 24.00
Florentine No.2, Salt & Pepper, Green 30.00
Florentine No.2, Sherbet, Green 6.50
Florentine No.2, Soup, Cream, Blue 35.00
Florentine No.2, Soup, Cream, Green .... 8.50 To 10.50
Florentine No.2, Tumbler, Blue, 4 In. 50.00
Florentine No.2, Tumbler, Footed, Green, 3 1/4 In. 10.00
Florentine No.2, Tumbler, Green, 4 In. 11.00
    FLOWER BASKET, see No. 615
Flower Garden With Butterflies, Candy Jar, Blue 65.00
Flower Garden With Butterflies, Candy Jar, Cover, Yellow 165.00

Flower Garden, Tray, Pink, 10 In. 53.00
Fortune, Plate, Pink, 6 In. 2.00
    FOSTORIA, see American
    FROSTED BLOCK, see Beaded Block
Fruits, Saucer, Green 2.00
Georgian, Bowl, Green, 6 1/2 In. .... 25.00 To 40.00
Georgian, Butter, Cover, Pink 55.00
Georgian, Cup, Green 5.00
Georgian, Plate, Green, 8 In. 5.00
Georgian, Platter, Green, 11 1/2 In. 45.00
Georgian, Sherbet, Green 5.00
Georgian, Sugar & Creamer, Cover, 3 In. 29.00
Georgian, Sugar, Green 4.00
Georgian, Tumbler, Green, 4 In. 28.00
Georgian, Tumbler, Green, 5 1/4 In. 65.00
    GLADIOLI, see Royal Lace
Grape, Salt & Pepper, Green 15.00
    HAIRPIN, see Newport
    HANGING BASKET, see No. 615
Harp, Ashtray, Crystal 1.25
Harp, Ashtray, Iridescent 2.50
Harp, Cake Plate, Crystal .... 10.00 To 13.00
Harp, Cake Plate, Iridescent 22.00
Harp, Cup, Pink 4.50
Harp, Plate, Pink, 7 In. 3.00
Harp, Tray, Rectangular, Crystal, Gold Trim 12.00
Heritage, Berry Bowl, Crystal, 5 In. 3.00
Heritage, Creamer, Crystal 18.00
Heritage, Cup & Saucer, Crystal .... 3.00 To 3.50
Heritage, Plate, Crystal, 9 1/4 In. 5.50
    HEX OPTIC, see Hexagon Optic
Hexagon Optic, Pitcher, Pink, 9 In. 24.00
    HINGE, see Patrician
Hobnail, Cup & Saucer, Pink 4.00
Hobnail, Cup, Pink 3.00
Holiday, Butter, Cover, Pink 35.00
Holiday, Chop Plate, Pink, 13 3/4 In. 70.00
Holiday, Creamer, Pink 5.00
Holiday, Cup & Saucer, Pink 7.00
Holiday, Pitcher, Pink, 4 3/4 In. 48.00
Holiday, Plate, Pink, 9 In. 9.00
Holiday, Sherbet, Pink .... 3.50 To 5.00

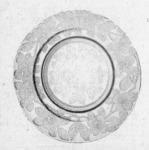

Dogwood

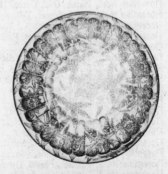

Floral

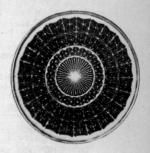

Florentine No. 1   Florentine No. 2   Holiday

Holiday, Soup, Dish, Pink	32.50
Holiday, Sugar, Cover, Pink	16.50
Holiday, Tumbler, Pink, 4 In.	14.00
Homespun, Butter, Cover, Pink	37.50
Homespun, Tumbler, Footed, Pink, 4 In.	6.00
HONEYCOMB, see Hexagon Optic	
HORIZONTAL FINE RIB, see Manhattan	
HORIZONTAL RIBBED, see Manhattan	
HORIZONTAL ROUNDED BIG RIB, see Manhattan	
HORIZONTAL SHARP BIG RIB, see Manhattan	
HORSESHOE, see No. 612	
IRIS & HERRINGBONE, see Iris	
Iris, Bowl, Beaded Edge, Iridescent, 8 In.	9.50
Iris, Bowl, Crystal, 9 1/2 In.	6.50
Iris, Bowl, Ruffled, Crystal, 5 In.	5.50
Iris, Bowl, Ruffled, Iridescent, 11 In.	6.00
Iris, Butter, Cover, Iridescent	25.00 To 32.00
Iris, Candy Jar, Cover, Crystal	70.00
Iris, Creamer, Crystal	4.00
Iris, Cup & Saucer, Crystal	12.00
Iris, Goblet, Crystal, 4 Oz., 5 3/4 In.	10.00
Iris, Pitcher, Iridescent	25.00
Iris, Plate, Crystal, 5 1/2 In.	4.00
Iris, Plate, Crystal, 8 In.	40.00
Iris, Sherbet, Iridescent, 2 1/2 In.	9.00
Iris, Tumbler, Footed, Crystal, 6 In.	10.00
Iris, Water Set, Crystal, 9 Piece	85.00
JADITE, see also Jane–Ray	
Jadite, Casserole, 1 Qt.	12.50
JANE–RAY, see also Jadite	
Jane–Ray, Cup & Saucer, Jadite	2.75
Jane–Ray, Eggcup, Jadite	3.50
Jane–Ray, Mug, Jadite	3.50
Jane–Ray, Plate, Jadite, 7 In.	3.00
Jane–Ray, Plate, Jadite, 9 In.	2.75
Jane–Ray, Soup, Dish, Jadite	5.00
Jane–Ray, Sugar & Creamer, Cover, Jadite	9.00
Jubilee, Cup & Saucer, Yellow	15.00
Jubilee, Plate, Yellow, 7 In.	7.25
Jubilee, Sugar, Yellow	16.50
KNIFE & FORK, see Colonial	
LACE EDGE, see also Coronation	

Lace Edge, Bowl, Pink, 6 3/8 In. 5.50
Lace Edge, Bowl, Pink, 7 3/4 In. 10.00
Lace Edge, Butter, Cover, Pink .... 42.50 To 50.00
Lace Edge, Cup & Saucer, Pink .... 21.00 To 22.00
Lace Edge, Grill Plate, Pink 10.00
Lace Edge, Plate, Pink, 7 1/4 In. .... 12.50 To 13.00
Lace Edge, Platter, 5 Sections, Pink 15.00
Lace Edge, Platter, Pink, 12 3/4 In. 25.00
Lace Edge, Relish, 5 Sections, Pink 14.00
Lace Edge, Tumbler, Footed, Pink, 5 In. 43.00
Lace Edge, Vase, Pink, 7 In. 165.00
    LACY DAISY, see No. 618
Laurel, Cup, Jade 2.50
    LILY MEDALLION, see American Sweetheart
    LINCOLN DRAPE, see Princess
    LITTLE HOSTESS, see Moderntone
    LOOP, see Lace Edge
    LORAIN, see No. 615
    LOUISA, see Floragold
    LOVEBIRDS, see Georgian
    LYDIA RAY, see New Century
Lydia Ray, Butter, Cover, Green 45.00
Lydia Ray, Salt & Pepper, Green 25.00
Madrid, Bowl, Amber, 8 In. 15.00
Madrid, Butter, Cover, Amber .... 37.50 To 55.00
Madrid, Cake Plate, Amber 10.00
Madrid, Candlestick, Pink, Pair 13.00
Madrid, Cookie Jar, Cover, Amber .... 30.00 To 37.50
Madrid, Creamer, Amber .... 4.00 To 5.00
Madrid, Cup & Saucer, Crystal 5.00
Madrid, Cup, Amber 4.50
Madrid, Cup, Pink 4.00
Madrid, Pitcher, Green, 8 In. 65.00
Madrid, Pitcher, Ice Lip, Amber, 8 1/2 In. 85.00
Madrid, Plate, Amber, 6 In. 1.75
Madrid, Plate, Green, 7 1/2 In. 4.50
Madrid, Platter, Amber, 11 1/2 In. 10.00
Madrid, Salt & Pepper, Footed, Green 75.00
Madrid, Sherbet, Cone Shape, Amber 5.50
Madrid, Soup, Dish, Amber 7.50
Madrid, Sugar, Amber 3.50
Madrid, Sugar, Green 4.50
Madrid, Tumbler, Green, 5 1/2 In. 23.00
    MAGNOLIA, see Dogwood
Manhattan, Berry Bowl, Pink, 5 3/8 In. 3.00
Manhattan, Bowl, Crystal, 4 1/2 In. 3.50
Manhattan, Candlestick, Square, Crystal, Pair 5.00
Manhattan, Cup & Saucer, Crystal 12.00
Manhattan, Plate, Crystal, 14 In. 8.50
Manhattan, Relish, 4 Sections, Crystal, 14 In. 6.00
Manhattan, Saucer, Crystal, 4 1/2 In. 3.50
Manhattan, Sugar, Pink .... 3.00 To 4.50
    MANY WINDOWS, see Roulette
    MAYFAIR, see Mayfair Open Rose
Mayfair Federal, Sugar & Creamer, Amber 18.00
Mayfair Open Rose, Bowl, Pink, 7 In. 11.50
Mayfair Open Rose, Bowl, Vegetable, Blue, 10 In. 37.00
Mayfair Open Rose, Butter, Cover, Blue .... 200.00 To 225.00
Mayfair Open Rose, Butter, Cover, Pink 45.00
Mayfair Open Rose, Cake Plate, Pink .... 12.00 To 20.00
Mayfair Open Rose, Candy Jar, Cover, Pink .... 26.00 To 32.50
Mayfair Open Rose, Cookie Jar, Cover, Blue 100.00
Mayfair Open Rose, Cookie Jar, Cover, Pink 27.50
Mayfair Open Rose, Cup & Saucer, Pink 14.00

Mayfair Open Rose, Cup, Blue .... 25.00 To 30.00
Mayfair Open Rose, Decanter, Stopper, Pink ....95.00 To 100.00
Mayfair Open Rose, Goblet, Pink, 4 1/2 In. 40.00
Mayfair Open Rose, Grill Plate, Pink 22.00
Mayfair Open Rose, Pitcher, Blue, 8 In. ....90.00 To 125.00
Mayfair Open Rose, Pitcher, Pink, 6 In. 25.00
Mayfair Open Rose, Plate, Pink, 8 1/2 In. .... 12.00 To 16.00
Mayfair Open Rose, Plate, Pink, 9 1/2 In. .... 29.50 To 35.00
Mayfair Open Rose, Relish, 4 Sections, Pink 16.00
Mayfair Open Rose, Salt & Pepper, Pink .... 33.00 To 40.00
Mayfair Open Rose, Sandwich Server, Green 37.00
Mayfair Open Rose, Sherbet, Footed, Pink, 3 In. 10.00
Mayfair Open Rose, Soup, Cream, Pink .... 28.00 To 32.50
Mayfair Open Rose, Sugar & Creamer, Pink 28.50
Mayfair Open Rose, Sugar, Pink ....8.00 To 14.00
Mayfair Open Rose, Tumbler, Footed, Pink, 6 1/2 In. 20.00
  MEADOW FLOWER, see No. 618
  MEANDERING VINE, see Madrid
  MISS AMERICA, see also English Hobnail
Miss America, Berry Bowl, Green, 4 1/2 In. 5.00
Miss America, Butter, Cover, Pink 250.00
Miss America, Cake Plate, Pink 20.00
Miss America, Candy Jar, Cover, Pink .... 68.00 To 75.00
Miss America, Celery Dish, Pink, 10 1/2 In. 18.00
Miss America, Creamer, Pink 10.00
Miss America, Cup, Green 15.00
Miss America, Jam Jar, Cover, Green 35.00
Miss America, Plate, Crystal, 10 1/4 In. 6.00
Miss America, Plate, Green, 6 3/4 In. 6.00
Miss America, Platter, Oval, Pink 16.00
Miss America, Relish, Crystal, 11 3/4 In. ....8.00 To 12.00
Miss America, Salt & Pepper, Pink 40.00
Miss America, Saltshaker, Pink 20.00
Miss America, Sherbet, Pink .ₐ 10.00
Miss America, Tumbler, Pink, 4 1/2 In. 20.00
  MODERNE ART, see Tea Room
Moderntone, Ashtray, Pink .... 45.00 To 52.00
Moderntone, Creamer, Cobalt Blue .... 6.00 To 7.50
Moderntone, Cup & Saucer, Cobalt Blue 9.00
Moderntone, Cup, Cobalt Blue 7.50
Moderntone, Custard Cup, Amethyst 12.00
Moderntone, Plate, Amethyst, 10 1/2 In. 12.50
Moderntone, Platter, Cobalt Blue, 11 In. 30.00
Moderntone, Punch Cup, Cobalt Blue 6.50
Moderntone, Salt & Pepper, Cobalt Blue .... 23.00 To 27.50
Moderntone, Salt & Pepper, Platonite 10.00
Moderntone, Salt & Pepper, Yellow .... 20.00 To 25.00
Moderntone, Sugar & Creamer, Cobalt Blue 15.00
Moondrops, Butter, Cover, Cobalt Blue 280.00
Moondrops, Butter, Cover, Red .... 280.00 To 300.00
Moonstone, Plate, Crystal, 8 1/2 In. 9.00
Moonstone, Powder Box, Crystal 12.50
Moonstone, Relish, Divided, Crystal, 7 3/4 In. 7.50
Moonstone, Sherbet, Crystal 6.00
Moonstone, Vase, Crystal, 5 1/2 In. 5.50
Moonstone, Vase, Green, 5 1/2 In. 5.00
Mt.Pleasant, Creamer, Cobalt Blue 6.00
Mt.Pleasant, Cup & Saucer, Cobalt Blue 6.00
Mt.Pleasant, Saucer, Amethyst 8.00
Mt.Pleasant, Saucer, Cobalt Blue 2.00
Mt.Pleasant, Sherbet, Cobalt Blue 6.00
Mt.Pleasant, Sugar & Creamer, Cobalt Blue 12.00
New Century, Creamer, Green 3.00
New Century, Plate, Green, 6 In. 1.50

New Century, Salt & Pepper, Green 25.00
New Century, Sugar, Green 4.00
Newport, Cup, Amethyst 6.00
    NO. 601, see Avocado
No.610, Tumbler, Footed, Green, 8 Oz. 25.00
No.612, Berry Bowl, Green, 9 1/2 In. 25.00
No.612, Creamer, Green 10.00
No.612, Creamer, Yellow 15.00
No.612, Cup & Saucer, Green 7.50
No.612, Plate, Green, 8 3/8 In. 6.00
No.612, Relish, Yellow 21.00
No.612, Sherbet, Green 7.00
No.612, Sugar, Green 7.00
No.615, Cup & Saucer, Yellow 12.00
No.615, Plate, Green, 10 1/4 In. 27.00
No.615, Plate, Yellow, 8 In. 7.00
No.615, Tumbler, Footed, Green 17.00
No.618, Sugar & Creamer, Amber 10.00
No.620, Berry Bowl, Amber, 9 In. 17.00
No.620, Sugar & Creamer, Amber 12.00
    NO. 622, see Pretzel
Normandie, Cup & Saucer, Pink .... 5.50 To 7.00
Normandie, Grill Plate, Iridescent 7.00
Normandie, Pitcher, Amber 50.00
Normandie, Plate, Pink, 8 In. 5.00
Normandie, Tumbler, Amber, 4 1/4 In. 8.50
Old Cafe, Bowl, Pink, 5 1/2 In. 3.00
Old Cafe, Candy Dish, Cover, Crystal 4.00
Old Cafe, Cup, Pink 3.00
Old Cafe, Sherbet, Pink 4.50
Old Cafe, Tumbler, Pink, 3 In. 4.00
Old English, Pitcher, Green 38.00
    OLD FLORENTINE, see Florentine No. 1
    OPALESCENT HOBNAIL, see Moonstone
    OPEN LACE, see Lace Edge
    OPEN ROSE, see Mayfair Open Rose
    OPEN SCALLOP, see Lace Edge
    ORIENTAL POPPY, see Florentine No. 2
    OVIDE, see New Century
Oyster & Pearl, Bowl, Pink, 6 1/2 In. 5.00
Oyster & Pearl, Relish, Pink 5.00
    PANELED ASTER, see Madrid

Iris, Beaded Edge   Madrid   Mayfair Open Rose

PANELED CHERRY BLOSSOM, see Cherry Blossom
PANSY & DORIC, see Doric & Pansy
PARROT, see Sylvan
Patrician, Bowl, Amber, 6 In. .... 6.00 To 8.00
Patrician, Bowl, Green, 8 1/2 In. 25.00
Patrician, Butter, Cover, Green 90.00
Patrician, Creamer, Green 9.00
Patrician, Cup, Amber 4.00
Patrician, Grill Plate, Amber 7.50
Patrician, Jam Jar, Amber 14.00
Patrician, Plate, Amber, 10 1/2 In. 3.00
Patrician, Saltshaker, Green 25.00
Patrician, Saucer, Amber 1.00
Patrician, Sherbet, Amber 6.50
Patrician, Sherbet, Green .... 5.00 To 6.00
Patrician, Soup, Cream, Green .... 10.00 To 12.00
Patrician, Sugar & Creamer, Green 18.00
Patrician, Sugar, Amber .... 5.00 To 6.50
Patrician, Tumbler, Amber, 4 In. 15.00
Patrician, Tumbler, Green, 4 1/2 In. 18.50
PETAL, see Petalware
PETAL SWIRL, see Swirl
Petalware, Bowl, Pink, 5 3/4 In. 5.00
Petalware, Creamer, Cobalt Blue 7.00
Petalware, Creamer, Pink 8.00
Petalware, Cup & Saucer, Monax 5.50
Petalware, Lamp Shade, Monax, 6 3/8 In. 4.00
Petalware, Plate, Colored Rings, 11 In. 10.00
Petalware, Plate, Pink, 9 In. 6.50
Petalware, Platter, Pink 10.00
Petalware, Saucer, Cobalt Blue .... 1.50 To 2.00
Petalware, Sugar, Pink 5.75
PINEAPPLE & FLORAL, see No. 618
PINWHEEL, see Sierra
POINSETTIA, see Floral
POPPY NO. 1, see Florentine No. 1
POPPY NO. 2, see Florentine No. 2
Pretzel, Celery Dish, Crystal .... 1.50 To 2.00
Pretzel, Creamer, Crystal 3.00
Pretzel, Pitcher, Crystal 65.00
Pretzel, Sugar, Crystal 3.00
PRIMUS, see Madrid
Princess, Bowl, Octagonal, Green, 9 In. 22.50
Princess, Bowl, Pink, 10 In. 12.50
Princess, Butter, Cover, Green 50.00
Princess, Cookie Jar, Cover, Pink 37.50
Princess, Cup & Saucer, Green 9.00
Princess, Cup & Saucer, Topaz 10.00
Princess, Grill Plate, Topaz .... 3.00 To 4.50
Princess, Pitcher, Green, 6 In. 37.00
Princess, Plate, Green, 5 1/2 In. 3.00
Princess, Plate, Yellow, 8 In. 6.00
Princess, Plate, Yellow, 9 In. 7.00
Princess, Platter, Green 20.00
Princess, Sherbet, Pink 11.00
Princess, Sherbet, Topaz 20.00
Princess, Sugar, Cover, Green 18.00
Princess, Tumbler, Green, 4 In. 15.00
PRISMATIC LINE, see Queen Mary
PROVINCIAL, see Bubble
PYRAMID, see No. 610
Queen Mary, Berry Bowl, Pink, 8 3/4 In. 4.50
Queen Mary, Bowl, Pink, 4 In. 2.00
Queen Mary, Bowl, Pink, 6 In. 5.00

Miss America

Moderntone

Queen Mary, Butter, Cover, Pink	75.00
Queen Mary, Candy Dish, Cover, Crystal	14.00
Queen Mary, Creamer, Pink	4.00
Queen Mary, Plate, 9 3/4 In.	20.00
Queen Mary, Plate, Pink, 12 In.	6.50
RASPBERRY BAND, see Laurel	
REX, see No. 610	
RIBBED, see Manhattan	
RIBBON CANDY, see Pretzel	
Ribbon, Berry Bowl, Green, 4 In.	7.00
Ribbon, Candy Dish, Cover, Green	18.00 To 20.00
Ribbon, Plate, Green, 6 1/4 In.	1.00
Ribbon, Sherbet, Green	1.50 To 2.50
Ribbon, Sugar & Creamer, Green	6.00
Ribbon, Sugar, Green	4.50
Ring, Whiskey, Crystal	3.00
Rock Crystal, Bowl, Footed, Crystal, 12 1/2 In.	28.00
Rock Crystal, Compote, Amber	32.00
Rock Crystal, Goblet, Crystal, 7 1/2 In.	13.50
Rock Crystal, Relish, 6 Sections, Crystal	17.00
Rock Crystal, Sugar, Red	25.00
Rose Cameo, Sugar Shaker, Green	10.00
ROSE LACE, see Royal Lace	
ROSEMARY, see also Mayfair Federal	
Rosemary, Berry Bowl, Amber, 5 In.	4.50 To 5.00
Rosemary, Bowl, Oval, Green, 10 In.	12.50
Rosemary, Creamer, Amber	8.00
Rosemary, Cup & Saucer, Amber	12.00
Rosemary, Plate, Amber, 9 1/2 In.	5.25 To 8.50
Rosemary, Platter, Amber	9.00
Rosemary, Saucer, Green	2.00
Rosemary, Soup, Cream, Amber	10.00
Rosemary, Sugar & Creamer, Amber	18.00
Rosemary, Sugar & Creamer, Green	20.00
Rosemary, Sugar, Green	13.50
Roulette, Cup & Saucer, Green	5.50
Roulette, Plate, Green, 8 1/2 In.	5.00
Roulette, Whiskey, Pink	6.50
Royal Lace, Bowl, Footed, Cobalt Blue, 10 In.	42.50
Royal Lace, Bowl, Green, 10 In.	25.00
Royal Lace, Bowl, Oval, Pink, 11 In.	17.00
Royal Lace, Butter, Cover, Crystal	35.00

Royal Lace, Cookie Jar, Cover, Green .... 45.00 To 65.00
Royal Lace, Creamer, Cobalt Blue 27.50
Royal Lace, Cup & Saucer, Pink 12.00
Royal Lace, Grill Plate, Cobalt Blue 22.50
Royal Lace, Pitcher, Cobalt Blue, 48 Oz. 95.00
Royal Lace, Salt & Pepper, Pink 35.00
Royal Lace, Saucer, Cobalt Blue .... 6.00 To 6.50
Royal Lace, Soup, Cream, Cobalt Blue 20.00
Royal Lace, Soup, Cream, Pink 15.00
Royal Lace, Sugar & Creamer, Cobalt Blue 42.00
Royal Lace, Sugar, Cover, Crystal 29.50
Royal Lace, Tumbler, Green, 4 1/8 In. 20.00
    RUSSIAN, see Holiday
S Pattern, Sugar & Creamer, Yellow 10.00
S Pattern, Tumbler, Crystal, 3 1/2 In. 5.00
S Pattern, Water Set, Crystal, 7 Piece 85.00
    SAIL BOAT, see White Ship
    SAILING SHIP, see White Ship
Sandwich Anchor Hocking, Bowl, Red, 5 1/4 In. 10.00
Sandwich Anchor Hocking, Cup & Saucer, Amber 5.50
Sandwich Anchor Hocking, Plate, Green, 9 In. 25.00
    SAWTOOTH, see English Hobnail
    SAXON, see Coronation
    SHAMROCK, see Cloverleaf
Sharon, Berry Bowl, Amber, 5 In. 4.75
Sharon, Berry Bowl, Green, 5 In. 8.00
Sharon, Berry Bowl, Pink, 8 1/2 In. .... 13.00 To 17.25
Sharon, Bowl, Oval, Pink, 9 1/2 In. .... 14.00 To 16.00
Sharon, Bowl, Pink, 6 In. .... 14.50 To 15.00
Sharon, Butter, Cover, Amber .... 35.00 To 40.00
Sharon, Butter, Cover, Pink .... 37.00 To 45.00
Sharon, Cake Plate, Pink 25.00
Sharon, Candy Jar, Cover, Amber 27.50
Sharon, Creamer, Pink .... 7.00 To 9.50
Sharon, Cup & Saucer, Amber 11.00
Sharon, Cup & Saucer, Pink 12.50
Sharon, Pitcher, Ice Lip, Amber 80.00
Sharon, Plate, Green, 9 1/2 In. 13.00
Sharon, Plate, Pink, 6 In. .... 2.00 To 4.00
Sharon, Plate, Pink, 9 1/2 In. 9.50
Sharon, Salt & Pepper, Green .... 50.00 To 55.00
Sharon, Salt & Pepper, Pink .... 30.00 To 35.00
Sharon, Saltshaker, Amber 12.00
Sharon, Soup, Cream, Pink 25.00
Sharon, Sugar & Creamer, Amber 10.00
Sharon, Sugar, Cover, Pink 29.00
Sharon, Tumbler, Green, 5 1/4 In. 60.00
Sharon, Tumbler, Pink, 5 1/4 In. 22.00
    SHELL, see Petalware
Sierra, Butter, Cover, Green .... 45.00 To 47.00
Sierra, Cup & Saucer, Green 13.00
Sierra, Cup & Saucer, Pink 11.50
Sierra, Plate, Pink, 9 In. 9.75
Sierra, Platter, Pink 22.00
Sierra, Tumbler, Footed, Green, 4 1/2 In. 33.00
    SMOCKING, see Windsor
    SNOWFLAKE, see Doric
    SPIRAL OPTIC, see Spiral
Spiral, Ice Tub, Green 11.00
Spiral, Sherbet, Green .... 3.00 To 4.00
Spiral, Water Set, Green, 6 Piece 75.00
    SPOKE, see Patrician
Starlight, Cup, Crystal 1.50
Starlight, Salt & Pepper, Crystal 6.00

STIPPLED ROSE BAND, see S Pattern
Strawberry, Berry Bowl, Green, 7 1/2 In. 22.00
Strawberry, Berry Bowl, Pink, Small 10.00
Strawberry, Sherbet, Green 8.50
Sunflower, Cake Plate, Green .... 6.00 To 7.00
   SWEET PEAR, see Avocado
Swirl, Ashtray, Ultramarine 10.00
Swirl, Berry Set, Pink, 11 Piece 16.00
Swirl, Cake Plate, Ultramarine 10.00
Swirl, Creamer, Ultramarine 5.00
Swirl, Plate, Sandwich, Ultramarine, 12 1/2 In. 11.50
Swirl, Plate, Ultramarine, 9 1/4 In. 10.00
Swirl, Saucer, Ultramarine 1.00
Swirl, Sugar & Creamer, Ultramarine 19.00
Swirl, Vase, Ultramarine, 8 1/2 In. 15.00
   SWIRLED BIG RIB, see Spiral
   SWIRLED SHARP RIB, see Diana
Sylvan, Cup, Green 20.00
Sylvan, Grill Plate, Green 15.00
Sylvan, Salt & Pepper, Green 235.00
Sylvan, Sugar, Green .... 14.00 To 18.00
   TASSELL, see Princess
Tea Room, Cup & Saucer, Pink 12.50
Tea Room, Pitcher, Crystal 115.00
Tea Room, Salt & Pepper, Pink 25.00
Tea Room, Sugar & Creamer, Green, 4 1/2 In. 27.50
Tea Room, Tumbler, Footed, Green, 5 1/2 In. .... 12.00 To 14.00
Thistle, Cup, Green 17.00
Thistle, Plate, Pink, 8 In. .... 6.00 To 8.50
   THREADING, see Old English
   THREE PARROT, see Sylvan
Twisted Optic, Candy Jar, Cover, Green 18.00
Twisted Optic, Jam Jar, Green 14.00
Twisted Optic, Plate, Oval, Green, 7 1/2 In. 2.50
Versailles, Bowl, Blue, 5 In. 17.50
Versailles, Cruet, Blue 300.00
Versailles, Cup & Saucer, Blue 25.00
Versailles, Plate, Blue, 7 1/2 In. 8.00
Versailles, Relish, Divided, Blue 40.00
   VERTICAL RIBBED, see Queen Mary
   VIVID BANDS, see Petalware
   WAFFLE, see Waterford

Mt. Pleasant   No. 612   Normandie

Waterford, Berry Bowl, Crystal, 8 1/4 In. 4.00
Waterford, Goblet, 5 1/4 In. 9.50
Waterford, Relish, 5 Sections, Crystal .... 10.00 To 11.00
Waterford, Sherbet, Crystal 2.00
Waterford, Sugar, Cover, Crystal 3.00
    WEDDING BAND, see Moderntone
    WHITE SAIL, see White Ship
White Ship, Roly Poly, Blue 7.50
White Ship, Tumbler, Blue 10.00
    WILD ROSE, see Dogwood
    WILDFLOWER, see No. 618
    WILDROSE WITH APPLE BLOSSOM, see Flower Garden with Butterflies
Windmill, Cocktail Shaker, Stirrer, Blue 17.50
Windmill, Tumbler, Blue, 8 Oz. 10.00
    WINDSOR DIAMOND, see Windsor
Windsor, Berry Bowl, Pink, 4 3/4 In. 2.50
Windsor, Cup, Green 4.50
Windsor, Pitcher, Green, 6 3/4 In. 28.00
Windsor, Plate, Sandwich, Green, 10 1/4 In. 10.00
Windsor, Salt & Pepper, Green 30.00
Windsor, Sherbet, Pink 3.50
Windsor, Sugar, Cover, Pink 15.00
Windsor, Tumbler, Footed, Crystal, 7 1/4 In. 6.00
Windsor, Tumbler, Pink, 5 In. 12.00
    WINGED MEDALLION, see Madrid

Derby porcelain was made in Derby, England, from 1756 to the present. The factory changed names and marks several times. Chelsea Derby (1770–1784), Crown Derby (1784–1811), and the modern Royal Crown Derby are some of the most famous periods of the factory.

    DERBY, see also Chelsea; Crown Derby; Royal Crown Derby
DERBY, Candle Snuffer, Figural, Woman & Monk, 19th Century, Pair 750.00
Candlestick, Figural, Harlequin & Punch, C.1810, 9 7/8 In., Pair 5500.00
Chamberstick, Floral Sprigs, Octafoil, Green Stem Handle, 5 1/8 In. 715.00
Group, Ewe & Lamb, Low Mound Base, 4 3/4 X 5 1/4 In., Pair 1100.00
Plate, Floral Circular Center, Gold Wheat, C.1830, 5 In. 250.00
Sweetmeat Stand, Figural, Woman & Man, Carrying Shell, 9 5/8 In. 1450.00

The DeVilbiss Company has made atomizers of all types since 1888 but no longer makes the perfume bottle tops so popular with collectors. These were made from 1920 to 1968. The glass bottle may be by any of many manufacturers even if the atomizer says DeVilbiss.

DEVILBISS, Bottle, Atomizer, Art Deco, Paper Label, 4 In. 60.00
Bottle, Perfume, Atomizer, Pedestal, Amethyst, Paper Label 125.00
Bottle, Perfume, Atomizer, White Opalescent, Feather Swirl 45.00
Bottle, Perfume, Penguin 95.00
Bottle, Perfume, Plunger Type, Crackle Glass 75.00

The comic strip "Dick Tracy" started in 1931. He was the hero of movies from 1937 to 1947, starred in a radio series in the 1940s and a television series in the 1950s. Memorabilia from all these activities is collected.

DICK TRACY, Aurora Moon Model Kit .... 100.00 To 125.00
Badge, Detective Club, Gold, Red, Black, Metal Shield 15.00
Badge, Lieutenant/Secret Service Patrol 70.00
Book, Big Little Book, Chains of Crime, 1936 .... 20.00
Book, Big Little Book, Dick Tracy & Yogee Yamma 15.00
Book, Comic, Motorola TV 12.00
Book, Paint, 1935 .... 6.00
Book, Pop-Up, 1930s 95.00
Booklet, Big Thrill Chewing Gum, Vault of Death, No.3, 1934 .... 25.00
Button, Left Profile, Red, Blue, White Ground, 1 3/4 In. 25.00

Car, Marx, 20 In. 175.00
Code Maker, Box 14.00
Crime Stoppers Set 35.00
Dart Board, 1941 .... 25.00
Doll, Bonnie Braids, Dick's Baby, Keywind, Creeping Action, Marx 125.00
Film, Acme No.1, Box 15.00
Game, Crime Stopper, 1961 .... 20.00
Game, Dick Tracy The Master Detective, 1961 .... 10.00
Handcuffs, Tin, On Litho Card, 1950s 17.50
Kiddie Kamera & Film Viewer, 2 Films, 1934 .... 50.00
Kit, Fingerprint 6.00
Light Bulb, Christmas Tree, Dick Tracy 45.00
Lunch Box 25.00
Pin, Secret Service Patrol Member, Girls' Division, Metal 8.00
Pistol, Siren, Signed Chester Gould 125.00
Plate, Mugg & Tracy, Square, 9 In. 65.00
Pocket Knife 40.00
Poster, Tracy Versus Crime, 1930 .... 75.00
Submachine Gun, Picture On Gun, Dated 1951, Box 195.00
Target, 1941 .... 45.00
Toy, Car, Squad, Dick Tracy, No.1, Tin Litho, Marx .... 40.00 To 60.00
Toy, Copmobile, 24 In. 95.00
Wallet, Crime Stoppers, 1950s 7.50
Wristwatch, Leather Band, Box 135.00
   DICKENS WARE, see Royal Doulton; Weller

The Dionne quintuplets were born in Canada on May 28, 1934. The publicity about their birth and their special status as wards of the Canadian government made them famous throughout the world. Visitors could watch the girls play, reporters interviewed the girls and the staff, and thousands of special dolls and souvenirs were made picturing the quints at different ages. Emilie died in 1954, Marie in 1970. Yvonne, Annette, and Cecile still live in Canada.

DIONNE QUINTUPLETS, Album, Picture 25.00
Blotter, Portrait, 1935 .... 9.00
Book, We're Two Years Old 25.00
Calendar, 1938, Framed 35.00
Calendar, 1939, Full Color of Girls On Farm, We Are 5 .... 30.00
Calendar, 1950, Sweet Sixteen 15.00
Doll, 8 In.Quints & 12 In.Nurse, Composition, 1930s 1000.00
Doll, Composition, With 4 In.Nurse, Box, 1930s 175.00
Fan, 1936 .... 22.00
Magazine, Life, Quints On Cover, First Communion, 1940 .... 20.00
Paper Doll, With Clothes, Cut 95.00
Sheet Music 15.00
Spoon Set, 5 Piece 90.00

Walt Disney and his company introduced many comic characters to the world. Collectors search for examples of the work of the Disney Studios and the many commercial products modeled after his characters. These collectibles are called "Disneyana."

DISNEYANA, Alarm Clock, Bradley, Yellow & Red, Germany 115.00
Album, Snow White, Souvenir Song, 50 Pages, 1938, Walt Disney 45.00
Ashtray, Bambi, Goebel 125.00
Ashtray, Three Little Pigs, Lusterware China, 1930s 85.00
Ball, Mickey Mouse, Rubber, 5 In. 12.00
Bank, Donald Duck, Composition, Sailor, Lifesaver, 1930s 130.00
Bank, Donald Duck, Figural, Deerwood Coffee, Glass 75.00
Bank, Mickey Mouse, Phone 25.00
Bank, Mickey Mouse, Pride Lines, Mechanical 175.00
Bank, Uncle Scrooge, Ceramic, 1961, Box 15.00
Banner, Sunoco, Mickey Mouse, Canvas, 1935, 5 X 3 Ft. 750.00
Blocks, Puzzle, Snow White, Litho Paper On Wood, 6 Solutions 85.00
Book, Adventures of Mickey Mouse, No.1, Hardcover 65.00

Book, Bambi's Big Day, Pop–Up 10.00
Book, Coloring, Disneyland, 1961 .... 15.00
Book, Donald Duck, Bringing Up Boys 15.00
Book, Mickey Mouse, Coloring, Dot To Dot, Tracing, 1957 .... 9.00
Book, Mickey Mouse, Pop–Up, Circus, 1933 .... 300.00
Book, Mickey Sees The USA, Walt Disney Prod., Copyright 1944 .... 25.00
Book, Paint, 1937 .... 25.00
Book, Pluto The Pup, Big Little Book, Whitman, 1938 .... 22.00
Book, Walt Disney's Big Book, Whitman, 124 Pages, 1958 .... 10.00
Book, Your Visit To Walt Disney's Magic Kingdom, Photos, 1955 .... 35.00
Bookplates, Bookmark, Ruler, Walt Disney, Original Card, 1950s 27.00
Bottle, Donald Duck, 1957, 6 In. 75.00
Bottle, Soda, Donald Duck, 6 Pack 25.00
Bowl, Fantasia, Mushroom, Green, Vernon Kilns 120.00
Bowl, Fantasia, Winged Nymph, Pink, Vernon Kilns 175.00
Box, Crayon, Mickey Mouse & Donald, Tin, Dated 1939 .... 35.00
Button, Pinback, Walt Disney World Centennial Press Club 30.00
Camera, Donald Duck, Marked Walt Disney Production, Chicago 35.00
Camera, Mickey Mouse, Fisher Price 25.00
Car, Mickey Mouse, Windup, Marx, 4 In. 185.00
Car, Racing, Mickey Mouse, Windup, 4 In. .... 185.00 To 200.00
Card Table, Walt Disney 39.00
Card, Ichabod & Mr.Toad, Animated, Disney, 1949, 14 X 36 In. 45.00
Ceiling Fixture, Mickey Mouse, Reverse Painted 75.00
DISNEYANA, CEL, see Animation Art
Chalk & Alphabet Board, Mickey Mouse, 1940, 35 In. 75.00
Chest, Mickey Mouse, 1930s 185.00
Clock Radio, Mickey Mouse, G.E., 1952 .... 85.00
Clock, Alarm, Mickey Mouse, Arms Tell Time, Bradley 35.00
Clock, Wall, Mickey Mouse, Schoolhouse Type, Elgin 60.00
Cookie Jar, Dumbo's Greatest Cookies On Earth, 12 In. 45.00
Cookie Jar, Mickey Mouse, Walt Disney Production 40.00
Costume, Mickey Mouse, Ben Cooper, Box 20.00
Crayon Set, Donald Duck & Mickey Mouse, Box, Giant 55.00
Dish, Feeding, Baby's, Donald Duck, Warmer 45.00
Doll, Donald Duck, Knickerbocker, 17 In. 45.00
Doll, Donald Duck, Spring Arms & Neck, Marx 75.00
Doll, Horace Horsecollar, Stuffed, Hand Sewn, 1930s, McCall, 26 In. 215.00
Doll, Mickey Mouse, Playing Horn, Bisque, 3 1/2 In. 45.00
Doll, Mickey Mouse, Stuffed, 1940s, 14 In. 10.00
Doll, Minnie Mouse, 10 1/2 In. 7.50
Doll, Pinocchio, Wood, Jointed, 5 In. 55.00
Drum Set, Mickey Mouse, Foot Pedal, Wood, Metal, 10 X 19 In. 100.00
Ferris Wheel, Disneyland 345.00
Figure, Mickey Mouse, Fun–E–Flex, Wooden, 4 In. 135.00
Figurine, Donald Duck, On Scooter, Bisque, 3 1/2 In. 70.00
Figurine, Dopey, Bisque, 3 1/2 In. 35.00
Figurine, Dumbo, Reclining, American Pottery 65.00
Figurine, Goofy, Glass, Marked 30.00
Figurine, Mickey & Minnie Mouse, Porcelain, W.Disney, 6 In., Pair 80.00
Figurine, Mickey Mouse, Glass, Marked 30.00
Figurine, Mickey Mouse, Wood, Felt Ears, 3 In. 80.00
Figurine, Minnie Mouse, Wooden, June–Flex 100.00
Figurine, Pinocchio, Pewter 35.00
Figurine, Pluto, Sniffing, Pottery 125.00
Figurine, Snow White, Chalkware 45.00
Figurine, Snow White, With Wishing Well, Enesco 45.00
Film, Movie, Mickey Mouse, 1930, Miniature 15.00
Fixture, Ceiling, Mickey Mouse, Donald Duck & Pluto, Box 185.00
Flashlight Gun, Mickey Mouse, Display Card 80.00
Fork, Baby, Mickey Mouse, Silver, 1930s 22.00
Fork, Mickey Mouse, Fairfield 25.00
Game, Bad Wolf, Silly Symphony, Disney 110.00
Game, Card, Hoffman's Ice Cream Premium 35.00

Game, Croquet, Mickey Mouse, Withington, Box 48.00
Game, Donald Duck, For Young Folks, Box, 1930s 50.00
Game, Fantasyland, Walt Disney 25.00
Game, Mickey Mouse Circus 125.00
Game, Scatterball, Mickey Mouse, Box 95.00
Game, Snow White & 7 Dwarfs, Milton Bradley 55.00
Game, Zorro, Target, Box 50.00
Guidebook, To Disneyland, 1957 .... 30.00
Guidebook, To Disneyland, 1963 .... 15.00
Hairbrush, Mickey Mouse, Black Painted Wood, Aluminum Figure 85.00
Hand Puppet, Pluto, 1969 .... 13.00
Handcar, Mickey & Minnie Mouse, Red, Lionel, 1934 .... 1100.00
Holder, Birthday Candle, Mickey Mouse, Box 50.00
Holder, Toothbrush, 3 Little Pigs 55.00
Holder, Toothbrush, Donald Duck, Mickey & Minnie Mouse, 1930s 175.00
Horn, Mickey Mouse, Party 75.00
Lamp, 3 Mickey Mouse Figures, Metal, 7 In. 38.00
Lamp, Mickey Mouse, Ceramic, Parchment Shade, 1950, 18 In. 80.00
Lamp, Mickey Mouse, Figural, LaMode, 1938 .... 350.00
Lawn Mower, Goofy, Box 48.00
Lobby Card, Lady & The Tramp, Set of 9, 11 X 14 In. 75.00
Lobby Card, Pete's Dragon, Set of 9, 11 X 14 In. 45.00
Lunch Box, Aladdin 40.00
Map, Disneyland, 1966 .... 35.00
Marionette, Minnie Mouse, Composition 80.00
Mask, Dopey, Mask Face, Painted Cloth, Velvet Body, 13 In. 135.00
Mug, Mickey Mouse, White, Glass, Marked Pepsi 1955 .... 10.00
Mug, Snow White & 7 Dwarfs, Plastic 10.00
Music Box, Melody Player, Mickey Mouse, 12 Rolls 485.00
Pail, Sand, Donald Duck, 1938 .... 25.00
Pail, Three Little Pigs, Tin, Ohio Art Co. 100.00
Paint Set, Disney Character, Box, 1940s ....:... 11.00
Paint Set, Plastic Palette, Transogram 50.00
Paper Doll, Snow White & 7 Dwarfs 38.00
Pencil Sharpener, Goofy, Rectangular, Bakelite 50.00
Pencil Sharpener, Pinocchio, Figural, Stenciled, Bakelite, 1939 .... 15.00
Pencil, Mickey Mouse, 1930s 15.00
Pennant, Mouseketeer, Felt, Disney, 1930s 35.00

Save your doll's packaging, tags, and inserts; these can triple the price when the doll is sold.

Pitcher, Mickey Mouse, Figural, Japan 75.00
Planter, Donald Duck 25.00
Planter, Mickey Mouse, As Cowboy 35.00
Postcard, Snow White & Prince, English 28.00
Poster, Donald Duck, Cardboard, 1952, 10 X 8 In. 35.00
Poster, Fantasia, Original Release 400.00
Program, Fantasia, Movie 35.00
Puppet, Goofy, 1930s, Box 285.00
Puppet, Hand, Donald Duck, 1930s 85.00
Purse, Mesh, Mickey & Minnie Mouse 95.00
Puzzle, Mickey Mouse, Parker Bros. 35.00
Puzzle, Snow White Picture, Walt Disney Ent., 1938, 2 Piece 100.00
Radio, Emerson, Mickey Mouse, 1930s 900.00
Radio, Mickey Mouse, Mickey's Head Turns Dial, 1960s 95.00
Record Player, Mickey Mouse, Lionel 75.00
Record, 3 Little Pigs, Colorful Litho Cover, Disney, 78 RPM 22.50
Record, Mouseketeers Original Cast, Illustration Cover 10.00
Ring, Donald Duck, 1930 .... 95.00
Rocker, Donald Duck, Wooden, Donald Duck Paddling Canoe 550.00
Rug, Scatter, Mickey Engineer, Donald Conductor, 45 X 59 In. 35.00
Salt & Pepper, Pinocchio, Hand Painted, Japan, 5 In. 35.00
Sand Sifter, Pluto, Donald, Huey, Dewey & Louis, Ohio Art Co. 95.00
Scissors, Electric, Donald Duck, Box 45.00
Sheet Music, Alice In Wonderland, Title Song 12.00
Sheet Music, Snow White, Whistle While You Work 22.00
Sheet Music, Who's Afraid of The Big Bad Wolf 35.00
Soap, Donald Duck, Figural, 1930s 50.00
Soap, Snow White & 7 Dwarfs, Box, 1938 .... 295.00
Spoon, Baby, Mickey Mouse, Silver, 1930s 22.00
Stacking Blocks, Cardboard, 10 Disney Characters 35.00
Tablecloth, Mickey Mouse Club, Paper, 56 X 86 In. 28.00
Tea Set, China, Walt Disney Prod., Marx, Japan, 23 Piece 245.00
Tea Set, Snow White & 7 Dwarfs, C.1940, 12 Piece 95.00
Teapot, Child's, Mickey & Minnie Mouse, Japan, 1930s 25.00
Tie Clasp, Mickey Mouse 30.00
Tool Chest, Metal, Mickey Mouse 60.00
Top, Mickey & Friends, Tin, Walt Disney, Fritz Bueschel 145.00
Top, Mickey, Spinning, Tin 80.00
Toy Chest, Mickey Mouse, 1930 .... 275.00
Toy, Boat, Mickey Mouse, Windup 10.00
Toy, Car, Goofy's Sport 7.00
Toy, Car, Mickey Mouse, Parade, Marx, Box 339.00
Toy, Cinderella & Prince Irwin, Dancers, Windup 40.00
Toy, Disney Dancer, Mickey Mouse, Gabriel, 1975 .... 12.00
Toy, Donald Duck Duet, Donald On Drums, Goofy Dances, Marx 400.00
Toy, Donald Duck, Handcar, Tin, Papier-Mache, Windup Engine, Lionel .. 475.00
Toy, Donald Duck, Long Bill Opens & Closes, Schuco, 1930s 325.00
Toy, Donald Duck, Plays Drums, Linemar 225.00
Toy, Donald Duck, Rubber, Squeeze, Rempel Mfg., 1940s, 12 In. 39.00
Toy, Fire Engine, Mickey & Donald, Red, Rubber, 6 1/2 In. 25.00
Toy, Guitar, Mickey Mouse, 1950s 60.00
Toy, Gumball Machine, Mickey Mouse, Hasbro, 1968 .... 20.00
Toy, Handcar, Mickey Mouse, Original Track, Key, Lionel 750.00
Toy, Jack-In-The-Box, Mickey Mouse, Carnival Toys 12.00
Toy, Mickey & Minnie, Swing Set, Windup, Celluloid, Borgfeldt 395.00
Toy, Mickey Mouse On Scooter, Mavco 100.00
Toy, Mickey Mouse, Driving Fire Engine, Rubber, 6 1/2 In. 50.00
Toy, Mickey Mouse, Handcar, Box 725.00
Toy, Mickey Mouse, Rubber, Walt Disney, Hong Kong, 5 In. 35.00
Toy, Minnie Mouse, Knitting In Rocking Chair, Windup, Linemar 250.00
Toy, Minnie Mouse, Steiff, 5 In. 600.00
Toy, Piano, Mickey Mouse, Wooden, Marks Bros., 9 X 10 In. 1050.00
Toy, Pluto The Acrobat, Linemar 250.00
Toy, Pluto, Top Hat, Plastic, Marx, 10 1/2 In. 125.00

Toy, Print Shop, Mickey Mouse, Rubber Letters, Tray, Fulton 45.00
Toy, Seven Dwarfs, Seiberling Rubber, Set 350.00
Toy, Snow White & 7 Dwarfs, Geo.Borgfeldt, 1938, 5 & 7 In. 605.00
Toy, Van, Donald Duck's Ice Cream 8.00
Toy, Xylophone, Mickey Mouse, Fisher Price 135.00
Tumbler, All–Star Parade, 1939 .... 10.00
Umbrella, Mickey Mouse, 1930s 75.00
Vase, Bud, Double, 3 Little Pigs, Silver Plate 60.00
Wallet, Snow White & 7 Dwarfs, Plastic, Walt Disney 8.00
Wallpaper Trim, Mickey Mouse, Unused Roll, Original Box 30.00
Watch, Mickey Mouse Time Teacher, Box 40.00
Watch, Mickey Mouse, Animated Hands, Strap, Bradley, Wristwatch 22.00
Watch, Mickey Mouse, Animated, Feet Move, 1973 .... 45.00
Watch, Pocket, Ingersoll, Mickey Mouse 175.00
Watch, Pocket, Mickey Mouse, Bradley, Red Plastic Case 45.00
Watch, Pocket, Mickey Mouse, Ingersoll, 1932 .... 200.00
Watering Can, Donald Duck, 1938 .... 50.00
Wrapper, Chocolate, Mickey Mouse, 1930s 22.00
Wristwatch, Mickey Mouse, 50th Anniversary, Box 40.00
Wristwatch, Mickey Mouse, Elgin 27.00
Wristwatch, Mickey Mouse, Ingersoll, Box 200.00
Wristwatch, Mickey Mouse, Wide Bezel, Swiss Works, Bradley, 1972 .... 22.00
    DOCTOR, see Medical; Dental

Doll entries are listed by marks printed or incised on the doll, if possible. If there are no marks, the doll is listed by the name of the subject or country.

DOLL, A.B.G. 639, Child, 16 In. 825.00
A.B.G., Baby, Brown Sleep Eyes, 11 In. 225.00
A.B.G., Chunky Body, Blue Eyes, Nude, 34 In. 800.00
A.B.G.1123 1/2, Bisque, Leather Body, 1880s Clothes, 28 In. 1095.00
A.M., Baby, Blue Taffeta, Cream Satin, 44 In. 2500.00
A.M., Baby, Dome Head, Celluloid Hands, Cloth Body, Dressed, 9 In. 95.00
A.M., Dream Baby, 2 Lower Teeth, 15 In. 350.00
A.M., Dream Baby, Composition Hands, 12 In. 295.00
A.M., Florodora, 1910, 16 In. 395.00
A.M., Florodora, Blue Sleep Eyes, Leather Jointed Body, 12 In. 185.00
A.M., Florodora, Sleep Eyes, Long Curls, Kid Body, Old Clothes, 20 In. 295.00
A.M., Googly, Just Me, Bisque Head, Blue Eyes, 5 Piece Toddler, 9 In. 650.00
A.M., Human Hair Wig, Blue Silk & Cream Satin Dress, 24 In. 2500.00
A.M., Lily, 15 In. 195.00
A.M., Silk Dress, Long Hair, Bonnet, C.1898, 30 In. 784.00
A.M.241, Baby, Kiddiejoy, Bisque, Dressed, 12 In. 165.00
A.M.251, Toddler, Girl, 24 In. 1600.00
A.M.253, Googly, Twins, Watermelon Mouth, Cotton Outfits, 7 1/2 In. 1350.00
A.M.323, Googly, Baby Body, 12 In. 1000.00
A.M.323, Googly, Bisque, Blue Sleep Eyes, Strawberry Blond Hair, 7 In. 950.00
A.M.327, Baby, Bisque Head, Composition, Jointed, 15 In. 185.00
A.M.341, My Dream Baby, 11 In. 185.00
A.M.370, Bisque Head & Hands, Leather Jointed Body, 24 In. 550.00
A.M.370, Girl, Bisque, Leather Body, 1890, 18 In. 130.00
A.M.390, Bisque, 4 Teeth, Brunette Wig, Cotton Dress, Bonnet, 16 In. 250.00
A.M.390, Bisque, Jointed Body, Original Clothes, 26 In. 650.00
A.M.541, Infant, Composition Boy, Sleep Eyes, Painted Hair, 8 In. 225.00
A.M.985, Bent Limb Body, Long Christening Gown, Slip, Bonnet, 23 In. 550.00
A.M.990–6/0, Baby, Bisque Head, Sleep Eyes, Bent Limb Body, 10 1/2 In. 225.00
Advertising, Big Boy Set, Dolly, Big Boy & Nuggett, 3 Piece 9.00
Advertising, Borden's Elsie, Mooing Cow 65.00
Advertising, Burger King, 21 In. 20.00
Advertising, Campbell Kid, Cloth Body, Compositon Limbs, 10 In. 45.00
Advertising, Campbell Kid, Straw Stuffed, Painted Eyes, Jointed, 1909 .... 250.00
Advertising, Campbell Kids, Composition, 1947 .... 88.00
Advertising, Cliquot Kid, Display, Cloth Body, Mask Face, 24 In. 150.00
Advertising, Cream of Wheat, Man, 1930s 68.00

Advertising, Dutch Boy, Paint, Molded Face, 36 In.	195.00
Advertising, General Electric, Mr.Magoo, Holding Big Light Bulb	20.00
Advertising, Gerber, Baby, Atlanta Novelty Co., Black, Box, 1979	150.00
Advertising, Gerber, Baby, Black, Box	35.00
Advertising, Gerber, Baby, Sun Rubber	25.00
Advertising, Holland American Lines, Composition Head	30.00
Advertising, Keebler Elf	20.00 To 58.00
Advertising, Kellogg, Dinky Dog, Printed Cloth	30.00
Advertising, Kellogg, Freckles Frog, Uncut, 1935	75.00
Advertising, Kellogg, Tony The Tiger	22.00
Advertising, Kelly Girl, Knickerbocker, Cloth, 1978, 12 1/2 In.	6.00
Advertising, Levi, Rag	8.00
Advertising, Life Savers Candy, Box	12.00
Advertising, Little Miss Revlon, Clothes, Hats, Sayco	40.00
Advertising, Mohawk Carpets, Indian	10.00
Advertising, Pillsbury Dough Boy	7.00
Advertising, Pillsbury Dough Girl	7.00
Advertising, Quaker Crackles Doll, Cloth, Uncut, Dated 1930, 16 In.	50.00
Advertising, Quaker Puffed Rice, Puffy	125.00
Advertising, RCA, Radiotrons, Wooden, Cameo	450.00
Advertising, Sea Island Sugar, George The Grocer, Cloth, Uncut, 1934	42.00
Advertising, Uneeda, Popeye, 8 In.	8.00
DOLL, ALEXANDER, see Doll, Madame Alexander	
Amberg, Charlie Chaplin, Original Clothes, C.1919	525.00
Amish, Cloth, Gray Smock, Blue Apron, Black Bonnet, Stuffed, 20 In.	193.00
Amish, Cloth, Stuffed, For Sunday, Blue Shawl, Plaid Skirt, 8 1/4 In.	55.00
Amish, Cloth, Stuffed, Purple Bonnet, Gray Smock, 13 1/2 In.	110.00
Annie Oakley, Walking, Original Box, Tag, American Character	344.00
Appalachian, Lady, Carved Walnut, Bonnet, Black Apron, C.1920, 14 In.	467.00
Apple Head, Rag Body, Gold Fiber Hair, Silk Dress, 10 1/2 In.	55.00
DOLL, ARMAND MARSEILLE, see Doll, A. M.	
Arranbee, Baby, Cloth Body, Holding Molded Celluloid Bottle, 12 In.	265.00
Arranbee, Cloth Body, Sleep Eyes, Open Mouth, 9 1/2 In.	115.00
Arranbee, Nancy Lee, 14 In.	125.00
Articulated, Wooden, Flesh Colored Paint, 4 In.	60.00
Automaton, Bisque, Closed Mouth, Human Hair, Dressed, French, 23 In.	5750.00
Bahr & Proschild, 224, Bisque, Stationary Eyes, Dressed, 12 In.	550.00
Bahr & Proschild, 536, Character, Dimpled, Closed Mouth, 13 In.	3500.00
Bahr & Proschild, 585, Baby, Bisque, Crier, Dressed.C.1915, 17 In.	400.00
Bahr & Proschild, Bisque, Blond Human Hair, Ball–Jointed, 22 In.	500.00
Bahr & Proschild, Bisque, Open Mouth, 4 Teeth, Dressed, C.1895, 15 In.	375.00
DOLL, BARBIE, see Doll, Mattel, Barbie	
Bathing Beauty, Pebbly Suit, Arms Over Head, 4 3/4 In.	75.00
Bebe, Bisque Socket, Head, Paperweight Eyes, Ball–Jointed, 1880, 19 In.	3750.00
Bebe, Bisque, Closed Mouth, Paperweight Eyes, Silk Dress, Hat, 18 In.	1600.00
Bebe, Walking, Bisque Shoulder Head, Blond Wig, Cork Pate, 14 In.	3000.00
Belgium Clothes, Composition, 1930s, 8 In.	28.00
Belton, Brown Eyes, Original Blond Wig, Dressed, 12 In.	1450.00
Belton, Closed Mouth, Blue Eyes, Straight Wrist, 16 In.	1750.00
Belton, Composition Body, Blond, Original Clothes, 10 In.	550.00
Belton, Glass Set Eyes, Painted Stockings, Strap Shoes, 6 In.	125.00
DOLL, BERGMANN, see also Doll, S & H; Doll, Simon & Halbig	
Bergmann, Ball–Jointed, 23 In.	475.00
Bergmann, Brown Sleep Eyes, Bisque, 32 In.	995.00
Betsy McCall, Completely Jointed, Photo Essay, 22 In.	135.00
Betsy McCall, Jointed Waist, Ankles, All Original, 22 In.	125.00
Betsy McCall, Teenager, Vinyl Socket Head, Sleep Eyes, Box, 1958, 14 In.	225.00
Betty Boop, Bisque, 6 1/2 In.	20.00
Betty Boop, Hot Pink Dress, Long Satin Coat, 20 In.	75.00
Betty Boop, Soft Vinyl, 9 In.	12.00
Bing, Character, Boy, Cloth, Jointed, Black Lederhosen, 1920, 14 In.	775.00
Bisque Head, Open Mouth, Anvil Mark, Print Dress, Straw Hat, 18 In.	750.00
Bisque Shoulder Head, Kid Body, Celluloid Hands, Sailor Suit, 18 In.	625.00
Bisque, Black Boy, Curly Hair, Ball–Jointed, Marked O, 12 1/2 In.	495.00

Doll, Gebruder Heubach 7711, Bisque,
8 1/2 In.

Doll, Madame Alexander, Wendy
Ann, Swivel Waist, C.1940, 13 In.

Doll, Madame Alexander,
Red Boy, C.1972, 8 In.

Doll, Madame Alexander,
Indian Boy, Plastic Head,
C.1968, 8 In.

Doll, Madame Alexander,
Tyrolean Boy, C.1965,
8 In.

Bisque, Blond Human Wig, Printed Face, Nightgown, Germany, 1920, 4 In. 60.00
Bisque, Boy & Girl, Blond Modeled Hair, Undressed, 3 1/2 In., Pair 25.00
Bisque, Boy & Girl, Velvet & Lace Ethnic Costume, 4 1/4 In., Pair 425.00
Bisque, Bride & Groom, Glass Eyes, Swivel Neck, 4 1/4 In., Pair 800.00
Bisque, Character Face, Sleep Eyes, Open Mouth, Teeth, Human Hair, 5 In. 275.00
Bisque, Cloth Body, Molded Hair, Germany, 7 In. 75.00
Bisque, Girl, Glass Eyes, Human Hair Wig, Closed Mouth, Case, 5 1/2 In. 50.00

Bisque, Jointed Arms, Legs, Painted Eyes, 5 In.	55.00
Bisque, Sleep Eyes, Shy Expression, Original Wig, Clothes, 5 1/2 In.	375.00
Bisque, Socket Head, Long Brown Hair, Satin & Lace Dress, 1880s, 4 In.	400.00
Bisque, Swivel Neck, Inset Eyes, Silk Ethnic Costume, 4 1/4 In.	300.00
Black, Rag, Checked Cotton Dress, Apron, Stuffed, C.1870, 18 In.	750.00
Blondie & Dagwood, 19 In.	50.00
Blondie & Dagwood, 20 In., Pair	40.00
Bonnie Toddler, 1955, 16 In.	150.00
Borgfeldt, Princess, Ball-Jointed Body, 21 In.	375.00
Boudoir, Composition Head & Arms, Felt, Cloth Body, 26 In.	20.00
Boudoir, Half Doll, Flapper, Green Feathers & Silver Net, Gold Shoes	25.00
Bride & Groom, Wedding Cake, Wooden Heads, Crepe Paper Clothes	25.00
Brother Coos, Composition, 26 In.	125.00
Bru Jne, Bebe, Bisque Swivel Head, Paperweight Eyes, Kid Body, 21 In.	9000.00
Bru Jne, Bisque, Swivel Head, Kid Body, Dressed, C.1870, 15 In.	4000.00
Bru Jne, Nursing, Open Mouth, Paperweight Eyes, Leather Body, 13 In.	5000.00
Bru Jne, Nursing, Paperweight Eyes, Jointed Body, Dressed, 13 1/2 In.	4650.00
Bruckner, Black Head, Red Skirt, White Head, Blue Checks, 14 1/2 In.	500.00
Bubbles, 17 In.	185.00
Bucherer, Mutt & Jeff, Pair	1200.00
Buddy Lee, Boy, Railroad Uniform, Composition, 13 In.	200.00
Buddy Lee, Coca-Cola Uniform, Composition	475.00
Buddy Lee, Cowboy, Plastic, 12 In.	100.00
Buttercup, Cloth, Signed Jimmy Murphy, 1924	45.00
Bye-Lo, All Bisque, Original Clothing, Paper Label, 4 In.	325.00
Bye-Lo, Baby, Bisque, Muslin Body, Celluloid Hands, Dress, 10 In.	1100.00
Bye-Lo, Baby, Vinyl Head, Cloth Body, Composition Hands, 24 In.	245.00
Bye-Lo, Bisque, Baby Hair, Celluloid Hands, Long Dress, C.1923, 16 In.	800.00
Bye-Lo, Celluloid Hands, Original Dress, Hat Tagged, Stamped, 12 In.	350.00
Catterfelder Pappenfabrik, Bisque, 2 Teeth, Christening Gown, 23 In.	600.00
Celluloid Head, Czechoslovakia, 1930s, 10 In.	35.00
Chad Valley, Fox, Glass Eyes, Riding Habit Like King George, 18 In.	550.00
Chad Valley, Princess Elizabeth, Glass Eyes, All Original, 19 In.	415.00
Chase, Baby, Signed, 19 In.	500.00
Chase, Character, Cloth, Oil Painted Features, C.1910, 25 In.	400.00
China Head, Blond, Alphabet Body, 11 1/2 In.	125.00
China Head, Curly Blond, Glazed Boots, Velvet Gown, 1880, 7 In.	45.00
Cloth, Boy, Wavy Hair, Stuffed, Litho Colors, Pat.1902, 12 1/2 In.	110.00
Cloth, Painted Face, Black Hair, Dress, Red Socks, C.1875, 26 In.	1500.00
Cloth, Pebbles, Knickerbocker, 6 1/2 In.	15.00
Cloth, Stuffed, Painted Blue Eyes, Plaid Shift, 12 In.	27.00
Dakin, Oliver Hardy	6.00
Dancing Black Man, Military Uniform, Carved Wood, 1863, 9 In.	750.00
Darrow, Leather, Handspun Flax Body, Painted Face, C.1850, 18 In.	200.00
Deanna Durbin, 21 In.	175.00
Demacol, Googly, Flirty Eyes, Original Wig, Dressed, 10 In.	650.00
DEP 12, Bisque Head, Paperweight Eyes, Teeth, Ball-Jointed, 15 1/2 In.	715.00
DEP 24, Blond Human Hair, Composition French Body, Blue Eyes, 24 In.	1100.00
Dollhouse Family, Composition Head, Wire & Cloth Bodies, 5 In., 6 Pc.	80.00
Dolly Dear, Cloth, Uncut, Frances Brundage Creation, 1916, 21 X 33 In.	275.00
Door of Hope, Child, All Original, 8 1/2 In.	495.00
Door of Hope, Mission Bride, Carved Wood, Red Jacket, 1920, 10 In.	250.00
Dressel, Bisque, Stationary Eyes, Composition, Wooden Limbs, 20 In.	225.00
Dumbo, Character Novelty, Plush, 13 In.	20.00
E.D.Child, Black, Bisque Head, French, 17 In.	1795.00
Eden Bebe, Bisque Head, Blue Eyes, Cork Pate, French Body, 19 1/2 In.	1875.00
Effanbee, Anne Shirley, 17 In.	150.00
Effanbee, Anne Shirley, Composition, Yarn Hair, Pinafore, Shoes, 21 In.	165.00
Effanbee, Babe Ruth, Box, 15 1/2 In.	150.00
Effanbee, Baby, Composition, Cloth Body, Curly Mohair, Blue Eyes, 22 In.	35.00
Effanbee, Barbara Lou, Merry Christmas Socks, 21 In.	275.00
Effanbee, Betty, Composition, 16 In.	185.00
Effanbee, Bubbles, Composition Cloth Body, Bent Limbs, 28 In.	350.00
Effanbee, Captain Kidd, 11 In.	25.00

Doll, Mattel, Barbie,
Fashion, Brunette, 12 In.

Doll, Mattel, Barbie,
Fashion, Blonde, 12 In.

Doll, Puppet, Snarky Parker,
With Microphone

Effanbee, Charlie McCarthy, Composition, 20 In. 150.00
Effanbee, Cinderella, 13 In. 49.00
Effanbee, Clown, Boy, Box, 1981, 16 In. 45.00
Effanbee, Dydee Baby, Caracul Wig, 12 In. 40.00
Effanbee, Eleanor Roosevelt, 11 In. 65.00
Effanbee, Franklin D.Roosevelt, 16 1/2 In. 150.00
Effanbee, George & Marsha Washington, White Wig, 1932, Box, 10 In., Pair 650.00
Effanbee, Gigi, Through The Years, Box, 1979, 6 Piece 250.00
Effanbee, Groucho Marx, 17 In. 75.00
Effanbee, Hans Brinker, 11 In. 25.00
Effanbee, Honey, Walker, Plastic, Red & Silver Gown, Parasol, 25 In. 350.00
Effanbee, Huck Finn, 11 In. 58.00
Effanbee, Lambkins, 16 In. .... 175.00 To 205.00
Effanbee, Little Lady, All Original, 27 In. 275.00
Effanbee, Lucille Ball, Box, 15 1/2 In. 150.00
Effanbee, Mae West, 11 In. 65.00
Effanbee, Mae West, Box, 18 In. 125.00
Effanbee, Mark Twain, 11 In. 58.00
Effanbee, Mary Lee, 32 In. 300.00
Effanbee, Mickey, Flirty, All Original, 27 In. 235.00
Effanbee, Muhammed Ali, 11 In. 58.00
Effanbee, Old McDonald, 11 In. 25.00
Effanbee, Orphan Annie, 1965, 14 In. 200.00
Effanbee, Pat-O-Pat, 1939 .... 125.00
Effanbee, Patsy Ann, 19 In. 150.00
Effanbee, Patsy Mae, Dotted Swiss Dress, Velvet Coat & Hat, 30 In. 550.00
Effanbee, Patsy Ruth, Composition & Cloth Body, Heart Bracelet, 22 In. 300.00
Effanbee, Patsy, Composition, 5 Piece Body, Clothes, 2 Outfits, 9 In. 125.00
Effanbee, Patsyette, Composition Head, Molded Hair, C.1935, 9 In. 280.00
Effanbee, Prince Charming, 13 In. 48.00
Effanbee, Rapunzel, 11 In. 25.00
Effanbee, Sister, String Hair, 16 In. 95.00
Effanbee, Skippy, World War I Dough-Boy Uniform, Leggings 325.00
Effanbee, Suzie Sunshine, 19 In. 20.00
Effanbee, Theodore Roosevelt, 17 In. 150.00
Effanbee, Winston Churchill, 11 In. 65.00
Emmett Kelly, 14 In. 125.00
English, Bride, Poured Wax, Paperweight Eyes, Original Clothes, 24 In. 2450.00
English, Child, Poured Wax, Molded Teeth, Muslin Body, C.1890, 40 In. 500.00
English, Portrait, Poured Wax, Rooted Hair, Original Dress, 18 In. 300.00
Ertel & Schwab 165, Toddler, Sleep Googly Eyes, 10 In. 2500.00
F.G., Bisque Head, Composition Body, Gray Dress, Stripes, Lace, 18 In. 3000.00
F.G., Bisque, Paperweight Eyes, Brocade Dress, Bonnet, 18 In. 2750.00
F.G., Fashion Child, Linsey Woolsey Walking Suit, Complete, 13 In. 1600.00
F.G., French Fashion, Closed Mouth, Kid Body, Bisque Head, 18 In. 1495.00
Fanny Brice, Baby Snooks, Composition, Original Clothes, 12 In. 175.00
Fashion, Bisque, Human Hair, Leather Arms, Muslin Body, 1885, 20 In. 1300.00
Fashion, Portrait, Bisque, Brunette Human Hair, Costume, C.1875, 20 In. 1900.00
Fashion, Smiling, Kid & Twill Body, 19 In. 5500.00
Flapper, Felt, Lady of The 20s, 21 In. 165.00
Floradora, Original Clothes, Lace, Plumes, Germany, 18 In. 200.00
French, Bisque, Closed Mouth, Original Clothes, 6 In. 750.00
French, Bisque, Swivel Head, Almond Paperweight Eyes, 25 In. 325.00
French, Character, Felt Swivel Head, Muslin Body, C.1920, 22 In. 450.00
French, Child, Bisque, Blond Human Hair, Wooden Jointed Body, 11 In. 800.00
French, Closed Mouth, Paperweight Eyes, 13 In. 1500.00
French, Fashion, Blue Paperweight Eyes, Kid Body, 17 In. 2450.00
French, Glass Eyes, Kid Body, Papier-Mache Head, Dressed, 21 In. 950.00
French, Wrestler, All Bisque, 8 1/2 In. 1050.00
Frozen Charlie, Blond Hair, Tinted Face, 10 1/2 In. 475.00
Frozen Charlotte, Bisque, Golden Curly Hair, Blue Eyes, 3 In. 125.00
Frozen Charlotte, Black Hair, 5 1/2 In. 50.00
Frozen Charlotte, Blond, Glazed Stockings, Luster Boots, 3 1/2 In. 200.00
DOLL, FULPER, see also Doll, Horsman

Fulper, Character, Toddler, Sleep Eyes, 2 Teeth, Ball–Jointed, 17 In. 800.00
Fulper, Dollie Face, 19 In. 450.00
Furga, Boy, Brunette, 14 In. 22.00
G.I.Joe, Foot Locker, Accessories, 1964 .... 45.00
G.I.Joe, Land Adventurer, Hair & Beard, Box 40.00
Gaultier, Bebe, Bisque Head, Stockinette Body, Blond Hair, 24 In. 3750.00
Gaultier, Fashion Lady, Paperweight Eyes, Cork Pate, Kid Body, 22 In. 3100.00
Gaultier, Fashion, Bisque, Kid Body, Lavish Costume, C.1870, 26 In. 2000.00
Gebruder Heubach 7711, Bisque, 8 1/2 In. ....*Illus* 600.00
Gebruder Heubach 7636, Patty Cake, Open–Close Mouth, Smiling 525.00
Gebruder Heubach 7911, Character Boy, Dimples, Laughing Mouth 850.00
Gebruder Heubach, Ball–Jointed, Set Eyes, Original Clothes, 34 In. 995.00
Gebruder Heubach, Character Boy, Intaglio Eyes, Open–Close Mouth 750.00
Gebruder Heubach, Laughing Child, Intaglio Eyes, 11 In. 350.00
Gebruder Heubach, Tumblers, Boy & Girl, Bells Inside Torso, 9 In. 950.00
Geisha, Lacquered Wood, Ivory Head, Hands & Feet, 13 3/4 In. 1500.00
German, Baby, Bisque Swivel Head, Painted Features, Jointed, 11 In. 650.00
German, Baby, Celluloid Head, Flirty Eyes, Turtle Mark, C.1920, 18 In. 200.00
German, Bisque, Painted Hair, Muslin Body, Leather Arms, C.1880, 17 In. 275.00
German, Character, Bisque, Socket Head, Sleep Eyes, 25 In. 3500.00
German, Child, Papier–Mache, Painted Teeth, Dressed, C.1885, 20 In. 200.00
German, Girl, Walking, Painted Socks, Shoes, Underclothes, 11 1/2 In. 450.00
German, Googly, Bisque Head, Torso, Legs, Painted Socks, Shoes, 4 In. 190.00
German, Gusseted Kid Body, Bisque Hands, Human Hair, 1900, 28 In. 500.00
German, Porcelain, Molded Hair, Original Outfit, High Boots, 12 In. 250.00
German, Porcelain, Molded Hair, Painted Features, Calico Dress, 14 In. 300.00
German, Porcelain, Painted Features, Taffeta Gown, Lace Trim, 19 In. 300.00
German, Porcelain, Painted Hair, Curls, Muslin Body, C.1880, 33 In. 250.00
Greiner, Cloth Body, 1858 Label, 21 In. 1250.00
Greiner, Papier–Mache, Molded Hair, Muslin Body, C.1858, 18 In. 400.00
Hancock, Bisque, Girl, Pouty, Sleep Eyes, Dressed, 1914–18, 17 In. 575.00
Handwerck 99, Ball–Jointed Body, Sleep Eyes, All Original, 32 In. 1095.00
Handwerck 109, Bisque Head, Ball–Jointed, Open Mouth, 17 In. 200.00
Handwerck 109/12, Bisque, Composition & Wooden Jointed Body, 24 In. 500.00
Handwerck 119, Sleep Eyes, Original Wig & Clothes, 19 In. 395.00
Handwerck 183/29, Bisque, Ball–Jointed, Open Blue Eyes, Dressed 600.00
Handwerck, Child, Bisque Socket Head, Ball–Jointd Body, 30 In. 895.00
Handwerck, Child, Bisque, 4 Teeth, Mohair Wig, Dressed, C.1910, 20 In. 350.00
Handwerck, Child, Bisque, Wooden Jointed Body, Dressed, C.1900, 30 In. 600.00
Hasbro, Flying Nun, 1968, Original Box 25.00
Hasbro, Little Miss No Name 30.00
Hee–Bee, Sticker On Foot, 5 1/2 In. 175.00
Hendren, Baby, Life–Like, 26 In. 150.00
Hendren, Dutch Girl, 10 In. 45.00
Hertel Schwab 152, Baby, Sleep Eyes, Blond Human Hair, 19 In. 375.00
Hertel Schwab 152, Character Baby, Gray Eyes, 11 In. 225.00
Hertel Schwab 165, Googly Eyes, Jointed Toddler Body, 12 In. 2995.00
Heubach Koppelsdorf 312, Houndstooth Checked Coat & Hat, 23 In. 375.00
Heubach Koppelsdorf 320, Toddler 325.00
Heubach Koppelsdorf 399, Black Baby, 11 In. 325.00
Heubach Koppelsdorf 399, Black Baby, Composition Body, 10 In. 350.00
Heubach Koppelsdorf, Twins, Bisque, Baby Body, Flannel Gown, 9 In., Pair ... 350.00
Heubach, 275, Leather Body, Compositon Arms & Legs, Underwear, 20 In. 275.00
Heubach, Bisque Head, Kid Body, Original Clothes, Marked, 12 In. 200.00
Heubach, Boy, Bisque Head, Cloth Body, Molded Hair, 15 In. 750.00
Heubach, Character, All Bisque, Touseled Hair, Dressed, C.1910, 9 In. 600.00
Horsman, Baby Dimples, Composition, Original Clothes, 16 In. 165.00
Horsman, Cindy, All Original, 1957, Box, 19 In. 45.00
Horsman, Ella Cinders, Googly Eyes, Black Painted Hair, 1925, 18 In. 450.00
Horsman, Nude, Naughty, Composition, 1930s 290.00
Ideal, Anne Shirley, String Hair, 21 In. 275.00
Ideal, Bam–Bam, Animal Print Outfit, 17 In. 25.00
Ideal, Blipfert, Composition Head, Arms & Legs, Cloth Body, 1933 .... 30.00
Ideal, Bubbles, 24 In. 150.00

Ideal, Crissy, Gro–Hair, Fully Dressed, 20 In. 425.00
Ideal, Deanna Durbin, Painted Eyes, Original Wig, 21 In. 425.00
Ideal, Dopey, Composition, 1937 ...... 68.00
Ideal, Fanny Brice, As Baby Snooks, Composition, Wrist Tag 200.00
Ideal, Goody Two–Shoes, Long Eyelashes, 18 In. 25.00
Ideal, Harriet Hubbard Ayers, C.1953, 14 In. ...... 85.00 To 95.00
Ideal, Kissy, 22 In. 50.00
Ideal, Miss Revlon, 17 In. 110.00
Ideal, Mortimer Snerd, Dressed, 12 1/2 In. 285.00
Ideal, Petite Pudgie, 13 In. 250.00
Ideal, Saucy Walker, Hard Plastic, 16 In. 45.00
Ideal, Skippy, 14 In. 275.00
Ideal, Snoozie, Latex Stuffed, 1933, 20 In. 125.00
Ideal, Thumbelina, Box, 16 In. 15.00
Ideal, Tiny Tears, 1982, Box 15.00
Ideal, Toni, Bleached Hair & Lashes, 1949, 14 In. 25.00
    DOLL, INDIAN, see Indian, Doll
International, Gibson Girl 27.00
    DOLL, J.D.K., see also Doll, Kestner
J.D.K.245, Hilda, Composition, Jointed, Sleep Eyes, 1914, 24 In. 500.00
J.D.K.257, Jointed Toddler Body, Sleep Eyes, Original Clothes, 15 In. 795.00
J.D.K.260, Character, Brown Eyes, Jointed, Swivel Head, Dress, 28 In. 900.00
J.D.K.260, Child, Bisque, Blue Sleep Eyes, Original Wig, 16 In. 750.00
Japanese Boy, Festival, Seated Nobleman, Papier Mache Head, 14 In. 200.00
Japanese Girl, Eggshell Bisque, 8 In. 30.00
Jerri, Cinderella & Prince Charming 1350.00
Jerri, Little Red Riding Hood 500.00
Jerry Mahoney, Costumes, Box, 1950 ...... 20.00
John Wayne, Box, 18 In. 95.00
Juggler, China, Dances On Stand, Bells Ring, Original Clothes, 7 In. 490.00
Jumeau 15, Bisque, Brunette Human Hair, Antique Costume, 32 In. 3900.00
Jumeau 1907, Open Mouth, Long Curls, Jointed, Dress, Bonnet, 32 1/2 In. 2650.00
Jumeau, Bebe, Bisque Head, Inset Eyes, Human Hair, Jointed, 32 In. 1800.00
Jumeau, Bisque Head, Paperweight Eyes, Ball–Jointed, Dressed, 26 In. 3200.00
Jumeau, Bisque, Auburn Wig, Wooden Jointed Body, C.1880, 19 In. 2500.00
Jumeau, Bisque, Ball–Jointed, Underclothes, Silk Dress, Bonnet, 16 In. 2495.00
Jumeau, Bisque, Brunette, Composition, Wooden Jointed, Dressed, 22 In. 3100.00
Jumeau, Bisque, Closed Mouth, Ball–Jointed, Red Velvet Outfit, 19 In. 5750.00
Jumeau, Bisque, Open Mouth, Label, Ball–Jointed, Silk Dress, Hat, 19 In. 1150.00
Jumeau, Bisque, Open Mouth, Signed Body, Dressed, 15 In. 2250.00
Jumeau, Bisque, Paperweight Eyes, Ball–Jointed Body, 12 1/2 In. 7500.00
Jumeau, Bisque, Paperweight Eyes, Satin Dress, Lace, Bonnet, 18 1/2 In. 1195.00
Jumeau, Bisque, Sleep Eyes, Old Clothes, 1907, 31 1/2 In. 2200.00
Jumeau, Bisque, Wooden Jointed Body, Embroidered Dress, C.1880, 28 In. 3250.00
Jumeau, Black, Composition Body, Original Clothes, 17 In. 3395.00
Jumeau, Child, Bisque Head, Amber Eyes, Composition, Wood, 1800, 27 In. 5500.00
Jumeau, Open Mouth, Long Curls, Upper Teeth, Pink Moire Dress, 29 In. 2450.00
Jumeau, Portrait, Bisque Head, Paperweight Eyes, Dressed, 17 In. 5500.00
Juro, Pinky Lee, With Tag, 1950s, 25 In. 150.00
Just Me, Sleep & Side Look Eyes, Papier–Mache Body, 8 In. 550.00
K * R 22, Character Baby, Blue Eyes, Satin Finish Bisque, 23 In. 750.00
K * R 28/5/0, Tyrolean Boy, Celluloid, Glass Eyes, Dressed, 8 In. 150.00
K * R 53, Human Hair Wig, Sleep Eyes, Flowered Dress, 22 In. 375.00
K * R 100, Boy, Character, Bisque Head, Corduroy Outfit, 18 1/2 In. 650.00
K * R 114, Original Wig, Underwear, 16 In. 3500.00
K * R 117/A, Mein Leibling, Bisque, Wooden Jointed Body, 32 In. 5750.00
K * R 117N, Flirty Eyes, White Silk Dress, Original Shoes, 27 In. 1900.00
K * R 121, Character Baby, Sleep Eyes, Christening Dress, 14 In. 430.00
K * R 121, Toddler, Blue Eyes, Dimples, 28 In. 2200.00
K * R 121, Toddler, Original Clothes, 13 1/2 In. 1250.00
K * R 122, Toddler Baby, Dressed As Boy, 19 In. 1100.00
K * R 126, Open Mouth, Tremble Tongue, Ball–Jointed Toddler, 33 In. 880.00
K * R 403, Ball–Jointed Arms, Walker Legs, Dressed, C.1915, 18 In. 425.00
K * R 728, Toddler, Flirty, Composition Body, 25 In. 370.00

K * R, Bisque, Sleep Eyes, Doll Fit Into Trunk, Clothes, 4 1/2 In. 650.00
K * R, Blue Sleep Eyes, 4 Teeth, Ball–Jointed, 28 In. 525.00
K * R, Boy, Baby Body, Brown Glass Eyes, Turtle Mark, 10 In. 110.00
K * R, Child, Open Mouth, Lawn Dress, Tucks & Lace Inset, Box, 27 In. 800.00
K * R, Flirty–Eyed Girl, Painted Curly Lashes, 4 Teeth, 21 In. 525.00
K * R, Flossie Flirt, 17 In. 750.00
Kaiser, Baby, Brown Glass Eyes, 14 In. 1350.00
Kamkins, Cloth, 20 In. 650.00
Karl Hartman, Bisque, Composition, All Original, 22 In. 550.00
Kathe Kruse, Baby, DuMein, Cloth, 1920s, 14 In. 1200.00
Kathe Kruse, Boy, Mannequin, Blond, Dated 1940, 53 In. 1200.00
Kathe Kruse, Girl, Wig, Cloth, 20 1/2 In. 1095.00
Kathe Kruse, Sandy Baby, Open Eyes, Layette, Box 900.00
Kathe Kruse, Yorgel, 19 In. 325.00
DOLL, KESTNER, see also Doll, J.D.K.
Kestner 18, Bisque Head, Open Closed Mouth, Teeth, Paper Label, 20 In. 3025.00
Kestner 111, Googly, Sleep Eyes, Jointed Elbows & Knees, 5 1/2 In. 850.00
Kestner 133, Sister, Character, All Original, 6 1/4 In., Pair 675.00
Kestner 143, Blond Mohair Wig, Sleep Eyes, 24 In. 675.00
Kestner 146, Sleep Eyes, Ball–Jointed Body, Original Clothes, 28 In. 695.00
Kestner 150, Girl, Bisque, Sleep Eyes, Brown Print Dress, 5 1/2 In. 100.00
Kestner 152–13, Character Baby, Bent Limb, Chin Dimples, Red Hair 800.00
Kestner 154, Human Hair Wig, Ball–Jointed Arms, Kid Body, Dress, 27 In. 410.00
Kestner 154, Kid Body, Bisque Hands, Brown Eyes & Wig, 21 In. 250.00
Kestner 155, Bisque, Sleep Eyes, Original Wig, 8 1/2 In. 550.00
Kestner 164, Young Lady, Leghorn Hat, Blue Eyes, Blond Wig, 32 In. 1000.00
Kestner 166, Blue Sleep Eyes, Original Blond Wig, 17 In. 395.00
Kestner 167, Bisque Head, Stamped Body, Human Hair Wig, Dressed, 23 In. 425.00
Kestner 168, Blue Eyes, Molded Teeth, Curly Wig, Old Clothes, 20 In. 330.00
Kestner 171, Sleep Blue Eyes, Original Wig, 26 In. 700.00
Kestner 185, Glass Eyes, Closed Mouth, Ball–Jointed, 11 In. 1700.00
Kestner 189, Googly, Bisque, Swivel Head, Russian Costume, 5 In. 500.00
Kestner 195, Fur Eyebrows, Pin–Jointed Kid Body, Dressed, 22 In. 395.00
Kestner 196, Bisque, Fur Eyebrows, Original Wig, Old Clothes, 25 In. 695.00
Kestner 211, Baby, Sleep Eyes, Open–Close Mouth, Original Wig, 17 In. 700.00
Kestner 214, Child, Blue Sleep Eyes, Auburn Human Hair, 25 In. 600.00
Kestner 245, Child, Bisque, Jointed Body, Sleep Eyes, 24 In. 100.00
Kestner 257, Character Baby, Jointed Wrists, 18 In. 475.00
Kestner 260, Bisque, Glass Eyes, Jointed Body, Dress, Straw Hat, 36 In. 1450.00
Kestner 560, Baby, Blue Sleep Eyes, Antique Clothes, 13 In. 325.00
Kestner 639, French Fashion, Turned Head, Paperweight Eyes, 18 In. 785.00
Kestner, American School Boy, 15 In. 395.00

Doll, S.F.B.J. 60, Black, Bisque,
Moroccan Costume, C.1915, 14 In.

Doll, Simon & Halbig 1009,
Bisque Head, 23 In.

Doll, Simon & Halbig
1159, Bisque, 13 In.

Kestner, Baby Hilda, Bisque, Bent Limb Body, Gown, Slip, C.1915, 12 In.	2000.00
Kestner, Baby, Bisque, Sleep Eyes, Open Mouth, 2 Teeth, 16 In.	1400.00
Kestner, Baby, Kid Body, 5 Piece Baby Clothes, 1898, 30 In.	900.00
Kestner, Bisque Socket Head, Brown Inset Eyes, Ball-Jointed, 18 In.	1800.00
Kestner, Bisque, Kid Body, Open Mouth With Teeth, Cotton Dress, 16 In.	250.00
Kestner, Bisque, Leather Body, Brown Sleep Eyes, 20 In.	200.00
Kestner, Blond Mohair, Closed Mouth, Straight Wrists, 19 In.	1850.00
Kestner, Character Child, Open-Close Mouth, Blue Eyes, 11 In.	1850.00
Kestner, Closed Mouth, Sleep Eyes, Original Wig & Clothes, 13 1/2 In.	1250.00
Kestner, Fashion, Shoulder Head, Jointed Kid Body, Peach Dress, 16 In.	175.00
Kestner, Googly, Bisque Socket Head, Ball-Jointed, C.1915, 12 In.	5500.00
Kestner, Sleep Eyes, 4 Teeth, Painted Lashes, Blond, C.1910, 22 In.	850.00
Kestner, Sleep Eyes, Mohair Wig, Kid Gusset Jointed Body, 18 In.	525.00
Kestner, Turned Head, Closed Mouth, Ball-Jointed Arms, 23 In.	800.00
Kestner, Turned Head, Leather Body, Bisque Hands, Long Curls, 30 In.	895.00
DOLL, KEWPIE, see Kewpie, Doll	
Kley & Hahn 525, Baby Body, Character, Bisque Head, Character, 15 In.	600.00
Kley & Hahn 525, Toddler, Bisque, Open-Close Mouth, 14 In.	1050.00
Kley & Hahn, Bisque, 4 Teeth, Composition & Wood Body, Dress, 24 In.	475.00
Kley & Hahn, Bisque, Girl, Walker, Ball-Jointed, 24 In.	375.00
Kling 131, Unglazed Bisque, Glass Eyes, Molded Hair, Kid Body, 18 In.	495.00
Knickerbocker, Laurel & Hardy, 1966	35.00
Knickerbocker, Raggedy Andy, Brown Shoes, 32 In.	50.00
L W & Co., Bisque Head, Leather Body, Open Mouth, Blond Hair, 16 In.	55.00
L.& M.Roche, Colette, Wooden Body, 21 In.	395.00
Lanternier, Bisque, 5 Piece Composition Body, Lace Dress, 1910, 7 In.	500.00
Lehmann, Waltzing, Celluloid Head, Arms, 9 In.	900.00
Lenci 253, Mozart, Pink Waistcoat & Knickers, Italian, 1925-26, 21 In.	2300.00
Lenci, Amelia Earhart, 16 1/2 In.	2500.00
Lenci, Aurelia, Made For Enchanted Dollhouse	200.00
Lenci, Boy, Tyrolean Original Clothes, 16 In.	550.00
Lenci, Brown Curly Hair, Painted Eyes Glance To Side, 1925-26, 15 In.	990.00
Lenci, Child, Organdy Costume, Flower Trim, Matching Umbrella, 18 In.	2400.00
Lenci, Clown, Felt, Jointed Arms, Legs, Costume, 15 In.	750.00
Lenci, Coiled Braids, Pink Luster, Flat Heeled Shoes, 9 In.	850.00
Lenci, David Copperfield, Character, Felt Swivel Head, Cloth, 24 In.	275.00
Lenci, Felt Swivel Head, Closed Mouth, Blond, Label, C.1930, 17 In.	1500.00
Lenci, Girl, Bow Back of Hair, Felt Dress, Pinafore, 1930s, 14 In.	495.00
Lenci, Googly Eyes, Felt Swivel Head, Mohair Wig, C.1925, 20 In.	2500.00
Lenci, Lillian Gish, Theatrical Costume, Fabric Tag, 1930s, 23 In.	1650.00
Lenci, Mascot, Little Girl In Costume of Tuscany, 9 In.	200.00
Lenci, Spanish Lady, Swivel Waist, Wooden Accessories	1150.00
Lenci, Street Urchin, Felt, Red Hair, Side Glancing Eyes, 13 In.	900.00
Limoges, Paperweight Eyes, Character Type, 25 In.	475.00
Little Lulu, Molded Face, Stringed Hair, Original Dress	195.00
Louis Wolf, Bisque Head, Leather Body, Cloth Feet, Mohair Wig, 16 In.	60.00
LuAnn Simms, Hard Plastic, Blue Dress, Wrist Tag, Late 1940s, 20 In.	250.00
Madame Alexander, Alexander-Kins, Plastic, Walking Legs, C.1955, 8 In.	250.00
Madame Alexander, Alice In Wonderland, Hard Plastic, 1951, 14 In.	275.00
Madame Alexander, Amish Boy, 1966-69	450.00
Madame Alexander, Amy, Little Women, Bent Knee Walker, Tag, 8 In.	85.00
Madame Alexander, Argentine Boy, 1965-66	595.00
Madame Alexander, Baby Tears, Vinyl, Marked, 1965, 13 In.	65.00
Madame Alexander, Baby, Composition, 1936, 7 1/2 In.	78.00
Madame Alexander, Baby, Puddin, 21 In.	80.00
Madame Alexander, Baby, Pussycat, Pink, 20 In.	80.00
Madame Alexander, Baby, Victoria, 20 In.	75.00
Madame Alexander, Ballerina, Blue, 1983	100.00
Madame Alexander, Berry, 16 In.	150.00
Madame Alexander, Beth, Little Women, Original Dress, 14 In. .... 70.00 To 90.00	
Madame Alexander, Bride, Hard Plastic, Ivory Satin Gown, 1950, 18 In.	210.00
Madame Alexander, Bride, Wendy Ann, Composition, Tag, 18 In.	375.00
Madame Alexander, Brigetta, Sound of Music, 1964	225.00
Madame Alexander, Caroline, Wrist Tag, 15 In.	135.00

Madame Alexander, Chatterbox, 1961, 24 In.	145.00
Madame Alexander, Cissy, Fashion Parade, Gown, Fur Cape, 1956, 13 In.	625.00
Madame Alexander, Cissy, Formal Gown, 1955, 21 In.	200.00
Madame Alexander, Coco, All Original, Tagged, 21 In.	300.00
Madame Alexander, Cornelia, 1976, Box, 21 In.	350.00
Madame Alexander, Cowboy, 1967–69	500.00
Madame Alexander, Dennis The Menace, 13 In.	25.00
Madame Alexander, Easter Girl, Vinyl Head, Sateen Dress, 1968, 12 In.	350.00
Madame Alexander, Elise, Ballerina, 17 In.	95.00
Madame Alexander, Elise, Bridesmaid, 17 In.	125.00
Madame Alexander, Emily Dickinson, 14 In.	80.00
Madame Alexander, Fairy Godmother, 14 In.	80.00
Madame Alexander, First Lady, Caroline Harrison, 14 In.	150.00
Madame Alexander, First Lady, Frances Cleveland, 14 In.	150.00
Madame Alexander, Florence Nightingale, 14 In.	85.00
Madame Alexander, Gigi, 14 In.	80.00
Madame Alexander, Godey, Red Velvet Jacket & Hat, Box, 21 In.	550.00
Madame Alexander, Good Fairy, Hard Plastic, 1950s, 14 In.	350.00
Madame Alexander, Groom, Tag, 1953, 18 In.	500.00
Madame Alexander, Heidi, 14 In.	75.00
Madame Alexander, Indian Boy, Plastic Head, C.1968, 8 In. ....*Illus*	425.00
Madame Alexander, Jack, 8 In.	45.00
Madame Alexander, Jenny Lind, Vinyl Head, Long Gown, 21 In.	850.00
Madame Alexander, Jo, Blue Sleep Eyes, 5 Piece Body, C.1956, 12 In.	250.00
Madame Alexander, Kate Greenaway, Tagged Dress, Composition, 24 In.	250.00
Madame Alexander, Kelly, Vinyl Head, Blond Hair, 6 Piece Body, 21 In.	550.00
Madame Alexander, Lissy Coco, Box, 21 In.	2000.00
Madame Alexander, Little Genius, Tagged, Original Bottle, 8 In.	130.00
Madame Alexander, Little Nurse, Plastic, Sleep Eyes, 1958, 8 In.	400.00
Madame Alexander, Little Women, Tag, 1962, 11 1/2 In., 5 Dolls	900.00
Madame Alexander, Louisa, Sound of Music, Costume, 1971–73, 10 In.	100.00
Madame Alexander, Lucinda, Umbrella, 1969, 12 In.	200.00
Madame Alexander, Madame Alexander, 21 In.	395.00
Madame Alexander, Manet, 14 In.	60.00
Madame Alexander, Margaret O'Brien, Composition, 21 In.	350.00
Madame Alexander, Marie Antoinette, 21 In.	320.00 To 325.00
Madame Alexander, Marme, Storyland Doll, Tag, 12 1/2 In.	60.00
Madame Alexander, Mary Mine, 14 In.	90.00
Madame Alexander, McGuffey Ana, Plastic, Blond Braids, 1963, 8 In.	1600.00
Madame Alexander, Melanie, Pink, 21 In.	240.00
Madame Alexander, Miss Muffet	90.00
Madame Alexander, Morocco, Bent Knee, 8 In.	125.00
Madame Alexander, Penny, All Original, 34 In.	250.00
Madame Alexander, Pinky, Original Clothes, 1937, 19 In.	225.00
Madame Alexander, Pollyana, 14 In.	70.00
Madame Alexander, Prince Charming, 1950, Wrist Tag, 14 In.	425.00
Madame Alexander, Prince Edward, 2 Tags, 15 In.	1650.00
Madame Alexander, Pumpkin, 22 In.	85.00
Madame Alexander, Pussy Cat, 1972, Dark Hair, 14 In.	65.00
Madame Alexander, Queen Elizabeth II, Gown, Tiara, 21 In.	275.00
Madame Alexander, Queen of Hearts, 8 In.	48.00
Madame Alexander, Rebecca, 14 In.	70.00
Madame Alexander, Red Boy, C.1972, 8 In. ....*Illus*	50.00
Madame Alexander, Red Riding Hood, 8 In.	45.00
Madame Alexander, Renoir Girl, 1967, 14 In.	250.00

Don't comb your doll's hair or wash the dresses. Keep them mint.

Doll, Steiff, Felt,
Swivel Head, C.1910, 13 In.

Doll, Stuffed Cloth, Lithographed,
American, C.1900, 26 In.

Madame Alexander, Romeo & Juliet, Box, 8 In., Pair 3595.00
Madame Alexander, Sarah Bernhardt, 21 In. .... 300.00 To 325.00
Madame Alexander, Scarlett O'Hara, 21 In. 500.00
Madame Alexander, Shari Lewis, 1959, 14 In. 335.00
Madame Alexander, Sleeping Beauty, 13 In. ....75.00 To 125.00
Madame Alexander, Snow White, 14 In. 55.00
Madame Alexander, So Big, 22 In. 75.00
Madame Alexander, Sonja Henie, 18 In. .... 325.00 To 385.00
Madame Alexander, Toulouse Lautrec, 21 In. 325.00
Madame Alexander, Tyrolean Boy, C.1965, 8 In. ....*Illus*   90.00
Madame Alexander, Ventriloquist, Danny O'Day, Composition, 25 In. 95.00
Madame Alexander, Wendy Ann, Swivel Waist, C.1940, 13 In. ....*Illus* 700.00
Mae Starr, Composition, Sleep Eyes, Cloth Body, Talking, 27 In. 240.00
Man From Uncle, Llya Karjakin 30.00
Marionette, Dapper Dan Dancing 40.00
Marionette, Monkey 100.00
Marionette, Wooden Jointed Hands, Feet, & Face, 13 In. 75.00
Marotte, Bisque Head, Jester Costume, Germany, 20th Century, 14 In. 300.00
Marotte, Bisque Head, Stationary Glass Eyes, Silk Clothes, Tune, 13 In. 325.00
Marotte, Court Jester, Bisque Head, Mohair Wig, Marked 4/0, 13 In. 400.00
Marseille, Bisque Socket Head, Ball-Jointed, 4 Teeth, 43 In. 1700.00
Marseille, Black Baby, Bisque, Painted Hair, Dressed, C.1925, 14 In. 350.00
Marseille, Character, Bisque Socket Head, Bent Limb Baby, 1920, 18 In. 175.00
Mascotte, Bisque, Bulgy Glass Eyes, Underclothes, Socks, 23 In. 2495.00
Mattel, Allan, Box, 1963 .... 48.00
Mattel, Barbie, Ballerina, Germany, Box, 1983 .... 45.00
Mattel, Barbie, Black 30.00
Mattel, Barbie, Carrying Case, Gown, 1966 .... 60.00
Mattel, Barbie, Color 'N' Curl, 2 Heads, Accessories 300.00
Mattel, Barbie, Dramatic Living, Box, 1969 .... 65.00
Mattel, Barbie, Extra Head, Trunk, With Clothes, 1961, 11 1/2 In. 60.00
Mattel, Barbie, Fashion Jeans, 1982 .... 22.00
Mattel, Barbie, Fashion Queen, 3 Wigs, 1963 .... 165.00
Mattel, Barbie, Fashion, Blonde, 12 In. ....*Illus* 200.00
Mattel, Barbie, Fashion, Brunette, 12 In. ....*Illus* 200.00
Mattel, Barbie, Gold Medal, Green Leotard, 1972 .... 15.00
Mattel, Barbie, Growin' Pretty Hair, Bendable Knees 125.00
Mattel, Barbie, No.2, Ponytail, Curly Bands, Blond, Pearl Earrings 450.00
Mattel, Barbie, No.3, Brown Eye Shadow, Solo Outfit 100.00
Mattel, Barbie, No.3, Brunette, Gold Dress, Sunglasses, Box 100.00
Mattel, Barbie, No.4, Blond Ponytail, 1960 .... 50.00
Mattel, Barbie, Sun-Loving Malibu 18.00

Mattel, Barbie, Talking, Blond, Pink Bathing Suit, Net Top, 1969	30.00
Mattel, Barbie, Twist & Turn	35.00
Mattel, Charmin Chatty, Record, Talks, 25 In.	37.50
Mattel, Dr.Doolittle, With Parrot, 1967, Box, 6 In.	35.00
Mattel, First Step, 1964	18.00
Mattel, Julia, 1 Piece Nurse Outfit, Diahann Carrol, 1978	95.00
Mattel, Ken, Doctor's Uniform, Stand, 1961	60.00
Mattel, Ken, Molded Hair, 1960	28.00
Mattel, Ken, Talking, Bathing Suit, Wrist Tag	25.00
Mattel, Midge, Red Hair, 1963	48.00
Mattel, Shrinking Violet, Talks, Tag	40.00
Mattel, That-A-Way, Crawls, 1974	35.00
Mego, Dorothy, Wizard of Oz, 1974, Box, 8 In.	30.00
Mego, Laverne & Shirley, 1977, Box, 12 In., Pair	50.00
Mego, Star Trek, 1974, Box	20.00
Mickey, Monkees, 1970	44.00
Moon Mullins, Wood, Jointed, 6 In.	72.00
Morimura, Blond Human Hair, Elaborate Dress, Matching Bonnet, 22 In.	400.00
Morimura, Character Baby, 16 In.	295.00
Morimura, Character Toddler, Sleep Eyes, 22 In.	250.00
Mr.Magoo, 1967, 28 In.	35.00
Nancy Ann Storybook, Bisque, Black Lace Costume, Hat, 6 In.	40.00
Nippon, Bisque, 5 1/2 In.	40.00
Nippon, Happifats, Boy & Girl, 3 3/4 In., Pair	178.00
Nippon, Hilda, Bisque Head, Inset Eyes, Bent Limb Baby Body, 22 In.	650.00
Norah Wellings, Boy, Canadian Royal Mountie, Velvet Cloth, 14 1/2 In.	165.00
Norah Wellings, Dutch Boy, 9 In.	27.50
Norah Wellings, Royal Mountie, 15 In.	135.00
Orsini, Bisque, Sleep Eyes, Open–Close Smiling Mouth, 5 In.	1350.00
DOLL, PAPER, see Paper Doll	
Papier–Mache Head, Molded & Painted Hair, Wood Limbs, 1830, 7 3/4 In.	225.00
Papier–Mache Head, Muslin Body, Greiner–Type, C.1860, 30 In.	500.00
Papier–Mache, Brown Eyes, Original Clothes, 27 In.	2750.00
Papier–Mache, Girl, Side Glancing Eyes, Jointed, Wig, 1920s, 15 In.	45.00
Parian, Man, Painted Blond Hair, Black Velvet Suit, 1880–1900, 6 In.	20.00
Patti Playpal, 36 In.	125.00
Pierotti Type, Poured Wax, 24 In.	900.00
Pierotti, Baby, Wax, Box, 17 In.	2500.00
DOLL, PINCUSHION, see Pincushion Doll	
Pinocchio, Composition, Original Clothes, 18 In.	275.00
Pintel & Godchaux, Wooden Jointed Body, Dressed, C.1885, 20 In.	1800.00
Porcelain, Shoulder Head, Painted Hair, Dress, Germany, 1878, 20 In.	300.00
Puppet, Black Man, Wooden Head, Glass Eyes, Movable Mouth, 40 In.	650.00
Puppet, Papier–Mache Head, Wooden Feet, Straw Hat	65.00
Puppet, Snarky Parker, With Microphone ....*Illus*	2860.00
Rag, Amish, Blue Dress & Black Bonnet, 12 In.	75.00
Rag, Brown Dress, Velvet Shoes, Drawn Face, Hair Wig, 12 In.	50.00
Rag, Embroidered Face, Floss Hair, White Dress, 14 In.	85.00
Rag, Mennonite, Printed Face, Yarn Hair, Machine Sewn, 8 1/4 In.	5.00
Rag, Pencil Drawn Face, Appliqued Hair, Dress, Velvet Booties, 24 In.	85.00
Rag, Reversible, Black Girl 1 End, White Girl Other, 7 In.	75.00
Rag, Stuffed Black Knit, Embroidered Face, Dress, Petticoats, 15 In.	205.00
Rag, Stuffed Sateen & Knit, Chenille Hair, Embroidered Face, 15 In.	85.00
Raggedy Ann & Andy, Cloth, 15 In, Pair	30.00
Ravca, Old Man & Woman, Tag, Pair	125.00
Rohmer, Fashion, China Arms & Swivel Neck, Stamped Kid Body, 14 In.	3500.00
Rose O'Neill, Buddha, Smiling, Rubber, Cameo Doll Co.	35.00
Ruth Newton, So–Wee Sun Babe, 10 In.	20.00
DOLL, S & H, see also Doll, Bergmann; Doll, Simon & Halbig	
S & H 749, Paperweight Eyes, Jointed Body, Whitework Dress, 12 In.	2200.00
S & H 939, Paperweight Eyes, Pale Bisque, Regional Costume, 24 In.	2695.00
S & H 1079, Brown Bisque, Ball–Jointed Body, Dressed, C.1910, 13 In.	500.00
S.F.B.J. 3, Walker, Papier–Mache, Sleep Eyes, Sailor Outfit, 14 In.	275.00
S.F.B.J. 60, Bisque Head, Blue Silk Dress, Lace Trim, 22 In.	850.00

S.F.B.J. 60, Black, Bisque, Moroccan Costume, C.1915, 14 In. ....*Illus*	350.00
S.F.B.J. 227, Molded Hair, Blue Jewel Eyes, New Clothes, 21 In.	2250.00
S.F.B.J. 236, Character, Bisque, Dressed, Parasol, 14 In.	700.00
S.F.B.J. 236, Toddler, Auburn Wig, Brown Eyes, Antique Dress, 18 In.	1295.00
S.F.B.J. 236, Toddler, Bisque, Open Glass Eyes, Cotton Dress, 23 In.	1550.00
S.F.B.J. 301, Bisque, Jointed Wrists, Satin Dress, Velvet Trim, 33 In.	1295.00
S.F.B.J., Bisque, Glass Eyes, Molded Teeth, Pink & Ecru Outfit, 35 In.	1500.00
S.F.B.J., First Kiss, 22 In.	950.00
S.F.B.J., Gladdie, 23 1/2 In.	1150.00
S.F.B.J., Sleep Eyes, Open Mouth, Papier–Mache, 14 1/2 In.	225.00
S.F.B.J., Walker, Talks, Throws Kisses, 22 In. .... 1100.00 To	1250.00
Schmitt, Bisque Head, Pierced Ears, Fixed Wrists, Lace Dress, 23 In.	6000.00
Schoenau & Hoffmeister, Bisque, In Wooden Sleigh, All Original, Pair	700.00
Schoenau & Hoffmeister, Open Mouth, Sleep Eyes, 10 In.	135.00
Schoenau & Hoffmeister, Sleep Eyes, Ball–Jointed, Dressed, 28 In.	475.00
Schoenhut, Baby, 15 In.	45.00
Schoenhut, Boy, Walker, 11 In.	375.00
Schoenhut, Girl, Blue Eyes, Original Clothes, 14 1/2 In.	1650.00
Schoenhut, Nature Boy, Wooden, Painted Hair, Bent Limb, C.1917, 15 In.	300.00
Schoenhut, Pouty Character, Jointed Wooden Body, Intaglio Eyes, 16 In.	575.00
Schoenhut, Walking, Wooden, Dressed, C.1915, U.S.A., 14 In.	575.00
Schoenhut, Wellsley Girl, Wooden, Original Clothes, Box, 12 1/2 In.	150.00
DOLL, SHIRLEY TEMPLE, see Shirley Temple	
Shoulder Head, Cloth Body, Bisque Limbs, Shawl, 6 In.	100.00
DOLL, SIMON & HALBIG, see also Doll, Bergmann; Doll, S & H	
Simon & Halbig 886, Stationary Eyes, Swivel Neck, 5 1/2 In.	525.00
Simon & Halbig 919, Bisque, Blue Threaded Paperweight Eyes, 16 In.	4250.00
Simon & Halbig 921, Oriental Baby, Black Human Hair, 5 Piece, 10 In.	1600.00
Simon & Halbig 939, Socket Head, Spiral Eyes, Costume, C.1890, 20 In.	1400.00
Simon & Halbig 949, Bisque Shoulder Plate, Closed Mouth, 22 In.	800.00
Simon & Halbig 1009, Bisque Head, 23 In. ....*Illus*	1500.00
Simon & Halbig 1010, Child, Bisque Shoulder Head, Teeth, Braids, 10 In.	100.00
Simon & Halbig 1078, Sleep Eyes, Walker, Pierced Ears, 12 In.	695.00
Simon & Halbig 1079, Bisque Head, Open Mouth, Teeth, Jointed, 32 In.	650.00
Simon & Halbig 1079, Bisque, Sleep Eyes, 4 Teeth, Antique Dress, 34 In.	1400.00
Simon & Halbig 1159, Bisque, 13 In. ....*Illus*	650.00
Simon & Halbig 1160, Beaded Fringe Dress, 1880, 6 1/2 In.	500.00
Simon & Halbig 1170, Bisque, Set Eyes, Kid Body, 18 In.	75.00
Simon & Halbig 1329, Oriental, Bisque, Molded Eyebrows, 18 In.	2500.00
Simon & Halbig, Bisque Head, Brown Eyes, Jointed, Velvet Dress, 28 In.	600.00
Simon & Halbig, Bisque Head, Brown Mohair Wig, Open Mouth, 21 In.	250.00
Skippy, Composition, 12 In.	225.00
Skookum, Indian, Male & Female, Blanket Costume, 17 & 16 In., Pair	130.00
Steiff, Babette, Blond, Jointed, 21 In.	350.00
Steiff, Felt, Swivel Head, C.1910, 13 In. ....*Illus*	2600.00
Steiff, Mickey Mouse, 18 In.	1050.00
Steiff, Morning Gentleman, Felt, 8 In. .... 220.00 To	270.00
Steiff, Soldier, Signed Belt, C.1911, 11 1/2 In.	1950.00
Steiner, Antique Silk Dress, Bead Encrusted Ribbons, 30 In.	7500.00
Steiner, Baby, 5 Piece Composition Body, Open–Close Eyes, 8 In.	195.00
Steiner, Baby, Bisque Head, Closed Mouth, Blue Eyes, 12 In.	240.00
Steiner, Bisque Head, Paperweight Eyes, Cardboard Pate, 24 In.	4500.00
Steiner, Bisque, Paperweight Eyes, Dressed, 18 In.	6500.00
Steiner, Black, Open Mouth, Old Clothing, 11 In.	1600.00
Steiner, Boy, German Costume, Marked, 7 In.	100.00
Steiner, Infant, All Original, 12 In.	285.00
Steiner, Majestic, 19 In.	325.00
Steiner, Phoenix Bebe, Bisque, Jointed, Underclothes, Socks, 11 1/2 In.	1595.00
Stuffed Cloth, Lithographed, American, C.1900, 26 In. ....*Illus*	225.00
Sun Rubber, Baby, 1938, 16 In.	75.00
Swing & Sway With Sammy Kaye, Molded Hair, Dress, Composition, 12 In.	75.00
Terri Lee, Benji, Black, 16 In.	210.00
Terri Lee, Bonnie Lou, Black, 16 In.	125.00
Terri Lee, National Baby Sitter, Plastic, Talking, Box, 1955, 17 In.	625.00

If your doll body leaks sawdust, try patching the hole by putting a few drops of clear glue in the hole. If the hole is too large, patch it with a piece of muslin or kid cut from an old glove. Cut a circular patch and glue in place.

Tete Jumeau, Bisque Head, Paperweight Eyes, Under Clothes, 26 In.	3500.00
Tete Jumeau, Closed Mouth, Curly Blond Wig, Dressed, 26 In.	3500.00
Tete Jumeau, Open Mouth, Beige Velvet, Lace, Red Stamp On Head, 24 In.	1900.00
Tete Jumeau, Open Mouth, Pierced Ears, Original Wig, 19 In.	950.00
Tin Head, Boy, Dressed, 18 In.	65.00
Toni Tenille, 12 In.	20.00
Topsy–Turvy, Black & White, 1940	45.00
Twins, Bisque, Closed Mouth, Blond Braid, German Costume, 3 1/2 In., Pr.	200.00
Twins, Boy & Girl, Wooden Lamb On Leash, 1915 Style Clothes, 4 In., Pr.	170.00
Two–Face, Frowning & Smiling, Bisque Head, Silk Dress, German, 12 In.	600.00
Uncle Sam, Printed Cloth	110.00
Uneeda, Popeye & Sweet Pea, 8 In., Pair	16.00
Unis 251, Toddler, Bisque Head, Wobbly Tongue, Vest, Straw Hat, 27 In.	1550.00
Unis, Bisque Head, Original Costume, 5 1/2 In.	150.00
Unis, Boy Toddler, Ball–Jointed, Velvet Pants & Vest, 27 In.	1550.00
Unis, Composition, 20 In.	250.00
Ventriloquist, Dummy, Man, Wooden Hands, Body, Papier–Mache Head, 3 Ft.	750.00
Vogue, Baby Dear, Painted Eyes, 18 In.	125.00
Vogue, Dear One, 26 In.	295.00
Vogue, Ginny, Plastic, Blond Braids, 5 Piece, Walking Legs, C.1955, 8 In.	125.00
Vogue, Too Dear, Toddler, 23 In.	300.00 To 425.00
Wax Over Composition, Girl, Lever Opening Mouth, Jointed, 8 In.	150.00
Wax Over Papier–Mache, Wire–Eyed, 18 In.	2500.00
Wee Patsy, 6 In.	200.00
Wernicke, Ball–Jointed, White Dress, 17 In.	125.00
Wilhelm Dehler, Bisque, Long Dress, Incised W.D.2, 14 In.	450.00
Wood Body, China Head & Lower Limbs, C.1850, 7 In.	2200.00
Wooden, Papier–Mache Head & Bodice, Polychrome Paint, 5 1/2 In.	85.00
Woody Woodpecker, Talking, Hard Plastic, 18 In.	25.00
Wrestler, Yellow Shoes, Outfit, Earrings, 8 In.	850.00

DONALD DUCK, see Disneyana

Iron doorstops have been made in all types of designs. The vast majority of the doorstops sold today are cast iron and were made from about 1890 to 1930. Most of them are shaped like people, animals, flowers, or ships.

DOORSTOP, Amish Man & Woman, Red Shirts, Cast Iron, Pair	325.00
Aunt Jemima, Cast Iron, Littco Products	185.00
Basket of Cornflowers, Handle, Cast Iron, 9 1/2 In.	125.00
Basket of Fruit, Original Paint, 5 In.	85.00
Basket, Tulips, Red & Yellow, Iron, 8 1/2 In.	95.00
Beaux Art Design, Worn Pastel Colors, Cast Nickel Steel, 8 In.	10.00
Beginner, Young Boy, Knickers, Smoking Behind His Hat, Cast Iron	250.00
Bird, Cast Iron, Polychrome, 7 1/4 In.	75.00
Black Watermelon Eater, Watermelon Slice, Cast Iron, 9 In.	125.00
Carriage, Cinderella, Gold Repaint, 19 In.	90.00

Cat, Black & White, Cast Iron, 12 In.	35.00
Cat, Bow At Neck, Flat–Sided, 8 In.	95.00
Cat, Reclining, Black, Yellow Eyes, Red Bow, Hubley, 10 1/2 In.	110.00
Cat, Reclining, Full Figure, Cast Iron	80.00
Cat, Seated, Iron, 1910	110.00
Cat, Seated, Yellow Eyes, Cast Iron, 11 1/2 In.	95.00
Charles Lindbergh, Cast Iron	165.00
Charleston Dancers, Cast Iron	685.00
Child, Sailor Suit, Flat, Full Figure, Cast Iron, 8 3/4 In.	285.00
Cinderella Carriage, 9 3/4 X 19 In.	145.00
Cinderella Slipper ....65.00 To	150.00
Clipper Ship, Iron, 11 X 10 In.	50.00
Coach & Horses, Hubley	190.00
Coach, London Mail, Polychrome Paint, 7 3/8 In.	65.00
Cockatoo, Cast Iron, 12 In.	95.00
Cockatoo, Cast Iron, White Paint, 7 3/4 In.	80.00
Cockatoo, Full Figure, Polychrome Paint, 7 In.	35.00
Colonial Man, Red Cape, Brown Knickers, Cast Iron, 7 1/4 In.	475.00
Conestoga Wagon, Original Orange & Blue Paint, Oct.1930	150.00
Cosmos In Vase, Hubley, 17 3/4 In.	655.00
Cottage, Green Roof, White Picket Fence, Flowers, Cast Iron	115.00
Cottage, Iron, 6 In.	85.00
Crane & Urn, Cast Brass, 10 In.	65.00
Dog, Airedale, Cast Iron ....*Illus*	275.00
Dog, Boston Bulldog, Cast Iron, 9 In.	65.00
Dog, Boston Bulldog, Seated, Chalkware, 1930, 10 In.	28.00
Dog, Boston Bulldog, Spike Collar, Cast Iron, Black, 1935, 10 In.	65.00
Dog, Boston Terrier, Iron, Original Paint, 9 5/8 In.	175.00
Dog, Bulldog, Iron, 10 1/2 In.	75.00
Dog, Cocker Spaniel, Black, Cast Iron	275.00
Dog, Dachshund, Brass	45.00
Dog, English Pointer, Full Figure	85.00
Dog, Fido, Full–Bodied, Polychrome Paint, Cast Iron, 5 In.	55.00
Dog, Fox Terrier, Cast Iron	125.00
Dog, French Bulldog, Seated	80.00
Dog, German Shepherd, Cast Iron ....*Illus*	100.00
Dog, Greyhound, Full Figure, Lake City Malleable Co., 1930, 12 In.	45.00
Dog, Gutter Pup, Polychrome Paint, Wooden, Head Turns	85.00
Dog, Irish Setter, Cast Iron, 12 In.	260.00
Dog, Pekingese, Lifelike, Hubley, 14 1/2 In.	825.00
Dog, Police, Cast Bronze, 8 3/4 In.	60.00
Dog, Russian Wolfhound, Iron, Chain & Loop, Goes Around Doorknob	75.00
Dog, Scotty, At Fence, Cream Paint, Green Base, Cast Iron, 6 1/2 In.	35.00
Dog, Scotty, Cast Iron ....*Illus*	100.00
Dog, Scotty, Full Figure, Black Paint, Cast Iron, 8 1/2 In.	75.00
Dog, Scotty, Original Paint, 11 X 9 In.	150.00
Dog, Sealyham, Hubley, 14 In.	585.00
Dog, Spaniel, Full Figure, Black & White, Red Collar, 6 3/4 In.	35.00
Dog, Spring Spaniel, Iron, Original Paint, 6 3/4 X 7 In.	185.00
Dog, Whippet, 8 1/2 In.	345.00
Dog, Wolfhound, Full Figure, Iron, Gold Paint Over Black, 10 In.	175.00
Dog, Yawning Pup, Cast Iron	385.00
Dowager, Fat, 5 1/2 In.	45.00
Drum Major, 13 1/2 In.	435.00
Dwarf, Full Figure, Polychrome Repaint, Cast Iron, 9 3/4 In.	45.00
Eagle & Snake, Cast Iron, C.1848	185.00
Eagle, Full Figure, Gold Paint, Marked, B.S.Co., Cast Iron, 7 In.	55.00
Eagle, Spread Wings, Black, Cast Iron, 7 1/2 In.	75.00
El Capitan, Coffee Co., Lancaster, Cast Iron, Repainted	275.00
Elephant, 10 X 11 In.	285.00
Elephant, Taking Coconuts From Tree, Cast Iron, 14 In.	330.00
Fantail Fish, Nickel Plated, Original Paint, Hubley	165.00
Felix The Cat, Wooden	50.00
Fireplace, White & Black Paint, Cast Iron, 4 1/2 In.	50.00

Fisherman, Bearded, In Rain Gear, Cast Iron, 7 In. 75.00
Flower Basket, Iron, Bronze Plated, 9 1/2 In. 75.00
Flower Basket, Iron, Original Paint, Albany Foundry, 16 1/4 In. 325.00
Flower Basket, Next To Fence, 7 In. 70.00
Flower Basket, With Fence, Cast Iron, 7 X 6 In. 140.00
Flower, Oval, Iron, B & H 60.00
Flowers, Cast Iron, 10 1/2 In. 45.00
Football Player, Holding Football, Under Horseshoe, 4 X 4 1/4 In. 125.00
Frog, Light Green Porcelain Enamel, Iron, 6 In. 45.00
Frog, With Black Boy, 5 1/2 X 6 1/2 In. 655.00
Fruit Bowl, Cast Iron .... 75.00 To 115.00
Galleon, Cast Iron, Polychrome Repaint, 8 In. 35.00
Gazelle, Jumping, Cast Iron 85.00
Geese, Hubley, 8 X 8 In. 210.00
Geisha Girl, Iron, Hollow, Original Paint, 10 1/4 In. .... 230.00 To 245.00
Geisha, On Pillow, Red Costume, 7 X 6 In. 385.00
General Lee, Cast Iron 125.00
Gnome .... 285.00 To 325.00
Golfer, In Knickers, Cast Iron 250.00
Grapevine, Cast Iron, 1920s 140.00
Halloween Cat, Iron, Original Paint, Hubley, 9 1/4 In. 175.00
Hercules Wrestling Serpent, Bronze Wash, 17 In. 285.00
High Button Shoe, Cast Iron .... 55.00 To 100.00
Hip, Mayflower, Cast Iron 70.00
Horse, Cast Iron, Hubley .... 55.00 To 89.00
House, Cape Cod, Cast Iron, Hubley, 5 1/2 In. .... 155.00 To 265.00
Humpty-Dumpty, 4 1/2 In. 485.00
Indian Potter, Full Figure, Iron, Worn White Paint, 4 1/2 In. 175.00
Knight, Signed, 13 1/4 In. 225.00
Lighthouse, Signed, 7 3/4 In. 215.00
Lion, Cast Iron, Black Paint, Gold Highlights, 7 In. 70.00
Lion, Flat Back, Iron, St.Blazey Foundry, C.1850, 14 1/2 In. 150.00
Lion, Original Gold Paint, 7 X 8 In. 135.00
Little Red Riding Hood & Wolf, Cast Iron .... 345.00 To 450.00
Log Cabin, Albany Foundry, 4 5/8 X 10 In. 215.00
Mammy, Cast Iron, 8 In. .... 135.00 To 175.00
Man, In Tuxedo, Cast Iron, Polychrome Paint, 7 1/2 In. 55.00
Man, Standing, Fox's Head, Boots, Iron, Black Paint, 11 1/4 In. 85.00
Man, With Hatchet & Pipe, Dog & Tree, Cast Iron, 14 3/4 In. 85.00
Masonic, Emblems, Cast Iron, 6 X 7 In. 130.00
Monkey, Full Figure, Cast Iron, 8 In. 125.00
Old Salt, Fisherman, Cast Iron, 11 In. .... 135.00 To 175.00
Old Salt, Seated, Cape Cod Fisherman, Iron, 1928, 5 5/8 In. 35.00
Ornament, Marked Arthur Mfg.Co., Baltimore, Md, Iron, 8 1/2 In. 100.00
Ostrich, 8 1/2 In. 375.00
Owl, Cast Iron, Hubley 150.00
Owl, Cast Iron, Polychrome Paint, 5 1/8 In. 95.00
Parrot In Ring, Iron, Original Paint, B & H, 13 3/4 In. 355.00

Doorstop, Dog, Cast Iron

Parrot, In Medallion, Cast Iron, Creation Co., Lancaster 85.00
Parrot, Signed KS, Original Paint, 8 In. 80.00
Peacock, Cast Iron, 7 In. 125.00
Peacock, Cast Iron, Worn Polychrome Paint, 6 1/8 In. 175.00
Penguin, Top Hat, Cast Iron 425.00
Pheasant, Signed Fred Everett 160.00
Pied Piper, Cast Iron .... 165.00 To 190.00
Pirate, On Chest, Full Figure, Silver Paint, Cast Iron, 6 In. 55.00
Punch, Black Repaint, Cast Iron, 12 1/2 In. 75.00
Puppies, In Basket, Cast Iron 475.00
Quail, Iron, Original Paint, Hubley, Signed Fred Everett, 7 1/4 In. 395.00
Rabbit, Lying Down, Chalk, 4 1/2 In. 20.00
Rabbit, Paws Up, White, Cast Iron, 7 In. 140.00
Rabbit, Signed L.W.Cox, Cast Iron 220.00
Rabbit, With Top Hat, 10 In. 645.00
Ram, Cast Iron, White Paint Traces, 7 1/4 In. 185.00
Rattle Snake, Cast Iron 120.00
Rose Basket, Blue Ribbon, Cast Iron 150.00
Sailor, Cast Iron, Original Paint, 8 1/2 In. 145.00
Sheep, Iron, 7 In., Pair 85.00
Ship, American Flags, Cast Iron, Western Foundry, 11 3/4 In. 95.00
Snooper, Top Hat, Flashlight, Magnifying Glass, Cast Iron, 13 In. 175.00
Spanish Dancer, Porcelainized Finish, 10 In. 145.00
Spanish Girl, Iron, Original Paint, 9 1/2 In. 245.00
Spanish Guitar Player, Full Figure, Cast Aluminum, 10 3/4 In. 65.00
Spanish Guitarist, White Metal, Signed, 11 In. 475.00
Stagecoach, 11 X 6 In. 175.00
Sunbonnet Baby, Polychrome Paint, Cast Iron, 6 1/4 In. 145.00
Swallows, Iron, Original Paint, Hubley, 8 1/2 In. 445.00
Three Fish, Nickel Finish, Cast Iron, 9 1/2 In. 35.00
Tiger, Full Figure, Cast Iron, 13 1/2 In. 20.00
Topsy, Hubley, 6 In. 425.00
Tulips, Iron, Original Paint, Hubley, 10 In. 175.00
Twin Cats, 7 In. 345.00
Warrior, With Shield, Signed, 13 1/4 In. 725.00
Woman, With Muff, 9 1/4 In. 275.00
Zinnias, Hubley, Cast Iron, 7 1/4 In. 150.00

Doulton pottery and porcelain were made by Doulton and Co. of
Burslem, England, after 1882. The name "Royal Doulton" appeared
on their wares after 1902. Other pottery by Doulton is listed under
Royal Doulton.

DOULTON, Bowl, Flower, Pilgrims On Horses, Chaucer, 3 1/2 X 6 1/8 In. 175.00
Bowl, Turquoise & White Flowers, Tan, Gilt, Ethel Beard 75.00
Ewer, Blue Iris, Cobalt Blue Trim, Gold, Burslem, 6 3/4 In. 145.00
Foot Warmer, Logo In Black Transfer, Lambeth Mark 55.00
Humidor, Applied Fox Head Handles, Tavern Scene, Tan, 6 7/8 In. 60.00
Jug, Cats & Mottoes, Flow Blue, 8 1/4 In. 195.00
Jug, Embossed Man In Medieval Dress, Marked, 7 3/4 In. 165.00
Lamp, Fairy, Burmese Shade, Base Flowers, Ball & Claw Feet, 7 In. 660.00
Pitcher, Hot Water, Orlando, Forest Background, Marked, 7 In. 185.00
Pitcher, Madras, 7 1/2 In. 155.00
Teapot, Chariot Scene, Ecru & Cobalt Blue, Burslem 85.00
Teapot, Katherine 150.00
Teapot, Tapestry, Flowers & Leaves, Beige, Lambeth, Marked, 5 In. 125.00
Vase, Blackberries & Leaves, Handle, Lambeth, Signed, 11 In. 165.00
Vase, Circus Horses, Hannah Barlow, Lambeth, Marked, 12 3/8 In. 595.00
Vase, Commemorative, Disraeli, Portrait, Primroses, 1804, 4 In. 250.00
Vase, Flowers Outlined In Gold, Burslem, 5 1/4 In. 100.00
Vase, Isle of Man, Man With Cane On Front, Marked, 3 1/4 In. 70.00
Vase, Mottled Blue & Green, Tapestry Bottom, 10 1/4 In. 225.00
Vase, Pastel Flowers, Irregular Form, Gold Legs, Burslem, 4 1/2 In. 120.00
DR. SYNTAX, see Adams; Staffordshire

Clarice Cliff pieces marked in
black are worth two to three
times as much as pieces marked
in any other color.

Dresden, Plaque, Woman, Standing,
   Holding Basket, 7 X 5 In.

Moriage is a type of decoration on Japanese pottery. Raised white
designs are applied to the ware. Dragonware is a form of moriage
pottery. White dragons are the major raised decorations. The
background color is gray and white, orange and lavender, or orange
and brown. It is a twentieth–century ware.

DRAGONWARE, Chocolate Set, 9 Piece	195.00
Creamer	25.00
Mug, Nippon	95.00
Tea Set, Lithophane Teacups, 16 Piece	175.00
Vase, Gold Trim, 8 In.	95.00

Dresden china is any china made in the town of Dresden, Germany.
The most famous factory in Dresden is the Meissen factory.
Figurines of eighteenth–century ladies and gentlemen, animal groups,
or cherubs and other mythological subjects were popular. One
special type of figurine was made with skirts of porcelain–dipped
lace. Do not make the mistake of thinking that all pieces marked
"Dresden" are from the Meissen factory. The Meissen pieces usually
have crossed swords marks, and are listed under Meissen.

DRESDEN, Basket, Bonbon, 1790–1800	480.00
Candlestick, Floral, 6 1/2 In., Pair	100.00
Card Holder, Roses, Stems & Leaves Support Card, 5 In.	25.00
Clock, Applied Cupids, Porcelain Flowers, Signed, 14 1/2 In.	525.00
Compote, Nude Child, Holding Flowers, Pierced, Rococo Stand, 12 In.	150.00
Cup & Saucer, Dresden Rose, Stamped	20.00
Feeder, Invalid, Blue & White	55.00
Figurine, Angel Band, C.1900, 5 1/4 In., 8 Piece	125.00
Figurine, Ballerina, 7 1/2 In.	110.00
Figurine, Ballerina, At Rest, Blue, White Chair, Marked, 4 X 4 In.	99.00
Figurine, Colonial Children, Encrusted Flowers, Kister, 7 In.	225.00
Figurine, Monkey Band, 8 Piece	900.00
Figurine, Peasant Girl, Feeding Chickens, Carl Thieme, 4 1/2 In.	95.00
Ice Pail, Porcelain, Gilt Handles, Round Foot, Cobalt Blue, 7 In.	475.00
Loving Cup, Nymphs In Woodland Scene, Gold Trim, 6 1/2 In.	360.00
Mirror, Porcelain Roses, Leaves, Cupids, Easel Back, 16 In.	525.00
Plaque, Woman, Standing, Holding Basket, 7 X 5 In. ....*Illus*	375.00
Tea Set, Gilded Lappets, Floral Swags, C.1900, 9 Piece	350.00
Urn, Floral, 2 Panels of Lovers In Garden, Cover, C.1860, 12 In.	395.00
Vase, Raised Gold Beading, Center Medallion, Courting Scene, 8 In.	325.00

Duncan & Miller is a term used by collectors when referring to glass made by the George A. Duncan and Sons Company or the Duncan and Miller Glass Company. These companies worked from 1893 to 1955, when the use of the name "Duncan" was discontinued and the firm became part of the United States Glass Company. Early patterns may be listed under Pressed Glass.

DUNCAN & MILLER, Beaded Swirl, Cruet, Original Stopper, Green, Gold Trim	250.00
Canterbury, Ashtray, 3 In.	4.00
Canterbury, Compote, Ruby, 5 1/2 In.	85.00
Caribbean, Ashtray, Footed, 4 1/2 In.	15.00
Caribbean, Creamer, Blue	35.00
Caribbean, Fruit Bowl, Footed, Handles, Blue, 9 In.	65.00
Caribbean, Goblet, Water, Crystal	8.00
Caribbean, Jar, Cider, Cover, Ruby	95.00
Caribbean, Plate, Crystal, 7 1/2 In.	4.00
Caribbean, Punch Cup	5.00
Caribbean, Punch Set, Ruby Handles, 15 Piece	195.00
Caribbean, Sugar & Creamer, Blue	36.00
Chanticleer, Tumbler, Cobalt Blue	55.00
Chanticleer, Tumbler, Old Fashion, Cobalt Blue	60.00
Diamond Ridge, Punch Set, C.1900	135.00
Duck, Ashtray, 5 In.	18.00
Duck, Ashtray, 7 In.	22.00
Duck, Box, Cigarette, Cover, 6 In.	40.00
First Love, Goblet	25.00
First Love, Liqueur	25.00
Georgian, Vase, Ruby, 8 In.	85.00
Hobnail, Goblet, 10 Oz.	9.00
Hobnail, Plate, 7 1/2 In.	6.00
Hobnail, Plate, 8 1/2 In.	8.00
Hobnail, Sherbet, Crystal	8.00
Hobnail, Sugar & Creamer, Crystal	10.00
Hobnail, Top Hat, Crystal, 3 3/4 In.	20.00
Hobnail, Tray, Mint, Crystal, 6 In.	15.00
Indian Tree, Goblet, Water	13.00
Indian Tree, Tumbler, Iced Tea	13.00
Mardi Gras, Berry Bowl, 4 X 10 In.	60.00
Mardi Gras, Compote, 5 3/4 In.	26.00
Mardi Gras, Cracker Jar, Cover	110.00
Mardi Gras, Jug, Claret, 9 3/4 In.	65.00
Mardi Gras, Punch Set, 12 Cups	138.00
Mardi Gras, Salt & Pepper, Metal Tops	40.00
Mardi Gras, Toothpick	20.00
Mardi Gras, Vase, Cornucopia, 14 In.	48.00
Pall Mall, Swan, Ruby, 7 In.	36.00
Puritan, Dish, Cheese & Cracker, Cover, Ruby	275.00
Sandwich, Basket, Applied Handle, Flared, Amber, 10 In.	60.00
Sandwich, Bowl, Crimped, 11 In.	32.00
Sandwich, Bowl, Fluted, 12 In.	38.00
Sandwich, Cake Plate, 13 In.	35.00
Sandwich, Candelabrum, 2–Light, Pair	245.00
Sandwich, Celery, 10 In.	27.00
Sandwich, Goblet	8.50
Sandwich, Pickle, 7 In.	20.00
Sandwich, Plate, 8 In.	10.00
Sandwich, Plate, 16 In.	55.00
Sandwich, Plate, Deviled Egg	40.00
Sandwich, Relish, 3 Sections, 12 In.	35.00
Sandwich, Sugar & Creamer	12.00
Sandwich, Torte Plate, Amber, 12 In.	50.00
Sanibel, Bowl, Blue Opalescent, 14 In.	75.00
Shell & Tassel, Bowl, Footed, 2 Handles, 2 In.	30.00
Shell & Tassel, Cake Stand, Shell Corners, Square, 9 In.	85.00

Shell & Tassel, Compote, Shell Corners, Frosted, 5 In.	50.00
Shell, Platter, Blue, 15 In.	60.00
Spiral Flutes, Bowl, Console, Green, 11 3/4 In.	25.00
Spiral Flutes, Bowl, Grapefruit	4.00
Spiral Flutes, Pickle, Oval, 8 5/8 In.	16.00
Spiral Flutes, Plate, 7 1/2 In.	4.00
Spiral Flutes, Sherbet, Green, 3 3/4 In.	6.50
Spiral Flutes, Tumbler, Footed, Green	12.00
Spiral Flutes, Tumbler, Juice, Footed, Green	14.00
Swag Block, Creamer, Etched	42.50
Swan, Chartreuse, 7 In.	30.00
Swan, Crystal Neck, Red Body, 12 In.	48.00
Swan, Ice Blue, 5 1/2 In.	20.00
Swan, Red, 12 In.	65.00
Swan, Red, Clear Neck, 7 In.	30.00
Swan, Sapphire Blue, Crystal Neck, 10 1/2 In.	95.00
Swordfish, Martini Set, 7 Piece	80.00
Teardrop, Cruet, Stopper, Crystal	18.00
Teardrop, Relish, 2 Sections, Round	10.00
Terrace, Ashtray, Ruby, 3 1/2 In.	20.00
Terrace, Plate, Ruby, 6 In.	35.00
Viking, Sauceboat	225.00

Durand glass was made by Victor Durand from 1879 to 1935 at several factories. Most of the iridescent Durand glass was made by Victor Durand, Jr., from 1912 to 1924 at the Durand Art Glass Works in Vineland, New Jersey.

DURAND, Dish, Bridgeton Rose, 8 In.	150.00
Lamp, Boudoir, Frosted Green & Gold, 15 In.	565.00
Lamp, Pulled Feather & Threaded, Marble Base, 12 In.	850.00
Plate, Orange Pulled Feather, Blue Top, Dark Blue Interior, 11 In.	7995.00
Powder Box, Gold Iridescent, Star Center On Lid	550.00
Rose Bowl, Random Streaks, Blue Iridescent, 4 In.	375.00
Vase, Applied Opal Feather, Urn Shape, 5 In.	550.00
Vase, Beehive, Peacock Blue, Gold Trim, Signed, 6 In.	765.00
Vase, Blue Aurene, 11 In.	1075.00
Vase, Bulbous, Blue, Signed, 12 In.	750.00
Vase, Gold, Flared, Signed & Numbered, 7 1/2 In.	425.00
Vase, Inverted Pyriform, Amber Iridescent, Signed, 10 In.	715.00
Wine, Pulled Feather, Opalescent Stem, Emerald Green, 4 1/4 In.	200.00

Elfinware was made from about 1918 to 1940. It is a Dresden–like porcelain that was sold in dime stores and gift shops. Many pieces were decorated with raised flowers. The small pieces are marked with the name "Elfinware" or with a crown and M mark. The words "Germany" or "Made in Germany" also appear on some pieces.

ELFINWARE, Basket, Allover Spinach, Applied Rose, Twig Handle, 3 X 2 1/2 In.	60.00
Basket, Forget-Me-Nots, Flared High Handle, 2 1/2 In., 12 Piece	250.00
Basket, Rows of Applied Flowers & Spinach, 2 X 2 In., Pair	40.00
Box, Mixed Florals Cover, 2 1/2 X 1 1/2 X 1 3/4 In.	35.00
Figurine, Piano, Germany	22.00

Elvis Presley, the famous singer, lived from 1935 to 1977. He became famous by 1956. Elvis appeared on television, starred in twenty-seven movies, and performed in Las Vegas. Memorabilia from any of the Presley shows, his records, and even memorials made after his death are collected.

ELVIS PRESLEY, Book, Illustrated By Grosset & Dunlap, 1976	20.00
Card, Gum, Set of 60	12.00
Cards, Playing, Unopened	9.00
Doll, Black Clothes, World No.2, Box, 21 In.	125.00
Doll, Phoenix & Flame, World Doll, 21 In.	85.00
Doll, Plaid Shirt, Denim Pants, Blue Suede Shoes, Box	825.00
Game, Elvis, King of Rock	5.00

Magazine, Elvis The King, 66 Pages, 1977	7.00
Magazine, Movieland, Dated 1957	10.00
Magazine, Rock 'N' Roll Rivals, No.1 Issue, Dated 1957	9.00
Paper Doll, Elvis & Priscilla, Uncut, Movie Outfits	20.00
Poster, Wild In The Country, In Spanish	35.00
Record, Shake, Rattle & Roll, 45 RPM, RCA	8.00
Sheet Music, Love Me Tender	8.00
Toy, Tour Van, Plastic, Decals, Box	28.00

Russian, French, and English workmen of the eighteenth and nineteenth centuries made small boxes and table pieces of enamel on metal. One form of English enamel is called "Battersea" and is listed under that name.

ENAMEL, Bowl, Figures Design, Square, Chinese, 4 1/2 In.	10.00
Box, Blue Hinged Top, Footed, Velvet Lined, Birmingham, Oval	300.00
Decanter Set, Enameled Frames, Crystal, French, 11 Piece	110.00
Dessert Set, Kuznichev, Moscow, Russian, 1891, 12 Piece	1700.00
Egg, Easter, Mosaic Pattern, Gold, Champleve, Riga, C.1910, 1 3/4 In.	6600.00
Egg, Easter, Stylized Foliage, Silver–Gilt, Ruckert, C.1900, 2 1/2 In.	4675.00
Egg, Signed Aimfeldt, Russian	2750.00
Epergne Set, Gilt–Metal, Champleve, Elkington, C.1862, 5 Piece	3575.00
Frame, Pastels With Garnets, Oval, Russian, Marked, 7 In.	795.00
Mug, Figures In Formal Garden, Sprays On Handle, C.1770, 4 3/8 In.	605.00
Pedestal, Onyx, Female Medallions, Plinth Base, Champleve, 43 In.	2475.00
Pitcher, Handle, Thumbprint, Blue	300.00
Salt Set, Spoon, Silver Gilt, Flowers, Footed, Russian, 5 Piece	495.00
Salt, Viking Ship Shape, Blue, Sterling Silver, With Spoon	75.00
Vase, Bulbous Base, Brass Rim & Base, C.1860, 5 3/4 In.	750.00
Vase, Lake Scene, Maiden Portrait, Artist Signed, C.1860, 5 3/4 In.	725.00

ES Germany porcelain was made at the factory of Erdmann Schlegelmilch from 1861 to 1925 in Suhl, Germany. The porcelain was sold decorated or undecorated. Other pieces were made at the factory in Saxony, Prussia, and are marked "ES Prussia." Reinhold Schlegelmilch, a brother, made the famous wares marked "RS Germany."

ES GERMANY, Bowl, Floral, 10 1/2 In.	50.00
Dish, Marie Antoinette Portrait, 7 In.	40.00
Dish, Portrait, Lady With Dove, 9 In.	50.00
Tray, Dresser, Red Roses, Marked	55.00
Vase, Mythological Scene, 7 1/2 In.	100.00
ES PRUSSIA, Vase, Floral, 10 In.	150.00

All types of Eskimo artifacts are collected. Carvings of whale or walrus teeth are listed under Scrimshaw. Baskets are in the Basket category. All other types of Eskimo art are listed here.

ESKIMO, Basket, Chippewa, Quill, Tufted Moose Figure On Lid, 2 1/2 X 4 In.	50.00
Basket, Coil, Sealskin & Birdskin Design, 11 X 13 In.	170.00
Basket, Coiled Grass, Sealskin & Birdskin Embroidery, 14 X 8 In.	475.00
Basket, Cover, Yukon River, Turnbaugh & Turnbaugh, 3 1/2 X 7 In.	450.00
Basket, Lid, Braided Design, Makah, 2 X 2 1/2 In.	50.00
Basket, Lid, Braided Handle, Alaskan, 5 X 6 1/2 In.	150.00
Bow Drill, Ivory, Sea Mammals, Red & Black Pigment, Drilled, 15 In.	250.00
Box, Baleen Covered, Ivory Bottom, Polar Bear Handle, 2 X 2 1/2 In.	1155.00
Comb Set, Wood, Dyed With Carbon & Fish Oil, Framed, Pair	70.00
Cribbage Board, Ivory, Design of Walrus & Seal, C.1890, 11 1/2 In.	335.00
Doll Head, Ivory, Black & Red Patina, Bering Sea Culture, 2 1/4 In.	1250.00
Doll, Carved Ivory Head, Sealskin Hooded Parka, Mukluks, 6 In.	200.00
Doll, Wooden Face, Native Dress of Fur, C.1920, 10 1/4 In.	55.00
Game Board, Ivory	3410.00
Harpoon Head, Serpentine, Bone Handle Inset, 11 1/2 In.	90.00
Hook, Halibut, Carved, Figural, Nootka, 20th Century, 8 In.	39.00
Kayak, Sealskin, C.1930, 24 In.	375.00
Knife & Fork, Carved Handles Depicting Faces	1650.00

Knife, Hunting, All Carved Animal Bone	60.00
Marionette, Carved Ivory, Incised Face, Arms & Legs Move, 3 1/2 In.	660.00
Mask, White Chalk Paint, Brown Eyebrows & Lips, 10 1/4 In.	300.00
Model, Boat, Umiak, Painted Hide, Over Wooden Frame, Float, 29 In.	325.00
Model, Dogsled, Carved Ivory, Bone, Seal Carcass, Dog Team, 4 1/2 In.	350.00
Model, Kayak, Hunter, Seal Float, Inua Spirit, Bering Sea, 1982, 25 In.	650.00
Mukluks, Leather Sole, Trade Cloth Uppers, Fur Bands, 14 X 11 In.	150.00
Needlecase, Carved Ivory, Walrus Clutching Tusks, Toggle, 4 In.	350.00
Pipe, Human Effigy, Incised Story Scene, Walrus Ivory, C.1850	2200.00
Snow Goggles, Inuit, Tortoiseshell, Leather Strap Has Russell Adams	65.00
Snowshoes, Primitive, 29 X 9 In.	65.00
Tool Box, Wooden, Inlaid Beaded Cover, Red, Hide Thongs, 14 In.	400.00
Totem Pole, Bird, Clan Hats, Bear Figure, Haida, C.1920, 12 1/2 In.	100.00
Totem Pole, Northwest Coast, Hand Carved, 21 X 14 In.	1595.00
Toy, Dogsled, Team, Wooden Sled, 4 Rabbit Skin Dogs, Alaska, 12 In.	475.00
Tusk, Eskimo With Dogsled, 5 Husky Dogs, Omedelina, Nome, 26 1/2 In.	300.00

ETLING   FRANCE   Etling glass is very similar in design to Lalique and Phoenix glass. It was made in France for Etling, a retail shop. It dates from the 1920s and 1930s.

ETLING, Bowl, White Opalescent Fern Fronds, 14 In.	70.00

ФАБЕРЖЕ   КФ   Faberge was a firm of jewelers and goldsmiths founded in St. Petersburg, Russia, in 1842, by Gustav Faberge. Peter Carl Faberge, his son, was jeweler to the Russian Imperial Court from about 1870 to 1914.

FABERGE, Coffee & Tea Set, Ivory Finials & Handles, Silver, Marked, 4 Piece	8250.00
Cup, Silver–Gilt, Royal Blue Enameled, Nevalainen, C.1910, 1 5/8 In.	2310.00
Cup, Vodka, Silver, Enameled Red Band, Guilloche, Marked, 1 7/8 In.	3850.00
Figurine, Elephant	1650.00
Holder, Pencil, Silver, Palisander, Silver Flags, C.1900, 4 3/4 In.	4620.00
Inkstand, Rococo, Presentation, 2 Wells, Hinged Covers, 1910, 14 In.	9350.00
Jar, Crystal, Silver–Gilt, Paw Feet, Satyr Masks, C.1900, 6 1/4 In.	2750.00
Knife, Paper, Nephrite, Silver Gilt & Enamel, 11 In. *Illus*	2200.00
Locket, Silver, Enameled Flower, Sunburst, Hollming, 1 In.	4620.00
Pendant, Diamond, Moonstone, Gold, Chain, Wigstrom, 1 3/8 In.	4950.00
Pin, Diamonds, Red Enameled, Gold, Silver, Hollming, 2 In.	2310.00
Serving Set, Tapered Faceted Handles, Silver, Case, 1885, 19 Piece	3850.00
Tray, Laurel & Beaded Rim, C.1900, 25 Oz.	880.00
Vase, Silver, Flowering Vine, 3 Handles, Bulbous, C.1885, 4 5/8 In.	3300.00

Definitions of the words differentiating the types of pottery and porcelain are difficult because there is so much overlapping of meaning. Faience is tin-glazed earthenware, especially the wares made in France, Germany, and Scandinavia. It is also correct to say that faience is the same as majolica or Delft, although usually the term refers only to the tin-glazed pottery of the three regions mentioned.

FAIENCE, Figurine, Man Holding Basket, Lady Holding Chicken, Gien, Pair	55.00
Inkpot, Buildings, Man, Animals On Side Panels, Glazed, 3 3/4 In.	130.00
Pitcher, French, 12 1/2 In.	135.00
Pitcher, Green, California, 8 1/2 In.	125.00
Planter, Low, French, Flowers, Floral Design, Bracket Feet, 11 In.	700.00
Sweetmeat Stand, Figural, Triton, Green Tail, C.1760, 11 1/4 In.	5775.00
Tureen, Duck, Swimming, Cover, Letter I Mark, C.1760, 5 5/8 In.	1760.00
Vase, Glossy Blue, 4 1/2 In.	125.00

Fairings are small souvenir china boxes and figurines that were sold at country fairs during the nineteenth century. Most were made in Germany. Reproductions of fairings are being made, especially of the famous "twelve months of marriage" series.

FAIRING, Box, Black & White Kittens, Sitting, Dresser, Staffordshire, 7 In.	95.00
Box, Man Hunting With Dog, Cover	40.00
Box, Red Riding Hood & Wolf On Lid, Staffordshire	55.00

Box, Victorian Child On Cover, Staffordshire	75.00
Figurine, Last In Bed To Put Out Light	225.00
Figurine, Married For Money	175.00
Figurine, Three O'Clock In The Morning	145.00
Match Holder, Pig, 9 Strikers	100.00

FAMILLE ROSE, see Chinese Export

 Fans have been used for cooling since the days of the ancients. By the eighteenth century, the fan was an accessory for the lady of fashion and very elaborate and expensive fans were made. Sticks were made of ivory or wood, set with jewels or carved. The fans were made of painted silk or paper. Inexpensive paper fans printed with advertising were giveaways in the late nineteenth and early twentieth centuries.

FAN, Advertising, Cherry Blossom Cola, Bottle Picture	22.00
Advertising, Cherry Smash, Pilgrim Boy	25.00
Advertising, Colchester Rubber Co.	6.00
Advertising, Keen Kutter Kutlery, St.Louis Fair, 1904	35.00
Advertising, Morrel Meats, Paper	15.00
Advertising, New Home Sewing Machines	18.50
Advertising, Pevely Milk, Shaped Like Can, With Cow	22.00
Advertising, Red & White Food Store	18.50
Advertising, Schlitz, Japan, 1890s	85.00
Advertising, Tube Rose Snuff, Can Shape	22.00
Advertising, Union Pacific Tea, Paper	18.00
Bluebird, Flowers, Gold Ground, Black Lacquer Sticks, C.1900, 34 In.	95.00
Buster Keaton, Paper	10.00
Electric, Art Deco, Cast Iron	30.00
Electric, Brass Blades	29.50
Electric, G.E., Brass Blades, 13 In.	35.00
Electric, Polar Cub, A.C.Gilbert, 6 In.	60.00
Electric, Wagner, Brass Blades, 12 In.	35.00
Electric, Western Electric, Brass Blades, Oscillating, 10 In.	4.00
Feather, Ivory Handle, Bird Center, Victorian	65.00
Fuchsia Satin, Hand Painted Flowers & Bluebirds, 29 X 13 1/2 In.	75.00
Gold Mesh & Ribs, Diamonds, Emeralds, Sapphires, Rubies, Cartier, 1840	6000.00
Hot Air, Prototype, 1960s	250.00
Ivory Frame, Carved, Silk Tassels, Lacquered Box, Oriental	185.00
Ivory Handle, Fancy Top, Early 1860s	40.00
Joan Crawford, Paper	10.00
Lace & Silk, Painted Lady & Cupids, French, Presentation Box, 24 In.	55.00
Manhattan, No.3, Battery Operated	300.00

Faberge, Knife, Paper, Nephrite, Silver Gilt & Enamel, 11 In.

Fireplace, Andirons, Brass, Federal, 18 In., Pair

Maroon & Pink, Reverse Opening To Hand Painted Erotic Scene, 1890s	350.00
Ostrich Feathers, Celluloid Handle	67.50
Ostrich Feathers, Plum, Celluloid Handle, 1920s	40.00
Ostrich Feathers, White, Tortoise Ribs, 15 To 24 In.	58.00
Peacock Feather, Victorian, Ivory Handle, Painted	35.00
Pleated Paper, Quail, Hand Painted, Black Sticks, Oriental, 1900, 34 In.	95.00
Silk, Lotus Blossom, Embroidered, Japan, 1930s	45.00
White Net, Yellow, Orange Painted Flowers, Bone Sticks, 13 X 30 In.	75.00
Woodrow Wilson, Protection, Prosperity	25.00

> Federzeichnung is the very strange German name for a pattern of
> mother–of–pearl satin glass. The pattern had irregularly shaped
> sections of brown glass covered with a pattern of gold squiggle lines.
> It was first made in the late nineteenth century.

FEDERZEICHNUNG, Vase, Mother–of–Pearl, Brown, Gold, White Lining, 10 1/4 In.	1695.00
Vase, Mother–of–Pearl, Tri–Foil Top, 5 1/2 In.	1245.00

> Fenton Art Glass Company, founded in Martins Ferry, Ohio, by
> Frank L. Fenton, is now located in Williamstown, West Virginia. It
> is noted for early carnival glass produced between 1907 and 1920.
> Many other types of glass were also made.

FENTON, Acorn, Bowl, Marigold, Moonstone, Ruffled, 7 1/2 In.	400.00
Apple Blossom Crest, Cake Plate, Crimped, 13 In.	95.00
Apple Blossom Crest, Vase, 4 1/2 In.	55.00
Apple Blossom, Vase, 8 In.	70.00
Aqua Crest, Basket, 10 In.	85.00
Aqua Crest, Bonbon, 5 In.	25.00
Aqua Crest, Compote, 7 In.	27.50
Aqua Crest, Vase, Fan, 7 In.	30.00
Banded Laurel, Nappy, Persian Blue, 4 1/2 In.	15.00
Basket Weave, Candy Dish, Blue Satin	20.00
Basket Weave, Candy Dish, Rosalene	20.00
Beaded Melon, Jug, Gold Overlay, Handle, 6 In.	40.00
Beaded Melon, Pitcher, 4 In.	24.00
Bubble Optic, Vase, Blue, 8 1/2 In.	69.00
Bubble Optic, Vase, Honey Amber, 11 In.	90.00
Burmese, Bell, Sea Shells	40.00
Burmese, Lamp, Mariner, Sea Shells	350.00
Burmese, Pitcher, Roses, 4 In.	40.00
Burmese, Vase, Pink Dogwood, 5 1/2 In.	40.00
Butterfly & Berry, Vase, Green, 9 In.	190.00
Butterfly & Fern, Tumbler, Blue	40.00
Buttons & Braids, Pitcher, Blue	130.00
Cherry Circles, Sauce, White, Round	70.00
Coin Dot, Basket, Cranberry, 7 In.	75.00
Coin Dot, Bowl, Amethyst, 9 In.	32.00
Coin Dot, Creamer, Cranberry, 4 In.	55.00
Coin Dot, Cruet, Cobalt Blue	30.00
Coin Dot, Ewer, Handles, Cranberry Opalescent, 9 In.	65.00
Coin Dot, Lamp, Boudoir, 11 1/2 In.	85.00
Coin Dot, Pitcher, Cobalt Blue, 32 Oz.	22.00
Coin Dot, Pitcher, Cranberry, 6 1/2 In.	77.00
Coin Dot, Rose Bowl, Marigold	30.00
Coin Dot, Sugar & Creamer, Cranberry	100.00
Coin Dot, Tumbler, Blue, 3 3/4 In.	14.00
Coin Dot, Vase, Blue Opalescent, Crimped, 6 In.	35.00
Coin Dot, Vase, Blue, 5 In.	40.00
Coin Dot, Vase, Topaz, 11 In.	60.00
Coin Dot, Water Set, Cranberry, 1949, 7 Piece	300.00
Coinspot, Lamp, Cranberry, C.1950, 10 In.	200.00
Coinspot, Water Set, Green. 7 Piece	295.00
Crystal Crest, Bowl, 10 In.	65.00
Crystal Crest, Vase, 8 1/2 In.	70.00
Currier & Ives, Lamp, Fairy, White Satin	29.00

Daisy & Button, Bell, Blue Satin	20.00
Daisy & Button, Bell, Green	20.00
Daisy & Button, Boot, Orange	12.50
Daisy & Fern, Bottle, Barber, Vaseline	130.00
Dancing Ladies, Bowl, Console, Crystal	65.00
Dancing Ladies, Urn, Cover, Moonstone, 12 In.	300.00
Diamond Lace, Epergne, Blue Opalescent, 10 In.	125.00
Diamond Lace, Epergne, Blue, 10 In.	115.00
Diamond Optic, Compote, Dolphin Handles, Ruby, 7 1/2 In.	45.00
Diamond Optic, Creamer, Ruby Overlay	35.00
Diamond Optic, Vase, Cranberry, C.1953, 6 In.	75.00
Diamond Optic, Water Set, Ruby Overlay, 6 Piece	150.00
Dolphin, Bowl, Crimped Edge, Jade Green, 9 In.	20.00
Dolphin, Bowl, Oval, Ebony, 10 In.	58.00
Dolphin, Candy Dish, Diamond Optic, Footed, Green, 4 In.	55.00
Dot Optic, Bowl, Cranberry, 7 In.	45.00
Dot Optic, Water Set, Ruffled, Cranberry, 7 Piece	295.00
Dragon & Berry, Bowl, Ruffled, Marigold, 9 1/2 In.	100.00
Emerald Crest, Bowl, Underplate, 3 1/2 In.	25.00
Emerald Crest, Cake Plate, Pedestal	65.00
Emerald Crest, Plate, 8 1/2 In.	24.00
Figurine, Bunnie, Green	25.00
Figurine, Donkey & Cart, White	50.00
Figurine, Swan, Rosalene	25.00
Figurine, Whale, Dianthus, Crystal Velvet	15.00
Garland, Rose Bowl, Footed, Green	325.00
Georgian, Mug, Pink	38.00
Georgian, Pitcher, Ruby, 54 Oz.	40.00
Hanging Heart, Cruet, Turquoise	100.00
Hobnail, Ashtray, Fan Shape, Blue, 5 1/2 In.	9.00
Hobnail, Basket, Blue Opalescent, 4 In.	25.00
Hobnail, Basket, Blue, 8 In.	35.00
Hobnail, Basket, Cranberry, 10 In.	120.00
Hobnail, Basket, Opalescent Blue, 10 In.	70.00
Hobnail, Bowl, Cranberry, 5 In.	35.00
Hobnail, Bowl, Crimped, 11 In.	50.00
Hobnail, Box, Cigarette, Wooden Cover	18.00
Hobnail, Candy Dish, Cover, Footed, Blue, 7 X 4 3/8 In.	32.00
Hobnail, Chamberstick, Cranberry	35.00
Hobnail, Cigarette Holder, Hat Shape, 2 1/2 In.	22.00
Hobnail, Cruet, Cranberry	48.00 To 57.50
Hobnail, Cruet, Turquoise	47.50
Hobnail, Cruet, Vaseline	47.50
Hobnail, Dish, Heart, Topaz	40.00
Hobnail, Epergne, 8 1/4 X 7 In.	35.00
Hobnail, Ivy Bowl	12.50
Hobnail, Lamp, Fairy, Green	25.00
Hobnail, Lamp, Vanity, Electric, Pair	35.00
Hobnail, Lighter, Cigarette	10.00
Hobnail, Pitcher, Blue, 80 Oz.	125.00
Hobnail, Pitcher, Milk, Opalescent	25.00
Hobnail, Pitcher, Water, Cranberry	125.00
Hobnail, Plate, Green, 6 In.	10.00
Hobnail, Powder Box, Cover, Cranberry	38.00
Hobnail, Punch Set, Ladle, Green, 7 Qt., 15 Piece	265.00
Hobnail, Salt & Pepper, Cranberry	35.00
Hobnail, Sugar & Creamer, Blue, Miniature	15.00
Hobnail, Top Hat, Blue Opalescent, 1 In.	25.00
Hobnail, Tumbler, Juice, Opalescent	7.25
Hobnail, Vase, 5 1/2 In.	20.00
Hobnail, Vase, Fan, 10 X 8 1/4 In.	32.00
Hobnail, Water Set, Squat Pitcher, Opalescent, 7 Piece	70.00
Holly, Compote, Lime Green Opalescent, Stemmed	650.00
Holly, Hat, Ruffled, Marigold, Moonstone	275.00

Iris, Compote, Green	22.50
Ivory Crest, Bowl, With Epergne Lily & Candlesticks	100.00
June, Cocktail, Oyster, Blue	29.00
Lamp, Gone With The Wind, Blue Satin, 24 In.	225.00
Lincoln Inn, Cup & Saucer, Cobalt Blue	35.00
Lincoln Inn, Sugar & Creamer, Cobalt Blue	60.00
Lotus & Poinsettia, Sauce, Ruffled, Footed, Amberina	450.00
Mandarin, Candlestick, 8 In., Pair	113.00
Mirrored Lotus, Rose Bowl, White	375.00
Moonstone, Bottle, Cologne, Black Stopper	22.00
Moonstone, Bowl, Lotus, Silver Stork, Black Base	85.00 To 95.00
Moonstone, Rose Bowl, Oriental Scene	150.00
Mulberry, Vase, 4 1/2 In.	88.00
Orange Tree Scroll, Tankard Pitcher, Marigold	325.00
Orange Tree, Mug, Shaving, Emerald Green	500.00
Orange Tree, Mug, Shaving, Marigold	42.50
Orange Tree, Mug, Straight, Marigold	22.50
Owl, Lamp, Fairy, Green	25.00
Peach Crest, Basket, Crystal Handle, 7 In.	60.00
Peach Crest, Basket, Rose Crest, 10 In.	95.00
Peach Crest, Bowl, 6 3/4 In.	35.00
Peach Crest, Bowl, 13 In.	90.00
Peach Crest, Candlestick, 5 In.	23.00
Peacock & Grapes, Bowl, Blue, 9 In.	40.00
Peacock, Vase, Blue Satin	35.00
Persian Medallion, Basket, Ruby	26.00
Persian Medallion, Chalice, Custard Satin	25.00
Persian Medallion, Compote, Blue Satin	25.00
Persian Medallion, Lamp, Fairy, 3 Piece	40.00
Plum, Candlestick, 3 In., Pair	58.00
Plum, Vase, 11 1/2 In., Pair	58.00
Poinsettia, Cornucopia, Centerpiece, Satin Glass, 11 In.	14.00
Rib Optic, Bowl, Cranberry Opalescent, 11 In.	110.00
Rib Optic, Salt & Pepper, Cranberry	45.00 To 75.00
Rib Optic, Vase, Green, 9 1/4 In.	60.00
Rib Optic, Vase, Spiral, Cranberry, 6 1/2 In.	45.00
Rose Crest, Bowl, With Epergne Lily, 10 In.	45.00
Rose Crest, Candleholder, Cornucopia	30.00
Rose Crest, Vase, 5 In.	25.00
Rustic, Vase, Funeral, Green, Mid-Size	70.00
Silver Crest, Basket, Apple Blossom In Bottom, 8 In.	25.00
Silver Crest, Basket, Turquoise, Crystal Handle, 13 In.	175.00
Silver Crest, Cake Plate, Footed, 13 In.	35.00
Silver Crest, Compote, Label, 8 In.	20.00
Silver Crest, Epergne, 2 Piece	45.00
Silver Crest, Plate, 8 1/2 In.	12.50
Silver Crest, Sugar	15.00
Silver Crest, Tidbit, 2-Tier	27.00
Silver Crest, Tidbit, 3-Tier	35.00
Silver Crest, Vase, 8 In.	20.00
Spiral Optic, Vase, Cranberry, 9 1/2 In.	75.00
Spiral Optic, Vase, Flared, 10 In.	65.00

Fiesta pottery has been reproduced since 1985 but the new pieces are made in different colors from the old ones.

Stippled Rays, Bonbon, Tri–Fold, 6 1/2 In. 26.00
Stippled Rays, Sugar, Breakfast, Open, Vaseline, Marigold Overlay 65.00
Strawberry Scroll, Tumbler, Blue 85.00
Strawberry, Bell, Crystal Velvet 25.00
Strawberry, Bonbon, Amberina 125.00
Strawberry, Box, Heart Cover, Custard Satin 45.00
Stream of Hearts, Compote, Marigold 50.00
Swan, Bonbon, Green 20.00
Turtle, Ring Tree 20.00
Versailles, Bowl, Whipped Cream, Blue 125.00
Versailles, Cocktail, Oyster, Blue 25.00
Versailles, Cup & Saucer, Blue 26.95
Versailles, Plate, Blue, 9 In. 24.00
Versailles, Sherbet, Blue 38.00
Versailles, Sugar Pail, Blue 155.00
Waterlily, Basket, Custard Satin, 7 In. 35.00
Waterlily, Bowl, 3–Footed, Custard Satin 18.00
Waterlily, Candleholder, Lime Green, Pair 20.00
Waterlily, Candleholder, White Satin, Pair 30.00
Waterlily, Candlestick, Crystal Velvet, Pair 35.00
Waterlily, Candy Bowl, Green 29.50
Waterlily, Rose Bowl, Lime Green 10.00
Waterlily, Vase, Bud, Blue Satin 24.00
Waterlily, Vase, Bud, Lilac 26.00
Wisteria, Vase, Crimped, 5 In. 15.00
Wreath of Roses, Punch Cup, Vintage Interior, Marigold 22.00

Fiesta, the colorful dinnerware, was introduced in 1936 by the Homer Laughlin China Co., redesigned in 1969, and withdrawn in 1973. The simple design was characterized by a band of concentric circles, beginning at the rim. Cups had full–circle handles until 1969, when partial–circle handles were made. Harlequin and Riviera were related wares. For more information and prices of American dinnerware, see the book "Kovels' Depression Glass & American Dinnerware Price List."

FIESTA, Ashtray, Forest Green 18.00
Ashtray, Red .... 26.00 To 30.00
Bowl, Fruit, Chartreuse, 5 1/2 In. 12.00
Bowl, Fruit, Cobalt Blue, 8 1/2 In. 15.00
Bowl, Fruit, Ivory, 4 3/4 In. 8.00
Bowl, Fruit, Ivory, 8 1/2 In. 18.00
Bowl, Fruit, Medium Green, 8 1/2 In. 45.00
Bowl, Fruit, Red, 4 3/4 In. 20.00
Bowl, Fruit, Red, 9 1/2 In. 32.00
Bowl, Fruit, Rose, 5 1/2 In. 15.00
Bowl, Fruit, Turquoise, 5 1/2 In. 15.00
Bowl, Fruit, Yellow, 4 3/4 In. 13.00
Bowl, Fruit, Yellow, 9 1/2 In. 22.00
Bowl, Nesting, Red, 11 1/2 In. 120.00
Bowl, Salad, Footed, Red .... 165.00 To 175.00
Bowl, Soup, Onion, Cover, Turquoise 550.00
Candleholder, Bulb, Cobalt Blue, Pair 30.00
Candleholder, Bulb, Green, Pair .... 35.00 To 38.00
Candleholder, Bulb, Red, Pair .... 30.00 To 48.00
Carafe, Cobalt Blue .... 80.00 To 95.00
Carafe, Red .... 95.00 To 125.00
Carafe, Yellow 70.00
Casserole, Cover, Turquoise 33.00
Casserole, French, Cover, Yellow 160.00
Chop Plate, Cobalt Blue, 15 In. 12.00
Chop Plate, Gray, 13 In. 25.00
Chop Plate, Ivory, 15 In. 25.00
Chop Plate, Rose, 13 In. 12.00
Chop Plate, Turquoise, 13 In. 17.00

Chop Plate, Yellow, 15 In. 25.00
Coffeepot, Red ....75.00 To 125.00
Coffeepot, Yellow 48.00
Compote, Turquoise, 12 In. 50.00
Compote, Yellow, 12 In. .... 40.00 To 50.00
Creamer, Dark Green 12.00
Creamer, Ivory 10.00
Creamer, Yellow 10.00
Cup & Saucer, After Dinner, Cobalt Blue 38.00
Cup & Saucer, After Dinner, Red 40.00
Cup & Saucer, Gray 17.00
Cup & Saucer, Medium Green 20.00
Eggcup, Ivory 30.00
Eggcup, Red 40.00
Gravy Boat, Chartreuse 22.00
Gravy Boat, Ivory 18.00
Jam Jar, Cobalt Blue 100.00
Jam Jar, Yellow .... 90.00 To 95.00
Mixing Bowl, Green, Kitchen Kraft, 6 In. 37.00
Mug, Medium Green 45.00
Mug, Rose 29.50
Mustard, Cover, Cobalt Blue 95.00
Mustard, Cover, Yellow 50.00
Pepper Shaker, Gray 6.00
Pitcher, Disc, Chartreuse 65.00
Pitcher, Disc, Medium Green 210.00
Pitcher, Disc, Red 85.00
Pitcher, Ice Lip, Cobalt Blue 65.00
Pitcher, Ice Lip, Red .... 50.00 To 90.00
Pitcher, Ice Lip, Yellow 30.00
Plate, Calendar, 1955, Gold 27.50
Plate, Cobalt Blue, 10 In. 25.00
Plate, Forest Green, 7 In. 4.00
Plate, Gray, 9 In. 9.00
Plate, Ivory, 7 In. 2.50
Plate, Light Green, 10 In. 4.50
Plate, Medium Green, 9 In. 22.00
Plate, Red, 10 In. 28.00
Plate, Rose, 9 In. 18.00
Platter, Yellow, 12 In. 18.00
Relish, Red 95.00
Relish, Turquoise & Yellow 98.00
Salt & Pepper, Cobalt Blue 12.00
Salt & Pepper, Forest Green 22.00
Salt & Pepper, Ivory .... 10.00 To 11.00
Salt & Pepper, Red 22.50
Saltshaker, Gray 6.00
Soup, Cream, Chartreuse .... 20.00 To 39.00
Soup, Cream, Dark Green 38.00
Soup, Cream, Turquoise .... 18.00 To 30.00
Soup, Cream, Yellow 12.50
Soup, Onion, Cover, Cobalt Blue 175.00
Soup, Onion, Cover, Light Green 200.00
Soup, Onion, Cover, Red .... 225.00 To 325.00
Spoon, Kitchen Kraft, Cobalt Blue 40.00
Spoon, Kitchen Kraft, Red 60.00
Sugar & Creamer, Red 50.00
Sugar, Cobalt Blue 30.00
Sugar, Ivory 22.00
Syrup, Cobalt Blue 140.00
Syrup, Dark Green ....95.00 To 125.00
Syrup, Ivory 160.00
Teapot, Dark Green 45.00
Teapot, Medium Green 185.00

Tray, Figure 8 Shape, Cobalt Blue	30.00
Tumbler, Cobalt Blue, 10 Oz.	26.00
Tumbler, Ivory, 5 Oz.	12.00
Tumbler, Red, 5 Oz.	35.00
Tumbler, Rose, 5 Oz.	39.00
Vase, Bud, Light Green	20.00
Vase, Bud, Turquoise	25.00 To 28.00
Vase, Cobalt Blue, 10 In.	250.00
Vase, Red, 12 In.	370.00

Findlay, or onyx, glass was made using three layers of glass. It was manufactured by the Dalzell Gilmore Leighton Company about 1889 in Findlay, Ohio. The platinum, ruby, or black pattern was molded into the glass. The glass came in several colors, but was usually white or ruby.

FINDLAY ONYX, Celery Vase	145.00
Creamer, 4 3/4 X 4 In.	395.00
Creamer, Rose	945.00
Mustard, Ruby	850.00
Salt & Pepper	595.00
Spooner, Tulip, Daisy & Thistle, 4 1/2 In.	425.00
Sugar, White On Ruby, 3 3/4 In.	570.00
Toothpick	325.00

It is said that every little boy wanted to be a fireman or a train engineer 75 years ago and the collectors today reflect this interest. All types of firefighting equipment are wanted, from fire marks to uniforms to toy fire trucks.

FIREFIGHTING, Ax, Hickory Handle, 35 In.	40.00
Badge, Gary, Indiana	25.00
Bell, Brass, Oak Case, 15 In.	250.00
Bell, Engine, La France, Eagle, Bronze	450.00
Bell, Gamewell, Oak Case, 6 In.	535.00
Book, Haverille, Ma., History, Photos, 1897, 148 Pages	75.00
Bucket, Leather, Black Repaint, Label Dovor, V.R., 10 In.	150.00
Bucket, Leather, Green Paint, M.R.E. Stencil, 13 In.	150.00
Bucket, Leather, No. 3, H. Tomlin, C.1830	350.00
Bucket, Leather, Scene of Flaming House, Firemen, No.2, 1822	8500.00
Bucket, W. English	300.00
Button, Waterbury Co., Sharpsburg, Pa., Set of 6	25.00
Cart, Hose, 2 Large Wheels	85.00
Cart, Wheel Hose, Hose Roller, Equipment Box, C.1880, 6 Ft.	3900.00
Extinguisher, Blue Glass, 1888	70.00
Extinguisher, C.M.St.P.& P.Ry., Brass	65.00
Extinguisher, Ford, Script, 13 In.	55.00
Extinguisher, Fyr Fyter, All Brass, 16 In.	10.00
Extinguisher, Grenade, Harden Star, Ribbed, Blue, 6 In.	100.00
Extinguisher, John's Manville, Tubular, Tin, 22 In.	20.00
Extinguisher, Kerotest, Wooden Case, Yellow Letters, Red	175.00
Extinguisher, Korbeline, Grenade, Amber	85.00
Extinguisher, Liberty Brand, Tubular	45.00
Extinguisher, Miller Peerless, Brass, Pump–Type, 5 Gal.	25.00
Extinguisher, Presto Fire, Box, 6 In.	14.00
Extinguisher, Red Comet	22.00 To 37.00
Extinguisher, Security Presto Dry Chemical, 1930s	40.00
Extinguisher, Texaco, Brass	60.00
Fire Mark, 4 Clasped Hands, No.906, Cast Iron, 7 X 10 1/2 In.	300.00
Firehouse Gong, On Board, 6 In.	125.00
Firemark, Oval, Hydrant & Hose, Iron, 7 X 11 In.	165.00
Grenade, Harden, Star, Light Blue, Wire Loop, 3/4 Contents	30.00
Grenade, Red Comet, With Holder	25.00
Helmet, Leather Shield On Front, Black Leather	75.00
Helmet, Parade, Eagle, Columbia Hose No.1, Whitestone, N.Y.	150.00
Helmet, White, Brass Shield, Cast Letters	375.00

Ice Box, On Stand, Fire & Police, Cast Iron 375.00
Lantern, American LaFrance, Bracket .... 290.00 To 350.00
Lantern, Dewey Mill 35.00
Lantern, Dietz, Copper Bottom 75.00
Lantern, Dietz, Wizard 795.00
Lantern, Fireman's, Brass, Pat.1907 .... 375.00
Nozzle, Brass & Copper, 30 In. 115.00
Nozzle, Brass, 11 In. 18.00
Nozzle, Eastman Co., Brass 16.00
Photograph, Firefighter's Expo, Framed, 1888, 22 X 25 In. 50.00
Postcard, Fire Dept., Springfield, Mass., 4 Knox Trucks, 1915 .... 10.00
Trumpet, Presentation 1150.00

The fireplace was used to cook and to heat the American home in past centuries. Many types of tools and equipment were used. Andirons held the logs in place, firebacks reflected the heat into the room, and tongs were used to move either fuel or food. Many types of spits and roasting jacks were made and are listed under Kitchen.

FIREPLACE, Andirons, Baseball, Pitcher, Batter, Painted, 19th Century 1700.00
Andirons, Brass Rosette Finials, Wrought Iron, 27 In. 125.00
Andirons, Brass, Baroque, Ball & Disc Standards, French, 29 In. 1350.00
Andirons, Brass, Double Acorn Design, Arched Legs, 12 3/4 In. 325.00
Andirons, Brass, Federal, 18 In., Pair ....*Illus* 700.00
Andirons, Brass, Federal, Ball & Bell, Slipper Feet, C.1810, 18 In. 700.00
Andirons, Brass, Federal, Ball Finial, Baluster Shaft, 13 In. 192.00
Andirons, Brass, Green Column Design, Ball Top, 29 1/2 In. 150.00
Andirons, Brass, Hammered Ball & Column, 18 1/2 In. 30.00
Andirons, Brass, Knife Blade, Urn Finials, American, C.1780 .... 800.00
Andirons, Brass, Leaf Design Columns, Quilted, Paw Feet, 24 In. 150.00
Andirons, Brass, Penny Foot, American, 20 1/2 X 20 In. 825.00
Andirons, Brass, Steeple Top, 21 1/2 In. 1400.00
Andirons, Brass, Steeple Top, Lower Belted Ball, 23 1/2 In. 1200.00
Andirons, Cast Iron, Dachshund, 8 X 22 In. 40.00
Andirons, Wrought Iron, Full–Face Heads, Square Posts, 25 In. 100.00
Bellows, Oriental Fish, Brass, 21 In. 20.00
Bellows, Painting of Birds, Leather, Brass Nozzle, 11 1/2 In. 45.00
Bellows, Red Flowers, Leaves, Line & Scroll Design, 17 1/2 In. 165.00
Broiler, Iron, Slatted Top, Handles, 12 1/4 X 16 In. 137.00
Broiler, Rotating, Iron, S–Style Bars, 11 X 20 In. 280.00
Broiler, Stationary, Iron, 15 1/2 X 15 1/2 In. 150.00
Broom, 1930s 23.00
Brush, Hearth, Handle, Oval Brush, Original Horsehair, 22 1/2 In. 40.00
Chenet, Louis XVI, Female Form, Torch, Gilt–Bronze, 18 In., Pair 1650.00
Coal Carrier, Cast Brass Bale, Wooden Handle, Oval, Sheet Brass 30.00
Coal Scuttle, Brass, Wooden Feet, Shovel, English, 19th Century 297.00
Fan, Folding, Brass, 26 3/4 In. 200.00
Fender, Brass & Wire, Bow Front, 15 1/4 X 43 1/4 X 16 1/2 In. 385.00
Fender, Brass Ball, Tubular, 8 X 36 X 14 In. 154.00
Fender, Brass, 5 X 10 X 50 In. 100.00
Fender, Brass, Beaded Grill Design, 48 In. 20.00
Fender, Brass, Paw Feet, 8 X 26 In. 85.00
Fender, Brass, Wirework, Brass Top Rail & Double Scrolls, 44 In. 600.00
Fender, Copper, Spade & Flower, Canted Sides, C.1910, 68 In. 150.00
Fender, Nickel, Iron, Black Canted Sides, England, 68 X 16 In. 100.00
Fender, Pierced Brass, Ash Guard, 43 In. 154.00
Fender, Pierced Brass, Paw Feet, 60 In. 250.00
Fireback, Man, Horseback, Scrolled Crest, Cast Iron, 17 X 23 In. 200.00
Fireboard, Painted As Bird's–Eye & Curly Maple, C.1835 .... 900.00
Fireboard, Pine, Graining, Striping, Pine, 38 3/4 X 34 In. 90.00
Food Warmer, Geometric Floral Design, Tin, Iron Legs, 28 1/4 In. 725.00
Grate, Broiler, Revolving, 18th Century, Iron, 11 3/4 In. 165.00
Lifter, Kettle, Iron, 16 In. 185.00
Mantel, Oak, Electric Heater Inset 110.00
Meat Hook, 5 Hooks, Iron, Twisted Detail, 17 1/2 In. 65.00

Meat Hook, Ring With Bale & 6 Hooks, Iron, 20 X 15 In.	190.00
Pan, Chestnut Roasting, Long Handle	35.00
Peel, Cookie, Tapered Paddle, Early 1800s, 11 1/2 In.	75.00
Peel, Forged Cylindrical Handle, Ball Handle, Iron, 25 In.	88.00
Peel, Ram's Horn Finial, Iron, 46 In.	55.00
Poker & Tongs, Brass Finials, Iron, 20 & 29 In.	50.00
Screen, 2 Sliding Panels, English, Walnut	175.00
Screen, Brass, Victorian, Winged Animal, Pierced, 31 1/2 In.	715.00
Screen, Leather Panel, Oak, Gustav Stickley, 35 X 31 In.	2000.00
Screen, Louis XVI, Tulipwood, Fabric, Writing Shelf, 43 In.	605.00
Scuttle, Coal, Brass & Ceramic Handles, Copper, 13 In.	35.00
Shovel, Figural Open Heart Handle, Iron, 18th Century, 30 In.	150.00
Spit, With Trammel, Iron, 11 In.	65.00
Tongs, Brass Finial, 31 In.	75.00
Tongs, Ember, Coggle Type, Steel, 18th Century, Opens To 16 In.	350.00
Tongs, Ember, Penny–Shaped Bill Ends, Hand–Forged Iron, 14 In.	220.00
Tongs, Iron, 12 3/4 In.	500.00
Tongs, Iron, Spring Top, Knuckle Turnings, 23 In.	20.00
Tool Set, Brass, 2 Ball–Top Shovels, Tongs	165.00
Trammel, Hanging, Saw Tooth, Iron, 44 In.	85.00
Warming Pan, Wooden Handle, Brass & Copper, 43 In.	30.00

M F Porcelain was made in Herend, Hungary, by Moritz Fischer. The factory was founded in 1839 and continued working into the twentieth century. The wares are sometimes referred to as "Herend" porcelain.

FISCHER, Bowl, Enamel Design Inside & Out, Reticulated Wall, 7 1/2 In.	125.00
Bowl, Figural Butterfly, Reticulated, Marked, 11 1/2 X 10 1/2 In.	225.00
Cup & Saucer, Flower, Butterfly, Large	24.00
Eggcup, Chinese Bouquet, Double, Green	30.00
Ewer, Floral Design, Gold Trim, 15 3/4 In.	350.00
Figurine, Nude With Flowers, 12 In.	295.00
Plaque, Figural, Shell, 12 In.	250.00
Vase, Multicolored Designs, Open Work At Rim, Marked, 15 1/4 In.	310.00

Fishing reels of brass or nickel were made in the United States by 1810. Bamboo fly rods were sold by 1860, often marked with the maker's name. Metal lures, then wooden and metal lures were made in the nineteenth century. Plastic lures were made by the 1930s. All fishing material is collected today and even equipment of the past thirty years is of interest if in good condition with original box.

FISHING, Book, Hardy's Angler's Guide, 1951	20.00
Box, Bait, Worms, Maggots, Brass, Graduated Sizes	175.00
Box, Bobber, 18 Hand Painted Floats, Salesman's Sample, 1915–20	2640.00
Button, License, Michigan, Nonresident, 1930, 1 3/4 In.	21.00
Cabinet, Display, Eagle Claw Hooks, Eagle With Fish, Box	175.00
Catalog, Edward Vom Hofe Catalog, 1917, 171 Pages	405.00
Catalog, Edward Vom Hofe, 1941, 143 Pages	180.00
Catalog, H.H. Kifle Tackle, 1898, 166 Pages	240.00
Catalog, Payne Rod Co., 1968, 20 Pages	120.00
Catalog, Thomas Fishing Rods, 1914, 32 Pages, Centerfold	320.00
Catalog, Thomas J. Conroy Tackle, 1915, 272 Pages	210.00
Decoy, Brook Trout, Belly Weight, Oscar Peterson, 5 1/8 In.	1000.00
Decoy, Brook Trout, Tack Eyes, Belly Weight, Oscar Peterson, 9 In.	2400.00
Decoy, Brown Trout, Carved Eyes, 1940, Oscar Peterson, 6 In.	850.00
Decoy, Musky, Green, Yellow, Black Stripes, Glass Eyes, Tony Smith	70.00
Decoy, Rock Bass, Carved, Roseville, Mich., Jerry Adams, 8 In.	175.00
Decoy, Sturgeon, Black, White Spots, Stripes, 1940, Bob Beebe, 11 In.	25.00
Decoy, Sunfish, Gray, White, Pink, Glass Eyes, George Aho, 7 In.	80.00
Decoy, Sunfish, Tack Eyes, White, Red, Gold, Bill Faue, 7 In.	200.00
Decoy, Trout, Blended Green, Jess Ramey, 6 1/2 In.	600.00
Decoy, Trout, Brown, Copper Fins, Glass Eyes, Bob Beebe, 1930, 10 In.	125.00
Decoy, Trout, Red, White, Black, Aluminum Fins, Jess Ramey	280.00
Decoy, Turtle, Spearing, Copper Top, Lead Belly, Mel Aaserude, 5 In.	170.00

Decoy, Walleye, Gray & White, Elk Lake, Mi., George Aho, 16 In. 200.00
Decoy, Yellow–Belly Perch, Copper Fins, Glass Eyes, Jerry Adams 225.00
Display, Let's Go Evinruding, Paper, 17 X 37 In. 55.00
Display, Pflueger Fishing Tackle, 1930, 17 X 17 In. 350.00
Display, South Bend Bait Co., 3–Dimensional, 1927, 30 X 49 In. 525.00
Etching, Leaping Marlin, W.J. Schaldach, 14 X 17 In. 75.00
Fly Reel, Winchester, No. 1236 .... 70.00
Fly Rod, Horrocks & Ibbotson, Cascade Model, Split Bamboo, 4 Piece 100.00
Fly Rod, Mitchell, C.1870 .... 470.00
Fly Rod, Tosaku, Bamboo, Box 65.00
Lure, Chub Creek, Baby Pike Minnow 15.00
Lure, Cod Fish, Alaskan Whale Bone, 3 1/2 In. 425.00
Lure, Crawler, Heddon, Tin 10.00
Lure, Crazy Crawler, Heddon 50.00
Lure, Dalton Special, Box 24.00
Lure, Giant Flaptail, Heddon 35.00
Lure, Glutton Dibbler, C.E. Key, Box 24.00
Lure, Hopatcong Perch, Glass Eyes, 1910, 3 X 6 In. 700.00
Lure, Large Mouth Bass, Alton Buchman, C.1980 .... 412.50
Lure, Lucky Strike, Robertson, Stark 15.00
Lure, Minnow, Feathered Tail Hook, 3 1/2 In. 200.00
Lure, Minnow, Haskell, Pat. 1859, 4 1/2 In. .... 8400.00 To 9240.00
Lure, Minnow, Leather, Plug, Hand Painted, 4 In. 25.00
Lure, Minnow, Rainbow Finish, Glass Eyes, Winchester, No. 9016 .... 300.00
Lure, Multi–Wobbler No. 9201, Green, Gold, Yellow, Glass Eyes 450.00
Lure, Musky Spinner, Salt Water Size, 5 3/4 In. 55.00
Lure, Paw Paw Lucky Strike, Box 22.00
Lure, Pike Minnow, C.C.B. & Co., Box 24.00
Lure, River Runt, Heddon, Box 18.00
Lure, Spinner, Decker Wooden, White, 2 1/2 In. 800.00
Lure, Spinner, Pflueger, Luminous, Embossed Fish Head, 3 1/8 In. 80.00
Lure, Striking Bait, Chautauqua Weedless, Automatic, Aug. 31, 1909 .... 2500.00
Lure, Tack Eyes, Metal Fins, Peterson Body, 6 In. 550.00
Lure, W.D. Chapman Classic, Allure 2 .... 130.00
Lure, Weedless, Magnetic 15.00
Lure, Wiggler, Deep Diving, Green, Yellow & Black Spots, Heddon 40.00
Lure, Wilson Sizzler, Pat. Aug. 24, 1904, 3 In. 140.00
Minnow Trap, Checotah, Oklahoma, Glass 35.00
Mold, Sinker, Fish Shape, Brass, 2 Part 140.00
Photograph, Zane Gray With Fishing Trophy, Marlin 550.00
Plug, Charles Lane, Box 715.00
Plug, Codfish, Alaskan Whalebone, C.1780 .... 465.00
Plug, Minnow, Pal'O Mine, Painted Eye, Box, Pflueger, 3 1/4 In. 16.00
Plug, Salmon, Martin, Box 30.00
Postcard, Abbey & Imbrie, Tackle 25.00
Reel, A. Clerk & Co., N.Y., Ball Handle, 1870, No. 1 Size 962.00
Reel, B.C. Milam, No. 3 .... 990.00
Reel, Ball–Balance Handle, F.Vom Hofe & Son 715.00
Reel, Casting, South Bend, No. 550 .... 25.00
Reel, Edward Vom Hofe Restigouche, 1879, 6/0 Size 1200.00
Reel, Edward Vom Hofe, Model 621, Size 4/0 .... 190.00
Reel, Fly, Henry Parkhurst Wells, Marked, C.1885 .... 1870.00
Reel, Fly, Meek, No.44 .... 6000.00
Reel, Hendryx, Nickel, 1888 .... 25.00
Reel, Hydro–Film Control, Shakespeare, No.1974 .... 35.00
Reel, Oceanic, Pflueger, No. 2178 .... 40.00
Reel, Penn Delmar, No. 285 .... 18.00
Reel, Pontiac, No. 357, 4 Brothers, Brass 45.00
Reel, Progress, No. 1943, Pflueger 20.00
Reel, Rocket, No. 1375, Pflueger 55.00
Reel, Salmon, E. Vom Hofe Ristigouche 632.50
Reel, Salmon, Otto Zwarg, No. 2/0 .... 495.00
Reel, Salt Water, Mitchell, Size 9/0, Wooden Fitted Box 450.00
Reel, Shaker, Handmade, Wooden Rod, Hancock, Mass. 200.00

Reel, Shakespeare, Model HE, 1940 .... 35.00
Reel, Stenciled Label, Chas. H. Lewis, Wood, 14 In. 25.00
Reel, Sunnybrook, No. 75, Union Hardware, Telescoping Rod 30.00
Reel, Tripart, No. 580, 1909 .... 34.00
Reel, Trout, Model 44, B.F. Meek & Sons 6600.00
Reel, Trout, No. 1558, Pflueger, Brass 22.00
Reel, Trump, No. 1943, Pflueger 18.00
Repair Kit, Angler's, Pigskin, Made In England 75.00
Rod, Fly, Acorn Butt Cap, Jim Payne No. 202, Abercrombie & Fitch 3250.00
Rod, Fly, Split Bamboo, J.C. Higgins 75.00
Rod, Garrison, Model 220, 2 Piece, 2 Tip, 8 Ft. 1800.00
Rod, Gillum, Brown Wrap, Super Z–Ferules, 2 Piece, 8 1/2 Ft. 1900.00
Rod, Gillum, Light Salmon, Ser. No. 1–912, Removable Butt, 9 Ft. 900.00
Rod, Gillum, Super–Z Ferrules, 2 Tip Rod, 8 Ft. 9 In. 1600.00
Rod, H.L. Leonard, Short Cork Extension Butt, 8 1/2 Ft. 495.00
Rod, Jim Payne, Model 102, Trout Fly, 2 Piece, 8 Ft. 1500.00
Rod, John Hubbard, 2 Tip, 1934, 3 Piece, 7 1/2 Ft. 625.00
Rod, Leonard & Mills Co., Short Handle, 8 Ft. 100.00
Rod, Orvis Deluxe, Serial No. 43264, 2 Tip, 2 Piece, 6 1/2 Ft. 325.00
Rod, Orvis, Impregnated Pat. Pend, Battenkill, 2 Piece, 7 1/2 Ft. 340.00
Rod, Orvis, Superfine, Trout Rod, 2 Tip, 2 Piece, 7 Ft. 350.00
Rod, R.W. Summers, Model 82, Trout, 2 Piece, 8 1/2 Ft. 525.00
Rod, Thomas & Thomas, The Midge, 2 Tip, 2 Piece, 7 Ft. 600.00
Rod, Tru–Temper, Perfect Model, Steel, 5 Ft. 35.00
Rod, Wright & McGill, Super Rod, Water Seal, 3 Piece, 9 Ft. 110.00
Spear, 5 Prong, Cylindrical Mount, 19th Century, 24 1/2 In. 88.00
Trap, Eel, Woven Splint, Wooden Top, 17 1/2 In. 150.00
Trap, Minnow, Original Cap, Marked IBX–128 .... 85.00
Trap, Minnow, Shakespeare, Glass, Wire Frame 95.00

FLAG, see Textile, Fiag

Flash Gordon appeared in the Sunday comics in 1934. The daily strip started in 1940. The hero was also in comic books from 1930 to 1970, in books from 1936, in movies from 1938, on the radio in the 1930s and 1940s, and on television from 1953 to 1954. All sorts of memorabilia are collected, but the ray guns and rocket ships are the most popular.

FLASH GORDON, Book, Flash Gordon & The Baby Animals, 1956 .... 3.00
Book, Painting, 96 Pages, 1935, Large 85.00
Book, Pop–Up 40.00
Card, Christmas .... 10.00 To 17.00
Compass, Original Card 20.00
Game, Target, Graphics, Tin, Box 85.00
Glove, Baseball 25.00
Model Kit, Flash Gordon & Martian, Revell, Dated 1965 .... 100.00
Ray Gun, Arresting 135.00
Record, Picture, City of Sea Caves 50.00
Rocket Fighter 200.00
Rocket Fighter, Windup, Marx .... 225.00 To 350.00

Florence Ceramics were made in Pasadena, California, from World War II to 1977. Florence Ward created many colorful figurines, boxes, candleholders, and other items for the giftshop trade. Each piece was marked with an ink stamp that included the name Florence Ceramics Co. The company was sold in 1964 and although the name remained the same the products were very different. Mugs, cups, and trays were made.

FLORENCE CERAMICS, Ashtray, Clover Shape, Pink & Gray, Gold Trim, 6 1/2 In. ... 12.50
Figurine, Abigail, 8 1/2 In. .... 55.00 To 95.00
Figurine, Annabelle .... 115.00 To 125.00
Figurine, Colleen 95.00
Figurine, Delia 65.00
Figurine, Dolores, 8 1/2 In. 65.00
Figurine, Elaine, 6 In. 55.00
Figurine, Ethel, 7 1/2 In. 85.00
Figurine, Gary, 8 1/2 In. .... 65.00 To 85.00
Figurine, Irene, 6 In. .... 35.00 To 50.00
Figurine, Jim, Gray Suit 65.00
Figurine, Lea, 6 In. 65.00
Figurine, Lillian, 7 1/2 In. 63.00
Figurine, Louise, 7 1/4 In. .... 80.00 To 90.00
Figurine, Matilda, 8 In. 95.00
Figurine, Musetta, 9 1/2 In. 85.00
Figurine, Sue Ellen, 8 In. .... 45.00 To 85.00
Flower Holder, Chinese Couple, Black, White, 8 In., Pair 75.00
Mug, Pasadena, Birds, Tall 12.00
Planter, Girl, Flowered Dress, Pink Hair Bow, 6 In. 25.00
Planter, Woman's Bust 45.00

Flow blue, or flo blue, was made in England about 1830 to 1900. The plates were printed with designs using a cobalt blue coloring. The color flowed from the design to the white plate so that the finished plate has a smeared blue design. The plates were usually made of ironstone china.

FLOW BLUE, Bone Dish, Argyle, Grindley 45.00
Bone Dish, Diana, Meakin 38.00
Bone Dish, Duchess, Grindley 25.00
Bone Dish, Normandy 45.00
Bone Dish, Rose, Grindley 23.00
Bone Dish, Touraine 53.00
Bowl, Amoy, Davenport, 6 X 8 In. 180.00
Bowl, Conway, 9 In. 42.00
Bowl, Dahlia, 10 In. 85.00
Bowl, Duchess, Oval, Grindley, 5 3/4 In. 25.00
Bowl, Jenny Lind, Wilkinson, 7 1/2 In. 175.00
Bowl, La Francaise, Cover, Footed, 10 In. 150.00
Bowl, Lorne, Open, 10 In. 85.00
Bowl, Mongolia, Oval, 10 In. 65.00
Bowl, Nelson, New Wharf Pottery, 9 In. 35.00
Bowl, Oxford, Johnson Bros., Oval, 7 3/4 In. 20.00
Bowl, Portman, Cover, Oval, 12 1/4 In. 210.00
Bowl, Richmond, Burgess & Leigh, 8 In. 28.00
Bowl, Shanghai, Grindley, 9 In. 38.00
Bowl, St.Louis, Johnson Bros., 12 In. 90.00
Bowl, Touraine, Cover, Oval, 9 In. 200.00
Bowl, Watteau, Doulton, Footed, 10 1/4 In. 95.00
Butter Chip, Alaska, Grindley 22.00
Butter Chip, Argyle, Grindley 30.00
Butter Chip, Florida, Grindley 25.00
Butter, Blue Danube, Cover, Johnson Bros. 195.00
Butter, Kenworth, Cover .... 125.00 To 135.00
Butter, Osborne, Grindley, Drainer, Cover, 3 Piece 215.00
Butter, Richmond, Cover, Johnson Bros. 95.00
Cake Plate, Clayton, 10 1/4 In. 45.00
Chamber Pot, Festoon, Grindley 175.00
Charger, Tyrolean, 12 1/4 In. .... 105.00 To 115.00
Compote, Celtic 160.00
Compote, Watteau, Doulton, 6 1/2 In. 60.00

Cracker Jar, La Belle	195.00
Creamer, Lorne	95.00
Creamer, Marie, Grindley	85.00
Creamer, Muriel	65.00
Creamer, Nonpareil, Burgess & Leigh	145.00
Creamer, Richmond, Johnson Bros.	75.00
Creamer, Touraine, 4 1/2 In.	135.00
Creamer, Waldorf	130.00
Cup & Saucer, Amour, Handleless	95.00
Cup & Saucer, Chapoo, Boote	100.00
Cup & Saucer, Elgar, Demitasse	50.00
Cup & Saucer, Grenada, Alcock	40.00
Cup & Saucer, Lancaster, New Wharf Pottery	60.00
Cup & Saucer, Lorne, Grindley	65.00
Cup & Saucer, Lyndhurst	37.50 To 42.00
Cup & Saucer, Osborne, Ridgway	55.00
Cup & Saucer, Richmond, Johnson	45.00
Cup & Saucer, Touraine, Alcock	45.00
Cup, Watteau, 2 Handles, Doulton	55.00
Dinner Set, Oxford, Johnson, Service For 12, 122 Piece	2000.00
Eggcup, Madras, Doulton, 5 Piece	60.00
Gravy Boat, Alexandra, S. Hancock & Sons, 7 1/2 In.	30.00
Gravy Boat, Douglas	75.00
Gravy Boat, Dresden, Attached Underplate	27.00
Gravy Boat, Haddon, Grindley, 8 In.	32.50
Gravy Boat, Lorne	75.00
Gravy Boat, Marechal Niel	85.00
Gravy Boat, Melbourne, Grindley	65.00
Gravy Boat, Osborne, Ridgway	55.00 To 60.00
Gravy Boat, Sabraon	150.00
Gravy Boat, Verona, Meakin	85.00
Nappy, La Belle, 8 In.	40.00
Pitcher & Bowl, Carnation	155.00
Pitcher & Bowl, Saskia	500.00
Pitcher & Bowl, Tonquin, Adams	900.00
Pitcher, Alaska, Grindley, 6 3/4 In.	145.00
Pitcher, Astoria, Johnson, 5 1/2 In.	45.00
Pitcher, La Belle, 6 1/2 In.	145.00
Pitcher, Milk, Nonpareil, Burgess & Leigh, 5 3/4 In.	125.00
Pitcher, Milk, Paisley	145.00
Pitcher, Scinde, Alcock, 10 In.	750.00
Pitcher, Temple, 7 1/2 In.	265.00
Pitcher, Water, Touraine	175.00 To 340.00
Pitcher, Watteau, Doulton, 6 1/2 In.	75.00
Plate, Abbey, Jones, 10 In.	35.00
Plate, Alexandra, S. Hancock & Sons, 10 In.	12.00
Plate, Amoy, Davenport, 10 1/2 In.	100.00
Plate, Arabesque, Mayer, 10 1/2 In.	90.00
Plate, Baltic, Grindley, 10 In.	60.00
Plate, Candia, 7 1/2 In.	30.00
Plate, Canton Vine, 8 1/2 In.	45.00
Plate, China Aster, Minton, 10 1/2 In.	38.00
Plate, Clyde, New Wharf Pottery, 9 In.	35.00
Plate, Conway, 9 In.	45.00
Plate, Crumlin, 9 In.	28.00
Plate, Denang, Ridgway, 10 1/4 In.	85.00
Plate, Devon, 7 In.	28.00 To 30.00
Plate, Fairy Villas, Adams, 7 In.	20.00
Plate, Florida, Johnson, 10 In.	50.00
Plate, Geneva, New Wharf Pottery, 9 In.	40.00
Plate, Georgia, Johnson Bros., 10 In.	45.00
Plate, Gironde, Grindley, 9 In.	30.00
Plate, Grecian, Ridgway, 10 1/4 In.	25.00
Plate, Grenada, Alcock, 9 In.	30.00

Plate, La Belle, 8 1/2 In.	35.00
Plate, La Francais, 9 In.	20.00
Plate, La Hore, 7 1/2 In.	50.00
Plate, Lakewood, 7 3/4 In.	27.00
Plate, Linda, John Maddock & Sons, 6 1/2 In.	20.00
Plate, Manhattan, Alcock, 7 1/2 In.	30.00
Plate, Manilla, 10 In.	70.00
Plate, Martha Washington, 8 In.	85.00
Plate, Medway, Meakin, 8 In.	15.00
Plate, Mongolia, 10 In.	35.00
Plate, Nelson, New Wharf Pottery, 9 1/2 In.	45.00
Plate, Nonpareil, Burgess & Leigh, 7 1/2 In.	48.00
Plate, Normandy, Johnson Bros., 10 In.	45.00
Plate, Oxford, Johnson Bros., 8 In.	25.00
Plate, Peléw, Challinor, 9 In.	80.00
Plate, Phoebe, 9 1/2 In.	17.50
Plate, Portman, Grindley, 8 In.	42.00
Plate, Raleigh, 10 1/2 In.	25.00
Plate, Regent, Johnson Bros., 9 In.	35.00
Plate, Richmond, Johnson, 10 In.	55.00
Plate, Rose, Grindley, 6 1/2 In.	14.00
Plate, Scinde, Alcock, 7 In.	48.00
Plate, Shanghai, Grindley, 10 In.	45.00
Plate, Singan, Goodfellow, 8 1/4 In.	65.00
Plate, Singan, Goodfellow, 10 In.	85.00
Plate, Temple, 8 3/4 In.	55.00
Plate, Temple, 9 3/4 In.	75.00
Plate, Tonquin, Adams, 10 1/4 In.	95.00
Plate, Touraine, Alcock, 7 3/4 In.	28.00
Plate, Touraine, Stanley, 6 1/2 In.	20.00
Plate, Troy, Meigh, 9 1/4 In.	75.00
Plate, Tyrolean, 12 1/2 In.	125.00
Plate, Vermont, 10 In.	48.00
Plate, Versailles, Furnival, 7 1/2 In.	12.00
Plate, Watteau, Doulton, 9 In.	45.00
Plate, Weir, 9 1/2 In.	15.00
Plate, Yeddo, Royal Staffordshire, 10 In.	50.00
Platter, Alaska, 14 In.	70.00
Platter, Alexandra, S.Hancock & Sons, 14 X 11 1/2 In.	60.00
Platter, Amoy, Davenport, 13 1/2 In.	180.00
Platter, Argyle, Grindley, 10 1/2 X 15 In.	115.00
Platter, Blue Danube, Johnson Bros., 18 X 13 In.	150.00
Platter, Burleigh, Burgess & Leigh, 16 X 12 In.	115.00
Platter, Denton, 14 In.	105.00
Platter, Hartington, Grindley, 16 X 11 1/2 In.	87.50
Platter, Holland, Johnson Bros., 16 In.	115.00
Platter, Holland, Meakin, 16 In.	80.00
Platter, Indian Jar, 14 In.	195.00
Platter, Knox, New Wharf Pottery, 10 1/2 In.	95.00
Platter, La Belle, Oval, 14 1/2 X 10 In.	195.00
Platter, La Francais, 15 In.	100.00
Platter, Lotus, Grindley, 16 X 12 1/2 In.	125.00
Platter, Melrose, 14 X 10 1/2 In.	45.00
Platter, Messina, Cauldon, 15 In.	135.00
Platter, Neopolitan, Johnson Bros.	45.00
Platter, Osborne, Ridgway, 14 In.	65.00
Platter, Oxford, Johnson Bros., 14 In.	90.00
Platter, Richmond, Johnson Bros., 9 1/2 X 13 In.	75.00
Platter, Trent, New Wharf Pottery, 11 In.	65.00
Platter, Turin, 12 1/2 In.	35.00
Platter, Watteau, Doulton, 13 1/2 X 11 In.	95.00
Punch Bowl, Luneville	475.00
Relish, Florida, Grindley, 9 1/4 In.	80.00
Relish, Pekin, Dimmock	85.00

China can be washed in warm water with mild soapsuds. The addition of ammonia to the water will add that extra sparkle.

Sauce, Conway, 5 In.	18.00
Sauce, Oregon, Mayer, 5 In.	60.00
Sauce, Princeton, Johnson Bros.	10.00
Saucer, Amerillia, 6 In.	25.00
Saucer, Kenworth	10.00
Saucer, Normandy, Johnson Bros.	10.00
Saucer, Wentworth	9.00
Soup, Dish, Blossom, 9 In.	20.00
Soup, Dish, Fairy Villas, Adams	40.00
Soup, Dish, Lois, New Wharf Pottery, 8 3/4 In.	55.00
Soup, Dish, Richmond, Burgess & Leigh, 8 In.	20.00
Soup, Dish, Shanghai, Grindley	38.00
Soup, Dish, Watteau, Doulton, 7 1/2 In.	35.00
Sugar & Creamer, Melbourne, Grindley	250.00
Sugar & Creamer, Oxford, Johnson Bros., Cover	140.00
Sugar, Baltic, Grindley	60.00
Sugar, Muriel, Cover	135.00
Sugar, Naida	65.00
Sugar, Pelew	250.00
Sugar, Touraine	82.00
Syrup, La Belle, Gold Trim, 4 1/2 In.	80.00
Teapot, Cattail	35.00
Teapot, Sugar & Creamer, Peking, Podmore–Walker, C.1840	900.00
Tile, Shakespeare, Copeland, 6 In.	70.00
Tureen, Oxford, Ladle	295.00
Tureen, Regent, Meakin, Cover, Oval	115.00
Tureen, Sauce, Oregon	350.00
Tureen, Sauce, Underplate, Verona	155.00
Tureen, Soup, Colonial	275.00
Tureen, Soup, Montana, Johnson Bros.	250.00
Tureen, Soup, Rhoda	225.00
Tureen, Soup, Scinde, Alcock	650.00
Tureen, Soup, Vermont	245.00
Tureen, Vegetable, Clayton, Cover	155.00
Waste Bowl, Chen–Si	125.00
Waste Bowl, Oriental	75.00
Waste Bowl, Temple	175.00

FLYING PHOENIX, see Phoenix Bird

Folk art is listed in many sections of the book under the actual name of the object. See categories such as Box; Cigar Store Figure; Weather Vane; Wooden; etc.

FOLK ART, Bird, Natural Growth Head & Body, Tin Winds & Tail, 11 3/4 In.	105.00
Bird, Turned Base, Black Paint On Blue, 11 X 11 1/2 In.	115.00
Birdhouse, Mission Oak Porch, Electric, Large	995.00
Board, Carved Foliage, Painted Circles, 10 1/4 X 31 In.	205.00
Box, Dresser, Whimsey, Seashells, Shadowbox 3–D Jungle Design	72.00

Box, Long Drawer, Bull, 6 Point Star, C.1870, 13 X 9 In. 880.00
Box, Rope Trim, Applied Leaves, Lion's Heads, Wire Nails, 8 In. 55.00
Brass Shell, Engraved New Guinea Bob To Lois, World War II, 7 In. 21.00
Carving, Horse & Wagon, Wood, Original Paint, 20th Century, 14 In. 85.00
Carving, Rearing Blow Snake, Smiling, Red Glass Eyes, 17 In. 2200.00
Carving, Woodpecker, Wood, Painted, 17 In., Pair 400.00
Carving, Young Woman, Gold Painted Detail, Varnish, 10 3/4 In. 475.00
Checkerboard, Red & Black Repaint, Pine, 17 3/4 X 27 3/4 In. 125.00
Checkerboard, Salmon Gray Paint, Black Squares, 15 1/2 X 28 In. 90.00
Church, Made of 2600 Matches, Pews Inside, Altar Lights, 1925 .... 110.00
Cover, Table, Circular Medallion of Wool, Circles, 38 X 65 In. 100.00
Deer's Head, Carved Wood, Gustafson, 1925 .... 1800.00
Dominoes, Wooden, Box With Sliding Lid, Handmade 45.00
Double Monkey, On Stick, Mechanical, Jointed, Painted, 23 3/4 In. 450.00
Egg, Ostrich, Painted With Figure, Male, Female Ostrich, Nest, 8 In. 330.00
Figure, 2 Oxen, Driver, Wooden, Polychrome, 10 X 17 X 9 1/2 In. 350.00
Figure, 5 Bearded Men At Work, Mechanized, Painted, 18 1/2 In. 1200.00
Figure, Amish Man, Green Shirt, Black Hat, Board, Life-Size 500.00
Figure, Black Man, Eating Watermelon, Cutout Wood 65.00
Figure, Cat, Wood Carved, Glass Eyes, 12 3/4 In. 225.00
Figure, Daniel Boone, Carved, 7 In. 65.00
Figure, Dog, Seated, Relief Carved Detail, 11 In. 135.00
Figure, Eagle, Folded Wings, Wood, Gustafson, 17 1/2 In. 990.00
Figure, Horse, Hand Carved, Original Worn Paint, 7 In. 165.00
Figure, Male, Standing, Derby Hat, Wooden, 1910, 12 1/2 In. 1300.00
Figure, Man In Pilgrim Costume, Hardwood, 11 In. 55.00
Figure, Mr.Jiggs, Standing, Wooden Base, 31 In. 192.00
Figure, Mr.Magoo, Painted Wood, Ohio, 20th Century, 8 3/4 In. 110.00
Figure, Preening Goose, Carved, Black, White, Glass Eyes, 17 X 8 In. 135.00
Figure, Robin, On Authentic Branch, Wooden Carved, 7 In. 37.50
Figure, Shepherd Boy, Wooden, Continental, 19th Century, 26 In. 150.00
Figure, Uncle Sam, Silhouette, Jigsaw Cut, C.1940, 31 1/2 In. 33.00
Fruit, Stone, Banana, Orange, Lemon, Strawberry, 9 Piece 425.00
Horse, Free Standing, Cloth Saddle, Blanket, C.1840, 11 In. 5775.00
House, Model, Pine, Gray Peaked Roof, Pale Yellow, 8 X 15 In. 192.00
Marionette, Man, Wooden, Jointed 495.00
Noah's Ark, Noah, Wife, 110 Animals, Pairs, Wooden, 11 X 19 In. 3100.00
Paper Cut, Floral Design, Black Paper Back, 11 1/2 X 15 In. 210.00
Pipe Holder, Wood Carving, Pipe Shape, 18 In. 95.00
Plaque, Eagle, Relief Carved, Wooden, 28 3/4 X 17 In. 25.00
Rifle, Pine, Rudimentary Trigger & Brackets, Blue, 31 In. 770.00
Rooster, Standing, Mounted On Stand, 1920, 11 1/2 In. 850.00
Shelf, Hanging, Jigsaw Work, Black Paint, 9 X 16 1/2 In. 20.00
Shell, 830 Aerosquadron, Eagle, Names, World War I 95.00
Shoofly, Red Sleigh, Black Rockers, 2 Horses, 37 X 13 In. 495.00
Smoking Stand, Twig, House Cigarette Box 110.00
Table, Wooden Spools, Oval Top, 20th Century, 15 X 34 X 29 In. 25.00
Toby Mug, Carved Wood, Polychrome Alligatored Paint, 6 1/8 In. 500.00
Toy, Horse, Pull Toy, Papier-Mache, Leather Ears, 19 In. 300.00
Toy, Man On Trapeze, Original Red, Black & White Paint, 14 In. 45.00
Toy, Man, Standing, Jingle, Tin, On Iron Rod, 19th Century, 20 In. 1100.00
Walking Stick, Carved Wooden Deer Hoof, 35 In. 85.00
Whirligig, Black Man, Dancing, Pipe Frame, Painted, 1915–20, 28 In. 300.00
Whirligig, Black Man, Sorrowful, Iron Post, 20th Century, 62 In. 85.00
Whirligig, Black Man, Switch & Bucking Mule, Rider 350.00
Whirligig, Dewey–Boy, Sailor, Flat Hat, Painted Features, 15 In. 300.00
Whirligig, Dog, Tail, Tin Litho 18.00
Whirligig, Dutch Girl, Churning, 21 X 22 In. 80.00
Whirligig, Indian In Canoe, Paddle Arms, 17 In. 125.00
Whirligig, Keystone Cop 70.00
Whirligig, Mammy Hitting Uncle Tom Over Head With Rolling Pin 160.00
Whirligig, Man Chopping Wood, Large Propeller, C.1930, 34 In. 935.00
Whirligig, Old Man, Chasing Mule 250.00
Whirligig, Rooster, Wood, White, Red Comb & Crown, 1900, 20 X 14 In. 247.00

Whirligig, Sailor, Blue & White, Pivoting Arms, 8 In.	375.00
Whirligig, Soldier, Hinged Arms, Pine, Green Stain, 1900, 16 In.	440.00
Whirligig, Soldier, Paddle Hands, Red Hat	495.00
Wrench, Rope Bed, Carved Face of Man With Beard, 14 In.	225.00

Cold feet have been a problem for generations. Our ancestors had many ingenious ways to warm feet with portable foot warmers. Some warmers held charcoal, others held hot water. Pottery, tin, and soapstone were the favored materials to conduct the heat. The warmer was kept under the feet, then the legs and feet were tucked into a blanket, providing welcome warmth in a cold carriage or church.

FOOT WARMER, Buggy, Charcoal Clar Heater, No.7D	25.00
Carriage, Drawer, Brass, Rug Cover, Admiral Lamp Co., 7 X 13 In.	42.00
Copper, Paul Leistner Sons Mfg.Co., St.Charles, Mo.12 In.	25.00
Friesan Carving All Sides, Top, Dutch Inscription, 1829, 8 In.	250.00
Friesan Carving All Surfaces, Horse Design On Door, 7 In.	225.00
Glass Sides, Fold-Down Carpet Covered Top, Wood Case, 8 In.	105.00
Mortised Frame, Punched Heart & Circle Design, 7 1/2 In.	200.00
Pig Type, Upright Or Lay On Side, 5 1/2 X 11 In.	50.00
Pottery, Molded Leaves Around Top, 1 1/2 In.	75.00
Punched Tin, Birch Frame, 14 In.	45.00
Punched Tin, Circles & Diamonds, Wooden Frame, 8 1/2 In.	125.00
Punched Tin, Hearts, Wooden Frame, Trace of Old Red, 9 In.	155.00
Punched Tin, Mortised Wood Frame, With Pan, 9 In.	135.00
Punched Tin, Old Brown Finish, 9 In.	135.00
Punched Tin, Turned Wood, Hinged Door, Swing Handle, 6 X 9 In.	193.00
Soapstone, Horse Anchor	10.00
Stoneware, Langley, England	45.00
Stoneware, Logan, Blue & White	175.00
Tin Case, Oval Glass Sides, Wire Guards, Wood, 1863, 8 In.	205.00
Tin, Mortised Wooden Frame, Punched Heart Design, 8 X 9 In.	225.00
Tole, Wooden Top, Original Black Paint, 8 X 8 In.	65.00

Fostoria glass was made in Fostoria, Ohio, from 1887 to 1891. The factory was moved to Moundsville, West Virginia, and most of the glass seen in shops today is a twentieth-century product. The company was sold in 1983; and new items will be easily identifiable, according to the new owners, Lancaster Colony Corporation.

FOSTORIA, see also Milk Glass

FOSTORIA, American Lady, Cordial	50.00
American Lady, Goblet, Amethyst Bowl	18.00
American Lady, Goblet, Water	20.00
American, Appetizer Set, 7 Piece	200.00
American, Ashtray, Square, 2 3/4 In.	4.00
American, Basket, Reed Handle	65.00
American, Bowl, 4 3/4 In.	70.00
American, Bowl, 6 1/2 In.	22.00
American, Bowl, 7 In.	30.00
American, Bowl, Cover, 5 1/2 In.	12.00
American, Bowl, Flare, 5 1/4 In.	12.00
American, Bowl, Oval, 9 In.	30.00
American, Bowl, Pedestal, Handles, 8 In.	160.00
American, Box, Cigarette, Cover	40.00
American, Butter, Cover, 1/4 Lb.	20.00
American, Butter, Dome Cover	70.00 To 110.00
American, Cake Plate, 3-Footed, 12 In.	22.00
American, Cake Stand	45.00 To 75.00
American, Candleholder, Double, Pair	60.00
American, Candlestick, Octagon, 6 In., Pair	32.00 To 48.50
American, Candy Dish, 3 Sections, Cover	65.00
American, Cheese & Cracker Set	55.00
American, Coaster	4.50
American, Cocktail, Cone, 3 Oz.	13.00

American, Cocktail, Oyster	9.50
American, Compote, Jelly, Cover, Footed, 7 In.	20.00
American, Condiment Set, Tray, 6 Piece	325.00
American, Cookie Jar	295.00
American, Creamer, 3 1/2 In.	7.00
American, Creamer, Individual, 3 In.	6.00
American, Cruet, 5 Oz.	25.00
American, Cup & Saucer	12.00
American, Decanter, 10 In.	55.00
American, Dish, Pickle, 8 In.	7.00 To 8.00
American, Dish, Tricornered, 2 1/2 X 7 1/8 In.	15.00
American, Goblet, Flared Top, Footed, 8 Oz.	9.00
American, Goblet, Hexagonal Footed, 6 3/4 In.	9.50
American, Goblet, Water	9.00 To 14.00
American, Gravy Boat, 12 In.	15.00
American, Hat, 3 In.	15.00
American, Hat, 4 1/2 In.	35.00
American, Ice Bucket, Underplate	45.00
American, Ice Tub, 6 1/2 In.	45.00
American, Jam Set, 3 Piece	105.00
American, Lemon Dish, Cover	35.00
American, Mustard, Cover	115.00
American, Pin Box	90.00
American, Plate, 6 In.	6.25 To 8.00
American, Plate, 7 In.	6.50 To 8.00
American, Plate, 8 1/2 In.	8.00 To 12.00
American, Plate, 9 1/2 In.	10.00 To 20.00
American, Plate, Torte, 14 In.	22.00 To 30.00
American, Platter, 10 1/2 In.	35.00
American, Platter, 11 In.	55.00
American, Platter, 13 In.	60.00
American, Platter, Oval, 10 1/2 In.	30.00
American, Punch Bowl, Footed	107.50
American, Punch Bowl, Underplate, 10 Cups	325.00
American, Punch Cup, Flared, Set of 6	40.00
American, Punch Set, Flared Cup, Bowl, 18 In., 13 Piece	350.00
American, Relish, 3 Sections, 9 1/2 In.	15.00 To 17.50
American, Relish, 4 Sections, Square, 10 In.	59.50
American, Rose Bowl, 5 In.	30.00
American, Salver, Round, 10 In.	40.00
American, Saucer	3.00
American, Server, Center Handle, 12 In.	33.00
American, Serving Dish, Handle, 9 In.	45.00
American, Sherbet, 3 1/2 In.	5.00
American, Shrimp Bowl	265.00
American, Spooner, 3 3/4 In.	18.00
American, Straw Jar, Cover	250.00
American, Sugar & Creamer, Breakfast Tray	24.00
American, Sugar & Creamer, Small	15.00
American, Sugar, Cover	17.50
American, Tray, Cloverleaf	100.00 To 140.00
American, Tumbler, Iced Tea, Footed, 12 Oz.	12.00
American, Tumbler, Juice, 5 Oz.	13.00
American, Tumbler, Whiskey, 2 Oz.	12.50
American, Urn, Square, 7 1/2 In.	35.00

American, Vase, Bud, 6 In. 8.00
American, Vase, Flared, 7 1/4 In. 18.00
American, Vegetable, Oval, 2 Sections, 10 In. 30.00
Arcady, Champagne 13.00
Arcady, Goblet 18.00
Baroque, Ashtray, Blue, 5 1/2 In. 16.00
Baroque, Bowl, Handles, Yellow, 6 In. 11.00
Baroque, Candleholder, 3–Light, Amber, Pair 15.00
Baroque, Candlestick, 8 Lustres, 7 1/2 In., Pair 40.00
Baroque, Candlestick, Topaz, 5 In., Pair 30.00
Baroque, Candy Dish, Cover, Low, Amber 38.00
Baroque, Creamer ....9.00 To 22.00
Baroque, Cup 4.00
Baroque, Cup & Saucer, Topaz 15.00
Baroque, Goblet 14.50
Baroque, Goblet, Water 15.00
Baroque, Jam Jar, Cover, 7 1/2 In. 25.00
Baroque, Oyster Cocktail 12.50
Baroque, Plate, 10 1/4 In. 15.00
Baroque, Punch Cup, Blue 12.00
Baroque, Saucer 2.00
Baroque, Sugar 7.00
Baroque, Sugar & Creamer, Topaz 20.00
Baroque, Sugar, Cover, Red 33.00
Baroque, Sugar, Footed 6.00
Baroque, Vase, Blue, 7 In. ....36.00 To 40.00
Beverly, Cup & Saucer, Demitasse 22.00
Beverly, Plate, Green, 10 1/4 In. 27.00
Bookends, Eagle 95.00
Bookends, Horse, Rearing, Polished Base, 7 1/2 X 5 1/4 In. 110.00
Brocade, Bowl, Green, 12 In. 125.00
Buttercup, Goblet, Iced Tea 32.50
Buttercup, Pitcher 125.00
Cameo, Champagne, Green 25.00
Cameo, Goblet, Green 25.00
Castle, Plate, 7 1/4 In. 6.00
Century, Bonbon, 3–Footed 8.00
Century, Bowl, Rolled Rim, Footed, 11 In. 33.00
Century, Butter 18.00
Century, Cake Plate, Handle, 9 1/2 In. 27.00
Century, Candlestick, 4 1/2 In. 15.00
Century, Candy Jar, Cover 30.00
Century, Creamer, Heather Etch 12.00
Century, Cruet 35.00
Century, Cup & Saucer ....10.00 To 24.00
Century, Ice Bucket, Handles 38.00
Century, Mayonnaise Set, 3 Piece ....35.00 To 44.00
Century, Relish, 2 Sections ....5.00 To 16.00
Century, Relish, 3 Sections, 11 In. 27.50
Century, Sherbet 8.00
Century, Sugar & Creamer, Footed ....16.00 To 18.00
Century, Sugar, 4 In. 8.00
Century, Tumbler, Iced Tea, 12 Oz. 16.00
Chintz, Champagne 14.00
Chintz, Champagne, Saucer, 5 1/2 In. 10.00
Chintz, Creamer 8.00
Chintz, Cruet, 5 Oz. 50.00
Chintz, Cup & Saucer ....18.00 To 22.00
Chintz, Goblet, 9 Oz. ....12.00 To 20.00
Chintz, Goblet, Claret, 5 3/8 In. 15.00
Chintz, Plate, 7 1/2 In. 12.00
Chintz, Plate, 9 In. ....20.00 To 35.00
Chintz, Plate, Torte, 14 In. 40.00
Chintz, Server, Center Handle 22.00

Chintz, Sugar & Creamer .... 25.00 To 30.00
Chintz, Sugar, Individual 15.00
Coin, Bowl, Pedestal, 8 1/2 In. 25.00
Coin, Bowl, Red, 8 1/2 In. 45.00
Coin, Candleholder, Clear Coins, Amber, 4 1/2 In., Pair 20.00
Coin, Candy Dish, Footed, Cover, 8 1/2 In. .... 40.00 To 45.00
Coin, Condiment Set, Amber, 4 Piece 135.00
Coin, Decanter, Amber, 10 3/4 In. 50.00
Coin, Lamp, No.2, Amber 85.00
Coin, Salt & Pepper, Ruby 38.00
Coin, Vase, Bud, Blue, 8 In 38.00
Colony, Bowl, Footed, 7 1/2 In. 20.00
Colony, Bowl, Mayonnaise 5.00
Colony, Cake Stand 67.50
Colony, Cruet 25.00
Colony, Goblet, Footed, 9 Oz. 8.00
Colony, Jug, 2 Qt. 58.00
Colony, Pitcher, 1 Pt. .... 40.00 To 45.00
Colony, Plate, Torte, 13 In. 50.00
Colony, Salver, 12 In. 32.00
Colony, Sugar & Creamer .... 10.00 To 20.00
Colony, Tray, 7 In. 7.00
Colony, Tray, Luncheon, Handles, 11 In. 30.00
Colony, Vase, Bud, 6 In. 10.00
Comet, Plate, 7 In. 4.00
Coronet, Mayonnaise, Double, 2 Ladles 10.00
Coronet, Sugar & Creamer, Iridescent 11.00
Coronet, Tidbit, Crystal, 3–Footed, 8 1/4 In. 8.00
Corsage, Goblet, Wine, Crystal, 3 Oz. 13.00
Czarina, Toothpick 28.50
Dolly Madison, Goblet 36.00
Fairfax, Ashtray, Amber 8.00
Fairfax, Bowl, Green, 9 In. 15.00
Fairfax, Butter, Cover, Amber .... 63.00 To 70.00
Fairfax, Candy Dish, Cover, 3–Footed, Pink 41.00
Fairfax, Champagne, Blue 81.00
Fairfax, Cup & Saucer, Blue 14.00
Fairfax, Cup, Amber 5.00
Fairfax, Cup, Amber, Demitasse 10.00
Fairfax, Cup, Footed, Blue 5.00
Fairfax, Ice Bucket, Green 30.00
Fairfax, Pail, Whipped Cream, Amber 22.00
Fairfax, Plate, Amber, 6 In. 1.50
Fairfax, Plate, Amber, 8 In. 3.50
Fairfax, Plate, Blue, 8 In. 6.00
Fairfax, Platter, Blue, 15 In. 48.00
Fairfax, Salt & Pepper, Footed, Glass Tops 35.00
Fairfax, Salt & Pepper, Individual 33.00
Fairfax, Saucer, Amber 2.00
Fairfax, Sugar & Creamer, Footed, Ruby 13.00
Fairfax, Sugar, Cover 30.00
Fairfax, Sugar, Cover, Amber 25.00
Figurine, Deer, Blue, Label, 4 1/2 In. 30.00
Figurine, Deer, Standing 50.00
Figurine, Duck, Baby, Head Back 50.00
Figurine, Mermaid .... 127.50 To 150.00
Figurine, Rabbit, Stylized, Frosted 50.00
Golden Grail, Champagne 35.00
Golden Grail, Goblet 40.00
Grape, Bowl, Centerpiece, Oval, Green, 13 In. 75.00
Grape, Compote, Green, 7 In. 68.00
Heather, Celery, Oval, 8 In. 18.00
Heather, Sugar & Creamer, Footed 30.00
Heirloom, Bowl, Blue, 10 In. 30.00

Heirloom, Bowl, Pink, Square, 9 In.	22.00
Heirloom, Bowl, Square, 7 In.	20.00
Heirloom, Candleholder, Blue, 9 In., Pair	45.00
Heirloom, Candleholder, Green, Pair	25.00
Hermitage, Decanter, Green	35.00
Holly, Cocktail	10.00
Holly, Cup & Saucer	28.00
Holly, Goblet, 7 3/4 In.	21.00
Holly, Sherbet	15.50
Holly, Tumbler, Iced Tea	27.50
Jamestown, Goblet, Water, Pink	9.00
Jamestown, Plate, Pink, 8 In.	6.00
Jamestown, Tumbler, Juice, 5 Oz.	6.00 To 8.00
June, Ashtray, Amber	30.00
June, Champagne, Topaz	21.00
June, Cup & Saucer, Amber	22.00
June, Goblet, Water, Blue, 8 1/4 In.	32.00
June, Pail, Whipped Cream, Blue	135.00
June, Pitcher, Label, Ice Blue	300.00
June, Plate, Azure, 7 1/2 In., 8 Piece	60.00
June, Plate, Blue, 8 3/4 In.	20.00
June, Salt & Pepper, Glass Covers	80.00
June, Sherbet	12.00
June, Tumbler, Juice, Topaz, 5 Oz.	16.00
June, Tumbler, Topaz	17.00
Lafayette, Relish, 3 Sections, Topaz, 7 1/2 In.	10.00
Lido, Cake Plate	22.50
Lido, Compote, 5 1/2 In.	15.00
Lido, Sherbet	9.00
Lily Pond, Bowl, 12 In.	60.00
Louise, Sugar, Cover	22.00
Mardi Gras, Vase, Signed, 7 1/4 In.	88.00
Mayfair, Cruet, Stopper, Green	65.00
Mayfair, Relish, Divided, Topaz, 8 1/2 In.	10.00
Meadow Rose, Relish, 3 Sections, 10 In.	22.00
Meadow Rose, Sugar Shaker	25.00
Meadow Rose, Tumbler, Footed, 12 Oz.	18.00
Morning Glory, Candlestick, 5 1/2 In., Pair	35.00
Morning Glory, Cup & Saucer	12.00
Morning Glory, Plate, 10 1/2 In.	15.00
Mother of Pearl, Wine, 7 In.	18.00
Mystic, Goblet, Green	20.00
Navarre, Bell, Blue	25.00
Navarre, Bowl, Console, Octagonal, Green, 12 In.	15.00
Navarre, Candleholder, Double, 4 1/2 In., Pair	40.00
Navarre, Cordial	20.00
Navarre, Goblet, 7 1/2 In.	15.00 To 19.00
Navarre, Goblet, Clear Stem, Blue, 8 In.	25.00 To 30.00
Navarre, Nappy, Tricornered, 4 5/8 In.	8.00
Navarre, Plate, 9 In.	18.00
Navarre, Relish, 3 Sections	20.00
Navarre, Tumbler, Footed, 13 Oz.	16.00
Oak Leaf, Candleholder	10.00
Oriental, Champagne, Crystal, 5 Oz.	10.00
Panel & Bull's-Eye, Spooner, Footed, 7 1/2 In.	30.00
Paradise, Vase, Orchid, 8 In.	95.00
Pioneer, Ashtray, Green	5.00
Pioneer, Cup & Saucer, Green	8.00
Pioneer, Ice Bucket, Green	12.00
Pioneer, Sugar, Cover, Green	17.00
Priscilla, Butter, Green, Gold Cover	45.00
Priscilla, Sugar & Creamer, Amber	15.00
Priscilla, Syrup, Original Lid, Green, Gold Trim	375.00
Raleigh, Sugar & Creamer, Individual	8.00

Romance, Cocktail, 3 1/2 Oz. 15.00
Royal, Finger Bowl, Amber 16.00
Royal, Platter, 12 In. 45.00
Royal, Soup, Dish, Amber, 8 In. 15.00
Sunray, Bowl, 3–Footed, 7 In. 0.00
Sunray, Goblet, 9 Oz. 12.00
Sunray, Ice Bucket, Handles 17.00
Sunray, Nappy, Square, Handle 6.00
Sunray, Plate, 7 In. 4.00
Sunray, Salt 10.00
Sunray, Sherbet 8.00
Sunray, Sugar & Creamer 15.00
Trojan, Cup, Topaz 13.00
Trojan, Ice Bucket, Topaz 73.00
Versailles, Candy Box, Etched, Cover, Amber 47.00
Versailles, Cup & Saucer, Blue 30.00
Versailles, Pitcher, Water, Topaz 250.00
Versailles, Plate, Blue, 8 In. 11.25
Versailles, Plate, Pink, 8 3/4 In. 8.00
Versailles, Sugar Pail, Green 80.00
Versailles, Tumbler, Amber, 12 Oz. 20.00
Vesper, Candy Dish, Cover, Amber 125.00
Vesper, Cocktail, Oyster, Footed, Amber, 4 Oz. 10.00
Vesper, Cup & Saucer, Footed, Amber 22.50
Vesper, Goblet, Water, Stem, Amber 25.00
Vesper, Plate, Amber, 7 1/2 In. 7.50
Vesper, Plate, Amber, 8 1/2 In. 9.50
Vesper, Plate, Amber, 10 1/2 In. 35.00
Victory, Plate, 7 3/8 In. 14.00
Virginia, Goblet, Pink 5.00
Willowmere, Cocktail, Oyster 12.00
    FOVAL, see Fry Foval
    FRAME, see Furniture, Frame

 Francisware is a named glassware made by Hobbs, Brockunier and
Company of Wheeling, West Virginia, in the 1880s. It is a clear or
frosted hobnail or swirl pattern glass with amber–stained rim. Some
pieces were made by a pressed glass method, others were mold
blown.

FRANCISWARE, Bowl, 2 1/2 X 5 1/4 In. 40.00
  Creamer, Amber Rim, Frosted 45.00
  Pitcher, Water 30.00
  Spooner, Hobnail, Amber, Frosted 35.00
  Sugar, Cover 40.00
  Toothpick, Frosted Hob, Amber Rim 30.00
  Water Set, Hobnail, 5 Piece 215.00

When the weather is bad, the auction will probably be good. Brave
storms and cold and attend the auctions in bad weather when the
crowd is small and the prices low.

Frankart, Inc., New York, New York, mass–produced nude "dancing–lady" lamps, ashtrays, and other decorative Art Deco items in the 1920s and 1930s. They were made of white lead composition and spray–painted. "Frankart Inc." and the patent number and year were stamped on the base.

FRANKART, Bookends, Boy, Toy Ship, Pup	55.00
Bookends, Cocker Spaniel, Bronze, 5 3/4 In.	85.00
Bookends, Dog	50.00
Bookends, Female Head & Bust	95.00
Bookends, Lady's Head, Flowers In Hair	75.00
Bookends, Nudes, Painted Apple Green, 9 1/4 In.	225.00
Bookends, Springer Spaniel, Metal	40.00
Bookends, Stallion	45.00
Lamp, Lady Balancing On Hands	165.00
Lamp, No.L251, Nude, Stands Guard Over Light Globe, 11 In.	280.00
Lamp, Seated Nude, Green	145.00
Lamp, Women, Seated On Pillar, Holding Glass Ball	175.00

ORIGINAL CREATION by FRANKOMA

Frankoma Pottery was originally known as The Frank Potteries when John F. Frank opened shop in 1933. The factory is now working in Sapulpa, Oklahoma. Early wares were made from a light cream–colored clay, but in 1956 the company switched to a red burning clay. The firm makes dinnerwares, utilitarian and decorative kitchen wares, figurines, flowerpots, and limited edition and commemorative pieces.

FRANKOMA, Ashtray, Art Deco	10.00
Ashtray, Comma Handle	27.50
Ashtray, With Magazine Rack, Black	88.00
Bank, Pig With Basket, Yellow	30.00
Billiken	65.00
Bookends, Horse	45.00
Bowl, Blue, Dated 1904, 5 X 10 In.	65.00
Bowl, Willow Leaf, Flat, Jade Green, 9 1/2 In.	10.00
Candleholder, Black, Pair	10.00
Candleholder, Ram's Head, Orange–Brown Grainy Matte	70.00
Candlestick, Desert Sand, Pair	15.00
Candlestick, Woodland Moss, Pair	15.00
Cowboy Boot	8.00
Creamer, Wagon Wheel	35.00
Figurine, Candle Girl	48.00
Figurine, Coyote	20.00
Figurine, English Setter	50.00
Figurine, Flower Girl	65.00
Honey Pot, Bee On Top	15.00
Mug, Cowboy Shape, Orange, White, Tan	8.50
Mug, Donkey, 1975	24.00
Mug, Elephant & Donkey, Set of 4	200.00
Mug, Elephant, 1968 .... 45.00 To 50.00
Mug, Elephant, 1970	50.00
Mug, Elephant, 1978	12.00
Mug, Nixon–Agnew, Elephant, Red	45.00
Pitcher, Ada, Bronze & Green	10.00
Pitcher, Green & Brown	20.00
Pitcher, Honey, Green	20.00
Pitcher, Wagon Wheel, Green	18.00
Planter, Ada, Blue	12.00
Planter, Black, Marked	28.00
Planter, Blue, Oblong, 12 In.	10.00
Planter, Bowl Shape, Black, Marked	28.00
Plaque, Will Rogers	65.00
Plate, Christmas, 1966	80.00
Plate, Christmas, 1967 .... 50.00 To 90.00
Plate, Christmas, 1969	25.00

Plate, Easter, 1972	14.00 To 15.00
Plate, Oklahoma	12.00
Plate, Rural Mail Carrier	55.00
Salt & Pepper, Sitting Bull, Green	35.00
Salt & Pepper, Tepee, Prairie, Green	15.00
Spoon Rest, 6 In.	6.50
Sugar & Creamer, Wagon Wheel, Green, 4 In.	8.00
Table Set, Wagon Wheel, 5 Piece	150.00
Toby Mug, Uncle Sam	15.00
Tray, Blue, 8 X 5 In.	10.00
Trivet, American Eagle	9.00
Trivet, Flag	8.50
Trivet, Willa Cather	30.00
Tumbler, Lazy Bones	7.50
Vase, Bud, Cactus, Red, 5 In.	45.00
Vase, Bud, Flying Goose, Red, 5 In.	38.00
Vase, Flame, Bottle Shape, Mushroom Stopper, Late 1960s, 10 In.	22.00
Vase, Flying Goose, Green & Brown, Rectangular, Label, 6 1/2 In.	15.00
Vase, Ram's Head, Orange–Brown Grainy Matte, 5 3/4 In.	85.00
Wall Pocket, Boot, Green, 6 3/4 In.	15.00
Wall Pocket, Indian Maiden, 5 1/2 In.	20.00
Wall Pocket, Phoebe	60.00
Wall Pocket, Wagon Wheel	15.00

The Fraternal section lists objects that are related to the many different fraternal organizations in the United States. The Elks, Masons, Odd Fellows, and others are included. Furniture is listed in the Furniture section.

FRATERNAL, see also Shaving Mug

FRATERNAL, B.P.O.E., Photograph, Oh! How I Love An Elk	75.00
B.P.O.E., Plate, Elks Logo, Scammel Chain, Blue, Ivory Trim, 9 In.	18.00
B.P.O.E., Shaving Mug, Elk's Head, Roses & Wreaths, Germany	90.00
B.P.O.E., Spoon, Sterling Silver, Elk's Lodge, Kansas City, Kansas	45.00
Eastern Star, Earrings, Rhinestone	12.00
Eastern Star, Ring, Past Mistress	42.50
Eastern Star, Spoon, Masonic Home, Boone, Iowa, Sterling Silver	30.00
Eastern Star, Spoon, Symbols, Sterling Silver	25.00
Knights of Pythias, Sword, Ceremonial	30.00
Knights Templar, Figure, Man, Bobbing Head, Fez, 1962	23.00
Masonic, Ashtray, Pressed Wood	25.00
Masonic, Badge, Center Sapphire, Case, 14K White Gold	295.00
Masonic, Bench, Lodge, New Black Upholstery	225.00
Masonic, Champagne, New Orleans, 1910	55.00
Masonic, Display Case, Dudley, Yellow Gold Filled	2250.00
Masonic, Goblet, St.Paul, Ruby	60.00
Masonic, Medal, Star In Circle, Ribbon, Birmingham, 1920	65.00
Masonic, Mug, Indian Design, Glass, 1903	48.00
Masonic, Mug, Indian, Sword Handle, 1903	58.00
Masonic, Mug, Peter A.B.Widener Lodge, Anniversary, 1912–1978	5.00
Masonic, Mug, Shriner, Zagazig Temple, Des Moines, 1904	35.00
Masonic, Napkin Ring, Temple, Chicago, Enameled, Pressed Glass	28.00
Masonic, Plate, Putnam Lodge, 1854–1954	20.00
Masonic, Pocket Flap, O.A.Lodge 461, Brown Edge, Embroidered	25.00
Masonic, Ring, 10K Gold, Emblems, C.1896	85.00
Masonic, Ring, 10K Gold, Polished Black Onyx, C.1896	75.00
Masonic, Ring, 14K Gold, Square & Compass, Diamond, 6 In.	200.00
Masonic, Ring, Gold Emblem, Sterling Silver	30.00
Masonic, Shaving Mug, Insignia, F.K.Mickelmoit In Gold, French	50.00
Masonic, Spoon, Souvenir, Louisville, Symbols, 1901	28.00
Masonic, Stickpin, 14K Gold, Pearl Center	30.00
Masonic, Stickpin, 32nd Degree	8.00
Masonic, Sword, Dress, Ivory Handle, Sheath	160.00
Masonic, Tie Rack, Pressed Wood	45.00
Masonic, Trivet, Footed, Brass	35.00

Masonic, Watch Fob, Basket 2.00
Odd Fellows, Button, Reunion, Hershey, Pa., White Dove, 1 1/4 In. 3.00
Shriner, Bookends, Scimitar, Red Star, Signed L.V.Aronsen, 1922 .... 75.00
Shriner, Champagne, Carnival Glass, Clear, 1911 .... 40.00
Shriner, Glass, Scimitar, Crescent, Lion, 1899 .... 50.00
Shriner, Ring, 14K Gold, With .20 Diamond, W.G.Eagle 300.00
Shriner, Shot Glass, Fez, Louisville, Cranberry & Gold, 1909 .... 70.00
Shriner, Shot Glass, Rochester, Cranberry, Gold, Handle, 1911 .... 60.00
Shriner, Toothpick, Pittsburg, New Orleans, 1910 .... 38.00
Shriner, Tumbler, 1913 .... 95.00
Shriner, Wine, Commemorative, 1899 .... 85.00
Walking Stick, Odd Fellows, Diamonds, Knotted Tassle, 34 In. 400.00

Fry glass was made by the H. C. Fry Glass Company of Rochester, Pennsylvania. The company, founded in 1901, first made cut glass and other types of fine glasswares. In 1922, they patented a heat-resistant glass called "Pearl Oven glass." For two years, 1926-27, the company made Fry Foval, an opal ware decorated with colored trim. Reproductions of this glass have been made. The company also made Depression glass.

FRY FOVAL, Candlestick, Blue Wafers & Spirals, 8 3/4 In. 75.00
Compote, Footed, 6 3/4 X 4 3/4 In. 195.00
Cup & Saucer, Green Handle 65.00
Cup & Saucer, Pearl, Green Handle 50.00
Tea Set, Transparent Smoky White, Silver Banded Finials, 11 Pc. 685.00
Vase, Cobalt Blue Base & Trim, Footed, 10 In. 185.00
FRY, Cup, Measuring 40.00
Custard, Oven Ware 8.00
Goblet, Optic Rib, Vaseline, Green, Footed 17.00
Mug, Lemonade, Radio Ware, Handle, Green 125.00
Percolator Top 7.00
Pitcher, Water, Signed, 10 In. 185.00
Trivet, 3-Footed 9.00

Fulper is the mark used by the American Pottery Company of Flemington, New Jersey. The art pottery was made from 1910 to 1929. The firm had been making bottles, jugs, and housewares from 1805. Doll heads were made about 1928. The firm became Stangl Pottery in 1929. Fulper art pottery is admired for its attractive glazes and simple shapes.

FULPER, Bookends, Book, Green & Gray, 4 3/4 In. 45.00
Bottle, Musical, Pinched, Green Over Cream Glaze, 10 In. 75.00
Bowl, Blue & Green Glossy Glaze, Rolled Rim, Signed, 9 X 2 In. 60.00
Bowl, Cobalt, Shaded Blue & Cream Over Rose, 8 1/2 In. 95.00
Bowl, Effigy, Blue Glaze, Drip Top, Ink Mark, 1915-20, 7 1/2 In. 525.00
Bowl, Effigy, Plum & Brown Outside, Pink Inside 425.00
Bowl, Gray & Green, Flambe Glaze, 10 In. 45.00
Bowl, Green & White, 3 X 8 In. 42.00
Bowl, Green, 4 3/4 In. 50.00
Bowl, Green, 8 In. 75.00
Bowl, Pink Matte, 5 3/4 In. 60.00
Chamberstick, Arched Candle Shield, Loop Handle, Signed, 1915, 7 In. 60.00
Chamberstick, Lavender, 10 In. 130.00
Figurine, Cat, Mottled Brown & Cream, Paper Label, C.1915, 9 In. 375.00
Flower Frog, Lily Pad Shape, Purple Pink, Vertical Ink Stamp 35.00
Flower Frog, Nude Woman, 5 3/4 In. 68.00
Lantern, Hooded, 3 Leaded Glass Inserts, 10 1/2 In. 600.00
Mustard, Black Mirrored Flambe Glaze, Cover, 9 In. 260.00
Perfume Lamp, Cytharia, Large .... 900.00 To 950.00
Powder Jar, Art Deco Girl, Lavender Top .... 125.00 To 150.00
Powder Jar, Egyptian Girl On Top 250.00
Vase, Blue Shades, High Glaze, Raised Vertical Mark 185.00
Vase, Brown & Black Drip, Brown Top, Handles, Stamp, 8 1/4 In. 195.00
Vase, Buttressed, Cylindrical, Semigloss Glaze, 12 In. ....*Illus* 1400.00

Fulper, Vase, Buttressed,
Cylindrical,
Semigloss Glaze, 12 In.

Furniture, Washstand, Sheraton,
Mahogany, Carved Acanthus, 30 In.

Furniture, Washstand, Sheraton,
Tiger Maple, C.1800, 36 X 20 In.

Furniture, Washstand, Classical
Revival, Mahogany, 3 Drawers, 1815

Vase, Dark Flambe Over Green Gloss, Ovoid, Marked, 8 3/4 In.	175.00
Vase, Double Handle, Brown Glaze, 5 In.	95.00
Vase, Flambe, Mirrored Glaze, Embedded Crystals, 9 X 8 In.	225.00
Vase, Gray Black Glaze, 8 1/2 X 11 In.	135.00
Vase, Gray Flambe, Tan, 7 In.	80.00
Vase, Grecian, 3 Handles, Raspberry, 7 In.	65.00
Vase, Green To Purple, Handles, 5 In.	50.00
Vase, High Gloss, 11 X 10 In.	375.00
Vase, Impressed Bellflower, Green, With Brown Highlights, 8 In.	60.00
Vase, Lava Glaze, Rose Over Green, 6 X 7 In.	125.00
Vase, Leopard Glaze, Raised Design, Octagonal, Signed, 8 In.	375.00
Vase, Mirrored Flambe Glaze, 9 In.	245.00
Vase, Mythological Dragon Climbing Down Neck, 8 In.	250.00
Vase, Orange Glaze, Lamp Hole, 18 X 9 In.	395.00
Vase, Red & Green, 4 1/2 In.	60.00
Wall Pocket, Bird, Green, Signed	65.00
Wall Pocket, Blue Flowered Top, Paper Label	110.00
Water Cooler, Blue Flambe Over Green, Loop Handles, Cover, 15 In.	60.00

All types of furniture are listed in this section. Examples dating
from the seventeenth century to the 1950s are included. Prices for
furniture vary in different parts of the country. Oak furniture is
most expensive in the West; large pieces over eight feet high are
sold for the most money in the South where high ceilings are found
in the old homes. Condition is very important when determining
prices. These are NOT average prices but rather reports of unique

sales. If the description includes the word "style," the piece resembles the old furniture style but was made at a later time. It is not a period piece.

FURNITURE, Armchair, see also Furniture, Chair

FURNITURE, Armchair, 4 Slats, Mission Oak, Adjustable Back, 1910, 37 X 32 In.	350.00
Armchair, Adirondack, Youth's	200.00
Armchair, Adjustable Back, L.& J.G.Stickley, Spring Cushion Seat	2700.00
Armchair, American Renaissance, Marquetry Inlaid, C.1865, Pair	2970.00
Armchair, Arrowback, Bamboo Turning, Bentwood, 16 In.	150.00
Armchair, Arrowback, C.1820	185.00
Armchair, Arrowback, Child's, Red Paint, Over Green, 18 1/2 In.	175.00
Armchair, Banister Back, Splint Seat, Maple, C.1740 ....*Illus*	4950.00
Armchair, Barrel Back, Spring Cushion Seat, Plail Brothers, 1910	900.00
Armchair, Bow, G.Stickley, Cane, Web Seat, Dark Finish, Decal, 1905	5500.00
Armchair, Charles II, Walnut, Caned Seat, Pierced Top Rail	770.00
Armchair, Child's, Eastlake Style, Oak, Design Crest, 26 In.	50.00
Armchair, Child's, Ladder Back, 2 Slats, 21 1/2 In.	80.00
Armchair, Child's, Ladder Back, 3 Slats, Green Paint, 22 X 13 In.	200.00
Armchair, Chippendale, Hand Carved Mahogany Frame, 19th Century	225.00
Armchair, Chippendale, Mahogany, Pierced Splat, Serpentine	110.00
Armchair, Classical Revival, Mahogany, Slip Seat, Sabre, C.1820	275.00
Armchair, Continental Baroque, Walnut, Upholstered, Pair	2310.00
Armchair, Country, Ladder Back, Pine, Turned Legs, Woven Seat	40.00
Armchair, Empire, Mahogany, Gilt-Bronze, Square Upholstered, Pair	2475.00
Armchair, Flemish, Carved, Caned Back & Seat, 19th Century	150.00
Armchair, Fountain Elms Pattern, Belter, Carved Rosewood	9900.00
Armchair, Fruitwood, Biedermeier, Curved Back, Scrolled Arms	90.00
Armchair, G.Stickley, 5 Vertical Slats, Adjustable, Cushion, 1907	4500.00
Armchair, George II, Mahogany, Upholstered Back, 45 1/2 In.	650.00
Armchair, George III, Mahogany, Cartouche, Padded Arms, 1770, Pair	8250.00
Armchair, George III, Painted, Parcel Gilt, Padded Arms, C.1775	1430.00
Armchair, Hepplewhite, Martha Washington, Mahogany, Raw Silk	300.00
Armchair, Heywood-Wakefield, Painted, 3 Piece	1650.00
Armchair, Hitchcock Type, Ladder Back, Black Paint, Gold Design	125.00
Armchair, Italian Baroque, Walnut, Needlepoint, Straight Legs	605.00
Armchair, Italian Renaissance, Carved, Walnut, 49 1/2 In.	425.00
Armchair, J.& J.W.Meeks, Upholstered Seat, Back & Arms	4400.00
Armchair, Ladder Back, Added Rockers, 4 Slats, Woven Splint Seat	125.00
Armchair, Ladder Back, Black Over Red Paint	275.00
Armchair, Ladder Back, Maple, Hickory, Splint Seat, New England	880.00
Armchair, Leather Back, Open Arms, Cushion Seat, Limbert, C.1907	100.00
Armchair, Library, George III, Mahogany, Padded Arms, Upholstered	4400.00
Armchair, Library, George III, Mahogany, Upholstered, Flared Seat	1045.00
Armchair, Louis XV, Carved Summer Flowers, Upholstered, Walnut	450.00
Armchair, Louis XVI, Giltwood, Twisted Ribbon, Padded Arms, 4 Pc.	3850.00
Armchair, Louis XVI, Shield Back, Needlepoint Upholstery	130.00
Armchair, Maple, Slat Back, Turned Legs, New England, C.1700	2200.00
Armchair, Morris, Cushion Seat & Back, L.& J.G.Stickley	1700.00
Armchair, Napoleon III, Bulle Marquetry, Gilt-Bronze, Red, Pair	3300.00
Armchair, Napoleon III, Ebonized, Inlaid, Upholstered, 1870, Pair	1650.00
Armchair, Office, Arrow, Swivel, Pressed Back, Old Caned Seat	125.00
Armchair, Queen Anne, Spanish Feet, Vase Splat, Rose Head Nails	2000.00
Armchair, Regency, Lacquer, Caned, Pierced Horizontal Splat	7150.00
Armchair, Regency, Painted, Parcel Gilt, X Splat, Upholstered, Pr.	7425.00
Armchair, Renaissance Revival, Walnut, U-Shaped Back, 29 In.	120.00
Armchair, Rococo, Rosewood, Belter, Upholstered, C.1855, Pair	6875.00
Armchair, Rococo, Rosewood, Laminated, John Henry Belter, 1850	9250.00
Armchair, Stickley, Adjustable Back, Drop, C.1907, 32 1/2 In.	4500.00
Armchair, Stuart, Oak, Serpentine Crest Rail, Dated 1677, Pair	2090.00
Armchair, Twig, 1920s	175.00
Armchair, Twig, Child's	45.00
Armchair, Wainscot, Walnut, Cutout Heart, Turned Legs, C.1725	8000.00

Armchair, Wing, Canted Back, Red Leather Upholstered	3850.00
Armchair, Wing, Chippendale, Mahogany, Loose Cushion ....*Illus*	5775.00
Armchair, Wing, Chippendale, Mahogany, Scrolled Arms, C.1780	1210.00
Armchair, Wing, George III, Mahogany, Serpentine, Loose Cushion	2200.00
Armchair, Wing, William & Mary, Ebonized, Loose Cushion Seat, Pr.	1750.00
Armchair, Wingback, William & Mary, Upholstered Cotton Print	1300.00
Armchair, Woven Back, Old Hickory Furniture Co., Pair	375.00
Armchair, York County, Rush Set, Box Stretcher, 1770–80	1600.00
Armoire, Baroque, Arched Doors, 2 Drawers, Walnut, 94 3/4 In.	2800.00
Armoire, Canadian, Mustard & Red Paint, 2 Doors, C.1750	2300.00
Armoire, English, C.1835, 84 X 56 In.	1850.00
Armoire, Louis XVI, Walnut, 2 Doors, Drawer, Bun Feet, 6 Ft.10 In.	6600.00
Armoire, Rococo, Rosewood, Mahogany, Cabinet Doors, 81 1/2 In.	475.00
Armoire, Single Door, Painted, Austrian, C.1871, 45 X 76 In.	2500.00
Armoire, Walnut, Double Thumb Molded Cornice, 2 Doors, 7 Ft.7 In.	450.00
Baker's Rack, 4 Shelves, Metal & Oak, 72 In.	75.00
Barrel, Garden, Polychromed Porcelain, Birds, 14 1/2 In., Pair	270.00
Bed Step, Top Opening For Chamber Pot, Walnut & Burl Veneer	375.00
Bed, 1/2 Tester, Carved Rosewood	8800.00
Bed, Baby's, 4 Rails Each Side, Lattice Slats, 30 1/2 X 48 In.	65.00
Bed, Baby's, Square Posts, Walnut & Poplar, 27 X 22 X 38 In.	215.00
Bed, Ball Finials On Posts, Grain Painted, C.1825, 67 X 51 In.	2800.00
Bed, Brass Mounted Mahogany, Campaign, England, C.1830	1900.00
Bed, Brass, White Iron, C.1910	350.00
Bed, Bunkcountry Empire, Twin	900.00
Bed, Cannonball, Painted & Grained, C.1830, 56 In.	300.00
Bed, Canopy, Federal, Maple, Pine, Reeded Swelled Foot Posts, 1820	2000.00
Bed, Carved, Poppy Flower Inlay, Art Nouveau, Double Size	1500.00
Bed, Child's, Federal, Scrolled Headboard, Maple, 38 In., Pair	665.00
Bed, Child's, Inset Rockers, Removable Posts, Painted, 55 In.	600.00
Bed, Day, Curly Maple, Turned Posts, Rails, 77 In.	1600.00
Bed, Day, Windsor, Or Hired Man's, Pine, Chestnut, 8 Legs, 1810–20	3200.00
Bed, Federal, Grain Painted, Crest, Peg Feet, Child's, 36 X 31 In.	850.00
Bed, Four–Poster, Casters, Grain Painted, C.1830, 41 X 72 In.	800.00
Bed, Four–Poster, Federal, Curly Maple, 1815, 7 Ft.4 In.	4950.00
Bed, Four–Poster, Grain Painted, Arched Head, Pa., C.1840, 6 Ft.	1350.00
Bed, Half–Tester, Child's, Rosewood, C.1850	2420.00
Bed, Handmade, Spindle, Box Spring & Mattress, Walnut, Twin	400.00
Bed, Louis XV, Tulipwood Marquetry, Mahogany, 45 In., Pair	5500.00
Bed, Louis XVI, Gilt Bronze, Amboyna, Mahogany, C.1860, 6 Ft.	1650.00
Bed, Maple, Mushroom Posts, Full Size	286.00
Bed, Maple, Pine, Sponge Painted, C.1830, 47 X 54 X 78 In.	6050.00

Furniture, Armchair, Wing,
Chippendale, Mahogany,
Loose Cushion

Furniture, Bed, Sleigh, American, Carved Mahogany, C.1840

Bed, Maple, Removable Finial, Yellow Paint, 1835, 77 X 52 In. 2475.00
Bed, Mission, Mahogany, Oak, Straight Crest, 1912, 54 X 42 In., Pair 650.00
Bed, Renaissance, Applied Carvings & Finials, Walnut, Queen Size 150.00
Bed, Rococo, Walnut, Arched Headboard, C–Scrolls, Lower Footboard 550.00
Bed, Rope, Birch & Poplar, Extended Side Rails, 52 X 77 X 55 In. 200.00
Bed, Rope, Cannonball Finials, Scrolled Crest, Poplar, 49 1/4 In. 275.00
Bed, Rope, Cannonball Posts, Red Cherry Finish, 51 X 47 In. 200.00
Bed, Rope, Chestnut, Top Hat Finial, Pennsylvania 395.00
Bed, Rope, Curly Maple, High Turned Posts 925.00
Bed, Rope, Curly Maple, Turned Posts, Natural, 51 X 71 X 51 In. 900.00
Bed, Rope, Pa.German, Grotesque Carved Headboard, C.1840 .... 6200.00
Bed, Rope, Poplar, Worn Red Paint, Cannonball, 51 X 70 X 48 In. 160.00
Bed, Rope, Red & Black Graining, Pine & Poplar, 60 3/4 In. 250.00
Bed, Rope, Spool Turnings, Curly Maple, 93 X 71 1/2 X 51 3/4 In. 500.00
Bed, Rope, Trundle, Green Paint, 42 1/2 X 60 3/4 In. 175.00
Bed, Rope, Turned Posts & Finials, Blue Paint, 52 1/4 X 72 In. 500.00
Bed, Rope, Turned Posts & Spool, Maple & Poplar, 43 1/4 X 68 In. 90.00
Bed, Shaker, Walnut Stain, Pine & Ash, 31 1/2 X 74 In. 800.00
Bed, Shaker, Youth's, Shaped Headboard, Red 500.00
Bed, Sleigh, American, Carved Mahogany, C.1840 ....*Illus* 1800.00
Bed, Sleigh, Fruitwood, French, C.1820, 79 In., Pair 4600.00
Bed, Sleigh, Walnut, 44 3/4 X 51 1/2 X 70 In. 145.00
Bed, Tall Fluted Posts, Canopy Frame, Mahogany, 86 X 54 In. 7000.00
Bed, Tall Post, Curly Maple, Rope, Scroll Carved, 56 X 75 X 86 In. 1600.00
Bed, Tester, Carved Leaves On Foot Posts, Mahogany, 7 Ft.4 In. 2860.00
Bed, Tester, Stuart, Carved Oak, 17th Century, 4 Ft.3 In. 4950.00
Bed, Walnut, Country, Scratch Carved Folk Design, Post, 69 In. 250.00
Bed, Youth, Amish, Original Paint 595.00
Bed, Youth, Bow Foot, Brass 1800.00
Bedroom Set, Frank Lloyd, Dressing Table, Armoire, Bed 4750.00
Bedroom Set, Marble Top, Walnut Trim, Victorian, 9 Ft., 3 Piece 5500.00
Bedroom Set, Renaissance Revival, Gilt Leaf, Shell, Walnut, 2 Pc. 6600.00
Bedroom Set, Rococo, Walnut, Marble Top Stand, Leaf Handles, 3 Pc. 750.00
Bedroom Set, Sheraton, Veneers, Painted Florals, C.1920, 8 Piece 6000.00
Bedroom Set, Victorian, Marble Tops, 3 Piece 2200.00
Bedroom Set, Wheat Finish, Heywood Wakefield, 4 Piece 1000.00
Bench, Bootjack Feet, Mortised & Wedged Construction 100.00
Bench, Bucket, 2 Shelves, Arched Feet, Pine, 24 X 37 3/8 In. 412.00
Bench, Bucket, Brown Over Blue, Underslung Drawer, Pine, 57 In. 1400.00
Bench, Bucket, Child's, Grain Painted, 19th Century, 44 X 46 In. 1045.00
Bench, Bucket, Cutout Ends, Base Shelf, Wire Nails, 43 1/4 In. 125.00
Bench, Bucket, Gray Paint, Arched Feet, 19th Century, 32 X 61 In. 1650.00
Bench, Bucket, Square Nails, Gray Paint, 24 1/2 X 28 In. 190.00
Bench, Carved Legs, Cane Seat, 17 X 48 In. 55.00
Bench, Church, Mennonite, Yellow Grain Painted, 1850–70 .... 195.00
Bench, Cobbler's, Leather Seat, 3 Tools In Drawer, 37 1/2 In. 270.00
Bench, Curtain Pattern, Cast Iron 950.00
Bench, Deacon's, Arms, Yellow Grained, 10 Ft. 525.00
Bench, Deacon's, Plank Seat, Brown Paint, Pine, 8 Ft. 605.00
Bench, Deacon's, Plank Seat, Spindles, Scrolled Arms, C.1840, 8 Ft. 770.00
Bench, Deacon's, Spindles, Splats, Scrolled Arms, Red, 7 Ft.11 In. 715.00
Bench, Deacon's, Tole Painting 350.00
Bench, Dressing Table, Gilded, Green Velvet Cushion, Iron, 36 In. 155.00
Bench, Egyptian Style, Inlaid Mahogany, Cotton Webb, 1925, 34 In. 5500.00
Bench, Farm, French, C.1850, Pair 750.00
Bench, Flared Supports, Missouri, Painted Green, Pine, 5 Ft.2 In. 137.50
Bench, Florals, Green, Yellow Striping, Old Mustard Paint, 74 In. 975.00
Bench, Garden, Foliage Scroll, Dark Green Paint, Iron, 37 3/4 In. 550.00
Bench, Gothic, Cast Iron, C.1845 .... 2750.00
Bench, Grape Pattern, Cast Iron 800.00
Bench, Hitchcock Style, 1830–35 .... 2995.00
Bench, Kneeling, Pine, Cutout Feet, Red Coverlet Upholstered 60.00
Bench, Lift Seat, 6 Spindles, Recessed Back, Box Base, 40 X 46 In. 425.00
Bench, Mammy's, Original Stenciling, Black Over Red, C.1820 .... 875.00

It is safe to use spray or paste wax on your furniture, but be careful about changing brands. It is okay to put paste wax over spray wax. It is not safe to put spray wax over paste wax because it may soften the paste wax and spoil the finish.

Bench, Mormon, Plank Top, Rectangular Supports, Spine, 4 Ft.10 In.	137.50
Bench, Ohio, 19th Century, Painted Green, Pine, 4 Ft.2 In.	165.00
Bench, Piano, Oak, Tenoned Shelf, Roycroft, Logo, 20 X 36 X 16 In.	2400.00
Bench, Piano, Stickley, D–Shaped Handles, Label, 21 X 36 X 13 In.	800.00
Bench, Pine, Cutout Feet, Bead Edge Apron & Corner, 13 X 96 In.	195.00
Bench, Provincial, Oak, 19th Century, 18 1/2 X 6 Ft.6 In., Pair	335.00
Bench, School, Child's, Oak, Cathedral Back, 9 Ft.	180.00
Bench, Shaker, Apple, New Lebanon, Pine, Maple, C.1840, 4 Ft.9 In.	650.00
Bench, Twig, Cast Iron, Pair	2600.00
Bench, Water, 2 Shelves, Scalloped Back, Poplar, 31 1/4 X 31 In.	85.00
Bench, Water, 2 Stepped Shelves, Pine, 39 1/2 X 40 1/2 In.	175.00
Bench, Water, Scrolled Detail, Soft Wood, 29 X 30 In.	250.00
Bench, Water, Square Nail Construction, Poplar, 31 1/2 X 39 In.	275.00
Bench, Windsor, Bamboo, Plank Seat, Shaped Crest Back, 91 In.	900.00
Bench, Work, Pullout Drawer & Tray Each Side, Pine, 32 X 24 In.	350.00
Bergere, Louis XV, Giltwood, Upholstered Back, Seat, Flowers	325.00
Bergere, Maple, Art Deco, Pair	3520.00
Book Press, 2 Lower Drawers, Dutch, 18th Century	1500.00
Bookcase Cabinet, George III, Bowfront, Mahogany, 7 Ft.1 In.	7700.00
Bookcase Cabinet, Italian Baroque, Walnut, Grill Doors, 90 In.	9900.00
Bookcase, 1 Door, 16 Panes, Gustav Stickley, Red Stamp	1850.00
Bookcase, 2 Doors, Gustav Stickley, Leaded Glass, 1903	8000.00
Bookcase, 2 Doors, String Inlay, Mahogany, 50 X 55 In.	200.00
Bookcase, 2 Glass Doors, 4 Shelves, Mahogany, 53 1/2 X 38 In.	185.00
Bookcase, 2 Paned Glass Doors, 2 Shelves, Mirrored Back, 62 In.	270.00
Bookcase, Cylinder Front, Inlaid Mahogany, C.1780, 7 Ft.6 In.	8250.00
Bookcase, G.Stickley, 2 12–Paned Doors, Gallery, 56 X 54 In.	3600.00
Bookcase, G.Stickley, Gallery, 2 Glass Doors, Tenons, 44 X 36 In.	2200.00
Bookcase, G.Stickley, Single Door, Keyed Tenons, C.1906, 55 In.	2400.00
Bookcase, Georgian, Brass Trim, England, Mahogany	3400.00
Bookcase, Glass Doors, 2 Lower Drawers, Mahogany, 45 X 86 In.	450.00
Bookcase, Glazed Doors, 2 Lower Drawers, Carved Walnut	990.00
Bookcase, Incised, Ebonized Walnut, 4 Glass Doors, 1870, 5 X 7 Ft.	3025.00
Bookcase, L.& J.G.Stickley, Gallery, 16–Paned Doors, Label, 55 In.	2400.00
Bookcase, Open, Gustav Stickley, Keyed Tenon 5 Shelves, 56 In.	4850.00
Bookcase, Revival, Rosewood, Gothic Trefoils, Walnut, 87 1/2 In.	1700.00
Bookcase, Secretary, 3 Base Drawers, Fold Down Shelf, 91 In.	1050.00
Bookcase, Victorian, 2 Glass Doors Top, 2 Doors, Rosewood, 86 In.	550.00
Bookcase, Victorian, Walnut, 2 Glass Doors Top, Drawers	820.00
Bookrack, Table, G.Stickley, Adjustable Runners, 1910, 12 X 7 In.	150.00
Box Desk, On Base, Raised Gallery, Walnut, 34 X 31 1/4 X 25 In.	225.00
Box, Blanket, Cotterpin Hinged Top, Old Green, 7 X 11 1/2 In.	525.00
Box, Blanket, New England, Grain Painted, Pine, 20 X 38 1/2 In.	750.00
Box, Blanket, Putty Grained, American, C.1825, Miniature	1800.00
Box, Desk, Mixed Woods, Pinned Construction, Short Gallery, Shelf	250.00
Box, Sewing, Mother–of–Pearl, Fruitwood, 19th Century, 26 X 13 In.	1100.00
Bracket, George II, Carved & Giltwood Eagle, 13 In., Pair	5500.00
Breakfront Bookcase, Mahogany, English, C.1850, 92 1/2 In.	2900.00
Breakfront, George III, Mahogany, Crest, 4 Glazed Doors, 5 Ft.	2750.00
Buffet, Louis XV, Walnut, Round Corners, 2 Drawers, 2 Doors, 4 Ft.	3575.00
Buffet, Pine, 2 Drawers, 2 Doors, Saint–Vallier, Can., 51 X 58 In.	1000.00
Bureau Bookcase, George III, Oak, Slant Front, 6 Ft.3 In.	3300.00

Bureau Plat, Louis XV, Tulipwood, Leather Inset, 3 Drawers, 58 In. 3575.00
Bureau Plat, Louis XVI, Mahogany, Tulipwood, Leather Inset, 36 In. 1650.00
Bureau, Bowfront, Federal, Mahogany, 4 Graduated Drawers, C.1815 .... 850.00
Bureau, Bowfront, Mahogany, 4 Drawers, Upper Drawer Fall Front 2310.00
Bureau, Chippendale, 4 Drawers, Cherry & Pine, C.1780, 38 1/4 In. 4250.00
Bureau, Chippendale, Mahogany, Serpentine, Graduated Drawers, 1780 .... 5000.00
Bureau, Cottage, 4 Drawers, Pine, Shaped Apron, 36 X 38 In. 248.00
Bureau, George II, Kneehole, Walnut, Recessed Door, 7 Drawers 2750.00
Bureau, Hepplewhite, 4 Drawers, Tapered Legs 1595.00
Bureau, Maple, New England, 4 Drawers, Button Feet, C.1830, 37 In. 600.00
Bureau, Sheraton, Bowfront, Mahogany, Replaced Brasses, C.1810 .... 1795.00
Bureau, Sheraton, Bowfront, Mahogany, Rope Legs, 40 X 43 X 22 In. 825.00
Bureau, Slant Front, Fitted Stepped Interior, Walnut, 41 In. 5225.00
Bureau, Slant Front, Louis XV, Walnut, Tulipwood, Parquetry, 38 In. 1425.00
Cabinet, 2 Doors, Drawer, Marquetry, Dauler Close Co., 44 3/4 In. 200.00
Cabinet, Apothecary, 27 Drawers, Cherry, 47 X 39 1/2 In. 7250.00
Cabinet, Apothecary, Pine, Marble, Glass, 1800, 10 Ft.6 In.X 70 In. 7500.00
Cabinet, Apothecary, Shaker, Stained, 12 Drawers, 13 X 66 In. 385.00
Cabinet, Architect's, Drafting Board Top, 14 Drawers, Mahogany 850.00
Cabinet, Baroque, Carved Walnut, 4 Shelves, 2 Part, 90 In. 1800.00
Cabinet, Black Lacquer, Floral & Bird Paintings, China, 5 Ft. 8800.00
Cabinet, Bone Inlaid, Ebonized, 2 Doors, 1870, Italy, 7 Ft.X 42 In. 2475.00
Cabinet, Brass Mounts, Drawer, Stepback Top, Mahogany, 69 In. 1400.00
Cabinet, Continental, Brass Trim, 9–Light Door, Walnut, 14 In. 250.00
Cabinet, Corner, Dutch Baroque, Painted Scenes, 53 X 20 In. 200.00
Cabinet, Corner, Walnut, Marble, 2 Doors, French, 31 X 28 In., Pair 95.00
Cabinet, Curio, Beveled Glass, 2 Enclosed Sections, Walnut, 6 Ft. 3500.00
Cabinet, Curio, Chinese, Black Lacquer, Glass, American, C.1865 .... 1000.00
Cabinet, Display, Wall, Carved Rosewood, Chinese, 20 In. 95.00
Cabinet, Eastlake, Ebonized, Gallery, Mirrored Shelves, 5 Ft.4 In. 1325.00
Cabinet, Federal Pine, 2 Doors, 5 Shelves, Cream, 1800, 10 Ft. 3000.00
Cabinet, Federal, Cherrywood, 2 Paneled Cupboard Doors, 22 In. 1320.00
Cabinet, Filing, Walnut, 24 Drawers, Brass Handles, 1886, 60 In. 750.00
Cabinet, George III, Mahogany, 4 Drawers, Veneered Door, 27 In. 495.00
Cabinet, Gilt–Bronze, 2 Painted Doors, Shaped Sides, 1860, 56 In. 2200.00
Cabinet, Hardware, American Bolt & Screw Co., 104 Drawers, 1880 .... 2200.00
Cabinet, Hardware, Nuts & Bolts, A.R.Brown, 1901 .... 1425.00
Cabinet, Hardware, Octagonal, 80 Drawers, Rotates, Pine 1200.00
Cabinet, Hoosier, Porcelain Countertop, Oak 1125.00
Cabinet, Italian Renaissance, Walnut, Putti Heads, 4 Ft.10 In. 1430.00
Cabinet, Jacobean Style, Red Japanned Doors, Walnut, 64 In. 200.00
Cabinet, Jelly, Blue Paint, 3/4 Gallery, 1 Drawer, 56 X 45 In. 880.00
Cabinet, Jelly, Green, Mustard Paint, Drawer Over 2 Doors, 52 In. 550.00
Cabinet, Jelly, Walnut, 2 Doors, 1 Drawer, Virginia 550.00
Cabinet, Kitchen, White Paint, Porcelain, Sifter, Sugar, Wilson 150.00
Cabinet, Lawyer's, Walnut, Country Style 250.00
Cabinet, Marble Top, Glazed Doors & Sides, Tulipwood, 48 3/4 In. 1300.00
Cabinet, Music, Brass Tubular Ends, Beveled Glass Doors, Walnut 750.00
Cabinet, Oak, 3 Drawers Over 3 Carved Drawers, Turned Posts 150.00
Cabinet, On Stand, George III, Inlaid Satinwood, 2 Doors, 44 In. 1430.00
Cabinet, Panel of Warrior, Noblemen On Sides, Carved, 28 In. 200.00
Cabinet, Parlor, Renaissance, Carved Rosewood, 1865 .... 1000.00
Cabinet, Pietra Dura–Mounted, Marquetry, Bronze, Herter, 5 Ft. 4950.00
Cabinet, Pine, Poplar, 10 Drawers, Bootjack Feet, 26 X 22 X 5 In. 660.00
Cabinet, Red Lacquer, Mountains, Birds In Gold Lacquer 230.00
Cabinet, Red Lacquer, Reserves of Birds & Flowers, Low, 18 In. 800.00
Cabinet, Rococo Style, Upper & Lower Glass Doors, Walnut, C.1900 .... 1800.00
Cabinet, Set Back, Sheraton–Empire, Cherry, Blind Door 1100.00
Cabinet, Side, Napoleon III, Gilt Bronze, Ebonized, Marble, 4 Ft. 775.00
Cabinet, Side, Rosewood, Painted, D Shape, English, C.1780 .... 7700.00
Cabinet, Side, Stuart, Oak, Molded Top, 2 Drawers, 32 X 5 Ft.2 In. 1980.00
Cabinet, Stuart Style, Grill Door, Base Drawer, Oak, 92 1/2 In. 850.00
Cabinet, Upper Shelves, Brass Studs, Spanish, Walnut, 74 In. 185.00
Cabinet, Wall Hanging, Mirrored Back, Shelves, Carved Oak, 28 In. 880.00

Furniture, Chair,
American Oak

Furniture, Chair,
Windsor, Step Down,
Bamboo Turning

Furniture, Armchair, Banister Back,
Splint Seat, Maple, C.1740

Furniture, Chair, Federal,
Arrow–Back, Yellow,
Stencil Design

Furniture, Chair,
Scholar's, Rosewood,
Marble Panels,
Chinese

Furniture, Chair, Corner, Vase Form Splats,
Maple, 1750–80

Cabinet, Wall, Gilded, Floral Cornice, 4 Inside Shelves, 57 In. 750.00
Cabinet, Walnut, Carved, Inlaid, Paneled Door, Drawer, 1810, 35 In. 2420.00
Cabinet, Writing, Gateleg Stand, Coral Japanned, 5 Ft.7 In. 4400.00
Campaign, Mahogany, Brass Corners, English, 2 Part, 47 X 36 In. 1375.00
Canape A Orielles, Louis XIV, Triple Arched Back, Leather, 6 Ft. 3025.00
Canape, Louis XIII, Walnut, Needlepoint Upholstery, 6 Ft.7 In. 9350.00
Canape, Louis XV, Beechwood, Serpentine To Arms, 6 Ft.1 In. 5500.00
Canape, Louis XV, Beechwood, Serpentine, Cabriole Legs, 48 1/2 In. 4125.00
Candlestand, 2 Arms, Wallace Nutting 1450.00
Candlestand, Adjustable Arm, 19th Century, Wooden, 12 In. 65.00
Candlestand, American Queen Anne, Octagonal Top, C.1780 .... 1450.00
Candlestand, Beaded Tripod, Painted Brown Over Gray, C.1810 .... 1800.00
Candlestand, Bentwood Gallery, Drawer, 3 Inset Feet, 27 In. 400.00
Candlestand, Cabriole Leg, Maple & Birch, C.1770, 27 1/2 In. 1300.00
Candlestand, Carved Mahogany, English, C.1860, 43 In., Pair 6600.00
Candlestand, Cherry Snake Feet, Maple Scrolled Top, 26 1/2 In. 200.00
Candlestand, Chippendale, Maple, Pine, Turned Post, C.1800, 25 In. 200.00
Candlestand, Chippendale, Octagonal Top, Maple, C.1780, 27 3/4 In. 850.00
Candlestand, Chippendale, Walnut, Tilt Top, Birdcage, C.1775 .... 1760.00
Candlestand, Country, Turned Column, Pine, 24 1/2 In. 85.00
Candlestand, Federal, Birch, Shaped Top, Hexagonal Block, C.1810 .... 325.00
Candlestand, Federal, Oval, Inlaid Mahogany, C.1810, 28 1/2 In. 2800.00
Candlestand, Federal, Tiger Maple, Ovolo Corners, C.1810, 28 In. 1300.00
Candlestand, Federal, Tilt Top, Mahogany, Diamond Inlay, C.1810 .... 1600.00
Candlestand, Federal, Tilt Top, Mahogany, Vase Form, 1795 .... 2750.00
Candlestand, Federal, Tilt Top, Oval Top, Cherry, 28 3/4 In. 250.00
Candlestand, Hepplewhite, Birch & Cherry, Old Red, 27 In. 155.00
Candlestand, Hepplewhite, Bird's-Eye Maple, 15 X 21 X 29 In. 225.00
Candlestand, Hepplewhite, Drawer, Inlaid Top, Cherry, 26 3/4 In. 2600.00
Candlestand, Hepplewhite, Tilt Top, Cherry, 27 1/2 In. 250.00
Candlestand, Iron, Grease Pan, Twisted Tripod Base, Hooks, 41 In. 500.00
Candlestand, Iron, Twisted Post, Tripod Base, Electrified, 47 In. 375.00
Candlestand, Maple, Vase Pedestal, Hexagonal Block, 24 In. 440.00
Candlestand, Pilgrim, Brown Paint, Square Pedestal, 22 X 14 In. 770.00
Candlestand, Shaker, Tiger Maple, Enfield, C.1820, 26 1/2 In. 1600.00
Candlestand, Spiral Carved Baluster, Mahogany, 21 1/4 In. 880.00
Candlestand, Spring Operated Device, Iron & Brass, 5 Ft.4 In. 1400.00
Candlestand, Tilt Top, Mahogany, 15 1/4 X 28 1/2 In. 130.00
Candlestand, Tilt Top, Tripod Base, Spider Legs, 16 X 28 In. 325.00
Candlestand, Tripod Base, Cherry, 27 1/2 In. 85.00
Candlestand, Walnut, 3 Spindle Legs, New England, 25 X 16 In. 495.00
Canterbury, Regency, Rosewood, 1 Drawer, Casters, 21 X 18 In. 2850.00
Canterbury, Rosewood, Victorian, 1 Drawer, Tripartite Top, 20 In. 775.00
Cassone, Italian Baroque, Inlaid Walnut, Hinged Lid, 24 X 66 In. 1320.00
Cassone, Italian Renaissance, Walnut, Putti, 5 Ft.2 In.X 22 In. 2475.00
Cellarette, Octagonal Hinged Top, Brass Bands, C.1770, 27 3/4 In. 2000.00
Cellarette, On Stand, Inlaid Central Shell Top, Mahogany, C.1800 .... 770.00
Cellarette, Rosewood, 23 X 34 In. 2250.00
Chair, American Oak ....*Illus* 70.00
Chair, Arched Back, Pierced Wheel, Upholstered Seat, Mahogany 495.00
Chair, Arched Back, Serpentine Seat, Mahogany, 18th Century 1100.00
Chair, Arrow Form Spindles, Grain Painted, C.1825, 34 In., Pair 425.00
Chair, Arrow Form Spindles, Painted, C.1820, Pair 1900.00
Chair, Arrow-Back, Gray Paint, Green Striping, Red Stencil 125.00
Chair, Balloon Back, Painted, Gold Borders, Fruit, 6 Piece 2750.00
Chair, Balloon Back, Tulip Shaped Splat 30.00
Chair, Baroque Revival, Carved Frame, Dolphin Feet 400.00
Chair, Barrel, Louis XVI Style, Gilded, Caned Seat & Back 225.00
Chair, Barrel-Back, Upholstered, Cushion Seat, 44 X 35 In. 550.00
Chair, Belter, Rosalie Pattern, Rosewood, Pair 3960.00
Chair, Bible, English, Oak, 1720 .... 425.00
Chair, Biedermeier, Tablet Crest Rail, Fruitwood, C.1825 .... 600.00
Chair, Bone Inlaid, Ebonized, C Scroll Design, Square Seat, Italy 1200.00
Chair, Bowed Needlepoint Back & Seat, Stained Beechwood 700.00

Chair, Bowed Seat, Downswept Arms, Biedermeier, Fruitwood, C.1825 .... 2500.00
Chair, Camp, Folding, Union, Blue, Red, White, 1864, 32 In. 450.00
Chair, Canadian, Mortised & Pinned Construction, Blue 150.00
Chair, Caned Seat, Hip Huggers, Burled Walnut 150.00
Chair, Captain's, Child's, Black Paint, C.1870, 10 X 11 X 17 In. 190.00
Chair, Captain's, Pine, Turned Spindle Back, Irish Spinning 150.00
Chair, Captain's, Red & Black Paint, Yellow Striping 200.00
Chair, Carved Floral, Bamboo Foliage & Bark, Teak, Oriental 150.00
Chair, Carved Rails, Pierced Splat, Splint Seat, Mahogany, C.1780 .... 2300.00
Chair, Carved Slat Back, Rabbit Ears 1100.00
Chair, Carved Splat, Oak, England, C.1800, 37 In., 4 Piece 1400.00
Chair, Charles I, Oak Frame, Rope Spiral Carving, Leather Cover 45.00
Chair, Charles II, Oak, 3 Splat, Caned Seat, Paw Feet, Pair 770.00
Chair, Child's, 2 Slat Back, Woven Splint Seat, Bentwood Arms 80.00
Chair, Child's, Angora Goat, Horns Are Legs 2250.00
Chair, Child's, Bentwood, Cane Seat 65.00
Chair, Child's, Caned Saddle Seat, Arched Back, Dark Green 99.00
Chair, Child's, Desk, Swivel 39.00
Chair, Child's, Empire, Rush Seat, Gilt, E.Oliver On Back, C.1825 .... 550.00
Chair, Child's, Horn Frame & Legs, Upholstered Back & Seat, 1890 .... 440.00
Chair, Child's, Pierced Slat Back, Carved Crest Rail, Walnut 150.00
Chair, Child's, Pine, 3 Arched Splats, Woven Seat, Utah, 1860 .... 110.00
Chair, Child's, Plank Seat, Painted Floral, Leaves, C.1845 .... 660.00
Chair, Child's, Sheraton, Old Black Paint, Leather Seat 135.00
Chair, Child's, Shield of The Republic, Meeks 935.00
Chair, Child's, Thonet, Bentwood, Caned Seat, 24 In. 245.00
Chair, Child's, William & Mary, Velvet Upholstered, C.1680 .... 825.00
Chair, Chippendale Style, Pierced Splat, Mahogany, 7 Piece 425.00
Chair, Chippendale, Carved Ears, Pierced Splat, Cherry, C.1780 .... 650.00
Chair, Chippendale, Crest Rail, Pierced Splat, Rush Seat, C.1780 .... 425.00
Chair, Chippendale, Mahogany, Crest, Pierced Splat, Slip Seat, 1780 .... 500.00
Chair, Chippendale, Mahogany, Pierced Splat, 1780, 36 In. 1300.00
Chair, Chippendale, Pierced Carved Slat, Shaped Arms 1000.00
Chair, Chippendale, Ribbon Back, Rush Slip Seat, Cherry 500.00
Chair, Chippendale, Ribbon Back, Slip Seat, Birch 650.00
Chair, Chippendale, Upholstered Seat, Ribbon Back, Mahogany 550.00
Chair, Classical Revival, Cane Seat, Tiger Maple, C.1830, Pair 2400.00
Chair, Cockfighting, Off-White Leather 275.00
Chair, Commode, Pierced Splat, Slip Seat, English, Mahogany 350.00
Chair, Corner, Arms, Carved Mahogany, English, C.1780 .... 1750.00
Chair, Corner, Chippendale, Mahogany, Shaped Crest Rail, Arms, 1780 .... 1800.00
Chair, Corner, Oak, England, C.1780, 30 In. 675.00
Chair, Corner, Queen Anne Style, Rhode Island, Mahogany, C.1860 .... 500.00
Chair, Corner, Queen Anne, Outscrolled Arms, Vase Form Splats 5170.00
Chair, Corner, Vase Form Splats, Maple, 1750-80 ....*Illus* 3960.00
Chair, Corner, William & Mary, Painted Maple, 18th Century, 32 In. 2700.00
Chair, Ebonized, Inlaid Rosewood, New York, C.1870, Pair 1760.00
Chair, English Hepplewhite, Beaded Back Frame, Slats, Mahogany 95.00
Chair, Fanback, Cupid's Bow Crest 1050.00
Chair, Federal, Arrow-Back, Yellow, Stencil Design ....*Illus* 500.00
Chair, Federal, Campeachy, Upholstered Back, C.1820 ....*Illus* 5775.00
Chair, Federal, Cherrywood, 3 Stylized Vasiform Splats, Rush Seat 165.00
Chair, Fern Pattern, Cast Iron, Arms 900.00
Chair, Flemish Style, Carved Mahogany, High Back, Carved Arms, Pr. 300.00
Chair, Floral Bouquet Crest, Meeks, Arms 1650.00
Chair, Floral Carved Crest Rail, Needlepoint Seat, Walnut 85.00
Chair, Folding, Brass Mounts, Red Lacquer, Japan, 40 1/2 In. 475.00
Chair, Fountain Elms Pattern, Rosewood, Victorian, Pair 7975.00
Chair, French Style, Balloon Back, Victorian 105.00
Chair, Fretwork Stretchers & Legs, Needlepoint Seat, C.1830 .... 6400.00
Chair, G.Henkel, Rococo Revival, Carved & Laminated Rosewood 1100.00
Chair, G.Stickley, 5 Slats, Sticker 4000.00
Chair, G.Stickley, 9 Spindles, Upholstered Seat, C.1912 .... 650.00
Chair, G.Stickley, Morris, 5 Slats, Sticker 4000.00

Furniture, Chair, Federal, Campeachy, Upholstered Back, C.1820

Furniture, Chair, Louis XVI, Cane Back, Laurel Crest

Furniture, Chair, Louis XVI, Gilded Barrel, Cane Seat & Back

Chair, George I, Flared Upholstered Drop–In Seat, Mahogany	2090.00
Chair, George II, Padded Back, Dipped Rail, Outscrolled Arms	6600.00
Chair, George II, Silk Upholstered Seat, Carved Mahogany, Pair	1100.00
Chair, George III, Black Japanned, Triple Splat, C.1800, Pair	1650.00
Chair, George III, Inlaid Oval Medallion, Flared Seat, Mahogany	165.00
Chair, Gothic Revival, Carved Walnut, Tapered Legs, Side, 42 In.	3200.00
Chair, Gothic, Carved Walnut, Arched Crest, Trefoil Design, 44 In.	800.00
Chair, Gothic, Upholstered Seat, Carved Walnut, 45 1/2 In.	800.00
Chair, Hall, Carved Oak, Ornate	595.00
Chair, Henkel, Solid Rosewood Back	1000.00
Chair, Hepplewhite, Martha Washington, Line Inlay, Arms	2600.00
Chair, Hepplewhite, Shield Back, Mahogany, Serpentine Front Seat	1700.00
Chair, Hitchcock, Pillow Back	82.00
Chair, Inlaid Back Rail, Marquetry, Curved Legs	70.00
Chair, Iron & Brass X Frame, Italian, Cushion Seat, C.1920	950.00
Chair, Italian Baroque, Walnut, Parcel Gilt, Upholstered, Pr.	3300.00
Chair, Jacobean, Turned Legs, Pegged Construction, Pair	100.00
Chair, L.& J.G.Stickley, 8 Spindles, Leather Seat, C.1910	450.00
Chair, Ladder Back, Child's, Rush Seat, Painted Maple, C.1780	550.00
Chair, Ladder Back, Hickory, Turned Feet, 2 Slats, Splint Seat	95.00
Chair, Ladder Back, High Seat, Low Back, Paper Rush Seat	115.00
Chair, Ladder Back, Low Seat, 4 Flats, Acorn Finials, Cane Seat	45.00
Chair, Lifetime, Cube, Drop Arm, Spring Cushion, C.1910, 32 In.	800.00
Chair, Lolling, Arched Crest, Massachusetts, C.1815, 44 In.	5500.00
Chair, Lolling, Federal, Carved Mahogany, Shaped Arms, Ma., C.1795	4400.00
Chair, Lolling, Federal, Mahogany, Upholstered Arched Back, C.1805	9900.00
Chair, Lolling, Molded Arm Rests, Upholstered, Mahogany	4250.00
Chair, Louis XVI, Cane Back, Laurel Crest ....*Illus*	200.00
Chair, Louis XVI, Gilded Barrel, Cane Seat & Back ....*Illus*	225.00
Chair, Man of The Mountain, Lion Heads, Paw Feet, Leather Seat	270.00
Chair, Master's, Carved Acanthus Leaves, Arms, Mahogany, Pair	4950.00
Chair, Moravian, Whittled Legs, Plank Seat, Oak, Pair	50.00
Chair, Morris, Child's, Refinished, 27 1/2 In.Back	185.00
Chair, Morris, Oak, Mission, Nubbly Brown Seat, 1910	1430.00
Chair, Mother-of-Pearl Inlay, Ebonized, Caned Back & Arms	3850.00
Chair, Neoclassical, Crest Rail Over Lyre Splat, Walnut, C.1800	200.00
Chair, Neoclassical, Square Seat, Carved Frame, Mahogany, German	450.00
Chair, Oak, 5 Back Slat, Spring Cushion Seat, C.1910, Pair	375.00
Chair, Oak, Rush Seat, 2 Slats, Square Stiles, J.P.McHugh, C.1900	300.00
Chair, Organ, Oak, Mother-of-Pearl Inlay	70.00
Chair, Pierced Splat, Carved Crest, Upholstered Seat, Cherry	750.00

Chair, Potty, Wicker 80.00
Chair, Pressed Back, Spindle Back, Cane Seat 55.00
Chair, Queen Anne, Arched Padded Back, Upholstered Seat, Walnut 465.00
Chair, Queen Anne, Balloon Seat, Mahogany, N.Y., C.1760 ....*Illus* 3630.00
Chair, Queen Anne, Carved & Molded Yoke Crest, Vase Splat, Maple 2900.00
Chair, Queen Anne, Cherry, Needlepoint Seats, Carved Knees, Pair 1200.00
Chair, Queen Anne, Ladder Back, 4 Slats, Rush Seat, Pair 850.00
Chair, Queen Anne, Massachusets, Mahogany, Balloon Seat, C.1770 .... 7000.00
Chair, Queen Anne, Shell Crest, Slip Seat, Walnut, 18th Century 275.00
Chair, Queen Anne, Spanish Feet, Black & Red Graining, Crest 1450.00
Chair, Queen Anne, Spanish Feet, Paper Rush Seat, Maple 400.00
Chair, Queen Anne, Spanish Feet, Vase Splat, Cherry Color, Maple 5000.00
Chair, Queen Anne, Vasiform Slats, Rush Seat, C.1760, Pair 3800.00
Chair, Queen Anne, Walnut, Shell Crest, Slip Seat ....*Illus* 275.00
Chair, Queen Anne, Walnut, Vase Splat, Slip Seat, Trifid Feet, 1765 .... 3100.00
Chair, Recliner, Child's, Morris ....,..... 120.00
Chair, Regency, Mahogany, Spiral Rail, Caned Tablet Splat, C.1815 .... 220.00
Chair, Relief Carving, Dragon Back, Lion Finials, Gold Oak, Arms 250.00
FURNITURE, Chair, Rocker, see Furniture, Rocker
Chair, Rococo, Carved Rosewood ....*Illus* 9250.00
Chair, Rococo, Rosewood, Cartouche Upholstered, C.1855, Pair 1760.00
Chair, Scholar's, Rosewood, Marble Panels, Chinese ....*Illus* 525.00
Chair, Set, 2 Slats With Leather Insert, Stickley Bros., 1912, 6 .... 400.00
Chair, Set, 3 Slat Thumb Back, Rush Seats, Painted, Jennersville, 6 .... 4000.00
Chair, Set, Adirondack, Splint, Woven Back Panel & Seat, 6 .... 475.00
Chair, Set, Balloon Back, Pennsylvania, C.1830, 6 .... 695.00
Chair, Set, Bamboo Turned, Painted Maple, C.1825, 6 ....*Illus* 1210.00
Chair, Set, Child's, Elmwood, Plank Seat, 4 .... 154.00
Chair, Set, Designed Plant Seat, C.1840, 6 .... 990.00
Chair, Set, Dining, Brass Palmette, Stars, Mahogany, C.1810, 6 .... 6600.00
Chair, Set, Dining, Federal, Inlaid Mahogany, Armchairs, C.1800, 8 .... 8250.00
Chair, Set, Dining, Federal, Mahogany, Pierced Slat, Slip Seat, 8 .... 1980.00
Chair, Set, Dining, George III, C.1790, 6 Side & 2 Armchairs 7425.00
Chair, Set, Dining, Pierced Splat Backs, Acanthus Knees, 4 .... 900.00
Chair, Set, Dining, Queen Anne, Cabriole Legs, Pad Feet, 6 .... 5750.00
Chair, Set, Dining, Regency, Rosewood, Parcel Gilt, 2 Arm, 4 Side 5750.00
Chair, Set, Directoire Style, Squared Back, Carved Oak, 6 .... 285.00
Chair, Set, Elm, England, C.1780, 37 In., 4 .... 1800.00
Chair, Set, Federal, Mahogany, Serpentine Upholstered Seat, 4 .... 8250.00
Chair, Set, Fiddleback, Dark Finish, Natural Cane Seats, 6 .... 297.00
Chair, Set, Flemish Scroll, Cane Seat & Back, 4 .... 340.00
Chair, Set, G.Stickley, 3 Slats, 1 Armchair, Label, 1907, 5 .... 1700.00
Chair, Set, George III, 4 Vertical Bars, Plank Seat, Oak, 6 .... 1870.00
Chair, Set, George III, Mahogany, 2 Arm, 6 Side, 1800 .... 8800.00
Chair, Set, George III, Mahogany, Flared Seat, 2 Arm, 6 Side 9350.00
Chair, Set, George III, Spindle Backrest, Plank Seat, Elmwood, 4 .... 605.00
Chair, Set, George III, Tapered Splat Headed, Mahogany, C.1790, 6 .... 6600.00
Chair, Set, George III, Yoke Over Pierced Splat, Mahogany, 5 .... 2200.00
Chair, Set, Gustav Stickley, Wide Center Slat, C.1910, 6 .... 1900.00
Chair, Set, Hepplewhite, Mahogany, 2 Arm, 8 Side 850.00
Chair, Set, Hitchcock, 1828–32, Signed, 4 .... 900.00
Chair, Set, Hitchcock, Black Paint, Stencil, Rush Seat, 2 Arm, 6 .... 880.00
Chair, Set, Hitchcock, Grain Finish, Gilt Details, 6 ....*Illus* 750.00
Chair, Set, Ice Cream, Hairpin Back, 8 .... 200.00
Chair, Set, Ladder Back, Oak, 2 Arched Splats, Pa., Rush Seat, 4 .... 300.00
Chair, Set, Nipple Top Spindle Back, Rush Seat, England, C.1820, 8 .... 3600.00
Chair, Set, Painted Rosewood, Gold Stencil, Cane Seat, Wm.Coles, 6 .... 625.00
Chair, Set, Queen Anne, Pierced Splat, 2 Arm, 6 Side 400.00
Chair, Set, Renaissance Revival, Rosewood, 2 ....*Illus* 7000.00
Chair, Set, Rococo Revival, Rosewood, Upholstered, C.Baudouine, 6 .... 1550.00
Chair, Set, Rococo Revival, Walnut, Upholstered, 2 Arm, 4 Side 522.00
Chair, Set, Spanish Baroque, Walnut, Leather Back & Seat, 6 .... 2850.00
Chair, Set, Stenciled Adams Orange, New York, 8 .... 1100.00
Chair, Set, Windsor, Bow Back, Cream Color, Green Striping, 1810, 4 .... 8500.00

Chair, Shaker, 3 Arched Slats, Tape Seat, Label, Maple, C.1850	1500.00
Chair, Shaker, 3 Slats, Decal, Mt.Lebanon, Maple, 1900, 41 In., Pr.	2600.00
Chair, Shaker, Brother Perkins, Sister Barlow, Maple, C.1910	1000.00
Chair, Shaker, Brother's, Cane Seat, Maple, New Lebanon, N.Y.	3500.00
Chair, Shaker, Brother's, Taped Seat, Watervliet, N.Y., C.1830	700.00
Chair, Shaker, Cane Seat, Cherry, Harvard, Ma., 41 1/2 In.	4000.00
Chair, Shaker, Child's, Mt.Lebanon, Woven Reed Seat, 3 Slats, Maple	950.00
Chair, Shaker, John Lockwood, Mt.Lebanon, 1840	4000.00
Chair, Shaker, Lebanon, Tape Seat, Tiger Maple Posts, 32 3/4 In.	850.00
Chair, Shaker, Red Stain, Cane Seat, Tilts, New Lebanon, C.1830	1000.00
Chair, Shaker, Shawl Bar, Taped Seat & Back, Mt.Lebanon, Arms	1600.00
Chair, Shaker, Sister's, Cane Seat, Tilts, New Lebanon, C.1850	3500.00
Chair, Shaker, Sister's, Rush Seat, Watervliet, N.Y., C.1840, 39 In.	650.00
Chair, Shaker, Taped Seat, Maple, Watervliet, N.Y., C.1820, 41 In.	800.00
Chair, Shaker, Tilter, 3 Arched Slats, Tape Seat, Harvard, C.1850	2400.00
Chair, Shaker, Tilter, Enfield, 3 Slats, Maple, C.1850	775.00
Chair, Shaker, Tilter, Maple, 3 Slats, Rush Seat, Mt.Lebanon	600.00
Chair, Shaped Crest, Vasiform Splats, Rush Seat, C.1760, Pair	3800.00
Chair, Shaped Plank Seat, Short Arrow Spindles, Designs, 31 In.	300.00
Chair, Sheraton, Curly Maple, Turned Legs, Slat, Rush Seat, Pair	500.00
Chair, Sheraton, Scrolled Slat, All Curly Maple, Rush Seat	625.00
Chair, Shield Back, Drapery Carving, Upholstered, Pair	700.00
Chair, Shoeshine, Double, Marble Top	1500.00
Chair, Slip Seat, Pierced Splat, Curved Crest, Cherry, Pair	1150.00
Chair, Slipper, Victorian, Striped Damask Upholstered, Casters	440.00
Chair, Slipper, Victorian, Walnut, Crest, Beige Upholstery, 39 In.	70.00
Chair, Stepladder, Augustus Eliaers, Boston, C.1850	2850.00
Chair, Stickley Bros., Plank Seat, Inlaid Trees Back, 1910, 44 In.	9000.00
Chair, Tub, Upholstered, Reeded Circular Feet, C.1840	3850.00
Chair, Urn–Shaped Splat, Cane Seat, Tiger Maple	100.00
Chair, Victorian, Gold Brocade Upholstered, Walnut Finish	10.00
Chair, Victorian, Needlepoint Upholstery, Walnut	125.00
Chair, Wainscot, Carved, Scrolled Arms, Carved Finials	200.00
Chair, Wakefield Rattan Co., Lounge, Wicker	550.00
Chair, Wallace Nutting Carver, Rush Seat, C.1920, Mode.364, 47 In.	400.00
Chair, Weaver's, Refinished, Stamped W.M.White, Boston	55.00
Chair, William & Mary, Banister Back, Painted, C.1740, 45 In.	450.00
Chair, William & Mary, Caned Panel, Velvet Seat, Walnut, C.1680	468.00
Chair, William & Mary, Leather Covered, Painted Maple, C.1730	2250.00
Chair, William & Mary, Painted, 1720–40, Pair	7500.00
Chair, Windsor, 6 Spindles, Thumb Back, Grained, C.1825, Pair	650.00
Chair, Windsor, 9 Spindles, Continuous Arm, Black, Saddle, 1780	750.00

Furniture, Chair, Set, Bamboo Turned,
Painted Maple, C.1825, 6

Furniture, Chair, Set, Hitchcock, Grain Finish,
Gilt Details, 6

Furniture, Chair, Queen Anne,
Walnut, Shell Crest, Slip Seat

Furniture, Chair, Rococo,
Carved Rosewood

Furniture, Chair, Queen Anne,
Balloon Seat, Mahogany, N.Y., C.1760

Furniture, Chair, Set, Renaissance Revival, Rosewood, 2

Chair, Windsor, Arrow–Back, Joseph Jones	3500.00
Chair, Windsor, Bamboo Turning, Rabbit Ear Post, Black Repaint	250.00
Chair, Windsor, Bamboo Turnings, 7 Curved Spindles	50.00
Chair, Windsor, Bamboo, Cage–Type Back, Yellow Striping	100.00
Chair, Windsor, Bamboo, Saddle Seat, New England, 19th Century	440.00
Chair, Windsor, Bow Back, 6 Spindles, Shaped Arms, England, C.1780	800.00
Chair, Windsor, Bow Back, 7 Spindles, Knuckle Arms, Painted Black	1000.00
Chair, Windsor, Bow Back, 7 Spindles, Saddle Seat, American	1045.00
Chair, Windsor, Bow Back, 7 Spindles, Shaped Seat, Splayed Base	275.00
Chair, Windsor, Bow Back, 9 Spindles, Saddle Seat, Label, 1796	1550.00
Chair, Windsor, Bow Back, 9 Spindles, Splayed Base, Saddle Seat	325.00
Chair, Windsor, Bow Back, American Saddle Seat ....*Illus*	200.00
Chair, Windsor, Bow Back, Bamboo Turnings, Saddle Seat, Pair	1150.00
Chair, Windsor, Bow Back, Black Paint, C.1790	365.00
Chair, Windsor, Bow Back, English, Arms, Pair	1050.00
Chair, Windsor, Bow Back, Oval Saddle Seat, Knuckle Arms	6700.00
Chair, Windsor, Bow Back, Shaped Arms ....*Illus*	625.00
Chair, Windsor, Bow Back, Shaped Seat, Arms, Pair	3100.00
Chair, Windsor, Brace Back, 7 Spindles, Mahogany, C.1800, 37 In.	2500.00
Chair, Windsor, Brace Back, Refinished, 17 3/4 In.Seat	275.00
Chair, Windsor, Child's, 3 Vertical Splats, Plank Seat, Red Paint	88.00
Chair, Windsor, Child's, Bamboo Turned, Green Paint, Plank Seat	220.00
Chair, Windsor, Child's, Ring Turned Legs, 1815, 28 1/2 In.	1600.00
Chair, Windsor, Child's, Yewwood, Elm, Crest, Spindle Splats	1760.00
Chair, Windsor, Comb Back, 9 Spindles, Green Paint, Arms, C.1780	2500.00
Chair, Windsor, Comb Back, 9 Spindles, Painted, C.1775 ....*Illus*	3025.00
Chair, Windsor, Comb Back, 9 Tapered Spindles, Painted, C.1770	9900.00
Chair, Windsor, Comb Back, C.1900	350.00
Chair, Windsor, Continous Arm, Brace Back, Saddle Seat, C.1780	1600.00
Chair, Windsor, Continous Arm, J.Bertine, N.Y.	1760.00
Chair, Windsor, Country Bamboo, 16 3/4 In., Pair	200.00
Chair, Windsor, Curved Back Post, Bamboo, 17 1/4 In.	175.00

Chair, Windsor, Fanback, 6 Spindles, Pine, Round Seat, C.1760 .... 1800.00
Chair, Windsor, Fanback, 6 Spindles, Saddle Seat, W.W.Nolen 700.00
Chair, Windsor, Fanback, 7 Spindles, Plank Seat, Painted, C.1800 .... 3400.00
Chair, Windsor, Fanback, 9 Spindles, Splayed Base, Black Paint 375.00
Chair, Windsor, Fanback, Ash, Maple, Crest Rail, 7 Spindles, C.1760 .... 400.00
Chair, Windsor, Fanback, H & Side Stretcher, Signed Thayer 625.00
Chair, Windsor, Fanback, Splayed Base, H Stretcher, 7 Spindles 150.00
Chair, Windsor, Sack Back, Bamboo Legs, Levi Prescott, C.1799 .... 715.00
Chair, Windsor, Sack Back, Signed J.Henzey, 18th Century 5500.00
Chair, Windsor, Step Down, Bamboo Turning ....*Illus* 255.00
Chair, Windsor, Thumb Back, 5 Spindles, Rolled Plank Seat, Pair 800.00
Chair, Windsor, Writing Arm, Bamboo Turned Upright, Maple 800.00
Chair, Wing, Barley Twist Legs, Leather Cover, England, C.1860 .... 1350.00
Chair, Wing, Child's, Federal, New England, Mahogany, C.1770 .... 5500.00
Chair, Wing, Chippendale, Ball & Claw Feet, Damask Upholstered 250.00
Chair, Wing, Chippendale, Mahogany, Crewel Upholstery, American 3400.00
Chair, Wing, Chippendale, Upholstered, Rolled Arms, New Eng., 1810 .... 1800.00
Chair, Wing, Federal, Child's, New England, C.1770, 30 In. 5500.00
Chair, Wing, Pad Foot, Walnut, 42 In. 1200.00
Chair, Wing, Trifid Foot, Walnut, 39 In. 1200.00
Chair, Wing, Upholstered Back, Padded Sides, Armrests, Mahogany 2310.00
Chair, Woman's, Finger Roll, Hand Carved, Walnut, Victorian 400.00
Chair, Youth, Oak Swivel Seat, Iron 225.00
Chaise, Child's, Tufted, Upholstery, Eastlake Style, 21 X 29 In. 800.00
Chest, 1 Large & 3 Small Drawers, C.1840 .... 300.00
Chest, 3 Dovetailed Drawers, Pine, Red Frame Graining, 36 1/2 In. 1025.00
Chest, 3 Drawers, Serpentine Front, Ivory Pulls, Miniature 1540.00
Chest, 3 Drawers, Victorian, Oak, 20 In. 90.00
Chest, 4 Drawers, 3-Section Crest, Maple & Poplar, 45 1/2 In. 185.00
Chest, 4 Drawers, Banded Inlay At Base, Mahogany, 37 1/4 In. 450.00
Chest, 4 Drawers, Ebonized Trim, Cherry & Curly Maple, 48 In. 600.00
Chest, 4 Drawers, English, Walnut, 35 In. ....*Illus* 1400.00
Chest, 4 Drawers, French Feet, Scalloped Apron, Pine, 34 3/4 In. 400.00
Chest, 4 Drawers, Glove Boxes, Burled Walnut 310.00
Chest, 4 Drawers, Graduated, Brass Bail Handles, Mahogany, 29 In. 1540.00
Chest, 4 Drawers, Inlaid Diamond Escutcheons, Walnut, 46 In. 1500.00
Chest, 4 Drawers, Mahogany, Bracket Feet, 33 X 36 X 20 In. 1000.00
Chest, 4 Drawers, Red & Black Grained, 1 Small Chest Top 440.00
Chest, 4 Drawers, Round Brasses, Cherry, 35 1/2 X 40 3/4 In. 2400.00
Chest, 4 Drawers, Wire Nail Construction, Poplar, Miniature 165.00
Chest, 5 Drawers, 2 Short, 3 Long, Oyster Veneer Walnut, 34 In. 3850.00
Chest, 5 Drawers, Ebonized, 53 In. ....*Illus* 550.00

Furniture, Chair, Windsor,
Bow Back, American Saddle Seat

Furniture, Chair, Windsor,
Bow Back, Shaped Arms

Furniture, Chair, Windsor,
Comb Back, 9 Spindles,
Painted, C.1775

Chest, 5 Drawers, Graduated, Painted Birch & Pine, C.1780, 44 In. 6000.00
Chest, 6 Drawers, Cherry, Rope & String Inlay, C.1800, 47 1/2 In. 4200.00
Chest, 6 Drawers, Graduated, Tiger Maple, C.1790, 48 X 38 1/2 In. 5500.00
Chest, 6 Drawers, Rail At Top Sides, Walnut, 19th Century 2800.00
Chest, 6 Drawers, Rhode Island, Maple, C.1780, 53 3/4 In. 6500.00
Chest, 6 Drawers, Turned Pulls, Bird's–Eye Maple Veneer, Cherry 600.00
Chest, 7 Drawers, House Front Shape, German Spice Names 600.00
Chest, 7 Drawers, Victorian, Side Lock, Foldout Desk 850.00
Chest, American Chippendale, Flame Birch, Bracket Base, 1740–60 .... 3400.00
Chest, Amish, Brown Paint, 3 Graduated Drawers, C.1880, 36 In. 330.00
Chest, Bachelor's, Chippendale, Cherrywood, Writing Slide, C.1790 .... 6050.00
Chest, Bachelor's, Reeded Sides, Walnut, England, C.1840, 31 In. 3200.00
Chest, Blanket, 2 Bottom Drawers, 1852 .... 6600.00
Chest, Blanket, 2 Drawers, Original Red Paint, 38 3/4 In. 700.00
Chest, Blanket, 2 Drawers, Pine, Green Paint, Red Striping, 45 In. 850.00
Chest, Blanket, 2 Drawers, Pine, Lift Top, Strap Hinge, 43 X 19 In. 470.00
Chest, Blanket, 2 Drawers, Pine, Refinished, 1850, 39 X 41 X 18 In. 450.00
Chest, Blanket, 3 Drawers, Curly Maple Panels, Poplar & Butternut 650.00
Chest, Blanket, 4 Drawers, Graduated, Pilgrim 9900.00
Chest, Blanket, 6–Board, Pine, Floral, 19th Century, 44 X 19 In. 900.00
Chest, Blanket, Amana Colonies, Bracket Feet, Pine, 18 X 46 In. 220.00
Chest, Blanket, Arched Apron, Red Paint, American, 25 X 38 In. 357.50
Chest, Blanket, Brown Graining, Pine, Poplar, 26 1/2 X 35 3/4 In. 925.00
Chest, Blanket, Child's, Chippendale, Painted Red, 18th Century 1100.00
Chest, Blanket, European, End Drawer, Iron Hinges, 42 1/2 In. 145.00
Chest, Blanket, Federal, 2 Drawers, Grain Painted, 37 X 37 In. 1320.00
Chest, Blanket, Federal, 2 Drawers, Red Paint, 19th Century, 41 In. 660.00
Chest, Blanket, Federal, Divided Interior, Yellow Paint, 67 In. 825.00
Chest, Blanket, Flame Grained Panels, Pine, 20 1/2 X 43 1/2 In. 550.00
Chest, Blanket, Flame Graining, Till, Pine & Poplar, 23 3/4 In. 375.00
Chest, Blanket, Grain Painted Black, Red, Pine, 23 1/2 In. 1300.00
Chest, Blanket, Grain Painted, Lift Lid, Carved, 26 X 44 In. 4000.00
Chest, Blanket, Grain Painted, Pine, 1820, 18 X 12 In. 880.00
Chest, Blanket, Grain Painted, Pine, Drawer Stringed, 1820, 39 In. 1150.00
Chest, Blanket, Green Paint, John Frye, 1829 In Lid 2200.00
Chest, Blanket, Green Painted Top, Shoe Feet, Pine, 4 Ft.7 In. 330.00
Chest, Blanket, Lift Top, 2 Drawers, Strap Hinge, 43 X 43 X 19 In. 470.00
Chest, Blanket, Lift Top, Drawer, Painted Pine, C.1800, 37 1/2 In. 1700.00
Chest, Blanket, Lift Top, Grain Painted, C.1850, 27 In. 650.00
Chest, Blanket, Lift Top, Pine, Butt Hinges, 22 X 42 In. 275.00
Chest, Blanket, Lift Top, Pine, Florals, 1790, Pa., 24 X 51 In. 2200.00
Chest, Blanket, Lift Top, Pine, Mahogany, England, 1820, 38 In. 1250.00
Chest, Blanket, Lift Top, Ralph Cahoon Painting, 36 X 44 X 19 In. 1760.00
Chest, Blanket, Lift Top, Vinegar Painted, C.1830, 16 X 39 In. 1100.00
Chest, Blanket, Old Green Over Black, Pine, 23 1/2 X 43 In. 525.00
Chest, Blanket, Painted Wrigglework, Pa., 1840, 36 X 46 In. 2200.00
Chest, Blanket, Pine, Black Sponging, Signed Butler 1774, 21 In. 175.00
Chest, Blanket, Pine, Original Green Paint, Black Foot, 12 5/8 In. 400.00
Chest, Blanket, Poplar, 24 1/2 X 43 In. 250.00
Chest, Blanket, Poplar, Brown Flame Graining, Gray, 20 X 26 In. 250.00
Chest, Blanket, Poplar, Red Brown Finish, 36 X 20 In. 265.00
Chest, Blanket, Red Flame Graining, Till, Poplar, 21 3/4 In. 925.00
Chest, Blanket, Red Vertical Stripes, Poplar, 20 X 43 3/4 In. 245.00
Chest, Blanket, Red, Black, American, 24 X 41 In. 335.00
Chest, Blanket, Smoke Grained Paint, Poplar, 21 1/2 X 17 1/2 In. 700.00
Chest, Blanket, Sponge Red, Black, Geometric, Pa., 1834, 24 X 48 In. 3300.00
Chest, Blanket, Stylized Tulips, Dated 1815, 33 1/2 X 66 In. 400.00
Chest, Blanket, Till, Dovetailed Poplar, 52 In. 250.00
Chest, Blanket, Till, Original Lock & Hinges, Pine, 23 X 43 In. 350.00
Chest, Blanket, Till, Varnish Finish, Poplar, 22 X 38 1/4 In. 290.00
Chest, Blanket, Tulip Blossoms, Pine, New York, C.1810, 40 3/4 In. 8500.00
Chest, Blanket, Vinegar Graining, 3 Drawers, Brass Pulls, 51 In. 925.00
Chest, Blanket, Vinegar Graining, Bear Trap Lock, Key, 50 1/2 In. 475.00
Chest, Blanket, Vinegar Graining, Till, Pine, 41 3/4 In. 625.00

Furniture, Chest, 4 Drawers, English, Walnut, 35 In.

Furniture, Chest, Bow Front, Reeded Columns, Brass Ovals, 43 In.

Furniture, Chest, Sheraton Empire, Rope Twist Column, 22 X 43 In.

Furniture, Chest, Sheraton, Tiger Maple, Serpentine Front, 40 In.

Chest, Blanket, Walnut, Dovetailed, 24 X 40 X 19 In.	375.00
Chest, Blanket, Wicker, Cover, Leather Handles, 14 X 22 X 12 In.	45.00
Chest, Blanket, William & Mary, Pine, 2 Drawers, 1750, 44 X 40 In.	4400.00
Chest, Bombe, Dutch, 3 Drawers, Mahogany, C.1770, 33 X 37 1/2 In.	950.00
Chest, Bow Front, Crotch Mahogany Veneer, C.1790, 39 1/2 In.	3200.00
Chest, Bow Front, Federal, Mahogany, Robinson & Berwick, C.1790	4000.00
Chest, Bow Front, Mahogany, Flame Veneer Facade, 41 X 44 1/2 In.	550.00
Chest, Bow Front, Reeded Columns, Brass Ovals, 43 In. ....*Illus*	1200.00
Chest, Bow Front, Sheraton, Mahogany, 3 Drawers, 1815–25, 13 In.	2600.00
Chest, Camphorwood, Brass Corners, Studded, Handles, 41 In.	715.00
Chest, Carved Panels, Top Rail, English, 26 3/4 X 53 1/2 In.	375.00
Chest, Chinoiserie, Black, Mother-of-Pearl, 1 Drawer, Chinese	2750.00
Chest, Chippendale, 4 Graduated Drawers, Mahogany, C.1780, 34 In.	3500.00
Chest, Chippendale, 4 Graduated Drawers, Pine, C.1770, 40 In.	4125.00
Chest, Chippendale, 4 Graduated Drawers, Walnut, C.1780, 35 In.	3850.00
Chest, Chippendale, 5 Drawers, Maple, Bracket Feet, 1780, 51 In.	2700.00
Chest, Chippendale, 6 Drawers, Curly Maple Fronts, Cut Base	2500.00
Chest, Chippendale, 6 Drawers, Curly Maple, C.1775, 59 In.	2200.00
Chest, Chippendale, 6 Drawers, Maple, Bracket Feet, 42 1/2 In.	2700.00
Chest, Chippendale, Cherry, Ogee Bracket Feet	2750.00
Chest, Chippendale, Overlapping Drawers, Curly Maple, 47 In.	2500.00
Chest, Chippendale, Writing Slide, Bracket Footed	1500.00
Chest, Dome Top, Painted Design, Legs	4800.00
Chest, Dots On Low Domed Cover, Painted Red, 25 In.	200.00
Chest, Dower, Cromwellian, Oak, Mother-of-Pearl Inlay, 1655, 4 Ft.	1325.00
Chest, Dower, Lift Lid, 2 Short Drawers, Painted Pine, 1852	375.00
Chest, Dowry, Raised Panels, Floral, Painted, 1834	600.00
Chest, Ebony & Satinwood Trim, French, Cherry, C.1840, 31 In.	2600.00
Chest, Egg & Dart Border, Serpentine Front, Mahogany, 33 1/2 In.	6325.00
Chest, Elizabethan Revival, 22 X 24 In.	325.00
Chest, Empire Revival, 6 Drawers, Gallery, Beehive Brasses	275.00
Chest, Empire, 3 Drawers, Mahogany, Chamfered Drawer, Glass Pulls	600.00
Chest, Empire, 3 Drawers, Wooden Knobs, Red, Blue, 4 X 6 X 7 In.	350.00
Chest, Empire, 4 Drawers, Curly Maple Drawer Front	300.00
Chest, Empire, 4 Drawers, Walnut Pulls, Bird's-Eye Maple	775.00
Chest, Empire, 7 Drawers, Poplar, Curly Maple Fronts, 47 In.	375.00
Chest, Empire, Bird's-Eye Maple Drawer Front	65.00
Chest, Empire, Bird's-Eye Veneer Drawers, Maple & Birch, 42 In.	400.00
Chest, Empire, Brass Trim, French, Mahogany, C.1820, 32 In.	4000.00
Chest, Empire, Butted Crotch Mahogany Veneer Drawers	440.00
Chest, Empire, Cherry & Curly Maple	300.00
Chest, Empire, Cherry, 4 Bird's-Eye Maple Drawer Fronts, 49 In.	550.00
Chest, Federal, 4 Drawers, Maple, Painted, Crossbanded, 1800, 41 In.	3700.00
Chest, Federal, 4 Graduated Drawers, Bow Front, Curly Maple, 1813	2970.00
Chest, Federal, Bird's-Eye Veneer Drawers, Curly Maple, 41 In.	950.00
Chest, Federal, Cherrywood, Bow Front, New England	1500.00
Chest, Federal, Inlaid Cherrywood, Pa.	1500.00

Chest, G.Stickley, Cedar Lined, Loop Handles, 20 X 38 In. 9000.00
Chest, G.Stickley, No Mirror, C.1910, 30 X 36 X 16 In. 1200.00
Chest, George I, 2 Short, 3 Long Drawers, On Base, Walnut, 5 Ft. 3025.00
Chest, George II, 5 Drawers, Bracket Feet, Mahogany, 36 X 43 In. 1210.00
Chest, George III, 2 Short, 3 Long Drawers, Mahogany, 32 In. 4400.00
Chest, George III, 4 Drawers, Bow Front, Inlaid Mahogany, 36 In. 2420.00
Chest, George III, 4 Drawers, Serpentine Front, Mahogany, C.1770 .... 6325.00
Chest, George III, 6 Inlaid Drawers, Mahogany, 44 1/2 X 47 In. 850.00
Chest, George III, Beaded Drawers, Brass Handles, Mahogany, 43 In. 900.00
Chest, George III, Serpentine Front, Writing Slide, Mahogany 7150.00
Chest, Georgian, 6 Drawers, Walnut, 37 X 45 In. 1875.00
Chest, Hepplewhite, 4 Drawers, Bow Front, Inlaid Edging, English 600.00
Chest, Hepplewhite, 4 Drawers, Brasses, Curly Birch, 37 1/2 In. 950.00
Chest, Hepplewhite, 4 Drawers, French Feet, Cherry 1900.00
Chest, Hepplewhite, 7 Beaded Drawers, Pine, 47 X 20 X 48 In. 400.00
Chest, Hepplewhite, Bow Front, English, Mahogany, 48 In. 500.00
Chest, Hinged Top, 6–Board, Grain Painted, Pine, 24 X 47 3/4 In. 1800.00
Chest, Merchant's, 6 Drawers, Hidden Drawer, Japanese, 37 In. 700.00
Chest, Mule, 1 Drawer, 6–Board Construction, Old Red, 35 1/2 In. 800.00
Chest, Mule, 1 Drawer, Poplar, Applied Molding On Lid, 37 X 39 In. 275.00
Chest, Mule, 2 Drawers, Blue Green Paint 9500.00
Chest, Mule, 5 Drawers, 3 False Drawers, New England, Painted 1150.00
Chest, Norwegian, Key, Dated 1865, Small 465.00
Chest, Oxbow Front, Mahogany, French Feet, 19th Century, 28 In. 1650.00
Chest, Pennsylvania, Unicorn & Floral Repaint, Poplar, 50 1/2 In. 600.00
Chest, Polychrome Design, Harvest Revelry, Pine, 22 X 61 In. 700.00
Chest, Queen Anne, 2 Short, 3 Long Drawers, Crossbanded Walnut 3300.00
Chest, Queen Anne, 5 Graduated Drawers, Painted Maple, C.1750 .... 6500.00
Chest, Rhode Island Style, 3 Shell, Goddard Copy, C.1900 .... 2700.00
Chest, Scandinavian, Hinged Top, Iron Hinges, Pine, 40 In. 825.00
Chest, Shaker, 8 Drawers, Yellow & Brown, Poplar, Birch, 54 1/4 In. 3800.00
Chest, Shaker, Apothecary, 9 Drawers, Grained Red Paint, C.1830 .... 4000.00
Chest, Shaker, Blanket, 1 Drawer, B.Moore Estate, Pine, 1827, 30 In. 2000.00
Chest, Shaker, Blanket, 2 Drawers, Pine, Canterbury, N.H., C.1840 .... 3000.00
Chest, Shaker, Blanket, Child's, Red Paint, Sliding Drawer, C.1830 .... 1500.00
Chest, Shaker, Blanket, Red, Till, Pine, Church Family, C.1800 .... 8000.00
Chest, Shaker, Graduated Drawers, Union Village, Oh., 1840, 42 In. 1750.00
Chest, Sheraton Empire, Rope Twist Column, 22 X 43 In. ....*Illus* 600.00
Chest, Sheraton, 4 Drawers, Birch, 38 X 38 X 18 In. 1045.00
Chest, Sheraton, 4 Drawers, Bow Front, Mahogany, 39 1/3 In. 500.00
Chest, Sheraton, 4 Drawers, Mahogany, Swell Front, Reeded Posts 625.00

Furniture, Chest, 5 Drawers,
Ebonized, 53 In.

Furniture, Chest–On–Chest, Chippendale,
Mahogany, Pa., 1780, 6 Ft.

Chest, Sheraton, 4 Graduated Drawers, George Clark, 19th Century 4500.00
Chest, Sheraton, 4 Graduated Drawers, Walnut, Replaced Brasses 985.00
Chest, Sheraton, 5 Applied Edge Molding Drawers, Cherry, 44 In. 630.00
Chest, Sheraton, 5 Tiger Maple Drawers, Wooden Pulls, 45 X 17 In. 1155.00
Chest, Sheraton, 6 Drawers, Corner Posts, Cherry, 53 X 44 In. 700.00
Chest, Sheraton, Inlaid Mariner's Stars In Drawer, Walnut, 45 In. 1400.00
Chest, Sheraton, Tiger Maple, Serpentine Front, 40 In. ....*Illus* 2750.00
Chest, Spice, 5 Drawers, Red & Black Grain Painted, 1844, 11 In. 450.00
Chest, Storage, Japanese Lacquer, Rectangular, Black, 21 1/2 In. 75.00
Chest, Tall, Chippendale, 5 Drawers, Over 2 Split, Tiger Maple 7150.00
Chest, Tall, Chippendale, Maple, Molded Top, 7 Drawers, 63 1/2 In. 3950.00
Chest, Victorian, 2 Short, 3 Graduated Drawers, Walnut, 43 In. 247.00
Chest, Wedding, Hand Carved, Chinese, 1923 .... 5000.00
Chest, William & Mary, 3 Drawers, Oyster Veneer, 39 1/2 In. 5500.00
Chest, William & Mary, 4 Drawers, Brass Pulls, Walnut, 53 In. 125.00
Chest, William & Mary, 4 Drawers, Walnut & Oak, C.1700, 35 In. 1430.00
Chest–On–Chest, 2 Short, 3 Long Drawers, Mahogany, C.1785, 6 Ft. 5060.00
Chest–On–Chest, 5 Drawers, Base Drawer, Mahogany, C.1800, 71 In. 1600.00
Chest–On–Chest, 5 Drawers, Over 3 Drawers, Mahogany, 66 In. 4125.00
Chest–On–Chest, Chippendale, Bonnet, Cherrywood, Ct., C.1785, 7 Ft. 9350.00
Chest–On–Chest, Chippendale, Mahogany, Pa., 1780, 6 Ft. ....*Illus* 8800.00
Chest–On–Chest, Chippendale, Maple, Molded Cornice, C.1780, 78 In. 8750.00
Chest–On–Chest, George II, Mahogany, Bracket Feet, 5 Ft.7 In. 3300.00
Chest–On–Chest, George III, Mahogany & Satinwood, 74 1/2 In. 3800.00
Chest–On–Chest, George III, Mahogany, Dentil Cornice, 6 Ft. 4125.00
Chest–On–Chest, Satinwood Inlay, 8 Drawers, Mahogany, C.1780 .... 5600.00
Chest–On–Chest, Small Drawers Atop Large, Mahogany, C.1770, 6 Ft. 9900.00
Chest–On–Frame, Cherry, Pine & Sumac Inlay, 18th Century, 35 In. 8500.00
Chest–On–Frame, Paneled Drawers, Barley Twist Legs, Oak, 34 In. 225.00
Chest–On–Frame, Red & Black Graining, Pine, 29 X 26 In. 1600.00
Chest–On–Stand, William & Mary, 5 Drawers, Inlaid Walnut, 44 In. 3850.00
Chest–On–Stand, William & Mary, Fruitwood, Marquetry, 1690 .... 8800.00
Chiffonier, Pine, 3 Doors, 4 Graduated Drawers, English, 78 In. 1430.00
China Cabinet, 2 Glazed Doors, 3 Shelves, Pine, 5 Ft.5 In. 935.00
China Cabinet, L.& J.G.Stickley, 12 Leaded Panes, Glass Doors 1300.00
China Closet, G.Stickley, 1 Door, 12 Panes, 1910–12, 63 X 36 In. 3000.00
China Closet, L.& J.G.Stickley, C.1912, 58 X 44 In. 3900.00
China Closet, Mission Oak, 2 Doors, C.1910, 64 X 46 X 18 In. 350.00
Clothes Box, Needlepoint, Upholstered, Ebonized, C.1880, 32 In. 1980.00
Coatrack, Black, Yellow Carved Bird On Top 300.00
Coffer, Oak, Carved, Domed Top, Flowers, English ....*Illus* 175.00
Coffer, Stuart, Carved Oak, Paneled Hinged Lid, 31 X 67 X 24 In. 880.00
Coffin, 6 Metal Hand Holds, Pine Box, Skeleton, 1900s, 4 Ft.7 In. 2000.00
Commode Secretary, Marble Top, Bird's–Eye Maple, C.1825 .... 7950.00
Commode, Italian Rococo, Walnut, Parquetry, Serpentine, 4 Ft.7 In. 9350.00
Commode, Italian Rococo, Walnut, Serpentine Top, Scenes, 52 In. 5775.00
Commode, Lift Top, Pine, Paneled Door, 1 Drawer, 30 X 29 In. 150.00
Commode, Louis XV Style, Marble Top, Kingwood, 34 X 39 1/2 In. 1300.00
Commode, Louis XV, Inlaid Mahogany, Marble Top, Straight Legs 1925.00
Commode, Louis XV, Provincial, 3 Shaped Drawers, Walnut, 50 In. 4600.00
Commode, Louis XV, Walnut, Serpentine, 3 Long Drawers, 48 In. 4950.00
Commode, Louis XVI Style, Marquetry, Tulipwood, 41 X 35 1/2 In. 900.00
Commode, Louis XVI Style, Tulipwood & Parquetry, 38 1/2 In. 750.00
Commode, Louis XVI, Brass Mounted, Cherrywood, 25 3/4 In. 450.00
Commode, Louis XVI, Fruitwood, Marble Top, Inlaid Doors 4675.00
Commode, Louis XVI, Mahogany, Tulipwood, Gilt, Marble, 55 In. 8250.00
Commode, Neoclassical, 2 Drawers, Walnut, 30 1/4 X 21 In. 475.00
Commode, Pine, Gray, 1 Board Ends, Chamber Pot Door, 19 In. 55.00
Commode, Pine, Lift Top, Door, Drawer, American, 30 X 29 In. 143.00
Commode, Shaker, Hinged Slant Lid, Interior Shelf, Pine, 48 In. 4500.00
Commode, Stepped, Regency, Mahogany, English, 27 3/4 X 17 X 31 In. 523.00
Commode, Towel Rail, Stenciled Fruit, Yellow, Orange, 29 In. 150.00
Commode, Victorian, Walnut, Marble Top, 16 X 31 In. ....*Illus* 225.00
Console, Louis XVI, Gilt & Gesso, Mirror Back 1600.00

Furniture, Coffer, Oak, Carved, Domed Top, Flowers, English

Furniture, Commode, Victorian, Walnut, Marble Top, 16 X 31 In.

Console, Renaissance, Walnut, Marble Top, Shell, Scroll Feet, 7 In. 475.00
Console, Rococo, Parcel Gilt, Iron, Marble Top, 40 In.X 6 1/2 Ft. 2750.00
Console, William IV, Grain Painted, Acanthus Terminals, C.1835 .... 467.00
Costumer, Double, G.Stickley, 6 Hooks, Trestle Base, Decal, 66 In. 1300.00
Cradle, French Empire, On Stand, Mahogany, C.1810 .... 3250.00
Cradle, Grain Painted, Stencil, Mortise & Tenon, Pa., 1820–40 .... 525.00
Cradle, Hooded, Pin, Dovetailed, Pennsylvania, C.1860 .... 285.00
Cradle, Hooded, Rosewood Grained, Stencil, Blue Interior, New Eng. 425.00
Cradle, Mahogany, Hooded, Dovetailed, Shaped Rockers, 1800, 25 In. 300.00
Cradle, Old Red Repaint, Pine, 37 In. 125.00
Cradle, Pierced Handles, Scrolled Rockers, Yellow, 41 In. 330.00
Cradle, Pine, Flared Form, Sloping Sides, American, 23 X 15 In. 55.00
Cradle, Pine, Pierced End, Oval Handle, Early 19th Century, 46 In. 445.00
Cradle, Rockers, Pine, Red Paint, American, 19th Century, 40 In. 225.00
Cradle, Square Corner Posts, Pyramid Finials, Pine, 26 X 38 In. 45.00
Cradle, Walnut, Scalloped Sides, Cutout Heart Foot, 39 1/2 In. 200.00
Crib, G.Stickley, Spindle Sides, Red Decal, 1907, 34 X 56 X 35 In. 1400.00
Cupboard, 1 Board Ends, Scalloped Apron, Paneled Door, Pine, 3 Ft. 325.00
Cupboard, 1 Door, Plank Scrubbed Top, Green Paint, C.1820, 30 In. 467.00
Cupboard, 1 Door, Yellow Graining, Pine, 67 X 35 1/2 In. 300.00
Cupboard, 2 Doors, Brown Over Grayish Blue, Pine, 75 1/2 In. 650.00
Cupboard, 2 Doors, Cherry, 28 X 21 In. 295.00
Cupboard, 2 Doors, Open Shelves, Spice Drawers, Top Crest, 69 In. 725.00
Cupboard, 2 Doors, Pennsylvania Country, Original Paint, C.1850 .... 2500.00
Cupboard, 2 Doors, White Over Blue, 67 1/2 In. 110.00
Cupboard, 2 Drawers, Glass Top Doors, Wooden Doors, Walnut, 7 Ft. 750.00
Cupboard, 2 Drawers, Jelly, Paneled Doors, Walnut, 43 3/4 In. 375.00
Cupboard, 2 Drawers, Mustard Paint, Mortise & Tenon, 1840s 2600.00
Cupboard, 2 Glass Doors, Over Drawers, Fitted For Spools, 71 In. 100.00
Cupboard, 2 Glazed Doors, 3 Shelves, Grain Painted, C.1825, 87 In. 6000.00
Cupboard, 2 Lower Doors, Upper Glass–Paned Doors, Walnut, 83 In. 1400.00
Cupboard, 2 Paneled Doors, Pine, Brown Finish, 75 X 46 X 17 In. 880.00
Cupboard, 2 Paneled Doors, Pitch Pine, Turned Legs, 76 In., 2 Part 660.00
Cupboard, 2 Shelves, Corner, Cubbyhole, Painted Pine, 79 1/4 In. 3000.00
Cupboard, 2 Top Glass Doors, Pine, Cutout Feet, Beading, 83 In. 825.00
Cupboard, 3 Drawers, Brown Graining On Yellow, Poplar, 89 In. 2050.00
Cupboard, 4 Doors, Spoon Rack, Scalloped Apron Bottom, 7 Ft. 2750.00
Cupboard, Blue Paint, Swedish, 71 In. 2250.00
Cupboard, Board & Batten Door, Low Gallery, Pine, 28 1/2 X 26 In. 200.00
Cupboard, Bootjack Feet, Open Shelves, Cherry, 72 X 34 3/4 In. 775.00
Cupboard, Campaign, 2 Doors, 5 Drawers, Mahogany, 2 Piece, 78 In. 2750.00
Cupboard, Charles I, Oak, Inscribed FTS 1699, 2 Piece, 5 Ft.10 In. 1650.00
Cupboard, Cherry, 2 Peg & Dovetail Doors, 2 Upper Drawers 250.00
Cupboard, Cherrywood, Hanging, Swivel Lock, Red, Pa., 31 X 23 In. 440.00
Cupboard, Child's, 2 Drawers, Pine, Shelf, Doors, 24 In. 150.00
Cupboard, Child's, 2 Glazed Doors, Step Back, Pine, 24 X 23 In. 150.00
Cupboard, Chimney, 2 Vertical Doors, Blue Paint, 84 X 18 In. 650.00
Cupboard, Chimney, Brown & Mustard Graining 895.00

Cupboard, Chimney, Muskingum Valley, Ohio 625.00
Cupboard, Chimney, Rosehead Nails, Brown Paint 1375.00
Cupboard, Chimney, Single Door, Grain Painted 750.00
Cupboard, Chippendale, Walnut, Swan's Neck Top, 7 Ft.6 In., 2 Pc. 2750.00
Cupboard, Corner, 2 Glass Upper Doors, Pine, C.1820 .... 2100.00
Cupboard, Corner, 2 Glazed Doors, Federal, Cherry, C.1820, 89 In. 2200.00
Cupboard, Corner, 2 Panel Doors, 2 Drawers, Cherry & Pine 2860.00
Cupboard, Corner, 2 Upper Glass Doors, Walnut, Shelf, Small 80.00
Cupboard, Corner, Arcade Glass Door, Design, Pa., C.1840, 2 Part 4950.00
Cupboard, Corner, Cherry, Blind Front, 82 In. ....*Illus* 2200.00
Cupboard, Corner, Cherry, Paneled Door, Cornice, 25 X 37 In. 400.00
Cupboard, Corner, Chippendale, Blue Paint, Pa., C.1830, 99 X 43 In. 4125.00
Cupboard, Corner, Chippendale, Cherry, 1780, 8 Ft. ....*Illus* 5500.00
Cupboard, Corner, Hanging, Mirror, Oak 140.00
Cupboard, Corner, Hanging, Scalloped Top & Bottom, Poplar, 32 In. 120.00
Cupboard, Corner, Iron Thumb Latches, Cherry, 76 1/2 In. 1400.00
Cupboard, Corner, Pale Yellow Paint, Original Shelves 2750.00
Cupboard, Corner, Red & Black Graining, Pa., C.1840, 7 Ft.1 In. 3850.00
Cupboard, Corner, Salmon Paint, Mustard Interior 3300.00
Cupboard, Corner, Tiger Maple, Zoar, Ohio 4200.00
Cupboard, Corner, Walnut, Poplar, Blind Doors, Pennsylvania 2600.00
Cupboard, Corner, Walnut, Red Paint, Paneled Doors, Ohio, 82 In. 2800.00
Cupboard, Dutch, 3–Drawer Base, Cherry, 2 Piece 1850.00
Cupboard, Dutch, Pewter Rail, Spoon Racks, Walnut, 2 Piece 3700.00
Cupboard, Dutch, Poplar, Brown Over Yellow Simulated Oak, 2 Pc. 900.00
Cupboard, Federal, 4 Doors, Molded Top, Pennsylvania, 1820, 86 In. 1200.00
Cupboard, Flemish Baroque, Ebonized Oak, Fluted Pilasters, 80 In. 2750.00
Cupboard, French Baroque, Walnut, Cornice, Paneled Doors, 64 In. 2200.00
Cupboard, Green Paint, Raised Panel Doors, Pine, Poplar, 74 In. 700.00
Cupboard, Grilled & Paneled Door, Dark Brown, C.1840, 82 X 53 In. 1650.00
Cupboard, Hand Painted Designs, Dauler Close Furniture, 69 In. 350.00
Cupboard, Hanging, 2 Shelves, Drawer In Base, Pine, 37 3/4 In. 395.00
Cupboard, Hanging, Poplar, Red & White Repaint, Pa., 19 X 24 In. 400.00
Cupboard, Honey–Colored Patina, Pine, Late 19th Century, 90 In. 2600.00
Cupboard, Hoosier 360.00
Cupboard, Interior Shelves, Poplar, 44 X 86 In. 800.00
Cupboard, Italian Baroque, Walnut, 2 Grotesque Doors, 54 In. 6600.00
Cupboard, Jail, 2 Doors, Refinished, Dovetailed, Square Nails 950.00
Cupboard, Jelly, 1 Board Doors, Zigzag Crest, Old Red, 54 3/4 In. 305.00
Cupboard, Jelly, 1 Drawer Over Doors, Red Paint, 5 Ft.2 In. 440.00
Cupboard, Jelly, 2 Drawers, 2 Doors, Pine 895.00
Cupboard, Jelly, Gallery, Red Paint, N.J., C.1880, 46 X 42 In. 650.00

Furniture, Cupboard, Corner, Cherry,
Blind Front, 82 In.

Furniture, Cupboard, Corner, Chippendale,
Cherry, 1780, 8 Ft.

Cupboard, Jelly, Old Red Finish, Brass H Hinges, Poplar, 65 In.	200.00
Cupboard, Jelly, Walnut, Paneled Doors, 1 Board End, 50 1/2 In.	325.00
Cupboard, Lard, Gray Over Mustard, Ohio	695.00
Cupboard, Mohawk River Valley, Double Picture Molding, 1825–45	2950.00
Cupboard, Open Shelves Top, Carved Oak, 2 Piece	525.00
Cupboard, Open, Hinged Door Below, Pine, Red Paint, 79 In.	2090.00
Cupboard, Over Drawers, Hudson River Valley, C.1810, Blue, 77 In.	8800.00
Cupboard, Paneled Doors, Brown Graining, Pine, 65 1/2 X 48 In.	650.00
Cupboard, Paneled Doors, Drawer, Poplar & Butternut, 71 1/4 In.	450.00
Cupboard, Pedestal, Dark Red Paint, Pine & Poplar, 24 In.	250.00
Cupboard, Pewter, 2 Shelves Over Door, Green, 18th Century, 76 In.	1650.00
Cupboard, Pewter, Gray With Red Trim, Pine	6800.00
Cupboard, Pewter, Green Over Red Paint, Pennsylvania, 1850–60	1795.00
Cupboard, Pewter, Oxblood Paint, Tenon Shelves, 19th Century	2895.00
Cupboard, Pewter, Pine, Open, Batten Door Base, Primitive, 74 In.	800.00
Cupboard, Pewter, Single Board Door, Pine & Poplar, 72 1/2 In.	500.00
Cupboard, Pewter, Step Back, Grain Painted, C.1790, 70 1/2 In.	5100.00
Cupboard, Pine, Dark Brown, Stenciled, Decoupage, 17 X 12 X 31 In.	200.00
Cupboard, Pine, Dark Red Alligatored, Blue Interior, 79 X 44 In.	250.00
Cupboard, Pine, Dovetailed Drawers, Wisconsin, 1850–60, 2 Piece	1575.00
Cupboard, Pine, Gray Paint, Paneled Doors, 43 X 14 X 66 1/2 In.	435.00
Cupboard, Pine, Green Over Red Paint, C.1800, 75 1/2 In.	800.00
Cupboard, Poplar, Cutout Feet, Gallery Top Doors, 29 X 33 In.	575.00
Cupboard, Post Office, Raised Panel Oak, 8 Ft.	400.00
Cupboard, Pressed Carving On Doors	240.00
Cupboard, Raised Head Nail Construction, Pine, 18th Century	1620.00
Cupboard, Red & Black Graining, Paneled Doors, Pine, 71 In.	4050.00
Cupboard, Scalloped Crest, Board & Batten Door, Pine, 54 1/2 In.	125.00
Cupboard, Shaker, 1 Door, Blue Over Yellow, Alfred, Me., C.1840	1200.00
Cupboard, Shaker, 5 Drawers, Paneled Door, Pine, 5 Ft.4 In.	2500.00
Cupboard, Shaker, Blue Over Gray, Sectioned Drawer, Pine, 61 In.	2250.00
Cupboard, Shaker, Cloak, Door, Brass Hardware, Enfield, N.H., 67 In.	1700.00
Cupboard, Shaker, Hanging, 3 Shelves, New Lebanon, C.1830, 14 In.	700.00
Cupboard, Shaker, Hanging, Infirmary, Enfield, Butternut, C.1840	550.00
Cupboard, Shaker, Hanging, Pine, Enfield, N.H., C.1820, 29 1/2 In.	1100.00
Cupboard, Shaker, Paneled Door, 5 Shelves, Pine, 6 Ft.7 In.	1700.00
Cupboard, Shaker, Shelves, Painted Pine & Poplar, C.1830, 86 In.	3500.00
Cupboard, Shaker, Step Back, 3 Doors, Watervliet, C.1830, 7 Ft.	1800.00
Cupboard, Shaker, Step Back, 4 Doors, Canterbury, N.H., 1840, 59 In.	3250.00
Cupboard, Shaker, Step Back, Pine & Butternut, 73 1/2 In.	1300.00
Cupboard, Shaker, Storage, Pine, Alfred, Me., C.1860, 5 Ft.7 In.	1200.00
Cupboard, Shaker, Wash, Splash Board, New Lebanon, Poplar, C.1840	2500.00
Cupboard, Spice, Salt Box Base, Lift Lid, 6 Drawers, 16 3/4 In.	350.00
Cupboard, Square Nail Construction, Old Blue Paint, C.1800	1200.00
Cupboard, Step Back, 2 Base Doors, Open, Poplar, 38 X 69 In.	700.00
Cupboard, Step Back, 2 Doors, Gray Paint, New England, 72 X 35 In.	825.00
Cupboard, Step Back, Child's, Painted Red, Pine, 29 1/2 In.	355.00
Cupboard, Step Back, Chippendale, Pine, Stain, 18th Century, 86 In.	4950.00
Cupboard, Step Back, Federal, Cherrywood, 4 Doors, 2 Drawers, 7 Ft.	2475.00
Cupboard, Step Back, Open Top, Door Below, Pine, Miniature	1200.00
Cupboard, Step Back, Original Blue Paint, Walnut	2900.00
Cupboard, Step Back, Painted Pine, Canada, C.1800, 74 1/2 In.	4750.00
Cupboard, Step Back, Pine, Red Patina, Wisconsin, 1860, 87 In.	8500.00
Cupboard, Step Back, Wall, Shelves, Cherry, 82 1/2 In.	2100.00
Cupboard, Stripped, Original Gray Paint, Reversed Panel Doors	3100.00
Cupboard, Stripped, Waxed Pine, 3 Sets of 2 Doors, Irish, 80 In.	990.00
Cupboard, Tulipwood, 2 Glass Paned Top Doors, Refinished, 1820s	575.00
Cupboard, Under The Eaves, 1 Door, Mustard Paint, Early 1800s	1250.00
Cupboard, Wall, 2 Doors, 2 Drawers, Cherry, 84 1/4 X 47 In.	1250.00
Cupboard, Wall, Cherry, Poplar, Glass Doors, Theo Miller, 84 In.	1050.00
Cupboard, Wall, Grain Painted, Mid–19th Century, 48 X 18 In.	770.00
Cupboard, Wall, Green Paint Over Red, Pine, Center Hinged Doors	400.00
Cupboard, Wall, Lower Doors, 6 Panes of Glass, 3 Drawers, 80 In.	450.00
Cupboard–Bin, 2 Doors, Original Blue Paint, Amish, C.1875	2395.00

Daybed, Scrolled Headrest, Caned Body, Wicker 2425.00
Daybed, William & Mary, Walnut, Caned Seat, 17th Century, 5 Ft. 550.00
Decanter Case, On Stand, Ebony Inlaid Mahogany, C.1820, 33 In. 4450.00
Desk Box, Table, Red Repaint, Stand, Pine, 13 1/4 X 24 In. 125.00
Desk Cupboard, Sloping Top, Long Drawer, Gray Paint, 45 X 53 In. 440.00
Desk, 2 Drawers, Mahogany, Gallery, English, 19th Century, 44 In. 440.00
Desk, 3 Drawers, Pine, Allover Carved Design, Black Paint, Wylie 8250.00
Desk, 3 Molded Drawers, Sausage Legs, English, Oak & Walnut 250.00
Desk, 4 Drawers To Side, Utah, Pine, C.1860, 4 Ft.4 In. 715.00
Desk, 4 Drawers, Original Brasses, Mahogany, 31 3/4 X 40 In. 3250.00
Desk, Butler's, Ellis & Norton, Est.1838, Mahogany & Cherry 995.00
Desk, Child's, Drop Leaf, Old Blue Paint 275.00
Desk, Child's, Slant Front, Chippendale, Maple, C.1760, 22 X 17 In. 6050.00
Desk, Chippendale, Block Front, Mahogany, Valenced Pigeonholes 4950.00
Desk, Chippendale, Serpentine Front, Slant Front, Mahogany, 42 In. 6500.00
Desk, Chippendale, Slant Front, Maple, Fan Carved Interior 3800.00
Desk, Chippendale, Slant Lid, Original Brasses, Maple, C.1780 .... 3100.00
Desk, Clerk's, 2 Drawers, Poplar Sloped Top, Ash Base, 42 1/2 In. 200.00
Desk, Davenport, Walnut, Leather Slant Top, Rack, C.1850, 34 In. 775.00
Desk, Drop Front, Bookcase Sides, Brooks Furniture, Grand Rapids 3500.00
Desk, Drop Front, L.& J.G.Stickley, Bootjack Ends, 40 X 32 In. 650.00
Desk, Dutch, Marquetry, Removable Top, 3 Drawers, Letter Drawers 2250.00
Desk, Empire, Mahogany, Fall Front, Bird's-Eye Veneer, 41 In. 1000.00
Desk, Fall Front, Gustav Stickley, Oak, 1910, Marked, 36 In. 2475.00
Desk, Fall Front, Queen Anne, Frame, Maple, 2 Molded Drawers, 1760 ...... 2700.00
Desk, Flat Top, 2 Half Drawers, G.Stickley, 1907, 36 X 38 X 23 In. 1100.00
Desk, Flat Top, Gustav Stickley, No.708 .... 1650.00
Desk, French, Pine, Flat Top 750.00
Desk, G.Stickley, Center & 8 Drawers, Tenons, Decal, 54 X 30 In. 1400.00
Desk, G.Stickley, Letter Rail, V Side Panels, Keyed Tenons, 34 In. 800.00
Desk, George III, 2 Drawers, Cylinder Top, Inlaid Mahogany, 38 In. 7700.00
Desk, George III, Yewwood, Pedestal, Leather Top, 59 1/2 In. 1800.00
Desk, Kneehole, George III, Mahogany, 1 Long & 7 Short Drawers 3300.00
Desk, Kneehole, George III, Mahogany, 32 1/2 X 37 In. 650.00
Desk, L.& J.G.Stickley, 5 Compartment Top, 2 Drawers, 1905, 50 In. 550.00
Desk, Lady's, Doors, Enclosed Shelves, Mahogany & Marquetry, Dutch 900.00
Desk, Lady's, Japanese Style, Aesthetic, Oak, Ash, 1880, 48 In. 300.00
Desk, Lady's, Louis XV, Marquetry, 18 X 35 In. ....*Illus* 525.00
Desk, Lady's, Slant Front, Louis Philippe, Bronze, Porcelain, 1850 .... 4950.00
Desk, Lap, Folding, Rosewood, Fitted, Brass Mounts, 24 X 20 In. 880.00
Desk, Lap, Mahogany, Brass, Wm.Dobson, London, 6 X 60 X 20 In. 300.00
Desk, Lap, Mother-of-Pearl Inlay, Fitted Interior 40.00
Desk, Limbert, 1 Drawer, Shelf, Signed 650.00
Desk, Louis XVI Style, Upper 8 Drawers, Mahogany, 31 X 48 In. 250.00
Desk, Melodian, Mahogany, Tapered Rope Legs 700.00
Desk, Million Oak, 29 X 48 X 28 In. 200.00
Desk, Partner's, Chippendale, Mahogany, Cabriole Legs, Claw Feet 600.00
Desk, Partner's, George III, Mahogany, Pedestal, 19th Century 8800.00
Desk, Partner's, Georgian, Leather, 19th Century, 55 X 36 X 31 In. 1000.00
Desk, Partner's, Leather Top, 3 Drawers Each Side, Mahogany 5610.00
Desk, Partner's, Oak, Ball & Claw Feet, Grand Rapids 2195.00
Desk, Pedestal, George III, Mahogany, Leather Top, 4 Ft.9 In. 4400.00
Desk, Pedestal, Inlaid Mahogany, Leather Top, English, 4 Ft.10 In. 4950.00
Desk, Plantation, Fitted Interior, Cherry, 53 1/2 In. 395.00
Desk, Plantation, Fitted Interior, Lift Lid, Cherry, 73 In. 1000.00
Desk, Plantation, Gallery, Slant Front, Walnut 522.00
Desk, Portable, Slant Front, Fitted, Grain Painted, 13 X 20 In. 375.00
Desk, Post Office, Pigeonholes, Oak, 5 X 4 Ft. 395.00
Desk, Queen Anne, Drop Front, Walnut, England, C.1720, 39 In. 5800.00
Desk, Queen Anne, Slant Front, 11 Drawers, Maple, C.1780 .... 4800.00
Desk, Queen Anne, Slant Front, Cherry, New York, C.1760 .... 2900.00
Desk, Roll Top, C Roll, Pedestal, Oak, 1920 .... 1700.00
Desk, Roll Top, C Roll, Pedestal, Raised Panels, Swivel Chair, Oak 985.00
Desk, Roll Top, Child's, Maple 185.00

Furniture, Desk, Lady's, Louis XV,
Marquetry, 18 X 35 In.

Furniture, Desk, Writing, Louis XV,
Leather Top, 29 X 57 In.

Furniture, Desk,
Slant Front, Cherry,
American, C. 1880,
44 X 40 In.

Furniture, Desk,
Slant Front, 4 Drawers,
American, 40 X 20 In.

Desk, Roll Top, Oak, 4 Drawers 1 Side, 3 Other Side	525.00
Desk, Roll Top, S Roll, Oak, Raised Panel, Refinished, 48 X 30 In.	1500.00
Desk, S Roll Top, Raised Panel, Oak	2000.00
Desk, Schoolmaster's, Hepplewhite, Pine & Hardwood, 36 1/2 In.	215.00
Desk, Schoolmaster's, Hepplewhite, Pine, Poplar, 35 X 37 In.	200.00
Desk, Schoolmaster's, Pine, New England, C.1840, 40 X 37 In.	950.00
Desk, Schoolmaster's, Pine, Red Stain, Stretcher Base, 36 X 21 In.	440.00
Desk, Schoolmaster's, Pine, Slant Top, Lift Front, 48 X 30 In.	195.00
Desk, Schoolmaster's, Slant Front, Pine, Grain Painted, C.1830	750.00
Desk, Secretary, Art Nouveau, Cylinder	1450.00
Desk, Shaker, Table Top, Red Paint, Interior Drawer, Pine, C.1830	550.00
Desk, Shaker, Trustee's	3000.00
Desk, Slant Front, 1 Drawer, Fitted Interior, Oak, 37 X 27 1/2 In.	90.00
Desk, Slant Front, 3 Drawers, Fitted Interior, Walnut, 39 In.	160.00
Desk, Slant Front, 3 Interior Drawers, Mahogany, C.1780, 43 In.	5500.00
Desk, Slant Front, 4 Drawers, 12 Interior Drawers, Mahogany	1700.00
Desk, Slant Front, 4 Drawers, American, 40 X 20 In. ....Illus	3800.00
Desk, Slant Front, 4 Drawers, Cherry, Brass Knobs, 44 X 20 In.	940.00
Desk, Slant Front, 4 Drawers, Chippendale, Maple, 1790, 42 3/4 In.	2800.00
Desk, Slant Front, 4 Drawers, Chippendale, Oxbow, Mahogany, C.1780	4250.00
Desk, Slant Front, 4 Graduated Drawers, Chippendale, 1790	1600.00
Desk, Slant Front, Bracket Base, Curly Maple	9000.00
Desk, Slant Front, Bracket Feet, Cherry, Kentucky, C.1820, 33 In.	4450.00
Desk, Slant Front, Cherry, American, C.1880, 44 X 40 In. .... Illus	3000.00
Desk, Slant Front, Chippendale, Cherry	2000.00
Desk, Slant Front, Chippendale, Mahogany, Jos.Davis, C.1775, 44 In.	9350.00
Desk, Slant Front, Chippendale, Plum Pudding, 40 In.	4800.00
Desk, Slant Front, Crafters, Leaded Glass Doors, 1906, 46 X 42 In.	450.00
Desk, Slant Front, Curly Maple, 4 Graduated Drawers, Flared Base	9000.00
Desk, Slant Front, Federal, Inlaid Mahogany, 43 X 20 In.	950.00
Desk, Slant Front, Fitted Interior, Burl, Germany, 46 1/4 In.	550.00
Desk, Slant Front, Flame Graining, Birch, 18th Century	4250.00

Desk, Slant Front, Italian Baroque, 3 Drawers, Walnut, 37 In. 650.00
Desk, Slant Front, Oak, Floral Carved Sides, 19 X 16 X 10 In. 300.00
Desk, Slant Front, Pigeonholes, Faded Mahogany, 1830, 40 1/2 In. 995.00
Desk, Slant Front, Stepped Interior, Tiger Maple, C.1780, 41 In. 4500.00
Desk, Slant Front, Walnut, Replaced Hardware 1870.00
Desk, Slant Front, Welsh, 18th Century 2000.00
Desk, Slant Top, Mortised Apron, Scalloped Edge, Pine 600.00
Desk, Slanted Writing Lid, 4 Side Drawers, Burl Walnut, 33 In. 1900.00
Desk, Wicker, Kidney Shape, Letter Holder, 1 Drawer 350.00
Desk, Wicker, Natural, 2 Drawers 550.00
Desk, William & Mary, 5 Drawers, Vase Form Legs, English 300.00
Desk, Writing, 3 Drawers, Louis XV Style, Leather Top, 29 X 57 In. 1200.00
Desk, Writing, Inlaid, Zigzag Design, Drop Door, Spanish, 59 In. 225.00
Desk, Writing, Louis XV, Leather Top, 29 X 57 In. ....*Illus* 1200.00
Desk-On-Frame, Queen Anne, Slant Front, Cherry, 1765, 42 In., 2 Pc. 4675.00
Desk-On-Frame, Slant Front, Queen Anne, Maple, New Eng., C.1765 .... 4950.00
Dining Set, Eastlake, Table, 6 Chairs, Marble Top Sideboard 1950.00
Dining Set, Jacobean Style, 2 Servers, Table, Walnut, 6 Chairs 875.00
Dining Set, Queen Anne Style, Table, Server, Cherry, 6 Chairs 1100.00
Dining Set, Round Table, Buffet, Golden Oak, 6 Chairs 3500.00
Dough Box, Mortised & Pinned Sides, Breadboard Top, 27 3/4 In. 350.00
Dough Tray, Poplar, Tapered Legs, Pinned Construction 425.00
Dresser, 3 Upper Drawers, Open Below, Welsh, Original Brasses 2900.00
Dresser, 5 Drawers, Flanked By Cupboard Doors, Oak, 7 Ft. 2090.00
Dresser, Chest, Portable, Wooden, Fold Down Shaving Mirror 200.00
Dresser, Child's, Eastlake, Stenciled Design, Mirror Panel, 31 In. 75.00
Dresser, Empire, Carved Mahogany, Marble Top, 1840 .... 650.00
Dresser, Empire, Mahogany, 5 Drawers, Carved Columns, 44 X 22 In. 150.00
Dresser, George III, 2 Cupboards, Inside Shelf, Oak, 8 Ft. 4125.00
Dresser, Lancashire, Fielded Panel Doors, Oak, England, C.1760 .... 7200.00
Dresser, Marble Top, Candlestands, Teardrop Pulls, Burled Walnut 500.00
Dresser, Marble Top, Carved Walnut, Bird's-Eye Maple Interior 1550.00
Dresser, Milk, Welsh, Iron Hooks, England, C.1780, 67 In. 1200.00
Dresser, Original Iron Hardware & Key, French, Walnut, 80 In. 6000.00
Dresser, Pewter, Pine, Open Top, 3 Doors, English, 89 X 61 In. 1100.00
Dresser, Renaissance Revival, Marble Top, Rosewood 770.00
Dresser, Sheraton, Curly Maple, 2 Drawers, 33 X 19 X 48 In. 900.00
Dresser, Welsh, George III, Cut Frieze, 3 Shelves, Oak, C.1770 .... 3600.00
Dresser, Welsh, Shelves, 2 Drawers, Cupboards, Oak & Pine, 78 In. 1550.00
Dresser, Welsh, South Wales, Pot Rack, Oak, C.1760, 76 In. 4000.00
Dressing Table, Louis XVI, Jasperware Inlaid Cameos 4900.00
Dry Sink, 1 Drawer, Removable Top, Open Well, 29 X 30 In. 150.00
Dry Sink, 1 Drawer, Zinc Lined, Poplar, 36 1/2 X 54 3/4 In. 700.00
Dry Sink, 2 Doors, 2 Small Top Drawers, Blue Over Red, Amish 1985.00
Dry Sink, 2 Doors, Brown Paint, 19th Century, 53 X 28 In. 357.00
Dry Sink, 2 Panel Doors, Gallery, Green, Arched Feet, 38 X 55 In. 1550.00
Dry Sink, 3 Doors, Dovetailed Drawer, 7 Ft. 3200.00
Dry Sink, 3 Drawers, Grain Painted To Simulate Oak, 5 Ft. 1050.00
Dry Sink, Green & White Paint, Amish, 19th Century, 38 X 44 In. 875.00
Dry Sink, Poplar Door Panels, Curly Maple, 55 X 34 1/2 In. 2200.00
Dry Sink, S.M.Mason, Westfield, N.Y., August 6, 1874 .... 2400.00
Dry Sink, Shaker, Lift Top, Walnut & Poplar, Union Village, Ohio 2100.00
Dry Sink, Shaker, Putty, 1 Large Drawer 1250.00
Dry Sink, Splashboard, Brown & Yellow Grained, New Eng., 49 In. 770.00
Dumbwaiter, George III, Mahogany, 2 Graduated Platforms, 32 In. 495.00
Dumbwaiter, Oak, Stauffacher's Patent Model, 1900s 95.00
Easel, Oak, Brass Holder, Buttons 135.00
Easel, Oak, Fretwork 175.00
Easel, Walnut, Hand Carved, Victorian 220.00
Empire, Maple, Bird's-Eye Panels, Acorn Finial, 55 X 76 X 59 In. 550.00
Etagere, 2 Tiers, Satinwood, Victorian, Mirror Back, 4 Ft.7 In. 1540.00
Etagere, 3 Tiers, Rosewood, Adjustable Ratchet Top, Casters, 4 Ft. 1430.00
Etagere, 4 Tiers, Candle Scones, Carved & Gilded 350.00
Etagere, 4 Tiers, Carved Walnut, Beveled Glass 265.00

Etagere, Eastlake, Ebonized, 78 X 44 In.	1750.00
Etagere, Oak, Stuart, Foliate Chip–Carved Drawer, 39 X 15 In.	1325.00
Etagere, Rectangular Shelves, Grain Painted Pine, Poplar, 43 In.	450.00
Etagere, Rococo, Rosewood, Marble Top, Cabinet Base, N.Y., C.1850	2310.00
Etagere, Spindle Gallery, Oval Beveled Mirror, Doors, Oak, 70 In.	575.00
Footstool, Beveled Top, Brown Graining Over Red, 13 1/2 X 7 In.	85.00
Footstool, Birch, 10 3/4 X 9 1/2 X 17 1/4 In.	15.00
Footstool, Child's, Red Paint, Pine, 10 X 7 In.	30.00
Footstool, Curly Maple Legs, Removed Upholstery, 9 X 14 X 7 In.	30.00
Footstool, Cutout Feet & Apron, Hardwood, 8 3/4 X 16 In.	45.00
Footstool, G.Stickley, Flared Feet, 1907, 4 1/2 X 12 1/2 In.	350.00
Footstool, G.Stickley, Leather Top, 4 Flared Feet, C.1906, 12 In.	550.00
Footstool, G.Stickley, Leather Upholstered, 15 X 20 X 16 In.	1600.00
Footstool, G.Stickley, Leather, Mahogany, C.1907, 4 X 12 X 19 In.	275.00
Footstool, G.Stickley, Leather, Stretcher Through Tenons, Decal	2100.00
Footstool, G.Stickley, Mahogany, Leather Cover, 1905, 4 X 12 In.	900.00
Footstool, Gilt Geometric Design, 13 X 11 X 22 In.	50.00
Footstool, Gold Paint, Red Plush Cover, Cast Iron, 7 1/2 X 10 In.	75.00
Footstool, Gout, All Wood	95.00
Footstool, Gout, Original Cushions	40.00
Footstool, Gray Paint Over Olive Brown, 10 X 13 In.	70.00
Footstool, Inlaid Star In Top, Walnut, 8 X 8 X 14 In.	85.00
Footstool, Queen Anne, Spade Feet, Needlepoint Cover	72.50
Footstool, Red, Black Border, 1874, 7 In.	150.00
Footstool, Shaker, Decal, Pine & Maple, C.1870, 11 X 11 3/4 In.	445.00
Footstool, Shaker, Sister's, Mt.Lebanon, N.Y., Pine, 9 1/2 In.	450.00
Footstool, Stenciled Fruit & Foliage, Pine, 4 1/2 X 8 1/2 In.	200.00
Footstool, Stick Legs, Green Paint, Pine, 9 1/2 X 24 1/4 In.	55.00
Frame, Chip Carved, 9 X 9 In.	15.00
Garden Seat, Birds & Flowers, Blue Ground, Japanese, 19 In.	95.00
Garden Seat, Blazed Colors, Marked, Elephant Shape, 19 In.	55.00
Garden Seat, Oak, Oriental Porcelain Seat, Octagonal, 17 In.	425.00
Garden Seat, Pierced Geometric Design, Japanese, 18 1/2 In.	30.00
Garden Seat, Rose Mandarin, Scenes, Hexagonal, 1850, 18 In.	7250.00
Garden Set, Fern Pattern, Cast Iron, 3 Piece	3080.00
Garden Set, Settee & 2 Chairs, Iron, Wm.Adams Foundry	5500.00
Hall Seat, Fluted Carvings, Shelf Below Seat, Oak, English, 45 In.	300.00
Hall Seat, Victorian, Leafage & Spindle Back, Mahogany	550.00
Hall Stand, American Gothic, Carved Oak ....*Illus*	2200.00
Hall Stand, Iron Umbrella Pan, Marble Top, Glove Box, Walnut	1125.00
Hall Stand, Mirror, Umbrella Racks, Oak	650.00
Hall Stand, Oak, Arms, With Seat, Mirror	700.00

Furniture, Hall Stand, American
Gothic, Carved Oak

Furniture, Mirror, Federal,
Eglomise, Gilt Wood, 45 X 22 In.

Furniture, Mirror, Repousse,
Silver, Beveled Glass, 13 In.

Hall Stand, Renaissance, Carved Oak, Mirror	605.00
Hall Stand, Victorian, Mirror, Walnut	565.00
Hat Rack, Horseshoe Shape, 6 Horn Hooks, J.M.F.1904, 22 X 28 In.	60.00
High Chair, 2 Slats, Green Paint, Turned Posts, Splint Seat	205.00
High Chair, 4-Slat Back, Delaware Valley, Green, 18th Century	5500.00
High Chair, Fretwork Back, Carved, Needlepoint Cushion, C.1830	2800.00
High Chair, Rounded Low Back, Painted Flower Heads, 19th Century	245.00
High Chair, Spindle Back, Blue Repaint, Seat Dated 1855, 35 In.	50.00
High Chair, Turned Legs, Traces of Decoration, 37 In.	105.00
Highboy, Queen Anne Transitional, Mahogany, New Eng., 1760, 53 In.	1000.00
Highboy, Queen Anne, Bonnet, Curly Maple, Pinwheel Carved, 1770	3500.00
Highboy, Queen Anne, Carved Fan, Dovetailed Drawers, Maple	5600.00
Highboy, Queen Anne, Cherry, Fan Carved, Cabriole Legs, 1760	3500.00
Highboy, Queen Anne, Curly Maple, 10 Drawers, Old Brasses, 70 In.	5000.00
Highboy, Queen Anne, Maple, 5 Drawers, Pad Feet, 1770, 72 In.	9600.00
Highboy, Queen Anne, Scrolled Apron, 6 Drawers, Maple, Dated 1791	3700.00
Highboy, William & Mary, Tortoise Walnut Veneer	5800.00
Huntboard, Bennington Knobs, Pine & Curly Cherry	6800.00
Huntboard, Cherry, Tennessee, Dated 1820-30	4500.00
Huntboard, Poplar, 2 Drawers, Georgia, 43 X 58 X 22 In.	3500.00
Huntboard, Southern Pine, Mahogany, Georgia, C.1810, 46 In.	3000.00
Hutch Table, Hepplewhite, Pine, Red Paint, 26 In.	1950.00
Icebox, Oak, Victor, Painted	110.00
Jewelry Casket, Louis XVI Style, Inlaid Kingwood	1430.00
Kas, Cherry, Pine, Turned Feet, Molded Top, 1710-40	9900.00
Kas, Pine, Brown, Scalloped Crest, 2 Doors, E.E.R.1878, 78 In.	500.00
Kas, Yellow Graining, Red & Brown Striping, Pine, 72 3/4 In.	950.00
Ladder, Library, Seat, George III, Oak, 28 1/2 In.	440.00
Lamp Stand, Egyptian Revival, Tile Top, Cloisonne Column, Brass	425.00
Linen Press, 3 Drawers, Double Doors, Pine, 78 X 47 1/4 In.	1000.00
Linen Press, Federal, Mahogany, Cornice, C.1810, 89 In., 2 Piece	6600.00
Love Seat, Art Deco, French	375.00
Love Seat, Hand Carving, Rose Brocade Upholstery, Walnut, 62 In.	375.00
Love Seat, Medallion Back, Fruit Carving, Walnut	750.00
Lowboy, 3 Thumb Molded Drawers, Carved Fans, English, Oak, 33 In.	500.00
Lowboy, Mahogany, Chippendale Style, Brass Hardware	625.00
Magazine Carrier, Open 3 Slat Box, Mission Oak, Handle, 18 In.	450.00
Mirror & Console, Victorian, Leaf Carved, Mahogany	1375.00
Mirror, 4 Iron Hooks On Bottom, G.Stickley, 1905-07, 28 X 36 In.	1200.00
Mirror, Adams Style, Gilded, Green & Ivory, 56 X 26 In.	175.00
Mirror, Baluster Frame, Reverse Glass, C.1840, 39 1/2 X 20 In.	425.00
Mirror, Baroque, Beveled Glass, Carved & Gilded, 48 X 51 In.	600.00
Mirror, Baroque, Carved Walnut, Putti, Cartouche Shape, 4 Ft.4 In.	4400.00
Mirror, Beveled Glass, Engraved Frame, Octagonal, 36 X 2 In.	250.00
Mirror, Beveled Mahogany Frame, Carved Sunburst, 10 X 13 In.	125.00
Mirror, Beveled, 3 Circles At Top, Bentwood, C.1902, 41 1/2 In.	1650.00
Mirror, Carved & Gilded Baroque Shield, Floral Crest, 33 In.	225.00
Mirror, Carved Gilt Wooden Frame, 39 X 22 In.	17.50
Mirror, Cheval, Bronze, Ribbed Legs, Ruhlmann, Round, 1925, 17 In.	3025.00
Mirror, Cheval, Empire Revival, Late 19th Century	880.00
Mirror, Cheval, Empire, Gilt Bronze, Swivel, 7 Ft.4 In.X 38 In.	1980.00
Mirror, Cheval, Faux Bamboo Maple, C.1870	1100.00
Mirror, Cheval, Man's, C.1830, 5 Ft.9 In.	525.00
Mirror, Cheval, Sheraton, Claw Feet, Mahogany, C.1890	1200.00
Mirror, Chinese Chippendale, Carved & Gilded, 46 X 29 In.	350.00
Mirror, Chinese, Painted, Gilt Wood, Floral Urn Columns, 21 In.	300.00
Mirror, Chippendale, Broken Arch & Shell Crest, 40 X 22 In.	175.00
Mirror, Chippendale, Flame Mahogany Veneer, Pine, 33 1/2 In.	1100.00
Mirror, Chippendale, Mahogany, Gilt Phoenix Crest, C.1760, 3 Ft.	1900.00
Mirror, Classic Gilt Frame, Oval, 32 X 26 In.	20.00
Mirror, Continental, Baroque, Shell, Foliate Design, 46 X 24 In.	450.00
Mirror, Courting, Carved & Painted, Original Glass, 12 In.	4750.00
Mirror, Courting, Pine, Shaped Crest, 18th Century, 8 1/4 X 5 In.	1325.00
Mirror, Courting, Pressed Brass Borders, C.1820, 8 1/2 X 5 In.	300.00

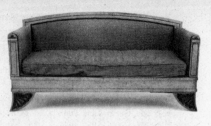

Furniture, Rocker, Comb
Back, 5 Arrowhead
Spindles, Painted, 1820

Furniture, Rocker,
L.& J.G.Stickley, Arms,
Leather Cushion, 40 In.

Furniture, Settee, Biedermeier, Burr Maple,
C.1830, 73 In.

Mirror, Cut & Engraved Design, Beveled Rim, Oval, 31 X 37 In. 325.00
Mirror, Dressing Table, Beveled, Swivel Supports, 25 3/4 In. 1200.00
Mirror, Dressing Table, Man's, Marquetry, 3 Drawers, 24 X 17 In. 715.00
Mirror, Dressing, George III, Inlaid Mahogany, 3 Drawers, 1800 .... 1100.00
Mirror, Dressing, George III, Mahogany, 18th Century, 24 In. 715.00
Mirror, Dutch Baroque, Gilt Brass, Floral Overlay, 46 In. 700.00
Mirror, Empire, Acanthus Leaves, Gilded, 32 1/4 X 22 1/4 In. 80.00
Mirror, Empire, Brass Rosettes, Black & Gold Paint, 31 3/4 In. 165.00
Mirror, Empire, Gilt, Split Baluster, 19th Century, 51 X 27 In. 400.00
Mirror, Empire, Parcel Gilt & Eglomise, C.1830, 20 X 10 3/4 In. 385.00
Mirror, Federal, Eglomise, Ebonized, Split Baluster, 19 X 11 In. 165.00
Mirror, Federal, Eglomise, Gilt Wood, 45 X 22 In. ....*Illus* 2640.00
Mirror, Federal, Fretwork, Mahogany, 43 X 21 In. 2500.00
Mirror, Federal, Gilt Carved Gesso Frame, 30 X 14 1/2 In. 60.00
Mirror, Federal, Gilt Gesso, Oval Drops, C.1820, 3 Ft. 150.00
Mirror, Federal, Urn of Wheat, Inlaid Mahogany & Gilt, 54 In. 6750.00
Mirror, Fireplace, Eagle Finial, Iron, Brass Finish, 30 X 28 In. 595.00
Mirror, Folding, Mahogany Case, Inlaid Lid Medallion, 3 X 6 In. 35.00
Mirror, Foliage Scrolls, Bids, Rococo Cast Plaster Frame, 47 In. 225.00
Mirror, George II, Leaf Border, Parcel Gilt Walnut, 19 X 43 In. 4675.00
Mirror, Gilded Rococo, Foliate Crest, 59 X 37 In. 750.00
Mirror, Ivory, Carved Leaves, Putti, Dieppe, 33 X 21 In., Pair 3300.00
Mirror, Louis XV, Carved & Gilt Trumeau, Canvas of Figures 1200.00
Mirror, Mahogany, Crest, Marquetry Panels, Crafters, 27 X 30 In. 750.00
Mirror, Mantel, Carved & Gilded, 34 1/2 X 63 In. 2450.00
Mirror, Mantel, Empire, Gilt Gesso Frame, 3 Sections, 25 X 66 In. 120.00
Mirror, Mantel, Federal, 3 Sections, Gilded Frame, 59 X 26 In. 100.00
Mirror, Mantel, George II, C.1870, 4 Ft.6 In. X 44 In. 1750.00
Mirror, Mantel, George II, Pine, Swan's Neck Crest, 53 X 60 In. 4400.00
Mirror, Mantel, George III, Gilt Spandrels, 36 1/2 In. 200.00
Mirror, Mantel, Victorian, Carved & Gilded, 1860 .... 1100.00
Mirror, Oak Frame, 11 1/2 X 14 1/2 In. 45.00
Mirror, Pier, Beveled Plate Glass, Marble Shelf, Mahogany, 101 In. 400.00
Mirror, Pier, Queen Anne, Parcel Gilt, 5 Ft.6 In. X 27 In. 2650.00
Mirror, Pier, Walnut & Rosewood, Arched, C.1900, 5 Ft.9 1/2 In. 2750.00
Mirror, Plateau, Applied Streamers, Bows, Double Beveled, 12 In. 75.00
Mirror, Plateau, Beveled, Ball-Footed, 10 In. 58.00
Mirror, Plateau, Beveled, Footed Frame, 14 In. 78.00
Mirror, Plateau, Beveled, Silver Plated Rim, 7 7/8 In. 70.00
Mirror, Plateau, Double Bevels, Scrolled Floral Sides, Tin Back 95.00
Mirror, Portrait Print of Hoyt Sisters, Nutting, 21 X 8 In. 100.00
Mirror, Puffed Figural Flowers, Double Beveled Glass, 14 In. 135.00
Mirror, Queen Anne, Molded Frame, Scrolled Crest, 24 1/2 X 13 In. 800.00
Mirror, Queen Anne, Shaped Crest, Gilt Designs, Japanned, 28 In. 2000.00
Mirror, Queen Anne, Walnut Veneer On Pine Frame, 31 1/4 X 13 In. 1750.00
Mirror, Queen Anne, Walnut Veneer, Gilt Liner, 22 3/4 X 13 In. 275.00
Mirror, Red Graining, Beveled Pine Frame, 12 1/4 X 16 1/4 In. 50.00
Mirror, Repousse, Silver, Beveled Glass, 13 In. ....*Illus* 150.00

Mirror, Repousse, Silver, Bevelled Glass, 13 In. ....*Illus* 150.00
Mirror, Scroll, Inlay & Gilded Lined Frame, 16 1/3 X 28 3/4 In. 450.00
Mirror, Scroll, Inlay Around Frame, Mahogany On Pine, 30 3/4 In. 1100.00
Mirror, Scroll, Mahogany, 19th Century, 19 1/2 X 13 1/4 In. 170.00
Mirror, Scroll, Molded Frame, Mahogany, 19 1/2 X 12 1/2 In. 225.00
Mirror, Shaving, 2 Drawers, Inlaid Frame, Bowed, Mahogany, 22 In. 75.00
Mirror, Shaving, Beveled Oval Turned Wooden Spindle, 14 In.Base 37.50
Mirror, Shaving, Bow Front, Flame Veneer On Drawers, Mahogany 75.00
Mirror, Shaving, Drawer, Turned Posts, Poplar, 13 3/4 In. 120.00
Mirror, Shaving, Folding, Celluloid, Milk Glass Bowl, Fuller Brush 35.00
Mirror, Shaving, Girl's Arms Hold & Encircle Mirror, 16 In. 95.00
Mirror, Shaving, Hepplewhite, Bow Front, Mahogany, 23 3/4 In. 305.00
Mirror, Shaving, Hepplewhite, Drawer, Inlaid & Reeded, Mahogany 175.00
Mirror, Shaving, Oak, Wall Mount, 2 Drawers 79.00
Mirror, Shaving, Queen Anne, Beveled, 9 Drawers, Walnut, 30 In. 600.00
Mirror, Shaving, Stand, Biedermeier, Ebonized Columns, 23 In. 225.00
Mirror, Shaving, White Paint, Shoe Feet, 1840, 22 X 10 3/4 In. 135.00
Mirror, Shield Form, Carved & Gilded, Plume Crest, 32 In. 175.00
Mirror, Tabernacle, Federal, Reverse Painted, Jos.Loring, 56 In. 200.00
Mirror, Tabernacle, Stenciled Gilt Floral, C.1830, 35 In. 325.00
Mirror, Table, Swivel, Arched Crest, Trestle Feet, C.1910, 20 In. 225.00
Mirror, Tin Frame With Leaves & Fruit, C.1800, 11 In. 45.00
Mirror, Top Panel Painting of Hunters With Hounds, 54 X 26 In. 150.00
Mirror, Vanity, Edge Cutting, Bird & Foliage 125.00
Mirror, Venetian, Etched Allegorical Woman Upper, 45 In., Pair 1100.00
Mirror, Victorian, Beveled, Gilt & Gesso Frame, 43 X 37 In. 40.00
Mirror, Victorian, Oval, Rosewood, Gold Liner, 19 X 16 In. 95.00
Mirror, William & Mary, Walnut Burl Veneer, England, 28 1/2 In. 2000.00
Music Stand, Empire, Canterbury Mahogany, Lyre Sides, 1 Drawer 32.00
Parlor Set, Egyptian Carved Design, Sofa & Armchair, C.1870 .... 1760.00
Parlor Set, Louis XV, Carved Fruitwood Frames, 3 .... 1000.00
Parlor Set, Mohair, Art Deco 1350.00
Parlor Set, Napoleon III, Ebonized, Upholstered, 1870, 5 .... 2750.00
Parlor Set, Renaissance, Carved Rosewood, 3 .... 5280.00
Parlor Set, Upholstered, Tasseled, Padded Arms, C.1840, 3 .... 1320.00
Parlor Set, Victorian, Mahogany, Cane Back & Seats, 4 .... 1500.00
Patio Set, Fanback Pattern, 7 .... 5100.00
Pedestal, Limbert, Oak, Square Top, Corbel Supports, C.1910, 36 In. 1600.00
Pedestal, Marble Top, Gilt–Mounted Satinwood, 43 In., Pair 1540.00
Pew, Church, Pine, Arms, Gothic Apron, Arched Feet, 4 Ft.6 In. 247.00
Pew, Church, Pine, Rectangular Arm Rests, Plank Seat, 4 Ft.6 In. 220.00
Pew, Church, Plain, 8 Ft. 40.00
Pew, Pine, Cutout Ends, Board Seat, Green Paint, 66 In. 55.00
Pie Safe, Drawer, 2 Doors, Punched Floral, Walnut & Poplar, 55 In. 650.00
Pie Safe, Hudson River Valley, Red Paint, 19th Century, 5 Ft. 412.00
Pie Safe, Painted Design, Pierced Tin Sides, Pennyslvania 2600.00
Pie Safe, Pecan & Pine, Rudolph Blaschke, Texas 4500.00
Pie Safe, Pine, 6 Punched Tin Panels, 2 Doors, 60 X 44 In. 495.00
Pie Safe, Punched Tin, Green Paint, 4 Doors, C.1870, 7 Ft.11 In. 1540.00
Pie Safe, Punched Tin, Masonic Symbols 530.00
Pie Safe, Punched Tin, Pine, Red & Blue Paint, Mo., 2 Doors, 47 In. 1540.00
Pie Safe, Wall Hung, Pierced Tin, Pine 700.00
Pie Safe, Walnut, Original Green Paint 1200.00
Plate Rack, Hanging, Doors, Center Medallion, England, C.1780 .... 1350.00
Pole Screen, George III, Late 18th Century 1800.00
Pole Screen, Victorian, Beaded, Brass, 3 Legs, Needlepoint, 5 Ft. 660.00
Potty Chair, Oval Back, Wooden Seat, Wicker, 20 1/2 In. 185.00
Potty Chair, Wainscot, Bottom Drawer, Chester County 5000.00
Rack, Clothes, Shaker, Wooden, Red Paint, 3 Hooks, 6 Ft.X 36 In. 2475.00
Rack, Coat & Hat, Brass Bark Style Hooks, Oak, 36 In. 65.00
Rack, Coat, Maple, Grain Painted, 5 Hooks, 19th Century, 4 X 49 In. 330.00
Rack, Drying, 4 Nails, Rounded Tops, Green Paint, 51 In. 550.00
Rack, Drying, Shaker, Enfield, N.H., 1840, 31 1/2 X 37 1/2 In. 650.00
Rack, Hat, Folding, Walnut, White Porcelain Knob Design 45.00

Furniture, Secretary, Federal, Mahogany,
C.1800, 54 In.

Furniture, Sideboard, Federal, Mahogany,
Gilt Wood, C.1820, 6 Ft.

Furniture, Sideboard, Mahogany,
Pineapple Carving, 59 X 53 In.

Furniture, Secretary, Federal, Mahogany, American, 81 In.

Furniture, Stand, 1 Drawer, Federal,
Mahogany, Inlaid Edge, 28 In.

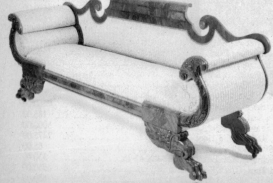

Furniture, Sofa, Empire, Hairy Paw Feet, Carved Fruit, 89 In.

Furniture, Stand, 2 Drawers,
Cherry & Tiger Maple, 28 X 22 In.

Rack, Magazine, L.& J.G.Stickley, Slats, 4 Shelves, 1910, 42 In. 1200.00
Rack, Magazine, Limbert, Caned Panels, 3 Shelves, 32 X 22 X 14 In. 475.00
Rack, Magazine, Limbert, Slat–Sided, Gallery, C.1910, 29 X 16 In. 468.00
Rack, Magazine, Oak, Hanging, Tin Litho Picture 50.00
Rack, Peg, New England, Green Paint, Pine, 40 3/4 In. 220.00
Rack, Smoking, Oak, 4 Portrait Panels, 22 In. 130.00
Rack, Spoon, Chip Carved Design, 3 Racks, 18th Century, 21 In. 1800.00
Rack, Towel, Shaker, Putty Gray Finish, Trestle Foot, Pine, 36 In. 450.00
Rail, Shaker, Herb Drying, 9 Pegs, South Family, C.1820, 34 1/2 In. 450.00
Raised Panel Door, 4 Removable Shelves, Pine, 59 3/4 In. 450.00
Recamier, Child's, Victorian, Mahogany, Upholstered, Brass Nail 450.00
Recamier, Upholstered Scrolled Sides, Brass Feet, Walnut, 7 Ft. 3025.00
Rocker & Footstool, Platform, Velvet Upholstery, Maple 50.00
Rocker, 4 Slats, Rush Seat, Ware Family, C.1840 .... 195.00
Rocker, 5 Arched Slats, Gold Design, Rush Seat, Arms 110.00
Rocker, Adirondack Twig, Splint Seat, 44 In. 130.00
Rocker, Bentwood Arms & Slats, Weathered Blue Paint, Splint Seat 75.00
Rocker, Bentwood, Signed Thonet, Child's 325.00
Rocker, Cane Back, Cutout Leaf Detail, Curly Maple 100.00
Rocker, Child's, 2 Slat Back, Arms, Tape Seat, Red Finish 75.00
Rocker, Child's, 4 Spindles, Tapestry Upholstered Seat 70.00
Rocker, Child's, Boston, Red Milk Paint 65.00
Rocker, Child's, Cane Back & Seat 80.00
Rocker, Child's, Cane Seat, Back, Victorian, Clinton, C.1860 .... 250.00
Rocker, Child's, Captain's Chair, Old Red, 14 3/4 In. 80.00
Rocker, Child's, Carved Elephant Sides, Painted, 19th Century 290.00
Rocker, Child's, Eastlake Style, Folding, Bamboo Turnings, 27 In. 125.00
Rocker, Child's, Eastlake, Walnut, Cane Seat, C.1880, 25 In. 300.00
Rocker, Child's, Empire, Mahogany, Vase Splat, Rush Seat, 22 In. 270.00
Rocker, Child's, G.Stickley, Open Arms, 3 Slats, Decal, 1904–06 .... 500.00
Rocker, Child's, G.Stickley, Original Leather Seat 550.00
Rocker, Child's, Golden Oak, Arms, Cane Seat, C.1890, 23 In. 350.00
Rocker, Child's, Ladder Back, 3 Slats, Turned Arms, Dark, 26 In. 150.00
Rocker, Child's, Old King Cole, Chestnut, Victorian, 28 In. 300.00
Rocker, Child's, Pressed Back, Bentwood Arms, Oak 120.00
Rocker, Child's, Pressed Back, Oak, Arms 300.00
Rocker, Child's, Rustic Bentwood, Arched Top, Arms, Woven Seat 330.00
Rocker, Child's, Shaker, Maple, No.1, Lebanon, N.Y., C.1870, 29 In. 1200.00
Rocker, Child's, Spindle Back, Needlepoint Seat 40.00
Rocker, Child's, Spindle Splats, Scrolled Arms, Painted Gray 385.00
Rocker, Child's, Stenciled & Grain Painted, 19th Century 165.00
Rocker, Chippendale, Vasiform Splat, Arms, Maple & Cherry, C.1800 .... 900.00
Rocker, Comb Back, 5 Arrowhead Spindles, Painted, 1820 ....*Illus* 2700.00
Rocker, Crest Rail Over Splat, Spindles, Plank Seat, Pine 165.00
Rocker, Double Seat, Pine, Peg Construction, Hickory Seat 525.00
Rocker, Folding, Writing Arm, Drawer Under Seat 160.00
Rocker, G.Stickley, Slat Sides, Arms, C.1900, 38 In. 400.00
Rocker, High Back, Curled Down Arms, C.1840 .... 175.00
Rocker, Hunzinger, Cloth Strap Back & Seat, Walnut, 31 1/2 In. 325.00
Rocker, L.& J.G.Stickley, Arms, Leather Cushion, 40. In. ....*Illus* 700.00
Rocker, Ladder Back, 4 Arched Horizontal Splats, Arms, Rush Seat 715.00
Rocker, Ladder Back, 4 Arched Slats, Woven Splint Seat 65.00
Rocker, Lady's, Bamboo Turnings, Maple, Rush Seat 110.00
Rocker, Lady's, Plank Seat, 1/2 Spindle Back, Stenciled Design 40.00
Rocker, Lincoln, Cane Seat 450.00
Rocker, Lincoln, S Curve Seat, Scroll Arms, Bootjack Splat 65.00
Rocker, Mammy's, Original Paint, 1820–30 .... 2100.00
Rocker, Maple, Hickory, Rush Seat, Green Paint, 18th Century 1100.00
Rocker, Morris Chair, L.& J.G.Stickley ....*Illus* 770.00
Rocker, Platform, Arms, Split Weave Wicker, White Paint 65.00
Rocker, Platform, Eastlake Style, Walnut, Red Velvet Upholstery 210.00
Rocker, Platform, Wicker, Pair 2100.00
Rocker, Pressed Back, Oak, Leather Seat 70.00

Rocker, Pressed Back, Oak, Painted Stencil, C.1900 .... 80.00
Rocker, Sewing, Cherry, Spindle Back, Cane Seat, Turned Posts 105.00
Rocker, Sewing, G.Stickley, Rush Seat, Decal, 1904–06, 31 X 17 In. 175.00
Rocker, Sewing, Green Stenciled Design, Black Paint, Shaped Seat 115.00
Rocker, Sewing, Leather Back & Seat, Burled 140.00
Rocker, Sewing, Plank Seat, Spindle Back, Shaped Crest 65.00
Rocker, Shaker, 4 Slats, Tape Seat, Shawl Bar, New Lebanon, C.1840 .... 1700.00
Rocker, Shaker, Dark, Back & Seat Reupholstered, Lebanon, No.3 .... 355.00
Rocker, Shaker, Ebony Finish, Rush Seat, No.2, Maple, 34 In. 800.00
Rocker, Shaker, Elder's, 4 Slats, New Lebanon, Tiger Maple, C.1820 .... 5500.00
Rocker, Shaker, Elder's, Arms, Cherry, Maple, Watervliet, C.1810 .... 5500.00
Rocker, Shaker, Elder's, Mushroom Arms, Shawl Bar 4000.00
Rocker, Shaker, Elder's, Splint Seat, Arms, New Lebanon, C.1820 .... 8600.00
Rocker, Shaker, Mt.Lebanon, Greenish Black Paint, C.1860 .... 8250.00
Rocker, Shaker, Mt.Lebanon, Original Woven Tape Seat 1650.00
Rocker, Shaker, Mushroom Hand Rests, Lebanon, No.7, Maple, 41 In. 1500.00
Rocker, Shaker, No.4, Wool Covered Seat, Shawl Bar, Maple, C.1870 .... 750.00
Rocker, Shaker, No.7, Decal, Mt.Lebanon, N.Y., C.1880, 41 In. 1000.00
Rocker, Shaker, No.7, Shawl Back .... 1050.00 To 1800.00
Rocker, Shaker, Sister's, Rush Seat, Maple, Watervliet, C.1820 .... 850.00
Rocker, Shaker, Slat Decal, Taped Seat, Mt.Lebanon, C.1880, 41 In. 1500.00
Rocker, Shaker, Youth's, 2 Slats, Canterbury, C.1820, 32 In. 4250.00
Rocker, Stencil Design, Greek Revival House, Arms, 44 In. 1000.00
Rocker, Thumb Molded Frame, Leaf Carvings, Upholstered, C.1860 .... 200.00
Rocker, Twig 400.00
Rocker, Wicker, Brown, C.1885 .... 420.00
Rocker, Wicker, Rolled Arms, Heart Back, Wakefield Style 215.00
Rocker, Windsor, Comb Back, 41 In. ....*Illus* 2700.00
Rocker, Windsor, Comb Back, 6 Spindles, Maple, Ash, Bamboo, 1760 .... 375.00
Rocker, Windsor, Comb Back, Arms, Painted, C.1830, 44 1/2 In. 325.00
Rocker, Windsor, Comb Back, Arms, Scalloped Crest 198.00
Rocker, Windsor, Plank Seat, 1/2 Spindles, 3 Slat Back 185.00
Rocker, Windsor, Rabbit Ear, Red Paint, Gold Striping 65.00
Rocker, Windsor, Writing Arm Swivels, Bamboo 275.00
Rocker, Writing Arm, Stenciled, C.1825 .... 895.00
Schrank, Dutch Baroque, Rosewood, Oak, Mid–17th Century, 7 1/2 Ft. 8250.00
Screen, 2–Panel, Hounds In Wooded Landscape, 82 X 47 In. 500.00
Screen, 2–Panel, Inlaid Birds, Flowers, Lacquered, 72 X 32 In. 275.00
Screen, 2–Panel, Watercolor Fowl, Grasses, 42 X 23 3/8 In. 275.00
Screen, 3–Panel, Carved Basket of Flowers, Red Fabric, Floor 400.00
Screen, 3–Panel, Painted Canvas, Deer, Hawk, Fledglings, 6 Ft.4 In. 2970.00
Screen, 6–Panel, Lakeside Retreat, Hills, Tanyu Hogen, 66 In. 3740.00
Screen, 8–Panel, Coromandel, Landscapes, Symbols, 6 Ft.3 In. 8800.00
Screen, Adjustable, Stenciled Flower, Wooden, Painted, 3 Ft.8 In. 550.00
Screen, Federal Style, Chinese Painting of Pigeon, Mahogany 175.00
Screen, Floral Needlepoint, Walnut Frame, 39 In. 200.00
Screen, Folding, Birds, Blossoms, Gold Ground, Section, 33 3/4 In. 45.00
Screen, Folding, Black Lacquer Frame, Silk Covered Panels, 67 In. 165.00
Screen, George III, Needlepoint Sample, Dated 1825, 51 In. 200.00
Screen, Louis XV, Ormolu, Birds, Floral, 3–Part Frames, Pair 650.00
Screen, Needlework, Ornate Walnut Frame, Rippled Glass, Stand 375.00
Screen, Stylized Greyhound, Iron, C.1925, 33 1/2 In. 4125.00
Seat, Wagon, Rush, 2 Chairs Joined By Middle Leg, 19th Century 795.00
Secretary Bookcase, Fitted Interior, English, C.1790 .... 6600.00
Secretary Bookcase, George III, Elmwood, C.1800, 7 Ft.5 1/2 In. 9900.00
Secretary Cabinet, Black Lacquer, Gilt, Chinese Export, 5 Ft. 7150.00
Secretary Desk, 16–Pane Doors, Slant Front Desk 950.00
Secretary Desk, Interior Compartments, Drawers, Mahogany, C.1800 .... 2750.00
Secretary, American Empire, Mahogany, Molded Cornice, 83 In. 2000.00
Secretary, Child's, 7 Secret Compartments, Philadelphia, 44 In. 3600.00
Secretary, Country, Drawers, Attached Top, Set–Back Doors, 62 In. 325.00
Secretary, Cupboard Top, 3 Shelves, Pine, C.1800, 84 1/2 In. 4250.00
Secretary, Curly Maple, 4 Drawers, Glass Doors, 77 In., 2 Piece 1500.00
Secretary, Cylinder Roll, Burl Walnut Drawer & Doors, 1880–90 .... 2100.00

Secretary, Cylinder Top, Glass Doors On Top, Walnut, 91 In. 2100.00
Secretary, Cylinder, Walnut, 7 Ft. 1800.00
Secretary, Doctor's, Ebony Pulls, Fretwork, Kneehole, 84 X 52 In. 3950.00
Secretary, Federal, Mahogany, American, 81 In. ....*Illus* 4000.00
Secretary, Federal, Mahogany, C.1800, 54 In. ....*Illus* 3700.00
Secretary, Grain Painted Over Putty Base, Red Wash Interior 9600.00
Secretary, Rococo Revival, Carved Mahogany, C.1870 .... 1650.00
Secretary, Sheraton, Arched Doors, Original Brasses, 2 Piece 1375.00
Secretary, Victorian, Burl Walnut Veneer, 90 X 45 In., 2 Piece 1800.00
Secretary, Wooton Patent, Renaissance Revival 7150.00
Server, Ash, Carved Heads, Gallery, Brasses 425.00
Server, Center Drawer, Side Drawers, Grain Painted, C.1830, 42 In. 1300.00
Server, Federal, Grain Painted, 1 Long Drawer, C.1840, 39 X 35 In. 715.00
Server, G.Stickley, 3 Drawers, Iron Hardware, 1907, 39 X 48 In. 1900.00
Server, G.Stickley, Oak, Gallery, 3 Half Drawers, 1907, 40 In. 7250.00
Server, L.& J.G.Stickley, No.752 .... 1540.00
Server, Pine, Original Apple Green Paint, Shaped Back 1050.00
Server, Stickley, 3 Drawer, Lower Shelf, Signed, 39 In. 1900.00
Settee, 3 Slats Over 12 Spindles, Painted, C.1825, 76 In. 2750.00
Settee, Biedermeier, Burr Maple, C.1830, 73 In. ....*Illus* 2200.00
Settee, George I, Upholstered Seat & Back, Scrolled Arms, Walnut 3100.00
Settee, George II, Mahogany, Scrolled, Upholstered, 5 Ft.7 In. 2850.00
Settee, George III, Mahogany, Chairback, Spade Feet, 38 X 44 In. 650.00
Settee, George III, Mahogany, Upholstered Seat, Serpentine, 56 In. 6600.00
Settee, George III, Painted Floral, Fruit Sprays, C.1800, 71 In. 2600.00
Settee, George III, Upholstered Back, Padded Arms, C.1785, 7 Ft. 4950.00
Settee, Georgian, Pierced Splats, Dolphin Feet, Shell & Feather 7700.00
Settee, Gilt Stencil, Cane Seat, Arms 3150.00
Settee, Louis XV Style, Ivory & Gold Fabric 325.00
Settee, Napoleon III, Gilt Bronze, Ebonized, Upholstered, C.1860 .... 550.00
Settee, Painted, Stencil Design, Arms, Plank Seat, 37 In. 2000.00
Settee, Regency, Rosewood, Brass Inlaid, Cushion Seat, 7 In. 7150.00
Settee, Rocking, Arrow–Back, Arms, Plank Seat, Black Paint, 52 In. 600.00
Settee, Rococo, Arcaded Back, Outscrolled Arms, Cast Iron 650.00
Settee, Rococo, Pierce Carved, Laminated, J & J Meeks, 1860, 5 Ft. 4400.00
Settee, Walnut, Eastlake 265.00
Settee, Windsor, Beaded Crest Rail, 16 Bamboo Spindles, C.1810 .... 2000.00
Settle, G.Stickley, 6 Panels, Short Posts, Decal, 41 X 84 X 34 In. 6250.00
Settle, Lifetime, Drop Arm, Spring Cushion, C.1910, 72 In. 1500.00
Settle, Pine, 4–Panel Back, Lift Seat, Brown Stain, 54 X 59 In. 610.00
Settle, Pine, 4–Panel Back, Stripped & Waxed, English, 42 X 59 In. 495.00
Settle, Pine, Grained Red Paint, Brass Molding, 62 X 47 In., Pair 990.00
Settle, Slat Back, L. & J.G. Stickley, Cushion, 1912, 34 X 76 In. 1500.00
Shelf, Black Paint, 3 Shelves, 19th Century, 17 X 43 In. 100.00
Shelf, Hanging, 3 Graduated Shelves, Grain Painted, 34 3/4 In. 1600.00
Shelf, Hanging, Canted, Old Finish, 19th Century, 21 X 25 In. 245.00
Shelf, Hanging, Mirror, Comb Case, Towel Bar, Pine, 9 X 25 In. 85.00
Shelf, Hanging, Pine, 3 Graduated Shelves, 1 Drawer, 34 X 23 In. 247.00
Shelf, Hanging, Pine, Folk Art, Fan & Sunburst, Dark, 9 X 20 In. 195.00
Shelf, Hanging, Walnut, Scrolled Back & Sides, 12 3/4 X 20 In. 125.00
Shelf, Pewter, 2 Shelves, Cutout Crest, 19th Century, 64 1/2 In. 475.00
Shelf, Plate, Scalloped Sides, 3 Shelves, 4 Iron Brackets, 38 In. 325.00
Sideboard, 2 Doors, 3 Drawers, Carved Facade, Oak, 64 1/2 In. 500.00
Sideboard, 4 Drawers Over 4 Doors, Cherry, 50 In. X 6 Ft. 2750.00
Sideboard, 5 Center Drawers, Side Cabinet Doors, Mahogany, 63 In. 150.00
Sideboard, American Rococo, Tiered Shelves, Mahogany 1550.00
Sideboard, Empire, Mahogany, Gallery, 2 Doors, 2 Drawers, 54 In. 200.00
Sideboard, Federal, Mahogany, 3 Drawers, Fluted Legs, 43 X 21 In. 450.00
Sideboard, Federal, Mahogany, 4 Top Drawers, C.1810 .... 3800.00
Sideboard, Federal, Mahogany, Gilt Wood, C.1820, 6 Ft. ....*Illus* 6600.00
Sideboard, Federal, Mahogany, Serpentine, 3 Frieze Drawers, 40 In. 1050.00
Sideboard, Federal, Medallion On Each Door, Mahogany, 72 1/2 In. 700.00
Sideboard, G.Stickley, 2 Half Drawers, Over Long Drawer, 60 In. 9500.00
Sideboard, Geometric Inlay, 2 Doors, 4 Drawers, Mahogany, 39 In. 950.00

Sideboard, George III, Mahogany, Pedestal, Brass Rail, 5 Ft.6 In. 2090.00
Sideboard, George III, Satinwood, Mahogany, Spade Feet, 7 Ft. 4950.00
Sideboard, Hepplewhite Style, Inlaid, Mahogany, 37 3/4 X 72 In. 700.00
Sideboard, Hepplewhite, 5 Drawers, Walnut, 37 X 58 3/8 In. 1600.00
Sideboard, Hepplewhite, Inlaid Tambour, Mahogany, 39 X 61 In. 2035.00
Sideboard, Hepplewhite, Inlay, Spade Feet, Mahogany, 66 1/2 In. 1500.00
Sideboard, Hepplewhite, Serpentine, Mahogany, 36 X 67 In. 300.00
Sideboard, Limbert, Plate Rail Over Mirror, 58 X 48 X 19 In. 475.00
Sideboard, Mahogany, Pineapple Carving, 59 X 53 In. ....*Illus* 1100.00
Sideboard, Marble Top, Beveled Mirror, Carved Griffins 1575.00
Sideboard, Mirror, Column Supports, 3 Lazy Susan Drawers, Oak 800.00
Sideboard, Mirrored Back, Carved Walnut 6600.00
Sideboard, Oak, Paneled Back Splash, 2 Doors, C.1910, 46 X 56 In. 900.00
Sideboard, Regency, Ebony–Inlaid Mahogany, C.1800, 6 Ft. 3850.00
Sideboard, Renaissance Revival, Mirror, 6 Drawers, 2 Cupboards 825.00
Sideboard, Victorian, Marble Top, Beveled Mirror 2700.00
Sideboard, Victorian, Walnut, Mirrored Gallery, 3 Drawers, 2 Doors 825.00
Sofa, Adirondack, Weathered Finish, 72 In. 70.00
Sofa, Agee Apron, Walnut Frame, Upholstered, 77 In. 675.00
Sofa, Chesterfield, Tufted Seat, Back & Arms, Leather 1000.00
Sofa, Empire, Hairy Paw Feet, Carved Fruit, 89 In. ....*Illus* 1600.00
Sofa, Empire, Horsehair, C.1825 .... 100.00
Sofa, Empire, Mahogany Trim, 4 Claw Feet 500.00
Sofa, Empire, Paw Feet, Tapestry Upholstered, Mahogany, 80 In. 290.00
Sofa, Federal, Mahogany, Acanthus, Hairy Paw Feet, 1825, 7 Ft.4 In. 1450.00
Sofa, Federal, Mahogany, Square Back, Maple Panels, 1815, 70 In. 1800.00
Sofa, Federal, Mahogany, Upholstered Arched Back, Square, 69 In. 800.00
Sofa, Fountain Elms Pattern, Velvet Upholstery, Victorian 9350.00
Sofa, Herter Bros., C.1865, 8 Ft. 4500.00
Sofa, Lyre Frame, Ram's Horn Finials, Oak, 61 In. 175.00
Sofa, Mahogany, Outscrolled Arms, Casters, 1820, 106 In. 2200.00
Sofa, Paw Feet With Cornucopias, Flame Grain Mahogany, 100 In. 800.00
Sofa, Philadelphia, Carved Mahogany, C.1830 .... 1050.00
Sofa, Rococo, Carved Mahogany, Medallion Back, 1850 .... 550.00
Sofa, Rosalie Pattern, Belter, Rosewood 6050.00
Sofa, Tete–A–Tete, Victorian, Walnut 2100.00
Sofa, Turned Back Rail, Scrolled Arms, Mahogany, C.1830, 88 In. 250.00
Stand, 1 Drawer, Cherry, Tiger Maple 275.00
Stand, 1 Drawer, Chestnut, Turned Legs, American, 29 In. 176.00
Stand, 1 Drawer, Federal, Mahogany, Inlaid Edge, 28 In. ....*Illus* 1540.00
Stand, 1 Drawer, Federal, Poplar & Mahogany, 30 1/2 In. 400.00
Stand, 1 Drawer, Hepplewhite, 3–Board Top, Walnut, 29 X 26 In. 275.00
Stand, 1 Drawer, Hepplewhite, Tiger Maple 225.00
Stand, 1 Drawer, Massachusetts, Cherry, Maple & Mahogany Inlaid 2900.00
Stand, 1 Drawer, Mission Oak, 1 Door, Shelf, 36 X 12 In. 300.00
Stand, 1 Drawer, Old Varnish Finish, Walnut 195.00
Stand, 1 Drawer, Painted Birch & Pine, Maine, C.1810, 26 3/4 In. 4000.00
Stand, 1 Drawer, Sheraton, Breadboard Ends, Pine, 30 1/4 In. 175.00

Furniture, Table, Baroque, Carved Oak,
Griffin Base, Lions, 54 In.

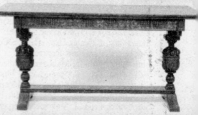

Furniture, Table, Refectory, Baroque,
Carved Oak, 66 In.

Stand, 1 Drawer, Sheraton, Drop Leaf Top, Walnut, 29 In.	350.00
Stand, 1 Drawer, Sheraton, Drop Leaf, Cherry	375.00
Stand, 1 Drawer, Sheraton, Tiger Maple, 31 X 21 In.	660.00
Stand, 2 Curly Maple Drawers, Walnut, 20 X 20 X 28 In.	300.00
Stand, 2 Drawers, Cherry & Tiger Maple, 28 X 22 In. ....*Illus*	500.00
Stand, 2 Drawers, Drop Leaf, Cherry, Mahogany Veneer, 18 X 19 In.	200.00
Stand, 2 Drawers, Drop Leaf, Cherry, Turned Legs, 19 X 21 3/4 In.	450.00
Stand, 2 Drawers, Drop Leaf, Mahogany Veneer, Cherry, 28 X 22 In.	345.00
Stand, 2 Drawers, Federal, Mahogany, Rope Turned Legs, 17 X 21 In.	300.00
Stand, 2 Drawers, Glass Knobs, Turned Legs, Walnut, 29 X 20 In.	100.00
Stand, 3 Splayed Legs, Square Top, Poplar, 18 In.	90.00
Stand, Adirondack, Canvas Covered Top, 26 1/2 In.	25.00
Stand, Bible, Iron Base, Oak Shelf	150.00
Stand, Black Crosshatched, Red Ground, 19th Century, 21 X 16 In.	3080.00
Stand, Blackamoor, Egg & Dart Border, Carved Walnut, 34 In.	1320.00
Stand, Cherry, Turned Legs, 2 Leaves, 16 X 24 In.	500.00
Stand, Dictionary, Floor Model	125.00
Stand, Dovetailed Drawer, Pullout Shelf, Cherry, 28 1/2 In.	400.00
Stand, Dragon Apron, Cloisonne Top, Rosewood, 36 1/2 In., Pair	375.00
Stand, Drawer, Ring-Turned Legs, Grained Rosewood, C.1830, 29 In.	6250.00
Stand, Drink, L.& J.G.Stickley, Original Finish, 27 In. ....*Illus*	450.00
Stand, Empire, Mahogany, Frame Veneer, Brass Ring Pulls, 29 In.	300.00
Stand, Fern, Victorian, Marble Top, Brass Mounts, 32 In.	30.00
Stand, Fern, Wicker, Square	50.00
Stand, Folio, G.Stickley, Slat Sides, 2 Shelves, 40 X 29 X 12 In.	3000.00
Stand, George III, Mahogany, Hinged Top, Scalloped Apron	357.00
Stand, Hepplewhite, Apron Banding, Drawer, Cherry, 25 3/4 In.	3100.00
Stand, Hepplewhite, Green Paint, Brass Pull, Cherry, 27 3/4 In.	500.00
Stand, Hepplewhite, Old Red, False Drawer, Cherry	375.00
Stand, Hepplewhite, Original 1-Board Oval Top, Curly Walnut	1225.00
Stand, Hepplewhite, Pencil Post Legs, Pine & Birch, 28 3/4 In.	150.00
Stand, Hepplewhite, Red Stain Base, Beaded Apron, Birch, 28 In.	190.00
Stand, Hepplewhite, Square Legs, Cherry, 26 5/8 In.	275.00
Stand, Kettle, George II, Mahogany, Dish Top, Columnar, 20 1/2 In.	4750.00
Stand, Light, Maple, Round Tapered Legs	1500.00
Stand, Little Journey, Oak, Keyed Tenons, Roycroft, 26 1/2 In.	275.00
Stand, Magazine, 5 Graduated Shelves, Cutout Sides, 46 X 20 In.	700.00
Stand, Magazine, Gustav Stickley, No.79	1980.00
Stand, Magazine, L.& J.G.Stickley, 3 Slat Sides, 4 Shelves, 42 In.	600.00
Stand, Magazine, Mission Oak, Cutout Arched Sides, 49 X 18 In.	500.00
Stand, Magazine, Mission, 3 Open Shelves, 37 X 14 X 18 In.	150.00
Stand, Maple & Pine, Vinegar Grain, Red Brown, C.1830, 30 In.	8600.00
Stand, Maple, Pine, Circular Top, Column, Rectangular Base, 22 In.	660.00
Stand, Marble Top, Claw & Ball Feet, Carved Rosewood, 32 In.	300.00
Stand, Music, Marquetry Lake Scene, Mahogany, C.1900, 4 Ft.8 In.	3025.00
Stand, Music, Tripartite Base, Ball Feet, Japan, 46 X 18 In.	400.00
Stand, Plant, Adirondack, Red Repaint, 26 1/2 In.	35.00
Stand, Plant, Cabriole Legs, Paw Feet, Mahogany, 34 3/4 In.	825.00
Stand, Plant, Cane Sides, Square Top, Corbels, 1910, 23 X 16 In.	475.00
Stand, Plant, Corner, Butterfly Design, Wire	300.00
Stand, Plant, Elephant Feet, Carved Open Work, India, 39 1/2 In.	65.00
Stand, Plant, Green Paint, 4 Graduated Curved Shelves, 3 X 4 Ft.	467.00
Stand, Plant, Marble Top, Cast & Gilded, 33 In.	90.00
Stand, Plant, Rustic Twig, Green Paint, Tripod, 29 X 15 1/2 In.	247.00
Stand, Plant, Tapering Legs, Shelf, G.Stickley, C.1905, 28 X 12 In.	70.00
Stand, Plant, Wicker, White, Side Handles	95.00
Stand, Plant, Wire, 3-Tiered	135.00
Stand, Plant, Wire, White Repaint, 36 X 31 1/2 In.	110.00
Stand, Plant, Wire, White, 3 Shelves, French, C.1870	785.00
Stand, Plant, Wooden, Old Green Paint, 1820s	625.00
Stand, Sewing, Drop Leaf, Sheraton, Mahogany, C.1800	8900.00
Stand, Shaker, 1 Drawer, Hancock, Mass., Cherry, 29 In.	2600.00
Stand, Shaker, 1 Drawer, Watervliet, Tiger Maple, C.1830, 27 In.	1600.00
Stand, Shaving, Mirror, Hepplewhite, Mahogany, 3 Drawers, 20 In.	225.00

Furniture, Table, Breakfast, Regency, Mahogany, 35 1/2 X 49 In.

Furniture, Table, Dining, Shaker, Tiger Maple, Cherry, 61 In.

Furniture, Tansu, 10 Drawers In Assorted Sizes, 45 X 39 In.

Stand, Shaving, Oak, Adjustable Mirror, 3 Legs, Compartment	265.00
Stand, Sheraton, 1 Drawer, Grain Painted	195.00
Stand, Sheraton, 2 Drawers, Cherry	265.00
Stand, Sheraton, 2 Drawers, Fluted Turned Legs	880.00
Stand, Sheraton, Cherry, Curly Maple Drawer & Legs	350.00
Stand, Sheraton, Cherrywood, Biscuit Corners, Reeded Legs	1095.00
Stand, Sheraton, Dovetailed Drawer, Curly Maple, 28 1/2 X 20 In.	875.00
Stand, Sheraton, Paint Design, Red Swirls On Black Ground	1950.00
Stand, Sheraton, Side Leaves, 3 Drawers, Writing Slide, Dated 1818	1350.00
Stand, Smoking, Oak, Marquetry, 4 Portrait Panels, 1910, 22 In.	130.00
Stand, Tripod, Regency, Mahogany, Brass, Removable Imari Charger	8800.00
Stand, Tripod, Urn & Column Standard, Mahogany, 27 In.	660.00
Stand, Turned Legs, Cherry, 29 X 19 1/4 X 19 1/4 In.	150.00
Steps, Bed, George III, Mahogany, Sliding Tambour Front	725.00
Stool Set, Soda Fountain, Brass, Oak & Porcelain, 5 Piece	170.00
Stool Set, Soda Fountain, Pedestal, Chrome, Cast Iron, 4 Piece	120.00
Stool, Backless, Armless, Keyhole Cutouts, Roycroft	3525.00
Stool, Bar, Revolving, Wooden, Iron	16.00
Stool, Cricket, Floral Needlepoint Upholstered, 12 In.	17.50
Stool, George I, Upholstered Seat, Cabriole Legs, Walnut, 23 In.	7425.00
Stool, George II, Mahogany, Rectangular Upholstered Seat	5500.00
Stool, George II, Padded Seat, Curule–Form Supports, Walnut	4125.00
Stool, Ice Cream, Wicker Seat	50.00
Stool, Joint, Mahogany, 21 X 11 X 18 In.	154.00
Stool, Louis XVII, Walnut, Upholstered, Block Turned Legs, 26 In.	1045.00
Stool, Milk, Round, Mustard Paint, 9 X 11 In.	95.00
Stool, Milk, Shaped Handle, Painted Blue, Pine, 19th Century	137.00
Stool, Oak, Joint, English, 18 1/4 X 16 1/2 X 12 1/4 In.	550.00
Stool, Oak, Stuart, Rectangular Top, Chip–Carved Foliate Border	1320.00
Stool, Organ, Spindle Back, Ball & Claw Feet	175.00
Stool, Oval Contoured Seat, 4 Legs, 29 1/4 In.	65.00
Stool, Piano, Carved Mahogany, Needlepoint Upholstery	125.00
Stool, Rococo Revival, Faux, Rosewood, Upholstered Seat, 21 In.	100.00
Stool, Semicircular Top, Turned Legs, English, Oak, 21 1/2 In.	250.00
Stool, Shaker, 2–Step, Arched Ends, Poplar, 9 X 11 3/4 In.	500.00
Stool, Shaker, 2–Step, Maple, 9 1/2 X 12 In.	400.00
Stool, Shaker, 2–Step, New Lebanon, Butternut, 20 In.	700.00
Stool, Shaker, 2–Step, Watervliet, N.Y., Pine, C.1820, 9 3/8 In.	500.00
Stool, Shaker, 3–Step, Arch Design, Butternut	9800.00
Stool, Shoe Polishing, Storage Section, 10 X 14 X 11 1/2 In.	15.00
Sugar Chest, Lift Top, 2 Upper Compartments, Cherry, 1840	4995.00
Table & Chair, Child's, Hickory, Splint Seat, 1940, 20 In., 2 Piece	250.00
Table, 1 Drawer, Oak Joined, England, C.1680, 27 In.	1200.00
Table, 1 Drawer, Traces of Green Paint, Pine, 27 3/4 X 20 In.	193.00
Table, 2 Drawers, Stuart, Oak & Elm, 28 1/2 X 67 In.	500.00
Table, 2 Tiers, Gilt–Bronze Mounts, Marquetry, C.1900, 31 In.	1320.00
Table, 5–Legged, Self–Storing Leaves, Oak	400.00
Table, American Empire, Marble Top, Walnut	550.00

Table, Art Deco, Parchment Covered, Rosewood, C.1925, 22 7/8 In.	2750.00
Table, Banquet, 2 Swing Legs, Oak, Pine Secondary Wood, 80 In.	650.00
Table, Banquet, Cherry, Rope Legs, Ogee Apron, Opens To 88 In.	900.00
Table, Banquet, Federal, Walnut, 1810, 27 3/4 In.	6200.00
Table, Banquet, George III, Mahogany, Drop Leaf, 29 In.	2900.00
Table, Baroque, Carved Oak, Griffin Base, Lions, 54 In. .... *Illus*	1550.00
Table, Boullework, Bronze Clad, Carved Legs	2860.00
Table, Brass Lion Head & Ring Handles, Walnut, 31 In.	100.00
Table, Breakfast, Regency, Mahogany, 35 1/2 X 49 In. .... *Illus*	550.00
Table, Breakfast, Regency, Mahogany, Ringed Turned Columnar, 1810	4125.00
Table, Breakfast, Regency, Yewwood Standard, Mahogany, 28 1/2 In.	2640.00
Table, Breakfast, Shallow Frieze, 3 Legs, Mahogany, 29 X 41 In.	2750.00
Table, Breakfast, Tilt Top, George III, Crossband Mahogany, 32 In.	3850.00
Table, Breakfast, William IV, Rosewood, C.1840, 4 Ft.5 In.	3080.00
Table, Card, Cherry, Inlaid, Chalk Signed, Royal B.Gould, Chester	4000.00
Table, Card, Console, American, C.1790, 28 1/2 In. .... *Illus*	1100.00
Table, Card, Federal, Demilune, Mahogany, D Top, C.1800, 33 In.	2750.00
Table, Card, Federal, Demilune, Mahogany, Satinwood, C.1800, 36 In.	5775.00
Table, Card, Federal, Inlaid Mahogany, 1790, 29 X 36 In. .... *Illus*	4675.00
Table, Card, Federal, Inlaid Mahogany, Satinwood, New Eng., C.1805	3300.00
Table, Card, Federal, Mahogany, Banded Inlay, Square Legs, 32 In.	140.00
Table, Card, Federal, Mahogany, D End, Flame Veneer, 17 X 36 In.	1100.00
Table, Card, Federal, Mahogany, D Top, Hinged Leaf, J.Baker, 1794	3575.00
Table, Card, Federal, Mahogany, Inlaid, Elliptic Front, C.1810	1000.00
Table, Card, Federal, Mahogany, Inlaid, Stringing, C.1790, 35 In.	2750.00
Table, Card, Federal, Mahogany, Serpentine, Hinged Top, 34 In.	825.00
Table, Card, Federal, Mahogany, Serpentine, McIntire, C.1830, 36 In.	2750.00
Table, Card, Flame Birch, Inlaid Mahogany, C.1805, 37 X 18 In.	7700.00
Table, Card, Geometric Stringing, Mahogany, C.1790, 35 1/2 In.	6500.00
Table, Card, George III, Inlaid Mahogany, Satinwood, C.1790, Pair	7425.00
Table, Card, Hepplewhite, Cherry, Inlay, 17 X 38 In.	1700.00
Table, Card, Hepplewhite, Drawer, Reeded Edge, Mahogany, 28 3/4 In.	450.00
Table, Card, Hepplewhite, Inlaid, Birdcage Tilt Top	850.00
Table, Card, Hepplewhite, Inlays At Edge, Skirt, Mahogany, C.1790	2350.00
Table, Card, Hepplewhite, Shaped Top, Oval & Square Inlaid Panel	2300.00
Table, Card, Hepplewhite, Tulip Inlays, Cherry, 28 3/4 X 36 In.	3250.00
Table, Card, Ovolo Corner Top, Flame Veneer, Medallions, 29 In.	1600.00
Table, Card, Rectangular Lift Top, Carved Pedestal, Mahogany	275.00
Table, Card, Sheraton, Mahogany, 6 Satinwood Panels, 1790–1810	5900.00
Table, Card, Sheraton, Mahogany, Satinwood Apron, Reeded Legs	2400.00
Table, Card, Tooled Leather Surface, Inlaid Rosewood, C.1820	3850.00
Table, Card, William IV, Plum Pudding, D Top, Leather, C.1835, Pair	5500.00
Table, Carved Frieze, 1 Shelf, Chinese, Teakwood, 31 1/2 In.	50.00
Table, Center, American Renaissance, Inlaid, Rectangular, C.1870	1750.00
Table, Center, American Rococo, Oval, Mahogany, Marble Top, 1860	550.00
Table, Center, Continental Baroque, Walnut, Molded Top, 52 In.	605.00
Table, Center, Empire, Mahogany, Gilt Bronze, Onyx Top, 1890, 32 In.	1650.00
Table, Center, Gothic Revival, Ogee Edge, Sleigh Feet, 42 In.	330.00
Table, Center, Grapes & Fruit, Marble Top, English, Walnut	1700.00
Table, Center, Iberian Baroque, Oak Chip–Carved, 3 Drawers, 81 In.	3025.00
Table, Center, Iberian Baroque, Walnut, 17th Century, 5 Ft.	4675.00
Table, Center, Inlaid Walnut, Octagon, Middle Eastern, 39 In.	1100.00
Table, Center, Louis XVI, Bronze, Marble, 19th Century, 42 In.	4675.00
Table, Center, Louis XVI, Marquetry, Gilt Bronze, Kingwood, Linke	3850.00
Table, Center, Mahogany, Circular Top, Scroll Feet, 29 1/2 In.	200.00
Table, Center, Napoleon III, Ebonized, Brass Inlaid, C.1860, 4 Ft.	1650.00
Table, Center, Pine, Red Paint, Splayed Legs, C.1800, 42 X 31 In.	1650.00
Table, Center, Rectangular Top, Onyx Panel, Carved, 1875, 42 In.	250.00
Table, Center, Regency, Flowers Above Plinth, Inlaid Rosewood	3850.00
Table, Center, Renaissance Revival, Gilt Incised Parcel Ebonized	3250.00
Table, Center, Rococo, Gilt & Painted, Turtle Top, Mother–of–Pearl	2750.00
Table, Center, Victorian, Rosewood & Parquetry Kingwood, 1850	2400.00
Table, Cherry, 18th Century .... *Illus*	9500.00
Table, Child's, Country, Drop Leaf, Walnut Legs, 24 X 28 In.	180.00

Furniture, Table, Card, Federal,
Inlaid Mahogany, 1790, 29 X 36 In.

Furniture, Table, Cherry, 18th Century

Furniture, Table, Federal, Mahogany,
3 Drawers, C.1805, 31 X 24 In.

Furniture, Table, Work, Curly Maple,
2 Drawers, 27 X 19 In.

Furniture, Table, Mission
Oak, Knockdown, Keyed
Tenons, 1910, 30 X 30 in.

Furniture, Table, Library, 1 Drawer, Ebonized,
Inlaid, C.1880

Furniture, Table, Pembroke, Mahogany,
Paw Feet, C.1800, 30 1/2 In.

Table, Child's, Red Paint, Frieze Overhang, Scrubbed Top, 28 In. 192.00
Table, Chinese Red Lacquer, Gold Design, Oriental, Low, Long 495.00
Table, Chippendale, Drop Leaf, Birch, Beaded Legs, C.1810, 44 In. 400.00
Table, Chippendale, Pembroke, Mahogany, Serpentine Leaves, C.1780 .... 1300.00
Table, Cincinnati, Dog, H.N.Wenning & Co., C.1869 .... 910.00
Table, Cocktail, Mahogany, Claw & Ball Feet, Carved Knees, Benton 625.00
Table, Coffee, Heywood–Wakefield, 16 1/2 X 19 X 36 In. 160.00
Table, Console, Adams Style, Demilune, Inlaid Bell Flowers, 62 In. 400.00
Table, Console, Central Drawer, Reeded Legs, 1820, 38 In. 2800.00
Table, Console, Drawer Over Mirrored Section, Mahogany, 40 In. 100.00
Table, Console, Eagle Form Standard, Ebonized, Marble Top, 4 Ft. 4950.00
Table, Console, Louis XV Style, Marble Top, Fruitwood, 31 1/2 In. 350.00
Table, Console, Louis XV Style, Marble Top, Oak, 38 In. 700.00
Table, Console, Marble Top, Bottom Planters, Mahogany, 48 1/4 In. 1100.00
Table, Console, Rococo Revival, Fluted Finial, Rosewood 770.00
Table, Console, String Inlay On Skirt, Mahogany, C.1800, 29 In. 8500.00
Table, Console, Victorian, Scroll Carvings, Shaped Front, 28 In. 120.00
Table, Copper Top, Limbert 880.00
Table, Cricket, Pine, Triangular Base, 3 Board Top, English, 31 In. 375.00
Table, Cutout Base, Limbert, Round, C.1905, 29 X 30 In. 1200.00
Table, Demilune, Chamfered Legs, Pegged, Blue–Green Finish 795.00
Table, Dining, 12 Leaves, Carved Oak, R.Horner, New York, C.1880 .... 6600.00
Table, Dining, 2 Pedestals, Carved Mahogany, 6 Ft.7 In. 3850.00
Table, Dining, 2 Pedestals, Rounded Corners, Mahogany, 69 1/2 In. 1100.00
Table, Dining, Black Lacquer Top, Rosewood, C.1930, 6 Ft.2 In. 5500.00
Table, Dining, Console, Cherry & Cherry Veneer, C.1800, 44 In. 600.00
Table, Dining, Duncan Phyfe, Double Pedestal, Mahogany, 116 In. 775.00
Table, Dining, Empire, Mahogany, Pedestal, Leaves, Extends 180 In. 775.00
Table, Dining, Federal, Cherry, Drop Leaf, 6 Legs, Opens 65 In. 650.00
Table, Dining, Federal, Drop Leaves, Painted Maple, C.1800 .... 4000.00
Table, Dining, Federal, Mahogany, Drop Leaves, 2 Swing Legs, 48 In. 450.00
Table, Dining, Federal, Walnut, Brown, Mo., 19th Century, 94 In. 1750.00
Table, Dining, G.Stickley, 6 Leaves, Paper Label, Round, 48 In. 2000.00
Table, Dining, George I, Rounded Corners, Walnut, 62 In. 750.00
Table, Dining, Georgian, Carved, 3 Pedestal, 4 Leaves 3100.00
Table, Dining, Hepplewhite Style, Inlaid, 5 Leaves, Mahogany 400.00
Table, Dining, Pedestal, 4 Radiating Legs, Hastings Co., 54 In. 1200.00
Table, Dining, Pullout Extension Either End, Rosewood, C.1930 .... 4950.00
Table, Dining, Queen Anne, Drop Leaf, Maple, C.1760, 50 In. 7500.00
Table, Dining, Shaker, Tiger Maple, Cherry, 61 In. ....*Illus* 8600.00
Table, Dining, Victorian, Mahogany, 1870–80, 10 Leaves 1050.00
Table, Dining, William & Mary, Gateleg, D Shaped Leaves, 1720–60 .... 3575.00
Table, Dining, William IV, 2 Pedestal, Mahogany, C.1840, 110 In. 1800.00
Table, Dough, Walnut, Planked Top, New Eng., 19th Century, 60 In. 880.00
Table, Dressing, Box Drawer, Painted Mustard Yellow, 30 X 35 In. 1800.00
Table, Dressing, Brass Trim, Inlaid, 29 X 15 X 22 In. 125.00
Table, Dressing, Federal, 1 Drawer, Painted, C.1820, 30 1/2 In. 1900.00
Table, Dressing, Fruitwood Marquetry, Walnut, C.1900, 5 Ft.1 In. 4125.00
Table, Dressing, George I, Walnut, 3 Drawers, Molded Edge, 29 In. 935.00
Table, Dressing, George III, English Satinwood, Fitted, 1910 .... 8250.00
Table, Dressing, Jacobean Style, Oak, 3 Drawers, Spool Legs, 31 In. 100.00
Table, Dressing, Kneehole, George I, Burl Walnut, C.1720, 29 In. 4950.00
Table, Dressing, Man's, Hinged Top, Inside Mirror, Mahogany, 36 In. 935.00
Table, Dressing, Man's, Mirror, Black Japanned, 5 Ft.8 In. 1045.00
Table, Dressing, Victorian, Mahogany, Pedestal Base, 34 X 53 In. 100.00
Table, Dressing, White Serpentine Marble Top, Walnut, 35 In. 150.00
Table, Drop Leaf, Acanthus Carved Shaft, Mahogany, 50 In. 1300.00
Table, Drop Leaf, Brass Mounted, Mahogany, C.1790, 28 In. 770.00
Table, Drop Leaf, Butterfly, Maple, Ring Turned Legs, 35 In. 385.00
Table, Drop Leaf, Cherry, 27 1/2 X 37 In. 150.00
Table, Drop Leaf, Child's, Country, Walnut, 24 X 28 X 21 In. 180.00
Table, Drop Leaf, Country, Walnut, 29 X 43 X 50 In. 200.00
Table, Drop Leaf, Curly Maple Top & Aprons, 29 1/2 In. 600.00
Table, Drop Leaf, Empire Style, 4 Carved Paw Feet, 29 X 46 In. 290.00

Table, Drop Leaf, Federal, Mahogany, Rounded Corners, 1820, 35 In.	605.00
Table, Drop Leaf, Federal, Swing Legs, Cherry, 48 1/2 X 48 In.	400.00
Table, Drop Leaf, Gateleg, Claw & Ball Feet, Walnut, 4 Ft.4 In.	2750.00
Table, Drop Leaf, Gateleg, William III, Oval, Oak, 5 Ft.5 In.	3300.00
Table, Drop Leaf, Mortised & Pinned Apron, Oak, 28 3/4 X 48 In.	100.00
Table, Drop Leaf, P.H.Powers, Hydetown, Pa., Cherry, 29 In.	500.00
Table, Drop Leaf, Pine, Rounded Corners, 19th Century, 40 In.	275.00
Table, Drop Leaf, Queen Anne, D Shaped Ends, Cabriole Legs, 5 Ft.	2750.00
Table, Drop Leaf, Swing Legs, Beaded Apron, Maple, 28 X 44 3/4 In.	1500.00
Table, Drop Leaf, Swing Legs, Leaves, Maple, 28 3/4 X 46 In.	600.00
Table, Drum, George III, Mahogany, Leather Inset, 4 False Drawers	7150.00
Table, Eagle Console, Gilded Wood, 48 In.Wingspan	825.00
Table, English Baroque, Triple Carved Frieze, Oak, 29 1/4 In.	935.00
Table, Federal, Mahogany, 3 Drawers, C.1805, 31 X 24 In. ....*Illus*	6325.00
Table, Federal, Painted Green, 1 Side Drawer, 29 X 27 In.	302.00
Table, Flip Top, Drawer, Biedermeier, Walnut	375.00
Table, Folding Base, Removable Top, Relief Carved, 24 In.	75.00
Table, Fruit, Foliage, Bats, Soapstone Inset, Chinese, Teak, 31 In.	145.00
Table, G.Stickley, Cut Corners, Lower Shelf, Decal, 1905–06, 30 In.	950.00
Table, G.Stickley, Leather Top, Hexagonal, Radiating Stretcher	7000.00
Table, G.Stickley, Lower Shelf, C.1910, 29 In.	250.00
Table, G.Stickley, Round Leather Top, Cross Stretchers, 36 In.	2100.00
Table, G.Stickley, Square, 1905, 29 In.	950.00
Table, G.Stickley, Trestle Base, Keyed Tenon Lower Shelf, 48 In.	700.00
Table, Galle, 2 Tiers, Commemorative Message, Mahogany, 30 In.	2500.00
Table, Galle, Winter Scene, Polar Bears of Inlay Woods, 29 In.	2000.00
Table, Game, Baize–Lined Playing Surface, Mahogany, C.1760	6050.00
Table, Game, Demilune, Inlaid Mahogany, C.1790, 29 X 35 In.	3960.00
Table, Game, Ebony Inlaid Mahogany, C.1810, 29 X 36 In.	5500.00
Table, Game, Edwardian, Marquetry, Interior Board, Inlaid, C.1890	225.00
Table, Game, George III, Painted & Inlaid Satinwood, 29 In.	5390.00
Table, Game, George III, Rosewood, Sliding Panel, C.1810	3300.00
Table, Game, Hepplewhite, Shaped Top, Oval & Square Apron	2300.00
Table, Game, Hinged Lid, Back Drawer, Walnut, C.1800, 45 1/2 In.	550.00
Table, Game, Hinged Top, Carved Knees, Mahogany, C.1770, 29 In.	2750.00
Table, Game, Inlaid Leather, Gold Scrolls, French	700.00
Table, Game, Louis XVI, Tulipwood & Marquetry, 19th Century	400.00
Table, Game, Mahogany, Foldover, Pedestal Base, Ball Feet, 1845	150.00
Table, Game, Mother–of–Pearl Inlay, 1 Drawer, Shelf, French	1100.00
Table, Game, Napoleon III, Bronze Mounts, Sevres Plaque Inset	770.00
Table, Game, Queen Anne, Concertina, Inlaid Burl Walnut, 32 In.	7150.00
Table, Game, Regency, Inlaid Rosewood, C.1820, 28 1/2 X 36 In.	2860.00
Table, Game, Regency, Rosewood, Leather Hinged Top, 36 In.	9900.00
Table, Game, Sheraton, Satinwood Apron, Mahogany	2400.00
Table, Game, Victorian, Inlaid Top, Rosewood	1595.00
Table, Gateleg, Curly Maple, Turned Legs, Feet & Stretcher, 43 In.	1500.00
Table, Gateleg, Drop Leaf, Maple, Gunstock Quality Curl Legs	425.00
Table, Gateleg, Stuart, Demilune, Oak, 17th Century, 35 X 16 In.	3575.00
Table, Gateleg, William & Mary, Walnut, Maple, New England, 41 In.	800.00
Table, George II Style, Tilt Top, Tripod, Mahogany, 28 In.	3300.00
Table, George II, Molded Tripod Legs, Walnut, 19th Century, 25 In.	495.00
Table, George III, Demilune, Inlaid Mahogany, 7 Ft.6 In.	1550.00
Table, George III, Drawer, Square Tapered Legs, Oak, 27 1/2 In.	200.00
Table, George III, Serpentine, Tapering Square Legs	495.00
Table, George III, Tambour Front, Doors, 1 Drawer, Mahogany, 31 In.	2640.00
Table, George III, Tilt Top, Tripod Pad Feet, Mahogany, 28 In.	275.00
Table, George III, Tilt Top, Waved Gallery, Mahogany, 28 1/2 In.	3750.00
Table, George III, Tripod, Fretwork Gallery, Mahogany, 28 In.	4625.00
Table, Gothic Style, Pedestal, Walnut, Extends To 16 Ft.	1100.00
Table, Hardwood, Marble Top, Paw Feet, Chinese, 19 In.	225.00
Table, Harvest, Canadian Pine, Red Paint, Scrubbed Top, 82 In.	1200.00
Table, Harvest, Drop Leaf, Pine, 1 Drawer With Original Pull	797.00
Table, Harvest, New England, Birch	750.00
Table, Harvest, Painted Salmon Base, Maple & Pine, 72 In.	2800.00

Table, Hepplewhite, Drop Leaf, Birch, Red Stain, 42 In. 425.00
Table, Hepplewhite, Nailed Mortises, Pine, 29 X 37 1/4 In. 175.00
Table, Hepplewhite, Pembroke, Mahogany, 1 Drawer, Ovolo Corners 450.00
Table, Hepplewhite, Swing Leg, Drop Leaf 990.00
Table, Hutch, Green Paint, Rectangular Plank Seat, 29 X 47 In. 1450.00
Table, Hutch, Red Paint, 3–Board Top, Pa., 19th Century, 60 In. 885.00
Table, Hutch, Red Paint, 4–Board Circular Scrubbed Top, 56 In. 1450.00
Table, Hutch, Round Lift Top For Seat, Red, New England 2500.00
Table, Hutch, Traces of Red, Handmade, 2–Board Top, 38 1/2 In. 300.00
Table, Hutch, William & Mary, Cherry & Pine, C.1750, 44 In. 6400.00
Table, Iberian Baroque, Walnut, Chip–Carved Drawers, 37 In. 2200.00
Table, Inlaid Sunburst Top, Brass Paw Feet, Mahogany, 34 In. 165.00
Table, Italian Renaissance, Drawer Each End, Walnut, 52 1/4 In. 550.00
Table, Kitchen, Drop Leaf, 2 Boards, Oak 210.00
Table, L.& J.G.Stickley, Lower Shelf, Cross Stretcher, 30 In. 550.00
Table, L.& J.G.Stickley, Trestle 750.00
Table, Lamp, Eastlake, Brown Marble Top 145.00
Table, Lamp, Oak, 2 Tiers, Glass Ball & Claw Feet, Square 105.00
Table, Leather Backgammon & Chessboard, Holly & Ebony, 1790 .... 5500.00
Table, Library, 1 Drawer, Ebonized, Inlaid, C.1880 ....*Illus* 5750.00
Table, Library, Aesthetic Movement, Drawer, Ebonized, Inlaid, 1880 .... 6325.00
Table, Library, Ebonized & Inlaid, American, New York, 1880 .... 5750.00
Table, Library, G.Stickley, 1907, 30 X 36 In. 1550.00
Table, Library, G.Stickley, 2 Drawers, Medial Shelf, 1904, 48 In. 1400.00
Table, Library, G.Stickley, Leather Top, Oak, Round, 48 In. 3800.00
Table, Library, Indiana Desk Co., 72 X 34 In. 125.00
Table, Library, Limbert, 1 Drawer, Lower Shelf, 42 X 29 X 30 In. 500.00
Table, Library, Oak, 3 Drawers, Reverse Faux Drawers, 1909, 58 In. 2600.00
Table, Library, Oak, Bookshelf Sides, Drop Down Doors, Desk 350.00
Table, Library, Oak, Lyre Pedestals 80.00
Table, Library, Oak, Pullout Shelf & Inkwell, Signed Limbert 180.00
Table, Library, Octagonal, 4 Drawers, Inlaid Mahogany, 46 In. 5500.00
Table, Library, Regency, Rosewood, Geometric Frieze, 1815, 37 In. 825.00
Table, Library, Renaissance Revival, Walnut, 2 Drawers 1045.00
Table, Library, Roycroft, Round 925.00
Table, Library, Stripped Walnut, Trestle Base, C.1900, 4 Ft. 358.00
Table, Limbert, Cross Stretcher, On Tapering Foot, C.1910, 24 In. 475.00
Table, Limbert, Cutout Sides, Oval, C.1907, 36 In. 2200.00
Table, Limbert, Octagonal 2200.00
Table, Limbert, Plate Rail, 2 Drawers, 2 Shelves, 43 X 40 In. 600.00
Table, Lobed Edge, Marble Inset, Mahogany & Beech, C.1900, 26 In. 3300.00
Table, Louis XV, Parquetry Inlaid 825.00
Table, Low, Chinese, Hardwood, Square, Marble Above, 18 In. 250.00
Table, Marble Top, Carved Quadripod Base, Walnut, 28 X 22 In. 100.00
Table, Mermaid, Conch Border, R.Cahoon, Painted, Pedestal, Round 2750.00
Table, Mission Oak, Knockdown, Keyed Tenons, 1910, 30 X 30 In. ....*Illus* 225.00
Table, Mission Oak, Leather, Copper Tacks, Tenoned Shelf, 26 In. 150.00
Table, Nesting, Hepplewhite, Mahogany Inlay, Set of 4 .... 175.00
Table, Onyx Top, Matching Inserts In Base Shelf, Gilt, 32 In. 95.00
Table, Parlor, Meeks, Victorian 4200.00
Table, Parlor, Roux, Victorian 1750.00
Table, Pembroke, Carved Legs, Brass Casters, Cherry, 28 3/4 In. 450.00
Table, Pembroke, Cherry, 10 In.Leaves, Drawer, Square Legs, 37 In. 825.00
Table, Pembroke, Crossbanded Top, Drawers, Mahogany, 28 In. 2475.00
Table, Pembroke, Drop Leaf Top, Mahogany, 28 3/4 In. 295.00
Table, Pembroke, Drop Leaf, Birch, 14 1/2 X 36 X 28 1/2 In. 550.00
Table, Pembroke, Drop Leaf, Single Drawer 750.00
Table, Pembroke, Federal, Mahogany, String Inlaid, C.1810, 38 In. 300.00
Table, Pembroke, Frieze Drawer, Shaped Platform, Mahogany, C.1780 .... 3025.00
Table, Pembroke, George III, Inlaid Mahogany, 3 Shaped Leaves 3740.00
Table, Pembroke, George III, Inlaid Mahogany, D End, 1 Drawer 9900.00
Table, Pembroke, George III, Mahogany, 1 Drawer, Pierced Gallery 1100.00
Table, Pembroke, George III, Mahogany, Square Legs, Casters, 28 In. 990.00
Table, Pembroke, George III, Oval, Inlaid Satinwood, C.1790 .... 4400.00

Table, Pembroke, Hepplewhite, Drop Leaves, 1 Drawer 300.00
Table, Pembroke, Hepplewhite, Pine Top, Red Paint, 13 In.Leaves 900.00
Table, Pembroke, Hepplewhite, Pine, 1 Board, Apron, 8 In.Leaves 325.00
Table, Pembroke, Mahogany, Paw Feet, C.1800, 30 1/2 In. ....*Illus* 1300.00
Table, Pembroke, Marquetry Inlaid Satinwood, 28 X 44 In. 4400.00
Table, Pembroke, New Eng., Tapered Hepplewhite Legs, 1790–1810 .... 650.00
Table, Pembroke, Pine, Leaves, Red Stained, 18 X 36 X 28 In. 300.00
Table, Pembroke, Pine, Leaves, Walnut Legs, 27 1/2 In. 225.00
Table, Pier, American Rococo, Carved Rosewood, Marble Top, 1850 .... 7150.00
Table, Pier, Bamboo, Painted 5830.00
Table, Pier, Scrolled Mahogany, Black, Tan, Gray Marble, 1835 .... 1000.00
Table, Pool, Brunswick Regina, Rosewood, Mahogany, 1920, 5 X 10 Ft. 5500.00
Table, Queen Anne, Drop Leaf, Duck Feet, Mahogany, 27 1/2 In. 6000.00
Table, Queen Anne, Drop Leaf, Hinged Oval Top, 18th Century 1760.00
Table, Queen Anne, Walnut, 1 Drawer, Box Stretcher, C.1750 .... 6600.00
Table, Queen Anne, Walnut, Shaped Top, Cabriole Legs, 23 X 16 In. 200.00
Table, Refectory, Baroque, Carved Oak, 66 In. ....*Illus* 325.00
Table, Refectory, English Baroque, Oak, 7 Ft.7 In. 2475.00
Table, Refectory, Italian Baroque, Walnut, Frieze, 2 Drawer, 79 In. 6325.00
Table, Regency, Bird's–Eye Maple, Rosewood, 6 Legs, C.1810 .... 5500.00
Table, Rounded Drop Leaves, Swing Legs, Mahogany, 27 X 36 1/2 In. 9000.00
Table, Sawbuck, Pine, 2–Board Top, 28 X 51 In. 400.00
Table, Sawbuck, Pine, 6 Ft. 1600.00
Table, Semicircular, 3 Legs, Pine & Poplar, 31 X 36 1/4 In. 100.00
Table, Serving, Federal, Mahogany, 3 Drawers, Reeded Legs, C.1820 .... 2750.00
Table, Serving, George III, Inlaid Mahogany, 4 Drawers, 8 Ft. 7700.00
Table, Settle, Folds Into Chair, Pine, 28 1/4 X 48 X 31 In. 300.00
Table, Sewing, Federal, Inlaid Curly Maple, 2 Drawers, C.1805 .... 7150.00
Table, Sewing, Regency Inlaid, Mahogany, 28 1/2 X 20 In. 750.00
Table, Shaker, Apple Sorting, Putty Gray, Pine & Chestnut, 5 Ft. 700.00
Table, Shaker, Cherry, Red Stain, Drawer, Tapered Square Legs 1210.00
Table, Shaker, Drop Leaf, Maple Top, Birch Legs, Alfred, Me., 1820 .... 1200.00
Table, Shaker, Green Over Red Paint, Maine, Poplar, Miniature 200.00
Table, Shaker, Pine & Birch, Red Stain, Canterbury, C.1820, 50 In. 1500.00
Table, Shaker, Pine, Butternut, Partial Red Paint, 35 In. 825.00
Table, Shaker, Red Paint, Drawer, Hancock, Ma., Cherry, Pine, 1830 .... 7750.00
Table, Shaker, Seed Sorting, Pleasant Hill, C.1840, 30 1/4 In. 1150.00
Table, Shaker, Sewing, 2 Drawers, Pine, Birch, Alfred, Me., 53 In. 3400.00
Table, Shaker, Sewing, Canterbury, N.H., Tiger Maple, Birch, C.1830 .... 8500.00
Table, Shaker, Work, 1 Drawer, Pine, Maple, Canterbury, N.H., C.1810 .... 700.00
Table, Shaker, Work, Kitchen, Pine & Birch, C.1840, 29 X 42 In. 1200.00
Table, Shaker, Work, Pine & Maple, Groveland, N.Y., 1840, 42 1/4 In. 550.00

Furniture, Table, Work, Crossbanded
Mahogany, C.1805, 28 3/4 In.

Furniture, Umbrella
Stand, Walnut

Furniture, Vargueno, On Stand,
Inlaid, Zigzag Design, 59 In.

Table, Sheraton, Drop Leaf, Curly Maple, Cherry, Refinished, 36 In.	525.00
Table, Sheraton, Drop Leaf, Cut Corners, Cherry, 28 3/4 X 44 In.	175.00
Table, Sheraton, Pembroke, Drop Leaf, Cherry, Red Finish, Leaves	850.00
Table, Snooker, Brunswick, 1912, 5 X 10 Ft.	6000.00
Table, Snooker, Mahogany	5900.00
Table, Sofa, False Drawers, Inlaid Mahogany, 4 Ft.10 1/2 In.	8800.00
Table, Sofa, George III, Mahogany, D Ends, 2 Drawers, 4 1/2 Ft.	1980.00
Table, Sofa, Regency, Inlaid Mahogany, C.1825, 4 Ft.5 In.	4300.00
Table, Sofa, Regency, Rosewood, Inlaid Brass, Leaves, 1815, 35 In.	4400.00
Table, Square Pedestal, Claw Feet, Oak, Round	280.00
Table, Square Top Over Open Section, Walnut, 29 In.	400.00
Table, Surrounding Ivory Medallions, Mahogany, C.1930, 29 3/8 In.	3300.00
Table, Swing Leg, Drop Leaf, Walnut, 6 Legs, Leaves, 24 X 45 In.	295.00
Table, Swing Leg, Tiger Maple	850.00
Table, Swivel Top, Eastlake Design, Oak, 42 In.	1750.00
Table, Tailor's, Shaker, Plank Top, 10 Drawers, X Legs, 61 X 31 In.	250.00
Table, Tavern, 2 Drawers, Walnut, Pa., Duck Feet, 54 X 29 In.	2420.00
Table, Tavern, Baluster Legs, English, Oak, 21 X 36 In.	100.00
Table, Tavern, Chippendale, Pine, Maple, Breadboard Ends, C.1780	550.00
Table, Tavern, Federal, Square Legs, Red Paint, New England, 37 In.	330.00
Table, Tavern, Maple, Scrubbed 2–Board Top, Breadboard Ends	2700.00
Table, Tavern, Pine, Red & Black Flame Graining, Stencil, 29 In.	1000.00
Table, Tavern, Queen Anne, Painted Maple, C.1765, 31 X 25 In.	7150.00
Table, Tavern, Queen Anne, Pine, Red Repaint, 25 X 42 X 27 In.	1400.00
Table, Tavern, Queen Anne, Refinished Maple, Oval Top, 26 X 40 In.	500.00
Table, Tavern, Queen Anne, Stippled Brown Over Mustard, C.1740	8500.00
Table, Tavern, Square Apron, 3–Board Top, Pine, 31 X 34 In.	275.00
Table, Tavern, William & Mary, Green Paint, Ball Feet, Oval, 34 In.	990.00
Table, Tavern, William & Mary, Philadelphia, 18th Century	7425.00
Table, Tavern, William & Mary, Pine & Maple, 1750, 25 In.	2500.00
Table, Tea, Chippendale, Birch, Serpentine Tilt Top, C.1780, 47 In.	800.00
Table, Tea, Chippendale, Mahogany, Pad Feet, 1780, 28 In.	1300.00
Table, Tea, Chippendale, Mahogany, Rectangular Dished Top, C.1770	3500.00
Table, Tea, Chippendale, Mahogany, Vasiform Standard, 1780, 35 In.	2100.00
Table, Tea, L.& J.G.Stickley, Lower Shelf Cross Stretcher, 24 In.	1000.00
Table, Tea, Mahogany, Tilt Top, Baluster, 28 1/2 X 31 1/4 In.	850.00
Table, Tea, Mahogany, Vase Turned Pedestal, Duck Feet, 28 X 40 In.	418.00
Table, Tea, Oak, Arched Skirt, Bowed Side Stretchers, 1910, 20 In.	225.00
Table, Tea, Oval Top, Red Finish, 28 1/2 X 21 X 26 In.	90.00
Table, Tea, Queen Anne, Maple, Tray Top, Shaped Skirt, 28 X 20 In.	7150.00
Table, Tea, Queen Anne, Painted Oak & Maple, C.1780, 33 1/2 In.	6600.00
Table, Tea, Queen Anne, Slate Top	4000.00
Table, Tea, Tilt Top, American, Mahogany, C.1780, 27 X 31 In.	1200.00
Table, Tea, Tilt Top, Chippendale, Mahogany, 1780, 27 In.	1000.00
Table, Tea, Tilt Top, Dutch, Mahogany & Marquetry, 27 5/8 In.	700.00
Table, Tea, Tilt Top, Vase Pedestal, Duck Feet, Mahogany, 28 In.	341.00
Table, Tea, Varnished, Peg Construction, English, 18th Century	1200.00
Table, Tilt Top, Chippendale, Mahogany, Tripod Base, 25 X 28 In.	700.00
Table, Tilt Top, Corner, Mahogany, English, C.1780	1100.00
Table, Tilt Top, George II, Piecrust Top, Mahogany, 29 In.	350.00
Table, Tilt Top, George III, Dished Top, Walnut, C.1770, 33 1/2 In.	450.00
Table, Tilt Top, George III, Mahogany, 3 Cabriole Legs, Snake Feet	1045.00
Table, Tilt Top, George III, Oak & Mahogany, C.1760, 26 In.	495.00
Table, Tilt Top, Mahogany, English, 25 X 29 1/2 In.	145.00
Table, Tilt Top, Mother–of–Pearl Inlaid & Painted, American	330.00
Table, Tilt Top, Papier–Mache	450.00
Table, Tilt Top, Snake Feet, Dish Top, Walnut, 19th Century, 28 In.	450.00
Table, Tilt Top, Walnut, 28 In.	200.00
Table, Tray, Drawer, Medial Shelf, Grain Painted, Maple, C.1820	3250.00
Table, Trestle, Italian Baroque, Walnut, Squared Supports, 6 Ft.	1760.00
Table, Trestle, Victorian Pine, Rectangular Top, 90 In.	500.00
Table, Twist–Fluted Standard, Tripod, Mahogany, 26 1/2 In.	3960.00
Table, Typing, 2 Drawers, Lyre–Style Side Legs, Collapses	195.00
Table, Victorian, 1 Drawer, Burled Walnut Panels, C.1875, 30 In.	150.00

Table, Wedding Couple Design, Removable Legs, Galle, 24 X 21 In. 1500.00
Table, Wicker, White, Bottom Shelf, Round 150.00
Table, Windsor, Birch, Natural, Chamfered, 17 X 26 In. 150.00
Table, Windsor, Red Paint, Breadboard Sides, C.1800, 24 X 18 In. 750.00
Table, Work, 2 Drawers, Original Brass Pulls, Painted, C.1825 .... 1000.00
Table, Work, 2 Drawers, Vinegar Painted Design, C.1830, 30 In. 2000.00
Table, Work, 2-Board Top, Pine, 28 3/4 X 26 1/2 X 48 In. 300.00
Table, Work, 3 Drawers, Removable Top, Walnut, 30 X 35 X 70 In. 500.00
Table, Work, 3-Board Scrubbed Top, 1 Drawer, Green Paint, 37 In. 825.00
Table, Work, 4-Board Top, Poplar, 30 3/4 X 95 1/2 In. 235.00
Table, Work, American, Mahogany, Drop Leaf, Acanthus Base, 1825 .... 500.00
Table, Work, Classical, Mahogany, Gilt Metal, 2 Drawers, 29 In. 5225.00
Table, Work, Crossbanded Mahogany, C.1805, 28 3/4 In. ....*Illus* 9900.00
Table, Work, Curly Maple, 2 Drawers, 27 X 19 In. ....*Illus* 300.00
Table, Work, Dovetailed Drawer Each End, Pine, 28 3/4 In. 475.00
Table, Work, Drawer, Removable Basket, Brass, Inlaid Rosewood, 1815 .... 2200.00
Table, Work, Drop Leaf, 2 Drawers, Sheraton, 17 X 16 X 8 1/2 In. 385.00
Table, Work, Drop Leaf, Mahogany & Mahogany Veneer, C.1820 .... 2600.00
Table, Work, Drop Leaf, Maple, 1 Drawer, American, 29 X 18 In. 308.00
Table, Work, Dutch, Inlaid Mahogany, Satinwood, 28 3/4 In. 950.00
Table, Work, Federal, 1 Drawer, Inlaid Legs, C.1800, Cherry, 28 In. 3500.00
Table, Work, Federal, Mahogany & Veneer, Storage Box, 1820 .... 800.00
Table, Work, Federal, Mahogany, 2 Drawers, Ball Feet, 1800, 22 In. 880.00
Table, Work, Federal, Mahogany, Bird's-Eye, C.1815, 29 X 19 In. 4675.00
Table, Work, Federal, Mahogany, Elliptical Top, Baize Lined, C.1805 .... 5775.00
Table, Work, Fitted Sliding Tray & Mirror, Carved Rosewood 2200.00
Table, Work, Hepplewhite, 1 Drawer, Pine, 29 1/2 X 43 In. 325.00
Table, Work, Hepplewhite, Poplar, Scrubbed Finish 375.00
Table, Work, Hepplewhite, Sawn Oak Top, Poplar, 29 3/4 X 62 In. 150.00
Table, Work, Hinged Top, Fitted Interior, Chinese Lacquer, 29 In. 2300.00
Table, Work, Inlaid Brass, Bronze Mounted Rosewood, 29 In. 7700.00
Table, Work, Mother-of-Pearl, Inlaid Black Lacquer, Papier-Mache 3100.00
Table, Work, Pine Top, Walnut, Ball Shaped Drawer Knobs, 6 Ft. 2000.00
Table, Work, Pine, Brown Paint, 1-Board Removable Top, 68 In. 375.00
Table, Work, Pine, Green Paint, 2-Board Scrubbed Top, 40 1/2 In. 385.00
Table, Work, Pine, Old Yellow, Apron, 2-Board Top, 27 X 39 X 30 In. 415.00
Table, Work, Poplar Base, Pine Top, Red & Gray Paint, 29 1/2 In. 500.00
Table, Work, Regency, Mahogany, Brass Inlaid, 1810, 32 X 22 In. 5500.00
Table, Work, Regency, Mahogany, D Leaves, 1 Shelf, C.1815, 13 In. 1210.00
Table, Work, Sheraton, 2 Drawers, Rope Turned Legs, 16 X 17 In. 385.00
Table, Work, String-Inlaid Edge, Cherry, New England, C.1800 .... 3500.00
Table, Work, William IV, 2 Drawers, Rosewood, D Flaps, 1815, 22 In. 995.00
Table, Writing, Chippendale, Red Paint, S.C., 1865, 35 In. 880.00
Table, Writing, George III, Mahogany, Tool Leather Top, 4 Ft. 9900.00
Table, Writing, Inlaid Crossbanded Satinwood, 27 1/2 In. 6600.00
Table, Writing, Lady's, Painted Satinwood, C.1775, 42 1/2 In. 7150.00
Table, Writing, Regency, 4 Drawers, Inlaid Mahogany, 4 Ft. 7700.00
Table, Writing, William IV, Rosewood, Leather, 1840, 4 Ft.6 In. 6050.00
Tabouret, G.Stickley, Arched Cross Stretchers, 1907, 16 X 14 In. 375.00
Tabouret, G.Stickley, Oak, Arched Cross Stretchers, 1905, 26 In. 1800.00
Tabouret, Limbert, Cutout 2530.00
Tansu, 10 Drawers In Assorted Sizes, 45 X 39 In. ....*Illus* 500.00
Tea Cart, Victorian, 3 Shelves, Wicker & Oak, 32 X 36 In. 200.00
Teble, Pembroke, Mahogany, Inlaid Tapered Legs, Oval Top 8000.00
Tray, Butler's, Folding Stand, Pierced Handles, Mahogany, 33 In. 1100.00
Tray, Butler's, Mahogany, Dovetailed, Added Base, 17 X 31 X 21 In. 165.00
Tray, Butler's, Stand With Wheels, Folding Supports, Mahogany 2420.00
Tray, Galle, Marquetry, Irises, Fruitwood, Signed, 20 X 13 In. 1200.00
Umbrella Stand, Ceramic, Leaves, Roses, Arts & Crafts, 27 In. 700.00
Umbrella Stand, Claw Feet, Oak 100.00
Umbrella Stand, G.Stickley, 4 Tapering Posts, C.1912, 33 X 11 In. 350.00
Umbrella Stand, Hammered Brass, Lion Head Handles, 23 In. 65.00
Umbrella Stand, Oak, Turned Legs, Rectangular Tray, 26 In. 20.00
Umbrella Stand, Porcelain, Multicolored Enamels, 24 1/2 In. 250.00

Umbrella Stand, Walnut ....*Illus*   650.00
Urn Stand, George III Style, Marquetry Top, Fruitwood, 31 In. 2310.00
Urn, Cast Iron, John Edgar, Pair 1500.00
Urn, Knife, Shield–Shaped Body, Inlaid Mahogany, C.1900, 25 In. 495.00
Vanity, Porcelain Plaques, Cherubs At Play, French, 30 X 14 In. 550.00
Vargueno, On Stand, Inlaid, Zigzag Design, 59 In. ....*Illus*   225.00
Vitrine, Line Inlay, Beveled Glass On All Sides, 18 X 30 In. 200.00
Vitrine, Lined Lower Section, Glass Sides, Mahogany, 23 1/4 In. 700.00
Vitrine, Louis XV, Mahogany Gilt Bronze, 3 Glazed Doors, 6 Ft. 2475.00
Vitrine, Louis XVI, Mahogany, Gilt Bronze, Marble, 2 Doors, 5 Ft. 4950.00
Vitrine, Napoleon III, Ormolu, Porcelain Mounted, Mahogany, 58 In. 2200.00
Wardrobe, 2 Inlaid Doors, 4 Drawers, Fruitwood, 82 X 74 In. 950.00
Wardrobe, American Pine, Murky Green Paint, C.1830 ....   3495.00
Wardrobe, G.Stickley, 2 Doors, 8 Narrow Drawers, 1904–06, 60 In. 3100.00
Wardrobe, Grain Painted, 2 Top Doors, Long Drawer, C.1880, 69 In. 525.00
Wardrobe, Lower Drawer, Inside Shelves, Maple, 6 Ft.7 1/2 In. 715.00
Wardrobe, Oak, 2 Side–By–Side Drawers Below, Crown, 8 Ft. 725.00
Wardrobe, Paneled Door, Inside Swivel Hooks, Poplar, 69 1/2 In. 250.00
Wardrobe, Paneled Doors, Shelf, Iron Hooks, Butternut, 80 1/4 In. 575.00
Wardrobe, Pine, Dark Finish, Tongue & Groove Doors, Brown, 71 In. 250.00
Wardrobe, Schrank, Pine, Raised Panels 1700.00
Wardrobe, Walnut, Scalloped Apron, Bracket Feet, Mo., 1850, 90 In. 1550.00
Wardrobe, William IV, Carved, Enclosed Shelves 750.00
Washstand, Base Shelf, 1 Drawer, Curly Maple, 32 1/4 X 19 In. 650.00
Washstand, Classical Revival, Mahogany, 3 Drawers, 1815 ....*Illus*   3600.00
Washstand, George III, 3 Wells, False Drawer Over Door, 32 In. 412.00
Washstand, Mahogany, Bird's–Eye Maple Drawer Front, C.1815 ....   3600.00
Washstand, Marble Top, Drawer Over 2 Doors, Casters, 33 X 17 In. 275.00
Washstand, Oak, Serpentine Drawer, Over 2 Doors 75.00
Washstand, Pine, Gray Paint Over Brown, 2–Board Top, Gallery 300.00
Washstand, Pink, Gray Paint, 1 Drawer, 1890s 235.00
Washstand, Scrolled Front Apron, Burl Veneer Drawer, Mahogany 2950.00
Washstand, Shaker, 1 Drawer, Pine, New Lebanon, N.Y., 1810, 33 In. 2300.00
Washstand, Shaker, Bowl Cut Out, Pine, Enfield, N.H., 1850, 31 In. 300.00
Washstand, Shaker, Gallery, Mt.Lebanon, C.1830, 32 X 31 In. 2200.00
Washstand, Sheraton, Mahogany, Carved Acanthus, 30 In. ....*Illus*   700.00
Washstand, Sheraton, Tiger Maple, C.1800, 36 X 20 In. ....*Illus*   700.00
Washstand, Stenciling, Drawer, Vinegar Painted, C.1825, 37 1/2 In. 375.00
Washstand, Towel Bar, Mirror, Oak, 3 Drawers, 1 Door 310.00
Washstand, Victorian, Marble, Walnut, 2 Doors, 32 X 29 X 16 In. 240.00
Washstand, Walnut, Marble Top & Splash, Original Drawer Pulls 490.00
Washstand, Walnut, Serpentine Base Shelf, Gallery, 1 Drawer 250.00
Whatnot, 5 Shaped Shelves, Spool Turned Supports, 58 In. 135.00
Window Seat, Black Japanned, Grospoint & Petitpoint Pad 665.00
Window Seat, Needlepoint Upholstery, Mahogany, 43 In. 3950.00
Wine Cooler, Regency, Inlaid Mahogany, Casters, 24 X 25 X 19 In. 2090.00
Workstand, Shaker, 1 Drawer, Watervliet, C.1870, Pine, 27 1/2 In. 550.00
Workstand, Shaker, Corner, 1/2–Gallery, Pine, Birch, Poplar, 24 In. 3000.00
Workstand, Shaker, Pine Top, Birch Legs, Red, 28 X 19 In. 550.00
Writing Stand, 3 Bird's–Eye Maple Veneer Drawers, Mahogany 4600.00
Writing Stand, Bird's–Eye Maple Veneer Drawers, Fitted Drawer 3000.00
Writing Stand, Sheraton, 2 Drawers, Lift Lid, Mahogany, 30 1/4 In. 3550.00

G–ARGY– Gabriel Argy–Rousseau, born in 1885, was a French glass artist who
ROUSSEAU produced a variety of objects in the Art Deco style. His mark, "G.
          Argy–Rousseau," was usually impressed.

G.ARGY–ROUSSEAU, Ashtray, Flower Shape, Double Tier Petals At Back, Signed 1200.00
Bowl, 2 Spiders & Webs Among Foliage 5500.00
Bowl, Butterfly, Outstretched Wings, Signed, C.1925, 3 In. 9350.00
Bowl, Grape Clusters, Leaves, Gray Ground, Signed, C.1925 ....   5500.00
Bowl, Stylized Florets Band, Chevron Ground, Signed, 5 In. 8250.00
Bowl, Stylized Florets, Swags, Signed, C.1925, 5 In. 8800.00
Box, Peaked Cover, Lunaria Pods, Signed, C.1925, 3 1/2 In. 4400.00
Paperweight, Butterfly, Wings Spread Over Beetle, 3 In. 2800.00

Pendant, Pate–De–Verre, Winged Beetle, Pierced 1000.00
Vase, Band of Rose Peonies, Signed, C.1920, 4 1/4 In. 6380.00
Vase, Berry Band, Violet Leaves, Signed, C.1925, 6 1/2 In. 4950.00
Vase, Color Streaked, Bouquets, Signed, C.1925, 7 1/8 In. 9900.00
Vase, Magenta Arrowheads, Chevrons, Signed, C.1925, 4 In. 5775.00
Vase, Pate–De–Verre, Gazelle, Signed, 3 3/4 In. 9900.00
Vase, Pate–De–Verre, Oranges, Signed, C.1925, 8 1/2 In. 8800.00
Vase, Rows of Semicircles, Signed, C.1925, 5 3/4 In. 6050.00
Vase, Spiders, Weaving Webs, Signed, C.1925, 4 3/4 In. 8250.00

Galle was a designer who made glass, pottery, furniture, and other Art Nouveau items. Emile Galle founded his factory in France in 1874. After Galle's death in 1904, the firm continued to make glass and furniture until 1931. The name "Galle" was used as a mark, but it was often hidden in the design of the object. Galle Pottery is listed above and his furniture is listed in the Furniture section.

Emile Galle, the famous French designer, made ceramics after 1874. The pieces were marked with the initials "E.G." impressed, "Em. Galle Faiencerie de Nancy," or a version of his signature. Galle is best known for his glass, listed in the next section.

GALLE POTTERY, Basket, Handle, 8 X 13 In. 750.00
  Bowl, Flowers, 5 X 8 In. 600.00
  Figurine, Cat, Flowers, 15 In. 1200.00
  Vase, Tree Trunk With Flowers, Branch Handle, 14 In. 1400.00
GALLE, Boat, Castles, Scrollwork, Gold Trim, Canoe Shape, Signed, 14 In. 975.00
  Box, Amethyst Flowers, Leaves, Frosted & Blue Ground, Signed, 7 In. 850.00
  Box, Floral, Amethyst & Blue Ground, Cover, Signed, Round, 7 In. 850.00
  Box, Marquetry Bird Scene On Hinged Lid, C.1900, 8 3/8 In. 990.00
  Dish, Serving, Enameled Floral, Scalloped, Amber, 10 In. 250.00
  Figurine, Rooster, Standing, Thistles, Mustard, Rust, Signed, 11 In. 990.00

Galle, Vase, Brown, Violet & Green Cameo, White Ground, 6 1/4 In.

Galle, Vase, Purple Foliage, Cameo, Pale Ground, 9 1/2 In.

Galle, Vase, Bud

Galle, Vase, Peach Leaves, Pale Ground, Grass Script, Cameo, 12 In.

Galle, Vase, Purple Hydrangea, Cameo, 7 1/2 In.

Galle, Vase, Purple & Green Foliage, 10 1/2 In.

Jug, Lotus Leaves, Brown Ground, Earth Tones, Marked, Squat, 7 In. 425.00
Lamp, Conical Shade, Pendant Cherry Blossoms, C.1900, 8 In. 9350.00
Perfume Bottle, Amethyst Floral, Foliage, Pink, White Cased, 4 1/2 In. 750.00
Pitcher, Carved Spirals, Tendrils Above Body, Signed, C.1894, 9 In. 5500.00
Pitcher, Exotic Inset, Flowering Plant, Brown Ground, Signed, 15 In. 1400.00
Plate, Flowers, Imari Colors, 9 1/2 In. 250.00
Prunus Blossoms, Dragonfly, Butterfly On Reverse, Signed, 5 1/8 In. 2475.00
Punch Bowl, Brown, Green Trees, Pink Sky, 9 1/2 In. 13200.00
Tray, Thistle Spray & Leaves of Inlay Woods, Signed, 24 X 16 In. 550.00
Vase, 3 Colors, Ovoid, 12 In. 1850.00
Vase, Amber Stripes, Purple Flowers, Carved Petals, Signed, 7 In. 9900.00
Vase, Amber Walls, Persian Horsemen, Beaded, Signed, C.1900, 4 1/4 In. 3575.00
Vase, Amberina, Enameled Florals, 6 Applied Feet, 6 X 5 In. 695.00
Vase, Applied Cabochons, Carved Poem, Signed, C.1900, 12 1/2 In. 8250.00
Vase, Banjo, Woodland Scene, 6 3/4 In. 800.00
Vase, Bleeding Hearts, 5 Layers of Cutting, Signed, 8 1/4 In. 1975.00
Vase, Blue Florals, Green Leaves, Signed, 5 3/4 In. 995.00
Vase, Bronze, Applied Yellow & Cream Orchids, Signed, 10 In. 325.00
Vase, Brown Leaves & Flowers, White Ground, 3 3/4 In. 350.00
Vase, Brown, Violet & Green Cameo, White Ground, 6 1/4 In. ....Illus 425.00
Vase, Bud ....Illus 70.00
Vase, Bud, Red Cameo Florals, Red Ground, 4 1/2 In. 345.00
Vase, Burgundy Florals, Frosted Ground, 14 In. 1250.00
Vase, Carved Yellow Leaves At Neck, Orange Base, 7 1/2 In. 950.00
Vase, Clematis Blossoms, Buds, Leaves, Signed, C.1925, 9 1/2 In. 6600.00
Vase, Dark Brown, Cameo, Bulbous, Signed, 4 1/2 In. 295.00
Vase, Dark Green Leaves, Light Green Ground, Cameo, Signed, 12 In. 950.00
Vase, Deep Brown, Gold, White, Green, Chartreuse, 9 3/4 In. 1750.00
Vase, Enameled River Landscape, Green, Signed, C.1900, 8 1/4 In. 3025.00
Vase, Flattened, Twining Flowers, Amber To White, Signed, 8 5/8 In. 650.00
Vase, Floral Carving, Fire Polished, Lime Green, 6 In. 685.00
Vase, Floral Sprays, Elliptical, Cut Away Rim, Signed, 13 1/4 In. 600.00
Vase, Floral, Amethyst, 6 1/2 In. 500.00
Vase, Floral, Pink, Red & Magenta, Signed, 10 In. 1225.00
Vase, Floral, Rose To Frosted White To Yellow, 10 1/2 In. 1125.00
Vase, Flowering Branches, Gilt Metal Rim, Signed, 13 1/4 In. 650.00
Vase, Frosted To Dark Green, Cameo, Signed, 8 In. 595.00
Vase, Fuchsia Blossoms & Leaves, Signed, C.1925, 11 3/4 In. 5720.00
Vase, Glass, Squat Bulbous Base, Apricot, Anemone, Cameo, 12 5/8 In. 575.00
Vase, Green To Purple Floral, Scalloped Rim, Signed, 13 1/2 In. 600.00
Vase, Green, Pink & Purple Floral, Signed, 24 In. 1700.00
Vase, Hydrangea Sprays, 2 Handles, Signed, C.1900, 7 7/8 In. 4675.00
Vase, Interior Silver Foil Inclusions, Lilies, C.1900, 5 1/4 In. 3300.00
Vase, Interior Silver Foil, Iris Blossoms, Signed, C.1900, 4 3/4 In. 5225.00
Vase, Leafy Cherry Branches, Yellow Walls, Signed, C.1925, 11 1/2 In. 7150.00
Vase, Lozenge Form, Fuchsia Blossoms, Signed, C.1900, 8 1/4 In. 1650.00
Vase, Mold–Blown, Pendent Fruiting Branches, Signed, C.1925, 11 In. 6600.00
Vase, Morning Glory Blossoms, Vines, Butterfly, Signed, 23 1/4 In. 4400.00
Vase, Mountains, Lake In Distance, Signed, C.1900, 14 In. 4125.00
Vase, Orange & Red Flowers, Leaves, Frosted Ground, Signed, 4 1/2 In. 365.00
Vase, Peach Leaves, Pale Ground, Grass Script, Cameo, 12 In. ....Illus 900.00
Vase, Pilgrim Shape, Leaves, Flowers, Pink Base, 6 1/2 In. 700.00
Vase, Pink Flowers, Olive Green, Blue Streaked, Bottle Shape, 9 In. 1750.00
Vase, Purple & Green Foliage, 10 1/2 In. ....Illus 900.00
Vase, Purple & Yellow, 13 1/2 In. 775.00
Vase, Purple Foliage, Cameo, Pale Ground, 9 1/2 In. ....Illus 800.00
Vase, Purple Hydrangea, Cameo, 7 1/2 In. ....Illus 800.00
Vase, Purple, Lavender, Flowers, Leaves, Gold Rising, 10 In. 2250.00
Vase, Quatrefoil Mouth, Bleeding Heart Blossoms, Signed, C.1900, 9 In. 3300.00
Vase, Ravens On Pine Bough, Silver Mounts, Signed, C.1900, 18 In. 5750.00
Vase, Red Amber Florals, Gold Ground, 11 X 11 In. 4950.00
Vase, Scenic, 14 In. 1950.00
Vase, Shoulder Handles, Enameled Flowers, Signed, C.1900, 9 3/4 In. 1500.00
Vase, Stick, Acid Cup, Yellow Ground, Violets, Leaves, 8 In. 675.00

Vase, Stick, Green Shades, Signed, 23 In. 1775.00
Vase, Wisteria, Green & Blue On Frosted Ground, Signed, 12 1/4 In. 850.00
Vase, Yellow Sides, Cherry Red, Carnations, Signed, 9 In. 2090.00
Wine, Enamel Leaf & Flower, Amber Tint, Signed, 2 3/4 In. 35.00

Game plates are plates of any make decorated with pictures of birds, animals, or fish. The game plates usually came in sets consisting of twelve dishes and a serving platter. These sets were most popular during the 1880s.

GAME PLATE, Field Dogs, Scalloped, Limoges, 12 In. 37.00
Gold Rococo Border, Pheasants, Quail, Limoges, 13 In., Pair 495.00
Pheasant, Scalloped, Limoges, 10 In. 80.00
Scalloped, Gold Border, Hand Painted, Limoges, 9 In., Set of 6 .... 475.00
GAME SET, Platter, Harker, 15 In., 5 Piece 145.00

Children's games of all sorts are collected. Of special interest are any board games or card games. Other games may be found listed under Toy, Card, or the name of the character or celebrity featured in the game.

GAME, Adventure, Milton Bradley, 1945 .... 13.00
American Baseball, Box, 1904 .... 100.00
Anagrams, Box, 1930 .... 18.00
Anagrams, Double Eagle, McLaughlin Bros., 1897 .... 30.00
Anagrams, Embossed Edition, Selchow & Righter Co., Box 25.00
Animal Bingo, Mechanical, Different Animals, Tin, Spinner, Box 35.00
Arabian Nights, National, C.1950 .... 40.00
Art Linkletter's People Are Funny, 1954 .... 15.00
Authors, 1888 .... 8.00
Authors, Fairchild 7.50
Authors, Whitman, Cards 22.00
Backgammon, Box, Leather Hinges, Wooden 125.00
Baseball, Electric Vibrating, Tudor, Box 35.00
Baseball, Roger Maris, 1962 .... 45.00
Batter-Up 30.00
Big League Baseball, 3M, 1967 .... 8.00
Billy Whiskers, 1923 .... 40.00
Bingo, Real, E.S.Lowe, With Birdcage, C.1950 .... 20.00
Bionic Woman, Box, 1976 .... 8.00
Black Sambo, Bowling 190.00
Board, Black Squares, Brown Paint, 144 Squares 1 Side, 64 Other 135.00
Board, Cribbage, Mahogany, Brass, 10 3/4 In. 45.00
Board, Family Card Game, Box, 1965 .... 25.00
Board, Little Orphan Annie's Treasure Hunt, 1933 .... 60.00
Board, Painted Yellow Striping, Pipes, American, 18 3/4 X 31 In. 325.00
Board, Parcheesi 1000.00
Board, Parcheesi & Checkers, Slate, C.1860, 23 X 23 In. 4400.00
Board, Parcheesi, Wood, Red, Green, Black, Orange, C.1870, 16 X 16 In. 3190.00
Bombs Away, Eagle Bombsight, Airplane View Target, Box, 1943 .... 150.00
Bowling, Arcade 135.00
Bridge For Two, Lowe, 1972 .... 7.00
Brownie Horseshoe 35.00
Camelot, Parker Brothers, Box, 1931 .... 16.00
Camp Granada, 1965 .... 10.00
Card, Beverly Hillbillies, 1963 .... 25.00
Card, Flags, U.S.Playing Cards, 1800s, Instructions, Box 48.00
Card, Foolish Questions, Rube Goldberg 35.00
Card, Laramie, Box, 1959 .... 25.00
Card, Munsters, Complete 40.00
Card, Old Maid, 1924, Complete 5.00
Card, Rook, 1910 .... 8.00
Card, Wall Street 12.00
Charlie Chan, Milton Bradley, 1937 .... 60.00
Checkerboard, Abalone & Black Glass, Cherry Frame, C.1900, 5 1/2 In. 135.00
Checkerboard, Applied Edge Molding, Black & White, 15 3/8 X 24 In. 175.00

Checkerboard, Applied Edge Strips, Red Paint, 13 1/4 X 23 In. 110.00
Checkerboard, Breadboard Ends All Sides, 12 3/4 X 14 1/2 In. 80.00
Checkerboard, Brown & Black Squares, Gray Ground, 1860–80, 19 X 16 In. 192.00
Checkerboard, Green, Light Green Squares, Backgammon Reverse, Square 550.00
Checkerboard, Inlaid, 12 3/4 X 13 In. 85.00
Checkerboard, Movable Parts, Rotating Squares, Wood, 17 X 14 In. 700.00
Checkerboard, Odd Fellows, Seeing Eye, Comic Heads, 26 X 15 In. 700.00
Checkerboard, Pink & Green Squares, Frank Pemruk, 1936, 19 X 20 In. 220.00
Checkerboard, Red & Black Paint, 2 Well Ends, 1880, 27 X 19 In. 330.00
Checkerboard, Red & Black Paint, Blue Stripe, Primitive, 14 X 15 In. 75.00
Checkerboard, Red & Black, Yellow Borders, C.1880, 26 X 15 1/4 In. 522.00
Checkerboard, Reverse of Painted Squares, 18 X 29 1/2 In. 850.00
Checkerboard, Yellow & Black Squares, Striped Border, Square, 17 In. 2200.00
Chess, Checkers, Dominoes, Backgammon, Milton Bradley, 1943, Box 35.00
Chinese Checkers, Akro Agate Marbles, Chein Steel Board 28.50
Chiromagica, McLaughlin Bros., 11 3/4 X 11 3/4 In. 180.00
Chutes & Ladders, Box, 1956 .... 16.00
Climbing Monkey, Lehmann, Box 210.00
Coon Chicken Inn, Optical Illusion 25.00
Croquet, Table, Wooden Box 75.00
Dark Shadows 20.00
Dart, Planet of The Apes, Transogram, 1967 .... 6.00
Dice Cage, With Bell, Painted Silver, Large 200.00
Dice, 3, In Case, Square Base, 1930s, 18 In. 100.00
Dig, Parker Brothers, 1939 .... 10.00
Dollhouse, Colleen Moore 75.00
Dominoes Set, Ivory & Ebony, Leather Case 45.00
Dominoes, Double Nine, Parker Brothers, 1940s 20.00
Dominoes, Embossing Co., Dovetailed Wooden Box, Instructions, 91 Piece 48.00
Dominoes, Halsam 5.00
Dominoes, Lone Star Embossing 15.00
Dragnet 22.00
Feeding Sambo, Pin Watermelon In Mouth, Lion Coffee, 1903, 12 X 20 In. 150.00
Fibber McGee, Wistful Vista Mystery, 1940 .... 25.00
Fish Pond, Magnetic, Parker Brothers, Box, 1938 .... 40.00
Fish Pond, Milton Bradley, Dated 1909 .... 12.00
Flintstone Stoneage 15.00
Flintstone Window Wacker, 1961 .... 35.00
Flip Your Wig, Complete, 1964 .... 35.00
Flying Goose, Target, Cast Iron, 8 3/4 In. 55.00
Football Spin A Game, Hasbro, C.1950 .... 13.00
Football–Baseball, Parker Brothers, 1926 .... 35.00
Frontierland 25.00
Game of The Rebellion, Civil War, New York Maker, 1861 .... 175.00
Gang Way, 1964 T.V.Show 22.00
Golf Clubs, Woodshaft, 20 Piece 10.00
Gomer Pyle 10.00
Grandma's Game of Useful Knowledge, 1910 .... 15.00
Great American Baseball Game, Tin, Wooden Base, 1925 .... 100.00 To 175.00
Groucho Marx TV Quiz, Magnetic 70.00
Gypsy Fortune Teller, Milton Bradley, Box, 1905 .... 42.00
H.R.Pufnstuff 10.00
Hats Off, Clown, Box, 1930s 35.00
Hearts, Letter Game, Box, 1914 .... 12.50
Hearts, Wooden Dice & Cup, Directions, Parker Brothers, 1914 .... 10.00
Hit 'N Run, Baseball, Motorized, Kenner, Box, 1962 .... 25.00
Hop–Ching Chinese Marbles, Pressman, Complete, Box 35.00
Horseshoes, Brownie 35.00
Hustler Baseball, Litho On Tin, Box, 1923 .... 280.00
I Win–You Lose, Card Game, 1911 .... 19.50
Jack & Jill, Milton Bradley 35.00
Jackstraws Set, Wooden 12.00
Jackstraws, Milton Bradley, Box, 1900s 55.00
Jamboree, Selchow & Righter 40.00

> **Watch out for exploding antiques! Any type of gun, shell, powder can, nitrate movie film, and some chemicals possibly left in old bottles or cans are dangerous. If you don't know about these items, contact your local police or fire department for help.**

James Bond, Road Race Set, 007, Box, Gilbert	100.00
James Bond, Secret Agent 007, Box, 1964	8.00
Kentucky Jones Horse Auction	18.00
Know Your States, Tip Top Bread	3.50
Kojak's Stake Out	7.00
Landy Andy Speedboat Races, Tin, Wolverine	35.00
Lawn Balls, Brunswick, Carrying Case	37.50
Li'l. Abner, Board	12.00 To 18.00
Little Black Sambo, Board, Box	75.00
Lotto, Trunk Design	10.00
Lucky Strike, Bowling, Wooden, Box, 1930s	19.00
Magic Dots, 1907	20.00
Mah–Jongg, Ivorene Counters, Racks, Leatherette Case, 1939, 19 3/4 In.	30.00
Mah–Jongg, Jr., Complete, 1923	19.00
Mah–Jongg, Leather Case, 5 Drawers, Ivory On Wood, 270 Piece	125.00
Mah–Jongg, Tin Tiles, Transfer Designs, Metal Money, Box	40.00
Man From U.N.C.L.E., Board, Box, 1965	25.00
Marble, Metal Bears, Arcade Label	85.00
Marble, Skillball, Marx, Box	30.00
Marble, Spot Shot, Sunny Andy, Wolverine, Box	37.00
McDonaldland, Box, Remco	25.00
Mighty Mouse Ring Toss, Terrytoons, 1964	35.00
Monopoly, Box, Board, Cardboard Money Holder, Early 1930s	25.00
Mr.Bug Goes To Town, Board, 1955	7.00
Number Please	17.00
O'Grady's Goat, Milton Bradley, Box, 1906	35.00
Old MacDonald's Farm	10.00
Operation, Box, 1965	8.00
Over The Garden Wall, Milton Bradley, Box, 1937	20.00 To 30.00
Pick–Up Sticks, Schoenhut	15.00 To 25.00
Pick–Up Sticks, Whitman	8.00
Pin The Tail On The Donkey, Printed Cloth, Early 20th Century	30.00
Pit, Card, Box, 1903	15.00
Planet of The Apes, Board, Box	8.00
Poker Chips, Clay, Leather Cover Case	26.00
Poker Chips, Ivory, Rack, 300 Piece	3500.00
Poker Chips, Slate, Box	125.00
Poker Chips, Wooden, Wooden Carrying Case	28.00
Poosh–M–Up, 5–Game Streamliner	35.00
Prince Valiant Game of Valor, Box	32.50
Punchboard, Chesterfield Cigarettes, 1 Cent, Unpunched	20.00
Punchboard, Lucky Strike Cigarettes, 1 Cent, Unpunched	20.00
Puzzle, Apollo 11	17.00
Puzzle, Blondie, Tillie The Toiler, Phila.Inquirer, 1933, Pair	30.00
Puzzle, Chase Dog Race, 4 Sets	7.00
Puzzle, Circus, Milton Bradley, Set of 4	55.00
Puzzle, Clark Gable, Original Envelope, 1930s	189.00
Puzzle, Daybreak, Maxfield Parrish, 16 X 25 In.	35.00
Puzzle, Dissected Map of The United States, Litho Cover, Mother, Girl	45.00
Puzzle, Hoods Rainy Day, Box	40.60
Puzzle, Katzenjammer Kids, 1942	25.00
Puzzle, Know Your Planes, Thompson Products, 18 X 10 1/2 In., 3 Piece	18.00
Puzzle, Little Black Sambo	35.00
Puzzle, Little Lady, Effanbee, Box, 14 In.	35.00
Puzzle, Mother Goose, Fern Bisel Peat Art, Saalfield, 1937, 3 Puzzles	15.00

Puzzle, Mother Goose, Nursery Rhyme Characters 15.00
Puzzle, Moving, Advertising, Bekins, Wooden, 1927 .... 18.00
Puzzle, Mr.Magoo, Box 20.00
Puzzle, Munsters, Box 40.00
Puzzle, Our Gang, Dated 1932, 11 X 14 In. 58.00
Puzzle, Skill Ball, Alice In Wonderland, Mad Tea Party Scene 15.00
Puzzle, Sohio, Standard Oil Co., Gene & Glenn, 1933 .... 20.00
Puzzle, Tales of Wells Fargo, Frame Tray, Dated 1958 .... 17.00
Puzzle, Tray, Zorro 8.00
Puzzle, Victory, Wooden, Circus, 12 Cutout Model Figures 45.00
Puzzle, Wedding, Parker Brothers, Box 85.00
Puzzle, White Sewing Machine & Bicycle 125.00
Quick Wit, Parker Brothers 8.00
Quiz Kids, Radio Question Box, 1945 .... 10.00
Raggedy Ann & Andy, 1941 .... 20.00
Red Ryder, Cardboard, Target, Whitman, Box, 1939 .... 75.00
Restless Gun, Board 25.00
Rin Tin Tin, Box 30.00
Rin Tin Tin, Cereal Giveaway, Metal, Pocket 11.00
Ring Toss, Box, 1937 .... 19.00
Ring Toss, Transogram Co., Dated 1947, Box 7.00
Robot Game 30.00
Rook Cards, 1931 .... 14.50
Roulette Wheel, Felt, Ball, Directions 45.00
Sambo, Metal Dartboard, Wyandotte 75.00
Say When 20.00
Scary Horror Rings, Display Box 35.00
Scribbage, Lowe, 13 Celluloid Dice, Instructions, Box 20.00
Secret Agent 007, Milton Bradley 18.00
Seven Keys, Ideal, 1961 .... 5.00
Shari Lewis In Shariland 15.00
Shoot A Crow, Target, Wood Crows, Box 18.00
Snaprazor, Straight, Keen Kutter, Black Handle, Box 5.00
Snuffy Smith's Bug Derby, Jaymar 10.00
Star Trek Super Phaser II Target, Laser Gun, Badge, Mego, Box, 1976 .... 60.00
Star Trek, Hasbro, 1974 .... 10.00
Star Trek, Milton Bradley, 1979 .... 8.00
Star Wars, Box 9.00
Starsky & Hutch 15.00
Stump The Stars 15.00
Sunken Treasure, Board, 1948 .... 13.00
Super Phaser II, Mego, Target, Unused, Box, 1976 .... 60.00
Swayze Television Game 15.00
Swing A Peg, Milton Bradley, Box, 1900s 55.00
Target, Steel, Bird At One End, Black Circles, 10 1/2 In. 10.00
Ten Pins, Dolly Dimples, C.1890 .... 110.00
Ten Pins, Wooden, Balls, Saginaw Wood Products 28.00
Tiddleywinks, Milton Bradley, 1940s ....8.00 To 16.00
Tiddleywinks, Tinker Belle, Box 45.00
Traffic, Matchbox, 1968 ....4.00 To 35.00
Trail Blazers, Fess Parker, Daniel Boone 10.00
Tripoly, Cadaco Ellis, 1957 .... 17.00
Uncle Wiggily 45.00
Uncle Wiggily, Board, Milton Bradley 12.00
Voyage To The Bottom of The Sea, Board 25.00
Welcome Back Kotter, 1976 .... 8.00
Where's Johnny, Box 25.00
Wonderful Game of Oz, 1921 .... 75.00

ГАРДНЕРЪ The Gardner porcelain works was founded in Verbiki, outside Moscow, by the English–born Francis Gardner in 1766. Gardner made porcelain tablewares, figurines, and faience.

GARDNER, Group, Man, Seated, Playing Accordion, Red Factory Mark, 6 3/4 In. 640.00
Group, Woman, Baby On Lap, Red Factory Mark, 6 3/4 In. 680.00

Gaudy Welsh, Bowl, Oyster Pattern, Footed,
6 X 10 1/2 In.

Grueby, Vase, Cabbage Form, Yellow,
Green Leaves, C.1905, 9 1/4 In.

Tea Set, Tray, Porcelain, Anthemion Borders, Green Ground, 16 Piece 1210.00

Gaudy Dutch pottery was made in England for America from about 1810 to 1820. It is a white earthenware with Imari–style decorations of red, blue, green, yellow, and black. Only sixteen patterns of Gaudy Dutch were made: Butterfly, Carnation, Dahlia, Double Rose, Dove, Grape, Leaf, Oyster, Primrose, Single Rose, Strawflower, Sunflower, Urn, War Bonnet, Zinnia, and No Name. Other similar wares are called "Gaudy Ironstone" and "Gaudy Welsh."

GAUDY DUTCH, Cup & Saucer, Dove 500.00
Cup & Saucer, Leaf, Blue, Rust & Lime Green 325.00
Plate, Carnation, 6 1/2 In. 185.00

Some collectors have named the ironstone wares with the bright Gaudy Dutchlike patterns "Gaudy Ironstone." There may be other examples found in the listing for Ironstone or under the name of the ceramic factory.

GAUDY IRONSTONE, Bowl, Spatterware, Stick, Blue Border, 10 3/8 In. 65.00
Dish, Shield Form, Flowers, Mason, Marked, 10 In., Pair 200.00
Pitcher & Bowl, Rose Design, Underglaze Blue, Red & Green 275.00
Pitcher, Floral, Staffordshire, 9 In. 150.00
Pitcher, Polychrome Floral, Purple Luster Band, 8 1/2 In. 35.00
Pitcher, Rose, Adams, 7 In. 200.00
Plate, Floral, Blue & Purple Luster, E.Walley, 8 1/2 In. 95.00
Plate, Flower Basket, 12–Sided, 8 7/8 In. 95.00
Plate, Morning Glory, 8 In. 85.00
Plate, Rose, Adams, 9 1/2 In. 125.00
Plate, Spatterware, Stick, Black Border, Wm.Adams, 8 3/8 In. 40.00
Platter, Strawberry, Crazing, 14 3/4 In. 335.00
Soup Dish, Floral, Staffordshire, 10 1/2 In. 75.00
Teapot, Floral, Staffordshire, 7 3/4 In. 180.00
Tureen, Tray, Imari Design, Marked, 7 3/4 In. 275.00

Gaudy Welsh is an Imari–decorated earthenware with red, blue, green, and gold decorations. It was made after 1820.

GAUDY WELSH, Bowl, Oyster Pattern, Footed, 6 X 10 1/2 In. .... *Illus* 220.00
Cake Plate, Self–Handles, Tulip, 1 In. 90.00
Cream Jug, Oyster Pattern, C.1820, 3 3/4 In. 80.00
Cup & Saucer .... 24.00 To 30.00
Cup & Saucer, Oyster Pattern 50.00
Mug, 3 In. 45.00

Mug, Blue Grape Leaves, Vine, Child's, 2 1/4 In.	60.00
Mug, Grape, Child's	75.00
Pitcher, Polychrome Floral, Embossed Band, 7 3/4 In.	75.00
Tea Set, Red, Gold, Oriental Mark	169.00
Tea Set, Wagon Wheel Pattern, Flow Blue, Child's	525.00
Toothpick, Oyster, 3 Handles	75.00

In the late nineteenth century Geisha Girl porcelain was made in Japan for export. It was an inexpensive porcelain often sold in dime stores or used as free premiums. Pieces are sometimes marked with the name of a store. Japanese ladies in kimonos are pictured on the dishes. Borders of red, blue, green, gold, brown, or several of these colors were used. Modern reproductions are being made.

GEISHA GIRL, Chocolate Pot, Blue Edge	79.00
Chocolate Pot, Red, Tall Cup & Saucer, Marked, 9 Piece	80.00
Chocolate Set, Pink Bushes, Blue Mountains, 7 Piece	100.00
Cookie Jar, Cobalt Blue	65.00
Creamer, Rust	6.00
Cup & Saucer	10.00
Hatpin Holder	40.00
Nut Bowl, Orange Red, Gold Trim, Nut Spoon, 4 Piece	60.00
Rose Bowl, Orange Red, Gold Trim	25.00
Salt & Pepper, Cobalt Blue Trim, 3 1/2 In.	15.00
Sugar & Creamer, Orange Red, Gold Trim, Pink Bushes	40.00
Tea Set, Dragon Pattern, Lithophane In Cup, 10 Piece	70.00
Tea Set, Green, Marked, 13 Piece, Large	80.00
Tea Set, Parasol Pattern, Red Trim, 13 Piece	90.00
Tea Set, Scenic, Red Trim, 4 Cups & Saucers	140.00
Tea Set, Shades of Orange, 5 Piece	85.00
Toothpick, 2 3/8 In.	8.00

Gene Autry was born in 1907. He began his career as the "Singing Cowboy" in 1928. His first movie appearance was in 1934, his last in 1958.

GENE AUTRY, Badge, Sheriff, Pinned On Braces	75.00
Book, Child's, Gene Autry Goes To The Circus, 1950	15.00
Book, Gene Autry & The Thief River Outlaws	10.00
Book, Golden Ladder Gang	5.00
Book, Gunsmoke, Bell 10 Cents, Fast Action, 1938	50.00
Book, March of Comics No.78, Child Life Shoes, 1951	35.00
Book, Painting, 1940, Large	25.00
Button, 1 1/4 In.	14.00
Button, Sunbeam Bread	2.00
Cap Gun	16.50
Guitar, Emenee	50.00
Guitar, Hollow Body, Wooden, Regulation Size	95.00
Guitar, Regulation Size	90.00
Holster, Double	12.00
Lunch Box	55.00
Mittens	25.00
Picture, Advertising, Oak Frame, 28 X 9 In.	85.00
Program, Souvenir, 1949	12.00
Record Album, Christmas	7.00
Record, Frosty The Snowman	6.00
Songbook, 1938	15.00
Tablet	9.00
Wristwatch, Animated, With Letter From Gene's Secretary, Box	175.00

Black and blue decorated Gibson Girl plates were made in the early 1900s. Twenty-four different 10 1/2-inch plates were made by the Royal Doulton Pottery at Lambeth, England. These pictured scenes from the book "A Widow and Her Friends" by Charles Dana Gibson. Another set of twelve 9-inch plates featuring pictures of the heads of Gibson Girls had all–blue decoration. Many other items also pictured the famous Gibson Girl.

GIBSON GIRL, Book, C.D.Gibson, 80 Drawings, C.1903	110.00
Plate, Calendar, 1909	16.00
Plate, Miss Babbles Brings Morning Paper	75.00
Plate, She Becomes A Trained Nurse, Royal Doulton, 10 In.	112.50
Plate, She Goes To Fancy Dress Ball As Juliet, 10 1/2 In.	80.00
Plate, She Looks For Relief Among Old Ones	80.00
Plate, Widow, 10 1/2 In.	160.00
Print, American Girl Abroad, Pencil, Ink, 1894, 17 X 26 1/2 In.	2640.00

GILLINDER   Gillinder pressed glass was first made by William T. Gillinder of Philadelphia in 1863. The company had a working factory on the grounds at the Centennial and made small, marked pieces of glass for sale as souvenirs. They made a variety of decorative glass pieces and tablewares.

GILLINDER, Figurine, Buddha, Red Amber, Signed	125.00
Mug, Snake Handle, Centennial Liberty Bell, Inscribed Bottom	495.00

The Girl Scout movement started in 1912, two years after the Boy Scouts. It began under Juliette Gordon Low of Savannah, Georgia. The first Girl Scout cookies were sold in 1928. Collectors search for anything pertaining to the Girl Scouts, including uniforms, publications, and old cookie boxes.

GIRL SCOUT, Ax	20.00
Badge, Chrome, St.Paul, 1932, Large	15.00
Camera, Flash, Official, Box	20.00
First Aid Kit, Tin	9.00
Handbook, 1917	18.00
Handbook, 1943	7.50
Handbook, Leadership of Girl Scout Troup, Intermediate, 1943	6.00
Kit, 1st Aid, Tin Box	25.00
Knife, 1950s	12.50
Knife, Pocket, Kutmaster	8.00
Pendant, Sterling Silver	6.00
Ring, Sterling Silver	35.00
Ring, Sterling Silver, Ribbed, Adjustable	12.00

GLASS, CONTEMPORARY, see Contemporary Glass

Eyeglasses, or spectacles, were mentioned in a manuscript in 1289 and have been used ever since. The first glasses with rigid side pieces were made in London in 1727. Bifocals were invented by Benjamin Franklin in 1785. Lorgnettes were popular in late Victorian times.

GLASSES, Chateline, Folding, Silver Plate, Ornate Case	30.00
Field, Brass	40.00
Granny, Case	25.00
Granny, Gold Filled, Glass Lens, 19th Century, 2 1/4 In.	25.00
Granny, Marked Hawkes, C.1900	20.00
Lorgnette, 14K Gold	425.00
Lorgnette, 14K Gold, Art Nouveau, Amethyst & 2 Diamonds Handle	1400.00
Lorgnette, 14K White Gold, Chain, 26 In.	200.00
Lorgnette, Telescoping Handle, Enameled Scenes, French, Le Fils	145.00
McKie Reid Spectacles, For Reading While Laying Down In Bed	25.00
Pince–Nez, 14K Gold, Black Leather Case	95.00
Pince–Nez, Chain, Bi–Focal Lens, Case	20.00
Pince–Nez, Folding, Chain, 12K Gold Filled	25.00
Pince–Nez, Folding, Chain, 14K Gold, Leather Case	35.00
Pince–Nez, Sterling Silver Frame & Chain, Case	12.50
Spectacles, J.Owen, Coin Silver, C.1830	195.00

W. Goebel Porzellanfabrik of Oeslau, Germany, now Rodental, West Germany, has made many types of figurines and dishes. The firm is

Goebel still working. The pieces marked "Goebel Hummel" are listed under Hummel in this book.

GOEBEL, Cigarette Set, Urn & 4 Ashtrays, Deco Dog, Marked	45.00
Doll, Perfume, Full Bee	85.00
Figurine, Boy Praying, Stamped VB, Signed	18.00
Figurine, Flapper, Playing Triangular Guitar, Marked, 10 In.	200.00
Figurine, Lady Dancer, 1930s, 10 In.	115.00
Figurine, Little Joe Otter, Signed, 7 In.	45.00
Figurine, Mama Bird Feeding Baby, Yellow, 1967	30.00
Figurine, Mary & Joseph, 1961, Pair	75.00
Figurine, Mother & Child On Donkey, Signed	45.00
Figurine, Puppies In Basket, Marked, 3 1/2 In.	68.00
Figurine, Rabbit, Ladybug On Tail, Brown, 1959	35.00
Figurine, Seated Nude, White Bisque	65.00
Figurine, Tinker Bell, Disney, 8 In.	175.00
Figurine, Upright Nude, White Bisque, 9 1/2 In.	85.00
Jar, Monk, Cover, Full Bee	25.00
Mustard, Monk	35.00
Pincushion Doll, Carrying Plate On Head	225.00
Pitcher, Milk, Googly-Eyed Girl, Impressed Mark	85.00
Reamer, Clown's Head, Blue, Impressed Mark, 4 X 5 X 6 1/2 In.	85.00
Salt & Pepper, Monk	25.00
Sign, Dealer's, Full Figure Bird	27.00
Sugar & Creamer, Monk	65.00
Sugar, Creamer & Tray, Monk, Full Bee	50.00

Porcelain has been made by three branches of the Goldscheider family. The family left Vienna in 1938 and started factories in England and in Trenton, New Jersey. The New Jersey factory started in 1940 as Goldscheider–U.S.A. In 1941 it became Goldscheider-Everlast Corporation. From 1947 to 1953 it was Goldcrest Ceramics Corporation. In 1950 the Vienna plant was returned to Mr. Goldscheider and the company continues in business. The Trenton, New Jersey, business is now Goldscheider of Vienna and imports all of the pieces.

GOLDSCHEIDER, Calling Card, Figural, Nude Lady, Standing, C.1900	1800.00
Candy Jar, Lady With Fan In Lid, 8 In.	85.00
Figurine, Chinese Girl With Fan, 12 In.	150.00
Figurine, Colonial Girl, Paper Label, 8 In.	55.00
Figurine, Colonial Lady, Pink	65.00
Figurine, Colonial Man, Pink	65.00
Figurine, Deco Dancer, 15 In.	250.00
Figurine, Easter Parade, Paper Label, 7 In.	65.00
Figurine, Everlast, Girl Figure, 8 In.	70.00
Figurine, Gentleman, Formal Dress	55.00
Figurine, Greyhound, 8 1/2 In.	150.00
Figurine, Juliet, With Doves, 3/4 Figure, 12 In.	125.00
Figurine, Lady Chrysanthemum, Label, 7 In.	65.00
Figurine, Lady Rose, 7 In.	50.00
Figurine, Lady, Fan, Rose In Blond Hair, Marked, 11 In.	125.00
Figurine, Love Letter, 7 1/2 In.	55.00
Figurine, Madonna, Teal Cowl	20.00
Figurine, Prince of Wales	45.00
Figurine, Russian Wolfhound, 10 X 11 In.	135.00
Figurine, Shepherd Dog	150.00
Figurine, Southern Belle, 10 1/2 In.	75.00
Figurine, Stork	250.00
Figurine, Venice, 12 In.	150.00
Figurine, Young Boy & Girl, Paper Label, Signed, 8 In.	325.00
Lamp, Man & Woman, Paper Label, 9 In., Pair	165.00
Mask, Madonna, Art Deco	95.00
Wall Mask, Orange, Green, 11 In.	350.00
GOLF, see Sports	

Lawton Gonder opened Gonder Ceramic Arts, Inc., in 1941. He worked in the old Peters and Reed pottery in Zanesville, Ohio. Gonder pieces include lamp bases marked "Eglee" and many wares with Oriental-type glazes.

GONDER, Figurine, Chinese Coolie, On Knees, Basket, 9 1/2 In.	22.00
Figurine, Horsehead	85.00
Figurine, Panther, Reclining	35.00
Ginger Jar, Crackle Glaze, Cover, Stand	30.00
Pitcher, Yellow, 8 1/2 In.	12.00
Sugar & Creamer, Mottled Brown	25.00
Vase, Floral, Pink Glaze, Label, 8 In.	15.00
Vase, Gourd Shape	15.00
Vase, Mauve, 2 Handles	7.00
GONDOR, Bookends, Oriental	22.00

Goofus glass was made from about 1900 to 1920 by many American factories. It was originally painted gold, red, green, bronze, pink, purple, or other bright colors. Many pieces are found today with flaking paint and this lowers the value.

GOOFUS GLASS, Bowl, Footed, 3 1/2 X 4 In.	15.00
Bowl, Ruffled, Roses, 9 In.	16.00
Compote, Cherries, Ruffled Rim, 10 In.	85.00
Compote, Fruit Design, 5 X 10 1/2 In.	65.00
Dish, Painted, Scalloped Rim, Square, 8 In.	12.00
Jar, Dresser, Allover Molded Roses, Red Paint, Gold Trim	23.50
Lamp, Oil, Nosegay Pattern	150.00
Plate, Grape Pattern, 10 In.	20.00
Plate, Palmer's Chocolates, 6 1/2 In.	37.50
Plate, Red Roses Center, Gold, 8 In.	20.00
Plate, Roses In Snow, 11 In.	14.00
Plate, Sunflower, 6 In.	6.00
Syrup, Rose & Lattice	43.50
Vase, Bird & Flowers, 12 In.	38.00
Vase, Bird, Grapes, Leaves, 9 In.	20.00
Vase, Grape, 12 1/2 In.	40.00
Vase, Iris, 12 In.	32.00
Vase, Parrot & Foliage, Gold, Red & Blue, 12 In.	60.00
Vase, Peacock, 10 1/2 In.	75.00
Vase, Purple, Grapes, 8 In.	15.00
Vase, Rose, 7 In.	35.00

Goss china has been made since 1858. English potter William Henry Goss first made it at the Falcon Pottery in Stoke-on-Trent. The factory name was changed to Goss China Company in 1934 when it was taken over by Cauldon Potteries. Production ceased in 1940. Goss china resembles Irish Belleek in both body and glaze. The company also made popular souvenir china, usually marked with local crests and names.

GOSS, Candle Snuffer, Aseroovey Crest, White, 2 1/4 In.	49.00
Character Jug, 3 In.	35.00
Creamer, Heraldic	60.00
Cup & Saucer, Coat of Arms	15.00
Ewer, Birmingham University, Roman Model, W.H.Goss, 4 In.	35.00
Figurine, Abbots Cup, Fountains Abbey	25.00
Figurine, Ancient Irish Bronze Pot, Ulster	20.00
Figurine, Eddystone Lighthouse, Herne Bay	45.00
Figurine, Old Salt Pot, Seven Oaks	20.00
Jardiniere, Argentina, Miniature	25.00
Night-Light, Robert Burns' House, 6 In.	140.00
Night-Light, Shakespeare's House	100.00
Plate, Armorial, 10 In.	20.00
Vase, Coronation, Amphora, C.1911, 4 In.	35.00

4 8
PLAZUID
GOUDA
Holland
A.M.P.smiT.

32V
BSK GOXMOVRN
WOLLRND
COREL
E

Pottery has been made in Gouda, Holland, since the seventeenth century. Two firms, the Zenith pottery, established in the eighteenth century, and the Zuid–Hollandsche pottery, made the brightly colored wares marked "Gouda" from 1880 to about 1940. Many pieces featured Art Nouveau or Art Deco designs.

GOUDA, Ashtray, 4 In.	35.00
Base, Starburst Floral, Multicolor, Bulbous, 10 In.	90.00
Basket, Regina, Frosted Floral, Twisted Handle, Gold Trim, 7 1/2 In.	45.00
Butter Chip, Zenith	7.00
Candle Lamp, Hooded	125.00
Candleholder, Shield, 9 In.	145.00
Candlestick, Art Deco, Spino Pattern, 7 1/8 In., Pair	165.00
Candlestick, Drip Pan, Multicolored, House Mark, 12 X 5 1/4 In.	125.00
Candlestick, Flared Base, Ring Handle, Marked, 7 In.	85.00
Chamberstick, Bird Design, Liberty & Co.Mark	55.00
Chamberstick, Ring Handle, Drip Guard, Marked, 7 1/4 In.	85.00
Chamberstick, Trumpet–Shaped Base, Drip Pan, Black Trim, 7 1/4 In.	95.00
Compote, Daisy, Handles, 5 X 7 1/4 In.	95.00
Dish, Boat Shape, Black Satin Ground, 3 1/4 X 8 In.	35.00
Figure, Woman's Head	65.00
Humidor, 8 Dutch Children, Scenic, Brass Lid	95.00
Humidor, Matte Design of Blue, Tan & Green, Signed	125.00
Jar, Scenic Windmills, Houses, Boats, Glossy, Cover, 4 1/2 In.	65.00
Lantern, 11 In.	80.00
Lantern, Art Nouveau Design, Plazuid House Mark, 6 In.	115.00
Lantern, Candle, Orange, Green, Blue & Yellow, 9 1/2 In.	110.00
Match Holder, Art Deco, Striker At Base, 2 1/8 In.	50.00
Powder Box, Handle On Cover, Black, Gold Design, 4 1/2 In.	75.00
Urn, Cover, Stylized Blossoms, Pods & Leaves, DAM, 16 1/2 In.	400.00
Vase, Black, White & Gold, Crown Royal, Artist Signed, 6 1/2 In.	85.00
Vase, Floral, Cloisonne Effect, Signed, 5 In.	40.00

Graniteware is an enameled tinware that has been used in the kitchen from the late nineteenth century to the present. Earlier graniteware was green or turquoise blue, with white spatters. The later ware was gray with white spatters. Reproductions are being made in all colors.

GRANITEWARE, Ashtray, Sullivan's Cigars, Red	20.00
Baking Pan, Thistle	38.00
Basin, Brown & White Swirl, 2 Handles	55.00
Basin, Wash, Brown Swirl	50.00
Bedpan, Blue	14.00
Bedpan, Cover	40.00
Bedpan, Cover, Gray, 14 X 16 In.	70.00
Bedpan, Navy Splatter	12.00
Bedpan, Urinal, Columbian Label, Gray	50.00

Graniteware and other enameled kitchenwares should be cleaned with water and baking soda. If necessary, use chlorine bleach.

Berry Bucket, Blue–Green & White 75.00
Berry Bucket, Gray, 3 In. 25.00
Berry Bucket, Gray, Cover, 3 1/2 In. 45.00
Berry Pail, Gray, 7 1/2 In. 26.00
Berry Pail, Green & White, Cover 135.00
Bowl, Gray, Royal Granite Steelware, Sample 70.00
Broiler, Thistle, Double 48.00
Bucket, Berry, Cover, Gray, 2 Gal. 38.00
Bucket, Brown, 1 Gal. 40.00
Bucket, Dinner, Gray 75.00
Bucket, Swirl, Cobalt Blue, Bail 55.00
Cake Pan, Iris, Blue Swirl, 8 1/2 X 13 In. 77.00
Cake Pan, Tube, Gray 44.00
Cake Pan, Tube, Gray, Octagonal, L & G Label 28.00
Cake Safe, Hinged Dome, Hasp Closing, 12 X 7 In. 150.00
Cake Safe, Snow On Mountain Finish, Dome Cover, 12 X 7 In. 150.00
Candleholder, Gray, Handle 55.00
Canister Set, Coffee, Sugar & Tea, Dutch, 3 Piece 125.00
Canister, Marked Tea, Cover, 5 1/2 In. 52.00
Coffee Boiler, Gray, Large 28.00
Coffee Boiler, Royal Label 30.00
Coffee Set, Blue, Miniature 275.00
Coffeepot, Castle Design, Pewter Top & Spout 210.00
Coffeepot, Curved Spout, Hinged Lid, Gray 32.00
Coffeepot, Dark Green & White Swirl 220.00
Coffeepot, Gooseneck Spout, Bail, Gray 30.00
Coffeepot, Gooseneck, Solid Red, Black Trim 14.00
Coffeepot, Gray, Manning Bowman, Pewter Trim 175.00
Coffeepot, Red 22.00
Coffeepot, White, 11 1/2 In. 38.00
Coffeepot, Wooden Bar Handle & Finial, Tin Top, Mulberry 65.00
Colander, Bail, Brown & White 14.00
Colander, Blue & White Swirl 35.00
Colander, Brown & White 24.00
Colander, Green 13.00
Cooler, Water, Cover, Brass Spigot, Gray, 5 Gal. 225.00
Cup & Saucer, Plate, Child's 35.00
Cup, Brown & White 20.00
Cup, Mush, Sky Blue, Copper Band 50.00
Dipper, Gray, 7 In. 22.00
Dipper, Gray, 14 1/2 In. 22.00
Dipper, Navy Splatter 7.00
Dipper, Water, Gray 20.00
Dish Pan, 14 In. 45.00
Dish Pan, Blue & White 40.00
Dish, Soap, Blue Swirl 65.00
Double Boiler, Cover, Gray 15.00
Filler, Fruit, Gray, 2 In. 15.00
Flask, Whiskey, Gray 85.00
Footbath, Gray 55.00
Funnel, Canning, Cobalt & White Swirl 195.00
Funnel, Cobalt Blue Swirl 36.00
Funnel, Gray Mottled 8.00
Funnel, Gray, Extra Agate, Small 38.00
Grater, Gray, Miniature 125.00
Kettle, Iris Blue Speckled, Cover 50.00
Kettle, Jelly, Brown & White Swirl, Bail Handle, Lift Tab 58.00
Ladle, White 8.00
Lunch Bucket, Dark Blue, White Specks, 9 X 6 In. 50.00
Measure, Cobalt & White Swirl, Pt. 225.00
Measure, Gray, 1 Gal. 47.00
Mirror, Shaving, Blue & White, Folding 49.00
Mold, Ring, Cream & Green 25.00
Mold, Ruffled, White 20.00

Mold, Turk's Head, Turquoise & White	200.00
Muffin Pan, 8 Holes, Iris Blue & White Mottled	75.00
Muffin Pan, 12 Hole, Gray	40.00
Mug, Child's, Green & White Swirl	95.00
Mug, Cobalt & White, Swirl, 1 X 1 In.	140.00
Pail, Milk, Gray, 2 Qt.	42.00
Pail, Utility, Bluish Gray	28.00
Pail, Wooden Handle, Gray, 9 1/2 X 11 In.	50.00
Pan, Frying, Cobalt Swirl	35.00
Pan, Milk, Red & White, Swirl	150.00
Pan, Sauce, Blue	18.00
Pan, Sauce, Turquoise & White Marbleized, 1 Qt.	10.00
Pan, Tube, Cobalt Blue & White Swirl	185.00
Pan, Tube, Gray, Round	24.00
Percolator, White Enameled, Foval Glass Dome, Footed	32.50
Pie Pan, Blue & White Interior, Germany, 1 X 4 In.	32.00
Pie Plate, Blue & White Swirl	20.00
Pitcher & Owl, Turquoise & White Swirl	165.00
Pitcher, Red & White	145.00
Pitcher, Water, Gray	55.00
Pitcher, Water, Gray, 10 1/2 In.	36.00
Pot, Mustard, Lidded, Ladle, 3 1/2 In.	78.00
Potty, Gray, Original Paper Label	20.00
Rack, Utensil, Gray	165.00
Roaster, Columbian Dark Blue	30.00
Roasting Pan, Black, Large	20.00
Salt Box, Wooden Lid, Blue	95.00
Salt, Hanging, Red & White	175.00
Scoop, Gray, Small	125.00
Skillet, Blue–Green & White Swirl	135.00
Skillet, Mottled Green, Black Trim	10.00
Slop Jar, Gray	15.00
Slop Jar, Green & Ivory	15.00
Spittoon, Aqua & White Swirl	50.00
Spittoon, Woman's, Blue & White	85.00
Spoon, Basting, Red & White	8.00
Spoon, Mixing, White, Long Handle	5.00
Strainer, Gray	30.00
Strainer, Gray, Small	9.00
Syrup, All Blue	65.00
Syrup, Handle, Gray	225.00
Tea Set, Child's, Blue & White, Box, 10 Piece	275.00
Tea Strainer, Sky Blue	35.00
Tea Strainer, Turquoise & White Swirl	175.00
Teapot, Blue & White	50.00
Teapot, Castle Scene, Pewter Trim	195.00
Teapot, Gray, 8 In.	25.00
Teapot, Gray, 9 In.	25.00
Teapot, Pewter Top, Copper Bottom	125.00
Teapot, Pewter Trim, Gray	165.00
Teapot, Sky Blue	35.00
Tray, Red & White, 18 In.	50.00
Utensil Rack, Gray	165.00
Washboard, Cobalt Blue, National Washboard Co.	50.00

Greentown glass was made by the Indiana Tumbler and Goblet Company of Greentown, Indiana, from 1894 to 1903. In 1899, the factory name was changed to National Glass Company. A variety of pressed, milk, and chocolate glass was made.

GREENTOWN, see also Chocolate Glass; Custard Glass; Holly Amber; Milk Glass; Pressed Glass

GREENTOWN, Berry Bowl, Leaf Bracket	20.00
Bowl, Herringbone Buttress, 7 1/2 In.	245.00
Bowl, Lily–of–The–Valley, Gold Rim, Wellsville	32.50

Bowl, Mitted Hand	25.00
Bowl, Pleat & Band, Cover, 7 1/8 X 6 3/4 In.	65.00
Bowl, Wildflower, Clear, Square	12.00
Butter, Dewey, Cover, Individual, Amber	50.00
Butter, Holly, Cover	75.00
Butter, Teardrop & Tassel, Cover, Blue	95.00 To 135.00
Chocolate, Nappy, Daisy, Cover	195.00
Compote, Amber, Holly, Open	1300.00
Compote, Clear, Teardrop & Tassel, Cover, Small	85.00
Compote, Pleat Band, Scalloped Rim, 8 1/2 In.	21.50
Compote, Teardrop & Tassel, 6 1/2 In.	50.00
Creamer, Amber	40.00
Creamer, Cobalt Blue, Brazen Shield	85.00
Creamer, Wildflower, Clear	22.50
Dish, Chicken On Nest, Amber	110.00
Dish, Hen Cover, Amber	125.00
Dish, Holly, Rectangular, 4 3/4 X 10 3/4 In.	115.00
Dish, Rabbit Cover, Amber	135.00
Goblet, Pleat Band	20.00
Mug, Amber, Serenade	90.00
Mug, Dewey, Handle, Amber	50.00
Mug, Dewey, Handle, Green	45.00
Mug, Elves, Green	65.00
Mug, Elves, Opaque Blue	34.00
Mug, Outdoor Drinking Scene, Nile Green	135.00
Mug, Serenade, Green	45.00 To 85.00
Nappy, Austrian, Cover	35.00
Pitcher, Water, Cord Drapery, Green	245.00
Pitcher, Water, Fleur–De–Lis	80.00
Pitcher, Water, Squirrel	200.00
Plate, Bread, Clear, God's Grapes, Motto	26.00
Plate, Serenade, Gilded Edge, 6 1/2 In.	45.00
Platter, Clear, Shell & Tassel, Oval	55.00
Punch Cup, Austrian, Crystal	10.00
Relish, Teardrop & Tassel	14.00
Relish, Teardrop & Tassel, Oval, Green	65.00
Sauce, Clear, Shell & Tassel, Square	10.00
Sauce, Teardop & Tassel, 3 5/8 In.	8.00
Spooner, Austrian	25.00
Stein, Serenade	35.00
Stein, Troubadour, Transparent Amber, 4 3/4 In.	67.50
Toothpick, Geneva	135.00
Toothpick, Leaf Bracket	350.00
Toothpick, Witch	175.00
Tumbler, Dewey, Amber	40.00
Tumbler, Dewey, Canary	65.00
Tumbler, Teardrop & Tassel	30.00
Vase, Austrian, Clear, 8 1/4 In.	45.00
Vase, Dewey, Green, 5 1/2 In.	22.50
Wine, Beehive	60.00
Wine, Herringbone Buttress, Green	160.00
Wine, Lattice	18.50
Wine, Shuttle	10.00

 Grueby Faience Company of Boston, Massachusetts, was incorporated in 1897 by William H. Grueby. Garden statuary, art pottery, and architectural tiles were made until 1920. The company developed a matte green glaze that was so popular it was copied by many other factories making a less expensive type of pottery. This eventually led to the financial problems of the pottery.

GRUEBY, Lamp, Matte Green Glaze, Tall Blades & Short Leaves, C.1910, 11 In.	1400.00
Paperweight, Scarab	225.00
Paperweight, Scarab, Mottled Green Glaze, Logo & Label, 2 3/4 In.	125.00
Tile, Green, Sterling Silver Frame, Ball Feet, Signed, 1910, 4 In., Pr.	200.00

Tile, Matte Green, Paper Label, C.1910, 6 In.	95.00
Vase, Alternating Buds & Leaves, Artist Initials, 11 7/8 In.	2600.00
Vase, Butterscotch Glaze, Bubble Burst Shoulder, 4 3/4 X 5 1/2 In.	450.00
Vase, Cabbage Form, Yellow, Green Leaves, C.1905, 9 1/4 In. ....*Illus*	4500.00
Vase, Elongated Neck, Green Cabbage Form, Yellow, C.1905, 9 1/4 In.	4500.00
Vase, Horizontal Ribs, Green Glaze, Signed, 8 In.	275.00
Vase, Mauve Yellow & Blue Narcissus, W.Post, 11 1/2 In.	5500.00
Vase, Molded Leaves, Short Neck Collar, Paper Label, 4 1/4 In.	275.00
Vase, Mottled Green Glaze, World's Fair St.Louis 1904 Label, 16 In.	4700.00
Vase, Mustard–Colored Glaze, 4 1/2 In.	325.00
Vase, Vertical Ribbed, Cylindrical, Artist MT, DV, 1905, 9 In.	650.00
Vase, Yellow Buds, Green Matte Glaze, Cylindrical, Artist, 10 1/4 In.	3000.00

 Included in this category are shotguns, pistols, and other antique firearms. Rifles are listed in their own section. Be very careful when buying or selling guns because there are special laws governing the sale and ownership. A collector's gun should be displayed in a safe manner, probably with the barrel filled or a part missing to be sure it cannot be accidentally fired.

GUN, BB, Daisy Model 96	275.00
BB, Daisy, Pump, Box	50.00
BB, Targeteer, Daisy No.118	45.00
Blank, Magic, Cast Iron, 3 1/2 X 6 1/2 In.	40.00
Blunderbuss, Flintlock, Brass Butt Plate, 1770–1800, 19 In.	725.00
Blunderbuss, Flintlock, H.W.Mortimer, C.1785, 26 3/4 In.	1650.00
Brass Starter Cannon, Black Powder, 6 In.Barrel	190.00
Buggy, Frank Wesson, Detachable Stock, Barrel 24 In.	450.00
Carbine, Gwyn & Campbell, Blue Finish, Civil War	2250.00
Carbine, Remington, Split Breech, Cavalry	875.00
Carbine, Sharps & Hankins, US Navy, Leather Covering, 24 In.	895.00
Carbine, Winchester, No.M1873, Saddle Ring, 1876	2100.00
Colt 51, Navy, Matched Numbers	475.00
Colt Peacemaker, 38–40 Caliber, 1902	650.00
Derringer, Sharp, C.1859	475.00
Flintlock, Pepperbox, 4–Shot, French, 1790–1810, 11 In.	3950.00
Flintlock, Walnut, Brass Tip, America, C.1775, 57 1/2 In.	1320.00
Marlin, 38 Caliber, 1878	175.00
Muff, Lady's, Baby Hammerless, 22 Caliber	120.00
Musket, 69 Cal., Percussion, Plate Jos.N.Nicholet, 23 In.Barrel	200.00
Musket, Indian Fur Trade, Walnut Stock, Dragon Plate, 1850s, 40 In.	2250.00
Musket, Springfield, Civil War	295.00
Musket, Springfield, Ramrod Bayonet, 1884	375.00
Pellet, Quackenbush	75.00
Pellet, Winchester, Model 425	250.00
Pistol, Colt, Automatic, 32 Caliber	140.00
Pistol, Colt, Single Action, 1887, 7 1/2 In.	1050.00
Pistol, Dueling, Flintlock, John Twigg, C.1783, 13 3/4 In.	660.00
Pistol, Flintlock, Navy, S.North, Walnut, 1808–10, 16 3/4 In.	3300.00
Pistol, Flintlock, Reeves, 7 In.	165.00
Pistol, Frank Wesson, Single Shot, 32 Caliber, Wire Stock	425.00
Pistol, Kilgore Federal, Box, Cast Iron	95.00
Pistol, Knuckleguard, Sure Defender No.93, 19th Century, 5 7/8 In.	880.00
Pistol, Lady's, Hopkins & Allen, Engraved, 32 Caliber	100.00
Pistol, Percussion Cap, Half Walnut Stock, French, 19th Century, 8 In.	1540.00
Pistol, Percussion, A.H.Waters, Single Shot, 54 Caliber, 1844, 14 In.	275.00
Pistol, Percussion, Ripol, Breech, Ramrod, 18th Century, 12 3/4 In.	990.00
Pistol, Pocket, Flintlock, Box Lock, Engraved G.I.Paris, 1800, 6 In., Pr.	770.00
Pistol, Service, Flintlock, Philip D'Auvergne, Henry Nock, C.1796, 12 In.	715.00
Pistol, Victor, Target, Box, Papers	350.00
Revolver, Colt, Army, Single Action, 45 Caliber, Thos.Howard, 5 1/2 In.	300.00
Revolver, Colt, Model 1849, 6 Shot, 31 Caliber, 6 In.	495.00
Revolver, French, Pinfire, 1864	300.00
Revolver, Iver–Johnson, 32 Caliber	37.00

Revolver, Navy, Percussion, Colt No.1851, 36 Caliber, 13 1/4 In. 1650.00
Rifle, Winchester, No.102 .... 750.00
Robbins & Lawrence, Pepperbox, C.1850 .... 185.00
Shotgun, Double Barrel, Muzzle Loading, Boy's 850.00
Shotgun, Hopkins & Allen, Single Barrel, 12 Gauge 75.00
Shotgun, Van Camp, 12 Gauge 27.50
Target Pistol, Percussion, Octagonal Barrel, 1830–40, French, 15 In., Pr. 3850.00
Winchester, Model 12, 20 Gauge, Gold Engraved 4500.00
Winchester, Model 21, 20 Gauge, Double Barrel 4250.00

Gunderson glass was made at the Gunderson–Pairpoint Glass Works of New Bedford, Massachusetts, from 1952 to 1957. Gunderson Peachblow is especially famous.

GUNDERSON, Compote, Ruby, 5 X 7 In. 80.00
Cornucopia, Marina Blue, 11 In. 135.00
Decanter, Peachblow, Raspberry To White, Shell Handle, 12 In. 750.00
Rose Bowl, Kensington, Engraved Waterbird, 1940s 97.50
Vase, Trefoil Shape, 9 1/4 In. 225.00

Gutta–percha was one of the first plastic materials. It was made from a mixture of resins from Malaysian trees. It was molded and used for daguerreotype cases, toilet articles, and picture frames in the nineteenth century.

GUTTA–PERCHA, Box, Odd Fellows 25.00
Case, Black, Indian Head, Young Man Tintype, 1 7/8 X 2 1/8 In. 50.00
Frame, Picture, Gold Foil, Velvet Interior, 4 In. 40.00
Match Holder, Globe Cycle Co. 65.00

Haeger Potteries, Inc., Dundee, Illinois, started making commercial art wares in 1914. Early pieces were marked with the name "Haeger" written over an "H." About 1938, the mark "Royal Haeger" was used. The firm is still making florist wares and lamp bases.

HAEGER, Ashtray, Gold Patina 10.00
Ashtray, No.138, Blue 6.50
Bowl, With Flower Frog, Green Swirl Glaze, Round, Marked 55.00
Candleholder, Green, 5 In., Pair 10.00
Flower Frog, Double Fish 15.00
Lighter, Cigarette, Aladdin Lamp 10.00
Pitcher, Flowers, White, 12 In. 15.00
Planter, Madonna & Child, White 10.00
Planter, Madonna, White, 6 X 9 In. 15.00
Planter, Turkey, Brown 10.00
Spittoon, Green 28.00
Vase, Nautilus Shell, Brown, Green 14.00
Vase, Pillow, Baby Rabbit Each End, Ivory, Sticker 15.00
Vase, Red, 12 In. 20.00
Vase, Ruffled, Cobalt Blue, 4 1/2 In. 7.00
Vase, Swan, Lavender, 8 3/4 In. 15.00

Hall China Company started in East Liverpool, Ohio, in 1903. The firm made all types of wares. Collectors search for the Hall teapots made from the 1920s to the 1950s. The dinnerwares of the same period, especially Autumn Leaf pattern, are also popular. The Hall

A hair dryer set for cool can be used to blow the dust off very ornate pieces of porcelain.

China Company is still working. Autumn Leaf pattern dishes are listed in their own category in this book.

HALL, Ashtray, Indian Head	10.00
Ashtray, Palmer House, Chicago, Blue Turquoise	10.00
Baker, French, Poppy	15.00
Bean Pot, 1 Handle	65.00
Bean Pot, Poppy & Wheat, 1 Handle	60.00
Bean Pot, Rose Parade, Tab Handle	35.00
Bowl, Cereal, Heather Rose, 6 1/4 In.	5.00
Bowl, Nesting, Cactus, Banded, 3 Piece	60.00
Bowl, Nesting, Morning Glory, 5 Piece	50.00
Bowl, Nesting, Poppy, 4 Piece	65.00
Bowl, Rose Parade, 6 X 9 1/2 In.	30.00
Bowl, Salad, Blue Bouquet	9.00
Bowl, Salad, Poppy	9.00
Bowl, Salad, Tavern	18.00
Cake Plate, Springtime	12.00
Casserole, Fantasy, Big Lip, Red Edge	33.00
Casserole, Flute, Handle, 7 1/4 In.	45.00
Casserole, G.E., Gray, Yellow Cover, 1 Qt.	35.00
Casserole, Morning Glory, Big Lip	30.00
Casserole, Pink Mums, Colonial	52.00
Casserole, Poppy, Cover	25.00
Casserole, Rose Parade	24.00 To 30.00
Casserole, Saf–Handle, Cover, Chinese Red	24.00
Casserole, Sunshine	35.00
Casserole, Tab Handle, Chinese Red	50.00
Coffeepot, Drip, Jewel Tea, 6 Cup	32.00
Coffeepot, Drip, Poppy	25.00
Coffeepot, Electric, Game Bird	90.00
Coffeepot, Maroon, Silver Trim	17.00
Coffeepot, Poppy, Gold Key	36.00
Coffeepot, Red Poppy	22.00
Coffeepot, Step Down, Red & Hi–White	30.00
Cookie Jar, Banded	45.00
Cookie Jar, Blue Blossom	185.00
Cookie Jar, Cactus, Banded	120.00
Cookie Jar, Flareware	15.00
Cookie Jar, Goldilocks	90.00
Cookie Jar, Grape, Yellow, Gold Trim	40.00
Cookie Jar, Zeisel, Turquoise, Gold Trim	15.00
Creamer, Springtime	5.00
Cup & Saucer, Pink Morning Glory	7.00
Cup, Heather Rose	4.00
Cup, Serenade	4.50
Custard, Poppy, Set of 3	10.00
Drip Jar, Poppy, Cover	17.00
Drip–O–Later, Gold Spot	35.00
Flour Shaker, Poppy & Wheat	20.00
Fruit Bowl, Heather Rose, 5 1/2 In.	3.50
Jug, Ball, Chinese Red	20.00
Jug, Ball, Chinese Red, No.4	13.00
Jug, Ball, Poppy	34.00
Jug, Ball, Red & Hi–White	30.00
Jug, Ball, Taverne	35.00
Jug, Banded, Chinese Red, 6 1/4 In.	15.00
Jug, Doughnut, Chinese Red	30.00
Jug, Poppy & Wheat, Cover	75.00
Jug, Red Poppy, Radiance	20.00
Jug, Rose Parade, 6 1/2 In.	20.00
Jug, Rose White	18.00
Jug, Shaggy Tulip, Cover	25.00
Leftover, Aristocrat, Canary, Oblong	9.00

Leftover, Taverne, Square 35.00
Match Holder, Red Poppy 22.00
Percolator, Pheasant Decal, Gold Trim 35.00
Pitcher, Milk, Red Poppy, 6 1/2 In. 15.00
Pitcher, Red Poppy, 7 In. 20.00
Pitcher, Taverne, Yellow 150.00
Pitcher, Tilt, Ice Lip, Red 8.00
Pitcher, Water, Ice Lip, Cobalt Blue 32.50
Pitcher, Water, Wards, Delphinium 24.00
Plate, Bouquet, Blue, 6 In. 3.00
Plate, Heather Rose, 6 1/4 In. 1.50
Plate, Heather Rose, 9 1/4 In. 5.00
Plate, Heather Rose, 10 In. 7.00
Plate, Pink Morning Glory, 9 In. 5.50
Plate, Salad, Cameo Rose 5.00
Plate, Wildfire, 9 In. 4.50
Platter, Bouquet, 15 In. 10.00
Platter, Caprice, Zeisel 5.00
Platter, Heather Rose, 13 In. 14.00
Platter, Red Poppy, 11 1/2 In. 8.00
Platter, Richmond, 13 In. 20.00
Pretzel Jar, Poppy .... 50.00 To 65.00
Pretzel Jar, Taverne 50.00
Refrigerator Jar, Yellow ....8.00 To 10.00
Refrigerator Set, Water Jug, Graduated Dishes, Assorted Colors, 5 Pc. 68.00
Rolling Pin, Taverne .... 53.00 To 90.00
Salt & Pepper, Poppy, Handles 20.00
Salt & Pepper, Rose White 15.00
Saltshaker, Crocus 7.00
Saucer, Heather Rose 1.50
Saucer, Red Poppy 1.00
Souffle, Crocus, 3 Pt. 28.00
Soup, Dish, Cameo Rose 10.00
Soup, Dish, Poppy 11.00
Soup, Dish, Wildfire, 8 1/2 In. 9.00
Sugar & Creamer, Blue Blossom 65.00
Sugar & Creamer, Cameo Rose 12.00
Sugar & Creamer, Colonial 35.00
Sugar & Creamer, Lipton, Black 10.00
Sugar & Creamer, Medallion, Lettuce Green 15.00
Sugar & Creamer, Pink Mums, Colonial 35.00
Teapot, Airflow, Cobalt Blue .... 30.00 To 45.00
Teapot, Airflow, Red 45.00
Teapot, Airflow, Turquoise, Gold Trim 45.00
Teapot, Aladdin, Black Luster, Gold Trim 35.00
Teapot, Aladdin, Canary Yellow, Gold, Round Infuser 21.00
Teapot, Aladdin, Cobalt Blue, Gold Trim 38.00
Teapot, Albany, Emerald Green, Gold Trim 25.00
Teapot, Automobile, Chinese Red 200.00
Teapot, Basket, Daffodil, Yellow, Platinum Trim 57.00
Teapot, Benjamin, Celadon Green 22.00
Teapot, Birdcage, Maroon 40.00
Teapot, Boston, Poppy 75.00
Teapot, Cameo Rose .... 20.00 To 38.00
Teapot, Cleveland, Maroon, Gold Trim 35.00
Teapot, Colonial, Ivory 10.00
Teapot, Cozy, Cover, Yellow 32.00
Teapot, Doughnut, Red 105.00
Teapot, Doughnut, Yellow, Gold Trim 135.00
Teapot, Fantasy 100.00
Teapot, French, Gold Flowers, Gold Label, 2 Cup 22.50
Teapot, French, Yellow, Gold, 10 Cup 32.00
Teapot, Globe, Gray, Gold Trim, Dripless 55.00
Teapot, Hollywood, Monterey Green, Gold Trim ....23.00 To 35.00

Teapot, Hook Cover, Chinese Red 30.00
Teapot, Lipton, Maroon 14.00
Teapot, Lipton, Yellow 18.00
Teapot, Los Angeles, Cobalt Blue .... 20.00 To 42.00
Teapot, Los Angeles, Yellow, Gold Trim 28.00
Teapot, McCormick, Green 24.00
Teapot, McCormick, Individual 30.00
Teapot, McCormick, Marine Blue 23.00
Teapot, Melody, Cobalt Blue, Gold Trim 90.00
Teapot, Moderne, Canary Yellow, Gold Trim 8.00
Teapot, Nautilus, Yellow, 6 Cup 90.00
Teapot, New York, Green, Gold Trim, 6 Cup 30.00
Teapot, Parade, Canary Yellow, Gold Trim .... 25.00 To 30.00
Teapot, Parade, Maroon, Gold Trim 35.00
Teapot, Philadelphia, Canary Yellow, Gold Trim 25.00
Teapot, Polka Dot 25.00
Teapot, Regal, Green, Gold Trim 120.00
Teapot, Rose Parade, Blue 17.50
Teapot, Saf–Handle, Canary Yellow, Gold Trim, 6 Cup 40.00
Teapot, Saf–Handle, Cobalt Blue 45.00
Teapot, Sani–Grid, Chinese Red, 6 Cup 22.00
Teapot, Sanka 28.00
Teapot, Star, Cadet Blue, Gold Trim 50.00
Teapot, Star, Green 32.00
Teapot, Streamline, Poppy 75.00
Teapot, Streamline, Yellow, Gold Trim 48.00
Teapot, Surfside, Emerald Green, Gold Trim .... 65.00 To 85.00
Teapot, T–Ball, Canary Yellow, Gold Tirm, Round 50.00
Teapot, Taverne 36.00
Teapot, Teamaster, Cobalt Blue, Twinspout 48.00
Teapot, Tip, On Stand 95.00
Teapot, Twinspout, Chinese Red, 4 Cup 80.00
Teapot, Westinghouse, Blue 35.00
Teapot, Windcrest, Yellow 55.00
Teapot, Windshield, Camellia Rose, Gold Trim 24.00
Teapot, Windshield, Gold Label 25.00
Toothbrush Holder, Little Red Riding Hood 76.00
Tricolator, Chinese Red 20.00

Halloween is an ancient holiday that has been changed in the last 200 years. The jack–o'–lantern, witches on broomsticks, and orange decorations seem to be twentieth–century creations. Collectors started to become serious about collecting Halloween–related items in the late 1970s. The papier–mache decorations, now replaced by plastic, and old costumes are in demand.

HALLOWEEN, Black Cat, Papier–Mache, 7 In. 45.00
Cat, Tall Neck, Papier–Mache, 6 1/2 In. 65.00
Centerpiece, Dennison, Box, With Cat Heads, Pumpkin, 1920s 95.00
Costume, Captain Hook, Box 10.00
Costume, Chief Smoke Smeller, Box 10.00
Costume, Flower, Crepe Paper & Cloth, Brown & Yellow 22.00
Costume, Jester, Orange & Black, Bells At Collar 35.00
Costume, Mickey Mouse, 1933 .... 125.00
Costume, Space Patrol, Box 40.00
Devil, Die Cut, German, 15 1/2 In. 20.00
Hat, 1920, German 10.00
Horn, Multicolored, Witches & Cats 10.00
Jack O'–Lantern, Face Both Sides, Papier–Mache, 10 1/2 In. 45.00
Jack O'–Lantern, German, Small 55.00
Jack O'–Lantern, Orange Cardboard, Tissue Eyes, Nose, 6 X 7 In. 35.00
Jack O'–Lantern, Orange Metal, 5 X 6 In. 32.00
Jack–O'–Lantern, Green Fabric Leaves, Orange, 3 In. 135.00
Jack–O'–Lantern, Papier–Mache, 9 In. 35.00
Lantern, Candle, With Devil, Witch & Cats, Germany, 1930s, 9 In. 95.00

Lantern, Cat, Papier–Mache	45.00
Lantern, Devil	195.00
Lantern, Devil, Papier–Mache	125.00
Lantern, Folding, Germany, 1930s, 9 In.	65.00
Lantern, Glass & Metal, 1950s	20.00
Lantern, Green & White Melon, Red Pickle Nose	395.00
Lantern, Green Melon, Green Fabric Leaves, 4 In.	195.00
Lantern, Hanging, Witches, Black Cats, Owl & Ghosts, 1920s	22.00
Lantern, Owl, Tin, 19th Century	185.00
Lantern, Pumpkin, Papier–Mache	23.50
Mask, Black Man, Bow Tie, Rubber	35.00
Mask, Daisy Mae, Rubber, Topstone	45.00
Mask, Mickey Mouse, Rubber, Spotlite Costume	58.00
Mask, Santa Claus, Pull–Over, Gauze Face, Wool Hair, 1920s	68.00
Mask, Witch, Papier–Mache	55.00
Noisemaker, Black Cat, Triple Ratchet, Germany, 6 In.	55.00
Noisemaker, Cat, Tin, Wooden	15.00
Noisemaker, Old Women On Orange Board, Wooden, 1930s	140.00
Noisemaker, Pumpkin Head, Paper Roll Out Blower, Papier–Mache	45.00
Noisemaker, Witch, Cardboard, Germany	22.00
Noisemaker, Witch, Tin ....5.00 To 20.00
Noisemaker, Wooden, 1920s, Germany	9.00
Pin, Pumpkin, Comic, 1920, Germány	8.00
Pumpkin, Pressed Cardboard, Paper Face	12.00
Pumpkin, Pressed Paper, White Eyes, Orange & Black, Stand–Up	85.00
Pumpkin, Tissue Paper, Cardboard Backing	55.00
Rattle, With Face, Drum Shape, Tissue Paper, Wooden, 8 In.	55.00
Sparkler, Witch, Box	40.00
Tambourine, Painted Witch's Head, Tin	28.00
Tambourine, Pumpkin & Black Cats, Tin	18.00
Tambourine, Pumpkin, Tin, 6 1/2 In.	20.00
Whistle, Cat, Papier–Mache, C.1900	115.00
Witch & Moon, Die Cut, Germany, 10 In.	28.00

Hampshire pottery was made in Keene, New Hampshire, between 1871 and 1923. Hampshire developed a line of colored glazed wares as early as 1883, including a Royal Worcester–type pink, olive green, blue, and mahogany. Pieces are marked with the printed mark or the impressed name "Hampshire Pottery" or "J.S.T. & Co., Keene, N.H."

HAMPSHIRE, Bowl, Bulb, Bud & Lily Pad Leaves Mold, Matte Green Glaze, 10 In. ...	100.00
Bowl, Mottled Matte Blue, 3 X 5 1/2 In.	75.00
Bowl, Oak Leaf Design, Matte Green, 2 3/4 X 6 In.	75.00
Chamberstick, Leaf Shape	65.00
Chamberstick, Shield Back, Green	90.00
Chocolate Pot, 9 1/2 In.	125.00
Creamer, Forest Green, Incised Mark	45.00
Dish, Shell, 8 In.	25.00
Mug, Matte Green, Marked, 6 In.	125.00
Mug, Scuttle, Blue Glaze, Gold Design Trim, Molded Ferns	68.00
Pitcher, Intertwined Vines Form Handle, Blue, 8 In. ....75.00 To 150.00
Plate, View of Central Square, 8 In.	25.00
Teapot, Butterfly	150.00
Vase, Green, 4 1/2 In.	37.50
Vase, Green, 7 In.	125.00
Vase, Matte Green, Handles, 4 1/2 In.	45.00
Vase, Overlapping Leaf Design, Blue–Green Mottled, 7 3/4 In.	425.00
Vase, Tulip, Green	150.00
Vase, Turquoise, Marked Galloway, 5 1/2 X 5 In.	45.00

Philip Handel worked in Meriden, Connecticut, from 1885 and in New York City from 1893 to 1933. His firm made art glass and other types of lamps. Handel shades were made not only of leaded glass in a style reminiscent of Tiffany but also of reverse painted glass. Handel also made vases and other glass objects.

HANDEL, Lamp, Arab & Camel, Signed, 18 In. 6500.00
Lamp, Bird of Paradise Shade, Signed 5250.00
Lamp, Birds & Trees, 10 In. 125.00
Lamp, Black–Eyed Susan Shade, 16 In. 2750.00
Lamp, Bronze Base, Leaded Shade ....*Illus* 2100.00
Lamp, Bronze Base, Leaded Shade, Baluster, Slag Glass, 27 X 25 In. 2000.00
Lamp, Bronze, Leaded Shade, Pink Flowers, 27 In. 2000.00
Lamp, Desk, Bronze Base, Green Shade, Signed 200.00
Lamp, Desk, Harp, Adjustable, Green Glass Shade, C.1920, 12 3/4 In. 750.00
Lamp, Desk, Persian Border 2475.00
Lamp, Dutch Seascape Shade, Blue Tones, 18 In. 3500.00
Lamp, Gone With The Wind, Ball Shade, Roses 400.00
Lamp, Goose Girl & Geese Park Scene, Shade, Signed, 14 1/2 In. 750.00
Lamp, Hanging, Parrots, Craquelle Globe, Amber Drops, Tassel, 10 In. 1750.00
Lamp, Library, Olive Green Shade 800.00
Lamp, Panel, Reverse Painted, Eagle Base 1550.00
Lamp, Persian Border 2475.00
Lamp, Reverse Rose, Beaded Texture, Signed, 18 In. 3900.00
Lamp, Summer Scene, Signed, 18 In. 3000.00
Lamp, Table, Large Dome Reverse Painted Shade, Flowerets, No.6004 .... 4500.00
Lamp, Treasure Island, 18 In. 7950.00
Lamp, Tropical Scene, Signed, 18 In. 1400.00
Lamp, Winter Scene, Signed, 16 In. 1800.00
Plaque, Reverse Painting, Trees, Mountain Lake, Signed, 25 X 13 In. 250.00
Sconce, 4 Amber Glass Etched Shades, Signed, Pair 275.00
Shade, Hanging, Grape & Leaf Pattern 2850.00
Tobacco Jar, Dogs On Front, Metal Cover, Green & Maroon, Signed 525.00
Tobacco Jar, Horse & Dog Heads, Pewter Lid With Pipe 275.00
Tobacco Jar, Owl On Front, Signed 550.00
Vase, Painted, 8 In. 350.00

Handel, Lamp, Bronze Base, Leaded Shade

Parchment lampshades can be cleaned with a cloth soaked in milk, then wipe dry with a clean cloth.

HARDWARE, see Architectural

Harker Pottery Company of East Liverpool, Ohio, was founded by Benjamin Harker in 1840. The company made many types of pottery but by the Civil War was making quantities of yellowware from native clays. They also made Rockingham–type brown–glazed pottery and whiteware. The plant was moved to Chester, West Virginia, in 1931. Dinnerwares were made and sold nationally. In

1971 the company was sold to Jeanette Glass Company and all operations ceased in 1972.

HARKER, Batter Set, Covers, Tulip	55.00
Bowl, Lisa, 9 In.	8.00
Cake Pan, Fruits, Square	12.00
Cake Plate, Mallow, Square	12.00
Cake Plate, Modern Tulip, 10 3/4 In.	7.00
Cake Plate, Tulip, Round	12.00
Cake Plate, Tulip, Square	12.00
Casserole, Lisa, 6 3/4 In.	7.00
Casserole, Lisa, 7 1/2 In.	12.00
Fork, Fruits	16.00
Fork, Petit Point	16.00
Jug, Refrigerator, Kelvinator	65.00
Lifter, Petit Point	12.00
Lifter, Tulip	12.00
Mixing Bowl, Amethyst	12.00
Mixing Bowl, Petit Point	10.00
Mug, Dog Handle, Deer Scene, Rockingham	20.00
Pie Pan, Fruits	12.00
Pie Pan, Mallow	12.00
Pie Pan, Petit Point	12.00
Pie Pan, Tulip	12.00
Pitcher, Lisa, 6 1/2 In.	10.00
Pitcher, Water, Iris, Purple	20.00
Plate, Cameo, 6 In.	1.50
Plate, Cameo, 11 In.	10.00
Plate, Cameo, Square, 8 In.	3.50
Plate, Utility, Cameo, Blue	12.00
Platter, Cameo, Teal, 11 3/4 In.	6.00
Ramekin, Apple, Handle, Cover	30.00
Rolling Pin, Amy	50.00
Rolling Pin, Fruits	65.00
Rolling Pin, Petit Point, White, Gold Trim	25.00
Rolling Pin, Taverne	65.00
Spoon, Fruits	14.00
Teapot, Cameo	20.00

Harlequin dinnerware was produced by the Homer Laughlin Company from 1938 to 1964, and sold without trademark by the F.W. Woolworth Co. It has a concentric ring design like Fiesta, but the rings are separated from the rim by a plain margin. Cup handles are triangular in shape.

HARLEQUIN, Ashtray, Basketweave, Turquoise	16.00
Bowl, Nut, Red	5.00
Bowl, Nut, Yellow	5.00
Butter, Cover, 1/2 Lb.	55.00
Creamer, Blue	25.00
Creamer, Chartreuse	4.00
Creamer, Cobalt Blue	4.00
Creamer, Spruce Green	4.00
Creamer, Turquoise	4.00
Cup & Saucer, Turquoise	5.00
Cup & Saucer, Yellow	5.00
Cup, Mauve	5.00
Cup, Medium Green	5.00
Cup, Red	5.00
Eggcup, Yellow	7.00
Figurine, Cat, Maroon	40.00
Figurine, Great Dane, 9 X 9 In.	175.00
Figurine, Horse, Rose	55.00
Gravy Boat, Gray	16.00
Gravy Boat, Mauve	8.00

Gravy Boat, Yellow 7.50
Jam Jar, Turquoise 55.00
Marmalade, Red 70.00
Pitcher, Ball, Chartreuse 58.00
Pitcher, Mauve, 22 Oz. 15.00
Pitcher, Water, Red 45.00
Pitcher, Yellow, 22 Oz. .... 15.00 To 25.00
Plate, Gray, 10 In. 5.00
Plate, Red, 10 In. 5.00
Plate, Rose, 10 In. 5.00
Plate, Turquoise, 9 In. 4.50
Plate, Turquoise, 10 In. 5.00
Plate, Yellow, 10 In. 5.00
Platter, Yellow, 13 In. 6.00
Soup, Cream, Turquoise .... 6.50 To 7.00
Spoon Rest, Yellow 95.00
Sugar & Creamer, Turquoise 12.00
Sugar, Cover, Rose 5.00
Sugar, Cover, Yellow .... 5.00 To 6.00
Sugar, Gray 6.00
Teapot, Red 30.00

Hatpins were fashionable from 1860 to 1920 when the large, heavy hat required special long–shanked pins to hold the hat in place. Naturally, hatpin holders were made during the same years. The hatpin holder resembles a large saltshaker, but it often has no opening at the bottom as a shaker does. Hatpin holders were made of all types of ceramics and metal. Look for other prices under the names of specific manufacturers.

HATPIN HOLDER, Child's, Blue Flowers 75.00
Floral, RS Germany, Green Mark, 7 In. 135.00
Geisha 45.00
Gold Beading, Open Top, Nippon, 4 3/4 In. 30.00
King & Queen, Double–Faced, Porcelain .... 265.00 To 325.00
Lady With Fan, Pink, Bisque, S & V 225.00
Large Flower, Full–Length, Holes In Top, 4 1/2 In. 32.00
Roses, Nippon 65.00
Shaded Beige, Pink Florals, 5 1/2 In. 40.00

Hatpins were popular from 1860 to 1920. The long pin, often over four inches, was used to hold the hat in place on the hair. The tops of the pins were made of all materials from solid gold and real gemstones to ceramics and glass. Be careful to buy original hatpins and not recent pieces made by altering old buttons.

HATPIN, Art Nouveau Lady, Sterling Silver .... 65.00 To 85.00
Bear, Standing By Tree, Sterling Silver 125.00
Depression Glass, Black Jets 16.00
Figural, Owl On Top, Sterling Silver, 3/4 In. .... 70.00 To 90.00
Floral Design, Satsuma 110.00
Glass, Aquamarine 24.00
Grape Leaf, Pearl–Type Grapes, 10 1/2 In. 38.00
Green–Eyed Snake, Holding Amethyst, 12 In. 85.00
Lady's Face, Art Nouveau, Sterling Silver 75.00
Oriental Design, Brass 12.50
Rhinestone, Swirled Pink Stones, 2 In. 12.00
Rhinestone, Triangular Shape, Filigree Border, 12 1/4 In. 135.00
Swastika, Red Enameled, 8 In. 5.00
Wire Flowers, Handmade, 18K Gold, 1852, 4 1/2 In. 335.00

HAVILAND & CO. Haviland china has been made in Limoges, France, since 1842. The factory was started by the Haviland Brothers of New York City. Other factories worked in the town of Limoges making a similar chinaware. It is possible to match existing sets of dishes through dealers who specialize in Haviland china. Listings of these china matching services can be found in "The Kovels' Collectors' Source Book." Porcelains made by other factories in Limoges, France, are listed in this book under "Limoges."

HAVILAND, Bowl, Vegetable, Ceylon, Cover	50.00
Bowl, Vegetable, Ganga, Cover	145.00
Butter, Pink Roses, Liner, Round, Cover	60.00
Chocolate Pot, Ladore	65.00
Chocolate Pot, Signed, 9 1/2 In.	125.00
Chocolate Set, Wedding Band, 6 Cups & Saucers	295.00
Coffeepot, Ganga	135.00
Cup & Saucer, Cobalt Blue, Gold Rim, Demitasse, 3 Sets	75.00
Cup & Saucer, Ganga	30.00
Cup & Saucer, Tea, Floral	20.00
Gravy Boat, Ganga	98.00
Ice Cream & Cake Set, Flowers & Butterflies	50.00
Ice Cream Set, Green & Yellow, Gold Trim, 9 Piece	130.00
Oyster Plate	58.00
Oyster Plate, Green & Brown Trim, Gold, 5 Sections, 8 5/8 In.	55.00
Pitcher, Duck, Yellow, Signed Sandoz	165.00
Plate, Blue Asters, 7 1/2 In.	15.00
Plate, Diana, Wide Cobalt Blue Bands, Gold Overlay, 7 1/2 In.	30.00
Plate, Luncheon, Chrysanthemum	8.00
Plate, Romeo Blank, Floral, Gold Border, 8 1/2 In.	20.00
Plate, Violets, Gold Lattice Rim, Signed, 6 1/4 In.	35.00
Platter, Ceylon, 14 In.	35.00
Platter, Floral, Gold Trim, Artist Signed, 16 X 10 In.	115.00
Platter, Flowers, Garland Border, Diamond, Seed Pearl, 14 1/2 In.	35.00
Platter, Ganga, 14 In.	76.00
Platter, Ganga, 16 In.	90.00
Platter, Princess, Star, 14 1/2 In.	35.00
Platter, Spring Bouquet, 16 In.	27.00
Ramekin, Orange & Green Floral Design, Gold Rim, Marked	65.00
Sugar & Creamer, Ceylon	95.00
Sugar & Creamer, Chrysanthemum	35.00
Sugar, Duck Cover, Yellow & White, Signed Sandoz, 7 In.	450.00
Tea Set, Forget–Me–Nots, Gold, 1894 Mark, Demitasse, 3 Piece	86.00
Tea Set, Gold Handles, Floral Rim, 4 Piece	60.00
Vegetable, Chrysanthemum, Clam Shape, Open	25.00

 T. G. Hawkes & Company of Corning, New York, was founded in 1880. The firm cut glass blanks made at other glassworks until 1962. Many pieces are marked with the trademark, a trefoil ring enclosing a fleur–de–lis and two hawks. Cut glass by other manufacturers is listed under either the factory name or the general category "Cut Glass."

HAWKES, Basket, Engraved Glass Insert, Silver Rim & Bail, Signed, Miniature	70.00
Bottle, Water, Signed, 8 In.	135.00
Bottle, Whiskey, Faceted Stopper, Signed, 12 1/2 In.	210.00
Bowl, Fruit, Hobstars, Kensington, 4 In.	765.00
Bowl, Scalloped, 9 In.	335.00
Bowl, Venetian, 3 1/2 X 8 1/4 In.	450.00
Box, Brilliant Cut, Lift–Off Lid, Signed, 3 1/2 X 6 1/2 In.	265.00
Box, Hinged Cover, Signed, 5 In.	310.00
Box, Millicent Pattern, Cover, Round, Signed, 4 1/2 X 9 In.	525.00
Bread Tray, Chrysanthemum Pattern, 11 X 7 1/2 In.	625.00
Candelabra, Signed, 9 In., Pair	800.00
Candlestick, Ring of Punties, Florals, Signed, 11 3/4 In., Pair	500.00
Candlestick, Yellow Cup & Foot, Crystal Twisted Stem, 10 In.	115.00
Candy Dish, Sterling Base, Signed	55.00
Candy Jar, Etched & Cut, Sterling Silver Top & Base, Signed, 11 In.	375.00
Carafe, Signed, 7 In.	135.00
Celery, Pinwheels & Hobstars, Signed, 4 1/2 X 12 In.	120.00
Champagne, Fern & Band	15.00

Champagne, Notched Stem, Signed, 7 In., 6 Piece 195.00
Champagne, Star, 5 Oz. 15.00
Cocktail Shaker, Golf Scene, Sterling Silver Top & Strainer 220.00
Compote, Scalloped Hobstar Foot, Hollow Teardrop Stem, Signed, 9 In. 725.00
Cruet, Etched Floral 70.00
Cruet, Etched Pattern, Sterling Silver Top, Pair 95.00
Cruet, Etched, Sterling Silver Stopper 250.00
Cruet, Oil & Vinegar, Sterling Top, Signed 115.00
Cruet, Sterling Silver Stopper, Signed & Dated 75.00
Cruet, Venetian Pattern, 6 In. 160.00
Cruet, Yale Pattern, Original Stopper 165.00
Decanter, Whiskey, Faceted Stopper, Square, Signed, 10 In. 175.00
Desk Set, Inkwell, Insert, Pen Tray & Letter Rack, Signed 250.00
Dish, Bird Etchings In Panels, Sterling Silver Top, Cover, 7 1/2 In. 110.00
Dish, Boat Shape, Harvard Pattern, Signed, 12 1/2 In. 195.00
Dish, Brazilian Pattern, 6 In. 85.00
Frame, Picture, Intaglio Roses & Strawberries, Oval, 5 X 7 In. 525.00
Goblet, Crisscross Cutting, 9 Oz. 14.00
Ice Bucket, Fighting Gamecocks, Sterling Silver Handle 90.00
Ice Bucket, Sterling Silver Mounts, Tongs & Strainer, 8 1/2 In. 425.00
Lamp, Cut Glass, Domed Shade, Pedestal, 20th Century, 17 3/4 In. 200.00
Nappy, Cut Glass 45.00
Nappy, Handle, Signed, 5 In. 65.00
Pitcher, Brilliant Period, Signed, 10 In. 475.00
Pitcher, Cocktail, Block Cut, Sterling Silver Top & Trim, Signed 235.00
Pitcher, Notched Cut Rim, Harvard Pattern, Signed, 5 X 5 1/2 In. 190.00
Pitcher, Satin Strips, Signed, 10 In. 325.00
Plate, Orpheus Pattern, Signed, 7 In. 250.00
Punch Bowl, Pedestal, Signed, 10 In. 475.00
Punch Cup, Handleless, Footed, Signed .... 85.00 To 90.00
Relish, Cornucopia, Fruit Baskets & Floral, Signed, 7 1/2 In. 55.00
Rose Bowl, Allover Rock Crystal Cutting, 5 1/2 X 6 1/2 In. 195.00
Sugar & Creamer, Stars & Stripes, 3 In. 250.00
Tankard, Crushed Fruit Drink, Engraved, 16 1/2 In. 235.00
Tray, Venetian, Signed, 12 In. 1250.00
Tumbler, Brunswick Pattern, 3 7/8 In. 75.00
Tumbler, Flying Duck Over Cattails, Signed 25.00
Tumbler, Queen's Pattern 58.00
Vase, Art Deco Shape, 10 In. 75.00
Vase, Baluster Form, Sterling Silver Collar, Etched Florals, 10 In. 95.00
Vase, Green, Gold Art Deco Design, Signed, 11 3/8 In. 165.00
Vase, Iris, Gravic Type, Signed, 20 In. 2000.00
Vase, Navarre, Signed, 16 In. 1000.00
Vase, Pedestal, Signed, 13 1/2 In. 175.00
Vase, Purple, Bird On Branch, 12 In. 250.00
Vase, Queen's Pattern, 14 In. 825.00
Vase, Trumpet, Cut Glass, Brunswick, Sawtooth Scalloped Rim, 12 In. 55.00

 Heintz Art Metal shop made jewelry, copper, silver, and brass in Buffalo, New York, from 1915 to about 1935. It became Heintz Brothers Manufacturers about 1935. The most popular items with collectors today are the copper desk sets and vases made with silver overlay designs.

HEINTZ ART, Ashtray, Attached Match Holder, 9 In. 90.00
Ashtray, Metal, Sterling Silver Trim, 9 In. .... 48.00 To 70.00
Box, Art Deco Silver Birds On Hinged Cover, 3 1/4 X 4 In. 95.00
Box, Sterling Silver Design On Bronze, Suede Lined, 9 In. 115.00
Cup, Westfield Tennis Club, Championship, 1920s 75.00
Desk Set, Sterling On Bronze, 3 Piece 150.00
Humidor 50.00
Vase, Golfer, Sterling Silver Overlay, Bronze, 2 Handles 245.00
Vase, Sterling Silver On Bronze, 10 In. 70.00
Vase, Sterling Silver Overlay On Bronze, Art Nouveau, 12 In. 125.00
Vase, Sterling Swirling Iris Design On Bronze, 4 1/2 In. 68.00

Vase, Stick, Sterling Silver Overlay, Bronze, 10 In. 110.00

Heisey glass was made from 1896 to 1957 in Newark, Ohio, by A. H. Heisey and Co., Inc. The Imperial Glass Company of Bellaire, Ohio, bought some of the molds and the rights to the trademark. Some Heisey patterns have been made by Imperial since 1960. After 1968, they stopped using the "H" trademark. Heisey used romantic names for colors such as "Sahara." Do not confuse color and pattern names.

HEISEY, see also Custard Glass; Ruby Glass

HEISEY, **Acorn,** Candlestick, Flamingo, Pair	180.00
Admiralty, Sherry	9.00
Albemarle, Goblet, Orange Flash	13.00
Albemarle, Tumbler, Iced Tea, Footed	20.00
Alexandrite, Plate, Marked, Square, Empress, 6 In.	35.00
Ambassador, Tumbler, 8 Oz.	14.50
Athena, Tray, 9 X 5 In.	10.00
Banded Flute, Candlestick, Saucer Foot, 2 In.	38.00
Banded Flute, Cup	10.00
Banded Flute, Wine, 3 Oz.	20.00
Bashful Charlotte, Figurine, Emerald Green, 13 In.	200.00
Beaded Flute, Candlestick, Saucer Foot, Pair	50.00
Beaded Panel & Sunburst, Bowl, Footed, 8 In.	75.00
Beaded Panel & Sunburst, Punch Cup	12.00
Beaded Swag, Berry Set, Crystal, Purple Flowers, 6 Piece	175.00
Beaded Swag, Bowl, Ruffled Point Scallop, Flat, 9 1/2 In.	45.00
Beaded Swag, Butter, Pink Rose, Cover	145.00
Beaded Swag, Mug, Etched Father, Mineola Fair, 1910	35.00
Beaded Swag, Mug, Etched Mother, Mineola Fair, 1910, Ruby Stain	35.00
Beaded Swag, Pitcher	100.00
Beaded Swag, Sugar, Pink Rose, Cover	125.00
Beaded Swag, Syrup, Etched Scrolling, Red Flash	195.00
Beaded Swag, Table Set, 4 Piece	375.00
Beaded Swag, Tankard Set, Opalescent, 4 Tumblers	300.00
Beaded Swag, Wine, Custard Glass	60.00
Bookends, Horsehead	195.00
Bowl, Salad Dressing, 2 Sections, 6 1/2 In.	35.00
Cabochon, Cocktail, Southwind Cut, 4 Oz.	10.00
Cabochon, Goblet, Southwind Cut, 10 Oz.	12.50
Cane With Rosette, Celery	35.00
Caprice, Cup & Saucer, Blue	32.00
Carcassone, Cigarette Holder, Cobalt Blue	75.00
Carcassone, Cocktail, Cobalt Blue	40.00
Carcassone, Cocktail, Oyster, Alexandrite, 3 Oz.	60.00
Carcassone, Decanter, 1 Pt.	160.00
Carcassone, Goblet, Sahara, 11 Oz.	12.00
Carcassone, Sherbet, Sahara	14.00
Cascade, Candleholder, 3–Light, Pair .... 140.00 To 145.00
Caswell, Sugar & Creamer, Flamingo, Silver Band	128.00
Cathedral, Vase, Flared, Arctic Etch	110.00
Charter Oak, Goblet, Moongleam, 8 Oz.	23.00
Chintz, Goblet, 8 In.	20.00
Classic, Candlestick, 1–Light, A Prisms, 16 In., Pair	40.00
Coarse Rib, Celery, Amber, 12 In.	22.00
Coarse Rib, Dish, Pickle, Handle, Pewter Frame, 6 In.	18.00
Coarse Rib, Pitcher, 3 Pt.	90.00
Coarse Rib, Sugar & Creamer, Moongleam	32.00
Coarse Rib, Tumbler, Soda, 9 Oz.	18.00
Colonial, Bowl, 8 1/2 In.	18.00
Colonial, Compote, Cupped, Footed, Marked, 4 1/2 In.	30.00
Colonial, Creamer, Marked	20.00
Colonial, Punch Bowl, 2 Part	145.00
Colonial, Punch Cup	10.00
Colonial, Salt, Footed	12.00

Colonial, Sugar & Creamer, Moongleam .... 50.00 To 55.00
Colonial, Vase, Trumpet, 15 In. 70.00
Columbia, Candlestick, Pair 40.00
Continental, Berry Set, Gold Trim, Marked, 6 Piece 65.00
Continental, Butter, Cover, Marked 60.00
Continental, Pitcher, Water 175.00
Crystolite, Ashtray, 3 1/4 In. 3.00
Crystolite, Candlestick, 3–Light, Pair 35.00
Crystolite, Candlestick, 4 In., Pair 26.00
Crystolite, Coaster, 3 1/2 In. 32.00
Crystolite, Coaster, Sahara, 3 1/2 In. 32.50
Crystolite, Coaster, Zircon, 3 1/2 In. 42.50
Crystolite, Cruet, Original Stopper, 3 Oz. 55.00
Crystolite, Dish, 2 Sections, Handle, 8 In. 20.00
Crystolite, Dish, Mustard, Amber 165.00
Crystolite, Dish, Pickle, Sterling Silver Overlay, Marked, 9 In. 50.00
Crystolite, Dresser Set, Powder Box, Cologne Bottle, Tray, 4 Piece 198.00
Crystolite, Pitcher, Water 75.00
Crystolite, Relish, 3 Sections, Oval, Marked, 13 In. 32.50
Crystolite, Relish, 5 Sections, 10 In. 23.00
Crystolite, Sherbet, 6 Oz. 12.00
Crystolite, Spooner 15.00
Crystolite, Sugar & Creamer .... 20.00 To 28.00
Crystolite, Syrup 55.00
Crystolite, Tumbler, Iced Tea, 12 Oz. 17.50
Diamond Optic, Sherbet, Moongleam, 4 1/2 In. 15.00
Diana, Tray, Center Handle, Heatherbloom 87.50
Dolphin, Pitcher, Sahara, Footed 135.00
Double Rib & Panel, Mustard, Cover, Flamingo 87.50
Duquesne, Cocktail, Normandy Etch 23.00
Duquesne, Goblet, 9 Oz. 9.50
Empress Etch, Plate, Moongleam, 8 In. 15.00
Empress, Basket, Floral, Butterfly Etch, 8 In. 180.00
Empress, Bowl, Flamingo, Footed, 2 Handles, 8 1/2 In. 35.00
Empress, Candlestick, Sahara, Pair 210.00
Empress, Creamer, Flamingo 75.00
Empress, Creamer, Sahara 75.00
Empress, Cruet, Flamingo 110.00
Empress, Cruet, Sahara 125.00
Empress, Dish, Pickle, Green, Gold Trim 110.00
Empress, Ice Bucket, Moongleam 95.00
Empress, Pitcher, Silver Overlay 50.00
Empress, Plate, Alexandrite, 7 1/2 In. 45.00
Empress, Plate, Chintz Etch, Flamingo, Square, 6 In. 10.00
Empress, Plate, Chintz Etch, Flamingo, Square, 7 In. 12.50
Empress, Plate, Square, 7 In. 8.00
Empress, Plate, Square, Tangerine 165.00
Empress, Relish, 2 Sections, Sahara 35.00
Empress, Relish, 3 Sections, Sahara 38.00
Empress, Sauce Dish, 4 1/2 In. 8.50
Empress, Sherbet, Sahara 29.50
Empress, Sugar & Creamer, Individual 27.00

Never put hot glass in cold water or cold glass in hot water; the temperature change can crack the glass.

Empress, Sugar & Creamer, Sahara .... 44.00 To 60.00
Empress, Tray, Center Handle, Sahara, 12 In. 70.00
Essex, Candlestick, 9 In., Pair 138.00
Eternal, Wine 24.00
Everglade, Compote, Oval 22.00
Fairacre, Bottle, Cologne, Flamingo 175.00
Fancy Loop, Bottle, Oil, Stopper 15.00
Fancy Loop, Bowl, 8 In. 32.00
Fancy Loop, Butter, Cover 125.00
Fancy Loop, Plate, Cheese, 8 In. 30.00
Fancy Loop, Toothpick 28.00
Fancy Loop, Vase, 8 In. 40.00
Fancy Loop, Vase, 10 In. 65.00
Fandango, Butter, Cover 90.00
Fandango, Compote, 8 In. 85.00
Fern, Candlestick, Bobeches & Prisms, Pair 72.50
Figurine, Asiatic Pheasant 275.00
Figurine, Bull, Marked 895.00
Figurine, Clydesdale Horse, Frosted 275.00
Figurine, Colt, Standing 55.00
Figurine, Colt, Standing, Amber 450.00
Figurine, Donkey 235.00
Figurine, Gazelle ....895.00 To 1050.00
Figurine, Giraffe, Head Back 165.00
Figurine, Girl, Dinkey Do 295.00
Figurine, Goose, Wings Halfway Up .... 70.00 To 75.00
Figurine, Goose, Wings Up 95.00
Figurine, Hen 325.00
Figurine, Mallard 95.00
Figurine, Mallard, Wings Down 220.00
Figurine, Mallard, Wings Up 155.00
Figurine, Piglets, Standing 65.00
Figurine, Pony, Rearing 135.00
Figurine, Pony, Standing, Amber 360.00
Figurine, Rabbit, Frosted, Small 120.00
Figurine, Ringneck Pheasant .... 125.00 To 150.00
Figurine, Rooster 418.00
Figurine, Scotty, 3 1/2 In. 145.00
Figurine, Swan, With 2 Cygnets, 7 X 8 1/4 In. 575.00
Figurine, Tropical Fish, Marked 895.00
Fine Tooth, Bowl, Low, 6 In. 15.00
Flamingo, Basket, 9 In. 75.00
Flamingo, Bowl, Nut, Octagonal, Individual 11.00
Flamingo, Plate, Marked, 8 In. 6.00
Flamingo, Punch Cup 25.00
Flamingo, Vase, Bud 50.00
Flat Panel, Bowl, Nut, Hawthorne, Individual 25.00
Flat Panel, Nappy, Marked, 7 1/2 In. 20.00
Flat Panel, Sugar & Creamer, Individual 40.00
Fox Chase, Tumbler, Old Fashioned, 8 Oz. 40.00
Gascony, Tumbler, Juice, Sahara 22.00
Gascony, Wine, Horse Scene 34.00
Gayoso, Cocktail, Flamingo 20.00
Glenford, Soda, 8 1/2 In. 35.00
Goose, Brandy 110.00
Goose, Cocktail, Frosted 110.00
Grape, Candlestick, 2–Light, Pair 175.00
Greek Key, Banana Boat 30.00
Greek Key, Butter Chip, 4 In. 13.00
Greek Key, Butter, Cover, Handle, Marked 95.00
Greek Key, Celery, 12 In. .... 40.00 To 48.00
Greek Key, Cruet, 4 Oz. 65.00
Greek Key, Cruet, 6 Oz. 47.50
Greek Key, Dish, Jelly, 2 Handles, Footed 40.00

Greek Key, Eggcup, 5 Oz. 60.00
Greek Key, Ice Bucket, Underplate 125.00
Greek Key, Nappy, Marked, 4 1/2 In. 12.00
Greek Key, Plate, 4 1/2 In. 10.00
Greek Key, Plate, 5 In. 10.00
Greek Key, Plate, 6 In. 12.00
Greek Key, Punch Set, 13 Piece 500.00
Greek Key, Sherbet .... 6.00 To 15.00
Greek Key, Soda, 5 Oz. 58.00
Greek Key, Sugar & Creamer 40.00
Greek Key, Tankard, 3 Pt. .... 198.00 To 200.00
Greek Key, Tray, French Bread .... 128.00 To 135.00
Groove & Slash, Pitcher 95.00
Half Circle, Sugar & Creamer 50.00
Half Circle, Sugar & Creamer, Sahara 98.00
Hartman, Candy Dish, Cover, Cut 70.00
Hawthorne, Bowl, 10 In. 35.00
Horn of Plenty, Tumbler, Marked, 5 In. 35.00
Horsehead, Box, Cigarette, 4 1/4 X 4 In. 65.00
Ipswich, Candy Dish, Cover 66.00
Ipswich, Candy Jar, Heather, Marked 75.00
Ipswich, Champagne, 4 Oz. 10.00
Ipswich, Sherbet 30.00
Iris, Soup, Dish 65.00
Jamestown, Champagne, Narcissus Cut, 6 Oz. 22.50
Jamestown, Goblet, Barcelona Cut, 9 Oz. 23.00
Jamestown, Goblet, Narcissus Cut, 10 Oz. 32.50
Jamestown, Oyster Cocktail 20.00
Kalonyal, Celery, 11 3/4 In. 58.00
Kenilworth, Cordial, 1 Oz. 75.00
Kohinoor, Sherbet 16.00
Kohinoor, Sherbet, Saturn Optic 19.00
Lariat, Basket, Bonbon, 7 1/2 In. 50.00
Lariat, Bonbon 23.50
Lariat, Bottle, Oil, Loop Stopper, Handle, Original Label, 4 Oz. 65.00
Lariat, Bowl, Cover, 7 In. 65.00
Lariat, Bowl, Crimped, Floral, 12 In. 20.00
Lariat, Bowl, Etched Flower, 11 In. 45.00
Lariat, Candleholder, 1 1/2 In., Pair 15.00
Lariat, Candlestick, 2-Light 53.00
Lariat, Candy Box, Cover, Round 5.00
Lariat, Claret, 4 Oz. 7.00
Lariat, Coaster .... 6.00 To 11.00
Lariat, Cocktail Shaker, Chrome Top, Ruby, 12 In. 45.00
Lariat, Cruet, 2 Oz. .... 35.00 To 37.00
Lariat, Cup 8.50
Lariat, Cup & Saucer 18.50
Lariat, Goblet, Moonglo Cut, 10 Oz. 19.50
Lariat, Lamp, Hurricane, No Globe, Handle 70.00
Lariat, Plate, Silver Overlay Design, 14 In. 55.00
Lariat, Platter, 13 In. 30.00
Lariat, Relish, Divided, Silver Overlay, 10 In. 50.00
Lariat, Sherbet, 6 Oz. 9.50
Lariat, Sugar & Creamer .... 16.75 To 19.00
Lariat, Torte Plate, 12 In. 21.00
Lariat, Vase, Crimped, 7 1/2 In. 65.00
Lariat, Vase, Fan, Footed, Etched, 7 In. 25.00
Lariat, Vase, Fan, Orchid, 7 In. 115.00
Leaf, Candleholder, 1-Light 55.00
Locket On Chain, Compote, 8 In. 110.00
Lodestar, Bowl, Dawn, 7 In. 75.00
Minuet, Goblet, Iced Tea 35.00
Minuet, Sugar & Creamer, Dolphin Feet 50.00
Minuet, Tumbler, Water, 9 Oz. 25.00

Narrow Flute, Bowl, Floral, 9 In.	39.50
Narrow Flute, Dish, Jelly, Handle, Marked, 5 1/2 In.	32.50
Narrow Flute, Dish, Nut, Moongleam	21.50
Narrow Flute, Dish, Strawberry, Rim	57.00
Narrow Flute, Tray, Sugar	35.00
National, Soda, Moonglo Cut, 10 Oz.	12.50
New Era, Candelabra, 2–Light, Bobeches, Prisms, Pair	75.00 To 110.00
New Era, Goblet	50.00
Nude Stem, Vase, Bud	100.00
Octagon, Jam Jar, Handles, Flamingo, 5 1/2 In.	12.50
Octagon, Plate, Center Handle, Empress Etch, Sahara, 10 1/2 In.	70.00
Octagon, Sugar & Creamer, Sahara	65.00
Old Colony, Compote, Etch, 7 In.	48.50
Old Colony, Vase, Empress, Sahara, 9 In.	125.00
Old Dominion, Champagne	20.00
Old Dominion, Goblet, Empress Etch, 10 Oz.	25.00
Old Sandwich, Ashtray, Individual	7.50
Old Sandwich, Beer Mug, Sahara	140.00
Old Sandwich, Candlestick, Pair	79.50
Old Sandwich, Candlestick, Sahara, Pair	150.00
Old Sandwich, Console Set, Frog Insert, Sahara	295.00
Old Sandwich, Cruet, Moongleam	95.00
Old Sandwich, Decanter, Sun–Colored Stopper, Cobalt Blue	450.00
Old Williamsburg, Candelabra, No.300, Prisms, Sahara, Pair	675.00
Old Williamsburg, Candelabrum, 2–Light	185.00
Old Williamsburg, Candelabrum, 3–Light	200.00
Old Williamsburg, Candlestick, 9 In., Pair	125.00
Old Williamsburg, Cordial, 1 Oz.	22.90
Old Williamsburg, Ice Bucket, Underplate	85.00
Old Williamsburg, Mustard, Cover, Spoon	25.00
Old Williamsburg, Pitcher, 3 Pt.	100.00
Old Williamsburg, Punch Bowl, Base	120.00
Old Williamsburg, Punch Cup	5.00
Orchid Etch, Ashtray, Square	30.00
Orchid Etch, Butter, Cover	130.00
Orchid Etch, Cake Plate, Footed, 13 1/2 In.	245.00
Orchid Etch, Candy Jar	40.00
Orchid Etch, Celery, 12 In.	45.00
Orchid Etch, Champagne	30.00
Orchid Etch, Cocktail, 4 Oz.	35.00
Orchid Etch, Cocktail, Flared	28.50 To 35.00
Orchid Etch, Compote, Low Footed, Waverly, 6 1/4 In.	48.00
Orchid Etch, Cordial, 1 Oz.	110.00 To 130.00
Orchid Etch, Cup & Saucer, Footed	55.00
Orchid Etch, Mayonnaise Set, 3 Piece	70.00
Orchid Etch, Plate, 7 1/4 In.	20.00
Orchid Etch, Relish, 4 Sections	70.00
Orchid Etch, Salt & Pepper, Waverly	60.00
Orchid Etch, Tumbler, Juice, Footed	55.00
Orchid Etch, Wine	55.00
Oxford, Cordial	22.50
Panel, Pitcher, Water	75.00
Peerless, Berry Set, Gold Trim, Marked, 7 Piece	95.00
Peerless, Goblet, 9 Oz.	20.00
Peerless, Pitcher, 2 Qt.	48.00
Peerless, Tankard	45.00
Peerless, Toothpick	29.50 To 32.00
Petticoat Dolphin, Candlestick, Pair	300.00
Pied Piper, Tankard	130.00
Pied Piper, Tumbler, 8 Oz.	12.00
Pillows, Jug, 3 Qt.	40.00
Pillows, Punch Set, Base & 6 Cups	400.00
Pillows, Spooner	50.00 To 98.00
Pillows, Sugar, Cover	45.00

Pillows, Vase, Ball, 4 1/2 In. 95.00
Pineapple & Fan, Berry Bowl, 8 In. 29.50
Pineapple & Fan, Butter, Cover, Green, Gold Trim 50.00
Pineapple & Fan, Salt & Pepper 55.00
Pineapple & Fan, Toothpick, Green, Gold Trim 195.00
Pineapple & Fan, Vase, Emerald Green, 8 In. 70.00
Pinwheel & Fan, Basket 295.00
Pinwheel & Fan, Sugar & Creamer .... 85.00 To 98.00
Pinwheel & Fan, Tumbler, 8 Oz. 22.00
Plain Panel, Cruet 45.00
Plantation II, Relish, 3 Sections 25.00
Plantation Ivy, Sherbet 1575.00
Plantation, Bowl, 3 X 7 In. 55.00
Plantation, Bowl, Gardenia, 9 1/2 In. 30.00
Plantation, Candlestick 38.00
Plantation, Candlestick, 2–Light, Pair 100.00
Plantation, Claret, 4 Oz. 37.50
Plantation, Cocktail, Ivy Etch, 4 1/2 Oz., 6 Piece 115.00
Plantation, Cruet ....95.00 To 135.00
Plantation, Goblet, Flared, 10 Oz. 21.00
Plantation, Jam Jar, Cover 90.00
Plantation, Plate, Luncheon, 8 1/2 In. 12.00
Plantation, Plate, Punch Bowl, 19 In. 80.00
Plantation, Punch Cup 20.00
Plantation, Salt & Pepper 50.00
Plantation, Sherbet, 4 Oz. 22.50
Plantation, Sugar & Creamer .... 38.00 To 40.00
Plantation, Syrup .... 75.00 To 95.00
Plantation, Tray, Oblong, 9 In. 35.00
Pleat & Panel, Cruet, Original Stopper, Pink 80.00
Pleat & Panel, Jam Jar, 2 Handles, Flamingo 25.00
Pleat & Panel, Pitcher, Moongleam 90.00
Prince of Wales, Berry Bowl, Gold Decal, 4 1/2 In. 12.50
Prince of Wales, Jug, Ruby Stain, 1/2 Gal. 125.00
Prince of Wales, Punch Set, 14 Piece 235.00
Priscilla, Jug, Crystal, 3 Pt. 80.00
Priscilla, Pitcher, 1 Qt. 95.00
Priscilla, Toothpick 18.00
Provincial, Cruet, Marked 35.00
Provincial, Relish 35.00
Punty & Diamond Point, Cruet 48.00
Punty & Diamond Point, Goblet, Water, Orchid Etch 25.00
Punty Band, Tumbler, Ruby Trim 45.00
Puritan, Carafe, Water 45.00
Puritan, Compote, Jelly, Marked, 5 In. 25.00
Puritan, Console Set, Square 10 In.Bowl 175.00
Puritan, Cordial 14.00
Puritan, Jug, 3 Pt. 55.00
Puritan, Punch Set, Footed, 13 In., 13 Piece 185.00
Puritan, Tankard, 1 Qt. 40.00
Quator, Creamer, Individual, Marked 18.00
Queen Ann, Candlestick, 1–Light, Orchid Etch, Pair 100.00
Queen Ann, Candlestick, Dolphin Footed, Sahara, Pair 175.00
Queen Ann, Flower Bowl, Dolphin Footed, 11 In. 45.00
Queen Ann, Jam Jar, Footed, Marked, 6 In. 50.00
Queen Ann, Plate, 10 1/2 In. 115.00
Queen Ann, Sherbet, Marked 22.00
Queen Ann, Torte Plate, 11 In. .... 85.00 To 95.00
Raised Loop, Creamer 35.00
Recessed Panel, Candy Dish, Cover, 3 Lb. 125.00
Reverse S, Candlestick, Double, Pair 80.00
Rib & Panel, Cruet, Original Stopper 57.50
Rib & Panel, Pitcher, Cover, 1 Qt. 125.00
Ribbed Octagon, Sugar & Creamer, Flamingo 45.00

Having trouble with a stain in a glass bottle or vase? Sometimes this type of stain can be removed. Fill the bottle with water, drop in an Alka-Seltzer, and let it soak for about 24 hours. Then rub the ring with a brush or a cloth. If the deposit is a chemical deposit, this treatment should remove it. If the ring is actually caused by etching of the glass, it cannot be removed unless the bottle is polished.

Ridgeleigh, Ashtray, Square, Individual	2.00 To 3.00
Ridgeleigh, Bonbon, Handles, 6 In.	9.00 To 11.00
Ridgeleigh, Bridge Set, Individual Ashtrays, Marked, 4 Piece	50.00
Ridgeleigh, Coaster, Zircon, 4 In.	35.00
Ridgeleigh, Compote, Jelly, 2 Sections, 6 In.	11.00
Ridgeleigh, Compote, Jelly, 6 In.	16.00
Ridgeleigh, Condiment Set, Signed	125.00
Ridgeleigh, Cruet, Blown, 2 Oz.	28.00
Ridgeleigh, Cruet, Pair	65.00
Ridgeleigh, Cup	7.00
Ridgeleigh, Decanter, 1 Qt.	95.00
Ridgeleigh, Fruit Bowl, 11 In.	21.00
Ridgeleigh, Fruit Bowl, Crimped & Flared, 12 In.	28.00
Ridgeleigh, Mayonnaise Set	24.00
Ridgeleigh, Punch Bowl, Underplate, 8 Cups	275.00
Ridgeleigh, Salt & Pepper, Glass Tops	25.00
Ridgeleigh, Sugar & Creamer, Tray	32.00 To 40.00
Ridgeleigh, Vase, Zircon, 8 In.	130.00 To 145.00
Ring Band, Butter, Hand Painted, Milk Glass	150.00
Rococo, Plate, Frosted, Marked, 12 In.	30.00
Rooster Head, Cocktail Shaker, Etched Horse, 2 Qt.	85.00
Rooster, Cocktail Shaker, 3 Part	80.00
Rooster, Cocktail, Amber	500.00
Rooster, Saltshaker	80.00
Rosalie, Cocktail, 3 Oz.	18.00
Rose Etch, Butter, Cover, Waverly	160.00
Rose Etch, Goblet, Waverly, 9 Oz.	37.50
Rose Etch, Plate, Waverly, 7 In.	20.00
Rose Etch, Plate, Waverly, 8 In.	25.00
Rose Etch, Relish, 3 Sections	60.00
Rose Etch, Salt & Pepper, Waverly	72.50
Rose Etch, Saltshaker	30.00
Rose Etch, Sherbet	27.00
Rose Etch, Sugar & Creamer, Waverly, Marked	65.00
Rose Etch, Tumbler, Iced Tea, Footed	33.00
Rose, Bowl, 9 1/2 In.	58.00
Rose, Candlestick, Pair	45.00
Rose, Candy Dish, Cover, Flat, Round, 5 1/4 In.	150.00
Rose, Claret	95.00
Rose, Compote, Jelly, Footed, 7 In.	35.00
Rose, Cordial, Stem	130.00
Rose, Cruet	90.00
Rose, Cup & Saucer, 16 Piece	360.00
Rose, Goblet	32.50 To 40.00
Rose, Mayonnaise, Footed	45.00
Rose, Plate, 8 In.	20.00 To 27.00
Rose, Platter, 13 In.	55.00

Rose, Salt & Pepper 30.00
Rose, Sherbet .... 25.00 To 35.00
Rose, Sugar & Creamer, Individual 85.00
Rose, Syrup 80.00
Rose, Tray, For Individual Sugar & Creamer 42.50
Rose, Tumbler, Iced Tea 38.00
Rose, Tumbler, Juice, Footed 35.00
Sahara, Sugar & Creamer 87.50
Saturn, Goblet, 10 Oz. 12.00
Saturn, Vase, Ball, 6 In. 50.00
Saturn, Vase, Limelight, Flared, 8 1/2 In. 165.00
Spanish, Cocktail, Cobalt Blue 110.00
Stanhope, Vase, Ivory Knobs, Handle, 9 In. 60.00
Star & Zipper, Bowl, Emerald, 8 In. 175.00
Suez, Cocktail, Belvedere Cut, Marked 7.50
Sunburst & Panel, Punch Bowl, Base 165.00
Sunburst, Relish 32.50
Sunburst, Salt & Pepper, No.2 Sanitary Tops 90.00
Sunburst, Tumbler, Marked 50.00
Swan Handle, Candlestick, Moongleam, Pair 280.00
Swan, Pink, Neck Sticker 100.00
Swirl, Ice Bucket, Tongs, Marked 85.00
Symphone, Cocktail, Renaissance Etch 30.00
Symphone, Goblet, Minuet Etch, 9 Oz. 25.00
Tally Ho, Cocktail Shaker, Rooster Stopper 165.00
Tally Ho, Decanter 140.00
Tally Ho, Stein, Amber, Clear Handle 33.00
Teapot, Rooster 50.00
Thumbprint & Panel, Bowl, Cobalt Blue, Flared, 11 In. 200.00
Thumbprint & Panel, Console Set, Candlesticks & 11 In.Bowl 55.00
Tom & Jerry, Mug 125.00
Touraine, Champagne 10.00
Touraine, Sherbet, Tangerine 270.00
Town & Country, Salad Bowl, 11 In. 30.00
Town & Country, Sandwich Plate, Dawn, 14 In. 50.00
Trident, Candleholder, 2–Light, Flamingo, Pair 110.00
Trident, Candleholder, 2–Light, Pair 115.00
Trident, Candleholder, 2–Light, Sahara, Pair 100.00
Trident, Candlestick, 2–Light, Orchid Etch, Pair 110.00
Trident, Candlestick, Etched, Pair 45.00
Trident, Candlestick, Moongleam, Pair 130.00
Trojan, Compote, Flamingo, 7 In. 35.00
Trojan, Goblet, Flamingo, 8 Oz. 19.50
Tropical Fish, Lamp, Signed 950.00
Tudor, Cigarette Box, Ashtray 98.00
Tudor, Cruet, Stopper, Marked 40.00
Tudor, Goblet, 8 Oz. 20.00
Tudor, Sherbet 6.00
Tulip, Vase, 9 In. 110.00
Tulip, Vase, Cobalt Blue, Marked, 9 In. 345.00
Twist, Berry Bowl, 4 1/2 In. 8.50
Twist, Bowl, Marigold, 12 In. 27.50
Twist, Bowl, Nut, Handle, Individual, Flamingo 17.50
Twist, Candlestick, Moongleam, Pair 42.00
Twist, Cocktail, Oyster, Marigold 29.50
Twist, Creamer, Individual 20.00
Twist, Cruet, Flamingo, 6 Oz. 85.00
Twist, Ice Bucket, Moongleam 52.00
Twist, Ice Tub, Marigold 100.00
Twist, Mustard, Moongleam 78.00
Twist, Nappy, Flamingo, 4 In. 6.00
Twist, Plate, Marigold, 6 In. 14.00
Twist, Plate, Pink, 8 In. 14.00
Twist, Relish, 2 Sections, Moongleam .... 22.00 To 47.00

Twist, Relish, 3 Sections, 13 In.	22.00
Tyrolean, Wine, Orchid Etch, 3 Oz.	55.00
Velvedere, Goblet, 10 Oz.	7.50
Victorian, Bell, Pink	10.00
Victorian, Champagne	27.50
Victorian, Cruet, French Dressing, Original Stopper	60.00
Victorian, Cruet, Original Stopper, 3 Oz.	47.50
Victorian, Eggcup	12.00
Victorian, Goblet, 2–Knob Stem	12.00
Victorian, Sugar & Creamer	18.00
Victorian, Wine, 2 1/2 Oz.	16.00
Victorian, Wine, 4 Oz.	16.00 To 20.00
Wabash, Goblet, Stem, Fontaine Etch	9.00
Waldorf, Cocktail, Tally Ho Etch, 3 Oz.	47.50
Wampum, Box, Cigarette, 4 Ashtrays	95.00
Wampum, Candlestick, 1–Light, Pair	52.50
Wampum, Candlestick, Pair	35.00
Wampum, Torte Plate, 14 In.	30.00
Warwick, Candlestick, 2–Light, Pair	50.00
Warwick, Vase, Cobalt Blue, 9 In.	165.00
Warwick, Vase, Cornucopia Shape, 9 1/2 In., Pair	75.00
Warwick, Vase, Sahara, 5 In.	75.00
Waverly, Bell, Dinner	125.00
Waverly, Bowl, 5–Crimped, 10 In.	75.00
Waverly, Bowl, Mayonnaise, Underplate, Footed, Marked	65.00
Waverly, Butter, Cover, Orchid Etch	165.00
Waverly, Butter, Cover, Rose Etch	165.00
Waverly, Compote, Footed, Low, 6 1/2 In.	40.00
Waverly, Cruet, Stopper	40.00
Waverly, Cup & Saucer	42.50
Waverly, Decanter, Cherry, Oval	250.00
Waverly, Dish, Mayonnaise, 3 Piece	92.50
Waverly, Knife Rest, Orchid Etch, 5 1/2 In.	50.00
Waverly, Plate, 7 1/2 In.	55.00
Waverly, Plate, 8 1/2 In.	22.50
Waverly, Plate, Luncheon, 8 In.	22.50
Waverly, Plate, Orchid Etch, 7 In.	15.00
Waverly, Plate, Salad, 7 In.	20.00
Waverly, Platter, 13 In.	55.00
Waverly, Relish, 3 Sections, Oblong, Orchid Etch, 11 In.	38.00
Waverly, Relish, 4 Sections, Round, 9 In.	95.00
Waverly, Salt & Pepper	72.50
Waverly, Sugar & Creamer	48.00 To 65.00
Waverly, Sugar & Creamer, Narcissus Cut	45.00
Waverly, Sugar & Creamer, Orchid Etch	42.00 To 60.00
Waverly, Torte Plate, Orchid Etch, 14 In.	75.00
Waverly, Vase, 7 In.	27.00
Whirlpool, Bowl, Nut, Individual	10.00
Whirlpool, Candy Dish, Cover, Footed, 5 1/2 In.	375.00
Whirlpool, Plate, Limelight, 8 In.	42.50
Whirlpool, Torte Plate, 13 In.	12.00
Wide Flat Panel, Stack Set	35.00
Wide Flute, Relish, 3 Sections	5.00
Will–O–The–Wisp, Goblet, Cut	25.00
Winged Scroll, Bowl, Emerald, 7 In.	60.00
Winged Scroll, Celery, Gold Trim	275.00
Winged Scroll, Compote, Ruffled Rim, 6 3/4 X 10 3/4 In.	495.00
World, Candelabra, 2–Light, Pair	295.00
Yeoman, Banana Split, Moongleam, Footed	35.00
Yeoman, Compote, Jelly, Floral Cut, 6 In.	17.50
Yeoman, Compote, Jelly, Gold Rim, Marked, 8 In.	25.00
Yeoman, Compote, Moongleam Stem & Foot	30.00
Yeoman, Cup & Saucer, Flamingo	12.00
Yeoman, Cup & Saucer, Moongleam	15.00

Yeoman, Finger Bowl, Coronation Etch 15.00
Yeoman, Perfume Bottle, Stopper, Gold Trim 75.00
Yeoman, Plate, Flamingo, 7 In. 9.00
Yeoman, Plate, Flamingo, 9 In. 9.50
Yeoman, Plate, Hawthorne, 6 In. 5.50
Yeoman, Powder Box, Cover 75.00
Yeoman, Relish, 3 Sections, Floral Etch, Flamingo 23.00
Yeoman, Soup, Cream, Green 15.00
Yeoman, Sugar & Creamer, Flamingo 55.00
Zodiac, Compote, Footed, 6 In. 40.00
    HEREND, see Fischer

Gebruder Heubach, a German firm working from 1820 to 1925, is best known for bisque dolls and doll heads, their principal products. They also manufactured bisque figurines, including piano babies, beginning in the 1880s, and glazed figurines in the 1900s. Dolls are not listed here, but are listed in the Doll section.

HEUBACH, Box, Trinket, Dutch Boy, Seated, Intaglio Eyes, Separates At Waist 450.00
    HEUBACH, DOLL, see Doll, Gebruder Heubach
Figurine, Baby, Green Tub, Marked, 2 In. 235.00
Figurine, Baby, Seated In Old Shoe, Toes Sticking Out, 7 In. 280.00
Figurine, Baby, Sitting, White Nightgown, Green, Marked, 7 1/2 In. 450.00
Figurine, Boy, Rugby Player, Blond, Impressed Sun Mark, 6 In. 75.00
Figurine, Dancing Girl, Gold & Black Design On Dress, 15 1/2 In. 765.00
Figurine, Dancing Girl, Pastel Dress, Pink Bow, Marked, 6 3/4 In. 88.00
Figurine, Dancing Girl, Pleated Skirt, Blue Trim, Blond, 6 3/4 In. 88.00
Figurine, Dutch Boy, Standing By Square Vase, 6 3/8 In. 110.00
Figurine, Dutch Children, Back To Back, Marked, 7 1/4 In. 145.00
Figurine, Dutch Children, Seated, Bisque, Marked, 7 1/4 In., Pair 245.00
Figurine, Dutch Girl, Blue Clothes, Marked, 4 In. 125.00
Figurine, Dutch Girl, Seated, Marked 65.00
Figurine, Fat Boy, 7 1/2 In. 85.00
Figurine, Fat Boy, Gray Coat, Black Hat & Boots, 4 1/2 In. 60.00
Figurine, Fisher Boy, Waders, Hat, Net With Fish & Lobster, 10 In. 150.00
Figurine, Girl, Pink Pleated Skirt, Marked, 5 3/4 In. 118.00
Figurine, Girl, Sitting, Blue Bonnet & Dress, Marked, 4 1/2 In. 125.00
Figurine, Mermaid, Purple Iridized Bowl 495.00
Figurine, Mother Mouse, Baby Squeezes Out Of Shoe, 3 1/4 X 5 In. 165.00
Figurine, Skye Terrier, Begging Position, White, 6 In. 85.00
Figurine, Street Sweeper, Trash Cart, Wheels, Marked, 2 X 1 1/2 In. 95.00
Figurine, The Bicyclist, Man, Victorian Dress, Signed, 11 1/2 In. 325.00
Figurine, Uncle Walt, Marked, 3 1/2 In. 85.00
Planter, 3 Bears & Tree 45.00
Planter, Pastoral Scene, Shepherdess With Staff, Signed, 11 In. 550.00
Soap Dish, Muzzled Pug Puppy, Seated In Dish, Intaglio Eyes, 4 In. 125.00

Higbee glass was made by the J. B. Higbee Company of Bridgeville, Pennsylvania, about 1900. Tablewares were made and it is possible to assemble a full set of dishes and goblets in some Higbee patterns. Most of the glass was clear, not colored.

    HIGBEE, see also Pressed Glass
HIGBEE, Bowl, Yoke & Circle, 9 In. 18.00
Table Set, Child's, Marked, 4 Piece 70.00
Table Set, Hawaiian Lei, Child's, Marked, 4 Piece 82.00
    HISTORIC BLUE, see Adams; Clews; Ridgway; Staffordshire

Hobnail glass is a pattern of glass with bumps in an allover pattern. Dozens of hobnail patterns and variants have been made. Clear, colored, and opalescent hobnail have been made and are being reproduced. Other pieces of hobnail are also listed under Carnival Glass, Hobnail.

    HOBNAIL, see also Fenton; Francisware
HOBNAIL, Bowl, Blue, Footed, 6 1/2 In. 5.00
Bowl, Crimped, Low, 4 1/2 In. 12.00

Celery, Bead & Ruffle Top	45.00
Creamer, Blue, Hobbs, Brockunier & Co.	165.00
Cruet, Cranberry Opalescent, Stopper, Hobbs, Brockunier & Co.	345.00
Lemonade Set, Clear & Frosted, Amber Stain, 5 Piece	450.00
Pitcher, Cranberry Opalescent, Ruffled, Crystal Handle, 5 3/4 In.	165.00
Pitcher, Water, Ruby Stain	45.00
Rose Bowl, Amethyst, Millersburg	375.00
Rose Bowl, Green, Millersburg	1550.00
Tray, Water, 8 1/2 X 12 1/2 In.	26.50
Tray, Water, Blue, 11 1/2 In.	55.00
Tumbler, Amber	20.00
Vase, Allover Hobs, White Lining, Crimped Ruffled Top, 5 1/4 In.	65.00
Vase, Frosted, Straight Crimped Top, Hobbs, Brockunier, 6 In.	35.00
Vase, Loving Cup, Cranberry	22.00
Wine, Amber	20.00

Hochst, or Hoechst, porcelain was made in Germany from 1746 to 1796. It was marked with a six-spoke wheel. Be careful when buying Hochst; many other firms have used a very similar wheel-shaped mark.

HOCHST, Chamberstick, Italian Landscape, Cartouche Foot, 3 1/6 In.	1550.00
Ewer, Cobalt Blue, Portrait Medallion, C.1780, 4 1/4 In.	1100.00
Figurine, Girl, Feeding Rooster, Hen & Chicks, 6 In.	295.00
Figurine, Girl, With Doll, Rose Jacket, C.1770, 4 3/8 In.	2310.00
Figurine, Jockey, Boy, Black Cap, Pink Jacket, 4 3/4 In.	1980.00
Figurine, Maiden, Lambs, 8 In.	250.00
Figurine, Youth, Holding Garland, C.1850, 7 In.	200.00
Group, Masquerading Children, Rocky Base, 1770–75, 7 In.	1430.00

Holly amber, or golden agate, glass was made by the Indiana Tumbler and Goblet Company of Greentown, Indiana, from January 1, 1903, to June 13, 1903. It is a pressed glass pattern featuring holly leaves in the amber-shaded glass. The glass was made with shadings that range from creamy opalescent to brown-amber.

HOLLY AMBER, Bowl, Opalescent, Beaded Rim, 7 In.	450.00
Butter, Cover	1100.00
Mug, Amber White Handle, Band Border, 4 1/2 In.	535.00
Nappy, Handle .... 375.00 To	550.00
Plate, Square	820.00
Relish, 9 In. .... 200.00 To	350.00
Toothpick .... 175.00 To	250.00
Tumbler	475.00
Vase, 6 In.	800.00

Hopalong Cassidy was named William Lawrence Boyd when he was born in Cambridge, Ohio, in 1895. His first movie appearance was in 1919, but the first Hopalong Cassidy film was not until 1934. Sixty-six films were made. In 1948, William Boyd purchased the television rights to the movies, then later made fifty-two new programs. In the 1950s, Hopalong Cassidy was seen in comics, records, toys, and other products. Boyd died in 1972.

HOPALONG CASSIDY, Bank, Plastic, Blue, 4 In.	25.00

Billfold	10.00
Binoculars, Box	225.00
Blotter, W.Boyd, Gabby Hayes Picture, Unused, Large	10.00
Book, Hoppy, Animated TV Screen On Cover, 1950s	25.00
Bottle, Dairy–Lea Milk, Black & Red Graphics, 1 Qt.	45.00
Bottle, Hair Trainer	35.00
Buckle, Scarf	12.00
Button, Savings Club, 3 In.	15.00
Cap Gun, Wyandotte, Metal Trigger, Leather Holster	250.00
Cap Pistol	25.00
Card Tray, Saddle Shape, Box	125.00
Card, Cereal, 1950s	5.00
Carton, Ice Cream, Unused, 1950s, 1 Qt.	14.00
Clock, Alarm, Ingraham	165.00
Coin, Good Luck	9.00
Cookie Jar, Cookie Corral .... 150.00 To 175.00
Cowboy Outfit	70.00
Crayon Set	65.00
Cup, Milk Glass, Black	16.50
Cup, Milk Glass, Green	11.00
Curtains, Yellow, Pictures, Plastic	100.00
Game, Board, Contents Sealed	95.00
Game, Chinese Checkers, Marbles	85.00
Gun & Holster	30.00
Gun, Zoomarang, Box	185.00
Handkerchief	13.00
Horn, Bicycle, Box	90.00
Horseshoe, Brand MKS, Auburn	45.00
Lamp, Wall, Aladdin	145.00
Lunch Box .... 18.00 To 25.00
Money Clip .... 15.00 To 25.00
Napkins, Package	15.00
Night–Light, Original Hoppy Shade, Aladdin	125.00
Pennant, Felt, 1950s, 8 X 19 In.	20.00
Pistol, Gold Plated, Box	200.00
Planter, Relief Design, Pottery	45.00
Plate, Birthday, 6 Piece	20.00
Plate, Hoppy On Topper Decal, W.S.George Ware, 9 1/4 In.	30.00
Postcard, Advertising, 1942 Chrysler	10.00
Puppet, Cloth Body, 15 In.	30.00
Radio, Arvin, Black, Foil Front	100.00
Record, Album, Singing Bandit, Book, 2 Records	65.00
Ring, Expansion, With Picture	15.00
Rug, Bath	40.00
Shoe Holder	90.00
Shooting Gallery, Automatic Toy Co., Box	225.00
Spoon	12.50
Suit, Play, Box, 1949	225.00
Sunglasses	25.00
Sweater, Child's, Short Sleeves, Hoppy On Front & Back	35.00
Thermos	28.00
Tin, Hoppy Popcorn	25.00
Wristwatch, Original Band .... 50.00 To 65.00

Howdy Doody and Buffalo Bob were the main characters in a children's series televised from 1947 to 1960. Howdy was a redheaded puppet. The series became popular with college students in the late 1970s when Buffalo Bob began to lecture on the campuses.

HOWDY DOODY, Bag, School, Full Figure of Howdy, It's Howdy Doody Time	25.00
Bank, Bust, Ceramic, 8 In.	35.00
Bank, CBS, Plastic	10.00
Barrettes, Hair	7.00
Book, Follow The Dots, Whitman, 1955	20.00

Book, Jack & Jill Magazine, Howdy Doody Cover, 1960 .... 16.00
Bottle, Welch's Grape Juice, Doodyville Circus, 4 Bottles 45.00
Crayon & Picture Set, Milton Bradley, C.1950 .... 25.00
Cup, Ovaltine, Bob Smith, Red Plastic, C.1950 .... 40.00
Doll, Clarabell Cow, Stuffed, Hand Sewn, McCall, 26 In. 210.00
Doll, Composition, Madame Alexander, 20 In. 185.00
Dummy, Suitcase & Clothes 150.00
Game, Flub–A–Dub Flip A–Ring, Package 10.00
Glass, Howdy & Friends At Picnic, Welch's Grape Juice 20.00
Lamp, Howdy Seated On Base, Light Inside 50.00
Lunch Box, Liberty, 1950s 30.00
Marionette, Compostion & Cloth, 17 1/2 In. 150.00
Marionette, Howdy, Flub–A–Dub, Mr.Bluster, Composition, 14 Pc. 275.00
Mug, Ceramic 20.00
Night–Light, Figural, Seated On Wooden Base, C.1950, 5 In. 55.00
Paint Kit, Bisque Figures, 4 Dolls, 6 3/4 In. 75.00
Paint Set, Oil, Box .... 45.00 To 65.00
Pencil, Howdy's Head On End 15.00
Phonograph, Box 250.00
Piano, Windup, Unique Art, Peanut Gallery On Back 125.00
Puppet, Hand 20.00
Sign, Howdy, Embossed, Tin, 4 X 12 In. 20.00
Stationery, Howdy's Characters On Paper, 3 Packs 25.00
Tee Shirt 10.00
Towel, Bath, Unused 27.50
Toy, Camera 35.00
Toy, Howdy Doody Band, Box 475.00
Toy, Howdy On Trapeze, Arnold .... 190.00 To 225.00
Tumbler, Face In Bottom 12.00
Washcloth, Mitten 28.00

Hull pottery was made in Crooksville, Ohio, from 1905. Addis E. Hull bought the Acme Pottery Company and started making ceramic wares. In 1917, A. E. Hull Pottery began making art pottery as well as the commercial wares. For a short time, 1921 to 1929, the firm also sold pottery imported from Europe. The dinnerwares of the 1940s, including the Little Red Riding Hood line, the high gloss artwares of the 1950s, and the matte wares of the 1940s, are all popular with collectors. The firm is still in business.

HULL, Bank, Little Red Riding Hood, Standing 200.00
Basket, Bow Knot, Pink Bow On Handle, Blue, 6 1/2 In. 75.00
Basket, Butterfly, White, 3 Handles, 10 1/2 In. 40.00
Basket, Capri, White 12.00
Basket, Dogwood, 7 1/2 In. .... 88.00 To 90.00
Basket, Ebb Tide, Green, Peach Trim 80.00
Basket, Iris, 7 In. 90.00
Basket, Open Rose, 8 In. 95.00
Basket, Parchment & Pine, Green, Black Interior, 16 1/2 In. 35.00
Basket, Parchment & Pine, Green, Brown, 8 In. 25.00
Basket, Serenade, Yellow, 7 In. 24.50
Basket, Sunglow, Pansies, Yellow, 6 1/2 In. 15.00
Basket, Woodland, 10 1/2 In. 55.00
Basket, Woodland, Gloss Pink, 8 3/4 In. 30.00
Bean Pot, Jewel Tea, 2 Handles 80.00
Bowl, Console Set, Butterfly, 3 Piece 60.00
Bowl, Console, Dogwood, 11 In. 68.00
Bowl, Console, Magnolia, Brown Base, 12 1/2 In. 35.00
Bowl, Ebb Tide, 15 In. 40.00
Bowl, Magnolia, 8 1/2 In. 24.00
Bowl, Pitcher, Serenade, Pink, Gold Trim, 10 1/2 In. 60.00
Bowl, Rose, Poppy, 4 3/4 In. 45.00
Candleholder, Blossom Flite, Blue, Pair 22.00
Candleholder, Serenade, Pink, 6 1/2 In., Pair 32.00

Candlestick, Butterfly, Pair	54.00
Candlestick, Open Rose, Pair	95.00
Candy Dish, Continental, Green	16.00
Canister, Coffee, Little Red Riding Hood	175.00
Chocolate Pot, Wildflower, 8 In.	125.00
Console Set, Blossom Flite, Pink & Blue, 3 Piece	30.00
Console Set, Butterfly, 3 Piece	38.00
Console Set, Parchment & Pine, Brown, 3 Piece	25.00
Console Set, Serenade	70.00
Console Set, Water Lily, Pink & Blue, 3 Piece	95.00
Cookie Jar, Barefoot Boy	195.00
Cookie Jar, Big Apple	16.00 To 34.00
Cookie Jar, Daisies	15.00
Cookie Jar, Duck	30.00
Cookie Jar, Goldilocks	45.00
Cookie Jar, Little Red Riding Hood, Closed Basket	77.00
Cookie Jar, Little Red Riding Hood, Open Basket	83.00
Cookie Jar, Little Red Riding Hood, Stenciled, 9 1/2 In.	135.00
Cookie Jar, Mother Bear	50.00
Cookie Jar, Old McDonald Barn	75.00
Cookie Jar, Pig	30.00
Cornucopia, Blue Flower, 8 1/2 In.	20.00
Cornucopia, Bow Knot, 7 1/2 In.	45.00 To 50.00
Cornucopia, Butterfly, 10 1/2 In., Pair	60.00
Cornucopia, Magnolia, Pink, 8 1/2 In.	18.00
Cornucopia, Pink & Blue, 10 In.	40.00
Cornucopia, Woodland, Matte, Green, Double, 1949, 8 1/2 In.	55.00
Cornucopia, Woodland, Rose, Speckled, 11 1/2 In.	18.00
Creamer, Little Red Riding Hood	40.00
Cup & Saucer, Bow Knot	65.00
Ewer, Butterfly, 10 In.	20.00
Ewer, Calla Lily, Green, 10 In.	80.00
Ewer, Dogwood, Peach, 4 3/4 In.	35.00
Ewer, Iris, 8 1/2 In.	48.00
Ewer, Iris, 13 1/2 In.	125.00
Ewer, Magnolia, Blue Gloss, 8 1/2 In.	18.00
Ewer, Mardi Gras, 10 In.	38.00
Ewer, Open Rose, 13 1/2 In.	150.00
Ewer, Rosella, Pink Gloss, 6 1/2 In.	15.00 To 20.00
Ewer, Wild Flower, Natural, 8 1/2 In.	50.00
Ewer, Wild Flower, Peach, 8 1/2 In.	65.00
Figurine, Prince Charming, 5 In.	15.00
Flowerpot, Bow Knot	55.00
Flowerpot, Sunglow, Pink	15.00
Grease Jar, Sunglow	13.00
Jar, Little Red Riding Hood, Yellow Basket At Feet, 9 In.	165.00
Jardiniere, Bow Knot, Pink & Turquoise, 5 1/2 In.	65.00
Jardiniere, Water Lily, 5 1/2 In.	25.00
Jug, Rosella, 7 1/2 In.	24.00
Lamp, Little Red Riding Hood	125.00
Lamp, Orchid	150.00
Magnolia, Teapot, Pink, 6 1/2 In.	55.00
Magnolia, Vase, Pink	125.00
Match Holder, Little Red Riding Hood	300.00
Mixing Bowl, Bouquet, Set of 3	50.00
Mug, Happy Days Are Here Again	9.00
Mustard, Little Red Riding Hood	75.00
Mustard, Poppy	100.00
Pitcher, Ice Lip, Quilted Pattern, Blue	20.00
Pitcher, Little Red Riding Hood, 7 In.	100.00
Pitcher, Magnolia	30.00
Pitcher, Milk, Little Bopeep	60.00
Pitcher, Milk, Little Red Riding Hood, 7 In.	110.00
Planter, Bow Knot, 6 1/2 In.	50.00

Planter, Dachshund	30.00
Planter, Lamb, Pink	22.00
Planter, Madonna & Child, Pink, Cream Matte, Marked	15.00
Planter, Madonna, White	18.00
Planter, Pheasant	10.00
Planter, Poodle Head	45.00
Planter, Rooster, Pink & Brown	14.00
Planter, St. Francis	25.00
Planter, Swan, White, No.23	16.00
Planter, Water Lily	40.00
Rose Bowl, Narcissus	25.00
Rose Bowl, Orchid	37.50
Salt & Pepper, Bouquet, 3 1/2 In.	10.00
Salt & Pepper, Little Red Riding Hood, 5 In.	30.00 To 78.00
Sugar & Creamer, Open Rose	45.00
Sugar & Creamer, Rosella	30.00
Sugar, Little Red Riding Hood, Crawling	65.00
Tea Set, Ebb Tide	95.00
Tea Set, Woodland, 3 Piece	45.00
Teapot, Little Red Riding Hood	85.00 To 120.00
Teapot, Sugar & Creamer, Magnolia, 3 Piece	90.00
Teapot, Sugar & Creamer, Woodland, Chartreuse & Rose	65.00
Teapot, Water Lily, Pink	70.00 To 85.00
Vase, Blossom Flite, 10 In.	20.00 To 28.00
Vase, Bow Knot, 8 1/2 In.	45.00 To 66.00
Vase, Bow Knot, Pink, 5 In.	34.00
Vase, Calla Lily, 8 In.	35.00
Vase, Dogwood, 6 1/2 In.	25.00
Vase, Dogwood, Peach, 6 1/2 In.	25.00
Vase, Fish, Ebb Tide, Turquoise, 11 In.	20.00
Vase, Iris, 4 3/4 In.	25.00
Vase, Magnolia, 6 1/2 In.	20.00
Vase, Magnolia, 13 In.	125.00
Vase, Magnolia, Blue & Pink, Matte, 16 1/2 In.	35.00
Vase, Magnolia, Blue To Pink, 6 1/4 In.	17.50
Vase, Magnolia, Matte, 6 1/4 In.	16.00
Vase, Magnolia, Matte, 15 In.	195.00
Vase, Magnolia, Pink, 12 1/2 In.	95.00
Vase, Magnolia, Pink, Blue & Coral, 8 1/2 In.	55.00
Vase, Mardi Gras, Blue Base, 9 In.	22.00
Vase, Open Rose, 6 1/2 In.	30.00
Vase, Open Rose, Pink & Blue, 8 In.	40.00
Vase, Orchid, 6 1/2 In.	45.00
Vase, Orchid, Pink, 6 In.	25.00 To 35.00
Vase, Parchment & Pine, 12 In., Pair	55.00
Vase, Parchment & Pine, Cream, Green & Brown, 7 1/2 In.	15.00
Vase, Pillow, Calla Lily, 9 In.	95.00
Vase, Poppy, 8 In.	40.00
Vase, Poppy, 10 1/2 In.	125.00
Vase, Rosella, Coral, 7 In.	40.00
Vase, Water Lily, 6 1/2 In.	25.00 To 28.00
Vase, Water Lily, Brown, 9 1/2 In.	60.00
Vase, Water Lily, Pink & Blue, 10 1/2 In.	67.00
Vase, Wild Flower, 5 1/2 In.	22.00
Vase, Wild Flower, 8 1/2 In.	36.00
Vase, Wild Flower, Pink, 7 1/2 In.	17.50
Wall Pocket, Bow Knot	40.00 To 60.00
Wall Pocket, Cup & Saucer, Pink & Blue, Sticker	90.00
Wall Pocket, Cup & Saucer, Sunglow	80.00
Wall Pocket, Goose	23.00
Wall Pocket, Little Red Riding Hood	225.00
Wall Pocket, Rosella, Pink, Gold Trim	28.00
Wall Pocket, Sunglow, Iron	15.00

Wall Pocket, Woodland, Blue, 7 1/2 In. 20.00
Window Box, Butterfly 21.00

Hummel figurines, based on the drawings of Berta Hummel, are made by the W. Goebel Porzellanfabrik of Oeslau, Germany, now Rodenthal, West Germany. They were first made in 1934. The mark has changed through the years. The following are the approximate dates for each of the marks: "Crown" mark, 1935 to 1949; "U. S. Zone, Germany," 1946 to 1948; "West Germany," after 1949; "full bee," with variations, 1950 to 1959; "stylized bee," 1960 to 1972; "three line mark," 1968 to 1979; "vee over gee," 1972 to 1979; "new mark," 1979 to present.

HUMMEL, Bank, No.118, Little Thirfty, Crown Mark 600.00
Bookends, No. 61A & 61B, Playmates & Chick Girl, Full Bee 595.00
Doll, Hansel, Box, 1950s 245.00
Figurine, No. 2/0, Little Fiddler, Full Bee 220.00
Figurine, No. 5, Strolling Along, Stylized Bee .... 80.00 To 120.00
Figurine, No. 9, Begging His Share, Stylized Bee 100.00
Figurine, No. 10, Flower Madonna, White, Full Bee 275.00
Figurine, No. 10/III, Flower Madonna, White, Full Bee 215.00
Figurine, No. 11/2/0, Merry Wanderer, Full Bee 125.00
Figurine, No. 11/2/0, Merry Wanderer, Stylized Bee .... 70.00 To 90.00
Figurine, No. 20, Before Battle, New Mark 98.00
Figurine, No. 21/0, Heavenly Angel, Crown Mark 295.00
Figurine, No. 23/I, Adoration, Stylized Bee 210.00
Figurine, No. 23/III, Adoration, Full Bee 458.00
Figurine, No. 30A & 30B, Ba–Bee–Ring, Full Bee 95.00
Figurine, No. 45/I, Madonna With Halo, Color, Full Bee 125.00
Figurine, No. 47/0, Goose Girl, Full Bee 125.00
Figurine, No. 49/0, To Market, Full Bee 510.00
Figurine, No. 49/0, To Market, Stylized Bee 119.00
Figurine, No. 51/3/0, Village Boy, Full Bee 95.00
Figurine, No. 56/A, Culprits, Crown Mark 650.00
Figurine, No. 57/0, Chick Girl, Full Bee 125.00
Figurine, No. 57/0, Chick Girl, Stylized Bee 130.00
Figurine, No. 58/0, Playmates, New Mark 70.00
Figurine, No. 58/0, Playmates, Stylized Bee 110.00
Figurine, No. 59, Skier, Crown Mark 395.00
Figurine, No. 59, Skier, Full Bee 285.00
Figurine, No. 65, Farewell, Full Bee 280.00
Figurine, No. 67, Doll Mother, Crown Mark 350.00
Figurine, No. 74, Little Gardener, New Mark 50.00
Figurine, No. 79, Globetrotter, Full Bee 225.00
Figurine, No. 82/2/0, School Boy, Stylized Bee 50.00
Figurine, No. 87, For Father, Stylized Bee 100.00
Figurine, No. 94, Surprise, Crown Mark 395.00
Figurine, No. 94, Surprise, Three Line Mark 140.00
Figurine, No. 97, Trumpet Boy, New Mark 40.00
Figurine, No. 99, Eventide 120.00
Figurine, No.109/0, Happy Traveller, Stylized Bee 200.00
Figurine, No.111/I, Wayside Harmony, Crown Mark 525.00
Figurine, No.112/I, Just Resting, Stylized Bee 70.00
Figurine, No.129, Band Leader, New Mark 65.00
Figurine, No.135, Soloist, Full Bee 125.00
Figurine, No.143, Boots, Full Bee 423.00
Figurine, No.143/0, Boots, Three Line Mark 125.00
Figurine, No.150/0, Happy Days, Full Bee 295.00
Figurine, No.152/B, Umbrella Girl, Stylized Bee 500.00
Figurine, No.152/II/B, Umbrella Girl, Three Line Mark 650.00
Figurine, No.171, Little Sweeper, Full Bee, 5 In. 125.00
Figurine, No.174, She Loves Me, She Loves Me Not, Full Bee 150.00
Figurine, No.175, Mother's Darling, Stylized Bee 100.00
Figurine, No.177/I, School Girls, New Mark 395.00
Figurine, No.185, Accordian Boy, Full Bee 150.00

| Hummel, Figurine, No.304, Artist, New Mark | Hummel, Figurine, No.321, Wash Day, Three Line Mark | Hummel, Figurine, No.361, Favorite Pet, Vee Over Gee | Hummel, Figurine, No.382, Visiting An Invalid, Three Line Mark |

Figurine, No.196/0, Telling Her Secret, Full Bee 325.00
Figurine, No.196/I, Telling Her Secret, Stylized Bee 400.00
Figurine, No.197/I, Be Patient, Three Line Mark 155.00
Figurine, No.198/2/0, Home From Market, Stylized Bee 60.00
Figurine, No.199/0, Feeding Time, Stylized Bee 60.00
Figurine, No.200/0, Little Goat Herder, Full Bee 235.00
Figurine, No.203/2/0, Signs of Spring, Full Bee 350.00
Figurine, No.262, Heavenly Lullaby, Three Line Mark 275.00
Figurine, No.304, Artist, New Mark ....*Illus* 135.00
Figurine, No.321, Wash Day, Three Line Mark ....*Illus* 150.00
Figurine, No.340, Letter To Santa Claus, Three Line Mark 138.00
Figurine, No.346, Smart Little Sister, Three Line Mark 95.00
Figurine, No.348, Ring Around The Rosie, New Mark 850.00
Figurine, No.361, Favorite Pet, Vee Over Gee ....*Illus* 175.00
Figurine, No.369, Follow The Leader, New Mark 475.00
Figurine, No.380, Daisies Don't Tell, New Mark 75.00
Figurine, No.382, Visiting An Invalid, Three Line Mark ....*Illus* 325.00
Figurine, No.391, Girl With Trumpet, New Mark 35.00
Holy Water Font, No. 26/0, Child Jesus, Stylized Bee 45.00
Holy Water Font, No. 36/0, Angel With Flowers, Stylized Bee 50.00
Holy Water Font, No. 75, White Angel, Stylized Bee 48.00
Holy Water Font, No.147, Devotion, Stylized Bee 50.00
Lamp, No. 44A, Culprits, Full Bee 275.00
Lamp, No. 44B, Out of Danger, New Mark 200.00
Plaque, No.180, Tuneful Goodnight, Three Line Mark 163.00
Plate, Anniversary, 1985 .... 140.00
Plate, Annual, 1971 .... 600.00
Plate, Annual, 1986 .... 75.00

Hutschenreuther Porcelain Company of Selb, Germany, was established in 1814 and is still working. The company makes fine quality porcelain dinnerwares and figurines. The mark has changed through the years, but the name and the lion insignia appear in most versions.

HUTSCHENREUTHER, Cup & Saucer, Cobalt Blue, Demitasse 35.00
Figurine, Deer, 8 X 5 1/2 In. 95.00
Figurine, Fisherman, 7 In. 95.00
Figurine, Girl With Butterfly, 6 1/2 In. 95.00
Figurine, Girl, Deer, All White, Signed, 8 In. 150.00
Figurine, Jungle Cat, 9 1/2 In. 250.00
Figurine, Kneeling Nude, White Bisque 85.00
Figurine, Musicians of Bremen, 8 In. 250.00
Figurine, Nude, On Gold Ball, 1930 .... 165.00
Figurine, Parakeet, Yellow, 6 In. 115.00
Figurine, Putti, With Pipes, Naked, 1920, 5 In. .... 100.00 To 120.00
Figurine, Robin, Brown 115.00
Figurine, Woman Tennis Player, Signed 395.00
Plate, Cherubs, Playing, Garden, Magenta Border, 8 1/2 In. 75.00

Plate, Cherubs, Pulling Cart, In Garden, Gold Border, 10 In. 110.00
Plate, Christmas, 1930 .... 175.00
Plate, Dutch Children, Playing, Beehive Mark, 10 In. 95.00
Plate, White & Pink Flowers, Green, Yellow Center, 8 In. 35.00
Tray, White & Orange Flowers, Pale Green Ground, Signed 75.00
Tureen, Vegetable, Squared Handles, Gold Trim, Cover 55.00

An icon is a special, revered picture of Jesus, Mary, or a saint. These are usually Russian or Byzantine. The small icons collected today are made of wood and tin or precious metals. Many modern copies have been made in the old style and are being sold to unsuspecting tourists in Russia and Europe.

ICON, Angels, In Archway, Greek, 27 In., Pair ....*Illus*   700.00
  Christ Pantocrator, Metal Riza, Boxed Frame, Russian, 10 X 9 In. 350.00
  Holy Visage, Silver–Gilt, Shaded Enamel, N.G., Moscow, 12 X 10 1/2 In. 3025.00
  Madonna & Child, Archangels, Michael & Gabriel, Wooden, Painted, 13 In. 200.00
  Mother of God, Chased Silver–Gilt, Tichvin, 1814, 12 1/4 X 10 1/2 In. 2640.00
  Painted & Gilded Angels, Within Column Archway, Greek, 27 In., Pair 700.00
  St.Nicholas, Egg Tempera, Silver Lacquer, Russian, 16 X 19 1/2 In. 3500.00
  Virgin & Christ Child, Boxed Frame, Russian, 10 X 8 1/2 In. 350.00
  Virgin & Christ Child, Russian, 19th Century, 12 1/2 X 10 In. 310.00
  Virgin & Christ Child, Surrounding Saints, Gesso Frame, Greek, 23 In. 400.00
  Virgin of Vladimir, Ivan Khlebnikov, C.1910, 10 1/2 X 8 3/4 In. 3850.00

Imari patterns are named for the Japanese ware decorated with orange and blue stylized flowers. The design on the Japanese ware became so characteristic that the name "Imari" has come to mean any pattern of this type. It was copied by the European factories of the eighteenth and early nineteenth centuries.

IMARI, Bowl, Blossoming Branches, Fruit Tree Design, 9 1/4 In. 275.00
  Bowl, Center Medallion, Cranes, 9 1/2 In. 275.00
  Bowl, Figures In Boat, Ukiyo–E Style, C.1840, 10 In. 357.50
  Bowl, Iron Red Cartouches, Branches, Fruit Tree Center, 9 1/4 In. 275.00
  Bowl, Lion, C.1790, 1 3/4 X 5 1/4 In. 200.00
  Bowl, Serving, Gilt Rim, Enameled Medallions, White, 12 1/2 In. 375.00
  Bowl, Serving, Low, Medallions, Gilt Rim, White Ground, 2 3/4 In. 375.00
  Charger, Basket of Flowers Center, 8 Floral Panels, C.1890, 12 In. 275.00
  Charger, Blue Design On Reverse, 19th Century, 16 In. 500.00
  Charger, Flower Center, Figures & Flowers, 24 1/2 In. 2200.00
  Charger, Gilt Rim, Stylized Landscape Center, 13 1/4 In. 200.00
  Charger, Peonies, Brocade Pattern, Floral Cartouche, 12 In. 330.00
  Charger, Phoenix Foliage, 12 In. 150.00

Icon, Angels, In Archway,
Greek, 27 In., Pair

Charger, Sunburst & Flowerhead Design, Blue & White, 16 3/8 In. 175.00
Cup, Chrysanthemum, C.1850, 2 3/4 In., Pair 350.00
Dish, Floral Alternate With Scenic Panels, Japan, 5 1/2 In. 20.00
Dish, Floral, Butterflies, Scalloped, 19th Century, Signed, 4 In. 30.00
Dish, Red, Gold & Aqua Design, Oval, 7 X 4 In. 30.00
Dish, Teppo, Gold & Aqua Design, Oval, 4 X 7 In. 7.50
Pitcher, Vertical Design of Flowers & Diapers, C.1885, 9 In. 425.00
Plate, Enameled, Gold, Gosai, 8 1/2 In. 165.00
Plate, Geometric Patterns, C.1850, 8 1/4 In. 250.00
Plate, Iron Red, Cobalt Blue, 8 1/2 In. 65.00
Plate, Landscape Scene, Impressed Seal, 8 1/2 In. 65.00
Plate, Panels of Flowering Branches Border, 18th Century, 12 1/2 In. 425.00
Plate, Rabbit, C.1790, 2 X 6 In. 375.00
Plate, Scalloped Brocade Rim, Dragon, Gold Trim, 8 1/4 In. 85.00
Plate, Wisteria & Peony, C.1850, 7 1/4 In. 275.00
Potpourri, Reticulated Silver Lid, Dragons, 3 Bracket Feet, 4 In. 200.00
Shaving Mug, Panels of Figures, 19th Century, 3 1/4 In. 100.00
Tray, Floral Design, Red, Blue & Gold, Square, 7 In. 5.00
Umbrella Stand, Landscape & Figural Scenes, Octagonal, 23 In. 1980.00
Urn, Cover, Paneled Hexagonal Form, Peony Plants, Florals, 18 1/2 In. 5500.00
Vase, Baluster, Blue, Enameled Red Iron, Cartouche Design, 8 In., Pr. 325.00
Vase, Dragon & Children, Bluish Celadon Ground, Bottle Shape, 13 In. 1650.00
Vase, Flared Rim, Baluster Body, Iron Red, Turquoise, Blue, 24 1/2 In. 1400.00
Vase, Floral Cartouches, Coiled Lizard, 13 In. 225.00
Vase, Floral Design, Cobalt Blue, Iron Red, Gilt, 6 1/8 In., Pair 225.00
Vase, Floral, Bottle Shape, 36 In. 2800.00
Vase, Flowers, Butterly & Bird, Black Ground, Gold Design, 17 In. 125.00
Vase, Palace, Dragon On Either Side, Floral, Fan & Bird, 49 1/2 In. 4600.00
Vase, Peonies, Gilt, Inverted Pyriform Body, Cover, C.1700, 11 In., Pair 3300.00
Vase, Stylized Floral Design, Gilt Highlights, 6 1/8 In., Pair 225.00
Vase, Stylized Floral, Cartouche Design, 19th Century, 8 1/2 In., Pair 325.00
Vase, Temple, Blue & White, C.1860, 5 In., 2 Piece 5060.00
Vase, Tube, Bird On Tree Design, 1920s, 9 In. 49.00

Imperial Glass Corporation was founded in Bellaire, Ohio, in 1901.
It became a division of Lenox, Inc., in 1977 and was sold to Arthur
R. Lorch in 1981. It was sold again in 1982. It went bankrupt in
1982 and some of the molds and assets have been offered to other
companies. The Imperial glass preferred by the collector is stretch
glass, art glass, carnival glass, and the top–quality tablewares.

IMPERIAL, Ashtray, Square, Purple Slap, 4 1/2 In. 28.00
Basket, Milk Glass, Marigold Top, Handle 475.00
Bookends, Concubine, Crystal Satin, Signed 285.00
Box, Duck Cover, Purple Slag 75.00
Candlestick, Dragon, Crystal Satin, Signed 115.00
Candlewick, Ashtray, Eagle, 6 1/2 In. 48.00
Candlewick, Ashtray, Pink, 6 In. 3.00
Candlewick, Basket, 6 1/2 In. 23.00
Candlewick, Basket, Beaded Handle, 5 In. 125.00
Candlewick, Bowl, 2 Handles, 7 In. 8.00
Candlewick, Bowl, 5 X 2 In. 5.00
Candlewick, Bowl, 8 In. 18.50
Candlewick, Bowl, Heart Shape, Handle, 9 In. 75.00
Candlewick, Bowl, Square, 7 1/2 In. 80.00
Candlewick, Butter, Silver Cover 45.00
Candlewick, Candleholder, Flower, 5 In. 35.00
Candlewick, Cocktail, 4 Oz. 12.00
Candlewick, Compote, 8 In. 80.00
Candlewick, Cordial .... 15.00 To 25.00
Candlewick, Cup & Saucer 10.00
Candlewick, Jam Jar, Cover 23.00
Candlewick, Ladle, Small 7.50
Candlewick, Lazy Susan 100.00
Candlewick, Mayonnaise Set, 4 Piece 38.00

Candlewick, Mirror, Round, 4 1/2 In. 70.00
Candlewick, Mustard 25.00
Candlewick, Nappy, Handle 25.00
Candlewick, Plate, 5 1/2 In. 20.00
Candlewick, Plate, 7 In. 8.00
Candlewick, Plate, 9 In. 11.00
Candlewick, Plate, 10 In. .... 18.00 To 20.00
Candlewick, Plate, Divided, Crystal, 10 1/2 In. 30.00
Candlewick, Relish, 3 Sections, 10 1/2 In. 22.00
Candlewick, Relish, 4 Sections, 12 In. 50.00
Candlewick, Sandwich Plate, Center Handle 23.00
Candlewick, Sherbet, 6 In. 11.00
Candlewick, Sugar & Creamer, 4 1/2 In. 22.50
Candlewick, Tumbler, Footed, 10 Oz. 11.00
Candlewick, Tumbler, Juice, 5 Oz. 8.00
Candlewick, Vase, Fan, 8 In. 85.00
Candlewick, Vase, Frosted Fern, Handle, 7 In. 30.00
Cape Cod, Bowl, 5 1/2 In. 5.00
Cape Cod, Bowl, 6 In. .... 6.00 To 7.00
Cape Cod, Bowl, Fruit, Footed, 9 In. 43.00
Cape Cod, Bowl, Handle, 7 1/2 In. .... 11.00 To 13.00
Cape Cod, Bowl, Vegetable, 10 In. 27.00
Cape Cod, Box, Cigarette, Cover, Handle 33.00
Cape Cod, Butter, Cover, 1/4 Lb. 40.00
Cape Cod, Cake Plate, 4-Footed, Square 148.00
Cape Cod, Cake Stand, 11 In. .... 35.00 To 45.00
Cape Cod, Coaster, 4 1/2 In. 7.00
Cape Cod, Compote, Cover, 6 In. .... 55.00 To 65.00
Cape Cod, Cordial, Black, 1 1/2 Oz. 25.00
Cape Cod, Creamer, Footed 6.00
Cape Cod, Cruet, Green, 4 Oz. 35.00
Cape Cod, Cruet, Stopper, Amber 17.00
Cape Cod, Goblet, 10 Oz. 5.00
Cape Cod, Jam Jar, Spoon, Cover 28.00
Cape Cod, Lamp, Hurricane, Chimney 98.00
Cape Cod, Mayonnaise, Liner 19.00
Cape Cod, Mug, 12 Oz. 12.00
Cape Cod, Mustard, Cover, Spoon 17.00
Cape Cod, Parfait, 6 Oz. 11.00
Cape Cod, Pitcher, Milk 22.00
Cape Cod, Plate, 8 In. .... 3.00 To 7.00
Cape Cod, Plate, 10 In. 12.00
Cape Cod, Plate, Cupped Edge, 16 In. 35.00
Cape Cod, Punch Bowl, 12 1/2 In. 43.00
Cape Cod, Relish, 3 Sections, Oval, 9 1/2 In. 35.00
Cape Cod, Salt & Pepper 12.00
Cape Cod, Sugar & Creamer 12.00
Cape Cod, Tumbler, 11 Oz. 5.00
Cape Cod, Tumbler, Footed, 6 Oz. 6.00
Cape Cod, Tumbler, Footed, 9 Oz. 4.00
Cape Cod, Tumbler, Juice 3.50
Grape, Plate, Purple, 6 1/2 In. 110.00
Paperweight, Advertising, Blue Ground 45.00
Paperweight, Logo Over Blue 100.00
Swan, Amber, 4 In. 25.00
Twisted Optic, Sugar & Creamer, Green 12.00
Vase, Funeral, Ripple, Marigold, Bubble Burst Rim, 15 X 4 3/4 In. 110.00
Vase, Hearts, Cobalt Blue, Paper Label, 10 In. 250.00
Vase, Hourglass Shape, Green Hearts & Vines, Pearl, Freehand, 9 In. 135.00
Wine, Star Cut, Clear 12.00

Indian Tree is a china pattern that was popular during the last half
of the nineteenth century. It was copied from earlier Indian textile
patterns that were very similar. The pattern includes the crooked

branch of a tree and a partial landscape with exotic flowers and leaves. Green, blue, pink, and orange were the favored colors used in the design.

INDIAN TREE, Cup & Saucer, Maddock 20.00
   Dessert Set, Coalport, 36 Piece 400.00
   Plate, Luncheon, Ironstone 15.00
   Plate, Soup 40.00
   Platter, 16 In. 32.50
   Soup, Cream, With Saucer 80.00
   Teapot, Sadler 30.00

Indian art from North America has attracted the collector for many years. Each tribe has its own distinctive designs and techniques. Baskets, jewelry, pottery, and leatherwork are of greatest collector interest. Eskimo art is listed in another section in this book.

INDIAN, Bag, Corn Husk, Nez Perce, Geometric Design Each Side, 18 X 24 In. 450.00
   Bag, Teton Sioux, Beaded, Blue Ground, Red, Green & Blue, 1890s, Pair 5000.00
   Basket Tray, Navajo, Wedding, 15 In. 145.00
   Basket, Apache, Burden, 15 1/4 In. 1050.00
   Basket, Apache, Burden, Twined, C.1910, 14 In. 700.00
   Basket, Apache, Coiled, 13 1/4 In. 850.00
   Basket, Apache, Coiled, 15 3/4 In. 2000.00
   Basket, Apache, Storage, 22 1/2 In. 6750.00
   Basket, Chippewa, Birch Bark, 12 X 9 X 14 In. 75.00
   Basket, Chitimacha, Square Base, Round Top, Colored Cane, 15 X 16 In. 65.00
   Basket, Coushatta, Pine Needle, Floral Trim, 2 1/2 X 4 In. 10.00
   Basket, Eastern Woodland, Cover, 5 In. 65.00
   Basket, Hupa, Finely Woven, 1910, 5 In. 125.00
   Basket, Klamath, 1910, 6 1/2 In. 120.00
   Basket, Klamath, Tule Fiber, Yellow Bird Quill In Design, 7 1/2 In. 150.00
   Basket, Makah, Cover, Twined Weave, Purple, Orange, 2 1/2 X 3 1/4 In. 45.00
   Basket, Makah, Trinket, Eagle Design Around Body, 2 1/4 X 3 3/4 In. 85.00
   Basket, Northwest Coast, Sweetgrass Plaited, Cover, Handle, 5 X 4 In. 70.00
   Basket, Paiute, Beaded, Cover, 6 In. 125.00
   Basket, Papago, Gathering, 10 X 8 In. 145.00
   Basket, Papago, Willow Coil, Braided Rim, 3 3/4 X 13 1/2 In. 800.00
   Basket, Penobscot, Rattlesnake Weave, Cover, 1890, 8 In. 125.00
   Basket, Pima, Radiating Lightning Design, C.1850, 16 3/4 In. 400.00
   Basket, Pine Needle, Palm Fiber Head Handle For Lid, 5 X 4 1/2 In. 35.00
   Basket, Potato Stamped, Self-Handles, 15 In. 168.00
   Basket, Quills, Salmon Paint, 3 1/2 X 7 In. 135.00
   Basket, Salishan, Gathering, Coiled, Step Design, 7 X 9 X 10 1/2 In. 150.00
   Basket, Seminole, Cover, Miniature 45.00
   Basket, Sewing, Aleutian, Rye Grass, Man, Geometric Design Lid, 4 In. 220.00
   Basket, Woodland, Splint Plaited, Carved Handle & Rim, 5 X 4 In. 70.00
   Basket, Woven Splint, Potato Stamp Design, Square, 9 X 13 X 13 In. 935.00
   Basket, Woven Splint, Potato Stamp, Geometric, 19th Century, 7 In. 138.00
   Basket, Yokuts, Bottleneck, Rattlesnake Design, 5 X 6 In. 450.00
   Belt, Navajo, Concha, Open Design Set, Central Turquoise, 36 In. 70.00
   Belt, Navajo, Concha, Silver, Spiderwork Turquoise 935.00
   Belt, Navajo, Concha, Silver, Stamped & Repousse, 1950s 440.00
   Belt, Navajo, Concha, Turquoise & Sterling Silver, 46 In. 175.00
   Birchbark Canoe, Chippewa, Wooden Slats, Reed, 1 Paddle, C.1890, 7 Ft. 500.00
   Blanket, Chimayo, Center Bird Design, C.1930, 47 X 84 In. 125.00
   Blanket, Eagle With Snake 48.00
   Blanket, Navajo, C.1924, 50 X 76 In. 995.00
   Blanket, Navajo, Double Saddle, 1940s 125.00
   Blanket, Navajo, Natural Hand Carded Yarn, C.1890, 40 X 55 1/2 In. 250.00
   Blanket, Navajo, Red, Brown & Cream, Gray Ground, 42 X 59 In. 240.00
   Blanket, Navajo, Saddle, Diamond Design, C.1950, 34 X 48 In. 115.00
   Blanket, Navajo, Saddle, Red, Natural White, Beige, 35 X 65 1/2 In. 50.00
   Blanket, Navajo, Turquoise, C.1910, 76 X 48 In. 175.00
   Book, Book of American Indian, H.Garland, Remington Pictures, 1923 .... 237.50

Bowl, Apache, Basketry, Coiled Sumac, Star Design, 15 1/2 In.	255.00
Bowl, Apache, Brown Geometric Pattern, 7 1/4 In.	100.00
Bowl, Apache, Coiled, Geometric Pattern, 15 In.	800.00
Bowl, Apache, Coiled, Polychrome Geometric Design, Flared, 9 In.	40.00
Bowl, Bulbous Round, Floral Bands, Hallmarked Silver, 4 7/16 In.	320.00
Bowl, Comanche, Pottery, Variegated Clay Colors, 10 In.	20.00
Bowl, Hopi, Geometric Design, Smoky Buff Slip, C.1920, 7 3/4 In.	150.00
Bowl, Hopi, Geometric Feather, Black, Brown, Over Tan Slip, 9 X 4 In.	110.00
Bowl, Hopi, Redware, Umber Design, White Outlined, Nampeyo, 5 X 10 In.	1225.00
Bowl, Isletta Pueblo, C.1900, 2 1/2 X 5 In.	75.00
Bowl, Northwest Coast, Facing Eagles, Wooden, 4 X 15 3/4 In.	425.00
Bowl, Northwest Coast, Nootka, Bird Shape, Inlaid Abalone, 13 In.	125.00
Bowl, Santa Clara, Black, Serpent, Signed Gregorita, 4 X 8 1/2 In.	250.00
Bowl, Santa Clara, Polished Blackware, 3 X 4 1/4 In.	65.00
Bracelet, Navajo, 3 Turquoise Stones, Sterling Silver	50.00
Bracelet, Navajo, Cluster, Baroque Nuggets, Set On Sterling Silver	360.00
Bracelet, Navajo, Silver, 9 Turquoise Stones	15.00
Bracelet, Navajo, Sterling Silver & Turquoise, Bennie Paheco	90.00
Bracelet, Navajo, Sterling Silver, Turquoise, Symbols, 1 1/4 In.	150.00
Bracelet, Southwest, Turquoise & Tortoiseshell Beads, Sterling	110.00
Bracelet, Zuni, Turquoise, Chain Thunderbird, Knife, Wing, Sunflowers	60.00
Bridle, Plains, Horsehair, Geometric Pattern, Tassel, C.1900, 16 In.	700.00
Bucket, Upper Missouri River, Rawhide Leather, Bentwood Rim, 18 In.	155.00
Burial Tag, Wyoming Territory	20.00
Canteen, Cream, Black & Orange, Pottery	125.00
Cape, Apache, Buckskin	75.00
Carving, Indian Warrior Head, Steer Thigh Bone, 19th Century, 5 In.	150.00
Chippewa, Moccasins, Blue, Green Beads, Geometric Design, Pair	45.00
Choker, Woven Bead, White	10.00
Cloak, Northwest Coast, Ceremonial, Purple Ground, 53 X 58 In.	875.00
Container, Woodland, Birchbark, Quill Work, Minneapolis, 7 1/4 In.	20.00
Container, Woodland, Birchbark, Splint Rim, Cattail Reed, 7 X 9 In.	20.00
Cradle Board, Leather Cover, Beaded, Bones, Weasel Tails, 13 X 33 In.	200.00
Cradle Cover, Arapaho, Beige Canvas, Wooden Frame, Quills	4600.00
Cradle, Penobscot, Doll's, Splint, C.1920	55.00
Cradleboard, Algonquin, Laced Face Guard & Footrest, 34 1/2 In.	350.00
Cradleboard, Iroquois, Flower & Vine Polychomed Carving	1600.00
Cradleboard, Plains, Quilled	2100.00
Cup, Plains, Buffalo Horn, Ceremonial, Beaded Deerskin Rim, 8 In.	250.00
Dance Stick, Beaded ....*Illus*	40.00
Doll, Bisque Socket Head, Closed Mouth, 5 Piece Composition, 5 In.	50.00
Doll, Cree, Buckskin Costume, Beaded, Fur, Papoose On Back, 11 1/2 In.	155.00
Doll, Kachina, Hopi, Dancing, Tablita Headdress, Fur Cape, 14 In.	160.00
Doll, Kachina, Hopi, Flattened, Feather Headpiece, Jointed, 11 In.	2800.00
Doll, Santee Sioux Boy, 1900, Buckskin With Beads, 15 In.	135.00
Doll, Seminole, Fern Root Body, Signed Osceola, C.1910, 11 1/2 In.	375.00
Doll, Seminole, Folk Art, 6 In.	9.00
Doll, Seminole, Palm Fiber Body, 1930s, 10 In.	40.00
Doll, Seminole, Palm Fiber, 5 1/2 In.	14.00
Doll, Seminole, Palm Fiber, Banded Cloth Costume, 4 In.	15.00
Doll, Seminole, Rosalie Osceola, Tag	350.00
Doll, Sioux, Beaded & Quill Dress, Buffalo Fur Stuffing, C.1870	1540.00
Doll, Sioux, Red Trade Cloth Dress, 19th Century	475.00
Doll, Skookum, Inca, Original Box, 16 In.	200.00
Doll, Wooden Legs & Feet	45.00
Fan, Dane, Athabascan, Basketry Center, Deer Hair Fringe, 14 In.	300.00
Figurine, San Ildefonso, Owl, On Branch, 5 1/4 In.	85.00
Figurine, Santa Clara, Beaver, Blackware, 3 1/4 In.	35.00
Game, Stick Toss & Catch, 15 In.	20.00
Gloves ....*Illus*	240.00
Hammer, Hand, Northwest Coast, T–Shaped Maul, 4 1/2 X 4 3/4 In.	450.00
Hammer, Stone, Northwest Coast, Bird Top, Phallic Shape, 7 5/8 In.	2200.00
Hat Band, Navajo, 12 Sterling Silver Conchas, Adjustable, 20 In.	45.00
Hat, Hupa, Basketry, Geometric Design, Tag, 19th Century	325.00

Indian, Dance   Indian, Gloves   Indian, Moccasins, Beaded, Burial

Hat, Huron, Scottish Style, Floral Embroidered, Moosehair, C.1850	5000.00
Headdress, Navajo, Feather	100.00
Headdress, Plains, Felt Wrapped Feathers, Felt Cap, C.1895, 18 In.	450.00
Hook, Halibut, Northwest Coast, Horned Mammal Shape, Wood, 10 In.	100.00
Hook, Halibut, Northwest Coast, Square Nail Barb, 1 Piece, 10 In.	100.00
Jacket, Plains, Beaded Design Depicting Warriors, Hunters & Game	2600.00
Jar, Acoma, Sloping Shoulder, Design On White Slip, C.1930, 6 In.	125.00
Jar, Isleta, Double Spout, White Slip, 3 1/2 X 4 In.	85.00
Jar, Jemez, Black Design On Red Slip, Signed Tonita, 7 In.	115.00
Jar, Pottery, Mask Handle, Snake Rim Lid, White Design, Footed, 6 In.	125.00
Jar, Santa Clara, Black, Anvanyu Design, Signed Minnie, 4 X 5 In.	150.00
Kachina Doll, Snake Dancer, Horsehair Fringe On Mask, 18 In.	575.00
Leggings, Half, Plains, Skin, Dyed Yellow, Geometric Bead Design	908.00
Mask, Portrait, Northwest Coast Kwakiutl	1500.00
Mat, Navajo, Black & Tan Geometric, Gray Ground, Woven, 16 X 27 In.	100.00
Moccasins, Beaded, Burial ....*Illus*	275.00
Moccasins, Blackfoot, Beaded	880.00
Moccasins, Blackfoot, Beaded On Toe & Perimeter, 10 In.	85.00
Moccasins, Chippewa, Blue & Green Beaded Geometric Design	45.00
Moccasins, Nez Perce, Child's, Beaded Floral Design On Toes, C.1890	150.00
Moccasins, Sioux, Allover Beaded, Red, White, Blue & Gold Designs	995.00
Moccasins, Sioux, Child's, Floral Beading, 7 1/4 In.	105.00
Moccasins, Sioux, Infant's, Fully Seed Beaded, 5 In.	195.00
Necklace, Hair Pipe, Plains, Womans, Beads, Fringe, Hide Amulet, 35 In.	325.00
Necklace, Lavender Beads & Leaves	25.00
Necklace, Navajo, Squash Blossom, Sterling Silver, Turquoise, 26 In.	375.00
Necklace, Navajo, Squash Blossom, Sterling, Turquoise, 27 In. .... 415.00 To 450.00	
Necklace, Navajo, Sterling Silver, Turquoise, Kingman Mine, Signed	70.00
Necklace, Northern Plains, Grizzly Claw, Brass Trade Beads, 36 In.	600.00
Necklace, Santo Domingo, Liquid Sterling Silver, 10 Strands, 26 In.	115.00
Necklace, Zuni, Squash Blossom, Sterling, Inlaid Bird, Naja, 27 In.	350.00
Painting, Kiowa, Warrior, Seated, Stephen Mopope, C.1930, 14 X 18 In.	105.00
Panel, Navajo, From Woman's Dress, Brown Center, Side Rows, Indigo	1200.00
Patch, Shoulder, Straight Arrow, Tribal, 1950	75.00
Photograph, Sioux & Crow, David Francese Barry, 1854–1934, 25 Piece	1100.00
Pincushion, Iroquois, Souvenir, Embossed Beadwork, 7 X 7 In.	10.00
Pipe Bag, Blackfoot, Finger Tab Top, Bead Panel Each Side	350.00
Pipe Bag, Plains Cree, Beaded	635.00
Pipe Bag, Sioux, Beaded Hide, Knife Sheath Front	1650.00
Pipe, Plains, Black Soapstone, Pewter Panels, Mid–19th Century, 5 In.	650.00
Pipe, Plains, Carved Open Work, Wooden Handle, Catlinite Bowl	550.00
Pipe, Quapaw, Effigy, Clay	45.00

Plaque, Northwest Coast, Carved Face ... In.	467.00
Postcard, Blackfoot, Dated 1907, Set of	45.00
Pot, Hopi, 2–Color Design, 19th Century	465.00
Pot, Hopi, Umber & Red Orange, Buff S	35.00
Pot, San Ildefonso, Black On Black, Small	175.00
Pot, Zia, Stylized Birds, 6 1/2 In.	495.00
Pot, Zuni, Heartline Deer, 1874, 6 In.	495.00
Pouch, Blackfoot, Tobacco, Fully Beaded, Fo	250.00
Pouch, Nez Perce, Belt, Corn Husk, 4 X 4 1	95.00
Pouch, Sioux, Beaded Buckskin, Draw–Closure	95.00
Pouch, Woodland, Beaded, Velvet, Shoulder St	350.00
Quiver, Cherokee	350.00
Rattle, Haida, Carved Wood, Raven Face 1 Side,	3085.00
Rattle, Iroquois, Turtle Shell, Red Pigment Design,	350.00
Rattle, Leg, Hopi, Turtle Shell, Cone & Dew Claw,	150.00
Rattle, Medicine Man's, Buffalo Horn, 11 In.	700.00
Raven Wand, Tlingit, Carved Wood, 19th Century	725.00
Ring, Navajo, Sterling Silver, Santo Domingo Turquoise	35.00
Ring, Zuni, Sterling Silver, Petit Point Turquoise, 1 X 1	75.00
Robe, Buffalo, Crow, Hunting & Battle Scenes	6875.00
Rug, Bolivia, Alpaca, Stylized Animals, 52 X 34 In.	125.00
Rug, Navajo, Crownpoint Rug Weavers Assn., New Mexic	125.00
Rug, Navajo, Crownpoint, Stepped Diamonds, Gold Ground	125.00
Rug, Navajo, Crystal Design, Feather Border, 38 X 62 In.	550.00
Rug, Navajo, Diamond Design, C.1950, 30 1/2 X 49 In.	00.00
Rug, Navajo, Ganado Design, C.1915, 40 X 60 In.	75.00
Rug, Navajo, Ganado Double Dye, Corner Tassels, C.1910, 4	5.00
Rug, Navajo, Germantown Style, 64 X 96 In.	0.00
Rug, Navajo, Hemp, Geometric Bands, Black, Red, On Neutral	5.00
Rug, Navajo, Klagetoh Sunrise Design, C.1930, 48 X 87 In.	0.00
Rug, Navajo, Natural White, Black & Gray, C.1880, 51 X 67 In.	0.00
Rug, Navajo, Red, Gray, Black, Natural Hand Corded, 1940, 29 X	0.00
Rug, Navajo, Sawtooth Diamond, Red, Brown, Tan & Cream, 48 X ᴏᴏ In.	400.00
Rug, Navajo, Serrate Design, C.1915, 37 X 57 In.	250.00
Rug, Navajo, Stepped Terraces, C.1940, 36 X 63 In.	75.00
Rug, Navajo, Storm Pattern, Wool, Brown, Black, Gray, White, 24 X 29 In.	300.00
Rug, Navajo, Two Gray Hills, Gray, Black & Natural, 39 X 57 In.	475.00
Rug, Navajo, Yei, 1940s, 31 X 33 In.	295.00
Sash, Dance, Hopi, Woven Cotton, Red, Black, White Ground, 5 X 108 In.	65.00
Sash, Portion, Choctaw, Brick Stroud Cloth, Beads, 19th Century	1200.00
Sheath, Knife, Crow, Geometric Sinew Sewn Seed Beads, C.1880, 15 In.	475.00
Sheath, Knife, Plains, Geometric Design, Sinew Sewn, 7 1/2 In.	260.00
Sheath, Knife, Sioux, Beaded, White Ground, Fringed, 4 3/4 In.	145.00
Shirt, War, Comanche, White Seed Beads, Fringe On Sleeves, C.1875	8500.00
Shirt, Woodlands, Man's, 2 Bead Mantle, Long Dangles, 1880	3500.00
Spear, Salmon, Northwest Coast	295.00
Spoon, Horn, Tlingit, Label Says Indian Spoon No.36 Mrs.Addison	1073.00
Staff, Haida, Human Figure, Eagle On Top of Figure, 49 1/2 In.	425.00
Staff, Haida, Speaker's, Alder, 23 In.	1350.00
Totem Pole, Haida, Argillite Model	2725.00
Totem Pole, Haida, Argillite, Eagle, Frog & Hawk, C.1900, 8 1/2 In.	600.00
Totem Pole, Northwest Coast, Carved Wood, Animal, Painted, 76 In.	600.00
Totem Pole, Northwest Coast, Cedar, Animals, 85 In.	1000.00
Totem Pole, Northwest Coast, Red Cedar, 22 Ft.	1950.00
Toy, Tepee, Crow, Red Trade Calico, C.1920, Miniature	350.00
Trade Beads, Dutch, Red, 21 In.	525.00
Tray, Apache, Basketry, Male & Female Figures, Horses, 9 1/4 In.	200.00
Tray, Apache, Coiled, 17 In.	2250.00
Tray, Apache, Coiled, Geometric Design, 8 In.	175.00
Tray, Apache, Geometric Pattern, Coiled, 11 1/2 In.	220.00
Tray, Basket, Yavapai, Double Rim, Figures & Burros, C.1890, 2 Ft.	6000.00
Tray, Navajo, Wedding, Basketry, Cloth Center, Sumac Design, 12 In.	140.00
Tray, Papago, Basket, Wedding, 12 In.	135.00
Tray, Pima, Coiled Basketry, Willow & Martynia, 8 In.	85.00

Vest, Child's, Sioux, Sinew Sewn Beading	1000.00
Vest, Santee Sioux, Beaded Crossed American Flags, C.1890	1100.00
Voucher, Indian Agency, Signed, Chief Horolish Wampo, With X, 1870	165.00

An inkstand was made to be placed on a desk. It held some type of container for ink, and possibly a sander, a pen tray, a pen, a holder for pounce, and even a candle to melt the sealing wax. Inkstands date to the eighteenth century and have been made of silver, copper, ceramics, and glass.

INKSTAND, 2 Urn Shaped Wells, Beaded, G.Keller, Paris, C.1900, 9 5/8 In.	1100.00
Counting House Form, S.Silliman & Co., Grain, Stencil, 3 X 5 In.	125.00
Elephant, Double, No Insert, 11 1/2 X 5 1/2 In.	55.00
Elk's Head, Covered Glass Well, Metal	49.50
Silver, Presentation, Lobed Border, Dish Top, K.P., Vienna, 18 In.	1450.00
Stag In Profile, Emerald Eye, Antlers, Cut Glass Inserts	85.00

Inkwells, of course, held ink. Ready–made ink was first made about 1836 and was sold in bottles. The desk inkwell had a narrow hole so the pen would not slip inside. Pottery, glass, pewter, silver, and other materials were used to make inkwells. Look in other sections for more listings of inkwells.

INKWELL, 2 Birds, Art Nouveau, Brass, No Insert, 8 X 4 In.	75.00
3 Nude Men, Retrieving Treasure Chest From Sea, Bronze, 11 In.	1210.00
Art Deco, Pyramid, Brass	40.00
Art Nouveau, Polished Bronze, Swirls, 4 3/4 X 3 In.	115.00
Basalt, Center Holder, 3 Quill Holder Holes, Marked, 2 1/4 In.	90.00
Beehive, Concentric Millefiori, 5 In.	395.00
Ben Franklin Type Man, Eating Turkey, Hinged Lid, Cast Iron	75.00
Beveled Glass, Brass, Crystal Pen Tray, C.1910, 12 In.	60.00
Bird, Bronze, Small	20.00
Boston Terrier, Head, Leather Collar, Silver Buckle, Wooden	575.00
Cat Seated On Cover, Daisy & Button, Glass	245.00
Center Fox Head, Crystal Insert, English, Brass, Square, C.1870	150.00
Chick Shape, Metal, Painted	11.00
Crab, Pan Am Exposition, Metal, 1901	40.00
Dachshund With Satchel, Bronze	260.00
Deer Shape, Cobalt Blue Base, Staffordshire, 6 X 6 1/2 In., Pair	248.00
Dog Pull, Brass, Cobalt Inkwell	37.50
Double, Art Nouveau, Bronze, Austrian, 11 1/2 X 9 In.	150.00
Double, Attached Tray, Vertical Ribbing, Gold, Porcelain, 6 In.	60.00
Double, Souvenir, New York City	55.00
Egyptian Head, Glass Insert, Brass	60.00
Elephant Head Form, Ivory Tusks, Bronze, 11 In.	850.00
Erotic, Male Torso, Primitive, Bone & Wood, 1 5/8 X 8 X 2 In.	115.00
Face of Black Boy, Lifts To Reveal Insert, Bronze, 3 X 6 In.	250.00
Floral, Gold Trim, 2 Pots, Pen Tray, Stamp Space, Marked Dresden	175.00
Gibraltar Flour, Paperweight	65.00
Grapes, Urn Shape, Bronze, Green Marble Base, 4 3/4 In.	125.00
Gustav Stickley, Hammered Copper, Hinged Cover	145.00
Head of Fox, Crystal Insert, Brass, C.1880, 6 In.	110.00
Hinged Lid, Viking Ships, Pen Tray, Jenning Bros., Bronze, 9 1/2 In.	95.00
Northern Salt Glaze, C.1870	62.00
Owl, Glass Eyes, Hinged Head, Carved Pen Rest, Wooden, 4 1/2 In.	45.00
Owl, Head, Glass Eyes, Bisque	195.00
Pen Rest, Glass Insert, Bronze, K.& Co., 2 1/2 X 2 1/2 In.	65.00
Pheasant, Figural, Polychromed, Austrian, Bronze, 8 In.	245.00
Reclining Figure On Cover, 2 Wells, 4 X 3 In.	95.00
Run Down Shoe & Sock, Hand Carved Wood	225.00
Sitting Child, Arms Raised, Body Hinged At Waist, Bronze, 6 In.	550.00
Soapstone, Black, 4 Quill Holders, Ribbed Dome Top, 2 1/2 In.	150.00
Sterling Silver, Art Nouveau, Gorham, C.1900, 6 1/2 X 11 1/2 In.	3100.00
Stoneware, Round, 3 3/8 X 1 7/8 In.	50.00
Swirl Design, Pressed Glass, Large	30.00
Victorian Boy At Well, Bronze	295.00

Whippet Shape, Cobalt Blue Base, Staffordshire, 5 X 7 In. 143.00
White Enamel Design, Hinged Top, 3 In. 95.00
Winged Lion Masks, Putti, Bronze, Triangular, 16th Century, 7 In. 1980.00
Woman's Head, Flowing Hair, Art Nouveau, Hinged, Cobalt Well, 9 In. 83.00
Wooden Bear, Pen Holder, Hand Carved, German, 8 In. 85.00

Insulators of glass or pottery have been made for use on telegraph or telephone poles since 1844. Thousands of different styles of insulators have been made. Most common are those of clear or aqua glass, most desirable are the threadless types made from 1850 to 1870.

INSULATOR, Ampersane, Aqua 15.00
Armstrong, Cherry 35.00
Buller's, Light Brown, Clay 10.00
California Electric, Aqua 85.00
Canadian Diamond, Yellowish Aqua, 2 Piece 18.00
Castle, Blue 225.00
Castle, Clear 225.00
Hemingray, No. 3, Cable With Drips 28.00
Hemingray, No.16, Green 10.00
Homer Brookes, Blue 20.00
Illinois, White, Underglaze Map 2.50
Imperial, White, Embossed 15.00
Knowles, Blue–Aqua 25.00
Locke, Dark Reddish Brown 5.00
Locke, White 2.00
Manhattan, Blue 35.00
Maydwell, No.20, Blue Milk Glass 20.00
O.B., Gray 5.00
Pyrex, No.661, Carnival Glass 38.00
Telegraphos, Dark Amber 10.00
Thomas, Cobalt Blue 4.00
Thomas, White 10.00
Westinghouse, Chocolate 2.50
Whitall Tatum, Amber 25.00
IRISH BELLEEK, see Belleek

Iron is a metal that has been used by man since prehistoric times. It is a popular metal for tools and decorative items like doorstops that need as much weight as possible. Items are listed here or under other appropriate headings such as Bookends, Doorstop, Kitchen, or Tool. The tool that is used for ironing clothes, an iron, is listed under Kitchen, Iron; or Kitchen, Sadiron.

IRON, Ashtray, Attached Match Holder, Griswold 60.00
Ashtray, Cupped Hands, Leaves & Gilt Grapes At Wrist, Black, C.1860 .... 50.00
Ashtray, Johnny Boy, Stand–Up 225.00
Ashtray, Prancing Horse 22.00
Ashtray, Skillet, Wagner Ware 8.00
Ball & Chain, Prisoner's, Barbell Shape, 15 Ft., Ankle Shackle, 49 Lb. 275.00
Bathtub, Baby's, Iron Stand 42.50
Boiler, Applied Swelling Cylindrical Handle, Ovoid, Marked 4 Qt. 88.00
IRON, BOOKENDS, see Bookends
Boot Scraper, Black Cat 175.00
Boot Scraper, Cat Silhouette, 15 X 12 In. 150.00
Boot Scraper, Mud, Horse 185.00
Bootjack, Beetle Shape 30.00
Bootjack, Cricket 24.00
Bootjack, Mermaid .... 18.00 To 45.00
Bootjack, Naughty Nellie, Dark Red & Gilt 85.00
Bootjack, Naughty Nellie, Old Polychrome Paint, 9 1/2 In. 200.00
Bracket, Scrolled Foliage, Black Over White, 21 X 25 In., Set of 4 .... 520.00
Bust, Abraham Lincoln, Architectural, 15 In. 125.00
Bust, Man With Beard, Other Without, Black Paint, Loops, 5 1/2 In., Pr. 30.00
Candleholder, Hooded Cobra, Cast Iron, 8 In. 75.00

Candleholder, Prong & Hook For Hanging	60.00
Candlestick, Spring Loaded, Pewter Fittings, 7 3/4 In.	100.00
Card Receiver, Ornate	8.00
Chair, Ice, Scrolled Frame, Arched Runner Base, 40 X 19 1/2 In.	220.00
Clipper, Cigar, Counter Top, Patent 1891	95.00
Cuspidor, Hat Shape, Bott Bros, Columbus, Ohio, 6 1/2 In.	155.00
Cutter, Empire Tobacco	40.00
Cutter, P.J.Sorg Tobacco Co., Arrow Base	225.00
Door Knocker, Butterfly	65.00
Door Knocker, Interior, Cherub, Victorian, Mother-of-Pearl	40.00
Door Knocker, Interior, Girl, Watering Flowers, Mother-of-Pearl	22.00
IRON, DOORSTOP, see Doorstop	
Eagle, Gold, Stepped Wooden Base, Architectural, 3 Sections, 31 In.	375.00
Figure, Barnyard Animals, Miniature, 8 Piece	22.00
Figure, Crane, Japanese, 12 3/4 & 25 In., Pair	350.00
Frame, Half Nude Body Top, Cherub Bottom, Easel, Gold Finish, 13 In.	100.00
Grill, Classical, Rayed Spears, Rectangular Frame, 22 X 33 3/4 In.	95.00
Hitching Post, Pineapple Finial, Set In Granite, C.1850, 5 Ft.2 In.	450.00
Incense Burner, Foo Dog	175.00
Jardiniere, Pierced Scrolled Handles, 1850	275.00
Lawn Sprinkling Tractor, Nelson	50.00
IRON, MATCH HOLDER, see Match Holder	
Mill Weight, Cow, Red & White, Green Base, 20th Century, 13 X 15 In.	550.00
Mirror, Cherubs, Fruit, Flowers, Gilt, 12 In.Mirror, 17 X 13 In.	50.00
Mirror, Dresser, Victorian, Ivy Design, Marble Base, 20 In.	99.00
Ornament, Quail, Hollow Sheet Metal, In Iron Frame, Hanging, 26 In.	200.00
Peel, Ram's Horn Handle, 47 In.	45.00
Pencil Sharpener, Lantern Shape	12.00
Planter, 9 Arms, 19th Century, 36 In.	150.00
Plaque, Band of Indians, Inscription, 32 X 18 In.	143.00
Rabbit, Garden Sculpture, Black, 12 In.	65.00
Rack, Utensil, Cutout Crest With Birds, Foliage, 7 Hooks, 27 In.	1250.00
Rack, Utensil, Late 19th Century, 18 X 18 In.	225.00
Shelf, Kettle, Pierced Top, Rectangular, 11 X 16 1/2 X 10 In.	70.00
Shelf, Warming, Hook For Andiron Rod, Scrolled Design, 12 X 23 1/2 In.	65.00
Skewer Set, Holder, Dipper, Tulip Finial, Inlaid Brass, T.Loose	30.00
Snow Eagles, With Metal Staves, Pair	25.00
Snuffer, Candle, Hand Forged, Scissor Shape, Rattail Handles	65.00
Snuffer, Candle, Scissor Shape, 18th Century	55.00
Spittoon, Turtle, Porcelain Lined	85.00
Sprinkler, Lawn, Heart Top	45.00
Sprinkler, Lawn, Turtle	185.00

Iron, Urn, Scrolled Eagle Supports,
N.A.Sweeney & Bro.

Iron, Windmill Weight, Indian, Hummer

Stand, Urn, Paint Stripped, 8 1/2 In., Pair 75.00
Target, Shooting Gallery, Clover, Large 135.00
Target, Shooting Gallery, Quail, Squirrel 35.00
Tazza, 4 Mythological Figures, Flowers, Vine, Marked Iron Art, 8 In. 16.00
Tobacco Cutter, Little Imp 100.00
Tool, Shaker & Lifter, Buck's Stove & Range Company, 15 In. 20.00
Toothpick Dispenser, Woodpecker 25.00
Trivet, & Swan Iron, Miniature 25.00
Urn, High Plinth, Scroll Handles, 49 In. 350.00
Urn, Made In 1 Piece, White Repaint, 15 1/2 X 21 1/4 In., Pair 350.00
Urn, On Plinth Base, 33 X 21 1/4 In. 225.00
Urn, Scroll Handles, Birds Against Pedestal, 6 Ft. 4070.00
Urn, Scrolled Eagle Supports, N.A.Sweeney & Bro. ....*Illus* 3500.00
Urn, Stewart Iron Works, Cincinnati, Ohio, 27 In., Pair 400.00
Windmill Weight, Bobtailed Horse .... 145.00 To 225.00
Windmill Weight, Eclipse of Moon ....50.00 To 150.00
Windmill Weight, Eclipse, Crescent, 10 1/4 In. 30.00
Windmill Weight, Horse .... 150.00 To 245.00
Windmill Weight, Horse, Marked 58G On Side, 16 1/2 In. 350.00
Windmill Weight, Horse, Short Tail, Dempster Mfg., 11 1/2 X 14 In. 250.00
Windmill Weight, Indian, Hummer ....*Illus* 450.00
Windmill Weight, Rooster, On Ball 440.00
Windmill Weight, Rooster, Rainbow Tail, No Paint 575.00

Ironstone china was first made in 1813. It gained its greatest popularity during the mid-nineteenth century. The heavy, durable, off-white pottery was made in white or was decorated with any of hundreds of patterns. Much flow blue pottery was made of ironstone. Some of the decorations were raised. Many pieces of ironstone are unmarked but some English and American factories included the word "Ironstone" in their marks.

IRONSTONE, see also Chelsea Grape; Chelsea Sprig; Gaudy Ironstone; Moss Rose; Staffordshire

IRONSTONE, Bowl, Blue Transfer, English University, Mason's, 9 1/2 X 10 In. 110.00
Bowl, Vegetable, Blackberry, Cover, Oval, White 40.00
Bowl, Vegetable, Cover, Oval, J.Meir & Son, C.1857, 11 3/4 In. 115.00
Chamber Pot, Ornate Finial, Embossed Handle, Meakin 35.00
Chamber Set, Etruscan, English, 4 Piece 275.00
Chop Plate, Polychrome Oriental Design, Ashworth, 12 1/2 In. 55.00
Coffeepot, Sugar & Creamer, Grapevine Design Handles, 3 Piece 20.00
Creamer, Grenade Shape, T & R Boote, 5 1/2 In. 60.00
Creamer, Wheat & Blackberry 65.00
Crock, Pennsylvania, Design, 20 Gal. 600.00
Cup & Saucer, Gaudy Floral, Handleless 65.00
Cup & Saucer, Handleless, Hyacinth Rim, Baker 30.00
Cuspidor, Woman's, Marked KT & K China, 8 In. 75.00
Dish, Blue & White Scene, Alcock, 9 X 5 In. 15.00
Dish, Mandalay Imari Pattern, 6 Sides, Mason's, 6 X 7 1/2 In. 45.00
Ewer, Corn & Oats, Wedgwood, 12 3/4 In. 150.00
Gravy Boat, Hyacinth 22.00
Gravy Bowl, Cover, Ladle, Syndenham Shape, T & R Boote, 1854 .... 75.00
Jam Jar, White 12.50
Jar, Spice, Blue & White, Floral, Gold Lettering, German, Set of 6 .... 50.00
Jug, Milk, Lily-of-The-Valley, 8-Sided 65.00
Match Safe, Slant Sided, Counter Model, Ribbed Striking Side 20.00
Mold, Food, Ear of Corn 55.00
Mold, Food, Grape Cluster, 9 X 7 3/4 X 4 In. 40.00
Pitcher & Bowl Set, White, Signed Royal V & B 75.00
Pitcher, Grape & Leaf Border, Allover Cottonplant, 8 In. 75.00
Pitcher, Milk, Paneled Grape, C.Meigh, 8 In. 55.00
Plate, Blue & White Sponge Spatter, 8 5/8 In. 125.00
Plate, Blue & White Sponge Spatter, 10 1/4 In. 280.00
Plate, Columbia, Blue Transfer, W.Adam & Son, 9 1/2 In. 5.00
Plate, Imari Design, Lion & Unicorn Mark, 9 1/8 In. 25.00

Plate, Scalloped Rim, Blue & White Sponge Spatter, 10 1/4 In. 175.00
Plate, Tonquin, 7 1/2 In. 60.00
Platter, Imari Design, Grape, 20 3/4 In. 250.00
Platter, Imari Design, Mason's, 13 1/4 In. 135.00
Platter, Light Blue Floral Transfer, 17 1/2 In. 65.00
Punch Bowl, Berry Cluster, Handles 125.00
Punch Bowl, Black Transfer Flowers, Birds, Ridgway, 7 X 16 In. 125.00
Punch Bowl, Scrolled Bubble, Parkhurst 195.00
Relish, Fluted Pearl, Reticulated Handles, Wedgwood 40.00
Relish, Wheat, Elsmore & Forster 30.00
Salt Box, Hinged Wooden Cover, Word Salt In Script 40.00
Sauce Boat, Columbia, Cover 125.00
Sauce Boat, Prairie, Cover, Ladle, Clementson 125.00
Sauce, Cover, Ladle, Baltic 95.00
Soup, Dish, Blue & White Sponge Spatter, Scalloped Rim, 9 1/8 In. 40.00
Soup, Dish, Niagara, Walley, 9 5/8 In. 15.00
Soup, Dish, Paneled Grape, J.F., 8 7/8 In. 12.00
Sugar, Cable & Ring, Cover 22.00

IRONSTONE, TEA LEAF, see Tea Leaf Ironstone

Tea Set, Child's, Punch & Judy, Red Transfer, 14 Piece 135.00
Teapot, Pearl Sydenham, J.& G.Meakin 75.00
Teapot, Signed Josiah Wedgwood 38.50
Toothbrush Holder, Bellflower, Cover, Burgess 45.00
Toothbrush Holder, Cable & Ring, Underplate, Cockson & Seddon 40.00
Toothbrush Holder, Hyacinth, Cover, Wedgwood 60.00
Tray, Mason's, 12 In. 150.00
Tray, Sandwich, Vista Pattern, Mason's Pat., 9 1/2 X 11 1/2 In. 16.00
Tumbler, Mason's, Black Ground, Polychrome Design, Set of 8 .... 250.00
Tureen, Moss Rose, Cover, 5 1/2 X 10 In. 52.00
Tureen, Savoy, Cover, T & R Boote 40.00
Tureen, Vegetable, Berlin Swirl, Cover, Mayer & Elliot 115.00
Tureen, Vegetable, Ceres, Elsmore & Forster .... 125.00 To 150.00
Tureen, Vegetable, Cover, Sydenham Shape, T & R Boote, Medium 175.00
Tureen, Vegetable, Ivy Wreath, Cover, John Meir 70.00
Tureen, Vegetable, Wheat, Clover & Bowknot, Turner & Tomkinson 75.00
Vase, Polychrome Oriental Design, Mason's, 7 3/4 In. 115.00
Vegetable, Oval, Cover, 11 X 6 In. 135.00
Wash Set, Blue & White, 1900s 295.00
Waste Bowl, Arched Forget–Me–Not, Elsmore & Forster 25.00

Ispanky Laszlo Ispanky began his American career as a designer for Cybis Porcelains. In 1966, he established his own studio in Pennington, New Jersey; and, since 1976, he has worked for Goebel of North America. He works in stone, wood, or metal, as well as porcelain. The first limited edition figurines were issued in 1966.

ISPANKY, Figurine, Awakening 175.00
Figurine, Ballerina ....900.00 To 1000.00
Figurine, Daffodils 900.00
Figurine, Forty–Niner, Colors 675.00
Figurine, Lancelot 400.00
Figurine, Madonna With Halo, White 275.00
Figurine, Maid of The Mist 750.00
Figurine, Narcissus 600.00
Figurine, Spring Fever 1000.00
Figurine, Swanilda 750.00

The tusk of an elephant is ivory, and to many that is the only true ivory. To most collectors, the term "ivory" also includes such natural materials as walrus, hippopotamus, or whale teeth or tusks, and some of the vegetable materials that are of similar texture and density. Other ivory items are listed under Scrimshaw or Netsuke.

IVORY, Beads, Graduating, Ivory Clasp, American, 24 In. 100.00
Box, Incense, Double T Fret Border, Phoenix Bird On Lid, 2 1/4 In. 75.00
Box, Monkey Design Cover, 4 1/2 In. 60.00

Bracelet, Design of African Woman, Hand Carved	65.00
Candle Shield, 1/2 Tusk, Nudes, Cupids, European, 11 In.	1250.00
Cannon, Stand, Ebony, Stylized Foliage, Lappets, 19th Century, 10 In.	1870.00
Card Case, Calling, Floral & Leaves Openwork	230.00
Case, Needle, Carved Figural Acorn Ends, Screw Off, 3 7/8 In.	75.00
Case, Needle, Eskimo Carved, Walrus Clutching Tusks, 4 In.	350.00
Chess Set, Japanese, Hand Carved, Wooden Box	800.00
Cigar Cutter, Boar Tusk, Mounted With Sterling Silver, 9 In.	175.00
Cigarette Holder, Carved Dragon	50.00
Cigarette Holder, Silver Tip	12.50
Cribbage Board, Open Carved Foliage, Brass Feet, Bone, 7 5/8 In.	65.00
Crucifix, Ebonized Cross, 17th Century, 14 3/4 In.	2090.00
Desk Set, Moose Antler, Deer, Used At Grand Canyon Hotel, 1900s	350.00
Dragon Boat, Dragon Prow, Phoenix Stern, Stand, 17 In.	350.00
Drill, Bow, Eskimo, Engraved, Sea Mammals, 15 In.	250.00
Figurine, 31 Human Figures, 20 Animals, 10 1/2 X 2 3/4 In.	500.00
Figurine, Apple, Scene of Pine Trees, Pagoda, Man On Horse, 3 In.	170.00
Figurine, Basket Seller, Signed, 5 In.	375.00
Figurine, Buddha, Wooden Base, 5 In.	110.00
Figurine, Child, Kneeling, Signed, Japan, 5 1/8 In.	660.00
Figurine, Chinese Peasant, With Dog, Wooden Stand, 4 1/4 In.	40.00
Figurine, Crocodile, Open Mouth, Carved Teeth, 17 In.	175.00
Figurine, Diana, Jean–Antoine Belletest, Late 18th Century, 4 7/8 In.	770.00
Figurine, Doctor's Lady, Head Pulls Off To Reveal Snuff Compartment	675.00
Figurine, European Matron, Skirt Opens, 3 Part Royal Throne Scene	550.00
Figurine, Farmer With Rabbit & Frog, 8 1/2 In. ....Illus	425.00
Figurine, Fisherman Displays Catch To Boy, Wooden Stand, 8 In.	375.00
Figurine, Fisherman, Carrying Pack of Fish, 5 1/2 In.	50.00
Figurine, Gardener, Carrying Basket of Flowers, 5 1/4 In.	50.00
Figurine, Geisha Girl, Flowing Robe, Obi, 5 In.	325.00
Figurine, Goddess, Indian, 7 In.	50.00
Figurine, Hotei, Fan, Sack, C.1900, 2 1/2 In.	300.00
Figurine, Japanese Lady, Holding Basket, Monkey At Feet, 5 In.	295.00
Figurine, King & Queen, C.1930, 24 In., Pair	1200.00
Figurine, Kneeling Old Man, 19th Century, 5 In.	325.00
Figurine, Kuan Yin, Holding Child, Wooden Base, Ming Dynasty, 11 In.	800.00
Figurine, Kwannon, Goddess of Mercy, Lotus Base, Bunshin, 6 1/2 In.	605.00
Figurine, Lady, Standing, With Parasol, Display Case, 12 5/8 In.	275.00
Figurine, Madonna, Standing In Prayer, Metal, Wood Case, 14 In.	700.00
Figurine, Man, With Tobacco Pipe, Holds Basket, Signed, 9 1/2 In.	700.00
Figurine, Musician, Playing Fool, 19th Century, Austrian, 5 1/8 In.	330.00
Figurine, Nubile Maiden, Standing, Carrying Water Dipper, Jug, 15 In.	375.00
Figurine, Okimono, Farmer With Rooster & Chick, 7 3/8 In. ....Illus	350.00
Figurine, Okimono, Warrior, Eagle, 6 1/2 In. ....Illus	475.00
Figurine, Oriental Fisherman, Bear Holding Fish, C.1900, 2 1/2 In.	70.00
Figurine, Oriental Man, Fossilized Tusk, 22 3/4 In.	700.00
Figurine, Peasant, Carrying Pack of Logs, 6 In.	45.00
Figurine, Sage, Holding Jui Scepter, 5 1/4 In.	250.00
Figurine, Soldier, Holding Ring, European Style, 9 3/4 In.	1100.00
Figurine, St.Margaret of Antioch, Standing On Dragon, C.1600, 5 In.	1100.00
Figurine, Street Vendor, Japanese, Signed, C.1900, 4 In.	375.00
Figurine, Tiger, Fighting Off Pack of Baboons, Japanese, 25 In.	300.00
Figurine, Woman, Floral Kimono, 19th Century, 9 1/2 In.	325.00
Figurine, Woman, With Flowers, Wooden Stand, 7 1/4 In., Pair	130.00
Fork, 3 Part Laminated Handle, Iron Pins, Bone, 5 3/8 In.	45.00
Glove Stretcher, Carved	39.00
Mallet, 4 1/8 In.	65.00
Medallion, Virgin, Onyx, Easel Brass Frame, L.O.Matei, French, 3 In.	95.00
Mirror, Oval, Leaves Border, Putti, Coat of Arms, 31 X 20 In., Pair	2200.00
Mystery Ball, 3 Elephants, Pedestal Base, 4 In.	80.00
Pail, Holy Water, 10th Century Style, Saints In Arcades, 9 In.	1600.00
Pipe Case, Applied Shell To Lacquer, Pipe, Hangs From Obi	467.50
Pipe Case, Grasses & Flowers, Stained, Hangs From Obi	325.00
Placecard Holder, Zaire, 6 Carved Pieces	525.00

Ivory, Figurine,
Okimono, Warrior,
Eagle, 6 1/2 In.

Ivory, Figurine,
Okimono, Farmer With
Rooster & Chick, 7 3/8 In.

Ivory, Figurine,
Farmer With Rabbit
& Frog, 8 1/2 In.

Poker Chip, Center Design, Green Rim, 1 1/2 In.	15.00
Poker Chip, Cherry & Leaf Design Center, Green Edge, 1 1/2 In.	14.00
Rattle, Blue & Amber Beads, 4 In.	150.00
Rule, Folding, Brass Fittings, 12 In.	125.00
Rule, Folding, Nickel–Plated Fittings, E.A.Stearns & Co., 12 In.	200.00
Skeleton, Anatomical, On Brass Rod, 18th Century, 6 5/8 In.	1100.00
Skull, German, 18th Century, 1 1/2 In.	660.00
Sphere, 2 Openings, Pastoral Scenes, Inlaid, Stone & Metal, Shibayana	725.00
Stein, Carved, Silver Mounts, Signed RC On Bottom, 8 1/8 In.	2500.00
Top, Octagonal, 1 1/4 In.	65.00
Travel Set, Clothespins, Leather Case	7.50
Tumbler, Relief Carved Village Scenes, Oriental, 2 7/8 In.	45.00
Tusk, Elephant, 2 X 23 In.	175.00
Whistle, 2 5/8 In.	85.00

 Jack Armstrong, the all–American boy, was the hero of a radio serial from 1933 to 1951. Premiums were offered to the listeners until the mid–1940s. Jack Armstrong's best–known endorsement is for Wheaties.

JACK ARMSTRONG, Airplanes, Model, Envelope, 1940s	50.00
Book, How To Fly Manual, 16 Pages	75.00
Cereal Box, Wheaties, 1939	40.00
Flashlight, Torpedo, Red Cardboard Body, Metal Ends, 1939	10.00
Game, Big Ten Football, Radio Premium, Mailer	15.00 To 50.00
Hike–O–Meter	12.00 To 35.00
Model, Pre–Flight Trainer, Unpunched, 1945	125.00
Ring, Dragon's Eye, Box	100.00
Ring, Siren	38.00
Secret Bomb Sight	48.00

 Jack–in–the–pulpit vases were named for their odd trumpetlike shape that resembles the wild plant called jack–in–the–pulpit. The design originated in the late Victorian years. Vases in the jack–in–the–pulpit shape were made of ceramic or glass.

JACK–IN–THE–PULPIT, Vase, Amberina, Gold Flowers & Leaves, 5 7/8 In.	210.00
Vase, Apple Green, Maroon Hobnail Edge, 7 1/2 In.	110.00
Vase, Blue Foot, Ruffled, Blue Opalescent, 6 1/2 In.	70.00
Vase, Clear Spirals, Cranberry, Clear Foot, 9 1/2 In.	118.00
Vase, Marigold, Carnival Glass, 10 3/4 In.	35.00
Vase, Pastel Stripes of Yellow, Pink & Blue, 10 In.	215.00
Vase, Spiral Glass Trim, Ruffled, Vaseline, 7 3/4 In.	85.00
Vase, Spirals, Glass Trim, Cranberry, 9 1/2 In.	118.00

Vase, White Exterior, Green Interior, 6 1/4 In. 95.00

Jackfield ware was originally a black glazed pottery made in Jackfield, England, from 1750 to 1775. A yellow glazed ware has also been called Jackfield ware. Most of the pieces referred to as "Jackfield" today are black-glazed, red-clay wares made at the Jackfield Pottery in Shropshire, England, in Victorian times.

JACKFIELD, Creamer, Cow, Gilt Trim, 6 3/4 In. 90.00

Two different minerals, nephrite and jadeite, are called jade. Nephrite is the mineral used for most early Oriental carvings. Jade is a very tough stone that is found in many colors from dark green to pale lavender. Jade carvings are still being made in the old styles, so collectors must be careful not to be fooled by recent pieces. Jade jewelry is found in this book under Jewelry.

JADE, Bowl, Mutton Fat 410.00
Figurine, Horse, Mutton Fat, Teakwood Stand, 5 1/2 X 6 1/2 In. 195.00
Teapot, Cover & Stand, White, 3 1/2 In. 650.00
Tree, 6 Multipetaled Flowers, Jade Pot, Turquoise Gravel, 17 In. 425.00

Japanese Coralene is a ceramic decorated with small raised beads and dots. It was first made in the nineteenth century. Later wares made to imitate coralene had dots of enamel. There is also another type of coralene that is made with small glass beads on glass containers.

JAPANESE CORALENE, Vase, Flowers, Green, Pink, Cobalt Trim, Handles, 12 In. 250.00
Vase, Flowers, Rust, Red, White Dot Trim, 12 In. 500.00
Vase, Iris, Lavender, Pink, Green, Gold Trim, 6 In. 75.00
Vase, Irises, Cobalt & Gold Trim At Top & Bottom, 9 In. 455.00

There are two types of jasperware. Some pieces have raised designs of white or a contrasting color made from colored clay. Other pieces are made by decorating the raised portions with a color.

JASPERWARE, see also various art potteries; Wedgwood
JASPERWARE, Biscuit Jar, Blue & White, Adams 200.00
Biscuit Jar, Dark Blue, Silver Mountings, Adams, 6 In. 135.00
Box, Powder, Kissing Children, Flower Garlands, Deep Blue, 4 In. 52.00
Box, Seashell Cover, Orchid & Sea Nymph Design, 3 3/4 In. 68.00
Cheese Dish, Domed Cover, Classical Figures On Blue, 8 1/2 In. 275.00
Creamer, Blue, Pink Figures 75.00
Humidor, Fox & Hound Design, Blue & White, Tunstall, 6 In. 187.00
Plaque, Cupid Pushing Another On Sleigh, German, 5 In. 75.00
Plaque, Young Man On Dock, Saying Goodbye To Girl, German, 6 In. 75.00
Teapot, Classical Figures On Blue, 8 In. 50.00
Urn, Fox Hunting Scene, Adams, 8 X 8 In. 195.00
Vase, Blue, White, Lilac Medallions, 10 In., Pair ....*Illus* 325.00
Wall Pocket, Classical Dance Figures, Green, 6 1/4 X 5 3/4 In. 115.00

Jewelry, if made from gold and precious gems or plastic and colored glass, is still popular with collectors. Values are determined by the intrinsic value of the stones and metal and by the skill of the craftsmen and designers. Victorian and older jewelry has been popular since the 1950s. More recent interests are Art Deco and Edwardian styles, Mexican and Danish silver jewelry, and beads of all kinds. Copies of almost all styles are being made.

JEWELRY, Bar Pin, Blue Enameled, 14K Gold, 2 1/4 In. 125.00
Bar Pin, Cobalt Blue Enameled, Victorian, 14K Yellow Gold Mounting 175.00
Bar Pin, Demantoid Garnet, Art Deco, Diamonds, Platinum Gold 4100.00
Bar Pin, Diamonds & Sapphires, White Gold Filigree 350.00
Bar Pin, Gold, Victorian, Etruscan Revival Design 150.00
Bar Pin, Micro-Mosaic Navette Plaque 225.00
Bar Pin, Rhinestone, Sterling Silver 20.00
Bar Pin, Sapphire Center, 14K Yellow & White Gold 175.00
Bar Pin, Victorian, 15K Gold, Onyx Plaque, Seed Pearl, Engraved 175.00

Bar Pin, Victorian, Garnets, Brass, 2 1/2 In.	45.00
Bar Pin, Victorian, Ruby & Diamond Ribbon	300.00
Beads & Earrings, Coal, 18 In.Strand	65.00
Beads, Garnet, 32 In.	145.00
Box, Victorian, Metal, Art Nouveau, 5 X 5 X 4 In.	85.00
Bracelet & Earrings, Black Glass Stones	35.00
Bracelet & Earrings, Rhinestone, Silver Hearts, Gold Filled	20.00
Bracelet, 10 Square Links of Carved Ivory, On Cord	75.00
Bracelet, 14K Yellow Gold, Rope Chain, Safety Lock, 9 In.	48.00
Bracelet, 18 Barrel–Form Sections, Red Molded Chevrons, Lalique	4950.00
Bracelet, 8 Linked Shilling Coins, Sterling Silver, 6 1/2 In.	22.00
Bracelet, Amber Rhinestones, Lisner	28.00
Bracelet, Art Deco, Link, 18K Gold, 3/4 In.Wide	395.00
Bracelet, Bangle, 3 Plaques & 3 Diamonds, 14K Gold	325.00
Bracelet, Bangle, Diamond, Pierced Gallery, Victorian, 18K Gold	900.00
Bracelet, Bangle, Enameled, Eisenberg	75.00
Bracelet, Bangle, Fluted Design, Tiffany, 18K Gold	950.00
Bracelet, Bangle, Opals & Diamonds, Silver, Arts & Crafts, 2 1/2 In.	2600.00
Bracelet, Bangle, Panels of 30 Small Diamonds, 14K Yellow Gold	270.00
Bracelet, Bangle, Sapphires, Gold	375.00
Bracelet, Bangle, Victorian, Pique, Hinged, Gold Beaded Inlay	475.00
Bracelet, Bangle, Victorian, Ruby, Diamond Crescent & Star, 18K Gold	600.00
Bracelet, Coin, Coro	12.00
Bracelet, Cuff, Silver, Georg Jensen	95.00
Bracelet, Emerald, 6 Silver Gilt Links, Pearls, 19th Century, 8 In.	990.00
Bracelet, Green Chalcedony, Silver Leafage, Jensen, 1926, 7 In.	990.00
Bracelet, Links, Joined By Channel–Set Rubies, 18K Gold, C.1940	1400.00
Bracelet, Marcasite, Mother–of–Pearl Cameo, Sterling Silver	75.00
Bracelet, Mesh, Black Enameled Border, Tassels, Victorian, 14K Gold	700.00
Bracelet, Mother–of–Pearl, Oriental Figures, 5 Glass Seals	150.00
Bracelet, Oval Piece of Ivory On Top, Hand Carved Floral, Silver	65.00
Bracelet, Rhinestone, 3 Rows, Weiss	40.00
Bracelet, Rhinestone, Ice Blue, Schiaparelli	75.00
Bracelet, Rhinestone, Silvertone, Gray & Aurora, Lisner	18.00
Bracelet, Sapphire, Diamonds, Victorian, 15K Yellow Gold	550.00
Bracelet, Slip On, Georg Jensen, 3/4 In.	195.00
Bracelet, Snake, Flexible Chain, 14K Gold	225.00
Bracelet, Sterling Silver Frames, 8 Ivory Enameled Domed Panels	85.00
Bracelet, Sterling Silver, Pierced Panels, Kalo, 7 1/2 In.	595.00
Bracelet, Sterling, Blue Square Rhinestones	45.00
Bracelet, Stippled Discs, Links, Small Diamond On Disc, 14K Gold	325.00
Bracelet, Topaz Colored Stone, Filigree	75.00
Bracelet, Wooden, 6 Coral Cabochons, Eggshell Ground, Lacquer, 4 In.	2300.00
Brooch, Circle, 2 Moonstones, Hollow, Georg Jensen	295.00
Brooch, Circle, Diamond & Platinum ....*Illus*	1200.00
Brooch, Drop, Garnets, Emeralds, England, 15K Gold, C.1845	2265.00
Brooch, Oval Onyx, Profile of Lady In White, 14K Gold Frame	300.00
Buckle, Shoe, Clip–On, Marcasite, Pair	18.00
Buckle, Shoe, Rhinestone, Pair	25.00
Buckle, Sterling Silver, Hammered, Kalo, 1 7/8 X 1 1/4 In.	150.00
Buckle, Victorian, Etched Foliate, 14K Gold	150.00
Cameo, 50 Seed Pearls, Pink & White, 10K Gold Frame	300.00
Cameo, Victorian Lady, Black & White Onyx, 14K Gold, C.1880	275.00
Cameo, Victorian Lady, Pink Ground, 10K Gold Frame .... 150.00 To	165.00
Chain, 10K Gold, 16 In.	25.00
Chain, 14K Gold, 14 In.	38.00
Chain, 14K Gold, 20 In.	65.00
Chain, Rope, 14K Gold, 25 In.	200.00
Chain, Rope, Safety Catch, 14K Gold, 18 In.	85.00
Chain, Solid Link, Anchor Pendant, 14K Gold, 24 In.	195.00
Chain, Sterling Silver, 20 In.	18.00
Chain, Watch, Gun In Holster Fob, Sterling Silver	42.00
Chain, Watch, Human Hair, Mother–of–Pearl & Brass Charms	50.00
Chain, Watch, Intricate Links, 14K Gold	400.00

Chain, Watch, Lady's, 14K Gold 125.00
Chain, Watch, Locket Fob, Rhinestone, Gold 65.00
Chain, Watch, Man's, Silver Plate 30.00
Chain, Watch, Sardonyx Fob 65.00
Chain, Watch, Simmons, With T–Bar, Gold Filled 30.00
Chain, Watch, Victorian, Diamond & Black Enameled, 14K Gold 1000.00
Chatelaine, Mesh Purse, 14K Yellow Gold 500.00
Cigarette Case, Rhinestone 45.00
Cigarette Case, Sterling Silver, 4 1/2 X 3 In. 98.00
Crucifix, Silver Filigree, On Velvet Ribbon 2.50
Cuff Links, Art Nouveau, Figures In Pink & Yellow Gold 400.00
Cuff Links, Cameo, Profile of 2 Gentlemen, Black Onyx, 14K Gold 315.00
Cuff Links, Figures In Pink, Yellow Gold, Art Nouveau 400.00
Cuff Links, Made From Butterfly Wings, Hoffman, Box, 1930s 18.00
Cuff Links, Mother–of–Pearl, Krementz 12.00
Cuff Links, Ruby, Mother–of–Pearl, 22K Gold Mounting 1300.00
Cuff Links, Square, Cut Diamond Center, 14K Gold 225.00
Ear Pendants, Amethyst, Emerald Cut, Suspended From Bow Motif 125.00
Ear Pendants, Carved Coral Putti, Victorian, Original Fitted Box 1800.00
Ear Pendants, Floral Etching, 14K Gold 275.00
Ear Pendants, Onyx, Suspended From Engraved 14K Rose Gold Plaque 275.00
Ear Pendants, Victorian, Pear Shaped Cameo, 14K Yellow Gold 500.00
Earrings, Butterfly, 39 Emeralds, 3 Pieces, Spain, 18th Century 3025.00
Earrings, Butterfly, Abalone, Mexican Sterling Silver 19.00
Earrings, Daisies, Cluster, Clip, Coro 7.00
Earrings, Etruscan Revival, Crescent Wire 225.00
Earrings, Full Cut Diamond, 14K White Gold, 3/4 Carat 1500.00
Earrings, Gold & Garnet, Emerald Cut, Gold Mounting 350.00
Earrings, Green Glass Stones, Gold Tone, Clip, Kreisler 18.00
Earrings, Ivory Dangle, Pineapple Shape, Screw 30.00
Earrings, Oak Leaf Design, Victorian, Sterling Silver 28.00
Earrings, Painter's Palette, Copper, Clip 15.00
Earrings, Rhinestone, Amber, Clip, Pell, 1940s 8.50
Earrings, Rhinestone, Weiss 15.00
Earrings, Silver, Loop, Georg Jensen 45.00
Earrings, Victorian, Gypsy, Loops, Red Coral Teardrops, 14K Gold 65.00
Hairpin, Cobalt Blue, Large 8.00
JEWELRY, HATPIN, see Hatpin
Heart, Black Metal, Art Nouveau, Lady In Center, 2 In. 32.00
JEWELRY, INDIAN, see Indian
Jabot, Arrow, Diamond, Channel Sapphires, Art Deco, 18K White Gold 800.00
Lapel Pin, Ladybug, Gold 20.00
Locket, 4 Mine Cut Diamonds, 18K Gold, C.1870 .... 275.00
Locket, Agate Cameo of Lady, Foliate Diamond, 14K Gold Frame 550.00
Locket, Amber Fossil Center, Victorian, Sterling Silver 70.00
Locket, Art Nouveau, Lady's Profile, Diamond Head Band, 18K Gold ... 325.00
Locket, Cameo, Agate, Lady, Foliate Diamond Set, 14K Gold Frame 550.00
Locket, Gold Serpent, Victorian, Scale Chain, 3 Emeralds 2100.00
Locket, Heart Shape, Mother–of–Pearl Front, Colored Rhinestones 12.00
Locket, Officer's Tintype, Opens, Young Lady, Civil War 125.00
Locket, Opens To 2 Pictures, Flower Etching, 3 Sets of 2 Rubies 45.00
Locket, Pendant, Easter Egg & Serpent, Diamond, C.1900, 1 In. 2750.00
Locket, Silver, Amber Fossil In Center, Victorian 70.00
Locket, Victorian, Center Arc, Pearls, 14K 2–Color Gold 250.00
Locket, Victorian, Chalcedony Lady Cameo, 14K Yellow Gold 250.00
Medal, Military, 25 Yrs.Faithful Service N.Y., Gold, Tiffany & Co. 595.00
Necklace & Bracelet, Brass, Borealis Stones, Coro 55.00
Necklace & Drop Earrings, Amber, Weiss 50.00
Necklace & Earrings, Black Jet, Gold Tone Metal, Trifari 45.00
Necklace & Earrings, Buffalo Horn 30.00
Necklace & Earrings, Rhinestone, Ice Blue, Screw Back 40.00
Necklace & Earrings, Sapphire Blue Crystal Beads, Lisner 28.00
Necklace & Earrings, Wooden Balls, Amber Cabochon, Eisenberg 75.00
Necklace, 4 Rows of Emerald Cut Rhinestones, Weiss 65.00

Necklace, Amber Beads, Graduated Ovals, 34 In. 110.00
Necklace, Baltic Amber, Cone Shaped Beads, 30 1/2 In. 90.00
Necklace, Black Jet Matchstick Beads, Frosted Beads, Open Circle 28.00
Necklace, Black Jet, Gold Tone Beads Between, 20 In. 27.00
Necklace, Blue Aurora Crystal Beads, Silver Links, 36 In. 40.00
Necklace, Braided, V Shaped, 14K 2–Colored Gold, 16 In. 75.00
Necklace, Carved Coral, Rock Crystal, Jade Mandarin, China 1800.00
Necklace, Chain of Bezel Set Marquis Diamonds, Amethyst, C.1915 .... 5600.00
Necklace, Crystal Beads, Graduated, 38 In. 25.00
Necklace, Gold, Onyx, Detachable Cameo Warrior Pin, 2 Tassels 1000.00
Necklace, Grapes Alternating With Leaves, Jensen, 16 In. 660.00
Necklace, Hobe, Pearl, Crystal, Rhinestone, 22 In. 120.00
Necklace, Honey Amber, With Fossils, Tie String, 24 In. 40.00
Necklace, Jet, Filigree Trim 15.00
Necklace, Jet, Gold Mounts, Victorian 175.00
Necklace, Lapis Beads & Discs 20.00
Necklace, Link Chain, Gucci, 18 In. 250.00
Necklace, Mexican Mask, Sterling Silver Chain, 3 Dimensional 45.00
Necklace, Pearl, Double Strand, Hattie Carnegie, 16 In. 45.00
Necklace, Peking Green Glass Beads, 1920s, 20 In. 55.00
Necklace, Pink Flat Oval Moonstone Beads, 25 In. 45.00
Necklace, Rhinestone, Clear & Red, Floral Pattern Center, 15 In. 10.00
Necklace, Rhinestone, Teardop Stones, Weiss 75.00
Necklace, Silver, Portrait of Gentleman, 18th Century Dress 100.00
Necklace, Snake Chain, Double, Trifari, 12 1/2 In. 45.00
Necklace, Victorian, Gold, Foxtail Link Tassels, Center Plaque 475.00
Necklace, White Gold, Yellow Gold Flowers, Red Center Stone 75.00
Pendant & Earrings, Amber Topaz, Chain, 14K Textured Gold 85.00
Pendant & Seed Pearl Chain, Diamond, Platinum Wires, Edwardian 650.00
Pendant, Art Nouveau, Design of Maiden, Webster Co., 3 X 2 In. 295.00
Pendant, Cameo, Lady Profile, Tortoiseshell Pierced Foliate Frame 225.00
Pendant, Cross Shape, Diamond, Pearl, Silver, 19th Century, 2 In. 440.00
Pendant, Filigree, Marcasite, Black Onyx Center, Silver Tone, 34 In. 48.00
Pendant, Gold & Nephrite, Green Enamel, Seed Pearls 350.00
Pendant, Head of Unicorn, Baguette & Trapezoid Diamonds, Gold 550.00
Pendant, Heart, 2 Diamonds, 14 Paved Diamonds, Platinum 600.00
Pendant, Jade, Foo Dog, 1 3/4 X 1 In. 70.00
Pendant, Marcasite, Sterling Silver Chain, Victorian, 1 1/2 In. 16.00
Pendant, Pearl Drop, Plique–A–Jour, Silver Chain, 1910, 15 In. 350.00
Pendant, Sterling Silver Chain, C.Horner, Blue Green Enameled 295.00
Pendant, Sterling Silver, Diamond Shape, Camel Design 10.00
Pendant, Winged Woman, Diamond, Pearl Drop, Gold Link, 1900, 2 In. 2200.00
Pin & Earrings, Eisenberg Ice, Box 67.50
Pin & Earrings, Gold Twisted Design, Hobe, Box, 1925–45 .... 55.00
Pin & Earrings, Rhinestone, Blue, Sterling Silver, Cart Art 35.00
Pin & Earrings, Rhinestone, Circles, Light Blue & Clear, Coro 18.00
Pin & Earrings, Rhinestone, Clear, Faux Pearls, Hattie Carnegie 30.00
Pin & Earrings, Rhinestone, Floral, Light Blue Cabochon, Judy Lee 28.00

Jewelry, Brooch, Circle, Diamond & Platinum

Pin & Earrings, Rhinestone, Frosted Leaves, Jomaz	28.00
Pin & Earrings, Rhinestone, Smoky Gray	35.00
Pin, 2 Onyx Cats, 14K Gold Frame, Glass Eyes, Victorian	300.00
Pin, 3 Ballerinas, 14K White Gold, Diamonds, Rubies, Sapphires	150.00
Pin, Arrow, Rhinestone, Art Deco, Celluloid	15.00
Pin, Art Deco, Inlay Metal, With Perfume Holder	38.00
Pin, Art Nouveau Lady, Butterfly Wings, Marcasite Border, Silver	110.00
Pin, Aurora Borealis, Joseph Warner	25.00
Pin, Bakelite, Carved Green Leaves, 1 1/2 In.	12.00
Pin, Bee Shape, 34 Diamonds, Diamond Eyes, Flaircraft, 7/8 In.	235.00
Pin, Bee Shape, 34 Diamonds, Emerald Eyes, 18K Gold, 15/16 In.	350.00
Pin, Bird, Figural, Metal, Rhinestones	22.00
Pin, Blue, Red, Green Stones, Rhinestone	55.00
Pin, Bow Shape, Platinum, Diamond, Seaman Schepps	4600.00
Pin, Boy & Scottie Dog, Sterling Silver, 1900	42.00
Pin, Brass, Abstract Leaf Design, G.W.Frost, 2 1/2 X 1 5/8 In.	75.00
Pin, Bumblebee, Sterling Silver, Enamel, Margot De Taxco	45.00
Pin, Butterfly Wings, Huffman	15.00
Pin, Butterfly, Amber Rhinestone, 2 In.	25.00
Pin, Calla Lily, Sterling Silver, 2 3/8 X 7/8 In.	195.00
Pin, Cameo, 10K Gold Bezel	100.00
Pin, Cameo, England, 15K Gold, C.1840	1600.00
Pin, Cameo, Frosted Glass, Black Ground, Brass Tone Mounting	18.00
Pin, Cameo, Shell, Victorian, Gold Plated Frame	100.00
Pin, Cameo, White Goddesses, Black Ground, Plastic, Celebrity	15.00
Pin, Castellani, Gold, Mosaic Center	500.00
Pin, Circle, 2 Moonstones, Georg Jensen, 1 5/8 In.	295.00
Pin, Circle, 5 Diamonds, 25 Marquises, 1 1/2 In. ....Illus	1200.00
Pin, Coral, Victorian, Young Girl Profile, 14K Yellow Gold Bezel	175.00
Pin, Crown, Sterling Silver, Trifari	125.00
Pin, Cupid, Victorian, Cupid Flying, With Torch, Sterling Silver	58.00
Pin, Daisy On Pearly Ground, Sulfide, Octagonal, 1 3/8 In.	27.50
Pin, Diamond, 2 Parts, Portuguese, Gold, 18th Century, 3 1/2 In.	1760.00
Pin, Diamond, Platinum, Edwardian, Rectangular Pierced Mounting	500.00
Pin, Dragonfly, Rhinestone, 2 In.	12.00
Pin, Elephant, Green, Rhinestone Trim, Hattie Carnegie, 2 In.	45.00
Pin, Flower, 3 Daisies, Gold Overlay, 3 Citrine Stones, Sterling	35.00
Pin, Flower, Porcelain, Staffordshire, 2 In.	12.00
Pin, Freshwater Pearls, Plique-A-Jour, Papyrus Leaves, 1 1/2 In.	200.00
Pin, Garnet, Letter M, Blood Red Rose Cut, Bohemian	115.00
Pin, Gold & Mosaic, Beetle Plaque, Gold Mounting	425.00
Pin, Gold Filled, For Double Photos, Victorian	35.00
Pin, Hat, Flower, Sterling Silver, 8 1/4 In.	36.00
Pin, Hat, Flying Dragon, Sword, 14K Gold, Garnets, Diamonds	750.00
Pin, Insect, Flying, Oval Black Glass Body, Gold Plated Wings	32.00
Pin, Knot Design, 14K Yellow Gold, Victorian	150.00
Pin, Lapel, American Legion, 14K Gold, 1/2 Carat Diamond	300.00
Pin, Leaf & Berry, Moonstone Cabochon, Sterling Silver, Ruopoll	275.00
Pin, Leaf, Sterling Silver, 2 In.	15.00
Pin, Mask Form, Silver-Gilt, Peruzzi, Boston	150.00
Pin, Micro-Mosaic, 2 Birds, Blue Sky, Roped Bezel, 18K Yellow Gold	1500.00
Pin, Mother-of-Pearl Leaves, Seed Pearls, Hobe	35.00
Pin, Oak Leaf, Diamond Center, 14K Gold	100.00
Pin, Opal, Snarling Creature, Lalique, Gold, 1900, 1 1/4 In.	8250.00
Pin, Ostrich, Rhinestone Feathers	35.00
Pin, Panda, Rhinestone, 2 In.	20.00
Pin, Pea Pod, Rhinestone, Pearls, Pannetta	18.00
Pin, Plaid, Highland Light Infantry, England, C.1870	475.00
Pin, Rose, Black Jet, Weiss	10.00
Pin, Sapphire, Pierced Platinum, Pearls & Diamonds, C.1900	3800.00
Pin, Scarecrow, Rhinestone, Faux Gemstones, Weiss	45.00
Pin, Siam Silver, Rectangle Shape, Open Filigree, 2 In.	30.00
Pin, Snowflake, Rhinestone, Weiss, 1 1/2 In.	30.00
Pin, Snowflake, Sterling Silver, A.Gotshall, 1 1/2 In.	50.00

> Beads that are stil strung on the original thread have more value than restrung pieces if you are a serious collector. If you plan to wear the jewelry, be sure the string has not weakened.

Pin, Sterling, Openwork Leaf, Cabochon of Carnelian, Gorham	275.00
Pin, Turtle, Aurora Borealis Rhinestone	12.00
Pin, Uncle Sam, Spanish–American War Era	55.00
Pin, Victorian Lady, 50 Seed Pearls, Pink & White, 10K Gold Frame	300.00
Pin, Victorian, 2 Beads Suspended, Foxtail Link Chain, 14K Gold	350.00
Pin, Victorian, Claw, Set In Etched Foliate 15K Gold	125.00
Pin, Victorian, Coiled Snake, Sapphire, Diamonds, 15K Yellow Gold	550.00
Pin, Victorian, Engraved Ribbon, Turquoise & 2 Tassels, 15K Gold	400.00
Pin, Victorian, Seed Pearls, French Hallmarks, 18K Gold, Box	800.00
Pin, Wasps, Wings Move, Rhinestone, Hattie Carnegie, 1 1/2 In.	35.00
Powder Case, Center Monogram Cartouche, 14K Gold, Octagonal	100.00
Ring, American Indian Head, 18K Gold, Rubies, Diamonds, C.1940	350.00
Ring, Biker's Skull, Helmet, Sterling Silver	30.00
Ring, Black Opal, Art Nouveau, 2 Diamonds, 14K Yellow Gold	900.00
Ring, Cameo, 14K, Antique, White Gold	125.00
Ring, Cameo, Woman's, 14K Gold	100.00
Ring, Center Cabochon Chrysoprase, 14K Yellow Gold	200.00
Ring, Child's, Signet, Victorian	35.00
Ring, Cultured Pearl, 2 Gray Baroque Pearls, 14K Gold Mounting	200.00
Ring, Diamond, Lozenge Shape Frame, Gold, Enameled, 18th Century	550.00
Ring, Dinner, Diamond Center, 8 Rubies, 14K Gold	250.00
Ring, Dinner, Emerald & Diamond, Platinum	1800.00
Ring, Dinner, Floral Design, 40 Point Diamond, 14K Gold	250.00
Ring, Dinner, Full Cut Diamond, 14K Gold, C.1940	3000.00
Ring, Emerald, Diamond, Enameled Gold, Sapphire, 19th Century	1210.00
Ring, Engagement, Prong Set Diamond, 14K Yellow Gold	165.00
Ring, French Cut Diamond, Rubies, .55 Ct., Marquise Shape, 14K Gold	300.00
Ring, Garnet, 10K Yellow Gold, Oval	48.00
Ring, Garnet, Cluster, 6 Marquise Shape Garnet Stones	249.00
Ring, Lava Scarab, In Revolving 14K Gold Mounting	100.00
Ring, Locket, Oval Stone, 14K Gold	200.00
Ring, Man's, 14K, 1/2 Carat Center Diamond	475.00
Ring, Man's, Adonis, Diamond Eyes, 16K Gold, C.1850	375.00
Ring, Man's, Two Dollar Gold Piece, 18K Gold	450.00
Ring, Man's, Victorian, 10K Gold, Carved Warrior Onyx	100.00
Ring, Masonic, Ruby, 14K Gold	135.00
Ring, Opal, Sterling Silver Filigree, C.1880	170.00
Ring, Oval, Black Onyx, Open Work, Marcasite Around	27.00
Ring, Princess Linear, 9 Rubies, 14K Yellow Gold	75.00
Ring, Reversible, Cameo One Side, Onyx On Reverse, 14K White Gold	100.00
Ring, Signet, Woman's, Victorian, Floral Shank Design, 14K Gold	75.00
Ring, Smoky Quartz, Turtle Set, Oval, 14K Yellow Gold Mounting	110.00
Ring, Square Cut Sapphire, Diamond, Platinum Mounting, C.1920	1000.00
Ring, Star Form Garnet Cluster, Victorian	325.00
Ring, Sterling, Marcasite Snake	50.00
Ring, Sterling, Marcasite, Butterfly, 6 Gemstones	79.00
Ring, Sugarloaf Cabochon Amethyst, Reeded Mounting, 18K Gold	450.00
Ring, Turquoise, Diamond & Peridot, 18K Gold	1100.00
Ring, Woman's, Basket Style Mounting, 33 Diamonds, Corner Pearls	350.00
Ring, Woman's, Canary Yellow Sapphire, 14K Gold, 1 Carat	300.00
Ring, Woman's, Citrine Stone, 16 Rubies, Filigree, 20K Gold, C.1850	450.00
Ring, Woman's, Polished Onyx, Garnet, 14K Gold, C.1870	110.00
Ring, Woman's, Rose Diamond, 18K Gold, C.1800	250.00
Ring, Woman's, Square Onyx, Diamond, Set In Filigree Platinum	695.00
Ring, Woman's, Victorian, 14K Gold, Pink Spine	55.00

Ring, Zircon & Garnet, 2 Brown Zircons, 2 Rhodolite Garnets, 18K 125.00
Slide, Jade, Mutton Fat, Language Symbols, On Cord With Beads 450.00
Stickpin, 1 Round Diamond Center, Black Enamel Trim, 2 1/2 In. 75.00
Stickpin, 22K Gold Nugget 75.00
Stickpin, Art Deco Brass, 7 Green Stones 15.00
Stickpin, Cameo, Shell, 10K Gold 95.00
Stickpin, Coral Rose, Gold Filled 32.00
Stickpin, Dog, 18K Gold 175.00
Stickpin, Rhinestones, Red, White & Blue 6.00
Stickpin, Sword, Pearl, Turquoise 40.00
Sweater Guard, Brass, Lady, Walking Hounds, Coro 45.00
    JEWELRY, WATCH, see Watch
Watch Pendant, Enamel & Silver, White Dial, Arabic Numbers 225.00

John Rogers statues were made from 1859 to 1892. The originals were bronze, but the thousands of copies made by the Rogers factory were of painted plaster. Eighty different figures were made. Similar painted plaster figures were made by some other factories. Never repaint a Rogers figure because this lowers the value to collectors.

JOHN ROGERS, Group, Charity Patient .... 650.00 To 850.00
Group, Going For The Cows 600.00
Group, Matter of Opinion 850.00
Group, Returned Volunteer 850.00
Group, Rip Van Winkle Returned 475.00
Group, School Examination 675.00
Group, Watch On The Santa Maria 475.00

Any memorabilia that refers to the Jews or the Jewish religion is collected. Interests range from newspaper clippings that mention eighteenth- and nineteenth-century Jewish Americans to religious objects, such as menorahs or spice boxes. Age, condition, and the intrinsic value of the material, as well as the historic and artistic importance, determine the value.

JUDAICA, Lamp, Hanging, Oil, Sabbath, Brass 150.00
Lamp, Hanukah, Sterling Silver 350.00
Plaque, Hebrew Inscription, Near East Scene, Copper On Wood 48.00
Plaque, House of David, Box, 10 In., Pair 50.00
Plaque, Rabbi, Silver, Framed, Boris Schatz, 2 3/4 X 2 In. 137.00
Plate, The Struggle, Silver, Bronze, Jacques Lipschitz, Box, 12 In. 225.00

Jugtown Pottery refers to pottery made in North Carolina as far back as the 1750s. In 1915, Juliana and Jacques Busbee set up a training and sales organization for what they named "Jugtown Pottery." In 1921, they built a shop at Jugtown, North Carolina, and hired Ben Owen as a potter in 1923. The Busbees moved the village store where the pottery was sold and promoted to New York City. Juliana Busbee sold the New York store in 1926 and moved into a log cabin near the Jugtown Pottery. The pottery closed in 1958. It reopened and is still working near Seagrove, North Carolina.

JUGTOWN, Bowl, Blue & Gray, Signed, 5 In. 25.00
Creamer, Orange 40.00
Cup & Saucer 12.50
Cup, Frogskin, Small 15.00
Jug, Finger, Stamped Ben Owen Master Potter 95.00
Pie Plate, Orange, Black Concentric Circles, 9 1/2 In. 65.00
Pitcher, Frogskin, Design By Juliana Busbee, C.1929 .... 115.00
Vase, Chinese Turquoise, Splotches of Red, 5 1/2 In. 165.00

Kate Greenaway, who was a famous illustrator of children's books, drew pictures of children in high-waisted Empire dresses. She lived from 1846 to 1901. Her designs appear on china, glass, and other pieces. Figural napkin rings depicting the Greenaway children are also to be found listed under Napkin Ring, Figural.

KATE GREENAWAY, Book, Little Folks, Painting, Hardcover 55.00
  Coloring Book, Sketches & Rhymes, 1952 .... 35.00
  Figurine, Rope Jumpers, 9 1/2 In., Pair 600.00
  Napkin Ring, Boy, Overcoat, Hat, Carrying Books 175.00
  Napkin Ring, Figural, Girl With Ring 125.00
  Salt & Pepper, Girl In Long Dress, Staffordshire, 3 1/4 In. 35.00
  Tile, Month, November, 1 In.Leaf Border, Wedgwood, 1880, 8 In. 135.00

"Kauffmann" refers to the type of work done by Angelica Kauffmann, a painter and decorative artist for Adam Brothers in England between 1766 and 1781. She designed small–scale pictorial subjects in the neoclassic manner. Most porcelains signed "Kauffmann" were made in the 1800s. She did not do the artwork on all pieces signed with her name.

KAUFFMANN, Bowl, Maidens & Cupid, Cranberry, Gold Border, Signed, 10 In. 85.00
  Cup & Saucer, Beehive, Royal Blue, Signed 100.00
  Demitasse Set, Beehive, 6 Cups & Saucers, Pot, Tray, Signed 950.00
  Ewer, Maiden & Cupid In Reserve, Gold, Maroon, 6 1/4 In. 195.00
  Holder, Condensed Milk, Underplate, Classical Figure, Signed 85.00
  Plate, Classical Scene, Maidens, Signed, 7 3/8 In. 90.00
  Plate, Maidens & Cupid Center, Gilt Roses, Green, Signed, 10 In. 65.00
  Sugar & Creamer 285.00
  Vase, Classical Scene, 4 Maidens, Signed, 20 In. 395.00
  KAYSERZINN, see Pewter

KELVA Kelva glassware was made by the C. F. Monroe Company of Meriden, Connecticut, about 1904. It is a pale, pastel–painted glass decorated with flowers, designs, or scenes. Kelva resembles Nakara and Wave Crest, two other glasswares made by the same company.

KELVA, Box, Dresser, Hinged Cover, Mottled Green, White, Florals, Marked, 8 In. 495.00
  Box, Flowers, Twigs, Gilded Rim, Green, Signed, Hinged Cover, 8 In. 475.00
  Box, Hinged Cover, Enameled Pink & White Flowers, 4 1/3 In. 150.00
  Box, Hinged Cover, Hand Painted Flowers, 4 1/2 In. 275.00
  Box, Hinged Cover, Mottled Sage Green, Poppy, Seed Pods, Round, 5 In. 300.00
  Box, Hinged Cover, Orange & White Floral, Octagonal Mold, 3 X 4 In. 335.00
  Box, Hinged Cover, Orange & White Flowers, Gilded Collar, 4 1/4 In. 325.00
  Box, Hinged Cover, Ormolu Collar, Mottled Green, Flowers, 4 In. 325.00
  Box, Hinged Cover, Pink & White Flowers, Marked, 8 In. 650.00
  Box, Hinged Cover, Poppies, Seed Pods, Vines, Lined, Marked 4 1/2 In. 300.00
  Box, Hinged Cover, Poppies, Trailing Stems, Lined, 4 1/2 In. 300.00
  Box, Hinged Cover, Variegated Flowers, Leaves, Gilt Collar, 8 In. 425.00
  Box, Hinged Cover, Variegated Poppies, Trailing Buds, 4 3/4 In. 295.00
  Box, Orange Flowers, Green, 4 1/2 In. 325.00
  Dish, Orchids, Hexagonal, 3 1/4 In. 30.00
  Fernery, Embossed, Ormolu Feet, Marked, 6 1/2 X 8 In. 600.00
  Humidor 500.00
  Tray, Mirror, Flowers On Blue Ground, Oval, 6 1/4 X 4 In. 500.00
  Vase, Pink Flowers, Green Ground, Ormolu Fittings, 17 1/2 In. 1150.00
  Vase, Scroll, Pink Flowers, Green Ground, 10 In. 450.00

Kemple glass was made by John Kemple of East Palestine, Ohio, and Kenova, West Virginia, from 1945 to 1970. The glass was made from old molds. Many designs and colors were made. Kemple pieces are usually marked with a "K" on the bottom. Many milk glass pieces were made with or without the mark.

KEMPLE, Dish, Cat Cover 55.00
  Dish, Rooster Cover, Amber, 8 In. 55.00

KEW-BLAS Kew Blas is the name used by the Union Glass Company of Somerville, Massachusetts. The name refers to an iridescent golden glass made from the 1890s to 1924. The iridescent glass was reminiscent of the Tiffany glass of the period.

KEW BLAS, Tumbler, Pinched Sides, Gold Iridescent, Signed, 4 In.	185.00
Vase, Blue Drapes, 6 In.	795.00
Vase, Gold Iridescent, Ruffled Everted Rim, Bell Form, 7 1/2 In.	350.00
Vase, Green & Gold Pulled Feather Design, Ivory Ground, 6 In.	550.00
Vase, Light Blue Pulled Loops, Dark Blue, Signed, 6 In.	825.00
Vase, Pulled Feathers, Apricot, Signed, 6 In.	850.00

Kewpies, designed by Rose O'Neill, were first pictured in the "Ladies' Home Journal." The pixielike figures were a success, and Kewpie dolls started appearing in 1911. Kewpie pictures and other items soon followed. Collectors search for all items that picture the little winged people.

KEWPIE, Bank, Black, Blue Wings, 12 In.	55.00
Bank, Clock Shape, Signed O'Neill	25.00
Bell, Brass	45.00
Button, Lapel	120.00
Candy Container, Bowl	65.00
Candy Container, Glass, Painted	110.00
Card, Merry Christmas, Kewpie In Tree, 23 X 31 In.	20.00
Clock, Mirror Side, Time Strike, Alarm, Ingraham	375.00
Doll, Arms Over Head, Label	125.00
Doll, Bisque Head, Molded Peak Hair, Toddler Body, Kestner, 12 In.	770.00
Doll, Bisque, Action, Seated, Arms Folded, Blue Wings, 4 1/2 In.	1600.00
Doll, Bisque, Blue Wings, Original Clothes, Sticker, O'Neill, 5 In.	125.00
Doll, Bisque, Jointed Arms, Starfish Fingers, Blue Wings, 10 In.	350.00
Doll, Bisque, O'Neill, 5 In.	225.00
Doll, Black Hot 'N Tot, Bisque	89.00
Doll, Boy, Going Fishing, 12 In.	20.00
Doll, Bride & Groom, Original Clothes, Glass Dome, O'Neill, 4 1/2 In.	225.00
Doll, Cameo, Vinyl, 24 In.	55.00
Doll, Celluloid, Green Wings, Marked Japan, 3 In.	10.00
Doll, Christmas Dress, Tree On Pocket, Bell, Cameo Marked, 14 In.	85.00
Doll, Composition, Original Clothes, 13 In.	125.00
Doll, Girl, Going Shopping, 12 In.	20.00
Doll, Huggero Signed, 1913	95.00
Doll, Kuddle, 14 In.	25.00
Doll, On Stomach, Signed, 4 In.	300.00
Doll, Ragsie, 12 In.	95.00
Doll, Sitting, Sucking Thumb, 3 In.	80.00
Doll, Standing, Bisque, Broom, Dust Bin, Label, 3 1/2 In. ....*Illus*	325.00
Doll, Thinker, Signed, 5 In.	235.00
Doll, Traveler With Doodle Dog, Japan	27.00
Doll, Traveler, Signed, 3 1/2 In.	200.00
Figurine, Bisque, Seated In Wicker Chair, Arms Folded, Governor	425.00
Figurine, Chalkware, 12 In.	60.00
Figurine, Heart Label, Rose O'Neill, Bisque, 5 3/4 In.	225.00
Figurine, Hot 'N Tot, Bisque	45.00
Figurine, Huggies, Bisque, 3 1/2 In.	85.00
Figurine, Kewpie Standing By Bucket, Painted	50.00
Figurine, Reclining, 6 In.	25.00
Figurine, Solid Brass, 4 In.	85.00
Figurine, Traveler, Molded Topknot, Brown Valise, C.1915, 2 1/2 In.	125.00
Figurine, Traveler, Umbrella, Suitcase, Rose O'Neill, 3 1/2 In.	225.00
Holder, Place Card, On Back, Legs In Air, Bisque, Rose O'Neill	110.00
Jar, Mayonnaise, Kewpie On Cover & Label	49.00
Mug, 5 Action Kewpies, Signed, Rose O'Neill, 3 1/4 In.	150.00
Music Box, Shamrock, Plays When Irish Eyes Are Smiling, 2 Kewpies	49.00
Perfume Bottle, Germany	140.00
Pin Tray, Marked Royal Austria	100.00
Pin, Celluloid, 1920, 1 In.	9.00
Planter, Pink	18.00

Kewpie, Doll, Standing, Bisque,
Broom, Dust Bin, Label, 3 1/2 In.

KPM, Plaque, Woman Hiding Cupid's
Bow, Signed Volk, 10 X 8 In.

Planter, Thinker, Blue Ceramic	35.00
Plate, 1973	20.00
Plate, 5 Kewpies Around Rim, Amid Trees, Rudolstadt, 7 1/2 In.	175.00
Postcard, Christmas, With Santa	18.00
Postcard, Easter	15.00
Spoon, Sterling Silver, Kewpie Handle	80.00
Stickpin, Celluloid	70.00
Tea Set, Doll's, Luster, Kewpie On Each Piece, Rose O'Neill, 7 Piece	295.00
Thimble, Marked Kewpie	18.00
Toothpick, Glass, Borgfeldt	85.00
Tray, Ice Cream, Montrose Dairy Parker–Brawner Co., Kewpie Eating	250.00
Valentine, Rose O'Neill	20.00
Watch Holder, Metal, With 2 Kewpies	125.00
Whistle, Figural, Brass	29.00

KIMBALL, see Cluthra
KING'S ROSE, see Soft Paste

All types of kitchen utensils, from eggbeaters to bowls, are collected today. Handmade wooden and metal items, like ladles and apple peelers, were made in the early nineteenth century. Mass–produced pieces, like iron apple peelers and graniteware, were made in the nineteenth century. Other kitchen wares are listed under manufacturers' names or under Iron; Advertising; Tool; or Wooden.

KITCHEN, %Iron, Brass, Dutch Style, Denmark, Early 1800s	67.50
%Iron, Charcoal, 1852	45.00
%Iron, Charcoal, 1916	50.00
%Iron, Charcoal, Brass	65.00
%Iron, Charcoal, Dolphin Handle	65.00
%Iron, Charcoal, Pat.Oct.3, 1916	35.00
%Iron, Charcoal, Red Wooden Handle	40.00
%Iron, Charcoal, Rooster Finial	45.00 To 50.00
%Iron, Child's, C & P Products Co., Electric, Miniature	25.00
%Iron, Curling, Solar, Electric	25.00
%Iron, Electric, Chevron, Fold Up	30.00
%Iron, Electric, Winchester	125.00
%Iron, Enterprise, Salesman's Sample	80.00
%Iron, Fluting, Indicator, Patent 1878, Ilion, N.Y., 2 Piece	75.00
%Iron, Fluting, Open Ring Handles, 12 In.	75.00
%Iron, Fluting, Patent Dates 1875–1880	64.50
%Iron, Fluting, Street Co., Hinged Bottom, Pat.1860, 2 Piece	52.50
%Iron, Fluting, The Best, 2 Piece	37.50
%Iron, Gas, Clothes, Blue Enamelware	35.00

%Iron, Gas, Coleman, Blue	35.00
%Iron, Gas, Imperial, 1903	40.00
%Iron, Gas, Montgomery Ward, Wooden Handle	30.00
%Iron, Goffering, Brass, & Iron Holder, 6 1/4 In.	125.00
%Iron, Goffering, Double, Brass On Iron Base, Oak Handle, 12 In.	250.00
%Iron, Goffering, Slug & Base Numbered 13, 7 X 15 In.	220.00
%Iron, Kerosene, Coleman, Measuring Can, Pump, Original Box	15.00
%Iron, Monitor, 1903	35.00
%Iron, Pierced Sides, Hinged Lid, Brass, Copper & Iron, 10 In.	125.00
%Iron, Sensible, No.6	60.00
%Iron, Sleeve, Iron Handle, 7 In.	45.00
%Iron, Steamomatic, Model 8200	18.00
%Iron, Tailor's	25.00
%Iron, Wafer, American	725.00
%Iron, Wafer, Cast Iron, Religious Symbols, Pat.Jul.26, '81, 34 In.	42.50
%Iron, Wooden Handle, S Scroll Brass Trim, 7 In.	435.00
Apple Corer, New Standard	5.00
Baker, Cornstick, Miracle Maize, Glass	15.00
Baker, Heart & Star, Griswold	130.00
Basket, Potato, Wire, Arched Handle, C.1800, 14 X 16 In.	190.00
Basket, Potato, Wire, Footed, Handle, Small	40.00
Bin & Sifter, Flour, Superior, 29 In.	250.00
Biscuit Pricker, Mushroom Knob, Metal Teeth, Birch, 4 X 4 1/4 In.	220.00
Biscuit Pricker, Turned Brass Handle & Teeth, Wooden, Round	140.00
Bluing Paddle, 1920s	6.00
Board, Bread, Shaped Handle, American, Pine, 19th Century, Round	88.00
Board, Noodle, Hanging Hole, Pine	100.00
Board, Oatmeal, Corrugated Board & Roller, 8 X 14 In.	90.00
Bootjack, Naughty Nellie	20.00
Bootjack, Pony Express Beetle	22.00
Bottle, Oil, Tin Pouring Spout, 1926, 1 Qt.	8.00
Bottle, Vacuum, Stanley, Chrome Cover	75.00
Bowl, Burl, Dark Patina, 15 1/2 X 6 1/2 In.	2000.00
Bowl, Dough, Carved Wood, Semicircular Handles, 25 1/8 In.	100.00
Box, Dough, Open Oval Ends, Slanted Sides, Blue Paint, 18 1/2 In.	65.00
Box, Pantry, Butter Carrier, Wire Bail, Wood Handle, 9 3/4 In.	165.00
Box, Pantry, Dry Chocolate Brown, Rose–Heads & Tacks, 12 3/4 In.	395.00
Box, Salt, Dovetailed, Blue Over Old Red, 19th Century, 10 In.	695.00
Braiser, Iron Pan Insert, Copper & Brass, 4 1/2 X 6 1/2 In.	20.00
Bread Box, Rolltop, Wooden Knob, Stainless Steel	50.00
Breaker, Seal For Fruit Jar, Jenney, Cast Iron	10.00
Broiler, Steak, Griswold	200.00
KITCHEN, BUTTER MOLD, see Kitchen, Mold, Butter	
Butter Spreader, Wooden, Primitive, 9 In.	6.00
Butter Stamp, 1 Side Sheaf, Reverse, Bird, Plants, 1883, 4 1/8 In.	175.00
Butter Stamp, Acorn, 1 Lb., 3 Piece	65.00
Butter Stamp, Apple & Leaves, Maple, Mushroom Knob Handle, 1800s	53.00
Butter Stamp, Beaver, 1 Piece	55.00
Butter Stamp, Bird, 2 1/2 X 3 1/2 In.	50.00
Butter Stamp, Carved Eagle, Chest Shield, 3 1/2 In.	225.00
Butter Stamp, Chip Carved, 2 Birds On Stylized Tree, Handle, 8 In.	350.00
Butter Stamp, Cow, 4 1/2 In.	90.00
Butter Stamp, Cow, Individual	9.50
Butter Stamp, Cow, Maple, 18th Century, 3 3/4 In.	395.00
Butter Stamp, Daisy & Leaf, Ribbed Border, 3 1/2 In.	65.00
Butter Stamp, Double Sheaf of Wheat, Hand Carved, Maple, C.1820	85.00
Butter Stamp, Double Star, Rectangular	120.00
Butter Stamp, Dove, 1 Piece	70.00
Butter Stamp, Eagle With Star, Handle, 4 1/4 In.	185.00
Butter Stamp, Eagle, Chest Shield, 3 1/2 In.	195.00
Butter Stamp, Eagle, Knob On Back, Unscrews, Half Circle	120.00
Butter Stamp, Fleur–De–Lis, Knob Handle, Wooden, 3 1/2 In.	85.00
Butter Stamp, Floral, Half Circle, Inserted Handle, 6 In.	245.00
Butter Stamp, Flower, Hand Carved, 3 X 4 In.	265.00

Butter Stamp, Geometric Floral Design, Handle, Round, 3 1/2 In. 45.00
Butter Stamp, Goat, With Bell, Individual 9.50
Butter Stamp, Heart Shaped Flower, Foliage, Handle, 4 7/8 In. 165.00
Butter Stamp, Heart, Knob On Back, Unscrews, Half Circle 119.00
Butter Stamp, Hearts, Pinwheel, Elliptical, 9 1/4 X 4 1/4 In. 750.00
Butter Stamp, Leaves & Ferns, Knob Handle, C.1830, 2 3/4 In. 75.00
Butter Stamp, Leaves, Wooden 75.00
Butter Stamp, Lentil Shape, Wooden 500.00
Butter Stamp, Morning Glory, Flat Back, 5 In. 40.00
Butter Stamp, Mushroom, Knob Handle, 3 3/4 In. 130.00
Butter Stamp, Oak Leaves, Hand Carved, 7 In. 135.00
Butter Stamp, Pineapple, 3 5/8 In. 70.00
Butter Stamp, Pineapple, Flat Back, Hand Carved, 1800, 4 In. 120.00
Butter Stamp, Pineapple, Handle, 4 1/4 In. 145.00
Butter Stamp, Roller, 6 Prints, C.1850 .... 155.00
Butter Stamp, Rooster, 1 Piece 67.00
Butter Stamp, Sheaves, Inserted Handle, Rectangular, 2 1/2 X 4 In. 35.00
Butter Stamp, Sheep, Small, 1 Piece 53.00
Butter Stamp, Star Flower Design, Self–Turned Handle, 3 5/8 In. 75.00
Butter Stamp, Strawberry, With Blossom, Small, 2 Piece 35.00
Butter Stamp, Swan 95.00
Butter Stamp, Tulip, Oval, Flat Back, Deeply Carved 75.00
Can Opener, Figural, Bull's Head, Extended Tail Handle, 6 In. 27.00
Can Opener, Figural, Steer's Head With Horns, Cast Iron 40.00
Can Opener, Keen Kutter, Cast Iron .... 17.50 To 22.50
Candlesnuffer, Scissors Type, Primitive, Pre–1800 .... 20.00
Canister Set, Green, Cover, Hocking, 5 Piece 130.00
Cap Lifter, Jar, Miracle Vacuum 3.00
Carving Set, Keen Kutter, Stag Handles, 3 Piece 40.00
Cherry Pitter, Dated 1917 .... 45.00
Cherry Pitter, Double, Goodell, C.1900 .... 35.00
Cherry Pitter, Enterprise, No.2 .... 32.50
Cherry Pitter, Kollman Mfg.Co., Spring Punch Type 18.00
Cherry Pitter, New Standard No.20, Mt.Joy 20.00
Chopper, Food, Foley 5.00
Chopper, Food, Hand Forged Iron, 1800s, Set of 4 .... 150.00
Chopper, Food, Hand Forged Iron, Steel Cutting Edge, 18th Century 35.00
Chopper, Food, Iron, Beech Handles, Brass Rivets, 6 1/2 X 6 1/2 In. 49.00
Chopper, Food, Rosewood Handle, 7 X 8 1/2 In. 55.00
Chopper, Food, Steel, 2 Blades, Horsehead Blade Ends, 12 1/4 In. 325.00
Chopper, Meat, Keen Kutter 40.00
Chopper, Onion, Federal, Label, Red Handle 17.00
Churn, Barrel, Mounted On Sawbuck Base 130.00
Churn, Blue Crown, Red Wooden Handles, 2 Gal. 45.00
Churn, Dasher, No Lid, Annapolis, Ind., 5 Gal. 90.00
Churn, Dazey, 1 Qt. 485.00
Churn, Dazey, 4 Qt. 37.00
Churn, Dazey, No.20, 1/2 Gal. 58.00
Churn, Dazey, No.4, Red Top 45.00
Churn, Dog Powered Treadmill Type 400.00
Churn, Elgin, Label, 2 Qt. 75.00
Churn, M.Brown & Co., Wapakoneta, Ohio, Bentwood, Stenciling 225.00
Churn, Orvus 45.00
Churn, Pine, Pierced Paddles, Crank, C.1870, 22 1/2 X 18 In. 165.00
Churn, Pins & Dasher, Traces of Red, Wooden, 34 In. 150.00
Churn, Planked, 4 Metal Bands, Late 19th Century, 22 In. 192.00
Churn, Poplar, Red Graining, Black Trim, Turned Handle, 35 In. 290.00
Churn, Red Cow On Back, R.B.Dunninger, Bangor, Maine 125.00
Churn, Square Case, Toledo, Ohio Maker 265.00
Churn, Swing, Davis, Yellow Paint, Black Stenciled Design, 1879 .... 265.00
Churn, Syllabub, Tin, 4 Looped Feet, Rectangular, C.1880, 5 X 8 In. 85.00
Churn, Table, Blue Paint, Stenciled Cow, Winchendon, 16 In. 150.00
Churn, Union, No.2, Floor Model, Patent 1864 .... 375.00

COLLECTOR'S GUIDE
TO MID-CENTURY COLLECTIBLES

Antiques collectors in the 1890s searched for furniture, statues, and coins dating from ancient Greece to the sixteenth century. Antiquities, not antiques, were considered important and anything less than 250 years old was trivial. Serious American collectors of the 1920s searched for the roots of the country in the furniture, paintings, and silver of the seventeenth and eighteenth centuries. Today there is instant communication, plus an international art market. There are still those who want Chippendale chairs or Federal silver, but the adventuresome collector is now exploring the decorative arts world from the 1920s to the 1960s. This is a guide to the recent past in decorative arts and collectibles. It ranges from Art Deco-inspired talcum powder cans to chairs designed by Frank Lloyd Wright.

Many decorative arts styles were popular in Europe and America from 1920 to 1960. They are so recent and so clear in our memory, still visible in old movies and television shows, that it is difficult to sort good from bad or one style from another. Collectors are now buying at all levels of the market, from the $209,000 Art Deco console by Pierre Legrain to free-form pottery lamps, mass produced for Woolworth's. Seven basic styles are listed here. Detailed makers' histories and prices of objects can be found in this book.

Galuchat and sycamore console, Pierre Legrain, c. 1920, $209,000. Courtesy Sotheby's, New York

Arts & Crafts, 1870-1930: William Morris, who started the Arts & Crafts movement in England, stressed handcrafted furniture, books, needlework, and accessories. In America the design theories were continued by Gustav Stickley, Roycrofters, and others under the name "Mission." Furniture was of heavy dark oak with exposed mortise and tenon joints. Copper hardware and vases, Indian-style rugs, and dark green pottery were favored accessories.

Wiener Werkstatte (Vienna Workshop), 1903-1930: A studio workshop founded by Josef Hoffmann, Koloman (Kolo) Moser, and others in Vienna, Austria. Made glass, silver, copper, wooden and metal furniture, and other decorative arts in geometric cubist designs. Many American artists were influenced by this group.

Art Deco, 1910-1930: The Paris Exposition Internationale des Arts Décoratifs et Industriels Modernes, or Art Deco, started in 1925. Characterized by straight lines, geometric shapes, light-colored wood, shiny black lacquer, blue mirrors, sharkskin, and frosted glass. Revived in the United States in the 1960s. Favorite colors: purple, peach, gray, green, turquoise, brown, mauve, white, black.

Bauhaus, 1919-1939: School of art and design founded in Germany in 1919. Called Bauhaus or International style. Influenced by industrial materials and machine production. Furniture of chrome, plastic, steel, glass, and bentwood. Best known for architecture.

Modern or Modernist, 1925-1950s: Style influenced by Art Deco and Bauhaus. Not accepted by the average American buyer until the 1950s when the "e" was dropped from "Moderne" and "Modern" was used to furnish "tract" houses. Bent plywood, laminated wood, wire furniture, Formica, chrome, plastic, steel, bean-shaped tables, wall-mounted shelves and storage systems. Free-form glass, geometric silver. Popular colors were pink, gray, lime green, turquoise, yellow, chocolate brown. The designs became popular immediately after World War II, then faded, but are now coming back.

Art Moderne, 1930-1940: A subdivision of Modern. The United States blend of French Art Deco and other styles, sometimes called Hollywood Art Deco because it was used for movie sets. Dramatic! Coffee tables, dressing tables, rounded upholstered chairs, glass-topped tables. Painted lacquer, Bakelite, and tubular steel. Black, white, gray, coral; few touches of bright colors; gold leaf; chrome.

Danish Modern or **Scandinavian Modern,** 1920s-1950s: Bauhaus design as interpreted in Sweden, Denmark, and Finland. Handcrafted. Exposed wood, curved corners, simple fabrics, blond wood, teak, walnut, pale colors, fiber glass, and wire. Heavy, free-form glass objects.

European Art Deco furniture originated with important designers. Leading artists in France, Austria, and Germany made sophisticated, plain-line furniture that contrasted with the flowing-line pieces of the preceding Art Nouveau period. Light-colored woods, black lacquer, mirrored surfaces, and new shapes (coffee tables and cocktail bars) were created. Daring American firms hired designers to create pieces for the mass market. Today's collector may not find a Legrain set, but Robsjohn Gibbings furniture for Widdicomb or Gilbert Rohde for Herman Miller is still in use. Learn to recognize designs, makers, and quality.

Furniture firms from the 1920s to 1960s made modern pieces, copies of traditional designs, and adaptations like "French Provincial" or "Chinese Modern." The 1930s "waterfall" furniture, with V-shaped patterned veneer sold well. Wicker appeared in new shapes. New weaving techniques and paper-wrapped wire "rush" were used.

The 1950s look included chairs made from wire with hammock-like canvas seats, steel tubing, sheet steel, molded plastic, aluminum, or bamboo. Fifties pieces can still be found in homes, estate auctions, and used furniture stores. Look for labeled pieces.

Below: Ivory-inlaid cabinet designed by Emile-Jacques Ruhlmann, c. 1922. Courtesy Sotheby's, New York. Right: Womb chair designed by Eero Saarinen, 1951. Below right: Diamond chair designed by Harry Bertoia, 1952. Courtesy Knoll International, New York

Alvar Aalto (1898-1976): Scandinavian. Worked for many U.S. firms. • **Harry Bertoia** (1915-1978): Associated with Knoll International. Best known for iron wire furniture. • **Donald Deskey** (1894-present): 1930 to 1934 designed for Ypsilanti Reed Furniture Co. of Michigan and S. Karpen & Bros. Used Bakelite, Formica, chrome-plated brass, aluminum foil, and reed. Designed Radio City Music Hall, New York. • **Charles Eames** (1907-1978):

Tableware by Russel Wright, 1950s.
Courtesy Woman's Day

In 1946-48 developed use of molded plywood for chairs. Laminated and bentwood pieces with metal bases. "Eames" chair. "Surf" coffee table (1948), storage units (early fifties). Furniture with natural finish, red or black stained. Aluminum group pieces and others manufactured by Herman Miller Co. • **Paul Frankl** (1886-1958): "Skyscraper" furniture (1926). Reed furniture for Ficks-Reed Furniture Co., Ypsilanti Reed Furniture Co., Heywood-Wakefield Co. Used wood, colored lacquer, mirrors, tubular chrome. • **Eileen Gray** (1878-1976): English. Used lacquer, exotic materials, tubular steel. Now being reproduced. • **Paul McCobb** (1917-1969): Worked in 1950s for Winchendon Furniture Co., Massachusetts. • **Isamu Noguchi** (1904-present): Knoll International (bean-shaped table) & Knorr; wood and glass tables for Herman Miller. • **Gilbert Rohde** (1894-1944): Heywood-Wakefield, Thonet Bros., and Koehler. Tubular chrome for Herman Miller Furniture Co., Troy Sunshade Co., John Widdicomb, Mutual Sunset Co. from 1934. Sectional furniture and bentwood chair. • **Emile-Jacques Ruhlmann** (1879-1933): French. Heavily veined hardwoods with ivory inlays and fittings. Used slender, often fluted legs. • **Eero Saarinen** (1910-1961): Knoll International. Cast aluminum, plastic pedestal furniture, "womb" chair of upholstered plastic with steel frame. • **Kem (Karl Emanuel Martin) Weber** (1889-1963): Used maple, birch, plywood, often lacquered. Introduced "bentlock," mass-produced furniture for Higgins Manufacturing Co., Oakland, California (1930); tubular metal furniture for Lloyd Manufacturing Co., Menominee, Michigan, and S. Karpen & Bros.; airplane chair for Airline Chair Co. (1934). • **Ludwig Mies Van der Rohe** (1886-1969): Cantilevered armchair (1927) still being made by Knoll; tubular steel furniture. • **Frank Lloyd Wright** (1869-1959): Heritage-Henredon Furniture Co. • **Russel**

Wright (1905-1976): "Flexible Modern" (sectional units) for Heywood-Wakefield (1931).

Look for blue mirrored glass furniture, chromed-steel designs popular 1920s to 1950s. Best by **Herman Miller Furniture Co.** (Michigan), **Troy Sunshade Co.** (Ohio), **Howell Co.** (Illinois), **Warren McArthur** (New York), **Deskey-Vollmer** (New York), **Kantack & Co.** (New York), **Robert Heller, Inc.** (New York). Beware. Many of the chairs are still being made. Chipped fiber glass can't be fixed. Chrome is expensive to refinish.

GLASS

The best high-style Art Deco glass was made in Europe. Strong sculptural shapes by Lalique, graceful vases of Venini, and latest style cameo glass by French manufacturers led the way. Most of this glass was marked. It was sold in American shops.

Cameo glass vases, ranging in price from $2,200 to $36,300. Courtesy Sotheby's, New York

Lalique vases, ranging in price from $2,200 to $53,900. Tiffany favrile glass vases, ranging in price from $880 to $11,550. Courtesy Sotheby's, New York

1920s. Lalique, France (1902-present): Heavy molded glass, usually frosted; premium prices for colored examples. Perfume bottles in demand. Objects marked "R. Lalique" before 1945, "Lalique" after 1945. • **Paolo Venini,** Italy (1895-1959): Handkerchief vase (1951); blown glass objects in modern styles. • French cameo glass: **Cristalleries de Nancy** (Daum Brothers) (1875-present); **Legras** (1864-1920); **Le Verre Francais,** from factory of C. Schneider (1920-1933). • **Pate-de-verre** (late 19th century): Powdered glass mixed into a paste and modeled. **Almeric Walter,** France (1859-1942); **Frederick Carder,** United States (1864-1963); **Charles Schneider** (Charder), France (1881-1962). • **J. & L. Lobmeyr,** Austria (1859-present): Vienna Workshop; geometric cut crystal. • **Marius-Ernest Sabino,** France (1920s-1930s/1960-present): Enameled glass, smoky white glass similar to Lalique. • **Czechoslovakian glass** (1918-present): Molded, cut, engraved in Art Deco designs. Not usually signed by the artist.

1930s. Look for commercial glasswares of the 1930s. Some in tradition of eighteenth-century designs, others inspired by Art Deco designs. • **Heisey** (1896-1957), **Imperial** (1904-1982): Traditional glass tablewares, stemware, modern, heavy, clear glass bowls and animal figurines. Marked "H" in a diamond, "Nuart," "Nucut," "IG," or "Imperial." • **Fenton Art Glass Company** (1905-present): Carnival glass, traditional tablewares, handmade contemporary glass (1925-1927). • **Fostoria** (1887-1983): Traditional tablewares, modern designs by George Sakier. Colored glass tablewares. • **Phoenix Glass Company** (1880-present): Sculptured glassware reminiscent of Lalique, 1930s-1950s. • **Steuben Glass Works** (1903-present):

Art glass, colored from early 1900s, including Cluthra, Cintra, Silverine, clear after 1918. Scandinavian-inspired modern glass after 1933. Marked "Steuben" or with a fleur-de-lis. • **Consolidated Lamp & Glass Company** (1894-1933; 1936-1967): Ruba Rombic pattern glassware, most modern of the 1920s American patterns, copies of Lalique. (Molds lent to Phoenix, 1933-c.1936.) • **Libbey Glass Company** (1888-present): Cut glass, traditional stemware, modern tablewares and stemwares, including Silhouette; purchased by Owens-Illinois in 1935. • **New Martinsville Glass Mfg. Co.** (1901-1944), became **Viking Glass Company** (1944): Tablewares, including Moondrops and free-form glass. • **Depression glass** (1930-1950s): Traditional patterns of inexpensive glass. Some modern designs such as Cubist, No. 610 (Pyramid), and Tea Room.

1950s "Contemporary Glass." **Orrefors**, Sweden (1898-present); **Val St. Lambert**, Belgium (1825-present); **Kosta**, Sweden (1742-present); **Blenko**, United States (1950-present). Other glass collectibles in demand are Venetian (**Murano**) glass figures; perfume bottles; and modern paperweights; by artists such as **Dominick Labino** (1963-1987) and **John Degenhart** (1947-1964).

POTTERY AND PORCELAIN

Pottery and porcelain design went in two directions during the 1920s to 1960s. Art Deco designs were made in Europe by **Robj, Sandoz,** and **Longwy,** while traditional designs were continued by factories like Wedgwood, Minton, and Haviland. American art potters made pieces that were influenced by European Deco styles. Many American potters were trained by **Wiener Werkstatte** artists. Collectors want everything from works by famous artists to kitchenwares, cookie jars, and dimestore dishes.

Artists. **Clarice Cliff**, England (1900-1972): Brightly colored pottery with abstract designs. Best known "Bizarre" and "Fantasque."

Lacquer vase, signed Jean Dunand, c. 1925, $28,600. Courtesy Sotheby's, New York

Clarice Cliff pitcher, nasturtium decoration, early 1930s. Courtesy Antique Collectors' Club, Suffolk, England

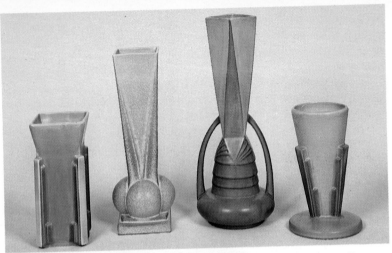

Roseville "Futura" vases. Courtesy Collection John P. Axelrod

Lacquered vases and covered boxes, ranging in price from $2,860 to $46,750. Courtesy Sotheby's, New York

• **Susie Cooper**, England (1903-present): Simple, monochromatic dinnerwares and vases. Worked for Gray Pottery and Wedgwood.
• **Bernard Leach**, England (1887-1979): Inspired by early Chinese pieces. Simple, earthtone pottery bowls and vases. • **Keith Murray**, England (1893-1981): Worked for Wedgwood, 1936; geometric shapes, green, white, gray vases and boxes. • **Robj**, France (1920s-1930s): Dealer making amusing stylized figurines, vases, and tablewares. Signed Robj. **Wiener Werkstatte** artists, Vienna (1903-1932): **Vally Wieselthier** (1895-1945), **Josef Hoffmann** (1870-1956), **Kolo Moser** (1868-1918), **Michael Powolny** (1871-1954).
• **Russel Wright**, United States (1904-1976): Designed first twentieth-century solid-colored dinnerware, "American Modern" (1939). It became the best-selling pattern in the world. Designs marked with his name. • **Eva Zeisel**, Germany, United States, England (1906-present): Modern-style ceramics. Worked for Rosenthal, Castleton China Co., Hall.

Many European factories had special lines of Art Deco-inspired wares. **Haviland**, France (1842-present) by Gerard Sandoz; **Royal**

Dux, Czechoslovakia (1860-present); **Zsolnay**, Hungary (1862-1962); **Sevres**, France (1769-present); **Bing & Grondahl**, Denmark (1853-present); **Rosenthal**, Germany (1879-present); **Boch Freres**, Belgium (1841-present); **Longwy**, France (1798-present); **Gouda**, Holland (1880-1940); **Societe Richard Ceramica, Ginori**, Italy (1896-present); **Meissen**, Germany (1710-present); **Goldscheider**, Austria, United States, England (1885-1953).

American art potteries produced a few high-style pieces. **Cowan** (1921-1930), **Pewabic** (1903-1961; 1968-present), **Rookwood** (1880-1960), **Roseville** (1890-1954), **Weller** (1873-1948), **Paul Revere** (1916-1942).

Inexpensive American dinnerwares inspired by Art Deco designs were made from the 1930s to 1960s. Solid color sets like Fiesta (1936-1973, 1986-present), Riviera (1938-1950), and Harlequin (1938-1964), free-form shapes like American Modern (introduced in 1939) or Hallcraft (1952), geometric shapes like Futura (1924), Moderne (1930), Lu-Ray (late 1930s), and imaginatively shaped **Hall** teapots (1920s).

Cookie jars, some **Royal Doulton** figurines and vases, pieces made in Czechoslovakia or Occupied Japan, and American pieces, such as **Kay Finch Ceramics** (1935-1963; c.1984-present), **Florence Ceramics** (1930s-c.1977), **Sascha Brastoff** (1953-present), and **Georges Briard** (1950-1960s) are now becoming collectible.

LAMPS AND LIGHTING

Electricity and the light bulb changed the appearance of lamps in the Art Nouveau period. Art Deco designers altered them even more. For the first time, lighting devices were designed to bounce the light off the ceiling. Colored glass shades were replaced by frosted glass. Bronze and stained glass went out of favor and painted metal, marble, lacquer, chrome, aluminum, and mirrors came into style.

G. Argy-Rousseau lamp, c. 1930, $50,600. Courtesy Sotheby's, New York

Lamp makers of the 1930s include **Venini** (Italy), **Val St. Lambert** (Belgium), **Lalique** (France), and **Phoenix** (United States). Some names on Art Deco lamps made in France are **Edgar Brandt, Damon, Daum, D.I.M., Edmond Etling & Co., Lalique, Sabino,** and **Robj**.

Lamps of the 1950s were more daring: asymmetrical shapes, amoeba-like pottery bases, pole lamps, vases with long wire legs, floor

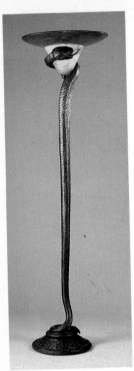

lamps with thin, swiveling and cantilevered arms. French and Italian designers led the way. **Isamu Noguchi** (United States) made a lamp of a paper cylinder held on three wooden legs (1948). **George Nelson** designed table lamps resembling suspended hot air bubbles. Copies of these were made in every price range.

Potteries made lamps that used a vase or figurine as the base. Chrome-plated domes hung from geometric stands; linear floor lamps and pivoting lamps on industrial-looking stands were popular. Plastic was often found on lamp bases. American designers and firms working before 1960 include **Donald Deskey, Walter von Nessen, Sun-Kraft, Inc., Polaroid Desk Lamp, Herman Miller Lamp Company**, and **Lightolier.**

Popular were lamps by the **Aladdin Lamp Company** (1909-1968); **Emeralite** (1909-1940s), featuring dark green glass shades; **Frankart, Inc.** (1920s-1930s), lamps of nude women and ball-shaped globes. Glass or alabaster plaques were illuminated from the rear. The "pole" lamp from the fifties had a pole with suction cups at the floor and ceiling and swiveling, cone-shaped lampshades. The 1960s lava lamp was an ever-moving glob of goo.

Serpent floor lamp, bronze by Edgar Brandt, mottled glass probably Daum Nancy, c. 1925, $38,500. Courtesy Sotheby's, New York

CLOCKS

Art Deco clockcases were created with geometric shapes, slim women, and simple lines. Wooden cases were less popular than chrome. Marble, bronze, and art glass clocks were copied in cheap bronzed pot metal, chrome, glass, and wood. Glass clockcases by Lalique, Sabino, and Daum, green metal figural clocks by Frankart, and silver and gold clocks set with precious jewels by Cartier and Tiffany were to be found. About 1930 the numerals on the clock were replaced by plain lines.

Clock design was revolutionized by Gilbert Rohde's digital clock in 1933. The numbers, and not the hands, moved. The traditional dial was gone. New clocks replaced the tick-tock with a hum and the bell chime became a buzz. Chrome, brass, copper, Formica, celluloid, or glass were used. The glass-faced clock had hands that seem suspended in the center of the clockface; no works can be seen. George Nelson designed the "ball" clocks in 1949; a black circle was surrounded by twelve black sticks, each holding a colored ball. It looked like the scientific model of an atom.

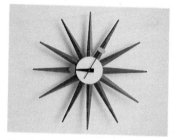

Clock by George Nelson, 1950s.
Courtesy Woman's Day

Lawson electric clock, designed by Kem Weber, c. 1933.
Courtesy Collection John P. Axelrod

Wrought and cast iron and marble mantel clock designed by Edgar Brandt, c. 1925. Courtesy Sotheby's, New York

SILVER

In the early 1900s Georg Jensen of Denmark began making silver in his own new shapes. Charles Rennie Mackintosh of Scotland and Henry Van de Velde of Belgium also began creating new metal forms. The English designers working in Art Nouveau and Liberty styles also created new forms. Shapes for teapots, bowls, even teaspoons were changed. By the 1920s the Art Deco designers of France began to make silver in their new style. American craftsmen were slow to accept the new forms and continued working in the earlier "colonial" style. By the late 1920s they began making modern pieces that were a combination of colonial and the Deco or "Modern Classic" style. In 1929 an American, William Spratling, founded a silver craft industry in Taxco, Mexico. His work was heavily influenced by the earlier Danish designs and the modern movement. Many Taxco shops made modern silver that was sold to tourists.

Important Companies, 1920s-1960s • **Cardeilhac**, France (c.1802); **Cartier**, France, United States, England (1857-present); **Christofle**, France (c.1839-present); **Gebelein Silversmiths, Inc.**, United States (1945-present); **Kalo Shop**, United States (1900-1970); **Marshall Field & Company Craft Shop**, United States (1904-1950); **Shreve, Crump & Low, Inc.**, United States (1869-present); **Tiffany & Co., Inc.**, United States (1848-present).

Important Artists, 1920s-1960s • **Jean Despres**, France (1889-1980); **Josef Hoffmann**, Austria (1870-1956); **Georg Jensen**, Den-

Danish silver centerpiece bowl, designed by Georg Jensen, c. 1925, $11,000. Seafood serving platter, stamped Georg Jensen, numbered 335, 1922, $22,000. Mantel clock, Georg Jensen Silversmithy, designed by Johan Rohde, c. 1945, $16,500. Courtesy Sotheby's, New York

mark, United States (1866-1935); **Arthur Nevill Kirk,** United States (1881-1958); **Erik Magnussen**, United States (1884-1961); **Koloman Moser**, Austria (1868-1918); **Harald Nielsen**, Denmark (1892-1977); **Dagobert Peche**, Austria (1887-1923); **Katherine Pratt**, United States (1891-1978); **Jean Puiforcat**, France (1897-1945); **Omar Ramsden**, England (1878-1939); **Eliel Saarinen**, United States, Finland (1873-1950); **Gerard Sandoz**, France (1902-present); **Jean Serriere**, France (c.1925); **William Spratling**, Mexico (1900-1967); **Harold Stabler**, England (1872-1945); **Arthur J. Stone**, United States (1847-1938); and **Kem Weber**, United States (c.1928-1939).

⊂• METAL: COPPER, CHROME, AND ALUMINUM •⊃

Designers in the 1920s searched for new materials like copper, aluminum, and iron. Chrome-plated steel and special alloys were incorporated in household goods. Of special interest are cocktail shakers and pieces embellished with plastic handles. Wall and table pieces of wirework were popular in the 1950s. Most were unsigned. Enameled ashtrays and candy dishes were a fad in the 1950s and 1960s.

Important Makers. **Bradley & Hubbard**, United States (1895-1930): Brass, plated metal lamps, bookends, decorative accessories. • **Edgar Brandt**, France, United States (1880-1960): Deco ironwork, lamps. • **Chase Chrome**, United States (1930-1942): Chrome and brass buffet, smoking, cocktail, and dressing table accessories created by American designers of the 1930s, including Russel Wright, Wal-

Wiener Werkstätte brass tea service designed by Josef Hoffmann, c. 1920, $11,000. Courtesy Sotheby's, New York

Polychromed bronze and ivory figure, Flame Leaper, inscribed F. Preiss, c. 1930, $24,200. Courtesy Sotheby's, New York

ter von Nessen, and Rockwell Kent.
• **Heintz Art Metal Shop**, United States (c.1915-1935): Copper, brass, silver on copper decorative accessories, vases, lamps, desk sets. • **Roycroft**, United States (1895-1938): Copper accessories, lamps. • **Dirk Van Erp**, United States (1860-1933): Copper work, lamps. • **Russel Wright**, United States (1905-1976): Spun aluminum serving pieces. • **Wiener Werkstatte**, Austria (1903-1932): Vienna workshop making jewelry, silver, many forms of metalwork.

Industrial design was a new idea in the 1920s. Designers became stars. Raymond Loewy, Russel Wright, Norman Bel Geddes, Donald Deskey, Walter Teague, and others were so well known their names helped to sell products. Designs for everything from automobiles and refrigerators to dinnerware and cameras were the province of these men. Collectors can find many examples of their unmarked works. The twenties to sixties were filled with well-designed everyday objects that will continue to interest serious collectors.

Jewelry. High-style Art Deco and forties-style precious gem pins, especially humorous animals and rings. Mexican silver jewelry (1920s-present); plastic pins and bracelets, especially Bakelite (1920-1950s); rhinestones; designer pieces from makers starting in the 1920s, such as Chanel, Schiaparelli, and Worth; 1930s, Molyneux, Eisenberg, Miriam Haskell; 1940s, Martha Sleeper, Trifari; 1960s, Kenneth Lane.

Paper. Don't forget disposable paper collectibles. Look for comic books, movie memorabilia; postcards; posters; pamphlets and cookbooks; Art Deco color prints by Parrish, Fox, and Icart; cardboard dollhouses; paper dolls.

Plastic. Plastic materials were used by artists in a variety of ways. Look for **Bakelite** (introduced in 1907) radios, jew-

Beau Brownie cameras, early 1930s. Courtesy Robert F. Grabosky, Provincetown, MA

Jewelry by Jean Desprès, ranging in price from $2,090 to $28,600. Courtesy Sotheby's, New York

Kitchen utensils, 1930s. Courtesy Woman's Day

Air King radio, red "Plaskon," c. 1934. Courtesy Robert F. Grabosky, Provincetown, MA

elry, dresser sets; **celluloid** (1869-1940s) dresser sets, toys, purse frames; "tortoiseshell" dresser sets; **Bandelasta** mottled dishes (1924); **Beetleware** such as Orphan Annie shakers (1930s-1940s); **Lucite** accessories (1940s-1970s). Also plastic animal napkin rings (1930s-1940s), Melamine dinnerwares (1950s), acrylic purses (1940-1950), pop-it beads (1950s), advertising giveaways, fountain pens, toys, eggbeaters, and kitchen spoons and forks with plastic handles.

Textiles. Pictorial rag rugs, especially marked Grenfell (c.1900-1930), Chinese Art Deco rugs (1916-1935), wearable clothing, Hawaiian printed shirts (1936-1960s), rayon gabardine bowling shirts (1930s-1960s), flower-printed tablecloths (1940s), printed handkerchiefs (1930s-1960s).

Toys. Robots from the 1950s and 1960s. Japanese lithographed tin toys of all types (1930s-1960s). Battery-operated toys (1920s-present). Celluloid toys of all types (1870s-present). Printed board games (1920s-1960s). Celebrity-related, full game with box and all board pieces are best. Disney-related toys, celebrity, movie and TV toys.

Wristwatches. Best are of unusual shape, have extra features like a calendar or stopwatch; top brands like Rolex and Patek Philippe.

Robot and trains, 1950s. Courtesy Woman's Day

Clothes Washer Stomper, 36 In.Handle 8.50
Clothespin, Bone, 3 In. 75.00
Clothespin, Bone, 4 3/4 In. 85.00
Coffee Dispenser, Clear & Frosted Glass, Metal, 16 X 30 In. 250.00
    KITCHEN, COFFEE GRINDER, see Coffee Grinder
Colander & Pestle, Green, Handle 8.00
Colander, High Loop Handle, Oval, Tin, 10 X 8 1/4 In. 40.00
Cooker, Swedish Pancake, Griswold 35.00
Cookie Board, Carved, Early Bicycle One Side, Horses Other, 14 In. 480.00
Cookie Board, Pineapple & Sunburst In Oval, C.1790, 7 1/2 X 9 In. 260.00
Cookie Board, Russian Turnip Domed Churches, Keg, Boot, 11 1/2 In. 60.00
Cookie Press, Child, On Potty Seat, Cast Iron, Oval 225.00
Corer, Pineapple, Iron 10.00
Cork Puller, English Pub, Bar Mounted, Brass, Wooden Handle 225.00
Cork Puller, Rapid, Pat.Apr.21, 1891, Pushes Bottle Away From Cork 275.00
Corker, For Bottle, Mechanical, Yankee Corker, Pat.1900 .... 150.00
Cup, Measuring, Fire King, Blue .... 10.00 To 12.00
Cup, Measuring, Kellogg, 3 Spouts, Green 15.00
Curtain Pull, Figural, Yellow 45.00
Cutter, Asparagus, Ward's Keen Edge, Wooden 85.00
Cutter, Biscuit & Doughnut, Rumford, Tin 15.00
Cutter, Biscuit, E–Z Bake 6.00
Cutter, Biscuit, Rumford .... 13.00 To 14.00
Cutter, Cabbage, 3 Blades, 28 In. 65.00
Cutter, Cabbage, Curly Maple, Arched Crest, 6 3/4 X 20 3/4 In. 200.00
Cutter, Cabbage, Heart Cutout In Crest, Maple, 15 1/2 X 7 In. 275.00
Cutter, Cabbage, New England, Pine, 18th Century, 21 In. 445.00
Cutter, Cabbage, Pine, Poplar, Dovetailed Hopper, 14 1/2 X 51 In. 100.00
Cutter, Cabbage, Walnut, 6 1/4 X 19 In. 20.00
Cutter, Cheese, Revolving, Iron & Wood 90.00
Cutter, Cookie, Acorn, Tin, 2 1/2 In. 5.00
Cutter, Cookie, Bear, Strap Handle 8.00
Cutter, Cookie, Bell, Tin, 2 1/2 In. 5.00
Cutter, Cookie, Bird In Flight 22.00
Cutter, Cookie, Cat, Tin, Strap Handle 8.00
Cutter, Cookie, Cornucopia, Tin, Rolled Edges, 3 1/2 In. 40.00
Cutter, Cookie, Dog, Flat Back 18.00
Cutter, Cookie, Fish, Tin, 6 In. 15.00
Cutter, Cookie, Garland Stoves & Ranges 30.00
Cutter, Cookie, Hackney Pony, Tin, C.1860, 5 1/2 X 6 1/2 In. 220.00
Cutter, Cookie, Hatchet, Tin, 2 Strap Handles, 7 In. 34.00
Cutter, Cookie, Heart, Red Handle, Tin 3.50
Cutter, Cookie, Hunter, Hat & Outstretched Gun, Tin, 4 1/2 In. 120.00
Cutter, Cookie, Mickey Mouse, Tin 20.00
Cutter, Cookie, Mother Hen, Strap Handle, Tin, C.1850 .... 10.00
Cutter, Cookie, Nesting, Geometric Flowers, Tin, Burlap Strip, 10 .... 30.00
Cutter, Cookie, Pigeon, Looking Backward, Tin, 3 1/2 X 4 1/2 In. 75.00
Cutter, Cookie, Pillsbury, Figure, Aluminum, 4 3/4 In. 6.00
Cutter, Cookie, Pipe, Tin, 4 In. 15.00
Cutter, Cookie, Reindeer, Handcrafted, 1840 .... 125.00
Cutter, Cookie, Robin Hood Flour, Figural .... 4.75 To 15.00
Cutter, Cookie, Rooster, Large Crimped Tail, Tin, 6 1/4 In. 150.00
Cutter, Cookie, Rooster, Tin, Copper Handle 6 X 6 In. 65.00
Cutter, Cookie, Santa Claus, Flat Back, Tin, Germany, 8 In. 130.00
Cutter, Cookie, Shamrock 12.00
Cutter, Cookie, Sheep, Flat Back 18.00
Cutter, Cookie, Tin, Animals, Birds, 4 In., Set of 9 .... 85.00
Cutter, Cookie, Top Hat, Tin, 4 In. 15.00
Cutter, Doughnut, Cottonlene Shortening 18.00
Cutter, Doughnut, Revolving, Tin, C.1910 .... 21.00
Dipper, Burl Maple, Dished Oval Form, Handle, 6 1/2 X 5 1/4 In. 88.00
Dipper, Coconut, Ivory & Ebony Inlaid Handle, 18 In. 125.00
Dipper, Iron Ferrule, Wooden Handle, Marked S.& T., 18 1/2 In. 17.50
Dipper, Maple, 23 In. 192.00

Dough Riser, Tin, Large 27.00
Dust Pan, Open Handle, Ruffled Rim, Hand Painted Flowers, 4 X 3 In. 18.00
Dust Pan, Salmon Paint, Gilt Stenciled Flowers, 5 X 7 1/2 In. 39.00
Dutch Oven, Griswold, No.8, Cover, Trivet .... 30.00 To 45.00
Dutch Oven, Renfrow Ware 30.00
Dutch Oven, Wagner Ware, Dripdrop, No.8 .... 30.00
Egg Cooker, Griswold 25.00
Egg Separator, Rumford 12.50
Egg Whip, Dunlap, Holes In Metal Strip 25.00
Eggbeater, A & J, Dated 1923 .... 12.00
Eggbeater, Child's, Wire 14.00
Eggbeater, Holt, 1899 .... 20.00
Eggbeater, Holt, Cast Iron & Tin, 1900 .... 18.00
Eggbeater, Merry Whirl, Jar, 1916 .... 22.00
Eggbeater, Peerless No.2, Iron Handle, Tin Beaters 25.00
Eggbeater, Rumsford, Spoon Shape 12.00
Eggbeater, Taplin, 1908 .... 15.00
Eggbeater, Tapper, Cast Iron 10.00
Eggbeater, Viko, Aluminum, Patent 1929 .... 6.00
Eggbeater, Yellow Bakelite Handle 22.00
Flue Cover, 2 Women In Boat 25.00
Flue Cover, Diamond Shape 20.00
Flue Cover, Victorian Child, Cat, Oval 10.00
Flue Cover, Victorian Children 30.00
Fork & Pie Crimper, Combined, Ivory, Wood Handle, 6 1/4 In. 250.00
Fork, 3-Tine, Embossed On Handle Rumford Baking Powder, 12 In. 18.00
Fork, Toasting, Twisted Shaft, Open Heart Handle, Iron, 33 In. 260.00
Fork, Turned Wooden Handle, Iron, 18 In. 17.50
Freezer, Ice Cream, White Mountain, Cedar Tub, Dated 1923, 2 Qt. 32.00
Funnel, Maple Syrup, Stave Constructed, Tubular Spout, Red Paint 65.00
Funnel, Tin, Painted Sunbonnet Babies, 10 In. 15.00
Glove Stretcher, Bone 7.50
Grater, Acme Safety 5.50
Grater, Nutmeg, Boye, Tin 65.00
Grater, Nutmeg, Flip Top, Hand Painted, Tin 16.00
Grater, Nutmeg, Hand Crank, Brown Japanning, 6 In. 175.00
Grater, Nutmeg, Hand Crank, Tin & Wood, 6 1/4 In. 85.00
Grater, Nutmeg, Mechanical, Edgar, 1896 .... 48.00 To 55.00
Grater, Nutmeg, Spring Loaded, Wood Handle, Tin, Patent 1877 .... 75.00
Grater, Nutmeg, Twined, Wooden, Brass Handle, 7 3/4 In. 275.00
Grater, Nutmeg, With Spring Loaded Nut Holder 42.50
Grater, Revolving, Iron, Lorraine 10.00
Griddle, Pancake, Erie Pattern, Griswold, No.7 .... 30.00
Griddle, Soapstone, Tin Band, Roud 25.00
Grinder, Cornmeal, Cast Iron 25.00
Grinder, Food, Climax 10.00
Grinder, Food, E.C.Simmons Keen Kutter, Pat.May 29, 1906 .... 15.00

Clean aluminum with fine steel wool or steel wool soap pads. To
remove discoloration, boil two teaspoons of cream of tartar and a
quart of water in the utensil. The acid from cooking tomatoes or
rhubarb in the pot may also remove the stain.

Grinder, Food, Griswold, No.2, Tinned 20.00
Grinder, Food, Keen Kutter .... 15.00 To 50.00
Grinder, Food, Universal L.F. & Co.No.2 .... 12.00
Grinder, Herb, Cast Iron, Wooden Handle, 7 1/2 In. 50.00
Grinder, Meat, Keen Kutter, No.22 .... 20.00
Grinder, Meat, Rollman Footed Chopper, No.11, 6 1/2 In. 35.00
Grinder, Poppy Seed, Iron & Wood 65.00
Herb Crusher, Iron, Boat Shape, Iron Cutting Wheel, Wooden Handle 495.00
Herb Dryer, Hangs From Beam, Oak, Bentwood, O Shape, 10 X 10 In. 11.00
Herb Press, 2 Shaped Sticks, Leather Top Hinge, Red, 18 1/2 In. 65.00
Ice Crusher, Chicago Precision 10.00
Icebox, 1 Door, Oak 240.00
Icebox, 2 Doors, Oak 240.00
Icebox, Lift Top, Oak 330.00
Ironing Board, Attaches To Hoosier Kitchen Cabinet, Wooden 28.00
Ironing Board, Wooden, Lower Shelf, Folds Up 55.00
Jar Wrench, Metal, Willson 5.00
Jar Wrench, Wizard, Metal, Hinged, 8 In. 4.50
Juicer, Meat, Iron, Pat.1884 .... 35.00
Kettle, Iron, Scrolled Hook, Swing Handle, 18th Century, 9 X 13 In. 440.00
Knife Sharpener, Ace 3.00
Knife Sharpener, Green & White Enameled, Advertising, Round 15.00
Ladle, Hook End, Tiger Maple, 18th Century, 5 X 11 In. 200.00
Lemon Squeezer, Hinged, Maple Wooden Handle, 2 Part 40.00
Lemon Squeezer, Pierced Cherry Insert, Hinged, Mid–1800s, 11 In. 65.00
Lemon Squeezer, Sunkist, Electric 22.00
Lemon Squeezer, Williams, Cast Iron, Clear Glass Insert 50.00
Lid Lifter, Woman's Figure 35.00
Lid, Skillet, George Washington, Griswold 125.00
Mangle Board, Original Paint, Dated 1802 .... 375.00
Masher, Potato, Wooden, 10 In. 9.00
KITCHEN, MATCH SAFE, see Match Safe
Measure, Gill, Gray 75.00
Measure, Grain, Bentwood, Round, 8 1/4 X 15 1/4 In. 55.00
Measure, Grain, Hexagonal, Poplar, 9 3/4 In. 35.00
Measurer, Coffee, Tin Spring 10.00
Meat Cleaver, W.Brady, Wooden Handle, 9 In.Blade, 18 In. 28.00
Meat Rack, Bull, Silvered Metal, 12 Hooks, 19th Century, 16 X 72 In. 302.00
Meat Tenderizer, Cast Iron, C.1850, 2 X 2 1/2 X 3 In. 40.00
Mixer, Milk Shake, Arnold, Model 15, Electric 55.00
Mixer, Milk Shake, Glass 11.00
Mixer, Milk Shake, Hamilton Beach, Porcelain, Green 75.00
Mixer, Milk Shake, Hamilton Beach, Triple Head, 3 Speeds, Green 185.00
Mixer, Milk Shake, Gilchrist No.22, Pat.1923 .... 85.00
KITCHEN, MOLD, see also Pewter, Mold; Tinware, Mold
Mold, Bread, Fish, For Lent, Tin 22.00
Mold, Butter, Bay Leaf, Wooden 15.00
Mold, Butter, Carved Cow, Round, 4 1/2 In. 125.00
Mold, Butter, Cow, 4 In. 90.00
Mold, Butter, Cow, Plunger Stick 225.00
Mold, Butter, Hand Carved Full Rose, Bud & Leaves, 1/2 Lb. 95.00
Mold, Butter, House, 2 Chimneys, Initialed D.J., 4 Part, 5 X 7 In. 215.00
Mold, Butter, Leaf, Rectangular, Handle, Round 75.00
Mold, Butter, Musk Melon, C.1830, 1/2 Lb. 35.00
Mold, Butter, Petaled Flowers, Plunger Type, 1 Lb. 45.00
Mold, Butter, Pineapple, Round, C.1866, 1 Lb. 75.00
Mold, Butter, Pomegranate, 4 In. 175.00
Mold, Butter, Standing Cow, Plunger Type, Wooden Handle 135.00
Mold, Butter, Stylized Eagle, Insert Handle, 4 In. 185.00
Mold, Butter, Swan, Plunger Type, Maple .... 55.00 To 100.00
Mold, Butter, Thistle, Handle, Round 75.00
Mold, Butter, Turned & Carved Cherrywood, 19th Century, 1 1/2 In. 100.00
Mold, Butter, Wheat, Handle, 2 1/2 In. 70.00

Mold, Cake, Lamb, Cast Aluminum 25.00
Mold, Cake, Lamb, Cast Iron .... 57.00 To 95.00
Mold, Cake, Lamb, Griswold .... 65.00 To 95.00
Mold, Cake, Rabbit, Cast Iron 125.00
Mold, Cake, Rabbit, Griswold 215.00
Mold, Cake, Santa Claus, 2 Part, Griswold, 12 In. 150.00
KITCHEN, MOLD, CANDLE, see Tinware, Mold, Candle
Mold, Candy, Lollipop, Santa Claus, Sheet Style 85.00
Mold, Candy, Maple Sugar, Hearts, Initials J.J., 6 1/4 X 28 1/2 In. 85.00
Mold, Chocolate, 4 Easter Eggs, Rabbits, Steel Frame, Tin, 15 In. 35.00
Mold, Chocolate, 4 Rabbits, 7 X 12 In. 60.00
Mold, Chocolate, 4 Witches, Hinged, 3 Peice 75.00
Mold, Chocolate, Baby Soccer Player, Tin, Folding, 4 5/8 In. 55.00
Mold, Chocolate, Bell, Holland 20.00
Mold, Chocolate, Crouching Rabbit, 3 1/2 X 4 1/2 In. 35.00
Mold, Chocolate, Duck, French, 5 X 5 In. 32.50
Mold, Chocolate, Heart & Cupid, Hinged 40.00
Mold, Chocolate, Heart & Flower, Sheet, Fabriek, 21 1/2 X 9 1/2 In. 125.00
Mold, Chocolate, Heart, 8 1/2 X 9 In., 3 Parts 40.00
Mold, Chocolate, Hen On Basket, Hinged, 3 X 3 1/2 In. 20.00
Mold, Chocolate, Rabbit, Epplesheimer, 9 1/2 X 18 In. 175.00
Mold, Chocolate, Rabbit, Standing, With Basket, 8 X 11 In. 60.00
Mold, Chocolate, Rabbit, Wooden, Round, Clamps Together 50.00
Mold, Chocolate, Rooster, Epplesheimer, 7 X 8 In. 110.00
Mold, Chocolate, Rooster, Tin, 3 3/4 In. 40.00
Mold, Chocolate, Scotty, Hinged, 11 X 9 In. 125.00
Mold, Chocolate, Squirrel, Bushy Tail, Acorn, Tin, 12 In. ....95.00 To 110.00
Mold, Chocolate, Zeppelin 275.00
Mold, Cookie, Butterfly, Oval, Albany Foundry, 1800s, 5 1/2 In. 175.00
Mold, Cookie, Double–Faced, Robin, Flowers, Graniteware, 1800s 120.00
Mold, Cookie, Horse, Stagecoach & Driver, Birch, 1800s, 3 X 4 In. 295.00
Mold, Cookie, Horse, Wooden, C.1880 .... 40.00
Mold, Cookie, Man, Flying Early Plane, Carved, 5 1/2 X 14 In. 200.00
Mold, Cookie, Pineapple, Geometric Border, Iron, 4 1/2 X 6 In. 110.00
Mold, Cookie, Revolutionary Soldier, Hand Carved, 10 1/2 X 3 In. 50.00
Mold, Cookie, Springerle, 4 Design, Screw–In Handle 62.00
Mold, Cookie, Turkey, Flat Backplate, 5 1/2 In. 95.00
Mold, Corn Bread, Marked Miracle Maize, Glass, 6 Piece 22.00
Mold, Corn Bread, Wagner Ware, 7 In. 95.00
Mold, Fish, Marked Kreamer, 11 In. 17.50
Mold, Fish, Tin, 9 1/4 In. 15.00
Mold, Fish, Tinned Copper, 6 1/2 In. 55.00
Mold, Food, Gothic Arch Pattern, Ring Handle, Copper, 5 1/2 In. 40.00
Mold, Food, Hen On Nest, Copper, 7 3/4 In., 2 Piece 135.00
Mold, Food, Indian, Copper, Legs, 7 3/4 In. 25.00
Mold, Food, Lion, Tin, Copper, Oval, 5 1/4 In. 120.00
Mold, Food, Scalloped, Embossed Fruit, Tin Lined, Copper, 11 1/2 In. 165.00
Mold, Food, Star, Tin 18.00
Mold, Food, Turk's Head, Geometric Design, 10 In. 65.00
Mold, Gelatin, Rabbit, Glass 12.00
Mold, Gelatin, Rabbits, Jell–O 15.00
KITCHEN, MOLD, ICE CREAM, see Pewter, Mold, Ice Cream
Mold, Maple Sugar, Gingerbread, Primitive 45.00
Mold, Maple Sugar, Maple Leaves, Rubber 22.00
Mold, Maple Sugar, Rooster, Pine, Square, 8 1/2 In. 240.00
Mold, Patty, Griswold, Box 32.00
Mold, Plum Pudding, Tin, England 12.00
Mold, Pudding, Full Figural, Pineapple Pattern, 4 1/4 X 6 In. 65.00
Mold, Sugar, 14 Hearts, 44 In. 195.00
Mold, Sugar, Hand Carved, Single Heart 125.00
Mold, Turk's Head, Bennington Type 50.00
Mold, Turtle, Copper, Tin Lining, 10 1/2 In. 165.00
Mortar & Pestle, Griswold 200.00
Mortar & Pestle, Iron, 6 1/2 In. 35.00

Mortar & Pestle, Iron, 7 In. 25.00
Mortar & Pestle, Iron, Old Gold Paint, 5 3/4 In. 10.00
Mortar, Pedestal Base, American, Ash, 18th Century, 6 X 6 1/2 In. 295.00
Noodle Maker, Cast Iron, Germany 45.00
Noodle Maker, Cast Iron, Tin, Cleveland, Oh., Pat.1908–20 .... 95.00
Noodle Roller, Corrugated Wood, 18 In. 32.00
Opener, Clam & Oyster, Brass 25.00
Opener, Jar, Metal, Aug.29, 1916 .... 6.00
Oven, Top of Stove, Tin, Temperature Gauge 50.00
Paddle, Butter, Carved Heart, Hex Signs, Wooden, 12 1/2 In. 375.00
Paddle, Butter, Wooden, Butter Stamp Handle 900.00
Paddle, Pine, Pierced Handle, 19th Century, 25 1/2 X 13 1/4 In. 66.00
Pan, Angel Food, Tin, Square 8.00
Pan, Biscuit, Cast Iron, Erie, No.2 .... 65.00
Pan, Bread, Isinglass Window 1 End, Double, Cover 5.00
Pan, Breadstick, Griswold 30.00
Pan, Brownie, Griswold No.9 .... 80.00
Pan, Cake, Brownie, Griswold 110.00
Pan, Cornstick, Cast Iron, 13 X 6 In. 16.00
Pan, Cornstick, Griswold 20.00
Pan, Cornstick, Wagner Krusty Korn Kobs, Aluminum, Patent 1920 ..... 15.00
Pan, Cornstick, Wheat Pattern, S.R.& Co., Cast Iron 22.00
Pan, Frying, Griswold No. 7, Red, Cover 40.00
Pan, Frying, Griswold, No. 8 .... 8.00
Pan, Frying, Griswold, No.10, Short Handle 22.00
Pan, Griddle, Erie No.737 .... 20.00
Pan, Ladyfinger, Tin 32.00
Pan, Loaf, Griswold 150.00
Pan, Muffin, 11 Holes, Cast Iron 35.00
Pan, Muffin, Cast Iron, Erie, No.10 .... 45.00
Pan, Muffin, Filley, No.9 .... 75.00
Pan, Muffin, Granite, Gray, 12 Hole 75.00
Pan, Muffin, Gray Enameled, 8 Hole 35.00
Pan, Muffin, Griswold, No.10 .... 40.00
Pan, Muffin, Wagnerware, Cutouts, Cast Iron, 1850s 60.00
Pan, Popover, 1890s 42.00
Pan, Popover, Griswold 55.00
Pan, Roasting, Wagnerware Magnalite, Sidney, Ohio, Large 35.00
Pan, Roll, Cast Iron, Erie, No.8 .... 75.00
Pan, Vienna Roll, Cast Iron, Erie, No.5 .... 75.00
Pan, Vienna Roll, Griswold, No.26 .... 50.00
Pantry Box, New Hampshire's Maker Embossed Name 80.00
Pat, Butter, Fleur–De–Lis Design, Wooden, 4 In. 55.00
Pea Huller & Bean Slicer, Vaughan 8.00
Peel, Bread, Wooden, 28 In. 20.00
Peel, Cookie, Hand Forged Iron, Ring Handle, 18th Century, 24 In. 130.00
Peeler, Apple, Iron 30.00
Peeler, Apple, Keen Kutter 100.00
Peeler, Apple, Lockey Howland, Cast Iron, 1856 .... 30.00
Peeler, Apple, Mechanical, Little Star, Cast Iron 85.00
Peeler, Apple, Reading Hardware Co., Table Model 50.00
Peeler, Apple, White Mountain .... 15.00 To 32.00
Pie Bird, Blackbird, White Base 39.00
Pie Bird, Goose 18.00
Pie Bird, Risden Mfg.Co., Brass, Dated 3/13/23 .... 75.00
Pie Bird, Rooster 17.50
Pie Crimper, All Tin, 7 3/4 In. 22.50
Pie Crimper, Fossilized Ivory, 5 1/4 In. 200.00
Pie Crimper, Ivory, 6 3/8 In. 95.00
Pie Crimper, Steel Wheel & Shank, Brass Ferrule, 8 3/4 In. 60.00
Pie Lifter, Wire, Wooden Handle 35.00
Pie Rack, Wire, 4 Tiers, 4 Tin Plates & Pie Lifter 55.00
Pitcher, Measuring, Glass Window, Mechanical, Copper, 7 1/2 In. 125.00
Pitcher, Milk, Priscilla, Kitchen Kraft 8.00

Cookie cutters can be dated by their construction methods. Old ones are soldered in spots—not a long thin solder joint. if the solder joins the cutting-edge piece to the back by a thin, barely visible line, it is less than fifty years old.

Platter Cover, Wire Screen, Ring Handle, 7 X 10 X 14 In.	85.00
Poacher, Fish, Tin, Oval, 27 In.	25.00
Pot Scrubber, Chain–Metal, Original Box, Pair	10.00
Pot, Cast Iron, Bail Handle, 3 Legs	45.00
Pot, Cooking, Iron, Hand Forged Bail, Early 19th Century, 7 1/2 In.	75.00
Potato Masher, 2 Grooved Bands, Tiger Maple, 10 1/2 In.	60.00
Potato Masher, Turned Wood, Primitive, 10 3/4 In.	9.00 To 10.00
Potato Ricer	5.00
Press, Cookie, Quaint Figures, Design, Beeswax, Germany	38.00
Press, Meat Juice, Cast Iron	65.00
Pressure Cooker, All American Steam, Aluminum, Books, 18 Qt.	50.00
Pumpkin Chopper, Hand Crank, Dated 1869	350.00
Rack, Drying, Clothes, Tin Canister	40.00
Rack, Drying, Mahogany, Folding, 3 Sections, 35 In.	100.00
Rack, Drying, Pine, Worn Red Paint, Shoe Feet, 34 X 37 In.	85.00
Rack, Dutch Oven, Griswold	225.00
Rack, Noodle Drying, Original Paint	435.00
Rack, Pie Cooling, Wire	35.00
Rack, Pine, 6 Scrolled Hooks, Chamfered Board, New England, 42 In.	304.00
Rack, Shoe, Pine, 6 Horizontal Shelves, Metal Rollers, 54 X 42 In.	165.00
Rack, Skillet, Griswold	100.00
Rack, Utensil, Country, Pine, Scalloped, 7 Iron Hooks, 27 In.	75.00
Raisin Seeder, Camping	22.00
Raisin Seeder, Enterprise, Mechanical, 1895	28.00
Raisin Seeder, Iron, Clamp-On, Iron Handle, Over Oval Tin Tray	260.00
Raisin Seeder, Wire Grid, Turned Wood Handle	55.00
Reamer, Black Glass	18.00
Rockabye Washing Machine, Smith Bros.Hardware, Columbus, Ohio	400.00
Rolling Pin, Baker's Lignum Vitae, 6 Lbs.	85.00
Rolling Pin, Bird's-Eye Maple	35.00
Rolling Pin, Blue Onion	140.00
Rolling Pin, Elongated Shaped Handles, Tiger Maple, 17 In.	95.00
Rolling Pin, General Store, Bradford, Iowa, Crockery	185.00
Rolling Pin, Glass, Dated 1879	40.00
Rolling Pin, Golden Grain Homemade Bread, Crockery, Brown On Gold	60.00
Rolling Pin, Harker, No.1, Petit Point	55.00
Rolling Pin, Harker, Silhouette	80.00
Rolling Pin, Harker, Tulip	65.00

Rolling Pin, Hot Springs, So.Dakota, Crockery 185.00
Rolling Pin, Kelvinator, China 45.00
Rolling Pin, Kelvinator, Milk Glass 68.00
Rolling Pin, Lake City, Iowa, Crockery 160.00
Rolling Pin, Marble, 14 In. 35.00
Rolling Pin, Pasta, Corrugated Ribbed Shaft, 11 In. 25.00
Rolling Pin, Ravioli, Wooden 45.00
Rolling Pin, Springerle, 16 Designs 58.00
Rolling Pin, Swivel Handles, Curly Maple, 24 In. 85.00
Rolling Pin, Tiger Maple, Knop Handles, 16 In. 85.00
Rolling Pin, Tin Cap, Paper Label, Columbus Baking Powder, 16 In. 135.00
Rolling Pin, White Ceramic, England 25.00
Rug Beater, Twisted Chain Wire, Wooden Handle, Oval, 29 In. 25.00
Sadiron, Asbestos, Sleeve Style, May 20, 1900 .... 37.50
Sadiron, Bentwood Detachable Handle 24.00
Sadiron, Child's, Arched Wooden Removable Handle, 3 1/2 In. 35.00
Sadiron, Child's, Wooden Handles, Reiss, Oct.7, 1879 .... 28.00
Sadiron, No.1, Raised Star & No.2 On Top, 7 1/4 In. 18.00
Sadiron, No.2, With Lever Release Handle 25.00
Sadiron, Scroll Handle, 6 1/2 In. 90.00
Sadiron, Wapak, Removable Walnut Handle, Footed Stand 22.00
Salt, Hanging, Laminated & Turned Light & Dark Wood, 9 In. 35.00
Saw, Meat, Winchester 37.00
Scale, Winchester 45.00
Scoop, Del Monico Ice Cream 90.00
Scoop, Dover Mfg.Co., 2–Way Action 100.00
Scoop, Flour, Pantry Box Type, Wooden, Signed Wilton, 5 1/2 In. 130.00
Scoop, Ice Cream, Ball Shape, Pewter, Japan 150.00
Scoop, Ice Cream, Banana Split, United Products 550.00
Scoop, Ice Cream, Benedict, No.16 .... 30.00
Scoop, Ice Cream, Chrome Plated Brass, Hamilton Beach No–Pak, 1932 .... 75.00
Scoop, Ice Cream, Clipper, Cone Shape, Squeeze Handle 100.00
Scoop, Ice Cream, Cone Shape, Dated 1876 .... 65.00
Scoop, Ice Cream, Cylinder Type, Made In Canada 250.00
Scoop, Ice Cream, Cylinder Type, Perfection Equipment Co. 400.00
Scoop, Ice Cream, Gilchrist No. 1 .... 32.50
Scoop, Ice Cream, Gilchrist No.30, Size 12 .... 48.00
Scoop, Ice Cream, Gilchrist No.31, Oval Bowl, 1915 Pat. 250.00
Scoop, Ice Cream, Gilchrist No.80 .... 45.00
Scoop, Ice Cream, Gilchrist, Nickel Over Brass 27.50
Scoop, Ice Cream, Gilchrist, Squeeze Handle 25.00
Scoop, Ice Cream, Hamilton Beach, 8 1/2 In. 8.00
Scoop, Ice Cream, Indestructo No.20 .... 14.00
Scoop, Ice Cream, Indestructo, Bakelite Handle 30.00
Scoop, Ice Cream, Mayer, Sandwich .... 135.00 To 145.00
Scoop, Ice Cream, Tin, Cone Shape, Revolving Handle 22.00
Scoop, Polar Pak Sandwich 250.00
Scraper, Dough, Copper Handle, Half–Circle Blade 95.00
Scraper, Dough, Iron, Brass Handle, Blade Engraved B.L.S.1868, 4 In. 325.00
Scraper, Dough, Iron, Brass Handle, Blade Engraved P.D.1850, 4 In. 425.00
Scrub Board, Name Alice Carved Above Opening For Soap, 29 In. 550.00
Shaver, Ice, Griswold 100.00
Sifter Mill, Flour, Hunter's, Cincinnati, Ohio 350.00
Sifter, Bean, Adjustable, Label, 1878 .... 150.00
Sifter, Flour Bin, Peerless, Patent 1885, Tin, 24 X 12 In. 120.00
Sifter, Flour, Arched Legs, Iron Beater Blades & Crank, Wood, 10 In. 260.00
Sifter, Flour, Hoosier, Metal 25.00
Sifter, Flour, Joseph Littlefield, Mass., 1865 .... 295.00
Sifter, Flour, Sawbuck Base, Old Red Paint, Pine, 43 1/2 X 60 In. 175.00
Sifter, Flour, Triple, Watkins 16.00
Skillet, Fish, With Lid, Griswold 175.00
Skillet, Griswold, Colonial 17.50
Skillet, Griswold, Glass Lid, With Emblem, Square 60.00
Skillet, Griswold, Iron, Cover, Pre–1900 .... 10.00

Skillet, Griswold, No.1 .... 120.00
Skillet, Griswold, Smoke Ring 20.00
Skillet, Impressed Good Health, Cast Iron, 7 In. 10.00
Slicer, Ice Cream, Ici Pi, Copyright 1925 .... 1250.00
Slicer, String Bean .... 48.00 To 65.00
Slicer, String Bean, Crank Handle 80.00
Smoothing Board, Horse Handle, Chip Carved, A.F.D.1787, 24 In. 1200.00
Smoothing Board, Horse Handle, Chip Carved, Painted, 23 1/2 In. 800.00
Smoothing Board, Oak, Hex Signed, Dark Finish, 5 1/4 X 31 In. 360.00
Smoothing Board, Primitive, Chip Carved Design, M.F.1886, 29 In. 95.00
Soap Saver, Wire, Wire Handle 15.00
Spice Box, 6 Graduated Sizes, Early 1800s, Stack of 6 .... 1100.00
Spice Box, 18 Drawers, Hanging 330.00
Spice Box, 8 Small Boxes, Black Lettering, Metal Bands, 10 Piece 165.00
Spice Box, Pinned Lid, Copper Fasteners, Oval, Wooden, 3 X 4 1/2 In. .. 120.00
Spice Cabinet, 3 Drawers 125.00
Spice Cabinet, 7 Drawers, Tin Plate Names, Wooden, 7 X 9 1/2 In. 95.00
Spice Cabinet, Pine, 12 Sections, New England, 19th Century, 19 In. .. 165.00
Spice Cabinet, Stenciled Spice Names On 8 Drawers 135.00
Spice Chest, Bride's, Vining Flowers, Pine & Cherry, 11 X 14 In. 2600.00
Spice Chest, Hanging, 6 Drawers, Pine & Walnut, C.1820, 8 X 11 In. ... 195.00
Spice Chest, Hanging, 8 Drawers, Scalloped Shelf Top, 20 X 14 In. 250.00
Spice Chest, Hanging, 8 Drawers, Scalloped Top, Wooden Knobs, 17 In. . 260.00
Spider, Brass, Handle, 18th Century, Round, 4 In.Handle, 3 3/4 In. ... 85.00
Spill Holder, Canary, White, Yellow, Brown Tree Stump, 5 3/4 In. 55.00
Spill Holder, Woodpecker, Blue, Green, Rust, Tree Stump, 7 In. 55.00
Spittoon, Griswold 1200.00
Spoon Rest, Figural, Elephant, Rosemeade, 6 In. 18.00
Spoon, Handmade, Wooden, Oiled Finish, 11 1/2 In. 4.50
Spoon, Slotted, Rumford 14.00
Spoon, Wire Handle Soldered To Slotted 4 X 4 In.Bowl 4.00
Spoon, Wooden, Handmade, 3 In.Bowl, 11 1/2 In. 4.50
Strainer, Cottage Cheese, Sliding Sides, Tin, American, 19 In. 77.00
String Holder, Apple, Chalkware 20.00
String Holder, Baker, Chalkware 25.00
String Holder, Ball, Cast Iron 42.00
String Holder, Beehive, Cast Iron .... 28.50 To 40.00
String Holder, Bell, Cast Iron 90.00
String Holder, Bulman, No.8, Cast Iron 35.00
String Holder, Cat On Ball, Chalkware 45.00
String Holder, Cat's Face, Hole In Ribbon For Scissors 20.00
String Holder, Chef 25.00
String Holder, Dutch Girl, Holding Flowers 49.00
String Holder, French Cook, Chalkware 20.00
String Holder, Girl Knitting Sock, Ceramic 25.00
String Holder, Head of Mexican, Chalkware 5.00
String Holder, Head, Bulldog 39.00
String Holder, Head, Sailor Boy, Plaster .... 38.00 To 55.00
String Holder, Lady, Full Figure, Ceramic 60.00
String Holder, Lovebirds, Ceramic 18.00
String Holder, Mammy, Hanging Or Counter 62.00
String Holder, Mexican Man .... 10.00 To 14.00
String Holder, Painted Blue & Red, Norwegian, Bentwood, 3 3/8 In. 137.00
String Holder, Post Toasties, Tin, Instructions 375.00
String Holder, Pumpkin Face, Ceramic 55.00
String Holder, Wall, Red & Yellow Apple, Green Leaves, Chalkware 35.00
String Holder, West Wind, Ceramic 65.00
String Holder, White Chef, Figural, Black Features 39.00
String Holder, Woman's Head, String Comes Out of Mouth, Cast Iron 350.00
Sugar Nipper, Iron, Incised Design, 7 In. 95.00
Sugar Nipper, Iron, Marked R.Simon & Son, Tooled, 9 In. 115.00
Sugar Nipper, Perfect 75.00
Sugar Shaker, Roses & Garland, Cream Ground, 6 In. 50.00

Sugar, Turned Burl, Ball Finial Cover, 19th Century, American, 5 In. 1980.00
Tea Set, Gold On Ivory, 21 Piece 210.00
Teakettle, Gooseneck Spout, Brass Finial & Swivel Handle, Copper 175.00
Teakettle, Gooseneck Spout, Swivel Handle, Zinc, 5 In. 100.00
Teakettle, Iron, Handle, Brass Finial, Gooseneck, Label, 11 In. 40.00
Teakettle, Turtle Head Shaped Spout, Iron 95.00
Teakettle, Wagner, Cast Iron, 1 Gal. .... 50.00 To 60.00
Teapot, Lipton 30.00
Thermometer, Candy, Betty Furness, Box, Unused 8.00
Thermometer, Candy, Taylor, 8 1/2 In. 35.00
Tie Back, Floral, Pair 35.00
Toast Rack, White Porcelain 50.00
Toaster, Iron, 15 3/4 In. 80.00
Toaster, Iron, 18 In. 175.00
Toaster, Marshmallow, Tin 60.00
Toaster, On The Stove, Bromwell 16.00
Toaster, Scrolled & Twisted Iron, Swivel End, 16 In. 200.00
Tray, Dough, Square Nails, Self-Handles, Pine 90.00
Trivet, Griswold 7.00
Trivet, Sadiron, Star & Fan Pattern, Cleveland Foundry Co. 15.00
Utensil Set, Child's, Blue Handles, White Trim, 6 Piece 100.00
Vacuum Cleaner, Bellows, Painted 95.00
Waffle Iron, 6 Different Squares & Patterns, 18 In. 130.00
Waffle Iron, Flip Over, Hearts 55.00
Waffle Iron, Foxall, Bail, Patent 1869 .... 20.00
Waffle Iron, Griswold, No.8 .... 25.00 To 45.00
Waffle Iron, Heart Design, Ring Handles 65.00
Waffle Iron, Heart Shape, Anderson 30.00
Waffle Iron, Hearts, Star In Center, Griswold, No.18 .... 70.00
Waffle Iron, Iron, 28-In. Handle, 4 1/2 X 8 In. 62.00
Waffle Iron, Keen Kutter .... 100.00 To 200.00
Waffle Iron, Late 1800s 45.00
Waffle Iron, Wagner, Cast Iron 125.00
Waffle Iron, Wagner, Miniature 135.00
Wash Boiler, Tin 35.00
Washboard, Blue Enamel 45.00
Washboard, Clear Glass 25.00
Washboard, Enamel King, Dark Blue Enamel 85.00
Washboard, Glass, Domestic Science Label, 17 X 8 In. 15.00
Washboard, Graniteware, Blue 77.50
Washboard, Lingerie, Columbus 13.00
Washboard, Marked Busy Bee, 18 X 9 In. 8.00
Washboard, Metal Surface, Name Midget In Soap Pocket, 18 In. 15.00
Washboard, Mother Hubbard, Turned Wooden Spindle 65.00
Washboard, Mother Hubbard, Wooden 85.00
Washboard, Real Silk Hosiery Mills, 5 X 7 In. 21.00
Washboard, Roller, Wooden, Primitive 105.00
Washboard, Shapleigh 35.00
Washboard, Soap Saver, Glass 15.00
Washboard, Wooden Spiral Rollers 90.00
Washboard, Word Alice On Top 605.00
Washing Machine, Copper Tub, Operated By Pushing & Pulling Lever 200.00
Whip, Cream & Egg, Brill Co., Flat Blades, Pat.1919 .... 9.00
Whip, Cream, Tin, Syllabub, Pat.Sept.14, 1875 .... 55.00
Whip, Wire, Omar Wonder Flour 5.00
Wrench, Fruit Jar, Triumph 18.00
Wringer Washer, Laundry Queen, 13 In. 225.00
Wringer, Rosewood & Brass, Salesman Sample 125.00

 In the 1960s, the United States government passed a law that required knife manufacturers to mark their knives with the country of origin. This seemed to encourage the collectors, and knife collecting became an interest of a large group of people. All types of knives are collected, from top quality twentieth–century examples to old bone– or pearl–handled knives in excellent condition.

KNIFE, Anheuser–Busch, Pocket	115.00
Anheuser–Busch, Silver Plate, Corkscrew, Stanhope, 3 Blades	95.00
Bakuba, Wood & Iron, Ribbed Leaf Shaped Blade, 14 1/2 In.	145.00
Barlow, Pocket, Prince Albert	12.00
Bowie, Mexican, Wood Grips, Black Leather Sheath, 21 In.	425.00
Buck Tapper, Commemorative, Winchester, Pocket, Box	70.00
Butcher, German, C.1890	25.00
Butcher, Russell–Green River Works, New John Russell, 10 In.	20.00
California, Bowie Shape, Coffin Handle, C.1850, Wostenholm & Son	2250.00
Camper's, 11 Implements	30.00
Case, No.62131, Etched On Blade, Carolina Butter Brand	85.00
Case, XX, Sheath	17.00
Dagger, Arab, Horn Grip, Curved Blade, Filigree Silver Sheath	125.00
Dagger, Black Wooden Handle, Double Edge Filigree Blade, 9 1/2 In.	50.00
Dagger, SS, Nazi, Walnut Handle	110.00
Dirk, Folding, Liberty & Union Guard, C.1840	750.00
Draw, Douglas Mfg.Co., Brass Ferrules & Tips, 11 In.	18.00
Draw, Winchester	75.00
Figural, Derringer Pistol, 1960s	12.25
Figural, Guitar, 1960s	13.25
Figural, Key, 1960	12.25
Figural, Lady's Shoe, Pocket	20.00
Fish, Sterling Silver, Ivory Handle, Arthur Stone, 1906, 11 1/4 In.	2600.00
Fruit, Mother–of–Pearl Handles, 5 Piece	20.00
Fruit, Tuft, 1877–1904, Set of 6	65.00
Golden Wedding Whiskey, Pocket	30.00
Hunting, Bear Head, Leather Handle, Schrader & Walden	35.00
Hunting, Western, No.F66	15.00
Indian Hunting, Leather Handle & Sheath, Leather Fringed Bottom	60.00
Jack, Easy Open, G.B.Kinney & Co. On Shield, Pocket	8.00
Jack, Keen Kutter, Bone Handle, 3 In.	25.00
Jack, Vulcan Cutlery, Signed, Miniature	12.50
Keen Kutter, Spirit of St.Louis, Box	30.00
Kentucky Riflemen, Half Horse & Half Alligator Design, 13 In.	2750.00
Lady's Shoe, Figural, Pocket	20.00
Marilyn Monroe Nude Picture, Pocket, 1950s	7.50
Peanut, Case XX	90.00
Pen, Cotton Belt	49.00
Pen, Kansas City, Pearl Handle, 2 3/4 In.	20.00
Pen, Sterlng Silver, 19th Century	37.50
Pocket, Camping, German, 4 In.	10.00
Pocket, Cast No.62000 1/2, 2 Blades	40.00
Pocket, Chrome, With Key Chain	10.00
Pocket, Daniel Boone, Rabbit's Foot, On Display Card	25.00
Pocket, Deputy Sheriff	17.00
Pocket, Keen Kutter, Spirit of St.Louis, Box	165.00
Pocket, Mother–of–Pearl, 4 In.	10.00
Pocket, Pearl Handle, Picture of City, Signed Erb	20.00
Pocket, Remington	25.00
Pocket, Remington, No.735	75.00
Pocket, Robeson	110.00
Pocket, Sheffield, Staghorn Handle, Hanging Loop, A.Allen Nameplate	150.00
Pocket, Souvenir, Atlantic City, Scenic	35.00
Pocket, Star Brand Shoes	100.00
Pocket, Syracuse, 2 Blades, Green	7.50
Pocket, Wostenholm, English Pence, 1943 Etched On Can Opener Blade	40.00
Remington, Circle Brand, Celluloid Handle	50.00
Sash, Ivory Clad, Carved 7 Household Gods, Japanese, 14 1/8 In.	175.00
Scout, Remington, Bone Handle	60.00
Swiss Army, Unused	15.00
Trapper, Case, No.6254	50.00

Traveler's Insurance, Nickel Silver, Pocket 75.00
U.S.1849 Rifleman's, Sheath, Ames Contract, Walnut Handle 3250.00
U.S.Bolo–Bayonet, Experimental, 1910, 14 In.Blade 2250.00
U.S.Navy, With Sheath 35.00
Utica, Fringed Buckskin Sheath, 7 In. 85.00
Watermelon, Folding, Diamond Edge, A102 .... 40.00
Winchester Experimental, Musket Bayonet, Sheath, Belt Hook 250.00
    KNOWLES, TAYLOR & KNOWLES, see KTK; Lotus Ware

KOCH   The name "Koch" is signed on the front of a series of plates decorated with fruit, vegetables, animals, or birds. The dishes date from the 1910 to 1930 period and were probably decorated in Germany.

KOCH, Pancake Cover, Apple 25.00
Plate, Grape 18.00
Sugar Shaker, Grapes 95.00
Syrup, Apple, Vine Handle, Cover 30.00
    KOREAN WARE, see Sumida

KPM

K.P.M   Most dealers and collectors use the term "KPM" to refer to Berlin porcelain, but the same initials were used alone and in combination with other symbols by several German porcelain makers. They include the Konigliche Porzellan Manufaktur of Berlin, initials used in mark, 1823–47; Meissen, 1723–24 only; Krister Porzellan Manufaktur in Waldenburg, after 1831; Kranichfelder Porzellan Manufaktur in Kranichfeld, after 1903; and the Kister Porzellan Manufaktur in Scheibe, after 1838.

KPM, Berry Dish 50.00
Bowl, Leaf, Figural, Bird, Nest With Eggs, Meissen, Pink, Blue, 3 In. 675.00
Figurine, Woman, Empire Style Dress, Black & Gold, Marked, 8 1/2 In. 235.00
Painting On Porcelain, Head of Lady, Plumed Hat, Signed 225.00
Plaque, 3 Children Dancing In The Wind, Marked, 5 3/4 X 8 In. 2000.00
Plaque, Bust, Elderly Woman, Elderly Man, Frame, 10 X 12 In., Pair 6000.00
Plaque, German Bride, Gold Cross, 9 3/8 X 6 1/4 In. 4290.00
Plaque, Gitana, With Red Cap, C.1900, 13 1/3 In. 8800.00
Plaque, Maiden, Long Blond Hair, Nude, 8 3/8 X 4 3/8 In. 1650.00
Plaque, Portrait of Woman, Signed Wagner, Oval, Frame, 13 1/2 X 11 In. 7000.00
Plaque, Ruth, Gray Gown, Wheat Sheath, Scepter, 16 X 10 5/8 In. 3575.00
Plaque, Shields & Verse, Blue & White, PUG, 10 1/2 In. 120.00
Plaque, Sistine Madonna, Scepter Mark, Oval, 10 1/2 In. 660.00
Plaque, Spring Time, Maiden, In Meadow, Scepter, 9 1/4 X 6 3/8 In. 2750.00
Plaque, St.Jerome, Bearded, Scepter Mark, 11 X 8 3/4 In. 1320.00
Plaque, Woman & 3 Cherubs, Signed A.Grisard, Frame, 9 1/4 X 6 In. 400.00
Plaque, Woman Hiding Cupid's Bow, Signed Volk, 10 X 8 In. ....*Illus* 4800.00
Plaque, Woman, Glancing Away, Blue Drapery, 9 1/2 In. 4500.00
Plaque, Young Girl, With Water Jug, Holds Bouquet In Apron, 13 X 8 In. 3600.00
Platter, C.1832, 10 X 13 1/2 In. 180.00
Shaving Mug, White, Gold Trim 24.00
Sugar & Creamer, White Flowers, Gold Handles 75.00
Teapot, Art Nouveau, Scepter Mark 55.00
Tile, 3 Boys, Accompanied By Dog, Playing Dice, 12 1/2 X 10 1/4 In. 3250.00
Tile, 4 Cherubs With Lamb, Gilded Frame, Marked, 10 1/4 X 9 In. 3800.00
Toothpick, Boots, With Clown In Center 65.00
Tray, Pin, 4 Children Eating 16.00
Vase, Figural, Cupid, Quiver of Arrows, Cornucopia, 23 3/4 In. 3190.00

Modern bleach can damage eighteenth-century and some nine-teenth-century dishes. To clean old dishes, try hydrogen peroxide or bicarbonate of soda. Each removes a different type of stain.

Vase, Young Napoleon, Signed Wagner, 6 In. 625.00

K.T.&K.
CHINA

KTK are the initials of the Knowles, Taylor & Knowles Company of East Liverpool, Ohio, founded by Isaac W. Knowles in 1853. The company made many types of utilitarian wares, hotel china, and dinnerwares. They made the fine bone china known as Lotus Ware from 1891 to 1896. The company merged with American Ceramic Corporation in 1928. It closed in 1934. Lotus Ware is listed in its own category in this book.

KTK, Bowl, Fruits, 9 In. 10.00
  Cup & Toothbrush Holder, Ironstone, 2 Piece Set 55.00
  Platter, Fruits, 13 In. 10.00
  Salt & Pepper, Fruits 8.00
  Syrup, Wild Rose Design, Pewter Top, 1872 .... 30.00
  Teapot, Pewter Lid, Double Scenic, Blue & White 85.00
  Vase, Hand Painted Rose, Green Ground, Fluted Rim, Handles, 11 In. 75.00

KKK

Any items relating to the Ku Klux Klan are now collected because of their historic importance. Literature, robes, and memorabilia are available. The Klan is still in existence, so new material is found.

KU KLUX KLAN, Book, The Clansman, Thomas Dixon Jr., 1905 .... 8.00
  Card, Membership, Donation Certificate, C.1940 .... 25.00
  Clip, Money 32.00
  Ring, Man's 135.00
  Robe, Hood, Pouch, Official Seal & Sword 350.00
  Sheet Music, Face Behind The Mask 25.00
  Uniform, With Ceremonial Book, 1930s 500.00

Kutani ware is a Japanese porcelain made after the mid–seventeenth century. Most of the pieces found today are nineteenth century. Collectors often use the term "kutani" to refer to just the later, colorful pieces decorated with red, gold, and black pictures of warriors, animals, and birds.

KUTANI, Bowl, 2 Carps, C.1850, 1 1/2 X 4 1/2 X 7 In. 450.00
  Bowl, Lady & Boy In Garden, On River Shore, Red & Gold, 7 1/2 In. 250.00
  Compote, 7 1/2 In. 145.00
  Garden Seat, Barrel Form, Children & Ladies In Garden, 18 In. 500.00
  Hair Receiver, Gold & Multicolor, 4 3/4 In. 65.00
  Salt & Pepper, Warrior 50.00
  Tea Set, Lotus Finial On Covers, 14 Piece 125.00
  Tea Set, Side Handle Pot, 4 Handleless Cups 45.00
  Toothpick, Multicolored, Floral, Signed, 2 X 2 In. 10.75
  Tray, Overall Nishikide Scenes of Children, 1910, 12 X 6 1/4 In. 60.00
  Vase, 6 Men, 3 Birds, Red & Gold, 5 1/2 In. 75.00
  Vase, Butterflies, Flowers, 3–Footed, Scalloped, 4 1/4 In. 125.00
  Vase, Double Gourd, Birds, Gold & Orange, C.1875, 10 In. 120.00
  Vase, Pagoda Scene, Signed, 7 1/2 In. 65.00
  Vase, Stick, Birds In Flight, Chrysanthemums, Signed, 3 1/2 In. 150.00

Lacquer is a type of varnish. Collectors are most interested in the Chinese and Japanese lacquer wares made from the Japanese varnish tree. Lacquer wares are made from wood coated with many coats of lacquer. Sometimes the piece is carved or decorated with ivory or metal inlay.

LACQUER, Box, Amber, Palace Scene, Japan, 8 1/2 X 3 1/2 In. 30.00
  Box, Chrysanthemums, Silver Mounts, Gold, 7 1/2 X 8 1/2 In. 2650.00
  Box, Cigarette, France 10.00
  Box, Fairy Tale, Russian, Pre–Revolution, Square, 5 1/4 In. 350.00
  Box, Fan, Cover, Chinoiserie Design, Black Ground, 19th Century 40.00
  Box, Gold, Plum Blossom, Wood Grain Surface, 18th Century, 2 In. 687.50
  Box, Rabbit, Moth, Bat, Floral, Geometric, Black, Silver Interior 330.00
  Box, Snakes, Frogs, Slugs, Wasps, Dragonflies, On Tray, Egg Shape 780.00
  Box, Storage, Scenic Design, Black Ground, Brass Latch, 7 X 9 In. 105.00
  Box, Swirling Brocade, 18th Century 605.00

Inro, Gold, Woman Asleep, Mt.Fuji, 4 Case, Kwansai I, 18th Century 2860.00
Inro, Spring Waterfall Landscape, Gold, 4 Case, Signed Shokasai 1100.00
Tea Caddy, Chinese, Domed Corner, Winged Dragon–Head Foot, 5 In. 275.00
Tea Set, Tray, Gold On Black, Kin Mi Ekie, 8 Piece 60.00
Tray, Peasant, Scene, Black, 13 1/2 In. 10.00

Lalique   Lalique glass was made by Rene Lalique in Paris, France, between
                        the 1890s and his death in 1945. The glass was molded, pressed, and
                        engraved in Art Nouveau and Art Deco styles. Pieces were marked
                        with the signature "R. Lalique." Lalique glass is still being made.
                        Pieces made after 1945 bear the mark "Lalique."

LALIQUE, Ashtray, Figural, Bird, 3 3/4 In. 50.00
Ashtray, Figural, Lovebirds, 4 In. 60.00
Ashtray, Figural, Swan, 4 In. 60.00
Ashtray, Lion, Signed 110.00
Ashtray, Louise, Opal & Black Enameling 110.00
Ashtray, Vezelay Pattern, Frosted 300.00
Bottle, Blue, Worth, France, Signed, 5 3/4 In. 650.00
Bottle, Perfume, Clear, Daisies 295.00
Bowl, Art Deco Gold Border, Signed, 12 X 2 1/2 In. 495.00
Bowl, Hounds, Embossed, Opalescent, Marked, 9 1/4 In. 450.00
Bowl, Rows of Overlapping Leaves, Signed, 3 1/2 X 8 In. 300.00
Bowl, Underplate, Dandelion 85.00
Bowl, Wide Bird Border, Low, 3 1/4 In. 100.00
Box, Fringed Flowers, Opalescent, C.1925, 5 1/2 In. 880.00
Box, Frosted, Ballerina, Wide Skirt Flaring, Green, Signed, 4 In. 880.00
Box, Peacocks Lid, Feathers Spread, Amber Wash, Signed, 2 3/4 In. 495.00
Box, Powder, 2 Mermaids Swimming, Bubbles, 1925, Signed, 4 In. 880.00
Candleholder, Hummingbird & Flowers, Pair 395.00
Champagne, Dessert, Nude Stem, Signed, 6 Piece 475.00
Chandelier, Clear Bowl, Vines, Brown Leaves, Silk Cords, 27 In. 4400.00
Clock, Drum Case, Florets, 1930, Marked, 4 1/2 In. 1540.00
Clock, Mantel, 2 Women Holding Round Clock, Metal, Glass, C.1925 .... 6875.00
Dish, Cigarette, Lion Pattern, Signed 85.00
Dresser Set, Frosted Birds, Powder Jar, 2 Colognes, Signed, 3 Piece 750.00
Figurine, Bull, 4 1/2 In. 149.00
Figurine, Cat, Frosted, 8 1/2 In. 310.00
Figurine, Child, Holding Bouquet of Flowers, Signed, 3 3/4 In. 115.00
Figurine, Fish, Oval Base, Signed, 6 1/2 In. 165.00
Figurine, Polar Bear, 5 3/4 In. 295.00
Figurine, Salamander, Green, 7 1/2 In. 150.00
Figurine, Toad, 4 1/8 In. 155.00
Figurine, Two Female Dancers, Signed, 9 1/2 In. 950.00
Figurine, Woman, Head Back, Clinging Dress, Signed, 5 1/2 In. 3575.00
Hood Ornament, Coq Nain, Rooster, Marked, 8 In. .... 675.00 To 695.00
Incense Burner, Frieze of Egyptian Dancers, Marked, 6 1/8 In. 935.00
Jar, Grecian Ladies, Signed, 1 1/4 X 2 In. 65.00
Lamp, Gros Poisson Vagues, Fish, Bronze Base, Signed, 15 1/2 In. 5000.00
Lighter, Cigarette, Florals, Brass Fittings, Signed, 4 1/4 In. 90.00
Paperweight, Deer, 4 1/2 In. 98.00
Pendant, 2 Nudes, Frosted, Cord, Signed 550.00
Pendant, Teardop Lilies, Green 650.00
Pendant, Woman With Doves, Frosted, Oblong 395.00
Perfume Atomizer, Frosted, Nude Maidens Holding Swag, Signed, 5 In. 1550.00
Perfume Atomizer, Ovoid, Frosted Sides, Blossoms, Leafy Vines, 5 In. 1200.00
Perfume Bottle, Blue Jade Stopper, Blue, Signed, 3 In. 110.00
Perfume Bottle, Coeur–Joie, Ricci, Heart Shape, Signed 225.00
Perfume Bottle, Dans La Nuit, Worth 250.00
Perfume Bottle, Double Dahlia, Original Stopper, Signed 125.00
Perfume Bottle, Epines, Brown Wash, Script Signed, 3 3/4 In. 350.00
Perfume Bottle, Frosted Back, Floral Flattened Stopper, 4 3/4 In. 4180.00
Perfume Bottle, L'Air Du Temps, Double Dove 125.00
Perfume Bottle, Lotus Helene, Frosted 750.00
Perfume Bottle, Molinard, Clear & Frosted 895.00

Perfume Bottle, Replique, Acorn, Pendant	275.00
Perfume Bottle, Ruffled Fan Devices, Green, 2 5/8 In.	1870.00
Perfume Bottle, Worth, Cobalt Blue, Light Blue Stopper	165.00
Plate, 3 Frosted Cherubs In Center, Signed, 7 3/4 In.	175.00
Plate, Annual, 1976	80.00
Plate, Annual, Dream Rose, 1966	150.00
Plate, Black, 7 1/2 In.	125.00
Plate, Black, 11 1/4 In.	175.00
Plate, Figures Et Fleurs, 6 3/4 In.	210.00
Platter, Spirales Pattern, 11 In.	425.00
Powder Box, D'Orsay	165.00
Powder Box, Dahlia Blossoms On Opalescent Cover, Signed, 8 1/4 In.	650.00
Punch Cup, Butterfly Handle	175.00
Ring Tree, Frosted Pheasant	55.00
Scent Burner, Sirens	1450.00
Vase, 3 Nude Boys In Relief, Signed	525.00
Vase, 4 Tiers of Leaves, Ovoid, Opalescent, C.1932, 9 In.	5500.00
Vase, Berry Laden Leafy Branches, Marked, 1932, 7 In.	715.00
Vase, Birds On Branches, Thick Angular Handles, Marked, 8 3/4 In.	3960.00
Vase, Birds, Signed, 5 In.	145.00
Vase, Blossom, Concentric Rings, Trumpet Form, Marked, 6 In.	1100.00
Vase, Branches, Brown Wash, Signed, 6 1/4 In.	600.00
Vase, Embossed Grapes & Vines, Signed, 6 1/4 In. .... 435.00 To	450.00
Vase, Embossed Leaves, Alternate Leaves Turned Down, 5 7/8 In.	395.00
Vase, Enameled Shoulder, Black, Zigzag, Signed, Bulging, 7 In.	4675.00
Vase, Escargot, Frosted, Signed, Block Letters, 7 1/2 In.	1750.00
Vase, Eucalyptus, Cylindrical, Leaves & Berries, Marked, 7 In.	450.00
Vase, Finches, Perched On Branches, Frosted, Marked, 8 In.	990.00
Vase, Fruit–Bearing Trees, Row of Ferns, Ovoid, C.1930, 6 5/8 In.	6380.00
Vase, Goldfish Design, France, 7 In.	400.00
Vase, Grasshoppers On Blade of Grass, Yellow, Signed, 11 In.	2200.00
Vase, Grasshoppers On Grasses, Sapphire, C.1932, Marked, 10 5/8 In.	6050.00
Vase, Gui Pattern, 6 1/2 In.	345.00
Vase, Laurel Leaves, Script Signed, 7 In.	550.00
Vase, Lovebirds On Flowering Branch, Deep Amber, Signed, 9 3/4 In.	4950.00
Vase, Overlapping Leafage, Turquoise, Marked, 1932, 6 In.	1210.00
Vase, Overlapping Wide Leaves, 1925, Marked, 6 1/2 In.	605.00
Vase, Protruding Embossed Nubs, Opalescent, Frosted, Marked, 7 In.	595.00
Vase, Protruding Fish, Raised Bubbles, Frosted, Signed, 5 1/2 In.	1500.00
Vase, Raisins, Molded Grapes, Signed	395.00
Vase, Ram, Bird & Fish, Signed, 6 1/4 In.	495.00
Vase, Stylized Leaves, Pedestal, 4 5/8 In.	150.00
Vase, Thistle, Charcoal, 8 1/2 In.	2400.00
Vase, Thorny Bramble Branches, Reddish Amber, Signed, 9 In.	1925.00
Vase, Thorny Branches, Brown, Signed, 9 In.	1250.00
Vase, Thorny Branches, Emerald Green, Signed, 8 In.	2750.00
Vase, Two Birds In Relief, 5 In.	145.00
Vase, Woody Branches, Blue, Signed, 9 In.	2750.00

Interest is strong in lamps of every type, from the early oil–burning Betty and Phoebe lamps to the recent electric lamps with glass or beaded shades. Fuels used in lamps changed through the years; whale oil (1800–40), camphene (1828), Argand (1830), lard (1833–63), turpentine and alcohol (1840s), gas (1850–79), kerosene (1860), and electricity (1879) are the most common. Other lamps are listed by manufacturer or type of material.

LAMP, 2–Light, Bronze & Champleve, Taoist Mask, 22 In.	165.00
2–Light, Enamel Bandings, Masks, Bronze, Japanese, 22 1/2 In.	145.00
A.W.Reisner, Peacock, Gate & Bush, Metal	170.00
Acanthus, Blue & Clambroth, Electrified, 19 1/2 In.	250.00
Aladdin, Alacite, Electric, Yellow & Cream, 1930s	45.00
Aladdin, B– 27, Simplicity, Gold Luster	120.00
Aladdin, B– 29, Simplicity, Ivory Alacite With Decal	75.00
Aladdin, B– 30, Simplicity, Log Cabin Shade	50.00

Aladdin, B– 30, Simplicity, Log Cabin Shade, Nashville Burner 110.00
Aladdin, B– 39, Washington Drape, Clear Beta Crystal Art Glass 90.00
Aladdin, B– 62, Lincoln Drape, Ruby, Short 350.00
Aladdin, B– 70, Solitaire, White Moonstone Art Glass 1100.00
Aladdin, B– 70, Solitaire, White Moonstone, Burners 920.00
Aladdin, B– 76, Lincoln Drape, Cobalt Blue, Crystal Art Glass 325.00
Aladdin, B– 76, Lincoln Drape, Cobalt, Scalloped Foot, Tall 400.00
Aladdin, B– 77, Lincoln Drape, Ruby, Crystal Art Glass, Tall 350.00
Aladdin, B– 81, Beehive, Green Beta, Crystal Art Glass 80.00
Aladdin, B– 85, Diamond Quilt, White Moonstone Art Glass 100.00
Aladdin, B– 87, Vertique, Rose Moonstone Art Glass 195.00
Aladdin, B– 88, Vertique, Yellow Moonstone Art Glass 350.00
Aladdin, B– 93, Vertique, White Moonstone Art Glass 325.00
Aladdin, B–110, Cathedral, White Moonstone Art Glass, Burners 140.00
Aladdin, B–115, Corinthian, Green Moonstone Art Glass .... 70.00 To 80.00
Aladdin, B–121, Majestic, Rose Moonstone Font 85.00
Aladdin, B–125, Corinthian, White Moonstone Bowl, Green Moonstone Base 75.00
Aladdin, B–126, White Moonstone Bowl, Rose Moonstone Base 75.00
Aladdin, Cupid, Alacite 100.00
Aladdin, G–271, Alacite, Swirl, Table 35.00
Aladdin, G–278, Alacite, Table 22.00
Aladdin, G–290d, Alacite With Decal, Table 32.00
Aladdin, Lincoln Drape, Original Burner, Chimney & Wick 425.00
Aladdin, Moonstone Font, Kerosene 80.00
Aladdin, No. 2, Table, Brass 125.00
Aladdin, No. 3, Table, International Gallery, Nickel, 4 Burners, 1908 .... 45.00
Aladdin, No. 6, Table, Font, With Burner, Nickel 65.00
Aladdin, No. 7, With 401 Shade 190.00
Aladdin, No. 7, With 416 Shade 400.00
Aladdin, No. 8, Bracket, 401 Shade 275.00
Aladdin, No. 12, Floor, With 616 Shade 275.00
Aladdin, No. 12, Wall Bracket, Font & Burner 110.00
Aladdin, No. 104, Colonial, Clear Beta Crystal Art Shade 50.00
Aladdin, No. 105, Colonial, Green Beta Crystal Art Shade 85.00
Aladdin, No. 108, Cathedral, Green Beta Crystal Art Shade 70.00
Aladdin, No.1242, Red Vase 200.00
Albertine, Hanging 475.00
Amberina Swirl, Miniature 100.00
Angle, Double, Opalescent Swirl Shades 325.00
Angle, Nickel Plated, Milk Glass Shade, Clear Glass Cover 77.00
Aquarius, Burner, Blue, 10 In. 140.00
Argand, Brass, Swans, Etched Shade, C.1850, 15 3/4 In., Pair ....*Illus* 1100.00
Argand, Double–Arm, Glass & Gilt Bronze, Pair 1540.00
Argand, Gilt Metal, Clear Shade, 16 In., Pair ....*Illus* 1430.00
Art Deco, Brass Woman's Figure, Marble Base, Marked Rembrandt 85.00
Art Deco, Dancing Nude, Glass, 11 In. 80.00
Art Deco, Figural, Parrot, Colorful, Glass, Black Base, 13 In. 200.00
Art Deco, Fish, Floating, Column Green Glass Shade 85.00
Art Deco, Illuminated Panels of Etched Nudes, Metal 100.00
Art Deco, Lady Dancer, Bronze Patinated, Alabaster Etched Base, 13 In. 250.00
Art Deco, Nude Lady, Sitting, Looking Upwards, Framed Silk Shade 240.00
Art Deco, Nude Lady, With Greyhound, White Metal 175.00
Art Deco, Nude Sitting On Pedestal, Green Globe, Bronze Wash 65.00
Art Deco, Nude, Leaded Glass Wings, Bronze, Signed Adolphi, 14 In. 1400.00
Art Deco, Spelter Lady, Kneeling, Holding Gold Glass Shade 55.00
Art Nouveau, Figural, Man & Woman, Fabrication Francaise, Paris, Pair 450.00
Art Nouveau, Pulled Green & Gold Feathers, Steuben Shade, Pair 450.00
Art Nouveau, White Metal, Bronze Gilding, Signed Causse 695.00
Baker's Oven, Iron, Hinged Lid 225.00
Banquet, Cupids On Ball Shade, Electrified, Brass Base & Stem, 29 In. 325.00
Banquet, Hand Painted Rural Scenes, Milk Glass 185.00
Banquet, Hand Painted Shades, Electrified 225.00
Betty, Hook & Wick Pick, American, 18th Century 275.00
Betty, Hook & Wick Pick, Tin, C.1810, 4 X 6 In. 165.00

Betty, Snake Feet Standard, 18th Century	1450.00
Betty, With Pick, Cast Iron, 8 In.	80.00
Boudoir, Figural, Girl, With Parasol Glass Shade, Pink Satin	20.00
Boudoir, Moe Bridges, Blue Scenic, 13 1/2 In.	315.00
Boudoir, Original Silk Shade, Pair	35.00
Boudoir, Woman's, Floral Cut Glass Shade, 1930s	25.00
Bracket, Cylindrical Bull's-Eye Cranberry Shade	325.00
LAMP, BRADLEY & HUBBARD, see Bradley & Hubbard, Lamp	
Buggy, Rayo, Kerosene, Wire Bail, 10 1/2 In.	65.00
Cabin Scene ....*Illus*	120.00
Cameo, 3 Graces Carved On Seashell, Bulbous, 1900-20, 4 X 6 1/2 In.	485.00
Candle, Coiled Ejector, Clear Glass Shade, Painted Green, Tin, 18 In.	900.00
Candle, Pierced Tin, Carrying Ring, Pierced Glass Panels, 8 3/4 In.	700.00
Carbide, Just-Rite, Brass, With Reflector, 4 In.	35.00
Carbide, Just-Rite, Reflector & Handle, 7 In.	55.00
Chandelier, 4-Light, Etched Glass, E.Brandt, D.Nancy, 1930, 34 In.	3850.00
Chandelier, 6-Light, Empire, Gilt-Bronze Eagle, C.1900, 4 Ft.9 In.	3575.00
Chandelier, 6-Light, George III, Diamond-Cut Sphere, Glass, 35 In.	3850.00
Chandelier, 6-Light, Louis XVI, Parcel Gilt, Center Term, 34 In.	1650.00
Chandelier, 9-Light, Tiers of Prisms, Crystal, 33 X 24 N.	150.00
Chandelier, 10-Light, Electric, Crystal, 20 X 27 In.	240.00
Chandelier, 15-Light, Animal Masks, Medallions, Gilt-Bronze, 36 In.	1100.00
Chandelier, 15-Light, Louis XV, Cut Glass, Beaded, Pendant, 51 X 37 In.	5500.00
Chandelier, 16-Light, Continental Baroque, Brass, Electric, 37 In.	3850.00
Chandelier, Hanging, Chains, Gilt Metal, 3 Glass Globes, C.1906, Bauer	1650.00
Chandelier, Steuben Petal Shades, Copper & Bronze, Signed, 20 In.	3000.00
Coach, Eagle Finial, Brass, For Interior Use, 28 1/2 In., Pair	50.00
Coleman Kerolite, Base	20.00
Columbian Coin, 8 1/2 In.	140.00
Cosmos, Miniature	225.00
Doll, Figural, Bisque, 12 1/4 In.	60.00
Electric, 3 Arms, Mica Shade, Old Mission Kopperkraft, 1910, 14 In.	2700.00
Electric, Baluster, Bamboo, Wooden Base, Pottery, 15 1/8 In.	125.00
Electric, Brass & Slag, Egyptian Scene On Shade, 28 3/8 In.	375.00
Electric, Child's, Dog Shape, 1940s	17.50
Electric, Cloisonne, Floral Design, Cobalt Blue Ground	175.00
Electric, Colonial Lady, Figural, Pink Glass, Umbrella Shade, Pair	78.00
Electric, Copper, Mica Panel Shade, Strap Handle Base, 1910, 14 3/4 In.	1400.00
Electric, Copper, Mother-of-Pearl Medallions, Cylindrical, 13 In.	400.00
Electric, Copper, Silver Design, Helmet Shade, C.1915, 10 3/4 In.	160.00
Electric, Delft Lady & Man, Brass Base, Occupied Japan, 7 1/2 In., Pr.	85.00
Electric, Desk, Gooseneck, Green Enameled Sight Craft Shade	60.00
Electric, Desk, Gooseneck, Pin Base, Metal Shade	35.00
Electric, Econolite, No.761, Revolving Action, Mountain Fire Scene	85.00
Electric, English Hobnail, Pink, 9 1/4 In.	65.00
Electric, Famille Noire, Porcelain, Floral, Wooden Base, 21 In., Pair	700.00
Electric, Floor, Gilt Bronze, Rope Twist Glass, Arched Base, 58 In.	475.00
Electric, Floor, Japanese Lacquer, Demons, Silk Shade ....*Illus*	600.00

Lamp, Argand, Brass, Swans, Etched Shade, C.1850, 15 3/4 In., Pair

Lamp, Argand, Gilt Metal, Clear Shade, 16 In., Pair

Lamp,
Cabin Scene

Lamp, Kerosene,
Lincoln Drape

Lamp, Electric, Floor, Japanese
Lacquer, Demons, Silk Shade

Electric, Floor, Torch, Art Deco, Oriental Design, Larged Fluted Shade	400.00
Electric, Green Onyx, 44 In.	175.00
Electric, Gustav Stickley, Floor	3300.00
Electric, Hall, Hanging, Cast Brass Frame, Curved Glass Panels, 25 In.	275.00
Electric, Hammered Copper, Conch Shell Bud, E.E.Burton, 1910, 24 In.	3400.00
Electric, Harlequin, Ivrene Face, Millefiori Shade, Marble Base, 1927	595.00
Electric, Hedi Schoop, Television, Comedy-Tragedy, Large	75.00
Electric, Lady At Well, Art Glass Shade, Signed, Bronze, 30 In.	950.00
Electric, Leaded Shade, Spiral Design, Scalloped Rim, Bronze, 21 In.	290.00
Electric, Lily Design, Baluster Base, Metal, Slag Glass Shade, 20 In.	400.00
Electric, Metal, Green Paint, 2 Arms, 21 In.	45.00
Electric, Mission Oak Slag Shade	305.00
Electric, Oak, Jigsaw Cut Design, Trapezoidal Shade, 21 X 17 In.	400.00
Electric, Oak, Trapezoidal Slag Glass Shade, 4 Branches, 14 X 18 In.	260.00
Electric, Owl, Figural, Cast Metal, 15 In.	30.00
Electric, Parker, White Glass, Blue Windmill & Sailboat, 29 In.	985.00
Electric, Patinated Metal, Tan Slag Glass Shade, Baluster, 23 1/2 In.	300.00
Electric, Peacock Feather, Amber, 10 In.	300.00
Electric, Puppy Dog, Black Base, Glass	195.00
Electric, Rock Crystal, Bird Shape, Gilt Leaf Base, Silk Shade, Pair	195.00
Electric, Roses, Metal Base, Porcelain, English, Bulbous, 12 In., Pair	225.00
Electric, Scotty, Chalkware, Glass Eyes, 1930s	20.00
Electric, Scrolled Foo Dog Head, Enamel On Bronze, Scene, 24 1/2 In.	375.00
Electric, Statue of Liberty, 1930s	35.00
Electric, Table, Silk Shade, With Painted Parrots, Beaded Fringe	225.00
Electric, Wicker, Dome Shade, Floor Model	425.00
Electric, Wicker, Latticework Shade, Splint Base, 1910, 24 X 18 In.	100.00
Electric, Wicker, Natural Brown, Silk Lining	225.00
Electric, Wooden Barrel Shaped Canteen, Blue, Homespun Shade, 19 In.	275.00
Electric, Yellow Slag Glass, Metal, Trapezoidal, C.1910, 23 X 14 In.	300.00
Entrance, Brass, Original Hanger, 18 In., Pair	253.00
Fairy, Bisque, Owl, Amber, Black Glass Eyes, Marked, 4 X 4 In.	345.00
Fairy, Clarke Base, Cranberry & White Verre Moire, 4 1/2 In.	175.00
Fairy, Clarke, Citron Nailsea, Clear Ribbed, Signed Base, 6 1/2 In.	145.00
Fairy, Cobweb, With Jewels, Brass	155.00
Fairy, Diamond-Quilted, Pyramid Shape, Clarke Base, 3 1/2 In.	145.00
Fairy, Jewels Hand From Leaf Top, 4 Chains, Brass	80.00
Fairy, Kitten's Head, Figural, Bisque, Green Eyes, Blue Collar	485.00
Fairy, Nailsea Shade, Signed Clarke Base	325.00
Fairy, Pyramid, Yellow & White, Verre Moire, Clarke Base	145.00
Fairy, Red Verre Moire Shade, Ribbed Dish Base, Signed	265.00
Fairy, Silver Inclusions, Green	135.00

Fairy, Swirl Mother-of-Pearl, Ruffled Edge At Base, 5 In. 455.00
Fairy, Verre Moire, Blue, Dome Shade, White Loops, 5 1/2 In. 425.00
Figural, Woman, With Urn, Glass Font, Metal Base, 23 In. 25.00
Finger, Double Wedding Ring, Flint 135.00
Finger, Kerosene, Coolidge Drape 85.00
Finger, Pressed Glass Font, Aqua, Shade, Polar Bear, English, 9 In. 78.00
Finger, Tin Bottom, Stamped Made In United States of America 28.00
Finger, Vapo Cresolene 28.00
Fluid, Brass, Miller Co., Chimney, 14 1/4 In. 55.00
Fluid, Elongated Loop Pattern, Square Base, Clear, 11 3/8 In. 275.00
Fluid, Four Printie Block, Amethyst, 12 In. 2100.00
Fluid, Four Printie Block, Clear, 12 1/4 In., Pair 450.00
Fluid, Four Printie Block, Pewter Collar, Purple, 10 3/4 In., Pair 3200.00
Fluid, Horn of Plenty, Pressed Lace Base 2800.00
Fluid, Kosmos, Plated Metal, Swivel Reflector, Chimney, 16 3/4 In. 132.00
Fluid, Loop & Ellipse, Hexagonal, Emerald Green, 8 5/8 In. 2200.00
Fluid, New England Glass Co., Sapphire Blue, 10 1/8 In., Pair 3100.00
Fluid, Octagonal Font, Flat & Concave Panels, Amethyst, 9 5/8 In., Pr. 3800.00
Fluid, Pewter, Smith & Co., 7 1/2 In. 275.00
Fluid, Pressed Glass Font, Milk Glass Base, 11 In. 121.00
Fluid, Pressed Glass, Ring Handle, 13 In. 44.00
Fluid, Punty & Ellipse, Amethyst, 10 In., Pair 4250.00
Fluid, Ruby Flash Glass, Brass Column Stem, Marble Base, 16 In., Pair 275.00
Fluid, Sweetheart Pattern, Clear, 10 7/8 In., Pair 1050.00
Fluid, Three Printie Block, Amethyst, 9 5/8 In. 2300.00
Fluid, Thumbprint Pattern, Brass Collar, Scalloped Base, Opalescent 1200.00
Fluid, Waffle Pattern, Clambroth, 11 5/8 In. 1100.00
Fluid, Whale Oil Burner, Brass Shade Ring, Flint, C.1840, 7 In., Pair 600.00
Gas, 6 Panel, 17 In. 265.00
Gas, Exit, Victorian, Bronze Frame, Glass Inset, Flowers 200.00
Gas, Hall, Hanging, Hexagonal Clear Globe, Frosted, Clear Floral, 33 In. 450.00
Gone With The Wind, Floral Hand Painted Shade, 21 In. 120.00
Gone With The Wind, Flowers, Web Design, Milk Glass, 18 In. 140.00
Gone With The Wind, Iris, Red Satin, Inverted Pear Font, 26 In. 595.00
Gone With The Wind, Red Satin Glass, Poppy Design, Brass, 1890s, 25 In. 800.00
Gone With The Wind, Red Satin Glass, Puffy, Brass Base, 27 1/2 In. 625.00
Gone With The Wind, Red Satin Glass, Quilted Diamond Drape, 27 In. 650.00
Gone With The Wind, Red Satin, Electric 400.00
Gone With The Wind, Tan Water Lilies 265.00
Grease, Pottery 360.00
Hand, Fishscale Pattern, Original Chimney & Reflector 285.00
Hand, Loop Pattern, Reverse Waisted, Clambroth, 4 9/16 In. 350.00
Hand, Purple Font, Fishscale, With Reflector 145.00
Hand, Vertical Ribs, Bulbous Foot, Blown Glass, 3 3/8 In. 225.00
     LAMP, HANDEL, see Handel, Lamp
Hanging, 4 Cherub Heads, Foliage, Carved ....*Illus* 150.00
Hanging, Cast Metal Filigree, Green Slag Glass, 6 Sides, 31 In. 90.00
Hanging, Copper Wheel Engraved Panels, Gilt Metal Frame, 12 3/4 In. 40.00
Hanging, Victorian, Cranberry Opalescent Shade, Small 375.00
Hearse, Beveled Glass Lens, Brass & Bronze, Pair 1500.00
Heating, Victorian, Copper, Reflector, Folding Handle In Back 125.00
Kerosene, Acme, Chimney & Reflector, Signed, Miniature 85.00
Kerosene, Apollo, Frosted Font & Stem, Canary, 12 In. 260.00
Kerosene, Blue Willow, Gold Edge, 9 In. 42.00
Kerosene, Brass Base, Floral Globe Shade, 22 In. 50.00
Kerosene, Brass, Marked Perkins House Safety Lamp, 8 3/4 In. 200.00
Kerosene, Bull's-Eye, Clear, Ruffled, 6 In. 65.00
Kerosene, Bull's-Eye, Green, 10 1/2 In. 175.00
Kerosene, Colonial Man & Lady, On Side of Pillar, Porcelain, 10 In. 24.00
Kerosene, Cosmos, Clear, 7 1/2 In. 125.00
Kerosene, Cosmos, No.S286, Pink, Miniature 275.00
Kerosene, Cosmos, No.S337, Miniature 285.00
Kerosene, Crossed Cannons, C.1860 .... 155.00
Kerosene, Daisy With Large Bull's-Eye Foot & Shoulders, Miniature 110.00

Kerosene, Figural, Colonial Man & Lady, Porcelain, 10 1/2 In.	24.00
Kerosene, Greek Key, 6 In.	95.00
Kerosene, Green Cut To Clear Font, Opaque White Foot, 9 5/8 In.	300.00
Kerosene, Green Opalescent Font, Hand Painted Shade, 20 In.	150.00
Kerosene, Hand, 4 Seasons, Emerald Green Glass	150.00
Kerosene, Hanging, Bristol Shade, Prisms, Electrified	500.00
Kerosene, Hobnail Base & Globe, Clear, 7 In.	22.00
Kerosene, Larkin, Hanging, Large Cabbage Roses On Shade, Font Prisms	300.00
Kerosene, Lincoln Drape ....*Illus*	800.00
Kerosene, Mother-of-Pearl, Pink, Melon Ribbed, Brass Foot & Top, 18 In.	895.00
Kerosene, Peachblow, Reverse Painted Winter Scene, Raspberry, 10 In.	295.00
Kerosene, Princess Feather, 12 In.	125.00
Kerosene, Sandwich Glass, Cranberry, Brass Column, Marble Base, 10 In.	578.00
Kerosene, Sawtooth & Thumbprint, Hexagonal Base, Flint, 8 3/8 In.	70.00
Kerosene, Silver Metal, Bird Handles, Red Millefiori Shade, 24 In.	375.00
Kerosene, Silver Plate, Pink Ribbed Overlay Shade, Burner, 11 In.	325.00
Kerosene, Student, Manhattan Brass, Pat.1876-79	425.00
Kerosene, Winged Lady, Metal Shade, White Metal, Paris Seal, 29 In.	1250.00
Lucerne, Brass, Snuffer, Wick Pick & Tweezers On Chains, 16 3/8 In.	50.00
Miner's, Chicken Finial, Iron, Twisted Hanger, 7 In.	75.00
Miner's, Coffepot Shape, 2 1/4 In.	35.00
Miner's, Fat Lamp, Copper Font, Tin Spout & Lid, Pat.May 1908	65.00
Miner's, Just-Rite, Carbide, Reflector	25.00
Miner's, Just-Rite, Hand, Hook, Box	75.00
Miner's, Safety, Davey, Brass	200.00
Miner's, Safety, Wolf, Brass & Iron	60.00
Miner's, Sunshine, Anton & Sons, Brass	80.00
Moe Bridges, Art Glass, Table Model	4000.00
Moe Bridges, Bronze, Art Deco	275.00
Moe Bridges, Greek Ruins, 18 In.	1850.00
Moe Bridges, Reverse Painted, Signed	2750.00
Night, White Opaque, Coolidge Drape	22.50
Oil, Alva, Blue Striped Font, Frosted Base	250.00
Oil, Amberette, Amber Bars, 10 In.	195.00
Oil, Black Glass, Acanthus Leaf Base, Pat.1890, 11 1/2 In.	150.00
Oil, Brass, 1877 Patent Date, Miniature	25.00
Oil, Bull's-Eye & Fleur-De-Lis, Brass Stem	110.00
Oil, Bull's-Eye, Miniature	25.00
Oil, Canadian Bull's-Eye, Blue Milk Glass, Base, Clear Font, 8 1/4 In.	800.00
Oil, Canadian Bull's-Eye, Burner, Green, 8 In.	125.00
Oil, Cast Metal, S.N.& H.C.Ufford, Boston, Pat.Feb.4, 1851	75.00
Oil, Cobalt Blue To Clear Font, Amethyst Foot, Brass Collar, 9 1/2 In.	150.00
Oil, Columbian Coin, 8 1/2 In.	125.00
Oil, Cosmos Variant, Green Band, Milk Glass	295.00
Oil, Daisy, Bull's-Eye Foot & Shoulder, Miniature	50.00
Oil, Diamond Thumbprint, Brass Stem, Marble Base	395.00
Oil, Double Spout, Saucer Base, Brass Plated, 7 1/2 In.	55.00
Oil, Enameling & Gilt, Overlay Luster Base, White To Cranberry, 37 In.	115.00
Oil, Glass, Coins Around Stem, Columbian Expo, 1492-1892, 9 1/2 In.	125.00
Oil, Hanging, Counterweighted, Milk Glass Shade, Brass Frame, 14 In.	425.00
Oil, Lion's Head, Glass, Pair	1800.00
Oil, Little Buttercup, Cobalt Blue, Miniature	95.00
Oil, Little Buttercup, No.36	70.00
Oil, Milk Glass, Block Pattern, Matching Shade, Miniature	95.00
Oil, Night, Little Harry's, Cobalt Blue, Brass, Chimney, 1877, 3 1/2 In.	225.00
Oil, Prince Edward, Pink Cased Glass, C.1890	1450.00
Oil, Princess Feather, Large	47.00
Oil, Princess, Pink Cased Glass, C.1890	1650.00
Oil, Rayo, Brass, Islamic Design, Paper Shade, 26 In., Pair	60.00
Oil, Repousse, Design On Scroll Feet, Electrified, Brass, 20 In., Pair	225.00
Oil, Roman Key, Miniature	40.00
Oil, Rosa Pattern, Satin Bowl With Leaves, Emerald Green	100.00
Oil, Sawtooth & Thumbprint Font, Hexagonal, Flint, 9 3/4 In.	110.00
Oil, Sheet Brass Spout, Weighted Base, 19 1/2 In.	25.00

Oil, Snowflake, Square Font, Blue Opalescent 375.00
Oil, Snuffer Cap, Iron Banded Base For Weight, Brass, 9 1/4 In. 375.00
Oil, Star & Punty 250.00
Oil, Student, Manhattan Brass, Shade, 1876–79 .... 330.00
Oil, Twinkle, Amethyst Clear, Miniature 195.00
Oil, U.S.Coin, Clear Coins, 9 1/2 In. 500.00
Oil, Venice, Clear Opalescent, Frosted Base 250.00
Oil, Waffle & Bull's–Eye, Metal Reservoir, 8 3/4 In. 600.00
Old Mission, Kopperkraft, Hammered Copper, 13 3/4 In. ....*Illus* 2700.00
     LAMP, PAIRPOINT, see Pairpoint, Lamp
Peg, Blown Glass, Tin Drop Burner, New Wooden Base, 8 In. 105.00
Peg, Cut Rayed Design, Clear, 5 1/4 In. 45.00
Peg, Lemon Yellow Swirl, Satin Glass, Mushroom Shades, 16 In., Pair ... 1195.00
Peg, Pewter Collar, Double–Drop Burner, 4 1/2 In., Pair 225.00
Perfume, Full Figured Eagle 250.00
Piano, Adjustable Foliate Font, Paw Feet, Bronze 225.00
Piano, Brass, Original Globe 395.00
Sconce, 2–Light, Brass, Star Shape, Rosette, Burnished, American, 12 In. ... 125.00
Sconce, 2–Light, Louis XVI, Painted Bronze, Female Mask, 27 In., Pair ... 2750.00
Sconce, 5–Light, Louis Philippe, Bronze, Winged Putti, 1840, 19 In., Pair ... 1540.00
Sconce, Candle, Crimped Reflector, Mirror Insert, C.1830, 14 In. 2950.00
Sconce, Candle, Hanging, Beaded Back Plate, C.1810, 11 1/2 In. 150.00
Sconce, Extended Hand Holding Cup, Plaster, Mirrored Back, 11 In., Pr. ... 2200.00
Sconce, Wall, Victorian, Brass, Cherubs, Mirrors, 2 Sockets, Pair 275.00
Sinumbra, Cornelius, Labeled, Original Chimney 2310.00
Sinumbra, Frosted Globe, Black Glass, 16 1/2 In. 7750.00
Skater's, Blue Globe, Marked Jewel, Tin, 7 In. 150.00
Skater's, Clear Globe, Brass, 6 7/8 In. 70.00
Skater's, Embossed Clear Globe, Perko Wonder, Junior, Tin, 6 1/2 In. 55.00
Sparking, Camphene, Single Tube With Cap, Pewter, 4 3/4 In. 260.00
Sparking, Handled Saucer Base, Cylindrical Font, Pewter, American 85.00
Street, Original Glass & Burner On Post, Ham, 1880s 295.00
Student, Brass, Converted To Electric, 21 In. 245.00
Student, Double, Cased Green Shades 500.00
Student, Double, Slag Glass, Oak, Trapezoidal Yellow Shades, 21 1/2 In. ... 250.00
Student, Gilt Metal, Cased Glass Shade 220.00
Student, Gooseneck, Custard Fluted Shade 38.00
Student, Green Cased Shade, All Original 495.00
Student, Miller Student Lamp, Brass, White Shade 450.00
Student, Perfection 1881, Green Glass Shade, 21 In. 950.00
     LAMP, TIFFANY, see Tiffany, Lamp
Torch, Dietz, For Repairs On Highway, Ball Type, 1920s 25.00

Lamp, Hanging,
4 Cherub Heads,
Foliage, Carved

Lamp, Old Mission,
Kopperkraft,
Hammered Copper,
13 3/4 In.

Lamp, Vapo–Cresolene

Torchere, Black & Gold Lacquer, Chinese Export, C.1850, Pair 7150.00
Torchere, Blackamoor, Standing, Shoulder Torch Stand, 5 Ft.2 In., Pair 4125.00
Torchere, Conical Metal Shade, Glass Cylinders, C.1930, 5 Ft.7 In. 2090.00
Torchere, Gilt Metal, Art Glass Shades, Pair 1450.00
Torchere, Louis XVI Style, 12 Light, 5 In., Pair 8800.00
Torchere, Renaissance Style, Leaded Stained Glass Panels, 78 In., Pr. 300.00
Vapo–Cresolene ....*Illus*   50.00
Wall Bracket, Brass, Cast Foliage, Adams & Westlake Co., 14 In. 60.00
Whale Oil, American, Tin, 1850s 60.00
Whale Oil, Apple Font, Brass, 8 In., Pair 475.00
Whale Oil, Double, Brass Wick, Attached Chain, 7 In. 165.00
Whale Oil, Ellipse & Bull's–Eye, 6–Paneled Hexagonal Fonts, 10 In. 650.00
Whale Oil, Heart Pattern, Sandwich Glass, 8 3/4 In. 125.00
Whale Oil, Loop Pattern, Pewter Collar, Emerald Green, 10 In. 7250.00
Whale Oil, Medallion Back, Italian Bronze, 4 In. 10.00
Whale Oil, Pewter, Ear Shaped Handle, American, 6 In. 150.00
Whale Oil, Star & Punty, Finger 400.00
Whale Oil, Star & Punty, Sandwich Glass, 11 In. 425.00
Whale Oil, Three Printie Block Pattern, Pewter Color, Blue, Pair 4600.00
Whale Oil, Three Printie Block, Emerald Green, 9 In. 1100.00
Whale Oil, Wall Mounted, Tin, C.1825 .... 135.00

A lantern is a special type of lighting device. It has a light source, usually a candle, totally hidden inside the walls of the lantern. Light is seen through holes or glass sections.

LANTERN, B & O RR, Cobalt Blue Glass 110.00
Barn, Black Painted Tin, Triangular, Late 19th Century, 22 In. 165.00
Bicycle, Solar, C.M.Hall Co., Red Lens 72.50
Candle, 3 Protruding Windows, Conical Top, Ring Handle, 9 In. 155.00
Candle, Bull's–Eye, Brass Trim, Reflectors, Hinged Door, 13 In. 75.00
Candle, Bull's–Eye, Punched Design, American, Tin, C.1800, 12 In. 650.00
Coal Mine, Safety, Clanny 125.00
Cole, No.1909, Brass, 13 In. 70.00
Copper, Glass, Top Hinge, Made For Over Post, 33 1/2 In. 125.00
Dark Room, Tin, Black, Striped, Carbutt's Dry Plate, 1882, 17 In. 55.00
Dietz, Kerosene, Acme Inspector Lamp, Tin, 14 1/4 In. 35.00
Dietz, King, American, LaFrance 180.00
Dietz, Little Wizard, Red Globe, 1923 .... 20.00
Dietz, Nickel Plated, Clear Lens, ɔ Filler Cap, 18 3/4 In. 22.00
Dietz, No.40, Gas Service 20.00
Dietz, Scout, Hand, Pat.July 26, 1904 .... 65.00
Domed Top, Pierced Tin, Hanging, Geometric, 19th Century, 18 In. 275.00
Folding, Stonebridge, Mica, Tin, 10 In. 48.00
Folding, Tin, 3 Sided Mica, Stonebridge Pat.1908, 10 In. 145.00
Hanging, Hexagonal Form, Twisted Arches, Italian, Iron, 40 In., Pair 500.00
Kerosene, Tin, U.S.Headlight Co.Decal, Wooden Base, 23 In. 65.00
L & N Extended Base Globe, Armspear Frame 80.00
Pierced Tin, Blown Glass, 10 1/2 In. 198.00
Pine, Glazed Panels, Metal Swing Handle, 19th Century, 13 X 6 In. 165.00
Rayo, No.15, Solid Brass 125.00
Rayo, No.77, Cold Blast Kerosene, Red Globe 25.00
Skater's, Brass, 7 In. 85.00
Skater's, Japanned, Candle Style 15.00
Slag Glass, Iron, Wall, Square Strapwork Form, C.1910, 21 1/2 In. 125.00
Tent, Collapsible, Dome Top, Tole, 1865 Patent, 3 X 5 In. 150.00
Tin, 7 Oblong Glass Inserts, 13 In. 70.00
Tin, Pressed Globe, Brass Top, S.Sargents, Pat.Sept.17, 1861, 13 In. 75.00
Tin, Whale Oil Burner, Ring Handle, Clear Blown Globe, 10 In. 365.00
Wabash, Blue Log Etched Globe, Marked Wabash Frame 300.00
Wooden Post, Pointed Finial, Black Paint, 36 In., Pair 225.00

Le Verre Francais Le Verre Francais is one of the many types of cameo glass made in France. The glass was made by the C. Schneider factory in Epinay-sur-Seine from 1920 to 1933. It is a mottled glass, usually decorated

Leeds, Bowl, Floral Design, Swan Finial,
Octagonal

Limoges, Plaque, Woman, Basket,
C.1900, 12 3/4 X 9 1/4 In.

with floral designs, and bears the incised signature "Le Verre Francais."

LE VERRE FRANCAIS, Bowl, Seed Pods, Red–Brown Exterior, 11 In. 860.00
Compote, 7 1/2 X 7 1/2 In. 450.00
Lamp, Band of Tulips, Matching Dome, Marked, 13 In. 2750.00
Lamp, Cats, Coolie Hat Form Shade, Yellow, Salmon, 15 In. 7700.00
Vase, Flying Geese, Yellow, Blue & Tortoiseshell, 10 In. 625.00
Vase, Geese In Flight, Rushes, Mottled Interior, 5 In. 700.00
Vase, Purple, Red & Burgundy Flowers, 11 In. 625.00

Leather is tanned animal hide and it has been used to make decorative and useful objects for centuries. Leather objects must be carefully preserved with proper humidity and oiling or the leather will deteriorate and crack. This damage cannot be repaired.

LEATHER, Belt, U.S.Infantry, Model 1856, Black, White Buff Inside, 1859–60 .... 165.00
Bird Calls, Mouth, Original Envelope, 12 Piece 4.00
Bull Whip, Braided 20.00
Case, Whiskey Bottle, 1932 .... 20.00
Chaps, Cowboy's, Latch Stitch, Bat Wings, Corner Buckle 225.00
Football Helmet, Wilson Pro–College, Black, Box, 1942 .... 145.00
Horse Collar 15.00
Money Belt, Adjustable 25.00
Pitcher, Labeled From Earl of Cravens, Warwickshire, 21 1/2 In. 50.00
Pocket Folder, Army Corp.Engineers, Blueprints, 1918 .... 35.00
Riding Crop, Leather Shaft, 14K Gold End 125.00
Saddle, 2 Hump Camel, Wooden 225.00
Saddle, U.S.Army, Leather Stirrups 100.00
Scabbard, For Rifle, Northwest, Floral Beadwood 850.00
Suitcase, Keen Kutter, Salesman's 350.00
Wallet, Lady's, Victorian 4.00

LEEDS POTTERY, Leeds pottery was made at Leeds, Yorkshire, England, from 1774 to 1878. Most Leeds ware was not marked. Early Leeds pieces had distinctive twisted handles with a greenish glaze on part of the creamy ware. Later ware often had blue borders on the creamy pottery.

LEEDS, Basket, Undertray, Lattice Cut Border, Creamware, C.1780, 9 1/4 In. 1200.00
Bowl, Floral Design, Swan Finial, Octagonal ....*Illus* 160.00
Dish, Swan Cover 750.00
Pepper Castor, Ribbed Green Band, Gray 70.00

Pepper Pot, Brown Enameled Bands, Creamware, 4 1/2 In. 125.00
Plate, Oriental, Blue Feather Edge, Soft Paste, 6 1/2 In. 150.00
Plate, Peafowl, 5 Colors, 8 In. 465.00
Pot, Peafowl 600.00

The Geo. Zoltan Lefton Company has imported porcelains to be sold in America since 1940. The pieces are often marked with the Lefton name. The firm is still in business. The company mark has changed through the years and objects can be dated accurately by the shape of the mark.

LEFTON, Bank, Cat 14.00
Compote, Flower, Openwork 15.00
Cookie Jar, Kitty, Blue 17.00
Cookie Jar, Tigger 32.00
Cookie Jar, Yogi Bear 35.00
Figurine, Bluebird, Marked, 1940s 72.00
Figurine, Boy, Wearing Cowboy Hat, Playing Guitar 9.00
Figurine, Doctor, Spanking New-Born, Label 22.50
Figurine, Kewpie, Bisque, Hand Painted 27.50
Figurine, Pheasant, Pair 35.00
Planter, Elephant 15.00
Planter, Madonna, White 10.00
Plaque, Fish 6.00
Plaque, Railroad Scene, Mountains, Hand Painted, 8 1/2 X 6 In. 15.00
Plaque, Relief Flowers, Hand Painted, Bisque 12.50
Salt & Pepper, Mr.& Mrs.Claus Heads 15.00
Sugar & Creamer, Monk, Goebel Type 17.50
Toby, Robert E.Lee 25.00
Tumble-Up, Pink Roses, White Ground, 7 1/2 In. 20.00
Tureen, Basket Weave, Ladle, Tray, Vegetables On Cover 35.00

Legras was founded in 1864 by Auguste Legras at St. Denis, France. It is best known for cameo glass and enamel-decorated glass with Art Nouveau designs. Legras merged with Pantin in 1920 and became the Verreries et Cristalleries de St. Denis et de Pantin Reunies.

LEGRAS, Bottle, Cameo, Lake Scene, 3-Sided Body, 3 3/4 In. ....*Illus* 250.00
Bowl, Ships, Mountains, Lakes, Orange Ground, Signed, 4 1/4 In. 275.00
Bowl, Winter Scene, Snow, Trees & Birds, Signed, 12 In. 750.00
Rose Bowl, Cameo Cut Leaves & Berries On Vines, Signed, 3 1/2 In. 375.00
Vase, Cameo Glass, Magenta Leaves, White To Orange, 11 1/2 In. 595.00
Vase, Cameo, Spring Scene, Tricornered, 4 In. 550.00
Vase, Enameled Scenic, 10 1/2 In. 185.00
Vase, Frosted Blue, Deer, Foliage, Trees, Birds, 9 In. 1250.00
Vase, Gray Pink, Overlay Red, Vine Design, Signed, 15 In. 500.00
Vase, Peachblow, 6 In. 310.00
Vase, Purple Grape Leaves, Vines Cut To Clear, 26 1/2 In., Pair 1400.00
Vase, Scenic, Silver Mounted, Signed, 12 In. 650.00
Vase, Winter Scene, Painted Snow At Base, Trees, Signed, 15 3/4 In. 325.00
Vase, Winter Trees, Stormy Ground, Birds, Signed, 7 In. 780.00

Walter Scott Lenox and Jonathan Cox founded the Ceramic Art Company in Trenton, New Jersey, in 1889. In 1906, Lenox left and started his own company. The company makes a porcelain that is similar to Irish Belleek. The marks used by the firm have changed through the years and collectors prefer the earlier examples.

LENOX, see also Ceramic Art Co.
LENOX, Bookends, Queen Nefertiti, Jade Green, 8 X 5 In., Pair 95.00
Bowl, Art Deco, Sterling Silver Overlay, Blue, Footed 115.00
Bowl, Pink, Ruffled, Green Mark, 6 In. 85.00
Bowl, Vegetable, Temple Blossom, Oval 54.00
Bowl, White, Gold, Footed, 11 In. 25.00
Box, Cover, Green, Gold Wash Handle, 7 In. 95.00
Bust, Woman, Profile, Deco, Green Mark, 4 In. 95.00

Cake Plate, Silver Overlay, 1st Mark, 1906, 10 1/2 In.	85.00
Candleholder, 3–Light, Art Deco, White	275.00
Candleholder, Dolphin, Ivory, Gold Trim	35.00
Candleholder, Pink & Gold, 3 1/4 In., Pair	65.00
Candlestick, Cream, Gold Trim, Palette Mark, 8 1/2 In., Pair	85.00
Candy Dish, Pedestal, Cover, Green, 4 1/4 In.	42.00
Candy Dish, Pink, Cover, Round, 7 1/2 In.	32.00
Chocolate Set, Silver On Brown, Wooden Handle, 3 Piece ....*Illus*	400.00
Coffeepot, Westwind	85.00
Compote, White, Gold, Flared	22.00
Cookie Jar, Blue Nob, White	50.00
Cup & Saucer, Cattail	14.00
Cup & Saucer, Deco, Inverted Heart, Silver Overlay, Palette Mark	40.00
Cup & Saucer, Sterling Silver Holder, Green Mark	37.50
Cup & Saucer, Temple Blossom	26.00
Dish, Leaf, Center Handle, Divided, Green Mark	55.00
Dish, Leaf, Pink, 9 1/4 In.	44.00
Dish, Lotus Leaf, Ivory, Gold Trim, Handle, 10 1/2 In.	70.00
Dish, Shell Shape, Ivory, 9 1/2 In.	10.00
Figurine, Bird, Coral Tree Stump, 5 1/2 In.	125.00
Jam Jar, Cover, Underplate, Fairmount Pattern	55.00
Jam Jar, Silver Overlay	75.00
Lamp, Figural, Nude Lady, Art Deco, 1929, 12 1/2 In.	675.00
Lamp, Figural, Nude, Art Deco, White Bisque, 11 In.	350.00
Mask, Male & Female, Square Base, Incised 1933, 8 In., Pair	495.00
Mug, Atlantic City, N.J., Imperial Council Session, 1933, Large	48.00
Mug, Harvard College, Green Mark, 1910, 5 1/4 In.	85.00
Pitcher, Cider, 3 Colors of Grapes	150.00
Pitcher, Lemonade, Hand Painted Lemons, Blossoms, Palette, 11 In.	195.00
Pitcher, Lemonade, Lemons, Leaves, Blossoms, Signed, 10 3/4 In.	235.00
Pitcher, Lemonade, Silver Overlay	225.00
Pitcher, Pink & White, 7 1/2 In.	35.00
Pitcher, Pink, Green Mark, 4 In.	45.00
Plate, Temple Blossom, 10 1/4 In.	18.00
Platter, Ming, 13 1/4 In.	40.00
Platter, Ming, 15 1/2 In.	60.00
Platter, Oak Leaf, White, Silver, 13 1/2 X 9 In.	28.00
Platter, Temple Blossom, 13 In.	75.00
Salt & Pepper, Nipper	50.00
Sherbet, Ear Handles, Ivory, Gilt Trim, Silver Frame, 10 Piece	350.00
Stein, Band of Flowers, Wide Band of Hanging Cherries, Marked, 7 In.	150.00
Stein, Monk, Hand Painted, Replaced Lid, 1/2 Liter	77.00

Lenox, Chocolate Set, Silver On Brown, Wooden Handle, 3 Piece

Low, Tile, Sheep, Village, Teal Blue, Signed A.D., 18 X 10 In.

Sugar & Creamer, Washington's Birthday, Cover	90.00
Sugar, Inverted Heart, Art Deco, Silver Overlay, Cover, Palette Mark	55.00
Swan, Gold Trim, Footed, 14K Gold Trim, 8 X 10 In.	135.00
Swan, Green Carnival, Imperial Label, 9 1/2 In.	28.50
Swan, Pink, Gold Trim	35.00
Swan, White, Gold Trim	25.00
Tankard, 3 Colors of Grapes, Palette Mark, 14 In.	275.00
Tankard, Green Handle, Lemon Foliage, Blossoms, Signed, 11 In.	245.00
Teapot, Mansfield	50.00
Teapot, Ming, Green Mark	45.00
Toby Jug, Marked Bailey Banks Biddle, Green Wreath	275.00
Toby Jug, William Penn, Treaty, White Indian Head Handle, Pink	165.00
Toby Jug, William Penn, Treaty, Indian Head Handle, All White	150.00
Vase, Bulbous Bottom, Pink, 7 1/2 In.	28.00
Vase, Bulbous, Medallions of Roses, Gold Trim, Marked, 7 1/2 In.	75.00
Vase, Fan Shape, Green, Marked, 7 1/4 In.	40.00
Vase, Meadowbrook, 10 In.	80.00
Vase, Peach, Enameled Daisies, 8 In.	95.00
Vase, Pink, 12 In.	70.00
Vase, Swan Handles, Ovington Label, Green Mark, 11 In.	125.00
Vase, Urn Shape, White, Green Wreath, 5 In., Pair	65.00

Letter openers have been used since the eighteenth century. Ivory and silver were favored by the well-to-do. In the late nineteenth century, the letter opener was popular as an advertising giveaway and many were made of metal or celluloid. Brass openers with figural handles were also popular.

LETTER OPENER, Alligator Head, Wooden	35.00
DuPont Explosives	30.00
Eagle Pencil, Pat.June 5, 1883	22.50
Fuller Brush	16.00
Head, Hammer Design, Union League Club, Sterling Silver, 1899	75.00
Illinois Traction System, Brass	65.00
Isaac Pincus & Sons, Hops, Tacoma, Wa.	14.00
Pittson Coal Co., Chicago, Bronze	9.00
Prudential Insurance, Fancy	35.00
Welsbach Gas Lights, Graphic	45.00
Yale Lock	32.00

The Libbey Glass Company has made glass of many types since 1888. Libbey made cut glass and tablewares that are collected today. The stemwares of the 1930s and 1940s are once again in style. The Toledo, Ohio, firm was purchased by Owens–Illinois in 1935 and is still working under the name "Libbey" as a division of that company.

LIBBEY, see also Amberina; Cut Glass; Maize

LIBBEY, Bowl, Finger, Underplate, Signed	75.00
Bowl, Glenda Pattern, Original Seal, C.1900, 9 In.	500.00
Bowl, Senora Pattern, Signed, 3 3/4 X 9 In.	475.00
Champagne, Figural, Squirrel	95.00
Compote, Turquoise Threading, Twisted Stem, 7 In.	225.00
Cordial, Concord Pattern, Signed	45.00
Cordial, Embassy Pattern, Signed, 6 3/4 In.	75.00
Cup, Figural, Leaf, World's Columbian Exposition	65.00
Decanter, Harvard Pattern, Pattern In Stopper, 13 In.	375.00
Decanter, Harvard Pattern, Spirit Jug, 14 In.	395.00
Decanter, Sultana Pattern, Cut Glass, Signed, 15 In.	875.00
Goblet, Blue Willow Border, 10 Oz.	8.00
Goblet, Corinthian Pattern, Notched Stem, Cut Base, Signed	57.50
Goblet, Opalescent Seated Cat Stem, Signed, 7 In.	125.00
Goblet, Water, Corinthian Pattern, Notched Stem, 7 Piece	400.00
Loving Cup, 3 Triple Notched Handles, Signed, 6 3/4 In.	910.00
Pitcher, Water, Libbey Pattern, 8 In.	535.00
Pitcher, Water, Signed, 10 1/2 In.	185.00

Pitcher, Wedgemere Pattern, Cut Glass, Signed, 6 3/4 X 6 In.	1450.00
Punch Set, Colonna Pattern, Signed, 8 Piece ...•..	540.00
Rose Bowl, Colonna Pattern, Sword Mark, Signed, 7 X 5 1/2 In.	450.00
Sauce Dish, Leaf Design	40.00
Sherry, Black Monkey Stem, 5 In.	85.00
Sugar & Creamer, Flute Pattern, High Standard, Signed	2450.00
Sugar & Creamer, Pinwheels, Triple Notched Handles, Globular Shape	175.00
Sugar Holder, For Cubes, Signed, 7 1/2 In.	65.00
Tray, Aztec Pattern, Cut Glass, Signed, 12 1/2 In.	4950.00
Tray, Brilliant Center, Engraved Rim, Signed, 12 In.	700.00
Tray, Colonna Pattern, Sword Mark, 10 X 7 1/2 In.	375.00
Tray, Libbey Pattern, Signed, Round, 12 In.	675.00
Tumbler, Juice, Harvard Pattern, Pair	75.00
Vase, Amberina, Signed, 11 1/4 In.	350.00
Vase, Bud, Floral Cut, Engraved, 12 1/2 In.	150.00
Water Set, Brilliant Cut, 5 Piece	495.00
Wine, Black Opaque Bear Stem, Signed	165.00
Wine, Opalescent Cat Stem, 7 In.	110.00

Cigarettes became popular in the late nineteenth century and with the cigarette came matches and cigarette lighters. All types of lighters are collected, from solid gold to the first of the recent disposable lighters. Most examples found were made after 1940.

LIGHTER, Brass, Souvenir 1918 Verdun	75.00
Butane, Cartier, Sterling Silver	60.00
Cat, Arched Back, Table	20.00
Cigar Store, With Cutter, Purple Globe, No.78, Patent 1901	425.00
Cigar, Art Nouveau Monkey	25.00
Cigar, Don Rosa, Cigar Cutter	180.00
Cigar, Electric, Walnut, Photograph Marquee, 1920s	75.00
Cigar, Jump Spark	375.00
Cigar, Lamp, C.1880	475.00
Cigar, Midland Spark, Battery Operated, C.1920, 7 1/2 X 16 In.	595.00
Cigar, Midland, Original Coil Works, Oak, 1910	325.00
Cigar, W.C.Fields, Electric	55.00
Cigar, Young Patriot, Marble Base, Gas Flame From Top of Flagpole	275.00
Cigarette, A & P Gas Lite	15.00
Cigarette, Automobile, Marked Lucky Car	125.00
Cigarette, Black Bartender, Ronson	65.00
Cigarette, Camel Cigarettes, Brass	45.00
Cigarette, Camera On Tripod, Occupied Japan	20.00
Cigarette, Canadian National Railways, Box	10.00
Cigarette, Chase Brass, 1965	20.00
Cigarette, Demley Surelite, Austria, Brass	10.00
Cigarette, Derringer Gun, Wooden Stand, Box, 6 In.	35.00
Cigarette, Dog, Bronze	15.00
Cigarette, Dow Oven Cleaner Can, Lighter On Top	12.00
Cigarette, Dunhill, Pistol	100.00
Cigarette, Evans, Case, Combination	7.50
Cigarette, Evans, Paperweight, Gold Swirls, Gold Dust, Ball Shape	45.00
Cigarette, Goodyear Tires, Bottle Shape, Cobalt Blue	35.00
Cigarette, Goodyear, Chrome, 1950 Time To Sell	15.00
Cigarette, Grizzley Brake Lining, Bear, Chrome Lever, 1940s	3.00
Cigarette, High–Top Shoe, Dated 1912	12.00
Cigarette, Kitty Clover Potato Chips	30.00
Cigarette, Lady's, Ronson, Art Deco	10.00
Cigarette, Lektrolite Flameless, Deco Style, 1930s, 15 In.	195.00
Cigarette, Miss Cutie, Lower Body	22.00
Cigarette, Nude On Front, 1930s	45.00
Cigarette, Parker Silent Flame, Nude	16.00
Cigarette, Pentax Camera Shape	10.00
Cigarette, RC Cola, Bottle Shape, 1930s, 2 1/2 In.	12.00
Cigarette, Revolving Space Capsule, With Music Box	15.00
Cigarette, Ronson, Footed, Beaded Swirl, Silver Plate	12.00

Cigarette, Ronson, Penciliter	50.00
Cigarette, Ronson, Sterling Silver	30.00
Cigarette, Roulette Wheel	12.50
Cigarette, Royal Crown, Bottle Shape	18.00
Cigarette, Sam Kelso, Figural	14.00
Cigarette, Scotty Dog, Figural	15.00
Cigarette, Sterling Silver, Okinawa, World War II	17.00
Cigarette, Texaco	5.00
Cigarette, Waterford, Table	50.00
Cigarette, Whip Wheel	7.00
Grizzley Brake Lining, Angelo Automotive, Chrome Thumb, 1940s	3.50
Nude, Figural	68.00
Pistol, Ronson, Pat.1910	95.00
Ronson, Chrome, Small	6.00
Ronson, Crown	10.00
Ronson, Touch–Type, Black & Chrome	50.00
Ship's Wheel, Chrome	12.00
Stove, Ronson Pist–O Liter, Cap Pistol Shape, Dated 1910	5.00
Telephones, Shows Phones From 1875 To 1964, Metal	35.00
Thanks, Jerry Vale, 14K Gold Plated	15.00

Lightning rods were placed on barns and wooden houses to protect the building from fire. Lightning rods are now favored by folk art collectors, although most were commercially made. The glass balls added to the rods were for decorative purposes only. The earliest glass balls for lightning rods date from the 1840s. Today most lightning rods have plastic instead of glass balls.

LIGHTNING ROD, Ball, Gold Mercury	25.00
Ball, Silver Mercury	20.00

Limoges porcelain has been made in Limoges, France, since the mid-nineteenth century. Fine porcelains were made by many factories including Haviland, Ahrenfeldt, Guerin, Pouyat, Elite, and others. Modern porcelains are being made at Limoges and the word "Limoges" as part of the mark is not an indication of age. Haviland is listed as a separate category in this book.

LIMOGES, Basket, Hand Painted Grapes, 10 1/4 In.	65.00
Box, Hand Painted, Floral Panel, Cobalt Blue Ground, Cover, 6 In.	40.00
Box, Yellow Roses, Brown To Ivory, 1911, 6 In.	35.00
Cake Plate, Cupid Scene	225.00
Candlestick, Floral Scalloped Top & Bottom, 5 1/2 In., Pair	65.00
Celery, Green Leaves, Pink Flowers, Gold Trim, 12 1/2 In.	40.00
Charger, Hand Painted Pansy Design, 16 In.	160.00
Cheese Dish, Flower Sprays, Underplate, Bud Finial Domed Cover	145.00
Chop Plate, Mauve Roses Center & Edge, Gold Scalloped Edge, 12 In.	55.00
Crucifix, Gilt Copper, Round Wooden Base, 13th Century, 8 1/4 In.	2090.00
Demitasse Set, Tray, 5 Cups & Saucers, Pot, 1900, Tressman & Vought	750.00
Dish, Lemon, Pink Wild Roses	30.00
Dresser Set, Roses, 3 Piece	110.00
Fernery, 4 Gold Rococo Legs, Roses On Turquoise, 8 In.	95.00
Finger Bowl, Lavender Flower, Gold Footed, Gold Trim, A.K.Co.	90.00
Fish Set, Scalloped Rim, Various Fish, Sprays, 9 1/8 In., 13 Piece	500.00
Inkwell, 3 Pen, Hand Painted, 4 In.	45.00
Inkwell, Floral Design, 1850–60	75.00
Jardiniere, Gold Elephant Head Handles, C.1910	295.00
Mirror, Painted, 5 In.	45.00
Mug, Blackberries & Foliage, Rococo Handle, Dated & Signed	55.00
Mug, Gooseberry Design, Autumnal Colors, 4 1/2 In.	50.00
Mug, Monk With Scroll, Cream & Brown	45.00
Oyster Plate, Flower Border	37.50
Pitcher, Berries, Blossoms & Leaves, Signed, 14 3/4 In.	195.00
Pitcher, Hanging Grapes In 3 Colors, Marked, 12 In.	165.00
Pitcher, Painted Cherries, Green Leaves, Gold Handle, 7 In.	45.00
Plaque, African Man, 1902, 18 In.	250.00

Always wash antique china in a sink lined with a rubber mat or towels; this helps prevent chipping. Wash one piece at a time. Rinse and let air dry. If you suspect a piece has been repaired, do not wash it. Clean with a soft brush dampened in a solution of ammonia and water.

Plaque, Cavalier, Coronet, Signed, 9 3/4 In.	165.00
Plaque, Fish, Signed, 10 In.	95.00
Plaque, Game, Gold Rococo Border, 13 1/2 In.	250.00
Plaque, Game, Underwater Fish & Foliage Scene, Signed, 11 3/4 In.	150.00
Plaque, Nole Me Tangere, Enameled, Wooden Frame, 10 1/2 X 8 1/4 In.	1100.00
Plaque, Wall, Birds, Natural Habitat, Marked, 11 1/2 In.	145.00
Plaque, Woman, Basket, C.1900, 12 3/4 X 9 1/4 In. ....Illus	350.00
Plaque, Young Women, Green Dress, Red Dress, Cherubs, 6 1/4 In., Pr.	500.00
Plate, Autumn Leaves, Berries, 8 1/2 In.	30.00
Plate, Fish, Hand Painted, 9 1/2 In.	35.00
Plate, Flying Game Bird, Rococo Gold Scalloped Rim, Coronet, 10 In.	105.00
Plate, Harvest Scene, Portrait, Enameled, 16th Century, 7 3/8 In.	935.00
Plate, Kitten, Butterfly, Hand Painted, L.Coudert, Coronet, 9 1/4 In.	45.00
Plate, Lady Portrait, Acorn Border, 9 1/2 In.	37.50
Plate, Monk, Coronet, Signed LePic, 9 In.	95.00
Plate, Mums, Rococo Border, Gold Trim, 6 In.	100.00
Plate, Portrait, By T.Leroy, Signed, 19th Century, 9 In.	225.00
Plate, Portrait, Lady, Gold On Red Border, 9 1/2 In.	195.00
Plate, Seafood, Shell Shape, Hand Painted, Gold Trim	35.00
Plate, Tiger & Leopard, Rococo Gold Edge, Pierced, 12 3/4 In., Pair	495.00
Punch Bowl, Hand Painted, 3–Color Grapes Inside & Out, 9 1/2 In.	175.00
Ring Tree, Figural, Hand, Black Lacy Design, Floral, Gold Edge	42.00
Ring Tree, Figural, Hand, Forget–Me–Nots	34.00
Sardine Set, Hand Painted, Fish & Shell, 3 Piece	200.00
Smoking Set, 1909, Cover, Artist Signed	89.00
Sugar Shaker, Mushroom Design, Gold Cover, E.M.Laughlin	60.00
Syrup, Corn, Hand Painted, Handle, 1906, 6 In.	125.00
Tankard, 3–Colored Hanging Grapes, Marked, 12 In.	145.00
Tankard, Flowers, Raised Gold, Gold Handles, 14 1/2 In.	210.00
Tankard, Fruits, Green Handle & Base, 11 In.	185.00
Tankard, Grapes, Red, Green, Purple, Dragon Handle, 14 1/2 In.	150.00
Tankard, Green & Purple Grapes, Artist Signed, C.1905, 13 1/2 In.	245.00
Tankard, Light, Dark Browns, Monkey Playing Fiddle, 12 1/2 In.	135.00
Tankard, Yellow, Red Roses, Dragon Handle, 11 1/2 In.	145.00
Tile, Portrait, Young Woman With Basket, C.1900, 12 3/4 X 9 1/4 In.	350.00
Tile, Portrait, Mother, Child, Porcelain, Signed Laroque, 6 X 13 In.	695.00
Tile, Roses, Green Ground, Gilt Frame, C.1907, 10 1/2 X 18 1/2 In.	475.00
Tray, Cigarette, Trees, Castle, Signed Luck	25.00
Tray, Dresser, Forget–Me–Nots, Blue, 16 X 14 In.	95.00
Tray, Dresser, Holly, Berries, Rust, Green, Signed, 13 X 16 In.	68.50
Tray, Dresser, Roses, Gold, Pastel, Kidney Shape, 13 X 9 In.	40.00
Tureen, Rose Drape & Garlands, 3 Handles, 12 In.	60.00
Urn, Chevrons, Starburst, Blue, White, Yellow, Foil Ground, 1925, 8 In.	2750.00
Urn, Colonial Family Scene, Signed, Dated 1898, 23 In., Pair	1500.00
Vase, Poppies, Stems, Black, Cylindrical, Art Nouveau, Guerin, 11 In.	80.00
Vase, Rose Design, Handle, Signed, 1907, 13 In.	70.00

In 1927, Charles Lindbergh, the aviator, became the first man to make a nonstop solo flight across the Atlantic Ocean. He was a national hero. In 1932, his son was kidnapped and murdered, and Lindbergh was again the center of public interest. He died in 1974. All types of Lindbergh memorabilia are collected.

LINDBERGH, Bookends, Airplane Design, Cast Iron 115.00
  Bookends, Bust 28.00
  Bookends, Spirit of St.Louis Plane, Cast Iron, 5 X 4 1/2 In. 40.00
  Bookmark, Woven Silk 40.00
  Box, Pencil, Spirit of St.Louis, Face of Lindbergh, Tin 40.00
  Button, Pinback 25.00
  Case, Pencil, Tin .... 35.00 To 45.00
  Handkerchief, Embroidered Plane, Spirit of St.Louis 24.00
  Lindy Air Mail Card Game 60.00
  Model Kit, North American F-86 Sabre Jet Fighter, 1952 .... 35.00
  Perfume Bottle, Lucky Lindy 12.00
  Photograph, Christening Ceremony, Airplane, City of Washington 5.00
  Photograph, News Release, Lindbergh Baby, 1932, 12 X 15 In. 25.00
  Pin, Spirit of St.Louis Center, Red, White & Blue, Oval, 1 In. 10.00
  Plane Kit, Spirit of St.Louis, Extra Parts 100.00
  Plate, New York To Paris, Picture 40.00
  Program, Souvenir, 1927 .... 27.00
  Scrapbook, Clippings For Atlantic Flight 45.00
  Sheet Music, Lindbergh The Eagle of U.S.A., Lindbergh Photo 20.00
  Tapestry, Bust In Center, New York & Paris Scene, 18 X 52 In. 45.00
  Toy, Plane, Spirit of St.Louis, Red Paint, Tin, 24 In.Wingspan 300.00
  Watch & Fob, Pocket, New York To Paris 225.00
  Watch, Pocket, New York To Paris, Ingraham 300.00

> Lithophanes are porcelain pictures made by casting clay in layers of various thicknesses. When a piece is held to the light, a picture of light and shadow is seen through it. Most lithophanes date from the 1825-75 period. A few are still being made. Many lithophanes sold today were originally panels for lampshades.

LITHOPHANE, Lamp, 3 Ships Scenes On Umbrella Shade, Column Base, 20 3/4 In. 1865.00
  Lamp, Harvard Student 1275.00
  Mug, 87 Regiment, Pewter Lid, With Soldier On Top, 1905-07 .... 475.00
  Mug, Edward VII Through Bottom 90.00
  Shade, 6 Trapezoid Panels, Children, Gilded Frame, 12 X 6 In. 675.00
  Shade, Ball, 3 Different Hunt Scenes 3875.00

> Liverpool, England, was the site of several pottery and porcelain factories from 1716 to 1785. Some earthenware was made with transfer decorations. Sadler and Green made print-decorated wares from 1756. Many of the pieces were made for the American market and feature patriotic emblems, such as eagles, flags, and other special-interest motifs.

LIVERPOOL, Bowl, Numerous Vessels Under Sail, 4 Wreathed Poems 385.00
  Jug, American Ship 1 Side, Rural Family Scene Other, 11 In. 2000.00
  Jug, Map of Newburyport Harbour, 9 1/4 In. 2500.00
  Jug, Woman Scene, 6 In. 275.00
  Pitcher, Liberty Independence, Washington, Sailing Ship, 7 In. 1000.00
  Pitcher, Washington & Lafayette, 1824 .... 550.00
  Pitcher, Young Boy, Bird's Nest, Girlfriend, C.1800, 6 1/2 In. 125.00
  Plate, Ship Scene, 9 In. 176.00

> Juan, Jose, and Vicente Lladro opened a ceramics workshop in Almacera, Spain, in 1951. They soon began making figurines in a distinctive, elongated style. In 1958 the factory moved to Tabernes Blanques, Spain. The company makes stoneware and porcelain vases and figurines in limited and nonlimited editions.

LLADRÓ°

LLADRO, Figurine, Aggressive Duck 310.00
  Figurine, Aroma of The Islands 300.00
  Figurine, Biking In The Country 360.00
  Figurine, Cinderella, No.4824, Box 85.00
  Figurine, Daisy 170.00
  Figurine, Fantasy 150.00
  Figurine, Feeding Time 260.00
  Figurine, Flapper 225.00

Figurine, Folk Dancing	250.00
Figurine, Girl, With Ducks	140.00
Figurine, Girl, With Parasol, No.49/2, Box	90.00
Figurine, Girl, With Swan & Dog	140.00
Figurine, Happy Birthday	100.00
Figurine, Lady, With Parasol	200.00
Figurine, Madam Butterfly, Oriental, With Fans	145.00
Figurine, Matrimony	180.00 To 385.00
Figurine, Midwife	175.00
Figurine, Mimi, No.4985	175.00
Figurine, My Hungry Brood	330.00
Figurine, Oriental Girl	350.00
Figurine, Polar Bear, 5 In.	80.00
Figurine, Reading	180.00
Figurine, Sunday In The Park	410.00
Figurine, Sweet Girl, No.4987	175.00
Figurine, Valencia Lady	450.00
Figurine, Wedding	125.00
Figurine, Windblown Girl	260.00
Plate, Christmas, 1971	35.00
Plate, Mother's Day, 1971	45.00

Locke Art is a trademark found on glass of the early twentieth century. Joseph Locke worked at many English and American firms. He designed and etched his own glass in Pittsburgh, Pennsylvania, starting in the 1880s. Some pieces were marked "Joe Locke," but most were marked with the words "Locke Art." The mark is hidden in the pattern on the glass.

LOCKE ART, Pitcher, Base Cut, 24 Ray Star, Vintage Pattern, Signed, 8 1/4 In.	425.00
Pitcher, Poppies Among Ferns, Scrolls On Handle, 9 3/4 In.	375.00
Salad Set, Bowl & Utensils, Sunset Lake Scene	150.00

Johann Loetz bought a glassworks in Austria in 1840. He died in 1848 and his widow ran the company; then in 1879, his grandson took over. Loetz glass was varied. Most collectors recognize the iridescent gold glass similar to Tiffany, but many other types were made. The firm closed during World War II.

LOETZ, Biscuit Jar, Irregular Threads, Silver Plate Fittings, 6 3/4 In.	118.00
Bowl, Amber, Silver Blue, Raised Pattern, Iridescent, 10 In.	1430.00
Bowl, Centerpiece, Wide Lip, Green, Signed, 6 1/2 X 8 In.	225.00
Bowl, Purple Blue, Green To Frosted Clear, 4 1/2 In.	160.00
Bowl, Ribbed, Pink, Scalloped, Iridescent	225.00
Candlestick, Iridescent Green, Pair	195.00
Compote, Hobnail Design, Metal Base, Amber, 12 1/2 In.	225.00
Compote, Metal Pedestal, 10 In.	210.00
Cookie Jar, Pewter Lid & Handle	675.00
Cornucopia, Gold, Circles, Applied Leaves, Iridescent, 17 In.	2500.00
Globe, Yellow, Green Stringing, Hemispherical, Iridescent, 10 In.	3025.00
Gold Iridescent, Green Rigaree, Signed, 10 1/2 In.	185.00
Inkwell, Art Nouveau, Iridescent Green, Metal Frame, 3 In.	200.00
Inkwell, Brass Lid, Blue & Purple, Iridescent	240.00
Inkwell, Copper Lid, Brass, Art Nouveau	325.00
Jack-In-The-Pulpit, Peacock Eye, Green, Flower, 8 1/2 In.	1500.00
Rose Bowl, Applied Pewter Rim, Grapes, Grape Leaves, Signed	225.00
Rose Bowl, Ribbed, Crystal & Green, Signed, 5 1/2 In.	175.00
Rose Bowl, Threaded Rigaree, Handles, Green, 8 In.	225.00
Spooner, Threaded, Cranberry, Signed, 5 1/2 In.	160.00
Sugar & Creamer, Inverted Thumbprint, Raised Enameling, Amber	175.00
Syrup, Green, 8 In.	185.00
Tumbler, Cobalt, Heart Shaped Leafage, Cameo Glass, 1910, 4 1/4 In.	2200.00
Vase, 3 Butterflies, Handkerchief Form, Signed, C.1900, 8 1/4 In.	1100.00
Vase, Amber, Blue, Butterflies, Ruffled, Iridescent, 1900, 10 In.	1210.00
Vase, Angled Feather Design, Brass Floral & Leaf Framing, Signed	350.00
Vase, Angled Pulled Feathers, Baluster Shape, Brass Frame, 12 In.	375.00

Legras, Bottle, Cameo, Lake
Scene, 3–Sided Body, 3 3/4 In.

Loetz, Vase, Bud, 5 In.

Loetz, Vase, Spiral Fluting,
Trumpet Shape, 11 In.

Vase, Art Nouveau Holder, Gourd Shape, 13 In. 425.00
Vase, Blown Out, Silver Green Outside, Amethyst Cased, Signed, 10 In. 210.00
Vase, Blue Mottled Exterior, Ruby Interior, Signed, 10 In. 750.00
Vase, Blue, Green, Purple, Ruffled, Crackle, Iridescent, Signed, 9 In. 275.00
Vase, Bud, 5 In. ....*Illus* 225.00
Vase, Coiled Ribbing, 3 Handles, Spherical Body, C.1900, 10 1/4 In. 2090.00
Vase, Drape Design, Signed, 6 In. 155.00
Vase, Egyptian Sprinkler Form, Yellow, Silver, Amber, Lilies, 9 In. 1980.00
Vase, Elephant Foot, Green Luster, Ruffled, Polished Pontil, 13 In. 150.00
Vase, Enameling, Frosted Green, Signed, 8 1/2 In. 140.00
Vase, Gold Spider Web, Applied To Outside, 8 In. 130.00
Vase, Gold, Indented, Square, Iridescent, Signed, 11 1/2 In. 185.00
Vase, Grape Pattern, Bronze Collar, 7 1/2 X 4 1/2 In. 350.00
Vase, Green & Silver, Tapering Form, Ruffled Edge, 9 1/2 In. 350.00
Vase, Green, Trumpet Shape, Iridescent, 11 In. 195.00
Vase, Green, White Threading, Iridescent, 4 In. 95.00
Vase, Inverted Form, Ruffled, Amber, Silver Spots, C.1900, 7 In. 2860.00
Vase, Lavender Fire & Drape Design, Amber, Signed, 8 1/4 In. 175.00
Vase, Orange, Purple, 12 In. 250.00
Vase, Pale Moss Green, Silver Spottings, Iridescent, 1900, 17 In. 1100.00
Vase, Purple, Green, Square, Ruffled Mouth, 12 In. 375.00
Vase, Red To Yellow, Angled Thumbprints, Iridescent, 8 1/4 In. 240.00
Vase, Red, Goldstones, Ruffled, Iridescent, 11 In. 395.00
Vase, Ribbed, Indented, Green, Gold, Signed, 5 1/2 In. 185.00
Vase, Silver Dragonflies On Lip, Pinch Bottom, Green, 4 X 5 In. 450.00
Vase, Spiral Fluting, Trumpet Shape, 11 In. ....*Illus* 425.00
Vase, Stylized Leaves, Ovoid, Marked, C.1900, 6 In. 1980.00
Vase, Tortoiseshell, Baluster Form, Opaline Trailed Design, 8 In. 375.00
Vase, Trefoil Crimped Top, Green, Corset Shape, 8 In. 75.00
Vase, Twisted Rainbow Iridescent, Art Nouveau, 12 1/2 In. 300.00
Vase, Violet, Pulled Feather, Iridescent, Signed, 4 3/4 In. 240.00
Vase, Warrior On Front, Amber, Signed, 8 1/2 In. 175.00

The Lone Ranger is a fictional character introduced on the radio in
1932. Over three thousand shows were produced before the series
ended in 1954. In 1938, the first Lone Ranger movie was made.
Television shows were started in 1949 and are still seen on some
stations. The Lone Ranger appears on many products and was even
the name of a restaurant chain for several years.

LONE RANGER, Advertising Display Card, 4 Badges 65.00
    Album, Souvenir 24.00

Atomic Bomb Ring	60.00
Badge, Deputy	4.00
Badge, Horseshoe, 1939	25.00
Badge, Silver Cup	25.00
Badge, Star, Bond Bread Safety Club, Golden, 1938	40.00
Badge, Victory Corps, 1942	30.00
Bank, 1938	50.00
Binoculars	45.00
Board, Dart, Tin & Rubber	55.00
Book, At Haunted Gulch, Striker, 1941	6.00
Book, Coloring, Whitman, Some Use	10.00
Book, Lone Ranger & Tonto, Signed Clayton Moore	25.00
Book, Paint, Whitman, 1940	17.00
Book, Ranger & The Outlaw Stronghold, 1936	15.00
Bookmark	18.00
Bullet, With Compass In Bottom	40.00
Button	5.00
Cap Gun .... 60.00 To	65.00
Card, Lobby, Lone Ranger & Tonto, Dated 1956	20.00
Clock, Alarm, 1980, Box	30.00
Costume, Leather Chaps & Vest, 1950s	50.00
Costume, Tonto, Picture On Box, C.1940	200.00
Dart Board, Tin, Graphic, 1938, 16 X 26 In.	62.00
Doll, Composition, Painted Face, Muslin Body, 1942, 16 In.	350.00
Doll, Tonto, 4 In.	4.00
Figurine, Lone Ranger & Silver, Hartland, 8 In.	65.00
First Aid Kit, Tin	40.00
Flashlight, Box, 1950s	25.00
Flashlight, Bullet Code, Box	35.00
Flashlight, Signal Siren, Silver Bullet Shaped Code Booklet	45.00
Game, Dart Board	50.00
Game, Guarding Mail Train	20.00
Game, Ring Toss	45.00
Game, Target	25.00
Globe, Snow	35.00
Guitar	45.00
Harmonica	18.00
Holster, Double	20.00
Lunch Box	15.00
Paperweight, Snow Inside	22.00
Pedometer .... 15.00 To	25.00
Pencil Box	15.00
Pencil, Silver Bullet	22.00
Photograph, Color, Lone Ranger & Silver, 1950s	35.00
Pin, Lone Ranger, On Horse	12.00
Pin, Safety Scout	12.00
Pistol, Clicker, Hi–Ho Silver, 1938	35.00
Printing Set, Box, 1939	22.00
Radio, Majestic	140.00
Ring, Atom Bomb, Radio Premium, Metal, Red Plastic End Bomb	31.00
Shirt	10.00
Sign, Merita Bread, Embossed Tin	400.00
Spoon, Hi–Ho Silver, Silvered Brass, 1938	40.00
Tattoos, Philadelphia Gum Co.	6.00
Toy, Astride Rearing Horse, Tin, Lithographed, Marx, 1938, 8 In.	90.00
Toy, Windup, Marx	70.00
Wristwatch, Bradley, Swiss Parts, Western Type Strap	23.00

 The Longwy Workshop of Longwy, France, first made ceramic wares in 1798. The workshop is still in business. Most of the ceramic pieces found today are glazed with many colors to resemble cloisonne or other enameled metal. The factory used a variety of marks.

LONGWY, Bowl, Aqua Outside, Cobalt Blue Inside, Red, Pink Flowers, 10 In. 285.00

Bowl, Enameled, Blue Basket Weave, Inside Floral, 2 Handles	235.00
Candelabra, 3–Light, Pottery Stem, Brass Foot, Pierced, 10 3/4 In.	110.00
Candlestick, Multicolored Floral, Brass Standard, Prisms, 9 3/4 In.	95.00
Candlestick, Prisms, Brass Standard, Pottery Base, 9 3/4 In., Pair	185.00
Charger, Firebirds, Flowers On Branches, Marked, 14 In.	900.00
Plate, Bird Center, 9 In.	55.00
Shoe, Allover Flowers, Turquoise, 6 In., Pair	100.00
Tile, Bird On Flowering Branch, Rocks, Lake, Square, 6 In.	110.00
Vase, Bird On White Beach, Palm Trees, Enameled Flowers, 7 In.	295.00
Vase, Circles, Waves, Dotted, Blue Ground, Marked, 11 In.	990.00
Vase, Turquoise Floral, 6 In.	30.00

The Lonhuda Pottery Company of Steubenville, Ohio, was organized in 1892 by William Long, W. H. Hunter, and Alfred Day. Brown underglaze slip–decorated pottery was made. The firm closed in 1896. The company used many marks; the earliest included the letters "LPCO."

LONHUDA, Bowl, Jessie Spaulding, Zanesville Mark, 1895, 7 In.	250.00
Vase, 3–Footed, 1895	225.00

Lotus Ware was made by the Knowles, Taylor & Knowles Company of East Liverpool, Ohio, from 1890 to 1900. Lotus Ware is a thin, Belleek–like porcelain. It was sometimes decorated outside the factory. Other types of ceramics that were made by the Knowles, Taylor & Knowles Company are listed under "KTK."

LOTUS WARE, Bowl, Florals, Buds & Leaves, Ruffled, Gold Beaded Top, 4 1/2 In.	510.00
Bowl, Flowers, Open Work Ends, White, Oval, 6 3/4 X 4 3/4 In.	650.00
Bowl, Pink Enamel Flowers, Crimped Rim & Handles	595.00
Creamer, Twig Base, Gold Tracing, Beaded, Turquoise, 3 1/2 In.	68.00
Cup & Saucer	80.00

Low art tiles were made by the J. and J. G. Low Art Tile Works of Chelsea, Massachusetts, from 1877 to 1902. A variety of art and other tiles were made. Some of the tiles were made by a process called "natural," some were hand–modeled, and some made mechanically.

LOW, Tile, Ivy, 3 X 6 In.	50.00
Tile, Sheep, Village, Teal Blue, Signed A.D., 18 X 10 In. ....*Illus*	650.00
LOY–NEL–ART, see McCoy	

Lunch pails and lunch boxes have been used to carry lunches to school or work since the nineteenth century. Today, most collectors want either early advertising boxes or children's lunch boxes made since the 1930s. The original Thermos bottle must be inside the box for the collector to consider it complete.

LUNCH BOX, Animal Cookie, Iten Biscuit Co., Omaha, Child's, Tin	88.50
Bagley's Wild Fruit	85.00
Blue Jay Tobacco	110.00
Bonanza	7.00
Brotherhood Tobacco	185.00
Burley Boy Tobacco	1125.00 To 1750.00
Central Union	30.00 To 60.00
Charlie's Angels	15.00
Cinco Tobacco	35.00
Dixie Kid Tobacco	175.00
Dixie Kid Tobacco, White Dude	600.00
Dixie Kid, Black	100.00 To 450.00
Dixie Kid, Blond	1000.00
Dixie Queen	140.00 To 150.00
Fashion Tobacco	145.00 To 195.00
Fat Albert	12.50
Fess Parker	20.00
Friends Tobacco	475.00
Gail & Ax Navy Tobacco	55.00

George Washington Tobacco .... 37.00 To 45.00
Gold Shore Tobacco, Tin 80.00
Great West Tobacco .... 125.00 To 130.00
Green Hornet, Thermos 50.00
Green Turtle Tobacco .... 135.00 To 195.00
Gunsmoke, 1959 .... 18.00 To 20.00
Handbag Tobacco .... 130.00 To 185.00
Ivins Biscuits 25.00
James Bond 15.00
Joe Palooka 40.00
Joe Palooka, Weston Biscuit Label, 1948, 7 In. .... 65.00 To 75.00
Junior Miss 15.00
Just Suits Tobacco .... 25.00 To 45.00
Kit Carson 22.00
Laredo Tobacco 70.00
Lorillard's Redi–Cut 85.00
Mickey Mouse Wonderful World, Thermos 20.00
Munsters, 1965 .... 45.00
North Pole Tobacco 485.00
Peanuts, 1965 .... 7.50
Peanuts, Baseball Scene 10.00
Pedro Tobacco 60.00
Penny Post 135.00
Peter Rabbit 30.00
Redicut Tobacco 100.00
Return of The Jedi, Thermos .... 8.00 To 20.00
Round Trip Tobacco, Battleship 145.00
School Bus, Walt Disney 20.00
Sensation Tobacco, Casket Shape .... 195.00 To 225.00
Sensible Tobacco .... 21.00 To 38.00
Star Wars 10.00
Sweet Cuba 30.00
Tiger Tobacco, Red 45.00
Tom Corbett, 1952 .... 30.00
U.S.Marine 295.00
U.S.Marine, Basket Weave 20.00
Union Leader Tobacco, Basket Weave 45.00
Union Leader Tobacco, Christmas Design 45.00
Union Leader Tobacco, Eagle, Red 22.00
Wild, Wild West, 1969 .... 25.00
Winner Tobacco, Race Cars 195.00
LUNCH PAIL, Aladdin, Fire Truck, Firemen At Work On Fire 30.00
Home Comfort Tobacco, Family, Paper Label, 1910 .... 75.00
Nigger Hair Tobacco 150.00
Pedro Tobacco 145.00

Luneville, a French faience factory, was established in 1731 by Jacques Chambrette. It is best known for its fine biscuit figures and groups and for large faience dogs and lions. The early pieces were unmarked. The firm was acquired by Keller and Guerin and is still working.

LUNEVILLE, Group, Girl, Boy, Child, Tree Stump, C.1770, 11 7/8 In., Pair ... 1100.00
Plate, Rooter, Stick & Spatter Edge 58.00

Lusterware was meant to resemble copper, silver, or gold. It has been used since the sixteenth century. Most of the luster found today was made during the nineteenth century. The metallic glazes are applied on pottery. The finished color depends on the combination of the clay color and the glaze.

LUSTER, Copper, Bowl, Wide Blue Flower Band, Copper Lined 69.00
Copper, Creamer .... 10.00 To 15.00
Copper, Creamer, Blue Ground 15.00
Copper, Creamer, Blue Leaf Design, Flared Lip, 5 1/2 In. 58.00
Copper, Creamer, Sanded Band, 3 In. 35.00

Copper, Cup, Satyr, Enameled Face, Frog Inside, 5 In.	95.00
Copper, Goblet, Sunderland Insets, Cream	45.00
Copper, Mug, Blue Band, 2 3/4 In.	40.00
Copper, Mug, Putty Band, Name Eliza Center, 2 1/2 In.	50.00
Copper, Pitcher, 2 Yellow Bands, Squiggly Luster Design, 4 1/2 In.	48.00
Copper, Pitcher, Black Transfer Clock Face, Riddle & Bryan, 5 In.	105.00
Copper, Pitcher, Blue Band, Raised Figures, 3 1/2 In.	14.00
Copper, Pitcher, Raised Floral Design, Numbered, 5 1/2 In.	45.00
Copper, Shaker, Sunderland Band, 4 In.	45.00
Copper, Shaker, Toby, 4 3/4 In.	75.00
Copper, Shaving Mug, House Pattern, Turquoise & Green Ground	55.00

LUSTER, COPPER, TEA LEAF, see Tea Leaf Ironstone

Copper, Teapot, Blue Band, Eagle Handle, 5 In.	30.00
Copper, Teapot, Blue Trim, English	20.00
Copper, Teapot, Floral Enamels	75.00
Copper, Teapot, White Grapes & Leaves, 4 Cup	50.00

LUSTER, FAIRYLAND, see Wedgwood

Gold, Pitcher, Raised Foxhunt Scene, Gold Handle, 8 In.	85.00
Pink, Creamer, Gold Flowers, Applied Cross On Bottom	40.00
Pink, Cup & Saucer, Gold Flowers	18.50
Pink, Cup & Saucer, Handleless, Florals In Medallion, Swagged Fern	45.00
Pink, Cup, Child's, Child Playing, Dog Dancing	10.00
Pink, Cup, Leaves, Gold Center Flowers, Gold Beaded Top	20.00
Pink, Mug, House Pattern, C.1820, 3 In.	85.00
Pink, Plate, Adams Rose Center, 6 3/4 In.	28.00
Pink, Plate, Florals In Medallion, Sagged Fern, 7 In.	25.00
Pink, Plate, Shepherd Boy, Center Transfer, C.1830, 7 3/4 In.	65.00
Pink, Salt Box, Cover, Germany	50.00
Pink, Tea Set, Child's, Floral, Germany, C.1890, 13 Piece	150.00
Silver, Creamer, Gadroon Top Border, Loop & Rib Pattern Base, 5 In.	85.00
Silver, Jug, Harlequin	135.00

LUSTER, SUNDERLAND, see Sunderland

Tan, Tea Set, Child's	27.50

Lustre Art Glass Company was founded in Long Island, New York, in 1920 by Conrad Vahlsling and Paul Frank. The company made lampshades and globes that are almost indistinguishable from those made by Quezal. Most of the shades made by the company were unmarked.

LUSTRE ART, Shade, Bell Shape, Gold Bands, Gold Lined, 5 In., Pair	350.00
Shade, Gold Feathery Design, 4 3/4 In. X 2 In.	98.00
Shade, Gold Opalescent Feather, Threaded, Signed, 5 1/4 In., Pair	300.00

Lustres are mantel decorations, or pedestal vases, with many hanging glass prisms. The name really refers to the prisms, and it is proper to refer to a single glass prism as a lustre. Either spelling, luster or lustre, is correct.

LUSTRES, Bohemian, Red, White, Clear, 13 In., Pair	500.00
Brass Stem of Child, Cut Prisms, 16 In., Pair	1200.00
Clear Candlesticks, Gilded Panels, Cut Prism Drops, 12 In., Pair	750.00
Cranberry, Gold, Overlay, C.1880, 12 In., Pair	1400.00

Petrus Regout established the De Sphinx pottery in Maastricht, Holland, in 1836. The firm was noted for its transfer–printed earthenware. Many factories in Maastricht are still making ceramics.

MAASTRICHT, Cup & Saucer, Brushed Green, Black & Orange, Demitasse	35.00
Gravy Boat, Blue Willow, Attached Underplate	40.00
Plate, Fluted Edge, 8 1/2 In.	15.00

Maize glass was made by W. L. Libbey & Son Company of Toledo, Ohio, after 1889. The glass resembled an ear of corn. The leaves were usually green, but some pieces were made with blue or red leaves. The kernels of "corn" were light yellow, white, or light green.

MAIZE, Bowl, 9 In.	40.00

Bowl, Centerpiece 100.00
Bowl, Green Husks, 9 In. 67.50
Celery .... 78.00 To 95.00
Pitcher, Water, Green Leaves, Opalescent White 550.00
Saltshaker, Ear of Corn, Gold–Edged Leaves, Brass Top, 4 In. 185.00
Sugar Shaker 60.00
Sugar Shaker, Custard Glass, Original Cover 145.00
Sugar Shaker, Green Trim 175.00
Syrup, Rows of Molded–In Kernels, Green Leaves, C.1889 .... 385.00

Majolica is a general term for any pottery glazed with an opaque tin enamel that conceals the color of the clay body. It has been made since the fourteenth century. Today's collector is most likely to find Victorian majolica. The heavy, colorful ware is rarely marked. Some famous makers include Wedgwood; Minton; Griffen, Smith and Hill (marked "Etruscan"); and Chesapeake Pottery (marked "Avalon" or "Clifton").

MAJOLICA, Ashtray, Figural, Camel 12.00
Bank, Dog, Sitting Up, Pink Jacket, 4 3/4 In. 55.00
Bank, Figural, Dog, Hat & Bow, Brown & Blue, 6 In. 65.00
Basket, Applied Roses & Leaves, 4 X 5 In. 18.00
Basket, Centerpiece, Begonia Leaf & Lily Pattern 200.00
Bowl, Bronze Rim, Wedgwood, 1870s, 4 1/2 X 10 In. .... 215.00 To 325.00
Bowl, Centerpiece, Basket Weave, Floral, Oak Branches ....*Illus* 950.00
Bowl, Floral & Bird Pattern, Wedgwood, 4 1/4 X 9 3/4 In. 80.00
Bowl, Green Leaf Center, Leaves On Side, Stippled Ground, 9 In. 95.00
Bowl, Portrait, Copper Luster Trim, 11 1/4 In. 325.00
Bowl, Raised Basket Design, Green Shaded To Brown, 3 1/4 In. 45.00
Bowl, Water Lily, Footed, 9 X 3 1/2 In. 30.00
Butter Chip, Begonia Leaf, Edge & Malkin 15.00
Butter, Floral, Cobalt Blue, Twig Handle, George Jones, 10 In. 160.00
Cake Stand, Maple Leaves, Tree Trunk & Ivy Base, Etruscan, 9 In. 145.00
Cake Stand, Pond Lily, 3 Crane Feet, Etruscan 210.00
Cake Stand, Strawberries, Blossoms, Pale Blue, Zell 65.00
Chamberstick, Leaf Design, Turquoise Ground, 6 In. 80.00
Charger, Ancient Warriors Attacking Fort, Signed, 8 In. 195.00
Charger, Grotesque Animals, Cavorting Putti, 1895, 28 In. 200.00
Charger, Snail, Worm, Butterfly & Crab, 6 In. 225.00
Cheese Keeper, Ivory Basket Weave, Red Lattice, Copeland 695.00
Compote, Rose, Classical Series, Etruscan 65.00
Compote, Stag, Doe & Rabbit, George Jones, 1871 .... 2795.00
Creamer, Brown & Cream Floral, 4 1/2 In. 46.00
Creamer, Corn 35.00
Creamer, Daisy, Brown 60.00
Creamer, Floral 48.00
Creamer, Pink Interior, Mottled Green & Brown, 4 1/2 In. 47.00
Creamer, Yellow & Pink Rose, Leaves & Banner, England, 6 In. 115.00

Majolica, Bowl, Centerpiece, Basket Weave, Floral, Oak Branches

Cup & Saucer, Cauliflower	185.00
Cup & Saucer, Open Rose	125.00
Dish, Begonia Leaf, Greens, Pink & White, 8 1/2 In.	75.00
Dish, Red & Green Floral Design, Molded Ground, 10 1/2 In.	20.00
Ewer, Green Floral, Left-Handed, 9 In.	75.00
Ewer, Paneled Flowers, 6 1/2 In.	55.00
Figurine, Black Man, Yellow Jacket, Lavender Accordion, 6 1/2 In.	58.00
Figurine, Parrot, 9 In.	165.00
Garden Seat, Rush Seat, Dragonflies, Birds, G.Jones, C.1874, Pair	9500.00
Humidor, Arab Head	50.00
Humidor, Brindled Bulldog, On Haunches, Pipe To Mouth, 8 In.	125.00
Humidor, Dutch Children, Figural Pipe On Cover, 4 1/2 In.	55.00
Humidor, Figural, Happy Hippo, 8 In.	135.00
Humidor, Monkey, French, 12 X 10 In.	385.00
Humidor, Scene of Dutch Children, Pipe On Lid, 4 X 3 In.	48.00
Jam Jar, Orange Shape, Marked	65.00
Jardiniere, Baby Satyr, Lion Head Supports, Minton, Pair	2200.00
Jug, Stylized Rose, Cartouche, Italy, 15th Century, 7 1/4 In.	495.00
Match Holder, Black Boy Smoking Pipe	475.00
Match Holder, Black Boy, With Ear of Corn	400.00
Match Holder, Monk Holding Beer Stein	225.00
Match Holder, Poor Boy, With Pockets Pulled Out	410.00
Match Holder, Ranger, With Rifle	500.00
Match Holder, Sailor Boy	375.00
Oyster Plate, Shell & Seawood Pattern, Minton, 12 Piece	1980.00
Pitcher, Avalon, Cream With Gold, 6 1/2 In.	38.00
Pitcher, Berry Design, Blue, 5 3/4 In.	25.00
Pitcher, Bird & Fan, 6 In.	150.00
Pitcher, Bird & Ribbon, 7 In.	155.00
Pitcher, Bird, 8 In.	175.00
Pitcher, Blackberry, 4 1/2 In.	85.00
Pitcher, Blossom Pattern, Brown Ground, Yellow Borders, 8 In.	70.00
Pitcher, Butterfly Lip, Etruscan, 5 In.	160.00
Pitcher, Corn, 7 1/2 In.	115.00
Pitcher, Corn, Lavender Interior, 4 In.	60.00
Pitcher, Corn, Light Color, English Registry Mark, 1869, 9 In.	145.00
Pitcher, Embossed Fish, 6 In.	45.00
Pitcher, Figural, Parrot, 11 In.	200.00
Pitcher, Figures Dancing Or Drinking, Cobalt, Minton, 1861, 13 In.	1430.00
Pitcher, Fish, 10 1/2 In.	130.00
Pitcher, Floral & Key, 8 In.	195.00
Pitcher, Floral, On Banded Tree Trunk Ground, 7 1/2 In.	60.00
Pitcher, Grapes, Pear, Apple, 8 1/2 In.	165.00
Pitcher, Green Palm Leaves On Brown, 6 1/4 In.	95.00
Pitcher, Hawthorne Patten, Mottled Colors, Etruscan, 5 In.	125.00
Pitcher, Leaf On Bark, 6 In.	70.00
Pitcher, Maple Leaf Design, 4 3/4 In.	50.00
Pitcher, Ostrich Design, 6 In.	60.00
Pitcher, Pineapple, Pewter Lid, 6 In.	235.00
Pitcher, Pink & Turquoise Flowers, Brown Tree Bark Ground, 7 In.	110.00
Pitcher, Pink Dogwood, Cream, Varicolored Leaves, 7 3/4 In.	85.00
Pitcher, Pink Rose & Banner, Pink Interior, 6 In.	45.00
Pitcher, Punch & Judy, Artist's Initials, 9 In.	225.00
Pitcher, Strawberries & Leaves, 9 In.	90.00
Pitcher, Water, Tan Texture, Blackberries, 9 1/2 In.	95.00
Pitcher, Yellow Star Design, Blue, 7 In.	35.00
Planter, Parrot, Incised Mark, 1930s, 13 In.	60.00
Planter, Parrot, Red, Blue, Yellow & Green, 13 In.	65.00
Plaque, Gentleman, Astride Horse, Green Ground, Oval, 9 X 11 In.	450.00
Plate, Asparagus, French	115.00
Plate, Avalon Faience, 8 In.	28.00
Plate, Bamboo, Marked, 8 1/2 In.	110.00
Plate, Begonia Leaf, 8 In.	18.00
Plate, Bird & Fan, Wedgwood, 9 In.	175.00

Plate, Bird In Flight, Turquoise, Holdcroft, 8 1/2 In., 12 Piece	1500.00
Plate, Cattle Scene, Black On White, Geo.Jones, 8 In.	105.00
Plate, Cauliflower, Etruscan, 9 In.	80.00
Plate, Fans, Butterflies, Wedgwood, 6 1/2 In.	55.00
Plate, Floral, 3 Leaves, 8 In.	40.00
Plate, Greek Key Reticulated Border, Wedgwood, 8 1/2 In.	125.00
Plate, Green & Brown Leaves, Etruscan, 8 7/8 In.	90.00
Plate, Green & Pink On Brown, Clover, 8 1/2 In.	35.00
Plate, Leaf & Floral, 10 In.	40.00
Plate, Leaf, 7 1/2 In.	30.00
Plate, Leaf, 8 1/2 In.	40.00
Plate, Leaf, Brown Ground, Etruscan, 9 In.	50.00
Plate, Mulberries, Leaves, Blossoms, Basket Weave Ground, 8 In.	40.00
Plate, Oak Leaf, Brown, With Green, 8 In.	55.00
Plate, Pear, Yellows, Green, Brown Ground, 8 In.	85.00
Plate, Running Stag & Dog, 8 In.	115.00
Plate, Seaweed, Etruscan Shell, 9 1/4 In.	145.00
Plate, Shell & Seaweed, Etruscan, 8 In.	100.00
Plate, Shell, Turquoise Ground, George Jones, 8 1/2 X 8 In.	30.00
Plate, Strawberries, Blossoms, Butterflies, Zell, 11 In.	48.00
Plate, Wasps Around Sunflower Center, 8 In.	40.00
Plate, Yellow Flowers, Pink Blossoms, Wedgwood, 8 7/8 In.	45.00
Platter, Asparagus, 16 In.	135.00
Platter, Harvest, 12 In.	150.00
Platter, Leaf Shape, Marked Etruscan, 9 1/2 X 12 In.	110.00
Platter, Wardle Bird & Fan, English Reg.Mark, 13 X 11 1/2 In.	100.00
Punch Bowl, Sunflower & Classical Urn Pattern, Samuel Lear	1200.00
Salad Bowl, Yellow, Festoons, Silver Plated Rim, Wedgwood, 8 In.	350.00
Saucer, Bamboo & Fern, Wardle, Marked	20.00
Server, Oyster, 3–Tiered, Revolving, Minton	3525.00
Shaving Mug, Pink Interior	110.00
Spooner, Shell & Seaweed, Albino	95.00
Stein, Molded Child's Head Front, Scrollwork, Yellow & Pink	285.00
Sugar & Creamer, Bird & Fan, Stippled Cobalt, Lavender Interior	185.00
Sugar & Creamer, Floral, Basket Weave, Iris Spout, Footed	45.00
Sugar, Bird & Fan, Wedgwood	125.00
Sugar, Cauliflower, Etruscan	145.00
Syrup, Etruscan	290.00
Syrup, Pineapple & Flower, Pewter Lid	175.00
Syrup, Shell & Seaweed, Etruscan	125.00
Tea Set, Shell & Seaweed, 23 Piece	1850.00
Teapot, Cabbage	35.00
Teapot, Drum Shape, Birds, Blossoms, Twig Handle, Cobalt Ground	95.00
Teapot, Sugar & Creamer, Spooner, Shell, Seaweed, Etruscan, 4 Piece	825.00
Tobacco Jar, Figural, Arab	95.00
Tobacco Jar, Figural, Irishman	100.00
Tobacco Jar, Figural, Scotsman	95.00
Toothpick, Figural, Mouse With Ear of Corn	135.00
Tray, Bread, Leaf, 13 In.	145.00
Urn, Cupids, Footed, 10 X 19 In.	295.00
Vase, Blown–Out Iris, Pink & Turquoise On Green, 10 1/2 In., Pair	225.00
Vase, Floral, Leaf Handle, 12 In.	70.00
Vase, Girl, In Wooden Shoes, Bowl of Fish, Vine Handle, 11 1/4 In.	155.00
Vase, Wishbone, Shells & Florals, 9 In.	38.50
Wall Pocket, 2 White Birds, Long Beaks, Foliage	145.00

Maps of all types have been collected for centuries. The earliest known printed maps were made in 1478. The first printed street map showed London in 1559. The first road maps for use by drivers of automobiles were made in 1901. Collectors buy maps that were pages of old books, as well as the multifolded road maps popular in this century.

MAP, Air Routes of The World, Air France, Old Airplanes	35.00
America, California As An Island, Seutter, Framed, C.1745, 19 X 23 In.	1500.00

Atlas, Railroad, 1901 .... 175.00
Beaver, East Coast, Newfoundland To Florida, 24 X 40 In. 2500.00
Chicago–Northwestern Railroad, Michigan, Wisconsin, 1925 .... 7.75
Countries Bordering On Mississippi & Missouri, 1821, 12 X 14 1/2 In. 140.00
Eastern & Middle States, Hand Drawn & Colored, C.1800, 21 X 25 In. 850.00
France, 1919 .... 15.00 To 18.00
German Railway System, World War II, 27 X 34 1/2 In. 25.00
Globe, Chein, 1933, 9 In. 22.00
Globe, Library, London Label 5100.00
Globe, New England, Land Masses, Mounted In Tripod, C.1810, 37 In. 5500.00
Globe, Terrestrial, Continental, Hand Painted, C.1611, 48 In. 4125.00
Globe, Terrestrial, London, Newton Son & Berry, 1836, 12 In. 1675.00
Globe, World, 1930s 47.00
Guide To Louisiana, Tourist & Shopper's, Rand McNally, Pocket, 1930 .... 10.00
Kling's Road Guide, 1913 .... 25.00
Montana, State Highway Commission, 1947 .... 2.00
North America, Canada, Mexico, Mounted On Canvas, J.Monk, 59 X 63 In. 275.00
Official Map of Georgia, Folded, Dept.of Agriculture, 1928, 28 X 36 In. 5.00
Road, Arkansas, Esso, 1947 .... 7.00
Road, Cleveland, Ohio, A.A.A., 1930s 3.00
Road, Farming, Illinois 17.00
Road, Iowa, Texaco 7.00
Road, Ohio, Dept.of Highways, 1933 .... 3.00
Road, Wisconsin, Pictures Wadham's Pump Globe 5.00
Santa Fe Lines, California, Dated 9/27/ 22, Folded, 8 X 9 In. 4.00
Soil, Grass Valley, California, Colored, 1918, 30 X 30 In. 8.50
Soil, Mississippi, 28 X 20 In. 7.50
Street Guide, Detroit, 157 Pages, 1924 .... 10.00
Tallis, Mexico, California & Texas, C.1850, 10 X 13 In. 200.00
Tennessee, Hand Colored, Linen Back, 1867, 20 X 48 In. 80.00
U.S., Union Pacific, Folded, 1947 .... 3.00
U.S.Military Forts, By Johnson & Browning, Dated 1861, 18 X 25 In. 60.00
United States & Canada, C.1850, 9 1/4 X 12 In. 90.00
United States, Hand Drawn, Color, Sarah J.Hunt, 1820, Framed, 18 X 22 In. 275.00
Unity Atlas, World, 32 Pages of Maps, 1899, 14 X 11 In. 18.00
Various Channels For Conveying Trade of Northwest To Atlantic, 1853 .... 85.00
Vicksburg, War, 1909 .... 16.00
Virginia & Maryland, N.& S.Carolina, Color, C.1831, 13 X 17 In. 50.00
Wall, Folds Into Book Cover, P.R.R., Dated 1907 .... 50.00
Washington City, Strangers Guide & Map, 1882 .... 20.00
Weber City, Amos & Andy, Original Envelope 35.00
Yellowstone National Park, Guide, 1920 .... 20.00

Marble is used in many ways on antiques. Marble tops are popular for tables because they resist stains and damage. Listed here are marble carvings, large or small figurines, and groups of people or animals that have been a special art form since the time of the ancient Greeks. Reproductions, especially of large Victorian groups, are being made of a mixture using marble dust. These are very difficult to detect and collectors should be careful. Other carvings are listed under Alabaster.

MARBLE CARVING, 5 Infant Musicians, Romanelli, Rectangular Base, 40 In. 4125.00
Bearded Man With Child, Lilies, 48 In. 300.00
Bust, Child, Young Boy, Smiling, 12 1/2 In. 330.00
Bust, David, 17 In. 250.00
Bust, Grecian Woman, White, R.Garella, 19th Century, 14 In. 650.00
Bust, Woman, Bare Breast, Socle, E.T.Waxler, 28 In., 2 Piece 2000.00
Bust, Woman, Face Pulled With Hands, Florence, Italy, 21 In. 300.00
Diana, Standing, Seated Hound, G.M.Benzoni, 1863, 4 Ft.4 In. 2750.00
Dog, Terrier, Reclining, White, 19th Century, 11 X 17 In. 225.00
Head, Youth, Classical Features, Concrete Socle, Italy, 9 In. 4125.00
Lady & Lion, Rossi, 26 In. 950.00
Lamb, Garden Sculpture, Lilies Support Body, 21 1/2 In. 1200.00
Lion, Guardian, Crouching, White, Chinese, 29 In. ....*Illus* 2400.00

Marble Carving, Lion, Guardian,
Crouching, White, Chinese, 29 In.

Marble Carving, Woman, Dove, Feccorelli,
23 X 25 In.

Madonna & Child, Standing, 14th Century, French, 13 1/4 In.	5500.00
Man, Seated In Boat, Marble Base, G.Colin, 17 1/8 In.	2475.00
Nude Woman, Standing On Clouds, H.Weigele, 46 In.	1925.00
Nude, Toe Into Water, Clutching Bath Sheet, 32 In.	1430.00
Pedestal, Gilt–Bronze Corinthian Capital, 1890, 47 In., Pair	6100.00
Pedestal, Green, Carved Garland Trim	550.00
Pedestal, Spiral Columnar, Green, Octagonal Base, 42 In.	250.00
Pedestal, Table, Rouge Fluted, Stepped Plinth, 13 In., Pair	1450.00
Prince Imperial, Leaning On Setter, Cauer, 1861, 30 In.	2475.00
Statue, Lady & Lion, Signed Rossi, 26 In.	950.00
Summer, Revealing Robes, Wheat In Hand, 19th Century, 36 In.	1450.00
Urn, Green Veined, Loop Handles, Ring Socle, 24 In., Pair	3575.00
Urn, Lamp Mounted, Stand, Electrified, Continental, 17 In.	1045.00
Urn, Tapered Body, Masks, Oak Leaves, Italy	320.00
Venus & Adonis, Paul–Louis Cyffle, 8 1/2 In.	880.00
Woman, Dove, Feccorelli, 23 X 25 In. ....*Illus*	1500.00
Woman, Seated On Rock, Bottinelli, 1854, 4 Ft.	4125.00

The game of marbles has been popular since the days of the ancient Romans. American children were able to buy marbles by the mid-eighteenth century. Dutch glazed clay marbles were least expensive. Glazed pottery marbles, attributed to the Bennington potteries in Vermont, were of a better quality. Marbles made of pink marble were also available by the 1830s. Glass marbles seem to have been made later. By 1880, Samuel C. Dyke of South Akron, Ohio, was making clay marbles and The National Onyx Marble Company was making marbles of onyx. The Navarre Glass Marble Company of Navarre, Ohio, and M. B. Mishler of Ravenna, Ohio, made the glass marbles. Ohio remained the center of the marble industry and the Akron-made Akro Agate brand became nationally known. The most expensive marbles collected today are the sulfides. These are glass marbles with frosted white figures in the center.

MARBLE, Agate, Carnelian, 1 5/8 In.	25.00
Agate, Tiger Eye, Second Eye, 15/16 In.	22.50
Banded Transparent, Red, Yellow, Blue Green, On Clear, 11/16 In.	5.00
Banded Transparent, Yellow & White, On Frosted, 3/4 In.	25.00
Cherry Carnelian, 7/8 In.	15.00
Clambroth, Black, White Lines, 7/8 In.	250.00
Clambroth, White, Red, Green, Blue Lines, 3/4 In.	280.00
Comic, Bimbo	50.00
Comic, Orphan Annie	50.00
Comic, Smitty	50.00

End–of–Day, 1 3/4 In.	450.00
Indian Swirl, Blue & White, On Black, 15/16 In.	160.00
Latticinio Swirl, 1 1/2 In.	75.00
Latticinio, 1 3/8 In.	68.00
Latticinio, Orange, 7/8 In.	38.00
Onionskin, Dark Blue, White, Red, 1 7/8 In.	270.00
Onionskin, Green, Brown, Lutz	295.00
Onionskin, Mica, Broken Cane, Blue, Orange, Yellow & White	325.00
Onionskin, Mica, Red & Yellow, 3/4 In.	25.00
Onionskin, Red, White & Blue, 2 1/4 In.	195.00
Onionskin, White & Light Green, 2 In.	80.00
Opaque Swirl, Red, White & Blue, 3/4 In.	20.00
Opaque, Black Glass, White Line, 5/8 In.	95.00
Opaque, Pink & Blue Banded, 1 1/4 In.	425.00
Peppermint Onion, 7/8 In.	35.00
Peppermint Swirl, 3/4 In.	50.00
Ribbon Core, 1 3/4 In.	90.00
Steelie, 1/2 In.	15.00
Steelie, 3/4 In.	20.00
Stone, 2 3/8 In.	85.00
Sulfide, Baboon, 1 3/8 In.	145.00 To 165.00
Sulfide, Bear, On All Fours, 1 1/2 In.	225.00
Sulfide, Bear, Sitting, 1 3/4 In.	125.00
Sulfide, Billy Goat, 1 3/4 In.	100.00
Sulfide, Bird, 1 7/16 In.	125.00
Sulfide, Boar, 1 1/2 In.	160.00
Sulfide, Bull, 2 1/8 In.	225.00
Sulfide, Camel, 1 1/2 In.	200.00
Sulfide, Cat, Pontil, 1 1/2 In.	90.00
Sulfide, Chicken, 1 1/2 In.	110.00
Sulfide, Child, With Ball & Mallet, 1 3/4 In.	1050.00
Sulfide, Classic Head	117.00
Sulfide, Cow, Grazing, 2 5/32 In.	225.00
Sulfide, Dog, Begging, 2 In.	115.00 To 125.00
Sulfide, Dog, Curled Tail, 1 1/5 In.	125.00
Sulfide, Dog, Lying Down, 1 3/4 In.	110.00 To 125.00
Sulfide, Dog, Standing, 1 3/8 In.	85.00
Sulfide, Donkey, 1 5/8 In.	100.00 To 125.00
Sulfide, Dove, On Post, 1 1/8 In.	145.00 To 185.00
Sulfide, Eagle, 1 5/8 In.	185.00
Sulfide, Elephant, 1 1/4 In.	85.00 To 200.00
Sulfide, Fish, 1 3/8 In.	125.00 To 200.00
Sulfide, Fox, Running, 1 7/16 In.	165.00
Sulfide, Frog, 1 7/16 In.	100.00 To 175.00
Sulfide, Goat, 2 1/32 In.	225.00
Sulfide, Hawk, 1 7/16 In.	175.00
Sulfide, Hen, On Nest, 1 1/2 In.	120.00
Sulfide, Hen, Pecking, 1 5/8 In.	110.00
Sulfide, Heron, 1 3/4 In.	150.00
Sulfide, Horse, Grazing, 1 3/8 In.	150.00
Sulfide, Lamb, 1 3/4 In.	125.00
Sulfide, Lion, 1 3/8 In.	75.00 To 275.00
Sulfide, Lion, 1 5/8 In.	175.00
Sulfide, Lion, Standing, 1 7/8 In.	125.00
Sulfide, Llama, 1 5/8 In.	90.00
Sulfide, Monkey, Sitting, 1 3/8 In.	135.00
Sulfide, Parrot, 2 3/8 In.	275.00
Sulfide, Pigeon, 1 3/8 In.	125.00
Sulfide, Prairie Chicken, 1 1/4 In.	325.00
Sulfide, Rabbit, Running, 1 3/8 In.	100.00 To 150.00
Sulfide, Ram, 2 1/8 In.	175.00
Sulfide, Rooster, 1 1/2 In.	100.00 To 135.00
Sulfide, Santa Claus, 2 In.	300.00
Sulfide, Sheep, 1 5/8 In.	110.00

Sulfide, Squirrel, Eating Nut, 1 1/2 In.	110.00
Sulfide, Steer	125.00
Sulfide, Turtle, 1 1/4 In.	125.00
Sulfide, Warthog, 2 1/4 In.	225.00
Sulfide, Whippet, 1 1/2 In.	120.00
Sulfide, Wild Boar, 1 1/2 In.	95.00 To 140.00
Swirl, 3 Gold Micas, 1 1/8 In.	55.00
Swirl, Clambroth, White & Green, Lines	185.00
Swirl, Divided Core, 1 1/2 In.	95.00
Swirl, End–O–Day, Cobalt, White, Pink & Green, 1 1/2 In.	35.00
Swirl, Lutz, Ribbon Core, Red & Blue, 1/2 In.	225.00
Swirl, Multi–Candy Stripe, Clear, 2 In.	120.00
Swirl, Net Core, Multicolored Outer Bands, 2 1/4 In.	240.00
Swirl, Red, White & Blue Stripes, Yellow Core, 2 In.	225.00
Swirl, White Latticinio Center, 1 7/8 In.	55.00
Transparent Swirl, Red, White & Blue, Divided Core, 2 3/8 In.	105.00
Transparent Swirl, White Latticinio Core, 2 1/16 In.	20.00
White Banded Opaque, 9 1/6 In.	110.00

The Marblehead Pottery was founded in 1905 by Dr. J. Hall as a rehabilitative program for the patients of a Marblehead, Massachusetts, sanitarium. Two years later it was separated from the sanitarium and it continued operations until 1936. Many of the pieces were decorated with marine motifs.

MARBLEHEAD, Candleholder, Blue, Scroll Handle, 3 In., Pair	150.00
Ginger Jar, Galleons, Circle & Scroll Band, No Lid, 1910, 7 In.	750.00
Tile, Flowers In Basket, Dark Brown, Framed, Logo, C.1910, 6 In.	125.00
Tile, Masted Ship, Waves, 4 Colors, C.1905, 6 In.	200.00
Tile, Painted Ship Seascape, Impressed Mark, Framed, 4 1/2 In.	150.00
Tile, Ship Design	350.00
Vase, Bulbous, Blue, 4 X 5 In.	70.00
Vase, Gray Floral Panels, Slate Ground, Artist, C.1905, 3 1/2 In.	275.00
Vase, Hanging Flowers, Gray Ground, Bulbous, Label, 6 In.	850.00
Vase, Olive Stylized Tree, Light Green Ground, C.1905, 6 In.	600.00
Vase, Purple Matte, 6 1/2 In.	95.00
Vase, Stylized Grape Design, Yellow, 3 1/2 X 3 1/2 In.	450.00
Vase, Stylized Green Bud & Stem, Dark Blue, HT, 1910, 3 1/2 In.	300.00
Vase, Stylized Leaf Panels, Brown Outlined, Bulbous, 1910, 6 In.	1300.00
Vase, Tapered Cylinder, Dark Green, 5 1/4 In.	68.00

R W Martin London Martinware is a salt–glazed stoneware made by the Martin Brothers of Middlesex, England, between 1873 and 1915. Many figural jugs and vases were made by the three brothers. Of special interest are the fanciful birds, usually made with removable heads.

MARTIN BROTHERS, Bird, Blue, Green, 1915, 7 1/2 In.	3500.00
Bird, Owl Form, 14 In.	4500.00
Flask, Stoneware, Molded Grinning Face, 1901, 9 In.	1400.00
Jar, Bird, Standing, Ocher, Navy, Chocolate, Signed, 9 In.	2100.00
Vase, Bird–Like Raised Face On Side, 1892, 8 1/2 In.	8000.00
Vase, Flowers, Leaves, 10 In.	200.00
Vase, Stoneware, Incised Frogs, Green, Brown, 1913, 5 In.	850.00

Mary Gregory glass is identified by a characteristic white figure painted on dark glass. It was made from 1870 to 1910. The name refers to any glass decorated with a white silhouette figure and not just to the Sandwich glass originally painted by Miss Mary Gregory. Many reproductions have been made and there are new pieces being sold in gift shops today.

MARY GREGORY, Bottle, Wine, Girl, Optic Effect, Faceted Stopper, Lime Green	145.00
Bowl, Ruffled, Sapphire Blue, Boy, Playing Instrument, 5 In.	195.00
Box, 2 Girls, Holding Flowers, Hinged Lid, Blue, 4 5/8 In.	395.00
Box, Boy Feeding Ducks, Royal Blue, White, 5 1/2 In.	630.00
Box, Boy In White On Cover, Lime Green, 3 X 3 3/4 In.	145.00
Box, Boy, Hoop & Stick, Lift–Off Lid, Lime Green, 2 3/8 In.	125.00

Spray the inside of a glass flower vase with a nonstick product, which is made to keep food from sticking to cooking pots. This will keep the vase from staining if water is left in the vase too long.

Box, Double Figure, Lift–Off Lid, Cranberry, 2 1/8 In.	175.00
Box, Girl Chasing Butterflies, Amethyst, 4 X 4 3/4 In.	450.00
Box, Girl, Butterfly, Cobalt Blue, Footed, 3 1/2 In.	165.00
Box, Hinged Cover, Boy With Flowers, Cranberry, 3 In.	215.00
Box, Hinged Cover, Boy, Foliage In White, Emerald Green, 3 In.	110.00
Box, Hinged Cover, Girl Feeding Bird, Sapphire Blue, 6 In.	475.00
Box, Hinged Cover, Girl In White, Sapphire Blue, 3 3/8 In.	150.00
Box, Hinged Cover, Girl, All White On Lid, Cobalt Blue, 4 In.	235.00
Box, Lift–Off Cover, Sprays, Boy, Cobalt Blue, 2 3/4 In.	135.00
Box, Running Boy On Cover, Flowered Base, Cranberry, 3 1/2 In.	275.00
Cruet, Boy On Fence, 2 Birds, Stopper, Amethyst, 8 1/2 In.	375.00
Cruet, Boy, Green Ground, Stopper, 8 1/4 In.	320.00
Cruet, Girl With Hoop, Blue	365.00
Cruet, White Scenic, Cobalt Blue	125.00
Decanter, Girl, Tinted Face, With Basket, Clear, 11 1/2 In.	135.00
Jar, Biscuit, Glass Cover, Boy, With Flesh Colored Face	150.00
Jug, White Boy, Gold Handle & Rim, Cranberry, 1 3/4 In.	225.00
Jug, White Figures of Boy, Cranberry, 2 In.	225.00
Lamp, Table, Enameled Glass, Wine, Figures, 20 In., Pair	300.00
Mug, Boy, Doffing Hat, Gold Trim, Amethyst	135.00
Mug, Young Boy, Clear Handle, Cranberry, 3 In.	70.00
Night–Light, Amethyst, Boy, Ormolu Mount, 9 1/4 In.	395.00
Perfume Bottle, Optic Panel, Girl, Blossoms, Cranberry	275.00
Pitcher, Boy, Gold Horn Around Neck, Gold Suit Trim, 7 In.	195.00
Pitcher, Boy, Green Handle, Optic Effect, Lime Green, 6 1/2 In.	125.00
Pitcher, Boy, With Kite, Emerald Green, 4 In.	65.00
Pitcher, Girl With Staff, Sapphire Blue, 10 In.	235.00
Pitcher, Girl, Bird In Hand, Applied Handle, Tankard, 7 1/8 In.	265.00
Pitcher, Girl, Lilies–of–The–Valley, Emerald, 7 5/8 In.	165.00
Pitcher, Lemonade, Girl, Fishing, Amber, 10 5/8 In.	185.00
Pitcher, Tankard Shape, Green Applied Handle, 6 In.	98.00
Pitcher, Water, Girl, Gold Dress, Sapphire Blue, 10 3/4 In.	275.00
Pitcher, Water, Squared Shape, Amber, 8 1/2 In.	275.00
Pitcher, Young Girl, Amber Handle, Olive Amber, 11 1/8 In.	225.00
Salt, Boy, Foliage In White, 2 1/4 In.	135.00
Sugar Shaker, Cobalt Blue, Tinted Face	80.00
Sugar Shaker, Optic Panel, Boy, Flowers, Cranberry, 5 In.	395.00
Tray, Card, Girl, Butterfly Net, Brass Stand, Cobalt Blue, 4 In.	135.00
Tray, Dresser, Boy Pulling Branch, Cobalt Blue, 7 X 10 In.	245.00
Tumbler, Boy Holding Flower, All White, 4 1/2 In.	75.00
Tumbler, Girl, Brown Hair, Feeding Birds, 5 In.	75.00
Tumbler, Juice, Girl, Birds, Cobalt Blue, 3 3/4 In.	50.00
Vase, All White Girl, Cranberry, 6 1/2 In.	98.00
Vase, Amethyst, Boy Holding Balloon, White Enameling, 8 In.	195.00
Vase, Boy & Girl, Facing, Amberina, 10 1/2 In., Pair	550.00
Vase, Boy Fishing, Fluted, Blue, 9 1/2 In.	110.00

Vase, Boy, All White, Cobalt Blue, 7 1/4 In.	110.00
Vase, Boy, Clear Handle, Lime Green, 6 3/4 In.	95.00
Vase, Boy, Scalloped, Sapphire Blue, 7 1/4 In.	135.00
Vase, Chalice Shape, Boy Tooting Bugle, Cranberry, 7 In.	135.00
Vase, Fluted Rim, Cobalt Blue, 10 In.	70.00
Vase, Girl & Basket, Boy, Hat & Cane, Cobalt Blue, 10 In., Pair	225.00
Vase, Girl Carrying Floral Bouquet, Amber, 6 3/8 In.	145.00
Vase, Girl Playing With Balloon, Cranberry, White, 8 1/2 In.	175.00
Vase, Girl With Dog, Black, 8 In.	45.00
Vase, Girl With Hat, Inverted Thumbprint, Cranberry, 6 In.	150.00
Vase, Girl, Flowers, Inverted Thumbprint, Cranberry, 9 3/4 In.	225.00
Vase, Girl, On Shore, Waving, Snail Handles, Green, 11 5/8 In.	275.00
Vase, Girl, White Enamel, Cranberry, 8 3/4 In.	175.00
Vase, Girls, Carrying Watering Cans, Cranberry, 8 7/8 In., Pr.	395.00
Vase, Girls, Hoops, Sticks, Mahogany Red, 12 1/2 In., Pair	425.00
Vase, Opaline, Green, 5 In.	45.00
Vase, Young Boy, All White, Sapphire Blue, 10 In.	75.00
Vase, Young Boy, Orange, 4 1/8 In.	85.00
Vase, Young Girl, Cranberry, 8 3/4 In.	175.00
Vase, Young Girl, Holding Branch, Cobalt Blue, 6 5/8 In.	95.00

MASONIC, see Fraternal

Massier pottery is iridescent French art pottery made by Clement Massier in Golfe–Juan, France, in the late nineteenth and early twentieth centuries. It has an iridescent metallic luster glaze that resembles the Weller Sicard pottery glaze. Most pieces are marked "J. Massier."

MASSIER, Knife Rest, Floral, Signed	20.00
Vase, Pansy Blossoms, Allover Magenta, Signed, 1891, 15 In.	3630.00

Large wooden matches were used in the nineteenth and twentieth centuries for a variety of purposes. The kitchen stove and the fireplace or furnace had to be lit regularly. One type of match holder was made to hang on the wall, another was designed to be kept on a tabletop. Of special interest today are match holders that have advertisements as part of the design.

MATCH HOLDER, 1 Open Pocket, 1 Self–Closing, Wall, Scalloped, C.1865, 9 In.	140.00
Acorns, Oak Leaves, Acorn Open Pocket, Wall, Brass, 6 1/2 In.	85.00
Aladdin	30.00
Alligator	60.00
American Steel Farm Fences, Wall	45.00
Amish Man, Shield, Cast Iron, 6 X 4 1/2 In.	45.00
Beetle, Figural, Lead, 4 1/4 In.	22.00
Bird, Secures Match With Bill, Iron	47.00
Boot, Iron	165.00
Bryant & May Limited, Gold Paint, Tin, 1 3/4 X 1 3/8 In.	9.50
Camel, Brass	25.00
Child, Carrying Wood, Cast Iron	40.00
Combination Salt & Pepper, Home Bakery, So.Ottumwa, Iowa, Tin	50.00
Dead Stock Removed Blue Earth Rendering, Wall	50.00
DeLaval Cream Separator	75.00
Devil, Iron	65.00
Dockash Stove Factory, Wall	40.00
Dog Dressed As Man, Smoking Pipe, Bisque, 4 In.	85.00
Dog On Lid, Rectangular, Ribbed, Cast Iron, 1860, 4 In.	65.00
Fatty Arbuckle, Bisque	50.00
Figural, Bird Secures Match With Bill, Iron	48.00
Flower Spray On Red Horseshoe, Good Luck, Newguay, 1 3/4 In.	25.00
Frog, Iron	125.00
Game Pouch, Brass	55.00
Gothic Arch Pattern, Cast Iron, Wall, 3 1/2 In.	53.00
Juicy Fruit Gum	75.00
King Tut, Art Deco, Brass	20.00
Lax–Ets	38.50

J.Massier fils

Leering Old Man, Chalkware, 4 In. 27.00
Log Cabin, Roof Hinged To Lift, Cast Iron, C.1860 .... 130.00
Michigan Stove Co., Cast Iron, Wall .... 60.00 To 65.00
Monkey, Cigarette 30.00
Moxie, Tin 195.00
Old Judson Whiskey 80.00
Open Umbrella, Black Metal 15.00
Pabst's Okay Specific, Celluloid On Metal, 1931 Calendar 12.50
Pointer Stoves & Ranges, Cast Iron, Wall 60.00
Rockford Watches, Tin .... 275.00 To 350.00
Safety First, Tin 38.50
Sharples Separator 151.00
St.Louis Fair, Tin, 1904 .... 25.00
Swisher Coal, Lima, Ohio, Tin 34.00
Top Hat, Horseshoe, Iron, Wall 13.00
Vulcan Farm Machinery, Man, Die Cut Tin, Wall 295.00
Wagon & Horses, Porcelain 15.00
Woman, Next To Wicker Basket, Clear Glass, 5 In. 57.00
Woman, Windsor & Co.Insurance, Tin 65.00

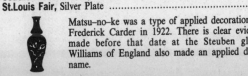

Early matches were made with phosphorus and could ignite
unexpectedly. Match safes were designed to be carried in the pocket.
The matches were safely stored in the tightly closed container.
Examples were made in sterling silver, plated silver, or other metals.
The English call these "vesta boxes."

MATCH SAFE, Alligator Route 275.00
Arm & Hammer, Gutta–Percha 55.00
Art Nouveau Stylized Flowers, Loop, German Silver 75.00
Bell's Waterproof Wax Vestas 5.00
Black Man Seated On Stump 35.00
Blue Willow, Porcelain, Bailey Walker, 3 1/4 X 6 In. 60.00
Boot Shape, Figural, Brass 14.00
Diamond Horseshoes, Sapphire, Gold Button, Gunmetal 325.00
Dr.Shopps Coffee 90.00
Embossed Hunt Scene, Sterling Silver 125.00
Facing Donkeys, Table Model, When We Meet Again, Zinc, 9 1/4 In. 85.00
GAR 28th Encampment 85.00
Hercules Powder, Celluloid 40.00
Hinged Top Striker Plate, Bakelite 38.00
Horse Hoof, Figural, Top Opens, Striker On Bottom, Silver Plate 125.00
Hunt Scene, Victorian, Sterling Silver 175.00
Huntley & Palmer, Top Opens, Striker On Bottom, 2 In. 135.00
Indian, Motorcycle 65.00
International Tailoring Co. 28.00
John Treber Wholesale Liquor & Cigars, Deadwood, S.D. 32.00
Kerr, 5 Cherubs, Angels, Wishbone, Sterling Silver 350.00
Klinger Funeral Home, Springfield, Missouri 35.00
Lapis With Brass, Cylindrical Hinged Top, 2 5/8 X 7/8 In. 350.00
Marbles Co. 23.00
Mouse, Pewter, 2 In. 145.00
Nouveau Scrollwork, Sterling Silver 75.00
Oak Hall, Wanamaker & Brown, Brass, Pocket 28.00
Pabst Beer, Brass 25.00
Pig, Fat & Chubby, Stand On 4 Legs, Silver Metal, 2 1/4 In. 95.00
Pointers, With Quail 20.00
Skull, Figural, Top Opens, Striker Under Chin, Brass, 1 3/4 In. 145.00
Southern Blue Coals, Brass 35.00
St.Louis Fair, Silver Plate 20.00

Matsu–no–ke was a type of applied decoration for glass patented by
Frederick Carder in 1922. There is clear evidence that pieces were
made before that date at the Steuben glassworks. Stevens &
Williams of England also made an applied decoration by the same
name.

MATSU–NO–KE, Candy Dish, Cover, Clear Bowl, Green Stem, Steuben, 6 1/2 In. 175.00

MATT MORGAN
–CIN. O–
ART POTTERY C°

Matt Morgan, an English artist, was making pottery in Cincinnati, Ohio, by 1883. His pieces were decorated to resemble Moorish wares. Incised designs and colors were applied to raised panels on the pottery. Shiny or matte glazes were used. The company lasted only a few years.

MATT MORGAN, Jug, Liquor, Cornstalks, Blue Glaze, Chain, Tag, C.1885, 7 In. 450.00
Vase, Incised Flowers, 8 In. 475.00

McCoy

McCoy pottery is made in Roseville, Ohio. The J. W. McCoy Pottery was founded in 1899. It became the Brush McCoy Pottery Company in 1911. The name changed to the Brush Pottery in 1925. The word "Brush" was usually included in the mark on their pieces. The Nelson McCoy Sanitary and Stoneware Company, a different firm, was founded in Roseville, Ohio, in 1910. The firm made art pottery after 1926. In 1933 it became the Nelson McCoy Pottery. Pieces marked "McCoy" were made by the Nelson McCoy Company.

MCCOY, Bank, Piggy, Large 20.00
Bank, Smile, Yellow 10.00
Basket, Acorns, Oak Leaves, Twig Handle, Marked, 7 1/2 In. 17.00
Bowl, Amaryllis Raised Design, Pastel Colors, Footed, Large 18.00
Bowl, Onyx, Rust, Beige, Dark Brown, 5 In. 32.00
Coffeepot, El Rancho 35.00
Cookie Jar, Asparagus, 1977–1979 .... 27.00 To 39.00
Cookie Jar, Bananas, 1950–1952 .... 27.00 To 40.00
Cookie Jar, Barn 57.00
Cookie Jar, Barrel, Signed 18.00
Cookie Jar, Bear, Upside Down, Black & White, Red Tongue, Marked 32.00
Cookie Jar, Betsy Baker, 1975 ....   45.00
Cookie Jar, Bobby Baker, 1974–1975 .... 22.00 To 30.00
Cookie Jar, Boy On Baseball, Marked, 1978 ....   59.00
Cookie Jar, Boy On Football, 1978 ....   15.00
Cookie Jar, Caboose, 1961 ....   50.00
Cookie Jar, Chef, Bust, 1962–1964 .... 35.00 To 45.00
Cookie Jar, Chipmunk, 1959–1962 ....   40.00
Cookie Jar, Christmas Tree, 1959 .... 175.00 To 210.00
Cookie Jar, Christmas Tree, Marked 300.00
Cookie Jar, Circus Horse, 1962 .... 45.00 To 100.00
Cookie Jar, Clown, Bust, 1943–1949 ....   55.00
Cookie Jar, Clown, In Barrel, 1953–1956 ....   32.00
Cookie Jar, Coffee Grinder, 1961–1968 .... 18.00 To 25.00
Cookie Jar, Coffee Mug, 1963–1966 ....   10.00
Cookie Jar, Cookie Bank, 1961 .... 30.00 To 50.00
Cookie Jar, Cookie Cabin, 1957–1960 ....   45.00
Cookie Jar, Cookie Churn, 1977, 1987 ....   29.00

Figurines are often damaged. Examine the fingers, toes, and other protruding parts for damage or repairs.

Cookie Jar, Cookie Safe, 1962–1963 .... 20.00
Cookie Jar, Covered Wagon, 1962 .... 18.00 To 38.00
Cookie Jar, Davy Crocket, 1957 .... 375.00
Cookie Jar, Dog On Basket Weave, 1956–1957 .... 30.00 To 39.00
Cookie Jar, Dutch Boy, 1946 .... 25.00
Cookie Jar, Dutch Treat Barn, 1968–1973 .... 25.00 To 30.00
Cookie Jar, Early American, Frontier Family, 1964–1971 .... 25.00
Cookie Jar, Engine, 1963–1964 .... 35.00 To 75.00
Cookie Jar, Fortune Cookies, Marked, 1965, 1968 .... 39.00
Cookie Jar, Globe, 1960 .... 125.00
Cookie Jar, Grandfather Clock, 1962–1964 .... 35.00 To 45.00
Cookie Jar, Granny, Gold Rim Glasses, 1974–1975 .... 45.00 To 62.00
Cookie Jar, Hamm's Bear, 1972 .... 55.00
Cookie Jar, Hobby Horse, 1948–1953 .... 70.00
Cookie Jar, Honey Bear, 1953–1955 .... 25.00 To 45.00
Cookie Jar, Hound Dog, Thinking Puppy, 1977–1979 .... 25.00 To 27.00
Cookie Jar, Indian, 1954–1956 ....90.00 To 180.00
Cookie Jar, Kettle, Black, 1962–1964 .... 15.00 To 25.00
Cookie Jar, Kittens & Yarn, 1954–1955 .... 30.00
Cookie Jar, Kittens On Basket Weave, 1956–1969 .... 30.00
Cookie Jar, Koala Bear, Marked, 1983–1985 .... 39.00
Cookie Jar, Kookie Kettle, 1959–1977 .... 18.00 To 25.00
Cookie Jar, Lamb On Basket Weave, 1956–1957 .... 10.00 To 25.00
Cookie Jar, Little Clown, Decorated, 1945 .... 35.00
Cookie Jar, Lollipops, 1958–1960 .... 10.00
Cookie Jar, Mac Dog, 1967 .... 35.00
Cookie Jar, Monk, Thou Shalt Not Steal, 1968–1973 .... 30.00 To 35.00
Cookie Jar, Oaken Bucket, Marked, 1961–1971 .... 12.00
Cookie Jar, Old Fashioned Auto, Touring Car, 1961–1964 .... 25.00 To 60.00
Cookie Jar, Owl, 1976 .... 25.00
Cookie Jar, Pepper, Yellow, Marked, 1972–1980 .... 24.00
Cookie Jar, Pineapple, 1955–1957 .... 22.00 To 30.00
Cookie Jar, Rocking Chair, Dalmatians, 1961 .... 150.00
Cookie Jar, Sad Clown, 1970–1971 .... 48.00
Cookie Jar, Snoopy, 1970 .... 135.00
Cookie Jar, Spaceship, Friendship 7, 1962–1963 .... 50.00
Cookie Jar, Strawberry, 1955–1957 .... 15.00 To 30.00
Cookie Jar, Tepee, 1957–1959 ....67.50 To 155.00
Cookie Jar, Time For Cookies, Mouse On Clock, 1968–1973 .... 22.00 To 24.00
Cookie Jar, Timmy Tortoise, 1977–1980 .... 17.00 To 39.00
Cookie Jar, W.C.Fields, 1972–1974 .... 55.00 To 80.00
Cookie Jar, Wishing Well, Wish I Had A Cookie, 1961–1970 ...... 14.00 To 33.00
Cookie Jar, Wren House, 1959–1960 .... 75.00
Creamer, Hershey's 10.00
Figurine, Dutch Shoe, Aqua 6.00
Figurine, Mother Goose 22.00
Figurine, Panther, Art Deco, 17 In. 23.00
Flowerpot, Basket Weave Pattern, Green 7.50
Flowerpot, Basket Weave Pattern, Pink 5.50
Jar, Pretzel, Buccaneer, Green 70.00
Jardiniere, Copper Mums, Brown To Dark Green, Loy–Nel–Art, 4 1/2 In. 60.00
Jardiniere, Pansies, Loy–Nel–Art, 5 In. 75.00
Jardiniere, Sylvan 65.00
Lamp, Cowboy Boots, Brown, No Shade, 6 3/4 In. 18.00
Lamp, Stylized Gazelle 55.00
Mug, Buccaneer, Green 12.00
Mug, Little Boy Blue, Brush 38.00
Mug, Peter Pan, Brush 38.00
Mug, Robin Hood, Brush 38.00
Mustache Cup, Father's 10.00
Pitcher, Barrel, Green Band, Nelson 35.00
Pitcher, Buccaneer, Green 70.00
Pitcher, Chicken 22.00
Pitcher, Donkey 15.00

Pitcher, Fish	15.00
Pitcher, Parrot	15.00
Pitcher, Sunfish Design	30.00
Planter, Basket Weave	9.50
Planter, Carriage Umbrella	30.00
Planter, Frog With Umbrella	35.00
Planter, Liberty Bell	50.00
Planter, Scotty's Head	17.50
Planter, Spinning Wheel	18.00
Planter, Triple Lily, 1953	45.00
Planter, Uncle Sam	10.00
Planter-Bookends, Floral Mold, Green & Yellow	15.00
Stein, Buccaneer, Green	10.00
Sugar & Creamer, Elsie & Elmer	40.00
Vase, Cascade, High Gloss, 7 In.	25.00
Vase, Fan, Chartreuse & Green, 8 1/2 In.	12.00
Vase, Onyx, Rust, Beige & Dark Brown, 5 In.	32.00
Vase, Springwood, Pink, 10 In.	20.00
Vase, Wild Roses, Loy-Nel-Art, 13 In.	325.00
Wall Pocket, Clock	24.00
Wall Pocket, Owl	65.00
Wall Pocket, Violin	10.00
Wall Pocket, Woman Clown, Ruff & Hat	19.50
Watering Can, Turtle	15.00

PRESCUT The McKee name has been associated with various glass enterprises in the United States since 1836, including J. & F. McKee (1850), Bryce, McKee & Co. (1850 to 1854), McKee and Brothers (1865), and National Glass Co. (1899). In 1903, the McKee Glass Company was formed in Jeanette, Pennsylvania. It became McKee Division of the Thatcher Glass Co. in 1951 and was bought out by the Jeanette Corporation in 1961. Pressed glass, kitchenwares, and tablewares were produced.

MCKEE, see also Custard Glass

MCKEE, Apollo, Toothpick, Pink	34.00
Autumn, Banana Bowl, Green	25.00
Bowl, Dots, Red, 9 In.	11.00
Bowl, Laurel, Ivory, 11 In.	21.50
Bowl, Laurel, Multicolor, 4 1/2 In.	12.00
Box, Salt, Yellow	95.00
Cake Plate, Harp	6.00
Candlestick, Rock Crystal, Amber, 9 In., Pair	130.00
Canister, Coffee, Jadite	25.00
Canister, Word Cereal	30.00
Celery, Rock Crystal, Oblong, 12 In.	18.00
Champagne, Rock Crystal, 6 In.	11.00
Cooler, Water, Vaseline, Spigot, 21 In.	295.00
Creamer, Comet	40.00
Cruet, Torquay, Red	140.00
Cup & Saucer, Laurel	18.00
Goblet, Rock Crystal, Stem, 8 Oz.	12.00
Pitcher, Aztec, 5 In.	15.00
Pitcher, Toltec	40.00
Plate, Moonstone, 10 1/2 In.	10.00
Punch Bowl, Aztec	90.00
Reamer, Jade	10.00
Salt & Pepper, Jadite	25.00
Sherbet, Clico Line, Green Bowl, Black Footed, 6 Piece	76.50
Sherbet, Rock Crystal, Plain Edge, 4 Piece	20.00
Shot Glass, Coaster, Green, Set of 4	250.00
Skillet, Range-Tec, Glass, 6 In.	20.00
Sugar, Open, White	20.00
Syrup, Petticoat, Vaseline	130.00
Tom & Jerry Set, White, Black Letters, 7 Piece	20.00

Toothpick, Champions, Green	35.00
Toothpick, Rock Crystal	35.00
Toothpick, Teutonic, Green	45.00
Tumbler, Orange Juice	35.00
Vase, Chalaine, Nude, 8 1/2 In.	165.00
Vase, Nude, Green, 8 In.	129.00

MECHANICAL BANK, see Bank, Mechanical

 All types of equipment used by doctors or hospitals are included in this section. Medical office furniture, operating tools, microscopes, thermometers, and other paraphernalia used by doctors are included. Medicine bottles are listed under Bottle. There are related collectibles listed under Dental.

MEDICAL, Almanac, Burdock Blood Bitters, 1888, 32 Pages	7.50
Almanac, Hostetter's For 1901	4.00
Backbar, Apothecary's Dispensing Unit, 10-11-1871	4500.00
Bag, Doctor's, Alligator	30.00
Beaker, Apothecary, Pedestal, Glass, 32 Oz.	10.00
Bleeder, 10 Blades, Brass, 1 5/8 In.	185.00
Bleeder, 3 Shark Teeth Shaped Blades, Horn Grip, 3 In., 3 Piece	38.00
Bleeder, Bone Handle, 3 Blades	95.00
Bleeder, Brass, Leather Box	90.00
Book, People's Medical Advisor, Pierce, 1909	8.50
Bottle, Drug, Cobalt Blue, Ground Stopper, 7 In.	35.00
Box, File, Druggist's, Filled With Prescriptions, Dated 1924	115.00
Breast Pump	9.00
Case, Black Leatherette, 8 Glass Vials, Labels, Pocket, C.1900	10.00
Case, Doctor's, Leather, Pullman Style	44.00
Case, Leather, Folding, Original Bottles, Civil War	22.50
Chart, Eye, Wall Hung, Wood Rolls, 7 Ft.	45.00
Electric Nerve Stimulator, E.J.Colby	175.00
Eyecup, Embossed Safe Guard, Cobalt Blue	10.00
Eyecup, John Bull, Cobalt Blue, 1917	35.00
Eyecup, John Bull, Green	32.00 To 40.00
Eyecup, McKesson's, Tin	5.00
Eyecup, Pedestal, Embossed, Green, Made In England	20.00
Eyecup, Pedestal, Fluted, Embossed Base, British	14.00
Eyecup, Picture of Eye On Side, Dated 1937	17.50
Eyecup, Reservoir Type, Medium Green, England	19.00
Eyecup, Wyeth, Blue	5.00 To 33.00
Fleam, 3 Blades, Folding Brass Frame, 1 X 3 In.	65.00
Haemometer Set, Complete, Original Case	25.00
Hot Water Bottle, Child's, Cat Shape	18.00
Hot Water Bottle, Child's, Mary Had A Little Lamb	15.00
Hot Water Bottle, Child's, Nursery Rhyme	10.00
Inhaler, Eagle Menthol, Tubular Glass, Cork Ends, Label, 3 3/4 In.	3.50
Instrument, Electraply, Battery Operated, Quack, Box	45.00
Knife, Bleeder, 18th Century	20.00
Knife, Blood Letting, Fleam, Wooden Handle, 6 In.	30.00
Kystoskop, Urologist's, C.1910, Box	75.00
Leg, Artificial, Leather, Metal & Wood	15.00
Machine, EKG, Cardiotron, Model PC2, Wooden Case	150.00
Machine, Electreat Roller, Chrome, Uses Batteries, Quack Device	35.00
Master Violet Ray Machine, Quack	30.00
Medeotronics Electric Shock Pulsator, Chiropractic, Model 50	140.00
Mortar & Pestle, Cast Iron, 4 7/8 In.	15.00
Mortar & Pestle, Iron, Clark & Co., 8 In.Pressed Glass Pestle	28.00
Mortar & Pestle, Lignum Vitae	300.00
Mortar, Pharmacy Display, Embossed RX, White Ceramic, 7 In.	45.00
Pill Baller, Cherry Treenware, Turned Pedestal Base, 4 In.	150.00
Prescription, Medicinal Liquor, U.S.Government, 1932, 4 X 5 1/2 In.	4.00
Quassia Cup, Pharmacist's, Wooden, Bitter Water, For Fever Cure	35.00
Roller, Pharmaceutical Pills	78.00
Saddlebag, With Bottles & Instrument, Set	195.00

Saw, Surgeon's, Brass Frame, 11 In.	110.00
Spoon, Dose, Metal, Rubber Bulb	20.00
Spoon, Glass, Bovinine Embossed On Handle, 5 3/4 In.	4.00
Spoon, Medicine, Folding, Sterling Silver	65.00
Sterilizer, Renwal, Ceramic	12.50
Stretcher, Bunion	25.00
Table, Chiropractor's, Oak & Leather, Folds Into Carrying Case	50.00
Tumbler, Dose, A.H.Lewis Medicine Co., Bolivar, Mo., 8 Tsps.	8.00
Tumbler, Medicine, Doctor's, 1 Oz.	4.00
Urinometer, Glass	4.00
Vaporizer, Cresolene	35.00
Wheelchair, 3rd Wheel, Small	100.00

Meerschaum pipes and other pieces of carved meerschaum, a soft mineral, date from the nineteenth century to the present.

MEERSCHAUM, Cigar Holder, Hunter With Dog	175.00
Pipe, Art Nouveau, Devil	250.00
Pipe, Bear Bowl	60.00
Pipe, Bearded Men With Turbans, White	75.00
Pipe, Bird's Claw Holding Pipe Bowl, White, Fitted Case	45.00
Pipe, Boy & Top Hat	450.00
Pipe, Boy With Mandolin, 12 In.	143.00
Pipe, C.P.F.Carved Fox Extending Bowl, 7 1/2 In.	120.00
Pipe, Calabash, 2 3/4 In.Bowl, Walnut Stand, Austria	39.00
Pipe, Cheroot, Coal Miner Digging Coal	225.00
Pipe, Dog, Ivory, Amber	75.00
Pipe, Hand Holding Corn	375.00
Pipe, Lady, Figural	45.00
Pipe, Laughing Bacchus	38.00
Pipe, Lion's Head, Leather Case	65.00
Pipe, Man's Face Bowl, 13 In.	95.00
Pipe, Raised Floral & Gold Work	150.00
Pipe, Slave Man & Woman, Chased By Dogs, 1850, 7 1/2 In.	650.00
Pipe, Sultan's Head, 13 In.	125.00
Pipe, Sultan's Head, Amber Stem	70.00
Pipe, Turk's Head	85.00
Pipe, Turkish Holy Man, Turban, Fitted Case, Unused, 6 In.	35.00

Meissen is a town in Germany where porcelain has been made since 1710. Any china made in the town can be called Meissen, although the famous Meissen factory made the finest porcelains of the area. The crossed swords mark of the great Meissen factory has been copied by many other firms in Germany and other parts of the world.

MEISSEN, Basket, Reticulated, Blue & White, Florettes, C.1765, 9 7/8 In.	495.00
Bowl, Allover Gold Encrusted Floral Design, Marked, 10 1/2 In.	135.00
Bowl, Bird Over Nest, Eggs, Ferns, Allover Beading, Marked, 13 In.	675.00
Bowl, Kakiemon Style, Branches, Powdered Puce, Crossed Swords, 8 In.	2000.00
Bowl, Oriental Flowering Plants, Phoenix Interior, 9 5/8 In.	1200.00
Bowl, Raised Gold, White Leaf Design At Rim, Marked, 10 1/2 In.	175.00
Box, Cover, Marked, Round, 2 In.	60.00
Box, Flowers, Gilt Borders, White With Magenta, Marked, 3 1/2 In.	425.00

A vase that is drilled for a lamp—even if the hole for the wiring is original—is worth 30 to 50 percent of the value of the same vase without a hole.

Box, Polychrome Scene On Lid, Youth, Maidens, 3 1/2 In.	275.00
Candelabra, Figural, Jupiter, 2–Light, Crossed Swords, 15 In., Pair	4100.00
Candleholder, 2–Light, Tree Trunk Support, 13 1/2 In., Pair	575.00
Chocolate Pot, Cover, Branch Molded Spout & Handle, 6 3/4 In.	1650.00
Clock, Jupiter & Prometheus, Pastel Flowers, Crossed Swords, 32 In.	4125.00
Clock, Rococo, Figures, Flowers, Scrolls, Blue, White, 17 In.	2100.00
Compote, Boat Pedestal, Venus, King Neptune, 11 X 15 In.	750.00
Corkscrew, Scent Bottle, Stays In Cork After Opened, 1860	290.00
Cup & Saucer, Magenta, Gold Handle, Demitasse	45.00
Cup & Saucer, Snake Handle, Blue Crossed Swords Mark	75.00
Cup & Saucer, Yellow Floral, Demitasse	45.00
Cup, Chocolate, Purple Stag, Double Scroll Handle, 3 In.	650.00
Dish, Shell Handle, 12 In.	100.00
Figurine, Allegorical Spring Maiden, White Robe, 1750, 5 9/16 In.	1100.00
Figurine, Bear, Standing, Brown, 7 1/2 In.	200.00
Figurine, Blackamoor, White Headdress, C.1740, 5 5/8 In.	825.00
Figurine, Children, Dancing, Colonial Costumes, Marked, 7 1/2 In.	250.00
Figurine, Cupid, Standing, Pushing Cart, Spoke Wheels, Marked, 9 In.	325.00
Figurine, Cupids Painting On Easel, 6 X 6 1/2 In.	450.00
Figurine, Dr.Boloardo, Italian Comedy, Peter Reinicke, 5 3/8 In.	2200.00
Figurine, Goat Scene With Children, 7 X 8 1/2 In.	450.00
Figurine, Goat, Brown Streaked Shaggy Coat, C.1745, 5 5/8 In.	1210.00
Figurine, Hare, Crouching, Gray, Pink Tinged Ears, 1745–50, 4 1/8 In.	1760.00
Figurine, Sawyer, White Sawhorse, J.J.Kaendler, C.1745, 5 In.	1320.00
Figurine, Winged Cupid, Pushing Cart, Roses On Wheels, Marked, 9 In.	295.00
Gravy Boat, Attached Liner, Florals, Gold, 19th Century	175.00
Group, 18th–Century Dress, Sheep, Statue of Pan, 13 In.	800.00
Group, Harlequin & Columbine, Crossed Swords, 1913, 10 5/8 In.	2530.00
Group, Hercules & Omphales As Children, 1760, Crossed Swords, 5 In.	770.00
Group, Monkey Band, 24 Piece, 4 In.	5775.00
Perfume Bottle, Pilgrim, Flask, Quatrefoil Panel, 1725, 3 1/4 In.	9350.00
Perfume Bottle, Rococo Cartouche Shape, Stopper, 1745, 3 13/16 In.	3500.00
Plaque, Military, Blue & White, PUG, 10 In.	160.00
Plate, Central Rose, White Ground, 7 3/4 In., 6 Piece	180.00
Plate, Courting Couple, Pierced Edge, Augustus Rex, 8 3/8 In.	225.00
Plate, Fliegender Hund, Bird In Flight, 1735–40, 9 3/8 In.	770.00
Plate, French Opera, Signed, 8 1/2 In.	30.00
Plate, Gold Morning Glories, Deep Yellow Scalloped, 11 1/2 In.	165.00
Plate, Kakiemon, 3 Friends, Crossed Swords, C.1740, 9 1/4 In.	1100.00
Platter, King Louis XIV & Marie–Therese, Crossed Swords, 20 In.	1750.00
Platter, Spring Flowers, White Ground, 19th Century, 19 In.	450.00
Platter, White, Blue Edge, Waves, Oval, 1900, 13 In.	715.00
Snuffbox, Lady Portrait, Silver Gilt, Oval, 1740–45, 2 13/16 In.	4950.00
Tea Caddy, Armorial, Figures & Animal, Cover, 1735–39, 4 1/8 In.	6600.00
Tea Set, Sprays of Flowers, Rococo Gold, Serpent Spout, 3 Piece	400.00
Teabowl & Saucer, Amorous Couple, Landscape, 1725–35, 3 1/8 & 5 In.	995.00
Toothpick, Clown	55.00
Tray, Bread, Cobalt Blue, Gold, White, 12 X 7 1/2 In.	250.00
Tureen, Duck Cover, White, Delineated Plumage, 1790–1810, 8 5/16 In.	880.00
Tureen, Underglaze Blue Design, Gilt, 6 1/4 In., Pair	70.00
Urn, Cherubs, Allover Porcelain Flowers, Marked, 12 In.	400.00
Vase, Harbor Scene, Men & Women, Gold Rim, Cover, C.1880, 8 3/4 In.	175.00
Vase, Snowball Pattern, Grapevines, Songbirds, Marked, 13 In.	755.00
Waste Bowl, Chinoiserie, Figures, Interior, River Landscape, 7 In.	1200.00

Mercury, or silvered, glass was first made in the 1850s. It lost favor
for a while but became popular again about 1910. It looks like a
piece of silver.

MERCURY GLASS, Candleholder, Allover Foliage, 10 In.	30.00
Candlestick, 9 1/2 In., Pair	200.00
Figurine, Stork, Germany, 4 In., Pair	50.00
Rose Bowl	20.00
Vase, Floral Design, Pedestal Base, 10 1/4 In.	32.00
Vase, Flower, Bird, Silver, Pair	25.00

Mettlach, Germany, is a city where the Villeroy and Boch factories worked. Steins from the firm are known as Mettlach steins. They date from about 1842. PUG means "painted under glaze." The steins can be dated from the marks on the bottom which include a date–number code. Other pieces may be listed in the Villeroy & Boch category.

METTLACH, Beaker, No.1785, 4 Helmeted Heads Support Cup, 17 In. 500.00
Charger, Cameo, Green, White, Figures At Harvest, 17 In. ....*Illus* 650.00
Charger, No.1676, Bird On Branch Center, Signed Hein, 19 In. 1320.00
Charger, No.7036, 4 Figures At Harvest, 17 1/2 In. 650.00
Mug, Boy, Hires Root Beer 125.00
Pitcher, Applied Green Leaves, Branch Handle, Gray, 8 1/2 In. 235.00
Pitcher, Milk, Art Nouveau, 7 In. 110.00
Pitcher, No.2076, 3 Liter, Ivory Cameo of Owls, Eagles 650.00
Plaque, No.1044/191, Stuttgart Church, PUG, 12 In. 88.00
Plaque, No.1044/201, House Scene, PUG, 12 In. 248.00
Plaque, No.1044/291, City Wall Scene, PUG, 12 In. 187.00
Plaque, No.1108, Castle On Rhine, Gold Edge, Marked, 17 In. 850.00
Plaque, No.1365, Castle Scene, 17 In. ....495.00 To 795.00
Plaque, No.2195 & 2196, Drinking Cavaliers, 17 In., Pair 550.00
Plaque, No.2305Y, Boat Scene, Matte Finish, 10 1/4 In. 85.00
Plaque, No.2442, Trojan Warriors On Boat, Dated 1899, 18 In. 1100.00
Plaque, No.7074, Cupid & Lady Scene, Square, 1907, 8 In. 375.00
Plaque, No.9032 & 9033, Pheasants, PUG, 14 In., Pair 303.00
Plate, Art Deco, Stylized Blue Flowers, 7 In. 50.00
Plate, Horseman Scene, Divided, Black On White, 11 In., 6 Piece 345.00
Pokal, No. 454, 1 1/2 Liter, King Fills Walking Stein, Pair 347.00
Stein Set, No.2893/1200, State Shields, PUG, 7 Piece 578.00
Stein, Inlaid Top, Pewter Fittings, Etched Scene, 9 7/8 In. 375.00
Stein, Knights & Horses, Scene On Body & Lid, 10 In. 375.00
Stein, No. 24, 1/2 Liter, Cavaliers 198.00
Stein, No. 171, 1/4 Liter, Gray & Tan, Blue Band, Mark 175.00
Stein, No. 171, 1/4 Liter, Raised Figures, Mercury Mark, 5 3/4 In. 175.00
Stein, No.1028, 1/2 Liter, Tree Trunk, Goddess of Wind ....165.00 To 185.00
Stein, No.1074, 1 Liter, Peasant Smoking Pipe 385.00
Stein, No.1266, 1/2 Liter, Man Drinking, Gray, Stars, Grapes, 6 In. 175.00
Stein, No.1403, 1/2 Liter, People, Tavern Keeper, Inserted Lid 475.00
Stein, No.1476, 1/2 Liter, Gnomes At Work, Etched, Pewter Lid 468.00
Stein, No.1526, 1/2 Liter, Fraternal Crest, Hand Painted 215.00
Stein, No.1526, 3/10 Liter, Rochester Brewing Co., PUG 50.00
Stein, No.1526, Berlin Scenes 210.00

Mettlach, Charger, Cameo, Green, White,
Figures At Harvest, 17 In.

If you have unopened bottles of drugs or other pharmaceuticals, be sure to check for ether or picric acid. These can explode spontaneously and are dangerous to keep.

Stein, No.1526/592, 1/2 Liter, Cavalier, Maiden & Verse, PUG	165.00
Stein, No.1526/600, 1 Liter, Cavalier & Verse, PUG	143.00
Stein, No.1533, 1/2 Liter, Man Drinking, Signed Warth	88.00
Stein, No.1536, 1/2 Liter, Man Drinking, Signed Warth	275.00
Stein, No.1642, 1/2 Liter, Man Drinking, Eagle	425.00
Stein, No.1643, 1/2 Liter, Student, Tapestry, Verse, Pewter Lid	230.00
Stein, No.1646, 1/2 Liter, Man Drinking, Funny Hat	226.00
Stein, No.1647, 1/2 Liter, Innkeeper, Drinking From Stein	242.00
Stein, No.1734, 2 Liter, Lovers, Etched, Signed Warth	468.00
Stein, No.1745, 1/2 Liter, Ring of Dots, Brown & Green	175.00
Stein, No.1863, 1/2 Liter, Village Scene, Garden, Band, Pewter Lid	475.00
Stein, No.1909, Procession of People, Green, Pewter Top, 9 In.	225.00
Stein, No.1909/612, 4/10 Liter, Munich Child Holding Shield	100.00
Stein, No.1909/715, 1/2 Liter, Drunken Revelers, PUG	198.00
Stein, No.1909/727, 1/2 Liter, Dwarfs Bowling, PUG	220.00
Stein, No.2001, Scholar, Philosopher	485.00
Stein, No.2002, 1 Liter, Munich Stein	330.00
Stein, No.2002, 1/2 Liter, Munich Scene	338.00
Stein, No.2018, 1/2 Liter, Pug Dog, Stoneware	250.00
Stein, No.2025, 1/2 Liter, Cherubs Dancing	440.00
Stein, No.2035, 1 Liter, Bacchus, Etched	495.00
Stein, No.2090, 1/2 Liter, Club, Man At Table, Smoking Pipe	425.00
Stein, No.2184/966, 1/2 Liter, Dwarfs, PUG	358.00
Stein, No.2211, 3/10 Liter, Bowling Scene In Relief	300.00
Stein, No.2327/1187, 1/4 Liter, Girl, With Basket, PUG, Beaker	61.00
Stein, No.2368, 1/4 Liter, Elks Club, PUG, Beaker	55.00
Stein, No.2384/1143, 2 1/4 Liter, Zecher Gesellschaft	480.00
Stein, No.2391, 1 Liter, Lohengrin Scene, Castle Lid, Etched	1045.00
Stein, No.2520, 1 Liter, Student & Barmaid, Signed H.S.	578.00
Stein, No.2520, 1/2 Liter, Student & Barmaid	595.00
Stein, No.2530, 1 Liter, Boar Hunt Scene	750.00
Stein, No.2717, 1 Liter, Nude In Front At Target	4620.00
Stein, No.2778, 1/4 Liter, Carnival Players, Signed, 6 3/8 In.	750.00
Stein, No.2882, 1/2 Liter, Der Durstige Retter	875.00
Stein, No.2967, Seated Men, Basket of Piglets, Pewter Top, 9 In.	275.00
Stein, No.2994, 1/4 Liter, Art Nouveau Design	209.00
Stein, No.3078/419, 1/2 Liter, Owl & Wreath	100.00
Stein, No.3191, 1/2 Liter, Man With Beaker, Signed FR	440.00
Stein, No.3424, 1 Liter, San Miguel Beer, Manila, P.I., 87–04	250.00
Stein, No.4526–95, 1/2 Liter, John C.White, 6 1/2 In.	350.00
Tea Set, Silver On Relief, 3 Piece	187.00
Tumbler, Boy With Violin	50.00
Vase, Cherubs As 4 Seasons, Marked, 14 In., Pair	650.00
Vase, Floral, Gray Ground, Green & Gold Leaves, Marked, 9 1/2 In.	345.00
Vase, No.1978, Grecian Woman Medallion, Pedestal, Marked, 13 In.	750.00
Vase, No.2706, Rookwood Style, 13 In.	385.00
Vase, No.2856, Rust, Incised Turquoise Design, Gold, 10 1/2 In.	175.00

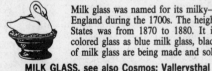

Milk glass was named for its milky–white color. It was first made in England during the 1700s. The height of its popularity in the United States was from 1870 to 1880. It is now correct to refer to some colored glass as blue milk glass, black milk glass, etc. Reproductions of milk glass are being made and sold in many stores.

MILK GLASS, see also Cosmos; Vallerysthal

MILK GLASS, Ashtray, Sailboat	10.00
Banana Boat, White, Footed	25.00
Bottle, Statue of Liberty	140.00
Box, Dog Cover, Blue & White, 4 3/8 In.	55.00
Box, Dresser, Scalloped, Fruit & Leaves, 2 1/2 X 5 X 7 1/4 In.	48.00
Box, Jewelry, Heart Shape, Raised Flowers, 3 Sections, 7 X 8 In.	40.00
Box, Sculptured Fruit & Flowers, Oval	25.00
Bread Plate, Three Graces	245.00
Butter, Cover, Child's, Wild Rose With Scrolling	60.00
Butter, Cover, Cosmos	125.00 To 150.00

Butter, Cover, Lacy Dewdrop	35.00
Butter, Rooster Cover, Blue, White Head, Red Trim	40.00
Butter, Wild Iris	55.00
Cake Plate, Grape	30.00
Cake Stand, Hand With Bracelet Stem, Ribbed Base, 11 1/2 In.	125.00
Candlestick, Crucifix, 9 1/2 In., Pair	325.00
Candlestick, Crucifix, 10 In.	95.00
Candy Dish, Cover, Grape, Westmoreland	18.00
Candy Dish, Cover, Old Quilt, Cambridge	18.00
Candy Dish, Cover, Paneled Grape	18.00
Candy Dish, Shell Finial, Shells Around Bowl, 3–Footed	38.00
Compote, File & Fan, Marigold, Ruffled, Westmoreland	310.00
Compote, Jenny Lind	150.00
Compote, Oak Leaf, Footed	22.50
Creamer, Cosmos	125.00
Creamer, Flute & Crown	20.00
Creamer, Lacy Dewdrop	20.00
Creamer, Menagerie, Owl	70.00
Creamer, Paneled Wheat	40.00
Creamer, Peacock & Drape, Blue	45.00
Creamer, Swan	37.00
Cruet, Cactus	24.00
Cruet, Forget–Me–Not	55.00
Cup, Punch, Grape	5.00
Decanter, Jenny Lind, Blue	75.00
Dish, American Hen Cover	50.00 To 60.00
Dish, Battleship Cover, Uncle Sam On Ship	50.00 To 100.00
Dish, Bird On Nest Cover, Footed, Blue, Westmoreland	52.00
Dish, Birds In Kerchief Cover	225.00
Dish, British Lion Cover	100.00
Dish, Cat Cover, White Head, Blue Base, Wide Rib	65.00
Dish, Cat On Drum Cover	55.00
Dish, Chick On Eggs Cover, Lacy Edge Pedestal Base, 7 In.	135.00
Dish, Chicken On Nest Cover, Glass Eyes, Red Comb, 7 In.	165.00
Dish, Crawfish Cover, 4 X 7 1/2 In.	135.00
Dish, Fish Cover, Entwined Rim, Dated 1889	145.00
Dish, Hen Cover, Blue Head, White, 5 1/2 In.	35.00
Dish, Lamb Cover, Blue & White	112.50
Dish, Lion Cover, Blue Picket Base	85.00
Dish, Lion Cover, Reclining, Ribbon Edge, Dated 1889	160.00
Dish, Owl Cover, 6 1/2 In.	125.00
Dish, Pekingese Cover, Diamond Diapered Base	260.00
Dish, Pickle, Bird	50.00
Dish, Pin, Fleur–De–Lis Shape, Palm Trees Center	14.00
Dish, Quail Cover, On Nest	120.00 To 165.00
Dish, Rabbit Cover, Square	95.00
Dish, Turtle Cover	85.00
Dish, Walking Elephant Cover, 4 X 8 In.	95.00
Eggcup, Birch Leaf, Flint	42.50
Epergne, Hobnail, 3 Lilies, 8 In.	12.00
Figurine, Swan, Raised Wing, Lacy Base	90.00
Flask, Eye Opener, Original Closure, 5 In.	90.00
Fruit Jar, Owl Shape, Eagle On Lid, Held By Tin Ring, 6 3/8 In.	115.00
Goblet, Grape, Footed	95.00
Goblet, Paneled Grape, Westmoreland, 6 In.	9.00 To 10.00
Jar, Enameled Dutch Girl Panel On Lid, Square, 3 In.	18.00
Jar, Roosevelt Bears Cover, 3 1/2 In.	155.00
Lamp, Block, Miniature	90.00
Lamp, Cosmos, Miniature	55.00
Lamp, Courting, Hobnail	95.00
Lamp, Elephant, Original Burner, Miniature	385.00
Lamp, Finger, Embossed Tulips & Leaves, Green, Miniature	250.00
Lamp, Swan, Brass Collar & Burner, Clear Chimney, 4 In.	275.00
Lighter, Cigarette, Hobnail	10.00

Match Holder, Divided Suitcase	65.00
Muffineer, Quilted Phlox	50.00
Mug, Child's, Bull & Elk, 2 In.	30.00
Mug, Robin, Pink	30.00
Mustard, Bull's Head, Ladle	150.00
Pitcher, Baby's Head Shape, Green Trim, 6 In.	95.00
Pitcher, Grape, 9 In.	19.50
Pitcher, Water, Blackberry, Applied Handle, Dated Feb.1870	450.00
Plate, Capital of Iowa, Gold Tassel Edge, 7 1/2 In.	35.00
Plate, Columbus 1492–1892, Lattice Rim, 9 1/2 In.	35.00
Plate, Cupid & Psyche, 7 1/2 In.	16.50
Plate, Indian Chief, Beaded Loop, 7 In.	23.00 To 35.00
Plate, Rabbit Chariot, 6 1/2 In.	67.50
Plate, Serenade, 6 In.	35.00
Plate, Serenade, 8 In.	30.00
Platter, Liberty Bell, Hancock Signature	295.00
Punch Bowl, Child's, Nursery Rhymes	185.00
Punch Cup, Child's, Hooks, 6 Piece	240.00
Punch Cup, Grape	5.00
Punch Cup, Little Red Riding Hood, Blue	30.00
Punch Set, Wild Rose, White, Child's, 7 Piece	240.00
Rolling Pin, Sailing Ship Decal, Verse, Dated 1856	110.00
Rose Bowl, Sawtooth Pattern, Pedestal	20.00
Salt & Pepper, Columbian Expo., Painted, Embossed, Egg Shape	155.00
Salt & Pepper, Embossed Fish On Corners	125.00
Salt & Pepper, Rabbit	49.00
Salt & Pepper, Raised Rabbits, Chickens & Chicks, 3 In.	135.00
Salt, Flying Fish, White, Master, 2 1/2 X 4 5/8 In.	30.00
Saltshaker, Grape, 4 Sides, 3 1/4 In.	25.00
Sauce, Hobstar Fruit, Ruffled, Marigold, Westmoreland	325.00
Sauce, Primrose & Pearls	50.00
Shaving Mug, Viking Pattern, 3 1/4 In.	80.00
Sleigh, Westmoreland, 9 In.	30.00
Spittoon, Red & Black Stripes	50.00
Spooner, Cosmos	125.00
Spooner, Paneled Wheat, Scalloped Rim	40.00
Sugar & Creamer, Cover, Crown Knobs	50.00
Sugar & Creamer, Cover, Pheasant	55.00
Sugar & Creamer, Ivy	30.00
Sugar & Creamer, Oakleaf, Westmoreland	27.50
Sugar Shaker, Leaning Pillars, Blue	55.00 To 65.00
Sugar Shaker, Pink, Metal Top, 4 In.	45.00
Sugar, Wild Rose, Child's	65.00
Syrup, Alba, Floral Spray	50.00
Syrup, Blue, Gold & Yellow Stained, Pewter Lid, Marked 1885	100.00
Syrup, Torquay, Yellow Design	80.00
Table Set, Cosmos, 4 Piece	600.00
Table Set, Delaware, Rose Flash, 4 Piece	400.00
Table Set, Guttate, Gold Trim, 4 Piece	350.00
Table Set, Ribbed, Lacy Rim, 4 Piece	95.00
Table Set, Shoshoni, Gold Trim, 4 Piece	300.00
Tile, Owl, On Branch In Relief, Square, 6 In.	65.00
Toothpick, Basket	20.00
Toothpick, Horseshoe & Clover	30.00
Toothpick, One–O–One, Blue	65.00
Toothpick, Scrolled Shell, Enameled Design	20.00
Toothpick, Swan & Cattail	20.00
Toothpick, Wicker Base, Handles	20.00
Tray, Dresser, Chrysanthemum, 7 1/2 X 10 In.	25.00
Tray, Oval, 11 In.	35.00
Tray, Pin, Blue	22.00
Tumbler, Danish National Festival Twin Cities	20.00
Vase, Gilded Exotic Bird & Floral, Propeller, 9 1/4 In.	225.00
Vase, Goddess of Liberty, 2 Faces, 8 In.	95.00

Old milk glass is slightly opalescent at the edge if held up to a strong light; new glass is not.

Vase, Hat Shape, Pink Inside, Crimped, Clear Edge, 3 1/2 In.	20.00
Vase, Paneled Grape, 5 1/4 In.	15.00
Vase, Quilt Block, 6 1/2 In.	11.50

Millefiori means, literally, a thousand flowers. It is a type of glasswork popular in paperweights. Many small flowerlike pieces of glass are grouped together to form a design.

MILLEFIORI, Bell, Clown Top, 6 In.	65.00
Button, Multicolor Design, 1 1/2 In., Set of 5	45.00
Dish, Swan Shape, Gold Flecks, Applied Eyes, 5 In.	65.00
Powder Jar, Cover, 4 In.	55.00
Rose Bowl, Crimped Rim, Small	75.00
Vase, 2 Handles, 6 In.	85.00

Minton china has been made in the Staffordshire region of England from 1793 to the present. The firm became part of the Royal Doulton Tableware Group in 1968, but the wares continued to be marked "Minton." Many marks have been used. The one shown dates from about 1873 to 1891, when the word "England" was added.

MINTON, Bowl & Pitcher, Child's, Pink Rosebuds, White, C.1906	450.00
Coffeepot, Marlowe, Multicolored Flowers, Demitasse	50.00
Compote, Mermaid & Shell	950.00
Dresser Set, 1898, 3 Piece	250.00
Eggcup, Marlowe, Florals	12.50
Ewer, Raised Fleur–De–Lis, Smiling Gargoyle At Lip, Signed	550.00
Jug, Parian, Ribbed, Greek Key Design, C.1852, 6 1/2 In.	90.00
Oyster Plate, Gold Enameling, White	60.00
Oyster Plate, Shell & Fish, White, 10 1/2 In.	49.00
Plate, Bird, Hand Painted, A.H.Wright, For Tiffany, 9 1/2 In., 7 Pc.	325.00
Teapot, Figural, Chinese Man	1980.00
Tile, Hunting Dog, Foliage, Turquoise, 8 In., Pair	100.00
Tile, Trinity Church Scenes, Adamantine Frame, 22 X 8 In., 3 Piece	150.00
Vase, Molded As Bamboo Tied With Sash, Marked, C.1862, 15 1/2 In.	150.00
Vase, Potpourri, 3 Profile Portraits, Cover, 10 In., Pair	2310.00

MIRROR, see Furniture, Mirror

Mochaware is an English–made product that was sold in America during the early 1800s. It is a heavy pottery with pale coffee–and–cream coloring. Designs of blue, brown, green, orange, black, or white were added to the pottery.

MOCHA, Bowl, Blue Band, Black Stripes, 6 1/2 X 3 1/2 In.	35.00
Bowl, Blue Spray, 13 In.	325.00
Bowl, Seaweed Design, White Band, 4 1/2 X 9 In.	130.00
Bowl, Seaweed, 12 In.	175.00
Castor, Herringbone Band, Yellow, 4 1/2 In.	418.00
Creamer, Banded Smoke, 3 3/4 In.	385.00
Cup, Green & Brown Glaze, Demitasse	25.00
Mug, Blue Band, Dark Brown Stripes, 3 In.	75.00 To 135.00
Mug, Brown & Blue Checkers, Fluted Band, White, 3 3/4 In.	220.00
Mug, Earthworm, Tan, Brown, Blue & White, 5 7/8 In.	275.00
Mug, Leaf Design, Brown, Tan, Qt.	500.00

Mug, Seaweed, Blue Green Band, Stripes, 4 3/4 In., Pt.	65.00
Mustard Pot, Blue Dotted Bands, 3 3/4 In.	330.00
Pitcher, Earthworm, Brown, Blue, Ocher, White, 6 3/8 In.	425.00
Pitcher, Tulip, Embossed Bands, Green, Brown, Blue, White, Beige, 7 In.	825.00
Punch Bowl, Cat's-Eye, Tan Band, 10 In.	1000.00
Punch Bowl, Cat's-Eyes Over Earthworm Band, 10 In.	700.00
Shaker, Earthworm, Gray Band, Dome Top, 4 1/2 In.	525.00
Shaker, Seaweed, White Bands, Dome Top, 4 3/8 In.	375.00
Shaker, Spice, Blue Glaze, Pear Shape, Band, Cat's-Eye, Footed, 4 In.	350.00
Spill Holder, Herringbone Bands, Seaweed, Soft Paste, 5 1/8 In.	275.00
Spittoon, Blue	128.00
Sugar, 2 Handles, Marbelized, 4 3/8 In.	375.00

Monmouth Pottery Company started working in Monmouth, Illinois, in 1892. The pottery made a variety of utilitarian wares. They became part of Western Stoneware Company in 1906. The maple leaf mark was used until 1930. If the word "Co." appears as part of the mark, the piece was made before 1906.

MONMOUTH, Bean Pot, Maple Leaf	30.00
Bowl, Blue Band, Fluted Sides, 7 In.	35.00
Bowl, Mix With Us, Blue Lettering	60.00
Bowl, No.9, Blue & Rust, Mottled, Wide Blue Band	40.00
Cookie Jar, Bail Handle, Word Cookies, Tan	15.00
Cookie Jar, Black	20.00
Stein, Ducks	135.00
Vase, Green, 5 In.	35.00
Vase, Mottled Brown On Orange, Handles, Labels, 8 In.	25.00

MONT JOYE, see Mt. Joye

William Moorcroft managed the art pottery department for James MacIntyre & Company of England from 1898 to 1913. In 1913, he started his own company, Moorcroft Pottery, in Burslem, England. He died in 1945, but the company continues. The earlier wares are similar to those made today, but color and marking will help indicate the age.

MOORCROFT, Box, Floral On Lid, Paper Label, 3 X 4 In.	85.00
Dish, Red & Blue Poppies, Blue-Green Ground, 8 1/2 In.	145.00
Ginger Jar, Dark Blue, 6 X 5 In.	95.00
Jar, Cover, Wisteria, Green, 5 In.	135.00
Lamp, Brown, Reds & Yellows, Paper Label, 25 In.	600.00
Lamp, Bulbous Base, Hibiscus, Cobalt Blue, Label, 13 1/2 In	275.00
Lamp, Iris, Multicolored, Cobalt Blue Ground, 10 3/4 In.	300.00
Nappy, Royal Blue & Pink Flower Inside, 4 In.	35.00
Pitcher, Bulbous, Orchids, Cobalt Blue, 5 In.	85.00
Plate, Blue & Red Flower, White, 4 1/2 In.	15.00
Saltshaker, Burslem, Blue & White	65.00
Vase, Allover Peach Poppies, Olive Green, 7 In.	190.00
Vase, Bulbous, Poppies, 7 In.	185.00
Vase, Cobalt Blue, 8 1/2 In.	135.00
Vase, Flared Rim, Pansies, Cobalt Blue, Signed, 8 In.	135.00
Vase, Floral On Blue Ground, 5 In.	55.00
Vase, Garland of Roses, Forget-Me-Nots, Gold Trim, 7 In.	495.00
Vase, Orchids On Dark Blue, 3 X 4 In.	125.00
Vase, Pansies On Cobalt Blue, 7 1/2 In.	55.00
Vase, Pansies, Reddish Purple, Dark Blue Ground, 1913, 6 In.	290.00
Vase, Pomegranate, Marked, C.1918, 7 In.	285.00

Some types of Japanese pottery and porcelain are decorated with a special type of raised decoration known as moriage. Sometimes pieces of clay were shaped by hand and applied to the item; sometimes the clay was squeezed from a tube in the way we apply cake frosting. One type of moriage is called dragonware and is listed under that name.

MORIAGE, Chocolate Pot, Flower Medallions, Matte Green	230.00

Ewer, Allover Turquoise Beading, Floral Medallions, 9 1/4 In. 170.00
Ewer, Medallions of Hand Painted Flowers, Pedestal, 12 In. 350.00
Hatpin Holder, Red Flower, Green Beading 65.00
Mug, Greek Key Border, Light Green Ground, 5 1/2 In. 145.00
Pitcher, Roses, Handle, Squat, 6 1/2 In. 250.00
Powder Jar, Floral Medallion 75.00
Tea Set, Mauve Ground, Red Roses, White, 5 Piece 650.00
Vase, Asters On Autumn Green, 10 3/4 In. 135.00
Vase, Floral Medallion, Low Handles, Dark Green Ground, 7 1/2 In. 195.00
Vase, Flower Cartouche, Blue Green Ground, Handles, 10 1/2 In. 255.00
Vase, Flowers, Birds In Flight, Green, 6 1/2 In. 235.00
Vase, Rainbow Slipworks, Medallions, Handles, Bottle Shape, 10 In. 180.00
Vase, Red Medallions, Green, White Lining, 2 Handles, 7 In. 95.00

The Mosaic Tile Company of Zanesville, Ohio, was started by Karl
Langerbeck and Herman Mueller in 1894. Many types of plain and
ornamental tiles were made until 1959. The company closed in 1967.
The company also made some ashtrays, bookends, and related gift
wares. Most pieces are marked with the entwined MTC monogram.

MOSAIC TILE CO., Cookie Jar, Mammy, Yellow Dress 200.00
Figurine, Dog, Attached Card Tray, Glossy Black 135.00
Figurine, German Shepherd, Marked 40.00
Frame, Floral, Brass Easel Back, 2 1/2 In. 75.00
Tile, Lincoln, White Head, Blue Ground, 3 1/2 In. 30.00
Tile, Longfellow's Home, Square, 6 In. 22.50

Moser glass is made by Ludwig Moser und Sohne, a Bohemian
glasshouse founded in 1857. Art Nouveau–type glassware and
iridescent glassware were made. The most famous Moser glass is
decorated with heavy enameling in gold and bright colors. The firm
is still working in Czechoslovakia. Few pieces of Moser glass are
marked.

MOSER, Bowl, Acorn Design, Enameled Oak Leaves, Gold Foliage, 5 5/8 In. 1050.00
Bowl, Chestnut Design, Reverse Painted, 12 In. 685.00
Bowl, Etched Gold Band, Maidens, Plants, Black Amethyst, 7 In. 75.00
Bowl, Gold Greek Design Band, Ribbed Bottom, Marked, 4 1/2 X 10 In. 585.00
Box, Enameled Floral, 4-Leaf Clovers, Cranberry, 3 X 5 In. 235.00
Box, Pin, Cavalier Portrait, Blue–Green, Marked, 4 In. 145.00
Box, Pink Berries On Cover, Green, 2 1/8 X 3 3/8 In. 265.00
Box, Salamanders On Cover, Salamanders Form Feet, 4 1/2 X 4 1/2 In. 600.00
Box, Trinket, Enameled Portrait, Crystal, Green, Marked 135.00
Box, Trinket, Ruby, Cover, 5 1/2 In., Pair 185.00
Compote, Egyptian, Sphinx Base, Cover, 7 In. 155.00
Cracker Jar, Applied Bees, Marked, Blue 285.00
Cruet, Amber Body, Bees, Moths, Butterflies, Dragonflies, Shell Feet 725.00
Cup & Saucer, Raised Ruby Panels, Faceted Rims 185.00
Decanter, Applied Glass Medallion, Woman, Gold Scrolling 295.00
Decanter, Blue Pedestal, Clear Base, Handle & Stopper, 12 In. 165.00
Decanter, Cobalt Blue, Enameled Grape Leaves, Stopper, 17 In. 1100.00
Decanter, Enameled Cameos, Oriental Style, Cut Glass Stopper, Marked 125.00
Decanter, Enameled, Green, 13 In. 1250.00
Decanter, Wine, Blue & Clear, Bubble Stopper, Marked, 12 In. 165.00
Decanter, Wine, Raised Enameled Coat of Arms, Marked, 10 In. 150.00
Ewer, Enameled Flowers, Multicolord Glass Beads, Marked, 11 1/2 In. 710.00
Finger Bowl, Underplate, Cut Bottom, Marked 225.00
Finger Bowl, Underplate, Incised, Louis XV Pattern, Marked 80.00
Goblet, Acorn Design, Oak Leaves Outlined In Gold, 5 3/8 In. 375.00
Goblet, Green Enameled Oak Leaves, Gold Foliage, Footed, 5 In. 275.00
Goblet, Presentation, Cameo Appliques, Gold Luster, 13 In., Pair 300.00
Liqueur Set, Pedestal Glasses, Intaglio Leaves, Birds, 3 Piece 295.00
Liqueur Set, Tray, Cranberry, Marked, 8 Piece 335.00
Perfume Bottle, Amethyst, Prism Cut, 3 In. 185.00
Perfume Bottle, Cobalt Blue, Enameled Berries, Stopper, 5 1/2 In. 135.00
Perfume Bottle, Gold, Warrior Banding, Atomizer, 9 1/4 In. 225.00

Pitcher, Diamond Design, Enameled Floral, Clear To Cranberry, 8 In. 195.00
Pitcher, Lavender Flowers, Brass Handle, Spout Lid, Marked, 12 In. 315.00
Punch Set, Geometric Enameling, Pedestal Cups, Smoked Crystal, 6 Pc. 365.00
Rose Bowl, Crimped, Enameled Scene, Garden, Maiden, Marked 115.00
Rose Bowl, Florals, Marked, Amber, 7 In. 275.00
Toothpick, Cranberry Cut Panels, Embossed Gold Band 65.00
Tumbler, Water, Little Girls, Gold Cartouches, Cranberry 235.00
Tumbler, White Flowers, Blue, 7 In. 65.00
Urn, Deer In Forest, Scalloped Base, Cover, 11 1/2 In. 195.00
Urn, Renaissance Wedding Feast, Brass Pedestal, Marked, 10 In. 275.00
Vase, 2 Protruding Stems, Raised Enameling, Blue, Marked, 9 1/2 In. 185.00
Vase, 3 Amber Feet, Cranberry Pedestal, Marked, 9 1/2 In. 235.00
Vase, Alexandrite, Gold Warrior Band, Marked, 10 In. 750.00
Vase, Amber, Satyr With Nudes, Gold Cameo Border, Marked, 4 In. 90.00
Vase, Amber, Swans, Cloud, Gold, Artist Marked, 6 In. 215.00
Vase, Black Amethyst, Cameo Cut Gold Border, Dragons, Flared, 10 In. 175.00
Vase, Bud, Enameled Cranberry, Floral Design, 2 Handles, 7 In. 350.00
Vase, Bulbous, Raised Florals, Ruby, Marked, 15 X 9 In. 190.00
Vase, Cathedral, White Cut To Cranberry, Gold, Marked, 14 In. 265.00
Vase, Cobalt Blue, Gold Trim, Marked, 9 1/2 In. 135.00
Vase, Cranberry To Clear, Gold Top Band, Marked, 13 1/2 In. 535.00
Vase, Cut Panel, Enameled Foliage, Marked, 8 1/2 In. 150.00
Vase, Cylinder, Gold Leaves & Sprays, Butterfly, Glass Acorns, 4 In. 95.00
Vase, Elephants In Jungle, Enameled, Amber Ground, Marked, 12 In. 950.00
Vase, Enameled Aztec Sun, Spanish Crown, Helmet, Spear, Marked, 7 In. 175.00
Vase, Enameled Oak Leaves, Glass Acorns, Gold Foliage, 9 1/4 In. 525.00
Vase, Floral Enameled Design, Emerald Green, 9 1/2 In., Pair 350.00
Vase, Floral Enameled, Marked, 13 In., Pair 450.00
Vase, Floral, Gold & Silver Leaves, Sapphire Blue, 12 In. 800.00
Vase, Frosted Green, Gold Florals, Metal Holder, Marked, 10 1/2 In. 350.00
Vase, Frosted White, Green & Gold, Metal Stand, Marked, 10 1/2 In. 365.00
Vase, Gold Ornaments, Pedestal, Green, 15 1/4 In. 165.00
Vase, Grape Leaves, Gold Foliage, Sapphire Blue, 4 1/4 In. 365.00
Vase, Green To Clear, Red, Yellow Poppies, Leaves, 10 In. 325.00
Vase, Hawk & 3 Mallard Ducks, 10 Panels, Oval, 11 In. 1485.00
Vase, Intaglio Pedestal, Clear To Apricot, Marked, 10 1/2 In. 250.00
Vase, Marquetry, Green Leaves, Red Flowers, Marked, 9 1/2 In. 1025.00
Vase, Nudes, Grapes In Relief, Marked, 5 In., Pair 275.00
Vase, Portrait, Art Nouveau Lady, Profile On Gold, Marked, 8 1/2 In. 260.00
Vase, Portrait, Brass Pedestal, Cranberry, Marked, 11 In. 400.00
Vase, Portrait, Cameo, Cranberry, Brass Pedestal, Marked, 14 In. 285.00
Vase, Portrait, Cranberry, Porcelain Medallion, Marked, 13 1/2 In. 350.00
Vase, Portrait, Lady, Cranberry, Marked, 15 In. 335.00
Vase, Raised Gold, White Florals, Marked, 14 In. 240.00
Vase, Scalloped Rim, Amethyst, Gold Design, Marked, 15 1/4 In. 215.00
Vase, Shaded Rose, Enameled, Marked, 11 1/2 In. 185.00
Vase, Tower, Floral Enameling, Clear To Cranberry, Marked, 12 In., Pr. 295.00
Vase, Trumpet, Cranberry, Cameo, Jewels, Marked, 13 In. 160.00
Vase, Trumpet, Enameled Flowers & Swags, 13 In. 100.00
Vase, Trumpet, Gold Design, Marble Cameo of Man, Jewels, Marked, 11 In. 130.00
Vase, Turquoise Sides, Enameled Florals, 25 1/2 In., Pair 1800.00
Vase, Yellow & White Flowers, Frosted, Green, 12 In. 95.00
Water Set, Cranberry, Applied Open Handle, 8 1/2 In. Pitcher, 3 Pc. 290.00
Water Set, Diamond Design, Raised Florals, Marked, 7 Piece 210.00
Water Set, White Enameled, Blue, Marked, 8 In. Pitcher, 3 Piece 210.00

> Moss rose china was made by many firms from 1808 to 1900. It has
> a typical moss rose pictured as the design. The plant is not as
> popular now as it was in Victorian gardens, so the fuzz–covered bud
> is unfamiliar to most collectors. The dishes were usually decorated
> with pink and green flowers.

MOSS ROSE, Pitcher & Bowl Set, Alfred Meakin, 7 Piece 275.00
Sauce, Johnson Brothers 10.00
Tea Set, Child's, 23 Piece 45.00

Tea Set, Child's, 26 Piece 75.00

Mother-of-pearl glass, or pearl satin glass, was first made in the 1850s in England and in Massachusetts. It was a special type of mold-blown satin glass with air bubbles in the glass, giving it a pearlized color. It has been reproduced. Mother-of-pearl shell objects are listed under Pearl.

MOTHER-OF-PEARL, Basket, Herringbone, Salmon Outside, Crimped, 9 1/2 In. 635.00
    Bowl, Diamond-Quilted, Coralene Design, 4 1/2 X 8 In. 685.00
    Creamer, Blue Ribbon, Frosted Foot & Handle, 2 7/8 In. 245.00
    Cruet, Blue Coralene Design 250.00
    Ewer, Diamond-Quilted, Blue, Melon, 7 In. 188.00
    Fairy Lamp, Blue Swirl, Ruffled, White Lining, 6 In. 450.00
    Finger Bowl, Underplate, Amberina, Cream Lining, 4 1/2 In. 900.00
    Lamp, Peg, Ruffled Shade, Metal Holder, Blue Swirl, 16 In. 760.00
    Perfume Bottle, Diamond-Quilted, Blue To White, 3 In. 385.00
    Perfume Bottle, Lay Down, Swirl, Pink Satin, 5 1/2 In. 445.00
    Pitcher, Water, Raindrop, Handle 350.00
    Pitcher, White Cased, 9 In. 300.00
    Rose Bowl, Diamond-Quilted, Rainbow, Signed 450.00
    Rose Bowl, Egg Shape, White Lining, 4 Crimp, 3 1/2 In. 168.00
    Rose Bowl, Herringbone, 8 Crimp, Apricot, 3 1/2 In. 195.00
    Rose Bowl, Moire, White Lining, 8 Crimp, 3 In. 495.00
    MOTHER-OF-PEARL, SATIN GLASS, see Satin Glass; Smith Brothers; etc.
    Tumbler, Diamond-Quilted, Blue To Pearl White, Enameled 285.00
    Tumbler, Diamond-Quilted, Pink To White 85.00
    Tumbler, Diamond-Quilted, Yellow To White 85.00
    Tumbler, Herringbone, Yellow Top Band 165.00
    Vase, Bud, Ribbon, Blue, Metal Holder, 8 1/4 In. 230.00
    Vase, Bulbous, Frosted Rim, White Lining, Blue, 8 1/4 In. 225.00
    Vase, Coralene On Snowflake, 3 1/8 In. 425.00
    Vase, Diamond-Quilted, Lemon, 6 1/8 In. 158.00
    Vase, Diamond-Quilted, Square Folded-Over Top, 6 1/4 In. 155.00
    Vase, Drape, Rose To Pink, 5 1/2 In. 260.00
    Vase, Fan, Drape, Ruffled Top, Rose To Pink, 6 In. 225.00
    Vase, Flared, Gold Rim, 4 X 7 In. 275.00
    Vase, Fluted Top, Pedestal Foot, Blue Swirl, 6 1/4 In. 165.00
    Vase, Garlands & Medallions, Roman Gold, 6 1/2 In. 895.00
    Vase, Green Moire, Allover Blown Flower, 6 In. 550.00
    Vase, Rainbow, Blue Coralene Design, 10 1/2 In. 295.00
    Vase, Ribbon, Gold Prunus Blossoms, 3 In. 395.00
    Vase, Rivulet, 4-Petal Top, Blue, 5 3/8 In. 210.00
    Vase, Star-Shaped Top, 9 In., Pair 350.00
    Water Set, Raindrop, Pink, 7 Piece 1500.00
    MOUSTACHE CUP, see Mustache Cup

Mt. Joye is an enameled cameo glass made in the late nineteenth and the twentieth centuries by Saint-Hilaire Touvoir de Varraux and Co. of Pantin, France. This same company made De Vez glass. Pieces were usually decorated with enameling. Most pieces are not marked.

MT.JOYE, Pitcher, Gold Florals, Frosted Green, Metal Top, 12 In. 210.00

Planter, Frosted Amethyst, Green Leaves, Signed, 7 1/2 X 4 In.	245.00
Planter, Gold, Green, Signed, 7 1/2 In.	250.00
Vase, Art Nouveau Poppy Design, Enameled Gilt, Signed, 9 3/4 In.	325.00
Vase, Cameo, Poppy Design, Frosted Ground, 11 1/8 In.	425.00
Vase, Enameled Flowers, Frosted, Gold Trim, Signed, 8 3/4 X 4 In.	250.00
Vase, Gold Oak Leaves, Silvered Acorns, Emerald Green, 25 1/4 In.	900.00
Vase, Red & Green, Floral Design, Chipped Ice Ground, 9 1/2 In.	425.00
Vase, Rubina, Swallows, 10 In.	175.00

The Mt. Washington Glass Works started in 1837 in South Boston, Massachusetts. In 1869 the company moved to New Bedford, Massachusetts. Many types of art glass were made there to the 1890s. These included Burmese, Crown Milano, Royal Flemish, and others.

MT.WASHINGTON, Berry Set, Burmese, 10 Piece	3500.00
Biscuit Jar, Floral, Brass Lid & Bail	185.00
Biscuit Jar, Florals, Signed In Lid, 7 In.	195.00
Biscuit Jar, Opaque White, Signed	195.00
Bottle, Lotion, Egg Shape, Blackberries & Leaves	350.00
Bowl, Burmese, Rigaree Rim, 2 1/2 X 6 1/2 In.	345.00
Bowl, Peppermint Stick, Cutting, 8 1/2 In.	98.00
Bowl, Random Bouquets, Pansies, Gold Chain Border, Signed	1275.00
Bowl, Winged Griffins & Shields, Pink & White, 9 In.	795.00
Bride's Bowl, Lavender & Gold, Orange Flower Sprays, 14 In.	695.00
Castor, Pickle, Gold Bands, Enameled Dot Flowers, 14 1/2 In.	345.00
Cracker Jar, Blown-Out Flowers, Lakeshore Scene, Signed	575.00
Creamer, Pear Shape, Burmese	385.00
Creamer, White Ribbed Surface, Applied Handle, 3 In.	350.00
Cruet, Cranberry, Inverted Thumbprint, White Daisies, 5 In.	275.00
Cruet, Melon-Ribbed, Burmese, 6 1/2 In.	945.00
Egg, Lay Down Egg, Columbian Exposition, Libbey, 1893	120.00
Fernery, Pink Rococo, Florals, Signed, 5 X 9 In.	195.00
Finger Bowl, Crimped Top, Blown Quilted Design, 4 3/8 In.	225.00
Flower Frog, Mushroom, Leaf & Foliage Design, White	125.00
Lamp, Delft, Windmills & Sailing Ships, Signed, Miniature	450.00
Perfume Bottle, Alabaster Egg, Maroon Berries, White Flowers	495.00
Pitcher, Burmese, Egyptian Style, Yellow Square Handle	985.00
Pitcher, Inverted Thumbprint, Amberina	450.00
Salt & Pepper, Burmese	235.00
Salt & Pepper, Burmese, Ribbed	325.00
Salt & Pepper, Chick, Egg-Shaped Body, Flowers, 2 1/2 In.	675.00
Salt & Pepper, Egg In Cup	195.00
Salt & Pepper, Egg, Sailor Brownie, Anchor & Boat	235.00
Salt & Pepper, Pewter Chicken Heads	675.00
Salt Dip, Melon, Forget-Me-Not Design	68.00
Saltshaker, 6-Melon Rib, Forget-Me-Nots	38.00
Saltshaker, 6-Melon Rib, Pansies, Blue	38.00
Saltshaker, Cranberry, White Violets	95.00
Saltshaker, Egg, Rooster	245.00
Saltshaker, Egg, Yellow Blend	55.00
Saltshaker, Pansy Design	125.00
Saltshaker, Upright Egg Shape, Enameled Flowers	48.00
Saltshaker, White Opal, Enameled Florals	90.00
Shade, Burmese, Optic Diamond-Quilted, 5 1/4 In.	285.00
Shade, Burmese, Ruffled, 4 1/2 In.	285.00
Sugar & Creamer, White Opal, Flowers, Silver Plate	325.00
Sugar Shaker, Egg Shape, Metal Pronged Top, 4 In.	585.00
Sugar Shaker, Egg Shape, Pansies & Leaves	185.00
Sugar Shaker, Egg, Enameled Forget-Me-Nots	145.00
Sugar Shaker, Egg, Ferns, White	275.00
Sugar Shaker, Egg, Melon-Ribbed	485.00
Sugar Shaker, Fig, Oak Leaf, Raised Blueberries	495.00
Sugar Shaker, Pansies, Ostrich Egg, Royal Flemish Glass	495.00
Sugar, Peachblow, Paper Label	1750.00

Syrup, Gold Traced Panels, Floral Design, Hinged Lid, 4 In.	395.00
Toothpick, Burmese, Blue & Pink Flowers, Yellow Rim	465.00
Toothpick, Burmese, Enameled Daisies & Stems	385.00
Toothpick, Burmese, Optic Diamond–Quilted, Label, 2 1/2 In.	485.00
Toothpick, Opalescent Satin, Yellow Finish, Dotted Rim	195.00
Toothpick, Raised Spider Web, Enameled Pine Cone	210.00
Tumbler, Peachblow, Blue–Gray Band At Base	1450.00
Vase, Burmese, Gourd Shape, 7 3/4 In.	395.00
Vase, Coralene, Flowers In Sections, Stars, Circles, 6 In.	895.00
Vase, Florals Outlined In Gold, 14 In.	350.00
Vase, Gourd, Burmese, 1880s, 9 In.	395.00
Vase, Lava Glass, Jet Black, 5 1/2 In.	935.00
Vase, Lily, Enameled Forget–Me–Nots, Alabaster, 10 In.	495.00
Vase, Peachblow Coloring, White Ground, White Lining, 12 In.	435.00
Vase, Refired Rim, Gilded Metal Holder, Cherubs, 9 1/2 In.	425.00
Vase, Trumpet, Lemon Yellow Rim, 8 In.	345.00
Water Set, Burmese, 7 Piece	2250.00

Mud figures are small Chinese pottery figures made in the twentieth century. The figures usually represent workers, scholars, farmers, or merchants. Other pieces are trees, houses, and similar parts of the landscape. The figures have unglazed faces and hands but glazed clothing. They were originally made for fish tanks or planters. Mud figures were of little interest and brought low prices until the 1980s. When the prices rose, reproductions appeared.

MUD FIGURE, Boat, Man Seated At End, 8 In.	110.00
Chinese Man, Cobalt Robe, Green Hat, Sitting On Stump, 5 1/2 In.	75.00
Elder, With Fish, China, Cobalt Blue, 6 In.	65.00
Fisherman, Chinese, 4 1/2 In.	13.00
Man Holding Large Urn, 8 In.	30.00
Man, China, 4 In.	30.00
Man, Seated On Rock, 3 1/2 In.	48.50
Man, Seated, Umbrella, Woman, Seated, Fan, 8 In., Pair	100.00
Peasant, 3 1/2 In.	20.00
Shoe, China, 4 In.	22.00

Mulberry ware was made in the Staffordshire district of England from about 1850 to 1860. The dishes were decorated with a transfer design of a reddish brown, now called "mulberry." Many of the patterns are similar to those used for flow blue and other Staffordshire transfer wares.

MULBERRY, Bowl & Pitcher, Jeddo, Adams	525.00
Bowl & Saucer, Temple, Handleless	100.00
Bowl, Vegetable, Cologne, Cover, Alcock, Large	175.00
Bowl, Vegetable, Cyprus, Cover	175.00
Bowl, Vegetable, Sitka, Cover, Staffordshire	50.00
Coffeepot, Genoa, Davenport, 9 7/8 In.	175.00
Creamer, Bleeding Heart	85.00
Creamer, Rhone Scenery, T.J. & J.Mayer, 5 1/4 In.	110.00
Creamer, Vincennes, J.Alcock, 5 1/4 In.	85.00
Creamer, Washington Vase, Podmore, Walker, 5 1/4 In.	60.00 To 75.00
Cup & Saucer, Handleless, Hyson	45.00
Cup & Saucer, Handleless, Washington Vase, Podmore, Walker	55.00
Cup & Saucer, Royal Rose	45.00
Cup Plate, Vincennes, Alcock	25.00

Don't store dishes for long periods of time in old newspaper wrappings. The ink can make indelible stains on the china.

Cup, Handleless, Deer, Violet, Staffordshire	25.00
Fruit Bowl, Melbourne, Footed, Staffordshire	50.00
Gravy Boat, Peru, 8–Sided, Holdcroft, 4 5/8 In.	65.00
Nappy, Peruvian, Wedgwood, 5 1/8 In.	15.00
Pitcher & Bowl, Corean, Bowl, 13 1/2 In.	450.00
Pitcher & Bowl, Corean, With Hot Water Pitcher	700.00
Pitcher & Bowl, Jeddo, Adams	495.00
Plate, Baronial, Meyer, 10 In.	35.00
Plate, Bologna, Adams, 7 In.	25.00
Plate, Castle Scenery, Furnival, 7 1/4 In.	25.00
Plate, Chusan, Podmore, Walker, 8 1/4 In.	25.00
Plate, Corean Pattern, Ironstone	27.50
Plate, Corean, 8 1/2 In.	30.00
Plate, Corean, Clementson, 9 1/2 In.	20.00
Plate, Peruvian, 12–Sided, Wedgwood, 9 3/8 In.	18.00
Plate, Rhone Scenery, T.J.& J.Mayer, 9 5/8 In.	35.00
Plate, Temple, Podmore, Walker, 8 3/4 In.	30.00
Plate, Ventura, 10 1/2 In.	45.00
Plate, Washington Vase, 8 3/4 In.	30.00
Plate, Washington Vase, 9 3/4 In.	38.00
Plate, Washington Vase, Podmore, Walker, 8 In.	30.00
Platter, Ferrara, Wedgwood, 16 X 14 In.	85.00
Platter, Octagonal, P & W Co., 15 3/4 X 12 In.	100.00
Platter, Rose, Walker, 15 1/2 In.	125.00
Platter, Washington Vase, 16 X 12 In.	170.00
Sauce, Beauties of China, Cover, Mellor, Venables & Co.	150.00
Soup, Dish, Foliage, Walley, 9 1/4 In.	35.00
Soup, Dish, Wreath, Furnival, 10 1/2 In.	35.00
Sugar, Corean, Lion Head Handles	125.00
Sugar, Vincennes	85.00
Teapot, Corean, Pedestal, Podmore, Walker, 9 1/4 In.	125.00
Teapot, Corean, Podmore, Walker, 8 In.	225.00
Teapot, Vincennes	125.00
Tureen, Sauce, Ladle & Undertray, Vincennes	395.00
Tureen, Sauce, Ladle, Blossom, Ashworth	185.00

Muller Freres, French for Muller Brothers, made cameo and other glass from the early 1900s to the late 1930s. Their factory was first located in Luneville, then in nearby Croismaire, France. Pieces were usually marked with the company name.

MULLER FRERES, Bowl, Fruit, Satin Glass, Cream To White, Iron Basket, Signed	175.00
Lamp, Cobalt To Pink, Abstract Design Shade, Signed, 20 In.	135.00
Lamp, Mottled Shade, 3–Arm Support, Marked, C.1925, 22 In.	2475.00
Lamp, Orange, Mottles, 14 In.	1200.00
Shade, 3–Light, Ceiling, Bronze Chain Links, 16 In.	400.00
Vase, 4 Colors, Fishermen On Lake, Trees, Squat, 2 1/2 In.	525.00
Vase, Cameo, Cream, Burgundy, Green, 4 1/4 In. ....*Illus*	440.00
Vase, Cameo, Trees, 2 1/2 In.	195.00
Vase, Continuous Shore Scene, Yellow, Signed, 3 5/8 In.	325.00
Vase, Double, Scenic, 9 In.	895.00
Vase, Fisherman & Woman, White Ground, 6 1/4 In.	1250.00
Vase, Mottled Yellow, Orange & Purple, 8 In.	145.00
Vase, Poppies, Frosted Gold Ground, Signed, 6 3/4 In.	1950.00
Vase, River Scene, Dutch Village, Signed, C.1920, 17 3/4 In.	2750.00
Vase, Scene, Trees, Mountains, Lake, Signed, 13 1/2 In.	1800.00
Vase, Shepherd & Flock of Sheep, Tree, Signed, 6 1/2 In.	1150.00
Vase, Sprays of Rosebuds, Blossoms, Signed, C.1920, 11 In.	2475.00

The Muncie Clay Products Company was established by Charles Benham in Muncie, Indiana, in 1922. The company made pottery for the florist and gift shop trade. The company closed by 1939. Pieces are marked with the name "Muncie" or just with a system of numbers and letters like "1A."

MUNCIE, Basket, Drip Rose, 11 In.	85.00

If you have an old piano, beware
of moths; they sometimes infest
the interior fabrics.

Muller Freres, Vase, Cameo, Cream,
   Burgundy, Green, 4 1/4 In.

Bowl, Drip Glaze, Pumpkin & Green	30.00
Figurine, Canoe & Frog, Matte Green	55.00
Flower Frog, Pink, Green, Oval, 6 1/2 In.	10.00
Vase, Black & Yellow Flambe Glaze, 8 In.	45.00
Vase, Lavender & Green, Handle, 6 1/2 In.	35.00
Vase, Narrow Top, Wide Shoulders, Matte Streaks, Gold, 6 In.	35.00
Vase, Pillow, Goldfish, Large	65.00
Vase, Stick, Purple & Green, Double Handle	35.00

Music boxes, musical instruments, and sheet music are listed in this
section. Phonograph records, jukeboxes, and phonographs are listed
in other sections in this book.

MUSIC, Accordion, Concertone, Mother-of-Pearl Buttons	65.00
Accordion, Cucinelli, Professional Model	750.00
Album, Rotating Pictures, Photos Rotate On Band	850.00
Autoharp, Zimmerman	40.00 To 55.00
Automaton, 7 Piece Orchestra, Bisque, German, C.1890, 16 X 17 X 12 In.	4200.00
Automaton, Acrobat, Jumeau Head, Turning Head, Decamps, 21 In.	4125.00
Automaton, Bellringers, 2 Children, Heubach, 1900, 10 X 6 In.	1600.00
Automaton, Bird In Cage, Rococo Design, Mechanical, 22 In. ....*Illus*	2200.00
Automaton, Bird In Cage, Tweets, Germany	235.00
Automaton, Bird Perching On Leafy T–Bar, Key, French, 19 In.	495.00
Automaton, Bird Popping Up, Moving, Singing, Sterling Silver, 4 In.	1295.00
Automaton, Lady Waving Fan, Lorgnette To Eyes, L.Lambert, 19 In.	2750.00
Automaton, Monkeys Turning Crank, Playing Instruments, German, 1910	1395.00
Automaton, Mother Rocking Baby, Oak Base, Key, German, 12 1/2 X 11 In.	700.00
Automaton, Polar Bear, Musical, Fur Covered, 22 In.	1600.00
Automaton, Singing Birds, In Birdcage, 22 In.	2200.00
Banjo Mandolin, Gibson, 4 String	325.00
Banjo, J.M.Turner, New York, 5 String, Rosewood Neck, 1870, 11 7/8 In.	425.00
Banjo, Lyon & Healy Tenor, Resonator	125.00
Banjo, Minstrel, 4 Strings, C.1880	175.00
Bass Drum, Primitive Painted Eagle, C.1812	2420.00
Bass Fiddle, Seth Elias, Poplar, Beech, Pine, Dated 1838, 30 7/8 In.	150.00
Box, Ariston, Cardboard Discs, 13 In.	200.00
Box, Baker Troll, 12 Tune, 13 In.Cylinder, Original Tune Card	1200.00
Box, Bremond, Interchangeable Cylinders, Matching Table, 5 Cylinders	5700.00
Box, Calliope, Upright, 12 Saucer Bells, 20 1/2 In.	4200.00
Box, Capital, Model A, 6 Cuffs, Oak	1800.00
Box, Children Scene, English, Mahogany, Tin Discs, 11 1/2 In.	1300.00
Box, Cigarette, Harry Lauder, I Love A Lassie, Crown Devon, 3 X 4 In.	175.00
Box, Criterion, Disc, 20 In.	2200.00

Box, Cylinder, Rosewood Cover, Rectangular Case, 20 1/4 In. 275.00
Box, Empress, Concert Grand, Floor Model 4500.00
Box, J.H.Heller, 9 Bells, Tune Card, Instructions, Inlaid Rosewood 1900.00
Box, Mermod Freres, Interchangeable Cylinders, Carved Oak Cabinet 2400.00
Box, Mira, Cherrywood Case, 10 Metal Discs 700.00
Box, Mira, Disc Console, Decals, 10 Discs, 18 1/2 In. 6500.00
Box, Model 40, Rookwood Art Case 6500.00
Box, Paillard, Interchangeable Cylinder, Table, Storage Drawer 4500.00
Box, Polyphon No.104, Upright, 19 5/8 In. 4650.00
Box, Polyphon, Upright, 19 5/8 In. 3800.00
Box, Regina, Coin–Operated, Oak, 15 1/2 In.Discs 1500.00
Box, Regina, Double Comb, Bird's–Eye Maple Case 2800.00
Box, Regina, No.17a, Upright Case, Double Comb, 17 Discs 2500.00
Box, Regina, No.40, Console, Short Bedplate, 15 1/2 In. 5200.00
Box, Regina, No.40, Rookwood Case, 15 1/2 In. 6500.00
Box, Regina, No.50, Double Comb, Mahogany Case, 22 Discs 2800.00
Box, Regina, No.50, Mahogany Serpentine Case, 25 Discs 3000.00
Box, Regina, No.61, Desk Style, Mahogany 8000.00
Box, Regina, Quarter–Sawed Oak, C.1900, 27 In.Disc, 7 Ft. 9995.00
Box, Regina, Single Comb, Mahogany, Disc, 15 1/2 In. 2000.00
Box, Regina, Sublima, Electric Drive, 3 Rolls 4500.00
Box, Regina, Sublima, No.24 .... 7500.00
Box, Stella, Console, Carved Oak Case, 17 1/4 In. 5000.00
Box, Stella, Double Comb, Bottom Drawer, Table Model, Mahogany 3200.00
Box, Swiss, 8 Tunes, Bells, Butterfly Striker, Bisque Doll, 18 1/2 In. 1000.00
Box, Swiss, Cylinder, 6 Bells With Bees 5500.00
Box, Symphonion No.106, Floor Model, Coin–Operated, 18 Discs 7350.00
Box, Symphonion No.192, Feet Drawer, 25 1/4 In. 8000.00
Box, Symphonion, Double Comb, Oak Case, 12 Discs, 9 X 18 In. 1495.00
Box, Symphonion, Imperial, Mahogany, 13 In.Disc 4000.00
Box, Symphonion, Wood, C.1896 .... 450.00
Box, Various Tunes, Walnut Inlaid Case, C.1840, 20 X 10 In. 800.00
Box, Victorian, 4 Cast Putti At Corners, Mechanical Bird, 9 In. 950.00
Bugle, U.S.Cavalry, Made In Japan 100.00
Calliope, Tangley, Roll, Whistles, All Pneumatic Parts 5800.00
Clarinet, Wm.S.Haynes Co., Silver, October 1933 .... 1400.00
Concertina, 20 Keys, German 30.00
Concertina, Honer, Box 60.00
Concertina, Rosewood, 6 Sides, Original Case, Key 125.00
Doghouse, With Dog, Tin, Switzerland, Large 40.00
Drum, Military, Flying Eagle, Federal Shield, 13 Stars 550.00
Drum, Snare, Tompkins, Hudson River Valley Scene, American Flags 500.00
Drum, U.S.Marine, Maple, Painted Eagle, 1859–61, Horstmann, 16 1/2 In. 7500.00
Fiddlette 385.00
Flute, Haynes, Sterling Silver, Case, August 1909 .... 2200.00
French Horn, King Instruments, U.S.M.C., 1890s .... 150.00 To 200.00
Guitar, Charles Stromberg 1000.00
Guitar, Martin, Tenor, 4 Strings, 1930 .... 450.00
Harmonette, Hohner, Harp Shape, Germany, Box 35.00
Harmonica, Echo, Box 15.00
Harmonica, Hohner, Echo Harp, Double Mouthpiece, Box 40.00
Harmonica, Hohner, El Centenario, Case, 1810–1910 .... 35.00
Harmonica, Little Lady, Miniature 20.00
Harmonica, Magnus, Duo–Tone 25.00
Harmonica, Marine Band 17.50
Harmonica, Masterphone 65.00
Harmonica, Silvertone 5.00
Harp, Clark, Irish, Celtic Monastic Designs, C.1915 .... 975.00
Harp, Gilded Gesso, Angels, Peacocks, J.S.Brown & Co., 67 In. 1000.00
Harp, Lap 200.00
Harp, Sebastian Erard, Neoclassical, C.1830 .... 3300.00
Hexaphone, No.102 .... 3950.00
Hurdy–Gurdy, 2 Wheeled Cart, 5 Christmas Songs, Spanish, 1860–80 .... 1400.00
Mandolin Harp, Lap, All Strings 125.00

Mandolin, Gibson, Kalamazoo, Mahogany, Ebony Fingerboard, 13 3/4 In. 225.00
Mandolin, Oliver Ditson, Gourd Shape, Original Cloth Case 90.00
Mandolin, Tater Bug, Dixon, Pearl Inlay 85.00
Melodeon, Brazilian Rosewood, 1866 .... 4800.00
Melodia, Hohner 20.00
Metronome, Seth Thomas, Mahogany Case 100.00
Metronome, Seth Thomas, Wooden Case .... 25.00 To 38.00
Nickelodeon, Coinola 3700.00
Nickelodeon, Coinola, Keyboard, Plays A Rolls 3500.00
Nickelodeon, Fox 4000.00
Nickelodeon, National, Mortier Orchestrion Facade 1500.00
Nickelodeon, National, Scopitone 700.00
Nickelodeon, Western Electric, Mascot, Model C 7000.00
Orchestrion, Barrel, With 2 Barrels, 6 Ft. 650.00
Organ, 4 Moving Figures, 2 Rank Barrel, Flute Clock, 8 Ft.8 In. 6500.00
Organ, Adler, Pump, Oak 950.00
Organ, Aeolian, Player, Model 1500 .... 1500.00
Organ, Barrel, De Keinst, 48 Keys, 101 Pipes, On Wagon, 36 X 36 In. 7300.00
Organ, Barrel, Flute Clock, 4 Moving Figures, 2 Rank 6500.00
Organ, Church, Seybold, 20 Stops, 440 Reeds, Oak, 1914 .... 1100.00
Organ, Coinola LX, With Xylophone 6800.00
Organ, Concert Roller, Cob, Oak, Dated 1913 .... 695.00
Organ, Crown, Walnut, With Mirror, C.1900 .... 2250.00
Organ, Estey, Beveled Mirror, Walnut 850.00
Organ, Estey, Pump, Hand Carved, 1869 .... 9950.00
Organ, Estey, Reed, 2 Manual, Gold Oak Case, C.1910 .... 2700.00
Organ, Gem, Roller, 3 Religious Cobs 300.00
Organ, Gem, Roller, Stenciled, 5 Cobs 375.00
Organ, Goodman, Pump, Gothic Style, Brass Pipes, 46 X 48 In. 3500.00
Organ, Hand Crank, Oil Paintings, French, C.1850 .... 3000.00
Organ, Hinners, Pump, Mission Oak, Bellows, 1910-20 .... 650.00
Organ, Mason & Hamlin, Pump, Ornate Top 250.00
Organ, Melody Grand, Foot Pumper, Burl Walnut, S Curve Sides 6500.00
Organ, Monkey, 15 Tunes, 89 Pipes 5200.00
Organ, Orguinette, Musette Mechanical, Gilt Stenciled, 6 Rolls 525.00
Organ, Packard, Walnut, Ft.Wayne, In., Late 1800s 600.00
Organ, Peloubet Pelton, Walnut, Refinished Fruitwood, Electrified 695.00
Organ, Pump, Oak, Spoon Carving, Shelves, Mirror 250.00
Organ, Pump, Victorian, Carved Case, Ivory Keys, Bench, Walnut 225.00
Organ, Regina Sublima, Rolls 5000.00
Organ, Seeburg, Model E, Flute Pipes 6200.00
Organ, Seybold, Church, 20 Stops, 440 Reeds, Oak, 1914 .... 1100.00
Organ, Street Barrel, 8 Tune, Front Crank, Marquetry, 23 X 17 X 37 In. 4950.00
Organ, Street Barrel, 9 Tune, Mahogany, Cloth Screen, 36 X 11 X 23 In. 4400.00
Organ, Street, Organo Grand No.15, 10 Tune, 33 3/4 X 23 X 48 3/4 In. 6050.00
Organ, Taylor & Farley, Cottage 250.00
Organ, W.W.Kimball, Walnut, Bench 850.00
Organ, William Thomson, Pump, 1920s 1200.00
Organ, Wurlitzer, Model 103, 55 Pipes, Drums, Cymbal, 10 Rolls 9500.00
Organette, McTammany, Paper Roll 300.00
Organette, Mignon, Ebonized Case, 5 1/4 In.Roll, 16 In. 605.00
Piano, A.G.Gale & Co., Grand, Signed, August, 1858 .... 5000.00
Piano, A.Lewandoski, Grand, Burled Walnut Case, 1849, 8 Ft. 3500.00
Piano, Behr Bros.& Co., Upright, Grand, Patent 1881 .... 800.00
Piano, Bradbury, Grand, Square, Full Size Keyboard 1500.00
Piano, Brambach, Baby Grand, Mahogany, Bench 450.00
Piano, Chickering, Ampico Grand, Reproducing, Art Case, Bench, Walnut 9500.00
Piano, Chickering, Grand, Rosewood, Refinished, Square, 1865 .... 7500.00
Piano, Chickering, Grand, Square, 1850 .... 1000.00
Piano, Chickering, Grand, Square, Rosewood, 1830 .... 3200.00
Piano, Cremona, Coin-Operated, 1905 .... 3000.00
Piano, Decker, Upright, Scroll Music Board, Black Walnut, 1888 .... 1950.00
Piano, Franklin, Ampico, Reproducing, Bench, Walnut Cabinet 1500.00
Piano, Franklin, Ampico, Upright, Reproducing, 1927 .... 4550.00

Piano, Haines Stoddard, Ampico, Reproducing, Upright 450.00
Piano, J.A.& W.Geib, Stool, C.1830, 33 X 57 In. ....*Illus* 1760.00
Piano, Kimball, Grand, Square, Carved, Walnut 2000.00
Piano, Knabe, Ampico B, Reproducing, Walnut Art Case 8500.00
Piano, Knabe, Ampico, Upright, Reproducing 1600.00
Piano, Knabe, Concert Grand, Square, Louis XIV Legs, Rosewood 700.00
Piano, Knabe, Grand, Square, Rosewood 1600.00
Piano, Lester Welte, Baby Grand, Bench 2100.00
Piano, Lyon & Healy, Resonator, 3/4 Keyboard, Cherry 500.00
Piano, Mason & Hamlin, Ampico Grand, Mahogany, Bench, Cabinet, 6 Feet 9100.00
Piano, Matushek, Grand, Rosewood Case, C.1875, 3 X 5 1/2 Ft. 3000.00
Piano, Melodigrand Jumbo, Foot Pumper, Burl Walnut, S Curved Sides 6500.00
Piano, Packard Co., Model 112137, Upright, Mission Oak, 58 In. 800.00
Piano, Player, Balwin Manualo, Hamilton, Rebuilt 1600.00
Piano, Player, Dynavoice, Sits On Keyboards, 1960s 195.00
Piano, Player, Hammond, Simplex, Electrified 1795.00
Piano, Player, Pianola, 64 Note, 1971 .... 1200.00
Piano, Player, Stroud, Upright, Duo-Art, Rolls 3200.00
Piano, Rehr Bros., Recordo, Upright 4000.00
Piano, Rosenkranz, Grand, Rectangular, C.1885 .... 1200.00
Piano, Seeburg, Model 53872, Coin-Operated, Stained Glass Windows 7500.00
Piano, Steinway, Duo-Art, Reproducing, Upright 5250.00
Piano, Steinway, Grand, Mahogany, Bench 6750.00
Piano, Steinway, Grand, Square, C.1874 .... 2500.00
Piano, Steinway, Grand, Square, Rosewood, C.1885 .... 6000.00
Piano, Stroud, Duo-Art, Reproducing, Upright 1100.00
Piano, Stroud, Duo-Art, Upright, Rolls 3200.00
Piano, Welte-Mignon, Baby Grand, Reproducing, Walnut, Bench 8000.00
Piano, Wurlitzer, Kingston Parlor Grand, Mahogany Case 380.00
Rolmonica, Chromatic, With Rolls 15.00
Rolmonica, Player Piano Type Rolls, 1926 .... 120.00
Rolmonica, Rolls, Box, Dated 1927 .... 125.00
Spinet, Thomas Hancock, Walnut, Cabriole Legs, C.1720, 6 Ft.6 In. 3520.00
Ukelin, With Bow, Music, Bill of Sale, 1926 .... 125.00
Violin, Amati, 2 Bowl, Case, 1894, 3/4 Size 775.00
Violin, August Gemunder, New York, 1877 .... 2000.00
Violin, D.Nocolaus Amati, Reddish-Brown 6000.00
Violin, Franz Diener, Baroque, Bohemia, C.1840 .... 2900.00
Violin, Ukes, With Music, Instruction Manual, Bow 45.00
Violincello, Mathias Neuner, 1813 .... 3400.00
Xylophone, Bedters, 25 Note, Rosewood 600.00
Xylophone, Litho Paper On Wood 65.00
Zither, Pillard, Polytype, Interchangeable Cylinders, Table 4500.00
Zonophone, Model B 1850.00

The mustache cup was popular from 1850 to 1900 when the large, flowing mustache was in style. A ledge of china or silver held the hair out of the liquid in the cup. This kept the mustache tidy and also kept the mustache wax from melting. Left-handed mustache cups are rare but are being reproduced.

MUSTACHE CUP, Floral Engraving, Tufts, Inscribed, 1869-87 .... 85.00
Hand Painted Violets, Bavaria 37.50
Raised Flowers, Love The Giver, Germany 50.00
Saucer, Hand Painted Violets, Gold Handle 35.00

"MZ Austria" is the wording on a mark used by Moritz Zdekauer on porcelains made at his works from about 1900. The firm worked in the town of Alt-Rohlau, Austria. The pieces were decorated with lavish floral patterns and overglaze gold decoration. Full sets of dishes were made as well as vases, toilet sets, and other wares.

MZ Austria

MZ AUSTRIA, Bowl, Flowers, 8 In. 150.00
Dish, Child's, Dogs, Cats, 7 In. 150.00
Hair Receiver, Cream Roses, 6 In. 30.00
Pitcher, Flowers, Pink, Red, Blue, Green, 8 In. 50.00

Nailsea glass was made in the Bristol district in England from 1788 to 1873. It was made by many different factories, not just the Nailsea Glass House. Many pieces were made with loopings of either white or colored glass as decoration.

NAILSEA, Bowl, White Looping, Crystal Handles & Feet, Sapphire, 6 1/4 In. 175.00
Cruet, Red & White Looping, Frosted 125.00
Flask, Perfume, Cobalt Blue, Pink & White Looping, 8 In. 245.00
Flask, Perfume, Pink & White Looping, Hand Blown, Pontil, 1800s 215.00
Flask, Perfume, Pink & White Looping, Horizontal Lines, 8 In. 235.00
Flask, Pink & White Looping, 5 3/4 In. 125.00
Flask, Pink Looping, White, 6 1/2 In. 160.00
Flask, Red, White & Blue Looping, Cased, 8 1/4 In. 125.00
Flask, White Looping, Clear 110.00
Lamp, Fairy, Blue & White, Upturned Ruffled Base, 6 X 6 1/2 In. 485.00
Lamp, Fairy, Lime Green, 3/4 X 4 In. 385.00
Lamp, Yellow 165.00
Spittoon 315.00

NAKARA Nakara is a trade name for a white glassware made about 1900 by the C. F. Monroe Company of Meriden, Connecticut. It was decorated in pastel colors. The glass was very similar to another glass made by the company called "Wave Crest." The company closed in 1916. Boxes for use on a dressing table are the most commonly found Nakara pieces. The mark is not found on every piece.

NAKARA, Bonbon, Octagonal, Bail 295.00
Box, Hand Painted Pink Roses, Green, Crown Mold, 9 In. 895.00
Box, Hinged Cover, Florals, Lined, Gold Washed Fittings, 3 3/4 In. 225.00
Box, Hinged Cover, Queen Louise, Blue, 4 1/2 In. .... 450.00 To 550.00
Box, Hinged Ormolu Cover, Dots, Poppies, Hexagonal, Signed, 6 1/2 In. 475.00
Box, Jewelry, Hinged Cover, Little Girls At Tea, 3 1/2 X 6 In. 300.00

Music, Piano, J.A.& W.Geib, Stool, C.1830, 33 X 57 In.

Box, Orchid Center of Cover, Lined, 3 1/2 X 6 1/2 In.	695.00
Box, Wild Roses, Beaded Ribbon, Octagonal, Marked, 3 1/2 X 6 In.	695.00
Box, Woman Scene Cover, Dots, Pink Roses, Green, Mirror, 8 X 3 3/4 In.	275.00
Case, Card, Flowers, Embossed, Beaded, Brass Trim, 2 1/2 X 4 1/2 In.	275.00
Dish, Pin, Flowers, Hexagonal, Signed, 3 In.	125.00
Hair Receiver, Bishop's Hat Mold, Apple Blossoms, Signed	225.00
Hair Receiver, Bishop's Hat, Floral Design, Pink Ground, Signed	345.00
Humidor, Indian Portrait, Cigars On Cover, C.F.M.Co., 5 3/4 In.	1150.00
Lamp, Daisies, Brass Base & Top, Opaque White, Russet, 23 In.	185.00
Mustard, Hexagonal, Enameled Daisies, Pink Ground	395.00
Vase, Hand Painted Roses, Dolphin Foot, 14 In.	495.00
Vase, Purple Iris, Metal Feet, Rust To Orange Ground, 13 1/2 In.	610.00

 Nanking is a type of blue-and-white porcelain made in Canton, China, since the late eighteenth century. It is very similar to Canton, which is listed under its own name in this book. Both Nanking and Canton are part of a larger group now called "Chinese Export" porcelain. Nanking has a spear-and-post border and may have gold decoration.

NANKING, Bowl, Mountains, Blue, White, 6 X 5 In.	1200.00
Dish, Hot Water, Pagoda Design, Floral Rim, Blue, White, 9 In.	170.00

 Napkin rings were in fashion from 1869 to about 1900. They were made of silver, porcelain, wood, and other materials. They are still being made today. The most popular rings with collectors are the figural napkin rings of silver plate. Small, realistic figures were made to hold the ring. Good and poor reproductions of the more expensive rings are now being made and collectors must be very careful, especially when buying any of the Kate Greenaway rings.

NAPKIN RING, Berries & Leaves, Chased Openwork, Sterling Silver, 1 3/4 In.	150.00
Cherub, Leash To Swan, Sterling, Wilcox	240.00
Clip, Monogram, Sterling Silver, Gorham, Set of 2	30.00
Figural, 2 Sailors Standing, Middleton	248.00
Figural, 2 Spread Winged Eagles, Meriden, 2 X 3 In.	80.00
Figural, 2 Turkish Dancers, Footed, Silver Plate	125.00
Figural, Baseball Player, With Bat, Silver Plate	225.00
Figural, Bird On Nest	90.00
Figural, Bird, Sterling Silver, Wood & Hughes	400.00
Figural, Boy, Dressed In Overcoat & Hat, Book Under Arm	255.00
Figural, Boy, Pulling Engraved Ring On Wheels, Silver Plate	245.00
Figural, Boy, Ruffled Collar, Hat, Stands At Front, Southington	255.00
Figural, Boy, Silver Plate	260.00
Figural, Bulldog, In House, Both Sides	125.00
Figural, Cart On Turning Wheels, Silver Plate	295.00
Figural, Cat On Pillow, Tail In Air	100.00
Figural, Cherubs Holding Dolls, Barrel Ring, Silver Plate	145.00
Figural, Chick, Wishbone, Best Wishes On Ring, Derby	40.00 To 90.00
Figural, Child of The Sea, Meriden	200.00
Figural, Child Sitting On Ring	185.00
Figural, Cockatoo On Branch, Meriden	120.00
Figural, Cow In Pasture	200.00
Figural, Dog Pulling Sled, Greyhounds On Side, Meriden	165.00
Figural, Dolphin Boy, Holding Trumpet, Silver Plate	180.00
Figural, Eagle, Both Sides, Meriden	72.00
Figural, Eagles, Holding Beaded Ring, Rockford Silver Plate	80.00
Figural, Elephant With Eye Rods, Catalin	25.00
Figural, Giraffe & Palm Tree, Silver Plate	360.00
Figural, Giraffe Eating Leaves	350.00
Figural, Girl Playing With Dog On Top, Silver Plate	125.00
Figural, Girl With Basket, Silver Plate	250.00
Figural, Girl, Silver Plate	225.00
Figural, Goat & Chariot, Silver Plate	325.00
Figural, Graceful Stork	350.00

Figural, Grizzly Bear 150.00
Figural, Horse Pulling Cart, Wheels Turn 350.00
Figural, Hunter & Dog, Silver Plate 425.00
Figural, Kate Greenaway Boy, Wing On His Back, Rogers & Bros. 87.50
Figural, Lily Pad, Engraved Ring, Middletown ....90.00 To 165.00
Figural, Lily, Meriden 45.00
Figural, Lion Pulling Cart 175.00
Figural, Lizard, Glass Eyes, Silver Plate 420.00
Figural, Marching Frog, Playing Drum, Reed & Barton 150.00
Figural, Monkey Dressed As Man, Tufts 265.00
Figural, Nude Male Runner, Holding Torch, Silver Plate, Square 195.00
Figural, Oak Leaves, Acorns At Side, Squirrel On Top, Tufts 78.00
Figural, Ostrich, Austrian 85.00
Figural, Rooster Pulling Cart, Wheels Turn 275.00
Figural, Sailor & Anchor, Silver Plate 375.00
Figural, Sailor With Rope, Barrel Ring, Stand, Silver Plate 175.00
Figural, Sheaf of Wheat 200.00
Figural, Small Goats Pulling Cart 259.00
Figural, Squirrel Eating Nut, Silver Plate 35.00
Figural, Turtle Crawling 170.00
Figural, Turtle, Sterling Silver 35.00
Figural, Water Lily Bud, Curling Stem On Leaf, Silver Plate 65.00
Figural, Winged Cherub On Top, Holds Chain To Bird, Sterling 235.00
Hammered Silver, Applied EB, Rectangular, 3 1/4 X 3/4 In. 195.00
Polar Bear's Face, Carved Bone 30.00
Sterling, Engraving, Shiebler 50.00
Woman, Sterling Silver, Unger, 1 1/2 X 1/4 In. 140.00

> Nash glass was made in Corona, New York, after 1919 by Arthur Nash and his sons. He worked at the Webb factory in England and for the Tiffany Glassworks in the United States.

NASH, Candlestick, Chintz, Red, 5 In., Pair 750.00
Compote, Chintz, Scalloped, Green, Zigzag, 4 In. 110.00
Compote, Chintz, Scalloped, Zigzag, Pedestal, Signed, 2 1/2 In. 110.00
Cordial, Chintz, 4 In. 55.00
Dish, Mint, Chintz, Scalloped, Radiating Stripes, 6 3/4 In. 75.00
Goblet, Chintz, Stem, 6 1/2 In. 60.00
Goblet, Pink Threaded, Clear Twisted Stem, Marked, 7 In. 145.00
Platter, Chintz, Allover Pattern, Green & Blue Bands, Signed, 8 3/4 In. 125.00
Vase, Blue Feather Strokes, Lime Streaks, Bulbous, Signed, 6 1/2 In. 395.00
Vase, Gold, Square Top, Signed, 6 1/4 In. 275.00

> Nautical antiques are listed in this section. Any of the many objects that were made or used by the seafaring trade, including ship parts, models, and tools, are included. Other pieces may be found listed under Scrimshaw.

NAUTICAL, Account Book, Whaling Co., E.Greenwich, R.I., 146 Pages, 1808–12 .... 5700.00
Barograph, Short & Mason 325.00
Bell, S.S.Ocean Bridge, Bronze, 14 1/2 In. 595.00
Bell, Ship's, Brass, Modern Wooden Mount, 19th Century, 8 X 8 In. 275.00
Bell, Ship's, Bronze, 10 In. 176.00
Binnacle, Engraved Compass, Brass, 19th Century, 9 1/2 In. 695.00
Binnacle, Wooden, Brass, 4 In. 800.00
Bottle Opener, Surinam Line, Brass 16.00
Butter Chip, White Star Line, Dated 1912 .... 65.00
Card, Admission, Aboard U.S.S.Wichita, Photo, 1939, 2 1/2 X 4 In. 4.00
Card, Playing, Canadian National Steamship Line, 1920s 20.00
Change Receiver, American Ship Line 50.00
Chart Tube, Bamboo, Leather Cap, China Trade, 19th Century, 27 In. 160.00
Chest, Canvas Top, Ship On Interior of Lid, Pine, 37 1/2 In. 125.00
Chest, Elmer A.Hall, Fitted Interior, Pine, Carved Lid, Small 375.00
Chest, Lift Top, Pine, Ditty Box Interior, Green Paint, 16 X 37 In. 165.00
Chest, Sea, Painting Inside, Ships, Roses, Mid-19th Century, 42 In. 4300.00
Chest, Seaman's, Maple, Carved, C.1860, 11 X 15 X 9 In. 695.00

Clock, Brass, J.E.Caldwell, Chelsea Movement, Bell, 8 In. 600.00
Clock, Brass, Kevin Bottomley, 5 In.Dial 176.00
Clock, Chelsea, U.S.Maritime, 12–Hour Dial 150.00
Clock, Fusee, Porcelain Dial, D.McGregor, Glasgow, C.1880, 10 In. 795.00
Clock, Seth Thomas, Bell Below, Brass 400.00
Compass, Brass, Oak Carrying Box, C.1940 .... 80.00
Compass, Convex Glass Lens, Paper Face, Wooden Case, 2 In. 150.00
Compass, Dinsmore 12.00
Creamer, New England Steamship Co. 35.00
Cup & Saucer, Cunard Steamship, Striped Cream, Foley, Demitasse 40.00
Cup & Saucer, Delta Lines, Demitasse 65.00
Decanter, Ship's, Glass, Squat, Unusual Handle 32.00
Ditty Bag, Sailor's 30.00
Eggcup, Luckenbach Line 26.00
Fog Horn, Ship's Emergency, Manual, Brass 95.00
Gun Sight, Brass, English, Early 20th Century, Wooden Case, 23 In. 88.00
Harpoon Gun, Greener Percussion, Brass, 1840s, 36 In. 2950.00
Harpoon Gun, S.S.Terra Nova, Dundee, Swivel & Mount, 34 In. 4000.00
Harpoon, Whaling, Greener, Charles W.Morgan Ship, 45 In. 950.00
Harpoon, Whaling, Ship's Name, B.K.Platina, Temple Iron, 39 In. 550.00
Helmet, Diving, Galeazzi 400.00
Inclinometer, Kelvin & Hughes, Beveled Glass, Brass, 12 In. 295.00
Inclinometer, U.S.Navy, 2–Tube Bubble, Moeller Instrument Co. 295.00
Lamp, Port & Starboard, Brass, C.1920, 12 In., Pair 275.00
Lamp, Ship, Brass, Glass Panels, Metal Handle, 1940s, 15 1/2 In. 185.00
Lamp, Whale Oil, 3 Fonts, English, Brass, C.1810 .... 165.00
Lantern, Kerosene, Round Clear Globe, Marked Perkins 8 .... 110.00
Lantern, Lifeboat, Brass, Round, 1940s, 11 X 14 In. 185.00
Lantern, Proctor, Blue Lens, Pat.1876 .... 38.00
Light, Masthead, Galvanized Metal, 16 In. 44.00
Light, Signal, Bridge–Mount, Brass, Iron Yoke, 22 X 12 In. 195.00
Menu, R.M.S.Olympic 8.00
Menu, S.S.Mariposa, 1938 .... 12.00
Mirror, Pocket, Scandinavian American Lines, Copenhagen 50.00
Model, 3–Masted Man–O'-War, Wooden, 20 In. 90.00
Model, Freighter, Electric Lamp In Bow, Wooden, 36 In. 170.00
Model, Gloucester Fishing Schooner, Columbia, 19th Century, 20 In. 900.00
Model, Italia Ocean Liner, Wood, Metal, Lifeboats, Case, 50 X 46 In. 300.00
Model, Man–O'-War, Boxwood, English, 19th Century, 13 1/2 In. 7150.00
Model, Marblehead Skiff, Half Model, Rob Napier, 14 1/2 In. 77.00
Model, P.T.64, Handmade, Wooden, Polychrome Paint, 49 In. 425.00
Model, Sailboat, Thyra, English, Large 2400.00
Model, Steam–Whaler Pioneer, French Prisoner of War, 26 1/4 In. 3000.00
Model, Warship, Prisoner of War, Bone, Ebony, 2 Decks 9000.00
Model, Whaler, Charles W.Morgan, Piel Craftsman, Wooden, 17 In. 195.00
Model, Yawl, Paper Sails, By Piel, Wooden, 11 1/4 In. 65.00
Paperweight, R.M.S.Cedric, Glass 25.00
Pipe, Boatswain's, Handwoven Cord, Silver 35.00
Postcard, White Star Line, Menu, Baltic, Aug.26, 1910 .... 6.00
Print, Aquitania, Cunard Line, Framed, 12 Ft. X 19 1/2 In. 75.00
Propellor, Ship's, 3 Blades, 24 In. 75.00
Rolling Ruler, Murray, Calcutta, Boxwood & Brass, C.1880, 33 In. 250.00
Sailor's Valentine, Octagonal, Double, 9 In. 1600.00
Sailor's Valentine, Shellwork, C.1870, 9 In. 525.00
Sign, Lusitania, Cunard Line, Tin, Litho, 1907, 26 X 35 In. 380.00
Sign, Scandinavian American Line, Self–Framed, Tin, 31 X 40 In. 475.00
Spoon, Alaskan Steamship Co., Sterling Silver 30.00
Tag, Baggage, Red Star Line, Card Stock 5.00
Telescope, Captain's, Canvas Cover, Knotwork At Ends, 32 In. 625.00
Telescope, Mahogany, Brass, Alvin Clarke & Sons, C.1870, 67 1/2 In. 3000.00
Timetable, New Haven Steamers, Summer 1882, 4 Pages, 3 1/2 X 5 In. 4.00
Tip Tray, American Line 75.00
Tip Tray, Cleveland & Buffalo Steamship, CB In Water 250.00
Trunk, Pierced Wood Handles, Painted Green, 13 1/4 X 32 In. 220.00

Trunk, Storage Area, Wood Handles, Green, 13 X 32 In. 250.00
Washstand, Ship's, Mahogany, Lift Top, Mirror, 1 Door, 33 In. 995.00
Watering Can, Queen Mary, Raised Figural Luxury Liner, 2 Sides 50.00
Wheel, Ship's, Hand Crafted, Inlaid, Brass Center, Stand, 24 In. 60.00
Whistle, Steam, Marked Lunkenheimer 46E, Bronze, 12 In. 295.00

Small ivory, wood, metal, or porcelain pieces were used as buttons on the end of the cord that held a Japanese money pouch. These were called "netsuke." The earliest date from the sixteenth century. Many are miniature, carved works of art.

NETSUKE, Brass, Badger Turning Into A Teapot 66.00
Brass, Urn, Dragon Handle 88.00
Bronze, Seed–Form Body, Silver & Gold Pomegranates 88.00
Gold, 3 Monkeys, Signed Kosai 357.00
Ivory, 2 Rats On Winnowing Basket, Kohosai 468.00
Ivory, 3 Puppies At Play, Inset Eyes, Signed Yoshimitsu 95.00
Ivory, Boy, Relieving Himself, Signed, 1 15/16 In. 85.00
Ivory, Courtesan, 19th Century 700.00
Ivory, Craftsman Weaving Mat, Signed 110.00
Ivory, Daruma Reads A Sutra, 18th Century 110.00
Ivory, Dog, Puppy On Back, Signed, Hole, 1 1/2 In. 29.00
Ivory, Dog, With Small Rabbit, Signed, Hole, 1 1/2 In. 32.00
Ivory, Dragon, Coiled Tail, Signed, 2 In. 50.00
Ivory, Drunken Man, Flowered Kimono, Signed Kyosen 70.00
Ivory, European Man, Rabbit Over Back, Signed, 2 1/2 In. 100.00
Ivory, Flying Bird, Dyed Brown, C.1850, 3/4 In. 65.00
Ivory, Fruits & Vegetables, 18th Century 200.00
Ivory, Goose, Inset Eyes 70.00
Ivory, Mask, Hannya, Jealous Woman, Signed, 2 1/2 In. 200.00
Ivory, Monk Asleep On His Drum, Signed Mitsutama 75.00
Ivory, Monkey, Tomokazu 330.00
Ivory, Old Man, Feeding Rooster, Signed, 2 In. 275.00
Ivory, Old Man, Kneeling By Sack 88.00
Ivory, Oni Carries Fukumusume On Back, 19th Century 70.00
Ivory, Plump Sleeping Kitten, Signed Daiban 80.00
Ivory, Rabbit, Inlaid Eyes, Signed 150.00
Ivory, Reclining Bull, 19th Century 90.00
Ivory, Scholar, 1 3/4 In. 30.00
Ivory, Skull, Rat On Top, Signed, 1 1/4 X 1 In. 325.00
Ivory, Soga Brothers, Ryuun, 19th Century 1250.00
Ivory, Squirrel On Grapes 143.00
Ivory, Wrestlers, Tomochika, 19th Century 1500.00
Lacquered Metal, Pistol, Matchlock 300.00
Lacquered Metal, Scholar, Peach Grove, Manju Form 176.00
Lacquered Wood, Shrub Design, Gold, Manju Form 220.00
Metal, Flower & Gourd, Latticed Wall, Silvered 143.00
Silver, Inlaid, Holy Man, Dragon, Sentoku 302.50

The rarest pieces of Azalea pattern Nippon china are said to be the fluted square plates, the scalloped and footed mayonnaise, the pancake jug, and the ashtray.

Silver, Lion Dancer, Signed	220.00
Wood, Bat & Shou Design	55.00
Wood, Gods of Good Luck, Wrestling, Signed Torinsai Toshinao	650.00
Wood, Grazing Horse, 19th Century	1000.00
Wood, Human Skull, Without Lower Jaw, Signed, 1 3/4 In.	70.00
Wood, Kappa, Water Imp, Sitting With Lotus Flower, 1 3/8 In.	50.00
Wood, Karako, Minko, 18th Century	1800.00
Wood, Monkey & Young, 19th Century	1000.00
Wood, Pair of Rats On Bale of Rice, 2 In.	200.00
Wood, Rat, Sitting On Winnowing Mushroom Basket, C.1800	770.00
Wood, Shishi, Head Resting On Reticulated Ball, 1 5/8 In.	175.00

New Hall Porcelain Manufactory was started at Newhall, Shelton, Staffordshire, England, in 1782. Simple decorated wares were made. Between 1810 and 1825, the factory made a glassy bone porcelain sometimes marked with the factory name. Do not confuse New Hall porcelain with the pieces made by the New Hall Pottery Company, Ltd., a twentieth-century firm.

NEW HALL, Bowl, Flower Sprigs, 6 In.	100.00
Cup & Saucer, Chinese Man, Woman, Orange, Blue, Green	125.00

The New Martinsville Glass Manufacturing Company was established in 1901 in New Martinsville, West Virginia. It was bought and renamed the Viking Glass Company in 1944 and is still producing fine glasswares.

NEW MARTINSVILLE, Bookends, Elephant	50.00
Bookends, Horse	25.00
Bookends, Sailing Ship, Crystal	95.00
Bookends, Seal & Ball	125.00
Bookends, Ship	15.00
Bride's Basket, Ruffled, Gold Luster Inside, 10 In.	475.00
Butter, Cover, Moondrops, Cobalt Blue	295.00
Cake Stand, Prelude, 11 1/2 In. .... 55.00 To 65.00
Cup & Saucer, Moondrops, Dark Green	6.50
Dish, Cheese, Cover, Peachblow	195.00
Figurine, Angel Fish, 8 1/4 In.	40.00
Figurine, Baby Chicks	25.00
Figurine, Hen	40.00
Figurine, Hunter, Round Base	75.00
Figurine, Pelican	25.00
Figurine, Penguin	25.00
Figurine, Rooster	55.00
Figurine, Seal	25.00
Figurine, Seal, Baby, Frosted Body, Crystal Ball, 4 1/2 In.	55.00
Figurine, Squirrel, Sticker, 5 1/4 In.	38.00
Figurine, Wolfhound	44.00
Perfume Bottle, Queen Anne, Amber, Pair	50.00
Sugar, Moondrops, Floral Design, Ruby	22.50
Tumbler, Moondrops, Ruby, 5 1/8 In.	16.00

Newcomb Pottery was founded by Ellsworth and William Woodward at Sophie Newcomb College, New Orleans, Louisiana, in 1896. The work continued through the 1940s. Pieces of this art pottery are marked with the printed letters "NC" and often have the incised initials of the artist as well. Most pieces have a matte glaze and incised decoration.

NEWCOMB, Candlestick, Mottled, Modified Espanol Design, Sadie Irvine, Hunt	995.00
Jardiniere, Irene Borden Keep, 1901	4950.00
Mug, Joseph Meyer, C.1902	2200.00
Mug, Sunflower, Hi-Glaze	1000.00
Mug, Sunflowers, Black Outlined, Ada W.Lonnegan, 1901, 4 1/4 In.	1600.00
Pot, Cypress Trees, Underglaze, 1903, 5 In. .... Illus	3800.00
Tea Set, Incised Roses, 6 Piece .... Illus	5100.00
Tile, Round, 6 In.	450.00

Newcomb, Pot, Cypress Trees, Underglaze, 1903, 5 In.

Newcomb, Tea Set, Incised Roses, 6 Piece

Vase, Bayou Scene, Moon, Sadie Irvine, 1930, 7 In.	2800.00
Vase, Blue, White Flowers, Blue Green Leaves, 5 1/5 In.	737.00
Vase, Carved White Flowers Collar, Matte Blue, AFS, 1925, 5 3/4 In.	250.00
Vase, Cypress Trees, Spanish Moss On Tree, Blue, Green, 7 In.	935.00
Vase, Floral Band, Mossy Trees, Sadie Irvine, 8 In.	800.00
Vase, Gray & Pink, Bailey, 1 5/8 In.	475.00
Vase, Hi–Glaze, Blue & Gray, 3 1/2 In.	175.00
Vase, Moonlight Through Moss, Signed, 6 1/4 X 3 1/2 In.	1300.00
Vase, Pink & Gray Flowers, Bailey, 1 5/8 X 3 5/8 In.	295.00
Vase, Pink Flowers, Blue, 4 Handles, Bailey, C.1922, 4 In.	425.00
Vase, Scenic, 6 In.	950.00
Vase, Spanish Moss On Tree, A.F.Simpson, 1914	2640.00
Vase, Spanish Moss, Full Moon, Squat, Bulbous, Initials KS, 5 In.	700.00

Niloak Pottery (Kaolin spelled backward) was made at the Hyten Brothers Pottery in Benton, Arkansas, between 1909 and 1946. Although the factory did make cast and molded wares, collectors are most interested in the marbelized art pottery line made of colored swirls of clay. It was called "Mission Ware."

NILOAK, Bowl, Swirl, 7 1/2 In.	65.00
Candleholder, Swirl, Label, Signed, 12 In., Pair	260.00
Candlestick, Marbelized, 8 1/2 In.	110.00
Jar, Marbelized, Cover, Cone, Tab Handle, Glossy Interior, 3 X 4 In.	325.00
Pitcher Set, Hywood, 5 Piece	45.00
Pitcher, Rose, Bulbous, 7 In.	15.00
Pitcher, Yellow, 5 In.	8.00
Planter, Camel, Blue	25.00
Planter, Camel, White	20.00
Planter, Deer	8.50 To 14.00
Planter, Elephant On Drum	18.00
Planter, Fawn	25.00
Planter, Kangaroo, Brown	22.00
Planter, Marbelized, 3 Triangular Openings	65.00
Planter, Squirrel, Rose Matte	15.00
Planter, Swan, Blue, 4 In.	17.00
Powder Jar, Cover, Marbelized	225.00
Sugar & Creamer, Blue	15.00
Toothpick, Marbelized	25.00
Vase, Aqua, Paper Label, 8 In.	16.00
Vase, Blue Glaze, Footed, Flared, Y Shaped Handles, 6 1/2 In.	20.00
Vase, Blue, 9 1/2 In.	25.00
Vase, Blue, Tulip Shape, Marked, 4 In.	12.50

Vase, Bud, Paper Label, 4 In.	12.00
Vase, Chartreuse Matte, Ear Handles, Crimped, 6 1/2 In.	20.00
Vase, Handles, Maroon, 7 In.	16.00
Vase, Hywood, Folded Sides, Pre–1930, 6 1/2 In.	25.00
Vase, Marbelized, 4 1/2 In.	48.00
Vase, Marbelized, 8 In.	85.00
Vase, Marbelized, 9 In.	85.00 To 150.00
Vase, Marbelized, Amphora Shape, 5 In.	70.00
Vase, Marbelized, Blue, Brown & Beige, Marked, 6 In.	40.00
Vase, Marbelized, Cream Terra–Cotta, Green & Blue, 7 1/2 In.	85.00
Vase, Marbelized, Flange Rim, 6 1/2 In.	45.00
Vase, Persian Rose, 2 Handles, 7 1/2 In.	32.50
Vase, Teardrop, 5 In.	50.00
Vase, Wing, Green	15.00

Nippon–marked porcelain was made in Japan from 1891 to 1921. "Nippon" is the Japanese word for "Japan." A few firms continued to use the word "Nippon" on ceramics after 1921 as a part of the company name more than as an identification of the country of origin. More pieces marked Nippon will be found in the Dragonware, Moriage, and Noritake sections.

NIPPON, Ashtray, Butterfly	35.00
Ashtray, Squirrel Scene, Woods	55.00
Berry Set, Turquoise Beading, Roses, Gold Trim, 6 Piece	85.00
Biscuit Jar, Florals, Green Leaves, Gold Trim, 3–Footed	80.00
Bowl, Blown–Out Nut, 6 Sides, 7 In.	95.00
Bowl, Blown–Out Peanuts, Jeweled Handles	45.00
Bowl, Gold Filigree, Flowers, Black Ground, Marked, 2 1/2 X 8 In.	175.00
Bowl, Gold Interior, Gold Moriage Around Medallions, 7 1/2 In.	125.00
Bowl, Ice Blue, 9 In.	395.00
Bowl, Lake Scene, Mountains, Moriage Trim, Maple Leaf, 7 3/4 In.	75.00
Bowl, Multicolor Florals, 2 Gold Handles, Green Mark, 8 In.	30.00
Bowl, Oak & Acorn Scene, Bisque, 1 1/2 X 6 In.	25.00
Bowl, Pastel Scene, Self Handles, Green Wreath Mark, 7 In.	35.00
Bowl, Phoenix Type Bird, Beaded, Footed, Green Wreath Mark, 7 1/4 In.	60.00
Bowl, Portrait, Gold Trim, 10 1/2 In.	160.00
Bowl, Red Poppies, Gold, Gaudy, Beading, Royal Kinran, 7 1/2 X 2 In.	149.00
Bowl, Roses, Gaudy, Gold Beading, Pink Ground, 10 In.	140.00
Bowl, Ruffled, Green, Gold Trim, 2 X 8 In.	325.00
Bowl, Scalloped, Magenta & Gold, Green Trim, White Dots, 9 3/4 In.	170.00
Bowl, Woodland Scene, Marked, 7 In.	159.00
Box, Sardine, Figural, Marked	150.00
Box, Stamp, 2 Compartments, Scenic, Green Mark	95.00
Cake Plate, Gold Leaves, Flowers, 13 In.	15.00
Cake Set, Pink Floral Border, Raised Gold, Handles, 7 Piece	95.00
Candlestick, Scenic, Black, Gold, Mark No.47, 6 In.	250.00
Celery Set, Bowl, 6 Salts, Allover Floral Design, Boat Shape, 7 Piece	95.00
Charger, Egyptian Design, People In Gondola, Marked, 11 1/4 In.	125.00
Chocolate Pot, Beaded Panels, Sailboats At Sea, Hexagonal	175.00
Chocolate Pot, Cobalt, Gold Geisha, Marked, 10 In.	55.00
Chocolate Pot, Pink & Red Roses, Gold	150.00
Chocolate Set, Gold Floral, Blue Matte Ground, 7 Piece	400.00
Chocolate Set, Gold Medallions & Trim, Marked, 7 Piece	250.00
Chocolate Set, Turquoise, White & Black, 13 Piece	225.00
Chocolate Set, Violets, 9 Piece	225.00
Chocolate Set, Yellow Roses, Marked, 9 Piece	175.00
Compote, Floral, 9 In.	22.00
Compote, Ostriches, Jewels, Pink Roses, Cobalt Blue, 10 In.	175.00
Cordial, Squirrel Handle	45.00
Cracker Jar, Footed, Blue Mark, 8 In.	90.00
Cracker Jar, Geisha, Melon, Ribbed	185.00
Cracker Jar, Orange Pomegranate, Gold Trim, Scalloped Shape, 7 In.	165.00
Creamer, Blown–Out Baby Doll	45.00
Dish, Capitol Building Center, VP Mark 31, Oblong	50.00

Dish, Souvenir, Nipper On Edge, Phonograph Horn	200.00
Dresser Set, Floral Medallions	110.00
Fernery, Bead & Jewel Border, 4 Scenic Panels, 5 3/4 X 10 1/2 In.	225.00
Fernery, Lakeside Scene, Jeweled Gilt Grapes, Leaves, Footed	150.00
Fernery, Purple Grapes, Green Leaves, Gold Stems, Molded Handles	125.00
Fernery, Raised Grapes & Outlines, Drab Green	45.00
Fernery, Stylized Lions, Bisque, 7 In.	180.00
Gravy Boat, Cream, Gold Floral, 3 Piece	40.00
Hair Receiver, Beaded Gold, White Swirls, Footed	20.00
Hatpin Holder, Beaded Gold Top & Bottom, Green Mark	50.00
Hatpin Holder, Cylinder Shape, Green Mark, 4 3/4 In.	45.00
Hatpin Holder, Egyptian Scenic	85.00
Hatpin Holder, Gold Top & Bottom, Blue Mark, 4 Sides, 4 3/4 In.	45.00
Hatpin Holder, Pink Flowers, Blue Borders, Gold Trim, 4 1/2 In.	90.00
Hatpin Holder, Roses, Footed, Aqua, Gold Trim, 4 1/2 In.	85.00
Hatpin Holder, Roses, Gold, 3–Footed, Marked	60.00
Humidor, Blown–Out Bulldog With Pipe, Cover	345.00
Humidor, Blown–Out Dog	90.00
Humidor, Cottage On Lake, Beaded, Green Mark, 5 1/2 In.	85.00
Humidor, Dragon, 8 In.	32.00
Humidor, Indian In Canoe, Geometric Jeweling, 6 Sides, Marked	185.00
Ice Cream Set, 5 Piece	595.00
Match Holder, Airplane Design	40.00
Match Holder, Cigarette & Match Design	25.00
Mustard Pot, Floral, Underplate, Green Wreath Mark	20.00
Nappy, Pink Floral, Handles, 7 In.	68.00
Nut Set, Blown–Out Design, Marked, 5 Piece	98.00
Nut Set, Pedestal, Magenta Wreath Mark, 7 Piece	55.00
Nut Set, Tree Scene, Gold Footed, 7 Piece	85.00
Nut Set, White, Raised Gold, 6 Piece	30.00
Pitcher, White Rose, Green, Gold Trim, 6 In.	80.00
Plaque, Blown–Out Buffalo Design, 10 1/2 In.	550.00
Plaque, Blown–Out Indian On Horseback, 10 1/2 In.	475.00
Plaque, English Riding Scene, Marked, 9 1/2 In.	175.00
Plaque, Happy Fat Boy, Blue Mark, 6 1/2 In.	35.00
Plaque, Indians, Blanket Wrapped, Headdress, Horses, 10 1/2 X 8 In.	245.00
Plaque, Man Poling Boat, 10 In.	175.00
Plaque, Moose, 10 In.	185.00
Plaque, Squirrel, 10 1/2 In.	900.00
Plaque, Sunset & Sailboat Scene, 8 In.	75.00
Plaque, Woodland Scene, Green Wreath Mark, 10 In.	250.00
Plate, Fish Shape, Floral, Enameled, Beaded, Blue Mark, 15 In.	175.00
Plate, Floral Border, Gold, Enameled, Green Mark, 7 1/2 In.	65.00
Plate, Flying Geese, Jeweled, 8 1/2 In.	125.00
Plate, Wisteria Blossoms, Gold Border, 10 In.	50.00
Rose Bowl, Tapestry Roses, Cobalt Blue, Footed	135.00
Smoke Set, Arab Astride Camel, 7 Piece	675.00
Stein, Man On Camel Scene, Green Mark, 7 In.	450.00
Sugar & Creamer, Pastel Roses, Matte Finish, Jewel Trim, 4 1/2 In.	145.00
Sugar Shaker, Encrusted Gold Design, White, Marked, Corset Shape	75.00
Sugar Shaker, Poppies, Gold Beaded, Hexagonal	75.00
Syrup, Underplate, Gold Design, White Ground	55.00
Tea Set, Egyptian Nile Scene, 19 Piece	275.00
Tea Set, Gold Encrusted, White, 3 Piece	85.00
Tea Set, Green, Gold Trim, 3 Piece	410.00
Tea Set, Houses, Boats, Crown Mark, 3 Piece	45.00
Vase, Basket, Pink Roses, Gold Ground, Stippled, Cover, 7 1/2 In.	280.00
Vase, Blown–Out Acorns & Leaves, Marked, 7 In.	525.00
Vase, Blown–Out Floral, Top & Bottom, Green Wreath Mark, 11 In.	200.00
Vase, Blown–Out Hunt Scene, Stag & Hounds, 2 Handles, 9 In.	500.00
Vase, Clipper Ship At Sea, Marked, 12 In.	180.00
Vase, Cobalt Blue, Floral, 2 Handles, Blue Maple Leaf Mark, 9 In.	175.00
Vase, Egyptian Design, 2 Handles, 7 3/8 In.	295.00
Vase, Enameled Leaves On Trees, Gold, 9 In.	225.00

Vase, Floral & Gold Gilt, Ram's Head Handles, 8 1/2 In.	85.00
Vase, Floral, Top & Bottom, Gold Trim, BML Mark, 9 In.	155.00
Vase, Gold, Scenic, Greek Key Design, Top & Bottom, 12 In.	695.00
Vase, Hand Painted Violet & Green Flowers, 3 Handles, 12 In.	145.00
Vase, Lake & Boat Scene, Gold Trim, Square Handle, Round, 12 In.	295.00
Vase, Lavender Flowers, Brown Ground, Black Enamel Outlining, 7 In.	135.00
Vase, Mountain, Flowers, Gold Collar, Beaded, Ring Handles, 8 1/4 In.	195.00
Vase, Orchids, Gold Trim, Marked, 11 1/2 In.	235.00
Vase, Pink Roses, White Ground, Gold Trim, 2 Handles, 5 1/2 In., Pair	95.00
Vase, Purple Wisteria, Leaf, Beaded, 3 Gold Handles, 11 1/2 In.	150.00
Vase, Rider, Camel, Moriage Palm Tree Scene, Footed, Handles, 14 In.	455.00
Vase, Roses, White Ground, Brown Handles, 6 In.	35.00
Vase, Vintage Airplane Design, 3 In.	125.00
Vase, Yellow & Red Bittersweet, Gold Trim, 12 In.	50.00
Vase, Yellow Roses, Moriage Top, 12 In., Pair	250.00
Wall Pocket, Butterfly Design, Royal Blue, Pair	47.00

Nodders, or nodding figures, or pagods, are porcelain figures with heads and hands that are attached to wires. Any slight movement causes the parts to move up and down. They were made in many countries during the eighteenth and nineteenth centuries. A few Art Deco designs are also known. Copies are being made.

NODDER, Andy Gump, Bisque, Germany	85.00
Baby, Pulling Off Sock, Pink & White Gown, 4 1/2 In.	175.00
Bakerman, Porcelain, 6 In.	20.00
Bellhop, Mortimer Snerd Type, Bisque, Japan, 3 1/2 In.	54.00
Black Boy, Bisque, Germany	125.00
Bum, Barefoot	28.00
Canadian Mountie	13.00
Cat, Black, Ceramic	25.00
Chester Gump, Bisque, Germany	75.00
Chicago Cubs, Composition	25.00
Chinese Man & Woman, Side To Side, 15 In., Pair	1250.00
Chubby Chaney, Bisque, Germany	95.00
Daddy Warbucks, Bisque, Germany	175.00
Denny Dimwit	300.00
Doctor, With Red Nose	15.00
Foxy Grandpa, Hand Painted	100.00
Girl, Standing, White Dress, Cobalt Blue, China, 7 3/8 In.	110.00
Golfer, Hole In One, Bank	35.00
Goose, Celluloid, Germany, U.S.Zone	28.00
Happy Hooligan, Papier–Mache	45.00
Indian, Japan, Pair	75.00
Jeff, Bisque, Germany	150.00 To 160.00
Kayo, Bisque, Germany	60.00 To 65.00
Ma Winkle, Germany	75.00
Mama Katzenjammer, Bisque, Seated, Germany, 4 3/4 In.	225.00
Mickey Mantle, Composition	125.00
Minnesota Vikings, Football, Composition	55.00
Moon Mullins, Bisque, Germany	25.00
Oriental Man, Bisque, C.1950	125.00
Pa Winkle, Germany	55.00
Player, Football, On Top of Radio, Composition	85.00
Rachel, Bisque, Germany	95.00
Retriever, Pheasant, White, Black, Clay, Glass Eyes, 5 X 15 In.	42.00
Seattle Seahawks, Football, Plastic, Box	40.00
Skulls, Salt & Pepper, In Holder	30.00
Sultan, Sitting, Mustache, Turban, Peach Bisque, 3 1/2 In.	70.00
Uncle Bim, Bisque	135.00
Uncle Walt, Bisque, Germany	85.00 To 100.00

Noritake–marked porcelain was made in Japan after 1904 by Nippon Toki Kaisha. The best–known Noritake pieces are marked with the M in a wreath for the Morimura Brothers, a New York

City distributing company. This mark was used until 1941. Another famous Noritake china was made for the Larkin Soap Company from 1916 through the 1930s. This dinnerware, decorated with azaleas, was sold or given away as a premium. There may be some helpful price information in the Nippon category since prices are comparable.

NORITAKE, Ashtray, Desert Scene, 4 In. 65.00
Ashtray, Figural, Clown, Art Deco .... 125.00 To 175.00
Asparagus Set, 7 Piece 195.00
Bonbon, Azalea, Side Handle, 6 1/4 In. .... 20.00 To 45.00
Bowl, Azalea, Open Handles, Round, 10 In. 30.00
Bowl, Nut, Azalea, Shell Shape, 7 3/4 In. 175.00
Bowl, Salad, Azalea, Handles, Round, 10 In. 36.00
Bowl, Tree In Meadow, 2 Handles, Oval, 7 1/2 In. 12.50
Bowl, Tree In Meadow, 6 In. 24.00
Bowl, Tree In Meadow, Divided, Oblong, 8 In. 20.00
Bowl, Vegetable, Azalea, Oval, 10 1/2 In. .... 30.00 To 40.00
Box, Clown, Red Polka Dot Suit, 5 1/2 In. 225.00
Box, Desert Scene, Hand Painted, Cover, 7 1/4 In. 175.00
Butter Tub, Azalea, With Insert .... 35.00 To 38.00
Butter Tub, Tree In Meadow, 5 1/2 In. 40.00
Cake Plate, Azalea, 10 In. 30.00
Card Holder, Girl Playing Cards, Red Flower In Hair, Art Deco 115.00
Casserole, Azalea, Cover, Handles, 10 3/4 In. 90.00
Celery, Azalea, Handles, 12 1/2 In. .... 32.00 To 40.00
Celery, Tree In Meadow 45.00
Chocolate Set, White, Gold Trim, 7 Piece 275.00
Compote, Cobalt Blue, Gold, 9 In. 75.00
Condiment Set, Azalea, 5 Piece 45.00
Condiment Set, Red, Blue, Yellow, Birds, 4 Piece 75.00
Cracker Jar, Mosaic Pattern, Silver-Plated Fittings, Marked 125.00
Cruet, Azalea, Stopper, 6 1/4 In. .... 150.00 To 160.00
Cruet, Tree In Meadow 75.00
Cup & Saucer, Azalea .... 12.00 To 17.00
Cup & Saucer, Baroda 14.00
Cup & Saucer, Holly 8.00
Cup, Tree In Meadow, Demitasse 22.50
Dish, Mayonnaise, Azalea 20.00
Dish, Oatmeal, Azalea, 5 1/2 In. 20.00
Eggcup, Azalea, 3 1/8 In. .... 45.00 To 50.00
Fernery, Landscape 75.00
Gravy Boat, Azalea, Attached Stand .... 30.00 To 32.00
Gravy Boat, Baroda 20.00
Humidor, Blown-Out Bulldog, Smoking Pipe 495.00
Humidor, Indian With Feather Headdress, Beaded, Jeweled 325.00
Humidor, Tree In Meadow 345.00
Jar, Mottled Mauve, Gold Veined, Bouquet Finial, 9 1/4 In. 175.00
Match Holder, Beehive Shape, Striker, Gold Luster 47.00
Match Holder, Figural, Polar Bear 95.00
Mayonnaise Set, Azalea, 3 Piece .... 25.00 To 35.00
Mayonnaise Set, Basket & Cherries On Cover, 3 Piece 75.00
Mayonnaise Set, White, Black, Gold Trim, Green Wreath, 3 Piece 35.00

> If you have to pack or store an oddly shaped antique, a footed bowl, or an unsteady figurine, try this trick. Get a damp polyurethane sponge, preferably the two-layer type with a stiffer bottom layer. Put the piece on the wet sponge. It will make the proper shaped indentation and when the sponge dries, the piece will be held safely in one position.

Mustard, Gold, Flowers, Underplate, Spoon 55.00
Napkin Ring, Portrait 45.00
Napkin Ring, Victorian Scene, Dandy In Cape & Top Hat 15.00
Nut Set, Molded Peanut, Small Peanut-Shaped Dishes, 7 Piece 125.00
Plaque, Cottage, Greens, Flowers, Brown Rim, 10 In. 65.00
Plate, Azalea, 6 1/2 In. .... 6.50 To 7.00
Plate, Azalea, 9 3/4 In. .... 18.00 To 22.00
Plate, Azalea, Divided, 10 1/4 In. 18.00
Plate, Lake, Sunset & Reflection, Marked, 7 7/8 In. 10.00
Plate, Lemon, Azalea, Side Ring Handle, 5 1/2 In. 22.50
Plate, Phoenix, 10 1/2 In. 12.00
Plate, Tree In Meadow, 7 1/2 In. .... 5.00 To 8.50
Plate, Victorian Cartouche, Light Green & Beige Border, 8 In. 6.00
Platter, Asparagus, Attached Sauce Dip, 6 Plates 190.00
Platter, Azalea, 12 In. .... 35.00 To 50.00
Platter, Azalea, 14 In. 50.00
Platter, Baroda, 14 In. 15.00
Platter, Dresalda, 13 1/2 In. 25.00
Relish, Azalea, 4 Sections 120.00
Salt & Pepper, Azalea, Bulbous, 3 In. 25.00
Salt & Pepper, Azalea, Individual, 2 1/2 In. 20.00
Salt & Pepper, Floral, Pink, Gold Tops, 3 In. 15.00
Salt & Pepper, Tree In Meadow 5.00
Saucer, Azalea 6.00
Shaving Mug, Stalking Tiger, Pierced Soap Compartment 110.00
Spoon Holder, Roses, Gold Rim & Handles 50.00
Sugar & Creamer, Azalea, Cover, 3 1/8 In. .... 20.00 To 26.00
Sugar & Creamer, Cottage, Lake, Water Lilies 40.00
Sugar & Creamer, Lake & Trees Scene 55.00
Sugar Shaker, Azalea, 6 1/2 In. 65.00
Syrup, Bluebird Finial 48.00
Tea Set, Art Deco, Luster, Chinese Bird Finials, 17 Piece 250.00
Tea Tile, Azalea, Round, 6 In. .... 40.00 To 45.00
Teapot, Azalea, 5 Cup, 4 1/2 In. 25.00
Teapot, Tree In Meadow 35.00
Toast Rack, Figural, Bird 65.00
Toothpick, Azalea, 6 Sides, 2 1/2 In. .... 75.00 To 98.00
Vase, Flowers, Hand Painted, Allover Gold, 10 In. 150.00
Vase, Tree In Meadow, Fan Shape, 8 In. 40.00
Wall Pocket, House & Tree Scene, Blue Luster 75.00
Wall Pocket, Ship & Seagulls, Tan Luster 75.00

The Norse Pottery Company started in Edgerton, Wisconsin, in 1903. In 1904 the company moved to Rockford, Illinois. The company made a black pottery which resembled early bronze relics of the Scandinavian countries. The firm went out of business in 1913.

NORSE, Vase, 4 In. 150.00
Vase, Horned Owls, Rose Bowl Shape 165.00

The North Dakota School of Mines was established in 1892 at the University of North Dakota. A ceramic course was included and pieces were made from the clays found in the region. Students at the university made pieces from 1909 to 1949. Although very early pieces were marked "U.N.D.," most pieces were stamped with the university seal.

NORTH DAKOTA SCHOOL OF MINES, Bottle, Water, Sioux, Calendar 225.00
Coaster, Oxen & Wagon In Relief, 4 In. 195.00
Figurine, Turkey, Signed, 3 1/2 In. 220.00
Lamp, Incised Cowboys On Horses, 7 1/2 In. 500.00
Mustard, Handles, 4 In. 35.00
Paperweight, Blue On Chocolate Clay 85.00
Pitcher, Ball, Black, Signed Belle Sheppard 135.00
Pitcher, Maroon, 8 1/2 In. 110.00

Planter, Green, Pair	230.00
Plate, Ruffled, Butt, 10 In.	48.00
Rose Bowl, Concentric Rings, Blue & Rust	45.00
Sugar & Creamer, Decal	55.00
Vase, Blue & Yellow, 4 In.	25.00
Vase, Blue On Blue Drip Glaze, 1928, 6 In.	65.00
Vase, Butterfly, Flowers, Marked, 1953, 9 In.	185.00
Vase, Concentric Rings, Blue & Rust, 4 In.	65.00
Vase, Dark & Light Blue, 6 In.	55.00
Vase, Drip From Shoulder, 3 In.	150.00
Vase, Incised, Cable, 7 In.	200.00
Vase, Lavender & Pink, Signed FW, 7 In.	95.00
Vase, Lavender, Pink Glaze, Signed, 8 In.	125.00
Vase, Matte Glaze, Marked, 2 1/2 X 3 In.	75.00

The Harry Northwood Glass Company was founded by Harry Northwood, a glassmaker who worked for Hobbs, Brockunier and Company, La Belle Glass Company, and Buckeye Glass Company before founding his own firm. He opened one factory in Sinclaire, Pennsylvania, in 1896, and another in Wheeling, West Virginia, in 1902. Northwood closed when Mr. Northwood died in 1923. Many types of glass were made, including carnival, custard, goofus, and pressed. The underlined N mark was used on some pieces.

NORTHWOOD, Berry Set, Paneled Holly, Green, Gold Trim, 7 Piece	300.00
Bowl, Daisy & Plume, Opalescent, 3 Footed	45.00
Bowl, Embroidered Mums, Light Marigold, Ruffled	140.00
Bowl, Heart & Flowers, Ruffled, Emerald Green	775.00
Bowl, Ice Cream, Peacock & Urn, Master, 10 In.	170.00
Bowl, Pearl Stretch, 13 In.	65.00
Bowl, Poinsettia & Lattice, Footed	45.00
Bushel Basket, Blue, Signed	110.00
Butter, Bella Donna, Green, Enameled Floral, Cover	60.00
Butter, Cherries, Green, Cover	47.50
Butter, Intaglio, Custard, Cover	285.00
Butter, Jackson, Vaseline, Cover	225.00
Butter, Millard, Ruby Stain, Cover	65.00
Butter, Teardrop Flower, Blue, Gold Trim, Cover	150.00
Candy Jar, Jade Green	35.00
Compote, Blue Iridescent, Twig Base	29.00
Compote, Daisy & Plume, Amethyst	45.00
Compote, Grape & Cable, Marigold, Small	30.00
Compote, Grape & Cable, Purple	400.00
Cracker Jar, Grape & Cable, Purple	400.00
Creamer, Leaf Umbrella, Cranberry	200.00
Creamer, Memphis, Green, Gold Trim	40.00
Creamer, Posies & Pods, Green, Gold Trim	55.00 To 65.00
Creamer, Strawberry & Cable, Ruby, Gold Trim	70.00
Cruet, Fluted Scrolls, Enameled, Blue	195.00
Cruet, Leaf Umbrella, Cranberry Spatter, Clear Stopper	350.00
Cruet, Palm Beach	45.00
Cruet, Snail, Crystal	85.00
Cup, Grape & Cable, Amethyst, 3 1/4 In.	95.00
Decanter, Whiskey, Memphis, Clear	125.00
Finger Bowl, Leaf Umbrella, Blue	85.00
Jam Jar, Intaglio, Blue	68.00
Mug, Dandelion, Knights Templar Advertisement, Marigold	385.00
Mug, Singing Birds, Green	155.00
Mug, Singing Birds, White	500.00
Pitcher, Water, Apple Blossom	85.00
Pitcher, Water, Fine Ribbed, Clear Handle, Cranberry	325.00
Pitcher, Water, Leaf Mold, Cranberry, White Spatter, Mica Flecks	250.00
Pitcher, Water, Peach, Green, Gold Trim	90.00
Pitcher, Water, Poinsettia, Dark Blue, Cobalt Blue Handle	345.00
Pitcher, Water, Royal Ivy, Frosted Rubina	265.00

Pitcher, Water, Wavering Quill, Green	45.00
Rose Bowl, Daisy & Plume, Green, Footed, Rayed Interior	47.50
Rose Bowl, Drapery, Aqua Opalescent	250.00
Rose Bowl, Leaf Mold, Vaseline	95.00
Rose Bowl, Pulled Feathers, Crimped Top, Marked, 3 In.	1100.00
Rose Bowl, Spatter Case, 4 In.	135.00
Salt & Pepper, Leaf Umbrella, Pewter Lids	85.00
Salt Dip, Flute, Master, Vaseline	140.00
Saltshaker, Paneled Holly, Green, Gold Trim	50.00
Sauce, Imperial Flute, Purple	35.00
Sauce, Shell, Footed	24.00
Spoon Holder, Cherry & Thumbprint	30.00
Spoon Holder, Hobnail	35.00
Spoon Holder, Holly, Green	40.00
Spoon Holder, Memphis, Green, Gold Trim	40.00
Spoon Holder, Peacock At The Fountain, Marigold	55.00
Sugar & Creamer, Memphis, Green, Gold Trim	90.00
Sugar, Memphis, Green, Gold Trim	60.00
Table Set, Grape & Gothic Arches, Green, Gold, 4 Piece	165.00
Table Set, Leaf Mold, Cranberry, 4 Piece	750.00
Table Set, Royal Ivy, Cranberry, Frosted, 4 Piece	750.00
Toothpick, Inverted Fan & Feathers, Pink	200.00
Tray, Card, Argonaut Shell, Vaseline	75.00
Tray, Card, Grape & Cable, Mid–Size	75.00
Tray, Condiment, Sapphire Blue	75.00
Tumbler, Dandelion, Ice Blue	170.00
Tumbler, Drapery, Blue	45.00
Tumbler, Grape & Cable, Amethyst, Bronze Overlay	100.00
Tumbler, Grape & Cable, Marigold	45.00
Tumbler, Oriental Poppy, Emerald, Gold Trim	32.00
Tumbler, Paneled Cherry	45.00
Tumbler, Singing Bird, Marigold	45.00
Vase, Diamond Point, Blue, 10 In.	38.00
Vase, Drapery, Purple, 8 1/2 In.	100.00
Vase, Flower, Striped, Pink, Pull Up Ruffle, 10 1/2 In.	650.00
Water Set, Drapery, 7 Piece	375.00
Water Set, Flute, Green, Gold Trim, 6 Piece	145.00
Water Set, Interior Poinsettia, 6 Piece	225.00
Water Set, Memphis, Green, Gold Trim, 7 Piece	175.00
Water Set, Regent, Amethyst, Gold Trim, 7 Piece	295.00
Water Set, Regent, Emerald Green, Gold Trim, 7 Piece	275.00

NUART   Nu–Art was a trademark registered by the Imperial Glass Company of Bellaire, Ohio, about 1920.

NU–ART, Ashtray, Standing Nude, Bronze Wash Finish	175.00
Bookends, Comical Dog	32.00
Bowl, Rosemarie, Crystal, Footed, Imperial, 8 1/2 In.	40.00
Figurine, Nude Juggler, Stepped Base	185.00
Lamp, Kneeling Nude	85.00
Lamp, Sitting Nude, Dark Bronze Wash Base, Mercury Glass Globe	225.00
Lamp, Sitting Nude, Green Glass Shade	165.00
Shade, Electric, Smoky Green, Iridescent, Art Glass, Signed	85.00
Shade, Gas, Smoky Green, Iridescent, Art Glass, Signed	135.00

Nutcrackers of many types have been used through the centuries. At first the nutcracker was a fancy hammer; but by the nineteenth century, many elaborate and ingenious types were made. Levers, screws, and hammer adaptations were the most popular. Because nutcrackers are still useful, they are still being made, some in the old styles.

NUTCRACKER, Alligator, 1915, Brass	40.00
Bulldog, Cast Iron, 1910	65.00
Cherub Design, Brass	75.00
Crocodile, 1920, 8 In.	38.00
Dog, Cast Iron, 11 1/2 In.	35.00 To 40.00
Dog, Cast Iron, 13 In.	75.00
Dog, Marked Grand Rapids Brass Co.	135.00
Eagle's Head, Feather As Handle, Cast Iron, Dated 1860	250.00
Eagle, Hand Carved, Wooden	120.00
Fagin & Sikes, Brass, 5 In.	33.00
Lady's Leg, Bronze, 1890	55.00
Laughing Monk's Head, Carved, Wooden, Italy, 1726, 9 3/4 In.	385.00
Man's Head, Rolled Queue, Hinged Jaw, Wooden, 1799, 9 In.	715.00
Mythological Bird, Betel Nuts	48.00
Naughty Nellie, Cast Aluminum, 4 1/2 In.	9.50
Old Dog Tray, Cast Iron	45.00
Parrot, Brass, 6 In.	22.00
Perfection, Nickel Plated, 1915	16.00
Punch & Judy, Brass, 1900	100.00
Ram, Carved Wood, Glass Eyes, 8 1/2 In.	65.00
Sailor & Lady, Kiss When Handles Close, Brass, 6 1/4 In.	50.00
Sailor, Seated On Barrel, Brass	250.00
Shell & Thread, Sterling Silver	200.00
Shouting Boy At Top, Cast Iron	20.00
Squirrel, Cast Iron, 1910	65.00 To 75.00
Squirrel, Cast Iron, Black Tail, 4 1/4 X 5 1/4 In.	35.00
Squirrel, Cast Iron, Patent 1913	25.00
St.Bernard, Bronze	50.00
St.Bernard, Cast Iron	45.00 To 60.00
Whippet, Running, 1890, Bronze	90.00
Woman, For Pecans, Walnut	65.00

The Nymphenburg porcelain factory was established at Neudeck-ob-der-Au, Germany, in 1753 and moved to Nymphenburg in 1761. The company is still in existence. Modern marks include a checkered shield topped by a crown, and a crowned "CT" with the year and a contemporary shield mark on reproductions of eighteenth-century porcelain.

NYMPHENBURG, Dish, 7 Floral Sprigs, Gold Bands, Oval, C.1765, 10 7/16 In.	4180.00
Figurine, Cupid As Actor, Mask, Cartouche Shape, C.1760, 4 In.	5225.00
Figurine, Mythological Flora, Spring, Putto, C.1760, 3 15/16 In.	665.00
Figurine, Peacocks, 8 1/2 In., Pair ....*Illus*	130.00
Tureen, Cover, Lemon Finial, Flowers, Gilt, 11 1/2 In.	495.00

The words "Occupied Japan" were used on pottery, porcelain, toys, and other goods made during the American occupation of Japan after World War II, from 1945 to 1952. Collectors now search for these pieces. The items were made for export.

OCCUPIED JAPAN, Bowl, Lattice Sides, Hand Painted Fruit, Gold Trim, 6 In.	18.00
Bowl, Rice, Cloisonne, 4 In.	50.00
Clock, Electric, Bluebirds, Roses, Chikusa, 6 X 6 In.	75.00
Cracker Jar, Wicker Handle, 3 Birds In Flowering Tree, 5 In	45.00
Creamer, Cow	23.00
Cup & Saucer, Dragon	25.00
Cup & Saucer, Yellow, White, Gold, Petal Form, Kipp Ceramics	18.00
Figurine, Ballerina, Outstretched Arms, 7 In.	15.00
Figurine, Bride & Groom, 4 In.	22.50
Figurine, Bust, Madonna, Bisque, 7 In.	45.00

Figurine, Cupid, With Horn, Bisque, 3 1/4 In. 12.50
Figurine, Girl, Barefoot, Basket At Feet, Bisque, 5 1/4 In. 25.00
Figurine, Lady, With Basket, 8 In. 30.00
Figurine, Man & Woman, Victorian Clothes, 6 In. 20.00
Figurine, Rabbit, Dressed For School 10.00
Musicians, Porcelain, 6 In., Pair 33.00
Planter, Duck 5.00
Planter, Elephant 9.00
Planter, Lady & Man, Shell Bowls, Bisque, 6 X 6 In. 95.00
Planter, Zebra 8.00
Plaque, Oriental Man & Woman, 6 X 6 In. 35.00
Salt & Pepper, Figural, Strawberries, 3 3/4 In. 16.00
Stein, Tavern Scene, Blue, Brown Trim 24.00
Tea Set, Tomato, Pot, Jam Jar, Sugar & Creamer, Large 60.00
Tray, Floral, Hand Painted, 14 X 12 In. 35.00

 George E. Ohr, a true eccentric, made pottery in Biloxi, Mississippi, between 1883 and 1918. The pottery was made of very thin clay that was twisted, folded, and dented into odd, graceful shapes. Some pieces were lifelike models of hats, animal heads, or even a potato. Some pieces were decorated with folded clay "snakes." Although reproductions would be almost impossible to make, there have been some reworked pieces appearing on the market. These have been reglazed, or snakes and other embellishments have been added.

OHR, Mug, Cobalt Blue & Yellow, Signed 395.00
Mug, Crumpled, Paper–Thin 1400.00
Mug, Puzzle 145.00
Mug, Red, Green Glaze Rim, Dated 3/18/96 .... 2300.00
Mug, Skull, 4 1/2 In. 450.00
Vase, Black Glaze, Piecrust Rim, Bulbous, 5 X 5 In. ....*Illus* 5000.00
Vase, Brown Green Glaze, Bulbous Elongated Neck, Squat, Signed, 4 In. 750.00
Vase, Bulbous, Dented & Deformed, Mottled Pink, 7 In. 3850.00
Vase, Incised Mud From New Orleans Street, 1905, 2 1/2 X 4 In. 260.00

 OLD IVORY 84 Old Ivory china was made in Silesia, Germany, at the end of the nineteenth century. It is often marked with a crown and the word "Silesia." Some pieces are also marked with the words "Old Ivory." The pattern numbers appear on the base of each piece.

OLD IVORY, Berry Bowl, No.84, 10 In. 85.00
Berry Set, No.11, 7 Piece 150.00
Berry Set, No.16, Silesia, 7 Piece 165.00
Berry Set, No.75, 7 Piece 175.00
Berry Set, No.84, 7 Piece 225.00
Biscuit Jar, No.16 .... 275.00 To 295.00
Bowl, No.10, Silesia, 10 In. .... 60.00 To 65.00
Bowl, No.11, 9 1/2 In. 65.00
Bowl, No.15, 10 1/4 In. 115.00
Bowl, No.16, 9 1/2 In. 115.00

Ohr, Vase, Black Glaze, Piecrust Rim, Bulbous, 5 X 5 In.

Bowl, No.32, Silesia, 6 1/2 In. 35.00
Bowl, No.73, Silesia, 9 1/2 In. 45.00
Bowl, No.82, Hand Painted Yellow Rose, Silesia, 9 1/2 In. 195.00
Cake Plate, No. 15, 10 In. 115.00
Cake Plate, No. 84, Pierced Handles, 11 In. .... 75.00 To 95.00
Cake Plate, No.200, Silesia 85.00
Cake Set, No.41, 5 Piece 125.00
Cake Set, No.75, Silesia, 5 Piece 145.00
Cake Set, No.84, 7 Piece 225.00
Celery, No.15 .... 75.00
Celery, No.84 .... 75.00 To 85.00
Chocolate Pot, No.11 .... 350.00
Chocolate Pot, No.15 .... 250.00
Chocolate Set, No.84, 11 Piece 495.00
Chop Plate, No.16, 13 In. 195.00
Cracker Jar, No.16 .... 275.00
Creamer, No.16, Silesia 60.00
Creamer, No.84, Silesia 35.00
Cup & Saucer, No. 11 .... 40.00
Cup & Saucer, No. 16, Silesia .... 45.00 To 55.00
Cup & Saucer, No. 84 .... 45.00 To 55.00
Cup & Saucer, No.204, Silesia, Demitasse 22.50
Jam Jar, No.100, Signed 195.00
Plate, No. 10, 6 1/2 In. 35.00
Plate, No. 11, 7 1/2 In. 24.00
Plate, No. 15, 7 1/2 In. 30.00
Plate, No. 16, 8 1/4 In. 50.00
Plate, No. 28, 7 3/4 In. 35.00
Plate, No. 73, 6 1/2 In. 24.00
Plate, No. 75, 7 3/4 In. 26.00
Plate, No. 84, 9 1/2 In. 125.00
Plate, No. 84, Fluted, 7 1/2 In. .... 30.00 To 40.00
Plate, No.200, 6 In. 20.00
Plate, No.200, 8 3/4 In. 35.00
Platter, No.16, 11 1/2 In. 125.00
Relish, No.15 .... 36.00
Relish, No.84 .... 40.00 To 45.00
Salt & Pepper, No.16 .... 90.00 To 125.00
Soup, Dish, No.84, Silesia 85.00
Sugar & Creamer, No.11, Silesia 120.00
Sugar & Creamer, No.15 .... 115.00
Sugar Shaker, No.84, Silesia 285.00
Sugar, No.16, Silesia, Cover 62.50
Sugar, No.33, Silesia 35.00
Tea Set, No.84, 11 Piece 695.00
Teapot, No.84 .... 175.00 To 295.00
Tray, Dresser, No.84 .... 125.00

OLD SLEEPY EYE, see Sleepy Eye

Onion pattern, originally named "bulb pattern," is a white ware decorated with cobalt blue or pink. Although it is commonly associated with Meissen, other companies made the pattern in the late nineteenth and the twentieth centuries. A rare type is called "red bud" because there are added red accents on the blue and white dishes.

ONION, Bowl, Reticulated, Oval, Double Crossed Swords, 6 X 9 In. 160.00
   Butter Chip 25.00
   Canister, Rice 50.00
   Canister, Tea, Blue 50.00
   Chamberstick, Blue & White, Germany 45.00
   Funnel 60.00
   Grill Plate 15.00
   Knife Rest, Crossed Sword, 4 Piece 125.00
   Knife Rest, Meissen 65.00

Mustard, Attached Plate, Ladle, Crossed Swords 125.00
Pie Crimper 60.00
Plate, Crossed Swords, 8 1/4 In. 35.00
Plate, Crossed Swords, 9 1/2 In. 55.00
Plate, Crossed Swords, 10 1/4 In. 65.00
Plate, Meissen, Crossed Swords, 9 1/2 In. 35.00
Plate, Reticulated, Double Crossed Swords, 8 1/4 In. 180.00
Platter, Fish, Double Crossed Swords, 22 X 10 1/2 In. 375.00
Platter, Fish, Double Drain, Meissen, C.1900, 23 1/2 In. 465.00
Platter, Hot Water, Child's, Pewter Base, Marked WMF 90.00
Platter, M In G Mark, Round, 12 In. 110.00
Platter, Meissen, Crossed Swords Mark, 11 In. 85.00
Platter, Meissen, Crossed Swords Mark, 18 In. 250.00
Platter, Oval, Meissen, 15 X 9 In. 95.00
Platter, Scalloped Rim, Meissen, 21 In. 300.00
Salad Set, Sterling Silver Base & Rim, Porcelain Handled Servers 250.00
Sauceboat, Scalloped Rim, Meissen 60.00
Soup, Dish, Crossed Swords, 9 1/4 In. 65.00
Soup, Dish, Crossed Swords, 10 1/2 In. 95.00
Soup, Plate, Meissen, 9 1/4 In. 20.00
Spice Jar, Allspice 39.00
Spice Jar, Ginger 39.00
Spice Jar, Nutmeg 39.00
Spoon Holder, Hanging 79.00
Toothpick, 3-Footed, Pedestal Base 95.00
Tray, Dresser, 8-Fold Edge, Crossed Swords, 11 X 9 In. 85.00
Trivet 35.00
Tureen, Cover, Meissen, 12 X 10 X 5 1/2 In. 495.00
Utensil Holder, Hanging, 15 Slots 150.00

> Opalescent glass is translucent glass that has the tones of the opal
> gemstone. It originated in England in the 1870s and is often found
> in pressed glassware made in Victorian times. Opalescent glass was
> first made in America in 1897 at the Northwood glassworks in
> Indiana, Pennsylvania. Some dealers use the terms "opaline" and
> "opalescent" for any of these translucent wares.

OPALESCENT, see also Northwood; Pressed Glass; Spanish Lace
OPALESCENT, Banana Boat, Argonaut & Shell, 8 1/2 In. 47.50
Banana Boat, Jewel & Fan, Green 90.00
Basket, Hobnail, Blue, 4 In. 25.00
Berry Bowl, Alaska, Blue, Individual 20.00
Berry Bowl, Beatty Rib, Master 50.00
Berry Bowl, Everglades, Oval, Blue, Master 110.00
Berry Bowl, Everglades, Vaseline, Individual 23.00
Berry Bowl, Flora, Master 95.00
Berry Bowl, Inverted Fan & Feather, White, 6 1/2 In. 20.00
Berry Bowl, Iris With Meander, Green, Master 85.00
Berry Bowl, Palm Beach, Blue, Individual 20.00
Berry Bowl, Tokyo, Green, 6 1/2 In. 15.00
Berry Bowl, Tokyo, Green, Master 50.00
Berry Bowl, Wreath & Shell, Blue 22.50
Berry Set, Alaska, Blue, 7 Piece 350.00
Berry Set, Jeweled Heart, Ruffled, 7 Piece 95.00
Berry Set, Kokomo, Green, 7 Piece 85.00
Berry Set, Palm Beach, Vaseline, 7 Piece 295.00
Berry Set, Paneled Ribs, 1889, Blue, 7 Piece 95.00
Bottle, Barber, Hobnail, Blue .... 110.00 To 155.00
Bottle, Barber, Polka Dot, Blue 110.00
Bottle, Barber, Stars & Stripes, Crystal .... 145.00 To 155.00
Bowl, Astro, Ruffled, 8 In. 45.00
Bowl, Beaded Star, 7 1/2 In. 20.00
Bowl, Beatty Swirl, 8 In. 45.00
Bowl, Grape & Cherry, Intaglio, Ruffled, Blue, 10 In. 95.00
Bowl, Jolly Bear, Crimped Fluted Rim, Blue, 8 1/2 In. 110.00

If you have jalousie or casement windows, remove the handles to make them more burglarproof.

Bowl, Keyhole, White, 9 In. .... 30.00 To 35.00
Bowl, Leaf & Beads, Fluted, Twig Feet, Blue, 8 In. 37.50
Bowl, Leaf Medallion, Clear, Gold Trim, 9 In. 30.00
Bowl, Many Loops, Green, 8 In. 30.00
Bowl, Vegetable, Maple Leaf 22.00
Bride's Bowl, Jeweled Heart, Blue 60.00
Bride's Bowl, Keyhole, Crystal 45.00
Butter, Cover, Beatty Swirl, Blue 95.00
Butter, Cover, Circle Scroll 175.00
Butter, Cover, Everglades, Blue, Gold Trim 200.00
Butter, Cover, Fleur-De-Lis Drape 68.00
Butter, Cover, Flora, Blue 225.00
Butter, Cover, Flora, Vaseline 210.00
Butter, Cover, Tokyo, Green 50.00
Butter, Cover, Wild Bouquet, Blue 350.00
Butter, Fluted Scroll, Blue, Gold Trim 145.00
Butter, Jeweled Heart, Gold 75.00
Butter, Regal, Cover, Green, Gold Trim 135.00
Candlestick, Dolphin Petticoat, Vaseline 120.00
Celery, Atlas, Blue 85.00
Compote, Argonaut Shell, Canary 50.00
Compote, Jelly, Everglades, Vaseline 125.00
Compote, Jelly, Intaglio 40.00
Compote, Jelly, Maple Leaf, Blue 35.00
Compote, Jelly, Ribbed Swirl, Blue 75.00
Compote, Jelly, Swag With Brackets, Blue 32.00
Compote, Jelly, Swag With Brackets, Green 20.00
Creamer, Child's, Beatty Swirl, Blue 30.00
Creamer, Child's, Twist, Blue 75.00
Creamer, Circled Scroll, Blue 85.00
Creamer, Fluted Scrolls, Green 40.00
Creamer, Intaglio, Crystal 30.00
Creamer, Jewel & Flower, Vaseline, Gold Trim 70.00
Creamer, Jewel & Flower, White 40.00
Creamer, Reverse Swirl, Blue, 4 1/2 In. 45.00
Creamer, Wild Bouquet, Blue 48.00
Creamer, Wreath & Shell, Blue 110.00
Cruet, Alaska, Blue .... 175.00 To 350.00
Cruet, Alaska, Vaseline 225.00
Cruet, Argonaut Shell, Blue 275.00
Cruet, Christmas Bead & Panel, Green 195.00
Cruet, Daisy & Fern, Blue .... 110.00 To 135.00
Cruet, Daisy & Fern, Crystal 75.00
Cruet, Intaglio, White 55.00
Cruet, Regal, Green 215.00
Cruet, Scroll With Acanthus, Blue 245.00
Cruet, Tokyo, Blue 150.00
Cruet, Wild Bouquet, Blue .... 175.00 To 245.00
Dish, Leafy Chalice, Footed, Blue 75.00
Dish, Tokyo, Green, 6 In. 58.00
Lamp, Boudoir, Dot Optic, 11 1/2 In. 85.00
Muffineer, Coin Dot, Blue 75.00

Mug, Singing Bird, Blue 195.00
Pitcher, Christmas Snowflake, Blue 335.00
Pitcher, Daisy & Fern, Bulbous, Square Top, Blue 125.00
Pitcher, Daisy In Crisscross, Blue 295.00
Pitcher, Poinsettia, Blue 155.00
Pitcher, Reverse Swirl, Bulbous, White 110.00
Pitcher, Water, Alaska, Blue .... 325.00 To 550.00
Pitcher, Water, Beatty Swirl, Blue .... 100.00 To 185.00
Pitcher, Water, Buttons & Braids, Blue 80.00
Pitcher, Water, Buttons & Braids, Green 150.00
Pitcher, Water, Dahlia, Blue 225.00
Pitcher, Water, Daisy & Fern, Yellow 70.00
Pitcher, Water, Dolly Madison, Blue, Gold Trim 125.00
Pitcher, Water, Drape, Blue 165.00
Pitcher, Water, Honeycomb & Clover, Green 175.00
Pitcher, Water, Intaglio, Blue 150.00
Pitcher, Water, Jewel & Flower, Gold Trim 115.00
Pitcher, Water, Jeweled Heart, Straw Marks, Green 50.00
Pitcher, Water, Pressed Optic, Vaseline 250.00
Pitcher, Water, Swag With Brackets, Vaseline .... 180.00 To 195.00
Plate, Water Lily & Cattail, White, 11 In. 15.00
Powder Jar, Cover, Fluted Scrolls, Vaseline 65.00
Rose Bowl, Bars & Beads, Threaded Outside, Blue, 4 1/2 In. 55.00
Rose Bowl, Beaded Cable, Candy Ribbon Edge, Green 35.00
Rose Bowl, Leaf & Beads, Blue 69.00
Salt & Pepper, Vaseline 70.00
Saltshaker, Jewel & Flower, Blue 50.00
Saltshaker, Sheli & Coral, Blue 35.00
Spittoon, Woman's, Wreath & Shell, Vaseline 110.00
Spooner, Alaska, Blue .... 50.00 To 95.00
Spooner, Flora, Vaseline 70.00
Spooner, Shell, Blue 75.00
Spooner, Swag With Brackets, Blue 65.00
Spooner, Tokyo, Blue .... 67.50 To 95.00
Spooner, Windows, Blue 55.00
Spooner, Wreath & Shell, Footed, Vaseline 75.00
Sugar Shaker, Daisy & Fern, Blue 45.00
Sugar, Cover, Alaska, Blue 150.00
Sugar, Cover, Beatty Rib, Blue 125.00
Sugar, Cover, Chrysanthemum Base Swirl, Crystal 120.00
Sugar, Cover, Flora, Vaseline 110.00
Sugar, Cover, Jewel & Flower, White 60.00
Sugar, Cover, Wild Bouquet 45.00
Sugar, Sunburst & Shield, Blue 45.00
Table Set, Beatty Rib, Blue, 4 Piece 265.00
Table Set, Fluted Scrolls, Vaseline, 4 Piece 295.00
Table Set, Iris With Meander, Vaseline, 4 Piece 475.00
Table Set, Jewel & Flower, 4 Piece 245.00
Table Set, Paneled Holly, 4 Piece 245.00
Table Set, Swag With Brackets, Green, 4 Piece 350.00
Toothpick, Iris With Meander, Blue 75.00
Toothpick, Iris With Meander, Green .... 35.00 To 65.00
Toothpick, Lattice, Cranberry 125.00
Toothpick, Reverse Swirl, Vaseline 95.00
Toothpick, Ribbed Lattice, Blue 95.00
Toothpick, Tokyo, Green 110.00
Toothpick, Twist, Blue 60.00
Toothpick, Wreath & Shell, Enameled, Vaseline 195.00
Tray, Water, Beatty Swirl, Blue 55.00
Tray, Water, Ribbed Spiral, Blue 55.00
Tumbler, Acanthus With Scroll, Green 32.00
Tumbler, Drapery, Blue, Northwood 45.00
Tumbler, Wreath & Shell, Blue .... 50.00 To 60.00
Vase, Inverted Fan & Feather, Green, 8 1/2 In. 45.00

Water Set, Button & Braids, Blue, 5 Piece 225.00
Water Set, Daisy & Fern, White, 7 Piece 265.00
Water Set, Drapery, Blue, 7 Piece 295.00
Water Set, Tokyo, Blue, 7 Piece 850.00

> Opaline, or opal glass, was made in white, green, and other colors. The glass had a matte surface and a lack of transparency. It was often gilded or painted. It was a popular mid–nineteenth–century European glassware.

OPALINE, Biscuit Jar, Medallion With 2 Cherubs Under Blankets, Wreath 150.00
Cup & Saucer, White, Gold, Fruit Design, Germany, Set of 6 .... 65.00
Perfume Bottle, Ball Feet, Florals At Collar, Brass Lid, 4 1/4 In. 175.00
Perfume Bottle, Blue, Pink Spiral On Neck, Teardrop Stopper, 7 In. 100.00
Pitcher, Water, Large Blue Iris, Outlined In Gold 95.00
Vase, Enamel & Gold Design, Tan, 10 In., Pair 78.00
Vase, Floral, Gold, 10 In., Pair 125.00
Vase, Hand Painted White Rose, White Cased, 9 In. 42.00

> The stage is a long way from some of the seats at a play or an opera, so the patrons sometimes carried special opera glasses in the nineteenth and early twentieth centuries. Mother–of–pearl was a popular decoration.

OPERA GLASSES, Au Demair, Paris, Leather Case 50.00
Brass, Iridescent 40.00
Brass, Long Handle, Cobalt Blue Star Trim, Paris 75.00
Brass, Marked Cross, Small 39.00
Brass, Mother–of–Pearl, Lorgnette Handle 75.00
Enameled Handle, Silver Stars, Woman's Portrait At Lens 325.00
French, Case, 19th Century 25.00
Gold Plated, Marked Zeiss 95.00
Gold, Set With Diamonds 3300.00
Luniere Pearl 40.00
Mother–of–Pearl Portraits, Signed Duchesse, French 175.00
Mother–of–Pearl, LeMaire, Paris 30.00
Vesta, Red & Silver Brocade Snap–Up Case 30.00

> Little Orphan Annie first appeared in the comics in 1924. The redheaded girl and her friends have been on the radio and are still on the comic pages. A Broadway musical show and a movie in the 1980s made Annie popular again and many toys, dishes, and other memorabilia are being made.

ORPHAN ANNIE, Baking Set, Box 45.00
Book, In The Circus 30.00
Book, Little Orphan Annie & The Big Train Robbery 9.50
Book, Orphan Annie & Ghost Gang, 1935 .... 12.00
Book, Pop–Up, 1935 .... 35.00
Book, Shipwrecked 30.00
Booklet, Secret Society, Radio, 1937 .... 25.00
Bracelet, Identification, Disc 15.00
Decoder, 1936 .... 20.00 To 30.00
Decoder, 1937 .... 20.00 To 30.00
Decoder, 1939 .... 35.00
Doll, Nodder 65.00
Doll, Wood, Jointed, 6 In. 125.00
Game, Knitting, Box 40.00
Game, Treasure Hunt, Ovaltine, Envelope, 1933 .... 35.00 To 45.00
Lunch Box, Thermos 15.00
Mug, Beetleware 25.00
Mug, Ovaltine 40.00
Pin, Radio Orphan Annie Secret Society, Bronze 23.00
Puzzle, Jigsaw, 1940s 45.00
Puzzle, Joe's Lunch, Annie As Waitress, Box, 22 X 14 In. 45.00
Ring, Look Around 35.00
Ring, Orphan Annie Mystic Eye 80.00

Salt & Pepper, Annie & Sandy	30.00
Sunday Full Page Comic, Harold Gray, 1940s	7.00
Toy, Stove .... 18.00 To 22.00	
Whistle, Lithographed, Tin, Member The Safety Guard," 1942	40.00
Wristwatch, Oblong, 1930s	75.00
Wristwatch, Sandy, Box	45.00
Wristwatch, Signed Harold Gray	75.00

The Orrefors Glassworks, located in the Swedish province of Smaaland, was established in 1898. The company is still making glass for use on the table or as decorations. There is renewed interest in the glass made in the modern styles of the 1940s and 1950s. Most vases and decorative pieces are signed with the etched name.

ORREFORS, Ashtray, Free-Form, Red, 1950s	70.00
Bowl, Fruit, Lead Crystal, 1900	75.00
Bowl, Red, 5 In.	100.00
Candleholder, Eden, Pair	65.00
Decanter, Engraved Design, Signed, 9 In.	125.00
Figurine, Bear, Sitting, Signed, Sticker, 3 5/8 In.	45.00
Paperweight, Owl, Clear, Signed, 6 1/2 In.	100.00
Perfume Bottle, 2 Birds	95.00
Plate, Clear, Polished Pontil, Signed, 7 1/4 In., Pair	25.00
Plate, Etched Eagle In Flight, Signed Gilbert, 10 1/4 In.	115.00
Vase, Engraved Ship, Marked, 7 1/2 In.	145.00
Vase, Etched Tropical Fish Swimming, Coral, 6 1/2 In.	85.00
Vase, Female Figures Holding Drapery, Scalloped Rim, 5 In.	2750.00
Vase, Fish, Swimming Amongst Sea Grass, Signed, 7 In.	495.00
Vase, Frosted Nude, Signed, Numbered, Crystal, 8 1/4 In.	170.00
Vase, Kneeling Girl, Birds, Etched, Signed, 5 In.	210.00
Vase, Nude Children Carrying Basket of Flowers, 7 X 5 X 3 In.	300.00
Vase, Paperweight, Green Underwater Scene, Marked, 4 1/2 In.	565.00
Vase, Swirl, Signed, 8 In.	150.00

Ott & Brewer Company operated the Etruria Pottery at Trenton, New Jersey, from 1863 to 1893. They started making belleek in 1882. The firm used a variety of marks that incorporated the initials O & B.

OTT & BREWER, Creamer, Enameled Flowers, Gold Trim, Marked, 3 1/2 In.	150.00
Cup & Saucer, Denver 1892	75.00
Demitasse Set, Cedar Rapids, Gold Letters, Pink Trim	125.00
Plate, Polychrome Flowers, Gold Paste Foliage, 8 1/2 In.	110.00

The four Overbeck sisters started a pottery in Cambridge City, Indiana, in 1911. They made all types of vases, each one-of-a-kind. Small, hand-modeled figurines are the most popular pieces with today's collectors. The factory continued until 1955 when the last of the four sisters died.

OVERBECK, Candlestick, Green, Finger Handle	55.00
Figurine, Camel, Multicolored, 4 1/2 In.	260.00
Figurine, Cello Player, 4 1/2 In.	300.00
Figurine, Colonial Girl, Hoop Skirt	285.00
Figurine, Farmer Eating Watermelon, 4 1/2 In.	275.00
Figurine, Mother of Katzenjammer Kids, 4 1/2 In.	140.00
Figurine, Pelican, 4 1/2 In.	150.00
Figurine, Robin, Signed	365.00

Owens Pottery was made in Zanesville, Ohio, from 1891 to 1928. The first art pottery was made after 1896. Utopian Ware, Cyrano, Navarre, Feroza, and Henri Deux were made. Pieces were usually marked with a form of the name "Owens." About 1907, the firm began to make tile and discontinued the art pottery wares.

OWENS, Jardiniere, Art Nouveau, Crazed, Marked, 8 3/4 X 12 In.	295.00
Jardiniere, Marked Cyrano	150.00

Jardiniere, Matte Green, 8 In.	48.00
Jardiniere, Standard Glaze, 12 In.	110.00
Lamp, Oil, Utopian, Blue To Blue Gray, Spider Mums, S.Timberlake, 8 In.	695.00
Mug, 3 Handles, Dark Green Mottled Glaze	65.00
Pitcher, Utopian	150.00
Vase, Art Nouveau, Frolicking Nudes, Flowers, 14 In.	495.00
Vase, Bud, Utopian, 6 In.	60.00
Vase, Magnolia Design, Brown Glaze, Signed Lewis, 13 In.	85.00
Vase, Seafoam & Dragon, 9 1/2 In.	45.00
Vase, Utopian, 9 In. .... 120.00 To	125.00
Vase, Utopian, Autumn Leaves On Dark Brown, Signed, 3 1/2 X 5 1/2 In.	175.00
Vase, Utopian, Marked, Sticker, 11 In.	225.00
Vase, Woman's Profile, Henri Deux Mark, 8 In.	325.00

Oyster plates were popular from the 1880s. Each course at dinner was served in a special dish. The oyster plate had indentations shaped like oysters. Usually six oysters were held on a plate. There is no greater value to a plate with more oysters although that myth continues to haunt antiques dealers. There are other plates for shellfish including cockle plates and whelk plates. The appropriately shaped indentations are part of the design of these dishes.

OYSTER PLATE, Mottled Green & Brown, White Shells, Minton, Majolica, 9 In.	195.00
Seaweed, Half Moon, Majolica	155.00
Shells Around Center, Scalloped, Germany, 9 In.	50.00

Paden City Glass Manufacturing Company was established in 1916 at Paden City, West Virginia. It is best known for glasswares but also produced a pottery line. The firm closed in 1951.

PADEN CITY, Bowl, American Rose, 9 In.	11.50
Bowl, Frost Etch, Crystal, 12 In.	40.00
Candy Dish, Ardith, Yellow	70.00
Compote, Cover, Wild Roses, Amethyst, 6 In.	45.00
Condiment Set, Green Glass, Metal Holder	17.50
Cup & Saucer, Crowfoot, Red	25.00
Decanter, Etched, Crystal, 1 Qt.	80.00
Figurine, Chinese Pheasants, Clear, 13 3/4 In., Pair	40.00
Goblet, Pennyline, Amethyst, Low, 5 1/2 In.	8.00
Napkin Holder, Green	85.00
Pitcher, Batter, Black Cover	35.00
Plate, American Rose, 6 In.	8.50
Plate, Bowl, Gazebo, 10 In.	25.00
Plate, Crowfoot, 6 In.	25.00
Plate, Pennyline, Amethyst, 7 1/2 In.	5.00
Platter, Crowfoot, 11 In.	20.00
Samovar, Blue, Bird Etched	295.00
Saucer, American Rose	6.00
Sherbet, Gothic Garden, Footed, Low	9.00

Don't put crazed pottery or porcelain in the dishwasher. It will often break even more.

Sherbet, Pennyline, Amethyst, 4 In.	5.00 To 6.00
Sugar & Creamer, Crowfoot, Footed	50.00
Sugar & Creamer, Gazebo, Crystal	30.00
Sugar, Nora Bird, Round Handles, Pink	15.00
Tumbler, Aristocrat, Flat, 12 Oz.	8.00
Tumbler, Pennyline, Amethyst, Flat, 3 1/2 In.	6.50
Tumbler, Pennyline, Amethyst, Flat, 5 1/4 In.	8.00
Vase, Lela Bird, Pink, 10 In.	70.00

The paintings listed in this book are not works by major artists but rather decorative paintings on ivory, board, or glass that would be of interest to the average collector. To learn the value of an oil painting by a listed artist you must contact an expert in that area.

PAINTING, On Academy Board, Haying Beside Lake, Oil, Framed, 10 X 14 3/4 In.	105.00
On Canvas, Cows In Stream, Oil, Frame, 30 X 35 3/4 In.	95.00
On Canvas, Mountain Landscape, Cattle, Oil, Gilt Frame, 18 X 24 In.	175.00
On Canvas, Rowboat, Wilderness River, T.Snow, Oil, 13 1/2 X 17 In.	175.00
On Canvas, Sunset On California Coast, Robert Wood, 20 X 24 In.	7000.00
On Canvas, Winter Landscape, Oil, Gilt Frame, 17 1/2 X 22 1/2 In.	65.00
On Celluloid Ivory, Moses Cleveland, F.M.Wassallo, 1856, 7 In.	175.00
On Copper, 5 Running Horses, Signed Moses, Gold Frame	100.00
On Glass, Maiden & Courier, Chinese Export, Framed, 15 X 11 In.	2860.00
On Ivory, 2 Women Disrobing, Ivory Frame, 4 1/2 X 5 5/8 In.	85.00
On Ivory, Child, Red Dress, Braided Hair, Case Back, 2 3/8 X 3 In.	400.00
On Ivory, Child, Short Blond Hair, Lacquered Frame, 4 3/4 X 5 In.	300.00
On Ivory, Gentleman, Embossed Floral Edge, 2 5/16 X 2 3/4 In.	150.00
On Ivory, Gentleman, Signed George Einsle, 1831	135.00
On Ivory, Lady With Spaniel Dog, Ivory Frame, 4 5/8 X 5 3/4 In.	145.00
On Ivory, Lady, Edwardian Dress, Ivory Frame, 4 5/8 X 5 3/4 In.	165.00
On Ivory, Lady, Quarter Right, Ruff Collar, Black Dress, 2 3/4 In.	275.00
On Ivory, Lady, White Cap, Glasses, Leather Case, 2 1/4 X 2 3/4 In.	100.00
On Ivory, Liszt Portrait, Signed, Brass, Ivory & Tortoise Frame	125.00
On Ivory, Mother & Child, Signed Ferruzi, 2 3/4 In.	42.00
On Ivory, Napoleon, Signed	195.00
On Ivory, Woman's Portrait, Signed Brun, French Brass Frame	150.00
On Ivory, Woman, Brass Mirrored Frame, Signed Ullrich, 1860, 8 In.	295.00
On Ivory, Woman, Plumed Hat, Brass Frame, Signed Wys, 6 In.	325.00
On Ivory, Woman, Signed Naztler, Framed	130.00
On Ivory, Young Man, Blue Eyes, Gold Finish Case, E.D.W., 2 In.	550.00
On Ivory, Young Man, Frock Coat, Silver Case, 1849, 2 5/8 X 3 In.	175.00
On Ivory, Young Woman, Engraved Ivory Frame, 4 1/2 X 5 3/4 In.	65.00
On Ivory, Young Woman, Gold Jewelry, Frame, 4 7/8 X 5 5/8 In.	350.00
On Mirror, Lady, Art Deco Clothes, Auto Ground, Framed, 12 X 16 In.	75.00
On Paper, Watercolor, Geo.H.Harper Family, Data, 11 1/2 X 15 In.	800.00
On Pine Board, Boy, Oil, 8 3/4 X 10 3/4 In.	400.00
On Porcelain, Copy of Madonna of The Chair, Ivory Frame, 6 In.	75.00
On Porcelain, Wagner Portrait, Gold Frame, 4 X 5 In.	950.00
On Silk, Empress On Moonlight Night, 15x 18 In.	75.00
On Silk, Mogul Emperor On His Throne, 20 X 15 In.	130.00
On Silk, Queen Victoria, Chromolith	65.00
On Tin, Portrait of Young Man, Oil, Framed, 31 X 25 1/2 In.	180.00
On Tin, Portrait, Man, Gilt Frame, 1829, 11 3/4 X 9 3/4 In.	450.00
On Velvet, Village Scene, Framed, 27 X 21 1/2 In.	192.50
Reverse On Glass, Allegorical Scene, Chinese, 35 X 17 1/2 In.	200.00
Reverse On Glass, Church, Trees, Beveled Frame, 9 3/8 X 11 3/8 In.	300.00
Reverse On Glass, Country Scene, On Foil, Floral, Bubble, 10 In.	35.00
Reverse On Glass, God Bless Our Home, Religious, Tinsel	45.00
Reverse On Glass, House In Field, Framed, 20 X 27 In.	90.00
Reverse On Glass, London Bridge, Wooden Frame, 48 X 24 In.	375.00
Reverse On Glass, Mounted Dignitary, Warriors, 10 X 26 1/2 In.	225.00
Reverse On Glass, Portrait, Rachel, Orange Ground, 4 X 5 1/8 In.	135.00
Reverse On Glass, Spring & Summer, Framed, 11 3/4 X 15 3/4 In.	375.00
Reverse On Glass, Woman Bathing In Sea, 11 1/2 X 9 1/2 In.	150.00
Reverse On Glass, Women & Cat, Visit, Framed, 22 X 27 3/4 In.	225.00

The Pairpoint Manufacturing Company started in 1880 in New Bedford, Massachusetts. It soon joined with the glassworks nearby and made glass, silver plated pieces, and lamps. Reverse-painted glass shades and molded shades known as "puffies" were part of the production until the 1930s. The company reorganized and changed its name several times but is still working today.

PAIRPOINT, Bowl, Center, Cut, 14 1/2 In.	50.00
Bowl, Nut, Squirrel Sits On Bowl, Formed of Leaves, Buds	95.00
Box, Jewelry, Rotating	325.00
Candlelamp, Puffy, Pink Pansies On Shade, Signed, 7 1/4 In.	425.00
Candlestick, Blue Bobeche, Bubble Ball Connector, 4 In., Pair	115.00
Cardholder, Glass, Footed, Cranberry Base, 3 Piece	125.00
Castor Set, 5-Bottle, Etched Bottles	95.00
Castor Set, 6-Bottle, Silver Plate, Ruby Cut To Clear, 19 In.	325.00
Chandelier, 2-Light, Aladdin Lamp Shape, Steuben Shades, Signed	395.00
Coffee Urn, Silver Plate, Marked, 15 In.	55.00
Compote, Amethyst, Engraved Grape, 10 X 5 In.	145.00
Compote, Brass Claw Feet, Onyx Base, Acanthus Leaf Band, 6 In.	180.00
Compote, Bubble Ball Connector, Green, 7 X 8 In.	135.00
Compote, Bubble Ball Stem Connector, Green, 6 1/2 In.	55.00
Compote, Bubble Ball, Amber, 8 In.	65.00
Compote, Bubble Stem, Chartreuse, 6 1/4 X 6 1/2 In.	70.00
Compote, Buckingham, Cut Stem, 6 X 6 1/2 In.	80.00
Compote, Chelsea, 8 X 6 3/4 In.	97.50
Compote, Engraved Florals, Triple Controlled Bubbles, 8 In.	75.00
Compote, Flemish Green, Clear Stem, 6 In.	65.00
Compote, Vintage, Swirl Connector	50.00
Compote, Wilton Pattern, Bubble Ball Connector & Finial, Cover	325.00
Console Set, Cranberry Holder For Bowl, Oranges, Blossoms, 3 Pc.	1275.00
Console Set, Ruby Glass, Controlled Bubble, Cornucopia	250.00
Cornucopia, Crimped Rim, Bubble Ball, 8 In.	50.00
Dish, Metal Holder, Cover, 9 1/2 In.	335.00
Ewer, Gold Lotus Branch Handle, Signed	550.00
Fernery, Hand Painted Lilies, Peach Ground, Signed, 6 X 4 1/2 In.	275.00
Lamp, 4 Portraits On Shade, Yellow To Red, Signed, 5 1/2 In.	550.00
Lamp, Blown-Out Lilacs, Wooden Base, 7 3/4 In., Pair	1950.00
Lamp, Buffet, Amber Cut Glass Shade, Handle, Signed, 18 In., Pair	500.00
Lamp, Farm Scene Shade, Brass Base, Signed, 22 1/2 In.	2900.00
Lamp, Golden Birds, Reverse Painted, Signed, 20 In.	1900.00
Lamp, Hanging, 3 Piece	1100.00
Lamp, Harbor Scene, Shade, Signed Macy, 20 1/2 In.	2200.00
Lamp, Landscape, Birch Trees, Lakes, Mountain, Marked, 22 In.	1800.00
Lamp, Puffy, Blue Butterflies, Violet Pansies, Boudoir, 14 In.	2400.00
Lamp, Puffy, Yellow & Orange Roses, 2 Handle Urn Form, 10 1/2 In.	650.00
Lamp, Scenic, 18 In.	1600.00
Lamp, Ship Harbor Scene, Artist Macy, 20 1/2 In.	2200.00
Lamp, Silver Plate, Etched Shade	125.00
Lamp, Snow Covered Landscape, Frosted, 18 In.	1400.00
Lamp, Sunset Night Scene, Castle, Artist Fisher, 20 In.	1400.00
Lamp, Table, Autumn Harvest Scene Shade, 20th Century, 22 In.	1600.00
Lamp, Table, Floral Font & Shade, Orchids, 3 Arms, 23 1/2 In.	2000.00
Paperweight, Airtrap Design, 3 1/2 In.	20.00
Perfume Bottle, Controlled Bubbles In Base & Stopper, 5 1/2 In.	75.00
Pitcher, Turquoise, Paper Label, 3 In.	50.00
Plate, Murillo, Serrated Rim, 10 In.	250.00
Shade, Green Palm Scene, Signed, 22 In.	500.00
Syrup, Floral, 4 3/4 In.	42.50
Toothpick, Figural, Barrel With Spigot, Fireman's Helmet	165.00
Vase, Bud, Silver Plated Frame, Etched, 12 In.	48.00
Vase, Gladiolus, Maiden of The Desert, Flirting, Signed, 15 In.	1250.00
Vase, Gladiolus, Winged Cherub, Pink Scarf, Handles	150.00
Vase, Ribbed, Trumpet Shape, Ball Connector, Green	80.00

> **To protect your investment in household furnishings: Rewire any lamps in your home that are fifteen or more years old; cords crack and are a fire hazard.**

Vase, Trumpet, Amethyst Base, Bubble Connector, 12 In.	65.00
Vase, White Opaque Flower, Slender Neck, Signed, 10 1/2 In.	120.00

PALMER COX, BROWNIES, see Brownies

 The first paper dolls were probably the pantins, or jumping jacks, made in eighteenth–century Europe. By the 1880s, sheets of printed paper dolls and clothes were being made. The first paper doll books were made in the 1920s. Collectors prefer uncut sheets or books or boxed sets of paper dolls. Prices are about half as much if the pages have been cut.

PAPER DOLL, 3 Girls, 1 Boy, Black Lady, Handmade, Framed, 12 X 15 In.	130.00
Amy Carter, Uncut	12.50
Ann Sothern, 1943, Uncut	20.00
Ann Sothern, 1959, Uncut	40.00
Annie Oakley, 1956, Uncut	40.00
Ava Gardner, Violets On Cover, 1952, Uncut	135.00
Baby–Alive, Whitman, Uncut	15.00
Barbara Britton, 1954, Uncut	110.00
Barbie Going Camping, Uncut	15.00
Barbie's Boutique, Uncut	15.00
Betsy McCall	1.50
Betty Bonnet Goes To A Wedding, Ladies Home Journal, 1918	12.00
Betty Bonnet's Army & Navy Cousins, 1917	26.00
Betty Bonnet's Best Friend	12.00
Betty Bonnet's Bride & Groom	8.00
Betty Bonnet's Household Servants, 1918	16.00
Betty Grable, 1953, Uncut	125.00
Beverly Hillbillies, Uncut	30.00
Black Butler, Cream of Wheat, Uncut	125.00
Blondie, 1945, Uncut	85.00
Blondie, 1949, Uncut	85.00
Bride, Sally, Queen Holden, Whitman, 1950	18.00
Career Girls, Whitman, 1944, Uncut	20.00
Carnival Doll, Saalfield, 1941, Uncut	18.00
Carol Lynley, 1960, Uncut	40.00
Carolyn Lee, Queen Holden	20.00
Claire McCardell, Whitman, 1956, Uncut	30.00
Claudette Colbert, 1943, Uncut	250.00
Clyde Beatty, Envelope	25.00
College Girls, Campus Cutout, Lowe	30.00
Cowgirls, Abbott Co., Kenosha, Wisconsin, Uncut	25.00
Debra Paget, 1957	30.00
Diana Lynn, 1953, Uncut	35.00
Dilly Dolly Twins, National Games, Package, Unused	10.00
Dinah Shore & George Montgomery, Whitman, 1959, Uncut	70.00
Dionne Quintuplets, Colgate–Palmolive Premium, 1937, Uncut	75.00
Dolly Dimple, No.3, Chubby Caroline, Dresses, Hats, Box, 1910	95.00
Donna Reed, Paste Stick, 15 In.Doll, 1964	16.00
Doris Day, Whitman, Uncut	30.00
Elizabeth Taylor, Whitman, Uncut	30.00
Esther Williams, Merrill, 1953, Uncut	65.00
Freckles & Sniffles, Uncut	8.00

Gail Storm, Whitman, 1958, Uncut	65.00
Girl Pilots of The Ferry Command, Uncut	10.00
Girl Pilots, World War II, 1943	65.00
Good Neighbor, Saalfield, 1941, Uncut	10.00
Grace Kelly, 1956, Uncut	75.00
Heavenly Twins & Their Guardian Angels, Merrill, 1948	15.00
Hedy Lamarr, 1951, Uncut	175.00
Hour of Charm, 1943	25.00
Indian & Cowboy, Platt & Munk, 1934, Uncut	34.00
Introducing Lettie Lane, George Jacobs Co., 288 Piece	80.00
Jack & Jill, 1946–52	4.00
Jane & Michael, From Mary Poppins, Whitman, 1964	25.00
Jane Russell, With Coloring Book, Saalfield, No.4451, Uncut	85.00
Juliet Jones, Uncut, 1955	30.00
Lettie Lane, Doll Party, 1909	12.00
Little Dreamer, 6 Outfits, Cut, 34 In.	75.00
Little Orphan Annie, Hinges, Envelope	25.00
Look Who I Am, Girl Changes Outfits As Pages Turn, 1952	12.00
Loretta Young, Uncut, 1956	60.00
Mary Martin, Star of South Pacific, Saalfield, No.1539, Uncut	125.00
Mary Poppins, Whitman, 1982	25.00
Miss America 1972, Uncut	12.50
Monk & Platt, 1968, Uncut	7.00
Mother Goose, Lion Coffee	23.00
Mother Goose, Pre–1900, Uncut	50.00
Munsters, 1966, Uncut	65.00
My Little Margie, 1954, Uncut	95.00
Natalie Wood, Whitman, Uncut	30.00
National Velvet, 1961	8.00
Navy Girls, World War II, 1943	65.00
Pat Boone, 1959, Uncut	25.00
Pat Crowley, 1955, Uncut	65.00
Patience & Prudence, 1958, Uncut	30.00
Piper Laurie, 1953, Uncut	75.00
Polly Pratt, 8 Pages	50.00
Quiz Kids, Saalfield, 1942, Uncut	35.00
Raggedy Ann & Raggedy Andy, 1968	15.00
Raphael Tuck, 3 Dresses, 1 Hat	75.00
Rhonda Fleming, Uncut	40.00
Robin Hood & Maid Marian, 1956, Uncut	20.00
Rosemary Clooney, 1959, Uncut	55.00
Roy Rogers & Dale Evans, 1952, Uncut	90.00
Simple Simon, Lion Coffee	23.00
Sleeping, Queen Holden, Partially Cut	18.00
Snow White & 7 Dwarfs, Tomart, Uncut	125.00
Sweet Alice, Tuck, Original Envelope, Dated 1894	125.00
Teddy Bear & His Friends To Dress, 1920s	50.00
Teddy Bear, Outfits, 2 Bears, McLaughlin	45.00
That Girl Marlo, Uncut	10.00
Tricia Nixon, Uncut	12.50
United We Stand, Children In Uniform, 1940, Uncut	55.00
United We Stand, World War II, 1943, Uncut	50.00
Vera Miles, 1957, Uncut	100.00

Paper collectibles, including almanacs, catalogs, children's books, stock certificates, and other paper ephemera, are listed here. Paper calendars are listed separately under Calendar Paper.

PAPER, Album, Fish From American Waters, Allen & Ginter	35.00
Album, Games & Sports, Goodwin & Co.	450.00
Almanac, A.T.&T., Bell System, 1934	6.00
Almanac, Dr.D.Jayne's Medical Almanac, Guide To Health, 1912, 32 Pgs.	3.50
Almanac, Dr.Miles, New Weather, 1939	3.50
Almanac, Elgin Watch, 1876	10.00
Almanac, Family Christian Almanac, 1862, 60 Pages	5.00

Almanac, Farmers Yearbook & Almanac, 1912, 95 Pages 5.00
Almanac, Hostetter's Illustrated US Almanac, 1897, 32 Pages 4.00
Almanac, Simon's Liver Regulator, 1882–83 .... 7.50
Almanac, Swamp Root, 1927 .... 5.00
Almanac, Swamp Root, Indian Maiden Cover, 1915, 8 1/2 X 6 In. 9.00
Almanac, Watkins, 1915 .... 10.00
Appraisal, Slave, Drafted To Work At Lynchburg, Va., 1864 .... 40.00
Atlas, Long's, 1856 .... 85.00
Atlas, World, 1930, 15 X 11 In. 20.00
Baggage Label, Zeppelin, Blue, Yellow, White, Circular, Unused, 4 In. 15.00
Blotter, Arm & Hammer Soda, Unused 2.50
Bond, Shell Oil Co., 14 1/2 Debenture, Woman With Globe, 1980s 4.00
Bond, Vacuum Oil Co., Pane, Company Name, Gargoyles, 1866 .... 14.00
Book, Animal Farm, George Orwell, Dust Jacket, 1st American Edition 200.00
Book, Arco Wand Vacuum Cleaners, 1913, 32 Pages 22.00
Book, Big Little Book, Phantom & The Girl of Mystery 12.50
Book, Bring 'Em Back Alive, Wild Elephants, Buck, Premium, 1934 .... 35.00
Book, Coloring, Bambi, Unused, 1942 .... 75.00
Book, Coloring, Betty Grable, Unused, 1951 .... 75.00
Book, Coloring, Bob Hope, 1954 .... 10.00
Book, Coloring, Cinderella, 1938 .... 10.00
Book, Coloring, Debbie Reynolds, Unused, 1954 .... 45.00
Book, Coloring, Esther Williams, Unused, 1950 .... 65.00
Book, Coloring, Eve Arden, Unused, 1953 .... 30.00
Book, Coloring, Gene Autry, Unused, 1950 .... 50.00
Book, Coloring, Gone With The Wind, 2 Pages Part Colored, 1940 .... 125.00
Book, Coloring, June Allyson, Unused, 1952 .... 35.00
Book, Coloring, Piper Laurie, Unused, 1953 .... 45.00
Book, Favorite Stove Facts, 1900, 16 Pages 12.00
Book, Franklin Sewing Machine, Operating Instructions, Sears 8.00
Book, Giant Airship, Zeppelin 12.00
Book, Paint, Red Ryder, 1940 .... 15.00
Book, Pop–Up, Avon, Cowboys & Indians, 1951 .... 75.00
Book, Pop–Up, Goldilocks, 1934 .... 70.00
Catalog, American Bicycles, High Wheels, 1885, 32 Pages 90.00
Catalog, Appleton Cornhusker, 1920 .... 10.00
Catalog, Chicago Mail Order Co., Fall & Winter, 1928–29 .... 25.00
Catalog, Colt Revolvers, Pistols, 1912, 40 Pages 24.00
Catalog, Electric Ranges, Hotpoint, Original Envelope, 1926, 35 Pages 25.00
Catalog, Fireworks & Novelties, Brazel Novelty Co., 1915, 40 Pages 30.00
Catalog, Kodak, 1910, 64 Pages 30.00
Catalog, Montgomery Ward, 1905, 1124 Pages 55.00
Catalog, Montgomery Ward, 1908 .... 45.00
Catalog, Montgomery Ward, 1931 .... 25.00
Catalog, Montgomery Ward, Fall & Winter, 1954 .... 14.00
Catalog, Montgomery Ward, Spring & Summer, 1923 .... 40.00
Catalog, Montgomery Ward, Spring & Summer, 1945 .... 22.00
Catalog, Remington Gun, 1919, 108 Pages 25.00
Catalog, Savage, Fall & Winter, 1927 .... 35.00
Catalog, Sears, Roebuck, 1902 .... 45.00
Catalog, Sears, Roebuck, 1931 .... 30.00
Catalog, Sears, Roebuck, Christmas, 1967 .... 20.00
Catalog, Sears, Roebuck, Fall & Winter, 1940–41 .... 22.00
Catalog, Sears, Roebuck, Vehicles, Buggies, 1908, 72 Pages 40.00
Catalog, Shipmates Stove, 1929, 52 Pages 20.00
Catalog, Spalding, Fall & Winter, 1915, 159 Pages 40.00
Catalog, Spiegel's Christmas, 1930 .... 15.00
Catalog, Wards, Summer, 1926, 122 Pages 6.00
Catalog, Winchester, Salesman's, Leather Bound, 1914 .... 175.00
Certificate, 1st Communion, Hand Colored, Deep Frame, 1864 .... 35.00
Certificate, Cities Service Co., Logo, Man & Woman, Tanker, 1910 .... 14.00
Cutout, Lovebirds, Hearts, Foliage, Black Ground, 10 3/4 X 12 In. 200.00
Easter Egg, Elf, In Egg House, Cardboard, Germany, 1900s, 11 X 8 In. 45.00
Envelope, Air Mail, Blue Calligraphy & Birds, 1900s 25.00

Paper, Fraktur, Christian Grof, Watercolor, Ink, 1790, 13 X 15 In.

Family Record, Cutout, W.M.Addicott, Floral, Framed, 1804, 23 X 34 In. 325.00
Flight Schedule, Zeppelin, South American, 1934 .... 35.00
Folder, Wilson Sewing Machine, 1880 .... 8.00
Fraktur, 1826 Birth, Pennsylvania, Vining Flowers, Framed, 16 X 18 In. 225.00
Fraktur, Birth Certificates, Reiter Family, Berks County, Pa., 1847 .... 875.00
Fraktur, Birth In Lecha County, Pennsylvania, 1846, 15 3/4 X 19 In. 225.00
Fraktur, Birth, Baptism, 1839 Birth In Centre County, Pa., 16 X 19 In. 135.00
Fraktur, Birth, Pennsylvania German, Angels, 1807, Framed, 14 X 17 In. 400.00
Fraktur, By Baltzer Heydrich, Montgomery Ct., Pa., Framed, 1845 .... 7600.00
Fraktur, Christian Grof, Watercolor, Ink, 1790, 13 X 15 In. ....*Illus* 4400.00
Fraktur, F.Sauno, 1813, Carlisle, Birds & Flowers, Framed, 16 X 18 In. 85.00
Fraktur, Geburts Und Taufschein, 1840 Birth Record, 20 X 18 In. 65.00
Fraktur, Haus Segen, Zigzag Border, Hearts, Framed, 16 X 18 3/4 In. 325.00
Fraktur, J.Schneider, 1790, Birth, F.Krebs Label, Framed, 16 X 19 In. 650.00
Fraktur, Johann Sala Druckter, Wooster, Ohio, 14 3/4 X 18 3/4 In. 350.00
Fraktur, Joseph, July 19, 1932, Pen, Ink, Watercolor, 10 X 13 1/2 In. 4300.00
Fraktur, Marriage Certificate, Written In German, 1876, 12 X 29 In. 75.00
Fraktur, Marriage, Framed, 1890, 16 X 21 In. 75.00
Fraktur, Stylized Floral, Rebecca Snyder, Watercolor, Ink, 8 X 9 In. 3700.00
Gum Wrapper, Film Comics, Caricatures of Movie Stars, 1935, 1 Cent 80.00
Magazine, Life, April 20, 1959, Marilyn Monroe Cover 15.00
Magazine, Sports Illustrated, 1st Issue, With Baseball Cards 135.00
Menu, Hotel New Yorker, Steel Engraving of N.Y.View, Envelope, 1941 .... 15.00
Menu, Jack Dempsey's Bar & Cocktail Lounge, 1939 .... 22.00
Menu, University of Buffalo, 21st Annual Banquet, Mar.24, 1891, 7 In. 1.50
Pamphlet, Anti–Prohibition, Cartoons, Sample Ballot 5.00
Program, Army–Navy Football, With Full Page Ads, 1937 .... 15.00
Program, Bijou Theatre, NYC, November 1905, Music Master, 16 Pages 3.00
Program, Buffalo Bill, 1897 .... 45.00
Program, Circus, Adam Forepaugh & Sells Bros., 1905 .... 60.00
Program, Circus, Barnum & Bailey, 1904 .... 60.00
Program, Circus, Cole Bros., With Clyde Beatty, 1935 .... 35.00
Program, Circus, Ringling Bros., 1924 .... 45.00
Program, Commencement, Yale University, Blue Leather, 1932 .... 8.00
Program, Music Hall, Boston, Rosenthal Recital, Nov.1896, 8 Pages 3.00
Program, World Series, 1976 .... 10.00
Punchboard, 2 Treasure Chests As Prizes, Unpunched, 16 X 12 1/2 In. 135.00
Punchboard, 2 Venus Dolls As Prizes, Unpunched, 15 X 13 In. 195.00
Slave Sale, Virginia 1801, Bill of Sale On Negro Woman Named Caty 40.00
Stock Certificate, Bingham Oil Co., Denver, Oil Rigs, Gusher, 1902 .... 18.00
Stock Certificate, Burlington & Northwestern RR, 1876 .... 15.00
Stock Certificate, Crown Central Petroleum Corp., Logo At Top, 1937 .... 12.00

Stock Certificate, Dorris Oil Co., Dunkard Creek, Lincoln Portrait 135.00
Stock Certificate, Hartford Oil Co., Oil Rigs, Gold Seal, 1901 .... 22.00
Stock Certificate, Maracaibo Oil Exploration Corp., Allegorical 3.00
Stock Certificate, New York & Franklin Oil Co., Revenue Stamp, 1865 .... 40.00
Stock Certificate, Ohio & California Refining Oil Co., 1903 .... 24.00
Stock Certificate, Texas & Gulf Coast Oil, Fields Company, 1919 .... 15.00
Stock Certificate, Wilkes Mining, 1901 .... 3.25

Paperweights must have first appeared along with paper in ancient Egypt. Today's collectors search for every type from the very expensive French weights of the nineteenth century to the modern artist weights or advertising pieces. The glass tops of the paperweights sometimes have been nicked or scratched and this type of damage can be removed by polishing. Some serious collectors think this type of repair is an alteration and will not buy a repolished weight; others think it is an acceptable technique of restoration that does not change the value. Baccarat paperweights are listed separately under Baccarat.

PAPERWEIGHT, Advertising, Bausch & Lomb Optical, Brass 30.00
Advertising, Chalmer's Motor Co., Early Autos, Factory, Bronze 55.00
Advertising, Colonial Chair Co., Chicago, Red Chair, Brass 27.50
Advertising, Crane Co., Metal, 1930 .... 8.00
Advertising, Dutch Boy Paints, Lead, Figural 60.00
Advertising, Globe Tool & Engineering, Leather Pillow 25.00
Advertising, Holt Motor Service, Miniature Motor, Iron 30.00
Advertising, Lion, Wabash Baking Powder, Bronzed Iron 20.00
Advertising, Mascot Mines, 1910 .... 18.00
Advertising, Moore Pen, Reverse Painted, 9 X 3 In. 40.00
Advertising, Moorman's Chick Champ, Cast Iron, 1957 .... 15.00
Advertising, Mounty, Northwest Paper, Bronze, 1948, 3 In. 38.00
Advertising, National Cash Register .... 50.00 To 60.00
Advertising, Newman Brothers Brewery, Pittsburgh, Pa., Glass 65.00
Advertising, Orange Crush, Bottle, Salesman's Sample, 5 In. 20.00
Advertising, Pegasus, O.R.Cote Co. Mobil Gas, Bronze 150.00
Advertising, Portland Cement Co., 100 Cement Chunks In Glass 20.00
Advertising, Prudential Life Insurance, 1892 .... 30.00
Advertising, Scottish Union & National Insurance Co. 25.00
Advertising, Sweetheart Flour 24.00
Advertising, Thatcher's Stoves 40.00
Advertising, White Mountain Refrigerator 55.00
Advertising, Wincroft Stove Works 20.00
Advertising, Words Rotary International, Emblem 12.50
Amethyst To Clear Cut, Circular & Star Pattern, 3 X 4 In. 40.00
Ayotte, Oriole, Baltimore, Black-Eyed Susans, 3 1/4 In. 550.00
Ayotte, Parrot, Scarlet Chest, Amherstias, White, 3 5/8 In. 500.00
Ayotte, Rabbit, Cotton Tail, Spring Flowers, Butterfly, 3 In. 450.00
Banford, Blacksnake, Coiled, Red Flowers, Sand Ground, 2 3/4 In. 600.00
Banford, Floral Bouquet, Purple, White, Diamond Cut Base, 3 In. 600.00
Banford, Flower, Turquoise, Yellow, Star Cut Base, 2 3/4 In. 600.00
Blenko, Blue Spiral Column, Clear, 4 1/2 In. 25.00
Clichy Type, Millefiori, Faceted Double Overlay, 3 1/4 In. 600.00
Clichy, Cherry Blossom, Pink, White, High Crowned, 2 1/2 In. 800.00
Clichy, Space Millefiori, 21 Canes, 2 Roses 625.00
Columbian Exposition, Mines & Mining Building, 1893 .... 25.00
Daum, Owl, Clear, 3 1/2 In. 35.00
Ed-E-Langbein, Pink Floral Design, Green Leaves, 3 In. 45.00
Electric Light Bulb, Lucite, Filaments, Socket Threads, 4 In. 75.00
Faneuil Hall 25.00
Gillinder, Abe Lincoln, 1876 Centennial, Opaque 110.00
Gillinder, Floral On Canes, Latticinio Ground, 2 5/8 In. 300.00
Ginori, Millefiori, Blue Center, White 35.00
Home Sweet Home, Cottage, Tree, Man, White Ground, 3 X 4 In. 195.00
Horseshoe, Glass, Dated Oct.3, 1899 .... 65.00
Iron, Mating Chickens 45.00

Kaziun, Morning Glory, Leaves, Pedestal Base, Signed, 2 In.	350.00
Lundberg, Fish, Ocean Floor, Seaweed Design, 1981, 2 3/4 In.	125.00
Lundberg, Orchid, Stylized, Buds, Dark Blue Ground, 3 1/4 In.	145.00
Lundberg, Rose, Pink, Stem, Green Leaves, 3 In.	200.00
Millefiori, Concentric Flowers, Heart & Star Centers, 3 In.	175.00
Millefiori, Concentric Rings, Latticinio Strips, 3 In.	75.00
Murano, Concentric Millefiori, 3 1/2 In.	25.00
Murano, Gold & Green Swirled Design, 4 In.	25.00
Murano, Pink Latticinio, Millefiori Stripes, Dome, 4 1/2 In.	35.00
New England, Life-Sized Pear, Natural Yellow, 2 1/2 In.	1200.00
New York Central, Engine & Coal Car, Cast Iron	75.00
Pan-American Expo., Glass, N.& S.America Girl Shape, 3 In.	13.00
Pansy, Full Bloom, White Center Cane, 3 Leaves, 1 Stem, 3 In.	250.00
Perthshire, Bouquet, Large Flowers, Deep Blue Ground, 2 7/8 In.	300.00
Perthshire, Faceted Pansy, Millefiori Canes, 1971, 2 3/4 In.	180.00
Perthshire, Flowers In Basket, Violet, White Basket, 2 3/4 In.	100.00
Perthshire, Golfer, Latticinio, Millefiori Canes, Faceted, 3 In.	160.00
Perthshire, Pink Dahlia, 4 Large Side Facets, 1972, 3 In.	325.00
Perthshire, Pink Flower, Burgundy On White, Faceted, 2 7/8 In.	500.00
Perthshire, Railway Engine, Millefiori, Latticinio, 2 In.	160.00
Perthshire, Scottish Broom, Dark Green Base, Faceted, 2 1/2 In.	375.00
Perthshire, Strawberries, Faceted, Strawberry Cut Base, 3 In.	400.00
Perthshire, Swan In Pond, Star Cut Base, 3 In.	350.00
Pig, Cast Iron, Painted	15.00
Rosenfeld, 2 Purple Plums, Pear, Red Cherries, Clear, 3 In.	250.00
Rosenfeld, Flowers, 2 Pink & 4 Buds, 2 1/2 In.	200.00
Rosenfeld, Rose Bouquet, Green Leaves, Crystal, 2 3/4 In.	300.00
Rosenfeld, Strawberries, Leaves, Blossoms, Marked, 2 5/8 In.	200.00
Sandwich, Pink Rose, Full Blossom, 2 Green Leaves, 2 7/8 In.	725.00
Sandwich, Poinsettia, Pink, Green, White, 5 Leaves, 2 7/8 In.	750.00
Sandwich, Poinsettia-Type, White Latticinio Ground, 2 3/4 In.	400.00
Sandwich, Wild Rose, Rose, Blue, Pink, 8 Leaves, 3 In.	110.00
Scrutton, Concentric Millefiori, 6 Circles, Canes Center, 3 In.	175.00
Scrutton, Garland, Purple, Blue, Green, White Clichy Roses, 3 In.	210.00
Scrutton, Scattered Millefiori, Canes In Muslin, Crystal, 3 In.	190.00
St.Louis, Basket of Fruit, Cherries, Pears, Plums, Apple, 3 In.	600.00
St.Louis, Bellflowers, Green Stem, Crystal, Cane, 2 7/8 In.	380.00
St.Louis, Blue Carpet, Millefiori, Blue Ground, Cane, 2 7/8 In.	440.00
St.Louis, Bouquet, Tricolor, Cane, Crystal, 2 7/8 In.	490.00
St.Louis, Flowers, Leaves, Powder Blue, Faceted, Cane, 3 1/8 In.	400.00
St.Louis, Garland of Canes	475.00
St.Louis, Looped Garland, Aqua Ground, 28 Cane Center, 3 In.	1500.00
St.Louis, Pink & White Jasper	80.00
St.Louis, Red Dahlia, Faceted Glass, 1970, 3 1/4 In.	300.00
St.Louis, Statue of Liberty, Gold Head, Red, White Stars, 3 In.	440.00
St.Louis, Torsade, Blue Cane, Red, White, Blue Ground, 3 In.	800.00
St.Louis, White Flower, Stems, Blue Ground, Faceted, Cane, 3 In.	375.00
St.Louis, White Latticinio Snake, Pewter Head, 1852, 3 In.	460.00
Star Cut Base, Emerald Overlay, Domed, Late 19th Century	75.00
Stourbridge, 3 Silvery Florals, Green Bullet Shape, 5 In.	125.00
Tarsitano, Spider, Fly, Web, Pink Flowers, Green Leaves, 4 In.	1450.00
Trabucco, Magnum Bouquet, Pin Roses, Yellow, Blue Flowers, 4 In.	1000.00
Turtle, Moving, A Fortune In A Junk Pile	85.00
White Rose, Striping, Leaves On Green Stem, 3 In.	500.00
Whitefriars, Modern Design, Multicolored Canes, Rectangular	20.00
Ysart, Fish, Blue Jasper Ground, 8 Complex Canes, 2 3/4 In.	650.00
Ysart, Millefiori, Deep Blue Ground, 3 In.	550.00
Ysart, Pink Flower, On Orange Millefiori Cane Basket, 3 In.	125.00

 Papier-mache is made from paper mixed with glue, chalk, and other ingredients, then molded and baked. It becomes very hard and can be painted. Boxes, trays, and furniture were made of papier-mache. Some of the nineteenth-century pieces were decorated with mother-of-pearl.

PAPIER–MACHE, see also Furniture
PAPIER–MACHE, Liqueur Set, Decanter, Lacquered, Tray, 6 Cups, Russian .... | 125.00
Man, Jointed Arms, Legs, Curly Wig, Dressed For Fishing, 1910 .... | 160.00
Tea Tray, Landscape, People Lunching, Grain Harvest, 31 In. .... | 400.00
Tray, Gilt Birds, Flowers, Black Paint, 30 In. .... | 5500.00
Tray, On Stand, Gilt Oak Leaves, Faux Bamboo Legs, 30 In. .... | 990.00
Tray, Painted Bay Scene, 19th Century, 31 1/4 X 26 1/2 In. .... | 1870.00
Tray, Polychrome Country House, Gentleman, 15 3/4 In. .... | 100.00
Tray, Regency, Tropical Scene, 2 Men, Octagonal, 21 3/4 In. .... | 375.00
   PARASOL, see Umbrella

Parian is a fine–grained, hard–paste porcelain named for the marble it resembles. It was first made in England in 1846 and gained in favor in the United States about 1860. Figures, tea sets, vases, and other items were made of Parian at many English and American factories.

PARIAN, Bottle, Hand Painted, G.Jones .... | 75.00
Bowl, Figural, 2 Classical Maidens, Pink, Copeland, C.1870, 18 In. .... | 715.00
Bust, Charles Sumner, 10 1/2 In. .... | 95.00
Bust, George Stephenson, L.W.Wyon Sculptor 1858, 10 1/4 In. .... | 35.00
Bust, Lafayette, Framed, 18 1/2 X 15 In. .... | 209.00
Bust, Mendelssohn, German, 5 1/2 In. .... | 90.00
Bust, Profile of Woman, Intaglio, Oval, 2 X 1 1/2 In. .... | 25.00
Bust, Shakespeare, 7 1/4 X 5 1/2 In. .... 58.00 To 60.00
Candle Screen, General Winfield Scott Portrait, Adjustable, 17 In. .... | 150.00
Figurine, Gentleman, Seated, Holding Papers, 10 In. .... | 110.00
Figurine, Gypsy Maiden, Standing, Kerchief, Beads, Bangles, 18 In. .... | 110.00
Figurine, Rebecca At The Well, Outstretched Arms .... | 55.00
Figurine, Woman and Child, Rustic Dress, Child On Shoulders, 16 In. .... | 80.00
Group, Owls Sitting On Branch, Match Making, 5 1/2 X 7 In. .... | 245.00
Jug, Bark In Relief, Vines, Lavender, 7 5/8 In. .... | 145.00
Jug, Bearded Man's Face On Handle, Lavender, 9 3/4 In. .... | 155.00
Match Holder, Dog, Beside Hydrant, Saucer .... | 20.00
Pitcher, Classically Posed Women, Rope Knot Mark, 1862, 7 In. .... | 90.00
Pitcher, Naomi & Daughters–In–Law, Lavender Under White, Alcock .... | 120.00
Toothpick, Child With Basket .... | 30.00

Vieux Paris, or Old Paris, is porcelain ware that is known to have been made in Paris in the eighteenth or early nineteenth century. These porcelains have no identifying mark but can be identified by the whiteness of the porcelain and the lines and decorations.

PARIS, Basket, Reticulated, White Biscuit Cupid Stand, Pair .... | 1100.00
Cup & Saucer, Handleless, Pink Floral, C.1840 .... | 225.00
Jar, Apothecary, Cover, Signed, 1850 .... | 250.00
Tureen, Cover & Undertray, Gilt & White, C.1840 .... | 495.00
Urn, 8 1/4 In. .... | 125.00
Vase, Castle Scene, 12 In. .... | 90.00
Vase, Cupid, Flowers, Pastels, White Ground, Signed, Dated, 13 In. .... | 260.00

Pate–de–verre is an ancient technique in which glass is made by blending and refining powdered glass of different colors into molds. The process was revived by French glassmakers, especially Galle, around the end of the nineteenth century.

PATE–DE–VERRE, Perfume Bottle, Atomizer, Red Berries, A.Walter .... | 1250.00

Pate–sur–pate means paste on paste. The design was made by painting layers of slip on the ceramic piece until a relief decoration was formed. The method was developed at the Sevres factory in France about 1850. It became even more famous at the English Minton factory about 1870. It has since been used by many potters to make both pottery and porcelain wares.

PATE–SUR–PATE, Box, Medallion of Cupids, Blue & White, C.1870, 4 1/4 In. .... | 175.00
Perfume Bottle, Atomizer, Nudes, Blue–Green, Art Deco, Limoges .... | 185.00
Plaque, Morning & Night, Velvet, Framed, Schenck, 23 X 13 In. .... | 910.00

Vase, Cupid Chasing Butterfly, George Jones, 6 In. 550.00

 Paul Revere pottery was made at several locations in and around Boston, Massachusetts, between 1906 and 1942. The pottery was operated as a settlement house program for teen–aged girls. Many pieces were signed "S.E.G." for Saturday Evening Girls. The artists concentrated on children's dishes and tiles. Decorations were outlined in black and filled with color.

PAUL REVERE POTTERY, Blue Lotus, White Band, SEG, 1910, 2 1/2 X 4 In. 100.00
Blue, Beige, Tree Border, Forest Green, 1911, 8 In. 350.00
Blue, Chartreuse Pock Marks, Marked, 5 In. 45.00
Bowl, Geese, Blue & Green Ground, SEG, 1915, 5 X 11 In. 600.00
Bowl, Gunmetal Gray, Turquoise Inside, SEG, 6 X 12 In. 90.00
Breakfast Set, Child's, Chicks, SEG, 1912, 3 Piece 225.00
Chicks & Wheat Shafts, White, SEG, 1911, 8 In. 325.00
Child's Set, Sir & Lady Rabbit, SEG, 1917, 3 Piece 2100.00
Mug, Brownies, Gold Handle, SEG, 1903, 3 7/8 In. 235.00
Pitcher, Green & Blue Drip Glaze Band, 1920, 7 1/2 In. 150.00
Pitcher, Round Medallion, Blue, Bulbous, 1923, SEG, 7 In. 50.00
Pitcher, Tortoise & Hare, SEG, 1909, 4 1/2 In. 850.00
Pitcher, Viking Ships, Pale Blue Ground, SEG, 9 3/4 In. 950.00
Plate, Flying Goose, Incised Landscape, 1924, 8 In. 400.00
Plate, Owl, White & Yellow Bands, 1925, 7 3/4 In. 200.00
Plate, Pigs, Center Monogram, SEG, 1910, 8 1/2 In. 900.00
Plate, Repeating Pigs, Monogram, SEG, 8 1/2 In. 1300.00
Plate, Tree Border, Forest Green, Monogram, 1911, 8 In. 350.00
Plate, Trees, House, Lake, Goose, Blue, Green, Yellow, 8 In 400.00
Squirrels, Green Band, SEG, 1909, 6 In. 300.00
Tile, Incised Rabbits, Brown Glaze On Green, 5 1/4 In. 110.00
Tile, Tea, Green Trees, Blue Lake, Round, 1914, 5 In. 325.00
Trivet, Geometric Bands, Overlapping Squares, 5 In. 150.00
Vase, Glaze, Signed SEG, 5 1/2 In. 75.00
White Lotus Border, Blue, 1915, 8 1/2 In. 140.00

 Peachblow glass originated about 1883 at Hobbs, Brockunier and Company of Wheeling, West Virginia. It is a glass that shades from yellow to peach. It was lined with white glass. New England peachblow is a one–layer glass shading from red to white. Mt. Washington peachblow shades from pink to blue. Reproductions of all types of peachblow have been made. Some are poor and easy to identify as copies, others are very accurate reproductions and could fool the unwary.

PEACHBLOW, Bowl, World's Fair, 1893, 2 Handles, Signed, 2 1/2 In. 425.00
Celery, New England .... 525.00 To 925.00
Cracker Jar, Enameled Floral, Silver Plated Fittings 325.00
Creamer, Bulbous, Shiny Finish, 4–Cornered Top, Wheeling, 4 In. 435.00
Cruet, Wheeling, Drape Pattern, Ruffled Top, 7 1/2 In. 1500.00
Cruet, Wheeling, Teardrop, Amber Handle, Hand Crafted 1185.00
Cruet, Wheeling, White Interior, Trefoil Top 1285.00
Decanter, Imperial, Paper Label 95.00
      PEACHBLOW, GUNDERSON, see Gunderson
Lamp, Hanging, New England 650.00
Mustard, Wheeling, Metal Lid & Handle 750.00
Pear, New England, Glossy, Stem 155.00
Pitcher, Hand Blown, Paper Sticker, 3 1/2 In. 65.00
Pitcher, Milk, New England, Elongated Crimp Forms Spout 1285.00
Pitcher, Milk, Wheeling, 5 In. 850.00
Pitcher, Sandwich, Slender Neck, Camphor Edge & Handle, 8 In. 125.00
Pitcher, Wheeling, Drape 1150.00
Pitcher, Wheeling, Mahogany To Amber, Acid Finish 1100.00
Punch Cup, New England .... 235.00 To 250.00
Punch Cup, New England, Gold Trim, World's Fair, 1893 .... 400.00
Punch Cup, New England, Reeded Handle & Bottom, 2 3/4 In. 385.00
Rose Bowl, New England, 7–Crimp Top, 2 3/4 X 3 In. 485.00

The best cleaner for your cut glass is a perfume-free, softener-free dishwasher detergent. Ammonia is too strong; scented softeners sometimes leave an oily film.

Rose Bowl, New England, 7–Crimp Top, Cream To Rose, 3 1/2 In.	325.00
Rose Bowl, New England, Siamese, White Floral Prunts, 3 1/8 In.	325.00
Salt & Pepper, Wheeling	220.00
Salt & Pepper, Wheeling, Ox Heart Cherries	435.00
Sock Darner, New England	120.00
Sock Darner, Pink To White, 2 1/2 X 6 In.	145.00
Spooner, New England, Wild Rose Pattern	385.00
Sugar & Creamer, Ribbed, White Handles	1100.00
Sugar & Creamer, White Handle	750.00
Toothpick, New England	385.00
Tumbler, New England	275.00
Tumbler, Wheeling, 3 3/4 In.	275.00
Tumbler, White To Raspberry, 3 3/4 In.	295.00
Tumbler, Wild Rose, 3 3/4 In.	350.00
Vase, Coralene Design, White Interior, 11 In.	375.00
Vase, Enameled Prunis Flowers & Beading, 10 1/2 In.	250.00
Vase, Lily, 5 1/4 In.	375.00
Vase, Lily, New England, 10 In.	1250.00
Vase, Lily, New England, Satin Finish	645.00
Vase, New England, Ball–Shaped Base, 6 1/4 In.	565.00
Vase, Pink To Cream, Blue Flowers, Branches, P.F.K., 12 1/2 In.	650.00
Vase, Sandwich, 2 Frosted Thorn Handles, 4 1/4 In.	185.00
Vase, Stick, Wheeling, Chocolate & Mahogany Colors, 8 1/2 In.	385.00
Vase, Wheeling, Drape, Ruffled, Pink To Yellow, Cylindrical	650.00

PEACHBLOW, WEBB, see Webb Peachblow

Listed under Pearl are items made of the natural mother–of–pearl from shells. The glassware known as mother–of–pearl is listed by that name. Opera glasses made with natural pearl shell are listed under Opera Glasses. Natural pearl has been used to decorate furniture and small utilitarian objects for centuries.

PEARL, Case, Calling Card	40.00
Case, Card, Divided Interior	17.50
Scissors, Cigar Cutter, Brass	38.00
Seal, Wax	10.00

 Peking glass is a Chinese cameo glass first made popular in the eighteenth century. The Chinese have continued to make this layered glass in the old manner, and many new pieces are now available that could confuse the average buyer.

PEKING GLASS, Bowl, Floral, Butterfly, Teakwood Stand, 7 X 3 In.	210.00 To 250.00
Snuff Bottle, Imitation of Agate, 19th Century	30.00
Vase, Bonsai Tree, Monkey In Branches, White Ground, 10 In.	340.00
Vase, Carved Flowers & Ducks, Imperial Yellow, 11 In.	250.00
Vase, Heads In Relief, Foo Dogs, White, 3 1/4 In.	60.00
Vase, Relief Monkey On Tree, Yellow On White, 10 In., Pair	300.00
Vase, Relief Peacock & Tree Peony Design, 9 7/8 In., Pair	375.00
Vase, Royal Blue Peony & Cicada Design, 8 7/8 In., Pair	400.00

Peloton glass is a European glass with small threads of colored glass rolled onto the surface of clear or colored glass. It is sometimes called spaghetti, or shredded coconut, glass. Most pieces found today were made in the nineteenth century.

PELOTON, Biscuit Jar, Yellow & White Coconut Strings Allover, 5 1/2 In.	575.00
Bowl, Pinched–In Top, Colored Strands, Orchid Lining, 2 1/2 In.	185.00
Cookie Jar	400.00
Dish, Sweetmeat, Robin's–Egg Blue, Silver Plated Fittings, 5 In.	585.00
Pitcher, Multicolored Spaghetti, Amber, 7 In.	295.00
Rose Bowl, 6–Crimp Top, Applied Coconut Strings, 2 1/4 In.	225.00
Vase, Colored Coconut & Threading, 4–Point Rim, Footed, 3 3/4 In.	265.00

The first steel pen point was made in England in 1780 to replace the hand–cut quill as a writing instrument. It was 100 years before the commercial pen was a common item. The fountain pen was invented in the 1830s but was not made in quantity until the 1880s. All types of old pens are collected.

PEN, Bat, Wood, Chicago White Sox	30.00
Cartier, Ballpoint, Sterling Silver	100.00
Conklin Crescent, Fountain	25.00
Desk, Bakelite, Black & Yellow, Spenco On Nib	35.00
Diamond, Fountain, 14K Gold Point, LF Marbelized	35.00
Dip, Mother–of–Pearl & Gold Handle, Silk Lined Case	55.00
Drexel, Fountain, Pencil, 14K Gold, Set	26.00
Eversharp, Art Deco, Red & Black, 6 In.	12.00
Eversharp, Skyline, Gold Filled Cap, New Bladder	60.00
Eversharp, Skyline, Green Stripes	15.00
Eversharp, Skyline, Navy Stripes	12.00
Eversharp, Skyline, With Pencil, 14K Gold	525.00
Eversharp, Symphony, Navy Chromium Cap, FGT	49.00
Eversharp, Woman's, Gold Filled	28.00
Keystone, Black Ribbon Design, 1917	15.00
Lady Webster, Gold Trim, Fountain	20.00
Leeds, Green Case, Fountain	15.00
Moore, Navy, Light Blue Cap & End	30.00
Moore, Retractable Point, Velvet Lined Box	500.00
Morrison, Fountain, Navy Emblem On Top	20.00
Parker, Duofold Jr., Orange, Engraved	22.00
Parker, Duofold Jr., Pump, Mandarin Yellow, Clip Dated 1919	95.00
Parker, Duofold, Desk Set, Incised Base, 7 X 11 In.	75.00
Parker, Duofold, Lucky Curve, Chinese Red	90.00
Parker, Duofold, Mother–of–Pearl Inlay	30.00
Parker, Lucky Curve No.28, Black, 1912	150.00
Parker, No.45, Fountain	12.00
Parker, No.51, Black, Gold Filled Cap	38.00
Parker, No.51, On Green Onyx Base, Brass Holder	12.00
Parker, Pump, 1928	95.00
Parker, Vacuum Black, Brass Filigree	35.00
Sentinel, White Dot, Green, Chromium Cap	48.00
Sheaffer, 14K Gold Nib, Fountain	25.00
Sheaffer, Feather Touch, Black, Box, New	48.00
Sheaffer, Fineline, Ballpoint, Original Store Card	12.00
Sheaffer, Lifetime	40.00
Sheaffer, No.400, Brown & Yellow	9.00
Sheaffer, No.400, Green	8.00
Sheaffer, White Dot, With Pencil, Box	40.00
Stratford, Mechanical, With Pencil	12.00
Swan, Self Filling, Black, Wide Gold Band, Mabel Todd, N.Y.	35.00
Valiant, White Dot, Green	55.00
Wahl, Bronze, Brown, Transparent Barrel, Pinch Filler	28.00
Wahl, Gold Filled, Fountain	35.00
Wahl, Oxford, Fountain	35.00
Wahl, Rosewood, Gold Trim	58.00
Wahl, Sterling Silver	65.00
Waterman, 14K Gold Nib, Sticker, Box	25.00

Waterman, 14K Solid Gold, Matching Pencil, Fountain, Spiegel, 1940s 325.00
Waterman, Barrel, Gold Filled 50.00
Waterman, No.52 .... 20.00
Waterman, No.54 .... 24.00
Wearever, Green & Black Case, Fountain 8.50

The pencil was invented, so it is said, in 1565. The eraser was not added to the pencil until 1858. The automatic pencil was invented in 1863. Collectors today want advertising pencils or automatic pencils of unusual design. Boxes and sharpeners for pencils are also collected.

PENCIL, Bullet, John Deere 5.00
Bullet, Mechanical Times Table, German 6.75
Bullet, Pacific Mutual Insurance Co., Railroad Department 6.00
Calendar, 1917, Advertising 6.00
Cross, Gold Filled, Ring Top, Short 35.00
Eversharp, Automatic, Engraved, 14K Gold, Dated 1919 .... 175.00
Eversharp, Blue, Brass 12.00
Eversharp, Sterling Silver, Label & Price 20.00
Lion, Silver Plate 10.00
Mechanical, Brotherhood of Railroad Trainmen, Pearlized 10.00
Mechanical, National Refining Company, Products, En–Ar–Co Boy 20.00
Mechanical, S.S.Ocean Monarch, Floats In Oil 15.00
Parker, Duofold Sr., Mechanical, Patent 1916 .... 50.00
Parker, Duofold, Emerald Green, 1916 .... 25.00
Pen–O–Pencil, 14K Gold Point 8.00
Sterling Silver, Collapsible, Loop, Closed, Tiffany, 2 1/4 In. 65.00
Wahl, Art Deco, Gold Filled 20.00
Wahl, Eversharp, Gold Filled, Chain 35.00
Wahl, Eversharp, Gold Filled, Loop 14.00
Wahl, Eversharp, Sterling Silver, Mechanical 35.00

Pennsbury Pottery The Pennsbury Pottery worked in Morrisville, Pennsylvania, from 1950 to 1971. Full sets of dinnerware were made as well as many decorative items. Pieces are marked with the name of the factory.

PENNSBURY, Ashtray, Advertising, Doyletown National Bank & Trust Co. 19.50
Ashtray, Girl, Saying 25.00
Ashtray, It Wonders Me, 5 In. 14.00
Ashtray, Pennsylvania R.R. 25.00
Bowl, Amish Family, Barn, 3 X 12 In. 45.00
Bowl, Dutch Design, 9 In. 25.00
Bowl, Rooster, 2 1/2 X 5 1/2 In. 22.00
Bowl, Vegetable, Divided, Red Rooster, 9 1/2 In. 25.00
Butter, Cover, Lovebirds 12.50
Butter, Cover, Red Rooster 25.00
Cigarette Box, Cover 18.00
Compote, Rooster, Handles 40.00
Cookie Jar, Amish 100.00
Creamer, Red Rooster .... 10.00 To 15.00
Cruet, Amish Man & Woman, Pair 40.00
Cruet, Oil & Vinegar, Gay Nineties 110.00
Cup & Saucer, Red Rooster 10.00
Letter Holder, 2 Ladies Under Tree 39.50
Mug, Amish Figure .... 17.50 To 22.00
Mug, Barbershop Quartet 22.50
Mug, Eagle & Shield, 4 1/2 In. .... 22.00 To 40.00
Mug, Geometric Hex–Like Design, Brown Ground, Stein, 4 1/2 In. 30.00
Mug, Here's Looking At You .... 14.00 To 22.50
Pin Tray, Horse, 3 X 5 In. 20.00
Pitcher, Amish Couple, 1 Qt. 45.00
Pitcher, Amish, 4 In. 18.00
Pitcher, Rooster, 6 1/2 In. 45.00
Pitcher, Water, Iris 18.00
Plaque, 100th Anniversary 35.00

Plaque, Central Pacific Railroad, C.P.Huntington	45.00
Plate, Amish Couple & 2 Children, 8 In.	20.00
Plate, Annual, 1935	35.00
Plate, Christmas, 1960, 8 In.	25.00
Plate, Christmas, 1964	15.00
Plate, Christmas, 1965	15.00
Plate, Harvest, With Amish, 11 In.	22.00
Plate, Lower Bucks County, 1952	35.00
Plate, U.S.Steel Corp.	15.00
Platter, Oval, 10 3/4 In.	15.00
Platter, Red Rooster, 13 1/2 In.	40.00
Salt & Pepper, Rooster	20.00
Sugar, Rooster, Cover	20.00
Teapot, Rooster, 2 Cup	45.00
Tray, Eagle & Shield, Small	22.00
Tray, Laurel Ridge	29.00 To 30.00

 Pepsi–Cola, the drink and the name, was invented in 1898 but was not trademarked until 1903. The logo was changed from an elaborate script to the modern block letters in the 1970 Pepsi label. All types of advertising memorabilia are collected and reproductions are being made.

PEPSI–COLA, Bag, Cloth, Holds 6 Bottles	35.00
Bottle, Block Letters	15.00
Bottle, Cincinnati Reds, World Series, Contents, 1975	30.00
Bottle, Embossed, Skirted, 6 1/2 Oz.	38.00
Bottle, Paper Label, 1930	45.00
Bottle, Paper Label, C.1910	30.00
Bottle, Stretch, Cork Stopper, 19 In.	19.00
Cake Carrier, 1960s	35.00
Calendar, 1931, From Local Bottler, Full Pad	65.00
Calendar, Sportsman, 1940	27.50
Can Set, Denver Nuggets Basketball, 1972, 15 Cans	50.00
Carrier, 6 Pack	18.00
Carton, With 6 Glass Bottles, 3 In.	23.00
Clock, Curved Glass, 1950, 15 In.	125.00
Clock, Electric, 13 1/2 X 20 1/4 In.	35.00
Clock, Electric, 2 Dots	85.00
Clock, Say Pepsi Please, Electric, Rectangular	75.00
Cooler, Blue & White Logo In Relief, Metal	40.00
Dispenser, Drink Pepsi–Cola, Ice Cold, Raised Letters, 1950s	425.00
Ice Chest, Blue, 1930s	50.00
Lighter, Metal	17.50
Mirror, Girl, 1950s, 13 1/2 X 6 In.	25.00
Pen, Fountain, 1930, 6 In.	45.00
Pencil, Mechanical, Miniature Bottle On Top	15.00
Pin, Hanging Baseball	35.00
Radio, Bottle Shape	10.00
Sign, Bottle Cap, 16 In.	45.00
Sign, Bottle Cap, Tin, 30 In.	85.00
Sign, Bottle Shape, 1920s, 44 X 13 In.	195.00
Sign, Cardboard, 1940s, 12 X 24 In.	50.00
Sign, Lunch Counter, Cardboard, 1956, 22 X 7 In.	15.00
Sign, Say Pepsi Please, Tin, Framed	25.00
Sign, School Crossing, Figural, Drive Slow Please, Tin	75.00
String Holder, 5 Cent, 1930s, 14 X 20 In.	375.00
Thermometer, 1930s	135.00
Thermometer, 1950s	18.00
Thermometer, Bottle Cap On Top & Bottom, 27 X 8 In.	35.00
Tray	15.00
Tray, Beach Scene, Round	8.00
Tray, Enjoy Pepsi–Cola, 13 X 13 In.	20.00
Tumbler, Embossed	35.00

Cut glass, pressed glass, art glass, silver, metal, enamel, and even plastic or porcelain perfume bottles have been made. Although the small bottle to hold perfume was first made before the time of ancient Egypt, it is the nineteenth- and twentieth-century examples that interest today's collector. Examples with the atomizer top marked "DeVilbiss" are listed under that name. Glass or porcelain examples will be found under the appropriate name such as Lalique, Czechoslovakia, etc.

PERFUME BOTTLE, Arden, 6 Women's Faces Molded On Sides, Frosted, 5 In.	45.00
Art Deco, Green Glass, Square, Cube Top, Ground Stopper	34.00
Art Glass, Navy Over Red, Elongated Ovals	95.00
Babs, Forever Yours, Heart Shape, Hands Under Glass Dome	95.00
Balenciaga, Le Dix, Stopper, Half Contents, Box, 2 3/4 In.	40.00
Bell & Flowers Design, Dauber, Signed Wells, 2 1/2 In.	60.00
Caron, Farnesiana, Green Shaded Box	115.00
Charisma, Gold Plastic Head, Label, Avon, 2 1/4 In.	20.00
Chevalie, De La Nuit, 1925	150.00
Clear Cut Swirl, Gold & Colored Enamel, 6 1/4 In.	150.00
Cobalt Blue Cut Overlay, Tapered, 7 1/2 In.	85.00
Coin Spot, White	45.00
Coty, Pyramid Shape, Frosted Stopper, Label, 2 1/2 In.	22.00
Crystal, Ribbed Bottom, Heart Stopper	10.00
Cupid's Breath, Elizabeth Arden	65.00
Cut Glass, Brilliant, Large	95.00
Cut Glass, Floral, Iridescent Amber, 6 1/2 In.	90.00
Cut Glass, Gold Intaglio Cameo, Amber To Clear, 5 1/4 In.	80.00
Cut Glass, Ice Blue, Pointed Geometric Stopper, 4 In.	45.00
Cut Glass, Prism Design, Minuet, 6 1/2 In.	75.00
Cut Glass, Sterling Collar, Stopper, English Hallmark	110.00
Cut Glass, Sterling Silver Openwork Cased, 8 In.	69.00
Czechoslovakia, Crystal, Blue, Signed	85.00
Czechoslovakia, Cut Glass, Amber To Clear, Etched, 7 7/8 In.	140.00
Czechoslovakia, Cut Glass, Floral Intaglio Stopper, 4 In.	35.00
Czechoslovakia, Iridescent Amber, Atomizer, 6-7/8 In.	90.00
Czechoslovakia, Prism Allover Cut, Long Stopper, 8 In.	125.00
Czechoslovakia, Yellow, Orange, Black, Design, Atomizer, 5 In.	65.00
DeVilbiss, Atomizer, Coin Spot, Marked	45.00
DeVilbiss, Atomizer, Gold Crackle Glass, Flower Top, 5 In.	48.00
DeVilbiss, Blue Opalescent, Coin Spot	55.00
DeVilbiss, Yellow, Gold & Black Design, Atomizer, 4 1/8 In.	135.00
Diamond Optic, Dauber, 6 1/4 In., Pair	95.00
Dunhill, Brass Case, Art Deco, 2 In.	30.00
Embossed Cathedral, Kolnisch Wasser, Sterling Top, Meissen	55.00
Enameled Floral, Coat of Arms, Silver Top, Dark Green, 1850	115.00
Fenton, Ribbed Opals, Crimped Rim, Blown Out, 5 1/2 In.	40.00
Figural, Black Woman, Head Detaches, 4 In.	16.50
Ft.Levenworth, Pottery, 4 In. ....*Illus*	15.00
Galle, Cameo, 8 1/2 In. ....*Illus*	500.00
Galle, Cameo, Purple Flowers, Yellow, 7 In. ....*Illus*	725.00
Garwood's Forest Blossoms, Etched	10.00
Goebel Crown, Dachshund Shape, Green	75.00
Golliwog, Black Glass, Googly Eyes, C.1920, 3 In. ....*Illus*	350.00
Guerlain, Fan Shape, Blue Stopper, Crystal, Marked, 4 In.	20.00
Heart, Blown Glass, Blue Lines, Brass Screw Top, 1 3/8 In.	35.00
John Block & Sons Perfumers, Etched Base, Faceted Stopper	18.00
Le Dandy, D'Orsay, Black Glass, Octagonal, Box	95.00
Lundberg, Iridescent, 6 In.	85.00
Marcel Franck, Pressed Glass, Atomizer, 3 7/8 In.	80.00
Mary Chess, Figural, Frosted, French, 3 1/2 In.	100.00
Molinard, Madrigal, C.1930, Box, 2 In.	85.00
Nuit De Noel, Dark Glass, Caron, France, 3 In.	40.00
Ooloo, Figural, Black Cat ....54.00 To 68.50
Palmer, Emerald Green, Cylindrical, Flat Front, 4 3/4 In.	6.00

Peach, Engraved Brass Neck, Atomizer, Glass Tube, 6 1/2 In.	90.00
Prism Design, Cut, 6 /12 In.	75.00
Raquel, Fragrance of The Night, Crackle Glass, 1930, 6 In.	75.00
Rosemary Cologne, Jug, Cork, Gold Tassels, Ceramic, 6 In.	15.00
Schiaparelli, Dress Form Shape, 1 3/4 Oz.	55.00
Shalimar, Baccarat Bottle, Fitted Box, Guerlain, 3 3/4 In.	65.00
Shalimar, Numbered & Signed, Guerlain, 5 7/8 In.	40.00
Shocking, Tape Measure Neck, Flowers, Schiaparelli, 6 In.	160.00
Silver Overlay, Green, 3 1/2 In.	200.00
Silver Plate, Atomzier, Original Glass Tube, 6 3/8 In.	165.00
Sterling Silver Overlay, 3 3/4 In.	40.00
T.I., Clear, Lacquered Box, Fitted, Lined, 1 7/8 In., 2 Piece	100.00
Teddy Bear, Schuco, 1913	475.00
Victorian Scenes, Blue, White, Stopper, Bavarian Signed	24.00
Woodhue, Faberge, Velvet Covered Cap, 3 1/4 In.	10.00

Peters & Reed Pottery Company of Zanesville, Ohio, was founded by John D. Peters and Adam Reed in 1897. Chromal, Landsun, Montene, Pereco, and Persian are some of the art lines that were made. The company became Zane Pottery in 1920, Gonder Pottery in 1941, and closed in 1957. Peters & Reed was unmarked.

PETERS & REED, Bookends, Indian Head In Relief, Red Matte Ground, 5 In.	65.00
Bowl, Aztec Pinecone, Signed Ferrell, 3 X 6 1/4 In.	50.00
Candlestick, Black Mirror, 10 In., Pair	18.00
Ewer, Brown, 17 In.	175.00
Jar, Landsun, Cover, Small	25.00
Jug, Brown Glaze, Grapes, Leaves, Bulbous, 6 1/2 In.	70.00
Umbrella Stand, Moss Aztec	125.00
Vase, Drip Glaze, 4 1/2 In.	28.00
Vase, Lake Scene, Chromal	145.00
Vase, Landsun, 6 In.	15.00
Vase, Moss Aztec, 11 1/2 In.	55.00

Perfume Bottle, Galle, Cameo, 8 1/2 In.

Perfume Bottle, Golliwog, Black Glass, Googly Eyes, C.1920, 3 In.

Ft. Levenworth, Pottery, 4 In.

Perfume Bottle, Galle, Cameo, Purple Flowers, Yellow, 7 In.

Vase, Moss Aztec, Embossed Flowers, 7 3/4 In.	48.00
Vase, Mt.Fujiyama, Chromal, Drilled, 13 In.	200.00
Wall Pocket, Egyptian Ware, Green	75.00
Wall Pocket, Moss Aztec, Grape Cluster, Signed Ferrell, 8 In.	50.00

PETRUS REGOUT, see Maastricht

The Pewabic Pottery was founded by Mary Chase Perry Stratton in 1903 in Detroit, Michigan. The company made many types of art pottery including pieces with matte green glaze and an iridescent crystalline glaze. The company continued working until the death of Mary Stratton in 1961. It was reactivated by Michigan State University in 1968.

PEWABIC, Bowl & Plate	75.00
Tile, Candle Blower, Artist Signed	125.00
Tile, Cherubs, Artist Signed	110.00
Tile, Detroit Women's League, Multicolored, Round, 4 In.	130.00
Tile, Oriental Dolphin, Burgundy & Turquoise, 5 1/4 In.	210.00
Tile, Owl, Square, 3 In.	55.00

Pewter is a metal alloy of tin and lead. Some of the pewter made after 1840 has a slightly different composition and is called "Britannia metal." This later type of pewter was worked by machine; the earlier pieces were made by hand.

PEWTER, Ashtray, Nude Lady & Ram, Norway, Pair	20.00
Basin, Fein Block Zinn, Engraved Initials On Rim, Germany, 13 In.	150.00
Basin, S.Kilbourn, Baltimore, 2 5/8 In.	900.00
Beaker, James Weeks, Straight Line Touch, Footed, 3 3/4 In.	600.00
Bedpan, Thomas D.Boardman, Screw–Off Handle, 12 In.	90.00
Bowl, Flagg & Woman, 3 X 5 1/2 In.	95.00
Bowl, Mess, Marked London, 5 1/2 X 2 1/4 In., Pair	110.00
Bowl, Raised Water Lily Center, Dragonflies, Kayserzinn, 10 In.	75.00
Candlestick, Elephant Type Figure, Base, Chinese, C.1820, 17 1/2 In.	121.00
Candlestick, Figural, Maiden, Wrapped About Stalks, 13 In, Pair	1760.00
Candlestick, Handmade, Double Greyhound Base, Unique, 5 In., Pair	5.00
Candlestick, Push Rod Ejector, C.1820, 8 1/2 In.	150.00
Candlestick, Silver Plated, 9 3/4 In.	450.00
Chalice, American, 5 1/4 In., Pair	300.00
Chalice, Communion, 6 1/8 In., Pair	350.00
Chamberstick, Scalloped & Beaded Edge, 5 1/4 In.	95.00
Chamberstick, Whale Oil Burner, 2 1/8 In.	175.00
Charger, Broad Flat Rim, Gray Stain, 19th Century, English, 17 In.	215.00
Charger, Compton, London, 12 1/8 In.	185.00
Charger, English, 13 1/2 In.	175.00
Charger, Gersham Jones, Providence, R.I., 13 1/2 In.	1200.00
Charger, Partial Name, Crowned Rose Mark, 16 3/4 In.	125.00
Charger, Reeded Edge, Stuart, Late 1600s, 18 In.	660.00
Charger, Rim Engraved M.S., English, Marked, 12 1/2 In.	95.00
Clock, Copper Face, Brass, Abalone Inlaid, 1900, Liberty & Co., 9 In.	995.00
Coffeepot, Engraved Design, Cast Flower Finial, H.Homan, 9 1/2 In.	95.00
Coffeepot, Lighthouse Shape, Gooseneck Spout, Scroll Handles, 15 In.	95.00
Communion Set, Reed & Barton, 15 1/2 In.Flagon, Chalice, 3 Piece	150.00
Cup, Wine Taster, Lobe & Flute Pattern, Snake Handle, French, 1870	75.00
Cup, Wine Taster, Neptune On Horseback, Shell Handle, French, 1920	45.00
Desk Set, 2 Hinged Lids, Removable Baffle, High Footed, 5 X 7 In.	95.00
Dish, Hinged Lid, Ashbil Griswold, 1 3/4 X 4 3/8 In.	220.00
Dish, Oval, English, 10 5/8 X 15 1/8 In.	175.00
Dish, Reeded Rim, Deep, Thomas Danforth II, 1770–90, 9 1/2 In.	375.00
Flagon, Boardman & Co., 9 1/4 In.	2000.00
Flagon, Communion, From Church In Minersville, Ohio, 14 In.	700.00
Flagon, Communion, Marked Sellew & Co., Cincinnati, 10 1/4 In.	250.00
Flagon, Communion, T.T. & S.Stafford, Hinged Lid, 10 1/4 In.	6000.00
Flagon, Double Acorn Thumbpiece, French, 10 1/8 In.	87.50
Flagon, Shell Thumbpiece, Crowned Rose Mark, 10 In.	175.00
Flagon, Sunburst Thumbpiece, Angle Mark, 9 3/4 In.	65.00

Flask, Whiskey, Large	75.00
Inkwell, Flat Base, Cover, 4 3/4 In.	25.00
Inkwell, Hinged Lid, English, 2 1/2 X 4 In.	55.00
Inkwell, Hinged Lid, Marked V.R., 2 1/8 X 3 3/8 In.	40.00
Jar, Glass, 3–Footed Frame, Spoon, Peter Behrens, Holland, 6 1/4 In.	450.00
Jar, Rose Petal, Shields & Diamonds On Sides, 5 1/2 In.	5.00
Ladle, Turned Wooden Handle, English, 15 1/2 In.	35.00
Lamp, Fluid, 2 Magnifying Lens, Domed Base, London, 10 3/4 In.	247.50
Lamp, Gimbal, Fluid Burner, With Homemade Lead Snuffer, 6 1/2 In.	65.00
Measure, Side Spout, Engraved R.W., Marked Pint, English, 4 7/8 In.	35.00
Measures, English, 1 5/8 To 3 3/4 In.	195.00
Mirror, Maple Leaves, Buds, Exaggerated Tendrils, 1900, 18 In.	750.00
Mirror, Zachary Taylor, Old Rough 'N Ready, 2 Circular Halves, 1848	275.00
Mold, Candle, Grained Black Paint, Green Ground, Dated 1835, 12 In.	770.00
Mold, Ice Cream, Banana Shape	33.00
Mold, Ice Cream, Basket	40.00
Mold, Ice Cream, Basket of Flowers, 2 7/8 In.	32.00
Mold, Ice Cream, Bassinet	45.00
Mold, Ice Cream, Calla Lily, 3 Sections	40.00
Mold, Ice Cream, Cannon	35.00
Mold, Ice Cream, Champagne Bottle	45.00
Mold, Ice Cream, Cottage	88.00
Mold, Ice Cream, Duck, Hinged, 3 X 2 1/2 In.	48.00
Mold, Ice Cream, Easter Lily	55.00
Mold, Ice Cream, George Washington, Marked F.C.Cassel, 5 5/8 In.	30.00
Mold, Ice Cream, Golfer In Knickers	75.00
Mold, Ice Cream, Kewpie, Dated 1913, E & Co., 6 In.	180.00
Mold, Ice Cream, Peanut, 3 1/2 X 3 1/2 In.	24.00
Mold, Ice Cream, Puss In Boots, E & Co., 657	46.00
Mold, Ice Cream, Rabbit, 11 In.	85.00
Mold, Ice Cream, Rabbit, Eppelsheimer, 4 1/2 In.	40.00
Mold, Ice Cream, Race Car	50.00
Mold, Ice Cream, Santa Claus, 4 1/2 In.	45.00
Mold, Ice Cream, Soldier Boy	65.00
Mold, Ice Cream, Strawberry	25.00
Mold, Ice Cream, Turkey, Hinged, 5 X 4 In.	65.00
Mold, Ice Cream, Walnut, 3 1/4 X 3 1/2 In.	24.00
Mold, Ice Cream, Witch On Broom	95.00
Pitcher, Mephistopheles, Kayserzinn, Signed & Numbered, 10 In.	185.00
Pitcher, Revere Style, Concord Pewter Co., 7 In.	30.00
Pitcher, Simpson C.Heald, Engraved Under Spout, 6 3/4 In.	240.00
Pitcher, Thermal, Universal, 1917, 6 1/12 In.	30.00
Plate, Ashbil Griswold, 7 7/8 In.	310.00
Plate, Boardman & Co., New York, Marked, 9 3/8 In.	300.00
Plate, Circular Flame Design, Wide Chased Rim, 12 In.	80.00
Plate, John Danforth, Connecticut, 9 In.	575.00
Plate, Marked Smith & Feltman, Albany, 10 1/4 In.	200.00
Plate, Scalloped Rim, Reeded, Zinklinging, 9 3/4 In.	195.00
Plate, Scalloped, Engraved NE.K.M., Germany, 9 1/4 In.	85.00
Plate, Stamped N.W., English, 12 1/4 In.	150.00
Plate, Thomas D.Boardman, 9 3/8 In.	300.00
Plate, William Will, Philadelphia, Marked M.S.1784, 9 1/2 In.	1175.00
Platter, English, 13 3/4 X 18 In.	300.00
Porringer Set, R.Gleason, 2, 3, 3 7/8, 4 3/8 & 5 1/8 In., 5 Piece	2000.00
Porringer, Basin Style, Handle, Thomas Danforth, Boardman, 4 In.	250.00
Porringer, Domed Base, Thomas Danforth, 4 1/2 In.	200.00
Porringer, Handles, English, 1 1/2 X 5 1/2 In.	25.00
Porringer, Heart Handle	120.00
Porringer, Molded Handles, Samuel Danforth, 3 3/4 In.	175.00
Porringer, Rhode Island Handle, S.Hamlin Jr. Mark, 4 1/4 In.	400.00
Pot, G.Richardson, Glenmore Co., No.3, 10 1/2 In.	425.00
Punch Bowl, Figure of Child On Lid, Ball & Claw Feet, Kayserzinn	575.00
Salt & Pepper, C.1880	75.00
Salt Box, Hanging, Applied Cast Head On Crest, French, 7 1/4 In.	45.00

Silent Butler, Wooden Handle 8.00
Soup Dish, Love Touch, 11 X 1 1/2 In. 300.00
Stein, Glass Bottom, Engraved Dartmouth 1955, English 25.00
Stein, Indian Bust, Full Headdress Finial, Dated 1904, 7 1/2 In. 175.00
Syringe, Turned Wooden Plunger, 15 In. 35.00
Tankard, Cylindrical, Flared Lip, Recurved Handle, English, 1/2 Pt. 60.00
Tankard, Hallmark, C.1780, 1 Qt. 150.00
Teakettle, Gooseneck Spout, Swivel Handle, Rose Mark, 7 In. 85.00
Teapot, Melon Ribbed, James Dixon & Sons, Footed, 7 1/8 In. 95.00
Teapot, Paw Feet, Squat Form, Dixon & Smith, 6 1/2 In. 110.00
Teapot, Putnam, 11 In. 358.00
Teapot, Ribbed, Ivory Wafers On Handle, Scotland, 8 1/4 In. 150.00
Teapot, Wooden Handle & Finial, Dutch, 8 3/4 In. 85.00
Teapot, Wooden Handle, Finial, Marked James Dixon & Sons, 10 3/4 In. 85.00
Teaspoon, Cast Handle, Charles Parker & Co., 5 7/8 In., Pair 110.00
Tray, Floral, Open Handles, Orivit, 12 In. 38.50
Tray, Panama Pacific Expo, '15, 3 1/2 X 9 In. 15.00
Tumbler, Marked A.G., Ashbil Griswold, 3 In. 25.00
Tureen, Cover, Underplate, Kayserzinn 375.00

Phoenix Bird, or Flying Phoenix, is the name given to a blue–and–white kitchenware popular between 1900 and World War II. A variant is known as Flying Turkey. Most of this dinnerware was made in Japan for sale in the dime stores in America. It is still being made.

PHOENIX BIRD, Creamer, 2 3/4 In. 18.00
Eggcup, Double 15.00
Plate, 6 In. ....6.50 To 12.00
Plate, 7 1/4 In. 7.50
Plate, 8 3/8 In. 12.50
Platter, 12 1/2 X 8 1/2 In. 35.00
Platter, Oval, 12 In. 20.00
Platter, Oval, 14 In. 35.00
Salt & Pepper 20.00
Sugar & Creamer ....40.00 To 45.00
Teapot 50.00
Teapot, 2 3/4 X 7 In. 60.00
Teapot, 7 X 7 In. 55.00

Phoenix Glass Company was founded in 1880 in Pennsylvania. The firm made commercial products such as lampshades, bottles, and glassware. Collectors today are interested in the sculptured glassware made by the company from the 1930s until the mid–1950s. The company is still working.

PHOENIX, Basket, Pink & Amethyst Dogwoods, 4 1/2 In. 55.00
Bowl, Green Lovebirds, Boat Shape, 15 In. ....265.00 To 275.00
Compote, Pedestal Foot, Green, Orchids, 4 1/2 In. 68.00

When restoring antiques or houses, take color pictures before and after for records of colors used, exact placement of decorative details, and insurance claims.

Lamp, Blue Foxgloves & Leaves, White Ground, No Shade, 23 In. 105.00
Lamp, Blue Peonies Inserts, 13 In. 95.00
Lamp, White Glass, Iron Base 75.00
Plate, Bird of Paradise In Center, Purple, Florals, 8 1/4 In. 85.00
Rose Bowl, Sculptured White Stars, Flowers, 7 In. 65.00
Vase, 7 Dancing Nudes, Pan Playing Pipes, 12 In. 500.00
Vase, Birds & Flowers, Amber, 6 1/2 In. 40.00
Vase, Blue Grasshopper, Brown Reeds, Cream Ground, 7 1/2 In. 125.00
Vase, Dancing Nudes With Pan, Frosted, 11 1/4 In. 350.00
Vase, Dogwoods On White, Sculptured Coral & Green, 11 In. 275.00
Vase, Flying Geese, Blue Ground, White Figures, Pillow Shape 165.00
Vase, Gilded Roses On White, 9 1/2 In. 125.00
Vase, Gold Peonies, White Ground, 6 In. 55.00
Vase, Goldfish Swimming, 8 3/4 In. 325.00
Vase, Iridescent White Flowers, 3 White Ribs, Label, 7 1/2 In. 155.00
Vase, Madonna, Sculptured, White, Ribbed Sides, Deep Blue, 10 1/4 In. 250.00
Vase, Owl, Caramel, 6 In. 87.00
Vase, Pillow, Flying Geese, Yellow Iridescent 230.00
Vase, Pillow, Lovebirds On Branches, Coral Flowers, 6 1/2 In. 85.00
Vase, Pink Flying Geese, White Ground, Label, 9 1/2 X 12 In. 210.00
Vase, Sculptured Leafy Form On White, Label, 6 In. 75.00
Vase, Sculptured White Pinecones, Green, Label, 5 In. 55.00
Vase, White Fern Fronds On Brown Ground, Label, 7 In. 75.00
Vase, Yellow Peonies, Leaves, White Ground, 12 In. 95.00
Vase, Zodiac, 4 Different Cameo Medallions, 10 In. 700.00

The phonograph, invented by Thomas Edison in the 1880s, has been made by many firms. This section also includes other items associated with the phonograph. Records are listed in their own section.

PHONOGRAPH, Brunswick, Upright, Lower Record Case, Oak 75.00
Cixreol VI, Table Model, Oak 150.00
Columbia, Regent Model, Desk 350.00
Columbia, Type A 275.00
Doll, Dancer, Siam Soo 575.00
Edison, Amberola X, Recorder Attachment, Box, 1913 .... 525.00
Edison, Concert, Model D, 1899 .... 1750.00
Edison, Cylinder, 90 Cylinder Records 1000.00
Edison, Cylinder, Amberola Model 50 .... 400.00
Edison, Cylinder, Mahogany Horn, 20 Records, Table Model 2500.00
Edison, Diamond Disc 350.00
Edison, Diamond Disc, Model 250, Shipping Crate 400.00
Edison, Fireside 375.00
Edison, Gem, Cylinder, Oak Case 450.00
Edison, Gem, Key Wind, Brass Horn, Oak 550.00
Edison, Gem, Morning Glory Horn 75.00
Edison, Home Model, No.H54389, Cylinder Type, Horn, Oak Case 200.00
Edison, No.A–80, Table Model, Diamond Disc 225.00
Edison, Recording, Class M 6500.00
Edison, Table Model, Cylinder Type, Oak Case 100.00
Edison, Table Model, No.715759D, Horn, Oak Case 275.00
Gramophone, Klingsor, 11 In.Table, Horn, 1910, 35 X 17 X 12 In. 550.00
Gramophone, Stylus Arm, Metal Horn, Speed Regular, Wood, 1900s 220.00
Harp, Brass 475.00
Home, Long Box 400.00
Jukebox, AMI, D–40 .... 600.00
Jukebox, AMI, No.B, Plays 45s 900.00
Jukebox, Bing Crosby Jr. 650.00
Jukebox, Coinola, Model LX, Xylophone 6800.00
Jukebox, Electramuse, Restored, 1929 .... 4500.00
Jukebox, Gabel's Jr., 12 Plays, 1930s 750.00
Jukebox, Mills, Throne of Music 750.00

Jukebox, Mills, Violano Virtuoso, Mahogany Case 9750.00
Jukebox, Rockola, 1948 .... 4100.00
Jukebox, Rockola, Counter Top Model, 1940 .... 2000.00
Jukebox, Rockola, Fireball 120, Model 1436 .... 490.00
Jukebox, Rockola, Lights Up 1500.00
Jukebox, Seeburg, Audiophone, 1928 .... 1750.00
Jukebox, Seeburg, Audiophone, 8 Selections, 1920s 2800.00
Jukebox, Seeburg, Model E, With Flute Pipes 6200.00
Jukebox, Seeburg, Model E, With Xylophone 5800.00
Jukebox, Wall Box, Mills, Violano 250.00
Jukebox, Wurlitzer, Model 24 .... 1500.00 To 1800.00
Jukebox, Wurlitzer, Model 53, 1800 Series 600.00
Jukebox, Wurlitzer, Model 600 .... 2000.00
Jukebox, Wurlitzer, Model 800 .... 2950.00 To 3500.00
Jukebox, Wurlitzer, Model 1015, 24 Selections, C.1946, 60 In. 9350.00
Jukebox, Wurlitzer, Model 1015, 45 RPM 3995.00
Jukebox, Wurlitzer, Model 1015, One More Time, New 3800.00
Jukebox, Wurlitzer, Model 1100 .... 4500.00
Jukebox, Wurlitzer, Model 2100, 200 Selections 350.00
Jukebox, Wurlitzer, Model 4000 .... 350.00
Klingsor, Stained Glass Doors 1700.00
Knabe, Upright, Ampico, Baltimore 1600.00
Linephone, Oak, Upright, 1910 .... 195.00
Lioret, Spring Driven, Brass & Celluloid Cylinders, 1900 .... 4500.00
Lundstrom Converto, Little Falls, New York, Oak 155.00
Lyra, Cylinder Records, Instructions, 12 In.Top of Horn 302.00
Radio, Atwater Kent, Tapestry Front, 1920s 200.00
Stella, Table Model, Drawer For Disks, Mahogany, 17 1/4 In. 4200.00
Victor II, Windup, Morning Glory Horn 575.00
Victor Talking Machine, Floor Model 75.00
Victor VI 155.00
Victor, Mahogany Horn 875.00
Victrola, 3rd Style, VTLA 2500.00
Victrola, Edison, Model D–2, 3 Reproducers, 150 Records 950.00
Victrola, Model M, Eldrige R.Johnson 1150.00
Victrola, Model VV–X–A, Oak 275.00
Wax Cylinder, Rosenthal, Original Box, 1898 .... 10.00
Zonophone, Nickel Plated Horn 385.00

 The first photograph was a view from a window in France taken in 1826. The commercially successful photograph started with the daguerreotype introduced in 1839. Today all sorts of photographs and photographic equipment are collected. Albums were popular in Victorian times. Cartes de visite were cardboard–mounted photographs popular in the years after the Civil War. Stereo views are listed under Stereo Card.

PHOTOGRAPHY, Album, Carpet Velvet, Fancy Metal, Latch & Stand 60.00
Album, Clasp On Cover, 12 Photos, C.1884, 4 1/2 X 6 In. 60.00
Albumen, 100 Firemen, Pumper Behind, Anderson, 1886, 20 X 34 In. 100.00
Albumen, Abraham & Tad, Oval Frame, 7 1/2 X 5 1/4 In. 280.00
Albumen, Mt.Harvard, Valley of Arkansas, W.Jackson, 17 X 22 In. 350.00
Albumen, Steamship Zenobia, Civil War, 12 3/4 X 19 In. 280.00
Ambrotype, 2 Union Officers, Civil War, 4 X 5 1/2 In. 225.00
Ambrotype, 5 Men & Union Soldier, Framed, 3 1/4 X 4 1/4 In. 125.00
Ambrotype, Blacksmith, Tools & Anvil, 1/4 Plate 170.00
Ambrotype, Hunter, Wide Brim Hat, Shotgun, 1850s, 2 1/2 X 3 In. 74.50
Ambrotype, Large House With Widow's Walk, 1/4 Plate 70.00
Ambrotype, Union Artilleryman, Bouquet, Civil War, 2 1/2 In. 195.00
Board, Trimming, Kodak, No.1 .... 10.00
Cabinet Card, 2 Men Holding Shotguns, Studio Backdrop, C.1880 .... 10.00
Cabinet Card, Cowboy Wearing Fringe, Colt Revolvers, Rifle 150.00
Cabinet Card, Dead Man In Casket, Albumen, 4 X 5 1/2 In. 25.00
Cabinet Card, Funeral Mourning Wreath, Engraved At Rest 10.00
Cabinet Card, Hudson River Steamboat, Albany, New York, 2 Pc. 30.00

Proper storage of old photographs is important because they can be damaged by acidic paper, glue on envelope seams, ink from ball-point pens, chemicals in glassine, moisture that can collect in plastic sleeves, and so forth.

Cabinet Card, Laguna Pueblo, Indians Dancing, Cal Brown & Co.	100.00
Cabinet Card, Pitchfork Ben Tillman, South Carolina Governor	20.00
Cabinet Card, Sarah Bernhardt, Sarony Photo, N.Y., Dated 1887	280.00
Cabinet Card, Sightseeing Washington, Wade's Hotel, 8 X 10 In.	20.00
Cabinet Card, Train Wreck	10.00
Camera, Agfa, Folding, Case	20.00
Camera, Ansco Viking, Case	23.00
Camera, Ansco, Extra Lens, Case, C.1926	100.00
Camera, Ansco, With Plates & Box of Film, C.1926	100.00
Camera, Anscoflex II, Case	17.50
Camera, Brownie, 2A, Model C, Wooden Case	25.00
Camera, Brownie, Brown On Box	95.00
Camera, Conley Safety, Wide Angle Lens	50.00
Camera, Eastman View No.2-D, Tripod, Wollenaak Lens	275.00
Camera, Eho, Germany, 2 1/2 X 2 1/4 In.	45.00
Camera, Goerz, 1913	15.00
Camera, Kodak Bantam, Box, Instructions, 1939	30.00
Camera, Kodak Jr., Autographic, No.2C	20.00
Camera, Kodak Pony, No.828	17.00
Camera, Kodak, Autographic, 1930	20.00
Camera, Kodak, Duraflex, Box	15.00
Camera, Kodak, Folding, 1930	15.00
Camera, Kodak, Folding, Vest Pocket, Early 1900s	65.00
Camera, Kodak, Girl Scout, Case, Instruction Book, 1930	115.00
Camera, Kodak, Model 1-A, Pigskin Color, Folding, C.1924	25.00
Camera, Kodak, Pocket Autographic, Cardboard Case, Patent 1910	25.00
Camera, Kodak, Rainbow Hawkeye, Folding, No.2A, Green, Case	55.00
Camera, Minolta, 16, Midget	22.50
Camera, Norton, 1934 Century of Progress Decal	195.00
Camera, Prontor, 125, Germany	10.00
Camera, Rolleicord II, Case	75.00
Camera, Tisdell & Whittelsey, Detective	750.00
Camera, Tower, 35 Mm, Japan	25.00
Carte De Visite, Abraham Lincoln	50.00
Carte De Visite, Andrew Johnson	12.50
Carte De Visite, Charles Sumner	14.00
Carte De Visite, Charleston Ruins, Beckett	150.00
Carte De Visite, Civil War Soldier, Amputated Arm	145.00
Carte De Visite, Florence Nightingale	28.00
Carte De Visite, Fort Sumter, Beckett	150.00
Carte De Visite, Haddon Spurgeon	35.00
Carte De Visite, Photographer Standing By Studio Camera	350.00
Carte De Visite, Rancher, Jackson, Waco, Texas	22.50
Carte De Visite, Sir Rowland Hill	30.00
Carte De Visite, Washington	12.50
Carte De Visite, Wild Bill Hickok, Ames Capitol Gallery	3850.00
Daguerreotype, Butcher Holding Cleaver Knife, 1/6 Plate	400.00
Daguerreotype, Captain Cole, By Wm.Wilgus, 1839, 1/4 Plate	2800.00
Daguerreotype, Charles Calistis, Abolitionist, 1/2 Plate	4950.00
Daguerreotype, Fire Brigade Pumper, 35 Men, 1/2 Plate	2200.00
Daguerreotype, Fireman, Washington No.5, 1/6 Plate	350.00
Daguerreotype, Gold Mining Scene, 1/4 Plate	1300.00

Daguerreotype, Jenny Lind, Swedish Nightingale, 1/2 Plate 1900.00
Daguerreotype, Old Woman, Lace Bonnet & Collar, 1/4 Plate 190.00
Daguerreotype, Side View of Church, 1/6 Plate 280.00
Glass Slide, Elmo Lincoln, Movie, Adventures of Tarzan 50.00
Glass Slide, Magic Lantern, World War I, 3 X 4 In., 6 Piece 15.00
Glass Slide, Rudolf Valentino, Movie, The Shiek 30.00
Lenseometer 75.00
Magic Lantern, 50 Slides, Hand Crank, Box 250.00
Magic Lantern, Astronomy Glass Slides, Case 100.00
Magic Lantern, Edison, 17 In. 125.00
Magic Lantern, German Cinematograph, 17 Slides, 4 Rolls 175.00
Magic Lantern, Glass Slides, Germany, 1866 .... 195.00 To 215.00
Magic Lantern, Glass Slides, Keystone, Box, Set of 25 .... 45.00
Magic Lantern, School Projector, Delineascope 65.00
Magic Lantern, Standard E.P., Screen & 21 Slides 195.00
Microprojector, Spencer, C.1924 .... 500.00
Photograph, Abraham Lincoln, Mathew Brady, 10 1/4 X 8 In. 1100.00
Photograph, Babe Ruth, Get Well Quick, Signed Babe Ruth 860.00
Photograph, Black Child, Oval Metal Frame, 19th Century, 19 In. 225.00
Photograph, Capitol Building, Framed, Feb.1906, 12 1/2 X 14 In. 30.00
Photograph, Chinese Man Holding Fish Catch, 7 X 5 In. 8.00
Photograph, Cooper Post Office, Attica, Ohio, 5 X 7 In. 6.50
Photograph, Edwin Booth, Framed, Signed, Dated 1892, 13 X 10 In. 750.00
Photograph, Firemen, Hose Carts, Uniform, 1900s, 10 X 12 In. 15.00
Photograph, Man Next To Racing Bike, Studio View, 1900 .... 12.50
Photograph, Niagara Falls, Panoramic View, 1913, 10 X 58 In. 90.00
Photograph, Nurse, Full View, Black & White, 1920, 4 X 5 1/2 In. 6.00
Photograph, Reading Railroad, Engine, William Rittase, 1928–29 .... 1350.00
Photograph, Saloon, Men, Ornate Bar, Matted, 1920, 5 X 8 In. 25.00
Photograph, Sampson Truck, Moving House, C.1915, Large 20.00
Photograph, Samuel Clemens, Signed Mark Twain, 3 1/4 X 5 In. 325.00
Photograph, Stone Cutters, Quarry, Matted, 1900, 8 X 10 In. 15.00
Photograph, Tom Thumb, Lady At His Side, 10 1/2 X 15 In. 450.00
Photograph, Ulysses S.Grant, Signed, Framed, 3 3/4 X 2 1/2 In. 1500.00
Photograph, Winston S.Churchill, Signed, Framed, 6 X 3 3/4 In. 2000.00
Platinum, Geronimo, F.A.Rinehart, Omaha, Copy.1898, 9 X 7 In. 400.00
Projector, Air–O–Quip, Slide 35.00
Projector, Ansco, Memoscope, Electric 25.00
Projector, Argus 300, Slide 35.00
Projector, Bell & Howell, Camera, Model 253, 8mm, 2 Piece 45.00
Projector, Illustravox, Jr., Filmstrip, Turntable, C.1928 .... 125.00
Projector, Keystone Moviegraph, No.154 .... 50.00
Projector, Keystone, 16mm, C.1930 .... 45.00
Projector, Keystone, 1931 .... 28.00
Projector, Kinetescope 385.00
Projector, Magic Lantern, Dual Commercial, 1870 .... 225.00
Salt Print, 2 Firemen, Holding Fire Horns, 1850s, 6 X 7 1/2 In. 150.00
Scale, Chemical, Kodak 55.00
Scale, Kodak, Avoirdupois 45.00
Timer, Darkroom, Kodak, Cast Iron 35.00
Tintype, 3 Young Men, Visored Hats, 1870s, 2 1/2 X 3 1/2 In. 24.50
Tintype, Annie Oakley, 2 X 3 In. 125.00
Tintype, Black Civil War Veteran, G.A.R.Medal, 2 1/2 In. 59.50
Tintype, Charles Sumner, Black & White, Frame, 1 1/5 X 5 In. 28.00
Tintype, Civil War Prostitutes, Whiskey Bottle, 2 In. 79.50
Tintype, Civil War Soldier, Case, 3 1/4 X 4 1/4 In. 65.00
Tintype, Civil War Soldier, Frock Coat, Tinted, Framed, 2 In. 32.50
Tintype, Civil War Soldier, Gun In Belt, 2 1/2 X 3 1/2 In. 75.00
Tintype, Civil War Soldier, On Trunk, Buckle, 3 1/4 X 4 1/4 In. 220.00
Tintype, Civil War Soldier, Shell Jacket, Tinted, 2 1/2 In. 34.50
Tintype, Civil War Soldiers, Playing Cards, 6 1/2 X 8 1/2 In. 195.00
Tintype, Civil War, Musician 15.00
Tintype, Fireman, 2 X 3 In. 68.00
Tintype, Fireman, Holding Presentation Fire Trumper, Tinted 75.00

Tintype, Gold Miners, Western Clothes, 1870s, Framed, 4 X 5 In.	395.00
Tintype, Horse & Buggy, Family & Small Child, 8 1/2 X 11 In.	30.00
Tintype, Man Holding Rifle, Gold Foil Frame, 4 X 5 1/2 In.	40.00
Tintype, Man, In Open Auto, Derby Hat, 1905, 2 1/2 X 3 1/2 In.	17.50
Tintype, Officer, Standing, Hard Hat, Civil War, 4 X 2 In.	75.00
Tintype, Photographer, Standing Next To Camera On Tripod	85.00
Tintype, Pretty Lady, Victorian, Oval, 8 X 6 In.	15.00
Tintype, Union Lieutenant, Upper Body, Frock Coat, 2 1/2 In.	27.50
Tintype, Union Soldier Holding Revolver Across Chest	75.00
Tintype, Woman Wearing Brooch, 6 1/2 X 8 1/2 In.	14.50
Tintype, Woman's Image, Decorative Mound, 2 1/2 X 4 In.	6.00
Tintype, Woman, Full Plate	15.00
Tintype, Young Girl, Doll & Letter	55.00

About 1880, the well-decorated home had a shawl on the piano. Bisque piano babies were designed to help hold the shawl in place. They range in size from 6 to 18 inches. Most of the figures were made in Germany. Reproductions are being made. Other piano babies are listed under manufacturers' names.

PIANO BABY, Blue Trimmed Gown, Bonnet, Heubach	65.00
Crawling, 3 1/2 X 4 1/2 In.	40.00
Crawling, 5 In.	65.00
Crawling, Gown Frilled, Blue Back Bow, Heubach, 5 In.	200.00
Crawling, Kicking Legs, White Gown, Heubach, 5 1/2 X 8 In.	415.00
Crying Face, Holding Plate, Germany, 4 3/4 In.	70.00
Fingers Extended, Bisque, 7 1/2 In.	175.00
Holding Bunny Rabbit, White Gown, Pink Trim, Hat, 6 1/4 In.	195.00
Holding Foot, 3 In.	38.00
In Shoe, Heubach, Signed	185.00
Lying On Back, 5 1/4 In.	65.00
Lying On Back, Arms & Legs Raised, Nightgown, Bonnet, 9 1/2 In.	185.00
Lying On Back, Heubach, 4 In.	95.00
Lying On Back, Signed, Heubach, 5 1/2 In.	125.00
On Left Hip, Leaning On Elbow, Both Arms Up, Marked 370, 4 In.	118.00
Papa's Darling, 5 1/2 In.	38.00
Sitting Toddler, Huge Bonnet, Pulling Off Sock, Heubach	350.00
Sitting Up, Legs Crossed, Arms Raised, 9 In.	75.00
Sitting, 4 1/2 In.	40.00
Sitting, Arms Raised, 4 1/2 In.	65.00
Sitting, Bonnet & Gown, 3 X 5 In.	85.00
Sitting, Heubach, 6 1/2 In.	295.00
Surprised Mouth, Intaglio Eyes, Signed, Heubach, 5 In.	275.00

Pickard China Company was started in 1898 by Wilder Pickard. Hand-painted designs were used on china purchased from other sources. In the 1930s, the company began to make its own china wares. The company now makes many types of porcelains including a successful line of limited edition collector plates.

PICKARD, Basket, Mauve With Gold Tracery Exterior, Gold Handle & Interior	65.00
Berry Bowl, Blackberry Fruit & Leaf Design, Signed, 7 In.	45.00
Bowl, Deserted Garden, Pedestal, Signed Vokral, 8 In.	125.00
Bowl, Nut, Signed Vokral, 8 X 6 1/2 In.	130.00
Cake Plate, Hanging Basket of Flowers, Open, Signed	45.00
Candlestick, Gold Embossed, Signed, 8 1/2 In., Pair	210.00
Chamberstick, Floral, Gold, Iridescent, Signed Talley, 7 1/4 In.	229.00
Chop Plate, Violets & Foliage, Gold Border, 12 In.	135.00
Coffeepot, Sugar & Creamer, Podlaha	325.00
Creamer, Dutch Scene, Hand Painted, Signed	50.00
Cup & Saucer, Floral, Signed James	40.00
Cup & Saucer, Gold & Blue Bands, Flowers, Gold Handles, C.1919	30.00
Dish, Mayonnaise, Attached Underplate, Daylilies, Gold Border	165.00
Hatpin Holder, Iris, Green Leaves, Bud, Gold Trim	75.00
Mug, Berry Design, Gold Handle & Rim, 5 1/2 In.	150.00
Pitcher, Maple Leaf, Stylized Floral, Gold, 10 Cup	265.00

Pitcher, Moonlight Garden Scene, Marked, Matte Finish 495.00
Pitcher, Scenic, Challinor, 8 In. 535.00
Plate, Autumn Scenic, Open Handles, Signed, 10 1/2 In. 195.00
Plate, Blue, Moon Over Lake, 8 1/2 In. 150.00
Plate, Card, Heart Shape, Flowers, Gold, 5 X 4 In. 55.00
Plate, Gazebo, Trees & Moon, Signed, Square, 5 1/2 In. 150.00
Plate, Gold & Turquoise Art Nouveau Design, 8 3/8 In. 50.00
Plate, Hand Painted Center Scene, 11 In. 395.00
Plate, Poppies, Gold Tracery & Border, Challinor, 8 1/2 In. 159.00
Plate, Scenic, Matte Finish, Signed, 8 3/4 In. 155.00
Plate, Sesquicentennial, 1968, Made For Marshall Fields 55.00
Plate, Violets, Hand Painted, Gold, Lemke, 8 1/2 In. 62.50
Punch Bowl, 14 In. 665.00
Salt & Pepper, Gold Band With Clusters of Flowers, C.1910 .... 45.00
Sugar & Creamer, Dutch Girl, Cover 95.00
Sugar & Creamer, Violets 75.00
Tea Set, Art Deco, 3 Piece 250.00
Tea Set, Etched Gold & Blue, Cover, 1919 .... 195.00
Tea Set, Gold, Art Deco Engraved, 3 Piece 120.00
Teapot, Aura Argenta Linear, Signed Hessler, 5 In. 100.00
Tray, Gold Trim, Double Circle Mark, 11 X 8 In. 65.00
Vase, Art Nouveau, Red Poinsettias, Marked, 1905–10, 17 1/2 In. 640.00
Vase, Deserted Garden Scene, Gold Ground, Marked, 6 1/2 In. 195.00
Vase, Etched Floral, Overall Gold, Flared Top, 7 In. 75.00
Vase, Etched Gold, Green Interior, Scalloped, 1925, 9 1/2 In. 75.00
Vase, Purple Grapes, Gold & Black, Marked, 8 In. 135.00
Vase, Roses, Shaded Green Ground, Gold Trim, 7 3/4 In. 245.00
Vase, Shaded Mums On Turquoise Ground, Gold Rim, 1905, 8 1/2 In. 150.00

PICTURE FRAME, see Furniture, Frame

Silhouettes and small decorative pictures are listed here. Some other types of pictures are listed under Print or Painting.

PICTURE, Embroidered, Biblical Scene, George III, C.1780, 17 X 16 In., Pair 1760.00
Embroidered, Boy, Seated, Under Tree, Silk, Framed, Oval, 9 X 10 In. 121.00
Embroidered, Maiden, With Trumpet, Silk, Sally Fairchild, 1800, 8 In. 715.00
Embroidered, Stumpwork, Abraham, Charles II, 1660, 11 X 10 X 7 In. 2850.00
Embroidered, Woman, Seated, Landscape, Silk, Framed, 1807, 3 X 8 In. 2200.00
Hair Wreath, Ornate, In Shadow Box 125.00
Needlepoint, Fruit, On Hillside, Embroidered, Silk, 1821, 9 X 11 In. 6325.00
Needlework, 2 Ladies, Parasol, Embroidered, Framed, 6 X 7 1/2 In. 2860.00
Needlework, Embroidered, Maidens, Garden, Silk, 28 1/4 X 24 1/4 In. 880.00
Needlework, Painted Features, Floral, Drape Needlework, 25 X 27 In. 3000.00
Petit Point, Silk, Man, Woman, Animals, English, 17th Century, 19 In. 2200.00
Silhouette, Cat, Free Cut, Signed T.G.Brooks, C.1840, 8 X 6 1/2 In. 225.00
Silhouette, Children On Ink Wash Ground, 9 3/4 X 15 1/4 In. 180.00
Silhouette, Deverell Family, 1783, 4 X 19 In., Set of 6 ....*Illus* 200.00
Silhouette, Family, Full Length, 7 People, Dog, Cat, 14 X 30 In. 1600.00
Silhouette, Gentleman, Glass Eyes, E.Fecit, 1830, Framed, 10 X 14 In. 550.00
Silhouette, Gentleman, Profile, Wig & Bow Tie, Ruffled Jabot, 5 In. 125.00
Silhouette, Girl With Umbrella & Dog 35.00
Silhouette, Girl, Holding Doll, Dog, Sarah Ann Emerson, Age 10, 1852 .... 225.00
Silhouette, Hollow Cut, Sewall P.Barnes, 1846, Framed, 4 1/8 X 5 In. 115.00
Silhouette, Lady, Piled Ribboned Hair, Signed J.Bruce, 1819, London 200.00
Silhouette, Man, Hollow Cut, Black Cloth Back, Framed, 5 X 6 In. 50.00
Silhouette, Memorial, Eagle, Framed, H.P.H., 1833, 19 X 15 In. 500.00
Silhouette, Portly Gentleman, Ink Wash Ground, Framed, 10 X 13 In. 135.00
Silhouette, Robert Burns, Profile, C.1840, 18 1/2 X 20 In. 350.00
Silhouette, Young Man In Top Hat, Walnut Frame, 6 X 7 In. 65.00
Silhouette, Young Man, Gilded Detail, Rosewood Frame, 5 7/8 X 7 In. 150.00
Silhouette, Young Man, Profile, Cut–Away Coat, Tall Hat, 10 1/4 In. 200.00
Theorem, Bowl of Melons, Plums, Velvet, Frame, 9 3/4 X 13 1/2 In. 1400.00
Theorem, Fruit Filled Compote, Linen, 19th Century, 7 X 9 In. 250.00
Theorem, Rose Floral Wreath, Gilt Framed, 1835, 9 X 9 In. 150.00
Tinsel, Different Colored Rose–Like Flowers, Bowl, 11 X 14 In. 29.00

Picture, Silhouette, Deverell Family, 1783,
4 X 19 In., Set of 6

Picture, Silhouette,
New Orleans Dandy,
A. Edouart, 10¾ X 6⅜ In.

Tinsel, Footed Bowl of Flowers, Framed, 10 X 13 1/2 In. 105.00

The Pigeon Forge Pottery was started in Pigeon Forge, Tennessee, in 1946. Red clay found near the pottery was used to make the pieces. Molded or thrown pottery with matte glaze and slip decoration was made. The pottery is still working.

PIGEON FORGE, Coaster, Gray & Green, Box 12.50
Figurine, Owl 14.00
Sugar & Creamer, Aqua 12.00

The Pilkington Tile and Pottery Company was established in 1892 in England. The company made small pottery wares like buttons and hatpin heads but soon started decorating vases purchased from other potteries. By 1903, the company had discovered an opalescent glaze that became popular on the Lancastrian pottery line. The manufacture of pottery ended in 1937 but decorating continued until 1948.

PILKINGTON, Vase, Iridescent, Artist Charles Cudall, 1910, 7 1/2 In. 225.00

The pincushion doll is not really a doll and often was not even a pincushion. The top half of the doll was made of porcelain. The edge of the half-doll was made with several small holes for thread, and the doll was stitched to a fabric body with a voluminous skirt. The finished figure was used to cover a hot pot of tea, a powder box, a pincushion, a whiskbroom, or a lamp. They were made in sizes from less than an inch to over 9 inches high. Most date from the early 1900s to the 1950s.

PINCUSHION DOLL, Arms On Hips, Brown Hair, Yellow Bodice, Germany, 3 In. 32.00
Arms Open Akimbo, Satin & Lace Cushion, 4 1/2 In. 25.00
Baby Head, Smiling, Curl On Forehead, Blond, Germany 55.00
Bathing Beauty, Nude, Blond Hair, Hose & Shoes, 2 1/4 In. 85.00
Bisque, Goebel, 3 In. 95.00

Black Girl, Print Fabric	32.50
Blond Hair, Hands Upraised, Right Over Left, 2 5/8 In.	40.00
Blond Sausage Rolls, White Gown, Germany, 3 In.	37.00
Blue Bodice, Blond, Beaded Tiara, Arms At Body, 4 5/8 In.	50.00
Blue Bodice, Painted Pink Neck Tassel, Germany, 3 In.	25.00
Braids Coiled Over Ears, 5 In.	230.00
Child, Both Arms Away, Curled Hair Over Ear, Germany	200.00
Composition Head, Satin Body, 9 In.	10.00
Coquette, Jointed Arms, Intaglio Eyes, Headband, Heubach	150.00
Court Lady, Hair Ornament, Holding Letter, 3 1/2 In.	68.00
Court Lady, On Cushion, Attached Legs, 2 5/8 In.	68.00
Dutch Girl, Blue	35.00
Dutch Hat, Arms Away, Germany, 2 3/4 In.	85.00
Dutch Maid, Lace Dress	65.00
Fan–Tan Hat, Plume, 3 In.	65.00
Flapper Legs, 2 1/4 In.	25.00
Flapper, 4 In.	75.00
Flapper, Dangly Earrings, Hands At Side of Head, 3 In.	68.00
Flapper, Hands On Head, Painted Pink Headband, Germany	40.00
Flapper, Holding Fan, Russet Hat, Yellow Bodice, 2 1/2 In.	22.00
Flapper, Red Headband, Cushion, Scratching Back, 2 1/2 In.	55.00
Flapper, Rose In Hair, Flesh Glaze, 3 In.	62.00
Flapper, Senorita Type, Rose In Black Hair, 3 In.	58.00
Flowers In Hair & At Bosom, 3 3/4 In.	62.50
Gray Hair, Blue Bodice, Arms Away, 4 1/8 In.	80.00
Hair Under Cap, Holding Tray of Hot Chocolate, 5 In.	250.00
Hand Placing Rose In Hair, Other In Front, 7 In.	65.00
Holds Gilt Opera Glasses, Green Blouse, 11 In.	200.00
Lady Holding Fan, Bow In Hair, Flared Base, 2 1/4 In.	35.00
Long Gray Curls, Incised 3305, 2 5/8 In.	55.00
Marie Antoinette, White Hair, 3 1/4 In.	125.00
Mermaid, Flapper, Germany, 3 1/2 In.	95.00
Nude, Hair Away From Face, Arms Away & Folded, 4 1/2 In.	80.00
Nude, Molded Hair, Arms Away, Curled Fingers, 3 1/2 In.	100.00
Nude, Sculpted Hair, Arms Away, Holding Yellow Posy, 4 In.	100.00
Nymph, Kneeling, Holds Bouquet of Flowers, 2 Holes, 2 In.	150.00
Plumes In Gray Hair, Arms Away, 4 3/8 In.	75.00
Red Cloche Hat, Fan In Right Hand, Left On Bosom	37.00
Silver Wig, Papier–Mache, Germany	20.00
Spanish Dancer, Germany	35.00

PINK SLAG, see Slag, Pink

Pipes have been popular since tobacco was introduced to Europe by Sir Walter Raleigh. Meerschaum pipes are listed under Meerschaum.

PIPE, Ben Wade, Volcano Shaped Bowl, Rocker Bottom, Unused, 7 1/2 In.	195.00
Briar Bowl, Metal, Plastic Tip, Unused, 1950s, 3 In.	9.00
Caminetto, Apple, Business No.121, 5 1/2 In.	60.00
Carved Man's Head, Handlebar Mustache, Burl, 3 1/2 In.	45.00
Character, Man Under Barrel, Porcelain, 10 In.	110.00
Dog Face, Clay, Germany	18.00
Dunhill, Shell Briar, Dated 1955, 6 1/2 In.	195.00
Dunhill, Virgin Conquest, Cone Shaped Bowl, Bird's–Eye Grain, 6 In.	50.00
Foxes, German Stanhope, Carved	48.00
Graf Zeppelin, Porcelain, 9 In.	143.00
Knute, Egg Shaped Bowl, Partial Bent Shank & Stem, 7 In.	29.00
Opium, Silver On Bamboo, Silver Hearts & Flowers, 25 In.	165.00
Pistol Shape	45.00
Relief Floral, Porcelain, 12 In.	105.00
Sasieni, Briar, Appledore, 4–Dot, 5 1/4 In.	50.00
Sasieni, Briar, Billiard, Original Saddle Bit, 5 In.	90.00
Sasieni, Briar, Heathcote, Tapered Stem, 4–Dot, 6 In.	75.00
Sasieni, Briar, Tapered Stem, H.Simmons, 1–Dot, 5 1/2 In., C.1920	145.00
Savinelli, Straight Shank, Autograph No.4, 7 In.	79.00
Stanwell, Bent Freehand, Design Choice No.63M, 5 3/4 In.	37.00

Tamp, Ivory Handle, Serrated Brass Surface, 3 In. 60.00

Pirkenhammer is a porcelain manufactory started in 1802 by Friedrich Holke and J. G. Lilst. It was located in Bohemia, now Brezova, Czechoslovakia. The company made tablewares usually decorated with views and flowers. Lithophanes were also made. The mark of the crossed hammers is easy to remember as the Pirkenhammer symbol.

PIRKENHAMMER, Cup & Saucer, Musical Cherubs, Hand Painted, C.1850 .... 45.00
Egg Server, Gold & Silver Birds & Insects, 11 X 7 1/2 In. 85.00
Figurine, Girl, Nude, Hands Over Head, Seated 300.00

Pisgah pottery pieces that are marked "Pisgah Forest Pottery" were made in North Carolina from 1926. The pottery was started by Walter R. Stephen in 1914, and after his death in 1941, the pottery continued in operation. The most famous types of Pisgah Forest ware are the cameo type with designs made of raised glaze and the turquoise crackle glaze wares.

PISGAH FOREST, Bowl, Cameo, Pioneer Scenes All Around, 2 1/2 X 7 In. 280.00
Candlestick, Handle, Green, Pair 30.00
Creamer, Dated 1939 .... 18.00
Creamer, Turquoise Crackle, Pink Interior, Stephen, 1941 .... 32.00
Jar, Cover, Turquoise, Glaze, 1942, 4 In. 35.00
Mug, Cameo, Dancing Couple On Platform 285.00
Mug, Cameo, Dated 1951 .... 350.00
Pitcher, Green, 5 In. 55.00
Pitcher, Green, Yellow Interior, 1951, 6 1/2 In. 50.00
Plate, Rose, Green, 5 In. 45.00
Sugar & Creamer, Crackle Cover, 1941 .... 45.00
Sugar & Creamer, Maroon & Turquoise 22.00
Sugar & Creamer, Pink, 1942 .... 38.00
Urn, Experimental Crystalline, Pre–1927, 10 In. 275.00
Vase, Chinese Crackle Glaze, 7 In. 75.00
Vase, Experimental, Molded Flowers, Nancy Jones, 1940 .... 335.00
Vase, Green, Pink, 1939 Mark, 4 1/2 In. 25.00
Vase, Mottled Green, Dated 1929 .... 190.00
Vase, Thrown Green, Handle, 5 In. 22.00
Vase, Turquoise To Plum, Flared, 5 In. 35.00

Planters Nut and Chocolate Company was started in Wilkes–Barre, Pennsylvania, in 1906. The Mr. Peanut figure was adopted as a trademark in 1916. National advertising for Planters Peanuts started in 1918. The company was acquired by Standard Brands, Inc., in 1961. Some of the Mr. Peanut jars and other memorabilia have been reproduced and, of course, new items are being made.

PLANTERS PEANUTS, Ashtray, Figural, Mr.Peanut Center, Silver Finish, 1909–56 ..... 50.00
Bank, Mr.Peanut, 11 In. 20.00
Bank, Vendor, With Key 200.00
Book, Coloring, Dedicated To Children of America, 1950 .... 28.00
Book, Guide To Tennis, Mr.Peanut 5.00
Bookmark, Mr.Peanut, Greetings From World's Fair 1939 .... 25.00
Box, Jumbo Block, Cardboard, Winter–Summer, 1941, 14 In. 95.00
Bracelet, 6 Figural Charms 34.00
Display, Store, Removable Top, 11 In. 35.00
Doll, Mr.Peanut, Cloth, 19 In. 27.50
Doll, Mr.Peanut, Jointed, Wooden, 9 In. .... 150.00 To 165.00
Figure, Mr.Peanut, Cast Iron, 42 In. 2800.00
Grinder, Nut 25.00
Hat, Knit 12.50
Jar, 1940, Leap Year, Cover 100.00
Jar, Corner, Original Clasp 285.00
Jar, Counter Display, Peanut Finial, Lid, 13 1/2 In. 120.00
Jar, Embossed, 2 Gal. 50.00
Jar, Mr.Peanut Decal, Lid 45.00

Jar, Mr.Peanut, 75th Anniversary	4.00
Jar, Red & White Frosted, Box	100.00
Knife, Mr.Peanut	6.00
Letter Opener, Celluloid	25.00
Nut Dish, Divided, Red, Plastic	15.00
Nut Set, 6 In.Bowl, 4 Servers	29.00
Nut Set, Cocktail, Tin, 6 Bowls, 3 In.	15.00
Paddle & Ball Toy	24.00
Pail, Litho Comic, Tin, Bail Handle, 1 Lb.	425.00
Peanut Wagon, Mr.Peanut, Plastic, 1950s	165.00
Picks, Set of 6	10.00
Punchboard, Cocktail Peanuts, 8 X 8 In.	60.00
Salt & Pepper, Glass, Monocle, Ceramic	60.00
Salt & Pepper, Mr.Peanut, Black & Mustard, 4 In.	9.00
Scale, Penny, Large Figure of Mr.Peanut	5200.00
Spoon, Mr.Peanut	6.00 To 20.00
Spoon, Serving, Red Plastic	12.50
Stirrer, Mr.Peanut	6.00
Tin, Planters Ice Cream Topping, Chopped Nuts, Mr.Peanut	75.00
Tray	25.00
Tumbler, Mr.Peanut Circus	150.00

> Plated amberina was patented June 15, 1886, by Edward D. Libbey and made by the New England Glass Works. It is similar in color to amberina, but is characterized by a cream colored or chartreuse lining (never white) and small ridges or ribs on the outside.

PLATED AMBERINA, Punch Cup, Vertical Rib, Applied Handle	1700.00
Tumbler, 4 In.	2500.00
Vase, 4 In.	1000.00
Vase, 8 In.	2000.00

> Plique–a–jour is an enameling process. The enamel is laid between thin raised metal lines and heated. The finished piece has transparent enamel held between the thin metal wires. It is different from cloisonne because it is transparent.

PLIQUE–A–JOUR, Box, Flower Finial On Lid, Floral Design, 1 3/4 X 2 1/4 In.	730.00

> All types of political memorabilia are collected, from buttons to banners. Items related to presidential candidates are the most popular, but collectors also search for material related to state and local offices. Many reproductions have been made.

POLITICAL, Ashtray, I Like Ike, Elephant Head, Chalkware, 4 X 3 1/2 In.	28.00
Badge, T.Roosevelt, Progressive Party, New York Delegate, 1912	68.00
Badge, Truman For President, Picture, 3 In.	75.00
Bandana, Al Smith, 14 In.	55.00
Bandana, Cleveland & Stevenson, Red Flags, White Silk, 1892	100.00
Bandana, Grover Cleveland, Framed, 28 X 26 1/4 In.	225.00
Bandana, Herbert Hoover	40.00
Bandana, Teddy Roosevelt	70.00
Bank, Donkey, Figural, Humphrey, Muskie, 1968	20.00
Banner, George Washington, Horse, On Printed Fabric, 23 1/2 In.	225.00
Banner, To The Irishmen Jas.Boyle O'Reilly, 34 X 39 In.	75.00
Book, Photo, Louisville Convention, Wallace, President, 72 Pages	15.00
Book, Republican Pledge Card, 1936	9.50
Book, Wendell Willkie, One World, Autographed Presentation	12.50
Booklet, Hood's Political Points For 1888, Cleveland, Harrison	7.50
Booklet, Teddy Roosevelt, Candidacy, 1 X 1 In.	38.00
Bookmark, Figural, Bear, Teddy Roosevelt, Aluminum, 2 3/4 In.	165.00
Broadside, Valedictory of Henry Clay, Silk, 1842, 14 X 18 In.	110.00
Brooch, Gold Bug, McKinley Campaign, 1896	22.00
Bust, Abraham Lincoln, Parian, Hadley, 12 X 8 In.	650.00
Bust, Abraham Lincoln, Plaster, Boston Sculpture Co., 1923, 32 In.	350.00
Button, Abraham Lincoln Picture, Lincoln & Hamlin Words, Donut	200.00
Button, Abraham Lincoln, Photo, Gold & Onyx Star, 3/4 In.	500.00

Button, America Needs Carter, A Man of The Soil, Picture	1.00
Button, America Needs Johnson, Picture, 3 In.	7.00
Button, Bell & Everett, 2 Sided, Brass Frame	50.00
Button, C D C For J F K, California Democratic Council	25.00
Button, Cleveland & Hendricks, Raised Letters, Brass	15.00
Button, Davis, Bryan, 7/8 In.	1800.00
Button, Debs, For President, Convict No.9653, 1900–20	605.00
Button, Dewey, Bricker	25.00
Button, Dick's Listening, Nixon With Headphones, Caricature	1.75
Button, Dwight D.Eisenhower, Picture, 1 In.	5.00
Button, Elephant, Wearing Eye Glasses, Goldwater	4.00
Button, FDR, Garner, Jugate, Blue & Gold, 1 1/4 In.	1000.00
Button, Figural, Bear, Roosevelt, Tin	85.00
Button, For President, Charles Curtis, Photo Center, 1 1/4 In.	7.00
Button, Goldwater, Miller	1.25
Button, Governor Richard Celeste For President, State Outline	1.50
Button, Grant & Colfax, Jugate, Brass, Shell Frame	120.00
Button, Grant, Colfax, Jugate, Oval Picture, Ferro, Rectangular	285.00
Button, Grant, Ferro, Large, Square	200.00
Button, Haig, Full Color	2.00
Button, Hat, Lyndon B.Johnson, All The Way, Brown Yellow, 4 In.	10.00
Button, Hoover, Curtiss, Double S, St.Louis	675.00
Button, Hubert Humphrey, For Senator, Portrait	15.00
Button, Hughes, Fairbanks, Jugate, 7/8 In.	3000.00
Button, Humphrey In '68, Picture, 2 1/8 In.	30.00
Button, I Am No Crook, I Will Not Resign, Caricature of Nixon	2.50
Button, I'm A Democrat For Goldwater	2.50
Button, I'm A Truman Democrat, Blue Tone, 1 1/2 In.	125.00
Button, I'm For Willkie, Joe Louis Picture, 1 In.	500.00
Button, I'm Wit Choo Ike	5.00
Button, Impeach Nixon!	2.50
Button, Irish For President Nixon, 2 1/2 In.	3.00
Button, Jimmy Carter For President In '76, Picture	1.00
Button, Jobs, Not Relief With Willkie	5.00
Button, John F.Kennedy, Man For The 60s, Flasher, Portrait	15.00
Button, Kefauver For President, Celluloid, 1 In.	6.00
Button, Kennedy & Johnson	5.00
Button, Land On Washington	800.00
Button, Landon Knox Out Roosevelt, Sunflower ....*Illus*	1361.00
Button, Landon, GOP, Knox, Elephant Picture	6.50
Button, McCarthy, Remember November	8.00
Button, McKinley, Carnation	25.00
Button, McKinley, Dinner Pail	35.00
Button, McKinley, Roosevelt & VanZant, Trigate	30.00
Button, McKinley, Tanner, Jugate	30.00
Button, Nix On Nixon	3.00
Button, President Nixon, Now More Than Ever	3.00
Button, Progressive Party, LaFollette & Wheeler, Bronze, 1924	50.00

Political, Button, Landon Knox Out
Roosevelt, Sunflower

Condition, size, and small details determine the value of political buttons. To be sure the description is accurate for buying, selling, or insurance, just put the buttons on the glass top of a photocopy machine. Get copies of both the front and the back.

Button, Ribbon, Bull Moose Progressive Party, 1912, 5/8 In. 26.00
Button, Robert F.Kennedy, President, Picture .... 2.00 To 3.00
Button, Rockland, McGovern, 10 Dollar Club 2.00
Button, Ron Paul, Libertarian For President 1.50
Button, Roosevelt, Wallace, 1 In. 300.00
Button, Stevenson For President, Center Picture, Date 1960 .... 4.00
Button, Taft Picture In Wishbone, 1 1/4 In. 95.00
Button, Taft, Well I Should, Cartoon 285.00
Button, Teddy Roosevelt, Charles Fairbanks, Jugate, Photo, 7/8 In. 16.50
Button, Teddy Roosevelt, Photo Center, 1 1/4 In. 11.75
Button, Truman, Civil Rights, 2 In. 135.00
Button, Ulysses S.Grant & Schuyler Colfax, Jugate, 7/8 In. 125.00
Button, Uncle Sam Hanging Hitler, Animated 20.00
Button, Vote Carter, Remember Watergate 1.50
Button, Warren G.Harding, Miniature 37.50
Button, Washington, Roosevelt, Party 9.00
Button, Westchester For Willkie & McNary, 3 1/2 In. 110.00
Button, William Harding, Portrait 12.00
Button, Wilson, Picture, 2 1/4 In. 180.00
Button, Winning Team, Wallace, Le May, Pictures 2.00
Button, Woodrow Wilson, Portrait 12.00
Cane, Bryan Head, Eagles & Shield, Free Coinage, Prosperity 110.00
Cane, Wm.H.Harrison, Branch, Eagle, Barrel Handle, 1840s, 35 In. 170.00
Card, Calvin Coolidge, White House, Autograph 195.00
Cartoon, Clay Coming In, Jackson Going Out, 1837, 7 1/2 X 12 In. 180.00
Charm, McKinley 25.00
Cigar Band, Teddy Roosevelt, Rough Rider Brand, C.1900 .... 5.00
Cup, Bouillon, F.D.Roosevelt, Yalta Conference, Gold Trim 495.00
Doll, Goldwater, Remco 25.00
Doll, Johnson 25.00
Earrings, Ike, Rhinestone 9.00
Face Mask, Carter 75.00
Face Mask, Nixon 75.00
Fan, Goldwater Fan Club, Elephant With Winking Eyes 5.00
Flask, McKinley & Roosevelt, Our Candidates, Round, Pocket, 5 In. 380.00
Flyer, Campaign, Dewey, Warren, Printed In Chinese For Chinatown 7.50
Glass, Wendell Willkie, 1940 .... 9.00
Handkerchief, Roosevelt, Battle Flag, 1912 .... 75.00
Handkerchief, Silk, American Flag, Printed, Framed, 19 X 19 In. 30.00
Hat, Campaign, John F.Kennedy 10.00
Invitation, J.F.Kennedy Inauguration, 1961, 6 X 10 In. 5.00
Jug, Landon, Knox, Miniature 30.00
Key Chain, Robert F.Kennedy, Picture 4.50
Knife, Woodrow Wilson, Bust of Wilson, White House, Pocket 20.00
Lamp, Figural, F.D.R.Base, Man of Hour, Bronze, Spelter, 11 In., Pr. ... 100.00
Lapel Pin, Nixon 2.25
Leaflet, We Want Willkie, Wendell Willkie, 4 Pages, 9 X 12 In. 10.00
License Plate, Landon For President 22.00
License Plate, Willkie For President 22.00
Light Bulb, Elephant & G.O.P.Inside, When Lights Up 65.00
Matchbook, Stevenson & Nixon 4.00
Mug, Nixon, Agnew, Blue, 1973 .... 50.00
Nodder, Teddy Roosevelt, Standing, Papier–Mache, 10 In. 190.00
Pamphlet, T.Roosevelt, Commencement Address, U.of California 30.00
Pennant, Dewey For President 20.00
Photograph, Barry Goldwater, Color, Signed, 8 X 10 In. 20.00
Photograph, Edmund S.Muskie, For President, Signed, 8 X 10 In. 10.00
Photograph, Frank & Eleanor Roosevelt, 1941, Framed, 8 X 10 In. 950.00
Photograph, John F.Kennedy, Inscribed, Framed, 10 X 8 In. 1500.00
Picture, Woodrow Wilson, Signed, 16 X 21 In. 40.00
Ping–Pong Paddles, Caricature of Nixon & Mao 10.00
Plaque, McKinley & Theodore Roosevelt, Artist Signed 300.00
Plate, Taft & Sherman, Jugate, China 40.00
Postcard, Roosevelt, Teddy's Bears 112.00

Program, Inaugural, Roosevelt, Garner, March 4, 1933	65.00
Puzzle, Jigsaw, Spiro Agnew, 1970	15.00
Puzzle, Nixon, Agnew, 2–Sided	12.00
Ribbon, Douglas, Little Giant	240.00
Ribbon, Gen.Eisenhower	45.00
Ribbon, Henry Clay, The People's Choice, Silk	200.00
Ribbon, Mourning, President Harrison, Framed, 1841	68.00
Ring, Hoover	20.00
Scarf, President Eisenhower	30.00
Sheet Music, March To Eisenhower, Ike's Photo Cover, 1953	10.00
Sheet Music, Roosevelt, Wallace	27.50
Sheet Music, We'll Link His Name With Lincoln, W.Wilson Photo	9.50
Stickpin, Grant & Colfax, Jugate	90.00
Stud, G.O.P. Elephant	3.50
Tie Clip, Wallace, 1968	4.50
Toy, Elephant, Mechanical, Barry Goldwater's Campaign, 10 In.	225.00
Trash Can, Spiro Agnew	20.00
Watch Fob, Democratic Convention, St.Louis, Brass, 1916	35.00
Watch Fob, Parker & Davis	22.00
Watch Fob, Teddy Roosevelt, Fairbanks, 1905	12.50
Watch Fob, Teddy Roosevelt, Picture, Multicolored, 1 1/4 In.	40.00
Wristwatch, Carter & Mondale, With Pocket Knife	35.00
Wristwatch, Dickey Nixon, Nixon On Dial	45.00
Wristwatch, George Wallace, 1970	35.00
Wristwatch, GOP, Elephant On Dial	35.00
Wristwatch, Nixon, Animated, I'm Not A Crook, American Time	85.00
Wristwatch, Spiro Agnew, Dirty Time	65.00
Wristwatch, Spiro Agnew, Sheffield Watch Co.	35.00

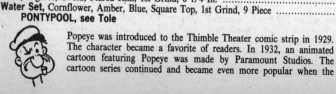

Pomona glass is a clear glass with a soft amber border decorated with pale blue or rose–colored flowers and leaves. The colors are very, very pale. The background of the glass is covered with a network of fine lines. It was made from 1885 to 1888 by the New England Glass Company. First grind was made from April 1885 to June 1886. It was made by cutting a wax surface on the glass, then dipping it in acid. Second grind was a less expensive method of acid etching that was then developed.

POMONA, Bowl, Cornflower, Ruffled, Petaled Base, 5 3/4 X 2 1/2 In.	350.00
Bowl, Ruffled, Amber Edge, 1st Grind	65.00
Cruet, Pansy & Butterfly, 2nd Grind, 7 1/4 In.	465.00
Pitcher, Diamond Quilted, 2nd Grind, Amber Band At Neck, 8 In.	225.00
Pitcher, Lemonade, Cornflower, 12 In.	185.00
Pitcher, Maidenhair Fern, Green & Jade, 7 In.	385.00
Pitcher, No Tint, 12 In.	75.00
Pitcher, Water, Acorn & Leaf	95.00
Pitcher, Water, Amber Stain Rim, Clear Handle, 1st Grind, 6 1/2 In.	185.00
Punch Cup, Blue Cornflower, Clear Handle, 1st Grind, 2 1/2 In.	295.00
Punch Cup, Cornflower Design, 1st Grind	180.00
Toothpick	60.00
Toothpick, Amber Ruffled Rim, Applied Rigaree	225.00
Toothpick, Rigaree Collar, 1st Grind	265.00
Tray, Ice Cream, Cornflower, 12 1/2 X 7 1/2 In.	395.00
Tumbler, 1st Grind	90.00
Tumbler, 2nd Grind	90.00
Tumbler, Blueberry, 2nd Grind	165.00
Tumbler, Cornflower	110.00
Vase, Rigaree, Ovoid, Flared Rim, 1st Grind, 6 1/4 In.	285.00
Water Set, Cornflower, Amber, Blue, Square Top, 1st Grind, 9 Piece	950.00

PONTYPOOL, see Tole

Popeye was introduced to the Thimble Theater comic strip in 1929. The character became a favorite of readers. In 1932, an animated cartoon featuring Popeye was made by Paramount Studios. The cartoon series continued and became even more popular when the old movies were used on television starting in the 1950s. The full-length movie with Robin Williams as Popeye was made in 1980.

POPEYE, Backpack, 1979	15.00
Bank, Dime Register	30.00 To 55.00
Bank, Knockout, Replaced Bruno, Mechanical, Tin Litho, 4 1/2 In.	341.00
Boat, Corgi	15.00
Book, Adventures of Popeye, Saalfield, 1934	22.00
Book, Comic, No.25, 1939	50.00
Book, Popeye Story Book, Whitman, 1937	17.00
Bowl, Cereal, Dated 1935	58.00
Bubble Set, 1935	30.00
Candy, Cigarettes	5.00
Car, Spinach Wagon, Matchbox	7.00
Card, Playing, King Features Syndicate, 1938	18.00
Charm, Celluloid, 1920s	5.00
Cookie Jar	250.00
Costume, Halloween, Pants, Jacket, Hat & Mask, 1935	65.00
Doll, Box, Uneeda, 1979, 8 In.	12.00
Doll, Brutus, Muscular, 22 In.	28.00
Doll, Olive Oyl & Sweet Pea, Rubber, 9 1/2 In.	10.00
Doll, Olive Oyl, 19 In.	25.00
Doll, Wooden Jointed Body, J.Chein, For 1933 World's Fair, 8 In.	300.00
Doll, Wooden, Jointed, 5 In.	45.00
Eggcup, Figural, China	120.00
Figurine, Mechanical, Celluloid, 1929, Large	225.00
Figurine, Olive Oyl, 5 In.	75.00
Game, Adventures of Popeye	28.00
Game, Juggler, Glass Covered	55.00
Game, Pipe Toss	25.00
Game, Popeye Goes Duck Hunting, Whitman, 1937	20.00
Game, Popeye The Skater, Linemar	795.00
Game, Popeye's Treasure Map, 1977	9.00
Game, Ring Toss, 1950s	35.00
Game, Skeet Shoot, Box, Late 1950s	80.00
Kazoo	15.00
Lamp, Figural, Electric, Chalkware	67.50
Lamp, Original Shade, 1935	200.00
Paint Book, 6 Colored Pages, 1936, 96 Pages	45.00
Paint Box, Tin	20.00
Paint Set, American Crayon Co., Color Litho, Popeye, Olive, 1933	10.00
Paint Set, Presto, 1961, Box	32.50
Pen, Fountain, 1930s	45.00 To 85.00
Pencil Box, 1933	20.00
Pencil Case, Contents, Hassenfeld Bros., 1950s	12.50
Pencil, Eagle	45.00
Pencil, Mechanical, 1930s	40.00
Phone	30.00
Pipe Kazoo	20.00
Pipe, Patent 1934	32.00
Pistols, 1961, Box	35.00
Punching Bag	650.00
Soap, On A Rope	20.00
Table Cover, Paper, Tuttle Press Co., 36 X 72 In.	15.00
Telephone, Figural, Push Button	30.00
Tie Clip	45.00
Toss Game, Box	18.00
Toy, Airplane, Box	525.00
Toy, Dippy Dumper, Celluloid Figure, Windup, Marx	85.00
Toy, Express, Box, 1930s	975.00
Toy, In Rowboat	1800.00
Toy, Lantern, Linemar, Box	225.00
Toy, Motorcycle, Large	500.00
Toy, Olive Oyl, Popeye Dances, Olive Plays Accordion, Key, 9 In.	650.00

Porcelain, Charger, 5 Children,
Signed Lobrichon, 22 In.

Porcelain, Plaque, Cherub With Lute, Oval,
3 1/2 In.

Toy, Parrot Cage, Windup, Marx	175.00
Toy, Pilot	495.00
Toy, Popeye & Olive Oyl On Roof, Marx	650.00 To 900.00
Toy, Popeye & Parrot	400.00 To 425.00
Toy, Popeye Express, Tin, Windup, 2 Planes, Olive & Popeye, Marx	600.00
Toy, Popeye Jitter Bug Band, 2 Kazoos, Cymbals, Box, 1930s	85.00
Toy, Popeye On Roof	350.00
Toy, Popeye Pouch, 1929	30.00
Toy, Pull, Fisher–Price, 1933	60.00
Toy, Skater, Linemar	900.00
Toy, Teeter–Totter, Sand Toy, Tin, Olive, Popeye, 1930, 9 1/4 In.	225.00
Toy, Turn Over Tank, Linemar	225.00 To 250.00
Toy, Walking, With Parrots, Windup, Marx, 1935	245.00
Vase, Bud, Figural, Glazed Ceramic, 1930s	45.00
Whistle Flashlight, On Original Display Card	125.00

Major porcelain factories are listed in this book under the factory name. This section lists pieces that are by the less well–known factories.

PORCELAIN, Barrel, Garden, Bronze Form Urns Filled With Flowers, 17 In.	400.00
Basket, Floral Sprigs, Reticulated, Ludwigsburg, 7 1/8 In.	1320.00
Bottle Stopper, Lady's Head, German	145.00
Bowl, Blue & White Floral, Dragons, Oriental, 7 3/4 In.	17.50
Bowl, Irises, Phoenix Interior, Enameled, Gilt, Fukagawa Si, 10 In.	1135.00
Bowl, Polychrome Enameled Figural Panels, Oriental, 7 1/2 In.	125.00
Bowl, Polychrome Enameled Scene, Wisteria & Hen, 14 1/4 In.	195.00
Bowl, Samurai, Hunting, Floral & Diaper Border, Artist, 11 In.	225.00
Bowl, Sang–De–Boeuf Glaze, Crackle Base, Stand, 7 1/8 In.	440.00
Box, White & Gold Design, Painted Young Girl On Lid, 3 In.	195.00
Bust, Nouveau Maiden, Rose In Hair, Blue & Green, Wahliss, 10 In.	700.00
Charger, 5 Children, Signed Lobrichon, 22 In. ....*Illus*	600.00
Charger, Group of Children, Hand Painted, J.Pascault, 22 In.	600.00
Charger, Stylized Foliage, Priest, Nobleman, Kuznetzov, 17 7/8 In.	3850.00
Cricket Cage, Blue & White, Oriental, 3 1/2 X 5 In.	25.00
Cup & Saucer, Demosthenes Medallion, Furstenberg, C.1780, 6 In.	3080.00
Cup & Saucer, Handleless, Leaves, Beige, Fluted, Chinese Mark	15.00
Cup, Dancing Couple, Hausmaler, 2 Handles, 1730–40, 3 5/8 In.	935.00
Dish, Carp, Fish, Red, Green, Gray, Yellow, Gilt, Meiji, 24 In.	1400.00
Dish, Serving, Trees, Gold Ground, Flowers, Russian, 1825, 14 In.	3555.00
Figurine, Actress, Brown Skirt, Hat, Wallendorf, 4 15/16 In.	770.00
Figurine, Bird On Stump, Blue, White & Gray, French, 6 In.	45.00
Figurine, Boy Guard, Bearskin Hat, Gilt, 6 3/4 In.	40.00

Figurine, Boy, Playing Pipe, Yellow Pants, Ludwigsburg, 4 1/8 In. 440.00
Figurine, Dog & Shepherd, Playing Flute, Signed Karl Ens 135.00
Figurine, Elder, On Stand, Cobalt Blue, China, 9 1/2 In. 65.00
Figurine, Female Dwarf, Green & Yellow Cap, Dog, Doccia, 3 1/8 In. 2750.00
Figurine, Flower Sellers, Boy, Girl, Frankenthal, 1765, 4 In., Pair 1875.00
Figurine, Gardener, Young Man, Frankenthal, C.1770, 4 In. 1985.00
Figurine, Girl, Carrying Wood, White Apron, Ludwigsburg, 4 1/2 In. 990.00
Figurine, Hotteuse, Woman, Mobcap, White, Chantilly, 10 7/16 In. 1980.00
Figurine, Keramische Lady, On Fancy Chair, Kunst, 1920, 9 In. 325.00
Figurine, Man, In Robes, French Inscription, 11 3/8 In. 65.00
Figurine, Monkey Band, 16 Piece 605.00
Figurine, Monkey Musicians, German, 5 3/8 In.Conductor, 4 In. 425.00
Figurine, Monkey, Polychrome Glaze, Chinese, 11 3/4 In. 75.00
Figurine, Musician, With Flute, Polychrome Enamel, 14 In. 25.00
Figurine, Parrot, Perched On Porcelain Wreath, 75 In., Pair 2750.00
Figurine, Peacock, Nymphenberg, 8 1/2 In., Pair ....*Illus* 130.00
Figurine, Pillow, 3 1/2 X 5 1/2 X 3 3/4 In. 650.00
Figurine, Rooster, Rock Base, Polychromed, Chinese, 17 In., Pair 253.00
Figurine, Singing Peasant, White Biscuit, French, 1770s, 7 1/2 In. 330.00
Figurine, Turkish Boy, White Turban, Frankenthal, 1765, 4 1/8 In. 450.00
Group, Children, Biscuit, On Rocks, Frankenthal, 5 1/2 In., Pair 825.00
Group, Dancers, Salmon Skirt, Yellow Tunic, Ludwigsburg, 5 7/8 In. 1100.00
Group, Gentleman Helps Lady Mount Horse, Sitzendorf, 14 1/2 In. 375.00
Group, Monkey Musicians, Germany, 19th Century, 5 3/8 In., 9 Piece 425.00
Inkstand, Floral Guilloches, Portrait, Frankenthal, 8 3/4 In. 1870.00
Jar, Beehive Shape, Kangxi, C.1720, 3 1/2 In. 650.00
Jar, Cover, Painted Foliate Reserves, Chinese, 11 1/2 In. 550.00
Jar, Ginger, Prunus Blossoms, Blue Ground, 8 1/4 In., Pair 75.00
Jar, Landscape, Figures, Hexagonal, Cover, Yabu Meizan, 5 1/2 In. 3410.00
Jar, Woman & Child On Horseback, Oriental, 7 1/2 In. 75.00
Jardiniere, Exterior Figures, Interior Gold Fish, 18 1/2 In. 500.00
Jardiniere, Red, Gray, Gilt, Blue Ground, Petal Form, Signed, 16 In. 1650.00
Jardiniere, River Landscape, Yellow, Vieux Paris, 7 3/8 In., Pair 1650.00
Jug, Floral Panels, Cover, Gilt Metal Hinge, Kangxi, C.1700, 7 In. 1350.00
Night–Light, Brown Collie Dog, Amber Eyes, Germany, 8 In. 145.00
Pillow, Flowers, Insects, Peacocks, Chinese, 6 X 15 In. 200.00
Pillow, Opium, Blue & White 145.00
Plaque, Blossom, Blond Hair To Shoulders, Wagner, 13 3/4 In. ....*Illus* 5775.00
Plaque, Cherub With Lute, Oval, 3 1/2 In. ....*Illus* 200.00
Plaque, Courtyard Scene, Figures At Game Table, French 50.00
Plaque, Grapes On Vine, Giltwood Frame, C.1900, 16 3/4 X 13 In. 170.00
Plaque, Lady Suffolk, Peach Bonnet, Signed Wagner, 7 X 5 1/8 In. 2475.00
Plaque, Moorish Scene, Women, Courtyard, Birds ....*Illus* 1000.00
Plaque, Portrait of Lady, Signed Wagner, 3 3/4 In. 200.00
Plaque, Saint & Child, Signed Balquer 80.00
Plaque, Sistine Madonna, Pope Sixtus II, German, 14 X 11 3/8 In. 1540.00
Plaque, Village Street Scene, Giltwood Frame, C.1900, 15 1/4 In. 130.00
Plate, Bird, Hand Painted, Alexander Pope Sr., 9 1/2 In., 5 Piece 200.00
Plate, Gilt Rim, Raised Floral Volutes, White, 10 1/4 In., 12 Pc. 250.00
Plate, Japanese Scene, Mice, Faux Japanese Mark, 9 In., 6 Piece 500.00
Plate, Mythological Maiden Scene, Meshcheriakov, 9 3/4 In., 4 Pc. 6600.00
Plate, Polychrome Floral, Chinese, 8 1/2 In., Pair 90.00
Plate, Topographical Scenes, Doccia, 1790–1810, 9 1/2 In., 12 Pc. 1540.00
Salt & Pepper, Hugging Bunnies 15.00
Samovar, Mythological Scenes, Scroll Handles, Alexaev, 21 3/4 In. 8250.00
Tea Set, Child's, Victorian Children, Germany, C.1890, 21 Piece 225.00
Tea Set, Child's, Victorian Girl, Washing, Germany, C.1885, 21 Pc. 300.00
Tea Set, Fuji Village Scene, Toii Mark, 1922, 21 Piece 98.00
Tea Set, Gardner, Deep Green Ground, Anthermion, Russian, 17 Pc. 1210.00
Teapot, Ducks 1 Side, Bird Reverse, Mennecy, C.1760, 4 3/16 In. 1760.00
Teapot, Floral Landscape, Blue, Domed Cover, 18th Century, 9 In. 198.00
Teapot, Polychrome Enameled Design, Japanese, 3 7/8 In. 10.00
Teapot, Rope Handle, Blue & White, Oriental, 3 3/4 In. 20.00
Teapot, Scene of Tritons & Mymphs, Blue & White, C.1760 .... 850.00

Toast Rack, Swan, Figural, White & Gold, Oval, 4 X 4 X 7 1/4 In. 70.00
Tureen, Soup, Cover, Birds, Trees, Ludwigsburg, 11 3/4 In. 2750.00
Tureen, Underplate, Boulevard, Belleek, Coxon 900.00
Umbrella Stand, Flowering Landscape, Blue & White, Japanese 130.00
Umbrella Stand, Small Building, Snow-Capped Mountains, 24 In. 200.00
Urn, Cover, Quatrefoil Reserves, Figures, Landscapes, 19 3/4 In. 3520.00
Urn, Domed Cover, Gilt On Magenta, Kuche, Toast Und Musik, 14 In. 850.00
Urn, Empire, Cobalt Blue, Ram's Head, Putti, 22 In., Pr. ....*Illus* 2200.00
Urn, Ormolu, Gilded Bronze Finial, Cover, Handles, 16 1/2 In. 650.00
Vase, 2 Cranes, Pine Trees, Pink, White, Blue, Signed, 17 In. 4675.00
Vase, 5 Doves, Ovoid, Meiji-Taisho Period, Impressed Mark 2722.00
Vase, Birds & Flowers, Yellow Ground, German, 6 In. 12.50
Vase, Blue & White Design, Reserves of Birds, Japanese, 12 In. 45.00
Vase, Bottle Shape, Clair-De-Lune, Qianlong Mark, 15 1/4 In. 330.00
Vase, Chinese Blue Souffle-Glazed, Pierced Base, 12 1/2 In., Pr. 8800.00
Vase, Floral Design, Pastels, Marked T.B.France, 11 In. 10.00
Vase, Garniture, Figural Garden Landscape, Blue, White, 9 1/8 In. 150.00
Vase, Gilt Bronze, 2 Handles, 19th Century, 32 In., Pair 7150.00
Vase, Incised & Enameled Pink Flowers, Blue, Baluster, 1880, Pair 250.00
Vase, Lamp Mount, Turquoise, Crackled, Baluster, China, 18 In., Pr. 935.00
Vase, Polychrome Enameled Scenes, Floral, Fish, Birds, 15 5/8 In. 45.00
Vase, Potpourri, Wicker Basket Shape, Cover, St.Cloud, 5 In., Pair 1750.00
Vase, Temple, Famille Noire, Exotic Birds, 25 1/2 In., Pair 400.00
Wall Pocket, Pierrette, Orange Dress, Black Mask, Germany 120.00

Postcards were first legally permitted in Austria on October 1, 1869.
The United States passed postal regulations allowing the card in
1872. Most of the picture postcards collected today date after 1910.
The amount of postage can help to date a card. The years the rates
changed and the rates are: 1872 (1 cent), 1917 (2 cents), 1919 (1
cent), 1925 (2 cents), 1928 (1 cent), 1952 (2 cents), 1959 (3 cents),
1963 (4 cents), 1968 (5 cents), 1973 (8 cents), 1975 (7 cents), 1976

Porcelain, Plaque, Moorish Scene, Women,
Courtyard, Birds

Porcelain, Figurine, Peacock, Nymphenberg,
8 1/2 In., Pair

Porcelain, Urn, Empire, Cobalt Blue,
Ram's Head, Putti, 22 In., Pr.

(9 cents), 1978 (10 cents), 1981 (12 cents), 1981 (13 cents), 1985 (14 cents), 1988 (15 cents).

POSTCARD, 60th Anniversary, Italia Airship Polar Expedition, Blue & White	3.00
Advertising, Rockford Watches	10.00
Aloha Hawaiian Islands, Passed By Army Examiner, 1943, 18 Piece	4.00
America's Exposition, Hollywood Motion Picture Hall of Fame	1.50
Buffalo Bill's Grave, Lookout Mountain, Photo, Black & White, 1920	6.00
Case Steam Tractor	8.00
Celluloid, 1912	25.00
Christmas, St.Nick & Elves, Signed R.Tuck	22.50
Clinton Oil Co., Omaha, Neb., Logo Upper Left Corner, 1902	5.00
Colfax, Iowa, East Howard Street	12.50
Comic, Motorcycle, Linen, Signed By Munson, 1930–40	1.00
Coon Chicken Inn, Pictures All 3 Restaurants	20.00
Cracker Jack Bears, No.15	12.50
Disneyland, Sleeping Beauty's Castle, 1955	7.50
Enrico Caruso Memorial, 1921	10.00
Father Christmas, Green Suit, Carrying Tree, Bag of Toys, 1908	20.00
Fisk Tires, Norman Rockwell, 1924	7.00
Flood, Men In Storefront, Watching Main Street Flood, Photo, 1910	5.00
German Cruiser Bremen, 1909	4.00
Gold Dust Twins Washing Powder, 1910, Set of 4	95.00
Graf Zeppelin, 1931 Arctic Flight, 1981, 4 1/8 X 6 1/2 In.	5.00
Halloween, Witch Chasing Boy, Pumpkin Head Stirring Pot, 1900s	7.50
Heinz, Pavilion In Atlantic City, 1910	10.00
Her Game, Tennis, Harrison Fisher	10.00
Hinds Face Cream, 1907	10.00
Hold To Light, Washington's Birthplace, Color, Postmarked 1914	17.50
Horn & Hardart Automats, How An Automat Works	2.00
Indy 500, Track & Leading Racers, Photo, Black & White, ·1920–30	7.50
Jack Dempsey, Broadway Restaurant	6.00
Keen Kutter, Panama–Pacific International Exposition, 1915	40.00
Leather, Scenes, Sayings, 25 Piece	115.00
Lincoln's Funeral Car, Photo, Unused, 1908	5.00
Little Nemo & Princess At Court, Color, 1907	65.00
Man–O–War Racehorse, Black Stableman, Photo, Black & White, 1919	10.00
Mechanical, Tobacco Advertising, Black, 1901	100.00
Mormon, Brigham Young's Office, Salt Lake, Utah Territory, 1874	50.00
National Corn Expo, Unused, 1911	2.50
Norway Royal Family, 1905	4.00
O'Neill Wireworks of Ohio, Unused	2.50
Office, Fire Boss, Anthracite Coal Mine, J.W.Evans Olyphant, 1914	5.00
Pilgrim, With Bell, Red Nose, Brundage	8.00
Pincushion, Lady's Leg, People Go Crazy After Seeing This	9.50
Pincushion, Reclining Bather, Writing In Sand	17.50
Polar Route Flight, Blue, Red On White, 1982	3.00
R.M.S.Queen Mary, 1 Cent Stamp	2.00
Red Star Line, SS Belgenland	5.00
Riverview Park, Chicago, Carousel & Circle Swing, Postmark 1913	8.00
Round Oak Stoves, Hunting Moon	12.00
Round–The–World Flight of Graf Zeppelin, 1981, 6 1/8 X 3 5/8 In.	7.50
San Francisco Disaster By Quake & Fire, 1906 Copyright	15.00
Santa Claus, Christmas Tree Behind Him, Pullout	30.00
Santa Claus, Full Color, 1930s	3.25
Santa Claus, Leather	15.00
Santa Claus, Red Silk Suit	25.00
Shredded Wheat, Niagara Falls 1 Corner, Factory, Bisquit Picture	4.00
Sing Chong Co., San Francisco	10.00
Stegmaier Brewing	5.00
Street Scene, Aurora, Indiana, Store Fronts, C.1909	6.00
Suffragette, 2 Women, Horse & Buggy, Bags Say Vote Women	6.00
Teddy Bear Santa Claus	25.00
Teddy Roosevelt Bear	6.00

Poster, Minstrel, 1870's

Ten Commandments, Original Envelope, Tuck, Set of 10 .... 100.00
Top Aviators In Flight, Monotones, French, 1909–13, 3 Piece 35.00
Trailways, Silver Eagle, Dexter Press Chrome, 1965 .... 1.25
U.S.Highway, 36 Scenes, Bathing Beauty, Folded, 1951 Roadsign 2.00
Ute Chief Mineral Water Co., Colorado, Indian & Geyser 4.50
Van Briggle Factory 12.00
Vanderbilt Race, Race Car, 1908 .... 35.00
West Point Scenes, C.1930, 13 Pieces 12.00
World War I, Embroidered 6.50

 Posters have informed the public about news and entertainment events since ancient times. Nineteenth–century advertising or theatrical posters and twentieth–century movie and war posters are of special interest today. The price is determined by the artist, the condition, and the rarity. Other posters are listed under Advertising, World War I, and World War II.

POSTER, A & P, Food Products of All States, World's Fair, 34 X 44 In. 85.00
    American Airlines To Chicago, McKnight Kauffer, 1948, 40 X 30 In. 175.00
    American Red Cross Carries On, Wyeth, 19 X 15 In. 88.00
    American War Relief, Europeans Receiving Help, Sperry, 37 X 26 In. 27.00
    Anheuser–Busch Centennial, Colored, 20 X 3 In. 10.00
    Apostle of Prosperity, Drawing of Teddy Roosevelt, 24 X 33 In. 25.00
    Arm & Hammer, Birds, Insect Border, 20 X 40 In. 65.00
    Baldwin's, 1905, 26 X 20 In. 35.00
    Barnum & Bailey, Show With 7 Dens of Beasts, 1891, 145 X 79 In. 4250.00
    Baseball, 1910–11, 21 X 14 In. 18.00
    Beach Boys, Die Cut, 2 Sides, 1977, 19 X 19 In. 15.00
    Blood Or Bread, Save Food, Henry Raleigh, 1918, 29 X 21 In. 30.00
    Blue Mouse, Madge Lessing, 3 Color, 28 X 10 1/2 In. 25.00
    Bonal, Friend of Sportsmen, Rugby, C.B.Lemmel, 1935, 31 X 23 1/2 In. 40.00
    Brooklyn Academy of Music, Comic Figures, Caniff, 1981, 34 X 24 In. 50.00
    Buffalo Bill, Astride Palomino, Litho, Strobridge, 1908 .... 1500.00
    Calling Dr.Kildare, Lew Ayres, Lana Turner, 1939, 14 X 22 In. 30.00
    Carlisle Rye, Dogs, Gambling, Smoking, Drinking, 1910, 30 X 12 In. 225.00
    Caswell Runyan Cedar Chests, 13 X 20 1/2 In. 110.00
    Christmas, Scribners, 1897, 22 X 14 In. 900.00
    Cleveland War Fund, Soaring Eagle, N.A.Arend, 1918, 22 X 14 In. 20.00
    Clipper Machines, Mower & Reaper, S.W.Green, 1870s, 19 X 24 In. 80.00
    Columbia Chainless Bicycles, J.Ottman Co., Colored, 87 X 40 In. 1980.00
    Dodge's Paste Kalsomine, Color Chart, Framed, 21 7/8 X 14 In. 130.00
    For Every Fighter A Woman Worker, Adolph Treidler, 40 X 29 In. 90.00
    Ford Tri–Motor Plane, Exploring Earth From Airplane 125.00

Freedom of Speech, Rockwell, 40 X 28 In. 250.00
Genevieve, Guitry, French Performer, Girbalo, 1920s, 47 X 31 1/2 In. 120.00
Gentleman With Cold Drink, Penfield, Harper's, 1898, 11 X 14 In. 145.00
George Roo's Brewery & Sale Stables, Black & White, 15 X 18 In. 300.00
Give 'Em Both Barrels, Soldier & Riveter, 1941, 15 X 20 In. 110.00
Give! American Red Cross, N.C.Wyeth, 15 X 19 In. 12.00
Glen Turner Scotch Whiskey, Marilyn Monroe, Lighted Ground, 3–D 75.00
Hershey Chocolate, Colored, 1935, 35 X 41 In. 28.00
Indian Root Pills, Framed, 1920s, 24 X 16 In. 135.00
Jack Hoxie, Downie Bros.Circus, Man On Horse, 1935, 28 X 41 1/2 In. 70.00
Join The Quarter–Master Corps, Uncle Sam, 1919, 26 X 17 In. 90.00
Kar–Mi, The Indian Prince, Philadelphia, Selma Illusion, 22 X 14 In. 150.00
Lady In Scarlet, Reginald Denny, Patricia Farr, 1935, 11 X 14 In. 35.00
Le Nil Cigarette Papers, Litho, Linen Back, French, 58 X 47 In. 195.00
Leroy Cigars, Color, 1929, 36 X 48 In. 46.00
Little Rascals, 1951, 42 X 26 In. 35.00
Lottie The Poor Saleslady, Theater, 1907 .... 1320.00
Marine Recruiting, World War I, J.M.Flagg, 40 X 29 In. 225.00
Mazda Lamps, Popeye, Cardboard, 1934, 21 X 31 In. 55.00
McCormick & Co., Our Country Right Or Wrong, Rough & Ready, C.1847 .... 495.00
McCormick Farm Machinery, Farmer, Framed, 1900, 25 X 35 In. 550.00
Mercy From The Skies, Betsy Ross Corps, C.1943, 20 1/2 X 13 In. 25.00
Montana, Errol Flynn, 1949, 27 X 41 In. 90.00
Moulin Rouge Follies, Raymond Maillet, 59 X 39 In. 50.00
Moving Picture Exhibition, Sears, Roebuck, Chicago, 21 X 28 In. 78.00
Murad Cigarettes, Doughboys, Winners Everywhere, 1919, 16 X 33 In. 200.00
Narragansett Brewing Co., Lager & Ale, C.W.Girsch, 1898, 15 X 18 In. 750.00
National Parks, Monuments, Pueblos of Southwest, 1930s, 40 X 27 In. 110.00
Navy Recruiting, Cartoon Style, 1919, 22 X 14 In. 20.00
O'Malley of The Mounted, George O'Brien, Irene Ware, 1936, 36 In. 25.00
Old Cornelius Whiskey, Framed, 1900, 24 X 20 In. 650.00
On With Roosevelt, Anti–Hoover, Dewey & Brickner, Remember Me 61.00
Orange Crush, Woman, Pier, Cardboard, 1920s, 12 X 18 In. 28.00
Over The Top For You, Marion, Liberty Loan, Reisenberg, 30 X 20 In. 35.00
Pierrefort, Gallery, Henri Ibels, 1897, 11 1/2 X 15 1/2 In. 80.00
Prince of Pilsen, Stone Litho, 1900s, 28 X 42 In. 125.00
Proclamation For Thanksgiving, R.Draper, 15 1/2 X 18 In. 775.00
Recruiting, Cavalry Service, Horse & Rider, 23 X 36 In. 50.00
Rising Sun Stove Polish, Woman, Factory, Linen Backed, 29 X 13 In. 220.00
Salvation Army, 2 Men & Woman Faces, 1948, 25 1/2 X 19 1/2 In. 40.00
Sarah Bernhardt, American Tour, 2 Sheet 4675.00
Saturday Evening Post, Big Business, Crime, Canvas, 1925, 3 X 4 Ft. 225.00
Schlitz Beer, Horse Festival Parade, Schlitz Logo, 49 X 22 In. 18.00
Smile, 1930s, 31 X 24 In. 60.00
Smokey The Bear, Color, 1947, 26 X 18 In. 20.00
Sorrows of Satan, Gould, Jr., Marie Corelli Novel, 1897, 13 X 10 In. 72.00
Star Spangled Girl, Tomi Ungerer, Neil Simon Play, 22 X 14 In. 26.00
Student Nurse, Signed Dan Smith, 18 X 26 In. 75.00
Sutro Baths, Full Color, 6 1/2 X 6 1/2 In. 2000.00
Temple In The Snow, Hasui, 24 X 18 In. 18.00
Ten Commandments, Full Color, 60 X 40 In. 150.00
This Man Is Your Friend, Russian Soldier, U.S.Govt., 1942, 10 In. 54.50
University of Virginia, Signed Richard Rummell, 1907, 14 X 28 In. 40.00
Women 20 To 36 Earn A Navy Rating, Waves, 1943, 20 X 14 In. 50.00
World Champions & Past Greats of Prize Ring, 1940s, 22 X 28 In. 21.00
World's Columbian Exposition, Uncle Sam, 1893, 16 X 23 In. 150.00
Your Country Is At War, Navy Recruiting, 1917, 33 X 23 In. 30.00

A potlid is just that, a lid for a pot. Transfer–printed potlids had
their heyday from the 1840s to the early 1900s. The English
Staffordshire potteries made ceramic containers with decorative lids
for bear's grease, shrimp or meat paste, cold cream, and toothpaste.
Printed advertising and pictures of historical events, portraits of
famous people, or scenic views were designed in black and white or

color. Reproductions have been made. The most famous potlids were
made by Pratt and are listed in that section.

POTLID, Areca Nut Tooth Paste, Black & White	30.00
Army & Navy's Cherry, Black & White	25.00
Bear Attacked By Dogs, Colors, Small	750.00
Clayton's Taraxacum Dandelion Cocoa, Star, Black & White	75.00
Gothic Archway, Colors, Small	1500.00
Skaters, Colors	250.00
Taylor's Saponaceous Shaving Compound, With Jar	45.00
Wellington, Colors	175.00

Pottery and porcelain are different. Pottery is opaque; you can't see
through it. Porcelain is translucent. If you hold a porcelain dish in
front of a strong light you will see the light through the dish.
Porcelain is colder to the touch. Pottery is softer and easier to break
and will stain more easily because it is porous. Porcelain is thinner,
lighter, and more durable. Majolica, faience, and stoneware are all
pottery. Many types of pottery are listed in this book under the
factory name.

POTTERY, Ashtray, Blue Concentric Circles, Glidden	25.00
Ashtray, Flamingo Center, Pink, Brown, 3 In.	22.00
Beer Set, Polychrome Transfer Scenes, Pewter Lids, German, 7 Piece	375.00
Bell, Winter Belle, Blue, Ceramic Art Studios	30.00
Biscuit Jar, Floral, Brass Cover, 6 In.	5.00
Bottle, Bird & Foliage Design, Blue & White, Japan, 3 In., Pair	20.00
Bowl, Catalina Pattern, White Satin, Oblong, 1 1/4 X 6 X 10 In.	8.00
Bowl, Gay Plaid, Blair China, 4 In.	4.00
Bowl, Green Mottling, Brown Drip, Prang, 2 X 6 In.	65.00
Bowl, Hand Painted Floral, Blue, Glidden, 8 1/2 X 6 1/2 In.	20.00
Bowl, Mixing, Newton Mfg.Co., Advertising Specialties, Iowa, 9 In.	50.00
Bowl, Painted Floral Medallions, Floral Rim, American, 17 1/2 In.	88.00
Bowl, Virginia Rose, Homer Laughlin, Oval, 9 1/2 In.	7.00
Bust, Madonna, Lenci	75.00
Candleholder, Green Ash Glaze, Lanier Meaders, 3 3/4 In.	40.00
Candlestick, Double, Orange, Pacific Pottery	25.00
Chamber Set, Child's, Blue Roses, White, German, Box, Label, 6 Piece	275.00
Cheese Dish, Floral, Cream, Handle, Cover, English, 7 3/4 X 9 In.	75.00
Cheese Dish, Wedgwood-Style, Light Brown, White, Cover, 8 5/8 In.	198.00
Children's Set, Laurel, Ivory, Scotty Dog Decal, 14 Piece	350.00
Cookie Jar, Paris Garden, Bamboo Handle	165.00
Cookie Jar, Peek-A-Boo, Van Tellingen	300.00
Creamer, Cow, Cream, Caramel & Green Glaze, 7 In.	50.00
Creamer, Georgian, Eggshell, Pink Flowers, Homer Laughlin	4.00
Crock, Brown & White, Roosevelt	45.00
Cup & Saucer, Pink Trim Over Gray, Hadley	16.00
Cuspidor, Fleur-De-Lis Pattern, Blue	45.00
Dish, Cheese, Swan Top, Blue, Gold Trim, Daisies, English, 7 In.	175.00
Ewer, Handle, Stopper, Stahl	510.00
Ewer, Olive Green, Rust, Bulbous, Pine Ridge Sioux, Artist, 4 1/4 In.	28.00
Ewer, Song-Style, Small Spout, Black Glaze, Handles, 12 In.	350.00
Figurine, Bird, Brayton Laguna, 15 In.	75.00
Figurine, Boy & Girl Elephant, Polka Dots, 3 1/2 In., Pair	38.00
Figurine, Boy, Riding Snail, Nude, Bent Head, 1910, 9 In.	1500.00
Figurine, Cat, Standing, Black, Hagenauer, 2 1/4 X 4 In.	120.00
Figurine, Chicken, Unglazed, Stahl, 4 In.	75.00
Figurine, Quail Family, Mamma & 2 Babies, Howard Pierce, 3 Piece	38.00
Humidor, Indian ....*Illus*	70.00
Jar, Blue, Copper Trim, Scroll Footed, Cover, Bulbous, Stamped, 5 In.	50.00
Jar, Edgefield, Signed Chandler Maker, 1850-54, Large	1700.00
Jar, Green Ash Glaze, Southern, 12 3/4 In.	55.00
Jardiniere, Yellow Daffodils, Louwelsa, 8 In.	75.00
Jug, Gray, Dark Glaze, Ovoid, 8 In.	30.00
Jug, Grotesque, 2-Face, Green Ash Glaze, Lanier Meaders, 8 3/4 In.	550.00

Jug, Grotesque, Green Ash Glaze, Lanier Meaders, 10 1/4 In.	525.00
Jug, Incised High Bridge Glens, Miniature	65.00
Lamp, Figural, Owl, Standing, Rocky Base, Glass Eyes, 18 In.	220.00
Mug, Beige, S.S.Christopher Columbus, Chicago–Milwaukee Route	125.00
Mug, Fred Tehring Brewing Co., 1868–1904, 2 1/4 In.	115.00
Mug, Grape, Light Brown	15.00
Panther, Black, Green Rhinestone Eyes, 20 In.	35.00
Pitcher, Castle, Brown, 6 In.	45.00
Pitcher, Cobalt Blue Daffodils & Dahlias, 7 3/4 In.	95.00
Pitcher, Fanny Flagg, Blue & White	215.00
Pitcher, Monk, Blue & White, 9 3/4 In.	225.00
Pitcher, Wash, Roses & Lily–of–The–Valley, Blue & White	90.00
Pitcher, Windy City, Blue & White	215.00
Planter, Duck, Gray, Rosemeade, 6 X 2 1/4 In.	18.00
Planter, Elephant, Seated, Brayton Laguna, 5 In.	28.00
Planter, Green, Deer, Howard Pierce	50.00
Planter, Lady's Shoe, 1942, 3 3/4 In.	18.00
Plate, Christmas, Santa Claus, Kay Finch	60.00
Plate, No Pattern, Pink, Purple, Hand Thrown, Brayton Laguna, 10 In.	32.00
Plate, Reticulated, Basket Weave, Marked Don Pottery, C.1790, 9 In.	150.00
Plate, Salad, Morning Glory, 7 1/2 In.	45.00
Plate, Sgraffito, Yellow Slip Design, Stahl	500.00
Plate, Virginia Rose, Homer Laughlin, 10 1/2 In.	6.00
Plate, Wall, A.L.Hamburg, Wartburg Castle, Hand Painted, 10 In.	165.00
Platter, Luray, Aqua, 13 In.	12.00
Pot, Blue, Brown & Gray, Belgium, 4 In.	18.00
Salt & Pepper, Bears, Brown & Black, Van Tellingen	14.00
Salt & Pepper, Bears, Huggies, Van Tellingen	15.00 To 18.00
Salt & Pepper, Bendel Love Bugs, Van Tellingen, 3 1/2 In.	26.00
Salt & Pepper, Black Boy With Dog, Van Tellingen	20.00
Salt & Pepper, Dutch Couple	25.00
Salt & Pepper, Dutch Couple, Huggies, Van Tellingen	19.00 To 22.50
Salt & Pepper, Egg Shaped Heads, 1 Winking, Hat, Suit Bodies	25.00
Salt & Pepper, Figural, Spaniel, Rosemeade	35.00
Salt & Pepper, Figural, Whippet, Rosemeade	35.00
Salt & Pepper, Girl & Lamb, Huggies, Van Tellingen	85.00
Salt & Pepper, Girls, With Head Scarves, Mittens, Van Tellingen	14.00
Salt & Pepper, Huggie Bears, Yellow, Van Tellingen	18.00
Salt & Pepper, Mermaid & Sailor, Van Tellingen	20.00 To 55.00
Salt & Pepper, Peek–A–Boo, Huggies, Van Tellingen	55.00
Salt & Pepper, Peek–A–Boo, Van Tellingen	100.00

Pottery, Humidor, Indian

Salt & Pepper, Pheasant	15.00
Salt & Pepper, Rooster	30.00
Salt, Reddish–Brown	425.00
Sugar Shaker, Dutch Men, Green, Silver Plated, Tunncliffe, 6 In.	65.00
Sugar, Cover, Bright Blue Glaze, Dated Feb.26, 1942, Stahl	250.00
Tea Set, Child's, Floral, Glazed, Japan, 7 Piece	75.00
Teapot, Blue, Dryden	28.00
Teapot, Lorine Pattern, Blue Ridge	15.00
Teapot, Oriental, Wrapped Twig Handle	105.00
Teapot, Sugar & Creamer, Apples, Puritan, 3 Piece	35.00
Tray, Tidbit, 2–Tier, Poppytrail	12.00
Urn, Dark Blue Glaze, 2 Handles, Stahl	975.00
Urn, Dark Blue Green Glaze, 2 Handles, Stahl, Marked IS	340.00
Vase, 2 Female Heads, Flowers, Iridescent, Purple, Blue, Green, 9 In.	385.00
Vase, 3 Open Crocus, Mottled Green Glaze, Merrimac, 1843, 4 3/8 In.	400.00
Vase, Clematis, Yellow, Roosevelt, 12 In.	75.00
Vase, Dutch Girl Scene, West Coast Pottery	25.00
Vase, Geometric, Green Matte Glaze, SP Mark, 1906, 6 In.	200.00
Vase, Indian Effigy, Lizard, Missouri Valley, 6 In.	550.00
Vase, Mission, Ivory Matte, Jade Blue Interior, Poxon, 1924, 9 In.	230.00
Vase, Pillow, Blue, Glidden	25.00
Whimsey, Bird Finial, Brown Glaze, 5 In.	95.00

Powder flasks and powder horns were made to hold the gunpowder used in antique firearms. The early examples were made of horn or wood; later ones were of copper or brass.

POWDER FLASK, Colt, Navy, Brass, 6 3/4 In.	150.00
POWDER HORN, Carved End Has Series of Rings, 13 1/4 In.	105.00
Carved Initials J.D. On Wooden Plug, 12 1/2 In.	85.00
Copper, Allover Oak Leaf Design, Telescopic Spout	59.50
Elk, Swimming, 3 Dogs Attacking In Water, French, 7 In.	49.50
Embossed Dog & Partridge, Copper, Brass	30.00
Philadelphia View, DuMont, 1750–60	6500.00
Royal Arms, DuMont, Relief Ring & Octagon Spout, 1757, 14 In.	2750.00
Stork, Standing, Long Bill, Lacquer Finish, Wreath Border, 8 In.	84.50
Stylized Tulips On Wooden Plug, J.Munro, 9 1/2 In.	85.00
U.S., Metal, Black Leather Band, Hall Patent Breech, 11 In.	2250.00
Violin Shape, Original Lacquer Finish, 8 1/2 In.	64.50

PRATT
FENTON

Pratt ware means two different things. It was an early Staffordshire pottery, cream–colored with colored decorations, made by Felix Pratt during the late eighteenth century. There was also Pratt ware made with transfer designs during the mid–nineteenth century in Fenton, England. Reproductions of the transfer–printed Pratt are being made.

PRATT, Creamer, Cow, Hobbled, Cover, 1785–1800	2250.00
Lid, Prince of Wales, Visiting Tomb of Washington	195.00
Pitcher, Seashell Design, Pewter Lid	200.00
Potlid, Rivals, 4 In.	85.00
Potlid, Strasbourg Scene	250.00
Tea Caddy, Original Lid	775.00
Watch Stand, Ralph Wood	1650.00

Pressed glass was first made in the United States in the 1820s after the invention of glass pressing machines. Hundreds of patterns of pressed glass were made in complete table settings. Although the Boston and Sandwich Works was the most famous of the pressed glass factories, there were about sixteen other factories making pressed glass from 1830 to 1850, and still more from 1850 to 1900, when pressed glass reached its greatest popularity. It is now being widely reproduced. The pattern names used in this listing are based on the information in the book "Pressed Glass in America" by John and Elizabeth Welker. There may be pieces of pressed glass listed in this book in other sections. See Lamp, Ruby, Sandwich, and Souvenir.

100–EYE, see Hundred Eye
100–LEAVED ROSE, see Hundred Leaved Rose
1000–EYE, see Thousand Eye
101, see One–Hundred–One
8–0–8, see Eight–0–Eight
ACANTHUS, see Ribbed Palm

PRESSED GLASS, Acorn, Creamer, Child's	125.00
Acorn, Goblet	35.00
Actress, Bowl, 9 1/2 In.	68.00
Actress, Bread Plate, Oval, 12 3/4 In.	68.00
Actress, Cake Stand, 9 1/2 In.	135.00
Actress, Celery, Frosted	155.00
Actress, Compote, Cover, 11 1/2 In.	125.00
Actress, Compote, Cover, 4 X 8 1/2 In.	75.00
Actress, Compote, Cover, Frosted, 10 In.	200.00
Actress, Compote, Frosted Dome, 6 1/4 X 9 1/2 In.	95.00 To 135.00
Actress, Creamer	40.00 To 100.00
Actress, Dish, Cheese	195.00
Actress, Goblet	70.00 To 90.00
Actress, Jam Jar	95.00 To 125.00
Actress, Sauce	20.00 To 25.00
Actress, Sauce, Footed, 4 In.	10.00
Actress, Sherbet, Footed	29.50
Actress, Spooner	45.00 To 90.00
Actress, Sugar, Pedestal, Frosted Faces	45.00
Ada, Vase, 8 1/2 In.	20.00
ADMIRAL DEWEY, see Spanish American	
Adonis, Compote, Cover, 7 In.	45.00
Alabama, Butter, Cover	75.00 To 80.00
Alabama, Castor Set, 4–Bottle, Green	450.00
Alabama, Castor Set, Green, 5 Piece	550.00
Alabama, Celery, Ruby & Amber Stain	135.00
Alabama, Syrup, Hinged Lid	65.00 To 95.00
Alabama, Toothpick	75.00
Alaska, Berry Set, Green, Gold Enameled, 5 Piece	245.00
Alaska, Butter, Cover, Gold & Enamel Trim	125.00
Alaska, Celery	45.00
Alaska, Celery, Vaseline	165.00
Alaska, Creamer, Emerald Green	42.50
Alaska, Saltshaker, Blue Opalescent	35.00
Alaska, Sugar, Cover, Blue	135.00
Albany, Butter, Cover	36.00
Albany, Pitcher, Water	30.00
Albany, Sugar, Cover	31.50
Albany, Wine	12.50
Almond Thumbprint, Goblet, Flint	40.00
Almond Thumbprint, Tumbler, Footed, Flint	30.00
Almond Thumbprint, Wine	14.50
Almond Thumbprint, Wine, Flint	18.00
Amazon, Butter, Cover	55.00
Amazon, Creamer	25.00 To 42.50
Amazon, Cruet, Amber	125.00
Amazon, Goblet	32.50
Amazon, Syrup	45.00
Amberette, Berry Set, Flat Base, 9 Piece	300.00
Amberette, Bowl, 2–Collared, 8 1/2 In.	200.00
Amberette, Butter, Cover	215.00
Amberette, Butter, Cover, Amber, Frosted	365.00
Amberette, Creamer	225.00
Amberette, Punch Cup, Amber, Frosted	110.00 To 150.00
Amberette, Relish, Boat Shape	245.00

Actress   Arched Fleur–de–Lis   Artichoke, frosted

Amberette, Sugar, Frosted Amber Cross, Cover 150.00
Amberette, Syrup 800.00
Amberette, Toothpick, Frosted, Amber 395.00
Amberette, Vase, Trumpet Style, 10 1/2 In. 160.00
Ambidextrous, Spooner 28.00
    AMERICAN BEAUTY, see La France
American Flag, Bread Tray 50.00
American Shield, Dish, Pickle .... 55.00 To 85.00
American Shield, Relish, Scalloped, 7 1/2 X 5 In. 125.00
American Shield, Table Set, 4 Piece 1900.00
Apollo, Cake Stand, 10 In. 60.00
Apollo, Creamer, Etched 45.00
Apollo, Cruet, Rose, Original Stopper 65.00
Apollo, Syrup, Frosted, Spring Lid 110.00
Arch & Forget–Me–Not Bands, Spooner 28.00
Arched Fleur–De–Lis, Bowl, 8 In. 25.00
Arched Fleur–De–Lis, Cruet 395.00
Arched Grape, Celery 40.00
Arched Ovals, Toothpick, Green, Gold Trim 30.00
Arched Ovals, Wine, Rose Flashed 17.00

Atlas   Austrian   Barberry

Argonaut Shell, Tumbler, Custard 40.00
Argus, Eggcup, 3 3/8 In. 5.00
Argyle, Bread Plate, 12 1/2 In. 55.00
Argyle, Goblet 25.00
    ARROWHEAD IN OVAL, see Style
Art, Banana Stand .... 75.00 To 95.00
Art, Bowl, Footed, 2 1/2 X 7 In. 25.00
Art, Butter, Cover 60.00
Art, Cake Stand, 10 1/2 In. 65.00
Art, Celery .... 30.00 To 35.00
Art, Compote, Cover 115.00
Art, Creamer 60.00
Art, Goblet .... 33.00 To 58.00
Art, Honey, Square 125.00
Art, Sauce, Footed, 4 In. 12.00
Art, Spooner .... 25.00 To 28.00
Art, Sugar, Cover 48.00
Artichoke, Berry Set, Frosted, 7 Piece 90.00
Artichoke, Cruet, Frosted 150.00
Ashburton, Celery, Scalloped Top 135.00
Ashburton, Claret, Flint, 5 1/4 In. 50.00
Ashburton, Creamer, Flint, 5 3/4 In. 95.00
Ashburton, Decanter, Bulbous Lip, Flint, 8 In. 55.00
Ashburton, Eggcup .... 25.00 To 35.00
Ashburton, Goblet .... 48.00 To 50.00
Ashburton, Goblet, Flint 35.00
Ashburton, Tumbler, Buttermilk 45.00
Ashburton, Wine, Flint, 4 1/8 In. 45.00
Ashman, Salt & Pepper, Amber 22.00
Atlanta, Celery 65.00
Atlanta, Celery, Frosted Base 45.00
Atlanta, Compote, Cover, 9 1/2 In. 125.00
Atlanta, Pitcher, Water, Sqaure 145.00
Atlas, Cake Stand 32.00
Aurora, Wine 14.00
Austrian, Compote, 8 In. 65.00
Austrian, Punch Cup, Gold 15.00
Austrian, Sugar, Cover 52.00
Austrian, Wine, Vaseline 110.00
Aztec, Bowl, Fruit, Cover, 8 1/2 In. 75.00
Aztec, Goblet .... 22.00 To 32.50
Aztec, Toothpick 30.00
Baby Face, Compote, 12 In. 395.00
Baby Face, Sugar, Cover 175.00
    BABY THUMBPRINT, see Dakota
    BALDER, see Pennsylvania
    BALKY MULE, see Currier & Ives
Ball & Bar, Tumbler 8.00
Ball & Swirl, Cake Stand .... 30.00 To 55.00
Ball & Swirl, Plate, Bread, Tiffin, 1888, 10 7/8 In. 285.00
Baltimore Pear, Bread Plate 40.00
Baltimore Pear, Butter, Cover 30.00
Baltimore Pear, Creamer .... 15.00 To 55.00
Baltimore Pear, Spooner 30.00
Baltimore Pear, Sugar, Cover .... 20.00 To 41.50
    BANDED BEADED GRAPE MEDALLION, see Beaded Grape Medallion,
    Banded
Banded Buckle, Spooner 30.00
Banded Grape, Butter, Cover 62.50
Banded Grape, Compote, Cover, 11 In. 60.00
Banded Grape, Creamer 55.00
Banded Grape, Spooner 40.00
Banded Grape, Sugar, Open 37.50
Banded Grape, Toothpick, Green 55.00

Block & Fan

Buckle

Beaded Grape

Banded Icicle, Celery	35.00
Banded Icicle, Tumbler, Dewey Portrait Base	40.00
BANDED PORTLAND, when flashed with pink, is sometimes called "Maiden Blush."	
Banded Portland, Bottle, Cologne, With Gold	51.00
Banded Portland, Goblet	32.50
Banded Portland, Jar, Dresser, Cover, 2 5/8 In.	33.50
Banded Portland, Pitcher, Water, Maiden Blush, Miniature	30.00
Banded Portland, Toothpick	35.00
Banded Raindrop, Sauce, Footed	8.00
OTHER BANDED PATTERNS, see under name of basic pattern: e.g., Banded Honeycomb, see Honeycomb, Banded	
BAR & DIAMOND, see Kokomo	
Barberry, Celery, 7 1/2 In.	50.00
Barberry, Compote, Cover, 8 In.	95.00
Barberry, Eggcup, Oval	16.50
Barberry, Pitcher, Applied Handle, 9 1/2 In.	85.00
Barberry, Plate, 6 In.	25.00
Barberry, Spooner	30.00
Barberry, Tumbler, Footed	24.00
BARLEY & OATS, see Wheat & Barley	
BARLEY & WHEAT, see Wheat & Barley	
Barley, Butter, Cover	25.00
Barley, Compote, 6 1/4 In.	18.00
Barley, Creamer	20.00
Barley, Goblet	25.00
Barley, Pitcher, Water	45.00
Barred Forget–Me–Not, Plate, Handle, 9 In.	32.50
Barred Hobnail, Cake Stand	28.00
Barred Hobnail, Pitcher, Water	32.50
Barred Ovals, Cruet, Frosted	85.00
BARREL HONEYCOMB, see Honeycomb	
BARRELED BLOCK, see Red Block	
Basket Weave, Goblet, 8 1/2 In.	10.00
Basket Weave, Pitcher, Water, Amber	40.00
Bead & Scroll, Butter, Cover	115.00
Bead & Scroll, Compote, Jelly, Etched	30.00
Bead & Scroll, Table Set, Child's, 4 Piece	275.00
Beaded Acorn, Goblet	14.00
BEADED BULL'S–EYE & DRAPE, see Alabama	
Beaded Circle, Spooner, Gold & Enamel Design, Green	45.00
BEADED DEWDROP, see Wisconsin	

Beaded Fine Cut, Creamer 32.00
Beaded Grape Medallion, Celery, 8 1/4 In. 65.00
Beaded Grape Medallion, Goblet, Buttermilk, Banded 40.00
Beaded Grape Medallion, Spooner .... 24.00 To 50.00
Beaded Grape, Creamer, Opalescent 100.00
Beaded Grape, Sugar, Cover, Sapphire Blue 650.00
Beaded Heart, Toothpick 35.00
Beaded Loop, Cruet 35.00
Beaded Loop, Dish, Pickle 18.00
Beaded Loop, Goblet .... 28.50 To 35.00
Beaded Loop, Pitcher, Milk 35.00
Beaded Loop, Sugar, Cover, Ruby Stain 48.00
Beaded Medallion, Goblet 30.00
Beaded Mirror, Goblet 30.00
Beaded Mirror, Pitcher, Water 100.00
Beaded Oval & Scroll, Goblet 16.00
Beaded Ovals In Sand, Cruet, Green, Original Stopper 135.00
Beaded Ovals In Sand, Pitcher, Water, Green 85.00
Beaded Panel & Sunburst, Creamer, Heisey, Miniature 45.00
Beaded Rosette, Wine, Findlay 30.00
Beaded Scroll, Creamer 13.00
Beaded Swag, Butter, Cover 125.00
Beaded Swag, Punch Cup 16.00
Beaded Swag, Spooner, Flower Design 42.50
Beaded Swag, Toothpick 28.00
Beaded Swirl, Butter, Child's, Cover 45.00
Beaded Swirl, Cruet, Original Stopper, Ruby Stain 75.00
Beaded Swirl, Sugar, Child's, Cover 35.00
Beaded Tulip, Bowl, Oval, 6 5/8 X 9 1/2 In. 10.00
    BEARDED HEAD, see Viking
    BEARDED MAN, see Queen Anne
Beatty Swirl, Water Tray, Vaseline 65.00
Beautiful Lady, Celery 28.00
Beggar's Hand, Toothpick 25.00
Belladonna, Butter, Cover, Green 65.00
Bellflower, Compote, Scalloped Rim, Flint, 5 1/4 X 7 3/4 In. 85.00
Bellflower, Eggcup, Pedestal 38.00
Bellflower, Goblet, Flint 30.00
Bellflower, Spooner, Flint 38.00
Bellflower, Syrup 350.00
Bellflower, Tumbler, Veined Leaves 75.00
    BENT BUCKLE, see New Hampshire
Bethlehem Star, Goblet .... 15.00 To 24.50
Bethlehem Star, Pitcher, Water 52.00
Bethlehem Star, Spooner 26.50
    BEVELED DIAMOND & STAR, see Albany
Beveled Star, Celery, Green 45.00
Beveled Star, Creamer, Green 40.00
Beveled Star, Spooner, Green, 1890 .... 50.00
    BIG BLOCK, see Henrietta
Big Button, Table Set, Amber, 4 Piece 150.00
Big Button, Water Set, Amber, 5 Piece 165.00
Bigler, Goblet, Flint 42.50
Birch Leaf, Goblet 25.00
Bird & Strawberry, Berry Set, Footed, 7 Piece 200.00
Bird & Strawberry, Bowl, Footed, 8 In. 58.00
Bird & Strawberry, Bowl, Footed, Oval, 6 X 9 1/2 In. 65.00
Bird & Strawberry, Butter, Cover 100.00
Bird & Strawberry, Cake Stand, 9 1/4 In. 50.00
Bird & Strawberry, Compote, Cover 115.00
Bird & Strawberry, Creamer .... 48.00 To 60.00
Bird & Strawberry, Platter, 12 In. 75.00
Bird & Strawberry, Punch Cup 18.00
Bird & Strawberry, Spooner 55.00

Bird & Strawberry, Sugar, Cover .... 65.00 To 80.00
Bird & Strawberry, Table Set, 4 Piece 300.00
Bird & Strawberry, Wine .... 45.00 To 65.00
    BIRD IN RING, see Grace
Bird In Roses, Champagne 34.00
Birds In Swamp, Goblet 35.00
Bismarc Star, Wine 24.00
Blackberry, Goblet 25.00
Blaze, Wine 55.00
Blazing Cornucopia, Toothpick, Purple Eyes 15.00
Bleeding Heart, Cake Plate, Pedestal 25.00
Bleeding Heart, Creamer 38.00
Bleeding Heart, Goblet, Buttermilk 20.00
Bleeding Heart, Mug 37.00
Bleeding Heart, Mug, White Opaque 85.00
Bleeding Heart, Wine 175.00
    BLOCK & CIRCLE, see Mellor
Block & Double Bar, Tumbler, Ruby Stained 30.00
    BLOCK & FAN, see Romeo
    BLOCK & FINE CUT, see Fine Cut & Block
    BLOCK & LATTICE, see Big Button
Block & Rosette, Spooner, Gold Trim 25.00
    BLOCK & STAR, see Valencia Waffle
Block & Thumbprint, Bowl, Scalloped, Footed, Flint, 7 7/8 In. 12.50
    BLOCK WITH STARS, see Hanover
Block, Bowl, Scalloped Rim, Flint, 8 1/4 In. 32.50
Block, Butter, Cover, Frosted, Amber Stained 45.00
Block, Butter, Cover, Ruby Stained 55.00
Block, Creamer, Frosted, Amber Stained 38.00
    BLOCKHOUSE, see Hanover
Blue Heron, Pitcher 150.00
Blue Heron, Sugar, Cover 55.00
    BLUEBIRD, see Bird & Strawberry
Bohemian, Berry Bowl, Green, Gold Trim 20.00
Bohemian, Pitcher, Cranberry, Gold Trim 295.00
Bordered Ellipse, Butter, Cover 65.00
Bosworth, Goblet, Scalloped Foot 25.00
Bow–Knot, Cruet, Frosted, Goofus Design 80.00
Bowtie, Candy Dish, 4 X 7 In. 25.00
Bowtie, Compote, High Standard, 9 In. 50.00
Bowtie, Creamer 45.00
Bowtie, Goblet 55.00
Bowtie, Salt, Master 45.00
Box–In–Box, Butter, Cover, Ruby Stained 110.00
Box–In–Box, Tumbler, Ruby Stained 40.00
Branched Tree, Pitcher .... 80.00 To 90.00
Brazen Shield, Tumbler, Blue 47.50
Brickwork, Creamer, Individual 12.00
Broken Column, Berry Bowl, 8 In. 35.00
Broken Column, Cake Stand 70.00
Broken Column, Celery, Cobalt Blue 48.00
Broken Column, Compote 120.00
Broken Column, Compote, Ruby Flashed 175.00
Broken Column, Cruet, Ruby Stained 75.00
Broken Column, Cup, Cobalt Blue 55.00
Broken Column, Goblet 22.00
Broken Column, Goblet, Cobalt Blue 65.00
Broken Column, Pitcher, Water .... 70.00 To 95.00
Broken Column, Plate, Red Notches, 8 In. 44.00
Broken Column, Spooner .... 30.00 To 32.00
Broken Column, Sugar, Cover 60.00
Broken Column, Tumbler, Cobalt Blue 55.00
Broken Column, Wine 85.00
    BROUGHTON, see Pattee Cross

BRYCE, see Ribbon Candy
BUCKET, see Oaken Bucket

Buckingham, Toothpick, 3 Handles, Gold Trim	26.00
Buckle With Star, Cake Stand	36.50
Buckle With Star, Creamer, Footed	28.00
Buckle, Butter, Cover, Acorn Finial, Flint	40.00
Buckle, Compote, Open, 10 In.	45.00
Buckle, Goblet	18.00 To 20.00
Buckle, Goblet, Flint	32.00
Buckle, Spooner, Flint	34.00
Buckle, Sugar, Cover, Flint	48.00
Budded Ivy, Champagne	32.50
Budded Ivy, Compote, Open	45.00
Bull's-Eye & Daisy, Berry Set, 8 Piece	95.00
Bull's-Eye & Daisy, Goblet, Red Eyes	20.00
Bull's-Eye & Daisy, Sugar, Handles	25.00
Bull's-Eye & Daisy, Water Set, 6 Piece	125.00
Bull's-Eye & Daisy, Wine, Green	20.00
Bull's-Eye & Fan, Butter, Green, Gold Trim	75.00
Bull's-Eye & Fan, Creamer, Blue, Gold Trim	45.00
Bull's-Eye & Fan, Pitcher, Water	38.00
Bull's-Eye & Fan, Spooner, Blue, Gold Trim	45.00
Bull's-Eye & Fan, Sugar, Cover, Blue, Gold Trim	35.00 To 55.00
Bull's-Eye & Fan, Toothpick	15.00
Bull's-Eye & Spearhead, Compote, Findlay, 7 1/2 In.	55.00
Bull's-Eye & Spearhead, Wine, Findlay	15.00
Bull's-Eye Band, Cake Stand	75.00
Bull's-Eye Band, Compote, Etched, 8 In.	60.00
Bull's-Eye Band, Fruit Stand	65.00
Bull's-Eye Band, Goblet	95.00
Bull's-Eye Band, Plate, 7 In.	65.00
Bull's-Eye Band, Sauce	10.00
Bull's-Eye Band, Sugar, Cover	80.00
Bull's-Eye Variant, Spooner	26.00
Bull's-Eye Variant, Wine	15.00 To 32.00
Bull's-Eye With Diamond Point, Celery	150.00
Bull's-Eye With Diamond Point, Goblet, Flint	110.00
Bull's-Eye With Diamond Point, Tumbler, Bar, Flint	165.00
Bull's-Eye With Diamond Point, Whiskey	150.00
Bull's-Eye, Cruet	25.00
Bull's-Eye, Eggcup, Flint, 3 1/4 In.	253.00
Bull's-Eye, Goblet, Flint, 6 1/4 In.	154.00
Bull's-Eye, Toothpick, Marked St.Louis	32.50
Bull's-Eye, Wine	25.00
Bullet, Spooner	165.00
Bunker Hill, Bread Plate, 13 X 9 In.	75.00
Butterflies & Flowers, Compote, Ruffled, Open	45.00
BUTTERFLY & FAN, see Grace	
Butterfly, Tray, Sandwich, Oval, 7 3/4 In.	150.00
Button Arches, Berry Set, 7 Piece	180.00
Button Arches, Creamer, Ruby Stained	20.00 To 40.00
Button Arches, Spooner, Platinum Band	45.00
Button Arches, Sugar, Cover, Platinum Band	65.00
Button Arches, Toothpick, Ruby Stained, 1899	38.00
Button Arches, Tumbler, Frosted Band, Ruby Stained	30.00
Button Arches, Water Set, Ruby Stained, 7 Piece	250.00
Button Arches, Wine	15.00
Buzz Saw, Creamer	15.00
Buzz Star, Punch Bowl	65.00
Buzz Star, Punch Cup	15.00
Buzz Star, Spooner, Child's	14.00
Cabbage Leaf, Bowl, Cover, Frosted Bunny Heads	275.00
Cabbage Rose, Bowl, Oval, 5 1/2 X 8 In.	27.50
Cabbage Rose, Compote, Wafer Base, Cover, Flint, 11 In.	110.00

Bull's–Eye & Daisy

Cathedral

Ceres

Classic

Columbian Coin

Dahlia

Cabbage Rose, Creamer, Applied Handle 58.50
Cabbage Rose, Spooner 35.00
Cable With Ring, Sugar, Flint 88.00
Cable, Bowl, Flint, 8 In. 45.00
Cable, Butter, Cover, Flint 75.00
Cable, Compote, 8 1/4 X 4 3/8 In. 65.00
Cable, Eggcup, Flint .... 40.00 To 50.00
Cable, Goblet, Flint 45.00
Cable, Goblet, Flint, 5 1/2 In. 75.00
Cable, Spooner, Flint 35.00
Cactus, Toothpick, Chocolate 55.00
Cadmus, Goblet 15.00
  CALIFORNIA, see Beaded Grape
Canadian, Goblet 45.00
Canadian, Pitcher, Water .... 90.00 To 95.00
Canadian, Wine 40.00

The pressed glass pattern sometimes called Candlewick is listed in
this section as Banded Raindrop. There is also a pattern called

"Candlewick" which has been made by Imperial Glass Corporation since 1936. It is listed in this book under Imperial, Candlewick.

CANDY RIBBON, see Ribbon Candy

Cane & Rosette, Celery	30.00
Cane Horseshoe, Sugar	10.00
Cane, Canoe, Blue	50.00
Cane, Creamer	20.00
Cane, Perfume Bottle, Canary Yellow	450.00
Cane, Pickle, Castor, Flint, Amber	115.00
Cane, Pitcher, Water, Blue	60.00
Cape Cod, Bread Plate	40.00
Cape Cod, Compote, Cover	70.00
Cape Cod, Goblet	45.00
Capitol Building, Goblet	35.00

CARDINAL, see Cardinal Bird

Cardinal Bird, Creamer	40.00
Cardinal Bird, Goblet	20.00 To 45.00
Carnation, Pitcher, Water	35.00
Carolina, Wine	28.50
Cathedral, Cake Stand, Vaseline	62.00
Cathedral, Compote, Amethyst, 6 3/4 In.	50.00
Cathedral, Compote, Blue, 9 1/2 In.	65.00
Cathedral, Compote, Ruffled Rim, Amber	55.00
Cathedral, Goblet	65.00
Cathedral, Relish, Fish Shape, Blue	30.00 To 38.00
Cathedral, Wine	32.00
Cathedral, Wine, Amber	43.00

CENTENNIAL, see Liberty Bell; Washington Centennial
CHAIN WITH DIAMONDS, see Washington Centennial

Chain With Star, Bread Plate	33.00
Chain With Star, Cake Plate	38.00
Chain With Star, Goblet	20.00 To 25.00
Chain, Salt, Master	20.00
Chain, Wine	15.00 To 22.00
Chandelier, Butter, Cover	65.00
Chandelier, Celery	36.50
Chandelier, Creamer, Etched	50.00
Chandelier, Goblet	30.00 To 65.00
Chandelier, Inkwell	75.00
Chandelier, Pitcher, Water	60.00
Chandelier, Spooner, Etched	25.00
Chandelier, Sugar, Cover	35.00
Cherry, Goblet	35.00

CHURCH WINDOWS, see Tulip Petals

Circled Scroll, Creamer, Green Opalescent	40.00
Civil War, Tumbler, Flint, Bumper To The Flag, Large	225.00
Civil War, Tumbler, Flint, Bumper To The Flag, Small	135.00
Classic Medallion, Creamer	25.00
Classic Medallion, Sherbet, Footed	8.50
Classic Medallion, Spooner	25.00
Classic, Berry Bowl	80.00
Classic, Bread Plate, Warrior	170.00
Classic, Celery, Collar	100.00
Classic, Celery, Log Feet	135.00
Classic, Pitcher, Water	600.00
Classic, Plate, Portrait, Signed Jacobus	165.00
Classic, Sauce, Log Feet	18.00
Classic, Spooner, Collar	100.00
Clear & Diamond Panels, Creamer, Child's	25.00
Clear & Diamond Panels, Table Set, Child's	115.00
Clear Diagonal Band, Compote, 7 X 8 1/2 In.	20.00
Clear Diagonal Band, Pitcher, Water	25.00
Cleat, Pitcher, Water, Flint	150.00

Coal Bucket, Toothpick, Amber 30.00
Coarse Zig–Zag, Wine 10.00
    COIN SPOT, see Coin Spot Category
Colonial, Goblet 25.00
Colonial, Toothpick 22.00
Colonial, Wine, Green, Gold Flashed 20.00
Colorado, Berry Set, Green, Gold Trim, 7 Piece 175.00
Colorado, Bowl, Blue, Gold Trim, 11 In. 35.00
Colorado, Bowl, Green, Gold Trim, Footed, 9 In. 40.00
Colorado, Butter, Cover, 6 1/2 In. 65.00
Colorado, Butter, Green, Cover, Gold Trim 70.00
Colorado, Creamer, Beaded Edge, Footed, Green, Gold Trim 70.00
Colorado, Creamer, Green, Flat, Souvenir, Individual 27.50
Colorado, Nappy, Blue, Gold Trim 38.00
Colorado, Punch Cup, Souvenir, Footed 20.00
Colorado, Sauce, Green .... 15.00 To 25.00
Colorado, Sherbet, Green, Gold Trim 30.00
Colorado, Table Set, Green, Gold Trim, 4 Piece .... 275.00 To 355.00
Colorado, Toothpick, Elks Carnival, Green, 1902 .... 28.00
Colorado, Toothpick, Gold Trim 21.00
Colorado, Toothpick, Green, 2 7/8 In. 40.00
Colorado, Tray, Card, Green, Gold Trim 45.00
Colorado, Vase, Blue, Footed 80.00
Colorado, Water Set, Green, Gold Trim, 7 Piece 375.00
Columbian Coin, Creamer, Gold Trim 70.00
Columbian Coin, Toothpick, Frosted .... 24.50 To 75.00
Columbian Coin, Toothpick, Gold Coins 165.00
Columbian Coin, Tumbler, Gold Coins 55.00
Columbian, Goblet 22.00
Columned Thumbprints, Celery 15.00
Comet, Goblet, Flint ....85.00 To 100.00
    COMPACT, see Snail
Constitution, Bread Plate 58.00
Constitution, Bread Plate, Liberty & Freedom, 1776 .... 55.00
Corcoran, Wine 15.00
Cord & Tassel, Cake Stand, 10 In. 65.00
Cord & Tassel, Compote, Cover 100.00
Cord & Tassel, Goblet 20.00
Cord & Tassel, Spooner 18.00
Cord & Tassel, Wine 40.00
Cord Drapery, Butter, Cover 45.00
Cord Drapery, Dish, Pickle, Cobalt Blue 100.00
Cord Drapery, Pitcher, Water, Amber 135.00
Cord Drapery, Relish, 4 X 7 In. 20.00
Cord Drapery, Sugar, Cover 40.00
Cordova, Punch Cup 8.00
Cordova, Toothpick 25.00
Corner Medallion, Creamer, Etched 15.00
Cornucopia, Sugar & Creamer, Cover, Blue 25.00
    COSMOS, see Cosmos Category
Cottage, Bowl, Oval, 7 X 9 In. 32.00
Cottage, Cake Stand, 10 In. 45.00
Cottage, Celery 32.50
Cottage, Goblet .... 18.50 To 28.00
Cottage, Plate, Ruby Stained, 5 1/8 In. 20.00
Cradle, Salt, Open, Amber 40.00
    CRANE, see Stork
Croesus, Berry Bowl, Amethyst, Gold Trim, Master 155.00
Croesus, Berry Set, Gold Trim, All Footed, 7 Piece 300.00
Croesus, Butter, Cover 195.00
Croesus, Butter, Cover, Purple 150.00
Croesus, Creamer, Green, Gold Trim 100.00
Croesus, Cruet, Purple, Gold Trim 50.00
Croesus, Pitcher, Water, Green, Gold Trim 225.00

Croesus, Pitcher, Water, Purple, Gold Handle 150.00
Croesus, Plate, Green 195.00
Croesus, Plate, Purple 245.00
Croesus, Salt & Pepper, Gold Trim, Amethyst 145.00
Croesus, Salt & Pepper, Purple, Gold Trim, Original Lids 135.00
Croesus, Sauce, Green, Gold Trim 25.00
Croesus, Spooner, Green, Gold Trim 110.00
Croesus, Spooner, Purple, Gold Trim 85.00
Croesus, Sugar, Cover, Green, Gold Trim 95.00
Croesus, Sugar, Cover, Purple, Gold Trim 90.00
Croesus, Table Set, Green, Gold Trim, 4 Piece 575.00
Croesus, Toothpick, Amethyst 95.00
Croesus, Tray, Kidney Shape, Green, 9 1/4 In. 25.00
Crossbar & Fine Cut, Celery 20.00
Crossed Fern, Bowl, Opaque Green, Footed, 7 In. 45.00
Crowfoot, Butter, Cover 40.00
Crowfoot, Compote, Cover, 12 In. 80.00
Crowfoot, Creamer 22.00
Crowfoot, Goblet 28.00
Crowfoot, Pitcher, Water 55.00
Crowfoot, Spooner 35.00
Crowfoot, Sugar & Creamer 30.00
  CROWN JEWELS, see Chandelier; Queen's Necklace
Crystal Band, Goblet 12.00
Crystal Wedding, Banana Stand .... 45.00 To 75.00
Crystal Wedding, Bowl, Cover, Square, 5 In. 62.50
Crystal Wedding, Cake Stand, Square, 9 In. 60.00
Crystal Wedding, Goblet 65.00
Crystal Wedding, Spooner, Amber Stained 45.00
  CUBE WITH FAN, see Pineapple & Fan
Cube, Butter, Cover 40.00
Cube, Punch Bowl 150.00
  CUPID & PSYCHE, see Psyche & Cupid
Cupid & Venus, Bread Plate, 11 1/2 In. 60.00
Cupid & Venus, Cake Plate, Handles 45.00
Cupid & Venus, Celery 55.00
Cupid & Venus, Cordial 85.00
Cupid & Venus, Creamer 36.50
Cupid & Venus, Goblet 50.00
Cupid & Venus, Jam Jar 85.00
Cupid & Venus, Mug, Child's 20.00
Cupid & Venus, Pitcher, Water .... 55.00 To 60.00

Deer & Dog

Diamond Thumbprint

Diamond Point

Cupid & Venus, Spooner 32.00
Cupid's Hunt, Bread Plate, Virginia Dare Center .... 65.00 To 75.00
Currant, Butter Chip 4.00
Currant, Butter, Cover 75.00
Currant, Cake Stand, 11 In. 55.00
Currier & Ives, Banana Boat .... 28.00 To 35.00
Currier & Ives, Compote, Cover, Amber, 11 1/2 In. 145.00
Currier & Ives, Cup 12.00
Currier & Ives, Finger Bowl 42.00
Currier & Ives, Goblet 24.00
Currier & Ives, Pitcher, Milk 50.00
Currier & Ives, Tray, Donkey & Cart 75.00
Currier & Ives, Wine 22.50
Curtain Tieback, Cake Stand, Pattern On Foot, 9 In. 23.00
Curtain Tieback, Goblet .... 11.00 To 25.00
Curtain Tieback, Pitcher .... 50.00 To 55.00
Curtain, Cake Stand, 9 In. 45.00
Curtain, Compote, 8 In. 30.00
Curtain, Mug, Amber 65.00
Cut Log, Cake Stand, 9 In. 45.00
Cut Log, Compote, 5 In. 35.00
Cut Log, Compote, Cover, 7 In. 35.00
Cut Log, Creamer, Individual .... 12.00 To 15.00
Cut Log, Cruet, Original Stopper 35.00
Cut Log, Dish, Olive 20.00
Cut Log, Goblet 60.00
Cut Log, Nappy 18.50
Cut Log, Pitcher, Water, Tankard Style 60.00
Cut Log, Sugar, Cover, Individual 18.00
Cut Log, Wine .... 15.00 To 38.00
Dahlia With Petal, Berry Bowl, Master, Green, Gold Trim 45.00
Dahlia With Petal, Wine 18.00
Dahlia, Bread Plate, Grape Handles, Oval 45.00
Dahlia, Cake Stand, 8 3/4 In. 40.00
Dahlia, Mug 32.50
Dahlia, Pitcher, Water .... 27.00 To 45.00
DAISIES IN OVAL PANELS, see Bull's—Eye & Fan
Daisy & Button With Crossbar, Cruet 75.00
Daisy & Button With Crossbar, Cruet, Amber 110.00
Daisy & Button With Crossbar, Goblet, Yellow 35.00
Daisy & Button With Crossbar, Pitcher, Water, Amber 90.00
Daisy & Button With Crossbar, Sauce, Amber, Footed 12.00
Daisy & Button With Crossbar, Tumbler, Blue 30.00
Daisy & Button With Crossbar, Water Set, Canary, 7 Piece 250.00
Daisy & Button With Narcissus, Cup & Saucer 18.00
Daisy & Button With Narcissus, Water Set, 6 Piece 100.00
Daisy & Button With Narcissus, Wine 22.00
Daisy & Button With Thumbprint, Pitcher, Water, Amber Trim 90.00
Daisy & Button With V—Ornament, Celery 18.00
Daisy & Button With V—Ornament, Toothpick, Amber 35.00
Daisy & Button With V—Ornament, Tumbler, Amber 22.00
Daisy & Button With V—Ornament, Tumbler, Vaseline 35.00
Daisy & Button, Basket, Nickel Silver Handle, C.1880, 6 In. 125.00
Daisy & Button, Berry Set, Blue, 7 Piece 85.00
Daisy & Button, Canoe, Sapphire, 8 In. 60.00
Daisy & Button, Celery 15.00
Daisy & Button, Creamer, Individual 20.00
Daisy & Button, Dish, Fan Shape 14.00
Daisy & Button, Goblet, Amber .... 20.00 To 30.00
Daisy & Button, Jug, Cover 25.00
Daisy & Button, Plate, Blue, 10 In. 35.00
Daisy & Button, Powder Jar, Amber 28.00
Daisy & Button, Salt Dip, Sapphire 12.00
Daisy & Button, Shot Glass, Blue 12.00

Daisy & Button, Table Set, Child's, Pink, 3 Piece 40.00
Daisy & Button, Toothpick, Flared Rim, Amber 30.00
Daisy Band, Cup & Saucer 20.00
Daisy, Wine, Amethyst Eyes 25.00
Dakota, Butter, Cover .... 40.00 To 45.00
Dakota, Butter, Cover, Etched 65.00
Dakota, Celery, Etched 45.00
Dakota, Compote, 9 X 9 In. 55.00
Dakota, Creamer, Etched 55.00
Dakota, Goblet, Etched, Souvenir 35.00
Dakota, Goblet, Fern Etched, Ruby Flashed 75.00
Dakota, Pitcher, Etched Bird On Tree, Florals 125.00
Dakota, Pitcher, Milk, Etched Fish, Lily Pads & Cattails 350.00
Dakota, Sauce, Footed, 4 In. 24.50
Dakota, Sugar & Creamer, Etched 75.00
Dakota, Tray, Water, 13 1/2 In. 120.00
Dakota, Tumbler, Etched 40.00
Dakota, Wine .... 20.00 To 22.50
Dakota, Wine, Etched Design 30.00
Dart, Creamer, Pedestal, 6 3/4 In. 20.00
Deer & Dog, Goblet .... 45.00 To 70.00
Deer & Dog, Goblet, Etched 60.00
Deer & Oak Tree, Pitcher, Water, Findlay 155.00
Deer & Pine Tree, Butter, Cover 95.00
Deer & Pine Tree, Cake Plate 120.00
Deer & Pine Tree, Celery, Frosted, Round 45.00
Delaware, Banana Bowl, Rose, Gold Trim 48.00
Delaware, Berry Bowl, Green, 8 In. 60.00
Delaware, Bowl, Green, Gold Trim, 9 1/2 In. 35.00
Delaware, Bowl, Green, Octagonal, 9 In. 65.00
Delaware, Bowl, Side Spouts, Green, Gold Trim, 11 3/4 In. 35.00
Delaware, Celery, Green, Gold Trim 60.00
Delaware, Creamer, Green, Gold Trim .... 45.00 To 50.00
Delaware, Cruet, Green, Gold Trim 145.00
Delaware, Pitcher, Claret, Green, Gold Trim 165.00
Delaware, Powder Box, Jeweled Cover, Gold Trim 195.00
Delaware, Punch Cup, Rose 24.00
Delaware, Sauce, Green, Round, 4 In. 35.00
Delaware, Spooner, Green, Gold Trim 45.00
Delaware, Sugar & Creamer, Cranberry 95.00
Delaware, Sugar, Cover, Green, Gold Trim 45.00
Delaware, Sugar, Green, Gold Trim 28.00
Delaware, Table Set, Ruby Flashed, 4 Piece 400.00
Delaware, Toothpick, Green, Gold Trim .... 75.00 To 85.00
Delaware, Tumbler, Green, Gold Trim 22.00
Delaware, Vase, Rose, Gold Trim, 6 In. .... 50.00 To 65.00
Dewdrop & Raindrop, Wine .... 20.00 To 22.00
Dewdrop In Points, Compote 40.00
Dewdrop With Sheaf of Wheat, Bread Tray, 10 In. 30.00
Dewdrop With Star, Compote, Cover, 12 In. .... 24.00 To 25.00
Dewdrop, Relish, Campbell Glass Co., C.1877 .... 22.00
Dewdrop, Tumbler 8.00
      DEWEY, see also Spanish American
Dewey, Butter, Cover, Green 45.00
Dewey, Creamer, Yellow 27.50
Dewey, Pitcher, Amber, 5 In. 50.00
Diagonal Band & Fan, Compote, Cover, 10 1/2 In. 50.00
Diagonal Band & Fan, Pitcher, Milk 38.00
Diagonal Band & Fan, Wine 20.00
Diagonal Sawtooth Band, Champagne, Flint 45.00
Diamond & Sunburst, Bowl, Cover, 8 In. 35.00
      DIAMOND CUT WITH FAN, see Holbrook
Diamond Cut With Leaf, Sugar, Cover, Amber 65.00
Diamond Cut With Leaf, Wine 15.00

Excelsior with Maltese Cross   Fine Cut & Block   Fan with Diamond

DIAMOND HORSESHOE, see Aurora
DIAMOND MEDALLION, see Grand
Diamond Point Discs, Spooner 12.00
Diamond Point Loop, Sugar, Cover, Amber 32.00
Diamond Point With Panels, Tumbler, Footed, Flint 35.00
Diamond Point, Goblet, 6 1/2 In. 15.00
Diamond Point, Goblet, Flint 35.00
Diamond Point, Wine, Flint 65.00
DIAMOND PRISMS, see also Albany
Diamond Prisms, Sugar, Cover 12.00
Diamond Prisms, Wine 18.50
Diamond Quilted, Goblet, Amber .... 30.00 To 50.00
Diamond Quilted, Goblet, Blue 35.00
Diamond Quilted, Goblet, Vaseline 35.00
Diamond Quilted, Sauce, Footed, Amethyst 25.00
Diamond Quilted, Wine, Amber 20.00
Diamond Shield, Goblet 18.00
Diamond Sunburst, Compote, Cover 48.00
Diamond Sunburst, Compote, Jelly 15.00
DIAMOND SWAG, see Fandango
Diamond Thumbprint, Creamer, Flint, 6 In. 95.00
Diamond Thumbprint, Sauce, Footed, Flint 45.00
Diamond Thumbprint, Tumbler, Flint .... 90.00 To 95.00
Diamond, Butter, Cover, Blue 85.00
Diamonds & Clubs, Water Set, Green, Gold Trim, 5 Piece 160.00
Diamonds With Double Fans, Goblet 15.00
Dice & Block, Cruet 125.00
Dice & Block, Cruet, Amber 85.00
Dickinson, Spooner 22.00
Diedre, Goblet 13.00
Dolphin, Bread Plate, Frosted Center, Dolphin Feet, Oval 225.00
DORIC, see Feather
Double Beetle Band, Goblet, Amber 35.00
Double Beetle Band, Mug, Child's 25.00
Double Beetle Band, Wine, Blue 22.00
DOUBLE DAHLIA WITH LENS, see Dahlia with Petal
DOUBLE DAISY, see Rosette Band
Double Fan, Creamer 18.00
DOUBLE LOOP, see Ribbon Candy
DOUBLE VINE, see Bellflower, Double Vine
DOUBLE WEDDING RING, see Wedding Ring
Doyle's Doyle, Goblet 13.50

Flattened Diamond & Sunburst   Frosted Circle   Frosted Eagle

Doyle's Shell, Wine	15.00
DRAPERY BAND WITH STARS, see Doyle's Doyle	
Drum, Butter, Cover, Child's	135.00
Drum, Punch Cup	20.00
Drum, Sugar & Creamer	90.00
Drum, Sugar, Cover, Child's	110.00
Duchess, Creamer, Green, Gold Trim	95.00
Duquesne, Goblet	15.00
E PLURIBUS UNUM, see Emblem	
EARL, see Spirea Band	
Eastern Star, Goblet	15.00
Egg In Sand, Bread Plate	25.00 To 45.00
Egg In Sand, Goblet	20.00 To 25.00
Egyptian, Bread Plate, Cleopatra Center	30.00
Egyptian, Bread Plate, Mormon Temple Center	200.00
Egyptian, Celery	95.00
Egyptian, Creamer	31.00 To 37.50
Egyptian, Goblet	30.00 To 65.00
Egyptian, Relish	12.00 To 15.00
Egyptian, Spooner, Footed	30.00
Egyptian, Sugar, 5 In.	30.00
Eight-O-Eight, Plate, 5 1/2 In.	20.00
Eight-O-Eight, Wine	15.00
Electric, Compote, Jelly, Green	18.50
Elephant Toes, Relish	7.00
Elephant Toes, Toothpick	40.00
EMBLEM, see also American Shield; Bullet	
Emblem, Relish	50.00
Emerald Green Herringbone, Cruet, Original Stopper, Green	95.00
Emerald Green Herringbone, Pitcher, Milk, Green	75.00
Empress, Spooner, Green, Gold Trim	48.00
Empress, Sugar & Creamer, Emerald, Gold Trim, Northwood	140.00
Empress, Tumbler	40.00
ENGLISH HOBNAIL CROSS, see Amberette	
Esther, Butter, Cover, Green, Gold Trim	110.00
Esther, Compote, Jelly, Green	30.00 To 55.00
Esther, Cruet, Green	80.00
Esther, Spooner, Green, Gold Trim	65.00
Esther, Sugar, Cover, Green, Gold Trim	115.00
Esther, Toothpick, Green, Gold Trim	75.00
Esther, Wine	17.50
ETCHED DAKOTA, see Dakota	

ETCHED FERN, see Crossbar & Fine Cut

Eureka, Bread Plate	30.00
Eureka, Compote, Jelly	75.00
Eureka, Goblet, Flint	19.00
Eureka, Spooner, Flint	42.00
Everglades, Bowl, Vaseline, Gold Trim, 5 In.	23.50
Everglades, Sugar, Opalescent, Cover, Blue	95.00
Excelsior With Maltese Cross, Cake Stand, 9 1/2 In.	125.00
Excelsior, Goblet	50.00
Excelsior, Wine	25.00 To 42.50
Eyewinker, Butter, Cover	50.00 To 75.00
Eyewinker, Celery	40.00
Eyewinker, Saltshaker	30.00
Eyewinker, Saucer	20.00
Eyewinker, Syrup	100.00

FAGOT, see Vera

Faith, Hope & Charity, Pat.Nov.23, 1875	85.00
Fan & Flute, Butter, Cover, Etch	100.00
Fan & Flute, Goblet	65.00
Fan & Flute, Pitcher, Water, Ruby Stained	98.00
Fan & Flute, Tumbler, Ruby Stained	30.00 To 47.50

FAN WITH DIAMOND, see Shell

Fandango, Cruet	27.50
Feather Band, Pitcher, Water	20.00
Feather Duster, Bread Plate	22.00
Feather Duster, Cake Stand, 8 1/2 In.	20.00
Feather Duster, Creamer, Green	35.00
Feather Duster, Water Set, Green, 6 Piece	160.00
Feather, Butter, Cover	45.00
Feather, Cake Stand, 11 In.	40.00
Feather, Cake Stand, Green, 9 1/2 In.	78.00
Feather, Celery	35.00
Feather, Cruet	20.00 To 50.00
Feather, Goblet	57.00
Feather, Pitcher, Water	48.50 To 60.00
Feather, Pitcher, Water, Green	200.00 To 215.00
Feather, Plate, 10 In.	40.00
Feather, Spooner	25.00
Feather, Sugar, Cover	33.00 To 50.00
Feather, Tumbler	45.00
Feather, Wine	32.00 To 45.00
Fern Garland, Creamer	15.00
Fern Garland, Pitcher	45.00
Fern Garland, Sherbet	13.00
Fern Garland, Spooner	30.00
Fern Garland, Sugar, Cover	35.00
Fern Garland, Tumbler	15.00
Fern, Compote, Etched	20.00
Fernland, Table Set, Child's, 4 Piece	65.00

FESTOON & GRAPE, see Grape & Festoon

Festoon, Bowl, 5 X 8 In.	25.00
Festoon, Cake Stand	38.00
Festoon, Sugar, Cover	58.00
Festoon, Table Set, Ruby Stained, 4 Piece	145.00
Festoon, Tray, Water	55.00
Festoon, Tumbler	15.00
File, Creamer	23.00
Fine Cut & Block, Cordial, Blue & Clear	65.00
Fine Cut & Block, Goblet	28.00
Fine Cut & Block, Pitcher, Blue	90.00
Fine Cut & Block, Pitcher, Buttermilk, Blue Blocks	45.00
Fine Cut & Block, Spooner	35.00
Fine Cut & Block, Tray, Blue, 14 1/2 X 12 1/2 In.	75.00

FINE CUT & FEATHER, see Feather

Fine Cut & Panel, Bread Plate 27.50
Fine Cut & Panel, Cake Stand, Vaseline 45.00
Fine Cut & Panel, Goblet, Blue 30.00
Fine Cut & Panel, Tray, Water, Canary, 12 In. 50.00
Fine Cut, Creamer, Blue 35.00
Fine Cut, Plate, Amber, 7 In. 12.50
Fine Cut, Toothpick, Hat Shape, Amber 20.00
Fine Cut, Tumbler, Gold Eyes, Blue 35.00
Fine Rib, Cordial, Flint, 3 1/4 In. 145.00
Fine Rib, Sugar, Cover, Flint ..,.. 175.00
Fine Rib, Wine, Flint 43.50
Fishscale, Bowl, Cover, 7 In. 55.00
Fishscale, Compote, Jelly 16.00
Fishscale, Pitcher, Milk 35.00
Flamingo Habitat, Compote, Etched, 7 1/2 X 8 In. 45.00
Flamingo Habitat, Creamer 25.00
Flamingo Habitat, Dish, Cheese, Cover 70.00
Flamingo Habitat, Tumbler, Etched 22.00
Flamingo, Goblet 45.00
Flattened Diamond & Sunburst, Cake Stand 39.50
Flattened Diamond & Sunburst, Creamer 15.00
Flattened Diamond & Sunburst, Punch Cup, Child's 5.00
Fleur–De–Lis & Drape, Wine 25.00
Fleur–De–Lis, Creamer 150.00
Fleur–De–Lis, Toothpick 25.00
Fleur–De–Lis, Wine 14.00
Florida Palm, Compote 25.00
    FLORIDA, see Emerald Green Herringbone
    FLORODORA, see Bohemian
Flower & Pleat, Cruet, Stopper, Clear & Frosted 115.00
Flower & Pleat, Mustard, Amber Flowers 45.00
Flower Band, Creamer, Frosted 110.00
Flower Band, Spooner, Frosted 68.00
    FLOWER FLANGE, see Dewey
Flower Medallion, Goblet, Flint 50.00
    FLOWER PANELED CANE, see Cane & Rosette
Flower Pot, Creamer 30.00
Flute, Berry Set, Child's 55.00
Flute, Bottle, Bar, Flint, 1 Qt. 75.00
Flute, Bottle, Bar, Straight Flutes 70.00
    FLYING ROBIN, see Hummingbird
Flying Stork, Castor, Pickle 125.00

Garfield Drape

Grape & Festoon

Horn of Plenty

Hamilton   Inverted Fern   Jeweled Heart

Flying Stork, Spooner	55.00
Forget–Me–Not, Butter, Cover, Paneled	65.00
Forget–Me–Not, Condiment Set, White, 4 Piece	70.00
Forget–Me–Not, Plate, Kitten Center, Handles, 9 In.	27.50
French Centennial, Compote	85.00
FROSTED PATTERNS, see also under name of main pattern	
Frosted Circle, Cake Stand	35.00
Frosted Circle, Spooner	25.00
FROSTED CRANE, see Frosted Stork	
Frosted Eagle, Bowl, Braided Rope Trim, Cover, 8 In.	395.00
Frosted Eagle, Celery	140.00
Frosted Eagle, Creamer, Etched	48.00
Frosted Eagle, Sugar, Cover	235.00
FROSTED FLOWER BAND, see Flower Band, Frosted	
Frosted Leaf, Eggcup, Flint	85.00
Frosted Leaf, Goblet, Flint	120.00
FROSTED LION, see Lion, Frosted	
FROSTED RIBBON, see Ribbon, Frosted	
FROSTED ROMAN KEY, see Roman Key, Frosted	
Frosted Stork, Bread Plate, One–O–One Border, 11 1/2 X 8 In.	70.00
Frosted Stork, Bread Plate, Scenic Border, 11 1/2 X 8 In.	90.00
Frosted Stork, Creamer	45.00
Frosted Stork, Goblet	75.00
Frosted Stork, Waste Bowl	35.00
FROSTED WAFFLE, see Hidalgo	
Gaelic, Toothpick	26.50
Gaelic, Toothpick, Gold Trim	28.50
Gaelic, Water Set, 5 Piece	75.00 To 100.00
Galloway, Butter, Cover	50.00
Galloway, Celery	18.50
Galloway, Dish, Sardine	16.00
Galloway, Goblet	75.00
Galloway, Pitcher, Milk	72.00
Galloway, Salt & Pepper	35.00
Galloway, Toothpick	35.00
Galloway, Water Set, Gold Trim, 7 Piece	165.00
Galloway, Wine	38.00 To 43.50
Garden Fruits, Goblet, Etched	13.00
GARDEN OF EDEN, see also Lotus & Serpent	
Garden of Eden, Bread Plate	20.00
Garden of Eden, Mug	37.00
Garden of Eden, Pitcher, Water, 8 1/2 In.	75.00

Garfield Drape, Compote, Cover, 8 In. 135.00
Garfield Drape, Creamer 38.50
Garfield Drape, Goblet .... 30.00 To 50.00
Garfield Drape, Pitcher, Water .... 70.00 To 95.00
Garfield Drape, Spooner ....•.............. 22.00
Garfield Memorial, Bread Plate 60.00
Gathered Knot, Spooner 20.00
Gatling Gun, Toothpick, Blue 25.00
George Peabody, Cup & Saucer 195.00
Giant Bull's–Eye, Cracker Jar 45.00
Giant Sawtooth, Cruet 30.00
Giant Sawtooth, Goblet, Flint 145.00
Giant Sawtooth, Spill Holder, Flint, 5 1/4 In. 35.00
Girl With Fan, Goblet .... 32.50 To 45.00
Gladiator, Tumbler, Green With Gold 25.00
Golden Rule, Plate 110.00
  GOOD LUCK, see Horseshoe
Gothic Arch, Relish, 7 In. 90.00
Gothic Arches, Castor, 3–Bottle, Original Metal Holder 60.00
Gothic, Bowl, Footed, Flint, 8 In. 60.00
Gothic, Eggcup, Flint 35.00
Gothic, Spooner, Flint 35.00
Grace, Bread Tray, Oval, 11 In. 30.00
Grace, Celery 40.00
Grace, Pitcher, Water 110.00
Grand, Bread Plate 21.50
Grand, Goblet 21.50
  GRAPE & CABLE, see Northwood's Grape
Grape & Cherry, Creamer, Blue 30.00
Grape & Festoon, Goblet, Stippled .... 26.50 To 35.00
Grape & Festoon, Sauce, Set of 4 .... 55.00
Grape & Festoon, Spooner, Stippled 21.00
Grape & Gothic Arches, Creamer, Green, Gold Trim 45.00
Grape & Gothic Arches, Table Set, Green, Northwood, 4 Piece 235.00
Grape & Gothic Arches, Water Set, Green, Gold Trim, 7 Piece 200.00
Grape Band, Compote 20.00
Grape Band, Goblet 18.00
Grape Band, Spooner 18.00
Grape Bunch, Wine 22.00
Grape Vine With Ovals, Butter, Cover, Child's 60.00
Grape Vine With Ovals, Spooner 55.00
Grape Vine With Ovals, Sugar, Child's 60.00
Grape With Scroll Medallion, Creamer, 1870s 20.00
Grape With Scroll Medallion, Sugar, Grape Cluster Handles 25.00
Grape With Thumbprint, Pitcher, Water, Cover 35.00
  GRAPE, see also Beaded Grape; Beaded Grape Medallion; Magnet &
    Grape; Magnet & Grape with Frosted Leaf; Paneled Grape
Grape, Wine, Stemmed, Pittsburgh 25.00
Grasshopper, Spooner 25.00
Grasshopper, Sugar, Cover 40.00
Gridley, Pitcher 140.00
Gridley, Pitcher, Water 85.00
Grooved Bigler, Goblet, Flint 48.00
Gypsy, Goblet 13.00
Hairpin With Thumbprint, Goblet, Flint 35.00
Hairpin, Compote, Scalloped, 10 1/2 In. 300.00
Hairpin, Spoon, Flint 35.00
Halley's Comet, Goblet 45.00
Halley's Comet, Syrup .... 48.50 To 50.00
Halley's Comet, Wine 30.00
Hamilton, Goblet, Flint 45.00
Hamilton, Spooner, Flint 22.00
Hand & Bar, Jam Jar, Cover 65.00
Hand, Bread Plate 23.00

Hand, Celery .... 32.00 To 41.50
Hand, Compote, Electric Blue 145.00
Hand, Jam Jar .... 35.00 To 48.00
Hand, Tumbler 135.00
Hanging Basket, Pitcher, Water 140.00
Hanover, Celery 25.00
Hanover, Sugar, Cover 24.50
Harvard, Saltshaker, Original Top 18.00
Hawaiian Lei, Spooner 18.50
Hawaiian Lei, Sugar, Handles, Open 24.50
Hawaiian Lei, Wine .... 25.00 To 35.00
Heart In Sand, Cruet 75.00
Heart Stem, Compote, Cover, 7 In. 115.00
Heart With Thumbprint, Bowl, 9 1/2 In. 41.50
Heart With Thumbprint, Cordial, Clear, 3 1/4 In. 150.00
Heart With Thumbprint, Cruet 45.00
Heart With Thumbprint, Goblet, Gold Trim .... 55.00 To 56.50
Heart With Thumbprint, Plate, 10 In. 25.00
Heart With Thumbprint, Punch Cup, Green 22.50
Heart With Thumbprint, Sugar, Pewter Band, Green 40.00
Heart With Thumbprint, Syrup, Pewter Lid 125.00
Heart With Thumbprint, Tumbler .... 30.00 To 65.00
Heart With Thumbprint, Vase, 6 In. .... 15.00 To 18.00
Heart With Thumbprint, Wine, Gold Trim 42.00
Henrietta, Sugar Shaker, Original Top 12.50
Hero, Butter, Cover 35.00
Herringbone, Berry Set, Emerald Green 125.00
Herringbone, Cruet, Emerald Green, Stopper 125.00
Herringbone, Pitcher, Water, Emerald Green .... 45.00 To 48.00
Herringbone, Plate, Green, Upturned Corners, 9 In. 37.50
Herringbone, Table Set, Green, 4 Piece 175.00
Hexagon Block, Butter, Cover, Etched Bird, Ruby Stained 78.00
Hickman, Cake Stand, 6 1/2 In. 32.00
Hickman, Compote, Open, 9 In. 45.00
Hickman, Goblet 28.00
Hickman, Relish, Green, Gold Trim 24.50
Hickman, Sauce, 8 In. 15.00
Hickman, Toothpick 45.00
Hidalgo, Butter, Cover, Etched Bellflower 50.00
Hidalgo, Celery, Etched 25.00
Hildago, Goblet, Etched 20.00
    HINOTO, see Diamond Point with Panels
    HOBNAIL, see Hobnail category
    HOBNAIL & BARS, see Barred Hobnail
Hobnail With Curved Bars, Pitcher, Water 35.00
Hobnail With Thumbprint Base, Butter, Cover, Child's, Blue 95.00
Hobnail With Thumbprint Base, Creamer, Child's, Blue 45.00
Hobstar, Goblet 25.00
Holbrook, Castor, Pickle, Metal Holder 95.00
Holly, Bowl, Rectangular, 4 X 10 In. 110.00
Holly, Relish, Amber 275.00
Holly, Sauce, Amber 135.00
Honeycomb Band, Goblet 15.00
Honeycomb, Celery .... 28.00 To 65.00
Honeycomb, Goblet, Flint .... 18.00 To 25.00
Honeycomb, Spooner 18.00
Horizontal Threads, Sugar, Child's, Cover 30.00
Horizontal Threads, Table Set, Child's, 4 Piece 110.00
Horn of Plenty, Creamer, Flint 185.00
Horn of Plenty, Eggcup .... 37.50 To 55.00
Horn of Plenty, Goblet, Flint .... 60.00 To 85.00
Horn of Plenty, Shot Glass, 3 In. 165.00
Horn of Plenty, Spooner, Yellow 225.00
Horn of Plenty, Sugar, Cover, Flint .... 70.00 To 110.00

Horse Mint, Wine 22.00
Horseshoe, Bowl, Oval, 9 In. 20.00
Horseshoe, Bread Plate, Horseshoe Handles, 14 X 10 In. 65.00
Horseshoe, Cake Stand, 10 In. 55.00
Horseshoe, Creamer .... 36.00 To 45.00
Horseshoe, Goblet, Knob Stem .... 30.00 To 36.50
Horseshoe, Pitcher, Milk ....95.00 To 125.00
Horseshoe, Pitcher, Water 65.00
Horseshoe, Sugar 35.00
Horseshoe, Tray, Double Handles 65.00
Huber, Eggcup 8.00
    HUCKLE, see Feather Duster
Hummingbird, Celery, Amber 65.00
Hummingbird, Goblet, Amber 65.00
Hummingbird, Goblet, Blue 70.00
Hummingbird, Pitcher, Water, Blue 125.00
Hummingbird, Table Set, Amber, 4 Piece 285.00
Hummingbird, Tray, Amber 175.00
Hundred Eye, Wine 9.50
Hundred–Leaved Rose, Bowl, 4 In. 5.00
Icicle With Chain Band, Goblet, Flint 48.00
Icicle With Star, Pitcher 30.00
    IDA, see Sheraton
Illinois, Pitcher, Silver–Plated Top 105.00
    INDIANA SWIRL, see Feather
Indiana, Tumbler 30.00
Indiana, Water Set, 7 Piece 95.00
Intaglio Sunflower, Pitcher, Water .... 45.00 To 60.00
Interlocking Hearts, Butter, Cover .... 35.00 To 38.00
Interlocking Hearts, Creamer 30.00
Inverted Fan & Feather, Berry Bowl, Green, Gold Trim 20.00
Inverted Fan & Feather, Tumbler .... 10.00 To 15.00
Inverted Fern, Eggcup 30.00
Inverted Fern, Sugar, Cover 85.00
Inverted Prism, Goblet, Etched 25.00
Inverted Strawberry, Berry Set, Child's, 5 Piece 125.00
Inverted Strawberry, Compote, 5 In. 21.50
Inverted Thumbprint With Star, Goblet 35.00
Inverted Thumbprint, Cruet, Vaseline 100.00
Inverted Thumbprint, Goblet, Canary 22.50
Inverted Thumbprint, Pitcher, Water, Square Top, Amber 50.00
Inverted Thumbprint, Syrup, Pinched Base, Blue 125.00
Ionia, Goblet 23.00
Iowa, Sugar, Pink Blush, Cover 22.00
Iris, Pitcher, Water, Gold Trim 85.00
Iris, Tumbler, Apple Green 98.00
Isis, Pitcher, Water 20.00
Isis, Wine 22.00
Ivanhoe, Spoon Tray, Gold Trim 30.00
Ivy In Snow, Dish, Honey, Cover, Green, Red Stained 95.00
Ivy In Snow, Goblet 25.00
Ivy In Snow, Syrup, Original Lid, Ruby Stained 295.00
Ivy Leaves, Cup & Saucer, Child's 29.00
Ivy, Relish, Handle 12.00
Jacob's Coat, Sugar, Cover, Amber 65.00
Jacob's Ladder With Maltese Cross, Butter 75.00
Jacob's Ladder With Maltese Cross, Sugar, Cover 65.00
Jacob's Ladder, Bowl, Oval, 6 1/2 X 10 1/2 In. 28.50
Jacob's Ladder, Celery .... 40.00 To 55.00
Jacob's Ladder, Celery, 1870, 9 In. 40.00
Jacob's Ladder, Compote, Cover, 8 1/2 In. 128.00
Jacob's Ladder, Creamer .... 30.00 To 40.00
Jacob's Ladder, Dish, Pickle 24.00
Jacob's Ladder, Goblet .... 50.00 To 62.00

Jacob's Ladder, Pitcher, Water 95.00
Jacob's Ladder, Plate, 1870, 6 1/4 In. 20.00
Jacob's Ladder, Relish, Maltese 'Cross In Handle .... 18.00 To 20.00
Jacob's Ladder, Salt, Footed 24.00
Jacob's Ladder, Spooner .... 30.00 To 35.00
Jacob's Ladder, Syrup 95.00
Jacob's Ladder, Wine .... 25.00 To 35.00
Jefferson's Optic, Cruet, Enamel & Gold, Amethyst 40.00
Jefferson's Optic, Toothpick, Green 45.00
Jenny Lind, Compote 145.00
Jewel & Dewdrop, Bread Plate, Our Daily Bread 36.00
Jewel & Dewdrop, Butter, Cover 55.00
Jewel & Dewdrop, Cake Stand, 9 In. 50.00
Jewel & Dewdrop, Creamer 35.00
Jewel & Dewdrop, Pitcher, Water .... 45.00 To 60.00
Jewel & Dewdrop, Toothpick 85.00
Jewel & Dewdrop, Wine 70.00
    JEWEL & FESTOON, see Loop & Jewel
Jewel Band, Sugar, Cover 35.00
Jeweled Drapery, Goblet 14.00
Jeweled Heart, Creamer, Gold Trim 25.00
Jeweled Heart, Creamer, Opalescent Green 95.00
Jeweled Heart, Pitcher, Water, Sapphire Blue 145.00
Jeweled Heart, Water Set, Gold Trim, 6 Piece 200.00
    JEWELED MOON & STAR, see Moon & Star Variant; Moon & Star
    JOB'S TEARS, see Art
    JUBILEE, see Hickman
Jumbo, Creamer 140.00
Jumbo, Sugar, Barnum Head, Cover 450.00
Kaleidoscope, Creamer 30.00
    KAMONI, see Pennsylvania
    KANSAS, see Jewel & Dewdrop
Kentucky, Toothpick, Green, Gold Trim 95.00
Kentucky, Wine, Green .... 30.00 To 35.00
Keystone Grape, Goblet 25.00
King's 500, Cup, Cobalt Blue 42.50
King's 500, Nappy, Handle, Cobalt Blue 27.50
King's 500, Tumbler, Cobalt Blue, Gold Trim 40.00
    KING'S CROWN, see also Ruby Thumbprint
King's Crown, Bowl, Flat, 9 3/4 In. 39.50
King's Crown, Cake Stand, Pedestal, Amber 35.00
King's Crown, Compote, 5 In. 32.00

Jumbo

Klondike

Leaf & Dart

Liberty Bell

Lincoln Drape

Magnet & Grape
with Stippled Leaf

King's Crown, Cup & Saucer 58.00
King's Crown, Goblet 25.00
King's Crown, Pitcher, Water, Tankard 95.00
King's Crown, Toothpick 26.50
King's Crown, Water Set, 6 Piece 295.00
King's Crown, Wine .... 22.00 To 28.00
    KLONDIKE, see Amberette
Kokomo, Compote, 8 In. 45.00
Kokomo, Wine 22.00
La France, Tumbler, Maiden Blush & Gold 30.00
Lace Band, Punch Cup 18.00
Lacy Daisy, Butter, Cover 47.00
Lacy Daisy, Sugar, Open 36.50
Lacy Dewdrop, Creamer, Opaque White, 4 1/2 In. 25.00
Lacy Dewdrop, Goblet 32.50
    LACY MEDALLION, see Princess Feather
Ladder With Diamond, Cruet 30.00
Lamb, Creamer, Child's 75.00
Late Block, Spooner 25.00
Leaf & Dart, Butter, Cover 77.00
Leaf & Dart, Goblet .... 25.00 To 40.00
Leaf & Dart, Pitcher, Water 95.00
Leaf & Dart, Sugar, Cover 45.00
Leaf & Flower, Pitcher, Water, Amber Stained 95.00
Leaf & Star, Pitcher, Water, Ice Lip 28.50
Leaf Medallion, Bowl, 9 In. 30.00
Leaf Medallion, Creamer, Cobalt Blue, Gold Trim 95.00
Leaf Medallion, Spooner 65.00
Leaf Medallion, Table Set, Amethyst, Gold Trim, 4 Piece 445.00
    LENS & STAR, see Star & Oval
Liberty Bell, Butter, Cover .... 135.00 To 140.00
Liberty Bell, Butter, Cover, Child's 75.00
Liberty Bell, Creamer, Twist Handle 125.00
Liberty Bell, Goblet .... 22.00 To 41.50
Liberty Bell, Pitcher, Water .... 545.00 To 850.00
Liberty Bell, Plate, 6 In. 60.00
Liberty Bell, Plate, 10 In. 110.00
Liberty Bell, Plate, Signers Border, 10 1/4 In. .... 85.00 To 90.00
Liberty Bell, Relish 30.00
Liberty Bell, Spooner .... 70.00 To 95.00
Liberty Bell, Table Set, Child's, 4 Piece 400.00
Lily-of-The-Valley, Compote, Cover, 8 In. 145.00

Lily–of–The–Valley, Creamer, Footed 50.00
Lily–of–The–Valley, Eggcup 65.00
Lily–of–The–Valley, Goblet, Etched 30.00
Lily–of–The–Valley, Pitcher, Milk 125.00
Lincoln Drape With Tassel, Goblet 125.00
Lincoln Drape, Compote 100.00
Lincoln Drape, Compote, Flint 50.00
Lincoln Drape, Goblet, Flint .... 80.00 To 90.00
Lincoln Drape, Spooner, Flint 65.00
Lincoln Drape, Syrup, Applied Handle, Tin Lid, 7 In. 115.00
    LION'S LEG, see Alaska
Lion, Bread Plate, Frosted 65.00
Lion, Butter, Cover, Child's 100.00
Lion, Celery 78.00
Lion, Compote Set, Frosted, 6 Sherbets 115.00
Lion, Compote, Cover, Frosted Head Finial, 11 3/4 In. 95.00
Lion, Compote, Cover, Frosted Lion Finial, Rope Edge, 9 In. 30.00
Lion, Creamer, Crimped Handle, Flint 45.00
Lion, Creamer, Frosted .... 52.50 To 75.00
Lion, Cup & Saucer, Child's 55.00
Lion, Cup & Saucer, Frosted 70.00
Lion, Dish, Rampant Lion Finial, Oval, 8 1/2 In. 150.00
Lion, Eggcup, Frosted ....48.00 To 110.00
Lion, Goblet 60.00
Lion, Jam Jar, Frosted Cover & Base, Rampant Lion Finial 100.00
Lion, Pitcher, Water, Frosted, Berry & Fern Etched 395.00
Lion, Plate, Grieving Lion Center 95.00
Lion, Punch Cup, Child's 35.00
Lion, Spooner .... 27.00 To 31.00
Lion, Sugar, Child's 35.00
Lion, Sugar, Rampant Lion Finial, 8 3/4 In. 150.00
Lion, Table Set, Child's, 4 Piece 365.00
    LIPPMAN, see Flat Diamond
Locket On Chain, Cake Stand 145.00
Locket On Chain, Wine ....80.00 To 110.00
Log & Star, Condiment Set, Amber 170.00
Log & Star, Cruet Set, Pedestal Base, Amber, 4 Piece 125.00
Log Cabin, Compote, High Standard, Cover 550.00
Log Cabin, Compote, Luden's Cough Drops, Cover 800.00
Log Cabin, Creamer .... 120.00 To 135.00
Log Cabin, Dish, Cottage, Cover 55.00
Log Cabin, Jam Jar, Cover, Amber 500.00
Log Cabin, Pitcher, Water 375.00
Log Cabin, Spooner ....95.00 To 120.00
Log Cabin, Table Set, 4 Piece 690.00
Loop & Block, Water Set, Ruby Stained, 7 Piece 275.00
Loop & Dart With Diamond Ornaments, Butter, Cover 45.00
Loop & Dart With Diamond Ornaments, Sugar, Cover 23.50
Loop & Dart With Round Ornaments, Butter Chip 12.00
Loop & Dart With Round Ornaments, Butter, Cover 85.00
Loop & Dart With Round Ornaments, Eggcup 22.50
Loop & Dart With Round Ornaments, Goblet 45.00
Loop & Dart, Creamer 28.00
Loop & Dart, Goblet .... 16.00 To 25.00
Loop & Dart, Spooner 20.00
Loop & Dart, Tumbler, Buttermilk, Flint 40.00
Loop & Jewel, Creamer, Individual 35.00
Loop & Petal, Salt, Flint, 2 5/8 In. 10.00
Loop & Pyramid, Wine 16.50
    LOOP WITH STIPPLED PANELS, see Texas
    LOOP, see also Seneca Loop
Loop, Compote, 9 1/2 In. 115.00
Loop, Vase, Crimped Rim, Sapphire Blue, Hexagonal, 9 5/8 In. 225.00
    LOOPS & DROPS, see New Jersey

Lorne, Butter, Cover, Bryce Bros.	42.50
Lotus & Serpent, Bread Plate	45.00
Louis XV, Pitcher, Green, Gold Trim, 5 In.	55.00
Madison, Sugar, Cover, Flint	150.00
Magnet & Grape With Frosted Leaf, Decanter, Flint, Pair	330.00
Magnet & Grape, Eggcup	20.00
MAIDEN BLUSH, see Banded Portland	
Maiden Fern, Goblet, Stippled	22.00 To 25.00
Maine, Berry Bowl, Green, Master	30.00
Maine, Bread Plate	26.00
Maine, Cake Stand, Green, 8 In.	58.00
Maine, Compote, Open, Green, 7 In.	35.00 To 58.00
Maine, Relish, Oval, 8 In.	12.00
Maine, Wine, Green	50.00
Maltese Cross, Bowl, Flat, Amber Flash, 8 1/2 In.	50.00
Mandolin, Toothpick, Gold Trim, Ruby Stained	30.00
Manhattan, Bread Plate	20.00
Manhattan, Creamer	15.00
Manhattan, Cruet	48.50
Manhattan, Goblet, Gold Rim	28.00
Manhattan, Plate, Oval, Gold Trim, 7 1/2 In.	15.00
Manhattan, Sugar & Creamer, Individual	30.00
Manhattan, Toothpick, Gold Trim	22.00
Manhattan, Vase, 6 1/4 In.	13.00
Maple Leaf, Creamer, Frosted	65.00
Maple Leaf, Oval, 13 1/4 In.	35.00
March Pink, Saltshaker	21.00
Mario, Syrup	65.00
Marlboro, Wine	20.00
Marquisette, Goblet	27.00
Marquisette, Spooner	25.00 To 30.00
Marquisette, Sugar, Cover	40.00
Marsh Fern, Pitcher, Water	70.00
Maryland, Bread Plate	40.00
Maryland, Goblet	25.00
Maryland, Pitcher, Water	58.00
Mascotte, Butter, Cover	35.00
Mascotte, Butter, Cover, Etched	50.00
Mascotte, Cake Basket	50.00 To 60.00
Mascotte, Pitcher, Water, Etched	55.00 To 65.00
Mascotte, Sugar, Cover	35.00
Masonic, Spooner, Footed	15.00
Massachusetts, Banana Boat	38.00 To 55.00
Massachusetts, Butter, Cover	52.00
Massachusetts, Butter, Cover, Green	60.00
Massachusetts, Rum Jug	80.00 To 165.00
Massachusetts, Tumbler, Flared, Gold Trim, 3 1/2 In.	15.00
Massachusetts, Vase, Gold Trim, 6 3/4 In.	21.00
McKinley, Bread Plate, 10 1/2 In.	45.00
Medallion Sunburst, Creamer, Double Lipped	12.50
Medallion Sunburst, Pitcher, Water	32.00
Medallion, Dish, Pickle, Amber	22.00
Medallion, Goblet	25.00
Medallion, Spooner	10.00
Medallion, Tumbler, Gold Trim, Pink Flower	10.00
Mellor, Celery	23.00
Melrose, Cake Stand, 9 3/4 In.	45.00
Melrose, Goblet	20.00 To 60.00
Melrose, Pitcher, Water	24.00 To 45.00
Melton, Celery	60.00
Menagerie, Creamer, Owl, Amber, Child's	135.00
Menagerie, Mustard, Bear, Child's	295.00
Menagerie, Spooner, Fish, Amber, Child's	85.00 To 130.00
Menagerie, Table Setting, Child's, 4 Piece	1500.00

Mephistopheles, Goblet 45.00
Michigan, Bowl, 8 In. 28.50
Michigan, Creamer, Child's 35.00
Michigan, Goblet, Amber 27.00
Michigan, Goblet, Green Wash, Enamel Design 48.00
Michigan, Mug, Lemonade, Enameled Daisy, Yellow Flashed 33.00
Michigan, Pitcher, Water .... 35.00 To 75.00
Michigan, Salt & Pepper, Pewter Lids, Individual 75.00
Michigan, Sugar, Red Flashed 200.00
Michigan, Toothpick, Yellow Flashed 38.00
Michigan, Tumbler .... 30.00 To 32.00
Mikado Fan, Bowl, Rectangular, 8 1/4 In. 20.00
Mikado Fan, Goblet 20.00
Milton, Goblet 15.00
Milton, Wine 22.00
Minerva, Bread Tray, Motto 70.00
Minerva, Cake Stand, 9 X 6 1/2 In. .... 110.00 To 115.00
Minerva, Compote, Cover, 10 1/2 In. 85.00
Minerva, Creamer .... 25.00 To 50.00
Minerva, Goblet 95.00
Minerva, Pitcher, Water .... 150.00 To 235.00
Minnesota, Mug, Large 16.00
Minnesota, Wine 25.00
Mirror & Fan, Wine 16.00
Mirror Star, Table Set, Gold Trim, 4 Piece 120.00
Mirror, Goblet, Knob Stem, Flint 45.00
Missouri, Butter, Cover 55.00
Missouri, Creamer 25.00
Missouri, Doughnut Stand 32.50
Missouri, Pitcher, Water 40.00
Missouri, Relish, Rectangular 28.00
Missouri, Syrup .... 60.00 To 75.00
Mitered Bars, Goblet 24.50
Mitered Bars, Wine 15.00
    MITERED DIAMOND POINTS, see Mitered Bars
Mitered Diamond, Tumbler, Amber .... 15.00 To 20.00
Mitered Diamond, Water Set, Blue, 7 Piece 195.00
Mitered Prisms, Compote, Open, 6 In. 20.00
Model Peerless, Jug, Original Stopper 35.00
Monkey, Mustard, 3 Sitting Up, Frosted, 4 In. 25.00
Monkey, Spooner 100.00
Monkey, Tumbler, Footed, Flint, Clear, 3 3/4 In. 95.00

Maine

Mitered Diamond

Moon & Star

Moon & Star Variant, Goblet	28.00
Moon & Star, Cake Stand, 10 In.	35.00 To 60.00
Moon & Star, Celery	21.00
Moon & Star, Compote, Cover, 10 In.	68.00
Moon & Star, Compote, Open	45.00
Moon & Star, Cruet, Original Stopper	125.00 To 150.00
Moon & Star, Sauce, Pedestal, Frosted	15.00
Moon & Star, Spill, Flint	55.00
Moon & Star, Sugar, Cover, Flint	195.00
Moon & Star, Toothpick	26.50
Moon & Star, Wine, Frosted	30.00
Morning Glory, Compote, Flint, 5 X 7 3/4 In.	300.00
Morning Glory, Eggcup, Flint	45.00
Nail, Butter, Cover, Etched	85.00
Nail, Cake Stand, Etched	40.00
Nail, Compote, Jelly	55.00 To 95.00
Nail, Goblet	70.00
Nail, Pitcher, Water, Ruby Stained	125.00
Nail, Saltshaker, World's Fair, 1893, Ruby Stained	45.00
Nail, Syrup	48.00
Nail, Table Set, Etched, 4 Piece	175.00
Nail, Tumbler, Ruby Stained	62.50
Nailhead, Butter, Cover	46.50 To 47.00
Nailhead, Celery	55.00
Nailhead, Creamer	22.00
Nailhead, Goblet	15.00 To 25.00
Nailhead, Pitcher, Water	25.00 To 35.00
Nailhead, Plate, Square, 7 1/8 In.	15.00
Nailhead, Wine	18.50
Narcissus Spray, Tumbler, Enameled Design	14.50
Narrow Swirl, Creamer	20.00
NAUTILUS, see Argonaut Shell	
Near Cut, Butter, Cover	75.00
NEBRASKA, see Bismarc Star	
Nellie Bly, Bread Plate	350.00
Nestor, Compote, Jelly, Amethyst	47.50
Nestor, Creamer, Blue, Gold Trim	45.00
Nestor, Toothpick, Blue	60.00
Nestor, Water Set, Green, Gold & Enamel Trim, 7 Piece	315.00
Netted Oak, Spooner, Northwood	45.00
New England Pineapple, Creamer, Flint	125.00
New England Pineapple, Eggcup	50.00
New England Pineapple, Goblet, Amber	75.00
New England Pineapple, Spooner	65.00
New England Pineapple, Sugar, Flint	60.00
New Hampshire, Creamer, Individual	10.00 To 25.00
New Hampshire, Goblet, Cranberry	48.00
New Hampshire, Pitcher, Water	37.00
New Hampshire, Sugar & Creamer	15.00
New Hampshire, Syrup	48.00
New Hampshire, Wine, Gold Flashed	28.50
New Jersey, Bowl, Flared, 9 1/4 In.	27.50
New Jersey, Bread Plate	22.00 To 30.00
New Jersey, Butter, Cover, Gold Trim	68.00
New Jersey, Creamer, Gold Trim	24.00
New Jersey, Goblet, Gold Trim	36.50
New Jersey, Pitcher, Water	48.00
New Jersey, Saltshaker	35.00
New Jersey, Sugar, Cover, Gold Trim	40.00
New Jersey, Table Set, Gold Trim, 4 Piece	140.00
New Jersey, Toothpick, Gold Trim	58.00
New Jersey, Vase, Emerald Green, 11 In.	55.00
New Jersey, Water Set, Gold Trim, 7 Piece	150.00
Newport, Goblet, Lavender Eye	20.00

New England Pineapple   Paneled Forget–Me–Not   Pleat & Panel

Niagara Falls, Tray, Water 85.00
Northwood's Grape, Goblet 28.00
Nursery Tales, Berry Bowl, Child's 10.00
Nursery Tales, Berry Set, Child's, 6 Piece 100.00
Nursery Tales, Butter, Cover, Child's 75.00
Nursery Tales, Creamer, Child's .... 40.00 To 50.00
Nursery Tales, Punch Set, Child's, 7 Piece 220.00
Nursery Tales, Water Set, Child's, 6 Piece 160.00
Oak Leaf, Bowl, Lacy, 7 1/8 In. 50.00
Oak Leaf, Compote, Cover, Acorn Finial 60.00
Oak Leaf, Pitcher 95.00
Oaken Bucket, Butter, Cover, Blue 85.00
Oaken Bucket, Creamer, Child's 45.00
Oaken Bucket, Pitcher, Water, Amber .... 65.00 To 85.00
Oaken Bucket, Pitcher, Water, Amethyst 75.00
Oaken Bucket, Spooner, Vaseline 25.00
Odd Fellows, Goblet 49.00
Ohio Star, Punch Bowl 65.00
Ohio, Goblet, Etched 35.00
Ohio, Sugar 40.00

Primrose   Princess Feather   Rexford

OLD ABE, see Frosted Eagle
Old State House, Bread Plate	75.00
Old State House, Tray, Sapphire Blue	195.00
Old State House, Tray, Water	75.00
One–Hundred–One, Bread Plate, Farm Production Center, Round	42.50
One–Hundred–One, Bread Plate, Give Us The Day, 11 In.	35.00
One–Hundred–One, Creamer	32.00 To 34.50
One–Hundred–One, Goblet	35.00 To 38.00
One–Hundred–One, Pitcher, 9 3/4 In.	65.00
One–Hundred–One, Plate, 8 In.	22.00

ONE–O–ONE, see One–Hundred–One
ONE–THOUSAND EYE, see Thousand Eye
Oneata, Spooner, Gold Trim	40.00
Open Rose, Eggcup	23.00
Open Rose, Goblet	30.00
Opposing Pyramids, Creamer	30.00
Opposing Pyramids, Salt & Pepper	30.00
Opposing Pyramids, Wine	14.00
Optica, Table Set, Sapphire Blue, Gold Trim, 4 Piece	300.00
Orange Peel, Spooner	28.50

OREGON, see also Beaded Loop
Oregon, Butter, Cover	45.00
Oregon, Celery	45.00
Oregon, Compote, Open, 8 1/8 In.	35.00
Oregon, Cruet, Original Stopper	30.00
Oregon, Pitcher, Milk	45.00 To 55.00
Oregon, Salt & Pepper	45.00
Orinocho, Goblet	16.00

ORION, see Cathedral
Oval Panel, Goblet, Amber	18.50 To 19.00
Oval Star, Punch Bowl, Child's, Gold Trim	26.00
Oval Star, Sugar, Cover, Child's	15.00
Oval Star, Water Set, Child's, 5 Piece	125.00

OWL, see Bull's–Eye with Diamond Point
Owl & Possum, Goblet	110.00

OWL IN FAN, see Parrot
Palm Beach, Compote, Flint, C.1850	65.00
Palm Beach, Sugar, Cover	45.00
Palm Leaf Fan, Salt	15.00
Palm Stub, Goblet	20.00
Palmette, Creamer	35.00
Palmette, Goblet	32.00 To 35.00
Palmette, Sugar	25.00
Paneled 44, Butter, Gold Trim	50.00
Paneled 44, Pitcher, Water, Platinum Band	135.00
Paneled Acorn Band, Creamer	28.50
Paneled Cane, Goblet	25.00
Paneled Cane, Tray, Water	12.00
Paneled Cherry, Sugar, Cover, Gold Trim	35.00
Paneled Cherry, Tumbler	12.50
Paneled Daisy, Berry Set, 7 Piece	75.00
Paneled Daisy, Cake Stand, 10 1/2 In.	45.00
Paneled Daisy, Relish, Amber	15.00
Paneled Dewdrop, Celery	24.00 To 38.00
Paneled Dogwood, Cruet, Original Stopper	35.00
Paneled Flowers, Goblet	17.00
Paneled Forget–Me–Not, Celery	30.00 To 32.00
Paneled Forget–Me–Not, Compote, 7 X 10 In.	25.00
Paneled Forget–Me–Not, Creamer	35.00
Paneled Forget–Me–Not, Jam Jar	60.00 To 70.00
Paneled Forget–Me–Not, Spooner	30.00
Paneled Forget–Me–Not, Sugar, Cover	30.00 To 40.00

Paneled Grape, Butter, Cover 25.00
Paneled Grape, Cheese Dish 28.50
Paneled Grape, Goblet, Water 9.00
Paneled Heather, Creamer 11.00
Paneled Herringbone, Berry Set, Green, 7 Piece 100.00
Paneled Herringbone, Goblet, Green 35.00
Paneled Holly, Pitcher, Water 125.00
Paneled Iris, Wine .... 15.00 To 22.00
Paneled Ivy, Bowl, Scalloped Collared Base, 10 In. 25.00
Paneled Jewels, Goblet 25.00
Paneled Nightshade, Goblet, Amber 40.00
Paneled Nightshade, Wine 15.00
Paneled Palm, Water Set, Pink, Gold Trim, 7 Piece 175.00
Paneled Sawtooth, Creamer 25.00
Paneled Star & Button, Creamer 19.00
    PANELED STIPPLED BOWL, see Stippled Band
Paneled Thistle, Bowl, 8 In. 22.00
Paneled Thistle, Bread Plate 25.00
Paneled Thistle, Compote, Jelly 10.00
Paneled Thistle, Wine, 4 Piece 75.00
Paris, Goblet 20.00
Parrot, Goblet .... 30.00 To 48.00
Pathfinder, Goblet 22.00
Pathfinder, Pitcher, Water 35.00
Pattee Cross, Cruet 22.00
Pattee Cross, Goblet, Amethyst Cross, Gold 15.00
Pattee Cross, Pitcher, Water, Child's 40.00
Pattee Cross, Pitcher, Water, Rose Stained 55.00
Pattee Cross, Water Set, Gold Trim, Child's, 7 Piece 85.00
Pavonia, Cake Stand, Etched, 9 1/2 In. 45.00
Pavonia, Creamer, Etched 42.50
Pavonia, Goblet, Etched Maple Leaf 18.50
Pavonia, Pitcher, Water, Ruby Stained 95.00
Pavonia, Salt & Pepper, Etched 18.00
Pavonia, Tray, Water, Etched 55.00
Pavonia, Tumbler, Etched .... 25.00 To 33.00
Pavonia, Water Set, Ruby Stained, 6 Piece 250.00
Peacock Feathers, Bowl, 7 1/2 In. .... 35.00 To 40.00
Peacock Feathers, Cup Plate 35.00
Peacock Feathers, Pitcher, Water 50.00
Peacock Feathers, Sandwich Plate, Flint 35.00
    PEACOCK'S EYE, see Peacock Feathers
Peacock, Cruet, Frosted 60.00
Pearl, Table Set, Ruby Stained, 4 Piece 265.00
    PEERLESS, see also Model Peerless
Peerless, Creamer, Crimped Handle 28.00
Peerless, Wine 20.00
Pennsylvania, Butter, Cover 175.00
Pennsylvania, Celery 31.00
Pennsylvania, Creamer, Child's, Green 95.00
Pennsylvania, Goblet, Gold Trim 15.00
Pennsylvania, Salt & Pepper, Pewter Tops 27.00
Pennsylvania, Wine 15.00
Persian, Goblet 25.00
Petal & Loop, Compote, Hexagonal Stem, Green, 6 3/4 In. 155.00
Petticoat, Berry Set, Vaseline, Gold Trim, 6 Piece 225.00
Philadelphia Centennial, Goblet 40.00
Picket, Compote, Open, 7 In. 24.00
Picket, Pitcher, Water 85.00
Pigs In Corn, Goblet 185.00
    PILLAR & BULL'S–EYE, see Thistle
Pillar, Celery, 8 Ribs, Footed, 9 In. 145.00
Pillar, Cruet, 15 Ribs, Original Stopper, 9 In. 165.00
Pillar, Syrup, 12 Ribs, Strap Handle, Pewter Lid 125.00

Ribbon Candy   Roman Rosette   Rose in Snow

Pillow Encircled, Butter, Cover	85.00
Pillow Encircled, Cruet, Faceted Stopper, Ruby Stained	60.00
Pillow Encircled, Water Set, Etched Fern & Leaf, 6 Piece	120.00
PINAFORE, see Actress	
Pineapple & Fan, Butter, Cover	35.00
Pineapple & Fan, Celery	45.00
Pineapple & Fan, Ice Cream Set, Tray, 10 Plates	120.00
Pineapple, Cake Stand	50.00
PLAIN SMOCKING, see Smocking	
Pleat & Panel, Celery	35.00 To 40.00
Pleat & Panel, Pitcher, Water	85.00
Pleat Band, Goblet	20.00
Plume, Berry Bowl, Master	35.00
Plume, Bowl, Stippled, 8 1/8 In.	225.00
Plume, Goblet	55.00
Plume, Sauce, Green, 4 1/2 In.	25.00
Pogo Stick, Bowl, 8 1/2 In.	15.00
Pogo Stick, Pitcher	40.00
Pointed Jewel, Goblet	15.00
POINTED THUMBPRINT, see Almond Thumbprint	
Polar Bear, Goblet	95.00
Polar Bear, Tray, Frosted	95.00
Popcorn, Cake Stand, 11 In.	60.00 To 78.00
PORTLAND WITH DIAMOND POINT BAND, see Banded Portland	
Portland, Berry Set	75.00
Portland, Goblet	38.00
Portland, Pin Dish, Oval, Ruby Stained	16.50
Portland, Pitcher, Water	45.00
Portland, Saltshaker	16.00
Portland, Toothpick	23.00
Portland, Vase, Bud	20.00
POTTED PLANT, see Flower Pot	
Powder & Shot, Eggcup	50.00
Powder & Shot, Goblet, Flint	75.00
Powder & Shot, Spooner, Flint	40.00 To 50.00
PRAYER RUG, see Horseshoe	
Pressed Diamond, Compote, Open, Amber, 10 In.	35.00
Pressed Diamond, Cruet, Amber	65.00
Pressed Diamond, Salt & Pepper, Vaseline	40.00
Pressed Diamond, Sugar, Cover, Amber	35.00 To 45.00
Pressed Leaf, Eggcup, Flint	15.00
Pressed Leaf, Wine, Flint	35.00

Pressed Optic, Cruet, Vaseline 50.00
Primrose, Pitcher, Milk 24.00
Primrose, Pitcher, Water 46.50
Primrose, Wine, Blue .... 38.00 To 45.00
Princess Feather, Bowl, 7 1/2 In. 25.00
Princess Feather, Bowl, Amethyst Tint, 8 5/8 In. 100.00
Princess Feather, Goblet 28.00
Princess Feather, Pitcher, Water 95.00
Princess Feather, Tumbler, Bar, Oval Panels, Gilt Trim 150.00
Priscilla, Bowl, 8 In. 37.50
Priscilla, Compote, Scalloped Rim, 4 In. 25.00
Priscilla, Creamer, Individual, 3 1/4 In. 25.00
Priscilla, Mustard 20.00
Priscilla, Spooner 28.50
Priscilla, Sugar, Cover 25.00
Priscilla, Table Set, 4 Piece 175.00
Priscilla, Wine 35.00
Prism & Broken Column, Wine 15.00
Prism & Diamond Band, Goblet .... 15.00 To 22.50
Prism & Diamond Band, Wine 32.00
Prism & Diamond Point, Tumbler, Flint 50.00
Prism & Herringbone, Wine 22.00
Prism & Sawtooth, Goblet, Flint 30.00
Prism Arc, Celery .... 19.00 To 20.00
Prism Arc, Wine 22.00
Prism, Cruet, Flint 60.00
Prism, Spooner, Rayed Bottom, Flint 32.00
Prism, Wine, Engraved 30.00
Prisms & Hexagons, Goblet 22.50
Prize, Butter, Cover 115.00
Prize, Celery, Green, Gold Trim 75.00
Prize, Cruet, Original Stopper, Green 175.00
Prize, Tumbler, Ruby Stained 42.50
Prize, Wine, Green, Gold Trim 45.00
Proud Lion, Bread Plate 60.00
Psyche & Cupid, Creamer .... 40.00 To 50.00
Psyche & Cupid, Goblet .... 35.00 To 45.00
Psyche & Cupid, Pitcher, Water 70.00
Puffed Bands, Goblet 25.00
Queen Anne, Creamer 32.00
Queen Anne, Salt, Master, 3 In. 45.00
Queen's Necklace, Toothpick 60.00

Sawtooth

Shell & Tassel

Shrine

Queen, Creamer, Gold Trim 35.00
Queen, Goblet, Blue 30.00
Queen, Pitcher, Water, Amber 65.00
Quixote, Wine 14.50
Railroad Train, Bread Plate, 12 X 9 In. 135.00
Ranson, Creamer, Vaseline, Gold Trim 38.00
Ranson, Toothpick 50.00
Rayed Flower, Water Set, 7 Piece 65.00
    RECESSED OVALS WITH BLOCK BAND, see Melton
Red Block, Goblet, Ruby Stained 25.00
Red Block, Spooner, 2 Handles 30.00
Red Block, Table Set, Ruby Stained, 4 Piece 205.00
Red Block, Wine .... 35.00 To 37.50
    REGENT, see Leaf Medallion
Regina, Wine 16.50
Reverse Swirl, Celery, Vaseline 35.00
    REVERSE TORPEDO, see Bull's–Eye Band
Rex, Water Set, Child's, 7 Piece 125.00
Rib & Bead, Saltshaker 35.00
Rib & Bead, Toothpick, Ruby Stained 60.00
Rib Band, Celery 20.00
Ribbed Droplet Band, Spooner, Amber Stained, Frosted 45.00
Ribbed Forget–Me–Not, Butter, Cover 115.00
Ribbed Forget–Me–Not, Creamer, Individual 20.00
Ribbed Ivy, Goblet, Flint 28.00
Ribbed Palm, Bowl, Footed, Scalloped, 8 1/2 X 4 5/8 In. 80.00
Ribbed Palm, Creamer, Flint 105.00
Ribbed Palm, Goblet, Water, Flint 35.00
Ribbed Palm, Pitcher, Applied Handle, 9 1/4 In. 165.00
Ribbed Palm, Pitcher, Water, Flint 250.00
Ribbed Palm, Spooner, Scalloped, 6 In. 45.00
Ribbed Palm, Sugar, Open, 5 5/8 In. 30.00
Ribbed Palm, Tumbler, 3 1/2 In. 30.00
Ribbon Candy, Cake Stand, 9 In. 30.00
Ribbon Candy, Cake Stand, Green, Child's .... 55.00 To 60.00
Ribbon Candy, Compote, Open 20.00
Ribbon Candy, Creamer 17.00
Ribbon Candy, Goblet, Stippled 47.50
Ribbon Candy, Spooner .... 15.00 To 20.00
Ribbon, Celery, Pedestal, Frosted 37.00
Ribbon, Compote, Dolphin Stem, Frosted 65.00
Ribbon, Creamer, Frosted 65.00
Ribbon, Spooner .... 12.00 To 18.00
Ribbon, Spooner, Frosted 25.00
Ring & Block, Goblet 50.00
Rising Sun, Butter, Cover, Green 40.00
Rising Sun, Pitcher, Water 45.00
Rising Sun, Vase, Gold Trim, 6 In. 25.00
Rising Sun, Water Set, Gold Trim, 7 Piece 95.00
Rising Sun, Wine, Purple Suns 15.00
Robin Hood, Compote, 9 In. 22.50
    ROCHELLE, see Princess Feather
Rock of Ages, Tray, Bread, Milk Glass Center 185.00
Roman Key, Eggcup, Frosted .... 30.00 To 55.00
Roman Key, Goblet, Flint 40.00
Roman Key, Spooner, Flint 40.00
Roman Key, Wine, Frosted 55.00
Roman Rosette, Celery 95.00
Roman Rosette, Compote, Circular Foot, 6 1/8 In. 250.00
Roman Rosette, Compote, Jelly 20.00
Roman Rosette, Dish, Scalloped, 6 In. 50.00
Roman Rosette, Plate, 9 3/8 In. 175.00
Roman Rosette, Relish, 6 In. 10.00
Romeo, Cake Stand, 10 In. 23.50

Squirrel

Star Medallion

Three Face

Romeo, Celery	25.00 To 30.00
Romeo, Goblet	20.00
Rooster, Butter, Cover, Child's	145.00
Rooster, Sugar, Cover, Child's	135.00
Rope & Thumbprint, Creamer, Blue	30.00
ROPE BANDS, see Argent	
Rose Band, Wine	20.00
Rose In Snow, Bread Plate	30.00
Rose In Snow, Butter, Cover	48.50
Rose In Snow, Creamer	15.00 To 30.00
Rose In Snow, Dish, Pickle, Double	95.00
Rose In Snow, Goblet, Amber	40.00
Rose In Snow, Mug, In Fond Remembrance	30.00
Rose In Snow, Spooner	12.00 To 20.00
Rose In Snow, Tumbler	37.00
Rose Sprig, Cake Stand, Blue	80.00
Rose Sprig, Celery	25.00 To 30.00
Rose Sprig, Goblet	35.00
Rose Sprig, Pitcher, Milk	45.00
Rosette & Palms, Cake Stand, 8 1/2 In.	20.00
Rosette & Palms, Compote, 8 In.	16.50
Rosette & Palms, Compote, 9 In.	18.00
Rosette & Palms, Wine	22.00 To 27.50
Rosette Band, Sugar, Creamer & Spooner	75.00
ROSETTE MEDALLION, see Feather Duster	
Rosette, Cake Stand, 10 1/2 In.	30.00
Rosette, Creamer	15.00
Rosette, Pitcher, Milk	32.00 To 50.00
Royal Ivy, Berry Bowl, Rainbow Cased, Master	150.00
Royal Ivy, Butter, Cover, Clear To Cranberry	195.00 To 225.00
Royal Ivy, Pitcher, Water, Cased Spatter	285.00
Royal Ivy, Pitcher, Water, Clear & Frosted	95.00
Royal Ivy, Pitcher, Water, Clear To Cranberry	195.00 To 265.00
Royal Ivy, Pitcher, Water, Rainbow Cased	285.00
Royal Ivy, Rose Bowl, Rainbow Spatter	165.00
Royal Ivy, Salt & Pepper, Rainbow Spatter	175.00
Royal Ivy, Syrup, Frosted, Brass Lid	175.00
Royal Ivy, Table Set, Frosted, 4 Piece	475.00
Royal Oak, Butter, Cover	65.00
Royal Oak, Creamer, Frosted	85.00
Royal Oak, Pitcher, Water	285.00
Royal Oak, Spooner	55.00

Thumbprint   Tree of Life   U.S. Coin

Royal Oak, Sugar Shaker	225.00
RUBY ROSETTE, see Hero	
RUBY THUMBPRINT, see also King's Crown	
Ruby Thumbprint, Berry Bowl, Boat Shape	125.00
Rustic, Spooner	25.00
S–Repeat, Cruet Set, Blue, 5 Piece	155.00
S–Repeat, Fruit Bowl, Amethyst, Gold Trim, 8 In.	65.00
S–Repeat, Salt & Pepper, Original Tops, Blue	55.00
S–Repeat, Saltshaker	12.50
S–Repeat, Saltshaker, Blue	30.00
S–Repeat, Spooner, Amethyst	38.00
SANDWICH LOOP, see Hairpin	
Sawtooth & Star, Tumbler, Ruby Stained	30.00
SAWTOOTH BAND, see Amazon	
Sawtooth, Celery, Knob Stem	40.00
Sawtooth, Compote, Cover, 8 X 14 In.	55.00
Sawtooth, Cordial, Ruby Stained	38.00
Sawtooth, Creamer, Child's	30.00
Sawtooth, Salt, Master, Cover, Footed, Flint	35.00
Sawtooth, Spill	46.50
Sawtooth, Spooner, Child's	26.00
Sawtooth, Spooner, Flint	35.00
Sawtooth, Sugar, Flint, 7 1/2 In.	25.00
Sawtooth, Wine, Flint	15.00
Scalloped Swirl, Goblet	60.00
SCALLOPED TAPE, see Jewel Band	
Scroll With Acanthus, Sugar & Creamer, Green, Gold, Northwood	110.00
Scroll With Cane Band, Toothpick	50.00
Scroll With Flowers, Bread Plate .... 22.00 To 36.50	
Scroll With Flowers, Creamer .... 24.00 To 28.00	
Scroll With Flowers, Spooner .... 17.00 To 18.00	
Scroll, Goblet	15.00
SEDAN, see Paneled Star & Button	
Seneca Loop, Compote, Flint, 6 1/2 X 9 1/2 In.	110.00
Seneca Loop, Decanter, Original Stopper	130.00
Seneca Loop, Spooner, Flint	34.50
Sequoia, Compote, Cover, Square	40.00
Serrated Prism, Syrup .... 30.00 To 35.00	
Serrated Rib & Finecut, Goblet	10.00
Sheaf & Block, Celery	35.00
Sheaf & Block, Pitcher, Water	65.00

SHEAF OF WHEAT, see Wheat Sheaf

Shell & Jewel, Berry Set, 9 Piece 55.00
Shell & Jewel, Creamer 30.00
Shell & Jewel, Pitcher, Water .... 32.50 To 45.00
Shell & Jewel, Pitcher, Water, Green 40.00
Shell & Jewel, Tumbler .... 12.50 To 13.00
Shell & Jewel, Water Set, With Tray, Green, 7 Piece 245.00
Shell & Tassel, Butter, Cover 120.00
Shell & Tassel, Compote, 7 1/2 In. 45.00
Shell & Tassel, Compote, 9 1/2 In. 82.00
Shell & Tassel, Creamer, Square 48.00
Shell, Eggcup 30.00
Shell, Pitcher, Buttermilk 22.00
Shell, Spooner, Blue, Gold Trim .... 50.00 To 55.00
Shell, Spooner, Green, Gold Trim 28.00
Shell, Wine 22.00
Sheraton, Butter, Cover 45.00

SHOSHONE, see Victor

Shrine, Carafe 41.50
Shrine, Celery 22.00
Shrine, Pitcher, Water, Frosted Moons 165.00
Signers, Bread Plate 60.00
Signers, Table Set, 4 Piece 425.00
Simple Scroll, Toothpick 25.00
Smocking, Sugar, Cover, Flint 42.00
Snail, Butter, Cover .... 60.00 To 85.00
Snail, Celery 48.50
Snail, Compote, 9 3/4 X 7 1/4 In. 95.00
Snail, Creamer 58.00
Snail, Cruet 350.00
Snail, Sugar, Cover 50.00
Snail, Syrup 100.00
Snail, Table Set, 4 Piece 275.00
Snail, Tumbler, Ruby Stained 62.50
Snail, Vase, 17 In. 65.00
Snail, Waste Bowl 135.00
Snakeskin With Dot, Creamer .... 20.00 To 30.00
Snowflake & Sunburst, Pitcher 35.00
Southern Ivy, Pitcher, Water 55.00
Spanish American, Dish, Cover, Figural, Amber 230.00
Spanish American, Pitcher, Tumbler, 2 Piece 95.00
Spanish American, Pitcher, Water, Stacked Cannonballs 55.00
Spanish American, Tumbler .... 20.00 To 38.00

SPANISH COIN, see Columbian Coin

Spectre Block, Butter, Cover, Westmoreland 48.00
Spirea Band, Compote, Cover, Low Stand, Amber, 7 In. 55.00
Spirea Band, Goblet, Amber .... 32.50 To 33.00
Spirea, Wine 18.50
Split Diamond, Goblet 25.00
Sprig, Cake Plate 46.00
Squared Star, Goblet 20.00
Squirrel, Butter, Cover 275.00
Squirrel, Mug 23.00
Squirrel, Pitcher, Water .... 90.00 To 175.00
Staggered Prism, Goblet 15.00
Star & Bar, Creamer, Child's, Blue 15.00
Star & Bar, Cruet Set, Blue 150.00
Star & Bar, Sugar, Open, Child's 15.00
Star & Crescent, Butter, Cover, Gold Trim 75.00
Star & Crescent, Creamer, Gold Trim 50.00
Star & Ivy, Cup & Saucer 35.00
Star & Oval, Celery 25.00
Star & Oval, Tumbler, Frosted Band 12.50

STAR & PUNTY, see Moon & Star

STAR BAND, see Bosworth

Starred Cosmos, Water Set, 6 Piece	120.00
Starred Loop, Goblet	25.00
Stars & Bars, Butter, Cover, Etched	45.00
Stars & Bars, Goblet	25.00
Stars & Bars, Table Set, Amber, 4 Piece	165.00
Stars & Stripes, Toothpick	22.00

STATES, see The States

Statue of Liberty, Pickle Jar, Brown Stain	95.00

STAYMAN, see Rustic

Stippled Band, Spooner	15.00
Stippled Chain, Goblet	17.00
Stippled Chain, Spooner	21.00

STIPPLED DAHLIA, see Dahlia

Stippled Diamond, Creamer, Child's	30.00
Stippled Fleur–De–Lis, Pitcher, Water, Green	75.00
Stippled Fleur–De–Lis, Tumbler, Blue	30.00
Stippled Forget–Me–Not, Cup & Saucer	45.00
Stippled Fuchsia, Goblet	32.00
Stippled Ivy, Sugar, Cover	30.00

STIPPLED PANELED FLOWER, see Maine
STIPPLED SCROLL, see Scroll

Stippled Star, Spooner	30.00

STIPPLED VINE & BEADS, see Vine & Beads

Stork, Goblet	60.00
Stork, Pitcher, Water, Etched	85.00
Strawberry & Currant, Goblet	20.00 To 25.00
Strawberry With Roman Key Band, Goblet	38.00
Style, Sugar & Creamer, Child's	45.00
Style, Wine	18.00
Sunk Daisy, Cake Stand, 7 1/2 In.	25.00
Sunk Daisy, Cracker Jar	48.00
Sunk Daisy, Plate, 8 In.	24.00
Sunk Honeycomb, Creamer, Souvenir, Vernon, South Dakota	35.00
Sunk Honeycomb, Cup & Saucer, Ruby Stained, B.H.Stone	35.00

SUNRISE, see Rising Sun

Swag With Brackets, Butter, Cover, Amethyst	75.00
Swag With Brackets, Salt & Pepper, Amethyst	50.00
Swag With Brackets, Spooner	65.00
Swag With Brackets, Toothpick, Amethyst, Gold Trim	75.00
Swag With Brackets, Water Set, Olive Green, Gold Trim, 7 Pc.	100.00
Swan, Bread Plate, Head Handles	185.00
Swan, Compote, Open	60.00
Swan, Creamer	45.00
Swan, Pitcher, Water	50.00
Swirl & Ball, Creamer, Footed	35.00
Swirl & Diamond, Pitcher, Water, Ruby Stained	225.00
Swirl, Cake Stand	23.00
Swirl, Hat, Polished Pontil, 2 1/4 X 3 In.	55.00
Sydney, Bowl, 8 In.	23.00
Tandem Bicycle, Celery	35.00
Tandem Bicycle, Goblet	32.00
Tappan, Butter, Cover, Amber, Child's	40.00
Tappan, Creamer, Amber, Child's	30.00
Tappan, Sugar, Cover, Amber, Child's	30.00
Tappan, Table Set, Child's, 4 Piece	60.00
Tarentum's Atlanta, Table Set, Ruby Stained, 4 Piece	245.00

TEARDROP, see Teardrop & Thumbprint

Teardrop & Tassel, Bowl, Sea Green, 7 1/2 In.	35.00
Teardrop & Tassel, Butter, Cover	35.00
Teardrop & Tassel, Compote, Nile Green, 7 X 7 1/4 In.	265.00
Teardrop & Tassel, Creamer	20.00 To 35.00
Teardrop & Tassel, Pitcher, 8 In.	40.00
Teardrop & Tassel, Tumbler	20.00

Teardrop & Tassel, Tumbler, Cobalt Blue	45.00
Teardrop & Thumbprint, Wine	16.50
Teardrop, Syrup	34.00
Teardrop, Wine, Souvenir, Indianapolis, Ruby Stained	18.00
Tennessee, Cake Stand, 8 1/2 In.	48.00
Tennessee, Goblet	55.00
Tennessee, Pitcher, Milk	50.00
Tepee, Nappy	25.00
Tepee, Salt & Pepper	31.50
Tepee, Toothpick	22.00
TEXAS BULL'S–EYE, see Bull's–Eye Variant	
Texas, Cake Plate	45.00
Texas, Relish	26.50 To 28.00
Texas, Toothpick	25.00 To 27.00
Texas, Vase, 7 In.	20.00
Texas, Vase, 9 3/4 In.	35.00
The States, Creamer, Green, Gold Trim, Individual	30.00
The States, Goblet	35.00
The States, Plate, 8 In.	70.00
The States, Plate, Liberty Bell, 10 In.	75.00
The States, Punch Cup	12.50
The States, Syrup	95.00
The States, Wine	25.00
The States, Wine, Green	20.00
Theodore Roosevelt, Bread Plate	150.00
Theodore Roosevelt, Bread Plate, Frosted	98.00
Thistle, Bowl, 8 In., Pair	200.00
Thistle, Celery	40.00
Thistle, Creamer	50.00
Thousand Eye, Butter, Cover	47.50
Thousand Eye, Butter, Cover, Apple Green	75.00
Thousand Eye, Cake Stand, Knob Stem, 9 In.	80.00
Thousand Eye, Celery, Green	65.00
Thousand Eye, Cruet, Stopper, Vaseline	95.00
Thousand Eye, Goblet	20.00 To 30.00
Thousand Eye, Goblet, Amber	25.00 To 36.00
Thousand Eye, Mug, Amber, 4 In.	18.00
Thousand Eye, Plate, Folded Corners, 10 In.	32.50
Thousand Eye, Spooner	30.00
Thousand Eye, Spooner, Amber	25.00
Thousand Eye, Sugar & Creamer, Cover, Amber	80.00
Thousand Eye, Toothpick, Blue	30.00 To 40.00
Thousand Eye, Tumbler, Amber	25.00
Thousand Eye, Water Set, Knob Stem, Vaseline, 7 Piece	300.00
Thousand Eye, Wine, Blue	40.00
Thousand Eye, Wine, Vaseline	42.50
Three Birds, Pitcher, Water	100.00
Three Face, Cake Stand, 9 In.	155.00
Three Face, Cake Stand, Frosted Base & Pedestal, 9 3/8 In.	150.00
Three Face, Claret, Clear & Frosted, 5 Oz.	145.00
Three Face, Compote, Cover, 6 In.	125.00
Three Face, Compote, Cover, Frosted Finial, Base, 12 1/2 In.	225.00
Three Face, Goblet	85.00
Three Face, Salt & Pepper	75.00 To 175.00
Three Face, Spooner	250.00
Three Face, Spooner, Frosted	45.00
THREE GRACES, see also Three Face	
Three Graces, Bread Plate, Dated 1875	65.00
Three Graces, Bread Plate, Milk Glass Center	245.00
Three Panel, Berry Bowl, Master, Amber	35.00
Three Panel, Berry Bowl, Master, Blue	55.00
Three Panel, Creamer	25.00
Three Panel, Creamer, Amber	40.00
Three Panel, Creamer, Blue	45.00 To 50.00

Waffle & Thumbprint   Washington Centennial   Westward Ho

Three Panel, Fruit Bowl, Blue, 10 3/4 In. .... 38.00 To 50.00
Three Panel, Goblet, Amber .... 21.00 To 35.00
Three Panel, Goblet, Vaseline 40.00
Three Panel, Sugar, Cover 45.00
Three Panel, Sugar, Cover, Blue 65.00
Three Presidents, Bread Plate, Frosted Center .... 65.00 To 85.00
Three Presidents, Goblet 325.00
    THREE SISTERS, see Three Face
Thumbprint, Bowl, Cover, Flint, 7 3/8 In. 45.00
Thumbprint, Bowl, Ruby, 6 3/8 In. 45.00
Thumbprint, Celery, Ruby 48.00
Thumbprint, Compote, Cover, Flint, 10 In. 135.00
Thumbprint, Compote, Flint, 9 In. 35.00
Thumbprint, Cup & Saucer, Ruby Stained 45.00
Thumbprint, Goblet 25.00
Thumbprint, Pickle, Ruby Stained 30.00
Thumbprint, Spooner, Flint 45.00
Thumbprint, Toothpick, Etched, Ruby Stained 30.00
Thumbprint, Wine, Flint 55.00
    TIDY, see Rustic
Tiny Lion, Celery, Etched 50.00
Tiny Lion, Pitcher, Water 45.00
    TOBIN, see Leaf & Star
Toltec, Tumbler 25.00
Torpedo, Berry Bowl, 9 1/4 In. 33.00
Torpedo, Celery 41.50
Torpedo, Compote, 7 In. 42.00
Torpedo, Decanter, Faceted Stopper 45.00
Torpedo, Goblet 54.00
Torpedo, Pitcher, 11 3/4 In. 60.00
Torpedo, Pitcher, Milk, Ruby Stained, 8 1/2 In. 88.00
Torpedo, Punch Cup 20.00
Torpedo, Salt, Master 65.00
Torpedo, Sugar, Cover 80.00
Torpedo, Syrup 75.00
Torpedo, Tray, Water 65.00
Tree of Life, Bread Plate 60.00
Tree of Life, Compote, Hand Pedestal, 9 In. 80.00
Tree of Life, Creamer 45.00
Tree of Life, Finger Bowl, 2 3/4 X 3 3/4 In. 35.00
Tree of Life, Pitcher, Water 78.00
Tree of Life, Salt, Master, Salt Impressed On Bowl 135.00

Tree of Life, Spooner	45.00
Triangular Prism, Goblet, Flint	30.00
Triple Triangle, Butter, Cover	75.00
Triple Triangle, Butter, Cover, Ruby Stained	65.00
Triple Triangle, Cake Stand, Ruby Stained	30.00
Triple Triangle, Table Set, Ruby Stained, 4 Piece	225.00
Triple Triangle, Water Set, 6 Piece	210.00
Triple Triangle, Wine, Ruby Stained	38.00
Truncated Cube, Wine, Ruby Stained	35.00
Tulip & Honeycomb, Butter, Cover, Child's	30.00
Tulip & Honeycomb, Creamer, Child's	22.00
Tulip & Honeycomb, Sugar & Creamer	36.00
Tulip & Honeycomb, Sugar, Cover, Child's	25.00 To 32.00
Tulip Petals, Table Set, Rainbow Colors, 4 Piece	225.00
Tulip Variant, Tumbler	12.50
Tulip With Sawtooth, Celery, Flint	60.00
Tulip With Sawtooth, Creamer	35.00
Tulip With Sawtooth, Spooner, Flint	27.00
Tulip, Compote, 8 In.	95.00
Tulip, Vase, Flint, Canary Yellow, 10 1/4 In., Pair	1000.00
Twin Snowshoes, Creamer, Child's	15.00
TWINKLE STAR, see Utah	
Two Band, Creamer	28.00
Two Band, Creamer, Child's	40.00
Two Panel, Bowl, Oval, Apple Green, 9 X 7 1/2 In.	37.50
Two Panel, Compote, Cover, Oval, Apple Green, 7 3/8 X 9 In.	125.00
Two Panel, Creamer, Blue, Gold Trim	35.00
Two Panel, Goblet, Blue	45.00
Two Panel, Goblet, Green	26.00 To 30.00
Two Panel, Spooner, Green	37.00
U.S.Coin, Bread Tray, Frosted	450.00
U.S.Coin, Compote, Cover, Frosted Coins, Dollar Finial, 9 In.	295.00
U.S.Coin, Dish, Pickle, Frosted	195.00
U.S.Coin, Epergne, Frosted Coins	1000.00
U.S.Coin, Sauce	40.00
U.S.Coin, Sugar, Cover	400.00
U.S.Coin, Toothpick, Dollar Obverse & Reverse	105.00
U.S.Coin, Tumbler, Frosted Dollar In Bottom	240.00
U.S.Peacock, Punch Bowl, 12 Cups	39.00
U.S.Rib, Cruet, Green, Original Stopper	70.00
U.S.Rib, Sauce, Green, Gold Trim	15.00
U.S.Rib, Sugar & Creamer, Breakfast, Emerald	75.00
Utah, Goblet, Blue	26.00
Utah, Pitcher, Water	45.00
Valencia Waffle, Celery, 6 1/2 In.	35.00
Valencia Waffle, Celery, Blue	35.00
Valencia Waffle, Compote, Cover, Blue, 8 1/4 In.	75.00
Valencia Waffle, Goblet	27.00
Vera, Berry Set, Clear & Frosted, 7 Piece	165.00
Vera, Cake Stand, Folded Sides, Clear & Frosted	30.00
Vermont, Berry Set, Green, 7 Piece	30.00
Vermont, Butter, Cover, Blue Trim	150.00
Vermont, Goblet, Green, Gold Trim	65.00
Vermont, Toothpick, Blue	33.50
Vermont, Toothpick, Gold Trim	45.00
Vermont, Toothpick, Green, Gold Trim	55.00
Vermont, Water Set, Green, Gold Trim, 6 Piece	265.00 To 275.00
Victor, Cake Stand	22.50
Victor, Cake Stand, Green	28.00 To 40.00
Victor, Celery	85.00
Victor, Creamer, Green	37.50
Victor, Spooner	35.00
Viking, Bread Plate	68.00
Viking, Creamer	35.00 To 60.00

Viking, Sugar, Cover, Bearded Man 60.00
Vine & Beads, Creamer, Child's, Green 85.00
Vine & Beads, Spooner, Child's 60.00
Vine & Beads, Sugar, Cover, Child's 80.00
    VIRGINIA, see Galloway
Waffle & Thumbprint, Goblet 60.00
Waffle & Thumbprint, Wine, Flint 50.00
Waffle With Points, Celery 25.50
Waffle, Bowl, Vegetable, Scalloped Corners, Green, 8 3/16 In. 100.00
Waffle, Celery 65.00
Waffle, Celery, Flint 120.00
Waffle, Champagne, Flint 135.00
Waffle, Eggcup, Flint 24.50
Waffle, Salt 3.25
Washboard, Plate, Green, 10 In. 27.00
Washington Centennial, Bread Plate, Bear Paw Handles 60.00
Washington Centennial, Cake Stand, 8 1/2 In. 40.00
Washington Centennial, Castor, Pickle, Claws, 1776–1876 .... 42.00
Washington Centennial, Goblet .... 38.00 To 40.00
Washington Centennial, Pitcher, Water 100.00
Washington, Table Set, 4 Piece 165.00
Way's Currant, Wine 18.00
Wedding Bells, Butter, Cover 45.00
Wedding Ring, Goblet 45.00
Wedding Ring, Wine, Flint 55.00
Wee Branches, Butter, Cover, Child's 150.00
Wee Branches, Plate, Child's .... 50.00 To 60.00
Wee Branches, Spooner, Child's .... 65.00 To 95.00
Wee Branches, Sugar, Cover, Child's 100.00
Westward Ho, Bowl, Gillinder, 4 X 7 X 9 In. 290.00
Westward Ho, Bread Plate, 13 X 9 In. 170.00
Westward Ho, Butter, Cover, Scalloped Base 100.00
Westward Ho, Compote, Cover, 6 In. 200.00
Westward Ho, Creamer .... 95.00 To 120.00
Westward Ho, Goblet 80.00
Westward Ho, Goblet, Frosted 75.00
Westward Ho, Pitcher, Water .... 145.00 To 165.00
Westward Ho, Sauce 15.00
Westward Ho, Spooner, Footed 95.00
Westward Ho, Sugar, Cover, 4 1/2 In. 200.00
Wheat & Barley, Compote, Amber, 8 1/4 In. 75.00
Wheat & Barley, Creamer 21.00

Wedding Ring

Wildflower

If you move glass in cold weather be sure to let it sit at room temperature for several hours before you try unpacking it. The glass will break more easily if there is an abrupt temperature change.

Wheat & Barley, Creamer, Amber	35.00
Wheat & Barley, Doughnut Stand, Blue	58.00
Wheat & Barley, Goblet	30.00
Wheat & Barley, Goblet, Amber	38.50
Wheat & Barley, Pitcher, Milk	38.50 To 78.00
Wheat & Barley, Spooner	20.00
Wheat Sheaf, Bread Plate, Give Us This Day, 13 X 9 In.	80.00
Wheat Sheaf, Pitcher, Water	48.00
Wheat Sheaf, Punch Set, Child's, 7 Piece	65.00
Wheat, Plate, 6 1/4 In.	100.00
WHIRLIGIG, see Buzz Star	
Wild Rose With Bow-Knot, Mustard, Cover, Clear & Frosted	40.00
Wildflower, Amber, Tumbler	40.00
Wildflower, Bowl, Blue, Square, 7 1/2 In.	35.00
Wildflower, Bread Plate	28.50
Wildflower, Compote, Cover, 8 In.	28.50
Wildflower, Compote, Footed, Amber, 6 In.	40.00
Wildflower, Creamer, Footed	35.00
Wildflower, Creamer, Green	50.00
Wildflower, Goblet	20.00
Wildflower, Goblet, Vaseline	40.00
Wildflower, Pitcher, Water	35.00
Wildflower, Salt, Green, Octagon, 2 1/2 X 3 1/4 In.	20.00
Wildflower, Syrup, Amber	150.00
Wildflower, Syrup, Blue	90.00
Wildflower, Water Set, Green, 8 Piece	325.00
Willow Oak, Cake Stand, Amber	60.00
Willow Oak, Compote, Amber	40.00
Willow Oak, Compote, Heisey, 7 In.	20.00
Willow Oak, Goblet	32.50
Willow Oak, Goblet, Amber	50.00
Willow Oak, Plate, Closed Handles, 9 In.	30.00
Willow Oak, Spooner	22.00
Willow Oak, Sugar, Cover	40.00
Willow Oak, Waste Bowl, Amber	48.00
Windflower, Compote, 8 In.	16.50
Winged Scroll, Match Holder	145.00
WINONA, see Barred Hobnail	
Wisconsin, Cake Stand	40.00
Wisconsin, Celery	45.00
Wisconsin, Compote, Jelly	20.00
Wisconsin, Dish, Rectangular, 5 7/8 X 8 1/4 In.	22.00

Wisconsin, Pickle	25.00
Wisconsin, Pitcher, Water	36.00
Wisconsin, Toothpick	40.00
Wisconsin, Wine	78.00
WOODEN PAIL, see Oaken Bucket	
Wreath & Bars, Goblet	21.00
Wreath & Shell, Celery, Blue	75.00
Wreath & Shell, Spittoon, Woman's, Enameled	65.00
Wyoming, Butter, Cover	95.00
Wyoming, Cake Stand, 9 3/4 X 4 In.	55.00
Wyoming, Goblet	55.00
Wyoming, Tankard, Cover, Individual	45.00
Wyoming, Tumbler	85.00
X–Ray, Berry Set, Green, Gold Trim, 7 Piece	155.00
X–Ray, Breakfast Set, Emerald Green, 4 Piece	320.00
X–Ray, Butter, Cover, Amethyst, Gold Trim	200.00
X–Ray, Butter, Cover, Gold Trim	75.00
X–Ray, Carafe, Green	35.00
X–Ray, Salt & Pepper, Original Tops	15.00
X–Ray, Toothpick, Green	58.00
X–Ray, Water Set, Green, Gold Trim, 7 Piece	235.00
YALE, see Crowfoot	
Yazoo City, Sherbet	50.00
Zippered Swirl & Diamond, Salt & Pepper, Glass Stand	55.00

 Print, in this listing, means any of many printed images produced on paper by one of the more common methods, such as lithography. The prints listed here are of interest primarily to the antiques collector, not the fine arts collector. Many of these prints were originally part of books. Other prints will be found in the sections headed Currier & Ives, Advertising, and Poster.

Audubon bird prints were originally issued as part of books printed from 1826 to 1854. They were issued in two sizes, 26 1/2 in. by 39 1/2 in. and 11 in. by 7 in. The quadupeds were issued in 28 in. by 22 in. size prints. Later editions of the Audubon books were done in many sizes and reprints of the books in the original size were also made. The bird pictures have been so popular they have been copied in myriad sizes by both old and new printing methods. This list includes originals and later copies because Audubon prints of all ages are sold in antiques shops.

PRINT, A.B.Frost, Monroe Doctrine, 1906, 16 X 10 3/4 In.	10.00
Armstrong, Seminude Lady Holding Egyptian Tray, Blue, Gold	90.00
Arthur, Child of The Forest, Indian Maiden, 11 X 14 In.	75.00
Audubon, Baltimore Oriole, C.1860, 25 X 38 1/4 In.	100.00
Audubon, Black Vulture, Chromolithograph, C.1860, 22 X 36 In.	450.00
Audubon, Grey Fox, C.1845, 17 3/4 X 23 3/4 In. ....*Illus*	2090.00
Audubon, Jay's Flycatcher, Male & Female, No.59	125.00
Audubon, Muskrats, Chromolithograph, Framed, C.1843, 21 X 27 In.	400.00
Audubon, Muskrats, Framed, 1843, 28 X 22 In.	400.00
Audubon, Pectoral Sandpiper, Framed, 28 X 22 In.	385.00
Audubon, Raccoon, Chromolithograph, 1845, 17 X 24 In.	375.00
Audubon, Ruffed Grouse, No.9, 26 1/2 X 39 1/2 In.	3900.00
Audubon, Slender–Billed Guillemot, Frame, 26 1/2 X 39 1/2 In.	850.00
Audubon, Stanley Hawk, 38 1/2 X 25 3/8 In. ....*Illus*	1500.00
Audubon, Virginia Partridge, No.16, 26 1/2 X 39 1/2 In.	4000.00
Audubon, White–Headed Eagle, 38 1/8 X 25 1/8 In. ....*Illus*	2750.00
Audubon, Wood Wren, No.119	125.00
Babes In The Woods, Girls With Fawns, Framed, 31 X 24 In.	65.00
Bachmann, Panorama of New York & Vicinity, 21 X 35 In. ....*Illus*	4950.00
Baillie, Gen.George Washington, Black Frame, 12 5/8 X 16 5/8 In.	40.00
Bartlett, Boston & Bunker Hill	147.50
Bartlett, Faneuil Hall, From The Water, Boston	147.50
Bartlett, Ferry At Brooklyn, New York	147.50

Print, Audubon, Grey Fox, C.1845, 17 3/4 X 23 3/4 In.

Bartlett, Outlet of Niagara River, Lake Ontario In The Distance	127.50
Bartlett, Railroad Scene, Little Falls	127.50
Bartlett, Schuylkill Water Works, Philadelphia	147.50
Bartlett, View From West Point	127.50
Bartlett, Landing On The American Side, Niagara Falls, 1838	18.00
Bartlett, Trenton Falls, View Down Ravine, Framed, 1839, 4 3/4 X 7 In.	25.00
Bartlett, View On Erie Canal, 1839, 4 3/4 X 7 In.	18.00
Beal, Before The Hurricane, 1929, 7 X 11 In.	120.00
Beal, Catch of The Day, 7 X 11 In.	130.00
Beal, In Tow, 1929, 7 X 11 In.	120.00
Beal, Summer Breezes, 1929, 8 X 11 In.	130.00
Bearden, Dreams of Exile, 22 X 16 In.	400.00
Becker, Terrier Puppy, Feeding Bottle To Baby, Framed	45.00
Benson, Ducks Alighting, 1921, 6 X 4 In.	125.00
Benson, Rippling Water, 1920, 9 X 8 In.	325.00
Benson, The River, 1916, 10 X 7 In.	350.00
Brown & Bigelow, Lights of Home	165.00
Brown & Bigelow, Quiet Solitude	45.00
Brown & Bigelow, Sheltering Oaks	45.00
Brown & Bigelow, Sun Up	165.00
Brown & Bigelow, Twilight	45.00
Bumbeck, Shadows, 8 X 10 In.	80.00
Burr, Desert Arizona, 1926, 6 X 8 In.	500.00
Chamberlain, Auxerre, 1931, 6 X 8 In.	160.00
Chinese, Begonia, Yu Zhizhen, Silk Scroll Mounting, 37 1/2 X 15 In.	125.00
Chinese, Pink Plum Blossoms, He Xiangning, Silk Mounting, 67 X 19 In.	200.00
Chinese, Spring Rain On Li River, Xu Beihong, Mounting, 65 X 31 In.	225.00
Christy, Sailing Close	15.00
Drayton, Scotty Dog	35.00
Earl Christy, My One Rose, 14 X 22 In.	95.00
Eby, Cider Mill, 7 X 13 In.	110.00
Edwards, English Hunting Scene, 15 X 21 In.	150.00

English, Football, Officers Playing, Dated 1827, 8 1/4 X 12 1/2 In.	100.00
Fisher, A Morning Greeting, 1904, 13 X 17 In.	45.00
Fisher, Evening Hour, Framed, 8 X 11 In.	45.00
Fisher, King of Hearts, Framed, 11 X 13 In.	65.00
Fox, 2 Summer Landscapes, 9 1/2 X 21 In.	50.00
Fox, Clipper Ship	55.00
Fox, Country Garden, Framed	35.00
Fox, Daydreams, 14 X 12 In.	75.00
Fox, Garden of Romance, 22 X 14 In.	35.00
Fox, Glorious Vista, 17 X 29 In.	35.00 To 55.00
Fox, Hearts Desire	25.00
Fox, Land of Dreams	30.00
Fox, Love's Paradise, 1925, 10 X 18 In.	225.00
Fox, Midsummer Magic, 22 X 14 In.	35.00
Fox, Peace & Sunshine, Framed, 21 X 33 In.	90.00
Fox, Spirit of Youth, 1926, 12 X 20 In.	225.00
Fox, Sunset Dreams, 10 X 17 In.	40.00
Fox, Sweet Dreams, Framed	50.00
Frahm, Fences, Framed	35.00
Gevin, Position Pour Le Garde, 1763, Framed, 10 1/2 X 15 1/2 In.	75.00
Gillray, Bear and His Leader, 9 X 13 In.	50.00
Gillray, John Bull and The Sinking Fund, 13 X 9 In.	70.00
Gillray, Political Amusements For Young Gentlemen, 10 X 13 In.	80.00
Gillray, Power of Beauty, St. Cecilia Charming The Brute, 9 X 13 In.	120.00
Gillray, Shrine At St. Ann's Hall, 10 X 14 In.	70.00
Gillray, State Waggoner and John Bull, 10 X 14 In.	60.00
Gropper, Dream, 1962, 11 X 15 In.	300.00
Gropper, Tailor, 1966, 13 X 16 In.	250.00
Grossman, 2 Girls In Garden Being Serenaded, 17 X 29 In.	75.00
Grosz, Fata Morgana, 11 X 9 In.	290.00
Gutmann, A Little Bit of Heaven, Framed, 11 X 14 In.	35.00 To 65.00
Gutmann, Awakening, Framed, 11 X 14 In.	35.00

Print, Audubon, Stanley Hawk,
38 1/2 X 25 3/8 In.

Print, Audubon, White-Headed Eagle,
38 1/8 X 25 1/8 In.

Gutmann, Colonial Lavender & Old Lace 75.00
Gutmann, First Dancing Lesson, 1923, 21 X 14 In. 80.00
Gutmann, Girl Sleeping, Dolly & Teddy Bear, 1907 .... 150.00
Gutmann, Good Morn 125.00
Gutmann, Harmony, No.802 .... 75.00
Gutmann, New Love, Framed, Small 45.00
Gutmann, On Dreamland's Border, Framed, 14 X 17 1/2 In. 45.00
Gutmann, Punishment 125.00
Gutmann, Reward 125.00
Gutmann, Television, 21 X 14 In. 75.00
Homer, Battle of Bunker Hill, 1875 .... 65.00
Homer, Fishing Party, 1869 .... 150.00
Homer, Morning Bell, 1873 .... 100.00
Homer, Station House Lodgers, 1874 .... 70.00
Homer, Waiting For A Bite, 1874 .... 275.00
Humphrey, Baby, On Floor With Roses 40.00
Humphrey, Children, Reading Newspaper, C.1897, 8 X 10 In. 210.00
Humphrey, Tea & Gossip, From Little Grown–Ups 40.00
Icart, Angry Steed, Signed, 1917, 16 X 10 In. 1650.00
Icart, Awakening, Signed, 1925, 15 1/2 In. 1100.00
Icart, Basket of Apples, Signed, 1924, 17 X 13 In. 1200.00
Icart, Bird of Prey, Signed, 1918, 18 X 13 In. 1450.00
Icart, Calmady Children, Framed 50.00
Icart, Casanova, Signed, 1928, 21 X 14 In. 1100.00
Icart, Chestnut Vendor, Signed, 1928, 19 X 14 In. 1200.00
Icart, Cinderella 1000.00
Icart, Flower Seller, Signed, 1928, 19 X 15 In. 1100.00
Icart, Girl In Crinoline, Signed, 1937, 23 X 19 In. 1325.00
Icart, Girl, Leaving Coach, Windmill Mark 1000.00
Icart, Gossip 900.00
Icart, Joy of Life, Signed, 1929, 24 X 16 In. 3025.00
Icart, Le Jardin Japonais 395.00
Icart, Open Cage, Signed, 1926, 17 X 13 In. 1210.00
Icart, Orange Seller, Signed, 1929, 19 X 14 In. 990.00
Icart, Silk Robe, Signed, 1926, 15 X 18 In. 1550.00
Icart, Sleeping Beauty, Signed, 1927, 15 X19 In. 1550.00
Icart, Smoke, Signed, 1926, 14 X 20 In. 1750.00
Icart, The Embrace, Signed, 1926, 15 X 18 In. 990.00
Icart, The Four Dears, Signed, 1929, 22 X 15 In. 1550.00
Icart, The Peacock, Signed, 1925, 19 X 15 In. 1980.00
Icart, White Underwear, Signed, 1925, 15 X 19 In. 1045.00
Icart, Woman In Wings, Signed, 1936, 7 X 9 In. 6600.00

Japanese prints are listed as follows: Print, Japanese, name of artist, title or description, type, and size. Dealers use the following terms: Tate–e is a vertical composition. Yoko–e is a horizontal composition. The words Aiban (13 by 9 inches), Chuban (10 by 7 1/2 inches), Hosoban (12 by 6 inches), Oban (15 by 10 inches), and Koban (7 by 4 inches) denote size.

Japanese, Chikanobu, True Beauties, 1897 .... 550.00
Japanese, Eisen, Floating World, C.1840 .... 1600.00
Japanese, Fishing Lake Matsubara Shunsu Province, Kawade 298.00
Japanese, Harbor Scene, Signed Hasui, 14 X 9 In. ....*Illus* 125.00
Japanese, Hasui, Evening At Ushibori, 1930, 16 3/4 X 12 In. 300.00
Japanese, Hiroshige, Shrine At Yushima, 1856 .... 2500.00
Japanese, Hiroshige II, Sumida River 1600.00
Japanese, Hiroshige, Cherry Blossoms, 1856 .... 4000.00
Japanese, Hiroshige, Fujikawa, 1834 .... 3600.00
Japanese, Hiroshige, Futagawa, 1834 .... 2000.00
Japanese, Hiroshige, Goyu, 1834 .... 4500.00
Japanese, Hiroshige, Sakai Ferry, 1857 .... 2200.00
Japanese, Hiroshige, Shono, 1834 .... 6000.00
Japanese, Hokusai, Famous Bridges, C.1832 .... 9000.00

Print, Bachmann, Panorama of New York & Vicinity, 21 X 35 In.

Print, Japanese, Harbor Scene,
Signed Hasui, 14 X 9 In.

Japanese, Horses, Framed, 20th Century, 18 X 12 1/2 In.	10.00
Japanese, Kiso River, Hiroshi Yoshida, 1928	633.00
Japanese, Kiyochika, Rickshaw Scene, C.1881	2500.00
Japanese, Kunickika, Famous Actors, C.1865	400.00
Japanese, Kuniyoshi, Heroes of Suikoden, C.1830	1200.00
Japanese, Kuniyoshi, Kisokaido Road, 1852	900.00
Japanese, Kuniyoshi, Mountain & Oceans, 1852	1200.00
Japanese, Kuniyoshi, Two Warriors, C.1850	1200.00
Japanese, Shinsui, Hand Mirror, 1925, 15 1/4 X 10 1/2 In.	300.00
Japanese, Snake & Melons, Hokkei	198.00
Japanese, Tominobu, Floating World, C.1838	1500.00
Japanese, Toyokuni III, 47 Ronin, 1864	500.00
Japanese, Toyokuni III, Sumo Wrestler, C.1859	600.00
Japanese, Yoshida, Bridge At Kameldo, 1927, 15 3/4 X 10 3/4 In.	250.00
Japanese, Yoshida, Glittering Sea, 1926, 16 X 10 1/2 In.	300.00
Japanese, Yoshida, Hirosaki Castle, 15 3/4 X 10 3/4 In.	250.00
Japanese, Yoshitoshi, Archer, Goddess, Battling Tidal Wave	440.00
Japanese, Yoshitoshi, Enjoyable Type, 1888	1500.00
Japanese, Yoshitoshi, Flute Players, 1886	1500.00
Japanese, Yoshitoshi, Heavy Type, 1888	2000.00
Japanese, Yoshitoshi, Spending Type, 1888	1800.00
Kahn, Child and The Bridge, 19 X 25 In.	110.00
Kellogg, Feeding The Pigeons, Mahogany Frame, 12 1/2 X 16 1/2 In.	25.00
Kellogg, Washington Family, Mahogany Veneer Frame, 17 3/4 X 13 In.	90.00
Kenyon, My Bluebird, 10 X 13 In.	45.00
Klabunde, Poseidon, 1976, 17 X 11 In.	80.00
Lazzell, Provincetown Studios, 1936, 11 X 7 In.	7300.00
Leyendecker, Discus–Thrower, Collier & Son, 1906, 11 1/2 X 10 In.	40.00
Little, Harbor Scene, 12 X 9 In.	50.00
MacLaughlan, Tennessee Pike, 8 X 13 In.	50.00
Melrose, Harbor of New York & Battery, 22 X 36 In. ....*Illus*	1320.00
Nast, Twas The Night Before Christmas, Harpers Weekly, Page, 1876	20.00
Nutting, Apple Tree Bend, Framed, 7 X 9 1/2 In.	36.00
Nutting, Autumn Processional, Framed, 7 1/2 X 9 1/2 In.	35.00
Nutting, Hollyhock Cottage, Framed, 4 X 6 In.	32.00
Nutting, Homeward Bound, Framed, 1918, 7 1/4 X 9 1/4 In.	42.00
Nutting, Hunter's Island, 4 X 10 In.	40.00
Nutting, Larkspur, 17 1/2 X 21 In.	115.00
Nutting, Lingering Waters, 7 1/2 X 9 1/2 In.	105.00
Nutting, Nearing The Crest, Framed, 1910, 4 X 9 1/2 In.	38.00
Nutting, Sheep At Pasture & Prayer, Dated 1901, 7 X 7 In.	10.00
Nutting, Swimming Pool, Framed, 14 X 17 1/2 In.	75.00

Nutting, Way Through The Orchard, Framed, 1915, 7 1/2 X 9 1/2 In. 38.00
Parr, An Inside View of Rotunda, Ranelagh Gardens, 10 X 16 In. 90.00
Parrish, Air Castles, 11 X 16 In. 125.00
Parrish, Brazen Boatman, Framed, 9 X 11 In. 85.00
Parrish, Canyon, 12 X 15 In. 175.00
Parrish, Contentment, With Edison–Mazda Calendar, 14 X 23 In. 190.00
Parrish, Dawn, Framed, 14 X 19 In. 150.00
Parrish, Daybreak, Framed, 10 X 18 In. 150.00
Parrish, Daybreak, Framed, 6 X 10 In. 45.00
Parrish, Dinkey Bird, Framed, 11 X 16 In. 95.00
Parrish, Dreaming, 10 X 18 In. 130.00
Parrish, Dreamlight, Edison–Mazda Calendar, 1925 .... 750.00
Parrish, Ecstasy 195.00
Parrish, Evening, 1922, 12 X 15 In. 125.00
Parrish, Fisk Tire Ad, Fit For A King, Framed 45.00
Parrish, Garden of Allah, Framed, 15 X 30 In. .... 175.00 To 180.00
Parrish, Garden of Opportunity, Framed, 8 X 7 In. 40.00
Parrish, Hilltop, 6 X 10 In. .... 90.00 To 165.00
Parrish, King of The Black Isles, 9 1/2 X 11 1/2 In. 50.00
Parrish, Lute Players, Framed, 18 X 30 In. 375.00
Parrish, Old King Cole, Framed, 25 X 6 In. 275.00
Parrish, Pierrot's Serenade, Bookplate 50.00
Parrish, Rubaiyat, Framed, 8 X 30 In. 320.00
Parrish, Solitude, With Edison–Mazda Calendar, 14 X 23 In. 265.00
Parrish, Spirit of Transportation, 16 X 20 In. 500.00
Parrish, Village Brook, 15 X 11 In. 150.00
Parrish, Wild Geese, Framed, 12 X 15 In. 120.00
Parrish, Wynken, Blynken & Nod, Matte Signed, Framed, 1912 .... 375.00
Pease, Good Morning, 11 X 14 In. 69.00
Pease, My Baby, 11 X 14 In. 69.00
Pennell, Woolworth Building, 1915, 11 X 7 In. 350.00
Petty, Girl, Large Hat & Telephone, 12 X 19 In. 33.00
Petty, Girl, Reclining, Book & Telephone, 12 X 19 In. .... 35.00 To 39.00
Picasso, Matador & 2 Figures, Signed L.R., Framed, 18 X 24 In. 50.00
Picasso, Mother & Child, Framed, 19 1/2 X 15 In. 75.00
Piranesi, Architectural Fantasy, 15 X 21 In. 170.00
Pope, The Black Duck, 1879, 13 X 20 In. 225.00
Prang, Carnations & Mignonette, After Lunzer, 7 1/2 X 10 1/2 In. 14.00
Prang, Home of Abraham Lincoln, 14 X 16 In. 70.00
Prang, Mother & Small Child In Hammock, 1888, 10 1/2 X 12 3/4 In. 20.00
Prang, Mother, Watching Child Picking Flowers, 10 1/2 X 12 3/4 In. 20.00
Prang, Rest On The Roadside, After Niles, Framed, 7 1/2 X 9 1/2 In. 95.00

Print, Melrose, Harbor of New York & Battery, 22 X 36 In.

Prang, Whittier's Barefooted Boy, Framed, 1868, 10 X 13 In. 110.00
Remington, Spanish Escort, 9 X 11 In. 15.00
Remington, When Tracts Spell Meat 25.00
Rinehart, Apache Women, Walnut Frame, 1899, 13 1/2 X 16 1/2 In. 65.00
Robinson, Portrait of Walt Whitman, 9 X 13 In. 150.00
Rockwell, Getting The Marriage License, Autograph 350.00
Rockwell, Shuttleton's Barber Shop, Matted 45.00
Rockwell, Truth About Santa, Autograph 350.00
Rowlandson, Crimping A Quaker, 9 X 13 In. 50.00
Rowlandson, Defrauding The Customers, 8 X 13 In. 170.00
Rowlandson, Macassar Oil, 13 X 9 In. 90.00
Rowlandson, Norwich Bull Feast, 9 X 14 In. 50.00
Rowlandson, Sagacious Buck, 10 X 13 In. 60.00
Rowlandson, Soldiers On The March, 9 X 13 In. 110.00
Rowlandson, Visit To The Uncle, 6 X 8 In. 70.00
Schmidt, Three Hunchbacked Dwarfs, 8 X 9 In. 90.00
Stern & Hacker, Enchantment, Original Frame, 15 X 23 In. 35.00
Sterner, Nocturne No.2, 1920, 12 X 16 In. 70.00
Thompson, Woodland Splendor, Framed 20.00
Turner, Calla Lilies, Mirrored Frame 60.00
Voodrous, Beach Scene, 1936, 9 X 10 In. 170.00
Wengeroth, Flack's Cove, 1966, 10 X 15 In. 350.00
Wengeroth, Matriarch, 1970, 13 X 11 In. 300.00
West, Pogy Boat, 9 X 11 In. 110.00
Wireman, Springtime, 3 Children, Garden, Rabbits, 1928 .... 75.00
Woodcut, Owl, 4 X 4 In. 2.00
Worth, A Clean Sweep, Black Comic, 11 3/4 X 15 3/4 In. 230.00
Worth, Darktown Fire Brigade, Saved, To The Rescue, Black Comic, Pair 390.00

How to carry a handkerchief and lipstick is a problem today for
every woman, including the Queen of England. The purse has been
recognizable since the eighteenth century. Leather and needlework
purses were preferred. Beaded purses became popular in the
nineteenth century, went out of style, but are again in use. Mesh
purses date from the 1880s and are still being made.

PURSE, Allover Beaded Loops, Pin & White, Snap 32.00
Art Deco, Black Cloth, Gold Frame 22.00
Art Deco, Handles, Celluloid, Rialto, New York 30.00
Art Deco, Rust Plastic, Brass, Book Type 24.00
Art Deco, Whiting & Davis 50.00
Bag, Pearlized Strip Trim, Inside Mirror, Comb, Black Velvet, Ingber 18.00
Beaded, Blue Iridescent, 8 In. 35.00
Beaded, Copper, Box Type, Carnival, Bent Handle, 5 1/2 X 5 In. 65.00
Beaded, Egyptian Design 39.00
Beaded, Flapper Style, Iridescent Blue 30.00
Beaded, Floral Design, Fringe 4.00
Beaded, Glass, Lady Bug, Lined, Metal Frame, 3 In. 8.00
Beaded, Iridescent, Green Celluloid Clasp & Chain 45.00
Beaded, Midnight Blue, Stylized Florals, Jeweled Clasp, 6 X 6 1/2 In. 45.00
Beaded, Multicolor, Mirror, French, 8 X 6 1/2 In. 100.00
Beaded, Ornate Silver Frame, Diamond & Floral Pattern, Art Nouveau 100.00
Brocaded With Silver Mesh, India, 8 X 5 In. 45.00
Bronze Carnival Glass Beads, 7 X 4 In. 22.00
Bugle Beads 16.00
Carved Nephrite, Gold Mount, Diamond Set Ribbons, Russian, 4 In. 6000.00
Cigarette, Gold Mesh 15.00
Clutch, Black Beaded, 1950s 18.00
Clutch, Foldover, Dark Iridescent Beaded, Small 18.00
Clutch, Inside Coin Purse, Mirror, Brown Satin 13.00
Crochet, Petit Point, Floral Design 30.00
Cut Steel, Gray & Black, 10 In. 35.00
Drawstring, Beaded, 7 1/2 X 9 1/2 In. 85.00
Flame Stitch, Crewel Yarns & Cut Steel Beads, Silk Lined, 7 X 5 In. 175.00
Flame Stitch, Crewel Yarns, Each Side Different, 5 3/4 X 6 3/4 In. 150.00

Flame Stitch, Envelope Style	40.00
Flame Stitch, Wool Yarns, Calamanco Lining, 4 1/4 X 7 3/4 In.	500.00
Leather, Jemco, 8 X 6 In.	28.00
Mesh, 14K Gold, Amethyst Closure, Garnets, Diamonds, Gold Finger Ring	1150.00
Mesh, 14K Gold, Square, 42 Grams	300.00
Mesh, 14K Gold, Square, Cabochon Sapphire Closure, Link Chain	300.00
Mesh, Art Deco Frame, Floral, Heavy Handle, 5 X 9 In.	85.00
Mesh, Bearded Man's Face, 2 Cupids, Both Sides, Sterling Silver, 1901	300.00
Mesh, Braided Chain, Mirror & Compact In Top, 4 1/2 X 2 1/2 In.	75.00
Mesh, Brass Tone, Whiting & Davis, Braided Handle, Fringe, 7 1/2 In.	15.00
Mesh, Chain Strap, German Silver, 1920s, 7 X 6 In.	15.00
Mesh, Comb, Mirror, Whiting & Davis, 1920s	45.00
Mesh, Embossed Mythological Bearded God, Bulrushes, Silver, German	85.00
Mesh, Floral, Whiting & Davis, 6 X 3 1/2 In.	35.00
Mesh, Metal Beaded Floral Design, Chain Strap	15.00
Mesh, Painted, Lined, Whiting Davis	95.00
Mesh, Platinum, Gold, Sapphire, Channel Set Sapphires & Diamonds	1500.00
Mesh, Sapphire Clasp, German Silver	100.00
Mesh, Silver Plated Top, Mirror, Original Lining	140.00
Mesh, Silver Top, Black, Pink & White Design	70.00
Mesh, Silver, Sapphire Clasp, German	100.00
Mesh, Silver, With Tassel, German	38.00
Mesh, Sterling Silver Engraved Frame	145.00
Mesh, Sterling Silver, 5 X 7 In.	125.00
Mesh, White, Summer, Celluloid Frame, Whiting & Davis	25.00
Mesh, Wrist, 14K Gold, Seed Pearls, Sapphire In Clasp, Leather, 7 In.	1200.00
Miser's, Marcasite Trim	110.00
Mottled Gray, 2 Rows of Rhinestones, Oval, Bakelite	23.50
Pearl Shell, Brass Hinge & Catch, Lined, Silk Cord, 2 X 3 1/2 In.	25.00
Pouch, Marcasite	150.00
Rhinestone, By Audrey Bedford, Austria	125.00
Rhinestone, French	60.00
Shell, Child's, Merry Christmas 1883	38.00
Silveroid Beads, 6 X 4 In.	20.00
Straw, Flowers, Art Deco, 1937	18.00
Victorian, Necessary, Rhinestones, Silver & Silver Plate	95.00
Wire Mesh, Art Deco, Chain Handle, Butterfly Design	38.50

Quezal   Quezal glass was made from 1901 to 1920 by Martin Bach, Sr., in Brooklyn, New York. Other glassware by other firms, such as Loetz, Steuben, and Tiffany, resembles this gold–colored iridescent glass. After Martin Bach's death in 1920, his son continued the manufacture of a similar glass under the name "Lustre Art Glass."

QUEZAL, Candle Lamp, Shade, Signed	250.00
Candy Bowl, Ribbed, Ruffled Squared Top, 2 1/2 X 4 1/2 In.	175.00
Candy Dish, Thin Stem, Signed, 5 In.	250.00
Chandelier, 4 Gold Shades, 1 Large Center Shade, Signed, 16 In.	850.00
Compote, Gold, Ribbed, Signed, 2 3/4 In.	550.00
Compote, Iridescent Swirls, Gold Stem & Foot, Signed, 6 3/4 In.	495.00
Cup & Saucer, S Shaped Handle, Gold, Signed	475.00
Shade, Aurene Platinum Feather, Green, Aurene	525.00
Shade, Fishnet Design, Opal Ground, Gold Interior, Ruffled, 7 In.	685.00
Shade, Gold Pulled Feathers On Calcite, Signed, 6 X 4 1/2 In., Pair	260.00
Shade, Opalescent & Green Snakeskin	95.00
Shade, Pulled Feather, Cobalt Blue, 4 Piece	1100.00
Shade, Tulip Shape, 2–Sided	150.00
Shade, White Snakeskin On Gold Upper, Green Lower Body, Signed, Pr.	275.00
Vase, Allover Design, Gold Feather Oval, Signed, 9 In.	975.00
Vase, Bud, Gold Trim, Signed, 12 In.	800.00
Vase, Bud, Gold, Signed, 12 In., Pair	825.00
Vase, Gold Hooked Feathers, Bulbous, Signed, 4 1/2 In.	1175.00
Vase, Gold Hooked Feathers, Green, Diamond Pattern, Signed, 5 In.	2250.00
Vase, Green, Gold, Feather, Signed, 7 1/2 In.	975.00
Vase, Jack–In–The–Pulpit, 1905, Amber, Alabaster, 11 In.	3300.00

Vase, Pulled Green Feather, Gold Lacing, Signed, 6 1/2 In. 1475.00
Vase, Purple Iridescent, Green Spangling, 6 1/2 In. 195.00
Vase, Rainbow, Gold Iridescent, Ruffled, Raised Design, Signed, 8 In. 375.00
Vase, Sweet Pea, Signed, 6 In. ....995.00 To 1100.00

 Quilts have been made since the seventeenth century. Early textiles were very precious and every scrap was saved to be reused. A quilt is a combination of fabrics joined to a filler and a backing by small stitched designs known as quilting. An appliqued quilt has pieces stitched to the top of a large piece of background fabric. A patchwork, or pieced, quilt is made of many small pieces stitched together. Embroidery can be added to either type.

QUILT, Appliqued, 4 Stylized Floral Medallions, 76 X 80 In. 165.00
Appliqued, American Star of Bethlehem, Red, Green, White, 90 X 89 In. 1000.00
Appliqued, Basket Pattern, Blue, Goldenrod, 82 X 82 In. 450.00
Appliqued, Butterflies, White Muslin, 1940s, 84 X 104 In. 65.00
Appliqued, Carolina Lily, Red & Blue Calico, 73 X 73 In. 350.00
Appliqued, Conventional Rose, Calico Patches, Border, 80 X 84 In. 425.00
Appliqued, Currants & Cockscomb, Twin 675.00
Appliqued, Double Irish Chain, Pink & Green Calico, 78 X 87 In. 185.00
Appliqued, Double Wedding Ring, Scalloped, 62 X 80 In. 110.00
Appliqued, Dutch Doll, Red, Pastels, 79 X 65 In. 125.00
Appliqued, English Rose Pattern, Tulip Border, C.1870, 90 X 88 In. 1000.00
Appliqued, Feathered Circles, White, Signed, 6 Ft.9 In.X 6 Ft.11 In. 330.00
Appliqued, Floral Medallion, Red, Green, 1859, 89 X 89 In. 950.00
Appliqued, Floral, Red, Green, Buds In Border, Puffed, 90 X 96 In. 360.00
Appliqued, Flying Geese, Blue, White, 19th Century, 51 1/2 X 58 In. 495.00
Appliqued, Geese In Flight, Missouri, C.1890, 80 X 86 In. 1100.00
Appliqued, Geometric Stylized Foliage Medallion, 100 X 102 In. 700.00
Appliqued, Linsey-Woolsey, 12 Star Medallions, Olive, 67 X 82 In. 75.00
Appliqued, Lone Star, 62 X 71 In. 175.00
Appliqued, Monkey Wrench, Yellow, White Ground, C.1930, 78 X 69 In. 660.00
Appliqued, Pinwheel Flowers, Machine & Hand Sewn, 1963, 84 X 84 In. 175.00
Appliqued, Red Tulips, Calico Goldenrod, White Ground, 83 X 83 In. 250.00
Appliqued, Rob Peter To Pay Paul, Red, White, 1880, 77 X 87 In. 675.00
Appliqued, Sampler, Different Maker's Names, C.1920, 80 X 62 In. 468.00
Appliqued, Snowball, 1930, 69 X 72 In. 125.00
Appliqued, Star, C.1880, 96 X 98 In. 650.00
Appliqued, Stylized Floral Design, Foliage Scrolls, 86 X 100 In. 275.00
Appliqued, Stylized Floral Medallions, Acorns, Berries, 82 X 82 In. 225.00
Appliqued, Stylized Florals, Trapunto Wreaths, 96 X 96 In. 500.00
Appliqued, Stylized Medallions, Red Calico, Vine Border, 82 X 89 In. 200.00
Appliqued, Trip Around The World, Signed, Dated 1961, Crib 170.00
Appliqued, Tulip Pattern, 80 X 100 In. 275.00
Appliqued, Wedding Ring, Lavender, 88 X 68 In. 235.00
Appliqued, White Stylized Flowers, Blue Ground, 76 X 90 In. 200.00
Appliqued, Yellow Sun Medallions, Red Rays, 87 X 88 In. 350.00
Embroidered, Animals, Cross-Stitched, 57 X 42 In. 195.00
Patchwork, 4 Rows of 4 Stars, Cotton, Blue Ground, 43 X 41 In. 660.00
Patchwork, 4 Rows of Diamond Patches, 6 Ft.4 In. X 6 Ft.5 In. 165.00
Patchwork, 9 Patches, Indigo Calico, Hand Sewn, C.1900, Crib 295.00
Patchwork, Album, Embroidered Names, Dated 1892, 70 X 72 In. 425.00
Patchwork, American, Mosaic, Greek Key Border, 42 X 44 In. ....Illus 1800.00
Patchwork, Amish, Diagonal, Blue, Lavender Border, 72 X 72 In. 250.00
Patchwork, Amish, Diamond In Square, Wool, Feather Stitch, 76 X 76 In. 4400.00
Patchwork, Amish, Grandmother's Flower Garden, Wool, 1910, 50 X 42 In. 2475.00
Patchwork, Amish, Lightning Pattern, Wool, Cotton, Indiana, 70 X 90 In. 675.00
Patchwork, Amish, Puzzle, Maroon & White, 60 X 64 In. 95.00
Patchwork, Amish, Star Medallions, Snyder Co., Pa., 80 X 94 In. 450.00
Patchwork, Amish, Star, Borders, Mrs.C.B.Miller, 1910-20, 84 X 73 In. 1870.00
Patchwork, Bars of Alternating Red & Green Calico, 84 X 86 In. 60.00
Patchwork, Basket, Green On Pink, White Ground, 86 X 72 In. 300.00
Patchwork, Bear Paw, Geometric, Chintz, 7 Ft.1 In.X 6 Ft.4 In. 1045.00
Patchwork, Birds In Flight, Multicolored Prints, 78 X 78 In. 285.00

Quilt, Patchwork, Mosaic, Greek Key
Border, 42 X 44 In.

Quilt, Patchwork, Tree, Hovering Hawks,
White, C.1880, 74 X 76 In.

Patchwork, Blue & White Cotton Squares, Homespun, 87 X 76 In. 413.00
Patchwork, Bowtie, Crib 35.00
Patchwork, Bowtie, Handmade, Dated 1962, 65 X89 In. 300.00
Patchwork, Bowtie, Turquoise, Beige & Blue, 76 X 86 In. 100.00
Patchwork, Broken Star, Star Point Borders, 78 X 82 In. 535.00
Patchwork, Broken Star, White Ground, 69 X 69 In. 175.00
Patchwork, Calico Baskets, Flower Design Quilting, 70 X 86 In. 225.00
Patchwork, Calico Pinwheels, Yellow Grid, Green Ground, 82 X 92 In. 350.00
Patchwork, Calico Star, Zigzag Border, 6 Ft.7 In. X 5 Ft.2 In. 495.00
Patchwork, Checkerboard Square, Green & Orchid, 84 X 106 In. 225.00
Patchwork, Checkerboard, Multicolored Prints, 76 X 82 In. 95.00
Patchwork, Chevron, Red, White, Corners Cutout For Posts, 76 X 83 In. 250.00
Patchwork, Crazy, Dated 1925, 89 X 76 In. 125.00
Patchwork, Crazy, Prints & Solids, Embroidery, 54 X 61 In. 145.00
Patchwork, Crazy, Velvet, Multicolor, 52 X 60 In. 250.00
Patchwork, Crown of Thorns, Cotton, C.1920, 80 X 69 In. 522.00
Patchwork, Democratic Donkey, 65 X 83 In. 60.00
Patchwork, Diamond & Squares, Red & Yellow Borders, Pa, 89 X 48 In. 1100.00
Patchwork, Diamond, Calico, Mustard, Green, Missouri, 1900, 74 X 60 In. 330.00
Patchwork, Dresden Plate, Scalloped, Yellow Ground, 76 X 95 In. 225.00
Patchwork, Dutch Doll, Red & Pastels, 79 X 65 In. 125.00
Patchwork, Family, Signatures Embroidered On Squares, 83 X 69 In. 600.00
Patchwork, Fan, 9 Patch, 1917, 68 X 82 In. 600.00
Patchwork, Fan, Pastels & Black On Yellow, 65 X 76 In. 125.00
Patchwork, Floral Design, Beige Ground, 84 X 93 In. 400.00
Patchwork, Flower Basket Center, Gold Border, C.1940, 80 X 84 In. 125.00
Patchwork, Flower Garden, 60 X 84 In. 250.00
Patchwork, Flower Garden, 90 X 103 In. 375.00
Patchwork, Four Patch, C.1835, 88 X 98 In. 325.00
Patchwork, Geometric Medallions, Square Centers, 76 X 90 In. 175.00
Patchwork, Geometric, Bear Paw, Chintz, Cotton, 7 Ft. X 6 Ft.4 In. 1045.00
Patchwork, Geometric, Pink, Red & Yellow, 77 X 86 In. 475.00
Patchwork, Giant Dahlia, Scalloped Edge, 72 X 75 In. 335.00
Patchwork, Goldenrod & Solid Blue, Homespun Back, 16 1/2 X 21 In. 300.00
Patchwork, Hand of Friendship, Quarter Circles, C.1875, 82 X 69 In. 295.00
Patchwork, Irish Chain, 54 X 42 In. 175.00
Patchwork, Irish Chain, Blue & White Border, 75 X 72 In. 325.00
Patchwork, Irish Chain, Pastel Floral Prints, 85 X 85 In. 175.00
Patchwork, Irish Chain, Red & Green Calico, Ivory Ground, 84 X 84 In. 325.00
Patchwork, Lightning Bars, Calico, 82 X 84 In. 325.00
Patchwork, Linsey-Woolsey, Swags, Foliage, 78 X 100 In. 150.00
Patchwork, Log Cabin, Barn Raising, Ohio, 1880, 88 X 72 In. 500.00

Patchwork, Log Cabin, Blue Ground, 6 Ft.7 In. X 5 Ft.4 In.	357.00
Patchwork, Log Cabin, Calico & Prints, 82 X 82 In.	350.00
Patchwork, Log Cabin, Prints & Solids, 76 X 78 In.	125.00
Patchwork, Log Cabin, Solid Green, A.J.Ericson, 68 X 72 In.	400.00
Patchwork, Mennonite, Embroidered Animals, Stars, 1907, 78 X 78 In.	1870.00
Patchwork, Mennonite, Embroidered, Dated 1907, Square, 6 1/2 Ft.	1870.00
Patchwork, Mennonite, Multicolored Prints, Calico, Penn., 65 X 65 In.	140.00
Patchwork, Mennonite, Patchwork, Blue & White, Children, 26 X 34 In.	150.00
Patchwork, Monkey Wrench, Calico, C.1910, 78 X 80 In.	250.00
Patchwork, Monkey Wrench, Solid Colors, Ohio, 85 X 85 In.	160.00
Patchwork, Mosaic, Calico, White Cotton, Chintz Border, 110 X 116 In.	770.00
Patchwork, Mosaic, Greek Key Border, 42 X 44 In. *Illus*	1800.00
Patchwork, Nine Patch Pattern, 42 X 43 In.	375.00
Patchwork, Nine Patch, Calicos & Solids, 86 X 86 In.	180.00
Patchwork, Nine Patch, Feather Circles, 20 1/2 X 20 1/2 In.	95.00
Patchwork, Ocean Wave, Red & White, 76 X 78 In.	250.00
Patchwork, Optical Star Design, White, Yellow & Purple, 72 X 82 In.	200.00
Patchwork, Pieced Chintz, Orange, Blue, White, Floral, 7 X 6 Ft.	1045.00
Patchwork, Pine Tree, Pink, White, Calico, 5 Ft.7 In.X 6 Ft.6 In.	247.00
Patchwork, Pink Triangle, Green, Pink, R.A.Smith, 1900, 78 X 80 In.	145.00
Patchwork, Pinwheel Medallion, Geometric Borders, Calico, 71 X 74 In.	770.00
Patchwork, Pinwheel, Periwinkle Blue Squares, 1930s, 73 X 86 In.	295.00
Patchwork, Prince's Feather, American, C.1880, 80 X 75 In. *Illus*	1650.00
Patchwork, Princess Feather, Vine Quilting, C.1930, 7 X 6 Ft.10 In.	770.00
Patchwork, Printed Diamond, Radiating Star, Red Band, 1920, 7 X 7 Ft.	715.00
Patchwork, Rail Fence Pattern, 66 X 82 In.	200.00
Patchwork, Round The Mountain, Multicolors On Red, 62 X 80 In.	95.00
Patchwork, Sampler, Calico, Red Printed Border, C.1920, 84 X 72 In.	1100.00
Patchwork, Sampler, Center Medallion, C.1870, Square, 96 In.	1000.00
Patchwork, Schoolhouse Squares, Pink, Blue Band Borders, 65 X 74 In.	715.00
Patchwork, Schoolhouse, Houses Face Same Way, Calico, 58 X 76 In.	1500.00
Patchwork, Six Kittens, 54 X 36 In.	185.00

Quilt, Patchwork, Prince's Feather, American, C.1880, 80 X 75 In.

Patchwork, Six Pointed Star, 90 X 108 In.	325.00
Patchwork, Snowflake, Goldenrod, Red & Blue, 69 X 90 In.	300.00
Patchwork, Square In Square, White Stripes, 66 X 76 In.	150.00
Patchwork, Star of Bethlehem, Red, Yellow & Green Calico, 28 In.	400.00
Patchwork, Star, Brown Print Ground, 72 X 86 In.	275.00
Patchwork, Star, C.1880, 96 1/2 X 98 In.	650.00
Patchwork, Star, Calico & Chintz, 90 X 102 In.	400.00
Patchwork, Star, Multicolored Prints, 66 X 78 In.	185.00
Patchwork, Star, Plaid Backing, 76 X 79 In.	150.00
Patchwork, Star, Red & Blue Calico, Binding, 1900s, 85 X 77 In.	125.00
Patchwork, Star, White Ground, 67 X76 In.	450.00
Patchwork, Star, White, Blue, Maroon, Homespun Back, 80 X 80 In.	225.00
Patchwork, Stars, Multicolored, White Ground, 1920, 77 X 93 In.	450.00
Patchwork, Steeplechase, Blue Calico, White, 1900, 68 X 84 In.	525.00
Patchwork, Sunbonnet Sue, Circular Quilting, C.1920, 65 X 79 In.	250.00
Patchwork, Sunburst Medallions, White Ground, 88 X 88 In.	375.00
Patchwork, T–Block, Diamond Border, Red, Blue, White, 1876, 72 X 72 In.	625.00
Patchwork, Tree of Life, Red Bar Borders, Cotton, 81 X 69 In.	467.00
Patchwork, Tree of Paradise, Linen Backing, C.1800, 83 X 68 In.	450.00
Patchwork, Tree, Hovering Hawks, White, C.1880, 74 X 76 In. ....*Illus*	2750.00
Patchwork, Triangles, Multicolored Prints, Pennsylvania, 78 X 78 In.	350.00
Patchwork, Triangles, Squares & Rectangles, 6 Ft.3 In. X 5 Ft.	440.00
Patchwork, Tumbling Pinwheel Blocks, Green Ground, 72 X 94 In.	155.00
Patchwork, Wedding Ring, Lavender, 88 X 68 In.	235.00
Patchwork, Wedding Ring, Orange & Green, 83 X 68 In.	235.00
Patchwork, Windmill, Multicolored, 70 X 78 In.	100.00
Pieced, Red Schoolhouse, Navy Border, 30 X 21 In.	500.00

Tin–glazed, hand–painted pottery has been made in Quimper, France, since the late seventeenth century. The earliest firm, founded in 1685 by Jean Baptiste Bousquet, was known as HB Quimper. Another firm, founded in 1772 by Francois Eloury, was known as Porquier. The third firm, founded by Guillaume Dumaine in 1778, was known as HR or Henriot Quimper. All three firms made similar pottery decorated with designs of Breton peasants and sea and flower motifs. The Eloury (Porquier) and Dumaine (Henriot) firms merged in 1913. Bousquet (HB) merged with the others in 1968. The group was sold to a United States family in 1984. The American holding company is Quimper Faience Inc., located in Stonington, Connecticut. The French firm has been called Societe Nouvelle des Faienceries de Quimper HB Henriot since March 1984.

HR
Quimper

QUIMPER, Bowl, Peasant Woman, 5 In.	20.00
Creamer, Stylized Floral, Cruet Shape	60.00
Cruet, Oil & Vinegar, Peasant, 6 In., Pair	110.00
Cup & Saucer, Heart Shape	65.00
Cup & Saucer, Peasant Figure	35.00
Cup, Peasants, Yellow Ground	24.00
Egg Plate, Hen In Relief	65.00
Eggcup, Attached Saucer, Boy & Girl On Front, Marked	50.00
Figurine, Girl & Boy Dancing, Signed Beldelcourt, 10 1/2 In.	500.00
Figurine, Girl With Umbrella, 10 In.	295.00
Inkstand, Double, Henriot, France	225.00
Inkwell, Porcelain, Small	40.00
Jar, Peasant With Basket, Cover, Signed, 4 1/2 In.	95.00
Jug, 4–Spout, 5 1/4 In.	55.00
Knife Rest, Henriot	45.00
Mayonnaise Set, Square Bowl & Underplate, Ladle, Signed, 4 In.	85.00
Mustard, Peasant, Yellow Ground, Cover	50.00
Pitcher, Girl's Head, No.228	175.00
Plate, Blue, 7 In.	65.00
Plate, Girl Carrying Umbrella & Basket, 11 1/2 In.	175.00
Plate, Peasant Man, Blue Concentric Bands, Yellow, Marked, 9 1/2 In.	22.50
Plate, Peasant Woman, Signed	38.00
Plate, Peasants, Yellow Ground, 6 In.	20.00

Plate, Rooster & Floral Design, Signed, 8 In.	65.00
Porringer, Henriot, Small	45.00
Salt & Pepper, On Donkey Pulled By Man, Signed Maillard	200.00
Salt, Celtic Bagpipe, Double, Signed	85.00
Salt, Double Swans, Peasant, Floral	65.00
Salt, Double, Swan	95.00
Sauce, Blue Design, Pink, Scalloped, 3 1/2 In.	15.00
Snuff Jar, Man, Bagpipe, Signed	315.00
Sugar & Creamer, Peasant, Yellow Ground, Cover	95.00
Tile, 5 1/2 In.	85.00
Tray, Male & Female Bust Center, Round, 12 In.	165.00

Radford pottery was made by Alfred Radford in Broadway, Virginia, Tiffin and Zanesville, Ohio, and Clarksburg, West Virginia, from 1891 until 1912. Jasperware, Ruko, Thera, Radera, and Velvety Art Ware were made. The jasperware resembles the famous Wedgwood ware of the same name.

RADFORD, Jardiniere, Brown, Tulips, Leaves, 8 1/2 In.	125.00
Vase, Floral Design, Matte Green Ground, Marked, 12 1/2 In.	450.00
Vase, Jasper, Cameo Panels of Angels, Volcanic Overglaze, 17 In.	275.00

The first radio broadcast receiving sets were sold in New York City in 1910. They were used to pick up the experimental broadcasts of the day. The first commercial radios were made by Westinghouse Company for listeners of the experimental shows on KDKA Pittsburgh in 1920. Collectors today are interested in all early radios, especially those made of Bakelite plastic or decorated with blue mirrors.

RADIO, Addison, Marbelized Red & Yellow	750.00
Addison, Swirled Green & Yellow, Bakelite	550.00
Admiral, Super Airoscope, Table, Standard Broadcast	65.00
Apex, 3 Dials, 3 Tubes	150.00
Arvin, Clock, Pink	35.00
Atwater Kent, Cathedral, No.84	150.00
Atwater Kent, Model 20	60.00 To 100.00
Atwater Kent, Model 46	45.00
Atwater Kent, Oriental Cabinet	500.00
Atwater Kent, Outside Horn	75.00
Atwater Kent, Speaker, 1927	175.00
Belmont, White Plastic, Streamlined, 1930s	65.00
Bendix, 2–Color	325.00
Bendix, Bakelite	40.00
Buckingham, Model 30, Inside Speaker	115.00
Capheart, Portable, Electric & Battery, AM & FM	20.00
Chelsea, Transcontinental, Model ZR–4	175.00
Coronado, White, Blue Marbelized Knobs & Handle	95.00
Crosley, Art Deco, Plastic, Green	30.00
Crosley, External Musicone Type D Speaker	95.00
Crosley, Grandfather Clock	250.00 To 350.00
Crosley, Maroon, Plastic	36.00
Crosley, Model 51	85.00
Crosley, Model 52, 3 Tubes	58.00 To 80.00
Crosley, Pup 1925	320.00
Crosley, White Plastic, Table Model	50.00
Crosley, White, Brass	95.00
Crystal Set, Brunswick	175.00
Crystal Set, Ealter Electrical Mfg.	240.00
Crystal Set, Federal, 1917	200.00
Crystal Set, World	80.00
Dayfan, 1920s	60.00
Delco, Floor Model	85.00
Delco, Table Model	25.00
Delco, Wooden	20.00

Dewald, Cream, Caramel Knobs	65.00
Emerson, Art Deco, Red Plastic, Table Model	25.00
Emerson, Model 157, Black Plastic, 1937	55.00
Fada, Art Deco, White, Table	35.00
Fada, Bakelite	21.00
Fada, Maroon & Orange, Bakelite	95.00
Federal Crystal Set	200.00
Firestone, Air Chief, Red Plastic, Table Model	55.00
Garod, Lunchbox Style, Fuchsia, Ivory Trim, Plastic	400.00
Gas Pump Shape, Standard Oil, Christmas Box & Paper	25.00
General Electric, Brown Bakelite	30.00
General Electric, Model 404, Plastic	50.00
Gilfillan, Bakelite	30.00
Hospix Bedside, Television & Radio	57.00
Hotel Radio Corp., Detroit, Michigan, Coin–Operated, Floor Model	250.00
John Wayne, AM	35.00
Lafayette, Console, 16–Tube	175.00
Majestic, Cathedral	275.00
Majestic, Figure, Eagle, Papier–Mache, 2 Ft. X 40 In.	850.00
Majestic, Grandfather Clock	675.00
Majestic, Table Model, Wooden	55.00
Marconi, 1934	145.00
McMurdo, Silver V	750.00
Metrodyne, Single Dial, Battery, Walnut Case	55.00
Midgette, Cathedral	110.00
Motorola, Green	26.00
Motorola, Model 58LII, Electric Qr Battery, Red, 6 1/2 X 8 In.	45.00
Motorola, Portable, Looks Like Wicker Suitcase	45.00
Murdock Neutrodyne, Battery Operated	120.00
Northome, Model VI, Speaker, 1920s	48.00
Paragon, RD5/10R	800.00
Philco Junior, Cathedral Model 81	120.00
Philco, Art Deco, Tan, Top Dial, Model 52–940	40.00
Philco, Baby Grand, 1931	125.00
Philco, Brown Bakelite, 1948	15.00
Philco, Cathedral, No.21	395.00
Philco, Cathedral, No.37	85.00
Philco, Cathedral, No.50	195.00
Philco, Cathedral, No.90	395.00
Philco, Lights Up, 1928	200.00
Philco, Model PT30, Plastic	50.00
Philco, Table, Wooden, Art Deco Style	24.00
Philco, Transitone, Table Model, Wooden	50.00
Princeton, Floor Model, Trapezoid Shape, C.1929, 21 In.	225.00
Radiola, RCA, Model 60, 9 Tubes	495.00
Radiola, With Phonograph, Model RE–73	85.00
RCA Golden Throat, Bakelite	295.00
RCA, 3–Band, Marbelized, Brown	70.00
RCA, Building Kit, Child's, 1939	65.00
RCA, Table, Ivory Bakelite, 66 X 12 In.	18.00
Remler, Scotty Dog Logo	150.00
Scott, Model C	1200.00
Sentinel, Black Plastic, 1950s, Small	25.00
Silvertone, Farm, Art Deco, World's Fair, 1933	225.00
Silvertone, Red Bakelite	30.00
Spartan, 1930, Blue Cloisonne Front, Yellow Catlin Back	1800.00
Speaker, Tower Adventure, Cast Iron, Round, With Ship	85.00
Steinite, Beehive	198.00
Stewart Warner, 10 Tube Tombstone	195.00
Texaco, Oil Filter, Box	20.00
Truetone, Bakelite	50.00
Ward's, Cloth Covered Speaker, Table Model, 13 X 9 X 6 In.	40.00
Ward's, Wood Case, 1940s	25.00
Westinghouse, Jukebox Shape, Die Cast, Tube	49.00

Westinghouse, Model H–171, Brown Plastic, 1946	30.00
Zenith, 3 Band, AC–DC, 1935	125.00
Zenith, Clock, Brown Bakelite	45.00
Zenith, Clock, Green, 1940s	20.00
Zenith, Farm, 6 Volt, Large Face, 22 X 16 1/4 In.	70.00
Zenith, Tombstone, Large Round Dial	135.00
Zenith, Transoceanic, Model 8G005	80.00
Zenith, Transoceanic, Model G 500	85.00
Zenith, Tube, Cloth Grill, Wood Cabinet, Table Model	55.00

Railroad enthusiasts collect any train memorabilia. Everything is wanted, from oilcans to whole train cars. The Chessie system has a store that sells many reproductions of their old dinnerware and uniforms.

RAILROAD, Ashtray, Cobalt Blue, Gold Design, Hall China	67.50
Ashtray, Great Northern, Pine Tree, Goats	130.00
Ashtray, Santa Fe	10.00
Ashtray, Southern Railway, Engraved Logo	150.00
Badge, Police, Illinois Central, Nickel Star ....75.00 To	100.00
Badge, Police, New Jersey Central, Nickel Shield	40.00
Badge, Special Officer, Atchison, Topeka & Santa Fe, Nickel	75.00
Blanket, New York Central, Wool	85.00
Blanket, Pullman	115.00
Blotter, Missouri Pacific Lines, Red Sunburst, White, Unused	4.00
Blotter, Santa Fe Logo, Unused, 6 X 3 1/4 In.	3.00
Bottle Opener, B & O, Metal	11.00
Bowl, California Poppy A.T.S.F., 5 1/4 In.	22.50
Box, Cash & Ticket, L.I., 966, Tin, Red, 1870s	100.00
Bucket, Fire, Conical, Handle, Hanging Circle, Tin, Red	75.00
Butter Chip, New York Central Logo, Silver Plate	45.00
Butter Chip, Santa Fe	37.50
Button, Brakeman, Star, Silver, 7/8 In.	3.00
Button, Coat, H.B.& T.R.R.	6.00
Button, Conductor, Rock Island Lines, Star, Silver, 5/8 In.	3.00
Button, Lapel, Burlington Route	35.00
Button, Uniform, C.V., Silver, Ring Back, 3/4 In.	3.00
Button, Uniform, Canadian Pacific, Domed Style, Gold, 1/2 In.	3.50
Button, Uniform, Central Vermont, Silver, 3/4 In.	3.00
Button, Uniform, Rock Island Lines, Star, Silver, 1/2 In.	3.50
Chest, Hinged Top, Illinois Central, J.T.Tucker, Agent, 25 In.	412.00
Chimes, Dining Car, 4 Notes	79.00
Clock, Locomotive, Seth Thomas, Brass, Dated 1876	75.00
Coffeepot, Pennsylvania R.R., International Silver Co., 10 Oz.	85.00
Compote, Union Pacific, Scammel, Pair	98.00
Creamer, Marked Pullman, Small	100.00
Creamer, Southern Pacific R.R.	8.00
Cup & Saucer, Canadian National Railroad	40.00
Cup, Chessie	68.00
Cup, Southern Pacific, Prairie Mountain Wildflower	35.00
Cuspidor, Union Pacific, Brass & Copper	90.00
Dish, Sauce, Northern Pacific, Monad	35.00
Fan, Pennsylvania R.R., Red Keystone, Cardboard, 14 In.	20.00
Fan, Wabash, Paper, Dated 1954	11.00
Fire Extinguisher, B & O, Green Glass, Star In Circle	150.00
Fire Extinguisher, L.& N. R.R., Copper	50.00
Goblet, Rock Island, Etched	12.00
Handkerchief, Chesapeake, Kittens, Linen	25.00
Hard Hat, C & O R.R., Chessie The Cat	20.00
Hat, Brakeman's, New York Central, 1940	85.00
Headrest Cover, Central Georgia	10.00
Iron Insulator, Central Pacific, Transcontinental Telegraph, 1868	150.00
Jacket, Conductor's, Chicago Northwestern	45.00
Kit, First Aid, Pennsylvania R.R., Metal, Unopened	28.00
Knife, Pocket, Cotton Belt R.R.	25.00

Lamp, Angled Double Burner	250.00
Lamp, Caboose, Aladdin, Paper Shade	65.00
Lamp, Model A, Union Carbide, Oxweld Co., White Metal, Handle	45.00
Lamp, Switch, Dressell	120.00
Lantern, A.T.& S.F.R.R., Kerosene, Clear Globe, Dated 1928	45.00
Lantern, Adlake P.R.R.	35.00
Lantern, Adlake, Amber Globe, Etched, I.C.R.R.	65.00
Lantern, Adlake, Cast Globe, Pennsylvania, 5 3/8 In.	100.00
Lantern, Atlantic Coastline R.R.	37.50
Lantern, B.& O. Logo, Reliable Frame	95.00
Lantern, B.& O., Cobalt Blue	155.00
Lantern, B.& O., Red Globe	70.00
Lantern, Blue Wabash Logo, Bell Bottom, Handlan Buck Frame	300.00
Lantern, Boston & Maine R.R.	37.50
Lantern, Brakeman's, Pennysylvania R.R., Clear	48.00
Lantern, C.C.C. & St.Louis, Handlan	55.00
Lantern, C.M. & ST.P, Brass Top Bell, Embossed Globe	150.00
Lantern, Dietz, Fire King, Copper & Tin, Dated 1907	75.00
Lantern, Dietz, No.6, Red Globe, New York Central Bell Bottom	65.00
Lantern, Dressel AT & SF R.R., Short Red Globe	55.00
Lantern, E.J.& E., Bell Bottom, Cast Globe	150.00
Lantern, E.R.R.Co., Red Cast, Erie Frame	90.00
Lantern, Erie, Letter E Etched Globe	45.00
Lantern, Globe, Clear, B.& M. R.R	39.00
Lantern, Globe, Ruby, 7 In.	29.00
Lantern, Illinois Central	35.00 To 50.00
Lantern, Inspector's, Etched D.L.& W.	25.00
Lantern, Joliet & Eastern R.R., Elgin, Cast Globe	175.00
Lantern, N.& W. Ry., Kerosene, Metal Frame, Bail Handle, 5 1/2 In.	75.00
Lantern, New York Central, Ruby Globe, Wire Frame	40.00
Lantern, Ovoid Clear Glass Globe, Painted, American, 20th Century	275.00
Lantern, Pennsylvania & St.Louis	20.00
Lantern, Pennsylvania, Red Globe	25.00
Lantern, Post & Co., Cincinnati, Ohio, Brass, Bell Bottom	495.00
Lantern, S.M.& St.P.Ry., Globe, Brass Top, Bell Bottom	120.00
Lantern, Santa Fe Logo, Globe, Bell Bottom Frame	120.00
Lantern, Switch, Adlake, Bull's-Eye	225.00
Lantern, Switch, Adlake, Oil Burning	150.00
Lantern, Switch, K.C.S.	75.00
Lantern, Tall Globe, Pennsylvania R.R.	58.00
Lock, B.& B.R.R., Stamped	100.00
Lock, C.P.R.R., Brass, Heart Shape, Stamped	100.00
Lock, O.C.R.R., Brass, Heart Shape, Embossed	150.00
Lock, P.R.R. In Script, Brass, Heart Shape, Key	95.00
Lock, Signal, P.R.R., Iron	20.00
Lock, South Pacific Co., Brass	90.00
Lock, Switch, Adlake, Rock Island Railroad	10.00
Lock, Switch, Hansel, Heart Shape, Brass	20.00
Lock, Ukelele, Harold Teen, Comic Characters Picture, 1920s, 21 In.	175.00
Lock, Union Pacific West, Brass, Unmarked Key	75.00
Mug, California Poppy, A.T.& S.F.	20.00
Plate, Animals, Mountain Goat, Logo, Great Northern R.R., 8 In.	95.00
Plate, Atlantic Coast Line, 10 In.	27.50
Plate, Atlantic Coast Line, Oval, Back Stamp, 9 1/2 In.	8.00
Plate, Atlantic Coast, 9 In.	20.00
Plate, B.& O. R.R., Centennial, Lamberton	45.00
Plate, C.& O. R.R., George Washington, Box	650.00
Plate, Centennial, B.& O. R.R., Potomac Valley	35.00
Plate, Charlottesville, C.& O., 8 In.	150.00
Plate, Dinner, Penn., Mt. Laurel	42.00
Plate, Eagle Streamliner, State Capitol Border, 11 In.	350.00
Plate, Harper's Ferry, W.Va.Center, Baltimore & Ohio, 9 In.	60.00
Plate, Indian Tree, N.H.& H. R.R., 9 In.	100.00

> **Rusty tin may be helped. Rinse the metal, scrub, dry, then coat with a thin layer of Vaseline.**

Plate, Missouri Pacific, 10 1/4 In.	225.00
Plate, Missouri Pacific, State Flower, Steamer, 10 5/8 In.	75.00
Plate, Moore–McCormick Lines, 10 In.	20.00
Plate, Mountain Laurel, Pennsylvania R.R., 10 In.	40.00
Plate, Santa Fe, Mimbreno, 10 In.	45.00
Plate, State Flower, Steamer, Missouri Pacific Lines, 10 5/8 In.	175.00
Plate, Union Pacific, Cobalt & Gold, Long Train, 1972	37.50
Plate, Union Pacific, Streamliner Logo On Front, 10 1/2 In.	35.00
Plate, Western Pacific, 9 1/2 In.	175.00
Platter, Aristocrat, Burlington R.R., 12 X 8 1/2 In.	185.00
Platter, Capitol, B.& O., Oval, 15 In.	200.00
Platter, Great Northern, Mountains & Flowers, 9 X 7 In.	75.00
Platter, Milwaukee Road, China, 10 In.	40.00
Platter, Union Pacific, White, Blue Trim, 6 In.	20.00
Postcard, Illinois Central Railroad, 3 Piece	5.00
Postcard, Pere Harquette Car Ferry, Lake Michigan, Saginaw, Linen	1.25
Postcard, Union Pacific, Hermitage, Ogden Canyon, Double Card	5.00
Postcard, Union Pacific, Logo, Rocky Mountain Nat'L Park, Double	5.00
Poster, $1000 Reward, Mobile & Ohio R.R., Holdup, Pinkerton, 1912	97.50
Print, Morning On The Mohawk, N.Y. Central, W.Greene, 19 X 24 In.	21.00
Print, Pennsylvania R.R., Ready To Go.1936, 17 X 24 1/2 In.	50.00
Print, Westward Bound, Mohawk, N.Y. Central, W.Greene, 19 X 23 In.	21.00
Roly Poly, P.R.R.Red Freight Train, 5 Oz.	10.00
Shovel, B.& O. R.R.	25.00
Shovel, Track, G.N.R.R.	15.00
Sign, Railway Express Agency, Hanging, Metal Edge	30.00
Sign, Stop, Look, Listen, Iron, Oval, 42 In.	145.00
Spittoon, Pullman	65.00
Spoon, Iced Tea, Erie R.R.	20.00
Spoon, Mt.Lowe Railway, Sterling Silver	35.00
Spoon, P.R.R., Silver Plate	8.00
Step Stool, Passenger, Erie	200.00
Stock Certificate, Atchison & Nebraska R.R.1880s	10.00
Stock Certificate, Cleveland, Painesville & Ashtubula	25.00
Stop Sign, Round, White Ground	145.00
Switch Lock Key, Stamped P.C. R.R., Adlake, Brass	12.00
Switch Lock, Illinois Central Railroad	15.00
Teaspoon, Sante Fe, Marked	9.00
Time Clock, Chicago Minute Man, Leather Carrying Case	75.00
Timetable, Baltimore & Ohio, 1929	12.00
Timetable, Boston, Revere Beach & Lynn, 1939	10.00
Timetable, Burlington Route, 1960s	2.00
Timetable, Delaware & Hudson	25.00
Timetable, Hudson River R.R., Summer 1881, 2 3/4 X 3 3/4 In.	4.00
Timetable, Hudson River Railroad, 2 3/4 X 3 3/4 In.	4.50
Timetable, N.Y. Central Lines	22.00
Timetable, New Haven, 1925	15.00
Timetable, New Haven, 1926	12.00
Timetable, Old Colony, Providence Division, 1889	10.00
Timetable, Pennsylvania, 1924	12.00
Timetable, Pennsylvania, Feb.17, 1932	10.00

Timetable, Southern Pacific	15.00
Timetable, St.Johnsbury & Lamoille County, 1955	5.00
Timetable, Winona Interurban Railway Co., Nov.17, 1912	6.00
Token, Union Pacific, Golden Gate Exposition, 1939, Aluminum	6.50
Tongs, Sugar, Southern R.R.	26.00
Tool, Press, Lead Seal, Iron, Pliers Shape, B.& M. R.R., 10 In.	25.00
Tool, Sealer, Boxcar, Lead Slug, RUT Impressed, 5/8 In.	1.00
Toothpick, Cloisonne, Santa Fe	25.00
Towel, New Haven R.R., 15 X 22 In.	10.00
Towel, Pullman Co., Blue & White	8.00
Tumbler, P.R.R.	40.00
Tumbler, Union Pacific R.R., Clear	5.00
Uniform, Conductor's, C.& N.W., Blue, Old Style, 4 Piece	85.00
Uniform, Conductor's, Milwaukee Road, Blue, 4 Piece	85.00
Watch Fob, Brotherhood of Railroad Trainmen	25.00
Whistle, Caboose, Brass, 1910	35.00
Whistle, P.R.R., Police, Brass	25.00
Whistle, Peanut, Caboose, Brass	15.00
Whistle, Steam, Brass, Sherbourne Co.	35.00
Wrench, Pipe, Stillson, N.H.R.R., 18 In.	35.00

The razor was used in ancient Egypt and subsequently wherever shaving was in fashion. The metal razor used in America until about 1870 was made in Sheffield, England. After 1870, machine–made hollow–ground razors were made in Germany or America. Plastic or bone handles were popular. The razor was often sold in a set of seven, one for each day of the week. The set was often kept by the barber who shaved the well–to–do man each day in the shop.

RAZOR, Auto Strop Safety Valet, Box, 2 Box of Blades	20.00
Blade Sharpener, Edge–Bak	7.50
Bow, Wade & Butcher, Celluloid	28.00
Gem, Box	8.00
Gillette, U.S.Service, Metal Case	12.50
Peter's Shoes, Leather Box	15.00
Rolls, England, 2 Strops, Case, 1927	20.00
Safety, Gem Junior, Brass	10.00
Safety, Keen Kutter, Box of Blades, Instructions Booklet	20.00
Safety, Larkin, Metal Case	14.00
Schick, Electric, Leather Case	30.00
Straight, Art Nouveau, Lady's Head, Flowing Hair, Celluloid	22.00
Straight, Bird With Fish In Mouth	24.00
Straight, Buckeye–Busch	16.00
Straight, Bust of Bismarck, Box	18.00
Straight, Celluloid, Original Holder, 12 Piece Set	75.00
Straight, Damascus, Sea Bird With Fish In Mouth	45.00
Straight, Defender, Girl Playing Harp	45.00
Straight, Engstrom, Box, 1881	15.00
Straight, Floral Design, Spencer & Barltett, Celluloid	20.00
Straight, Gold Blade, Kaufmann	26.00
Straight, H.B.W.Special	7.50
Straight, H.Boker & Co., S.S.St.Louis On Blade, Black Handle, Case	22.00
Straight, Improved Eagle, Plastic Handle, Germany	5.50
Straight, Kaufmann, Gold Blade, Box	45.00
Straight, Keen Kutter, Black Handle, Simmons Hardware Co., Germany	25.00
Straight, Keen Kutter, No.88, Hone	45.00
Straight, Keen Kutter, No.K–46	40.00
Straight, Landers, Faux Tortoiseshell Handle, Blade, Palmer, Chicago	28.00
Straight, Maher & Grosh, Toledo, Ohio, Box	30.00
Straight, Marbleized Brown	15.00
Straight, Norvell Shapleigh, Celluloid Handle, Silver Inlaid Peacock	75.00
Straight, Nude Handle	40.00 To 55.00
Straight, Shapleigh Hardware, Imitation Ivory Handle	50.00
Straight, W.R.Case & Sons, Bone Handle	125.00
Straight, W.R.Case & Sons, Bradford, Pa., Box	50.00

Straight, Wadsworth, Ivory Handle, Nude, French Stag, Germany	65.00
Straight, Winchester, Celluloid	60.00
Straight, Winchester, No.8536	50.00
Strip, Kriss Kross, Box	12.00
Strop, K 94	25.00
Twinplex, Mechanical, Strap, Box, 1924	4.00

Reamers, or juice squeezers, have been known since 1767, although most of those collected today date from the twentieth century. Figural reamers are among the most prized.

REAMER, Blue Delphite	40.00
Boat Shape, White Clambroth	185.00
Clown, Ceramic	42.00
Crisscross, Green	12.00
Double Handle, Wooden	50.00
Little Handy Lemon Squeezer, Figural, Silver & Co., Glass	85.00
Milk Glass, Light Blue	135.00
Monkey, Germany	70.00
Radiant, Crystal	65.00
Sunkist, Blue Milk Glass	70.00
Sunkist, Orange, Electric	175.00
Sunkist, White	14.00
Sunkist, Yellow	38.00 To 50.00
Tab Handle, Cobalt Blue, Small	40.00
Will & Finch, Lime	165.00
Wolverine, Zippy	55.00

The cylinder–shaped phonograph record for use with the early Edison phonograph was made about 1889. Disc records were first made by 1894; the double–sided disc by 1904. The high–fidelity records were first issued in 1944, the first vinyl disc in 1946, the first stereo record in 1958. The 78 RPM became the standard in 1926 but was discontinued in 1957. In 1932, the first 33 1/3 RPM was made but was not sold commercially until 1948. In 1949, the 45 RPM was introduced.

RECORD, Album, Countess From Hong Kong, Charles Chaplin, Decca, 1967	10.00
Album, Doctor Dolittle, Rex Harrison, 20th Century Fox, 1967	10.00
Album, Hits of Judy Garland, Capitol	10.00
Album, Nostalgic Railroad Sounds, Jim Ameche, 33 1/3 RPM, 1959	12.00
Album, Sounds of Vanishing Era, Steam & Diesel, 33 1/3 RPM, 1957	15.00
Basin Street Blues, Cab Calloway, 78 RPM	7.00
Begin The Beguine, Artie Shaw, 78 RPM	5.00
Chelsea Morning, Joni Mitchell, 45 RPM	7.00
Gone With The Wind, Warners Bros.Centennial Recording, 1961	25.00
Great Balls of Fire, Jerry Lee Lewis, 45 RPM	7.50
I've Got A Note, Johnny Mercer, 78 RPM	7.00
It's My Party, Lesley Gore, 45 RPM	5.50
Ken Maynard Bar–K, Talking Story, Red Plastic, 1940s	20.00
Louisiana Mama, Gene Pitney, 45 RPM	9.00
Loveless Love, Jack Teagarden, 78 RPM	25.00
Monday Monday, Mamas and Papas, 45 RPM	5.00
On The Sentimental Side, Billie Holiday, 78 RPM	3.00
Over The Rainbow, Judy Garland, 78 RPM	3.00
Rudolph The Red–Nosed Reindeer, Gene Autry	20.00
Shanghai Honeymoon, Lawrence Welk, 78 RPM	30.00
Splish Splash, Bobbie Darren, 45 RPM	7.00
Three Little Words, Gene Krupa, 78 RPM	8.00
Voices of Victory, Gem Razor Blades For Savings Bonds, Envelope	12.00
Walk Like A Man, Four Seasons, 45 RPM	5.50

The Red Wing Pottery of Red Wing, Minnesota, was a firm started in 1878. It was not until the 1920s that art pottery was made. It closed in 1967. Rumrill pottery was made for George Rumrill by the Red Wing Pottery and other firms. It was sold in the 1930s.

RED WING, Ashtray, Commemorative, General Electric 15.00
    Ashtray, Donkey, Rose 38.00
    Ashtray, Minnesota Twins, World Series, 1965 .... 60.00
    Ashtray, Open Book 14.00
    Bean Pot 75.00
    Bean Pot, Advertising 45.00
    Beater Jar, Blue Bands 50.00
    Beater Jar, Hustisford, Minn., Seefeldt's 75.00
    Beater Jar, Logo & Minnesota Advertising 95.00
    Beater Jar, You Beat Eggs, We Beat Prices, Star Grocery, Iowa 75.00
    Beaver On Football, Dated 1939 .... 85.00
    Bowl, 9 1/2 In. 17.00
    Bowl, 15 1/2 In. 85.00
    Bowl, Blue & Rust Sponge, 8 In. 45.00
    Bowl, Earling, Iowa, Sponge Band, Signed 75.00
    Bowl, Geometric Rim, Art Pottery, Green Glaze, Marked, 10 In. 10.00
    Bowl, Gray, 11 In. 30.00
    Bowl, Lu Ray, Yellow, 8/4 In. 7.00
    Bowl, Spongeware, Paneled, 7 1/2 In. 40.00
    Bowl, Spongeware, White, Red & Blue, 9 1/4 In. 75.00
    Bowl, Vegetable, Divided 12.00
    Bowl, Vegetable, Divided, Driftwood 12.00
    Bread Tray, Capistrano 5.00
    Casserole, White, Pink Spongeware, Painted Bird, Cover 15.00
    Centerpiece, Deer Frog, Ivory, 15 In. 25.00
    Churn, Bail Handles, 4 Gal. 175.00
    Churn, Cover, 2 Gal. 50.00
    Churn, Small Wing, 2 Gal. 90.00
    Churn, Wing, 5 Gal. 80.00
    Clock, Kitchen, Black Mammy, Electric, 1940s 100.00
    Console Set, Leaf Design, Brushed Brown, Rolled Rim, Ivory, 3 Pc. 125.00
    Cookie Jar, Baker, Beige 40.00
    Cookie Jar, Baker, Blue 46.00
    Cookie Jar, Black Cat 35.00
    Cookie Jar, Blue & Rust Red Spongeware 120.00
    Cookie Jar, Bunch of Bananas 22.00
    Cookie Jar, Cattail, Green 250.00
    Cookie Jar, Cow Jumped Over The Moon 35.00
    Cookie Jar, Dutch Girl, Blue 25.00
    Cookie Jar, Dutch Girl, Yellow .... 32.00 To 40.00
    Cookie Jar, French Chef, Cream Color 28.00
    Cookie Jar, Gray Line, Cover 275.00
    Cookie Jar, Katrina, Green 47.50
    Cookie Jar, Monk, Green 95.00
    Cookie Jar, Monk, Thou Shalt Not Steal, Yellow .... 30.00 To 50.00
    Cookie Jar, Pineapple, Aqua .... 18.50 To 25.00
    Cookie Jar, Pink Rooster 60.00
    Cookie Jar, Saffron Ware 95.00
    Cookie Jar, Sponge Band 100.00
    Cooler, Cover, Commemorative, Red Wing Society, 1985 .... 75.00
    Creamer, Ribbed, Oatmeal 7.00
    Crock, Bail, Union Stoneware, 15 Gal. 140.00
    Crock, Beehive, 5 Gal. 175.00
    Crock, Black Birch Leaves, Oval, 3 Gal. 25.00
    Crock, Blue Birch Leaves, Oval, 2 Gal. 30.00
    Crock, Butter, Blue Stripes, Bail Handle, 3 Lb. 65.00
    Crock, Butter, Large Wing, 20 Lb. 285.00
    Crock, Dated 1915, 10 Gal. .... 45.00 To 48.00
    Crock, No.2 Target, Salt Glaze, Marked 100.00
    Crock, Small Wing, Oval, 2 Gal. 30.00
    Crock, Target, Salt Glaze, 3 Gal. 175.00
    Cup, Iris 6.00
    Dispenser, Lye, McCormick Deering 175.00
    Egg Plate, Pink Spice 18.00

Check the metal strips holding any heavy wall-hung shelves. After a few years, the shelf holder may develop "creep" and gradually bend away from the wall.

Feeder, Ko–Rec, 2 Piece, 1 Gal.	40.00 To 50.00
Figurine, Lady, With Tambourine	85.00
Figurine, Man, Brown, With Accordion	35.00
Flower Bowl, Bear Flower Frog, Matte Beige & Brown Glaze	50.00
Flower Frog, With Base, Deer, Ivory	28.00
Flowerpot, Orange, 2 1/4 In.	8.00
Jar, Applesauce, Large Wing, Wire Clamp, 5 Gal.	115.00
Jar, Canning, Apple Butter	115.00
Jar, Fruit, 1/2 Gal.	95.00
Jar, Fruit, Blue Writing, 1 Qt.	110.00
Jar, Fruit, Mason, 1 Gal.	110.00 To 315.00
Jar, Fruit, Mason, Square, 1 Qt.	125.00
Jar, Mason, Stoneware, 1 Qt.	100.00
Jar, Mason, Stoneware, Black Lettering, 1/2 Gal.	85.00
Jar, Pantry, Wire Bail, 1/2 Gal.	40.00
Jar, Preserve, Stoneware, Mason, Zinc Lid	150.00
Jar, Refrigerator, Grayline, Cover, Marked, 3 1/2 X 3 1/4 In.	350.00
Jardiniere, Green, Brushware, Pedestal	450.00 To 500.00
Jug, Beehive, Large Wing, 5 Gal.	120.00 To 165.00
Jug, Beehive, Salt Glaze, Lazy 8, 5 Gal.	300.00
Jug, Birch Leaves Design, Union Stoneware, 5 Gal.	140.00
Jug, Blue Band, Marked, 1 Gal.	295.00
Jug, Brown, Top Wing, 1/2 Gal.	120.00
Jug, Eleda Vinegar, Milwaukee, 1/4 Pt.	50.00
Jug, Liquor, I.Miller, Sioux City, Iowa	120.00
Jug, No.8, 1 Gal.	50.00
Jug, Shoulder, Oval, 5 Gal.	35.00
Jug, Strap Handle, Stopper, 3 Gal.	45.00
Jug, White Shoulder, 1/2 Gal.	25.00
Jug, White, Vinegar, Bail Handle, 1 Gal.	65.00
Pie Plate, Brown, Original Label	70.00
Pitcher & Bowl Set, Painted, Applied Handles	45.00
Pitcher, Castle, Blue & White, 12 In.	165.00
Pitcher, Cherries & Leaves	85.00
Pitcher, Green, 6 In.	35.00
Pitcher, Lexington, 10 1/2 In.	5.00
Pitcher, Lotus, 10 1/2 In.	5.00
Pitcher, Montmartre, 1 Qt.	15.00
Pitcher, Water, Anton Hommerberg, Ballaton, Minnesota	135.00
Planter, Pear Shape, Blue	15.00
Planter, Piano	30.00
Planter, Wall, Violin, Rust Color	18.00
Plate, Green Flowers On Brown Branch, Hand Painted, 9 In.	18.00
Plate, Morning Glory, 6 1/4 In.	2.00
Plate, Morning Glory, 10 1/2 In.	4.00
Plate, Morning Glory, Blue, 7 1/2 In.	4.00
Platter, Lu Ray, Green, Oval, 12 In.	7.00

Platter, Morning Glory, 13 In. 8.00
Reamer, Sponge Band 300.00
Salad Bowl, Montmartre, 12 In. 25.00
Salt & Pepper, Bird 34.00
Salt & Pepper, Orleans 5.00
Saucer, Iris 4.00
Saucer, Lotus .... .50
Server, 3–Tier, Tampico 20.00
Spoon Rest, Capistrano 7.00
Teapot, Figural, Girl, Dark Blue 40.00
Teapot, Tampico 21.00
Teapot, Yellow Rooster, Gold Trim 50.00
Tray, French Bread, Geometric Design, 5 X 23 In. 12.00
Vase, Brown Panels, Green Ground, 10 In. 20.00
Vase, Double Handles, White, 7 1/2 In. 10.00
Vase, Egyptian Style, Green & White, 12 In. 30.00
Vase, Figural, Elephant Head, Shoulder Handles, Green, 6 1/4 In. 32.00
Vase, Leaves, Ivory, Rose Interior, 7 1/2 In. 15.00
Vase, Lotus, 10 In. 20.00
Vase, Morning Glory, Green Exterior, Yellow Interior, 8 1/2 In. 10.00
Vase, Mottled Green & Brown, Matte Glaze, 10 In. 35.00
Vase, Sitting Rabbit, Maroon, Signed, 5 1/2 X 5 1/2 In. 39.50
Water Cooler, Cover, 3 Gal. .... 300.00 To 395.00

> Redware is a hard, red stoneware that originated in the late 1600s
> and continues to be made. The term is also used to describe any
> common clay pottery that is reddish in color.

REDWARE, Bank, Apple 75.00
Bank, Beehive Shape, Unglazed 65.00
Bank, Figural, Clam, Original Paint 55.00
Bank, Hen On Nest, Greenish Glaze Top, Unglazed Base, 3 1/8 In. 60.00
Basin, Milk Cooling, 15 1/2 X 5 3/4 In. 120.00
Bean Pot, Clear Lead Glaze, 5 1/2 In. 35.00
Birdhouse, 6 X 10 1/2 In. 75.00
Bottle, Hot Water, Flat Circular Shape, 4 1/2 X 8 In. 80.00
Bottle, Ink, Brown Glaze, Small Mouth, 2 1/2 In. 95.00
Bowl, Coggled Edge, Swirled Yellow Slip, Shallow, 11 1/2 In. 275.00
Bowl, Cream Slip Inside, 7 X 14 In. 75.00
Bowl, Milk, Tooled Dot Line, 7 In. 225.00
Bowl, Mixing, Partial Glazed Interior, Tapered, 19th Century, 14 In. 99.00
Bowl, Tapering Inward Sides, Manganese Splotches, 11 1/2 In. 200.00
Creamer, Brown Glaze, C.1820, 5 1/2 In. 220.00
Cuspidor, Embossed Lion's Heads, 6 In. 65.00
Flask, Clear Lead Glaze, 8 In. 85.00
Flowerpot, Attached Saucer, Yellow Slip Stripes, Brown, 4 1/4 In. 135.00
Flowerpot, Coggled Edge, Greenish Brown Glaze, 9 In. 85.00
Flowerpot, Yellow Slip, Green & Brown, Shenandoah, 8 1/2 In. 500.00
Garden Seat, Elephant, White Celadon, China, 16 X 22 In., Pair 225.00
Jar, Apple Butter, 7 1/4 In. 120.00
Jar, Apple Butter, Interior Glaze, 8 1/8 In. 65.00
Jar, Apple Butter, Strap Handle, 7 In. 70.00
Jar, Finger Crimped Side Handles, Brown Glaze, Cover, 12 In. 10.00
Jar, Green Glaze, Red Highlights, Embossed Bands, 6 1/4 In. 375.00
Jar, Greenish Gray Slip, Brown Highlights, 10 1/4 In. 400.00
Jar, Impressed John Bell, Waynesboro, Interior Glaze, 8 3/4 In. 150.00
Jar, Uneven Brown Glaze, Strap Handle, Cover, 9 In. 45.00
Jug, Molded Dragon In Relief, Blue Stain, 3 1/2 In. 30.00
Jug, Oversize Handle, Black Glaze, 8 5/8 In. 35.00
Jug, Puzzle, Pierced Design, Thumb Piece, 6 7/8 In. 100.00
Loaf Pan, Yellow Slip Design 175.00
Mold, Cookie, Grizzly Bear, 18th Century, 3 1/2 X 5 In. 440.00
Mold, Heart Shape, Man On Steed In Relief, Medford, Pa., 1823 .... 275.00
Mold, Turk's Head, Coggled Edge, Scalloped Rim, 7 1/4 In. 55.00
Mold, Turk's Head, Dark Brown Sponging, Clear Glaze, 8 3/4 In. 45.00

Mold, Turk's Head, Dark Green Glaze, 8 In. 35.00
Mold, Turk's Head, Yellow & White Slip 85.00
Mug, Applied Star Design, 5 1/4 In. 125.00
Mug, Multicolored Glaze, 4 In. 60.00
Pie Plate, Coggled Edge, 3 Line Yellow Slip Design, 8 In. 75.00
Pie Plate, Coggled Edge, 3 Line Yellow Slip Design, 9 1/4 In. 200.00
Pie Plate, Coggled Edge, Brushed Brown Leaf Design, 9 In. 45.00
Pie Plate, Coggled Edge, Mustard Yellow Glaze, 11 In. 275.00
Pie Plate, Coggled Edge, Yellow Glaze 65.00
Pie Plate, Coggled Edge, Yellow Slip Design, 8 In. 85.00
Pie Plate, Stylized Tulips 950.00
Pie Plate, Yellow & Green Slip, W.Smith, Womelsdorf, 8 1/2 In. 1300.00
Pitcher, Bulbous, Albany Brown Glaze, Early 1800s, 1 Pt. 225.00
Pitcher, Dark Brown Glaze, 10 1/4 In. 30.00
Pitcher, Sgraffito Dragonfly, Applied Handle, E.Chaplet, 9 1/2 In. 150.00
Pitcher, Sponge Design, Incised Bottom 10, 7 3/4 In. 250.00
Pitcher, Yellow Slip, Green & Brown, Shenandoah, 6 1/2 In. 500.00
Plate, Coggled Edge, Pinwheel In Yellow Slip, 12 1/4 In. 325.00
Platter, Coggled Edge, Green Slip Marbelized, 13 1/2 X 10 1/4 In. 2600.00
Pot, Brown Sponging, Rim Spout, 5 In. 50.00
Pot, Open Handles, , Dark Brown Glaze, 13 X 16 In. 130.00
Pot, Strap Handle & Spout, Amber Olive Glaze, Cover, Ohio, 3 3/4 In. 37.50
Sugar, Dome Cover, Ball Finial, Applied Handles, Red Ground, 12 In. 3410.00
Tea Set, Dragon Design, Pewter, Waste Bowl, China, 5 Piece 45.00
Teapot, Black Cat 14.00
Tobacco Jar, White Clay Floral, Ribbed Finial, 3 Part, 11 In. 45.00
Vase, Multicolored, Coggled Edge, 7 In. 185.00
Vase, Rustic Design, Masonic Emblem, Brown Matte Glaze, 9 In. 50.00
Vase, Triangular Mouth, Greenish Black Glaze, 4 1/4 In. 85.00
    REGOUT, see Maastricht

"Richard" was the mark used on acid–etched cameo glass vases, bowls, night–lights, and lamps made in Lorraine, France, during the 1920s. The pieces were very similar to the other French cameo glasswares made by Daum, Galle, and others.

RICHARD, Shade, Hanging, Butterflies & Pinecones, Original Fittings, 15 In. 2350.00
Vase, Light & Dark Brown Foliage, Cut To Green, Signed, 12 1/2 In. 675.00
Vase, Scarf Dance, Lady, Roses & Leaves, Green To Peach, 9 7/8 In. 995.00
Vase, Scene of House, Arched Bridge, River, Navy Blue, Signed, 8 In. 550.00
Vase, Scenic, Brown Cut To Orange, 8 1/2 In. 475.00
Vase, Village & Mountains Scene, Trees, Brown, Tan, Orange, 10 In. 1100.00

Ridgway pottery has been made in the Staffordshire district in England since 1808 by a series of companies with the name Ridgway. The transfer–design dinner sets are the most widely known product. They are still being made. Other pieces of Ridgway are listed under Flow Blue.

RIDGWAY, Ale Set, Coaching Days, Silver Luster Trim, Marked, 7 Piece 295.00
Ale Set, Coaching Days, Silver Luster Trim, Tray, 8 Piece 295.00
Biscuit Jar, Coaching Days, Rattan Handle, 6 1/2 In. 230.00
Bowl, Coaching Days, Silver Trim, 9 1/2 In. 60.00
Coffeepot, Coaching Days, Silver Trim 75.00
Compote, Oriental Pattern, Cover, 8 1/2 X 11 In. 70.00
Compote, Oriental Pattern, Cover, 9 X 8 In. 70.00
Cup & Saucer, Coaching Days, Demitasse 30.00
Cup & Saucer, Royal Vista 20.00
Jug, Coaching Days, Black Scene On Gold, Marked, 5 1/2 In. 75.00
Jug, Milk, Coaching Days, South Work Scene 85.00
Lemonade Set, Royal Vista Sailing Scene, 7 Piece 250.00
Mug, Coaching Days, Silver Luster Trim 55.00
Mug, Mormon Square, Salt Lake City, 4 1/2 In. 35.00
Mug, Polar Bear & Car, Silver Trim, 4 1/2 In. 45.00
Mush Set, Juvenile, Golliwogs, 3 Piece 98.00
Mustard, Silver Trim, Wooden Spoon, 3 In. 45.00

Pitcher, Bamboo, 7 In.	75.00
Pitcher, Cider, Coaching Days, Black Scenes, Silver Handle, 7 In.	75.00
Plaque, Coaching Days, Taking Up The Mails, 12 In.	130.00
Plaque, Norman House, Christ Church, Gold Trim, 9 In.	75.00
Plate, 2nd Avenue Center, Sepia Tone, 9 In.	34.00
Plate, Child's, Jolly Jinks, 3 Bears, Rabbits, Squirrels On Border	48.00
Plate, Coaching Days, A Clandestine Interview, 8 In.	30.00
Plate, Coaching Days, A Snapped Pole, 10 In.	35.00
Plate, Oriental, Green, 9 1/4 In.	30.00
Platter, Blue Willow, Rectangular, Deep Well, 12 X 9 1/2 In.	45.00
Platter, Grecian Pattern, Scalloped Edge, 12 X 15 In.	125.00
Platter, Mottled Blue On White, 19th Century, 17 1/2 X 14 In.	247.00
Platter, Turkey, Sprigs of Rust Roses, Foliage, 17 1/2 X 13 In.	60.00
Sugar & Creamer, Oriental Pattern, 5 In.	60.00
Tankard Set, Coaching Days, Silver Luster Bands, Tray, 8 Piece	195.00
Tankard, Coaching Days, Silver Trim, 4 In.	35.00
Teapot, Sugar & Creamer, Grecian Pattern, Bulbous, 3 Piece	300.00
Tumbler, Black Transfer of Great Stone Face, Silver Rim	40.00
Tureen, Oriental, Pattern Inside & Out, 10 In.	75.00
Tureen, Sauce, Blind Boy, Blue, Cover, Ladle, Undertray	275.00
Tureen, Soup, Classic Pattern	175.00

A rifle is a firearm that has a rifled bore and that is intended to be fired from the shoulder. Other firearms are listed under Gun.

RIFLE, Breech Loading, A.Sander, Brown Twisted Barrel, Walnut, 42 1/8 In.	2475.00
Kentucky Long Flintlock, Converted To Percussion Gun, Tiger Maple	467.00
Kentucky, Lock Signed I.Keller, Curly Maple Stock, 56 In.	250.00
Kentucky, Norristown, Pa., 1830s	800.00
Kentucky, Signed Leman, Curly Maple Stock, Lancaster, Pa., 52 In.	1300.00
Marlin, Lever Action, 32 Caliber, Model 92	150.00
Percussion, Target, N.Y., N.Angell, Remington Cast Steel, 1850–60	550.00
Percussion, Target, S.C.Miller, German Silver Mounts, 1850–60, 44 In.	1210.00
Percussion, Whitney–Plymouth, Navy, 69 Caliber, Bayonet Stud, Sling	2950.00
Sharps Borchardt Military	895.00
Sharps, No.1853, Carbine, 52 Cal., Patch Box, 21 1/2 In.Barrel	1150.00
Sharps, No.1859, Carbine, Chief Crow King, 22 In.Buttstock	250.00
Spencer, Repeating Carbine, 52 Cal., Chief Gall Hunkpapas, 20 In.	800.00
Spencer, Repeating Carbine, 52 Cal., Confederate States, 20 In.Barrel	650.00
Springfield 1808, Musket, Percussion, 69 Cal., 29 In.Barrel	150.00
Training, Reguarth Gun By Pettibone Bros., Mfg.Co., Civil War	160.00
Winchester 1873, 38–40 Caliber	350.00
Winchester, 405 Caliber, Model 1895	995.00
Winchester, Carbine, Plate, Avenger of Gen.Custer, 1873, 20 In.Barrel	750.00
Winchester, Model 1873, 44/40 Caliber	360.00
Winchester, Model 1886, Deluxe, Takedown, 33 Caliber	1870.00
Winchester, Model 1905, Semiautomatic	295.00
Winchester, Model 64, Standard, 30/30 Caliber	410.00
Winchester, Model 70, Bolt Action, 220 Swift Caliber	385.00
Winchester, Model 71, Deluxe, 348 Caliber	1045.00
Winchester, Model 92, Trapper Carbine, Registration Papers	1540.00
Winchester, No.66, 44 Caliber, Engraved Thomas Howard, 24 In.Barrel	300.00

Riviera dinnerware was made by the Homer Laughlin Co. of Newell, West Virginia, from 1938 to 1950. The pattern was similar in coloring and in mood to Fiesta and Harlequin. The Riviera plates and cup handles were square.

COLONIAL

RIVIERA, Bowl, Red, 9 In.	12.00
Casserole, Yellow, Cover	42.50
Soup Dish, Red	8.50
Sugar & Creamer, Blue, Cover	12.50
Syrup, Cover, Red	40.00

Rockingham, in the United States, is a brown glazed pottery with a tortoiseshell–like glaze. It was made from 1840 to 1900 by many

American potteries. Mottled brown Rockingham wares were first made in England at the Rockingham factory. Other types of ceramics were also made by the English firm.

ROCKINGHAM, Bookends, Young Girl With Books, 7 1/2 In.	260.00
Bottle, Embossed Morning Glories, 8 1/4 In.	85.00
Bottle, Toby, 9 1/2 In.	150.00
Bowl, 12 X 3 3/8 In.	105.00
Bowl, 2 5/8 X 9 3/4 In.	50.00
Bowl, Canted Side, 7 1/2 In.	50.00
Bowl, Double Arches, 11 X 5 In.	95.00
Bowl, Embossed Exterior, 4 1/4 X 9 3/4 In.	20.00
Bowl, Embossed Foliage Scroll Design, 8 3/4 X 2 3/8 In.	80.00
Bowl, Oval, 10 1/2 In.	85.00
Creamer, Embossed Rim Band, 4 5/8 In.	45.00
Cuspidor, Embossed Diamond Design, 8 1/8 In.	20.00
Cuspidor, Embossed Shells, 10 1/2 In.	20.00
Cuspidor, Shells Pattern, Mottled Glaze	125.00
Dish, Soap, Oval, 4 3/4 In.	85.00
Flask, Embossed Leaf, 7 1/2 In.	35.00
Flask, Lady's High Shoe, Tortoiseshell, Bennington Type, 6 In.	295.00
Inkwell, Sleeping Figure, 4 In.	100.00
Jar, Impressed Handles, 2 7/8 In.	15.00
Jug, Hound Dog	45.00
Jug, Milk, Anchor Pattern, Bulbous, 7 3/4 In.	60.00
Jug, Milk, Anchor Pattern, Bulbous, 8 1/2 In.	115.00
Mold, Food, Turk's Head, 3 1/2 X 8 1/8 In.	90.00
Mug, 3 7/8 In.	60.00
Mug, Acanthus Leaf Pattern, 5 In.	150.00
Pie Plate, 9 3/4 In.	80.00
Pie Plate, Brown & Yellow Marbelized, 10 1/2 In.	95.00
Pitcher, Embossed Horsehead, Hunting Scene, Marked, 8 In.	125.00
Pitcher, Embossed Hunting Scenes, 8 In.	145.00
Pitcher, Hound Handle, Embossed Hanging Game, 7 1/4 In.	75.00
Pitcher, Hunt Scene, 8 1/2 In.	55.00
Pitcher, Hunter & Hounds	140.00
Pitcher, Man Smoking & Woman Taking Snuff Scene, Lid, 9 In.	130.00
Pitcher, Milk, Brown To Yellow, Bulbous, 1 1/2 Qt., 8 1/2 In.	60.00
Pitcher, Tulip, 9 3/4 In.	95.00
Plate, Gothic Arch Pattern, 8 3/4 X 8 3/4 In.	55.00
Soap Dish, 12 Panels On Bottom Half, Drain Holes, 4 1/8 In.	60.00
Soap Dish, Oval, 5 1/8 In.	85.00
Teapot, Rebecca At The Well, 9 In.	40.00

ROGERS, see John Rogers

Rookwood pottery was made in Cincinnati, Ohio, from 1880 to 1960. All of this art pottery is marked, most with the famous flame mark. The R is reversed and placed back to back with the letter P. Flames surround the letters. After 1900, a Roman numeral was added to the mark to indicate the year. The name and some of the molds were purchased in 1984; new items will be clearly marked.

ROOKWOOD, Ashtray, 71st Anniversary, Cincinnati, Ohio, Turquoise, 6 In.	45.00
Ashtray, Figural, Owl, Blue, Numbered, 1931	87.50
Ashtray, Figural, Rook	125.00
Ashtray, Heart Shape	20.00
Ashtray, Incised Flower, Pink, 1931	45.00
Ashtray, Romulus & Remus Devil, 1920, 6 In.	125.00
Ashtray, Rook	60.00 To 75.00
Ashtray, Yellow & Green	12.00
Bookends, Owl, Tan High Glaze	97.00
Bookends, Rook, White Matte	125.00
Bookends, Wallflower	185.00
Bowl, Brown, Pink Matte, 1917, 5 In.	48.00
Bowl, Cabbage Leaves Shape, No.5533, 1947, Large	95.00

Some tea and coffee stains on dishes can be removed by rubbing them with damp baking soda.

Rookwood, Vase, Iris Glazed, Swamp Scene, Geese Flying, 9 X 5 In.

Rookwood, Vase, Landscape, Vellum, Birch Trees, Mountains, 9 In.

Bowl, Cover, Amelia B.Sprague, 3 1/2 X 3 1/2 In.	195.00
Bowl, Flower Bud & Stem, Stipple Interior, 10 In.	195.00
Bowl, Flower Frog, Pink & Yellow	35.00
Bowl, Maroon, 1914, 3 In.	30.00
Bowl, Purple Outside, Yellow Inside, Dated 1921, 8 In.	38.00
Bowl, Relief Pattern, Woodrose Matte Glaze, 2 1/2 X 12 In.	51.00
Candleholder, Aladdin's Lamp, Floral, Brown	185.00
Candleholder, Dark & Light Blue, C.1920, 5 X 2 In., Pair	75.00
Candleholder, Lily Pad, 1923	45.00
Chamberstick, Hooded, Matte Pink To Olive, 7 1/2 In.	50.00
Cookie Jar, Betsy Ross, Sewing Flag, Red, White & Blue	55.00
Creamer, Birch Catkins, Yellow, Angled Handle, O.G.R., 4 1/4 In.	175.00
Creamer, Black & Gray	15.00
Creamer, Butterfly Handle, Columbine, C.1900	185.00
Creamer, Fluted, Golden Flowers, Amelia B.Sprague, 4 In.	98.00
Creamer, Mary Perkins, Dated 1891	200.00
Creamer, Pale Blue	15.00
Cup & Saucer, Blue, Green, White	40.00
Cup & Saucer, Sailing Ship, Blue & White	45.00
Dish, Nut, Half Shell, High Glaze Interior	250.00
Eggcup, Aventurine Glitter Glaze, 1933	50.00
Ewer, Glaze, Burnt Orange, Yellow Green, Leaves, Berries, 9 In.	345.00
Ewer, Leaves & Berries, Dated 1900, 9 1/4 In.	350.00
Ewer, Nasturtiums, Gloss Glaze, Signed, 1902, 8 3/4 In.	575.00
Ewer, Signed Virginia Demerest, 1902, 7 In.	235.00
Ewer, Standard Glaze, Variegated Leaves, Hanging Berries, 1900	295.00
Ewer, Trefoil Top, Leaves & Berries, Signed, Dated 1900, 9 1/4 In.	325.00
Ewer, Yellow, Olive Green, C Scroll Handle, 14 In.	5775.00
Figurine, Rooster, Green Glaze, Dated 1928, 5 1/4 In.	110.00
Flower Frog, Kingfisher, 1927	150.00
Inkwell, Tray, Silver Overlay, C.Baker, 1899, 10 1/2 In.	1950.00
Jar, Drugstore, Decorette, 8 Sides, 10 In.	135.00
Jug, Brown Butterfly, High Glaze, 1884, Signed MR, 4 3/4 In.	585.00
Lamp, Apple Blossom Design, Brass Mountings, WPMcD, 19 In.	200.00
Lamp, Scenic, Vellum, 9 1/2 In.	450.00
Mug, Floral, S.Toohey	275.00
Mug, Green, Matte, 1904	95.00
Mug, Medallion, Advertisers Club, Cincinnati, Red, 5 In.	60.00
Mug, Portrait, Mountaineer Smoking Pipe, Bruce Horsfall, 5 In.	1100.00
Mug, Siebel Institute, 1948	25.00
Paperweight, Bird Perched On Square Block, Blue, 3 1/2 In.	60.00
Paperweight, Penguin, No.2727, White Matte, 1934	95.00

Pin Tray, Mouse, Standard Brown Glaze, A.M.Valentien, 1888, 7 In.	250.00
Pitcher, 3–Spout, Matte, 1905, 8 1/4 In.	225.00
Pitcher, Blue Dogwood Blossoms, White, 1883, 6 3/4 In.	250.00
Pitcher, Brown To Sky Blue, Spray of Dogwoods, 6 In.	450.00
Pitcher, Ivory Green Spout, Matte, 1929, 5 In.	65.00
Pitcher, Signed WPMcD, 12 X 12 In.	1000.00
Pitcher, Trefoil Rim, Loop Handle, Marsh Grasses, MLN, 1882, 6 In.	750.00
Pitcher, Tulip & Bird Design, Loop Handle, Sara Sax, 1890, 7 In.	50.00
Pitcher, White Fern Fronds, Artist S.N.M., Chocolate Color, 5 In.	500.00
Plaque, Country Road, Vellum Glaze, Sara Sax, 1914	3850.00
Plaque, Scenic, Signed, 1917, 8 X 6 In.	1500.00
Plate, Swirl Design, Blue To Peach, White Flowers, 7 In.	50.00
Postcard, Dated 1921	10.00
Sign, Dealer, Starkville, Mississippi, Blue Glaze	40.00
Stein, Wiedemann Brewing Co., Eagle On "W", Pewter Top, 5 1/2 In.	150.00
Sugar, Leaves & Berries, Cover, 1893	75.00
Tea Set, Yellow, 1918, 3 Piece	425.00
Tile, Herschede Clock Advertisement, 6 In.	95.00
Tile, Test New Glaze Formulas, 1930s, Square, 6 In.	87.50
Tray, Pin, Round, Yellow Mouse, Brown, 7 In.	250.00
Trivet, 4–Color, 1920	80.00
Trivet, Bluebird	125.00
Trivet, Butterflies & Flower Basket	100.00
Trivet, High Glaze, 1925	105.00
Trivet, Tea, Parrot, Rose, Lilac, Perched On Rose Trellis, 5 X 5 In.	50.00
Vase, 6 Panels, Baluster Form, 1920, 5 In.	90.00
Vase, Art Moderne, No.6706, 1945	45.00
Vase, Art Nouveau Strapwork, Silver Overlay, C.C.L., 7 1/4 In.	1600.00
Vase, Aztec, 11 In.	160.00
Vase, Beige Roses Base To Rim, Kataro Shirayamadani, 14 In.	3650.00
Vase, Blue Iris, Blue To Pink Ground, Cylindrical, 1929, 17 In.	950.00
Vase, Blue, Green, Brown, Birch Trees, Lake, 7 In.	1210.00
Vase, Blue, Large Handles, Bulbous, 5 1/2 In.	65.00
Vase, Brown Textured Matte, Purple Accent, 1911, 8 3/4 In.	125.00
Vase, Bulbous, Charles Dubowski, 1894, 5 1/2 In.	3850.00
Vase, Bulbous, Slender Neck, Caramel, 9 3/4 In.	60.00
Vase, Butterflies & Birds In Relief, Green Matte, 1933, 5 In.	55.00
Vase, Butterflies, Shaded From Rose To Blue, Dated 1890, 6 In.	65.00
Vase, Celadon Poppies, Green Matte Glaze, Logo, C.1929, 12 In., Pair	150.00
Vase, Cherries, Laura Lindeman, 1897, 5 1/2 In.	350.00
Vase, Cherry Blossom Branches, Artist Signed, 5 In.	295.00
Vase, Chrysanthemums, Crashing Surf, Arthur Conant, 9 In.	5500.00
Vase, Cream, Grapes & Leaves Around Top, Marked, 6 In.	17.50
Vase, Daffodils, Mary Norse, 10 In.	3850.00
Vase, Dark Blue, Band of Rooks Top, 1915, 5 1/4 X 4 1/2 In.	28.00
Vase, Dark Green Matte Glaze, Art Deco, Bulbous, 1923, 5 In.	50.00
Vase, Dark Purple, 1924, 5 1/2 In.	45.00
Vase, Dark Purple, 1924, 6 1/4 In.	75.00
Vase, Deep Blue, Green, Red Design On Top, 7 1/2 In.	100.00
Vase, Deer & Foliage, Cream, 1929, 7 1/2 In.	95.00
Vase, Embossed Florals, Rose To Green, 1928, 8 1/2 In.	50.00
Vase, Embossed Mexican Designs, Blue, 1950s, 5 1/2 In.	60.00
Vase, Fern Fronds, Green, Signed Albert Pons, 1908, 11 In.	495.00
Vase, Fish Swimming, Brown, Green Ground, 1906, 7 In.	1430.00
Vase, Floral Bouquets, Mottled Aqua Ground, MHM, 1938, 5 1/2 In.	175.00
Vase, Floral Design, High Gloss Glaze, Signed, Sarah Sax, 10 In.	575.00
Vase, Floral Vellum, 1930, 50th Anniversary Kiln Mark, 5 1/2 In.	150.00
Vase, Floral Vellum, Pink Flowers On Peach, 1915, 11 In.	400.00
Vase, Floral, Dark Standard Glaze, Artist Signed, 1904, 7 In.	385.00
Vase, Floral, Standard Glaze, Signed, Dated 1902, 5 1/2 In.	225.00
Vase, Florals, Matte Glaze, Dated 1929, S.E.Coyne, 8 In.	450.00
Vase, Geese Flying, Swamp Scene, Iris Glazed, 9 1/4 In. .... *Illus*	6250.00
Vase, Gray Merging Into Coral, 1929, 10 1/2 In.	65.00
Vase, Green Floral, Wax Matte, Signed MHM, 1928, 7 1/2 In.	200.00

Vase, Green, Rose Matte, 1924, 3 5/8 In.	35.00
Vase, Handle, Blue Matte, 1922, 8 In.	175.00
Vase, Holly Leaf & Berries, Upright Mold, 1916, 9 1/4 In.	150.00
Vase, Iris Glazed, Swamp Scene, Geese Flying, 9 X 5 In. ....*Illus*	6250.00
Vase, Iris, Gray To Orchid To Black, Berries, Sara Sax, 8 3/4 In.	1100.00
Vase, Lamb & Flowers, Beige, 4 1/2 X 5 1 2 In.	65.00
Vase, Landscape, Iris Glaze, 9 In.	4400.00
Vase, Landscape, Vellum, Birch Trees, Mountains, 9 In. ....*Illus*	1700.00
Vase, Lavender, Gray, Blue, Green, Oyster, 1903, Marked, 9 In.	1045.00
Vase, Leaf & Pod Design, 1940, 5 1/2 In.	70.00
Vase, Leaping Gazelles, 1929, 7 1/2 In.	110.00
Vase, Leaves & Blackberries, Wax Matte Blue, Rose, 1926, 9 3/4 In.	490.00
Vase, Leaves & Blueberries, Sallie Toohey, 1900, 10 3/4 In.	600.00
Vase, Marine Scene, Carl Schmidt, 9 In.	3300.00
Vase, Maroon Tulips, Teal Leaves, Turquoise, Jeweled, 1904, 7 In.	1400.00
Vase, Molded Butterflies, Green Matte Glaze, 5 In.	32.00
Vase, Mountain Scene, Vellum, Harriet E.Wilcox, 1918, 8 In.	850.00
Vase, Nasturtiums, Burnt Orange & Brown, Artist, 1900, 7 In.	275.00
Vase, Orange Poppy, Brown, Elongated Neck, AMV, 1899, 19 In.	1300.00
Vase, Pillow, Honeysuckle & Bellflowers, Gold, 1889, 14 X 12 In.	1000.00
Vase, Pink Flowers On Branch, Irish Glaze, 1904, 5 In.	225.00
Vase, Poppies, Watery Glaze, Irene Bishop, 1902, 10 In.	350.00
Vase, Purple, Green, Blue Peacock Feathers, Marked, 10 In.	600.00
Vase, Purple–Blue Wisteria, Leaves, Cylinder, 12 In.	3450.00
Vase, Rust Drip Over Ochre, Beaded Neck & Base, 1926, 4 In.	20.00
Vase, Rust Flowers, Green Stems, Green To White, Marked, 12 In.	800.00
Vase, Scenic Vellum, Lake, Mountains, Edward Diers, 7 In.	750.00
Vase, Scenic, Trees, E.T.Hurley, 1940, 11 X 5 In.	1000.00
Vase, Shades of Black, Yellow & Chartreuse, Signed, 1906–07, 7 In.	395.00
Vase, Standard Glaze, 1901, 9 In.	300.00
Vase, Stylized Flowers, Handles, High Glaze, 1924, 10 In.	425.00
Vase, Vellum, Pinecone, 1910, 5 In.	160.00
Vase, Violets, Yellow, Long Neck, Bulbous, ZEG, 1893, 6 1/4 In.	125.00
Vase, Wax Matte Floral, L.N.Lincoln, 1920, 6 In.	200.00
Vase, White Sailboat, Black, Ball Shape, Signed L.H., 1954, 4 In.	175.00
Vase, Yellow Flowers, Signed A.M.V., 9 X 5 In.	295.00
Vase, Yellow Iris Blossoms, Brown Stalks, 1886, 13 In.	1320.00
Vase, Yellow Jonquils, Brown Ground, Dated 1899, 3 1/2 In.	325.00
Vase, Yellow Roses, Signed, E.Felton, 1897, 6 1/2 In.	265.00
Vase, Yellow, Amber, Spray of Yellow Flowers, 8 In.	285.00
Wall Pocket, Locust, Brown, 1917	175.00
Wall Pocket, Praying Saint, Deep Rose, 9 In., Pair	250.00

ROSALINE, see Steuben

Rose bowls were popular during the 1880s. Rose petals were kept in the open bowl to add fragrance to a room, a popular idea in a time of limited personal hygiene. The glass bowls were made with crimped tops, which kept the petals inside. Many types of Victorian art glass were made into rose bowls.

ROSE BOWL, Drapery & Prunts, Footed, Cranberry	325.00
Frosted Daisy & Fern, Cranberry	90.00
Quilted Mother–of–Pearl, Satin Glass Outside, 5 1/2 In.	640.00
Shell & Seaweed, Blue & White, 1880s	275.00

If you are the victim of a theft be sure to give the police complete information about your antiques. You should have a good description, a photograph, and any known identifying marks.

Rose Canton china is similar to Rose Medallion, except no people are pictured in the decoration. It was made during the nineteenth and twentieth centuries in greens, pinks, and other colors.

ROSE CANTON, Platter, Reticulated, 11 In. 185.00
Tea Set, Porcelain, 7 3/4 In.Teapot, 3 Piece 325.00
Teapot, Cylinder Shape, Reed Handle, 7 In. 100.00

Rose Medallion china was made in China during the nineteenth and twentieth centuries. It is a distinctive design picturing people, flowers, birds, and butterflies. Pieces are colored in greens, pinks, and other colors.

ROSE MEDALLION, Bowl, Birds, Butterflies, Mandarin Scenes, 5 3/8 In. 50.00
Bowl, Butterflies, Mandarin Scenes, 8 1/2 In. 65.00
Bowl, Flowers, Birds, Butterflies, 8 1/2 In. 35.00
Bowl, Flowers, Birds, Mandarin Scenes, 4 3/4 In. 10.00
Bowl, Ladies & Flowers, Fluted, 4 1/2 In. 30.00
Bowl, Reticulated, 10 1/2 In. 650.00
Bowl, Set In Pewter, Artist Signed, 6 In. 55.00
Candlestick, Panels of Oriental People, Flowers, 8 1/2 In. 145.00
Charger, 12 In. 175.00
Charger, 14 In. 200.00
Chop Plate, Flower, Bird, Mandarin Scenes, 14 1/2 In. 350.00
Creamer, Flowers, Birds, Mandarin Scenes, 3 1/2 In. 65.00
Cup & Saucer .... 45.00 To 65.00
Cup & Saucer, Paneled Saucer, Mandarin Scenes 25.00
Cup & Saucer, Scalloped Rim 35.00
Cup & Saucer, Scalloped, Birds, Butterflies, Scenes 30.00
Cup & Saucer, Scalloped, Flowers, Birds, Scenes 25.00
Cup, Saki, Ladies & Flowers, Footed 16.00
Dish, Kidney Shape, Mandarin Scenes, 7 7/8 X 10 1/4 In. 235.00
Dish, Quatre–Foil Shape, Mandarin Scenes, 9 1/2 X 10 In. 50.00
Dish, Quatre–Foil Shape, Mandarin Scenes, Cover, 9 3/4 In. 300.00
Dish, Serving, Oval, 8 3/4 X 11 In. 135.00
Dish, Serving, Square, 8 3/4 In. 30.00
Flowerpot, Saucer, Continous Mandarin Scenes, 7 1/4 In. 425.00
Flowerpot, Separate Saucer, Flowers, Birds, Scenes, 3 7/8 In. 115.00
Ginger Jar, Gold Overlay On Foo Dog, Marked, 15 In., Pair 350.00
Jar, Flowers, Mandarin Scenes, 4 5/8 In. 85.00
Pitcher, Handle, Flowers, Birds, Scenes, 13 In. 600.00
Plate, Birds, Flowers, Bats, Fan In Border, 8 1/2 In. 35.00
Plate, Dessert, 7 1/4 In., 8 Piece 220.00
Plate, Floral Design, Circled By Butterflies, 8 1/2 In. 20.00
Plate, Hot Water, Cover, Mandarin Scenes, Orange Peel Glaze 375.00
Platter, 18 1/2 In. 750.00
Platter, Butterflies, Scenes, Orange Peel Glaze, 10 X 13 In. 125.00
Platter, Flowers, Birds, Mandarin Scenes, 17 3/4 In. 100.00
Platter, Flowers, Butterflies, Scenes, 6 Sections, 16 1/4 In. 350.00
Platter, Late 19th Century, 8 1/2 X 11 In. 150.00
Punch Bowl, Flowers, Birds, Butterflies, Scenes, 13 3/8 In. 500.00
Soup, Dish, Roses, Birds & Butterflies 225.00
Soup, Plate, Flower, Bird, Butterfly, Scenes, 9 In. 15.00
Tea Set, Teapot, 2 Handled Cups, Fitted Wicker Basket 250.00
Teapot & Cup, In Lined Wicker Caddy 225.00
Teapot, Flowers, Birds, Scenes, Wire Handle,, 5 1/4 In. 65.00
Tray, Genre Scenes, Floral Panels, Scalloped, 11 X 14 In. 275.00
Tureen, Birds, Butterflies, Scenes, 8 1/2 X 11 3/4 In. 1200.00
Umbrella Stand, Genre Scenes, Floral Panels, 24 1/2 In. 850.00
Vase, Flowers, Birds, Mandarin Scenes, 4 1/2 In. 200.00
Vase, Flowers, Butterflies, Dragons, Scenes, 10 1/4 In. 225.00
Vase, Gold Overlay Rim, 4 Panels, 18 In., Pair 550.00
ROSE O'NEILL, see Kewpie

Rose Tapestry porcelain was made by the Royal Bayreuth factory of Tettau, Germany, during the late nineteenth century. The surface of the porcelain was pressed against a coarse fabric while it was still damp, and the impressions remained on the finished porcelain. It looks and feels like a textured cloth. Very skillful reproductions are being made that even include a variation of the Royal Bayreuth mark, so be careful when buying.

ROSE TAPESTRY, Ashtray, Pink & White Roses, Signed, 4 3/4 In.	145.00
Basket, Roses Inside & Out, Royal Bayreuth, 4 3/8 In.	275.00
Creamer, Pinched Spout, Dogs, Swimming Stag, Blue Mark	200.00
Creamer, Pinched Spout, Royal Bayreuth, 3 1/2 In.	225.00
Creamer, Pink Roses, Gold Squared Spout & Handle	125.00
Dish, Mint, Palette Shape, Blue Mark, 4 1/2 X 4 In.	135.00
Fernery, 3–Color Roses, Gold Ring Handles	245.00
Hair Receiver, Footed, Royal Bayreuth, Blue Mark	199.00
Hair Receiver, Pink Roses, Gold Feet	125.00
Hatpin Holder, Christmas Cactus, Blue Mark	395.00
Jar, Biscuit, Ornate Top & Bail, Anchor & Sword Mark	135.00
Pitcher, Pinched, Pink, 3 In.	140.00
Plate, Cavaliers, 9 1/2 In.	225.00
Salt, 3–Color Roses, Gold Rim, Scalloped	195.00
Slipper, Roses, Gold Trim, Holes For Shoestring, 2 1/3 In.	265.00
Toothpick, 3–Color Roses, Gold Handles, Blue Mark	495.00
Toothpick, Coal Scuttle Shape, Pheasant Scene	395.00
Toothpick, Pink Roses, 2 Handles, Royal Bayreuth, 2 5/8 In.	175.00
Tray, Country Scene, Blue Mark, 11 X 8 In.	290.00
Tray, Dresser, 3–Color Roses, 11 X 7 3/4 In.	300.00
Tray, Dresser, Alternating Panels of Roses, 11 X 7 3/4 In.	295.00
Tray, Sheep In Meadow, Blue Mark, Royal Bayreuth, 11 X 8 In.	295.00
Vase, 4–Color Roses, Bulbous Shoulder, Narrow Neck, 5 1/2 In.	295.00
Vase, Gold Handles, Ruffled, Gold Beading, Marked, 4 1/4 In.	350.00
Vase, Matte Black Base, Yellow Roses, 4 1/2 In.	100.00
Vase, Pink Roses, Squared Handles, 3 In.	125.00
Vase, Reverse Cone Shape, Royal Bayreuth, 6 1/2 In.	275.00
Vase, Tavern Scene, 2 Handles, 8 In.	210.00

Rosenthal porcelain was made at the factory established in Selb, Bavaria, in 1880. The factory is still making fine–quality tablewares and figurines. A series of Christmas plates was made from 1910. Other limited edition plates have been made since 1971.

ROSENTHAL, Bonbon, Winifred Pattern, Moss Rose, 2 1/2 X 5 1/4 In.	25.00
Bowl, Grapes, Leaves, Gold Handles, Cream Ground, 9 In.	165.00
Chocolate Set, Isolde, 5 Piece	75.00
Clock, Nude Female On Top, Turquoise & Gilt, 14 1/2 In.	3850.00
Coffee Set, Hand Painted Orchids, Gold Trim, Pre–1950, 40 Piece	425.00
Cup & Saucer, Donatello Pattern, Demitasse	15.00
Cup & Saucer, Rosenthal Rose	30.00
Dish, Girl, With Lambs, Green Transfer, Gilt Trim, Marked, 9 In.	30.00
Dish, Overall Design of Roses, White Ground, Square, 9 X 9 In.	85.00
Figurine, Bear, Standing, 3 1/2 In.	40.00
Figurine, Child Feeding Pigeons, 4 1/4 In.	75.00
Figurine, Dancing Girl, On One Knee, Sybille Spalinger, 9 In.	250.00
Figurine, Draped Standing Nude, R.Kresbach, 21 1/2 In.	750.00
Figurine, Elephant, Circus Ball	68.00
Figurine, Finch, Signed, 4 1/2 In.	55.00
Figurine, Girl With Fawn, 6 1/4 In.	155.00
Figurine, Goose, 4 1/4 In.	50.00
Figurine, Lady, Art Deco, Signed	125.00
Figurine, Lillian Harvey, 12 In.	200.00
Figurine, Naked Boy Holding Goat, 6 1/2 In.	135.00
Figurine, Naked Boy With Wolfhound, 8 In.	300.00
Figurine, Nubian Musicians, Meisel, 8 In., Pair	300.00

Figurine, Nubian, White Turban, Pantaloons, Playing Mandolin	105.00
Figurine, Poodle, 6 In.	45.00
Figurine, Rabbit, 2 In.	24.00
Figurine, White Rabbit, 5 In.	75.00
Group, Fantail Pigeons, Aqua Base, Artist Signed, 15 In.	325.00
Plaque, Hussar Regiment, Blue & White, PUG, 9 1/2 In.	120.00
Plate, Christmas Madonna, Dillingen, 1947	575.00
Plate, Christmas, 1920	175.00
Plate, Christmas, 1969	90.00
Plate, Rosenthal Rose, 10 1/4 In.	21.00
Plate, Scalloped, 2 In.Cobalt Blue Border, Green Ground, 9 In.	45.00
Plate, Windmill, 6 3/4 In.	30.00
Powder Bowl, Deco, Lime Green, Pink & Brown	75.00
Relish, Floral, Handle, 9 1/4 In.	25.00
Teapot, Holland Windmill Scene, White, Gold Trim	50.00
Vase, Entwining Vines, Grapes, Cream, Artist Signed, 7 In.	65.00
Vase, Lithophane, Blown–Out Ivory Herons, Grasses, 9 In.	325.00
Vase, Onion Form, Variegated Brown Lines, Signed, 8 In.	300.00
Vase, Tulip, Allover Pastel, Floral, Signed Walters, 9 1/2 In.	78.00

Roseville U.S.A.

The Roseville Pottery Company was organized in Roseville, Ohio, in 1890. Another plant was opened in Zanesville, Ohio, in 1898. Many types of pottery were made until 1954. Early wares include sgraffito, Olympic, and Rozane. Later lines were often made with molded decorations, especially flowers and fruit. Pieces are marked "Roseville."

ROSEVILLE, Arranger, Flower, Tuscany, Blue	23.00
Ashtray, Bushberry, Blue	50.00 To 65.00
Ashtray, Bushberry, Brown, 5 1/4 In.	45.00
Ashtray, Magnolia, 2 Handles	135.00 To 145.00
Ashtray, Magnolia, Brown, 7 In.	45.00
Ashtray, Match Holder, Fatima Cigarettes, Creamware	90.00 To 125.00
Ashtray, Snowberry, Orange & Green	35.00 To 45.00
Bank, Buffalo	65.00 To 85.00
Bank, Frog	65.00 To 95.00
Bank, Lion Head	95.00
Bank, Pig	95.00 To 100.00
Basket, Blackberry, 9 In.	425.00
Basket, Bushberry, Blue, 8 In.	60.00 To 70.00
Basket, Bushberry, Green, 12 In.	150.00
Basket, Cosmos, Blue, 12 In.	135.00
Basket, Donatello, Ribbon Handle	200.00
Basket, Freesia, Green, 7 In.	45.00
Basket, Hanging, Apple Blossom, 8 In.	75.00
Basket, Hanging, Clematis	45.00
Basket, Hanging, Corinthian, 8 In.	70.00
Basket, Hanging, Dahlrose	125.00
Basket, Hanging, Florentine, Brown	75.00
Basket, Hanging, Pine Cone, Green, Paper Label	85.00
Basket, Hanging, Thorn Apple, Pink	110.00
Basket, Hanging, Vista, 12 In.	125.00
Basket, Imperial I, 13 In.	120.00
Basket, Jonquil, 8 In.	185.00
Basket, Magnolia, Blue, 10 In.	75.00 To 125.00
Basket, Magnolia, Brown–Orange, 14 In.	65.00
Basket, Magnolia, Green, 7 In.	45.00
Basket, Ming Tree, White, 14 In.	125.00
Basket, Peony, Yellow, 8 In.	45.00
Basket, Peony, Yellow, 10 In.	90.00
Basket, Pine Cone, Blue, 10 In.	185.00
Basket, Snowberry, Green, 10 In.	45.00
Basket, Snowberry, Pink, 10 In.	65.00 To 75.00
Basket, Vista, 9 1/2 In.	145.00

Go outside and try to read your house numbers from the street. If you can't read them, get new, larger ones. Police responding to an emergency must be able to see the numbers in your address.

Basket, Water Lily, Green, 8 In.	50.00
Basket, Wincraft, Blue, 12 In.	52.50
Basket, Wincraft, Green, 8 In.	45.00
Basket, Zephyr Lily, Green Handle, 7 In.	45.00
Bookends, Bittersweet	50.00
Bookends, Ming Tree, Blue	80.00 To 85.00
Bookends, Snowberry, Blue	47.50 To 75.00
Bookends, Snowberry, Rose	55.00
Bookends, Wincraft, 6 In.	27.00
Bookends, Zephyr	55.00
Bottle, Monkey, Brown, 5 1/2 In.	65.00
Bowl, Blackberry, 8 In.	95.00
Bowl, Clematis, Blue, 6 In.	22.00
Bowl, Clematis, Brown, 10 In.	30.00 To 40.00
Bowl, Clematis, Green, 14 In.	35.00
Bowl, Cosmos, Green, 4 In.	42.50
Bowl, Cremona, Pink, 9 In.	25.00
Bowl, Donatello, Rolled Edge, Pedestal, 12 In.	175.00
Bowl, Earlam, 5 1/2 In.	65.00
Bowl, Florentine, Brown, 8 In.	35.00
Bowl, Florentine, Tan & Brown, 9 In.	36.00
Bowl, Flower Frog, Futura, 12 X 5 X 3 1/2 In.	225.00
Bowl, Foxglove, Matte Green Shaded To Pink, 2 1/2 X 11 In	49.00
Bowl, Freesia, Brown, 8 In.	35.00
Bowl, Fruit, Mock Orange, 12 In.	50.00
Bowl, Futura, Blue, 3 X 6 In.	150.00
Bowl, Imperial I, Brown, 8 In.	40.00
Bowl, Iris, Pink, 5 In.	40.00
Bowl, Ixia, 7 In.	95.00
Bowl, Magnolia, Blue, 6 In.	32.50
Bowl, Ming Tree, Blue, 10 In.	50.00
Bowl, Moss, 10 In.	28.00
Bowl, Mostique, 5 1/2 In.	25.00 To 30.00
Bowl, Mostique, 8 In.	75.00
Bowl, Pine Cone, Blue, 3 In.	30.00
Bowl, Pine Cone, Boat Shape, Blue, 10 In.	100.00
Bowl, Royal Capri, 9 In.	200.00
Bowl, Rozane, 3 In.	45.00
Bowl, Thorn Apple, Brown, 7 In.	40.00
Bowl, Thorn Apple, Pink, 8 In.	100.00
Bowl, Topeo, Blue, Oblong	60.00
Bowl, Tourmaline, 8 In.	30.00
Bowl, Velmoss Scroll, 8 In.	30.00
Bowl, White Rose, 10 In.	55.00
Butter, Cover, Raymor, Green	30.00
Candleholder, 3–Light, Pine Cone, Brown	65.00
Candleholder, Apple Blossom, Green, Pair	25.00
Candleholder, Bittersweet, Gray, 3 In.	20.00
Candleholder, Cherry Blossom, 4 In., Pair	95.00
Candleholder, Clematis, Blue, 2 1/2 In.	12.00
Candleholder, Creamware, Florals, Gold Trim, 12 In.	65.00
Candleholder, Gardenia, Gray, Pair	27.00

Candleholder, Lotus, Blue & Cream, Pair 48.00
Candleholder, Pine Cone, Brown, 2 1/2 In., Pair 60.00
Candleholder, Rozane, Pair 75.00
Candleholder, Thorn Apple, Brown, 5 In. 40.00
Candleholder, Tuscany, Pink, 3 In., Pair 38.00
Candleholder, Velmoss Scroll, 9 In., Pair 80.00
Candleholder, White Rose, Brown, 2 In., Pair 25.00
Candleholder, Zephyr Lily, 4 1/2 In., Pair 40.00
Casserole, Raymor, Brown, Individual 17.50
Chamberstick, Earlam, Green, 4 In. 125.00
Cider Set, Bushberry, Brown, 7 Piece .... 400.00 To 450.00
Compote, Carnelian, Footed, Green, Tan 38.00
Compote, Cover, Volpato, Footed, White, 3 1/2 In. 50.00
Compote, Donatello, 5 In. 45.00
Compote, Rozane, 6 1/2 In. 75.00
Console Set, Corinthian, 3 Piece 150.00
Console Set, Freesia, Brown, 3 Piece 70.00
Console Set, Freesia, Green, 3 Piece 82.00
Console, Wisteria, 12 In. 75.00
Cookie Jar, Magnolia, Blue 110.00
Cornucopia, Bittersweet, Green 55.00
Cornucopia, Fuchsia, Brown, 6 In. 50.00
Cornucopia, Pine Cone, Brown, 8 In. 65.00
Cornucopia, Primrose, Pink 28.00
Creamer, Egypto, 3-Way, 3 1/2 In. 155.00
Creamer, Florentine, Footed, Brown 33.00
Creamer, Freesia, Blue 15.00
Creamer, Holly, 4 In. 325.00
Creamer, Juvenile, Fat Puppy, 3 In. 110.00
Creamer, Juvenile, Rabbits 55.00
Creamer, Landscape, Blue Ship 52.00
Creamer, Wincraft 18.00
Crocus Pot, Jonquil, 7 In. 150.00
Cup & Saucer, Raymor 15.00
Cup, Raymor, Brown 8.00
Cuspidor, Mostique 125.00
Dish, Feeding, 4 Rabbits, Rolled Edge 55.00
Dish, Feeding, Baby Bunting 85.00
Dish, Feeding, Hickory Dickory Dock 52.00
Dresser Set, Forget-Me-Not, 5 Piece 395.00
Ewer, Apple Blossom, Blue, 15 In. 125.00
Ewer, Apple Blossom, Pink, 15 In. 150.00
Ewer, Bittersweet, Gold, 8 In. 60.00
Ewer, Bleeding Heart, Blue, 10 In. .... 85.00 To 95.00
Ewer, Clematis, Blue, 10 In. 60.00
Ewer, Columbine, Brown, 7 In. 45.00
Ewer, Freesia, Blue, 15 In. 180.00
Ewer, Iris, Pink & Green, 10 In. 150.00
Ewer, Magnolia, Brown, 10 In. 95.00
Ewer, Magnolia, Green, 6 In. 35.00
Ewer, Mock Orange, Pink, 16 In. .... 160.00 To 195.00
Ewer, Poppy, Pink, 10 In. 80.00
Ewer, Silhouette, Turquoise, 10 In. 60.00
Ewer, Snowberry, Pink, 10 In. 65.00
Ewer, Wincraft, 18 In. 165.00
Fernery, Mock Orange 28.50
Flower Frog, Bleeding Heart, Pink 35.00
Flower Frog, Clematis, Brown 21.00
Flower Frog, Magnolia, Brown, 5 In. 30.00
Flowerpot, Cherry Blossom, 4 In. 75.00
Flowerpot, Freesia, Coral, Brown, Signed 50.00
Flowerpot, Underplate, Bleeding Heart 75.00
Flowerpot, Underplate, Ixia, Green 42.00
Ginger Jar, Tourmaline 300.00

large Pot or Stand for Plants

Jardiniere, Apple Blossom, Blue, 8 In.	165.00
Jardiniere, Baneda, 4 In.	30.00
Jardiniere, Blackberry, 8 1/4 X 10 3/4 In.	200.00
Jardiniere, Bushberry, 8 In.	425.00
Jardiniere, Cherry Blossom, Brown, 6 In.	80.00
Jardiniere, Cherry Blossom, Pink, Foil Label, 4 In.	100.00
Jardiniere, Clematis, Pedestal, Green	435.00
Jardiniere, Corinthian, 5 In.	48.00
Jardiniere, Dahlrose, Blue, 7 In.	50.00
Jardiniere, Donatello, 8 In.	70.00
Jardiniere, Freesia, Blue, 4 In.	32.00
Jardiniere, Freesia, Pedestal, Green	575.00
Jardiniere, Futura, 6 In.	225.00
Jardiniere, Landscape, Pedestal, Artist Signed, 44 In.	600.00
Jardiniere, Primrose, Blue, 8 In.	175.00
Jardiniere, Rozane, 8 In.	65.00
Jardiniere, Snowberry, Pedestal, Blue, 8 In.	415.00
Jardiniere, Stork	50.00
Jardiniere, Sunflower, 6 In.	65.00
Jardiniere, Vista, 8 1/2 X 10 1/2 In.	175.00
Jardiniere, White Rose	185.00
Jardiniere, Wisteria, 6 1/2 In.	50.00
Jardiniere, Zephyr Lily, Pedestal, Green	395.00
Lamp, Aztec, Blue	275.00
Lamp, Carnelian II, 2–Light, Rose Tones	85.00
Lamp, Futura, Beehive	325.00
Lamp, Savona, Green, 12 In.	95.00
Match Holder, Pine Cone, Brown	90.00
Mug, Bushberry, Rust, 3 1/2 In.	30.00
Mug, Dutch, Creamware	55.00
Mug, Juvenile, Chick	60.00
Mug, Monk, Creamware	165.00
Mug, Pine Cone, Brown	100.00
Pitcher & Bowl, Dutch	300.00
Pitcher, Aztec, Blue	150.00
Pitcher, Freesia, Blue, 10 In.	70.00
Pitcher, Landscape, 7 1/2 In.	60.00
Pitcher, Peony, Gold, Ice Lip	80.00
Pitcher, Pine Cone, Branch Handle	42.50
Pitcher, Pine Cone, Green, 9 1/2 In.	150.00
Pitcher, Tulip	45.00 To 50.00
Pitcher, Vista	65.00
Pitcher, White Rose, Blue	57.00
Planter, Apple Blossom, Blue, 10 In.	45.00
Planter, Bittersweet	45.00
Planter, Hanging, Bushberry, Blue	110.00
Planter, Lotus, 10 In.	65.00
Planter, Luffa, Brown, 10 In.	55.00
Planter, Ming Tree, Blue, 10 In.	50.00
Planter, Ming Tree, Ivory, 8 In.	30.00
Planter, Ming Tree, White	25.00
Planter, Persian, 5 In.	95.00 To 115.00
Planter, Pine Cone, Bark Handle, Green, 12 In.	65.00
Planter, Pine Cone, Green	50.00
Planter, Silhouette, White, Footed, Rectangular	36.00
Plate, Juvenile, Chicks, 6 1/2 In.	32.00
Plate, Juvenile, Ducks With Boots, Rolled Edge, 6 1/2 In.	50.00
Plate, Lily, Leaf Shape, 14 In.	25.00
Pot, Pedestal, Donatello, Pot, 23 In.	275.00
Powder Jar, Donatello	225.00
Rose Bowl, Pine Cone, Blue, 4 In.	110.00
Rose Bowl, Silhouette, Nude, White & Aqua, 6 In.	120.00
Rose Bowl, Tourmaline, 4 In.	22.00
Salt & Pepper, Snowberry, Blue, 8 In.	395.00

Sign, Dealer, Script In Blue	425.00
Spittoon, Fern Trail, Brown Glaze	65.00
Strawberry Pot, Earlam, 8 In.	55.00
Sugar & Creamer, Cover, Raymor	32.00 To 35.00
Sugar & Creamer, Freesia, Green	40.00
Sugar & Creamer, Magnolia, Blue	55.00
Sugar & Creamer, Winfield	12.00
Tankard Set, Indian, Creamware, 7 Piece	1800.00
Tankard, Rozane, Cherry Decal, 11 In.	185.00
Tankard, Rozane, Marked, 16 In.	525.00
Tea Set, Bushberry, Green, 3 Piece	165.00
Tea Set, Snowberry, Green, 3 Piece	105.00 To 110.00
Teapot, Della Robbia, 6 In.	450.00
Teapot, Snowberry, Green	30.00
Teapot, Wincraft, Brown & Apricot	40.00
Tray, Spoon, Corn Shape, Advertising, Marion, South Dakota	35.00
Tray, Zephyr Lily, 14 1/2 In.	40.00
Tumbler, Dutch	70.00
Tumbler, Pine Cone, Brown, 3 1/4 In.	90.00
Umbrella Stand, Pine Cone	600.00
Urn, Carnelian II, 1915, 8 In.	75.00
Urn, Clematis	20.00
Urn, Earlam, 6 In.	60.00
Urn, Ferella, Raspberry, 6 In.	175.00
Urn, Morning Glory, 10 In.	225.00
Urn, Tourmaline, Blue, 5 In.	48.00
Vase, Apple Blossom, Blue, 7 In.	45.00
Vase, Apple Blossom, Pink, 12 In.	100.00
Vase, Aztec, Blue, 10 1/4 In.	325.00
Vase, Baneda, Pink, 10 In.	235.00
Vase, Baneda, Red, 10 In.	265.00
Vase, Bittersweet, Gray, 8 In.	35.00
Vase, Blackberry, 5 In.	100.00 To 110.00
Vase, Blackberry, 6 In.	95.00 To 125.00
Vase, Blackberry, 8 In.	175.00
Vase, Blackberry, 10 In.	225.00
Vase, Bleeding Heart, Green, Double, 4 1/2 In.	45.00
Vase, Bushberry, Blue, 6 In.	30.00
Vase, Bushberry, Brown, 10 In.	95.00
Vase, Bushberry, Brown, 15 In.	150.00
Vase, Bushberry, Green, 18 In.	195.00
Vase, Carnelian I, Blue-Green, 8 In.	34.00
Vase, Carnelian, Fan Shape, Green Drip, 8 In.	40.00
Vase, Cherry Blossom, Brown, 4 1/2 In.	95.00
Vase, Cherry Blossom, Brown, 5 In.	80.00
Vase, Cherry Blossom, Pink & Green, 8 In.	225.00
Vase, Cherry Blossom, Tan & Cream, 12 In.	325.00

If photographing antiques for insurance records use a Polaroid camera. There will be no negatives, and no one else has to see your treasures.

Vase, Clemana, Brown, 12 In. .... 195.00 To 200.00
Vase, Clematis, Blue, 16 In. 185.00
Vase, Clematis, Pink Flowers, Green, 1944, 15 1/2 In. 160.00
Vase, Clematis, Tan, 8 In. 29.00
Vase, Columbine, Blue, 3 In. 20.00
Vase, Columbine, Blue, 14 In. 150.00
Vase, Columbine, Handles, 12 In. 55.00
Vase, Corinthian, Double, 4 1/2 In. 28.00
Vase, Cremona, Green, 12 In. 80.00
Vase, Cremona, Pink, 10 In. 68.00
Vase, Dawn, Green, 4 In. 40.00
Vase, Dogwood I, 9 1/2 In. 65.00
Vase, Dogwood II, 8 In. 55.00
Vase, Dogwood II, 14 1/2 In. 225.00
Vase, Donatello, 8 In. 70.00
Vase, Egypto, 7 In. 175.00
Vase, Falline, Blue, 6 In. .... 150.00 To 225.00
Vase, Falline, Brown, 6 In. 175.00
Vase, Ferella, Brown, 10 1/4 In. 395.00
Vase, Ferella, Raspberry, 6 In. 120.00
Vase, Ferella, Red, 4 In. 125.00
Vase, Ferella, Red, 8 1/4 In. .... 190.00 To 215.00
Vase, Florane, Brown, 10 In. 100.00
Vase, Florentine, 6 In. 20.00
Vase, Florentine, 8 In. 30.00
Vase, Foxglove, Green & White, 10 In. 125.00
Vase, Foxglove, Green, 14 In. 165.00
Vase, Freesia, Blue, 7 In. 35.00
Vase, Freesia, Brown, 8 In. 60.00
Vase, Fuchsia, Brown, 6 In. 40.00
Vase, Fuchsia, Green, 6 In. 40.00
Vase, Futura, Pink & Gray, 8 In. 195.00
Vase, Gardenia, 8 In., Pair 75.00
Vase, Imperial II 145.00
Vase, Imperial II, 5 1/2 In. 75.00
Vase, Ivory II, Flowerpot Shape 30.00
Vase, Ixia, Blue, 7 In. 50.00
Vase, Jonquil, Bulbous, 10 1/2 In. 120.00
Vase, Laurel, Green, 6 In. 40.00
Vase, Luffa, Brown & Green, 6 In. 80.00
Vase, Luffa, Brown, 6 In. 45.00
Vase, Luffa, Bulbous, Green, 8 1/2 In. 85.00
Vase, Luffa, Green, 7 In. .... 60.00 To 70.00
Vase, Magnolia, Blue, 14 In. 195.00
Vase, Magnolia, Brown, 8 In. 42.00
Vase, Magnolia, Coral, Green, 8 In. 30.00
Vase, Mayfair, Scalloped Rim, 10 In. 65.00
Vase, Ming Tree, Blue, 12 In. 85.00
Vase, Ming Tree, Blue, 15 1/2 In. 180.00
Vase, Moderne, Beige, 8 In. 40.00
Vase, Monticello, Aqua, 4 In. 55.00
Vase, Morning Glory, White, 6 In. 135.00
Vase, Morning Glory, White, 8 1/2 In. 200.00
Vase, Mostique, Gray, 6 In. 20.00
Vase, Orian, Blue, 6 In. 60.00
Vase, Orian, Raspberry, 7 In. 95.00
Vase, Orian, Yellow, 6 In. 65.00
Vase, Peony, Blue, 14 In. 110.00
Vase, Peony, Double Handles, Yellow, 8 In. 48.00
Vase, Peony, Green, 14 In. 105.00
Vase, Pine Cone, Blue, 12 In. 150.00
Vase, Pine Cone, Blue, 14 In. 295.00
Vase, Pine Cone, Blue, 2 Handles, 8 1/2 In. 70.00

Vase, Pine Cone, Brown, 6 In.	60.00
Vase, Pine Cone, Brown, 12 In.	160.00 To 165.00
Vase, Pine Cone, Green, 6 1/2 In.	35.00
Vase, Pine Cone, Green, Paper Label, 10 In.	125.00
Vase, Poppy, Blue, 6 In.	40.00
Vase, Poppy, Gray, 18 In.	175.00 To 235.00
Vase, Rosecraft, Handles, Blue, 6 In.	24.00
Vase, Rozane, Blue, 9 In.	35.00
Vase, Russco, Blue, 6 1/2 In.	40.00
Vase, Russco, Blue, 12 In.	72.00
Vase, Savona, Blue, 8 In.	175.00
Vase, Silhouette, Blue–Green, 5 In.	20.00
Vase, Silhouette, Fan Shape, White Nude, 7 In.	105.00
Vase, Silhouette, Maroon, 8 In.	30.00
Vase, Silhouette, Nude, White & Aqua, 6 In.	100.00
Vase, Snowberry, Blue, 15 In.	150.00
Vase, Thorn Apple, Pink, 9 1/2 In.	75.00
Vase, Topeo, Blue, 8 1/2 In.	75.00
Vase, Topeo, Blue, 10 In.	115.00
Vase, Topeo, Red, 6 In.	85.00
Vase, Topeo, Red, 9 In.	135.00
Vase, Tourmaline, Blue, 8 In.	30.00
Vase, Velmoss II, Aqua, 8 In.	60.00
Vase, Velmoss II, Pink, 8 In.	65.00
Vase, Velmoss Scroll, 10 In.	70.00
Vase, Water Lily, Brown, 14 In.	155.00
Vase, White Rose, Blue, 6 In.	40.00
Vase, Wincraft, Chartreuse, 14 In.	150.00
Vase, Wincraft, Peach, 10 In.	35.00
Vase, Wisteria, Blue, 10 In.	125.00
Vase, Wisteria, Brown, 7 In.	75.00
Vase, Zephyr Lily, Blue, 12 1/2 In.	50.00
Vase, Zephyr Lily, Brown, 18 1/2 In.	165.00
Vase, Zephyr Lily, Green, 15 In.	155.00 To 165.00
Wall Pocket, Blackberry, Gold Sticker, 8 1/2 In.	245.00 To 255.00
Wall Pocket, Carnelian I, Blue	45.00
Wall Pocket, Carnelian I, Green On Green	125.00
Wall Pocket, Cherry Blossom	250.00
Wall Pocket, Clematis, Blue	45.00
Wall Pocket, Columbine	75.00
Wall Pocket, Corinthian	30.00 To 65.00
Wall Pocket, Dahlrose, Black Sticker, 8 1/2 In.	70.00
Wall Pocket, Dahlrose, Green	85.00
Wall Pocket, Dogwood II, 15 In.	85.00
Wall Pocket, Donatello, 10 In.	80.00
Wall Pocket, Ferella, Brown	395.00
Wall Pocket, Florentine, 7 In.	50.00
Wall Pocket, Florentine, 12 In.	150.00
Wall Pocket, Foxglove, Blue, 8 1/2 In.	70.00
Wall Pocket, Freesia, Blue	60.00
Wall Pocket, Gardenia, Orange	105.00
Wall Pocket, Imperial I	100.00
Wall Pocket, Imperial II	140.00
Wall Pocket, Jonquil	90.00
Wall Pocket, La Rose, 12 In.	165.00
Wall Pocket, Lombardy, Straight Lipped, Blue & Gray	250.00
Wall Pocket, Lotus	150.00
Wall Pocket, Magnolia, Blue	88.00
Wall Pocket, Mostique, 9 1/2 In.	135.00
Wall Pocket, Peony, Gold	68.00
Wall Pocket, Peony, Pink & Green, 8 In.	34.00
Wall Pocket, Pine Cone, Double, Green	95.00
Wall Pocket, Pine Cone, Triple	225.00
Wall Pocket, Poppy	125.00

Wall Pocket, Primrose, Brown 110.00
Wall Pocket, Rosecraft Vintage 135.00
Wall Pocket, Rosecraft, Yellow 165.00
Wall Pocket, Snowberry, Pink, Blue & Green 70.00
Wall Pocket, Sunflower 45.00
Wall Pocket, Thorn Apple, Brown 110.00
Wall Pocket, Velmoss Scroll 125.00
Wall Pocket, White Rose, 9 In. 90.00
Wall Pocket, Wincraft, Brown, 4 In. 85.00
Wall Pocket, Wisteria, 8 In. 285.00
Wall Pocket, Zephyr Lily, Green 48.00
Window Box, Apple Blossom, 12 In. 65.00
Window Box, Cosmos, Brown, 9 In. 30.00
Window Box, Gardenia, Gray 28.00
Window Box, Pine Cone, 12 In. 225.00
Window Box, Wincraft, Blue, 13 In. 70.00

Rowland & Marsellus Company is a mark which appears on historical Staffordshire dating from the late nineteenth and early twentieth centuries. Rowland & Marsellus is believed to be the mark used by the British Anchor Pottery Co. of Longton, England, for some pieces made for export to a New York firm. Many American views were made. Of special interest to collectors are the rolled edge, blue and white plates.

ROWLAND & MARSELLUS, Cup & Saucer, City Scene, Blue 50.00
Plate, Battle of Lake Erie, Multicolor, 10 In. 55.00
Plate, Charles Dickens, Blue, 10 In. 50.00
Plate, Cleveland, Ohio, Rolled Edge, 10 In. 60.00
Plate, Grand Rapids, Blue 15.00
Plate, Independence Hall, Philadelphia, 10 In. 25.00
Plate, Indianapolis, Soldiers, Sailors Monument, 10 In. 30.00
Plate, Phoenix, Arizona, Rolled Edge, 10 In. 55.00

Roy Rogers was born in 1911 in Cincinnati, Ohio. In the 1930s, he made a living as a singer; and in 1935, his group started work at a Los Angeles radio station. He appeared in his first movie in 1937. From 1952 to 1957, he made 101 television shows. Roy Rogers memorabilia is collected, including items from the Roy Rogers restaurants.

ROY ROGERS, Bandana, Red, Trigger 25.00
Bank, Boot 12.00
Bank, Horseshoe 28.00
Bank, Roy & Trigger, Ceramic 30.00
Bedspread, Child's, With Trigger, Red & White 45.00
Binoculars 48.00
Blanket 150.00
Book, Coloring, 4 Colors, 1946 .... 30.00
Book, Coloring, Unused, 1944 .... 50.00
Book, Gopher Creek Gunman, 1945 .... 10.00 To 12.50
Book, Roy Rogers Favorite Stories 12.00
Camera .... 22.00 To 25.00
Chaps 45.00
Clock, Alarm, Windup, Animated, Roy & Trigger, Ingraham, 1951 .... 150.00
Comic Book, Dale Evans, D.C.No. 3, 1949 .... 50.00
Comic Book, No.82 .... 20.00
Costume, Dale Evans, Complete 75.00
Costume, Leather Chaps & Vest, 1950s 50.00
Desk Set, Pewter 36.00
Dinner Set, Western, No.4579 .... 100.00
Flashlight, Box 70.00
Gun & Holster 45.00
Gun, Six-Shooter, Holster 45.00
Handkerchief 13.00
Harmonica .... 8.00 To 15.00

Horseshoe, Trigger's Lucky Horseshoe	45.00
Lamp, Figural, Original Shade	150.00
Lantern .... 18.00 To 20.00
Lunch Box, Dale Evans	20.00
Mug, Figural	14.00
Paper Doll, Roy Rogers & Dale Evans, 1954	20.00
Photograph, Roy, With Trigger, Autograph	15.00
Pinback, 1953, Tin, Grape–Nuts	24.00
Pitcher & Mug, Child's, Plastic, 3 1/2 In.	15.00
Poster, 3 To 1 Odds	8.00
Poster, Roll On Texas Moon, Dale Evans, Trigger, Gabby Hayes	47.00
Print, Lithograph, Roy On Rearing Trigger	5.00
Raincoat	67.00
Record, Lore of The West, Gabby Hayes, 1949	65.00
Reel, View–Master	4.00
Ring, Neckerchief, Star, Metal, Roy's Signature, Sides, 1 1/2 In.	25.00
Ring, Saddle, Sterling Silver	75.00
Scarf, Head	12.50
Sharpener & Pencil	10.00
Sheet Music, 1952	10.00
Toothbrush	18.00
Toy, Pull, Chuck Wagon, Gong Bell, Litho Paper On Wood, 1950	145.00
Toy, Pull, Roy Riding Trigger	150.00
Wallet	25.00
Wristwatch, Dale Evans .... 42.00 To 45.00
Wristwatch, Roy On Trigger, 1950	70.00
Yo–Yo .... 18.00 To 20.00

The Royal Bayreuth factory was founded in Tettau, Bavaria, in 1794. It has continued to modern times. The marks have changed through the years. A stylized crest, the name "Royal Bayreuth," and the word "Bavaria" appear in slightly different forms from 1870 to about 1919. Later dishes may include the words "U.S. Zone," the year of the issue, or the word "Germany" instead of "Bavaria."

ROYAL BAYREUTH, see also Rose Tapestry; Sand Babies; Snow Babies; Sunbonnet Babies

ROYAL BAYREUTH, Ashtray, Elk	35.00
Ashtray, Hunting Scene	25.00
Ashtray, Pastoral Sheep, Blue Mark	70.00
Bell, Nursery Rhymes, Jack & The Beanstalk	285.00
Biscuit Jar, Enameled Ivory	290.00
Bowl, Floral & Gold Design, White, Blue Mark, 10 1/4 In.	185.00
Bowl, Floral Mold, Cherry Blossoms, Blue Mark, 9 In.	115.00
Bowl, Flowers Inside, Gold Trim, Ruffled, 10 1/2 In.	150.00
Bowl, Pastel Pink Roses, Blue Mark, 10 1/2 In.	175.00
Bowl, Red Poppy Mold, Green Leaf Base, Blue Mark, 9 1/2 In.	138.00
Bowl, Tomato, Blue Mark, 4 1/2 In.	40.00
Box, Tomato, Cover, Blue Mark, 3 3/4 X 4 1/2 In.	50.00
Bread Tray, Oak Leaf, Blue Mark	175.00
Cake Plate, Roses, Raised Gold In V Form, 10 In.	60.00
Candleholder, Brittany Girl, Signed, 4 1/4 In.	45.00
Candleholder, Children, 4 1/4 In., Pair	65.00

When you cancel your paper before you leave on a trip, do not tell why you want the paper stopped. Call to restart it when you return.

Candleholder, Corinthian, Black & White, Handle, 5 1/2 In.	50.00
Candy Dish, Devil & Cards, Blue Mark	240.00
Candy Dish, Nouveau Lady, Blue Mark	450.00
Celery, Roses, 13 X 5 1/4 In.	89.00
Celery, Shell	110.00
Chamberstick, Cows In Pasture, Handle, Dark Green, Blue Mark	135.00
Chocolate Pot, Floral, Domed Lid, Handle, Blue Mark	175.00
Chocolate Pot, Pink Roses, Creamy Yellow Ground	235.00
Chocolate Pot, Poppy, Blue Mark	550.00
Clock, Christmas Cactus Pattern, Blue Mark	395.00
Compote, Tomato, Leaves Base, 3 3/4 X 5 1/2 In.	65.00
Conch Shell, Pearlized, Blue Mark	35.00
Cracker Jar, Grape, Pearlized Yellow, Signed	375.00
Cracker Jar, Lobster	250.00
Cracker Jar, Orange Poppies, White To Yellow	85.00
Cracker Jar, Tomato, Blue Mark	265.00
Creamer, Alligator	165.00
Creamer, Apple, Blue Mark	60.00 To 80.00
Creamer, Bear	295.00
Creamer, Bellringer	175.00
Creamer, Bird of Paradise	250.00 To 285.00
Creamer, Black Crow, Blue Mark	120.00
Creamer, Bull	87.00 To 145.00
Creamer, Cat	85.00
Creamer, Cavaliers, 4 1/2 In.	69.00
Creamer, Children, 3 1/2 In.	42.00
Creamer, Coachman	84.00 To 200.00
Creamer, Cockatoo	190.00
Creamer, Corinthian, Black	50.00
Creamer, Corinthian, Red	75.00
Creamer, Cow, Black	165.00
Creamer, Crow	175.00
Creamer, Dachshund	115.00 To 165.00
Creamer, Devil & Cards, 4 3/4 In.	85.00 To 145.00
Creamer, Eagle, Blue Mark	175.00
Creamer, Elk, Blue Mark, 4 In.	80.00 To 85.00
Creamer, Fish, Open Mouth	60.00
Creamer, Fox, Red, Marked	475.00
Creamer, Frog, Dark Blue	185.00
Creamer, Girl Holding Candle	75.00
Creamer, Ibex, Stirrup	175.00
Creamer, Jack Horner, 5 In.	72.00
Creamer, Kangaroo, Blue Mark	550.00 To 875.00
Creamer, Lamplighter	95.00 To 175.00
Creamer, Lobster	50.00 To 75.00
Creamer, Melon, Blue Mark	140.00
Creamer, Monkey, Green, 3 3/4 In.	145.00
Creamer, Moose, Blue Mark	70.00
Creamer, Mountain Goat	95.00 To 220.00
Creamer, Mouse	650.00 To 750.00
Creamer, Musicians	40.00 To 48.00
Creamer, Old Man of The Mountain	65.00 To 75.00
Creamer, Orchid, Blue Mark	395.00
Creamer, Pansy, Blue Mark	125.00
Creamer, Parakeet	115.00 To 165.00
Creamer, Pear	135.00
Creamer, Pelican	110.00
Creamer, Platypus	250.00 To 370.00
Creamer, Poodle, Gray	150.00
Creamer, Robin	105.00 To 145.00
Creamer, Shell, Blue Mark	75.00
Creamer, St.Bernard	145.00 To 220.00
Creamer, Strawberry, Blue Mark	70.00

Creamer, Turtle, Marked 250.00
Cup & Saucer, Apple, Demitasse 45.00
Cup & Saucer, Rose, Pink 240.00
Dish, Figural Leaf Handle, Blue Mark, 4 In. 18.00
Dish, Juvenile, Girl With Dog 135.00
Dresser Set, Hair Receiver, Powder Box, Hatpin Holder 200.00
Figurine, Musicians, Blue Mark, 6 Piece 550.00
Hair Receiver, Golden Roses 95.00
Hatpin Holder, Attached Saucer, Musicians, Blue Mark 250.00
Hatpin Holder, Penguin, Blue Mark 495.00
Hatpin Holder, Poppy, Blue Mark, 4 1/4 In. .... 275.00 To 350.00
Hatpin Holder, Red Poppy, Blue Mark 145.00
Humidor, Lamplighter, Blue Mark 695.00
Humidor, Portrait of Woman With Fan, 2 Handles 185.00
Inkwell, Moose 75.00
Jam Jar, Shell 100.00
Match Holder, Cavalier Scene, Ball Shape, 3 1/4 In. 88.00
Match Holder, Corinthian, Hanging 110.00
Match Holder, Mountain Goat, Hanging .... 195.00 To 395.00
Match Holder, Poppy, Red, Hanging 65.00
Match Holder, Stork, Yellow, Hanging 250.00
Matchbox, Cavaliers, Hanging, Dixon, Blue Mark 185.00
Mayonnaise Set, Red Poppy, Signed 95.00
Mug, Devil & Cards, Small 40.00
Mug, Jack & The Beanstalk .... 45.00 To 47.00
Mug, Sand Babies 60.00
Mustard, Grape, Yellow, Blue Mark 95.00
Mustard, Lemon, Lid & Spoon, Blue Mark .... 75.00 To 95.00
Mustard, Tomato, Blue Mark 35.00
Nappy, Arab, Tapestry, Lemon, Blue Mark 125.00
Nappy, Jack & The Beanstalk 58.00
Pitcher, Apple, Blue Mark, 5 In. 150.00
Pitcher, Arab & Camel, 5 1/2 In. 45.00
Pitcher, Babes In Woods, Child Holds Doll, 5 In. 205.00
Pitcher, Border of Cows, Sunset Background, Marked, 5 In. 85.00
Pitcher, Brittany Girls, 5 In. 75.00
Pitcher, Cat, Red Around Inside Top, Grays, 3 In. 85.00
Pitcher, Cavaliers, Pinched Snout, Signed, 7 1/4 In. 450.00
Pitcher, Clown, Red, Blue Mark, 4 1/2 In. 250.00
Pitcher, Coachman, Blue Mark, 5 In. 325.00
Pitcher, Coachman, Blue Mark, 7 In. .... 495.00 To 550.00
Pitcher, Conch Shell, Lobster Handle, 7 In. 350.00
Pitcher, Cow's Head, Dark Brown, Light Gray, 3 3/4 In. 65.00
Pitcher, Devil & Cards, Blue Mark, 5 In. .... 230.00 To 235.00
Pitcher, Duck, Blue Mark, 5 In. 145.00
Pitcher, Fighting Cocks, 5 In. 65.00
Pitcher, Girl Holding Candle, 5 In. 95.00
Pitcher, Hunt Scene, 4 In. 48.00
Pitcher, Hunt Scene, Apple Green, Blue Mark, 7 1/2 In. 150.00
Pitcher, Hunting, 6 3/4 In. 67.00
Pitcher, Little Miss Muffet, 4 1/2 In. 58.00
Pitcher, Lobster, 7 In. .... 225.00 To 395.00
Pitcher, Men In Sailboat, Blue Mark, 6 In. 65.00
Pitcher, Monkey, 5 In. 250.00
Pitcher, Musicians, 6 In. 210.00
Pitcher, Netherlands Scene, Blue Mark, 5 In. 85.00
Pitcher, Orange, 5 In. 135.00
Pitcher, Parakeet, 5 In. 85.00
Pitcher, Poppy, White Satin, Blue Mark, 7 In. 435.00
Pitcher, Rural Scene, Pinched, Green, 3 1/2 In. 50.00
Pitcher, Shell, Murex, 7 In. 375.00
Pitcher, Snake, Blue Mark, 4 In. 500.00
Pitcher, St.Bernard, 5 In. 225.00
Pitcher, Steer's Head, Red, Inscription, 4 1/2 In. 65.00

Pitcher, Tomato, Blue Mark, 7 In. 275.00
Pitcher, Water Buffalo, Gray Finish, Black Trim, 3 3/4 In. 85.00
Pitcher, White Satin, 5 In. 125.00
Plate, Corinthian, White Figures, Salmon Ground, 9 1/2 In. 75.00
Plate, Goose Girl, 6 In. 70.00
Plate, Hunter With Dog, Blue Mark, 7 1/2 In. 55.00
Plate, Jack & The Beanstalk, Marked, 6 In. 55.00
Plate, Lettuce, Yellow Flowers, Ring Handle, Blue Mark, 7 In. 40.00
Plate, Roses, Gold Trim & Tracery, Blue Mark, 9 In. 43.00
Plate, Tomato, 8 3/4 In. 30.00
Powder Jar, Rose Tapestry, Footed, Cover, Blue Mark 175.00
Salad Set, Lettuce Leaf 250.00
Salt & Pepper, Clown 90.00
Salt & Pepper, Grape, Purple 95.00
Salt & Pepper, Red Poppy, Green & Tan Centers, 2 1/4 In. 75.00
Salt & Pepper, Tomato 20.00
Salt, Lobster Claw 38.00
Sauceboat, Underplate, Poppy 90.00
Shoe, Lady's, Black, High Top, Pair, Signed 135.00
Shoe, Oxford 85.00
Strawberry Set, Green Leaf Shape Bowls, 6 Piece 190.00
String Holder, Hanging, Rooster, Blue Mark 225.00
Sugar & Creamer, Conch Shell 185.00
Sugar & Creamer, Farmer & Turkeys, Blue Mark 195.00
Sugar & Creamer, Musician's, Blue Mark 120.00
Sugar & Creamer, Roses, Blue Mark 295.00
Sugar & Creamer, Shell, Blue Mark 70.00
Sugar & Creamer, Tomato 85.00
Sugar, Apple, Cover, Blue Mark 80.00
Sugar, Cover, Tomato, Blue Mark, 2 1/2 X 4 In. 40.00
Sugar, Grape, Purple, Cover 65.00
Sugar, Lobster, Cover 55.00
Sugar, Poppy, Cover, Blue Mark 140.00
Sugar, Tomato, Cover 40.00
Sugar, Tomato, Underplate 80.00
Tankard, Sailing Ship, 6 In. 125.00
Tea Set, Tomato, Blue Mark 185.00
Teapot, Apple 145.00
Teapot, Grape, Blue Mark 275.00
Teapot, Orange, Blue Mark 240.00
Teapot, Tomato 80.00
Toothpick, 3 Handles, Corinthian Ware 65.00
Toothpick, Brittany Woman, 3–Footed, Blue Mark 125.00
Toothpick, Elk, Blue Mark ....95.00 To 125.00
Toothpick, Lamplighter 95.00
Tray, Dresser, Corinthian, 10 In. 95.00
Tray, Dresser, Devil & Cards, Blue Mark 495.00
Tray, Lily Pad, Handle, 5 1/2 In. 25.00
Vase, Double Portrait, 4 3/4 In. 150.00
Vase, Floral, Blue Mark, 7 X 5 In. 175.00
Vase, Landscape With Sheep, Tapestry, 4 In. 7.00
Vase, Pheasant, Cobalt Blue & Gold, Blue Mark, 6 X 9 In. 165.00
Vase, Portrait In Medallion, Gold Framed, 5 1/4 In. 165.00
Vase, Portrait, 4 3/4 In. 90.00
Vase, Roses, Foliage, Gold Scrolling, Bulbous, 3 1/2 X 3 In. 75.00
Wall Pocket, Devil 200.00
Wall Pocket, Grape, Green 195.00

Royal Bonn is the nineteenth– and twentieth–century trade name for the Bonn China Manufactory. It was established in 1755 in Bonn, Germany. A general line of porcelain was made. Many marks were used, most including the name "Bonn," the initials "FM," and a crown.

ROYAL BONN, Biscuit Jar, Flowers Outline In Gold, Marked, 7 1/2 In. 125.00

Biscuit Jar, Flowers, Green Leaves, Brass Rim, Handle, Lid, 7 In. 100.00
Clock, Ansonia, 4 X 7 In. 125.00
Dish, Cheese, Sloping Cover, Floral, 7 1/2 X 6 1/2 In. 35.00
Urn, Cover, Tapestry, Signed, 14 In. 750.00
Vase, Art Nouveau, 12 In. 250.00
Vase, Birds, Flowers, Reticulated Handles, Gilt, 9 1/4 In. 175.00
Vase, Blue, Gold, 8 In. 43.00
Vase, Bluebird, Autumn Flowers, Gold Handle, 10 In. 125.00
Vase, Floral, Green & Yellow Ground, Handle, 13 In. 100.00
Vase, Flowers & Leaves Covered With Gold, Ivory Ground, 12 In. 145.00
Vase, Flowers, Leaves, Multicolored, Cream Ground, Marked, 12 In. 145.00
Vase, Gilt Tracery Over Florals, Hand Painted, 7 In. 65.00
Vase, Green, Roses, Slim Top & Bottom, Bulbous Middle, 9 In. 50.00
Vase, Hand Painted, 8 In. 85.00
Vase, Old Dutch, Arabesque & Floral Design, 10 In. 225.00
Vase, Pink Roses, 9 1/2 In. 65.00
Vase, Portrait, Artist Signed, 19th Century 125.00
Vase, Purple Ground, Yellow Irises, 8 In. 150.00
Vase, Red & White Roses, Gold Handles, Molded Gold Rings, 14 In. 35.00
Vase, Roses, 5 1/2 In. 85.00
Vase, Scenic, 4 Handles, Artist Signed, 13 1/2 In. 625.00
Vase, Tapestry, Floral & Gold 140.00
Vase, Tapestry, Multicolored Flying Bird, Frogs, 12 In. 235.00
Vase, Victorian Woman, 6 In. 170.00

Royal Copenhagen porcelain and pottery have been made in Denmark since 1772. The Christmas plate series started in 1908. The figurines with pale blue and gray glazes have remained popular in this century and are still being made. Many other old and new style porcelains are made today.

ROYAL COPENHAGEN, Ashtray, Seated Ape, Stares At Hissing Serpent, 5 In. 200.00
Candleholder, Blue, White, 9 In., Pair 200.00
Compote, Floral, Rose Center, Low, 7 1/2 In. 30.00
Compote, Fruits, Footed, Openwork Rim, Pair 750.00
Cruet, Pink Roses, Lavender & Green Design, Gold Stopper 18.00
Figurine, Boy Leading Sow, No.848, 7 1/4 In. 195.00
Figurine, Boy, With Calf 250.00
Figurine, Boy, With Lunch Box, Artist Initials, No.865 .... 145.00
Figurine, Dog, Chewing On Master's Slipper, 4 1/2 In. 90.00
Figurine, Duck, No.829 .... 175.00
Figurine, Foal 85.00
Figurine, Goose Girl, No.528 .... 95.00
Figurine, Pan, Piping, Lizard At Base, 8 In. 185.00
Figurine, Polar Bear, Marked 1137 GHK, 11 In. 145.00
Figurine, Siamese Cat, Seated, No.3281, 8 In. 95.00
Figurine, Stallion 300.00
Plaque, Classical Figures, Bisque, 5 1/2 In., Pair 80.00
Plate, Christmas, 1928 .... 100.00
Plate, Christmas, 1948 .... 225.00
Plate, Christmas, 1951 .... 215.00 To 250.00
Plate, Christmas, 1962, Little Mermaid .... 125.00 To 175.00
Plate, In The Desert 20.00
Platter, Flora Danica, No.3521, Oval, 20 1/2 In. 2200.00
Platter, Flora Danica, Pink Border, Marked, 15 In., Pair 2750.00
Vase, Hand Painted Shore Scene, Flared Rim, C.1929, 16 In. 700.00
Vase, Sailboat, Sea Scene, 7 X 6 In. 60.00

Royal Copley china was made by the Spaulding China Company of Sebring, Ohio, from 1939 to 1960. The figural planters and the small figurines, especially those with Art Deco designs, are of great collector interest.

ROYAL COPLEY, Ashtray, Leaf Shape, Bird Perched On Rim 10.00
Figurine, Bird, On Birdhouse 38.00
Figurine, Cockatoo, Pink, Green 30.00

Figurine, Deer & Fawn, 9 In.	10.00
Figurine, Dove, 5 In.	10.00
Figurine, Hen, White	20.00
Figurine, Kinglet	5.00
Figurine, Lark, Yellow, Green & Cobalt Blue, 5 In.	4.00
Figurine, Little Wren, Maroon, Yellow & Brown, 3 1/2 In.	6.00
Figurine, Panda, On Stump	32.00
Figurine, Parrot, Green, 8 In.	22.00
Figurine, Planter, Kinglet, 5 In.	6.00
Figurine, Rooster, With Wheelbarrow	38.00
Figurine, Skylark, 6 1/2 In.	8.00
Figurine, Tanager	6.00
Figurine, Titmouse, 8 In.	10.00
Figurine, Warbler	5.00
Figurine, Wrens, 6 1/4 In.	8.00
Pitcher, Blown–Out Dogwood, 8 In.	30.00
Pitcher, Dogwood	30.00
Planter, Bear With Mandolin	30.00
Planter, Bear, Small	20.00
Planter, Bird On Bowl	15.00
Planter, Black Cat & Tub	6.00
Planter, Cat, At Fence	6.50
Planter, Cat, By Book	7.50
Planter, Deer & Fawn	10.00
Planter, Dog & Mailbox	18.00
Planter, Elephant, Green Circles	25.00
Planter, Elephant, With Ball	12.00
Planter, Girl With Pigtails	8.00
Planter, Jumping Salmon	20.00
Planter, Oriental Girl, Basket Ground, Turquoise & Rust	6.00
Plate, Christmas, 1959	80.00
Vase, Doe & Fawn, 9 1/2 In.	15.00
Vase, Dogwood, Yellow, Green & Rose, 6 1/2 In.	8.00
Vase, Gold Fish, 8 1/4 In.	15.00
Vase, Maroon & Gray, Flowing Leaves, Paper Label	12.00
Wall Pocket, Cocker Spaniel Heads, Pair	25.00
Wall Pocket, Hat, Wide Brim, Pink, Yellow Flowers	12.00
Wall Pocket, Pirate	15.00

Royal Crown Derby Company, Ltd., was established in England in 1876. There is a complex family tree that includes the Derby, Crown Derby, Worcester, and Royal Crown Derby porcelains. The Royal Crown Derby mark includes the name and a crown. The words "Made in England" were used after 1921.

ROYAL CROWN DERBY, Cup & Saucer, Imari Pattern, Demitasse	65.00
Cup & Saucer, Mikado	18.00
Cup & Saucer, Ponxton Roses	18.00
Liqueur Set, China, 1934, 6 Piece	65.00
Plate, Mikado, 8 In.	9.00
Rose Bowl, Hand Painted Gold Flowers, Cover, 4 In.	135.00
Vase, Gold Florals, Pink, Gold Handles, 4 1/4 In.	195.00
Vase, Jeweled Berries, Flowers, Yellow Ground	265.00

"Royal Doulton" is the name used on Doulton and Company pottery made from 1902 to the present. Doulton and Company of England was founded in 1853. Pieces made before 1902 are listed under Doulton. Royal Doulton collectors search for the out–of–production figurines, character jugs, and series wares. For a complete listing, see "Kovels' Illustrated Price Guide to Royal Doulton."

ROYAL DOULTON, Animal, Dog, Bulldog, Brindle, HN 1043	225.00
Animal, Dog, Bulldog, HN 1074	65.00
Animal, Dog, Cocker Spaniel, HN 1078	95.00

Animal, Dog, Dalmation, Goworth Victor, HN 1113, 5 3/4 In.	75.00
Animal, Dog, Doberman Pinscher, Rancho Dobe's Storm, HN 2645	65.00
Animal, Dog, English Setter, Maesydd Mustard, HN 1050	125.00
Animal, Dog, Sealyham, Scottia Stylist, HN 1031, Medium	165.00
Animal, Drake Mallard, HN 2555, 6 In.	250.00
Animal, Drake, Standing, No.137, Flambe, 6 In.	80.00
Animal, Horse, Chestnut Mare & Foal, HN 2522	475.00
Animal, Mallard, HN 2556	250.00
Animal, Penguin, K 23	105.00
Animal, Snowy Owl, Male, HN 2669	950.00
Ash Pot, Auld Mac, D.6006, A Mark	95.00
Ash Pot, Parson Brown, D.6008	95.00
Ashtray, Gillette Razors & Blades, Blue & White, 1938	115.00
Ashtray, Parson Brown	90.00
Biscuit Box, Mother Goose Commode	215.00
Biscuit Jar, Floral Bouquets, Cream, Silver Plated, 8 In.	190.00
Bowl, Burslem, Blue & White, 15 3/4 In.	100.00
Bowl, Falstaff, 9 1/4 In.	145.00
Bowl, Moreton Hall, Oval, 11 In.	50.00
Bowl, Rosalind, Marked, 10 In.	70.00
Bowl, Shakespeare, Shylock, 10 In.	35.00
Bust, General Gordon, B.Stocks, 1885, 15 In.	350.00
Butter, Cobalt Dragons, Orange Flowers	65.00
Candlestick, Dutch Series, 6 1/2 In.	55.00

Character jugs are the modeled head and shoulders of the subject. They are made in four sizes: large, 5 1/4 to 7 inches; small, 3 1/4 to 4 inches; miniature, 2 1/4 to 2 1/2 inches; and tiny, 1 1/4 inches. Toby jugs depict a seated, full figure.

Character Jug, 'Ard of 'Earing, Large	850.00 To 1100.00
Character Jug, 'Arriet, Large	200.00
Character Jug, 'Arriet, Small	80.00 To 100.00
Character Jug, 'Arriet, Tiny	125.00 To 210.00
Character Jug, 'Arry, Large	125.00 To 165.00
Character Jug, 'Arry, Small	125.00
Character Jug, Anne of Cleves, Large	60.00
Character Jug, Aramis, Large	95.00
Character Jug, Artful Dodger, Tiny	38.00
Character Jug, Auld Mac, A Mark, Miniature	35.00
Character Jug, Auld Mac, Tiny	175.00 To 225.00
Character Jug, Bacchus, Miniature	30.00
Character Jug, Barleycorn, Large	115.00
Character Jug, Beefeater, A Mark, Small	50.00
Character Jug, Beefeater, Large	100.00
Character Jug, Blacksmith, Large	75.00 To 85.00
Character Jug, Bootmaker, Large	85.00
Character Jug, Bootmaker, Miniature	35.00
Character Jug, Captain Ahab, Small	45.00
Character Jug, Captain Hook, Large	475.00
Character Jug, Cardinal, Large	125.00 To 155.00
Character Jug, Cardinal, Miniature	45.00 To 55.00
Character Jug, Cardinal, Tiny	180.00 To 225.00
Character Jug, Cavalier, Large	115.00 To 145.00
Character Jug, Clown, Red Hair, Large	2400.00
Character Jug, Clown, White Hair, Large	920.00 To 1050.00
Character Jug, Dick Turpin, Gun Handle, Small	65.00 To 70.00
Character Jug, Dick Turpin, Horse Handle, Small	50.00
Character Jug, Dick Whittington, Large	375.00 To 425.00
Character Jug, Drake, Hatless, Large	4100.00 To 4800.00
Character Jug, Falstaff, Large	35.00
Character Jug, Farmer John, Large	125.00
Character Jug, Farmer John, Small	60.00
Character Jug, Fat Boy, Miniature	60.00 To 100.00
Character Jug, Fat Boy, Small	90.00 To 100.00

Character Jug, Field Marshall Smuts, Large 1600.00
Character Jug, Fortune Teller, Large .... 385.00 To 495.00
Character Jug, Fortune Teller, Miniature .... 325.00 To 350.00
Character Jug, Friar Tuck, Large .... 365.00 To 440.00
Character Jug, Gardener, Large .... 125.00 To 150.00
Character Jug, Gardener, Miniature 40.00
Character Jug, Gladiator, Large .... 575.00 To 595.00
Character Jug, Gladiator, Small .... 325.00 To 395.00
Character Jug, Gondolier, Large .... 295.00 To 600.00
Character Jug, Gondolier, Small 310.00
Character Jug, Gone Away, Large .... 65.00 To 75.00
Character Jug, Granny, Toothless, Large 1050.00
Character Jug, Guardsman, Miniature .... 35.00 To 45.00
Character Jug, Gulliver, Large .... 490.00 To 575.00
Character Jug, Gulliver, Small .... 375.00 To 385.00
Character Jug, Gunsmith, Large 75.00
Character Jug, Henry V, Large 200.00
Character Jug, Henry VIII, Large .... 35.00 To 60.00
Character Jug, Izaak Walton, Large .... 69.00 To 75.00
Character Jug, Jarge, Large 295.00
Character Jug, Jarge, Small .... 175.00 To 185.00
Character Jug, Jockey, Large .... 265.00 To 275.00
Character Jug, John Barleycorn, Miniature .... 45.00 To 50.00
Character Jug, John Barleycorn, Small 60.00
Character Jug, John Doulton, 8 O'Clock, Small 100.00
Character Jug, John Peel, Large .... 125.00 To 150.00
Character Jug, John Peel, Tiny .... 180.00 To 225.00
Character Jug, Johnny Appleseed, Large .... 295.00 To 350.00
Character Jug, Lawyer, Large 35.00
Character Jug, Lobster Man, Small 40.00
Character Jug, Lord Nelson, Large .... 265.00 To 325.00
Character Jug, Lumberjack, Large 75.00
Character Jug, Mad Hatter, Large .... 40.00 To 85.00
Character Jug, Mephistopheles, Small ....*Illus* 750.00
Character Jug, Mikado, Large .... 435.00 To 525.00
Character Jug, Mikado, Small .... 265.00 To 395.00
Character Jug, Mine Host, Large 65.00
Character Jug, Mr.Micawber, Tiny ....65.00 To 100.00
Character Jug, Mr.Pickwick, Large 135.00
Character Jug, Mr.Pickwick, Tiny .... 180.00 To 235.00
Character Jug, Night Watchman, Large .... 40.00 To 75.00
Character Jug, Old Charley, A Mark, Small .... 45.00 To 55.00
Character Jug, Old Charley, Miniature .... 25.00 To 60.00
Character Jug, Old Charley, Tiny ....65.00 To 100.00
Character Jug, Old King Cole, A Mark, Large 285.00
Character Jug, Old King Cole, Large .... 235.00 To 255.00
Character Jug, Paddy, A Mark, Large 140.00
Character Jug, Paddy, A Mark, Miniature .... 45.00 To 50.00

Royal Doulton, Character Jug, Mephistopheles,
Small

Future Royal Doulton collectors will be able to easily identify character jugs and figurines made before 1984. As of this year, the words "hand made" and "hand decorated" are added above the lion and crown mark in the shape of an arch.

Character Jug, Paddy, Tiny ....65.00 To 100.00
Character Jug, Parson Brown, Large .... 125.00 To 135.00
Character Jug, Pied Piper, Large 70.00
Character Jug, President Reagan, Large 365.00
Character Jug, Punch & Judy Man, Large 475.00
Character Jug, Punch & Judy Man, Miniature 365.00
Character Jug, Regency Beau, Large ....850.00 To 1050.00
Character Jug, Regency Beau, Small .... 500.00 To 625.00
Character Jug, Robin Hood, Large .... 115.00 To 125.00
Character Jug, Robin Hood, Small .... 40.00 To 55.00
Character Jug, Robinson Crusoe, Large 70.00
Character Jug, Sairey Gamp, A Mark, Large .... 60.00 To 90.00
Character Jug, Sairey Gamp, Miniature 30.00
Character Jug, Sairey Gamp, Tiny ....75.00 To 110.00
Character Jug, Sam Weller, Large 125.00
Character Jug, Sam Weller, Miniature .... 35.00 To 60.00
Character Jug, Samuel Johnson, Large 255.00
Character Jug, Sergeant Buz Fuz, Small ....65.00 To 105.00
Character Jug, Scaramouche, Large 695.00
Character Jug, Simon The Cellarer, Large .... 115.00 To 150.00
Character Jug, Simon The Cellarer, Small .... 57.00 To 65.00
Character Jug, Simple Simon, Large .... 495.00 To 520.00
Character Jug, Sleuth, Large 60.00
Character Jug, St.George, Large 290.00
Character Jug, Tam O'Shanter, Miniature 45.00
Character Jug, Toby Philpots, Large .... 119.00 To 125.00
Character Jug, Tony Weller, Tiny 85.00
Character Jug, Touchstone, Large .... 190.00 To 195.00
Character Jug, Town Crier, Large 235.00
Character Jug, Town Crier, Small .... 125.00 To 130.00
Character Jug, Trapper, Small 60.00
Character Jug, Ugly Duchess, Small 245.00
Character Jug, Uncle Tom Cobbleigh, Large .... 345.00 To 365.00
Character Jug, Veteran Motorist, Large 80.00
Character Jug, Vicar of Bray, Large .... 180.00 To 210.00
Character Jug, Viking, Large 170.00
Character Jug, Viking, Miniature .... 110.00 To 115.00
Character Jug, Walrus & Carpenter, Large 115.00
Character Jug, Yachtsman, Large 100.00
Child's Set, Bunnykins 50.00
Chocolate Pot, Gleaners & Gypsies 155.00
Chop Plate, Jackdaw of Rheims, 13 In. 85.00
Cigarette Lighter, Beefeater 225.00
Coffeepot, Chelsea Rose 95.00
Coffeepot, Moorish Scene, 7 X 3 3/4 In. 145.00
Coffeepot, Shakespeare Ware, Orlando, 7 1/2 In. 150.00
Cookie Jar, Enameled Medallions, Pale Orange, Silver Bail 75.00
Cup & Saucer, Christmas Series, Journey To Bethlehem 38.00
Cup & Saucer, Coaching Days 25.00
Cup & Saucer, Flambe, Landscape 65.00
Cup & Saucer, Northwest Orient Airlines, Gold Lettering 45.00
Dish, Child's, Little Miss Muffet 40.00
Eggcup, Glamis Thistle 20.00
Figurine, A'Courting, HN 2004 .... 395.00 To 450.00
Figurine, Abdullah, HN 2104 .... 450.00 To 545.00
Figurine, Adrienne, HN 2152 ....98.00 To 155.00
Figurine, Afternoon Tea, HN 1747 .... 195.00
Figurine, Alexandra, HN 2398 .... 170.00
Figurine, Alice, HN 2158 .... 110.00 To 125.00
Figurine, Annabella, HN 1872 ....*Illus* 525.00
Figurine, Anthea, HN 1527 .... 655.00
Figurine, Apple Maid, HN 2160 .... 400.00
Figurine, Autumn Breezes, HN 1913 .... 150.00
Figurine, Baby Bunting, HN 2108 .... 245.00 To 300.00

Royal Doulton, Figurine

Top O' The Hill, HN 1833, Spring Morning, HN 1922,
Annabella, HN 1872, Irene, HN 1952, Penelope, HN 1901

Figurine, Balinese Dancer, HN 2808	300.00
Figurine, Ballerina, HN 2116	235.00 To 275.00
Figurine, Balloon Seller, HN 583	545.00
Figurine, Barbara, HN 1432	525.00
Figurine, Bather, HN 687	500.00
Figurine, Bather, HN 773	1400.00
Figurine, Beggar, HN 2175	355.00
Figurine, Belle O' The Ball, HN 1997	180.00
Figurine, Belle, HN 754	550.00 To 795.00
Figurine, Bess, HN 2002	235.00
Figurine, Blithe Morning, HN 2021	150.00 To 175.00
Figurine, Blithe Morning, HN 2065	190.00
Figurine, Bluebeard, HN 2105	225.00
Figurine, Bon Appetit, HN 2444	185.00
Figurine, Breton Dancer, HN 2383	315.00
Figurine, Bride, HN 2166	165.00 To 225.00
Figurine, Bridesmaid, HN 2196	115.00 To 125.00
Figurine, Bridget, HN 2070	225.00
Figurine, Broken Lance, HN 2041	475.00
Figurine, Camille, HN 1648	430.00
Figurine, Captain Cook, HN 2889	190.00 To 200.00
Figurine, Captain MacHeath, HN 464	695.00
Figurine, Captain, HN 2260	145.00 To 200.00
Figurine, Carolyn, HN 2112	275.00 To 325.00
Figurine, Carolyn, HN 2974	110.00 To 135.00
Figurine, Carpet Seller, HN 1464	190.00 To 245.00
Figurine, Cavalier, HN 2716	135.00 To 180.00
Figurine, Centurion, HN 2726	145.00 To 150.00
Figurine, Charmian, HN 1568	595.00
Figurine, Christmas Morn, HN 1992	145.00
Figurine, Christmas Parcels, HN 2851	155.00 To 250.00
Figurine, Christmas Time, HN 2110	300.00 To 335.00
Figurine, Cicely, HN 1516	650.00 To 750.00
Figurine, Clare, HN 2793	155.00 To 165.00
Figurine, Clarinda, HN 2724	150.00
Figurine, Cleopatra, HN 2868	900.00 To 1400.00
Figurine, Clockmaker, HN 2279	190.00 To 225.00
Figurine, Clown, HN 2890	160.00
Figurine, Coachman, HN 2282	310.00 To 385.00
Figurine, Cobbler, HN 1706	185.00 To 200.00
Figurine, Columbine, HN 2185	185.00
Figurine, Coppelia, HN 2115	545.00

Figurine, Craftsman, HN 2284 .... 400.00
Figurine, Cup of Tea, HN 2322 .... 110.00 To 145.00
Figurine, Cymbals, HN 2699 .... 465.00
Figurine, Daffy Down Dilly, HN 1712 .... 235.00 To 275.00
Figurine, Dainty May, HN 1639 .... 260.00
Figurine, Dancing Years, HN 2235 .... 230.00
Figurine, Debutante, HN 2210 .... 335.00
Figurine, Deidre, HN 2020 .... 275.00 To 310.00
Figurine, Delight, HN 1772 .... 175.00
Figurine, Delphine, HN 2136 .... 200.00 To 250.00
Figurine, Denise, HN 2273 .... 225.00 To 250.00
Figurine, Detective, HN 2359 .... 160.00
Figurine, Doctor, HN 2858 .... 165.00
Figurine, Dorcas, HN 1491 .... 495.00
Figurine, Dorcas, HN 1558 .... 145.00 To 350.00
Figurine, Doreen, HN 1389 .... 575.00
Figurine, Dreamweaver, HN 2283 .... 115.00 To 210.00
Figurine, Drummer Boy, HN 2679 .... 325.00 To 370.00
Figurine, Duke of Edinburgh, HN 2386 .... 475.00
Figurine, Dulcinea, HN 1343 .... 950.00
Figurine, Easter Day, HN 1976 .... 425.00
Figurine, Easter Day, HN 2039 .... 185.00 To 285.00
Figurine, Eleanor of Provence, HN 2009 .... 475.00
Figurine, Elizabeth, HN 2946 .... 200.00
Figurine, Ermine Coat, HN 1981 .... 185.00 To 310.00
Figurine, Ermine, M 40 .... 425.00
Figurine, Evelyn, HN 1622 .... 1250.00
Figurine, Family Album, HN 2321 .... 350.00
Figurine, Farmer's Wife, HN 2069 .... 350.00
Figurine, Fiona, HN 2694 .... 165.00
Figurine, Fleur, HN 2368 .... 125.00
Figurine, Flora, HN 2349 .... 195.00
Figurine, Flute, HN 2483 .... 850.00
Figurine, Fortune Teller, HN 2159 .... 325.00 To 500.00
Figurine, Forty Winks, HN 1974 .... 165.00 To 200.00
Figurine, Four O'Clock, HN 1760 .... 475.00
Figurine, French Peasant, HN 2075 .... 455.00 To 495.00
Figurine, Friar Tuck, HN 2143 .... 325.00
Figurine, Gaffer, HN 2053 .... 400.00
Figurine, Gentlewoman, HN 1632 .... 550.00
Figurine, Giselle, HN 2139 .... 288.00
Figurine, Golliwog, HN 2040 .... 185.00 To 245.00
Figurine, Good Catch, HN 2258 .... 150.00
Figurine, Good King Wenceslas, HN 2118 .... 225.00
Figurine, Gossips, HN 1429 .... 595.00
Figurine, Gossips, HN 2025 .... 275.00 To 325.00
Figurine, Grand Manner, HN 2723 .... 175.00
Figurine, Grandma, HN 2052 .... 275.00
Figurine, Granny's Heritage, HN 2031 .... 375.00
Figurine, Granny's Shawl, HN 1647 .... 395.00
Figurine, Greta, HN 1485 .... 245.00 To 275.00
Figurine, Griselda, HN 1993 .... 420.00 To 475.00
Figurine, Guy Fawkes, HN 98 .... 1250.00
Figurine, Gwynneth, HN 1980 .... 200.00
Figurine, Gypsy Dance, HN 2230 .... 235.00
Figurine, Harp, HN 2482 .... 850.00
Figurine, Helen of Troy, HN 2387 .... 750.00 To 850.00
Figurine, Henrietta Maria, HN 2005 .... 575.00
Figurine, Her Ladyship, HN 1977 .... 260.00 To 295.00
Figurine, Hornpipe, HN 2161 .... 550.00
Figurine, Hostess From Williamsburg, HN 2209 .... 150.00
Figurine, Huntsman, HN 2492 .... 140.00 To 175.00
Figurine, Ibrahim, HN 2095 .... 575.00

Figurine, In The Stocks, HN 2163 .... 595.00
Figurine, Indian Brave, HN 2376 .... 5700.00
Figurine, Invitation, HN 2170 .... 100.00 To 125.00
Figurine, Irene, HN 1621 .... 325.00 To 395.00
Figurine, Irene, HN 1952 ....*Illus* 800.00
Figurine, Jacqueline, HN 2000 .... 475.00 To 655.00
Figurine, Jacqueline, HN 2001 .... 525.00
Figurine, Janet, M 75 .... 250.00
Figurine, Janice, HN 2022 .... 350.00
Figurine, Jean, HN 2032 .... 320.00
Figurine, Jersey Milkmaid, HN 2057 .... 275.00
Figurine, Joan, HN 2023 .... 295.00
Figurine, Jolly Sailor, HN 2172 .... 450.00 To 470.00
Figurine, Jovial Monk, HN 2144 .... 150.00 To 200.00
Figurine, Kate Hardcastle, HN 1718 .... 695.00
Figurine, Kurdish Dancer, HN 2867 .... 600.00
Figurine, Lady April, HN 1958 .... 245.00 To 300.00
Figurine, Lady Betty, HN 1967 .... 225.00 To 245.00
Figurine, Lady Charmian, HN 1948 .... 175.00 To 230.00
Figurine, Lady Clare, HN 1465 .... 695.00 To 750.00
Figurine, Lady From Williams, HN 2228 .... 150.00
Figurine, Ladybird, HN 1638 .... 2100.00
Figurine, Leisure Hour, HN 2055 .... 325.00 To 350.00
Figurine, Leopard On Rock, HN 2638 .... 850.00
Figurine, Lilac Time, HN 2137 .... 245.00
Figurine, Lily, HN 1798 .... 195.00
Figurine, Lion On Rock, HN 2641 .... 850.00
Figurine, Lisa, HN 2310 .... 145.00 To 195.00
Figurine, Little Bridesmaid, HN 1433 .... 145.00 To 160.00
Figurine, London Cry, Turnips & Carrots, HN 752 .... 725.00
Figurine, Long John Silver, HN 2204 .... 340.00 To 375.00
Figurine, Love Letter, HN 2149 .... 235.00
Figurine, Lucy Ann, HN 1502 .... 275.00
Figurine, Lunchtime, HN 2485 .... 145.00 To 160.00
Figurine, Margaret, HN 1989 .... 220.00 To 300.00
Figurine, Marguerite, HN 1928 .... 285.00 To 500.00
Figurine, Marietta, HN 1341 .... 500.00 To 840.00
Figurine, Marietta, HN 1446 .... 475.00
Figurine, Marigold, HN 1447 .... 495.00
Figurine, Market Day, HN 1991 .... 350.00
Figurine, Mary Jane, HN 1990 .... 325.00 To 450.00
Figurine, Masque, HN 2554 .... 200.00
Figurine, Masquerade, HN 2251 .... 275.00
Figurine, Master Sweep, HN 2205 .... 400.00 To 495.00
Figurine, Matilda, HN 2011 .... 510.00
Figurine, Maureen, HN 1770 .... 250.00 To 275.00
Figurine, Mayor, HN 2280 .... 345.00 To 350.00
Figurine, Memories, HN 2030 .... 275.00 To 500.00
Figurine, Mendicant, HN 1365 .... 285.00
Figurine, Mexican Dancer, HN 2866 .... 600.00
Figurine, Midinette, HN 2090 .... 265.00 To 295.00
Figurine, Miss Demure, HN 1402 .... 150.00 To 245.00
Figurine, Miss Muffet, HN 1936 .... 180.00
Figurine, Miss Muffet, HN 1937 .... 195.00 To 265.00
Figurine, Mr.Pickwick, HN 556 .... 350.00
Figurine, Mr.Pickwick, HN 2099 .... 265.00 To 295.00
Figurine, Mrs. Bardell, M 86 ....*Illus*   45.00
Figurine, Mrs.Fitzherbert, HN 2007 .... 950.00
Figurine, New Bonnet, HN 1728 .... 675.00
Figurine, New Companions, HN 2770 .... 120.00 To 160.00
Figurine, Newsboy, HN 2244 .... 450.00
Figurine, North American Indian Dancer, HN 2809 .... 315.00
Figurine, Officer of The Line, HN 2733 .... 150.00
Figurine, Old King Cole, HN 2217 .... 625.00

Figurine, Old Meg, HN 2494 .... 225.00
Figurine, Old Mother Hubbard, HN 2314 .... 225.00
Figurine, Olga, HN 2463 .... 160.00 To 165.00
Figurine, Olivia, HN 1995 .... 490.00
Figurine, Orange Lady, HN 1759 .... 185.00 To 215.00
Figurine, Orange Lady, HN 1953 .... 225.00
Figurine, Organ Grinder, HN 2173 .... 550.00 To 575.00
Figurine, Paisley Shawl, HN 1392 .... 425.00 To 495.00
Figurine, Paisley Shawl, HN 1987 .... 175.00 To 195.00
Figurine, Paisley Shawl, HN 1988 .... 135.00 To 150.00
Figurine, Pantalettes, HN 1362 .... 300.00
Figurine, Pantalettes, HN 1412 .... 350.00 To 355.00
Figurine, Parson's Daughter, HN 564 .... 350.00
Figurine, Past Glory, HN 2484 .... 140.00 To 165.00
Figurine, Patchwork Quilt, HN 1984 .... 300.00 To 375.00
Figurine, Patricia, HN 1431 .... 445.00
Figurine, Pauline, HN 1444 .... 400.00
Figurine, Pearly Boy, HN 1547 .... 400.00
Figurine, Pearly Girl, HN 1483 .... 245.00
Figurine, Pecksniff, HN 535 ....*Illus* 60.00
Figurine, Peggy, HN 1941 .... 125.00 To 135.00
Figurine, Penelope, HN 1901 ....*Illus* 250.00
Figurine, Pensive Moments, HN 2704 .... 140.00 To 190.00
Figurine, Pied Piper, HN 2102 .... 200.00 To 220.00
Figurine, Pierrette, HN 644 .... 675.00
Figurine, Pirouette, HN 2216 .... 200.00
Figurine, Polish Dancer, HN 3836 .... 450.00
Figurine, Polka, HN 2156 .... 200.00
Figurine, Polly Peachum, HN 549 .... 295.00
Figurine, Polly Peachum, HN 698 .... 385.00
Figurine, Potter, HN 1493 .... 200.00
Figurine, Prince Charles, HN 2803 .... 325.00
Figurine, Prince of Wales, HN 1217 .... 1100.00
Figurine, Prized Possessions, HN 2942 .... 425.00
Figurine, Prue, HN 1996 .... 235.00 To 265.00
Figurine, Punch and Judy Man, HN 2765 .... 150.00
Figurine, Queen Elizabeth II, HN 2878 .... 395.00
Figurine, Queen of Sheba, HN 2328 .... 750.00 To 850.00
Figurine, Reflections, HN 1848 .... 1125.00
Figurine, Repose, HN 2272 .... 135.00 To 215.00
Figurine, Reverie, HN 2306 .... 195.00
Figurine, Rosabell, HN 1620 .... 595.00 To 625.00

Think about security when you landscape your house. Cut bushes low under windows. Don't plant trees or bushes near doors where prowlers can hide. Place decorative lights in the yard to illuminate windows and doors. You might try the early 19th-century style of landscaping in the Midwest farm areas—no shrubbery plantings but flowers near the house.

Figurine, Rosemary, HN 2091	375.00
Figurine, Rowena, HN 2077	425.00 To 550.00
Figurine, Royal Governor's Cook, HN 2233	450.00
Figurine, Sabbath Morn, HN 1982	250.00
Figurine, Sairey Gamp, HN 558	450.00
Figurine, Sam Weller, HN 531 ....*Illus*	60.00
Figurine, Santa Claus, HN 2725	150.00
Figurine, Sea Harvest, HN 2257	185.00
Figurine, Seafarer, HN 2455	225.00
Figurine, Shepherd, HN 751	900.00
Figurine, Silversmith of Williamsburg, HN 2208	155.00
Figurine, Spring Flowers, HN 1807	275.00
Figurine, Spring Morning, HN 1922 ....*Illus*	195.00
Figurine, Spring Morning, HN 1923	275.00
Figurine, St.George, HN 2051	340.00
Figurine, Suitor, HN 2132	345.00 To 350.00
Figurine, Summer's Day, HN 2181	325.00
Figurine, Summer, HN 2086	395.00
Figurine, Sunday Best, HN 2206	150.00 To 225.00
Figurine, Suzette, HN 2026	225.00 To 300.00
Figurine, Sweet & Twenty, HN 1298	270.00
Figurine, Sweet Anne, HN 1318	195.00 To 325.00
Figurine, Sweet Anne, HN 1496	135.00 To 200.00
Figurine, Sweet Anne, M 5	225.00
Figurine, Sweet April, HN 2215	300.00
Figurine, Symphony, HN 2287	250.00 To 275.00
Figurine, Tiger On Rock, HN 2639	850.00
Figurine, Tinsmith, HN 2146	450.00
Figurine, Top O' The Hill, HN 1833 ....*Illus*	200.00
Figurine, Toymaker, HN 2250	300.00 To 340.00
Figurine, Uncle Ned, HN 2094	290.00
Figurine, Uriah Heep, HN 2101	325.00
Figurine, Veronica, HN 1517	265.00 To 285.00
Figurine, Vivenne, HN 2073	240.00
Figurine, Votes For Women, HN 2816	150.00 To 195.00
Figurine, Wardrobe Mistress, HN 2145	350.00 To 435.00
Figurine, Willy–Won't He, HN 2150	410.00
Figurine, Yeoman of The Guard, HN 2112	695.00
Humidor, After The Hunt	125.00
Jardiniere, Gold Scroll Body, 3 Handles, Signed, 7 In.	450.00
Jardiniere, Pierced Rim, Tapestry Design, 7 1/2 In.	200.00
Jug, DeWar's Whiskey, Brown & Tan, 5 1/4 In.	85.00
Jug, Gleaners, Corinth Shape, 5 1/2 In.	90.00
Jug, Jackdaw of Rheims, Came Limping, Herrick Shape, 5 In.	95.00
Jug, Portia, Shakespeare Ware, Marked, 6 3/8 In.	110.00
Jug, Sea Shanty, Sailors, Ship, Verses All Around, 6 3/4 In.	150.00
Jug, Welsh Ladies, Front & Back, Marked, Miniature	85.00
Jug, Welsh Ladies, Simon Shape, 6 1/2 In.	105.00
Lamp, Lambeth, Milk Glass Umbrella Shade, 12 1/4 In.	580.00
Loving Cup, Nelson	975.00
Match Holder, Dutch People, Marked, 2 3/4 In.	88.00
Match Holder, Striker, Raised Floral, Incised Leaves	85.00
Mug, Dutch Boy & Girl On Front, Boy On Back, 1 7/8 In.	50.00
Pitcher, Alfred Jingle, Dickens Ware, Square, Marked, 7 3/8 In	125.00
Pitcher, Dutch People, Man On Front, Woman On Back, 2 5/8 In.	60.00
Pitcher, Floral Center, Gold Neck & Handles, 5 In.	235.00
Pitcher, Golfer, 9 In.	495.00
Pitcher, Hogarth, Would You Know The Value of Money, 7 In.	200.00
Pitcher, Kingsware, 7 In.	200.00
Pitcher, Moorish Gate Series, 4 3/4 In.	85.00
Pitcher, Mr.Micawber, Dickens Ware, Square, Marked, 5 3/4 In.	95.00
Pitcher, Old Bob Ye Guard, Pinched Sides, 8 In.	95.00
Pitcher, Robin Hood, King of The Archers, 7 In.	145.00
Pitcher, Trotty Veck, Dickens Ware, Square, Marked, 6 5/8 In.	118.00

Plate, Automotive Series, Blood Money, 10 1/2 In. 295.00
Plate, Babes In Woods, Girl With Basket, 8 3/4 In. 230.00
Plate, Bill Sykes, Noke, 11 In. .... 55.00 To 65.00
Plate, Coach, 8 In. 22.00
Plate, Countess, 7 1/2 In. 12.00
Plate, Gibson Girl, Message From Outside World, 10 1/2 In. 85.00
Plate, Gibson Girl, Mrs.Diggs Is Alarmed, 10 1/2 In. 85.00
Plate, Gleaners, Reticulated Border, 9 1/2 In. 35.00
Plate, Robert Burns, 10 1/2 In. 50.00
Plate, Romeo, 10 In. 65.00
Plate, Sam Weller, 8 1/2 In. 58.00
Plate, Titanian, 8 3/4 In. 55.00
Plate, Tony Weller, 13 1/2 In. 125.00
Plate, Welsh Ladies, Women & Child Walking, Chapel, 10 In. 70.00
Platter, Bristol Pattern, 15 In. 45.00
Salt, Master, Devil & Cards 85.00
Sugar & Creamer, Cardinal 130.00
Sugar & Creamer, Teatime Sayings 75.00
Sugar, Sairey Gamp 350.00
Tankard, Christmas, 1971 .... 75.00
Tankard, Fisherfolk, 5 1/2 In. 75.00
Teapot, Fisherwomen Series, Sailboats, Marked, 5 1/2 X 9 In. 195.00
Teapot, Hunting, Lambeth 90.00
Teapot, Kirkwood Pattern 45.00
Teapot, Sugar & Creamer, Nursery Series 155.00
Teapot, White Flowers, Trimmed In Gold, Blue, 4 1/2 X 8 In. 85.00
Tobacco Jar, Hunting, Lambeth 80.00
Tobacco Jar, Raised Figures Smoking, Drinking, Marked, 5 In. 118.00
Toby Jug, Best Is None Too Good, 4 In. 250.00
Toby Jug, Cliff Cornell, Brown, 9 In. 250.00
Toby Jug, Double XX, 6 1/2 In. 375.00
Toby Jug, Falstaff, 5 1/4 In. 95.00
Toby Jug, Falstaff, A Mark, 8 1/2 In. 175.00
Toby Jug, Old Charley, 5 1/2 In. 125.00
Toby Jug, Old Charley, 8 3/4 In. 175.00
Toby Jug, Sam Weller, 4 1/2 In. 100.00
Toby Jug, Sir Winston Churchill, 5 1/2 In. 48.00
Tray, Egyptian, 7 1/2 X 12 In. 80.00
Tray, Koala Bear, Embossed Leaves At Rim, Marked, 5 5/8 In. 275.00
Tray, Rustic England, 5 X 10 1/2 In. 50.00
Tray, Sandwich, Bill Sykes, Dickens Ware, 5 5/8 X 11 In. 88.00
Vase, Arthur Barlow, 8 1/2 In. 150.00
Vase, Babes In Woods, Girl With Doll, 5 1/4 In. .... 265.00 To 275.00
Vase, Blacksmith Fixing Horse's Shoe, 7 1/4 In. 75.00
Vase, Cavalier, Motto, 9 In. 80.00
Vase, Dickens Ware, 2 Handles, 7 1/2 In. 145.00
Vase, Donkeys, Hannah Barlow, 12 In. 350.00
Vase, Flambe, Camels, People, Palm Trees, Pre–1930, 6 In. 400.00
Vase, Flambe, Landscape Scene, Signed, & In. 300.00
Vase, Flambe, Man Fishing In Stream, 13 1/4 In. 280.00
Vase, Flambe, Veined Sung, 7 In. 165.00
Vase, Gallant Fishers, 2 1/2 In. 70.00
Vase, Goats, Hannah Barlow, 8 1/2 In. 250.00
Vase, Gold Scroll At Top, Cobalt & White Neck, 11 In., Pair 600.00
Vase, Horses, Hannah Barlow, 13 In. 395.00
Vase, Horses, Sheep, Hannah Barlow, 12 In. 325.00
Vase, Kingfisher, Yellow Luster, 10 In. 85.00
Vase, Old Peggoty, Dickens Ware, Marked, 5 1/4 In. 79.00
Vase, Robin Hood Series, Flattened Shape, Marked, 5 1/2 In. 95.00
Vase, Sung, Flambe, 10 In. 215.00
Vase, Welsh Ladies & Childen, Walking On Path, 7 In. 165.00
Vase, Welsh Ladies, Ladies & Dog On Front, Marked, 2 1/2 In. 85.00
Wall Pocket, Owl 225.00

Royal Dux, Figurine, Man, Harlequin, Dances With Lady, 19 In.

Smoking is bad for the health of your antiques. Smoke causes discoloration and weakens textiles. Another reason to stop smoking.

The Duxer Porzellanmanufaktur was founded in Dux, Bohemia, in 1860 by E. Eichler. By the turn of the century, the firm specialized in porcelain statuary and busts of Art Nouveau–style maidens, large porcelain figures, and ornate vases with three–dimensional figures climbing on the sides. The firm is still in business.

ROYAL DUX, Basket, Flowers, Copper Wheel, Engraved, Pat.Marked, 11 In. 75.00
Basket, Handle, Young Boy, Hanging Berries, Gold Trim, 12 In. 225.00
Bowl, Young Woman, 2 Cherubs Supporting Shell Overhead, 20 In. 445.00
Bust, Shakespearean, Mask With Dagger Base, Pink Triangle, 12 In. 325.00
Candleholder, Lady, Pants Suit, Pink, Marked 250.00
Centerpiece, Nouveau Maidens Holding Shell, 2 X 16 In. 650.00
Centerpiece, Nude Women Kneeling, Art Deco, Off–White, 7 3/4 In. 375.00
Figurine, Bird, Black & White, Art Deco, 8 3/4 In. 63.00
Figurine, Boy & Girl, Playing Instrument, 11 In. 795.00
Figurine, Camel With Rider, 17 In. 395.00
Figurine, Chariot & Horses 300.00
Figurine, Courting Couple, Pink Triangle Mark, Sticker 450.00
Figurine, Courting Couple, Red & Gold Dress, Triangle Mark 275.00
Figurine, Fisherman, Boots, Net In Hat, Marked, 18 In. 635.00
Figurine, Girl, Green, Water Lily, Oval Pond, Signed, 6 In. 175.00
Figurine, Girl, With Flower, Book, On Knee, 6 In. 330.00
Figurine, Lady, Decorating Pottery, Pink Triangle, 8 X 6 In. 450.00
Figurine, Lady, Reading Book, 19 In. 750.00
Figurine, Maiden Victorian, Pink & Green Frilly Dress, 22 In. 650.00
Figurine, Maiden, Reading 850.00
Figurine, Maiden, Sits On Tree Trunk, Feet In Pool, Marked, 13 In. 750.00
Figurine, Maidens, Holding Shell, Nouveau, 22 X 16 In. 650.00
Figurine, Man, Bearded, Caftan, Camel, Servant, Marked, 24 In. 825.00
Figurine, Man, Harlequin, Dances With Lady, 19 In. .... *Illus* 325.00
Figurine, Man, Seated, Working On Pottery Jugs, 6 X 4 In. 415.00
Figurine, Mother, Child & Basket, Triangle Mark, 8 1/2 In. 395.00
Figurine, Peasant Boy & Girl, Bohemia, Satin, 11 1/2 In., Pair 550.00
Figurine, Peasant Boy & Girl, Marked, 11 1/2 In., Pair 550.00
Figurine, Polar Bear, 7 X 14 In. 185.00
Figurine, Polar Bear, Art Deco, White, 8 X 13 In. 265.00
Figurine, Shepherdess, Toga, Sheepskin Robe, Goats, 14 3/4 In. 575.00
Figurine, Victorian Woman, Rose Dress, Turquoise Bow, 14 In. 500.00
Figurine, White Owl, 12 In. 75.00
Figurine, White Polar Bear, 20 In. 475.00
Figurine, Woman With Fan, Man With Basket, Marked, 7 1/4 In., Pr. 275.00
Figurine, Woman With Lyre, Man Holding Medieval Ax, 12 In., Pr. 400.00

Figurine, Woman, Getting Dressed, No.3396, 7 3/4 In. 125.00
Group, Man, Dressed As Harlequin, Dances With Lady, 19 In. 325.00
Pitcher, Applied Fruits & Flowers, 11 In. 125.00
Plate, Figural, Rhino–Beetle, Signed, 5 X 3 1/2 In. 125.00
Vase, Art Nouveau, Dolphin Handles, 13 X 5 1/2 In. 195.00
Vase, Children, With Garlands of Flowers, Beige, Matte, 20 In. 400.00
Vase, Cyclamens In Relief, Pink Triangle Mark, 10 In. 105.00
Vase, Figures, Earth Tones, 2 Handles, Triangle Mark, 12 In. 450.00
Vase, Nouveau, Dolphin Handles, Green, Gold Trim, 13 In. 195.00
Vase, Posey, Hand Painted, 4 1/2 In. 45.00

Royal Flemish glass was made during the late 1880s in New Bedford, Massachusetts, by the Mt. Washington Glass Works. It is a colored satin glass decorated with dark colors and raised gold designs. The glass was patented in 1894. It was supposed to resemble stained glass windows.

ROYAL FLEMISH, Biscuit Jar, Roman Coins On Angular Panels, 9 3/4 In. 1450.00
Bowl, 7 Ducks, Frosted White, Signed, 9 In. 575.00
Vase, 5 Roman Medallions, Gold Bordered Panels, C.1890 .... 1985.00
Vase, Dragon Head Medallions, Rose Colored Sections, 11 In. 1700.00
Vase, Peacock On Raised Gold Bough, Jeweled Eyes, 13 In. 6750.00
Vase, Winged Gargoyle, Gold Panel Dividers, 8 In. 2450.00
  ROYAL HAEGER, see Haeger
  ROYAL IVY, see Pressed Glass, Royal Ivy
  ROYAL OAK, see Pressed Glass, Royal Oak
  ROYAL RUDOLSTADT, see Rudolstadt
  ROYAL VIENNA, see Beehive

Worcester porcelains were made in Worcester, England, from about 1751. The firm went through many different periods and name changes. It became the Worcester Royal Porcelain Company, Ltd., in 1862. Today collectors call the porcelains made after 1862 "Royal Worcester." In 1976, the firm merged with W. T. Copeland to become Royal Worcester Spode. Some early products of the factory are listed under Worcester.

ROYAL WORCESTER, Basket, Red, Blue, 1891, 12 In. 325.00
Biscuit Jar, Cobalt Blue Leaves On White Bamboo, 7 In. 350.00
Biscuit Jar, Embossed Swirl Ribs, Flowers, 7 1/4 In. 295.00
Bowl, Oriental Rust & Cream Flowers, Silver Plated, 6 In. 247.00
Candelabra, Child Musicians, 3–Light, 1889, 20 1/2 In., Pair 1980.00
Candleholder, Horn, Ivory With Gold Trim, C.1889 .... 175.00
Candlesnuffer, Monk 38.00
Candlesnuffer, Plumed Hat, White, Pink 65.00
Candlestick, Figural, Green Mark, Boy, Girl, Pug Dog, 12 In. 250.00
Coffeepot, Matte Finish, Lid, Marked 1876, 9 In. 175.00
Creamer, Lydia 25.00
Dish, Phoenix On Cover, Blue, White, Elephant Handles 250.00
Egg Coddler, Blue Willow, Ring Finial, 1927, 2 5/8 In. 35.00
Ewer, Flying Swans, Matte Blue Ground, Marked, 1895, 17 In. 1210.00
Ewer, Lighthouse Shape, Gold Flowers, Purple Mark, 10 In. 225.00
Figurine, Anne Boleyn, Blue Gown, Gold Coat, 8 1/2 In. 350.00
Figurine, Eastern Water Carrier, C.1895, 10 1/2 In. 500.00
Figurine, Eastern Water Carriers, Colored, 21 In., Pair 1850.00
Figurine, Grandmother's Dress, Green 55.00
Figurine, Indian, Rifle, Flowing Robe, C.1890, 19 In., Pair 1500.00
Figurine, Ireland, No.3178, 1936 .... 225.00
Figurine, Joan 90.00
Figurine, Mary, Queen of Scots, Floral Dress, 8 1/2 In. 350.00
Figurine, Parakeet, Blue, On Flowered Stump, 1940s 85.00
Figurine, Persian Kitten, Blue 3 1/2 In. 65.00
Figurine, Ring, Rider On 3 Circus Horses 1200.00
Figurine, Sleepy Boy 125.00
Figurine, Sweet Anne, No.3630 .... 110.00 To 150.00
Game Plate, Fish, 10 1/2 In. 25.00

Gravy Boat, Lavinia	35.00
Jar, Cover, Butterfly & Flowers, 1850, 3 In.	95.00
Jardiniere, Reticulated Design, Roses, Gilt, 1909, 14 In.	1200.00
Loving Cup, Florals, Beige Ground, Gold Handles, 7 1/2 In.	215.00
Pitcher, Bundled Vines Handle, Ivory Ground, 10 1/4 In.	60.00
Pitcher, Florals, Cream, Orange Gold Handle, 8 In.	185.00
Pitcher, Flowers, Red Trimmed Gold Ribbing, 10 1/4 In.	235.00
Pitcher, Gold Outlined Flowers, 1901, 4 1/4 In.	88.00
Pitcher, Gold Outlined Pink Flowers, Marked, 6 In.	125.00
Pitcher, Hot Milk, Floral, Metal Lid, 8 In.	175.00
Pitcher, Ivory, Flat Back, Gold Floral Gold, 1894, 5 In.	40.00
Pitcher, Lighthouse, Gold Flowers, Purple Mark, 10 1/4 In.	235.00
Pitcher, Lion Head Spout, Paw Handle, Registry Mark, 7 In.	325.00
Pitcher, Reptile Handle, Ivory, 19th Century, 7 In.	90.00
Plaque, Highland Cattle Grazing, River, Misty, Oval, 10 In.	2200.00
Plate, Bicentennial, Eagle, Gold Trim, 10 1/2 In.	85.00
Plate, Landscape Scene, Blue & Gilt Rim, Marked, 8 7/8 In.	49.00
Plate, Man, Fishing, Trees, Mountain Tops, 9 1/2 In.	250.00
Platter, Lavinia, 13 1/2 In.	35.00
Pot, Woman's Head Spout, Cover, Basket Weave Handle	750.00
Sugar Shaker, Figural, Girl, Hat, Gold Trim, 7 1/2 In.	395.00
Teapot, Lydia	55.00
Toby, Jester	125.00
Vase, Blue Flowers, Tan Leaves, Salamander Handle, 9 In.	450.00
Vase, Elephant Head Handles, C.1895, 9 1/4 In., Pair	400.00
Vase, Floral, Gilded, Reticulated Handles, C.1890, 14 In.	475.00
Vase, Hand, Parian, Registry Mark, 1864, 6 In.	75.00
Vase, Irises, Ivory Ground, Bulbous, Cover, Handle, 12 In.	375.00
Vase, Landscape, Peacocks, Pierced Cover, C.1903, 8 1/2 In.	1300.00
Vase, Reticulated, 8 1/4 In.	225.00
Wall Pocket, Cherub Attacks Net On Fruit Tree, 8 1/2 In.	225.00

Roycroft products were made by the Roycrofter community of East Aurora, New York, in the late nineteenth and early twentieth centuries. The community was founded by Elbert Hubbard, famous philosopher, writer, and artist. The workshops owned by the community made furniture, metalware, leatherwork, embroidery, and jewelry. A printshop produced many signs, books, and the magazines that promoted the sayings of Elbert Hubbard. Furniture by the Roycroft community is listed in the furniture section.

ROYCROFT, Ashtray, Floor, Copper, Oak, Strap Handle On Matchbox, Logo, 29 In.	175.00
Ashtray, Stacking, Stylized Flower, Squat, Logo, 4 In., 2 Piece	40.00
Bookends, Embossed Poppies, Brass On Copper, 5 In.	250.00
Bookends, Floral Design, 5 X 4 1/2 In.	65.00
Bookends, Hammered Copper, 6 7/8 X 8 1/2 In.	30.00
Bookends, Semicircular Arch, Rectangular Plate, Washed, 3 1/2 In.	125.00
Bookends, Stylized Repousse Flower, Hammered, 8 1/2 X 5 3/4 In.	55.00
Bowl, Dark Brown Glossy Glaze, 5 X 10 1/2 In.	90.00
Box, Cigar, Copper, Medallion, Cedar Lined, Logo, 1910, 2 X 9 X 6 In.	400.00
Box, Cigarette, Hinged	60.00
Box, Stamp, With Penholder, Marked	130.00
Candelabra, 2 Short Arms, Twisted Standard, Logo, 20 X 9 In., Pair	750.00
Candelabra, 3–Light, Twisted Signed, 20 In., Pair	750.00
Candlestick, Flattened Rim, Cylindrical Standard, 10 In., Pair	300.00
Candlestick, Hammered Copper, Cylindrical Stem, Signed, 8 In., Pair	150.00
Candlestick, Twist Standard Base, 12 3/4 In., Pair	135.00
Catalog, Leather Copper Mottos, Elbert Hubbard, 1910, 9 In.	40.00
Console Set, Square Flowers, Silver Washed, Square Candlesticks	250.00
Frame, Picture, Brass, Desk Size	30.00
Inkwell, Glass Insert, Brass	40.00
Jar, Tan, Cover, 4 3/4 In.	18.00
Jug, Little Brown, Marked	24.00
Lamp, Hammered Copper, Mica Paneled Dome, Logo, C.1910, 13 3/4 In.	950.00
Lamp, Kerosene, Sweetheart	150.00

Mustard, Cover	38.00
Platter, Handle, Oval, 22 In.	175.00
Vase, Bellflower, 6 In.	185.00
Vase, Copper, 4 1/2 In.	190.00
Vase, Hammered Copper, Embossed Band, Signed, 4 5/8 X 4 5/8 In.	125.00

ROZANE, see Roseville

RRP is the mark used by the firm of Robinson–Ransbottom. It is not a mark of the more famous Roseville Pottery. The Ransbottom brothers started a pottery in 1900 in Ironspot, Ohio. In 1920, they merged with the Robinson Clay Product Company of Akron, Ohio, to become Robinson–Ransbottom. The factory is still working.

RRP CO., Ashtray, Anniversary, 1951	12.00
Bowl, Blue, 6 In.	35.00
Cookie Jar, Cow Jumped Over The Moon, Gold Trim	75.00
Cookie Jar, Peter, Peter	50.00
Pitcher, Blue, Raised Flowers, 8 In.	45.00

The RS Germany mark was used on porcelain made at the factory of Reinhold Schlegelmilch from about 1910 to 1956 in Tillowitz, Germany. It was sold decorated and undecorated. The Schlegelmilch family made porcelains marked in many ways. Each type is listed separately. See also ES Germany, RS Poland, RS Prussia, RS Silesia, RS Suhl, and RS Tillowitz.

RS GERMANY, Ashtray, Red Poppies	35.00
Basket, Lily–of–The–Valley, Gold Edge, 4 1/2 X 5 1/2 In.	155.00
Berry Set, Pink & Gray Floral, 7 Piece	120.00
Bowl, Floral Design, Marked, 10 1/2 In.	50.00
Bowl, Lady With Cows, Near Cottage, Handles, 10 In.	255.00
Bowl, Pheasants, Allover Color, 10 In.	195.00
Bowl, Pink, White Floral On Cream To Blue, Gold, 9 In.	75.00
Bowl, Scattered Flowers, Marked, 9 1/2 In.	85.00
Bowl, Water Lilies, Gold Water Design, Steeple Mark, 10 1/2 In.	600.00
Cake Plate, 2 Parrots, Yellow	185.00
Cake Plate, Multicolored Bouquet, Greens & Browns Ground	50.00
Cake Plate, Parrots, On Vine, Yellow, Open Handles, Green Mark	225.00
Cake Plate, White Carnations On Green, 10 In.	75.00
Candy Dish, White Camellias, Green & White, Handles, 8 X 4 In.	35.00
Cheese Server, Orange Tulip, Art Deco	70.00
Chocolate Pot, White Rose Florals, Blue Mark, Demitasse	85.00
Chocolate Set, Lacy Gold Borders, Gray Ground, 7 Piece	285.00
Coffeepot, Cobalt Blue, Steeple Mark	395.00
Cracker Jar, Roses	65.00
Creamer, Cabbage Leaf	30.00
Cup & Saucer, Chocolate, Roses, Gold Trim, Blue Mark, Set of 6	75.00
Dish, Cheese & Cracker, Roses, Stems, Leaves, 2–Tiered	70.00
Dresser Set, Pink Tulip Design, Hatpin Holder, Marked, 3 Piece	175.00
Dresser Set, Sweet Pea Design, Marked, 3 Piece	175.00
Dresser Set, Tulip Design, Green Mark, 3 Piece	175.00
Hair Receiver, Lilies, Footed	95.00
Hatpin Holder, Floral	59.50
Holder, Condensed Milk, Underplate, Bands of Gold, 5 In.	145.00
Holder, Toothbrush, Yellow Floral	49.50
Jam Jar, Underplate, Violets	125.00
Lamp, Fairy, Owl, Pair	565.00
Mustard, Cover, Roses	22.00
Nut Set, Master Bowl, 6 Matching Bowls	300.00
Plate, Floral, Gold Beading, Marked, 6 1/2 In.	100.00
Plate, Flowers, Saying, Hand Painted, 2 Handles, 9 1/2 In.	40.00
Plate, Snowbird, Marked, 8 1/8 In.	175.00
Relish, Florals, 8 1/2 In.	22.00
Relish, Orange Poppies, Gray Ground, Open Handles, 11 In.	60.00
Relish, Pansies, Beaded Edge, Oval, Open Handles	85.00

Relish, Pansy Design, Scalloped, Oval	45.00
Sugar & Creamer, Iris, 2 1/2 In.	30.00
Sugar & Creamer, Peonies, Pink	55.00
Sugar & Creamer, Violets, Pink Roses	75.00
Sugar & Creamer, White, Purple Iris, 2 1/2 In.	47.00
Syrup, Mill Scene, Green Mark	75.00
Toothpick, Day Lily, White & Green Ground, 3 Handles	100.00
Toothpick, Florals, 2 Handles	65.00
Tray, Pink & White Roses, Shadowy Flowers, 12 1/2 In.	45.00
Tray, Sheepherder & Mill Scene, Handles, 11 1/2 X 7 1/4 In.	255.00

The RS Poland (German) mark was used by the Reinhold Schlegelmilch factory at Tillowitz from about 1945 to 1956. This is one of many of the RS marks used. See also ES Germany, RS Germany, RS Prussia, RS Silesia, RS Suhl, and RS Tillowitz.

RS POLAND, Dresser Set, Floral Pinks & Greens, 12 In.Tray, Marked	345.00
Flower Holder, Brass Frog Insert, Pheasants, Marked	675.00
Planter, Pink Floral Band, Gold Highlights, Pedestal, 6 3/4 In.	230.00
Plate, Dogwood & Pine, 8 In.	95.00
Vase, Roses In White & Beige, Gold & Brown Ground, 8 3/4 In.	148.00
Vase, Swan, Lake & Trees, 7 In.	275.00

"RS Prussia" is a mark that appears on porcelain made at the factory of Reinhold Schlegelmilch from the late 1870s to 1914 in Tillowitz, Germany, or on items made at the Erdmann Schlegelmilch factory in Suhl, Germany, from about 1910 to 1956. It was sold decorated or undecorated. The factories were owned by brothers. See also ES Germany, RS Germany, RS Poland, RS Silesia, RS Suhl, and RS Tillowitz.

RS PRUSSIA, Bell, Dinner, Pink, Green Stem, Wooden Clapper, 3 1/2 In.	215.00
Berry Bowl, Blown-Out Iris, Pink Roses, Daisies, Marked, 10 In.	285.00
Berry Bowl, Pink Roses & Chrysanthemums, Scalloped Border	125.00
Berry Bowl, Swans On Lake, Swallows Overhead, Red Mark	220.00
Berry Set, Blown-Out Iris, Carnations, Greens, Red Mark, 5 Piece	295.00
Berry Set, Red & Pink Roses, 7 Piece	350.00
Bone Dish, Flowers, Red Mark	85.00
Bowl, 5 Medallion Border, Grapes, Gold Pleated, 10 1/2 In.	220.00
Bowl, 7 Bluebirds Over Cottage, Pointed Edge, Red Mark, 11 In.	475.00
Bowl, Beaded Rim, Center Poppies, Gold Trim, 9 1/4 In.	125.00
Bowl, Blown-Out Iris Mold, Red Mark, 10 In.	225.00
Bowl, Bowl-In-Bowl, Poppies, Gold Trim, Red Mark	135.00
Bowl, Bust of Woman Center, 10 1/2 In.	100.00
Bowl, Carnation Mold, Blue & Pink Poppies, 3 X 11 1/2 In.	400.00
Bowl, Carnation Mold, Pink & White Roses, Red Mark, 10 1/4 In.	235.00
Bowl, Carnation Mold, Pink Roses, Green, Red Mark, 12 In.	375.00
Bowl, Carnation, Pink & Yellow Roses, Red Mark, 14 3/4 In.	775.00
Bowl, Centerpiece, Carnation Mold, Center Poppies, 11 1/2 In.	400.00
Bowl, Cluster of Roses, Red Mark, 10 1/4 In.	90.00
Bowl, Dogwood, 4 Foot, Ruffled, Red Mark, 6 1/2 In.	75.00
Bowl, Dogwood, Lustre Finish, Green Tints, Red Mark, 10 X 3 In.	179.00
Bowl, Floral Spray In Ivory Field, Red Mark, 10 1/2 In.	90.00
Bowl, Floral, Blown-Out Rim, Green & White, 9 In.	95.00
Bowl, Floral, Cobalt Blue, Double Circle Mark, 9 1/2 In.	95.00
Bowl, Floral, Footed, 3 1/2 X 7 In.	125.00
Bowl, Floriform, Young Woman, Ribbon In Hair, 10 In. ....*Illus*	400.00
Bowl, Gold Star Royal Berlin Mark, 5 In.	175.00
Bowl, Green, White, 5 In.	18.00
Bowl, Hanging Basket of Flowers, Shadows, Red Mark, 11 In.	250.00
Bowl, Lavender Flowers & Trim, Red Mark, 11 In.	175.00
Bowl, Lavender, Blue, Gold, Floral, 4 Footed, 9 X 7 In.	210.00
Bowl, Mill Scene, Oval, Yellow & Brown Tints, 13 X 8 1/4 In.	595.00
Bowl, Molded Poppy, Pink Shading, Gold Trim, 9 1/2 In.	140.00
Bowl, Pedestal, Red Roses In & Out, Red Mark, 9 In.	135.00
Bowl, Pink Roses, Daisies, Gold, Tulip Mold, Red Mark, 10 3/4 In.	95.00

Bowl, Pink Roses, Shadow Leaves, Handle, Red Mark, 3 X 6 1/4 In. 150.00
Bowl, Pink, Red Roses, Gold Tracery, Blown–Out Irises, 10 In. 199.00
Bowl, Poppies, Gold Trim, Red Mark, 9 1/4 In. 150.00
Bowl, Poppy Mold, 14 1/2 In. ....*Illus* 1200.00
Bowl, Portrait of Woman, Ribbon In Hair, 10 1/2 In. 400.00
Bowl, Ribbon & Jewel Mold, Roses, Red Mark, 9 In. 130.00
Bowl, Ripple & Quilt Mold, Roses, Red Mark, 10 3/4 In. 170.00
Bowl, Rose Design On White Ground, Red Mark, 10 In. 110.00
Bowl, Roses, Blown–Out Lily Pads, 10 In. 50.00
Bowl, Satin Finish, Molded Points & Scallops, 11 In. 295.00
Bowl, Scattered Flowers, Red Mark, 10 1/2 In. 110.00
Bowl, Spiky Leaves, Cobblestone Rim, Red Mark, 10 In. 265.00
Butter, Liner, Cream, Melon Ribbed, Wild Roses, Blue Daisies 275.00
Cake Plate, 4 Swans, Red Mark 350.00
Cake Plate, Barnyard, Pheasant, Icicle Mold, Wheelock, 10 In. ..../ 750.00
Cake Plate, Deep Yellow, Parrots, Hanging Leaf Vine, Marked 225.00
Cake Plate, Fan Shaped Rim Designs, Roses, Red Mark, 10 3/4 In. 175.00
Cake Plate, Floral, Red Mark, 9 1/2 In. 85.00
Cake Plate, Icicle Mold, Blown Flowers, Handles, Red Mark, 10 In. 160.00
Cake Plate, Icicle Mold, Poppies, Pierced Handles, 11 In. 145.00
Cake Plate, Icicle Mold, Swans, Lily Pads, Red Mark, 10 3/4 In. 475.00
Cake Plate, Jonquils, Cobalt Blue 245.00
Cake Plate, Pink & Yellow Roses, Pearlized, Red Mark, 11 In. 235.00
Cake Plate, Pink Poppy On Green, Red Mark, 10 In. 185.00
Cake Plate, Pink Roses, Scalloped Border, Red Mark 37.00
Cake Plate, Scalloped, Open Handles, Roses, Red Mark, 11 1/2 In. 135.00
Cake Plate, Sunflower Mold, Open Handles, 11 In. 350.00
Celery, 3 Swans, Lake, 13 1/2 X 6 3/4 In. 750.00
Celery, Blown–Out Carnation Mold, Roses, Red Mark, 12 1/2 In. 145.00
Celery, Blown–Out Iris, Fall Season, Red Mark 750.00
Celery, Lily Mold, Green Shadows, Roses, 12 1/2 In. 75.00
Celery, Roses, Pink Ground, Red Mark, 14 X 7 In. 170.00
Celery, Sunflower, Pink & White Roses, Red Mark, 12 1/2 In. 2200.00
Chocolate Pot, Calla Lily, Satin Finish, Red Mark 310.00
Chocolate Pot, Cottage Scene, Browns, Red Mark 775.00
Chocolate Pot, Florals, Red Mark, 8 1/2 In. 145.00
Chocolate Pot, Flowers Reflected In Water, Red Mark, 10 1/2 In. 225.00
Chocolate Pot, Hand Painted & Transfer, Gold Handle, Red Mark 1000.00
Chocolate Pot, Ivy Design, 10 In. 295.00
Chocolate Pot, Pink Roses, Red Mark, 10 In. 175.00
Chocolate Pot, Roses, Purple & Green Luster, Red Mark, 10 In. 595.00
Chocolate Set, Brown & Tan, With Snowballs, Red Mark, 6 Piece 900.00

RS Prussia, Bowl, Floriform, Young Woman,   RS Prussia, Plate, Woman, Dogwood Flowers,
Ribbon In Hair, 10 In.   7 In.

Chocolate Set, Carnation Mold, Red Mark, 11 Piece	895.00
Chocolate Set, Dogwood Blossoms, Green Luster, Red Mark, 7 Pc.	925.00
Chocolate Set, Lavender Floral, Red Mark, C.1870, 8 Piece	1800.00
Chocolate Set, Pink Flowers, Dark Green, Red Mark, 9 Piece	800.00
Cocoa Set, Dark Green, Pink Bachelor Button Flowers, Red Mark	800.00
Compote, Christmas Roses & Holly Berries, Red Mark	195.00
Compote, Green Floral, Signed, 4 In.	85.00
Cracker Jar, Melon Boy, Red Mark	1350.00
Cracker Jar, Pink Roses, Fleur-De-Lis Feet, Crown Mark	325.00
Cracker Jar, Reflecting Roses, Red Mark	325.00
Creamer, Blue & Pink, Gold Handle, 3 In.	65.00
Creamer, Cottage Scene, Green, Red Mark	185.00
Creamer, Mill Scene, Paneled Foot	80.00
Creamer, Pink & White Roses, Gold Swags, Green Ground, 6-Footed	55.00
Creamer, Underplate, Pastels, Red Mark, 5 In.	175.00
Cup & Saucer, Coca, Swan Design, Water, Mountain, Castle, Marked	235.00
Cup & Saucer, Floral, Gold Trim, Red Mark, Demitasse	125.00
Cup & Saucer, Iris Mold, Green Shadows, Pink Poppies, Demitasse	75.00
Cup & Saucer, Jeweled Satin Floral, Demitasse, 6 Piece	300.00
Cup, Ornate Roses, Footed, Red Mark .... 35.00 To 55.00
Dish, Christmas Rose, Footed, Red Mark, 10 In.	215.00
Dish, Cover, Floral Design, Orange Ground, Green Mark, 5 1/2 In.	80.00
Dish, Fleur-De-Lis Around Edge, Red Mark, 13 1/2 X 6 1/2 In.	175.00
Dish, Olive, Purple Azaleas, Red Mark, 9 In.	135.00
Dish, Pin, Hidden Image, Pink Orchids, Cover, Gold Trim	135.00
Dish, Pin, Sheepherder	145.00
Ewer, Girl In Landscape, Holding Bough, Red Mark, 6 In.	325.00
Fernery, Yellow, Pink Roses, Red Star Mark	225.00
Hatpin Holder, Attached Underplate, Flowers, Red Mark	65.00
Hatpin Holder, Bluebird Scene, 6 Sides, Red Mark	275.00
Hatpin Holder, Cottage Scene, With Bluebirds, Red Mark	425.00
Hatpin Holder, Floral Design, White Ground, Marked, 4 1/2 In.	95.00
Hatpin Holder, Floral Designs On White, Red Mark, Wreath, 4 In.	95.00
Hatpin Holder, Roses, Luster Finish, Scalloped Base, 4 3/4 In.	235.00
Hatpin Holder, Roses, Signed, 4 In.	215.00
Hatpin Holder, Snow & Ice Design	3400.00
Muffineer, Scalloped Base, Roses, Pearlized, 5 In.	235.00
Mustard, Floral, Cover, Spoon, 6 Foot, Red Mark	85.00
Mustard, Red & Pink Roses, Green Footed, Red Mark	175.00
Mustard, Spoon, Underplate, Dogwood Blossoms, Gold Enameled	165.00
Nut Dish, Christmas Roses, White, Footed, Red Mark, 3 X 6 In.	65.00
Nut Set, Calla Lily Pattern, 5 Piece	165.00
Pickle, Roses, Blues, Scalloped, Red Mark	67.50
Pitcher, Lemonade, Carnation Mold, Pink Roses, Red Mark, 9 In.	650.00
Pitcher, Milk, Blown-Out Iris Mold, Steeple Mark, 10 In.	350.00
Pitcher, Milk, Pink & White Flowers, Red Mark, 6 In.	285.00
Pitcher, Water, Roses On Shaded Ground, Red Mark, 6 1/2 In.	95.00
Plate, 3 Cherubs, Satin Finish, 2 Handles, Signed, 11 In.	295.00
Plate, 3 Kittens, Red Mark, 8 1/2 In.	130.00
Plate, 6 Scallops, Artist Signed, 11 In.	225.00
Plate, Cake, Gaston Mold, Pansies On Green, Gold, 11 In.	275.00
Plate, Carnation Mold, Pierced Handle, Red Mark, 10 1/2 In.	125.00
Plate, Castle Scene, Browns & Yellows, Red Mark, 10 1/2 In.	550.00
Plate, Cherub & Floral, Red Mark, 11 In.	300.00
Plate, Fall Season, Iris Mold, 9 In.	325.00
Plate, Gaston Mold, Purple Daisies On Green, 8 In.	135.00
Plate, Icicle Mold, Sitting Basket of Flowers, 10 1/4 In.	300.00
Plate, Jewel & Ribbon Mold, Open Handle, Red Mark, 10 1/2 In.	265.00
Plate, Jonquils, Cobalt, 10 In.	295.00
Plate, Lily Design, Blue Mark, 8 1/2 In.	50.00
Plate, Monk, Dark Green, Gold Deco, St.Kilian Mark, 10 In.	300.00
Plate, Old Man of The Mountain, Scenic Cove, Red Mark, 8 1/2 In.	325.00
Plate, Red Roses, Gold, 10 In.	150.00
Plate, Ribbons & Jewels, Gold Outlined, 10 1/2 In.	240.00

RS Prussia

Tankard, Poppy Mold, Gold Design, Bowl, Poppy Mold, 14 1/2 In.,
Tankard, Satin, 6 Flower Design

Plate, Shell & Leaf Design, Inner Rim Shells, Red Mark, 11 In.	155.00
Plate, Spring Season, Lily Mold, Red Mark, 8 3/4 In.	750.00
Plate, Summer Season, Iris Mold, 8 In.	750.00
Plate, Tankard, White Snowballs, 10 1/2 In.	300.00
Plate, White Flowers, Scalloped Gold Edge, Handle, 9 1/2 In.	95.00
Plate, Woman, Dogwood Flowers, 7 In. ....*Illus*	500.00
Powder Box, Roses, Pearl Finish, Red Mark	110.00
Relish, Center Roses, Pink Border, Sawtooth Mold, 9 1/2 In.	175.00
Relish, Green, Dark Green Leaves, Tiffany Finish Edge, Red Mark	45.00
Relish, Open Roses, Foliage, Gold Stenciled, Red Mark, 12 1/2 In.	90.00
Relish, Winter Season, Iris Mold, Oblong	500.00
Salad Bowl, Roses, White Ground, Red Mark, 10 In.	325.00
Sugar & Creamer, Carnation Mold, Lavender, Red Mark	295.00
Sugar & Creamer, Floral, Green Base, Red Mark	100.00
Sugar & Creamer, Lilies-of-The-Valley, Gold Stems, Red Mark	250.00
Sugar & Creamer, Pearlized Dogwood, Gold Trim, Red Mark	150.00
Sugar & Creamer, Pedestal, Roses, Pink, Red Mark	195.00
Sugar & Creamer, Pink Roses, Gold Tracery, Pedestal, Red Mark	95.00
Sugar & Creamer, Pink Roses, Small Footed, Red Mark	325.00
Sugar & Creamer, Poppy Design, Light Green, White & Red	95.00
Sugar & Creamer, Roses, Red Star Mark	135.00
Sugar & Creamer, Water Lilies, Footed Icicle Mold, Red Mark	275.00
Sugar, Cover, Swan, Pedestal, Red Mark	275.00
Sugar, Green Florals, Gold, Fleur-De-Lis Shaped Feet, Red Mark	125.00
Sugar, Scalloped Seashells, Pedestal, Turquoise & Yellow	75.00
Syrup, Canterbury Bells, Red Mark	135.00
Syrup, Medallion Mold, Diana The Huntress, Red Mark	300.00
Syrup, Underplate, Turquoise, Gold Trim, Red Mark	225.00
Tankard, Cobalt Blue, Victorian Lady Watering Flowers, 14 In.	2100.00
Tankard, Poppy Mold, Gold Design ....*Illus*	750.00
Tankard, Rose & Snowball, Marked, 11 In.	425.00
Tankard, Satin, 6 Flower Design ....*Illus*	800.00
Tea Strainer, With Undercup, Pink Flowers, 6 In.	150.00
Tea Tile, Peach, Tan, White Snowballs, Round, Marked	150.00
Teapot, Dogwood, 6 In.	225.00
Teapot, Foliate Form, 6 In.	90.00
Teapot, Iris Mold, Pink Roses, Red Mark	300.00
Teapot, Roses, Satin Finish, Pale Peach, 6 1/4 In.	245.00
Toothpick, Blue, Roses, 2 Handles	95.00
Toothpick, Double Handles, Jeweled Feet, Roses, Shadows	250.00
Tray, Blown-Out Iris, Red Mark, 5 1/2 In.	105.00
Tray, Bun, Melon Boy, Brown, Red Mark	650.00
Tray, Center Scene of Mill, Scalloped, Red Mark, 10 1/2 In.	140.00
Tray, Dresser, Floral, Irregular Edge, 7 1/4 X 11 3/4 In.	110.00
Tray, Dresser, Hidden Image, Art Nouveau Woman, Handles, Marked	255.00
Tray, Dresser, Point & Clover, Roses, Red Mark, 11 X 7 3/4 In.	135.00
Tray, Dresser, Poppies, Carnation Mold, Red Mark	330.00

Tray, Hidden Image, Blown–Out Lily Mold, 7 X 10 1/2 In.	325.00
Tray, Hidden Image, Iris, Head of Woman, 10 X 7 In.	295.00
Tray, Lily Pads On Water, Handles, Red Mark, 11 1/2 X 7 1/2 In.	95.00
Tray, Point & Clover, Pink Roses, Red Mark, 11 1/2 X 7 3/4 In.	145.00
Tray, Portrait, Floral Border, 11 3/4 In.	400.00
Urn, Portrait, Belles of Linden	625.00
Vase, Cottage Scene, Green Tint, Blown–Out Lily, 9 1/4 In.	450.00
Vase, Lady With Fan, Cobalt Blue, Floral Mold, 8 1/2 In.	595.00
Vase, Poppies, Double Scroll Handles, Red Mark, 9 In., Pair	375.00
Vase, Purple Bottom, Shaded To Shadow Leaves Top, Roses, 6 In.	325.00
Vase, Roses, Scalloped Base, Neck, Gold Handles, 9 In.	345.00
Vase, Sheepherder, Pink Flowering Trees, Red Mark, 9 1/2 In.	700.00
Vase, Spring Season, 2 Handles, Keyhole, 10 In.	825.00

The RS Silesia mark appears on porcelain made at the Reinhold Schlegelmilch factory in Tillowitz, Germany, from about 1920 to the mid–1930s. The Schlegelmilch family made porcelains marked in many ways. Each type is listed separately. See also ES Germany, RS Germany, RS Poland, RS Prussia, RS Suhl, and RS Tillowitz.

RS SILESIA, Cake Set, Red Fuchsia, 7 Piece	65.00
Syrup, Floral, Cream To Brown, Marked	35.00

RS Suhl was a mark used by the Erdmann Schlegelmilch factory in Suhl, Germany, from c.1900 to the mid–1920s. The factory worked from 1861 to 1925. The Schlegelmilch family made porcelains in many places. See also ES Germany, RS Germany, RS Poland, RS Prussia, RS Silesia, and RS Tillowitz.

RS SUHL, Bowl, Open Roses, White, Pink, Green Border, 9 1/4 In.	65.00
Cup & Saucer, Portrait	100.00

The RS Tillowitz mark was used by the Reinhold Schlegelmilch factory at Tillowitz, near Silesia, from about 1920 to the mid–1930s. Table services and ornamental pieces were made. See also ES Germany, RS Germany, RS Poland, RS Prussia, RS Silesia, and RS Suhl.

RS TILLOWITZ, Sugar & Creamer, Pink Roses	55.00
Sugar & Creamer, Yellow & Salmon Roses	45.00
Tea Set, Art Deco	75.00
Tray, Fuchsias, 10 1/2 In.	35.00
Vase, Floral, 8 In.	85.00

Rubena Verde is a Victorian glassware that was shaded from red to green. It was first made by Hobbs, Brockunier and Company of Wheeling, West Virginia, about 1890.

RUBENA VERDE, Ashtray, 4 X 8 1/2 In.	60.00
Bowl, Honeycomb, Rolled Rim, Footed, 9 X 5 1/4 In.	100.00
Bowl, Opalescent Crimped Top, Rigaree, Shell Feet, 5 1/2 In.	95.00
Butter, Cover, Inverted Thumbprint	85.00
Creamer	40.00
Cruet, Inverted Thumbprint	125.00
Epergne, Lily, Applied Rigaree, 16 In., Pair	495.00
Pitcher, Blown Glass, Dark Red To Dark Green, 9 In.	65.00
Pitcher, Bull's-Eye .... 285.00 To 300.00	
Pitcher, Inverted Thumbprint, Quadruple Top, 6 1/2 In.	260.00
Vase, 12 In. .... 65.00 To 75.00	
Vase, Applied Gold Design, Polished Pontil, 12 3/4 In.	150.00
Vase, Jack–In–The–Pulpit, 7 1/4 In.	135.00
Vase, Ruffled Top, 6 In.	115.00

Rubena is a glassware that shades from red to clear. It was first made by George Duncan and Sons of Pittsburgh, Pennsylvania, about 1885. This coloring was used on many types of glassware. The pressed glass patterns of Royal Ivy and Royal Oak are listed under Pressed Glass.

RUBENA, Compote, Blown, Gold Enameled Flowers, 5 In.	85.00
Compote, Honeycomb, Low, Footed	95.00
Cruet, Baby Thumbprint, Original Stopper	60.00
Cruet, Petticoat, Inverted Thumbprint, Original Stopper	385.00
Jam Dish, Silver Plated Basket Holder, Cranberry Insert, 6 In.	110.00
Mug, Marked Brother, Clear Handle	55.00
Pitcher, Beater, Clear Reeded Handle, 10 In.	185.00
Pitcher, Etched Design, 8 1/2 In.	175.00
Pitcher, Hobnail, Bulbous Bottom, Quatrefoil Rim, Hobbs	175.00
Pitcher, Inverted Thumbprint	150.00
Pitcher, Optic Rib, Applied Clear Handle, 5 1/2 In.	75.00
Pitcher, Water, Opalescent Stripe, Burlington Mark	215.00
Pitcher, Water, Quatrefoil, Daisy, Bulbous	55.00
Pitcher, Water, Scottish Moor	225.00
Salt, Petal Top Insert, Crystal Collar, Basket Holder, 3 1/2 In.	130.00
Shade, Ruffled, Allover Floral Design, 7 5/8 In.	175.00
Vase, Bud, Rose, Gold Overlay, 7 In.	45.00
Vase, Melon, Ribbed, Ruffled Top, Beaded, Floral Design, 6 In.	310.00
Vase, Primrose, Blown, 7 In.	125.00
Vase, Verde, Enameled Gold Foliage, 10 In.	150.00
Water Set, Floral Design, Outlined In Gold, Crystal Handle, 7 Piece	880.00

Ruby glass is the dark red color of the precious gemstone known as a ruby. It was a popular Victorian color that never went completely out of style. The glass was shaped by many different processes to make many different types of ruby glass. There was a revival of interest in the 1940s when modern shaped ruby table glassware became fashionable. Sometimes the red color is added to clear glass by a process called flashing or staining. Flashed glass is clear glass dipped in a colored glass, then pressed or cut. Stained glass has color painted on a clear glass. Then it is refired so the stain fuses with the glass. Pieces of glass colored in this way are indicated by the word "stained" in the description.

RUBY GLASS, see also Cranberry Glass; Pressed Glass; Souvenir

RUBY GLASS, Bell, Enameled Floral Design, Gold Handles, Set of 4	20.00
Berry Bowl, Master, Fancy Diamonds	30.00
Berry Set, Thumbprint, 13 Piece	525.00
Butter, Fern & Berry, Cover, Daisy & Fern, O'Hara Diamond, Stain	110.00
Butter, Fleur-De-Lis, Gold Trim, Cover	75.00
Butter, O'Hara Diamond, Etched, Cover	110.00
Butter, Prize, Cover	75.00
Butter, Royal Crystal, Stained	175.00
Butter, Thumbprint, Cover	140.00
Compote, Clear Controlled Bubble Stem, Polished Pontil	95.00
Compote, Double Daisy, Open	155.00
Compote, Scalloped 6-Point, Open	65.00
Compote, Thumbprint Etched, Stained, 7 3/8 X 7 In.	145.00
Cordial, Thumbprint, Stained	40.00
Cracker Jar, Beaded Drapery	185.00
Creamer, Button Arches, Souvenir	45.00
Creamer, Frost Crystal With Gold	45.00
Creamer, O'Hara Diamond	65.00
Creamer, Thumbprint With Fern & Berry	45.00
Creamer, Triple Triangle	60.00
Creamer, Truncated Cube, Miniature	35.00
Cruet, 7 In.	95.00
Cruet, Beaded Swirl & Lens, Original Stopper	75.00
Cruet, Button Arches, Frosted Band, Gold Trim	175.00
Cruet, Flower & Pleat	165.00
Cruet, Inverted Thumbprint	225.00
Cruet, Original Stopper, Red Stained	135.00
Cup, Souvenir, Mary, 1897, Stained	42.00
Goblet, Henrietta	45.00
Goblet, Loop & Block	35.00

Goblet, Red Block	48.00
Goblet, Ruby Thumbprint, Souvenir, Janesville, Wisconsin	45.00
Goblet, Triple Triangle	59.00
Jar, Sweetmeat, Bale	265.00
Mug, Bordered Ellipse, Handle	35.00
Mug, Bordered Ellipse, Souvenir, Annie Leonard	30.00
Mug, Diamond Pet, Etching, Small	15.00
Nappy, Tarentum's Verona, Handle	45.00
Perfume Bottle, Enameled Foliage, Roses, Jewels, Ball Stopper	118.00
Perfume Bottle, Hobnail Pattern, Flash & Clear, 4 5/8 In.	225.00
Pitcher, Esther, 6 1/4 In.	30.00
Pitcher, Milk, Hobnail & Thumbprint, Red Stained	50.00
Pitcher, Water, Sunk Honeycomb	87.00
Pitcher, Water, Tankard, Hexagon Block	95.00
Pitcher, Water, Torquay	140.00
Relish, Barred Ovals	50.00
Salt & Pepper, Fleur-De-Lis, Enameled Flowers, Original Lids	150.00
Salt & Pepper, Heart Band	55.00
Salt & Pepper, Thumbprint	65.00
Sauce, Footed, Etched, Millard	25.00
Sauce, Shoshone	23.00
Sauce, Sweet Sixty-One	16.00
Spooner, Barred Ovals	65.00
Spooner, Block & Fan	45.00
Spooner, Diamonds With Double Fans	45.00
Spooner, Double Daisy	55.00
Spooner, Ivy In Snow	395.00
Spooner, Nail	55.00
Spooner, New Jersey	415.00
Spooner, O'Hara Diamond	50.00
Spooner, O'Hara Diamond, Etched	55.00
Spooner, Paneled Dogwood	25.00
Spooner, Royal Crystal, Stained	75.00
Spooner, Thumbprint With Fern & Berry	55.00
Spooner, Thumbprint, Stained, Etched	30.00
Spooner, Triple Triangle	60.00
Sugar, Cathedral, Cover	60.00
Sugar, Loop & Block, Cover, Stained	65.00
Sugar, Mardi Gras, Open	35.00
Sugar, Triple Triangle, Cover	75.00
Syrup, Majestic	160.00
Syrup, Millard, Etch	195.00
Syrup, Scroll & Net With Cosmos, Frosted Handle	575.00
Syrup, Sunk Honeycomb	130.00 To 140.00
Table Set, Riverside Victoria, Stained, 4 Piece	375.00
Table Set, Scalloped Swirl, Stained, 4 Piece	385.00
Table Set, Triple Triangle, 4 Piece	250.00
Toothpick, Double Arches, Stained	110.00
Toothpick, Exposition, 1893	45.00
Toothpick, Thompson 77	35.00
Toothpick, Thumbprint, Stained	35.00
Toothpick, Truncated Cube	30.00
Tray, Wine, Aurora	45.00
Tumbler, Commemorating Little America, Penguin	10.00
Tumbler, Diamond Peg, Indiana, 1910	35.00
Tumbler, Oregon	45.00
Tumbler, Pleating	33.00
Tumbler, Royal Crystal	15.00
Tumbler, Zipper Slash	35.00
Vase, Gold Panels & Scrolls, Enameled Flowers, 2 5/8 In., Pair	50.00
Water Set, Pillow Encircled, 5 Piece	165.00
Water Set, Thumbprint, Stained, Tankard, 6 Piece	245.00
Wine, Triple Triangle, Stained	38.00
Wine, Truncated Cube	35.00

Rudolstadt was a faience factory in the Thuringia region of Germany from 1720 to about 1791. In 1854, Ernst Bohne began working in the area. From about 1887 to 1918, the New York and Rudolstadt Pottery made decorated porcelain marked with the RW and crown familiar to collectors. This porcelain was imported by Lewis Straus and Sons of New York, which later became Nathan Straus and Sons. The word "Royal" was included in their import mark. Collectors often call it "Royal Rudolstadt." Late nineteenth- and early twentieth-century pieces are most commonly found today.

RUDOLSTADT, see also Kewpie

RUDOLSTADT, Bowl, Gold Pie Crust Rim, Poppies & Foliage, 10 In.	40.00
Bowl, Hand Painted Poppies, Footed, Signed, 8 3/8 In.	65.00
Bowl, Roses, 9 3/4 In.	42.00
Cake Plate, Pink & White Roses, Gold Rim & Handles, Marked	40.00
Cake Plate, Spray of Roses Top, Man & Woman In Boat, Marked	60.00
Celery, Roses, Gold Trim, Open Handles, 12 1/2 X 5 1/2 In.	70.00
Chocolate Pot, Pink Rose, Green Leaf, 10 In.	95.00
Chocolate Pot, Rose Design, Green Leaf & White Flower, 10 In.	150.00
Chop Plate, Poppies, 13 In.	95.00
Cocoa Set, White Roses On Pastel Ground, 5 Piece	140.00
Cup, Saucer & Plate, Happifats	50.00
Dresser Set, Kewpie, Tray, 10 X 7 In., 5 Piece	950.00
Nut Dish, Underplate, Ball Footed	97.00
Nut Set, Roses, Fluted, Footed, Blue Mark, 7 Piece	250.00
Pitcher, Bulbous, Gold & Jeweled Flowers, Signed, 15 1/2 In.	285.00
Plaque, Cupid, Pulled By Dragonflies, Wedgwood Blue, 11 X 6 In.	375.00
Plate, Couple In Boat, Mountains, Blue Mark, 8 1/2 In.	50.00
Plate, Embossed Beading, Scalloped, Cabbage Roses, 8 1/2 In.	30.00
Plate, Poppy, 9 In.	58.00
Relish, 3 Rose Bouquets, 6 Single Roses, Marked, 4 1/8 X 8 In.	12.50
Sugar & Creamer, Marked	75.00
Tray, 8 Kewpies, Signed Rose O'Neill, Gold Rim, 10 In.	295.00
Tray, Dresser, Bluebirds, Branches, Blue Rim, 12 1/2 X 7 3/4 In.	120.00
Tray, Dresser, Day Lilies	45.00
Tray, Dresser, Floral	55.00
Tray, Pin, Kewpie	400.00
Vase, Enameled Floral, Gold Beading, Cobalt Ground, 7 In.	153.00
Vase, Enameled Florals, Gold Beading, Gold Handles, 6 1/2 In.	155.00
Vase, Floral Design, Elephant Handles, 4 In.	90.00
Vase, Flowers, Yellow & Beige Ground, Blown-Out Leaves, 12 In.	70.00
Vase, Girl Feeding Birds, Copper Luster, 13 In.	90.00
Vase, Pastel Flowers, Cream Ground, Handles, Worcester Type	125.00

Rugs have been used in the American home since the seventeenth century. The Oriental rug of that time was often used on a table, not on the floor. Rag rugs, hooked rugs, and braided rugs were made by housewives from scraps of material.

RUG, Afshar, Multicolored Pear Pattern, 9 Ft.4 In. X 4 Ft.11 In.	50.00
Afshar, Rows of Palmettes, Wool, 3 Ft.11 In. X 4 Ft.11 In.	2000.00
Afshar, Sawtooth Design, Ivory Ground, Brown, Rust, Red, 6 X 4 Ft.	750.00
Anatolian, Double Iche, Banded By S-Designs, 4 Ft.6 In. X 6 Ft.6 In.	8500.00
Anatolian, Prayer, Mihrab With Hanging Lamp, 5 Ft.10 In. X 3 Ft.1 In.	800.00
Animal Figures, Brown Field, 19th Century, 3 Ft.1 In. X 5 Ft.	1600.00
Baluch, Diagonal Square Lattice, 2 Ft.9 In. X 5 Ft.4 In.	550.00
Baluch, Diamond Lattice, Blossoming Trees Border, 4 Ft. X 4 Ft.9 In.	475.00
Baluch, Octagonal Lattice Inset With Squares, 4 Ft. X 2 Ft.9 In.	650.00
Bidjar, Cartouche of Herati Design, Floral Field, 8 Ft.6 In. X 4 Ft.	600.00
Bidjar, Herati-Filled Stepped Medallion, 11 Ft.8 In. X 7 Ft.4 In.	3000.00
Bidjar, Single Blue Sawtooth Medallion, 5 Ft.8 In. X 4 Ft.6 In.	2000.00
Bokhara, Central Medallion, Crimson Ground, 4 X 7 Ft.	175.00
Braided, Concentric Oval Bands, Oval, 7 Ft.11 In. X 5 Ft.7 In.	245.00
Braided, Dark Colors, Oval, Handmade, 31 X 55 In.	95.00
Caucasian, 3 Hexagons, Trees, Floral & Animals, 6 Ft. X 3 Ft.9 In.	1300.00

Caucasian, 4 Lesghi Stars, Polygons, 3 Ft.5 In. X 6 Ft.1 In.	2100.00
Caucasian, Akstafa, Blue, Ivory, Cornflower, Medallions, 10 X 4 Ft.	8250.00
Caucasian, Blue Field, 3 Hooked Medallions, 7 Ft.2 In. X 4 Ft.5 In.	350.00
Caucasian, Gird of Lesghi Stars, 5 Ft.4 In. X 3 Ft.5 In.	6300.00
Chinese, Abstract Bands & Waves, Blue Field, 6 Ft.9 In. X 4 Ft.	4500.00
Chinese, Center Fretwork Roundel, Animals, 6 Ft.10 In. X 8 Ft.10 In.	1100.00
Chinese, Gold Field, Blossoms, Blue Border, Pink, Green, 9 X 11 In.	175.00
Chinese, Ivory Foo Dogs, Branches, 11 Ft.6 In. X 6 Ft.4 In.	300.00
Chinese, Rows of Circular Medallions, Silk, 8 Ft.2 In. X 9 Ft.1 In.	2700.00
Dergazine, Floral Spray, Rose Ground, 9 X 12 Ft.	200.00
Ersari, 3 Center Medallions, Surrounded By Zigzag, 5 Ft.3 In. X 3 Ft.	700.00
Ersari, 3 Rows of 7 Guls, Diamond Lattice Border, 11 Ft. X 8 Ft.4 In.	650.00
Ersari, Allover Mina Khani Design, 3 Ft.3 In. X 1 Ft.6 In.	650.00
Ersari, Luminous Stepped Diamonds, Sawtooth, 1 Ft.1 In. X 4 Ft.8 In.	425.00
Ersari, Mina Khani Design, 4 Ft.11 In. X 2 Ft.9 In.	550.00
Ersari, Plain & Patterned Horizontal Bands, 3 Ft.5 In. X 5 Ft.9 In.	325.00
Felt Penny, Embroidered, Vase, Floral Sprigs, 20th Century, 28 X 34 In.	467.00
Feraghan, Center Arrow Medallion, 4 Ft.10 In. X 3 Ft.7 In.	550.00
Feraghan, Pinecone Pear Pattern, 12 Ft.8 In. X 6 Ft.	200.00
Gorevan, Blossoming Trees, Serrated Leaves, 11 Ft.6 In. X 7 Ft.4 In.	3000.00
Gulistan, Sarouk Pattern, 3 X 9 Ft.	105.00
Hamadan, Allover Floral Sprays, Ivory Field, 9 Ft.10 In. X 7 Ft.4 In.	500.00
Hamadan, Floral Medallion, Cream Cartouche, 5 Ft.6 In. X 9 Ft.10 In.	1800.00
Hamadan, Herati Design, Corner Spandrels, 6 Ft. X 6 Ft.8 In.	400.00
Hamadan, Herati Design, Vine & Boteh Border, 6 Ft.7 In. X 4 Ft.8 In.	475.00
Hamadan, Ivory Medallion, Floral Cartouche, 5 Ft.3 In. X 3 Ft.5 In.	350.00
Hamadan, Multicolored Herati Design, 21 Ft. X 9 Ft.10 In.	3250.00
Hamadan, Repeated Foliate Design, Red Ground, 3 Ft.5 In. X 6 Ft.10 In.	325.00
Hamadan, Scalloped Floral Medallion, 18 Ft.1 In. X 9 Ft.8 In.	650.00
Hamadan, Stylized Floral & Geometric Design, 7 Ft.3 In. X 3 Ft.9 In.	675.00
Handmade, Oval, Braided, 28 In.	12.50
Heriz, Blue, Red, Ivory, Red Floral Ground, 12 X 8 Ft.	1400.00
Heriz, Floral Medallion, Boteh Cartouche, 11 Ft.4 In. X 9 Ft.3 In.	4000.00
Heriz, Medallion On Rust Cartouche, 9 Ft. X 7 Ft.7 In.	2700.00
Heriz, Red Ground, Green, Gold, Peach, Ivory Border, 8 X 11 Ft.	4500.00
Heriz, Stepped Floral Medallions, 4 Ft.5 In. X 6 Ft.7in.	1400.00
Hooked, 8-Point Stars, Trellis Border, C.1900, 26 X 47 1/2 In.	220.00
Hooked, Alternating Gray & Blue Braided Squares, American, 51 X 72 In.	77.00
Hooked, American Eagle, Holding Arrow With Feet, Stars, 23 X 35 In.	385.00
Hooked, Amish, Acorns, Oak Leaves, Rag & Yarn, 25 X 63 In.	65.00
Hooked, Amish, Blue Foliage Scrolls, 24 X 40 In.	55.00
Hooked, Amish, Floral Design, 22 X 43 1/2 In.	40.00
Hooked, Amish, Geometric Design, 26 X 37 1/2 In.	350.00
Hooked, Amish, Geometric Floral Design, 25 X 40 In.	225.00
Hooked, Ban, Farmer With Sheaves of Corn, C.1880, 26 X 42 In.	395.00
Hooked, Black Dog, 21 X 35 In.	95.00
Hooked, Black Dog, Beige, Gray Ground, 34 X 56 In.	750.00
Hooked, Black, White, Gray, Red, Beige, Farm Scene, 19 X 34 In.	1430.00
Hooked, Bopeep, Garden Scene, Oval, 32 In.	60.00
Hooked, Brown Dove, On Red Heart, Other Hearts, 31 X 32 In.	242.00
Hooked, Burlap, 2 Black Cats, Whiskers, Gray, Tan, 31 X 36 In.	325.00
Hooked, Central Green Striped Panel, Black, Blue, Fringed, 76 X 27 In.	77.00

Turn your rag rug upside down the day before you plan to clean it— some of the loose dirt will fall out.

Hooked, Dog, Blue & Black Striped, Cotton, 19th Century, 16 X 30 In. 625.00
Hooked, Eagle, Rocks Underneath, Beige Ground, 20 X 38 1/2 In. 425.00
Hooked, Earth Tones, Design, 33 X 58 In. 100.00
Hooked, Floral & Foliage, Gold, Brown, Gray & Green, 25 X 48 In. 55.00
Hooked, Floral Blocks, Black Border, Cloth Back, 1930, 8 X 10 Ft. 995.00
Hooked, Floral, Beige, Foliage Border, 40 X 70 In. 75.00
Hooked, Flower Basket, Oval, 35 X 23 In. 65.00
Hooked, Geometric Design, Flowers, 22 1/2 X 32 In. 125.00
Hooked, Green, Red, Black, Fringe, 5 X 7 Ft. 750.00
Hooked, Grenfell, Cabin In Snow, Framed, 11 X 13 In. 125.00
Hooked, Home Sweet Home, Flowers, 21 X 34 In. 110.00
Hooked, Horse, Black, Gray, Red Outline, Abstract, 1900, 22 X 38 In. 495.00
Hooked, House Scene, Blue Ground, 22 X35 In. 85.00
Hooked, House, Apple Trees, Chicken, 25 X 36 In. 215.00
Hooked, Irish Setter, Vegetable Dyes, 34 X 24 In. 185.00
Hooked, Light & Shadow Design, 32 X 63 In. 325.00
Hooked, Lion Profile, Standing, American, Late 19th Century, 31 X 39 In. 275.00
Hooked, Moss Green Dog, Variegated Stripe Border, 2 Ft.7 In. X 5 Ft. 600.00
Hooked, Mother Cat, 3 Kittens, Mouse, 19th Century, 26 X 52 In. 695.00
Hooked, Multicolored Flowers, 1930s, 25 X 46 In. 82.00
Hooked, Owl, 19 X 24 In. 20.00
Hooked, Pictorial Cottage Scene, 18 X 16 In. 60.00
Hooked, Polo Player In Black, 19 X 37 In. 175.00
Hooked, Red Barn Scene, Ducks, Chicks, Pa., 20th Century, 11 X 39 In. 275.00
Hooked, Red Rose Design, 1920s, 25 X 45 In. 68.00
Hooked, Rooster, Weather Vane, 44 X 36 In. 65.00
Hooked, Scene, House & Trees, Border, 33 X 38 1/2 In. 45.00
Hooked, Scotty, Red Ribbon, Gray Ground, Brown Border, 20 1/2 X 38 In. 75.00
Hooked, Shell Border, 25 X 45 In. 125.00
Hooked, Stripes, Machine Sewn Binding, 15 X 29 In. 70.00
Hooked, Stylized Floral Center, Fish Scale Design Border, 38 X 41 In. 25.00
Hooked, Stylized Floral, Red, Blue, White & Black, 25 X 48 In. 175.00
Hooked, Sunbonnet Girl, Ice Skating, Square, 17 In. 50.00
Hooked, Winter Scene, 2 Cabins & Man, American, 21 1/2 X 30 In. 100.00
Hooked, Zigzag & Diamond Design, 24 X 36 In. 45.00
Indian Oriental, Floral Medallion, Ivory, Floral Border, 9 X 12 Ft. 200.00
Ingrain, Central Medallions, Loop & Hooked Square, 75 X 108 In. 175.00
Karabagh, Center Diagonal Stripes, 8 Ft.3 In. X 3 Ft.10 In. 2000.00
Karabagh, Geometric Designs, Cream Field, 7 Ft.8 In. X 4 Ft.9 In. 600.00
Karabagh, Ivory Medallion, Gold Gables, 6 Ft.9 In. X 4 Ft.3 In. 1300.00
Kashan, Blue Cartouche, Tendrils, Animal Figures, 10 Ft.8 In. X 7 Ft. 4800.00
Kazak, Abrashed Center Panel, Medallions, 6 Ft.8 In. X 3 Ft.5 In. 550.00
Kazak, Blue Abrashed Field, 4 Medallions, 7 Ft.10 In. X 4 Ft.6 In. 750.00
Kazak, Cruciform Medallion, Abrashed Field, 7 Ft.1 In. X 4 Ft.9 In. 2500.00
Kazak, Eagle Style Medallions, 6 Ft.2 In. X 3 Ft.5 In. 375.00
Kazak, Geometric Medallions, 6 Ft.3 In. X 4 Ft.4 In. 1000.00
Kazak, Latch–Hook Medallions, 5 Ft.2 In. X 4 Ft.8 In. 200.00
Kazak, Long Stepped Medallion, 19th Century, 6 Ft.6 In. X 4 Ft.8 In. 2100.00
Kazak, Lori Pambak, Medallions, Red Field, 4 Ft.7 In. X 6 Ft.4 In. 3500.00
Kazak, Shield–Like Medallions, Red Field, 8 Ft. X 4 Ft.7 In. 1800.00
Kazak, Stepped Polygons, Animal & Human Figures, 6 Ft.11 In. X 3 Ft. 650.00
Kelim, 3 Ivory & Purple Squares Center, 11 Ft. X 5 Ft.4 In. 950.00
Kelim, Caucasian, Stepped Diamonds, 4 Ft.7 In. X 9 Ft.8 In. 400.00
Khorossan, Ivory Herati Stepped Diamond Medallion, 16 X 13 Ft. 2420.00
Khotan, 3 Medallions, Rust–Red Field, 4 Ft.4 In. X 7 Ft.8 In. 3400.00
Khotan, 3 Roundels, Ying–Yang Symbols, Wave Border, 12 X 6 Ft. 3100.00
Kilim, Overall Multicolored Geometric, 8 Ft. X 8 Ft.4 In. 200.00
Kirman, Allover Palmettes, Vines, 20th Century, 12 X 18 Ft. 3800.00
Kirman, Blue, Green, Red, Floral Medallion, 11 Ft.6 In. X 8 Ft.7 In. 500.00
Kirman, Center Medallion, Gold Field, Burgundy, Blue, Mauve, 4 X 6 Ft. 225.00
Kirman, Floral Medallion, Wine Red Field, 7 X 10 Ft. 900.00
Kirman, Floral Medallions, Burgundy, Green, Gold, Blue, 7 X 4 Ft. 1000.00
Kirman, Florals, Blue Field, Hand Knotted, 30 X 63 In. 350.00
Kirman, Ivory Center, Floral Design, 7 Ft.8 In. X 4 Ft.10 In. 800.00

Kirman, Ivory Field, Flowering Trees, 11 Ft.3 In. X 2 Ft.10 In.	375.00
Kirman, Repeating Floral Medallions, Burgundy, Green, Gold, 7 X 4 Ft.	1000.00
Konya, Gold Star In Hooked Medallion, Blue Floral Field, 8 X 6 Ft.	1400.00
Konya, Pictorial, Octagons On Yellow Field, 4 Ft.3 In. X 7 Ft.9 In.	8000.00
Konya, Turkic Design, 6 Ft.6 In. X 4 Ft.11 In.	6000.00
Kuba, Blue Ground, Tulip Design, Red, Blue, 6 X 9 Ft.	90.00
Kurdish, Animal & Human Figures, 3 Ft. X 7 Ft.6 In.	250.00
Kurdish, Center Panel, Vertical Stripes, 8 Ft.7 In. X 3 Ft.2 In.	700.00
Kurdish, Gold Field, Stepped Diamond Lattice, 3 Ft.11 In. X 9 Ft.	400.00
Lillihan, Open Floral Design, Corner Spandrels, 6 Ft.8 In. X 5 Ft.	950.00
Malayer, Overall Mustaffi Design, 12 Ft.4 In. X 8 Ft.8 In.	1800.00
Mashad, Medallion On Floral Cartouche, 5 Ft.10 In. X 4 Ft.3 In.	475.00
Moghan, Columns of Stepped Octagons, 8 Ft.6 In. X 3 Ft.5 In.	2000.00
Penny, Appliqued, Embroidered, Floral Sprigs, White, Iowa, 32 X 63 In.	275.00
Penny, Star & Floral Medallion, Appliqued Felt, Octagonal, 1900, 35 In.	165.00
Persian, Black Medallion, Green Border, Ivory Guard, 12 X 14 In.	1200.00
Persian, Narrow Stripes, Diamond Lattice Corners, 5 Ft.7 In. X 12 Ft.	3400.00
Sarouk, Allover Blossoming Vines, 6 Ft.4 In. X 4 Ft.3 In.	925.00
Sarouk, Allover Floral Sprays, Blue Field, 6 Ft.3 In. X 4 Ft.1 In.	325.00
Sarouk, Blossoming Palmette, Sprays, 4 Ft.11 In. X 3 Ft.3 In.	850.00
Sarouk, Blue Abrashed Center, Floral Sprays, 3 Ft.3 In. X 4 Ft.8 In.	700.00
Sarouk, Blue Medallion, Rose Arabesques, 12 Ft.4 In. X 8 Ft.8 In.	3750.00
Sarouk, Elongated Medallion On Floral Field, 3 Ft.5 In. X 5 Ft.	1600.00
Sarouk, Empty Taupe Cartouche, Palmettes Border, 4 Ft. X 6 Ft.3 In.	1500.00
Sarouk, Floral Medallion On Cartouche, 6 Ft.4 In. X 4 Ft.3 In.	2000.00
Sarouk, Floral Medallion, Blue Field, 5 Ft.10 In. X 4 Ft.4 In.	200.00
Sarouk, Floral Sprays, Vine Border, 4 Ft.9 In. X 3 Ft.2 In.	750.00
Sarouk, Medallion On Taupe, Floral Field, 4 Ft.9 In. X 3 Ft.6 In.	1600.00
Sarouk, Overall Floral Spray & Bouquet Design, 11 Ft.9 In. X 9 Ft.	2400.00
Sarouk, Overall Floral Spray Design, 11 Ft.4 In. X 8 Ft.5 In.	2000.00
Sarouk, Red Field, Allover Floral Design, Leaves, 8 Ft. X 12 Ft.	500.00
Sarouk, Red Field, Floral Sprays, 8 Ft.11 In. X 6 Ft.2 In.	1500.00
Sarouk, Small Cartouches, Flowering Sprays, 2 Ft.8 In. X 10 Ft.	650.00
Scandanavian, Hemp, Flat Weave, Yellow Band, Striated Ground, 9 X 12 Ft.	200.00
Serab, Continuous Sawtooth Medallions, 9 Ft.8 In. X 3 Ft.	700.00
Serapi, Serrated Reserve, Hooked Medallion, 8 Ft.7 In. X 11 Ft.8 In.	6000.00
Shiraz, Allover Hooked Diamonds, 10 Ft.6 In. X 6 Ft.5 In.	1900.00
Shirvan, Repeating Diamond-Shaped Flowers, 3 Ft.11 In. X 2 Ft.4 In.	900.00
Soumak, Arrowhead Medallions, 3 Ft.10 In. X 5 Ft.7 In.	2300.00
Soumak, Red Square Field, Diamond Medallions, 8 Ft.2 In. X 8 Ft.8 In.	3250.00
Sultanabad, Allover Leafy Vines, Floral Border, 12 Ft. X 8 Ft.10 In.	5000.00
Tabriz, Pendented Medallions, 11 Ft.1 In. X 14 Ft.5 In.	1800.00
Tabriz, Red Field, Ivory Floral Center, Peach & Gold, 4 X 5 Ft.	950.00
Tabriz, Taupe Medallion On Blue Cartouche, 4 Ft.5 In. X 5 Ft.10 In.	1600.00
Tekke Bokhara, Octagons On Red Field, 2 Ft.8 In. X 3 Ft.10 In.	350.00
Tekke, Rows of Guls, Sunburst Border, Red Field, 6 Ft. X 3 Ft.8 In.	950.00
Ushak, Floral Gold Border, 20th Century, 13 Ft.3 In. X 8 Ft.4 In.	2000.00
Ushak, Floral Lattice, Palmettes, Vines, 13 Ft.10 In. X 10 Ft.7 In.	2800.00
Wool, Handwoven, Bird & Snake, Brown Ground, Peruvian, 50 X 76 In.	125.00
Wooven, Stripes of Red, White & Blue, 9 X 12 Ft.	450.00
Yastik, Red Octagon, Smaller Octagons & Squares, 34 X 22 In.	375.00
Yomud, 4 Rows of 12 Tauk-Nauska Guls, 5 Ft.8 In. X 9 Ft.3 In.	1700.00
Yoruk, Rose Ground, Blue, Gray, Gold Brown, Coral Border, 7 X 3 Ft.	300.00
Yoruk, S Designs & Polygons, 2 Ft.10 In. X 8 Ft.9 In.	1200.00

RumRill   Rumrill Pottery was designed by George Rumrill of Little Rock, Arkansas. From 1930 to 1933, it was produced by the Red Wing Pottery of Red Wing, Minnesota. In 1938, production was transferred to the Shawnee Pottery in Zanesville, Ohio. Production ceased in the 1940s.

RUMRILL, Beverage Server, Uranium Red, Copper Neck Ring, Handle, Cover	22.50
Pitcher, Ball, Closed Top, Mauve	20.00
Pitcher, Ball, Ice Lip, Matte Green	20.00
Pitcher, Tilt, Green	12.50

Pitcher, Tilt, Red	17.50
Vase, 2 Full Nudes As Handles, 11 1/2 In. .... 150.00 To	175.00
Vase, Blue, Squared Handles, 13 In.	35.00
Vase, Cornucopia Shape, 7 In.	25.00
Vase, Urn Shape, White, Blue Interior, Handles	30.00
Vase, White Exterior, Blue Interior, Handles, 5 1/2 In.	15.00
Vase, White Exterior, Turquoise Interior, Handles, Rings, 7 In.	18.00

Ruskin is a British art pottery of the twentieth century. The Ruskin Pottery was started by William Howson Taylor; his name was used as the mark until about 1899. The factory, at West Smethwick, Birmingham, England, stopped making new pieces in 1933 but continued to glaze and sell the remaining wares until 1935. The art pottery is noted for the exceptional glazes.

RUSKIN, Vase, Metallic Lavender, Dated 1913, 6 In.	55.00
Vase, Purple, 1913, 6 In.	95.00

Russel Wright designed dinnerwares in modern shapes for four companies. Iroquois China Company, Harker China Company, Steubenville Pottery, and Justin Therod and Sons made dishes marked "Russel Wright." The Steubenville wares, first made in 1938, are the most common today. This section lists the dinnerwares by Wright. He was a designer of domestic and industrial wares, including furniture, aluminum, radios, interiors, and glassware.

RUSSEL WRIGHT, Ashtray, Bauer, Tan	195.00
Bowl, Cereal, Grass	6.00
Bowl, Cereal, Iroquois, Brown	5.50
Bowl, Cover, Grass, 9 1/2 In.	25.00
Bowl, Vegetable, Divided, American Modern, Gray	25.00
Bun Warmer, Aluminum .... 35.00 To	78.00
Butter, Cover, Iroquois, Nutmeg, 1/2 Lb.	55.00
Butter, Iroquois, Charcoal	50.00
Carafe, Iroquois, Charcoal	65.00
Carafe, Wine, Iroquois, Oyster	30.00
Celery, American Modern, Granite Gray	21.00
Chop Plate, American Modern, Coral .... 18.00 To	20.00
Clock, Black Face, Harker	50.00
Coffeepot, American Modern, Chartreuse, After Dinner	35.00
Creamer, American Modern, Chartreuse	5.00
Creamer, American Modern, Coral .... 5.00 To	7.50
Creamer, American Modern, Gray	5.00
Creamer, Stack, Iroquois, Aqua	12.00
Cup & Saucer, American Modern, Coral	19.00
Cup & Saucer, American Modern, Granite Gray	8.50
Cup & Saucer, Grass	3.50
Cup & Saucer, Iroquois, Charcoal .... 7.50 To	12.50
Cup, Iroquois, Sugar White	10.00
Dish, Fruit, American Modern, Coral	8.00
Gravy Boat, American Modern, Gray .... 12.00 To	18.00
Gravy, American Modern, Coral .... 8.00 To	14.00
Pickle, American Modern, Cedar Green	6.00
Pitcher, Black Chutney	60.00
Pitcher, Cover, Iroquois, Sugar White	60.00
Pitcher, Seafoam	38.00
Pitcher, Water, American Modern, Coral	38.00
Pitcher, Water, American Modern, Gray	24.00
Pitcher, Water, American Modern, Seafoam	40.00
Pitcher, Water, American Modern, White	52.00
Pitcher, Water, Coral	26.00
Plate, American Modern, 10 In.	5.00
Plate, American Modern, Coral, 6 1/4 In.	1.50
Plate, Dinner, American Modern, Coral	45.50
Plate, Grass, 6 1/4 In.	3.50
Plate, Grass, 10 1/2 In.	6.50

> A quilt that is not in use should be aired each year. Open up and put flat on the floor for a few days. A quilt that is used on a bed or hung should be taken down and rested every six months.

Plate, Iroquois, Aqua, 7 1/2 In.	6.00
Plate, Iroquois, Cantelope, 9 1/2 In.	6.25
Plate, Iroquois, Ice Blue, 10 In.	8.00
Platter, American Modern, Cantelope, 12 In.	15.00
Platter, American Modern, Chartreuse, 14 In.	17.50
Platter, American Modern, Coral, 10 1/2 In.	12.00
Platter, American Modern, Coral, 13 1/2 In.	15.00
Platter, American Modern, Seafoam, 13 1/2 In.	15.00
Platter, Grass, 13 In.	15.00
Platter, Iroquois, Brown, 12 1/2 In.	10.00 To 20.00
Relish, American Modern, Chartreuse, 13 In.	18.00
Salt & Pepper, Coral	6.00
Salt & Pepper, Gray	6.00
Salt & Pepper, Green	6.00
Salt & Pepper, Pink	12.00
Salt & Pepper, Seafoam	12.00
Saucer, Grass	2.00 To 6.00
Sherbet, American Modern, Chartreuse	15.00
Shot Glass, Ellipse	5.00
Soup, Dish, Lug, Sea Foam, Chartreuse	6.50
Stack Set, Chartreuse	95.00
Sugar & Creamer, Stack, Iroquois, Apricot	12.00
Sugar, American Modern, Bean Brown	15.00
Sugar, American Modern, Granite Gray	8.50
Sugar, Cover, Chartreuse	10.00
Sugar, Cover, Grass	12.50
Sugar, Iroquois, Brown, Cover	16.50
Sugar, Open, Grass	8.00
Teapot, American Modern, Coral	36.00 To 37.00
Teapot, American Modern, Gray	38.00 To 40.00
Teapot, Iroquois, Charcoal	75.00
Teapot, Steubenville, Blue–Green	35.00
Teapot, Woodfield, Rose	12.00
Teapot, Yamoto, Porcelain	1000.00
Vegetable, Brown, 2 Sections, Large	20.00

SABINO FRANCE

Sabino France

Sabino glass was made in the 1920s and 1930s in Paris, France. Founded by Marius–Ernest Sabino, the firm was noted for Art Deco lamps, vases, figurines, and animals in clear, colored, and opalescent glass. Production stopped during World War II but resumed in the 1960s with the manufacture of nude figurines and small opalescent glass animals. The new pieces are a slightly different color and can be recognized.

SABINO, Bottle, Perfume, Nudes Bathing, Powder Blue, 5 1/2 In.	135.00
Bottle, Perfume, Nudes Dancing, Signed, 6 1/2 In.	105.00
Bottle, Perfume, Quilted Drape, Bulbous, Signed, 5 1/2 In.	75.00
Pitcher, Orange With Green, Handle, 7 1/ 2in.	75.00

Salopian ware was made by the Caughley factory of England during the eighteenth century. The early pieces were blue and white with some colored decorations. Another ware called "Salopian" today is a tableware decorated with color transfers. This ware was made during the late nineteenth century.

SALOPIAN, Cup & Saucer, Ship Transfer, Turquoise	75.00
Cup & Saucer, View of Inn, Sign & Figures, C.1820	85.00

Plate, Toddy, Black Transfer, Crow's Feet Center, 5 1/4 In. 85.00
SALT & PEPPER, see Porcelain; Pressed Glass; etc.

Salt glaze has a grayish–white, pitted, orange–peel–textured surface. It is a method of decoration that has been used since the eighteenth century. Salt–glazed pieces are still being made.

SALT GLAZE, Bottle, Ink, Conical 5.00
Churn, Blue Leaf, 6 Gal. 200.00
Churn, Butter, I.A.Bauer Pottery, Blue Stencil, Ovoid, 2 Gal. 165.00
Creamer, Cow 30.00
Creamer, Floral Dividers, American Eagle On Side, 4 3/4 In. 75.00
Creamer, Gothic Design, Deer, Pewter Lid, 5 1/2 In. 75.00
Crock, Blue Floral Sprig, Gray, Loop Handles, 13 1/2 In. 357.00
Crock, Cobalt Blue Design Over Front, Brown Lining, 4 Gal. 145.00
Crock, Cobalt Blue Markings, No.2, Ears 45.00
Crock, Double Stamped, 3 Gal. 175.00
Crock, Finger Painted Acorns, Branch, No.4, Ear Handles, 4 Gal. 95.00
Crock, Jacob Fisher, Lyons, N.Y., Late 19th Century, 2 Gal. 195.00
Crock, Loop Handles, Stylized Floral Sprig, 13 1/2 In. 357.00
Crock, Ornate Front Design, Brown Lining, 4 Gal. 200.00
Crock, Rib Cage & Target, Minnesota, Split Oval, 4 Gal. 300.00
Dish, Reticulated, Scalloped Rim, 18th Century, 10 1/2 In. 200.00
Jar, Butterfly, 6 Gal. 180.00
Jar, Double Rib Cage, 6 Gal. 140.00
Jug, Beehive, Bangor, Maine, C.1895, 9 1/2 In. 95.00
Jug, Cobalt Blue Butterfly, New York Stoneware, 1 Gal. 140.00
Jug, Incised Bangor, Maine, 1 Gal. 85.00
Jug, Naomi's Daughters–In–Law, April, 1847, 9 1/4 In. 118.00
Jug, Rampant Lion, Bellarmine, Rhenish, 18th Century, 12 1/4 In. 1100.00
Jug, Threshing, Rib Cage & Target Design, 2 Handles, 10 Gal. 2200.00
Jug, Universe, Wreathed Medallion of People, Animals, 9 5/8 In. 295.00
Match Holder, Side Striker, American Brewing Co. 65.00
Pitcher, Cattail 145.00
Pitcher, Fern Pattern, Pewter Cover 125.00
Pitcher, Gothic, Virgin Scenes, Charles Meigh, 1946, 8 1/8 In. 70.00
Pitcher, Gray, Applied White Floral Design, Imperial, 8 1/4 In. 75.00
Pitcher, Rose On Trellis, 8 1/2 In. 175.00
Pitcher, Stylized Floral Design, Pewter Lid, 1903, 14 In. 65.00
Syrup, Pewter Lid, Bacchanalian Deign, Meigh 150.00
Tankard, Birds, Goat, Stylized Foliage, Pewter Mounted, 8 3/8 In. 550.00

Samplers were made in America from the early 1700s. The best examples were made from 1790 to 1840. Long, narrow samplers are usually older than square ones. Early samplers just had stitching or alphabets. The later examples had numerals, borders, and pictorial decorations. Those with mottoes are mid–Victorian.

SAMPLER, ABC, Brown Linen, Sarah P.Carr, Age 9 Years, 1837, 19 X 17 In. 1430.00
Adam & Eve, Elizabeth Bray, 1833, 13 X 16 In. 675.00
Alphabet & Verse, Islip, N.Y., Dated 1820, 13 X 9 In. 300.00
Alphabet, 2–Story House, Pious Verse, Linen, C.1830, 19 X 20 In. 3600.00
Alphabet, Church, Houses, Floral Border, Maple Frame, 16 X 18 In. 350.00
Alphabet, Cross–Stitch, 1927, 18 X 14 In. 40.00
Alphabet, Crowns, H.Millar, Millar's School, 1844, 15 3/4 X 19 In. 295.00
Alphabet, Eleanor Davies, 10 Years, 1826, Framed, 18 3/4 X 15 In. 275.00
Alphabet, Eliza B.Unwin, 7 Years, 1845, Framed, 14 X 14 1/2 In. 450.00
Alphabet, Flowers, Homespun, Bird's–Eye Veneer Frame, 13 X 16 In. 385.00
Alphabet, Flowers, Margret Millne Cooper, 1859, 14 X 19 In. 65.00
Alphabet, Isabella Ann Kay, 11 X 11 1/2 In. 300.00
Alphabet, Numbers, House, Trees, Birds, Dated 1817, 7 X 16 In. 375.00
Alphabet, Numbers, Verse, Floral Border, 16 X 12 In. 375.00
Alphabet, Red Wool, Linen, Frame Signed, 1840s, 15 1/2 X 16 1/2 In. 695.00
Alphabet, Verse, Mary Hornblower, 1769, Framed, 10 X 15 1/2 In. 350.00
Alphabet, Numerals, Birds, Mary Smith, 1701, Framed, 21 X 8 5/8 In. 440.00
Alphabet, Numerals, Hepza R.Hurley, C.1880, 8 X 7 1/2 In. 137.00

Sampler, Nancy Womersley, 1830, 25 X 26 In.

Caroline Crook Stourport, 1829, 25 X 17 In. ....*Illus*   375.00
Eliza Romaine, 5 Alphabets, Dated 1812, 11 X 20 In. 375.00
Family Record, C. Squire, Fairfield, 1827, 17 X 18 In. .... *Illus* 2200.00
Flowers, Pot, Olive Homespun, Lucy Nichols, 1800, Framed, 22 X 23 In. 2250.00
Gennett Clapp, 18 Years, Norwich, Ohio, 1839, 19 3/8 X 19 3/4 In. 3900.00
Geometric & Floral Sprig, Hepza Hall, C.1830, 13 1/8 X 8 1/2 In. 330.00
Geometric, Stylized Flowers, Animals, Homespun, Framed, 23 X 33 In. 195.00
Harriet Ann Dockum, No.13, Portsmouth, N.H., 1825, 26 X 21 1/2 In. 2200.00
Harriet N.Atwood Cornish, 12 Years, New Eng., Framed, 12 X 16 In. 2200.00
Harriet Wetherall May, Age 10 Years, 1830, 16 1/4 X 16 1/2 In. 1900.00

Sampler, Caroline Crook Stourport, 1829,
25 X 17 In.

Sampler, Family Record, C. Squire, Fairfield,
1827, 17 X 18 In.

Human Figures, Apple Trees, Dated 1746, 11 X 12 In. 575.00
Martha Morrisons, 9 Years, AD 1826, Frame, 13 X 12 12 In. 695.00
Mary Hillebraun, Age 13, 1821, 16 X 17 1/2 In. 550.00
Mary Rice, Born March 23rd, 1791, 9 X 6 1/2 In. 650.00
Nancy Womersley, 1830, 25 X 26 In. ....*Illus* 700.00
Needlepoint, Alphabet, Adam & Eve, Crucifixion, 1851, 24 X 25 In. 125.00
Needlework, Mary Webb, 1779, Silk Yarn, On Wool, England, 14 X 12 In. 350.00
Punch Paper, Cross–Stitch, Richard Johnson, Departed 1849, 17 In. 250.00
Rosamunda Heidelbach, Letters, Numbers, Linen, 1827, 11 X 16 In. 495.00
Rowe Family, Elizabeth, Age 11, C.1830, Framed, 16 3/4 X 15 In. 1320.00
Silk Thread On Linen, Orissa Willard, Sterling, 1815, 16 X 19 In. 2250.00
Spain, Lohize Re–Medios Herreran Rojas, 9 3/4 X 24 1/4 In. 75.00
Susannah Styles, Finished Work In 10th Year, 1800, Square, 13 In. 1000.00
Vanity of Wealth, Margaret C.Dye, 1827, 2–Story House, 26 X 19 In. 880.00
Verse, Houses, Martha Nash, 1831, 15 X 15 In. 250.00
Verse, My Bird Is Dead, C.W.Wakhouse, 10, 1834, 22 X 7 1/2 In. 467.00

Samson and Company, a French firm specializing in the reproduction of collectible wares of many countries and periods, was founded in Paris in the early nineteenth century. Chelsea, Meissen, Famille Verte, and Chinese Export porcelain are some of the wares that have been reproduced by the company. The firm uses a variety of marks on the reproductions. It is still in operation.

SAMSON, Bowl, Louis XVI, Lapis, Blue, Lobed Sides, 1900, 12 X 16 In. 3850.00
Group, Good Mother, Sleeping Baby, C.1870, Psuedocrowned, 7 7/8 In. 220.00
Vase, Armorial, Cover, Lowestoft Type, Early 19th Century 185.00

Sand Babies were used as decorations on a line of children's dishes made by the Royal Bayreuth China Company. The children are playing at the seaside. Collectors use the names "Sand Babies" and "Beach Babies" interchangeably.

SAND BABIES, Creamer, Blue Mark 55.00
Cup & Saucer 50.00
Dish, 6 Sides, 4 X 5 In. 65.00
Match Holder, Wall, Blue Mark 225.00
Tray, Pin, Blue Mark 75.00

Sandwich glass is any one of the myriad types of glass made by the Boston and Sandwich Glass Works in Sandwich, Massachusetts, between 1825 and 1888. It is often very difficult to be sure whether a piece was really made at the Sandwich factory because so many types were made there and similar pieces were made at other glass factories.

SANDWICH GLASS, see also Pressed Glass, etc.
SANDWICH GLASS, Bottle, Whiskey, Cut Panels On Neck & Body, 12 1/2 In. 295.00
Bowl, Finger, Ruby Cut To Clear, 3 In. 95.00
Bowl, Hairpin Pattern, Scalloped, 8 1/4 In. 240.00
Bowl, Lacy, Crossed Peacock Feathers, Oval, 2 X 6 In. 135.00
Bowl, Princess Feather Medallions, 9 7/8 In. 175.00
Compote, Curled Leaf 70.00
Compote, Frosted Dog, Cover 115.00
Compote, Girl With Goose, Cover, Frosted 125.00
Compote, Lacy, 9 1/2 In. 750.00
Compote, Lacy, Clear, 4 1/16 X 6 5/8 In. 2000.00
Compote, Lacy, Footed, Low, Miniature 110.00
Compote, Princess Feather Medallion & Fleur–De–Lis, 9 In. 700.00
Creamer, Star & Buckle 450.00
Cup & Saucer, Lacy, Miniature 165.00
Dish, Vegetable, Lacy Pattern, Oval, 3 X 2 In. 135.00
Jar, Pomade, Bear, Amethyst, 3 1/2 In. ....300.00 To 400.00
Jar, Pomade, Punty & Plume, Pewter Cover, C.1830, 2 1/2 In. 195.00
Lafayette, Salt, Boat, Blue 400.00
Lamp, Acorn, Clear, Amethyst Base 195.00
Lamp, Clambroth, Gold Trim, Column Stem, C.1830, 12 In. 595.00

Lamp, Fluid, Hexagonal Looped Font, Blue, 10 In., Pair	1100.00
Lamp, Sweetheart Pattern, Grapevine Pattern Shade, 19 In.	185.00
Lamp, Whale Oil, Blown Font, Pressed Base, 9 In.	165.00
Perfume, Artichoke, Matching Stopper, 4 1/2 In.	495.00
Plate, Peacock Eye & Thistle, 8 In.	145.00
Plate, Scotch Plaid, 9 1/2 In.	120.00
Platter, Lacy, Oval, 2 7/8 X 1 7/8 In.	75.00
Relish, Gothic Arches, Oblong, 7 1/2 In.	135.00
Salt, Christmas, Agitator, Dated 1877, Amber	80.00
Salt, Christmas, Cobalt Blue, Agitator, Dated Top	110.00
Salt, Gothic Arch, Lacy	300.00
Salt, Lacy, Cobalt Blue	500.00
Salt, Peacock Blue	750.00
Salt, Shell, Clear	175.00
Salt, Shell, Medium Blue	75.00
Salt, Shell, Opalescent	450.00
Salt, Strawberry Diamond	35.00
String Holder, Bull's-Eye, Cased Ruby On Clear	195.00
Sugar, Cover, Gothic Arch, Canary Yellow	700.00
Tie Back, Apple Green, Pewter Stem, 3 1/2 In.	35.00
Tie Back, Ruby To Amber, Pewter Stem, 3 1/2 In., Pair	62.00
Tray, Paneled, 2 X 2 In.	95.00
Tray, Scalloped Edge, Oblong, 10 3/4 X 9 In.	650.00
Vase, Frosted Thorn Handles, Peachblow, 4 1/4 In.	185.00
Vase, Trumpet, Etched Ferns, Polished Pontil, 10 In., Pair	95.00
Whiskey Taster, Scalloped Base, Emerald Green	300.00

 Utzschneider and Company, a porcelain factory, made ceramics in Sarreguemines, Lorraine, France, from 1770. Transfer-printed wares and majolica were made in the nineteenth century. The nineteenth-century pieces, most often found today, usually had colorful transfer-printed decorations showing peasants in local costumes.

SARREGUEMINES, Invalid Feeder, Embossed Flower At Top, White	38.00
Jar, Pomade, Cover, Advertising	45.00
Jardiniere, Allover Enameled Lily Pads, Brown, 1952, 12 In.	150.00
Mug, Character, Woman With Mole	55.00
Mustard, Tan & Brown	48.00
Plate, French Nations, 7 In.	25.00
Plate, Fruit, Majolica, 7 1/2 In.	10.00
Sugar, Mocha, Cover, Marbelized Red & Black, White, 6 In.	176.00
Vase, Gargoyles, Lizards, Avocado, Signed, 8 1/2 In.	125.00
Wall Pocket, Diaper Style, Floral In White	37.00

 Satin glass is a late nineteenth-century art glass. It has a dull finish that is caused by a hydrofluoric acid vapor treatment. Satin glass was made in many colors and sometimes had applied decorations. Satin glass is also listed by factory name or in the mother-of-pearl category in this book.

SATIN GLASS, Baby Set, 2 Covered Jars, Tumbler, Powder, Cover, Wicker Tray	85.00
Basket, Herringbone, Deep Pink To Light, Wishbone Handle, 5 In.	315.00
Bell, Thumbprint, Dusty Rose, Wheat Handle, 6 1/2 In.	55.00
Biscuit Jar, Beaded Drape, Silver Plated Lid & Bail	250.00
Biscuit Jar, Florette, Glass Lid	60.00 To 80.00
Biscuit Jar, Open Heart Arches, Enameled Florals	225.00
Bowl, Blue, Ruffled, Ormolu Foot, White Flowers, 5 3/8 In.	295.00
Box, Light Blue, Enameled Pink Roses, 3 3/4 X 5 3/4 In.	240.00
Cookie Jar, Pink	165.00
Cracker Jar, Pulled Feather Design, Ice Blue, Art Glass	285.00
Cruet, Diamond-Quilted Mother-of-Pearl, Reed Handle, 7 In.	630.00
Epergne, Lily, Blue	30.00
Ewer, Diamond-Quilted, Apricot Shaded, Thorn Handle, 9 1/2 In.	255.00

Jam Jar, Gold & Orange Floral, Silver Plated Lid & Bail 215.00
Jar, Pulled Feather, Hand Blown, Flowers, Butterfly, Ice Blue 285.00
Nappy, Diamonds, Pink, 2 Handles, 6 In. 47.50
Pitcher, Diamond–Quilted, Blue, Reed Handle, 3 Spouts, 8 In. 250.00
Pitcher, Diamond–Quilted, Foliage, Flowers, Blue, 8 In. 350.00
Pitcher, Flowers & Leaves Outlined In Gold, 7 In. 225.00
Pitcher, Water, Mother-of-Pearl, Raindrop, 9 In. 550.00
Powder Box, Colonial Man, Woman & Child On Lid, Pink 50.00
Rose Bowl, 8–Crimp Top, Egg Shape, Flowers, Foliage, Blue, 6 In. 135.00
Rose Bowl, 8–Crimp, Enameled Flowers, 4 3/4 X 5 1/2 In. 150.00
Rose Bowl, Cranberry 60.00
Rose Bowl, Diamond–Quilted, Yellow To White 65.00
Rose Bowl, Embossed Flowers, 8–Crimp Top, 3 7/8 In. .... 118.00 To 125.00
Rose Bowl, Enameled Floral, White To Blue, 5 1/2 X 21 In. 115.00
Rose Bowl, Flowers & Leaves Overlay, Blue, 3 3/8 In. 118.00
Rose Bowl, Leaf Feet, Jewel Center Daisies, Blue, 4 1/4 In. 135.00
Rose Bowl, Quilted, Pink, Footed 375.00
Rose Bowl, Rose, Egg Shape, White Lining, 6–Crimp, 3 3/4 In. 148.00
Rose Bowl, Trumpet Flower, Leaves, Frosted Feet, 5 1/2 In. 135.00
Rose Bowl, White Flowers, Gold Leaves, 8–Crimp, 4 1/4 In. 110.00
Salt & Pepper, Melon Ribbed, Enameled Florals, 3 1/4 In. 90.00
Sugar & Creamer, Blue Beetles, Flowers, Square Tops, 3 In. 510.00
Toothpick, Grecian Column, Blue 110.00
Tumbler, Diamond–Quilted, Blue To White 85.00
Vase, Coin Spot, Ruffled, Peach, 8 1/2 In. 550.00
Vase, Diamond–Quiled, Frosted Ruffle, Handle, Blue, 7 1/2 In. 85.00
Vase, Herringbone, Blue, 3 X 4 In. 125.00
Vase, Melon Ribbed, Applied Handle 125.00
Vase, Mother-of-Pearl, Bridal Ribbon, Medallions, 6 1/2 In. 895.00
Vase, Rose, Ribbed, Square, Bulbous, White Lining, 7 3/4 In. 145.00
Water Set, Herringbone Pattern, Square Top, Blue, 6 Piece 445.00
SATIN GLASS, WEBB, see Webb

> Satsuma is a Japanese pottery with a distinctive creamy beige
> crackled glaze. Most of the pieces were decorated with blue, red,
> green, orange, or gold. Almost all the Satsuma found today was
> made after 1860. During World War I, Americans could not buy
> undecorated European porcelains. Women who liked to make hand–
> painted porcelains at home began to decorate plain Satsuma. These
> pieces are known today as "American Satsuma."

SATSUMA, Base, Warriors On 1 Side, Man & Woman On Other, 14 In. 185.00
Bowl, Flowers, Gold Highlights, 8 1/2 In. 225.00
Bowl, Men, Dragon, C.1890, 4 In. 90.00
Bowl, Tea, Gosu & Colros, Takan Design, Mid–19th Century 350.00
Box, Children, Temple, Interior Geisha, Cover, Hankinzan, 4 In. 2860.00
Box, Flowers & Butterflies, C.1915, Cover, 2 1/2 In. 125.00
Box, Gold Mums, Shaded Leaves, Double Domed Lid, C.1830, 4 1/2 In. 275.00
Burner, Incense, Cover, Karako & Sages, Signed, 5 1/2 In. 50.00
Charger, Warriors In Battle, Gilt Accents, 18 1/2 In. 500.00
Cup & Saucer, Scenes of Warriors, Cobalt Blue, Demitasse 210.00
Cup & Saucer, Thousand Faces, Marked 115.00
Feeder, Cricket, Warriors In Bowl, Marked, 1 1/2 X 1 1/4 In. 42.00
Ginger Jar, Domed Lid, Knop Finial, Gilt Figures, 7 1/2 In. 275.00
Incense Burner, Chrysanthemum Design, Cover, C.1860, 5 1/2 In. 990.00
Incense Burner, Phoenix & Shishi Design, Cover, C.1860, 6 In. 1980.00
Jar, 1000 Lohan's Design, Rectangular Form, 4 In. 357.50
Jar, Cover, Overall Nishikide Raised Design, 1890, 7 In. 165.00
Jar, Pierced Metal Cover, Globular, C.1850, 6 In. 770.00
Jar, Temple, Seated Girl, Holds Dog, Finial On Cover, 29 In. 1200.00
Jar, Vertical Panels of Cloisonne Design, 7 1/2 In. 275.00
Plaque, Samurai Warriors, Rust, Maroon, Black, Cream, 12 In. 165.00
Plate, Birds, Floral, Blue & Gold Ground, Kinkozan, C.1880, 8 1/2 In. 140.00
Plate, Scenic Design, Fluted, 19th Century, 7 In. 75.00
Plate, Two Sumurai Under Tree, On Knees, Seashore, 9 In. 275.00

Salt, Cream, Gold Flowers, Mother–of–Pearl Spoon, Square	30.00
Tazza, Floral Design, 19th Century, 5 1/2 X 8 3/4 In.	185.00
Teapot, Shishi Design, Gosu Cross & Circle, Early 19th Century	695.00
Tray, Cranes In Relief, Floral Design, 19th Century, 7 In.	595.00
Urn, Bird Handle, Geisha Girl Scene, 1920, 14 In., Pair	265.00
Urn, Hanging, Warrior & Flowers, 10 In.	50.00
Vase, 2 Reserves of Noblemen & Samurai, Floral Ground, 38 In. ....*Illus*	2100.00
Vase, 28 Faces, Dragons, Signed, 8 In. .... 325.00 To	350.00
Vase, Allover Flying Birds, Gold Borderwork, Artist, 4 1/2 In.	275.00
Vase, Applied Blossom Handle, Floral Scenes, 16 7/8 In., Pair	350.00
Vase, Baluster, Millefiori Patterns, Gilt Landscapes, 9 1/2 In.	800.00
Vase, Blue, Pink & Yellow Flowers, Foliage, Signed, 9 In.	95.00
Vase, Bulbous Form, Figural Design, Brown Ground, 5 In.	225.00
Vase, Carp Form, Standing On Tail, Signed, 17 3/4 In.	800.00
Vase, Dragon Around Neck & Body, 28 Arhats, 8 In. .... 350.00 To	395.00
Vase, Faces, Dragons, Signed, 8 In.	325.00
Vase, Floral Design, 19th Century, 8 1/2 In., Pair	'55.00
Vase, Flowers Outlined In Gold, Trees, Streams, Hill, 7 1/4 In.	325.00
Vase, One Thousand Butterflies, 6 In.	375.00
Vase, Panels of Mother & Child, Gold Florals, C.1900, 2 3/4 In.	95.00
Vase, Pear Shape, C.1860, 5 In.	225.00
Vase, Polychrome Figural Panels, Geometric Ground, 4 1/2 In.	150.00
Vase, Rakan, Dragons, Black, Red, Brown & Gold, Signed, 1925, 6 1/2 In.	295.00
Vase, Scenes of Civil Wars of Shogunate Period, Signed, 8 In.	1800.00
Vase, Thousand Faces, Gilt Robes, Enameled Dragons, 9 5/8 In., Pair	1200.00
Vase, Thousand Gold Cranes, Black Ground, 9 In.	195.00
Vase, Tiger, Characters With Halos, 9 1/2 In.	190.00
Vase, Warrior Design In Gilt, Brown Ground, Bulbous, 9 1/2 In.	350.00
Vase, Woman In Landscape, 6 Color, Enameled, 15 In.	130.00
Vase, Woman, On Dragon, On Elephant, Blown–Out, Cobalt, 6 In., Pair	125.00

Special scales have been made to weigh everything from babies to gold. Collectors search for all types. Most popular are small gold–dust scales and special grocery scales.

SCALE, A.D.Jennings, White Porcelain	1200.00
A.D.Jennings, Lollipop, White Porcelain	1000.00
Agile Dile, Open Face & Mirror, Base	500.00
American Scale Co., Fortunes, Coin–Operated	140.00
Anderson Computing Scale Co., Candy, 2 Lbs.	250.00
Apothecary, Traveling, Gold, Brass Fittings, Weights In Pine Box	175.00
Baby, Wicker	45.00
Balance, Cast Iron Base, Tin Pans, 22 In.	60.00
Balance, Oak Base, Chocolate Marble Top, Indicator Window, No Pans	150.00
Balance, Wrought Iron, 23 In.	5.00
Bathroom, Art Deco, Cast Iron, 300 Lbs.	40.00
Buffalo Hide, 1860s .... 65.00 To	100.00
Butter, Square Platform, All Wooden, 27 In.	75.00

Some tea and coffee stains on dishes can be removed by rubbing them with damp baking soda.

Satsuma, Vase, Noblemen, Samurai,
Floral, 38 In., Pair

Candy, Brass	45.00
Cast Iron, 1800s	25.00
Chatillon Spring Balance, Brass Face, Weights To 144 Lbs., 17 In.	60.00
Child's, Cast Iron, Scoop & Weights	25.00
Coin–Operated Machine, Talking	8500.00
Cow Chow Makes More Milk At Less Cost, Purina, Cow	35.00
Dayton, Meat, White Enamel	200.00
Dayton, No.166, Brass Pan, Brass, 14 1/2 In.	200.00
Detectogram, Candy, Brass Pan, Weights, Iron, 1930s	135.00
Egg, Single	20.00
Enterprise, Candy, Nickel Plated Brass, Panto 2 Lbs.	62.00
Gold Miner's, Portable, Hand Held Brass Balance, Tole Box, Pocket	150.00
Gold, Virginia City, Nevada, Weights, Brass	495.00
Hanging, Brass Face, Small	10.00
Hanson, Postal, 1st Class, 5 Cent	5.00
Horse Teather, Brass, 7 Lbs., 7 In.	40.00
Jeweler's, Marble Top, Brass Scales & Weights, Wood & Glass Case	250.00
Jiffy Way, Egg	12.00
Liberty Postal, Platform, Flat, 4 X 5 1/2 In.	28.00
Lollipop, White, 1 Cent ....950.00 To 1000.00	
Milk, Brass, Box	95.00
Mills Fat & Lean, Lollipop, 1 Cent	750.00
Mills, 1 Cent	750.00
National Store Co., Candy, Tin Pan, Weights To 2 Lbs., C.1910	85.00
National, Candy Store	250.00
National, Candy, No.6, Brass Tray	225.00
National, Claw Foot, Fancy Round Stand	750.00
National, Pepsi Design	250.00
Oak, Rose Marble Top, Brass Weights In Oak Box	120.00
Peerless Weighing Machine, Lollipop, Honest Weight 1 Cent, 1968	635.00
Pharmacy, Beveled Glass, Marble, Oak, 1800s	295.00
Pioneer, Balance, Pocket	5.00
Postal, 2 Drawers, 3 Pen Holders, Double Inkwell	55.00
Postal, Celluloid Advertising Badge Front	19.00
Rheva, Cast Iron, Brass Pan, 4 Weights	88.00
Standard Comp., Candy, Brass Scoop	185.00
Steelyard, Iron, 3 Hooks, 21 In.Weight	25.00
Stimpson Meat Store, No Glass Plate, 1912	150.00
Store, Glass Encased, Balance Beam, Tray	27.50
Toledo, Candy, Burgandy	625.00
Toledo, Counter, Blue & Chrome With Tan	165.00
Toledo, Porcelain Pan, Brass, 30 In.	350.00
Toledo, White Enamel, 3 Lbs. Limit, Pan	60.00
Trener, Candy, Counter Top, Brass Arm & Scoop	125.00
Use Purina Pail Hook, Brass, Use Purina, 4 1/2 X 15 In.	75.00
Walla–Walla Gum, Restored	500.00
Watling, 1 Cent	1375.00
Watling, Fortune, Coin–Operated, 1 Cent	250.00
Weight, Drug Store, Porcelain, Brass Foot Piece, 1 Cent, 72 In.	195.00
Wells Fargo	295.00
Wrigley's Gum, Tin, Brass	175.00
Wrigley's Spearmint Pepsin Gum	185.00

Schafer & Vater, makers of small ceramic items, are best known for their amusing figurals. The factory was located in Volkstedt–Rudolstadt, Germany, from 1890 to 1962. Some pieces are marked with the crown and R mark, but many are unmarked.

SCHAFER & VATER, Candlestick, Yellow Lion, White Eyes, Cube Shape, 5 3/4 In. ...	95.00
Creamer, Bear With Muff, 5 In.	95.00
Creamer, Chinaman & Monkey, 5 1/2 In.	95.00
Creamer, Cow In Dress, Blue	90.00
Creamer, Cow, Blue & White, 4 In.	50.00
Creamer, Dutch Girl, Purse, Jug	65.00
Creamer, Girl With Basket	85.00

Creamer, Goose In Bonnet	100.00
Creamer, Maid With Jug & Keys, 3 1/3 In.	85.00
Creamer, Mother Goose, 5 1/2 In.	95.00
Creamer, Seated Goat, Boutonniere, 5 1/2 In.	95.00
Figurine, Hobo, Bearded, Comic, 8 In.	60.00
Figurine, Lady, On Resting Camel, Ivory, Gold, 6 1/2 In.	125.00
Figurine, Young Girl, Holding 2 Large Shoes, 4 1/2 In.	95.00
Flask, Comic Figure, Just A Little Nip	40.00
Hatpin Holder, Egyptian Ladies, Jewels In Hair, 4 1/2 In.	145.00
Holder, Calling Card, Bisque, Cameo, Cupid Kissing Venus	90.00
Match Holder, Man With No Moustache	80.00
Nodder, Black Girl On Dish, Bisque	185.00
Nodder, Grinning Monkey, Apple In Hand, 4 1/4 In.	175.00
Pitcher, Chinese Man, Holding Baby, Queue Is Handle	75.00
Pitcher, Milk, Milkmaid, Blue, White	100.00
Pitcher, Milk, Oriental Woman, Crying Child	120.00
Pitcher, Milkmaid	32.00
Salt & Pepper, Smiling Apple & Pear	75.00
Teapot, Smiling Apple	100.00
Toothpick, Bulging Loops, Green	35.00
Toothpick, Skull	22.50
Toothpick, Smiling Pig	75.00
Urn, Jasperware, Cherubs, Scrolled Handles, 7 1/2 In.	95.00
Vase, Medallion of Grecian Lady's Head, 4 3/4 In.	55.00

Schneider Schneider Glassworks was founded in 1903 at Epinay-sur-Seine, France, by Charles and Ernest Schneider. Art glass was made between 1903 and 1930. The company still produces clear crystal glass.

SCHNEIDER, Bowl, Amber, Signed, 10 In.	145.00
Bowl, Marbled Charcoal, Signed, 8 1/4 In.	175.00
Candleholder, Paperweight, Double Clematis, Signed, 5 1/2 In.	165.00
Compote, Orange Mottling, Iron Stem, Balls, Signed, 6 1/2 In.	275.00
Compote, Peach Bowl, Blue Rim, Amethyst Base & Stem, 7 1/2 In.	380.00
Compote, Pink To Purple, Pedestal, Signed	295.00
Lamp Base, Inlaid Candy Cane, Orange Design, 8 1/2 In.	250.00
Paperweight, Pulled Feather Design, Signed	195.00
Vase, Bright Pink, 10 In.	135.00
Vase, Cameo, Lemon Yellow, Purple, Chocolate, Orange, Signed, 12 In.	1430.00

Scrimshaw is bone or ivory or whale's teeth carved by sailors and others for entertainment during the sailing-ship days. Some scrimshaw was carved as early as 1800. There are modern scrimshanders making pieces today on bone, ivory, or plastic.

SCRIMSHAW, see also Ivory, Nautical

SCRIMSHAW, Antler, Nautical Map, Symbols, 10 In.	425.00
Bone, Ship Model, Made By French Prisoners, In England, 19 In.	5000.00
Bone, Whimsies, Lady, At Spinning Wheels, Crank, With Gears, 5 In.	1400.00
Box, Wooden Bottom & Top, 3 Ships, Compass, Oval, 6 1/2 In.	200.00
Cane, Walrus Ivory Handle, Elephant's Head, Wooden	1000.00
Corkscrew, Dated 1871	275.00
Ivory Husk, Washington, Schooner, Capitol, Hancock, 13 In.	500.00
Ivory, Woman's Brush, Indian With Harpoon Design, 8 3/4 In.	325.00
Thimble, Ship, Flowers	15.00
Tooth, British & American Naval Battle 1 Side, 1825-50, 7 In.	6000.00
Tooth, Doorknob, Engraved, 5 To 6 In., Set of 4	2100.00
Tooth, Ship, Clouds, Gulls, 2 1/4 In.	32.00
Tooth, Whale Chewing Man & People, People Under Umbrellas, 6 In.	400.00
Tooth, Whale Destroying Boat, J.Pinkham Memorial, 1824, 7 1/8 In.	4250.00
Tooth, Woman, Seated In Chair, Polychrome, 6 1/2 In.	1650.00
Walrus Tusk, Snow Goose, Eskimo, 3 1/8 In.	396.00
Walrus Tusk, Whaling Ship, Bird, Men In Boats, Dated 1842	1000.00
Watch Holder, French Prisoner of War	950.00
Whale Bone, Dolphin, Ship, Bust of Man, Dated 1864, 13 1/4 In.	450.00

Whale Bone, Harbor Scene, 15 In. 375.00
Whale Bone, Hunting Scene, 2 Stalking Eskimos, Spears, 13 In. 300.00
Whale Bone, Knitting Needles, Clenched Fist End, Wood, 12 In., Pr. 2600.00
Whale Bone, Man Riding Sperm Whale, 7 In. 350.00
Whale Bone, Panel, Map, Sites & Symbols, 4 In. 200.00
Whale Bone, Plaque, Ship Saracen, 1880, 5 In. 250.00

Prescott W. Baston made the first Sebastian miniatures in 1938 in Marblehead, Massachusetts. More than 400 different designs have been made and the collectors search for the out-of-production models. The mark may say "Copr. P. W. Baston U.S.A.," or "P. W. Baston, U.S.A.," or "Prescott W. Baston." Sometimes a paper label was used.

SEBASTIAN MINIATURES, Abraham Lincoln, Purple Label 18.00
    Andrew Jackson, Blue Label 18.00
    Annie Stuyvesant 40.00
    Aunt Betsy, 1946 .... 30.00
    Aunt Polly .... 26.00 To 35.00
    Barkis, Green Label 26.00
    Becky Thatcher, Orange Label 18.00
    Ben Franklin & Press, Signed 160.00
    Betsy Ross 40.00
    Clown .... 100.00 To 119.00
    Colonial Blacksmith, Blue Label 18.00
    Colonial Blacksmith, Green Label 26.00
    Dahl's Fisherman, Signed 160.00
    Dame Van Winkle, Signed 140.00
    David Copperfield & Wife 50.00
    Doctor 65.00
    Dutchman's Pipe .... 185.00 To 200.00
    Family Picnic, Box 10.00
    Farmer & Wife, Pair 110.00
    Forty-Niner, Signed 20.00
    Gathering Tulips 200.00
    George Washington, Blue Label 16.00
    George Washington, Yellow Label 18.00
    Henry VIII, Anne Boleyn, Pair 110.00
    Home From The Sea 45.00
    Huckleberry Finn, Blue Label 18.00
    Huckleberry Finn, Green Label 26.00
    Ichabod Crane, Purple Label 30.00
    Ichabod Crane, Signed 140.00
    In The Candy Store 65.00
    Jack & Jill Went Up The Hill, 1949 .... 75.00
    John & Priscilla Alden 75.00
    John Alden, Marblehead 40.00
    John F. Kennedy 30.00
    John Smith .... 40.00 To 70.00
    Judge Thatcher .... 36.00 To 75.00
    Knickerbocker, Signed 140.00
    Lobsterman 52.00
    Madonna of The Chair 40.00
    Martha Washington 45.00
    Mr. Obocell .... 85.00 To 125.00
    Penny Shop, Blue Label 18.00
    Peter Stuyvesant 40.00
    Pilgrims .... 26.00 To 45.00
    Praying Hands 235.00
    Sam Weller, Green Label 26.00
    Sampling The Stew 70.00
    Shaker, Man & Woman, Pair 150.00
    Shepherds, Green Label 26.00
    Shoemaker, Blue Label 18.00
    Sidewalk Days, Boy, Green Label .... 48.00 To 60.00

Sidewalk Days, Girl, Green Label .... 48.00 To 60.00
Skipper .... 45.00 To 55.00
Swan Boat, Orange Label 18.00
Swan Boat, Purple Label, Signed 26.00
Switching The Freight, Orange Label, Signed 30.00
Thomas Jefferson, 1949 .... 65.00
Tom Bowline Ashore 35.00
Trout Fisher, Box 10.00
Will Rogers, Signed 140.00
Williamsbury Lady 130.00
Yankee Sea Captain .... 26.00 To 35.00
   SEG, see Paul Revere Pottery

Sevres porcelain has been made in Sevres, France, since 1769. Many copies of the famous ware have been made. The name originally referred to the works of the Royal Porcelain factory. The name now includes any of the wares made in the town of Sevres, France. The entwined lines with a center letter used as the mark is one of the most forged marks in antiques. Be very careful to identify Sevres by quality, not just by mark.

SEVRES, Bowl, Cover, Footed, 9 1/2 In. 350.00
Bowl, Venus, On Dolphins, Pierced Border, Term Handles, Maglin, 22 In. 1980.00
Box, Jewelry, Courting Scene On Lid, Florals, C.1844, 7 1/2 X 5 In. 495.00
Casket, 2 Maidens, Musician, Gilt Metal, Cover, Signed Lauque, 12 In. 1450.00
Centerpiece, Tureen, 6–Light, Porcelain, Cover, Raised Base, 21 In. 4950.00
Coffee Can & Saucer, Scattered Rose Sprigs, 1775–76, 2 5/8 In. 885.00
Coffee Set, Portraits, Napoleon, Josephine, Marie Louise, 10 Piece 1600.00
Cruet, Gold Scrolls & Florals, Free–Form Handle, Label, 8 1/2 In. 435.00
Cup & Saucer, Cupids In Panel, Pink, Gold, White Border, Signed 48.00
Dish, Condiment, Trefoil, Cup At Corners, Floral Bouquets, 1760 .... 425.00
Garniture, 3–Light Candelabra, Marie Antoinette Bust Clock, 3 Piece 5500.00
Garniture, 5–Light Candelabra, Clock, Cupids, 22 In.Clock, 3 Piece 1100.00
Garniture, Brass Footing & Finial, Boy Playing Flute, Marked 175.00
Pedestal, Putti Panels, Border, Ebonized Wood Top & Base, 46 In., Pr. 1210.00
Pillbox, Floral, Green & Gold Enameled, Signed 85.00
Plate, 18th Century Lovers, Scalloped, Morin, 9 1/2 In., 12 Piece 2200.00
Plate, Chateau St.Cloud, Couple In Garden, Gold Rim, 8 In. 75.00
Plate, Elongated Oval Reserves, Flowers In Gilt Frames, 14 3/4 In. 550.00
Plate, Grape Leaves, Gold Grapes, Cranberry, 7 1/2 In. 12.00
Plate, Jeweled, Silver Overlay, Signed Cagnet, Dated 1844 .... 125.00
Plate, Madame De Montespan, Gold Encrusted, Signed, 9 1/2 In. 135.00
Plate, Madame Lavalliere, Gold Scalloped Rim, Signed, 9 1/2 In. 125.00
Plate, Napoleon At Battle of Austerlitz, Gold Leaf Rim, 9 1/2 In. 250.00
Saucer, Ornithological, Puce Flowering Plant, C.1795, 5 9/16 In. 935.00
Seau Crenele, Floral Sprays, Scroll Handles, Gilt Edge, 11 5/8 In. 1875.00
Urn, Gold Scrolling, Floral, Portrait, Scenic Reverse, C.1890, 9 In. 255.00
Urn, Maiden, Standing, Ormolu Handle, Cover, 1890s 235.00
Urn, Palace, Maiden With Cupid, Marked, 21 1/2 In. 165.00
Urn, Pineapple Finial, Portrait Bust, Cover, 13 1/2 In., Pair 275.00
Urn, Yellow, Gold Trim, Colonial Lady, Blue Forget–Me–Nots At Top 245.00
Vase, Bleu Celeste Ground, Vessel, Portrait, Cover, 20 1/2 In., Pair 1450.00
Vase, Flower Sprays, Gilt, Satyr's Mask Handles, Poitevin, 18 In., Pr. 1100.00

To remove fresh food stains from rugs and upholstery, sprinkle cornmeal on the spot. It will act like a blotter. Vacuum.

Vase, Maiden, 2 Cupids, Ovoid, Bronze Mounted, Cover, 1910, 29 1/4 In. 1350.00
Vase, Round Bird Panel, Blue Celeste Ground, Knop Cover, 16 In., Pair 4100.00
Vase, Snowy White Spider, Chrysanthemum, Yellow, 1902, 24 In. 2750.00
Vase, Urn, Gilt Bronze, Artist Poitevin, 19th Century, 46 In. 4500.00

> Sewer tile figures were made by workers at the sewer tile and pipe factories in the Ohio area during the late nineteenth and early twentieth centuries. Figurines, small vases, and cemetery vases were favored. Often the finished vase was a piece of the original pipe with added decorations and markings. All types of sewer tile work are now considered folk art by collectors.

SEWER TILE, Birdhouse, Glazed 135.00
Bookends, Gorillas, Tooled Coats, Superior Clay Corp., 15 In. 700.00
Cat, Sitting, Painted 50.00
Cuspidor, Tooled Bark–Like Finish, 3 1/4 X 5 In. 25.00
Dog, Incised Design, 10 In. 110.00
Dog, Seated, Bottom Initialed D.G., 8 In. 75.00
Lamp Base, Stump, Applied Vining, Animal At Knot Hole, 9 In. 150.00
Lion, Lying Down, Base 125.00
Lion, Reclining, Brown 125.00
Match Holder, Stump, Incised W.A.Baker, 12 X 11 X 28 In. 25.00
Planter, Stump, Tooled Bark, Knot Holes, 18 In. 40.00
Solid Log, Tooled Bark, 2 Unglazed Areas, 7 1/2 In. 10.00

> All types of sewing equipment are collected, from sewing birds that held the cloth to old wooden spools.

SEWING, Basket, 2 Pillow & 2 Strawberry Pincushions, Wicker, 6 1/4 In. 85.00
Basket, Shaker, Wooden 155.00
Bird, Clamp, C.1810 .... 220.00
Bottle, Travelers Sewing Machine Oil, Clear, Cork, Case, 1 2/3 In. 4.00
Box, Lacquer, Figural Cover, Mother–of–Pearl, Black, Japan, 5 X 13 In. 132.00
Box, Teak Panels, Animals & Flowers, Ivory, Paw Feet, 7 X 18 In. 1750.00
Box, William IV, Brass Inlaid, Rosewood, Ring Handles, 1835, 7 In. 825.00
Box, Wooden, Painted Village Scene, Sliding Cover, 3 X 7 X 10 In. 950.00
Caddy, Pincushion, Metal, Thread Revolving, 1900 .... 25.00
Case, Fitted, Scissors, Thimble, Needle Case, Stiletto 125.00
Case, Needle & Thread, F.Schneider, Jeweler, 1912 Calendar, 3 X 5 In. 3.00
Case, Needle, Gold & Enameled, Female Figures, Swiss, 1800, 4 3/8 In. 4180.00
Cupboard, Belding Silk Thread, Inside Shelves, Oak, 39 X 35 In. 395.00
Darner, Glove, Repousse Mums, Sterling Silver, 4 In. 48.00
Darner, Glove, Repousse Scrolls, Sterling Silver, 4 1/2 In. 45.00
Darning Egg, Silver Handle 22.00
Dress Form, Dated 1906 .... 75.00
Dress Form, Victorian, Cast Iron Feet, Wire Construction 30.00
Egg, Engraved, Sterling Silver 140.00
Hem Marker, Metal, Adjustable Arm For Chalk, Pat.1905, 7 1/2 In. 15.00
Holder, Needle & Shuttle, Boye Brand 95.00
Holder, Thimble, Acorn, Vegetable Ivory 85.00
Holder, Thimble, Carved Vegetable Ivory, With Thimble 95.00
Holder, Thimble, Hinged Cover, Embossed Berries, Sterling Silver 95.00
Holder, Thread, Repousse, Sterling Silver, Marked, 1 1/2 X 1 In. 115.00
Kit, Schoolhouse Shape, Beaded Bamboo 22.00
Lamp, Massive Greek Key, Glass 110.00
Machine, Buttonhole, Treadle, 1867 .... 175.00
Machine, Cast Iron, Ornate Base, Claw Feet, German, 11 X 7 X 9 In. 125.00
Machine, Electric, Berling, Miniature 55.00
Machine, Howe Treadle 75.00
Machine, Label, Star Shuttle, Cleveland, Ohio, Cast Iron, 10 X 21 In. 185.00
Machine, New Home 35.00
Machine, Singer, Child's, Black 32.50
Machine, Singer, Portable 125.00
Machine, Singer, Treadle, Oak Cabinet 30.00
Machine, Singer, Walnut Portable Case, Pre–1900 .... 95.00

Machine, Wilcox & Gibbs, Foot Pedal, Walnut Carrying Case, Electric 495.00
Machine, Singer, Child's, Box 35.00
Model, Milliner's, 15 1/4 In. 350.00
Needle Book, Army & Navy, Iowa, Germany 2.00
Needle Book, Globe Fertilizer 4.00
Needle Book, Happy Home, 3 1/2 X 6 In. 5.50
Needle Case, Barrel Shape, Wooden, Germany 20.00
Needle Case, Boye Co., 40 Containers & Needles, Metal, Round, 16 In. 135.00
Needle Case, Brass, 3 3/4 X 2 1/2 In. 60.00
Needle Case, Figural, Acorn, Vegetable Ivory, 2 3/4 In. 75.00
Needle Case, Figural, Fish, Embedded Metal Dots, Bone, 3 1/4 In. 70.00
Needle Case, Figural, Umbrella, Wood & Bone, 4 In. 95.00
Needle Case, Ivory, 13 Eyelet Punch, 4 Ribbon Needles, 2 1/2 In. 35.00
Needle Case, Umbrella, Celluloid, Ivory & Black 45.00
Needle Threader, Champion Oil, Metal 8.50
Needlebook, Blue Ribbon, Steeplechase Scene 4.50
Pin Casket, Leaf Slide Lid, Beaded, Pratt & Farmer, 1822, 2 3/4 In. 125.00
   SEWING, PINCUSHION DOLL, see Pincushion Doll
Pincushion, Beaded, Dated 1838, 2 In. 45.00
Pincushion, Celluloid, Canoe Shape 12.50
Pincushion, Lady, Holding Spear, Bronze, French 175.00
Pincushion, Man's Shoe, Silver, Over Light Oak, English, 5 X 2 In. 150.00
Pincushion, Metal Heeled Shoe 15.00
Pincushion, Metal Slipper, 4 In. 20.00
Pincushion, Prudential Girl 8.00
Pincushion, Rocking Chair 12.00
Pincushion, Star Shape, Velvet Floss Stitches, Tassels 15.00
Pincushion, Vegetable Ivory, Miniature 35.00
Punch, Eyelet, Gauge Relief Engraved Handle, Sterling Silver 30.00
Scissors, Bird Shape 12.00
Scissors, Buttonhole, Peters Brothers 12.00
Scissors, Embroidery, Repousse Handle, Marked 32.00
Scissors, Sterling Silver, 4 1/2 In. 25.00
Sewing Box, Mother-of-Pearl Inlay, Thos.Spurlin, 1898, 12 X 9 In. 2100.00
Sewing Egg, Sterling, Engraved, With Thimble 140.00
Sewing Machine, Child's, Reliable, Original Wooden Box 100.00
Sewing Machine, Folding, Light Oak, Attachments, Box 12.50
Shears, Pinking, Gem, 3 Cutting Wheels 37.50
Shears, Tailor's, To Mayor Andrew Johnson, 1834, Bronze & Steel 850.00
Shuttle, Tatting, Ivory 14.00
Shuttle, Tatting, Sterling Silver 95.00
Spool Holder, Barrel Shape, Carved Walnut, Ivory Holes, 3 Sections 85.00
Tape Measure, Akron Truss Co. 12.00
Tape Measure, Alarm Clock, Celluloid, Germany, 2 In. 65.00
Tape Measure, Alligator 55.00
Tape Measure, Apple, With Fly Pull 45.00
Tape Measure, Barrel, Niagara Falls Views, Stanhope 85.00
Tape Measure, Basket of Fruit, Celluloid 25.00
Tape Measure, Bear 55.00
Tape Measure, Boot & Shoe Workers Union, Metal, Celluloid, 60 In. 25.00
Tape Measure, Chicken & Chicks, Celluloid 45.00
Tape Measure, Clock 22.00
Tape Measure, Crown Flour 30.00
Tape Measure, Dog, Waving 45.00
Tape Measure, Engraved Piercing, Carved Vegetable Ivory 45.00
Tape Measure, Esso, Bakelite Case, Retractable, 2 In. 12.00
Tape Measure, Fab 12.00
Tape Measure, Fab Washing Powder, 1 1/2 In. 10.00
Tape Measure, Fab, Celluloid 12.00
Tape Measure, Fish, Celluloid, 4 1/2 In. .... 20.00 To 28.00
Tape Measure, Frigidaire, Cloth Tape, Man Carrying Block of Ice 10.00
Tape Measure, General Electric Refrigerator, Celluloid 25.00
Tape Measure, Hat 65.00
Tape Measure, John Deere 20.00

The early 1840s were the time of pressed glass table settings. The early patterns were simple, with heavy loops or ribbed effects. The 1870s meant more elaborate naturalistic patterns. Clear and frosted patterns with figures were in style during the 1870s. Overall patterns that were slightly geometric in feeling were in style by 1880, and patterns such as Daisy and Button and Hobnail came into vogue. Colored pressed glass patterns became popular after the Civil War.

Tape Measure, Lewis Lye, 1918 .... 23.00 To 35.00
Tape Measure, Lydia Pinkham, Portrait, Celluloid 45.00
Tape Measure, Mead Johnson, Small 15.00
Tape Measure, Penguin 65.00
Tape Measure, Pierced Vegetable Ivory, Windup Knob 55.00
Tape Measure, Pierrot Playing Mandolin, Porcelain 45.00
Tape Measure, Pig, Brass .... 70.00 To 95.00
Tape Measure, Pumpkin End of Tape, Celluloid 12.50
Tape Measure, Puppy, Straw Filled 12.00
Tape Measure, Robin Hood 10.00
Tape Measure, Sailing Ship, Celluloid, Japan .... 35.00 To 42.00
Tape Measure, Seagram's VO 12.00
Tape Measure, Silver Plated Flask, Logo, Textured 65.00
Tape Measure, Stromberg Carburator 45.00
Tape Measure, Woman's Head, Papier-Mache 35.00
Thimble, 14K Gold, Straw Case Design, Set 125.00
Thimble, Fries Celebrated, Registerd Ice Cream, Red Band, Aluminum 12.00
Thimble, Gold, In Sweet Grass Basket Case 150.00
Thimble, Jewel Stoves & Ranges, Aluminum 8.00
Thimble, Kurtz's Liver Tablets, Yellow Band, Aluminum 6.00
Thimble, Racine Feet Hosiery, Black Band, Aluminum 9.00
Thimble, Scenic Band, Barn, Silo, House, Sterling Silver, Size 7 .... 38.00
Thimble, Sterling Silver, C.1900 .... 20.00
Thimble, Sterling, Lily of The Valley, 1890's 90.00

Shaker-produced items are characterized by simplicity, functionalism, and orderliness. There were many Shaker communities in America from the eighteenth century to the present day. The religious order made furniture, small wooden pieces, and packaged medicines, herbs, and jellies to sell to "outsiders." Other useful objects were made for use by members of the community.

SHAKER, Basket, 4 Carved Handles, Maple Splint, Square, 8 X 11 X 11 In. 2600.00
Basket, Berry, Made By Brother David Johnson, 5 1/2 X 5 1/4 In. 600.00
Basket, Berry, Woven Splint, Splint Handle, 3 1/2 X 3 1/4 In. 138.00
Basket, Carved Handles, Gray Paint, Maple Splint, 6 1/2 X 12 In. 150.00
Basket, Double Wrapped Rim, Inverted Bottom, Maple & Ash, 21 In. 350.00
Basket, Feather, Signed Ann Sater, Brother David Johnson, C.1872 .... 600.00
Basket, Fruit, Carved Handles, Enfield, Maple, Black Ash, 15 1/4 In. 450.00
Basket, Gathering, Hoop Handle, Ash Splint, 13 1/2 X 11 1/2 In. 350.00
Basket, Hoop Handle, Interwoven Splint, Maple, Black Ash, 5 In. 100.00
Basket, Hoop Handle, R.N.Canterbury, N.H., Maple Splint, 11 In. 600.00
Basket, Kitten Head Shape, Wrapped Rim, Maple & Black Ash 850.00
Basket, Laundry, 4 Handles, Maple, Black Ash, Enfield, 22 1/2 In. 2900.00
Basket, Laundry, Wrapped Rim, Double Bottom, Handles, Ash, 13 X 24 In. 550.00
Basket, Orchard, Enfield, NH., Maple & Ash Splint, 15 1/2 X 21 In. 800.00
Basket, Sewing, Double Attached Lid, Pine Bottom, Oval, 6 X 5 1/2 In. 300.00
Basket, Sewing, Sliding Lid, Star Design Top, Maple & Ash, 11 1/2 In. 700.00

Basket, Sewing, With Pincushion, Needles Case & Wax Acorn	325.00
Basket, Sewing, Woven Splint & Sweet Grass, Silk Handles, Miniature	100.00
Basket, Single Wrapped Rim, Hickory Handled, Ash, 9 X 15 1/2 In.	600.00
Basket, Splint, Lid Slides Up Arched Handle, Square Bottom, 10 In.	430.00
Basket, Wool Gathering, Maple & Black Ash Splint, Enfield, C.1840	1600.00
Beater, Rug, Metal Holder, Hickory, Maple, Canterbury, N.H., 27 1/2 In.	210.00
Bonnet, Cotton, Summer, Brim, Collapsible, 1/2 Rows Poplar Stays	38.00
Bonnet, Field, Woven Herringbone Straw Brim, Brown Cotton	100.00
Bonnet, Straw, Dated 1863	75.00
Book, Almanac, Medical & Formulation Advice, 1884, 7 7/8 X 6 In.	77.00
Book, Portraiture of Shakerism, Mary M.Dyer,, 446 Pages, 1822	175.00
Bowl & Herb Masher, Enfield, N.H., Yellow Birch, 15 1/2 In.	400.00
Bowl, Bread, Handles, Canted Sides, Watervliet, C.1840, 21 1/2 In.	600.00
Bowl, Carved Lozenge Shape, Black Ash, C.1840, 12 X 21 In.	300.00
Bowl, Chopping, Original Red Paint, Ash, 7 X 19 In.	200.00
Box, 3–Finger, Cherry Top, Maple & Pine, Oval, 4 1/2 In.	500.00
Box, 3–Finger, Fitted Cover, Sarah S.Woods, Canterbury, 3 1/2 In.	1300.00
Box, 3–Finger, Oval, Maple & Pine, 1 5/8 X 3 5/8 In.	900.00
Box, 3–Finger, Red Paint, Oval, Maple, Pine, C.1830, 2 1/8 X 6 1/4 In.	1250.00
Box, 4–Finger, Blue–Green Paint, Alfred, Me., Maple, Pine, Oval, C.1830	3750.00
Box, 4–Finger, Green Paint, Oval, Maple & Pine, C.1830, 10 1/2 In.	850.00
Box, 4–Finger, Maple & Pine, Natural Finish, Maine, 12 3/4 In.	200.00
Box, 4–Finger, Original Blue Paint, Oval, Pine & Maple, 4 3/4 In.	7000.00
Box, 4–Finger, Sewing, Pincushion, Needle Case, Beeswax, Oval, 1870	600.00
Box, 5–Finger, Maple & Pine, 5 3/4 X 13 1/4 X 9 1/2 In.	475.00
Box, Apple, Pumpkin Paint, Canted Sides, Mt. Lebanon, 9 3/4 X 9 In.	600.00
Box, Blanket, Brass Escutcheon, Enfield, Pine, C.1860, 24 1/2 X 24 In.	1100.00
Box, Blanket, Orange Paint, Bootjack Ends, Poplar, 21 1/2 X 39 In.	800.00
Box, Blue Paint, Iron Escutcheon Plate, Pine, 21 X 21 In.	400.00
Box, Comb, Hanging, Painted Green, Signed Wallace, Poplar, 5 X 9 In.	250.00
Box, Dark Green, Cover, 3 X 4 In.	300.00
Box, Document, Harvard, Mass., Walnut, C.1840, 5 1/4 X 13 In.	300.00
Box, Fitted Cover, Painted Border, Oval, Putty Grained, 4 3/8 In.	3300.00
Box, Glove, Brown Stain, Poplar, Harvard, Mass., C.1820, 12 1/4 In.	350.00
Box, Grained, Initials On Cover, Round	3630.00
Box, Herb, Extract of Butternut Label, New Lebanon, 6 1/2 X 10 In.	1100.00
Box, Iron Diamond Bail Plate, Pine & Maple, 5 X 4 3/4 In.	175.00
Box, Knife, Dovetailed Construction, Maple, 3 1/2 X 15 1/2 X 9 In.	250.00
Box, Orange Stain, Papered Interior, Pine, 18 3/4 In.	800.00
Box, Oval, Salmon Color, C.1837	2860.00
Box, Papered Interior, Red Paint, Pine, 9 X 21 X 12 3/4 In.	1200.00
Box, Red Paint, Pine, Alfred, C.1820, 9 1/2 X 10 1/2 In.	175.00
Box, Salmon Color, Date Pricked Onto Lid, 1837	2860.00
Box, Seed, Gray Paint, Double Lid, Birch & Poplar, 33 1/4 X 8 In.	400.00
Box, Sewing, 2–Step, Pine & Birch, 13 X 13 3/4 X 14 In.	900.00
Box, Sewing, 4–Finger, Swing Handle, Sabbath Day Lake, Maple, Pine	200.00
Box, Sewing, Clock Mechanism On Top, 2 Drawers, Walnut, 13 1/2 In.	750.00
Box, Sewing, Pincushion Lid, Brother F.Harris, Harvard, 1850, 6 In.	400.00
Box, Sewing, Satin Lined, Signed J.A., Watervliet, 12 In.	3080.00
Box, Side Handles, Inside Shelf, Pine, 9 X 19 1/4 In.	350.00
Box, Straight Lap, Copper Nails, 2 1/4 X 5 1/2 In.	85.00
Box, Utility, 4–Finger, Painted, 19th Century, 4 3/4 X 12 In.	700.00
Box, Wood, Porcelain Knobs, New Lebanon, Butternut, C.1830, 32 In.	1000.00
Box, Wrought Iron Straps, Poplar, C.1840, 22 In.	400.00
Box, Yellow Paint, Pine, Enfield, Conn., C.1830, 17 3/4 In.	600.00
Bucket, Berry, Carrier, Slatted Bottom, Poplar & Ash, 5 1/2 X 23 In.	450.00
Bucket, Berry, Green Paint, Diamond Bail Plate, Pine, 7 X 5 1/2 In.	600.00
Bucket, Berry, Red Exterior, Blue Interior, Diamond Bail Plate, Pine	425.00
Bucket, Berry, Red Paint, Diamond Bail Plate, Iron Bands, Pine, 6 In.	325.00
Bucket, Berry, Red Paint, Iron Bands & Bail Plate, Pine, 5 1/2 In.	325.00
Bucket, Black Bands, Enfield, N.H., Pine, C.1850, 9 X 9 3/4 In.	500.00
Bucket, Brass Wraps & Bail Plate, Pine, 6 1/4 X 5 1/2 In.	425.00
Bucket, Cover, Apple Green, Diamond Bail Plate, Enfield, N.H., C.1830	550.00
Bucket, Cover, Iron Bands, Swing Handle, Oak, Watervliet, N.Y., C.1840	275.00

Bucket, Diamond Bail Plates, Chrome Yellow, Pine, 9 X 11 3/4 In. 225.00
Bucket, Dome Cover, Knob Design, Tapered Sides, Red, 10 In. 150.00
Bucket, Grain, Swing Handle, Ash, Maple, New Lebanon, C.1850, 10 In. 200.00
Bucket, Green Paint, Iron Bands, Lid, Canterbury, N.H., 9 1/2 In. 400.00
Bucket, Painted Blue Exterior, Hoops & Handles, Pine, 5 X 10 In. 500.00
Bucket, Plugged Lid, Canted Sides, Pine, 9 1/2 X 11 1/2 In. 250.00
Bucket, Stenciled W.H.Berry, Yellow Grained Paint, Pine, C.1850 .... 175.00
Bucket, Teardrop Bail Plate, Blue, Canterbury, C.1820, 11 1/2 In. 550.00
Bucket, Water, Hickory Bands, Iron Bail Handle, Pine, C.1830, 13 In. 400.00
Butter Mold, Box, Brass Hardware 55.00
Card, Stereopticon, Shaker & Building, Elders, Canterbury, Enfield 300.00
Carrier, 2-Finger, Fixed Handle, Oval, Maple, Pine, 6 1/4 X 9 3/4 In. 800.00
Carrier, Double Lid, Pine, Sabbath Lake, C.1830, 12 X 18 3/8 In. 800.00
Carrier, Hickory Handle, Mt.Lebanon, Pine, Square, C.1870, 10 1/4 In. 800.00
Case, Herb Drying, 6 Flat Drawers, Sophia Wood, Enfield, 1847, 17 In. 1900.00
Case, Medicine Bottle, Slide Lid, Church Family, Black Walnut, C.1820 .... 300.00
Cloak, Child's, Red Wool, Lined Hood, E.Canterbury, N.H., 30 In. 700.00
Cloak, Red, French Wool, Label, Sabbathday Lake 500.00
Cradle, Doll's, Red Stain Finish, Pine, 7 1/2 X 17 3/4 In. 250.00
Dipper, Flour ....95.00 To 185.00
Drainer, Cheese, Tin, Pierced, 18 In. 225.00
Dryer, Clothes, 4 Vertical Folding Arms, 3 Horizontal Bars, C.1860 .... 400.00
SHAKER, FURNITURE, see Furniture
Ironing Board, Wool & Leather Binding, Mt.Lebanon, Pine, 56 In. 175.00
Ladder, Folding, 10 Ft, 6 In. 715.00
Mortar & Pestle, Chrome Yellow Wash, Canterbury, Maple, C.1840 .... 800.00
Motto, God Is Our Hope, Walnut Frame, Canterbury, 8 3/4 X 20 1/2 In. 200.00
Pail, Mustard Paint, Ginger, House E, Dated 1868, Cover, 8 1/2 In. 600.00
Peeler, Apple, Stamped JS, Maple & Poplar, C.1820, 14 3/4 In. 250.00
Picture, Silhouette, Eldress Rachael Baker, Wisdom's Valley, 15 In. 800.00
Picture, Watercolor, Wreath of Flowers Shape, Mt.Lebanon, 1865 .... 935.00
Pie Lifter, Wooden Handle, Brass Ferrule 53.00
Rolling Pin, Tiger & Bird's-Eye Maple, 10 In. 225.00
Rug, Hooked, Red Border, Multicolored Field, Cotton, Wool, 35 X 18 In. 425.00
Rug, Sheared Wool, Cross With 5 Circles, 5 Ft. 8 In. X 3 Ft. 550.00
Rug, Woven & Clipped Wool, Multicolored Center, 42 X 18 1/2 In. 725.00
Scoop, Carved From 1 Piece Maple, Mt.Lebanon, C.1850, 14 In. 525.00
Scoop, Flour, Turned Handled, Carved Finger Grip 150.00
Scoop, Flour, Wooden Threaded Handle, Copper Fasteners, 8 X 13 In. 50.00
Shawl, Plaid, Fringed All Sides, Wool, 19th Century, 60 X 60 In. 150.00
Shawl, Sister's, Black & White Fringe, Wool, Label, MB 78, 9 Ft.6 In. 1000.00
Shovel, Grain, Carved 1 Piece, Maple, Harvard, Mass., C.1820, 35 In. 550.00
Spinning Wheel, Flex, Bone Collar, Birch, Hickory & Oak, Enfield 600.00
Spinning Wheel, Flex, Canterbury, Maple, Oak, C.1820 .... 600.00
Spinning Wheel, Oak & Maple, Marked SR AL 900.00
Spool Holder, Velvet Pincushion, Spool Spikes, Maple, Cherry, 6 In. 225.00
Stereoscope, Folding, Butternut, Tin & Brass, Label, 1872, 15 1/2 In. 600.00
Stick, Tailoring, Hand Numbered, Cherry, Mt.Lebanon, C.1830, 38 In. 700.00
Swift, Original Mustard Paint, Maple, 27 In. 300.00
Swift, Original Yellow Varnish, 16 In. 150.00
Swift, Wooden Thumb Screws, Hancock, Mass., Maple & Poplar, 27 In. 300.00
Thread Reel, Enfield, C.1860 .... 875.00
Traveler, Wrought Iron Wheel, New Lebanon, N.Y., C.1800, 15 1/2 In. 400.00
Trunk, Dome Lid, Leather Covered, Canterbury, N.H., C.1820, 9 X 20 In. 500.00
Wagon Seat, Rush, Tapered Posts, New Lebanon, C.1850, 28 X 33 1/2 In. 750.00
Yarn Winder, Dark Green Paint, Arched Trestle Base, 20 X 18 In. 330.00
Yarn Winder, Maple, Butternut, 6 Arms, Red Paint, 3 1/2 Ft. 200.00

 Shaving mugs were popular from 1860 to 1900. Many types were made, including occupational mugs featuring pictures of men's jobs. There were scuttle mugs, silver plated mugs, glass-lined mugs, and others.

SHAVING MUG, 2 Entwined Flags, Letter H, Name In Gold, Words Rah!Rah! 325.00
Black Glass, Satin Lined Leather Case, Unused 24.00

Brother In Gold Letters, Pink Roses, Blue Flowers, Germany	45.00
Eagle Medallion, Flags, Leon Henry Berry, Gold Trim, Limoges	150.00
Embossed Roses, Gold Washed Insert	85.00
English Ironstone, With Man's Name, Maddock & Sons	25.00
Floral, Prussian Mark 14, 2 1/2 In.	35.00
Fraternal, B.P.O.E.	85.00 To 125.00
Fraternal, F.O.E.	250.00
Fraternal, Italian Ethnic	300.00
Fraternal, Knights of Columbus, Gold Name	75.00
Fraternal, Knights of Pythias, Skull	95.00
Fraternal, Masonic	100.00
Fraternal, Oddfellow	225.00
Fraternal, P.O.S.A.	175.00
Fraternal, S.O.V.	375.00
Head of Bay Horse, Bridled, Transfer, White China	48.00
Hinged Lid, Victorian, Original Glass Liner, Sterling Silver	85.00
Hunter With Dog, Shooting Gamebird, Limoges, Gold Name	220.00
Male & Female Moose, Dresden	95.00
Moose	85.00
Occupational, Bartender	400.00
Occupational, Blacksmith At Work	375.00
Occupational, Buggy	250.00
Occupational, Butcher, Longhorn Cow	275.00
Occupational, Butcher, Tools	275.00
Occupational, Caboose	300.00
Occupational, Carpenter	325.00
Occupational, Carpenter, Tools	250.00
Occupational, Dr.A.W.Harrington, Masonic Symbols, Gold Trim	275.00
Occupational, Druggist	250.00
Occupational, Farmer Plowing Field	350.00
Occupational, Harness Maker At Work	400.00
Occupational, Horse-Drawn Hearse	235.00
Occupational, Letter Carriers Association	110.00
Occupational, Man Driving Black Horse Cab	325.00
Occupational, Man On Wagon, With Team	350.00
Occupational, Pile Driver, On River Barge	375.00
Occupational, Plasterer	275.00
Occupational, Race Horse	350.00
Occupational, Railroad Steam Engine	225.00
Occupational, Red Caboose & Name	85.00
Occupational, Sewing Machine	300.00
Occupational, Shoe Salesman	300.00
Occupational, Sulky Driver	200.00
Occupational, Telegraph Key	300.00
Occupational, Trumpet	325.00
Occupational, Violin & Bow	300.00
Palmer Cox	90.00
Scuttle, Figural, Dog Head, Tan & White, Black Eyes, 4 1/2 In.	135.00
Scuttle, Figural, Fish, Gold Trim, 4 1/2 In.	135.00
Stoneware, Brown Albany Slip, 4 5/8 In.	25.00
Washington Dairy Lunch, Geo.Washington's Picture & Flags	100.00

Most shaving mug reproductions are imaginative copies of old mugs that would not fool a serious collector. There is often no space for the owner's name. Some examples are marked Brandenburg. Copies include designs such as Currier and Ives prints, a hearse drawn by horses, and trade names such as Peddler, Fireman, or Painter.

The Shawnee Pottery was started in Zanesville, Ohio, in 1935. The company made vases, novelty ware, flowerpots, figurines, dinnerwares, and cookie jars. Shawnee produced pottery for George Rumrill during the late 1930s. The company stopped working in 1961.

SHAWNEE, Bank, Smiley, Gold Trim	112.00
Bowl, Corn King, 6 In.	13.50
Bowl, Corn King, 8 In.	20.00
Butter, Corn King, Cover	30.00
Butter, Corn Queen, Cover	22.00
Casserole, Corn	37.50
Casserole, Corn King, Large	25.00 To 35.00
Cookie Jar, Cat	30.00
Cookie Jar, Clown	60.00
Cookie Jar, Cookie House	250.00
Cookie Jar, Corn King	65.00
Cookie Jar, Donkey	45.00
Cookie Jar, Dutch Boy, Patches On Pants, Gold	90.00
Cookie Jar, Dutch Girl	22.50 To 45.00
Cookie Jar, Fruit Basket	20.00 To 45.00
Cookie Jar, Milk Wagon	45.00
Cookie Jar, Mugsy, Gold	95.00
Cookie Jar, Owl	35.00 To 75.00
Cookie Jar, Pink Elephant	35.00
Cookie Jar, Sailor Boy, Decals, Gold Trim	135.00
Cookie Jar, Smiley Pig	75.00
Cookie Jar, Smiley Pig, Gold Trim, Salt & Pepper, 3 Piece	105.00
Cookie Jar, Smiley Pig, Gold Trim, Smiley Written Across Stomach	100.00
Cookie Jar, Smiley Pig, Pink Flowers, Gold Trim	100.00
Cookie Jar, Smiley Pig, Shamrocks	40.00
Cookie Jar, Smiley Pig, Shamrocks, Gold Trim	80.00
Cookie Jar, Winnie Pig, Clover Flowers	32.00
Cookie Jar, Winnie Pig, Green Collar, Marked	67.00
Cookie Jar, Winnie Pig, Shamrocks On Hat & Coat	80.00
Cookie Jar, Yogi Bear	47.00
Creamer, Cat, Gold Trim	85.00
Creamer, Corn King	12.00 To 15.00
Creamer, Elephant	12.00 To 18.00
Creamer, Elephant, Gold Flowers	57.00
Creamer, Puss 'N Boots	12.00 To 15.00
Creamer, Salt & Pepper, Puss 'N Boots, 3 Piece	20.00
Creamer, Smiley Pig	12.00
Creamer, Smiley Pig, Yellow, Gold Trim	60.00
Cup & Saucer, Corn King	15.00 To 22.50
Mixing Bowl, Corn King, No.6	17.00
Mixing Bowl, Corn King, No.8	18.00 To 20.00
Mug, Corn King	25.00
Mug, Hammered Ground, Copper Luster, 5 3/4 In.	20.00
Pitcher, Chanticleer, Outlined In Gold	45.00 To 60.00
Pitcher, Corn King, 8 In.	35.00 To 42.00
Pitcher, Elephant	15.00
Pitcher, Green, Dragon Handle	12.00
Pitcher, Large, Gold Trim	65.00
Pitcher, Little Boy Blue	24.00
Pitcher, Little Boy Blue, 7 In.	30.00
Pitcher, Milk, Bopeep	22.50 To 45.00
Pitcher, Smiley Pig	45.00
Pitcher, Water, Corn King	35.00
Pitcher, Water, Raised Colored Fruits	35.00
Planter, 4 Chickadees On Stump	20.00
Planter, Alarm Clock	6.00
Planter, Bowknot	5.00
Planter, Boy With Fishing Pole	6.00

Planter, Deer	6.00
Planter, Doe & Log	18.00
Planter, Donkey & Cart	7.00
Planter, Duck	6.00
Planter, Elf On Shoe	12.00
Planter, Fawn	10.00
Planter, Globe	20.00
Planter, Hound & Pekingese	6.00
Planter, Oriental, With Basket	4.00
Planter, Pekingese	8.00
Planter, Polynesian Girl	10.00 To 15.00
Planter, Pup Pushing Cart	12.00
Planter, Rickshaw	4.00
Planter, Skunk, Gold Trim	10.00
Planter, Toy Horse, Gold Trim	9.00
Planter, Water Trough & Pump	12.00
Planter, Water Wheel	9.00
Planter, Wishing Well, Dutch Boy & Girl	12.00 To 24.00
Relish, Corn King	13.00 To 15.00
Relish, Corn Queen	10.00
Salt & Pepper Mugsy, Gold Trim	23.00
Salt & Pepper, Bopeep	12.00
Salt & Pepper, Chanticleer, Large	10.00
Salt & Pepper, Corn King, Large	14.00 To 18.00
Salt & Pepper, Corn King, Small	8.50 To 12.00
Salt & Pepper, Corn Queen	16.00
Salt & Pepper, Dutch Boy & Girl	14.00 To 20.00
Salt & Pepper, Fruit	18.00
Salt & Pepper, Lobster	15.00
Salt & Pepper, Milk Can	9.00 To 12.00
Salt & Pepper, Mugsy, Large	10.00 To 17.50
Salt & Pepper, Mugsy, Small	5.00
Salt & Pepper, Owl	10.00 To 12.00
Salt & Pepper, Puss 'N Boots	10.00
Salt & Pepper, Sailor Boy & Bopeep	7.50
Salt & Pepper, Smiley Pig	10.00 To 20.00
Salt & Pepper, Swiss Children, Gold Trim	20.00
Salt & Pepper, Winnie Pig	10.00 To 15.00
Sugar Shaker, Corn King	35.00
Sugar, Cover, Corn King	15.00 To 20.00
Syrup, Blue & White	14.00
Teapot, Corn King	35.00 To 45.00
Teapot, Corn King, No.65, Individual	60.00
Teapot, Daisy	25.00
Teapot, Elephant	55.00
Teapot, Granny Anne	26.00 To 40.00
Teapot, Pied Piper	30.00
Teapot, Tom, Tom, The Piper's Son	35.00
Teapot, With Flower	20.00
Vase, Leaf, Green & Tan, 9 In.	15.00
Vase, Twin Doves, Yellow	15.00

The Shearwater pottery is a family business started by Mr. and Mrs. G. W. Anderson, Sr., and their three sons. The local Ocean Springs, Mississippi, clays were used to make the wares in the 1930s. The company is still in business.

SHEARWATER, Mug, Sea Horse Handle, Blue	15.00
Vase, Ribbed, Turquoise, 6 1/2 In.	24.00

Sheet music from the past centuries is now collected. The favorites are examples with covers featuring artistic or historic pictures. Early sheet music covers were lithographed but by the 1900s photographic reproductions were used. The early music was larger than more recent sheets and you must watch out for examples that were trimmed to fit in a twentieth–century piano bench.

SHEET MUSIC, A March For Mickey Mouse, Rifle On Shoulder, 1934	17.50
A Night At The Opera, Marx Brothers, 1935	20.00
A Perfect Day, Laurel & Hardy Photo, 11 X 14 In.	5.00
A Wonderful Guy, Rodgers & Hammerstein, 1949	1.00
Ac–Cent–Tchu–Ate The Positive, Mercer, Arlen, 1944	.75
Adoring You, Ziegfeld Follies, Vargas Cover, 1924	20.00
Am I To Blame?, 1934	3.00
America Here's My Boy, 1917	10.00
Animal Crackers, Marx Brothers, 1935	20.00
As Time Goes By, Bogart	25.00
Babe Ruth, Babe Ruth, We Know What You Can Do, Drawing, 1928	20.00
Ballad of Davy Crockett	8.00
Banjo Pickaninnies, Barefoot Black Boys Playing Banjo	15.00
Barney Google	12.00
Battle of Gettysburg, Full Color Battle Scene, 1917	15.00
Belle of Cuba Quickstep, Arthur Cohen, Bromo–Seltzer Ad, 1895	15.00
Breeze, Picture of Blacks	5.00
Buy War Bonds, Uncle Sam	4.00
By Radio Phone, Girl Operator On Cover, 1922	10.00
By The Beautiful Sea, 1914	10.00
Carioca, Fred Astaire	6.00
Casey Jones, Train Front	6.00
Chicago Day Waltz, Columbian Expo	8.00
Columbia The Gem of The Ocean, Dated 1843, 30–Star Flags	57.50
Confederacy March, Dedicated To Pres.Jefferson Davis, 1861	125.00
Cotton States Rag, Croft, Thomasville, Ga., 1910	17.00
Darktown Strutters Ball, Color, 1917	9.50
Dearly Beloved, Jerome Kern, Johnny Mercer	1.25
Don't Fence Me In, Cole Porter, Hollywood Canteen, 1944	.45
Don't Hang Your Dreams On A Rainbow, Eddie Cantor, 1929	1.25
Don't Worry, Marty Robbins	5.00
Donkey Serenade, Rudolf Friml, Herbert Stothart	.75
Dragnet Theme, Jack Webb On Cover, 1953	4.00
Dusky Stevedore	3.00
Eagle of U.S.A., Lindbergh	12.00
Edelweiss, Rodgers & Hammerstein, 1959	.75
Fashion Rag, Couple Steppin' Out, Dressed Up Pug Dog, 1897	25.00
Flying Down To Rio, Fred Astaire	6.00
Funeral March, James A.Garfield	10.00
General Grant's Richmond March, Civil War, 1865, 8 Pgs.	79.50
General McClellan's Grand March, Civil War, 1861, 6 Pgs.	57.50
Gentlemen Prefer Blondes, Marilyn Monroe, Jane Russell Cover	15.00
Get 'Em In A Rumble Seat	12.00
Go U Northwestern, 1933	6.00
Gold Mine In The Sky, Kate Smith Cover, 1937	10.00
Gold Rush In The Dakotas, 6 Stanzas, Mid–1870s, 5 X 8 In.	39.50
Good Ship Lollipop, Shirley Temple's Picture On Cover	10.00
Goona Goo, Blacks Depicted, 1936	15.00
Grand March of The Southern Confederacy, Dated 1861, 4 Pgs.	84.50
Guitar Songbook, Youngblood & Bone, Covington, Ind., 1912, 7 In.	5.00
Half As Much, Rosemary Clooney	5.00
Henry's Made A Lady Out of Lizzie	12.00
Here's Your Mule, Civil War Camp Song, 1862	12.50
Hot Time In The Town of Berlin	3.00
Hunting The Hun, Maroon Cover, Pilsner Beer Keg	15.00
I Found You Among The Roses, 1916	10.00
I Love You Truly, Carrie Bond	2.00
I Scream For Ice Cream, Pictures, 1927	7.00
I Want My Mammy, Eddie Cantor	6.00
I Whistle A Happy Tune, Rodgers & Hammerstein, 1951	.35
I Will Care For Mother Now, Civil War, Penny Song Sheet	6.00

I'm A Lonely Little Petunia, Lawrence Welk	4.00
I'm Always Chasing Rainbows, Dolly Sisters	.50
I've Got A Pocketful of Dreams, Burke, Monaco, 1938	1.25
In An Airplane, Wright Bros.Type Plane, 1910	15.00
It's A Long Way To Tipperary, Dated 1912	15.00
Later Tonight, Sonja Henie	10.00
Laugh Clown Laugh, Lon Chaney Sr., 1928	5.00
Laura, Gene Tierney, 1945	5.00
Little French Mother Goodbye, Norman Rockwell Cover, 1919	18.00
Little Nemo, 1908	25.00
Lonely Little Melody, Albert Vargas, Ziegfeld Follies, 1924	20.00
Lover Come Back To Me, Frank Mandel, Oscar Hammerstein	.75
Meet Me In St.Louis	4.00
Midnight Fire Alarm, Arranged By E.T.Paull	20.00
Midnight Flyer March, E.T.Paull, Photo Cover, 1902	20.00
Mohawk Trail, Indian Picture	3.00
My Foolish Heart	.50
My Man, Fanny Brice Cover	12.00
Oh Lucindy, Black Cover, 1917	10.00
Ol' Man River, Hammerstein, Kern, 1927	.65
Over The Rainbow, Cast of Wizard of Oz On Cover, 1939	20.00
Over The Rainbow, Judy Garland	10.00
Over There, Norman Rockwell Cover, Signed	45.00
Passage To Marseille, Bogart	8.00
Perfect Song, Amos & Andy, Pepsodent Hour	20.00
Pickaninny Lullaby	4.00
Plume Polka, Litho of Birds, Copyright 1853	40.00
Radiant Youth, Rolf Armstrong	40.00
Rock Around The Clock, Bill Haley & Comets On Cover	17.50
Rock-A-Bye-Baby, Effie I.Canning, 6 Pgs., 1886	17.50
Rum & Coca-Cola, Pictures Andrews Sisters, 1944	20.00
Sailors Beware, Rolf Armstrong	15.00
Shadow Waltz, Al Dubin, Harry Warren, Gold Diggers, 1933	1.00
She'll Always Remember, Kate Smith	5.00
Singin' In The Rain, Arthur Free, N.H.Brown, 1929	.35
Snow White	35.00
Song of The Vagabonds, Rudolf Friml, Post & Hooker, 1925	.50
Sonny Boy, Al Jolson, 1928	10.00
Stars & Stripes Forever, John Philip Sousa, 1897	12.00
Step Rag, Banjo Player Caricatures	15.00
Stormy Weather, Lena Horne, Black Caricatures	15.00
Sweetheart of Sigma Chi, 1927	6.00
Teddy Bear Pieces, Feares	8.75
Tell Me Little Gypsy, Irving Berlin, Ziegfeld Follies, 1920	1.00
The American Flag, Dedicated To M.G.Winfield Scott, Civil War	79.50
The Drummer Boy of Shiloh, Confederate Soldier, 1863, 6 Pgs.	175.00
Thinking of You, Rolf Armstrong	20.00
Three Little Words, Amos & Andy	15.00
Tramp! Tramp! Tramp! Prisoners Hope, Dated 1864, 6 Pgs.	29.50
Two Step Rag, Banjo Player Caricature	10.00
Uncle Remus Said, Johnny Lange, Song of The South, 1946	1.00
Virginia Blues, Picture of Blacks	5.00
Whistle While You Work, From Snow White & 7 Dwarfs, 1938	12.00
White Christmas, Irving Berlin, 1942	1.00
Who's Afraid of The Big Bad Wolf, 3 Little Pigs, Disney, 1933	12.00
Wilson's Call, World War I, Wilson Cover, 1917	15.00
With Kind Permission of The Cotton Belt Route, Framed, 1901	20.00
Wreck of Titanic	12.50
Yes We Have No Bananas Today, 1922	7.00

SHEFFIELD, see Silver–English; Silver Plate

Shirley Temple, the famous movie star, was born in 1928. She made her first movie in 1932. Thousands of items picturing Shirley have been and still are being made. Shirley Temple dolls were first made in 1934 by Ideal Toy Company. Millions of Shirley Temple cobalt blue glass dishes were made by Hazel Atlas Glass Company and U.S. Glass Company from 1934 to 1942. They were given away as premiums for Wheaties and Bisquick. A bowl, mug, and pitcher were made as a breakfast set. Some pieces were decorated with the picture of a very young Shirley, others used a picture of Shirley in her 1936 "Captain January" costume. Although collectors refer to a cobalt creamer it is actually the 4 1/2 inch high milk pitcher from the breakfast set. Many of these items are being reproduced today.

SHIRLEY TEMPLE, Album, Song, Photos, 1935	45.00
Birthday Album, 21st, Dell	12.00
Book, Big Little Book, Little Colonel	12.00
Book, Capt.January & Little Colonel, Random House	11.00
Book, Coloring, Large Size, 1936	50.00
Book, Poor Little Rich Girl, Saalfield, 1936	12.00
Book, Rebecca of Sunnybrook Farm	11.00
Book, Shirley Temple At Play	35.00
Book, Shirley Temple In Stowaway, 1937	20.00
Book, Spirit of Dragonwood	25.00
Book, Wee Willie Winkie, 1937	25.00
Bowl, Cereal	36.50
Bowl, Mug & Pitcher, Cobalt Blue, 3 Piece	135.00
Creamer	32.00 To 38.50
Doll, 1958	30.00
Doll, 1972	60.00
Doll, 4 Outfits, Purse, Wrist Tag, Display Box, 1957, 12 In.	295.00
Doll, Baby, Flirty Eyes, Molded Hair, Dress & Bonnet, 17 In.	495.00
Doll, Blue & White Stand Up & Cheer Dress, 1934, 17 In.	395.00
Doll, Celluloid, Knitted Blue Dress, 1936, 9 1/2 In.	475.00
Doll, Composition, Jointed, Sleep Eyes, 13 In.	75.00
Doll, Composition, Sleep Eyes, Ideal, C.1935, 12 In.	475.00
Doll, Hard Plastic, Vinyl, 1950, 12 In.	95.00
Doll, Heidi, Pink Dress, 2 Extra Dresses, 1960, 36 In.	1100.00
Doll, Horsman, Original Clothes, 13 In.	125.00
Doll, Ideal, 1984 Limited, 36 In.	175.00
Doll, Ideal, 20 In.	250.00
Doll, Ideal, Composition Head, Real Lashes, C.1938, 13 In.	600.00
Doll, Ideal, Composition, Sleep Eyes, 1938, 13 In. ....*Illus*	600.00
Doll, Ideal, Plastic, Smiling, Rooted Curls, C.1958, 12 In.	150.00
Doll, Madame Alexander, 17 In.	150.00
Doll, Madame Alexander, Box, 12 In.	150.00
Doll, Montgomery Ward, Box, 1972, 14 In.	150.00
Doll, Vinyl, 1952, 17 In.	125.00
Doll, Vinyl, All Original, 1957, 17 In.	225.00
Game, The Little Colonel, Selchow & Righter, 1935	70.00
Handkerchief, Little Colonel, Linen, White	25.00
Mirror, Pocket	10.00
Mug, Cobalt	48.50
Paper Doll, 1976	15.00
Paper Doll, Cardboard, Dollhouse, Saalfield, 1935	145.00
Paper Doll, Wigged, Box, Gabriel	45.00
Paper Dolls, Cut, 1937	45.00
Photo, Shirley Holding Doll, Glass Frame, Chrome Corners	15.00
Picture, Framed, 5 X 7 In.	20.00
Pin, Silvertone, Blue Enameled	48.00
Pitcher, Cobalt Blue	29.00 To 50.00
Postcard, Dutch, 1930s	10.00
Poster, Autographed, 24 X 30 In.	250.00
Poster, Little Miss Broadway, 1937, 8 X 11 In.	110.00
Ring, Picture, 1930s	15.00
Sheet Music, Animal Crackers In My Soup	16.00
Sheet Music, Little Colonel, 1935	18.00
Stationery Box, Shirley Cutout On Top, Cardboard, 1936	17.50

Shirley Temple,
Doll, Ideal,
Composition, Sleep Eyes,
1938, 13 In.

Tea Set, Plastic, Pink, Box 125.00
Toy Cosmetics, Beauty Bar, Gabriel Industries, Box 85.00
Trunk, Doll's, 1934, 13 In. 150.00
Wristwatch 30.00
   SHRINER, see Masonic

Silver deposit glass was made during the late nineteenth and early twentieth-centuries. Solid sterling silver was applied to the glass by a chemical method so that a cutout design of silver metal appeared against a clear or colored glass. It is sometimes called silver overlay.

SILVER DEPOSIT, Plate, Handles, 11 In. 65.00
   Plate, Sterling, Black Amethyst, 8 In. 10.00
   Vase, Bird, Black Amethyst, 12 In. 40.00
   Vase, Cyclamen Flowers, Black Amethyst, Squat, 4 1/2 In. 95.00
   Vase, Emerald Green, Silver Flowers, Vines, 10 In. ....*Illus* 425.00
   Vase, Silver Dragonfly, Coquere, 16 In. ....*Illus* 1200.00

Listed in this section are many of the current and out-of-production silver and silver plated flatware patterns made in the past eighty years. Other silver is listed under Silver-American, Silver-English, etc. Most silver flatware sets that are missing a few pieces can be completed through the help of one of the many silver matching services listed in "The Kovels' Collectors' Source Book."

SILVER FLATWARE SILVER PLATE, Adam, Salad Fork 3.00
   Adam, Soup Spoon, Oval, 1917 .... 12.50
   Alhambra, Bouillon Spoon 7.00

Silver Deposit, Vase, Emerald Green,
Silver Flowers, Vines, 10 In.

Silver Deposit, Vase, Silver Dragonfly,
Coquere, 16 In.

Alhambra, Dinner Fork	6.00
Alhambra, Fruit Spoon	6.00
Alhambra, Salad Fork	6.00
Anniversary, Cocktail Fork, Box, 6 Piece	22.00
Anniversary, Tablespoon	3.00
Berkshire, Butter Knife, Rogers	10.00
Bird of Paradise, Salad Fork	4.00
Charter Oak, Butter Knife, Rogers	16.00
Charter Oak, Cold Meat Fork, Rogers	45.00
Charter Oak, Dinner Fork, Rogers	14.00
Charter Oak, Ice Cream Spoon, Rogers	16.00
Charter Oak, Sugar Shell, Rogers	15.00
Coronation, Bonbon Spoon	6.00
Coronation, Butter Knife	4.50
Coronation, Service For 12, Oneida, 76 Piece	225.00
Easter Lily, Ice Cream Fork, Gold Wash	16.50
Erminie, Pie Fork, 6 Piece	45.00
Eternally Yours, Fruit Spoon	8.00
Eternally Yours, Soup Spoon, Oval, 1941	20.00
Fairoaks, Demitasse Spoon	7.00
Flower, Pickle Fork	15.00
Grenoble, Butter Knife, Rogers	10.00
Grenoble, Dessert Spoon, Rogers	7.00
Grenoble, Pea Server, Pierced, Rogers	30.00
King Edward, Iced Tea Spoon, National	4.00
King Edward, Soup Spoon, National	3.00
La Vigne, Soup Ladle, Rogers, 10 1/2 In.	110.00
La Vigne, Sugar Shell, Rogers	6.50 To 10.00
La Vigne, Tablespoon, Rogers	11.00
LaConcorde, Pie Server, Rogers, 9 3/8 In.	30.00
LaConcorde, Sugar Shell, Rogers	10.00
Laurel, Nut Pick, Rogers, 6 Piece	24.00
Marcella, Nut Spoon, Rogers	7.00
Mayfair, Cocktail Fork, Rogers	3.00
Meadowbrook, Serving Spoon, Salad	8.00
Meadowbrook, Tongs	10.00
Medallion, Butter Knife, Rogers	5.00
Moselle, Meat Fork	45.00 To 48.00
Mystic, Dinner Fork, Rogers	4.00
Newport, Soup Ladle, Rogers, 13 In.	55.00
Noblesse, Iced Tea Spoon	7.50
Noblesse, Salad Fork	4.50
Old Colony, Gravy Ladle, Rogers	22.00
Old Colony, Meat Fork	20.00
Orange Blossom, Butter Spreader, Rogers	3.50
Orange Blossom, Dinner Fork, Rogers	9.00
Orleans, Gravy Ladle, 1901	6.00
Oxford, Gravy Ladle, 1901	4.50
Oxford, Oyster Fork	10.00
Pansy, Gravy Ladle	10.00
Saratoga, Punch Ladle, Rogers	65.00
Southgate, 55 Piece	225.00
Unique, Pickle Fork, Reed & Barton	10.00
Unique, Preserve Spoon, Reed & Barton	12.00
Vendome, Fruit Spoon, R.C.Co.	2.00
Vendome, Salad Fork, R.C.Co.	4.00
Venetian, Fruit Spoon, Gold Wash, Rogers	4.00
Victorian Rose, 48 Piece	100.00
Vintage, Cheese Scoop, Rogers	48.00
Vintage, Cocktail Fork	13.00
Vintage, Tomato Server	145.00
Westminster, Mustard Spoon	15.00
Yale, Cream Ladle, Rogers, 6 In.	15.00
SILVER FLATWARE STERLING, 1690, Lemon Fork	15.00

1690, Nut Spoon 18.00
Abbottsford, Tomato Server, International 75.00
Adam, Ladle, Whiting, Monogram, 12 In. 195.00
Aegean Weave, Tablespoon, Slotted, Wallace 40.00
Ailanthus, Berry Spoon, Kidney Shape, Tiffany 495.00
American Beauty, Ice Cream Spoon, Schiebler 28.00
American Beauty, Lettuce Fork, Schiebler 55.00
American Beauty, Sardine Fork, Schiebler 65.00
American Classic, Cold Meat Fork, Easterling 35.00
American Victorian, Teaspoon, Lunt 15.00
Angelique, Service For 10, International, 69 Pc. 875.00
Angelo, Salad Set, Wood & Hughes 275.00
Antique, Pie Server, Gorham 85.00
Apollo, Sardine Fork, Alvin 55.00
Arabesque, Pie Server, Whiting 175.00
Aristocrat, Fruit Spoon 14.00
Arlington, Meat Fork, Large, Towle 125.00
Athenian, Horseradish Spoon, Reed & Barton 42.00
Awakening, Cold Meat Fork, Towle 35.00
Awakening, Gravy Ladle, Towle 35.00
Baltimore Rose, Citrus Spoon, Schofield 30.00
Baltimore Rose, Salad Fork, Schofield 35.00
Baronial, Youth Set, Frank M.Smith, Box, 3 Piece 225.00
Bead, Aspic Knife, Whiting 48.00
Beaumont, Soup Spoon, Gorham, 1915 .... 5.00
Beekman, Soup Ladle, Tiffany 350.00
Berry, Salad Serving Set, Whiting 290.00
Bridal Rose, Berry Spoon, Alvin 65.00
Bridal Rose, Butter Pick, Alvin .... 65.00 To 75.00
Bridal Rose, Salad Set, Alvin .... 375.00 To 495.00
Broom Corn, Olive Spoon, Tiffany 95.00
Buttercup, Bouillon Ladle, Gorham, 8 1/4 In. 235.00
Buttercup, Butter Spreader, Gorham 15.00
Buttercup, Cream Scoop, Gorham 22.00
Buttercup, Cucumber Server, Gorham 100.00
Buttercup, Dinner Fork, Gorham .... 21.00 To 25.00
Buttercup, Ice Cream Server, Gorham, 12 1/4 In. 295.00
Buttercup, Iced Tea Spoon, Gorham 28.00
Buttercup, Sardine Fork, Gorham 125.00
Buttercup, Service For 8, Gorham, 32 Piece 640.00
Buttercup, Soup Ladle, Gorham 295.00
Buttercup, Soup Spoon, Oval, Gorham 26.00
Buttercup, Tomato Server, Gorham 110.00
Buttercup, Youth Set, Gorham, 3 Piece 75.00
Cambridge, Butter Spreader, Gorham, Individual 25.00
Cambridge, Lettuce Spoon, Gorham 95.00
Cambridge, Tablespoon, Gorham 32.00
Camella, Sugar Spoon, Gorham 19.00
Candlelight, Service For 6, Towle, 30 Piece 450.00
Canterbury, Cold Meat Fork, Towle 95.00
Canterbury, Food Pusher, Whiting 32.00
Canterbury, Sardine Fork, Towle 55.00
Casa Grande, Iced Tea Spoon, Oneida 15.00
Cat Tails, Seafood Fork, Durgin 45.00
Celtic Weave, Cold Meat Fork 35.00
Celtic Weave, Iced Tea Spoon 18.00
Celtic Weave, Lemon Fork 18.00
Chantilly, Asparagus Fork, Gorham 350.00
Chantilly, Chocolate Spoon, Gorham .... 45.00 To 48.00
Chantilly, Cream Soup Spoon, Gorham 28.00
Chantilly, Mayonnaise Ladle, Gorham 65.00
Chantilly, Pie Server, Gorham 22.00
Chantilly, Soup Ladle, Gorham 325.00
Chantilly, Sugar Sifter, Gorham 145.00

Chantilly, Tomato Server, Gorham	125.00
Chantilly, Youth Set, Gorham	70.00
Chapel Bells, Tablespoon, Alvin	29.00
Chapel Bells, Teaspoon, Alvin	11.00
Charlemagne, Soup Spoon	20.00
Charles II, Sugar Sifter, Dominick & Haff	75.00
Charter Oak, Butter Knife, Rogers	15.00
Chased Romantique, Service For 8, Alvin, 40 Piece	500.00
Chatham, Bouillon Spoon, Durgin	22.00
Chatham, Butter Spreader, Durgin, Individual	19.00
Chelsea Manor, Dinner Fork, Gorham	25.00
Chelsea Manor, Sugar Spoon, Gorham	15.00
Chippendale, Cream Soup Spoon, Towle	27.00
Chippendale, Fish Server Fork, Gorham	85.00
Chrysanthemum, Cheese Scoop, Gorham	85.00
Chrysanthemum, Citrus Spoon, Durgin, 6 Piece	240.00
Chrysanthemum, Dinner Fork, Durgin, 6 In.	27.00
Chrysanthemum, Tablespoon, Gorham	29.00
Chrysanthemum, Teaspoon, Durgin	25.00
Cinderella, Cream Soup Spoon, Gorham	15.00
Classic Rose, Butter Knife, Reed & Barton	18.00
Classic Rose, Gravy Ladle, Reed & Barton	30.00
Classique, Lemon Fork, Gorham	12.00
Classique, Sugar Spoon, Gorham	15.00
Clover, Dinner Knife, Hollow Handle, Gorham	16.00
Cluny, Bonbon Spoon, Gorham	125.00
Cluny, Butter Knife, Gorham	95.00
Cluny, Ice Cream Slice, Gorham	385.00
Cluny, Luncheon Fork, Gorham	45.00
Colonial Thread, Cocktail Fork	12.00
Colonial, Cream Ladle, Gorham	8.00
Colonial, Sugar Spoon, Gorham	17.00
Contessina, Butter Knife	12.00
Contessina, Pickle Fork	12.00
Contessina, Tablespoon	35.00
Contour, Cold Meat Fork, Towle	42.00
Cordova, Asparagus Fork, Towle	155.00
Cordova, Cream Ladle, Towle	35.00
Country Manor, Butter Spreader	6.00
Crest of Arden, Gravy Ladle, Tuttle	40.00
Crystal, Teaspoon, International	14.00
Cupids, Food Pusher, Unger	75.00
Damask Rose, Gravy Ladle, Oneida	47.00
Damask Rose, Meat Fork, Oneida	45.00
Danish Baroque, Dinner Fork	20.00
Debussy, Grapefruit Spoon, Durgin	40.00
Debussy, Teaspoon, Towle	22.00
Dresden, Gravy Ladle, Whiting	85.00
Dresden, Sugar Shaker, Whiting	45.00
Duchess, Teaspoon, Gorham	13.00
Duke of York, Tablespoon, Whiting	32.00
Duvaine, Olive Fork, Unger	65.00
Eloquence, Berry Spoon, Lunt	98.00
Empire, Cucumber Server, Whiting, 1892, 5 3/4 In.	75.00
Etruscan, Butter Pick, Gorham	65.00
Etruscan, Dinner Fork, Gorham	23.00
Etruscan, Service For 8, Luncheon, Gorham, 48 Pc.	850.00
Evangeline, Salad Fork, Alvin	9.00
Fairfax, Coffee Spoon, Durgin	7.00
Federal Cotillion, Service For 8, Smith, 48 Piece	960.00
Fiddle Thread, Macaroni Server, Gale & Willis	325.00
Florence Nightingale, Butter Knife, Alvin	16.00
Florentine Lace, Salad Set, Reed & Barton	295.00
Fontaine, Service For 12, International, 72 Piece	1440.00

Clean silver with any acceptable commercial polish. Don't use
household scouring powder on silver no matter how stubborn the
spot may be. Use a tarnish-retarding silver polish to keep your silver
clean. It will not harm old solid or plated wares. Do not use "instant"
silver polishes.

Francis I, Ice Cream Fork, Reed & Barton	35.00
French Provincial, Lemon Fork	15.00
Frontenac, Asparagus Fork, International	450.00
Frontenac, Berry Spoon, International, 9 In.	150.00
Frontenac, Butter Pick, International	65.00
Frontenac, Cheese Scoop, International	115.00
George & Martha, Dinner Fork, Westmoreland	58.00
Georgian Rose, Cocktail Fork, Reed & Barton	15.00
Georgian, Bouillon Spoon, Towle, 12 Piece	360.00
Georgian, Cold Meat Fork, Towle	125.00
Gossamer, Teaspoon, Gorham	15.00
Grand Colonial, Service For 8, Gorham, 55 Piece	795.00
Grande Baroque, Wallace, 162 Piece	2400.00
Hampshire, Cold Meat Fork, Durgin	35.00
Hampton Court, Butter Knife, Reed & Barton	15.00
Heiress, Vegetable Spoon, International	34.00
Heraldic, Tea Strainer, Whiting	75.00
Hizen, Sugar Tongs, Gorham	115.00
Hunt Club, Cream Ladle, Gorham	32.50
Imperial Chrysanthemum, Dinner Fork, Gorham	24.00
Imperial Chrysanthemum, Luncheon Fork, Gorham	18.00
Imperial Chrysanthemum, Tomato Server, Gorham	125.00
Imperial Queen, Bouillon Ladle, Whiting	275.00
Imperial Queen, Strawberry Fork, Whiting	32.00
Imperial, Sugar Shell, Whiting	38.00
Intaglio, Teaspoon, Reed & Barton	12.00
Irian, Berry Spoon, Wallace	165.00
Irian, Butter Knife, Wallace	95.00
Iris, Salad Set, Durgin, 9 1/4 In.	475.00
Iris, Soup Ladle, Durgin	650.00
Iris, Strawberry Fork, Durgin	60.00
Isis, Berry Spoon, Gorham	250.00
Japanese, Nut Pick, Whiting	45.00
John & Priscilla, Soup Spoon, Oval, Westmoreland	15.00
Jubilee, Berry Spoon, Reed & Barton	50.00
Kensington, Sardine Fork, Gorham	27.00
Kimberly, Cold Meat Fork, Lunt	40.00
King Edward, Cold Meat Fork, Whiting, 1901	125.00
King Edward, Luncheon Knife, Gorham	26.00
King Richard, Dinner Fork, Towle	25.00
King Richard, Teaspoon, Towle	16.00 To 24.00
La Modele, Tablespoon, Gorham	25.00
La Parisienne, Cheese Scoop, Reed & Barton	125.00
La Rochelle, Luncheon Fork, Gorham	14.00
La Salle, Gravy Ladle, Dominick & Haff	38.00
La Scala, Fork, Gorham	25.00
Labors of Cupid, Dessert Spoon, Dominick & Haff	55.00
Lady Diana, Tomato Server, Towle	35.00
Lady Mary, Bouillon Spoon	10.00
Lady Mary, Service For 6, Towle, 36 Piece	300.00
Lafayette, Cucumber Server, Towle	30.00
Lancaster Rose, Tablespoon, Gorham, 8 1/2 In.	24.00

Lancaster, Chocolate Spoon, Gorham	25.00
Lancaster, Soup Ladle, Gorham	375.00
Legato, Steak Knife, Guard	17.00
Les Six Fleurs, Butter Knife, Reed & Barton	95.00
Lily of The Valley, Berry Spoon, Whiting	185.00
Lily, Berry Spoon, Gorham	150.00
Lily, Teaspoon, Whiting	28.00
Litchfield, Ice Cream Fork, International	35.00
Louis XIV, Service For 12, Towle, 48 Piece	720.00
Louis XV, Tablespoon, Whiting	32.00
Love Disarmed, Asparagus Server, Reed & Barton	160.00
Love Disarmed, Cold Meat Fork, Reed & Barton	134.00
Love Disarmed, Ice Cream Slicer, Reed & Barton	170.00
Luxembourg, Sauce Spoon, Gorham	12.00
Lyric, Teaspoon	11.00
Mademoiselle, Tablespoon, Slotted, International	34.00
Marguerite, Soup Ladle, Gorham	295.00
Martha Washington, Meat Fork, Dominick & Haff	42.00
Mary Chilton, Service For 8, Towle, 32 Piece	550.00
Mary Warren, Cold Meat Fork, Manchester	35.00
Maryland, Service For 8, Kirk, 32 Piece	1050.00
Mazarin, Strawberry Fork, Dominick & Haff	20.00
Medallion, Berry Spoon, Gorham	195.00
Medallion, Tomato Server, Gorham	275.00
Medici, Dinner Fork, Gorham	28.00
Medici, Teaspoon, Gorham	16.00
Moonbeam, Service For 8, International, 48 Piece	600.00
Moonglow, Berry Spoon, International	40.00
Morning Glory, Cold Meat Fork, Alvin	85.00
Mount Vernon, Tablespoon, Lunt	32.00
Mythologique, Fish Fork, Gorham	75.00
New Queens, Ice Cream Fork, Durgin, 6 Piece	185.00
New Standish, Tomato Server	55.00
Newport Shell, Tablespoon, Pierced	45.00
Norfolk, Soup Ladle, Gorham	295.00
Old English, Lettuce Fork, Towle, 8 3/4 In.	42.00
Old French, Vegetable Fork, Gorham, 10 In.	125.00
Old Lace, Gravy Ladle, Towle	45.00
Old Lace, Service For 6, 24 Piece	400.00
Old Lace, Sugar Spoon, Towle	20.00
Old London, Soup Spoon, Gorham	15.00
Old Master, Bonbon Spoon, Towle	34.00
Old Master, Service For 8, Towle, 32 Piece	850.00
Old Newbury, Tablespoon, Towle	32.00
Orange Blossom, Cold Meat Fork, Alvin	225.00
Orange Blossom, Sardine Fork, Alvin	95.00
Pine Tree, Service For 12, International, 60 Pc.	875.00
Pirouette, Sugar Spoon, Alvin	13.00
Plymouth, Luncheon Fork, Gorham	20.00
Pomona, Ice Cream Fork, Towle	35.00
Pomona, Teaspoon, Towle	15.00
Pompadour, Crumber, Whiting	175.00
Poppy, Jelly Server, Gorham	30.00
Portsmouth, Berry Spoon, Gorham	40.00
Prelude, Feeding Spoon, Infant, International	25.00
Prince Eugene, Butter Knife, Alvin	28.00
Prince Eugene, Service For 8, Alvin, 56 Piece	1230.00
Prince Eugene, Sugar Spoon, Alvin	27.00
Princess Patricia, Dinner Knife, Gorham, 9 In.	28.00
Putnam, Sugar Tongs, Watson	48.00
Queen Anne, Cream Soup Spoon, Dominick & Haff	20.00
Queen's Lace, Gravy Ladle, International	37.00
Renaissance, Sugar Spoon, Reed & Barton	22.00
Repousse, Asparagus Server, Kirk	250.00

Repousse, Baby Fork, International 35.00
Repousse, Butter Knife, Kirk 25.00
Rhapsody, Vegetable Spoon, Slotted, International 42.00
Riviera, Service For 8, International, 54 Piece 725.00
Romantique, Jelly Server, Alvin 16.00
Rose Marie, Salad Fork, Gorham 20.00
Rose Tiara, Salad Fork, Gorham 22.00
Royal Danish, Cold Meat Fork, International 95.00
Royal Danish, Tablespoon, Wallace 65.00
Royal Windsor, Teaspoon 10.00
Rustic, Strawberry Fork, Towle, 6 Piece 155.00
Sculptured Rose, Iced Tea Spoon 14.00
Sea Rose, Teaspoon, Gorham 13.00
Silver Flutes, Tablespoon 50.00
Silver Plumes, Cold Meat Fork, Towle 38.00
Silver Plumes, Salad Fork 16.00
Silver Spray, Salad Fork 12.00
Spanish Provincial, Dinner Knife, Towle 17.00
Spanish Provincial, Salad Fork, Towle 19.00
Spanish Tracery, Dinner Fork, Gorham 24.00
St.Cloud, Dinner Fork, Gorham 35.00
St.Cloud, Fish Serving Fork, Gorham 195.00
St.Cloud, Teaspoon, Gorham 10.00
Stanton Hall, Cake Server, Oneida 16.00
Stradivari, Luncheon Knife, Wallace 25.00
Strasbourg, Beef Fork, Gorham 75.00
Strasbourg, Cucumber Fork, Gorham 125.00
Strasbourg, Lettuce Fork, Gorham 95.00
Strasbourg, Pastry Fork, Gorham 38.00
Strasbourg, Service For 8, Gorham, 48 Piece 960.00
Symphony, Jelly Spoon, Towle 15.00
Theseum, Cold Meat Fork, International 42.00
Trianon, Sugar Spoon, International 20.00
Versailles, Butter Knife, Gorham 40.00
Vintage, Butter Knife, Rogers 14.00
Violet, Butter Pick, Wallace 95.00
Violet, Cold Meat Fork, Wallace 85.00
Violet, Sauce Ladle, Wallace 45.00
Virginian, Gravy Ladle 38.00
Virginiana, Strawberry Fork, Gorham 25.00
Wadefield, Berry Spoon, Kirk 44.00
Warwick, Tongs, International 30.00
Washington, Carving Set, Wallace 70.00
Washington, Sauce Ladle, Wallace 34.00
Watteau, Dinner Fork, Durgin 32.00
Wedgwood, Service For 8, International, 57 Piece 969.00
White Paisley, Sugar Spoon, Gorham 23.00
William & Mary, Service For 12, Towle, 48 Piece 850.00
William & Mary, Teaspoon, Lunt 20.00
Willow, Gravy Ladle, Gorham 37.00
Winslow, Bouillon Spoon, Kirk 21.00
Woodlily, Cream Soup Spoon, F.Smith 29.00
York, Asparagus Server, Gold Wash, Blackinton 95.00
Zodiac, Teaspoon, Gorham 45.00

Ⓔ Ⓟ Ⓝ Ⓢ   Silver plate is not solid silver. It is a ware made of a metal, such as nickel or copper, that is covered with a thin coating of silver. The letters "EPNS" are often found on American and English silver plated wares. Sheffield silver is a type of silver plate.

SILVER PLATE, Ashtray, Leaf Shape, Individual, England, 3 1/2 In., 8 Piece 20.00
  Basket, Bread, Victorian, Filigree, Floral Design 48.00
  Basket, Etched Cupid Design, Swing Handle, 9 1/2 In. 80.00
  Basket, Flower, 17 In. 65.00
  Basket, Leaf & Acorn Design On Rim, Swing Handle, 11 1/2 In. 35.00

Basket, Pierced Design On Sides, Marked England, 10 1/2 In.	35.00
Basket, Swing Handle, Scalloped Rim, Reed & Barton, 7 1/2 In.	75.00
Basket, Victorian, Monogrammed B, Meriden	30.00
Beaker, Embossed Floral Design, C.1845, 7 In.	70.00
Beaker, Floral & Leaf Design, Top & Bottom Brass Band, 6 In.	75.00
Bonbon, Boat Shape, Pierced Sides, Gadroon, English, 6 In., Pair	20.00
Bottle Stopper, Black & White Agate Handle, C.1900	30.00
Bowl, Arabic Design, Cone-Shaped Lid, Brass Handles, 8 In.	35.00
Bowl, Chased Design Border, Reed & Barton, 10 In.	20.00
Bowl, Floral Scroll Relief Rim, Homan, 9 1/2 X 6 In.	5.00
Bowl, Pierced, 4 Claw Feet, Derby Silver, Square, 9 1/2 In.	10.00
Box, Biscuit, Footed, Cover, C.1860	1375.00
Box, Glove, Applied Florals, Swirls, Wilcox, 12 In.	165.00
Box, Raised Figural Design, Dutch, 6 1/2 X 3 X 3 In.	35.00
Butter, Engraved Banding, Insert, Knife Rest, Cover	45.00
Butter, Handles, Knife Rest, Ice Insert, Wilcox, Cover, 7 In.	65.00
Butter, Insert, Roll-Type Cover	38.50
Butter, Oval, Scroll Feet, Sheffield, Cover, 5 1/4 In.	75.00
Butter, Pierced, Engraved, Blue Glass Liner, Cover, C.1860, Oval	600.00
Candelabra, 4-Light, 2 Maidens, Robes, 19 In., Pair	5775.00
Candlestick, Danish Modern, 1950s, 6 1/4 In., Pair	65.00
Candlestick, Danish Modern, 9 In., Pair	75.00
Candlestick, Leaf & Grape Design, Sheffield, 14 In., Pair	175.00
Candy Dish, Filigree, Sectional Glass Liner, Handle, 9 In.	15.00
Casserole, Cover, Handles, Meriden & Co., 9 1/2 In.	10.00
Cigar Case, Figural, 3 Mold, Hinged, Scroll Engraving	35.00
Coaster, Wine, Gadroon Rim, Sheffield, C.1820, 6 1/8 In., Pair	522.00
Cocktail Shaker, Penguin, Napier	225.00
Coffee Service, Trumpet Form, Berry Leaves, German, 5 Piece	3300.00
Coffee Urn, Reed & Barton, 17 1/2 In.	55.00
Coffeepot, Chased Floral Design, 12 1/2 In.	35.00
Coffeepot, Washington Pattern, Rogers, 9 1/2 In.	5.00
Compote, Genre Scene, Pierced Rim, Dutch, 12 1/2 X 5 1/4 In.	10.00
Compote, Reticulated Base, 10 3/4 X 11 In.	45.00
Cup, Little Boy Blue	12.00
Desk Stand, Footed Plateau, 2 Glass Bottles, English, 13 In.	50.00
Dish, Entree, Cover, Gadroon Rims, Sheffield, 11 1/2 In., 4 Pc.	1750.00
Dish, Entree, Cover, Warming Stand, English, C.1815, 14 In.	775.00
Dish, Sardine, Cover, English, Glass Liner	10.00
Dish, Serving, Shell Shape, Chased Floral, England, 10 1/2 In.	205.00
Epergne, Grapevine Borders, Putti Base, H.Wilkinson, 36 In.	1650.00
Flask, Golfer's, Fluted Edge, Engraved Golfer In Knickers	140.00
Grape Shears, Gnarled Wood-Design Handle	55.00
Gravy Boat, Tray, Reed & Barton, Marked Mayflower 500	30.00
Hair Receiver, Beaded, Wilcox, 4 1/4 In.	35.00
Junior Set, Active Elves, 3 Piece	45.00
Measuring Spoon, Great Atlantic & Pacific Tea Company	10.00

When buying silver with bright cut design, avoid worn pieces. The best prices are paid for silver with clear, crisp designs.

Mirror, Plateau, Beveled Glass, Signed, 6 In.	45.00
Mirror, Plateau, Victorian, Signed, 5 In.	60.00
Mug, Engraved Handle, Sheffield, 19th Century, 3 1/2 In., Pair	20.00
SILVER PLATE, NAPKIN RING, see Napkin Ring	
Pitcher, Grape & Leaf Design, International, 10 1/2 In.	70.00
Pitcher, Water, First Flight Trophy, L.C.A., 1918, 8 In.	5.00
Punch Bowl, Coin, Gadrooned, Ring Handles, 7 1/4 X 10 1/2 In.	302.00
Punch Bowl, Undertray, Floral Rims, Engraved, 10 1/2 In.	195.00
Sauceboat, Tapered Body, Sheffield, C.1830, 4 1/4 In.	90.00
SILVER PLATE, SPOON, SOUVENIR, see Souvenir, Spoon, Silver Plate	
Spooner, Victorian, Handles, Footed, Bridgeport Silver Co.	45.00
Stamp Dispenser, Desk Size, 1890s	20.00
Sugar Bowl, Egg, Chick On Irregular Top, 5 3/8 In.	110.00
Sugar Bowl, Spooner, Bird Finial, Handles, 12 Hooks, Columbia	125.00
Tea Ball, With Chain, Matching Stand, Dutch	30.00
Tea Kettle, Stand, Bright Cut Floral Design, Victorian, 13 In.	25.00
Tea Set, Chippendale, Matching Tray, 24 In., 4 Piece	75.00
Tea Set, Engraved Floral, Walter & Hall, Sheffield, 4 Piece	200.00
Tea Set, Meriden, Gold Wash Interior, Bright Cut Floral	155.00
Tea Set, Old Sheffield Pattern, Community, 5 Piece	350.00
Tea Set, Rogers Smith & Co., 6 Piece	300.00
Tea Strainer, Costumed Man & Woman Finial, Dutch	25.00
Toothpick, Boy, Heavy Clothing, Struggling With Crate	80.00
Toothpick, Chick On Wishbone	30.00
Toothpick, Fat Pig, Glass Eyes, Engraved Boston Baked Beans	85.00
Toothpick, Kate Greenaway, Tufts	275.00
Toothpick, Monkey With Rifle, Dog, Rabbit, Tree Stump, Tufts	245.00
Toothpick, Sailor Boy, Shooting Cannon, Reed & Barton	350.00
Toothpick, Wheelbarrow, Simulated Birch Log, Signed Tufts	110.00
Tray, Bead Feet, Sheffield, Dixon & Sons, C.1835, 28 1/2 In.	465.00
Tray, Butler's, Gadroon & Floral Rim, Bright Cut, 24 In.	25.00
Tray, Card, Chased Center, Vines, Leaves On Border, 7 In.	45.00
Tray, Center Bowl For Dip, Wm.Rogers, 15 In.	5.00
Tray, Galleried, Oak Base, English, 22 1/2 In.	495.00
Tray, Heppelwhite Pattern, 6 1/2 In.	5.00
Tray, Marked Made In England, Handles, 26 X 15 In.	100.00
Tray, Meat & Vegetable, Well, Victorian Rose, Wm.Rogers, 22 In.	45.00
Tray, Reed & Tie Handles, Sheffield, C.1830, 28 1/2 In.	1100.00
Tray, Scrolls & Foliate, Handles, 32 X 21 In.	275.00
Tray, Tea, Bracket Handles, Medallions, Sheffield, 14 X 19 In.	302.00
Tray, Tea, Foliage At Intervals, Sheffield, C.1815	1100.00
Tureen, Cover, Fluted, Paw Feet, Sheffield, 8 X 11 1/2 In.	825.00
Tureen, Shell & Scroll Handles, Sheffield, C.1830, 15 1/2 In.	1540.00
Tureen, Soup, Cover, Foliage Handles, Knowles, C.1835, 15 In.	1320.00
Tureen, Soup, Domed Cover, Floral, Shellwork, Sheffield, 15 In.	1980.00
Tureen, Turtle Soup, Detachable Hinged Lid, 20 X 14 In.	1760.00
Umbrella Stand, Interlaced Flowering Branches, 20 1/2 In.	220.00
Urn, Hot Water, Continental, Scroll Handles, 15 In.	325.00
Urn, Tea, 3 Putti, Baby Centaur Picking Grapes, 15 1/2 In.	605.00
Urn, Tea, Lion Paw Feet, Attached Plate, 15 1/2 In.	247.50
Vase, Chased Leaf & Grape Design, Sheffield, 14 In., Pair	150.00
Vase, Trumpet Shape, Etched Design At Rim, 8 In.	20.00
Vase, Trumpet, Raised Vine & Grape Design, 27 In.	60.00
Victorian Rose, Well & Tree Platter, Rogers	65.00
Watch Holder, Kate Greenaway, Tufts	300.00
Wine Bucket, Spherical Handles, Christofle, C.1935, 8 1/4 In.	1650.00
Wine Cooler, Inverted Pear Shape, Sheffield, 9 In., Pair	5500.00
SILVER, SHEFFIELD, see Silver Plate; Silver–English	

 The silver listed in this book is subdivided by country. Silver–American is the first listing, followed by Silver–Austrian, Silver–Canadian, Silver–Chinese, Silver–Danish, etc. There are also other pieces of silver and silver plate listed under special categories, such as Napkin Ring or Tiffany, and under Silver Flatware.

SILVER–AMERICAN, see also Tiffany Silver; Silver–Sterling

SILVER–AMERICAN, 4 Piece Set, Hammered, Marshall Field, Monogram, 1911	495.00
Basket, Floral & Lattice Design, Bailey, Banks & Biddle	725.00
Basket, Relish, Gorham, Pierced Rigid Handle, 24 1/2 Oz.	325.00
Bonbon, Heart Shape, Gorham	1100.00
Bonbon, Old London, Gorham	30.00
Bowl, Adam Pattern, Footed, Shreve & Co., 9 In.	660.00
Bowl, Center, Oak Lead & Acorn Design, 14 1/4 In.	605.00
Bowl, Center, Pierced Skirt Rim, Graff, Washbourne & Dunn	495.00
Bowl, Centerpiece, Chrysanthemums, 1898, Billings, 17 In.	6650.00
Bowl, Chased Stylized Foliage Rim, Gorham, 11 In.	275.00
Bowl, Colonial Revival, Footed, F.J.R.Gyllenberg, 4 5/8 In.	1650.00
Bowl, Copper Exterior, Rolled Rim, Bulbous, Gebelein, 4 In.	90.00
Bowl, Engraved Eugene Rockwell, Matson, 2 1/2 X 5 1/4 In.	50.00
Bowl, Frank Whiting Co., 10 In.	115.00
Bowl, Fruit, Beaded Rim, Ball Feet, Shreve, 1920, 5 X 9 In.	1200.00
Bowl, Fruit, Openwork Sides, Gorham, 10 In.	330.00
Bowl, Hammered, G.W.Shiebler, C.1880, 4 3/8 In. ....*Illus*	715.00
Bowl, Handles, International, 11 1/2 In.	357.50
Bowl, Inscription, Footed, 1931, A.J.Stone, 4 X 9 1/2 In.	1300.00
Bowl, Louis XIV, Towle, C.1920, 14 In.	220.00
Bowl, Marie Antoinette, Gorham, 10 In.	340.00
Bowl, Paul Revere, 19 Troy Ounces, 8 In.	250.00
Bowl, Pierced Sides, Beaded Rim, Gorham, 12 1/2 In.	275.00
Bowl, Pierced, Unger Bros., 2 5/8 X 6 In., Pair	350.00
Bowl, Revere Style, Dominick & Haff, 5 1/2 X 11 In.	440.00
Bowl, Ribbed Band, Concave Rim, Gebelein, 1929, 4 X 5 In.	125.00
Bowl, Studded Cross, Hammered Strap, Shreve, 1 X 5 1/2 In.	165.00
Bowl, Triple Rib Border, H.Taylor, Stone, Lobe Shape, 8 In.	225.00
Box, Gorham, Stylized Grecian Key, 5 X 3 In.	175.00
Box, Letter, Red Leather, D–Shape, 4 Sections, Mauser, 8 In.	825.00
Box, Pill, Monogram Cover, H.Taylor, Stone, 1 X 1 3/4 In.	300.00
Box, Rose, Foliate Areas, Cover, Barbour Silver, 7 1/4 In.	335.00
Breakfast Set, Ebony Handle, Monogrammed, Watson, 4 Piece	275.00
Cake Basket, Rococo, Pierced, Handle, Frank W.Smith, 15 In.	1550.00
Cake Plate, Basket of Flowers On Sides, Dominick & Haff	445.00
Cake Plate, Domed Base, Strapwork, Monogram, Shreve, 10 In.	300.00
Cake Plate, Or Vegetable Dip, Fluted, JP, Lebolt, 10 3/4 In.	350.00
Cake Plate, Petaled Interior, Black, Starr & Frost, 10 In.	175.00
Calendar, Desk, Repousse, Signed Samuel Kirk, 4 X 3 1/2 In.	125.00
Candlestick, 1–Light, Shreve & Co., 13 In., 4 Piece	1870.00
Candlestick, Adam Pattern, Shreve & Co., 14 In., 4 Piece	2200.00
Candlestick, Bailey Banks & Biddle, 9 1/2 In., Pair	130.00
Candlestick, Black, Starr & Frost, C.1900, 10 5/8 In., Pair	900.00
Candlestick, Flared Nozzles, Shreve & Co., 15 In., 4 Piece	2100.00
Candlestick, Fluted, H.B.Stanwood, C.1850, 10 1/4 In., Pair	1300.00
Candlestick, LaSalle Pattern, Dominick & Haff, 1933, 4 Pc.	375.00
Carving Set, Embossed Scroll, Floral, Case, Gorham, 3 Piece	58.00
Caster, Zachariah Brigden, Boston, C.1770	1210.00
Centerpiece, Chased Anemones, Gorham, 1900, 4 X 13 X 11 In.	2750.00
Centerpiece, Grapevine Feet, Gilt Interior, Gorham, 37 Oz.	1540.00
Child's Set, Nursery Scenes, Names, Matthews Co., 3 Piece	247.50
Chocolate Pot, Bud Finial, Long Neck, Melon, Gorham, 11 In.	3500.00
Chop Plate, Relief Scroll Border, Harris & Shafer, 16 In.	900.00
Coaster, Wine, Grapes, Monogram, E.G.Webster, 1890, 6 1/2 In.	185.00
Coffee Set, Iris Pattern, Martele, Gorham, 4 Piece ....*Illus*	9350.00
Coffeepot, Demitasse, Whitney Co., 1858, 8 In. ....*Illus*	2970.00
Coffeepot, Rope Border On Lid, Ivory Heat Stops, Durgin	200.00
Compote, Adam Pattern, Shreve & Co., 11 1/4 In.	550.00
Compote, Circular Base, Shreve & Co., 15 1/2 In.	825.00
Compote, Pierced, Floral Swags, Black, Starr & Frost, 12 In.	2750.00
Compote, Square Top, Floral Design, Dominick & Haff, 8 In.	385.00
Creamer & Bowl, C.L.Boehme, Melon Shape, C.1812	2150.00
Crumber, A.Coles, Castle Scene Center, C.1850, 13 1/4 In.	295.00

Silver–American

Ewer, Hyde & Goodrich   Coffeepot, Demitasse, Whitney Co., 1858, 8 In., Tea Caddy, Basket Shape, Whitney Co., 3 1/2 In., Bowl, Hammered, G.W.Shiebler, C.1880, 4 3/8 In.

Cup, 3 Handles, Wavy Rim, Reed & Barton, C.1900, 9 1/2 In.	2750.00
Cup, Baby, Raised Cattail & Leaf, Mitchell & Tyler, 3 In.	20.00
Cup, Bright Cut Medallion, Braverman & Levy, 3 1/4 In.	137.00
Cup, Julep, A.Metcalfe Steele, 3 1/2 In.	400.00
Cup, Julep, Engraved Charley, 3 7/8 In.	225.00
Cup, Julep, Engraved Kit, Marked W.R.Evans, 3 7/8 In.	425.00
Cup, Julep, Engraved P.E.C., 3 5/8 In.	500.00
Cup, Julep, Footed, N.Harding & Co., Boston, 4 1/2 In.	325.00
Cup, Julep, Friendship & Brotherly Love, 3 5/8 In., Pair	850.00
Cup, Julep, Graverman & Levy, Tooled Design, 3 3/4 In.	300.00
Cup, Julep, John A.Steele Jr., 3 1/2 In.	400.00
Cup, Julep, McDonald, Premium, 3 5/8 In., Set of 6	2850.00
Cup, Julep, Reeded Top & Base, S.Kirk & Son, C.1932	135.00
Cup, Julep, To Nephew Jefferson Bettmann, 4 1/8 In.	225.00
Cup, Julep, W.C.A.Society 1st Premium, 3 1/2 In.	400.00
Cup, To My Janie, 1868, F.H.Clark & Co., 3 1/8 In.	325.00
Dish, Asparagus, Liner, Pierced, Handles, F.Fuchs, 9 1/2 In.	1100.00
Dish, Floral Rim, Black, Starr & Frost, C.1900, 10 3/4 In.	450.00
Dish, Footed, Reed & Barton, Shell Shape, 8 In.	35.00
Dish, Ivory Finial Cover, Arthur Stone, 1916–21, 4 X 7 In.	1400.00
Dish, Lord Saybrook Pattern, International, 12 In., Pair	275.00
Dish, Nut, Open Oyster Shape, Shells, Gorham, 1890, 4 X 4 In.	125.00
Dish, Scroll Border, Weighted Base, Whiting	20.00
Ewer, Engraved SWCP, 1850, New Orleans, 15 1/2 In.	5750.00
Ewer, Hyde & Goodrich ....*Illus*	5750.00
Flask, Glass, Silver Base, Bicycle Race, 8 In.	2090.00
Fork, Bailey & Co., Fiddle Thread, C.1848, 6 3/4 In.	30.00
Fork, Beaded Edge, Crane & Co., C.1842, 7 7/8 In.	45.00
Fork, Floral & Scroll Pattern, Backman, C.1850, 7 3/4 In.	25.00
Fork, Juvenile, Olive Pattern, Wriggins & Warden, C.1850	30.00
Fork, Meat, Bunker Hill, Watson	50.00
Fork, Olive, S.Wilmot, 6 7/8 In.	60.00
Fork, Pickle, Bailey & Co., Philadelphia, C.1860	135.00
Fork, Prince Albert, Lincoln & Reed, 7 3/4 In.	35.00
Goblet, Cocktail, Gilt Interior, Shreve & Co., 6 In., 6 Pc.	136.50
Goblet, Wine, Rooster Stem, Reed & Barton, 4 Piece	80.00
Gravy Boat, Georgian Pattern, Underplate, Poole, 14 Oz.	200.00
Holder, Ramekin, German Ceramic Liners, Watson, Set of 12	135.00
Ice Bucket, Tab Handles, Kalo, 1918, 5 3/8 In.	1600.00
Inkwell, Art Nouveau, Martele	3100.00
Jar, Condiment, Engraved, Hawkes	85.00
Jar, Hinged Lid, Floral, Jacobi & Jenkins, 3 1/4 In.	200.00

Jar, Jam, Spoon, Enameled, M.P.Winlock, 1901–27, 2 X 5 In.	500.00
Jar, Powder, Cover, PPG Initials, Howard Co., 3 1/4 X 4 In.	175.00
Julep Cup, Hudson & Dolfinger, Reeded Top Band, C.1854	650.00
Julep Cup, Jones, Shreve, Brown & Co., 2 7/8 In.	450.00
Knife & Fork, P.Dirder, Philadelphia, Pa., Bright Cut	60.00
Knife & Fork, Youth, Beaded Josephine, H.L.Webster, 1850	38.00
Ladle, Broad Handle, Robert Keyworth, 12 3/4 In.	575.00
Ladle, Condiment, Fiddle Tip, Palmer & Batchelder	30.00
Ladle, Fiddle & Threaded, Double Struck, New Orleans	325.00
Ladle, Fiddle Thread, Hyde & Goodrich, C.1829, 14 In.	625.00
Ladle, Flared Handle, H.Fletcher, C.1818, 13 3/4 In.	750.00
Ladle, Gold Washed Bowl, N.G.Wood & Son, 8 1/2 In.	80.00
Ladle, Gravy, Art Nouveau, Unger Bros.	50.00
Ladle, Gravy, H.Porter & Co., C.1830, 7 1/4 In.	110.00
Ladle, Gravy, O & AK Childs, Pinched Fiddle, C.1847	375.00
Ladle, Gravy, P.Huntington, Finless Fiddle, C.1815, 8 In.	125.00
Ladle, Gravy, Thistle, Blackinton	40.00
Ladle, King's Pattern, Penfield & Co., Savannah, Georgia	895.00
Ladle, McMullin, C.1790, 14 1/8 In.	750.00
Ladle, Mustard, Bright Cut, J.F.Butler, Utica, N.Y., C.1860	40.00
Ladle, Mustard, Coffin Fiddle, J.Boutier, New York, C.1810	58.00
Ladle, Mustard, Coin Silver, J.A.Coles, C.1840	45.00
Ladle, Mustard, J.Blackman & Co., Bridgeport, Ct., C.1835	30.00
Ladle, Sauce, Basket of Flowers Handle, A.G.Storn	75.00
Ladle, Sauce, Basket of Flowers Handle, E.Whiton, 7 In.	95.00
Ladle, Sauce, Olive Pattern, S.T.Crosby, C.1850	45.00
Ladle, Sauce, T.K.Emery, Boston, C.1810	75.00
Ladle, Sauce, Wadefield, S.Kirk, C.1920, 5 3/8 In.	25.00
Ladle, Soup, Grape Pattern, Farrington & Hunnewell, 1860	195.00
Ladle, Soup, J.A.Fogg, Ribbed, Salem, Mass., C.1850, 5 In.	245.00
Ladle, Soup, R.Wilson, Coin Silver, 1830s	250.00
Letter Opener, Floral Edge, Kirk	45.00
Loving Cup, Annual Cruise N.Y.Yacht Club, 1st Prize, 1903	125.00
Loving Cup, Tulip Form, Foliage, Gorham, 12 1/8 In.	2200.00
Marrow Scoop, Double Scoop, Script Engraving, 10 1/8 In.	325.00
Mirror, Hand, Curling Handle, Marine Design, 1900, 9 In.	660.00
Mirror, Hand, International	30.00
Muddler, Norfolk	75.00
Nut Set, Etruscan Revival Pattern, Gorham, Spoon, 12 Picks	160.00
Paddle, Bailey & Co., Bright Cut, Twist Handle, C.1850	325.00
Pepper Box, Andrew Tyler, Boston, C.1730	3190.00
Pitcher & Tray, Chrysanthemum & Foliate Border, Circular	850.00
Pitcher, Classical Revival Baluster Form, Gorham	350.00
Pitcher, Ear-Shaped Handle, J.B.Akin, 10 5/8 In.	1300.00
Pitcher, Helmet Form, Beaded Rim, Goodnow & Jenks, 34 Oz.	825.00
Pitcher, Lobed Baluster Form, Grapevine, Gorham, 54 Oz.	6875.00
Pitcher, Marked P.Revere Reproduction, 7 3/4 In.	275.00
Pitcher, Milk, N.Harding & Co., Boston, Repousse, C.1850	535.00
Pitcher, Repousse Floral, S.Kirk & Sons, 7 5/8 In.	900.00
Pitcher, S Handle, Tooled Bands, Edw.Kinsey, 13 7/8 In.	5100.00
Pitcher, Tooled Foot Band, Kinsey, Engraved Rose, 8 1/4 In.	800.00
Pitcher, Water, Engraved Shield, Jones & Co., 1840, 11 In.	935.00
Pitcher, Water, Gadroon Rims, Harp Handle, Gorham, 8 In.	660.00
Pitcher, Water, Ivory, Floral, Gorham, C.1900	2750.00
Pitcher, Water, Medallion, W.K.Vanderslice, 1870–74, 12 In.	1320.00
Pitcher, Water, Monogram, Porter Blanchard, 8 3/8 In.	1750.00
Pitcher, Water, Octagonal, Kalo	1900.00
Pitcher, Water, Oval Cartouche, Reed & Barton, 30 Oz.	550.00
Plate, Bread & Butter, Shreve & Co., 7 1/8 In., 16 Piece	1650.00
Plate, Nursery Rhyme Figures Around, Gorham, 1885, 7 In.	115.00
Platter, Engraved Crests, S.Kirk, 12 1/4 In., Pair	385.00
Platter, Foliage, Oval, 1898–1904, Gorham, 15 In.	3025.00
Platter, Meat, Plymouth Pattern, Gorham	350.00
Porringer, Bartholomew Schotts, New York, C.1725	1980.00

Porringer, John Edwards, Lion Crest Top, C.1724	2700.00
Porringer, Josiah Austin, Charlestown, C.1750	1320.00
Punch Bowl, Chased & Pierced, Duhme Co., 14 In.	2750.00
Rattle, Coral Handle, Signed M.B., Dated 1766, 6 1/4 In.	2250.00
Salt & Pepper, Chased Shoulder, Gorham, 7 In., Pair	550.00
Salt & Pepper, Panel Form Around Bottom, Kalo, 4 3/8 In.	375.00
Salt, Adam Pattern, Liner, Shreve & Co., 2 3/4 In., Pair	110.00
Salver, 3 Floral & Shell Feet, Bailey & Co., 6 5/8 In.	495.00
Salver, Applied Cartouches & Scroll Rim, Gorham, 13 In.	467.50
Salver, Engraved, Border, Lincoln & Foss, 1856, 7 3/4 In.	350.00
Sauceboat, Ball–Black & Co., 2 Eagles, 5 3/4 X 9 In., Pair	1500.00
Scrolling Foliage, Footed Bowl, Schulz & Fischer, 8 In.	302.00
Server, Butter, Dome Top, Pierced Sterling Liner, Gorham	275.00
Server, Ice Cream, Mazerin, Dominick & Haff	125.00
Shaker, Pepper, Diamond Cover, Baluster, A.Stone, 4 1/4 In.	225.00
Shears, Grape Tool, Silver Blades, U.S., C.1900	165.00
Spoon, Baby's, Rabbit, Pierced, Artist E, A.J.Stone, 4 In.	275.00
Spoon, Basket Handle, J.J.Low, 7 In.	32.00
Spoon, Basket Handle, P.Field, 7 1/2 In.	30.00
Spoon, Coin Silver, Shepard & Boyd, 1810–30, 6 Piece	200.00
Spoon, Dessert, Downturned Fiddle, E.Rockwell, C.1830	30.00
Spoon, Dessert, Fiddle, D.B.Hempsted, C.1840, 7 1/4 In.	40.00
Spoon, Dessert, H.P.Buckley, C.1850, 7 In.	45.00
Spoon, Dessert, J.Lockwood, N.Y.C., C.1800	35.00
Spoon, Dessert, Overlap Fiddle, W.W.White, C.1830	35.00
Spoon, Dessert, Upturned Fiddle, W.Kendrick, C.1840	35.00
Spoon, Martini, G.C.Erickson, 12 1/2 In.	195.00
Spoon, Medicine, Folding, E.Todd, Tablespoon & Teaspoon	60.00
Spoon, Preserve, Raised Strawberries On Handle	85.00
Spoon, Radish, Oakland Horse, Watson	45.00
Spoon, Salt, Engraved M, T.C.Garrett & Co., 4 In., Pair	100.00
Spoon, Salt, Flower Petal Bowl, N.Munroe, C.1825, 4 1/8 In.	45.00
Spoon, Salt, Shell Bowl, Levi Drummond, C.1842	30.00
Spoon, Salt, Shell Bowl, Standish Barry, C.1795, 3 7/8 In.	75.00
Spoon, Salt, Towle & Jones, Newburyport, Mass., C.1855, Pair	95.00
Spoon, Serving, Abraham Forbes, N.Y., Coin Silver, 1790–95	135.00
Spoon, Serving, Allover Flowers & Fruits, Kirk, Large	175.00
Spoon, Serving, Cantwell Douglas, C.1799, 9 3/4 In.	155.00
Spoon, Serving, Fiddle, E.E.Bailey, C.1830, 8 1/2 In., Pair	55.00
Spoon, Serving, Marguerite, Wood & Hughes	70.00
Spoon, Soup, Mayflower, Kirk	55.00
Spoon, Stuffing, P.Krider, C.1860, 13 1/2 In.	350.00
Spoon, Victorian, Fruits, Flowers, Kirk	150.00
Stand, Bowl, Pierced Scrolled, Flared, Reed & Barton, 7 In.	150.00
Stand, Cream Soup, Lenox China Liners, Watson, Set of 12	180.00
Stand, Sherbet, Cut Glass Liner, Watson No.5, Set of 4	75.00
Strainer, Wine, Ecclesiastical, Gold Washed Bowl, Gorham	110.00
Sugar & Creamer, Repousse, J.E.Caldwell, C.1880, 5 In.	600.00
Sugar & Creamer, Threaded Handle, E.Cole, C.1820	150.00
Sugar & Creamer, Twisted Line Design At Base, Towle	40.00
Sugar Shell, Currier & Trott, Boston, C.1830	35.00
Sugar Shell, Fiddle Thread, T.Evans & Co., 1857, 6 3/8 In.	110.00
Sugar Shell, George L.Ames & Bro., C.1850, 6 1/2 In.	45.00
Sugar Shell, N.G.Wood, Coin Silver	18.00
Sugar Shell, Scalloped Rib Bowl, N.Harding & Co.	28.00
Sugar Shell, Twist Handle, Keller & Bros., C.1860	35.00
Sugar Sifter, Bailey & Kitchen, Philadelphia, C.1840	95.00
Sugar Sifter, Fiddle Thread, Bailey & Co., C.1840	135.00
Sugar Spoon, Shell Bowl, Basket Handle, Manning, 6 1/4 In.	40.00
Sugar Tongs, Acorn Nippers, I.& S., C.1795, 5 3/4 In.	195.00
Sugar Tongs, Basket of Flowers, P.Kum, Coin Silver, 1825–30	210.00
Sugar Tongs, Scalloped Bonnet, Stevens & Lakeman, C.1830	75.00
Sugar, Bud Finial Cover, Handles, Gebelein, 1929, 5 1/2 In.	250.00
Sugar, Flower Finial, A.E.Warner, Jr., C.1865, 5 1/2 In.	525.00

Tablespoon, A.X.F.Shepard, C.1815, 8 1/2 In. 45.00
Tablespoon, Clark, Rackett & Co., C.1840, 8 1/4 In. 125.00
Tablespoon, Cowles, Cleveland, Ohio, 1850, 8 1/2 In., 4 Pc. 125.00
Tablespoon, Fiddle Tip, Hyde & Goodrich, 8 1/4 In. 38.00
Tablespoon, Fiddle Tip, J.Conning 75.00
Tablespoon, H.Evans, Newark, C.1830 .... 35.00
Tablespoon, P.Lupp, New Brunswick, N.J., C.1760 .... 375.00
Tablespoon, Sheaf of Wheat, Moses Eastman, 8 3/4 In. 135.00
Tablespoon, W.Cornell, Providence, Rhode Island, C.1780 .... 150.00
Tankard, Bear On Top of Lid, Gorham, 13 In. 250.00
Tazza, Center Block Style, Reeded, E.E., Lebolt, 4 X 7 In. 350.00
Tea & Coffee Set, Adam Pattern, Shreve & Co., 6 Piece 2750.00
Tea & Coffee Set, Georgian, Pear Shape, T.B.Starr, 6 Piece 3200.00
Tea & Coffee Set, Tray, Crisscross, A.G.Shultz, 6 Piece 8250.00
Tea & Coffee Set, Tray, Inverted Pear Shape, Gorham, 8 Pc. 6600.00
Tea Caddy, Basket Shape, Whitney Co., 3 1/2 In. ....*Illus* 3410.00
Tea Set, Ebony Handles, Holloware, C.1927, Gorham, 6 Piece 5400.00
Tea Set, Grapes, Leaves, Tendrils, Shreve & Co., 3 Piece 450.00
Tea Strainer, Louis XV, Whiting 125.00
Tea Strainer, Over–The–Cup, Gorham 225.00
Teapot, Art Nouveau, Vines, Shreve & Co., 9 1/2 In. 385.00
Teapot, Chicken Legs, Ivory Handle, Gorham 900.00
Teapot, Domed Bud Finial Cover, Monogram, C.1835, 9 1/2 In. 425.00
Teapot, Shoulder Design, Hinged Lid, R & H Farnam, 1807 .... 495.00
Teaspoon, B.H.Tisdale, Newport & Providence, C.1820 .... 21.00
Teaspoon, Basket of Flowers Handle, Griffen & Son, 6 In. 25.00
Teaspoon, Basket of Flowers, Henry Gooding, C.1830 .... 30.00
Teaspoon, Basket of Flowers, J.S.Mott., C.1825 .... 40.00
Teaspoon, Beaded Edge, Joel N.Freeman, C.1860, 6 1/4 In. 25.00
Teaspoon, Bird Back, W.Haverstick, Jr., Lancaster, Pa., 1795 .... 85.00
Teaspoon, Bright Cut, B.Wenman, New York City, C.1790 .... 75.00
Teaspoon, Bright Cut, Underhill & Bernon, N.Y.C., C.1785 .... 75.00
Teaspoon, Cambridge, Gorham, 5 1/4 In. 8.00
Teaspoon, Canfield Bros., Baltimore, C.1830, 6 Piece 95.00
Teaspoon, Clipped Fiddle, E.P.Lescure & Son, C.1820 .... 18.00
Teaspoon, Coffin Fiddle, B.Cleveland, C.1805, 6 Piece 250.00
Teaspoon, Coin Silver, Engraved Ida, H & S, 6 Piece 54.00
Teaspoon, Coin Silver, Engraved Myra, Duhme & Co., 6 Piece 60.00
Teaspoon, D.B.Nichols, Oval Drop, C.1820, 5 7/8 In. 55.00
Teaspoon, E.Darby, Elizabeth, N.J., C.1830 .... 30.00
Teaspoon, Eagle Back, J.Kucher, Philadelphia, C.1790 .... 95.00
Teaspoon, Fiddle Tip, D.B.Hempsted, 6 1/8 In. 20.00
Teaspoon, Isaac Reed & Son, C.1830, 6 Piece 125.00
Teaspoon, J.S.Walter, Matawan, C.1815 .... 32.00
Teaspoon, N.Coleman, Burlington, C.1790 .... 95.00
Teaspoon, Oval, Thread, G.Spence, Newark, C.1855 .... 25.00
Teaspoon, Pelletreau Bennett & Cooke, 6 1/8 In., 4 Piece 260.00
Teaspoon, Pointed Fiddle, Browne & Seal, C.1815 .... 18.00
Teaspoon, R.Smith, Newark, N.J., C.1845 .... 25.00
Teaspoon, S.Baker & Son, New Brunswick, N.J., C.1840, 6 Pc. 195.00
Teaspoon, Short Midrib, F & H.Clark, C.1830, 5 1/2 In. 35.00
Teaspoon, T.Bradbury, Newburyport, Mass., C.1810 .... 32.00
Teaspoon, W.H.Hoyt, New York City, C.1820 .... 21.00
Teaspoon, W.Lupp, New Brunswick, N.J., C.1815 .... 75.00
Tongs, Asparagus, Bailey & Co., C.1850 .... 475.00
Tongs, Asparagus, Schmitz Moore & Co., N.Y., C.1915 .... 70.00
Tongs, Basket of Flowers, Stebbins & Howe, 6 In. 125.00
Tongs, H.Lewis, Philadelphia, Pa., C.1815 .... 75.00
Tongs, Ice, Chased Rib Border, Pierced Bowl, Kalo, 8 In., Pr. 600.00
Tongs, King Pattern, Bailey & Kitchen, Philadelphia 95.00
Tongs, Serving, Bailey & Co., C.1865 .... 225.00
Tongs, Sugar, Coleman, Floral Engraving, 5 5/8 In. 15.00
Tongs, Vegetable, Wood & Hughes 175.00
Tray, Adam Pattern, Handles, Shreve & Co., 27 In. 7150.00

Tray, Alternating Squiggle & Circle, A.J.Stone, 11 In. 1650.00
Tray, Applied Band Around Rim, G.C.Erickson, 7 X 4 1/8 In. 275.00
Tray, Bread, Strap Border, Hammered, Shreve, 14 1/4 In. 450.00
Tray, Card, Wavy Edge, Pad Feet, Oval, A.Stone, 5 1/4 In. 400.00
Tray, Chippendale, Plain, Circular Border, Gorham, 14 In. 660.00
Tray, Engraved Scroll, Gorham, C.1932, 12 3/8 In. 300.00
Tray, Footed, Sheffield, 1835 Mark, 11 1/2 In. 295.00
Tray, Presentation, Shreve & Co., Dated 1915, 16 3/4 In. 357.50
Tray, Stieff, 2 1/2 X 5 In. 30.00
Tray, Undulating Wavy Flange, Gebelein, Round, 15 1/2 In. 2250.00
Tureen, Chased Peapods, Turtles, Whiting, Cover, 46 Oz. 8850.00
Tureen, Soup, Georgian, Cover, Black, Starr & Frost, 17 In. 3100.00
Urn, Hot Water, Berries, Wood & Hughes, C.1870, 20 In. 935.00
Vase, Pierced, Engraved Foliage, Whiting, 1913, 24 1/8 In. 2090.00
Water Set, Engraved B, Kalo, 9 In.Pitcher, 6 Goblets 3950.00
SILVER–AUSTRIAN, Cup, Cherubs, Swans, Swags, 1866, 7 3/8 In. ....*Illus* 1700.00
   Gravy Boat, Attached Tray, Helmet Form, Schwartz & Steiner 467.00
   Kettle, Hot Water, Ivory Finial, Stand, 10 3/4 In. 1200.00
   Mirror, Dressing Table, Monogram, Easel, 1910, 18 In. 1650.00
   Plate, Dinner, Undulating Rims, G.H., 1791, 9 3/4 In., 12 Pc. 8250.00
   Tray, Tea, Rococo Revival, Handles, J.G.Klingkosch, 26 In. 2200.00
SILVER–BELGIAN, Chafing Dish, Pierced Border, Scroll Feet, Masks, 6 3/4 In. 1980.00
SILVER–CHINESE, Belt, Braided Link, Fancy Container End, 30 In. 135.00
   Box, Incense, Hut Shape, Windows, Hinged Door, 2 X 2 X 2 In. 225.00
   Cocktail Set, Bamboo Design Rim, Blown–Out Dragons, 8 Piece 750.00
SILVER–CONTINENTAL, Beaker, Vermeil Interior, Scenic Design, 2 1/2 In. 90.00
   Box, Singing Bird, Dancing Couple, Musicians, 1900, 4 In. 2750.00
   Centerpiece, Beaded, Fluted, Wood Handles, Corona, 9 In. 1350.00
   Centerpiece, Fortune Finial, Breast Handles, 23 In. 4450.00
   Creamer, Foliate Handle, Lobed Melon Shape, 3 3/4 In. 137.50
   Creamer, Neoclassical, Helmet Form, Monogram, 4 1/4 In. 110.00
   Decanter Set, 3–Bottle, 4 Putti Around Goat, 11 In. 880.00
   Dish, Reticulated Design of Birds, Flowers, 8 In. 100.00
   Ewer, Gilt, Rock Crystal, Satyrs, Serpent Handles, 7 In. 3575.00
   Figurine, Eagle, Marble Plinth, Engraved, 1900, 14 In. 2475.00
   Holder, Tea Glass, Heart Shaped Loops, 3 1/2 In. 180.00
   Salt & Pepper, Pheasant, 6 In., 8 Sets 495.00
   Spoon Warmer, Nautilus Shell, Standing Goose, 14 In. 2900.00
   Sugar & Creamer, Rococo Design 100.00
   Tea Set, 19th Century, Scenes of Putties, 5 Piece 1200.00
   Wine Nef, Fully Rigged Sailing Ship Form, 14 1/2 In. 2200.00
SILVER–DANISH, Bar Knife, Georg Jensen 65.00

Silver–Austrian, Cup, Cherubs, Swans, Swags,
1866, 7 3/8 In.

Blossom, Salad Set, Georg Jensen 600.00
Bottle Opener, Bloch Pattern, Georg Jensn 65.00
Bowl, Hammered, 8 Foliate Supports, Georg Jensen, 6 1/2 In. 1760.00
Box, Ribbed, Foliage, Amber Buds, Georg Jensen, 1939, 5 X 6 In. 3300.00
Candlestick, Grape Bunches, Georg Jensen, 19 1/8 In., Pair 4675.00
Coffee Service, Hammered Surface, Georg Jensen, 3 Piece 3400.00
Coffee Service, Ivory Handles, Oval Tray, Georg Jensen, 7 Pc. 6000.00
Coffee Set, Blossom Pattern, Ivory Handles, G.Jensen, 3 Pc. 2750.00
Compote, Band of Leaves, Cushion Foot, Michelsen, 12 1/2 In. 775.00
Compote, Bonbon, Calyx Leaves Support, Georg Jensen, 4 In. 665.00
Compote, Grapevine, Fluted Stem, Georg Jensen, 5 In. 1100.00
Compote, Openwork Stem, Georg Jensen, C.1934, 12 1/2 In. 4950.00
Compote, Openwork Stem, Oblong Bowl, Cohr, 5 1/2 In. 192.50
Compote, Presentation, Georg Jensen, C.1934, 8 3/4 In. 2530.00
Ladle, Acorn Pattern, Georg Jensen, 5 1/2 In. 65.00
Pastry Server, Blossom, Georg Jensen 350.00
Pitcher, Bud Design, Bone Handle, Georg Jensen, 1930, 8 In. 1210.00
Pitcher, Hammered Surface, Georg Jensen, 9 In. 2090.00
Salt, Acorn & Scroll, Georg Jensen 45.00
Sardine Fork, Cactus, Georg Jensen 32.00
Sauceboat, Ladle, Georg Jensen 1100.00
Server, Fish, Engraved Tendrils, Georg Jensen, C.1937 .... 1875.00
Spoon, Berry, Blossom–Like Pattern, Georg Jensen 192.00
Sugar Tongs, Acorns, Georg Jensen .... 60.00 To 75.00
Tray, Beaded Foliage, Hammered, Georg Jensen, 13 3/8 In. 3850.00
Tray, Hammered, Lappet Border, Oval, 1930, Georg Jensen, 23 In. 3950.00
Tray, Openwork Gallery, Handles, Georg Jensen, 13 5/8 In. 4950.00
SILVER–DUTCH, Biscuit Box, Beaded Rims, Hinged Cover, Middelhysen, 6 1/4 In. 1750.00
Cake Basket, Pierced Sides, Boat Shape, Jan Buysen, 15 3/4 In. 4125.00
Caster, Festoons & Beaded Borders, Vase Form, Sondag, 9 In. 7150.00
Creamer, Pyriform Body, Cabriole Legs, 1793, 6 In. 247.50
Fork & Spoon, Salad, Crowned Lion Crest, Basket of Fruit 247.50
Pepper Mill, C.1910 .... 65.00
Scoop, Marrow, Double Ends, Amsterdam, 18th Century, 9 1/4 In. 357.50
Server, Vegetable, Turning Blade Windmill End, Export Mark 110.00
Tea Kettle, Lampstand, Bombe Oval, Logerath, 14 1/2 In. 3850.00
Teapot, Chased Spiral Flutes, Inverted Pear Shape, 4 5/8 In. 3575.00
Tray, Riveted Rows Beading, Ribbon Handles, Stolting, 20 In. 4950.00

English silver is marked with a series of four or five small hallmarks. The standing lion mark is the most commonly seen sterling quality mark. The other marks indicate the city of origin, the maker, and the year of manufacture. These dates can be verified in many good books on silver.

SILVER–ENGLISH, Basket, Glass Liner, Henry Chawner, 1791, 6 In. 1650.00
Bowl, Punch, Victorian, 1889, Stuart Harris 2100.00
Bowl, Vegetable, Leaf Finial, Flowers, Shells, 1850, 11 In. 935.00
Box, Document, Rectangular, Oak Leaf Sprays, 6 X 18 X 12 In. 700.00
Box, Jewelry, Wood Panels, Scroll Feet, 1900, Comyns, 7 In. 1430.00
Brush Set, British Sterling Hallmark, Case, 6 Piece 495.00
Cake Basket, Rococo Scrollwork, R.& S.Garrard, 15 In. 4675.00
Cake Basket, Swing Handle, Foliage, Birds, W.H.& Son, 1919 .... 302.50
Candlestick, Molded Rim, 1826, 10 1/8 In., Pair 2850.00
Candlestick, Tendrils Support Sconce, 4 3/4 In., Pair 995.00
Case, Cigarette, Engraved Florals 40.00
Coaster, Wine Bottle, Wooden Bottom, 4 5/8 In., Pair 85.00
Coaster, Wine, George III, Gadroon Borders, 6 5/8 In., Pair 1325.00
Coffee Service, Button Design, Wood Handles, 1933, 4 Piece 665.00
Coffeepot, George IV, Melon Shape, Wooden Handle, Wm.Fell 550.00
Coffeepot, Hinged Cover, Pear Shape, 11 5/8 In. 715.00
Creamer, George II, Rococo, Leaf Capped Handle, 3 3/4 In. 137.00
Creamer, George III, Neoclassical, Strap Handle, 2 7/8 In. 137.00
Creamer, George IV, Ribbed Panels, Pear Shape, P.Storr, 5 In. 2200.00
Cup, Celtic Revival, Handle, Chester, 1908–09 .... 130.00

Silver–English, Dish, Serving, Foliate Handle,
Sheffield, 16 In.

Always repair dented silver.
Cleaning a piece with a dent can
eventually lead to a hole.

Cup, Cover, Baluster Finial, Scroll Handle, 10 5/8 In., Pair	935.00
Cup, Spiral Fluted Edge, C.E., 1897, 2 3/4 In., Pair	137.50
Cup, Trophy, Mappin & Webb, Date, Inscription, 49 Oz., Pair	1100.00
Dish, Cover, Foliate & Shell Design, Sheffield, 17 In.	250.00
Dish, George III, Cheese, Hinged Domed Cover, 10 1/4 In.	275.00
Dish, Serving, Foliate Handle, Sheffield, 16 In. ....*Illus*	1500.00
Dressing Spoon, Fiddle, Thread & Shell, S.Hayne & D.Cater	330.00
Dressing Spoon, George Gray, 1791	110.00
Egg Caddy, Center Post, Loop Handle, 6 Cups & Shell Spoons	165.00
Fruit Basket, Scrolls, Garlands, R.Hennell, 1820, 14 3/4 In.	4950.00
Inkstand, 2 Glass Bottles, Silver Tops, 1908	250.00
Inkstand, George II, Gadroon Rim, 3 Galleries, 8 5/8 In.	2310.00
Marrow Scoop, Thomas Chawner, 1774, 9 In.	250.00
Marrow Scoop, Thomas Northcote, 1779, 8 3/4 In.	225.00
Mug, Queen Anne, Molded Borders, Cylindrical, Timbrell, 4 In.	1200.00
Mustard, Hinged Cover, Repousse, Spoons, Pair	190.00
Picture Frame, Flowering Branches, Birmingham, 1910, 9 In.	885.00
Picture Frame, Head of Maiden, Birmingham, 1905, 8 In.	880.00
Picture Frame, Maidens Picking Flowers, Birmingham, 13 In.	2475.00
Picture Frame, Repousse, Enameled Butterfly, 5 In.	150.00
Platter, Meat, George II, Serpentine Ends, Feline, 19 1/4 In.	2425.00
Platter, Meat, On Stand, Dome Cover, Sheffield, 26 In.	450.00
Platter, Molded Rim, Engraved Crest On Border, 15 3/4 In.	250.00
Salt, George III, Boat Shape, Engraved Crest, 4 Piece	825.00
Salt, George III, Cobalt Blue Liner, Engraved Design	50.00
Salver, Ebenezer Coker, Shells, 1762, 14 5/8 In.	2860.00
Salver, Gadrooned Rim, Robert Salmon, C.1792, 8 In.	425.00
Sauce Tureen, Cameo Shaped Body, Cover, 9 In., Pair	4700.00
Sauceboat, Rococo Design, Scrolled Rim, Boat Shape, 8 In.	275.00
Sauceboat, Shell Supports, Scalloped Rim, A.Killick, 8 In.	1050.00
Server, Fluted Cover, Ribbed Legs, Divided, Ovoid, 13 In.	295.00
Soap Dish, Hammered, Inlaid Gold, Crest, Hallmark, 1869	125.00
Soap Dish, Hinged, Gold Wash Interior, London Mark, 1863	95.00
Spoon, Platter, Victorian, Fiddle & Thread, JW & JW	137.00
Spoon, Serving, Basket Handle, Gilded Bowl, 9 In.	65.00
Spoon, Stuffing, George III, Armorial, William Fearn, 1774	220.00
Spoon, Stuffing, Thomas Wallis & Jonathan Hayse, 1814	250.00
Sugar Tongs, Hester Bateman	175.00
Tablespoon, Robert Bowers, 1825, Pair	100.00
Tankard, Rococo, Handle, B.Cartwright, 4 3/4 In.	995.00
Tankard, Scroll Handle, W.Kidney, 1742, 4 3/4 In.	715.00
Tea & Coffee Service, Tray, English, 6 Piece	3800.00
Tea & Coffee Set, George III–Style, Marked E.V., 7 Piece	2350.00
Tea Caddy, George III, William Sumner, 1788, 12 Oz.	2100.00
Tea Set, Open Sugar, Creamer, Boat Shape, Grapevine Handles	700.00
Tea Set, Oval Form, Oak Leaf Engraving, London, 1808	1100.00
Teapot, Federal, Gadroon Trim, Sheffield, C.1780, 6 1/2 In.	400.00
Teapot, Leaf Capped Spout, Gadrooning, W.Shaw II, 6 1/2 In.	605.00

Tongs, Asparagus, Fiddle, Thread & Shell, WW/BT, 1903, 10 In.	247.50
Tray, George III, Rosettes, Leaves, W.Tweedie, 33 Oz.	550.00
Tray, Scrolled Feet, Strapwork Designs, RFF, 28 1/2 X 20 In.	5500.00
Tray, Tea, Bunches of Roses, Scroll Handles, J.Figg, 31 In.	8850.00
Tray, Tea, Edwardian, Gadroon, Slot Handles, Sheffield, 26 In.	2200.00
Tray, Tea, George IV, Flowers, Handles, Wm.Eley II, 31 In.	6325.00
Tumbler Cup, Hammered Sides, C.1680	247.50
Tureen, Sauce, Cover, Loop Handles, Charner, 1788, 30 Oz., Pr.	2100.00
Urn, Tea, George III, Gadroon & Shell, R.Sibley, 15 1/2 In.	9350.00
Vase, Trumpet Shape, Embossed Design, Cupids, 6 3/4 In.	95.00
SILVER—FINNISH, Sugar & Creamer, Matching Tray, Antler Form Handles, 3 Pc.	225.00
SILVER—FRENCH, Ashtray, Cover, Vertical Flutes, Cartier, C.1930, 4 3/8 In.	2860.00
Ashtray, Pearl Inlaid, Cigarette Holder, 1925, 13 In.	2750.00
Basket, Pierced Sides, Swing Handle, 4 Busts, 4 3/8 In.	137.00
Box, Enameled Hinged Cover, Roses, Leaves, 1/2 X 1 5/8 In.	110.00
Butterfield, Sundial & Compass, Pocket, Cover, Leather Bag	1540.00
Case, Cigarette, Black Enamel Lid, Gold Panel, 3 1/2 X 3 In.	660.00
Case, Cigarette, Niello Cover, Leaves, Flowers, 3 1/2 X 3 In.	165.00
Centerpiece, Beaded Borders, Leaf Handles, G.J.A.B., 12 In.	1100.00
Centerpiece, Wood Knop, 12 Sides, Puiforcat, 15 In.	3350.00
Coffee Service, Wood Handles, Puiforcat, 4 Piece	3850.00
Compote, Cut Glass, Putti Stem, Odiot, C.1860, 8 1/2 In., Pair	3025.00
Compote, Glass Liner, Cabriole Leg Table Shape, 4 X 5 In.	330.00
Condiment Stand, Double, Loop Handle, Marked LD, 7 X 8 In.	192.00
Cup, Wine Taster, Convex Bottom, Thumb & Ring Handle, 1838	350.00
Cup, Wine Taster, Grapes & Vines, Louis XV, 1838, 4 In.	450.00
Cup, Wine Taster, Snake Handle, Minerva Mark, 1838, 2 1/4 In.	375.00
Desk Set, Japanese Style, Insects & Flowers, LB Mark, 3 Piece	495.00
Dish, Pierced Rim, Engraved Shells, Fluted, 9 1/8 In., Pair	880.00
Porringer, French Coin Center, Stamped 1790, 3 1/8 In.	125.00
Salt Stand, Master, Rococo, Shell Shaped Bowl, 4 3/4 In., Pair	125.00
Salver, 4 Scroll Feet, Octagonal, Puiforcat, 11 In.	995.00
Tea & Coffee Set, Baluster, Monogram, Odiot, C.1880, 4 Piece	1650.00
Tureen, Domed Cover, Foliate Knops, Marked, 1819, 11 In.	2090.00
Tureen, Soup, Cluster Design, Tapered, 1930, Keller, 18 In.	9350.00
Urn, Cover, Ovolo Rim, Cone Finial, Pierced Body, 8 In.	1760.00
Vase, Flared Sides, 2 Gilt Bands, 1940, Puiforcat, 6 In.	7125.00
SILVER—GERMAN, Beaker, Matted Band, Cylindrical, Busch I, C.1660, 3 5/8 In.	2250.00
Belt Buckle, Horse, Cowboy, Cald	27.00
Bottle Stopper, Horse, Rearing, Marked 800	25.00
Bowl, Centerpiece, Repousse Genre Scenes, Pierced, 11 X 4 In.	225.00
Bowl, Neoclassical, Acanthus Leaves Band, 5 X 4 3/4 In.	165.00
Box, Biscuit, Repousse, Putti, Musical Instruments, 8 1/2 In.	775.00
Box, Snuff, 7 Years War Victory, Enameled, C.1757, 3 3/8 In.	1760.00
Box, Sugar, Bombe, Footed, Domed Cover, I.G.I., 1776–91, 5 In.	1200.00
Bread Basket, Kneeling Suitor, Alpine Landscape, 15 In.	522.50
Cake Basket, Foliage & Pheasants Panels, 10 1/2 In.	467.50
Chalice, Cover, Pineapple Lobes, Lizard On Stem, 10 1/4 In.	715.00
Coffee & Tea Set, Rococo Style, Shaped Oval Tray, 5 Piece	1000.00
Compote, Fan & Diamond Cutting, Scroll Handles, 6 3/8 In.	475.00
Cup & Napkin Ring, Baby's, Bremerhaven, Engraved, 1890s	95.00
Dish, Serving, Threaded Indented Rim, E.Meyer, 10 3/4 In., Pr.	665.00
Ecuelle, Fleur–De–Lis Handles, Lobed Cover, C.1700, 4 3/4 In.	2425.00
Figurine, Musician, Barrel Shape, Heads Revolve, 7 In.	850.00
Nef, Movable Wheels & Rudder, Full Sail, Figures, 18 In.	3575.00
Pencil Holder, Egyptian Revival, Enameled Mummy, Loop	150.00
Plaque, Adoration of Magi, Virgin, C.1600, 4 3/8 X 3 3/8 In.	6100.00
Plate, Portrait, Karl Wilhelm & 18th Century Lady, 9 In., Pr.	357.00
Sweetmeat, Lobed Oval, Lovebirds, Basket, 17th Century, 8 In.	4125.00
Sweetmeat, Lobed Oval, S–Scroll Handles, C.1660, 4 3/4 In.	2860.00
Tazza, Glass Bowl, Medallion 1 Side, Floral Basket, 10 In.	165.00
Tea & Coffee Set, Silver Mounted Wood Tray, 5 Piece	3300.00
Tea & Coffee Set, Slip–On Covers, Jung, Mannheim, 1790, 4 Pc.	2850.00
Tea & Coffee Set, Tray, Trumpet Form, C.1900, 5 Piece	2975.00

Tea & Coffee Set, Vertical Matted Flutes, C.1790, 4 Piece	2850.00
SILVER–HUNGARIAN, Box, Sugar, Leaf & Berry Finial, J.Blettel, 1790, 5 1/4 In.	1550.00
SILVER–IRANIAN, Candlestick, Rococo Style, Round Pedestal, 7 1/4 In., Pair	467.00
SILVER–IRISH, Coaster, Wine, George III, Pierced, Wood Base, Haines, 5 In., Pr.	2200.00
Cup, Cartouche, Leafage, Handles, Lamp & Flame Finial, 13 In.	665.00
Jug, Cream, George II, Helmet Form, John Moore, 3 7/8 In.	880.00
SILVER–ITALIAN, Box, Cigarette, Rape of Europa, M.Minotto, 5 1/2 In.	500.00
SILVER–JAPANESE, Punch Set, Ladle, Plain Bowl, Ring Foot, C–Handles, 12 Cups ...	665.00
Tray, Rectangular, Bleeding Hearts, Beetle, 1880, 7 In.	1100.00
Vase, Pricked Chrysanthemum, Baluster Base, 9 1/4 In., Pair	935.00
SILVER–MEXICAN, Bowl, Applied Scroll Border, Small	32.50
Bowl, Egg Shape, Lift–Off Lid, 2 3/8 In.	75.00
Bowl, Kidney Shape, 3 Cast Feet, 6 X 8 3/4 In.	225.00
Butter, Cover, Signed AVA, C.1940, 10 1/2 In.	125.00
Candlestick, 3–Light, Pedestal Base, 10 In., Pair	900.00
Pitcher, Water, Ice Lip, Melo Ribs, 12 In.	575.00
Tea Set, Turquoise Finials, Miniature, 7 Piece	250.00
SILVER–MEXICO, Dish, Serving, Retangular, Scroll Rim, 2 Sections	325.00
SILVER–NORWEGIAN, Dresser Set, 4 Pieces In Blue Enamel, 8 Piece	150.00
Goblet, Liquer, Gilt Interior Bowl, 3 3/4 In., 12 Piece	467.50
Ladle, Soup, Neoclassical, Monogram, J.Tostrup, 15 3/4 In.	110.00
Salt, Viking Ship, Vermeil & Rust, Spoon	120.00
Spoon, Strapwork Border, Plumeion, Fig Shape Bowl, 6 In.	2000.00
Tea Kettle, Stand & Sugar, Melon Shape, David Andersen	1100.00
SILVER–PERUVIAN, Beaker, Ceremonial, Janus Head Design, 4 1/4 X 3 1/2 In.	355.00
Bowl, Hammered Finish, Scalloped Rim, 13 3/4 In.	247.50

Russian silver is marked with the cyrillic, or Russian, alphabet. The numbers 84, 88, or 91 indicate the silver content. Russian silver may be higher or lower than sterling standard. Other marks indicate maker, assayer, or city of manufacture. Many pieces of silver made in Russia are decorated with enamel.

SILVER–RUSSIAN, Basket, Naplin Overlaid, Cable Handle, Footed, 1886, 17 In.	2200.00
Box, Cigar, Table, Sunburst Design, 6 3/4 In.	5500.00
Box, Cigar, Woodgrain, Engraved, St.Petersburg, 1890, 8 In.	5775.00
Cake Basket, Repousse Border, Nicholls & Plinke, 12 In.	2530.00
Cake Basket, Swing Handle, Leafage, 1870, 12 In.	2530.00
Candleholder, Attached Match Box, Shell–Shaped Saucer	125.00
Candlestick, Carayatid Stems, Masks, Dietrich, 9 3/4 In., Pr.	2860.00
Case, Cigarette, Green Cabochon Stone, 1925	665.00
Case, Cigarette, Red Stone Knob, Dated 1915, 4 X 3 In.	225.00
Case, Cigarette, Table, Wood Grain, 1890, 4 3/4 In.	2425.00
Casket, Stylized Foliage, Enameled, N.Zverev, 4 1/8 In.	3100.00
Chalice, Leave Borders, Enameled Plaques, Grigoriev, 14 In.	4125.00
Figurine, Dog, Raised Head, Marked PED, 15 3/4 In.	1430.00
Flask, Scene, Enameled Floral Band, Baluster, K.S., 2 3/4 In.	1650.00
Ice Bucket, Repousse, Continuous View Kremlin, 1885, 11 In.	3750.00
Jug, Milk, Enameled Boyar, Fruit Vine Handle, 1900, 4 1/2 In.	2425.00
Kovsh, Enameled Foliage, Blue Beads, Saltykov, 8 1/2 In.	6650.00
Samovar, Inverted Pear Shape, 4 Ball Feet, V.K.Mark, 14 In.	3300.00
Smoker's Set, Tray, Scrolling Foliage, A.Kuzmichev, 5 Piece	1100.00
Spoon, Niello, Gold Wash, Moscow, C.1888	80.00
Tea Caddy, Flowers, Chinese Figure, Pipe, Shchetinin, 6 In.	1985.00
Tray, Tea, Entwined Strapwork Handles, Monogram, Sper, 31 In.	2750.00
Tray, Tea, Scrolling Foliage, 2 Handles, C.1856, 31 In.	2750.00
SILVER–SCOTCH, Bowl, Armorial Engraving, C.1734, 4 1/2 In.	495.00
Chocolate Pot, Pyriform, Robert Gray & Son, 1804, 11 1/2 In.	770.00
Dressing Spoon, Fiddle, Heron, 1835, 13 In.	110.00
Tea Caddy, 2–Sections, Chinese Figures, J.Mithell, 1851, 8 In.	2475.00
SILVER–SIAMESE, Bowl, Animal Frieze, Floral Border, 4 3/4 X 9 In.	200.00

Sterling silver is made with 925 parts silver out of 1,000 parts of metal. The word "sterling" is a quality guarantee used in the United States after about 1860. The word was used much earlier in England

and Ireland. Pieces listed here are not identified by country. Other pieces of sterling quality silver are listed under Silver–American, Silver–English, etc.

SILVER–STERLING, Basket, Edwardian, Pierced Border, 6 In.	30.00
Basket, Fruit, Stationary Openwork Handle, 26 1/2 Oz.	400.00
Basket, Handle, 3 1/2 X 6 In.	20.00
Belt Buckle, Art Nouveau, Floral Design	100.00
Bowl, Underplate, Monogram, Flared, Reed & Barton, 5 X 6 In.	50.00
Bowl, Vegetable, Divided, Lebkuecher & Co., C.1896	475.00
Box, Enameled, Pale Amethyst Top, Unger, 3 In.	175.00
Buckle, Belt, Ladies, Floral Design, Art Nouveau	100.00
Butter Spreader, Victorian, Large	32.00
Candelabra, 3–Socle, Column Form, Sheffield, 19 In.	450.00
Candy Dish, Pierced & Chased Border, 5 1/2 In., Pair	25.00
Carving Set, Violet, Wallace, 2 Piece	110.00
Case, Calling Card, Dated Dec.12, 1886	75.00
Case, Cigarette, C.1941	22.00
Case, Cigarette, Enameled Nude On Cover	1600.00
Case, Cigarette, Female Photograph Cover, England, 1909	1100.00
Case, Cigarette, Hammered Design, Initials On Cover	45.00
Case, Cigarette, Man's, Large	45.00
Chatelaine, With Book, Perfume, Pencil On Cherub Clip	300.00
Child's Set, Knife, Fork & Spoon, Engraved Bobby	58.00
Clip, Blanket Or Bib, Enameled, Little Boy Blue, Monogram A	125.00
Comb, Chignon, 1890s	60.00
Compote, Raised Floral Design, S.Kirk & Son, 11 1/2 In.	275.00
Compote, Repousse Rose & Mum, Steiff, 5 1/2 In.	80.00
Compote, Simpson Hall Miller, 5 Oz.	75.00
Cordial, Weighted Base, 3 7/8 In., 10 Piece	120.00
Crimper, Hair, Repouse Scrolled Handle, Mother–of–Pearl	30.00
Cup, Wine Tasters	25.00
Cutter, Cigar, 6 In.	65.00
Dish, Nut, Heart Shape, Pierced, 5 1/2 In., 4 Piece	247.00
Door Knocker, Arab Heads, Monogram Space, Pair	650.00
Figurine, Elephant, Raised Trunk, 4 1/2 X 3 In.	225.00
Fork, Baby's, 1900s	20.00
Fork, Baby's, Victorian	25.00
Funnel, Cap Lifter & Sheath, Leather Case, C.1900, 4 Piece	125.00
Funnel, Perfume	38.00
Glove Stretcher, Art Nouveau	85.00
Holder, Cigarette, Chased Hands, Marble Base, 4 In., Pair	175.00
Holder, For Lady's Fan, Telescoping	65.00
Kettle, Water, On Stand, Octagonal Burner, 1920, 11 1/2 In.	375.00
Ladle, Gold Wash, Embossed, Monogram, 11 In.	225.00
Loving Cup, Shincook Hills Golf Course, 2 Handles, 1899	150.00
Mustache Spoon, Manchester Sterling Mark, 4 1/2 In.	55.00
Pitcher, Water, Wiedlich, Large	340.00
Plate, Bread, S Monogram, 6 In., Set of 8	240.00
Rattle, With Bells & Whistle, Red Coral Handle, 3 1/2 In.	235.00
Salad Server, Art Nouveau, Venus & Cupid, 10 1/2 In., 2 Pc.	385.00
Salt, Oval, Blue Glass Liner, 3 In., 4 Piece	120.00
Serving Set, Fish, Engraved Fish & Seaweed, Bone Handles	200.00
Shoe Horn, Floral Design, Ornate Handle	38.00
Shoe Horn, Victorian, Floral Design	45.00
Sipper, Spoon End, Dangling Oriental Items, 9 In., Set of 6	75.00
Spoon, Art Nouveau, Nude Lady In Handle	75.00
Spoon, Baby's, Curved Handle	25.00
Spoon, Condiment, Pierced, Gothic Pattern, Marked, 4 1/4 In.	60.00
Spoon, Engraved E.D.R.On Handle	50.00
Spoon, Nude Lady In Handle, Art Nouveau	75.00
SILVER–STERLING, SPOON, SOUVENIR, see Souvenir, Spoon, Sterling Silver	
Sugar & Creamer, Strap Design Rim, Bulbous, 1915, 3 3/4 In.	150.00

Tea Ball, Snowflake Design, Chain, Ring, Marked, 1 3/4 In.	36.00
Tea Infuser, Chain, Tea Kettle Shape	45.00
Tea Strainer, 2 Handles	32.50
Tea Strainer, Art Nouveau	65.00
Tea Strainer, Turned Wooden Handle, 6 1/2 In.	30.00
Teapot, Ribbed Bowl, Foliage Handle & Top Rim, 6 1/2 In.	425.00
Tray, 4 Squash Blossoms Rim, Indented Center, 10 In.	700.00
Tumbler, Hammered, Applied Initial G, 1915, 3 5/8 In.	150.00
Watch Holder, Cherubs, Ribbons & Wreath, Easel Back	475.00
SILVER–SWEDISH, Spoon, Serving, Plique–A–Jour & Gilt, Fig–Shaped Bowl	246.50
Sugar, Pad Feet With Leaves, Scroll Handles, 5 In.	192.00
Tankard, Plant Sprays, Handle, Cap Cover, Wibeck, 7 5/8 In.	9350.00
SILVER–VIENNESE, Ewer, Neptune 1 Side, Draped Female Other, Ovoid, 10 In.	3850.00
Salt, 3 Shell Feet, Chased Shell & Floral Design, Pair	450.00

Sinclaire cut glass was made by H.P. Sinclaire and Company of Corning, New York, between 1905 and 1929. He cut glass made at other factories until 1920. Pieces were made of crystal as well as amber, blue, green, or ruby glass. Only a small percentage of Sinclaire glass is marked with the S in a wreath.

SINCLAIRE, Decanter, Whiskey, Thistle Pattern, Square, Teardrop Stopper, Pair	425.00
Jar, Copper Wheel Engraving, Amber, Cover, 14 1/2 In.	135.00
Vase, Fan, Green Glass, Engraved, 7 1/2 In.	65.00

SKIING, see Sports

Slag glass resembles a marble cake. It can be streaked with different colors. There were many types made from about 1880. Pink slag was an American Victorian product of unknown origin. Purple and blue slag were made in American and English factories. Red slag is a very late–Victorian and twentieth–century glass. Other colors are known but are of less importance to the collector.

SLAG, Black, Dish, Hen, White Head, Atterbury, Small	150.00
Blue, Hen On Nest	29.00
Blue, Humidor, Drum Shape, Cap–Shaped Finial, 6 1/2 In.	345.00
Blue, Lamp, Desert Scene, Building, Gilded Cast Iron Base, 21 In.	165.00
SLAG, CARAMEL, see Chocolate Glass	
Green, Jar, Owl, 7 In.	20.00
Pink, Cruet, Inverted Fan & Feather, Clear Stopper	995.00
Pink, Tumbler, Inverted Fan & Feather, 3 7/8 In.	350.00
Purple, Butter, Cover, Rooster	135.00
Purple, Cake Stand, Plain Baluster	95.00
Purple, Celery, Daisy Block, Rowboat, 12 In.	135.00
Purple, Celery, Jewel Pattern	85.00
Purple, Compote, Beaded Hearts, 4 1/2 X 5 In.	68.00
Purple, Compote, Jelly, Threaded	55.00
Purple, Compote, Jenny Lind Pattern	150.00
Purple, Compote, Marked, 7 In.	65.00
Purple, Compote, Open, Threaded & Fluted Top	125.00
Purple, Dish, Hen Cover, Basket, 6 1/2 In.	65.00
Purple, Dish, Horse Cover, Nest	22.00
Purple, Doorstop, Alley Cat, Fenton	50.00
Purple, Figurine, Chessie Cat, Fenton	50.00
Purple, Humidor, Fenton	75.00
Purple, Mug, Robin	30.00
Purple, Ornament, Obelisk, 8 In.	95.00
Purple, Salt, Urn Shape, 2 Handles, Embossed Ribbing, 2 1/4 In.	55.00
Purple, Soap Dish, Ribbed	25.00
Purple, Spooner, Oval Panel	60.00 To 65.00
Purple, Spooner, Scroll With Acanthus	65.00 To 75.00
Purple, Toothpick	18.00
Purple, Tumbler, Present From Bristol Expo, 1893	45.00
Red, Basket	30.00
Red, Bowl, Mandarin, Black Amethyst Base, Fenton, 13 In.	195.00
Red, Cornucopia, Imperial	15.00

Red, Fruit Bowl, 8 1/2 In.	25.00
Red, Mug, Robin, Imperial	28.00
Red, Vase, Crimped Top, Footed, 12 In.	50.00
White, Dish, Hen, Black Head, Atterbury	190.00
Yellow, Green Edge, Corinthian Column, Gold, 26 In.	300.00

Sleepy Eye collectors look for anything bearing the image of the 19th– century Indian chief with the drooping eyelid. The Sleepy Eye Milling Co., Sleepy Eye, Minnesota, used his portrait in advertising from 1883 to 1921. It offered many premiums, including stoneware and pottery steins, crocks, bowls, mugs, and pitchers, all decorated with the famous profile of the Indian. The pottery was popular and was made by Western Stoneware and other potteries long after the flour mill went out of business in 1921. Reproductions of the pitchers are being made today. The original pitchers came in only five sizes: 4 in., 5 1/4 in., 6 1/2 in., 8 in., and 9 in. The Sleepy Eye image was also used by companies unrelated to the flour mill.

SLEEPY EYE, Bread Board Scraper, To Be Sure, Use Sleepy Eye Flour	395.00
Card, Advertising Flour & Cereal	40.00
Creamer, Blue On White, 1/2 Pint	120.00
Crock, Butter, Blue On Gray .... 395.00 To	445.00
Crock, Salt, 6 1/2 In.Diam.	375.00
Fan, Hand	75.00
Flour Sack	75.00
Letter Opener	18.00
Mirror, Pocket .... 15.00 To	35.00
Mug, Blue On White, 4 1/2 In. .... 150.00 To	175.00
Mug, Convention, 1976, Set of 6	550.00
Mug, Gray & Blue	225.00
Mug, Signed Monmouth, 4 1/2 In. .... 125.00 To	135.00
Picture, 1st Convention Edition, Oak Frame, 19 X 24 In.	95.00
Pillow Cover, Chief Before President Monroe, Square, 20 1/2 In.	450.00
Pillow Top, Portrait	350.00
Pitcher, Blue & White, Signed Western Stoneware, 4 In.	140.00
Pitcher, No.1, Blue & White, 4 In.	60.00
Pitcher, No.1, Blue On White, 4 In. .... 125.00 To	150.00
Pitcher, No.2, Blue & White, 5 1/4 In.	75.00
Pitcher, No.2, Blue On White, 5 1/4 In. .... 80.00 To	150.00
Pitcher, No.3, Blue & White, 6 1/2 In.	225.00
Pitcher, No.4, Blue On White, 8 In. .... 84.00 To	91.00
Pitcher, No.5, Blue On Gray, 9 In.	225.00
Pitcher, Set of 5	850.00
Pitcher, Western Stoneware, Blue On White, 4 In.	145.00
Postcard, Indian Artist	65.00
Salt, Bowl, Blue On Gray .... 425.00 To	450.00
Sign, Flour, Indian	1250.00
Sign, Flour, Scenes Around Indian	5000.00
Sign, The Meritorious Flour, Tin, Litho ....*Illus*	3600.00
Spoon	100.00
Stein, Blue & Gray, 1979, 7 3/4 In.	200.00
Stein, Blue & Gray, 7 3/4 In.	550.00
Stein, Blue On Gray Stoneware ....*Illus*	675.00
Stein, Blue On Gray, 7 3/4 In.	500.00
Stein, Blue On White, 7 3/4 In.	490.00
Stein, Blue, 7 3/4 In.	275.00
Stein, Brown On White, 7 3/4 In. .... 210.00 To	250.00
Stein, Brown, 1952, 40 Oz.	350.00
Sugar & Creamer, Gray & Blue	700.00

Slip is a thin mixture of clay and water, about the consistency of sour cream, that is applied to pottery for decoration. It is a very old method of making pottery and is still in use.

SLIPWARE, Charger, Coggled Edge, Large	350.00
Dish, Unicorn, Galloping, Running Dog Rim, 17th Century, 12 1/4 In.	1200.00

Pan, Loaf, Dark & Light Double Cross Lines, 11 3/4 X 14 In. 750.00
    SLOT MACHINE, see Coin–Operated Machine

Smith Brothers glass was made after 1878. Alfred and Harry Smith had worked for the Mt. Washington Glass Company in New Bedford, Massachusetts, for seven years before going into their own shop. They made many pieces with enamel decoration.

Smith Bros. Co.

SMITH BROTHERS, Cookie Jar, Melon Ribbed, Design 360.00
  Herons, Butterscotch, 6 In. 100.00
  Humidor, Barrel Shape, Yellow Ground, Daisies, Signed, 7 In. 165.00
  Jar, Dresser, Pansies, Melon–Ribbed, 3 3/4 X 5 1/2 In. 285.00
  Plate, Santa Maria, Dated 1893, Signed, 7 In. 285.00
  Saltshaker, Stork In Marsh Scenic, Pewter Top 50.00
  Sugar & Creamer, Ribbed, Flowers, Silver–Plated Parts, 3 In. 410.00
  Sugar & Creamer, White, Yellow & Orange Flowers, Marked 410.00
  Toothpick, Pastel Flowers, Blue Dot Rim, White Ribbed 125.00
  Toothpick, Pastel Flowers, Dots, 2 1/4 In. 135.00
  Vase, Blue Floral, Gilded Leaves, Swirl, Signed, 6 3/4 In. 425.00
  Vase, Clamatis Blossoms, Raised Gold Rim, 8 3/4 In. 385.00
  Vase, Enameled Stork In Marsh, Silver Plated Holder, 4 In. 100.00
  Vase, Floral Design, Peach Ground, C.1885, 8 X 3 In. 145.00
  Vase, Herons, Butterscotch, 6 In. 100.00
  Vase, Wisteria Traced In Gold, Gold Beading, 7 1/4 X 8 In. 1215.00

Snow Babies, made from bisque and spattered with glitter sand, were first manufactured in 1864 by Hertwig and Company of Thuringia. Other German and Japanese companies copied the Hertwig designs. Originally, Snow Babies were made of candy and used as Christmas decorations. There are also Snow Babies tablewares made by Royal Bayreuth. Copies of the small Snow Babies figurines are being made today and can easily confuse the collector.

SNOW BABIES, Candlestick, Riding On Sled, Royal Bayreuth, 6 1/2 In. 125.00
  Night–Light, Seated, Legs Out, Ice Skates, Heubach, 3 1/2 In. 450.00
  On Sled, 1 1/2 In. .... 38.00 To 42.00
  On Snowball, 1 1/2 X 3 In. 55.00
  On Snowball, 2 In. 55.00
  On Stomach 46.00
  On Stomach, 1 1/2 In. 40.00
    SNUFF BOTTLE, see Bottle, Snuff

Sleepy Eye, Sign, The Meritorious Flour, Tin, Litho   Sleepy Eye, Stein, Blue On Gray Stoneware

Taking snuff was popular long before cigarettes became available. The snuff was kept in a small box. The gentleman or lady would take a small pinch of the ground tobacco or snuff in the fingers, then sniff it and sneeze. Snuffboxes were made of many materials, including gold, silver, enameled metal, and wood. Most snuffboxes date from the late eighteenth or early nineteenth century.

SNUFFBOX, Agate & Gold Colored Metal, Oval, 1 1/2 X 2 In.	55.00
Brass Lid, Ship, Swan & Geometric Design, Tooth, 4 1/4 In.	725.00
Brass, Incised David Williams, 1895, English	55.00
Classical Scene On Cover, Gold & Enamel, Swiss, C.1810	1350.00
Enameled Inlay, Brass, Signed Paris	85.00
Enameled, 2 Headed Eagle, Gold On Silver, Comma Shape, 2 3/4 In.	375.00
Engraved Flower Head On Cover, Red Paint, American, 3 1/4 In.	100.00
George IV, Gold & Silver Medallion, Tortoise Trim, 1 X 3 In.	770.00
Gold Snake, Enamel Scales, Gold & Beryl, C.1940, 2 1/4 In.	2530.00
Heart, Heart Carved, Chamfered Slide Cover, 18th Century, 1 Piece	150.00
Ivory, Figures In Landscape, Geometric Borders, 2 3/8 In.Diam.	137.50
Ivory, Painted Brunette Lady, French, 2 5/8 In.Diam.	137.50
Naval Battle On Lid, Papier–Mache, 3 5/8 In.	35.00
Painted Cover of People Playing Cards, C.1740, 3 1/4 In.	825.00
Papier–Mache, Girl In Dressing Gown Painted On Lid, 2 3/4 In.	150.00
Queen Victoria, Portrait As Young Girl On Lid, Tin	60.00
Shoe Shape, Hinged Lid, Upturned Toe, 2 3/4 X 8 In.	65.00
Silver, Bombe Sides, Romantic Scene Hinged Lid, German, 2 1/4 In.	225.00
Silver, Engraved, Presentation, Hinged Lid, 1800s, 2 X 3 In.	275.00
Statue, Peter The Great, Silver & Niello, 1823, 3 1/2 X 2 5/8 In.	825.00
Twist Wire Framing, Hinged Lid, Eagles & Crown, Gilt On Silver	235.00

Soapstone is a mineral that was used for foot warmers or griddles because of its heat–retaining properties. Soapstone was carved into figurines and bowls in many countries in the nineteenth and twentieth centuries. Most of the soapstone seen today is from China or Japan. It is still being carved in the old styles.

SOAPSTONE, Bookends, Floral Relief Design, 6 In.	20.00
Box, Chinese Figures, In Garden, 5 In.	90.00
Figurine, Buddha, Light Green, 6 In.	60.00
Figurine, Horses, On Base, 5 1/2 X 7 1/2 In.	95.00
Figurine, Oriental Girl, Basket of Fish, 11 In.	45.00
Group, Cupid & Sleeping Putto, Pedestal, Biagini, 31 In., Pair	2860.00
Inkwell, Center Well, 4 Corner Quill Holders, Geometric Design	150.00
Teapot, Dragon, Carved, Cut–Outs, Fitted Cover, Green, 7 In.	170.00
Toothpick, 3 Monkeys	10.00
Urn, Cover, Carved Foliage, Mounted As Lamps, 11 1/2 In., Pair	605.00
Vase, Double, Monkey, Pig & Bird, Dark Brown, 19th Century, 8 In.	145.00
Vase, Red, Bird & Fruit Tree Around Base, China, 5 1/2 X 6 In.	40.00
Vase, World's Fair, N.Y., China, 1939, 8 1/2 In.	125.00

Soft paste is a name for a type of pottery. Although it looks very much like porcelain, it is a chemically different material. Most of the soft–paste wares were made in the early nineteenth century. Other pieces may be listed under Gaudy Dutch or Leeds.

SOFT PASTE, Bowl & Saucer, Shipwrecked Figures, C.1765	380.00
Compote, Lion Head Finial, River Scene, Ruins, Oval, 7 1/2 In.	110.00
Creamer, Diamond Design	75.00
Creamer, House Design	115.00
Creamer, King's Rose	117.50
Cup & Saucer, Sprig Pattern, Adams	22.00
Figurine, Boy & Dog, Flower Bower, Staffordshire, 4 5/8 In.	155.00
Pitcher, Blue Sponged, Green Embossed Bands, 5 1/4 In.	75.00
Plate, Sprig Pattern, Adams	28.00
Shaker, Blue Feather Band, 4 1/2 In.	90.00
Sugar, Blue Transfer, Scenes of Shepherd, 4 1/2 In.	25.00

Sugar, Floral Design, Swan Form Finial, English, 19th Century	225.00
Sugar, King's Rose, Davenport, 4 1/2 In.	55.00
Teapot, Floral, Almond Shape, Scalloped Rim, 7 1/4 In.	75.00
Vase, Mountainous Landscape, Blue & White, Chinese, 15 3/4 In.	650.00

What could be more fun than to bring home a souvenir of a trip? Our ancestors enjoyed the same thing and souvenirs were made for almost every location. Most of the souvenir pottery and porcelain pieces of the nineteenth century were made in England or Germany, even if the picture showed a North American scene. In the twentieth century, the souvenir china business seems to have gone to the manufacturers in Japan, Taiwan, Hong Kong, England, and America. Another popular souvenir item is the souvenir spoon, made of sterling or silver plate. These are usually made in the country pictured on the spoon.

SOUVENIR, see also Coronation; World's Fair

SOUVENIR, Ashtray, Launching of Moore–McCormack, Sterling Silver, 1958	40.00
Ashtray, Minnesota Centennial, State Shape	33.00
Ashtray, Rio Grande, Denver	9.00
Ashtray, University of Illinois, Metal, Blue, 1937	9.00
Ashtray, Visit of Norwegian Training Ship To U.S.A., Silver	45.00
Bandanna, Jake Kilrain, Portrait, Pugilist	275.00
Bowl, Haitian Coin, Small Silver Spoon, 1887	40.00
Button, Confederate Veteran's Convention, Dallas, 1902	20.00
Comb, Sterling Silver, San Francisco Bay Expo, Metal Case	25.00
Creamer, Blue, Tell City, Ind.	50.00
Cup, Red, Mary, 1897	55.00
Dish, 1st Lunar Landing, 6 Panels, Black, Gold, House of Art, Penn.	75.00
Figurine, Mouse, Topo Gigio, Bisque, Pink, Ed Sullivan Show, 4 In.	10.00
Handkerchief, Linen, Map of Minnesota, Towns & Building Pictures	15.00
Mirror, Pine, Four State Seal Corners, 1860s, 19 X 14 In.	280.00
Mug, Pottery, Remember The Maine, Battleship Scene	40.00
Pencil, Golden Gate Exposition, Figural, 1939, Box	16.00
Pitcher, Norris Dam, Blue, 5 1/2 In.	10.00
Plate, Bulldog, I Bark For Mazepa, Minn.	16.00
Plate, Conneaut Lake Exposition, Lacy Edge, Clear, 1895	25.00
Plate, Harvard University, Maroon & White, 10 In., 12 Piece	235.00
Plate, Niagara Falls, American Falls, Cobalt Blue Border, 6 In.	7.00
Plate, Rose Parade, 1975	140.00
Ribbon, Red Silk, Utica Daily Press, Excursion, Beacon Beach, 1885	5.00
Salt & Pepper, Mormon Tabernacle & Temple, Metal	11.00
Shoe, Woman's Pump, Glass, Cleveland, Ohio	12.00
Shot Glass Set, Zeppelin Airship, Europe, Columbia & America, Box	100.00
Spoon, Silver Plate, Berry Lou	9.00
Spoon, Silver Plate, Colorado Springs	18.00
Spoon, Silver Plate, Dewey, Hero of Manilla	15.00
Spoon, Silver Plate, Golden Gate Exposition, 1939	10.00
Spoon, Silver Plate, Grant's Tomb, 1897	15.00
Spoon, Sterling Silver, Alamo, San Antonio, TX, Gold Wash Bowl	15.00
Spoon, Sterling Silver, Albuquerque, N.M., Alvarado Hotel	28.00
Spoon, Sterling Silver, Alexandria, Virginia, Cutout Handle	19.00
Spoon, Sterling Silver, Arizona, Indian Symbols	25.00
Spoon, Sterling Silver, Atlantic City, Indian Head	38.00
Spoon, Sterling Silver, Atlantic City, Seashell Bowl	28.00
Spoon, Sterling Silver, August, Birgo, Mermaid On Stem	35.00
Spoon, Sterling Silver, Baltimore	35.00
Spoon, Sterling Silver, Bear, California	25.00
Spoon, Sterling Silver, Belleville, Illinois, City Hall	30.00
Spoon, Sterling Silver, Bethesda Spring, Waukesha	25.00
Spoon, Sterling Silver, Black Boy, Sunny South, Fort Worth, Fla.	45.00
Spoon, Sterling Silver, Boston, Massachusetts, Trinity Church	22.00
Spoon, Sterling Silver, Brooklyn Bridge	37.50
Spoon, Sterling Silver, Buffalo, N.Y., Buffalo In Bowl	15.00
Spoon, Sterling Silver, Bullfighter Handle	52.00

Spoon, Sterling Silver, California	22.00
Spoon, Sterling Silver, Camel Handle, Coin, Bolivia, Set	90.00
Spoon, Sterling Silver, Carleton College	25.00
Spoon, Sterling Silver, Carnegie Library, Mt.Carmel, Ill.	25.00
Spoon, Sterling Silver, Catalina Island	15.00
Spoon, Sterling Silver, Chicago Children's Home, Fair, 1892	40.00
Spoon, Sterling Silver, Chicago, Grant's Monument In Bowl	20.00
Spoon, Sterling Silver, Chippewa Falls, Wisconsin, High School	32.00
Spoon, Sterling Silver, Colorado Springs	35.00
Spoon, Sterling Silver, Colorado, Capitol In Bowl	20.00
Spoon, Sterling Silver, Colorado, Deer Hunting	75.00
Spoon, Sterling Silver, Columbian Hotel, Picture In Bowl	25.00
Spoon, Sterling Silver, Cripple Creek, Colorado	45.00
Spoon, Sterling Silver, Dallas, Texas, Scottish Rite Cathedral	25.00
Spoon, Sterling Silver, Deadwood, South Dakota	25.00
Spoon, Sterling Silver, Decatur, Illinois	40.00
Spoon, Sterling Silver, Denver, Colorado	20.00
Spoon, Sterling Silver, Denver, Mule With Pack In Bowl	25.00
Spoon, Sterling Silver, Des Moines, Soldiers & Sailors Monument	22.50
Spoon, Sterling Silver, Garden of The Gods	25.00
Spoon, Sterling Silver, Halifax, Nova Scotia	35.00
Spoon, Sterling Silver, Harper, Kansas, Poppy Handle	17.50
Spoon, Sterling Silver, Harrah's	35.00
Spoon, Sterling Silver, Hiawatha, Minnehaha Falls	40.00
Spoon, Sterling Silver, Huron, So.Dakota, Ralph Voorhees Hall	35.00
Spoon, Sterling Silver, Indiana, Boshen In Bowl	18.00
Spoon, Sterling Silver, Indianapolis, State Capitol, 6 In.	65.00
Spoon, Sterling Silver, Iowa State College, Indian Chief Head	27.00
Spoon, Sterling Silver, Jamestown Exposition	35.00
Spoon, Sterling Silver, Kansas City, Convention Hall Bowl, 4 In.	35.00
Spoon, Sterling Silver, Kansas, Plow, Farmer, Oil Well In Bowl	38.00
Spoon, Sterling Silver, Kentucky, Daniel Boone On Handle	20.00
Spoon, Sterling Silver, Keokuk, Iowa	52.00
Spoon, Sterling Silver, Lake George, Sports & Pleasures	12.00
Spoon, Sterling Silver, Lake Louise	16.00
Spoon, Sterling Silver, Lake Okaboji, Iowa, Indian Head In Bowl	45.00
Spoon, Sterling Silver, Last Sacrifice, Embossed Bowl	75.00
Spoon, Sterling Silver, Los Angeles, Mission	25.00
Spoon, Sterling Silver, Manilla, Iowa, School	35.00
Spoon, Sterling Silver, Manitou, Colorado, Struck It At Last	50.00
Spoon, Sterling Silver, Manufacturing & Liberty Arts, 6 In.	65.00
Spoon, Sterling Silver, McKinley Top, Temple of Music, Buffalo	26.00
Spoon, Sterling Silver, Merry Christmas, Dated 1899	55.00
Spoon, Sterling Silver, Michigan	25.00
Spoon, Sterling Silver, Minnesota	25.00
Spoon, Sterling Silver, Mississippi	35.00
Spoon, Sterling Silver, Mt.Pleasant, Iowa, Court House	8.00
Spoon, Sterling Silver, Nebraska	22.00
Spoon, Sterling Silver, New Orleans	26.00 To 35.00
Spoon, Sterling Silver, New York, Flat Iron Building	22.50
Spoon, Sterling Silver, New York, Grant's Tomb, Picture In Bowl	25.00
Spoon, Sterling Silver, New York, Standing Buffalo In Bowl	20.00
Spoon, Sterling Silver, New York, Statue of Liberty	40.00
Spoon, Sterling Silver, Niagara Falls, Kneeling Indian Top	30.00
Spoon, Sterling Silver, Ohio State University, Cutout Handle	19.00
Spoon, Sterling Silver, Ohio, Paul Revere	15.00
Spoon, Sterling Silver, Oklahoma	45.00
Spoon, Sterling Silver, Olin, Iowa, School	35.00
Spoon, Sterling Silver, Ottawa, Demitasse	16.00
Spoon, Sterling Silver, Paris, Enameled	25.00
Spoon, Sterling Silver, Parkersburg, Iowa, Word Iowa In Bowl	15.00
Spoon, Sterling Silver, Pasadena, California	35.00
Spoon, Sterling Silver, Philadelphia, Pennsylvania	35.00
Spoon, Sterling Silver, Portland, Oregon, Mt.Hood In Bowl	35.00

Spoon, Sterling Silver, Prentice High School, 1910	25.00
Spoon, Sterling Silver, Prentice, Wisc.High School In Bowl	24.00
Spoon, Sterling Silver, Providence, R.I., State Capitol	35.00
Spoon, Sterling Silver, Providence, Rhode Island	45.00
Spoon, Sterling Silver, Rolex Watch	25.00
Spoon, Sterling Silver, Rushville, Illinois	32.00
Spoon, Sterling Silver, Salt Lake City	35.00
Spoon, Sterling Silver, San Antonio, Texas	35.00
Spoon, Sterling Silver, San Diego	25.00
Spoon, Sterling Silver, San Francisco, Mission Dolores, 1776	38.00
Spoon, Sterling Silver, Saratoga Indian, Kneeling, Turtle Handle	30.00
Spoon, Sterling Silver, Saugatuck, Michigan	15.00
Spoon, Sterling Silver, Seattle, King Country Court House	25.00
Spoon, Sterling Silver, Sioux City	35.00
Spoon, Sterling Silver, Skagway Bay, Totem Pole, Engraved Bowl	50.00
Spoon, Sterling Silver, Skyline, Detroit Harbor	60.00
Spoon, Sterling Silver, Springfield, Ohio	38.00
Spoon, Sterling Silver, St.Augustine, Totem Pole Handle	20.00
Spoon, Sterling Silver, St.Louis, Design Front & Back	25.00
Spoon, Sterling Silver, St.Louis, Mo., Union Station	22.50
Spoon, Sterling Silver, Teddy Roosevelt, Riding Horse, Front, Back	85.00
Spoon, Sterling Silver, Temple of Music, McKinley Handle	50.00
Spoon, Sterling Silver, Toronto, Canada	20.00
Spoon, Sterling Silver, U.S.Battleship, Maine	15.00
Spoon, Sterling Silver, Utah, Temple In Bowl	22.00
Spoon, Sterling Silver, Virginia	20.00
Spoon, Sterling Silver, Washington, D.C., Buildings	37.00
Spoon, Sterling Silver, Washington, D.C., McKinley Handle	26.00
Spoon, Sterling Silver, Winona Hotel, Indiana	35.00
Spoon, Sterling Silver, Wyoming	25.00
Spoon, Sterling Silver, Yellowstone, Bear On Handle	24.00
Toothpick, Watkins Glen, N.Y., Urn Shape, Green, Gold Handles	12.00
Toy, Girl On Potty, Mouse, Mechanical, Tin, Yellowstone, Pre–1918	125.00
Tray, Desk, Pony Express, 80th Anniversary, F.D.Roosevelt, 14 In.	90.00
Tumbler, Kentucky Derby Engraved, Sterling Silver, 1983	115.00
Tumbler, Lacy Medallion, Atlantic City, Father, 1901, 3 1/2 In.	45.00
Tumbler, Rangeley Lakes, Maine, Heisey, Custard Glass	42.00
Tumbler, San Francisco, 1894	28.00

Spangle glass is multicolored glass made from odds and ends of colored glass rods. It includes metallic flakes of mica covered with gold, silver, nickel, or copper. Spangle glass is usually cased with a thin layer of clear glass over the multicolored layer.

SPANGLE GLASS, see also Vasa Murrhina

SPANGLE GLASS, Basket, Applied Handle, Multicolored, 11 X 7 In.	125.00
Basket, White Case, Swirl Rib Body, Silver Flecking, 7 In.	110.00
Cruet, Crystal, Blue Base, Silver Mica Flakes	435.00
Pitcher, Cranberry	175.00

If you have old laces and ribbons, press them by pulling them over a warm electric light bulb. Limp lace can be washed, then sprayed with starch or sizing. Lace can be colored by a quick dip in tea.

Spanish lace is a type of Victorian glass that has a white lace design. Blue, yellow, cranberry, or clear glass was made with this distinctive white pattern. It was made in England and the United States after 1885. Copies are being made.

SPANISH LACE, Biscuit Jar, Vaseline	65.00
Bowl, 8 1/2 In.	25.00
Cake Stand, Silver Crest, 11 In.	25.00
Cruet, Vaseline	160.00
Pitcher, Opalescent	90.00
Pitcher, White	125.00
Rose Bowl, Aqua	30.00 To 40.00
Rose Bowl, Blue	50.00
Rose Bowl, Crystal	55.00
Saltshaker, Vaseline	85.00
Sugar Shaker, Wide Waist, Vaseline	135.00
Vase, Blue, 6 In.	95.00
Water Set, Green, 7 Piece	525.00
Water Set, Northwood, Green, 7 Piece	490.00

Spatter glass is a multicolored glass made from many small pieces of different colored glass. It is sometimes called "End–Of–Day" glass. It is still being made.

SPATTER GLASS, Basket, Clear Ruffled Edge, Thorn Handle, 7 1/2 In.	158.00
Basket, Clear Ruffled Edge, Thorn Handle, 8 1/2 In.	175.00
Basket, Ruffled, Thorn Handle, Pink, White & Tan, 5 In.	175.00
Bowl, 5 1/2 In.	12.00
Bowl, Red, 5 In.	125.00
Dove On Nest, Double	30.00
Figurine, Rabbit, 5 In.	82.50
Salt & Pepper, Leaf Mold, Vaseline	225.00
Salt, Crystal Shell Trim At Top, 1 1/2 In.	50.00
Sugar Shaker, Cranberry	95.00
Tumbler, Cranberry, White Spatter	60.00
Vase, Jack–In–The–Pulpit, Quilted, Sapphire Blue, 7 In.	110.00
Water Set, Embossed Swirl, Overlay, 7 7/8 In.Pitcher, 5 Piece	325.00

The creamware or soft-paste dinnerware decorated with spatter designs in color is called, of course, spatterware. The earliest pieces were made in the late eighteenth century, but most of the spatterware found today was made from about 1800 to 1850 or is a late nineteenth– and twentieth–century form of kitchen crockery that has added spatter designs. The early spatterware was made in the Staffordshire district of England for sale in America. The kitchen type is an American product.

SPATTERWARE, Bowl, Plate, Rooster, Red Border, Blue Shield Mark, 8 1/2 In.	99.00
Bowl, Swirled Fluted Rim, Blue & White, 9 3/4 In.	135.00
Bowl, Vegetable, Blue & White, 7 3/8 X 9 3/4 In.	180.00
Chop Plate, Gaudy Floral, Stick, 16 1/2 In.	145.00
Coffeepot, Red & Blue Stripes, C.1840, 9 In.	886.00
Creamer, Peafowl	240.00
Creamer, Pineapple, Blue	1400.00
Creamer, Red & Green, Blue Border Stripe, Stick, 4 1/2 In.	85.00
Crock, Butter, Brown & White	85.00
Cup & Saucer, Handleless, Rainbow, Red, Green	70.00
Cup & Saucer, Rose, Blue, Adam	135.00
Cup, Handleless, Thistle, Black	120.00
Cup, Parrot	150.00
Dish, Dessert, Peafowl, Blue, Red & Yellow, 4 In.	145.00
Dish, Soup, Peafowl, Red, Adams, 9 1/2 In.	105.00
Funnel, Large	50.00
Pitcher, Blue & White, 12 In.	100.00
Pitcher, Hunt Scene, Cream With Cobalt, 12 In.	125.00
Pitcher, Milk, Green & Brown, 6 In.	60.00
Pitcher, Swirled Ribs, Pink, Yellow, 9 In.	125.00
Plate, Blue & White, 9 In.	85.00

Plate, Blue Transfer Eagle & Shield, Blue, 8 1/4 In.	100.00
Plate, Castle Design, Red, 8 3/8 In.	400.00
Plate, Gaudy Floral, Stick, 8 1/8 In.	75.00
Plate, Gaudy Floral, Stick, 10 In.	115.00
Plate, Peafowl, Heath, 9 1/2 In.	45.00
Plate, Peafowl, Red, 8 1/4 In.	50.00
Plate, Purple & Blue Edge, Tulip, Cotton & Barlow, 10 1/2 In.	325.00
Plate, Rose, Blue, 9 1/4 In.	175.00
Plate, Tulip, Blue, 9 3/8 In.	220.00
Platter, Stick, Red, Green, Blue, 11 5/8 In.	125.00
Saucer, Blue, Pomegranate	10.00
Saucer, Schoolhouse Pattern, 3 In.	55.00
Saucer, Star, Blue & White Border, English, C.1840, 6 In.	88.00
Soup, Dish, Gaudy Floral Design, Belgium, 10 3/4 In.	95.00
Soup, Dish, Tulip, Red & Blue Rim, Cotton & Barlow, 10 5/8 In.	125.00
Sugar, Drape Design, Red & Blue, 4 1/2 In.	80.00
Sugar, Red & Green, Oversize Cover, 5 1/4 In.	70.00
Tea Bowl, Saucer, Reindeer In Saucer	125.00
Tray, Blue & White, 13 3/4 In.	210.00
Tray, Scalloped Rim, Blue & White, 11 1/4 In.	175.00

Spelter is a synonym for a zinc alloy. Figurines, candlesticks, and other pieces were made of spelter and given a bronze or painted finish. The metal has been used since about the 1860s to make statues, tablewares, and lamps that resemble bronze. Spelter is soft and breaks easily. To test for spelter, scratch the base of the piece. Bronze is solid; spelter will show a silvery scratch.

SPELTER, Bookends, Bust of Lincoln, Parsons Casket Hdw. Co., 5 1/2 In.	58.00
Bookends, Thinker, Bronze Finish, 7 In.	55.00
Figurine, Angel Cherub, 14 In.	350.00
Figurine, Charlemagne, 5 1/2 In.	32.00
Figurine, Le Siffleur, C.1890, 17 /12 In.	250.00
Figurine, Man Leading Horse, Black Paint, Wooden Base, 16 1/2 In.	100.00
Figurine, Marley Horse, Signed Costeau, 14 In.	400.00
Figurine, Peasant Woman, Outstretched Arms, Basket On Back, 7 In.	135.00
Figurine, Woman, Art Deco, Arms Forward, Leg Raised, C.1922, 10 In.	60.00
Lamp, Oil, Peasant Girl, Flower Basket On Head, 13 In.	45.00
Lamp, Statue of Liberty, Light On Torch, Bronze Finish, 12 In.	55.00

The old spinning wheel in the corner has been the symbol of earlier times for the past 100 years. Although spinning wheels date back to medieval times, the ones found today are rarely more than 200 years old. Because the style of the spinning wheel changed very little, it is often impossible to place an exact date on a wheel.

SPINNING WHEEL, Flax Holder, Wooden, 11 In.	95.00
Green Paint, Baluster Spokes, Trestle Stretcher, 30 In.	192.00
Wooden Spokes, Trestle Stretcher, 19th Century, 28 In.	357.00
Wooden, Blue Paint, Turned Cylindrical Legs, C.1860, 35 In.	440.00
Wooden, Yellow Paint, 41 In.	60.00

Spode pottery, porcelain, and bone china were made by the Stoke-on-Trent factory of England founded by Josiah Spode about 1770. The firm became Copeland and Garrett from 1833 to 1847, then W.T. Copeland or W.T. Copeland and Sons until 1976. It then became Royal Worcester Spode Ltd. The word "Spode" appears on many pieces made by the factories. Most collectors include all the wares under the more familiar name of Spode. Porcelains are listed in this book by the name that appears on the piece.

SPODE, see also Copeland; Copeland Spode

SPODE, Berry Bowl, Cowslip	13.50
Bowl, Chestnut, Reticulated, Willow Pattern, C.1820, 10 In.	450.00
Butter Chip, Wickerdale	7.50
Casserole, Florence, Rectangular, 2 Piece	155.00
Casserole, Florence, Round, 2 Piece	155.00

Look for a sunken hole on the inside of a Sleepy Eye pitcher where the handle is attached. This indicates a reproduction. Old pitchers are smooth.

Spongeware, Casserole, Cover, 4 1/2 X 7 In.

Coffee Can & Saucer, Imari, 1804, 2 5/8 In.Can, 5 3/8 In.Saucer	230.00
Cup & Sacuer, Windsor	35.00
Cup & Saucer, Blue Tower	24.00
Cup & Saucer, Charlene	20.00
Cup & Saucer, Newburyport, Red	45.00
Eggcup, Buttercup	20.00
Jam Jar, Rosebuds, Green Leaves Form Band, Marked, 3 1/2 In.	48.00
Pitcher, Fortuna, 6 1/2 In.	85.00
Plate, Bird & Flowers, Polychrome, 8 In.	65.00
Plate, Charlene, 8 In.	10.00
Plate, Dessert, Arcadia, Set of 8	80.00
Plate, Dessert, Fruit Pattern, Signed J.Pierce, 9 In., Set of 12	60.00
Plate, Dinner, Cowslip	22.00
Plate, Luncheon, Cowslip	18.00
Plate, Luncheon, Fitzhugh	10.00
Plate, Newburyport, Red, 10 1/4 In.	45.00
Platter, Cut Corners, Stylized Floral Design, C.1815, 16 X 20 3/4 In.	300.00
Platter, Newburyport, Red, 14 In.	120.00
Sugar & Creamer, Fleur-De-Lis	17.00
Syrup, Tree, 6 Ladies, White Handle, Pewter Lid, 6 In.	87.00
Teapot, Blue Tower	95.00

Spongeware is very similar to spatterware in appearance. The designs were applied to the ceramics by daubing the color on with a sponge or cloth. Many collectors do not differentiate between spongeware and spatterware and use the names interchangeably. Modern pottery is being made to resemble the old spongeware, but careful examination will show it is new.

SPONGEWARE, Bean Pot, Light Rust, Green	85.00
Beater Jar, Brown, Green & Yellow	85.00
Bowl, Blue & White, 7 In.	65.00
Bowl, Blue & White, 8 X 12 1/4 In.	125.00
Bowl, Brown & Green On Yellow, 9 In.	78.00
Bowl, Brown & Yellow, 3 1/4 X 6 1/4 In.	30.00
Bowl, Green, Yellow Rim, 9 3/4 In.	25.00
Bowl, Light Green & Brown On Cream, 7 In.	65.00
Bowl, Marked Lincoln Malt Co., 7 In.	40.00
Bowl, Mixing, Blue & White, 11 In.	135.00
Bowl, Mixing, Wide Rim, Clear & Blue Bands	295.00
Bowl, Yellow & Rust, 9 1/2 In.	65.00
Cake Plate, Side Handles, Blue & White, 10 1/2 In.	75.00
Casserole, Cover, 4 1/2 X 7 In. ....*Illus*	50.00
Casserole, Green & Brown, Cover	85.00
Crock, Word Butter, Blue & White	155.00
Cup, Custard, Blue & White	60.00
Cuspidor, Blue & White	85.00
Custard, Original Metal Holder, 5 Piece	150.00
Pitcher & Bowl Set, Blue & White, Large	145.00

Pitcher, Blue On Blue, 10 In.	165.00
Pitcher, Blues & Browns, 9 In.	85.00
Pitcher, Blues, Early 19th Century, 9 X 7 In.	595.00
Pitcher, Bulbous, Blue On Blue, Small	190.00
Pitcher, Cherry Cluster & Basketweave	195.00
Pitcher, Cobalt Blue, Knowles, 4 1/2 In.	35.00
Pitcher, Green & Brown, 4 1/2 In.	45.00
Pitcher, Light Green & Brown On Cream, 7 1/2 In.	85.00
Pitcher, Milk, Kansas Dairy	25.00
Pitcher, Swastika, Blue & White, 8 In.	125.00
Pitcher, Tan, Green, Orange & Gold, 7 In.	75.00
Pitcher, Yellow & Rust, 6 1/2 In.	95.00
Platter, Blue & White, 10 X 13 In.	200.00
Platter, Foliate Chain, Elsmore & Foster, 13 1/4 X 10 1/4 In.	110.00
Platter, Scalloped Edge, Blue & White, 10 1/4 In.	125.00
Salt & Pepper, Green, Amber & White Design, Hand Thrown	95.00
Salt Box, C.1885	95.00
Spittoon, Blue & White	125.00
Teapot, Brown, Cream	68.00
Teapot, Elevator Advertising, Brown, Rust & Cream	67.50
Water Cooler, Blue, Woman At The Well, 5 Gal.	450.00

> Sporting goods, equipment, brochures, and related items are listed
> here. Other sections of interest are Bicycle, Fishing, Gun, Rifle,
> Sword, Toy, and Weapons.

SPORTS, Baseball Bat, Jim McNut, Campbell Pork & Beans	15.00
Baseball Bat, Jimmy Dykes, 1930s	20.00
Baseball Bat, Mountain Dew	35.00
Baseball Mitt, Nellie Fox, No.1759, J.C.Higgens	20.00
Baseball, Ty Cobb, Joe DiMaggio, 8 Other Signatures	185.00
Bat Rack, 19 Bats of National League Teams, Plastic, 1960s, Small	17.00
Figure, Atlanta Braves, Bobbing Head, 1967	29.00
Figure, White Sox, Bobbing Head, 1967	24.00
Figurine, Nellie Fox, Baseball, Hartland	90.00
Fishing Lure, Creek Chub Dingbat, Glass Eyes	25.00
Fishing Lure, Wood, South Bend	5.00
Fishing Reel, Bronson Meteor No.1500	30.00
Fishing Reel, Cascade, Jeweled	30.00
Fishing Reel, Casting, Fox, Gun Co.	35.00
Fishing Reel, Kalamazoo, Model B	15.00
Fishing Reel, Keen Kaster, Shapleigh DR4	85.00
Fishing Reel, Pennell Keystone, Jeweled	40.00
Fishing Reel, Pflueger Pakron No.3178	45.00
Fishing Reel, Saltwater, Fox	46.00
Fishing Reel, Shapleigh, SR10 Black Prince	50.00
Fishing Reel, South Bend, No.775	12.50
Fishing Reel, Sport King, No.22	10.00
Fishing Reel, Thos.Wilson Co., No.H646	40.00
Fishing Reel, Trolling, Pfleuger, Sal–Trout	30.00
Fishing Reel, Winchester, No.4161	75.00
Fishing Reel, Wm.Shakespeare Jr., No.2 Quad	95.00
Fishing Rod, Bamboo, 17 Ft.	90.00
Fishing Rod, Richardson, Wooden Handle, Case	40.00
Fishing Rod, Union Hardware, Iron	25.00
Fishing Rod, Winchester, Model 6055	185.00
Fly Rod, Weber	85.00
Fly Rod, Winchester, Model No. 6055	195.00
Football Helmet, Wilson Pro–College, Leather, 1942	85.00
Ice Skates, Black Painted Steel, Wood, Spade Shape, C.W.Wirt, 13 In.	192.00
Ice Skates, Forged Iron, Bird's Head, On Front Curl, 18th Century	260.00
Ice Skates, Leather Toe & Heel Straps, Wood Footrest, 11 In., Pair	88.00
Ice Skates, Pine, Carved, Painted, Steel Blades, Brass Designs, 12 In.	247.00
Ice Skates, Winchester, Shoe	30.00
Menu, Steamship Lines, Signed Babe Ruth	650.00

Mug, Milwaukee Braves, 1957 .... 20.00
Muscle Builder, For Progressive Chest Pulls, Whitely, Box, 1920s 20.00
Newspaper, Babe Ruth, Sultan of Swat, Yankees To Victory, 1932 .... 375.00
Oar, Pine, Green Paint, American, 20th Century, 5 Ft.6 In. 44.00
Paper, Game of Golf For Women, From Ladies Home Journal, 1894 .... 11.50
Pennant, Yankee, Team Picture Insert, Felt, Dated 1967 .... 35.00
Photograph, Babe Ruth, Signed, Suss, 9 1/2 X 7 1/2 In. 650.00
Program, Official, Indy 500, 1958 .... 6.00
Pump, For Inflating Footballs, Joe Palooka 45.00
Ring, Baseball, World's Champion, Gold & Silver, Zircon, 1948 .... 1000.00
Roller Skates, Globe Skate Corp., Steel Wheels 6.50
Roller Skates, Union Steel 12.50
Roller Skates, Winchester .... 15.00 To 60.00
Scorebook, Columbus, Ohio, Redbirds, Louisville, 15 Pgs., 1942 .... 9.00
Scorecard, Mystic B.B.C. & Torrnentor B.B.C., N.Y., Sept.10, 1868 .... 150.00
Ski Sled, Raised Seat, On Post, Red Paint, New England, 20 X 42 In. 357.00
Tray, Minnow, C.F.Orvis, Glass 50.00
Tray, Minnow, Checotah, Oklahoma, Glass 30.00
Yearbook, Chicago Cubs, 1985 .... 3.00
Yearbook, Philadelphia Athletics, 1953 .... 18.00
Yearbook, Washington Senators, 1952 .... 18.00

 Pottery and porcelain have been made in the Staffordshire district in England since the 1700s. Hundreds of kilns are still working in the area. Thousands of types of pottery and porcelain have been made in the many factories that worked and still work in the area. Some of the most famous factories have been listed separately, such as Adams, Davenport, Ridgway, Rowland & Marsellus, Royal Doulton, Royal Worcester, Spode, Wedgwood, and others. Some Staffordshire pieces are listed under sections like Fairing, Flow Blue, Shaving Mug, etc.

STAFFORDSHIRE, see also Flow Blue; Mulberry
STAFFORDSHIRE, Bowl, Lovejoy–Tyrant's Foe, Light To Medium Blue, 10 In. 150.00
Bowl, Vegetable, Columbia, Blue, Adams, 11 X 8 3/4 In. 85.00
Box, Port Scene, Florals On Sides & Base, 2 3/4 X 3 1/2 In. 400.00
Bust, John Wesley, Black Clothes, Marbelizbase, 11 1/2 In. 175.00
Chimney Piece, Scottish Couple, 7 1/5 In. 350.00
Creamer, Beehives & Garden, Mulberry, 3 In. 130.00
Creamer, Cow, Stopper, Pink Luster, Red Iron Paint, C.1830 .... 275.00
Creamer, Cow, Willow, Blue, Removable Back Cover, 5 1/4 In. 350.00
Creamer, Cumberland 25.00
Creamer, Medium Blue, Floral, Stone China, 5 In. 55.00
Crock, Butter, Lid, Bail, Handle, Blue & White 110.00
Cup & Saucer, Handleless, Dark Blue, Harbor Scene, Wood 125.00
Cup & Saucer, Handleless, Lafayette At Franklin Tomb 250.00
Cup & Saucer, Moral Maxims, Black Transfer, Handleless 60.00
Cup & Saucer, Pansies, Demitasse 9.00
Cup & Saucer, Pink, Franklin's Moral Pictures, C.1835 .... 85.00
Cup & Saucer, Stauton's Church & Octagon Church, Black 110.00
Cup Plate, Fairmount 65.00
Cup, Yellow Transfer, A Rabbit For William 325.00
Dish, Blue Willow, Blue & White, Cover, 8 X 9 In. 10.00
Dish, Cheese, Blue, Thatched House, Man On Horse, Trees, Church 80.00
Dish, Hen On Basket, White Bisque Top, Oval Base, 6 1/4 In. 175.00
Dish, Hen On Nest Cover, Yellow Bottom, Marked, 5 In. 175.00
Dish, Salt Glaze, Leaf Shape, Veined, 1755–60, 6 7/16 In. 1430.00
Dog, 3 3/4 In. 45.00
Dresser Set, With Candlesticks & Stickpin Holder, 7 Piece 550.00
Figurine, Boy On Elephant, 4 In. 65.00
Figurine, Boy, With Horse, 6 1/2 In. 220.00
Figurine, Cat, Glass Eyes, Charcoal Gray, 12 X 8 1/2 In. 200.00
Figurine, Cat, Seated, Black, White, Ochre Ribbon, 3 3/4 In. 195.00
Figurine, Cavaliers, On Horseback, 15 In., Pair 330.00
Figurine, Cows, 7 1/2 In., Pair 578.00

Figurine, Dog, Copper Luster Spots, Collar & Chain, 8 In., Pr. 250.00
Figurine, Dog, Dalmation, Seated, 4 In. 50.00
Figurine, Dog, Green Luster Spots, 12 In., Pair 265.00
Figurine, Dog, Polychrome Enameling, 8 3/4 In. 350.00
Figurine, Dog, White Body, Rust Trim, Miniature, Pair 250.00
Figurine, Dolly Petreath, Last One To Speak Cornish, 6 In. 110.00
Figurine, General Jackson, Hero of New Orleans, 8 In. 410.00
Figurine, Girl, Basket, Berries, Dog At Feet, 7 In. ....*Illus* 105.00
Figurine, Girl, On Rock, With Open Book, 5 1/2 In. 105.00
Figurine, Hereford Cow, 9 In. 95.00
Figurine, Hereford Cow, Full-Bodied, Rust & White, 7 1/2 In. 85.00
Figurine, Lamb, Lying Down, 3 1/4 X 2 1/4 In. 65.00
Figurine, Lion, Brown Glass Eyes, 10 1/2 X 9 1/2 In., Pair 350.00
Figurine, Lion, Brown, White, With Black, 3 1/4 In. 165.00
Figurine, Little Red Riding Hood, 4 1/2 In. 55.00
Figurine, Maiden On Tree Trunk, Dog, Bowl, 8 In. ....*Illus* 425.00
Figurine, Man Holding Dog, Woman, Lamb, 9 In., Pair ....*Illus* 105.00
Figurine, New Marriage Act, 10 In. 500.00
Figurine, Scotsmen, On Horseback, 15 In., Pair 330.00
Figurine, Scottish Girl, Holding Dog In Arms, 6 1/2 In. 75.00
Figurine, Spaniel, 11 In. 110.00
Figurine, Spaniel, Black & White, Yellow Eyes, 4 In., Pair 85.00
Figurine, Spaniel, Copper Over White, 9 In., Pair 180.00
Figurine, Spaniel, Gold, 7 In., Pair 150.00
Figurine, Spaniel, On Pillow, Gilt Bow, 13 In., Pair 375.00
Figurine, Victoria & Albert, 10 In., Pair 775.00
Flagon, Wine, Allegorical Figures, Pewter Mounts, Yellow 175.00
Gravy Tureen, Underplate, Blue Scenic Lid 68.00
Group, Burns & His Army, 11 3/4 In. 35.00
Group, Children, On Horseback, Coming Home, 8 In. 176.00
Group, Sailor Boy, With Girl, 8 In. 209.00
Group, Youth & Maiden, Polychrome Enameling, 8 1/4 In. 100.00
Hatpin & Ring Holder, Blue, Signed 50.00
Inkwell, Bird In Nest With Chicks & Worm 135.00
Inkwell, Man With Pipe 125.00
Jug, Jack Frost Attacking Boy In Russia, Pearl, 5 1/4 In. 995.00
Jug, Mr.Pickwick, A.S.Wilkinson, 7 In. 20.00
Jug, Robin, Floral Sprays, Silver Luster Ground, 4 3/8 In. 775.00
Mug, Black Train Transfer, Fury, Blue Band, 3 3/4 In. 140.00
Mug, Child's, Children Playing, Purple Transfer, 2 1/2 In. 75.00
Mug, Child's, Circus Scenes 20.00

Staffordshire, Figurine

Girl, Basket, Berries,   Maiden On Tree Trunk,   Man Holding Dog, Woman, Lamb, 9 In., Pair
Dog At Feet, 7 In.   Dog, Bowl, 8 In.

Mug, Child's, Cock Crowed 17.00
Mug, Child's, Franklin's Maxims, Black Transfer, 2 1/2 In. 85.00
Mug, Child's, Hop–Picker 20.00
Mug, Drinking Scenes, Interior Frog, 3 7/8 In. 100.00
Mug, Frog Bottom, Brown Transfer Country Scene, 9 1/4 In. 25.00
Pepper Pot, Allover Brown Transfer, Castle, Trees, 5 In. 130.00
Perfume Bottle, Floral, Fruit, Bird, Dotted Ground, 3 1/4 In. 225.00
Pitcher & Bowl, Basket & Vase Pattern, Medium Blue 550.00
Pitcher, Babes In The Woods, Periwinkle Blue, C.1850 .... 150.00
Pitcher, Floral Design, Gaudy, 9 3/4 In. 95.00
Pitcher, Lord Nelson, 11 1/2 In. 275.00
Pitcher, Pink Transfer, Albany, N.Y., 10 In. 225.00
Pitcher, Strawberry & Vine, Pink, Georgian Handle, 9 In. 325.00
Pitcher, Water, Nursery Rhyme, 4 1/4 In. 65.00
Plate, Alphabet, Independence Hall, 7 In. 225.00
Plate, American Villa, Fruit & Foliage Border, 7 1/2 In. 75.00
Plate, Andalusia, Pink Transfer, 10 1/2 In. 50.00
Plate, Boston Mails, Black, Edwards, 8 1/4 In. 55.00
Plate, Carmine, View Near Conway, N.H., Brown, White, Adams 95.00
Plate, Catskill Mountain House, Pink, 10 3/8 In. 75.00
Plate, Cave Castle, Yorkshire, Medium Blue, Stevenson, 8 In. 55.00
Plate, Center Rose, A.B.Smith, 8 In. 75.00
Plate, City of Albany, 10 In. 475.00
Plate, Columbia College, Stevenson, 6 1/4 In. 525.00
Plate, Columbus, Ohio, Scene, 10 In. 3800.00
Plate, Commodore MacDonnough's Victory, Deep Blue, 7 1/2 In. 110.00
Plate, Dark Blue Transfer, Couple, In Garden, 8 1/2 In. 75.00
Plate, Dark Blue Transfer, Hospital, Boston, 9 In. 250.00
Plate, Dark Blue, Baltimore & Ohio Railroad, 9 1/8 In. 550.00
Plate, Dark Blue, La Grange Residence of Marquis Lafayette 225.00
Plate, Downtown Scene, New Orleans, Dark Blue, C.1900, 10 In. 55.00
Plate, Embossed Border, Present For John Independence, 7 In. 125.00
Plate, Fairmount Near Philadelphia, Blue Transfer, 10 In. 185.00
Plate, Fishkill, Hudson River, Clews, 10 1/2 In. 95.00
Plate, Greek Statue, Medium Blue, Rogers, 9 3/4 In. 48.00
Plate, Indians Hunting, Purple, Adams, 9 1/2 In. 75.00
Plate, Ladies Cabin, Black, Edwards, 8 1/4 In. 55.00
Plate, Lewis & Clark Centennial, 1905, 10 In. 50.00
Plate, Library, Philadelphia, Medium Blue, Ridgway, 8 1/8 In. 110.00
Plate, Millenium, Black, Stevenson, 10 1/4 In. 75.00
Plate, Nahant Hotel, Boston, Dark Blue, Stevenson, 8 1/2 In. 385.00
Plate, Peace & Plenty Pattern, Clews, 10 1/4 In. 260.00
Plate, Penn's Treaty, Black, Green, 8 1/4 In. 55.00
Plate, Sancho & Priest & Barber, Dark Blue, 7 1/2 In. 80.00
Plate, Seasons, February, Pink, Adams, 8 1/2 In. 55.00
Plate, Swiss Scenery, Blue, 10 1/2 In. 50.00
Plate, Toddy, Embossed Floral Border, Green & Yellow, 5 In. 115.00
Plate, Transylvania University, Lexington, Blue, 1830, 9 In. 225.00
Plate, View Near Conway, N.H., Red Transfer, 9 In. 575.00
Plate, West Point, Hudson River, Purple, Clews, 8 In. 120.00
Plate, Winter View, Pittsfield, Conn., Blue, Clews, 7 In. 240.00
Plate, Wm.Penn's Treaty, Brown Transfer, 7 1/2 In. 55.00
Platter, American Cities & Scenery, Boston, Blue, 14 X 18 In. 90.00
Platter, Caledonia, Red & Green Transfer, Adams 55.00
Platter, Christianburg, Africa, Shell Rim, E.Wood, 14 X 18 In. 700.00
Platter, Dark Blue, Landing of Lafayette, Clews, 15 1/4 In. 850.00
Platter, Dark Blue, Niagara From American Side, 38 1/2 In. 1000.00
Platter, Dr.Syntax, Harvest Home, 16 In. 2250.00
Platter, Town, River, Floral Rim, Marked, C.1825, 12 X 15 In. 225.00
Platter, Tree & Well, Bridge Over River Schuylkill, 18 In. 950.00
Punch Set, Nursery Rhyme, 5 Cups 135.00
Snuffbox, Blue Dotted Ground, Landscape, 19th Century, 2 In. 175.00
Soup, Dish, Dark Blue Transfer, Seashell, Stubbs, 9 3/4 In. 110.00
Soup, Dish, Dark Blue, La Grange, Marquis Lafayette, 10 In. 250.00

Soup, Dish, Headwaters of Juniata, Adams, 10 1/2 In. 100.00
Soup, Dish, Sancho Meets Dapple, Clews, 8 3/4 In. 165.00
Soup, Dish, Sepia, Spanish Convent, Adams, 10 3/4 In. 35.00
Tea Set, Child's, Boy & Dog Brown Stenciled, C.1875, 24 Piece 225.00
Tea Set, Child's, Pearlware, Peafowl, 11 Piece 750.00
Tea Set, Child's, Punch & Judy Stenciled, 1875, 18 Piece 400.00
Tea Set, Girl, Dog & Cat Scene, Burgundy, White, 12 Piece 135.00
Tea Set, Little May, Child's, 11 Piece 135.00
Teapot, Blue Transfer, English Country House, 10 In. 100.00
Teapot, Dark Blue Transfer, Lafayette At Franklin Tomb 250.00
Teapot, Dark Blue, Valentine, Wilkie Series, 7 3/4 In. 275.00
Teapot, Pink Transfer, The Servers 225.00
Teapot, Rose Transfer Design, Cream Ground 250.00
    STAFFORDSHIRE, TOBY JUG, see Toby Jug
Tray, Dog, 7 In. 20.00
Tureen, Pagoda, Cover, Blue & White, Octagon, 4 1/2 X 5 In. 29.00
Tureen, Sauce, Underplate, Dog Head Design, 1825, 5 X 8 In. 150.00
Tureen, Soup, India Temple, Light Blue, Rose Handles, 1814-30 .... 995.00
Tureen, Soup, Lion Finial, Lion Head Handles, 13 1/2 In. 550.00
Vase, Black, Leaf, Berry, Twisted Vines, 9 In. 100.00
Vase, Spill, Daisy Bell Bicycle Built For 2 .... 55.00
Whippet, 7 1/2 In., Pair 264.00

The Fulper Pottery had a long history that entwined with the Stangl Pottery in 1910 when Johann Martin Stangl started work. He bought into the firm in 1913, became president in 1926, and in 1929 changed the company name to Stangl Pottery. The pottery made dinnerwares and a line of limited-edition bird figurines. The company went out of business in 1972.

STANGL, Ashtray, Canvasback Duck, No.3915G 35.00
Ashtray, Duck 22.00
Ashtray, Pheasant 22.00
Bird, Bird of Paradise, No.3408 .... 60.00 To 65.00
Bird, Bluebird, No.3453, 6 1/2 In. 70.00
Bird, Bluebirds, No.3276D 145.00
Bird, Bluejay & Leaf, No.3716 .... 300.00
Bird, Bluejay & Peanut, No.3715 .... 300.00
Bird, Broadbill Hummingbird, No.3629 .... 85.00
Bird, Broadtail Hummingbird, No.3626 .... 115.00
Bird, Cardinal, No.3444 .... 45.00 To 80.00
Bird, Cardinal, No.3596 .... 77.00
Bird, Cerulean Warbler, No.3456 .... 50.00
Bird, Chickadee, No.3581 .... 145.00
Bird, Cock Pheasant, No.3492 .... 135.00 To 160.00
Bird, Cockatoo, No.3405D, Pair 85.00
Bird, Cockatoo, No.3405 .... 32.00 To 42.00
Bird, Cockatoo, No.3584, Label, 12 In. .... 225.00 To 250.00
Bird, Cockatoos, No.3405D .... 75.00 To 125.00
Bird, Duck, No.3443 .... 235.00
Bird, Evening Grosbeak, No.3813 .... 100.00
Bird, Flying Duck, No.3443 .... 185.00 To 235.00
Bird, Goldfinch, No.3635 .... 185.00
Bird, Hen Pheasant, No.3491 .... 75.00 To 175.00
Bird, Hen, No.3446 .... 150.00 To 175.00
Bird, Hummingbirds, No.3599D .... 235.00 To 250.00
Bird, Indigo Bunting, No.3589 .... 37.00 To 72.00
Bird, Kentucky Warbler, No.3598 .... 70.00
Bird, Key West Quail Dove, No.3454 .... 275.00
Bird, Kingfisher, No.3406 .... 45.00 To 65.00
Bird, Lovebirds, No.3404D 80.00
Bird, Magpie Jay, No.3578 .... 650.00
Bird, Orioles, No.3402D 100.00
Bird, Owl, No.3407 .... 300.00
Bird, Painted Bunting, No.3452 .... 85.00 To 125.00

Bird, Parakeet, No.3582 ....95.00 To 125.00
Bird, Parakeets, No.3582D 95.00
Bird, Parrot, No.3400 .... 23.00
Bird, Parula Warbler, No.3583 .... 35.00 To 40.00
Bird, Penguin, No.3274 .... 295.00 To 325.00
Bird, Pheasant, Male, Brown, No.3492 .... 90.00
Bird, Red-Headed Woodpecker, Double, No.3752 .... 325.00
Bird, Rooster, No.3445 ....80.00 To 150.00
Bird, Rufous Hummingbird, No.3585 .... 25.00 To 55.00
Bird, Scissortail Flycatcher, No.3757 .... 350.00
Bird, Wilson Warbler, No.3597 .... 72.00
Bird, Wrens, No.3401D ....65.00 To 95.00
Bowl, Holly, 9 3/4 In. 15.00
Bowl, Salad, Golden Harvest, 8 In. 2.50
Box, Apple Tree On Lid, Green Bottom, White & Gold Trim, 5 1/4 In. 20.00
Box, Cigarette, Ivy 15.00
Box, Magnolia, Cover, 1/2 X 4 In. 10.00
Bread Tray, Golden Harvest 10.00
Candy Dish, Caribbean, Cover 10.00
Charger, Magnolia, 14 In. 20.00
Clock, Golfer, Daddy, Clubhouse Lights 45.00
Coffeepot, Fruit Pattern, 8 Cup 20.00
Creamer, Magnolia 5.00
Creamer, Prelude 4.00
Cup & Saucer, Blueberry 8.00
Cup & Saucer, Prelude 5.00
Cup, Amber Glo 3.00
Flowerpot, 6 3/4 In. 25.00
Flowerpot, Rose 18.00
Gravy Boat, Magnolia 12.00
Gravy Boat, Orchard Song 5.00
Jug, Turquoise, Brushed Gold, 6 In. 35.00
Mold, Dessert, Fluted, 6 In. 20.00
Mug, Henpecked 60.00
Pitcher, Black Gold, 12 In. 12.00
Pitcher, Red, 10 In. 35.00
Pitcher, Thistle, 3 Cup 12.00
Planter, Swan, Blue & Gold 17.00
Plate, Engraved Design, Gold, Green & Tan, 14 1/4 In. 25.00
Plate, Fruit, 8 In. 5.00
Plate, Orchard Song, Metal Base, 10 In. ....3.00 To 3.75
Plate, Prelude, 8 In. 4.00
Plate, Prelude, 10 In. 5.00
Plate, Terra Rose, Yellow Tulip, 10 In. 5.00
Plate, Tidbit, Dogwood, White 6.50
Plate, Windfall, 3 7/8 In. 8.00
Plate, Windfall, 4 3/4 In. 65.00
Reamer, With Pitcher, Town & Country, Spatterware 1.00
Saucer, Amber Glo 5.00
Soup, Dish, Lug, Magnolia 25.00
Teapot, Fruit 15.00
Teapot, Thistle 20.00
Vase, Cornucopia, Terra Rose, Dark Blue, 6 1/2 In. 40.00
Vase, Granada, Hand Painted, 22K Gold Trim, 20 In. 200.00
Vase, Horsehead, Terra Rose, 12 1/4 In. 110.00
Vase, Silver Overlay, Trumpet Shape, 6 Panels, Yellow, 11 In. 5.00
Vase, Terra Rose, Paper Label, Yellow, 3 In. 30.00
Vase, Willow, Sunflower, Blue, Terra Rose, 12 In. 15.00
Warmer, Coffee 150.00
Wig Stand, Red Hair ....

We named Star Holly in an article in the 1950s. It was thought to
be an early nineteenth-century art glass, but it is really a type of
milk glass made by the Imperial Glass Company of Bellaire, Ohio,

in 1957. The pieces were made to look like Wedgwood jasperware. White holly leaves appear against colored borders of blue, green, or rust. It is marked on the bottom of every piece. Some identical molded glass was made without the added color. Unfortunately, misinformation is difficult to correct, and even some museums have mislabeled the Star Holly as earlier than 1957.

STAR HOLLY, Plate, Green, White	85.00
Sherbet, Footed, Blue	75.00

Steins have been used by beer and ale drinkers for over 500 years. They have been made of ivory, porcelain, stoneware, faience, silver, pewter, wood, or glass in sizes up to nine gallons. Although some were made by Meissen, Capo-di-Monte, and other famous factories, most were made in Germany. The words "Geschutz" or "Musterschutz" on a stein are the German words for patented or registered design, not company names. Steins are still being made in the old styles.

STEIN, Air Corps, Nazi Emblems, No.2962, Stoneware, 1/2 Liter	468.00
Albert Jacob Thewalt, 1/8 Liter, Pre-1950	15.00
Artillery Regiment, Maneuver Scenes, Pottery, 1/2 Liter	160.00
Artillery Shell, 75mm., Handmade, 1/2 Liter	61.00
Ball Pattern, Pressed Glass, 4/10 Liter	17.00
Barroom Scene, Eva Vom Lande, Pewter, 1/5 Liter	110.00
Black Fraternity Student, Earthenware, 1/2 Liter	176.00
Blown Glass, Blown, Enameled Floral, Biedermeier, 1/2 Liter	248.00
Blown Glass, Cut Oval Designs, Prism Lid, 1/2 Liter	138.00
Bowling Scene, Stoneware, 1/2 Liter	77.00
Brunhilde & Siegfried, Pottery, Signed KB, 1/2 Liter	44.00
Budweiser, Chicago, Skyline & Clydesdales, 1980, 7 1/4 In.	75.00
Budweiser, Holiday, Champion Clydesdales, 1980, 5 In.	20.00
Budweiser, Holiday, Clydesdales, Winter, 50th Anniversary, 1933-83	75.00
Card Playing, Merkelbach & Wick, 3/10 Liter	61.00
Carved Ivory Neptune & Woman, Putti, Silver, C-Scroll Handle, 14 In.	5225.00
Cavalier & Maiden, Merkelbach & Wick, 1 Liter	160.00
Cavaliers, Shooting Dice, J.W.Remy, No.1360, Etched, 2 Liter	358.00
Celebrating Olympics, No.3188, Marzi & Remy, 3/4 Liter	40.00
Christmas, Nazi Emblems, Stoneware, 1/2 Liter, 1939	292.00
City of Altdorf, Pottery, 1/4 Liter	50.00
Cobalt & Violet Glaze Design, Stoneware, Westerwald, 1 Liter	248.00
Columbus, Egg Shape, Pottery, Reinhold Hanke, 1/2 Liter	550.00
Drunken Knights, Girmscheid No.926, 3/10 Liter	99.00
Drunken Monkey, Holding Bottle, No.833, 1/2 Liter, 8 3/4 In.	195.00
Drunken Monkey, R.P.M., 1/2 Liter	115.00
Egyptian Scenes, Pottery, Relief, 1/2 Liter	77.00
Faience, Floral Design, Hungarian, 1/2 Liter	275.00
Faience, Man With Basket, 1 Liter	105.00
Field Artillary, Maneuver Scenes, Porcelain, 1/2 Liter	358.00
Fireman, Character, Stoneware, 1/2 Liter	275.00
Gambrinus Parade, Pewter Lid, Marzi & Remy, 1/2 Liter	77.00
Glass, Enameled Floral, Lustered, 1/2 Liter	105.00
Glass, Enameled Moose, 1/2 Liter	105.00
Glass, Enameled Munich Child, Amber, 4 3/4 In.	138.00

Do not have old monograms removed from silver. It lowers the value. If it bothers you to have an old initial, don't buy the piece. We like to tell people it belonged to a great-aunt with that initial.

Glass, Occupational, Wagon Builder, Enameled, 1/2 Liter	385.00
Glass, Relief Metal Handle, Neck & Lid, Amber, 12 In.	286.00
Glass, Relief Pewter Handle, Neck & Lid, Green, 11 1/2 In.	275.00
Happy Radish, Musterschutz	375.00
Heidelberg Student, Porcelain, 1/2 Liter	154.00
Hooded Monk, Gray, Purple Robe, Pottery, German, 1/2 Liter	175.00
Hunter, Eckhardt & Engler, Pottery, 1/2 Liter	127.00
Infantry Regimental, Darmstadt, Porcelain, 1/2 Liter, 1895	275.00
Initials HB, Brown & Blue, Stoneware, 1/2 Liter	35.00
King, Engraved Lid, Pottery, 1/2 Liter	50.00
Log Cabin Gun Club, 1918, Reed & Barton, Pewter, 1/2 Liter	44.00
Lowenbrau Muenchen, Matching Lid, Pottery, 1/2 Liter	105.00
Lowenbrau Muenchen, Merkelbach & Wick, Stoneware, 1/2 Liter	143.00
Ludwig & Bavarian Shields, Regensburg, Stoneware, 1/2 Liter	88.00
Machine Gun Company, O.2871, Marzi & Remy, Stoneware, 1/2 Liter	275.00
Malling, Willow Encircling, C.1949, 4 1/2 In.	55.00
Man Drinking, Hand Painted, Pottery, 1 Liter	175.00
Man, Top Hat, Lady, Curtains Around Body, Risque, Al.Thewalt, 1/2 Liter	145.00
Mandolin Player & Maidens, Etched, Signed Brandl, 1/2 Liter	275.00
Maneuver Scenes, Karlsruhe, Porcelain, 1900–03, 1/2 Liter	468.00
Men At Table, Hand Painted, Pottery, Gerz, 1/2 Liter	72.00
STEIN, METTLACH, see Mettlach, Stein	
Military Head, Porcelain, Schierholz, ECS 322, 1/2 Liter	688.00
Miller, Holiday, Holly Leaf Border, 1984, 6 1/2 In.	13.00
Monkey & Missing Link, Pottery, 1/2 Liter	237.00
Monkey, Black Top Hat, German Inscription, Pewter Thumb Lift, 9 In.	255.00
Muchener Burger Brau, Matching Lid, Pottery, 1/2 Liter	105.00
Munchener Kindl & L.L., Pewter, Nouveau Design, C.1900, 10 3/4 In.	300.00
Munich Child With Lithophane, Porcelain, 1/2 Liter	303.00
Munich Child, Eckhardt & Engler, Pottery, 1/2 Liter	143.00
Munich Child, Pottery, 1/2 Liter .... 50.00 To 66.00	
Munich Child, Schierholz, 1/2 Liter	215.00
Munich Maid, Enameled, Pewter Lid & Thumbpiece, 14 1/2 In.	495.00
Munich Tower, Stoneware, 1 Liter	275.00
Musical, Nobody Knows How Dry I Am	95.00
Nun, No.67, Imperial, Germany	188.00
Nun, Pottery, 1/2 Liter	187.00
Picture of Hotel Grunewald, New Orleans, Pewter Lid, Germany, 7 In.	195.00
Pig With Pipe, Porcelain, Schierholz, ECS 54, 1/2 Liter	495.00
Pottery, Bicycling, All Heil, Pewter Lid, Germany, 1/2 Liter	195.00
Pottery, Story of Tower Sentry's Daughter, Signed KB, 2 Liter	275.00
Pressed Glass, Pewter Lid, C.1860, 1/4 Liter	55.00
Pschorr–Brau, Munche With Matching Lid, Pottery, 1/2 Liter	171.00
Regimental, 1 Pioneer, Ingolstadt, Porcelain, 1910, 1/2 Liter	160.00
Regimental, 13 Field Art.Reg.Tannstatt, 1911–13, 1/2 Liter	209.00
Regimental, German Reservist, Bottom Lithophane, 1907–10	450.00
Regimental, Hand Painted, German, 1906–08, 12 1/2 In.	375.00
Regimental, Porcelain, Lithophane, Rider & Horse Finial, 10 3/4 In.	475.00
Regimental, Telegraph Line Scenes, Pottery, 1896–98, 1/2 Liter	374.00
Sad Radish, Beige, Musterschutz, 1/2 Liter, 7 In.	325.00
Sad Radish, Leaves Finial, Musterschutz, 7 In.	300.00
Scenes, Gymnastics, Pottery, 1/2 Liter	77.00
Scratch Work, Cobalt Design, Stoneware, Westerwald, 3/4 Liter	275.00
Scratch Work, Cobalt Design, Stoneware, Westerwald, C.1860, 1/2 Liter	175.00
Singing Pig, Musterschutz	400.00
Skull, Bisque, 1/2 Liter, 5 1/4 In.	298.00
Skull, Musterschutz	325.00
Stoneware, Munich Tower, 1/2 Liter	99.00
Stroh's Holiday, Heritage Series I, Horse & Wagon, 1984, 7 1/2 In.	12.00
Stroh's Statue of Liberty, Ellis Island, Limited Edition	50.00
Tavern Scene, Pewter Lid & Finger Grip, German, 7 In.	50.00
Tigerbaus, Matching Lid, Merkelbach & Wick, Pottery, 1/2 Liter	330.00
Trumpeter, Reinhold Merkelbach No.960, 4/10 Liter	66.00
University of Budweiser, Concepts, Red Lettering On Handle, 6 In.	12.50

Viking & Maiden Scenes, Pottery, 1/2 Liter	72.00
Wayne Brewing Co., Maddock's Son's, 1/2 Liter	66.00
Werner Corzellus of Hohr, Castle Shape, Pre–1950, 7 Liter, 26 In.	375.00
Woman Character, Flower In Mouth, Pottery, 1/2 Liter	132.00
Woman Character, No.488, Thewalt, 1 Liter	385.00
Woman, No.429, Musterschutz	325.00

Stereo cards that were made for stereopticon viewers became popular after 1840. Two almost identical pictures were mounted on a stiff cardboard backing so that, when viewed through a stereoscope, a three–dimensional picture could be seen. Value is determined by maker and by the subject. These cards were made in quantity through the 1930s.

STEREO CARD, 4th of July, Young Man, Lighting Large Firecracker, Tinted	10.00
Charleston Navy Yard	5.00
Dead Rebel Soldier In Trenches, 1865	27.50
Deer Hunters, Photos By Kilburn, Dated 1876 & 1890, Pair	8.00
Gettysburg, Table Rock At Devil's Den	12.00
Hunting Scenes, Color, C.1895, 36 Piece	120.00
Kickapoo Indian Camp, 1877	21.00
Miners, To Climb Golden Stairway, Chilkoot Pass, Alaska, 1898	9.00
New Orleans, Steamboat, 1885	10.00
Northern Pacific R.R., Marked Dakota Territory, 6 Piece	75.00
Old Israel, 1897	25.00
President McKinley & His Cabinet, 1900	10.00
Rochester, Minn., Cyclone, Houses In Ruins, J.C.Cook, 1883, Pair	16.00
San Francisco Earthquake, Color, Set of 60	175.00
Sears, Roebuck, Chicago, 48 Piece	50.00
Steam Train Through Royal Gorge, Copy, 1897	3.00 To 4.00
View of Ferris Wheel, Chicago World's Fair, 1893	10.00
Vigilante Hanging, 1898	35.00
White House, '04	10.00

The stereoscope, or stereopticon, was used for viewing stereo cards. The hand viewer was invented by Oliver Wendell Holmes, although more complicated table models were used before his was produced in 1859.

STEREOSCOPE, Abby Becarers, Patent 1857	400.00
Viewer, Keystone 235, Tour of World Cards, 47 Assorted Cards	130.00

STERLING SILVER, see Silver–Sterling

Steuben glass was made at the Steuben Glass Works of Corning, New York. The factory, founded by Frederick Carder and T. C. Hawkes, Sr., was purchased by the Corning Glass Company. They continued to make glass called "Steuben." Many types of art glass were made at Steuben. The firm is still making exceptional quality glass but it is clear, modern–style glass.

STEUBEN, see also Aurene

STEUBEN, Ashtray, Amber, Applied Green Leaf, Stamped, 4 In.	160.00
Ashtray, Crystal, Signed, 3 1/2 In.	25.00
Ashtray, Diamond–Quilted, Topaz, Leaf Shape, Leaf Handles, Signed	125.00
Basket, Gold Aurene, Signed, 6 In.	825.00
Bowl, Alabaster, Rosaline On Ruffled Rim, 7 In.	75.00
Bowl, Applied Swirled Base, Crystal, 6 X 9 1/2 In.	85.00
Bowl, Aurene, Gold Iridescent, Signed, 10 In.	335.00
Bowl, Aurene, Gold Top, Footed, Signed, 8 In.	395.00
Bowl, Blue Threaded, Signed, 12 In.	265.00
Bowl, Burgundy Swirl, 12 1/2 In.	290.00
Bowl, Centerpiece, Gold Aurene & Calcite Deco	250.00
Bowl, Grotesque, Cobalt Blue Shading To Clear, Signed, 6 X 8 In.	160.00
Bowl, Jade, Italian Blue, 10 3/4 In.	495.00
Bowl, Plum Jade Acid Cut Back, 5 3/4 In.	1850.00
Bowl, Ribbed, Turned–Out Collar, Amber, Signed, 14 In.	175.00
Bowl, Swirled Base, Crystal, 4 X 7 In.	80.00

Bowl, Underplate, Rosaline, Alabaster Foot, Signed 125.00
Box, Black Threading, Faceted Handle, Marked, Cover, 6 In. 245.00
Box, Faceted Crystal Knob On Cover, Threaded Bottom, 4 1/2 In. 125.00
Candleholder, Gold Aurene, Signed, 10 In., Pair 950.00
Candleholder, Mushroom, Green, Signed, 4 1/2 In., Pair 135.00
Candlestick, Blue Aurene, Twisted Stem, Signed & Numbered 725.00
Candlestick, Flying Saucer Shape, Aurene & Calcite, 5 In., Pair 750.00
Candlestick, Gold Aurene, Calcite, Mushroom Shape 425.00
Candlestick, Gold Aurene, Iridescent, Twisted Stem, Signed, 8 In. 950.00
Candlestick, Marina Blue, Crystal Inset, Signed, 12 In., Pair 850.00
Candlestick, Purple, Signed, 6 In., Pair 270.00
Candlestick, Rosaline & Alabaster, Twisted, 10 In. 1200.00
Candlestick, Topaz, Double Domed Foot, Twisted Stem, Signed, 12 In. 95.00
Candy Dish, Clear, Blue Stripes, Signed Carter, 5 1/4 X 7 In. 225.00
Candy Dish, Ribbed Amethyst, Clear Stem, Turned Over Rim, 7 In. 95.00
Champagne, Gold Ruby Swirl Ribbed Top, Clear Twisted Stem 85.00
Champagne, Green Jade, Alabaster, Twisted Stem, Signed 110.00
Champagne, Green Top & Bottom, Crystal Twisted Stem, Pair 125.00
Compote, Calcite & Gold Aurene, 8 In. 385.00
Compote, Crystal, Celeste Blue, 7 1/2 In. 165.00
Compote, Gold Aurene On Calcite, Paper Label, 4 X 4 In. 160.00
Compote, Ribbed Amethyst, Clear Stem, Signed, 7 1/4 X 3 1/2 In. 95.00
Compote, Scalloped Rim, Signed, Amber, 4 X 7 1/2 In. 80.00
Console Set, Oriental Jade, Signed, 3 Piece 2750.00
Cordial, Twisted Stem, Gold Aurene, Marked, 3 1/2 In. 275.00
Decanter, Ship's, Signed, 10 In. 395.00
Figurine, Dinosaur, 12 3/4 In. 1500.00
Figurine, Diving Girl, Frosted, With Stand, 14 In. 2250.00
Figurine, Elephant, Trumpeting, 7 1/2 In. 750.00
Figurine, Horse Head, No.7779, 5 In. 325.00
Figurine, Owl, 5 1/4 In. 500.00
Figurine, Songbird, 4 1/2 In. .... 250.00 To 350.00
Figurine, Songbird, No.8112 .... 250.00
Figurine, Squirrel, 5 In. 500.00
Figurine, Water Bird, Signed Lloyd Atkins 600.00
Flower Frog, Blue Aurene 185.00
Flower Frog, Buddha Figure, Green 360.00
Goblet, Aurene, Gold Twisted Stem, 6 In. 265.00
Goblet, Champagne, Oriental Poppy, Green Stem, Signed, 6 1/4 In. 350.00
Goblet, Green Bowl, Intaglio Thistles & Leaves, Square Foot, 6 In. 250.00
Goblet, Oriental Poppy, Signed 485.00
Goblet, Water, Oriental Jade, Braided Stem, 8 In. 475.00
Jar, Green, Amber Finial, Cover, 3 1/4 In. 77.00
Lamp, 2 Nudes, Bronze, Art Deco, Moss Agate Shade 1750.00
Lamp, Art Deco, Bronze Kneeling Nude, Shade, Marble Base 1850.00
Lamp, Black Jade Over Pomona Green, Original Fittings, Glass Base 2650.00
Lamp, Centra, Green Cut To Alabaster, Bronze Fittings, 32 In. 1950.00
Lamp, Fan Shape, Jade Cut To Alabaster 650.00
Lamp, Mansard Pattern, Black To Pomona Green, All Fittings, 32 In. 2850.00
Lamp, Opalescent White, Spanish Green, Signed 1500.00
Nut Dish, Blue Aurene, 3 Foot, Signed, 3 1/2 In. 325.00
Perfume Bottle, Atomizer, Blue Aurene .... 325.00 To 350.00
Perfume Bottle, Atomizer, Blue Aurene, Amber Finial, 8 In. 475.00
Perfume Bottle, Aurene, Blue, Steeple Stopper 465.00
Perfume Bottle, Blue Aurene, 7 In. 350.00
Perfume Bottle, Crystal, Gold Ruby, Shape No.1455 .... 485.00
Perfume Bottle, Figurine, Gazelles, Pair 950.00
Perfume Bottle, Gold, Ruby & Crystal, Steeple Stopper 485.00
Perfume Bottle, Jewel Top, Blue Aurene 650.00
Perfume Bottle, Oriental Poppy, Petal-Shaped Stopper, 5 1/4 In. 250.00
Perfume Bottle, Threaded, Flat Stopper, 3 1/2 In. 350.00
Perfume Bottle, Verre De Soie, Nile Green, Steeple Stopper, 10 In. 395.00
Perfume Bottle, Wisteria, Square, Threading 395.00
Plaque, Display, Goose & Gander, Clear 225.00

Plate, Serving, Aurene, Gold, Paper Label, 8 In., Pair	350.00
Rose Bowl, Calcite, 6 1/2 In.	450.00
Rose Bowl, White Exterior, Gold Aurene Interior, 5 In.	135.00
Rose Bowl, White Exterior, Gold Interior, 4 In.	350.00
Salt & Pepper, Crystal, Silver Top	35.00
Salt, Gold Calcite, Iridescent, Pedestal, 1 1/2 In.	250.00
Salt, Master, Iridescent Gold, 3–Footed, Signed, 3 1/2 In.	225.00
Salt, Open, Verre De Soie	110.00
Salt, Ribbed, Amethyst, Roll Over Rim	18.00
Salt, Rosa	95.00
Shade, Gold Aurene Interior, Calcite Ribbed, Pair	150.00
Shade, Green Feather On Pale Yellow Ground, Signed, Pair	230.00
Sherbet, Calcite, Gold, 2 Piece	155.00
Sherbet, Underplate, Blue Threaded, Signed	95.00
Sherbet, Verre De Soie	15.00
Sugar & Creamer, Crystal	295.00
Vase, 3–Pronged Tree Trunks, Amber Crystal, Signed, 6 In.	150.00
Vase, 3–Pronged Tree Trunks, Green Jade, Signed, 5 1/2 In.	225.00
Vase, Amber, Pedestal Foot, Signed, 7 In.	95.00
Vase, Aquamarine, Turquoise Band, 7 In.	225.00
Vase, Art Deco, Tiered, Ruffled, Turquoise Threading, Signed, 7 In.	100.00
Vase, Aurene, Pinch Type At Bottom, Signed, 3 1/2 X 5 1/2 In.	395.00
Vase, Black, Jade Trim, Appled Foot, Signed, 8 1/2 In.	240.00
Vase, Blue Aurene, 10 In.	950.00 To 1150.00
Vase, Blue Aurene, Ruffled Top, 10 In.	850.00
Vase, Bristol Yellow Body, Pomona Green Foot, Signed, 8 In.	125.00
Vase, Bud, Aurene, Gold, Signed & Numbered	285.00
Vase, Cluthra, 8 In.	625.00
Vase, Cluthra, Cream To Mottled Design, Marked, 8 1/2 In.	510.00
Vase, Cypriote, 8 1/8 In.	105.00
Vase, Diagonal Rib, Cone Shape, Green, Signed, 9 1/4 In.	195.00
Vase, Diagonal Rib, Pedestal Foot, Selenium Red, Signed, 12 In.	275.00
Vase, Diagonal Ribbed Body, Amber Foot, Signed, 10 In.	125.00
Vase, Diagonal Ribbed, Blue, 7 In.	135.00
Vase, Diagonal Ribbed, Hexagon Shape, Yellow Body, 8 In.	125.00
Vase, Embossed Swirl, Blue Aurene Foot, 8 In.	875.00
Vase, Fan, Amethyst, 8 1/4 In.	85.00
Vase, Fan, Blue, 6 In.	95.00
Vase, Fan, Etched Ship, Green, 8 3/4 In.	295.00
Vase, Fan, Pomona Green Stem & Base, Topaz, 6 In.	145.00
Vase, Gold Aurene, Pinched Sides, 3 Handles, Signed, 8 1/4 In.	850.00
Vase, Jack–In–Pulpit, Ivrene, 6 1/2 In.	650.00
Vase, Millefiori, Signed, 3 In.	1100.00
Vase, Oriental Poppy, Mounted In Signed Tiffany Base, 19 In.	1850.00
Vase, Ribbed, Rectangular, Signed, Jade Green, 9 1/2 In.	125.00
Vase, Rosaline, Carved Alabaster Handle, 18 In.	450.00
Vase, Rosaline, Pink Jade, Signed, 6 In.	150.00

The blue Staffordshire patterns were the earliest, with both black and blue transfer designs used during the eighteenth century. Pink, green, or brown transfer designs were used about 1820, and the combination of several colors began about 1820.

Vase, Rosaline, Signed, Bud, 8 In. 200.00
Vase, Scalloped, Random Controlled Bubble, Clear & Amber, 6 3/4 In. 125.00
Vase, Smoky Green, Oval Lipped Shape, Signed, 11 X 7 1/2 In. 150.00
Vase, Strawberry Mansion, Cut & Engraved 1430.00
Vase, Stump, Aurene, 3 Stem 295.00
Vase, Stylized Leaves, Angular Branches, Footed, C.1930, 7 3/4 In. 9075.00
Vase, Topaz Crystal, Jade Vertical Stripes, Signed, 12 In. 525.00
Vase, Tree Trunk, Iridescent, Signed, 6 In. 950.00
Vase, Upright Handles, Ivrene, C.1930, 10 1/2 In. 350.00
Wine, Rosaline, Cone Shape, Twisted Alabaster Stem, Signed 165.00

Stevengraphs are woven pictures made like fancy ribbons. They were manufactured by Thomas Stevens of Coventry, England, and became popular in 1862. Most are marked "Woven in silk by Thomas Stevens" or were mounted on a cardboard that tells the story of the Stevengraph. Other similar ribbon pictures have been made in England and Germany.

STEVENGRAPH, Bookmark, A Wish 35.00
Columbus Leaving Spain, World's Fair, 1893 .... 150.00
Declaration of Independence, 1893 .... 150.00
George Washington, 1776–1876 .... 95.00
Lord's Prayer, Schmieder Bros., Framed, 16 X 14 In. 20.00
Present Time, Framed 325.00
The Death, Framed 325.00

Stevens & Williams of Stourbridge, England, made many types of glass, including layered, etched, cameo, and art glass, between the 1830s and 1930s. Some pieces are signed "S & W." Many pieces are decorated with flowers, leaves, and other designs based on nature.

STEVENS & WILLIAMS, Basket, Applied Pink Flowers, Triangle Handle, Signed 165.00
Basket, Cream, Applied Green & Amber Leaves, 9 In. 365.00
Biscuit Jar, Applied Leaves, Silver Plated Fittings 275.00
Bonbon, Threaded Rose & Clear, Flared, 5 1/2 In., Pair 90.00
Bowl, 3–Lily, Rigaree On Trumpets, Vaseline, 24 X 12 In. 425.00
Bowl, Crimped, Flower Prunt, Allover Bamboo, 3 1/2 In. 595.00
Bowl, Gold Swirl, Mother–of–Pearl, Lining, Crimped, 4 In. 850.00
Bowl, Pink Center, Green Fluted Top, 9 In. 245.00
Bride's Bowl, Amber Trim, Candy Ribbon Rim 375.00
Bride's Bowl, Design, Triangular 375.00
Bride's Bowl, Frosted Fuchsia, Plated Stand, Signed 175.00
Candy Box, Cover, Alabaster Foot & Finial, 6 1/2 In. 185.00
Cheese Dish, Applied Mice 350.00
Jar, Biscuit, Cranberry To Vaseline, Plated Lid, 7 In. 610.00
Lamp, Fairy, Crimped Shade, Clarke Base, 4 1/2 In. 295.00
Pitcher, Peachblow Over Opaline, Clear Handle, Signed 240.00
Plate, Strawberries, Amber Handle, 4 1/2 X 10 In. 730.00
Rose Bowl, Arboresque, Ruffled, Green, White, 3 1/4 In. 75.00
Rose Bowl, Box Pleated Top, Basket Weave Overlay, 6 In. 395.00
Rose Bowl, Crimped, White Blossoms, Green Leaves, 5 In. 145.00
Rose Bowl, Honeycomb Pattern, Bow Pleated Top, 4 In. 110.00
Rose Bowl, Mother–of–Pearl, Diamond–Quilted, Miniature 1045.00
Rose Bowl, Peachblow, Matsu–No–Ke, Crimped, 5 3/4 In. 1345.00
Rose Bowl, Striped, Swirl Allover, 8–Crimp Top, 3 In. 175.00
Sweetmeat Jar, Glass Leaves, Silver Plated Fittings 195.00
Tumbler, Flowers & Ovals, Royal Blue To Pink, 4 In. 65.00
Vase, Amber Scalloped Top, Opaque, Signed, 10 1/2 In. 190.00
Vase, Applied Flowers, Amber Branches, 6 3/8 In. 175.00
Vase, Applied Flowers, Branches, White Lining, 8 1/4 In. 295.00
Vase, Applied Fruit, Amber Handle & Branch, 8 In. 100.00
Vase, Applied Salamander, Rigaree, Amber, Signed, 10 In. 325.00
Vase, Egg Shape, Pink Flowers, Amber Branches, 4 1/2 In. 245.00
Vase, Flowers, Leaves, Snail Feet, Pink, 3 7/8 In. 195.00
Vase, Fluted, Pink Flowers, Leaves, Signed, 3 3/4 In. 1250.00
Vase, Gold Applied Leaves & Acorns, Amber Feet, 10 In. 195.00

Stiegel Type, Bottle, Blue, 4 In.   Stiegel Type, Bottle, Brown, Bird & Flower,
Enameled, 4 In.

Vase, Gourd Shape, Matsu–No–Ke Trim, 11 1/2 In. 650.00
Vase, Green Jade, 10 In. 300.00
Vase, Intaglio Cut, Blue Overlay, Vines, 9 1/2 In. 495.00
Vase, Intaglio Cut, Ruffled Top, Pink Outside, 5 1/8 In. 275.00
Vase, Molded Drapery, Coral Pulled Lines, 6 3/4 In. 1100.00
Vase, Mother–of–Pearl, Tangerine, White Lining, 11 In. 265.00
Vase, Multicolor Swirls, Enameled Flowers, 13 In. 275.00
Vase, Opaque White, Amber Leaves, Signed, 10 In. 190.00
Vase, Ruffled, Applied Leaf, 8–Crimp, Cream, 6 1/2 In. 145.00
Vase, Swans In Water At Top, Clear Bottom, 7 1/2 In. 495.00
Vase, White Threaded, Cranberry Petal Top, Signed, 8 In. 130.00
Vase, White, Amber, Pink Flowers, Opaque White, 9 In. 115.00

Henry William Stiegel, a colorful immigrant to the colonies, started
his first factory in Pennsylvania in 1763. He remained in business
until 1774. Glassware was made in a style popular in Europe at that
time and was similar to the glass of many other makers. It was
made of clear or colored glass and was decorated with enamel
colors, mold blown designs, or etching. It is almost impossible to be
sure a piece was made by Stiegel, so the knowing collector now
refers to this glass as Stiegel type.

STIEGEL TYPE, Bottle, Blue, 4 In. ....*Illus* 150.00
  Bottle, Brown, Bird & Flower, Enameled, 4 In. ....*Illus* 400.00
  Dish, 200 Years of American Blown Glass 400.00
  Mug, Bird, Enameled, Strap Handle, 1760s 850.00

Stoneware is a coarse, glazed, and fired potter's ceramic that is used
to make crocks, jugs, bowls, etc. It is often decorated with cobalt
blue decorations. Stoneware is still being made.

STONEWARE, Ashtray, Anniversary, Norton Red Wing, 1953 .... 30.00
  Bank, Tiered Top, Incised Eliza Arkenburgh, 6 3/4 In. 600.00
  Batter Jug, Blue Flower, Salt Glaze 325.00
  Batter Jug, Cowden & Wilcox, Harrisburg, Cobalt Blue Flower 1995.00
  Batter Jug, Dutch Man & Woman Holding Baby, Windmill, 7 3/4 In. 155.00
  Batter Jug, Flower, 1 Gal. 357.00
  Bean Jar, Brown & Cream 45.00
  Bean Pot, Raised Design, Words Boston Baked Beans, 6 1/2 In. 100.00
  Beater Jar, Blue Band 23.00
  Beater Jar, Gray, Blue Band 35.00
  Beater Jar, Montezuma, Iowa, Blue Stripe 60.00
  Beater Jar, Use This Jar For Beating, Toma's Groceries 70.00
  Bed Warmer, Vent Hole, Open Handle, Jager Co., 7 1/2 X 9 1/2 In. 220.00

Bottle, Bulbous Cobalt Blue Lip, P.Mansfield, 6 5/8 In. 55.00
Bottle, Medicine, Habits of Drink, Label, Fulham, C.1800, 6 In. 65.00
Bottle, Mercury, 5 1/2 In. 10.50
Bottle, Ogdensburg Ginger Beer Works, H.N.Daniels, Proprietor 30.00
Bottle, Walter's Distillery Pure Canada Malt Whiskey, 1 Qt. 80.00
Bowl, Berry, Flying Bird, Blue & White 85.00
Bowl, Blue & White Sponge Spatter, 4 3/4 X 13 3/4 In. 230.00
Bowl, Blue Stripes On White, 9 In. 72.00
Bowl, Chain Link, Solid Blue, 8 1/2 In. 17.00
Bowl, Embossed Exterior, Blue & White Spatter, 10 1/8 In. 105.00
Bowl, Mixing, Blue & White Sponge Spatter, 6 1/4 X 13 In. 160.00
Bowl, Mixing, Dark Blue, Scalloped, Large 85.00
Bowl, Mixing, Embossed Exterior, Blue, White Spatter, 12 1/4 In. 125.00
Bowl, Mixing, Orange Rush Sponge Design, 7 1/4 In. 90.00
Bowl, Nesting, Wedding Ring, 3 Piece 225.00
Bowl, Oxford Ware, Blue, 8 3/4 In. 35.00
Bowl, Roberts Cottage Cheese, 2 Lb. 20.00
Bowl, Tan & Blue Spatter, Advertising Transfer Inside, 7 3/4 In. 50.00
Bowl, Wedding Ring, Blue & White, 5 In. .... 40.00 To 95.00
Bowl, West End Grocery, Waukon, Iowa, Blue & White, 7 In. 55.00
Bowl, Wildflower, 10 In. 125.00
Box, Salt, Blue & White Sponge Spatter, Embossed Label, 6 In. 215.00
Butter, Apple Blossom, Blue & White, Cover 275.00
Butter, Apple Blossom, Cover 155.00
Butter, Apricot, Bail, Cover 200.00
Butter, Apricot, Blue & White, Cover .... 175.00 To 195.00
Butter, Colonial Pattern, Blue & White 130.00
Butter, Cows & Columns, Cover 185.00
Butter, Daisy & Trellis, Blue & White, Cover 140.00
Butter, Dutch Couple, Blue & White 155.00
Butter, Eagle, Blue & White, Cover 425.00
Butter, Grapes & Leave, Blue & Gray, Cover 195.00
Butter, Hand Painted Flowers, Blue & White 150.00
Butter, Printed Cows, Blue & White, Cover 120.00
Canister, Coffee, Basket Weave, Blue & White 125.00
Canister, Marked McNaughton, Clarington, Ohio 185.00
Canister, Tea, Basket Weave 85.00
Canister, Tea, Basket Weave, Blue & White, Cover 195.00
Chamber Pot, Open Rose, Blue & White 115.00
Chicken Waterer, Brown Glaze, W.R.& Co., Akron, Ohio, 1895 .... 150.00
Churn, Blue, 1 Gal. 18.00
Churn, C.W.Braun 1050.00
Churn, Cobalt Blue Floral, No.4, Wooden Lid & Dasher, 16 1/2 In. 275.00
Churn, Lid, Homemade Dasher, Western Stoneware 50.00
Churn, Shield Flanked By Lion & Beaver, Ovoid, 18 1/4 In. 850.00
Churn, White's, Utica, Stylized Design, Dated 1876, 6 Gal. 850.00
Coffeepot, Peacock, Blue & White 1150.00
Coffeepot, White Top, Blue Bottom, Blue Band 275.00
Container, Razorbrite, Cover 24.00
Cooler, 2 Loop Handles, Blue Design, Flowers, 1855, 21 In. 8000.00
Cooler, Blue & White, Polar Bear, Brass Spigot, 3 Gal. 825.00
Cooler, Blue Band, Steel Spigot, Cover, Crown Mark, 6 Gal. 10.00
Cooler, Cobalt Blue Tulip, Handles, C.1850, 32 In. 800.00
Cooler, Cupid, Blue & White 750.00
Cooler, Frank Jones Old Fashioned Lively Ale, Spigot, C.1910 .... 375.00
Cooler, Lady At Well, Cabin In Background, Flowers 395.00
Cooler, Westhafer & Lambright, Tulips, 1866, 24 3/4 In. 800.00
Cracker Jar, Wildflower, Blue & White, Cover 225.00
Creamer, Arc & Leaf Paneled, Blue 48.00
Crock, Alexis Pottery Co., Illinois 95.00
Crock, An Ideal Fat Food For Children & Invalids 35.00
Crock, Bird, Haxton, 1 Ear 195.00
Crock, Blue Fern & Leaf Design, Gray, 2 Gal. 150.00
Crock, Blue Leaf Design, Signed Geddes, Eared, Gray, 2 Gal. 150.00

Crock, Brown Glaze, Picton, Canada West, C.1840 .... 375.00
Crock, Butter, Apricot, Bail 175.00
Crock, Butter, Blue & White Sponge Spatter, 3 3/4 X 6 In. 165.00
Crock, Butter, Ft.Dodge, Brown, 3 Lb. 50.00
Crock, Butter, Swastika, Wire & Wood Bail, 5 X 6 In. 150.00
Crock, C.Crolius, N.Y., Ovoid, Handles, 3 Gal. 467.00
Crock, Chain Pattern, Blue & Gray, 5 In. 30.00
Crock, Chandler Gilt Edge Creamery, Ogdensburg, N.Y., 1 Gal. 70.00
Crock, Cobalt Bands, Butter In Raised Letters, Gray, 1 Gal. 95.00
Crock, Cobalt Blue Bird, Farrar Co., Geddes, N.Y., 1 Gal. 600.00
Crock, Cobalt Blue Gooseberries, Handles, New Eng.1847, 2 Gal. 275.00
Crock, Cobalt Blue Stag, Standing, Fort Edward Pottery, 5 Gal. 5775.00
Crock, Coffeepot, Bohemian Pottery, Zanesville, Ohio, Brown, 10 In. 75.00
Crock, Diamond Ink Co., Bail Handle, Clamp Closing, 1 Gal. 75.00
Crock, Domser's Creamery, Utica, N.Y., Blue Lettering, 1 Gal. 70.00
Crock, Fort Dodge, Iowa, Brown, Brown Lining, 1 Gal. 35.00
Crock, Fort Edward Pottery Co., Stylized Deer, 4 Gal. 3410.00
Crock, Geo.Johnston, Clarksburg, W.Va., Stenciled, 2 Gal. 275.00
Crock, Grease, Flying Bird, 2 Gal. 125.00
Crock, Hanging, Butterfly, Wooden Lid, 2 Gal. 125.00
Crock, Horseradish 40.00
Crock, Illinois Map, Cobalt Blue, 2 Gal. 30.00
Crock, Inverted Picket Fence Design, Blue, 3 X 5 In. 75.00
Crock, J.& E.Norton, Blue Stag In Fenced Area, 2 Gal. 1200.00
Crock, J.Burger Jr.Rochester, N.Y., 2, Cobalt Blue Slip, 9 1/4 In. 175.00
Crock, J.Burger, Bird & Foliage, 5 Gal. 1550.00
Crock, J.S.Taft & Co., Keene, N.H., Cobalt Blue Floral, 12 1/2 In. 120.00
Crock, Krisch's Goodies, 1 Gal. 50.00
Crock, Leaves, J.McKenzie, Beaver, Pa., 8 Gal. 192.50
Crock, Lion, Handles, 4 Gal. 9250.00
Crock, Maple Leaf, 2 Gal. 35.00
Crock, McComb, 1 Gal. 18.00
Crock, N.A.White & Son, Utica, N.Y., 4 Gal. 700.00
Crock, Peoria, Brown, 1 Gal. 25.00
Crock, Pickle, Blue Band, Bail, National Pickle Co., 5 Gal. 150.00
Crock, Pickle, Dodson & Braun's, 3 Gal. 125.00
Crock, Red Rose Dog & Puppy Chow, 7 1/2 X 3 1/2 In. 32.00
Crock, Saddle Club Farms, Cordovia, Illinois, Tan, 1 Gal. 45.00
Crock, Somerset Potters Works, 4 Gal. 2420.00
Crock, Syracuse Guernsey Dairy Co-Op, Inc., 1 Gal. 70.00
Crock, White, Utica, Deer Design, 3 Gal. 1950.00
Cup, Bowtie, Rose Decal 35.00
Cuspidor, Blue & White Sponge 85.00
Cuspidor, Sunflowers, Blue & White 110.00
Dish, Cobalt Blue Stripes, Albany Slip Interior, 3 3/4 X 7 In. 275.00
Dish, Soap, Lion, Blue & White 100.00
Dispenser, Ice Water, Blue Band, White 75.00
Inkwell, 2 Quill Holes, Olive Mustard Glaze, Round, 3 1/2 In. 130.00
Jar, Ballock Hardware, Cover 75.00
Jar, Bennington, Bird On Stump, 5 Gal. 797.00
Jar, Blue & White Sponge Spatter, Cover, 6 In. 140.00
Jar, Blue Swirls, Gray, 3 3/4 In. 30.00
Jar, Brushed Cobalt Floral, Applied Handles, No.20, 25 In. 1550.00
Jar, Brushed Floral Design, Polka Dots, No.4, Ovoid, 14 1/4 In. 85.00
Jar, Canning, Union Stoneware RW, Minnesota, 1 Gal. 145.00
Jar, Canning, Blue Slip Wavy Lines, 8 In. 45.00
Jar, Canning, Blue Song Bird On Branch, Gray, 2 Gal. 495.00
Jar, Canning, Tin Lid, 8 1/2 In. 45.00
Jar, Canning, Weil Lock, Western, 1/2 Gal. 28.00
Jar, Cobalt Blue Dog, Edwards & Co., Flat Ear Handles, 9 1/2 In. 2530.00
Jar, Ear Handles, 7 1/4 In. 80.00
Jar, Flemish Gray & Cobalt Blue, 8 In. 72.00
Jar, Food Storage, Cobalt Blue Floral, Dated 1865, 23 In. 1200.00
Jar, Hamilton & Jones Label, Cobalt Blue Stencil, 9 In. 150.00

Jar, Hamilton & Jones, No.3, Stenciled & Brush Design	95.00
Jar, Herring, Western, Cover	205.00
Jar, L.N.Yeager & Co., Allentown, Pa., Flower, Ovoid, 6 3/4 In.	295.00
Jar, Label J.F.Brayont & Co., Utica, Cobalt Flower, Ovoid, 12 In.	325.00
Jar, Label, S.Purdy, Ohio, 3, Cobalt On Handles, 12 In.	85.00
Jar, Louis C.Wheeler, 1892 Salineville, Ohio, Brown, 4 In.	30.00
Jar, Moore, Nichols & Co., Cobalt Blue Flower, Ovoid, 8 In.	150.00
Jar, New York Stoneware Co., Fort Edward, N.Y.2, Bird, 11 1/2 In.	295.00
Jar, T.F.Rypert, Greensboro, Pa., Number 4, Ovoid, 15 3/4 In.	200.00
Jar, Williams & Reppert, Greensboro, Pa., 5, Wavy Lines, 16 In.	95.00
Jug, 2–Tone Blend Brown Glaze, Handle, 1 Qt.	65.00
Jug, A.B.Wheeler & Co., Number 4 In Cobalt Blue Slip, 17 In.	65.00
Jug, B.Lemann & Bros., Donaldsonville, Louisiana, 16 In.	85.00
Jug, Beehive, Brown Glaze, Marked B, 1/2 Gal.	18.50
Jug, Beehive, Brown, Minnesota Stoneware Co., 1 Gal.	40.00
Jug, Beehive, Salt Glaze, 1 Gal.	40.00
Jug, Bird, Spotted Body, Blue, 2 Large Flowers, Marked, 17 In.	5300.00
Jug, Blue Advertising, Greensboro, Pa., Strap Handle, Gray, 2 Gal.	250.00
Jug, Blue Flower Leaf, Blue & Gray, 1 Gal.	175.00
Jug, Brown Glaze, Ovoid, 11 1/2 In.	25.00
Jug, Brown Over White, Western Stoneware, 1 Gal.	22.50
Jug, Brushed Cobalt Blue Floral, No.3, 16 In.	125.00
Jug, C.Crolius, Manhattan, Wells, New York, C.1797, 11 1/2 In.	550.00
Jug, Cobalt Blue Bird, W.H.Farrar & Co., C.1845, 1 Gal.	4200.00
Jug, Copal Varnish No. 1, Lucins H.Pratt, Floral, 14 1/2 In.	400.00
Jug, E.E.Hall & Co., Boston 2, Floral, Cobalt Blue, 13 1/2 In.	325.00
Jug, Eagle, Norton, 1 Gal.	6050.00
Jug, F.H.Cowden, Harrisburg, Stenciled Blue Design, 11 1/4 In.	95.00
Jug, Feather, Nichols & Boynton, Burlington, Vt., C.1856, 2 Gal.	300.00
Jug, Fort Edward Pottery Co., Chicken In Yard, 4 Gal.	1650.00
Jug, Geddes, N.Y., Hearts, 2 Gal.	3025.00
Jug, George H.Goodman Co., Red Rock, Evansville, Ind.3 Gal.	65.00
Jug, Gray, 2 Handles, Cobalt Design, 24 In.	910.00
Jug, Griesel Bros., Winona, Minnesota, Brown Top, 1 Gal.	45.00
Jug, H.D.Block, Wine & Liquors, Louisville, Dark Brown, 1 Gal.	115.00
Jug, Impressed Havens, No.2, Brushed Cobalt Blue, 11 1/2 In.	55.00
Jug, J.& E.Norton, Bennington, Vt., Blue Highlights, 10 3/4 In.	85.00
Jug, J.& E.Norton, Cobalt Blue Butterfly, Swirls, 1 Gal.	215.00
Jug, J.& E.Norton, Eagle Design, Spread Wings, 1 Gal.	6050.00
Jug, Jack Daniels' Fine Goods, Lynchburg, Tennessee, 2 Gal.	675.00
Jug, Jack Daniels, Old Time Distillery, Blue Ink Stamp, 1 Gal.	225.00
Jug, Jas.Hamilton & Co., Cobalt Blue Stenciled Label, 14 In.	200.00
Jug, John L.Smith & Co., Wheeling, W.Va., 3 Gal.	350.00
Jug, Leaves, Scrolls & Dots, Blue Slip, 2 Gal.	260.00
Jug, M.D.Breen, Albany, N.Y., Stenciled Letters, 1 Gal.	110.00
Jug, N.A.White & Son, Stenciled Lettering, 2 Gal.	225.00
Jug, New York Stoneware Co., Cobalt Leaves, Floral, 1 Gal.	185.00
Jug, Norton & Bennett, Brantford C.W.3, Cobalt Flower, 16 3/4 In.	175.00
Jug, Norton & Co., Bennington, Ovoid, 14 1/2 In.	175.00
Jug, Old Continental Whiskey, 1/8 Pt.	30.00
Jug, Ottman Bros. & Co., Fort Edward, N.Y., 16 In.	55.00
Jug, Ovoid, Brownish Tan Glaze, 8 1/2 In.	85.00
Jug, Rhode Island State, Bluebird, Gray, 2 Gal.	395.00
Jug, Stetzenmeyes, Floral Design, 2 Gal.	1500.00
Jug, T.C.Taylor, Stylized Bird, 2 Gal.	1815.00
Jug, T.Harrington, Star–Face, 4 Gal.	4500.00
Jug, Triple Flower, Leafy Wreath Design Over All Front, 2 Gal.	1650.00
Jug, Vinegar, Blue & Gray, 1 Gal.	225.00
Jug, Vinegar, Clark Bros., Zanesville, Ohio, 1899, 1 Gal.	35.00
Jug, W.H.Farrar, Flower & 3 Blossoms, Gray, 11 1/2 In.	275.00
Jug, Whiskey, Glen Garry Highland, Dundas Pottery Co., 9 X 18 In.	150.00
Jug, Whiskey, Maple Leaf, 1 Gal.	65.00
Jug, White Rock, Distillery, Kansas City, Mo., Bail Handle, 2 Gal.	65.00

Jug, White's, Utica, Blue Poppy & Leaves, 1 Gal. 190.00
Jug, White's, Utica, Fantail Peacock, Turned Head, 1885, 15 In. 1600.00
Jug, White's, Utica, Leafy Branch, 3 Flowers, C.1880, 1 Gal. 250.00
Jug, White's, Utica, N.Y., Leaves, Butterfly, 3 Gal. 192.50
Loaf Dish, Slip Design, 17 3/4 X 12 1/2 In. 3200.00
Match Holder, Beehive 70.00
Match Holder, Striking Surface 12.50
Meat Tenderizer, Buff Salt Glaze, Wooden Handle, Pat.1877, 10 In. 75.00
Mold, Ice Cream, Wheat Design, Tan, 8 1/2 In. 35.00
Mold, Pudding, Fluted, Yellow, 9 In. 65.00
Mug & Bowl, Child's, Flying Bird, Blue & White 200.00
Mug, Basket Weave, Blue & White 65.00
Mug, Buckeye Root Beer 45.00
Mug, Flying Bird, Brown 145.00
Mug, Grape & Leaf, Green, 5 In. 20.00
Mug, Grapes In Shield, Green 28.00
Mug, Keg Shape, Embossed Cobalt Blue Bands, 4 1/2 In., Pair 70.00
Mug, Toby, Applied Handle, G.Priest, Canton, 7 1/2 In. 225.00
Mug, Windy City .... 135.00 To 150.00
Pail, Batter, Wildflower 250.00
Pie Plate, Star, Blue & White 150.00
Pitcher & Bowl, Bowtie, Blue & White 150.00
Pitcher, American Beauty Rose, Blue & White 300.00
Pitcher, American Beauty Rose, White 175.00
Pitcher, Apricot, Blue & White 125.00
Pitcher, Barrel Shape, 6 Mugs, Blue & White 395.00
Pitcher, Basket Weave, Morning Glories, Blue & White, 10 In. 200.00
Pitcher, Beer, Blue & Gray 600.00
Pitcher, Blue & White Sponge Spatter, 8 7/8 In. 185.00
Pitcher, Bluebird, Blue & Gray, 8 In. 250.00
Pitcher, Bluish-Brown Glaze, Flecks, Albany Slip Inside, 14 In. 60.00
Pitcher, Bowknot, Cobalt Decal, Blue & White, 10 In. 85.00
Pitcher, Boy & Girl, Blue & White, 10 In. 200.00
Pitcher, Butterfly, Blue & White, 8 In. 165.00
Pitcher, Butterfly, Blue, Gray, 8 In. 195.00
Pitcher, Castle, Blue & White, 7 In. 125.00
Pitcher, Cattail, 7 1/2 In. 150.00
Pitcher, Cattail, Blue & White, 9 In. 95.00
Pitcher, Cattails & Dragonfly, Wide Grasses, Blue, White, 7 In. 68.00
Pitcher, Cherry Band, Advertising, Blue & White, 7 In. 250.00
Pitcher, Cherry Cluster, Blue & Gray, 8 1/2 In. 95.00
Pitcher, Cobalt Blue Surface, Salt Glaze, Handle, 1855, 8 1/4 In. 2200.00
Pitcher, Courtship, Matrimony, Caricature, England, 6 1/2 In. 350.00
Pitcher, Cow, Blue & White, 8 In. .... 175.00 To 235.00
Pitcher, Cow, Brown, Green & Tan, 7 In. 215.00
Pitcher, Cow, Brown, Green & Tan, 8 In. 150.00
Pitcher, Cow, Cream & Green, 7 In. 125.00
Pitcher, Doe & Fawn, Blue & White, 8 In. 200.00
Pitcher, Double Spout, Rust, Brown & Green Spatter, 6 In. 65.00
Pitcher, Dutch Boy & Girl Kissing, Blue & White, 8 In. 145.00
Pitcher, Dutch Boy & Girl With Dog, Blue & White, 8 In. 160.00
Pitcher, Dutch Farm, Blue & White, 8 In. 175.00

Wash Sumida ware carefully. The orange red color is only lightly fired and will wash off.

Pitcher, Dutch Printed Landscape, Blue & White, 10 In. 175.00
Pitcher, Eagle, Blue & White, 12 In. 500.00
Pitcher, Edelweiss, Blue & White, 6 In. 78.00
Pitcher, Flemish Peasant, Blue & Gray, 6 In. 120.00
Pitcher, Flemish Tavern Scene, Blue & Gray, 6 In. 175.00
Pitcher, Flowers, Blue & Gray, 14 In. 150.00
Pitcher, Flying Bird, Blue & White, 14 In. 400.00
Pitcher, Grape & Shield, Green & Yellow, 8 In. 85.00
Pitcher, Grape & Trellis, Blue, 7 In. 110.00
Pitcher, Grape Cluster In Shield, Green & Ivory, 8 1/2 In. 75.00
Pitcher, Gray–Brown Glaze, 11 In. 40.00
Pitcher, Hunting Scene, Lambeth, 9 X 10 1/2 In. 230.00
Pitcher, Indian & Waffle, 8 In. 300.00
Pitcher, Indian Head, Blue & White, 8 In. 275.00
Pitcher, Indian, Blue & White, 7 In. 300.00
Pitcher, Leaping Deer, Blue & White, 8 In. .... 150.00 To 225.00
Pitcher, Lee & Watkins, Ashton, South Dakota, 8 1/2 In. 147.50
Pitcher, Lincoln, No.2, Blue & White, 5 1/2 In. .... 225.00 To 250.00
Pitcher, Lovebirds, Blue & White, 8 In. 250.00
Pitcher, Monk, 8 In. 300.00
Pitcher, Monmouth, Aqua, 6 In. 12.50
Pitcher, Northstar Grape & Rickrack, 6 In. 80.00
Pitcher, Poinsettia, Blue & White, 8 In. .... 185.00 To 250.00
Pitcher, Puzzle, Lambeth, Writings & Sayings, 9 In. 225.00
Pitcher, Rose On Trellis, Blue & Gray, 9 In. .... 120.00 To 135.00
Pitcher, Sawtooth, Blue, 7 In. 120.00
Pitcher, Sawtooth, White, Hall, 7 In. 95.00
Pitcher, Scenes of Country Life, Blue & White, 6 7/8 In. 75.00
Pitcher, Scoll & Leaf, Advertising, Blue & White, 10 In. 300.00
Pitcher, Scroll & Leaf, Steamboat Rock, Iowa, Blue & Gray, 10 In. 195.00
Pitcher, Star, Embossed Grapes, Leaves, Brown, 6 In. 50.00
Pitcher, Swastika, Blue & White, 8 In. 145.00
Pitcher, Tulip, Blue & White, 10 In. 225.00
Pitcher, Vinegar, Brown Glaze, 6 In. 15.00
Pitcher, Wild Rose, Sponge, Blue & White, 10 In. 275.00
Pitcher, Windmill & Bush, Blue & White, 8 In. .... 120.00 To 140.00
Pitcher, Windmill, Blue & White, 8 In. 160.00
Pitcher, Windmill, Blue & White, 10 In. 275.00
Rolling Pin, Advertising, Solma & Son, Pontiac, Ill. 75.00
Rolling Pin, Guenthers Sells It For Less, Lake City, Iowa 165.00
Rolling Pin, Polar Bear Flour Is King, Tulsa Feed Store 150.00
Rolling Pin, Wildflower, Blue & White .... 100.00 To 235.00
Salt Box, Brown, Raised Grape Design, Hanging 38.00
Salt Box, Green Key, Blue 275.00
Salt Box, Waffle, Hanging, Wooden Lid 98.00
Salt, Apricot 100.00
Salt, Bluebirds 65.00
Salt, Butterfly, Blue & White, Cover 155.00
Salt, Daisy On Snowflakes, Blue & White, Cover .... 210.00 To 220.00
Salt, Eagle, Blue & White, Cover 325.00
Salt, Hanging, Grape Pattern 95.00
Soap Dish, Beaded Rose 95.00
Soap Dish, Blue & White 145.00
Soap Dish, Brown Albany Glaze, Hole Drip Shelf, 1800, 3 X 5 In. 220.00
Soap Dish, Cat's Head, Blue 90.00
Soap Dish, Flower Scale, Brown 100.00
Soap Dish, Lion, Blue & White 125.00
Soap Dish, Rose & Leaves In Beading, Blue & White, 4 3/4 In. 80.00
Soap Dish, Rose, Blue & White 125.00
Spittoon, Brown 35.00
Spittoon, Daisy, Brown 50.00
Spittoon, Gray, Blue Band, Small 32.50
Spittoon, Green & Gold Glaze, 7 1/4 X 5 In. 12.50
Spittoon, Lily & Plume 90.00

Don't send your antique white linen or cotton items out to be dry cleaned; the chemicals will yellow the fabric. Hand wash them in soap, nonchlorine bleach, and tepid water. Be sure to rinse until all soap is removed.

Spittoon, Sponged Blue Earthworm Pattern, Blue & White	120.00
Syrup, Brown & Cream	35.00
Tankard, Bacchantic, James Dixon & Sons, C.Meigh, 1844, 7 1/2 In.	475.00
Teapot, Brown, Green & Cream, Advertising	85.00
Teapot, Bud Finial, Painted Swag, England, C.1790, 7 1/2 In.	500.00
Toothbrush Holder, Bow, Stenciled Flower	50.00
Umbrella Stand, Blue, White, Oak Leaves & Animals, 20 3/4 In.	350.00
Vase, 2 Lions, Cobalt Blue, Slate Gray, R.G.Crook, 9 1/2 In.	750.00
Vase, Bulb, Hyacinth, Brown Glaze Inside, 8 1/2 In.	65.00
Wedding Bowl, 5 In.	55.00

Most items found in an old store are listed under advertising in this book. Store fixtures, cases, cutters, and other items that have no advertising as part of the decoration are listed here.

STORE, Bin, Grain, Raised Trough, Legs Extend To Support, 30 X 15 In.	165.00
Bin, Roast Coffee, Counter, 13 X 9 3/4 X 12 In.	125.00
Cabinet, Nuts & Bolts, 104 Drawers, Revolves On Base, Pine	1200.00
Display Case, Counter Top, Hinged Fold–Down Shelves, Oak, 6 Ft.	350.00
Display Case, Door In Back, Oak Frame, 10 1/2 X 14 3/4 X 16 1/2 In.	115.00
Display Case, Jewelry, Rings, Hand Rotated, 3 Sections	48.00
Display Case, Slant Glass Front, Counter Top, Hinged Shelves, 4 Ft.	350.00
Icebox, Walk–In, McCray, Frigidaire Unit, 8 Ft. X 9 Ft. 4 In.	4800.00
Light, Exit, Red, Round	40.00
String Holder, Counter Top, Cone Type	28.00

Stoves have been used in America for heating since the eighteenth century and for cooking since the nineteenth century. Most types of wood, coal, gas, kerosene, and even some electric stoves are collected.

STOVE, 4 O'clock, Leibrandt & McDowall, Iron, Ornate, 23 X 12 X 15 In.	325.00
Child's, Empire Works, Electric, 1930s	125.00
Coal, Tiles With Pineapple Design, Cast Iron, European, 37 In.	275.00
Cook, American Stove Co., No.501–1, Top Warmers	2000.00
Cook, Buck Junior, Cast Iron, Sample, 22 In.	500.00
Cook, Buck, No.4, Nickel Plated, Sample, 11 X 16 X 22 In.	700.00
Cook, Reservoir, Porcelain, Wood Burning	500.00
Haller, Kerosene, 3 Burners, Green	125.00
Home Comfort Range, Water Reservoir, Gray Enamel, Grates	950.00
Imperial Universal, Nickel, Isenglass, Gargoyle Design	4500.00
Kerosene, Graniteware, Brown, Single Burner, With Tea Kettle	125.00
Kitchen, Wood Burning, Range, Eternal, 30 X 18 In.	995.00
Kitchen, Wood Burning, Water Reservoir, Shelf	350.00
Majestic, Wood Burning, Water Reservoir, 1930s	700.00
Parlor, Gothic Style, Victorian	130.00
Parlor, Little Flower No.2, Cast Iron, Dated 1859, 21 In.	250.00
Parlor, Victorian, Chrome & Iron, Moores Air Light, 58 In.	750.00
Shaker, Black Finish, Cast Iron, C.1840, 23 X 34 In.	350.00

Shaker, Cast Iron, High Pipe Legs, Ring Handle Door	525.00
Shaker, Lift Lid Opening, Cast Iron, 20 1/2 X 33 In.	800.00

STRAWBERRY, see Soft Paste

> Stretch glass is named for the strange stretch marks in the glass. It was made by many glass companies in the United States from about 1900 to the 1920s. It is iridescent. Most American stretch glass is molded; most European pieces are blown and may have a pontil mark.

STRETCH GLASS, Basket, Butterfly & Berry, Rose	30.00
Basket, Gray, 10 1/2 In.	70.00
Bell, Star Crimped, Blue	35.00
Bell, Star Crimped, Purple	30.00
Bowl, Amethyst Base, Imperial	15.00
Bowl, Crystal, 7 1/2 In.	11.00
Bowl, Footed, Orange, 9 3/4 In.	48.00
Bowl, Iridescent, 10 In.	25.00
Bowl, Red, 3 1/2 X 7 In.	55.00
Candlestick, Florentine, Blue, Gold Trim, 10 In., Pair	65.00
Candlestick, Green, 9 3/4 In., Pair	32.00
Candy Dish, Cover, Purple Iridescent	25.00
Candy Dish, Dolphin, Cover, 75th Anniversary, Rose	35.00
Candy Dish, Yellow	35.00
Compote, Cover, Celeste Blue, Fenton	24.00
Compote, Cumula, Ice Green	18.00
Compote, Paneled, White, 7 In.	18.00
Compote, Persian Medallion, Blue	20.00
Compote, White, 4 1/2 X 9 In.	32.00
Console, Rose	30.00
Lamp, Gone With The Wind, Blue	200.00
Plate, 14–Panel, Amberina, 8 1/4 In.	40.00
Plate, Gold Iridescent, 12 In.	59.00
Powder Jar, Cover, Vaseline, Fenton	25.00
Powder Jar, Vaseline, Footed, Small	25.00
Salt, Master, Flute, Celeste Blue, Northwood	45.00
Vase, Dolphin Handles, Pink, 6 In.	50.00
Vase, Fan, Dolphin, Rose	30.00
Vase, Fan, Ice Blue	20.00

> Sumida, or Sumida Gawa, is a Japanese pottery. The pieces collected by that name today were made about 1895 to 1970. There has been much confusion about the name of this ware, and it is often called "Korean Pottery" or "Poo ware." Most pieces have a very heavy orange–red, blue, or green glaze, with raised three–dimensional figures as decorations.

SUMIDA, Basket, Applied Monkey & Dog, Handle, Kiln Mark	185.00
Bowl, Boy On Rim, 5 In.	90.00
Tankard, Applied Children Seal Signature, 12 1/2 In.	549.00
Tankard, Applied Monkeys, Seal Mark, 12 3./4 In.	265.00
Vase, Applied Figure, Red Ground, Kiln Mark, 7 In.	145.00
Vase, Applied Figures, Black Ground, Kiln Mark, 10 In.	250.00

> Sunbonnet Babies were first introduced in 1902 in the "Sunbonnet Babies Primer." The stories were by Eulalie Osgood Grover, illustrated by Bertha Corbett. The children's faces were completely hidden by the sunbonnets. The children had been pictured in black and white before this time, but the color pictures in the book were immediately successful. The Royal Bayreuth China Company made a full line of children's dishes decorated with the Sunbonnet Babies. Some Sunbonnet Babies plates have been reproduced but are clearly marked.

SUNBONNET BABIES, Book, Grover, 1928	45.00
Book, Sunbonnet Babies In Mother Goose Land, 1938	35.00
Bowl, Cereal, Washing & Ironing, 7 In.Underplate	385.00

Bowl, Mending, On Porch, 6 In. 80.00
Candleholder, Hooded, Royal Bayreuth 320.00
Candlestick, Fishing, Pair 325.00
Candlestick, Sewing, Pair 325.00
Candlestick, Sweeping 250.00
Candlestick, Washing, Pair 325.00
Candy Dish, Cleaning, Club Shape, Royal Bayreuth 235.00
Cookie Plate, Royal Bayreuth 245.00
Creamer, Sewing, Bulbous 140.00
Creamer, Sewing, Cylinder Shape 150.00
Creamer, Sweeping 150.00
Cup & Saucer, Mellor Ironstone 35.00
Cup & Saucer, Sewing, Coffee 145.00
Cup & Saucer, Washing, Coffee 145.00
Cup, Saucer, Creamer & Teapot, Sledding, Royal Bayreuth 210.00
Dish, Cleaning, Spade 155.00
Dish, Farming, Heart 155.00
Dish, Feeding 190.00
Dish, Feeding, Sewing, Child 165.00
Dish, Fishing, Spade 155.00
Dish, Sewing, Diamond 155.00
Dish, Sweeping, Spade 155.00
Hair Receiver, Cleaning 325.00
Mug, Sewing, Child's 150.00
Mug, Sweeping, Royal Bayreuth, Blue Mark 95.00
Nappy, Cleaning House 195.00
Nappy, Sewing, Handle 155.00
Pitcher, Cleaning, Blue Mark, 4 X 3 In. 195.00
Pitcher, Milk, Fishing, Turned-In Lip, Blue Mark 175.00
Pitcher, Milk, Washing 235.00
Pitcher, Sweeping, Royal Bayreuth, 4 1/2 In. .... 195.00 To 225.00
Plate, 7 3/4 In. 95.00
Plate, Cleaning, 7 In. 100.00
Plate, Ironing, 5 In. 115.00
Plate, Open Handles, 10 1/2 In. 175.00
Plate, Staffordshire, 8 1/2 In. 65.00
Plate, Three of Us 50.00
Plate, Washing, 7 In. 100.00
Plate, Washing, 8 In. 100.00
Print, 7 Days of The Week, Set of 7 .... 75.00
Relish, Fishing, Open, Handle, 8 In. 175.00
Sugar & Creamer, Cleaning, Boat Shape 300.00
Sugar & Creamer, Ironing, Washing, Pedestal, Marked, 5 In. 385.00
Sugar, Royal Bayreuth, Blue Mark 45.00
Tile, Washing, Royal Bayreuth, Blue Mark 295.00
Toothpick, Cleaning, Basket Shape, 3 Handles, Blue Mark 425.00
Toothpick, Cleaning, Bulbous Base, Narrow Top, Handles 395.00
Wall Pocket, Cleaning, Royal Bayreuth, Blue Mark 495.00

Sunderland luster is a name given to a special type of pink luster made by Leeds, Newcastle, and other English firms during the nineteenth century. The luster glaze is metallic and glossy and appears to have bubbles in it.

SUNDERLAND, Bottle, Bottle 85.00
Jug, Luster, Pink 325.00
Plaque, Black Transfer, Thou God Seest Me, Copper Luster, 8 In. 65.00
Poem, Ship Success To Coal Trade, 1844, 5 5/8 In. 660.00
Teapot 60.00

Superman was created by two seventeen-year-olds in 1938. The first issue of "Action" comics had the strip. Superman remains popular and became the hero of a radio show in 1940, cartoons in the 1940s, a television series, and several major movies.

SUPERMAN, Action Comics, No.61	280.00
Bank, Dime Register	90.00
Belt, Leather, Buckle, 1940	75.00
Book, Action Comics, No. 2	4500.00
Book, Action Comics, No. 3	3400.00
Book, Action Comics, No. 4, First Mention of The Daily Planet	1450.00
Book, Action Comics, No. 6, Introducing Jimmy Olsen	2500.00
Book, Action Comics, No.20, Clark Kent Works At The Daily Star	805.00
Bubble Bath, Figural, Avon, Box	20.00
Button, Kellogg's Pep	15.00
Button, Supermen of America, Pin Back	4.00
Card, Trade, Superman, Carrying Lois, Color, 1949	45.00
Chalkboard, Figural	20.00
Clock, 1970s, Large	20.00
Clock, Alarm	550.00
Cookie Jar, Box	175.00
Cookie Jar, Ceramic	30.00
Curtain Panel, 1978, 2 X 5 Ft.	16.00
Doll, 12 In.	30.00
Figure, With Original Cape, Ideal	800.00
Figurine, Wood, Pressed, 5 3/4 In.	350.00
Game, Card	15.00
Game, Quoit Set, Box	1265.00
Gum Cards, 1 To 48	600.00
Gun, Krypto–Ray, Black, Metal	175.00
Machine Gun, Prototype, Plastic, Tag, Marx	550.00
Night–Light, 1977	35.00
Patch, Superman of America, Premium	200.00
Pen, Ballpoint, 1960s	15.00
Pencil Box	65.00
Puzzle, Jigsaw, Superman Saves The Streamliner, 1940, 12 X 16 In.	65.00
Radio, Telephone Booth, 1978	15.00
Raygun, Krypto, Daisy	85.00
Secret Code, Folder	25.00
Spoon, Stainless, 1966	3.00
Sunday Section Comic, 1/2 Page, 1940s	8.00
Thermos	26.00
Toy, Airplane, Windup, Marx	225.00
Toy, Tank Turn Over	325.00
Tumbler, Pepsi–Cola Series, Glass, 1976	15.00

In 1933, the Kraft Food Company began to market cheese spreads in decorated, reusable glass tumblers. These were called "Swankyswigs." They were discontinued from 1941 to 1946, then made again from 1947 to 1958. Then plain glasses were used for most of the cheese, although a few special decorated Swankyswigs have been made since that time. A complete list of prices can be found in "Kovels' Depression Glass & American Dinnerware Price List."

SWANKYSWIG, Antique, Black	1.25 To 3.00
Band No. 2, Black & Red	2.00 To 4.00
Bustlin' Betsy, Blue	1.25 To 1.75
Centennial, Texas, Blue	25.00
Circle & Dot, Green	2.50 To 3.50
Kiddie Cup, Black	1.25 To 1.50
Kiddie Cup, Red	1.75
Posy Cornflower No. 2, Dark Blue	2.00
Posy Cornflower No. 2, Yellow	2.00
Posy Forget–Me–Not, Blue	2.50 To 3.00
Sailboat No. 1, Blue	8.50 To 12.00
Star, Black	2.50

Tulip No. 3, Yellow .... 2.00 To 3.00

All types of swords are of interest to collectors. The military dress sword with elaborate handle is probably the most wanted. Be sure to display swords in a safe way, out of reach of children.

SWORD, Bayonet, Confederate, Brass Hilt, Cook & Brother, 19 In.Blade	550.00
Bayonet, Springfield Armory, For 69 Caliber Hardin No.10	750.00
Bayonet, William Rose, Philadelphia, 18th Century, 15 In.Blade	550.00
British Infantry, Officer's, Scabbard, Pierced VR, 32 In., Wilkinson	135.00
Cast Brass Hilt, 24 1/2 In.	40.00
Confederate Cavalry Saber, Nashville Plow Works, 35 In.Blade	1850.00
Confederate Officer's	345.00
Dragon Saber, Calvary, Tiffany & Co., Scabbard	450.00
Duelling Rapier, Scrolling Foliage, Toledo, 19th Century, 35 In., Pair	1870.00
Kuba, Iron & Wood, Ribbed Blade, Turned Wood Handle, 27 In.	90.00
Officer's, Metal Scabbard, C.R.Thayer, Co.H 33d Wisconsin Volunteers	300.00
Officer's, Presentation, German, Scabbard, Case, 1880, 30 In.Blade	880.00
Oriental, Repousse Silvered Scabbard, 46 In.	225.00
Saber, Cavalry, Civil War, 1840	225.00
Saber, Cavalry, Civil War, 1860	200.00
Samurai, Katana	465.00
Sergeant's, Scabbard, U.S., 1864, Ames, Brass Mounts	375.00
Stiletto, Gilt Silver, Chased Jeweled Sheath, Grip, Russia, 8 5/8 In.	1100.00
Trowel Bayonet, Scabbard, Marked U.S.Pat.1866, Indian War	125.00
Tsuba, Akasaka Style, Iron, 18th Century, 3 In.	500.00
Tsuba, Butterfly & Grasshopper, Iron, Copper, 18th Century, 3 1/4 In.	1000.00
Tsuba, Heian Style, Iron, Brass, 18th Century, 3 1/4 In.	900.00
Tsuba, Nara School, Brass, Copper, 19th Century, 2 3/4 In.	900.00
Tsuba, Treasure–Bag & Hotei, Copper, Iron, 18th Century, 2 1/4 In.	500.00
U.S.Cavalry, Scabbard, Brass Hilt, Mansfield & Lamb, 1864	375.00
U.S.Infantry, Officer's, 33 In.Scimitar–Like Blade, War of 1812	550.00
U.S.Infantry, Officer's, Scabbard, Ames, Chicopee, Mass, 30 In.Blade	695.00
U.S.Navy, Officer's, Scabbard, Civil War, Ames, Mass.	595.00
U.S.Officer, Presentation, Brass Hilt, Tiffany, 1865, 32 3/4 In.	2300.00
Virginia Manufactory Arms, Scabbard, Curved, 36 In.	1950.00

SYRACUSE China — Syracuse is a trademark used by the Onondaga Pottery of Syracuse, New York. The company was established in 1871. It is still working. The name became the Syracuse China Company in 1966. It is known for fine dinnerware and restaurant china.

SYRACUSE, Creamer, Westvale	9.00
Cup & Saucer, Old Ivory, Demitasse	12.50
Cup & Saucer, Suzanne	21.00
Dinner Service, California Poppy, 50 Piece	200.00
Dinner Service, Indian Tree, 36 Piece	300.00
Plate, Marietta, 6 1/2 In.	8.00
Plate, Marietta, 10 1/4 In.	15.00
Plate, Suzanne, 8 In.	15.00

Tea Caddy, Hepplewhite, Walnut, Ball Feet

Plate, Suzanne, 10 1/2 In.	15.00
Platter, Westvale, Platter, 14 In.	22.00
Sugar, Westvale, Cover	11.00

TANKARD, see Stein

TAPESTRY, PORCELAIN, see Rose Tapestry

A tea caddy is a small box made to hold tea leaves. In the eighteenth century, tea was very expensive and it was stored under lock and key. The first tea caddies were made with locks. By the nineteenth century, tea was more plentiful and the tea caddy was larger. Often there were two sections, one for green tea, one for black tea.

TEA CADDY, Acorn & Oak Leaf Medallions On Lid, Satinwood, 4 3/4 In.	440.00
Beveled Side & Lid, Diamond Shaped Ivory Escutcheon, Mahogany	25.00
Black Painted Edge Scallops, Bird's–Eye Veneer, 10 In.	275.00
Blue Willow, Square, C.1885	40.00
Burl Walnut, Dated 1892	300.00
Cherry, Satinwood Panels, Tiger Maple Corners, C.1815	1250.00
Chippendale, Mahogany, English, 6 1/2 X 9 1/2 X 5 1/4 In.	220.00
Floral Stencil, Ivory Escutcheon, Brass Handles, 7 X 12 In.	440.00
Flower, Apple Shape, Japanese	45.00
Fruitwood, Yellow, Hinged, Apple Shape, 19th Century, 5 3/4 In.	3080.00
George II, Inlaid Satinwood, Later Stand, C.1800, 24 X 14 In.	605.00
George II, Walnut, Brass, Bombe Case, 18th Century, 5 1/2 In.	880.00
Hepplewhite, Stringing & Cross Banding, Mahogany, 10 In.	145.00
Hepplewhite, Walnut, Ball Feet *Illus*	145.00
Line Edge Inlay, Diamond Escutcheon, Mahogany, 4 7/8 In.	25.00
Mahogany, George III, Brass Handle, 5 X 9 In.	250.00
Mahogany, Rectangular, Brass Handle, 6 3/8 In.	150.00
Painted Flowers & Leaves, Cover, Oval, Tin, 5 1/4 In.	30.00
Pear Shape, Wooden, Painted, Late–19th Century, Germany	1090.00
Pink To Yellow, Gold Trim On Collar & Lid, Signed LE, 4 3/4 In.	75.00
Regency, English, Pewter Lined, Mahogany, 6 In., Pair	660.00
Rosewood, Inlaid Pearl Escutcheon, Silver Tea Scoop, 8 In.	160.00
Screw–Off Cap, Pear Shape, Treen, 5 1/8 In.	350.00
Shell Inlaid, English Style, Dated 1862	175.00
Silver, Beaded Rims, Ribbonwork, Dutch, Nieuwenhuys, 4 1/8 In.	2400.00
Silver, Engraved Garlands of Flowers, Durgin Mark, 5 In.	165.00
Silver, George III, Bright Cut, Hinged Cover, W.Vincent, 6 In.	1650.00
Silver, Grapevine Finial, Egg Shape, Footed, 4 5/8 X 6 1/8 In.	250.00
Tole, Dark Brown Japanned, Floral, 5 1/4 In.	25.00
Tortoiseshell Front, Divided, 2 Lids, Ivory Handles, 7 1/2 In.	550.00
Tortoiseshell, Rectangular, Pewter Lined, C.1800, 4 1/2 In.	440.00

There was a superstition that it was lucky if a whole tea leaf unfolded at the bottom of your cup. This idea was translated into the pattern of dishes known as "tea leaf." By 1850, at least twelve English factories were making this pattern; and by the 1870s, it was a popular pattern in many countries. The tea leaf was always a luster glaze on early wares, although now some pieces are made with a brown tea leaf.

TEA LEAF IRONSTONE, Baker, Pepper Leaf, Oval	80.00
Baker, Wilkinson	25.00
Bone Dish, Leaf Shape, Grindley	17.50
Bone Dish, Meakin	42.50
Bowl, Apple, Ruffled, Shaw	60.00
Bowl, Vegetable, Cover, Bamboo, Meakin	40.00
Bowl, Vegetable, Cover, Fish Hook, Meakin	65.00
Bowl, Vegetable, Cover, Lily–of–The–Valley, Shaw	65.00
Bowl, Vegetable, Scalloped, Square, Meakin	17.50
Bowl, Wash, 14 3/4 In.	145.00
Butter Chip, Meakin	12.00
Butter Chip, Meakin, 4 Piece	42.50
Butter Chip, Wilkin	40.00

Butter, Cover, Bamboo, Meakin	45.00
Butter, Cover, Drain, Square, Wedgwood	120.00
Cake Plate, Cloverleaf	7.50
Cake Plate, Fish Hook, Meakin	32.50
Chamber Pot, Meakin	188.00
Coffeepot, Fish Hook, Meakin	75.00 To 120.00
Coffeepot, Lily-of-The-Valley	50.00
Coffeepot, Wedgwood	20.00
Creamer, Bamboo, Grindley	45.00
Creamer, Basket Weave, Shaw	72.50
Creamer, Fish Hook, Meakin	27.50
Creamer, Gothic Shape	75.00
Creamer, Mellor Taylor	27.50
Cup & Saucer, Barrel Shape, Wedgwood	55.00
Cup & Saucer, Burslem, Anthony Shaw, C.1850	90.00
Cup & Saucer, Cable, Shaw	80.00
Cup & Saucer, Corn, W & E	55.00
Cup & Saucer, Davenport, Variant	45.00
Cup & Saucer, Handleless, Chinese Shape	80.00
Cup & Saucer, Handleless, Lily-of-The-Valley	75.00
Cup & Saucer, Handleless, Walley, C.1850	95.00
Cup & Saucer, Meakin	47.50
Cup & Saucer, Niagara Shape, Walley	40.00 To 60.00
Cup & Saucer, Pepper Leaf Variant, Elsmore & Forster	35.00
Cup Plate, 3 1/2 In.	45.00
Eggcup	35.00
Ewer, Large	200.00
Gravy Boat, Meakin	35.00
Gravy Boat, Wedgwood	35.00
Jug, Milk, Blanket Stitch, Alcock, 8 3/8 In.	100.00
Jug, Milk, Dolphin, Edwards, 8 1/8 In.	150.00
Jug, Pinwheel	147.50
Mug, Child's, Copper	165.00
Mug, Shaving, Cloverleaf, K T & K	32.50
Mug, Shaving, Lily-of-The-Valley, Shaw	52.50
Nappy, Chinese Shape, Shaw	18.00
Nappy, Hanging Leaves, Shaw	12.00
Nappy, Meakin, Square, Meakin	16.00
Pitcher & Bowl, Wedgwood	155.00
Pitcher, Bowl & Chamber Pot	250.00
Pitcher, H.Burgess, 13 In.	215.00 To 225.00
Pitcher, Meakin, 6 In.	80.00
Pitcher, Square Bottom, Meakin, 5 1/2 In.	34.50
Pitcher, Water, Burgess	25.00
Plate, 7 1/2 In.	10.00
Plate, 8 3/4 In.	15.00
Plate, Luncheon, Niagara Shape, Walley, 4 Piece	50.00
Plate, Teaberry, Clementson	5.00
Platter, Meakin, 10 X 14 In.	30.00
Relish, Fish Hook, Meakin, Rectangular	25.00
Relish, Powell Bishop	25.00
Relish, Reticulated Handle, Oval, Wilkinson	50.00
Sauce, Fish Hook, Meakin	95.00
Saucer	12.00
Shaving Mug, Meakin	75.00
Soap Dish, Cover, Drainer, Combo Type Finial	95.00
Soup, Dish, Fan, Shaw, C.1858, 9 1/2 In.	27.00
Soup, Dish, Luster Bands, Davenport, C.1871, 10 In.	18.00
Soup, Dish, Shaw, 8 3/4 In.	10.00 To 15.00
Soup, Teaberry, Clementson, 4 Piece	70.00
Sugar Bowl	50.00
Sugar, Bamboo, Meakin, Small	55.00
Sugar, Cover, Meakin	45.00
Sugar, Cover, Meller Taylor	20.00

Teco, Vase, Leaves, Green, Ribbed,
  Flared Rim, 11 1/2 In.

Sugar, Daisy, Shaw	7.50
Sugar, Fish Hook, Meakin, Large	55.00
Sugar, Teaberry, Clementson	20.00
Sugar, Wedgwood	12.50
Teapot, Bamboo, Grindley	45.00
Teapot, Mellor Taylor	70.00
Teapot, Morning Glory	80.00
Toothbrush Holder, Shaw	150.00
Tureen, Cover	130.00
Tureen, Sauce, Lion Head, Mellor Taylor	295.00
Tureen, Soup, Powell Bishop	65.00 To 95.00
Tureen, Vegetable, Cover, Wedgwood, Rectangular	80.00
Vase, Low, K T & K	25.00
Waste Bowl, Chinese Shape, Shaw	60.00
Waste Bowl, Pepper Leaf Variant, Elsmore & Forster	70.00

Teco is the mark used on the art pottery line made by the American
Terra Cotta and Ceramic Company of Terra Cotta and Chicago,
Illinois. The company was an offshoot of the firm founded by
William D. Gates in 1881. The Teco line was first made in 1885 but
was not sold commercially until 1902. It continued in production
until 1922. Over 500 designs were made in a variety of colors,
shapes, and glazes. The company closed in 1930.

TECO, Ashtray, Organic Design, Octagonal	800.00
Bowl, Berries & Leaves, Sticker, 9 In.	395.00
Bowl, Bulb, Green, 2 X 9 In.	175.00
Pitcher, Cylindrical, Curving Handle, Impressed Mark, 9 In.	150.00
Vase, 4 Arms At Top, 10 In.	2090.00
Vase, 6 Points, Elongated, Fluted, 10 In.	475.00
Vase, 6 Points, Pinched Rim, Lobes, Bulbous Base, Marked, 10 1/2 In.	475.00
Vase, Brown Matte Glaze, 4 Angled Handles, Elongated Neck, 7 1/4 In.	650.00
Vase, Bud, 4 Buttress Handles To Base, Cylindrical, 1910, 7 In.	400.00
Vase, Bud, Yellow, Onion Shape, Impressed Mark, 4 1/2 X 5 1/2 In.	375.00
Vase, Buff Color, Handle, Marked, 9 In.	575.00
Vase, Cooling Tower, Double Stamp, 13 In.	495.00
Vase, Cylindrical Neck, 3 Section Splayed Feet Base, 1910, 15 3/4 In.	400.00
Vase, Double Mark, 5 1/4 In.	135.00
Vase, Gourd Shape, Double Stamp, 4 1/2 In.	295.00
Vase, Gourd Shape, Double Stamp, 7 In.	495.00
Vase, Green Glaze, Angled Shoulder, 2 Angular Handles, C.1910, 7 In.	350.00
Vase, Leaves, Green, Ribbed, Flared Rim, 11 1/2 In. ....*Illus*	7000.00
Vase, Sea Green Glaze, Squat, 5 In.	325.00

Vase, Wall, Artichoke Design, 16 In.	950.00
Wall Pocket, Arts & Craft Design, Square Top, Circular Bottom	485.00
Wall Pocket, Indian Peace Sign	495.00
Wall Pocket, Medallion In Relief, 6 1/2 X 6 1/2 In.	595.00

 The first teddy bear was a cuddly toy said to be inspired by a hunting trip made by Teddy Roosevelt in 1902. Morris and Rose Michtom started selling their stuffed bears as "Teddy bears" and the name stayed. The Michtoms founded the Ideal Novelty and Toy Company. The German version of the teddy bear was made about the same time by the Steiff Company. There are many types of teddy bears, all collected, and the old ones are being reproduced.

TEDDY BEAR, Amber, Red & Green Plush, Christmas, Straw Filled, 1920, 14 In.	225.00
Amber, Snout Nose, Embroidered, Hump, Straw Filled, C.1915, 19 In.	300.00
Bat Ears, Yellow Gold Long Mohair, Jointed, Tail, 1940s	175.00
Black Silk Plush, Growler, Germany, 1940s	285.00
Blond, Mohair, Jointed, Shoebutton Eyes, 17 In.	275.00
Brown, Jointed, Tan Snout, Pads, Excelsior Stuffed, 1940s, 15 In.	175.00
Buster, Straw Stuffed, Metal Wheels, Rubber Tires, 1930s, 15 In.	245.00
Cinnamon Mohair, Shoebutton Eyes, Swiss, C.1915, 17 In.	575.00
Columbia, Glass Eyes, Orange, Mohair, Milk Glass Teeth, 17 In.	475.00
Dean, Brown, With Growler, 24 In.	75.00
Electric, Tree Stump, Turtleneck Sweater, Turns Circles, 27 In.	295.00
Farnell Alpha, White Mohair, Blue Pads, Foot Tag, 1940s, 12 In.	125.00
Fiddle Faddle	17.00
Gold Mohair, Jointed, Black Paws & Ears, C.1915, 24 In.	450.00
Gold Mohair, Straw Filled, Glass Eyes, Jointed, 1920s, 20 In.	350.00
Gold Plush, Fully Jointed, Glass Eyes, England, 12 In.	135.00
Gold To Gray Mohair, Hump, Pointed Nose, Black Emblem, 12 In.	395.00
Gold, Button & Tag, Glass Eyes, Brown Lederhosen, 1934, 16 In.	950.00
Herman Co., Jointed, 1930s, 11 In.	250.00
Hermann, Cinnamon, 1950s, 17 In.	285.00
Hermann, Light Beige, Growler, 1950s, 12 In.	185.00
Hermann, Long Red Mohair, 1950s, 9 In.	150.00
Hump Back, Mohair, Straw Stuffed, Glass Eyes, 29 In.	395.00
Humped Back, Mohair, 29 In.	350.00
Ideal, Short Mohair, Silver Sheen, Red Nose, Hard Stuffed, 24 In.	595.00
Jointed Limbs, Stitched Features, Glass Eyes, 12 In.	225.00
Jointed, Leather Pads, Tan, 15 1/2 In.	195.00
Jointed, Straw Stuffed, Exaggerated Hump, 18 In.	450.00
Jointed, Straw Stuffed, Growler, 17 In.	325.00
Jointed, Straw Stuffed, Growler, 27 In.	395.00
Mohair, Straw Stuffed, Glass Eyes, Jointed, 10 1/2 In.	148.00
Mohair, Straw Stuffed, Shoebutton Eye, Hump, 1920, 17 In.	275.00
Muff, Steiff	325.00
Nested, Goldielocks, Wooden, 5 Piece	45.00
Pale Brown, Button Eyes, Jointed, Black Ears, Paws, 1900, 10 In.	192.00
Schlummi, Steiff, 22 In.	200.00
Schuco, Fully Jointed, 2 1/2 In.	110.00
Schuco, Yes–No, 5 In.	550.00
Steiff, 3 In.	57.00
Steiff, Amber, Ear Button, Paper Tag, 3 1/2 In.	130.00
Steiff, Brown Mohair, Jointed, Chest Tag, Tea Party Set, 6 In.	85.00
Steiff, Caramel, U.S.Zone, 8 In.	345.00
Steiff, Cosy, Caramel, 7 1/2 In.	97.00
Steiff, Dark Brown, Fully Jointed, 1920s, 25 In.	345.00
Steiff, Gold Mohair, Brown Glass Eyes, Button, 20 In.	2400.00
Steiff, Gold Mohair, Shoebutton Eyes, Button, C.1915, 18 In.	2100.00
Steiff, Gold, Brown Lederhosen, Button & Tag, C.1934, 16 1/2 In.	950.00
Steiff, Gold, Jointed, 17 In.	225.00
Steiff, Golden Hair, Jointed, Glass Eyes, Open Mouth, 14 In.	90.00
Steiff, Hump, Growler, Long Arms, 1920, 20 In.	650.00
Steiff, Long Arms, Pointed Nose, Button, 13 In.	450.00
Steiff, Mr.Cinnaman, 13 In.	200.00

Steiff, Tan, Jointed, 3 In.	145.00
Steiff, Twins, Yellow Mohair, Silent Squeaker, 1950's, 13 In., Pr.	900.00
Steiff, White Mohair, Brown Glass Eyes, C.1910, 10 In.	1100.00
Swivel Head, Googly Eyes, Movable Tongue, 18 In. ....*Illus*	3000.00
Yellow Fur, Leather Soles On Feet, Plastic Eyes, C.1925	160.00
Yellow Plush Fur, Movable Limbs, Felt Pads, Voice Box, 20 In.	95.00

The first telephone may have been made in Havana, Cuba, in 1849, but it was not patented. The first publicly demonstrated phone was used in Frankfurt, Germany, in 1860. The phone made by Alexander Graham Bell was shown at the Centennial Exhibition in Philadelphia in 1876, but it was not until 1877 that the first private phones were installed. Collectors today want all types of old phones, phone parts, and advertising.

TELEPHONE, Ashtray, Mountain States Telephone & Telegraph Co.	50.00
Automatic Electric, 1950s	75.00
Badge, Southern California Telephone Co., Bell Shape, Enamel	35.00
Booth, Fan, Light, Maple, 1950s	850.00
Booth, Oak	650.00
Candlestick, AT & T, 1892	85.00
Candlestick, Brass	125.00
Candlestick, Dial, Black	78.00
Candlestick, French, 1914 ....225.00 To	250.00
Candlestick, Nickel Plated	70.00
Candlestick, Pay, Dial, Black, 3 Slot, Half Wood	109.00
Candlestick, Ringer Box	115.00
Candlestick, Strombert, Oak Ringer Box	100.00
Candlestick, Western Electric, Pat.1904	125.00
Carlson–Stromberg, Short Box	145.00
Century, Tapered Shape	375.00
Desk, Cradle, Dovetailed Oak	65.00
French Horn, Danish, 1913	55.00
Kellogg, Wall, Wood	260.00
Mickey Mouse, Push Button, AT & T, Box	75.00
Mirror, Pocket, AT & T, Nebraska Telephone Co.	30.00
Oak, 6 X 8 1/2 X 10 In.	95.00
Paperweight, Advertising, New York Telephone Co., Belsey, Blue	90.00
Paperweight, Bell System, New York Telephone	85.00
Paperweight, C & T Bell System, Blue Glass	100.00
Pay, 3–Slot, Half Wood	109.00
Pay, 5 Cent, 10 Cent & 25 Cent	135.00
Pay, Hotel, 1898	650.00

If the teddy bear needs washing, do it very carefully. First vacuum the fur, then mix water and liquid detergent, and brush the detergent through the fur. Dry with a towel, then a hair dryer on low. Let dry completely and comb with a dog comb.

Teddy Bear, Swivel Head, Googly Eyes, Movable Tongue, 18 In.

Scissor, Western Electric	75.00
Sign, General Telephone System, Porcelain, 12 X 12 In.	135.00
Sign, Public Telephone Bell System, Porcelain, 2 Sides, 18 In.	95.00
Sign, Public Telephone, Porcelain, 8 In.Diam.	40.00
Spoon, Souvenir, Telephone Girl, Tri–State, Silver Plate	50.00
Wall, Oak, Swedish–Made, 35 In.	250.00
Wall, R.C.A.American Electric Co.	265.00

 Teplitz refers to art pottery manufactured by a number of companies in the Teplitz–Turn area of Bohemia during the late nineteenth and early twentieth centuries. The Amphora Porcelain Works and the Alexandra Works were two of these companies.

TEPLITZ, Basket, Enameled Flowers, Cobalt Blue Rim, Amphora, 3 3/4 X 4 In.	50.00
Bowl, Girl Pulling Rooster's Tail, 5 1/2 In.	65.00
Bowl, Pink Florals, Beige, Brown Ground, Gold, Jeweling, 6 X 8 In.	195.00
Bowl, Portrait, Cover, 4 1/2 In.	75.00
Box, Turtle Shape, 2 Children On Back Cover, Marked, 5 1/2 X 9 In.	365.00
Bust, Young Girl, Art Nouveau, 17 In.	950.00
Candlestick, Camel, Amphora, 6 X 4 In.	45.00
Candlestick, Yellow, Amphora, 12 In.	85.00
Ewer, Floral Design, Raised Beading, Ivory Ground, Amphora, 9 In.	225.00
Ewer, Purple Poppies, Gold On Cream Ground, Marked, 9 In.	90.00
Ewer, Trees, Fish Form, Gold Handle, Mottled Green, Amphora	165.00
Fernery, White Basket Weave, Gold Trim, Gold Cupid, Amphora	225.00
Figurine, Maiden Flowers In Her Hair, Marked, 15 In.	425.00
Jar, 3 Elephants, Trunks Down, Cover, Amphora, 9 In.	880.00
Pitcher, Hound Handle, Signed	135.00
Pitcher, Portrait, Arab On Horseback	60.00
Vase, 2 Enameled Scenes, Amphora, Crown Mark, 16 1/2 In.	250.00
Vase, 4 Spouts, Stylized Enameled Flowers, Double Handle, 13 In.	295.00
Vase, Art Nouveau, Flowers & Birds, Amphora, 4 X 5 1/2 In.	75.00
Vase, Black, Gold Flowers, Green & Blue, Applied Cupids, 15 In.	295.00
Vase, Blown–Out Multicolor, Amphora, 10 1/2 In.	80.00
Vase, Blue Poppy, Amphora, 4 Handles, 7 1/2 In., Pair	150.00
Vase, Blue, Snake Coiled Around, Leaves, Art Deco, Bulbous, 7 1/2 In.	295.00
Vase, Children Playing Grown–Up, Handles, 6 In.	95.00
Vase, Cobweb Design, Painted Flowers, Amphora, 13 In.	350.00
Vase, Crimped Sides, Flowers, Berries & Leaves, Amphora, 7 1/4 In.	155.00
Vase, Cupid, Center, Double Handles, Green, Lavender Ground, 16 In.	375.00
Vase, Double, Blue Matte Ground, Portrait Medallion, 7 In.	35.00
Vase, Egyptian Design, Blue, 3 In.	75.00
Vase, Enameled Floral, 7 In.	125.00
Vase, Enameled Tree Design, Gilt Sunburst, Insects, 10 In., Pair	700.00
Vase, Female Face Molded In Relief, Turquoise, 12 In.	295.00
Vase, Figural, Pierced, Tree Trunks, Pheasant, Amphora, 16 1/2 In.	950.00
Vase, Flowers Outlined In Gold, Marked, 7 1/4 In.	110.00
Vase, Flowers, Leaves, Bird On Branch, 4 Handles, Amphora, 8 1/2 In.	145.00
Vase, Gold Enameled Flowers, Double Handles, 15 1/2 In.	325.00
Vase, Gold Grapes, Purple & White, Amphora, 9 X 7 In.	225.00
Vase, Pierced Work, Roman Gold Trim, 11 3/8 In.	175.00
Vase, Poppies, Gold Outlining & Trim, Marked, 17 1/4 In., Pair	475.00
Vase, Portrait, Woman, Exotic Headdress, Amphora, 10 1/2 In.	400.00
Vase, Squirrel In Bushes, Reds, Greens, Golds, Amphora, 8 In.	375.00
Vase, Swirl, Twisted Lobes, Green Dandelion Puffs, Blue, 6 1/8 In.	50.00
Vase, Urn Type, 2 Handles, Gold, Brown Leaves, Amphora, 8 In.	65.00

Terra–cotta is a special type of pottery. It ranges from pale orange to dark reddish–brown in color. The color comes from the clay, which is fired but not always glazed in the finished piece.

TERRA–COTTA, Bust, Abraham Lincoln, From Life, 1860	1200.00
Bust, Empress Josephine, Jos.Chinard, Dated 1805–06, 11 1/4 In.	3300.00
Bust, Lady, With Primroses, Gilt Dress, Verrocchio, 22 3/4 In.	715.00

Bust, Nobleman, Marbelized Circular Base, 27 1/2 In	4125.00
Figure, Angel, Creche, Gilt, Painted, Neopolitan, 15 1/2 In., Pair	4950.00
Figure, Devil, Over Rock, 18th Century, 9 5/8 In.	880.00
Figure, Woman, Crouching, Giambologna, 10 1/8 In.	445.00
Head, St.Denis, Gilt Mitre In Hand, 18th Century, 21 1/2 In.	3025.00
Pitcher, Hound, Game In Relief	60.00
Plaque, 2 Cupids Fight Over A Fallen Heart, 18 In.	550.00
Plaque, Castle Scene, Border, 24 In.Diam., Pair	248.00
Plaque, Postman, At Table, With Ladies, Jon Maresch, 19 In.Diam.	176.00
Tankard, Dragon Around Base, Claw Forms Handle, C.1860, 11 In.	275.00

Textile includes many types of printed textiles, table and household linens, and clothing. Some other textiles will be found under Clothing, Coverlet, Rug, Quilt, etc.

TEXTILE, Antimacassar Set, White Cupid Design, 3 Piece	95.00
Bedspread, Art Deco, Pansies, Basket, Muslin, Fringed, 80 X 92 In.	30.00
Bedspread, Battenberg–Type Lace, 95 X 95 In.	460.00
Bedspread, Candlewick Pot of Flowers, Tied Fringe, 80 X 92 In.	135.00
Bedspread, Cream Fillet Flowers, Squares, 68 X 104 In.	90.00
Bedspread, Crocheted, Homespun Flax, Braden, 1833, 86 X 76 In.	165.00
Bedspread, Crocheted, Popcorn & Diamond, 95 X 108 In.	210.00
Bedspread, Crocheted, Popcorn & Diamond, 95 X 99 In.	150.00
Bedspread, Crocheted, Popcorn Stitch, 80 X 90 In.	160.00
Bedspread, Crocheted, Popcorn Stitch, Ecru, 100 X 78 In.	250.00
Bedspread, Crocheted, Sunflower Design, 100 X 90 In.	140.00
Bedspread, Embroidered Doves, Flowers, Fringe, Silk, 74 X 86 In.	225.00
Bedspread, Embroidered, Linen, Lace Insertions, Shams, 92 X 96 In.	245.00
Bedspread, Embroidered, Owl & Pussycat Center, Double Size	55.00
Bedspread, French Lace, Twin, Pair	175.00
Bedspread, Machine Woven, Popcorn Design, Chenille, 80 X 104 In.	125.00
Bedspread, Marseilles Geometric Pattern, Border, 80 X 90 In.	25.00
Blanket, Homespun, Blue & White Plaid, Linen, Wool, 7 X 6 Ft.	330.00
Blanket, Homespun, Blue Star & Pine Trees, Wool, 70 X 108 In.	75.00
Blanket, Homespun, Mustard, Tomato, Red & Black Wool, 70 X 82 In.	265.00
Blanket, Mexican, Serape Style, 60 X 92 In.	75.00
Blanket, Mexican, Turquoise, Gray & Natural, 63 X 98 In.	90.00
Blanket, Pendleton, Double Weave, Gold, Red, Green, Brown, 60 X 80 In.	75.00
Blanket, U.S.Cavalry, Gray–Blue Wool, Santiago, 1898, 64 X 84 In.	1250.00
Blanket, Wool, Natural, Red, 62 X 77 In.	115.00
Canvas, Painted Target Clown, Carnival, Wooden Base, 1900, Pair	85.00
Chair Pad, Child's, Hooked, Dog, Seated, With Box, 12 X 12 1/2 In.	165.00
Chair Pad, Hooked, Rose Center, Brown & Tan, 18 1/2 In.	45.00
Chairback Set, Crocheted, Pineapple Design, 3 Piece	15.00
Comforter, Patchwork, Log Cabin Pattern, Knotted Yarn, 72 X 84 In.	115.00
Commode Splash Cloth, With Hunter, Turkey Red, 29 X 19 In.	20.00
Cover, Piano Bench, Hunting Dog Scene, Fringed, Blue, 21 X 40 In.	23.00
Curtains, Cotton, Stylized Flower, Corded, C.1900, 51 X 90 In., Pair	100.00
Doilie, Battenburg, 10 In.Diam.	6.00
Doilie, Tatted, 22 In.Diam.	22.50
Doilie, Tatted, 32 In.Diam.	27.50
Flag, American, 46 Stars, 5 X 8 Ft.	80.00
Flag, American, 48 Stars, 5 X 8 In.	29.00
Flag, American, 48 Stars, 5 X 10 In.	15.00
Flag, N.Vietnam, 3 X 5 Ft.	20.00
Hammock, Child's, White & Beige Design, Wood Frame, Iron Fittings	65.00
Handkerchief, Embroiderd, Linen, Swiss	25.00
Hanging, Chinese, Embroidered Silk, Court Figures, 7 X 3 Ft.	125.00
Mat, Pictorial, Spot Designs, Grenfell, Newfoundland, 20 X 26 In.	2400.00
Mattress Cover, Homespun, Red Embroided Initials, 66 X 78 In.	25.00
Mattress Cover, Tape Ties, Initials, C.A.R.G., 126 X 76 In.	105.00
Napkin, Damask, Figural Border, Dogs, Women, 27 In., 12 Piece	30.00
Panel, Aubusson, Rose Bouquet, 11 Ft.9 In.X 5 Ft.8 In.	2750.00
Panel, Bands of Hexagons, Shahsavan Mafrash, 1 Ft.10 In. X 3 Ft.	350.00
Panel, Cupid & Floral Design, 8 In.	95.00

Fresh air and limited sunlight are good for fabrics. Cotton and linen should be washed once a year, even if stored in a drawer, because dirt will cause damage. Dry clean wool and silk if cleaning is needed. Protect fabrics from moths with the usual precautions. Paradichlorobenzene will do the job.

Panel, Embroidered Design, Apricot Ground, Silk, 12 X 13 1/2 In.	40.00
Panel, Embroidered Lakeside Scene, Silk, Japanese, 33 X 57 1/4 In.	95.00
Panel, Hooked, Horse & Buggy Scene, Iowa, C.1900, 16 X 18 In.	192.00
Panel, Silk Embroidered Vines, Center King & Queen, 5 1/2 X 7 In.	450.00
Pillow Sham, Beige Linen, Cutwork, Satin Ruffle, Pair	65.00
Pillow Sham, Cutwork, Beige Linen, Over Blue Satin, 23 In., Pair	72.00
Pillow Sham, Embroidered, C.1915	60.00
Pillow Sham, Floral & Bow, Lace Inserts, French, Pair	395.00
Pillow Sham, Patchwork & Embroidered, 27 X 27 In., Pair	335.00
Pillow Sham, Patriotic, World War II	7.00
Pillow, Beadwork, Floral, Green Velvet, Victorian, 15 X 15 In., Pair	990.00
Robe, Buggy, Dog Picture	65.00
Runner, Embroidered Panels, Florals, Anatolian, 39 X 17 In.	300.00
Scarf, Battenburg Lace, 54 X 18 In.	85.00
Sheet, Homespun Wool, 67 X 78 In.	45.00
Sheet, Homespun, Pennsylvania, 76 X 100 In.	40.00
Sheet, Homespun, Red Embroidered Initials, 38 X 90 In.	45.00
Sheet, Linen, Hand Hemmed, 74 X 76 In.	45.00
Tablecloth, Anatolian, Embroidered, Khaki, Olive Green, 18 X 25 In.	95.00
Tablecloth, Baskets & Daisies, Scalloped Edge, Square, 35 In.	42.00
Tablecloth, Baskets, Flowers, Cutwork, 6 Napkins, Round, 52 In.	58.00
Tablecloth, Battenburg Lace, 42 X 42 In.	95.00
Tablecloth, Battenburg Lace, 6 X 8 Ft.	225.00
Tablecloth, Battenburg, Grapes & Leaves, Round, 72 In.	195.00
Tablecloth, Battenburg, Linen Center, Grapes, Vines, Round, 70 In.	195.00
Tablecloth, Border of Daisies, Leaves, 10 Napkins, Round, 70 In.	85.00
Tablecloth, Crewel, Stylized Trees, Natives, 66 X 96 In.	350.00
Tablecloth, Crocheted, Ecru, 60 X 80 In.	60.00
Tablecloth, Crocheted, Pinwheel & Spider Web, 45 X 82 In.	65.00
Tablecloth, Crocheted, Rose Fillet, Dancing Figures, 45 X 58 In.	65.00
Tablecloth, Crocheted, Round Medallion, 80 X 66 In.	325.00
Tablecloth, Crocheted, Spider Web Pattern, 64 X 80 In.	150.00
Tablecloth, Cross-Stitch, Linen, 56 X 74 In.	75.00
Tablecloth, Cutwork & Lace, Ecru Linen, 12 Napkins, 62 X 130 In.	200.00
Tablecloth, Cutwork, 4 Napkins, 96 X 64 In.	60.00
Tablecloth, Cutwork, Embroidered, Center & Edge Design, 60 X 94 In.	75.00
Tablecloth, Cutwork, Fillet Lace, 12 Napkins, 76 X 116 In.	310.00
Tablecloth, Drawn Work, 54 X 56 In.	85.00
Tablecloth, Drawn Work, 76 X 92 In.	175.00
Tablecloth, Embroidered & Crocheted, Blue Linen, 49 X 66 In.	10.00
Tablecloth, Embroidered, Floral Squares, White Lace, 100 X 68 In.	75.00
Tablecloth, Embroidered, Lace Inserts, 8 Napkins, 70 X 108 In.	270.00
Tablecloth, Embroidered, Madeira, 12 Napkins, 68 X 100 In.	225.00
Tablecloth, Embroidered, Scalloped, Green On White, 58 X 84 In.	45.00
Tablecloth, Eyelet Embroidery, French Knots, Square, 52 In.	56.00
Tablecloth, Homespun Linen, Stylized Floral Tree, 58 X 74 In.	45.00
Tablecloth, Irish Linen, Hand Crocheted Inserts, 60 X 102 In.	110.00
Tablecloth, Lace, Italian Point De Venize, 108 X 64 In.	250.00
Tablecloth, Linen, Beige, Cross-Stitching, Full Size	22.50
Tablecloth, Linen, Chinese Cutwork, 12 Napkins, 64 X 96 In.	230.00
Tablecloth, Linen, Embroidered Corners, 12 Napkins, 124 X 38 In.	85.00
Tablecloth, Linen, Embroidered Yellow Chrysanthemums, 1915, 36 In.	75.00

Tablecloth, Linen, Peach, Patterned Border, 8 Napkins, 70 X 90 In. 38.50
Tablecloth, Madeira, Embroidered, 4 Napkins, Square, 44 In. 50.00
Tablecloth, Overshot, Brown & White, 40 X 60 In. 100.00
Tablecloth, Paisley, 19th Century, 71 X 71 In. 125.00
Tablecloth, Paisley, Multicolored, 132 X 63 In. 140.00
Tablecloth, Quaker, White Lace, 48 X 74 In. 75.00
Tablecloth, Satin, Embroidered Flowers, Cord Edge, 80 X 68 In. 440.00
Tablecloth, Spirit of St.Louis Plane In Center, 17 X 25 In. 62.00
Tablecloth, Suede, Egyptian Rev.Scarab Design, 1904, 54 X 17 In. 275.00
Tablecloth, White Damask, Irish Linen, 6 Napkins, 55 X 70 In. 65.00
Tablecloth, White Embroidery, Drawn Work, Square, 144 In. 185.00
Tablecloth, White Lace, Figures, 19th Century, 87 X 58 In. 1980.00
Tapestry, Cephalus & Procris, In Woods, 18th Century, 8 X 10 Ft. 4400.00
Tapestry, Deer Scene, 50 X 24 In. 65.00
Tapestry, Floral, Embroidered, Lavender Silk, C.1880, 84 X 70 In. 1870.00
Tapestry, Lawn Party, Victorian Gowns, Belgium, 19 X 39 In. 75.00
Tapestry, Park Landscape, Aubusson Verdure, 8 Ft.5 In.X7 Ft.8 In. 5225.00
Tapestry, Tavern Scene, Grays & Beige, French, 18 X 52 In. 40.00
Tapestry, Young Woman, Attendants, Courtyard, Aubusson, 54 X 79 In. 1400.00
Towel, Homespun, Embroidered Initials A.N.& N.J., 18 X 42 In. 35.00
Towel, Homespun, Red Embroidered Initials, 20 X 19 In. 40.00
Towel, Linen Homespun, Tied Fringe One End, 18 1/2 X 25 In. 45.00
Towel, Tea, Linen, Children In Watermelon Patch, 28 X 15 In. 30.00

The thermometer was invented in 1731. It measures temperature of either water or air. All kinds of thermometers are collected, but those with advertising messages are the most popular.

THERMOMETER SET, Westinghouse, Betty Furness, Box, Unused 10.00
THERMOMETER, 7–Up, 27 In. 35.00
Abalone, Gold Filled Pen–Like Case 95.00
Atwater Kent, Wooden, 14 In. 50.00
Barometer, Wall, Carved Walnut, 36 In. 132.00
Bavarian Cabin, Man & Woman Come Out, Wooden, 5 1/2 In. 15.00
Belfast Root Beer 27.00
Bireley's Soda Pop, Pictures, Bottle 49.00
Camel Cigarettes, Raised Pack, Extended Cigarette, 13 1/2 In. 40.00
Camel Cigarettes, Tin, 13 In. 22.00
Candy, Copper 65.00
Chesterfield Cigarettes 35.00
Dad's Root Beer, Metal 35.00
Dad's Root Beer, Tin, 24 In. .... 30.00 To 35.00
Dr Pepper, Drink Dr Pepper Good For Life, Clock At Top, 1940 .... 68.00
Ex–Lax, 3 Ft. 95.00
Ex–Lax, Porcelain, C.1920, 8 X 36 In. 120.00
Farmers Union Oil Co., Key Shape, Plastic, 9 In. 8.00
Goodyear, Flying Foot Emblem, Goodyear Flag, 10 In.Diam. 40.00
Hills Brothers Coffee, Porcelain .... 185.00 To 275.00
J.H.Tiemeyer Carpet Co., Wooden 42.50
Jewelry & Watch Repair, Porcelain, Yellow & Black 195.00
John Deere 11.00
Kenmore Clothes Washing, Tin, Paddle Shape 35.00
Kenmore Scientific Washing, Tin, Paddle Shape 20.00
La–Fendrich, Cigar Around Glass Tube, 9 1/2 X 25 1/2 In. 55.00
Lee Batteries, Tin, Car Battery Picture .... 40.00 To 45.00
Mahn Funeral Home, DeSota, Missouri, Tin 17.00
Mail Pouch Tobacco, Porcelain 250.00
Maple Syrup, Copper 45.00
Mason's Root Beer, Tin 7.00
McLaughlin Undertaker, Wooden 42.50
Morton Salt, Tin 35.00
Nature's Remedy, Porcelain .... 125.00 To 150.00
Nesbitt Orange, Enameled On Metal, 1938, 27 X 7 In. 85.00
Nesbitt, Picture of Bottle, 20 X 5 In. 45.00
None–Such New England Mincemeat, Figural, 1888, 9 3/4 In. 300.00

Occident Flour, Wooden, Old Paint 45.00
Ohio Match 18.00
Old Dutch Cleanser, Porcelain 375.00
Orange Crush, It Tastes Better, Shows Amber Bottle, C.1940 .... 45.00
Peters Shoes, Black On Red On White, Porcelain 85.00
Potosi Lager Beer, Porcelain 165.00
Prestone Antifreeze, Porcelain, Tin, 34 In. 42.00
Princeton, Illinois, Wooden 4.50
Purolator 30.00
R.C.Cola 35.00
Railway Express 40.00
Ramon's Brown Pills For Kidneys, Doctor With Bag, Wooden 265.00
Red Seal Battery, Porcelain 75.00
Rislone Oil, Porcelain, 25 1/2 X 9 3/4 In. .... 55.00 To 75.00
Simonds Saws, Tin, Shows Saw Blades 65.00
Standard Oil, 1959 ....5.00 To 15.00
Sun Crest Pop, 1950s, 16 X 6 In. 30.00
Sunbeam Bread, Miss Sunbeam, 1970 .... 65.00
Texaco, Round, Porcelain, 8 In. 38.00
Vita–Var, Wooden 12.00
Wanda Oil Co., Round 25.00

Tiffany glass was made by Louis Comfort Tiffany, the American glass designer who worked from about 1879 to 1933. His work included iridescent glass, Art Nouveau styles of design, and original contemporary styles. He was also noted for his stained glass windows, his unusual lamps, bronze work, pottery, and silver. Other types of Tiffany are listed under Tiffany Pottery, Tiffany Silver, or at the end of this section under Tiffany. The famous Tiffany lamps are under Tiffany, Lamp. Reproductions of some types of Tiffany are being made.

TIFFANY GLASS, Bonbon, Leaves, Intaglio Butterfly, Signed, 5 3/4 In. 575.00
Bonbon, Ruffled Top, Gold Iridescent, 5 In. 175.00
Bonbon, Threaded, Applied Teardrops At Lower Half, Signed 235.00
Bowl, Center Well, Footed Base, Blue, Signed, 10 In. 950.00
Bowl, Centerpiece, Scalloped, Ribbed Body, Signed, 3 1/4 In. 700.00
Bowl, Flower, Intaglio Lily Pad, Signed 1750.00
Bowl, Flower, Vine & Lily Pad Design, Flower Holder Center 1250.00
Bowl, Gold Footed, Iridescent, Swirled, Scalloped, 7 1/2 In. 650.00
Bowl, Green & Silver Tones, Short Base, Ruffled, 2 1/2 In. 500.00
Bowl, Intaglio Cut Butterfly, Foil Label, 3 1/2 X 12 In. 1100.00
Bowl, Iridescent, Swirled, Scalloped, Gold, Footed, 7 In. 650.00
Bowl, Lavender Inside, Clear Out, Ribbed, Signed, 5 In. 325.00
Bowl, Nut, Scalloped Rim, Signed, 2 1/2 X 4 1/2 In. 375.00
Bowl, Prunts, Threading On Bottom Half, Signed, 4 3/4 In. 295.00
Bowl, Ribbed & Scalloped, Signed, 8 1/2 In. 575.00
Bowl, Ruffled Rim, Fluted, Twisted Stem, Marked, 5 3/4 X 6 In. 500.00
Bowl, Scalloped, Gold Iridescent, Signed, 5 In. 225.00
Butter Chip, Scalloped Rim, Gold Iridescent, Paper Label 175.00
Candlestick, Green, Removable Bobeche, Blown Out, 17 1/2 In. 900.00
Candlestick, Magnolia, Bronze, Apple Green, Flared, 17 1/2 In. 2000.00
Champagne, Blue, Red & Violet Tones, Signed, 6 In. 250.00
Compote, Melon Ribbed, Pedestal Base, Blue–Green, 5 1/2 In. 525.00
Compote, Scalloped Rim, Signed, 2 3/4 X 4 3/4 In. 375.00
Creamer, Pink & White, Signed, 3 1/4 In. 425.00
Decanter, Gold Iridescent, Applied Pig Tails, 10 1/2 In. 695.00
Decanter, Yellow, Brown, Swirl, Glass Stopper, 11 1/2 In. 2500.00
Dish, Mint, Scalloped, Center Well, Gold Iridescent, Signed 110.00
Dish, Nut, Gold Iridescent, Flared, Ribbed, Signed, 3 In. 175.00
Finger Bowl & Plate, Gold Iridescent, Signed 275.00
Finger Bowl, Flower Center, Signed 775.00
Finger Bowl, Ruffled, Underplate 350.00
Flower Frog, Double, Vine & Leaf Design, 10 In. 1495.00
Goblet, Chintz Pattern, Blue, Green, Signed, 6 1/4 In. 60.00

Goblet, Gold Iridescent, Circular Base, Signed, 5 1/4 In. 250.00
Goblet, Turquoise Opalescent, Set of 8 .... 5000.00
Jar, Dimpled, Blue Edged Cover, Handle, Signed, 3 1/2 In. 1100.00
Parfait, Yellow, Marked, 6 In. 300.00
Perfume Bottle, Amber, Green Leaves, Vines, 1918, 5 In. 1870.00
Perfume Bottle, Leaf & Vine, Knobbed Stopper, Signed, 4 In. 2000.00
Pitcher, Peacock Blue, Purple At Bottom, Signed, 4 In. 550.00
Plate, Raised Star Center, Gold Iridescent, 6 1/2 In. 265.00
Plate, Scalloped Indentation At End, Favrile, 8 In. 175.00
Plate, Scalloped, Gold Iridescent, Signed, 6 In. 185.00
Punch Cup, Gold, Scroll Handle, Signed 325.00
Punch Cup, Spreading Hollow Stem, Signed, 3 1/2 In. 150.00
Salt, Bowl Shape, Pedestal, Gold Iridescent, Signed 185.00
Salt, Gold Iridescent, 4 Twisted Prunts, Signed, Round 185.00
Salt, Gold Iridescent, Highlights, Favrile, Master, 1 1/2 In. 235.00
Salt, Gold Iridescent, Ruffled, Signed .... 135.00 To 150.00
Shade, Pulled-Up Feather, Scalloped, Yellow, 3 In. 245.00
Sherbet, Gold Iridescent, Hollow Pedestal, Signed, 3 1/2 In. 225.00
Tile, Opalescent, Dated 1881, Square, 3 1/2 In. 230.00
Toothpick, Fishtail Teardrops, Amber, Corset Shape, Signed 290.00
Toothpick, Pinched, Gold, Signed, 3 In. 245.00
Tumbler, Liquor, Pinched Bottom, Gold, 1 3/4 In. 160.00
Tumbler, Pinched Bottom, Gold Iridescent, Signed, 3 3/4 In. 185.00
Urn, Blue Favrile, Threaded Handles, Baluster, 11 5/8 In. 425.00
Vase, Amber Iridescent, Favrile, 1892-1928, Signed, 8 In. 1210.00
Vase, Amber, Concentric Bands, Scrolls, 1899-1920, 5 In. 990.00
Vase, Amber, Festoons, Olive Green, Pearly, 1895, 4 In. 1650.00
Vase, Amber-Blue Iridescent, Carmel Ground, 1910, 3 In. 1430.00
Vase, Bottle Shape, 3-Sectioned Body, Agate, Signed, 5 In. 875.00
Vase, Bud, Gold Dore, Iridescent, Bronze Base, 16 In., 2 Piece 495.00
Vase, Bulbous, Flared Ruffled Top, Gold Iridescent, 4 3/4 In. 550.00
Vase, Bulbous, Ribbed, Pinched-In Dimples, Signed, 4 1/2 In. 500.00
Vase, Cobalt Blue Iridescent, Marked, 3 1/2 In. 165.00
Vase, Cypriote, Rough Textured, Signed, 5 1/4 In. 850.00
Vase, Double Gourd Form, Yellow, Caramel, Blossoms, 12 In. 6100.00
Vase, Favrile, Gold Iridescent, Green Leaf, Vine, 9 In. 1600.00
Vase, Feather Design, Applied Wafer Pontil, Signed, 6 1/4 In. 750.00
Vase, Floriform, Bulging Cup, Signed, C.1892, 13 In. 1430.00
Vase, Floriform, Green Vertical Bands, Carmel Base, 17 In. 1550.00
Vase, Floriform, Knopped Standard, Signed, C.1906, 15 3/4 In. 2200.00
Vase, Floriform, Onion Form Cup, Green, Amber, 1906, 11 In. 1925.00
Vase, Flower Form, Gold Iridescent, Ribbed, Signed, 6 1/4 In. 550.00
Vase, Flower Form, Ribbed, Opal Color, Signed, 11 1/2 In. 2000.00
Vase, Gladioli, Paperweight, White Blossoms, Signed, 16 In. 4100.00
Vase, Gold Favrile, Baluster, Short Neck, Green Design, 6 In. 650.00
Vase, Gold Iridescent, 2 Handles, Signed, 3 1/4 In. 300.00
Vase, Gold Iridescent, Bud, Signed, 12 In. 625.00
Vase, Gold Iridescent, Ribbed, Highlights, Favrile, 4 1/2 In. 500.00
Vase, Gold, Flower Form, Pineapple Base, 14 In. 1100.00
Vase, Gourd Shape, Gold Iridescent, Highlights, Favrile, 5 In. 475.00
Vase, Green & Gold Feather, Opalescent Ground, 14 1/2 In. 1950.00
Vase, Green Aventurine, Allover Feathering, Signed, 4 1/2 In. 850.00

A signature adds 25 percent to the value of the glass.

Vase, Green Feather, White, Flower Form, Favrile, 11 In. 1400.00
Vase, Green Leaf & Trailing Vines, Signed, 3 1/2 In. 1300.00
Vase, Intaglio Cut, Footed, Signed, 8 1/2 In. 850.00
Vase, Iridescent Gold, Lappet Design, 21 1/2 In. 6000.00
Vase, Leaves Around Body, Vines, 3 Arms, Signed, 7 1/2 In. 2500.00
Vase, Onionskin, Butterscotch Iridescent, Signed, 4 3/4 In. 525.00
Vase, Outlined Leaves, Blue, Bulbous, Favrile, 3 X 3 1/2 In. 1400.00
Vase, Paperweight, Blossoms, Leaves, Green, Olive, 1905, 12 In. 6875.00
Vase, Paperweight, Red, With Flower Frog, 11 In. 1295.00
Vase, Paperweight, Vertical Panels, Signed, C.1905, 8 1/2 In. 1925.00
Vase, Paperweight, Yellow Blossoms, Signed, C.1919, 11 In. 9900.00
Vase, Poppies, Double–Ringed Neck, Signed, C.1909, 9 5/8 In. 5500.00
Vase, Pulled Handles, Gold Favrile, Signed, 3 1/4 In. 475.00
Vase, Pulled Leaf Design, Green Trim, Green, Signed, 6 1/4 In. 725.00
Vase, Shaded Blue To Purple, Swirled Neck, Signed, 3 1/2 In. 750.00
Vase, Striated Feathering, Signed, C.1918, 10 3/4 In. 3300.00
Vase, Swirl Design, Applied Flowers, Bands, Signed, 10 In. 1250.00
Vase, Trumpet, Iridescent Blue, 1917, Signed, 18 In. 1100.00
Vase, Trumpet, Pulled Feathers, Green & Gold, Signed, 14 In. 1600.00
Vase, Wave Design, Gold Ground, Ribbed Body, Signed, 8 1/4 In. 750.00
Vase, Yellow & Green Line Design, Black, 3 1/2 X 5 In. 950.00
Whiskey, Gold Iridescent, Dimpled, Signed, 2 1/4 In. 150.00
Whiskey, Gold Iridescent, Pigtail Twist At Bottom 150.00
Wine, Chintz, Blue, Green, Signed, 3 3/4 In. 55.00
Wine, Yellow, Purple Iridescent, Signed 285.00
TIFFANY POTTERY, Vase, Artichoke, Raised Leaves, Hourglass Shape, 11 In. 1500.00
Vase, Cylindrical, Green Exterior, Spotted Interior, 7 In. 350.00
Vase, Green Glaze, Bottom Yellow Streaks, Signed, 10 In. 550.00
Vase, Iridescent Flowers, 4 1/2 In. 950.00
Vase, Narrow Neck, Green Top, Yellow Streaks, 10 In. 550.00
Vase, Narrow Neck, Iridescent, Signed, 4 1/2 In. 500.00
Vase, Overlapping Leaves, Green Inside, Signed, 3 1/4 In. 750.00
Vase, Raised Blossoms, Stems, Unglazed Outside, 13 1/4 In. 900.00
Vase, Silver, Green Inside, Signed, 16 1/2 In. 2500.00
Vase, Tulips In Relief, Stems To Base, Signed, 7 In. 1200.00
Vase, Unglazed, Blossoms From Branches At Center, 4 In. 300.00
TIFFANY SILVER, Ashtray, Match Holder 68.00
Ashtray, Shell Shape, Small 35.00
Berry Spoon, Ailanthus Conch 495.00
Bowl, Gravy, Richelieu 100.00
Bowl, Leaves, Stems & Flowers On Pierced Rim, 9 In. 635.00
Bowl, Petal Shape, 3 1/2 X 9 1/4 In. 495.00
Bowl, Rococo Shell Border, Oval, 15 In. 1000.00
Bowl, Spun, Enameled Medallion, 2 1/4 X 7 7/8 In. 300.00
Butter, Pedestal, Dome Cover, Cupid Knob, 1865–70 .... 715.00
Buttonhook, Marked 60.00
Candelabra, 5–Light, Beaded Edge Design, 14 In. 1400.00
Candle Snuffer, 12 In. 65.00
Coffee Set, Berries, Foliage, Buds, 1902, 3 Piece 4070.00
Coffee Set, Colonial Design, Wooden Handles, 4 Piece 935.00
Coffee Set, Persian Style, 1907, 4 Piece 3200.00
Cold Meat Fork, Canterbury 165.00
Desk Set, Abalone Design, Signed, 1900–20, 7 Piece 1650.00
Dish, Nut, Octagonal, 3 1/2 In. 75.00
Dish, Turtle Shell, 6 X 4 3/4 In. 225.00
Finger Bowl, Cylindrical Shape, 1907, 5 In., 12 Piece 1650.00
Fish Server, Antique Ivy 275.00
Fish Set, Serving, Vine 750.00
Fish Set, Young & Ellis 500.00
Fish, Knife, Wave Edge Pattern, Set of 6 .... 400.00
Fork, Asparagus, Olympian 695.00
Fork, Olive, English King 85.00
Inkwell, Grotesque Griffins On Sides, Signed, 4 1/4 In. 550.00
Knife, Cheese, Points, English King 175.00

Tiffany Silver, Tray, Chippendale Style,
Cyma Edge, 8 In.

Tiffany Silver, Tazza, 2 Birds On Rim, 1873–91, 12 1/2 In.

Ladle, Claret, Chrysanthemum	175.00
Ladle, Gravy, Flemish	85.00
Ladle, Soup, English King	695.00
Ladle, Soup, Richelieu	450.00
Marrow Spoon, Colonial, Individual, 1895	65.00
Mug, Engraved William Shields Davis, March 17, 1923	145.00
Platter, Molded Rim, Plain Surface, 1907, 13 In.	605.00
Prayer Book, Lavender Enamel, Sterling, 1900	1000.00
Ruler, 2 1/4 Troy Oz.	75.00
Salver, Threaded Rim, Double Tab Feet, 14 1/4 X 10 1/4 In.	770.00
Scoop, Cheese, Wave Edge	295.00
Server, Pea, Olympian	495.00
Server, Tomato, Florentine	250.00
Server, Tomato, Pierced, Hampton	235.00
Shade, Acorn & Leaf, 3 3/4 In.	495.00
Soup, Dish, Engraved Crest, 1947, 8 7/8 In., 12 Piece	3520.00
Spoon, Bonbon, English King	165.00
Spoon, Demitasse, Holly	55.00
Spoon, Tea Caddy, Jockey Cap	95.00
Spoon, Twisted Stem, Demitasse, 12 Piece	245.00
Sugar Sifter, Persian	195.00
Sugar Sifter, Vine, Gold Wash Bowl	225.00
Sugar Sifter, Wave Edge	175.00
Sugar Tongs, Gramercy Pattern	75.00
Tazza, 2 Birds On Rim, 1873–91, 12 1/2 In. ....*Illus*	1430.00
Tea Strainer, Over The Cup, Monogram	95.00
Teapot, Sugar & Creamer, Cover, 1910–20	750.00
Teapot, Sugar & Creamer, Mt. Vernon Pattern	275.00
Tongs, Ice, Wave Edge	395.00
Tray, Chippendale Style, Cyma Edge, 8 In. ....*Illus*	275.00
Tray, Desk, Square Well & Oil Lamp, 20th Century	850.00
Tray, Monogram TLK, Special Hand Work, 5 3/8 X 4 1/2 In.	395.00
Tray, Scroll Design Edge, Marked, 3 1/2 In.	45.00
Tray, Smoking, Handles, Cord Rim, Lighter & Cutter, 15 In.	1450.00
Tray, Wave Form Rim, Oval, Early 20th Century, 18 In.	950.00
Tureen, Soup, Dome Lid, Engraved Foliage, Sheep Finial	2250.00
Vase, Comedy & Tragedy Mask, Columbian Expo, 13 3/8 In., Pr.	6050.00
Vase, Trumpet, Floral Design, Monogram, 11 1/2 In.	450.00
Waffle Server, Wave Edge	395.00
Wine Tester, 3 In.	140.00
Youth Set, Audubon, Japanese Style, 3 Piece	350.00

Tiffany objects made from a mixture of materials, such as bronze
and glass boxes, are listed here. Tiffany lamps are included in this
section.

TIFFANY, Ashtray, Match Holder, Zodiac, Bronze, Signed	95.00
Ashtray, Nest, Gold Dore, Scalloped Raised Rim, Bronze, 4 Piece	350.00
Basket, Favrile Glass & Bronze, Handle, Signed, 7 In.	450.00
Blotter Ends, American Indian, 4 Piece	250.00
Blotter Ends, Venetian, 4 Corner, Signed, 4 3/4 X 4 3/4 In., 4 Piece	200.00
Bookends, Figure of Buddha, Bronze, Signed, 6 X 5 1/2 In.	275.00 To 350.00
Bookends, Line & Leaf Design, Bronze & Abalone, Signed, 5 1/2 In.	650.00
Bookends, Relief Figures, Curved Ribbed Line Design, Signed, 6 In.	350.00
Bookrack, Bronze & Abalone, Iridescent Discs, 14 1/2 X 10 In.	850.00
Bowl, Dore Bronze, Band of Repeating Pierced Flowers, 8 3/4 In.	100.00
Bowl, Flower, Raised Leaf Pattern, Glass & Holder Insert, 10 In.	1600.00
Bowl, Lattice & Floral Design, Bronze, Signed, 9 In.	90.00
Bowl, Ruffled Trim, Bronze, Blue, Gold, 5 In.	250.00
Box, Abalone Discs In Leaf Pattern, Hinged Lid, Bronze, 5 1/2 In.	500.00
Box, Adam, Bronze, Oval, Hinged Cover, 4 X 3 1/2 X 2 1/2 In.	250.00
Box, Art Deco Pattern, Hinged Cover, Bronze, Signed, 2 1/2 X 4 In.	225.00
Box, Azalea, Bronze, Green Slag Glass, Ball Feet, Square, 7 In.	750.00
Box, Jewelry, Pine Needle, Bronze & Glass, Signed, 9 1/4 X 6 In.	975.00
Box, Pine Needle, Bronze, Green Slag Glass, 9 1/2 X 7 X 3 In.	950.00
Box, Stamp, Pine Needle, Bronze & Glass, 2 1/4 X 4 In.	350.00
Box, Zodiac, Hinged Cover, Gold Dore, 4 1/2 X 3 1/2 X 2 In.	350.00
Candelabrum, 6–Light, Bronze, Gold Dore Finish, Signed, 3 1/2 In.	1800.00
Candelabrum, 8–Light, Bobeches, Bronze, Signed, 15 1/2 In.	2500.00
Candlestick, 2–Light, Bronze, Enameled Bobeches, 16 In.	2500.00
Candlestick, 3–Light, Bronze, Urn Form, 1899–1920, Signed, 12 In.	1320.00
Candlestick, Bronze, Orange–Green Enameled Top, 10 In.	450.00
Candlestick, Bud Form Candle Socket, Green Glass, Bronze, 20 In.	200.00
Candlestick, Removable Bobeche, Bulbous Socket, Bronze, 19 In., Pair	1100.00
Card & Letter Holder, Grapevine, Bronze, Beaded, 5 1/2 In.	475.00
Chandelier, 4–Light, Amber, Yellow, 1899, 30 In.	4400.00
Chandelier, 6 Green & Opalescent Lily Shades, 29 In.	6050.00
Chandelier, Bronze Acorn, Yellow, Green, Beaded Border, 21 In.	8250.00
Chandelier, Turtleback Tile, Bronze & Glass, Signed, 1920, 20 In.	8800.00
Clock, Carriage, Sedan Chair Form, Repeat, Crown Finial, 11 3/8 In.	2200.00
Clock, Mantel, Gilt Bronze, Champleve Enameled, Columns, 19 1/2 In.	4125.00
Clock, Medallion Design, Bronze & Enamel, Key, Signed, 6 In.	975.00
Clock, Multicolored Enamel Design, Bronze, 5 1/2 X 5 1/2 In.	975.00
Clock, Tall Case, Westminster & Whittington Chimes, Oak, C.1890	8400.00
Compote, Engraved Geometric Rim, Bronze, Footed, Signed, 4 1/2 In.	225.00
Compote, Indian Design, Bronze, 10 In.	250.00
Compote, Raised Rim, Etched Design, Bronze, 3 1/4 X 6 In.	175.00
Console Set, Rope Candlesticks, Black Base, Amberina, Bowl 11 In.	95.00
Desk Set, Adam, Bronze, Letter Rack, Inkwell, Blotter Ends	450.00
Desk Set, Pine Needle, Slag Glass, Bronze, 9 X 5 1/2 In.	1800.00
Desk Set, Zodiac, Bronze, 7 Piece	850.00
Dish, Chased Border, Bronze, Marked, 7 1/2 In.	75.00
Figurine, Draped Female, Leaning On Urn & Pedestal, Bronze, 5 Ft.	5500.00
Finger Bowl, Underplate, Gold, Signed, 4 1/2 In., Pair	550.00
Frame, Flower & Leaf Design, Bronze, Abalone, Easel Style, 6 1/2 In.	425.00
Frame, Gold Dore Finish, Abalone Discs, Bronze, 10 1/4 X 7 1/4 In.	1200.00
Frame, Gold Dore Finish, Zodiac, Bronze, Signed, 7 X 8 In.	750.00
Frame, Grapevine, Bronze & Glass, Oval Opening, 4 X 5 1/2 In.	950.00
Frame, Zodiac, Symbols, Bronze, Signed, 8 X 10 In.	1200.00
Goblet, Applied Lily Pads, Gold Iridescent, Signed, Set of 6	1900.00
Goblet, Engineers Club December 9th, 1907, Bronze, 7 1/2 In.	325.00
Hatpin Holder, Swirled, Bronze	185.00
Holder, Note Pad, Grapevine, Signed, 7 1/2 X 4 1/2 In.	300.00
Humidor Ashtray, Bronze, Matchbox Holder, Signed, 7 X 5 In.	325.00
Humidor, Pine Needle, Bronze & Glass, Signed, 4 1/4 In.	750.00
Inkwell, Bronze Lace Over Green, Hinged Top, Signed, 7 In.	425.00

Inkwell, Bronze Raised Dragons, Top Hinged Cover, 4 1/2 X 6 In. 650.00
Inkwell, Bronze Turtle Back, Tile Covered, Signed, 1899, 3 3/4 In. 2750.00
Inkwell, Bronze, Green Glass Blown Through Openings, 3 1/2 In. 1500.00
Inkwell, Bronze, Overall Moor Design, Abalone Circles, 4 1/2 In. 200.00
Inkwell, Bronze, Paw Feet, Leaf Designed Hinged Top, Signed 600.00
Inkwell, Grapevine, Amber Slag Glass, Bronze, Signed, 7 In. 700.00
Inkwell, Nautical, Gold Dore, Dolphin Feet, 5 1/4 X 3 1/2 In. 650.00
Inkwell, Pine Needle, Bronze & Glass, Signed, 7 In. 700.00
Inkwell, Venetian, Bronze, 2 Glass Wells, Gold Dore, 5 X 3 X 3 In. 550.00
Inkwell, Zodiac, Cover, Gold Finish, 4 In. 175.00
Jam Jar, Sterling Silver Rim & Handle, Glass Insert, Signed 550.00
Lamp, 2-Arm, Green Feather Shades, Bronze, Signed, 14 1/2 In. 3500.00
Lamp, 3 Arms Support Bronze Shade, Bronze, Signed, 10 1/2 In. 850.00
Lamp, Acorn, Stained Glass Shade, Bronze, Signed, 15 In. 4500.00
Lamp, Base, 6-Light, Squares, Diamonds Bronze Base, Signed, 28 In. 3850.00
Lamp, Blue Dragonfly, Bronze, Table 6600.00
Lamp, Bridge, Adjustable, Bronze Base, Bell-Shaped Shade, 48 In. 1800.00
Lamp, Bridge, Ribbed Body, Curved Arm Holds Shade, Signed, 48 In. 1800.00
Lamp, Bronze Base, Bell-Shaped Favrile Shade, Signed, 12 1/2 In. 975.00
Lamp, Candlestick, 2-Arm, Chinese Gold Shades, Bronze, 18 3/4 In. 2500.00
Lamp, Candlestick, Bronze, Favrile, Gold Iridescent, 15 In., Pair 1500.00
Lamp, Candlestick, Gold Iridescent Shade, Bronze, Signed, 15 In. 800.00
Lamp, Candlestick, Green Feather Design Shade, Bronze Base, 15 In. 1200.00
Lamp, Desk, Bronze Square Base, Geometric Design, 13 1/2 In. 975.00
Lamp, Desk, Counterweight, Bronze Base, Curved Arm, Blue, Violet 3800.00
Lamp, Desk, Geometric Pattern On Base, Bronze, Signed, 14 1/2 In. 2200.00
Lamp, Desk, Glass, Enameled, Gilt Bronze, Signed, 14 1/4 In. 7700.00
Lamp, Desk, Kapa Shell Shade, Bronze, Signed, 56 In. 2200.00
Lamp, Desk, Lily, 3-Light, Bronze .... 1350.00 To 1650.00
Lamp, Desk, Raised Leaf Design In Bronze, Leaded Shade, Signed 1800.00
Lamp, Desk, Sapphire Blue, Vertical Bands, Harp Shape, 17 In. 5500.00
Lamp, Desk, Wave Design On Bronze Base, Harp, Signed, 19 1/2 In. 3000.00
Lamp, Desk, Zodiac, Adjustable Oval Bronze Shade, Signed, 10 In. 950.00
Lamp, Enameled Copper, Alternating Dandelions, Leaves, 1900, 15 In. 3700.00
Lamp, Fabrique, Amber, Bronze Base, Ribbed Platform, Signed, 20 In. 4000.00
Lamp, Fleur-De-Lis, Leaded Shade, Bronze Base, Urn Shape, 21 In. 5000.00
Lamp, Floor, Green Glass Shade, Bronze 2640.00
Lamp, Geometric Pattern, Green On White, Bronze Base, 24 In. 6500.00
Lamp, Geometric, Gridwork Shade, Bronze, Signed, 1899, 22 1/2 In. 6600.00
Lamp, Green Pulled Feather, Shade, 15 In. 3200.00
Lamp, Leaf Pattern Shade, Signed, 18 In. 8500.00
Lamp, Lily, 3-Light, Bronze Base, Favrile Shades, Signed, 12 In. 3500.00
Lamp, Lily, 7-Light, Bronze, Yellow, Green Shade, 19 In. 7700.00
Lamp, Mosque, Gold, Green Feather Shade, Bronze Base, 8 1/2 In. 2000.00
Lamp, Mushroom, Interlocking Coils, Marked, Glass & Gilt Bronze 3850.00
Lamp, Nautilus, Opalescent Tiles, Glass & Bronze, Marked, 12 1/4 In. 5500.00
Lamp, Nautilus, Shell Form Shade, Green, Bronze, 14 In. 8800.00
Lamp, Palm Tree, Bronze Base, Gold Sphere Shade, Signed, 32 In. 4500.00
Lamp, Reading, No.418, Harp Holder, Damascene Shade 2450.00
Lamp, Scarab Mold, 2 Branches, Green-Blue Favrile Glass, 8 1/2 In. 3000.00
Lamp, Student, Bronze Base, Adjustable Arm, Signed, 19 1/2 In. 2500.00
Lamp, Student, Gold Dore, Signed, 24 In. 1600.00
Lamp, Student, Turtleback Tile, Glass & Bronze, 14 7/8 In. 3025.00
Lamp, Table, 3-Lily Light, Quezal Shades, Bronze Base 1450.00
Lamp, Table, Swirling Leaf Pattern, Bronze 7150.00
Lamp, Urn Style Body, 4 Legs, Shade, Bronze, Signed, 14 In. 1500.00
Lamp, Wire Jacket Over Blown Glass Shade, 3 Arms, Signed, 21 In. 3500.00
Letter Holder, Ninth Century, 14K Gold Plate, Bronze & Jeweled 4450.00
Letter Opener, Abalone Discs, Gold Dore Finish, Signed, 10 In. 225.00
Letter Opener, Bookmark, Gold Dore, Symbol On Handle, 10 1/2 In. 195.00
Letter Opener, Chinese, Both Sides of Handle, Signed, 11 In. 175.00
Letter Opener, Graduate, Gold Dore Finish, Signed, 9 In. 95.00
Letter Opener, Grapevine, Green Glass In Handle, Signed, 9 In. 250.00
Letter Opener, Indian, Signed, 10 1/2 In. 150.00

Letter Opener, Pine Needle, Glass In Handle, Signed, 9 In.	250.00
Letter Opener, Venetian, Gold Dore, Signed, 10 1/4 In.	165.00
Letter Opener, Zodiac, Signed, 10 1/2 In.	150.00
Letter Rack, Bronze, Gold, Blue & Red Enameled, 9 1/2 X 5 1/2 In.	350.00
Letter Rack, Bronze, Venetian, 2 Sections, Gold Dore, 10 X 3 X 6 In.	400.00
Letter Rack, Chinese, Bronze, Gold Dore, 3 Sections, 12 X 8 X 3 In.	500.00
Letter Rack, Nautical, Wave Border, 2 Sections, 11 X 7 X 2 1/2 In.	650.00
Letter Rack, Raised Dragons, Spanish, 10 In.	650.00
Letter Scale, Zodiac, Gold Dore Finish, 3 1/4 X 2 3/4 X 1 1/2 In.	350.00
Light, Ceiling, 2–Light, Jewels, Turtleback, Balls, Bronze, Signed	8000.00
Light, Ceiling, 31 Green Prisms, Original Fittings, 12 In.	750.00
Magnifying Glass, American Indian, Gold Dore Finish, Signed	295.00
Magnifying Glass, Grapevine, Amber Slag Glass, Gold Dore, 7 3/4 In.	395.00
Magnifying Glass, Venetian, Gold Dore Finish, Signed	295.00
Paper Clip, Adam, Gold Dore Finish, Signed	150.00
Paper Clip, American Indian, Gold Dore, Mask On Top, Signed	150.00
Paper Clip, Pine Needle, Over Amber Slag Glass, Beaded, Signed	200.00
Paper Clip, Venetian, Gold Dore Finish, Chain Link & Mink, Signed	200.00
Paperweight, Bronze, Owl, Dark Patina Finish, 3 X 1 1/4 In.	525.00
Paperweight, Dog, Pointer, Name Shando, Bronze, Signed, 3 1/2 In.	495.00
Paperweight, Lioness, Recumbent, Bronze, Gold Dore, Signed, 5 In.	495.00
Paperweight, Turtleback, Red, Bronze Base, Signed, 4 3/4 X 6 In.	975.00
Pen Tray, Chinese, Bronze, 2 Raised Sides, Signed, 12 X 3 3/4 In.	150.00
Pen Tray, Grapevine, 4 Ball Feet, Glass Insert, 3 In.	195.00
Pen Tray, Pine Needle, 3 Sections, 4 Ball Feet, 2 3/4 X 9 1/2 In.	225.00
Penholder, Nautical, Gold Dore Finish, 2 Pens, 8 X 4 1/2 In.	550.00
Planter, Glass & Bronze Turtleback Tile, Signed, 1899, 15 3/4 In.	4400.00
Planter, Grapevine, Amber Slag Glass, Gold Dore, 8 X 10 In.	1500.00
Plate, Optic, Onion Skin Edge, Aqua, Lavender, 8 In.	475.00
Platter, Deep Center Well, Gold Dore, Bronze, Signed, 9 In.	95.00
Platter, Radiating Sunburst Design, Pedestal, Bronze, Signed, 8 In.	225.00
Punch Cup, Applied Lily Pads, Pulled Stems, Signed	275.00
Punch Cup, Gold Iridescent, Hollow Stem, Signed, 3 1/2 In.	195.00
Rose Bowl, Diamond Quilted, Rainbow Colors, 5 In.	1400.00
Salt, Favrile, Iridescent Gold, Signed, 2 1/2 In.	125.00
Salt, Pulled Twisted Prunts	185.00
Scale, Postage, Zodiac Dore, Signed, Numbered	275.00
Sconce, 2–Light, Amber, Green Shade, Rope Twist Border, 15 In.	2200.00
Sconce, Turtleback, Wall, Electric, Signed, Pair	5000.00
Shade, Hanging, Red & Green, Signed, C.1922, 28 In.	4500.00
Shot Glass, Gold, Blue Highlights, Dimpled, Signed, 2 In.	140.00
Smoke Stand, 4 Removable Cups, Center Leaf Pattern, Signed, 27 In.	600.00
Smoke Stand, Cigarette Rests, Matchbox Holder, Bronze, Signed	550.00
Thermometer, Zodiac, Gold Dore Finish, 8 In.	450.00
Tray, Bookmark, Pattern In Center, Signed, 8 1/2 X 2 3/4 In.	125.00
Tray, Bronze, Gold Dore Finish, 8 In.Diam.	195.00
Tray, Card, Grapevine, Etched At Bottom, Bronze, Signed, 1 X 4 In.	225.00
Tray, Design On Rim, Gold Dore, Bronze, 14 In.	195.00
Tray, Etched Line & Circle Border, Bronze, Signed, 8 In.	195.00
Tray, Geometric Design Edge, Bronze, Pedestal, Signed, 10 In.	225.00
Tray, Gold Dore Finish, Red Jewels Set In Rim, Signed, 12 In.	250.00
Tray, Raised Border Design, Gold Dore Finish, Bronze, 12 In.	175.00
Tray, Venetian, Bronze, 2 Sections, Signed, 10 X 3 1/2 In.	150.00
Trivet, Mosiac, Bronze, Multicolored Ground, 1920, Signed, 6 In.	1870.00
Vase, Bronze, Green, Gold, Dore, Signed, 13 In.	1100.00
Vase, Bud, Favrile & Bronze, Byzantine Design, Signed, 2 1/4 In.	325.00

The Tiffin Glass Company of Tiffin, Ohio, was a subsidiary of the United States Glass Co. of Pittsburgh, Pennsylvania, in 1892. The U.S. Glass Co. went bankrupt in 1963, and the Tiffin plant employees purchased the building and the inventory. They continued running it from 1963 to 1966, when it was sold to Continental Can Company. In 1969, it was sold to Interpace; and in 1980, it was closed. The black satin glass, made from 1923 to 1926, and the stemware of the last twenty years are the best–known products.

TIFFIN, Bowl, Footed, Black Satin, 10 1/2 In.	30.00
Bowl, June Night, Crimp, 9 1/2 In.	55.00
Candleholder, Twist Stem, Black Satin, 7 1/2 In., Pair	35.00
Candlestick, Black Satin Cat, Pair	50.00
Candy Dish, Canary Yellow, Heart Shape, Cover, Signed	85.00
Candy Jar, Canterbury Contour, Twilight, Footed, Cover, 5 1/2 In.	120.00
Candy, Black Satin, Cover, 1/4 Lb.	55.00
Cocktail, Byzantine	15.00
Cocktail, Cherokee Rose	17.00
Compote, Autumn Leaf Design, 9 X 5 In.	45.00
Compote, Canterbury Contour, Twilight, Stem, 8 In.	87.50
Cordial, Cut Bubble Stem, Etched	25.00
Cordial, June Night	25.00 To 30.00
Creamer, Cherokee Rose	9.50
Goblet, Cherokee Rose	14.00
Goblet, Cherokee Rose, 9 Oz.	16.00 To 19.00
Goblet, Cocktail, June Night	15.00
Goblet, Water, Flanders, Crystal Stem	15.00
Goblet, Water, Flanders, Yellow Stem	17.00
Goblet, Water, Tempo	18.00
Juice, June Night, Footed, 5 In.	14.00
Lamp, Lovebirds	100.00
Plate, Cherokee Rose, 8 In.	7.00
Rose Bowl, Black	40.00 To 75.00
Saucer, June Night	16.00
Sherbet, Cherokee Rose	11.00 To 16.00
Sherbet, Dancing Shawl, Green Stem, Crystal, 7 Oz.	16.00
Sherbet, Flanders, Stem, Crystal	8.00
Sugar & Creamer, Cherokee Rose	23.00
Sugar, Creamer & Tray, Cerise	45.00
Tumbler, Ice Tea, June Night, Footed	18.00
Tumbler, Juice, June Night	12.00
Tumbler, Water, Flanders, Stem, Crystal	15.00
Tumbler, Water, Palais Versailles	45.00
Vase, Black Satin, Silver Overlay, 8 In.	95.00
Vase, Canterbury Contour, Twilight, 5 In.	55.00
Vase, Cherokee Rose, 8 In.	20.00
Vase, Coralene Bead, Daffodils, Iris, Black Satin, Bulbous, 6 1/2 In.	75.00
Vase, Coralene Bead, Daffodils, Iris, Black Satin, Bulbous, 8 In.	85.00
Vase, Flower Arranger, 8 1/2 In.	168.00
Vase, Poppy, Bulbous, 5 In.	27.50
Wine, Cherokee Rose	13.00 To 22.00

Tiles have been used in most countries of the world as a sturdy building material for floors, roofs, fireplace surrounds, and surface toppings. Many of the American tiles are listed in this book under the factory name.

TILE, Angelfish, Gladding, McBean, 6 X 6 In.	45.00
Blue & Yellow Bird In Birdcage, Dutch, 19th Century	1800.00
Calendar, 1895, Statehouse	48.00
Calendar, 1901, Harvard Stadium	48.00
Calendar, 1906, Jones, McDuffee & Stratton Co., Pottery Merchants	50.00
Calendar, 1907, Bunker Hill Monument	48.00
Calendar, 1929, House of Seven Gables	48.00
Calendar, 1929, Nebraska Advertising, Octagonal, 6 1/4 In.	45.00
Castle, Sailboats, Blue & White	15.00
Dog, By Beehive, Minton, Hollins, C.1880, 6 In.	45.00
Dutch Boy, With Pail, Batchelder	75.00
Faience, Half Octagonal, Turquoise, 6 1/2 In., Pair	27.50

Faience, Rounded Corners, Jade, 4 1/4 X 4 1/2 In. 15.00
Indian Head, Blown Out, Copper Luster Trim, 6 1/2 In. 40.00
Kittens Chasing Butterflies, Grasshoppers, Chinese, 22 X 15 In., Pair 200.00
Man & Cow, Maiden With Horse, Polychrome, Dutch, C.1800, Pair 3500.00
Menorah Design, Virgil Cantini, 5 1/2 In. 20.00
Middle Eastern Woman's Head, Green, Trent, 6 X 6 In. 85.00
Peacock, Grape Arbor, Mottled Blue, California Art, 7 3/4 X 11 1/2 In. 80.00
Pink Roses, Germany, Red Crown Mark 25.00
Portrait, Gilt Bronze Rococo Frame, Signed Rose, 3 1/4 X 2 1/2 In. 175.00
Statehouse, Augusta, Maine, Germany 25.00
Stove, Woman Peasant, Seated, Dog, Green Glaze, 7 7/8 X 7 1/2 In. 550.00
Tea, Faience, Flowers 295.00
Tea, Tea Tile, California, Faience 250.00
Transfer, Animal & Bird Scenes, Framed, Liverpool, 4 7/8 In., 4 Piece 400.00
Viking Ship, 5-Color, California, Faience 450.00
Woman With Bouquet of Flowers, Framed, English, 12 X 9 In. 325.00

 Tin has been used to make household containers in America since the seventeenth century. The first tin utensils were brought from Europe; but by 1798, tin plate was imported and local tinsmiths made the wares. Painted tin is called "tole" and is listed separately. Some tin kitchen items may be found listed under Kitchen. The lithographed tin containers used to hold food and tobacco are listed under Advertising, Tin.

TINWARE, Admiral's Hat, Anniversary, Chapeau De Bras, Ostrich Plume, 6 In. 250.00
Basket, Berry, Old Red Paint, C.1880, 4 1/2 X 3 1/2 X 4 1/2 In. 110.00
Biscuit Prick 85.00
Box, Beech-Nut Gum, Pastoral Scenes, Mohawk Valley 57.50
Box, Candle, Punched, Cylindrical 195.00
Box, Picnic, Nursery Rhyme, Wooden Swing Handles, Hinged Cover 22.50
Box, Punched Pattern, Circles & Panels, 22 X 11 X 10 In. 775.00
Calendar, 1943, Embossed Scotty Dog 12.00
Candleholder, Spike, Rolled Edges, Pointed End, Mantel, 1830, 3 In. 16.00
Candlestick, Cylindrical, Adjustable, Handle, 1 Shade, 19 In., Pair 770.00
Canteen, Punched Star & Circle Designs, 5 5/8 In. 95.00
Coffeepot, Floral, Loop Handle, Brass Finial, C.1848, 10 5/8 In. 1100.00
Coffeepot, Wrigglework, Tulips, Strap Handle, Flag Eagle, 12 In. 3080.00
Colander, 2 Handles, 11 X 6 In. 30.00
Drainer, Cheese 75.00
Edwards Marshmallow, Sugar Puff, Tin, Glass Lid 145.00
Frame, Picture, Victorian, 7 X 5 In. 38.00
Glycerole Shoe Polish, Trunk Shape, Tin 145.00
Lantern, Pierced, Carrying Loop & Collar, 5 1/2 X 16 In. 150.00
Licorice Lozenges, Glass Front, 5 Lb. 55.00
Lunch Bucket, Collapsible 26.00
Lunch Pail, Bail, Wooden Handle, Round 15.00
Matchbox, Hanging, Striker 13.00
Mold, Candle, 6 Tube 17.00
Mold, Candle, 8 Tube, Arched Base & Handle 220.00
Mold, Candle, 12 Tube ....75.00 To 125.00
Mold, Candle, 12 Tube, Handle, New England, 19th Century, 9 1/2 In. 88.00
Mold, Candle, 24 Tube 310.00
Mold, Candle, 24 Tubes, Signed P.Reams 1495.00
Mold, Cheese, Heart Shape 295.00
Mold, Fish, Curved, Hanging Hook, 8 X 10 In. 29.00
Mold, Pudding, Fluted, 2 Parts, Each With Handle, 5 X 8 In. 27.50
Old Gold Medals, Flat 50 .... 15.00
Pen, Waterman, Rectangular 15.00
Rexall Orderlies Laxative 5.00
Sconce, Box Shape, Polished Tin Reflectors, C.1830, Pair 900.00
Sconce, Candle, Crimped Oval Reflector, Black, Primitive, 8 In. 75.00
Sconce, Upright Leaf Shape, 12 In. 65.00
Snuffer, Candle, Twisted Wire, Hanging Loop, C.1840, 4 1/2 In. 44.00
Yellow Cab Cigar, Hinged Lid, Lettering, Dovetailed, Round 22.00

TOBACCO CUTTER, see Advertising

Because tobacco needs special conditions of humidity and air, it has been stored in special containers since the eighteenth century. The tobacco jar is often made in fanciful shapes.

TOBACCO JAR, Arab, Majolica	95.00
Bison, Brown	185.00
Chinese Man's Head, Moustache, Braid, Pottery, 5 3/4 In.	118.00
Cigars Tied With Yellow Bow, Pipe Lid, 6 1/2 In.	37.00
Coachman, Bavaria	95.00
Fish, Smoking Pipe, 4 1/2 In.	95.00
Gentleman With Cigar & Stein, Cigar Band–Type Base, Bohemia	105.00
Irishman, Majolica	95.00
Man, Drinks Aussig Pilsner, Cigars Base, Austrian	160.00
Owl, 6 1/4 In.	95.00
Peacocks, Art Deco, Noritake	115.00
Pipe On Lid, Man Smoking, Horse On Side, Majolica	225.00
Scotsman, Majolica	95.00
Skull & Cigarette, E.Diers, Rookwood, 1898	1650.00
Skull, 6 In.	85.00
Skull, Black & White Teeth, Black Eyes, Pottery, 5 1/2 In.	135.00
St.Bernard, 5 1/2 In.	95.00
Turk, Weller, Dickens Ware	450.00
White Figures, Dark Blue, Wedgwood, Marked	195.00

The toby jug is a very special form of pitcher. It is shaped like the full figure of a man or woman. A pitcher that shows just the top half of a person is not correctly called a toby. More examples of toby jugs can be found under Royal Doulton and other factory names.

TOBY JUG, General MacArthur, Occupied Japan	45.00
John Bull, Marked	30.00
McLean, C.1955, Large	20.00
Pearl Ware, Sponged Base, 1785–1800, 4 1/2 In.	1750.00
Peg Leg, Irate, On Sea Chest	75.00
Washington, C.1955, Large	20.00

Tole is painted tin. It is sometimes called "japanned ware," "pontypool," or "toleware." Most nineteenth–century tole is painted with an orange–red or black background and multicolored decorations. Many recent versions of toleware are made and sold.

TOLE, see also Tinware

TOLE, Box, Document, Dome Top, Black, Floral, Brass Bale Handle, 10 1/2 In.	250.00
Box, Document, Dome Top, Brown Japanning, Band of Fruit, 9 In.	105.00
Box, Document, Dome Top, Brown Japanning, Stenciled Floral, 10 In.	195.00
Box, Document, Dome Top, Wire Ring Handle, Floral Sprays, 8 3/4 In.	300.00
Box, Document, Red Berries, Green Leaves, New York, 3 In.	140.00
Box, Document, Red, Green, Yellow, 1850, 6 1/2 In.	85.00
Box, Document, Stenciled, Blue, Gold & Red On Black, 8 1/2 In.	60.00
Box, Spice, With 6 Square Canisters, Brown Japanning, 9 1/2 In.	55.00
Box, Worn Black Paint, Floral, Shell, Oval, 5 In.	225.00
Bread Tray, Victorian, Oriental Figures, Garden Setting, 13 3/4 In.	247.50
Candleholder, 2–Light, Adjustable Drip Plate, Conical Base, 15 In.	1200.00
Coal Bin, Domed Lid, Barnyard Scene, Gilt Handles, 16 X 16 In.	825.00
Coffeepot, Brown Japanning, Floral Design, Gooseneck Spout, 10 In.	650.00
Coffeepot, Flowers On Black Japanned Ground, Side Spout, Child's	225.00
Coffeepot, Gooseneck Spout, Floral Design, Yellow, Red, Brown, 1838	1550.00
Colander, Pierced, Canted, Strap Handle, Geometric, 7 X 10 In.	495.00
Comb & Brush Holder, With Mirror	20.00
Comb Case, Original Finish of Red Roses, Green Ground	20.00
Creamer, Dark Brown Japanning, Colored Design, 4 In.	90.00
Lantern, French ....*Illus*	350.00
Mug, Dark Brown Japanning, Floral, 4 1/4 In.	225.00
Plate, Union Pacific Tea Co., Girl Center, Bear Border, 8 In.	67.50

Pot, Floral & Foliage, 10 1/4 In. 500.00
Sconce, Dish Reflector, Cylindrical Cup, American, 13 1/4 In., Pair 1870.00
Screen, Mantel, Beveled Glass, Needlepoint, Pair 260.00
Spice Set, Original Paint, In Box With Brass Handle, Set of 6 .... 85.00
Sugar, Polychrome Design, 4 In. 500.00
Tea Bin, Chinese Design, Gold, Red, Black, J.Maund, London, 16 In., Pair 1180.00
Tea Bin, Painted, Mahogany Lid, English, 19th Century, 3 Ft., Pair 1270.00
Tea Caddy, Flower, Leaf & Bird, Cylindrical, Brown Ground, 4 1/2 In. 125.00
Tray, Apple, Coffin Shape, Yellow Leaves, Red Birds, 3 In. 1540.00
Tray, Classical Maiden, Flowing Gown, Cherub With Flute, 16 X 14 In. 55.00
Tray, Countryside Scene, 16 Sides, Victorian, 19th Century, 29 In. 5060.00
Tray, Floral Sprig, Black, Gilt Stenciled Border, 11 3/4 X 8 3/4 In. 44.00
Tray, Gold Design, 6 X 14 In. 7.50
Tray, Green, 19 1/2 X 27 In. 40.00
Tray, Regency, Dying Nelson, Deck of Ship, Officers, 29 X 20 In. 1800.00

Tom Mix was born in 1880 and died in 1940. He was the hero of over 100 silent movies from 1910 to 1929, and 25 sound films from 1929 to 1935. There was a Ralston Tom Mix radio show from 1933 to 1950, but the original Tom Mix was not in the show. Tom Mix comics were published from 1942 to 1953.

TOM MIX, Bandana 75.00
   Belt Buckle 38.00
   Belt Buckle, Tom Mix Secret 65.00
   Book, Big Little Book, Fighting Cowboy 25.00
   Book, Big Little Book, Terror Trail 25.00
   Book, Comic, Ralston Premium, No.3, 1941 .... 60.00
   Book, Draw & Paint, Whitman, 1935 .... 17.00
   Book, Tony & His Pals, Hardcover, Whitman, 144 Pages 30.00
   Bowl, Cereal, Ralston 10.00
   Cap Gun, H–O, With Holster 50.00
   Card, Arcade 5.00
   Catalog, Straight Shooters Premiums, Original Envelope 25.00
   Comic, 1/2 Page, Cincinnati Enquirer, Color, Oct.20, 1935 .... 15.00
   Compass, Straight Shooters, Brass, Magnifying Glass, 1940 .... 55.00
   Decoder 42.00
   Gold Sample, Radio Premium 17.00
   Gun, Wooden 75.00
   Knife, Pocket, Straight Shooter 30.00
   Magnifier 10.00
   Movie, Western 50.00
   Picture, Tom Mix & Horse, Name Incised In Stand–Up Silver Frame 65.00

Tole, Lantern, French   Tortoiseshell, Box, Dresser, Domed Lid, Ivory Ball Feet, 10 In.

Print, Ray–O 35.00
Ring, Look–In Picture, But No Picture, 1938 .... 45.00
Ring, Magnet, 1935 .... 45.00
Ring, Spy 39.00
Secret Writing Manual 22.00
Spinner, Good Luck 25.00
Watch Fob 60.00

Tools of all sorts are listed here, but most are related to industry. Other tools will be found listed under Iron; Kitchen; Tinware; and Wooden.

TOOL, Adze, Hand, Live Oak Handle, Blade, 4 1/2 In. 58.00
Adze, Keen Kutter, Handle 25.00
Adze, Ship, Forged 29.00
Anvil, Brass, 2 1/4 X 5 In. 35.00
Anvil, Watchmaker, Brass, 1 1/4 Lb. 15.00
Auger Brace, Winchester, 8 In. 50.00
Auger, Ship, Keen Kutter 10.00
Auger, Swan's Universal, Wooden Box, Instructions 170.00
Awl, Upholstery, Turned Wooden Handle, 17 In. 22.00
Ax, Broad, Diamond Edge 95.00
Ax, Camp, Marble Arms & Mfg. Co., Gladstone, Mich., Pat. 1898 ...... 110.00
Ax, Center Bit, Post Hole, Mortise, Brady, 9 In.Head 72.00
Ax, Double Bit, Post Hole, Mortise, Brady, 13 In.Head 88.00
Ax, Firestone 25.00
Ax, Goose Wing, Laid–On Steel Edge, 14 In.Blade 165.00
Ax, Single Bit, Handle, Keen Kutter 15.00
Ax, Wrought Iron, 5 1/2 In.Head, 3 1/4 In.Blade 72.00
Back Saw, Double Edge, Keen Kutter, Pat.Jan.9, '06 .... 80.00
Battery Tester, W.C.Fields, Red Nose Lights Up, Good Battery, 11 In. ... 8.50
Bee Smoker, Woodman's Famous Bee Smoker 18.00
Bellows, Blacksmith's, Red Paint & Leather, 36 X 65 In. 165.00
Bellows, Wig Powdering, Leather, 1800s, 6 1/2 In. 130.00
Bench, Scythe Sharpening, Dengelshtock Mounted In Bench, 22 X 18 In. ... 125.00
Bench, Work, Wooden, 2 Wooden Vises, 2 Metal Bench Stops, 23 X 96 In. ... 210.00
Bevel, Carpenter's, Cherry, U.S.Cent Inset Washer At Pivot End, 1840 ... 150.00
Bevel, Shipwright's, Solid Brass, 7 In. 95.00
Bitstock, Cherry, 17 In. 235.00
Bitstock, Quick Release, 10 In. 25.00
Blow Torch, Jim Dandy, Directions, Box 15.00
Book Press, Burrows Company, Cleveland, Ohio 175.00
Bootjack, Deer's Head, Original Paint 85.00
Bootjack, Maple, James A.Banister Co., Folding 20.00
Bootjack, Naughty Nellie, Original Paint 95.00
Bootjack, Pistol, Cast Iron 125.00
Bow Saw, Beech, 9 X 13 In. 65.00
Brace Bit, Winchester, No.12 .... 17.50
Brace, Darling, Bridgewater, Mass., Pat.Oct.20, 1868 .... 385.00
Brace, Deane & Co., Wooden 80.00
Brace, George Horton, Bronze, Rosewood, Sweep 1200.00
Brace, Keystone, Beech Handle, Ratchet Adjustment, Ives Mfg.Co., 13 In. ... 30.00
Brace, Sheffield, Brass Plates & Head, Beech 85.00
Brace, Stanley, No.313 .... 10.00
Brace, Stanley, No.915 .... 10.00
Brace, Ultimatum, William Marples, Ebony, Brass 450.00
Brace, Wimble, No.12W, Rosewood Handle & Head, Nickel Plating 45.00
Brace, Winchester, No.3504, 12 In. 60.00
Brace, With Bit, Sheffield, Maple, Ebony Handle 120.00
Brace, Wm. Marples & Sons, Brass, Rosewood 695.00
Brace, Wooden, Brass Trim, Signed J.Patterson 250.00
Branding Iron, V Shape 20.00
Bucket, Sugar, Natural, Metal Bands, Bail Handle, Stapled Lid, 8 In. 74.00
Bullet Opener, Lemp, Copper 35.00
Bung Start, Cooper's 38.00

Butt & Rabbet Gauge, Brass & Rosewood, Stanley No.92 .... 72.00
Calipers, A.J.Bruce, Metal 15.00
Calipers, Brass & Iron, London, 6 In. 22.00
Calipers, Legs, Iron, 3 3/4 In. 62.00
Can Opener, Cap Lifter & Piercer, French, C.1930 .... 10.00
Cart, Hand, Wooden Spoke Wheels, Red Paint, 28 X 36 In. 115.00
Chain, Surveyor's, Steel, Round Loop Handles, 33 1/3 In. 49.00
Chalk Line Reel, Stanley, With Scratch Awl, 7 In. 22.00
Chest, Carpenter's, Pine, Green Paint, Brushed Design, 46 1/2 In. 200.00
Chest, H.Julius Smith's Igniting Dynamo, Walnut, Patent 1895 .... 150.00
Chisel, Keen Kutter, 11 In. 20.00
Chisel, Wood, Leather Butt Handle, 3/4 In. 25.00
Clapboard Gauge, Oak, Dovetailed Scribe, 14 Steps, 8 In.Wide 62.00
Clapboard Slick, 3 3/4 In.Blade 39.00
Compass, Kieger & Faudt, Berling, Pocket 25.00
Compass, Plane, Stanley No.113, Sweetheart Blade 90.00
Corn Husker, Boss, Iron, Yellow Leather Handle 16.00
Corn Sheller, 1859 .... 200.00
Croze, Cooper's, 3 Steel Wear Plates, 6 X 17 In. 62.00
Cultivator, Horse Drawn, Wooden Frame, 6 Steel Blades, Sample, 5 In. 295.00
Cutter, Bolt, Porter's, Patent 1892 .... 15.00
Cutter, Stanley No.45, Screw Adjusting, Knob, 1895 .... 50.00
Divider, Wooden, Ram's Horn Nut, 30 In. 70.00
Dowel Jig, Stanley No.59, 5 Guides, Original Box & Directions 45.00
Drill, Push, No.75, Yankee 50.00
Fillister, Moving, Ohio Tool Co., Brass Depth Stop, Nickel 50.00
Flashlight, Hand Generator, Power, Squeeze Handle, Pygmy, Pocket, 1930s 65.00
Flashlight, Winchester, 3 Cell 75.00
Flax Separator, Cover, Hetchell, Small 28.00
Flax Wheel, Pennsylvania, Painted Red & Blue, 1890s 345.00
Funnel, Turned Walnut, Bell Shape, Hexagonal Spout, 6 X 4 1/4 In. 110.00
Gauge, Butt & Rabbet, Stanley, Dated 1892 .... 80.00
Gauge, C.Sholl, Mahogany, 4 Stem, 1800s Map of Mt.Joy, Pa. 375.00
Gauge, Clapboard, 15 Numbered Steps, Oak, 8 X 10 In. 45.00
Gauge, Farrier's, Shoe Fitting, John Hood Co., Boston, Iron Brass 95.00
Gauge, Marking, Squared Center, Brass Trim, Walnut, W.Tarring, 6 3/4 In. 60.00
Gauge, Mortise, Brass Fences & Trim, Rosewood, Patent 1867, 9 In. 55.00
Goffering Iron, Original Slug, 7 1/2 X 15 In. 220.00
Grain Probe, Brass, Large 150.00
Grinder, Bench, Hand, Keen Kutter 45.00
Grinding Wheel, Foot Operated, Seat 100.00
Gunsmith Float, Rosewood Handle, 2 Flat, 1 Round, 3 Piece, 10 In. 135.00
Hair Dryer, Mottled Red & Black Bakelite, 1930s 95.00
Hammer, Ball Peen, Keen Kutter, KM1 Shapleigh, 20 Oz. 25.00
Hammer, Goat Headed, With Tack Puller, Cast Bronze, 8 1/2 In. 125.00
Hammer, Mason's, Keen Kutter 50.00
Handcuffs, Iron Claw, Bronze 135.00
Handcuffs, Peerless, Key, Box 45.00
Handcuffs, Smith & Wesson, Nickel Plated, Leather Belt Carrier, Pair 12.00
Hatchet, Hewing, Keen Kutter 25.00
Hatchet, Hewing, Waters 15.00
Hatchet, Winchester .... 30.00 To 48.00
Hay Tester, Wrought Iron, Wooden Handle, 31 In. 22.00
Hod, Farrier's, Hoof Knife, Primitive 145.00
Hoe, Weeding, Winchester, No.10 .... 75.00
Hog Scraper, Wooden Handle 13.00
Ice Tongs, Wrought Iron, 6 1/2 In. 70.00
Jack, Conestoga Wagon, Signed P.N., Dated 1863, 22 In. 110.00
Jack, Wagon, Wood & Iron, Boston, Massachusetts 95.00
Jack, Wagon, Wrought Iron, Wood, Engraved H.Voigt, 1837, 31 In. 40.00
Jigsaw, Keen Kutter, No. 249, Electric 50.00
Jointer, Cooper's, Punch Design At Throat, Cherry, 3 X 3 X 46 In. 65.00
Jointer, Long, Chip Carving, Dated 1817, Europe, 48 In. 600.00
Kant Suck, To Keep Calf From Sucking, Cast Iron, Dated 1910 .... 30.00

Knife, Putty, Keen Kutter ....6.00 To 12.50
Lathe, Turning, Blacksmith, Wooden Bed, Flat Pulley, Jack Shaft, 6 Ft. 200.00
Lathe, Watchmaker's, Marshall 165.00
Lawnmower, Winchester 350.00
Level & Grade Finder, Helb's, Beech, Compass, 7–12–04, Inclinometer 335.00
Level, Carpenter's, Stanley, Brass Fittings, Cherry 5.00
Level, Davis & Cook, Brass & Mahogany, Patent 1886 .... 25.00
Level, Iron Filigree, M.W.Robinson Co., No.9 Davis Pat., 24 In. 95.00
Level, Keuffel & Esser 15.00
Level, Rosewood & Brass, Marked, Mackay & Co., 12 In. 125.00
Level, Stanley, No. 40, Round Ends, 3 1/4 In. 15.00
Level, Stanley, No. 41, Embossed Brass Top, Screw–On Clip 25.00
Level, Stanley, No.103, Brass Trim 45.00
Level, Stanley, No.237 .... 20.00
Level, Stratton Brothers, Rosewood, Brass, Pat.1872 & 1887, 22 In. 115.00
Level, Stratton Brothers, Rosewood, Brass, Pat.July 16, 1872, 10 In. 250.00
Level, Winchester, No.3028, Wood, Label 60.00
Log Auger, Iron Pump, Side Plate, 4 X 24 In., 3 Piece 175.00
Loom, Tape, Standing, 9 1/2 In.Board, 34 In. 525.00
Loop, Jeweler's, 10 Power, 14K Gold 350.00
Microscope, Brass, Bausch & Lomb, Fitted Wood Case 330.00
Miter Box & Saw, Keen Kutter 375.00
Miter Box, Craftsman, No.3646 .... 20.00
Miter Box, Langdon, Millers Falls 25.00
Miter Jack, Fruitwood, Victor Fautier & Fils, Paris, 27 In. 65.00
Mixing Stick, Pewter & Brass Wire, Wooden Black Handle, 13 1/2 In. 55.00
Mold, For Making Pewter Spoons, 8 In., 2 Piece 400.00
Mold, Tablespoon, Bronze, 18th Century 200.00
Monkey Wrench, Winchester, No.1001,6 In. 65.00
Nail Carrier, 8 Sections, Metal Hoop Handle, Wood 95.00
Needle Sharpener, From Phonograph Store, Hand Drill Shape, 5 In. 11.00
Niddy–Noddy, Turned Wood, Serpentine Ends, American, 18 X 12 In. 44.00
Niddy–Noddy, Walnut, Engraved Initials, 18 1/4 X 12 1/2 In. 77.00
Nippers, End, Winchester, 6 In. 32.00
Nippers, Nail, Farrier, Wrought, 14 In. 10.00
Nose Auger, Wrought Iron, 17 In.Wooden Cross Handle, 1 3/8 X 21 In. 12.00
Ovolo, Sash, Beech, 1 7/8 In. 45.00
Padlock, American Express, Key 125.00
Padlock, Iron, Y & T, Trefoil, Loxol, 2 In.Diam. 10.00
Padlock, Keen Kutter ....65.00 To 85.00
Padlock, Norvell Shapleigh Hardware Co. 250.00
Panel Gauge, Cabinetmaker's, Tiger Maple & Burl, C.1800, 13 1/2 In. 85.00
Pantograph, No.145, Maple, Mahogany Edges, Brass Points, 40 In. 30.00
Plane, Bailey, No.26 .... 25.00
Plane, Bench, Fales, Pat.Variable 900.00
Plane, Block, Diamond Edge, No.110 .... 40.00
Plane, Block, Keen Kutter, No. 60 .... 45.00
Plane, Block, Keen Kutter, No.129 .... 15.00
Plane, Block, Stanley, No. 60 .... 40.00
Plane, Block, Stanley, No.130 .... 20.00
Plane, Block, Winchester, 7 1/8 In. 50.00
Plane, Bridle Plow, Currie 200.00
Plane, Bull–Nosed Rabbet, Stanley No.90, 1936 .... 70.00
Plane, Cabinetmaker's Scraper, Stanley, No.85 .... 525.00
Plane, Chamfer, Booth Bros., Dublin, Beech, Brass Adjustment, 6 1/2 In. 85.00
Plane, Chamfer, Stanley, No.72 .... 200.00
Plane, Chariot, Slater, London, Rosewood Wedge, 4 In. 350.00
Plane, Coachman's, Moulson Brothers 22.00
Plane, Corebox, Stanley, No.56 .... 1300.00
Plane, Corner Rounding, 1/2 In.Cutter, Stanley No.144 .... 225.00
Plane, Fillister, Winchester, No.3201 .... 140.00
Plane, Fore, Edwin Hahn, No.10, 19 In. 85.00
Plane, Fore, Steere's, Pat No.307 .... 225.00
Plane, Grooving, Iron, Double Cutter, 3/8 In.Apart 12.00

Plane, Hollow Molding, E.W.Carpenter, No.18	49.00
Plane, Jack, Metallic Plane Co., Lever Actuated Blade, 15 In.	200.00
Plane, Jack, Stanley, No.5 1/4C, 18 In.	200.00
Plane, Jack, Stanley, No.5, High Knob, Label On Handle	28.00
Plane, Jack, Winchester, No.3045	90.00
Plane, Jointer, Stanley No.34	65.00
Plane, Low Angle Miter, Solid Brass, Made By P.Shea, Newton, Mass.	125.00
Plane, Molding, Impressed W.Wintkle, Clint.O., Wooden, 9 1/2 In.	17.50
Plane, Molding, Multiform, Brass Depth Stop, Pat.Aug.29, 1854, 2 In.	110.00
Plane, Molding, N.Weigle–Union Factory Warranteed, Wooden	23.00
Plane, Molding, Sargeant & Co., Wooden, Single Bit Type, 3/4 X 9 In.	18.00
Plane, Molding, Wm.C.Ross, Wooden, Double Bit Type, 7/8 X 9 1/2 In.	37.50
Plane, Pattern Maker's, Simplex, HS&CO., 5 Soles, 1837	195.00
Plane, Plank, Sandusky Tool Co., Ohio, Beech, Screw Arms, 14 In., Pair	125.00
Plane, Plough, W.Greenslade, Bristol, London, 1865	105.00
Plane, Plow, Auburn, No.90	135.00
Plane, Plow, Stanley, No.45	85.00
Plane, Rabbet, No.55	100.00
Plane, Rabbet, Stanley, No.278	100.00
Plane, Sash, Double, Beech, No.212, Boxwood Screw Arms, Union Factory	95.00
Plane, Scraper, Eclipse Plane Co., Pat.1874	400.00
Plane, Scraper, Stanley No.85	650.00
Plane, Smooth, Stanley Sweetheart, No.1	500.00
Plane, Smooth, Stanley–Bailey No.4	20.00
Plane, Smooth, Tower & Lyon	90.00
Plane, Stanley, No. 26	25.00
Plane, Stanley, No. 45	65.00 To 80.00
Plane, Stanley, No. 55, 3 Boxes of Blades	350.00
Plane, Stanley, No.444, Dovetail, Nickel Plating, 1910	585.00
Plane, Stanley–Wards Miter, No.7, Wooden, 21 In.	15.00
Plane, Victor Fore, No.6, 18 In.	250.00
Plane, Winchester, No.3005	50.00
Plane, Winchester, No.3030	70.00
Plane, Witchet, Wrought Iron Screws, 5 1/2 In.Blade, 7 1/2 X 10 In.	98.00
Plane, Wood Sash, Sandusky Tool Co., Double Iron, 1869–1920, 9 1/2 In.	90.00
Planter, Metal Hopper, Spring Loaded Metal Foot, 33 In.	55.00
Pliers, Needle Nose, Keen Kutter	19.00
Pliers, Winchester, 8 In.	16.00
Plumb, Carpenter's, Brass	20.00
Pulley, Wooden, Brass Disc Over Pulley Axle, 4 In.Block, 8 1/2 In.	16.00
Punch, Conductor's, Union Pacific	18.00
Rabbet, Side, Beech, Brass Plated Sole, 6 In.	75.00
Rake, Hay, Wooden, Branded M.B.Young, 67 In.	200.00
Razee Jointer, Gage Tool Co., Vineland, N.J., Mahogany	150.00
Reamer, Iron, Wooden, Makes 2 In.Holes, 13 In.	35.00
Reamer, Wheelwright's, Hooked, Weigler	70.00
Rope Twisting Machine, Brass & Iron, Handle, Mahogany, 4 3/8 In.	75.00
Router, Hand, Stanley, No.71 1/2	85.00
Rule, Angle, Goodell Pratt Co., Etched Owner's Name, Steel, 1900s	20.00
Rule, Folding, Ivory, Brass Joints, No.89, 4–Fold, 12 In.	150.00
Rule, Folding, Stanley, No.13 1/2, 2–Fold, 6 In.	35.00
Rule, Folding, Stanley, No.53 1/2, Architect's, 4–Fold, 12 In.	40.00
Rule, Folding, Stanley, No.55, Boxwood, Brass Tips, 4–Fold, 12 In.	25.00
Rule, Folding, Stanley, No.61	15.00
Rule, Folding, With Caliper, Stephens & Co., No.95, 6 In.	32.00
Rule, Interlox, Folding, 24 In.	25.00
Rule, Ivory, Stanley No.87	180.00
Rule, Miller Falls, Brass Tip, 6 Ft.	11.00
Rule, Stanley, No.62, Brass Bound	25.00
Safe, Barnes, Original Bill of Sale, 1895, 28 3/4 X 18 1/2 In.	125.00
Saw, Circular, Tyobi Industrial, 7 1/4 In.	45.00
Saw, Coping, Winchester	25.00
Saw, Hand, Diamond Edge, No.165	35.00
Saw, Hand, Keen Kutter, 22 In.	30.00

Saw, Hand, Winchester Old Trusty	85.00
Saw, Keyhole, Dated 1877	95.00
Saw, Tenon, Temple's Sheffield, Brass Backed	60.00
Saw, Winchester, No.10	40.00
Scissors, Buttonhole, Keen Kutter	25.00
Scissors, Winchester, No.9016, 9 In.	45.00
Scoop, Charcoal, Blacksmith's, Wrought Iron, 27 In.	22.00
Scoop, Cranberry, Blue Paint, Sharpened Spikes, Rod Handle, 18 X 15 In.	192.00
Scraper, Cabinet, Stanley No.85	625.00
Screwdriver, Archimedes, Lignum Vitae Head, Reid, Pa., Pat.Dec.1882	30.00
Scribe, Carpenter's, Wooden Bar & Thumbscrew, Measurements, 9 In.	9.00
Seeder, Cyclone, Hand Held	10.00
Shears, Tailor's	40.00
Shingle Slick, D Handle	40.00
Shovel, Grain, Open D Handle, Hand Carved Wood, C.1820, 36 In.	220.00
Side Snipe, Goodman, R.Nelson, London, 1823–52, 9 1/8 In.OAL	20.00
Skate Sharpener, Berghman, Box, 1920	35.00
Slide Rule, Keuffel & Esser, 1947	10.00
Slide Rule, Keuffel & Esser, Patent 1916	12.00
Slide Rule, Keuffel & Esser, Wood & Celluloid, Case, Dated 1900	35.00
Slide Rule, Pickett 160, Leatherette Case, 6 In.	10.00
Splint, Leg, Hinged Sides, Walnut, 23 1/2 In.	65.00
Spoke Shave, C.S.Osborne, Rosewood, 11 In.	32.00
Spoke Shave, Stanley, No.71	75.00
Sprayer, S.D.G.Ideal Spray Co., Brass, Steel, Pat.1927	55.00
Square, Cabinetmaker's, Adjustable, Stanley, No.18	12.50
Stanchion, Milking, Metal Hardware, 4 Styles, Salesman's Sample	225.00
Stave Finisher, Cooper's, Curved, 1 Brass Ferrule Split	25.00
Stretcher, Wire, Western Union	45.00
Swift, Table Clamp, All Wooden, Yellow Stain, 24 In.	125.00
Swift, Wooden Table Clamp, Folding, Yellow Varnish, 22 In.	200.00
T–Bevel, Brass & Ebony, 5 1/2 In.	65.00
Tap & Die Set, Peugeot Freres	475.00
Tatting Shuttle, Bone	20.00
Template, For Weather Vane, Running Horse, Tin	500.00
Tester, Hay, Hooked, Forged Iron, Wooden Handle, 31 In.	20.00
Tongs, Blacksmith, Cast Iron, 47 In.	40.00
Tongs, Pipe, Wrought Iron, 11 3/4 In.	60.00
Trammel Points, Stanley, Brass, 4 1/4 In.	35.00
Trammel, Chain Link, Wrought Iron, Twisted Design Back, 57 In.	25.00
Transit, Surveyor, Fairfield County, Ohio, Primitive, Handmade, 1870s	275.00
Transit, Surveyor, J.Prentice, N.Y., C.1850	250.00
Try Square, Cherry, Brass Bound, 12 In.	25.00
Utility Battery Filler, Glass Bottle, Hose, Cast Iron, 1910, 13 In.	35.00
Vise, Hand Forged, Wall, 1800s	75.00
Wax Seal, Ivory Handle, Monogram On Brass, 2 5/8 In.	200.00
Wheelbarrow, Flared Body, Stick Handles, Painted Red, 4 Ft.	192.00
Wheelbarrow, Toledo Clipper Stenciled On Sides, Dated 1882	325.00
Whetstone, Winchester	35.00
Whip Holder, Buggy, Wooden	15.00
Wrench, Adjustable, Billings Type, 3 In.	100.00
Wrench, Adjustable, Duffy, Bethlehem Wrench Co.	32.00

To restore old tools, wash wood with Murphy's oil soap, dry, sand with steel wool, apply two coats of Minwax or other oil, then use paste wax and buff. Clean metal parts, then coat with clear lacquer.

Wrench, Alligator, Keen Kutter, No. 40	60.00
Wrench, Alligator, Keen Kutter, No.120	75.00
Wrench, Irland Pipe Wrench Co., Boston, Mass.A, Pat.July 7, 1905, 14 In.	49.00
Wrench, Millwright's, With Cap Screw Tightener, 32 In.	45.00
Wrench, Open End, Winchester, No.1705	25.00
Wrench, Pipe, Keen Kutter, No.14	15.00
Wrench, Pocket, Adjustable, Iver Johnson	25.00
Wrench, Spark Plug, Tungsten	15.00
Yarn Winder, 3 Splayed Legs, Counting Mechanism In Case, Crank, 27 In.	50.00
Yarn Winder, Wooden, Red Painted Trestle, Metal Crank, 34 1/2 X 26 In.	165.00
Yoke, Ox, Double	120.00

 Toothpick holders are sometimes called "toothpicks" by collectors. The variously shaped containers made to hold the small wooden toothpicks are of glass, china, or metal. Most of the toothpick holders are Victorian.

TOOTHPICK, see also other categories such as Bisque; Silver Plate; Slag; etc.

TOOTHPICK, Allover Hobnail, Blue Opalescent	35.00
American, Fostoria	29.00
Arkansas	25.00
Blue Opalescent, Rising Sun	75.00
Boston Bean Pot, Green, Pink Figural Sitting Pig, Germany	35.00
Bulldog, Stands Next To Holder, Derby Silver Plate	50.00
Bunny, With Cart, Occupied Japan	12.50
Carnival Glass, Flute, Deep Orange	65.00
Carnival Glass, Kittens, Gold	135.00
Chick On Egg, Heart–Shaped Vase, Silver Plate	20.00
Cracked Egg, Bearded Elf, Sitting, Raised Silver Dots, Germany	55.00
Cut Glass, Etched Thistle Blossom	45.00
Cut Glass, Fluted Diamonds	38.00
Frisco	75.00
Frog	42.00
Frosted Coin, Silver Dollar	300.00
Heart Band, Souvenir, Beals, Maine, Gold Rim	25.00
Hobnail, Blue Ribbed Base	35.00
Jefferson Optic, Amethyst, Enameled	45.00
Kansas	55.00
Keokuk, Iowa, Custard Glass	21.00
Kitten On Pillow, Amber	85.00
Kitten On Pillow, Blue	95.00
Kradle, Crys–Tol, Flat	18.00
Mother, Custard Glass	10.00
Owl, With Top Hat	8.00
Paddlewheel & Star	35.00
Pink Cased, Pansy	87.50
Shoshone, With Gold	30.00
Souvenir, Dempsey, Gibbon Fight	75.00
Souvenir, Illinois State Fair, 1939	22.50
Swan, Milk Glass	19.00
Three Dolphin Base, Amber	55.00
Three–Faced Girl, 3 Different Smiles, Bonnet, Bisque	55.00
Two Roosters, Blue	85.00
Yellow Pig, With Basket	18.00

TORQUAY   Torquay is the name given to ceramics by several potteries working near Torquay, England, from 1870 until 1962. Until about 1900, the potteries used local red clay to make classical style art pottery vases and figurines. Then they turned to making souvenir wares. Items were dipped in colored slip and decorated with painted slip and sgraffito designs. They often had mottos or proverbs, and scenes of cottages, ships, birds, or flowers. The "Scandy" design was a symmetrical arrangement of brush strokes and spots done in colored slips. Potteries included Watcombe Pottery (1870–1962); Torquay

Terra–Cotta Company (1875–1905); Aller Vale (1881–1924); Torquay Pottery (1908–1940); and Longpark (1883–1957).

TORQUAY, Coffeepot, Black Cockerel, Verse On Back, Longpark, 6 1/2 In.	79.00
Creamer	25.00
Cruet, Seagull	75.00
Dish, Cheese	45.00
Dish, Scandy, Dust Pan Shape, Verse, Watcombe, 3 In.	50.00
Eggcup, Cottage	40.00
Hatpin Holder, Rooster, Keep Me On The Dressing Table, 5 In.	85.00
Jam Pot, Cottage, Handle, Words On Back, Watcombe, 3 1/4 In.	48.00
Jar, Cracker, Milk Glass, Hand Decorated	75.00
Match Holder, Motto Ware, Scandy	60.00
Mug, Pixie, Yellow, Motto Ware	55.00
Pitcher, Aller Vale, Motto Ware, 4 Line, 5 3/4 In.	60.00
Pitcher, Purple & Green Floral, Motto Ware, 3 1/2 In.	55.00
Plate, Dartmouth Cottage, Motto Ware, 6 1/2 In.	25.00
Plate, Dartmouth Cottage, Motto Ware, 8 In.	45.00
Plate, Dartmouth Cottage, Motto Ware, 10 In.	55.00
Puzzle Jug, Sailboat, Motto Ware, 4 In.	55.00
Teapot, Cockerel, Motto Ware	30.00
Teapot, Scandy, Wording On Back, Cream Ground, 4 1/2 In.	55.00
Tile, Quotation, 5 X 7 1/2 In.	100.00
Vase, Daffodils, Green Leaves, Top Opening For Flowers, 5 1/2 In.	55.00
Vase, Double Handles, 8 In.	65.00
Vase, Flowers, Leaves, Brown Glaze, Longpark, 10 In.	50.00
Vase, Kersall Daisy, 3 Handles	45.00
Vase, Sailboats, Wording On Back, Pierced Top, 6 1/4 In.	50.00

Tortoiseshell glass was made during the 1800s and after by the Sandwich Glass Works of Massachusetts and some firms in Germany. Tortoiseshell glass is, of course, named for its resemblance to real shell from a tortoise. It has been reproduced.

TORTOISESHELL GLASS, Bottle, Snuff, Animal Design, Pear Shape, 2 5/8 In.	220.00
Bowl, Amber Feet, Footed, 4 X 7 3/4 In.	110.00
Bowl, Spangle Interior	50.00
Cruet, Cut Stopper	185.00
Finger Bowl, Undertray, Ruffled, 3 X 6 X 6 In.	275.00
Vase, 14 1/4 In.	275.00

The shell of the tortoise has been used as inlay and to make small decorative objects since the seventeenth century. Some species of tortoise are now on the endangered species list, and objects made from these shells cannot be sold legally.

TORTOISESHELL, Box, Dresser, Domed Lid, Ivory Ball Feet, 10 In. ....*Illus*	550.00
Box, Inlaid Silver Floral Spray, 3 1/2 In.	125.00
Case, Card, Mother–of–Pearl Inlay	70.00
Case, Cigarette, Erotic Painting In False Bottom, Meirling	175.00
Case, Dance Program, Monogram Cover, Ivory Stylus, 4 X 3 In.	10.00
Comb, 18K Gold Inlaid Butterfly, Stones	15.00
Dresser Set, 14K Gold Ovals, 5 Piece	85.00
Frame, Double, SS Hinged, Lock, SS Design, Cover	165.00

Toys are designed to entice children; and today, they have attracted new interest among adults who are still children at heart. All types of toys are collected. Tin toys, iron toys, battery operated toys, and many others are collected by specialists. Dolls, Games, Teddy Bears, and Bicycles are listed under their own categories. Other toys may be found under company or celebrity names.

TOY, %Iron, Besto	30.00
%Iron, Dolly Dell, Electric	7.50
%Iron, Electric, Nassau	15.00
%Iron, Electric, Robin's–Egg Blue Graniteware, 1920s	40.00
%Iron, Removable Wooden Handle, 5 In.	35.00

%Iron, Sunny Susy, Electric	7.00
%Iron, Westinghouse, Heats To Warm, Ohio Art Co.	12.00
%Iron, Wooden Handle, Sensible No.6, N.R.S.N. Co.	37.50
Acrobat, Merry–Go–Round, 3 Men Hang Onto Trapeze Bars, Tin, Windup	475.00
Adam The Porter, Frys Chocolates, Trunk On Dolly, Lehmann	1350.00
Adam The Porter, Pushes Cart, No Trunk, Windup, Lehmann	850.00
Aerial Ladder Truck, Windup, Steel, Keystone, 1930s, 23 In.	140.00
African Mailman, In Cart, Pulled By Ostrich, Windup, Lehmann	650.00
Airplane Kit, Spitfire, Megow Balsa Wood, 30–In. Wingspan, Box	48.00
Airplane, American Airlines, 28 In.	38.00
Airplane, American Flyer, Tin, 18–In. Wingspan	260.00
Airplane, Areo Speeder, Pull Lever To Make Plane Fly, Buffalo Toys	55.00
Airplane, Army Air, Metal, White Rubber Tires, Hubley, 6 X 8 In.	45.00
Airplane, Biplane, Yellow, Green, Tin, Key Wind, Wells, C.1933, 9 1/2 In.	200.00
Airplane, Boeing Strato Cruiser, Pressed Steel, Wyandotte, 13 In.	115.00
Airplane, Camouflage Colors, Tinplate, Key Wind, Marx, 13 In.	130.00
Airplane, China Clipper, Wyandotte, 10 In.Wing Span	50.00
Airplane, Circus, With Cloth, Japan Zone, 3 In.	40.00
Airplane, Delta, Fan Jet, On Stand, 35 In.	350.00
Airplane, Flying Bomb, Wyandotte, 18 In.	100.00
Airplane, Folding Wings, Hubley, 1950s	15.50
Airplane, Glider, Lindy, Rubber Tires, Dismountable Rider, Hubley, 1933	450.00
Airplane, Helicopter, Air Force, Viewable Piston, Friction, Japan, 11 In.	32.00
Airplane, Helicopter, Daily Planet, Corgi, Box	15.00
Airplane, Helicopter, G.I.Joe, With Doll, Yellow, 12 X 24 In.	40.00
Airplane, Helicopter, Sun Star, Strauss	50.00
Airplane, Japan Airlines, DC8, On Stand, 34 In.	350.00
Airplane, Mitsubishi, Prop Plane, 44 In.	850.00
Airplane, Monoplane, Single Prop, Wooden Wheels, C.1930	30.00
Airplane, Northeast, DC9, Aluminum, On Stand, 27 In.	350.00
Airplane, Pan American, Marx, 27–In. Wingspan	145.00
Airplane, Pull Toy, Tin, Litho Trans–Continental Airlines, Girard	275.00
Airplane, Seaplane, Red, Light Tan, Tin, Meccano, C.1935, 9 X 11 In.	325.00
Airplane, Single Engine, Iron, Hubley, 5–In. Wingspan	65.00
Airplane, Sky Ranger, Rotates Around Center Tower, Windup, Unique Art	225.00
Airplane, Sky Ranger, S–RS, Flying Roundabout, Tinplate, Marx, 9 In.	130.00
Airplane, Tri–Motor, Pathfinder, Windup, Katz Co., 22–In. Wingspan	450.00
Airplane, TWA, Aluminum Prop Plane, 26 1/2 In.	500.00
Airplane, U.S.Army, Rubber Tires, Hubley, 6 1/2 X 9 In.	18.00
Airplane, Wings Fold, Wheels Retract, Painted, Metal, Hubley	12.50
Alabama Coon Jigger, Oh My, Strauss, 1930s	600.00
Alley Oop, 2 Race Cars, Ramp, Tin Litho, Graphics On Box, Germany, 1920s	425.00
Alligator, Black Boy On Top, Tin, Chein	135.00
American Eagle Lunar Module, DSK, Box	150.00
Andy Gump, Cast Iron, Original Paint	295.00
Anxious Bride, Windup, Lehmann	1400.00
Armored Attack Set, Marx	75.00
Armored Fortress, World War II, H.G.Toys, Unopened Box, Late 1960s	30.00
Army Train, Marx	55.00
Army Wagon, Trico, 1930s	25.00
B.O.Plenty, Windup, Lithographed, 1940s, 8 1/2 In.	100.00
Badge, Man From U.N.C.L.E., Display Card, 12 Piece, Dated 1965	50.00
Bake Set, Like Mother's, Aluminum, Box	95.00
Balloon Man, Mickey Mouse On String, Windup, Germany	400.00
Barnacle Bill The Sailor, Walks, Talks, Windup, Chein, 1930	195.00
Barnacle Bill, Marx	135.00
Bartender, Face Turns Red, Smoke Comes Out of Ears, Battery Operated	50.00
Battleship, Clockwork, Painted Tin, 4 Funnels, Bing, C.1912, 32 In.	4950.00
Battleship, Key Wind, Hess	500.00 To 525.00
Battleship, Oregon, Wooden Wheels, Wood Cannons On Deck, C.1900, 24 In.	260.00
Bazooka, Bob Burns	17.50
TOY, BEAR, see also Teddy Bear	
Bear, Boxing, Mechanical, Cragstan	65.00
Bear, Dancing, Windup, Schuco	120.00

Toy, Grocer's Shop, Lithographed Paper, Wooden, 9 X 20 In.

Bear, Grandma, Knitting, Windup, Metal, Chein 40.00
Bear, Mama Bear Feeding Baby Bear, Battery Operated 65.00
Bear, Peanut Vendor, Battery Operated, Tin, 5 Actions, Cragstan 120.00
Bear, Sitting, Drinks Milk, Windup, Metal 30.00
Bear, Tumbling, Red & Gold Suit, Mohair Head, Key Wind, Schuco, 4 In. 350.00
Bear, Walking, Windup, Metal, Chien 25.00
Bed, Doll's, 4-Poster, Pine, Red, Patchwork Quilt, 1830, 18 X 11 In. 775.00
Bed, Doll's, Canopy, Maple, Spread & Canopy Cover, C.1910, 11 1/2 In. 225.00
Bed, Doll's, Painted White, Gold Knobs, Wooden 17.00
Bed, Doll's, Turned Posts, Walnut, 10 1/2 X 16 1/4 In. 250.00
Bed, Doll's, Victorian Gothic, Iron, White Paint, Mattress & Pillow 225.00
Bed, Doll's, Victorian, Iron, 10 X 16 In. 65.00
Bed, Doll's, Wood, Painted White, Gold Knobs 17.00
Bedrock Express, Flintstone, Box 245.00
Beer Drinker, Squeaker, Papier-Mache Face, Wine Glass 80.00
Beetle, Flaps Wigs, Tin, Windup, Shakes, Lehman 75.00
Bell Ringer, Landing of Columbus, Cast Iron 235.00
Bell Toy, Ding Dong Bell, Pussy's Not In Well, Clowns Rescuing, 1890s 1350.00
    TOY, BICYCLE, see Bicycle
Big Joe Chef, Windup, Tin Litho, Yone, Japan, 6 1/2 In. 135.00
Bird, Pecking, Multicolored, Windup, 1927 .... 40.00
Bird, Singing, Windup, Brass Cage, French, 1890s, 11 In. 275.00
Bird, Tin, Cardboard Wings, Lehman 475.00
Black Figure, Riding Alligator, Windup, Chein, Box 155.00
Black Man, Dancing On Street Corner, Windup, Tin, Celluloid 135.00
Black Man, Playing Piano 425.00
Blackboard, 13 X 16 In. 2.00
Blender, Battery Operated 35.00
Blimp, Tootsietoy 70.00
Blocks, Anchor, No.4 .... 90.00
Blocks, Animal, ABC, & Picture, Paper Covered, McLoughlin Bros., 4 Piece 85.00
Blocks, Building, Clay, Richter, Complete Set In Box, 1890s 335.00

Blocks, Building, Stone, Architector Jr., Wooden Box, Dated 1945	40.00
Blocks, Building, Wooden Box, DePage, Dated 1945	40.00
Blocks, Liberty, No.2, Phoenix	95.00
Blocks, New Rattle, ABC, Box, Germany	145.00
Blocks, Wooden, Halsom, Box	165.00
Blocks, Wooden, Paper Scene On Each Cube, Box, French, 8 1/2 X 10 In.	100.00
Blocks, Wooden, Paper, English Steam Engines, Box, Hameley, 1900s	185.00
Blocks, Wooden, Red & White, Embossed Designs, Set, 7 3/4 X 9 3/4 In.	125.00
Boat Carrier, Original Boats, Tin, Buddy L	45.00
Boat, Battleship, Tootsietoy, 1940s	24.00
Boat, Cannons, Waves, Lithograph Wood, Bliss, 1882, 31 In.	770.00
Boat, Ferry, Side–Wheeler, Cast Iron, Wilkins, 7 1/2 In.	165.00
Boat, Green, White, Man Steering, Tin, Windup, Germany, 8 In.	80.00
Boat, Liner, Bremen, Man Pops Out of Hatch, Tin, Windup, Germany, 14 In.	150.00
Boat, Motor Patrol, Dinky, Box	30.00
Boat, Passenger Liner, Falk, Tin, 4 Funnels, 1920, 12 In.	1100.00
Boat, S.S.Wolverine Luxury Liner, Windup, Tin, Box, 15 In.	75.00
Boat, Speedboat, Windup, Tin, Box, Chein, 14 In.	95.00
Boat, Steam Launch, H.E.Boucher Mfg.Co., N.Y.	750.00
Boat, Steam Power, Bowman, Brass & Wood, Box, 22 In.	825.00
Boat, Submarine, Tootsietoy, 1940s	15.00
Boat, Tin, Orkincraft, 17 In.	875.00
Boat, Transport, Tootsietoy, 1940s	24.00
Boat, Windrotoren, Carette, 1912, 11 In.	950.00
Boat, Yacht, Tootsietoy, 1940s	18.00
Bottle, Doll's, Milk Glass, Red Rubber Nipple, 1940	5.00
Bowler, Man Throws Clay Balls, Wooden Pins, Tin, Windup, Martin, 8 In.	1300.00
Box, Exercising, With 2 Balls, Guntherman, 1900	575.00
Boxing Gloves, 1890–1900, Set of 4	35.00
Boy, On Sled, Tin Litho, No Wheels, Hess, Germany, 6 1/2 In.	125.00
Bucket, Milk, Sunbonnet Girl, Milking Cow Scene, Tin, Bail Handle, Marx	40.00
Bucking Bronco, Rider, Celluloid, Windup, Occupied Japan, 6 X 6 In.	85.00
Bug, Windup, Wings Move, 6 Legs, Metal, English, C.1890	250.00
Bulky Mule, Lehmann, 1907	195.00
Bull, Bucking, Remote Control	22.00
Bulldozer, Battery Operated, Linemar ....30.00 To 40.00
Bulldozer, Dinky Supertoys, 5 1/2 In.	42.50
Bunny, Drumming, Battery Operated, Box	85.00
Bunny, Pushing Baby In Carriage, With Colored Eggs, Windup	95.00
Bus, Coast–To–Coast, Blue, Gold, Iron, Hubley, 1927, 13 In.	425.00
Bus, Double Decker, Kenton, 4 In.	75.00
Bus, Double Decker, Open Top, Red, Driver, Arcade, 1928, 8 In.	225.00
Bus, Double Decker, Red, Advertising Decals, Taylor & Barrett, 4 In.	325.00
Bus, Double Decker, Red, White Windows, Triang, 20 In.	225.00
Bus, Double Decker, Strauss	425.00
Bus, Greyhound Lines, Buddy L	160.00
Bus, Greyhound, Realistic Toy	30.00
Bus, Interstate, Stairs Leading To Top Deck, Strauss	380.00
Bus, Light Blue, Tin, Key Wind, Tippcar, Tippco, 9 In.	130.00
Bus, Mercedes Benz, Red, White, Swastika Eagle, Diecast, Conrad, 1938	500.00
Bus, Night Coach, Kenton, 5 3/4 In.	250.00
Bus, Paris, Tin, Key Wind, Dark Green, C.R.French, C.1929, 11 1/4 In.	1300.00
Bus, Trailways, Friction ....8.00 To 10.00
Bus, Wolverine, Tin	95.00
Bus, World's Fair, Cast Iron, Arcade, 1939	195.00
Butterfly, Pull Toy	62.50
Butterfly, Windup, Tin, Strauss	85.00
Cable Car, Lehmann, Box	20.00
Cable Car, Vinette, Lehmann	1250.00
Cackling Hen, Red, Fisher–Price	45.00
Camel, Cosy, 2 Humps, Steiff	115.00
Camel, On Platform, Iron Wheels, 23 X 18 1/2 In.	675.00
Camel, Straw Stuffed, Velvet Covered, Glass Eyes, Steiff, 13 In.	325.00
Camel, With Trappings, Synthetic Fur, Plastic Eyes, On Wheels, 3 Ft.	450.00

Camera, Flintstone, 1964 .... 35.00
Camera, Komic Kamera, Windup, Tin, 3 Rolls of Film, Box 75.00
Camera, Movie, Patte News, Pressed Steel, Marx, 10 In. 135.00
Camera, Newsreel, Mattel, 1965 .... 35.00
Cannon, Big Bank, 18 In. 75.00
Cannon, Bronze, Cast Iron Carriage, 9 In. 40.00
Cannon, Cast Iron, Brass, Green Carriage, 14 1/4 In. 250.00
Cannon, Cast Iron, Swivels On Carriage, Spoked Wheels, 13 In. 150.00
Cannon, Movable Brass Barrel, Wheels, Made In USA, 8 In. 60.00
Cannon, Tin, 5 1/2 In. 40.00
Canteen, Daniel Boone 15.00
Cap Gun, Army, Cast Iron 25.00
Cap Gun, Banjo, Stevens, Box 50.00
Cap Gun, Brass Lock & Key Shape, Hubley 75.00
Cap Gun, Cast Iron, 1878 .... 75.00
Cap Gun, Cheyenne Shooter, Ivory Grips, Western Style 40.00
Cap Gun, Colt, Patent June 17, 1880, 2 3/4 X 5 1/2 In. 40.00
Cap Gun, Cowboy King, Cast Iron 50.00
Cap Gun, Cowboy, Revolving Cylinder, Hubley, 11 1/2 In. 35.00
Cap Gun, Fanner, Mattel 15.00
Cap Gun, Flintlock Jr., Hubley, 7 1/2 In. 35.00
Cap Gun, Flintlock, Double Barrel, Double Hammer, Hubley 50.00
Cap Gun, Futuristic Strato, Repeater 25.00
Cap Gun, Invincible 50 Shot Cast Iron Cap Pistol, Original Paint 45.00
Cap Gun, Invincible, Kilgore 22.00
Cap Gun, J.E.Stevens .... 25.00 To 32.00
Cap Gun, Kit Carson, Kilgore 30.00
Cap Gun, Lion's Head, C.1890 .... 165.00
Cap Gun, National, Box 40.00
Cap Gun, Nichols Stallion, 1950 .... 18.00
Cap Gun, Pistol, Border Patrol, Kilgore 17.50
Cap Gun, Plastic Handle, Applied Steer Heads, Pot Metal, Hubley 12.00
Cap Gun, Pluck, P15 .... 35.00
Cap Gun, Ric–O–Shay, 45, Hubley 50.00
Cap Gun, Scout, Single Shot, Stevens, Dated 1890, 7 In. 20.00
Cap Gun, Secret Agent, Box 25.00
Cap Gun, Tex, Embossed Bull On Handle, 5 1/2 In. 8.00
Cap Gun, Texan, 50 Shot Repeater, Hubley, Box 60.00
Cap Gun, Thundercap, Several Rolls, Box 15.00
Cap Gun, Trooper, Hubley 12.00
Cap Gun, Villa, V3 .... 33.00
Cap Gun, Wild Bill Hickok .... 15.00 To 35.00

Toy, Hobbyhorse, Articulated Ears, Tail,
Cloth Saddle, Pine, 44 In.

Cap Gun, Wyatt Earp, Pearl Handle 25.00
Car, 1908 Model T Ford, Brown Wheels & Seat, Dinky 70.00
Car, 1962 Impala, HO Slot, Atlas 28.00
Car, 2–Door Coupe, Red & Brown, Tin Wheels, Windup, Tin 160.00
Car, Ambulance, Friction, Box 35.00
Car, Amos & Andy Taxicab, Tin, Windup, Autographed Marx, 7 1/2 In. 750.00
Car, Andy Gump Driving, Tootsietoy 275.00
Car, Aston Martin, James Bond, Gold, Corgi 65.00
Car, Austin Healey, Friction 75.00
Car, Bandi, Mustang, Convertible, Red, 1965, 12 In. 75.00
Car, Buick Century, White Top, Green, Tootsietoy, 5 1/2 In. 15.00
Car, Cab, Yellow, A Century of Progress, Chicago 1933, Arcade 340.00
Car, Cadillac, Convertible, Gama, 1950s 550.00
Car, Cadillac, Eldorado, Promotion, 1976 .... 18.00
Car, Cadillac, Friction, Gama, West Germany, 1950s 735.00
Car, Cadillac, Tin, Ichiko, 1961, 20 In. 585.00
Car, Combinato No.4003, Schuco, Box 115.00
Car, Convertible, Wyandotte, 10 In. 45.00
Car, Corvette, Eldon, 1968 .... 35.00
Car, Crazy, Mortimer Snerd, Marx, 1930s 575.00
Car, Duesenburg, Rubber Tires, Hubley, 12 1/2 In. 65.00
Car, Fire Chief, Pull Toy, Bell, Marx 85.00
Car, Firebird, 1965, Box 100.00
Car, Ford, 1951, Windup, Tin, Guntherman, 11 In. 250.00
Car, Golden Arrow Racer, Kingsbury, Pressed Steel, Driver, 19 1/2 In. 440.00
Car, Grandpa's New Car, Tin, Windup, Mechanical, 5 1/2 In. 135.00
Car, Hansom Cab, Clockwork, Tin, Lehmann, Early 1900s, 5 3/4 In. 715.00
Car, Hi–Way Henry, 1920s 1450.00
Car, Hill Climber Roadster, Driver, C.1920, 11 In. 375.00
Car, Honk–Along Lincoln, Tin, Friction, 2 Tone Blue, Honks, Japan, Box 95.00
Car, Jaguar XK–120, Red, Dinky Toy 50.00
Car, Jaguar XKE, Green, Silver, Marx 15.00
Car, Jalopy, Half, Happy Bunny, Brake, Friction, Japan, 1950s 27.00
Car, James Bond, Gilbert 25.00
Car, Jeep, Searchlight Trailer, Marx 95.00
Car, Limosine, Driver, Kenton, Tin 550.00
Car, Lincoln & House Trailer, Blue, Silver, Smith–Miller 850.00
Car, Man From U.N.C.L.E., 1966 Corgi, Box 80.00
Car, Marklin, Windup, Tin, Bavaria, 1920s 795.00
Car, Mercedes Benz, Hardtop Roadster, White & Red, Corgi, Box 45.00
Car, Mercedes Polizei, Battery Operated, Tin Litho, Ichico, 13 In. 250.00
Car, Mercedes, Key Wind, Distler, Box 225.00
Car, Microracer, Mercer, Schuco 129.00
Car, Milton Berle, Windup, Marx 175.00
Car, Model T Ford, Black & Gray, White Rubber Tires, Arcade 1650.00
Car, Mustang Mach L, White, Racing Lettering, Taiyo, 10 In. 45.00
Car, Mustang, Electric Power, Plastic, 16 In. 150.00
Car, Naughty Boy, Goes Different Directions, Grabs Wheel From Father 1200.00
Car, Oldsmobile Toronado, Friction 135.00
Car, Packard, White Tires, Tootsietoy 75.00
Car, Police, Remote Control, Linmar 45.00
Car, Pop–Out Driver, Windup, Tin Litho, Breuete, 5 1/2 In. 145.00
Car, Porsche Yescha, Windup, Tin, Blue Paint, Germany 200.00
Car, Racing, Clockwork, Tinplate, John Cobb, English, 10 In. 200.00
Car, Racing, Cooper Maserati, Corgi 20.00
Car, Racing, Indianapolis, Hubley 80.00
Car, Racing, Lotus, Dinky 18.00
Car, Racing, Mercedes Benz, Silver, Tin, Battery Operated, Marusan, 10 In. 150.00
Car, Racing, No.5, Hubley 40.00
Car, Rambler Station Wagon, Tootsietoy 18.00
Car, Reversible Coupe, Art Deco, Marx 225.00
Car, Roadster, 1925 Model T, Laurel & Hardy 30.00
Car, Roadster, Tin, Windup, White Rubber Wheels, Kingsbury Toys, 12 In. 185.00
Car, Rolls–Royce, Friction, Tin, Japan 150.00

Car, Rolls–Royce, Silver Shadow, Corgi, Box 25.00
Car, Rolls–Royce, Touring, Friction, Tin, Linemar 65.00
Car, Schuco, Model No.1001, Tin, U.S.Zone Germany 50.00
Car, Scooter Bumper, Lusse, Full–Size 950.00
Car, Sedan, Convertible, Removable Top, Windup, Maroon, 1922, Gunthermann 225.00
Car, Sedan, Lime Green, Cream, Driver, Key Wind, Tinplate, English, 13 In. 225.00
Car, Sheriff Sam Whoopee, Windup, Marx 145.00
Car, Skeeter Bug, Windup 60.00
Car, Space Computer, Windup 65.00
Car, Sportster, Convertible, Red, Cream Lighograph, Push Toy, Marx, 20 In. 70.00
Car, Station Wagon, Maroon & Tan, Wooden, Buddy L 260.00
Car, T–Bird, Tootsietoy 15.00
Car, Touring, Franklin, Cast Iron, Dent, 9 In. 500.00
Car, Touring, Trunk Rack, Clockwork, Tin, Germany, 1900s, 8 X 6 1/2 In. 3575.00
Car, Volkswagen, Police, Dutch Version, Corgi 50.00
Car, Volkswagen, Windup, Schuco .... 40.00 To 45.00
Car, Windup, Convertible, Black, Lady Driver, Bing 395.00
Car, Winnebago, Motor Home, Tonka, Tootsietoy 45.00
Car, Yellow Top, Blue Body, Sun Rubber, 4 In. 35.00
Carousel, Clockwork, 3 White Horses, Painted, Germany, 12 In. 1540.00
Carousel, Music Box, Boys, Girls, Ponies, Boats, Windup, 17 In. 650.00
Carousel, Sailway, Unique Art, Windup, Marx 45.00
Carpet Sweeper, Bissell Little Gem 55.00
Carpet Sweeper, Happy Time, Sears & Roebuck 30.00
Carpet Sweeper, Pretty Maid, Sparks 40.00
Carpet Sweeper, Sally Ann 50.00
Carpet Sweeper, Sunshine, Gilt Script Name, Varnished, 1900s, 30 In. 30.00
Carriage, Doll's, Corduroy Lined, With Coverlet, Pillow, Wicker, 35 In. 120.00
Carriage, Doll's, Red, Wooden Wheels, Leatherette, 19th Century, 30 In. 275.00
Carriage, Doll's, Surrey, Orange, Yellow Design, Black Top, Wooden Wheels 250.00
Carriage, Doll's, Victorian, Wire 325.00
Carriage, Doll's, Wicker, Corduroy Lined, Side Windows, 1900, 34 X 29 In. 220.00
Carriage, Doll's, Wicker, Glass Windows Hood, South Bend Toy Co., 23 In. 120.00
Carriage, Doll's, Wicker, Victorian, 2 Small, 2 Large Wheels, 1890, 27 In. 375.00
Carriage, Doll's, Wicker, White Corduroy Lined, 35 In. 120.00
Carriage, Doll's, Wire & Mesh, Black Paint, 23 In. 135.00
Carriage, Doll's, Wooden, Black Leather Sunshade, C.1875, 38 In. 375.00
Carriage, Doll's, Wooden, Stenciled, 1880, 51 X 44 In. ....*Illus* 500.00
Cart, Bouncing Bunny, Fisher–Price 65.00
Cart, Chester Gump, Arcade, Cast Iron 425.00
Cart, Donkey, Girl Driver, 6 1/2 In. 225.00
Cart, Horse Drawn, Passenger, Iron, Stanley, 11 1/2 In. 80.00
Case, Doll's, Sedan Chair, White Silk Upholstered, Glass Sides, 35 In. 495.00
Cash Register, Buddy L, 9 X 11 In. 135.00
Cash Register, Kamlap, Tin, Gray & Red, 9 In. 22.00
Cash Register, Little Learners, Chrome, Metal & Glass, Red 18.00
Cash Register, Tom Thumb .... 10.00 To 25.00
Cat, Angora, Steiff 150.00
Cat, Cheshire, Steiff 65.00
Cat, Clockwork, Fur Cover, Opens Mouth To Squeak, France, 10 1/2 In. 175.00
Cat, Susie, Steiff, 7 1/2 In. 100.00
Cavalry, 8 Riders & 8 Walking, Horses, Elastolin, 5 1/4 In., 16 Piece 175.00
Cement Mixer, Buddy L, 1926 .... 125.00 To 250.00
Chair, Doll's, H–Stretcher, 8 In. 95.00
Chair, Doll's, Ladderback, Bittersweet Paint, Leather Seat, 11 1/4 In. 110.00
Chair, Doll's, Sheraton, Black Paint, Gold Striping, Needlework Seat 135.00
Chair, Rocker, Horse Form Sides, Wooden, 27 X 42 In. 250.00
Chariot, Horse Drawn, Kenton, 8 In. 265.00
Charley Weaver Bartender, Battery Operated, Box 30.00
Chemistry Set, Boy Scientist Pictured, 1937, Unused, Box 25.00
Chest, Doll's, Victorian, Oak Stain, 3 Drawers, Gallery, 18 1/2 In. 90.00
Chicken & Rabbit, Pull Toy, Painted Wood, American, C.1900, 12 1/2 In. 110.00
Chicken, Lays Eggs, Windup, Baldwin 40.00
Child, On Folding Wire Trapeze, Windup, Celluloid, 12 In. 10.00

Toy, Player Piano, Side Wind, Schoenhut, 8 X 12 In.

Church, Litho Paper On Wood, 13 Red Finials, Bliss, C.1880 .... 1850.00
Circus Wagon, Animal Haulers, Tandem, Iron Wheels, Rubber Tires, 4 Pc. 5000.00
Circus Wagon, Bear, Pulled By 2 Horses, With Driver, Cast Iron, 14 In. 300.00
Circus, Humpty Dumpty, Patented 1903, Electric 3750.00
Clicker, Felix The Cat 18.00
Clicker, Snapping Bug, Tin, Ladybug Picture, 1946 .... 7.00
Clock, Punch Out, Capt. Kangaroo's Grandfather, Premium, 1956 .... 25.00
Clothes Washer, Wringer, Princess, Steel, Cream Color, 12 In. 60.00
Clown, Articulated Arms & Legs, Paper Covered Wood, 17 In. 50.00
Clown, Beating Drums, Original Clothes, Hand Painted, Germany 375.00
Clown, Dances, Plays Violin, Windup, Schuco, 1930s 85.00
Clown, In Barrel, Windup, Chein 165.00
Clown, Jack–In–The–Box, 4 In. 110.00
Clown, Jester, Chein 115.00
Clown, Musical, Roly Poly, Schoenhut 195.00
Clown, On Mule Wagon, Windup, Tin, Lehman, 1910 .... 295.00
Clown, On Roller Skates, Windup, Japan 150.00
Clown, On Stilts, Playing Violin, Cloth Costume, Tin, Windup, 8 3/4 In. 35.00
Clown, Plays Violin & Dances, 1935, Schuco, 4 1/2 In. ....85.00 To 125.00
Clown, Spinning Flag On Head, Celluloid & Fabric, Windup, 13 1/2 In. 140.00
Clown, Suspended On Rod, Mechanical Action, Tin, Penny Toy 225.00
Clown, With Stubborn Donkey, In Cart, Lehmann 320.00
Coach, 2 Horses, Driver, 2 Passengers, Cast Aluminum, Stanley, 12 In. 25.00
Coach, Oxford London Mail, Wood, Driver, Passenger, 12 1/2 In. 110.00
Conestoga Wagon, Horses, Metal, Wooden, Fabric, Canton, Ohio, 1910, 19 In. 225.00
Construction Set, Wooden, Arkitoy, Box, 1930s 29.00
Constructioneer, Metal Building Set, No.8, Metal Case, Electric Motor 75.00
Costume, Bat Masterson 10.00
Cottage, Wood & Papier–Mache, Marked Elastolia, Germany, 8 1/4 In. 70.00
Couch, Doll's, Fainting Couch, Carved 110.00
Cow, Bessie, Mohair, Steiff 200.00
Cow, Pull Toy, Hide Cover, Horns, Red Grained Base, American, 8 X 11 In. 440.00
Cow, Pull Toy, Suede Covered, Bell, Flap For Milking, C.1885, 14 In. 375.00
Cradle, Doll's, Arched Hood, Bells Mounted Underside, American, 14 In. 135.00
Cradle, Doll's, Brown Paint, Dark Green Banding, American, 15 3/8 In. 165.00
Cradle, Doll's, Brown Paint, Scrolled Edges, Heart Cutout Sides, Pine 115.00
Cradle, Doll's, Hooded, Grained Mahogany, Putty Inside, 1840, 11 X 19 In. 275.00
Cradle, Doll's, Jenny Lind, Rope Style, Green Paint 50.00
Cradle, Doll's, Pine, Red, 19 1/2 In. 40.00
Cradle, Doll's, Square Nail Construction, Poplar, 12 In. 135.00
Cradle, Doll's, Wicker, 7 1/2 X 8 In. 90.00
Crapshooter, Battery Operated, Cragstan .... 40.00 To 55.00

Crazy Clown, In Car, Windup, Palan, Box 20.00
Crib, Wooden, String, Tinkertoy, 1919 .... 15.00
Crocodile, Celluloid, Box 55.00
Croquet Set, Steel, Miniature, 13 Piece 25.00
Cupboard, Doll's, Wooden, Cream Paint, 4 Doors, 1920s, 5 3/4 X 3 5/8 In. 45.00
Cupboard, Pressed Design, Oak, 1900, 46 X 24 In. 350.00
Cutouts, Toonerville Town, Vaseline, Cardboard, 1930s 75.00
Cymbal Player, Circus, Schoenhut 150.00
Dandy Jim, Dancing Clown, Key Wind, Tin, Unique Art, 9 In. .... 250.00 To 325.00
Dennis The Menace Mischief Kit, Box 50.00
Desk, Blackboard, Roller, President McKinley, Oak, 47 In. 160.00
Dinosaur, Dino, Battery Operated, 17 In. 225.00
Dippee Bug, Pull Toy 20.00
Dirigible, Akron, Pull Toy, Tin, 25 1/2 In. 185.00
Dish Set, Akro Agate, Box, 16 Piece 90.00
Dishes, Doll's, Circus Pattern, Box, Ohio Art Co., 31 Piece 45.00
Dishes, Doll's, Pinnochio, Ohio Art, Tin, 5 Piece 9.00
Doctor Doodle, Fisher-Price 75.00
Dog, Blue, Walks When Pulled, Hand Painted, Spring Tail, 1950s 55.00
Dog, Boxer, Button, Leather Collar, Signed Steiff 160.00
Dog, Bulldog, Moving Legs, Platform Toy, Hustler Toy Co., 1920s 75.00
Dog, Buttons Puppy With A Brain, Battery Operated, Marx, 12 In. 85.00
Dog, Cocker Spaniel, Rider, Voice, Steiff 375.00
Dog, Collie, Steiff, 16 In. 125.00
Dog, Collie, Windup, Tin & Plush, Walks & Wags Tail 1100.00
Dog, Collie, Windup, Tin, Plush 150.00
Dog, Dancing, Lindstrom 45.00
Dog, Flippo The Jumping, Windup, Marx 85.00
Dog, Old Faithful, Rubber, Squeeze Bulb, With Tube, Japan, Box 6.00
Dog, On Iron Wheels, Steiff 275.00
Dog, Poodle, Black Fleece, Stuffed, Floppy Ears, Alexander, C.1935, 17 In. 175.00
Dog, Poodle, Black, Steiff, 14 In. .... 65.00 To 75.00
Dog, Poodle, Gray Mohair, Jointed, Steiff, 9 In. 58.00
Dog, Poodle, Iron Wheels, Button, Squeaker, Steiff, 1908, 15 X 16 In. 695.00
Dog, Poodle, Jointed, Glass Eyes, Red Neck Strap, Steiff, 13 In. 95.00
Dog, Poodle, Stuffed, Beige Flannel, Tufted Yarn Ears, Tail & Legs, 7 In. 65.00
Dog, Puppy, Red Collar, Steiff, Ear Tag, 7 In. 50.00
Dog, Scotty, Battery Operated, Walking Barking, Cragstan 50.00
Dog, Terry, Steiff Button, 10 In. 139.00
Dog, Windup, Flat Tin, Barking, Schriner's Hat, Germany 245.00
Dog, Yorkshire Terrier, Stuffed, Squeaks, 1940s 45.00
    TOY, DOLL, see Doll
Dollhouse, 1 Room Bungalow, Schoenhut, Decal Label 250.00
Dollhouse, 2 Stories, Side Openings, Bliss, 24 X 18 In. 900.00
Dollhouse, Bliss Type, Paper, Wood, Furniture, Dolls, Germany, 11 X 8 In. 350.00
Dollhouse, Bliss, 3-Story, Victorian 6000.00
Dollhouse, Bliss, Victorian, Litho Wood, C.1908, 17 1/2 In. 465.00
Dollhouse, Colonial Style, 2-Story, Wood, Schoenhut, 20 X 12 X 18 In. 250.00
Dollhouse, Dunham, 4 Paper-Covered Rooms, Made From Packing Crate 315.00
Dollhouse, Furniture, Bathroom Fixture, Wooden, Toilet, Tub & Wash Basin 150.00
Dollhouse, Furniture, Bathroom Set, White Wood, Strombecker, 5 Piece 20.00
Dollhouse, Furniture, Bedroom & Living Room, Tootsietoy, 13 Pieces 95.00
Dollhouse, Furniture, Bedroom Set, Crib, Chair, 1930-40, Tynietoy, 7 Piece 200.00
Dollhouse, Furniture, Bedroom Set, Pink, Metal, Tootsietoy 30.00
Dollhouse, Furniture, Bentwood Set, Cane Seats, Gilded Metal, 8 Piece 175.00
Dollhouse, Furniture, Birdcage, Brass, Bird Inside, On Stand, 7 In. 120.00
Dollhouse, Furniture, Bookcase, Cupboard, 3 Tables, Chairs, Rug, Shackman 30.00
Dollhouse, Furniture, Buffet, 3 Shelves, Columns, Biedermeier, 6 In. 400.00
Dollhouse, Furniture, Chandelier, Brass, Gilded Wood, Candles, 5 In. 30.00
Dollhouse, Furniture, Chifferobe, Vanity & Stool, Barbie, Dated 1964 .... 35.00
Dollhouse, Furniture, Dining Room, Mission, Oak, 7 Piece 75.00
Dollhouse, Furniture, Dining Table & 2 Chairs, Walnut, Strombecker 20.00
Dollhouse, Furniture, Fireplace Mantel, Chair, Petite Princess 18.00
Dollhouse, Furniture, Garden Set, Tin Litho, 6 Piece 70.00

Dollhouse, Furniture, Garden Set, Umbrella, Table, 3 Chairs, Metal 75.00
Dollhouse, Furniture, Kitchen, Cream, Aqua Trim, Iron, Arcade, 1920s, 3 Pc. 550.00
Dollhouse, Furniture, Living Room, Victorian, Velvet Upholstery, 6 Piece 1400.00
Dollhouse, Furniture, Occasional Chair, Ottoman, Petite Princess 10.00
Dollhouse, Furniture, Parlor Group, Bliss 125.00
Dollhouse, Furniture, Salon Coffee Table Set, Petite Princess 10.00
Dollhouse, Furniture, Sideboard, Rococo, Ivory, Biedermeier, 6 1/2 In. 250.00
Dollhouse, Furniture, Sofa, Rococo, Tin, Rock & Grenier, 8 1/4 In. 1000.00
Dollhouse, Furniture, Table & Chair, Tin, Rock & Grenier, 3 9/16 In. 450.00
Dollhouse, Furniture, Table, 6 Chairs, Bentwood, Velour Trim, 7 Piece 75.00
Dollhouse, Furniture, Table, Drop Leaf, Tin, Stevens & Brown, 2 7/8 In. 100.00
Dollhouse, Furniture, Telephone Set, Fantasy, Petite Princess 10.00
Dollhouse, Schoenhut, 2–Story, Front Porch 1050.00
Dollhouse, Tynie, Wood, Colonial, 2–Story, 6 Rooms, 48 X 16 X 30 In. 800.00
Dollhouse, With Furniture, Strombecker, Box 275.00
Dollhouse, Wood, 2 Rooms, Furniture, German, 19th Century, 55 In. 1600.00
Donkey, Gray Plush, Button Eyes, Red Felt Saddle, Red Bridle, 8 In. 15.00
Donkey, Pull Toy, Carved Body, Plinth On 4 Wheels, Pine, 12 3/4 In. 78.00
Drawing Kit, Spooky Kopee, Harvey Character, 1959 .... 18.00
Drill, John Deere 45.00
Drum, Charlie Brown, Chein 32.00
Drum, Metal, Ohio Art 25.00
Drum, National Biscuit, Tiny Tot, Cardboard, 6 X 4 In. 29.00
Drum, Ringling, Barnum & Bailey Circus, Tin, 6 1/4 In. 35.00
Drummer Boy, Windup, Marx 85.00
Drunkard, Le Pochard, Windup, Martin, France 380.00
Duck, Battery Operated, Remco Co. 15.00
Duck, Lariat, Cowboy Outfit, Windup, Tin, C.1930 .... 75.00
Duck, Mallard, Tin, Windup, Lithographed, Germany, 8 In. 175.00
Duck, On Wheels, Pull, Triangle Brand Shoes 50.00
Duck, On Wooden Wheel, Button, Steiff, 1913 .... 125.00
Duck, Waddling, Celluloid, On Tin Platform, Pull Toy, Box 125.00
Duck, Windup, Occupied Japan, Box, 4 In. 25.00
Eggbeater, Tin, Wooden Handle 10.00
Electric Wizard, Box, Marx 25.00
Elephant, Blanket, Circus, Schoenhut 145.00
Elephant, Gray Mohair, Felt Tusks, Jointed, Ear Button, Steiff, 1910 .... 695.00
Elephant, Musical, Fisher–Price 145.00
Elephant, On Wheels, Circus Wagon, Steiff .... 250.00 To 300.00
Elephant, Pulling Wagon, Cairo Express, 10 In. 80.00
Elephant, Red Blanket, Straw Stuffed, Button & Tag, Steiff, 8 X 11 In. 95.00
Elephant, Standing, White, Riding, Stuffed, Wheels, Germany, 21 X 23 In. 550.00

Toy, Tea Set, Porcelain, Gebruder Heubach, C.1900, 23 Piece

Toy, Train

Locomotive, No.700E,
NY Central Tender, Steam

No.255E, Lionel, Engine, No.263W Tender, Gray,
No.238E, Lionel, Engine, No.225W Tender, Streamlined

Elephant, Steiff, U.S.Zone, 4 In.	97.00
Elephant, Wooden Wheels, Pull String Voice, Button, Tag, Steiff, 21 In.	695.00
Elf, Rubber Face, Red Beard, Felt Body, Felt Suit, Steiff, 12 In.	85.00
Erector Set, A.C.Gilbert Co., 1929	30.00
Erector Set, Gilbert No.7 1/2, Engineer's, Instruction Book	50.00
Erector Set, Gilbert, Electric Motor, Metal Chest	160.00
Erector Set, Gilbert, Manual, Blue Box, 1938	75.00
Erector Set, Gilbert, No.3, Instructions, Cardboard Box	100.00
Erector Set, Gilbert, No.7 1/2, Red Metal Box	150.00
Farm Set, Kansas City, 1930s	150.00
Felix The Cat, Chasing Mice, Pull Toy	385.00
Felix The Cat, Jointed, Black Paint, Dated On Foot, 1924–25, 4 1/4 In.	100.00
Felix The Cat, Jointed, Wooden, 1925, 8 1/2 In.	355.00
Felix The Cat, White, Green Velvet, Straw Stuffed, C.1910, 10 3/4 In.	137.00
Ferris Wheel, 5 Chairs, Tin, Windup, 11 1/4 In.	175.00
Ferris Wheel, Hercules, Windup, Tin, Donald Duck, Pluto On Seats, Chein	135.00
Ferryboat, Tin, Windup, Lithographed, Yellow, Red, Walbert, 13 In.	200.00
Fido Zilo, Fisher–Price	65.00
Field Phone, Monkey Division, Remco, 1964	35.00
Fingerprint Set, G–Men, Graphic, Dated 1937, Box	95.00
Fire Engine, Drawn By 3 Horses, Cast Iron, Kenton	850.00
Fire Engine, Hook & Ladder, Driver, Clockwork, Litho, Tin, 18 In.	385.00
Fire Engine, Pump, Rubber Wheels, Cast Iron, 6 In.	98.00
Fire Engine, Snorkel, Corgi, Box	40.00
Fire Engine, Tin, Red & Gilt, Early 20th Century, American, 20 In.	330.00
Fire Pumper, Drawn By 3 Horses, Cast Iron, Hubley, 1920s, 18 In.	230.00
Fire Station, Volunteer, Marx	32.00
Fire Station, With Pumper, Wilkins, Kingsbury	750.00
Fire Truck, Aerial Hose, Steel, Red, Copper Tank, Keystone, 32 In.	550.00
Fire Truck, Aerial Ladder, Sheet Metal, Structo, 31 In.	27.50
Fire Truck, Aerial Ladder, Smith–Miller	500.00
Fire Truck, Hook & Ladder, B, M.I.C.Tires, Smith–Miller	495.00
Fire Truck, Hook & Ladder, Tonka	150.00
Fire Truck, Hydraulic Ladder, Structo, 1940s	110.00
Fire Truck, Keystone, 1920s, 28 In.	550.00
Fire Truck, Ladders, Oh–Boy, 17 In.	45.00
Fire Truck, Short Ladder, Kilgore, Iron, 1928, 8 In.	375.00
Fire Truck, Toy, Trolley, Toonerville, Tinplate, 5 In.	150.00
Fire Truck, Water Tower, Keystone	650.00
Fireboat, Carette, 1905, 11 In.	950.00
Flashlight, Tom Cobett, Space Cadet Signal Siren, Box, 1950s	45.00
Ford Mustang, Battery Operated, Plastic, 1967	190.00

Fort Apache Indian Stockade, Marx, Original Box 45.00
Fort Cheyenne, Ideal, Vinyl Carrying Case, Opens To Fort, 39 Piece 25.00
Foxy Grandpa, Mechanical, Push Chest & He Crashes Cymbals, 1910, 11 In. 250.00
Freddie The Freeloader, Rubber, Rempel, 1940s 20.00
Frog, Green Velvet, Button & Tag, Steiff, 4 1/2 In. 50.00
Frog, Jolly Jumper, Pull Toy, Fisher-Price 15.00
Frog, Windup, Kellerman 150.00
Funny Andy, Zilotone Player, Tin, 2 Discs, Wolverine, Box, 7 1/2 In. 400.00
G.I.Joe & Bouncing Jeep, Windup, Unique Art .... 100.00 To 125.00
G.I.Joe & K-9 Pups, Tin, Windup, Unique Art, 8 In. ....80.00 To 175.00
     TOY, GAME, see Game
Garage, 2-Door, Penny Toys 200.00
Garage, 3 Cars, Toy Town 925.00
Giraffe, Circus, Schoenhut 275.00
Giraffe, Steiff, 11 In. 55.00
Goat, Pull Toy, Felt Covered, Tin Wheels, Germany, 1930s 210.00
Goat, Squeak, Schuco 390.00
Goggles, Steve Canyon, On Original Card 65.00
Golden Goose, Windup, Tin, Marx, No.87 .... 195.00
Goldilocks & 3 Bears, Steiff, Box 595.00
Goofy, Rides Unicycle, Windup, Linemar 350.00
Goose, Red Felt Jacket, Black Plush Hat, Windup Music Box, 17 In. 25.00
Goose, Windup, Tin, Unique, 8 3/4 In. 45.00
Graf Zeppelin, Tin, Windup, 9 In. 175.00
Grinder, Food, Arcade 24.00
Grocer's Shop, Lithographed Paper, Wooden, 9 X 20 In. ....*Illus* 800.00
Gun & Holster Set, Johnny Ringo, TV, Marx 32.00
Gun Set, Western, Marx, 2 Cap Guns, Black Plastic Holster & Belt 50.00
Gun, Bang, Newman's Shoe Store, 1930s 4.00
Gun, BB, HyScorem, No.808 .... 45.00
Gun, BB, Red Ryder, Box, 1960s 35.00
Gun, Click, Tin, Dated 1916 .... 75.00
Gun, Clicker, Advertising, Gerber Foods 5.00
Gun, Daisy Jr., Air Force Rocket Command Signal Gun, Box 125.00
Gun, Pop Pistol, Daisy Zooka, Metal, Red, Yellow, Blue, Buck Rogers Type 60.00
Gun, Red Ryder, BB, Box, 1960s 35.00
Gun, Repeater, G-Man, Flint Sure Shot, Chein, On Card 30.00
Gun, Ring, 007 Secret Agent, 1960s 12.00
Gun, Signal, Daisy Jr.Air Force Rocket Command, Box 145.00
Gun, Space, Sparkling, Windup, Marx, 1950 .... 75.00
Gun, Tommy, Hogue Co. 100.00
Gun, Tommy, Unique Art 100.00
Ham & Sam, Minstrels, Musical, Tin, Key Wind, Strauss, 7 In. .... 350.00 To 700.00
Hand Clapper, Frog, Old Reliable Coffee 10.00
Hand Puppet, Dennis The Menace 22.00
Handcar, Mechanical, Girard 150.00
Handcar, Moon Mullins & Kayo, Tin, Windup Engine, 6 In. 625.00
Happy Hooligan, Windup, Tin, Chein 200.00
Harbor Set, Lighthouse, Warehouse, Ships, Pier, Painted Wood, Germany 100.00
Harold Lloyd, Walks, Makes Faces, Windup, Marx, 1920, 11 In. .... 225.00 To 350.00
Hauler, Machinery, Flat Bed, Red & Yellow, Structo, 12 1/2 In. 45.00
Hedgehog, Steiff, 7 In. 35.00
Hen, Lays Marble Eggs, Wyandotte 33.00
Hen, Mohair, Steiff 85.00
Highchair, Doll's, Metal, Blue & Yellow, Amsco 15.00
Highchair, Doll's, Pink, Wooden, 16 In. 35.00
Highchair, Doll's, Strombecker 25.00
Highchair, Doll's, Victorian, 14 In. 55.00
Hippopotamus, Circus, Schoenhut 245.00
Hobbyhorse, Glider, Painted Wood, Trestle, 19th Century, 28 X 34 In. 770.00
Hobbyhorse, Prancing, Pine, Leather Saddle, 19th Century, 36 X 44 In. 935.00
Hobbyhorse, Articulated Ears, Tail, Cloth Saddle, Pine, 44 In. ....*Illus* 1320.00
Hobbyhorse, Glass Eyes, Leather Mane, Stenciled Design, 33 X 39 In. 600.00
Hobbyhorse, Leather Harness, Burlap Covered, 19th Century, 25 1/2 In. 715.00

Hoisting Tower, Original Chutes, Buddy L 1075.00
Hoky–Poky, Windup, Wyandotte, Tin ....85.00 To 135.00
Hook & Ladder, Cast Iron, 2 Teams of Black Horses, Ladders, 37 In. 325.00
Hoop–O–Loop, Wolverine, Partial Box, 1925 .... 65.00
Horse & Cart, Painted Wood, Black Leather Saddle, C.1920, 17 X 44 In. 522.00
Horse & Sulkey, Papier–Mache, Tin, Plastic & White Metal, Box, 6 1/2 In. 185.00
Horse & Wagon, Ladder, Cast Iron, 1870s, 30 In. 1250.00
Horse & Wagon, Mohair, Off–Center Wheel Under Horse, Gallops, 30 In. 610.00
Horse & Wagon, Pull Toy, Gibbs, 20 In. 300.00
Horse Trailer, Metal, Rubber Tires, Tonka, 9 X 9 In. 17.50
Horse Wagon, Harrison Circus, Tin, 12 3/4 In. 55.00
Horse, Cart, With Chester Gump, Arcade, 8 In. 350.00
Horse, Coal Wagon, Polychrome Paint, Tin, Pull Toy, 25 1/2 In. 2600.00
Horse, Felt, Wooden Wheels, Printed Button, Steiff, 1915 .... 725.00
Horse, Ice Wagon, Lithographed, Converse, 1920s, 13 In. 225.00
Horse, On Iron Wheels, Steiff 1495.00
Horse, On Metal Wheels, Wagon, Black Composition, French, 12 In. 395.00
Horse, Paper On Wood, Pulling Tin Cart, Iron Wheels, Gibbs Co. 125.00
Horse, Pull Toy, Papier–Mache, Standing, Brown Burlap Cover, 1890, 15 In. 375.00
Horse, Pull Toy, Wooden, Red Wheels, Horsehair Mane & Tail, 1885, 16 In. 550.00
Horse, Riding & Pull, Bells, Litho Head, Hampton Gong Bell Mfg.Co. 60.00
Horse, Riding, 4 Wheels, Expert Toy, 1930s, 20 In. 110.00
Horse, Riding, Wheels, Whinny, Steiff 475.00
Horse, Rocking, Back Legs On Iron Spring, Front Legs Up, Wooden, 47 In. 700.00
Horse, Rocking, Black Velvet, Red Wooden Frame, 1880, 14 X 29 X 33 In. 650.00
Horse, Rocking, Brown, Orange Saddle, 4 Wheels, 1900, 3 X 4 Ft. 2475.00
Horse, Rocking, Carved, Painted, On Stand, 49 X 57 In. 900.00
Horse, Rocking, Pine, Black & Red, Long Rockers, 1800–20, 22 1/2 X 46 In. 885.00
Horse, Rocking, Red, Black & White, Delphous Toys, 1940s 145.00
Horse, Rocking, Wooden, Iron Spring, 47 In. ....*Illus* 700.00
Horse, Rocking, Wooden, Leather Saddle, Horsehair Tail, German, C.1880 .... 750.00
Humpty–Dumpty Circus, Tent, Animals, Performers, Electric, Pat.1903 .... 3750.00
Ice Skates, Doll's, Metal, Engraved Sonja Henie, 1938, 2 In. 14.00
Indian, Crazy, Windup, Marx 55.00
Ironing Board, Wooden, Folding, C.1920, 10 X 24 In. 19.00
Jack–In–The–Box, Chinaman, Papier–Mache, English, 18th Century, 8 In. 440.00
Jazzbo Jim, Dances On Roof of Cabin, Windup, Marx .... 300.00 To 485.00
Jazzbo Jim, Playing Violin 750.00
Jeep, Army, Wood Commodities Corp., Cannon, Drab, Wooden, 23 In. 110.00
Jeep, Nellybelle, Marx, Factory Sealed 135.00
Jeep, Red & Yellow, Marx 50.00
Jeep, Rodeo Joe, Windup, Tin, Unique Art 85.00
Jeep, Spotlight, Marx, Box 95.00
Jeep, U.S.Army Mobile Radar, Trailer, Hood Opens, Marx, 1942, Box 120.00
Jeep, Willys, Marx 15.00
Jiggle, Man, Standing, Pine, Painted, American, 19th Century, 13 In. 2970.00
Jocko, Steiff, Zoned Germany Tag, 18 In. 250.00
Jumpin' Jeep, 4 Soldiers, Windup, Marx 85.00
Jumping Jack, Wooden Head, Mechanical, C.1820 .... 300.00
Jungle Shooting Range, Marx 50.00
Jupiter Rocket, Friction, Tin Litho, Box 35.00
Kaleidoscope, Bush, 1875 .... 1000.00
Kazooka Bazooka, Bob Burns, Tin, Advertising Decal 125.00
Kicker, Football, Cast Iron 345.00
Kiddy Car, Keystone R.R., Red & Black Paint, Sheet Metal, 26 3/4 In. 105.00
Kit, Aircraft, AT–6, Texan 8.00
Kit, Boeing 727, United Jetliner, 1962 .... 10.00
Kit, Indy Racer, Metal, Unassembled, Hubley 95.00
Kit, Mitsubishi Zero, 1962 .... 10.00
Kit, Model, Atom Powered Submarine, Revell 25.00
Kit, Model, Swept Wings Sabre Jet, Famous Fighters, Aurora F–86D 30.00
Kit, U.S.Navy, A3J, Vigilante, 1959 .... 10.00
Kitty, Movable Legs & Head, Steiff, 9 X 15 In. 150.00
Klippity–Klop Cowboy Action Sand Toy, Rowley, Box 5.00

Knitting Kit, Barbie's, 1962	10.00
Lady Acrobat, Schoenhut	185.00
Lady Circus Rider, Schoenhut	225.00
Ladybug, Windup, Franomia	20.00
Ladybug, Windup, Tin, Japan, 4 3/4 In.	65.00
Lamb, Wooden Legs, German, 3 In.	22.00
Lawn Mower, Marx, 24 In.	40.00
Li'L Abner Dogpatch Band, Windup, Unique Art, 1945, 8 In. .... 225.00 To 495.00
License Plate, Man From U.N.C.L.E., Metal, Marx	10.00
Lincoln Logs Set, Fort Dearborn	100.00
Lincoln Tunnel, Unique Art	250.00
Lion, Plush Coat, Green Glass Eyes, Steiff, 31 In.	135.00
Little Miss Seamstress, Mechanical, Kanto Toys	65.00
Little Snoopy, Pull Toy, Fisher-Price	18.00
Lizzy Lizard, Steiff, 8 In. .... 195.00 To 285.00
Long Tom Disappearing Gun, Copyright 1916	35.00
Louis Armstrong, Windup, Box	200.00
Luncheon Set, White Porcelain, Christmas, Germany, C.1900, 11 Piece	200.00
Luxury Liner, Windup, Wolverine, Box	145.00
Machine Gun, Sparking, Ronson	50.00
Machine Gun, Untouchables, Battery Operated	50.00
Maggie & Jiggs, Windup, Nifty	1395.00
Magic Set, Man From U.N.C.L.E., Box, 1965	35.00
Mammy, Sweeping, Windup, Tin, Lindstrom	75.00
Man On Horse, Pull Toy, Polychrome Paint, 14 In.	675.00
Man On Tricycle, Ives, Windup, 1875	950.00
Man, Black, Dancing, Articulated Wooden Figure, On Paddle, 10 3/4 In.	35.00
Manure Spreader, Arcade, 1930s	97.50
Manure Spreader, John Deere	37.50
Mask, Gorilla, Papier-Mache, Polychrome Design, 1920's	65.00
Merry Makers Noise Band, Marx, 11 In. .... 695.00 To 895.00
Merry-Go-Around, Hand Painted, Bing	2500.00
Mickey The Musician, Zylophone, Celluloid, Louis Marx, C.1950, 11 In.	450.00
Microscope & Lab Set, Gilber, No.13013, Box	45.00
Mikado Family, 3 Figures, Carrying Box, Lehmann	2800.00
Minky Zotty, Steiff	275.00
Miss American, Pull Toy, Gong Bell Co.	55.00
Mister Robot, Cragstan	325.00
Mobile, Marx, Tin Litho, Metal, Electric, Unopened, Box	350.00
Molding & Coloring Set, Tom Corbett, Kay Stanley, Box	75.00
Molly Moo Cow, Fisher-Price	45.00
Monkey, Climbing Coconut Tree, Tin, 21 In.	55.00

Toy, Train, No.260, Lionel, No.263 Tender, No.1685 Passenger

Monkey, Crap Shooting, Battery Operated, Cragstan 75.00
Monkey, Drummer, Tin, Windup, Marked Germany, 7 3/4 In. 145.00
Monkey, Jocko, Merry Organ Grinder, Distler, 6 In. 100.00
Monkey, Jocko, Drinking, Battery Operated, Linemar 65.00
Monkey, Jocko, Squeaker, Jointed, Open Mouth, Steiff, 12 In. 100.00
Monkey, Loop The Loop, Battery Operated 40.00
Monkey, Metal Face, Brown Mohair, Schuco, 3 1/2 In. 125.00
Monkey, Morrie The Drummer, Windup 20.00
Monkey, On Stump, Windup 100.00
Monkey, On Tricycle, Steiff, 1920s, 9 In. 110.00
Monkey, Perfume Container, Mohair, Jointed, In Removable Head, Schuco 300.00
Monkey, Plays Drum, Windup, Schuco, Box 80.00
Monkey, Rock N' Roll, Battery Operated, Box 225.00
Monkey, Tumbling, Mohair, Bellhop Outfit, Gerbruder Bing, 1920s 210.00
Monkey, With Trumpet, Battery Operated, Plush, Tin Litho, Alps, 9 1/2 In. 225.00
Monkey, Yes/No, Felt Face, Glass Eyes, Cloth, Steiff, 9 In. 250.00
Monkey, Yes/No, Schuco, Glass Eyes, 14 1/2 In. .... 180 .00
Motor Home, Winnebago, Tonka 25.00
Motorcycle Driver, Curvo 1000, Schuco, U.S.Zone 195.00
Motorcycle, Champion, Cast Iron 70.00
Motorcycle, Clockwork, Tin, Driver, Passenger In Sidecar, Germany, 8 In. 2850.00
Motorcycle, Driver, Harley Davidson, Cast Iron 175.00
Motorcycle, Driver, Sidecar, Windup, 1960s, Russia, 8 1/2 In. 165.00
Motorcycle, Driver, Swerves, Curvo 1000, Windup, Schuco, 1930s, 5 In. 175.00
Motorcycle, Mobo 165.00
Motorcycle, Policeman, Balloon Tires, Marx, 8 1/2 In. 100.00
Motorcycle, With Driver, Technofy, No.4 .... 295.00
Motorcycle, With Officer, Marx 225.00
Motorcycle, With Policeman, White Rubber Tires, Cast Iron, Hubley 225.00
Motorcycle, With Sidecar, Hubley, Cast Iron 695.00
Motorcycle, With Sidecar, Marx 125.00
Motorcycle, With Sidecar, Windup, Tin, Marx, 1930s 185.00
Mouse, Walker, Wooden, Leather Ears, 1920s, 5 In. 60.00
Moxie, Pull Toy, Lithographed Tin, American, Early 1900s, 8 1/2 In. 275.00
Mr.Fox The Magician, Windup, Box 120.00
Mule, Balky, 1910 .... 275.00
Mule, Pull Toy, Flocked Coat, Wood & Papier–Mache, 5 1/4 In. 105.00
Music Box, Children Playing In Band, Tin, Ohio Art, Round 22.00
Musicians, Mouse, Monkey & Clown, Tin Litho, Key Wind, Schuco, 4 1/2 In. 450.00
Naughty Boy, Tin, Windup, Lehmann, 4 5/8 In. .... 275.00 To 900.00
Neanderthal Man, Tooth Necklace, Steiff, 7 1/2 In. 132.00
Newsboy, Bell, Waves Extra Newspaper, Windup, Occupied Japan, 6 In. 75.00
Noah's Ark, 12 Animals, Converse 325.00
Noah's Ark, 25 Wooden Animals, Flat Bottom Style, C.1890 .... 325.00
Noah's Ark, Paper Lithographed, Bliss 320.00
Nursing Bottle Sterilizer, Blue Enameled, Amsco, Complete 65.00
Old Jalopy, Tin Litho, Windup, Marx 225.00
Oven, Suzy Homemaker, Plug In, 1968 .... 65.00
Owl, With Nut, Steiff, 5 1/2 In. 35.00
Ox Cart, Pulled By 1 Ox, Harris, Cast Iron, 11 In. 200.00
Paddy & The Pig, Tin, Windup, Lehmann, 5 1/2 In. 300.00
Pail, Sand, Humpty–Dumpty, Castle Wall, Tin, Ohio Art, Large 15.00
Pail, Sand, Wizard of Oz 55.00
Paint Box, Alice In Wonderland 39.00
Paint By Number, Casper, Around The World 20.00
Paul's Soap Circus, Litho On Wood, Ark, On Wheels, Box 150.00
Peacock, Steiff, Life–Size 750.00
Pedal Car, 1929 Packard 4500.00
Pedal Car, 1940 Lincoln, Zephyr 450.00
Pedal Car, Airflow, Steelcraft, 1935 .... 1750.00
Pedal Car, American National, Headlights, Motor Meter, Brake, 1921 .... 3800.00
Pedal Car, Auburn, Super Charged, White 3750.00
Pedal Car, Cadillac, 1953 .... 600.00
Pedal Car, Casey Jones, Garton's 425.00

Toy, Train

No.5149, Lionel, Boxcar,   No. 10, Lionel, Locomotive,
Ivory, Peacock Roof   Whistle, Brass Inserts

No.513, Lionel, Cattle Car,   No.515, Lionel, Tank Car,
Green, Orange Roof   Orange, Brass Rails

Pedal Car, Chevrolet, Gendron, 1936	1750.00
Pedal Car, Fire Chief, Mexico, 1950s	175.00
Pedal Car, Ford, 1936	800.00
Pedal Car, Jet Sweep, AMF, Model 501	95.00 To 100.00
Pedal Car, LaSalle, 1939	1750.00
Pedal Car, Lincoln Zephyr, 1940	450.00
Pedal Car, Mustang, 1966	275.00
Pedal Car, Packard, 1932	1850.00
Pedal Car, Red, Yellow Striping, Sheet Metal, American National, 41 In.	1450.00
Pedal Car, Sprint Racer, 1930	650.00
Pedal Car, Studebaker, Convertible, 1930s, Skippy	350.00
Pedal Car, Stutz Tandem, 2 Passenger, 2–Tone Blue	5000.00
Pedal Car, U–Haul, Trailer	150.00
Pencil Set, Mickey Mantel, Sealed, 1962	15.00
Pete The Talking Parrot, Battery Operated, Tin, C.1950, 18 In.	400.00
Peter Pan Play, With Sandy Duncan	10.00
Petite Princess, Carrying Case, Opens, 2–Story House, 13 Pc.Furniture	95.00
Piano, Baby Grand, 8 Keys, Painted Wood, Japan, 1950s	38.00
Piano, Baby Grand, Tin & Wood, Black, Tapering Cylindrical Legs	27.50
Piano, Biedermeier Style, Wooden Keys, 6 In.	550.00
Piano, Flintstones, Stoneway	15.00
Piano, Player, Chein	150.00
Piano, Player, Mahogany Finish, 11 Wooden Keys, Schoenhut, C.1900, 12 In.	200.00
Piano, Tootsietoy	25.00
Pig, Glass Eyes, Pink & Black, Schoenhut	375.00
Pig, Waddling, Windup, Tin, Chein, 5 In.	22.50
Pinocchio, Acrobat, Marx	165.00
Pip–Squeak, Baby, In Cradle, Wood, Cardboard, Papier–Mache, 5 1/2 In.	300.00
Pip–Squeak, Bird, Feeding Young, Papier–Mache, Animated Wings, 5 1/4 In.	350.00
Pip–Squeak, Chicken Coop, Feather Covered Rooster Pops Out, 5 3/4 In.	75.00
Pip–Squeak, Dog, Papier–Mache, 5 3/4 In.	40.00
Pip–Squeak, Hen With Ducklings, Polychrome Paint, Glass Eyes, 6 In.	300.00
Pip–Squeak, Parrot, In Top Hat, Papier–Mache, Leather On Bellows	225.00
Pip–Squeak, Rabbit, Lying, Animated Ears, Papier–Mache, Gray, 2 3/4 In.	125.00
Pip–Squeak, Robin Redbreast, Papier–Mache, 19th Century, 4 3/4 In.	100.00
Pip–Squeak, Robin, Painted Wood, 8 In.	300.00
Pip–Squeak, Rooster, Papier–Mache, Feathers, Coiled Wire Legs, 5 In.	225.00
Pipe Organ, Musical, Hand Crank, Arched, J.Chein & Co.	50.00
Pistol, Cap, Dragnet, Red, Black & Gold, Plastic, Knickerbocker, 6 In.	15.00
Pistol, Cap, Pluck, Cast Iron, Stevens, 1895, 3 1/2 In.	29.00
Pistol, Cork, Tin	15.00
Pistol, Dart, Tin	12.00

Pistol, Water, Daisy, 1917, Metal 42.00
Pistol, Water, Daisy, 1926 .... 35.00
Pistol, Water, Dragnet 35.00
Pitching Machine, Tin, Marx 60.00
Player Piano, Side Wind, Schoenhut, 8 X 12 In. ....*Illus* 200.00
Pluto, Pop–Up, Wooden String, Fisher–Price 45.00
Pogo Stick, Wooden, Cast Iron Foot Rest, 1880s 125.00
Polar Bear, Standing Upright, Deans Rag Book Co., 1920s, 19 In. 550.00
Polar Bear, Stuffed, England, 18 In. 550.00
Police Patrol Motorcycle, Friction, Japan, Box 100.00
Pool Players, Tin, Windup, Lithograph, C.1925, 12 X 5 In. 200.00
Porter, Pushes 2 1/2 In.Trunk, Windup, Germany, 1930s 140.00
Postal Station, Playskool 18.00
Potty, Doll's, Strombecker 15.00
Printing Block Set, Wooden, Tin Ink Pad, 1900s, Box 15.00
Puppet Theater, Animated, Pillsbury, Puppets, Cardboard, '36 .... 75.00
Puppet, Crocodile, White Teeth, Green Paint, Wooden, C.1930, 15 In. 330.00
Puppet, Little Ricky Ricardo, Original Box, 1953 .... 65.00
Puppet, Mammy Yokum, Hand, Box 35.00
Puppet, Possy, Hand, Steiff, Button, Tag 55.00
Puppet, Punch & Judy, Carved Wooden Heads, Hands, Cloth Body, 11 Piece 375.00
Puppet, Wooden, Cloth Costume, Movable Arms, Head, Eyes & Mouth, 23 In. 225.00
Purse, Doll's, Leather 20.00
Purse, Doll's, Metal Mesh 20.00
Queen Buzzy–Bee, Fisher–Price 15.00
Quilt, Doll's, Plaid, 18 X 18 In. 35.00
Rabbit, Flipping, Key Wind, Schuco 40.00
Rabbit, Musical, Windup, Box 50.00
Rabbit, Pushing Egg On Wheels, Chein 22.00
Radio, Fred Flintstone, Box 18.50
Railroad Station, Domed Glass, Iron, Passengers, Germany, 1910, 14 In. 775.00
Ram, Snucki, Chest Tag, Raised Button, Steiff 95.00
Ram, Tin, Pull Toy, 10 In. 730.00
Refrigerator, Snow White, Wolverine 36.00
Reindeer, Renny, Raised Button, Steiff, 9 In. 225.00
Rickshaw, Doll's, Painted Tin, Fabric Top & Upholstery, 9 X 15 In., Pair 325.00
Riding Cowboy, Legs Move, Windup, Celluloid, Occupied Japan 100.00
Rifle, Daniel Boone, Flintlock, Cap Shooting, Pinback, Manual, 43 In. 35.00
Ring, Gabby Hayes, Cannon 40.00
Ringmaster, Circus, Schoenhut 225.00
Robot, Answer Machine, Box 550.00
Robot, Dr Pepper, Zeroilas, Battery Operated, Ideal 60.00
Robot, Lost In Space, AHI, Box, 1977 .... 85.00
Robot, Marvelous Mike 135.00
Robot, Planet, Windup 175.00
Robot, R–35, Linemar 400.00
Robot, Radio, Starroid, Box 30.00
Robot, Sparky, Box 215.00
Robot, Super Astronaut, Battery Operated .... 67.00 To 95.00
Robot, Super Rotate–O–Matic Astronaut, Battery Operated, Box 125.00
Robot, Swinging Baby, Box 325.00
Robot, Tommy Verbot, Battery Operated, 10 In. 15.00
Robot, Zeroild, Battery Operated, Ideal, 1968 .... 15.00 To 35.00
Rocker, Doll's, Adirondack, 12 In. 55.00
Rocker, Doll's, Bentwood Back, Original Blue Paint, 7 1/4 In. 110.00
Rocker, Doll's, Chestnut, Rolled Arms, Paper Litho, C.1890, 12 In. 550.00
Rocker, Doll's, Pine, Arms, 3 Spindle, Pale Green, 15 1/4 In. 88.00
Rocker, Doll's, Tufted Red Velvet Seat & Back 95.00
Rocker, Doll's, Woven Cane Seat 40.00
Rocket Ship, Tom Corbett, Space Cadet, Windup, Marx 175.00
Rocket, Riding, Metalcraft, 24 In. 150.00
Rodeo Joe, Cowboy, Crazy Car, Windup, Tin, Unique Art 90.00
Roller Chimes, Fisher–Price 68.00
Roller Coaster, Chein .... 60.00 To 95.00

Rooster, Mohair, Steiff	85.00
Royal Air Force, Britain, Set 2011, 22 Piece	300.00
Sadiron, Trivet, Child's, Dover, No.602, 4 Piece	50.00
Sailboat, Wooden, Marked Birkenhead, England, 11 1/2 In.	15.00
Sand Sifter, Horace, Clarebell, Mickey & Pluto, Ohio Art	205.00
Santa Claus, Celluloid Head, Tin, Windup, Box	50.00
Santa Claus, Rings Bell, Windup, Papier–Mache, Celluloid, 6 1/2 In. ...	65.00
Santa Claus, Steiff, Box, 1953	85.00
Santa Claus, Waving, Mechanical, 1950s, 36 In.	75.00
Santa Claus, With Phone, Plastic Head, Felt Costume, Windup, Tin, 7 In.	35.00
Satchmo, Brown Skin, Older Man, Head Moves, Key Wind, Tin, 10 In.	325.00
Saw, Power Mite, Ideal	10.00
Saxaphone, Playsax, Mechanical, 20 Music Rolls, Box	200.00
Saxophone, Part Brass, Hohner, 18 In.	35.00
Scarab, Red, Buddy L	125.00
School Bus, Strasburg School District, GMC, Hubley	24.00
School Bus, Yellow, Hubley	50.00
Seal, Mohair, On Wheels, Post–War Button, Steiff, 15 X 32 In.	500.00
Sedan, Lime Green, Silver Grill, Tin, Key Wind, English, 13 1/2 In.	225.00
Seesaw, Circus, 3 Monkeys, Windup, Tin, Lewco Products, Box	40.00
Sewing Machine, Betsy Ross, Metal, Gibraltar Mfg.Co., Box	25.00
Sewing Machine, Casige, Germany .... 14.00 To 18.00
Sewing Machine, Decal, Black, Stitchwell	85.00
Sewing Machine, Doll's, Renwal	15.00
Sewing Machine, Gateway	18.00
Sewing Machine, Little Betty, Hand Operated, Straco, England	65.00
Sewing Machine, Little Miss, Necchi, Box	22.00
Sewing Machine, Little Mother .... 20.00 To 25.00
Sewing Machine, Sewette, Ideal, Battery Operated .... 18.00 To 40.00
Sewing Machine, Sewmaster, Kayanee .... 15.00 To 30.00
Sewing Machine, Singer Sewhandy	40.00
Sewing Machine, Singer, Hem Gauge, Bakelite Handle, 1930s	95.00
Sewing Machine, Stitch Mistress	25.00
Sewing Machine, Touch & Sew	15.00
Sheep, Pull Toy, Wool Coat, Wood & Papier–Mache, Tin Wheels, 10 In.	455.00
Sheep, Wool Coat, Brass Horns, Wood & Papier–Mache, 7 1/2 In., Pair	100.00
Shooting Gallery, Man From U.N.C.L.E., Box	150.00
Signal Man, Railroad Crossing, Red & Silver, Plastic & Tin, Marx	25.00
Singing Canary, Windup, Tin, Kohler	65.00
Sled, 3 Runner Kids, Cannon Ball	75.00
Sled, Belly Flopper, C.1890	130.00
Sled, Flexible Flyer, Airline Junior	300.00
Sled, Flexible Flyer, Pre–1945	65.00
Sled, Iron Tipped Runners, Red & Green Paint, Striping, 29 In.	130.00
Sled, Oak, Wrought Iron, Late 19th Century, Paris Mfg.Co., 26 In.	495.00
Sled, Pine, Metal, Red Painted Seat, Black Runners, American, 35 X 13 In.	300.00
Sled, Pine, Wrought Iron, American, 38 X 17 In.	247.00
Sled, Wooden, Signed W.Bub	75.00
Sleigh, 2 Horses, Balance Wheel, Lady Driver, Iron, Hubley, 1921, 15 In.	550.00
Sleigh, Doll's, Metal & Wood	225.00
Sleigh, Iron, 1880, 7 In.	90.00
Smitty On Scooter, Marx, 1930 .... 950.00 To 1450.00
Smoking Bear, Battery Operated	85.00
Smoking Grandpa, Battery Operated	45.00
Soldier, American Indian, Marx, Tin, Flat, 3 1/2 In.	4.50
Soldier, American Infantry, Doughboy, Tin, Flat, Marx, 3 1/2 In.	4.50
Soldier, Britain, Grenadier Guard, No.1238, Box, Set of 8	85.00
Soldier, Bugler, Grey Iron Casting Co.	12.00
Soldier, Deep Sea Diver, Silver, Manoil, 1930s	18.00
Soldier, Lancer, India's Empress, Troopers, Horse, C.1930, 5 Piece	285.00
Soldier, Machine Gunner, Grey Iron Casting Co.	12.00
Soldier, Marching Band, Foot Soldiers, Elastolin, 3 7/8 In., 30 Piece	175.00
Soldier, Paper, Wood Back, Germany, Otto Joachin, 1920s	10.00
Soldier, Radio Operator, Grey Iron Casting Co.	23.00

Soldier, U.S.Marines, Marching, Blue Tunics, Peaked Caps, 8 Piece 105.00
Space Cruiser, Windup, Box 100.00
Space Rocket Solar–X, Battery Operated, Japan, Box 125.00
Space Tank, Battery Operated, Gyro–Action, China, Box 75.00
Spaceship, Revolving Astronaut, Box, Gemini 75.00
Spaceship, Tom Corbett, Box 1050.00
Sparkler, Hand, Chein, Box 20.00
Speedphone, Metal, Gong Bell Co., Box 10.00
Spidy Spider, Steiff, 4 In. 425.00
Spinner, Poll Parrot Shoes 15.00
Squirrel, Hopping, Windup, Box, Occupied Japan 25.00
Squirrel, In Cage, Martin 850.00
Station, Built–Rite Chrysler–Plymouth Garage Shell Station, Paper 170.00
Station, Shell Service, 1967 .... 100.00
Steam Engine, Jensen Co., 1940s 175.00
Steam Engine, Tin Litho, Bing, Germany, 1920s, 9 1/2 In. 450.00
Steam Engine, Weeden, Tin & Brass, 10 5/8 In. 40.00
Steam Roller, Diesel, Orange, Hubley, 9 X 3 1/2 In. 75.00
Steam Roller, Keystone, To Ride, 21 In. 195.00
Steam Shovel, Red & Black, Keystone, 1930s, 25 In. 150.00
Steam Shovel, Wooden Wheels, Structo 35.00
Stethoscope, Dr.Kildare Thumpy Heartbeat, Box 20.00
Stock Car Driver, Lady, Lehman .... 350.00 To 395.00
Stove, Crescent, Burner Covers, Cast Iron, 4 3/4 In. 95.00
Stove, Doll's, Metal, Electrified, Metal Ware, 8 1/2 X 4 X 8 In. 20.00
Stove, Double Oven & Burner, Empire, 14 X 15 In. 145.00
Stove, Empire, Electric, 1930s .... 72.00 To 125.00
Stove, Gas, White Star 95.00
Stove, Holly Hobbie, Electric 20.00
Stove, Kent, Green, Iron, 4 1/2 In. 35.00
Stove, Little Chef, Electric, 1940s, Box 48.00
Stove, Little Lady, Electric 20.00
Stove, Pretty Maid, 1950s .... 20.00 To 25.00
Stove, Queen, Black, Iron, Utensils, 6 1/2 In. 12.00
Stove, Refrigerator & Sink, Wolverine 45.00
Stove, Roper, Cast Iron, 6 In. 30.00
Stove, Wolverine, Snow White, Steel, Box, 15 In. 25.00
Streetcar, Clanging Bell, Wolverine, Tin, Box, 14 In. 485.00
Streetcar, Pacific Coast, Tin, Friction, Bell, 6 In. 25.00
Stroller, With Raggedy Ann & Raggedy Andy, Ohio Art 28.00
Submarine, Diving, Wolverine 65.00
Submarine, Windup, Wolverine, 13 In. .... 55.00 To 75.00
Super Jet, Fisher–Price 65.00
Swing, Doll's, 2 Seater, Swing, Wooden Construction, Red & Green, 1930s 110.00
Swing, Doll's, Lawn, Kilgore 22.00
Symmetroscope, C.1880 .... 275.00
Talking Alarm Clock, Star Wars, C3PO & R2D2, Box 25.00
Tank, Burnett, Windup, Tinplate, English, 7 1/2 In. 300.00
Tank, Cap Firing, Marx, Box 50.00
Tank, Combat, Tin Tires, Windup, 11 In. 180.00
Tank, Doughboy, Sparking, Marx, 10 In. .... 125.00 To 165.00
Tank, Flintstones, Turnover, Linemar 350.00
Tank, Mounted Gun & Soldier Top, Tin, Windup, Burnett, 7 1/2 In. 300.00
Tank, Pop–Up Soldier With Rifle, Windup, Tin, Marx, 10 In. 62.50
Tank, Rex Mars, Planet Patrol 125.00
Tank, Roll Over, Windup, Marx, Box 175.00
Tank, World War I Soldier & Flag, Marx 50.00
Tank, World War II, Wooden, Painted, Clicker Bottom, 8 X 4 In. 15.00
Tanker, Battery Operated, Lights, Holland, 21 In. 75.00
Tanker, Holland Oil, 1950s, 21 In. 50.00
Taxi, Amos & Andy 395.00
Taxi, Lupor, Windup 65.00
Taxi, Yellow Cab, Arcade, Cast Iron, 9 In. 535.00
Tea Set, Doll's, Floral Pattern, Marked Depon, 15 Piece 90.00

Tea Set, Doll's, Iridescent Yellow, Blue Trim, Japan, 20 Piece	20.00
Tea Set, Mother Goose, Tin, Ohio Art, 12 Piece	30.00
Tea Set, Pagoda With Trees, Blue, Service For 4	25.00
Tea Set, Porcelain, Gebruder Heubach, C.1900, 23 Piece ....*Illus*	230.00
Tea Set, Sterling Silver, Turquoise Stone Handles, Mexico, 1 1/2 In.	100.00
TOY, TEDDY BEAR, see Teddy Bear	
Teeter–Totter, Doll's, Gibbs, Tin, 14 1/2 In.	90.00
Teeter–Totter, Doll's, Kilgore	118.00
Telephone, Candlestick, Handi–Ocraft Co., Plastic	28.00
Telephone, Tin, Black, 1930	25.00
Telescope, Brass, Boy Detective, Box, 1930s, Germany, Extends 3 Ft.	20.00
Tiger, Kitten, Straw Stuffed, Green Glass Eyes, Steiff	85.00
Tiger, Pull Toy, Fisher–Price	10.00
Tiger, Pull Toy, Leather Cover, Wood & Papier-Mache, 14 3/4 In.	125.00
Tiger, Running, Blue Glass Eyes, Steiff, 3 1/2 X 8 In.	35.00
Toaster, Tin, Sunshine Miss, Ohio Art	5.00
Toe–Joe Man, On Trapeze, Spring Operated, Ohio Art	75.00
Toonerville Trolley, Clockwork, Tin, Fontaine Fox, C.1922, Box, 5 In.	675.00
Tootin Chuggin Loco, Battery Operated, Cragstan	28.00
Top, Aerial, Capt.Jack's	15.00
Top, Mexican Children, Ohio Art, Tin, Large	17.00
Tractor & Thresher, McCormick & Deering, Arcade	350.00
Tractor & Trailer, John Deere	45.00
Tractor & Wagon, Allis Chalmers, Cast Iron	85.00
Tractor Trailer, Jolly Green Giant, Tonka	45.00
Tractor Trailer, Smith Miller, 24 In.	95.00
Tractor Trailer, GMC Hi–Way, Red Cab, Wood Fences, Smith–Miller	150.00
Tractor Trailer, M.I.C. P.I.E, Red & Silver, Smith–Miller	490.00
Tractor, Blue Metal, Orange Wagon, Hubley, 5 X 3 In.	25.00
Tractor, Cast Iron, Arcade, 5 1/2 In.	125.00
Tractor, Caterpillar, Cast Iron, Metal Tracks, Arcade, C.1936, 8 In.	275.00
Tractor, Euclid Caterpillar, Corgi, Box	100.00
Tractor, Field Artillery, Dinky	15.00
Tractor, Ford, Blue & White, No.8600, 12 In.	35.00
Tractor, Golf Club, Metal & Rubber, Tonka	40.00
Tractor, International 656, Red, Rubber Wheels, Ertle Mfg., 5 In.	65.00
Tractor, John Deere, Cast Iron	20.00
Tractor, Massey–Ferguson, Corgi, Box	35.00
Tractor, Oliver, Arcade, 5 In.	125.00
Tractor, With Snowplow, Driver, Marx, Box	75.00
Train Set, Cast Iron Windup Engine, Late 19th Century, Marklin, Box	2100.00
Train Set, Key Wind, Litho Label On Box, Marklin	4500.00
Train Set, Lionel, No.1477s, Steam Pellets, Box	295.00
Train Set, Plastic Engine, Tin Cars, Windup, Marx	45.00
Train Set, Sparking, Windup, Marx, Box	80.00
Train Set, Union Pacific, Battery Operated, Mar Lines	45.00
Train, American Flyer, 175 Watt Transformer	60.00
Train, Cast Iron Windup Steam Engine, Marklin, Box, Late 19th Century	2100.00
Train, Cast Iron, Ives, Black & Red, 4 Passenger Cars, C.1895	1200.00
Train, City Of Los Angeles, Windup, Plastic, Engine, 3 Cars, Nosco, 1950s	18.00
Train, Day Coach, Dark Olive Green, New York Central, Lionel, C.1918	300.00
Train, Electric, O Gauge, Marked Jep, 1930s, 6 Piece	110.00
Train, Electric, Steam Engine No.1666, Tender, 5 Stock, Tracks, Lionel	225.00
Train, Engine & Tender, Buddy L	950.00
Train, Engine, Pennsylvania Railroad, Tootsietoy, 5 1/2 In.	30.00
Train, Engine, Santa Fe Freight Diesel, Lionel	45.00
Train, Engine, Steam, Junior Engineer Electric, Model SE–100	45.00
Train, Engine, Steam, Style 75, Jensen Mfg., Instruction Sheet	55.00
Train, Engine, With Passenger Car, Red & Black, Marked C.P.R.R.	150.00
Train, Freight, Complete, Lionel, 1930s	700.00
Train, Honeymoon Express, Tin, Windup, Marx, 1940s ....95.00 To 185.00	
Train, Loader, Railroad Derrick, Black & Red, Tin, Marx, Box	20.00
Train, Locomotive & Tender, Hillclimber, Tin, 27 In.	285.00
Train, Locomotive & Tender, NY Central, 3/4 In.Scale, Langworthy, 42 In.	3850.00

Train, Locomotive Engine, Friction, Black, Early 20th Century, 14 In. 275.00
Train, Locomotive, Bild–A–Loco Motor, Gray, Black, Lionel, Standard Gauge 375.00
Train, Locomotive, No.700E, NY Central Tender, Steam ....*Illus* 2000.00
Train, Locomotive, Riding, Keystone 325.00
Train, Locomotive, Steam Gauge I, Marklin, Black, Red Trim, C.1905, 12 In. 880.00
Train, Locomotive, Zephyr Style, Streamliner, Wolverine, Steel, 5 X 18 In 80.00
Train, No. 10, Lionel, Locomotive, Whistle, Brass Inserts ....*Illus* 140.00
Train, No.238E, Lionel, Engine, No.225W Tender, Streamlined ....*Illus* 185.00
Train, No.255E, Lionel, Engine, No.263W Tender, Gray ....*Illus* 795.00
Train, No.260, Lionel, No.263 Tender, No.1685 Passenger ....*Illus* 700.00
Train, No.513, Lionel, Cattle Car, Green, Orange Roof ....*Illus* 60.00
Train, No.5149, Lionel, Boxcar, Ivory, Peacock Roof ....*Illus* 50.00
Train, No.515, Lionel, Tank Car, Orange, Brass Rails ....*Illus* 50.00
Train, Overland Flyer, Marx, Set 65.00
Train, Passenger, Union Pacific Engine, M1005, 3 Cars, Streamline, Marx 75.00
Train, Pratt & Letchworth, Sheet Metal, Red Passenger Car 250.00
Train, Sante Fe, Windup, Box 25.00
Train, Super Yard Bird, Doepke, 6 Volt, Battery Operated 1100.00
Train, Tasty Food, Made From 4–2 1/2 Lb.Coffee Canisters 300.00
Train, Tin & Wood, Black Paint, Carlisle & Finch, 6 Piece, 5 Ft.7 In. 1100.00
Train, Union Pacific Streamline, Tin Litho, Windup, Marx, Box, 22 In. 700.00
Train, Union Pacific, Windup, Sheet Metal, Marx, 21 In. 30.00
Travel Chicks, Railroad Car, Windup, Tin, Strauss, Box 695.00
Trencher, Tonka, No.534 .... 40.00
Tricky Motorcycle, Police, Marx, Box 95.00
Tricky Taxi, Marx, Box .... 60.00 To 85.00
Trolley Car, Broadway Line 712, Red Paint, Iron, Wilkins, 12 In. 2000.00
Trolley Car, Friction, 1920s 140.00
Truck & Trailer, Lumber, B, Yellow, With Bulldog, Smith–Miller 525.00
Truck & Trailer, National Biscuit, Pull Toy, 5 Samples, 1930s, 26 In. 350.00
Truck, Aerial, Original Paint, Buddy L, Decals 525.00
Truck, Auto Transport, Tootsietoy, 9 In. 250.00
Truck, Bell Telephone, Cast Iron, Red, Hubley, 1930, 9 1/2 In. 375.00
Truck, Cab, Trailer, Van Lines, Orange, Black, Wooden, Buddy L 185.00
Truck, Cannon, Battery Operated, Cragstan 180.00
Truck, Carrier, Van Freight, Buddy L 125.00
Truck, Cement Mixer, Structo, 21 In. 155.00
Truck, Cement, Tonka, Red 65.00
Truck, Circus, Pulling Circus Wagon, Wyandotte, No.503 .... 195.00
Truck, Coal Dump, Rubber Wheels, Red, Cast Iron, Mack, 10 1/4 In. 130.00
Truck, Coal, Buddy L 1370.00
Truck, Coca–Cola, Buddy L, Box 325.00
Truck, Concrete Mixer, Structo 45.00
Truck, Concrete, Emmets 750.00
Truck, Cragstan Cannon, Battery, Box 200.00
Truck, Dark Green Canvas Back, Red, Tin, Key Wind, Schuco, 10 1/2 In. 350.00
Truck, Delivery Van, Buddy L, Steel, Black, Green, Door Opens, 25 1/4 In. 450.00
Truck, Drive–O–Dump, GMC, Remote, Red, Smith–Miller 300.00
Truck, Dump, Arcade, 11 In. 275.00
Truck, Dump, Back Lifts, Kingsbury, Tin, Cast Iron Driver, 9 1/2 In. 250.00
Truck, Dump, Blue & Red Body, Kilgore, 8 1/2 In. 350.00
Truck, Dump, Buddy L, 1940s 125.00
Truck, Dump, Cast Iron, Kilgore 260.00
Truck, Dump, Clip–On Headlights, Turner, 1920s, 27 In. 165.00
Truck, Dump, Lift Mechanism, Original Paint, Buddy L 225.00
Truck, Dump, Metal, Keystone, 1930s, 27 In. 300.00
Truck, Dump, Metal, Tin Litho, Red, 1920s, Marx 50.00
Truck, Dump, Orange, Wooden Wheels, Wyandotte, 7 In. 90.00
Truck, Dump, Pressed Steel, Structo, Orange & Black, 11 In. 650.00
Truck, Dump, Steel, Windup, Orange, Black, Structo, 11 In. 650.00
Truck, Dump, Structo, 1920s 125.00
Truck, Dump, Structo, 1960s 25.00
Truck, Dump, Tiang, 18 In. 150.00
Truck, Dump, Windup, Marx 35.00

Truck, Dump, Windup, Structo, 1950s, 9 In. 60.00
Truck, Dump, Wood, Playskool 15.00
Truck, Dumper, Structo, 1960s 25.00
Truck, Earth Mover, Structo 65.00
Truck, Electric Dairy Van, Dinky Toys, No.30V 21.00
Truck, Extension Ladder, Red, 1947, Buddy L 145.00
Truck, Farm, Merchants Trouser, Tin, Windup, Marx, 10 1/2 In. 145.00
Truck, Fast Freight, White Cab, Orange Carrier, Buddy L 50.00
Truck, Forklift, Friction, Celluloid Driver, Linemar 31.00
Truck, Garbage, Steel, Structo, 21 In. 165.00
Truck, GMC Wrecker, Red & White, Sides, Replaced Cord, Smith–Miller 375.00
Truck, GMC, Box, Buddy L, 1956 .... 145.00
Truck, Grader, Euclid, Doepke 85.00
Truck, Grader, Tonka, No.510 .... 40.00
Truck, Heinz Pickle, White, Metalcraft 135.00
Truck, Howard Johnson, Marx, Box, 1940s 70.00
Truck, Hubley, Post Hole Auger, 3 Digging Tools, 2 Ladders, 10 In. 645.00
Truck, Hydraulic Dump, Tonka ....30.00 To 40.00
Truck, Hydraulic Hauling Dumper, Buddy L, 21 In. 35.00
Truck, Hydraulic, Buddy L, 1950s 55.00
Truck, International Car Carrier, Tootsietoy, C.1947 .... 15.00
Truck, International, Arcade, Iron, 9 In. 95.00
Truck, Log Hauling Structo 45.00
Truck, M.I.C.Lift Gate, Red & Black, Smith–Miller 500.00
Truck, Mack, Stake, Nickel Spoke Sheels, Arcade, Cast Iron, 12 In. 2000.00
Truck, Merry–Go–Round, Buddy L, 1950s 65.00
Truck, Milk, Wooden, Buddy L 110.00
Truck, Motor Dispatch, Structo, Original Price Tag, 20 In., 1930s 120.00
Truck, Moving, With Trailer, Marshall Field & Co., Sheet Metal, 1940s 45.00
Truck, Oil Tanker, Cast Iron, 1930s, 5 1/2 In. 45.00
Truck, Oil Tanker, Texaco, Pressed Steel, 24 In. 60.00
Truck, Pickup, Cab Delivery, Ford Model T, Iron, 9 In. 130.00
Truck, Pickup, Hinged Tailgate, Iron, Vindex, 8 In. 225.00
Truck, Pickup, Original Decal, Cast Iron, Arcade, 5 In. 65.00
Truck, Pumper, American LaFrance, Sturditoy, No.7 .... 325.00
Truck, Railway Express, Milk & Ice Cream Advertising, Buddy L, 21 In. 125.00
Truck, Railway Express, Painted, Steelcraft, 24 In. 675.00
Truck, Road Grader, State Highway Department, Metal & Rubber, Tonka 45.00
Truck, Scoop & Load, Cream Body, Green Scoop, Buddy L, 16 In. 25.00
Truck, Stake, Wyandotte, 1930s, 12 In. 37.50
Truck, Steam Shovel, Bulldog Mack, Rubber Tires, 10 In. 45.00
Truck, Steam Shovel, Steel Plate, Black, Red Roof, Keystone, 20 In. 82.00
Truck, Tank, Mobil Gas, Friction, Japan, 1950s, 9 1/2 In. 28.00
Truck, Telephone Company, Steel, Structo, 1940s, 12 In. 30.00
Truck, Texaco, Tin, Buddy L, 1950s, 23 In. 35.00
Truck, Tow, 1934, Detachable Grille, Chassis, Red, Champion, 5 In. 400.00
Truck, Tow, Buddy L, 1928 .... 265.00
Truck, Tow, Detachable Chassis, Iron, Hubley, 5 In. 345.00
Truck, Tow, Red, Structo, 12 In. 45.00
Truck, Tow, Sit & Ride, Buddy L, 21 In. 85.00
Truck, Wabco, Plastic Wheels, Ertle Mfg.10 X 4 1/2 In. 125.00
Truck, Wrigley's Spearmint, Buddy L 100.00
Trunk, Doll's, Domed Lid, Stenciled Paper, Plywood Banding, 9 X 14 In. 88.00
Trunk, Doll's, Dy–Dee, With Clothes, Effanbee 25.00
Trunk, Doll's, George Buroughs & Sons, Milwaukee, 4 Drawers, Hanger Rack 75.00
Trunk, Doll's, Original Paper Inside, Lift Out Tray, 16 X 11 In. 125.00
Trunk, Doll's, Steamer, 11 1/2 In. 15.00
Tub, Wringer, Washboard, 1920s 28.00
Tugboat, Betty Jane, Linemar 25.00
TV, Floor Model, Plastic, Knob Turns Picture, Ideal, 1950s 25.00
Typewriter, American Flyer ....25.00 To 55.00
Typewriter, Berwin 38.00
Typewriter, Dial, Marx 45.00
Typewriter, Jr., Marx, Box ....18.00 To 25.00

Typewriter, Simplex Model A, Box 24.00
Typewriter, Simplex, Model 240, Box 95.00
Typewriter, Unique Art 25.00
Typewriter, Visible Typewriter, American Typewriter Co., Case 85.00
Vanity, Doll's, Mirror, Drawer, Blue & Ivory, 11 X 12 In. 52.00
Viewmaster, 32 Reels, Hoppy, Space Cadet, Baseball, Original Box 75.00
Violin Player, Hat Moves Back & Forth, Clockwork, Tin, C.1900, 10 In. 825.00
Waffle Iron, Cast Aluminum 15.00
Waffle Iron, Wagner, Cast Iron 100.00
Wagon, Bliss, Complete With Blocks, 14 In. ....95.00 To 145.00
Wagon, Coaster, Iron, Champion Express, Green, Red Handle, White Wheels 55.00
Wagon, Delivery Truck In Red Paint, Varnished, Removable Sides, 36 In. 135.00
Wagon, Doll, American, Joe Ellis Style 180.00
Wagon, Dray, Double Team, Winkins, C.1910, 21 In. 275.00
Wagon, Express, Tin, C.1800, 31 X 16 In. 1995.00
Wagon, Fisher-Price, No.171 .... 100.00
Wagon, Marked Express, Metal, Replaced Wood Stick Handle, 16 X 30 In. 192.00
Wagon, Red, Gilt & Black Express Lettering, 69 In. 770.00
Wagon, Stanley Dump, 2 Horses, Driver, Cast Aluminum, 12 In. 15.00
Wagon, Stenciled The Detroit News, Wooden 95.00
Wagon, Trail Blazer, 1920s 185.00
Wallet, Official Wyatt Earp Set, 1958 .... 45.00
Wash Set, Doll's, Art Deco, Pink Enameled Metal, 3 1/2 In.Pitcher, 4 Pc. 120.00
Washboard, Child's, Little Housekeeper 15.00
Washboard, Midget Washer, All Glass 33.00
Washboard, Tin, Wooden, Wolverine 12.00
Washing Machine, Wringer & Tub, Wolverine 50.00
Watering Can, Indian, Duck, Ohio Art Co. 25.00
Western Suit, Cowhide Chaps, Vest, Gun, Belt, Gun, Eagle, Size 10 .... 35.00
Wheelbarrow, Arcade 25.00
Wheelbarrow, Squirrel On Sides, Paris Mfg.Co., No.2, Wooden 275.00
Whistle, Jack Webb Dragnet 6.00
Wolf, Black & Tan, White Mohair, Marked On Shoes, Schuco, 6 1/2 In. 85.00
Woman, Sweeping, Windup, Tin, Gunthermann 975.00
Woofy Waggerpull, Barks, Wags Tail, Fisher-Price 48.00
Wrecker, Words Repair Truck, Cast Iron, Buddy L 75.00
Wrecking Truck, Buddy L, Steel, Turning Crane, 28 In. 300.00
Xylophone, Stand, F.M.T., Japan, Box, 10 In. 12.00
Yellow Kid, Tin, Yellow Paint, Red Bowtie, 1930s, 6 In. 100.00
Zeppelin, Akron Steelcraft, 24 In. 300.00
Zeppelin, Graf Zeppelin, Steelcraft, 24 In. 200.00
Zeppelin, New York, Strauss, 10 In. 95.00

Toy, Carriage Drills, Wooden,
Stenciled, 1880, 51 X 44 In.

Zeppelin, Pull Toy, Steelcraft, 25 In.	85.00
Zeppelin, Push Type, Tin, Marx, 1930s	85.00
Zilotone, Wolverine	235.00 To 300.00

Tramp art is a form of folk art made since the Civil War. It is usually made from chip–carved cigar boxes. Examples range from small boxes and picture frames to full–sized pieces of furniture.

TRAMP ART, Box, 10 1/2 X 6 In.	35.00
Box, 2 Tiers, 3 Drawers, Old Varnish, 10 X 11 3/4 In.	70.00
Box, Cigar, Glass Windows On Side, Carved Tulip On Lid	45.00
Box, Cover, 4 X 8 X 7 In.	48.00
Box, Jewel, Chip Carved, Diamond Shape, Flared Base, 1930, 7 X 9 In	. 66.00
Box, Jewelry, 11 X 7 X 7 In.	125.00
Box, Jewelry, Satin Lined, Round	125.00
Box, To My Mother	185.00
Box, Wooden, 15 X 10 In.	60.00
Cupboard, Corner, Hanging, Black Paint, Print, C.1920, 24 X 13 In.	775.00
Frame, Center Mirror, 16 3/4 X 19 3/4 In.	20.00
Frame, Cross Corner, Natural Finish, 16 1/4 X 21 1/4 In.	25.00
Frame, Dark Paint, 22 X 18 In.	30.00
Frame, Mirror, 5 3/4 X 7 3/4 In.	45.00
Frame, Picture, Gold & Silver Paint Traces, 1 3/4 X 19 X 23 In.	25.00
Frame, Wooden Hearts At Corners, 8 X 10 In.	24.00
Magazine Rack, Wall, 7 Layer	75.00
Magazine Rack, Wall, Painted	175.00
Matchbox, 7 In.	18.00
Saltbox	145.00
Shelf, Carved Flower Design	115.00

Animal traps may be handmade. One of the most unusual is the mousetrap made so that when the mouse entered the trap, it was hit on the head with a mallet. Other traps were commercially manufactured and often are marked with the name of the manufacturer. Many traps were designed to be as humane as possible, and they would trap the live animal so it could be released in the woods.

TRAP, Bear, Newhouse, No.15, Safety Chain	195.00
Bear, Tempered Steel Springs, 36 In.	145.00
Bear, Triumph, Model 415X, 25 In.	165.00
Box, Hinged Cover, Pedestal Base, 5 Pyramids On Top, 9 X 7 In.	85.00
Cat, 1870s	25.00
Fly, Amethyst Glass, Victorian	165.00
Fly, Dome Shape, Screen, Bug & Fly Trap, Nesko, Shur Katch	45.00
Fly, Sur–Katchem, Screen, Tin Top, 6 X 10 1/2 In.	35.00
Jaw, Hand Forged, 8 In.	75.00
Minnow & Roaches, McSwain, Jonesboro, Arkansas, Glass	45.00
Mole, Cast Iron	30.00
Mole, Reddick	8.50
Mouse, 4 Hold, Wood	12.00
Mouse, Auto–Set	6.00
Mouse, Deadfall, Wood, 18th Century, 5 1/2 X 10 1/2 X 11 1/2 In.	450.00
Mouse, Ketch–All, Metal	22.00
Mouse, McGill, Metal	5.00 To 12.00
Mouse, Twisted Wire, 8 In.	65.00
Mouse, Victor, Metal	7.00
Oneida Victor No.2, Pa., Metal, Chain, 14 In.	15.00
Racoon, 2 Springs	4.00
Wolf, No.4 1/2	85.00

TREEN, see Wooden

Trivets are now used to hold hot dishes. Most trivets of the late nineteenth and early twentieth centuries were made to hold hot irons. Iron or brass reproductions are being made of many of the old styles.

TRIVET, Blue Willow, Wedgwood, Round, 6 In.	75.00
Brass, Wrought Iron Legs, Turned Wooden Handle, 12 1/2 In.	55.00
Broiler Shape, Heart–Like Handle Finial, Wrought Iron, 11 In.	225.00
Cathedral Pattern, Sadiron, 6 In.	15.00
Cleveland Foundry, Iron	19.50
Colebrookdale Iron Co.	18.00
Colt, Cast Iron	75.00
Compass, Star & Fans, Cast Iron, 9 1/2 In.	27.50
Engraved Slip, Paw Feet, Reticulated, English, Brass, 5 1/2 X 10 In.	55.00
Fireplace, Brass, Horse Center, 3 Legs, 3 1/2 X 6 In.	68.00
Folded Oak Leaf Design, Cast Iron, Footed, 19th Century	47.50
Foliage Scroll, Cast Brass, 9 7/8 In.	12.50
H In Center, W.H.Howell Co., Geneva, Illinois	12.00
Harp Shape, Brass & Iron, Penny Feet, Black Handle, 11 1/2 In.	55.00
Heart In Band, Odd Fellows Insignia, Cast Iron, 8 1/4 In.	20.00
Heart, 3 Footed, Wrought Iron, 4 1/4 X 7 In.	110.00
Heart, Cutout Design, Brass, 8 1/2 In.	60.00
Hearth, Triangular, Hand Forged Iron, Scalloped Sides, 3 X 11 In.	85.00
Horse Center, Brass, 6 In.	75.00
Horseshoe & Good Luck Center, 2 Horses, 4 1/2 X 8 1/2 In.	21.00
Horseshoe, God Bless Our Home, 1887	52.00
Horseshoe, Good Luck Horse At Top, 4 X 8 In.	20.00
I Want You, Cast Iron	18.00
Jenny Lind, Iron	28.00
Little Girl, House, Dog Carrying Hat, Handle, Cast Iron, 11 1/2 In.	260.00
Majolica, Lotus Blossoms, White, Meshed Wire Holder, 5 In.	55.00
Odd Fellows	15.00
Pinwheel & Heart Design, Cast Iron, Round, 7 In.	30.00
Reticulated Brass Top, Iron, Penny Feet, Wooden Handle, 15 X 12 In.	130.00
Scroll Detail, Wooden Handle, Brass Ferrule, Iron, 9 1/4 In.	30.00
Sliding Rest, Iron, C.1850	190.00
Star & Sunburst, Cleveland Foundry Co., Cast Iron	20.00
Triangular, Wrought Iron, 7 3/4 In.	20.00
Tulip, Round, Iron, 5 1/2 In.	50.00
Wilton, Black, Box, Miniature	5.00
Wooden Handle, Legs, Brass	20.00

Trunks of many types were made. The nineteenth–century sea chest was often handmade of unpainted wood. Brass–fitted camphorwood chests were brought back from the Orient. Leather–covered trunks were popular from the late eighteenth to mid nineteenth centuries. By 1895, trunks were covered with canvas or decorated sheet metal. Embossed metal coverings were used from 1870 to 1910. By 1925, trunks were covered with vulcanized fiber or undecorated metal.

TRUNK, Camelback, Child's, Wooden, 18 X 10 X 11 In.	75.00
Camphorwood, Lift Top, Brass Mounts, 12 1/2 X 30 X 15 In.	385.00
Doll's, Camelback, With Tray	250.00
Dome Top, Floral Medallions, Aurel 1850, Norwegian, 29 X 46 In.	550.00
Dome Top, Painted Leather, Armorial, Spanish Colonial, 24 X 47 In.	1430.00
Dome Top, Painted Swags, Feathers, Pine, Paper Lined, 5 X 12 X 6 In.	1375.00
Dome Top, Plain Interior, Sponge Painted, New England, 8 1/8 X 20 In.	165.00
Dome Top, Sponge Painted, Black & Brown, New England, 7 X 15 In.	137.00
Dome Top, Wood Slats, Leather Handles, Paper Lined, 21 X 32 In.	10.00
Dome Top, Wooden, Rollers, 24 In.	185.00
Handwrought Metal Work, Pine, 19th Century, 24 X 23 X 39 In.	250.00
Hide Covered, Dated October, 1830, Small	138.00
Immigrant's, Dome Top, Pine, Handles, Green–Brown Paint, 26 X 36 In.	66.00
Leather Covered, Green, Tan, Brass Studs, Brass Handle, 15 1/2 In.	350.00
Lift Top, Pine, Butt Hinge, Dovetail Construction, 14 X 27 In.	121.00
Oak, Spanish, Sculptured Front, Iron Hinges, 18th Century	2000.00
Polychrome Design, Leather Cover, Brassbound, China, 34 1/2 In.	75.00
Sea, Blue–Green Paint, White Interior, Handles, American, 16 X 41 In.	247.00

Sponge Painted, Domed, Spotted Red, Brown 165.00
Steamer, Original Wooden Hangers 18.00
Till, Divided Well, Painted Blue, 11 X 28 In. 195.00
Wrought Iron Strap Handles, Inscribed Adam Gates, 1848, 41 In. 605.00

Tuthill The Tuthill Cut Glass Company of Middletown, New York, worked from 1902 to 1923. Of special interest are the finely cut pieces of stemware and tableware.

TUTHILL, Bowl, Geometric, Intaglio, 8 In. 325.00
Bowl, Rex Pattern, Signed, 3 1/4 X 8 In. 2025.00
Bowl, Three Fruits, Vesicas, Signed, 8 1/4 In. 700.00
Bowl, Vintage Pattern, Band of Hobstars, Footed, Signed, 7 1/2 In. 495.00
Bowl, Vintage, Roll Over, Pedestal, Signed, 9 3/4 In. 595.00
Decanter, Thistle, Intaglio, Sterling Silver Stopper 325.00
Plate, Vintage, Signed, 10 In. 860.00
Plate, Wild Rose, Signed, 7 In. 485.00
Sugar & Creamer, Signed 125.00
Tray, Vintage Pattern, Geometric Cutting, Intaglio, Oval, 8 1/2 In. 525.00
Vase, Vintage Pattern, Signed, 12 In. 295.00

The first successful typewriter was made by Sholes and Glidden in 1874. Collectors divide typewriters into two main classifications: the index machine, which has a pointer and a dial for letter selection, and the keyboard machine, most commonly seen today.

TYPEWRITER, Blickensderfer, No.5 .... 125.00
Corona, Roller Folds Down Over Keys, 1917, 9 X 10 X 6 In. 50.00
Densmore 250.00
Folding, Types Polish, German, French, Accessories 500.00
Franklin 350.00
Hammond, Fold–Up Keyboard 80.00
Hammond, Multiplex, Multilingual .... 235.00 To 500.00
Monarch, Portable 35.00
Odell, No.4, Box 275.00
Remington Rand, No.5, Portable 35.00
Royal No.10, 1922 .... 45.00
Royal, Double Glass Sides 25.00
Royal, Portable 10.00
Smith, Premier, No.1 .... 245.00
Smith–Corona, Folding 45.00
Smith–Corona, Portable, Case, Instruction Book, 1920s 35.00
Stenotype, Case, 1911 .... 17.00
Underwood, Standard Portable, Green, Carrying Case 45.00

Uhl Pottery
hand-turned
Since 1850
Huntingburg Ind
Uhl pottery was made in Evansville, Indiana, in 1854. The pottery moved to Huntingburg, Indiana, in 1908. Stoneware and glazed pottery were made until the mid–1940s.

UHL, Bowl, Mixing, Blue, Small 15.00
Bowl, Pink, 11 In. 18.00
Casserole, Cover, Tan 25.00
Cookie Jar, Dutch Boy & Girl 30.00
Cookie Jar, Mulberry, Cover 45.00
Crock, 2 Gal. 15.00
Crock, 5 Gal. 35.00
Crock, 6 Gal. 45.00
Figurine, Shoe 245.00
Jug, Double Fisted, Company Name, 10 Gal. 130.00
Jug, Light Brown, Over White, 2 Gal. 65.00
Jug, Spherical, Rose 20.00
Jug, Water, Polar Bear, Blue 385.00
Mug, Barrel, Tan 7.00
Mug, Beer, Ink Stamp 15.00
Pitcher, Amber 48.00
Pitcher, Barrel, Pink 35.00
Pitcher, Dark Blue 35.00

Pitcher, Grape, Amber	22.00
Pitcher, Grape, Blue	90.00
Pitcher, Grapes On Lattice	75.00
Pitcher, Lincoln, Blue & White, 4 In.	325.00
Stein, Barrel Shape	15.00

The first known umbrella was owned by King Louis XIII of France in 1637. The earliest umbrellas were sunshades, not designed to be used in the rain. The umbrella was embellished and redesigned many times. In 1852, the fluted steel rib style was developed and that has remained the most useful style.

UMBRELLA, Black, Folding, Tag, Early 1940s	45.00
Carved Rabbit Handle	55.00
Celluloid Head At Tip, Child's	35.00
Champion Spark Plugs	20.00
Gold Handle, Ornate	45.00
Horsehead Handle, Red Eyes	22.50
Mary Poppins, Child's, Yellow	10.00
Nubby Handle, Ivory, Large Ring Handle	125.00
Oliver Tractor	45.00
Parade, N.E.Fat Man's Club, Picture of Fat Man, Oversized	60.00
Parasol, Child's, Black Silk Lace, Carved Wooden Handle	75.00
Parasol, Paper, Occupied Japan, 34 In.Diam.	25.00
Parasol, Pink Linen	40.00
Parosol, Black, Handle Folds	20.00
Repousse Silver Handle, Engraved Geroldine, Black	17.50
Woman's, White Linen, White Embroidered Flowers	175.00

The Union Porcelain Works was established at Greenpoint, New York, in 1848 by Charles Cartlidge. The company went through a series of ownership changes and finally closed in the early 1900s. The company made a fine quality white porcelain that was often decorated in clear, bright colors.

UNION PORCELAIN WORKS, Oyster Plate, 9 1/2 In.	110.00
Stein, Inlaid Lid, Jetter Brewing Co., C.1865	210.00

UNIVERSITY OF NORTH DAKOTA, see North Dakota School of Mines

Val St. Lambert Cristalleries of Belgium was founded by Messieurs Kemlin and Lelievre in 1825. The company is still in operation. All types of table glassware and decorative glassware were made. Pieces were often decorated with cut designs.

VAL ST.LAMBERT, Bottle, Perfume, 7 In.	65.00
Holder, Toothbrush, Signed	50.00
Lamp, Base, Muller Freres, Signed, C.1906, 14 In.	850.00
Paperweight, Ram	45.00
Pitcher, Diamond Shape, Signed	95.00
Powder Jar, Clear, Amber Stain, 2 1/2 In.	45.00
Ring Tree, Flowers, Acid Etched, Blue To Clear, 3 1/2 In.	175.00
Vase, Blue, Clear, Art Deco, Signed, 8 In.	225.00
Vase, Cameo, Flowers, Scrolled White Ground, Signed, 7 In.	475.00
Vase, Landscape, Leafy Trees, 2 Peacocks, Signed, 7 In.	605.00
Vase, Purple Tulips & Trim, Violet Shades, Signed, 9 In.	775.00
Wine, Intaglio Cut, Ribbons, Bowls, Cranberry, Set of 12	480.00

Vallerysthal Glassworks was founded in 1836 in Lorraine, France. In 1854 the firm became Klenglin et Cie. It made table and decorative glass, opaline, cameo, and art glass. A line of covered, pressed glass animal dishes was made in the nineteenth century. The firm is still working.

VALLERYSTHAL, Butter Dish, Radish, Signed	75.00
Candy Jar, Cover, Blue, Gold Trim, Signed	90.00
Dish, Dog Cover, Seated On Gun & Ammunition Pouch, 5 1/2 In.	125.00
Dish, Lemon, Cover, Yellow, Signed	50.00
Salt, Hen On Nest, Individual, Amber	14.00

Salt, Hen On Nest, Individual, Cobalt Blue 14.00
Vase, Stick, Dragonfly & Bullrushes, Intaglio Cut 750.00

 Van Briggle Pottery was made by Artus Van Briggle in Colorado Springs, Colorado, after 1901. Van Briggle had been a decorator at the Rookwood Pottery of Cincinnati, Ohio. He died in 1904. His wares usually had modeled relief decorations and a soft, dull glaze. The pottery is still working and still making some of the original designs.

VAN BRIGGLE, Ashtray, Blue 20.00
  Ashtray, Embossed Colorado 18.00
  Ashtray, Hopi Indian Maid, Blue 65.00
  Bookends, Bear On Stump, Turquoise 225.00
  Bookends, Owls, Spread Wings, Matte Green 68.00
  Bookends, Peacock .... 27.50 To 55.00
  Bookends, Ships, Maroon 55.00
  Bookends, Squirrels 70.00
  Boot, 2 1/4 In. .... 25.00 To 35.00
  Bowl, Acorn, Turquoise, No.734 .... 30.00
  Bowl, Centerpiece, With Flower Frog 65.00
  Bowl, Dragonflies, Flower Frog, Maroon 70.00
  Bowl, Dragonfly, Matching Frog, 9 In. 45.00
  Bowl, Green To Blue, Matte, 1908–11, 5 1/2 X 10 In. 895.00
  Bowl, Mottled Green Glaze, Bulbous, Short Neck, 4 X 7 In. 50.00
  Bowl, Tulips & Leaves, Ming, Oval, 19 Hole Frog, 8 1/2 In. 55.00
  Candleholder, Double, Persian Rose, Tulip, Pair 68.00
  Candlestick, Oakleaf & Acorn, C.1940, Pair 38.50
  Compote, Footed, Brown, Signed Anna 25.00
  Conch Shell, Aqua, 17 In. 65.00
  Console Set, Female Center Frog, Aqua, 14 In. 165.00
  Creamer, Melon Shape, Midnight Black Glaze 35.00
  Figurine, Elephant, Raised Trunk, Turquoise, Marked 90.00
  Figurine, Indian Maiden, Kneeling 100.00
  Flower Frog, Duck, Blue 45.00
  Flower Frog, Duck, Green 38.50
  Flower Frog, Turtle, Lady of The Lake, Turquoise 210.00
  Flower Frog, White Lotus, 3 X 6 In. 35.00
  Lamp, 2 Racing Deer, Ming Blue, 11 In. 125.00
  Lamp, Damsel, White 125.00
  Lamp, Moonglow Matte, Butterfly Shade, Carved, Signed, 18 In. 175.00
  Lamp, Night, Grass & Butterfly Shade, Turquoise 135.00
  Lamp, Persian Rose, Damsel of Damascus 205.00
  Lamp, Relief Molded Leaves, Ming Glaze, 14 In. 115.00
  Lamp, Squirrel, Cream 50.00
  Mug, Blue–Green, Signed, 4 1/2 In. 75.00
  Paperweight, Elephant, Green 65.00
  Pitcher, Horn Shape, Dark Blue 45.00

It is easy to glue pieces of broken china. Use a new fast setting but not instant glue. Position the pieces correctly, then use tape to hold the parts together. If the piece needs special support, lean it in a suitable position in a box filled with sand.

Pitcher, Ming Blue, Marked, 3 In.	21.00
Pitcher, Persian Rose	15.00
Planter, Conch Shell, Turquoise Ming Glaze, 12 In.	55.00
Rose Bowl, Turquoise	24.00
Salt & Pepper, Barrel Shape, Teal	30.00
Salt & Pepper, Persian Rose, Floral Design	42.00
Tankard, Inscribed The Gunters, Brown Glaze	70.00
Vase, Anemon, White, 5 In.	6.00
Vase, Boat Shape, Blue, 4 1/2 In.	20.00
Vase, Boot, Anna Van Briggle, 5 In.	25.00
Vase, Brown & Green, Handles, 10 X 12 In., Pre-1900	175.00
Vase, Brown Glaze, 1906, 7 1/4 In.	475.00
Vase, Bulbous, Blue & Green, Signed, 4 1/2 In., Pair	50.00
Vase, Butterfly, Maroon, Dated 1914, 4 In.	70.00
Vase, Candlestick, Blue & Green, C.1930, 9 In.	35.00
Vase, Copper, 1907-12, 5 In.	1050.00
Vase, Dark Maroon, Blue, 3 In.	20.00
Vase, Dark Pink Bottom, Purple Top, Dated 1917, 7 In.	160.00
Vase, Dragonflies, Maroon, 2 3/4 In.	125.00
Vase, Dragonflies, Turquoise Ming Glaze, 7 In.	48.00
Vase, Embossed Leaf, Maroon & Blue, 4 1/2 In.	65.00
Vase, Indian Heads, Ming Blue Glaze, 12 In.	70.00
Vase, Indian Heads, Turquoise Ming Glaze, 11 In.	95.00
Vase, Ivris, 2 Loop Handle, Blue, Marked, 13 In.	175.00
Vase, Long-Stemmed Flowers, 10 In.	95.00
Vase, Lorelei, 10 In.	100.00 To 150.00
Vase, Metallic Gray Glaze, Pre-1907, 10 In.	425.00
Vase, Ming, Turquoise, Stylized Flowers, 7 1/2 In.	115.00
Vase, Molded Flowers, Long Stem, Pale Blue Matte, Marked, 12 In.	150.00
Vase, Mottled Cream To Powder Blue, 1905, 6 In.	325.00
Vase, Persian Rose, 10 In.	95.00 To 108.00
Vase, Persian Rose, Leaf Design, 8 In.	70.00
Vase, Pink Matte Glaze, 1906, 10 X 8 In. ....*Illus*	275.00
Vase, Poppy Seed Pod Edge, Blue Matte, Signed, 1905, 5 1/2 In.	600.00
Vase, Tapered, Blue & Green, 9 In.	10.00
Vase, Turquoise, 2 Handles, 3 1/2 In.	30.00
Vase, Turquoise, Bud, 9 In.	30.00
Wall Pocket, Nouveau Relief, Turquoise Matte, 7 1/2 In.	75.00

Vasa Murrhina is the name of a glassware made by the Vasa Murrhina Art Glass Company of Sandwich, Massachusetts, about 1884. The glassware was transparent and was embedded with small pieces of colored glass and metallic flakes. Some of the pieces were cased. The same type of glass was made in England. Collectors often confuse Vasa Murrhina glass with aventurine, spatter, or spangle glass. There is much confusion about what actually was made by the Vasa Murrhina factory.

VASA MURRHINA, see also Spangle Glass

VASA MURRHINA, Basket, Blue & Aventurine Green, Handle, 11 In.	100.00
Basket, Brown & Orange Mica Flakes, Handle, Fenton	65.00
Basket, Jack-In-The-Pulpit	125.00
Basket, Melon Sectioned, Gold Mica Flakes, 8 1/2 X 10 In.	295.00
Basket, Mica Flakes, Clear Rim & Handle, Blue, 4 3/4 In.	125.00
Basket, Mica Flecked, Thorn Handle, Clear, Square	185.00
Basket, Silver Mica Flakes, Crimped Ruffled Top, 7 X 8 In.	235.00
Berry Bowl, Leaf Mold, Cranberry Spatter, Small	30.00
Bride's Bowl, Rainbow	85.00
Centerpiece, Rose, Ruffled, Ormolu Mount, White Lining, 18 In.	495.00
Creamer, Autumn Orange	66.00
Cruet, Powder Horn Shape	495.00
Figurine, Elephant, Orange & Brown	50.00
Figurine, Mushroom, Pink, Lavender & White	25.00
Pitcher, 3 Pouring Lips, Gold Mecca Dots, 8 1/2 In.	95.00
Pitcher, Orange, 5 1/2 In.	66.00

Pitcher, Water, Gold, Blue Spatter, Mica, Art Glass, Handle	85.00
Rosebowl, Rose, White Lining, Mica, 8 Crimp Top, 3 5/8 In.	110.00
Sugar Shaker, Leaf Mold, Cranberry Spatter, Original Lid	195.00
Sugar Shaker, Leaf Mold, Pink Spatter, Original Lid	195.00
Tumbler, Leaf Mold, Pink Cased	50.00
Vase, Blue & Aventurine, 14 In.	100.00
Vase, Blue Mist, 7 In.	58.00
Vase, Blue Mist, 8 In.	66.00
Vase, Fan, Fenton, C.1964, 7 In.	55.00
Vase, Fan, Rose Mist, 7 In.	58.00
Vase, Jack–In–The–Pulpit, Mica Flakes, White, 5 1/2 In.	110.00
Vase, Jack–In–The–Pulpit, Ruffled Top, Mica Flakes, 5 In.	110.00
Vase, Orange & Brown, 11 In.	75.00
Vase, Rose, Aventurine Green, 4 In.	75.00
Vase, Rose, Mica Flakes, Ruffled, Thorn Handles, 7 1/2 In., Pr.	225.00

Vaseline glass is a greenish–yellow glassware resembling petroleum jelly. Some vaseline glass is still being made in old and new styles. Pressed glass of the 1870s was often made of vaseline–colored glass. Some pieces of vaseline glass may also be listed under Pressed Glass in this book.

VASELINE GLASS, Basket, Drape Design, Opalescent Band, Thorn Handle, 7 In.	250.00
Berry Bowl, Petticoat, 8 In.	75.00
Berry Set, Daisy & Button, 13 Piece	225.00
Berry Set, Everglades, 7 Piece	375.00
Berry Set, Iris With Meander, 6 Piece	220.00
Berry Set, Maple Leaf, Oval, Footed, 7 Piece	115.00
Bonbon, Fluted Scrolls, 3–Footed, 7 1/2 In.	26.00
Bottle, Barber, Daisy & Fern, Opalescent	130.00
Bowl, Blown, 3 X 12 In.	45.00
Bowl, Daisy & Button, Square, 7 X 10 In.	20.00
Butter, Diamond Spearhead, Cover	195.00
Cake Stand, Wildflower	95.00
Candlestick, Caryatid Pattern, C.1870, 9 3/4 In., Pair	3500.00
Candlestick, Hexagonal, 7 1/2 In., Pair	650.00
Candlestick, Stretch, Fenton, 8 1/2 In., Pair	55.00
Celery, Boat Shape, Daisy & Button, 13 X 4 1/2 In.	110.00
Celery, Daisy & Button With Crossbar	36.00 To 42.50
Celery, Daisy & Button With V Shaped Panels, 6 1/2 X 5 In.	55.00
Celery, Leaf & Panel	35.00
Compote, Gothic Arch, Hexagonal Standard, Flint, 5 7/8 In.	1000.00
Cordial, Fringed Drape	35.00
Creamer, Daisy & Button With Crossbar	35.00
Cruet, Optic, Gold Trim, Original Stopper	110.00 To 125.00
Cruet, Swag With Brackets, Opalescent	195.00
Cruet, Swirl, Clear Handle & Stopper, 7 In.	75.00
Cruet, Tray, Optic, Original Stopper	175.00
Epergne, 4 Lilies, Opalescent	385.00
Jam Jar, Daisy & Button, 5 X 5 In.	125.00
Perfume Bottle, Swirl, Ground Lid, Glass Dauber, 6 In.	95.00
Pitcher, Daisy & Button, 5 In.	18.00
Pitcher, Everglades, Water	375.00
Pitcher, Ovals, Quilted Pattern, English, 3 1/2 In.	40.00
Pitcher, Water, Basket Weave	85.00
Pitcher, Water, Iris With Meander	215.00
Pitcher, Water, Iris With Meander, Opalescent	275.00
Pitcher, Water, Thousand Eye, Opalescent Rim, Handle, 8 In.	60.00
Relish, 3 Sections, Brass Basket, Marked Mt.Washington	40.00
Rose Bowl, Banners & Foliage, World's Fair, 1893, 3 In.	125.00
Salt & Pepper, Diamond & Fluted Panels, 3 3/4 In.	34.75
Salt, Daisy & Button	8.00
Salt, Tulip Shape	42.50
Spooner, Diamond–Quilted, Stemmed	48.00
Spooner, Iris With Meander	75.00

Spooner, Iris With Meander, Opalescent	85.00
Spooner, Petticoat Pattern	65.00
Sugar & Creamer	25.00
Sugar & Creamer, Opalescent, Hobnail, Footed, 3 1/2 In.	65.00
Sugar, Three Panel, Cover	58.00
Syrup, Pewter Top	45.00
Syrup, Ribbed, Blown, Silver Plated Holder	70.00
Syrup, Rope & Thumbprint	110.00 To 125.00
Table Set, Daisy & Button, 3 Piece	65.00
Table Set, Hobnail With Thumbprint, 4 Piece	335.00
Table Set, Hobnail, 4 Piece	370.00
Table Set, Swag With Bracket, 4 Piece	355.00
Toothpick, Iris With Meander, Opalescent	100.00
Toothpick, Ribbed Spiral	45.00
Toothpick, Wreath & Shell	88.00 To 195.00
Tray, Wildflower, 7 1/2 X 11 In.	45.00
Tumbler, Daisy & Button	60.00
Vase, Auto	28.00
Vase, Bar & Ellipse, 4 3/4 In., Pair	1600.00
Vase, Pedestal, Horn of Plenty In Hand	70.00
Water Set, Leaf Mold, Cranberry Spatter, 4 Piece	675.00
Water Set, Swag With Bracket, 7 Piece	375.00
Wine, King's Crown	10.00

Venetian glass has been made near Venice, Italy, from the thirteenth to the twentieth century. Thin, colored glass with applied decoration is favored, although many other types have been made.

VENETIAN GLASS, Bowl, Clear, Turquoise & Gold Flecks, 13 1/4 In.	15.00
Card Holder, Swan, Flecked Body, Opaque Green, C.1910, 5 In.	36.00
Figurine, Chubby Bird, Flared Tail, Gold Flecked Beak, 4 In.	40.00
Figurine, Crowing Rooster, Yellow Back & Tail, Flecks, 9 In.	75.00
Figurine, Dancing Figures, Swirled Ribbed Body, 8 1/4 In.	70.00
Figurine, Parrot, Ruby Body, Amber Tail & Head, 6 1/2 In.	30.00
Figurine, Rooster, Standing, 15 In., Pair	49.00
Figurine, Tuba Player, 6 1/2 In.	70.00
Lamp Base, Pink, Gold Flecks, Ormolu Mounted, 30 In.	75.00
Paperweight, Pear, Blown	37.50
Salt, Flecked Body, Opaque Green, 4 X 5 In.	35.00
Sherbet, Underplate	20.00
Swan, Gold Flecked, Ivory Beak, Black Eyes, Green, 9 X 4 In.	50.00
Vase, Berries, Quilted, Petal Stem, Goblet Shape, 10 1/2 In.	48.00

Verlys glass was made in France after 1931. It was made in the United States from 1935 to 1951. The glass is either blown or molded. The American glass is signed with a diamond–point–scratched name, but the French pieces are marked with a molded signature. The designs resemble those used by Lalique.

VERLYS, Ashtray, Birds	55.00
Ashtray, Duck	45.00
Bowl, Chrysanthemum, Frosted Crystal, 10 In.	125.00
Bowl, Console, Butterfly, 14 In.	125.00
Bowl, Cupid & Hearts, Crystal, 6 In.	45.00
Bowl, Cupid, Signed, 6 In.	65.00
Bowl, Dragonfly, Clear, 14 In.	150.00
Bowl, Frosted Chrysanthemum, Greek Key Base, 6 X 10 In.	50.00
Bowl, Frosted, Tassel, Signed, 11 1/2 In.	110.00
Bowl, Opalescent Bluebirds With Dragonflies, 12 In.	135.00
Bowl, Pinecone, Frosted, 6 In.	48.50
Bowl, Tassel, 12 In.	85.00
Bowl, Thistle, 8 In.	40.00
Bowl, Thistle, Cobalt Blue, 6 In.	65.00
Bowl, Thistle, Sapphire Blue, 12 In.	205.00
Bowl, Water Lilies, 13 In.	145.00
Box, Butterfly, Amber, Signed	375.00

Candleholder, Frosted Leaf, 3 In.	55.00
Charger, Gulls & Fish, Signed	175.00
Charger, Water Lily, 13 1/2 In. .... 170.00 To	200.00
Powder Box, Green	45.00
Shade, Raised Birds & Fish, Signed, Lavender, 3 5/8 In.	275.00
Vase, Fan, Clear & Frosted, Lovebirds, Signed, 5 X 6 In.	120.00
Vase, Gem, Frosted Ground, Brass Base, 6 3/4 In.	135.00
Vase, Thistles, Clear & Frosted, Signed, 10 In.	240.00
Vase, Thistles, White Opalescent & Clear, Signed, 6 1/2in.	95.00

Vernon Potteries, Ltd., started in Vernon, California, in 1931. It became Vernon Kilns by 1948. The company made dinnerware and figurines until it closed in 1958. Collectors search for the brightly colored dinnerware and the pieces designed by Rockwell Kent, Walt Disney, and Don Blanding.

VERNON KILNS, Ashtray, California, Square	7.00
Ashtray, Catalina Island, Gold	30.00
Ashtray, Kentucky, Red	18.00
Bowl & Frog, Poxon, Marked	45.00
Bowl, Chowder, Hawaiian Flowers, 6 In.	6.00
Bowl, Mushroom	135.00
Bowl, Organdie, 9 In.	10.00
Bowl, Salad, Vistosa, Yellow, Footed, 12 In.	45.00
Bowl, Vegetable, Homespun, 9 In.	10.00
Butter, Organdie .... 15.00 To	20.00
Carafe, Organdie .... 20.00 To	25.00
Casserole, Homespun	32.00
Chop Plate, California, 12 In.	15.00
Chop Plate, Casa California, 5–Color Floral	25.00
Chop Plate, Mayflower	15.00
Chop Plate, Organdie	15.00
Coaster, Gingham	5.00
Coffeepot, Hawaiian Flowers, Brown	75.00
Creamer, Homespun	8.00
Creamer, Moby Dick, Blue	48.00
Creamer, Organdie	4.00
Creamer, Plaid, Yellow & Green	4.00
Cup & Saucer, Santa Barbara, Demitasse	10.00
Cup & Saucer, Tam O'Shanter	10.00
Cup, Monterey	6.00
Eggcup, California	11.00
Eggcup, Double, Organdie	8.00
Figurine, Bits of The Old West, 8 1/2 In.	20.00
Figurine, Stage Arrival	20.00
Fruit Bowl, Hawaiian Flowers, 5 1/2 In.	4.00
Grill Plate, Monticello	12.50
Pitcher, Sherwood, 9 1/2 In.	10.00
Pitcher, Water, Organdie .... 18.00 To	22.50
Plaque, Salamina, 14 In.	235.00
Plate, Alabama, With Blacks, 10 In.	24.00
Plate, Barber of Seville, 8 1/2 In.	12.00
Plate, California, 10 In.	10.00
Plate, Flower Ballet, 9 1/2 In.	30.00
Plate, Hawaiian Flowers, Maroon, 9 1/2 In.	8.00
Plate, Homespun, 6 In.	4.00
Plate, Homespun, 9 1/2 In.	85.00
Plate, Moby Dick, Rockwell Kent, Blue, 9 1/2 In.	30.00
Plate, Organdie, 9 1/2 In.	4.00
Plate, Republican National Convention, 1956, 13 In.	70.00
Plate, Salamina, 12 In.	152.00
Plate, Tchaikovsky, 8 1/2 In.	18.00
Plate, Wyoming, With 8 Scenes	7.50
Platter, California, 12 In.	12.00
Salt & Pepper, Hawaiian Flowers	16.00

Salt & Pepper, Homespun	8.00
Sauceboat, Raffia	18.00
Sugar, Organdie	7.00
Syrup, Homespun	32.00
Syrup, Organdie	32.00
Teacup, Homespun	7.00
Tumbler, Blue, 13 Oz.	22.00
Tumbler, Yellow, 13 Oz.	22.00
Vase, Winged Pegasus, 7 3/4 X 12 In.	150.00

Verre de soie glass was first made by Frederick Carder at the Steuben Glass Works from about 1905 to 1930. It is an iridescent glass of soft white or very, very pale green. The name means glass of silk, and it does resemble silk. Other factories have made verre de soie, and some of the English examples were made of different colors. Verre de soie is an art glass and is not related to the iridescent, pressed, white Carnival glass mistakenly called by its name.

VERRE DE SOIE, see also Steuben

VERRE DE SOIE, Bottle, Perfume, Steeple Stopper, 10 In.	250.00
Powder Box, Gold, Red, Green, Beaded, Frosted, 4 X 4 1/2 In.	135.00

Vienna Art plates are round metal serving trays produced at the turn of the century. The designs, copied from Royal Vienna porcelain plates, usually featured a portrait of a woman encircled by a wide, ornate border. Many were used as advertising or promotional items and were produced in Coshocton, Ohio, by J.F. Meeks Tuscarora Advertising Co. and H.D. Beach's Standard Advertising Co.

VIENNA ART, Plate, Baker's Chocolate	225.00
Plate, Barbee Whiskey, 1905	300.00
Plate, Dr Pepper	175.00
Plate, Gypsy, 10 In.	50.00
Plate, Lady & Urn	55.00
Plate, Lady With Candle	65.00

VIENNA, see Beehive

The Villeroy & Boch Pottery of Mettlach was founded in 1841. The firm made many types of pottery, including the famous Mettlach steins. It is confusing for the collector because although Villeroy and Boch made most of its pieces in the city of Mettlach, Germany, they also had factories in other locations. There is a dating code impressed on the bottom of most pieces that makes it possible to determine the age of the piece.

VILLEROY & BOCH, see also Mettlach

VILLEROY & BOCH, Bowl, Vegetable, Willow Pattern, Rectangular, 11 X 10 In.	60.00
Charger, Castle On Elbe, 12 In.	175.00
Charger, Japanese Scene, Impressed Mark, 14 In.	250.00
Creamer, Aragon	15.00
Figurine, Chinaman, Seated, VB Mark, C.1740, 3 1/2 In.	6650.00
Holder, Onion, Hanging, White & Blue Lettering, Zwiebeln	55.00
Mug, Barrel Shape, Nude Handle, 4 In.	30.00
Mug, Hires Root Beer	100.00
Mug, Let's Drink	85.00
Mug, Roses, 2 Handles, 5 1/2 X 8 In.	65.00
Pitcher, Grapevines, People In Relief, Marked, 6 1/2 In.	175.00
Plaque, Marked 1044	125.00
Plate, Aragon, 10 1/4 In.	12.50
Plate, Commemorative, 1945, Germany	36.00
Plate, Dutch Boy & Girl, Seated On Bench, 4 1/2 In.	25.00
Plate, Moroco, No.2	60.00
Plate, Old Touring Car With Passengers, 8 1/2 In.	45.00
Plate, Tsar Bear	60.00
Tile, Dutch Scene, Windmills, Blue & White, 5 1/4 In.	40.00

Never stack cups or bowls inside each other.

Tile, Raleigh Tavern, 6 In.	50.00
Tray, Cavalier, PUG, 11 X 16 In.	154.00
Tureen, Nimrod, Cover	65.00

VOLKMAR Corona N.Y Volkmar pottery was made by Charles Volkmar of New York from 1879 to about 1911. He was associated with several firms, including the Volkmar Ceramic Company, Volkmar and Cory, and Charles Volkmar and Son. Volkmar had been a painter, and his designs often look like oil paintings drawn on pottery.

VOLKMAR, Charger, Mt.Vernon	150.00
Vase, Wine Color Glaze, 8 In.	225.00

Volkstadt was a soft–paste porcelain manufactory started in 1760 by Georg Heinrich Macheleid at Volkstadt, Thuringia. Volkstadt–Rudolstadt was a porcelain factory started at Volkstadt–Rudolstadt by Beyer and Bock in 1890. Most pieces seen in shops today are from the later factory.

VOLKSTADT, Figurine, Lady, White Robe, Hat, Holding Fan, 10 In.	125.00
Figurine, Veiled Lady, Holding Fan, All White, C.1910, 9 1/2 In.	95.00
Holder, Placecard, Applied Petals, Marked, 3 X 2 1/4 In.	50.00

WALLACE NUTTING photographs are listed under Print, Nutting. His reproduction furniture is listed under Furniture.

Walrath Pottery Frederich Walrath was a potter who worked in New York City, Rochester, New York, and at the Newcomb Pottery in New Orleans, Louisiana. He died in 1920. Pieces listed here are from his Rochester period.

WALRATH, Flower Holder, Figural, Nude Female, Kneeling, White, 8 Holes, 5 In.	375.00
Vase, Squat, Cylindrical, Orange Stylized Clover, Green Ground	1100.00

WALT DISNEY, see Disneyana
WALTER, see A. Walter

IOGA Warwick china was made in Wheeling, West Virginia, in a pottery working from 1887 to 1951. Many pieces were made with hand painted or decal decorations. The most familiar Warwick has a shaded brown background. The name "Warwick" is part of the mark and sometimes the word "IOGA" is also included.

WARWICK, Chocolate Pot, Red Currents, 8 In.	90.00
Dish, Underplate, Cover, Brown Red Rose Hips, IOGA, 12 1/4 In.	150.00
Gravy Boat, Handle, White, Green Trim	15.00
Jar, Tobacco, Woman's Portrait, Brown, IOGA	190.00
Jardiniere, Hunting Dog Decal, Signed Back	450.00
Jug, Spirit, Indian Decal	175.00
Jug, Spirit, Monk Decal	125.00
Mug, Singing Monk, Brown, 4 1/2 In.	45.00
Pitcher, Cider, Brown, Floral, IOGA, 7 In.	60.00
Plate, Herons On Green Ground, 10 In.	135.00
Plate, Monk Drinking Wine, Brown, 9 1/2 In.	75.00
Sauce, Oriental Poppy, Large	28.00
Stein Set, Elks, IOGA, 8 Piece	275.00
Tankard, Hunt Scene	375.00
Vase, Amaryllis–Type Flowers, Loop Handles, IOGA, 10 In.	70.00

Vase, Elks, 8 1/2 In., Pair 45.00
Vase, Girl, Flamingo Shading, Twig Handles, 10 1/2 In. 275.00
Vase, Girl, Red & Brown, IOGA, 11 1/2 In. 250.00
Vase, Gypsy Girl Portrait, Brown Shading, Twig Handles, 10 1/2 In. 150.00
Vase, Hibiscus, Brown, 10 In. 65.00
Vase, Monk Wearing Red Skull Cap, IOGA, 11 In. 140.00
Vase, Red Hibiscus On Brown, 11 In. 75.00
Vase, Verona Pattern, Ring Handles, Pine Cones, 11 3/4 In. 115.00

 Watch fobs were worn on watch chains. They were popular during
Victorian times and after. Many styles, especially advertising designs,
are still made today.

WATCH FOB, 1898 English Coin, Enameled, In Glass, Silver Bezel 55.00
369th American Expeditionary Force, World War I 10.00
Abraham Fur Company 85.00
Acme Cement Company 24.00
Adamant Suit 20.00
Alaska Pacific Expo, 3 Tier 45.00
Alaska-Yukon Pacific Exposition 65.00
American Bowling Congress, 18 .... 12.00
Anheuser Busch 750.00
Atlantic City Boardwalk Scene, Strap, 1910 .... 18.00
Austin Western 25.00
Avery Bulldog .... 65.00 To 90.00
B.P.O.E., Insignia 18.00
Battleship U.S.S.New York, Launched October 30, 1912 .... 15.00
Boston Red Socks, World Champions, 1915, 5 X 1 1/2 In. 4000.00
Bucyrus Erie 40.00
Buffalo Brand Rubber Boots 35.00
Buick Motor Cars 80.00
Bull Durham, 14K Gold 20.00
Caledonia Railway 165.00
Carnelian & Moonstone, 14K Gold, England, C.1850 .... 215.00
Case Knives 60.00
Case Threshing Machines 70.00
Case Tractor 60.00
Caterpillar 11.00
Chalmers Motor Co. 135.00
Cherry Smash 140.00
Chew Bulldog Twist 43.00
Clark Equipment 12.00
Clause Shear Co. 15.00
Cleveland State Convention, American Legion, 1946 .... 18.00
Comus Shirt 35.00
Cyrus McCormick Reaper, Brass 28.00
Damrow Creamery Equipment 22.00
Dead Shot, Winchester 125.00
DeLaval Cream Separator, Enameled 80.00
Delta Files, Enamel 32.00
Dodge Bros. 75.00
Double Locket, Brass, Dated 1916 .... 25.00
Douglas The Tailor 20.00
Drink Chero-Cola 55.00
Electrical Workers Union 15.00
Elk's Tooth, Gold 40.00
Empire State Numismatic Assoc. 10.00
Euclid Earth Moving Equipment 23.00
Fireman's Convention, 1938 .... 16.00
Germer Stove Company 32.00
Gold Dust Twins, Spinner 125.00
Good Luck, Celluloid Picture Inset 10.00
Goodrich Steamship Lines 45.00
Green River Whiskey .... 25.00 To 50.00

Harnischfeger Corp.	15.00
Heinz 57 Varieties	22.00 To 28.00
Heydt Bakery, St.Louis, 1908	18.00
Hohner Little Lady Harmonica	24.00
Hollister, Man Taking Whiskey Bottle From Box	30.00
Horsehead, Locket On Horsehair Chain, Garnet Set	95.00
Hudson Motor Car Co.	95.00
Hudson Valley Volunteer Firemans Assoc., 1926	30.00
Human Hair & Mother-of-Pearl, Brass Charm	37.50
Hunter Cream Flour, Hunter With Game	30.00
Illinois Steel Company, Enamel	22.00
Ingersoll-Rand, Construction Worker, Jackhammer, Strap	30.00
International Harvester	45.00 To 60.00
International Life Insurance Co., St.Louis	55.00
John Deere Centennial, Bronze	60.00
Jones Company Shoes, Brass, 1889	35.00
Keen Kutter Cutlery	55.00
Kellogg's Toasted Corn Flakes	75.00
Kentucky Whiskey, Strap	35.00
King Oscar Cigars, Established 1864, Brass & Red Glass	55.00
Koehring Equipment	14.00
Lincoln Insurance Co., Enamel	24.00
Link-Belt Shovel Crane	21.00
Lone Scouts of America	20.00
Luther Burbank	45.00
Mack Trucks	45.00
Majestic Stoves, Egyptian Designs, Columbian Exposition	44.00
Malleable Steel Range	27.00 To 30.00
Mamon Automobile	50.00
Massey-Harris Tractors	70.00
McCormick Deering, I.H.C.	90.00
Meyer Furnace Pipe & Fittings	27.00
Milwaukee Manufacturer, 1912, Enamel	19.00
Modern Woodsmen of America	20.00
Monarch Ranges, 1896	20.00
National American Radio Convention, 1921	30.00
National Sportsman, Deer Head, Brass	35.00
Nebraska Tractor & Equipment Company	35.00
New York State Fair, Syracuse, 1921	20.00
Ohio Varnishes	22.00
Old Dutch Cleanser	32.00
Oldsmobile, Olds Motor Works, Red & White Porcelain On Brass	125.00
OVB Hardware	60.00
Paris Expo, 1889, Engraved Brass	16.00
Pharmacist, Chain, 1898	55.00
Polarine Oils	45.00
Porter Hay Carrier	60.00
Railroad Telegrapher	35.00
Red Ball, Texarkana, Ark., Leather Strap	18.00
Shell Oil Co.	135.00
Silver Saws	18.00
Smith Oil & Gas Separator, Greenduck Co.	85.00
Studebaker Autos	40.00
Success Manure Spreader	35.00
Sun Insurance Company	30.00
Trader Trapper, Hunter	275.00
Truetone Blescher Band Instruments, Elkland, Indiana	28.00
U.S.Gypsum	23.00
U.S.Steel Service, 15 Year	18.00
Velvet Tobacco, Pouch Shape, Enamel On Bronze	85.00
Veterans of Foreign Wars, 21st Encampment, Rochester, N.H., 1941	20.00
Wallis Tractors	75.00
Ward's Tip Top Bread	20.00
Webb Motor Fire Apparatus Co., St.Louis, USA	45.00

Western Union Telegraph, Brass	35.00
Will Rogers Memorial Hospital, Saranac Lake, New York	10.00
Woodsmen of America	25.00
Zeppelin, Akron	45.00

 The pocket watch was important in Victorian times because it was not until World War I that the wristwatch was used. All types of watches are collected: silver, gold, or plated. Watches are listed by company name or by style.

WATCH, Advertising, Pocket, Dairy Ice Cream, New Haven, Train Engraved Case	100.00
Agassiz, Pocket, Gold Coin Form, Gilt Dial, 18K Gold	1760.00
Agnew, Wristwatch, Sheffield, 1970	48.00
Apple Form, Enameled Sprays, Gold & Enamel, Late 19th Century	2100.00
Arnex, Pocket, Skeleton, 17 Jewel, Hunting Case	35.00
Audemar Piquet, Wristwatch, 17 Jewel, Silvered Dial, Signed, C.1960	1210.00
Aurora, Pocket, 15 Jewel, Coin Silver Hunting Case	225.00
Babe Ruth, Wristwatch	135.00
Ball, Railroad, Open Face, 17 Jewel	245.00
Baylor, Wristwatch, Small Diamond Set In Dial, 14K Yellow Gold	185.00
Breitling, Wristwatch, Chronograph, 18K Gold, 17 Jewel, Black Dial	2640.00
Breitling, Wristwatch, Chronometer	145.00
Bulova Accutron, Wristwatch, Old Style, Railroad, Battery Operated	60.00
Bulova, Railroad, White Gold Filled Case, Battery Driven	55.00
Bulova, Wristwatch, Lady's, Platinum, Diamond Bracelet, 15 Jewel	700.00
Bulova, Wristwatch, White Gold Filled, Railroad Approved	55.00
Bulova, Wristwatch, Woman's, 16 Jewel, 1920s	85.00
Bulova, Wristwatch, Woman's, 23 Jewel, 24 Diamonds, 14K Yellow Gold	665.00
Bulova, Wristwatch, Woman's, Square, 23 Jewel, 18K Gold	35.00
Burlington, 21 Jewel, Hunting Case	55.00
C.Mairete, Pocket, No.31976, Key Wind, Enameled Gold Case, 2 3/8 In.	300.00
Calendar, Pocket, Repeating Caillon, Gold Hunting Case, C.1890	4125.00
Cartier, Bracelet, Lady's, 18K Gold Duo-Plan, C.1950	8800.00
Charles Humbert, Chronograph, Hunter Case, 18K Gold, Fitted Box	1540.00
Cinor, Lapel, Woman's, Sterling Silver Bezel	95.00
Columbus, Pocket, 17 Jewel, Silveroid Case, Steam Train Engraved	150.00
Cooper, Silver Plated, US Navy Officer's, Scene, Pocket, 2 In.	275.00
Corum, Wristwatch, 18K Gold, Black Lizard Strap ....*Illus*	400.00
Corum, Wristwatch, Man's, 18K Gold	600.00
Corum, Wristwatch, Mystery, Revolving Dial, Eagle Indicates Minutes	2200.00
Courvoisier & Comp, Quarter Repeating Carillon, Silver, C.1800	1650.00
Cresarrow, Wristwatch, 18K Gold, 15 Jewel, Gold Arabic Numbers, Ribbon	225.00
Dent, Pocket, Chronograph, Gold Hunter Case, 18K Gold, C.1890	1210.00
E.Howard, Pocket, Gold Filled, Series 5, 1912, Size 16	275.00
Edmunds, Pocket, Fusee, Sterling Silver, 1820	250.00
Elgin National, Pocket, Size 18, 17 Jewel, C.1918	70.00
Elgin National, Pocket, Sterling, Open Face, Stand, Size 18, 1869	450.00
Elgin, 15 Jewel, Gilt Dial, Silverine Case	15.00
Elgin, National, Pocket, Hunting Case, 1900s	85.00
Elgin, Pocket, 15 Jewel, 10K Gold Hunter Case	350.00
Elgin, Pocket, 15 Jewel, 18 Size	40.00
Elgin, Pocket, 16S, Open Face, Flip-Out Movement, Gold Steer Insert	140.00
Elgin, Pocket, 17 Jewel, 20 Year Gold Case, Green Crystal	85.00
Elgin, Pocket, 17 Jewel, Engraved Floral Design On Case	100.00
Elgin, Pocket, 17 Jewel, Gold Filigree Hands, Open Face	250.00
Elgin, Pocket, 17 Jewel, Gold Filled, Size 18, C.1918	70.00
Elgin, Pocket, 17 Jewel, Hunter Nickel Case, RN Dial	35.00
Elgin, Pocket, 18 Size, Key Wind, Key Set, Silveroid Case	95.00
Elgin, Pocket, 19 Jewel, 3/4 Movement, Gold Filled Case	85.00
Elgin, Pocket, Art Deco, Black & Chrome	65.00
Elgin, Pocket, Father Time, 16/S, 21 Jewel	100.00
Elgin, Pocket, Hunter's Case, 15 Jewel, Size 12	135.00
Elgin, Pocket, Hunting Case, Closed Face, 14K Gold, 1897	350.00
Elgin, Pocket, Key Wind, 1884	120.00
Elgin, Pocket, Lady's, Diamond In Hunter Case, 14K Gold	375.00

Watch

Movado, Wristwatch, Platinum, Diamonds, Glycine, Wristwatch, Platinum, Diamonds, Black Strap, Corum, Wristwatch, 18K Gold, Black Lizard Strap, Longines, Doctor's, Stainless Steel, Leather Strap, Rolex, Wristwatch, 14K, Blue Dial

Elgin, Pocket, Masonic, Brass, Chain	135.00
Elgin, Pocket, National, Roman Numerals, 17 Jewel	125.00
Elgin, Pocket, O Size, 14K Gold, Open Face	175.00
Elgin, Pocket, Open Face, 17 Jewel, Gold Filled	65.00
Elgin, Pocket, Pabst Seal, Gold, Initials G.L., 1899	875.00
Elgin, Pocket, Railroad, 21 Jewel, Yellow Gold Filled Case	100.00
Elgin, Pocket, Railroad, Sterling Silver Case, Key Wind, 1878	250.00
Elgin, Pocket, Size 18, 18K Gold, 17 Jewels	1500.00
Elgin, Pocket, Swing–Out Case, 18s, 21 Jewel	90.00
Elgin, Pocket, Veritas, 16/S, 23 Jewel, Yellow Gold Filled Case	225.00
Elgin, Pocket, Veritas, Yellow Gold Filled, 23 Jewel	275.00
Elgin, Wristwatch, K.S., Silveroid Case, Size 18, C.1885	90.00
Faivre Perrin, Pocket, Minute Repeating, 18K Gold, C.1890	4125.00
Glycine, Wristwatch, Platinum, Diamonds, Black Strap ....*Illus*	750.00
Graf Zeppelin, Pocket, Commemorative of Flight, Case, 1930	150.00
Gruen, Pocket, Musical, 17 Jewel, Open Face, Box	250.00
Gruen, Pocket, Veri–Thin, 17 Jewel	250.00
Gruen, Wristwatch, Veri–Thin, 14K Gold	325.00
Gubelin, Wristwatch, Moon Phases, Calendar, 18K Pink Gold	2750.00
Hamilton, Asymmetric, Electronic, 18K Gold, C.1950	1760.00
Hamilton, Military, Black Dial, Base Metal, Ordinance Markings	105.00
Hamilton, Pocket, 17 Jewel, Marked Union Special, New Metal Case	80.00
Hamilton, Pocket, 21 Jewel, Yellow Gold Filled	195.00
Hamilton, Pocket, 21 Jewel, Yellow Gold Filled Case	150.00
Hamilton, Pocket, Grade 910, 17 Jewel, Box	125.00
Hamilton, Pocket, No.6306, 17 Jewel, Lever Set	125.00
Hamilton, Pocket, No.922, 18K White Gold, 23 Jewel, Box, 1930	1250.00
Hamilton, Pocket, No.946, 23 Jewel	395.00
Hamilton, Pocket, No.992, 21 Jewel	125.00
Hamilton, Pocket, No.992, 21 Jewel, Lever Set, 1933	125.00
Hamilton, Pocket, No.992, 21 Jewel, Open Face, 14K Gold Filled	125.00
Hamilton, Pocket, No.992, Montgomery Dial, 21 Jewel, Gold Filled Case	115.00
Hamilton, Pocket, No.992–B, Gold Filled Case	185.00
Hamilton, Pocket, No.992E, 21 Jewel, Yellow Gold Filled Case	160.00
Hamilton, Pocket, No.993, Hunter Case, 21 Jewel, 14K Gold	500.00
Hamilton, Pocket, Railroad, 17 Jewel, Engraved Train On Reverse	100.00
Hamilton, Wristwatch, Navigator's, World War II, Black Dial, 22 Jewel	250.00
Hamilton, Wristwatch, Railroad, Stainless Steel, Battery Operated	55.00
Hamilton, Wristwatch, Size 16, 17 Jewel, 14K Gold Hunter Case	495.00
Hamilton, Wristwatch, Woman's, 52 Full Cut Diamonds, 14K Gold, 1930s	450.00
Hampden, Pocket, Enameled Face, Second Hand, Hunting Case	100.00
Hampden, Pocket, Ten Year Warranty Gold Case, 17 Jewel	125.00

Hampden, Pocket, William McKinley, 17 Jewel	60.00
Hampden, Pocket, William McKinley, 21 Jewel, Gold Filled Open Case	100.00
Hampden, Pocket, Woolworth Model, New York Watch Co., C.1876	225.00
Hampden, Wristwatch, Woman's, 15 Jewel, Yellow Gold Case	115.00
Herodia, Wristwatch, 18K Gold, Diamond Edge Face, Mesh Strap, C.1940	800.00
Howard, Pocket, Adjustable Gilt Movement, Open Face, Silveroid Case	325.00
Howard, Pocket, Bridge Model, 19 Jewel, Yellow Gold Filled Case	160.00
Howard, Pocket, Double Sunk Dial, Montgomery, 14K Gold Case	1000.00
Howard, Pocket, Model BB, 15 Jewel, 1912	98.00
Howard, Pocket, Series 11, 21 Jewel, Orginal Case	200.00
Howard, Pocket, Size 18, 19 Jewel, Case	375.00
Howard, Railroad, Size 16, 24 Hour Dial, 14K Gold Chain, Knife, Coin	1500.00
Howard, Wristwatch, Masonic Dial, 17 Jewel, White Gold Filled Case	165.00
Illinois, Pocket, Bunn Special, 21 Jewel, Yellow Gold Filled Case	160.00
Illinois, Pocket, Bunn Special, 60 Hour, 21 Jewel	350.00
Illinois, Pocket, Coin Silver, Gold Overlay, Size 18, Stand, 1880s	350.00
Illinois, Pocket, Gold Miner's, Nickeled Silver, 1870–80, 2 1/2 In.	450.00
Illinois, Pocket, Lady's Hunter Case, Yellow Gold Filled, Chain	250.00
Illinois, Pocket, Napolean, Enameled Face, Second Handle, 14K Gold	30.00
Ingraham, Pocket, New York To Paris	300.00
International, Wristwatch, 19 Jewel, 6 Adjustments, 18K Gold, C.1920	1320.00
Irish Spring Soap, Wristwatch, 1970s	20.00
J.A.Jaccard, Split Second Chronograph, 18K Gold, C.1890	2200.00
Jaeger Cartier, Wristwatch, Lady's, 18K Gold, 15 Jewel, C.1945	2200.00
Josephson, Pocket, No.4226, Silver Case, Key Wind, Enameled Face, 2 In.	325.00
Kermit The Frog, Wristwatch, Box	38.00
Lady's, Wristwatch, Platinum Face, Diamond Surrounds, 14K White Gold	1650.00
Lapel, Scarab Form, Jewel Set, Dial Beneath Wings, Diamonds, Garnets	5500.00
Le Coultre, Wristwatch, 17 Jewel, Moon Phases, C.1945	1760.00
Le Rayond Locle, Pocket, 19 Rubies, Gold Hands, 14K Gold Case	600.00
Longines, Doctor's, Stainless Steel, Leather Strap ....Illus	325.00
Longines, Lady's, Diamonds, Gold Metal Case, 14K Gold	800.00
Longines, Pocket, 15 Jewel	200.00
Lucerne, Pocket, Lady's, Pendant, Size 6	40.00
Lucerne, Wristwatch, Jump Hour Digital	20.00
Lucian Piccard, Wristwatch, Seashell Model, Gold Filled, Round	75.00
Marion, Pocket, 17 Jewel, Silver Over Nickel	350.00
Meylan, Pendant, Gold & Enamel Brooch, 1 Diamond, C.1900	2750.00
Military, 17 Jewel, Black Dial, Second Hand, Stainless Steel Case	40.00
Mobilis, Pocket, Tourbillion, 24 Hour Dial, Open Face, C.1900	1430.00
Movado, Wristwatch, Chronograph With Pulsemeter, 18K Gold, C.1940	2090.00
Movado, Wristwatch, Man's, 14K Gold, 1 Diamond	250.00
Movado, Wristwatch, Platinum, Diamonds ....Illus	2100.00
Omega, Wristwatch, Automatic, Gold Filled	115.00
Omega, Wristwatch, Man's, 14K Gold, Tank Style, Seconds Dial, Leather	350.00
Omega, Wristwatch, Military, Quebec, Canada, Metal Case, 1918	225.00
Omega, Wristwatch, Rhinestone Trim, 18K White Gold	200.00
Packard, Pocket, Presentation, 14K Gold	425.00
Packard, Pocket, Shell Oil Co., Presentation, Original Fob	250.00
Patek Philippe, Bracelet, Lady's, 18 Jewel, Set Within Bracelet, 1945	5500.00
Patek Philippe, Pocket, 14K Gold, 18 Jewel, Triple Signed, 1900	1895.00
Patek Philippe, Pocket, 18K Gold, Blue Enameled, Chain, 1908, Case	2500.00
Patek Philippe, Pocket, Double Balance Staff, C.1905	250.00
Patek Philippe, Pocket, Regulator, Imperial Monogram, C.1913	3850.00
Patek Philippe, Pocket, Second Chronograph, Open Face, 18K Gold, 1890	3025.00
Patek Philippe, Wristwatch, 18 Jewel, Hinged Case, Platinum, C.1930	8800.00
Patek Philippe, Wristwatch, 18K Gold, 18 Jewel, Signed, C.1940	2530.00
Patek Philippe, Wristwatch, 18K Gold, 18 Jewels, Gold Bracelet	4950.00
Patek Philippe, Wristwatch, Attached Bracelet, Stainless Steel	1250.00
Patek Philippe, Wristwatch, Gold Mesh Bracelet, C.1935	1200.00
Patek Philippe, Wristwatch, Gold Sweep Seconds, 18K Gold, C.1949	3025.00
Patek Philippe, Wristwatch, Lady's, 2–Tone 18K Gold, C.1945	2090.00
Patek Philippe, Wristwatch, Lady's, Platinum & Diamond, C.1929	3300.00
Patek Philippe, Wristwatch, Lady's, Rose Gold, Rubies, Diamonds	1800.00

Patek Philippe, Wristwatch, Man's, 18K Gold, Calendar, Date, Leather	2000.00
Patek Philippe, Wristwatch, Man's, Square, Leather Band, 18K Gold	2250.00
Patek Philippe, Wristwatch, Micrometer Regulator, 18 Jewel, Pink Gold	1980.00
Patek Philippe, Wristwatch, Micrometer Regulator, Self–Winding, Gold	2100.00
Patek Philippe, Wristwatch, Regulator, Platinum & Diamond, C.1950	9350.00
Patek Philippe, Wristwatch, Silver Dial, 18K Gold, 1946	2200.00
Patek Philippe, Wristwatch, Square Numerals, Stainless Steel, C.1950	2310.00
Patek Philippe, Wristwatch, Tachometer, 18K Gold, 23 Jewel, Signed	1210.00
Patek Philippe, Wristwatch, Ultra Thin, 18K Gold, Silvered Dial, 1970	2200.00
Paul Ditisheim, Wristwatch, Platinum, Diamond Numbers, 17 Jewel	1600.00
Pendant, Gold, Open Face, 18K Gold, Lady's Portrait, Rubies, Diamonds	1550.00
Pendant, Lady Bug, 17 Jewel, Wings Open Reveals Watch, Swiss	10.00
Pendant, Swiss, Lady's, 15 Jewel, Short Chain	15.00
Perret & Cie, Pocket, Quarter Repeating Chronograph, 30 Jewel, 1890	1870.00
Piaget Polo, Wristwatch, Quartz, Matching Bracelet, 2–Tone Gold	7150.00
Piaget, Wristwatch, Lady's, Folds Into Ten Dollar Gold Coin	1760.00
Pocket, Mother–of–Pearl, Human Hair, Gold Accents	50.00
Pocket, Pabst Seal On Back, Ornate Face, 1899	875.00
Railroad, Burling Special, 19 Jewel	145.00
Reconvilier W., Wristwatch, 14K Gold, 17 Jewel, Pierced Cover, C.1945	750.00
Rexton, Wristwatch, Lady's, 14K Gold, 1940s	35.00
Riverside, Pocket, Maximus, 23 Jewel	525.00
Rockford, Pocket, 15 Jewel, Arabic Dial, Silveroid Swing Ring Case	55.00
Rockford, Pocket, 17 Jewel, 20 Year Case Opens, Movement Side Swings	35.00
Rockford, Pocket, 21 Jewel, Open Face Case, Yellow Gold Filled	235.00
Rolex, Wristwatch, 14K, Blue Dial ....*Illus*	900.00
Rolex, Wristwatch, Cellini, 19 Rubies, White Gold Watch & Band	2475.00
Rolex, Wristwatch, Cellini, Asymmetrical Square, 18K Gold	1450.00
Rolex, Wristwatch, Oyster, Digital	750.00
Rolex, Wristwatch, Oyster, Enamel Dial, Cushion Form, 9K Gold, C.1925	1750.00
Rolex, Wristwatch, Oyster, Lady's, 18K Pink Gold, 18 Rubies, Bracelet	1750.00
Rolex, Wristwatch, Oyster, Perpetual Chronometer, Box	650.00
Rolex, Wristwatch, Oyster, Perpetual, Self–Winding, Pink Gold, C.1940	2550.00
Rolex, Wristwatch, Oyster, Perpetual, Self–Winding, Silver Case	1750.00
Rolex, Wristwatch, Oyster, Perpetual, White Gold, Signed	3025.00
Rolex, Wristwatch, Oyster, Tachometer & Telemeter, Stainless Steel	5500.00
Rolex, Wristwatch, Prince, Duo–Dial, 9K Gold, 15 Rubies, 1934	2310.00
Rolex, Wristwatch, Trigger Stem, Seconds, Self–Winding, 18K Gold	2310.00
Seth Thomas, Pocket, 15 Jewel, Gold Hands, Hunting Case, Keystone	135.00
Seth Thomas, Pocket, Locomotive Engrave On Silveroid Case, 15 Jewel	65.00
Snoopy, Wristwatch, Red, 1968	48.00
South Bend, Pocket, 15 Jewel, Hunting Case	175.00

Watch, Waltham, Pocket, 14K Gold,
Enameled Case

South Bend, Pocket, 21 Jewel, Pettibone Watch Fob 100.00
South Bend, Pocket, 25 Year, Yellow Gold Filled Hunter Case 125.00
South Bend, Pocket, Hunting Case, 14K Gold Filled, 15 Jewel, C.1903 .... 175.00
South Bend, Pocket, Montgomery Style, 21 Jewel 130.00
South Bend, Pocket, Pink Open Face, No.204, 15 Jewel 65.00
Sun, Wristwatch, Frank Buck, Explorer 45.00
Swiss, Pocket, Blue Enamel, Gold & Diamond Design On Back, 14K Gold 650.00
Swiss, Pocket, Lady's, 17 Jewel, Enameled Lilies 75.00
Tissot, Wristwatch, Man Or Woman's, Sterling Silver Bracelet 145.00
Vacheron & Constantin, Asymmetrical Double Dial, 18K Gold 4125.00
Vacheron & Constantin, Pocket, 21 Jewel, Gold Filled Case 325.00
Vacheron & Constantin, Pocket, Medical Chromograph, 18K Gold, C.1900 .... 1450.00
Vacheron & Constantin, Pocket, Split Second Chronograph, Silver 1430.00
Vacheron & Constantin, Wristwatch, Lady's, White Gold Bracelet 1650.00
Vacheron & Constantin, Wristwatch, Presentation, Gold, Steel 2475.00
Vacheron & Constantin, Wristwatch, Silvered Dial, 18K Gold, C.1955 .... 1100.00
Vacheron & Constantin, Wristwatch, Skeletonized, Sapphie Crown 6600.00
Waltham, 7 Jewel, 14K Gold Filled Case 85.00
Waltham, 7 Jewel, Silveroid Case, Marked Equity 20.00
Waltham, 11 Jewel, 14K Solid Gold Hunting Case 600.00
Waltham, 15 Jewel, 14K Solid, Multicolor Gold Hunting Case 2000.00
Waltham, 17 Jewel, Bartlett, Pocket 150.00
Waltham, 17 Jewel, Bond Street, Pocket 50.00
Waltham, 21 Jewel, Size 16, VP 7 Down Indicator, Gold Filled Case 335.00
Waltham, Pocket, 14K Gold, Enameled Case ....*Illus* 140.00
Waltham, Pocket, 15 Jewel, 25 Year Warranty Gold Case 135.00
Waltham, Pocket, 15 Jewel, Multicolor Dial, Open Face, Size 18 .... 245.00
Waltham, Pocket, 15 Jewel, Swing–Out Movement, Chain 75.00
Waltham, Pocket, 17 Jewel, Santa Fe Special, Logo, 1883 Model 425.00
Waltham, Pocket, 21 Jewel, Gold Jewel Settings, Arabic Dial 65.00
Waltham, Pocket, Broadway, 7 Jewel, Silveroid Case 60.00
Waltham, Pocket, Hunter Case, Engraved, Gold Filled 125.00
Waltham, Pocket, Hunter Case, Model 1889, 7 Jewel 375.00
Waltham, Pocket, Hunting Case, 17 Jewel, Gold Filled 100.00
Waltham, Pocket, Lady's, 3–Color Flowers On Lids, 7 Jewel 55.00
Waltham, Pocket, Premier, Open Face, Gold Filled, Montgomery Dial 225.00
Waltham, Pocket, Railroad, 21 Jewel, Train On Back, Gold Filled 200.00
Waltham, Pocket, Railroad, 17 Jewel, 10K Gold Filled Case 230.00
Waltham, Pocket, Riverside, Size 16, Yellow Gold Filled 210.00
Waltham, Pocket, Scalloped Case, Yellow Gold Filled Case 200.00
Waltham, Pocket, Vanguard, 23 Jewel, 10K Gold Case, Railroad 165.00
Waltham, Pocket, Vanguard, 23 Jewel, 20 Year Masonic Case 125.00
Waltham, Pocket, Vanguard, Up & Down Indicator 375.00
Waltham, Pocket, Vanguard, Wind Indictator 435.00
Waltham, Wristwatch, Vanguard, 21 Jewel, 14K Gold Flip–Out Case 475.00
William Ellery, Pocket, Key Wind & Set, 11 Jewel, Silver Cover 180.00
Winchester Store, Pocket 325.00

Waterford–type glass resembles the famous glass made from 1783 to 1851 in the Waterford Glass Works in Ireland. It is a clear glass that was often decorated by cutting. Modern glass is being made again in Waterford, Ireland, and is marketed under the name "Waterford."

WATERFORD, Bottle, Scent, Diamond Cut, 4 1/2 In. 70.00
Finger Bowl, Double Lip, C.1875 .... 150.00
Goblet, Kylemore 22.00
Snifter, Brandy, Colleen 35.00
Tumbler, Juice, Colleen, Footed, 12 Piece 185.00

The Watt family bought the Globe pottery of Crooksville, Ohio, in 1922. They made pottery mixing bowls and dishes of the type made by Globe. In 1935 they changed the production and made the pieces with the free hand decorations that are popular with collectors today. Apple, Star Flower, Rooster, Red & Blue Tulip, and Autumn Foliage are the best–known patterns. The plant closed in 1965.

WATT, Bean Pot, Apple, Cover, No.76	65.00
Berry Bowl, Morning Glory	35.00
Bowl, Apple, No.96	35.00
Bowl, Cereal, Apple	30.00
Bowl, Mixing, Orchardware, Leaf, No.110	32.00
Bowl, No.6	13.00
Bowl, Pansy, Small, 3 Piece	25.00
Bowl, Red Apple, Advertising, 5 In.	24.00
Bowl, Rooster, Advertising, Crowsfoot On Bottom	35.00
Bowl, Serving, Tulip, 9 In.	75.00
Bowl, Spaghetti, No.24	70.00
Bowl, Underplate, Spaghetti, Starflower	100.00
Casserole, Apple, Cover	45.00
Casserole, French, Raised Flower Design, Cover	85.00
Cassrole, Cover, No.601	40.00
Cookie Jar, Apple	85.00
Creamer, Apple	25.00
Creamer, Apple, Advertising	17.00
Creamer, Tulip, No.62	25.00
Cup & Saucer, Posey Pattern	75.00
Cup, Morning Glory	55.00
Dutch Oven, Apple	65.00
Ice Bucket, Apple	75.00
Mixing Bowl, Apple, No.9	45.00
Mixing Bowl, No.7	40.00
Mug, Starflower	50.00
Pie Plate, Apple, Green Band, Advertising	35.00
Pitcher, Apple, Ice Lip	75.00
Pitcher, Apple, Kewaunee Co–Op	40.00
Pitcher, Apple, No.16, Advertising	37.50
Pitcher, Apple, No.17	65.00
Pitcher, Apple, No.62, Advertising	30.00
Pitcher, Milk, Grain Company Advertising	40.00
Pitcher, No.15	26.00
Pitcher, No.62	30.00
Pitcher, No.62, Advertising	40.00
Pitcher, Red Apple, Advertising, Storm Lake, No.15	30.00
Pitcher, Tulip, No.62	30.00
Salad Set, Apple, Large Bowl & 8 Small Bowls	150.00
Saucer, Morning Glory, Watt	20.00
Vase, Apple, No.98	30.00

WAVE CREST WARE

Wave Crest glass is a white glassware manufactured by the Pairpoint Manufacturing Company of New Bedford, Massachusetts, and some French factories. It was decorated by the C. F. Monroe Company of Meriden, Connecticut. The glass was painted in pastel colors and decorated with flowers. The name "Wave Crest" was used after 1898.

WAVE CREST, Ashtray & Match Holder, Combination, Marked	450.00
Biscuit Jar, Barrel Shape, Hand Painted Orchids	130.00
Biscuit Jar, Barrel Shape, Pale Green To White, Wild Roses	130.00
Biscuit Jar, Egg Crate, Apple Blossom, Paper Label	225.00
Biscuit Jar, Egg Crate, Poppies, Marked	245.00
Biscuit Jar, Floral Scrolling, Sterling Silver Fittings, 6 In.	225.00
Biscuit Jar, White To Pink, Floral, Marked	185.00
Bottle, Perfume, Full–Figured Woman, Victorian Dress, Parasol	395.00
Bowl, Puffy Egg Crate, Flowers, Raised Beading, Marked, 6 1/2 In.	550.00
Bowl, Cherub, Rococo, Raised Enameling, Marked, 5 1/2 In.	300.00
Box, Allover Hand Painted Violets, Gold Outlined Leaves, 6 In.	545.00
Box, Collars & Cuffs, Brass Feet, Banner Mark ....*Illus*	625.00
Box, Cupids & Flowers, Scroll Mold, Pale Yellow, 3 X 5 In.	500.00

Wave Crest, Box, Collars & Cuffs, Brass Feet,
Banner Mark

Box, Double Shell, Blue Floral, Banner Mark, 2 3/4 X 3 1/4 In.	225.00
Box, Dresser, Hinged Lid, Beaded Collar, Floral, Trees, 9 1/2 In.	1200.00
Box, Enameling, Blue Florals, Marked, 7 In.	425.00
Box, Helmschmied Swirl, 5 In.	250.00
Box, Hinged Cover, 4 Ormolu Feet, Marked, 4 In.	315.00
Box, Hinged Cover, Egg Crate, Square, 3 X 3 In.	220.00
Box, Hinged Cover, Molded Florals, Silk Lining, 7 In.	175.00
Box, Hinged Cover, Puffy Loops, Flowers, 7 In.	275.00
Box, Hinged Cover, Word Cigars In Gold, Marked, 6 In.	595.00
Box, Hinged, Jewelry, Cherubs, Marked, 2 X 4 In.	250.00
Box, Hinged, Jewelry, Cover, Marked, 8 In.	485.00
Box, Jewelry, Child, Bow & Arrow Lining, 7 X 6 In.	1200.00
Box, Jewelry, Open, Ormolu Trim, Marked, 3 1/2 In.	140.00
Box, Pale Pink, Floral Enameling, Helmscheid, Large	450.00
Box, Pin, Ormolu Rim, Marked	75.00
Box, Pink, Enameled Flowers, Scrollwork, Marked, 4 1/2 In.	450.00
Box, Puffy, Beading, Small	210.00
Box, Ring, Painted Scene, Lake, Trees & House, 3 In.	195.00
Box, Rococo, 4–Footed, Marked, 5 X 6 In.	865.00
Box, Rococo, Raised Enameling, Round, 7 1/2 In.	350.00
Box, Rococo, Raised Florals, Lined, 5 1/4 In.	335.00
Box, Shell, Enameled Flowers, Cover, Marked, 2 1/2 X 4 In.	150.00
Box, Swirl, Cover, 4 In.	200.00
Box, Swirl, Daisies, Purple Asters, 6 1/2 In.	575.00
Box, Swirl, Enameled Jeweling, Square, 3 In.	140.00
Box, Swirled, Floral, Marked, 7 In.	350.00
Box, Trinket, Pale Blue, Pink & White Floral, Marked, 4 X 3 In.	225.00
Box, Violets, Rococo, Marked, 6 In.	260.00
Box, Wild Roses, Green Leaves, Figured Heads For Feet, 8 1/2 In.	875.00
Card Holder, Rococo, Pink, Metal Top, Red Banner Mark, 4 In.	245.00
Cracker Jar, Carnations, Leaves, Silver Plate Fittings	185.00
Dish, Dresser, Ormolu Collar, Swirl Ribs, Marked	115.00
Dish, Engraved Collar, Pink, Blue, Forget–Me–Nots, 4 1/4 In.	110.00
Dish, Pin, Ormolu Collar, Swirl Ribbing, Marked, 4 In.	115.00
Dish, Sweetmeat, Brass Top & Rim, Marked, 6 1/2 X 7 In.	290.00
Dish, Sweetmeat, Pink, Beige Enameling, Brass Rim, 7 1/2 In.	295.00
Dish, Sweetmeat, Rococo, Ornate Lid, Marked, 7 1/2 In.	295.00
Fernery, Egg Crate Design, Enameled, 4–Footed, 7 In.	310.00
Fernery, Floral Design, Blue & Ivory Panels, 4 1/2 X 8 In.	295.00
Fernery, Puffy Egg Crate, Blue Flowers	195.00
Finger Bowl, Underplate	295.00
Frame, Photograph, Masked Ormolu Footed, Florals, 3 3/4 X 5 In.	325.00
Hair Receiver, Hand Painted Flowers, Embossed	235.00
Holder, Cigarette, Pansies, Ormolu Tab Handles & Feet, 4 In.	295.00
Holder, Cigarette, Yellow & Pink Pansies, 4 In.	195.00
Letter Holder, Daisies, Puffy Egg Crate Mold	250.00
Match Holder, Ormolu Footed, Floral	125.00
Photo Holder, Beaded Rim, Baroque Scrolling, 6 1/4 X 3 1/4 In.	275.00

Plaque, Boat Scene, Wedgwood Blue Trim, 11 1/2 In.	1400.00
Plate, Floral Design, Ormolu Knob	450.00
Salt & Pepper, Artichoke, Blue Floral, Original Lids	95.00
Salt & Pepper, Bust of Cat, Swirled Necks, Wreath of Foliage	110.00
Salt & Pepper, Hunting Dogs, Foliage, Pair	110.00
Salt & Pepper, Swirl, Floral Enameling, Pewter Top	150.00
Salt & Pepper, Tiered Daisy Petal Pattern	95.00
Salt, Floral Design, Embossed Tulip Petal Base	165.00
Saltshaker, Shasta Daisy, 24 Petal Design, Pewter Top	285.00
Sugar & Creamer, Brass Handles & Cover, Pink Ground, Florals	265.00
Syrup, Pale Blue Ground, Enamel Design of Wild Roses	435.00
Toothpick, Blown Out, Puffy, Opalescent	125.00
Toothpick, Enameled Pansy, Ormolu Rim & Feet	145.00
Toothpick, Pansy Design, Ormolu Base	325.00
Tray, Pin, Swirl, Flowers, Handles, Banner Mark, 3 In.	125.00
Tray, Trinket, Puffed Panels, Beading At Top, Hand Painted	125.00
Tray, Trinket, Swirl, Red & White Daisies, Label, 6 1/2 In.	195.00
Urn, Floral, Ormolu Base, Black, Red Banner Mark, 14 1/2 In.	1150.00
Vase, Baroque Design, Floral Spray, Enameled Beading, 9 In., Pair	425.00
Vase, Baroque Scrolls, Floral Beading, Marked, 10 1/4 In.	325.00
Vase, Baroque Scrolls, Floral, Enameled Ormolu, Marked, 10 In.	365.00
Vase, Baroque Scrolls, Ormolu Neck & Handle, Marked, 7 1/2 In.	295.00
Vase, Baroque Scrolls, Yellow Ground, Burgundy & Pink, 10 In.	375.00
Vase, Florals On Sides, Raised Gold, 4 Ormolu Feet, 14 1/2 In.	1150.00
Vase, Niagara Falls Background, Brass Base, 6 1/2 In.	425.00
Vase, Ormolu Base & Handles Top, Hand Painted Flowers, 6 In.	285.00
Vase, Pink Daisies, Beaded, Red Mark, 9 In.	375.00
Vase, Pink Panels, Blue Flowers, White Ground, Marked, 7 In.	295.00
Vase, Pink Side Panels, Flowers, Ormolu Handle, 7 1/2 In.	295.00
Vase, Rococo, 4–Footed, Metal Stand, 10 1/2 In., Pair	795.00
Vase, Roses, Ornate Brass Base, Dolphin Feet, 13 1/2 In.	950.00
Vase, Spindrift Blown–Out Blank, Roses, Dolphin Base, 13 1/2 In.	825.00
Vase, White Enameled Flowers, Gold Scrolling, 10 1/2 In.	385.00
WEAPON, see also Gun; Rifle; Sword; etc.	
WEAPON, Nightstick, Police Officer's, William IV, C.1830, 28 3/4 In.	400.00
Sailor's Life Preserver, C.1840, 13 1/4 In.	195.00
Tipstaff, George III, C.1800, 8 In.	400.00
Tipstaff, Manchester Shield, Royal Arms, 1801–16, 13 In.	475.00
Tipstaff, Manchester, George III, C.1810, 11 1/2 In.	495.00
Tipstaff, Manchester, Rosewood, C.1820, 13 In.	525.00
Tipstaff, Manchester, William IV, C.1830, 12 1/4 In.	395.00
Tipstaff, Police Officer's, George IV, C.1820, 11 3/4 In.	495.00
Tipstaff, William IV, Painted, C.1835, 22 In.	450.00
Truncheon, Birmingham, Dated 1834, 21 In.	495.00
Truncheon, Hampshire Parish Constable's, C.1860, 17 1/4 In.	525.00
Truncheon, Police Officer's, William IV, London, C.1830, 18 1/2 In.	425.00
Truncheon, Police, Gloucester, C.1846, 18 In.	495.00

The earliest American weather vanes were used in seventeenth–century Boston. The direction of the wind was an indication of coming weather, important to the seafaring and farming communities. By the mid–nineteenth century, commercial weather vanes were made of metal. Today's collectors often consider weather vanes to be examples of folk art, even though they may not have been handmade.

WEATHER VANE, Apple Tree, Leaves, Fruit, Man, Ladder, Basket, Iron, 30 In.	5600.00
Arrow, Chamfered Edges, Wooden, 19th Century, 3 Ft.10 In.	200.00
Arrow, Directionals, Gilded Copper, Zinc Point, 71 1/4 In.	100.00
Arrow, Wrought Iron, Olive Brown Paint, J.P.N., 27 X 30 In.	105.00
Car, 1914, Driver, Rooster In Front, Copper, 3 Ft.	6250.00
Cast Head, Patchin, C.1870	3500.00
Cow, Molded Copper, 19th Century, 20 X 32 In. ....*Illus*	4950.00
Crowing Cock, Hollow, Copper, Old Gold Paint, 70 1/2 In.	800.00

Eagle, Cast Aluminum, Black & Gold Paint, 38 /12 In.	70.00
Eagle, Copper, Spread Wings, Resting On Sphere, 1880, 35 In.	1100.00
Eagle, On Orb, Copper	1250.00
Eagle, Spread Winged, On Sphere, Copper, 24 In. ....*Illus*	450.00
Figural, Gabriel, Sheet Iron, 17 1/2 In.	500.00
Fish, Carved, Gilded, Scales, Copper Fins, Metal, 33 In.	7150.00
Flying Goose, Elmer Rowell	7800.00
Full–Bodied Horse & Driver, Sulky, Iron Directionals, 36 In.	6000.00
Horse & Trainer, Sheet Copper, American, 19 X 29 In.	4000.00
Horse, Full–Bodied, Embossed Mane, Copper, 28 1/2 X 33 In.	4500.00
Horse, Prancing, Sheet Metal, Black Paint, 18 X 17 1/2 In.	22.00
Horse, Prancing, Tail Flowing, Copper, 33 In.	385.00
Horse, Prancing, Template, Tin	500.00
Horse, Racing, Jockey, Arrow, Wooden, Tin Tail, 11 X 17 In.	475.00
Horse, Running, 1870, Gold Leaf, 15 X 31 In.	1800.00
Horse, Running, Full–Bodied, Copper, 31 1/2 In.	5300.00
Horse, Running, Full–Bodied, Zinc Head, Copper, 18 X 39 In.	1900.00
Horse, Running, Jockey On Back, Late 19th Century, England	2200.00
Horse, Running, Molded Copper, Colonel Patchen, 20 1/2 In.	2650.00
Horse, Running, Molded Copper, Tail Broken Off, Ma., 28 In.	500.00
Horse, Running On Horse, Gilded Copper, Wooden Base, 20 X 30 In.	3025.00
Pike, Full–Bodied, Metal	3000.00
Pike, Northern, Copper, 36 In.	3300.00
Rooster, Arrow, American, Wooden, 19th Century, 4 Ft.9 In.	1400.00
Rooster, Copper, Metal Tail, Directionals, A.B.Jewel, 23 In.	1500.00
Rooster, Counter Balance, Embossed Zinc, Cast Iron, 21 3/4 In.	150.00
Rooster, Crowing, Full–Bodied	1800.00
Rooster, Flat, Metal	500.00
Rooster, Painted Pine, Silhouette, Wrought Iron Bands, 19 In.	1765.00
Rooster, Tin, C.1920	495.00
Stag, Leaping Position, Copper & Lead	3500.00
Stag, Leaping, Full–Bodied, Gilded, Zinc Head, 30 In.	4100.00

Weather Vane, Cow, Molded Copper, 19th Century, 20 X 32 In.

Weather Vane, Eagle,
Spread Winged, On
Sphere, Copper, 24 In.

Touring Car, Cast Iron Arrow, Glass Insert 195.00

Webb Webb glass was made by Thomas Webb & Sons of Stourbridge, England. Many types of art and cameo glass were made by them during the Victorian era. The factory is still producing glass. Webb Burmese and Webb Peachblow are special colored glasswares of the Victorian period.

WEBB BURMESE, Basket, Signed, 9 In. 450.00
   Bell, Wedding, Cranberry, Clear Handle, 9 1/2 In. 450.00
   Bowl, Floral, Applied Glass At Rim, Marked, 3 3/4 X 6 1/4 In. 1100.00
   Bowl, Ivy Leaves & Vine, 2 3/4 X 3 3/4 In. 325.00
   Bowl, Piecrust Rim, Marked, 2 1/4 In. 210.00
   Creamer, Flower Design, 2 5/8 In. 550.00
   Epergne, Bronze Holder, Miniature 150.00
   Fairy Lamp Epergne, 3 Metal Rings, Ruffled, 20 3/4 In. 2120.00
   Fairy Lamp, Clarke Insert & Cup, 6 1/8 In. 575.00
   Fairy Lamp, Clarke Insert, Marked, 5 5/8 In. 550.00
   Fairy Lamp, Pink, Cream, Dome Shade, Ruffled Base, 5 5/8 In. 550.00
   Fairy Lamp, Reversible Ruffled Base, Clarke Insert, 5 In. 550.00
   Fairy Lamp, Ruffled Bowl Base, Clarke Cup, 6 In. 475.00
   Rose Bowl, 5–Petal Flower, Leaves, Crimped Top, 2 7/8 In. 375.00
   Rose Bowl, 5–Petal Flowers, Leaves, 8–Crimp Top, 2 3/8 In. 295.00
   Shade, 5–Petal Flowers, Leaves, Signed, 6 5/8 In. 395.00
   Vase, 5–Petal Flowers, Green & Brown Leaves, 7 5/8 In. 475.00
   Vase, 5–Petal Flowers, Leaves, Yellow Handles, Marked, 5 In. 695.00
   Vase, 5–Petal Flowers, Ruffled Pedestal Foot, 3 5/8 In. 295.00
   Vase, Ball Shape, 6–Sided Top, Leaves, Flowers, 3 1/2 In. 295.00
   Vase, Brown Foliage, Enameled Flowers, Star–Shaped Top, 3 In. 295.00
   Vase, Flower Petal Top, Berries & Leaves, 3 3/8 In. 325.00
   Vase, Flower Petal Top, Marked, 2 3/4 In. 225.00
   Vase, Gold Leaves & Branches, Raised Berries, 9 1/4 In. 1100.00
   Vase, Green Ivy Leaves, Vines, Scalloped Top, 3 3/4 In. 395.00
   Vase, Green Leaves, Coral Flower Buds, 8 1/4 In. 695.00
   Vase, Green Leaves, Red Berries, Pedestal Foot, 3 3/4 In. 275.00
   Vase, Ivy Leaves, Acid Finish, Pedestal Foot, 4 1/2 In. 325.00
   Vase, Red Flowers, Brown Leaves, Bird, Marked, 7 5/8 In. 895.00
   Vase, Ruffled Pedestal Foot, Flowers, Leaves, 4 In. 300.00
   Vase, Salmon Pink To Lemon Yellow, Pedestal, 6 In. 295.00
   Vase, Yellow Ruffled Edge, 3 In. 295.00
WEBB PEACHBLOW, Bottle, Barber, Ribbed, Bulbous Bottom, Pair 285.00
   Ginger Jar, White Blossoms, Enameling 395.00
   Ivy Bowl, Enameled Floral, Coralene 135.00
   Owl, Applied Clear Branches, Leaves, Flowers, 5 X 4 5/8 In. 395.00
   Perfume Bottle, Flowers, Leaves, Enameled Design, 2 3/4 In. 650.00
   Perfume Bottle, Gold Blossoms, Silver Top, 4 1/2 In. 495.00
   Perfume Bottle, Lay Down, Gold Prunus, 3 3/4 In. 365.00
   Pitcher, Bulbous, Cream Inside, Clear Handle, 3 1/2 In. 225.00
   Vase, Applied Berries, Leaves & Flowers, 5 3/4 In. 550.00
   Vase, Beatles, Wildflowers, Square Flared Rim, 3 In. 240.00
   Vase, Blue, Square Bottom, 18 In. 245.00
   Vase, Bottle Shape, Gold Leaves, House Scene, 9 7/8 In. 395.00
   Vase, Bulbous, Signed, 10 In. 195.00
   Vase, Crystal Applique & Feet, Embossed Swirls, 5 3/4 In. 550.00
   Vase, Gold Flowers & Leaves, Gold Butterfly, 8 1/4 In. 475.00
   Vase, Horizontal Ribbing, Cased White, 8 In. 175.00
   Vase, Swirls, Clear Feet, Berries & Leaves, 5 3/4 In. 550.00
   Vase, White Cased, Acid Finish, 8 In. 175.00
WEBB, Bottle, Barber, 9 In. 150.00
   Bottle, Water, Tumbler, White To Yellow, Gold, Blue, Marked, 2 Piece 245.00
   Bowl, Fluted, 1 Side Folded, Amber Rim, Marked, 11 X 11 In. 175.00
   Bowl, Folded Scalloped Top, Strawberry, Pink Interior, 6 X 12 In. 225.00
   Bowl, Fuchsia Interior, Jagged Top, Brass Base, Marked, 11 X 11 In. 235.00
   Bowl, Honeycomb, White Interior, Pink Exterior, Marked, 8 1/2 In. 350.00

Webb, Salt, Cameo, Sterling Silver Rim, 1 1/2 In., Pair

Webb, Tumbler, Cameo,
Green Floral, 5 3/4 In.

Bowl, Pearlized & Overshot With Green, Marked, 5 X 6 In.	110.00
Bowl, Ruffled, White Flowers, Amber Rim, Blue, 9 In.	1150.00
Bowl, White Overlay Cut To Pink, Marked, 3 X 7 1/4 In.	635.00
Box, Butterscotch, Raised Enameled Cathedral Scene, Brass Frame	205.00
Bride's Basket, Gold Leaves, Birds, Silver Plated Holder	495.00
Bride's Basket, Pale To Deep Green, Gold, Metal Holder, 12 In.	235.00
Bride's Basket, Pink Ruffled, Metal Holder, 11 In.	235.00
Bride's Bowl, Fluted, Raised Enameling, Square Metal Holder, 11 In.	240.00
Bride's Bowl, Raised Enameling, Scalloped Top, White & Fuchsia	185.00
Bride's Bowl, Scalloped Top, Opaque White To Apricot, Marked, 11 In.	195.00
Bride's Bowl, Waffle Design Top, White, Pink, Marked, 9 1/2 In.	165.00
Bride's Bowl, White To Scalloped Pink Rim, Marked, 11 In.	145.00
Cameo, Vase, Cranberry, White Morning Glories, 8 1/2 In.	2250.00
Cameo, Vase, Frosted Red, White Butterfly, Flowers, 4 1/2 In.	1295.00
Cameo, Vase, Ivory, Crimped, Carved Leaves, Brown Stain, 4 7/8 In.	795.00
Fairy Lamp, Clarke Insert, Brass Dolphin Holder, 3 1/2 In.	1000.00
Fairy Lamp, Clear Marked Clarke Base, Mirror Plateau, 5 3/8 In.	465.00
Lamp, Cut Glass Shade, Signed, 18 In.	595.00
Lamp, Frosted White, Pale Green, Marble & Brass Base, 12 In.	425.00
Lamp, Kerosene, Black Porcelain, Brass Base, Marked, 21 In.	375.00
Perfume Bottle, Amber Cameo, White Florals, Sterling Silver Top	1250.00
Perfume Bottle, Blossoms, Blue Satin, Sterling Silver Top, 3 1/2 In.	875.00
Perfume Bottle, Butterfly, Amber, Brown & White, Sterling Silver Top	1350.00
Perfume Bottle, Flowers, Leaves, Carved X's At Neck, Marked, 5 1/2 In.	1320.00
Pitcher, Barn Swallow, Coralene Thorn Handle, Marked	200.00
Pitcher, Gold Raindrop Satin Glass, Square Top, Frosted Handle, 8 In.	325.00
Planter, Pink, Clear Ball Feet, Medallions, Button Mark, 6 In.	295.00
Rose Bowl, 8–Crimp Top, Gold Blossoms On Front, Blue, 2 1/2 In.	225.00
Rose Bowl, Beatles, Queen Anne's Lace, Blue To White, Marked	200.00
Rose Bowl, Egg Shape, Coin Gold Prunus Blossoms On Front, 3 3/4 In.	395.00
Salt, Butterfly, Marked	65.00
Salt, Cameo, Sterling Silver Rim, 1 1/2 In., Pair ....*Illus*	600.00
Shade, Coralene, Diamond–Quilted, Ruffled, 4 X 5 In.	195.00
Tumbler, Cameo, Green Floral, 5 3/4 In. ....*Illus*	250.00
Vase, 2–Color Flowers & Butterflies, 6 In.	1150.00
Vase, Basket Weave, Crimped Top, Blue Shades, Yellow Interior, 7 In.	295.00
Vase, Bird, Gold, Silver & White, Yellow Cased, Marked, 9 1/2 In.	410.00
Vase, Blue, Stick Top, Bulbous Bottom, Marked, 5 1/4 In.	115.00
Vase, Bulbous, Indented, Square, Blue, 18 In.	290.00
Vase, Bunches of Grapes, Tendrils, Daisies, Red Ground, Marked, 8 In.	3450.00
Vase, Butterflies Hovering About Branch, Blue Cased, 13 In.	1350.00
Vase, Calla Lily Blossoms, Butterfly On Reverse, C.1900, 8 3/4 In.	2200.00

Vase, Cameo, White Chrysanthemums, Butterfly, Blue, Marked, 7 1/2 In.	1450.00
Vase, Carved Flowers, Frosted Cranberry, Marked, 10 3/8 In.	2395.00
Vase, Coralene, Gold Flowers, Pink Ground, Marked, 10 In.	265.00
Vase, Florentine, Fuchsia, Signed, 8 1/2 In.	165.00
Vase, Folded Lemon Top, Blue Stars On White, Marked, 5 3/4 In.	170.00
Vase, Gold Prunus & Sunbrust Florals, Butterfly, 7 3/4 In.	485.00
Vase, Gold Seaweed, Butterscotch, Marked, 9 In., Pair	270.00
Vase, Gold Seaweed, Frosted White To Butterscotch, Marked, 9 In.	285.00
Vase, Leaves All Around, Clusters On Front, Cranberry, 5 In.	1850.00
Vase, Melon Rib, Ivory, Red Swirl, Gold Dragonfly Tracery, 8 1/2 In.	395.00
Vase, Mother-of-Pearl, 11 In.	395.00
Vase, Multicolor Coralene, Marked, 10 1/2 In.	265.00
Vase, Opaque White To Butterscotch, Bulbous, Marked, 11 1/2 In.	195.00
Vase, Pink Opalescent To Pale Green, 2 3/4 In.	58.00
Vase, Pink, Gold Design, Bulbous, 13 In., Pair	195.00
Vase, Prunus & Butterfly, Blue Overlay, Satin Glass, 8 In., Pair	395.00
Vase, Quilted Satin, Bulbous, White & Yellow, Marked, 11 In.	175.00
Vase, Satin Glass, Birds, Flowers, Blue & White, 6 In.	225.00
Vase, Simulated Ivory, Flower Petal Top, Signed, 2 3/4 In.	650.00
Vase, Sprays of Gold Prunus Blossom, Gold Bee, 8 1/4 In.	295.00
Vase, Stick, Gold Prunus & Butterfly Design, Cream Lining, 7 1/8 In.	350.00
Vase, Teardrop, Custard Yellow To Rose, Floral, 12 In.	750.00
Vase, White Chrysanthemum, Butterfly, Marked, 7 1/2 In.	1450.00
Vase, White Floral, Bee & Butterfly On Back, Blue Ground, 12 In.	3200.00
Vase, White Florals, Acorns, Frosted Lime, 8 1/2 In.	825.00
Vase, Yellow Diamond, Square Top, Marked, 10 1/2 In.	185.00

WEDGWOOD   Josiah Wedgwood, although considered a cripple by his brother and forbidden to work at the family business, founded one of the world's most successful potteries. The pottery was founded in England in 1759. A large variety of wares has been made, including the well-known jasperware, basalt, creamware, and even a limited amount of porcelain. There are two kinds of jasperware. One is made from two colors of clay, the other is made from one color clay with a color dip to create the contrast in design. The firm is still in business.

WEDGWOOD, Ashtray, Jasperware, Classical, Round, 4 1/2 In.	45.00
Ashtray, Spode Shape, Cupids, 4 1/2 In.	30.00
Biscuit Jar, Floral On Lavender, Acorn Finial, 7 3/4 In.	700.00
Biscuit Jar, Jasperware, Sage Green, Lavender, 6 1/4 In.	695.00
Biscuit Jar, Ladies Around Sides, Blue & White, 6 In.	145.00
Bowl, Amherst Pheasant, Fairyland Luster, Gold Trim, 8 5/8 In.	1650.00
Bowl, Blue Willow, Border Inside & Out, Octagonal, 7 3/4 In.	75.00

Wedgwood, Vase, Jasperware, Lilac Medallions, 10 In., Pair

Bowl, Butterfly Luster, Orange Exterior, Blue Interior, 6 1/2 In.	325.00
Bowl, Dragon Luster, Orange, Blue Interior, Peacocks, 7 In.	325.00
Bowl, Dragon Luster, Purple, Gold, 1 1/2 X 2 1/4 In.	150.00
Bowl, Fairyland Luster, Butterfly, 2 3/4 X 3 1/4 In.	195.00
Bowl, Fairyland Luster, Elves & Bell Branch Interior, 8 7/8 In.	1600.00
Bowl, Fairyland Luster, Green Inside, Flame Outside, Marked, 5 In.	775.00
Bowl, Fairyland Luster, Hummingbirds, Geese, Octagonal, 8 1/2 In.	650.00
Bowl, Fairyland Luster, Leapfrogging Elves, Marked, 4 3/4 In.	675.00
Bowl, Fairyland Luster, Leapfrogging Elves, Marked, 4 In.	450.00
Bowl, Fairyland Luster, Leapfrogging Elves, Marked, 5 1/2 In.	650.00
Bowl, Floral Design, Oriental Garden Scene, Luster, 9 1/4 In.	250.00
Bowl, Killarney, Etruria, 14 1/2 In.	15.00
Box, Dragon Luster, Mother-of-Pearl Luster Under Cover, 5 In.	395.00
Box, Scalloped, Duke of Edinburg, Royal Blue, Cover, 5 In.	150.00
Bread Tray, Raised Grapes, Leaves, Turquoise Ground, 10 X 12 In.	325.00
Bust, Bearded Man, Black Basalt, Marked, 4 3/8 In.	375.00
Bust, Dwight D.Eisenhower, Basalt, Limited Edition	95.00
Bust, John Bunyan, Black Basalt, Wedgwood Plinth, C.1850, 14 In.	1450.00
Bust, Prior, Black Basalt, 11 1/2 In.	695.00 To 750.00
Bust, William Shakespeare, Black Basalt, Plinth, C.1850, 13 In.	1250.00
Cake Plate, Black Jasperware, 9 In.	48.00
Candleholder, Queensware, 8 In., Pair	175.00
Candlestick, Dolphin, Black Basalt, Marked, 8 5/8 In., Pair	695.00
Candlestick, Jasperware, Classical Ladies, Green, 7 1/2 In., Pair	125.00
Candlestick, Jasperware, Dark Blue & White, Date, 7 3/4 In., Pair	585.00
Candlestick, Jasperware, White Figures, Green Ground, 6 In., Pair	75.00
Cheese Dish, Cover, Dark Blue, Acorn Finial	500.00
Cheese Dish, Cover, Ladies Around Sides, Blue & White, 9 In.	395.00
Cheese Dish, Dark Blue, White Classical Figures	300.00
Compote, Terra-Cotta	125.00
Cookie Jar, Jasperware, Classical Figures, Dark Blue & White	135.00
Cookie Jar, Raised Gilt Berries, Leaves, Urn Mark	145.00
Creamer, Coronation of Edward VIII, 1937	35.00
Creamer, Crest of Ontario, Maple Leaf, Marked	250.00
Creamer, Jasperware, White Classical Figures, Dark Blue	80.00
Creamer, Webbed, C.1785, 4 In.	125.00
Cup & Saucer, Creamware, Enameled Daisies	65.00
Cup & Saucer, Queensware, Demitasse	35.00
Dish, Heart Shape, Classical Design, 4 1/2 In.	30.00
Figurine, Elephant, Basalt, White Tusks	425.00
Figurine, Eros & Euphrosyne, Marked, 16 1/2 In.	875.00
Flower Frog, Seated Nude, Cream Color, 9 In.	225.00
Flower Holder, Hedgehog, Basalt, Marked	350.00
Flower Holder, Raised Flowers, Gray Ground, Salt Glaze, 5 3/8 In.	245.00
Flowerpot, Garlands of Grapes, Raised Lion's Head, 4 1/2 In.	145.00
Garden Seat, Red Gloss, Tufted Cushion & Tassels, 1886, 16 In.	850.00
Humidor, Tobacco, Bison Head	135.00
Jar, Cover, Jasperware, Coronation, Royal Blue, 1953, 4 In.	150.00
Jar, Jasperware, White On Blue, 4 In.	48.00
Jar, Potpourri, Cover, Dragon Luster, 17 1/8 In.	695.00
Jar, Preserve, 4 Classic Muses In Cartouches, Cover, 6 In.	195.00
Jardiniere, Lion's Head, Grapes & Leaves, Classical Figure, 4 In.	85.00
Jardiniere, Undertray, Lion's Head With Swags, Blue, 7 1/4 In.	250.00
Jug, Commemorative, Roger Williams	325.00
Jug, Jasperware, White & Yellow, Etruscan, 6 1/4 In.	385.00
Jug, Ladies Around Sides, Masked Horned Man Under Spout, 8 In.	145.00
Mug, Cream Color, Signed Keith Murray	65.00
Mug, Jasperware, Classical Figures, Dark Blue & White, 2 1/2 In.	85.00
Mug, Jasperware, Cupids, Classical Figures, Dark Blue, 3 In.	135.00
Mug, White Cameo, Washington, Franklin, Lafayette, Green, 4 In.	450.00
Pitcher & Bowl, White, Marked	90.00
Pitcher, Blue & White, 1/2 Moon Mark, 4 1/2 In.	295.00
Pitcher, Blue & White, 1/2 Moon Mark, 8 1/2 In.	425.00
Pitcher, Dark Green & White Slip, 1924, 6 In.	150.00

Pitcher, Grape Rim, Sacrifice Scene, Rope Handle, Green, 6 In.	110.00
Pitcher, Jasperware, Allegorical Design, Blue & White, 6 1/4 In.	75.00
Pitcher, Jasperware, Classical Ladies, Grapes, Leaves, 6 3/8 In.	110.00
Pitcher, Jasperware, Classical Ladies, Lavender, White, 6 In.	195.00
Pitcher, Jasperware, Rope Handle, Olive Green, 6 1/2 In.	130.00
Pitcher, Ladies & Cupids Around Sides, Blue & White, 6 1/2 In.	145.00
Pitcher, Longfellow's Picture Front, Keramos' Poem Back, 6 In.	125.00
Pitcher, Milk, Silver Round Handle, White, 5 In.	55.00
Pitcher, Rose & Butterfly, Marked, 5 In.	95.00
Pitcher, Sacrifice Scene, Rope Handle, Blue, 6 1/2 In.	130.00
Pitcher, Silver Luster, 4 In.	45.00
Plaque, Fairyland Luster, Picnic By A River, 10 X 4 1/2 In.	4500.00
Plaque, Jasperware, Cherubs Playing Blindman's Bluff, 13 3/8 In.	450.00
Plaque, Jasperware, Grapes, Maidens, Cupids, Lavender, 6 X 8 In.	145.00
Plaque, Jasperware, Hanging, Lilac, Medallion, Virgin Mary, 9 In.	135.00
Plaque, Jasperware, Mythological Figures, Green & White, 5 7/8 In.	150.00
Plate, Annual, 1969	215.00
Plate, Calendar, 1977, Children's Games	45.00
Plate, Capitol, Dark Blue, 9 1/4 In.	32.00
Plate, Chapel U.S.Naval Academy, Blue & White, 10 In.	30.00
Plate, Child's, Happy Children Red Transfer, Floral Rim	122.00
Plate, Chinese, Flow Blue, 10 1/4 In.	65.00
Plate, Christmas, 1969	75.00 To 150.00
Plate, Christmas, 1971	35.00
Plate, Columbia Series, Library, 10 1/2 In.	35.00
Plate, Columbian Expo, 1893	20.00
Plate, Fairyland Luster, Rim of Roses, Boys On Bridge, 10 5/8 In.	1250.00
Plate, Harvard, Rose, 1932, 8 3/4 In.	18.00
Plate, Harvard, Rose, 1941, 10 1/4 In.	20.00
Plate, Ivanhoe Series, Rebecca Repelling The Templar, 10 In.	55.00
Plate, Japan Pattern, Gold Designs, 1878, 9 1/4 In.	275.00
Plate, Polychrome Floral Border, Creamware, C.1820, 10 In.	60.00
Plate, Return of The Mayflower, Dark Blue, 9 1/4 In.	32.00
Plate, Shell, Jasperware, White, 9 In.	195.00
Platter, Cows, Flow Blue, 17 In.	55.00
Ring Tree, Jasperware, Dark Blue, Classical Scenes	175.00
Soup, Cream, Underplate, Ashford	25.00
Sugar & Creamer, Canadian Seal On Front, Thistle & Flowers	225.00
Sugar & Creamer, Classical Figures, Sage Green & White, Marked	125.00
Sugar & Creamer, Egyptian, Marked, C.1900	225.00
Tankard, Jasperware, Rope Handle, 8 1/2 In.	185.00
Tea Bowl & Saucer, Dr.Wall	100.00
Tea Caddy, Jasperware, Classical, Yellow, Gray, Marked, 6 In.	500.00
Tea Set, Jasperware, Sage Green, Washington, Franklin, 3 Piece	575.00
Tea Set, Jasperware, Yellow, Black & White, 3 Piece	700.00
Teapot, Jasperware, Sugar & Creamer, Lilac, Dated 1961	350.00
Teapot, Arabesque Scene, Dog Finial	225.00
Teapot, Bamboo, Primrose, Terra–Cotta	95.00
Teapot, Basalt, Canadian Emblem, Small	35.00
Teapot, Black Basalt, Enameled Flowers & Leaves, Marked, 4 1/4 In.	325.00
Teapot, Jasperware, Black & White, Large	385.00
Teapot, Jasperware, Classical Figures, Dark Blue & White	135.00
Tile, Calendar, Commonwealth Pier, 1914	45.00
Tile, Calendar, Federal Theater, 1897	65.00
Tile, Calendar, Harvard Medical Building, 1908	45.00
Tile, Dog & Bird, Framed	135.00
Tray, Comb, Jasperware, Dark Blue, Classical Scenes, 9 X 6 In.	185.00
Tray, Pin, Jasperware, 6 In.	40.00
Tureen, Underplate, Ladle, Black Wheel Border, Dahlia Design	375.00
Vase, Black & White, Bud	125.00
Vase, Blue, White, Floral, Ring Handle, Square Mouth, 8 In.	475.00
Vase, Chicoreus Shell, Coral Stand, Marked, C.1894, 7 In.	175.00
Vase, Classical Figures, Oak Leaf & Acorn, Marked, 5 1/4 In.	104.00
Vase, Classical Figures, White Relief, Blue, Stoneware, 10 In.	1600.00

Iridescent pottery such as Sicardo should be carefully cleaned. Wash in mild detergent and water. Rinse and dry by buffing vigorously with dry, fluffy towels. Then polish with a silver cloth as if it were made of metal. Buff again with a clean towel.

Weller, Vase, Louwelsa, Indian Portrait,
C.1915, 10 3/4 In.

Vase, Cover, Fairyland Luster, Fairy Under The Rainbow, 9 In.	2050.00
Vase, Dragon Luster, Gold Scenes To Rim, 8 In.	265.00
Vase, Fairyland Luster, Imps On Bridge, Gold Trim, 8 1/8 In.	1100.00
Vase, Fairyland Luster, Trumpet, Butterfly Women, Pixies, 7 7/8 In.	1150.00
Vase, Fish, Powder Blue Luster, 6 1/2 In.	800.00
Vase, Gold Enameled Pattern, Pair	210.00
Vase, Hummingbird Luster, Gold Outlined, Gold Trim, Marked, 5 In.	195.00
Vase, Jasperware, Classical Band, Blue, Gold, Tricolor, 3 3/4 In.	450.00
Vase, Jasperware, Lilac Medallions, 10 In., Pair ....*Illus*	325.00
Vase, Pendants of Leaf & Berry, Lilac & White, 10 In., Pair	325.00
Vase, Portland, White Raised Figures, Blue & White, 7 In.	350.00
Vase, White Flowers, Carved Leaves Band, Blue, Barnard, 12 1/2 In.	910.00
Waste Bowl, Jasperware, Classical, Deep Blue & White, 2 3/8 In.	70.00

LOUWELSA WELLER

Weller pottery was first made in 1873 in Fultonham, Ohio. The firm moved to Zanesville, Ohio, in 1882. Art wares were first made in 1893. Hundreds of lines of pottery were made, including Louwelsa, Eocean, Dickens, and Sicardo, before the pottery closed in 1948.

WELLER, Art Pottery, Vase, Burntwood, 3 1/2 In.	32.00
Basket, Hanging, Chelsea	195.00
Basket, Hanging, Flemish, 10 In.	80.00
Basket, Silvertone, 8 1/2 In.	80.00
Bowl, Atlas, Apricot, Ivory, 13 1/2 In.	17.50
Bowl, Claywood, 2 1/2 In.	5.00
Bowl, Claywood, 3 In.	40.00
Bowl, Coppertone, Flower Frog, 15 In.	138.00
Bowl, Copra, 9 In.	170.00
Bowl, Flower Frog, Golden Glow	135.00
Bowl, Flower Frog, Malvern, 10 In.	55.00
Bowl, Hudson, Blue & Gray, Footed, 12 In.	95.00
Bowl, Panella, Blue Matte, Footed, 7 In.	30.00
Bowl, Roma, 6 In.	17.00
Bowl, Woodcraft, 3 1/2 In.	50.00
Bowl, Woodcraft, 7 In.	42.00
Candlestick, Arcola, 12 In., Pair	60.00
Candlestick, Roma, Matte, Floral, F.Lorber, 9 1/2 In.	135.00
Clock, Louwelsa, 7 In.	375.00
Clock, Mantel, Louwelsa, Floral, 12 In.	950.00
Console, Wild Rose, Aqua	50.00
Cookie Jar, Mammy	325.00
Creamer, Zona	20.00
Ewer, Louwelsa, 22 In.	625.00
Ewer, Louwelsa, Marked Burgess, 6 In.	125.00
Ewer, Sabrinian, 9 In.	55.00
Ewer, Wild Rose, Aqua, 14 In.	50.00
Ewer, Wild Rose, Green, 7 In.	19.00
Figurine, Dachshund, 3 X 6 In.	55.00
Figurine, Frog On Lily Pad	50.00

Figurine, Nude Child	65.00
Figurine, Squirrel, Garden Ornament, Hanging, 13 1/2 In.	300.00
Figurine, Turtle, Coppertone	139.00
Flower Frog, 1920s Girl, Matte Turquoise, Hobart, 8 1/2 In.	75.00
Flowerpot, Forest, 4 1/2 In.	80.00 To 85.00
Garden Ornament, Rooster, 12 1/2 In.	550.00
Jardiniere, Aurelian, Brown Gloss Glaze, Florals, 4 In.	140.00
Jardiniere, Burntwood, Chickens All Around, 8 In.	250.00
Jardiniere, Cameo Jewell, 8 In.	95.00
Jardiniere, Dickens Ware, Portrait of Cavalier, Caramel	1000.00
Jardiniere, Eocean, Wildflowers, Cream To Turquoise, 6 3/4 In.	135.00
Jardiniere, Flemish, 8 In.	45.00
Jardiniere, Forest, 5 In.	35.00 To 45.00
Jardiniere, Louwelsa, Florals, Leaves, Pedestal Base, 31 In.	400.00
Jardiniere, Louwelsa, Ruffled, Poppies, 7 1/2 In.	150.00
Jardiniere, Roma, 9 1/2 In.	90.00
Jardiniere, Rosemont, Ivory, 4 1/2 In.	75.00
Jardiniere, Rosemont, White, 4 1/2 In.	58.00
Jug, Dickens Ware, Golfers	550.00
Jug, Dickens Ware, Monk, 6 In.	225.00
Jug, Louwelsa, Blackberry Design	120.00
Jug, Louwelsa, Cherry Design	125.00
Jug, Louwelsa, Leaf & Berries, 1900, 5 In.	200.00
Lamp Base, Arcola	40.00
Lamp Base, Silvertone, 12 In.	325.00
Lamp, Louwelsa, Autumn Leaves, 13 In.	285.00
Lamp, Oil, Dickens Ware, Orange Tree Leaves, J.W.Brooks, 6 X 11 In.	225.00
Lamp, Oil, Turada, Blue	650.00
Mug, Aurelian, Chestnut Leaves & Burrs, Handle, Artist K	195.00
Mug, Dickens Ware, 1st Line	145.00
Mug, Dickens Ware, Dumbey & Son, 5 5/8 In.	195.00
Mug, Etna, Grape Design, 6 In.	85.00
Pitcher, Kingfisher, Cobalt Blue, 1/2 Gal.	97.00
Pitcher, Louwelsa, 5 In.	120.00
Pitcher, Marvo, Green, 8 In.	65.00
Pitcher, Pierre, Pink	15.00
Pitcher, Zona, Duckling Splashing, 8 In.	110.00
Pitcher, Zona, Green	30.00
Planter, Duck	35.00
Planter, Roma, Square	20.00
Planter, Warwick, 3 1/2 In.	45.00
Planter, Woodcraft, 3 Foxes	135.00
Plaque, Lincoln, Bisque, 1904 Expo	115.00
Plate, Juvenile, Rolled Rim, Squirrels	25.00
Sugar, Pierre, Pink	4.00
Syrup, Mammy	210.00
Tankard, Etna, Cherries, 10 1/2 In.	275.00
Tankard, Floretta, Grapes, 10 1/2 In.	80.00
Tankard, Louwelsa, 17 In.	550.00
Teapot, Forest, High Glaze, Signed	165.00
Umbrella Stand, Ardsley	265.00
Vase, Ardsley, Footed, Green, 10 In.	55.00
Vase, Aurelian, Nasturtiums, Albert Haubrich, 15 1/2 X 5 1/2 In.	395.00
Vase, Bedford, Glossy, 8 In.	30.00
Vase, Blue Ware, 9 In.	120.00
Vase, Bonito, 7 In.	35.00 To 55.00
Vase, Bonito, 10 In.	75.00
Vase, Bouquet, Yellow, 5 In.	15.00
Vase, Bud, LaSa, 7 1/2 In.	100.00 To 110.00
Vase, Bud, Roma, Double, 8 In.	42.00
Vase, Burntwood, Floral, 5 In.	15.00
Vase, Cameo, Blue, 13 In.	50.00
Vase, Chengtu, 11 1/2 In.	85.00
Vase, Claywood, 3 1/2 In.	20.00

Vase, Copra, 9 In. 80.00
Vase, Dickens Ware, 2nd Line, Clown, 10 In. 575.00
Vase, Dickens Ware, Golfer, 10 In. 575.00
Vase, Etna, 10 In. 95.00
Vase, Fleron, 4 3/4 In. 25.00
Vase, Floral, Green, 4 1/2 In. 30.00
Vase, Floretta, Raised Roses, Matte Green, Salmon, 5 X 2 1/2 In. 45.00
Vase, Forest, 8 In. 60.00
Vase, Forest, 10 1/4 In. 85.00
Vase, Greenbriar, 3 In. 20.00
Vase, Hudson, 10 In. 125.00
Vase, Hudson, Blackberries & Blossoms, McLaughlin Initial, 8 In. 190.00
Vase, Hudson, Daisies, 7 In. .... 145.00 To 150.00
Vase, Hudson, Dogwood, Signed Walch, 6 1/2 In. 285.00
Vase, Hudson, Floral, Artist Signed, 7 In. 50.00
Vase, Hudson, Floral, Blue & Aqua, Rose Ground, 9 In. 195.00
Vase, Hudson, Iris, 9 1/2 In. 100.00
Vase, Hudson, Perfecto, Leaves, Berries, 5 1/2 In. 75.00
Vase, Hudson, Roses, Signed Pillsbury, 7 In. 350.00
Vase, Hudson, Wild Roses, Vines, Cream Ground, 6 Sides, 11 1/2 In. 250.00
Vase, Iridescent Floral & Scroll, Sicard, 4 3/4 X 8 In. 325.00
Vase, Jewell, 9 1/2 In. 85.00
Vase, Kenova, Cylindrical, 10 In. 85.00
Vase, L'Art Nouveau, Irises At Top, Marked, 11 In. 135.00
Vase, LaSa, 3 1/2 In. 105.00
Vase, LaSa, 6 In. 175.00
Vase, LaSa, Iridescent Water & Trees, 4 In. 185.00
Vase, LaSa, Luster, Signed, 7 1/2 In. 155.00
Vase, LaSa, Yellow, Blue & Red Layered Bands, C.1900, 6 1/4 In. 90.00
Vase, Louwelsa, Brown, Gold Trim, 12 In. 175.00
Vase, Louwelsa, Carnations, Lillie Mitchell, 9 In. 275.00
Vase, Louwelsa, Indian Portrait, C.1915, 10 3/4 In. ....Illus 475.00
Vase, Manhattan, Peach Matte, Signed O, 6 1/2 In. 15.00
Vase, Marengo, Hexagonal, 9 1/2 In. 160.00
Vase, Orris, Branches & Leaves In Relief, 10 In. 55.00
Vase, Panella, Yellow, Initial R, 5 In. 20.00
Vase, Patra, 7 In. 38.00
Vase, Patra, Handles, 5 In. 35.00
Vase, Roba, Blue, 8 In. 50.00
Vase, Roma, Blue, Square, 7 In. 15.00
Vase, Sicard, Amber Leaf & Dot Design, Maroon, C.1910, 10 3/4 In. 425.00
Vase, Sicard, Geometric Floral, Iridescent, Trefoil, 7 1/4 In. 225.00
Vase, Sicard, Gold Orchids, Turquoise & Rose Ground, Signed, 6 In. 395.00
Vase, Sicard, Poppy Design, Iridescent, 1910, 11 3/4 In. 225.00
Vase, Sicard, Rolled Lip, Design, Signed, 7 In. 625.00
Vase, Sicard, Signed, 6 1/2 In. 400.00
Vase, Silvertone, 6 3/4 In. 35.00
Vase, Silvertone, 11 1/2 In. 155.00
Vase, Silvertone, Fan Shape 60.00
Vase, Softone, Blue, 5 In. 12.00
Vase, Souevo, 6 In. 85.00
Vase, Souevo, 9 In. 130.00
Vase, Sydonia, Fan Shape, Green 30.00
Vase, Velva, Green, 6 In. 24.00
Vase, Voile, 6 1/4 In. 75.00
Vase, Warwick, 4 1/2 In. 50.00
Vase, Wild Rose, Green Matte Glaze, 8 In. 32.00
Vase, Xenia, Stylized, Floral, Blue Ground, 5 3 1/4 In. 150.00
Wall Pocket, Blue Drapery, Pair 75.00
Wall Pocket, Classic, Blue 40.00
Wall Pocket, Golden Glow 70.00
Wall Pocket, Roma, 8 In. 40.00
Wall Pocket, Souevo, 16 In. 95.00
Wall Pocket, Woodcraft, Florals 55.00

Wall Pocket, Woodcraft, Owl, 11 In. 85.00
Wall Pocket, Woodcraft, Squirrel, Cone Shaped Tree, 9 1/2 In. 129.00
Window Box, Forest, 5 X 14 In. 165.00
Window Box, Warwick, 9 In. 30.00

> Wemyss ware was made by Robert Heron in Kirkaldy, Scotland, from 1850 to 1929.

WEMYSS, Inkwell 325.00

> Willets Manufacturing Company of Trenton, New Jersey, worked from 1879. The company made belleek in the late 1880s and 1890s in shapes similar to those used by the Irish Belleek factory. They stopped working about 1912. Pieces were marked with a variety of marks, all including the name Willets.

BELLEEK
WILLETS

WILLETS, Bowl, Pink Fleur–De–Lis, Crimped Edge, Gold Handles, 7 1/2 In. 155.00
Creamer, Gold Dragon Handle 60.00
Cup & Saucer, 2 Handles, Flowers 45.00
Cup & Saucer, Mother–of–Pearl Luster, Ribbed, Belleek 75.00
Plate, Floral, 8 1/4 In. 95.00
Salt, Monogram C, Gold Trim, 2nd Mark 20.00
Salt, Open, Gold Ruffled Rim, Different Flowers, Red Mark, 12 Piece 180.00
Sugar & Creamer, Crimped Gold Rims & Handles 75.00
Sugar, Gold Dragon Handles, Flowers, Cover, Belleek, 1st Pink Mark 95.00
Tankard, Grapes, Applied Dragon Handle, Artist Signed, 1910, 15 In. 275.00
Vase, Nude Maiden Wrapped In Veil, Marked, 1910, 15 In. 850.00
Vase, Red Geranium, Belleek, 15 In. 275.00
WILLOW, see Blue Willow

> Stained glass and beveled glass windows were popular additions to houses during the late nineteenth and early twentieth centuries. The old windows became popular with collectors in the 1970s; today, old and new examples are seen.

WINDOW, Caramel & Green Slag, Geometric, C.1910, Oak Frame, 35 X 15 In., Pair   800.00
Fan, Louvered, Blue–Green, 61 In. 1500.00
Leaded, Blue Panels, 45 1/2 X 24 In., Pair 100.00
Leaded, Iridescent Panels, Clear Border, Elmslie, 50 X 35 In. 500.00
Leaded, Prairie Style, Greens, Ambers, Slag, 49 X 17 In., Pair 500.00
Leaded, Stained, Woman At Window, 72 X 64 In. 4400.00
Stained & Slag Glass, In Frame, C.1915, 3 1/2 X 3 Ft. 150.00
Stained Glass, Advertising, Broadway Brewing, Buffalo, 3 X 5 Ft. 1200.00
Stained Glass, Butterflies 175.00
Stained Glass, Chapel, 8 X 4 In. 2000.00

Wood Carving, War Horse, Tang, 41 In., Pair

Wood Carving, Women, Standing, Draped, 13 In., Pair

Stained Glass, Green Dragon, Elliptic, 13th Century, 8 X 14 In.	550.00
Stained Glass, Original Frame, 30 X 53 In.	100.00

> Wood carvings and wooden pieces are listed separately in this book. There are also wooden pieces found in other sections, such as Kitchen.

WOOD CARVING, American Eagle, Pine, Gilt, On Flattened Ball, 12 X 17 In.	1540.00
Angel, Curly Hair, Garland, Paint Traces, Italy, 22 In.	1100.00
Angel, Gilt, Spain, 17th Century, 12 3/8 & 12 5/8 In.	2970.00
Bear & Human Group, Platform, C.1900, 5 X 9 In.	350.00
Blow–Snake, Rearing, Root Carving, Brown Green Paint, 17 In.	2200.00
Boat, Lily Pad Shape, Chinese, 19 In.	20.00
Bowl, Queen Anne, Burl, 7 1/2 X 30 In.	3900.00
Box, Witch & Child, 19th Century, Round, Japan, 7 3/4 In.	143.00
Bridge, With 5 Elephants Crossing, Oriental, 1920s, 19 In.	35.00
Buddha, Seated On Rock Formation, Asian, 12 1/2 In.	125.00
Chain Links, Eyes, Walnut, 61 1/2 In.	700.00
Chain, Walnut	545.00
Christ Child, Curls, Painted, Iberian, 17th Century, 33 3/4 In.	2750.00
Diorama, Man In Armor, Notaries, Relief Carved, 22 X 38 In.	375.00
Dog, Black & White Paint, Leatherized Cloth Ears, 3 In.	75.00
Dog, Varnish Finish, Red Tongue, 9 In.	35.00
Dove, Full-Breasted, Spread Wings, Gray Over White, 10 3/4 In.	350.00
Eagle's Head, 10 1/2 In.	193.00
Eagle, 1 Piece Pine, Primitive, Weathered, 20th Century, 21 In.	375.00
Eagle, Crossed Flags & Shield, 1 Piece of Pine, 24 In.	2100.00
Eagle, Dark Brown, 20th Century, 37 1/2 In.	55.00
Eagle, Head Turned Left, Clutching Branch, Painted, 28 In.	1900.00
Eagle, Ships, Upraised Wings, Gold Leaf, 19th Century, 22 In.	2400.00
Eagle, Welcome Stranger Banner, Bellamy, Small	5610.00
Elder, With Pipe, Rosewood, 5 In.	37.50
Gama Sennin, Immortal, Holding Frog, Seiho, 7 1/2 In.	1540.00
Horse, Blue Blanket, Stylized Detail, 4 1/8 In.	445.00
Horse, Original Brown Paint, Black Trim, Gold Harness, 8 In.	400.00
Horse, Saddle & Bridle, Wooden Base, China, 23 1/8 In.	500.00
Horse, Standing, Painted & Gessoed, 19th Century, Italy, 14 In.	445.00
Horse, Standing, Painted, Horsehair Tail, C.1880, 7 Ft.10 In.	4500.00
Indian, Polychrome Paint, 20th Century, 74 In.	600.00
Intertwined Fish, Glass Eyes, 12 1/4 In.	30.00
Lamp, Standing Sennin, Holding Jar, Teak, 19th Century, 37 In.	500.00
Lion, 3 X 3 In.	10.00
Lions, Seated, C.1600, England, 27 1/2 In., Pair	6650.00
Madonna & Child, Painted, 17th Century, 16 3/4 In.	660.00
Male Acrobat, Handstand, Painted Black, 31 In.	2900.00
Male, Seated, Ribbed, Easter Island, 14 X 2 1/2 In.	2600.00
Mask, Dance, Mexican	175.00
Ornament, Bird, Exaggerated Wings, Yellow Ocher, 3 1/4 In.	900.00
Plaque, Motto, Oak, Arts & Crafts, GRG, 1915, 19 X 43 1/2 In.	300.00
Putto, Hands Folded, Painted, Italy, 18th Century, 17 In.	885.00
Quan Yin, Loose Robe, Lotus Base, 4 Ft.7 In.	800.00
Rabbit, Standing, Europe, Late 19th Century, 32 In.	1180.00
Sailor Boy, With Binoculars, Store Figure, 1850–1900, 40 In.	6000.00
Shorebird, Distressed Black Paint, Contemporary, 13 In.	85.00
Snake, Forked Tongue, Rattles, Joints At Head & Tail, 44 In.	450.00
Stand, Calling Card, Black Man, Cutout	95.00
Tang War Horses, Polychromed, Chinese, 41 In., Pair	800.00
Village & Farm Animals, Painted, English, Early 20th Century	200.00
War Horse, Tang, 41 In., Pair ....*Illus*	800.00
Women, Standing, Draped, 13 In., Pair ....*Illus*	100.00

 Wood was used for many containers and tools used in the early home. Small wooden pieces are called "treenware" in England, but the term "woodenware" is more common in the United States.

WOODEN, see also Kitchen; Advertising; Tool

WOODEN, Ashtray, Bellboy, Silhouette, Cutout, Tin Tray, 32 In. 85.00
  Ashtray, Black Man Bellhop, Cutout Arms, 30 1/2 In. 100.00
  Ashtray, Black Waiter, Polychrome Paint, Cutout, 34 1/2 In. 60.00
  Barrel, Banded Oak, Top, 19th Century 66.00
  Barrel, Red Stain, White Borders, Peg Handle, New England, 20 X 9 In. 88.00
  Bed Smoother, Trapezoidal Head, Wrigglework, Dated 1765, 18 In. 77.00
  Billy Club, Policeman's, Hand Painted Lettering, Dated 1900, 15 In. 20.00
  Bootjack, American Rococo, Carved, Carpet Pouch, 1845 .... 270.00
  Bowl, Apple, Treen, Flat Ends, 19th Century, 38 X 18 In. 225.00
  Bowl, Ash Burl, Footed, Inscription, 1796,, 5 1/2 In. 850.00
  Bowl, Ash Burl, Turned Lip, 4 3/4 X 13 3/4 In. 450.00
  Bowl, Blue Paint Over Earlier Green, 15 1/2 X 21 1/2 In. 150.00
  Bowl, Blue Paint, Almond Shape, 11 1/2 X 20 1/2 In. 225.00
  Bowl, Blue Paint, C.1830, 14 In. 175.00
  Bowl, Burl, Irregular Square Shape, 5 X 10 1/2 X 11 1/2 In. 100.00
  Bowl, Burl, Laced Copper Wire Repair At Rim, 12 In. 175.00
  Bowl, Burl, Open Bottom, Branded J.S.Edge, 8 3/4 X 4 In. 175.00
  Bowl, Burl, Protruding Rim Handles, Mustard Outside, 11 X 13 X 5 In. 450.00
  Bowl, Burl, Scrubbed Finish, 12 1/2 In. 145.00
  Bowl, Burl, Signed, 10 In. 85.00
  Bowl, Carrying Handles, 1 With Hole For Hanging, Burl, 22 1/2 In. 1600.00
  Bowl, Carved Semicircular Handles, Drilled For Hanging, 25 1/4 In. 192.50
  Bowl, Chip Carved Design of Flutes, Sunbursts, Oval, 8 1/4 X 12 In. 700.00
  Bowl, Chopping, Round, 6 In. 100.00
  Bowl, Curly Maple, Cracked, 12 1/4 X 12 3/4 X 1 7/8 In. 800.00
  Bowl, Deer Form, Allover Beaver Nails, 2 Stones, 9 X 11 In. 40.00
  Bowl, Dough, C.1875, Large 135.00
  Bowl, Dry Salmon Paint, Footed, 19th Century, 6 7/8 In. 150.00
  Bowl, Flaring Sides, American, Late 19th Century, 18 1/2 In. 110.00
  Bowl, Maple, Tool Marks, Oblong, 10 1/4 X 19 In. 175.00
  Bowl, Oblong, 4 3/4 X 10 3/4 X 24 In. 95.00
  Bowl, Painted Winter Scene Interior, Initials O.A., 11 X 12 In. 15.00
  Bowl, Poplar, 1 Piece, 24 X 8 In. 95.00
  Bowl, Red Exterior, 2 X 6 In. 285.00
  Bowl, Red Exterior, Oblong, Carved M.P. 1872, 10 X 13 1/2 In. 140.00
  Bowl, Scrubbed Interior, Green Paint, 16 1/2 In. 150.00
  Bowl, Scrubbed Interior, Oblong, 11 3/4 X 19 In. 125.00
  Bowl, Scrubbed White Surfaces, Burl, 5 3/8 X 17 In. 350.00
  Bowl, Spherical Body, Incised Line Design, Footed, Green, 3 3/4 In. 425.00
  Bowl, Sugar, Burl, Dome Top Cover, Incised Border, 6 In. 1980.00
  Bowl, Tooled Lip, Ash Burl, 1 3/4 X 5 In. 120.00
  Bowl, Turned Burlwood, Tapered, Small Circular Foot, 3 X 5 1/2 In. 192.00
  Bowl, Walnut, Engraved Stylized Floral Sprigs, 5 1/4 X 13 1/2 In. 220.00
  Box, Ditty, Sailor's, Chip Wood, Cover, 6 X 5 X 9 In. 425.00
  Box, Heart, Geometric Design, Pink & Maple, Lawton, C.1840, 7 1/2 In. 2300.00
  Box, Spice, 18 Drawers, Hanging 330.00
  Bucket, Blue Paint, 2 Bentwood Handles, New England, 10 X 12 In. 302.00
  Bucket, Lehnware, Leaf Design On Hoops 2100.00
  Bucket, Metal Bands, Wire Bail Handle, Old Yellow Paint 50.00
  Bucket, Peat, Brass Mounted, Mid–19th Century, 13 1/2 In. 935.00
  Bucket, Quince Butter, Lid & Bail, Label, Primitive, 8 In. 30.00
  Bucket, Sap, Hangs On Maple Tree, Tin, 8 In. 4.00
  Bucket, Stave, Interlaced Wooden Bands, Gray Paint, 14 3/4 In. 65.00
  Bucket, Sugar, Reddish Stain, Natural Bands, Copper Nails, 12 In. 145.00
  Bucket, Sugar, Stave Constructed, Copper Tacks, 9 3/4 In. 50.00
  Bucket, Sugar, Stave, Yellow Base, Worn Blue Painted Lid, 10 In. 90.00
  Butter Churn, Rocking, Oak 125.00
  Cabinet, Spice, 7 Drawers, Tin Name Plate, 7 X 9 1/2 X 3 In. 95.00
  Cabinet, Spice, 8 Drawers, Over Long Drawer, Red Stain, 15 X 14 In. 275.00
  Cake Stand, Pine Top & Base, Cherry Shaft, American, 18th Century 450.00
  Can, Kerosene, Tin Insert, Wire Bail, Round, 11 1/2 In., 1 Gal. 17.00
  Canteen, Birchbark, Cylindrical Top, Metal Loop Handle, 7 1/2 In. 110.00
  Canteen, Oval, Iron Bands & Handle, Wood Staved 89.00
  Canteen, Stave Constructed, Metal Bands, Compass Designs, 7 1/4 In. 150.00

Comb Case, Cutout Rabbit & Swan On Crest, Wire Nails, 9 In.	50.00
Cookie Board, Truck, With People, Animals, Flowers, 9 1/2 X 23 In.	470.00
Cookie Print, Pineapple & Leaves, Border, Pine, C.1820, 4 In.	120.00
Crate, Bottle, Stenciled Label, Blue Mountain Bitters, 12 3/4 In.	95.00
Dipper, Dished Bowl, Arched Cylindrical Handle, 19th Century, 23 In.	192.00
Dipper, Water, Burl, Large	350.00
Dough Box, Arched Ends, Painted Red, American, 19th Century, 27 In.	192.00
Dough Box, Old Red, Dovetailed Pine & Poplar, 34 1/2 In.	200.00
Dummy Board, Women, Colonial Dress, Selling Wares, 3 Ft.	1950.00
Firkin, Gray Paint, Cylindrical, Swing Handle, New Eng., 10 X 9 In.	138.00
Firkin, Plank, Bentwood Band, Black Paint, Cylindrical, Norway, 17 In.	110.00
Firkin, Staved, Carved Name Elizabeth, Handle, 2 1/3 In.	250.00
Firkin, Wooden Bail, Copper Fasteners, Staved, Blue, Gray, 9 3/4 In.	160.00
Game Rack, Pine, 8 Wrought Iron Hooks, Pendant Apron, 8 X 31 In.	302.00
Gun Case, Ornate Carving of Rifles, Foliage, Initials	525.00
Humidor, Hinged Lid, Lined, Oak, 11 1/2 X 8 X 8 In.	32.50
Jar, Turned, Poplar, 9 1/2 X 11 1/2 In.	235.00
Jar, Turned, Scrubbed White Finish, Pease, 5 3/4 In.	140.00
Keg, Iron Bands, Stave Construction, 10 1/2 In.	50.00
Ladder, Herb Drying, Birch, 3 Rungs, 18th Century, 11 X 28 In.	140.00
Measure, Dry, Bentwood, Cylindrical, Stylized Medallions, 5 X 13 In.	66.00
Mirror, Hand, Black Finish, Round, Turned Handle, 5 X 9 In.	75.00
Mold, Candle, Cherry Frame, 36 Pewter Holes, All Marked A.Brower	2500.00
Mold, Chocolate, 6 Carved Schoolhouse Pictures, 1 7/8 X 11 3/4 In.	137.00
Mortar & Pestle, Chip Carved Design, 7 In.	55.00
Mortar & Pestle, Copper Bands Marked Revere On Mortar, 7 1/4 In.	250.00
Mortar & Pestle, Poplar, 7 1/4 In.	75.00
Mortar & Pestle, Turned Pine, 7 X 5 In., 10 In.Pestle	247.00
Noggin, Pitcher, 5 5/8 In.	60.00
Paddle, Soap, 32 In.	22.00
Pail, Dovetailed, Rectangular	85.00
Peat Bucket, Concave Lip, Brass Body, Liner & Handle, Mahogany	1540.00
Pepper Can, Red Paint, Partial Paper Pepper Label, 19 X 14 In.	55.00
Plate, Poplar, 7 To 8 In., 6 Piece	450.00
Porringer, Tab Handles, Walnut, Round, C.1810, 4 1/2 In.	175.00
Rack, Utensil, Scalloped Crest, Chip Carved Bands, 31 In.	65.00
Rooster, High Red Comb, Black Bead, Gray Body, 32 In.	1300.00
Scoop, Burl Bowl, Raised Handle 1 Side, Late 18th Century, 8 In.	550.00
Scoop, Irregular Bowl, Bird's Head Handle, Maple Burl, 9 1/2 In.	400.00
Sheath, For Scythe, Animal Head End, Signed & Dated 1809, 29 1/2 In.	115.00
Spool, Mill, Wooden, Blue, 11 In.	5.00
Spreader, Butter, 9 In.	6.00
Tray, Dough, Snyder County	400.00
Tray, Knife, Red Painted Pine, Molded Rail Top, C.1830, 8 X 11 In.	120.00
Tray, Rose Mulled Design, Black Ground, 9 1/4 X 20 1/4 In.	85.00
Trencher, Blue, Hand Hewn, 19th Century, 21 1/2 X 11 X 6 In.	600.00
Tub, Oak, Iron Banding, English, 19th Century, 22 X 22 1/2 In.	66.00
Urn, Cover, Spire-Like Finial, Painted Circles, Pedestal, 7 3/4 In.	1900.00

Worcester porcelains were made in Worcester, England, from 1751.
The firm went through many name changes and eventually, in 1862,
became The Royal Worcester Porcelain Company Ltd. Collectors
often refer to Dr. Wall, Barr, Flight, and other names that indicate
time periods and artists at the factory. It became part of Royal
Worcester Spode Ltd. in 1976.

WORCESTER, see also Royal Worcester

WORCESTER, Bowl, Dr.Wall, Inside Line, Floral Spray On Bottom, 4 3/4 In.	125.00
Cup & Saucer, Spiral Flute, Cobalt Blue Trim, Demitasse, C.1793	55.00
Cup, Saucer & Tea Bowl, Dr.Wall, Bengal Tiger Pattern, C.1776	425.00
Jardiniere, View of Worcester, Gilt Scroll, C.1820, 9 1/4 In.	1300.00
Mug, Dr.Wall, Strap Handle, Rose Clusters, 1 Qt.	275.00
Mug, Roses, Buds, Butterfly, C.1770, 6 1/8 In. ....*Illus*	275.00
Plate, Dessert, Pink, Gold Border, Marked, 9 In., Set of 14	350.00
Snuffer, Candle, Figural, Woman In Bonnet, C.1887	110.00

Never move an object that might explode. Call the local police bomb squad. Many accidents are caused by old souvenir hand grenades and firearms.

Worcester, Mug, Roses, Buds, Butterfly, C.1770, 6 1/8 In.

Souvenirs of World War I and World War II are collected today. Be careful not to store anything that includes live ammunition. Your local police station will tell you how to dispose of the explosives.

WORLD WAR I, Belt, Cartridge, Canvas	15.00
Ashtray, Copper, Enameled Badge Center, City of Paris, Round	5.00
Backpack, U.S.105 Engineers Stenciled, Lt.'s Name	9.00
Belt, Sam Brown, Dyed Black	10.00
Bucket, Water, Canvas, Collapsible, Marked	26.00
Button, Eagle, With V, Initials	5.00
Courier Bag & Belt, Officer's	85.00
Desk, Military, Lap, Morocco Leather Cover, Plain Interfaces	30.00
Gas Mask Kit, Cased	350.00
Helmet, Soldier With Rifles, 4 Lb.	25.00
Helmet, U.S., Complete	23.50
Mirror, Trench	10.00
Poster, Are You In This, United Kingdom, B.Powell, 20 X 30 In.	125.00
Poster, Greatest Mother In World, Red Cross Nurse, 19 X 28 In.	50.00
Poster, Liberty Bonds, Hun His Mark, 30 X 20 In.	20.00
Poster, Save Your Cans, Doughboys, Machine Gun	35.00
Poster, Today Buy That Liberty Bond, Peeking Sun, 28 X 22 In.	20.00
Poster, U.S. Shipping Board, Rivets Are Bayonets, 30 X 20 In.	20.00
Poster, Victory Loan, They Said We Couldn't Fight, 41 X 30 In.	65.00
Pouch Folder, Cloth, Statue of Liberty, Flag, Contains Manuals	45.00
Sewing Kit, Leg Wrap	15.00
Surgeon's Field Instruments, Oak Case, German, 12 X 20 In.	1450.00
Wallet, Leather, Filled With Russian Scrip	12.50
WORLD WAR II, Badge, Cap, Royal Lancers, 17th, Death Or Glory	39.00
Bayonet, Nazi	30.00
Belt & Buckle, Luftwaffe	45.00
Belt & Buckle, Nazi, Army	20.00
Belt, Web, Nazi, Tropical	25.00
Binoculars, Navy, Bausch & Lomb, Case, 7 X 50 In.	100.00
Box, Doughboy Prophylactics, 5 Unopened Packages	25.00
Canteen, U.S.Coast Guard, Lifeboat, Tin, Unopened, 1944	35.00
Cap, Garrison, Khaki, E.M.	10.00
Card, Cigarette, Nazi Military Scenes, Set of 50	30.00
Card, Membership, Nazi Party, Dec.11, 1933	20.00
Creamer, U.S.Army Medical Dept., White, Maroon Logo, 2 1/2 In.	4.00
Cup & Saucer, Spitfire Emblem, Always Be An England, 1940s	28.00
Dagger, Nazi Labor Leaders	375.00
Dagger, Officer's Dress, Luftwaffe	125.00

Dagger, Sheath, Nazi 175.00
Dagger, SS Elite Guard, German 125.00
Duffel Bag, Arm, 1940s 15.00
Flag, Japanese Ball, Silk 30.00
Flag, Nazi Battle, 3 X 5 Ft. 20.00
Flag, Nazi, 30 X 46 In. 75.00
Flag, Nazi, Black Pennant, Juhnde 1/9/1932 .... 75.00
Flag, Red Cross, Cloth, 20 X 32 In. 7.50
Gas Mask, Rubber 4.00
Hat Insignia, Nazi Labor Corp., Back Broken Off, Hallmarked 10.00
Helmet, Italian, Complete 10.50
Helmet, Japan 15.00
Knife, Dinner, Eagle & Swastika, Nazi 15.00
Knife, Hitler Youth 30.00
Lanyard, Silver Braid, German 45.00
Medal, Iron Cross, German 12.00
Medal, Italian Facist Foreign Schools, Blue Ribbon 5.00
Paperweight, Hitler Face, Hog, Iron 35.00
Photograph, Aerial Recon, Framed 25.00
Photograph, All Black Regiment 30.00
Pin, British War Relief, Screw Back 5.00
Pin, Discharge, Ruptured Duck, Gold 10.00
Pin, Fourth Liberty Loan, Flag, 5/8 In. 2.00
Pin, Nurse's, Sterling Silver 20.00
Pin, Philadelphia Naval Shipyard Suggestion Award 5.00
Pin, Ship's For Victory 15.00
Pin, Veterans of Foreign Wars, Ribbon, Screw Back, 1943 .... 5.00
Pin, Women Unite Fight War & Fascism 1.50
Pincushion, Hitler 42.50
Postcard, Soldiers, Sailors, Air Raid Wardens, Comic, 16 Piece 9.00
Postcard, W.A.C., Comic, 3 Piece 3.00
Poster, Nurses Are Needed, 12 1/2 X 19 In. 15.00
Poster, Third Reich, Goeth, 9 1/2 X 13 1/2 In. 20.00
Poster, Third Reich, Goring, 9 1/2 X 13 1/2 In. 20.00
Poster, To Have & To Hold, Little Girl, 20 X 14 In. 25.00
Poster, We Caught Hell, 11 1/2 X 20 In. 20.00
Puzzle, Buy War Bonds, Soldiers In Action, Minuteman Box 10.00
Puzzle, Jigsaw, Total Warface, Victory Savings Bond Minuteman 10.00
Radio, Field Base Station, Tokyo Electric Co., Dec.1941 .... 370.00
Record, Voices of Victory, Gem Razor Blades, Savings Bonds 14.00
Salt & Pepper, Made From Bullets, English Coins On Feet 15.00
Shirt, Wool, Green, Man's 18.00
Surrender Leaflet, U.S.Forces, Pacific, 3 Languages, 5 X 8 In. 39.50
Telephone, Coded MD By National 110.00
Telephone, Field, Canvas Bag 20.00
Telephone, Field, Case 24.00
Tumbler, Remember Pearl Harbor, 6 Piece 50.00

Souvenirs of all world's fairs are collected. The first fair was the Great Exhibition of 1851 in London. Memorabilia of fairs include directories, pictures, fabrics, ceramics, etc.

WORLD'S FAIR, Ashtray, 1933, Aluminum, Chicago 10.00
Ashtray, 1939, New York, Metal 15.00
Bank, 1933, Canco 25.00
Bank, 1961, Mechanical 28.00
Bank, Typewriter, 1939, Remington Rand Hall, New York 38.00
Blotter, 1919, Ohio 3.00
Book, 1933, Official View, Original Mailing Box 12.50
Book, 1939, New York, Story of Lucky Strike 15.00
Book, Coloring, 1964, New York's Official 12.50
Booklet, 1933, Century of Progress, Church Latter Day Saints 5.00
Booklet, 1933, Wings of Century, Chicago, 14 Pages, 9 X 12 In. 4.00
Bottle, 1939, Milk Glass, 9 In. 10.00
Bracelet, 1933, Wrist Wrap, Silver, Century of Progress 35.00

Card, Playing, 1893	65.00
Card, Playing, 1933	28.00
Card, Playing, 1939, Double Deck, Box	28.00
Catalog, Map, 1893, Champion Harvest Machine Co.	20.00
Coaster, 1939, New York, Tin	9.00
Cocktail Shaker, 1933, Century of Progress, Aluminum, Scenes	48.00
Compact, 1893, Chicago	15.00
Cookbook, 1933	5.00
Cup & Saucer, 1933, Chicago Century of Progress, Golliwog	47.00
Cup & Saucer, 1939	50.00
Cup, 1904, Enameled	95.00
Cup, 1904, Tin	30.00
Dish, 1982, Knoxville, Tenn., Lefton, Hand Painted, 6 In.	15.00
Dish, Candy, 1939	25.00
Flyer, Pa.R.R., 1939, Excursions To Fair, Short Letter	10.00
Invitation, 1939, New York's Opening Fair, Engraved, 2 Piece	25.00
Kan–O–Seat, 1939, Cane Opens Into Spectator Chair	55.00
Key, 1934, Chicago World's Fair	7.00
Knife, 1904, 2 Blades, 5 Scenes, Germany	25.00
Knife, Pocket, 1933, Coca–Cola 5 Cents, Chicago	26.00
Knife, Pocket, 1934, Century of Progress, Chicago	12.00
License Plate, 1964, Child's, New York	3.75
Map, 1904, St.Louis, Westinghouse	15.00
Map, 1939, Souvenir, Useful Facts, Childs Restaurants	3.00
Map, 1940, New York, French Pavilion	7.00
Match Holder, 1933, Century of Progress	10.00
Match Safe, 1904, St.Louis, Sterling Silver	75.00
Mirror, 1939, New York, Mailing Box, 3 1/2 X 2 1/2 In.	14.00
Mirror, Pocket, 1904, Liberal Arts Building, Pastel Tan Tones	20.00
Mortar & Pestle, M04, St.Louis, Brass, Miniature	25.00
Official Guide, 1939, New York, First Edition	15.00
Paperweight, 1893, Impressed Columbus' Head, Glass	110.00
Paperweight, 1904, St.Louis	19.50
Pen, Desk, 1933, Chicago, Celluloid	55.00
Photograph, 1964, J.F.Kennedy, Other Dignitaries, 8 In., 2 Pc.	10.00
Pillow Cover, 1933, Century of Progress, Scenes	20.00
Plate, 1904, St.Louis, Gold Embossed Kittens	85.00
Plate, 1933, Brass, With Views, 5 In.	30.00
Plate, 1964, Color Scenes, Fluted Sides, Marked, 7 In.	5.00
Pocket Guide, 1893, Knox World Renowned Hats, 158 Pages	28.00
Postcard Folder, 1939, New York, 18 Color Tint Pictures	5.00
Postcard, 1933, Unused	2.25
Powder Box, 1893, Chicago, Heart	25.00
Print, 1904, St.Louis, Wood, We's Been To De World's Fair	40.00
Puzzle, Jigsaw, 1939, Sloan's Liniment, New York, Complete	20.00
Ring, 1934, Chicago	15.00
Salt & Pepper, 1933, Chicago, Black Bakelite	28.00
Salt & Pepper, 1934	6.00
Salt & Pepper, 1940, Golden Gate Expo	13.50
Salt, 1893, Columbian Exposition, Lay Down Egg, Blue, Libbey	120.00
Scarf, 1936, Views, Dated, 18 In.	25.00
Scarf, 1939, Scenic, Golden Gate International Expo.	25.00
Scarf, 1964, Silk, With Views, Green, 18 In.	20.00
Sewing Kit, Singer, 1933	9.00
Spoon Set, 1939, New York, Wooden Box, With Logo, 12 Piece	95.00
Spoon, 1893, Columbian Exposition, Ship Bowl, Sterling Silver	50.00
Spoon, 1893, Women's Bldg., Columbus Handle, Sterling Silver	50.00
Spoon, 1901, Pan America, Temple of Music, Sterling Silver	30.00
Spoon, 1915, Panama–San Francisco Expo, Sterling Silver	50.00
Spoon, 1933, Century of Progress, Silver Plate, Fair's Scenes	8.00
Spoon, 1933, Sterling Silver	28.00
Spoon, 1939, Albany, N.Y., Sterling Silver	15.00
Spoon, 1939, Silver Plate, Court of Pacifica	18.00
Spoon, Book & Stamp, 1893, Columbian Expo	40.00

Sugar Scoop, 1893, Doe Wah Jack 45.00
Tape Measure, 1933, Chicago 22.00
Thermometer, 1933, Chicago 24.00
Thermometer, 1933, Havoline Tower 13.00
Thermometer, 1933, Key Shape, Chicago 18.00
Ticket, Wallet, 1939, New York, 40 Tickets, ID Card 20.00
Tip Tray, 1904, Red Raven Splits 65.00
Token, 1939, New York, Brass, 150th Washington Inauguration 10.00
Towel, 1893, Columbian Expo, Red, Columbus Bust, Linen 18.00
Toy, Ferris Wheel, 1959, U.S.Royal Tire, Battery Operated 35.00
Tray, Change, 1904, Tin 40.00
Tumbler, 1939, Set of 6 .... 55.00
Tumbler, 1964, Kodak 7.50
Vase, 1893, Peachblow, Gourd, Gold Enameled Design 250.00
Vase, 1904, Purple Luster & Gold Picture, St.Louis, 6 In. 125.00
Viewer & Films, 1939, New York, Box 40.00
Water Bottle, 1933, Chicago 22.00

Yellowware is a heavy earthenware made of a yellowish clay. It varies in color from light yellow to orange–yellow. Many nineteenth– and twentieth–century kitchen bowls and jugs were made of yellowware. It was made in England and in the United States. Another form of pottery that is sometimes classed as yellowware is listed in this book under Mocha.

YELLOWWARE, Bank, Pig, Green & Amber Daubs, 5 In. 45.00
Bank, Pig, Stripe & Swirl Upper Body, Austria, 4 In. 50.00
Beater Jar, Brown Stripe, Pocahontas, Iowa Dairy 38.00
Bowl Set, Brown Stripes, Set of 4 .... 40.00
Bowl, 6 In. 22.00
Bowl, 8 In. 20.00
Bowl, 13 In. 60.00
Bowl, 2 Blue Bands, 8 1/2 In. 25.00
Bowl, 3 Brown Stripes, 9 In. 25.00
Bowl, 3 Brown Stripes, 10 In. 38.00
Bowl, 3 White Stripes, 10 1/2 In. 30.00
Bowl, Apricot, 9 1/2 In. 75.00
Bowl, Banded, Child's 38.00
Bowl, Batter, 11 1/2 In. 65.00
Bowl, Batter, Diamond Scalloped Sides, 10 In. 140.00
Bowl, Blue & Brown Sponged Spatter, 8 3/8 X 4 1/4 In. 45.00
Bowl, Blue Bands, 9 In. 30.00
Bowl, Blue Bands, 10 1/2 In. .... 30.00 To 35.00

Yellowware, Mold

Pinwheel, 2 1/2 In.& 6 In., 2 Piece, Grape Design, 6 X 7 In., Corn Cob Design, 5 X 7 In.

In snowy weather make tracks both in and out of your door. One set of tracks leaving the house is an invitation to an intruder. Or perhaps you could walk out of the house backward.

Yellowware, Salt, Hanging, 3 White Bands,
    6 1/2 X 6 In.

Bowl, Blue Bands, White Pinstripes, 4 3/4 In.	40.00
Bowl, Brown & White Stripes, 4 1/2 X 9 In.	42.00
Bowl, Brown & White Stripes, 6 3/4 X 13 3/4 In.	45.00
Bowl, Embossed Ribs, Blue Stripes, 6 1/4 X 11 1/2 In.	25.00
Bowl, Girl With Watering Can, 11 1/2 In.	55.00
Bowl, Grape Pattern, 10 In.	60.00
Bowl, Mixing, 2 Narrow & 1 Wide White Band, 11 3/4 In.	44.00
Bowl, Mixing, Brown, White Stripes, 15 In.	38.50
Bowl, White & Brown Bands, 12 In.	50.00
Bowl, White Band, 5 3/8 X 11 1/4 In.	30.00
Butter Churn, C.1870, 16 In.	225.00
Butter, Cover, Daisy	100.00
Casserole, Blue Bands	55.00
Casserole, Cover	75.00
Chamber Pot, Blue Sponged, Gold Trim, Cover	85.00
Chamber Pot, Wide White Band, Small Brown Bands, White	95.00
Colander	145.00
Crock, Butter, Green Stripe, 4 X 5 3/4 In.	57.00
Crock, Butter, White & Brown Bands, 5 1/4 In.	65.00
Crock, Butter, White Band, 2 Stripes	85.00
Crock, Butter, White Stripe, Butter In Black Lettering, Cover	95.00
Cup, Snail In Bottom, Child's	22.00
Cuspidor, Green, Blue & Tan Sponged, 5 X 7 1/2 In.	58.00
Custard Cup, Blue Striped, 6 Piece	60.00
Figure, Lamb, Old White Paint, 16 In.	500.00
Flowerpot	85.00
Jar, Blue Seaweed Design, White Bank, Brown Stripes, 7 X 6 In.	700.00
Jar, Brown Slip, 8 3/4 In.	525.00
Jar, Cover, Keg Shape, Blue, Green & Brown Run Glaze, 8 In., Pair	370.00
Jar, Pepper, Cover, White Band, 2 Stripes	85.00
Jar, Spice, Vented Knob Lid, 5 In.	85.00
Jug, Brown & White, Striping, 8 1/2 In.	375.00
Mixing Bowl, Embossed, Brown Bands, 12 1/4 X 6 1/2 In.	35.00
Mold, Corn Cob Design, 5 X 7 In. ....*Illus*	40.00
Mold, Grape Design, 6 X 7 In. ....*Illus*	85.00
Mold, Pinwheel, 2 1/2 In.& 6 In., 2 Piece ....*Illus*	105.00
Mug, Barrel Shape, White Interior	27.50
Mug, Bennington, Large	50.00
Mug, Blue Seaweed, White Band, Brown Stripes, E.Liverpool, 4 In.	325.00
Mug, Brown Dots, Roger Bacon Collection Label, 3 1/4 In.	675.00
Mug, Rockingham Glaze	75.00

Mug, White Band, Brown Stripes, 3 7/8 In.	95.00
Pie Plate, 9 1/2 In.	50.00 To 85.00
Pitcher Set, Buttermilk, Cow, Green, Graduated, 3 Piece	325.00
Pitcher, Ale	198.00
Pitcher, Grape Cluster On Shield, Green, Cream Ground	95.00
Pitcher, Green Tree Bark	95.00
Pitcher, Green, Basket Weave & Carnation	130.00
Pitcher, Keg Shape, Green & Brown Sponging, 7 3/8 In.	35.00
Pitcher, Milk, Blue & White Bands	75.00
Pitcher, Mottled Green & Brown, 4 1/2 In.	25.00
Plate, Henderson, C.1820, 8 In.	145.00
Plate, Westward Expansion, 1875–90	195.00
Rolling Pin	250.00 To 285.00
Rolling Pin, Blue Stripe	300.00
Salt, Hanging, 3 White Bands, 6 1/2 X 6 In.	*Illus* 200.00
Spittoon, Embossed Scrolling, Green	85.00
Tankard	205.00
Tobacco Jar, Bulldog Lid, English, 6 In.	175.00
Tobacco Jar, Hound & Fox Heads, Hare Finial, English, 7 3/4 In.	185.00
Tub, Banded In Brown & White, Cylindrical, 5 X 6 1/2 In.	60.00
Tumbler, Banded	65.00
Washboard, Pine Frame, Blue Sponge, C.1880	475.00

ZANE WARE

Zane Pottery was founded in 1921 by Adam Reed and Harry McClelland in South Zanesville, Ohio, at the old Peters and Reed Building. Zane pottery is very similar to Peters and Reed pottery, but it is usually marked. The factory was sold in 1941 to Lawton Gonder.

ZANE, Bowl & Flower Frog, Brown	45.00
Vase, Landsun, 5 In.	30.00

LA MORO

The Zanesville Art Pottery was founded in 1900 by David Schmidt in Zanesville, Ohio. The firm made faience umbrella stands, jardinieres, and pedestals. The company closed in 1962. Many pieces are marked with just the words "La Moro."

ZANESVILLE, Vase, La Moro, 8 In.	250.00

ZSOLNAY PÉCS

Zsolnay pottery was made in Hungary after 1862 and was characterized by Persian, Art Nouveau, or Hungarian motifs. A series of new Zsolnay figurines with green–gold luster finish is available in many shops today. Early Zsolnay was not marked; but by 1878, the tower trademark was used.

ZSOLNAY, Bowl, Centerpiece, Reticulated, Floral, Gold Trim, 5 X 4 In.	285.00
Compote, Floral Design, Hearts On Either Side, 4 1/2 In.	60.00
Dish, Fan Shape, Rolled–Over Rim, Reticulated, 8 1/2 In.	175.00
Figurine, Bison, Reclining, Bronze & Gold Glaze	85.00
Figurine, Nude, Pull Off Slip	225.00
Frog, Green, Large	185.00
Jardiniere, Blue Iridescent, Frolicking Bacchus, 1900, 13 In.	1980.00
Jug, Puzzle, Reticulated Roundels, Jeweling, Marked, 6 3/4 In.	135.00
Jug, Puzzle, Roundels, Looped Protrusions, Marked, 6 3/4 In.	115.00
Vase, Completely Reticulated, Double Walled, Marked, 6 1/2 In.	350.00
Vase, Figural, 2 Women, Chartreuse, Ocher, Gold, 1900, Marked, 10 In.	110.00
Vase, Reticulated Outer Layer, Brown & Green, Gold Trim, 3 3/4 In.	125.00
Vase, Woman Pulling Dress Over Head, Pedestal, Marked, 8 1/2 In.	240.00

KOVELS

ND ORDERS & INQUIRIES TO: **Crown Publishers, Inc.**
:5 Park Avenue South, New York, N.Y. 10003
TT: SALES DEPT.

SALES & TITLE INFORMATION
1-800-526-4264

AME _____

DDRESS _____

TY & STATE _____ ZIP _____

EASE SEND ME THE FOLLOWING BOOKS:

EM NO.	QTY.	TITLE		PRICE	TOTAL
985X	_____	Kovels' Antiques & Collectibles Price List 21st Edition	PAPER	$10.95	_____
66133	_____	Kovels' Bottles Price List Eighth Edition	PAPER	$12.95	_____
66966	_____	Kovels' Guide to Selling Your Antiques & Collectibles	PAPER	$9.95	_____
58718	_____	Kovels' Advertising Collectibles Price List 1st Edition	PAPER	$11.95	_____
01411	_____	Dictionary of Marks – Pottery and Porcelain	HARDCOVER	$10.95	_____
59145	_____	Kovels' New Dictionary of Marks	HARDCOVER	$17.95	_____
68659	_____	Kovels' Depression Glass & American Dinnerware Price List 3rd Edition	PAPER	$12.95	_____
5044X	_____	Kovels' Illustrated Price Guide to Royal Doulton 2nd Edition	PAPER	$10.95	_____
45012	_____	Kovels' Know Your Antiques Revised and Updated	HARDCOVER	$15.95	_____
36080	_____	Kovels' Know Your Collectibles	HARDCOVER	$18.95	_____
4668X	_____	American Country Furniture 1780 – 1875	PAPER	$14.95	_____

COMING IN THE SPRING

68829	_____	Kovels' American Silver Marks	HARDCOVER	$40.00	_____

_____ TOTAL ITEMS   TOTAL RETAIL VALUE _____

HECK OR MONEY ORDER ENCLOSED MADE PAYABLE TO
ROWN PUBLISHERS, INC., 225 Park Avenue South,
Jew York, N.Y. 10003
r telephone 1-800-526-4264
No cash or stamps, please)

Shipping & Handling
Charge $1.40 for one book;
60¢ for each additional book   _____

harge: ☐ MasterCard ☐ Visa ☐ American Express
ccount Number (include all digits)   Expires MO. YR.

TOTAL AMOUNT DUE _____

_____

PRICES SUBJECT TO CHANGE
WITHOUT NOTICE. If a more
recent edition of a price list has
been published at the same price, it
ignature _____   will be sent instead of the old edition.

Thank you for your order.